Organic Chemistry

Fourth Edition

Janice Gorzynski Smith
University of Hawai'i at Mānoa

CHEM 51 A/B/C
Study Guide / Solutions Manual
University of California - Irvine

Mc Graw Hill Education

1 2 3 4 5 6 7 8 9 0 KNG KNG 16 15 14 13

ISBN-13: 978-1-25-911225-6
ISBN-10: 1-25-911225-X

Learning Solutions Consultant: Kimberly Scheyving
Associate Project Manager: Vanessa Estrada
Cover Photo Credits: 009463.mod.tif © Creatas / PunchStock

Contents

Chapter 1 Structure and Bonding

Chapter Review

Important facts

- **The general rule of bonding:** Atoms strive to attain a complete outer shell of valence electrons (Section 1.2). H "wants" 2 electrons. Second-row elements "want" 8 electrons.

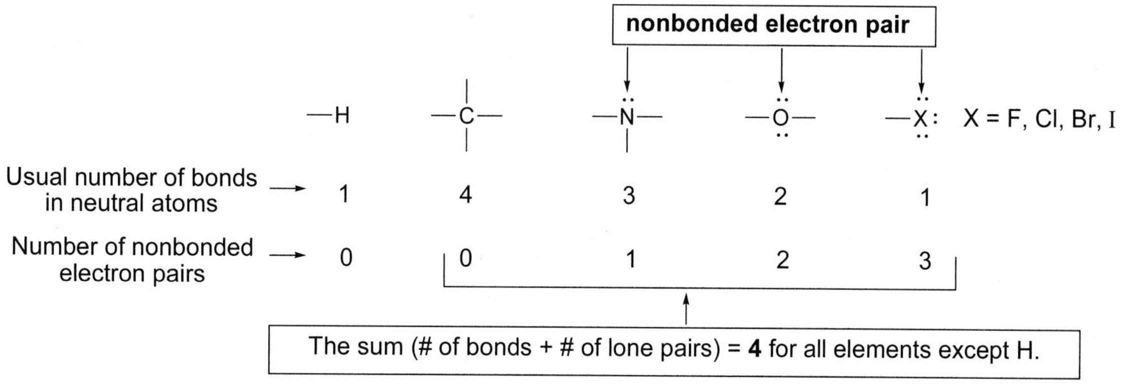

- **Formal charge** (FC) is the difference between the number of valence electrons on an atom and the number of electrons it "owns" (Section 1.3C). See Sample Problem 1.3 for a stepwise example.

Definition: **formal charge** = **number of valence electrons** – **number of electrons an atom "owns"**

Examples:

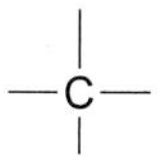

- C shares 8 electrons.
- C "owns" **4** electrons.
- FC = 0

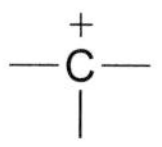

- C shares 6 electrons.
- C "owns" **3** electrons.
- FC = +1

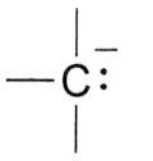

- C shares 6 electrons.
- C has 2 unshared electrons.
- C "owns" **5** electrons.
- FC = –1

- **Curved arrow notation** shows the movement of an electron pair. The tail of the arrow always begins at an electron pair, either in a bond or a lone pair. The head points to where the electron pair "moves" (Section 1.6).

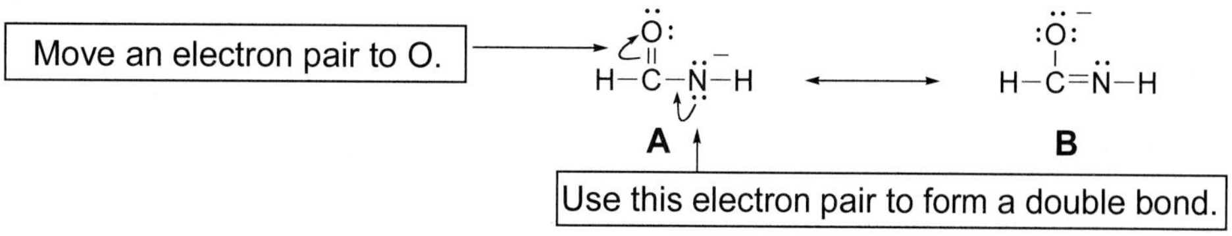

- **Electrostatic potential plots** are color-coded maps of electron density, indicating electron rich (red) and electron deficient (blue) regions (Section 1.12).

The importance of Lewis structures (Sections 1.3–1.5)

A properly drawn Lewis structure shows the number of bonds and lone pairs present around each atom in a molecule. In a valid Lewis structure, each H has two electrons, and each second-row element has no more than eight. This is the first step needed to determine many properties of a molecule.

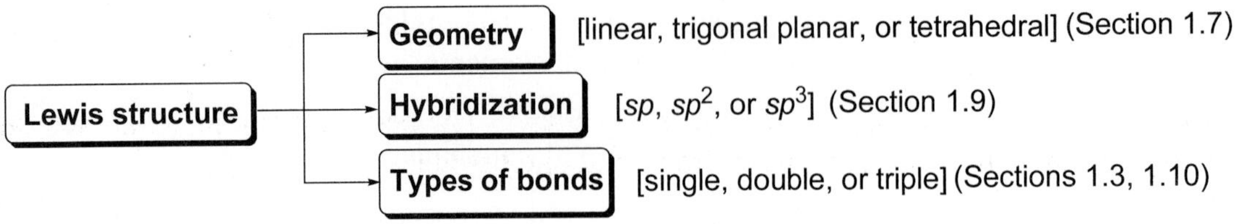
Lewis structure
Geometry
[linear, trigonal planar, or tetrahedral] (Section 1.7)
Hybridization
[sp, sp2, or sp3] (Section 1.9)
Types of bonds
[single, double, or triple] (Sections 1.3, 1.10)

Resonance (Section 1.6)

The basic principles:

- Resonance occurs when a compound cannot be represented by a single Lewis structure.
- Two resonance structures differ *only* in the position of nonbonded electrons and π bonds.
- The resonance hybrid is the only accurate representation for a resonance-stabilized compound. A hybrid is more stable than any single resonance structure because electron density is delocalized.

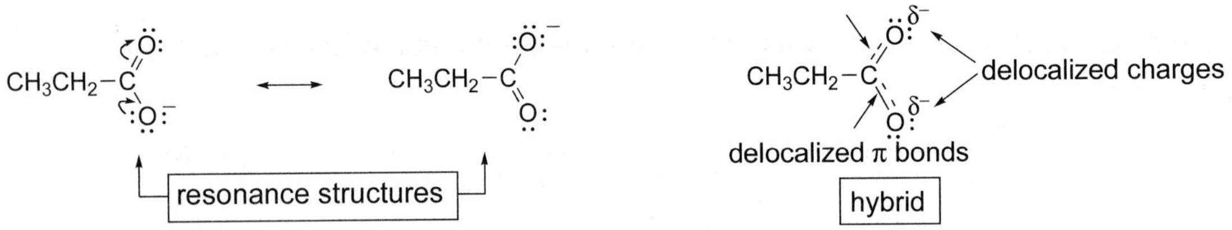
resonance structures
delocalized charges
delocalized π bonds
hybrid

The difference between resonance structures and isomers:

- Two **isomers** differ in the arrangement of *both* atoms and electrons.
- **Resonance structures** differ *only* in the *arrangement of electrons*.

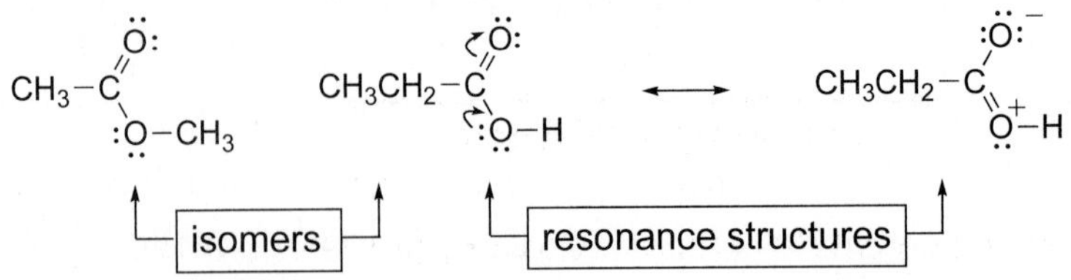
isomers
resonance structures

Geometry and hybridization

The number of groups around an atom determines both its geometry (Section 1.7) and hybridization (Section 1.9).

Number of groups	Geometry	Bond angle (°)	Hybridization	Examples
2	linear	180	*sp*	BeH_2, HC≡CH
3	trigonal planar	120	sp^2	BF_3, CH_2=CH_2
4	tetrahedral	109.5	sp^3	CH_4, NH_3, H_2O

Drawing organic molecules (Section 1.8)

- Shorthand methods are used to abbreviate the structure of organic molecules.

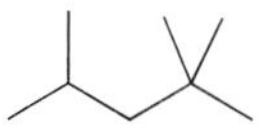

=

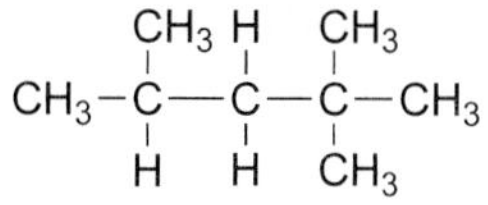
CH3 H CH3
CH3–C–C–C–CH3
H H CH3

= $(CH_3)_2CHCH_2C(CH_3)_3$

skeletal structure isooctane condensed structure

- A carbon bonded to four atoms is tetrahedral in shape. The best way to represent a tetrahedron is to draw two bonds in the plane, one in front, and one behind.

Four equivalent drawings for CH_4

Each drawing has two solid lines, one wedge, and one dashed line.

Bond length

- Bond length decreases across a row and increases down a column of the periodic table (Section 1.7A).

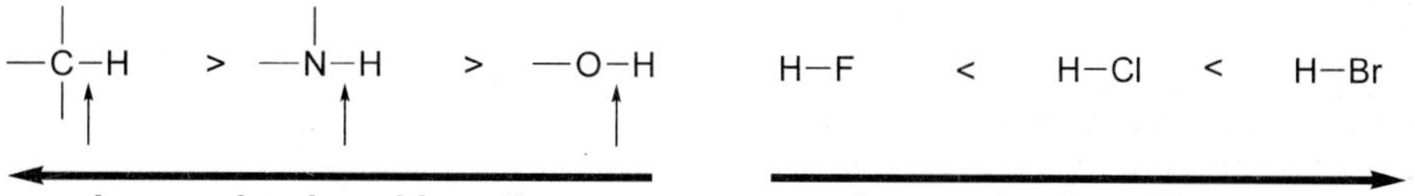
—C–H > —N–H > —O–H
H–F < H–Cl < H–Br

Increasing bond length **Increasing bond length**

- Bond length decreases as the number of electrons between two nuclei increases (Section 1.11A).

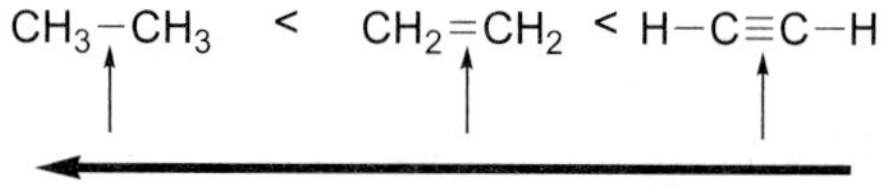
CH3–CH3 < CH2=CH2 < H–C≡C–H

Increasing bond length

- Bond length increases as the percent *s*-character decreases (Section 1.11B).

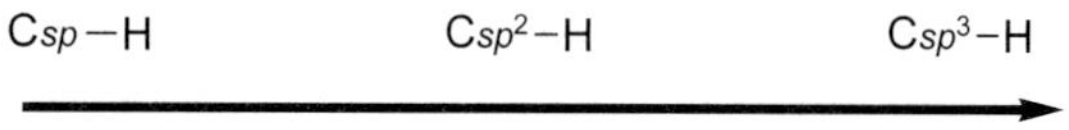
Csp–H
Csp2–H
Csp3–H

Increasing bond length

- Bond length and bond strength are inversely related. Shorter bonds are stronger bonds (Section 1.11).

longest C–C bond
weakest bond

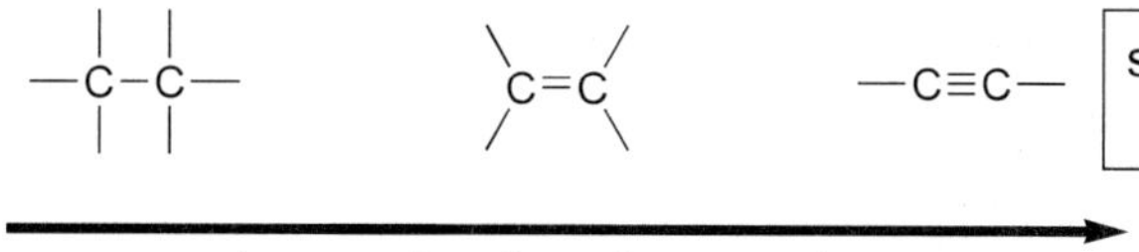
—C≡C—

shortest C–C bond
strongest bond

Increasing bond strength

- Sigma (σ) bonds are generally stronger than π bonds (Section 1.10).

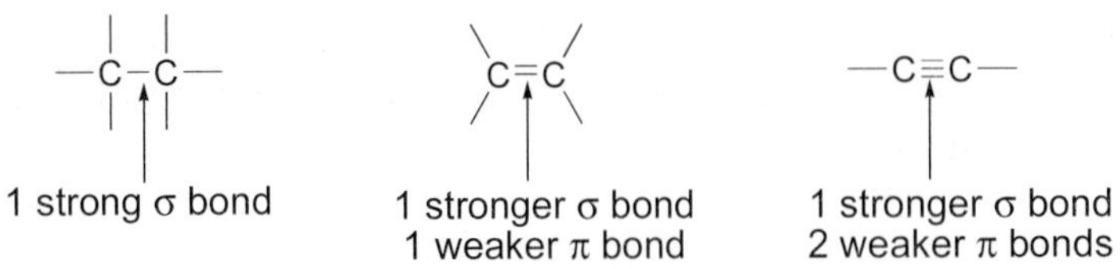
1 strong σ bond
1 stronger σ bond
1 weaker π bond
1 stronger σ bond
2 weaker π bonds

Electronegativity and polarity (Sections 1.12, 1.13)

- Electronegativity increases from left to right across a row and decreases down a column of the periodic table.
- A polar bond results when two atoms of different electronegativity are bonded together. Whenever C or H is bonded to N, O, or any halogen, the bond is polar.
- A polar molecule has either one polar bond, or two or more bond dipoles that reinforce.

Drawing Lewis structures: A shortcut

Chapter 1 devotes a great deal of time to drawing valid Lewis structures. For molecules with many bonds, it may take quite awhile to find acceptable Lewis structures by using trial-and-error to place electrons. Fortunately, a shortcut can be used to figure out how many bonds are present in a molecule.

Shortcut on drawing Lewis structures—Determining the number of bonds:

[1] Count up the number of valence electrons.

[2] Calculate how many electrons are needed if there are no bonds between atoms and every atom has a filled shell of valence electrons; that is, hydrogen gets two electrons, and second-row elements get eight.

[3] Subtract the number obtained in Step [1] from the sum obtained in Step [2]. **This difference tells how many electrons must be shared** to give every H two electrons and every second-row element eight. Since there are two electrons per bond, dividing this difference by two tells how many bonds are needed.

To draw the Lewis structure:

[1] Arrange the atoms as usual.

[2] Count up the number of valence electrons.

[3] Use the shortcut to determine how many bonds are present.

[4] Draw in the two-electron bonds to all the H's first. Then, draw the remaining bonds between other atoms making sure that no second-row element gets more than eight electrons and that you use the total number of bonds determined previously.

[5] Finally, place unshared electron pairs on all atoms that do not have an octet of electrons, and calculate formal charge. You should have now used all the valence electrons determined in the first step.

Example: Draw all valid Lewis structures for CH_3NCO using the shortcut procedure.

[1] Arrange the atoms.

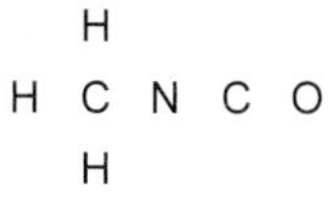
H
H C N C O
H

- In this case the arrangement of atoms is implied by the way the structure is drawn.

[2] Count up the number of valence electrons.

3H's	x	1 electron per H	=	3 electrons
2C's	x	4 electrons per C	=	8 electrons
1N	x	5 electrons per N	=	5 electrons
1O	x	6 electrons per O	=	+ 6 electrons
				22 electrons total

[3] Use the shortcut to figure out how many bonds are needed.

- Number of electrons needed if there were no bonds:

3 H's	x	2 electrons per H	=	6 electrons
4 second-row elements	x	8 electrons per element	=	+ 32 electrons
				38 electrons needed if there were no bonds

- Number of electrons that must be shared:

  38 electrons
  – 22 electrons
  16 electrons must be shared

- Since every bond takes two electrons, 16/2 = **8 bonds are needed.**

[4] Draw all possible Lewis structures.

- Draw the bonds to the H's first (three bonds). Then add five more bonds. Arrange them between the C's, N, and O, making sure that no atom gets more than eight electrons. There are three possible arrangements of bonds; that is, there are three resonance structures.
- Add additional electron pairs to give each atom an octet and check that all 22 electrons are used.

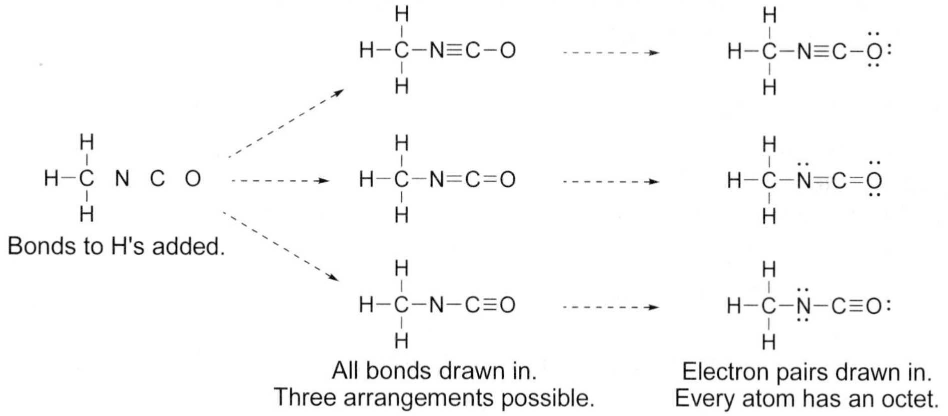
Bonds to H's added.
All bonds drawn in.
Three arrangements possible.
Electron pairs drawn in.
Every atom has an octet.

- Calculate the formal charge on each atom.

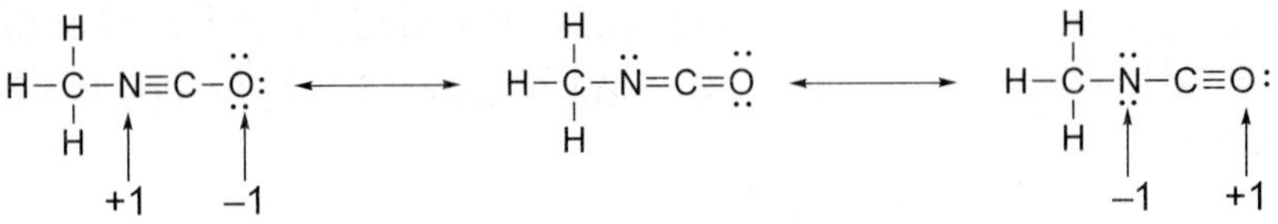

- You can evaluate the Lewis structures you have drawn. The middle structure is the best resonance structure, since it has no charged atoms.

Note: This method works for compounds that contain second-row elements in which every element gets an octet of electrons. It does NOT necessarily work for compounds with an atom that does not have an octet (such as BF_3), or compounds that have elements located in the third row and later in the periodic table.

Practice Test on Chapter Review

1. a. Which compound(s) contain a labeled atom with a +1 formal charge? All lone pairs of electrons have been drawn in.

1. 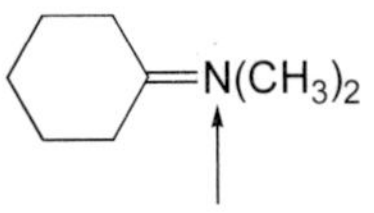 2. 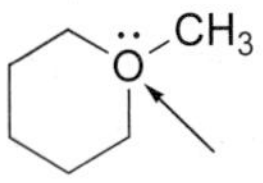 3. 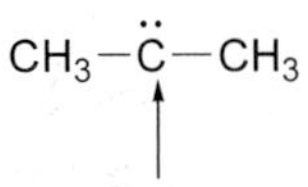

4. Both (1) and (2) have labeled atoms with a +1 charge.
5. Compounds (1), (2), and (3) all contain labeled atoms with a +1 formal charge.

b. Which of the following compounds is a valid resonance structure for **A**?

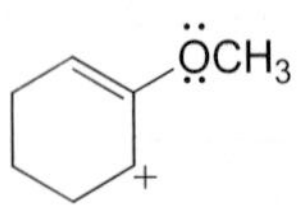
A

1. 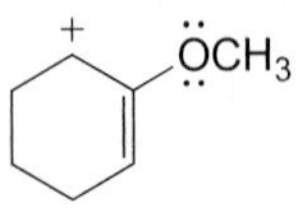 2. 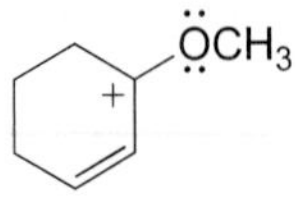 3. 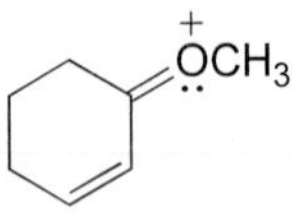

4. Both (1) and (2) are valid resonance structures for **A.**
5. Cations (1), (2), and (3) are all valid resonance structures for **A.**

c. Which species contains a labeled carbon atom that is *sp*² hybridized?

1. 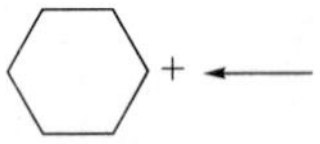 2. 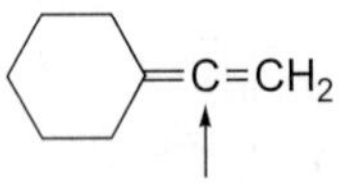 3. 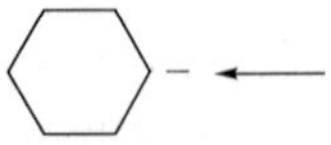

4. Both (1) and (2) contain labeled *sp*² hybridized atoms.
5. Species (1), (2), and (3) all contain labeled *sp*² hybridized carbon atoms.

d. Which of the following compounds has a net dipole?

1. $CH_3CH_2NHCH_2CH_3$
2. $CH_3CH_2CH_2OH$
3. $FCH_2CH_2CH_2F$
4. Compounds (1) and (2) both have net dipoles.
5. Compounds (1), (2), and (3) all have net dipoles.

2. Rank the labeled bonds in order of increasing bond length. Label the shortest bond as **1,** the longest bond as **4,** and the bonds of intermediate length as **2** and **3.**

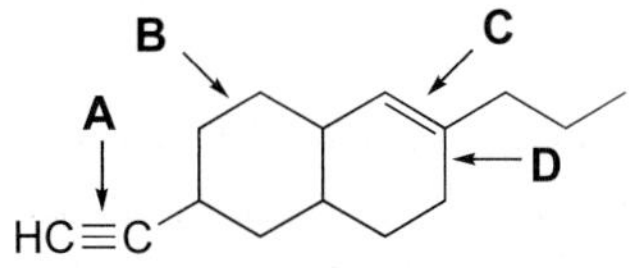

3. Answer the following questions about compounds **A–D.**

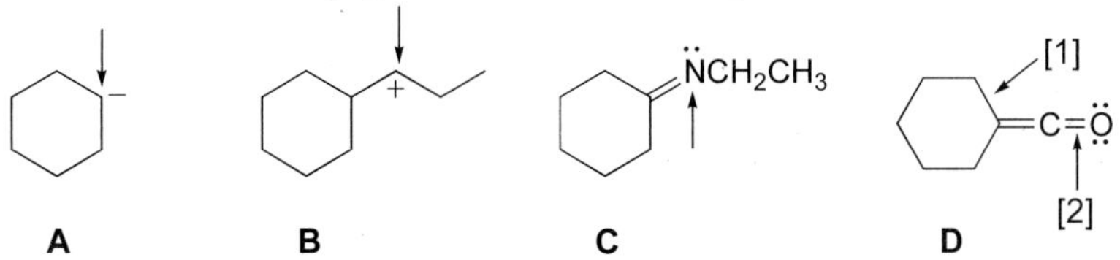

A **B** **C** **D**

a. What is the hybridization of the labeled atom in **A?**
b. What is the molecular shape around the labeled atom in **B?**
c. In what type of orbital does the lone pair in **C** reside?
d. What orbitals are used to form bond [1] in **D?**
e. Which orbitals are used to form the carbon–oxygen double bond [2] in **D?**

4. Draw an acceptable Lewis structure for CH_3NO_3. Assume that the atoms are arranged as drawn.

```
  H   O
H C O N O
  H
```

5. Follow the curved arrows and draw the product with all the needed charges and lone pairs.

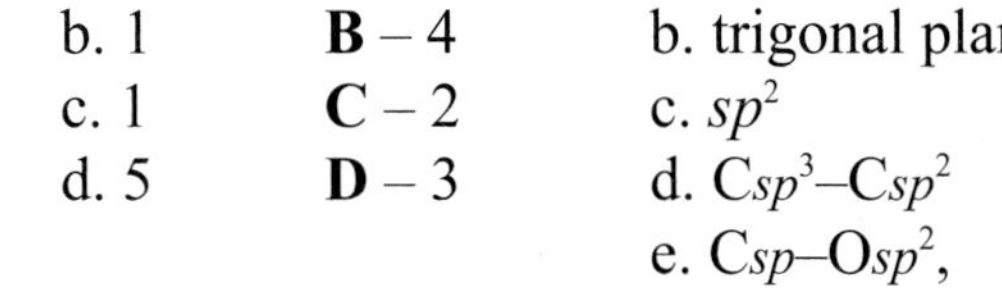

Answers to Practice Test

1. a. 4
   b. 1
   c. 1
   d. 5

2. **A** – 1
   B – 4
   C – 2
   D – 3

3. a. sp^3
   b. trigonal planar
   c. sp^2
   d. Csp^3–Csp^2
   e. Csp–Osp^2, Cp–Op

4. One possibility:

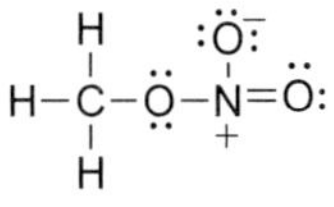

5.

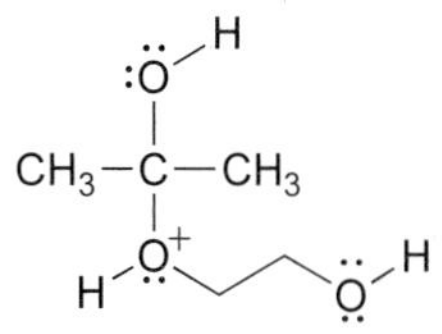

Answers to Problems

1.1 The **mass number** is the number of protons and neutrons. The **atomic number** is the number of protons and is the same for all isotopes.

	Nitrogen-14	Nitrogen-13
a. number of protons = atomic number for N = 7	7	7
b. number of neutrons = mass number – atomic number	7	6
c. number of electrons = number of protons	7	7
d. The group number is the same for all isotopes.	5A	5A

1.2 **Ionic bonds** form when an element on the far left side of the periodic table transfers an electron to an element on the far right side of the periodic table. **Covalent bonds** result when two atoms *share* electrons.

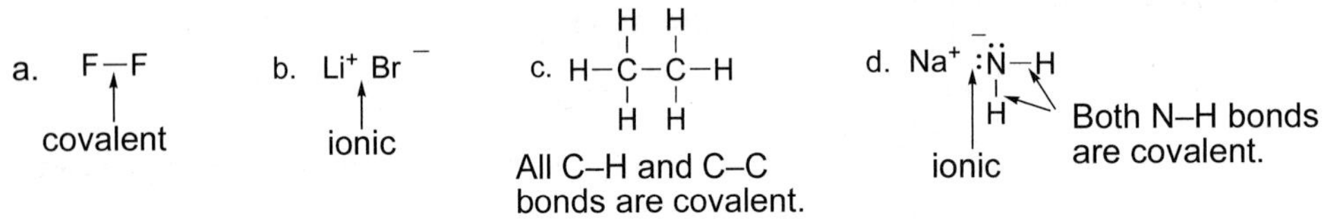
a. F–F
covalent
b. Li⁺ Br⁻
ionic
c.
All C–H and C–C bonds are covalent.
d. Na⁺
ionic
Both N–H bonds are covalent.

1.3 Atoms with one, two, three, or four valence electrons form one, two, three, or four bonds, respectively. Atoms with five or more valence electrons form [8 – (number of valence electrons)] bonds.

a. O 8 – 6 valence e^- = 2 bonds

b. Al 3 valence e^- = 3 bonds

c. Br 8 – 7 valence e^- = 1 bond

d. Si 4 valence e^- = 4 bonds

1.4 [1] Arrange the atoms with the H's on the periphery.
[2] Count the valence electrons.
[3] Arrange the electrons around the atoms. Give the H's 2 electrons first, and then fill the octets of the other atoms.
[4] Assign formal charges (Section 1.3C).

a. [1]
H H
H C C H
H H

[2] Count valence e^-.
2C x 4 e^- = 8
6H x 1 e^- = 6
total e^- = 14

[3]

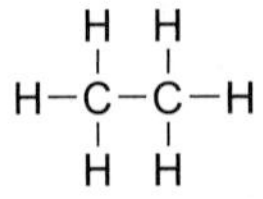

All 14 e^- used.
All second-row elements have an octet.

b. [1]
H
H C N H
H H

[2] Count valence e^-.
1C x 4 e^- = 4
5H x 1 e^- = 5
1N x 5 e^- = 5
total e^- = 14

[3]

12 e^- used.
N needs 2 more electrons for an octet.

c. [1] H
H C
H

[2] Count valence e⁻.
1C x 4 e⁻ = 4
3H x 1 e⁻ = 3
negative charge = 1
total e⁻ = 8

[3] 

6 e⁻ used.
C needs 2 more electrons for an octet.

[The –1 charge on C is explained in Section 1.3C.]

d. [1] H
H C Cl
H

[2] Count valence e⁻.
1C x 4 e⁻ = 4
3H x 1 e⁻ = 3
1Cl x 7 e⁻ = 7
total e⁻ = 14

[3] 

8 e⁻ used.
Cl needs 6 more electrons for an octet.

Complete octet.

1.5 Follow the directions from Answer 1.4.

a. HCN — H C N

Count valence e⁻.
1C x 4 e⁻ = 4
1H x 1 e⁻ = 1
1N x 5 e⁻ = 5
total e⁻ = 10

H−C−N — 4 e⁻ used.

H−C≡N: — Complete N and C octets.

b. H_2CO — H C O / H

Count valence e⁻.
1C x 4 e⁻ = 4
2H x 1 e⁻ = 2
1O x 6 e⁻ = 6
total e⁻ = 12

6 e⁻ used. — Complete O and C octets.

c. $HOCH_2CO_2H$ — H O / H O C C O H / H

Count valence e⁻.
2C x 4 e⁻ = 8
4H x 1 e⁻ = 4
3O x 6 e⁻ = 18
total e⁻ = 30

16 e⁻ used. — Complete octets.

1.6 **Formal charge** (FC) = number of valence electrons – [number of unshared electrons + (½)(number of shared electrons)]

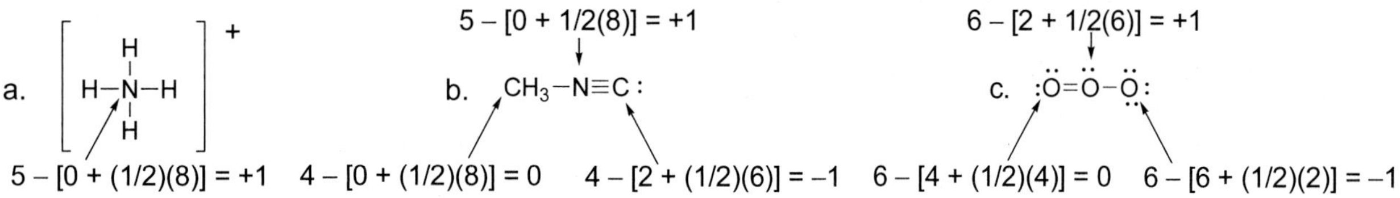
a.
b.
c.
5 – [0 + 1/2(8)] = +1
6 – [2 + 1/2(6)] = +1
5 – [0 + (1/2)(8)] = +1
4 – [0 + (1/2)(8)] = 0
4 – [2 + (1/2)(6)] = –1
6 – [4 + (1/2)(4)] = 0
6 – [6 + (1/2)(2)] = –1

1.7

a. CH_3O^- — [1] H / H C O / H

[2] Count valence e⁻.
1C x 4 e⁻ = 4
3H x 1 e⁻ = 3
1O x 6 e⁻ = 6
total e⁻ = 13
Add 1 for (–) charge = 14

[3] 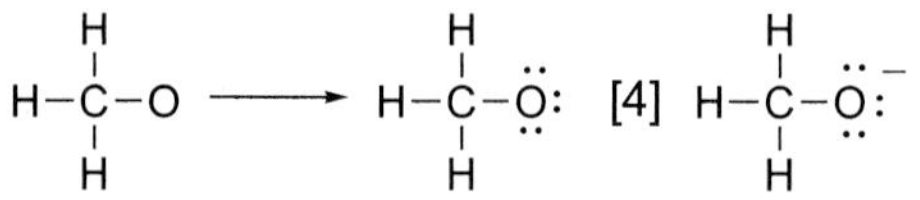

8 e⁻ used. — Assign charge.

b. HC_2^-

[1] H C C

[2] Count valence e⁻.
2C x 4 e⁻ = 8
1H x 1 e⁻ = 1
total e⁻ = 9
Add 1 for (–) charge = 10

[3] H–C–C ⟶ H–C≡C:
4 e⁻ used.

[4] H–C≡C:⁻
Assign charge.

c. $(CH_3NH_3)^+$

[1] H H
H C N H
H H

[2] Count valence e⁻.
1C x 4 e⁻ = 4
6H x 1 e⁻ = 6
1N x 5 e⁻ = 5
total e⁻ = 15
Subtract 1 for (+) charge = 14

[3] 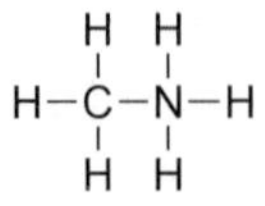
14 e⁻ used.

[4] 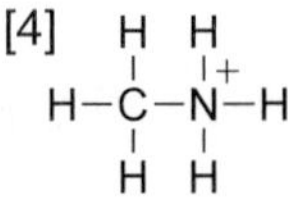
Assign charge.

d. $(CH_3NH)^-$

[1] H
H C N H
H

[2] Count valence e⁻.
1C x 4 e⁻ = 4
4H x 1 e⁻ = 4
1N x 5 e⁻ = 5
total e⁻ = 13
Add 1 for (–) charge = 14

[3] 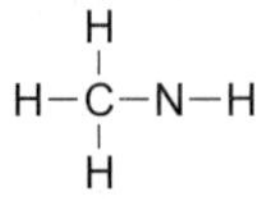
10 e⁻ used.

[4] 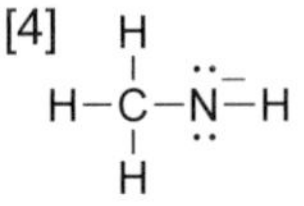
Complete octet and assign charge.

1.8

a. $C_2H_4Cl_2$ (two isomers)

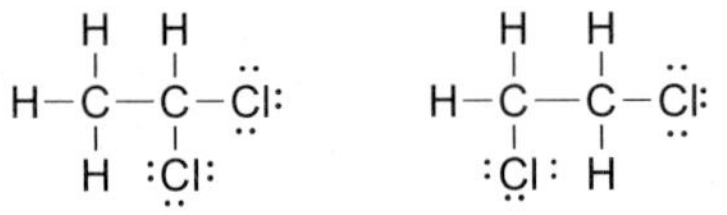

Count valence e⁻.
2C x 4 e⁻ = 8
4H x 1 e⁻ = 4
2Cl x 7 e⁻ = 14
total e⁻ = 26

b. C_3H_8O (three isomers)

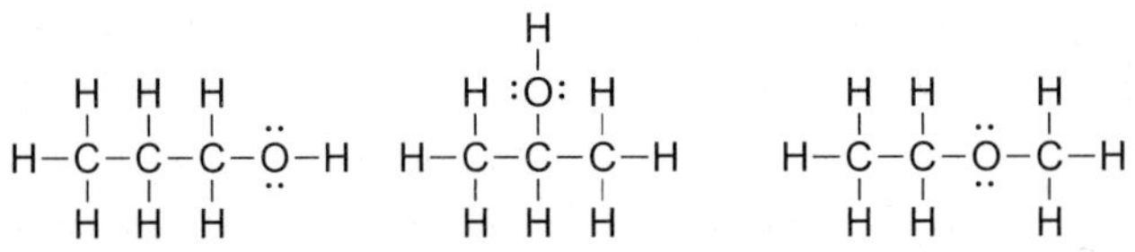

Count valence e⁻.
3C x 4 e⁻ = 12
8H x 1 e⁻ = 8
1O x 6 e⁻ = 6
total e⁻ = 26

c. C_3H_6 (two isomers)

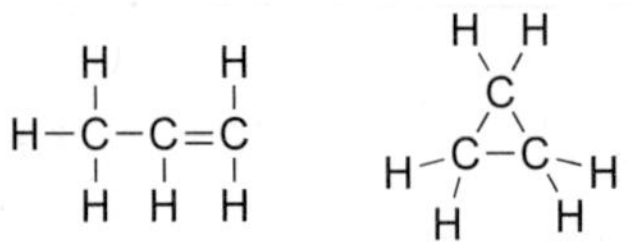

Count valence e⁻.
3C x 4 e⁻ =12
6H x 1 e⁻ = 6
total e⁻ = 18

1.9 Two different definitions:

- **Isomers** have the same molecular formula and a *different* arrangement of atoms.
- **Resonance structures** have the same molecular formula and the *same* arrangement of atoms.

a. 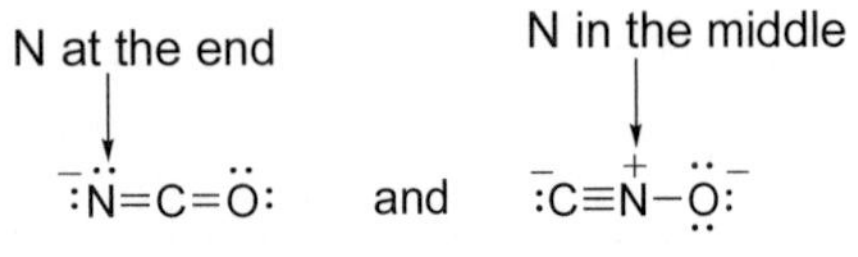
N at the end
N in the middle
and

different arrangement of atoms = **isomers**

b. 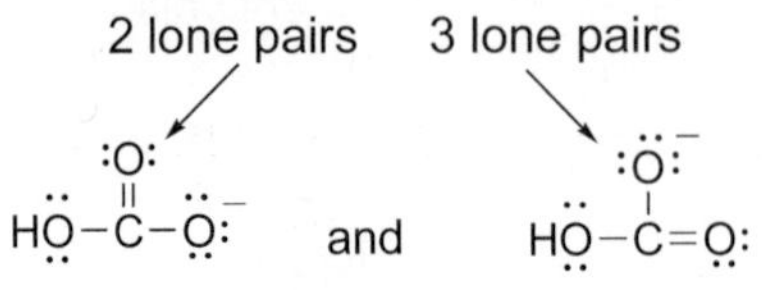
2 lone pairs
3 lone pairs
and

same arrangement of atoms = **resonance structures**

1.10 **Isomers** have the same molecular formula and a *different* arrangement of atoms. **Resonance structures** have the same molecular formula and the *same* arrangement of atoms.

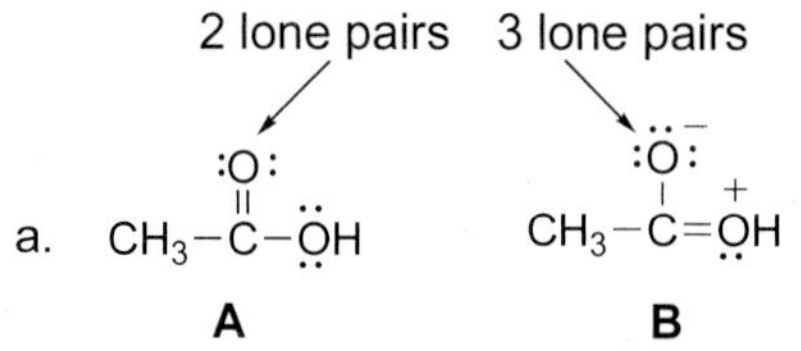

same arrangement of atoms = **resonance structures**

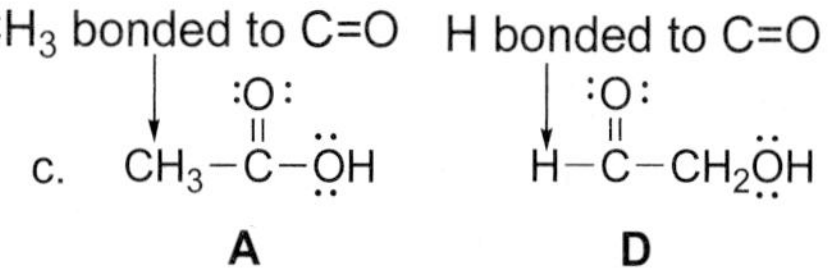

different arrangement of atoms = **isomers**

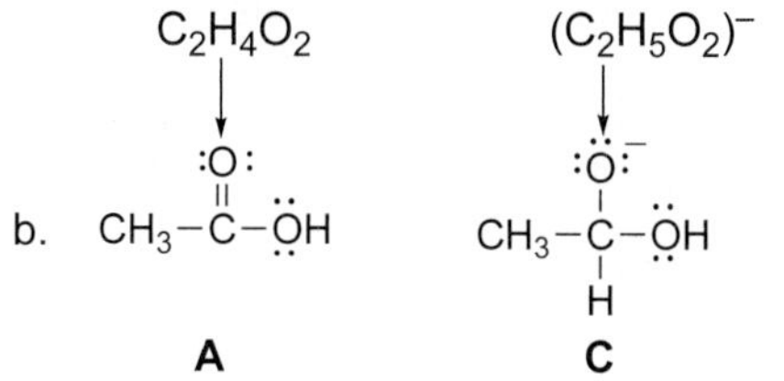

different molecular formulas = **neither**

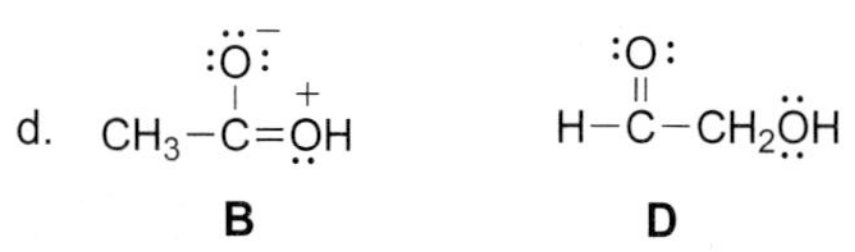

different arrangement of atoms = **isomers**

1.11 Curved arrow notation shows the movement of an electron pair. The tail begins at an electron pair (a bond or a lone pair) and the head points to where the electron pair moves.

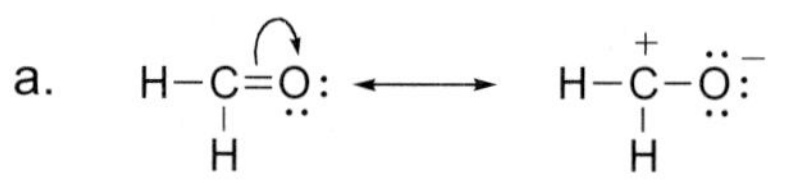

The net charge is the same in both resonance structures.

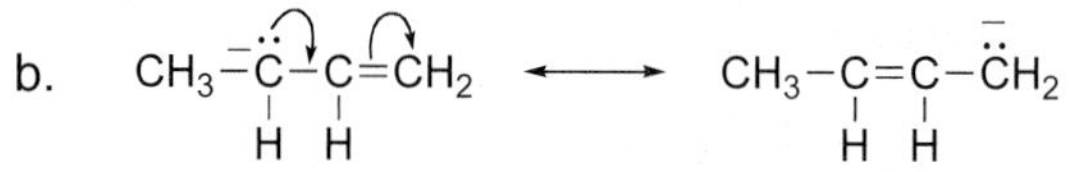

The net charge is the same in both resonance structures.

1.12 Compare the resonance structures to see what electrons have "moved." **Use one curved arrow to show the movement of each electron pair.**

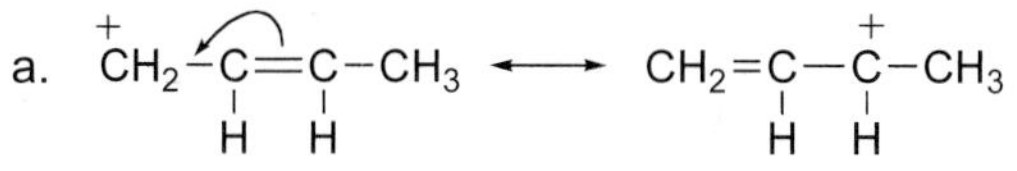

One electron pair moves: one curved arrow.

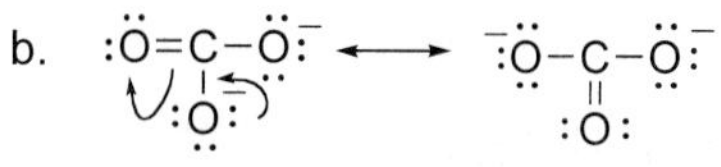

Two electron pairs move: two curved arrows.

1.13 To draw another resonance structure, **move electrons only in multiple bonds and lone pairs** and keep the number of unpaired electrons constant.

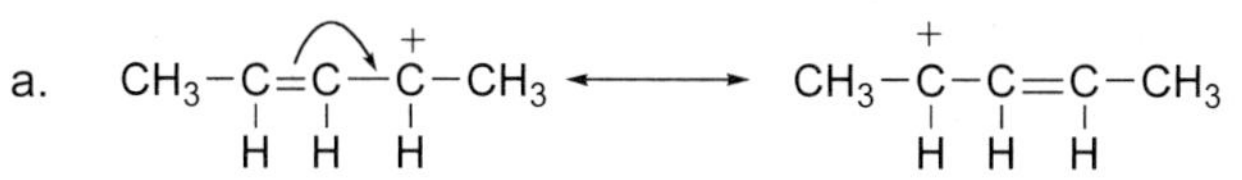

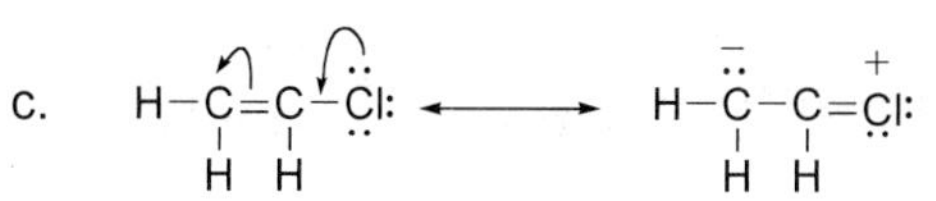

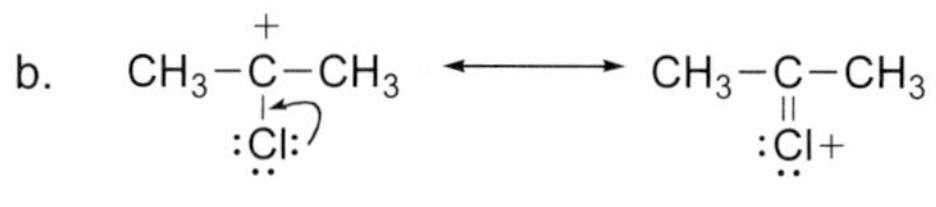

1.14 **A "better" resonance structure is one that has more bonds and fewer charges.** The better structure is the major contributor and all others are minor contributors. To draw the resonance hybrid, use dashed lines for bonds that are in only one resonance structure, and use partial charges when the charge is on different atoms in the resonance structures.

a. 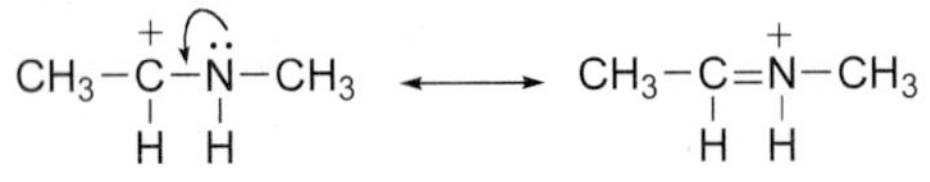

All atoms have octets.
one more bond
major contributor

hybrid:

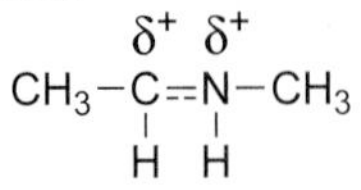

b. 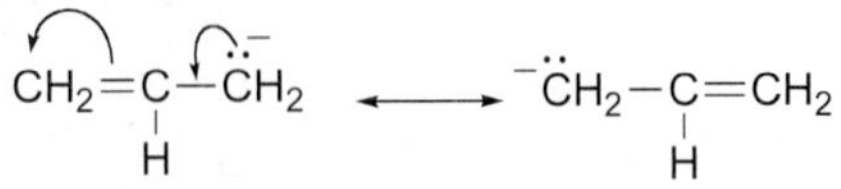

These two resonance structures are equivalent. They both have one charge and the same number of bonds. They are **equal contributors** to the hybrid.

hybrid:

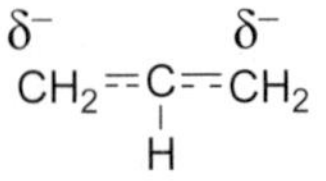

1.15 Draw a second resonance structure for nitrous acid.

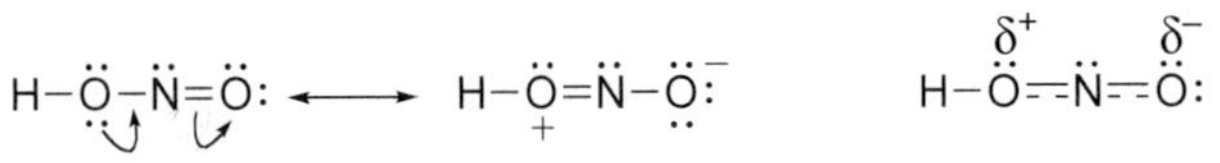

major contributor fewer charges — minor contributor — hybrid

1.16 All representations have a carbon with two bonds in the plane of the page, one in front of the page (solid wedge) and one behind the page (dashed line). Four possibilities:

1.17 To predict the geometry around an atom, **count the number of groups (atoms + lone pairs),** making sure to draw in any needed lone pairs or hydrogens: 2 groups = linear, 3 groups = trigonal planar, 4 groups = tetrahedral.

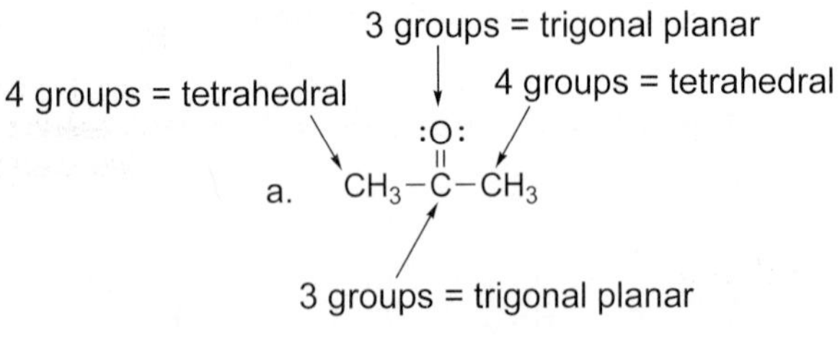

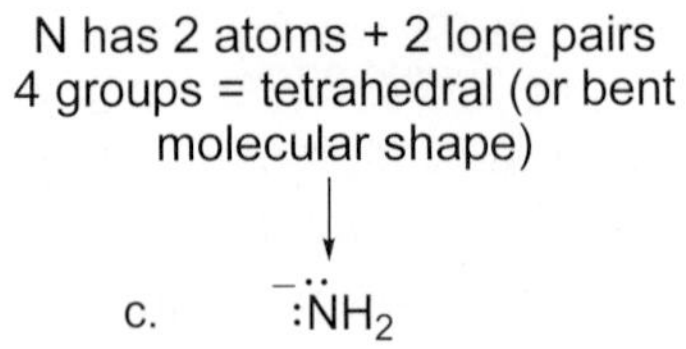

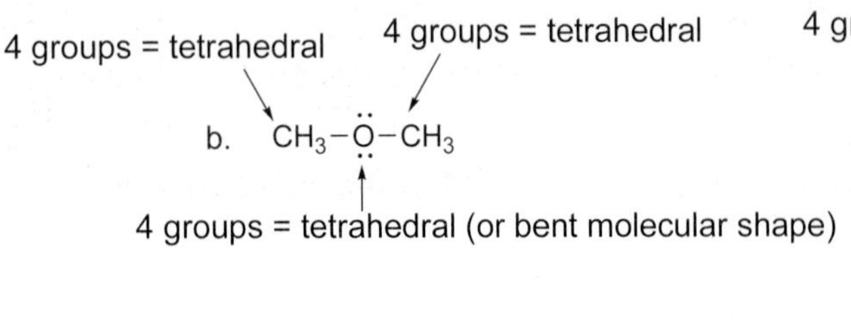

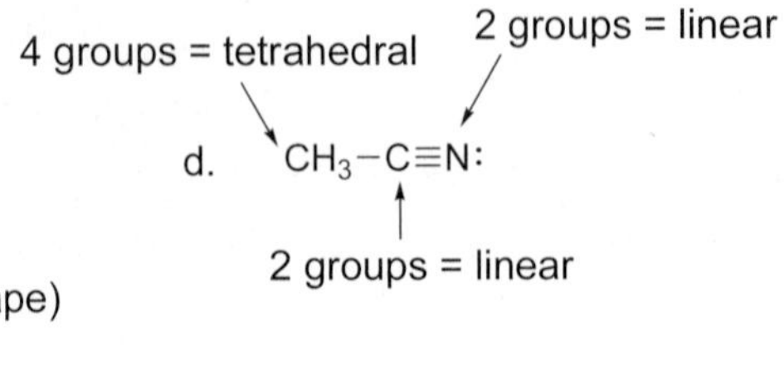

1.18 To predict the bond angle around an atom, **count the number of groups (atoms + lone pairs)**, making sure to draw in any needed lone pairs or hydrogens: 2 groups = 180°, 3 groups = 120°, 4 groups = 109.5°.

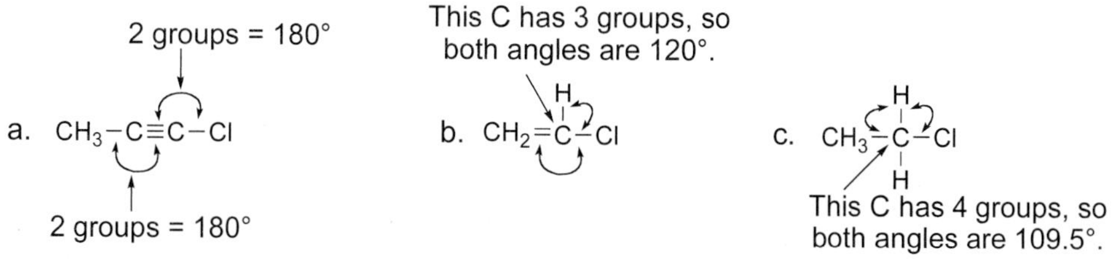
2 groups = 180°
a. $CH_3-C\equiv C-Cl$
2 groups = 180°
This C has 3 groups, so both angles are 120°.
b. $CH_2=C(H)-Cl$
c. CH_3-CH_2-Cl
This C has 4 groups, so both angles are 109.5°.

1.19 To predict the geometry around an atom, use the rules in Answer 1.17.

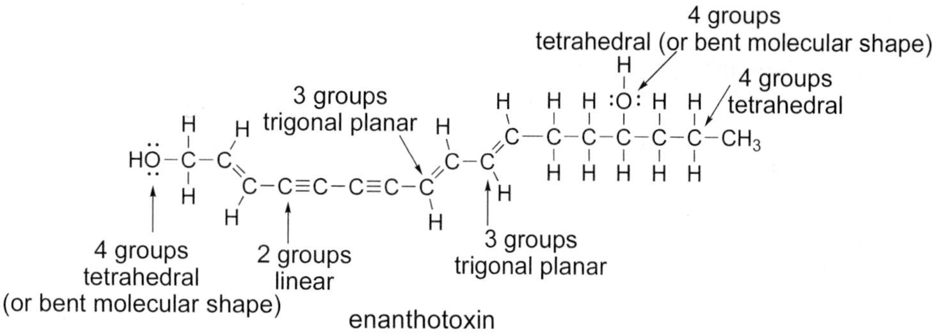
4 groups
tetrahedral (or bent molecular shape)
4 groups
tetrahedral
3 groups
trigonal planar
4 groups
tetrahedral
(or bent molecular shape)
2 groups
linear
3 groups
trigonal planar
enanthotoxin

1.20 Reading from left to right, draw the molecule as a Lewis structure. Always check that carbon has four bonds and all heteroatoms have an octet by adding any needed lone pairs.

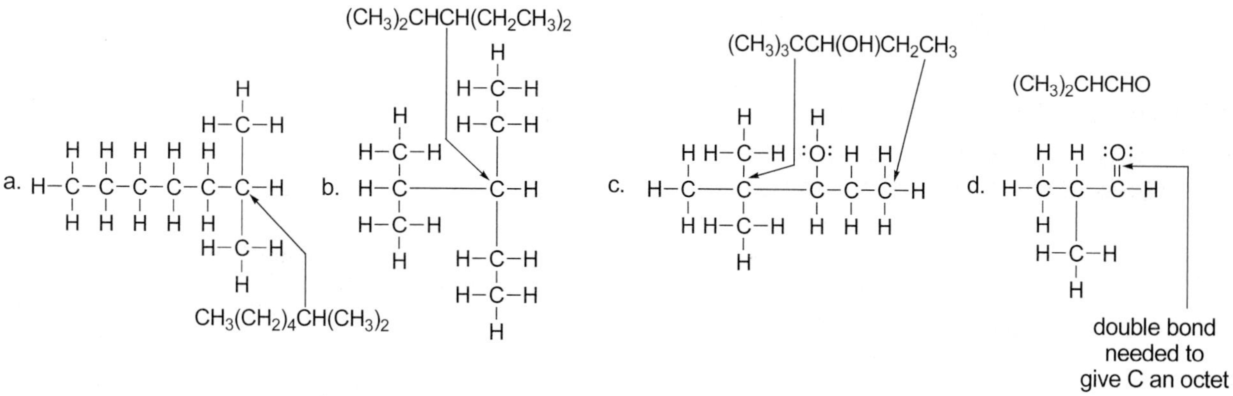
$(CH_3)_2CHCH(CH_2CH_3)_2$
$(CH_3)_3CCH(OH)CH_2CH_3$
$(CH_3)_2CHCHO$
a.
b.
c.
d.
$CH_3(CH_2)_4CH(CH_3)_2$
double bond needed to give C an octet

1.21 Simplify each condensed structure using parentheses.

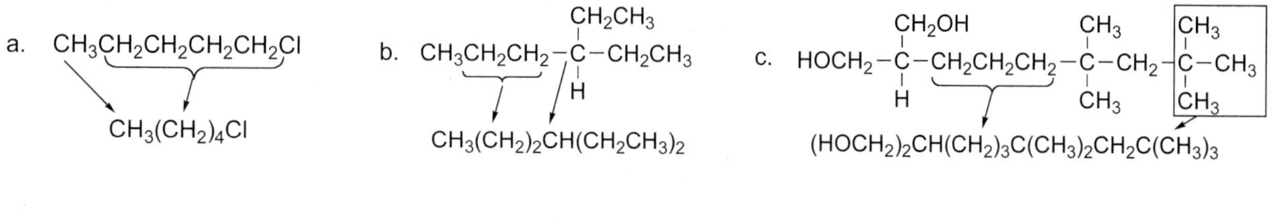
a. $CH_3CH_2CH_2CH_2CH_2Cl$
$CH_3(CH_2)_4Cl$
b. $CH_3CH_2CH_2-C(H)(CH_2CH_3)-CH_2CH_3$
$CH_3(CH_2)_2CH(CH_2CH_3)_2$
c. $HOCH_2-C(H)(CH_2OH)-CH_2CH_2CH_2-C(CH_3)_2-CH_2-C(CH_3)_2-CH_3$
$(HOCH_2)_2CH(CH_2)_3C(CH_3)_2CH_2C(CH_3)_3$

1.22 Draw the Lewis structure of lactic acid.

$CH_3CH(OH)CO_2H$ ⟶ 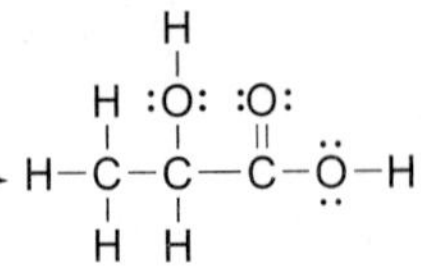

1.23 In shorthand or skeletal drawings, **all line junctions or ends of lines represent carbon atoms.** The carbons are all tetravalent.

a. 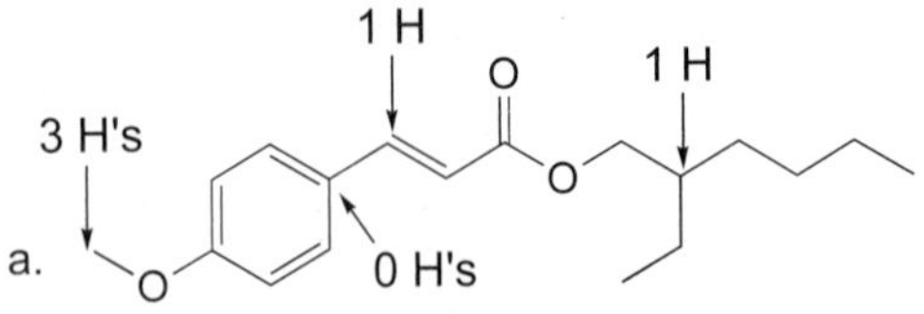

octinoxate
(2-ethylhexyl 4-methoxycinnamate)
$C_{18}H_{26}O_3$

b. 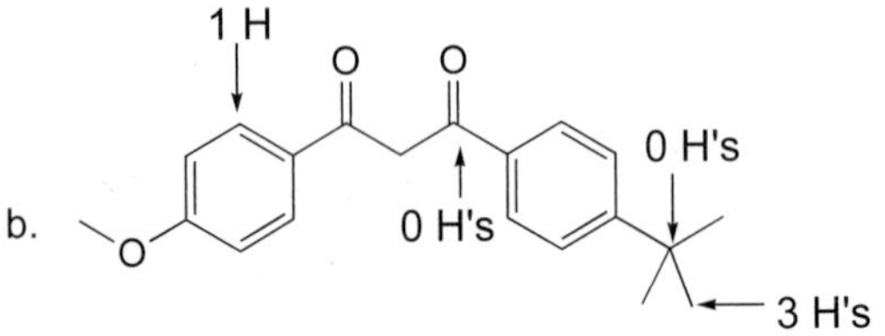

avobenzone
$C_{20}H_{22}O_3$

1.24 In shorthand or skeletal drawings, **all line junctions or ends of lines represent carbon atoms.** Convert by writing in all carbons, and then adding hydrogen atoms to make the carbons tetravalent.

a. 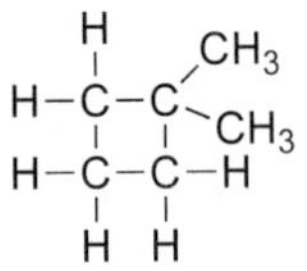

b. 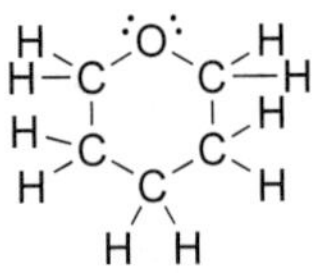

c. 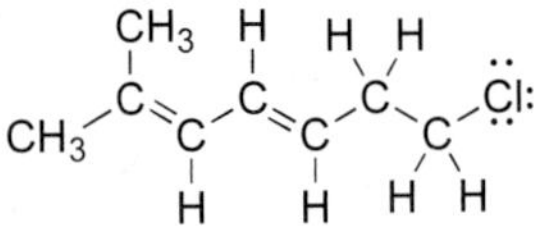

d. 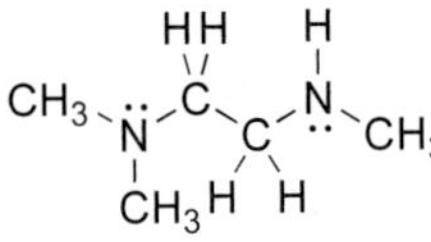

1.25 A charge on a carbon atom takes the place of one hydrogen atom. **A negatively charged C has one lone pair, and a positively charged C has none.**

a. 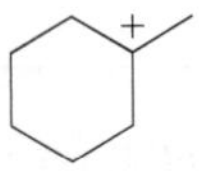

positive charge
no lone pairs
no H's needed

b. 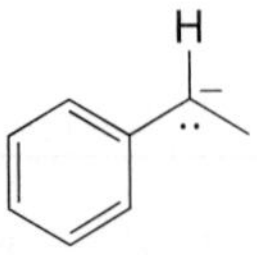

negative charge
one lone pair
one H needed

c. 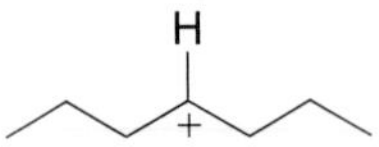

positive charge
no lone pairs
one H needed

d. 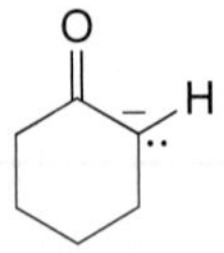

negative charge
one lone pair
one H needed

1.26 Draw each indicated structure. Recall that in the skeletal drawings, a carbon atom is located at the intersection of any two lines and at the end of any line.

a. $(CH_3)_2C{=}CH(CH_2)_4CH_3$ = 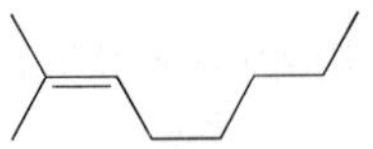

c. 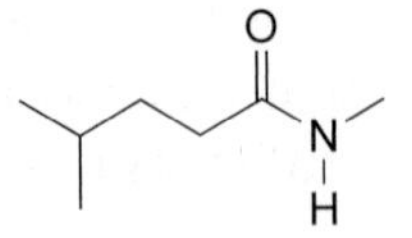 = $(CH_3)_2CH(CH_2)_2CONHCH_3$

b. 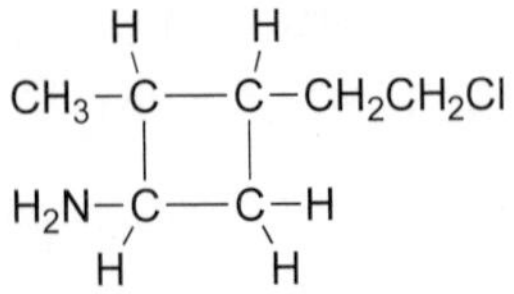 = 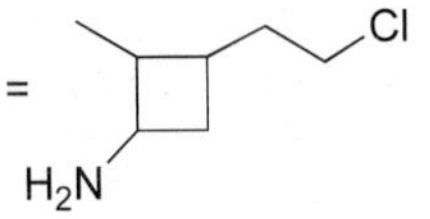

d. 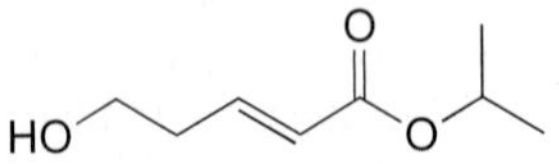 = $HO(CH_2)_2CH{=}CHCO_2CH(CH_3)_2$

1.27 To determine the orbitals used in bonding, **count the number of groups** (atoms + lone pairs): 4 groups = sp^3, 3 groups = sp^2, 2 groups = sp, H atom = $1s$ (no hybridization). All covalent single bonds are σ, and all double bonds contain one σ and one π bond.

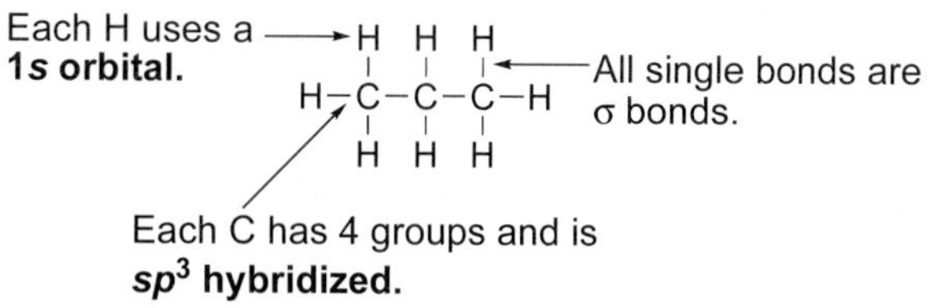

Each C–C bond is Csp^3–Csp^3.
Each C–H bond is Csp^3–$H1s$.

Total of 10 σ bonds.

1.28 [1] Draw a valid Lewis structure for each molecule.
[2] **Count the number of groups** around each atom: 4 groups = sp^3, 3 groups = sp^2, 2 groups = sp, H atom = $1s$ (no hybridization).

Note: **Be and B** (Groups 2A and 3A) do not have enough valence e^- to form an octet, **and do not form an octet in neutral molecules.**

a. [1]

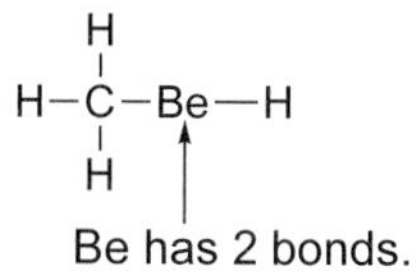

[2] Count groups around each atom:

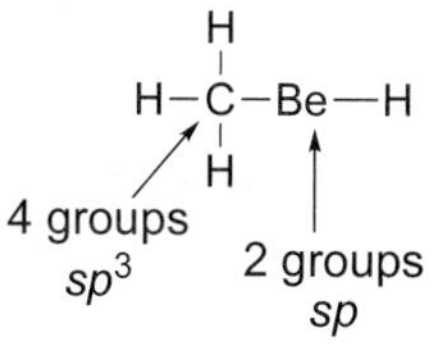

[3] All C–H bonds: Csp^3–$H1s$
C–Be bond: Csp^3–$Besp$
Be–H bond: $Besp$–$H1s$

b. [1]

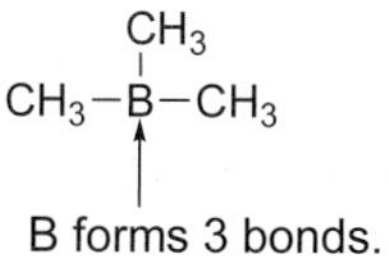

[2] Count groups around each atom:

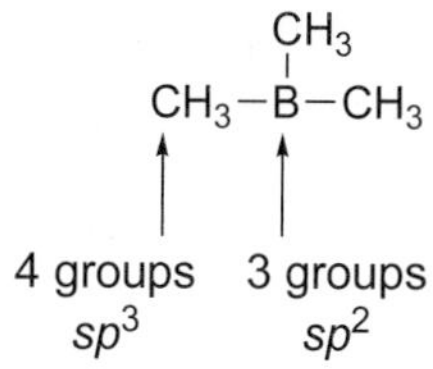

[3] All C–H bonds: Csp^3–$H1s$
C–B bonds: Csp^3–Bsp^2

c. [1]

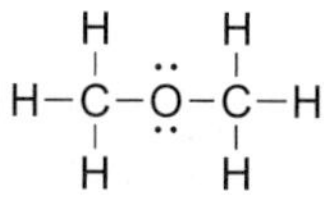

[2] Count groups around each atom:

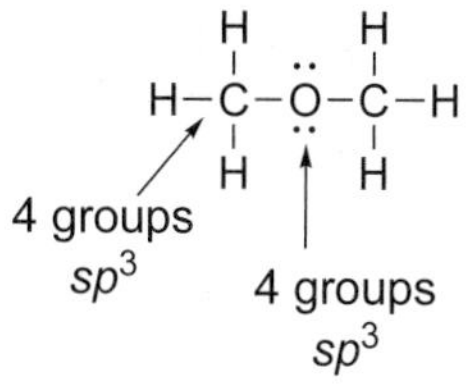

[3] All C–H bonds: Csp^3–$H1s$
C–O bonds: Csp^3–Osp^3

1.29 To determine the hybridization, **count the number of groups** around each atom: 4 groups = sp^3, 3 groups = sp^2, 2 groups = sp, H atom = $1s$ (no hybridization).

a.

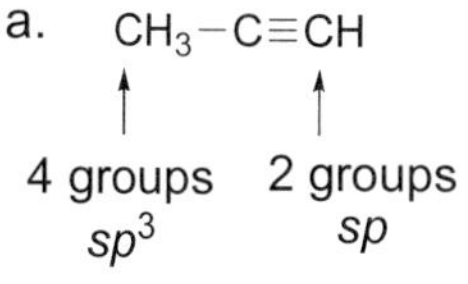

b.

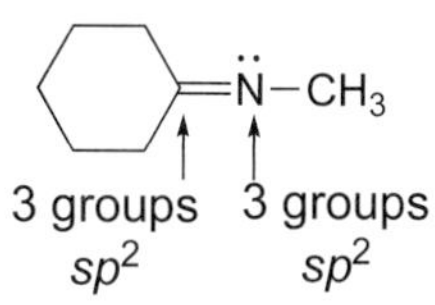

c.

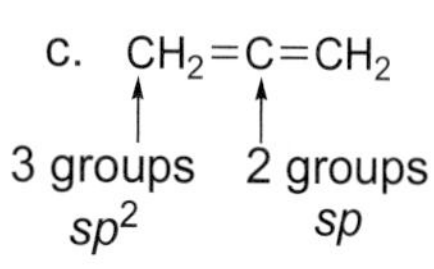

1.30 All single bonds are σ. Multiple bonds contain one σ bond, and all others are π bonds.

All C–H bonds are σ bonds.

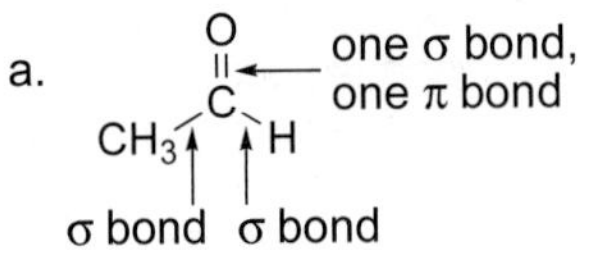
a.
one σ bond,
one π bond
σ bond σ bond

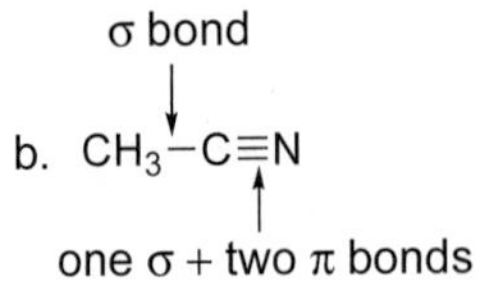
σ bond
b. CH_3–C≡N
one σ + two π bonds

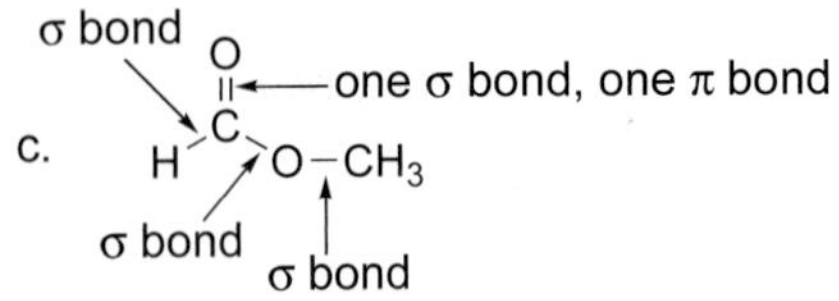
c.
σ bond
one σ bond, one π bond
σ bond
σ bond

1.31 Single bonds are weaker and longer than double bonds, which are weaker and longer than triple bonds. **Increasing percent *s*-character increases bond strength and decreases bond length.**

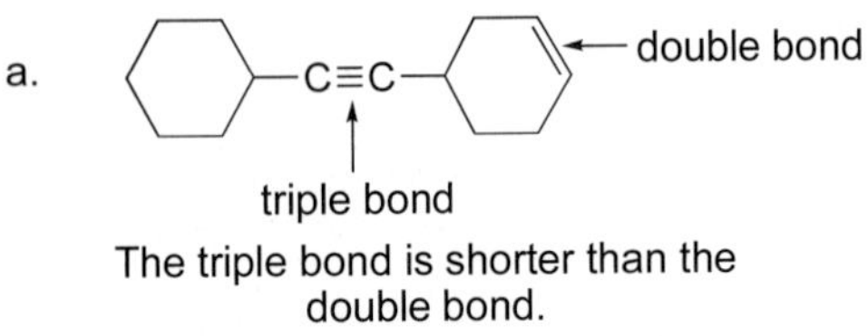
a.
double bond
triple bond
The triple bond is shorter than the double bond.

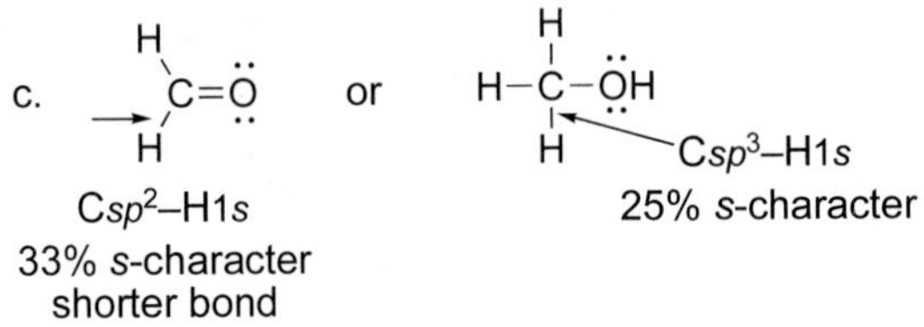
c.
or
Csp²–H1s
33% s-character
shorter bond
Csp³–H1s
25% s-character

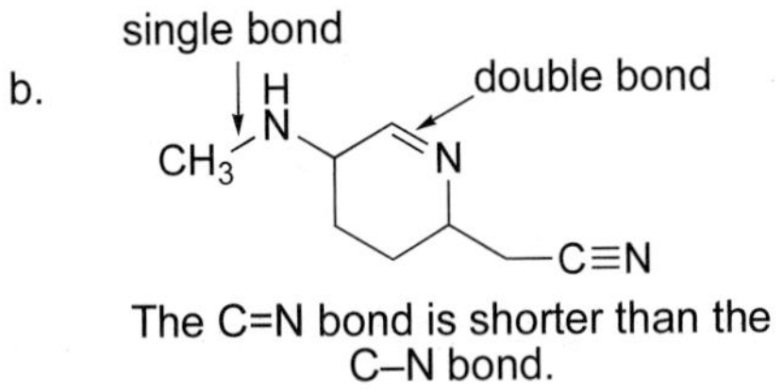
b.
single bond
double bond
The C=N bond is shorter than the C–N bond.

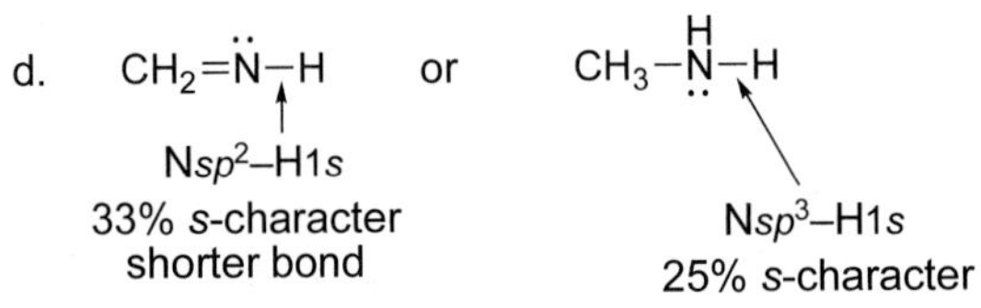
d.
or
Nsp²–H1s
33% s-character
shorter bond
Nsp³–H1s
25% s-character

1.32 Electronegativity increases from left to right across a row of the periodic table and decreases down a column. Look at the relative position of the atoms to determine their relative electronegativity.

a. most electropositive: Se; most electronegative: O — Se < S < O (increasing electronegativity →)

b. most electropositive: Na; most electronegative: Cl — Na < P < Cl (increasing electronegativity →)

c. most electropositive: S; most electronegative: F — S < Cl < F (increasing electronegativity →)

d. most electropositive: P; most electronegative: O — P < N < O (increasing electronegativity →)

1.33 Dipoles result from unequal sharing of electrons in covalent bonds. More electronegative atoms "pull" electron density towards them, making a dipole. **Dipole arrows point towards the atom of higher electron density.**

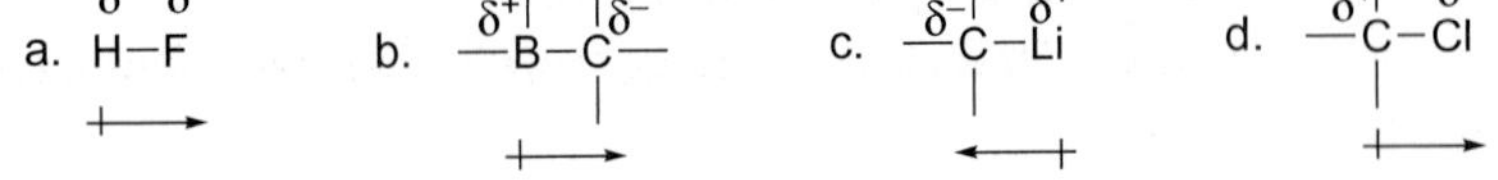
a. H–F
b.
c.
d.

1.34 Polar molecules result from a net dipole. To determine polarity, draw the molecule in three dimensions around any polar bonds, draw in the dipoles, and look to see whether the dipoles cancel or reinforce.

a.

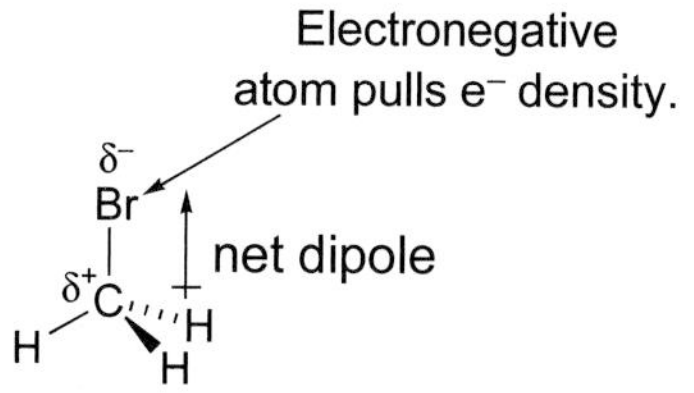

All C–H bonds have no dipole.
one polar bond
net dipole = **polar molecule**

c.

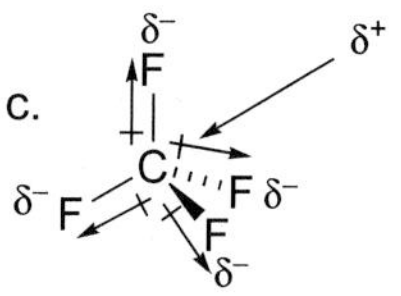

no resulting dipole =
nonpolar molecule

Four polar bonds cancel.

b.

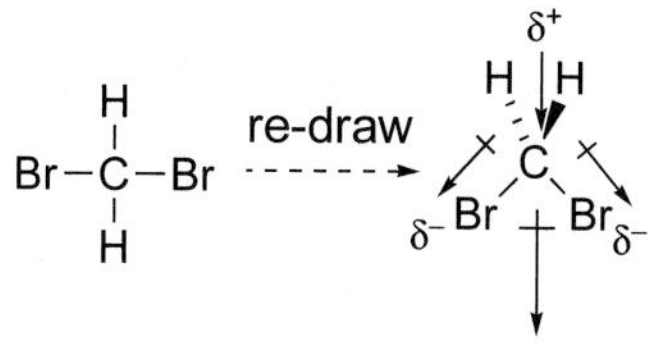

resulting dipole =
polar molecule

d.

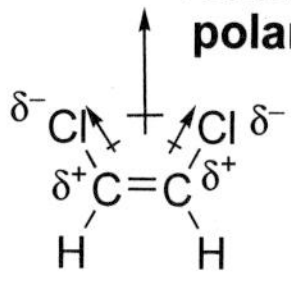

resulting dipole =
polar molecule

Note: You must draw the molecule in three dimensions to observe the net dipole. In the Lewis structure, it appears the dipoles would cancel out, when in fact they add to make a polar molecule.

e.

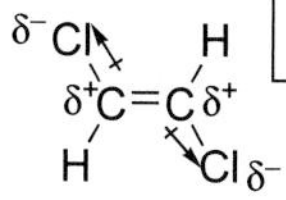

no resulting dipole =
nonpolar molecule

Two polar bonds are
equal and opposite
and cancel.

1.35

a. The two circled C's are *sp*^{3} hybridized.

b. All the C–H bonds are nonpolar. All H's bonded to O and N bear a partial positive charge (δ^+).

c.

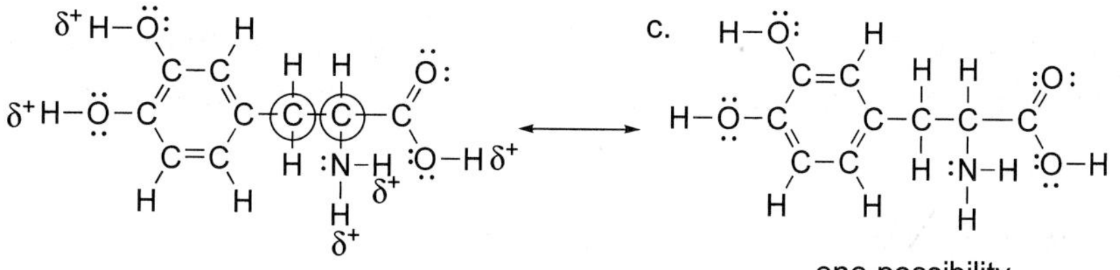

one possibility

1.36

a.

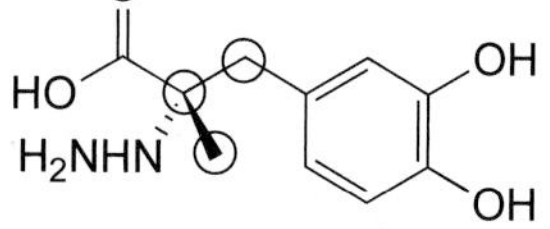

skeletal structure

b. Circled carbons are *sp*^{3} hybridized. All others are *sp*^{2} hybridized.

c. Each N is surrounded by three atoms and a lone pair, making it *sp*^{3} hybridized and trigonal pyramidal in molecular shape.

d.

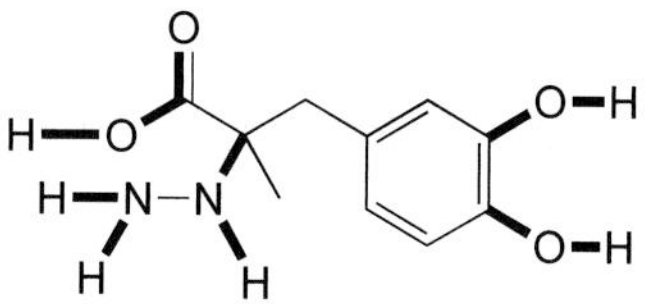

11 polar bonds shown in bold

1.37

a, b, c.

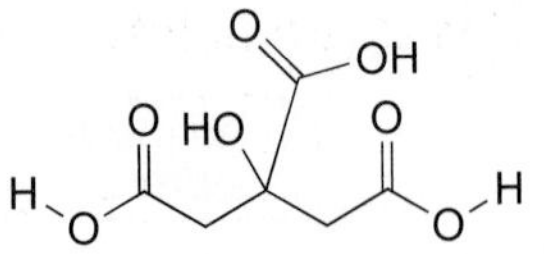

$C_6H_8O_7$

14 lone pairs, 2 lone pairs on each O

d. Each C that is part of a C=O is sp^2 hybridized, so there are three sp^2 C's.

e. Orbitals:

[1] C=O, Csp^2–Osp^2 and Cp–Op
[2] C–C, Csp^3–Csp^2
[3] O–H, Osp^3–H1s
[4] C–O, Csp^3–Osp^3

1.38

a, b, c.

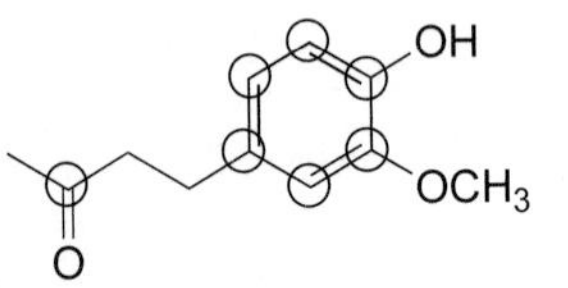

$C_{11}H_{14}O_3$

6 lone pairs, 2 lone pairs on each O

d. The sp^2 hybridized C's (seven) are labeled with circles.

e. Orbitals:

[1] C–C, Csp^3–Csp^2
[2] C–C, Csp^3–Csp^3
[3] C–H, Csp^3–H1s
[4] C–H, Csp^2– H1s

1.39 Use the definitions in Answer 1.1.

	Iodine-123	Iodine-131
a. number of protons = atomic number for I = 53	53	53
b. number of neutrons = mass number – atomic number	70	78
c. number of electrons = number of protons	53	53
d. The group number is the same for all isotopes.	7A	7A

1.40 Use bonding rules in Answer 1.2.

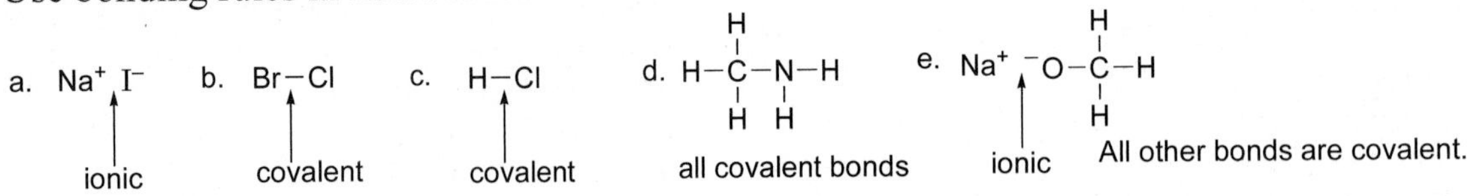
a. Na⁺ I⁻
ionic
b. Br–Cl
covalent
c. H–Cl
covalent
d.
all covalent bonds
e. Na⁺ ⁻O–
ionic
All other bonds are covalent.

1.41 **Formal charge** (FC) = number of valence electrons – [number of unshared electrons + (½)(number of shared electrons)]. C is in group 4A.

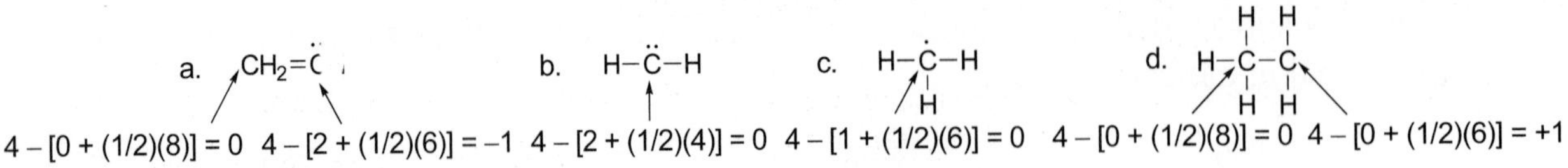
4 – [0 + (1/2)(8)] = 0
4 – [2 + (1/2)(6)] = –1
4 – [2 + (1/2)(4)] = 0
4 – [1 + (1/2)(6)] = 0
4 – [0 + (1/2)(8)] = 0
4 – [0 + (1/2)(6)] = +1

1.42 Formal charge (FC) = number of valence electrons – [number of unshared electrons + (½)(number of shared electrons)]. N is in group 5A and O is in group 6A.

a. 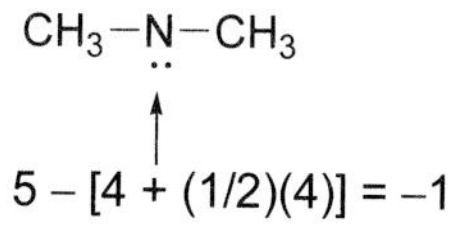
CH_3–N–CH_3
5 – [4 + (1/2)(4)] = –1

c. 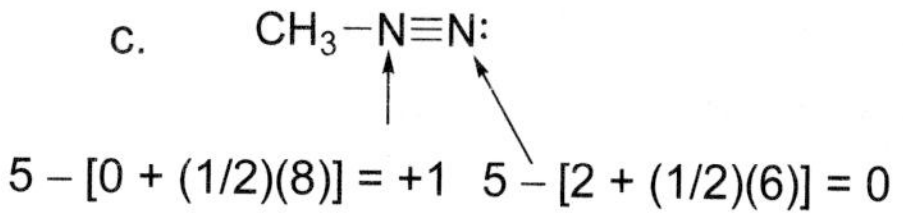
CH_3–N≡N:
5 – [0 + (1/2)(8)] = +1
5 – [2 + (1/2)(6)] = 0

e. 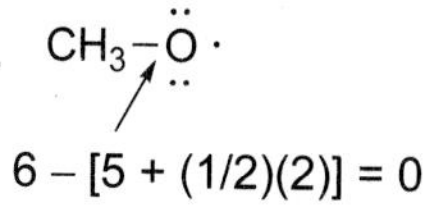
CH_3–O·
6 – [5 + (1/2)(2)] = 0

b. 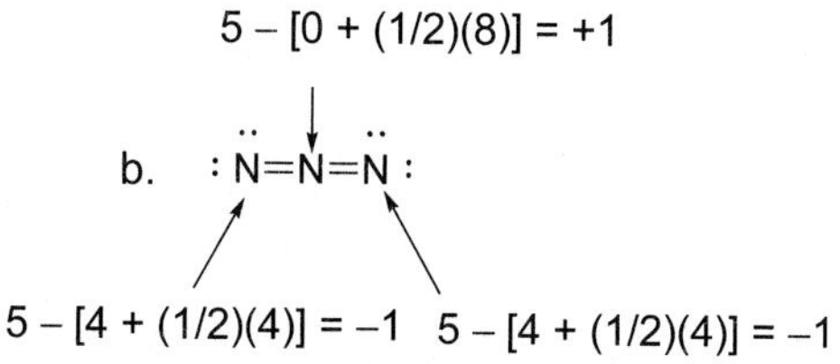
5 – [0 + (1/2)(8)] = +1
:N=N=N:
5 – [4 + (1/2)(4)] = –1
5 – [4 + (1/2)(4)] = –1

d. 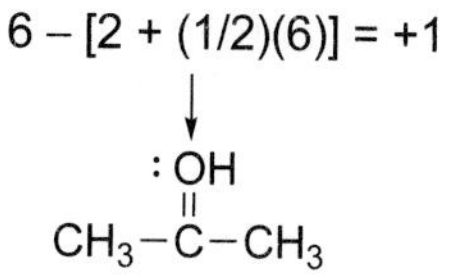
6 – [2 + (1/2)(6)] = +1
:OH
CH_3–C–CH_3

f. 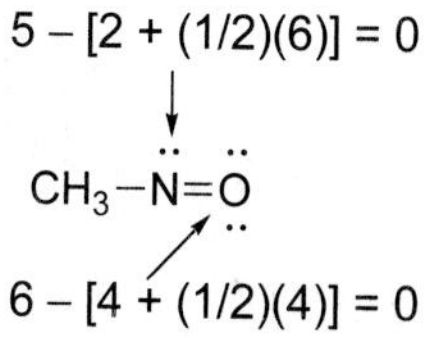
5 – [2 + (1/2)(6)] = 0
CH_3–N=O
6 – [4 + (1/2)(4)] = 0

1.43 Follow the steps in Answer 1.4 to draw Lewis structures.

a. CH_2N_2

valence e⁻	
1C x 4 e⁻ =	4
2H x 1 e⁻ =	2
2N x 5 e⁻ =	10
total e⁻ =	16

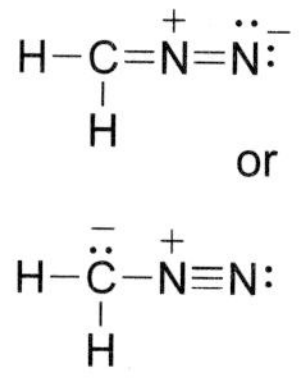
or

d. HCO_2^-

valence e⁻	
1C x 4 e⁻ =	4
1H x 1 e⁻ =	1
2O x 6 e⁻ =	12
1 for (–) charge =	1
total e⁻ =	18

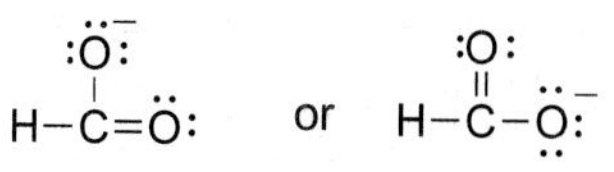
or

b. CH_3NO_2

valence e⁻	
1C x 4 e⁻ =	4
3H x 1 e⁻ =	3
1N x 5 e⁻ =	5
2O x 6 e⁻ =	12
total e⁻ =	24

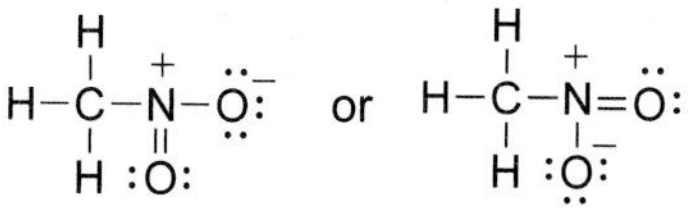
or

e. HCO_3^-

valence e⁻	
1C x 4 e⁻ =	4
1H x 1 e⁻ =	1
3O x 6 e⁻ =	18
1 for (–) charge =	1
total e⁻ =	24

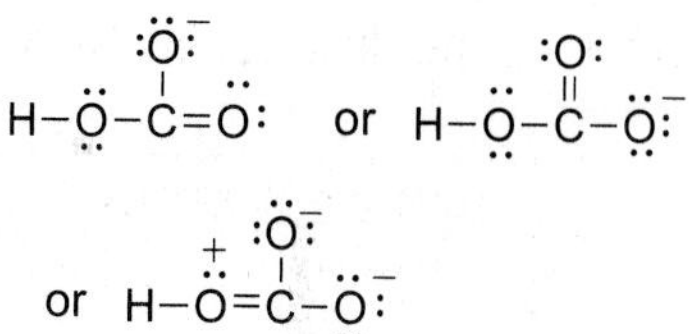
or
or

c. CH_3CNO

valence e⁻	
2C x 4 e⁻ =	8
3H x 1 e⁻ =	3
1N x 5 e⁻ =	5
1O x 6 e⁻ =	6
total e⁻ =	22

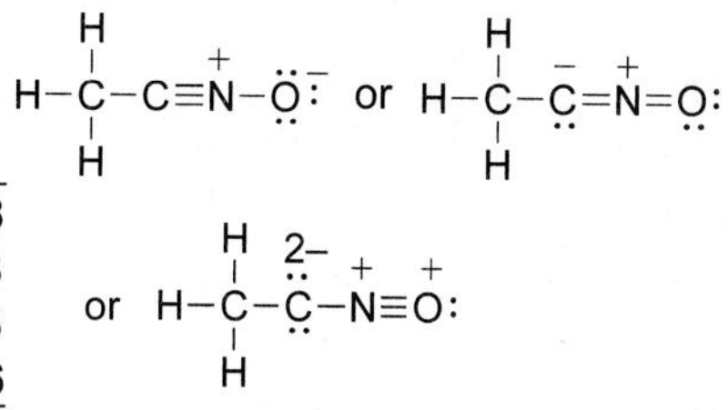
or
or

f. $^-CH_2CN$

valence e⁻	
2C x 4 e⁻ =	8
2H x 1 e⁻ =	2
1N x 5 e⁻ =	5
1 for (–) charge =	1
total e⁻ =	16

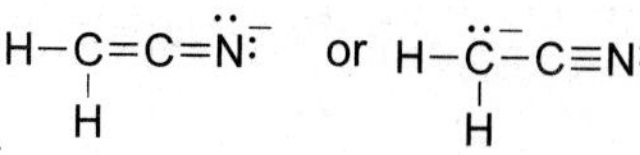
or

1.44 Follow the steps in Answer 1.4 to draw Lewis structures.

a. N_2

[1] N N

[2] Count valence e⁻.

2N x 5 e⁻ =	10
total e⁻ =	10

[3] N–N → :N≡N:

2 e⁻ used. Complete N octets.

b. $(CH_3OH_2)^+$ [1]
H
H C O H
H H

[2] Count valence e⁻.
1C x 4 e⁻ = 4
5H x 1 e⁻ = 5
1O x 6 e⁻ = 6
total e⁻ = 15
Subtract 1 for (+) charge = 14

[3] 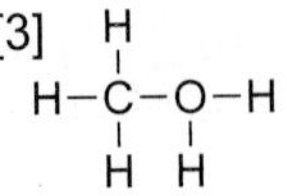
12 e⁻ used.

[4] 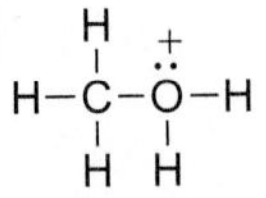
Add charge and lone pair.

c. $(CH_3CH_2)^-$ [1]
H
H C C H
H H

[2] Count valence e⁻.
2C x 4 e⁻ = 8
5H x 1 e⁻ = 5
total e⁻ = 13
Add 1 for (–) charge = 14

[3] 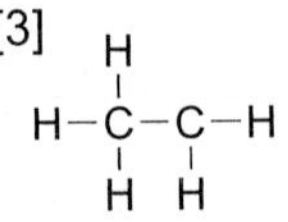
12 e⁻ used.

[4] 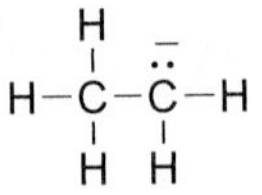
Add charge and lone pair.

d. HNNH [1] H N N H

[2] Count valence e⁻.
2H x 1 e⁻ = 2
2N x 5 e⁻ = 10
total e⁻ = 12

[3] H–N–N–H ⟶ H–N̈=N̈–H
6 e⁻ used.
Complete N octets.

e. H_6BN [1]
H H
H B N H
H H

[2] Count valence e⁻.
1B x 3 e⁻ = 3
6H x 1 e⁻ = 6
1N x 5 e⁻ = 5
total e⁻ = 14

[3] 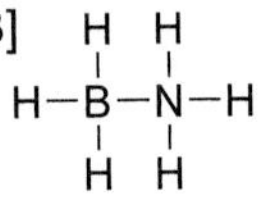
14 e⁻ used.

[4] 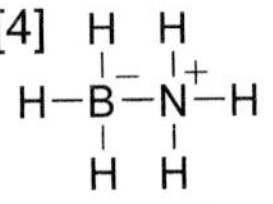
Add charges.

1.45 Follow the steps in Answer 1.4 to draw Lewis structures.

a. $(CH_3CH_2)_2O$ [1]
H H H H
H C C O C C H
H H H H

[2] Count valence e⁻.
1O x 6 e⁻ = 6
10H x 1 e⁻ = 10
4C x 4 e⁻ = 16
total e⁻ = 32

[3] 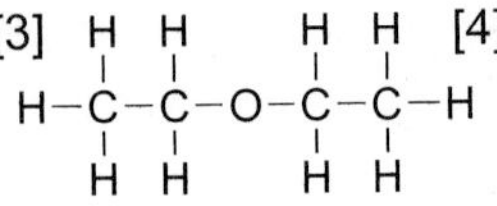
28 e⁻ used.

[4] 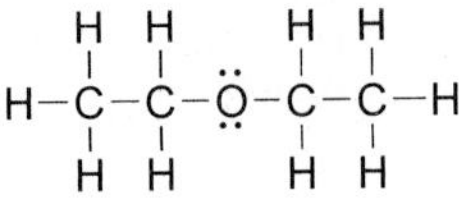
Add lone pairs.

b. CH_2CHCN [1]
H H
C C C N
H

[2] Count valence e⁻.
1N x 5 e⁻ = 5
3H x 1 e⁻ = 3
3C x 4 e⁻ = 12
total e⁻ = 20

[3] 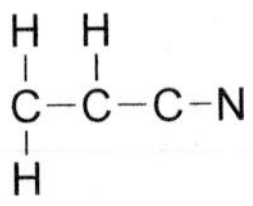
12 e⁻ used.

[4] 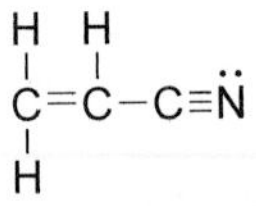
Add lone pairs and π bonds.

c. $(HOCH_2)_2CO$ [1]
H O H
H O C C C O H
H H

[2] Count valence e⁻.
3O x 6 e⁻ = 18
6H x 1 e⁻ = 6
3C x 4 e⁻ = 12
total e⁻ = 36

[3] 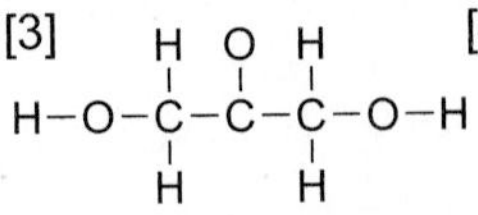
22 e⁻ used.

[4] 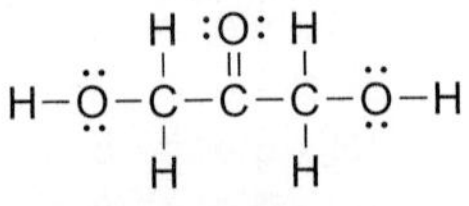
Add lone pairs and π bonds.

d. $(CH_3CO)_2O$ [1]
H O O H
H C C O C C H
H H

[2] Count valence e⁻.
3O x 6 e⁻ = 18
6H x 1 e⁻ = 6
4C x 4 e⁻ = 16
total e⁻ = 40

[3] 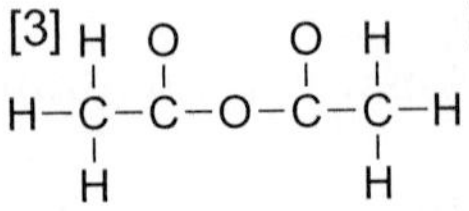
24 e⁻ used.

[4] 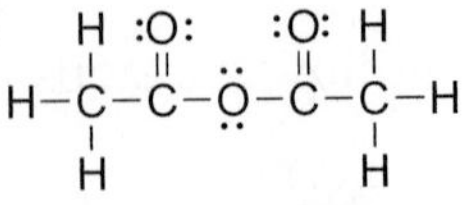
Add lone pairs and π bonds.

1.46

a.

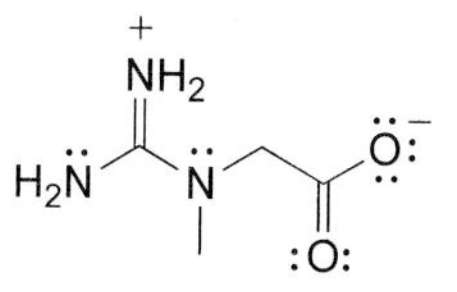

b. Two of the possible resonance structures:

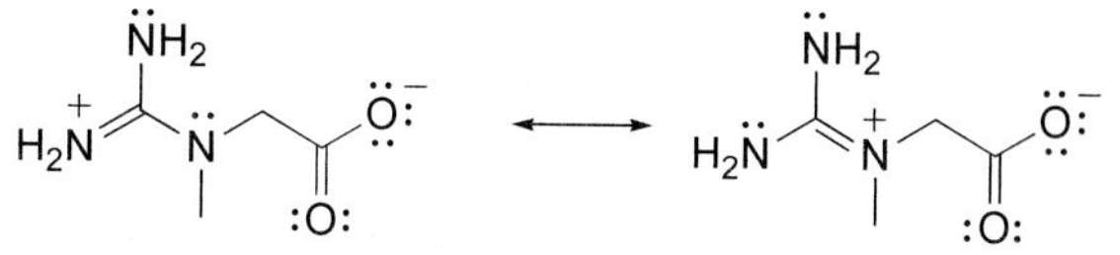

1.47 Isomers must have a different arrangement of atoms.

a. Two isomers of molecular formula C_3H_7Cl

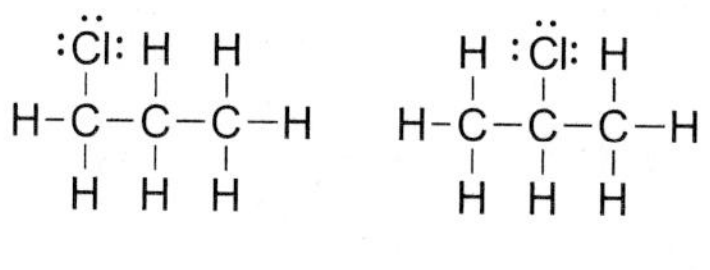

b. Three isomers of molecular formula C_2H_4O

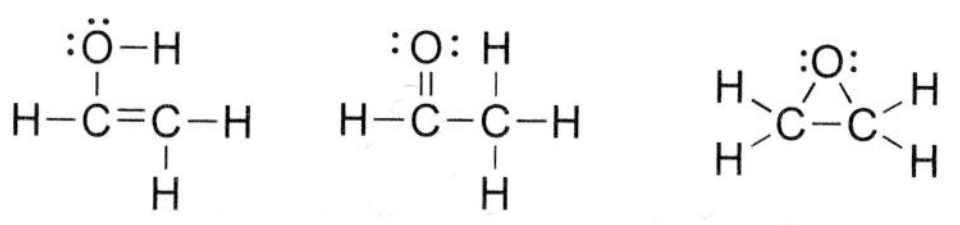

c. Four isomers of molecular formula C_3H_9N

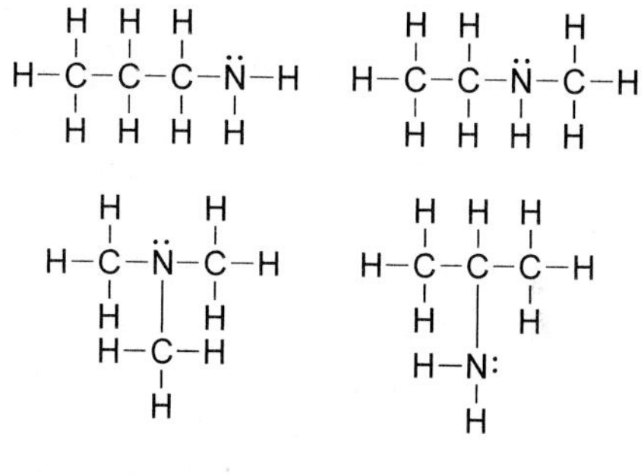

1.48

Nine isomers of C_3H_6O:

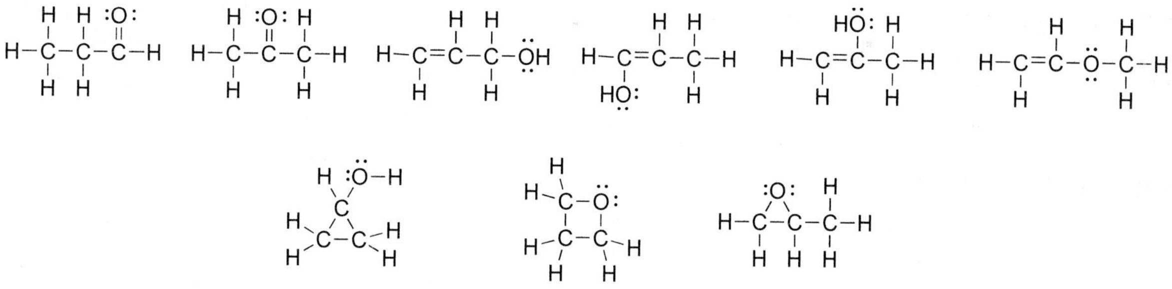

1.49 Use the definition of isomers and resonance structures in Answer 1.9.

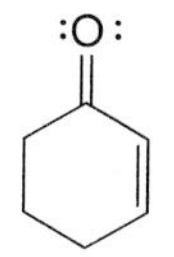

C_6H_8O

A

a.

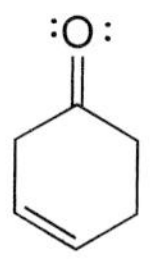

C_6H_8O
isomers

b.

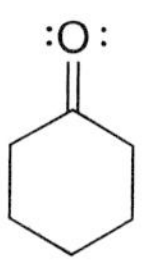

$C_6H_{10}O$
different molecular formula
neither isomers nor resonance structures

c.

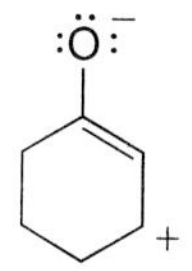

C_6H_8O
same arrangement of atoms
resonance structures

d.

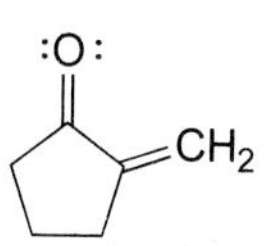

5 membered ring

C_6H_8O
different arrangement of atoms
isomers

1.50 Use the definitions of isomers and resonance structures in Answer 1.9.

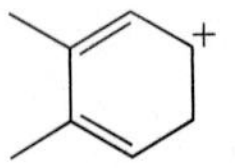

a. 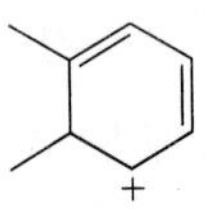

b. 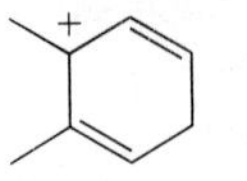

c. 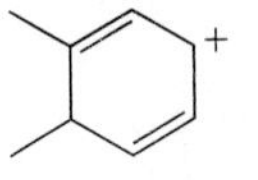

d. 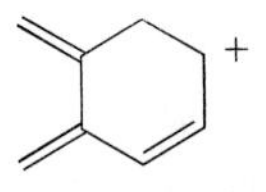

B	a.	b.	c.	d.
$(C_8H_{11})^+$	$(C_8H_{11})^+$	$(C_8H_{11})^+$	$(C_8H_{11})^+$	$(C_8H_9)^+$
B	different arrangement of atoms **isomers**	same arrangement of atoms **resonance structures**	different arrangement of atoms **isomers**	different molecular formula **neither**

1.51 Use the definitions of isomers and resonance structures in Answer 1.9.

a. 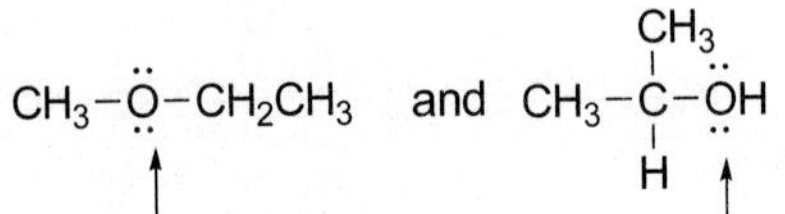

two C–O bonds; one O–H bond

Different arrangement of atoms.

Both have molecular formula C_3H_8O = **isomers**

b.  and 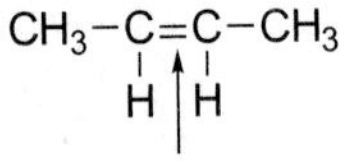

ring; double bond

Different arrangement of atoms.

Both have molecular formula C_4H_8 = **isomers**

c.  and 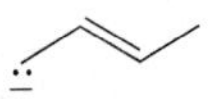

Same arrangement of atoms.

Both have molecular formula $(C_4H_7)^-$.

Different arrangement of electrons = **resonance structures**

d. $CH_3CH_2CH_3$ and $CH_3CH_2\ddot{C}H_2$

molecular formula C_3H_8 molecular formula $(C_3H_7)^-$

different molecular formulas = **neither**

1.52 Compare the resonance structures to see what electrons have "moved." **Use one curved arrow to show the movement of each electron pair.**

a. 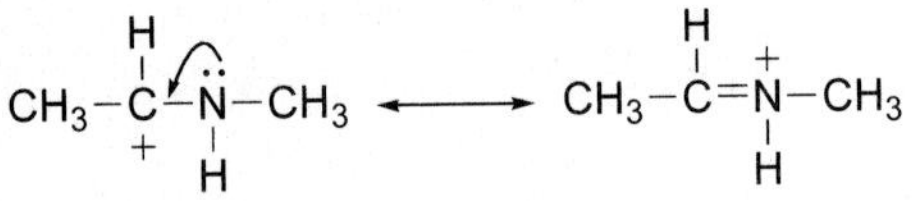

One electron pair moves = one arrow

b. 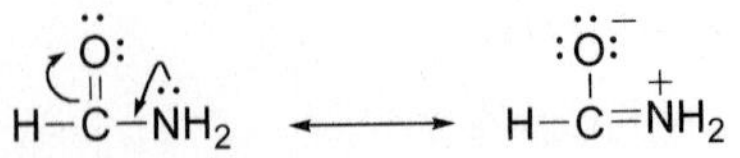

Two electron pairs move = two arrows

c. 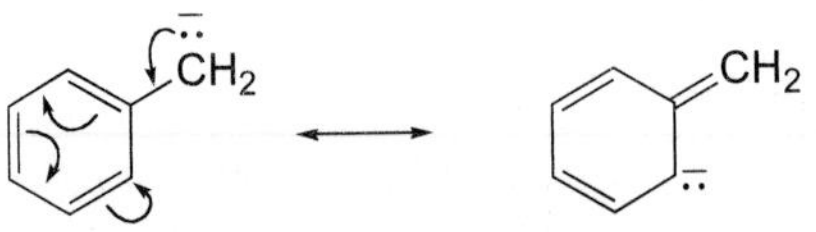

Four electron pairs move = four arrows

1.53 Curved arrow notation shows the movement of an electron pair. The tail begins at an electron pair (a bond or a lone pair) and the head points to where the electron pair moves.

a. 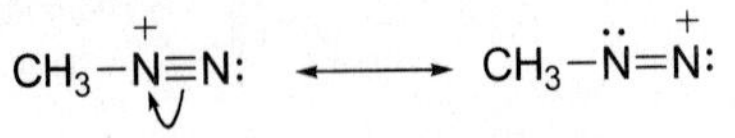

b. 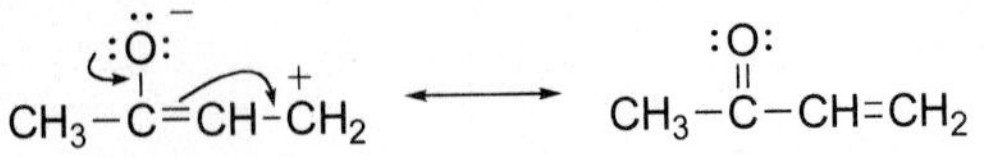

c. 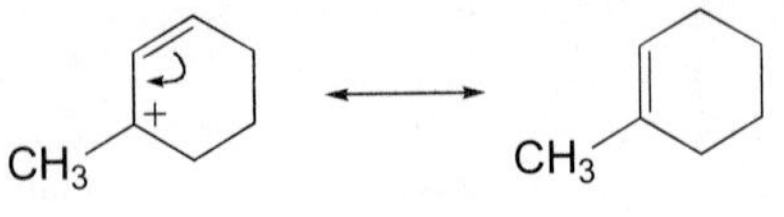

d. 

1.54 Use the rules in Answer 1.13.

a. 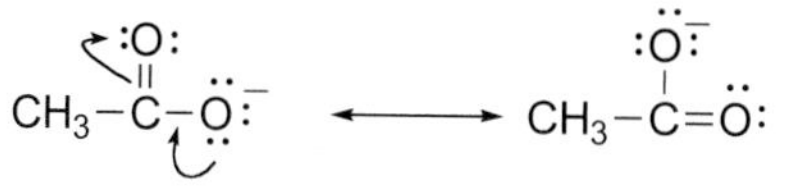

Two electron pairs move = two arrows

c. 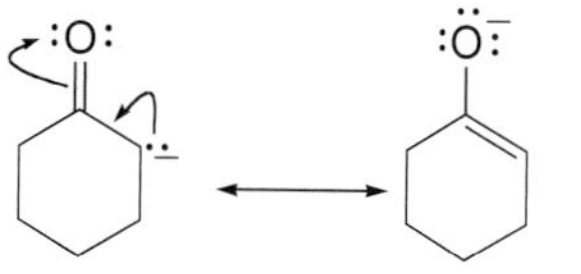

Two electron pairs move = two arrows

Charge is on both O's.

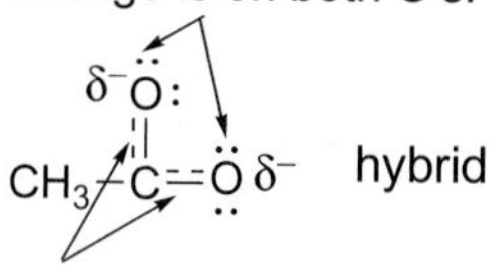

Double bond can be in 2 locations.

Charge is on both atoms.

Double bond can be in 2 locations.

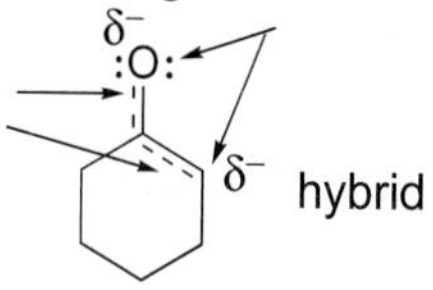

b. 

One electron pair moves = one arrow

partial double bond character

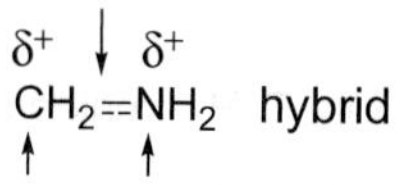

Charge is on both atoms.

d. 

One electron pair moves = one arrow

Charge is on both atoms.

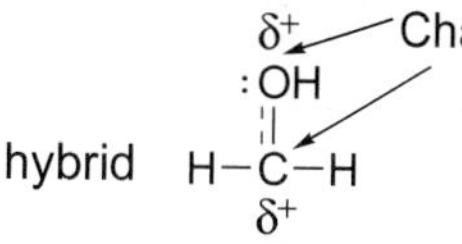

C–O bond has partial double bond character.

1.55 For the compounds where the arrangement of atoms is not given, first draw a Lewis structure. Then use the rules in Answer 1.13.

a. O_3

Count valence e^-.	
3O x 6 e^-	= 18
total e^-	= 18

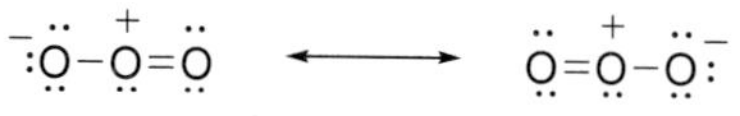

b. NO_3^- (a central N atom)

Count valence e^-.	
1N x 5 e^-	= 5
3O x 6 e^-	= 18
(–) charge	= 1
total e^-	= 24

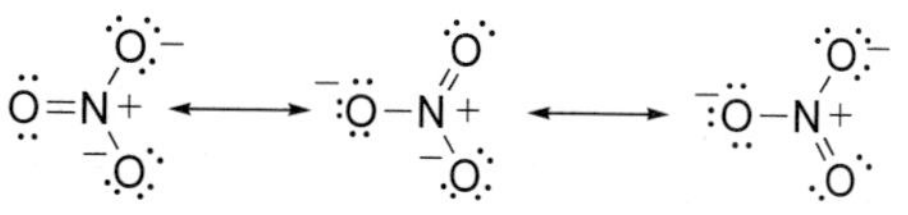

c. N_3^-

Count valence e^-.	
3N x 5 e^-	= 15
(–) charge	= 1
total e^-	= 16

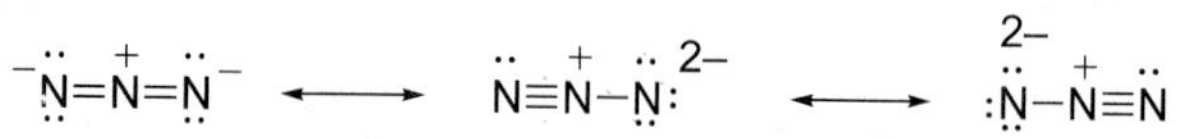

d. 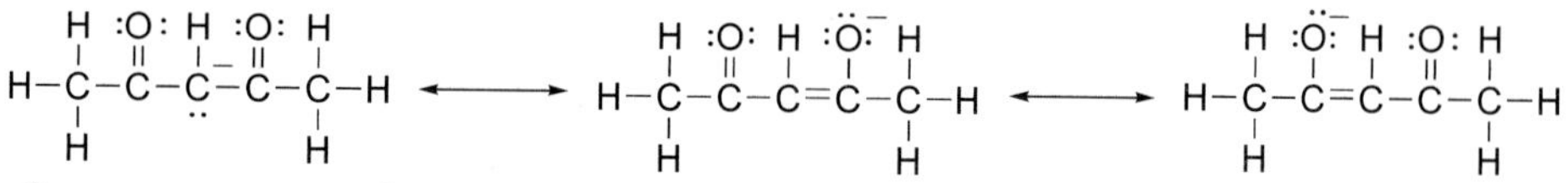

e. 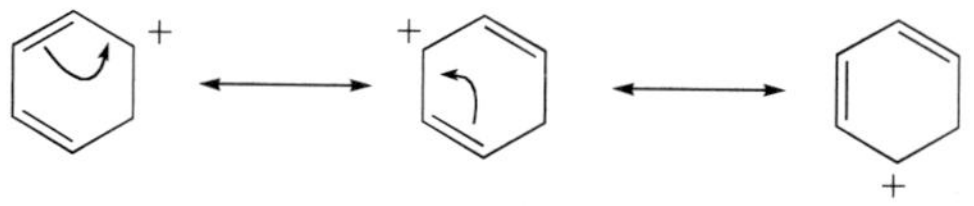

f. 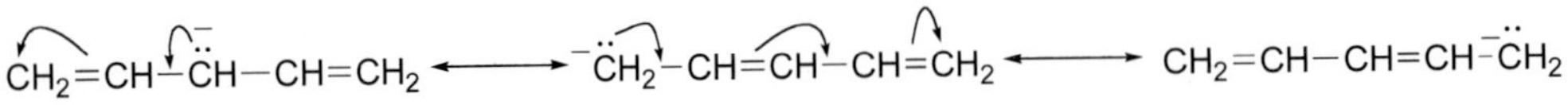

g. 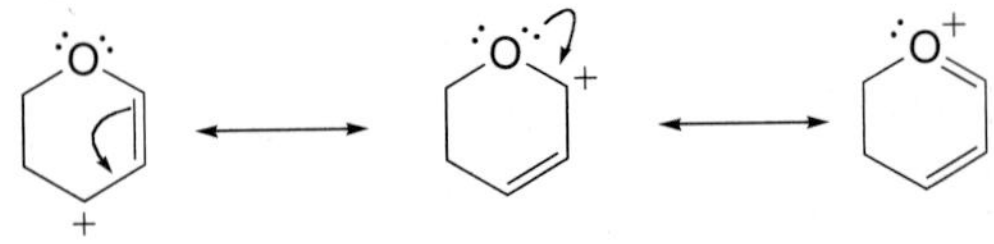

1.56 To draw the **resonance hybrid,** use the rules in Answer 1.14.

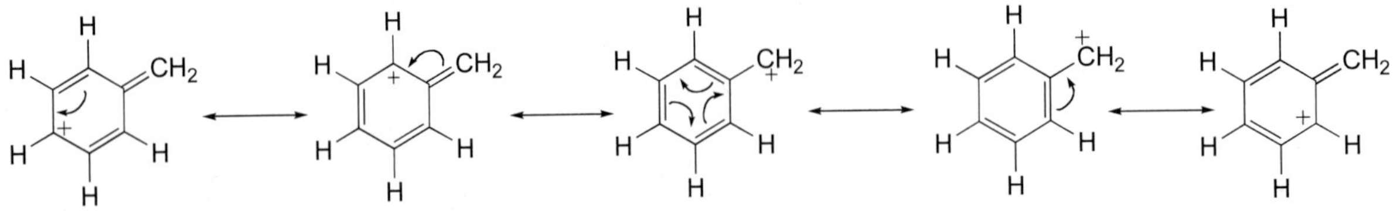

resonance hybrid

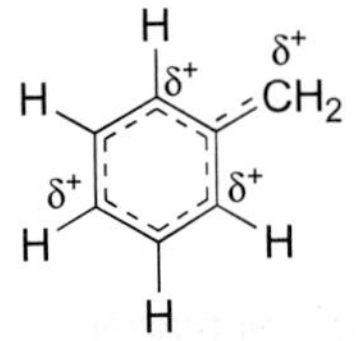

1.57 A "better" resonance structure is one that has more bonds and fewer charges. The better structure is the major contributor and all others are minor contributors.

a. 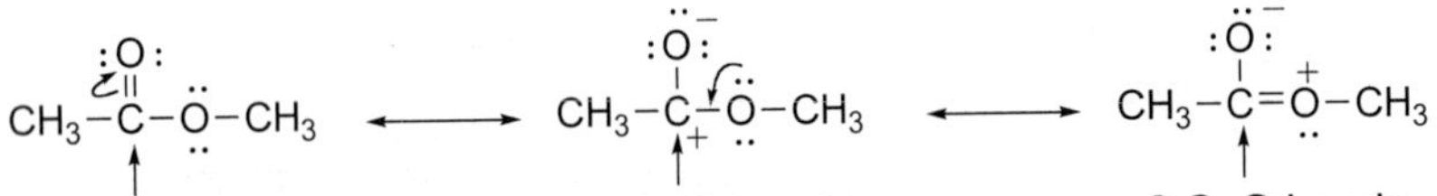

3 C–O bonds
no charges
contributes the most = **3**

2 C–O bonds
2 charges
contributes the least = **1**

3 C–O bonds
2 charges
2

b. 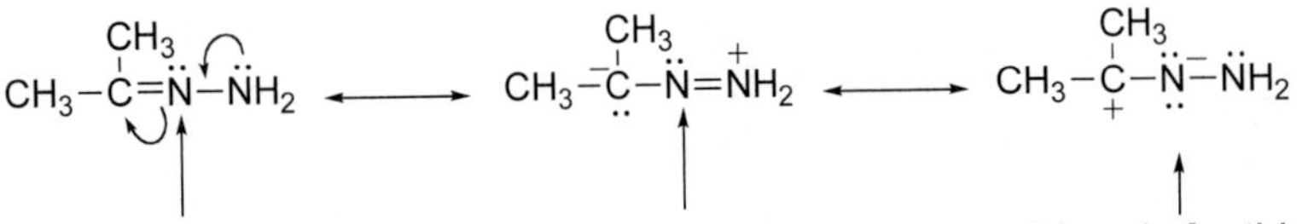

3 bonds for this N
no charges
contributes the most = **3**

3 bonds for this N
2 charges
2

2 bonds for this N
2 charges
contributes the least = **1**

1.58

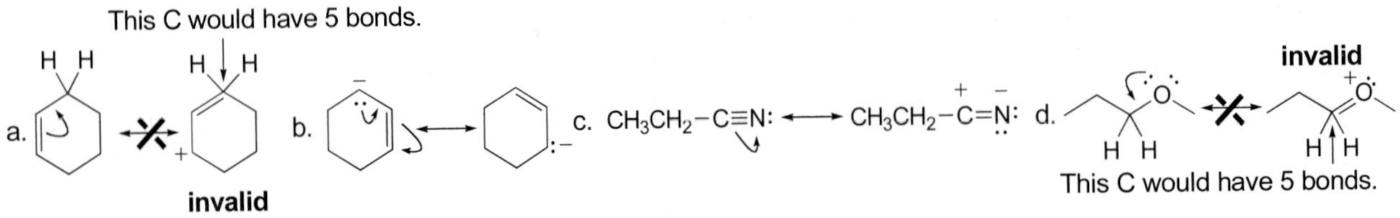
This C would have 5 bonds.
a.
invalid
b.
c. CH3CH2–C≡N: ⟷ CH3CH2–C=N:
d.
invalid
This C would have 5 bonds.

[Note: The pentavalent C's in (a) and (d) bear a (–1) formal charge.]

1.59 Use the rules in Answer 1.18.

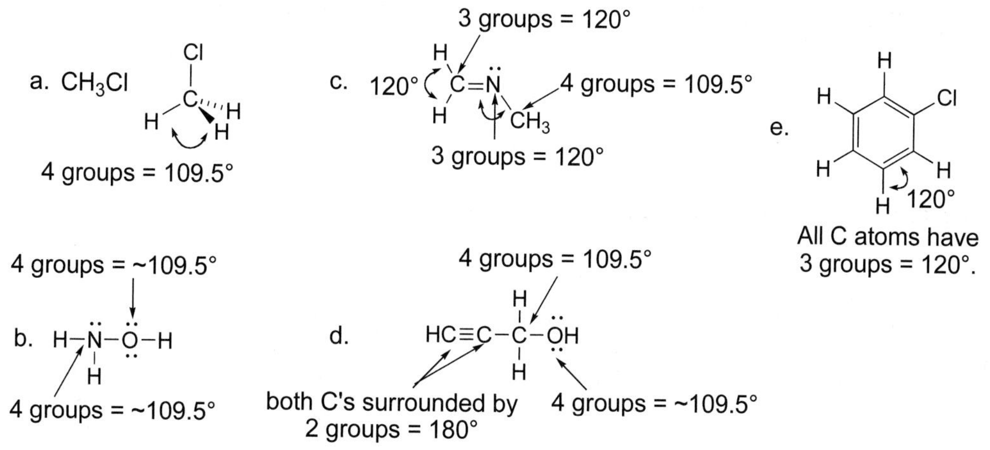

a. CH_3Cl
4 groups = 109.5°
c.
3 groups = 120°
120°
4 groups = 109.5°
3 groups = 120°
e.
All C atoms have
3 groups = 120°.
120°
b.
4 groups = ~109.5°
4 groups = ~109.5°
d.
4 groups = 109.5°
both C's surrounded by
2 groups = 180°
4 groups = ~109.5°

1.60 To predict the geometry around an atom, use the rules in Answer 1.17.

a. $CH_3CH_2CH_2CH_3$
4 groups
(4 atoms)
tetrahedral

b. $(CH_3)_2N^{-}$
4 groups
(2 atoms, 2 lone pairs)
tetrahedral
(bent molecular shape)

c. 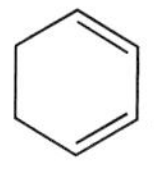
3 groups
(3 atoms)
trigonal planar

d. BF_4^-
4 groups
(4 atoms)
tetrahedral

e. $CH_3-C(=O)-OH$
3 groups
(3 atoms)
trigonal planar

f. $(CH_3)_3N$
4 groups
(3 atoms, 1 lone pair)
tetrahedral
(trigonal pyramidal molecular shape)

1.61 Each C has two bonds in the plane of the page, one in front of the page (solid wedge) and one behind the page (dashed line).

$CF_3CHClBr$

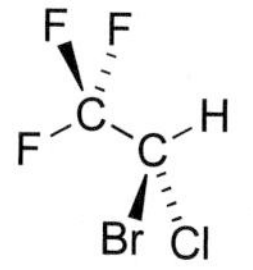

F
F
F
C
C
H
Br
Cl

1.62 In shorthand or skeletal drawings, **all line junctions or ends of lines represent carbon atoms.** The C's are all tetravalent. All H's bonded to C's are drawn in the following structures. C's labeled with (*) have no H's bonded to them.

a. 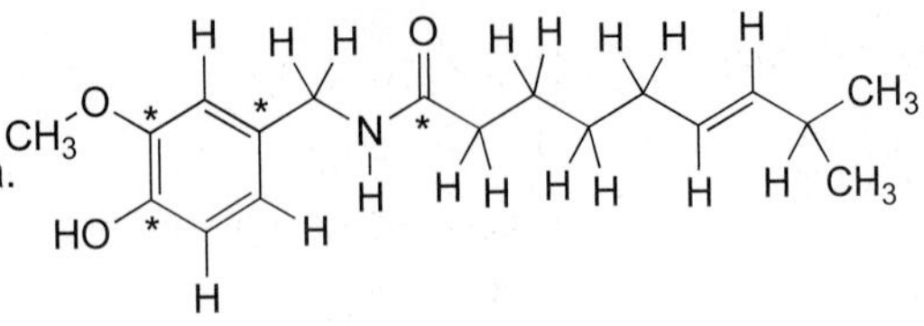

b. 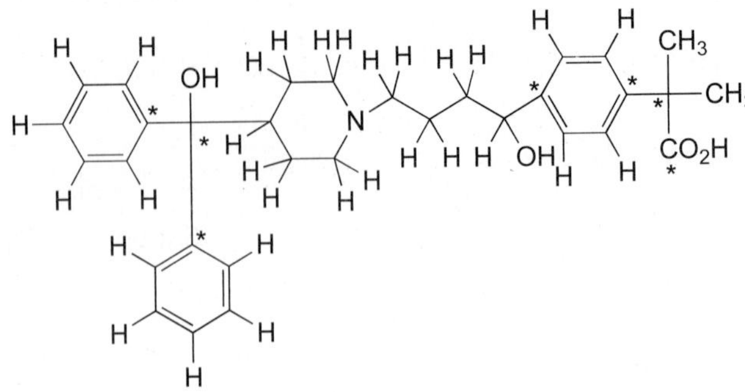

1.63 In shorthand or skeletal drawings, **all line junctions or ends of lines represent carbon atoms.** Convert by writing in all C's, and then adding H's to make the C's tetravalent.

a. 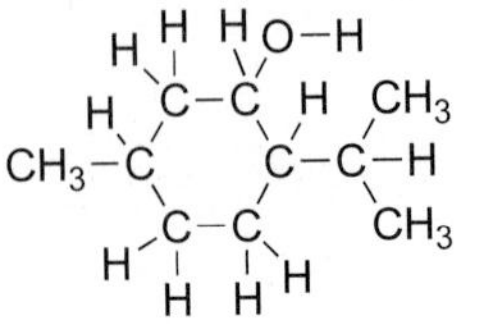

menthol
(isolated from peppermint oil)

b. 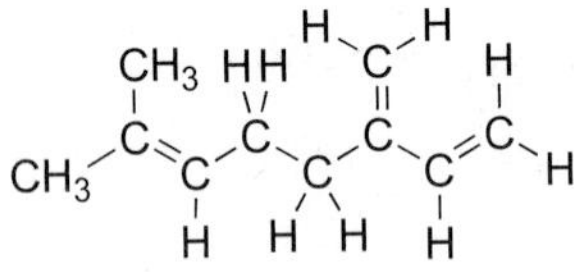

myrcene
(isolated from bayberry)

c. 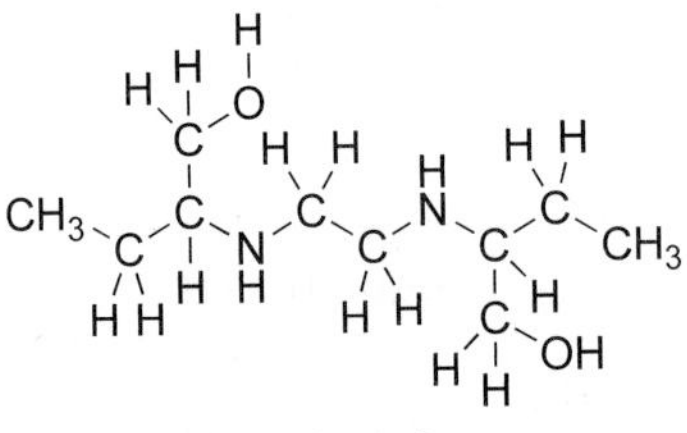

ethambutol
(drug used to treat tuberculosis)

d. 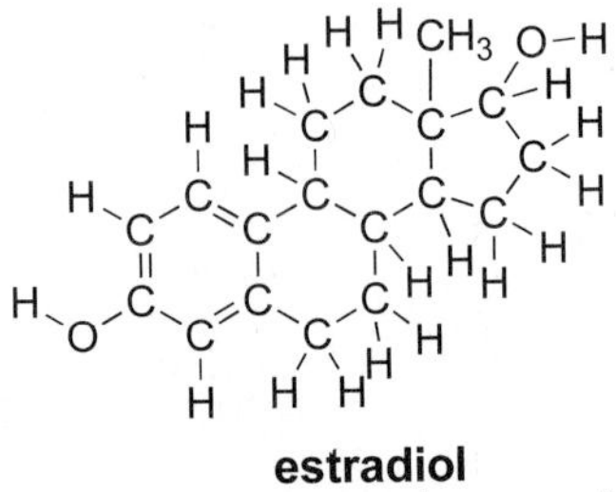

estradiol
(a female sex hormone)

1.64 In skeletal formulas, leave out all C's and H's, except H's bonded to heteroatoms.

a. $(CH_3)_2CHCH_2CH_2CH(CH_3)_2$

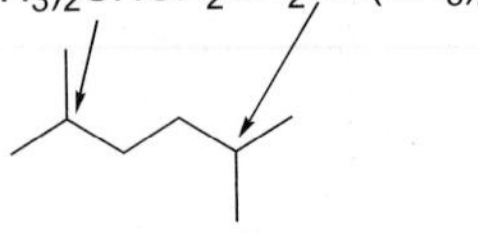

b. $CH_3CH(Cl)CH(OH)CH_3$

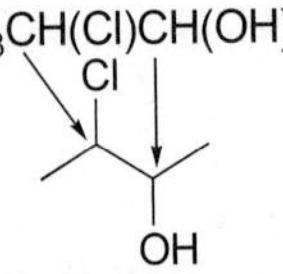

c. $(CH_3)_3C(CH_2)_5CH_3$

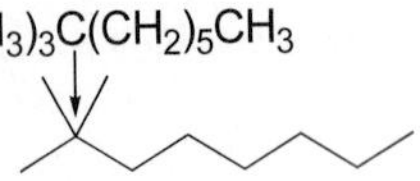

d. 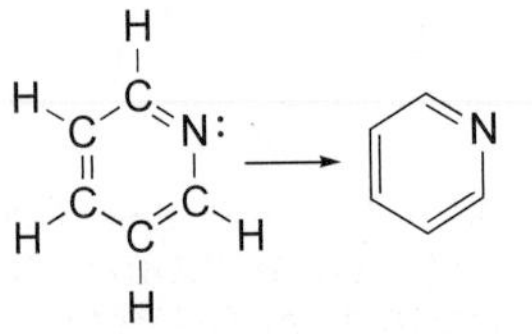

e. 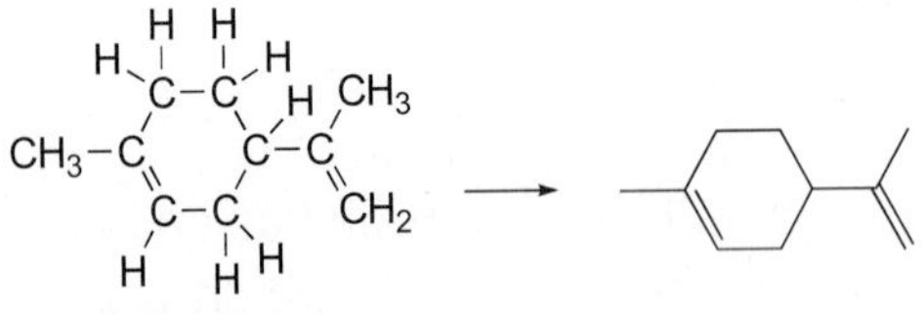

limonene
(oil of lemon)

f. $CH_3(CH_2)_2C(CH_3)_2CH(CH_3)CH(CH_3)CH(Br)CH_3$

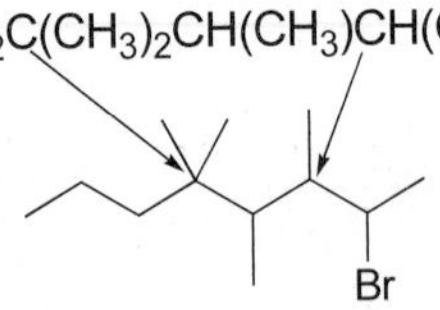

1.65 For Lewis structures, all atoms including H's and all lone pairs must be drawn in.

a. CH_3CH_2COOH

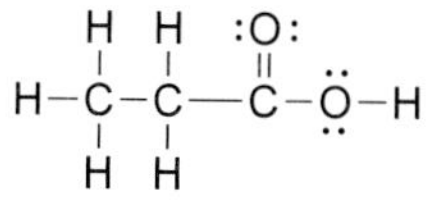

c. CH_3COCH_2Br

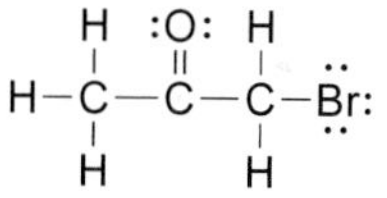

e. $(CH_3)_3CCHO$

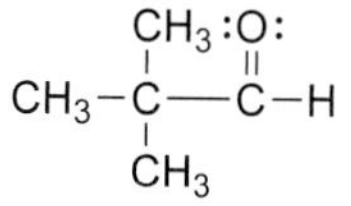

g. $CH_3COCH_2CO_2H$

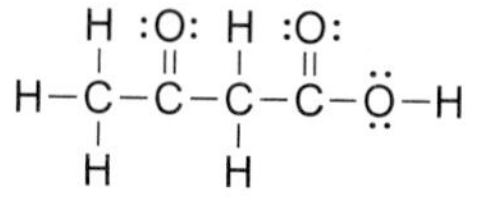

b. $CH_3CONHCH_3$

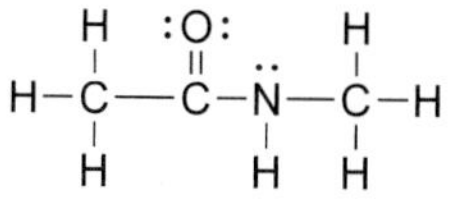

d. $(CH_3)_3COH$

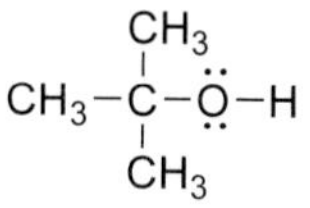

f. CH_3COCl

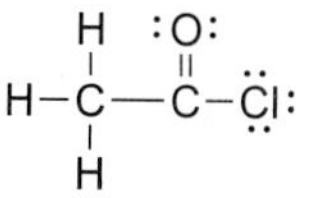

h. $HO_2CCH(OH)CO_2H$

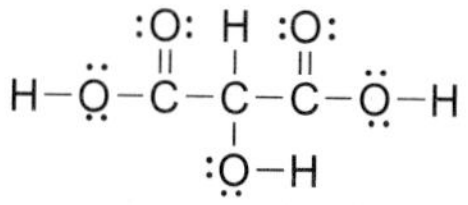

1.66 A charge on a C atom takes the place of one H atom. A negatively charged C has one lone pair, and a positively charged C has none.

a. 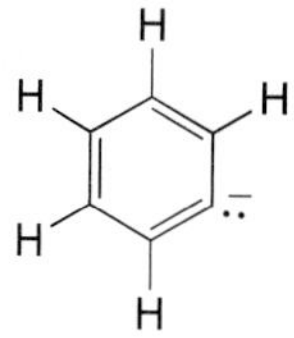

b. 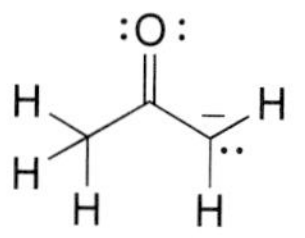

c. 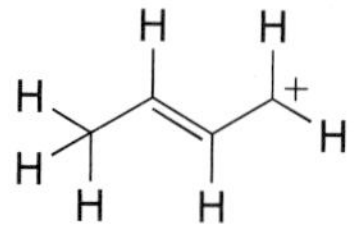

d. 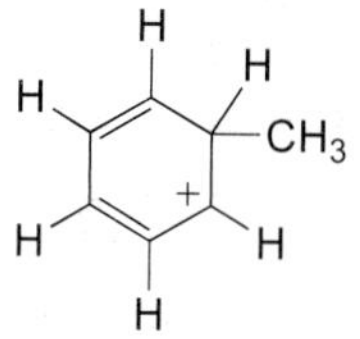

1.67

a. 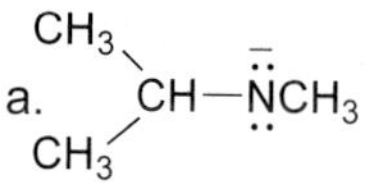

b. 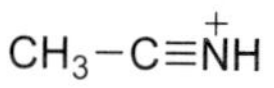

c. 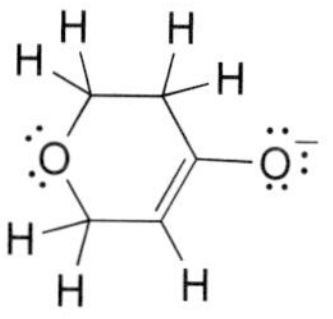

d. 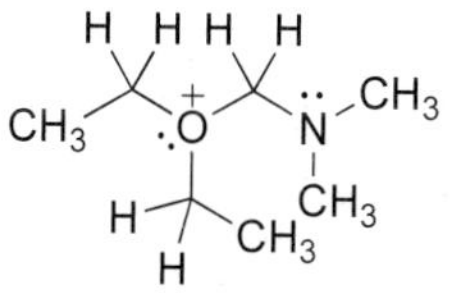

1.68 Examine each structure to determine the error.

a. $CH_3CH=CH=CHCH_3$

This C has 5 bonds.

b. $(CH_3)_3CHCH_2CH_2CH_3$

This C has 5 bonds.

c. 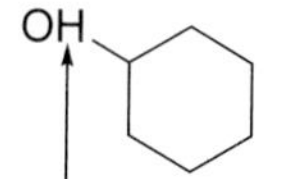

This H has 2 bonds. It should be HO–.

d. 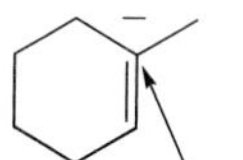

This C has 4 bonds. The negative charge means a lone pair, which gives C 10 electrons.

e. 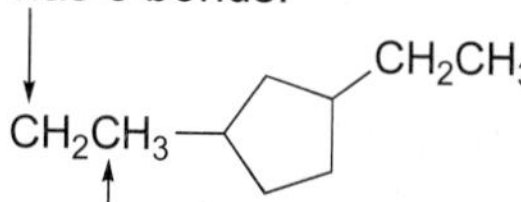

This C has 3 bonds.

This C has 5 bonds. It should be CH_3CH_2–.

1.69 To determine the hybridization around the labeled atoms, use the procedure in Answer 1.29.

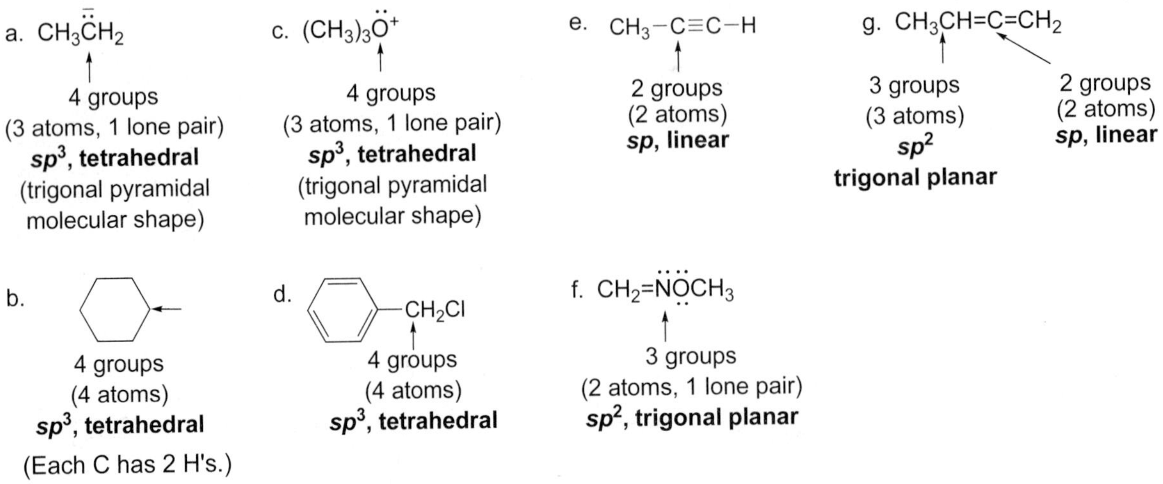
a. $CH_3\ddot{C}H_2$
4 groups
(3 atoms, 1 lone pair)
sp^3, tetrahedral
(trigonal pyramidal
molecular shape)
c. $(CH_3)_3\ddot{O}^+$
4 groups
(3 atoms, 1 lone pair)
sp^3, tetrahedral
(trigonal pyramidal
molecular shape)
e. $CH_3-C\equiv C-H$
2 groups
(2 atoms)
sp, linear
g. $CH_3CH=C=CH_2$
3 groups
(3 atoms)
sp^2
trigonal planar
2 groups
(2 atoms)
sp, linear
b.
4 groups
(4 atoms)
sp^3, tetrahedral
(Each C has 2 H's.)
d.
CH_2Cl
4 groups
(4 atoms)
sp^3, tetrahedral
f. $CH_2=\ddot{N}\ddot{O}CH_3$
3 groups
(2 atoms, 1 lone pair)
sp^2, trigonal planar

1.70 To determine what orbitals are involved in bonding, use the procedure in Answer 1.27.

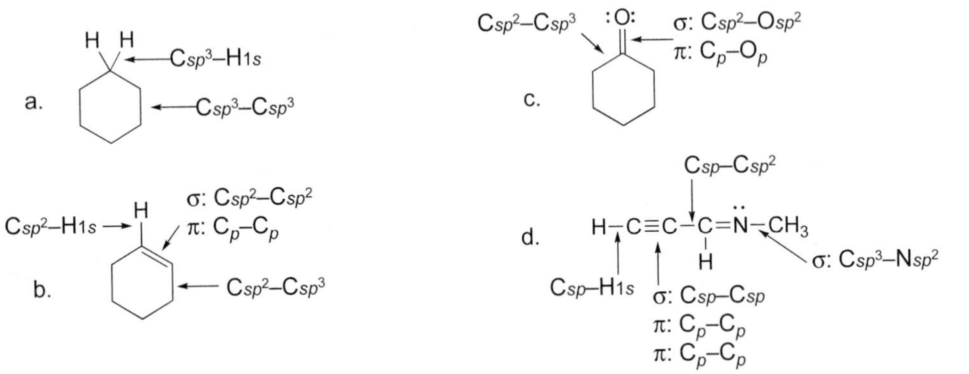
a.
H H
Csp^3–$H1s$
Csp^3–Csp^3
b.
Csp^2–$H1s$
H
σ: Csp^2–Csp^2
π: C_p–C_p
Csp^2–Csp^3
c.
Csp^2–Csp^3
:O:
σ: Csp^2–Osp^2
π: C_p–O_p
d.
Csp–Csp^2
H–C≡C–C=N–CH₃
H
Csp–$H1s$
σ: Csp–Csp
π: C_p–C_p
π: C_p–C_p
σ: Csp^3–Nsp^2

1.71

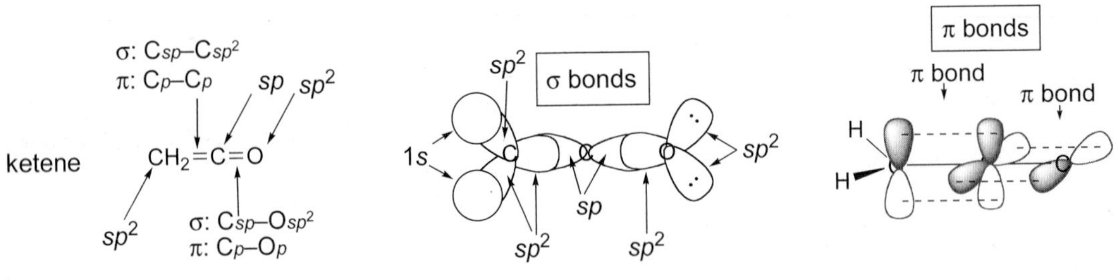
σ: Csp–Csp^2
π: Cp–Cp
sp
sp^2
ketene
$CH_2=C=O$
sp^2
σ: Csp–Osp^2
π: Cp–Op
sp^2
σ bonds
1s
sp
sp^2
sp^2
sp^2
π bonds
π bond
π bond
H
H

[For clarity, only the large bonding lobes of the hybrid orbitals are drawn.]

1.72

$CH_2=\overset{+}{C}H$
sp^2
sp
σ: Csp^2–Csp
π: Cp–Cp
$CH_2=\ddot{C}H$
sp^2
sp^2
σ: Csp^2–Csp^2
π: Cp–Cp

1.73 To determine relative bond length, use the rules in Answer 1.31.

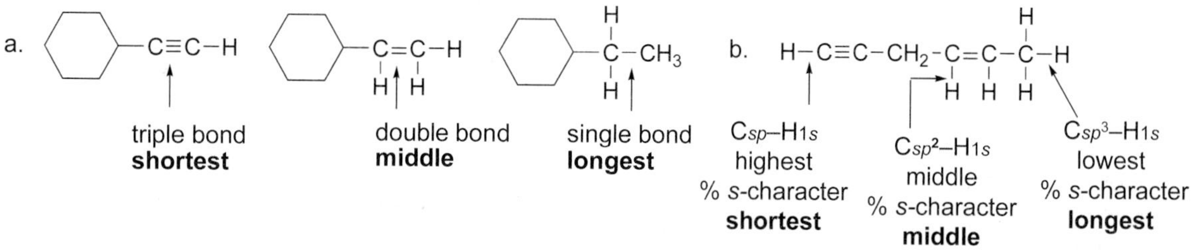
a.
C≡C–H
C=C–H
C–CH3
triple bond
shortest
double bond
middle
single bond
longest
b. H–C≡C–CH2–C=C–C–H
Csp–H1s
highest
% s-character
shortest
Csp²–H1s
middle
% s-character
middle
Csp³–H1s
lowest
% s-character
longest

1.74

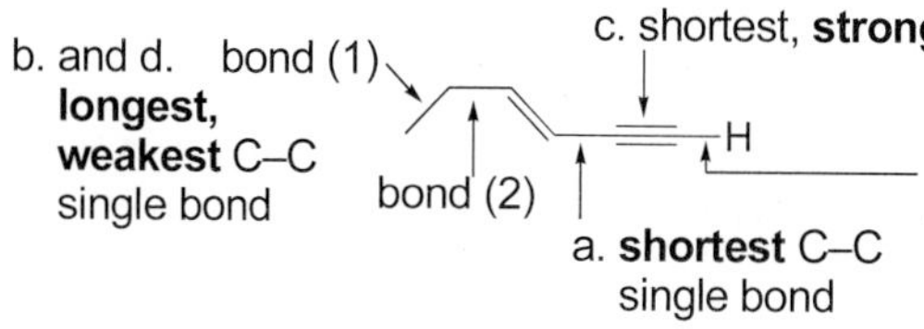
b. and d. bond (1)
longest,
weakest C–C
single bond
bond (2)
c. shortest, strongest C–C bond
H
e. strongest C–H bond
a. shortest C–C
single bond

f. Bond (1) is a C_{sp^3}–C_{sp^3} bond, and bond (2) is a C_{sp^3}–C_{sp^2} bond. Bond (2) is shorter due to the increased percent *s*-character in the sp^2 hybridized carbon.

1.75 Percent *s*-character determines the strength of a bond. **The higher percent *s*-character of an orbital used to form a bond, the stronger the bond.**

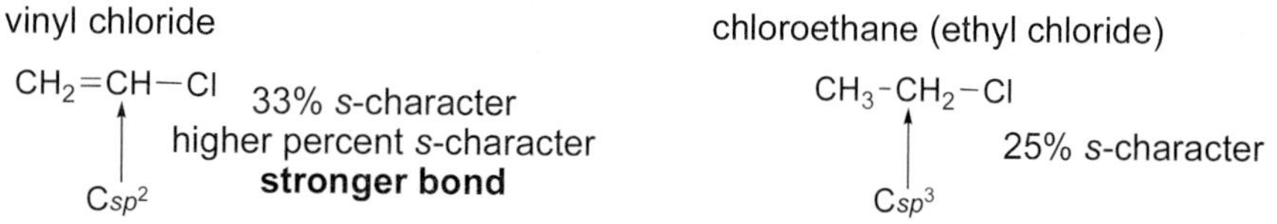
vinyl chloride
CH2=CH–Cl
33% s-character
higher percent s-character
stronger bond
Csp²
chloroethane (ethyl chloride)
CH3–CH2–Cl
25% s-character
Csp³

1.76 Dipoles result from unequal sharing of electrons in covalent bonds. More electronegative atoms "pull" electron density towards them, making a dipole.

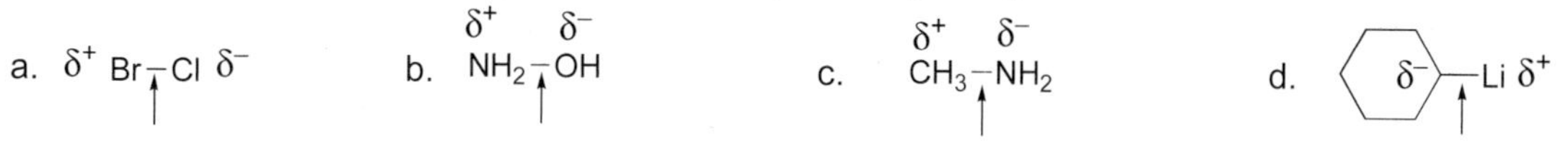
a. δ+ Br–Cl δ–
b. δ+ δ– NH2–OH
c. δ+ δ– CH3–NH2
d. δ– Li δ+

1.77 Use the directions from Answer 1.34.

a. $CHBr_3$

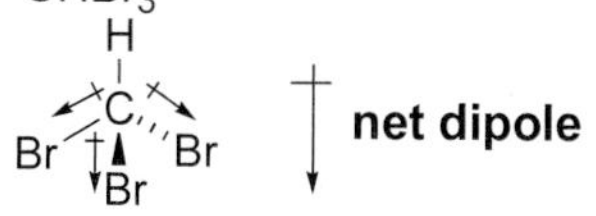
H
C
Br
Br
Br
net dipole

c. CBr_4

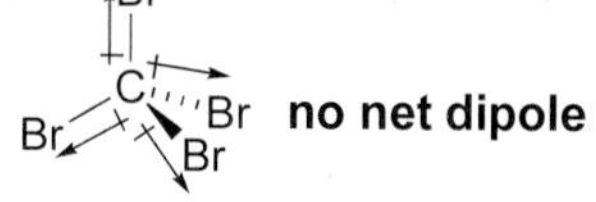
Br
C
Br
Br
Br
no net dipole

e.

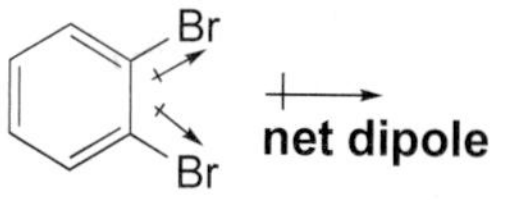
Br
Br
net dipole

b. $CH_3CH_2OCH_2CH_3$

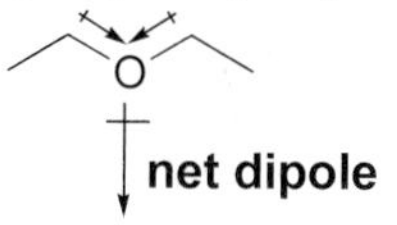
O
net dipole

d.

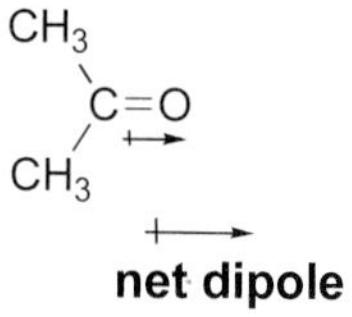
CH3
C=O
CH3
net dipole

f.

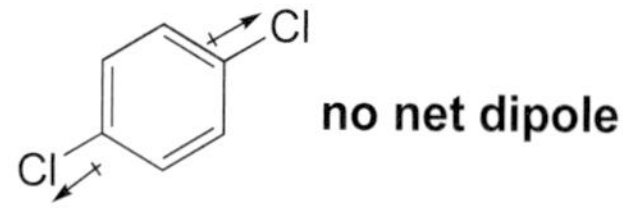
Cl
Cl
no net dipole

1.78

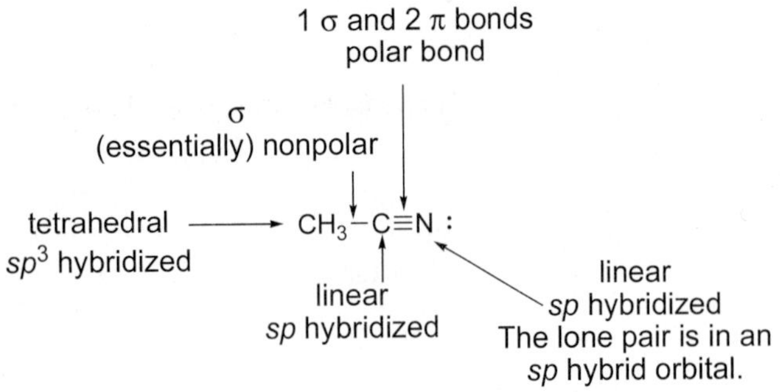
1 σ and 2 π bonds
polar bond
σ
(essentially) nonpolar
tetrahedral
sp^3 hybridized
CH_3–C≡N :
linear
sp hybridized
linear
sp hybridized
The lone pair is in an
sp hybrid orbital.

All C–H bonds are nonpolar σ bonds.
All H's use a 1*s* orbital in bonding.

1.79

a. sp^2
b. Each C is trigonal planar; the ring is flat, drawn as a hexagon.
c.

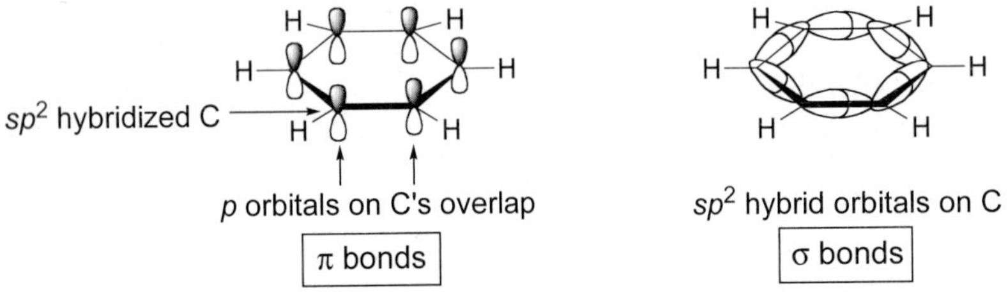
sp^2 hybridized C
p orbitals on C's overlap
π bonds
sp^2 hybrid orbitals on C
σ bonds

[Only the larger bonding lobe of each orbital is drawn.]

d.

e. Benzene is stable because of its two resonance structures that contribute equally to the hybrid. [This is only part of the story. We'll learn more about benzene's unusual stability in Chapter 17.]

1.80

a.

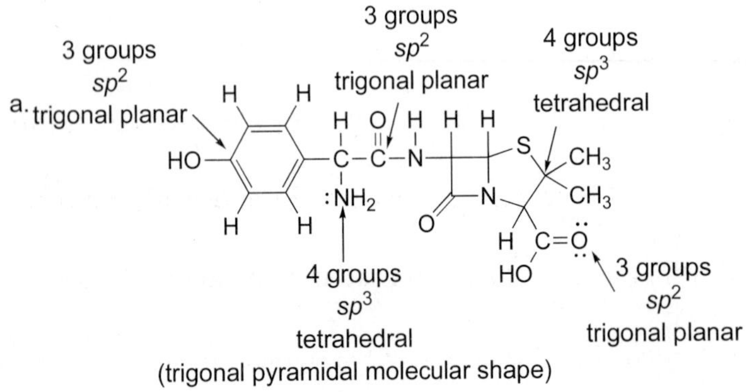
3 groups
sp^2
trigonal planar
3 groups
sp^2
trigonal planar
4 groups
sp^3
tetrahedral
4 groups
sp^3
tetrahedral
(trigonal pyramidal molecular shape)
3 groups
sp^2
trigonal planar

b.

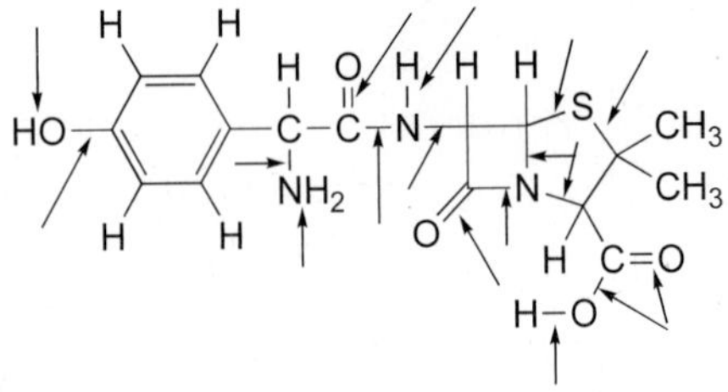

All C–O, C–N, C–S, N–H, and O–H bonds are polar and labeled with arrows.
All partial positive charges lie on the C.
All partial negative charges lie on the O, N, or S.
In OH and NH bonds, H bears a δ^+.

c. **skeletal structure:**

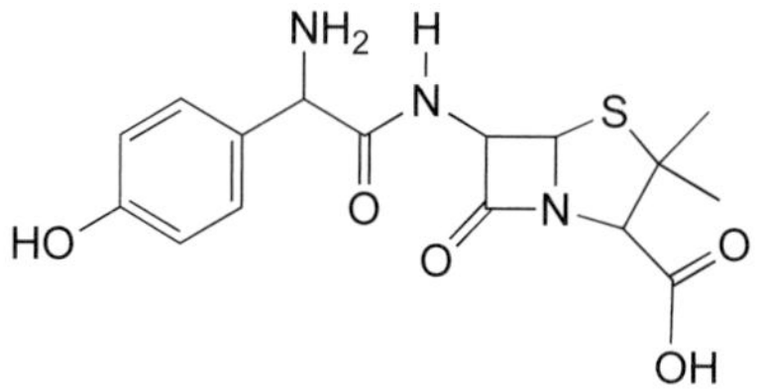

e. **33% *s*-character = sp^2 hybridized**

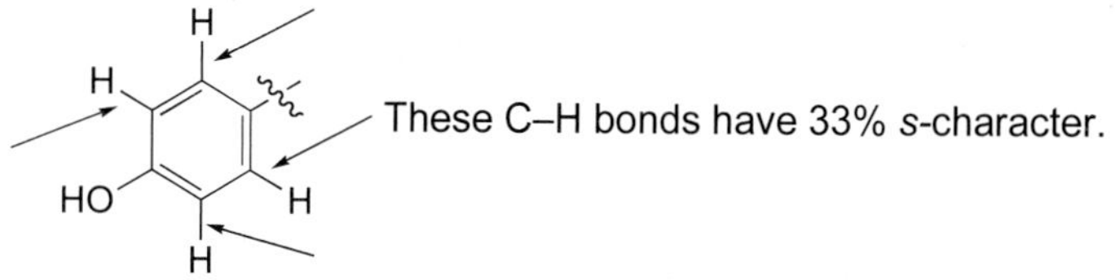
These C–H bonds have 33% *s*-character.

d.

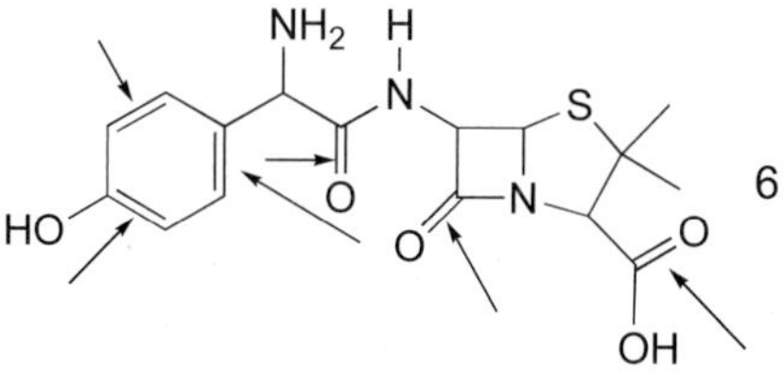

6 π bonds

1.81

a, b, c.

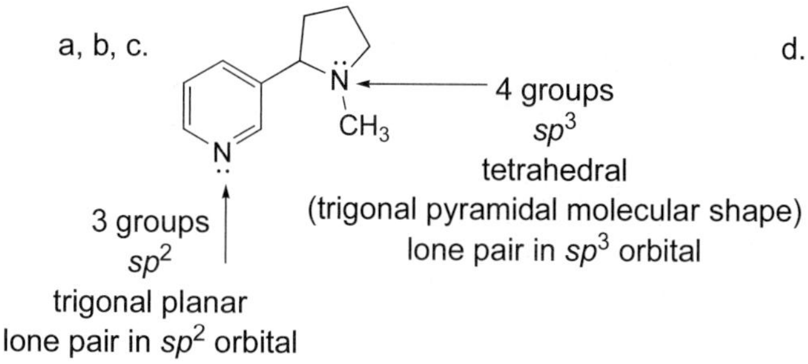
4 groups
sp^3
tetrahedral
(trigonal pyramidal molecular shape)
lone pair in sp^3 orbital
3 groups
sp^2
trigonal planar
lone pair in sp^2 orbital

d.

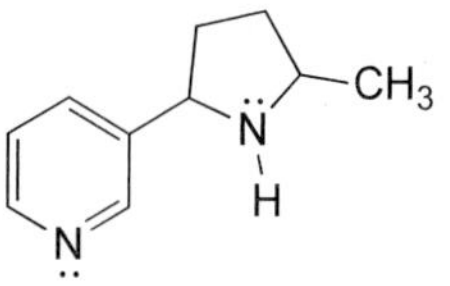

constitutional isomer

e.

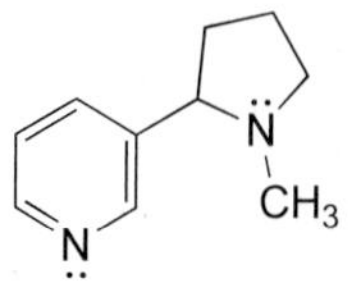

resonance structure

1.82 a.

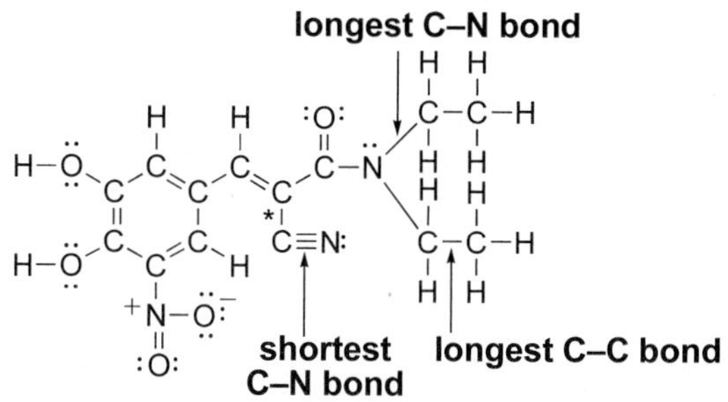
longest C–N bond
shortest C–N bond
longest C–C bond

b. The C–C bonds in the CH_2CH_3 groups are the longest because they are formed from sp^3 hybridized C's.

c. The shortest C–C bond is labeled with a (*) because it is formed from orbitals with the highest percent *s*-character (Csp–Csp^2).

d. The longest C–N bond is formed from the sp^3 hybridized C atom bonded to a N atom [labeled in part (a)].

e. The shortest C–N bond is the triple bond (C≡N); increasing the number of electrons between atoms decreases bond length.

f.

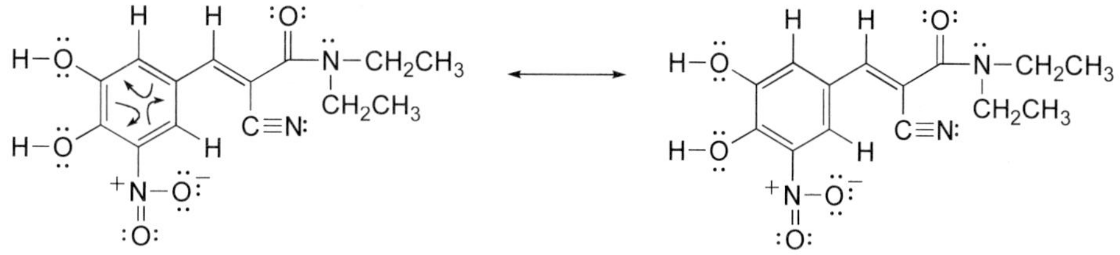

g. 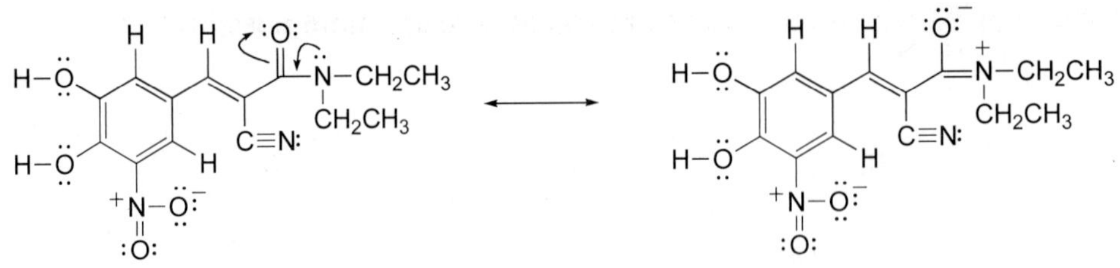

1.83

$\overset{+}{C}H_3$ 3 groups
sp^2 trigonal planar
plot **A**

The blue region is evidence of the electron-poor cation.

$\ddot{:}CH_3^-$ 4 groups
sp^3 tetrahedral
(The molecular shape is trigonal pyramidal.)
plot **B**

The red region is evidence of the electron-rich anion.

1.84 If the N atom is sp^2 hybridized, the lone pair occupies a *p* orbital, which can overlap with the π bond of the adjacent C=O. This allows electron density to delocalize, which is a stabilizing feature.

σ bonds in $–CONH_2$

π bonds in $–CONH_2$

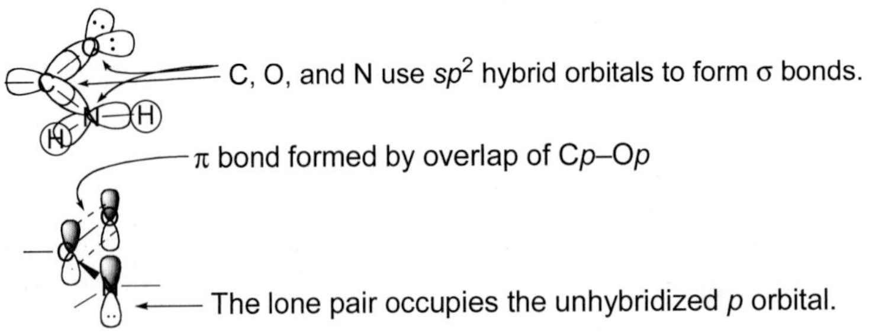
C, O, and N use sp² hybrid orbitals to form σ bonds.
π bond formed by overlap of Cp–Op
The lone pair occupies the unhybridized p orbital.

1.85

a.

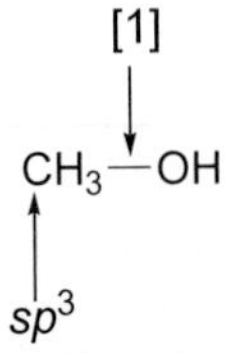
[1]
CH3—OH
sp3

25% *s*-character
The lower percent *s*-character makes this bond longer.

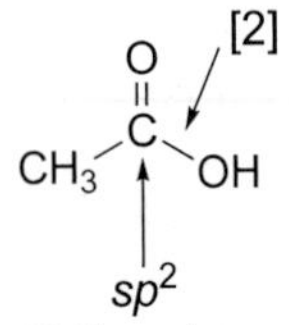
[2]
CH3
OH
sp2

33% *s*-character

b.

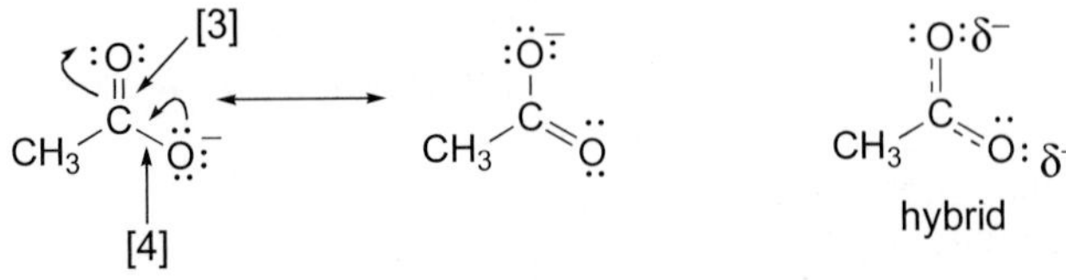
[3]
CH3
[4]
hybrid

two resonance structures

Bonds [3] and [4] are both equivalent in length, because the anion is resonance-stabilized, and the C–O bond of the hybrid is a composite of one single bond and one double bond. Both resonance structures contribute equally to the hybrid. Since each C–O bond in the hybrid has partial double bond character, it is shorter than the C–O single bond labeled [2].

1.86 Ten additional resonance structures are drawn. (There are more possibilities.)

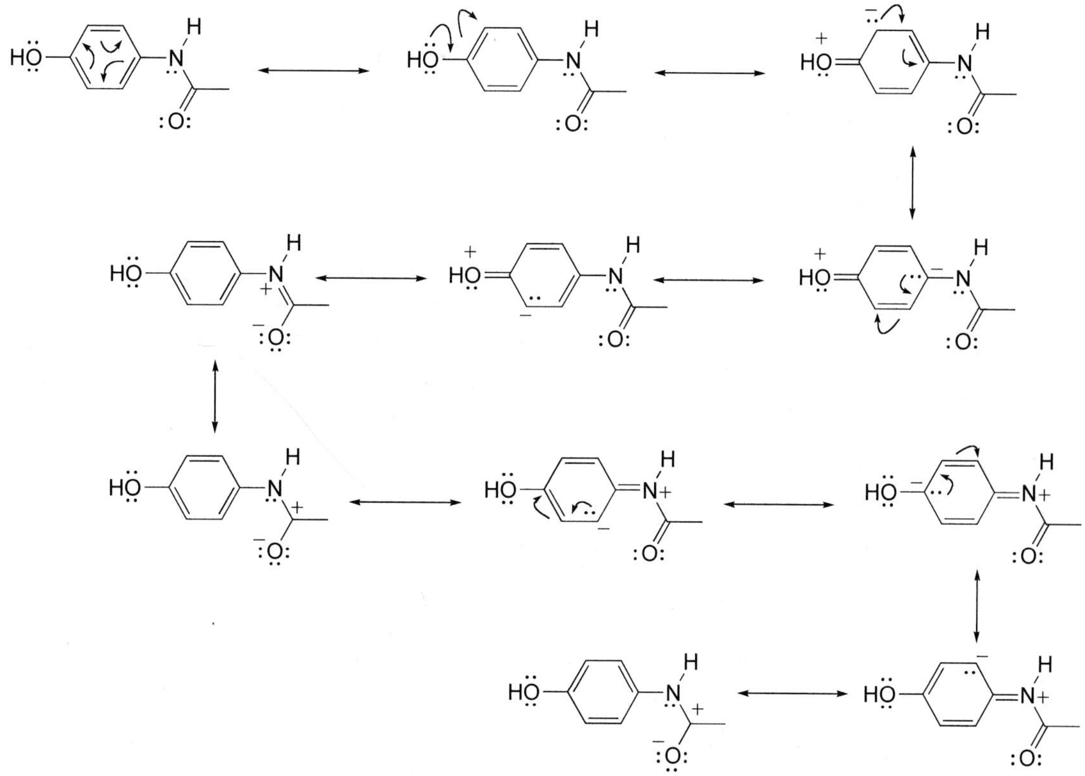

1.87 Polar bonds result from unequal sharing of electrons in covalent bonds. Normally we think of more electronegative atoms "pulling" more of the electron density towards them, making a dipole. In looking at a Csp^2–Csp^3 bond, the atom with a higher percent *s*-character will "pull" more of the electron density towards it, creating a small dipole.

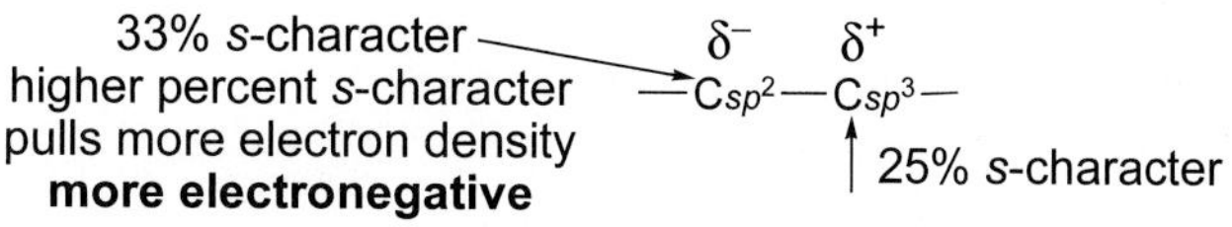
33% s-character
higher percent s-character
pulls more electron density
more electronegative
δ⁻ δ⁺
Csp²—Csp³
25% s-character

1.88

Isomers of C_4H_8:

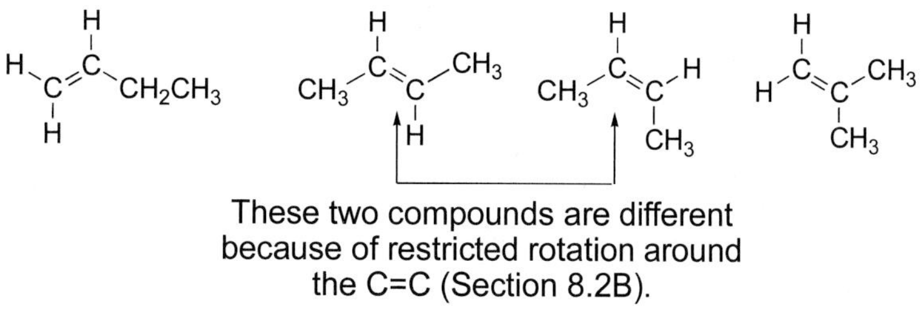
These two compounds are different
because of restricted rotation around
the C=C (Section 8.2B).

1.89 Carbocation **A** is more stable than carbocation **B** because resonance distributes the positive charge over two carbons. Delocalizing electron density is stabilizing. **B** has no possibility of resonance delocalization.

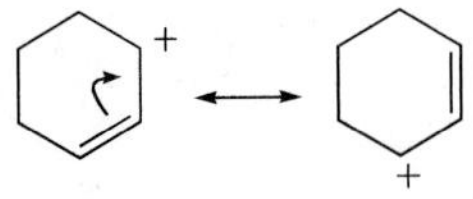

A

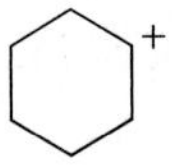

B

No resonance structures

1.90

a. 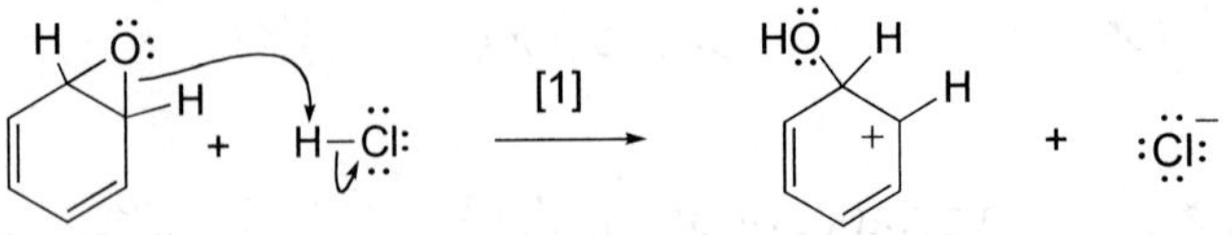

b. 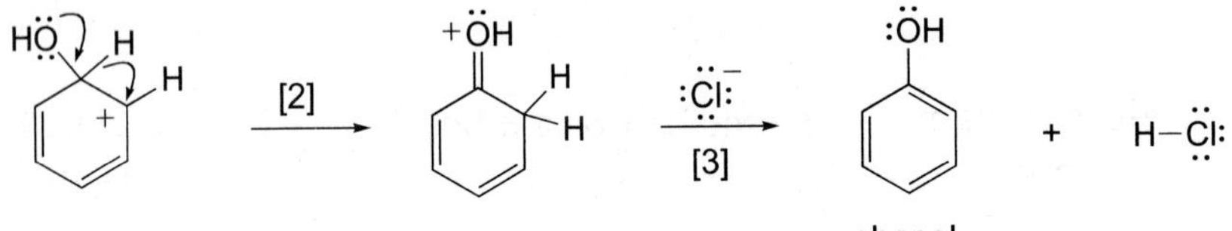

X

phenol

Chapter 2 Acids and Bases

Chapter Review

A comparison of Brønsted–Lowry and Lewis acids and bases

Type	Definition	Structural feature	Examples
Brønsted–Lowry acid (2.1)	proton donor	a proton	HCl, H_2SO_4, H_2O, CH_3COOH, TsOH
Brønsted–Lowry base (2.1)	proton acceptor	a lone pair *or* a π bond	^-OH, $^-OCH_3$, H^-, $^-NH_2$, $CH_2{=}CH_2$
Lewis acid (2.8)	electron pair acceptor	a proton, *or* an unfilled valence shell, *or* a partial (+) charge	BF_3, $AlCl_3$, HCl, CH_3COOH, H_2O
Lewis base (2.8)	electron pair donor	a lone pair *or* a π bond	^-OH, $^-OCH_3$, H^-, $^-NH_2$, $CH_2{=}CH_2$

Acid–base reactions

[1] A Brønsted–Lowry acid donates a proton to a Brønsted–Lowry base (2.2).

Example

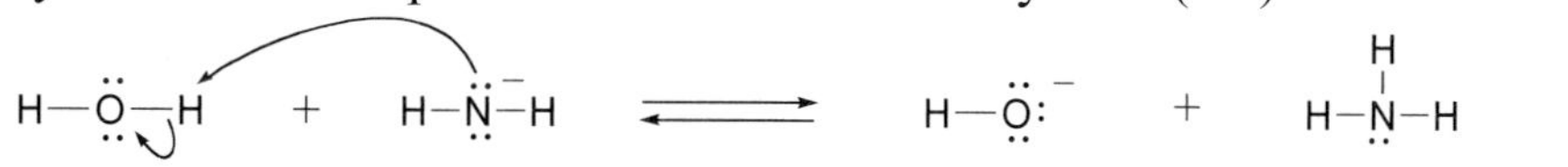

[2] A Lewis base donates an electron pair to a Lewis acid (2.8).

Example

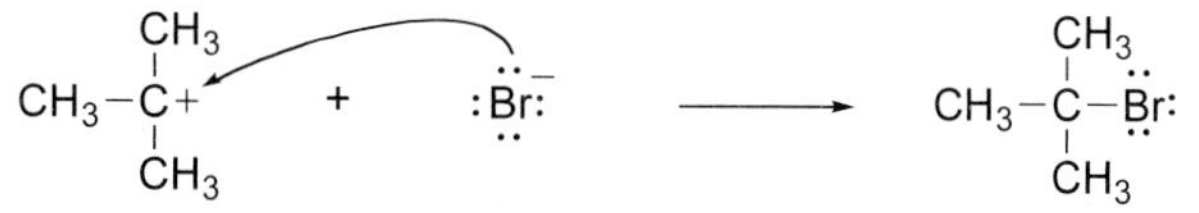

- Electron-rich species react with electron-poor ones.
- Nucleophiles react with electrophiles.

Important facts

- Definition: $\mathbf{p}\boldsymbol{K}_\mathbf{a} = \mathbf{-log}\ \boldsymbol{K}_\mathbf{a}$. The **lower the p$K_a$,** the **stronger** the acid (2.3).

NH_3	versus	H_2O
pK_a = 38		pK_a = 15.7
		lower pK_a = stronger acid

- The stronger the acid, the weaker the conjugate base (2.3).

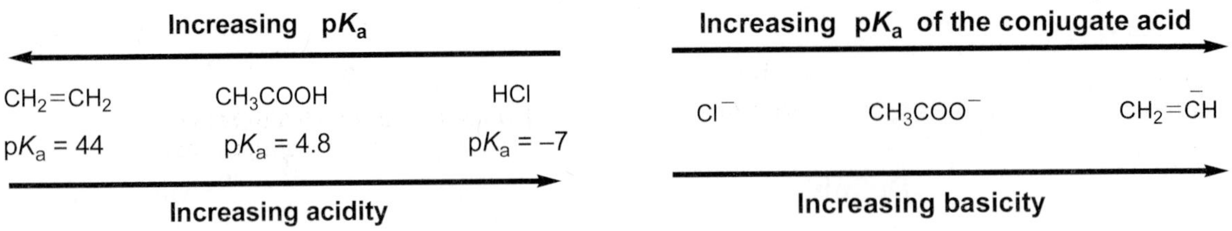

- In proton transfer reactions, equilibrium favors the weaker acid and the weaker base (2.4).

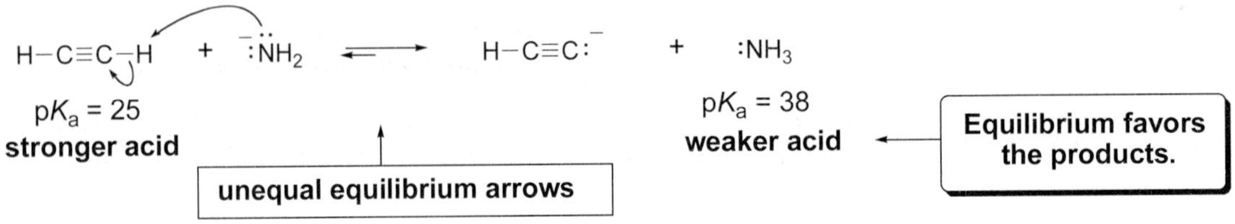

- An acid can be deprotonated by the conjugate base of any acid having a **higher p*K*a** (2.4).

Acid	pK_a	Conjugate base	
$CH_3COO–H$	4.8	CH_3COO^-	
$CH_3CH_2O–H$	16	$CH_3CH_2O^-$	These bases
HC≡CH	25	HC≡C^-	can deprotonate
H–H	35	H^-	$CH_3COO–H$.
	higher pK_a than $CH_3COO–H$		

Factors that determine acidity (2.5)

[1] **Element effects** (2.5A) The acidity of H–A increases both left to right across a row and down a column of the periodic table.

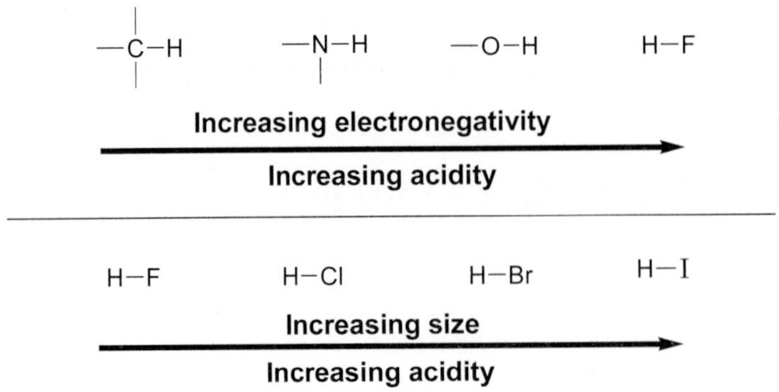

[2] Inductive effects (2.5B)

The acidity of H–A increases with the presence of electron-withdrawing groups in A.

CH_3CH_2OH → $CH_3CH_2O^-$

weaker acid

No additional electronegative atoms stabilize the conjugate base.

CF_3CH_2OH →

stronger acid

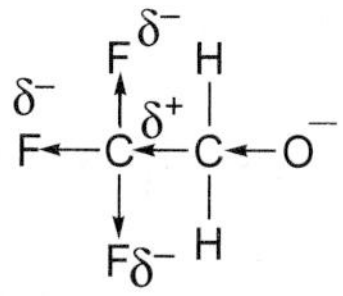

CF_3 withdraws electron density, stabilizing the conjugate base.

[3] Resonance effects (2.5C)

The acidity of H–A increases when the conjugate base A:⁻ is resonance stabilized.

$CH_3CH_2\ddot{O}–H$ → $CH_3CH_2\ddot{O}:^-$

ethanol

ethoxide
conjugate base

only **one** Lewis structure

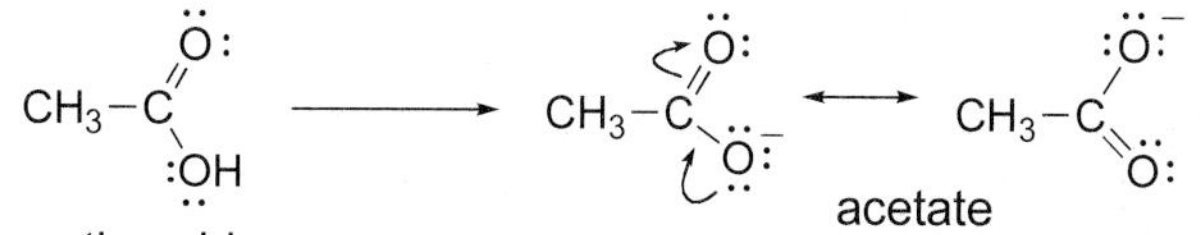

acetic acid
more acidic

acetate
conjugate base

two resonance structures

[4] Hybridization effects (2.5D)

The acidity of H–A increases as the percent *s*-character of the A:⁻ increases.

CH_3CH_3	$CH_2=CH_2$	$H–C\equiv C–H$
ethane	ethylene	acetylene
$pK_a = 50$	$pK_a = 44$	$pK_a = 25$

→

Increasing acidity

Practice Test on Chapter Review

1. a Given the pK_a data, which of the following bases is strong enough to deprotonate C_6H_5OH (pK_a = 10) so that the equilibrium lies to the right?

Compound	pK_a
H_3O^+	−1.7
NH_4^+	9.4
H_2O	15.7
NH_3	38

1. NaOH
2. $NaNH_2$
3. NH_3
4. Compounds (1) and (2) are strong enough to deprotonate C_6H_5OH.
5. Compounds (1), (2), and (3) are all strong enough to deprotonate C_6H_5OH.

b. Which of the following statements is true about pK_a, acidity, and basicity?
1. A higher pK_a means the acid is less acidic.
2. In an acid–base reaction, the equilibrium lies on the side of the acid with the higher pK_a.
3. A lower pK_a value for the acid means the conjugate base is more basic.
4. Statements (1) and (2) are both true.
5. Statements (1), (2), and (3) are all true.

c. Which of the following species can be Lewis acids?
1. BCl_3
2. CH_3OH
3. $(CH_3)_3C^+$
4. Both (1) and (2) can be Lewis acids.
5. Species (1), (2), and (3) can all be Lewis acids.

2. Answer the following questions about compounds **A–D**.

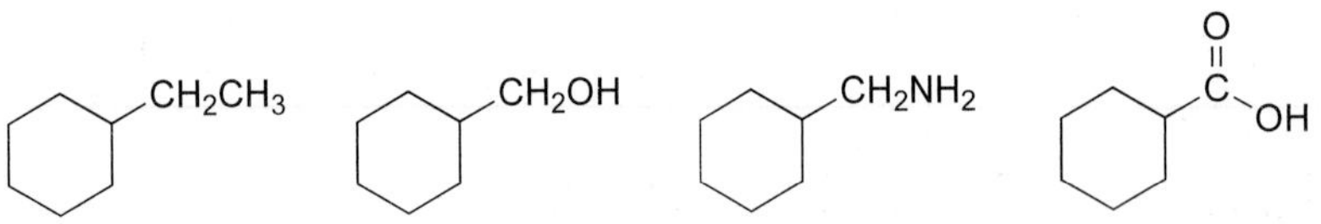

A **B** **C** **D**

a. Which compound is the strongest acid?
b. Which compound forms the strongest conjugate base?
c. The conjugate base of **C** is strong enough to remove a proton on which compound(s) such that the equilibrium favors the products?

3. (a) Which compound is the strongest Brønsted–Lowry acid? (b) Which compound is the weakest Brønsted–Lowry acid?

A **B** **C** **D**

4. Draw all the products formed in the following reactions.

a. 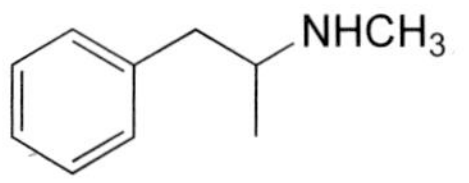 + HBr ⟶   b. 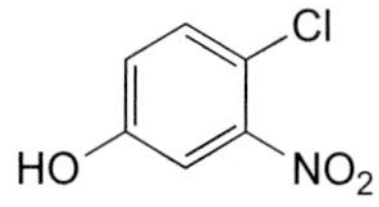 + $Na^+ \ ^-NH_2$ ⟶

5. Draw the product(s) formed in the following Lewis acid–base reaction.

$(CH_3)_2\overset{+}{C}H$ + CH_3OH ⟶

Answers to Practice Test

1. a. 4
   b. 4
   c. 5

2. a. **D**
   b. **A**
   c. **B, D**

3. a. **C**
   b. **B**

4. a. 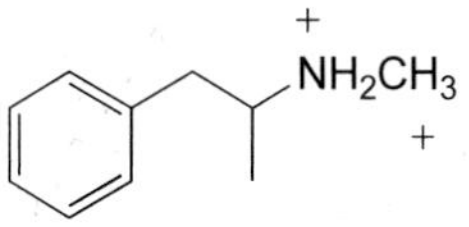 + Br^-

   b. 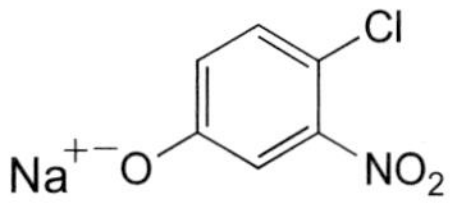 + NH_3

5. 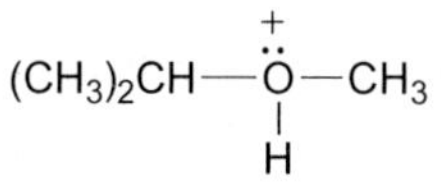

Answers to Problems

2.1 **Brønsted–Lowry acids** are **proton donors** and must contain a hydrogen atom. **Brønsted–Lowry bases** are **proton acceptors** and must have an available electron pair (either a lone pair or a π bond).

a. $H\ddot{B}r:$ — **acid**; $\ddot{N}H_3$ — **acid**; CCl_4 — not an acid—no H

b. CH_3CH_3 — no lone pairs or π bonds, not a base; $(CH_3)_3C\ddot{O}:^-$ — lone pairs on O, **base**; H–C≡C–H — **base**—π bonds

c. $CH_3CH_2\ddot{O}H$ — **base**—lone pairs on O, **acid**—contains H atoms; $CH_3CH_2CH_2CH_3$ — not a base—no lone pairs or π bonds, **acid**—contains H atoms; 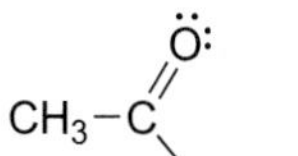 — **base**—lone pairs on O's, π bond, **acid**—contains H atoms

2.2 A Brønsted–Lowry base accepts a proton to form the conjugate acid. A Brønsted–Lowry acid loses a proton to form the conjugate base.

a. NH_3 ⟶ NH_4^+
Cl^- ⟶ HCl
$(CH_3)_2C=O$ ⟶ $(CH_3)_2C=\overset{+}{\ddot{O}}H$

b. HBr ⟶ Br^-
HSO_4^- ⟶ SO_4^{2-}
CH_3OH ⟶ CH_3O^-

2.3 The Brønsted–Lowry base accepts a proton to form the conjugate acid. The Brønsted–Lowry acid loses a proton to form the conjugate base. Use curved arrows to show the movement of electrons (***NOT protons***). Re-draw the starting materials if necessary to clarify the electron movement.

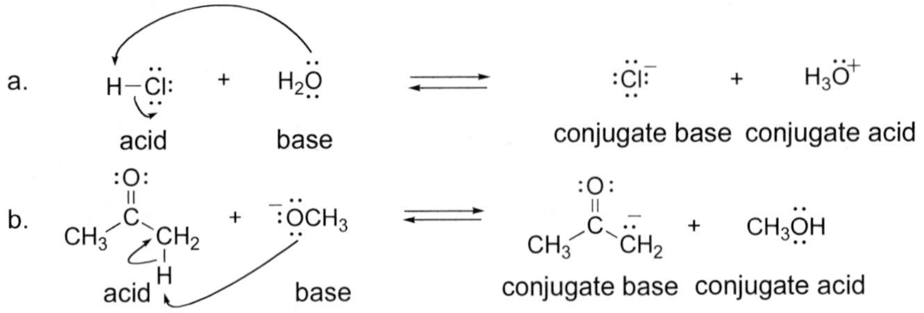
a.
acid
base
conjugate base conjugate acid
b.
acid
base
conjugate base conjugate acid

2.4 To draw the products:
[1] Find the acid and base.
[2] Transfer a proton from the acid to the base.
[3] Check that the charges on each side of the arrows are balanced.

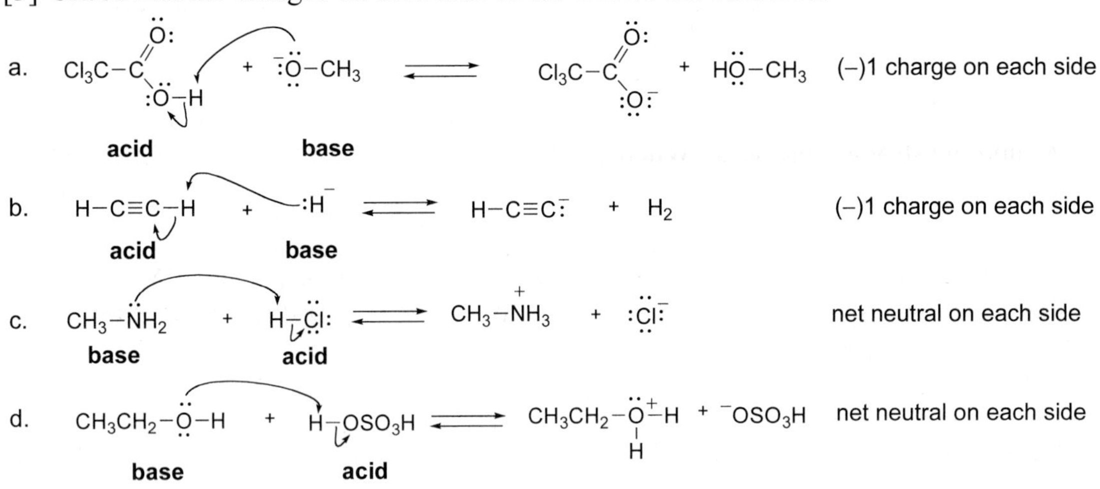
a.
acid
base
(–)1 charge on each side
b.
acid
base
(–)1 charge on each side
c.
base
acid
net neutral on each side
d.
base
acid
net neutral on each side

2.5 Draw the products in each reaction as in Answer 2.4.

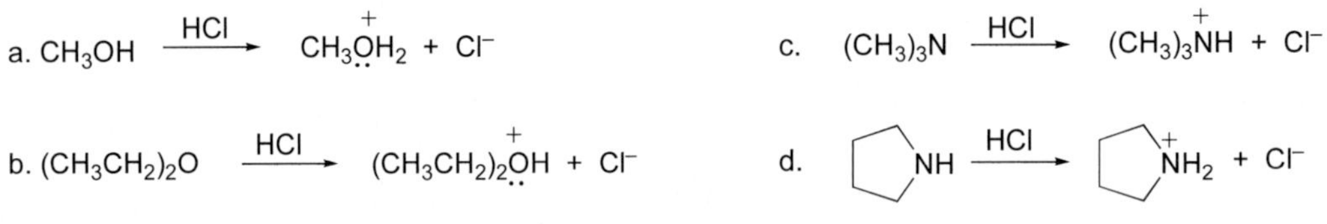
a. CH3OH
HCl
b. (CH3CH2)2O
HCl
c. (CH3)3N
HCl
d.
HCl

2.6 The smaller the pK_a, the stronger the acid. The larger the K_a, the stronger the acid.

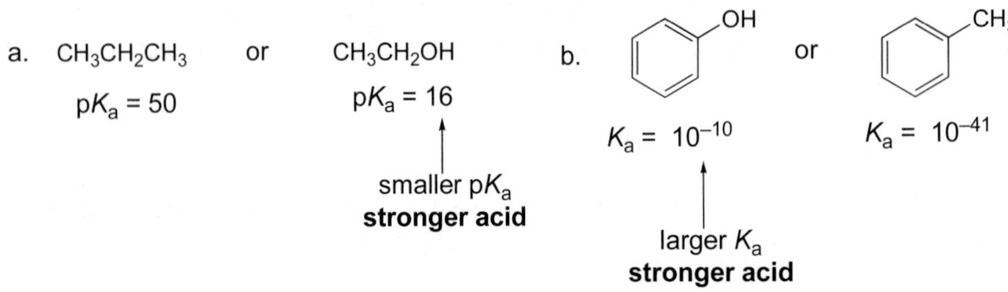
a. CH3CH2CH3
or
CH3CH2OH
pKa = 50
pKa = 16
smaller pKa
stronger acid
b.
or
Ka = 10–10
Ka = 10–41
larger Ka
stronger acid

2.7 To convert from K_a to pK_a, take (–) the log of the K_a; **pK_a = –log K_a.**
To convert pK_a to K_a, take the antilog of (–) the pK_a.

a. $K_a = 10^{-10}$ → pK_a = 10 $K_a = 10^{-21}$ → pK_a = 21 $K_a = 5.2 \times 10^{-5}$ → pK_a = 4.3

b. pK_a = 7 → $K_a = 10^{-7}$ pK_a = 11 → $K_a = 10^{-11}$ pK_a = 3.2 → $K_a = 6.3 \times 10^{-4}$

2.8 Since **strong acids form weak conjugate bases,** the basicity of conjugate bases increases with increasing pK_a of their acids. Find the pK_a of each acid from Table 2.1 and then rank the acids in order of increasing pK_a. This will also be the order of increasing basicity of their conjugate bases.

a. Increasing acidity ←
H_2O, NH_3, CH_4
pK_a = 15.7 38 50
conjugate bases: ^-OH, $^-NH_2$, $^-CH_3$
Increasing basicity →

b. Increasing acidity ←
HC≡CH, CH_2=CH_2, CH_4
pK_a = 25 44 50
conjugate bases: ^-C≡CH, ^-CH=CH_2, $^-CH_3$
Increasing basicity →

2.9 Use the definitions in Answer 2.8 to compare the acids. The smaller the pK_a, the larger the K_a and the stronger the acid. When a stronger acid dissolves in water, the equilibrium lies further to the right.

HCO_2H
formic acid
pK_a = 3.8

$(CH_3)_3CCO_2H$
pivalic acid
pK_a = 5.0

a. smaller pK_a = larger K_a
b. smaller pK_a = stronger acid
c. weaker acid = stronger conjugate base
d. stronger acid = equilibrium further to the right

2.10 To estimate the pK_a of the indicated bond, find a similar bond in the pK_a table (H bonded to the same atom with the same hybridization).

a. 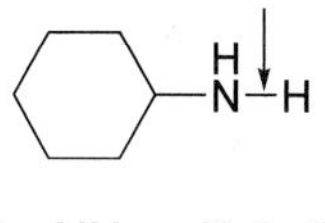
For NH_3, pK_a is 38.
estimated pK_a = 38

b. 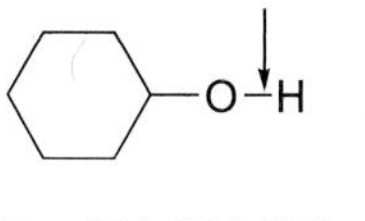
For CH_3CH_2OH, pK_a is 16.
estimated pK_a = 16

c. $BrCH_2COO$–H
For CH_3COOH, pK_a is 4.8.
estimated pK_a = 5

2.11 Label the acid and the base and then transfer a proton from the acid to the base. To determine if the reaction will proceed as written, compare the pK_a of the acid on the left with the conjugate acid on the right. **The equilibrium always favors the formation of the weaker acid and the weaker base.**

a. CH_2=CH_2 + $H:^-$ ⇌ CH_2=$\ddot{C}H^-$ + H_2

CH_2=CH_2	$H:^-$	CH_2=$\ddot{C}H$	H_2
acid	base	conjugate base	conjugate acid
pK_a = 44			pK_a = 35
weaker acid			

Equilibrium favors the **starting materials.**

b. CH_4 + $^{-}\ddot{O}H$ $\rightleftharpoons$ $^{-}:CH_3$ + $H_2\ddot{O}:$

- CH_4: acid, pK_a = 50, **weaker acid**
- $^{-}:\ddot{O}H$: base
- $^{-}:CH_3$: conjugate base
- $H_2\ddot{O}:$: conjugate acid, pK_a = 15.7

Equilibrium favors the **starting materials.**

c. CH_3COOH + $CH_3CH_2\ddot{O}:^{-}$ $\rightleftharpoons$ CH_3COO^{-} + $CH_3CH_2\ddot{O}H$

- CH_3COOH: acid, pK_a = 4.8
- $CH_3CH_2\ddot{O}:^{-}$: base
- CH_3COO^{-}: conjugate base
- $CH_3CH_2\ddot{O}H$: conjugate acid, pK_a = 16, **weaker acid**

Equilibrium favors the **products.**

d. $:\ddot{Cl}:^{-}$ + $CH_3CH_2\ddot{O}H$ $\rightleftharpoons$ $H\ddot{Cl}:$ + $CH_3CH_2\ddot{O}:^{-}$

- $:\ddot{Cl}:^{-}$: base
- $CH_3CH_2\ddot{O}H$: acid, pK_a = 16, **weaker acid**
- $H\ddot{Cl}:$: conjugate acid, pK_a = –7
- $CH_3CH_2\ddot{O}:^{-}$: conjugate base

Equilibrium favors the **starting materials.**

2.12 An acid can be deprotonated by the conjugate base of any acid with a higher pK_a.

CH_3CN
pK_a = 25
Any base having a conjugate acid with a pK_a higher than 25 can deprotonate this acid.

Base	Conjugate acid	pK_a
NaH	H_2	35
Na_2CO_3	HCO_3^{-}	10.2
NaOH	H_2O	15.7
$NaNH_2$	NH_3	38
$NaHCO_3$	H_2CO_3	6.4

Only NaH and $NaNH_2$ are strong enough to deprotonate acetonitrile.

2.13 The acidity of H–Z **increases left to right across a row and down a column** of the periodic table.

a. NH_3, H_2O ← H_2O: O is farther to the right in the periodic table. **stronger acid**

b. H_2S, HBr ← HBr: Br is farther across and down the periodic table. **stronger acid**

2.14 Compare the most acidic protons in each compound to determine the stronger acid.

a. $CH_3CH_2CH_2NH_2$ or $(CH_3)_3N$

- $CH_3CH_2CH_2NH_2$: N–H bond. N is farther to the right in the periodic table. **stronger acid**
- $(CH_3)_3N$: C–H bond

b. $CH_3CH_2OCH_3$ or $CH_3CH_2CH_2OH$

- $CH_3CH_2OCH_3$: C–H bond
- $CH_3CH_2CH_2OH$: O–H bond. O is farther to the right in the periodic table. **stronger acid**

2.15 Look at the element bonded to the acidic H and decide its acidity based on the periodic trends. **Farther to the right and down the periodic table is more acidic.**

a. $CH_3CH_2CH_2CH_2$**OH** (most acidic: the O–H hydrogen)
Molecule contains C–H and O–H bonds.
O is farther right; therefore, O–H hydrogen is the most acidic.

b. **HO**$CH_2CH_2CH_2NH_2$ (most acidic: the O–H hydrogen)
Molecule contains C–H, N–H, and O–H bonds.
O is farthest right; therefore, O–H hydrogen is the most acidic.

c. $(CH_3)_2NCH_2CH_2CH_2$**NH_2** (most acidic: the N–H hydrogens)
Molecule contains C–H and N–H bonds.
N is farther right; therefore, N–H hydrogen is the most acidic.

2.16 The acidity of HA increases left to right across the periodic table. Pseudoephedrine contains C–H, N–H, and O–H bonds. The O–H bond is most acidic.

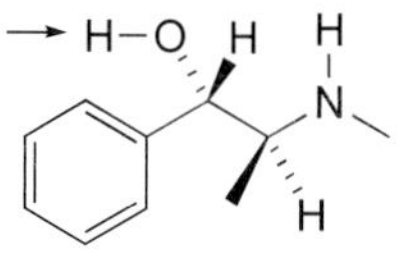

pseudoephedrine
skeletal structure

2.17 **More electronegative atoms stabilize the conjugate base, making the acid stronger.** Compare the electron-withdrawing groups on the acids below to decide which is a stronger acid **(more electronegative groups = more acidic).**

a. $ClCH_2COOH$ or FCH_2COOH
more acidic

F is more electronegative than Cl, making the O–H bond in the acid on the right **more acidic.**

b. Cl_2CHCH_2OH or $Cl_2CHCH_2CH_2OH$

Cl is closer to the acidic O–H bond. **more acidic**

Cl is farther from the O–H bond.

c. CH_3COOH or O_2NCH_2COOH
more acidic

NO_2 is electron withdrawing, making the O–H bond in the acid on the right **more acidic.**

2.18 **More electronegative groups stabilize the conjugate base, making the acid stronger.**

↓
$HOCH_2CO_2H$
an α-hydroxy acid
The extra OH group contains an electronegative O, which stabilizes the conjugate base.
stronger acid

CH_3CO_2H
acetic acid

2.19 HBr is a stronger acid than HCl because Br is farther down a column of the periodic table, and the larger Br^- anion is more stable than the smaller Cl^- anion. In these acids the H is bonded directly to the halogen. In HOCl and HOBr, the H is bonded to O, and the halogens Cl and Br exert an inductive effect. In this case, the more electronegative Cl stabilizes ^-OCl more than the less electronegative Br stabilizes ^-OBr. Thus, HOCl forms the more stable conjugate base, making it the stronger acid.

2.20 The acidity of an acid increases when the conjugate base is resonance stabilized. Compare the conjugate bases of acetone and propane to explain why acetone is more acidic.

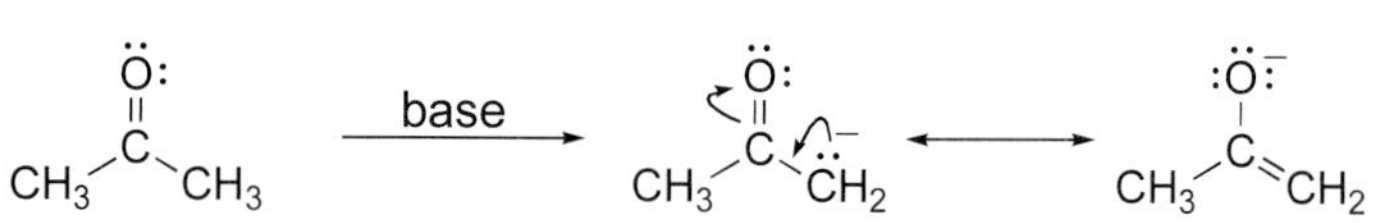

acetone
$pK_a = 19.2$

One resonance structure places the (–) charge on the more electronegative O atom. This is especially good.

2 resonance structures
more stable conjugate base
Acetone is more acidic.

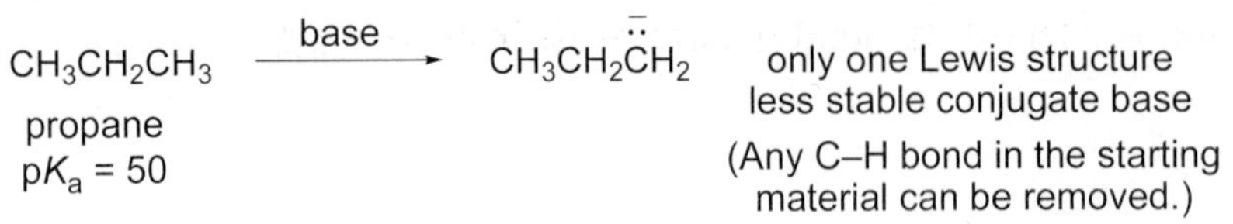
$CH_3CH_2CH_3$
base
$CH_3CH_2\ddot{C}H_2^-$
only one Lewis structure
less stable conjugate base
propane
$pK_a = 50$
(Any C–H bond in the starting material can be removed.)

2.21 The acidity of an acid increases when the conjugate base is resonance stabilized. Acetonitrile has a resonance-stabilized conjugate base, which accounts for its acidity.

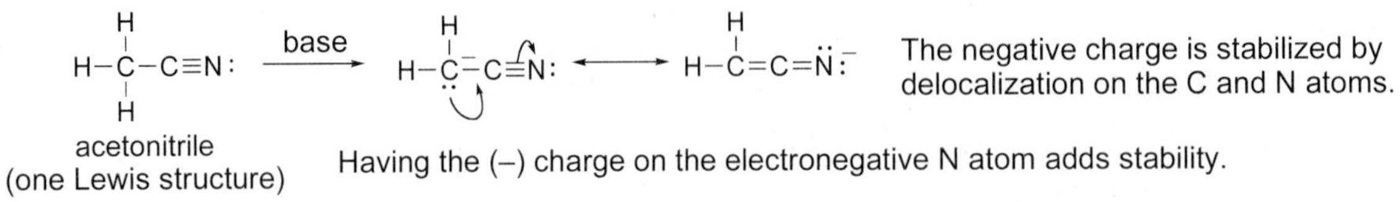
base
acetonitrile
(one Lewis structure)
The negative charge is stabilized by delocalization on the C and N atoms.
Having the (–) charge on the electronegative N atom adds stability.

2.22 **Increasing percent *s*-character makes an acid more acidic.** Compare the percent *s*-character of the carbon atoms in each of the C–H bonds in question. A stronger acid has a weaker conjugate base.

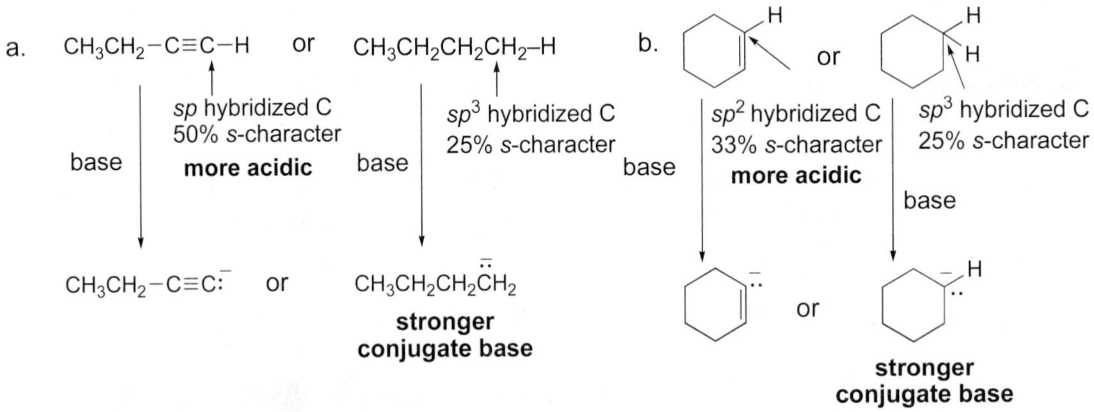
a.
$CH_3CH_2-C{\equiv}C-H$
or
$CH_3CH_2CH_2CH_2-H$
sp hybridized C
50% *s*-character
more acidic
sp^3 hybridized C
25% *s*-character
base
base
$CH_3CH_2-C{\equiv}C:^-$
or
$CH_3CH_2CH_2\ddot{C}H_2^-$
stronger
conjugate base
b.
or
sp^2 hybridized C
33% *s*-character
more acidic
sp^3 hybridized C
25% *s*-character
base
base
or
stronger
conjugate base

2.23 To compare the acids, first **look for element effects.** Then identify electron-withdrawing groups, resonance, or hybridization differences.

a. $CH_3CH_2CH_3$ — C is farthest left in the periodic table. **CH bond is least acidic.**

$CH_3CH_2NH_2$ — **intermediate acidity**

CH_3CH_2OH — O is farthest right in the periodic table. **OH bond is most acidic.**

b. $CH_3CH_2CH_2OH$ — OH group **least acidic**

CH_3CH_2COOH — **intermediate acidity**

$BrCH_2COOH$ — Br is electron withdrawing and the conjugate base is resonance stabilized. **most acidic**

c. $(CH_3)_3N$ — C is farthest left in the periodic table. **CH bond is least acidic.**

$CH_3CH_2NH_2$ — **intermediate acidity**

CH_3CH_2OH — O is farthest right in the periodic table. **OH bond is most acidic.**

2.24 Look at the element bonded to the acidic H and decide its acidity based on the periodic trends. **Farther to the right and down the periodic table is more acidic.**

a. 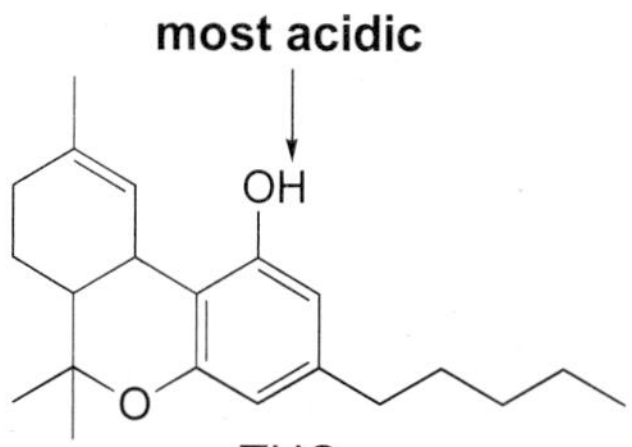
most acidic
OH
O

THC
tetrahydrocannabinol
The molecule contains C–H and O–H bonds.
O is farther right; therefore, O–H hydrogen is the most acidic.

b. 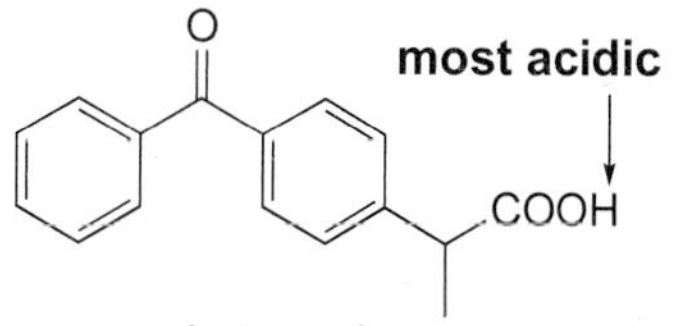
O
most acidic
COOH

ketoprofen
The molecule contains C–H and O–H bonds.
O is farther right; therefore, O–H hydrogen is the most acidic.

2.25 Draw the products of proton transfer from the acid to the base.

a. $(CH_3)_2CH\ddot{O}{-}H$ (acid) + $Na^+\ H:^-$ (base) ⇌ $(CH_3)_2CH\ddot{O}:^-\ Na^+$ (conjugate base) + H_2 (conjugate acid)

b. $(CH_3)_2CH\ddot{O}{-}H$ (base) + $H{-}OSO_3H$ (acid) ⇌ $(CH_3)_2CH\overset{+}{O}H_2$ (conjugate acid) + HSO_4^- (conjugate base)

c. $(CH_3)_2CH\ddot{O}{-}H$ (acid) + $Li^+\ ^-\ddot{N}[CH(CH_3)_2]_2$ (base) ⇌ $(CH_3)_2CH\ddot{O}:^-\ Li^+$ (conjugate base) + $H\ddot{N}[CH(CH_3)_2]_2$ (conjugate acid)

d. $(CH_3)_2CH\ddot{O}{-}H$ (base) + $H{-}OCOCH_3$ (acid) ⇌ $(CH_3)_2CH\overset{+}{O}H_2$ (conjugate acid) + $^-OCOCH_3$ (conjugate base)

2.26 To cross a cell membrane, amphetamine must be in its neutral (not ionic) form.

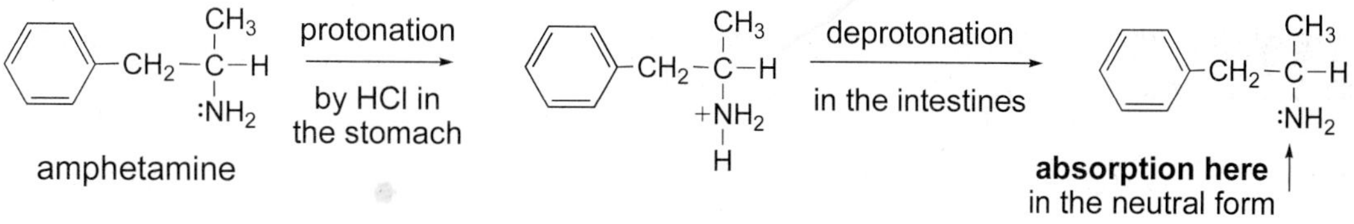
CH3
CH2–C–H
:NH2
amphetamine
protonation
by HCl in
the stomach
CH3
CH2–C–H
+NH2
H
deprotonation
in the intestines
CH3
CH2–C–H
:NH2
absorption here
in the neutral form

2.27 **Lewis bases are electron pair donors:** they contain a lone pair or a π bond.

a. $\ddot{N}H_3$ — **yes** - has lone pair

b. $CH_3CH_2CH_3$ — **no** - no lone pair or π bond

c. $H:^-$ — **yes** - has lone pair

d. $H{-}C{\equiv}C{-}H$ — **yes** - has 2 π bonds

2.28 **Lewis acids are electron pair acceptors.** Most Lewis acids contain a proton or an unfilled valence shell of electrons.

a. BBr_3	b. CH_3CH_2OH	c. $(CH_3)_3C^+$	d. Br^-
yes unfilled valence shell on B	**yes** contains a proton	**yes** unfilled valence shell on C	**no** no proton no unfilled valence shell

2.29 Label the Lewis acid and Lewis base and then draw the curved arrows.

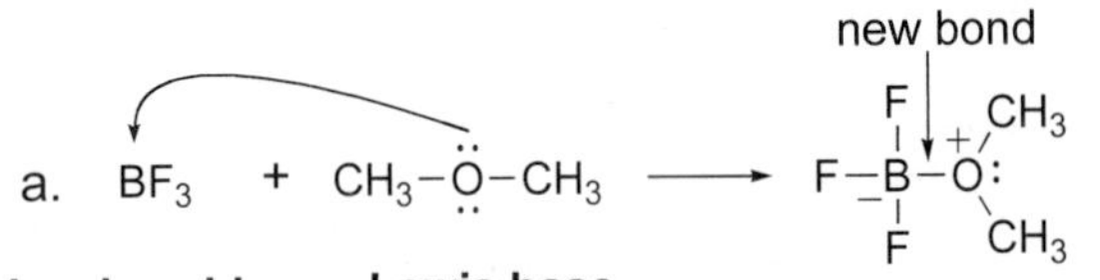

Lewis acid — unfilled valence shell on B
Lewis base — lone pairs on O

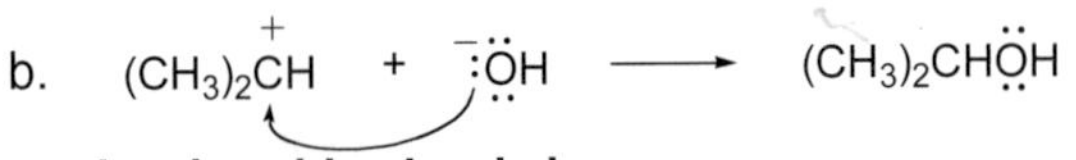

Lewis acid — unfilled valence shell on C
Lewis base — lone pairs on O

2.30 A Lewis acid is also called an **electrophile.** When a Lewis base reacts with an electrophile other than a proton, it is called a **nucleophile.** Label the electrophile and nucleophile in the starting materials and then draw the products.

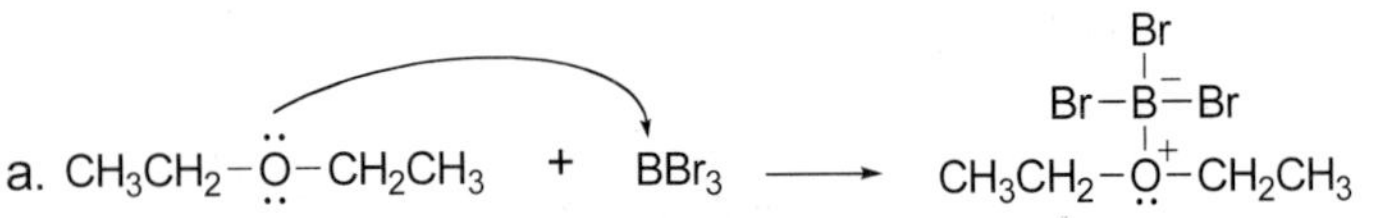

Lewis base — **nucleophile** — lone pairs on O
Lewis acid — **electrophile** — unfilled valence shell on B

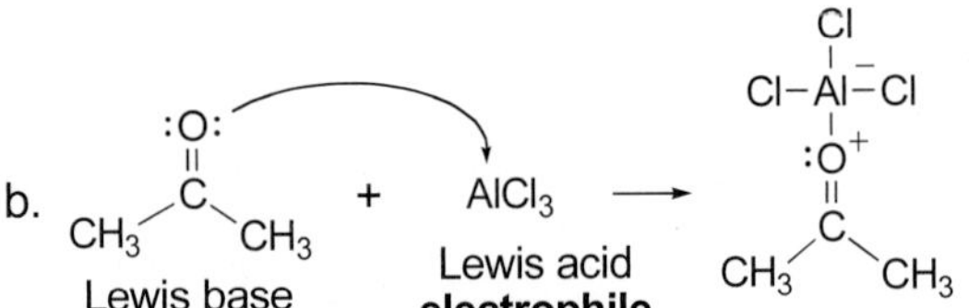

Lewis base — **nucleophile** — lone pairs on O
Lewis acid — **electrophile** — unfilled valence shell on Al

2.31 Draw the product of each reaction by using an electron pair of the Lewis base to form a new bond to the Lewis acid.

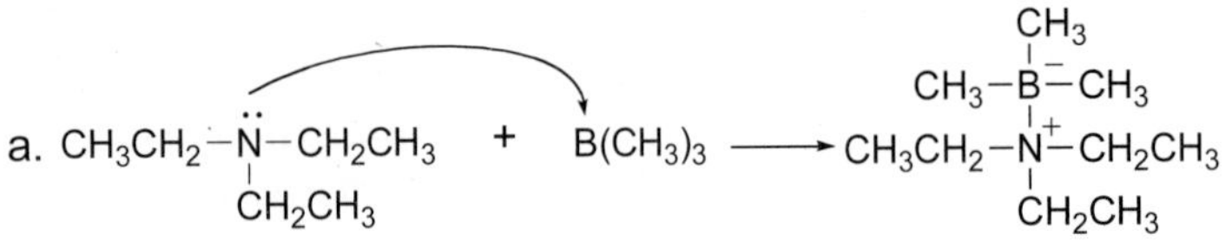

Lewis base — **nucleophile** — lone pair on N
Lewis acid — **electrophile** — unfilled valence shell on B

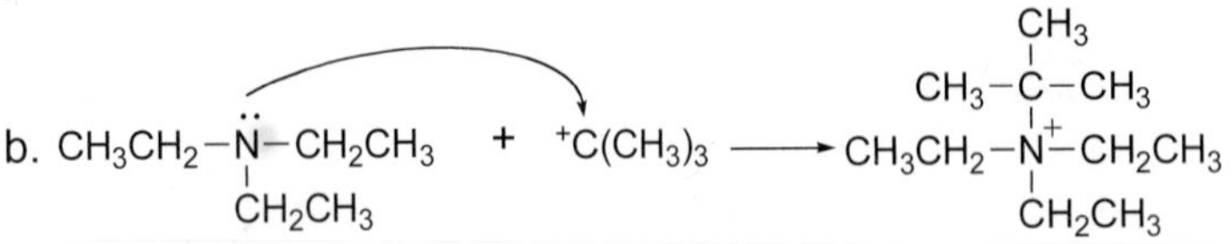

Lewis base — **nucleophile** — lone pair on N
Lewis acid — **electrophile** — unfilled valence shell on C

c.

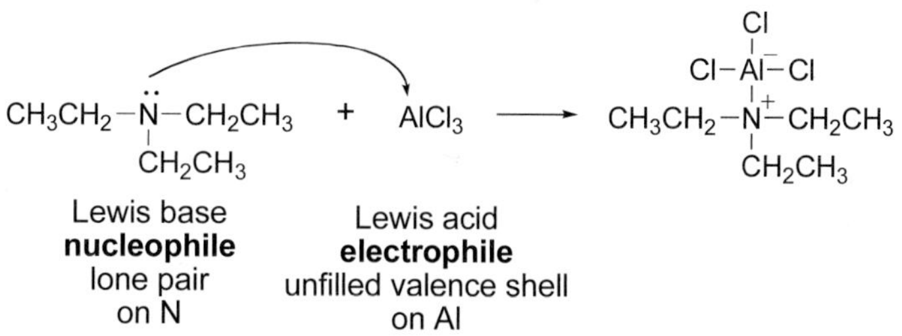

2.32 Curved arrows begin at the Lewis base and point towards the Lewis acid.

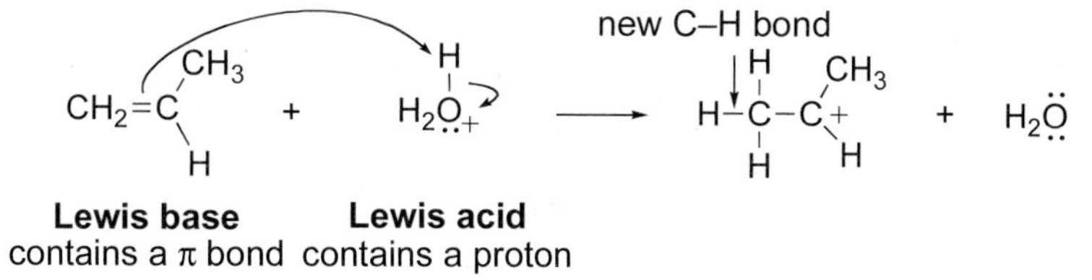

2.33 a, b. Since acidity increases from left to right across a row of the periodic table and propranolol has C–H, N–H, and O–H bonds, the O–H bond is most acidic. NaH is a base and removes the most acidic OH proton.

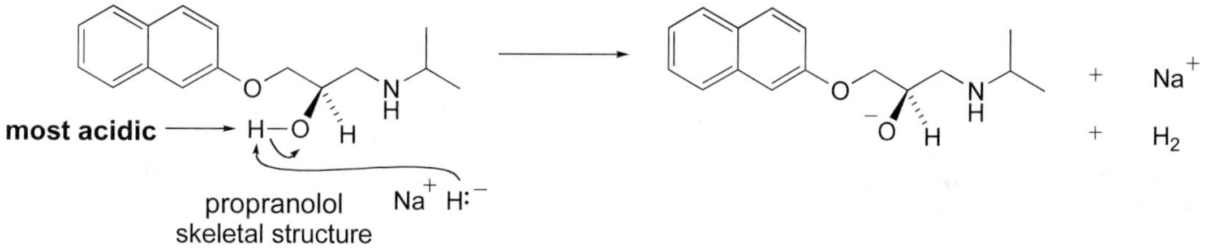

c, d. Of the atoms with lone pairs (N and O), N is to the left in the periodic table, making it the most basic site. HCl is an acid, which protonates the most basic site.

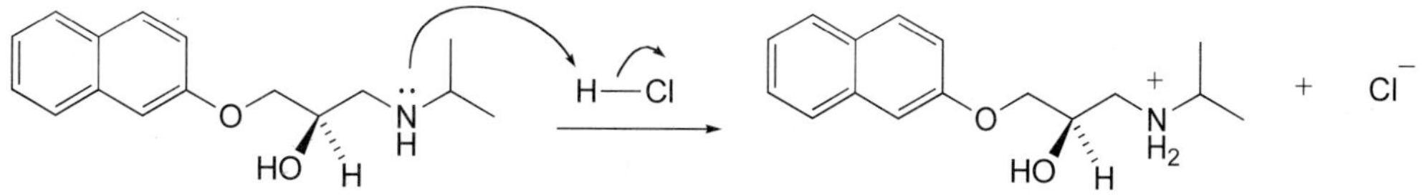

2.34 a, b. Using periodic trends, the N–H bond of amphetamine is most acidic. NaH is a base that removes a proton on N.

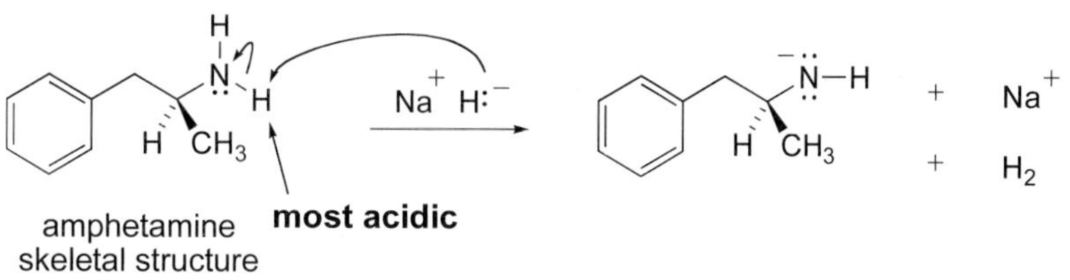

c. HCl protonates the lone pair on N.

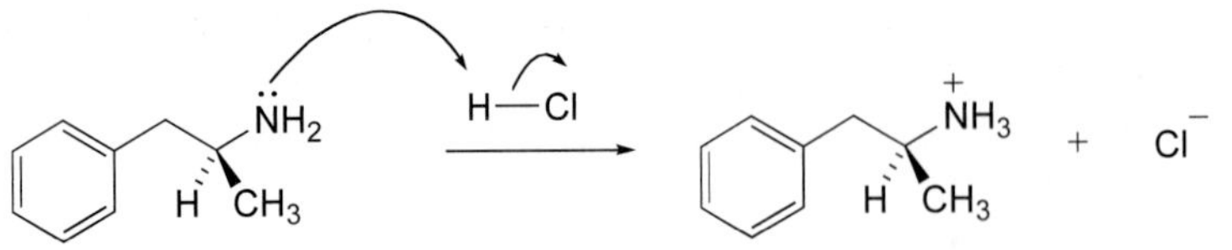

2.35 To draw the conjugate acid of a Brønsted–Lowry base, **add a proton to the base.**

a. $H_2\ddot{O}: \xrightarrow{H^+} H_3\ddot{O}^+$

b. $^-\!:\ddot{N}H_2 \xrightarrow{H^+} \ddot{N}H_3$

c. $HCO_3^- \xrightarrow{H^+} H_2CO_3$

d. $CH_3CH_2\ddot{N}HCH_3 \xrightarrow{H^+} CH_3CH_2\overset{+}{N}H_2CH_3$

e. $CH_3\ddot{O}CH_3 \xrightarrow{H^+} CH_3-\overset{+}{O}(H)-CH_3$

f. $CH_3COO^- \xrightarrow{H^+} CH_3COOH$

2.36 To draw the conjugate base of a Brønsted–Lowry acid, **remove a proton from the acid.**

a. $HCN \xrightarrow{-H^+} {}^-CN$

b. $HCO_3^- \xrightarrow{-H^+} CO_3^{2-}$

c. $(CH_3)_2\overset{+}{N}H_2 \xrightarrow{-H^+} (CH_3)_2NH$

d. $HC{\equiv}CH \xrightarrow{-H^+} HC{\equiv}C^-$

e. $CH_3CH_2COOH \xrightarrow{-H^+} CH_3CH_2COO^-$

f. $CH_3SO_3H \xrightarrow{-H^+} CH_3SO_3^-$

2.37 Use the definitions from Answer 2.2.

$CH_2{=}CH_2 \longrightarrow \overset{+}{C}H_2-CH_3$

ethylene — accepts a proton, conjugate acid

$CH_2{=}CH_2 \longrightarrow CH_2{=}\ddot{C}H^-$

loses a proton, conjugate base

2.38 To draw the products of an acid–base reaction, transfer a proton from the acid (H_2SO_4 in this case) to the base.

a.

b.

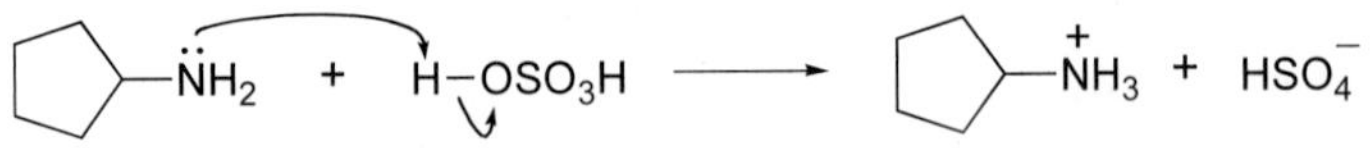

c.

d.

2.39 To draw the products of an acid–base reaction, transfer a proton from the acid to the base (^{-}OH in this case).

a. 

b. 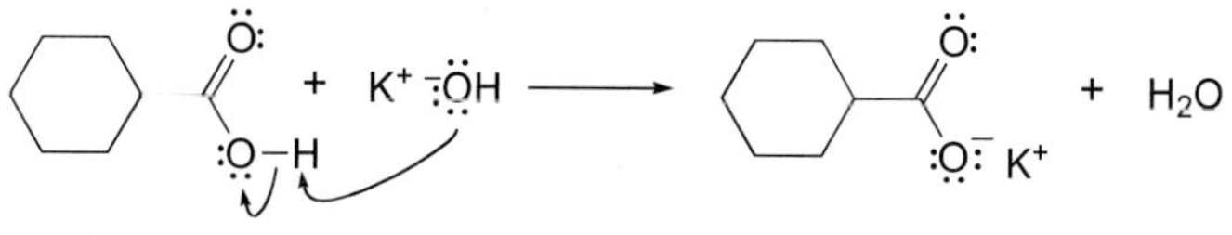

c. 

d. 

2.40 Label the Brønsted–Lowry acid and Brønsted–Lowry base in the starting materials and **transfer a proton from the acid to the base** for the products.

a. 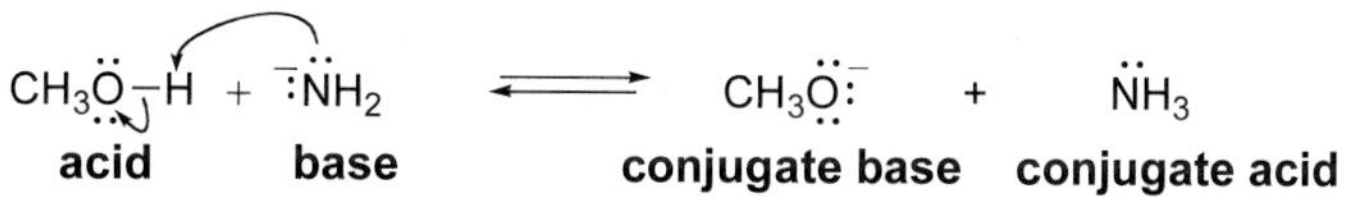
acid
base
conjugate base
conjugate acid

b. 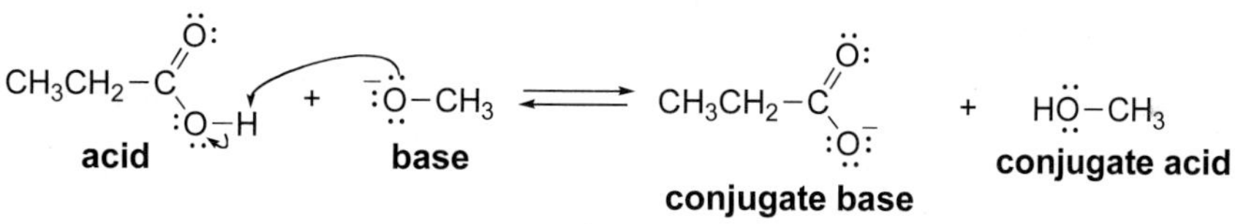
acid
base
conjugate base
conjugate acid

c. 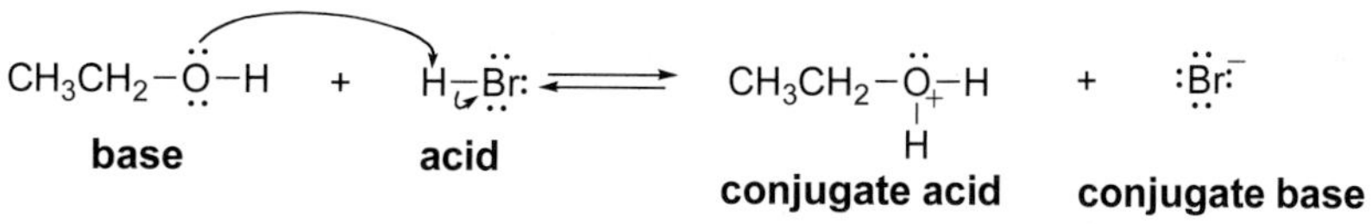
base
acid
conjugate acid
conjugate base

d. 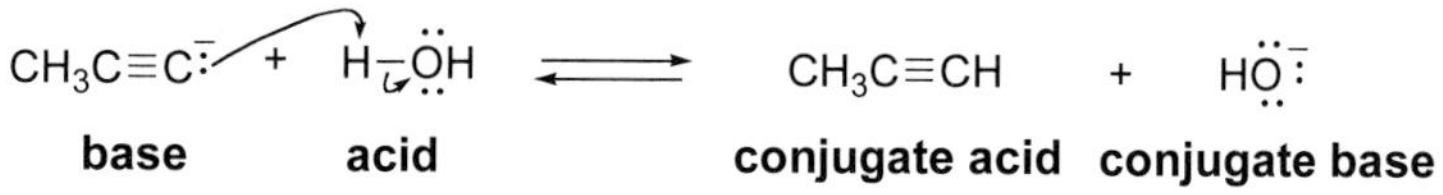
base
acid
conjugate acid
conjugate base

2.41 Label the acid and base in the starting materials and then draw the products of proton transfer from acid to base.

a. 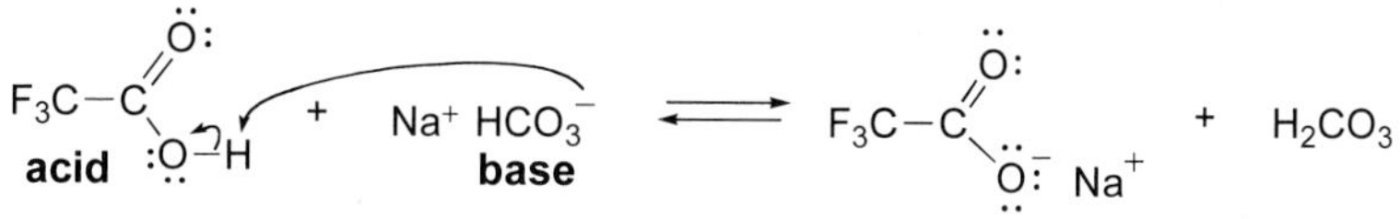
acid
base

b. 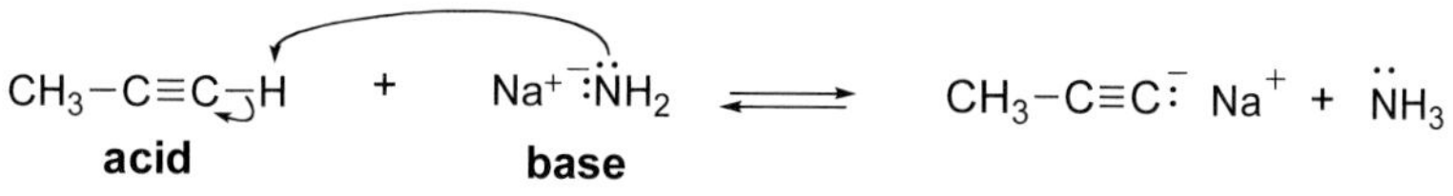
acid
base

c. 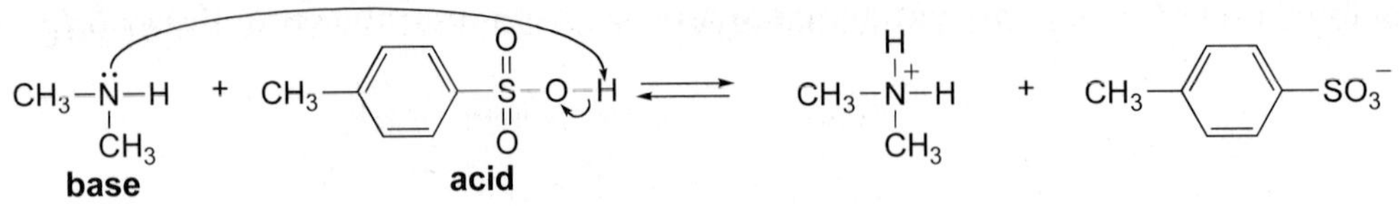

d. 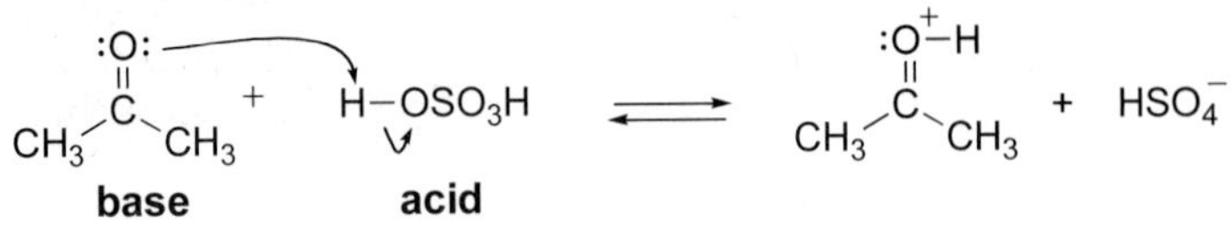

2.42 Draw the products of proton transfer from acid to base.

a. 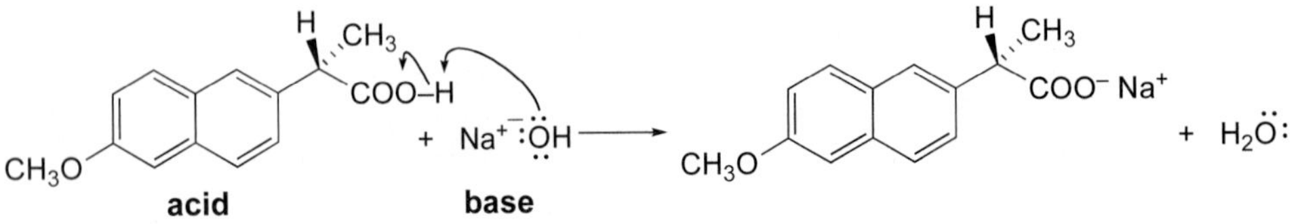

b. 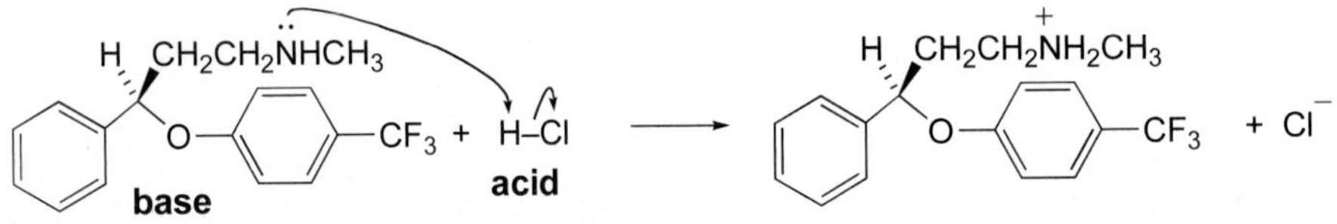

2.43 Draw the products of proton transfer from acid to base.

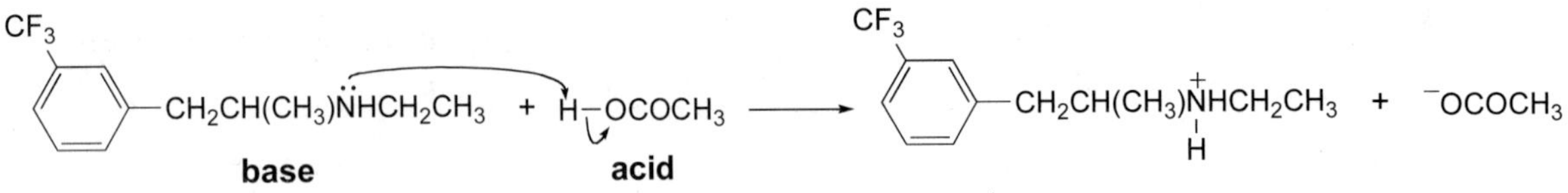

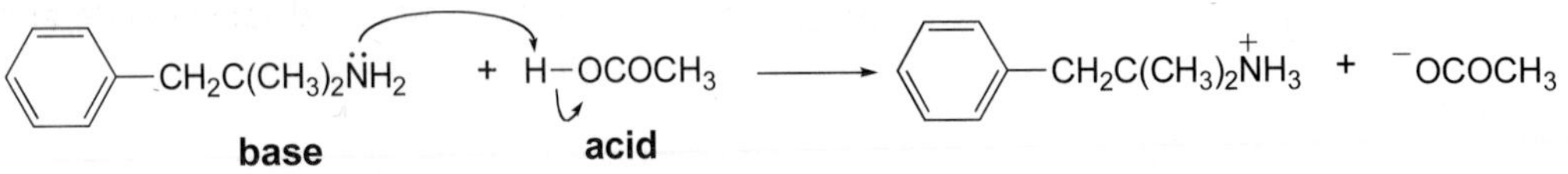

2.44 To convert pK_a to K_a, take the antilog of (–) the pK_a.

a. H_2S	b. $ClCH_2COOH$	c. HCN
pK_a = 7.0	pK_a = 2.8	pK_a = 9.1
$K_a = 10^{-7}$	$K_a = 1.6 \times 10^{-3}$	$K_a = 7.9 \times 10^{-10}$

2.45 To convert from K_a to pK_a, take (–) the log of the K_a; **pK_a = –log K_a.**

a. 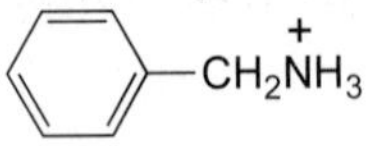

$K_a = 4.7 \times 10^{-10}$
pK_a = 9.3

b. 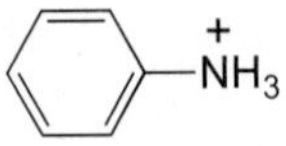

$K_a = 2.3 \times 10^{-5}$
pK_a = 4.6

c. CF_3COOH

$K_a = 5.9 \times 10^{-1}$
pK_a = 0.23

2.46 An acid can be deprotonated by the conjugate base of any acid with a higher pK_a.

$CH_3CH_2CH_2C{\equiv}CH$
pK_a = 25
Any base having a conjugate acid with a pK_a higher than 25 can deprotonate this acid.

Base	**Conjugate acid**	**pK_a**
H_2O	H_3O^+	–1.7
NaOH	H_2O	15.7
$NaNH_2$	NH_3	38
NH_3	NH_4^+	9.4
NaH	H_2	35
CH_3Li	CH_4	50

Only $NaNH_2$, NaH, and CH_3Li are strong enough to deprotonate the acid.

2.47 $^-$OH can deprotonate any acid with a pK_a < 15.7.

a. HCOOH
pK_a = 3.8
stronger acid
deprotonated

b. H_2S
pK_a = 7.0
stronger acid
deprotonated

c. 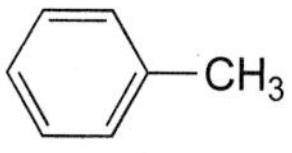
CH3
pK_a = 41
weaker acid

d. CH_3NH_2
pK_a = 40
weaker acid

These acids (c and d) are too weak to be deprotonated by $^-$OH.

2.48 Draw the products and then compare the pK_a of the acid on the left and the conjugate acid on the right. **The equilibrium lies towards the side having the acid with a higher pK_a (weaker acid).**

a. 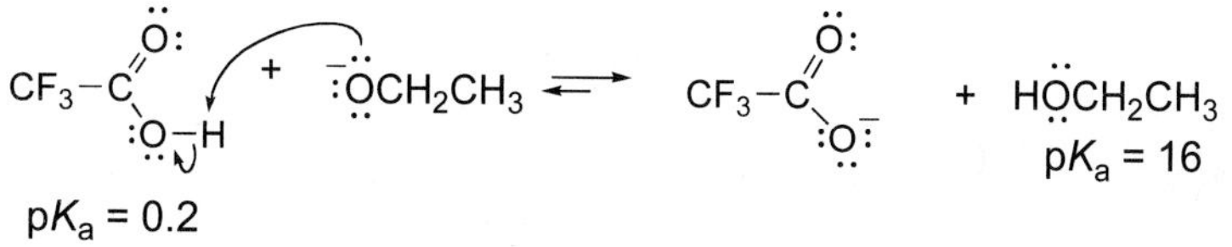
CF3–C
+
OCH2CH3
+ HOCH2CH3
pKa = 16
pKa = 0.2
products favored

b. 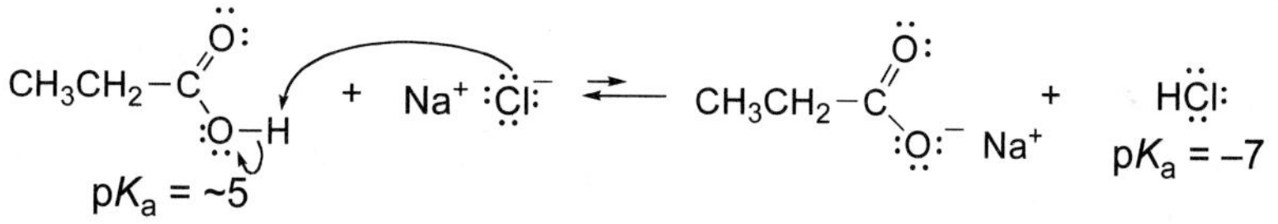
CH3CH2–C
+ Na+ Cl
CH3CH2–C
Na+
+ HCl
pKa = –7
pKa = ~5
starting material favored

c. 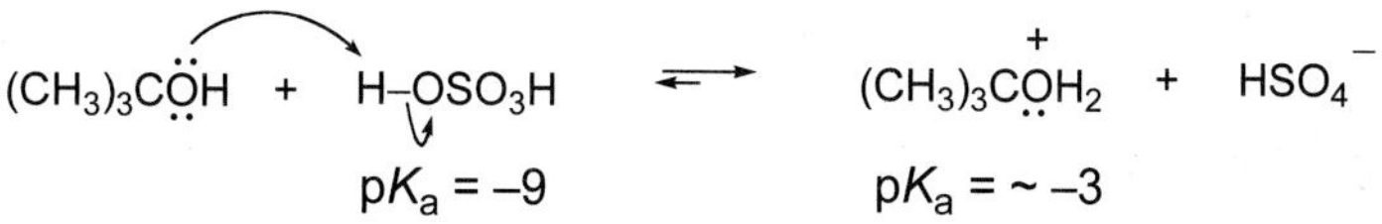
(CH3)3COH + H–OSO3H
pKa = –9
(CH3)3COH2 + HSO4
pKa = ~ –3
products favored

d. 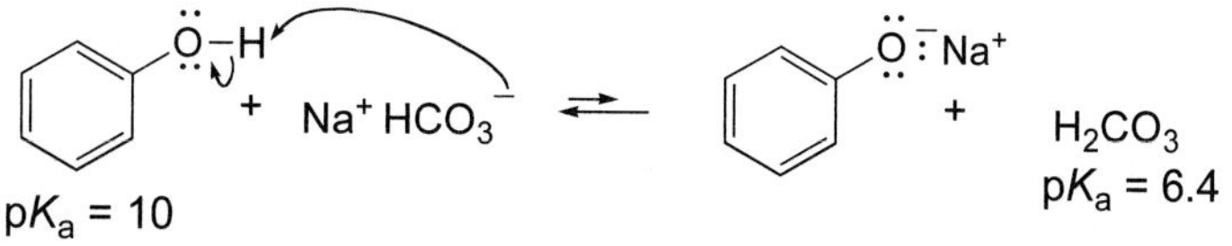
+ Na+ HCO3
Na+
+
H2CO3
pKa = 6.4
pKa = 10
starting material favored

e. 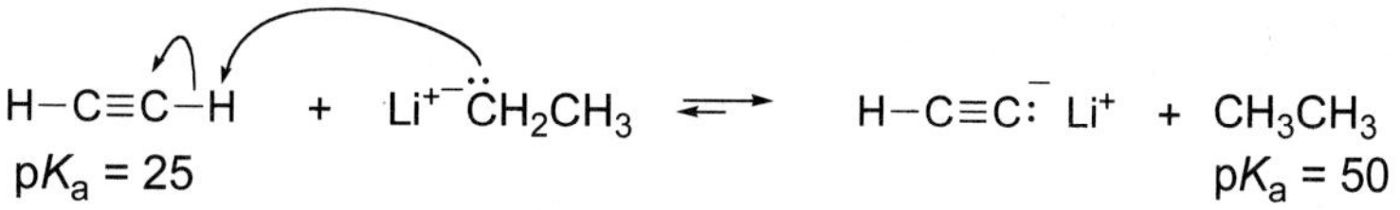
H–C≡C–H + Li+ CH2CH3
pKa = 25
H–C≡C: Li+ + CH3CH3
pKa = 50
products favored

f. 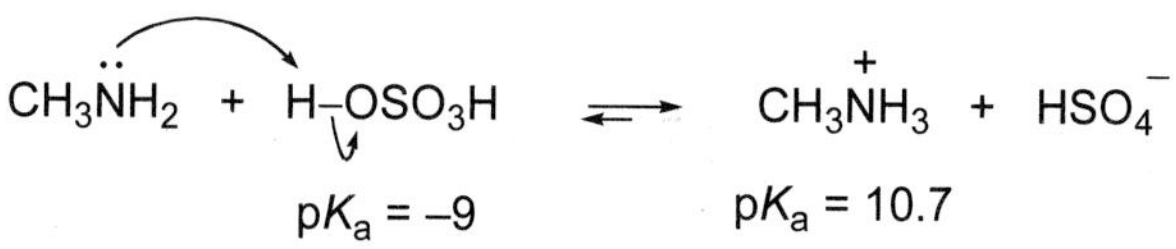
CH3NH2 + H–OSO3H
pKa = –9
CH3NH3 + HSO4
pKa = 10.7
products favored

2.49 Compare element effects first and then resonance, hybridization, and electron-withdrawing groups to determine the relative strengths of the acids.

a. Acidity increases across a row:
$NH_3 < H_2O < HF$

b. Acidity increases down a column:
$HF < HCl < HBr$

c. increasing acidity: $^{-}OH < H_2O < H_3O^+$

d. increasing acidity: $NH_3 < H_2O < H_2S$

Compare NH and OH bonds first:
acidity increases across a row.
OH is more acidic.

Then compare OH and SH bonds:
acidity increases down a column.
SH is more acidic.

e. Acidity increases across a row:
$CH_3CH_3 < CH_3NH_2 < CH_3OH$

f. increasing acidity: $H_2O < H_2S < HCl$

Compare HCl and SH bonds first:
acidity increases across a row.
H–Cl is more acidic.

Compare OH and SH bonds:
acidity increases down a column.
SH is more acidic.

g. $CH_3CH_2CH_3$, $ClCH_2CH_2OH$, CH_3CH_2OH

$CH_3CH_2CH_3$: only C–H bonds, **weakest acid**

$ClCH_2CH_2OH$: O–H bond and electron-withdrawing Cl, **strongest acid**

CH_3CH_2OH: O–H bond

increasing acidity: $CH_3CH_2CH_3 < CH_3CH_2OH < ClCH_2CH_2OH$

h. $HC{\equiv}CCH_2CH_3$ $CH_3CH_2CH_2CH_3$ $CH_3C{=}CCH_3$ (with H on each alkene C)

$HC{\equiv}CCH_2CH_3$: *sp* C–H, **strongest acid**

$CH_3CH_2CH_2CH_3$: all *sp*^{3} C–H, **weakest acid**

$CH_3CH{=}CHCH_3$: *sp*^{2} C–H

increasing acidity: $CH_3CH_2CH_2CH_3 < CH_3CH{=}CHCH_3 < HC{\equiv}CCH_2CH_3$

2.50 The strongest acid has the weakest conjugate base.

a. Draw the conjugate acid.
Increasing acidity of conjugate acids:
$CH_3CH_3 < CH_3NH_2 < CH_3OH$

increasing basicity: $CH_3O^- < CH_3NH^- < CH_3CH_2^-$

b. Draw the conjugate acid.
Increasing acidity of conjugate acids:
$CH_4 < H_2O < HBr$

increasing basicity: $Br^- < HO^- < {}^-CH_3$

c. Draw the conjugate acid.
Increasing acidity of conjugate acids:
$CH_3CH_2OH < CH_3COOH < ClCH_2COOH$

increasing basicity: $ClCH_2COO^- < CH_3COO^- < CH_3CH_2O^-$

d. Draw the conjugate acid.
Increasing acidity of conjugate acids:

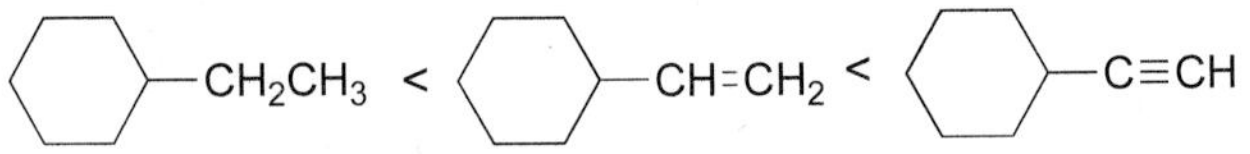

increasing basicity:

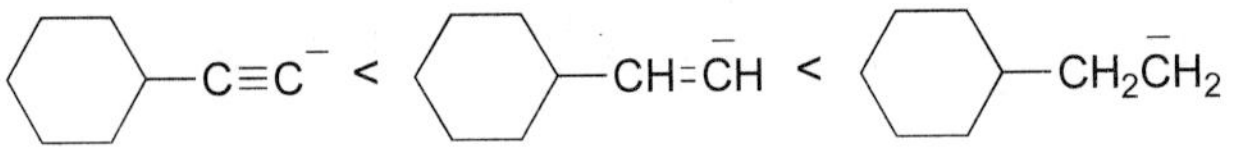

2.51 **More electronegative atoms stabilize the conjugate base by an electron-withdrawing inductive effect, making the acid stronger.** Thus, an O atom increases the acidity of an acid.

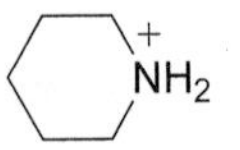

pK_a = 11.1

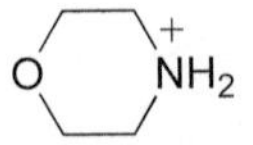

The O atom makes this cation the stronger acid.
pK_a = 8.33

2.52 In both molecules the OH proton is the most acidic H. In addition, compare the percent *s*-character of the carbon atoms in each molecule. Nearby C's with a higher percent *s*-character can help to stabilize the conjugate base.

$HC{\equiv}CCO_2H$

pK_a = 1.8

The *sp* hybridized C's of the triple bond have a higher percent *s*-character than an sp^3 hybridized C, so they pull electron density towards them, stabilizing the conjugate base.

stronger acid

$CH_3CH_2CO_2H$

pK_a = 4.9

2.53

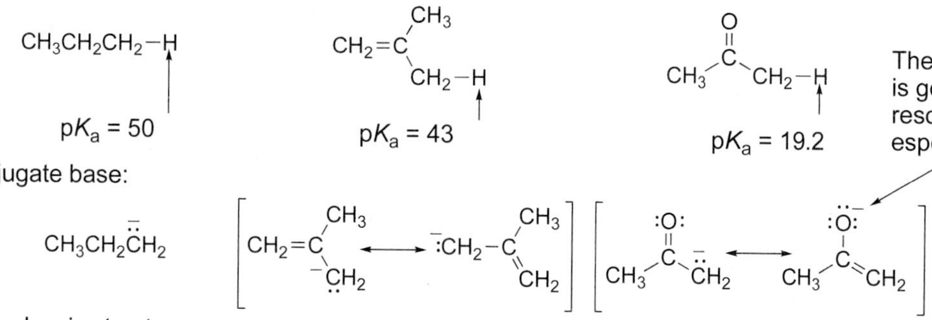

pK_a = 50 — pK_a = 43 — pK_a = 19.2

The negative charge on O is good. This makes this resonance structure especially good.

one Lewis structure
weakest acid

two resonance structures
negative charge delocalized on two carbons

two resonance structures
negative charge delocalized on one O and one C
strongest acid

2.54 To draw the conjugate acid, look for the most basic site and protonate it. To draw the conjugate base, look for the most acidic site and remove a proton.

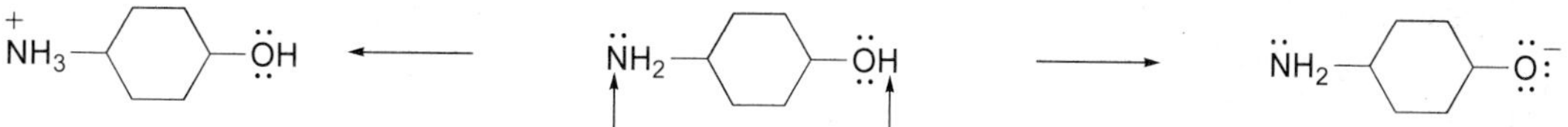

conjugate acid — most basic site — **A** — most acidic proton — conjugate base

2.55 Estimate the pK_a of **B** as 16. A difference of 10^5 in acidity is a difference of 5 pK_a units.

a.

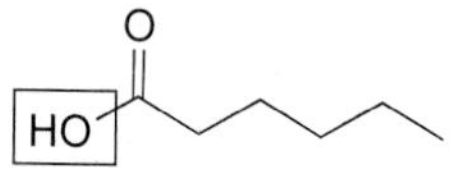

most acidic H
pK_a ~ 5

b.

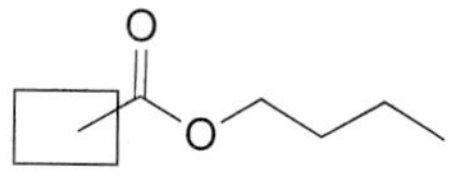

most acidic
pK_a ~ 25

c.

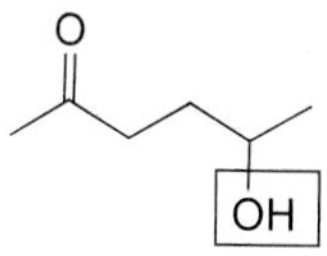

most acidic
pK_a ~ 16

2.56 Remove the most acidic proton to form the conjugate base. Protonate the most basic electron pair to form the conjugate acid.

a.

only O–H bond
most acidic proton

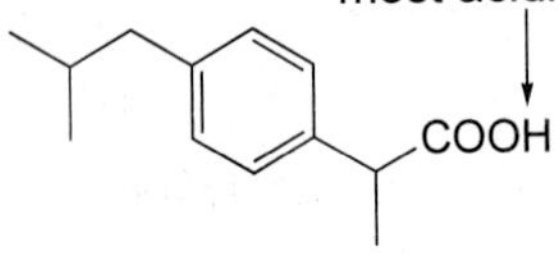
COOH

ibuprofen

conjugate base:

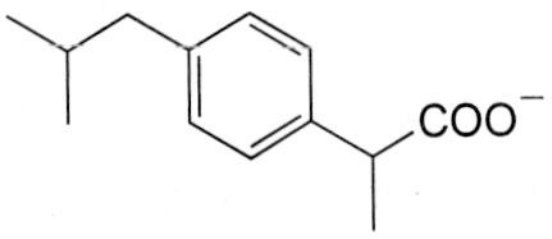
COO⁻

b.

most basic electron pair

Increasing basicity:

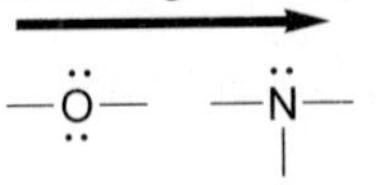

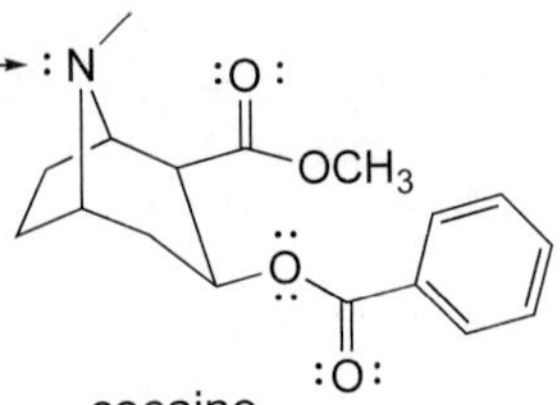
:N
:O:
OCH3
:O:

cocaine

conjugate acid:

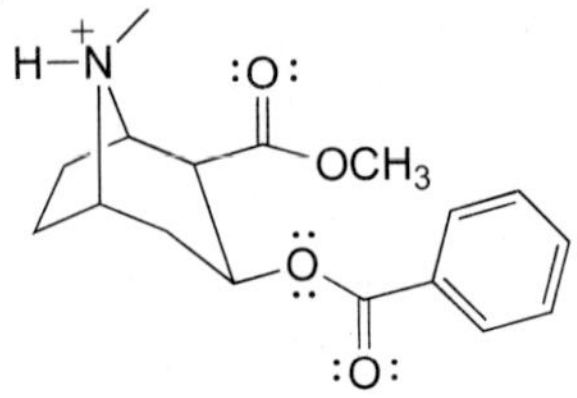
H–N
:O:
OCH3
:O:

2.57 Compare the isomers.

dimethyl ether CH_3OCH_3 CH_3CH_2OH ethanol

All H's are on C.

One O–H bond
O–H bonds are more acidic than C–H bonds.
more acidic

2.58 Compare the Lewis structures of the conjugate bases when each H is removed. The more stable base makes the proton more acidic.

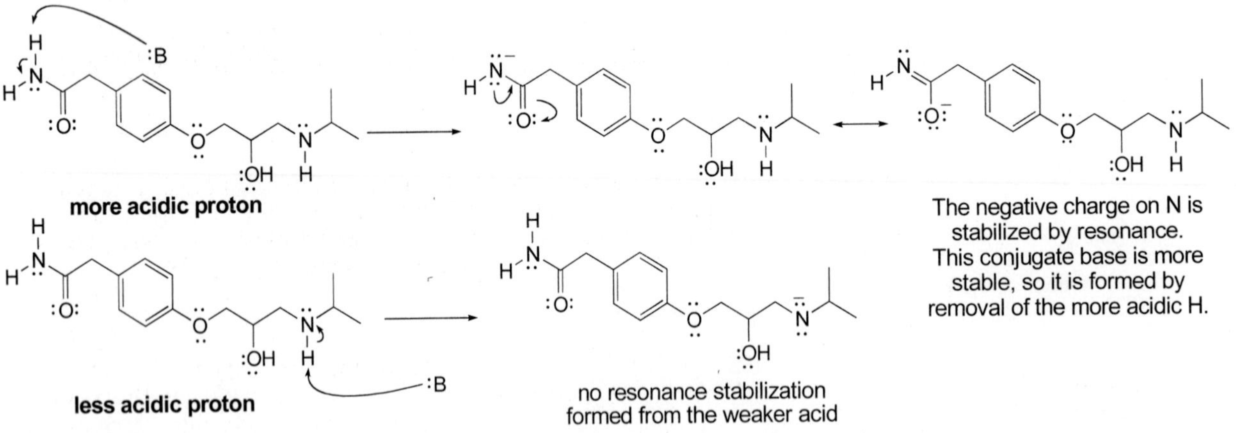
:B
:OH H
more acidic proton
:OH H
less acidic proton
:B
:OH
no resonance stabilization
formed from the weaker acid
The negative charge on N is stabilized by resonance.
This conjugate base is more stable, so it is formed by removal of the more acidic H.

2.59 Draw the conjugate base to determine the most acidic hydrogen.

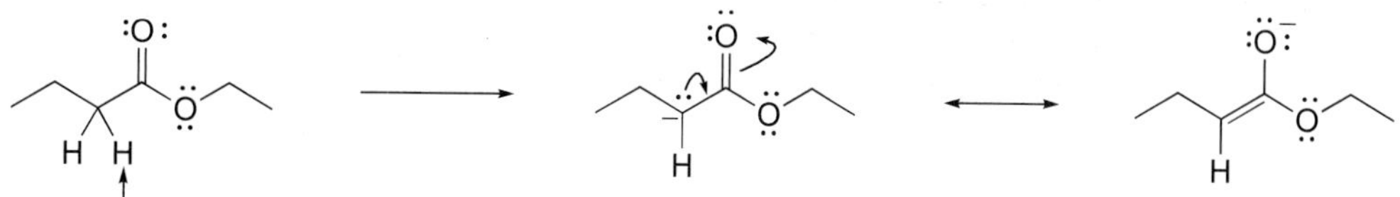

Resonance stabilization of the conjugate base makes this the most acidic proton.
In Appendix A, the closest compound for comparison is $CH_3CO_2CH_2CH_3$ with a pK_a of 24.5; therefore, the estimated pK_a of ethyl butanoate is 25.

resonance-stabilized conjugate base

2.60 Look at the element bonded to the acidic H and decide its acidity based on the periodic trends. **Farther to the right across a row and down a column of the periodic table is more acidic.**

a.

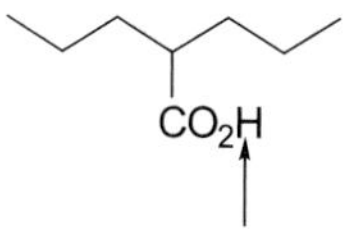

most acidic

The molecule contains C–H and O–H bonds. O is farther right in the periodic table; therefore, the O–H hydrogen is the most acidic.

b.

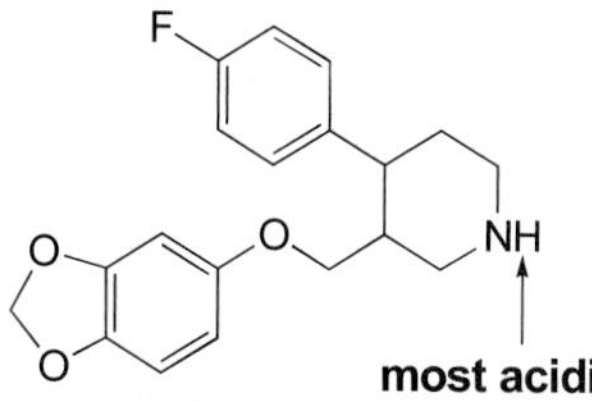

most acidic

The molecule contains C–H and N–H bonds. N is farther right in the periodic table; therefore, the N–H hydrogen is the most acidic.

c.

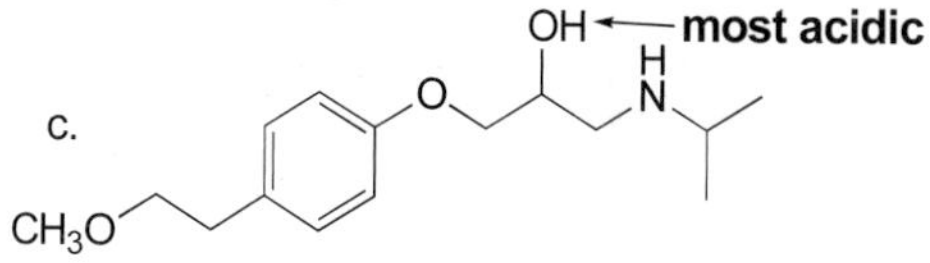

The molecule contains C–H, N–H, and O–H bonds. O is farthest right in the periodic table; therefore, the O–H hydrogen is the most acidic.

2.61 Use element effects, inductive effects, and resonance to determine which protons are the most acidic. The H's of the CH_3 group are least acidic since they are bonded to an sp^3 hybridized C and the conjugate base formed by their removal is not resonance stabilized.

lactic acid

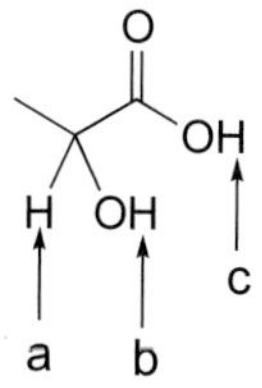

c > b > a
Both O–H protons [(b) and (c)] are more acidic than the C–H proton (a) by the element effect. The most acidic proton has added resonance stabilization when it is removed, making its conjugate base the most stable.

conjugate base by loss of (c):

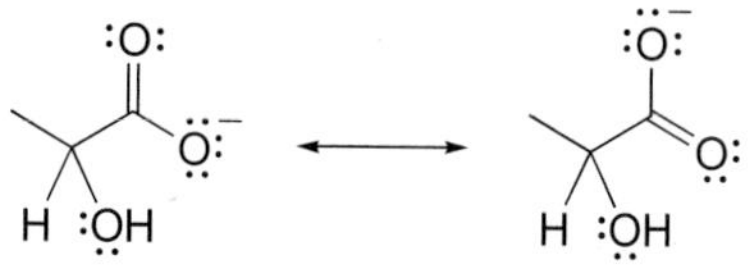

resonance stabilization
negative charge on O in both resonance structures
This makes (c) most acidic.

conjugate base by loss of (b):

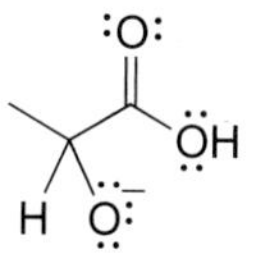

no resonance stabilization, but negative charge on O, an electronegative atom

conjugate base by loss of (a):

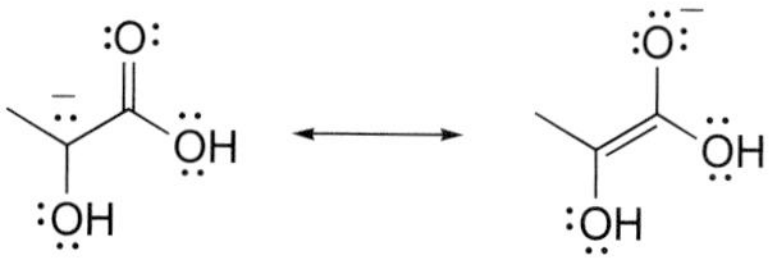

This conjugate base has two resonance structures, but one places a negative charge on C.

2.62 ***Lewis bases* are electron pair donors:** they contain a lone pair or a π bond. ***Brønsted–Lowry bases* are proton acceptors:** to accept a proton they need a lone pair or a π bond. This means Lewis bases are also Brønsted–Lowry bases.

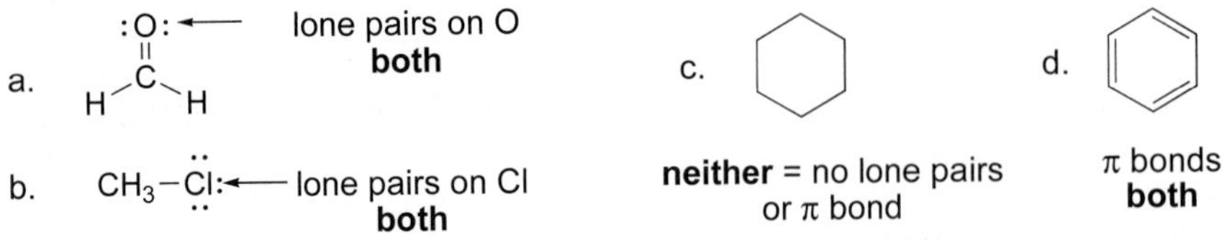
a.
lone pairs on O
both
b.
lone pairs on Cl
both
c.
neither = no lone pairs
or π bond
d.
π bonds
both

2.63 A ***Lewis acid* is an electron pair acceptor** and usually contains a proton or an unfilled valence shell of electrons. A ***Brønsted–Lowry acid* is a proton donor** and must contain a hydrogen atom. All Brønsted–Lowry acids are Lewis acids, though the reverse may not be true.

a. H_3O^+	b. Cl_3C^+	c. BCl_3	d. BF_4^-
both contains a H	**Lewis acid** unfilled valence shell on C	**Lewis acid** unfilled valence shell on B	**neither** no H or unfilled valence shell

2.64 Label the Lewis acid and Lewis base and then draw the products.

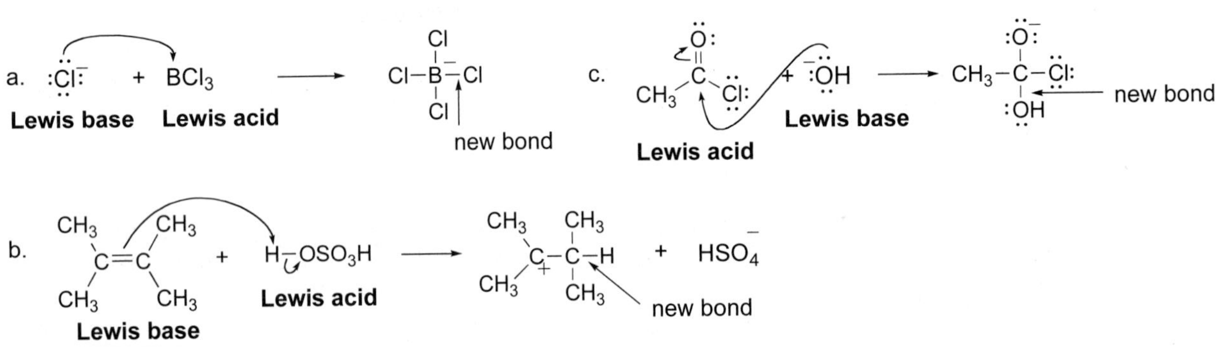
a.
Lewis base
Lewis acid
new bond
c.
Lewis acid
Lewis base
new bond
b.
Lewis base
Lewis acid
new bond

2.65 A Lewis acid is also called an **electrophile.** When a Lewis base reacts with an electrophile other than a proton, it is called a **nucleophile.** Label the electrophile and nucleophile in the starting materials and then draw the products.

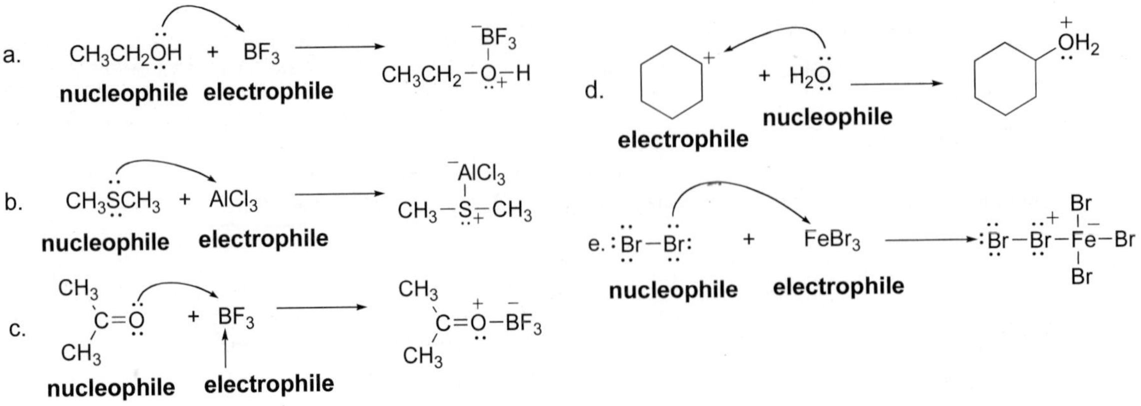
a.
nucleophile
electrophile
b.
nucleophile
electrophile
c.
nucleophile
electrophile
d.
electrophile
nucleophile
e.
nucleophile
electrophile

2.66 Draw the product of each reaction.

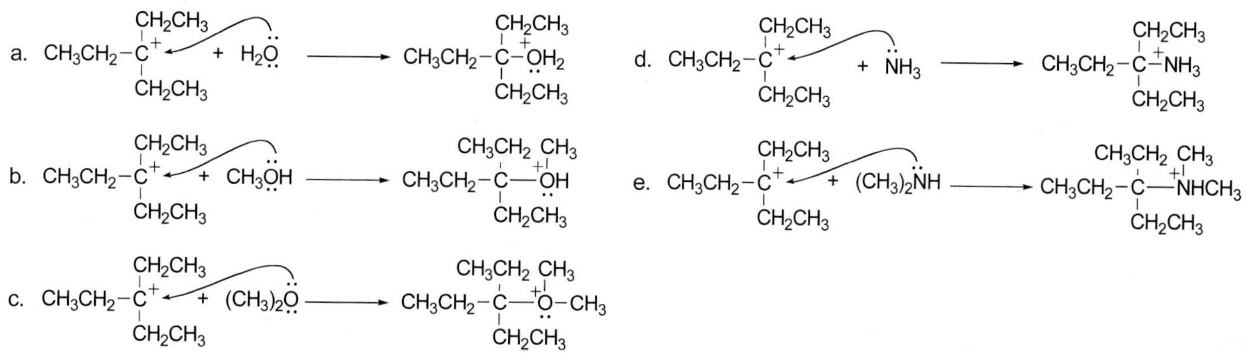

2.67

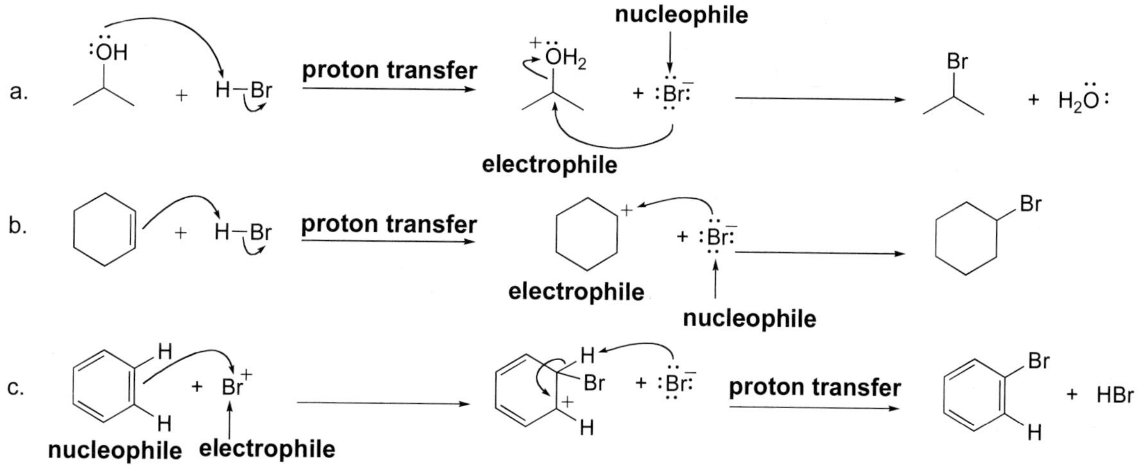

2.68 Draw the products of each reaction. In part (a), $^{-}$OH pulls off a proton and thus acts as a Brønsted–Lowry base. In part (b), $^{-}$OH attacks a carbon and thus acts as a Lewis base.

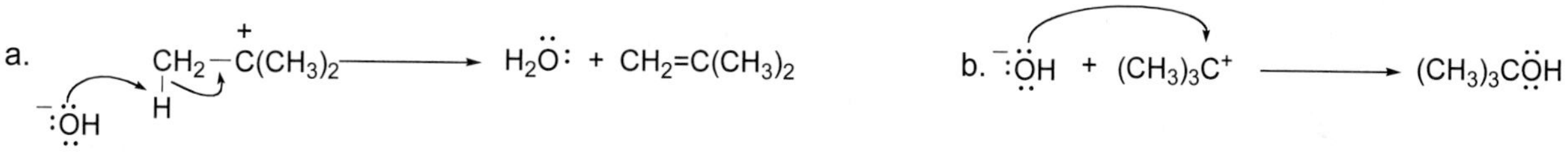

2.69 Answer each question about esmolol.

a.

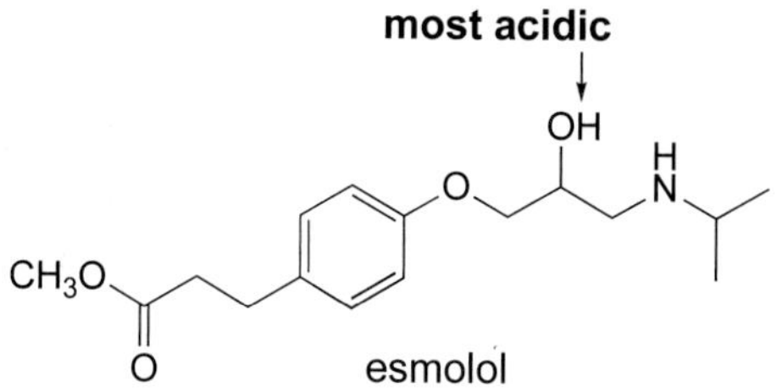

Esmolol contains C–H, N–H, and O–H bonds. Since acidity increases across a row of the periodic table, the OH bond is most acidic.

b.

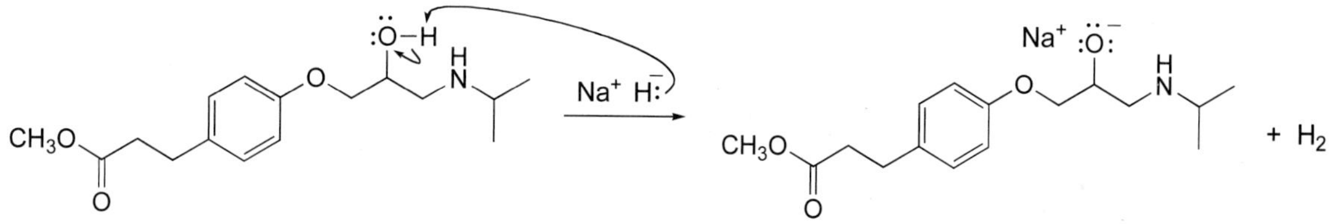

c.

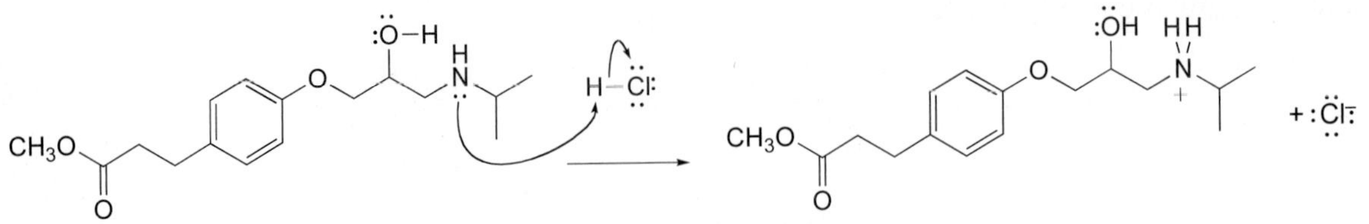

d, e, f.

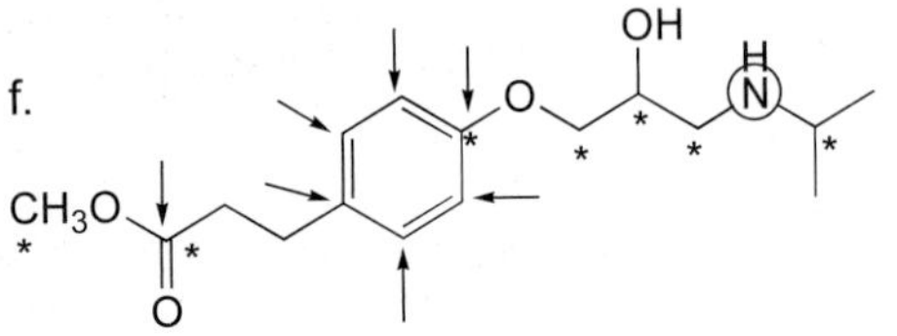

All sp^2 C's are indicated with an arrow.
The N is the only trigonal pyramidal atom.
The δ^+ C's are indicated with a (*).

2.70

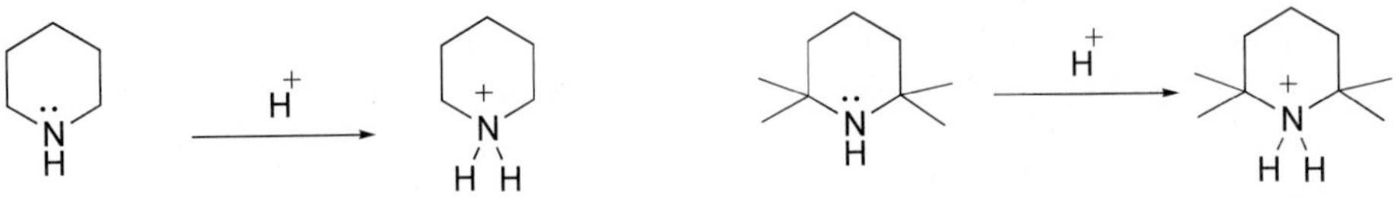

P

pK_a = 11.1

weaker base

Q

pK_a = 1.2
much lower pK_a
much stronger acid

The four CH_3 groups near the electron pair make it difficult to donate that electron pair to a proton. This makes the conjugate base of **Q** much weaker, and **Q** a stronger acid.

2.71

[1]

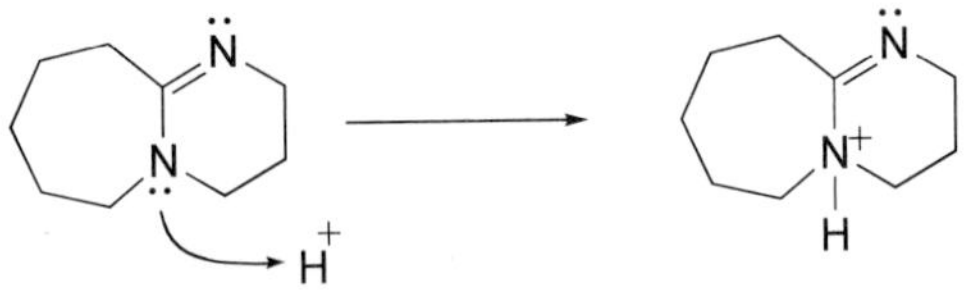

no additional stabilization

or

[2]

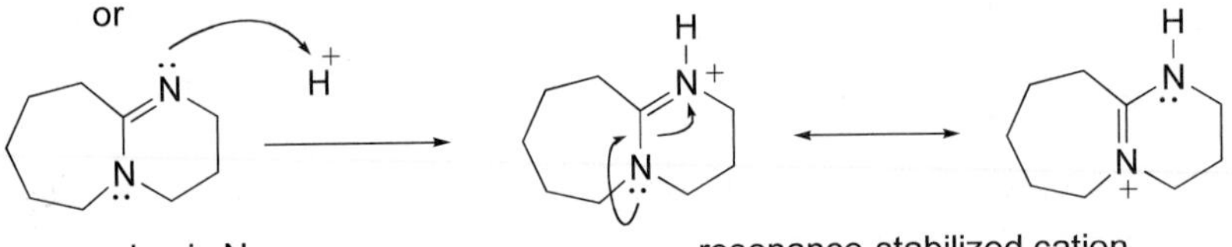

more basic N

resonance-stabilized cation

Path [2] is favored because a resonance-stabilized conjugate acid is formed. The N that is part of the C=N is therefore more basic.

2.72 Draw the product of protonation of either O or N and compare the conjugate acids. When acetamide reacts with an acid, the O atom is protonated because it results in a resonance-stabilized conjugate acid.

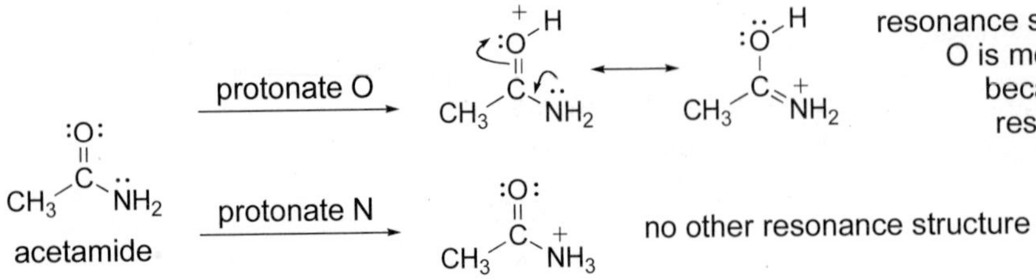

resonance stabilization of the + charge
O is more readily protonated
because the product is
resonance stabilized.

2.73

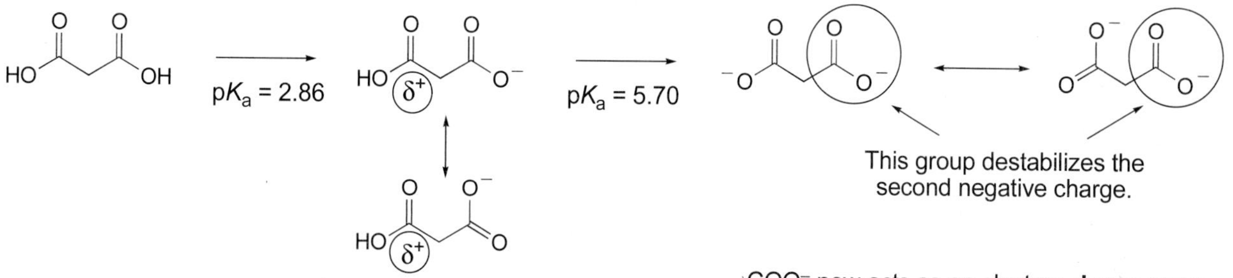
HO
OH
$pK_a = 2.86$
δ^+
$pK_a = 5.70$
This group destabilizes the
second negative charge.

δ^+ stabilizes the (–) charge of the conjugate base.

The nearby COOH group serves as an electron-**withdrawing** group to stabilize the negative charge. This makes the first proton **more** acidic than CH_3COOH.

COO^- now acts as an electron-**donor** group which destabilizes the conjugate base, making removal of the second proton more difficult and thus it is **less** acidic than CH_3COOH.

2.74 The COOH group of glycine gives up a proton to the basic NH_2 group to form the zwitterion.

a.

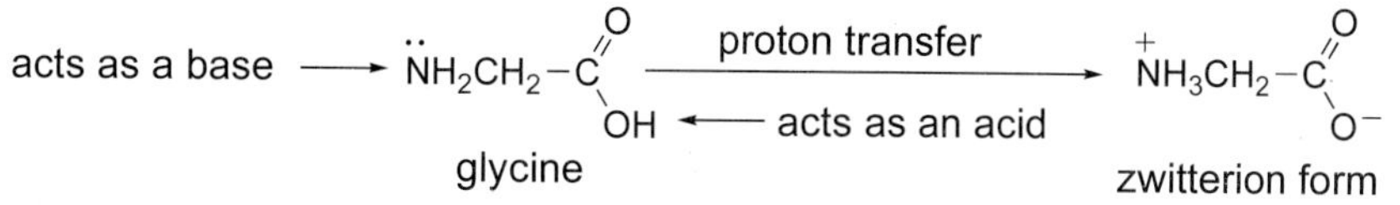
acts as a base
proton transfer
acts as an acid
glycine
zwitterion form

b.

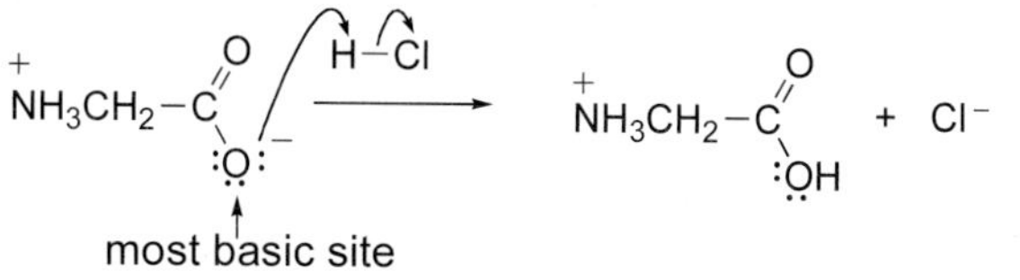
H–Cl
+ Cl⁻
most basic site

c.

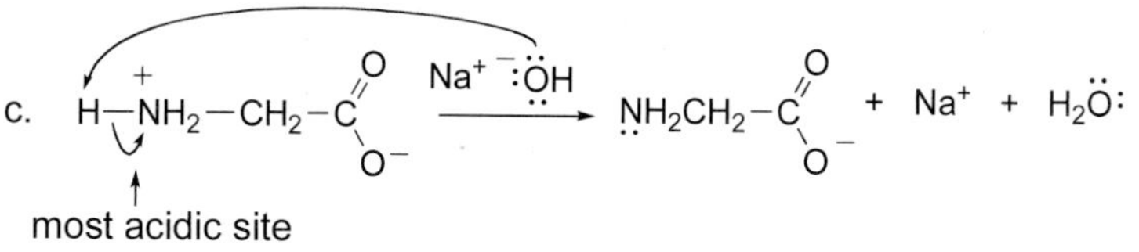
Na⁺ ⁻:ÖH
+ Na⁺ + H₂Ö:
most acidic site

2.75 Use curved arrows to show how the reaction occurs.

[1]

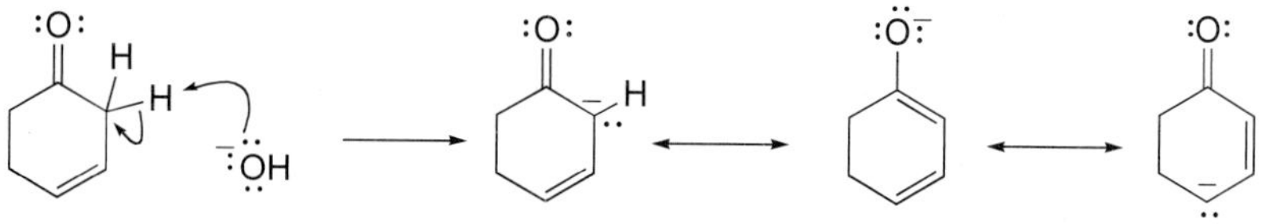

[2]

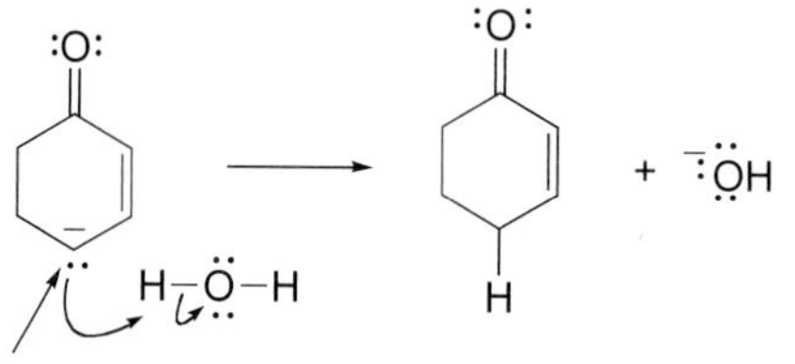

Protonate the negative charge on this carbon to form the product.

2.76 Compare the OH bonds in vitamin C and decide which one is the most acidic.

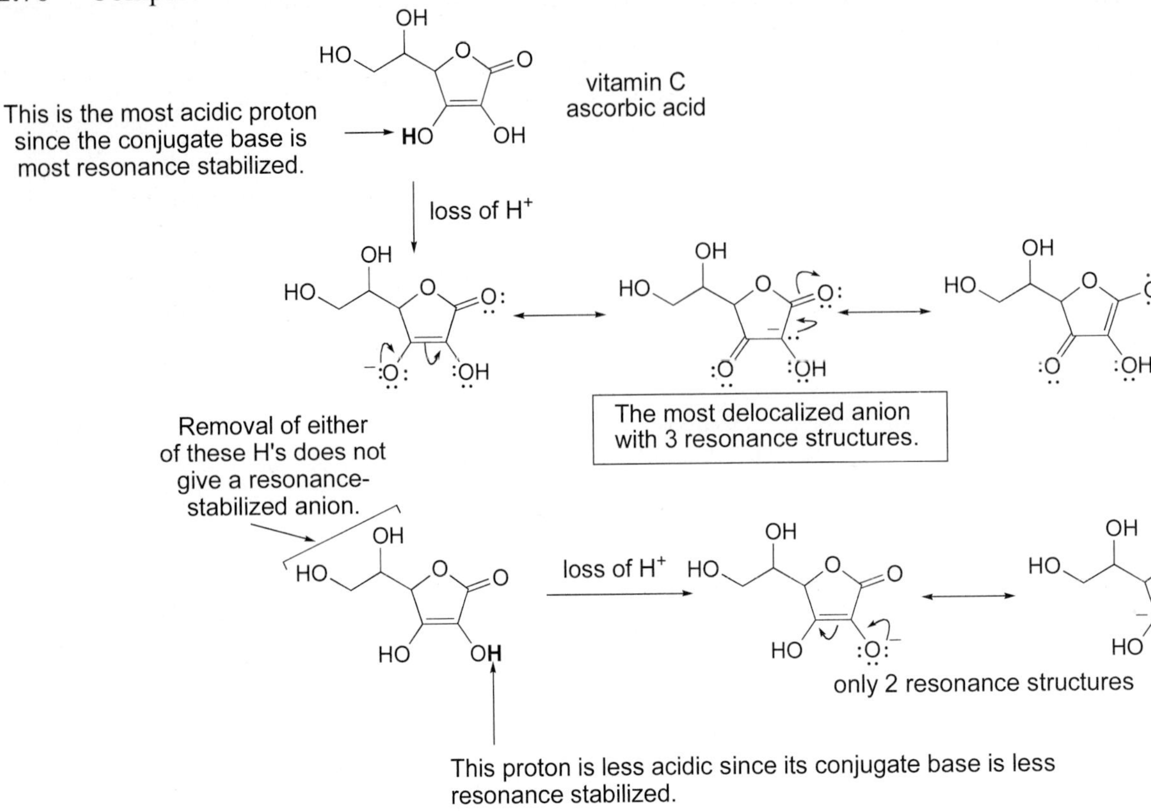
vitamin C
ascorbic acid
This is the most acidic proton since the conjugate base is most resonance stabilized.
loss of H+
Removal of either of these H's does not give a resonance-stabilized anion.
The most delocalized anion with 3 resonance structures.
loss of H+
only 2 resonance structures
This proton is less acidic since its conjugate base is less resonance stabilized.

2.77

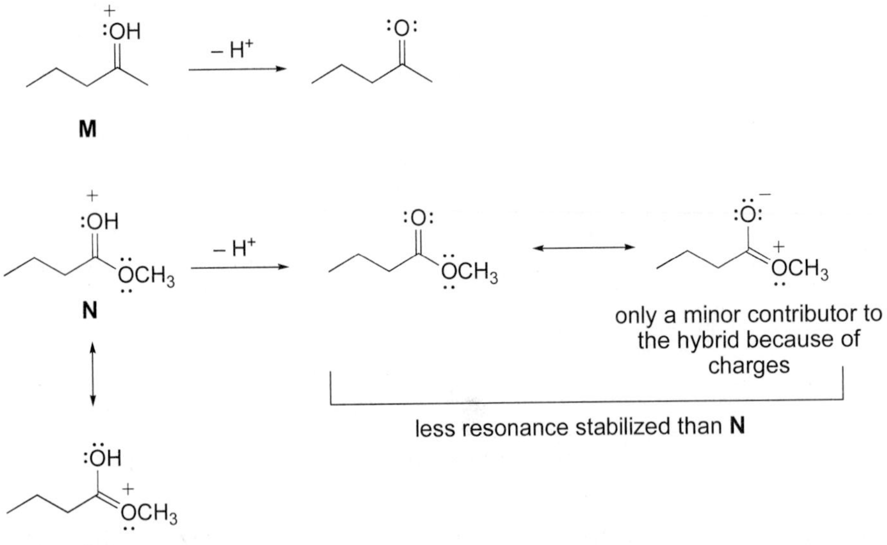
M
N
– H+
– H+
only a minor contributor to the hybrid because of charges
less resonance stabilized than N

N has two resonance structures with the same number of bonds and charges, so both contribute approximately equally to the hybrid. This makes **N** more resonance stabilized than its conjugate base, and less willing to give up a proton than **M,** which has no similar resonance stabilization. Thus **M** is a stronger acid than **N.** (Resonance structures that break the C=O bond are not drawn in this solution, since they are possible for each compound.)

Chapter 3 Introduction to Organic Molecules and Functional Groups

Chapter Review

Types of intermolecular forces (3.3)

Increasing strength ↓

Type of force	Cause	Examples
van der Waals (VDW)	Due to the interaction of temporary dipoles • Larger surface area, stronger forces • Larger, more polarizable atoms, stronger forces	All organic compounds
dipole–dipole (DD)	Due to the interaction of permanent dipoles	$(CH_3)_2C{=}O$, H_2O
hydrogen bonding (HB or H-bonding)	Due to the electrostatic interaction of a H atom in an O–H, N–H, or H–F bond with another N, O, or F atom.	H_2O
ion–ion	Due to the interaction of two ions	NaCl, LiF

Physical properties

Property	Observation
Boiling point (3.4A)	• For compounds of comparable molecular weight, the stronger the forces the higher the bp. $CH_3CH_2CH_2CH_2CH_3$ — VDW — MW = 72 — bp = 36 °C $CH_3CH_2CH_2CHO$ — VDW, DD — MW = 72 — bp = 76 °C $CH_3CH_2CH_2CH_2OH$ — VDW, DD, HB — MW = 74 — bp = 118 °C → **Increasing strength of intermolecular forces** **Increasing boiling point** • For compounds with similar functional groups, the larger the surface area, the higher the bp. $CH_3CH_2CH_2CH_3$ — bp = 0 °C $CH_3CH_2CH_2CH_2CH_3$ — bp = 36 °C → **Increasing surface area** **Increasing boiling point** • For compounds with similar functional groups, the more polarizable the atoms, the higher the bp. CH_3F — bp = –78 °C CH_3I — bp = 42 °C → **Increasing polarizability** **Increasing boiling point**

Property	Observation
Melting point (3.4B)	• For compounds of comparable molecular weight, the stronger the forces the higher the mp. $CH_3CH_2CH_2CH_2CH_3$ — VDW — MW = 72 — mp = –130 °C $CH_3CH_2CH_2CHO$ — VDW, DD — MW = 72 — mp = –96 °C $CH_3CH_2CH_2CH_2OH$ — VDW, DD, HB — MW = 74 — mp = –90 °C → **Increasing strength of intermolecular forces** **Increasing melting point** • For compounds with similar functional groups, the more symmetrical the compound, the higher the mp. $CH_3CH_2CH(CH_3)_2$ — mp = –160 °C $(CH_3)_4C$ — mp = –17 °C → **Increasing symmetry** **Increasing melting point**
Solubility (3.4C)	Types of water-soluble compounds: • Ionic compounds • Organic compounds having ≤ 5 C's, and an O or N atom for hydrogen bonding (for a compound with one functional group). Types of compounds soluble in organic solvents: • Organic compounds regardless of size or functional group. • Examples: 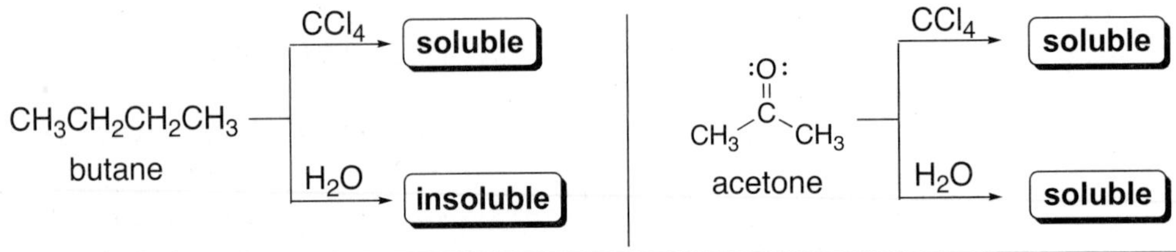 CCl4 soluble CH3CH2CH2CH3 butane H2O insoluble CCl4 soluble acetone H2O soluble
	Key: VDW = van der Waals, DD = dipole–dipole, HB = hydrogen bonding MW = molecular weight

Reactivity (3.8)

- **Nucleophiles react with electrophiles.**
- Electronegative heteroatoms create electrophilic carbon atoms, which tend to react with nucleophiles.
- Lone pairs and π bonds are nucleophilic sites that tend to react with electrophiles.

electrophilic site
basic and nucleophilic site

Practice Test on Chapter Review

1.a. Which of the following compounds exhibits dipole–dipole interactions?

1. 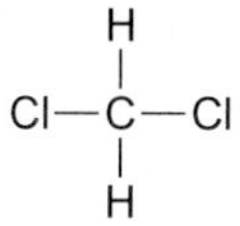

2. $CH_3—O—CH_3$

3. $CH_3CH_2CH_2—OH$

4. Compounds (1) and (2) both exhibit dipole–dipole interactions.

5. Compounds (1), (2), and (3) all exhibit dipole–dipole interactions.

b. Which of the following compounds can hydrogen bond to both another molecule like itself and to water?

1. 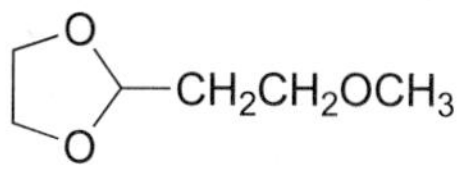

2. 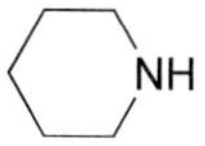

3. $CH_3C{\equiv}N$

4. Compounds (1) and (2) can each hydrogen bond to another molecule like itself and water.

5. Each of the three compounds, (1), (2), and (3), can hydrogen bond to another molecule like itself and to water.

c. Which of the following compounds has the highest boiling point?

1. $CH_3CH_2CH_2OCH_2CH_3$
2. $CH_3(CH_2)_4CH_3$
3. $CH_3(CH_2)_4NH_2$
4. $(CH_3)_2CHCH(CH_3)NH_2$
5. $(CH_3)_2CHCH(CH_3)_2$

d. Which statement(s) is (are) true about the following compounds?

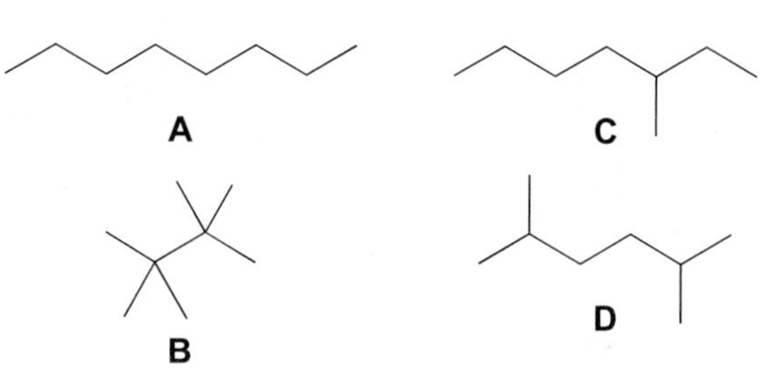

1. The boiling point of **A** is higher than the boiling point of **B.**
2. The melting point of **B** is higher than the melting point of **C.**
3. The boiling point of **A** is higher than the boiling point of **D.**
4. Statements (1) and (2) are both true.
5. Statements (1), (2), and (3) are all true.

2. Consider the anti-hypertensive agent atenolol drawn below.

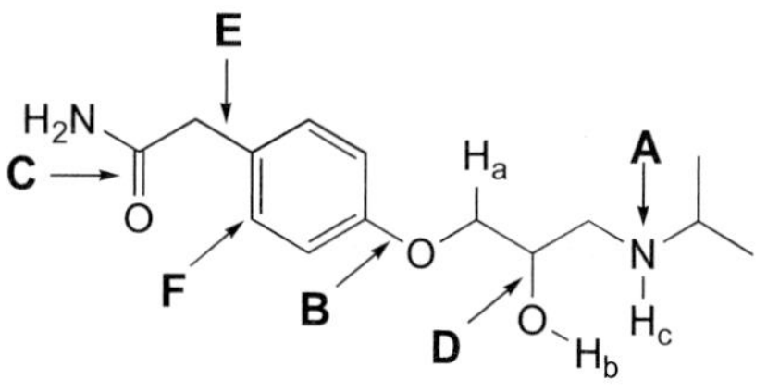

a. What is the hybridization of the N atom labeled with **A?**
b. What is the shape around the C atom labeled with **F?**
c. What orbitals are used to form the bond labeled with **E?**
d. Which bond (**B, C,** or **D**) is the longest bond?
e. Would you predict atenolol to be soluble in water?
f. Which of the labeled H atoms (H_a, H_b, or H_c) is most acidic?

Answers to Practice Test

1. a. 5
   b. 2
   c. 3
   d. 5

2. a. sp^3
   b. trigonal planar
   c. C_{sp2}–C_{sp3}
   d. **D**
   e. yes
   f. H_b

Answers to Problems

3.1

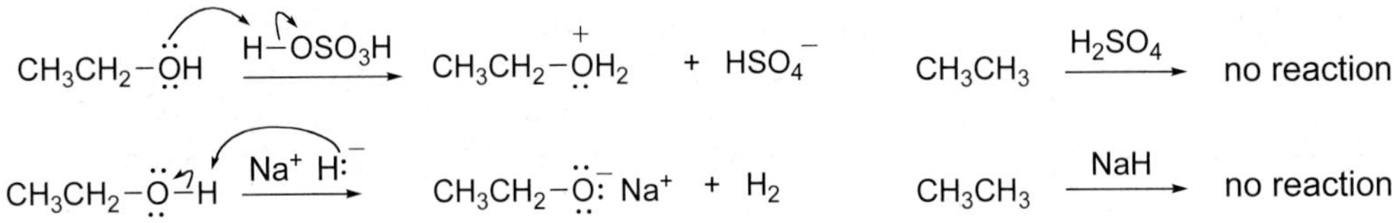

3.2 Identify the functional groups based on Tables 3.1, 3.2, and 3.3.

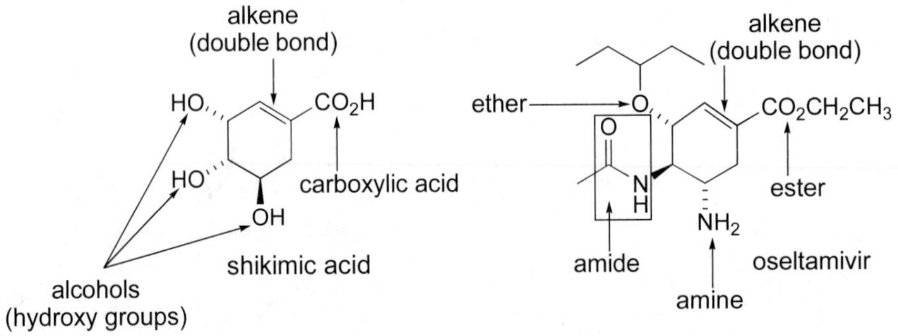

3.3 One possible structure for each functional group:

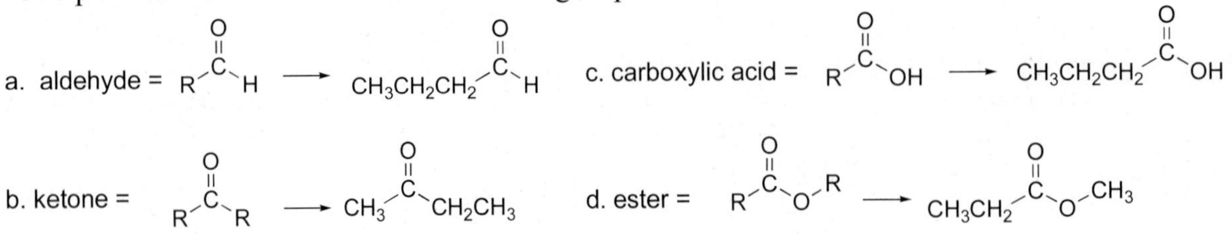

3.4 One possible structure for each description:

a. $C_5H_{10}O$

b. $C_6H_{10}O$

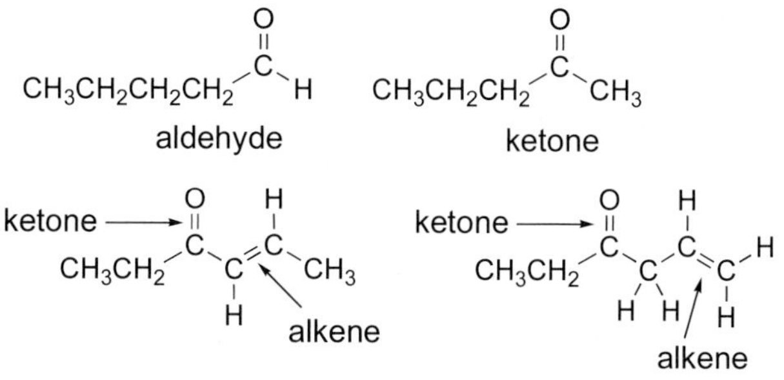

$CH_3CH_2CH_2CH_2$
aldehyde
$CH_3CH_2CH_2$
CH_3
ketone
ketone
CH_3CH_2
CH_3
alkene
ketone
CH_3CH_2
alkene

3.5 Summary of forces:

- **All compounds exhibit van der Waals forces (VDW).**
- **Polar molecules have dipole–dipole forces (DD).**
- **Hydrogen bonding (H-bonding)** can occur only when a **H is bonded to an O, N, or F.**

a. 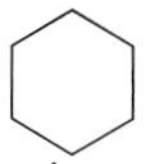

- only nonpolar C–C and C–H bonds
- **VDW only**

b. 

- **VDW forces**
- 2 polar C–O bonds and a net dipole – **DD**
- no H on O so no H-bonding

c. $(CH_3CH_2)_3N$

- **VDW forces**
- polar C–N bonds – **DD**
- no H on N so no H-bonding

d. $CH_2{=}CHCl$

- **VDW forces**
- polar C–Cl bond – **DD**

e. $CH_3CH_2CH_2COOH$

- **VDW forces**
- polar C–O bonds and a net dipole – **DD**
- H bonded to O – **H-bonding**

f. $CH_3{-}C{\equiv}C{-}CH_3$

- only nonpolar C–H and C–C bonds
- **VDW only**

3.6 One principle governs boiling point:

- **Stronger intermolecular forces = higher bp.**
  Increasing intermolecular forces: van der Waals < dipole–dipole < hydrogen bonding

Two factors affect the strength of van der Waals forces, and thus affect bp:

- **Increasing surface area = increasing bp.**
  Longer molecules have a larger surface area. Any branching decreases the surface area of a molecule.
- **Increasing polarizability = increasing bp.**

a. $(CH_3)_2C{=}CH_2$ or $(CH_3)_2C{=}O$

- $(CH_3)_2C{=}CH_2$: only VDW
- $(CH_3)_2C{=}O$: VDW and DD; polar, stronger intermolecular forces; **higher boiling point**

b. CH_3CH_2COOH or CH_3COOCH_3

- CH_3CH_2COOH: VDW, DD, and H-bonding; stronger intermolecular forces; **higher boiling point**
- CH_3COOCH_3: no H-bonding

c. $CH_3(CH_2)_4CH_3$ or $CH_3(CH_2)_5CH_3$

- $CH_3(CH_2)_5CH_3$: longer molecule, more surface area; **higher boiling point**

d. $CH_2{=}CHCl$ or $CH_2{=}CHI$

- $CH_2{=}CHI$: I is more polarizable. **higher boiling point**

3.7 Increasing intermolecular forces: van der Waals < dipole–dipole < hydrogen bonding

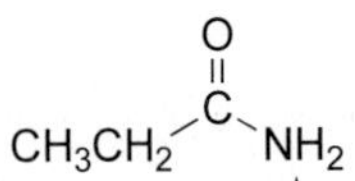

N–H bonds allow for hydrogen bonding.
stronger intermolecular forces
higher boiling point

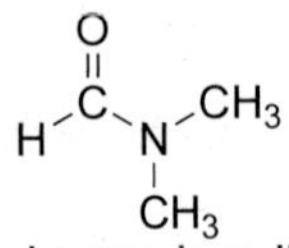

no hydrogen bonding
weaker intermolecular forces

3.8

a.  or 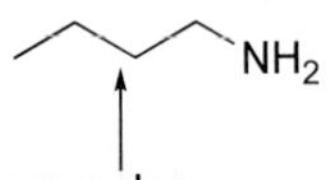

more polar
stronger intermolecular forces
(H-bonding)
higher mp

b. 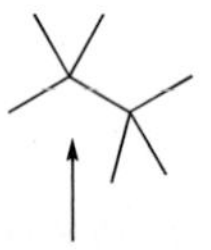 or 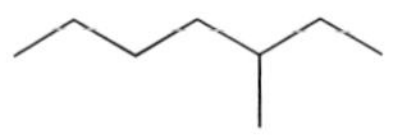

more spherical
packs better
higher mp

3.9 Compare the intermolecular forces to explain why sodium acetate has a higher melting point than acetic acid.

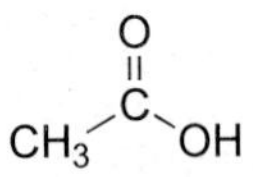

acetic acid

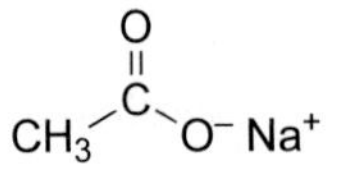

sodium acetate

a. VDW, DD, and H-bonding
b. not ionic, lower melting point

a. VDW, DD, ionic bonds
b. Ionic bonds are the strongest: **higher melting point.**

3.10 A compound is water soluble if it is ionic or if it has an O or N atom and ≤ 5 C's.

a. $CH_3CH_2OCH_2CH_3$

an O atom that
can H-bond with water
≤ 5 C's
water soluble

b. $CH_3CH_2CH_2CH_2CH_3$

nonpolar
not water soluble

c. $(CH_3CH_2CH_2CH_2)_3N$

an N atom that can
H-bond to H_2O, but
> 5 C's
not water soluble

3.11 **Hydrophobic** portions will primarily be hydrocarbon chains. **Hydrophilic** portions will be polar.

Circled regions are **hydrophilic** because they are polar.
All other regions are **hydrophobic** since they have only C and H.

a. 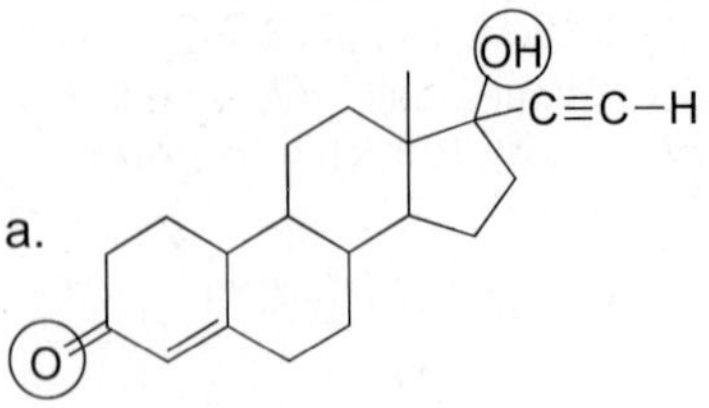

norethindrone

b. 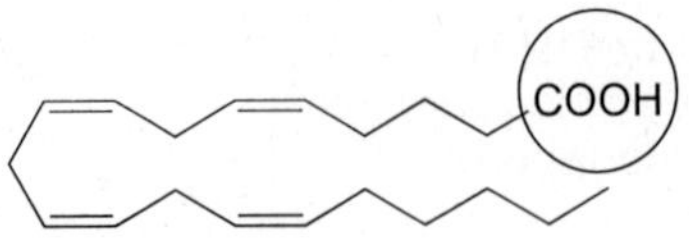

arachidonic acid

3.12 Like dissolves like.

- To be **soluble in water,** a molecule must be ionic, or have a polar functional group capable of H-bonding for every 5 C's.
- Organic compounds are generally **soluble in organic solvents** regardless of size or functional group.

a.

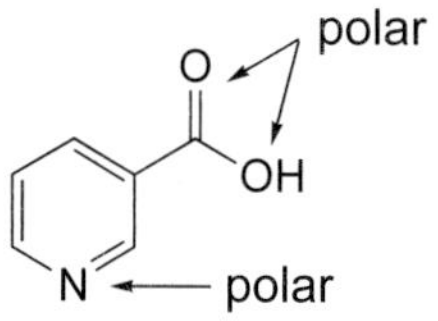

vitamin B_3
(niacin)

soluble in water due to two polar functional groups and only 6 C's in the molecule

b.

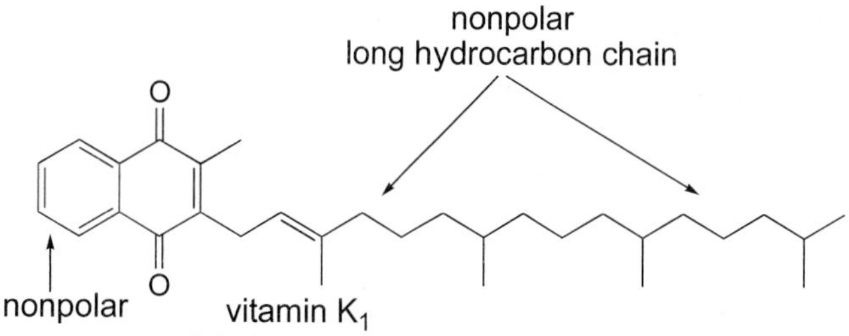

vitamin K_1
(phylloquinone)

soluble in organic solvents
two polar C–O bonds but the compound has > 10 C's
water insoluble

3.13 a.

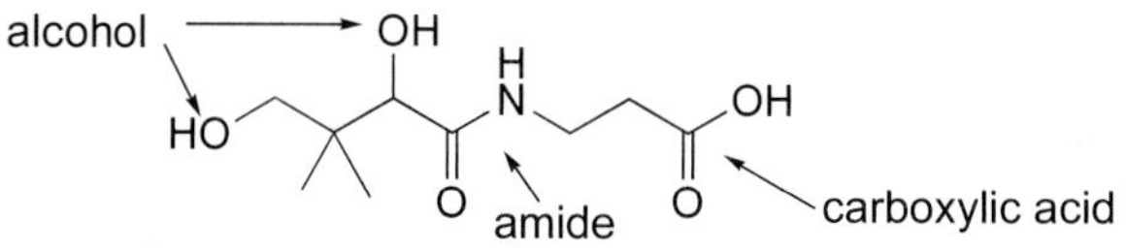

b. The amide, carboxylic acid, and both alcohols can all hydrogen bond with water.
c. Since pantothenic acid has only nine carbons with four functional groups that can hydrogen bond, pantothenic acid is a water-soluble vitamin.

3.14 A soap contains both a long hydrocarbon chain and a carboxylic acid salt.

a. $CH_3CO_2^-Na^+$
↑ short chain carboxylic acid salt

b. $CH_3(CH_2)_{14}CO_2^-Na^+$
ionic salt (at $CO_2^-Na^+$); long chain (at $CH_3(CH_2)_{14}$)
This is a soap because it contains both a long chain and a carboxylic acid salt.

c. $CH_3(CH_2)_{12}COOH$
↑ no salt

d. $CH_3(CH_2)_9CO_2^-Na^+$
ionic salt (at $CO_2^-Na^+$); long chain (at $CH_3(CH_2)_9$)
This is a soap because it contains both a long chain and a carboxylic acid salt.

3.15 Detergents have a polar head consisting of oppositely charged ions, and a nonpolar tail consisting of C–C and C–H bonds, just like soaps do. Detergents clean by having the **hydrophobic ends of molecules surround grease,** while the **hydrophilic portion of the molecule interacts with the polar solvent** (usually water).

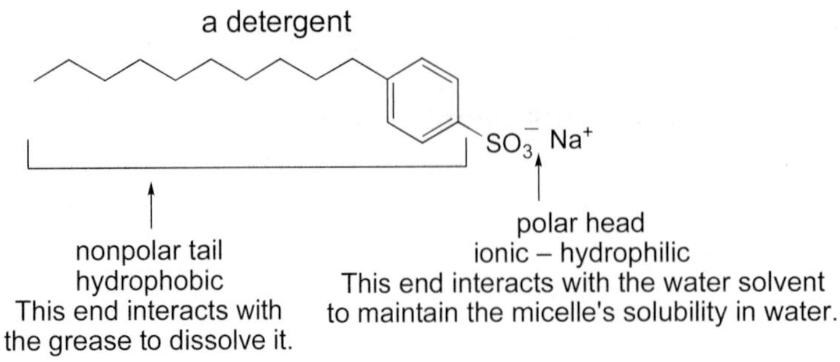

3.16

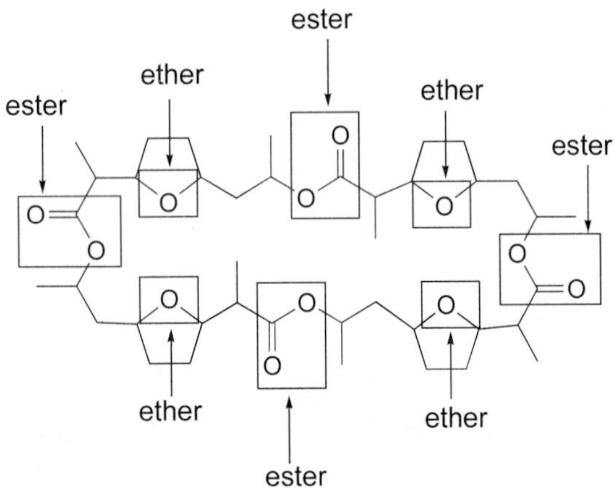

nonactin

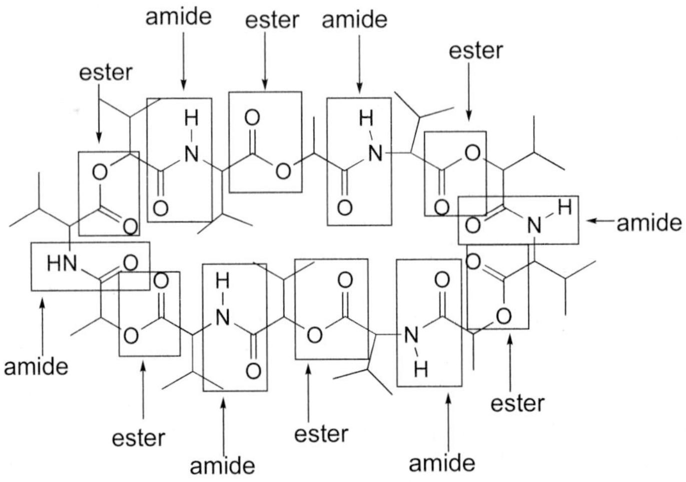

valinomycin

3.17 Because the interior of a cell membrane is nonpolar, aspirin crosses a cell membrane as a neutral carboxylic acid, by the general rule "Like dissolves like."

3.18 Electronegative heteroatoms like N, O, or X make a carbon atom an *electrophile.* A lone pair on a heteroatom makes it basic and nucleophilic. Pi (π) bonds create *nucleophilic* sites and are more easily broken than σ bonds.

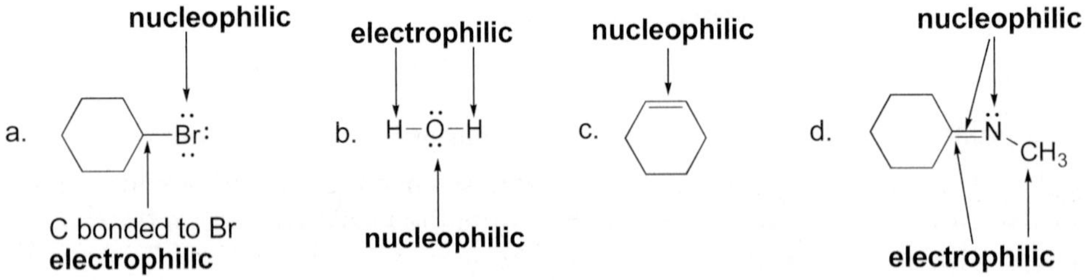

3.19 Electrophiles and nucleophiles react with each other.

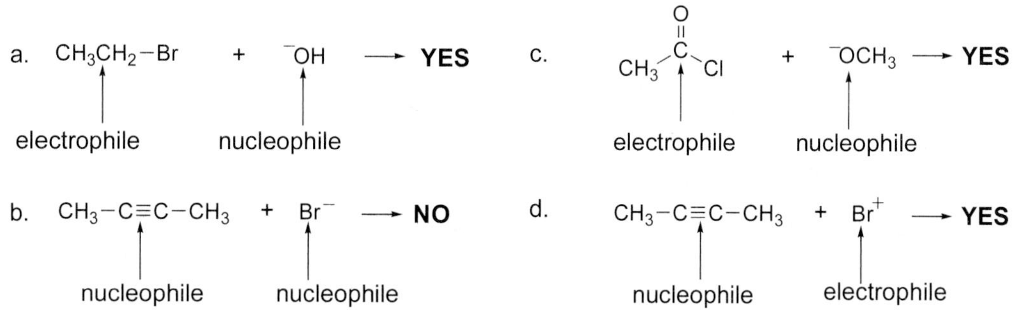

3.20

a.

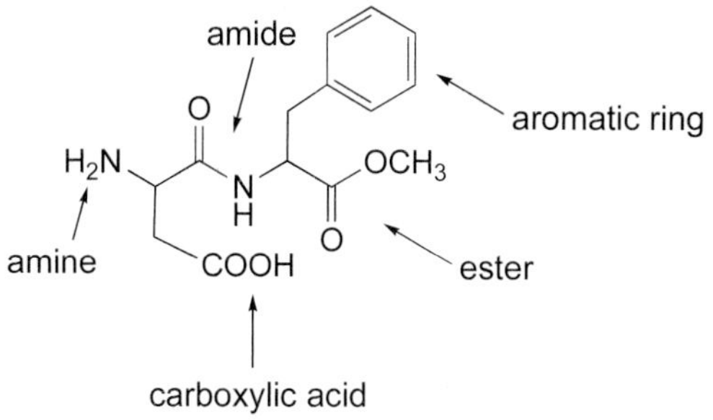

b, c.

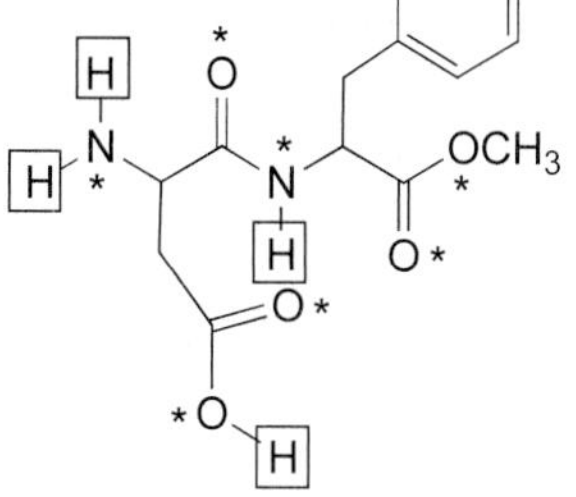

H's that are boxed in can hydrogen bond to O of H_2O.
Atoms labeled with (*) can hydrogen bond to H of H_2O.

3.21

a, c.

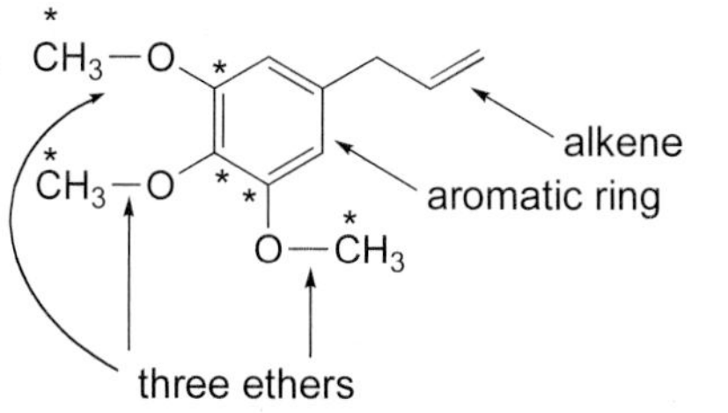

Electrophilic carbons are labeled with (*).

b.

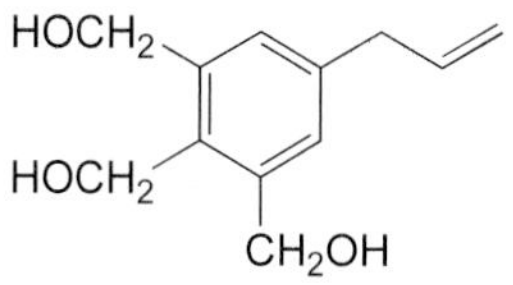

Three OH's allow for H-bonding.
Stronger intermolecular forces mean a higher bp and mp.

3.22

a, c.

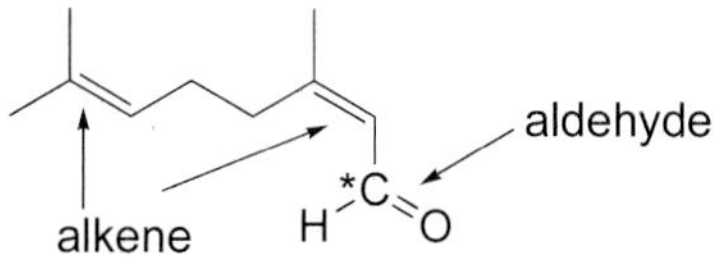

The most electrophilic C is labeled with *.

b.

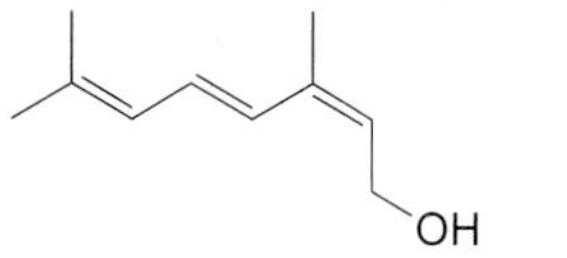

This isomer has an OH, more opportunities for H-bonding (through both O and H atoms), and so probably more H_2O soluble.

3.23 Identify the functional groups based on Tables 3.1, 3.2, and 3.3.

a.

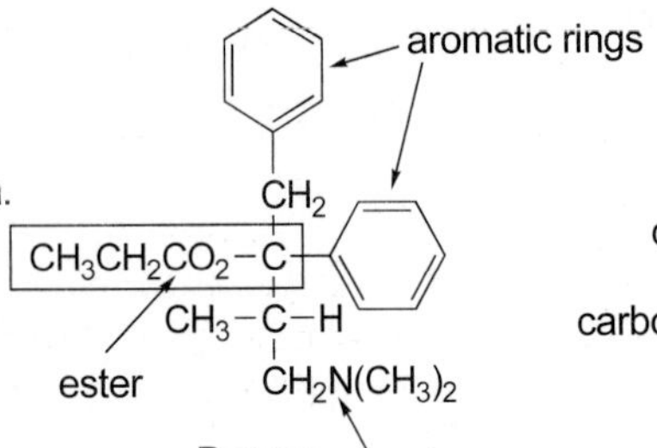
aromatic rings
ester
amine

Darvon

c.

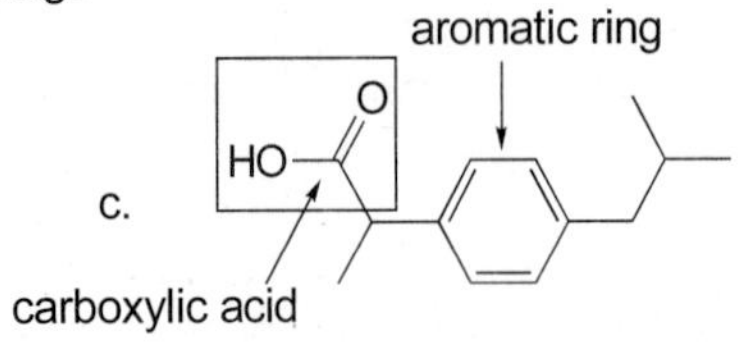
aromatic ring
carboxylic acid

ibuprofen

e.

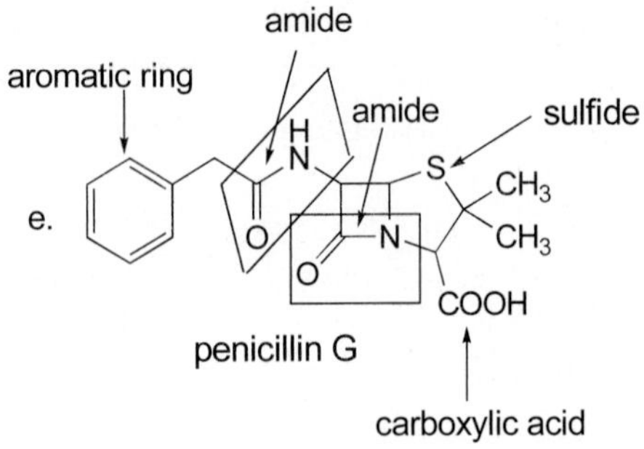
amide
aromatic ring
amide
sulfide
carboxylic acid

penicillin G

b.

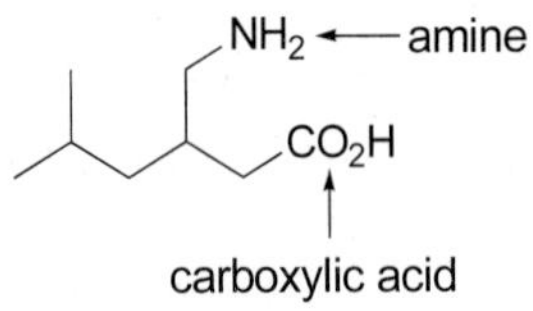
amine
carboxylic acid

pregabalin

d.

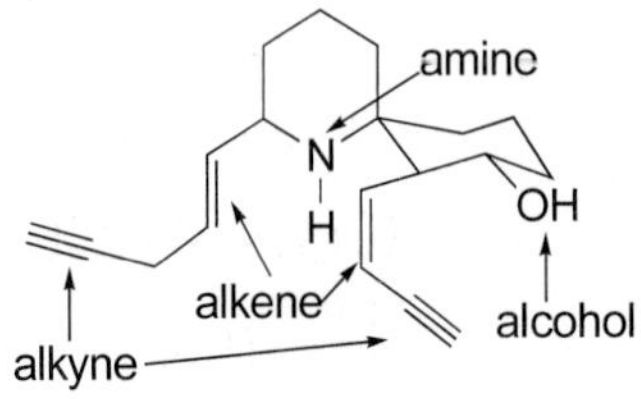
amine
alkene
alkyne
alcohol

histrionicotoxin

f.

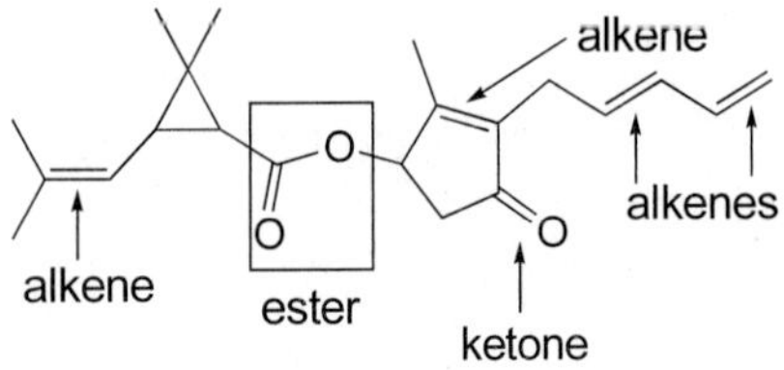
alkene
alkene
ester
ketone
alkenes

pyrethrin I

3.24

$CH_3-CH(OH)-CH_2-CH_3$	$CH_3CH_2CH_2CH_2-OH$	$CH_3-CH(CH_2OH)-CH_3$	$CH_3-C(CH_3)_2-OH$
alcohol	**alcohol**	**alcohol**	**alcohol**

$CH_3CH_2-O-CH_2CH_3$	$CH_3-O-CH(CH_3)-CH_3$	$CH_3-O-CH_2CH_2CH_3$
ether	**ether**	**ether**

3.25 A cyclic ester is called a lactone. A cyclic amide is called a lactam.

a. 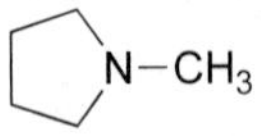

amine

b. 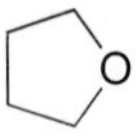

ether

c. 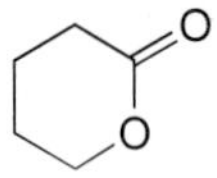

ester
lactone

d. 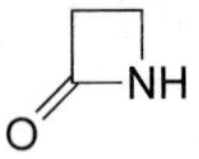

amide
lactam

3.26 Draw the constitutional isomers and identify the functional groups.

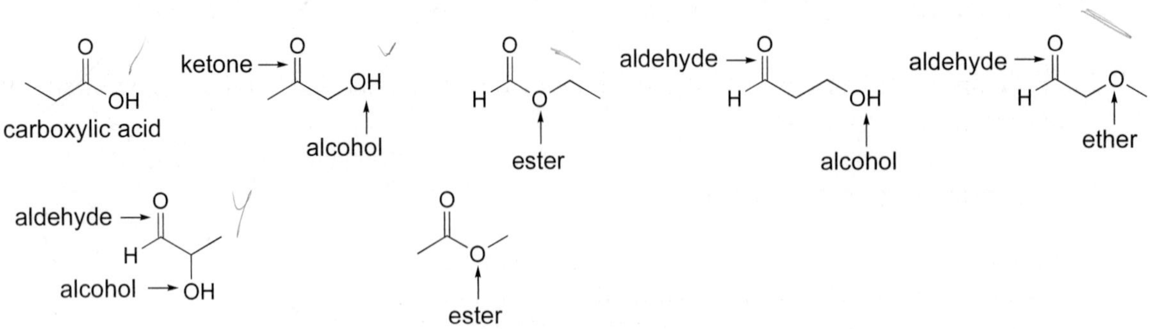
carboxylic acid
ketone
alcohol
ester
aldehyde
alcohol
aldehyde
ether
aldehyde
alcohol
ester

3.27 Use the rules from Answer 3.5.

a. 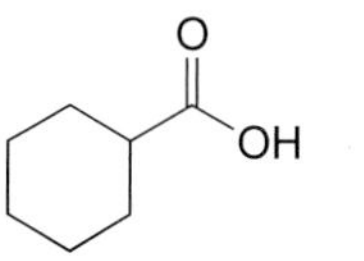

VDW
dipole–dipole
H-bonding (O–H bond)

b. 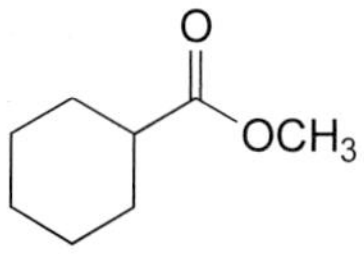

VDW
dipole–dipole
no H-bonding (no O–H bond)

c. 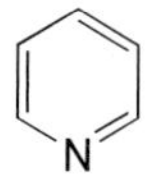

VDW
dipole–dipole
no H-bonding (no N–H bond)

d. 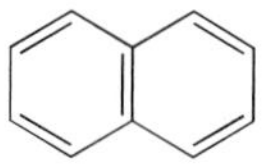

VDW
no dipole–dipole
(nonpolar C–C, C–H bonds)
no H-bonding (no O, N, F)

3.28 **Increasing intermolecular forces:** van der Waals < dipole–dipole < H-bonding

a. **increasing intermolecular forces:**

CH_3CH_3 < CH_3Cl < CH_3NH_2

- CH_3CH_3 ↑ VDW
- CH_3Cl ↑ VDW, dipole–dipole
- CH_3NH_2 ↑ VDW, dipole–dipole, H-bonding

b. **increasing intermolecular forces:**

CH_3Cl < CH_3Br < CH_3I

⟶

Increasing polarizability
stronger intermolecular forces

c. **increasing intermolecular forces:**

$(CH_3)_2C{=}C(CH_3)_2$ < $(CH_3)_2CHCOCH_3$ < $(CH_3)_2CHCOOH$

- $(CH_3)_2C{=}C(CH_3)_2$ ↑ VDW
- $(CH_3)_2CHCOCH_3$ ↑ VDW, dipole–dipole
- $(CH_3)_2CHCOOH$ ↑ VDW, dipole–dipole, H-bonding

d. **increasing intermolecular forces:**

CH_3Cl < CH_3OH < NaCl

- CH_3Cl ↑ VDW, dipole–dipole
- CH_3OH ↑ VDW, dipole–dipole, H-bonding
- NaCl ↑ ionic

3.29

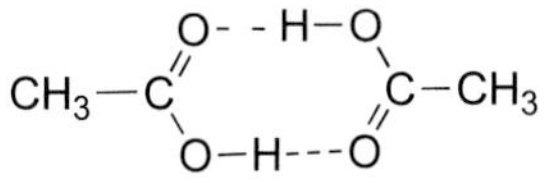

hydrogen bonding between
two acetic acid molecules

3.30 **A** = VDW forces; **B** = H-bonding; **C** = ion–ion interactions; **D** = H-bonding; **E** = H-bonding; **F** = VDW forces.

3.31

a.

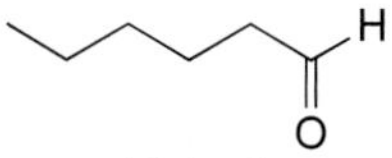

aldehyde

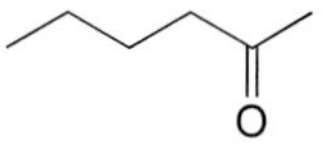

ketone

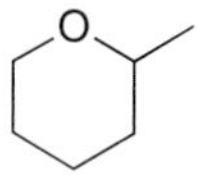

ether

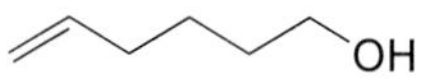

alcohol

b. The alcohol is the highest boiling since it is the only isomer that can hydrogen bond with another molecule like itself.

3.32 Use the principles from Answer 3.6.

a. $CH_3(CH_2)_4{-}I$ $\quad$ $CH_3(CH_2)_5{-}I$ $\quad$ $CH_3(CH_2)_6{-}I$

⟶

Increasing size, increasing surface area, increasing boiling point

b. $CH_3CH_2CH_2CH_3$ < $(CH_3)_3N$ < $CH_3CH_2CH_2NH_2$

$CH_3CH_2CH_2CH_3$	$(CH_3)_3N$	$CH_3CH_2CH_2NH_2$
VDW	VDW dipole–dipole	VDW dipole–dipole H-bonding

Increasing boiling point →

c. $(CH_3)_3COC(CH_3)_3$ < $CH_3(CH_2)_3O(CH_2)_3CH_3$ < $CH_3(CH_2)_7OH$

$(CH_3)_3COC(CH_3)_3$	$CH_3(CH_2)_3O(CH_2)_3CH_3$	$CH_3(CH_2)_7OH$
VDW dipole–dipole smaller surface area	VDW dipole–dipole larger surface area	VDW dipole–dipole H-bonding highest bp

Increasing boiling point →

d.

VDW | VDW, dipole–dipole | VDW, dipole–dipole, H-bonding | VDW, dipole–dipole, H-bonding, larger surface area

Increasing boiling point →

e.

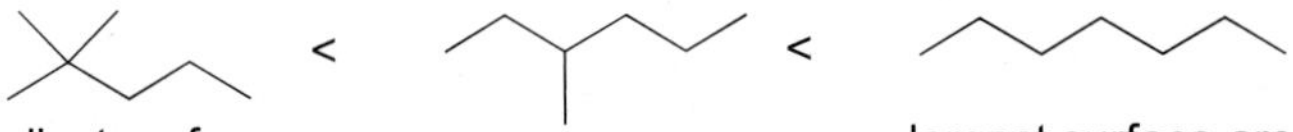

smallest surface area
most branching

largest surface area

Increasing boiling point →

f.

VDW | VDW, dipole–dipole | VDW, dipole–dipole, H-bonding

Increasing boiling point →

3.33 In $CH_3CH_2NHCH_3$, there is a N–H bond so the molecules exhibit intermolecular hydrogen bonding, whereas in $(CH_3)_3N$ the N is bonded only to C, so there is no hydrogen bonding. The hydrogen bonding in $CH_3CH_2NHCH_3$ makes it have much **stronger intermolecular forces** than $(CH_3)_3N$. As intermolecular forces increase, the boiling point of a molecule of the same molecular weight increases.

3.34 Stronger forces, higher mp.

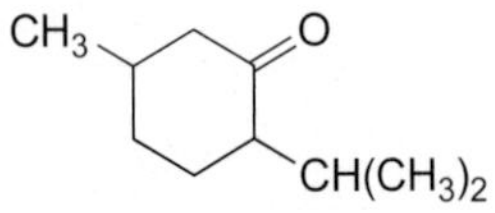

menthone
VDW
dipole–dipole
lower melting point

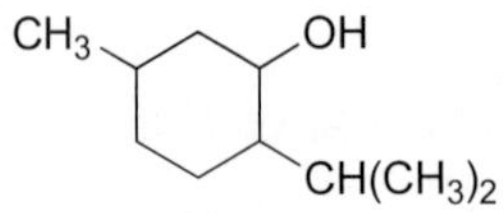

menthol
VDW
dipole–dipole
H-bonding
stronger forces
higher melting point

3.35 Stronger forces, higher mp. More symmetrical compounds, higher mp.

a. $(CH_3)_3CH$ < $(CH_3)_2C{=}O$ < $(CH_3)_2CHOH$

$(CH_3)_3CH$	$(CH_3)_2C{=}O$	$(CH_3)_2CHOH$
VDW	VDW DD	VDW DD H-bonding

Increasing intermolecular forces →
Increasing melting point

b. CH_3F < CH_3Cl < CH_3I

Increasing polarizability →
Increasing melting point

c.

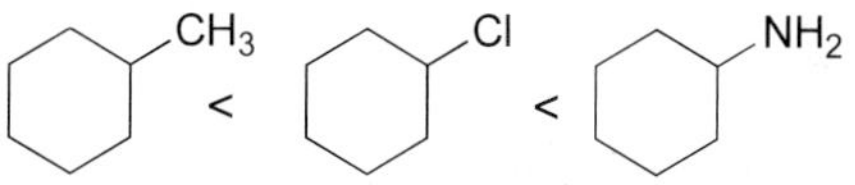

methylcyclohexane	chlorocyclohexane	cyclohexylamine
VDW	VDW DD	VDW DD H-bonding

Increasing intermolecular forces →
Increasing melting point

3.36

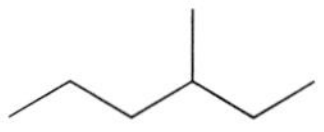

−119 °C
not symmetrical

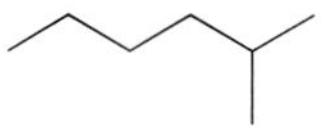

−118 °C
not symmetrical

In both compounds the CH_3 group dangling from the chain makes packing in the solid difficult, so the mp is low.

−91 °C
symmetrical
higher mp

This molecule can pack somewhat better since it has no CH_3 group dangling from the chain, so the mp is somewhat higher. It also has the most surface area and this increases VDW forces compared to the first two compounds.

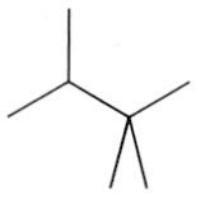

−25 °C
most spherical
highest mp

This compound packs the best since it is the most spherical in shape, increasing its mp.

3.37 **Boiling point is determined solely by the strength of the intermolecular forces.** Since benzene has a smaller size, it has less surface area and weaker VDW interactions and therefore a lower boiling point than toluene. The increased melting point for benzene can be explained by symmetry: benzene is much more symmetrical than toluene. More symmetrical molecules can pack more tightly together, increasing their melting point. Symmetry has no effect on boiling point.

benzene
bp = 80 °C
mp = 5 °C

very symmetrical
closer packing in solid form
higher mp

and

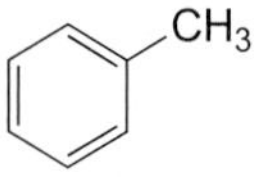

toluene
bp = 111 °C
mp = −93 °C

less symmetrical
lower mp

3.38 Increasing polarity = increasing water solubility.

Neither compound is very H_2O soluble.

a. $CH_3CH_2CH_2CH_3$ < $(CH_3)_3CH$ < $CH_3OCH_2CH_3$ < $CH_3CH_2CH_2OH$

$CH_3CH_2CH_2CH_3$	$(CH_3)_3CH$	$CH_3OCH_2CH_3$	$CH_3CH_2CH_2OH$
VDW	VDW more spherical (This nonpolar, hydrophobic molecule is more compact, making it more water soluble than its straight-chain isomer, drawn to the left.)	VDW DD	VDW DD H-bonding

b.

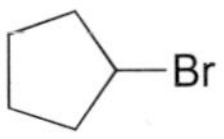

polar
no H-bonding

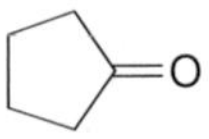

polar
H-bonding to H_2O, not itself

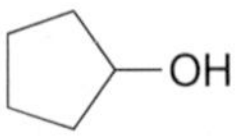

polar and
H-bonding
More opportunities for H-bonding with its O atom and its H on O.

3.39 Look for two things:

- To H-bond to another molecule like itself, the molecule must contain a **H bonded to O, N, or F.**
- To H-bond with water, a molecule needs **only to contain an O, N, or F.**

Each of these molecules can H-bond to another molecule like itself. Both compounds have N–H bonds.
b. CH_3NH_2, e. $CH_3CH_2CH_2CONH_2$

These molecules can H-bond with water. All of these molecules have an O or N atom.
b. CH_3NH_2, c. CH_3OCH_3, d. $(CH_3CH_2)_3N$, e. $CH_3CH_2CH_2CONH_2$, g. CH_3SOCH_3, h. $CH_3CH_2COOCH_3$

3.40 Draw the molecules in question and look at the intermolecular forces involved.

no H bonded to O

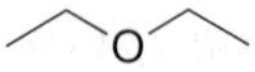

diethyl ether

VDW forces
dipole–dipole forces

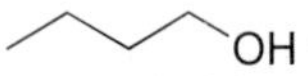

H bonded to O: hydrogen bonding

1-butanol

VDW forces
dipole–dipole forces
H-bonding

- Both have ≤ 5 C's and an electronegative O atom, so they can H-bond to water, making them soluble in water.
- Only 1-butanol can H-bond to another molecule life itself, and this increases its boiling point.

3.41 Use the solubility rule from Answer 3.12.

a.
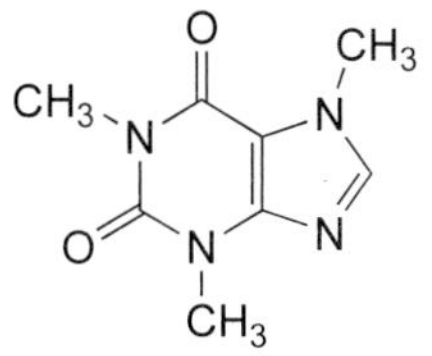
caffeine

many polar bonds with N and O atoms
many opportunities for H-bonding
water soluble

c.
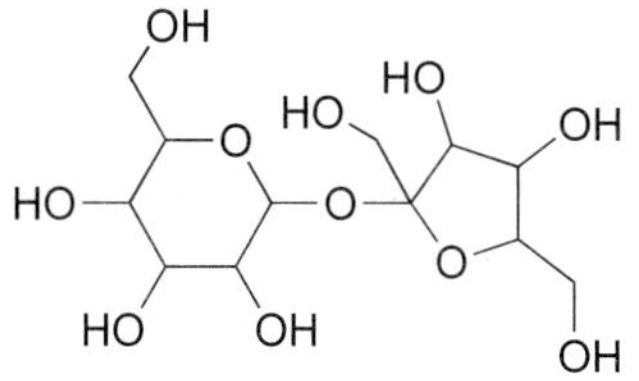
sucrose
many polar bonds with O
11 O's and 12 C's
many opportunities for H-bonding with H_2O
water soluble

b.
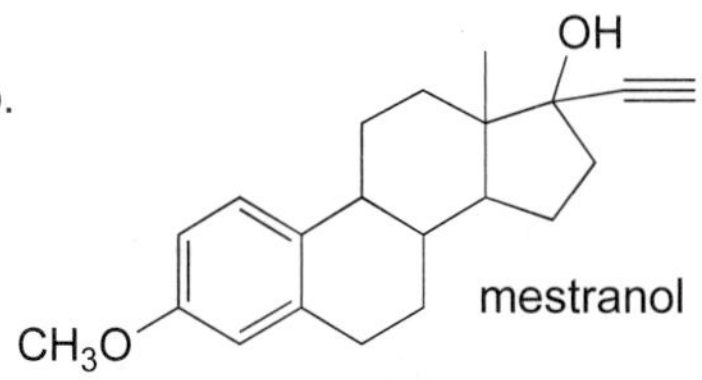
mestranol

2 polar functional groups
but > 10 C's
not water soluble

d.
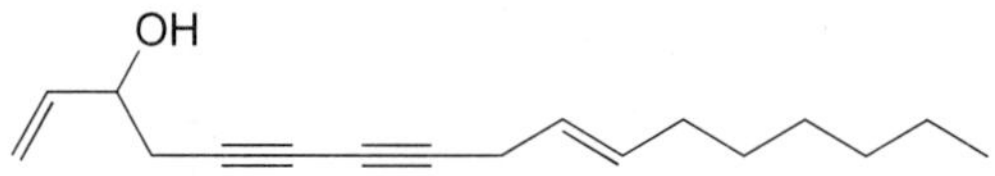
carotatoxin
1 polar functional group
but > 10 C's
not water soluble

3.42 Water solubility is determined by polarity. Polar molecules are soluble in water, while nonpolar molecules are soluble in organic solvents.

Arrows indicate polar functional groups.

a.
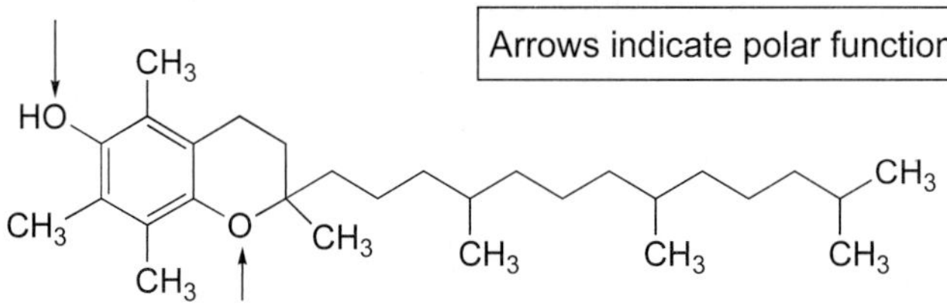
vitamin E

only 2 polar functional groups
many nonpolar C–C and C–H bonds (29 C's)
soluble in organic solvents
insoluble in H_2O

b.
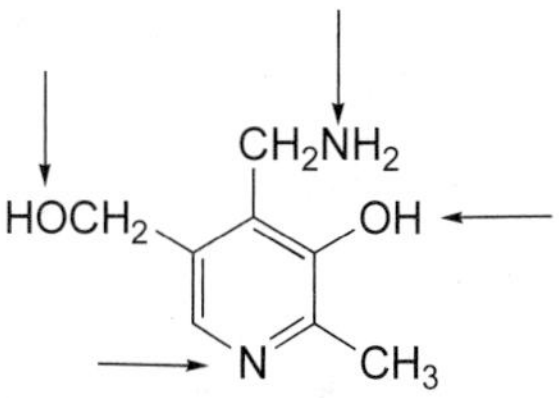
pyridoxine
vitamin B_6
many polar bonds and few nonpolar bonds
soluble in H_2O
It is also **soluble in organic solvents** since it is organic, but is probably more soluble in H_2O.

3.43 Compare the functional groups in the two components of sunscreen. Dioxybenzone will most likely be washed off in water because it contains two hydroxy groups and is more water soluble.

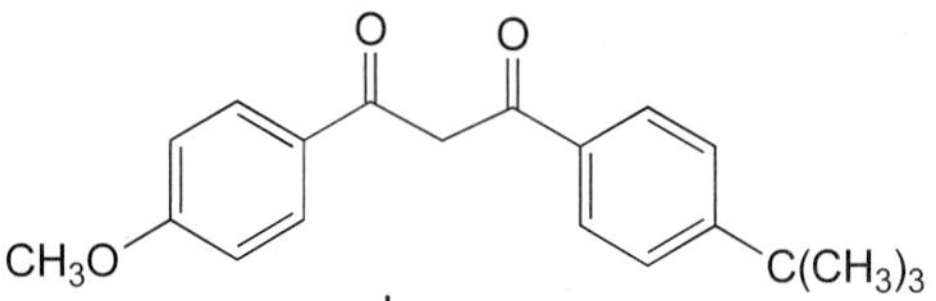
avobenzone
two ketones
one ether

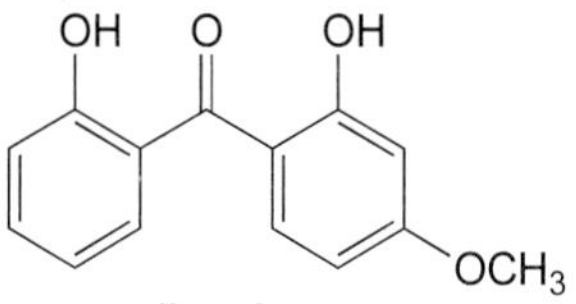
dioxybenzone
two hydroxy groups
one ketone
one ether
more water soluble

3.44 Because of the O atoms, PEG is capable of hydrogen bonding with water, which makes PEG water soluble and suitable for a product like shampoo. PVC cannot hydrogen bond to water, so PVC is water insoluble, even though it has many polar bonds. Since PVC is water insoluble, it can be used to transport and hold water.

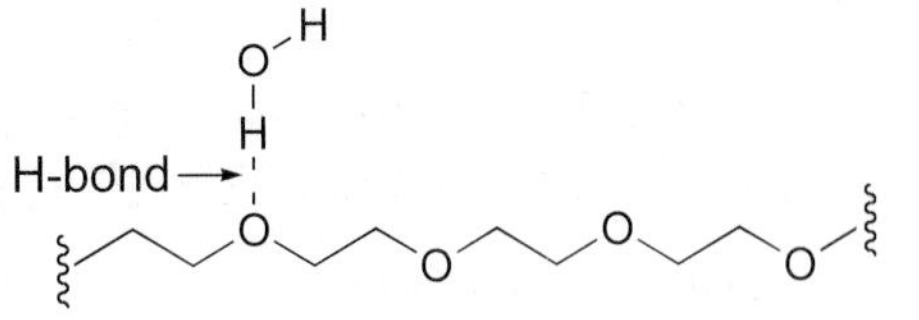

poly(ethylene glycol)
PEG
water soluble

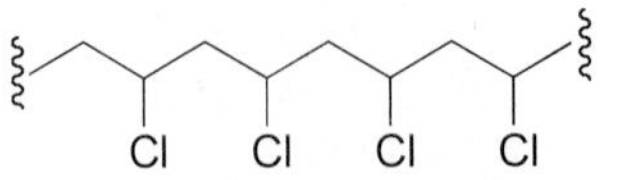

poly(vinyl chloride)
PVC
water insoluble

3.45 Molecules that dissolve in water are readily excreted from the body in urine, whereas less polar molecules that dissolve in organic solvents are soluble in fatty tissue and are retained for longer periods. Compare the solubility properties of THC and ethanol to determine why drug screenings can detect THC and not ethanol weeks after introduction to the body.

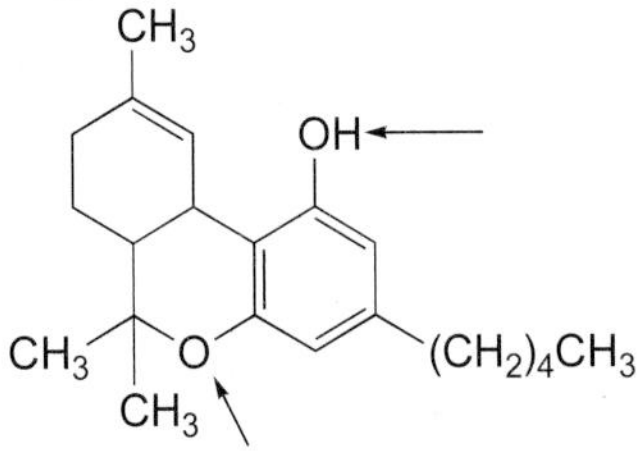

tetrahydrocannabinol
THC

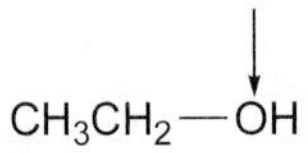

ethanol

THC has relatively few polar bonds compared to the number of nonpolar bonds, making it **soluble in organic solvents** and therefore **soluble in fatty tissue.**

Ethanol has 1 O atom and only 2 C's, making it **soluble in water.**

Due to their solubilities, **THC is retained much longer in the fatty tissue of the body,** being slowly excreted over many weeks, while ethanol is excreted rapidly in urine after ingestion.

3.46 Compare the intermolecular forces of crack and cocaine hydrochloride. Stronger intermolecular forces increase both the boiling point and the water solubility.

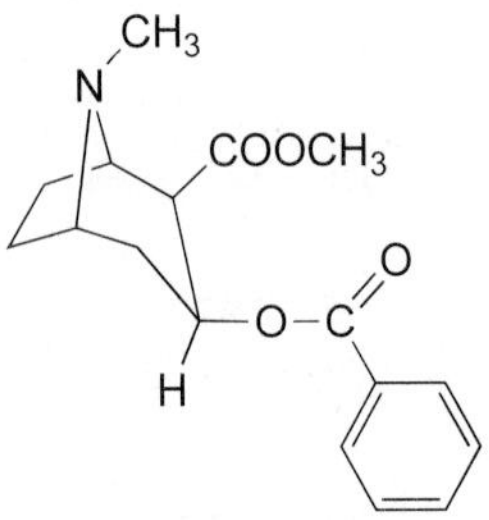

cocaine (crack)
neutral organic molecule

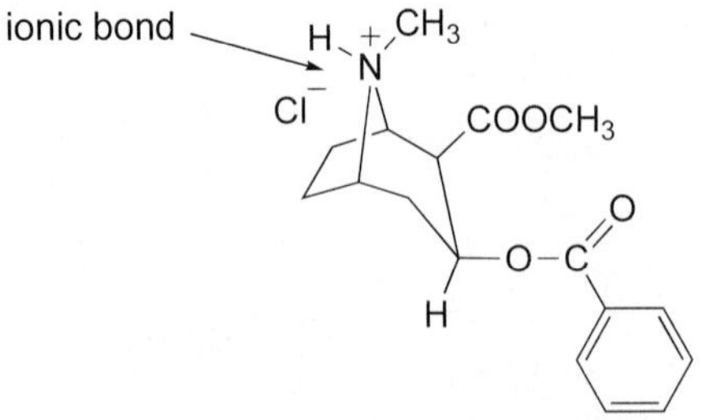

cocaine hydrochloride
a salt

The molecules are identical except for the ionic bond in cocaine hydrochloride. Ionic forces are extremely strong forces, and therefore the cocaine hydrochloride salt has a much **higher boiling point and is more water soluble.** Since the salt is highly water soluble, it can be injected directly into the bloodstream, where it dissolves. Crack is smoked because it can dissolve in the organic tissues of the nasal passages and lungs.

3.47 A laundry detergent must have both a highly polar end of the molecule and a nonpolar end of the molecule. The polar end will interact with water, while the nonpolar end surrounds the grease or other organic material.

a.
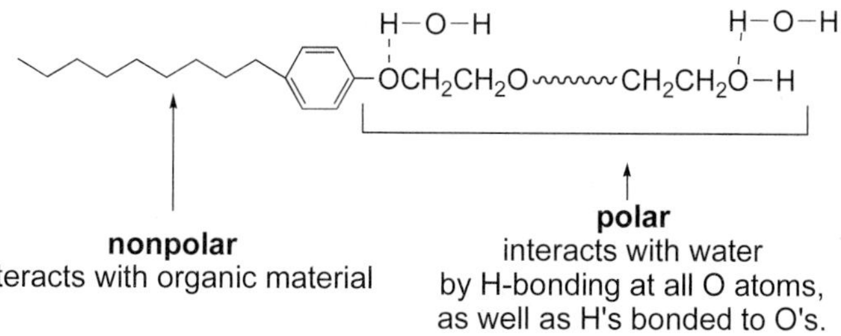
H–O–H
H–O–H
OCH2CH2O
CH2CH2O–H
polar
interacts with water
by H-bonding at all O atoms,
as well as H's bonded to O's.
nonpolar
interacts with organic material

b.
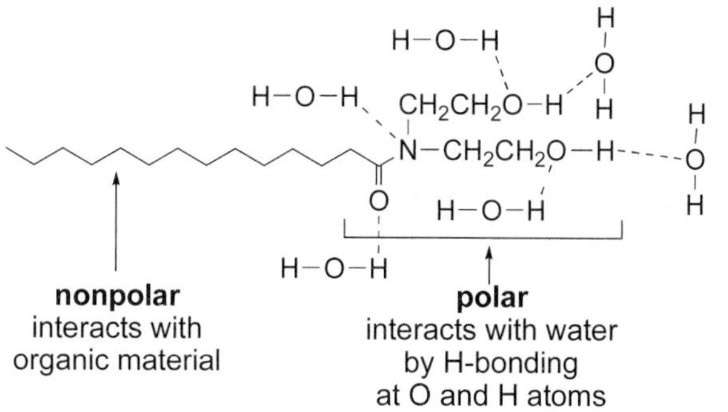
H–O–H
CH2CH2O–H
N–CH2CH2O–H
H–O–H
nonpolar
interacts with
organic material
polar
interacts with water
by H-bonding
at O and H atoms

3.48

a.
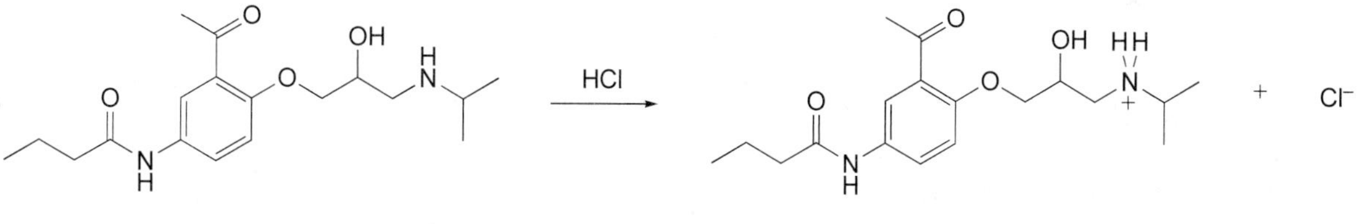
HCl
OH
OH HH
Cl–

b.
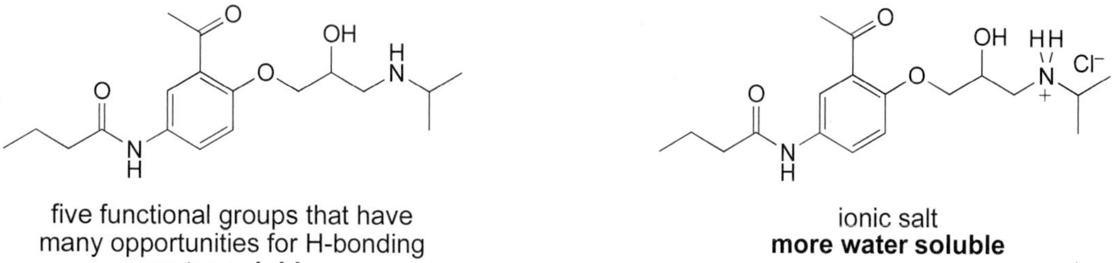
five functional groups that have
many opportunities for H-bonding
water soluble
ionic salt
more water soluble

c. Since the hydrochloride salt is ionic and therefore more water soluble, it is more readily transported in the bloodstream.

3.49 Use the rules from Answer 3.18.

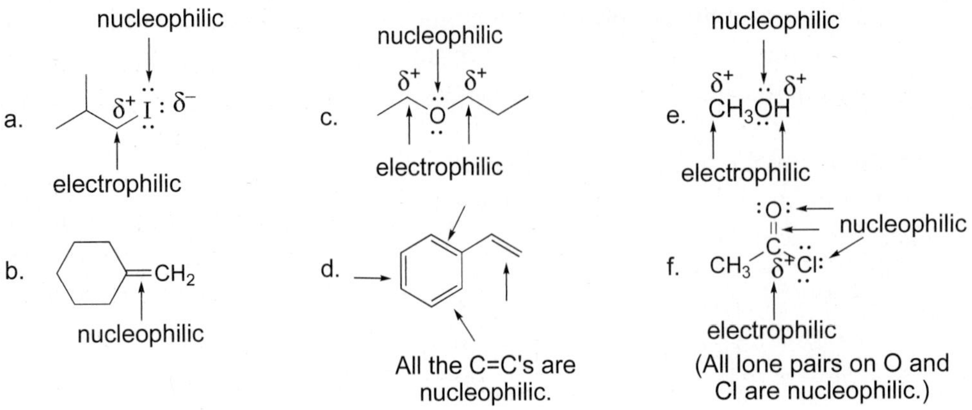
a.
nucleophilic
δ+ I : δ−
electrophilic
b.
CH2
nucleophilic
c.
nucleophilic
δ+ δ+
O
electrophilic
d.
All the C=C's are nucleophilic.
e.
nucleophilic
δ+ δ+
CH3OH
electrophilic
f.
:O:
nucleophilic
CH3 C δ+Cl:
electrophilic
(All lone pairs on O and Cl are nucleophilic.)

3.50

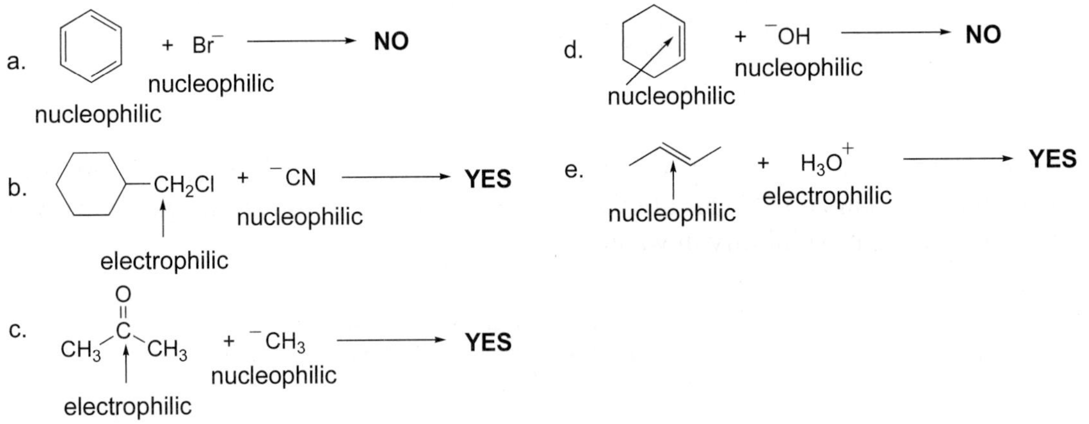
a.
+ Br−
NO
nucleophilic
nucleophilic
b.
CH2Cl
+ −CN
YES
nucleophilic
electrophilic
c.
O
CH3 C CH3
+ −CH3
YES
nucleophilic
electrophilic
d.
+ −OH
NO
nucleophilic
nucleophilic
e.
+ H3O+
YES
electrophilic
nucleophilic

3.51 More rigid cell membranes have phospholipids with *fewer* C=C's. Each C=C introduces a bend in the molecule, making the phospholipids pack less tightly. Phospholipids without C=C's can pack very tightly, making the membrane less fluid, and more rigid.

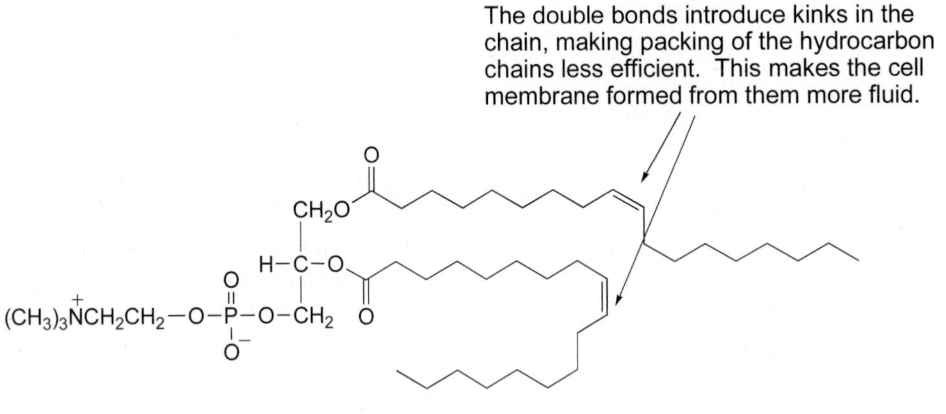
The double bonds introduce kinks in the chain, making packing of the hydrocarbon chains less efficient. This makes the cell membrane formed from them more fluid.
O
CH2O
H–C–O
O
(CH3)3N+CH2CH2–O–P–O–CH2
O
O−

3.52

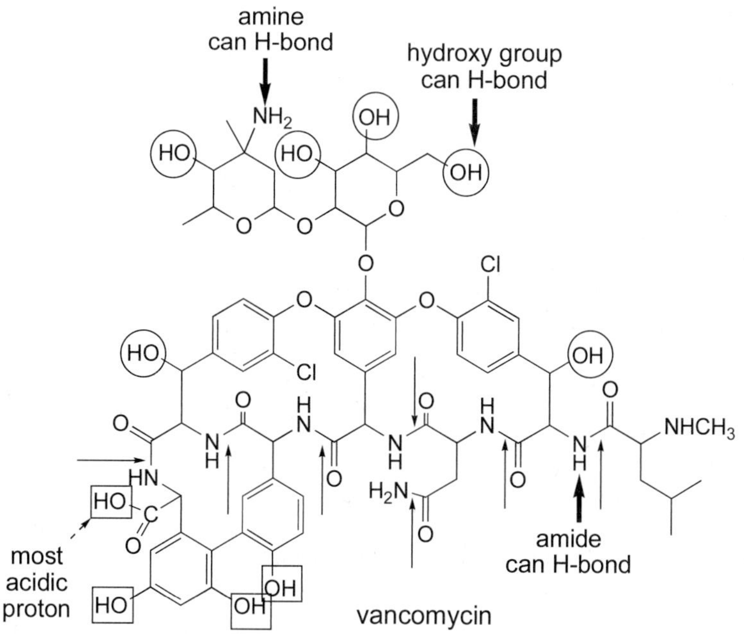
amine
can H-bond
hydroxy group
can H-bond
amide
can H-bond
most
acidic
proton
vancomycin

a. Seven amide groups [regular (unbolded) arrows]

b. OH groups bonded to sp^3 C's are circled. OH groups bonded to sp^2 C's have a square.

c. Despite its size, vancomycin is water soluble because it contains many polar groups and many N and O atoms that can H-bond to H_2O.

d. The most acidic proton is labeled (COOH group).

e. Four functional groups capable of H-bonding are ROH, RCOOH, amides, and amines.

3.53 Because the O atom in tetrahydrofuran is in a ring, the C atoms bonded to it are kept away from the lone pairs on O. This allows the O atom to more readily hydrogen bond with water, thus increasing its solubility in water.

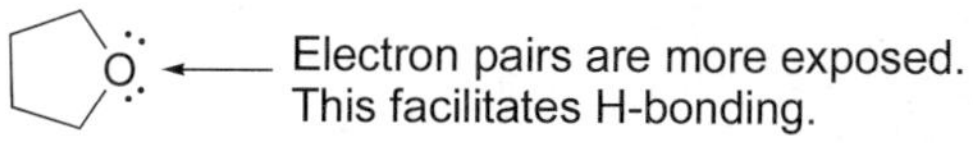
Electron pairs are more exposed.
This facilitates H-bonding.

3.54

a.

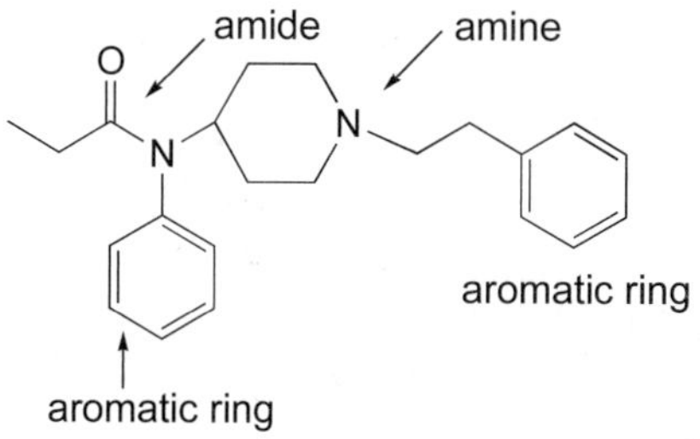
amide
amine
aromatic ring
aromatic ring

e. An isomer that can hydrogen bond should have a higher boiling point.

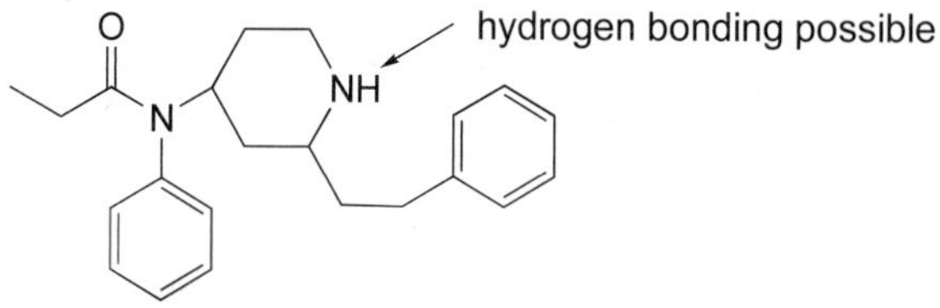
hydrogen bonding possible

b, c, f, g.

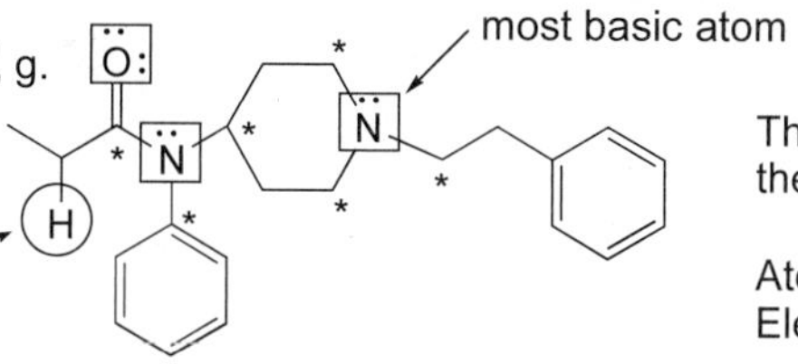
most basic atom

The N atom of the amide is less basic because the lone pair is part of resonance with the C=O.

Atoms that can hydrogen bond to H_2O are boxed in.
Electrophilic carbons are labeled with (*).

most acidic H, pK_a ~ 25
All H's are bonded to C's. Removal of the H on the C adjacent to the C=O results in a resonance-stabilized anion.

d. Fentanyl exhibits van der Waals and dipole–dipole interactions but no hydrogen bonding, since there is no H bonded to O or N.

3.55

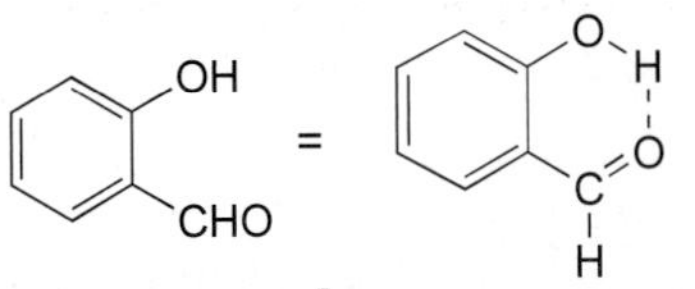

A

The OH and CHO groups are close enough that they can intramolecularly H-bond to each other. Since the two polar functional groups are involved in intramolecular H-bonding, they are less available for H-bonding to H_2O. This makes **A** less H_2O soluble than **B,** whose two functional groups are both available for H-bonding to the H_2O solvent.

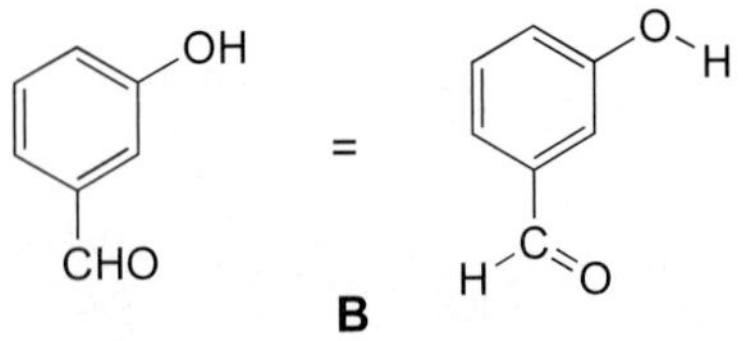

B

The OH and the CHO are too far apart to intramolecularly H-bond to each other, leaving more opportunity to H-bond with solvent.

3.56

a. melting point

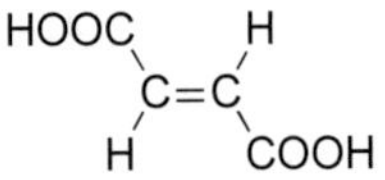

fumaric acid

Fumaric acid has its two larger COOH groups on opposite ends of the molecule, and in this way it can pack better in a lattice than maleic acid, giving it a **higher mp.**

b. solubility

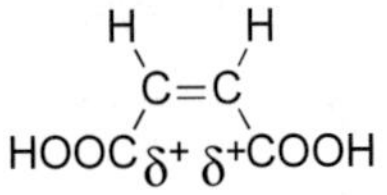

maleic acid

Maleic acid is more polar, giving it greater **H_2O solubility.** The bond dipoles in fumaric acid cancel.

c. removal of the first proton (pK_{a1})

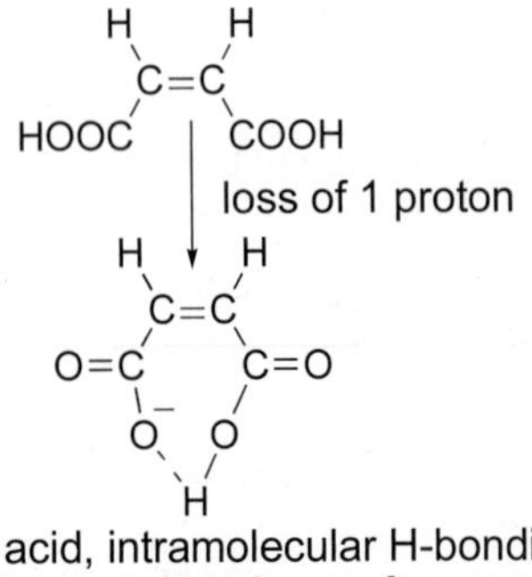
loss of 1 proton

In maleic acid, intramolecular H-bonding stabilizes the conjugate base after one H is removed, making maleic acid more acidic than fumaric acid.

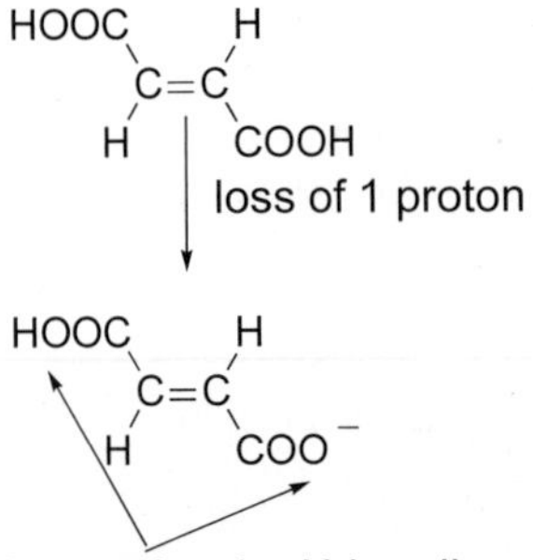
loss of 1 proton

Intramolecular H-bonding is not possible here.

d. removal of the second proton (pK_{a2})

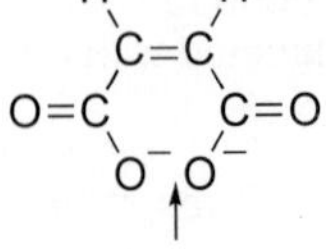

Now the dianion is held in close proximity in maleic acid, and this destabilizes the conjugate base. Thus, removing the second H in maleic acid is harder, making it a weaker acid than fumaric acid for removal of the second proton.

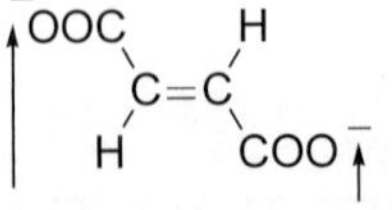

The two negative charges are much farther apart. This makes the dianion from fumaric acid more stable and thus pK_{a2} is lower for fumaric acid than maleic acid.

Chapter 4 Alkanes

Chapter Review

General facts about alkanes (4.1–4.3)

- Alkanes are composed of **tetrahedral, *sp*^{3} hybridized** C's.
- There are two types of alkanes: acyclic alkanes having molecular formula $\mathbf{C_nH_{2n+2}}$, and cycloalkanes having molecular formula $\mathbf{C_nH_{2n}}$.
- Alkanes have only **nonpolar C–C and C–H bonds** and no functional group so they undergo few reactions.
- Alkanes are named with the suffix ***-ane.***

Classifying C's and H's (4.1A)

- Carbon atoms are classified by the number of C's bonded to them; **a 1° C is bonded to one other C,** and so forth.

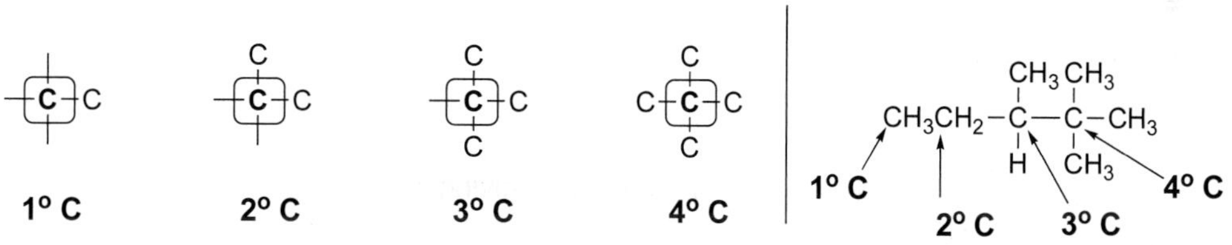

1° C
2° C
3° C
4° C
CH3 CH3
CH3CH2–C–C–CH3
H CH3
1° C
2° C
3° C
4° C

- Hydrogen atoms are classified by the type of carbon atom to which they are bonded; **a 1° H is bonded to a 1° C,** and so forth.

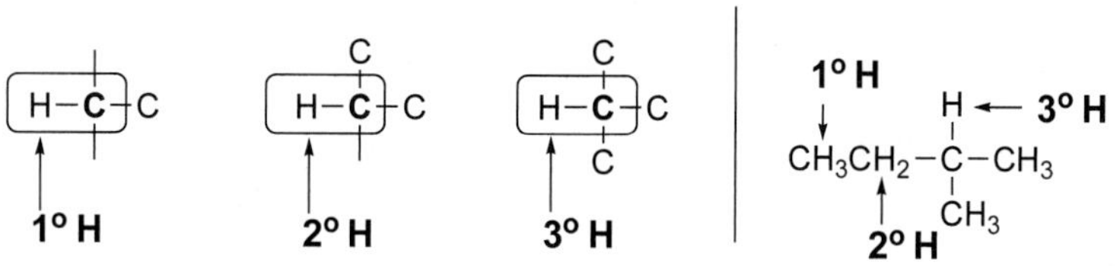

1° H
2° H
3° H
1° H
H ← 3° H
CH3CH2–C–CH3
CH3
2° H

Names of alkyl groups (4.4A)

CH_3— methyl	=	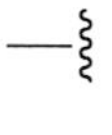	$CH_3CH_2CH_2CH_2$— butyl	=	
CH_3CH_2— ethyl	=	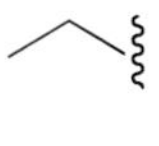	$CH_3CH_2CHCH_3$ (bond from CH) *sec*-butyl	=	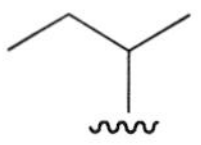
$CH_3CH_2CH_2$— propyl	=	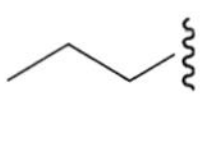	$(CH_3)_2CHCH_2$— isobutyl	=	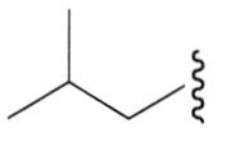
$(CH_3)_2CH$— isopropyl	=	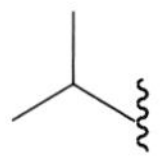	$(CH_3)_3C$— *tert*-butyl	=	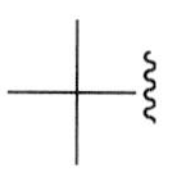

Conformations in acyclic alkanes (4.9, 4.10)

- Alkane conformations can be classified as **staggered, eclipsed, anti,** or **gauche** depending on the relative orientation of the groups on adjacent carbons.

eclipsed

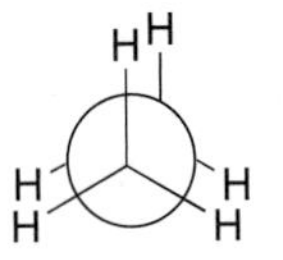

- Dihedral angle = 0°

staggered

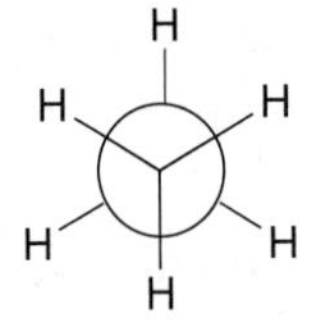

- Dihedral angle = 60°

anti

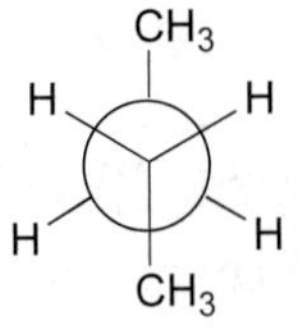

- Dihedral angle of 2 CH_3's = 180°

gauche

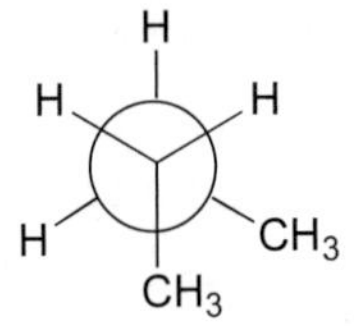

- Dihedral angle of 2 CH_3's = 60°

- A staggered conformation is **lower in energy** than an eclipsed conformation.
- An anti conformation is **lower in energy** than a gauche conformation.

Types of strain

- **Torsional strain**—an increase in energy due to eclipsing interactions (4.9).
- **Steric strain**—an increase in energy when atoms are forced too close to each other (4.10).
- **Angle strain**—an increase in energy when tetrahedral bond angles deviate from 109.5° (4.11).

Two types of isomers

[1] **Constitutional isomers**—isomers that differ in the way the atoms are connected to each other (4.1A).
[2] **Stereoisomers**—isomers that differ only in the way atoms are oriented in space (4.13B).

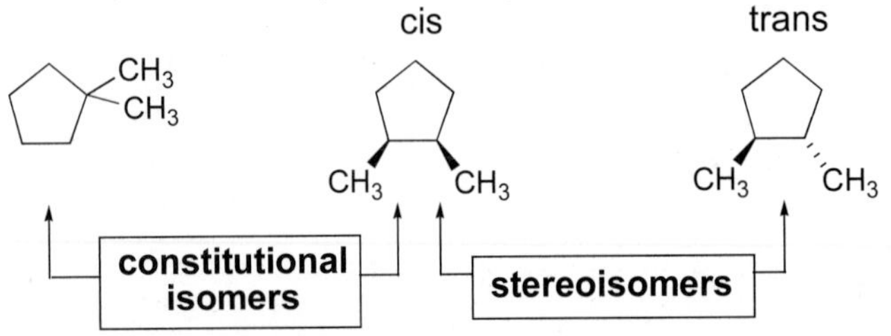

Conformations in cyclohexane (4.12, 4.13)

- Cyclohexane exists as **two chair conformations** in rapid equilibrium at room temperature.
- Each carbon atom on a cyclohexane ring has **one axial** and **one equatorial hydrogen.** Ring-flipping converts axial H's to equatorial H's, and vice versa.

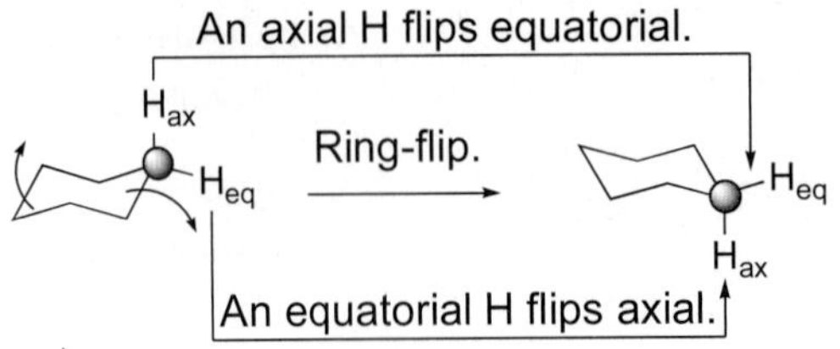

- In substituted cyclohexanes, groups larger than hydrogen are more stable in the **more roomy equatorial position.**

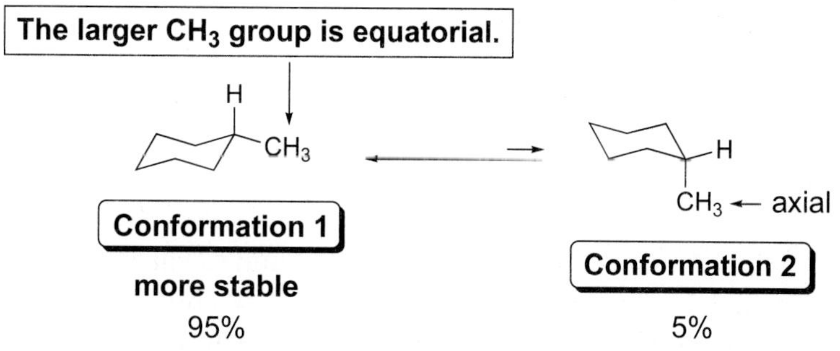
The larger CH_3 group is equatorial.
H
CH_3
Conformation 1
more stable
95%
H
CH_3 ← axial
Conformation 2
5%

- Disubstituted cyclohexanes with substituents on different atoms exist as two possible stereoisomers.
  - The **cis** isomer has two groups on the **same side** of the ring, either both up or both down.
  - The **trans** isomer has two groups on **opposite sides** of the ring, one up and one down.

CH_3
H
CH_3
H
CH_3
H
CH_3
H

trans isomer   **cis** isomer

Oxidation–reduction reactions (4.14)

- **Oxidation** results in an **increase in the number of C–Z bonds** or a **decrease in the number of C–H bonds.**

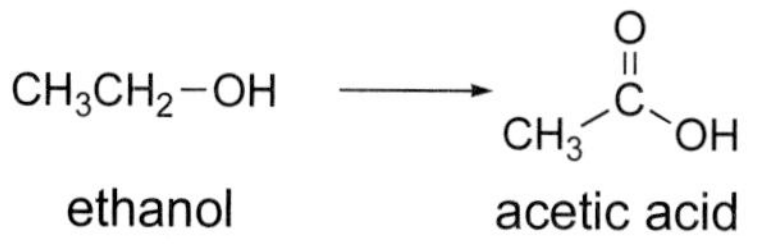
CH_3CH_2–OH
ethanol
O
CH_3
C
OH
acetic acid

Increase in C–O bonds = **oxidation**

- **Reduction** results in a **decrease in the number of C–Z bonds** or an **increase in the number of C–H bonds.**

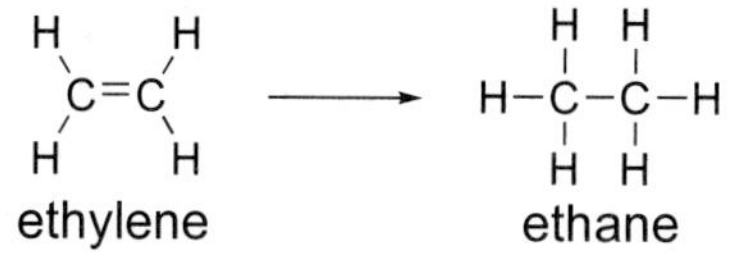
H H
C=C
H H
ethylene
H H
H–C–C–H
H H
ethane

Increase in C–H bonds = **reduction**

Practice Test on Chapter Review

1. a. Which statement is true about compounds **A–D** below?

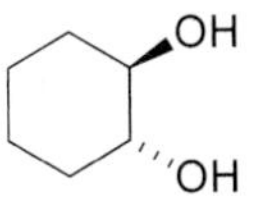

A

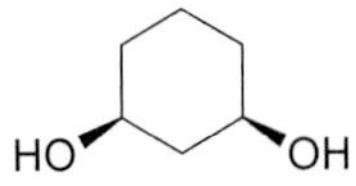

B

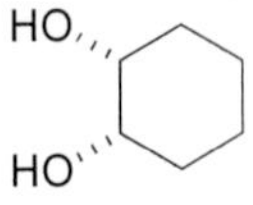

C

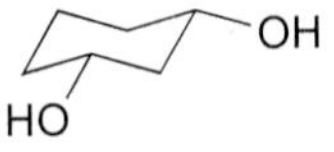

D

1. **A** and **C** are stereoisomers.
2. **B** and **D** are identical.
3. **A** and **B** are stereoisomers.
4. Statements (1) and (2) are both true.
5. Statements (1), (2), and (3) are all true.

b. Which of the following statements is true about *cis*-1-isopropyl-2-methylcyclohexane?
1. The more stable conformation has the isopropyl group in the equatorial position and the methyl group in the axial position.
2. The more stable conformation has both the methyl and isopropyl groups in the equatorial position.
3. *cis*-1-Isopropyl-2-methylcyclohexane is a meso compound.
4. Statements (1) and (2) are true.
5. Statements (1), (2), and (3) are all true.

c. Rank the following conformations in order of ***increasing energy.***

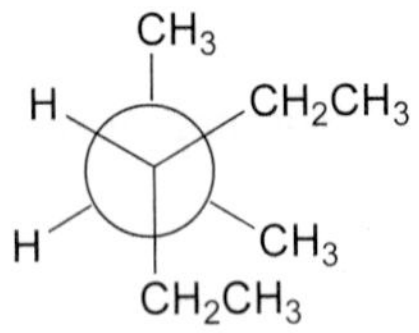

A

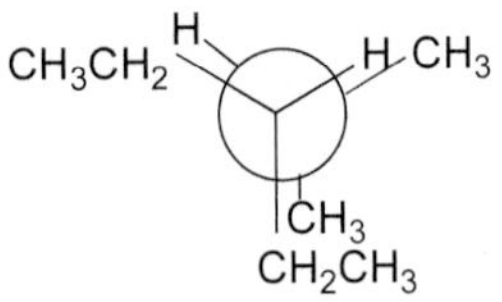

B

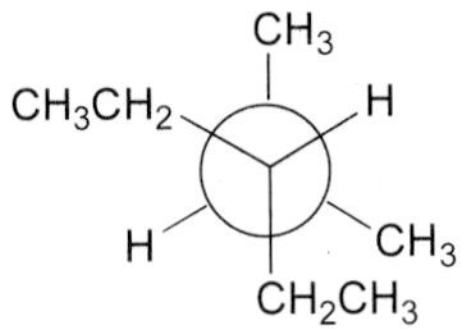

C

1. **C < B < A**
2. **C < A < B**
3. **A < C < B**
4. **B < A < C**
5. **A < B < C**

2. Give the IUPAC name for each of the following compounds.

a. 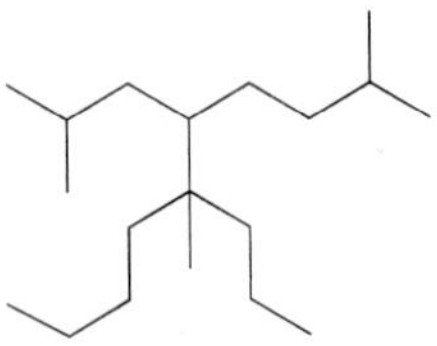

b. 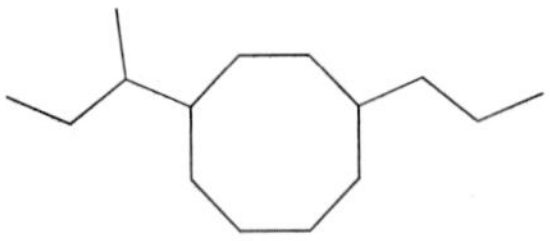

3. How are the molecules in each pair related? Are they constitutional isomers, stereoisomers, identical, or not isomers?

a. 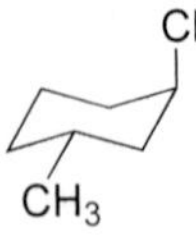

and

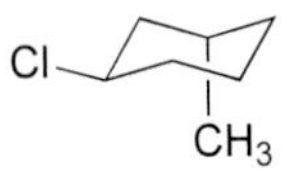

b. 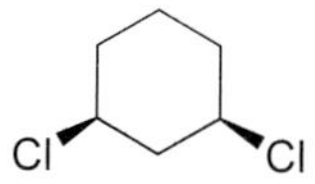
Cl
Cl
and
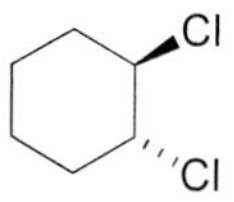
Cl
Cl

c. 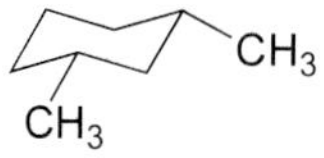
CH3
CH3
and
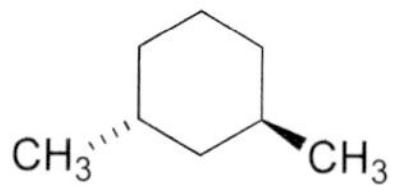
CH3
CH3

4. Rank the following conformations in order of increasing energy. Label the conformation of lowest energy as **1,** the highest energy as **4,** and the conformations of intermediate energy as **2** and **3.**

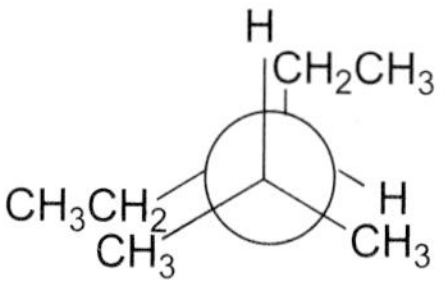
H
CH2CH3
CH3CH2
CH3
H
CH3

A

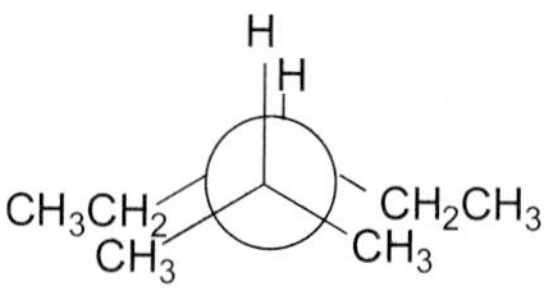
H
H
CH3CH2
CH3
CH2CH3
CH3

B

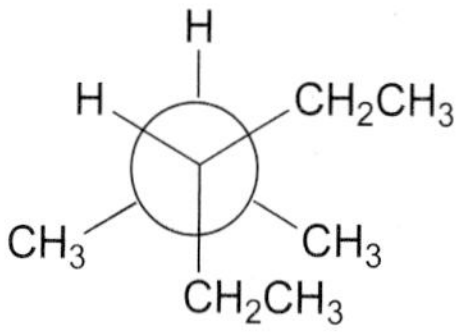
H
H
CH2CH3
CH3
CH3
CH2CH3

C

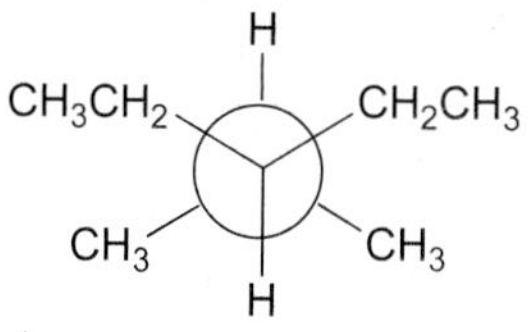
H
CH3CH2
CH2CH3
CH3
CH3
H

D

5. Consider the following disubstituted cyclohexane drawn below:

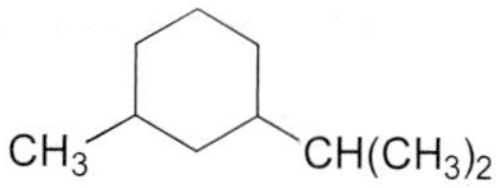
CH3
CH(CH3)2

a. Draw the more stable chair conformation for the cis isomer.
b. Draw the more stable chair conformation for the trans isomer.

Answers to Practice Test

1. a. 4
   b. 1
   c. 2

2. a. 5-isobutyl-2,6-dimethyl-6-propyldecane
   b. 1-*sec*-butyl-4-propylcyclooctane

3. a. identical
   b. constitutional isomers
   c. stereoisomers

4. **A**–3
   B–4
   C–2
   D–1

5. a. 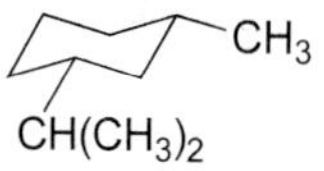
CH3
CH(CH3)2

   b. 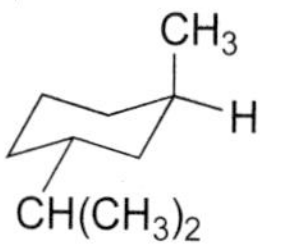
CH3
H
CH(CH3)2

Answers to Problems

4.1 The general molecular formula for an acyclic alkane is $\mathbf{C_nH_{2n+2}}$.

Number of C atoms = *n*	**2*n* + 2**	Number of H atoms
23	2(23) + 2 =	48
25	2(25) + 2 =	52
27	2(27) + 2 =	56

4.2 2-Methylbutane has 4 C's in a row with a 1 C branch.

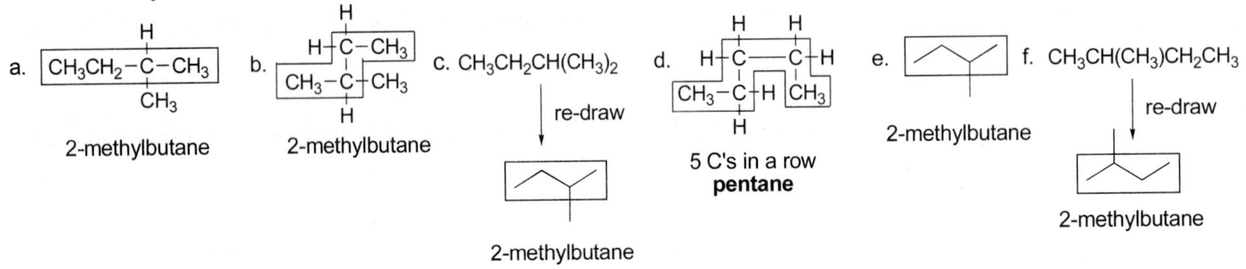
a.
2-methylbutane
b.
2-methylbutane
c. CH3CH2CH(CH3)2
re-draw
2-methylbutane
d.
5 C's in a row
pentane
e.
2-methylbutane
f. CH3CH(CH3)CH2CH3
re-draw
2-methylbutane

4.3 To classify a carbon atom as 1°, 2°, 3°, or 4° **determine how many carbon atoms it is bonded to (1° C** = bonded to **one** other C, **2° C** = bonded to **two** other C's, **3° C** = bonded to **three** other C's, **4° C** = bonded to **four** other C's). Re-draw if necessary to see each carbon clearly.

To classify a hydrogen atom as 1°, 2°, or 3°, **determine if it is bonded to a 1°, 2°, or 3° C (a 1° H is bonded to a 1° C; a 2° H is bonded to a 2° C; a 3° H is bonded to a 3° C).** Re-draw if necessary.

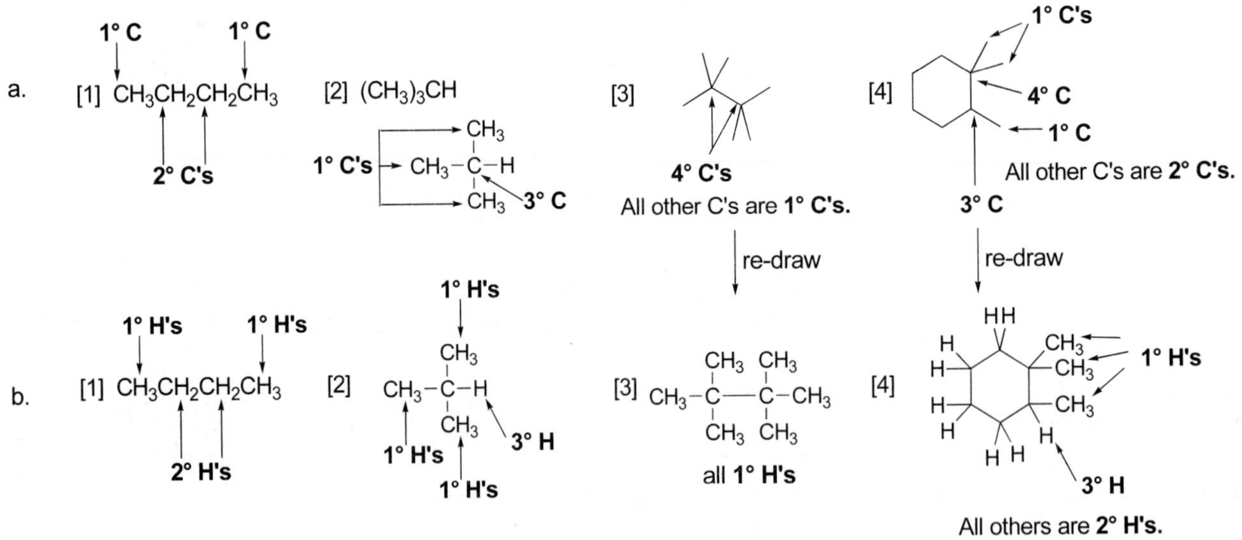
a.
[1] CH3CH2CH2CH3
1° C
1° C
2° C's
[2] (CH3)3CH
1° C's
3° C
[3]
4° C's
All other C's are 1° C's.
re-draw
[4]
1° C's
4° C
1° C
All other C's are 2° C's.
3° C
re-draw
b.
[1] CH3CH2CH2CH3
1° H's
1° H's
2° H's
[2]
1° H's
3° H
1° H's
1° H's
[3]
all 1° H's
[4]
1° H's
3° H
All others are 2° H's.

4.4 Use the definition of 1°, 2°, 3°, or 4° carbon atoms from Answer 4.3.

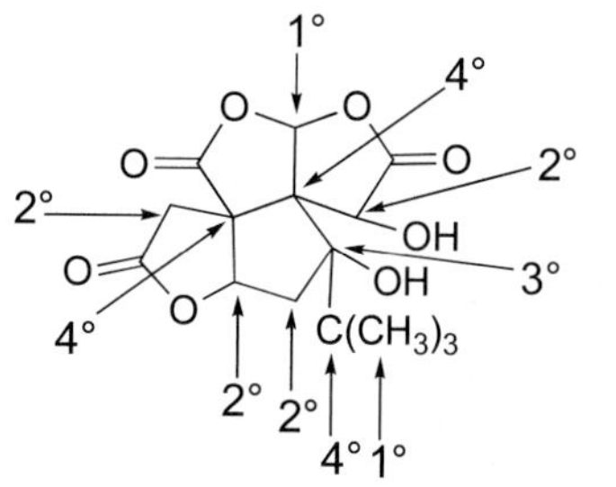
1°
4°
2°
2°
3°
4°
2°
2°
4° 1°
OH
OH
C(CH3)3

4.5 **Constitutional isomers differ in the way the atoms are connected to each other.** To draw all the constitutional isomers:
[1] Draw all of the C's in a long chain.
[2] Take off one C and use it as a substituent. (Don't add it to the end carbon: this re-makes the long chain.)
[3] Take off two C's and use these as substituents, etc.

Five **constitutional isomers** of molecular formula C_6H_{14}:

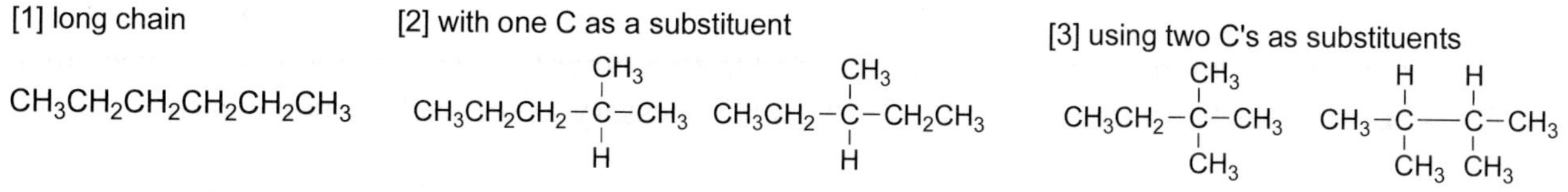
[1] long chain
[2] with one C as a substituent
[3] using two C's as substituents
CH3CH2CH2CH2CH2CH3
CH3CH2CH2–C(CH3)(H)–CH3
CH3CH2–C(CH3)(H)–CH2CH3
CH3CH2–C(CH3)(CH3)–CH3
CH3–C(H)(CH3)–C(H)(CH3)–CH3

4.6 Draw each alkane to satisfy the requirements.

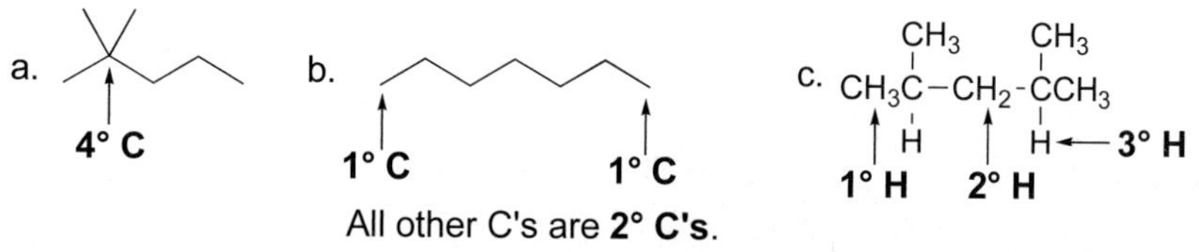
a.
4° C
b.
1° C
1° C
All other C's are 2° C's.
c.
CH3C–CH2-CCH3
CH3
CH3
H
H
1° H
2° H
3° H

4.7 Draw each compound as a skeletal structure to compare the compounds.

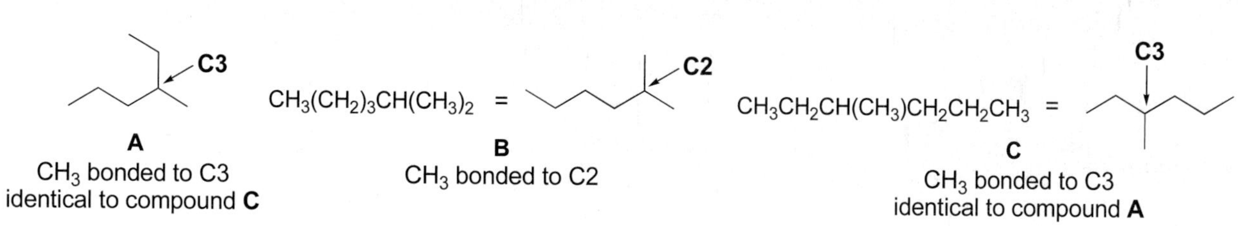
C3
A
CH3 bonded to C3
identical to compound C
CH3(CH2)3CH(CH3)2 =
C2
B
CH3 bonded to C2
CH3CH2CH(CH3)CH2CH2CH3 =
C3
C
CH3 bonded to C3
identical to compound A

4.8 Use the steps from Answer 4.5 to draw the constitutional isomers.

Five **constitutional isomers** of molecular formula C_5H_{10} having one ring:

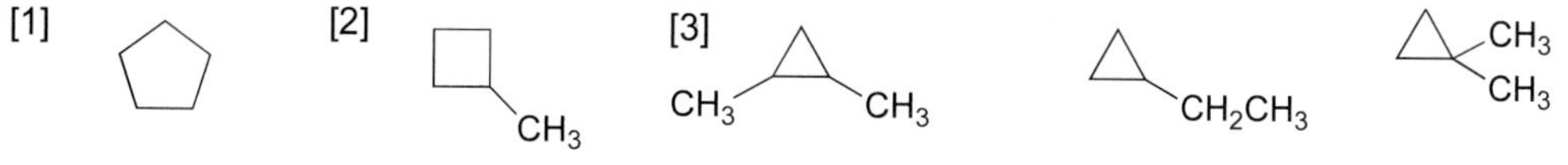
[1]
[2]
CH3
[3]
CH3
CH3
CH2CH3
CH3
CH3

4.9 Follow these steps to name an alkane:

[1] **Name the parent chain** by finding the longest C chain.

[2] **Number the chain** so that the first substituent gets the lower number. Then **name and number all substituents,** giving like substituents a prefix (di, tri, etc.).

[3] **Combine all parts,** alphabetizing the substituents, ignoring all prefixes except *iso*.

a. [1]

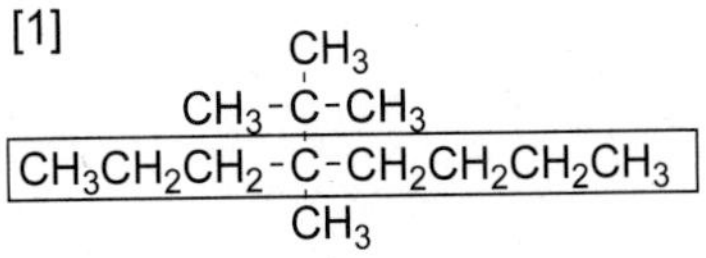

8 carbons = **octane**

[2]

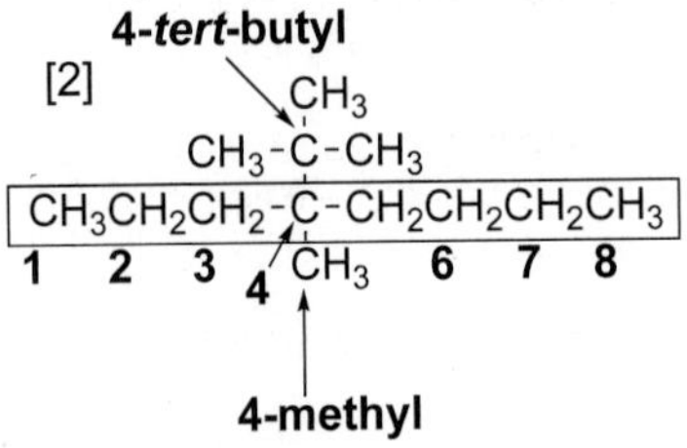

[3] **4-*tert*-butyl-4-methyloctane**

b. [1]

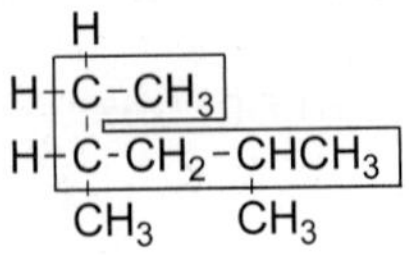

6 carbons = **hexane**

[2]

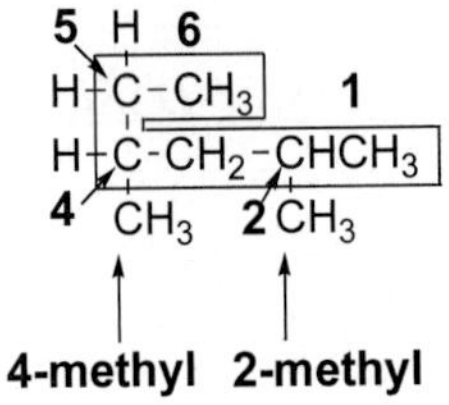

[3] **2,4-dimethylhexane**

c. [1]

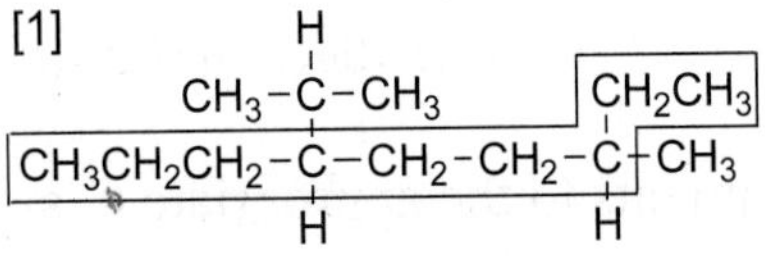

9 carbons = **nonane**

[2]

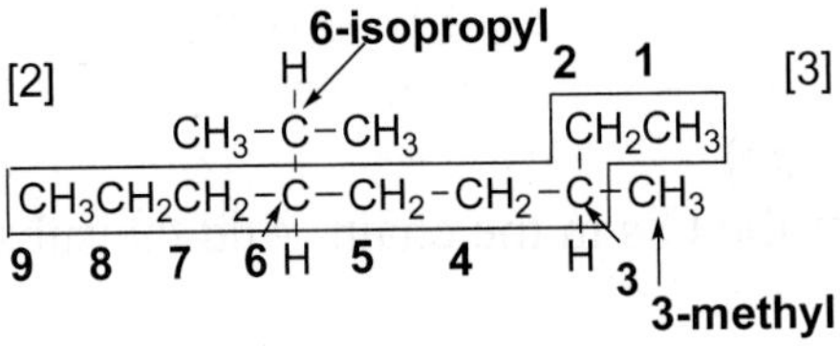

[3] **6-isopropyl-3-methylnonane**

d. [1]

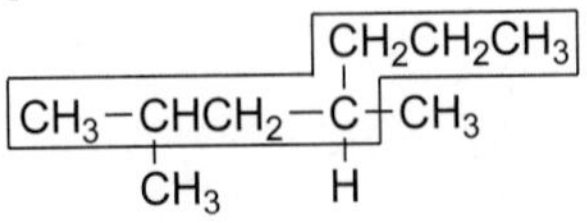

7 carbons = **heptane**

[2]

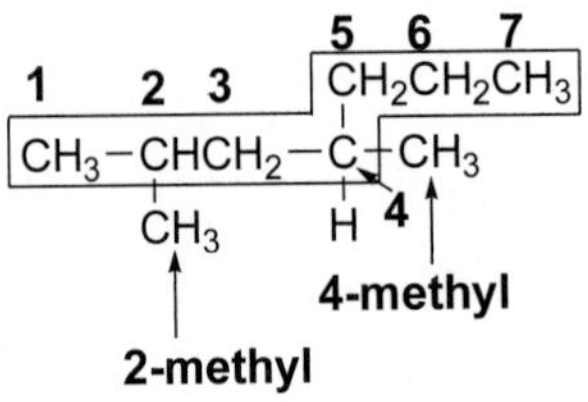

[3] **2,4-dimethylheptane**

4.10 Use the steps in Answer 4.9 to name each alkane.

a. $(CH_3)_3CCH_2CH(CH_2CH_3)_2$

re-draw

[1]

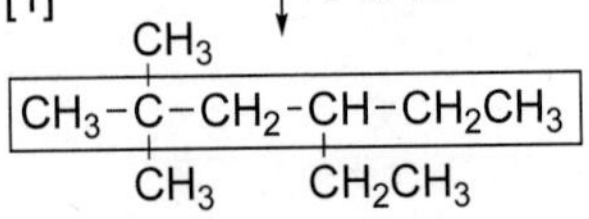

6 carbons = **hexane**

[2]

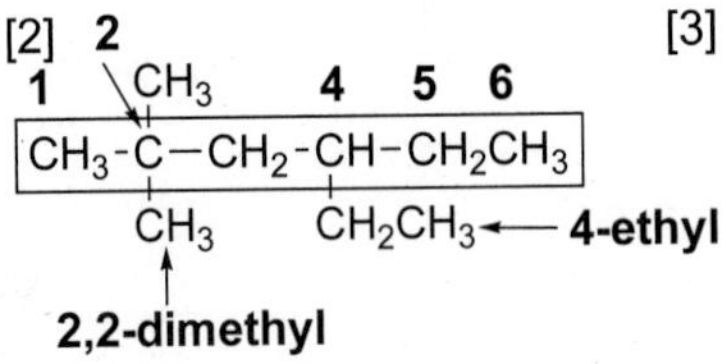

[3] **4-ethyl-2,2-dimethylhexane**

b. $CH_3(CH_2)_3CH(CH_2CH_2CH_3)CH(CH_3)_2$

re-draw

[1]

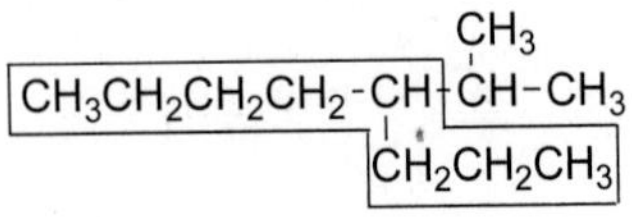

8 carbons = **octane**

[2]

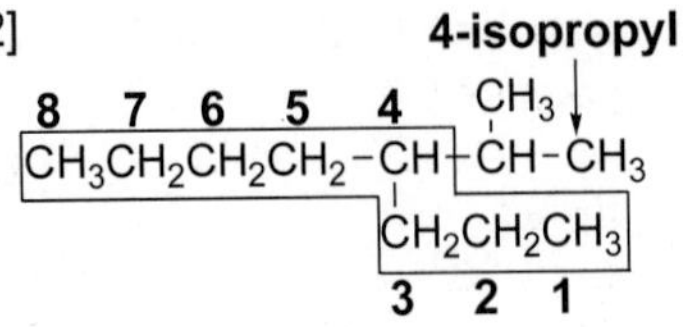

[3] **4-isopropyloctane**

c. [1]

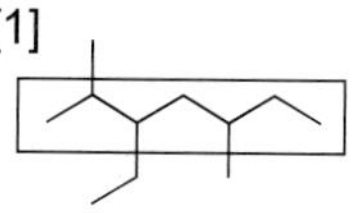

or

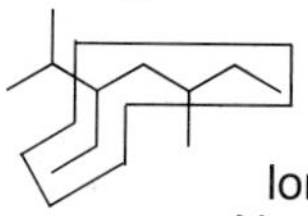

[2]

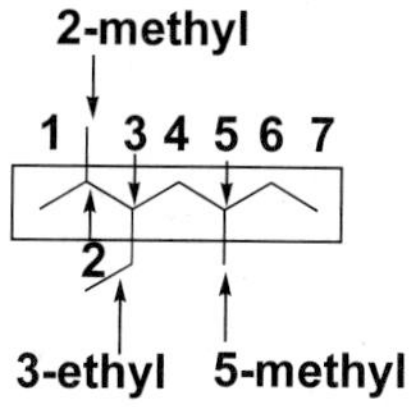
2-methyl
1
3 4 5 6 7
2
3-ethyl
5-methyl

[3] **3-ethyl-2,5-dimethylheptane**

longest chain = 7 carbons = **heptane**
Number so there are **more** substituents.
Pick the upper option.

d. [1]

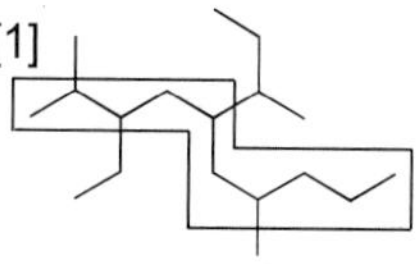

10 carbons = **decane**

[2]

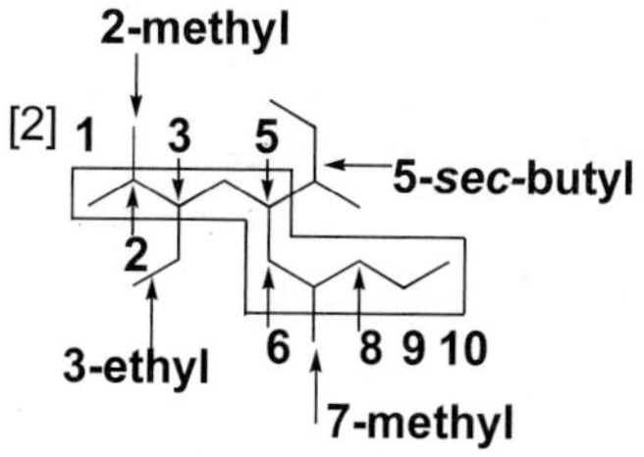
2-methyl
1
3
5
5-*sec*-butyl
2
3-ethyl
6
8 9 10
7-methyl

[3] **5-*sec*-butyl-3-ethyl-2,7-dimethyldecane**

4.11 To work backwards from a name to a structure:

[1] Find the parent name and draw that number of C's. Use the suffix to identify the functional group **(-ane = alkane).**
[2] Arbitrarily number the C's in the chain. Add the substituents to the appropriate C's.
[3] Re-draw with H's to make C's have four bonds.

a. 3-methyl**hexane**

[1] 6 carbon alkane

C–C–C–C–C–C

[2] CH_3 ← methyl on C3

C–C–C(CH3)–C–C–C

[3] $CH_3CH_2–CH(CH_3)–CH_2CH_2CH_3$

b. 3,3-dimethyl**pentane**

[1] 5 carbon alkane

C–C–C–C–C

[2] methyl groups on C3

C–C–C(CH3)(CH3)–C–C

[3] $CH_3CH_2–C(CH_3)_2–CH_2CH_3$

c. 3,5,5-trimethyl**octane**

[1] 8 carbon alkane

C–C–C–C–C–C–C–C

[2] methyl groups on C3 and C5

C–C–C(CH3)–C–C(CH3)(CH3)–C–C–C

[3] $CH_3CH_2–CH(CH_3)–CH_2–C(CH_3)_2–CH_2CH_2CH_3$

d. 3-ethyl-4-methyl**hexane**

[1] 6 carbon alkane

C–C–C–C–C–C

[2] ethyl group on C3

C–C–C(CH2CH3)–C(CH3)–C–C

CH_3 ← methyl group on C4

[3] $CH_3CH_2–CH(CH_2CH_3)–CH(CH_3)–CH_2CH_3$

e. 3-ethyl-5-isobutyl**nonane**

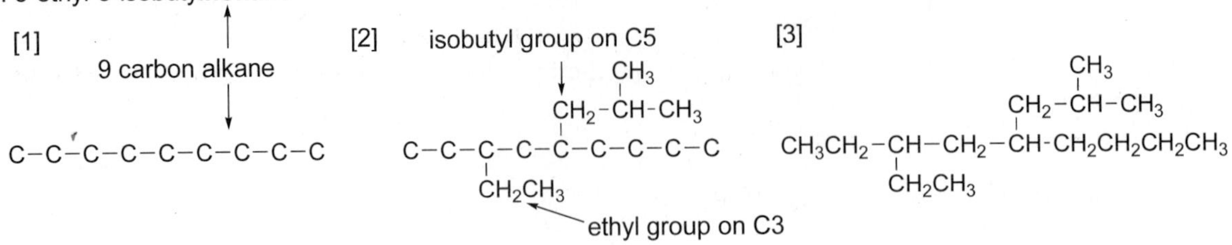

[1]
9 carbon alkane
[2]
isobutyl group on C5
ethyl group on C3
[3]

4.12 Use the steps in Answer 4.9 to name each alkane.

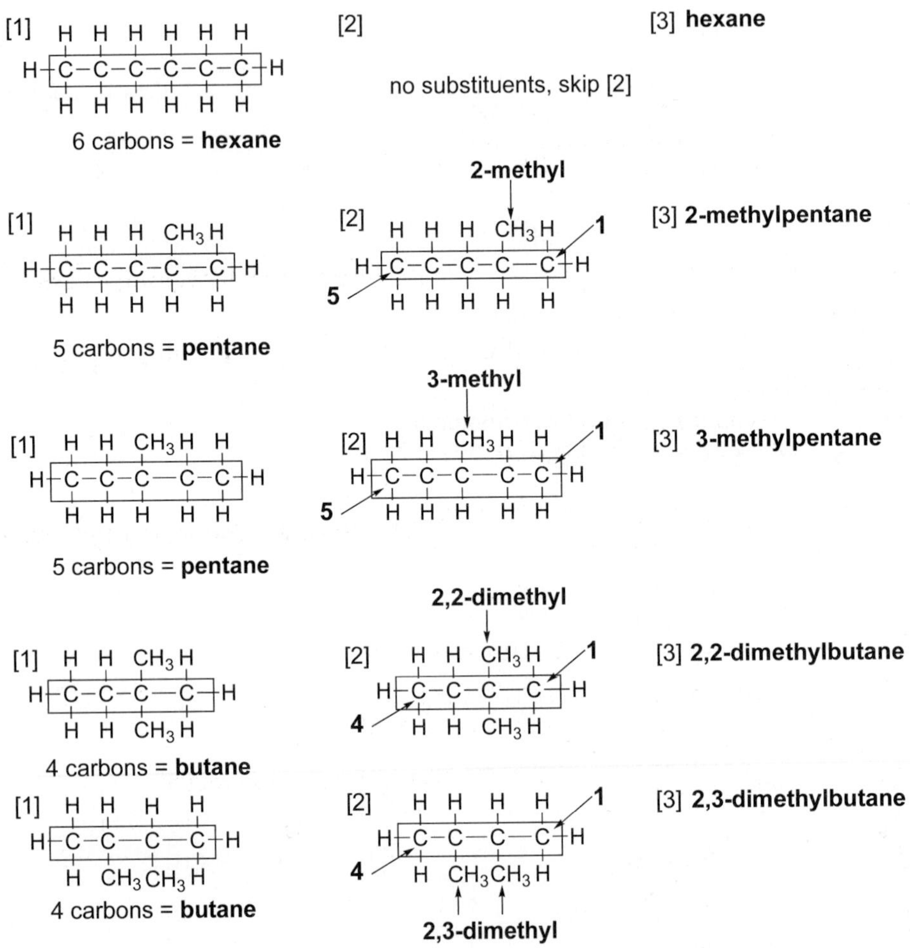

[1]
6 carbons = **hexane**
[2]
no substituents, skip [2]
[3] **hexane**
[1]
5 carbons = **pentane**
[2]
2-methyl
[3] **2-methylpentane**
[1]
5 carbons = **pentane**
[2]
3-methyl
[3] **3-methylpentane**
[1]
4 carbons = **butane**
[2]
2,2-dimethyl
[3] **2,2-dimethylbutane**
[1]
4 carbons = **butane**
[2]
2,3-dimethyl
[3] **2,3-dimethylbutane**

4.13 Follow these steps to name a cycloalkane:

[1] **Name the parent cycloalkane** by counting the C's in the ring and adding cyclo-

[2] **Numbering:**

[2a] Number around the ring beginning at a substituent and giving the second substituent the lower number.

[2b] Number to assign the lower number to the substituents alphabetically.

[2c] Name and number all substituents, giving like substituents a prefix (di, tri, etc.).

[3] **Combine all parts,** alphabetizing the substituents, ignoring all prefixes except *iso*.

(Remember: If a carbon chain has more C's than the ring, the chain is the parent, and the ring is a substituent.)

a. [1]

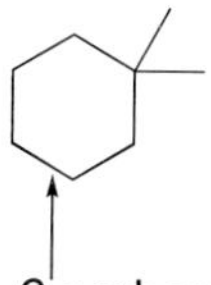

6 carbons in ring = **cyclohexane**

[2]

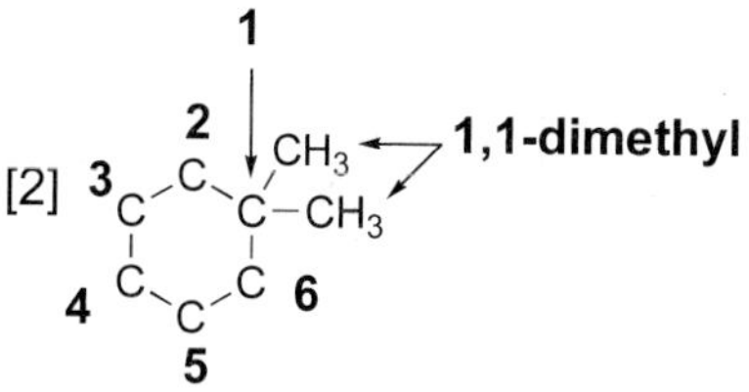

Number so the substituents are at C1.

[3] **1,1-dimethylcyclohexane**

b. [1]

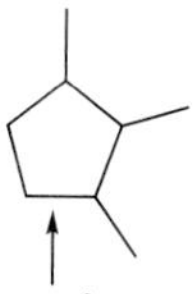

5 carbons in ring = **cyclopentane**

[2]

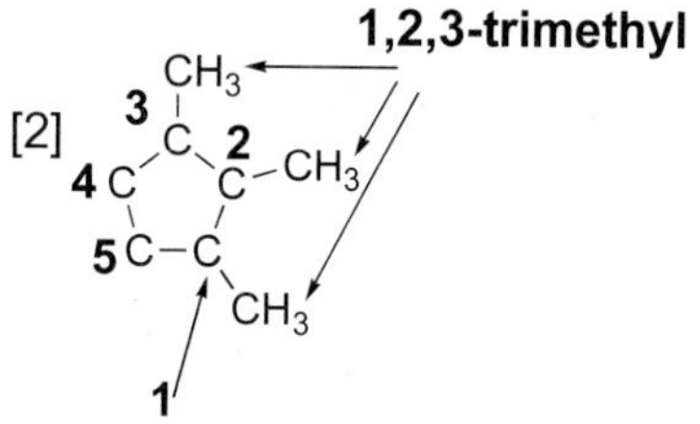

Number so the first substituent is at C1, second at C2.

[3] **1,2,3-trimethylcyclopentane**

c. [1]

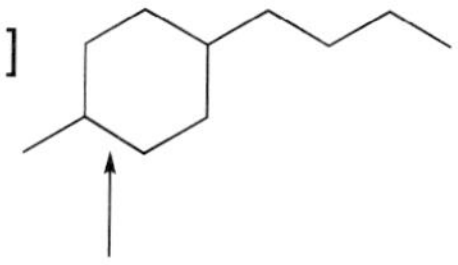

6 carbons in ring = **cyclohexane**

[2]

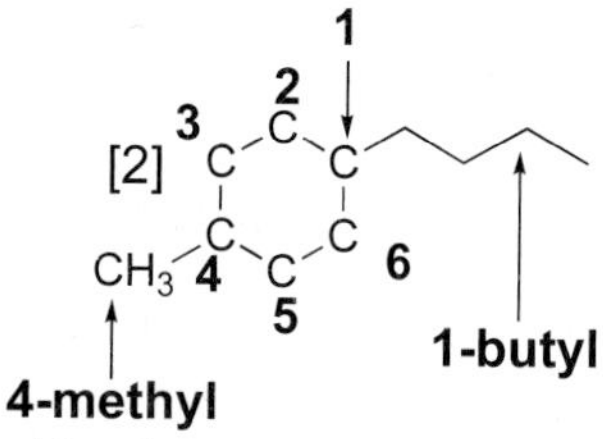

Number so the earlier alphabetical substituent is at C1, **b**utyl before **m**ethyl.

[3] **1-butyl-4-methylcyclohexane**

d. [1]

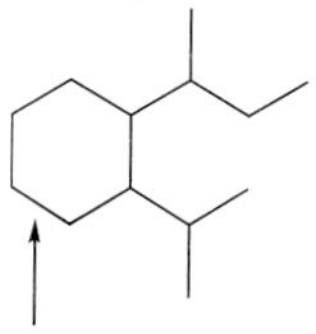

6 carbons in ring = **cyclohexane**

[2]

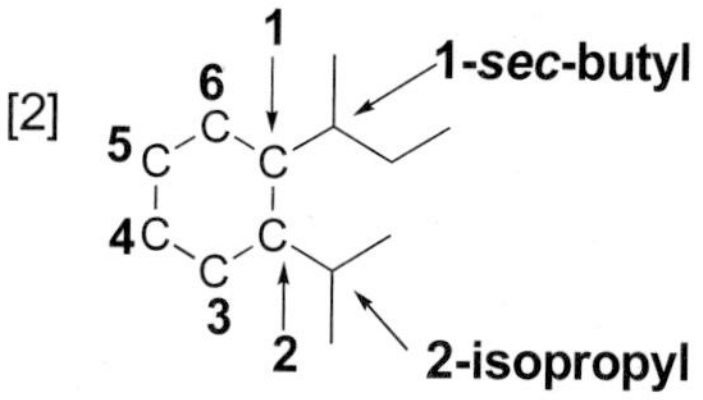

Number so the earlier alphabetical substituent is at C1, **b**utyl before **i**sopropyl.

[3] **1-*sec*-butyl-2-isopropylcyclohexane**

e. [1]

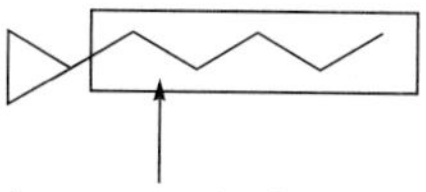

longest chain = 5 carbons = **pentane**

[2]

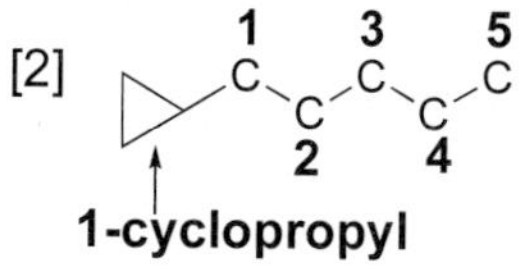

Number so the cyclopropyl is at C1.

[3] **1-cyclopropylpentane**

f. [1]

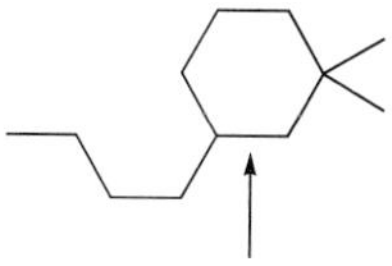

6 carbons in ring = **cyclohexane**

[2]

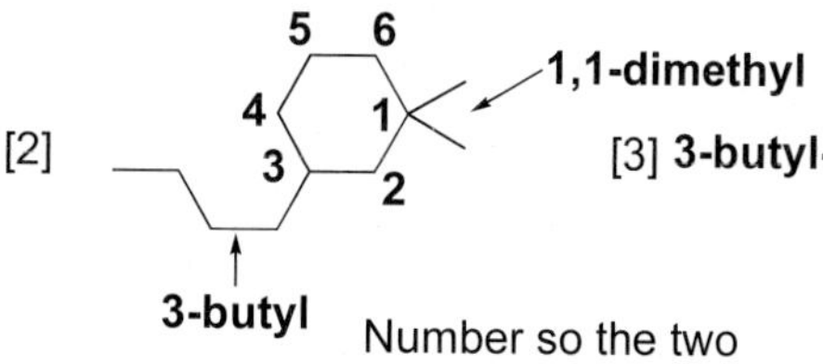

Number so the two methyls are at C1.

[3] **3-butyl-1,1-dimethylcyclohexane**

4.14 To draw the structures, use the steps in Answer 4.11.

a. 1,2-dimethyl**cyclobutane**

[1] 4 carbon cycloalkane

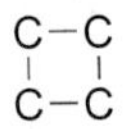

[2]

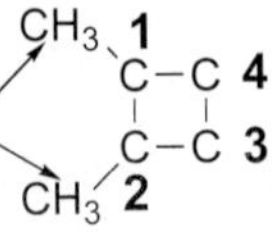
methyl groups
on C1 and C2

[3]

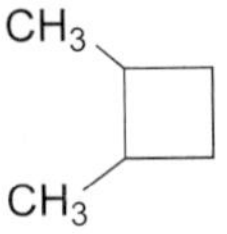

b. 1,1,2-trimethyl**cyclopropane**

[1] 3 carbon cycloalkane

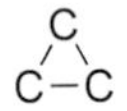

[2]

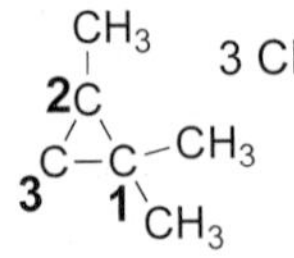
3 CH_3's

[3]

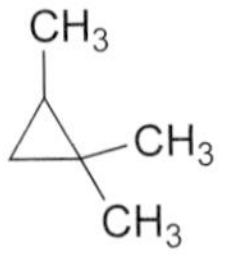

c. 4-ethyl-1,2-dimethyl**cyclohexane**

[1] 6 carbon cycloalkane

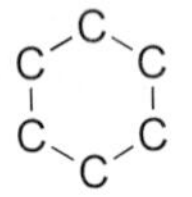

[2]

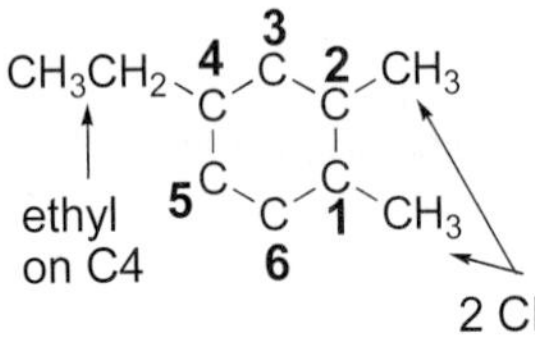
ethyl
on C4
2 CH_3's

[3]

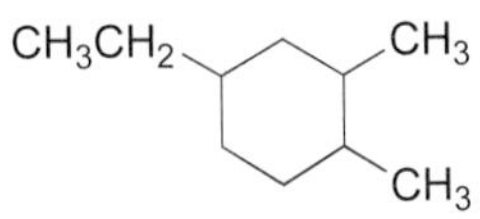

d. 1-*sec*-butyl-3-isopropyl**cyclopentane**

[1] 5 carbon cycloalkane

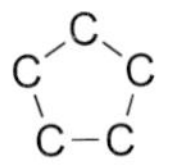

[2]

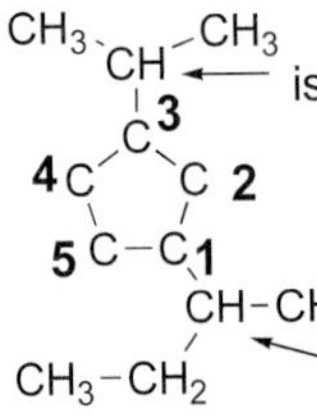
isopropyl
sec-butyl

[3]

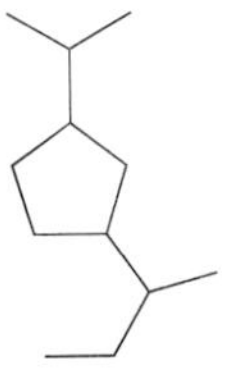

e. 1,1,2,3,4-pentamethyl**cycloheptane**

[1] 7 carbon cycloalkane

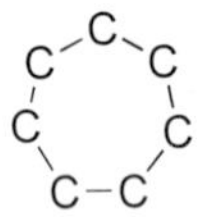

[2] 5 CH_3's

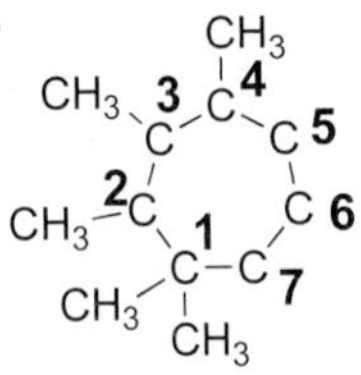

[3]

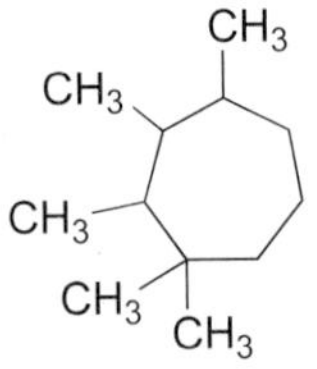

4.15 Compare the number of C's and surface area to determine relative boiling points. Rules:

[1] Increasing number of C's = increasing boiling point.

[2] Increasing surface area = increasing boiling point (branching decreases surface area).

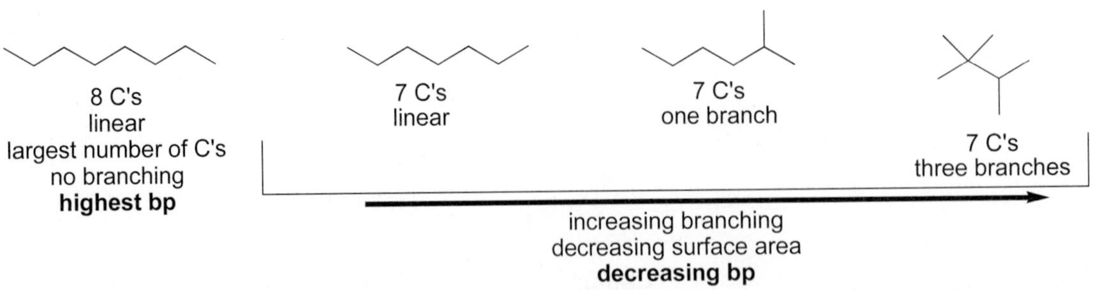
8 C's
linear
largest number of C's
no branching
highest bp
7 C's
linear
7 C's
one branch
7 C's
three branches
increasing branching
decreasing surface area
decreasing bp

Increasing boiling point: $(CH_3)_3CCH(CH_3)_2 < CH_3CH_2CH_2CH_2CH(CH_3)_2 < CH_3(CH_2)_5CH_3 < CH_3(CH_2)_6CH_3$

4.16 To draw a Newman projection, visualize the carbons as one in front and one in back of each other. The C–C bond is not drawn. There is only one staggered and one eclipsed conformation.

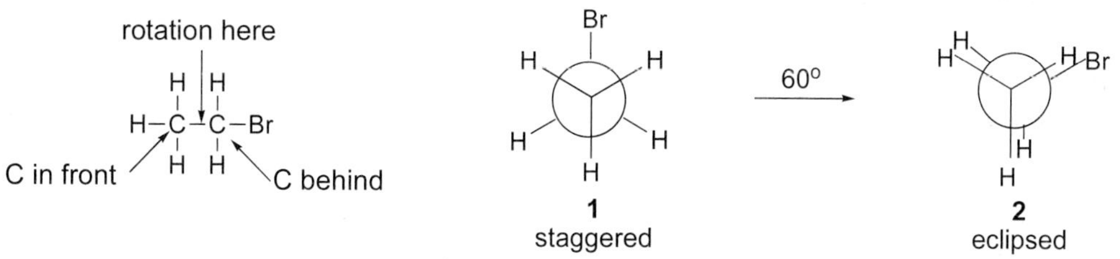

4.17

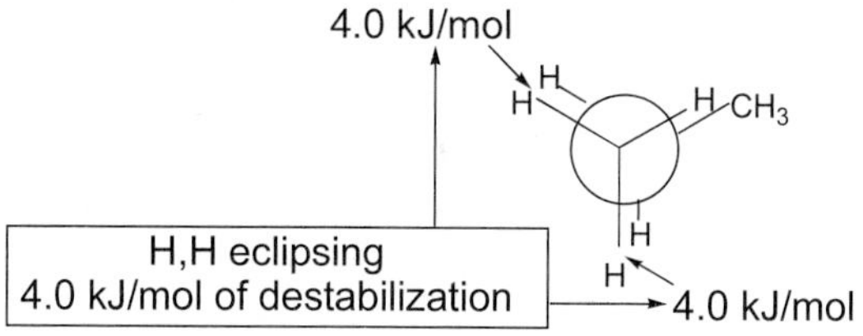

To calculate H,CH_3 destabilization:

14 kJ/mol (total) –
8.0 kJ/mol for 2 H,H eclipsing interactions
= **6 kJ/mol** for one H,CH_3 eclipsing interaction

4.18 To determine the energy of conformations keep two things in mind:

[1] Staggered conformations are more stable than eclipsed conformations.

[2] Minimize steric interactions: keep large groups away from each other.

The highest energy conformation is the eclipsed conformation in which the two largest groups are eclipsed. The lowest energy conformation is the staggered conformation in which the two largest groups are anti.

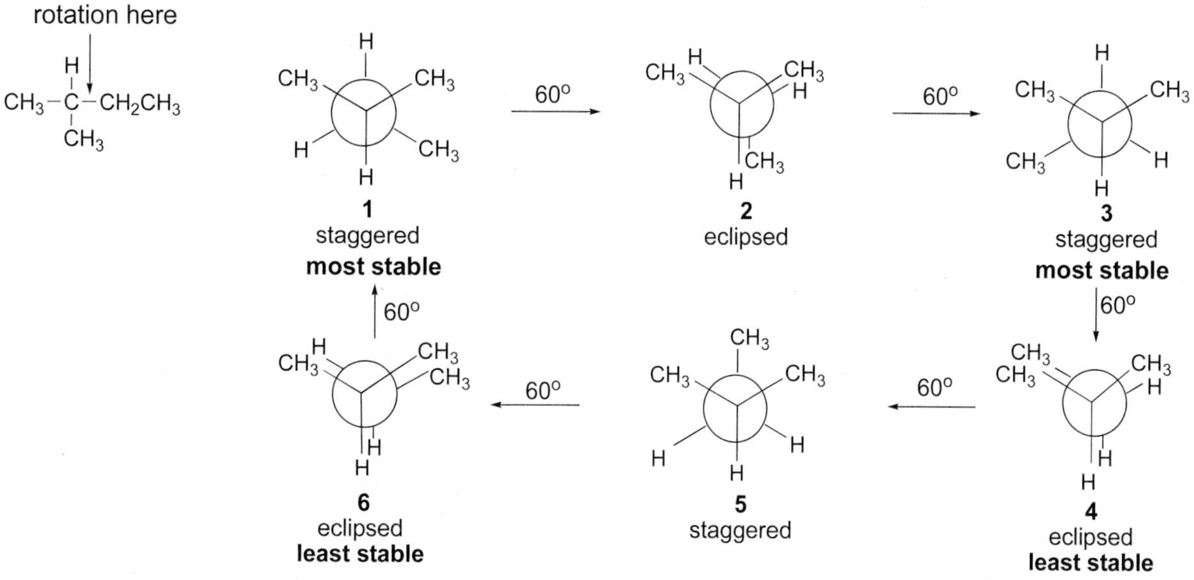

4.19 To determine the most and least stable conformations, use the rules from Answer 4.18.

a. **1,2-dichloroethane**

$ClCH_2-CH_2Cl$

rotation here

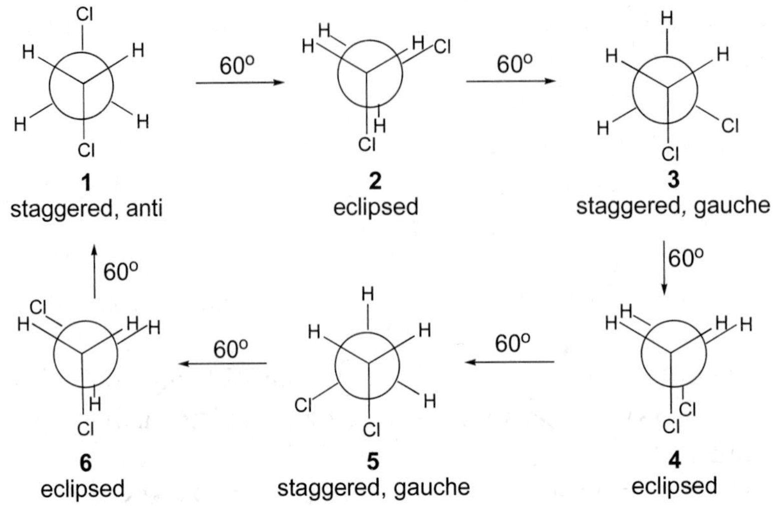

60°
1
staggered, anti
2
eclipsed
3
staggered, gauche
4
eclipsed
5
staggered, gauche
6
eclipsed

b.

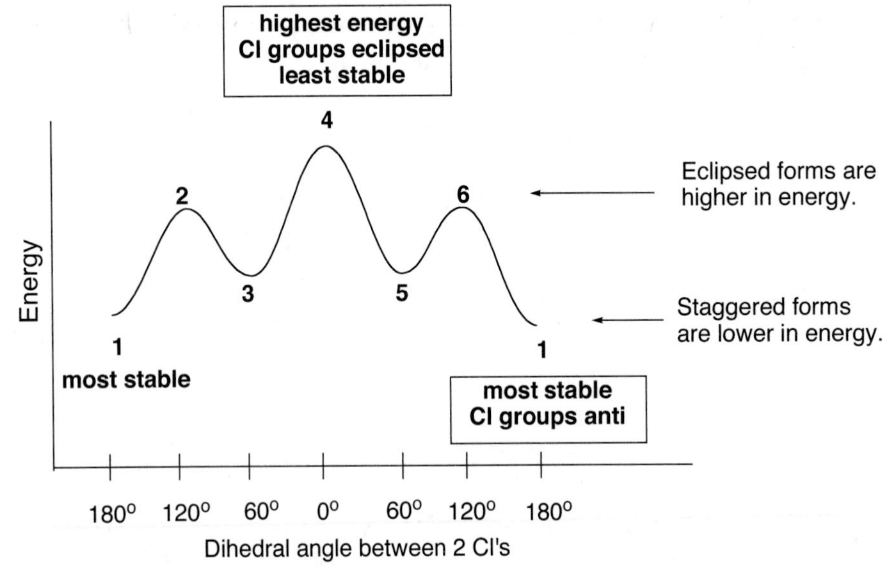

highest energy
Cl groups eclipsed
least stable
Energy
most stable
most stable
Cl groups anti
Eclipsed forms are higher in energy.
Staggered forms are lower in energy.
180° 120° 60° 0° 60° 120° 180°
Dihedral angle between 2 Cl's

4.20 Add the energy increase for each eclipsing interaction to determine the destabilization.

a.

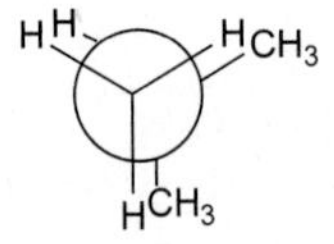

1 H,H interaction = 4.0 kJ/mol

2 H,CH_3 interactions (2 x 6.0 kJ/mol) = 12.0 kJ/mol

Total destabilization = 16 kJ/mol

b.

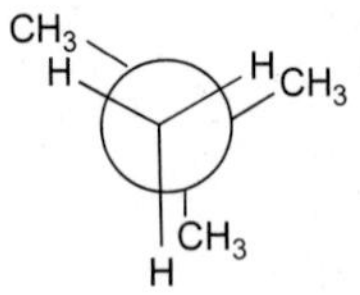

3 H,CH_3 interactions

(3 x 6.0 kJ/mol) = **18 kJ/mol**

Total destabilization

4.21 Two points:

- Axial bonds point up or down, while equatorial bonds point out.
- An *up* carbon has an axial *up* bond, and a *down* carbon has an axial *down* bond.

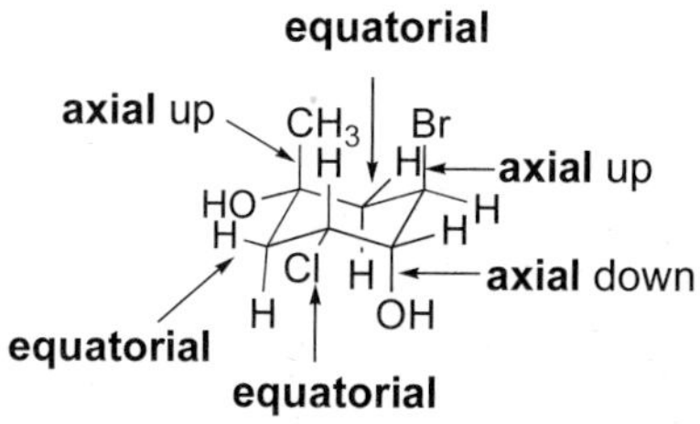

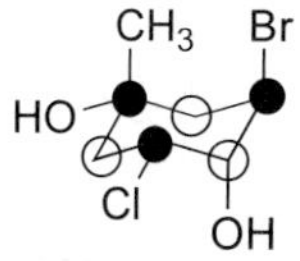

Up carbons are dark circles.
Down carbons are clear circles.

4.22 Draw the second chair conformation by flipping the ring.

- **The *up* carbons become *down* carbons, and the axial bonds become equatorial bonds.**
- **Axial bonds become equatorial, but *up* bonds stay *up*;** that is, an axial *up* bond becomes an equatorial *up* bond.
- The conformation with **larger groups equatorial is the more stable** conformation and is present in higher concentration at equilibrium.

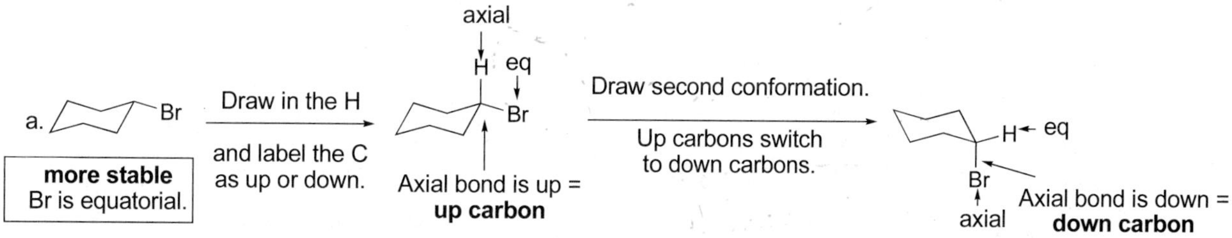

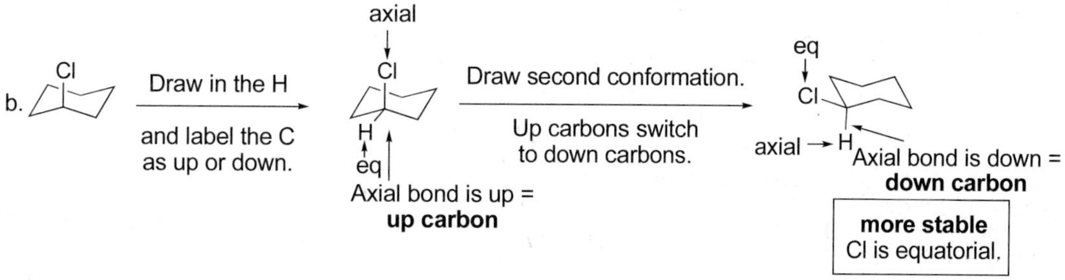

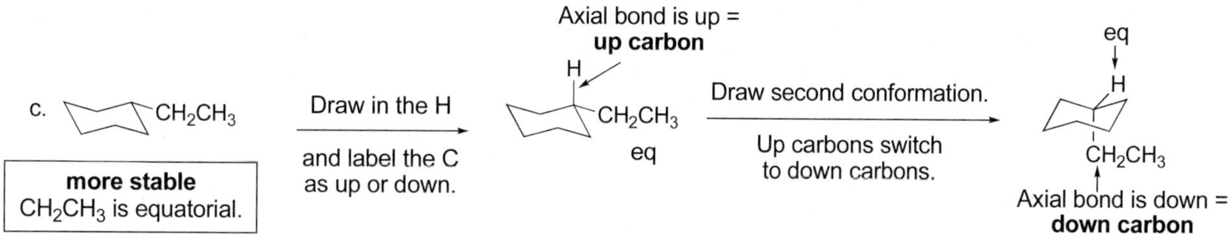

4.23 Larger axial substituents create unfavorable diaxial interactions, whereas equatorial groups have more room and are favored.

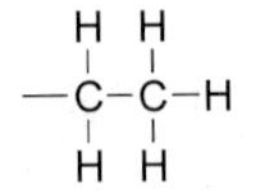

larger substituent
more important to be equatorial

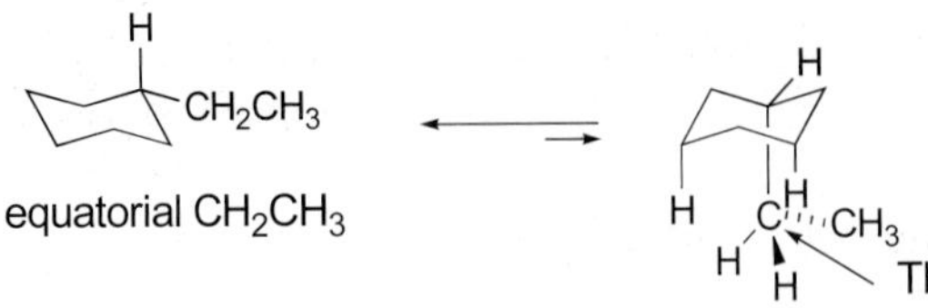

equatorial CH_2CH_3

The H's and CH_3 of the sp^3 hybridized C have severe 1,3-diaxial interactions with the two other axial H's.

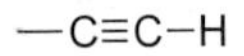

more compact substituent
less important to be equatorial

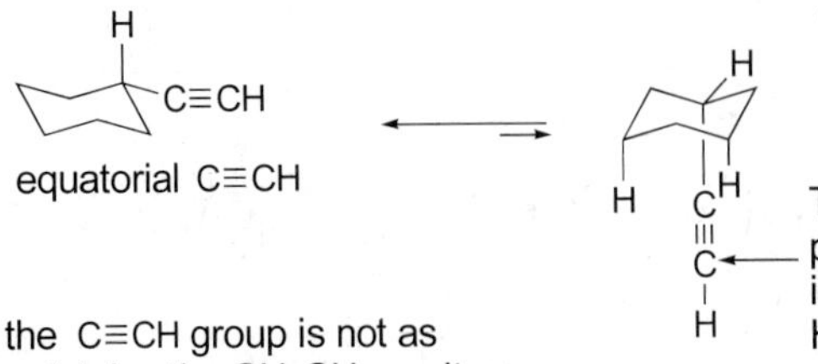

equatorial C≡CH

The *sp* hybridized C's are linear and point down. The 1,3-diaxial interactions with the two other axial H's are less severe.

The axial conformation containing the C≡CH group is not as unstable as the axial conformation containing the CH_2CH_3, so it is present in higher concentration at equilibrium.

4.24 Wedges represent "up" groups in front of the page, and dashes are "down" groups in back of the page. Cis groups are on the same side of the ring, and trans groups are on opposite sides of the ring.

a. ***cis*-1,2-dimethylcyclopropane**

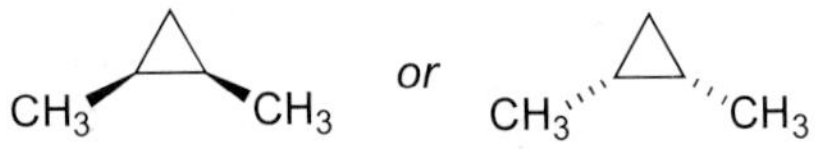

cis = same side of the ring
both groups on wedges or
both on dashes

b. ***trans*-1-ethyl-2-methylcyclopentane**

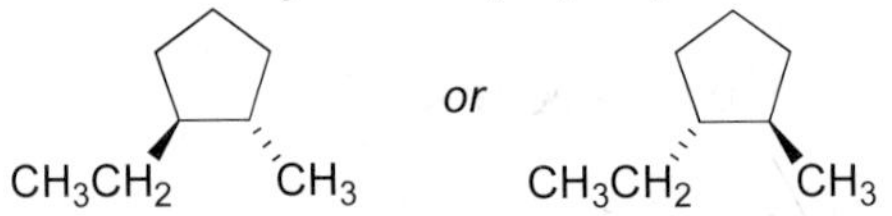

trans = opposite sides of the ring
one group on a wedge,
one group on a dash

4.25 Cis and trans isomers are stereoisomers.

***cis*-1,3-diethylcyclobutane**

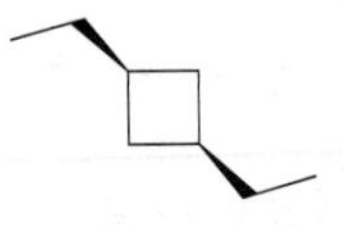

cis = same side of the ring
both groups on wedges or
both on dashes

a. ***trans*-1,3-diethylcyclobutane**

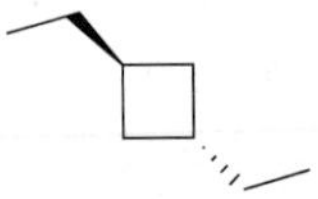

trans = opposite sides of the ring
one group on a wedge,
one group on a dash

b. ***cis*-1,2-diethylcyclobutane**

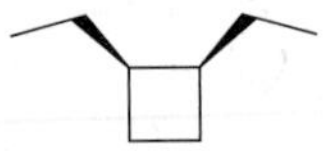

constitutional isomer
different arrangement of atoms

4.26 To classify a compound as a cis or trans isomer, **classify each non-hydrogen group as up or down. Groups on the same side = cis isomer; groups on opposite sides = trans isomer.**

a.

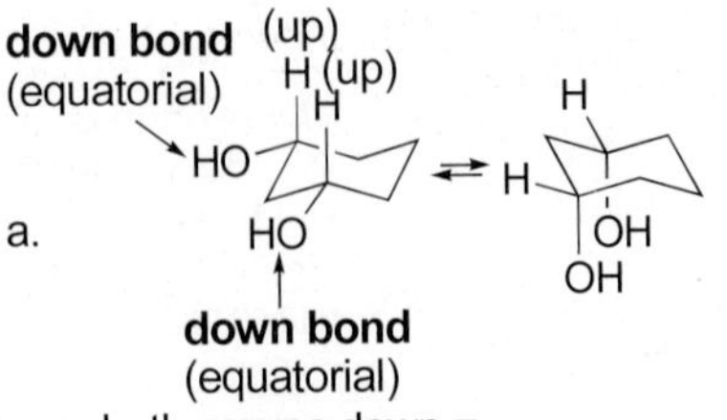

both groups down =
cis isomer

b.

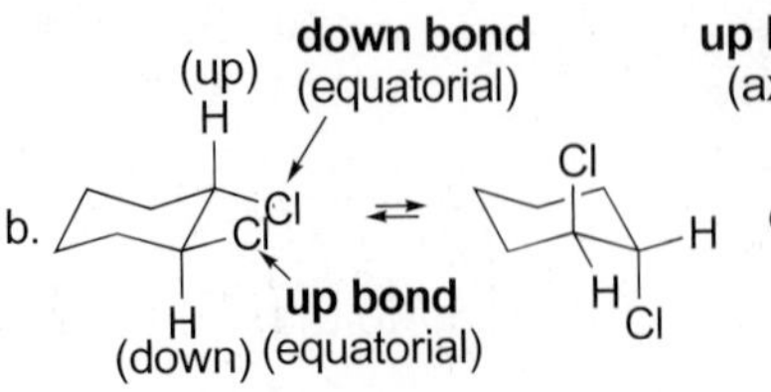

one group up, one down =
trans isomer

c.

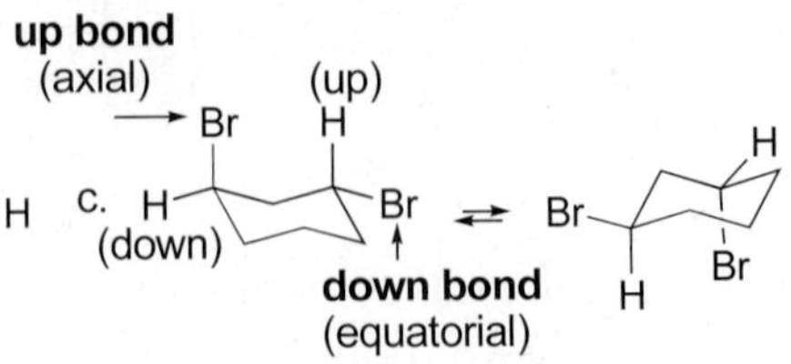

one group up, one down =
trans isomer

4.27

a.

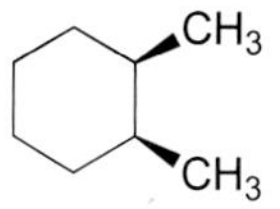

groups on same side
cis isomer

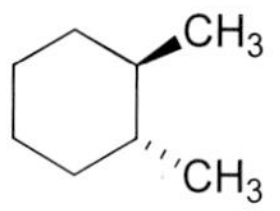

groups on opposite sides
trans isomer
(one possibility)

b. cis:

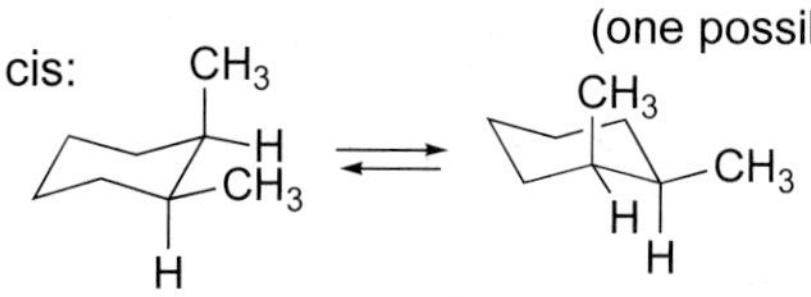

two chair conformations for the **cis isomer**

Same stability since they both have one equatorial, one axial CH_3 group.

c. trans:

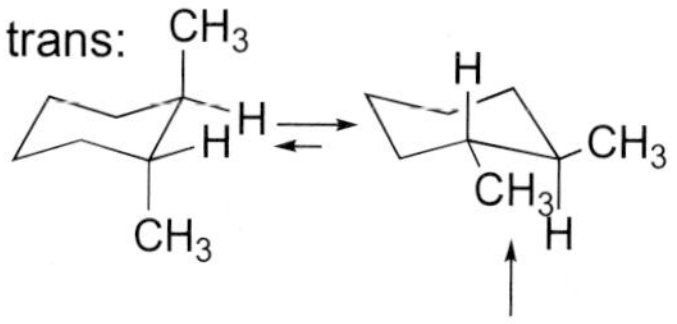

both groups equatorial
more stable

two chair conformations for the **trans isomer**

d. The **trans isomer is more stable** because it can have both methyl groups in the more roomy **equatorial** position.

4.28

a.

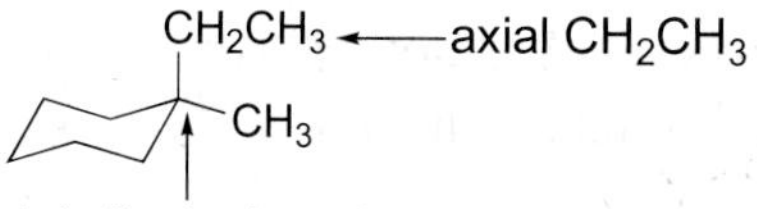

1,1-disubstituted

b.

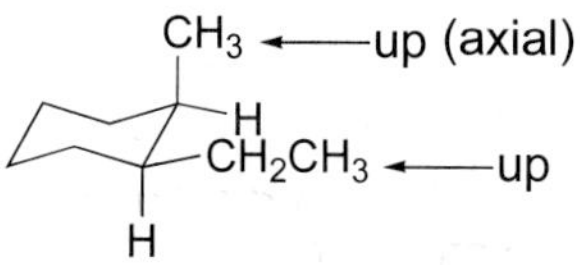

cis-1,2-disubstituted

c.

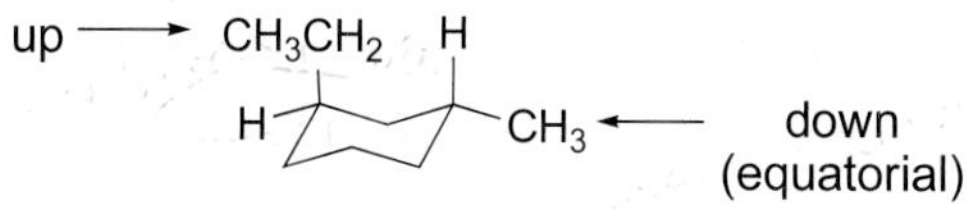

trans-1,3-disubstituted

d.

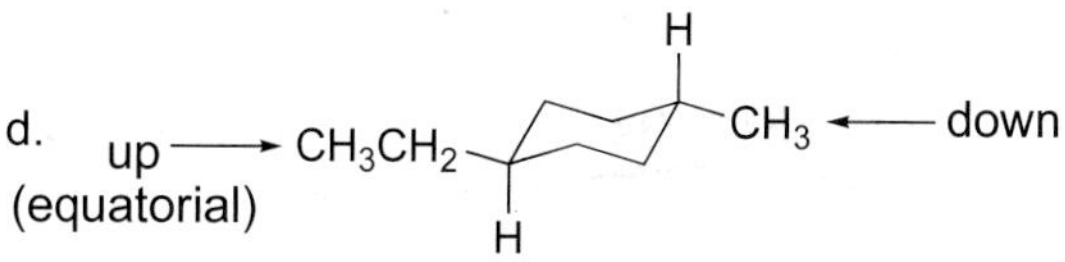

trans-1,4-disubstituted

4.29 *Oxidation* results in an *increase* in the number of C–Z bonds, or a *decrease* in the number of C–H bonds.

Reduction results in a *decrease* in the number of C–Z bonds, or an *increase* in the number of C–H bonds.

a.

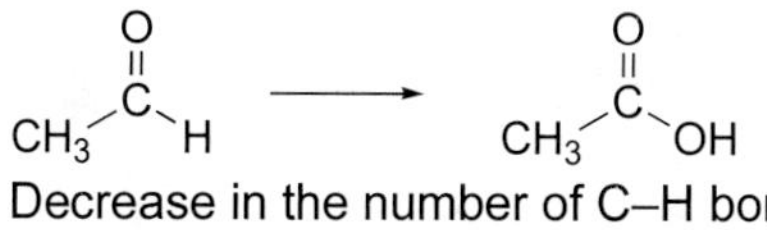

Decrease in the number of C–H bonds.
Increase in the number of C–O bonds.
Oxidation

b.

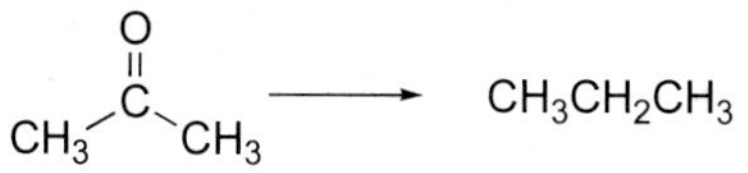

Decrease in the number of C–O bonds.
Increase in the number of C–H bonds.
Reduction

c.

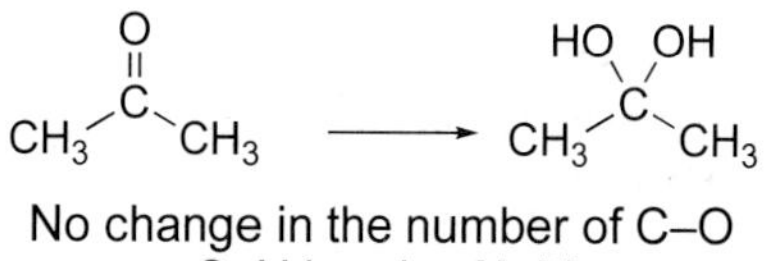

No change in the number of C–O or C–H bonds. **Neither**

d.

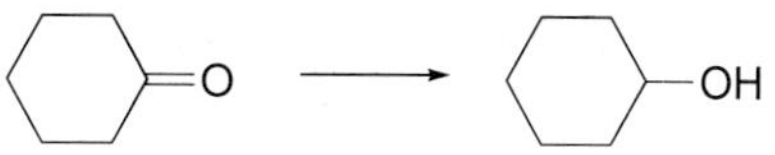

Decrease in the number of C–O bonds.
Increase in the number of C–H bonds.
Reduction

4.30 The products of a combustion reaction of a hydrocarbon are always the same: **CO_2 and H_2O.**

a. $CH_3CH_2CH_3 + 5\ O_2 \xrightarrow{\text{flame}} 3\ CO_2 + 4\ H_2O$ + heat

b. 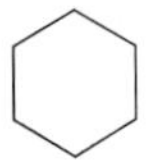 + 9 O_2 —flame→ 6 CO_2 + 6 H_2O + heat

4.31 "Like dissolves like." Beeswax is a lipid, so it will be more soluble in nonpolar solvents. H_2O is very polar, ethanol is slightly less polar, and chloroform is least polar. Beeswax is most soluble in the least polar solvent.

Increasing polarity ←

H_2O $\quad$ CH_3CH_2OH $\quad$ $CHCl_3$

→ Increasing solubility of beeswax

4.32 Re-draw the model as a skeletal structure. The longest chain has 15 C's, making it a derivative of pentadecane. Numbering from either direction gives the same numbers.

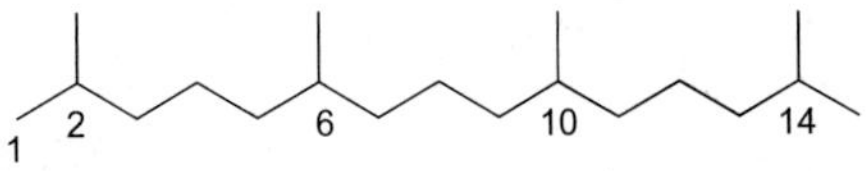

15 C's ----→ pentadecane

4 methyl groups at C2, C6, C10, and C14

2,6,10,14-tetramethylpentadecane

4.33 Re-draw each alkane as a skeletal structure, and use the steps in Answer 4.9 to name each compound. Use the definitions in Answer 4.3 to classify C's.

a.

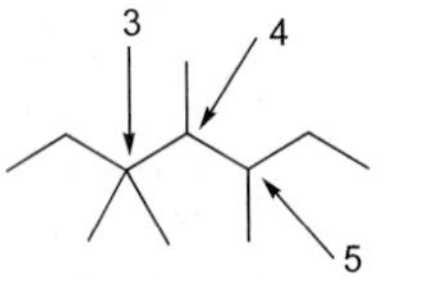

7 C's in longest chain = heptane
Number from left to right to put two substituents on C3.

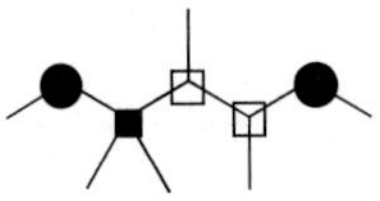

● = 2° C

□ = 3° C $\quad$ 1° C's unlabeled

■ = 4° C

Four CH_3 groups ----→ tetramethyl

Answer: **3,3,4,5-tetramethylheptane**

b.

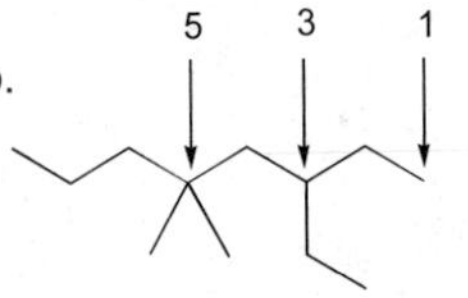

8 C's in longest chain = octane
Number from right to left to put first substituent at C3.

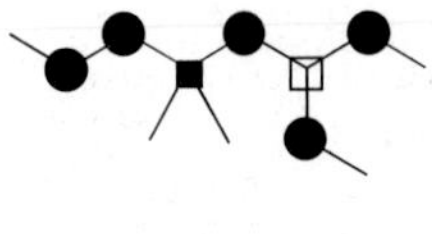

● = 2° C

□ = 3° C $\quad$ 1° C's unlabeled

■ = 4° C

ethyl at C3; 2 methyls (C5) ----→ dimethyl

Answer: **3-ethyl-5,5-dimethyloctane**

4.34 Re-draw the ball-and-stick model as a chair form.

a.

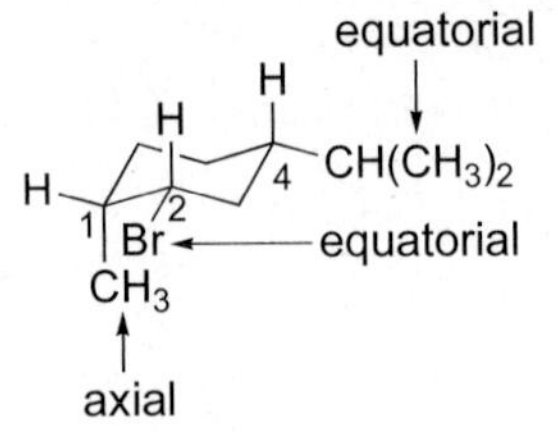

b. CH_3 on Cl and Br on C2 are both down, making them cis.
c. Br on C2 and $CH(CH_3)_2$ on C4 are both down, making them cis.

d. Second chair form:

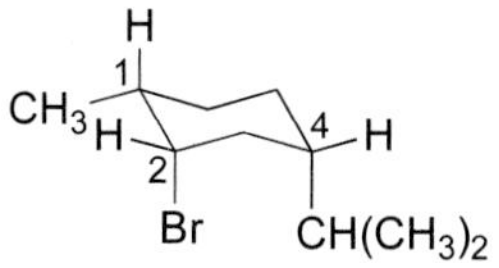

This chair form is less stable because two groups [Br and $CH(CH_3)_2$] are in the more crowded axial position.

4.35

a.

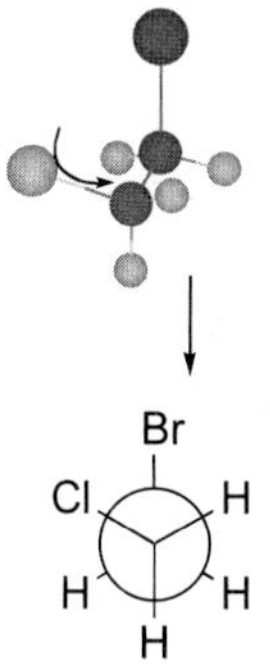

b.

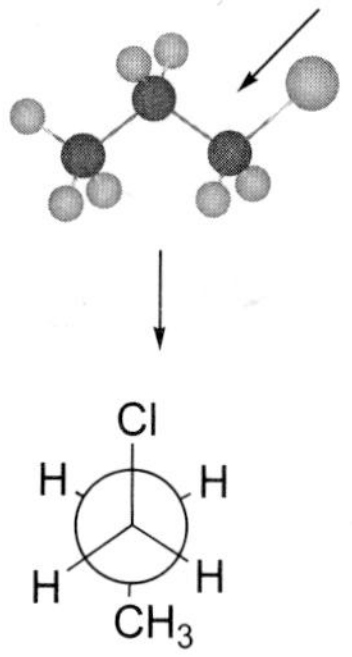

c.

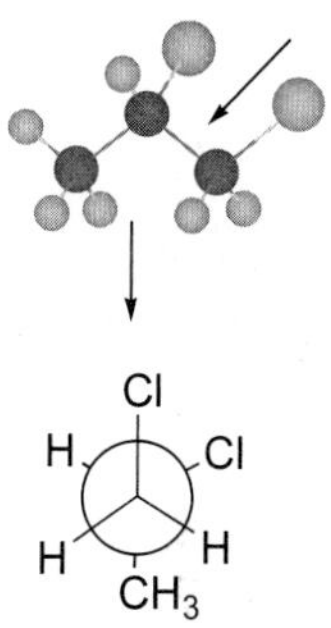

4.36 Use the rules from Answer 4.3.

a. [1]

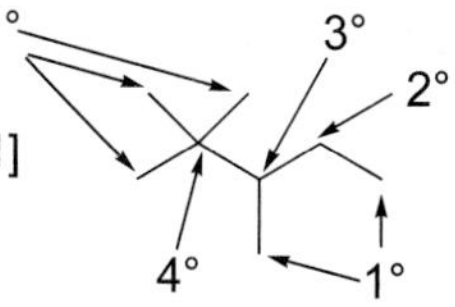

[2]

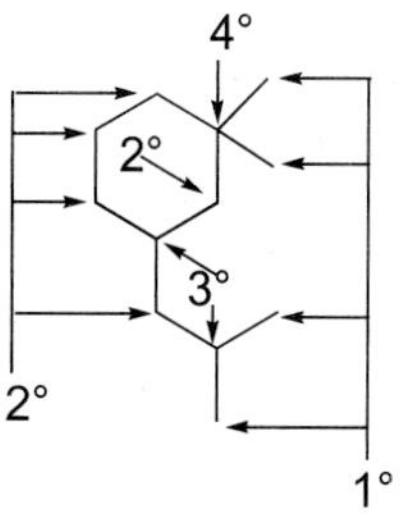

b. [1]

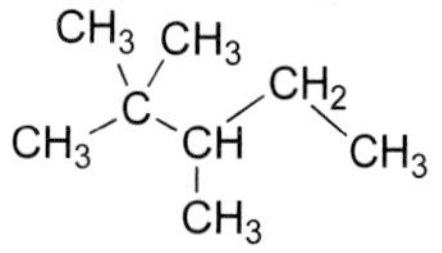

All CH_3's have 1° H's.
All CH_2's have 2° H's.
All CH's have 3° H's.

[2]

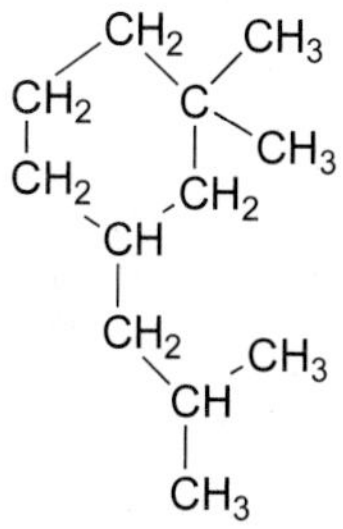

4.37

One possibility:

a.

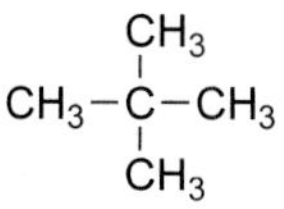

b.

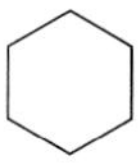

c. $CH_3CH_2CH_3$

d. $(CH_3)_3CH$

4.38

a. Five constitutional isomers of molecular formula C_4H_8:

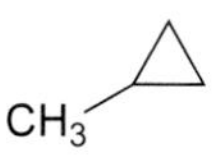

$CH_3CH{=}CHCH_3$ $CH_2{=}CHCH_2CH_3$

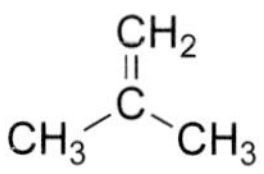

b. Nine constitutional isomers of molecular formula C_7H_{16}:

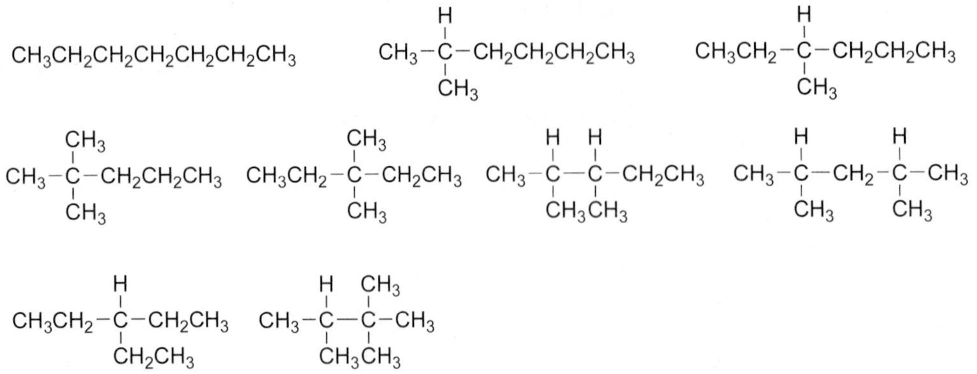

c. Twelve constitutional isomers of molecular formula C_6H_{12} containing one ring:

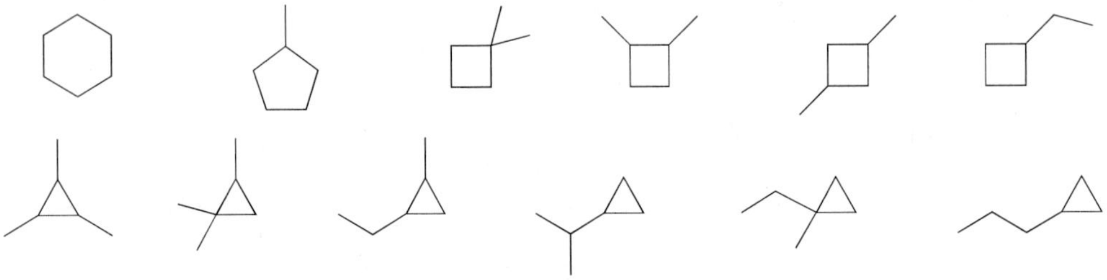

4.39 Use the steps in Answers 4.9 and 4.13 to name the alkanes.

a.

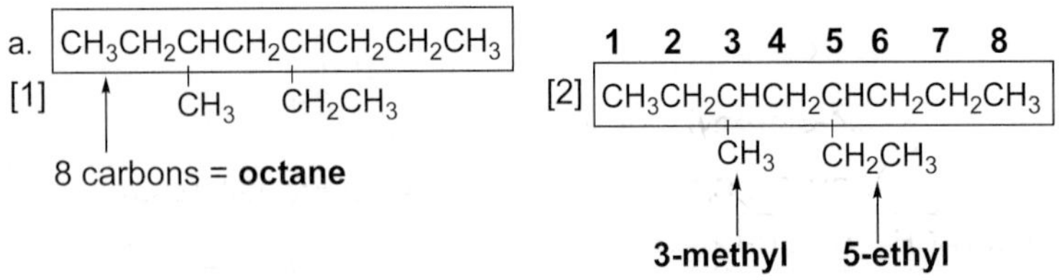
[1]
8 carbons = **octane**
[2]
1 2 3 4 5 6 7 8
3-methyl
5-ethyl

[3] **5-ethyl-3-methyloctane**

b.

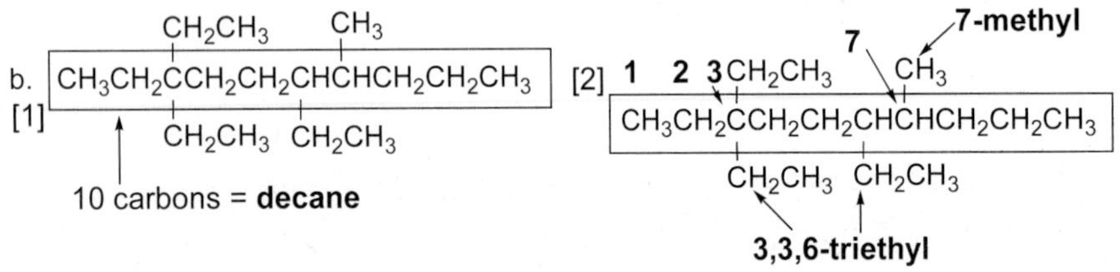
[1]
10 carbons = **decane**
[2]
7-methyl
3,3,6-triethyl

[3] **3,3,6-triethyl-7-methyldecane**

c. $CH_3CH_2CH_2C(CH_3)_2C(CH_3)_2CH_2CH_3$

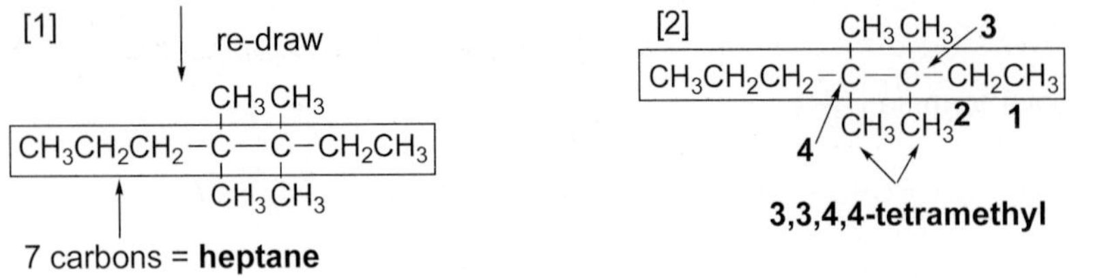
[1]
re-draw
7 carbons = **heptane**
[2]
3,3,4,4-tetramethyl

[3] **3,3,4,4-tetramethylheptane**

d. $CH_3CH_2C(CH_2CH_3)_2CH(CH_3)CH(CH_2CH_2CH_3)_2$

[1]
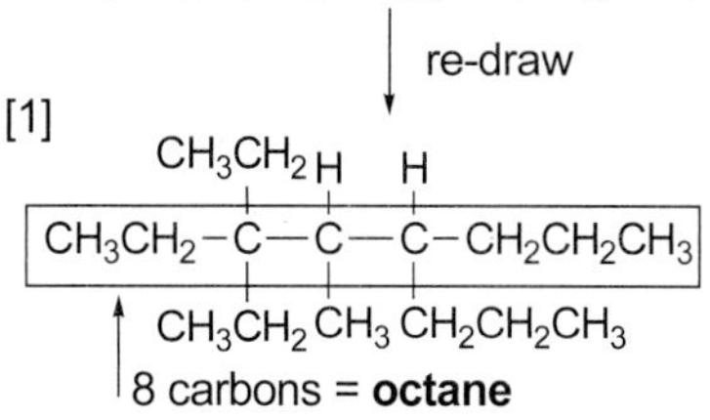
re-draw
8 carbons = octane

[2]
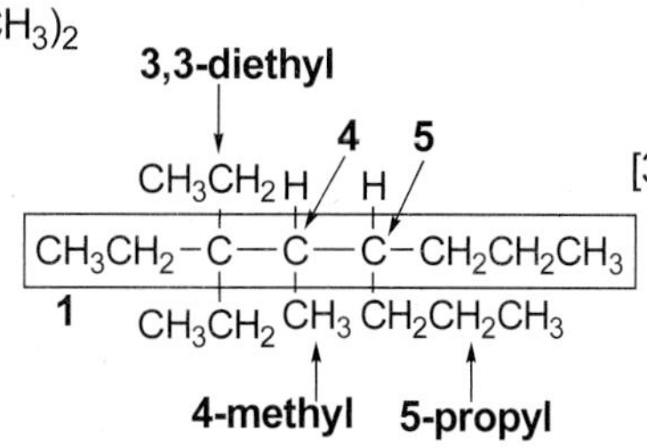
3,3-diethyl
4
5
1
4-methyl
5-propyl

[3] **3,3-diethyl-4-methyl-5-propyloctane**

e. $(CH_3CH_2)_3CCH(CH_3)CH_2CH_2CH_3$

[1]
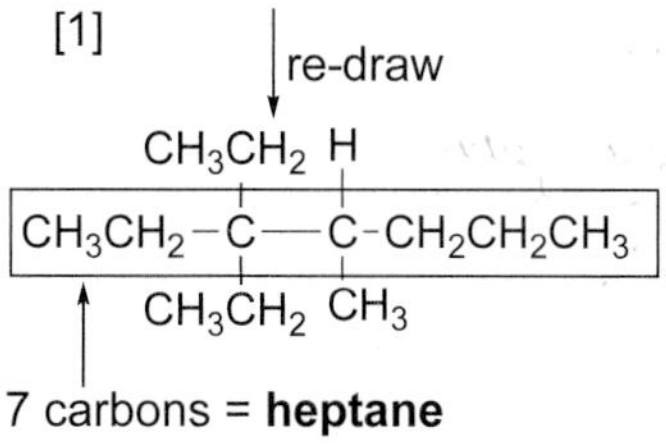
re-draw
7 carbons = heptane

[2]
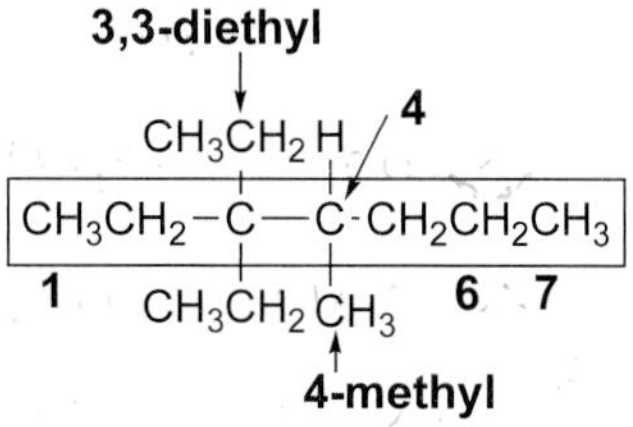
3,3-diethyl
4
1
6
7
4-methyl

[3] **3,3-diethyl-4-methylheptane**

f. $CH_3CH_2CH(CH_3)CH(CH_3)CH(CH_2CH_2CH_3)(CH_2)_3CH_3$

[1]
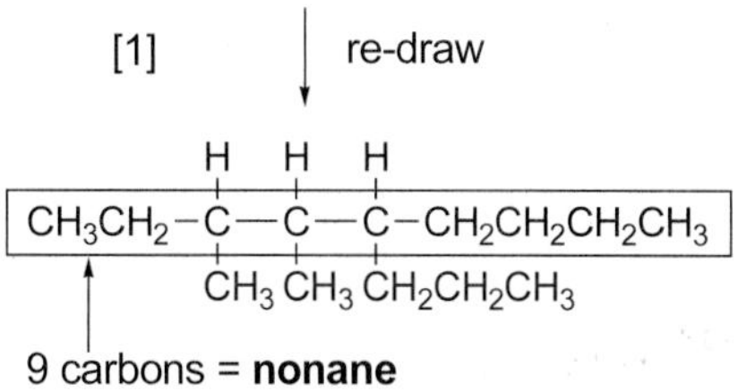
re-draw
9 carbons = nonane

[2]
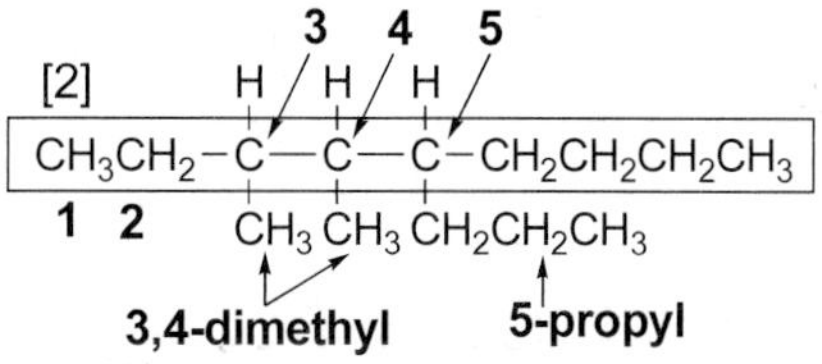
3
4
5
1 2
3,4-dimethyl
5-propyl

[3] **3,4-dimethyl-5-propylnonane**

g. $(CH_3CH_2CH_2)_4C$

[1]
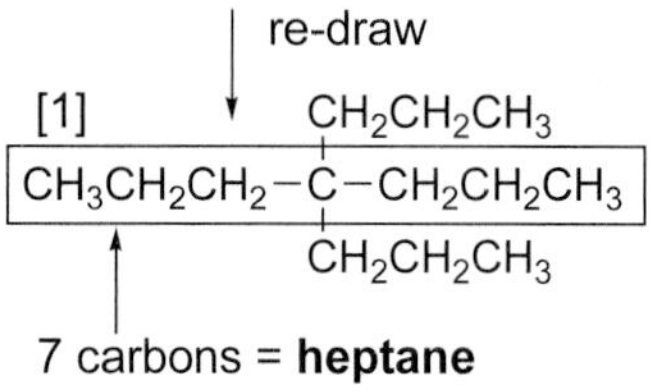
re-draw
7 carbons = heptane

[2]
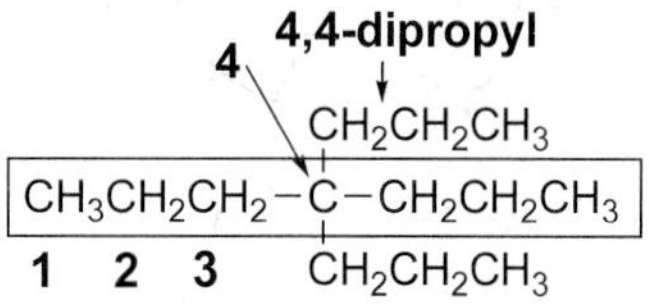
4,4-dipropyl
4
1 2 3

[3] **4,4-dipropylheptane**

h. [1]
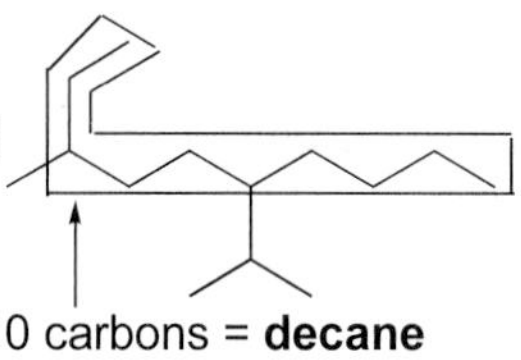
10 carbons = decane

[2]
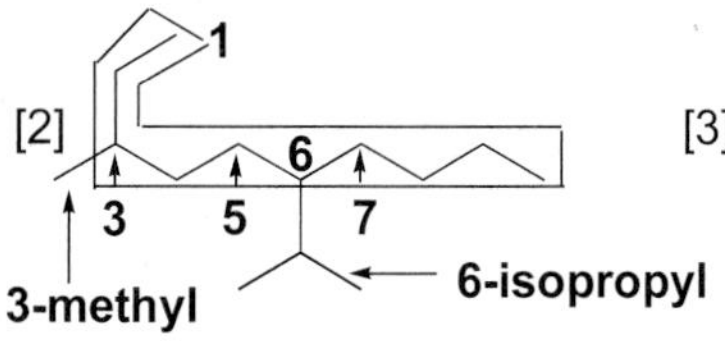
1
6
3
5
7
3-methyl
6-isopropyl

[3] **6-isopropyl-3-methyldecane**

i. [1]
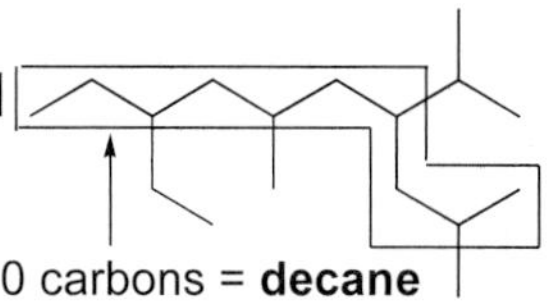
10 carbons = decane

[2]
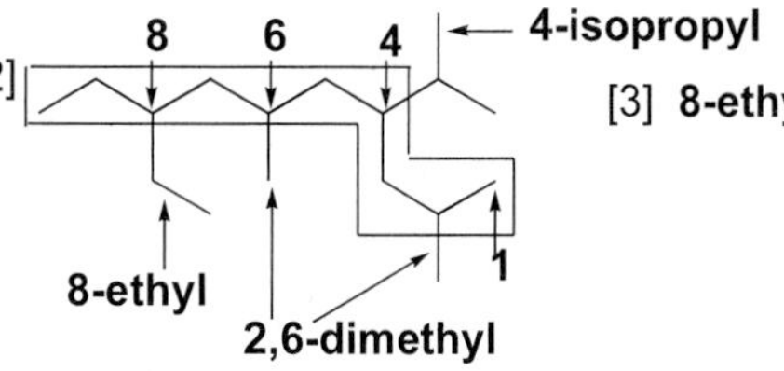
8
6
4
4-isopropyl
1
8-ethyl
2,6-dimethyl

[3] **8-ethyl-4-isopropyl-2,6-dimethyldecane**

j. [1]
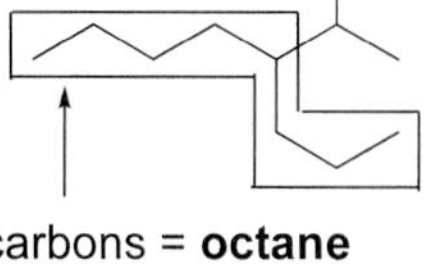
8 carbons = octane

[2]
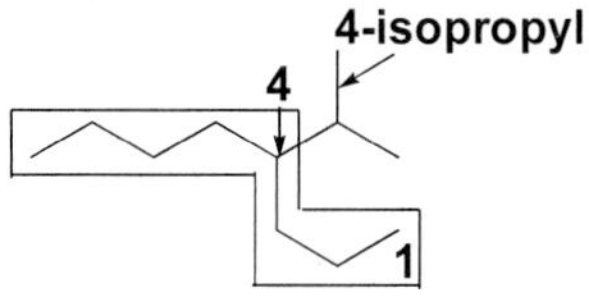
4-isopropyl
4
1

[3] **4-isopropyloctane**

k. 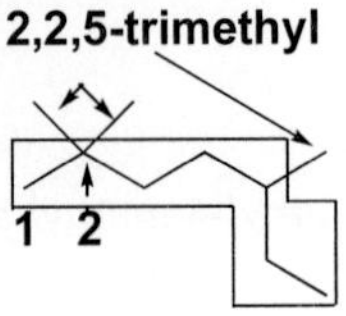
2,2,5-trimethyl
1 2
2,2,5-trimethylheptane

l. 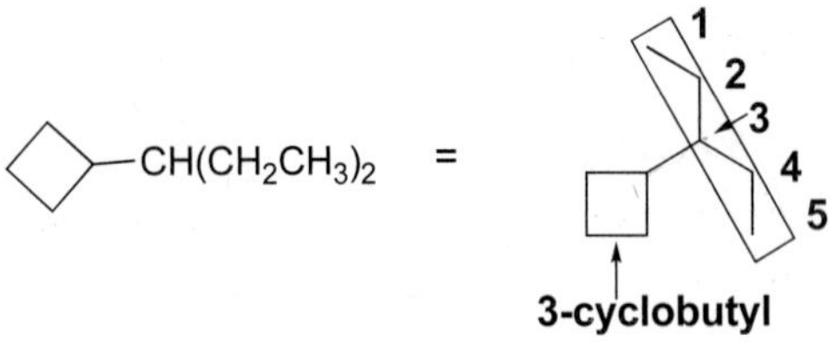
CH(CH2CH3)2
=
1
2
3
4
5
3-cyclobutyl
3-cyclobutylpentane

m. 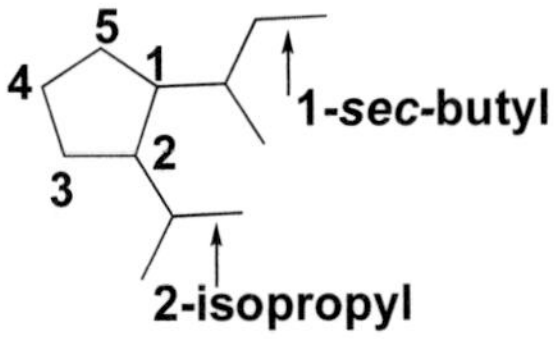
5
4
1
2
3
1-sec-butyl
2-isopropyl
1-*sec*-butyl-2-isopropylcyclopentane

n. 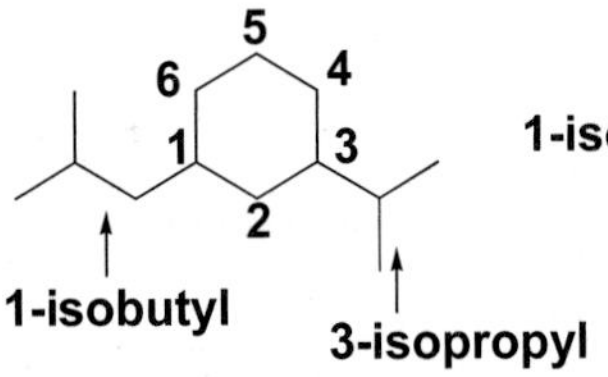
5
6
4
1
3
2
1-isobutyl
3-isopropyl
1-isobutyl-3-isopropylcyclohexane

4.40

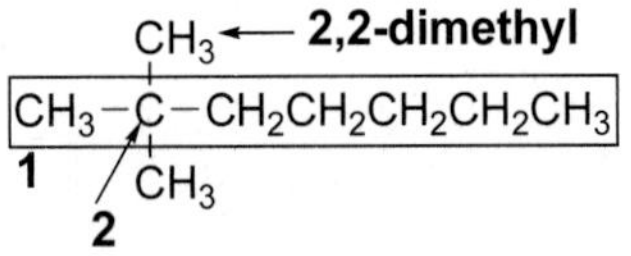
CH3 ← 2,2-dimethyl
CH3–C–CH2CH2CH2CH2CH3
1
CH3
2
2,2-dimethylheptane

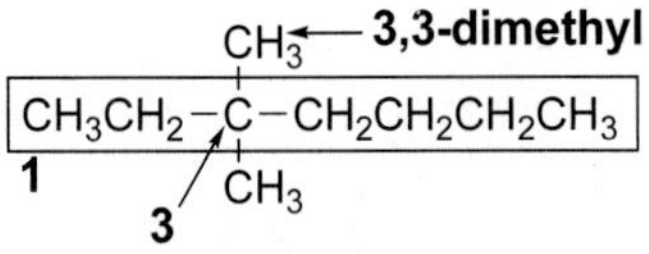
CH3 ← 3,3-dimethyl
CH3CH2–C–CH2CH2CH2CH3
1
CH3
3
3,3-dimethylheptane

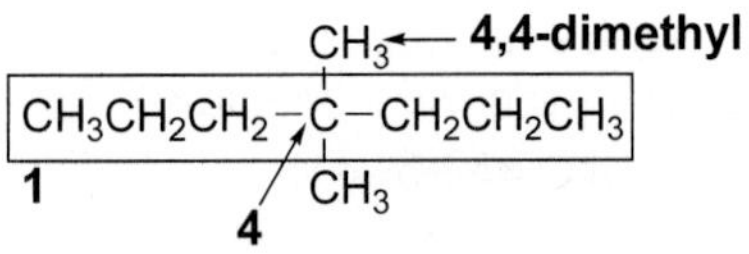
CH3 ← 4,4-dimethyl
CH3CH2CH2–C–CH2CH2CH3
1
CH3
4
4,4-dimethylheptane

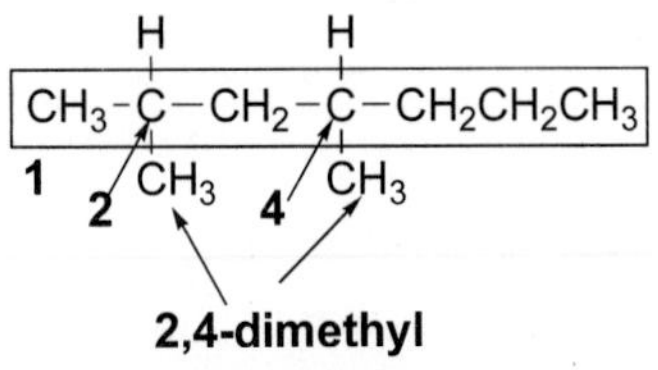
H H
CH3–C–CH2–C–CH2CH2CH3
1 2 CH3 4 CH3
2,4-dimethyl
2,4-dimethylheptane

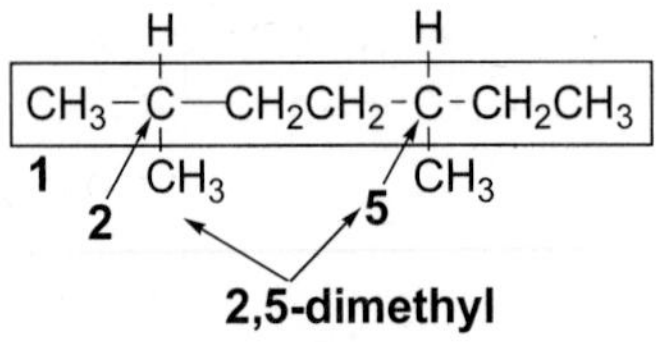
H H
CH3–C–CH2CH2–C–CH2CH3
1 CH3 CH3
2 5
2,5-dimethyl
2,5-dimethylheptane

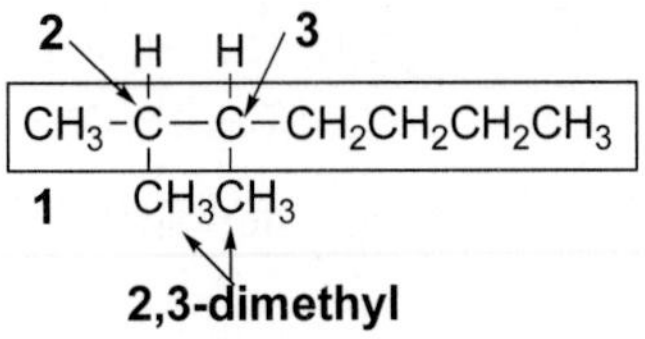
2 H H 3
CH3–C–C–CH2CH2CH2CH3
1 CH3CH3
2,3-dimethyl
2,3-dimethylheptane

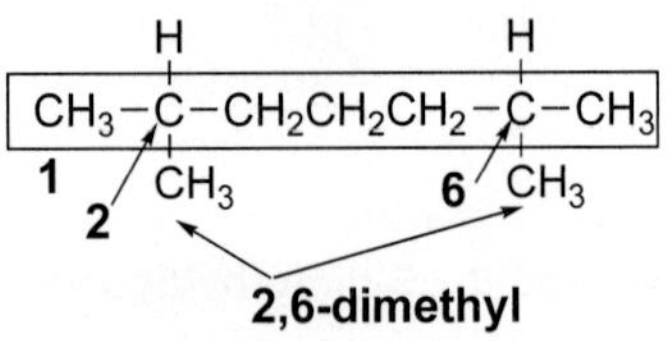
H H
CH3–C–CH2CH2CH2–C–CH3
1 CH3 6 CH3
2
2,6-dimethyl
2,6-dimethylheptane

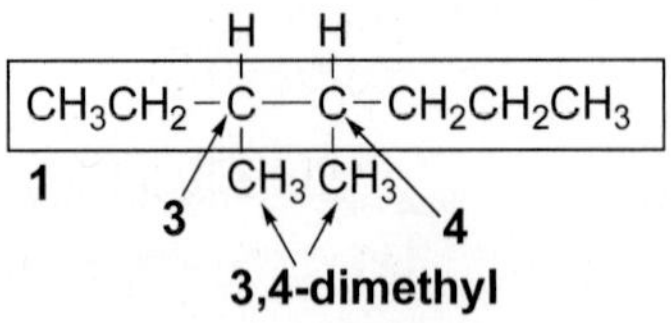
H H
CH3CH2–C–C–CH2CH2CH3
1 CH3 CH3
3 4
3,4-dimethyl
3,4-dimethylheptane

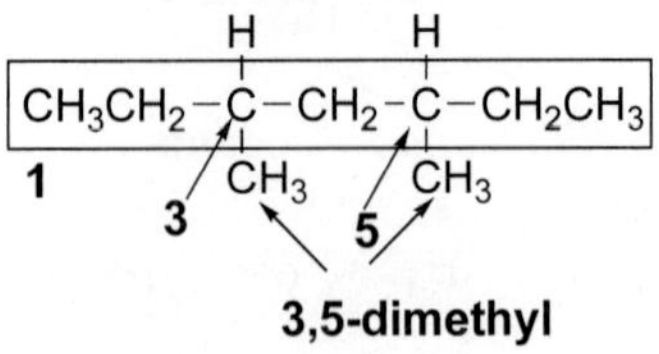
H H
CH3CH2–C–CH2–C–CH2CH3
1 CH3 CH3
3 5
3,5-dimethyl
3,5-dimethylheptane

4.41 Use the steps in Answer 4.11 to draw the structures.

a. 3-ethyl-2-methyl**hexane**

[1] 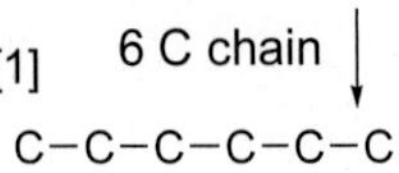
6 C chain
C–C–C–C–C–C

[2] 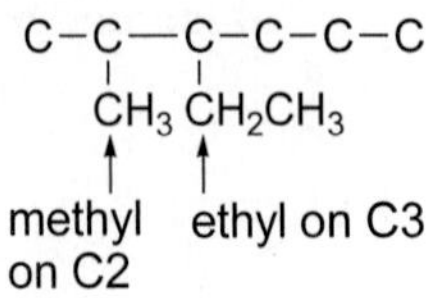
C–C–C–C–C–C
CH3 CH2CH3
methyl on C2
ethyl on C3

[3] 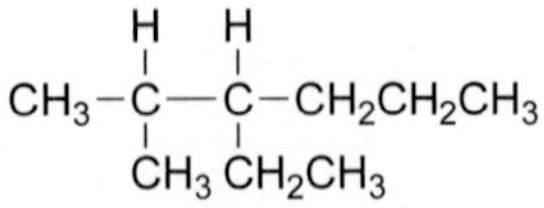
H H
CH3–C–C–CH2CH2CH3
CH3 CH2CH3

b. *sec*-butyl**cyclopentane**

[1]

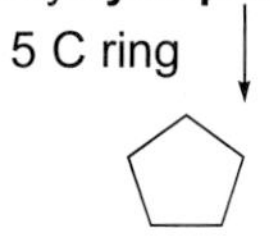
5 C ring

[2]

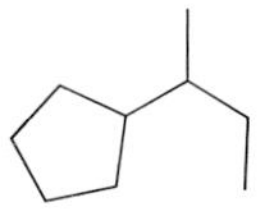

c. 4-isopropyl-2,4,5-trimethyl**heptane**

[1]

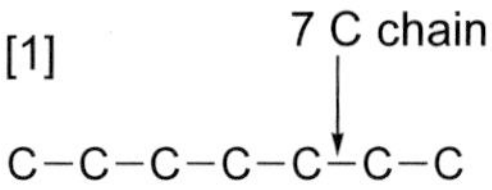
7 C chain

[2]

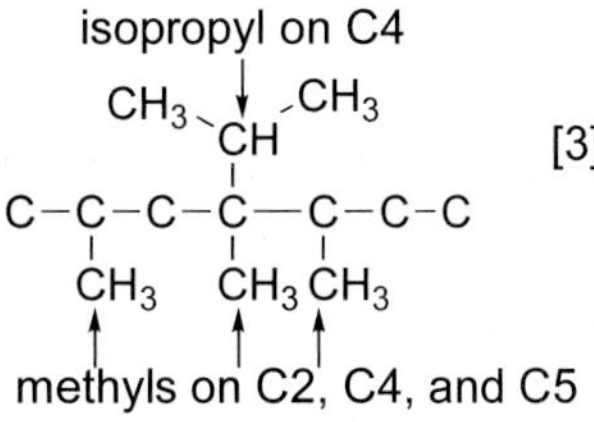
isopropyl on C4
methyls on C2, C4, and C5

[3]

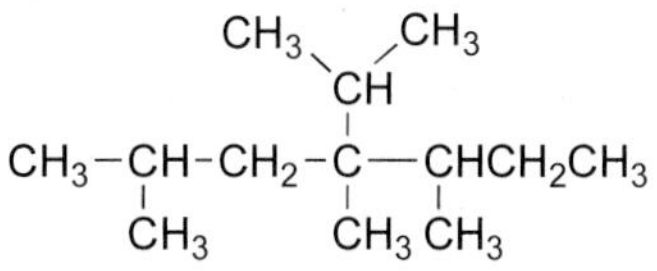

d. cyclobutyl**cycloheptane**

[1] 7 C cycloalkane

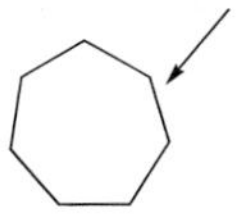

[2]

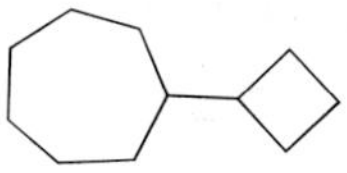

e. 3-ethyl-1,1-dimethyl**cyclohexane**

[1]

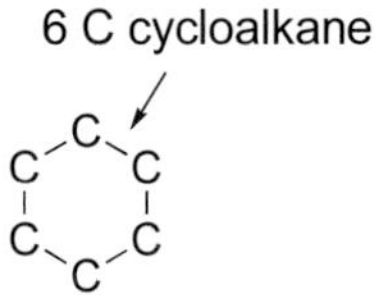
6 C cycloalkane

[2]

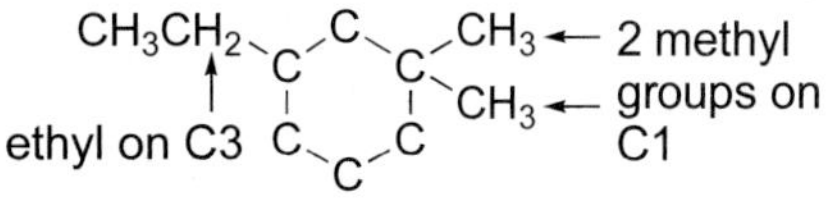
ethyl on C3
2 methyl groups on C1

[3]

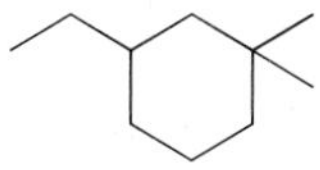

f. 4-butyl-1,1-diethyl**cyclooctane**

[1]

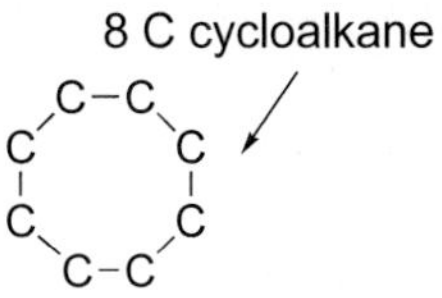
8 C cycloalkane

[2]

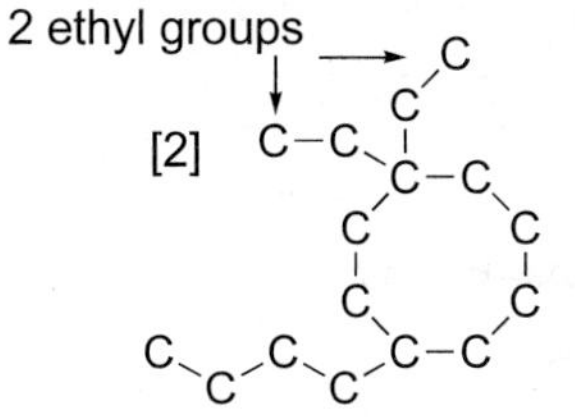
2 ethyl groups

[3]

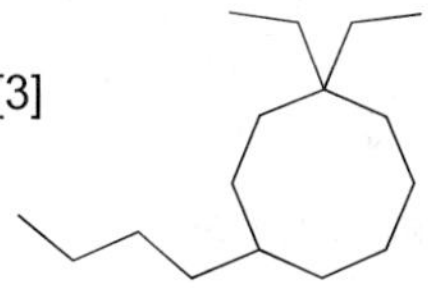

g. 6-isopropyl-2,3-dimethyl**nonane**

[1]

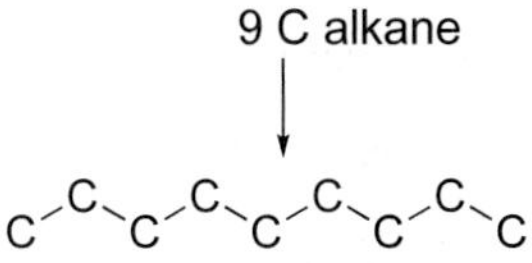
9 C alkane

[2]

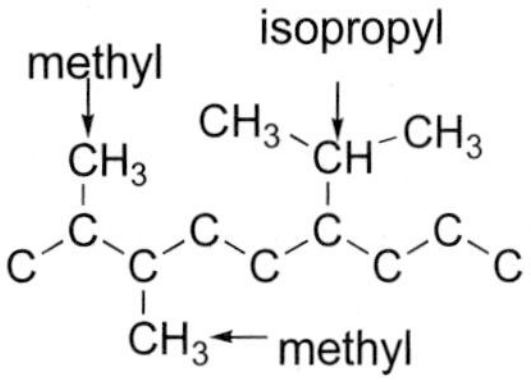
methyl
isopropyl
methyl

[3]

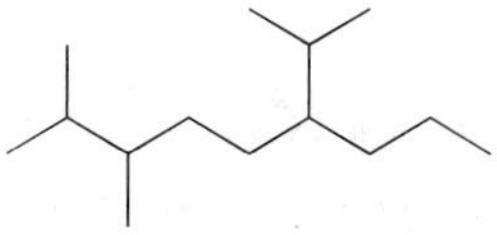

h. 2,2,6,6,7-pentamethyl**octane**

[1]

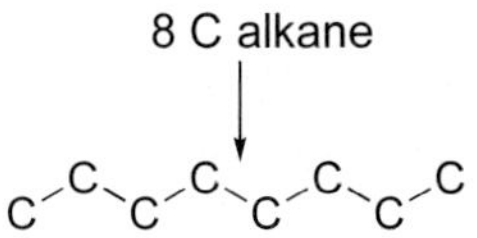
8 C alkane

5 methyl groups

[2]

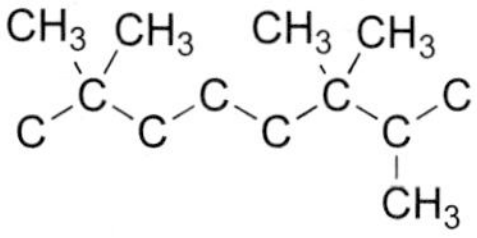

[3]

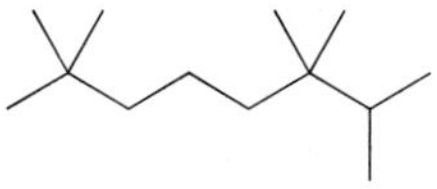

i. *cis*-1-ethyl-3-methyl**cyclopentane**

[1]

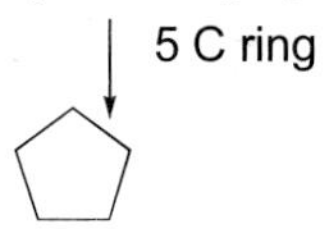
5 C ring

[2]

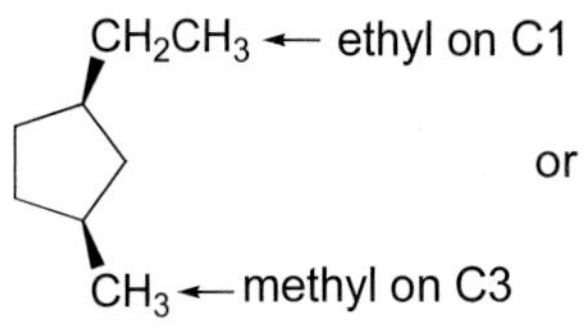
ethyl on C1
methyl on C3

or

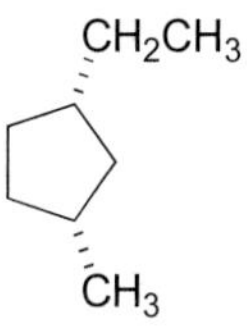

j. *trans*-1-*tert*-butyl-4-ethyl**cyclohexane**

[1] 6 C ring

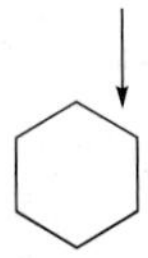

[2]

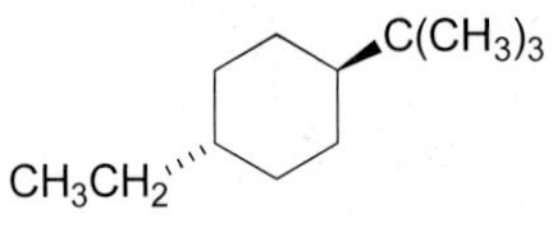
C(CH3)3
CH3CH2

4.42 Undecane has 11 C's in an unbranched long chain, with molecular formula $C_{11}H_{24}$. A compound that is not an isomer must have a different molecular formula. Only (c) has a different molecular formula.

a.

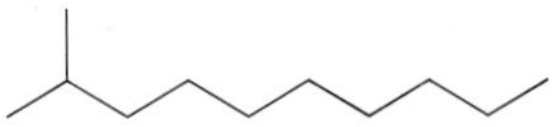

2-methyldecane
$C_{11}H_{24}$
isomer

b.

3,3-dimethylnonane
$C_{11}H_{24}$
isomer

c.

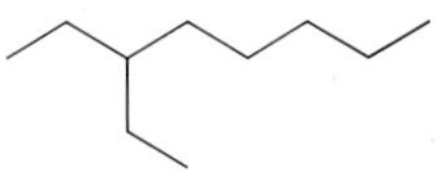

3-ethyloctane
$C_{10}H_{22}$
not an isomer

d.

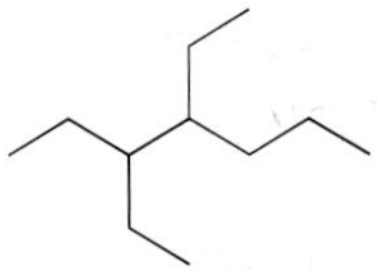

3,4-diethylheptane
$C_{11}H_{24}$
isomer

e.

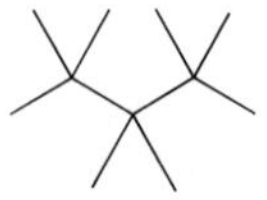

2,2,3,3,4,4-hexamethylpentane
$C_{11}H_{24}$
isomer

4.43 Draw the compounds.

a. 2,2-dimethyl-4-ethylheptane

alphabetized incorrectly
ethyl before **meth**yl

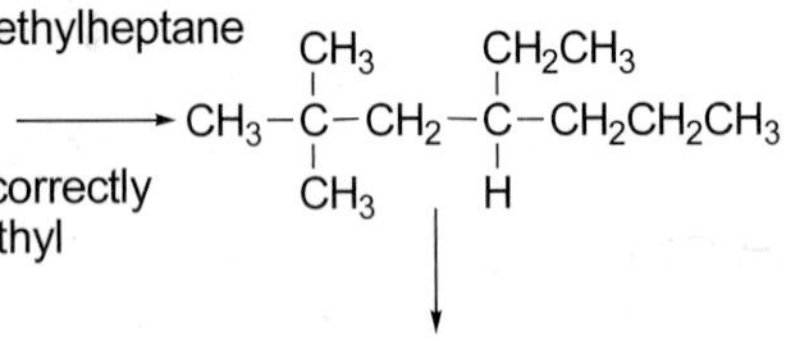
CH3 CH2CH3
CH3–C–CH2–C–CH2CH2CH3
CH3 H

4-ethyl-2,2-dimethylheptane

b. 5-ethyl-2-methylhexane

Longest chain was not chosen = **heptane**

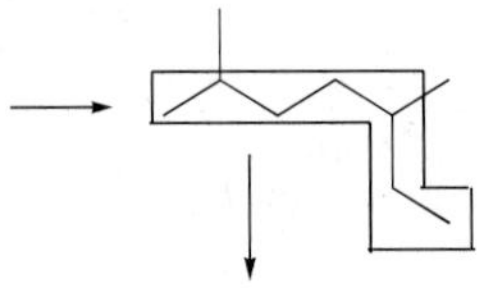

2,5-dimethylheptane

c. 2-methyl-2-isopropylheptane

Longest chain was not chosen = **octane**

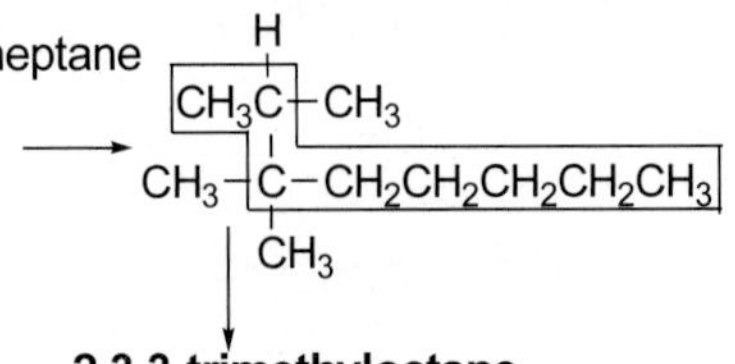
H
CH3C–CH3
CH3–C–CH2CH2CH2CH2CH3
CH3

2,3,3-trimethyloctane

d. 1,5-dimethylcyclohexane

Numbered incorrectly. Re-number so methyls are at C1 and C3.

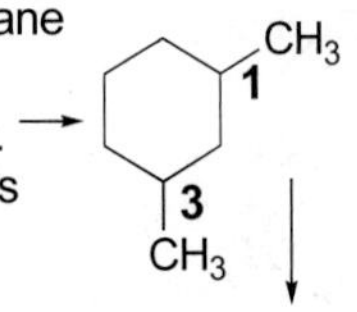
CH3
1
3
CH3

1,3-dimethylcyclohexane

e. 1-ethyl-2,6-dimethylcycloheptane

Numbered incorrectly. Re-number so methyls are at C1 and C4.

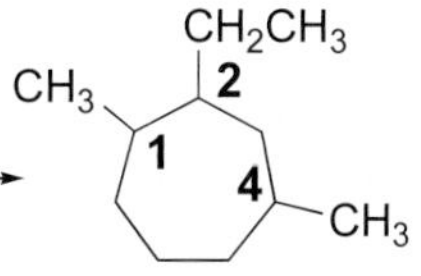
CH2CH3
2
CH3
1
4
CH3

2-ethyl-1,4-dimethylcycloheptane

f. 5,5,6-trimethyloctane

Numbered incorrectly. Re-number so methyls are at C3 and C4.

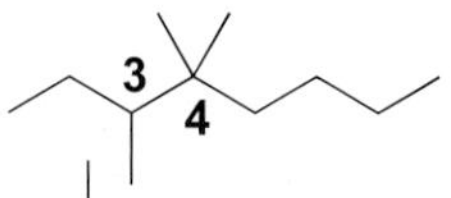
3
4

3,4,4-trimethyloctane

g. 3-butyl-2,2-dimethylhexane

Longest chain not chosen = **octane**

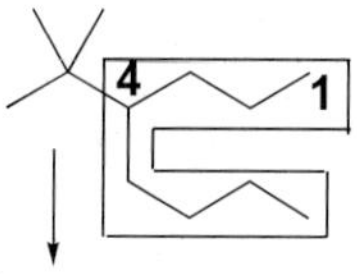
4
1

4-*tert*-butyloctane

h. 1,3-dimethylbutane

Longest chain not chosen = **pentane**

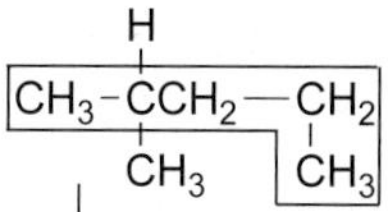
H
CH3–CCH2—CH2
CH3
CH3

2-methylpentane

4.44

a.

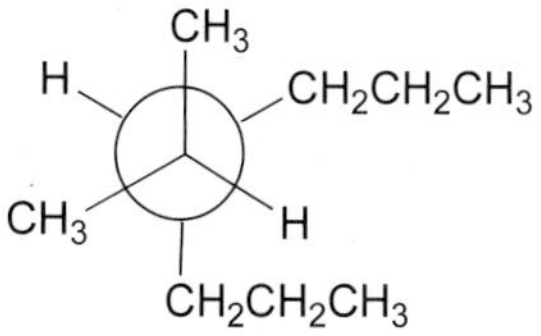
CH3
H
CH2CH2CH3
CH3
H
CH2CH2CH3

re-draw

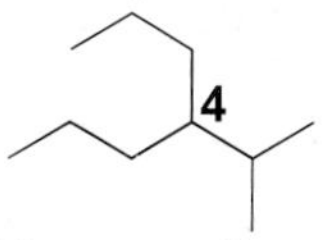
4

4-isopropylheptane

b.

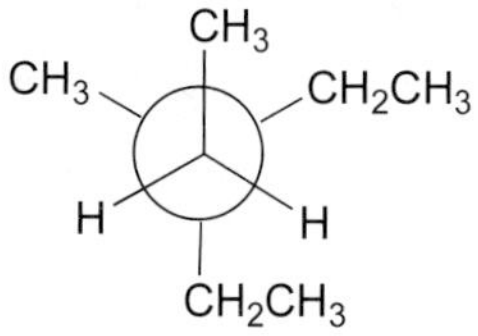
CH3
CH3
CH2CH3
H
H
CH2CH3

re-draw

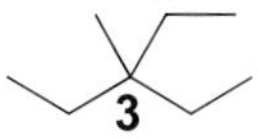
3

3-ethyl-3-methylpentane

c.

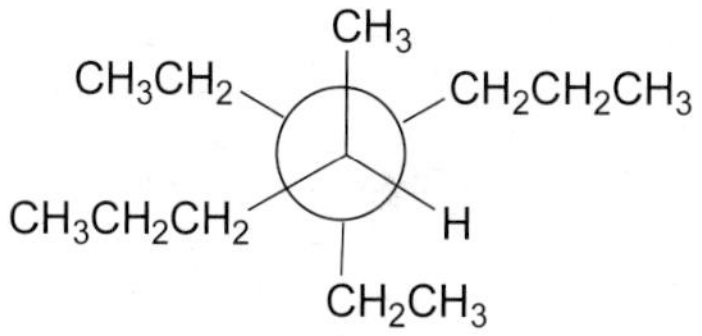
CH3
CH3CH2
CH2CH2CH3
CH3CH2CH2
H
CH2CH3

re-draw

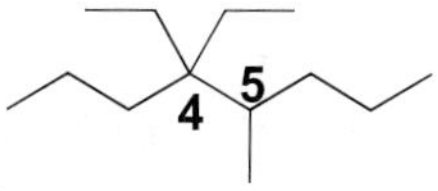
4
5

4,4-diethyl-5-methyloctane

4.45 Use the rules from Answer 4.15.

a. $CH_3CH_2CH_3$ (3C's, **lowest boiling point**) $CH_3CH_2CH_2CH_3$ (4 C's) $CH_3CH_2CH_2CH_2CH_3$ (5 C's, **highest boiling point**)

b. $(CH_3)_2CHCH(CH_3)_2$ (most branching, **lowest boiling point**) $CH_3CH_2CH_2CH(CH_3)_2$ $CH_3(CH_2)_4CH_3$ (least branching, **highest boiling point**)

4.46 a.

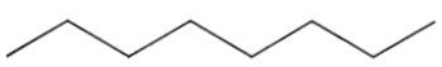

$CH_3(CH_2)_6CH_3$
no branching = higher surface area
higher boiling point

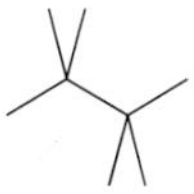

$(CH_3)_3CC(CH_3)_3$
branching = lower surface area
lower boiling point
more spherical, better packing =
higher melting point

b. There is a 159° difference in the melting points, but only a 20° difference in the boiling points because the symmetry in $(CH_3)_3CC(CH_3)_3$ allows it to pack more tightly in the solid, thus requiring more energy to melt. In contrast, once the compounds are in the liquid state, symmetry is no longer a factor, the compounds are isomeric alkanes, and the boiling points are closer together.

4.47

a.

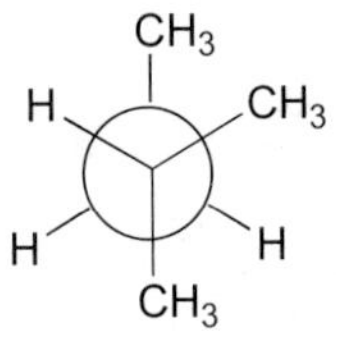

or

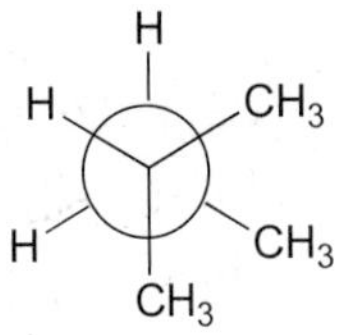

1 gauche CH_3,CH_3
= 3.8 kJ/mol
of destabilization

higher energy
2 gauche CH_3,CH_3
3.8 kJ/mol x 2 = 7.6 kJ/mol
of destabilization

Energy difference =
7.6 kJ/mol – 3.8 kJ/mol = **3.8 kJ/mol**

b.

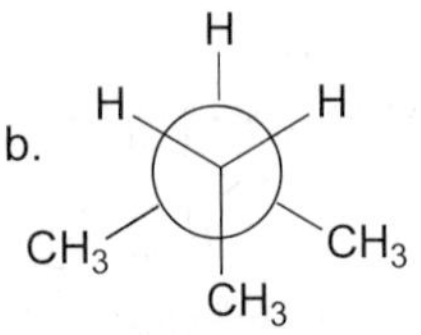

or

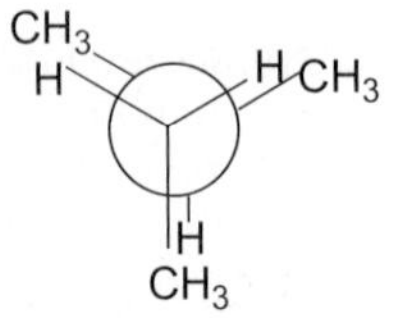

2 gauche CH_3,CH_3
3.8 kJ/mol x 2 =
7.6 kJ/mol
of destabilization

higher energy
3 eclipsed H,CH_3
6 kJ/mol x 3 = 18 kJ/mol
of destabilization

Energy difference =
18 kJ/mol – 7.6 kJ/mol = **10.4 kJ/mol**

4.48 Use the rules from Answer 4.18 to determine the most and least stable conformations.

a. $CH_3–CH_2CH_2CH_2CH_3$

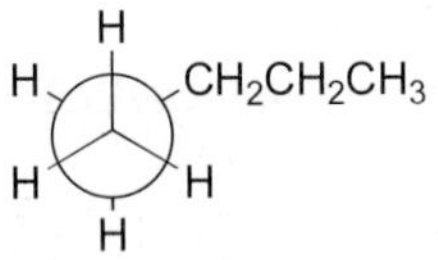

staggered
most stable

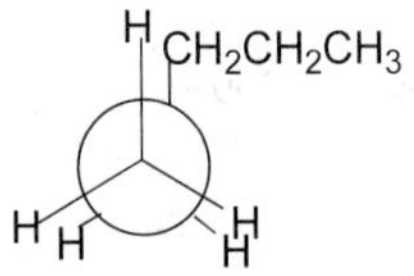

eclipsed
least stable

All staggered conformations are equal in energy.
All eclipsed conformations are equal in energy.

b. $CH_3CH_2CH_2–CH_2CH_2CH_3$

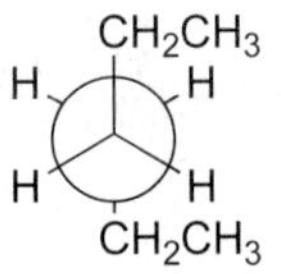

staggered
ethyl groups anti
most stable

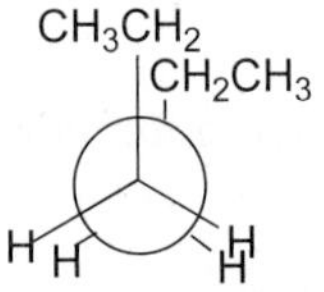

eclipsed
ethyl groups eclipsed
least stable

4.49

a.

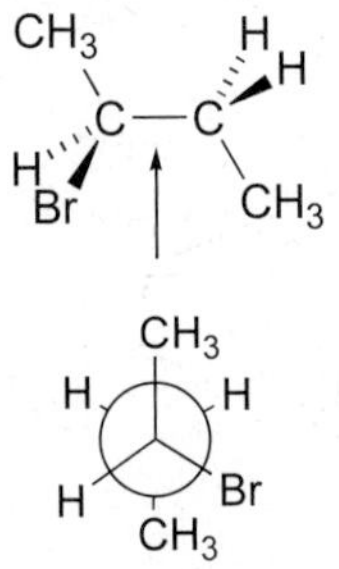

b.

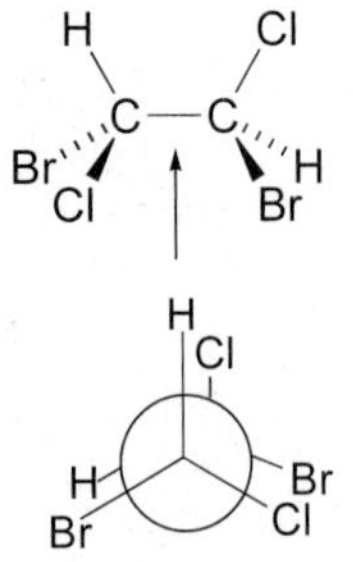

c.

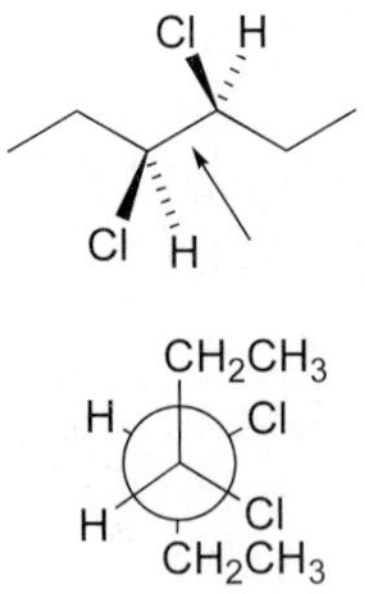

4.50

[1]

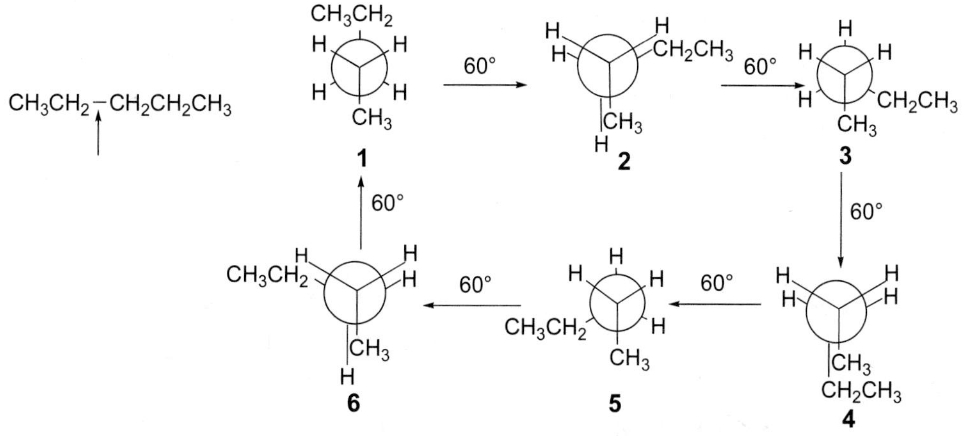
CH3CH2–CH2CH2CH3
60°
1
2
3
4
5
6

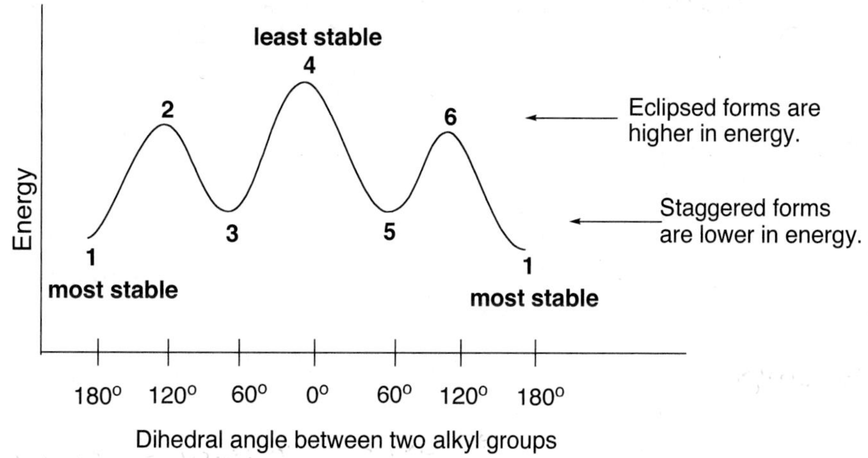
least stable
most stable
Eclipsed forms are higher in energy.
Staggered forms are lower in energy.
Energy
180° 120° 60° 0° 60° 120° 180°
Dihedral angle between two alkyl groups

[2]

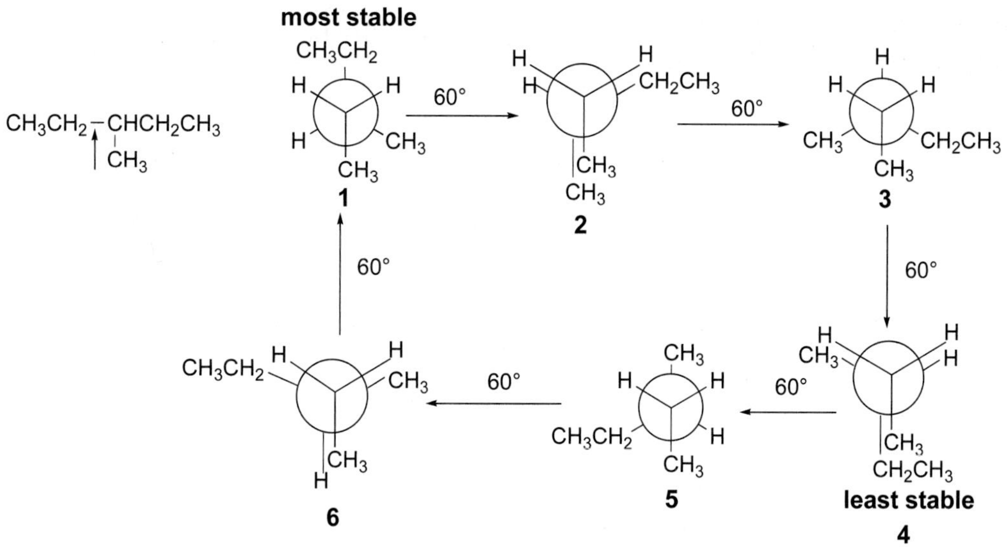
CH3CH2–CHCH2CH3
most stable
least stable
60°
1
2
3
4
5
6

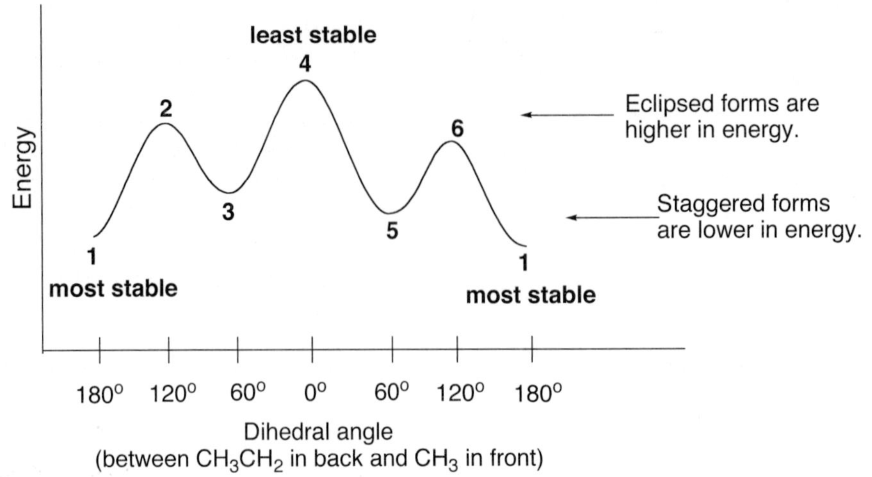

4.51 Two types of strain:

- *Torsional strain* is due to eclipsed groups on adjacent carbon atoms.
- *Steric strain* is due to overlapping electron clouds of large groups (e.g., gauche interactions).

a. 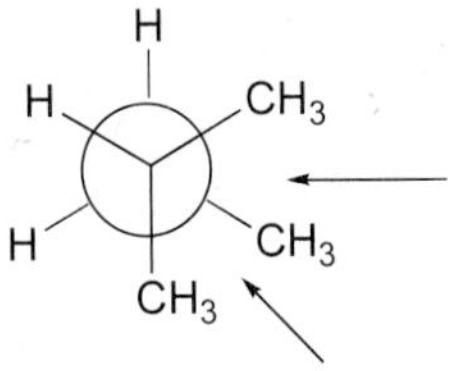

two sites
three bulky methyl groups close =
steric strain

b. 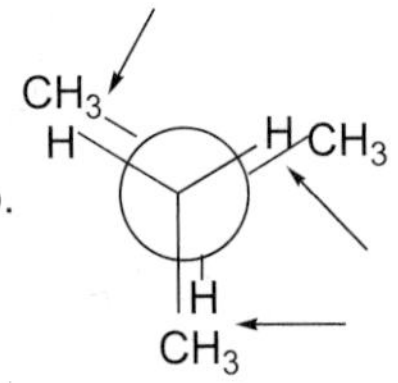

eclipsed conformation =
torsional strain

c. 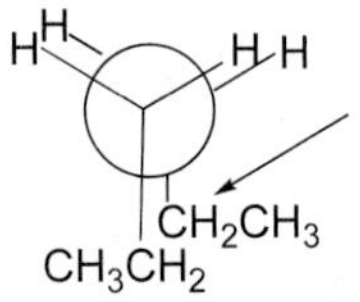

two bulky ethyl groups close =
steric strain
eclipsed conformation =
torsional strain

4.52 The barrier to rotation is equal to the difference in energy between the highest energy eclipsed and lowest energy staggered conformations of the molecule.

a. $CH_3-CH(CH_3)_2$

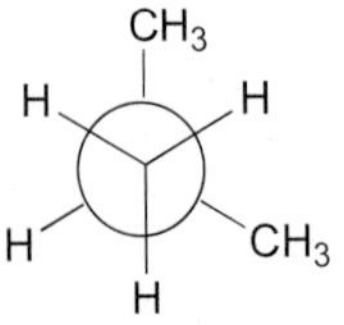

most stable

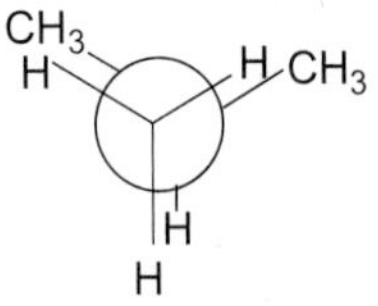

least stable

Destabilization energy =

2 H,CH_3 eclipsing interactions
2(6.0 kJ/mol) = 12.0 kJ/mol
1 H,H eclipsing interaction = 4.0 kJ/mol

Total destabilization = **16.0 kJ/mol**

16.0 kJ/mol = rotation barrier

b. $CH_3-C(CH_3)_3$

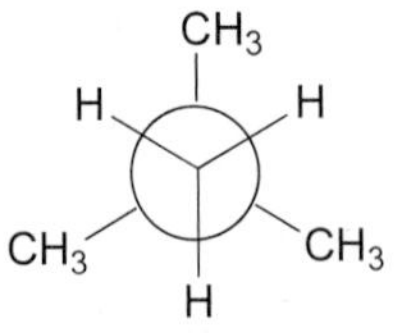

most stable

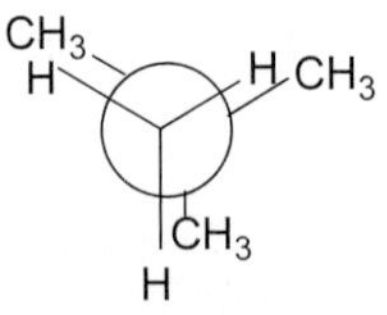

least stable

Destabilization energy =

3 H,CH_3 eclipsing interactions
3(6.0 kJ/mol) = 18.0 kJ/mol

Total destabilization = **18.0 kJ/mol**

18.0 kJ/mol = rotation barrier

4.53

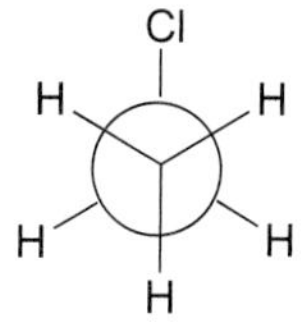

most stable

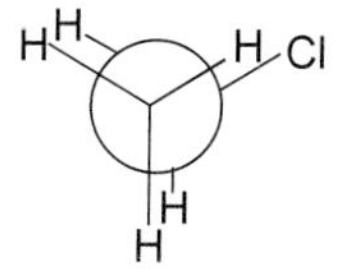

least stable

2 H,H eclipsing interactions = 2(4.0 kJ/mol) = 8.0 kJ/mol

Since the barrier to rotation is 15 kJ/mol, the difference between this value and the destabilization due to H,H eclipsing is the destabilization due to H,Cl eclipsing.

15.0 kJ/mol – 8.0 kJ/mol = 7.0 kJ/mol
destabilization due to H,Cl eclipsing

4.54 The gauche conformation can intramolecularly hydrogen bond, making it the more stable conformation.

$HOCH_2$–CH_2OH
rotation here

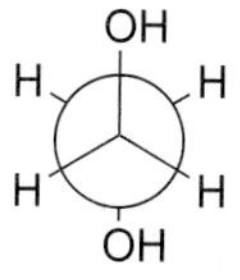

anti

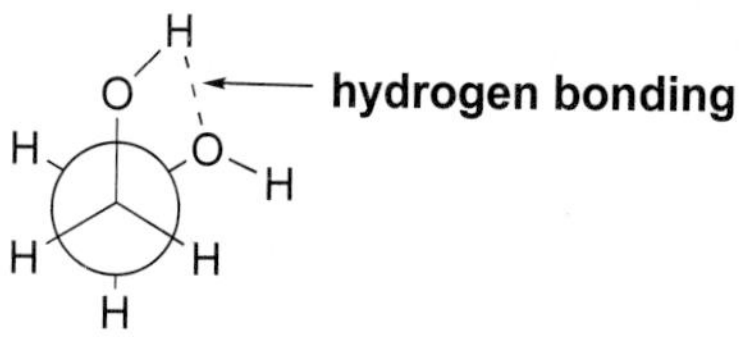

gauche

Hydrogen bonding can occur only in the gauche conformation, making it **more stable.**

4.55

[1] a.

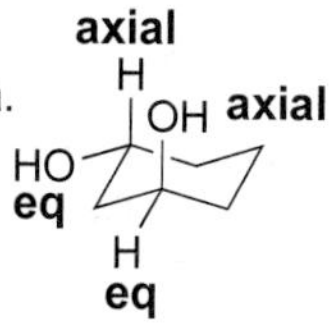

b.

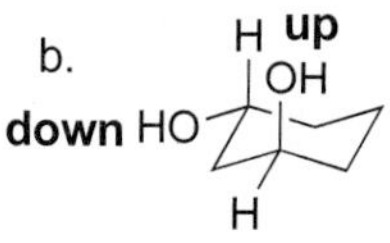

one up, one down =
trans

c.

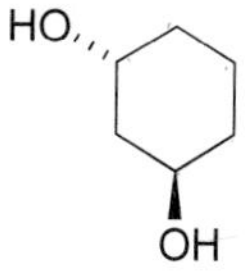

d.

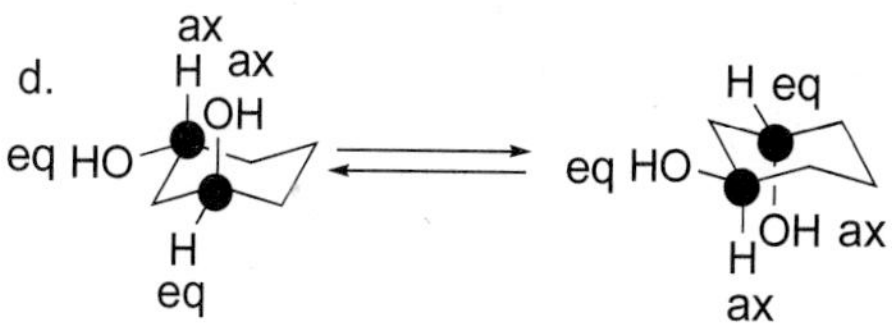

[2] a.

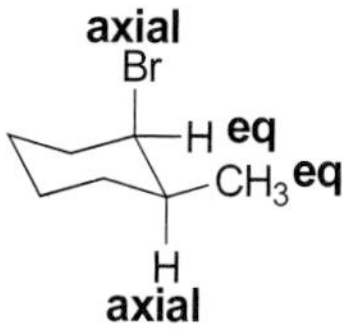

b.

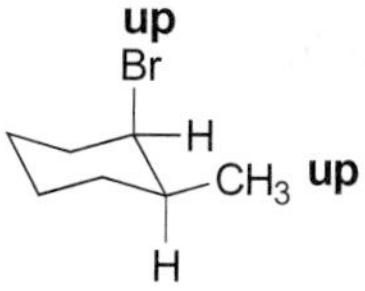

both up =
cis

c.

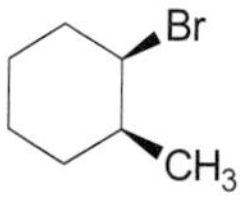

d.

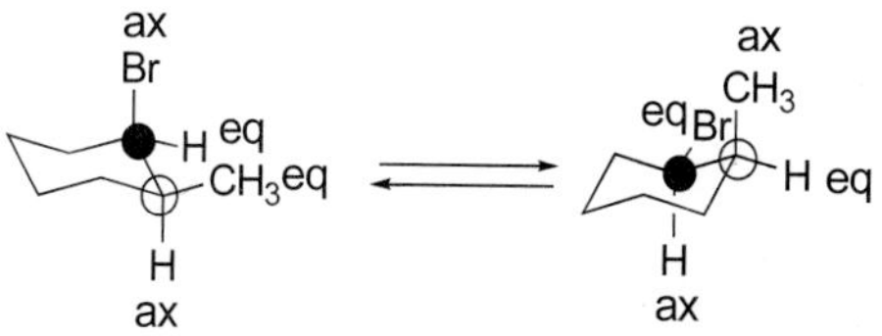

[3] a.

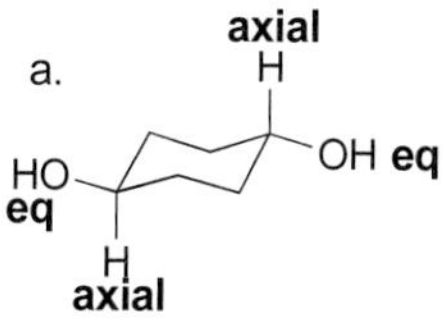

b.

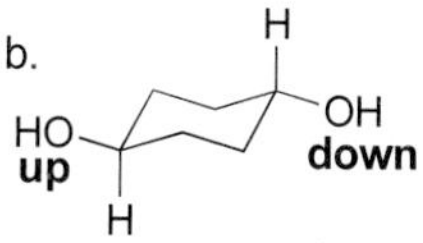

one up, one down =
trans

c.

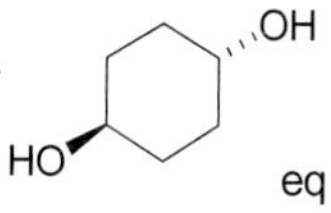

d.

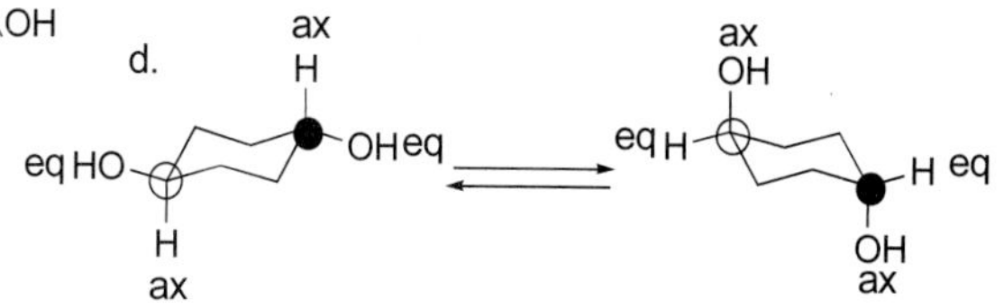

4.56

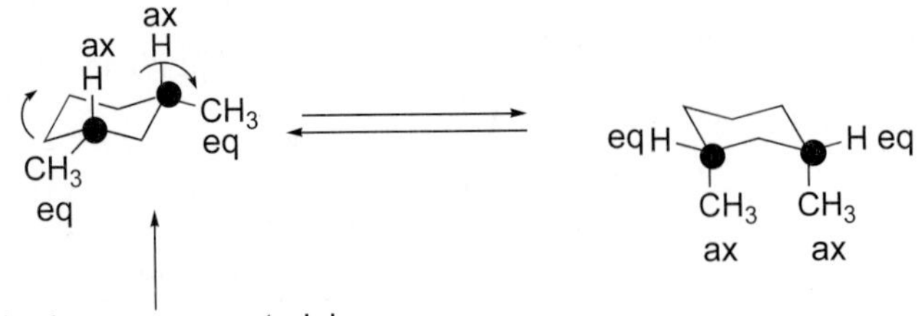

both groups equatorial
more stable

4.57 A **cis isomer** has two groups on the **same side** of the ring. The two groups can be drawn both up or both down. Only one possibility is drawn. A **trans isomer** has one group on one side of the ring and one group on the other side. Either group can be drawn on either side. Only one possibility is drawn.

[1] 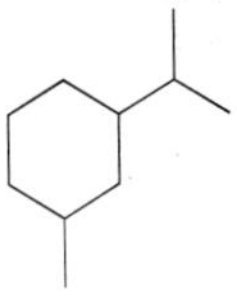

a. 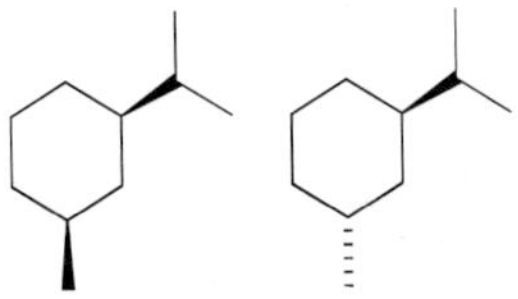

cis **trans**

b. cis isomer

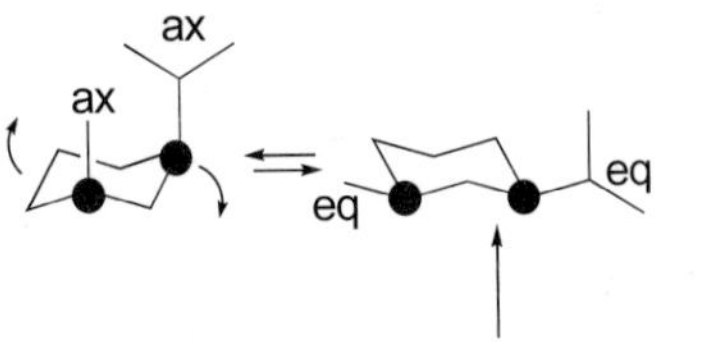

both groups equatorial
more stable

c. trans isomer

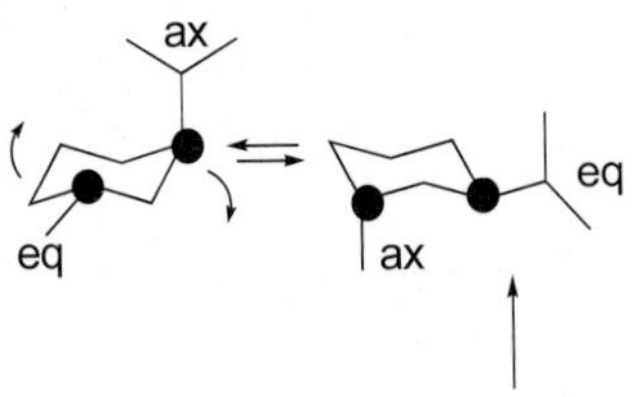

larger group equatorial
more stable

d. 

The cis isomer is more stable than the trans since one conformation has both groups equatorial.

[2] 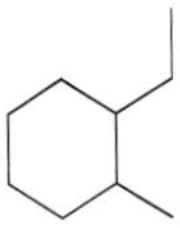

a. 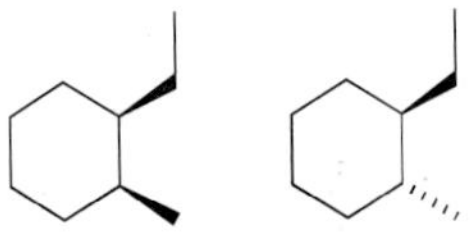

cis **trans**

b. cis isomer

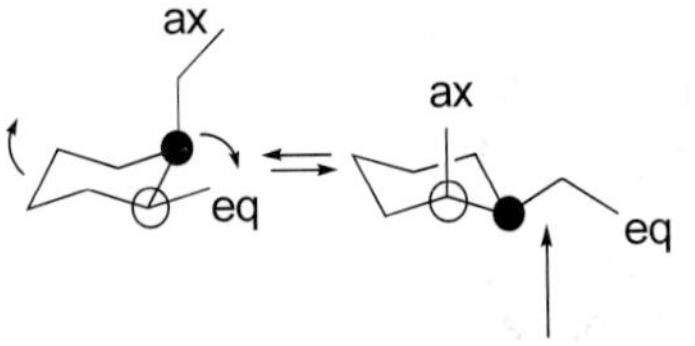

larger group equatorial
more stable

c. trans isomer

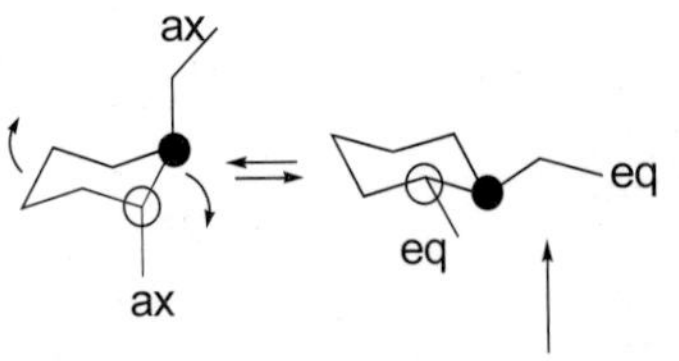

both groups equatorial
more stable

d. 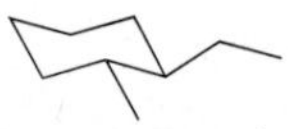

The trans isomer is more stable than the cis since one conformation has both groups equatorial.

[3] 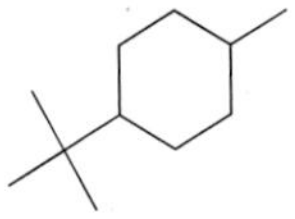

a. 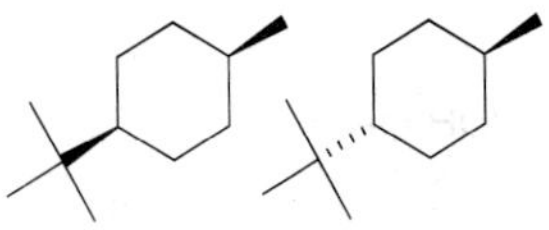

cis **trans**

b. cis isomer

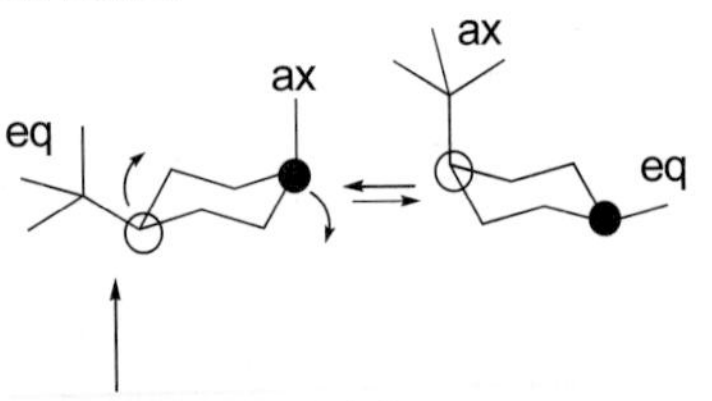

larger group equatorial
more stable

c. trans isomer

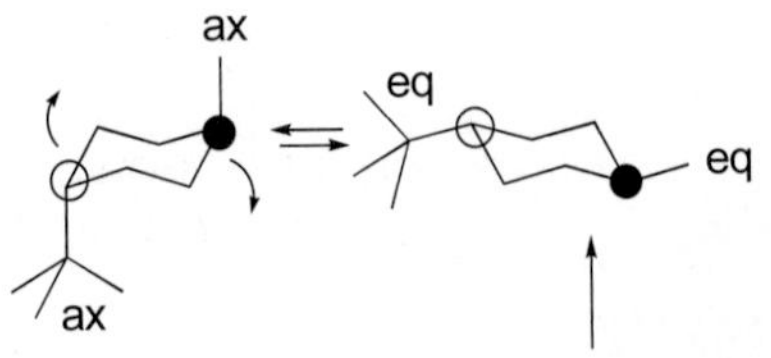

both groups equatorial
more stable

d. 

The trans isomer is more stable than the cis since one conformation has both groups equatorial.

4.58

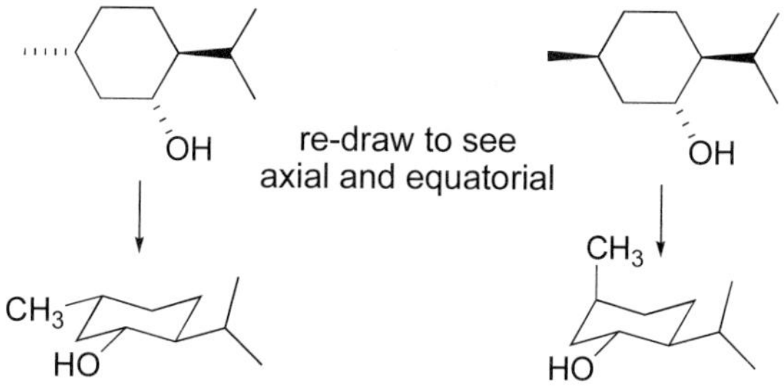
OH
re-draw to see
axial and equatorial
OH
CH3
CH3
HO
HO

all equatorial
menthol

4.59

a. 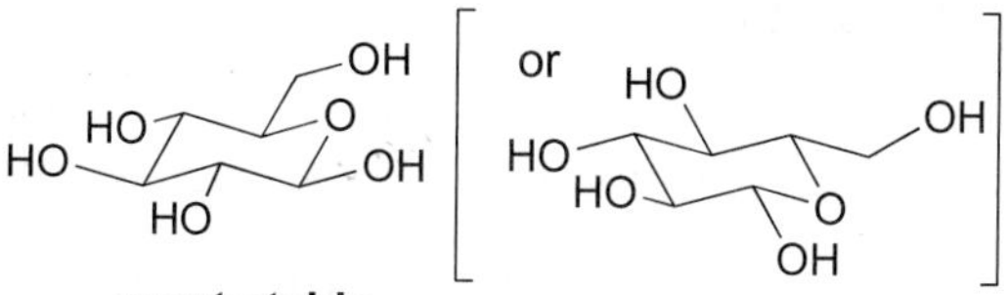
OH
HO
O
HO
OH
HO
or
HO
OH
HO
HO
O
OH

most stable
All groups are equatorial.

b. 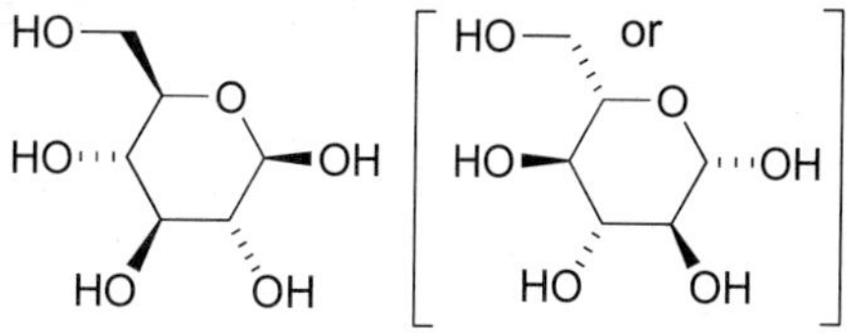
HO
O
HO
OH
HO
OH
HO
or
O
HO
OH
HO
OH

4.60

a. 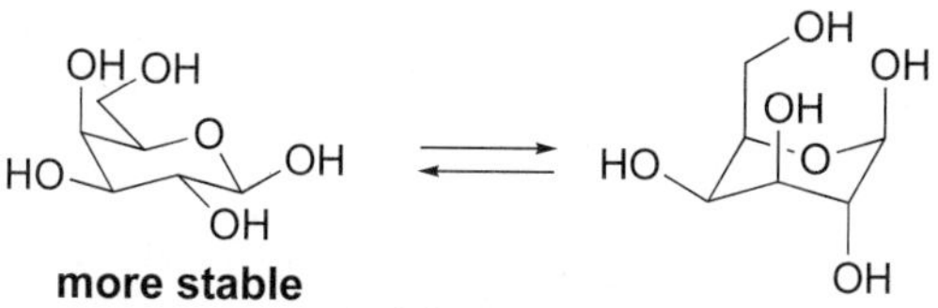
OH OH
O
HO
OH
OH
OH
OH
OH
HO
O
OH

more stable
More groups are equatorial.

c. 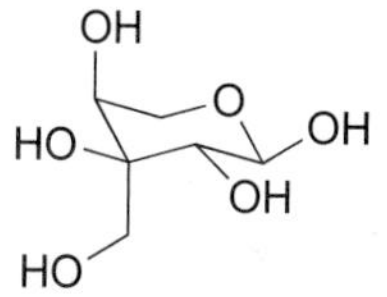
OH
O
HO
OH
OH
HO

constitutional isomer

b. 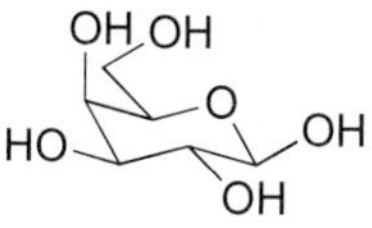
OH OH
O
HO
OH
OH

galactose

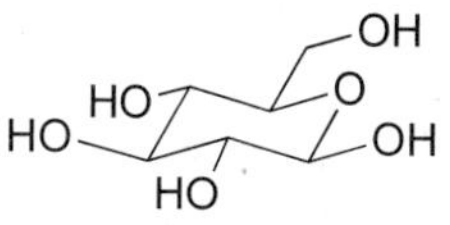
OH
HO
O
HO
OH
HO

glucose
All groups are equatorial.
more stable

d. 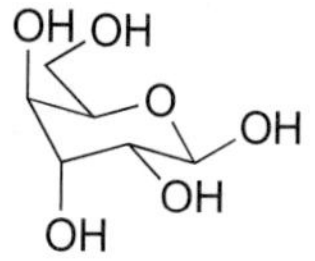
OH OH
O
OH
OH
OH

stereoisomer

4.61

a. 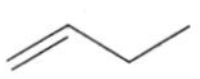 and 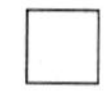

same molecular formula C_4H_8
different connectivity
constitutional isomers

b. 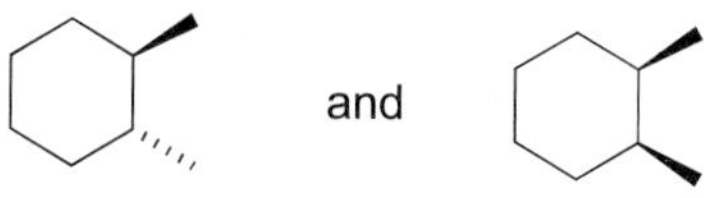
and

different arrangement in three dimensions
stereoisomers

c. 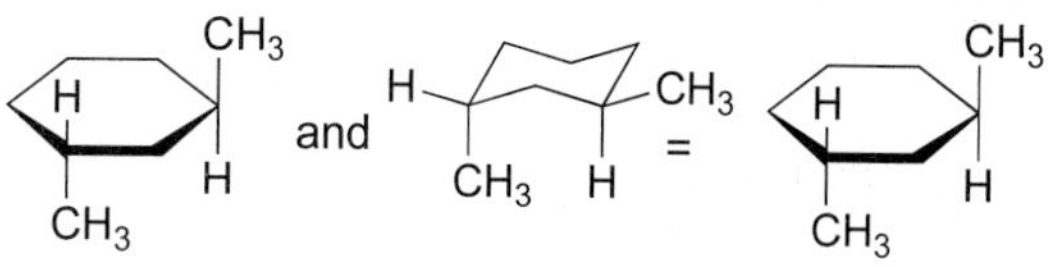
CH3
H
H
CH3
and
H
CH3
CH3
H
=
CH3
H
H
CH3

1 down, 1 up =
trans

1 down, 1 up =
trans

same arrangement in three dimensions
identical

d. 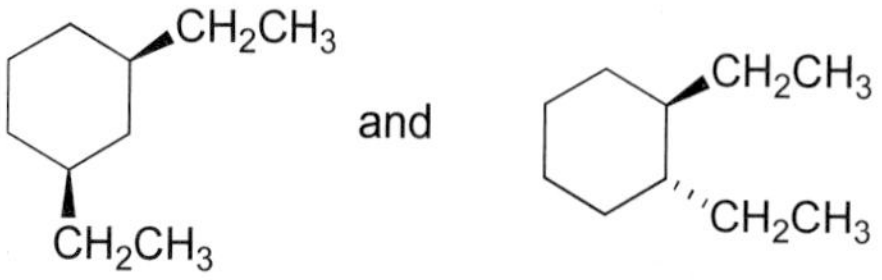
CH2CH3
CH2CH3
and
CH2CH3
CH2CH3

same molecular formula $C_{10}H_{20}$
different connectivity
constitutional isomers

e. 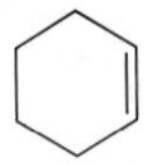 and 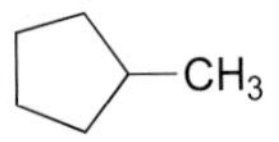
CH3

molecular formula: C_6H_{10} **molecular formula: C_6H_{12}**

different molecular formulas
not isomers

g. 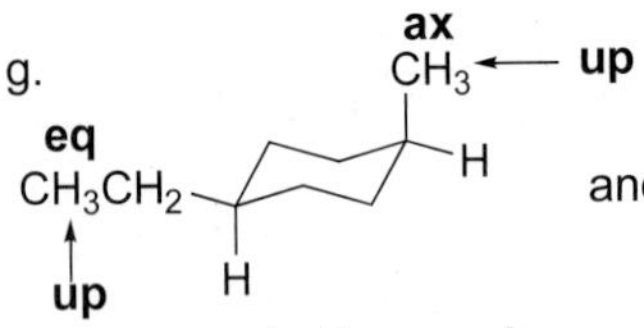
ax
CH3
up
eq
CH3CH2
H
up
H

and 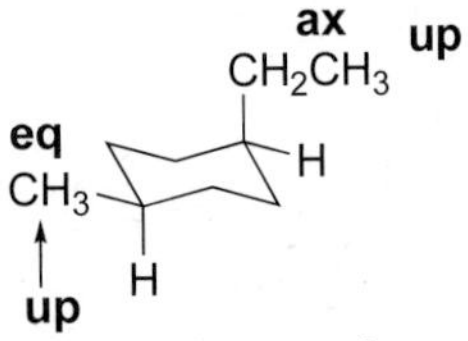
ax
up
CH2CH3
eq
CH3
H
up
H

both up = **cis** both up = **cis**

same arrangement in three dimensions
identical

f. 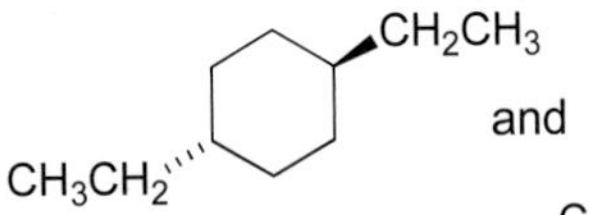
CH2CH3
CH3CH2

and 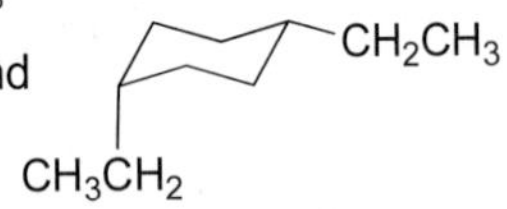
CH2CH3
CH3CH2

1 down, 1 up =
trans

both down =
cis

different arrangement in three dimensions
stereoisomers

h. 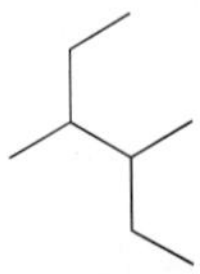 and 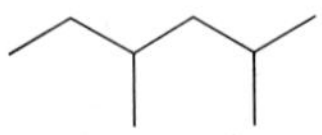

3,4-dimethylhexane **2,4-dimethylhexane**

same molecular formula C_8H_{18}
different IUPAC names
constitutional isomers

4.62

a. 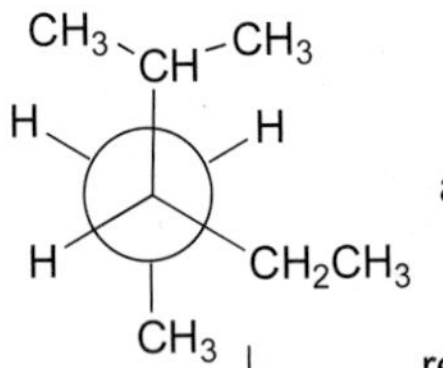
CH3
CH
CH3
H
H
H
CH2CH3
CH3

and 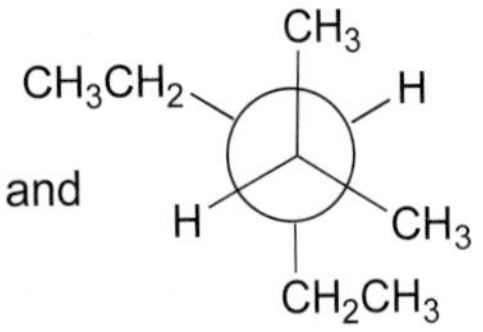
CH3
CH3CH2
H
H
CH3
CH2CH3

re-draw

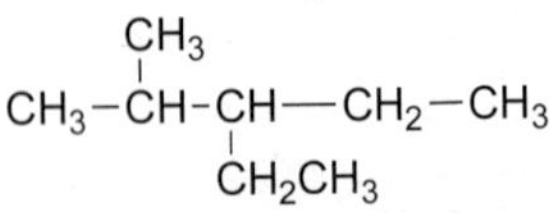
CH3
CH3–CH-CH—CH2–CH3
CH2CH3

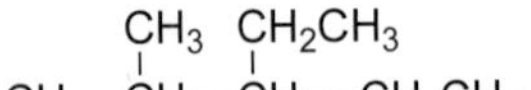
CH3 CH2CH3
CH3–CH—CH—CH2CH3

3-ethyl-2-methylpentane 3-ethyl-2-methylpentane

same molecular formula
same name
identical molecules

b. 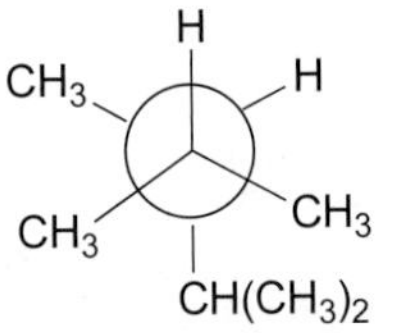
H
CH3
H
CH3
CH3
CH(CH3)2

and 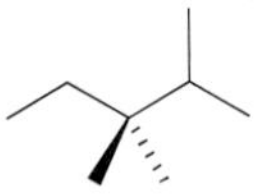

re-draw

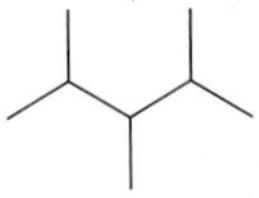

same molecular formula
different arrangement of atoms
constitutional isomers

4.63

One possibility: **constitutional isomer** **stereoisomer**

a. 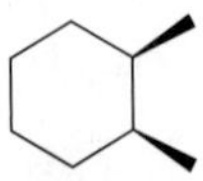 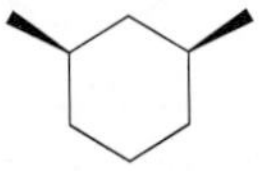 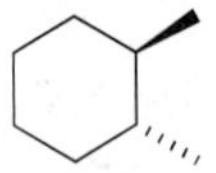

cis **trans**

b. 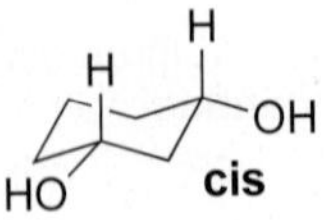
H
H
OH
HO

cis

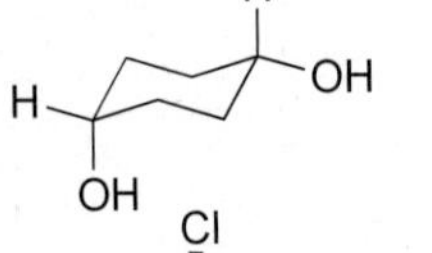
H
H
OH
OH

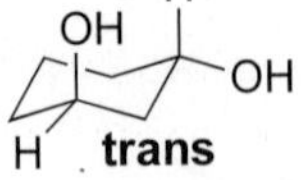
H
OH
OH
H

trans

c. 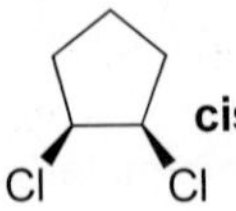
Cl
Cl

cis

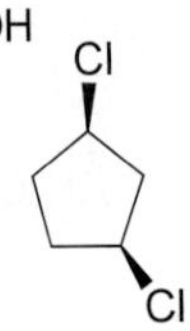
Cl
Cl

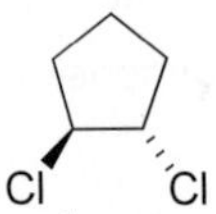
Cl
Cl

trans

4.64

Three constitutional isomers of C_7H_{14}:

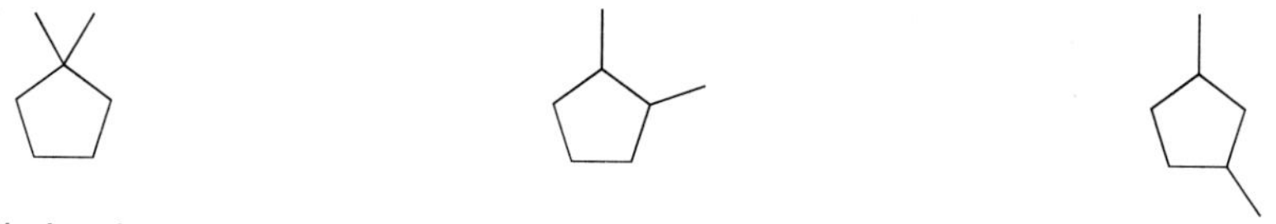

1,1-dimethylcyclopentane 1,2-dimethylcyclopentane 1,3-dimethylcyclopentane

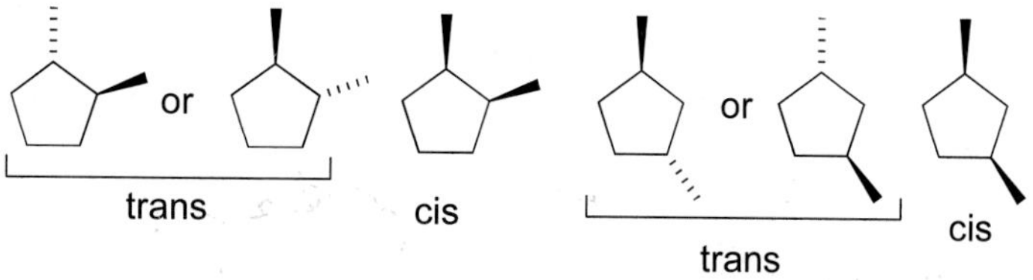

4.65 Use the definitions from Answer 4.29 to classify the reactions.

a. CH_3CHO = 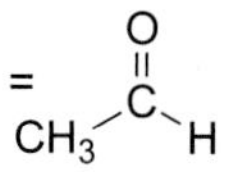 ⟶ CH_3CH_2OH

Decrease in the number of C–O bonds. **Reduction**

b. $CH_2{=}CH_2$ ⟶ $H{-}C{\equiv}C{-}H$

Decrease in the number of C–H bonds. **Oxidation**

c. 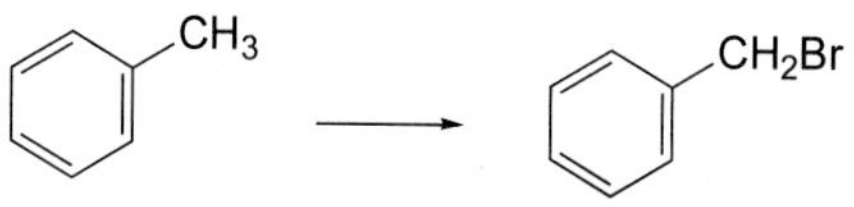

Increase in the number of C–Z bonds. **Oxidation**

d. CH_3CH_2OH ⟶ $CH_2{=}CH_2$

Loss of one C–O bond *and* one C–H bond. **Neither**

4.66 Use the rule from Answer 4.30.

a. $CH_3CH_2CH_2CH_2CH(CH_3)_2 \xrightarrow[11\ O_2]{\text{flame}} 7\ CO_2 + 8\ H_2O + \text{heat}$

b. 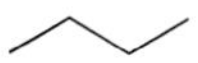 $\xrightarrow[(13/2)\ O_2]{\text{flame}} 4\ CO_2 + 5\ H_2O + \text{heat}$

4.67

a. 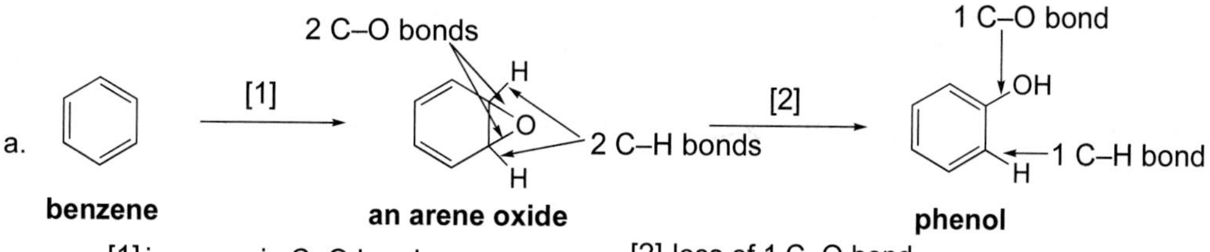

[1] increase in C–O bonds
oxidation reaction

[2] loss of 1 C–O bond,
loss of 1 C–H bond
neither

b. Phenol is more water soluble than benzene because it is **polar (contains an O–H group) and can hydrogen bond with water,** whereas benzene is nonpolar and cannot hydrogen bond.

4.68 Lipids contain many nonpolar C–C and C–H bonds and few polar functional groups.

a. 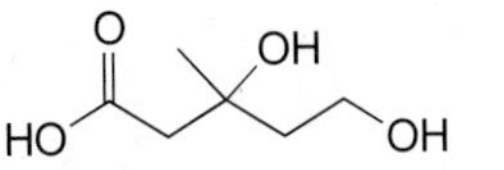

mevalonic acid

many polar functional groups
not a lipid

c. 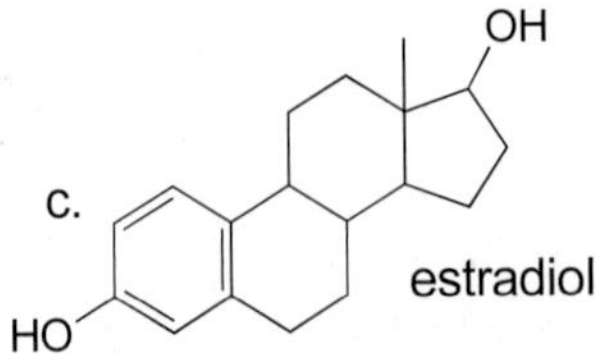

estradiol

few polar functional groups
a lipid

d. 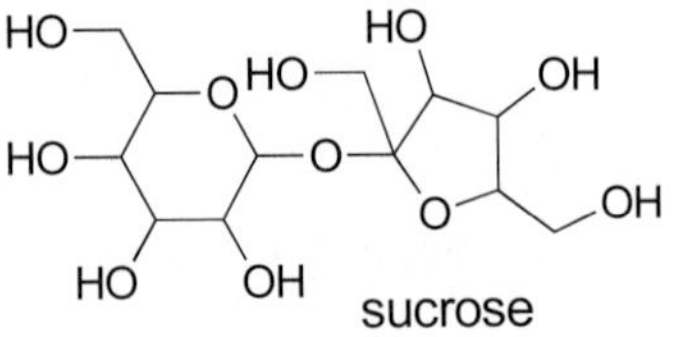

sucrose

many polar functional groups
not a lipid

b. 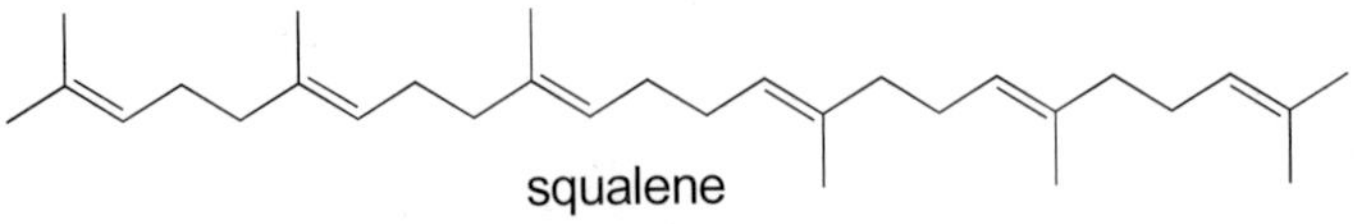

squalene
no polar functional groups
a lipid

4.69

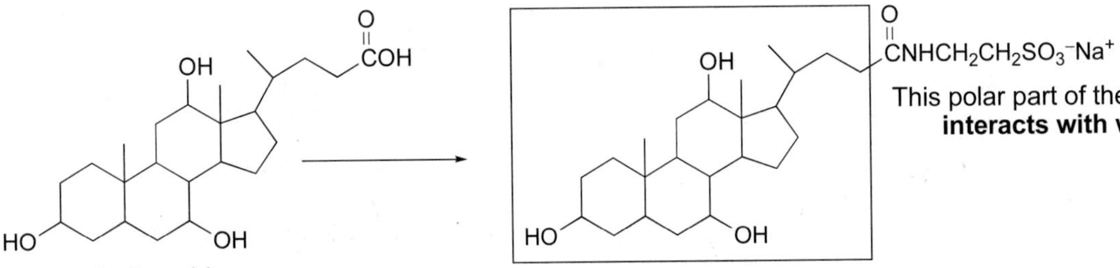

This polar part of the molecule **interacts with water.**

cholic acid
a bile acid

a bile salt

This nonpolar part of the molecule can **interact with lipids** to create micelles that allow for transport of lipids through aqueous environments.

4.70 The mineral oil can prevent the body's absorption of important fat-soluble vitamins. The vitamins dissolve in the mineral oil, and are thus not absorbed. Instead, they are expelled with the mineral oil.

4.71 Cyclopropane has larger angle strain than cyclobutane because the internal angles in the three-membered ring (60°) are smaller than they are in cyclobutane. Although cyclobutane is not flat, as shown in Figure 4.11, there are more C–H bonds than there are in cyclopropane, so there are more sites of torsional strain. Thus cyclopropane has more angle strain but less torsional strain. The result is that both cyclopropane and cyclobutane have roughly similar strain energies.

4.72 The amide in the four-membered ring has 90° bond angles giving it angle strain, which makes it more reactive.

amide

penicillin G

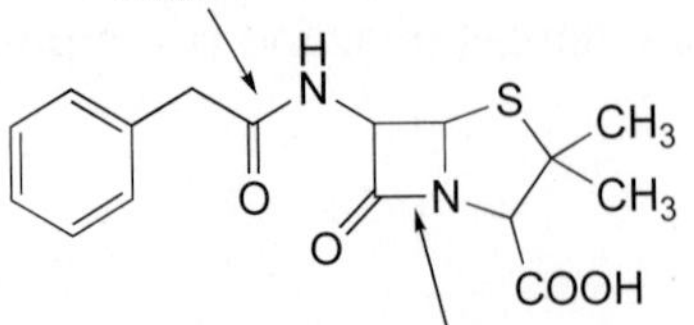

strained amide
more reactive

4.73

Example:

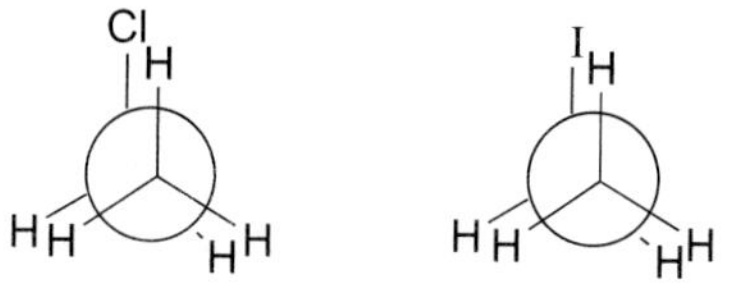

Although I is a much bigger atom than Cl, the C–I bond is also much longer than the C–Cl bond. As a result the eclipsing interaction of the H and I atoms is not very much different in magnitude from the H,Cl eclipsing interaction.

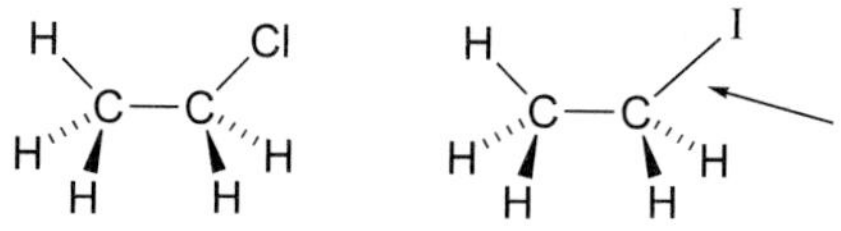
longer bond

4.74

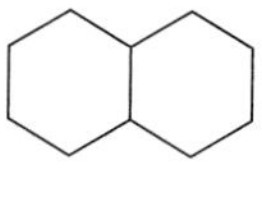

decalin

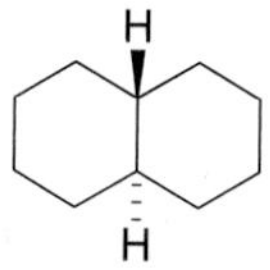

trans-decalin

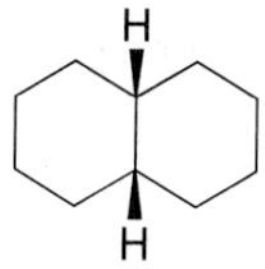

cis-decalin

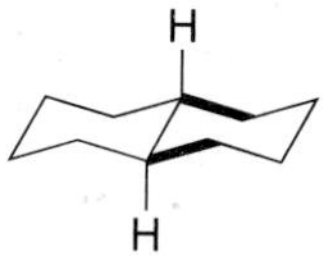

trans

The trans isomer is more stable since the carbon groups at the ring junction are both in the favorable equatorial position.

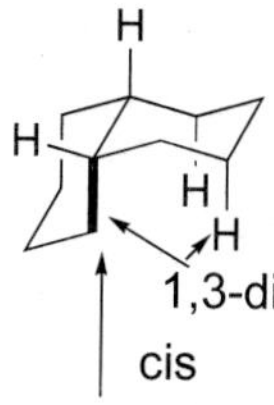
1,3-diaxial interaction

cis

This bond is axial, creating unfavorable 1,3-diaxial interactions.

4.75 Re-draw the ball-and-stick model using chair forms.

a.

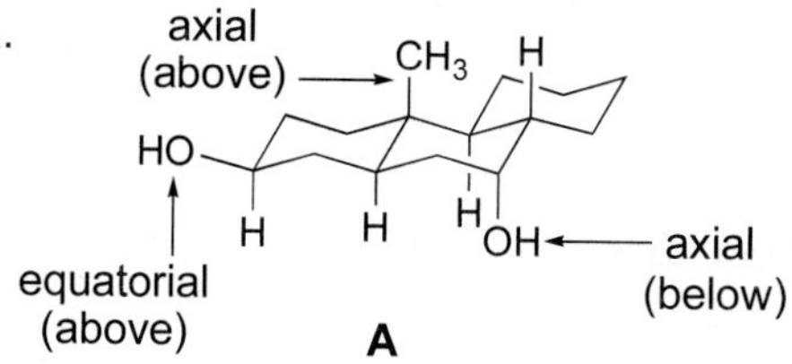
axial
(above)
equatorial
(above)
axial
(below)

A

b. All bonds above the ring are on wedges and all bonds below the ring are on dashed lines.

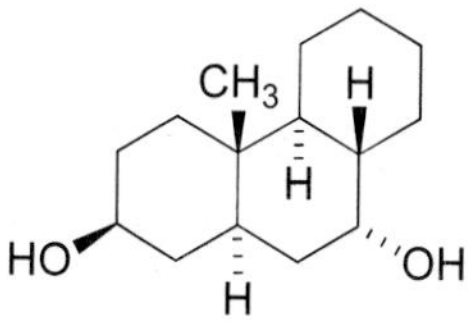

4.76

a, b.

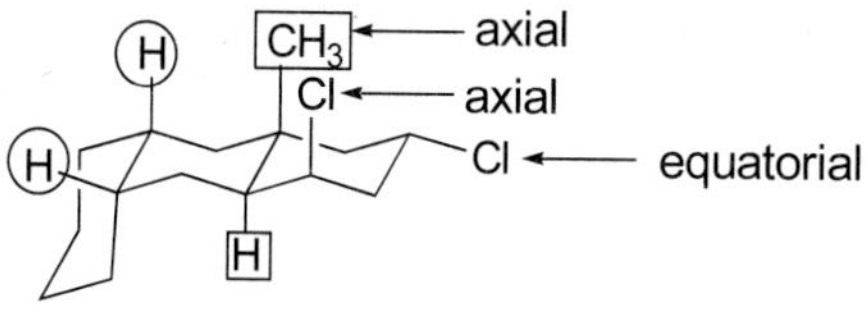
axial
axial
equatorial

B

c. The circled H's at one ring fusion are cis. The boxed in CH_3 and H at the second ring fusion are trans.

4.77

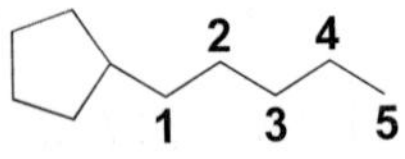

pentylcyclopentane

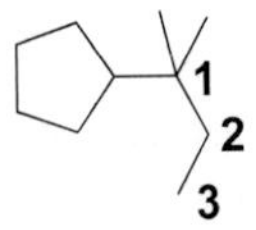

(1,1-dimethylpropyl)cyclopentane

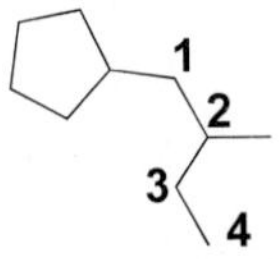

(2-methylbutyl)cyclopentane

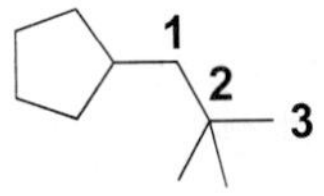

(2,2-dimethylpropyl)cyclopentane

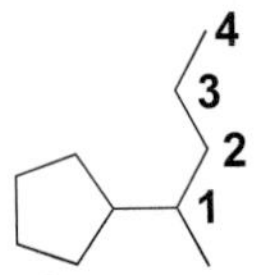

(1-methylbutyl)cyclopentane

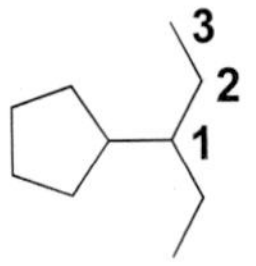

(1-ethylpropyl)cyclopentane

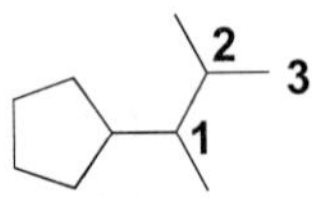

(1,2-dimethylpropyl)cyclopentane

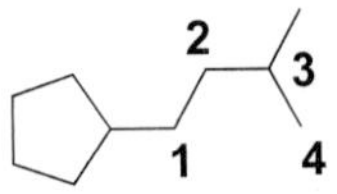

(3-methylbutyl)cyclopentane

4.78

a.

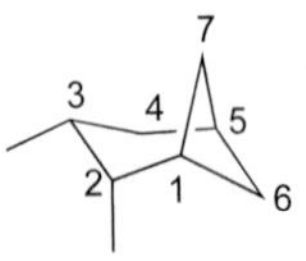

2,3-dimethylbicyclo[3.1.1]heptane

b.

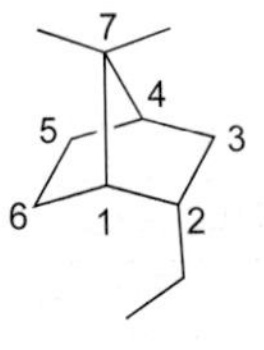

2-ethyl-7,7-dimethylbicyclo[2.2.1]heptane

c.

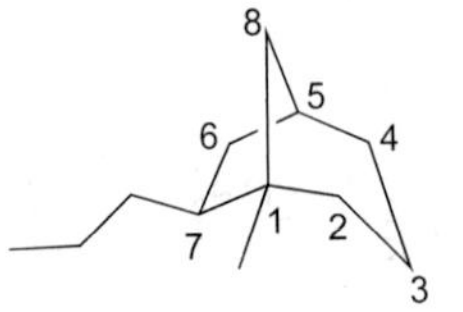

1-methyl-7-propylbicyclo[3.2.1]octane

d.

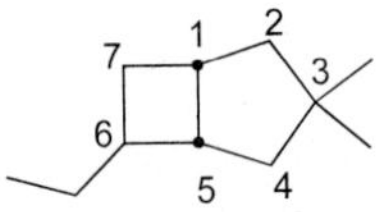

6-ethyl-3,3-dimethylbicyclo[3.2.0]heptane

Chapter 5 Stereochemistry

Chapter Review

Isomers are different compounds with the same molecular formula (5.2, 5.11).

[1] **Constitutional isomers**—isomers that differ in the way the atoms are connected to each other. They have:
- different IUPAC names
- the same or different functional groups
- different physical and chemical properties.

[2] **Stereoisomers**—isomers that differ only in the way atoms are oriented in space. They have the same functional group and the same IUPAC name except for prefixes such as cis, trans, *R*, and *S*.
- **Enantiomers**—stereoisomers that are nonsuperimposable mirror images of each other (5.4).
- **Diastereomers**—stereoisomers that are not mirror images of each other (5.7).

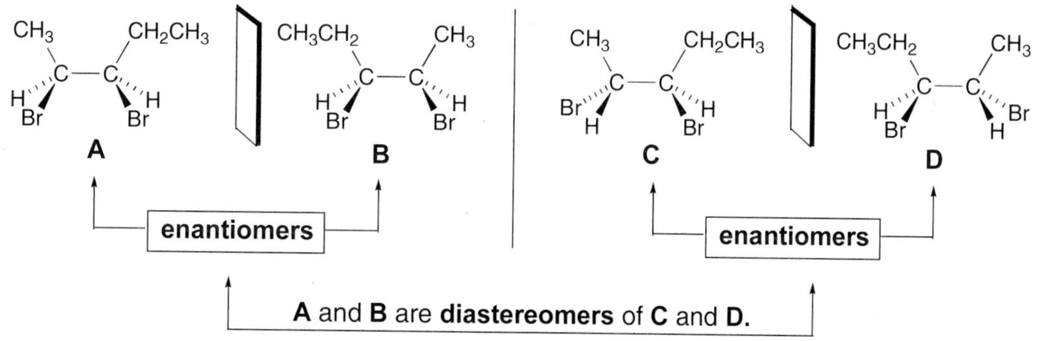

Assigning priority (5.6)

- Assign priorities (1, 2, 3, or 4) to the atoms directly bonded to the stereogenic center in order of decreasing atomic number. The atom of *highest* atomic number gets the *highest* priority (1).
- If two atoms on a stereogenic center are the *same*, assign priority based on the atomic number of the atoms bonded to these atoms. *One* atom of higher atomic number determines a higher priority.
- If two isotopes are bonded to the stereogenic center, assign priorities in order of decreasing *mass* number.
- To assign a priority to an atom that is part of a multiple bond, treat a multiply bonded atom as an equivalent number of singly bonded atoms.

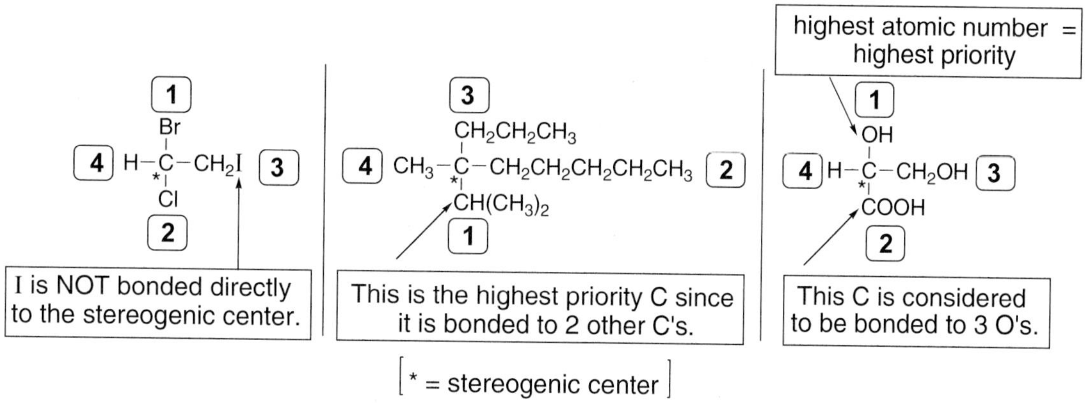

Some basic principles

- When a compound and its mirror image are **superimposable,** they are **identical achiral compounds.** A plane of symmetry in one conformation makes a compound achiral (5.3).
- When a compound and its mirror image are **not superimposable,** they are **different chiral compounds** called **enantiomers.** A chiral compound has no plane of symmetry in any conformation (5.3).
- A **tetrahedral stereogenic center** is a carbon atom bonded to four different groups (5.4, 5.5).
- For ***n*** **stereogenic centers,** the maximum number of stereoisomers is $\mathbf{2^n}$ (5.7).

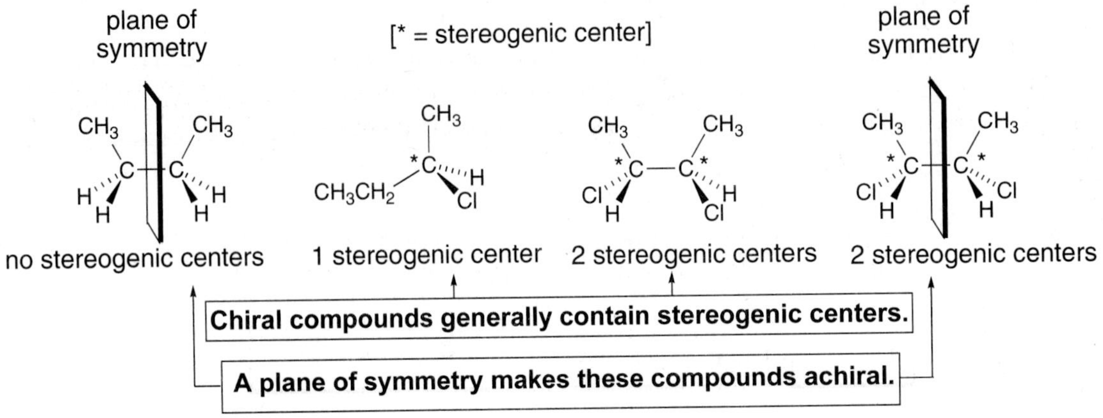

Optical activity is the ability of a compound to rotate plane-polarized light (5.12).

- An optically active solution contains a chiral compound.
- An optically inactive solution contains one of the following:
  - an achiral compound with no stereogenic centers.
  - a meso compound—an achiral compound with two or more stereogenic centers.
  - a racemic mixture—an equal amount of two enantiomers.

The prefixes *R* and *S* compared with *d* and *l*

The prefixes *R* and *S* are labels used in nomenclature. Rules on assigning *R,S* are found in Section 5.6.

- An enantiomer has every stereogenic center opposite in configuration. If a compound with two stereogenic centers has the *R,R* configuration, then its enantiomer has the *S,S* configuration.
- A diastereomer of this same compound has either the *R,S* or *S,R* configuration; one stereogenic center has the same configuration and one is opposite.

The prefixes *d* (or +) and *l* (or –) tell the direction a compound rotates plane-polarized light (5.12).

- *d* (or +) stands for dextrorotatory, rotating polarized light clockwise.
- *l* (or –) stands for levorotatory, rotating polarized light counterclockwise.

The physical properties of isomers compared (5.12)

Type of isomer	Physical properties
Constitutional isomers	Different
Enantiomers	Identical except the direction of rotation of polarized light
Diastereomers	Different
Racemic mixture	Possibly different from either enantiomer

Equations

- Specific rotation (5.12C):

$$\text{specific rotation} = [\alpha] = \frac{\alpha}{l \times c}$$

α = observed rotation (°)
l = length of sample tube (dm)
c = concentration (g/mL)

[dm = decimeter; 1 dm = 10 cm]

- Enantiomeric excess (5.12D):

$$ee = \text{\% of one enantiomer} - \text{\% of other enantiomer}$$
$$= \frac{[\alpha]\ \text{mixture}}{[\alpha]\ \text{pure enantiomer}} \times 100\%$$

Practice Test on Chapter Review

1.a. Which of the following statements is true for compounds **A–D** below?

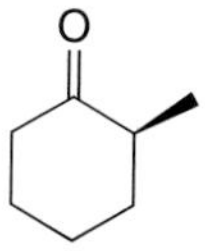

A

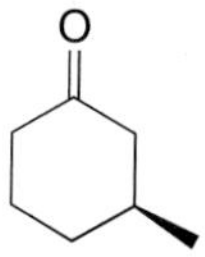

B

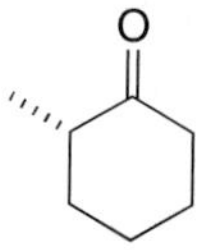

C

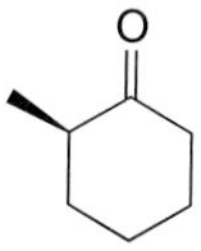

D

1. **A** and **B** are separable by physical methods such as distillation.
2. **A** and **C** are separable by physical methods such as distillation.
3. **A** and **D** are separable by physical methods such as distillation.
4. Statements (1) and (2) are both true.
5. Statements (1), (2), and (3) are all true.

b. Which of the following statements is true about compounds **A–C** below?

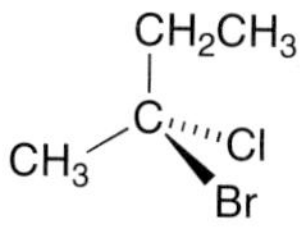

A

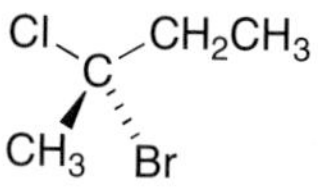

B

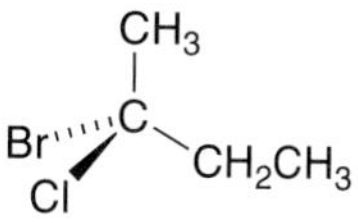

C

1. **A** and **B** are enantiomers.
2. **A** and **C** are enantiomers.
3. An equal mixture of **B** and **C** is optically active.
4. Statements (1) and (2) are true.
5. Statements (1), (2), and (3) are all true.

c. Which compound is a diastereomer of **A?**

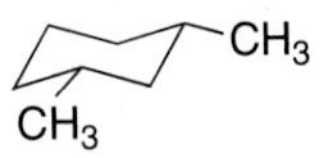
CH3
CH3

A

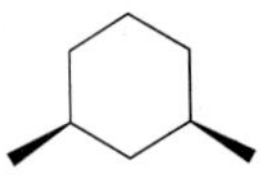

B

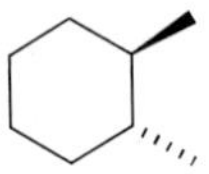

C

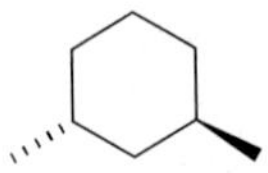

D

1. **B** only
2. **C** only
3. **D** only
4. Both **B** and **C**
5. Compounds **B, C,** and **D**

2. Rank the following four groups around a stereogenic center in order of decreasing priority. Rank the highest priority group as **1,** the lowest priority group as **4,** and the two groups of intermediate priority as **2** and **3.**

$-CH_2Cl$	$-CH_2CH_2Br$	$-COOH$	$-CH_2OH$
A	**B**	**C**	**D**

3. Label each stereogenic center in the following compound as *R* or *S*.

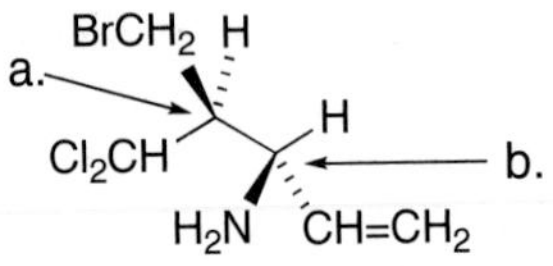
BrCH2 H
a.
H
Cl2CH
b.
H2N CH=CH2

4. State how the compounds in each pair are related to each other. Choose from constitutional isomers, enantiomers, diastereomers, or identical compounds.

a. 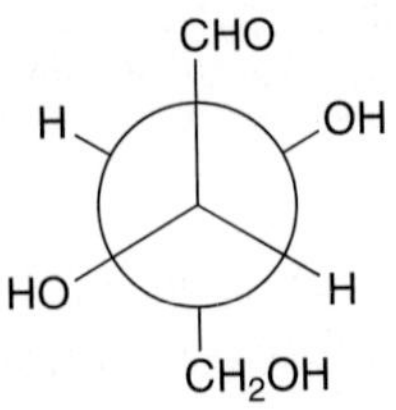
CHO
H
OH
HO
H
CH2OH

and

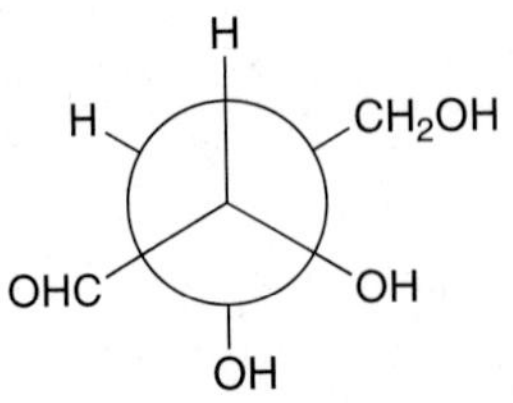
H
H
CH2OH
OHC
OH
OH

b. 
Cl

and

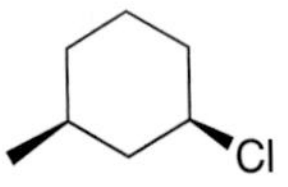
Cl

c. 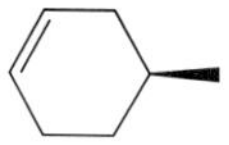 and 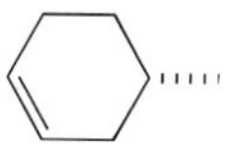

5. The enantiomeric excess of a mixture of **A** and **B** is 62% with **A** in excess. How much of **A** and **B** are present in the mixture?

Answers to Practice Test

1. a. 1	2. **A**–1	3. a. *S*	4. a. diastereomers	5. 81% **A**
b. 2	**B**–4	b. *S*	b. enantiomers	19% **B**
c. 3	**C**–2		c. identical	
	D–3			

Answers to Problems

5.1 Cellulose consists of long chains held together by intermolecular hydrogen bonds forming sheets that stack in extensive three-dimensional arrays. Most of the OH groups in cellulose are in the interior of this three-dimensional network, unavailable for hydrogen bonding to water. Thus, even though cellulose has many OH groups, its three-dimensional structure prevents many of the OH groups from hydrogen bonding with the solvent and this makes it water insoluble.

5.2 **Constitutional isomers** have atoms bonded to different atoms.
Stereoisomers differ only in the three-dimensional arrangement of atoms.

a. 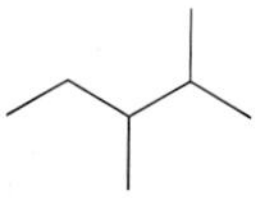 and 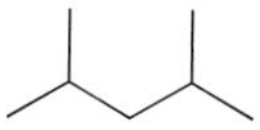

2,3-dimethylpentane 2,4-dimethylpentane

different connectivity of atoms
different names
constitutional isomers

b. 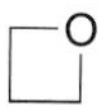

and 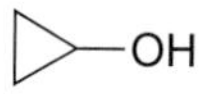

four-membered ring three-membered ring

different connectivity of atoms
constitutional isomers

c. 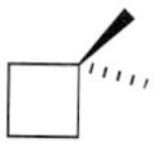 and 

different connectivity of atoms
constitutional isomers

d.  and 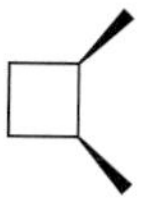

trans isomer cis isomer

Both are 1,2-dimethylcyclobutane,
but the CH_3 groups are oriented differently.
stereoisomers

5.3 Draw the mirror image of each molecule by drawing a mirror plane and then drawing the molecule's reflection. **A chiral molecule is one that is not superimposable on its mirror image.** A molecule with one stereogenic center is always chiral. A molecule with zero stereogenic centers is not chiral (in general).

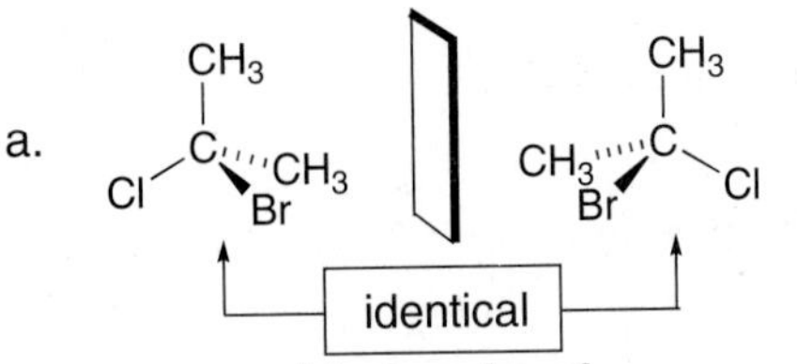

achiral molecule

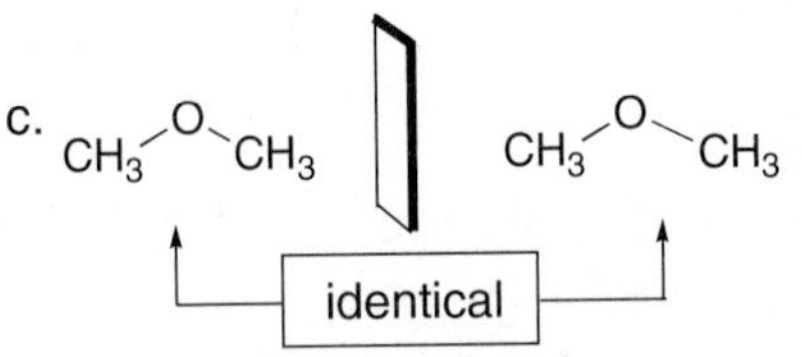

achiral molecule

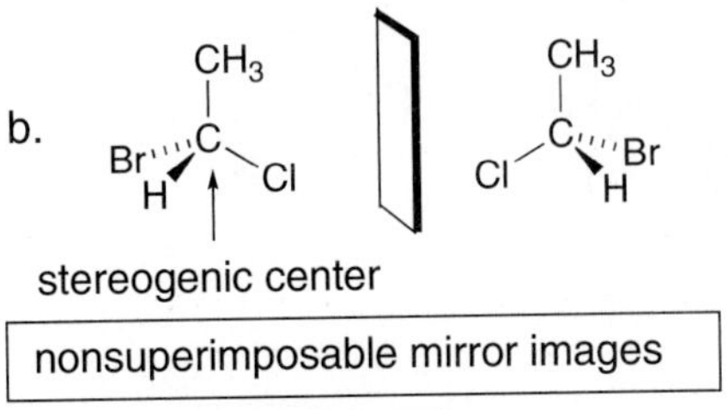

chiral molecules

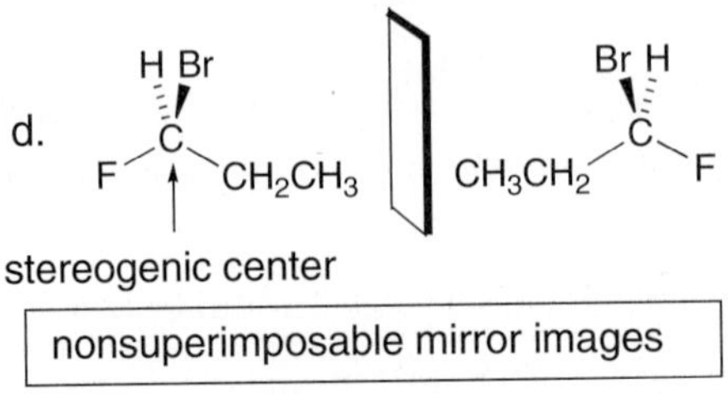

chiral molecules

5.4 A plane of symmetry cuts the molecule into **two identical halves.**

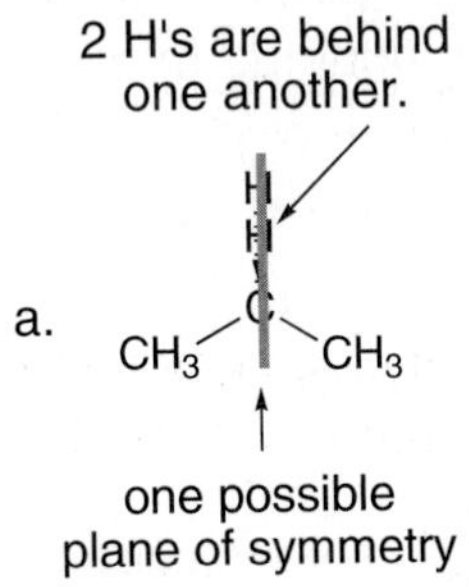

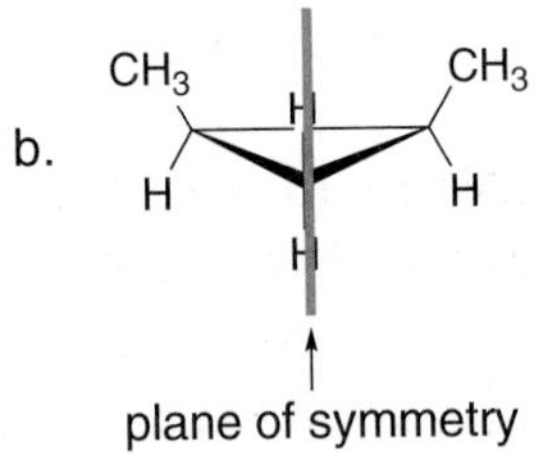

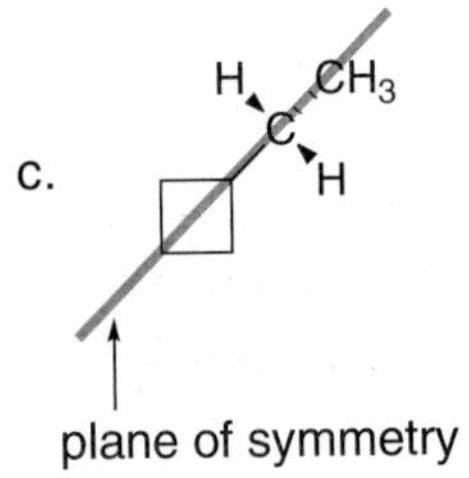

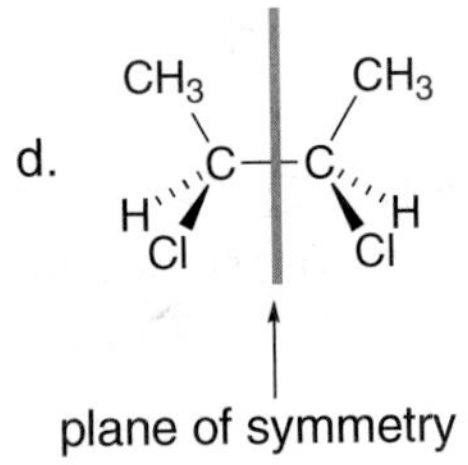

5.5 Rotate around the middle C–C bond so that the Br atoms are eclipsed.

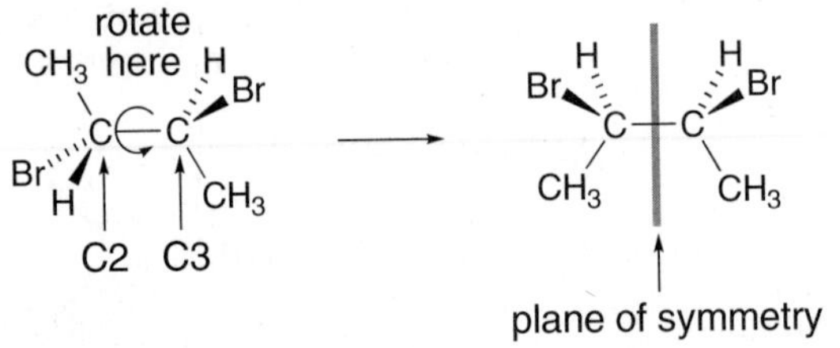

5.6 To locate a stereogenic center, omit all C's with two or more H's, all *sp* and sp^2 hybridized atoms, and all heteroatoms. (In Chapter 25, we will learn that the N atoms of ammonium salts [$R_4N^+X^-$] can sometimes be stereogenic centers.) Then evaluate any remaining atoms. A tetrahedral stereogenic center has a carbon bonded to **four different groups.**

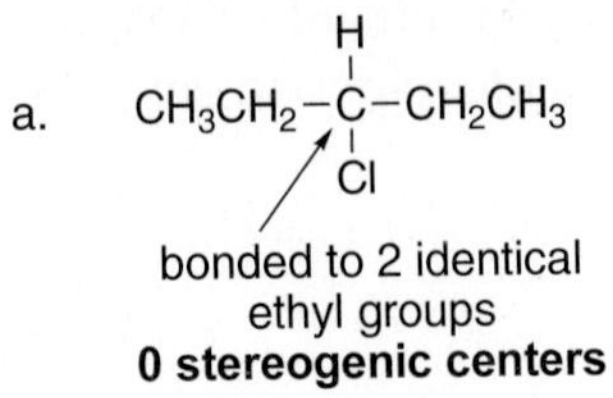

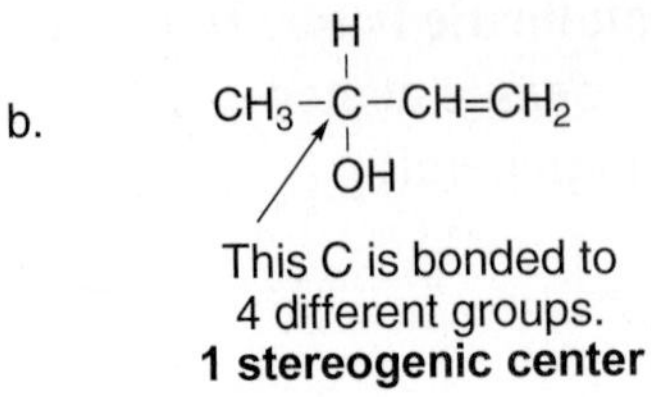

c. $CH_3CH_2CH_2OH$

0 stereogenic centers

d. 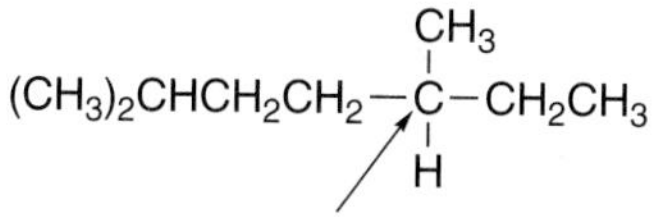

This C is bonded to
4 different groups.
1 stereogenic center

e. 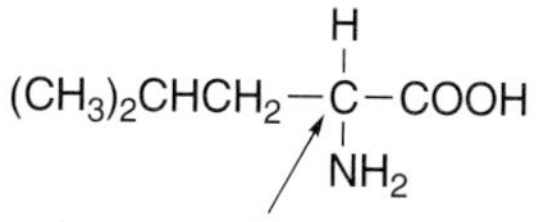

stereogenic center

f. 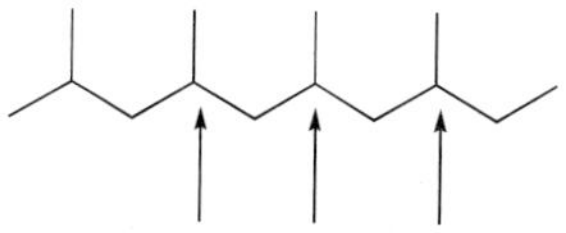

3 C's bonded to 4
different groups
3 stereogenic centers

5.7 Use the directions from Answer 5.6 to locate the stereogenic centers.

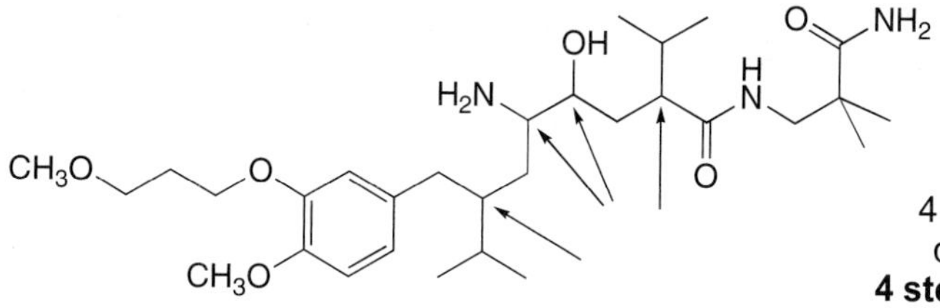

aliskiren

4 C's bonded to 4
different groups
4 stereogenic centers

5.8 Find the C bonded to four different groups in each molecule. At the stereogenic center, draw two bonds in the plane of the page, one in front (on a wedge), and one behind (on a dash). Then draw the mirror image (enantiomer).

stereogenic center

a. $CH_3CH(Cl)CH_2CH_3$

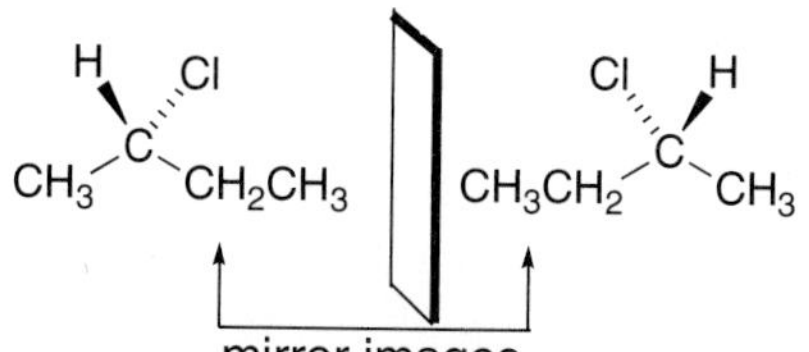

mirror images
nonsuperimposable
enantiomers

stereogenic center

b. $CH_3CH_2CH(OH)CH_2OH$

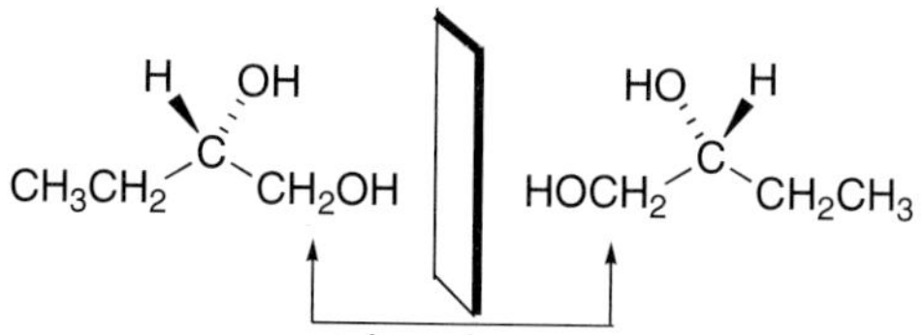

mirror images
nonsuperimposable
enantiomers

stereogenic center

c. $CH_3SCH_2CH_2CH(NH_2)COOH$

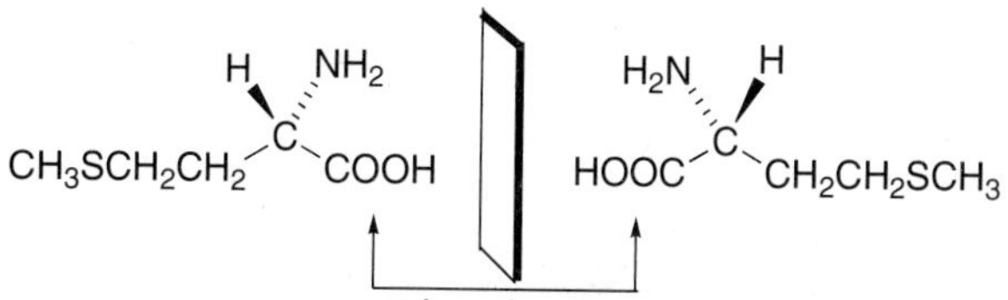

mirror images
nonsuperimposable
enantiomers

5.9 Use the directions from Answer 5.6 to locate the stereogenic centers.

a. 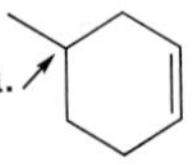 C bonded to H and 3 different C's: **1 stereogenic center**

c. 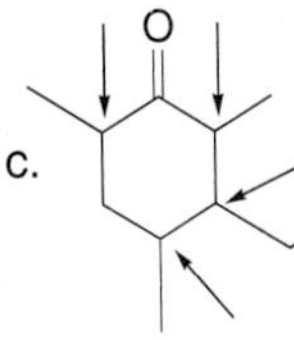 4 C's bonded to 4 different groups: **4 stereogenic centers**

e. 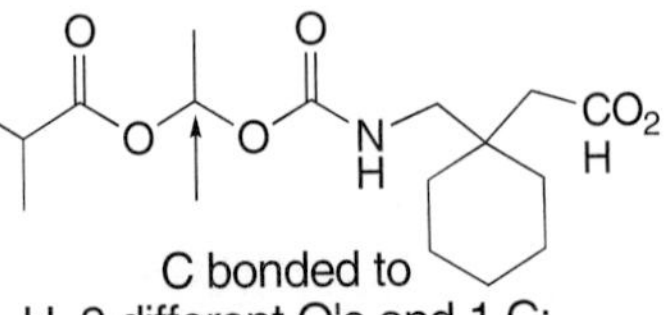

C bonded to H, 2 different O's and 1 C: **1 stereogenic center**

b. 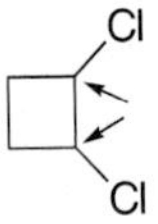

Each labeled C is bonded to: H, Cl, CH_2, CHCl: **2 stereogenic centers**

d. 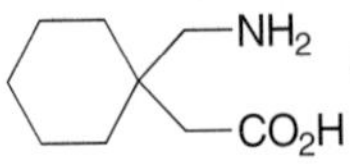

no stereogenic centers

5.10

a. 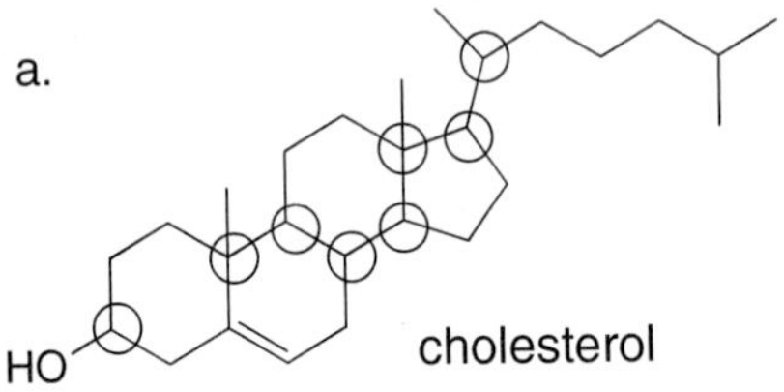

cholesterol

b. 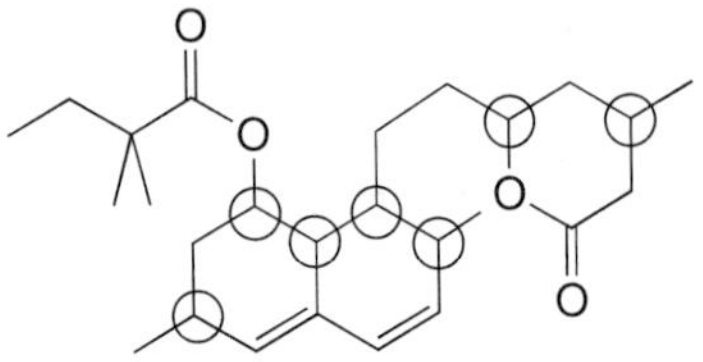

simvastatin

All stereogenic C's are circled. Each C is sp^3 hybridized and bonded to 4 different groups.

5.11 Assign priority based on atomic number: atoms with a higher atomic number get a higher priority. If two atoms are the same, look at what they are bonded to and assign priority based on the atomic number of these atoms.

a. $-CH_3$, $-CH_2CH_3$ ↑ **higher priority** ($-CH_2CH_3$)

b. –I, –Br ↑ **higher priority** (–I)

c. –H, –D ↑ higher mass **higher priority** (–D)

d. $-CH_2Br$, $-CH_2CH_2Br$ ↑ **higher priority** ($-CH_2Br$)

e. $-CH_2CH_2Cl$, $-CH_2CH(CH_3)_2$ ↑ **higher priority** ($-CH_2CH_2Cl$)

f. $-CH_2OH$, –CHO = H–C=O (2 C–O bonds) = H–C(–O)–O with C on O

$-CH_2OH$: 2 H's, 1 O; –CHO: **2 O's**, 1 H

C bonded to 2 O's has **higher priority.**

5.12 Rank by decreasing priority. Lower atomic number = lower priority.

Highest priority = 1, Lowest priority = 4

a.

		priority
–COOH	C = second lowest atomic number	3
–H	H = lowest atomic number	4
$-NH_2$	N = second highest atomic number	2
–OH	O = highest atomic number	1

decreasing priority: –OH, $-NH_2$, –COOH, –H

b.

		priority
–H	H = lowest atomic number	4
$-CH_3$	C bonded to 3 H's	3
–Cl	Cl = highest atomic number	1
$-CH_2Cl$	C bonded to 2 H's + **1 Cl**	2

decreasing priority: –Cl, $-CH_2Cl$, $-CH_3$, –H

c.		priority
$-CH_2CH_3$	C bonded to 2 H's + **1 C**	2
$-CH_3$	C bonded to 3 H's	3
–H	H = lowest atomic number	4
$-CH(CH_3)_2$	C bonded to 1 H + **2 C's**	1

decreasing priority: $-CH(CH_3)_2$, $-CH_2CH_3$, $-CH_3$, –H

d.		priority
$-CH=CH_2$	C bonded to 1 H + **2 C's**	2
$-CH_3$	C bonded to 3 H's	3
–C≡CH	C bonded to **3 C's**	1
–H	H = lowest atomic number	4

decreasing priority: –C≡CH, $-CH=CH_2$, $-CH_3$, –H

5.13 To assign *R* or *S* to the molecule, first rank the groups. The lowest priority group must be oriented behind the page. If tracing a circle from (1) → (2) → (3) proceeds in the clockwise direction, then the stereogenic center is labeled *R*; if the circle is counterclockwise, then it is labeled *S*.

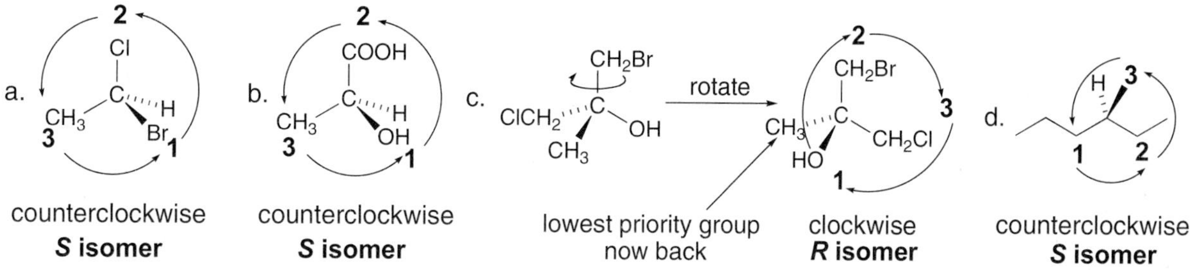
a.
counterclockwise
S isomer
b.
counterclockwise
S isomer
c.
rotate
lowest priority group
now back
clockwise
R isomer
d.
counterclockwise
S isomer

5.14

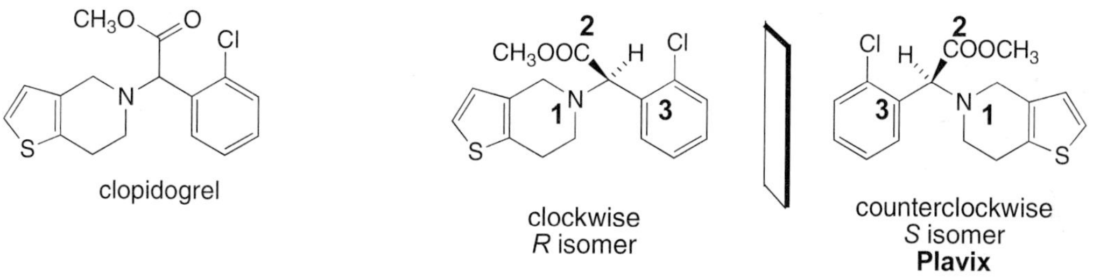
clopidogrel
clockwise
R isomer
counterclockwise
S isomer
Plavix

5.15 a, b. Re-draw lisinopril as a skeletal structure, locate the stereogenic centers, and assign *R*,*S*.

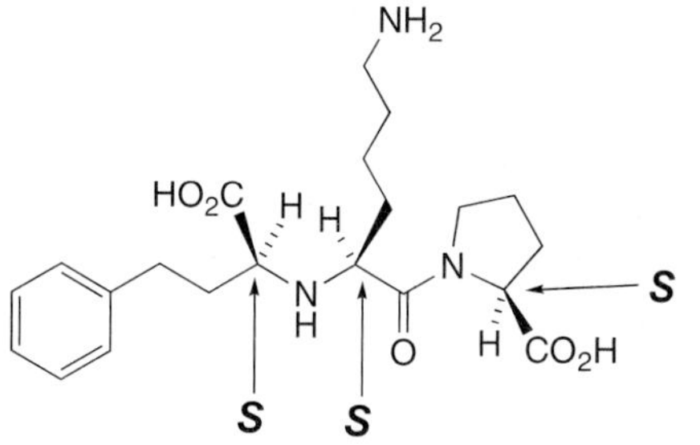

three stereogenic centers
All have the *S* configuration.

5.16 The maximum number of stereoisomers = 2^n where n = the number of stereogenic centers.

a. 3 stereogenic centers
2^3 = 8 stereoisomers

b. 8 stereogenic centers
2^8 = 256 stereoisomers

5.17

a. $CH_3CH_2CH(Cl)CH(OH)CH_2CH_3$

2 stereogenic centers = 4 possible stereoisomers

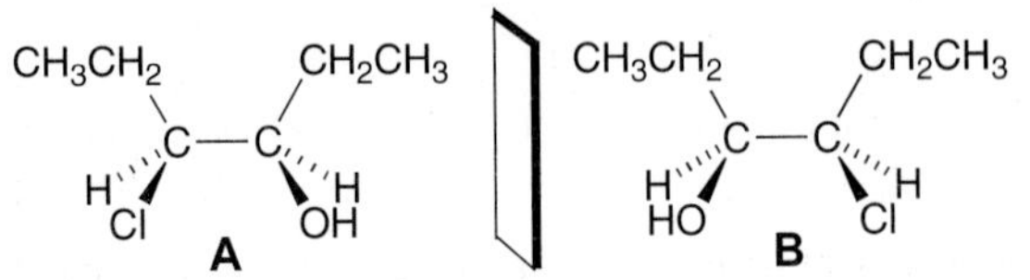

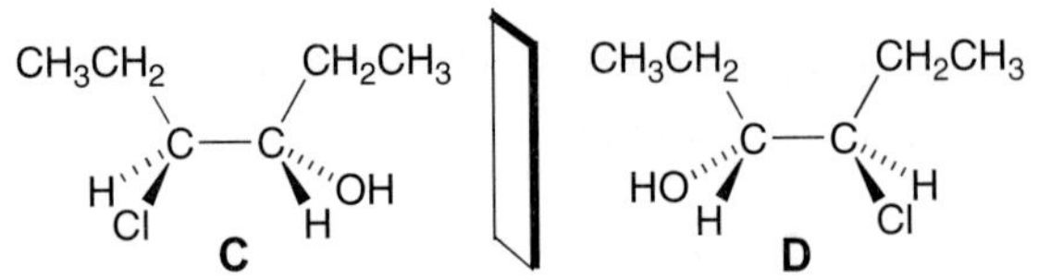

b. $CH_3CH(Br)CH_2CH(Cl)CH_3$

2 stereogenic centers = 4 possible stereoisomers

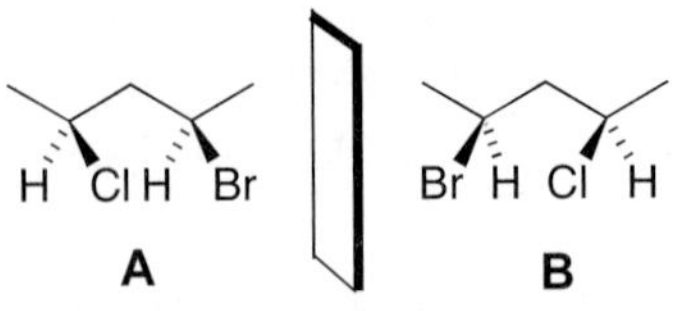

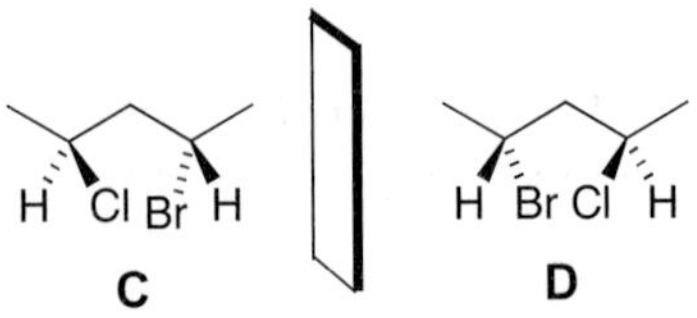

5.18

a. $CH_3CH(OH)CH(OH)CH_3$

2 stereogenic centers = 4 possible stereoisomers

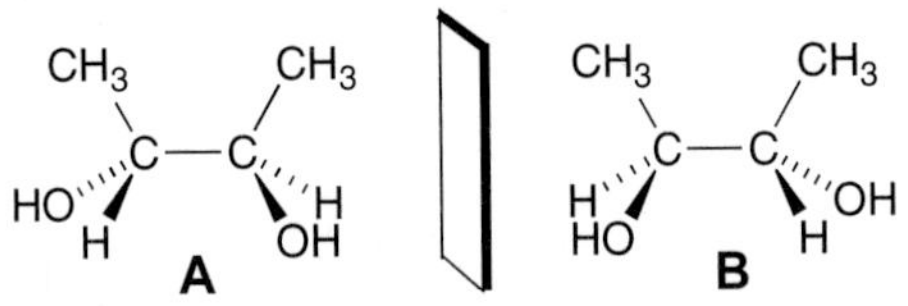

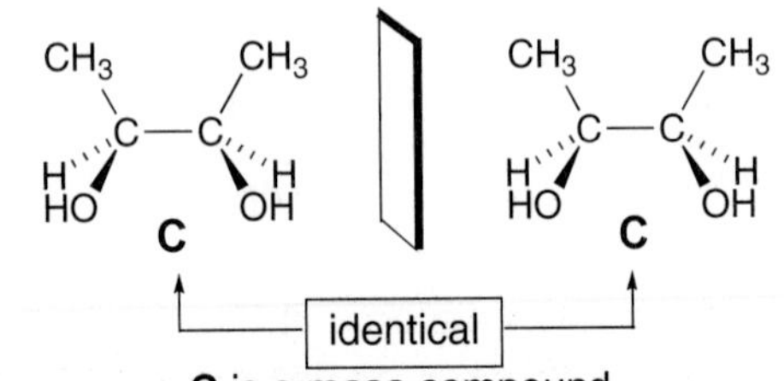

C is a meso compound.

A and **B** are enantiomers.

Pairs of diastereomers: **A** and **C**, **B** and **C**.

b. $CH_3CH(OH)CH(Cl)CH_3$

2 stereogenic centers = 4 possible stereoisomers

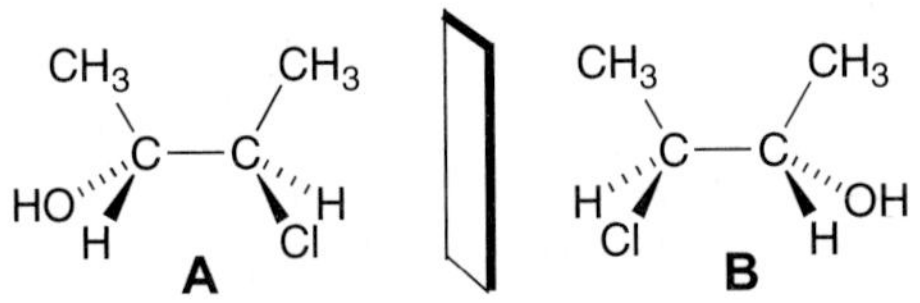

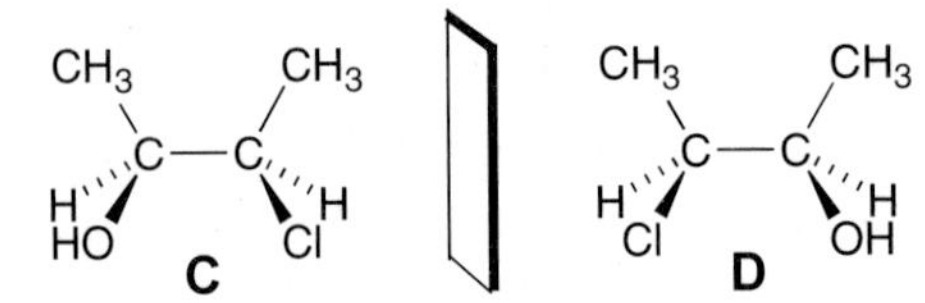

Pairs of enantiomers: **A** and **B**, **C** and **D**.

Pairs of diastereomers: **A** and **C**, **A** and **D**, **B** and **C**, **B** and **D**.

5.19 **A meso compound must have at least two stereogenic centers. Usually a meso compound has a plane of symmetry.** You may have to rotate around a C–C bond to see the plane of symmetry clearly.

a.

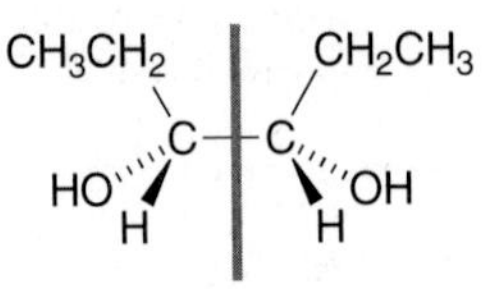

2 stereogenic centers
plane of symmetry
meso compound

b.

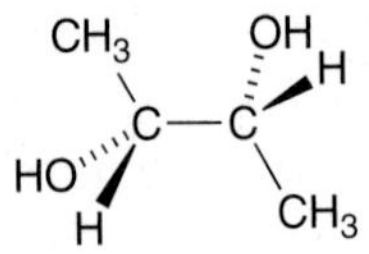

2 stereogenic centers
no plane of symmetry
not a meso compound

c.

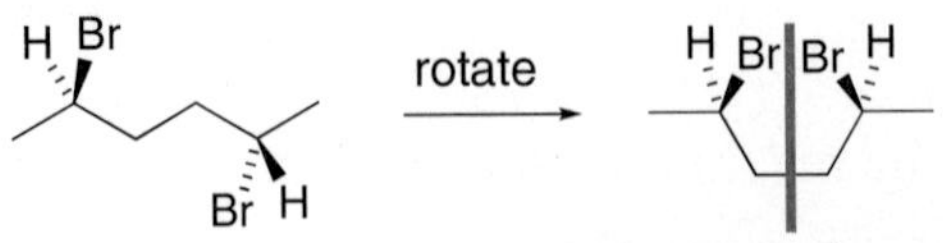

2 stereogenic centers
plane of symmetry
meso compound

5.20 Use the definition in Answer 5.19 to draw the meso compounds.

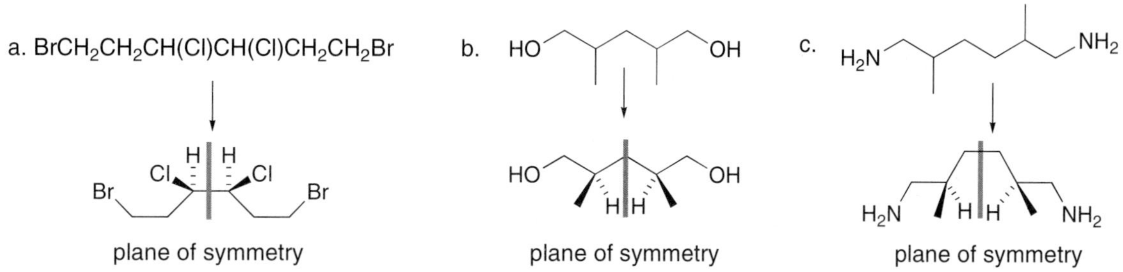
a. BrCH2CH2CH(Cl)CH(Cl)CH2CH2Br
b. HO OH
c. H2N NH2
H H
Cl Cl
Br Br
HO OH
H H
H2N NH2
H H
plane of symmetry
plane of symmetry
plane of symmetry

5.21 The enantiomer must have the exact opposite *R,S* designations. Diastereomers with two stereogenic centers have one center the same and one different.

If a compound is ***R,S:***

Its enantiomer is: ***S,R*** ← Exact opposite: *R* and *S* interchanged.

Its diastereomers are: ***R,R* and *S,S*** ← One designation remains the same, the other changes.

5.22 The enantiomer must have the exact opposite *R,S* designations. For diastereomers, at least one of the *R,S* designations is the same, but not all of them.

a. (2*R*,3*S*)-2,3-hexanediol and (2*R*,3*R*)-2,3-hexanediol
One changes; one remains the same:
diastereomers

b. (2*R*,3*R*)-2,3-hexanediol and (2*S*,3*S*)-2,3-hexanediol
Both *R*'s change to *S*'s:
enantiomers

c. (2*R*,3*S*,4*R*)-2,3,4-hexanetriol and (2*S*,3*R*,4*R*)-2,3,4-hexanetriol
Two change; one remains the same:
diastereomers

5.23 The enantiomer must have the exact opposite *R,S* designations. For diastereomers, at least one of the *R,S* designations is the same, but not all of them.

a. 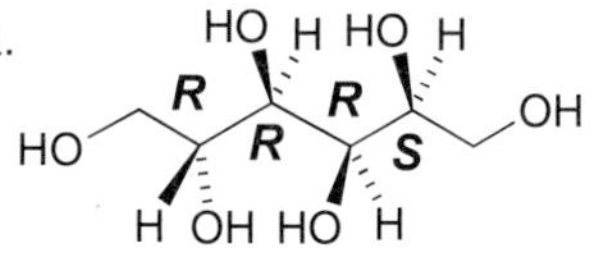
HO H HO H
R R
HO R S OH
H OH HO H

sorbitol

b. 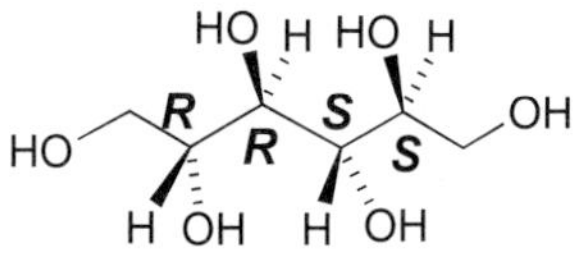
HO H HO H
R S
HO R S OH
H OH H OH

A

One changes; three remain the same.
diastereomer

c. 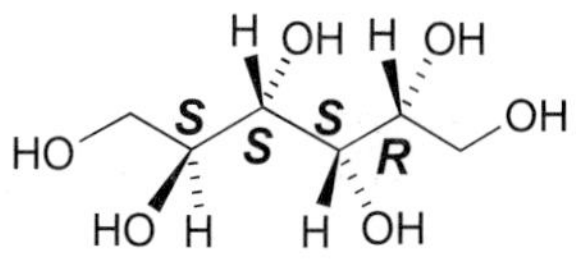
H OH H OH
S S
HO S R OH
HO H H OH

B

All stereogenic centers change.
enantiomers

5.24 Meso compounds generally have a plane of symmetry. They cannot have just one stereogenic center.

a. 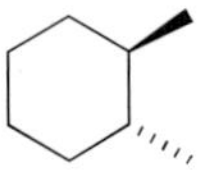

no plane of symmetry
not a meso compound

b. 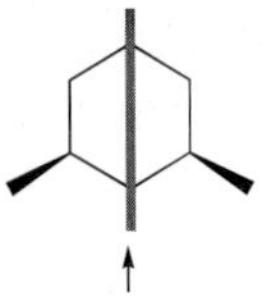

plane of symmetry
meso compound

c. 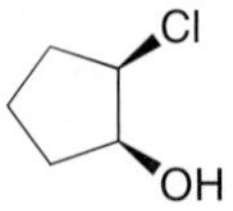

no plane of symmetry
not a meso compound

5.25

a. 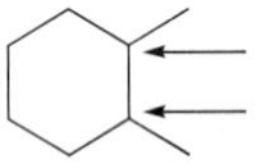

2 stereogenic centers =
4 stereoisomers maximum

Draw the cis and trans isomers:

cis

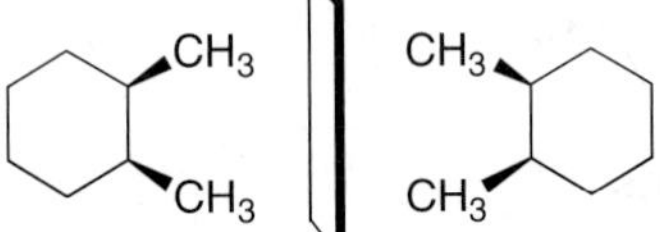

A identical

trans

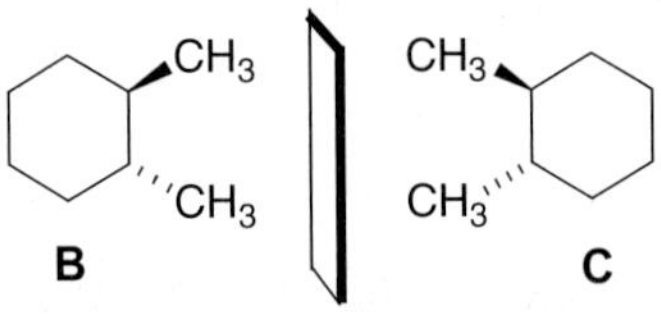

B **C**

Pair of enantiomers: **B** and **C.**
Pairs of diastereomers: **A** and **B, A** and **C.**

Only 3 stereoisomers exist.

b. 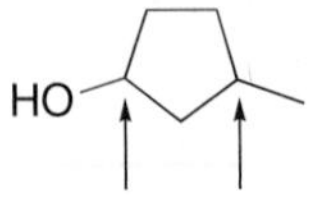

2 stereogenic centers =
4 stereoisomers maximum

Draw the cis and trans isomers:

cis

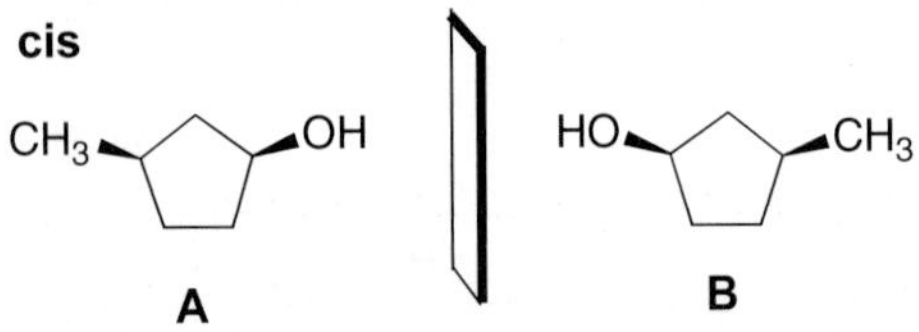

A **B**

trans

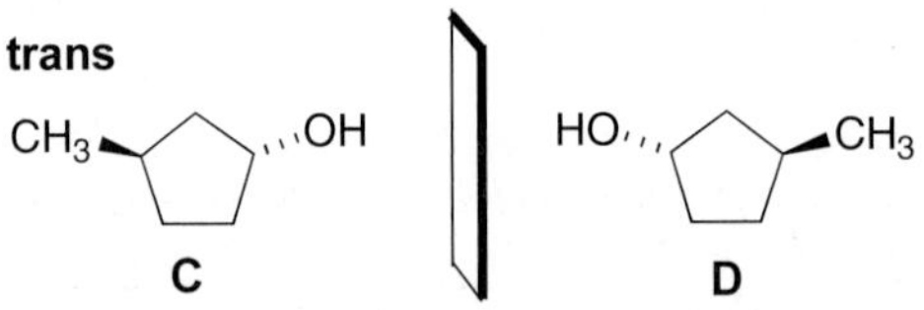

C **D**

Pairs of enantiomers: **A** and **B, C** and **D.**
Pairs of diastereomers: **A** and **C, A** and **D, B** and **C, B** and **D.**

All 4 stereoisomers exist.

c. 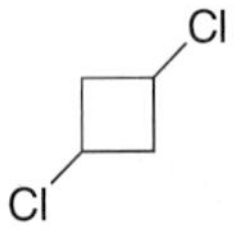

Draw the cis and trans isomers:

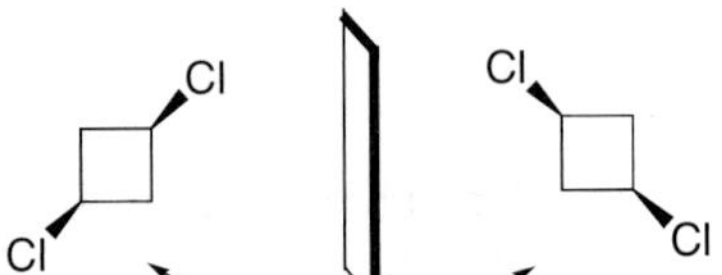

A identical

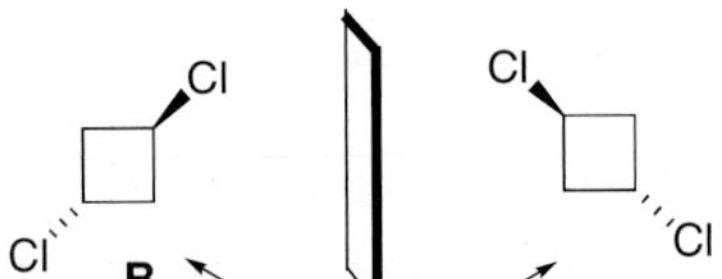

B identical

Pair of diastereomers: **A** and **B.**

Only 2 stereoisomers exist.

5.26 Four facts:

- **Enantiomers** are mirror image isomers.
- **Diastereomers** are stereoisomers that are not mirror images.
- **Constitutional isomers** have the same molecular formula but the atoms are bonded to different atoms.
- **Cis and trans isomers** are always diastereomers.

a.

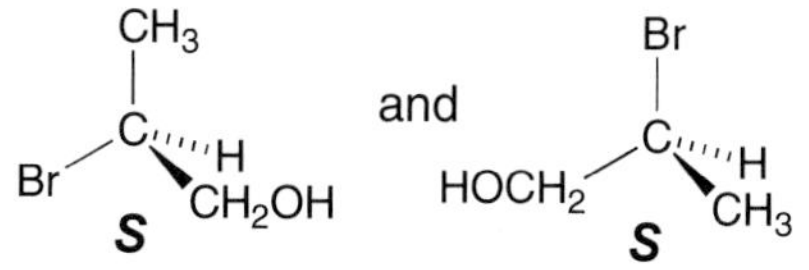

same molecular formula
same *R,S* designation:
identical

c.

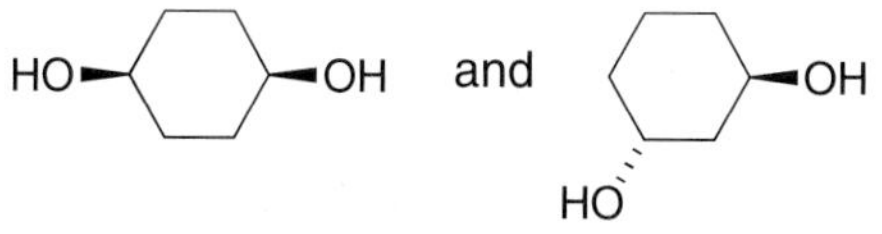

1,4- isomer
1,3-isomer
constitutional isomers

b.

same molecular formula,
opposite configuration at one
stereogenic center
enantiomers

d.

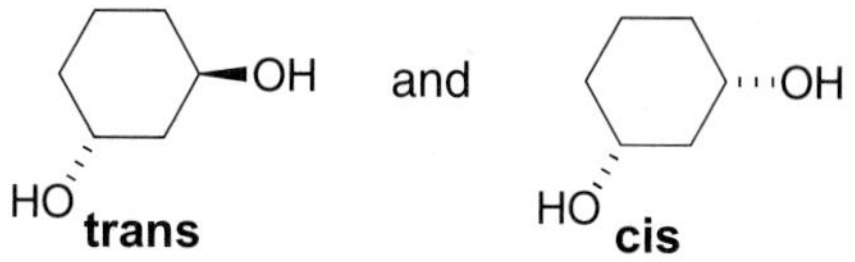

Both 1,3 isomers,
cis and trans:
diastereomers

5.27

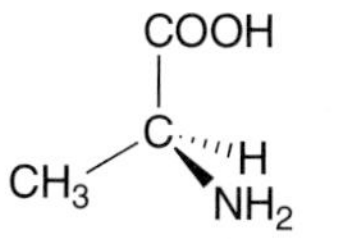

(*S*)-alanine
[α] = +8.5
mp = 297 °C

a. Mp = same as the *S* isomer.
b. The mp of a racemic mixture is often different from the melting point of the enantiomers.
c. –8.5, same as *S* but opposite sign
d. Zero. A racemic mixture is optically inactive.
e. Solution of pure (*S*)-alanine: **optically active**
Equal mixture of (*R*)- and (*S*)-alanine: **optically inactive**
75% (*S*)- and 25% (*R*)-alanine: **optically active**

5.28

$$[\alpha] = \frac{\alpha}{l \times c}$$

α = observed rotation
l = length of tube (dm)
c = concentration (g/mL)

$$[\alpha] = \frac{10°}{1 \text{ dm} \times (1 \text{ g}/10 \text{ mL})}$$ **= +100 = specific rotation**

5.29 Enantiomeric excess = *ee* = % of one enantiomer – % of other enantiomer.

a. 95% – 5% = **90% ee**

b. 85% – 15% = **70% ee**

5.30

a. 90% *ee* means 90% excess of **A** and 10% racemic mixture of **A** and **B** (5% each); therefore, **95% A and 5% B.**
b. 99% *ee* means 99% excess of **A** and 1% racemic mixture of **A** and **B** (0.5% each); therefore, **99.5% A and 0.5% B.**
c. 60% *ee* means 60% excess of **A** and 40% racemic mixture of **A** and **B** (20% each); therefore, **80% A and 20% B.**

5.31

$$ee = \frac{[\alpha]\text{ mixture}}{[\alpha]\text{ pure enantiomer}} \times 100\%$$

a. $\frac{+10}{+24} \times 100\% = 42\%\ ee$

b. $\frac{[\alpha]\text{ solution}}{+24} \times 100\% = 80\%\ ee$

$[\alpha]$ solution = +19.2

5.32

a. $\frac{[\alpha]\text{ mixture}}{+3.8} \times 100\% = 60\%\ ee$

$[\alpha]$ mixture = +2.3

b. % one enantiomer – % other enantiomer = *ee*
80% – 20% = 60% *ee*

80% dextrorotatory (+) enantiomer
20% levorotatory (–) enantiomer

5.33 • **Enantiomers have the same physical properties** (mp, bp, solubility), and rotate the plane of polarized light to an equal extent, but in opposite directions.
• **Diastereomers have different physical properties.**
• **A racemic mixture is optically inactive.**

trans isomers **cis isomer**

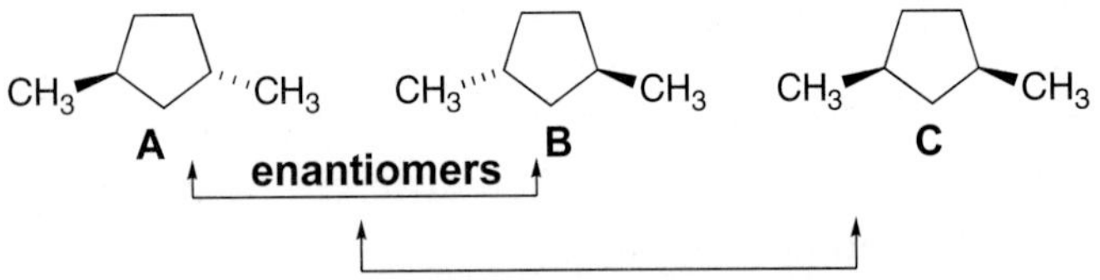

A and **B** are diastereomers of **C.**

a. The bp's of **A** and **B** are the same. The bp's of **A** and **C** are different.
b. Pure **A:** optically active
Pure **B:** optically active
Pure **C:** optically inactive
Equal mixture of **A** and **B:** optically inactive
Equal mixture of **A** and **C:** optically active
c. There would be two fractions: one containing **A** and **B** (optically inactive), and one containing **C** (optically inactive).

5.34

a, b.

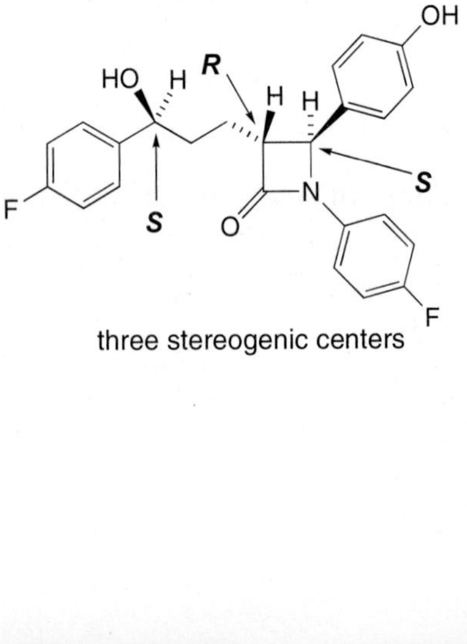

three stereogenic centers

5.35

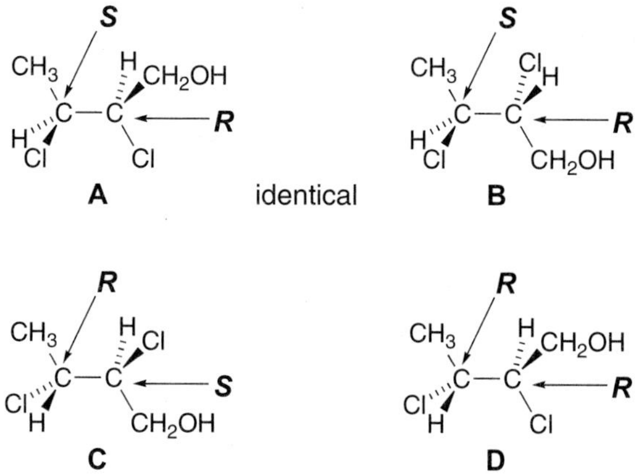

a. **A** and **B,** same *R,S* assignment, identical
b. **A** and **C,** opposite *R,S* assignment, enantiomers
c. **A** and **D,** one stereogenic center different, diastereomers
d. **C** and **D,** one stereogenic center different, diastereomers

5.36 Use the definitions from Answer 5.2.

a. 

same molecular formula C_4H_8O
different connectivity
constitutional isomers

c. 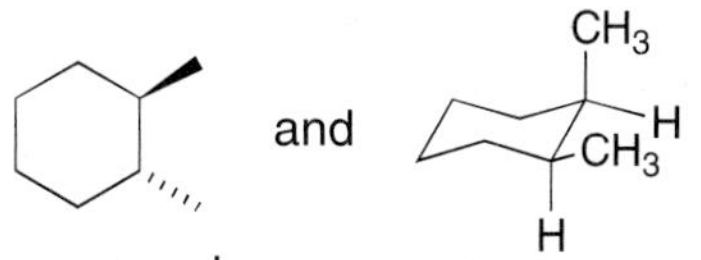

one up, one down **trans** — both up **cis**

Both compounds are 1,2-dimethylcyclohexane.
one cis, one trans = **stereoisomers**

b. 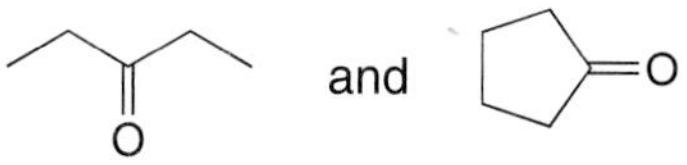

$C_5H_{10}O$ — C_5H_8O
different molecular formulas
not isomers

d. 

same molecular formula C_7H_{14}
different connectivity
constitutional isomers

5.37 Use the definitions from Answer 5.3.

a. 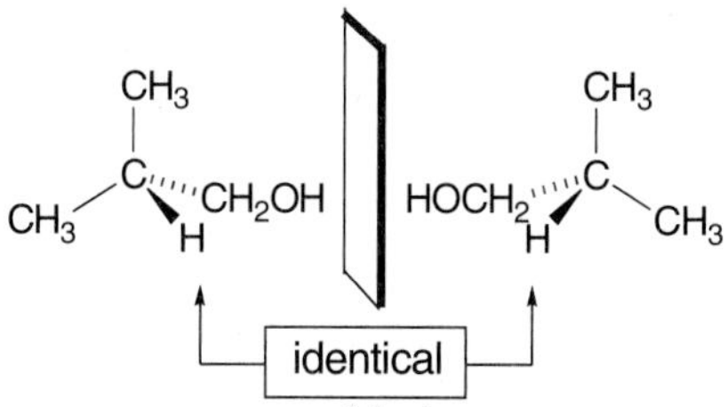

achiral

c. 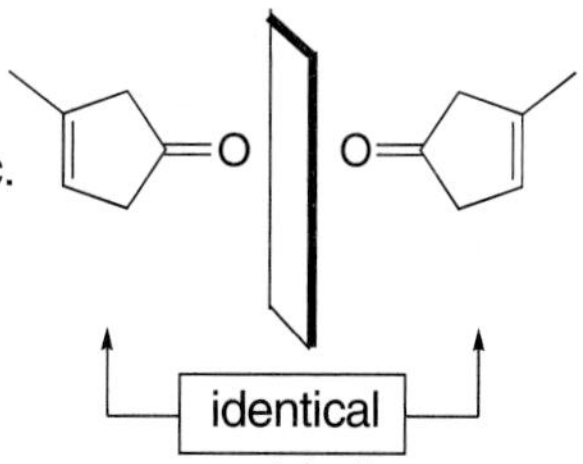

achiral

e. 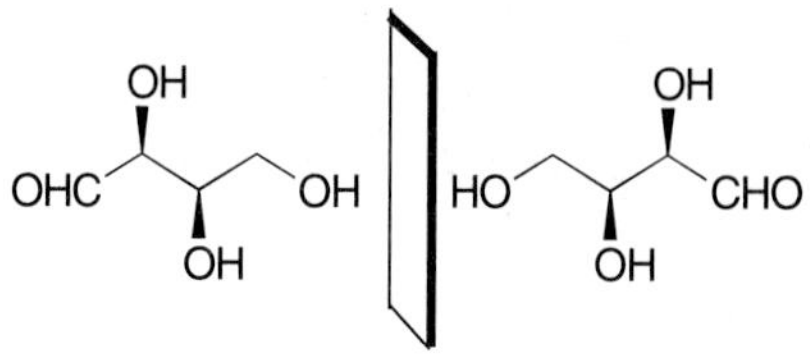

chiral

b. 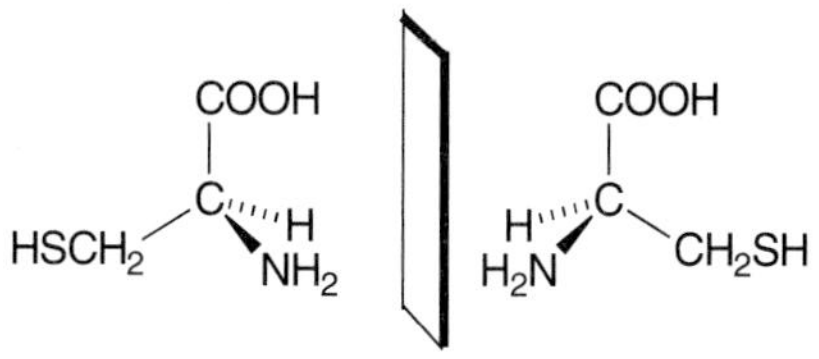

chiral

d. 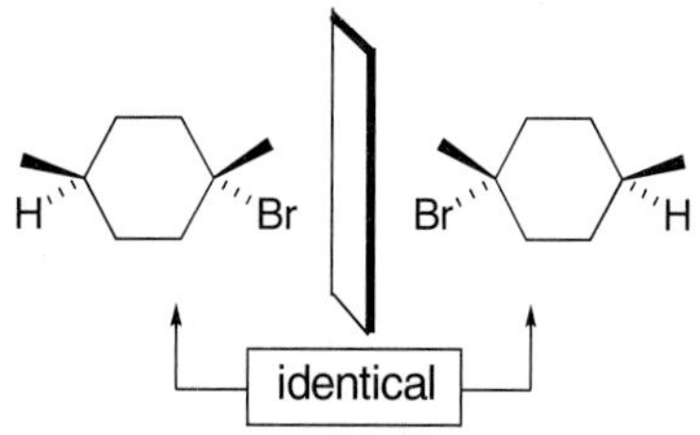

achiral

5.38

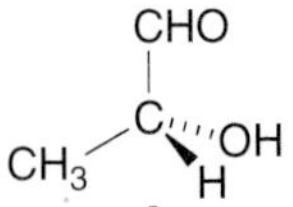
CHO
C
OH
CH3
H

A

R isomer

a. 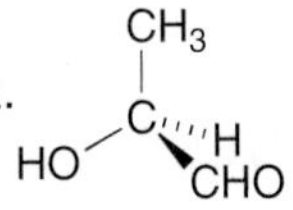
CH3
C
H
HO
CHO

S

enantiomer

b. 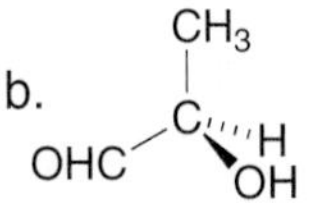
CH3
C
H
OHC
OH

R

identical

c. 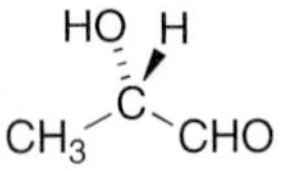
HO H
C
CH3
CHO

S

enantiomer

5.39 A plane of symmetry cuts the molecule into **two identical halves.**

a. 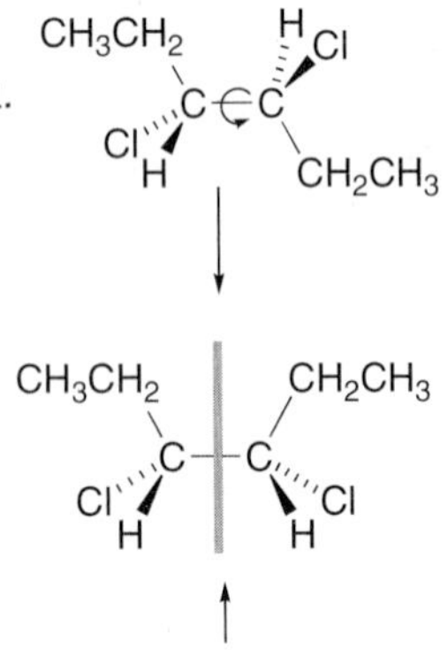
CH3CH2
H
Cl
C
C
Cl
H
CH2CH3
CH3CH2
CH2CH3
C
C
Cl
H
Cl
H

plane of symmetry

b. 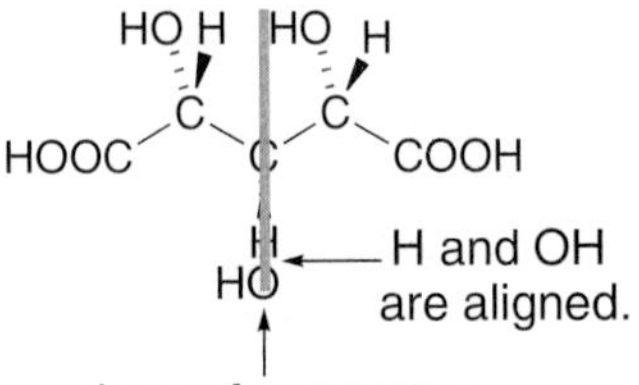
HO H
HO H
C
C
C
HOOC
COOH
H
HO
H and OH
are aligned.

plane of symmetry

c. 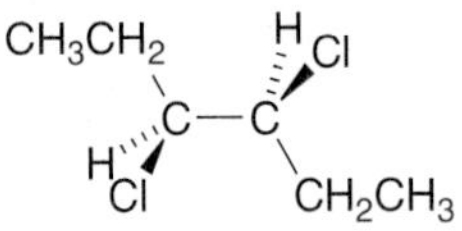
CH3CH2
H
Cl
C
C
H
Cl
CH2CH3

no plane of symmetry

d. 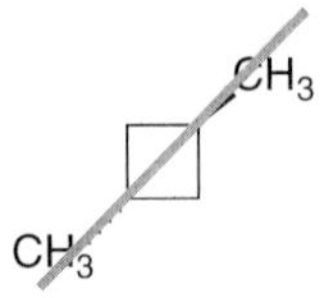
CH3
CH3

The plane of symmetry bisects the molecule.

e. 

no plane of symmetry

5.40 Use the directions from Answer 5.6 to locate the stereogenic centers.

a. $CH_3CH_2CH_2CH_2CH_2CH_3$

All C's have 2 or more H's.

0 stereogenic centers

b. 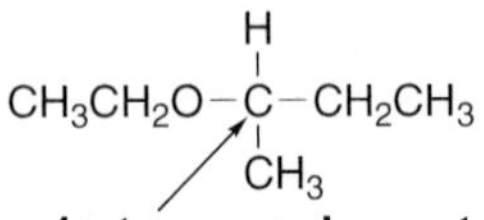
H
CH3CH2O
C
CH2CH3
CH3

1 stereogenic center

c. $(CH_3)_2CHCH(OH)CH(CH_3)_2$

0 stereogenic centers

d. 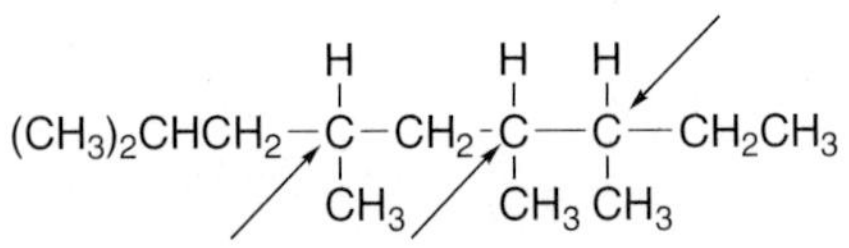
H
H
H
(CH3)2CHCH2
C
CH2
C
C
CH2CH3
CH3
CH3
CH3

3 stereogenic centers

e. 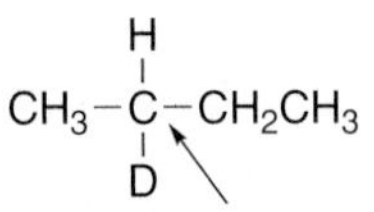
H
CH3
C
CH2CH3
D

bonded to 4 different groups

1 stereogenic center

f. 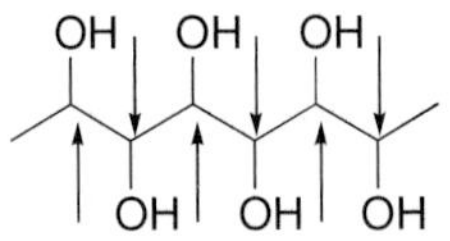
OH
OH
OH
OH
OH
OH

Each indicated C bonded to 4 different groups =

6 stereogenic centers

g. 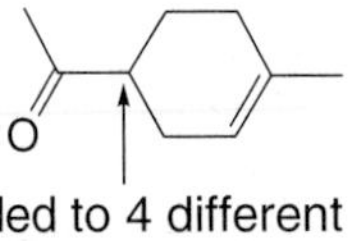
O

bonded to 4 different groups

1 stereogenic center

h. 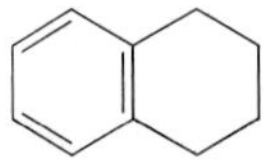

All C's have 2 or more H's or are sp^2 hybridized.

0 stereogenic centers

i. 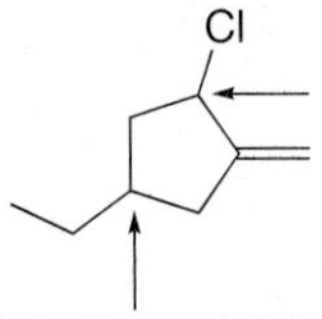
Cl

Each indicated C bonded to 4 different groups =

2 stereogenic centers

j.

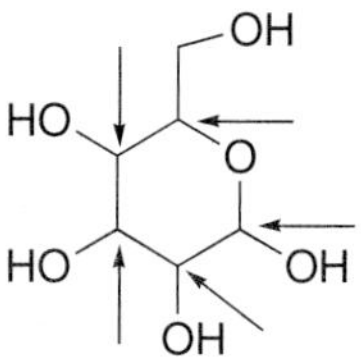

Each indicated C bonded to 4 different groups =
5 stereogenic centers

5.41 Stereogenic centers are circled.

Eight constitutional isomers:

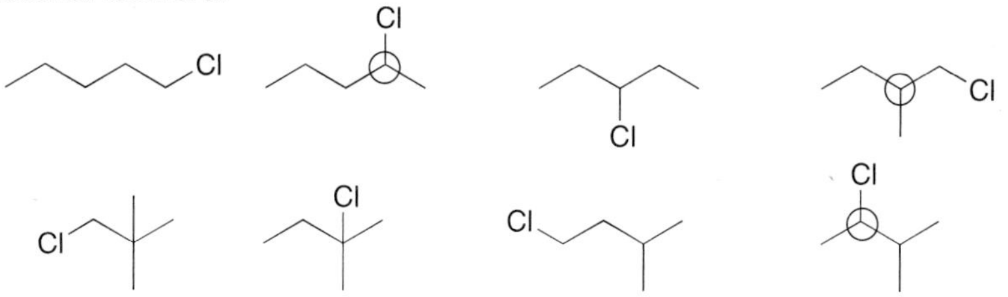

5.42

a.

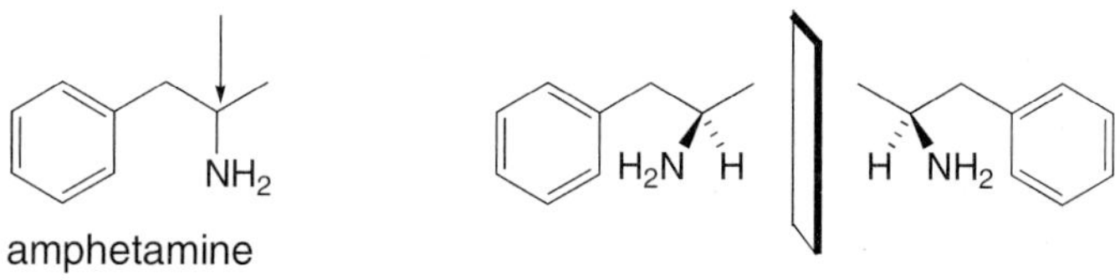

amphetamine

b.

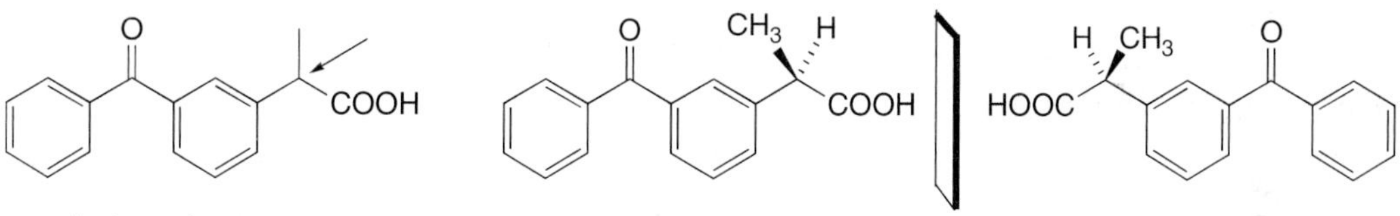

ketoprofen

5.43 Draw a molecule to fit each description.

a.

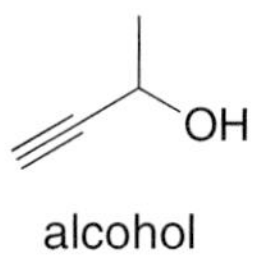

alcohol

b.

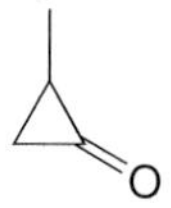

ketone

c.

cyclic ether

5.44 Assign priority based on the rules in Answer 5.11.

a. $-CD_3$, $-CH_3$

↑ D higher mass than H
higher priority

b. $-CH(CH_3)_2$, $-CH_2OH$

↑ C bonded to O
higher priority

c. $-CH_2Cl$, $-CH_2CH_2CH_2Br$

↑ C bonded to Cl
higher priority

d. $-CH_2NH_2$, $-NHCH_3$

↑ higher atomic number
higher priority

5.45 Assign priority based on the rules in Answer 5.11.

a. $-F > -OH > -NH_2 > -CH_3$

b. $-(CH_2)_3CH_3 > -CH_2CH_2CH_3 > -CH_2CH_3 > -CH_3$

c. $-NH_2 > -CH_2NHCH_3 > -CH_2NH_2 > -CH_3$

d. $-COOH > -CHO > -CH_2OH > -H$

e. $-Cl > -SH > -OH > -CH_3$

f. $-C{\equiv}CH > -CH{=}CH_2 > -CH(CH_3)_2 > -CH_2CH_3$

5.46 Use the rules in Answer 5.13 to assign *R* or *S* to each stereogenic center.

a.

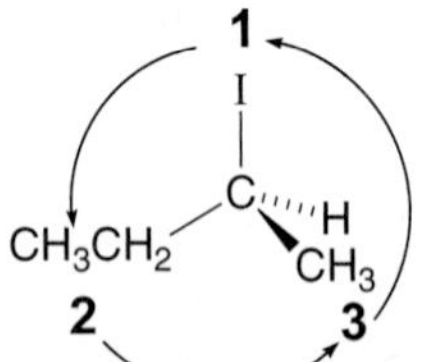

counterclockwise
***S* isomer**

c.

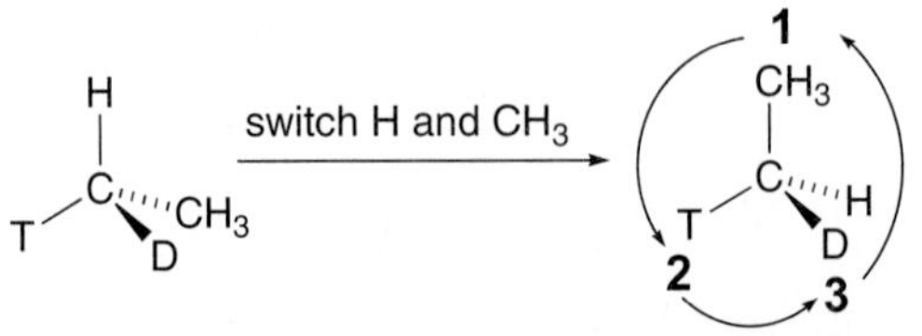

counterclockwise
It looks like an *S* isomer, but we must reverse the answer, *S* to *R*.
***R* isomer**

b.

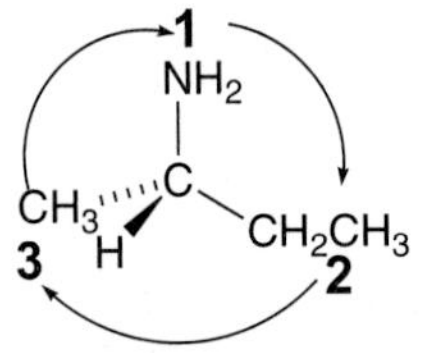

clockwise, but H in front
***S* isomer**

d.

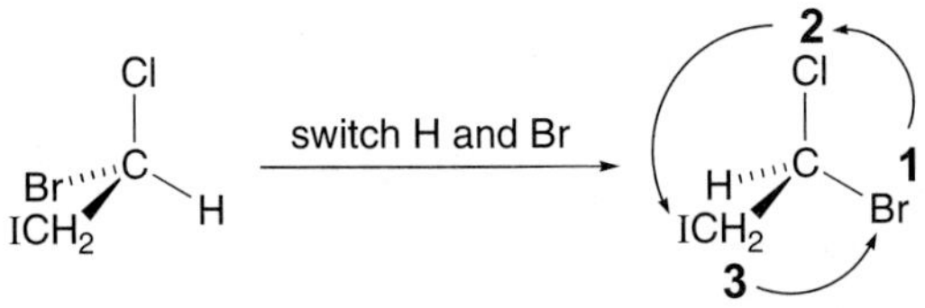

counterclockwise
It looks like an *S* isomer, but we must reverse the answer, *S* to *R*.
***R* isomer**

e.

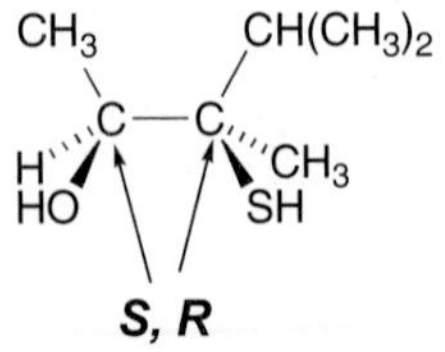

f.

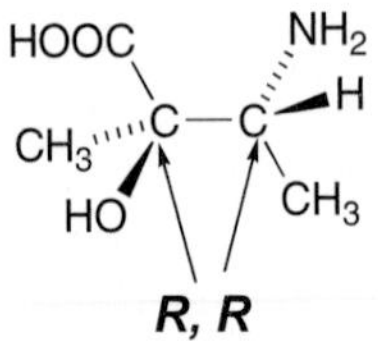

g.

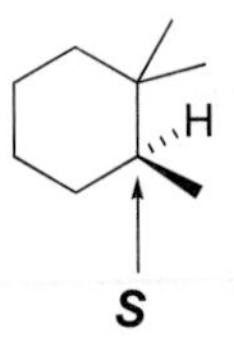

h.

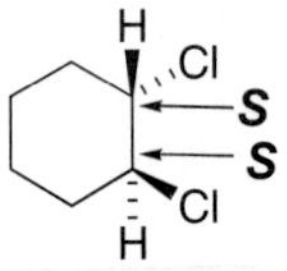

5.47

a. (3*R*)-3-methylhexane

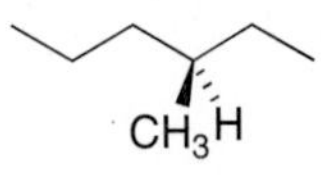

b. (4*R*,5*S*)-4,5-diethyloctane

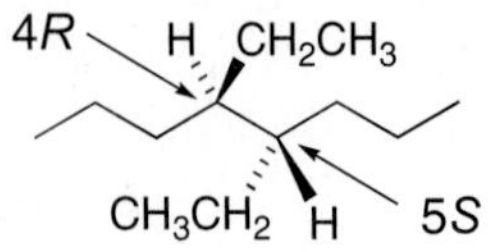

c. (3*R*,5*S*,6*R*)-5-ethyl-3,6-dimethylnonane

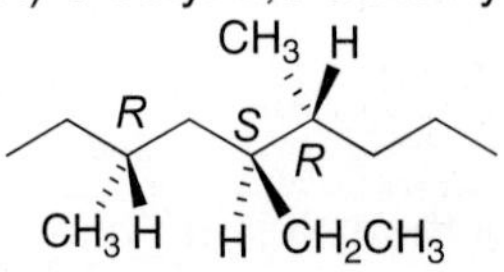

d. (3*S*,6*S*)-6-isopropyl-3-methyldecane

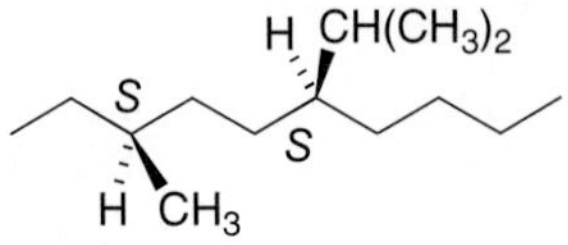

5.48

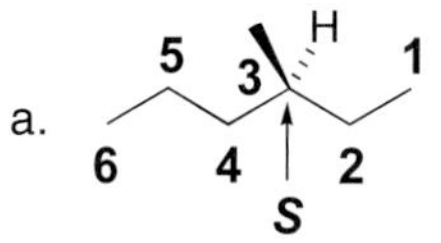

(3*S*)-3-methylhexane

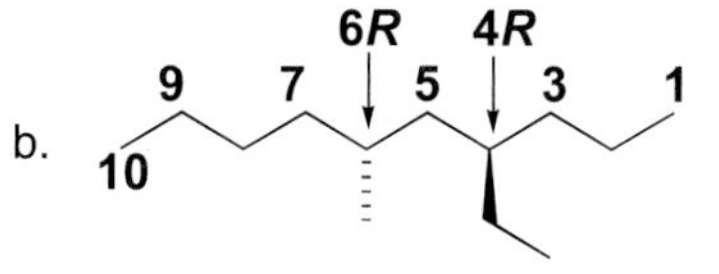

(4*R*,6*R*)-4-ethyl-6-methyldecane

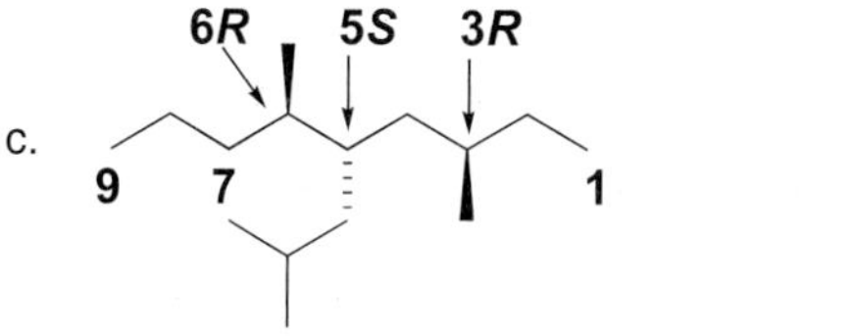

(3*R*,5*S*,6*R*)-5-isobutyl-3,6-dimethylnonane

5.49 Two enantiomers of the amino acid leucine.

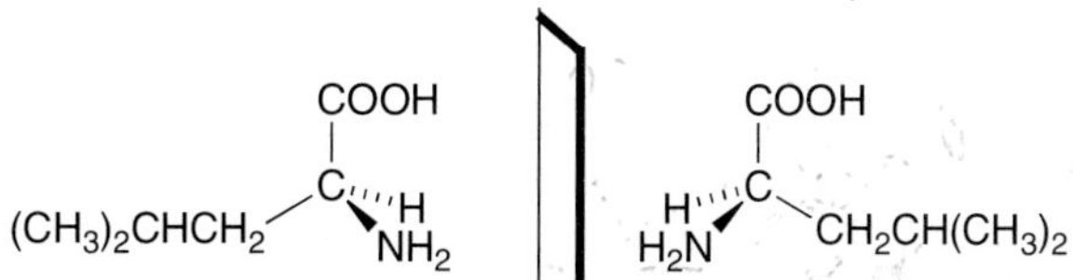

S isomer
naturally occurring

R isomer

5.50

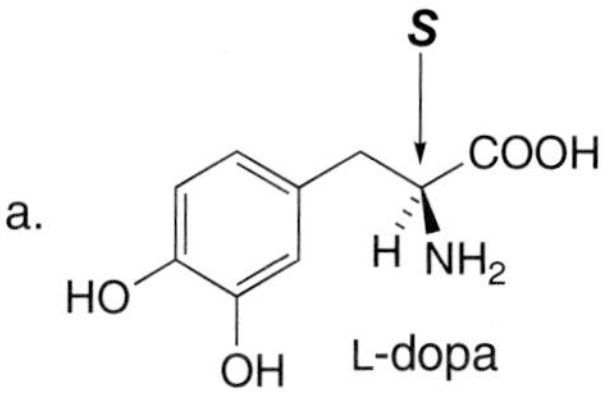

L-dopa

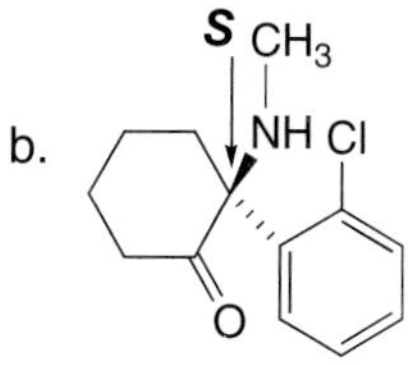

ketamine

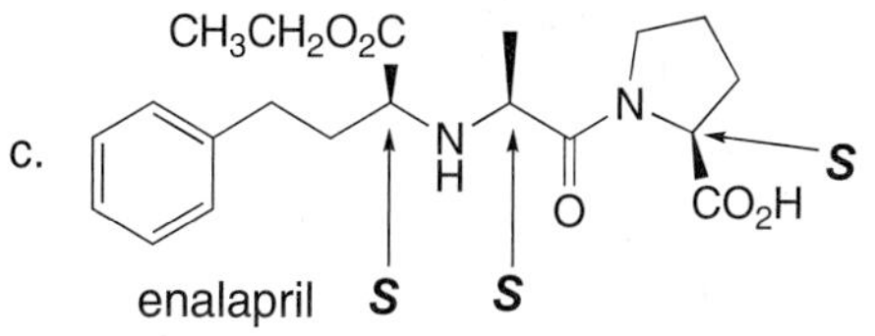

enalapril

5.51

a. 1*R*,2*S*

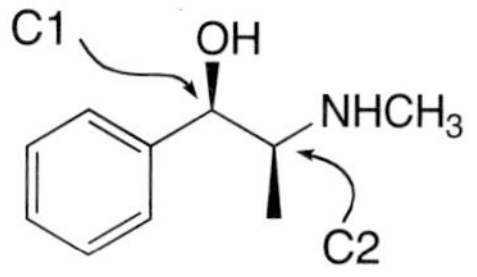

ephedrine

d.

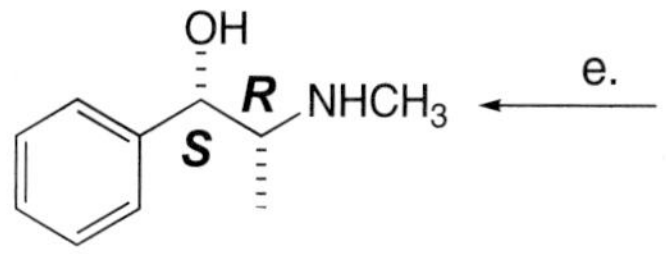

e.

enantiomer of (–)-ephedrine

b. 1*S*,2*S*

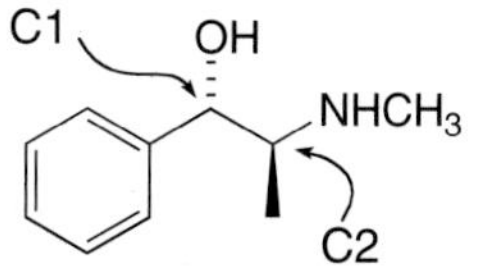

pseudoephedrine

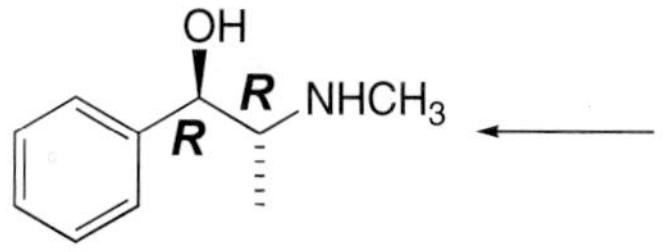

diastereomer of (–)-ephedrine

c. Ephedrine and pseudoephedrine are diastereomers (one stereogenic center is the same; one is different).

5.52

a.

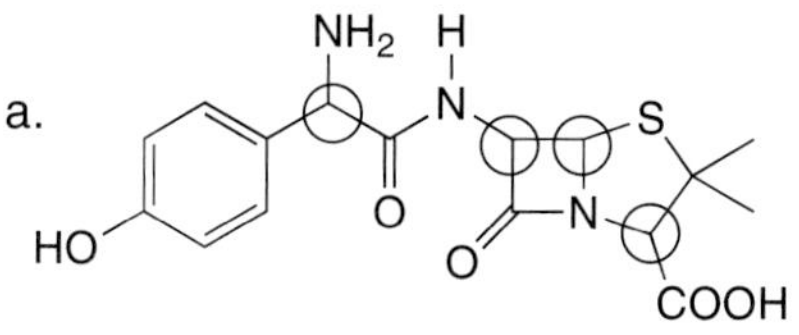

amoxicillin

b.

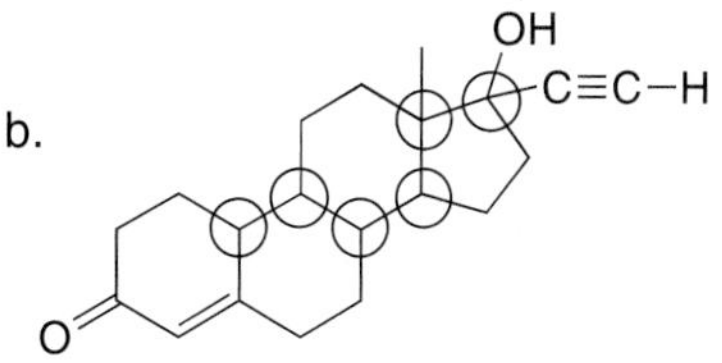

norethindrone

c.

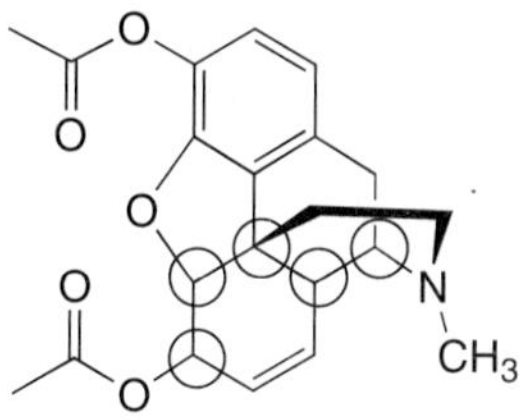

heroin

5.53

a. $CH_3CH(OH)CH(OH)CH_2CH_3$

2 stereogenic centers
$2^2 = 4$ possible stereoisomers

b. $CH_3CH_2CH_2CH(CH_3)_2$

0 stereogenic centers

c. 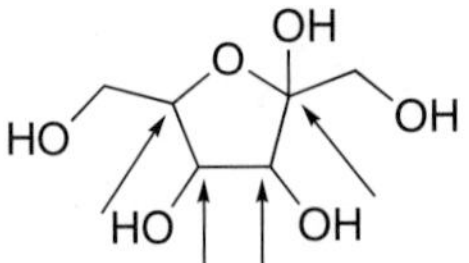

HO
O
OH
OH
HO
OH

4 stereogenic centers
$2^4 = 16$ possible stereoisomers

5.54

a. $CH_3CH(OH)CH(OH)CH_2CH_3$

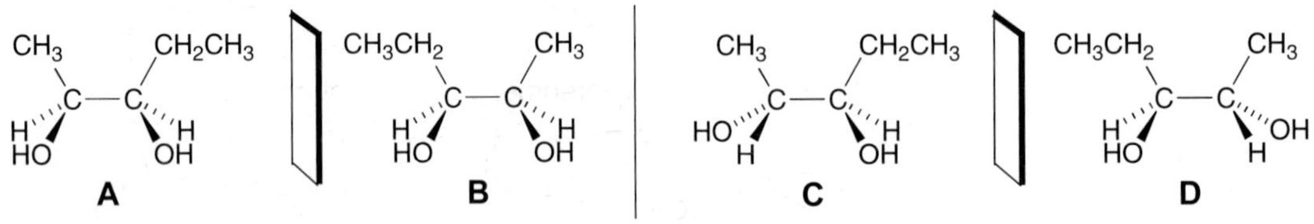

A
B
C
D

Pairs of enantiomers: **A** and **B, C** and **D.**
Pairs of diastereomers: **A** and **C, A** and **D, B** and **C, B** and **D.**

b. $CH_3CH(OH)CH_2CH_2CH(OH)CH_3$

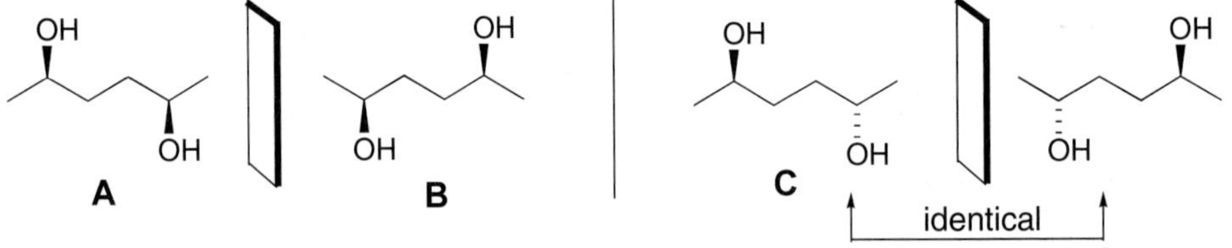

A
B
C
identical

meso compound

Pair of enantiomers: **A** and **B.**
Pairs of diastereomers: **A** and **C, B** and **C.**

c. $CH_3CH(Cl)CH_2CH(Br)CH_3$

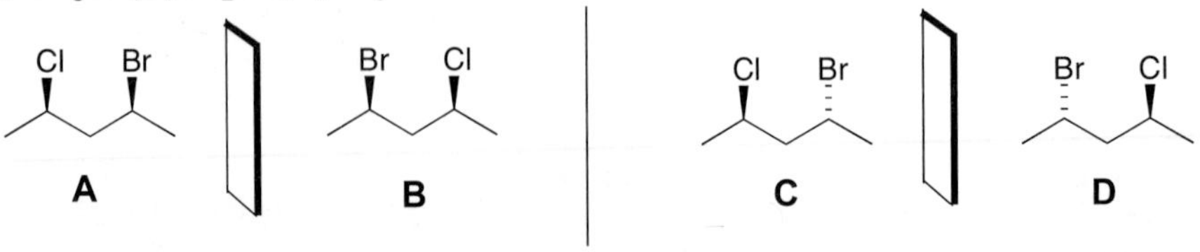

A
B
C
D

Pairs of enantiomers: **A** and **B, C** and **D.**
Pairs of diastereomers: **A** and **C, A** and **D, B** and **C, B** and **D.**

d. $CH_3CH(Br)CH(Br)CH(Br)CH_3$

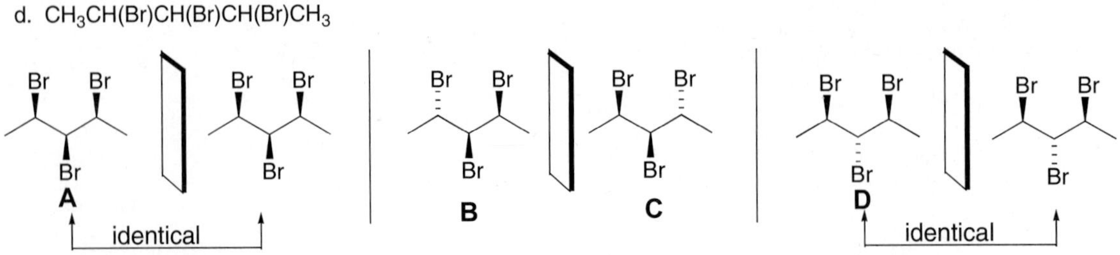

A
identical
B
C
D
identical

meso compound **meso compound**

Pair of enantiomers: **B** and **C.**
Pairs of diastereomers: **A** and **B, A** and **C, A** and **D, B** and **D, C** and **D.**

5.55

a.

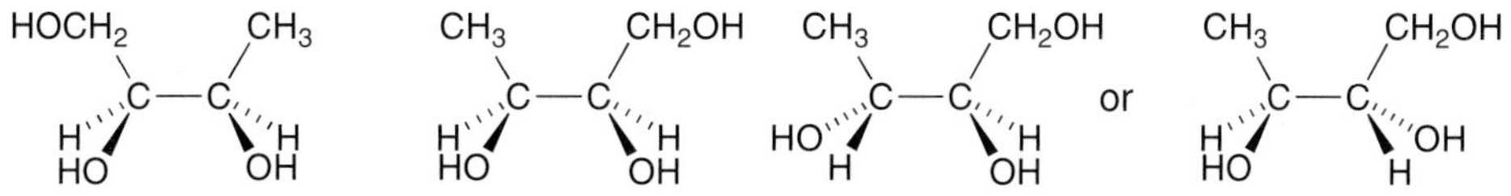

enantiomer diastereomer diastereomer

b.

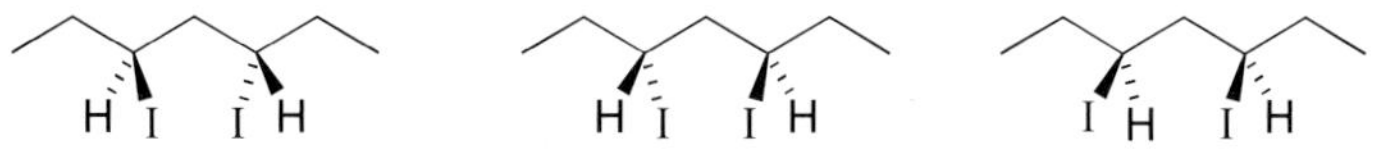

enantiomer diastereomer

c.

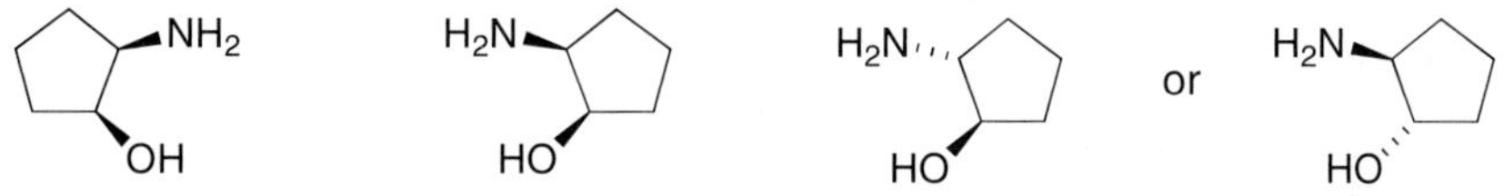

enantiomer diastereomer diastereomer

d.

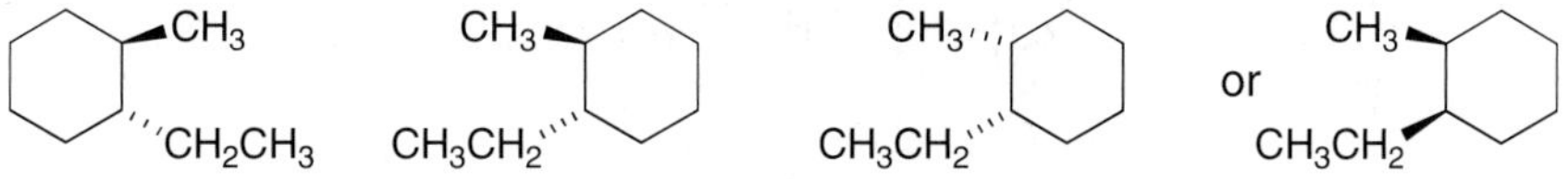

enantiomer diastereomer diastereomer

5.56

a.

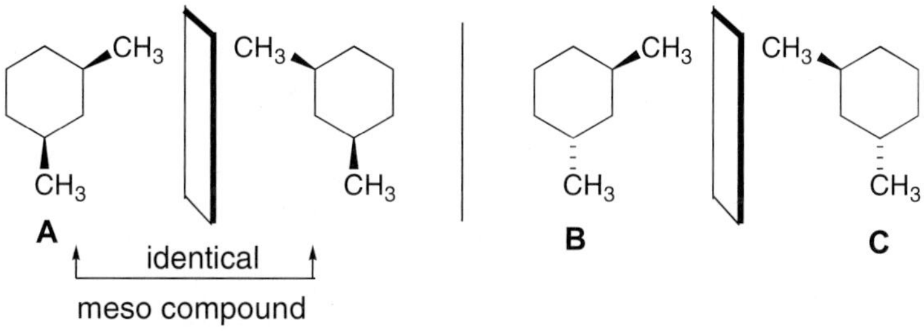

Pair of enantiomers: **B** and **C.**
Pairs of diastereomers: **A** and **B, A** and **C.**

b.

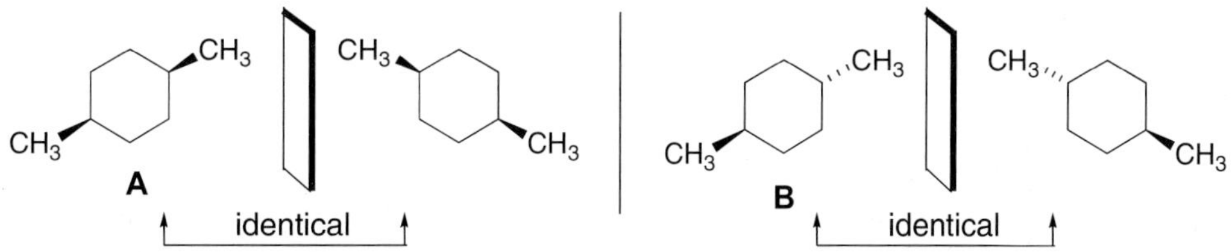

Pair of diastereomers: **A** and **B.**
Meso compounds: **A** and **B.**

c.

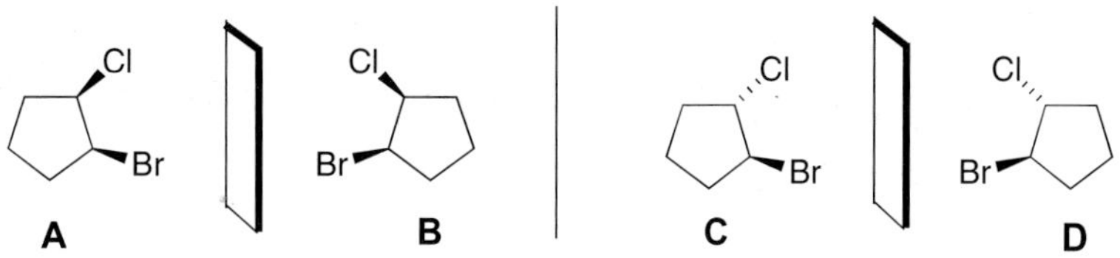

Pairs of enantiomers: **A** and **B, C** and **D.**
Pairs of diastereomers: **A** and **C, A** and **D, B** and **C, B** and **D.**

5.57

achiral achiral chiral chiral achiral achiral

5.58 Explain each statement.

a. 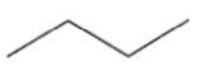

All molecules have a mirror image, but only chiral molecules have enantiomers. **A** is not chiral, and therefore, does not have an enantiomer.

b. 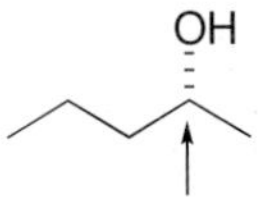

B has one stereogenic center, and therefore, has an enantiomer. Only compounds with two or more stereogenic centers have diastereomers.

c. 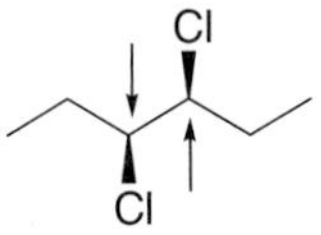

C is chiral and has two stereogenic centers, and therefore, has both an enantiomer and a diastereomer.

d. 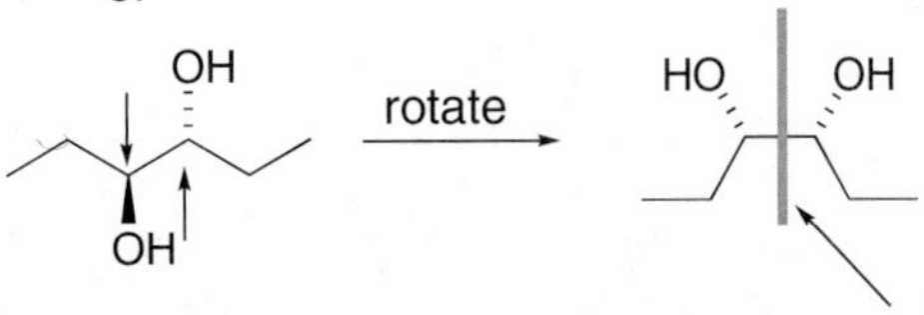

D has two stereogenic centers, but is a meso compound. Therefore, it has a diastereomer, but no enantiomer since it is achiral.

plane of symmetry

e. 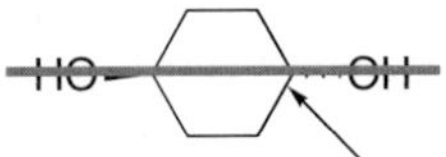

E has two stereogenic centers, but is a meso compound. Therefore, it has a diastereomer, but no enantiomer since it is achiral.

plane of symmetry

5.59

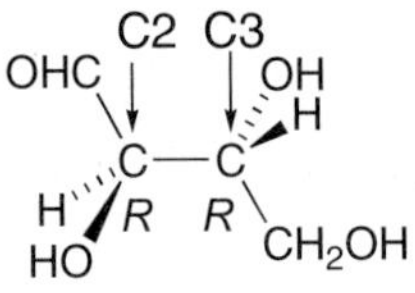

D-erythrose

2R,3R

a. 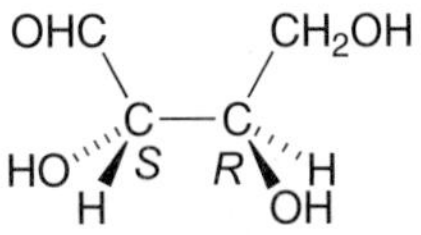

2S,3R
diastereomer

b. 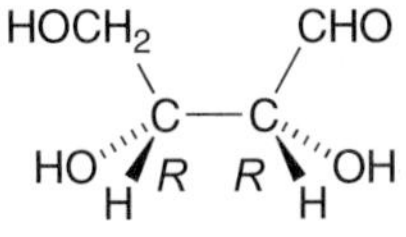

2R,3R
identical

c. 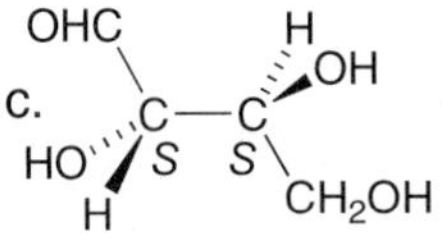

2S,3S
enantiomer

d. 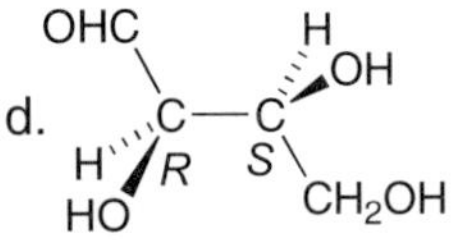

2R,3S
diastereomer

5.60 Re-draw each Newman projection and determine the *R,S* configuration. Then determine how the molecules are related.

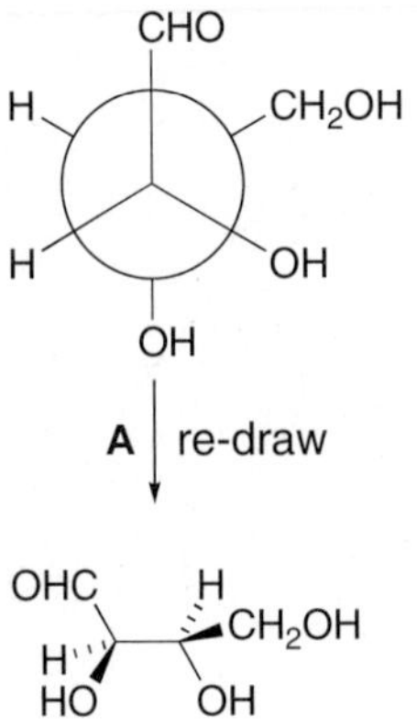

R,R

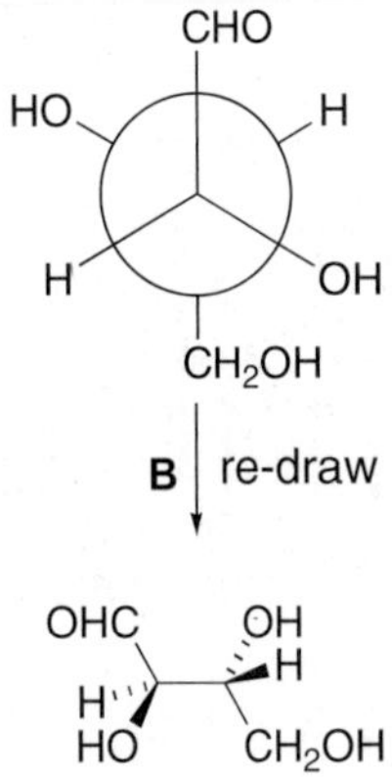

R,R

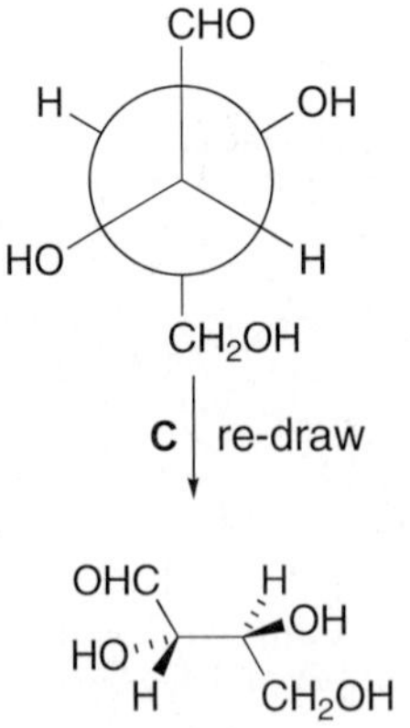

S,S

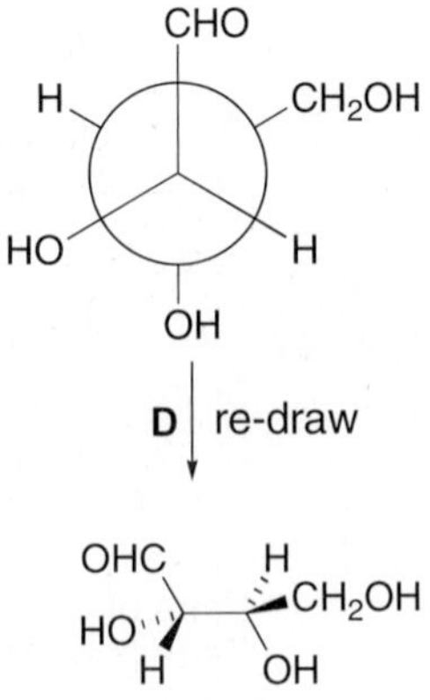

S,R

a. **A** and **B** are identical.
b. **A** and **C** are enantiomers.
c. **A** and **D** are diastereomers.
d. **C** and **D** are diastereomers.

5.61

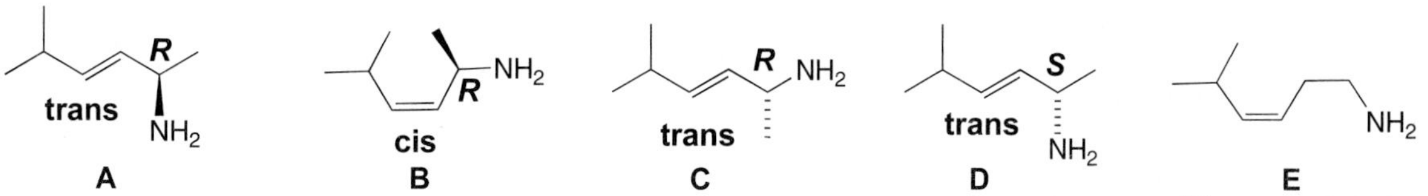

A **B** **C** **D** **E**

NH_2 group is in a different location.

A (trans, *R*) and **B** (cis, *R*) are diastereomers.
A (trans, *R*) and **C** (trans, *R*) are identical molecules.
A (trans, *R*) and **D** (trans, *S*) are enantiomers.
A (trans, *R*) and **E** are constitutional isomers.

5.62

a. 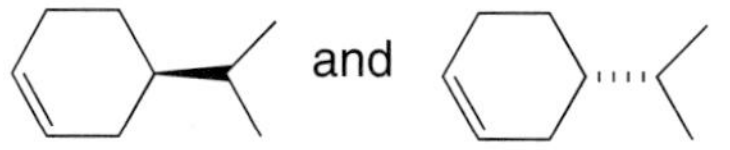

enantiomers

b. 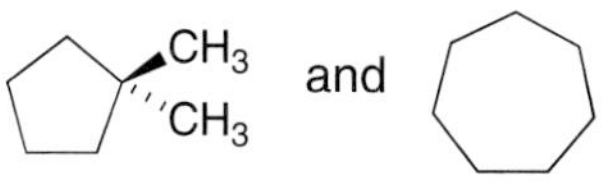

same molecular formula
different connectivity
constitutional isomers

c. 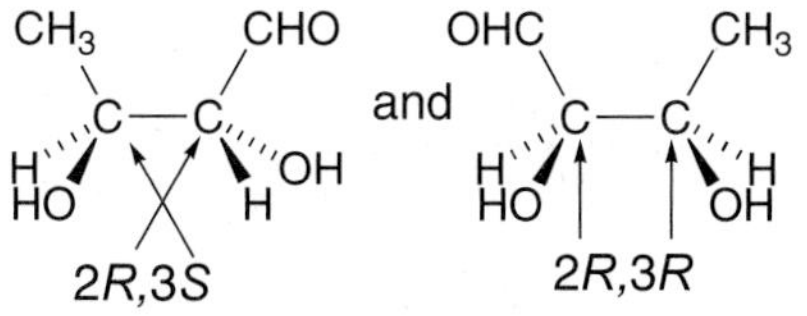

one different configuration
diastereomers

d. 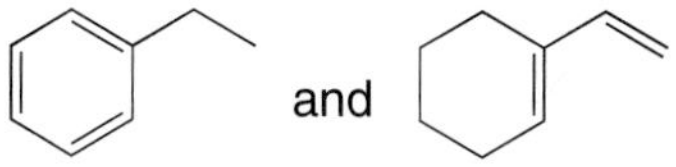

different molecular formulas
not isomers

e. 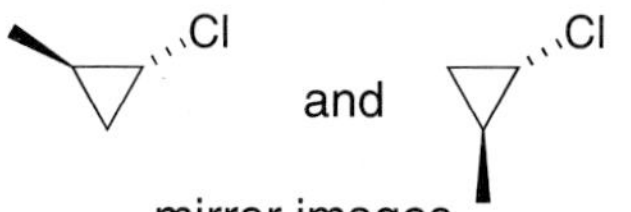

mirror images
not superimposable
enantiomers

f. 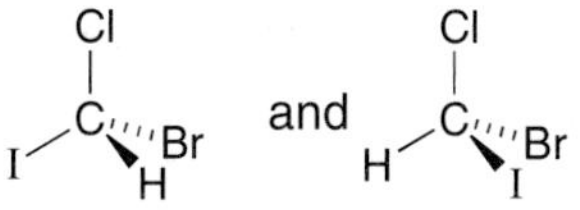

enantiomers

g. 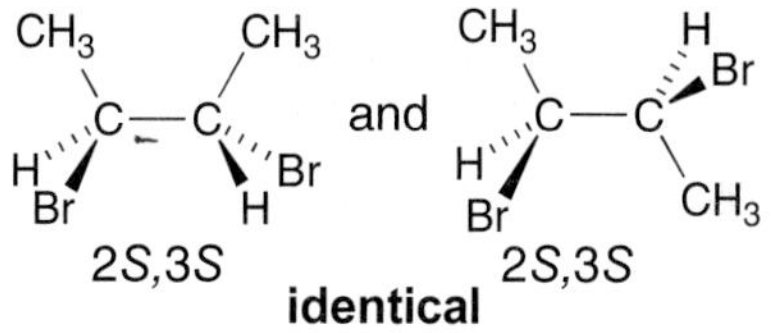

identical

h. 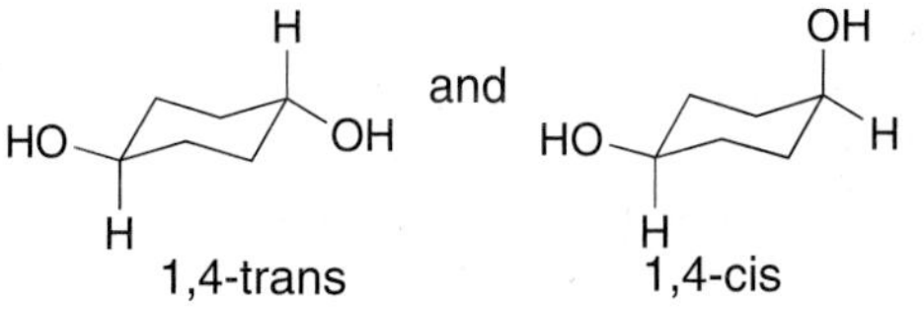

diastereomers

i. 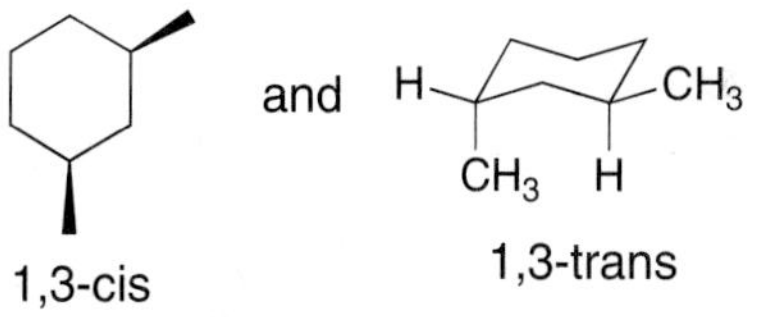

diastereomers

j. 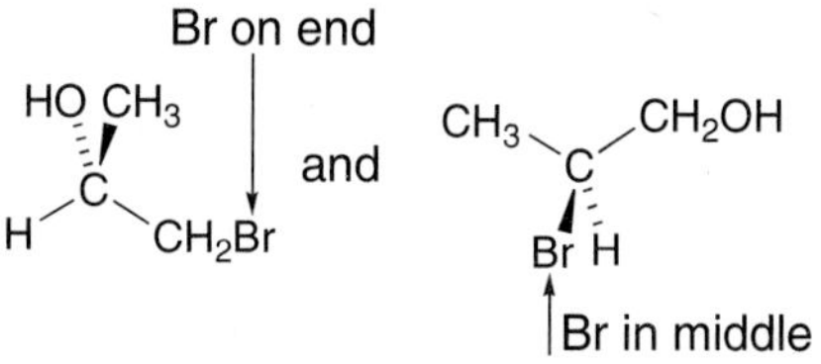

different connectivity
constitutional isomers

5.63

a. **A** and **B** are constitutional isomers.
A and **C** are constitutional isomers.
B and **C** are diastereomers (cis and trans).
C and **D** are enantiomers.

b.

plane of symmetry

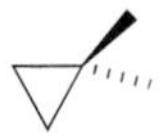

A

A has two planes of symmetry.
achiral

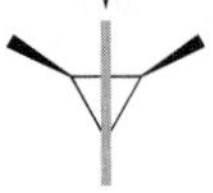

B

achiral

C

chiral

D

chiral

mirror images and not superimposable
enantiomers

c. Alone, **C** and **D** would be optically active.
d. **A** and **B** have a plane of symmetry.
e. **A** and **B** have different boiling points.
B and **C** have different boiling points.
C and **D** have the same boiling point.
f. **B** is a meso compound.
g. An equal mixture of **C** and **D** is optically inactive because it is a racemic mixture.
An equal mixture of **B** and **C** would be optically active.

5.64

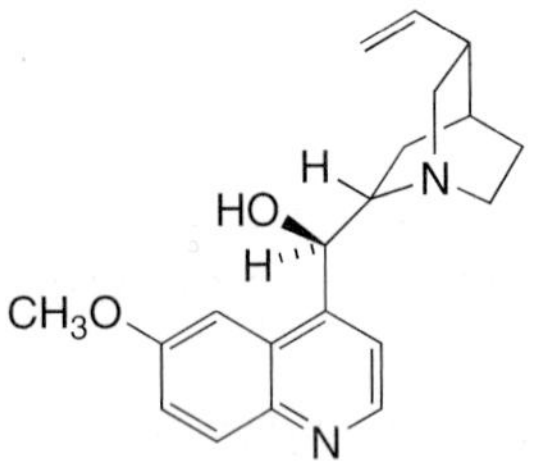

quinine

$$ee = \frac{[\alpha] \text{ mixture}}{[\alpha] \text{ pure enantiomer}} \times 100\%$$

quinine = **A**
quinine's enantiomer = **B**

a.

$$\frac{-50}{-165} \times 100\% = 30\%\ ee$$

b. 30% *ee* = 30% excess one compound (**A**)
remaining 70% = mixture of 2 compounds (35% each **A** and **B**)
Amount of **A** = 30 + 35 = **65%**
Amount of **B** = **35%**

$$\frac{-83}{-165} \times 100\% = 50\%\ ee$$

50% *ee* = 50% excess one compound (**A**)
remaining 50% = mixture of 2 compounds (25% each **A** and **B**)
Amount of **A** = 50 + 25 = **75%**
Amount of **B** = **25%**

$$\frac{-120}{-165} \times 100\% = 73\%\ ee$$

73% *ee* = 73% excess of one compound (**A**)
remaining 27% = mixture of 2 compounds (13.5% each **A** and **B**)
Amount of **A** = 73 + 13.5 = **86.5%**
Amount of **B** = **13.5%**

c. $[\alpha] = +165$
d. 80% – 20% = 60% *ee*

e. $$60\% = \frac{[\alpha] \text{ mixture}}{-165} \times 100\%$$

$[\alpha]$ mixture = –99

5.65

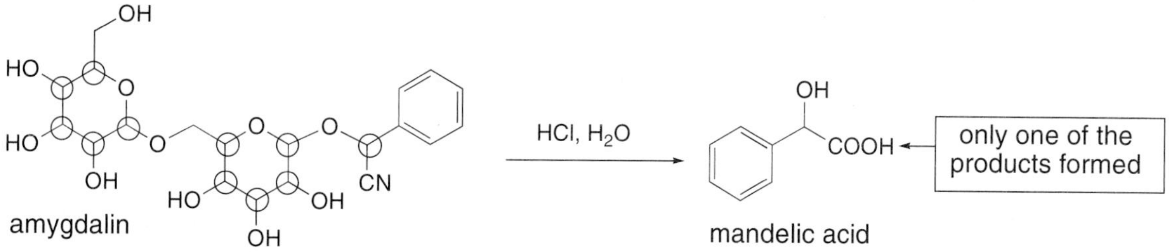

amygdalin　　　　mandelic acid

a. The 11 stereogenic centers are circled. Maximum number of stereoisomers = 2^{11} = 2048

b. Enantiomers of mandelic acid:

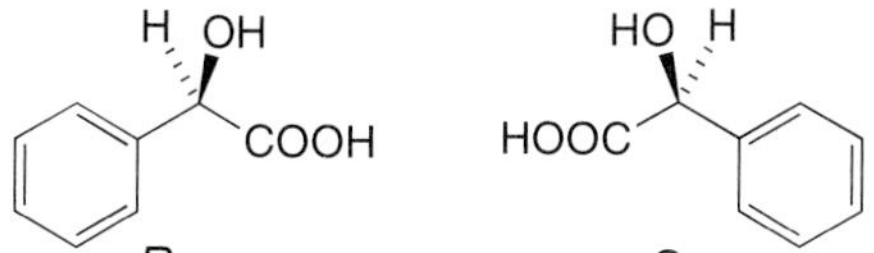

R　　　　*S*

c. 60% – 40% = 20% *ee*
20% = [α] mixture/–154 x 100%
[α] mixture = –31

d. $ee = \dfrac{+50}{+154} \times 100\% = 32\%\ ee$

[α] for (*S*)-mandelic acid = +154

32% excess of the *S* enantiomer
68% of racemic *R* and *S* = 34% *S* and 34% *R*

S enantiomer: 32% + 34% = 66%
R enantiomer = 34%

5.66

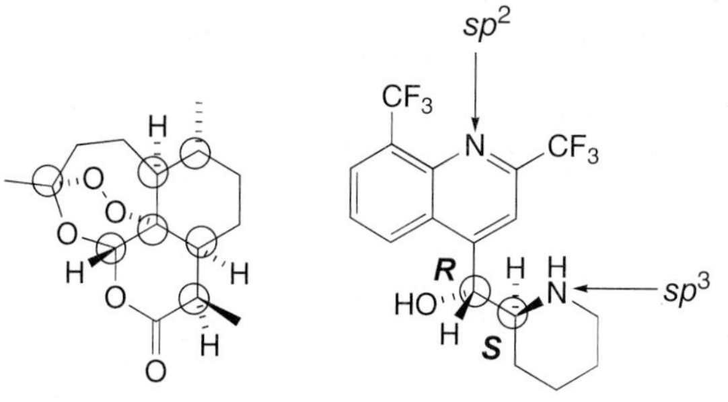

artemisinin　　　　mefloquine

a. Each stereogenic center is circled.
b. The stereogenic centers in mefloquine are labeled.
c. Artemisinin has seven stereogenic centers.
$2^n = 2^7 = 128$ possible stereoisomers
d. One N atom in mefloquine is sp^2 and one is sp^3.
e. Two molecules of artemisinin cannot intermolecularly H-bond because there are no O–H or N–H bonds.

f.

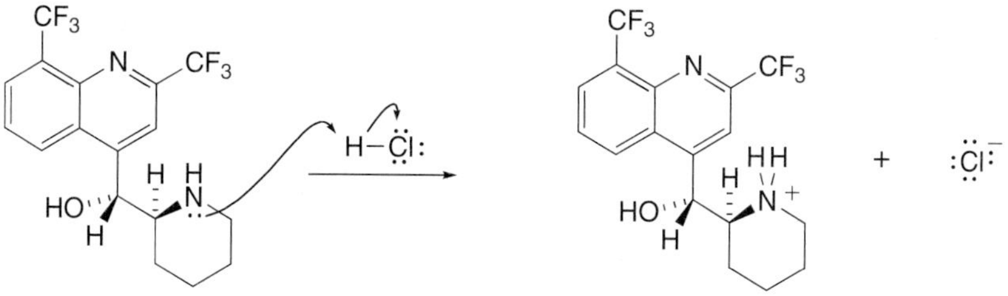

5.67

a. Each stereogenic center is circled.

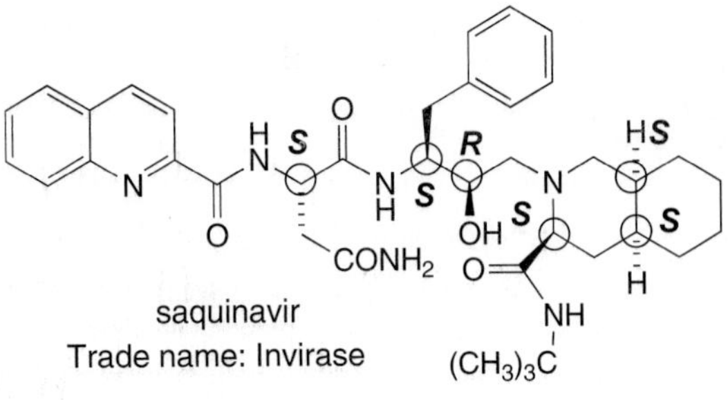

S
R
S
S
HS
S
S
CONH$_2$
OH
NH
(CH$_3$)$_3$C

saquinavir
Trade name: Invirase

c. diastereomer

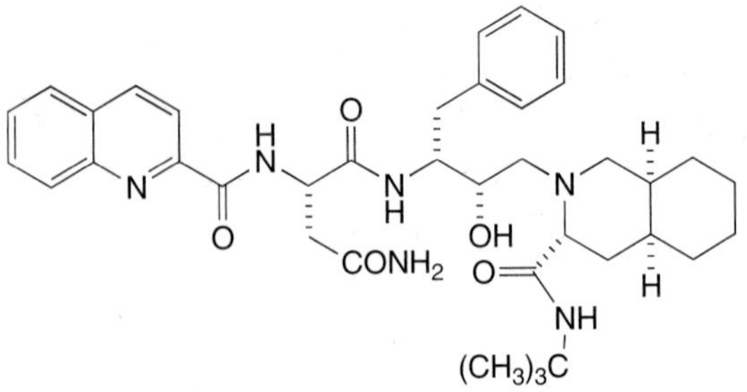

CONH$_2$
OH
NH
(CH$_3$)$_3$C

b. enantiomer

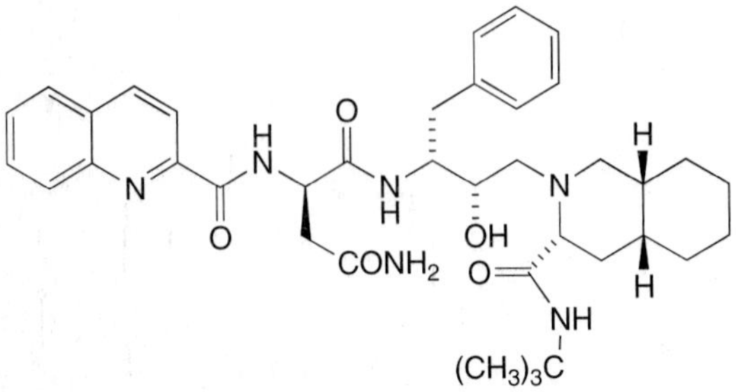

CONH$_2$
OH
NH
(CH$_3$)$_3$C

d. constitutional isomer

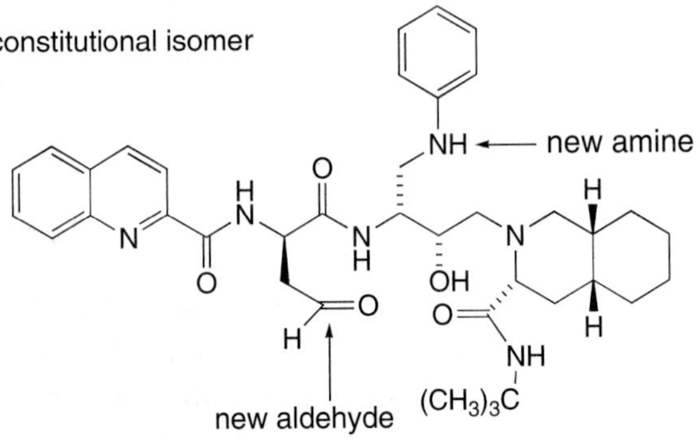

new amine
new aldehyde
OH
NH
(CH$_3$)$_3$C

5.68 Allenes contain an *sp* hybridized carbon atom doubly bonded to two other carbons. This makes the double bonds of an allene perpendicular to each other. When each end of the allene has two like substituents, the allene contains two planes of symmetry and it is achiral. When each end of the allene has two different groups, the allene has no plane of symmetry and it becomes chiral.

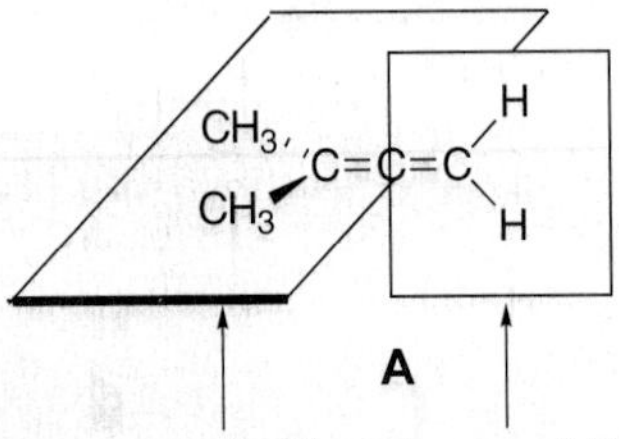

CH$_3$
CH$_3$
C=C=C
H
H

A

These two substituents are at 90° to these two substituents.
Allene **A** contains two planes of symmetry, making it **achiral.**

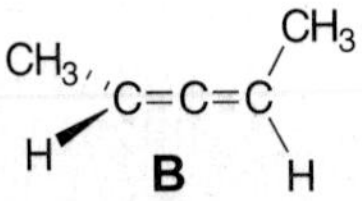

CH$_3$
CH$_3$
C=C=C
H
H

B

no plane of symmetry
chiral

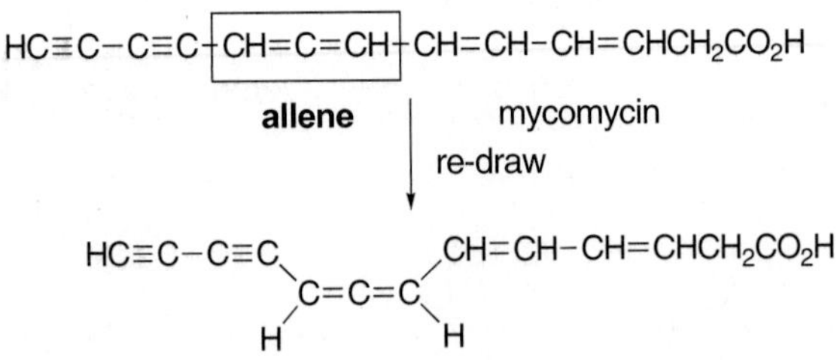

HC≡C–C≡C–CH=C=CH–CH=CH–CH=CHCH$_2$CO$_2$H
allene
mycomycin
re-draw
HC≡C–C≡C
CH=CH–CH=CHCH$_2$CO$_2$H
C=C=C
H
H

The substituents on each end of the allene in mycomycin are different. Therefore, mycomycin is **chiral.**

5.69

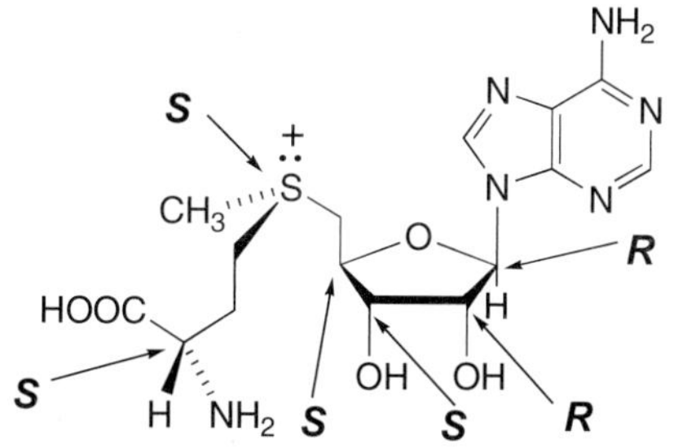

six stereogenic centers

5.70

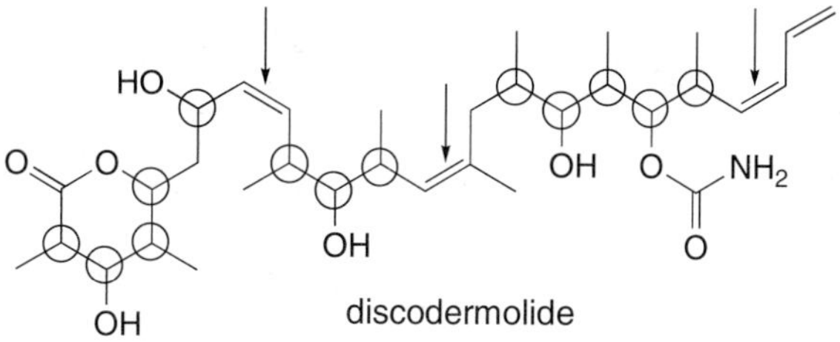

discodermolide

a. The 13 tetrahedral stereogenic centers are circled.

b. Because there is restricted rotation around a C–C double bond, groups on the end of the double bond cannot interconvert. Whenever the substituents on each end of the double bond are different from each other, the double bond is a stereogenic site. Thus, the following two double bonds are isomers:

These compounds are isomers.

There are three stereogenic double bonds in discodermolide, labeled with arrows.

c. The maximum number of stereoisomers for discodermolide must include the 13 tetrahedral stereogenic centers and the three double bonds. Maximum number of stereoisomers $= 2^{16} = 65,536$.

5.71 When the spiro compound has a plane of symmetry, it is achiral.

a. 

achiral

b. 

chiral

c. 

achiral

d. 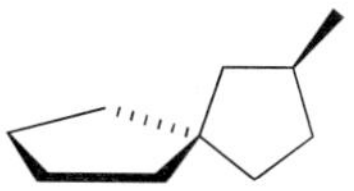

chiral

5.72

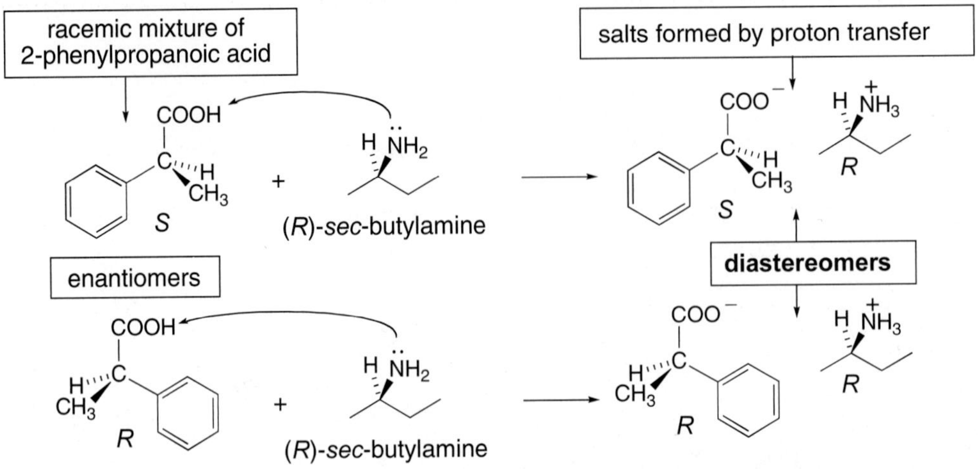

These salts are **diastereomers,** and they are now separable by physical methods since they have different physical properties.

Chapter 6 Understanding Organic Reactions

Chapter Review

Writing organic reactions (6.1)

- Use curved arrows to show the movement of electrons. Full-headed arrows are used for electron pairs and half-headed arrows are used for single electrons.

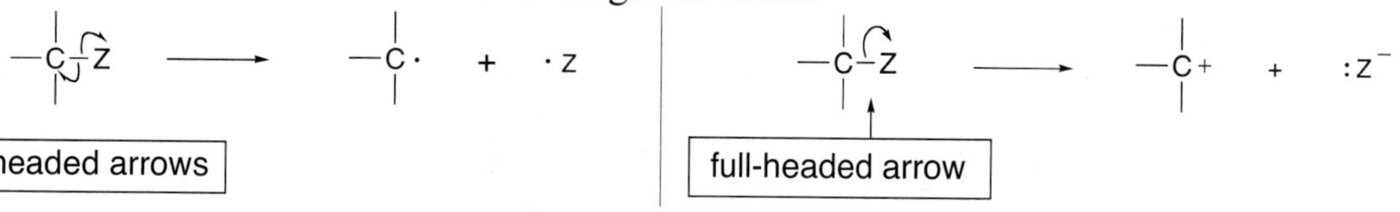
half-headed arrows
full-headed arrow

- Reagents can be drawn either on the left side of an equation or over an arrow. Catalysts are drawn over or under an arrow.

Types of reactions (6.2)

[1] Substitution	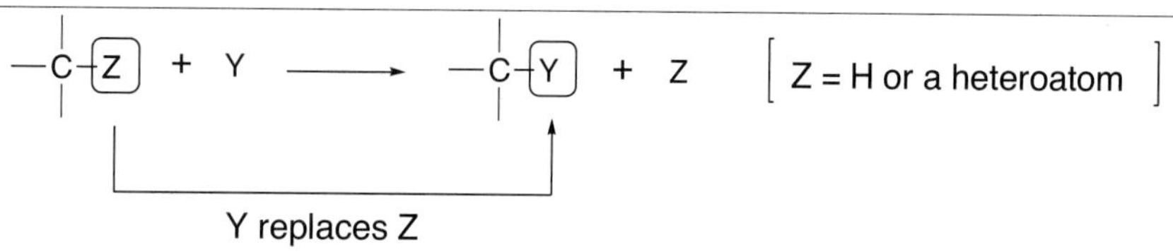 Z = H or a heteroatom Y replaces Z
[2] Elimination	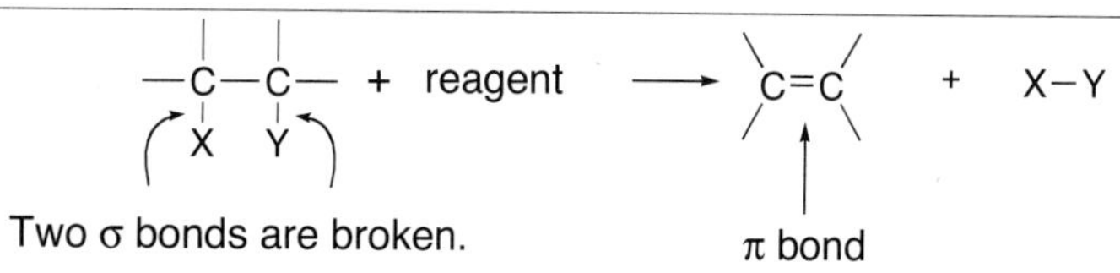 Two σ bonds are broken. π bond
[3] Addition	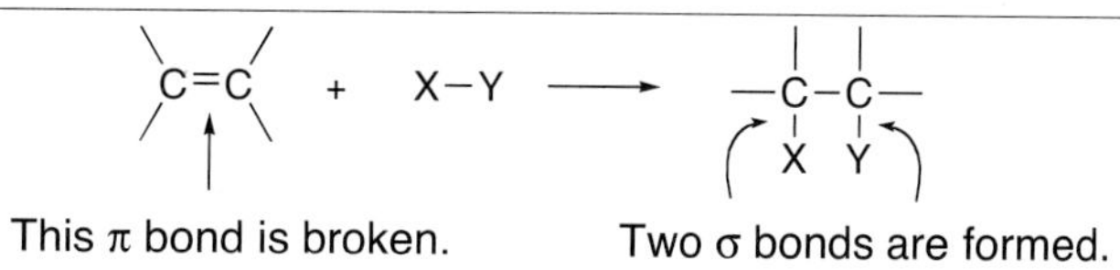 This π bond is broken. Two σ bonds are formed.

Important trends

Values compared	Trend
Bond dissociation energy and **bond strength**	The ***higher*** the bond dissociation energy, the ***stronger*** the bond (6.4). **Increasing size of the halogen** → CH_3-F CH_3-Cl CH_3-Br CH_3-I ΔH^o = 456 kJ/mol 351 kJ/mol 293 kJ/mol 234 kJ/mol ← **Increasing bond strength**

E_a and reaction rate	The ***larger*** the energy of activation, the ***slower*** the reaction (6.9A). 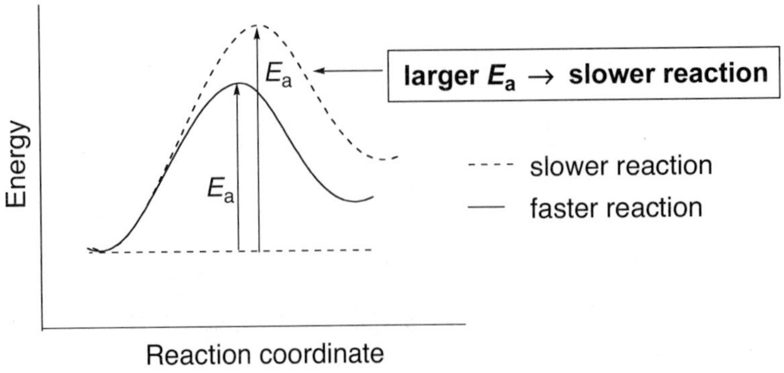
E_a and rate constant	The ***higher*** the energy of activation, the ***smaller*** the rate constant (6.9B).

Equilibrium always favors the species *lower* in energy.

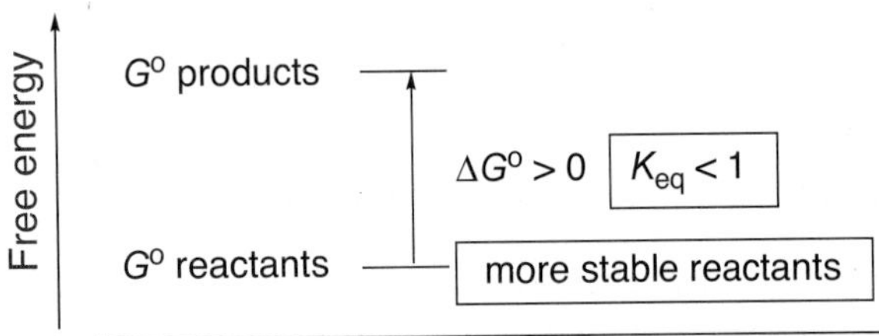

Equilibrium favors the starting materials.

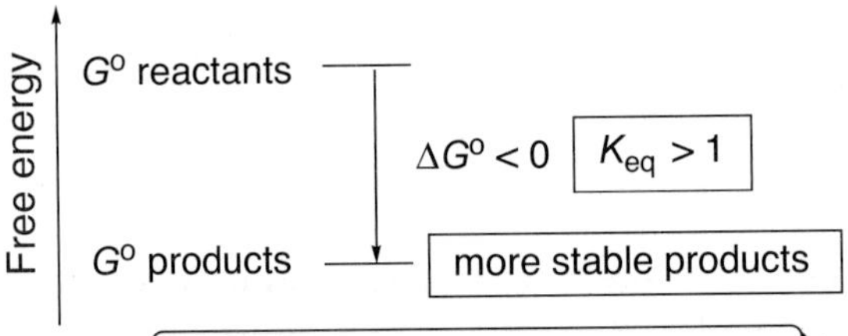

Equilibrium favors the products.

Reactive intermediates (6.3)

- Breaking bonds generates reactive intermediates.
- Homolysis generates radicals with unpaired electrons.
- Heterolysis generates ions.

Reactive intermediate	General structure	Reactive feature	Reactivity
radical	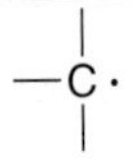	unpaired electron	electrophilic
carbocation	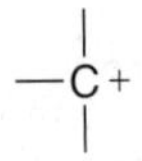	positive charge; only six electrons around C	electrophilic
carbanion	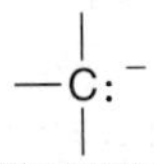	net negative charge; lone electron pair on C	nucleophilic

Energy diagrams (6.7, 6.8)

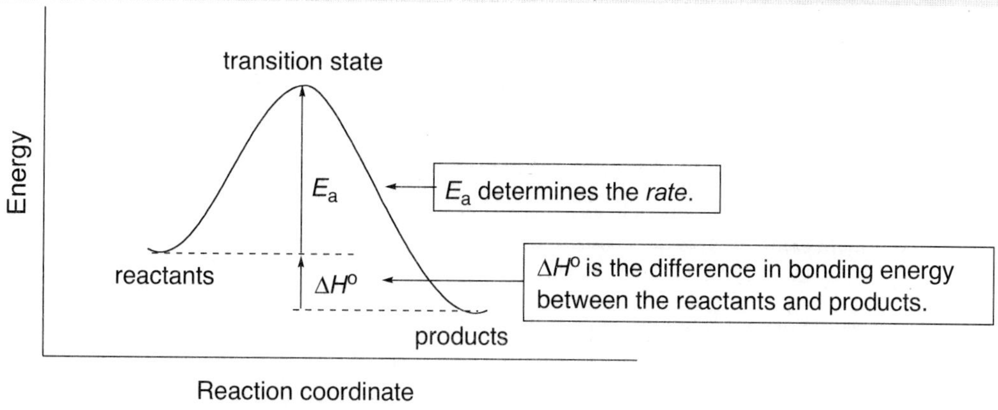

Conditions favoring product formation (6.5, 6.6)

Variable	Value	Meaning
K_{eq}	$K_{eq} > 1$	More product than starting material is present at equilibrium.
ΔG^o	$\Delta G^o < 0$	The energy of the products is **lower** than the energy of the reactants.
ΔH^o	$\Delta H^o < 0$	Bonds in the products are **stronger** than bonds in the reactants.
ΔS^o	$\Delta S^o > 0$	The product is **more disordered** than the reactant.

Equations (6.5, 6.6)

$$\Delta G^o = -2.303RT \log K_{eq}$$

K_{eq} depends on the energy difference between reactants and products.

[R = 8.314 J/(K•mol), the gas constant
T = Kelvin temperature (K)]

$$\Delta G^o = \Delta H^o - T\Delta S^o$$

- ΔG^o: free energy change
- ΔH^o: change in bonding energy
- $T\Delta S^o$: change in disorder

[T = Kelvin temperature (K)]

Factors affecting reaction rate (6.9)

Factor	Effect
energy of activation	higher E_a → slower reaction
concentration	higher concentration → faster reaction
temperature	higher temperature → faster reaction

Practice Test on Chapter Review

1. Label each statement as TRUE (T) or FALSE (F) for a reaction with $K_{eq} = 0.5$ and $E_a = 18$ kJ/mol. Ignore entropy considerations.

   a. The reaction is faster than a reaction with $K_{eq} = 8$ and $E_a = 18$ kJ/mol.
   b. The reaction is faster than a reaction with $K_{eq} = 0.5$ and $E_a = 12$ kJ/mol.
   c. $\Delta G°$ for the reaction is a positive value.
   d. The starting materials are lower in energy than the products of the reaction.
   e. The reaction is exothermic.

2. a. Which of the following statements is true about an endothermic reaction, ignoring entropy considerations?

   1. The bonds in the products are stronger than the bonds in the starting materials.
   2. $K_{eq} < 1$.
   3. A catalyst speeds up the rate of the reaction and gives a larger amount of product.
   4. Statements (1) and (2) are both true.
   5. Statements (1), (2), and (3) are all true.

   b. Which of the following statements is true about a reaction with $K_{eq} = 10^3$ and $E_a = 2.5$ kJ/mol? Ignore entropy considerations.

   1. The reaction is faster than a reaction with $E_a = 4$ kJ/mol.
   2. The starting materials are higher in energy than the products of the reaction.
   3. $\Delta G°$ is positive.
   4. Statements (1) and (2) are both true.
   5. Statements (1), (2), and (3) are all true.

3. a. Draw the transition state for the following reaction.

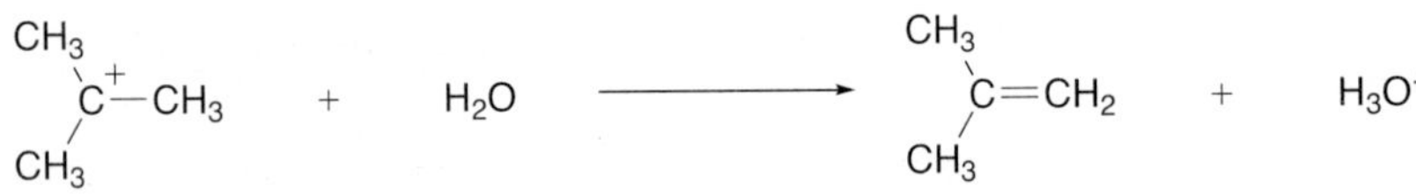

   b. Draw the transition state for the following one-step elimination reaction.

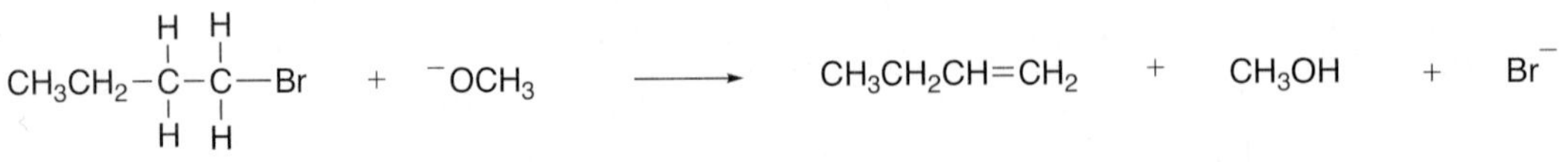

Answers to Practice Test

1. a. F
   b. F
   c. T
   d. T
   e. F

2. a. 2
   b. 4

3. a.

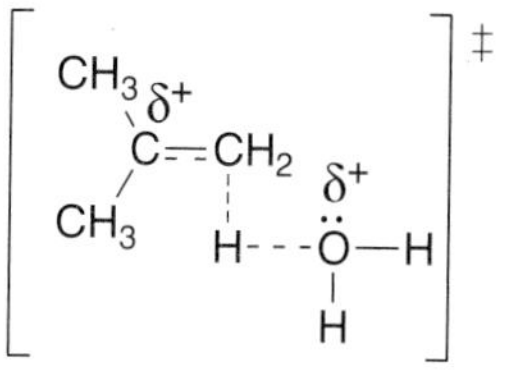

b.

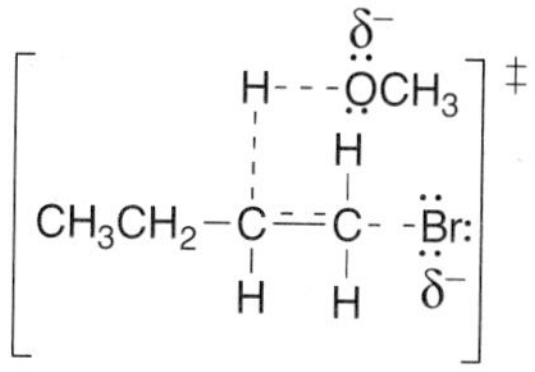

Answers to Problems

6.1 [1] In a **substitution reaction,** one group replaces another.
[2] In an **elimination reaction,** elements of the starting material are lost and a π bond is formed.
[3] In an **addition reaction,** elements are added to the starting material.

a.

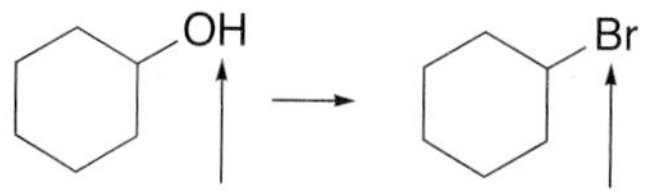

Br replaces OH =
substitution reaction

c.

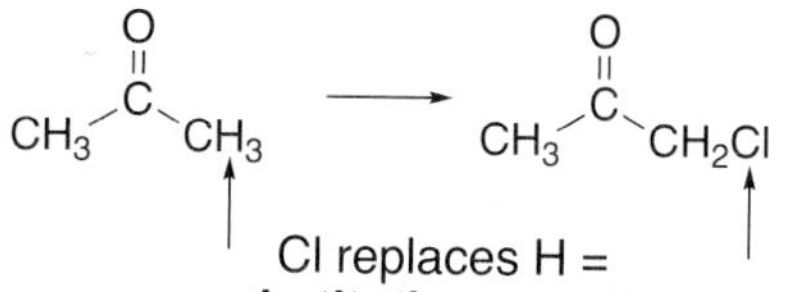

Cl replaces H =
substitution reaction

b.

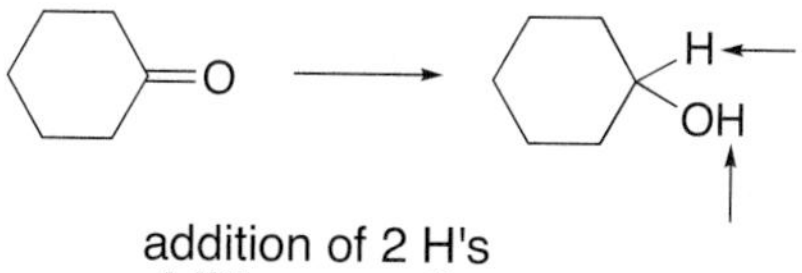

addition of 2 H's
addition reaction

d. $CH_3CH_2CH(OH)CH_3 \longrightarrow CH_3CH{=}CHCH_3$

elements lost (H + OH)
π bond formed
elimination reaction

6.2 **Heterolysis** means one atom gets both of the electrons when a bond is broken. A carbocation is a C with a positive charge, and a carbanion is a C with a negative charge.

a.

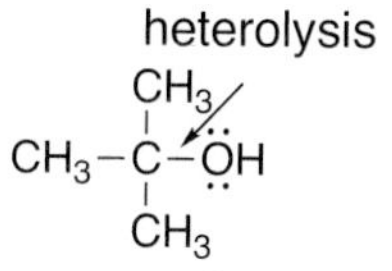

Electrons go to the more electronegative atom, O.

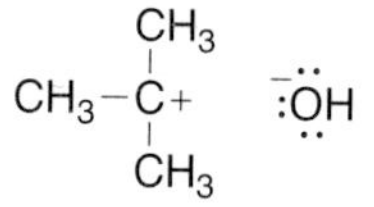

carbocation

b.

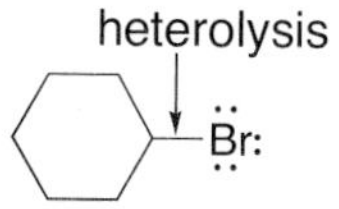

Electrons go to the more electronegative atom, Br.

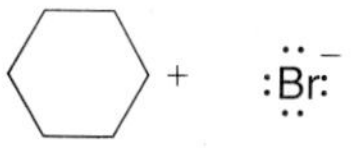

carbocation

c. heterolysis

CH_3CH_2–Li

Electrons go to the more electronegative atom, C.

$CH_3\ddot{C}H_2^{-}$ Li^{+}

carbanion

6.3 Use **full-headed arrows** to show the movement of electron pairs, and **half-headed arrows** to show the movement of single electrons.

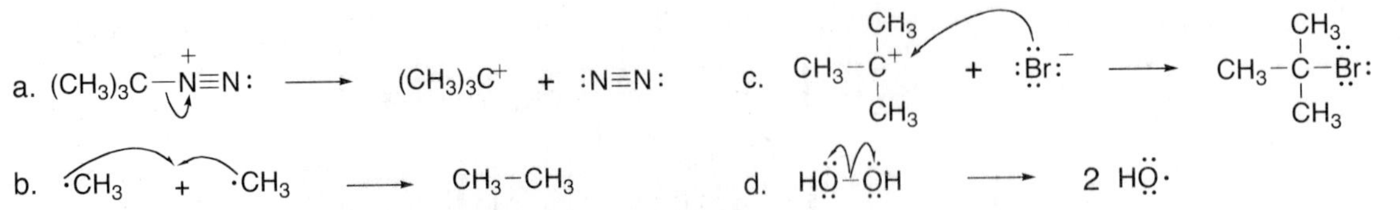
a. $(CH_3)_3C-\overset{+}{N}\equiv N:$ → $(CH_3)_3C^+$ + $:N\equiv N:$
b. $\cdot CH_3$ + $\cdot CH_3$ → CH_3-CH_3
c. $CH_3-\overset{CH_3}{\underset{CH_3}{C^+}}$ + :Br:⁻ → $CH_3-\overset{CH_3}{\underset{CH_3}{C}}-Br:$
d. HO–OH → 2 HO·

6.4 Increasing number of electrons between atoms = increasing bond strength = increasing bond dissociation energy = decreasing bond length.
Increasing size of an atom = increasing bond length = decreasing bond strength.

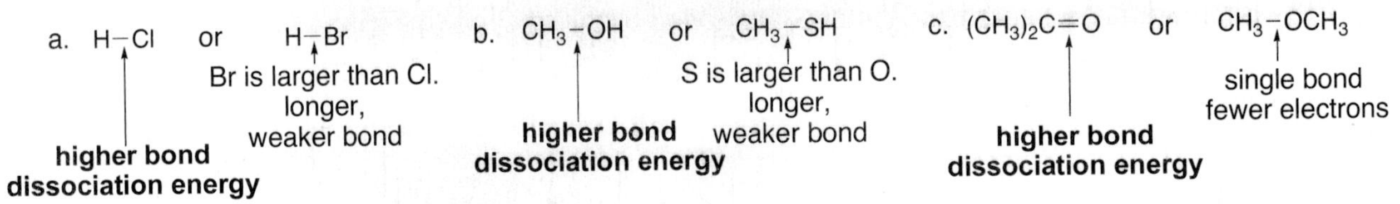
a. H–Cl or H–Br
Br is larger than Cl.
longer,
weaker bond
higher bond
dissociation energy
b. CH_3–OH or CH_3–SH
S is larger than O.
longer,
weaker bond
higher bond
dissociation energy
c. $(CH_3)_2C$=O or CH_3–OCH_3
single bond
fewer electrons
higher bond
dissociation energy

6.5 **To determine ΔH° for a reaction:**
[1] Add the bond dissociation energies for all bonds *broken* in the equation (+ values).
[2] Add the bond dissociation energies for all of the bonds *formed* in the equation (– values).
[3] *Add the energies together* to get the ΔH° for the reaction.
A positive ΔH° means the reaction is ***endothermic.*** **A negative ΔH°** means the reaction is ***exothermic.***

a. $CH_3CH_2-Br + H_2O \longrightarrow CH_3CH_2-OH + HBr$

[1] Bonds broken

	ΔH° (kJ/mol)
CH_3CH_2-Br	+ 285
H–OH	+ 498
Total	+ 783 kJ/mol

[2] Bonds formed

	ΔH° (kJ/mol)
CH_3CH_2-OH	– 393
H–Br	– 368
Total	– 761 kJ/mol

[3] Overall ΔH° =

sum in Step [1]
+
sum in Step [2]

+ 783 kJ/mol
– 761 kJ/mol

ANSWER: + 22 kJ/mol
endothermic

b. $CH_4 + Cl_2 \longrightarrow CH_3Cl + HCl$

[1] Bonds broken

	ΔH° (kJ/mol)
CH_3–H	+ 435
Cl–Cl	+ 242
Total	+ 677 kJ/mol

[2] Bonds formed

	ΔH° (kJ/mol)
CH_3–Cl	– 351
H–Cl	– 431
Total	– 782 kJ/mol

[3] Overall ΔH° =

sum in Step [1] + sum in Step [2]

+ 677 kJ/mol
– 782 kJ/mol

ANSWER: – 105 kJ/mol
exothermic

6.6 Use the directions from Answer 6.5. In determining the number of bonds broken or formed, you must take into account the coefficients needed to balance an equation.

a. $CH_4 + 2\,O_2 \longrightarrow CO_2 + 2\,H_2O$

[1] Bonds broken

	ΔH° (kJ/mol)	
CH_3–H	+ 435 x 4 =	+ 1740
O–O	+ 497 x 2 =	+ 994
Total		+ 2734 kJ/mol

[2] Bonds formed

	ΔH° (kJ/mol)
OC–O	– 535 x 2 = – 1070
HO–H	– 498 x 4 = – 1992
Total	– 3062 kJ/mol

[3] Overall ΔH° =

sum in Step [1] + sum in Step [2]

+ 2734 kJ/mol
– 3062 kJ/mol

ANSWER: – 328 kJ/mol

b. $2\,CH_3CH_3 + 7\,O_2 \longrightarrow 4\,CO_2 + 6\,H_2O$

[1] Bonds broken

	ΔH° (kJ/mol)
CH_3CH_2–H	+ 410 x 12 = + 4920
O–O	+ 497 x 7 = + 3479
C–C	+ 368 x 2 = +736
Total	+ 9135 kJ/mol

[2] Bonds formed

	ΔH° (kJ/mol)
OC–O	– 535 x 8 = – 4280
HO–H	– 498 x 12 = – 5976
Total	– 10256 kJ/mol

[3] Overall ΔH° =

sum in Step [1] + sum in Step [2]

+ 9135 kJ/mol
– 10256 kJ/mol

ANSWER: – 1121 kJ/mol

6.7 Use the following relationships to answer the questions:
If $K_{eq} = 1$, then $\Delta G° = 0$; if $K_{eq} > 1$, then $\Delta G° < 0$; if $K_{eq} < 1$, then $\Delta G° > 0$.

a. A negative value of $\Delta G°$ means the equilibrium favors the product and K_{eq} is > 1. Therefore, $K_{eq} = 1000$ is the answer.
b. A lower value of $\Delta G°$ means a larger value of K_{eq}, and the products are more favored. $K_{eq} = 10^{-2}$ is larger than $K_{eq} = 10^{-5}$, so $\Delta G°$ is lower.

6.8 Use the relationships from Answer 6.7.

a. $K_{eq} = 5.5$. $K_{eq} > 1$ means that the equilibrium favors the **product.**
b. $\Delta G° = 40$ kJ/mol. A positive $\Delta G°$ means the equilibrium favors the **starting material.**

6.9 When the *product* is lower in energy than the *starting material*, the equilibrium favors the *product.* When the *starting material* is lower in energy than the *product*, the equilibrium favors the *starting material.*

a. **$\Delta G°$ is positive,** so the equilibrium favors the starting material. Therefore the *starting material is lower in energy than the product.*
b. **K_{eq} is > 1,** so the equilibrium favors the product. Therefore the *product is lower in energy than the starting material.*
c. **$\Delta G°$ is negative,** so the equilibrium favors the product. Therefore the *product is lower in energy than the starting material.*
d. **K_{eq} is < 1,** so the equilibrium favors the starting material. Therefore *the starting material is lower in energy than the product.*

6.10

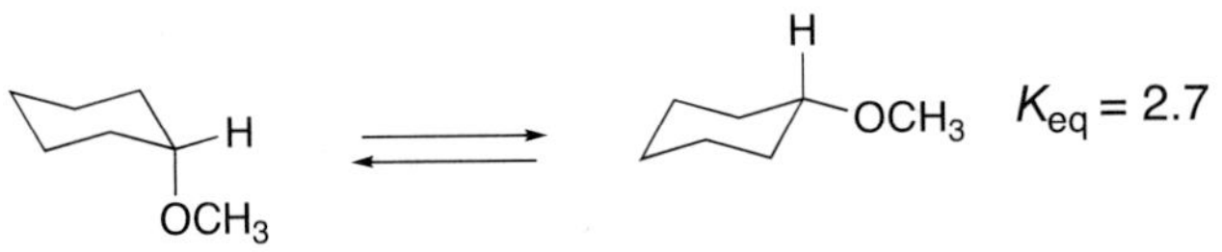

a. The K_{eq} is > 1, so the **product** (the conformation on the right) is favored at equilibrium.
b. The $\Delta G°$ for this process must be **negative,** because the product is favored.
c. $\Delta G°$ is somewhere between 0 and –6 kJ/mol.

6.11 A positive $\Delta H°$ favors the starting material. A negative $\Delta H°$ favors the product.
a. $\Delta H°$ is positive (80 kJ/mol). The starting material is favored.
b. $\Delta H°$ is negative (–40 kJ/mol). The product is favored.

6.12

a. **False.** The reaction is endothermic.
b. **True.** This assumes that $\Delta G°$ is approximately equal to $\Delta H°$.
c. **False.** $K_{eq} < 1$.
d. **True.**
e. **False.** The starting material is favored at equilibrium.

6.13

a. **True.**
b. **False.** $\Delta G°$ for the reaction is negative.
c. **True.**
d. **False.** The bonds in the product are stronger than the bonds in the starting material.
e. **True.**

6.14

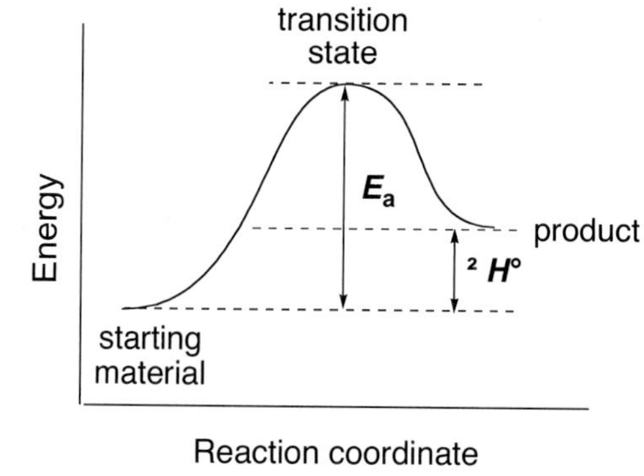

6.15 A transition state is drawn with dashed lines to indicate the partially broken and partially formed bonds. Any atom that gains or loses a charge contains a partial charge in the transition state.

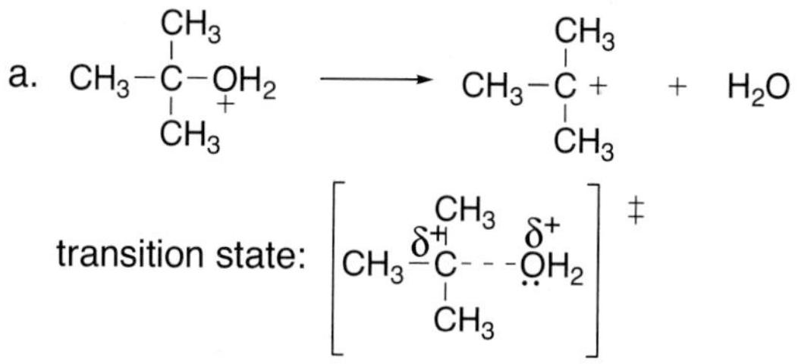

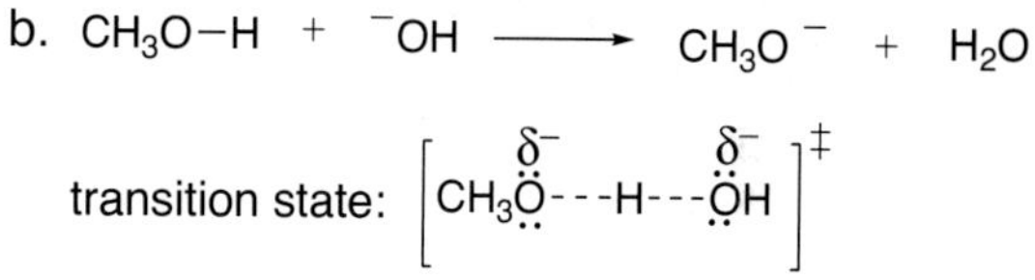

6.16

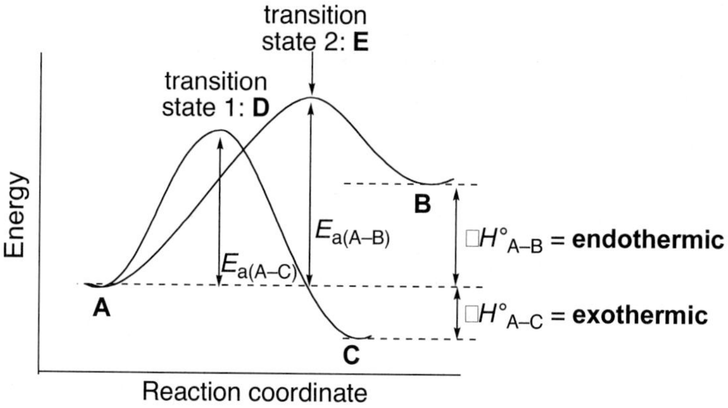

a. Reaction **A–C** is exothermic.
   Reaction **A–B** is endothermic.
b. Reaction **A–C** is faster.
c. Reaction **A–C** generates a lower-energy product.
d. See labels.
e. See labels.
f. See labels.

6.17

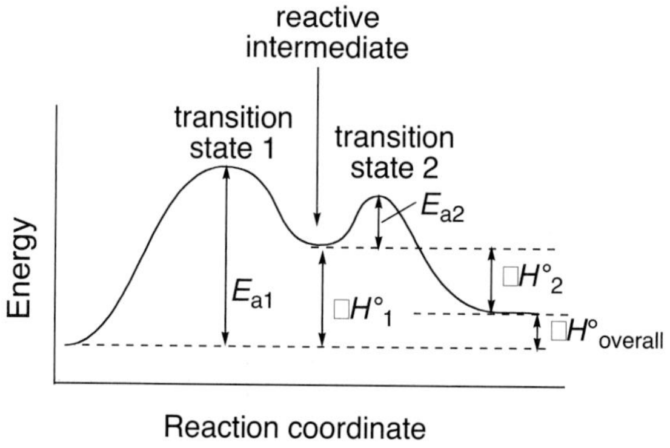

a. Two steps, because there are two energy barriers.
b. See labels.
c. See labels.
d. One reactive intermediate is formed (see label).
e. The first step is rate-determining, because its transition state is at higher energy.
f. The overall reaction is endothermic, because the energy of the products is higher than the energy of the reactants.

6.18

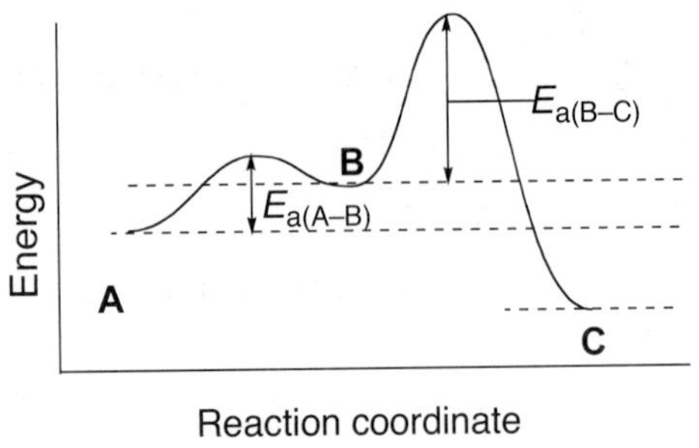

relative energies: C < A < B
B → C is rate-determining.

6.19 **E_a, concentration, and temperature affect reaction rate.** $\Delta H°$, $\Delta G°$, and K_{eq} do not affect reaction rate.

a. **E_a = 4 kJ/mol** corresponds to a faster reaction rate.
b. A temperature of **25 °C** will have a faster reaction rate, because a higher temperature corresponds to a faster reaction.
c. **No change:** K_{eq} does not affect reaction rate.
d. **No change:** $\Delta H°$ does not affect reaction rate.

6.20

a. **False.** The reaction occurs at the same rate as a reaction with K_{eq} = 8 and E_a = 80 kJ/mol.
b. **False.** The reaction is slower than a reaction with K_{eq} = 0.8 and E_a = 40 kJ/mol.
c. **True.**
d. **True.**
e. **False.** The reaction is endothermic.

6.21 All reactants in the rate equation determine the rate of the reaction.

[1] rate = $k[CH_3CH_2Br][^-OH]$

a. Tripling the concentration of CH_3CH_2Br only → **The rate is tripled.**
b. Tripling the concentration of ^-OH only → **The rate is tripled.**
c. Tripling the concentration of both $CH_3CH_2CH_2Br$ and ^-OH → **The rate increases by a factor of 9 (3 × 3 = 9).**

[2] rate = $k[(CH_3)_3COH]$

a. Doubling the concentration of $(CH_3)_3COH$ → **The rate is doubled.**
b. Increasing the concentration of $(CH_3)_3COH$ by a factor of 10 → **The rate increases by a factor of 10.**

6.22 The rate equation is determined by the rate-determining step.

a. $CH_3CH_2{-}Br + {}^-OH \longrightarrow CH_2{=}CH_2 + H_2O + Br^-$

one step
rate = $k[CH_3CH_2Br][^-OH]$

b. $(CH_3)_3C{-}Br \xrightarrow[\text{slow}]{} (CH_3)_3C^+ + Br^- \xrightarrow[\text{fast}]{^-OH} (CH_3)_2C{=}CH_2 + H_2O$

two steps
The slow step determines the rate equation.
rate = $k[(CH_3)_3CBr]$

6.23 A catalyst is not used up or changed in the reaction. It only speeds up the reaction rate.

OH and H are added to the starting material.

a. $CH_2{=}CH_2 \xrightarrow[H_2SO_4]{H_2O} CH_3CH_2OH$

H_2SO_4 is not used up = **catalyst.**

I^- not used up = **catalyst.**

b. $CH_3Cl \xrightarrow[^-OH]{I^-} CH_3OH$

^-OH substitutes for Cl^-.

H_2 adds to the starting material.

c.

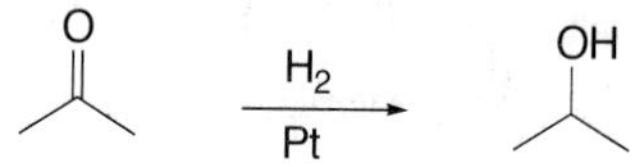

Pt not used up = **catalyst.**

6.24

a.

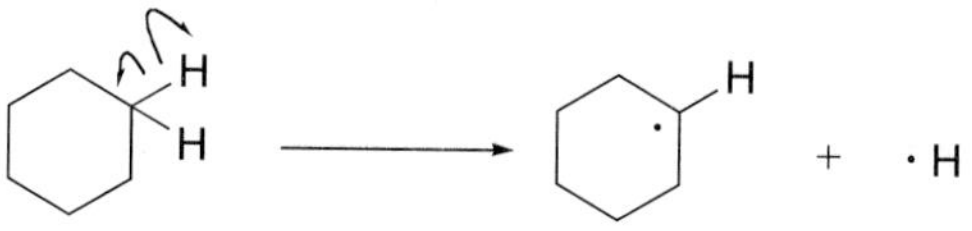

radical

b.

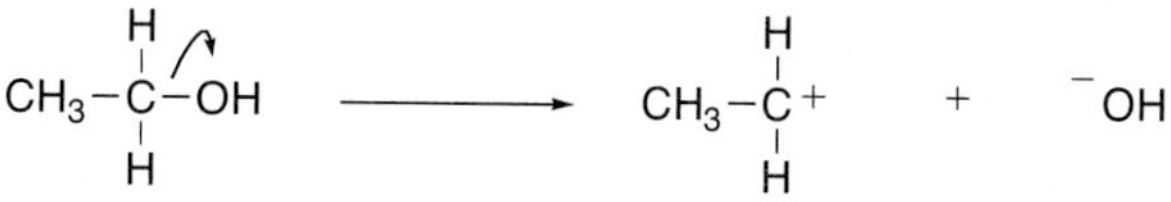

carbocation

6.25

propane

$CH_3{-}CH_2CH_3 \longrightarrow \cdot CH_3 + \cdot CH_2CH_3$

$\Delta H^o = 356$ kJ/mol
This bond is formed from two sp^3 hybridized C's.

propene

$CH_3{-}CH{=}CH_2 \longrightarrow \cdot CH_3 + \cdot CH{=}CH_2$

$\Delta H^o = 385$ kJ/mol
This bond is formed from one sp^2 and one sp^3 hybridized C. The higher percent *s*-character in one C makes a stronger bond; thus, the bond dissociation energy is higher.

6.26 Use the directions from Answer 6.1.

a.

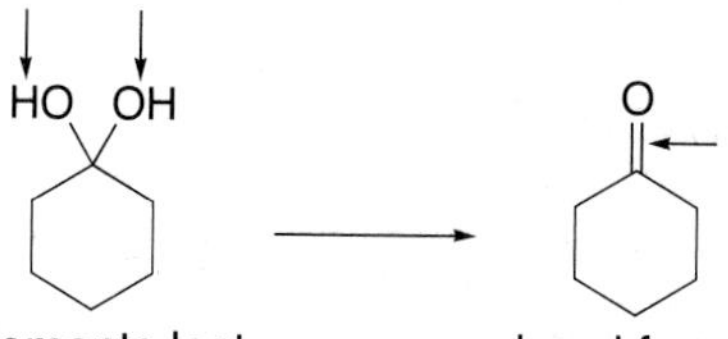

elements lost (H + OH)

π bond formed

elimination reaction

c.

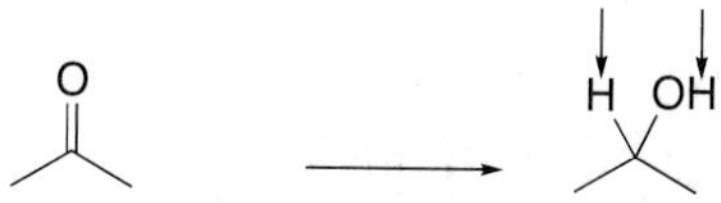

addition of 2 H's
addition reaction

b.

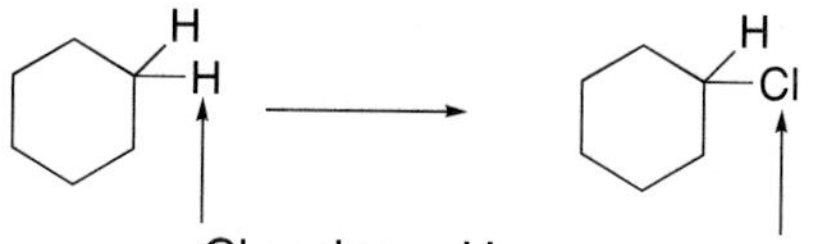

Cl replaces H =
substitution reaction

d.

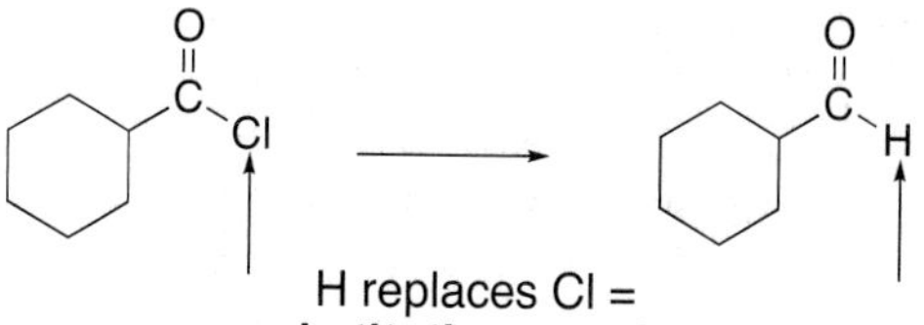

H replaces Cl =
substitution reaction

6.27 Use the rules in Answer 6.3 to draw the arrows.

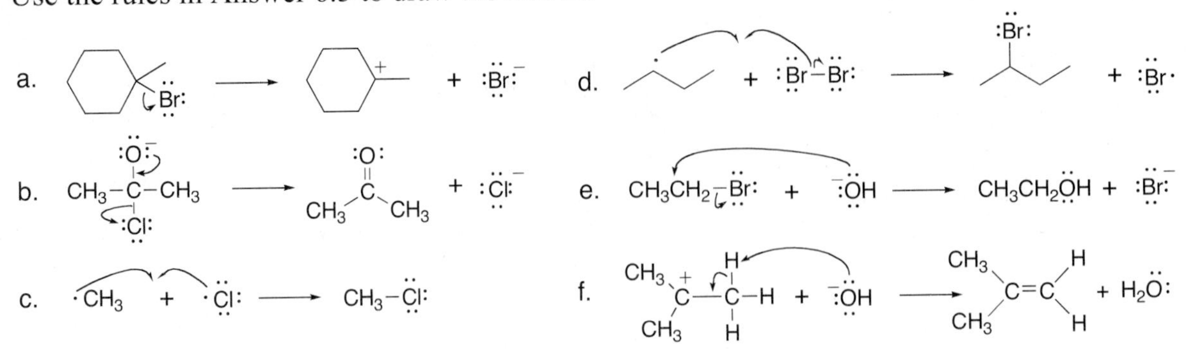

6.28

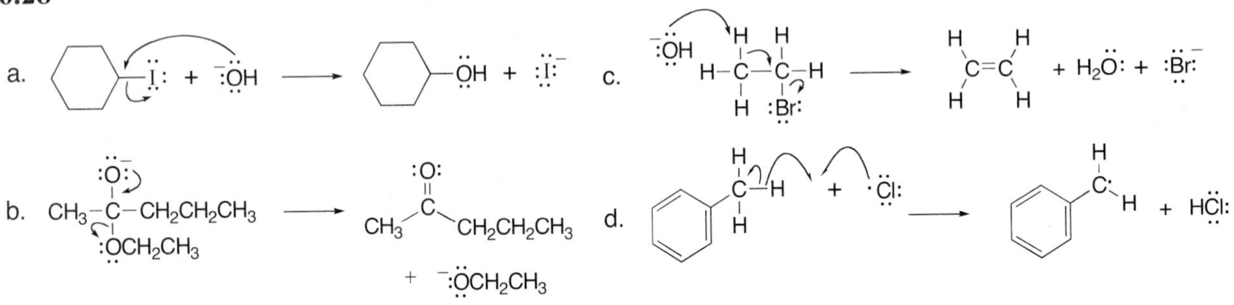

6.29 Draw the curved arrows to identify the product **X**.

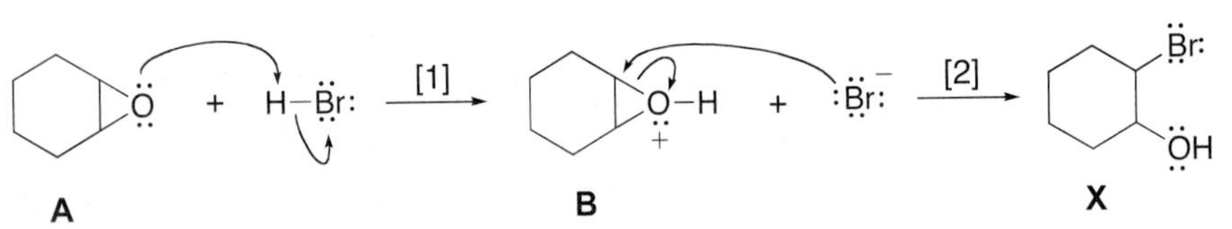

6.30 Follow the curved arrows to identify the intermediate **Y**.

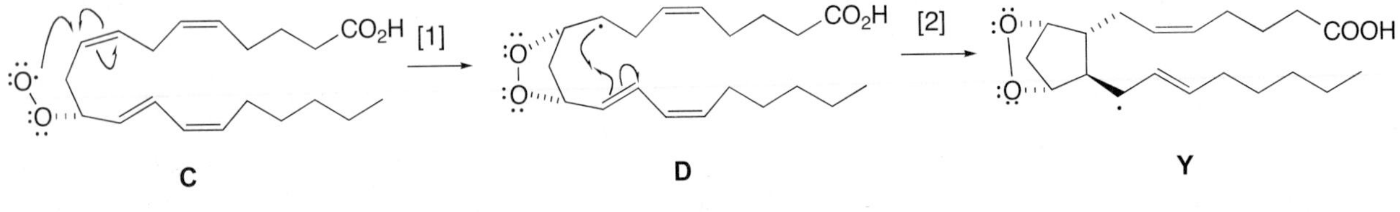

6.31 Use the rules from Answer 6.4.

a.
- I–CCl_3: largest halogen, **weakest bond**
- Br–CCl_3: **intermediate bond strength**
- Cl–CCl_3: smallest halogen, **strongest bond**

b.
- H_2N–NH_2: single bond, **weakest bond**
- HN=NH: double bond, **intermediate bond strength**
- N≡N: triple bond, **strongest bond**

6.32 Use the directions from Answer 6.5.

a. $CH_3CH_2{-}H + Br_2 \longrightarrow CH_3CH_2{-}Br + HBr$

[1] Bonds broken

	ΔH^o (kJ/mol)
$CH_3CH_2{-}H$	+ 410
$Br{-}Br$	+ 192
Total	+ 602 kJ/mol

[2] Bonds formed

	ΔH^o (kJ/mol)
$CH_3CH_2{-}Br$	– 285
$H{-}Br$	– 368
Total	– 653 kJ/mol

[3] Overall ΔH^o =

+ 602 kJ/mol
– 653 kJ/mol

ANSWER: – 51 kJ/mol

b. $\cdot OH + CH_4 \longrightarrow \cdot CH_3 + H_2O$

[1] Bonds broken

	ΔH^o (kJ/mol)
$CH_3{-}H$	+ 435 kJ/mol

[2] Bonds formed

	ΔH^o (kJ/mol)
$H{-}OH$	– 498 kJ/mol

[3] Overall ΔH^o =

+ 435 kJ/mol
– 498 kJ/mol

ANSWER: – 63 kJ/mol

c. $CH_3{-}OH + HBr \longrightarrow CH_3{-}Br + H_2O$

[1] Bonds broken

	ΔH^o (kJ/mol)
$CH_3{-}OH$	+ 389
$H{-}Br$	+ 368
Total	+ 757 kJ/mol

[2] Bonds formed

	ΔH^o (kJ/mol)
$CH_3{-}Br$	– 293
$H{-}OH$	– 498
Total	– 791 kJ/mol

[3] Overall ΔH^o =

+ 757 kJ/mol
– 791 kJ/mol

ANSWER: – 34 kJ/mol

d. $\cdot Br + CH_4 \longrightarrow \cdot H + CH_3Br$

[1] Bonds broken

	ΔH^o (kJ/mol)
$CH_3{-}H$	+ 435 kJ/mol

[2] Bonds formed

	ΔH^o (kJ/mol)
$CH_3{-}Br$	–293 kJ/mol

[3] Overall ΔH^o =

+ 435 kJ/mol
– 293 kJ/mol

ANSWER: + 142 kJ/mol

6.33

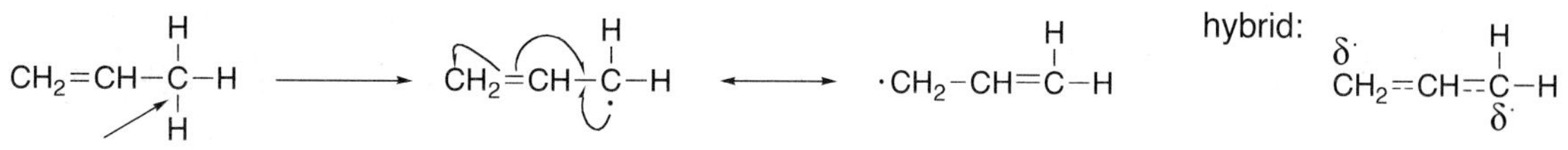

6.34 The more stable radical is formed by a reaction with a smaller $\Delta H°$.

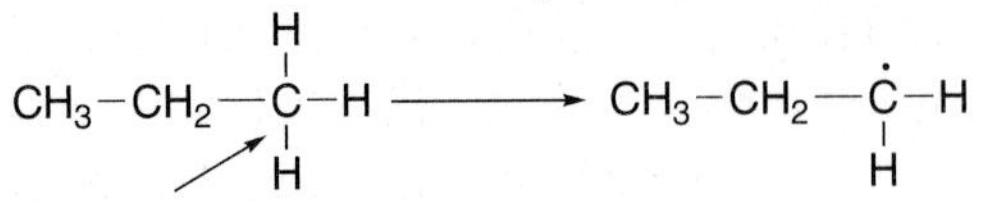

$\Delta H° = 410$ kJ/mol = less stable radical

This C–H bond is stronger.

A

$\Delta H° = 397$ kJ/mol = more stable radical

This C–H bond is weaker.

B

Because the bond dissociation for cleavage of the C–H bond to form radical **A** is higher, more energy must be added to form it. This makes **A** higher in energy and therefore less stable than **B.**

6.35 Use the rules from Answer 6.9.

a. $K_{eq} = 0.5$. K_{eq} is less than one, so the **starting material** is favored.
b. $\Delta G° = -100$ kJ/mol. $\Delta G°$ is less than 0, so the **product** is favored.
c. $\Delta H° = 8.0$ kJ/mol. $\Delta H°$ is positive, so the **starting material** is favored.
d. $K_{eq} = 16$. K_{eq} is greater than one, so the **product** is favored.
e. $\Delta G° = 2.0$ kJ/mol. $\Delta G°$ is greater than zero, so the **starting material** is favored.
f. $\Delta H° = 200$ kJ/mol. $\Delta H°$ is positive, so the **starting material** is favored.
g. $\Delta S° = 8$ J/(K•mol). $\Delta S°$ is greater than zero, so the **product** is more disordered and favored.
h. $\Delta S° = -8$ J/(K•mol). $\Delta S°$ is less than zero, so the **starting material** is more disordered and favored.

6.36

a. A negative $\Delta G°$ must have $K_{eq} > 1$. $K_{eq} = 10^2$.
b. K_{eq} = [products]/[reactants] = [1]/[5] = 0.2 = K_{eq}. $\Delta G°$ is positive.
c. A negative $\Delta G°$ has $K_{eq} > 1$, and a positive $\Delta G°$ has $K_{eq} < 1$. $\Delta G° = -8$ kJ/mol will have a larger K_{eq}.

6.37

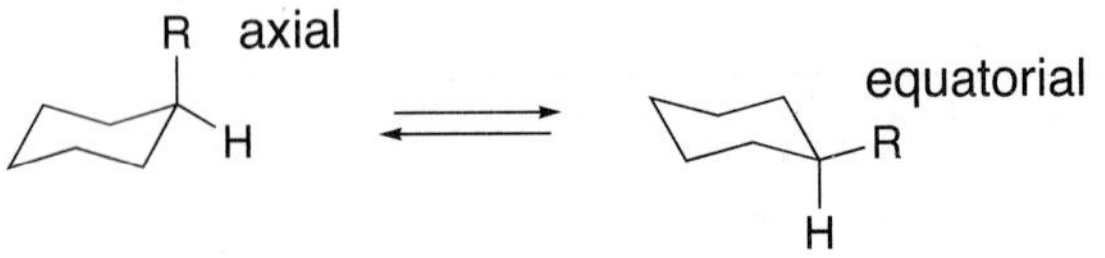

R	K_{eq}
$-CH_3$	18
$-CH_2CH_3$	23
$-CH(CH_3)_2$	38
$-C(CH_3)_3$	4000

a. The equatorial conformation is always present in the larger amount at equilibrium, because the K_{eq} for all R groups is greater than 1.
b. The cyclohexane with the $-C(CH_3)_3$ group will have the greatest amount of equatorial conformation at equilibrium, because this group has the highest K_{eq}.
c. The cyclohexane with the $-CH_3$ group will have the greatest amount of axial conformation at equilibrium, because this group has the lowest K_{eq}.
d. The cyclohexane with the $-C(CH_3)_3$ group will have the most negative $\Delta G°$, because it has the largest K_{eq}.
e. The larger the R group, the more favored the equatorial conformation.

f. The K_{eq} for *tert*-butylcyclohexane is much higher because the *tert*-butyl group is bulkier than the other groups. With a *tert*-butyl group, a CH_3 group is always oriented over the ring when the group is axial, creating severe 1,3-diaxial interactions. With all other substituents, the larger CH_3 groups can be oriented away from the ring, placing a H over the ring, making the 1,3-diaxial interactions less severe. Compare:

tert-butylcyclohexane

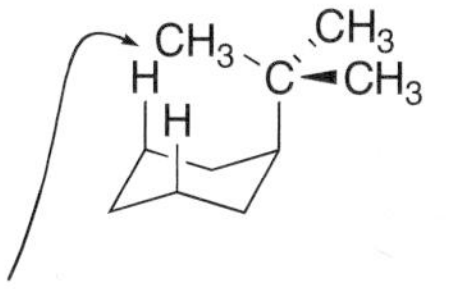

severe 1,3-diaxial interactions with the CH_3 group and the axial H's

isopropylcyclohexane

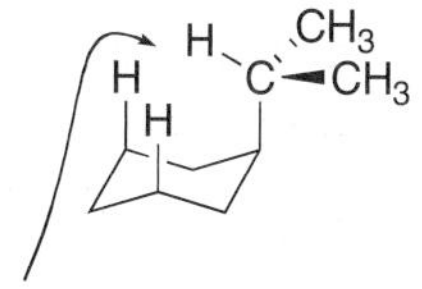

less severe 1,3-diaxial interactions

6.38 Calculate K_{eq}, and then find the percentage of axial and equatorial conformations present at equilibrium.

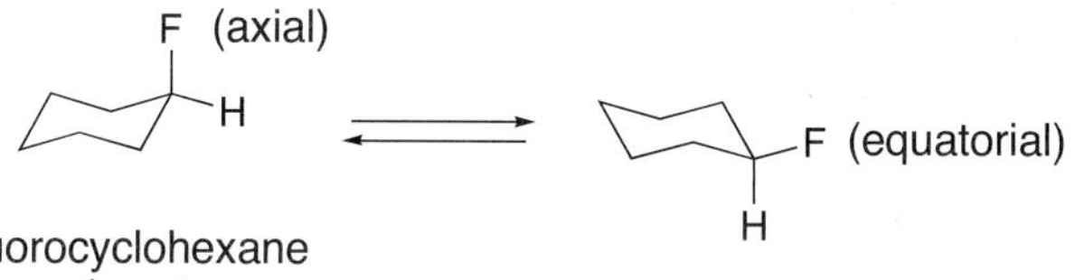

fluorocyclohexane
1 part

1.5 parts

a. $\Delta G° = -5.9 \log K_{eq}$
$\Delta G° = -1.0$ kJ/mol
-1.0 kJ/mol $= -5.9 \log K_{eq}$
$K_{eq} = 1.5$

b. K_{eq} = [products]/[reactants]
1.5 = [products]/[reactants]
1.5[reactants] = [products]
[reactants] = 0.4 = 40% axial
[products] = 0.6 = 60% equatorial

6.39 Reactions resulting in an increase in entropy are favored. When a single molecule forms two molecules, there is an increase in entropy.

a. 
increased number of molecules
ΔS° is positive.
products favored

b. $CH_3\cdot$ + $CH_3\cdot$ ⟶ CH_3CH_3
decreased number of molecules
ΔS° is negative.
starting material favored

c. $(CH_3)_2C(OH)_2$ ⟶ $(CH_3)_2C{=}O$ + H_2O
increased number of molecules
ΔS° is positive.
products favored

d. CH_3COOCH_3 + H_2O ⟶ CH_3COOH + CH_3OH
no change in the number of molecules
neither favored

6.40 Use the directions in Answer 6.15 to draw the transition state. Nonbonded electron pairs are drawn in at reacting sites.

a. 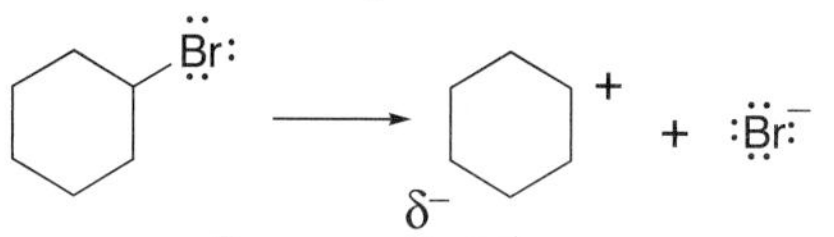

transition state:

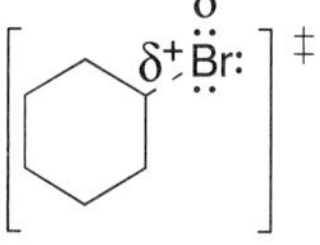

b. BF_3 + :Cl:⁻ ⟶ 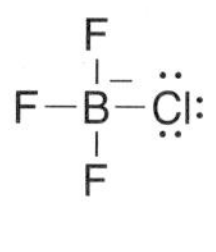

transition state:

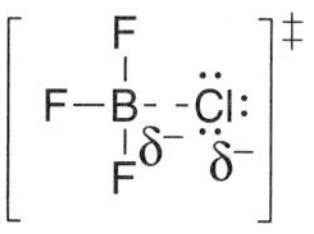

c. 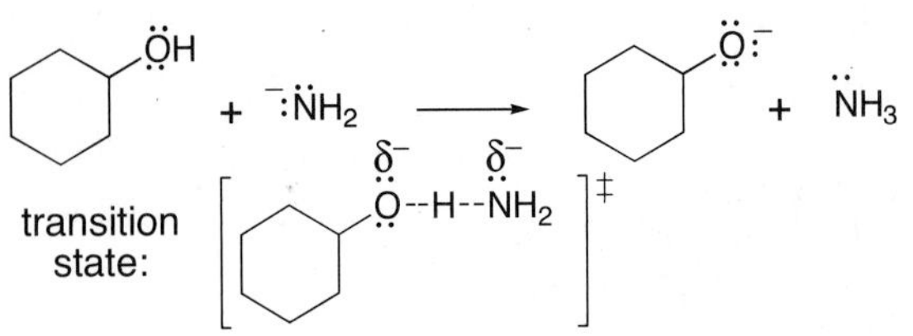

OH
+ :NH2
O:
+ NH3
δ−
δ−
O--H--NH2
‡
transition state:

d. 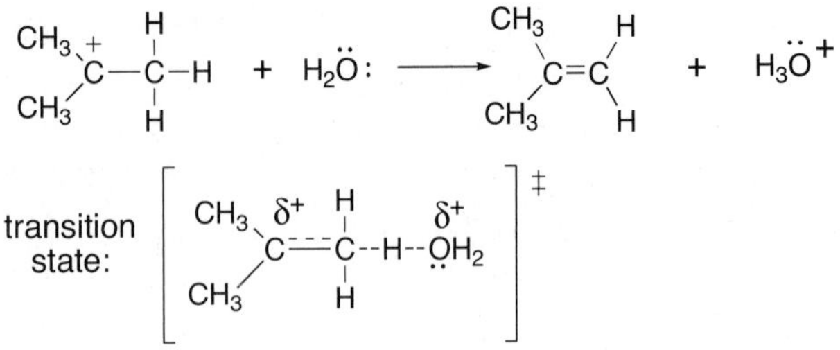

CH3
CH3
H
C—C—H
H
+ H2O:
CH3
H
C=C
CH3
H
+ H3O+
transition state:
CH3 δ+ H δ+
C==C--H--OH2
CH3 H
‡

6.41

a. 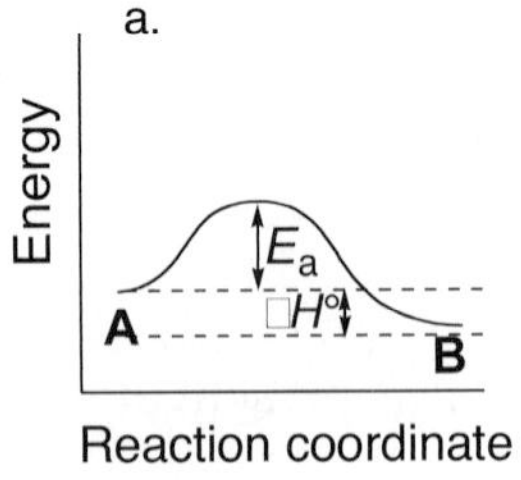

Energy
Ea
ΔH°
A
B
Reaction coordinate

- one step **A**→**B**
- exothermic since **B** lower than **A**
- low E_a (small energy barrier)

b. 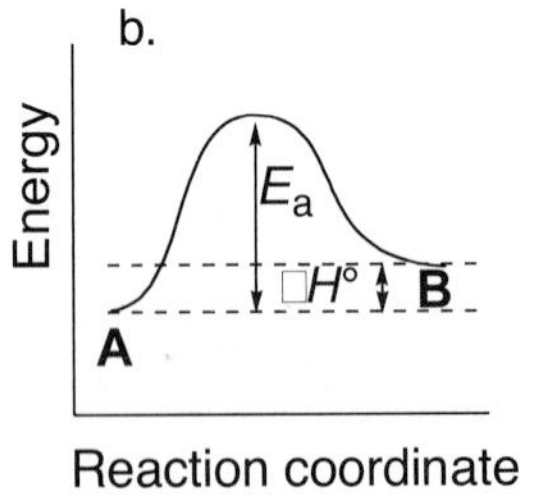

Energy
Ea
ΔH°
A
B
Reaction coordinate

- one step **A**→**B**
- endothermic since **B** higher than **A**
- high E_a (large energy barrier)

c. 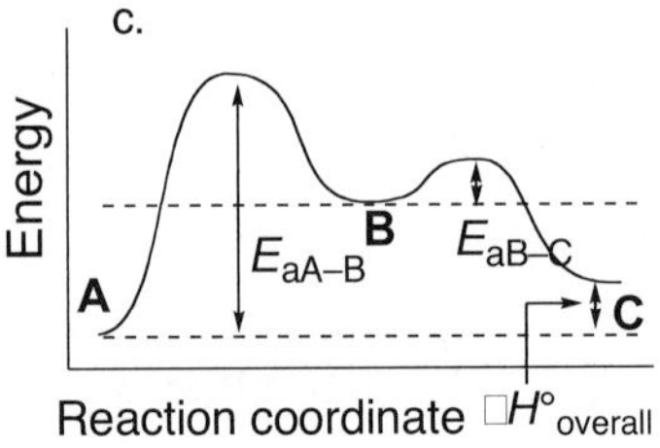

Energy
A
B
C
EaA–B
EaB–C
Reaction coordinate
ΔH°overall

- two steps
- **A** lowest energy
- **B** highest energy
- **$E_{a(A\text{-}B)}$ is rate-determining**, since the transition state for Step [1] is higher in energy.

d. 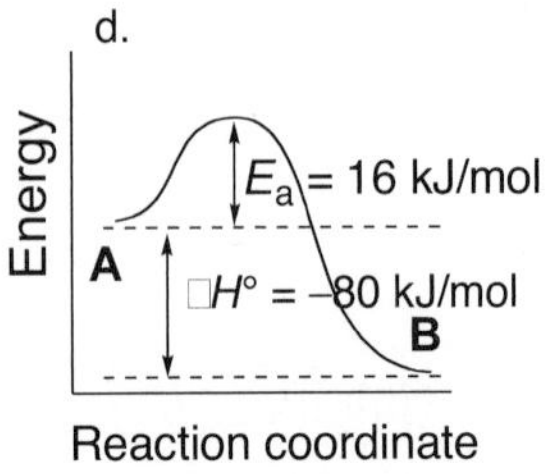

Energy
Ea = 16 kJ/mol
A
ΔH° = –80 kJ/mol
B
Reaction coordinate

- one step **A**→**B**
- exothermic since **B** lower than **A**

6.42

a. 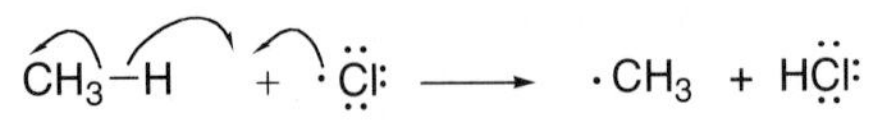

CH3—H + ·Cl:
·CH3 + HCl:

b. $\cdot Cl + CH_4 \longrightarrow \cdot CH_3 + HCl$

[1] Bonds broken

	ΔH^o (kJ/mol)
CH_3–H	+ 435 kJ/mol

[2] Bonds formed

	ΔH^o (kJ/mol)
H–Cl	– 431 kJ/mol

[3] Overall ΔH^o =

+ 435 kJ/mol
– 431 kJ/mol

ANSWER: + 4 kJ/mol

c. 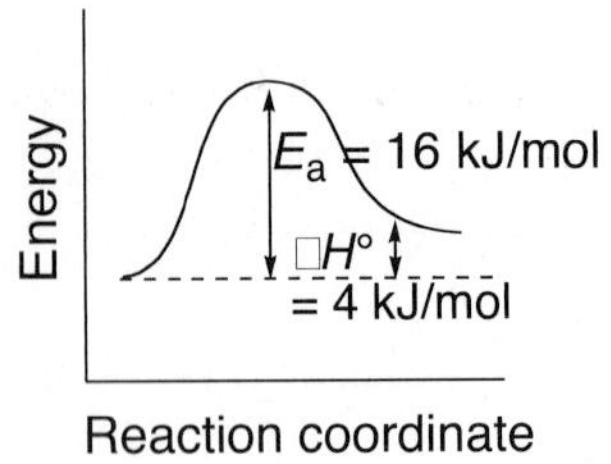

Energy
Ea = 16 kJ/mol
ΔH°
= 4 kJ/mol
Reaction coordinate

d. The E_a for the reverse reaction is the difference in energy between the products and the transition state, 12 kJ/mol.

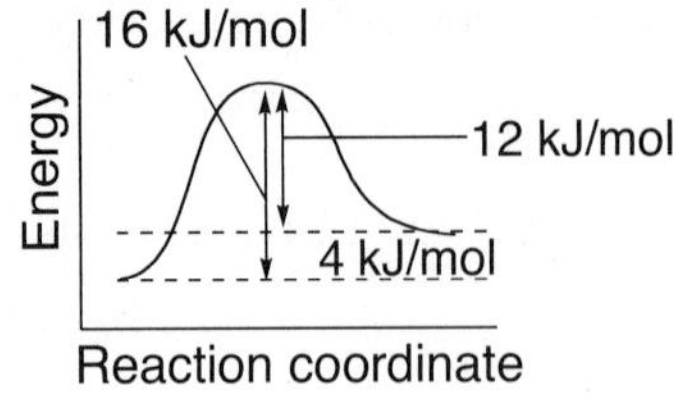

16 kJ/mol
12 kJ/mol
4 kJ/mol
Energy
Reaction coordinate

6.43

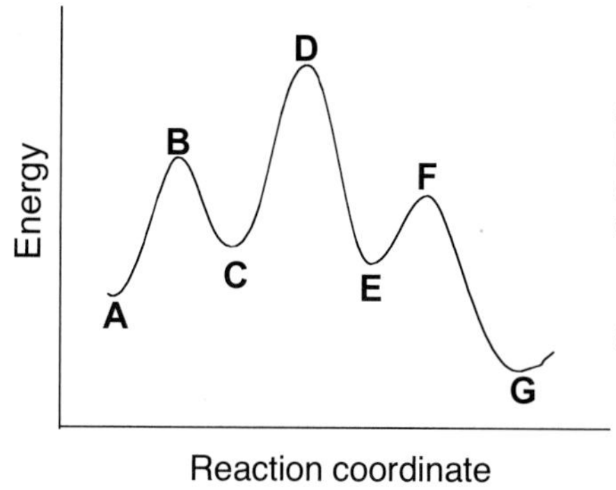

a. **B, D,** and **F** are transition states.
b. **C** and **E** are reactive intermediates.
c. The overall reaction has **three steps.**
d. **A–C** is endothermic.
   C–E is exothermic.
   E–G is exothermic.
e. The overall reaction is exothermic.

6.44

Since pK_a (CH_3CO_2H) = 4.8 and pK_a [$(CH_3)_3COH$] = 18, the weaker acid is formed as product, and equilibrium favors the products. Thus, $\Delta H°$ is negative, and the products are lower in energy than the starting materials.

transition state:

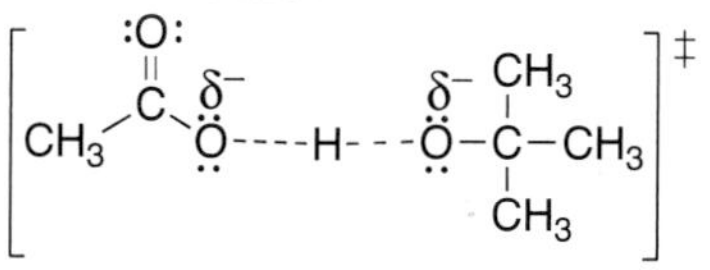

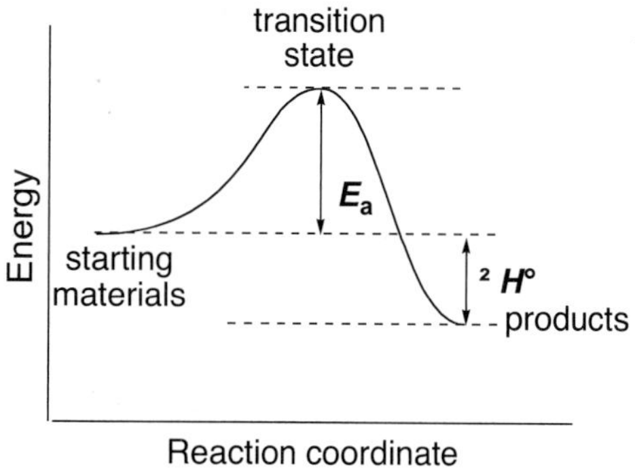

6.45

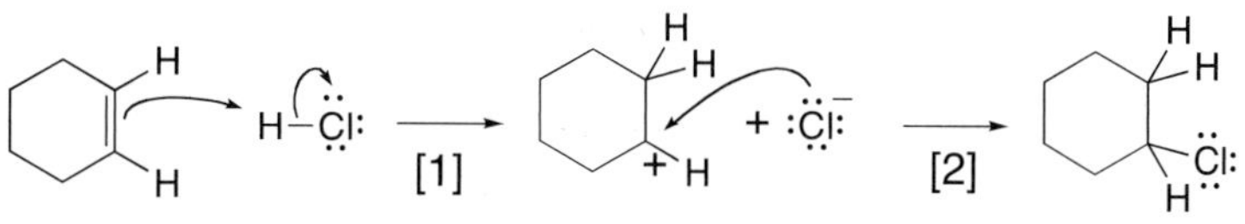

a. Step [1] breaks one π bond and the H–Cl bond, and one C–H bond is formed. The $\Delta H°$ for this step should be positive, because more bonds are broken than formed.
b. Step [2] forms one bond. The $\Delta H°$ for this step should be negative, because one bond is formed and none is broken.
c. Step [1] is rate-determining, because it is more difficult.
d. Transition state for Step [1]: Transition state for Step [2]:

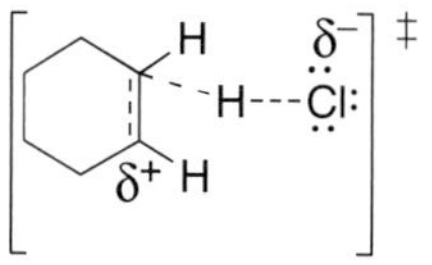

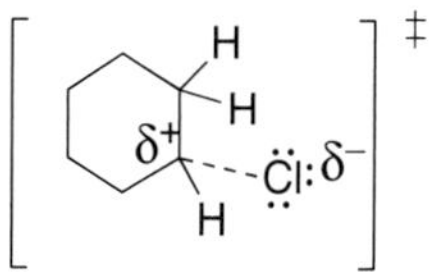

e.

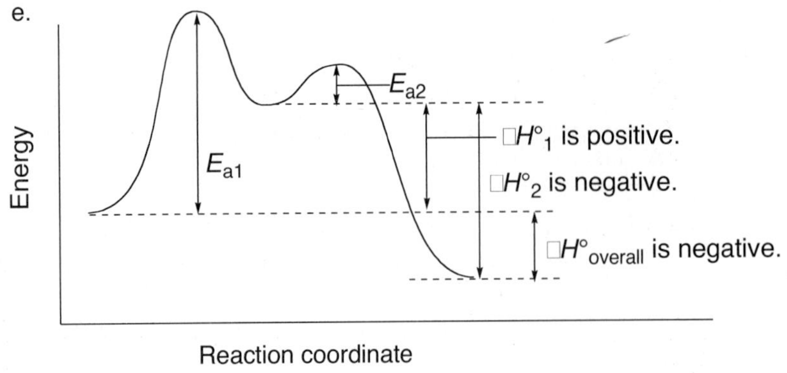

6.46

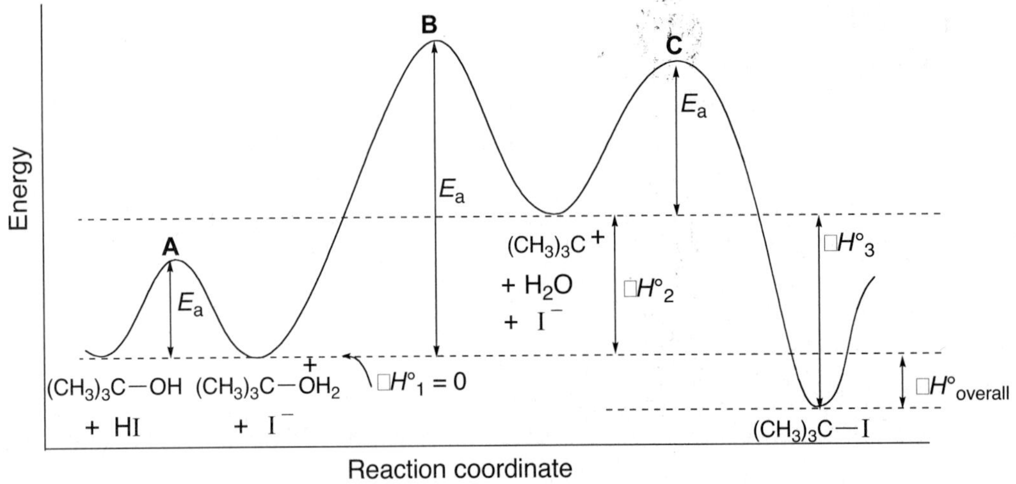

a. The reaction has three steps, because there are three energy barriers.
b. See above.
c. Transition state **A** (see graph for location): Transition state **B:** Transition state **C:**

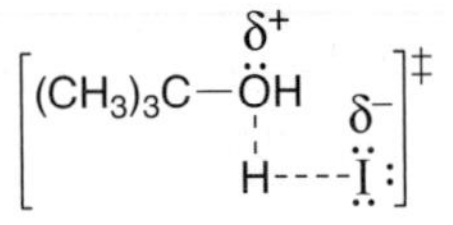

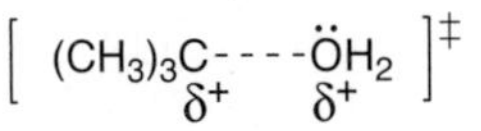

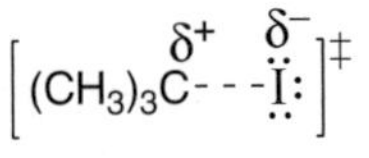

d. Step [2] is rate-determining, because this step has the highest energy transition state.

6.47 E_a, concentration, catalysts, rate constant, and temperature affect reaction rate so (c), (d), (e), (g), and (h) affect rate.

6.48

a. **rate = *k*[CH_3Br][NaCN]**
b. Double [CH_3Br] = **rate doubles.**
c. Halve [NaCN] = **rate halved.**
d. Increase both [CH_3Br] and [NaCN] by factor of 5 = [5][5] = **rate increases by a factor of 25.**

6.49

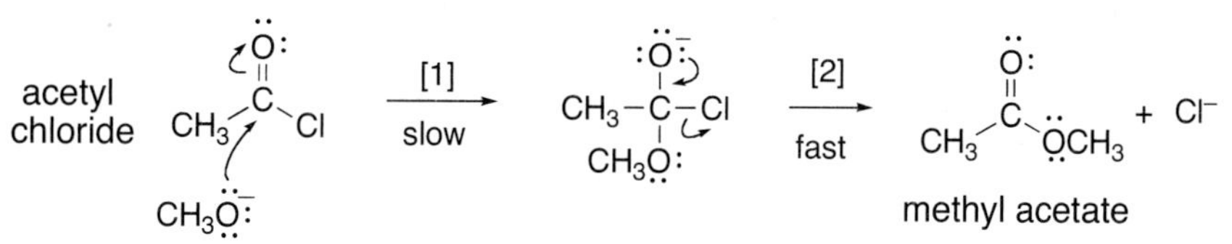

a. Only the slow step is included in the rate equation: **Rate = k[CH$_3$O$^-$][CH$_3$COCl]**
b. CH$_3$O$^-$ is in the rate equation. Increasing its concentration by 10 times would increase the rate by **10 times.**
c. When both reactant concentrations are increased by 10 times, the rate increases by **100 times (10 × 10 = 100).**
d. This is a **substitution reaction** (OCH$_3$ substitutes for Cl).

6.50

a. **True:** Increasing temperature increases reaction rate.
b. **True:** If a reaction is fast, then it has a large rate constant.
c. **False: Corrected**—There is no relationship between $\Delta G°$ and reaction rate.
d. **False: Corrected**—When the E_a is large, *the rate constant is small.*
e. **False: Corrected**—There is no relationship between K_{eq} and reaction rate.
f. **False: Corrected**—Increasing the concentration of a reactant increases the rate of a reaction *only if the reactant appears in the rate equation.*

6.51

a. The first mechanism has one step: **Rate = k[(CH$_3$)$_3$CI][$^-$OH]**
b. The second mechanism has two steps, but only the first step would be in the rate equation, because it is slow and therefore rate-determining: **Rate = k[(CH$_3$)$_3$CI]**
c. Possibility [1] is second order; possibility [2] is first order.
d. These rate equations can be used to show which mechanism is plausible by changing the concentration of $^-$OH. If this affects the rate, then possibility [1] is reasonable. If it does not affect the rate, then possibility [2] is reasonable.

e.

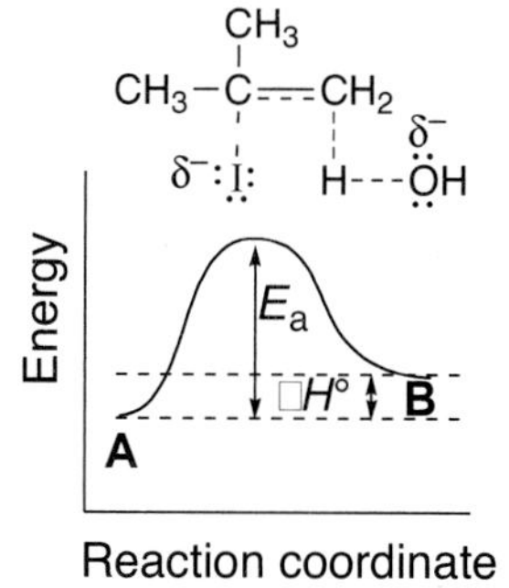

A = (CH$_3$)$_3$CI + $^-$OH
B = (CH$_3$)$_2$C=CH$_2$ + I$^-$ + H$_2$O

f.

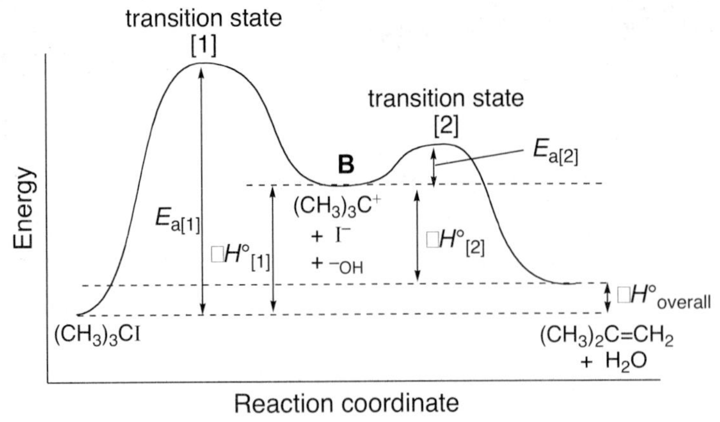

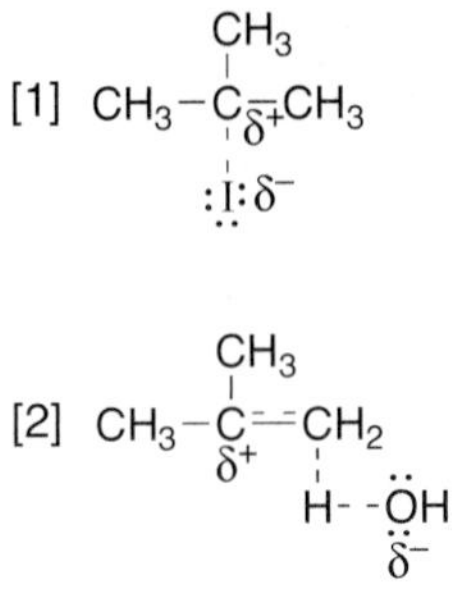

6.52 The difference in both the acidity and the bond dissociation energy of CH_3CH_3 versus HC≡CH is due to the same factor: percent *s*-character. The difference results because one process is based on homolysis and one is based on heterolysis.

Bond dissociation energy:

CH_3CH_2–H: *sp*^{3} hybridized, 25% *s*-character

HC≡C–H: *sp* hybridized, 50% *s*-character. Higher percent *s*-character makes this bond shorter and stronger.

Acidity: To compare acidity, we must compare the stability of the conjugate bases:

$CH_3\bar{C}H_2$: *sp*^{3} hybridized, 25% *s*-character

$HC{\equiv}C^-$: *sp* hybridized, 50% *s*-character. Now a higher percent *s*-character stabilizes the conjugate base making the starting acid more acidic.

6.53 a. Re-draw **A** to see more clearly how cyclization occurs.

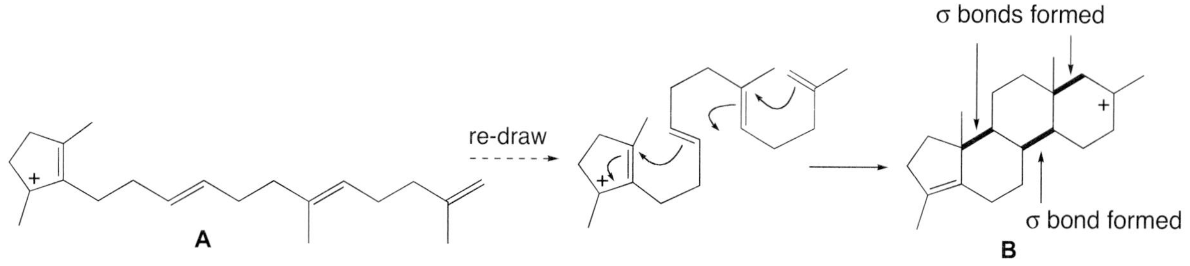
σ bonds formed
re-draw
A
σ bond formed
B

b.

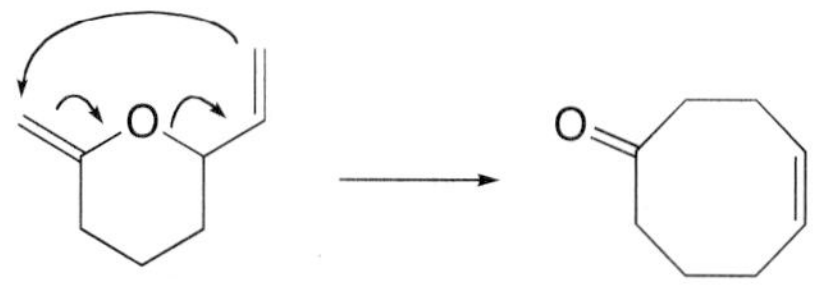

6.54

a.

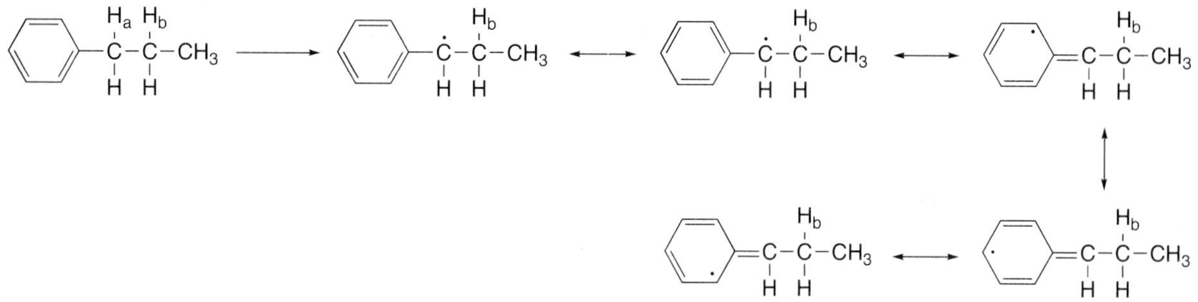

b.

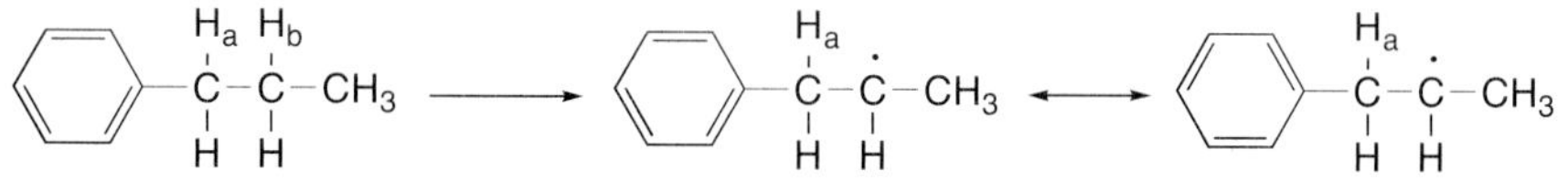

c. C–H$_a$ is weaker than C–H$_b$ since the carbon radical formed when the C–H$_a$ bond is broken is highly resonance stabilized. This means the bond dissociation energy for C–H$_a$ is lower.

6.55 In Reaction [1], the number of molecules of reactants and products stays the same, so entropy is not a factor. In Reaction [2], a single molecule of starting material forms two molecules of products, so entropy increases. This makes $\Delta G°$ more favorable, thus increasing K_{eq}.

6.56

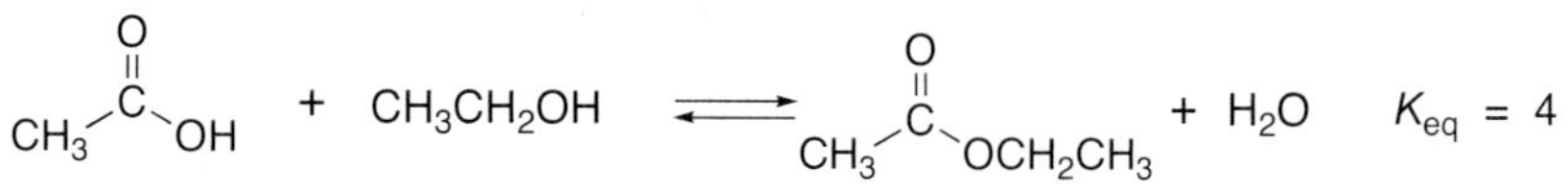
+ CH3CH2OH
+ H2O
Keq = 4

ethyl acetate

To increase the yield of ethyl acetate, H_2O can be removed from the reaction mixture, or there can be a large excess of one of the starting materials.

6.57

a. 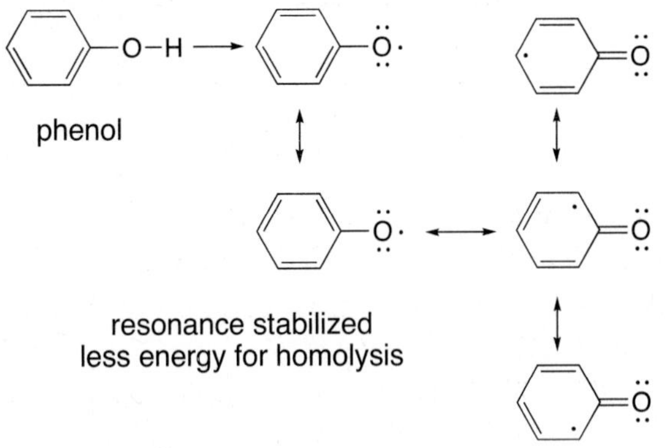

phenol

resonance stabilized
less energy for homolysis

$CH_3CH_2-\ddot{O}-H \longrightarrow CH_3CH_2-\ddot{O}\cdot$

ethanol — no resonance stabilization

Less energy is required for cleavage of $C_6H_5O{-}H$ because homolysis forms the more stable radical.

b. 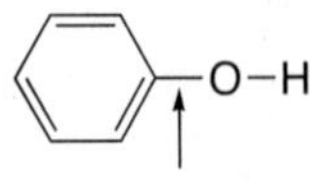

Csp^2–O
higher % *s*-character
shorter bond

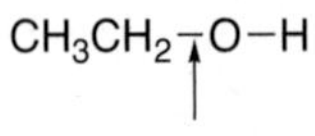

Csp^3–O
lower % *s*-character
longer bond

Chapter 7 Alkyl Halides and Nucleophilic Substitution

Chapter Review

General facts about alkyl halides

- Alkyl halides contain a halogen atom X bonded to an sp^3 hybridized carbon (7.1).
- Alkyl halides are named as halo alkanes, with the halogen as a substituent (7.2).
- Alkyl halides have a polar C–X bond, so they exhibit dipole–dipole interactions but are incapable of intermolecular hydrogen bonding (7.3).
- The polar C–X bond containing an electrophilic carbon makes alkyl halides reactive towards nucleophiles and bases (7.5).

The central theme (7.6)

- Nucleophilic substitution is one of the two main reactions of alkyl halides. A nucleophile replaces a leaving group on an sp^3 hybridized carbon.

$$R{-}X \quad + \quad :Nu^- \longrightarrow R{-}Nu \quad + \quad X:^-$$

nucleophile (:Nu⁻) — leaving group (X:⁻)

The electron pair in the C–Nu bond comes from the nucleophile.

- One σ bond is broken and one σ bond is formed.
- There are two possible mechanisms: S_N1 and S_N2.

S_N1 and S_N2 mechanisms compared

	S_N2 mechanism	S_N1 mechanism
[1] Mechanism	• One step (7.11B)	• Two steps (7.13B)
[2] Alkyl halide	• Order of reactivity: $CH_3X > RCH_2X > R_2CHX > R_3CX$ (7.11D)	• Order of reactivity: $R_3CX > R_2CHX > RCH_2X > CH_3X$ (7.13D)
[3] Rate equation	• rate = k[RX][:Nu⁻] • second-order kinetics (7.11A)	• rate = k[RX] • first-order kinetics (7.13A)
[4] Stereochemistry	• backside attack of the nucleophile (7.11C) • inversion of configuration at a stereogenic center	• trigonal planar carbocation intermediate (7.13C) • racemization at a stereogenic center
[5] Nucleophile	• favored by stronger nucleophiles (7.17B)	• favored by weaker nucleophiles (7.17B)
[6] Leaving group	• better leaving group → faster reaction (7.17C)	• better leaving group → faster reaction (7.17C)
[7] Solvent	• favored by polar aprotic solvents (7.17D)	• favored by polar protic solvents (7.17D)

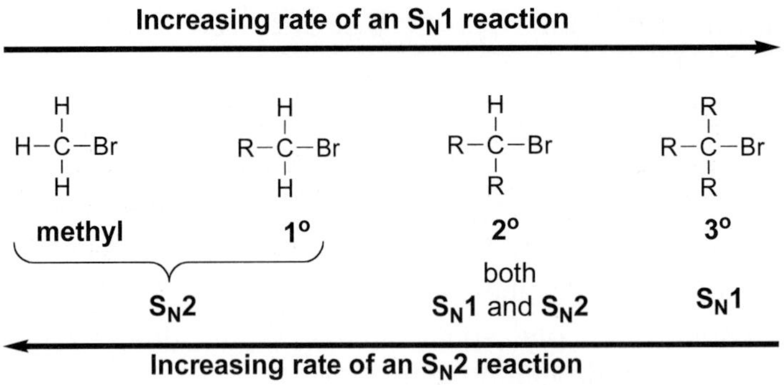

Important trends

- The best leaving group is the weakest base. Leaving group ability increases left to right across a row and down a column of the periodic table (7.7).

Increasing basicity ←

$:NH_3$ $H_2\ddot{O}:$

→ **Increasing leaving group ability**

Increasing basicity ←

F^- Cl^- Br^- I^-

→ **Increasing leaving group ability**

- Nucleophilicity decreases across a row of the periodic table (7.8A).

For 2nd row elements with the same charge:

CH_3^- $^-NH_2$ ^-OH F^-

← **Increasing basicity**
Increasing nucleophilicity

- Nucleophilicity decreases down a column of the periodic table in polar aprotic solvents (7.8C).

Down a column of the periodic table

F^- Cl^- Br^- I^-

← **Increasing nucleophilicity in polar aprotic solvents**

- Nucleophilicity increases down a column of the periodic table in polar protic solvents (7.8C).

Down a column of the periodic table

F^- Cl^- Br^- I^-

→ **Increasing nucleophilicity in polar protic solvents**

- The stability of a carbocation increases as the number of R groups bonded to the positively charged carbon increases (7.14).

$\overset{+}{C}H_3$	$R\overset{+}{C}H_2$	$R_2\overset{+}{C}H$	$R_3\overset{+}{C}$
methyl	**1°**	**2°**	**3°**

→ **Increasing carbocation stability**

Important principles

Principle	Example
• Electron-donating groups (such as R groups) stabilize a positive charge (7.14A).	• 3° Carbocations (R_3C^+) are more stable than 2° Carbocations (R_2CH^+), which are more stable than 1° carbocations (RCH_2^+).
• Steric hindrance decreases nucleophilicity but not basicity (7.8B).	• $(CH_3)_3CO^-$ is a stronger base but a weaker nucleophile than $CH_3CH_2O^-$.
• Hammond postulate: In an endothermic reaction, the more stable product is formed faster. In an exothermic reaction, this fact is not necessarily true (7.15).	• S_N1 reactions are faster when more stable (more substituted) carbocations are formed, because the rate-determining step is endothermic.
• Planar, *sp*^{2} hybridized atoms react with reagents from both sides of the plane (7.13C).	• A trigonal planar carbocation reacts with nucleophiles from both sides of the plane.

Practice Test on Chapter Review

1. Give the IUPAC name for the following compound, including the appropriate *R,S* prefix.

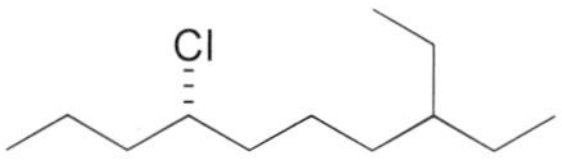

2. a. Which of the following carbocations is the most stable?

1. 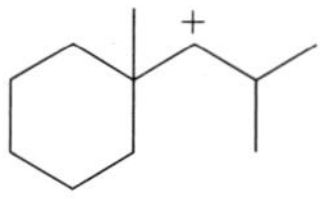
2. 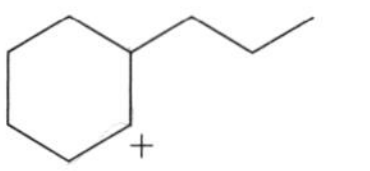
3. 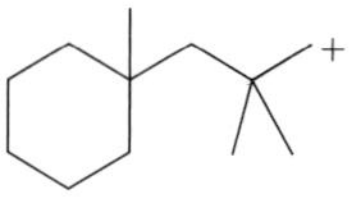
4. 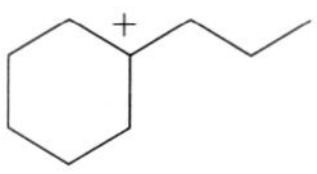
5. 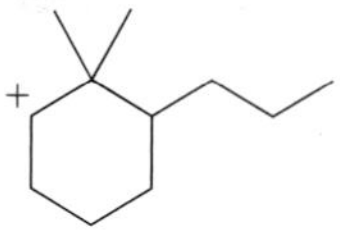

b. Which of the following anions is the best leaving group?

1. CH_3^- 2. ^-OH 3. H^- 4. $^-NH_2$ 5. Cl^-

c. Which species is the strongest nucleophile in polar protic solvents?

1. F^- 2. ^-OH 3. Cl^- 4. H_2O 5. ^-SH

d. Which of the following statements is true about the given reaction?

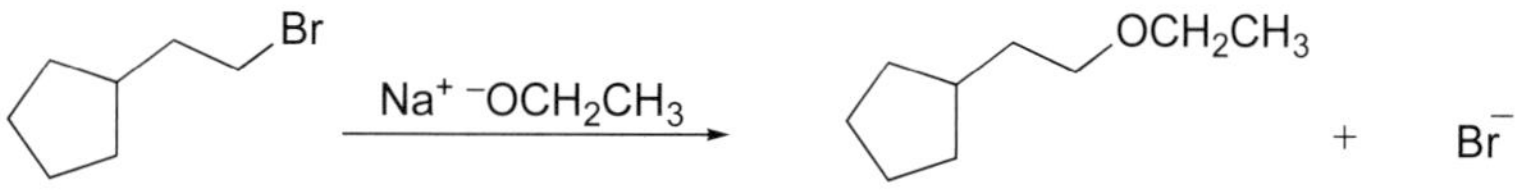

1. The reaction follows second-order kinetics.
2. The rate of the reaction increases when the solvent is changed from CH_3CH_2OH to DMSO.
3. The rate of the reaction increases when the leaving group is changes from Br to F.
4. Statements (1) and (2) are both true.
5. Statements (1), (2), and (3) are all true.

3. Rank the following compounds in order of ***increasing*** **reactivity in an S_N1** reaction. Rank the ***least reactive*** compound as **1,** the ***most reactive*** compound as **4,** and the compounds of intermediate reactivity as **2** and **3.**

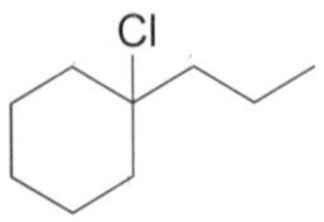
Cl

A

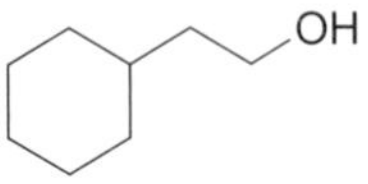
OH

B

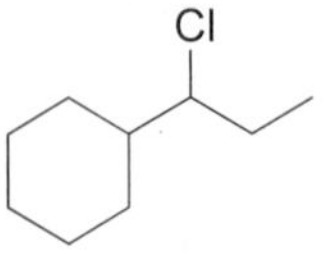
Cl

C

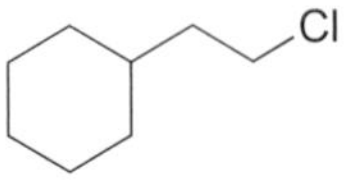
Cl

D

4. Consider the following two nucleophilic substitution reactions, labeled Reaction [1] and Reaction [2]. (Only the starting materials are drawn.) Then answer True (T) or False (F) to each of the following statements.

Reaction [1] $(CH_3CH_2)_3CBr$ + CH_3OH ⟶

Reaction [2] $CH_3CH_2CH_2Br$ + $^{-}OCH_3$ ⟶

a. The rate equation for Reaction [1] is rate = $k[(CH_3CH_2)_3CBr][CH_3OH]$.
b. Changing the leaving group from Br^- to Cl^- decreases the rate of both reactions.
c. Changing the solvent from CH_3OH to $(CH_3)_2S{=}O$ increases the rate of Reaction [2].
d. Doubling the concentration of both $CH_3CH_2CH_2Br$ and $^{-}OCH_3$ in Reaction [2] doubles the rate of the reaction.
e. If entropy is ignored and K_{eq} for Reaction [1] is < 1, then the reaction is exothermic.
f. If entropy is ignored and $\Delta H°$ is negative for Reaction [1], then the bonds in the product are stronger than the bonds in the starting materials.
g. The energy diagram for Reaction [2] exhibits only one energy barrier.

5. Draw the organic products formed in the following reactions. **Use wedges and dashes to show stereochemistry in compounds with stereogenic centers.**

a.
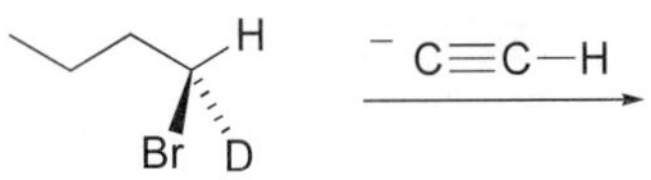
H
Br
D
⁻ C≡C–H

b.
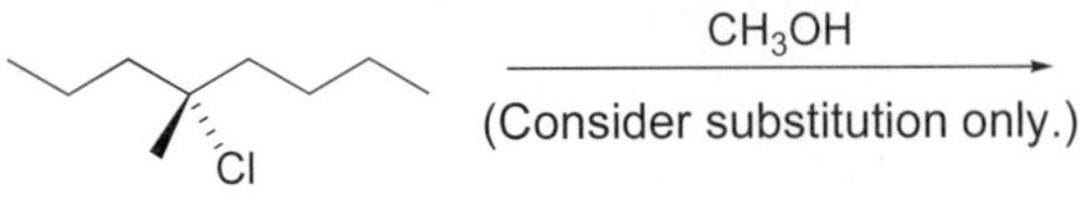
Cl
CH3OH
(Consider substitution only.)

c.
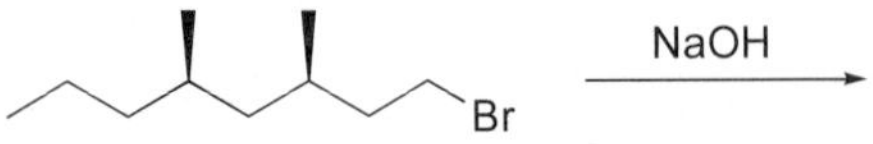
Br
NaOH

d. 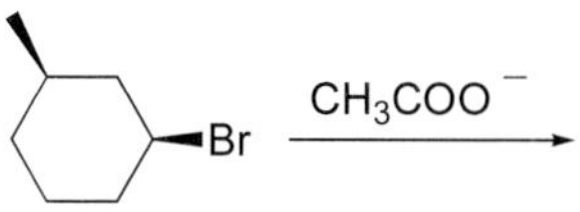
Br
CH_3COO^-

Answers to Practice Test

1. (7*S*)-7-chloro-3-ethyldecane

2. a. 4
   b. 5
   c. 5
   d. 4

3. **A**–4
   B–1
   C–3
   D–2

4. a. F
   b. T
   c. T
   d. F
   e. F
   f. T
   g. T

5. a. 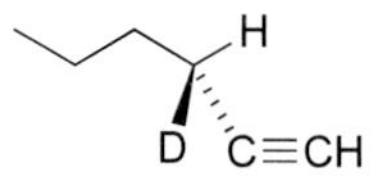
H
D
C≡CH

   b. 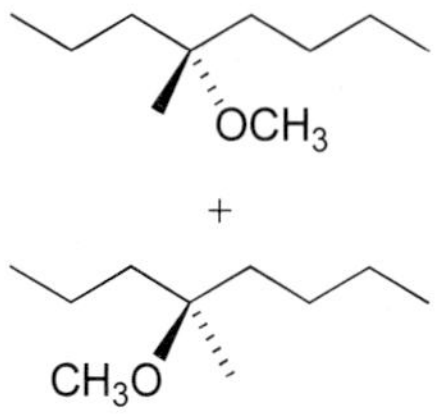
OCH3
+
CH3O

   c. 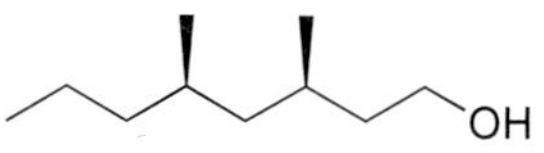
OH

   d. 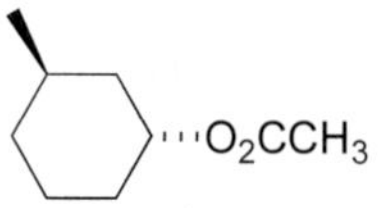
O2CCH3

Answers to Problems

7.1 Classify the alkyl halide as 1°, 2°, or 3° **by counting the number of carbons bonded directly to the carbon bonded to the halogen.**

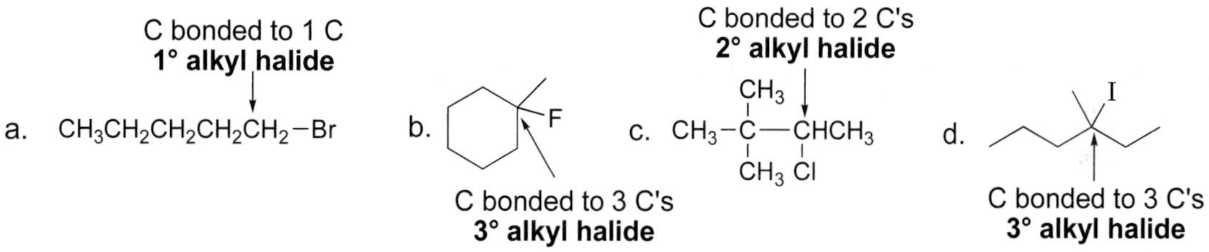
C bonded to 1 C
1° alkyl halide
a. CH3CH2CH2CH2CH2–Br
b.
F
C bonded to 3 C's
3° alkyl halide
C bonded to 2 C's
2° alkyl halide
c. CH3–C–CHCH3
CH3
CH3 Cl
d.
I
C bonded to 3 C's
3° alkyl halide

7.2 Use the directions from Answer 7.1.

a, b. 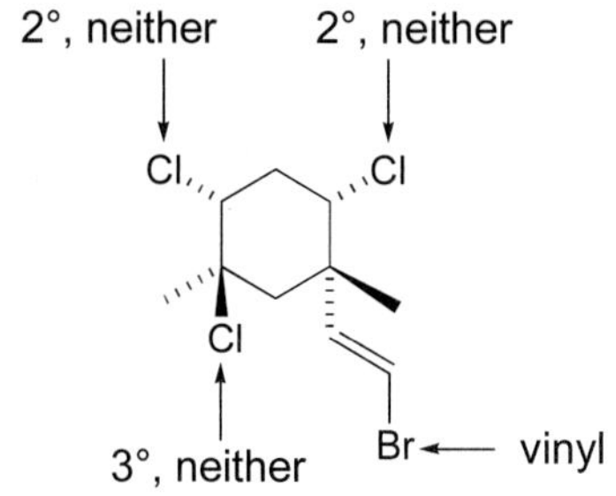
2°, neither
2°, neither
Cl
Cl
Cl
3°, neither
Br
vinyl

telfairine

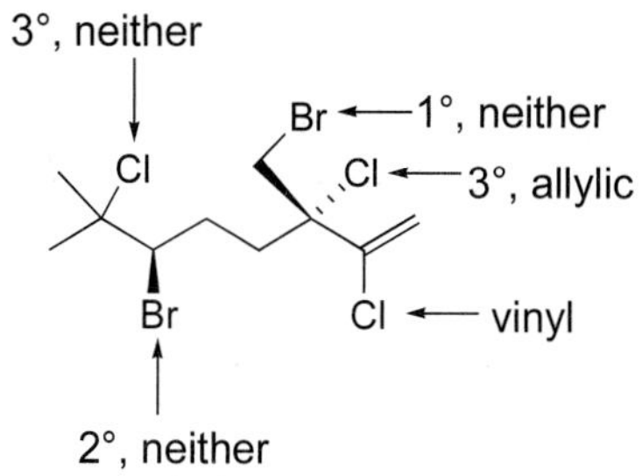
3°, neither
Cl
Br
1°, neither
Cl
3°, allylic
Br
Cl
vinyl
2°, neither

halomon

7.3 Draw a compound of molecular formula $C_6H_{13}Br$ to fit each description.

a. 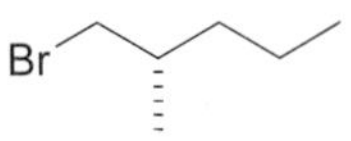
Br

1° alkyl halide
one stereogenic center

b. 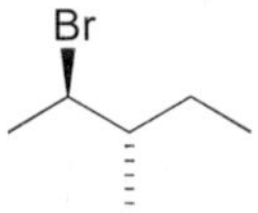
Br

2° alkyl halide
two stereogenic centers

c. 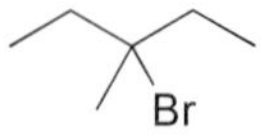
Br

3° alkyl halide
no stereogenic centers

7.4 To name a compound with the IUPAC system:

[1] **Name the parent** chain by finding the longest carbon chain.

[2] **Number the chain** so the first substituent gets the lower number. Then **name and number all substituents,** giving like substituents a prefix (di, tri, etc.). **To name the halogen substituent, change the *-ine* ending to *-o*.**

[3] **Combine all parts,** alphabetizing substituents, and ignoring all prefixes except iso.

a. $(CH_3)_2CHCH(Cl)CH_2CH_3$

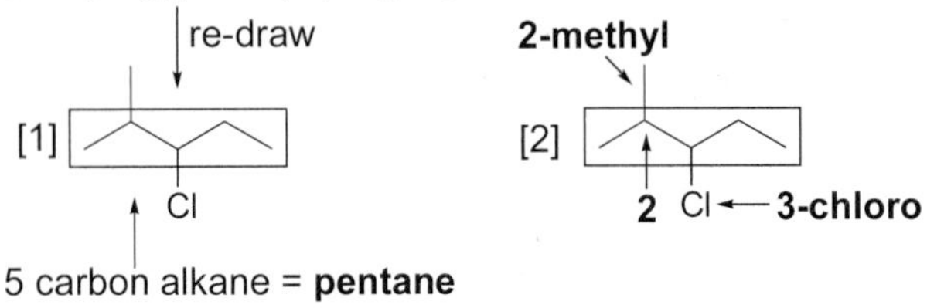
re-draw
[1]
Cl
5 carbon alkane = pentane
2-methyl
[2]
2
Cl
3-chloro

[3] **3-chloro-2-methylpentane**

b.

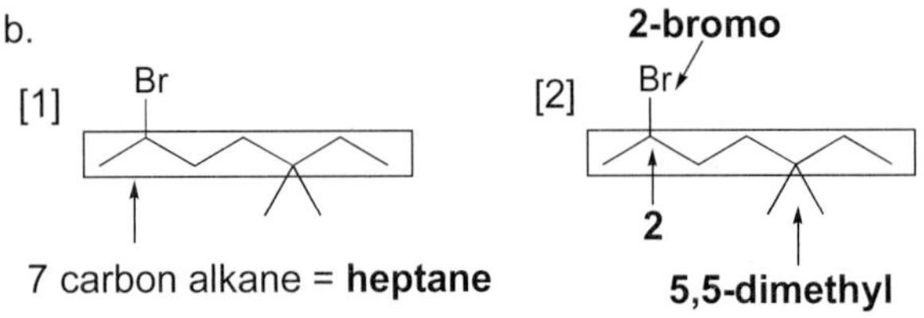
[1]
Br
7 carbon alkane = heptane
2-bromo
[2]
Br
2
5,5-dimethyl

[3] **2-bromo-5,5-dimethylheptane**

c.

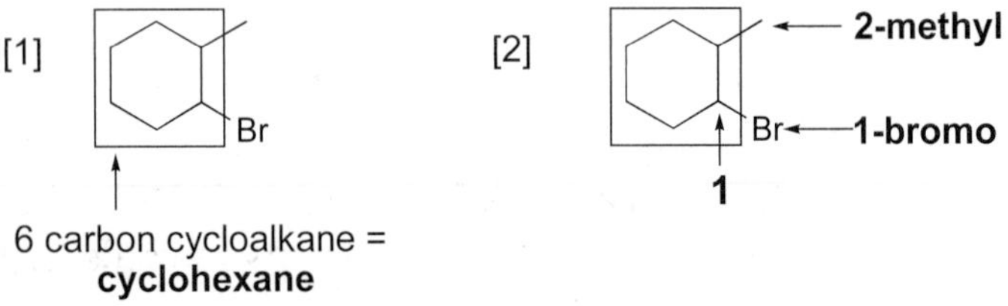
[1]
Br
6 carbon cycloalkane = cyclohexane
[2]
2-methyl
Br
1-bromo
1

[3] **1-bromo-2-methylcyclohexane**

d.

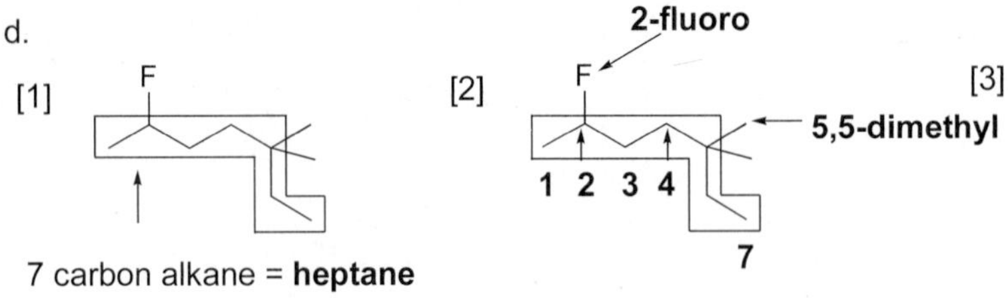
[1]
F
7 carbon alkane = heptane
2-fluoro
[2]
F
5,5-dimethyl
1 2 3 4
7

[3] **2-fluoro-5,5-dimethylheptane**

7.5 To work backwards from a name to a structure:

[1] Find the parent name and draw that number of carbons. Use the suffix to identify the functional group **(-ane = alkane).**

[2] Arbitrarily number the carbons in the chain. Add the substituents to the appropriate carbon.

a. 3-chloro-2-methyl**hexane**

[1] 6 carbon alkane

1 2 3 4 5 6

[2]

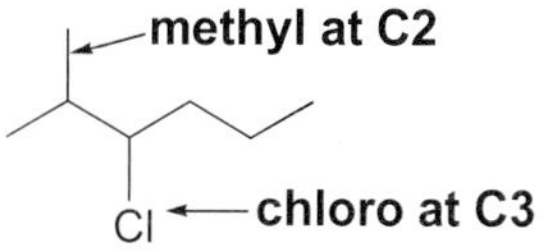
methyl at C2
Cl
chloro at C3

b. 4-ethyl-5-iodo-2,2-dimethyl**octane**

[1] 8 carbon alkane

1 2 3 4 5 6 7 8

[2]

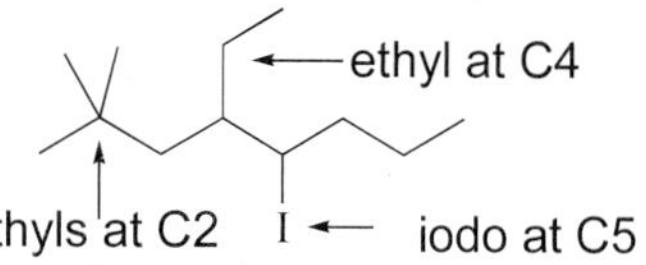
ethyl at C4
2 methyls at C2
I
iodo at C5

c. *cis*-1,3-dichloro**cyclopentane**

[1] 5 carbon cycloalkane

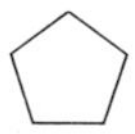

[2] chloro groups at C1 and C3, both on the same side

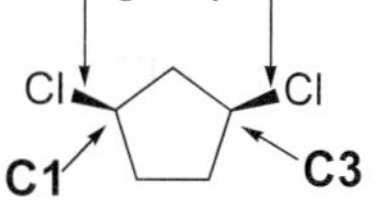
Cl
Cl
C1
C3

d. 1,1,3-tribromo**cyclohexane**

[1] 6 carbon cycloalkane

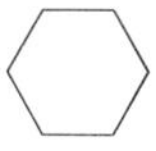

[2]

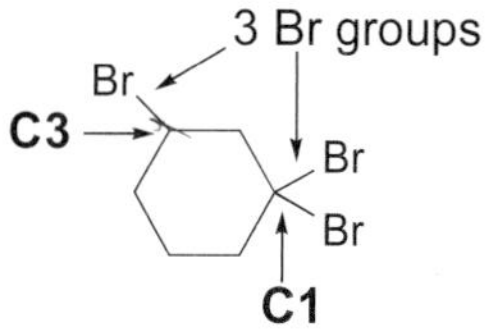
3 Br groups
Br
C3
Br
Br
C1

e. **propyl** chloride

[1] 3 carbon alkyl group

$CH_3CH_2CH_2$—

[2] **chloride on end**

$CH_3CH_2CH_2$–Cl

f. ***sec*-butyl** bromide

[1] 4 carbon alkyl group

CH_3–$\underset{|}{C}HCH_2CH_3$

[2] **bromide**

CH_3–$\underset{Br}{C}HCH_2CH_3$

7.6 a. Because an sp^2 hybridized C has a higher percent *s*-character than an sp^3 hybridized C, it holds electron density closer to C. This pulls a little more electron density towards C, away from Cl, and thus a Csp^2–Cl bond is less polar than a Csp^3–Cl bond.

b.

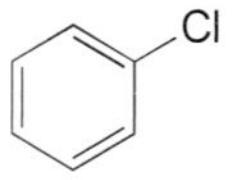
Cl

lowest boiling point

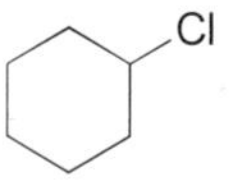
Cl

sp^3 C–Cl bond
intermediate boiling point

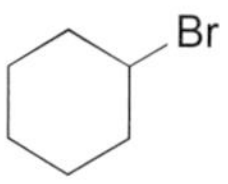
Br

larger halogen, sp^3 C–Br bond
highest boiling point

7.7 a. Since chondrocole A has 10 C's and only one functional group capable of hydrogen bonding to water (an ether), it is insoluble in H_2O. Because it is organic, it is soluble in CH_2Cl_2.

b.

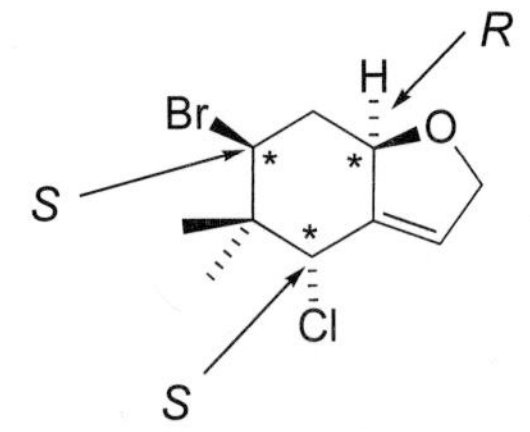

Three stereogenic centers are labeled with (*).

c.

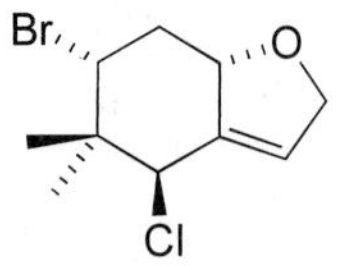

enantiomer

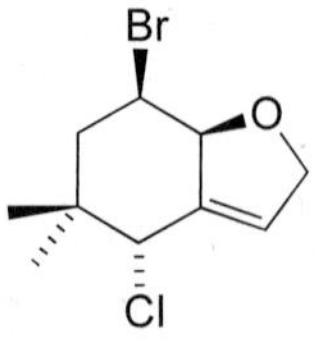

constitutional isomer

7.8 To draw the products of a nucleophilic substitution reaction:
[1] **Find the *sp*³ hybridized electrophilic carbon** with a leaving group.
[2] **Find the nucleophile** with lone pairs or electrons in π bonds.
[3] **Substitute the nucleophile for the leaving group** on the electrophilic carbon.

a.

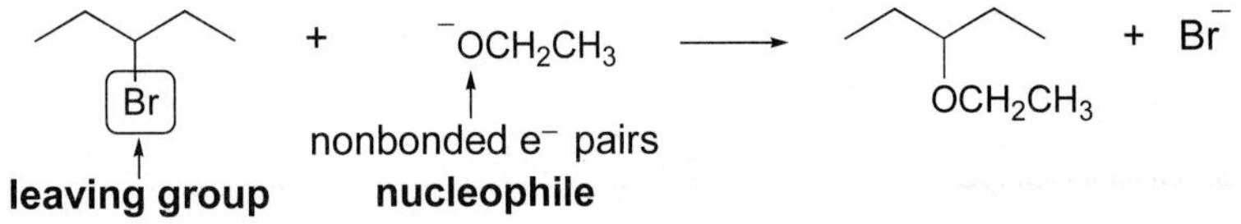

b.

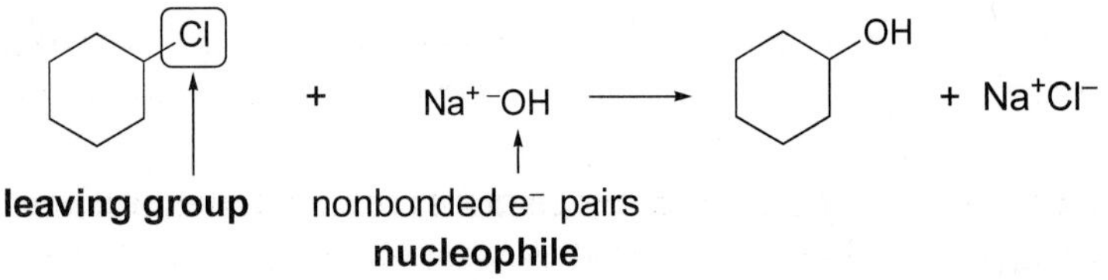

c.

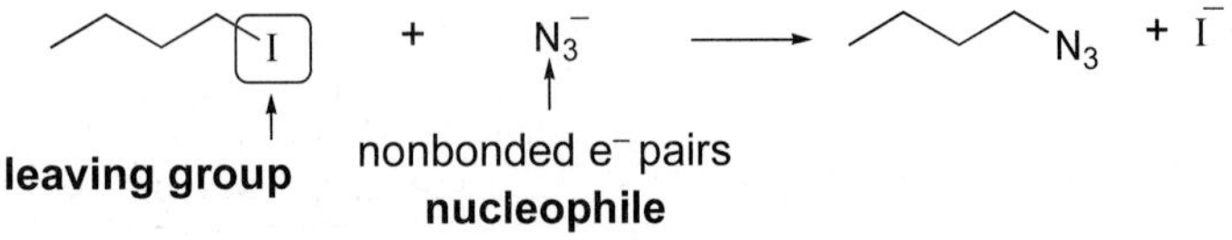

d.

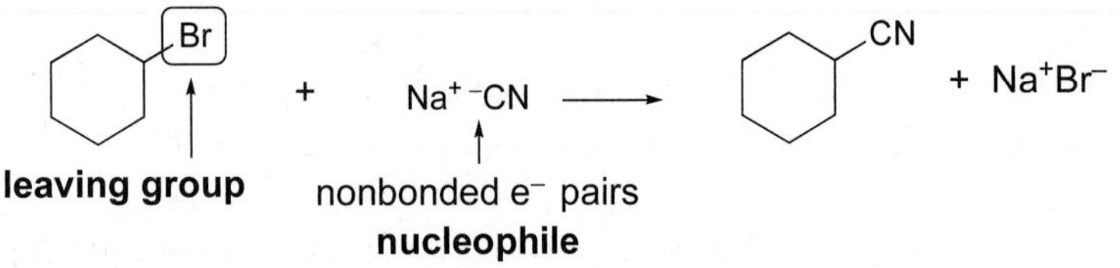

7.9 Use the steps from Answer 7.8 and then draw the proton transfer reaction.

a.

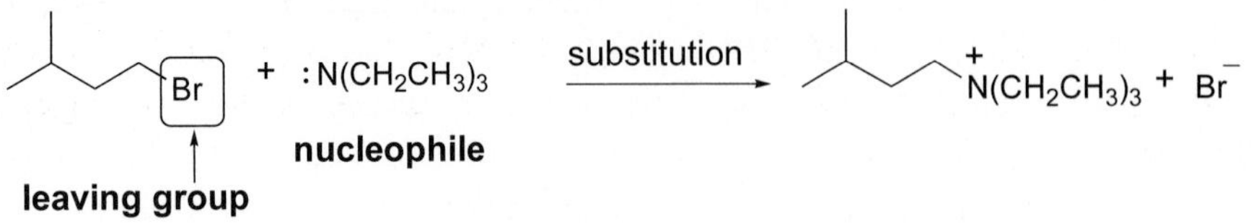

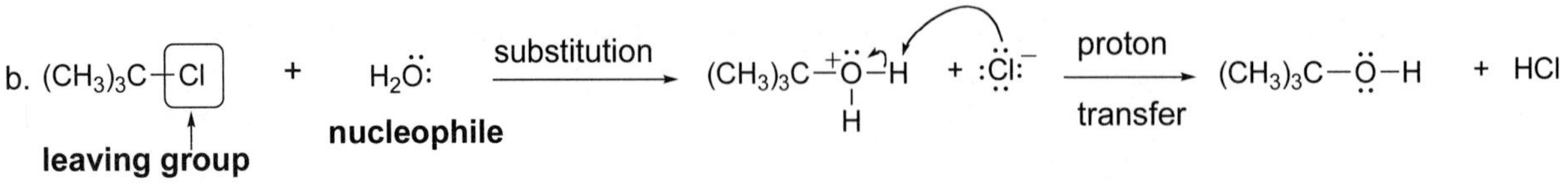

7.10 Draw the structure of CPC using the steps from Answer 7.8.

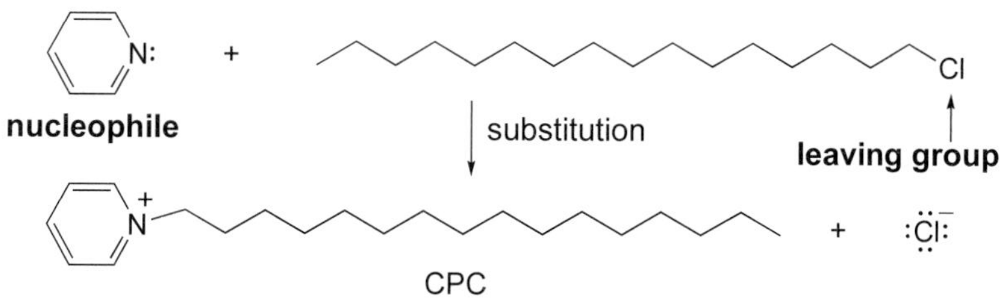

7.11 Compare the leaving groups based on these trends:
- Better leaving groups are weaker bases.
- A neutral leaving group is always better than its conjugate base.

a. Cl^-, I^- ↑ farther down a column of the periodic table, less basic, **better leaving group**

b. NH_3, NH_2^- ↑ neutral compound, less basic, **better leaving group**

c. H_2O, H_2S ↑ farther down a column of the periodic table, less basic, **better leaving group**

7.12 Good leaving groups include Cl^-, Br^-, I^-, and H_2O.

a. $CH_3CH_2CH_2$–Br — Br^- is a **good leaving group.**

b. $CH_3CH_2CH_2OH$ — No good leaving group. ^-OH is too strong a base.

c. $CH_3CH_2CH_2$–$\overset{+}{O}H_2$ — H_2O is a **good leaving group.**

d. CH_3CH_3 — No good leaving group. H^- is too strong a base.

7.13 To decide whether the equilibrium favors the starting material or the products, **compare the nucleophile and the leaving group.** The reaction proceeds towards the weaker base.

a. $CH_3CH_2-NH_2 + Br^- \longrightarrow CH_3CH_2-Br + {}^-NH_2$

Br^-: **nucleophile**, better leaving group, weaker base, pK_a (HBr) = –9

$^-NH_2$: **leaving group**, pK_a (NH_3) = 38

Reaction favors starting material.

b.

^-CN: **nucleophile**, pK_a (HCN) = 9.1

I^-: **leaving group**, better leaving group, weaker base, pK_a (HI) = –10

Reaction favors product.

7.14 It is not possible to convert $CH_3CH_2CH_2OH$ to $CH_3CH_2CH_2Cl$ by nucleophilic substitution with NaCl because ^-OH is a stronger base and poorer leaving group than Cl^-. The equilibrium favors the reactants, not the products.

$CH_3CH_2CH_2OH + Na^+\ Cl^- \not\longrightarrow CH_3CH_2CH_2Cl + Na^+\ {}^-OH$

Cl^-: weaker base

^-OH: stronger base

7.15 Use these three rules to find the stronger nucleophile in each pair:

[1] Comparing two nucleophiles having the ***same attacking atom*****, the stronger base is a stronger nucleophile.**

[2] **Negatively charged nucleophiles** are always **stronger than their conjugate acids.**

[3] **Across a row of the periodic table, nucleophilicity decreases** when comparing species of similar charge.

a. NH_3, NH_2^-

NH_2^-: A negatively charged nucleophile is stronger than its conjugate acid. **stronger nucleophile**

b. CH_3NH_2, CH_3OH

CH_3NH_2: Across a row of the periodic table, nucleophilicity decreases with species of the same charge. **stronger nucleophile**

c. 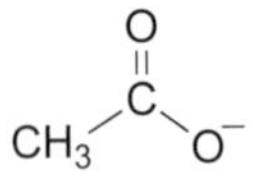

$CH_3CH_2O^-$

$CH_3CH_2O^-$: same attacking atom (O) stronger base **stronger nucleophile**

7.16 ***Polar protic solvents*** **are capable of hydrogen bonding,** and therefore must contain a **H bonded to an electronegative O or N.** ***Polar aprotic solvents*** **are incapable of hydrogen bonding,** and therefore do not contain any O–H or N–H bonds.

a. $HOCH_2CH_2OH$ — contains 2 O–H bonds **polar protic**

b. $CH_3CH_2OCH_2CH_3$ — no O–H bonds **polar aprotic**

c. $CH_3COOCH_2CH_3$ — no O–H bonds **polar aprotic**

7.17
- In ***polar protic solvents,*** **the trend in nucleophilicity is opposite to the trend in basicity** down a column of the periodic table so that nucleophilicity increases.
- In ***polar aprotic solvents,*** **the trend is identical to basicity** so that nucleophilicity decreases down a column.

a. Br^- and Cl^- in polar protic solvent

Br^-: farther down the column **more nucleophilic in protic solvent**

b. ^-OH and Cl^- in polar aprotic solvent

^-OH: farther up the column and to the left in the row more basic **more nucleophilic**

In polar aprotic solvents: nucleophilicity increases (← across: O F; ↑ up column: Cl) nucleophilicity increases

c. HS^- and F^- in polar protic solvent

HS^-: farther down the column and left in the row **more nucleophilic in protic solvent**

In polar protic solvents: nucleophilicity increases (← across: O F; ↓ down column: S) nucleophilicity increases

7.18 The stronger base is the stronger nucleophile except in polar protic solvents when nucleophilicity increases down a column. For other rules, see Answers 7.15 and 7.17.

a. H_2O — no charge — **weakest nucleophile**
^{-}OH — negatively charged — **intermediate nucleophile**
$^{-}NH_2$ — negatively charged, farther left in periodic table — **strongest nucleophile**

b. Br^{-} — Basicity decreases down a column in polar aprotic solvents. — **weakest nucleophile**
F^{-} — Basicity decreases across a row. — **intermediate nucleophile**
^{-}OH — **strongest nucleophile**

c. H_2O — **weakest nucleophile**
CH_3COO^{-} — weaker base than ^{-}OH — **intermediate nucleophile**
^{-}OH — **strongest nucleophile**

7.19 To determine what nucleophile is needed to carry out each reaction, look at the product to see what has replaced the leaving group.

a. $(CH_3)_2CHCH_2CH_2{-}Br \longrightarrow (CH_3)_2CHCH_2CH_2{-}SH$
SH replaces Br.
HS^{-} is needed.

b. $(CH_3)_2CHCH_2CH_2{-}Br \longrightarrow (CH_3)_2CHCH_2CH_2{-}OCH_2CH_3$
OCH_2CH_3 replaces Br.
$CH_3CH_2O^{-}$ is needed.

c. $(CH_3)_2CHCH_2CH_2{-}Br \longrightarrow (CH_3)_2CHCH_2CH_2{-}OCOCH_3$
$OCOCH_3$ replaces Br.
CH_3COO^{-} is needed.

d. $(CH_3)_2CHCH_2CH_2{-}Br \longrightarrow (CH_3)_2CHCH_2CH_2{-}C{\equiv}CH$
$C{\equiv}CH$ replaces Br.
$HC{\equiv}C^{-}$ is needed.

7.20 The general rate equation for an S_N2 reaction is rate = $k[RX][:Nu^{-}]$.

a. $[RX]$ is tripled, and $[:Nu^{-}]$ stays the same: **rate triples.**
b. Both $[RX]$ and $[:Nu^{-}]$ are tripled: **rate increases by a factor of 9 ($3 \times 3 = 9$).**
c. $[RX]$ is halved, and $[:Nu^{-}]$ stays the same: **rate halved.**
d. $[RX]$ is halved, and $[:Nu^{-}]$ is doubled: **rate stays the same ($1/2 \times 2 = 1$).**

7.21 The transition state in an S_N2 reaction has **dashed bonds to both the leaving group and the nucleophile,** and must contain partial charges.

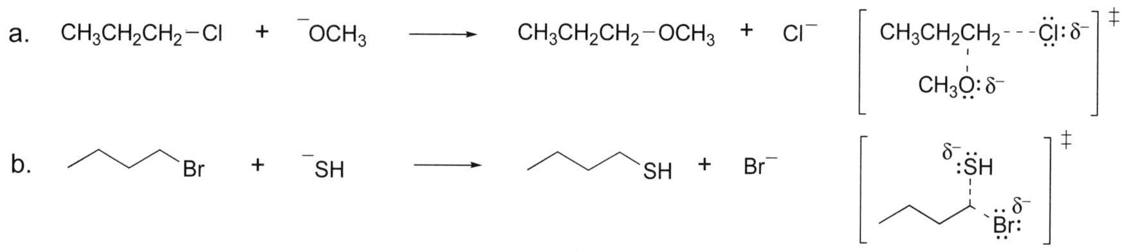
a.
CH3CH2CH2−Cl + −OCH3 → CH3CH2CH2−OCH3 + Cl−
CH3CH2CH2---Cl: δ−
CH3O: δ−
‡
b.
Br + −SH → SH + Br−
δ− :SH
δ− Br:
‡

7.22 All S_N2 reactions have one step.

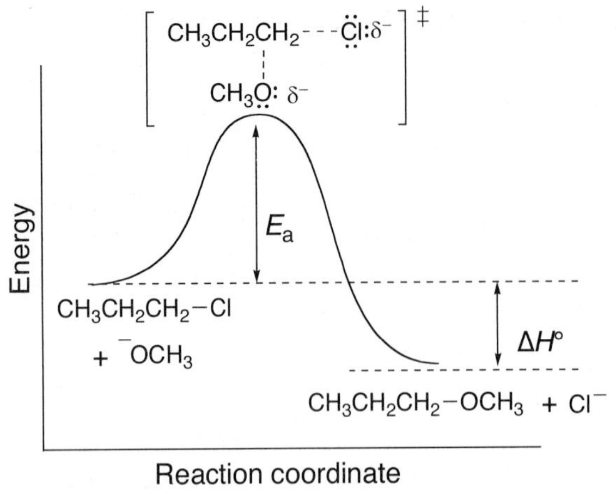
CH3CH2CH2---Cl:δ−
CH3O: δ−
‡
Energy
Ea
CH3CH2CH2−Cl
+ −OCH3
ΔH°
CH3CH2CH2−OCH3 + Cl−
Reaction coordinate

7.23 To draw the products of S_N2 reactions, **replace the leaving group by the nucleophile, and then draw the stereochemistry with *inversion* at the stereogenic center.**

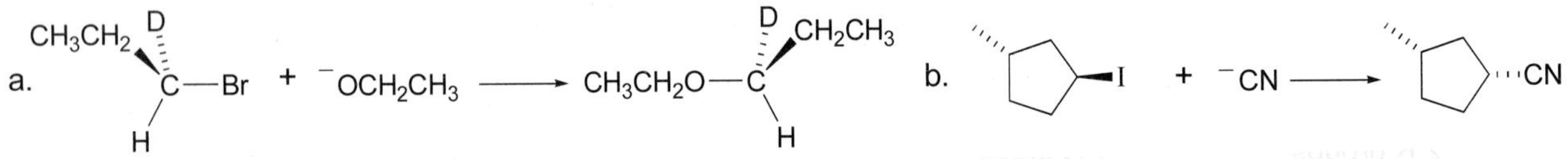
a.
CH3CH2
D
C—Br
H
+ −OCH2CH3
CH3CH2O—C
D
CH2CH3
H
b.
I
+ −CN
CN

7.24 *Increasing* the number of R groups *increases* crowding of the transition state and *decreases* the rate of an S_N2 reaction.

a.
Cl
or
Cl
2° alkyl halide
1° alkyl halide
faster reaction
b.
Br
or
Br
2° alkyl halide
faster reaction
3° alkyl halide

7.25

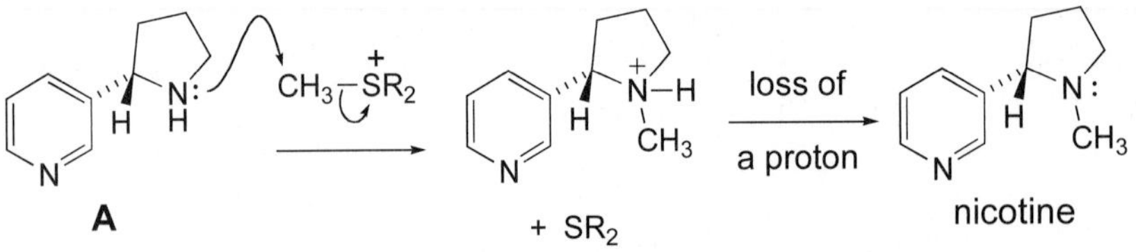
N:
H H
N
A
CH3−SR2
+
N−H
H
CH3
N
+ SR2
loss of
a proton
N:
H
CH3
N
nicotine

7.26 In a first-order reaction, **the rate changes with any change in [RX].** The rate is independent of any change in [:Nu⁻].

a. [RX] is tripled, and [:Nu⁻] stays the same: **rate triples.**

b. Both [RX] and [:Nu⁻] are tripled: **rate triples.**

c. [RX] is halved, and [:Nu⁻] stays the same: **rate halved.**

d. [RX] is halved, and [:Nu⁻] is doubled: **rate halved.**

7.27 In S_N1 reactions, racemization always occurs at a stereogenic center. Draw two products, with the two possible configurations at the stereogenic center.

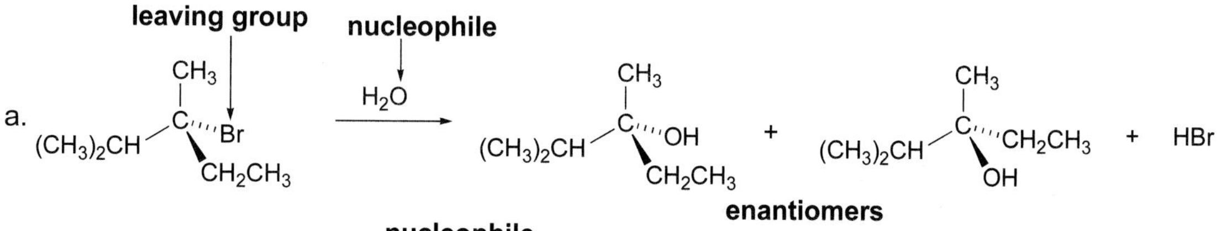

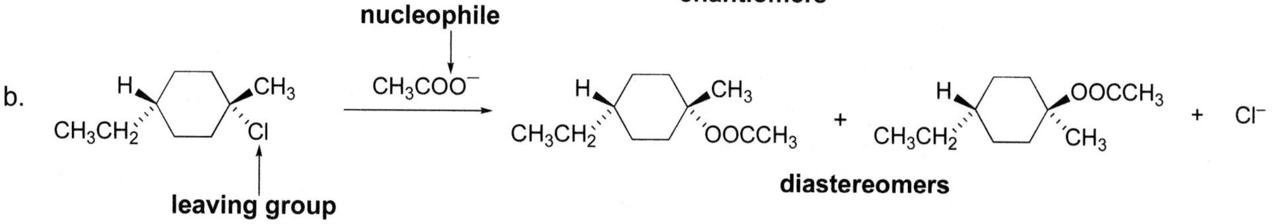

7.28 Carbocations are classified by the number of R groups bonded to the carbon: 0 R groups = methyl, 1 R group = 1°, 2 R groups = 2°, and 3 R groups = 3°.

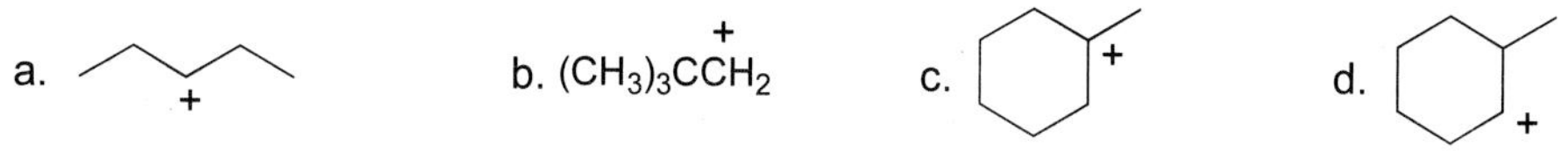

a.	b. $(CH_3)_3C\overset{+}{C}H_2$	c.	d.
2 R groups **2° carbocation**	1 R group **1° carbocation**	3 R groups **3° carbocation**	2 R groups **2° carbocation**

7.29 For carbocations: Increasing number of R groups = Increasing stability.

$CH_3CH_2CH_2\overset{+}{C}H_2$	$CH_3\overset{+}{C}HCH_2CH_3$	$CH_3-\overset{+}{C}(CH_3)-CH_3$
1° carbocation **least stable**	2° carbocation **intermediate stability**	3° carbocation **most stable**

7.30 For carbocations: Increasing number of R groups = Increasing stability.

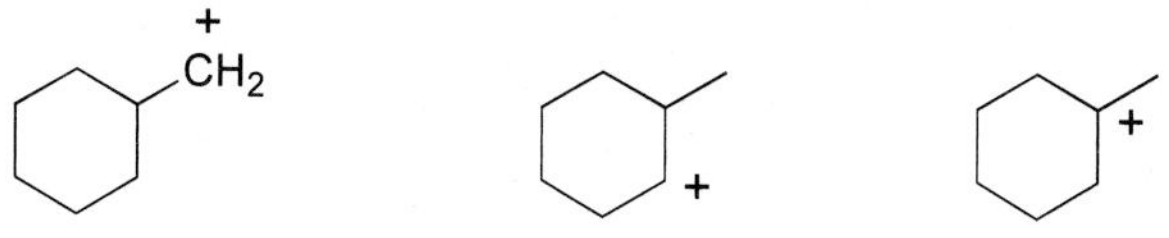

1° carbocation **least stable**	2° carbocation **intermediate stability**	3° carbocation **most stable**

7.31 The rate of an S_N1 reaction increases with increasing alkyl substitution.

a. $(CH_3)_3CBr$ or $(CH_3)_3CCH_2Br$

3° alkyl halide — **faster S_N1 reaction**; 1° alkyl halide — **slower S_N1 reaction**

b.

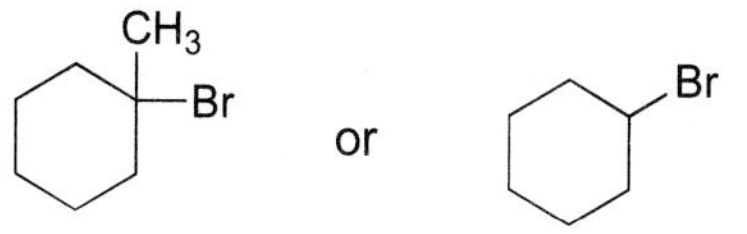

3° alkyl halide — **faster S_N1 reaction**; 2° alkyl halide — **slower S_N1 reaction**

7.32 • For **methyl and 1° alkyl halides,** only S_N2 will occur.
• For **2° alkyl halides,** S_N1 and S_N2 will occur.
• For **3° alkyl halides,** only S_N1 will occur.

a. 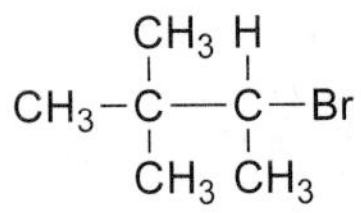

2° alkyl halide
S_N1 and S_N2

b. 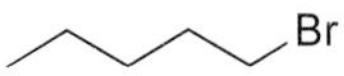

1° alkyl halide
S_N2

c. 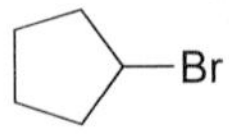

2° alkyl halide
S_N1 and S_N2

d. 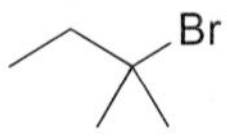

3° alkyl halide
S_N1

7.33 • Draw the product of nucleophilic substitution for each reaction.
• For **methyl and 1° alkyl halides,** only S_N2 will occur.
• For **2° alkyl halides,** S_N1 and S_N2 will occur and other factors determine which mechanism operates.
• For **3° alkyl halides,** only S_N1 will occur.

a. 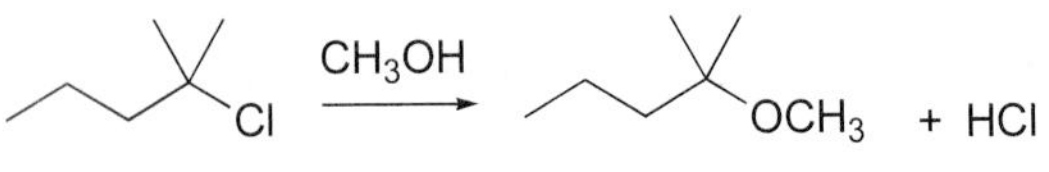

3° alkyl halide
only S_N1

c. Strong nucleophile
favors S_N2.

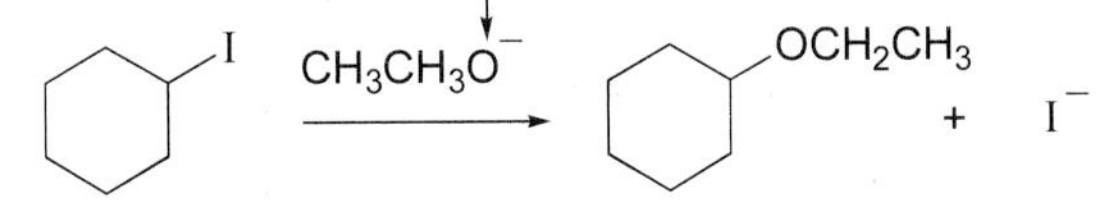

2° alkyl halide
Both S_N1 and S_N2 are possible.

b. 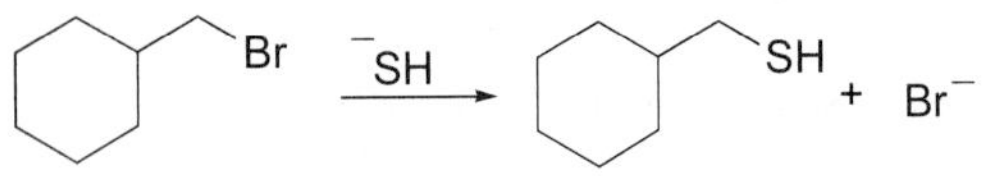

1° alkyl halide
only S_N2

d. Weak nucleophile
favors S_N1.

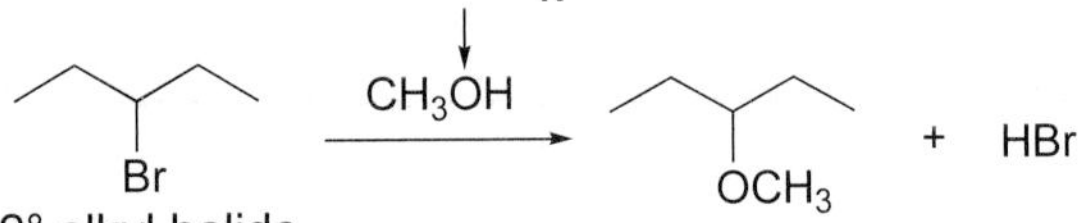

2° alkyl halide
Both S_N1 and S_N2 are possible.

7.34 First decide whether the reaction will proceed via an S_N1 or S_N2 mechanism. Then draw the products with stereochemistry.

a. 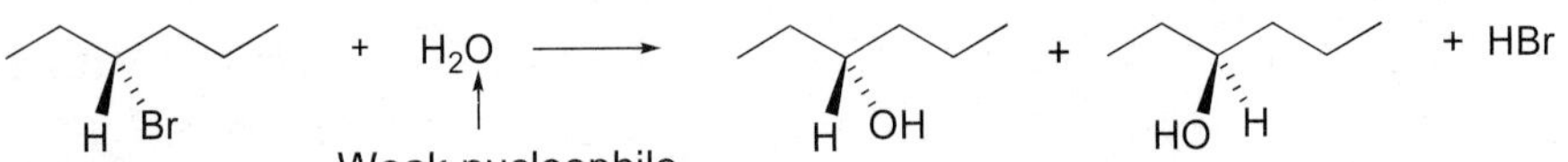

2° alkyl halide
S_N1 and S_N2

Weak nucleophile
favors S_N1.

enantiomers

S_N1 = racemization at the stereogenic C

b. 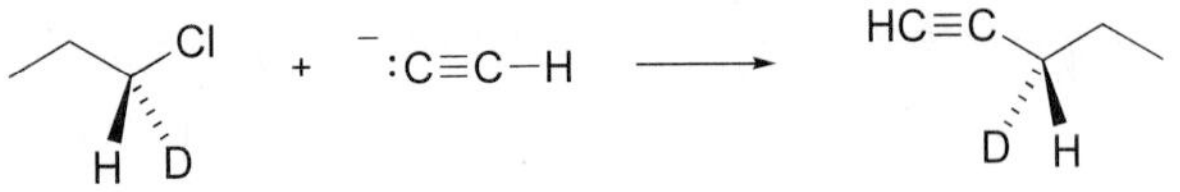

1° alkyl halide
S_N2 only

S_N2 = inversion at the stereogenic C

7.35 Compounds with better leaving groups react faster. Weaker bases are better leaving groups.

a. $CH_3CH_2CH_2Cl$ or $CH_3CH_2CH_2I$ ← weaker base, **better leaving group**

b. $(CH_3)_3CBr$ or $(CH_3)_3CI$ ← weaker base, **better leaving group**

c. $(CH_3)_3C{-}OH$ or $(CH_3)_3C{-}\overset{+}{O}H_2$ ← weaker base, **better leaving group**

d. $CH_3CH_2CH_2OH$ or $CH_3CH_2CH_2{-}OCOCH_3$ ← weaker base, **better leaving group**

7.36 • **Polar protic solvents** favor the S_N1 mechanism by solvating the intermediate carbocation and halide.

• **Polar aprotic solvents** favor the S_N2 mechanism by making the nucleophile stronger.

a. CH_3CH_2OH	b. CH_3CN	c. CH_3COOH	d. $CH_3CH_2OCH_2CH_3$
polar protic solvent	polar aprotic solvent	polar protic solvent	polar aprotic solvent
contains an O–H bond	no O–H or N–H bond	contains an O–H bond	no O–H or N–H bond
favors S_N1	**favors S_N2**	**favors S_N1**	**favors S_N2**

7.37 Compare the solvents in the reactions below. **For the solvent to increase the reaction rate of an S_N1 reaction, the solvent must be *polar protic.***

a.

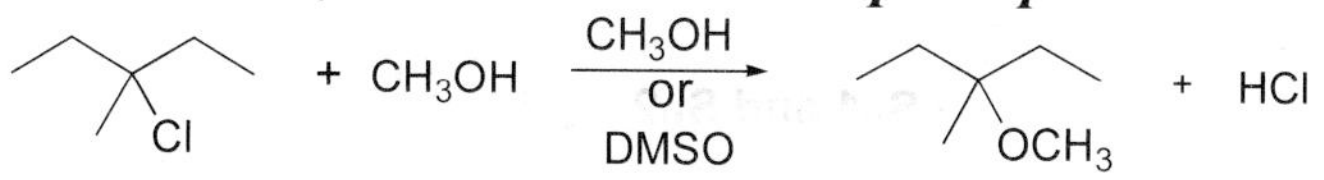

Cl
+ CH3OH
CH3OH
or
DMSO
OCH3
+ HCl

3° RX – S_N1 reaction

CH_3OH
Polar protic solvent
increases the rate of an S_N1 reaction.

b.

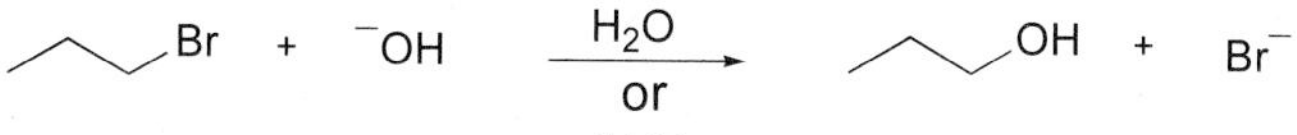

Br
+ ⁻OH
H2O
or
DMF
OH
+ Br⁻

1° RX – S_N2 reaction

DMF $[HCON(CH_3)_2]$
Polar aprotic solvent
increases the rate of an S_N2 reaction.

c.

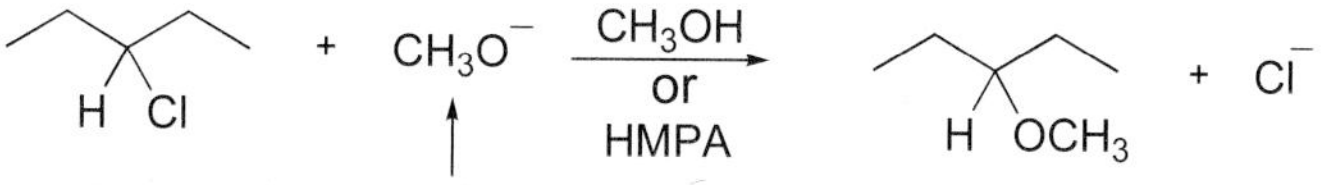

H Cl
+ CH3O⁻
CH3OH
or
HMPA
H OCH3
+ Cl⁻

2° RX strong nucleophile
S_N2 reaction

HMPA $[(CH_3)_2N]_3P{=}O$
Polar aprotic solvent
increases the rate of an S_N2 reaction.

7.38 To predict whether the reaction follows an S_N1 or S_N2 mechanism:

[1] **Classify RX as a methyl, 1°, 2°, or 3° halide.** (Methyl, 1° = S_N2; 3° = S_N1; 2° = either.)

[2] **Classify the nucleophile as strong or weak.** (Strong favors S_N2; weak favors S_N1.)

[3] **Classify the solvent as polar protic or polar aprotic.** (Polar protic favors S_N1; polar aprotic favors S_N2.)

a.

CH2Br
+ CH3CH2O⁻
CH2OCH2CH3
+ Br⁻

S_N2 reaction

1° alkyl halide
S_N2

b.

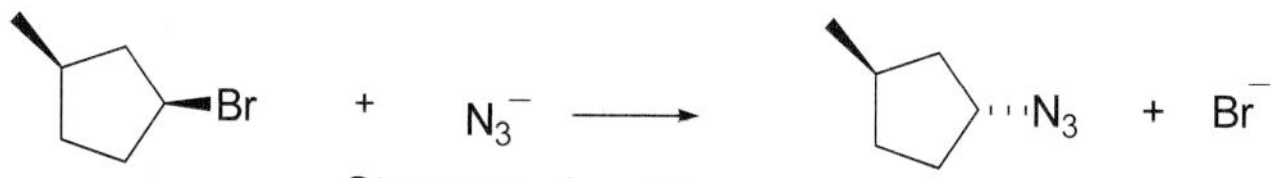

Br
+
N3⁻
N3
+ Br⁻

2° alkyl halide
S_N1 or S_N2

Strong nucleophile
favors S_N2.

S_N2 reaction = ***inversion*** at the stereogenic center
The leaving group was "up."
The nucleophile attacks from below.

c. 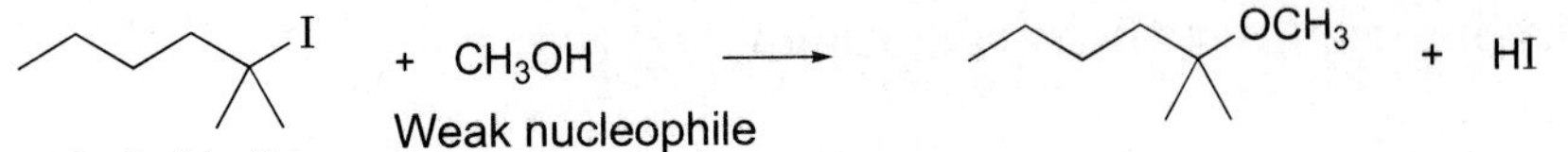
I
+ CH_3OH
OCH_3
+ HI

3° alkyl halide **S_N1** — Weak nucleophile **favors S_N1.** — S_N1 reaction

d. 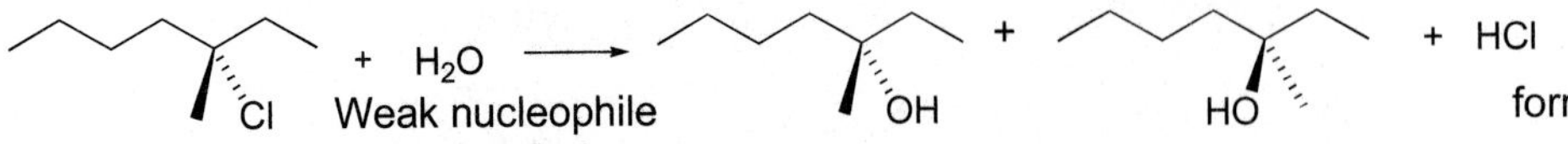
Cl
+ H_2O
OH
+
HO
+ HCl

3° alkyl halide **S_N1** — Weak nucleophile **favors S_N1.** — S_N1 reaction forms **two enantiomers.**

7.39 Vinyl carbocations are even less stable than 1° carbocations.

$CH_3CH_2CH_2CH_2CH{=}\overset{+}{C}H$	$CH_3CH_2CH_2CH_2CH_2\overset{+}{C}H_2$	$CH_3CH_2CH_2CH_2\overset{+}{C}HCH_3$
vinyl carbocation **least stable**	1° carbocation **intermediate stability**	2° carbocation **most stable**

7.40 Convert each ball-and-stick model to a skeletal or condensed structure and draw the reactants.

a. 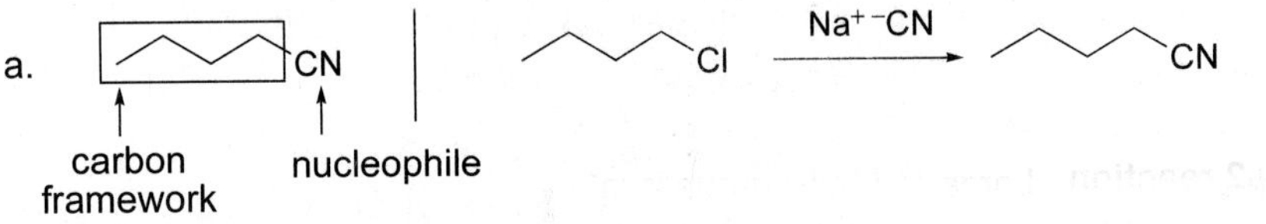
CN
carbon framework
nucleophile
Cl
$Na^+ {}^-CN$
CN

b. $(CH_3)_3CCH_2CH_2$–SH (carbon framework: $(CH_3)_3CCH_2CH_2$; nucleophile: SH)

$(CH_3)_3CCH_2CH_2-Cl \xrightarrow{Na^+ \; {}^-SH} (CH_3)_3CCH_2CH_2-SH$

c. 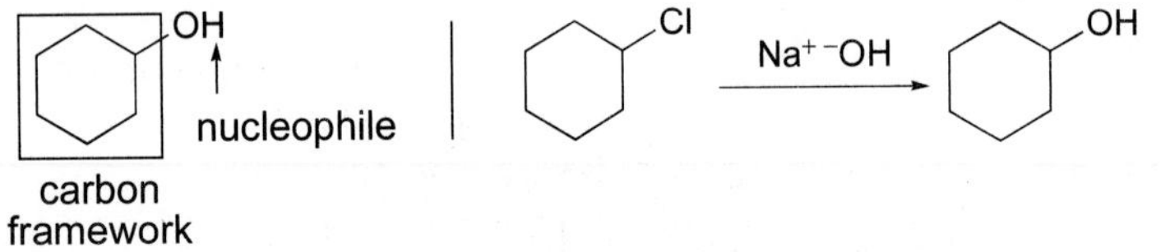
OH
nucleophile
carbon framework
Cl
$Na^+ {}^-OH$
OH

d. CH_3CH_2–C≡C–H (carbon framework: CH_3CH_2; nucleophile: C≡C–H)

$CH_3CH_2-Cl \xrightarrow{Na^+ \; {}^-C{\equiv}CH} CH_3CH_2-C{\equiv}C-H$

7.41

$CH_3\ddot{O}:^-$ + $Cl-CH_2CH_3$ → $CH_3\ddot{O}CH_2CH_3$
$CH_3CH_2\ddot{O}:^-$ + $Cl-CH_3$ → $CH_3\ddot{O}CH_2CH_3$

7.42 Use the directions from Answer 7.4 to name the compounds.

a.

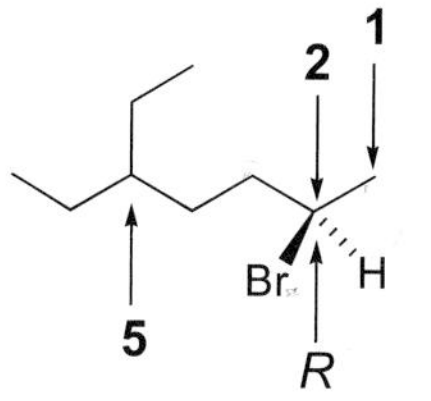
1
2
5
Br
H
R

7 C chain = heptane
bromo at C2
ethyl at C5
one stereogenic center–*R*
(2*R*)-2-bromo-5-ethylheptane

b.

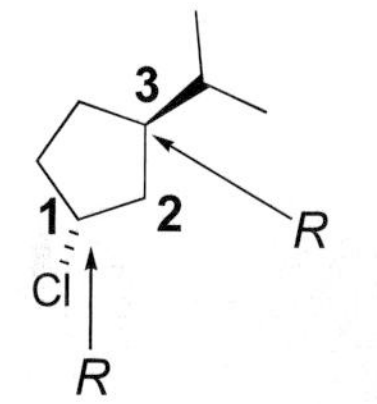
3
1
2
R
Cl
R

5 C ring = cyclopentane
chloro at C1
isopropyl at C3
trans isomer–one substituent up, one down
(1*R*, 3*R*)-*trans*-1-chloro-3-isopropylcyclopentane

7.43

a.

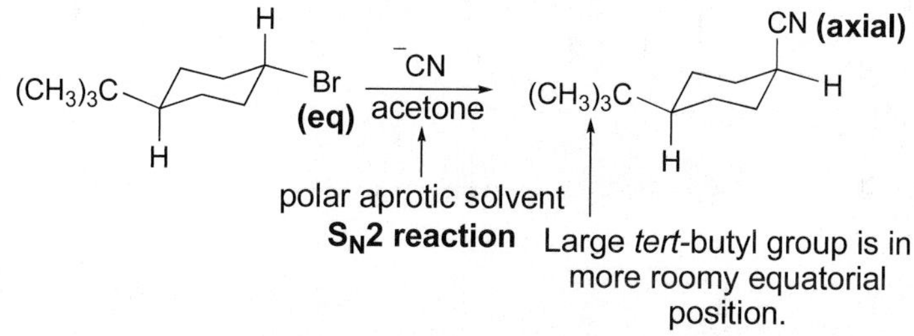
H
(CH3)3C
Br
(eq)
H
−CN
acetone
polar aprotic solvent
SN2 reaction
CN (axial)
(CH3)3C
H
H
Large tert-butyl group is in more roomy equatorial position.

inversion (equatorial to axial)

b.

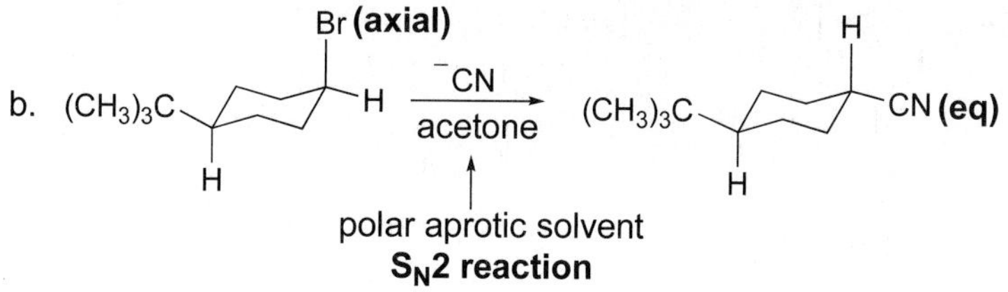
Br (axial)
(CH3)3C
H
H
−CN
acetone
polar aprotic solvent
SN2 reaction
H
(CH3)3C
CN (eq)
H

inversion (axial to equatorial)

7.44 Use the directions from Answer 7.4 to name the compounds.

a. [1]

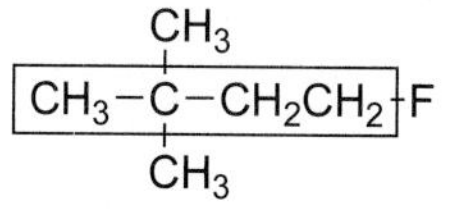
CH3
CH3–C–CH2CH2–F
CH3

4 carbon alkane = **butane**

[2]

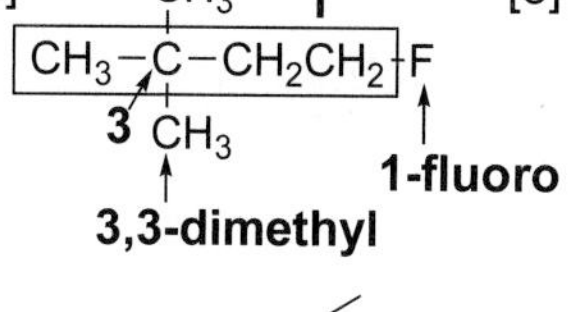
CH3
1
CH3–C–CH2CH2–F
3
CH3
1-fluoro
3,3-dimethyl

[3] **1-fluoro-3,3-dimethylbutane**

b. [1]

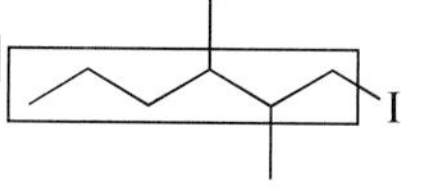
I

6 carbon alkane = **hexane**

[2]

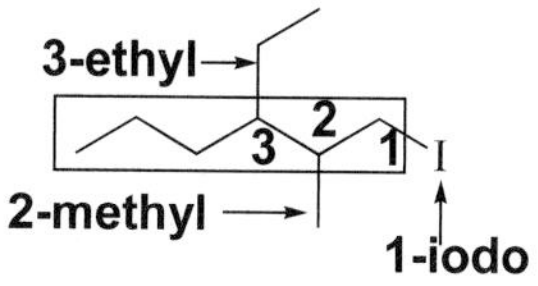
3-ethyl
3
2
1
I
2-methyl
1-iodo

[3] **3-ethyl-1-iodo-2-methylhexane**

c. [1] $(CH_3)_3CCH_2Br$

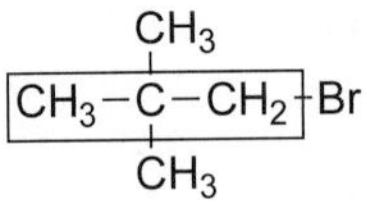
CH3
CH3–C–CH2–Br
CH3

3 carbon alkane = **propane**

[2]

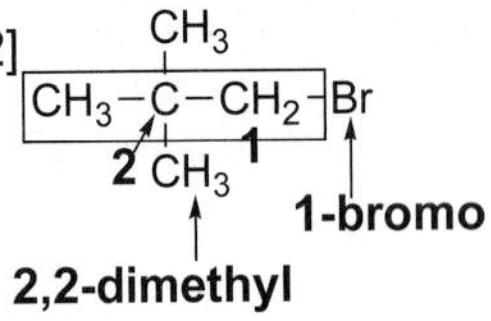
CH3
CH3–C–CH2–Br
2 CH3
1
1-bromo
2,2-dimethyl

[3] **1-bromo-2,2-dimethylpropane**

d. [1]

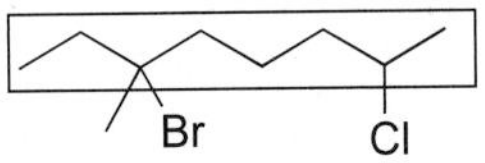
Br
Cl

8 carbon alkane = **octane**

[2]

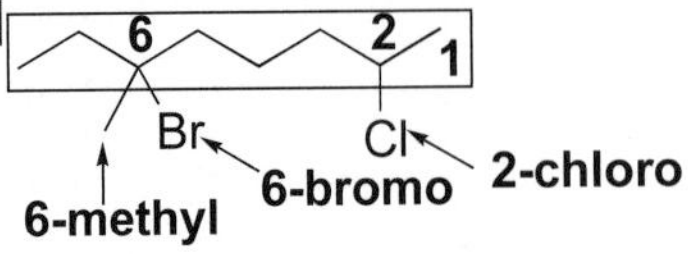
6
2
1
Br
Cl
6-methyl
6-bromo
2-chloro

[3] **6-bromo-2-chloro-6-methyloctane**

e. [1]

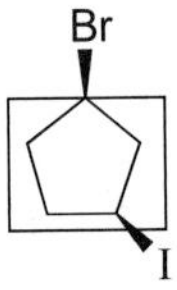
Br
I

5 carbon cycloalkane = **cyclopentane**

[2]

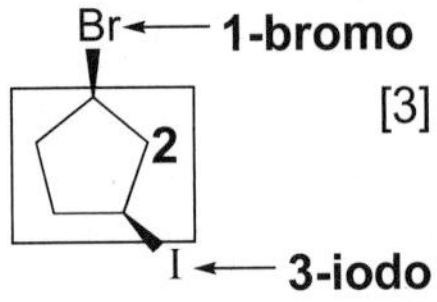
Br
1-bromo
2
I
3-iodo

[3] ***cis*-1-bromo-3-iodocyclopentane**

f. [1]

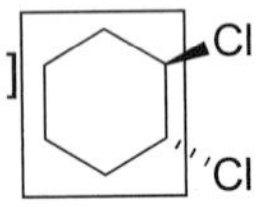
Cl
Cl

6 carbon cycloalkane = **cyclohexane**

[2]

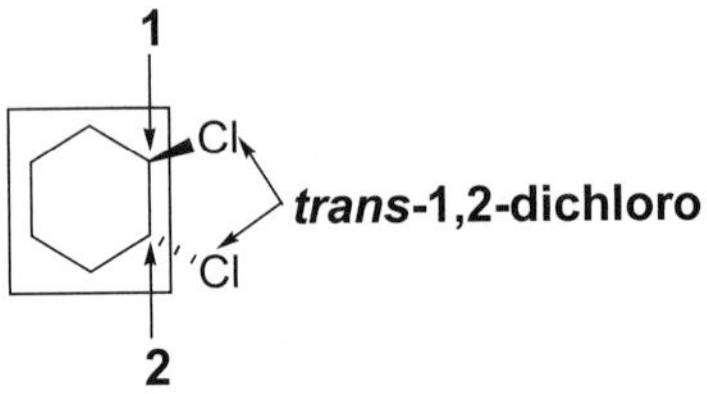
1
Cl
Cl
2
trans-1,2-dichloro

[3] ***trans*-1,2-dichlorocyclohexane**

g. [1] $(CH_3)_3CCH_2CH(Cl)CH_2Cl$

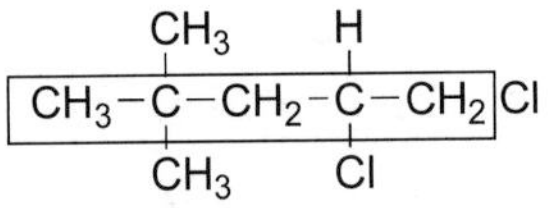
CH3 H
CH3–C–CH2–C–CH2Cl
CH3 Cl

5 carbon alkane = **pentane**

[2]

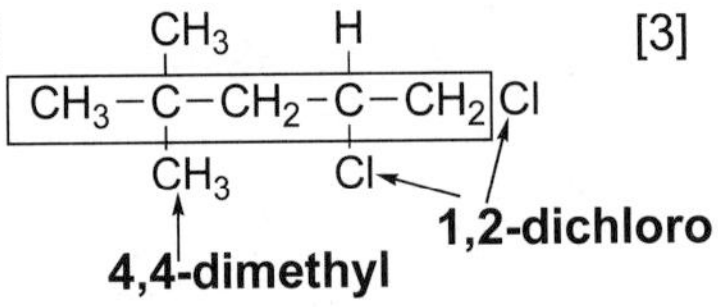
CH3 H
CH3–C–CH2–C–CH2Cl
CH3 Cl
1,2-dichloro
4,4-dimethyl

[3] **1,2-dichloro-4,4-dimethylpentane**

h. [1]

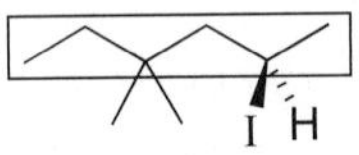
I H

6 carbon alkane = **hexane**
(Indicate the *R*,*S* designation also)

[2]

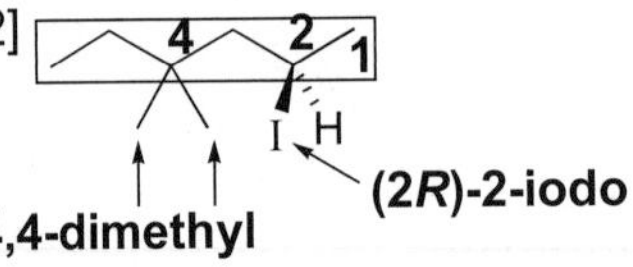
4
2
1
I H
4,4-dimethyl
(2R)-2-iodo

[3] **(2*R*)-2-iodo-4,4-dimethylhexane**

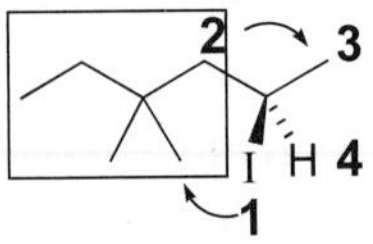
2
3
I H 4
1

Clockwise
R

7.45 To work backwards to a structure, use the directions in Answer 7.5.

a. **isopropyl** bromide

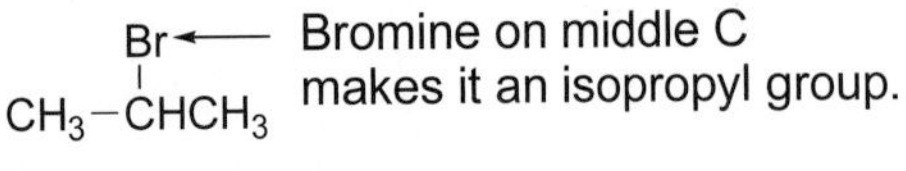
Br
CH3–CHCH3
Bromine on middle C
makes it an isopropyl group.

b. 3-bromo-4-ethyl**heptane**

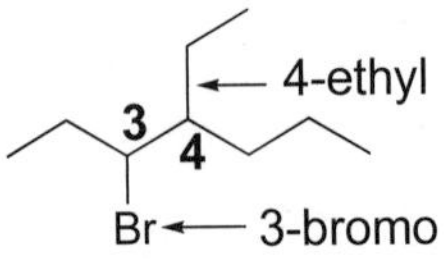
4-ethyl
3
4
Br
3-bromo

c. 1,1-dichloro-2-methyl**cyclohexane**

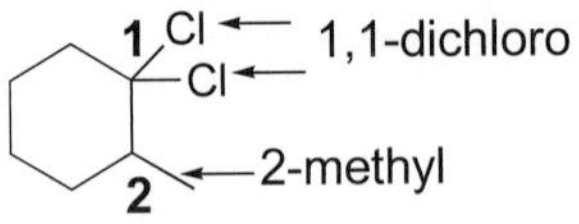
1
Cl
Cl
1,1-dichloro
2
2-methyl

d. *trans*-1-chloro-3-iodo**cyclobutane**

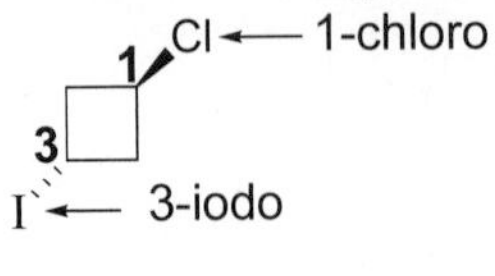
Cl
1-chloro
1
3
I
3-iodo

e. 1-bromo-4-ethyl-3-fluoro**octane**

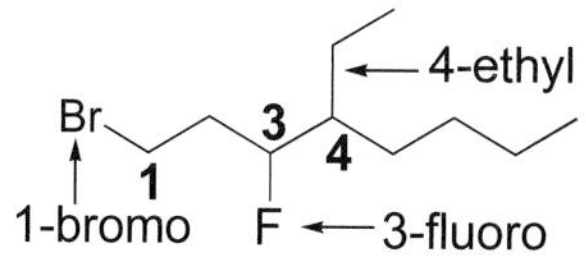
4-ethyl
Br
3
4
1
1-bromo
F
3-fluoro

f. (3*S*)-3-iodo-2-methyl**nonane**

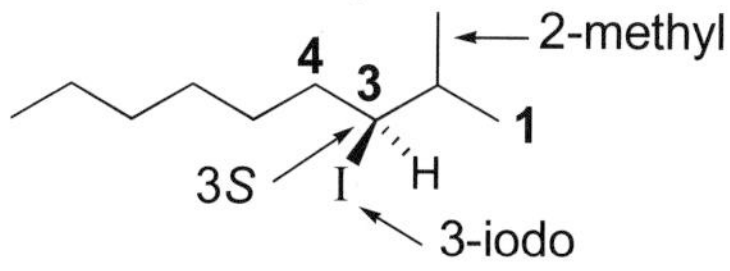
2-methyl
4
3
1
3S
I
H
3-iodo

g. (1*R*,2*R*)-*trans*-1-bromo-2-chloro**cyclohexane**

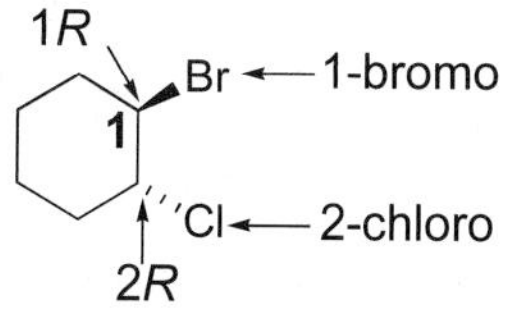
1R
Br
1-bromo
1
Cl
2-chloro
2R

h. (5*R*)-4,4,5-trichloro-3,3-dimethyl**decane**

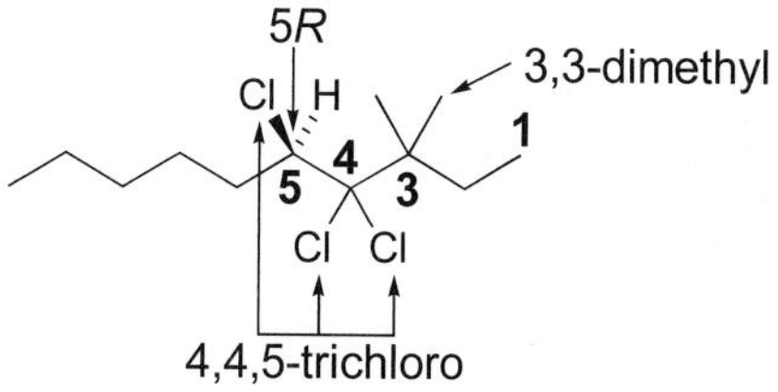
5R
Cl
H
3,3-dimethyl
1
4
5
3
Cl
Cl
4,4,5-trichloro

7.46

a.

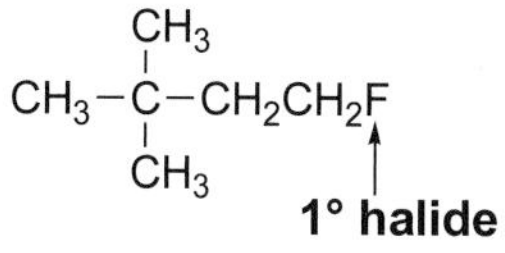
CH3
CH3–C–CH2CH2F
CH3
1° halide

b.

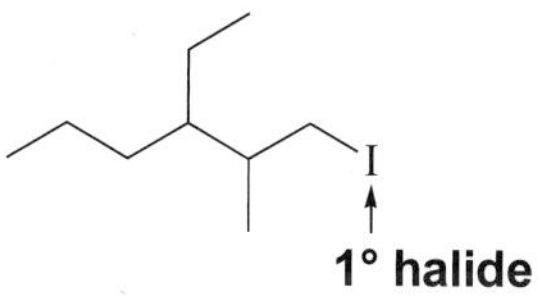
I
1° halide

c. $(CH_3)_3CCH_2Br$

1° halide

d.

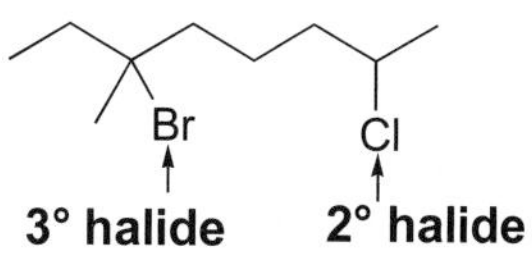
Br
Cl
3° halide
2° halide

e.

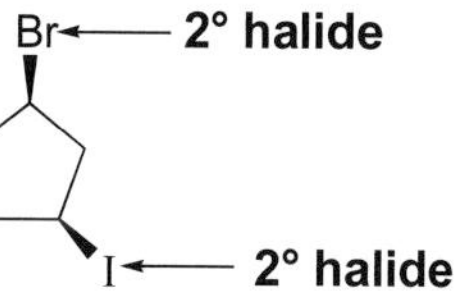
Br
2° halide
I
2° halide

f.

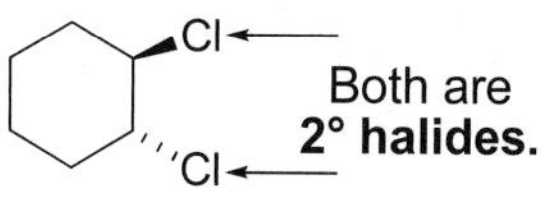
Cl
Both are
2° halides.
Cl

g.

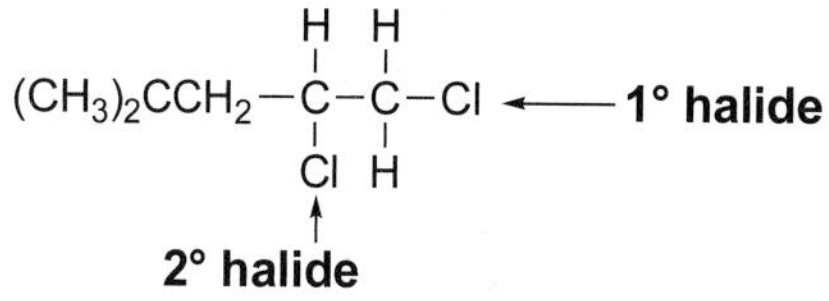
H H
(CH3)2CCH2–C–C–Cl
Cl H
1° halide
2° halide

h.

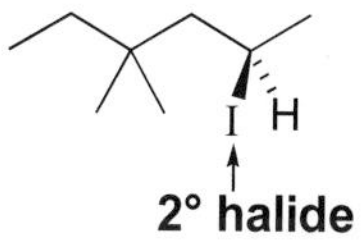
I
H
2° halide

7.47

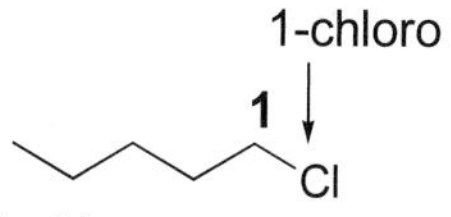
1-chloro
1
Cl

1-chloropentane

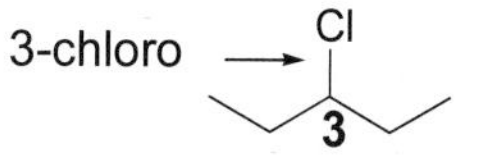
3-chloro
Cl
3

3-chloropentane

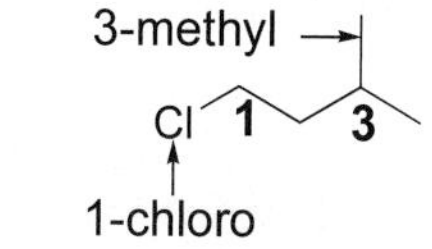
3-methyl
Cl
1
3
1-chloro

1-chloro-3-methylbutane

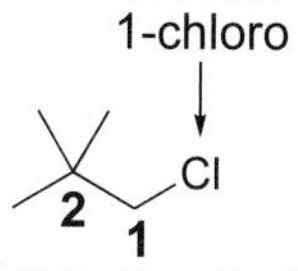
1-chloro
Cl
2
1

1-chloro-2,2-dimethylpropane

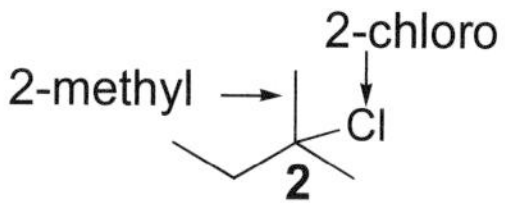
2-chloro
2-methyl
Cl
2

2-chloro-2-methylbutane

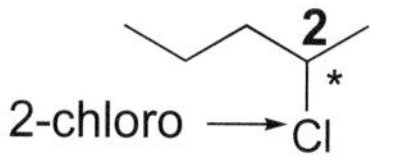
2
*
2-chloro
Cl

2-chloropentane

[* denotes stereogenic center]

Two stereoisomers

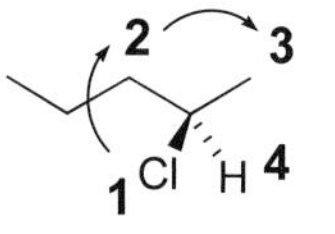
2
3
1
Cl
H
4

Clockwise
"4" in *back* =
R

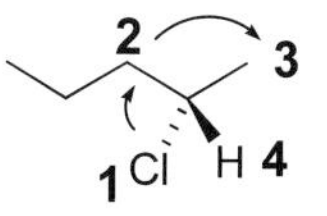
2
3
1
Cl
H
4

Clockwise
"4" in *front* =
S

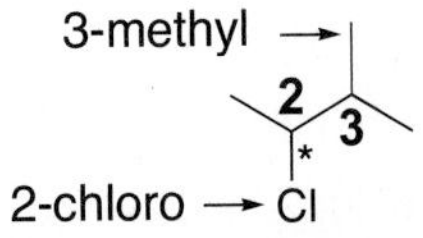

2-chloro-3-methylbutane
[* denotes stereogenic center]

Two stereoisomers

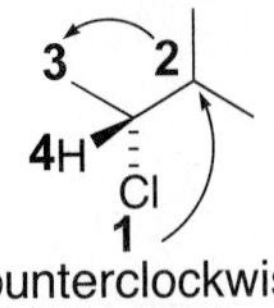

Counterclockwise
"4" in *front* =
R

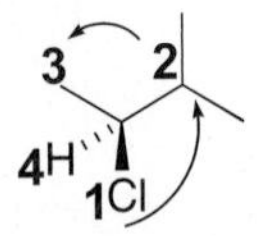

Counterclockwise
"4" in *back* =
S

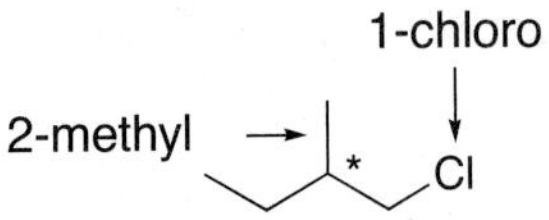

1-chloro-2-methylbutane
[* denotes stereogenic center]

Two stereoisomers

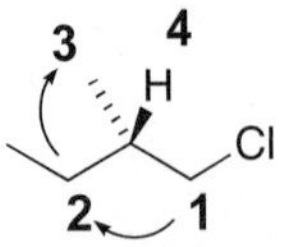

Clockwise
"4" in *front* =
S

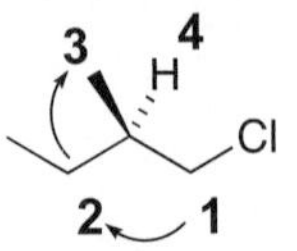

Clockwise
"4" in *back* =
R

7.48

a. $(CH_3)_3CBr$ or $CH_3CH_2CH_2CH_2Br$
↑
larger surface area =
stronger intermolecular forces =
higher boiling point

b.  or 
↑
larger halide = more polarizable =
higher boiling point

c. 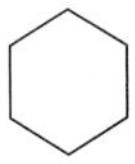 or 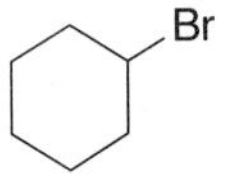

nonpolar
only VDW forces

more polar =
higher boiling point

7.49

a. $CH_3CH_2CH_2CH_2{-}Br + {}^{-}OH \longrightarrow CH_3CH_2CH_2CH_2OH + Br^{-}$

b. $CH_3CH_2CH_2CH_2{-}Br + {}^{-}SH \longrightarrow CH_3CH_2CH_2CH_2SH + Br^{-}$

c. $CH_3CH_2CH_2CH_2{-}Br + {}^{-}CN \longrightarrow CH_3CH_2CH_2CH_2CN + Br^{-}$

d. $CH_3CH_2CH_2CH_2{-}Br + {}^{-}OCH(CH_3)_2 \longrightarrow CH_3CH_2CH_2CH_2OCH(CH_3)_2 + Br^{-}$

e. $CH_3CH_2CH_2CH_2{-}Br + {}^{-}C{\equiv}CH \longrightarrow CH_3CH_2CH_2CH_2C{\equiv}CH + Br^{-}$

f. $CH_3CH_2CH_2CH_2{-}Br + H_2\ddot{O}: \longrightarrow CH_3CH_2CH_2CH_2\overset{+}{\underset{..}{O}}H_2 + Br^{-} \longrightarrow CH_3CH_2CH_2CH_2OH + HBr$

g. $CH_3CH_2CH_2CH_2{-}Br + \ddot{N}H_3 \longrightarrow CH_3CH_2CH_2CH_2\overset{+}{N}H_3 + Br^{-} \longrightarrow CH_3CH_2CH_2CH_2NH_2 + HBr$

h. $CH_3CH_2CH_2CH_2{-}Br + Na^{+}\,I^{-} \longrightarrow CH_3CH_2CH_2CH_2I + Na^{+}\,Br^{-}$

i. $CH_3CH_2CH_2CH_2{-}Br + Na^{+}\,N_3^{-} \longrightarrow CH_3CH_2CH_2CH_2N_3 + Na^{+}\,Br^{-}$

7.50 Use the steps from Answer 7.8 and then draw the proton transfer reaction, when necessary.

a. 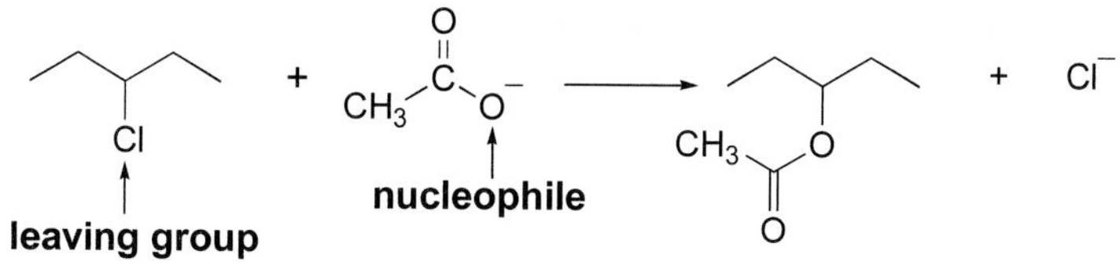

b. 

c. 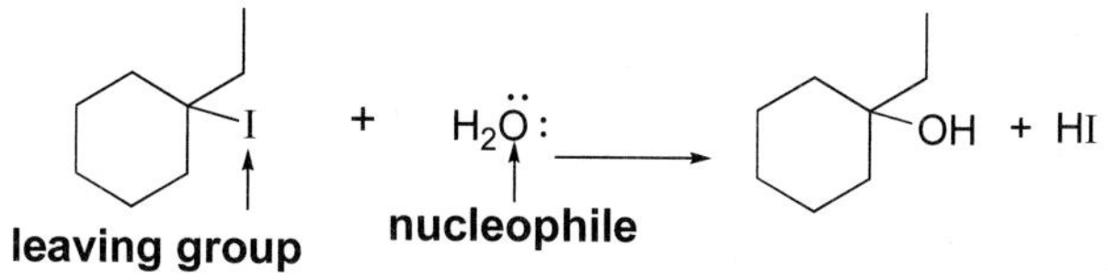

d. 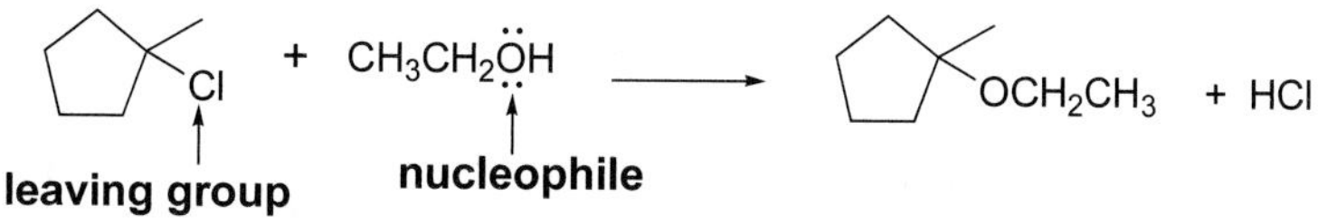

e. 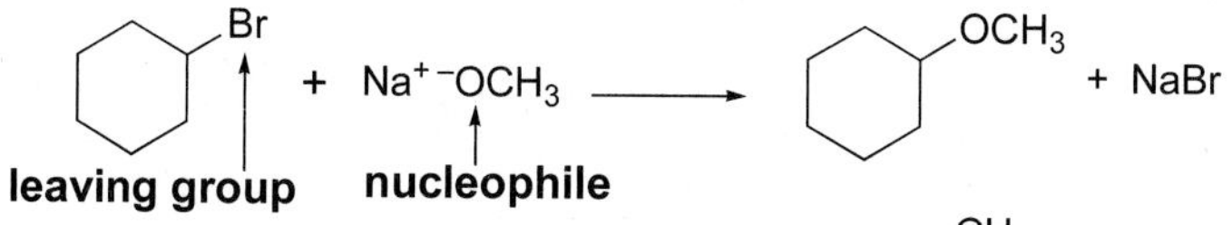

f. 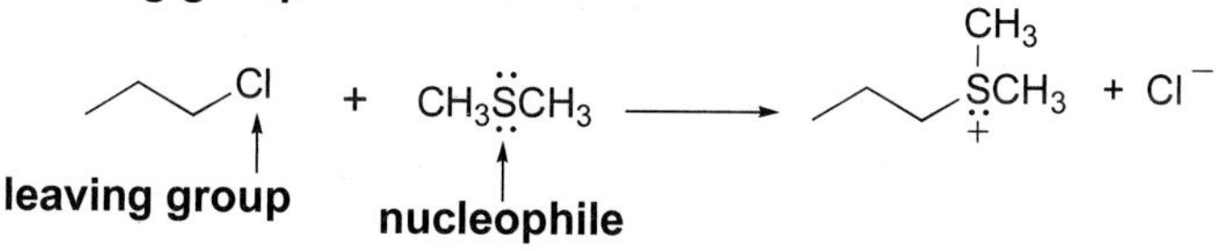

7.51 A good leaving group is a weak base.

a. 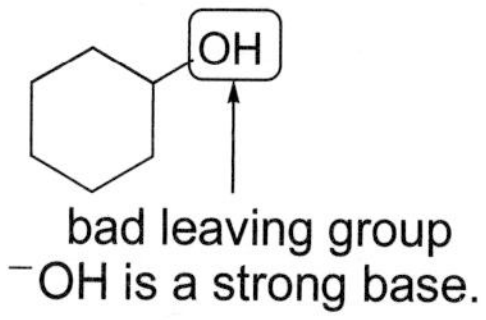

b. 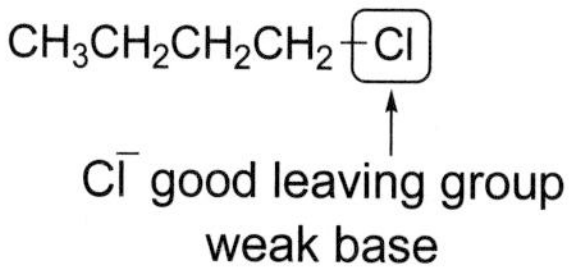

c. 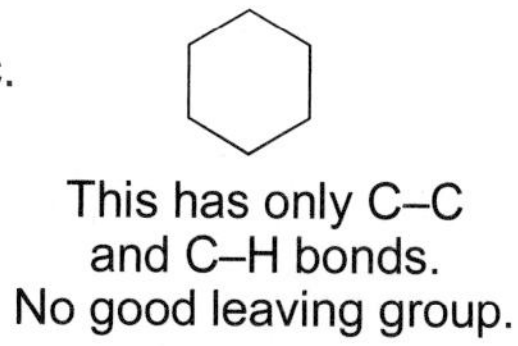

d. 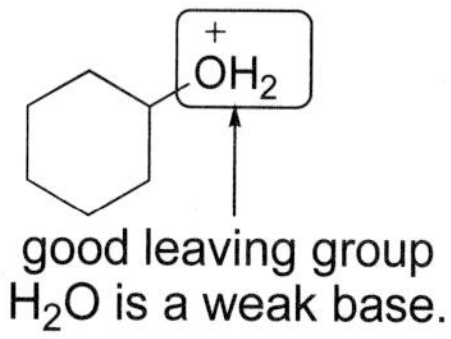

e. 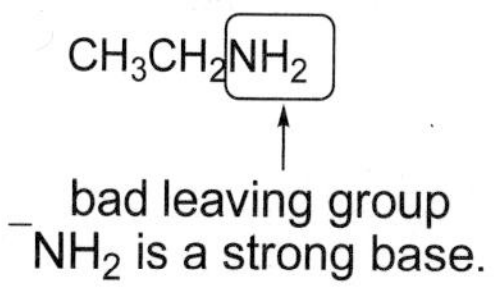

f. 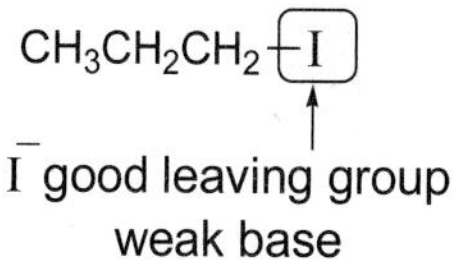

7.52 Use the rules from Answer 7.11.

a. increasing leaving group ability: $^{-}NH_2 < {}^{-}OH < F^-$

- $^{-}NH_2$: most basic, **worst leaving group**
- F^-: least basic, **best leaving group**

b. increasing leaving group ability: $^{-}NH_2 < {}^{-}OH < H_2O$

- $^{-}NH_2$: most basic, **worst leaving group**
- H_2O: least basic, **best leaving group**

c. increasing leaving group ability: $Cl^- < Br^- < I^-$
- Cl^-: most basic, **worst leaving group**
- I^-: least basic, **best leaving group**

d. increasing leaving group ability: $NH_3 < H_2O < H_2S$
- NH_3: most basic, **worst leaving group**
- H_2S: least basic, **best leaving group**

7.53 Compare the nucleophile and the leaving group in each reaction. The reaction will occur if it proceeds towards the weaker base. Remember that the stronger the acid (lower pK_a), the weaker the conjugate base.

a.
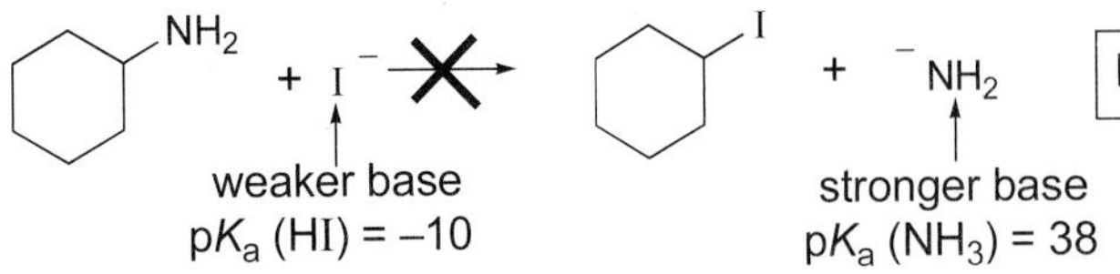

Reaction will not occur.

b. $CH_3CH_2I + CH_3O^- \longrightarrow CH_3CH_2OCH_3 + I^-$

CH_3O^-: stronger base, pK_a (CH_3OH) = 15.5; I^-: weaker base, pK_a (HI) = –10

Reaction will occur.

c.
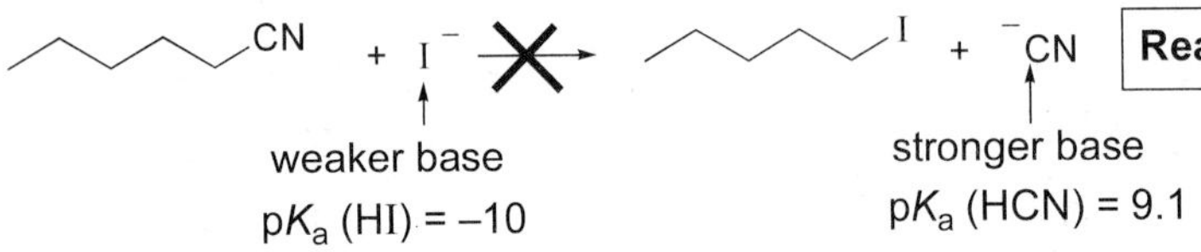

Reaction will not occur.

7.54 Use the directions in Answer 7.15.

a. Across a row of the periodic table nucleophilicity decreases.

$^-OH < ^-NH_2 < CH_3^-$

b. • In a **polar protic solvent** (CH_3OH), nucleophilicity *increases down a column* of the periodic table, so: ^-SH is more nucleophilic than ^-OH.
• *Negatively charged species* are more nucleophilic than neutral species so ^-OH is more nucleophilic than H_2O.

$H_2O < ^-OH < ^-SH$

c. • In a **polar protic solvent** (CH_3OH), nucleophilicity *increases down a column* of the periodic table, so: $CH_3CH_2S^-$ is more nucleophilic than $CH_3CH_2O^-$.
• For two species with the same attacking atom, the more basic is the more nucleophilic so $CH_3CH_2O^-$ is more nucleophilic than CH_3COO^-.

$CH_3COO^- < CH_3CH_2O^- < CH_3CH_2S^-$

d. Compare the nucleophilicity of N, S, and O. In a polar aprotic solvent (acetone), nucleophilicity parallels basicity.

$CH_3SH < CH_3OH < CH_3NH_2$

e. In a **polar aprotic solvent** (acetone), nucleophilicity parallels basicity. Across a row and down a column of the periodic table nucleophilicity decreases.

$Cl^- < F^- < ^-OH$

f. Nucleophilicity decreases across a row so ^-SH is more nucleophilic than Cl^-. In a **polar protic solvent** (CH_3OH), nucleophilicity increases down a column so Cl^- is more nucleophilic than F^-.

$F^- < Cl^- < ^-SH$

7.55 ***Polar protic solvents*** **are capable of hydrogen bonding,** so they must contain a H bonded to an electronegative O or N. ***Polar aprotic solvents*** **are incapable of hydrogen bonding,** so they do not contain any O–H or N–H bonds.

a. $(CH_3)_2CHOH$
contains O–H bond
protic

b. CH_3NO_2
no O–H or N–H bond
aprotic

c. CH_2Cl_2
no O–H or N–H bond
aprotic

d. NH_3
contains N–H bond
protic

e. $N(CH_3)_3$
no O–H or N–H bond
aprotic

f. $HCONH_2$
contains an N–H bond
protic

7.56

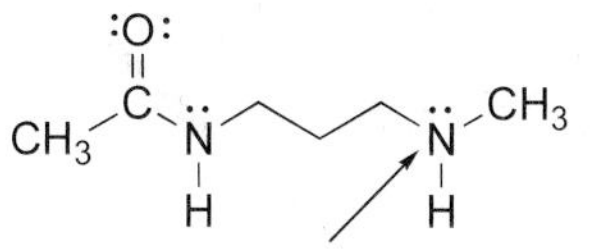

The amine N is more nucleophilic since the electron pair is localized on the N.

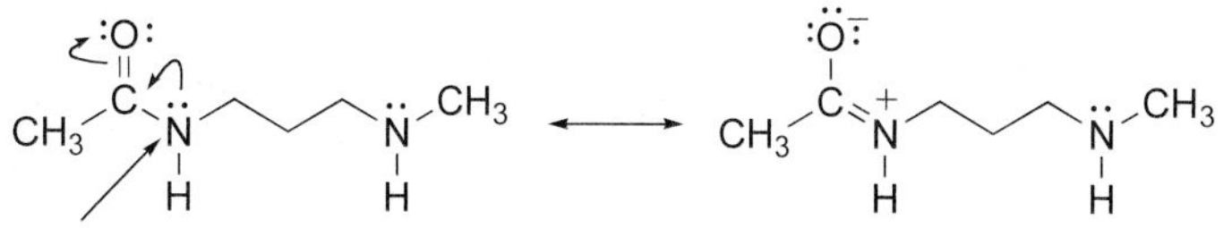

The amide N is less nucleophilic since the electron pair is delocalized by resonance.

7.57

1° alkyl halide
S_N2 reaction

a. Mechanism:

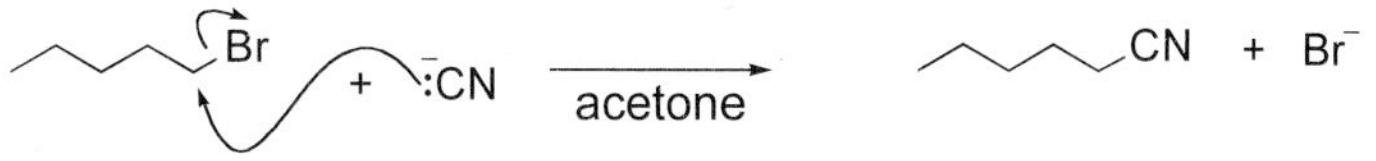

b. Energy diagram:

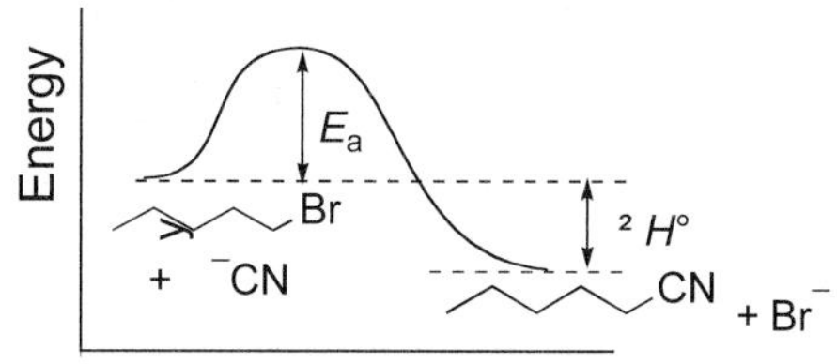

Reaction coordinate

c. Transition state:

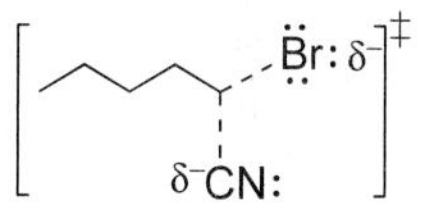

d. Rate equation: one-step reaction with both nucleophile and alkyl halide in the only step:
rate = k[R–Br][$^-$CN]

e. [1] The leaving group is changed from Br^- to I^-:
Leaving group becomes less basic → a better leaving group → faster reaction.
[2] The solvent is changed from acetone to CH_3CH_2OH:
Solvent changed to polar protic → decreases reaction rate.
[3] The alkyl halide is changed from $CH_3(CH_2)_4Br$ to $CH_3CH_2CH_2CH(Br)CH_3$:
Changed from 1° to 2° alkyl halide → the alkyl halide gets more crowded and the reaction rate decreases.
[4] The concentration of $^-$CN is increased by a factor of 5.
Reaction rate will increase by a factor of 5.
[5] The concentration of both the alkyl halide and $^-$CN are increased by a factor of 5:
Reaction rate will increase by a factor of 25 (5 x 5 = 25).

7.58 Use the directions from Answer 7.24.

a.

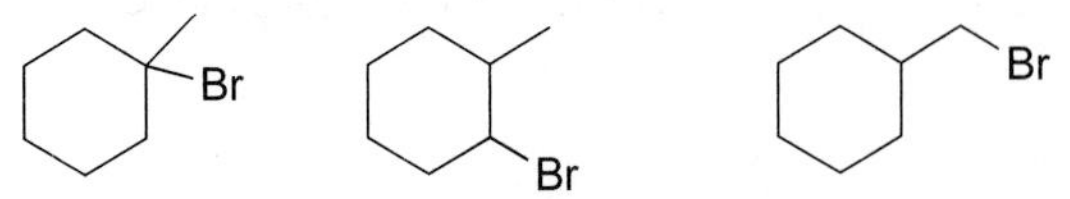
Br
Br
Br

3° alkyl halide **least reactive** | 2° alkyl halide **intermediate reactivity** | 1° alkyl halide **most reactive**

b.

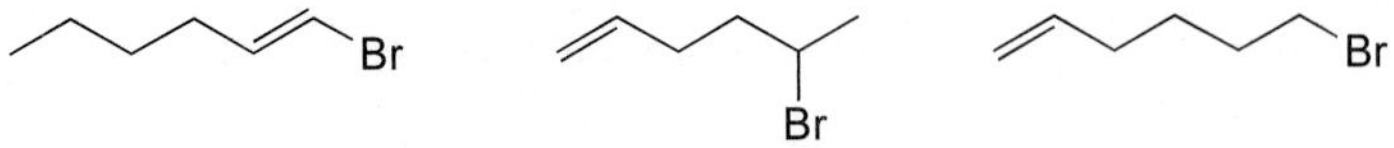
Br
Br
Br

vinyl halide **least reactive** | 2° alkyl halide **intermediate reactivity** | 1° alkyl halide **most reactive**

7.59

better leaving group

a. CH_3CH_2Br + ^-OH ⟶ **faster reaction**

CH_3CH_2Cl + ^-OH ⟶

stronger nucleophile

b.

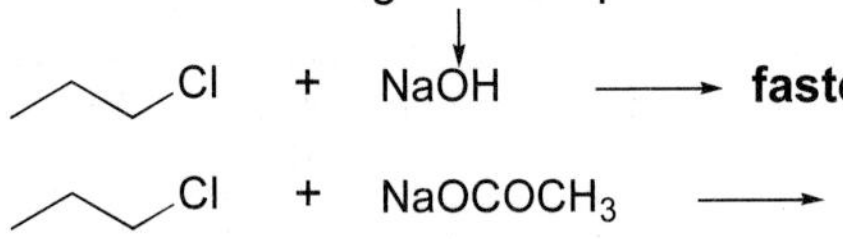
Cl
+
NaOH
Cl
+
NaOCOCH3

faster reaction (NaOH)

c.

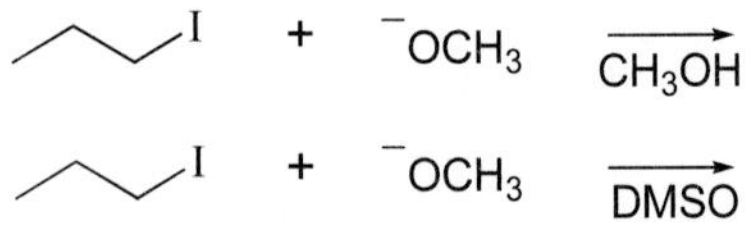
I
+
OCH3
CH3OH
I
+
OCH3
DMSO

faster reaction (DMSO)

polar aprotic solvent

less steric hindrance

d.

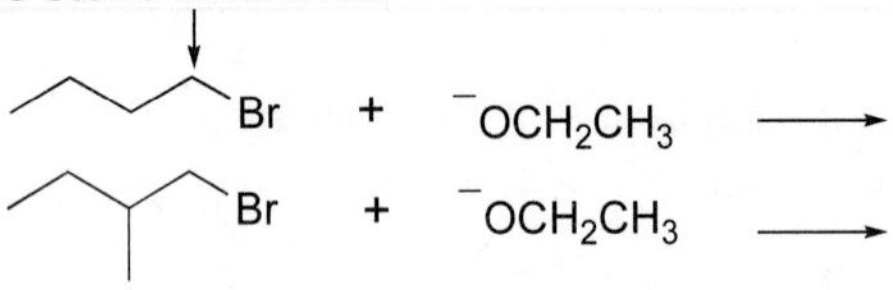
Br
+
OCH2CH3
Br
+
OCH2CH3

faster reaction (first)

7.60 All S_N2 reactions proceed with backside attack of the nucleophile. When nucleophilic attack occurs at a stereogenic center, inversion of configuration occurs.

a.

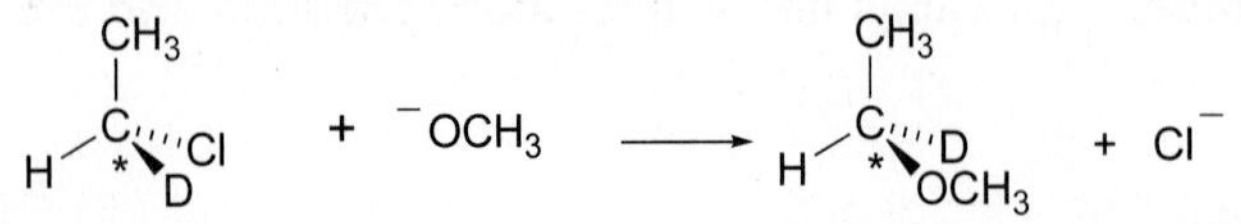
CH3
C
Cl
H
*
D
+
OCH3
CH3
C
D
H
*
OCH3
+ Cl

inversion of configuration

b.

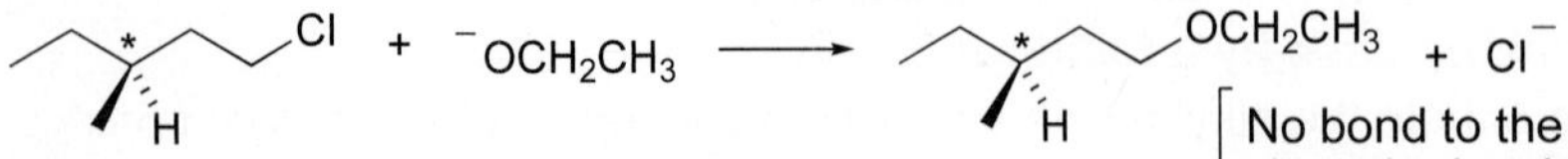
*
Cl
H
+
OCH2CH3
*
OCH2CH3
H
+ Cl

No bond to the stereogenic center is broken, since the leaving group is not bonded to the stereogenic center.

c.  inversion of configuration

[* denotes a stereogenic center]

7.61 Follow the definitions from Answer 7.28.

a. $CH_3CH_2\overset{+}{C}HCH_2CH_3$

2° carbocation

b. 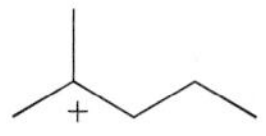

3° carbocation

c. 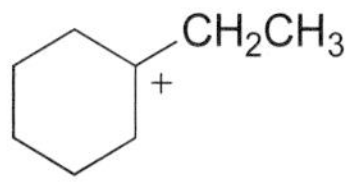

3° carbocation

d. 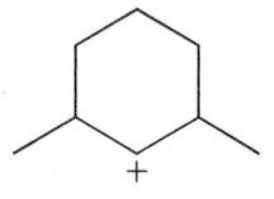

2° carbocation

e. 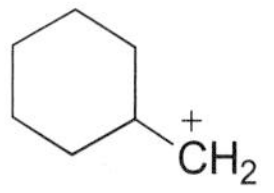

1° carbocation

7.62 For carbocations: **Increasing number of R groups = Increasing stability.**

a. 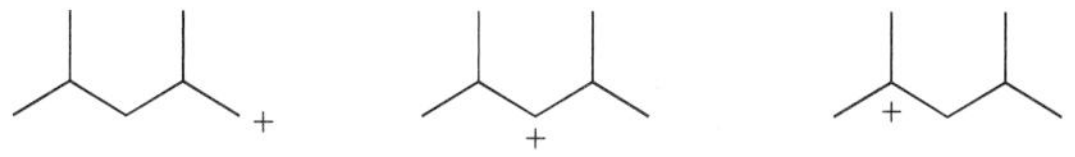

1° carbocation **least stable**; 2° carbocation **intermediate stablity**; 3° carbocation **most stable**

b. 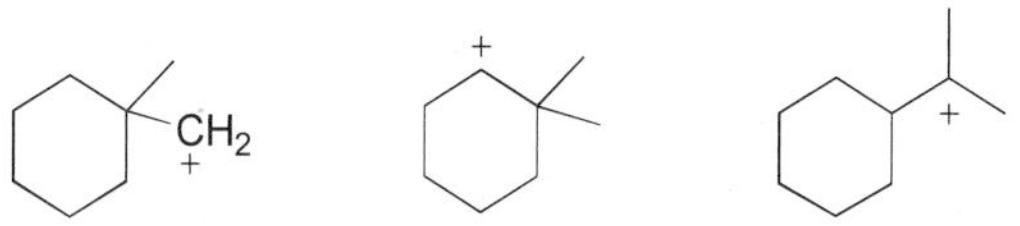

1° carbocation **least stable**; 2° carbocation **intermediate stablity**; 3° carbocation **most stable**

7.63 Both **A** and **B** are resonance stabilized, but the N atom in **B** is more basic and therefore more willing to donate its electron pair.

A 

B 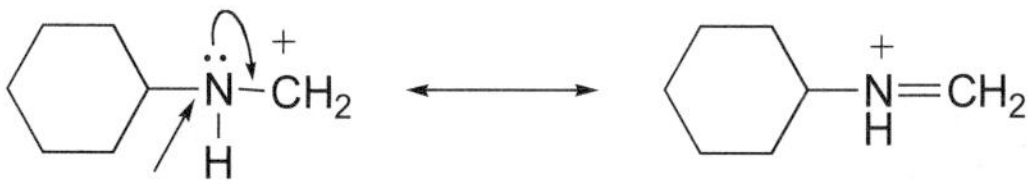

more basic N atom

This resonance form stabilizes the carbocation more than the equivalent resonance structure for **A**.

Thus, **B** is more stable then **A**.

7.64

a. Mechanism: **S_N1 only**

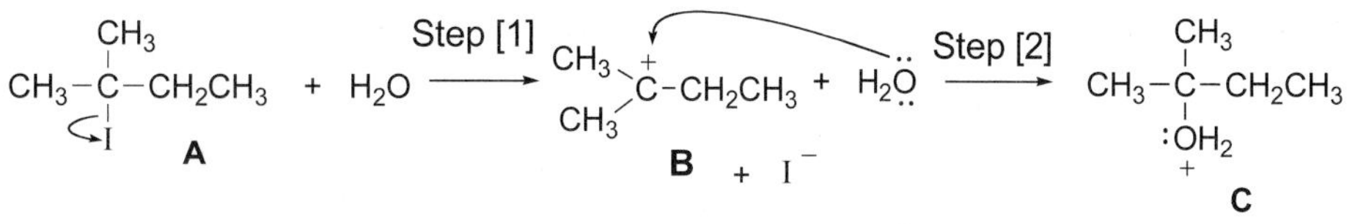

b. Energy diagram:

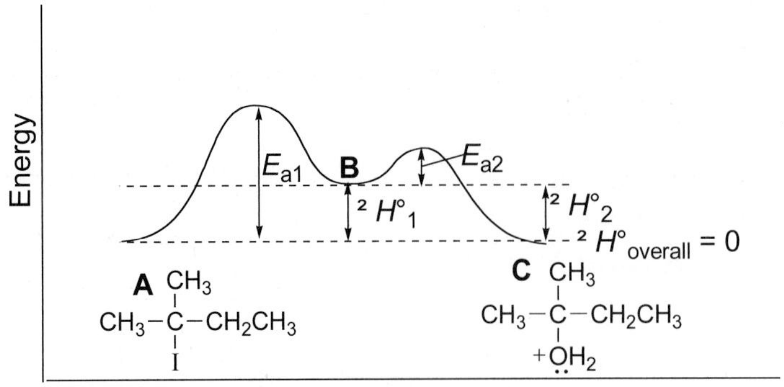

Energy
Ea1
B
Ea2
2 H°1
2 H°2
2 H°overall = 0
A CH3
CH3–C–CH2CH3
I
C CH3
CH3–C–CH2CH3
+OH2

Reaction coordinate

c. Transition states:

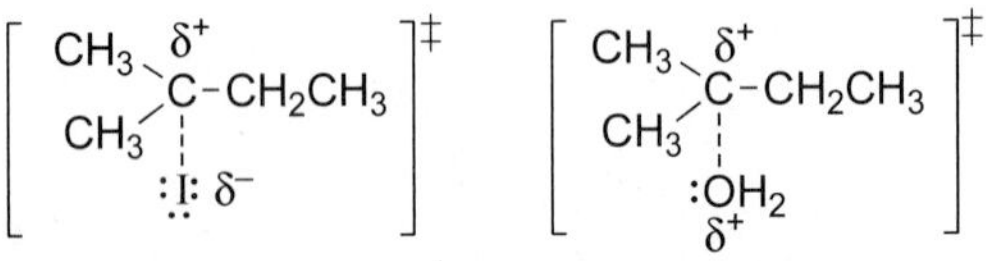

CH3 δ+
C–CH2CH3
CH3
:I: δ–
‡
CH3 δ+
C–CH2CH3
CH3
:OH2
δ+
‡

d. rate equation: **rate = k[$(CH_3)_2CICH_2CH_3$]**

e. [1] Leaving group changed from I^- to Cl^-: **rate decreases** since I^- is a better leaving group.
[2] Solvent changed from H_2O (polar protic) to DMF (polar aprotic):
rate decreases since polar protic solvent favors S_N1.
[3] Alkyl halide changed from 3° to 2°: **rate decreases** since 2° carbocations are less stable.
[4] [H_2O] increased by factor of five: **no change in rate** since H_2O is not in rate equation.
[5] [R–X] and [H_2O] increased by factor of five: **rate increases** by a factor of five. (Only the concentration of R–X affects the rate.)

7.65 The rate of an S_N1 reaction increases with increasing alkyl substitution.

a.

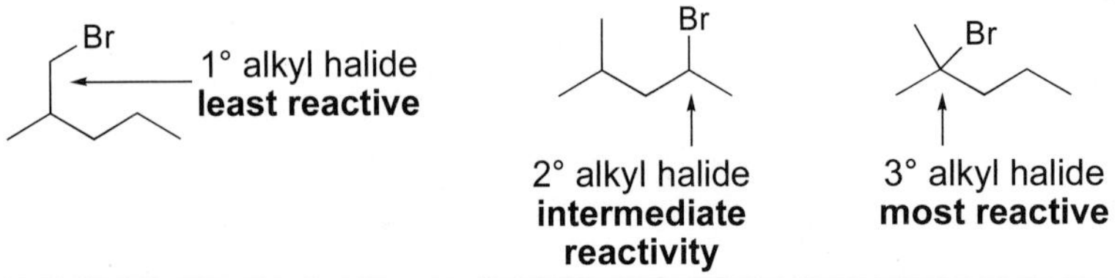

Br
1° alkyl halide
least reactive
Br
2° alkyl halide
intermediate
reactivity
Br
3° alkyl halide
most reactive

b.

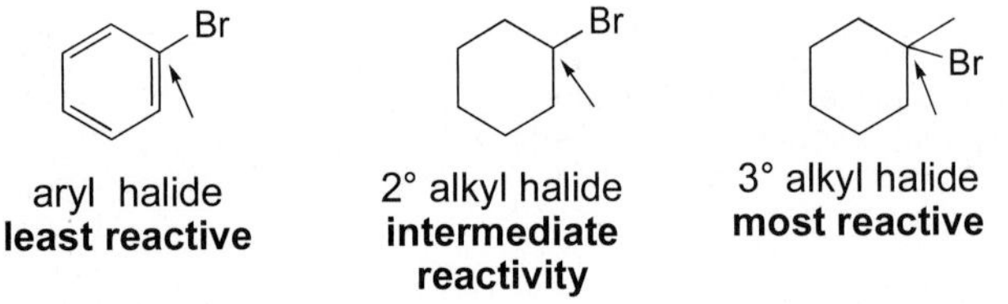

Br
aryl halide
least reactive
Br
2° alkyl halide
intermediate
reactivity
Br
3° alkyl halide
most reactive

7.66 The rate of an S_N1 reaction increases with increasing alkyl substitution, polar protic solvents, and better leaving groups.

a. $(CH_3)_3CCl + H_2O \longrightarrow$

$(CH_3)_3CI + H_2O \longrightarrow$ better leaving group **faster** reaction

b.

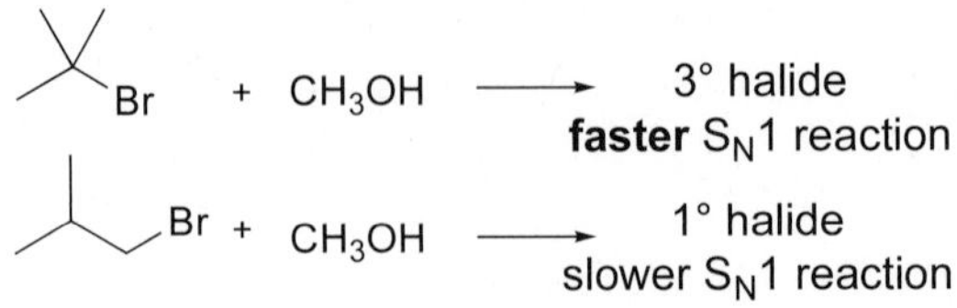

Br
+ CH3OH
3° halide
faster SN1 reaction
Br
+ CH3OH
1° halide
slower SN1 reaction

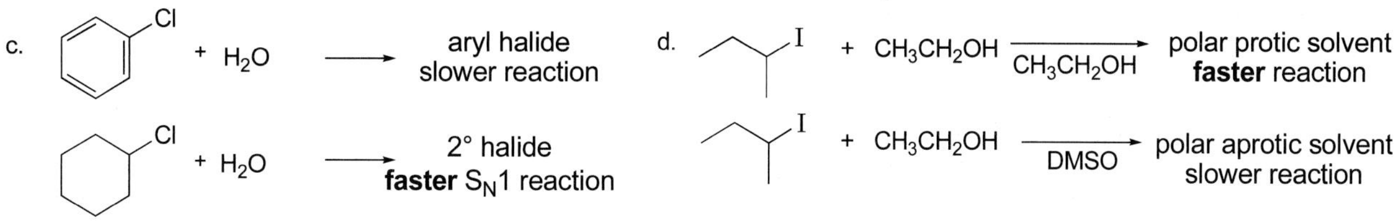
c.
Cl
+ H2O
aryl halide
slower reaction
Cl
+ H2O
2° halide
faster SN1 reaction
d.
I
+ CH3CH2OH
CH3CH2OH
polar protic solvent
faster reaction
I
+ CH3CH2OH
DMSO
polar aprotic solvent
slower reaction

7.67

a.

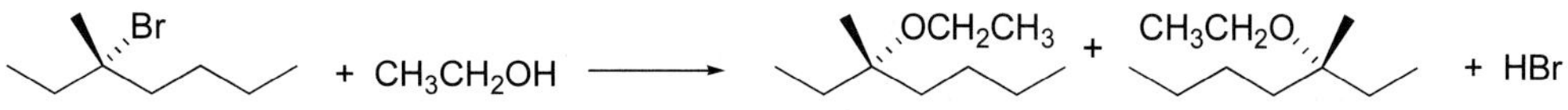
Br
+ CH3CH2OH
OCH2CH3
+
CH3CH2O
+ HBr

b.

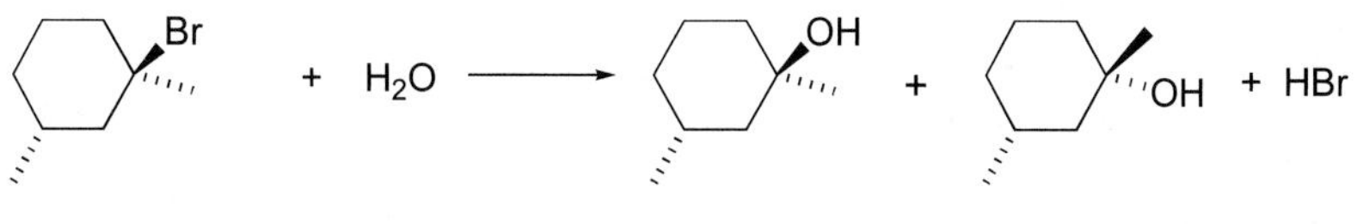
Br
+ H2O
OH
+
OH
+ HBr

7.68 The 1° alkyl halide is also allylic, so it forms a resonance-stabilized carbocation. Increasing the stability of the carbocation by resonance, increases the rate of the S_N1 reaction.

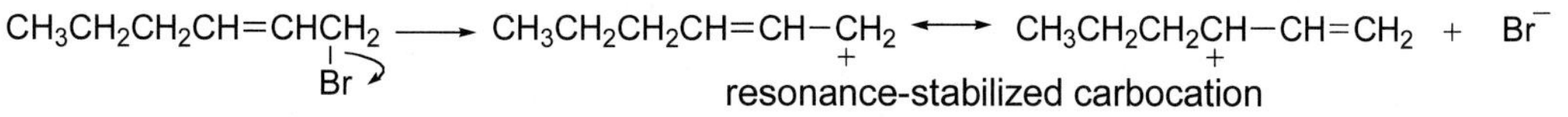
CH3CH2CH2CH=CHCH2
Br
CH3CH2CH2CH=CH–CH2
CH3CH2CH2CH–CH=CH2 + Br–
resonance-stabilized carbocation

Use each resonance structure individually to continue the mechanism:

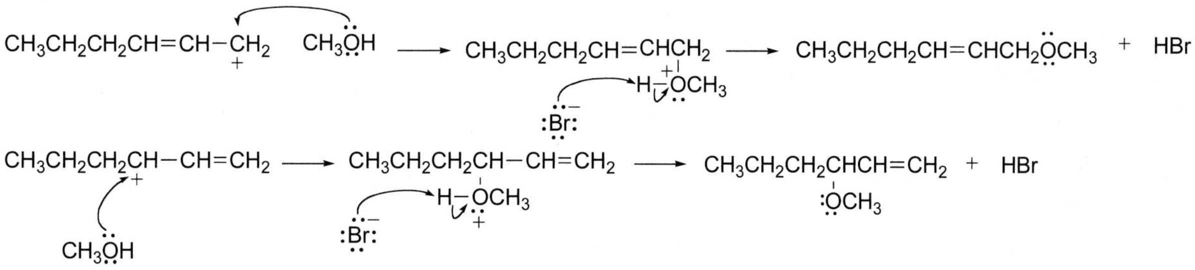
CH3CH2CH2CH=CH–CH2 CH3OH
CH3CH2CH2CH=CHCH2
H–OCH3
:Br:
CH3CH2CH2CH=CHCH2OCH3 + HBr
CH3CH2CH2CH–CH=CH2
CH3OH
CH3CH2CH2CH–CH=CH2
H–OCH3
:Br:
CH3CH2CH2CHCH=CH2 + HBr
:OCH3

7.69

a.

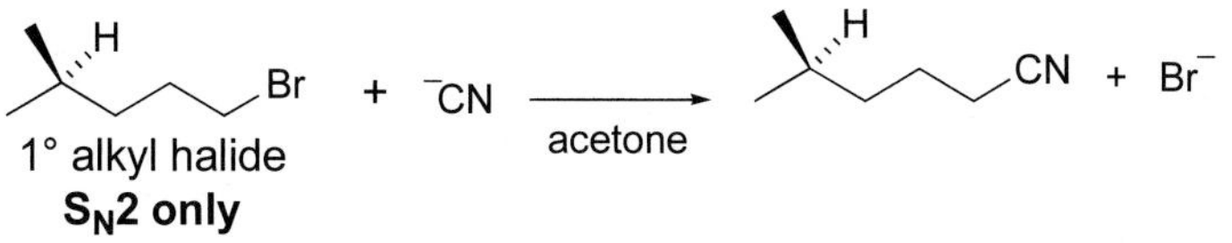
H
Br
+ –CN
acetone
H
CN + Br–
1° alkyl halide
SN2 only

b.

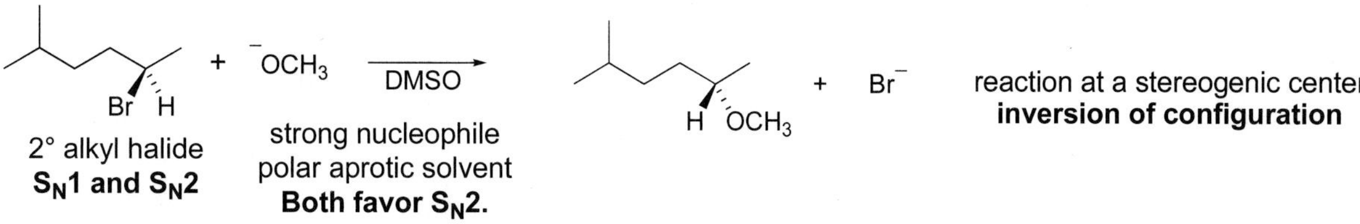
+ –OCH3
DMSO
Br H
2° alkyl halide
SN1 and SN2
strong nucleophile
polar aprotic solvent
Both favor SN2.
H OCH3
+ Br–
reaction at a stereogenic center
inversion of configuration

c.

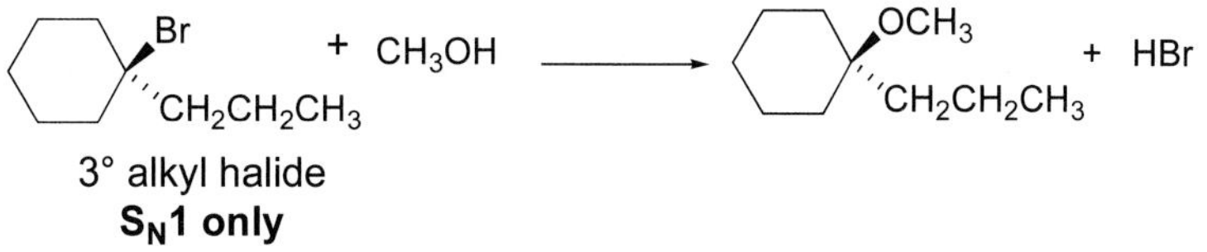
Br
+ CH3OH
CH2CH2CH3
3° alkyl halide
SN1 only
OCH3
+ HBr
CH2CH2CH3

d.

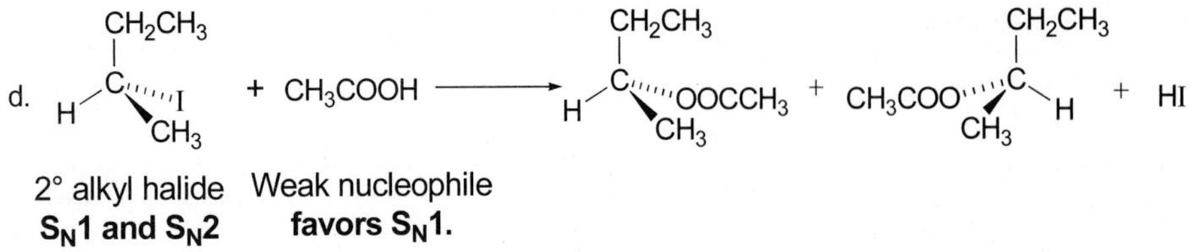

CH_2CH_3
+ CH_3COOH
$OOCCH_3$
CH_3COO
+ HI
2° alkyl halide
S_N1 and S_N2
Weak nucleophile
favors S_N1.

reaction at a stereogenic center
racemization of product

e.

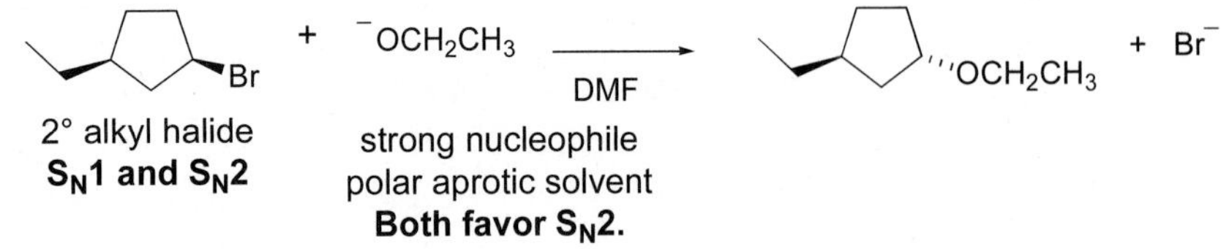

Br
+ $^-OCH_2CH_3$
DMF
OCH_2CH_3
+ Br^-
2° alkyl halide
S_N1 and S_N2
strong nucleophile
polar aprotic solvent
Both favor S_N2.

reaction at a stereogenic center
inversion of configuration

f.

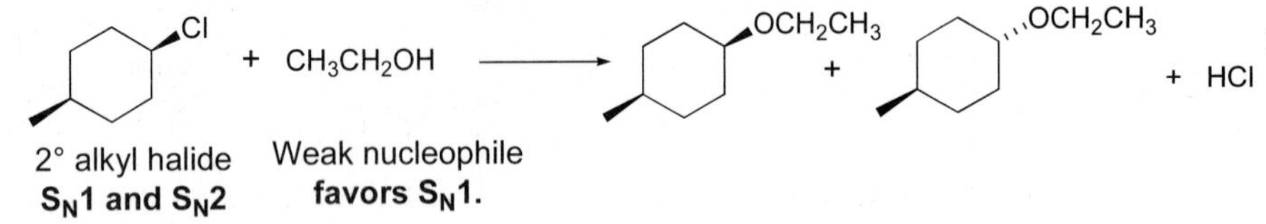

Cl
+ CH_3CH_2OH
OCH_2CH_3
+
OCH_2CH_3
+ HCl
2° alkyl halide
S_N1 and S_N2
Weak nucleophile
favors S_N1.

two products – **diastereomers**
Nucleophile attacks
from above and below.

7.70

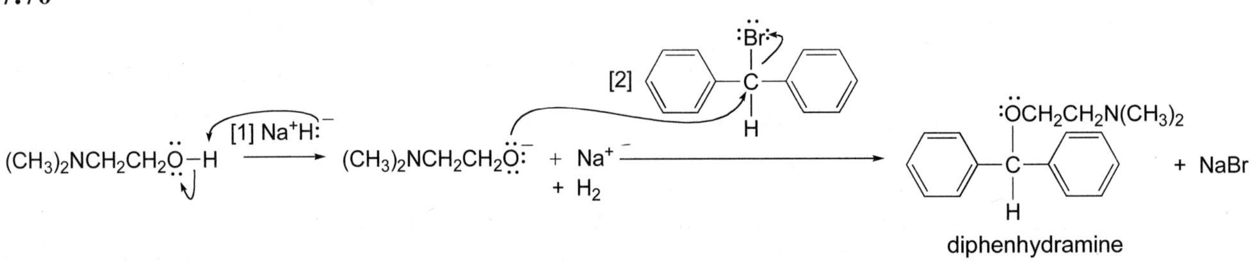

$(CH_3)_2NCH_2CH_2O–H$
[1] $Na^+H:^-$
$(CH_3)_2NCH_2CH_2O:^-$ + Na^+
+ H_2
[2]
:Br:
C
H
$:OCH_2CH_2N(CH_3)_2$
+ NaBr
diphenhydramine

7.71 First decide whether the reaction will proceed via an S_N1 or S_N2 mechanism (Answer 7.38), and then draw the mechanism.

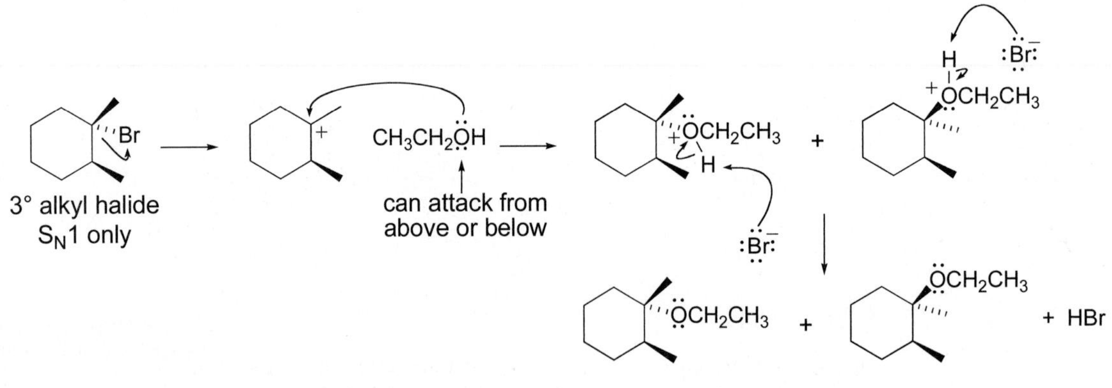

Br
3° alkyl halide
S_N1 only
$CH_3CH_2\ddot{O}H$
can attack from
above or below
OCH_2CH_3
H
:Br:
+
OCH_2CH_3
+ HBr

7.72

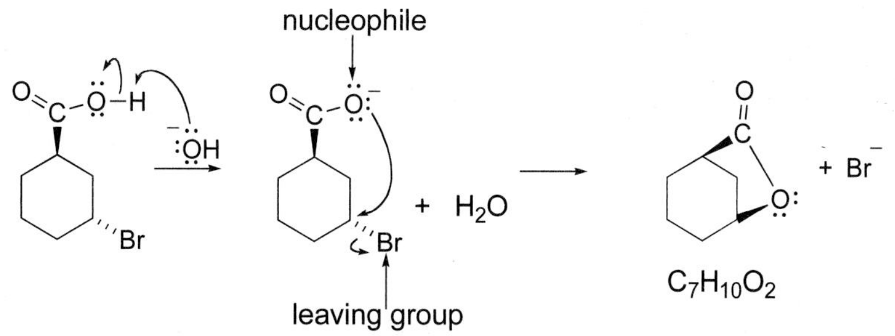

7.73

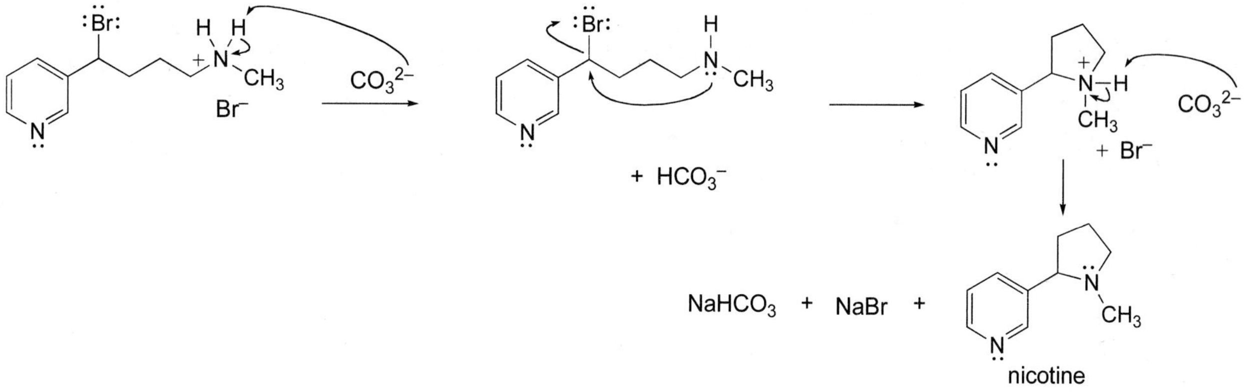

7.74

a. Two diastereomers (**C** and **D**) are formed as products from the two enantiomers of **A**.

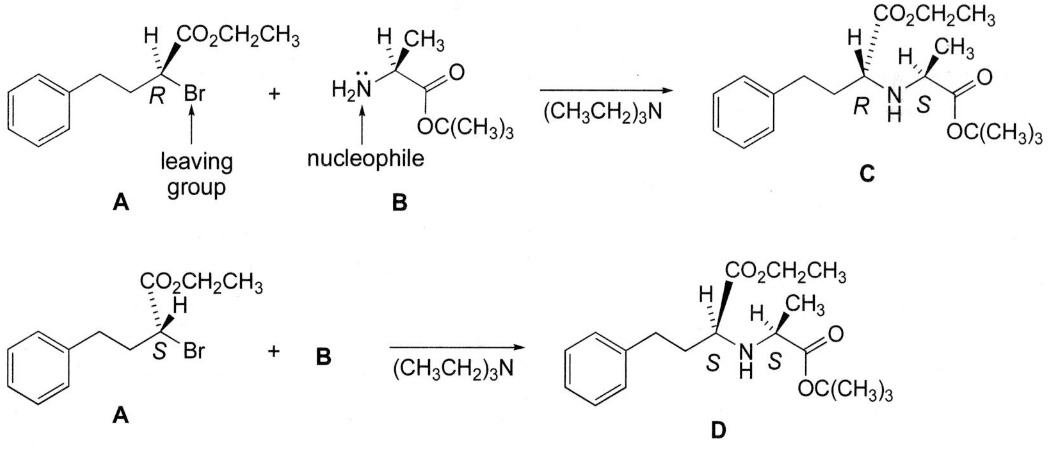

b.

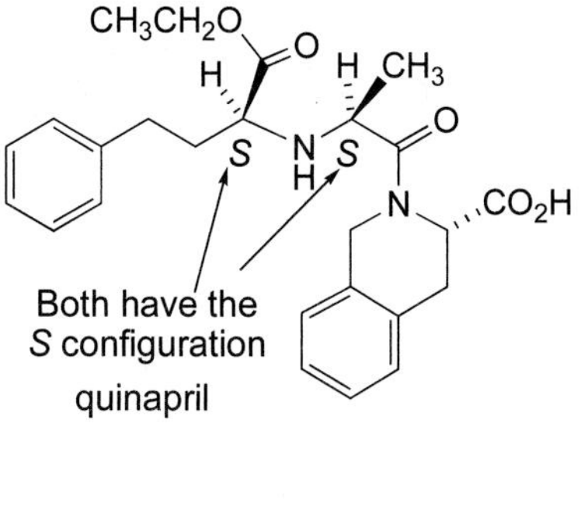

quinapril

Since both stereogenic centers in **D** have the *S* configuration and the corresponding stereogenic centers in quinapril are also *S*, **D** is needed to synthesize the drug.

7.75

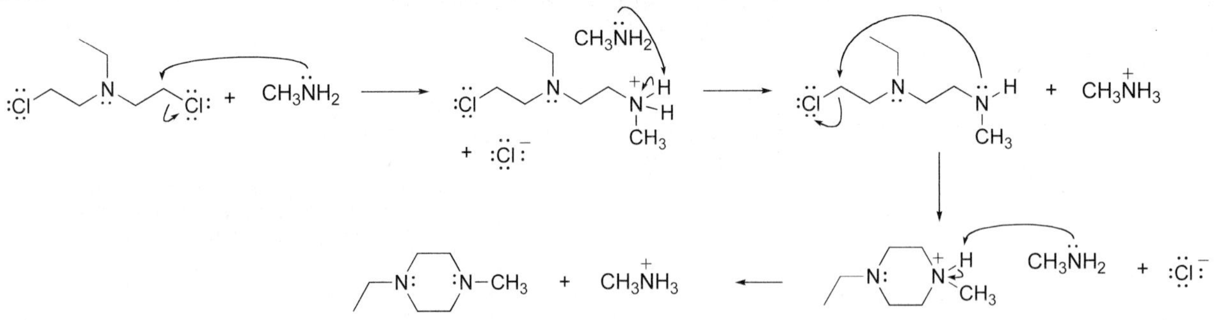
:Cl
N
Cl:
+ CH3NH2
CH3NH2
+ :Cl:⁻
N
H
CH3
+ CH3NH3
N: :N–CH3 + CH3NH3
H
CH3
CH3NH2 + :Cl:⁻

7.76 In the first reaction, substitution occurs at the stereogenic center. Since an achiral, planar carbocation is formed, the nucleophile can attack from either side, thus generating a racemic mixture.

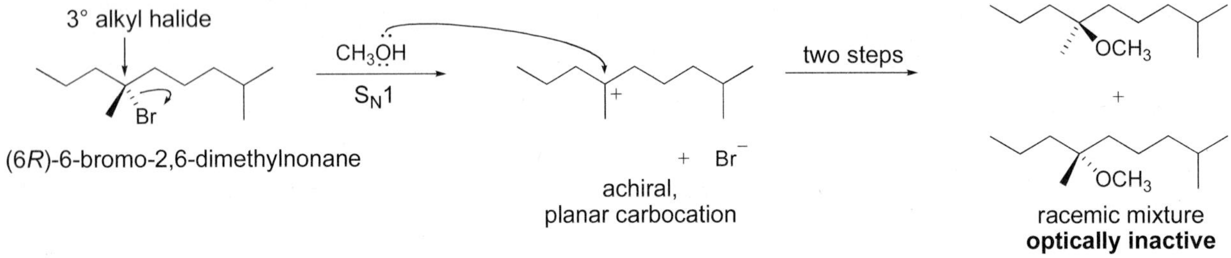
3° alkyl halide
Br
(6R)-6-bromo-2,6-dimethylnonane
CH3OH
SN1
+ Br⁻
achiral,
planar carbocation
two steps
OCH3
+
OCH3
racemic mixture
optically inactive

In the second reaction, the starting material contains a stereogenic center, but the nucleophile does not attack at that carbon. Since a bond to the stereogenic center is not broken, the configuration is retained and a chiral product is formed.

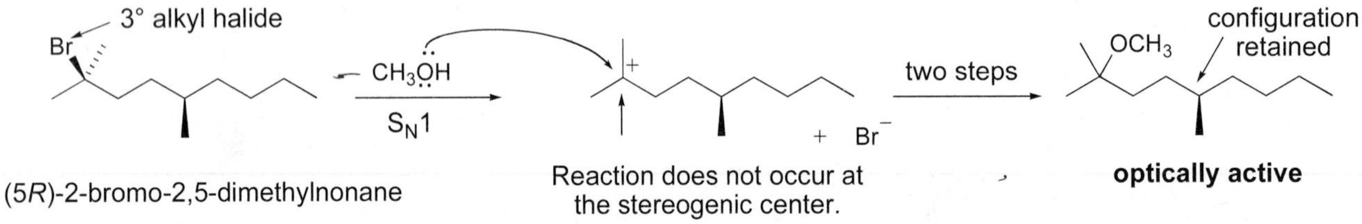
3° alkyl halide
Br
(5R)-2-bromo-2,5-dimethylnonane
CH3OH
SN1
+ Br⁻
Reaction does not occur at
the stereogenic center.
two steps
OCH3
configuration
retained
optically active

7.77

a.

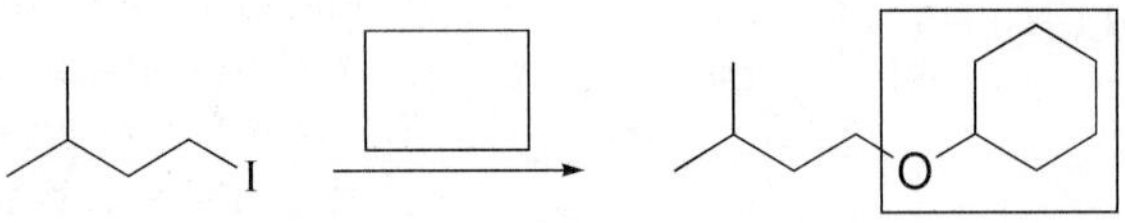
I
O

The nucleophile has replaced the leaving group.
Missing reagent:

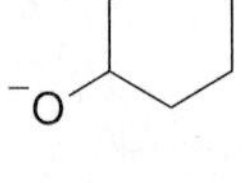
⁻O

b.

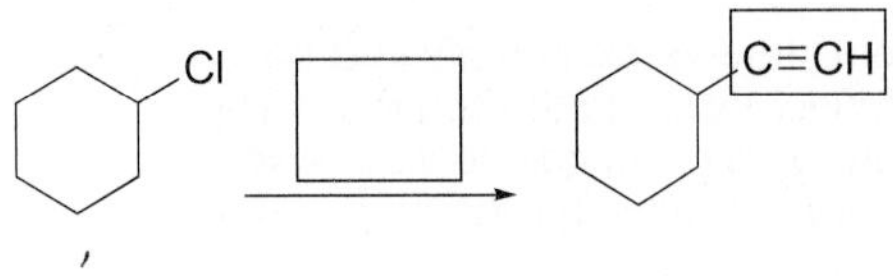
Cl
C≡CH

The nucleophile has replaced the leaving group.
Missing reagent: $^{-}C{\equiv}CH$

c. 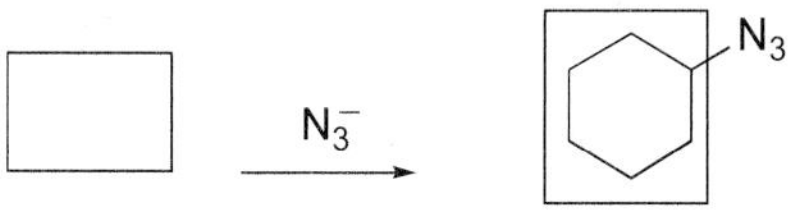
N3−
N3

The nucleophile has replaced the halide.
Starting material: 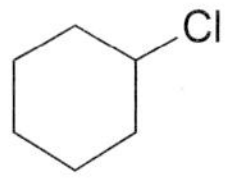
Cl

d. 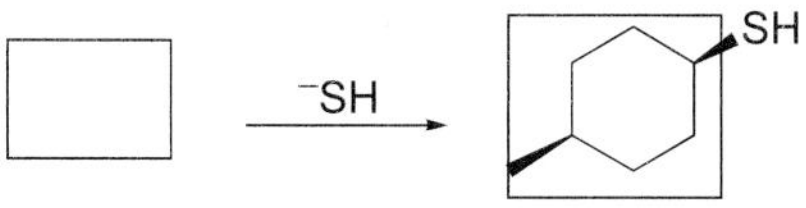
−SH
SH

The nucleophile has replaced the halide.
Starting material: 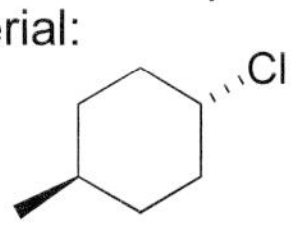
Cl

The leaving group must have the opposite orientation to the position of the nucleophile in the product.

7.78 To devise a synthesis, look for the carbon framework and the functional group in the product. **The carbon framework is from the alkyl halide and the functional group is from the nucleophile.**

a. 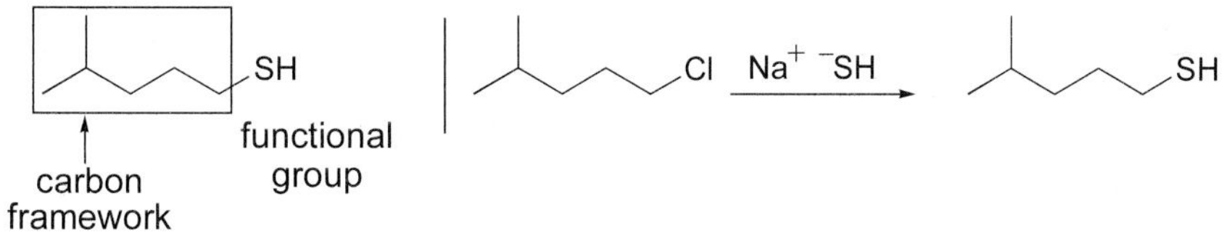
SH
functional group
carbon framework
Cl
Na+ −SH
SH

b. 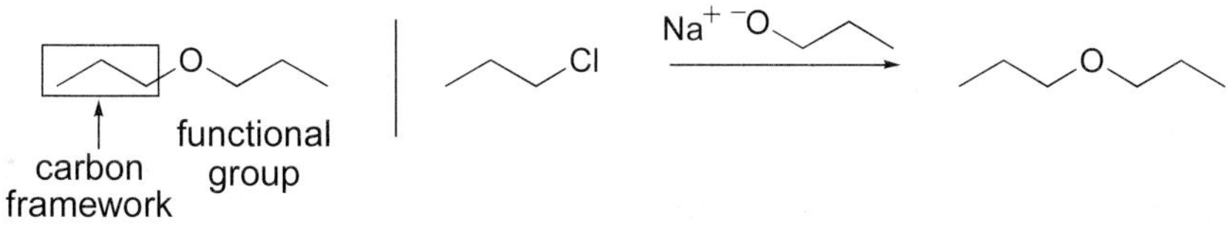
O
functional group
carbon framework
Cl
Na+ −O
O

c. 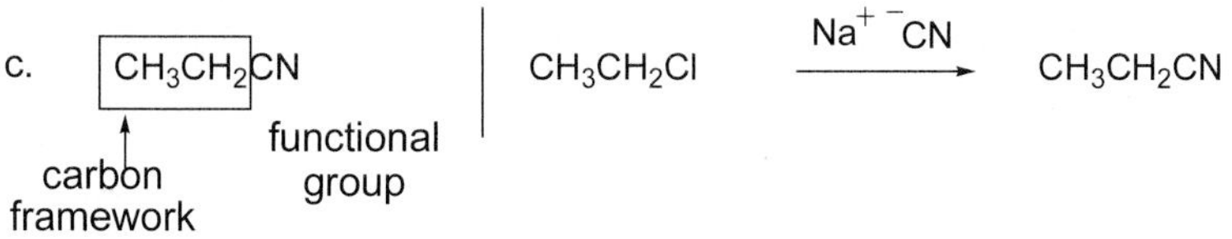
CH3CH2CN
functional group
carbon framework
CH3CH2Cl
Na+ −CN
CH3CH2CN

d. 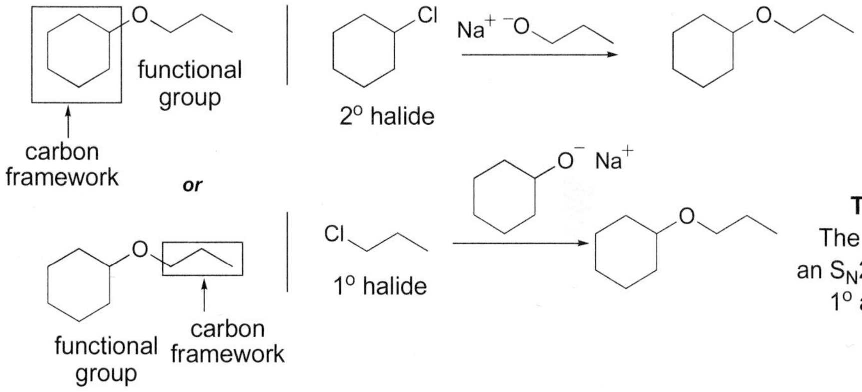
O
functional group
carbon framework
Cl
Na+ −O
2° halide
O
or
O− Na+
O
carbon framework
functional group
Cl
1° halide
O

This path is preferred.
The strong nucleophile favors an S_N2 reaction so an unhindered 1° alkyl halide reacts faster.

e. 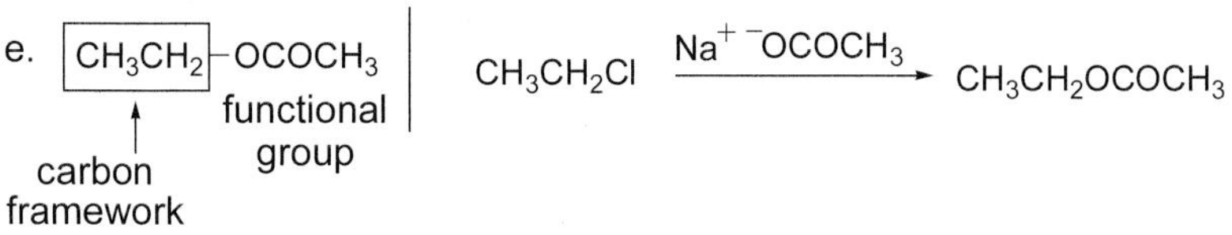
CH3CH2–OCOCH3
functional group
carbon framework
CH3CH2Cl
Na+ −OCOCH3
CH3CH2OCOCH3

7.79 Work backwards to determine the alkyl chloride needed to prepare benzalkonium chloride **A**.

a.
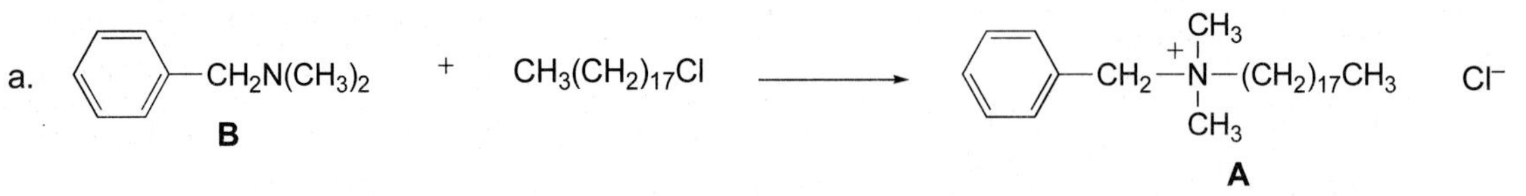
CH2N(CH3)2
B
CH3(CH2)17Cl
CH2–N–(CH2)17CH3
Cl⁻
A

b.
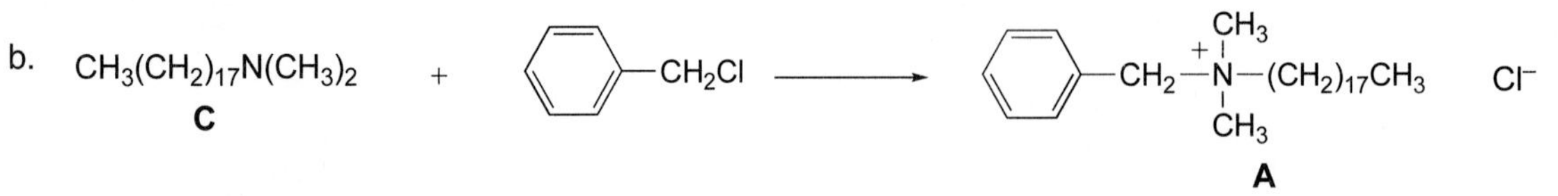
CH3(CH2)17N(CH3)2
C
CH2Cl
CH2–N–(CH2)17CH3
Cl⁻
A

7.80

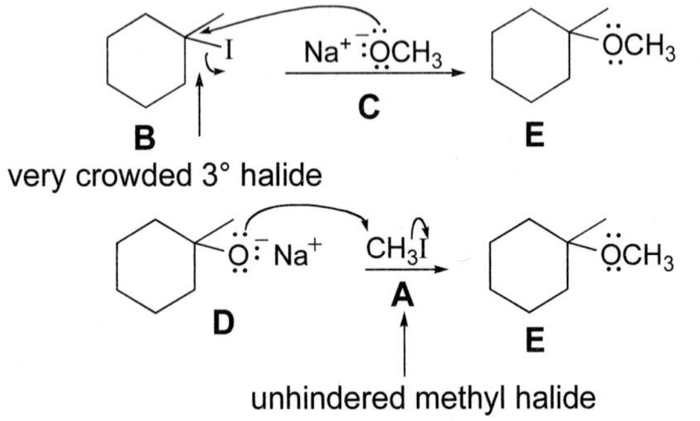
Na⁺ :OCH3
C
B
E
very crowded 3° halide
Na⁺
CH3I
A
D
E
unhindered methyl halide

preferred method
The strong nucleophile favors S_N2 reaction so the alkyl halide should be unhindered for a faster reaction.

7.81

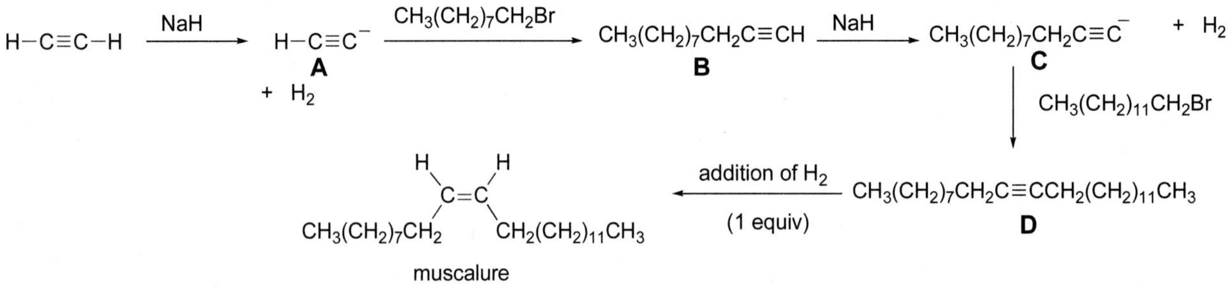
H–C≡C–H
NaH
H–C≡C⁻
A
+ H2
CH3(CH2)7CH2Br
CH3(CH2)7CH2C≡CH
B
NaH
CH3(CH2)7CH2C≡C⁻
C
+ H2
CH3(CH2)11CH2Br
CH3(CH2)7CH2C≡CCH2(CH2)11CH3
D
addition of H2
(1 equiv)
muscalure

7.82

a.
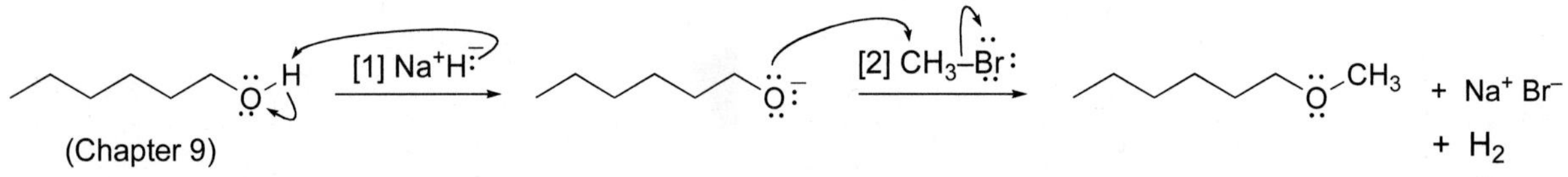
(Chapter 9)
[1] Na⁺H:⁻
[2] CH3–Br:
+ Na⁺ Br⁻
+ H2

b.
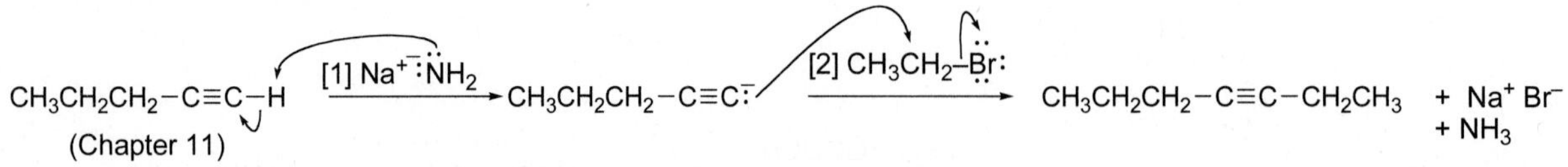
CH3CH2CH2–C≡C–H
(Chapter 11)
[1] Na⁺ :NH2
CH3CH2CH2–C≡C:⁻
[2] CH3CH2–Br:
CH3CH2CH2–C≡C–CH2CH3
+ Na⁺ Br⁻
+ NH3

c.
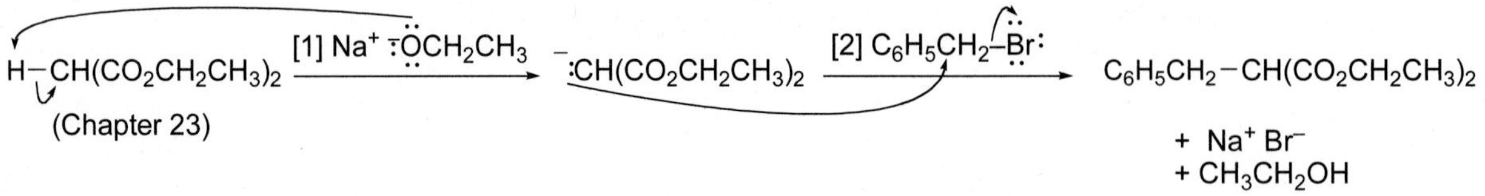
H–CH(CO2CH2CH3)2
(Chapter 23)
[1] Na⁺ :OCH2CH3
:CH(CO2CH2CH3)2
[2] C6H5CH2–Br:
C6H5CH2–CH(CO2CH2CH3)2
+ Na⁺ Br⁻
+ CH3CH2OH

7.83

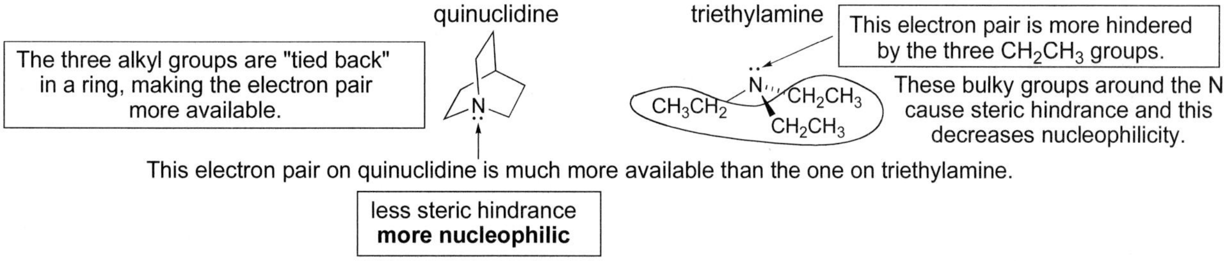
quinuclidine
triethylamine
The three alkyl groups are "tied back" in a ring, making the electron pair more available.
This electron pair is more hindered by the three CH_2CH_3 groups.
N
CH_3CH_2
CH_2CH_3
CH_2CH_3
These bulky groups around the N cause steric hindrance and this decreases nucleophilicity.
This electron pair on quinuclidine is much more available than the one on triethylamine.
less steric hindrance
more nucleophilic

7.84

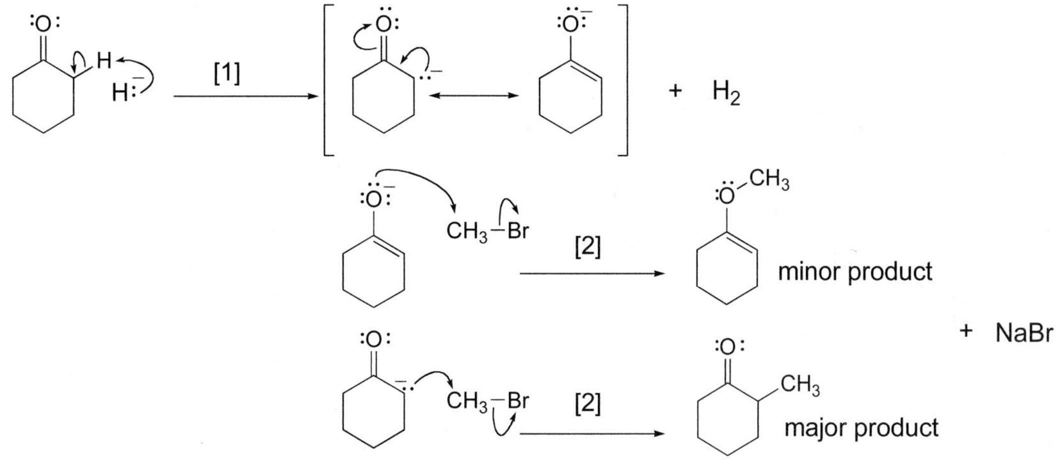
H
H:
[1]
+ H_2
CH_3–Br
[2]
CH_3
minor product
+ NaBr
CH_3–Br
[2]
CH_3
major product

7.85

a.

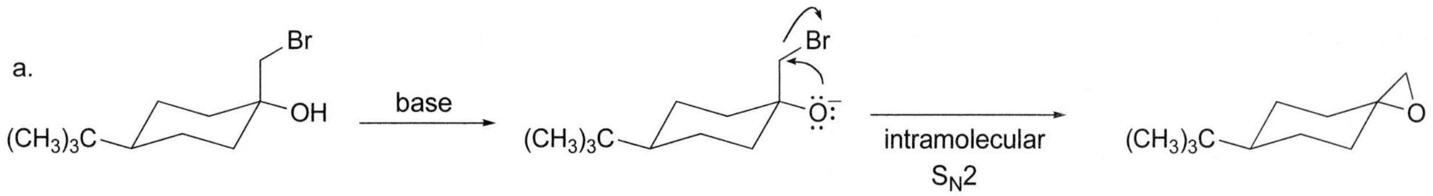
Br
OH
$(CH_3)_3C$
base
intramolecular
S_N2

b.

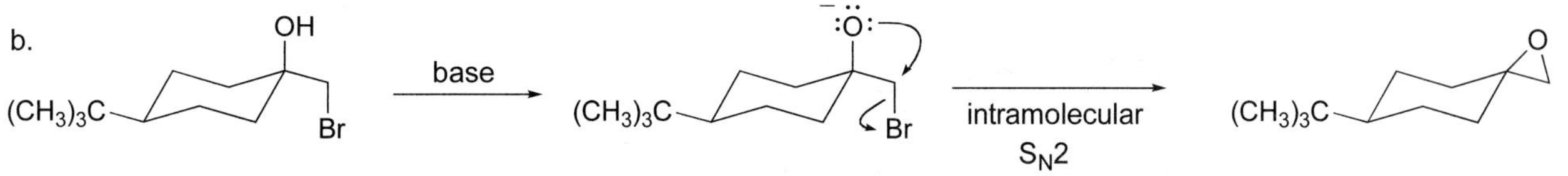
OH
Br
$(CH_3)_3C$
base
intramolecular
S_N2

c.

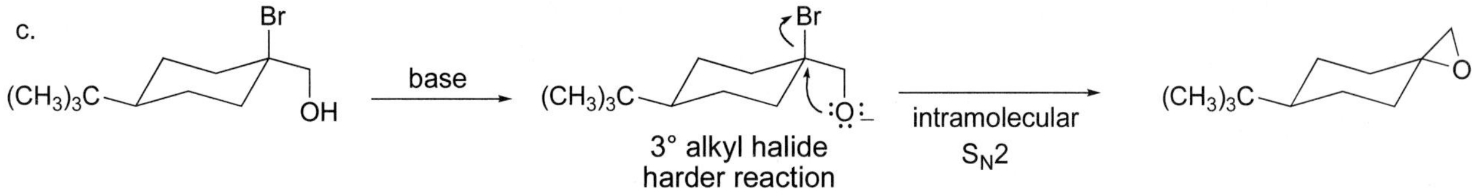
Br
OH
$(CH_3)_3C$
base
3° alkyl halide
harder reaction
intramolecular
S_N2

d.

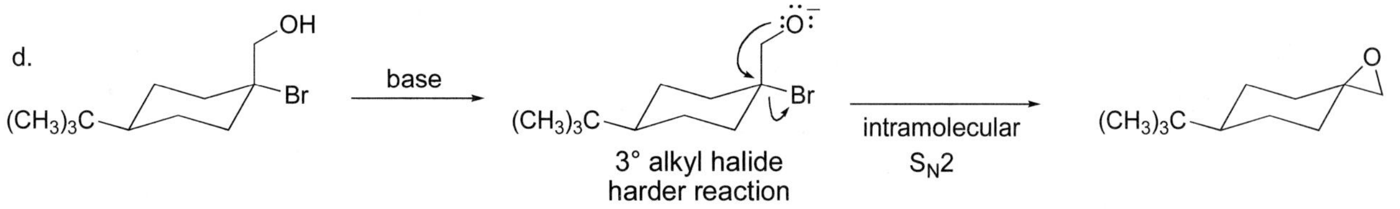
OH
Br
$(CH_3)_3C$
base
3° alkyl halide
harder reaction
intramolecular
S_N2

7.86

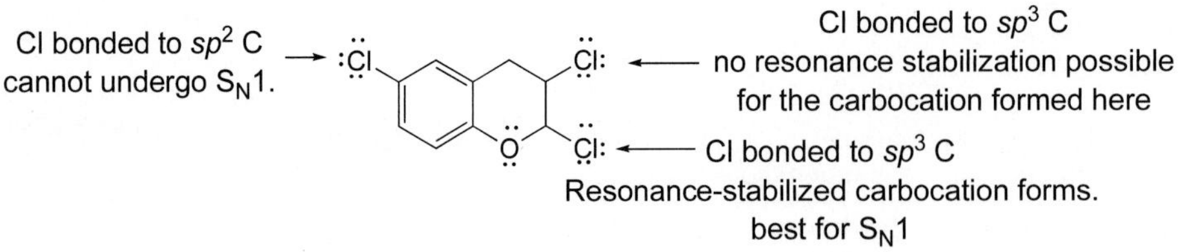
Cl bonded to sp^2 C
cannot undergo S_N1.
Cl bonded to sp^3 C
no resonance stabilization possible
for the carbocation formed here
Cl bonded to sp^3 C
Resonance-stabilized carbocation forms.
best for S_N1

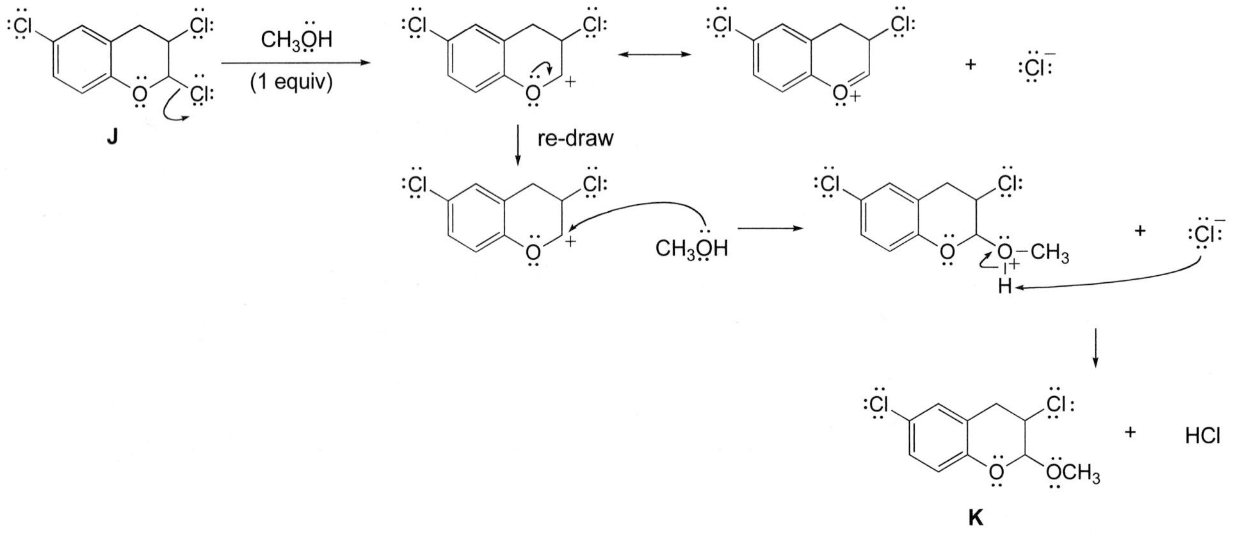
CH_3OH
(1 equiv)
J
re-draw
CH_3OH
HCl
K

7.87

a.

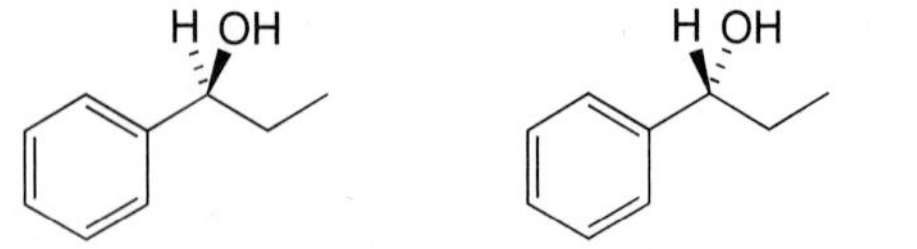

(*S*)-1-phenyl-1-propanol (*R*)-1-phenyl-1-propanol
[α] = –48 [α] = +48

$$ee = \frac{[\alpha] \text{ mixture}}{[\alpha] \text{ pure enantiomer}} \times 100\%$$

$$= \frac{+5.0}{+48} \times 100\% = 10.\% \text{ excess of } R \text{ isomer}$$

90% racemic mixture = 45% *R* and 45% *S*
Total *R* isomer = 45 + 10 = 55% *R* isomer

b. The *R* product is the product of inversion and it predominates.

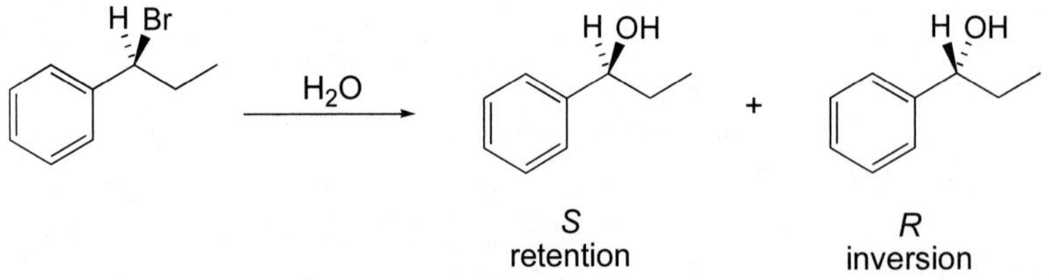
H_2O
S
retention
R
inversion

c. The weak nucleophile favors an S_N1 reaction, which occurs by way of an intermediate carbocation. Perhaps there is more inversion than retention because H_2O attacks the intermediate carbocation while the Br^- leaving group is still in the vicinity of the carbocation. The Br^- would then shield one side of the carbocation and backside attack would be slightly favored.

Chapter 8 Alkyl Halides and Elimination Reactions

Chapter Review

A comparison between nucleophilic substitution and β-elimination

Nucleophilic substitution—A nucleophile attacks a carbon atom (7.6).

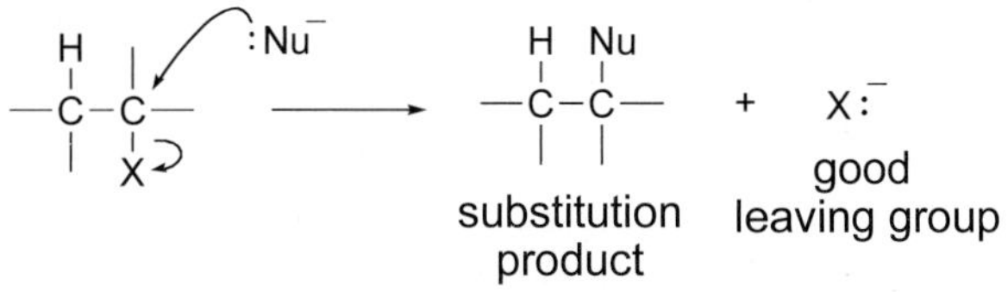

β-Elimination—A base attacks a proton (8.1).

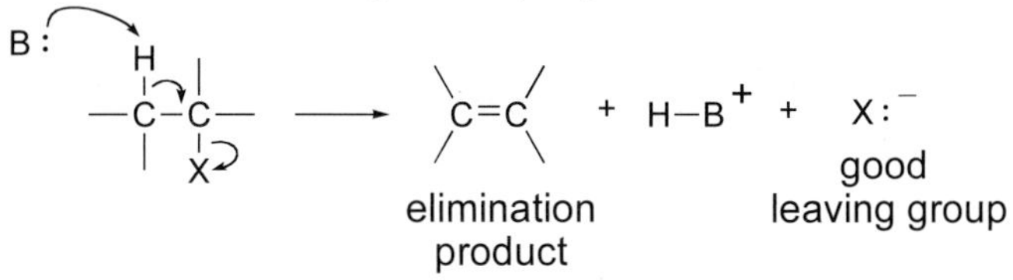

Similarities	Differences
• In both reactions RX acts as an electrophile, reacting with an electron-rich reagent. • Both reactions require a **good leaving group X:⁻** willing to accept the electron density in the C–X bond.	• In substitution, a nucleophile attacks a single carbon atom. • In elimination, a Brønsted–Lowry base removes a proton to form a π bond, and two carbons are involved in the reaction.

The importance of the base in E2 and E1 reactions (8.9)

The strength of the base determines the mechanism of elimination.

- Strong bases favor E2 reactions.
- Weak bases favor E1 reactions.

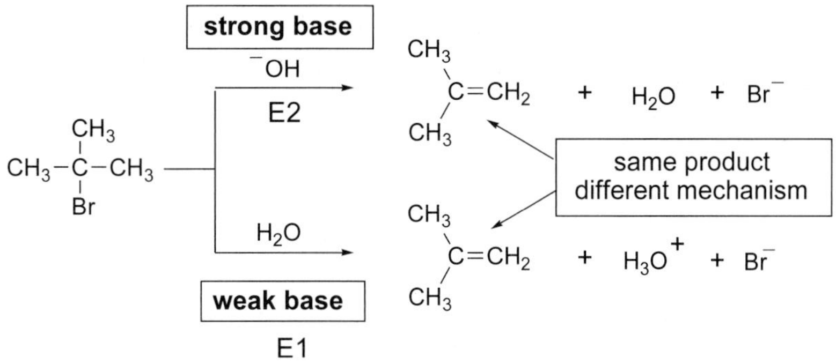

E1 and E2 mechanisms compared

	E2 mechanism	E1 mechanism
[1] Mechanism	• one step (8.4B)	• two steps (8.6B)
[2] Alkyl halide	• rate: $R_3CX > R_2CHX > RCH_2X$ (8.4C)	• rate: $R_3CX > R_2CHX > RCH_2X$ (8.6C)
[3] Rate equation	• rate = k[RX][B:] • second-order kinetics (8.4A)	• rate = k[RX] • first-order kinetics (8.6A)
[4] Stereochemistry	• anti periplanar arrangement of H and X (8.8)	• trigonal planar carbocation intermediate (8.6B)
[5] Base	• favored by strong bases (8.4B)	• favored by weak bases (8.6C)
[6] Leaving group	• better leaving group → faster reaction (8.4B)	• better leaving group → faster reaction (Table 8.4)
[7] Solvent	• favored by polar aprotic solvents (8.4B)	• favored by polar protic solvents (Table 8.4)
[8] Product	• more substituted alkene favored (Zaitsev rule, 8.5)	• more substituted alkene favored (Zaitsev rule, 8.6C)

Summary chart on the four mechanisms: S_N1, S_N2, E1, and E2

Alkyl halide type	Conditions	Mechanism
1° RCH_2X	strong nucleophile	**S_N2**
	strong bulky base	**E2**
2° R_2CHX	strong base and nucleophile	**S_N2 + E2**
	strong bulky base	**E2**
	weak base and nucleophile	**S_N1 + E1**
3° R_3CX	weak base and nucleophile	**S_N1 + E1**
	strong base	**E2**

Zaitsev rule

- β-Elimination affords the more stable product having the more substituted double bond.
- Zaitsev products predominate in E2 reactions except when a cyclohexane ring prevents trans diaxial arrangement.

Practice Test on Chapter Review

1. Which of the following is true about an E1 reaction?
   1. The reaction is faster with better leaving groups.
   2. The reaction is fastest with 3° alkyl halides.
   3. The reaction is faster with stronger bases.
   4. Statements (1) and (2) are true.
   5. Statements (1), (2), and (3) are all true.

2. Consider the S_N2 and E1 reaction mechanisms. What effect on the rate of the reaction is observed when each of the following changes is made? Fill in each box of the table with one of the following phrases: **increases, decreases,** or **remains the same.**

Change	S_N2 Mechanism	E1 Mechanism
a. The alkyl halide is changed from $(CH_3)_3CBr$ to $CH_3CH_2CH_2CH_2Br$.		
b. The solvent is changed from $(CH_3)_2CO$ to CH_3CH_2OH.		
c. The nucleophile/base is changed from ^-OH to H_2O.		
d. The alkyl halide is changed from CH_3CH_2Cl to CH_3CH_2I.		
e. The concentration of the base/nucleophile is increased by a factor of five.		

3. Rank the following compounds in order of ***increasing*** **reactivity in an E2 elimination** reaction. Rank the ***most reactive*** compound as **3,** the ***least reactive*** compound as **1,** and the compound of intermediate reactivity as **2.**

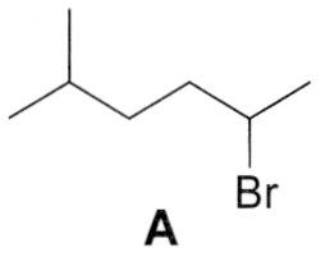

A

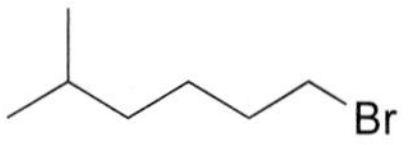

B

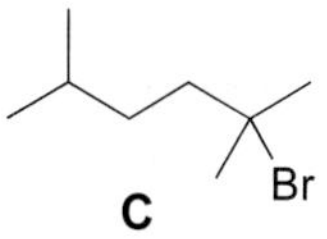

C

4. Draw the organic products formed in the following reactions.

a. 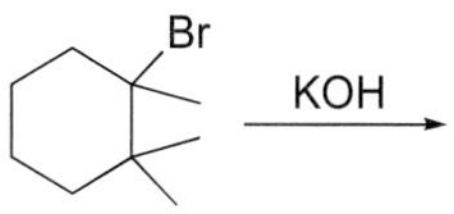

c. 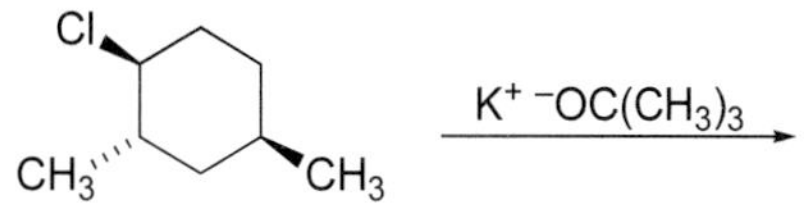

b. 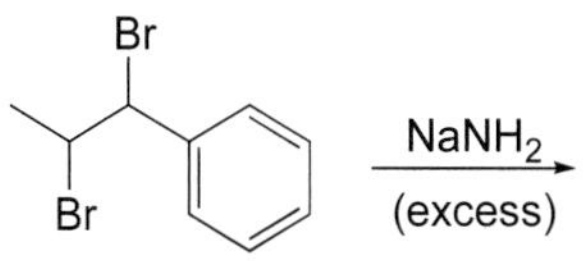

d. 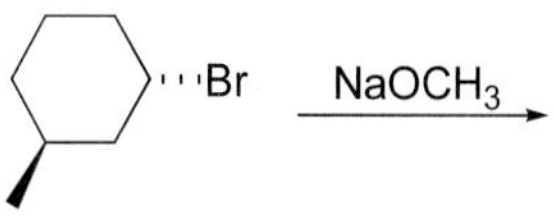

5. a. Fill in the appropriate alkyl halide needed to synthesize the following compound as a single product using the given reagents.

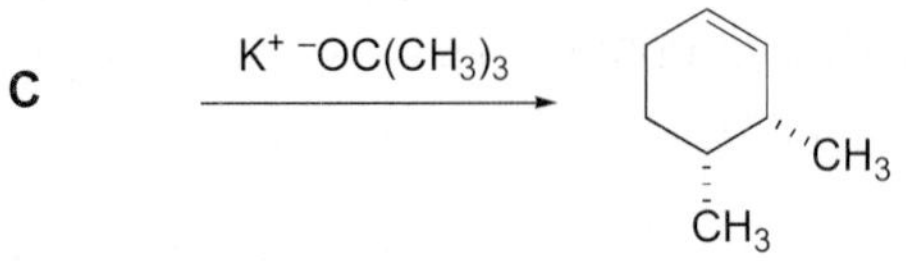

b. What starting material is needed for the following reaction? The starting material must yield product cleanly, in one step without any other organic side products.

D $\xrightarrow{K^+\ ^-OC(CH_3)_3}$ $CH_3CH_2CH{=}CHCH_3$
(cis and trans mixture)

6. Draw all products formed in the following reaction.

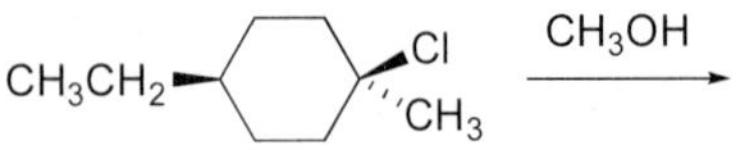

Answers to Practice Test

1. 4

2.

	S_N2	E1
a.	increases	decreases
b.	decreases	increases
c.	decreases	same
d.	increases	increases
e.	increases	same

3. **A**–2
   B–1
   C–3

4.

a. 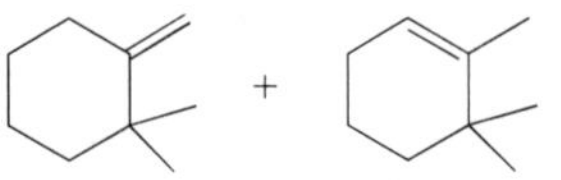

b. 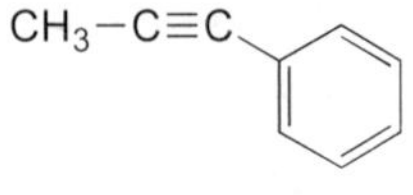

c. 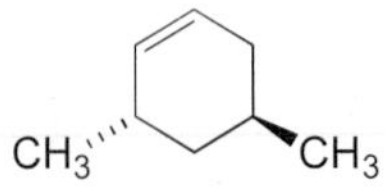

d. 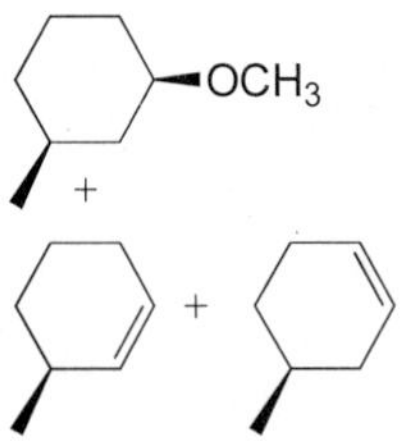

5.

a. 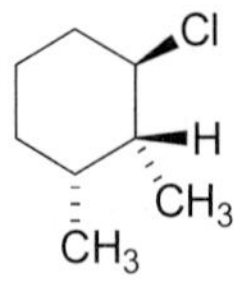

C

b. 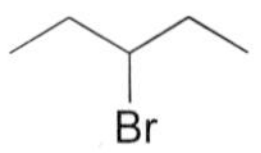

(or Cl or I)

D

6.

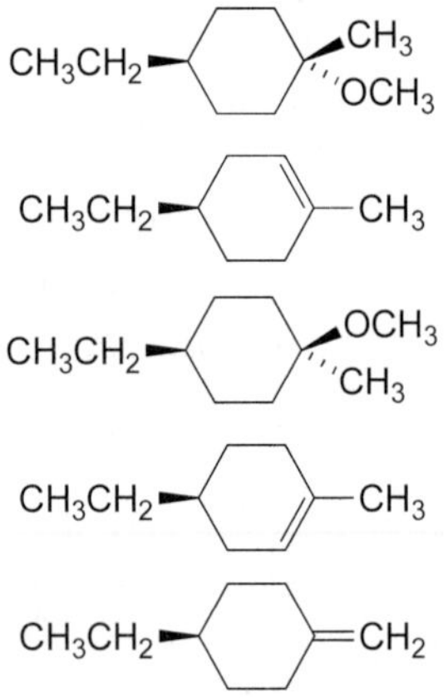

Answers to Problems

8.1 • The carbon bonded to the leaving group is the **α carbon.** Any carbon bonded to it is a **β carbon.**
• **To draw the products of an elimination reaction:** Remove the leaving group from the α carbon and an H from the β carbon and form a π bond.

a. $CH_3CH_2CH_2\overset{\beta}{C}H_2\overset{\alpha}{C}H_2{-}Cl \xrightarrow{K^{+}\,{}^{-}OC(CH_3)_3} CH_3CH_2CH_2CH{=}CH_2$

b. 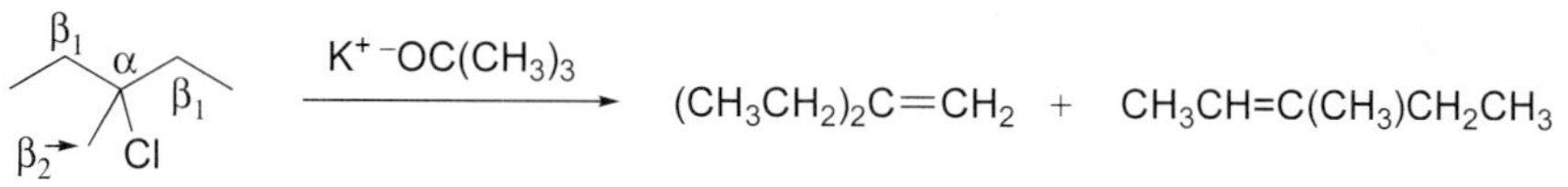
β1
α
β1
β2
Cl
K+ -OC(CH3)3
(CH3CH2)2C=CH2 + CH3CH=C(CH3)CH2CH3

c. 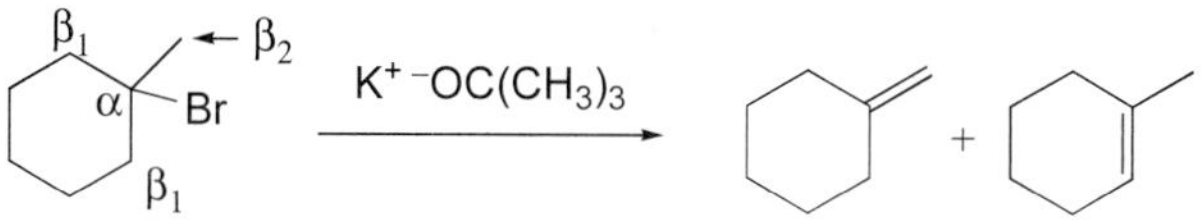
β1
β2
α
Br
β1
K+ -OC(CH3)3
+

8.2 **Alkenes are classified by the number of carbon atoms bonded to the double bond.** A monosubstituted alkene has one carbon atom bonded to the double bond, a disubstituted alkene has two carbon atoms bonded to the double bond, etc.

a. 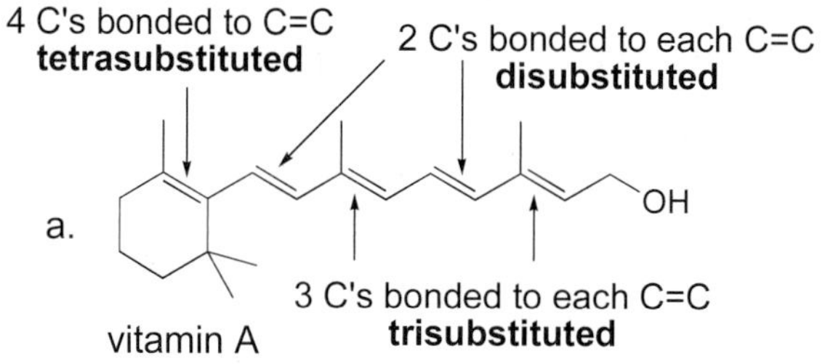
4 C's bonded to C=C
tetrasubstituted
2 C's bonded to each C=C
disubstituted
OH
3 C's bonded to each C=C
trisubstituted
vitamin A

b. 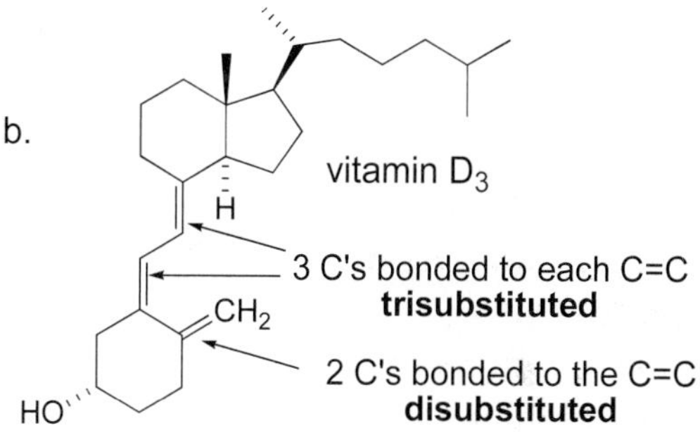
vitamin D3
H
3 C's bonded to each C=C
trisubstituted
CH2
2 C's bonded to the C=C
disubstituted
HO

8.3 To have stereoisomers at a C=C, the two groups on each end of the double bond must be different from each other.

a. 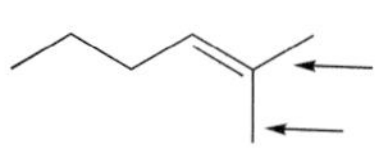

two CH_3 groups
no stereoisomers possible

b. two different groups (CH_3CH_2 and H) | two different groups (H and CH_3)

$CH_3CH_2CH{=}CHCH_3$

stereoisomers possible

c. two different groups (cyclohexyl and H) | two different groups (cyclohexyl and H)

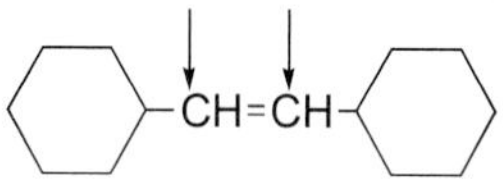
CH=CH

stereoisomers possible

8.4

a. 2 CH_3's on one end →

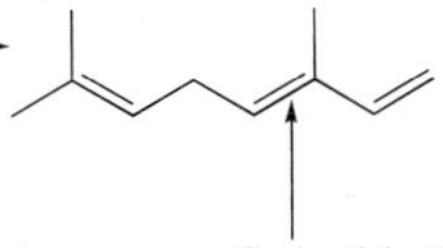

← 2 H's on one end

Only this C=C exhibits stereoisomerism.

b. A diastereomer has a different 3-D arrangement of groups but the carbon skeleton and the double bonds must stay in the original positions.

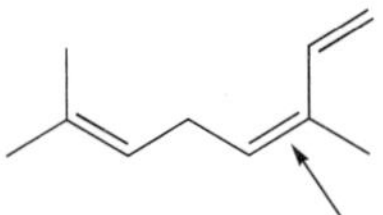

diastereomer

different arrangement of groups around this double bond

8.5 Two definitions:

- **Constitutional isomers** differ in the connectivity of the atoms.
- **Stereoisomers** differ only in the 3-D arrangement of the atoms in space.

a. 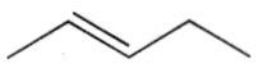 and 

different connectivity of atoms
constitutional isomers

b. 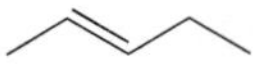 and 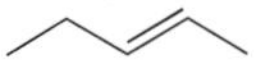

trans trans
identical

c.  and 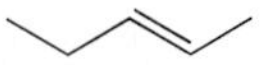

cis trans
different arrangement of atoms in space
stereoisomers

d. 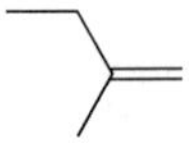 and 

different connectivity of atoms
constitutional isomers

8.6 Two rules to predict the relative stability of alkenes:
[1] Trans alkenes are generally more stable than cis alkenes.
[2] The stability of an alkene increases as the number of R groups on the C=C increases.

a. 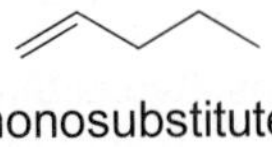 or 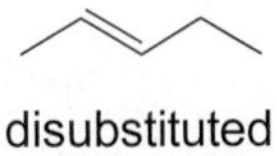

monosubstituted

disubstituted
more stable

b. 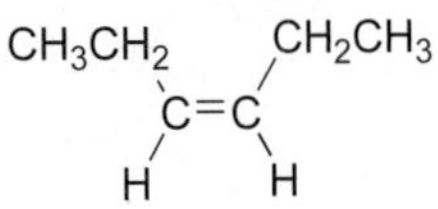

or

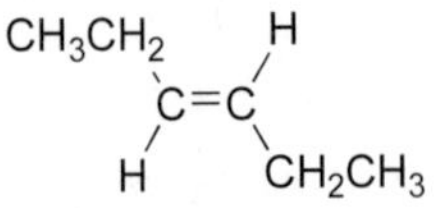

cis

trans
more stable

c. 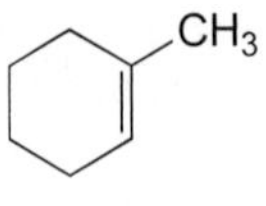

or

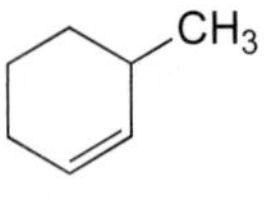

trisubstituted
more stable

disubstituted

8.7

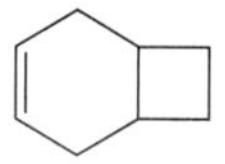

A

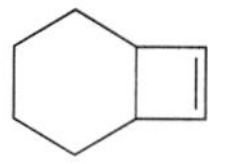

B

Alkene **A** is more stable than alkene **B** because the double bond in **A** is in a six-membered ring. The double bond in **B** is in a four-membered ring, which has considerable angle strain due to the small ring size.

8.8 In an E2 mechanism, four bonds are involved in the single step. Use curved arrows to show these simultaneous actions:

[1] The base attacks a hydrogen on a β carbon.
[2] A π bond forms.
[3] The leaving group comes off.

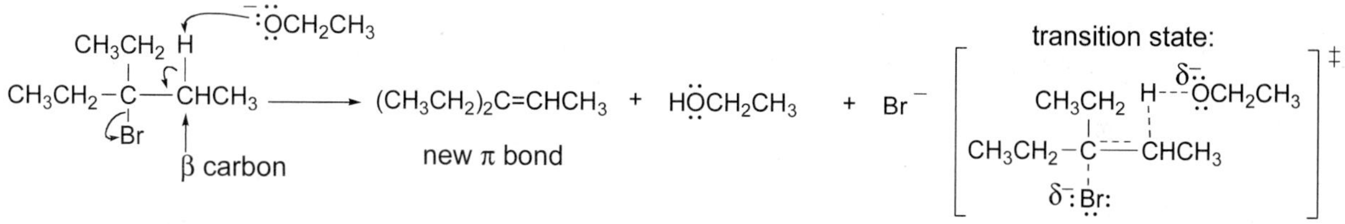

8.9 In both cases, the rate of elimination decreases.

a. stronger base, **faster reaction**

$CH_3CH_2{-}Br + {}^{-}OC(CH_3)_3 \longrightarrow$

$CH_3CH_2{-}Br + {}^{-}OH \longrightarrow$

b. better leaving group, **faster reaction**

$CH_3CH_2{-}Br + {}^{-}OC(CH_3)_3 \longrightarrow$

$CH_3CH_2{-}Cl + {}^{-}OC(CH_3)_3 \longrightarrow$

8.10 As the number of R groups on the carbon with the leaving group increases, the rate of an E2 reaction increases.

a.

$(CH_3)_2CHCH_2CH_2CH_2Br$	$(CH_3)_2CHCH_2CH(Br)CH_3$	$(CH_3)_2C(Br)CH_2CH_2CH_3$
1° alkyl halide **least reactive**	2° alkyl halide **intermediate reactivity**	3° alkyl halide **most reactive**

b.

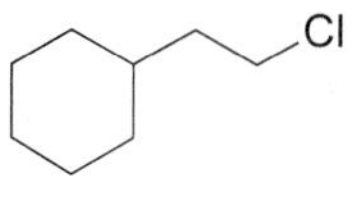

1° alkyl halide
least reactive

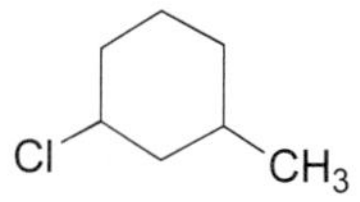

2° alkyl halide
intermediate reactivity

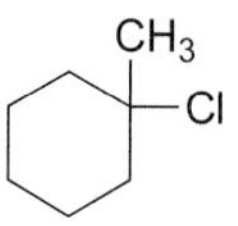

3° alkyl halide
most reactive

8.11 Use the following characteristics of an E2 reaction to answer the questions:

[1] E2 reactions are second order and one step.
[2] More substituted halides react faster.
[3] Reactions with strong bases or better leaving groups are faster.
[4] Reactions with polar aprotic solvents are faster.

Rate equation: rate = *k*[RX][Base]

a. tripling the concentration of the alkyl halide = **rate triples**
b. halving the concentration of the base = **rate halved**
c. changing the solvent from CH_3OH to DMSO = **rate increases** (Polar aprotic solvent is better for E2.)
d. changing the leaving group from I^- to Br^- = **rate decreases** (I^- is a better leaving group.)
e. changing the base from ^-OH to H_2O = **rate decreases** (weaker base)
f. changing the alkyl halide from CH_3CH_2Br to $(CH_3)_2CHBr$ = **rate increases** (More substituted halide reacts faster.)

8.12 The Zaitsev rule states: In a β-elimination reaction, the major product has the more substituted double bond.

a. 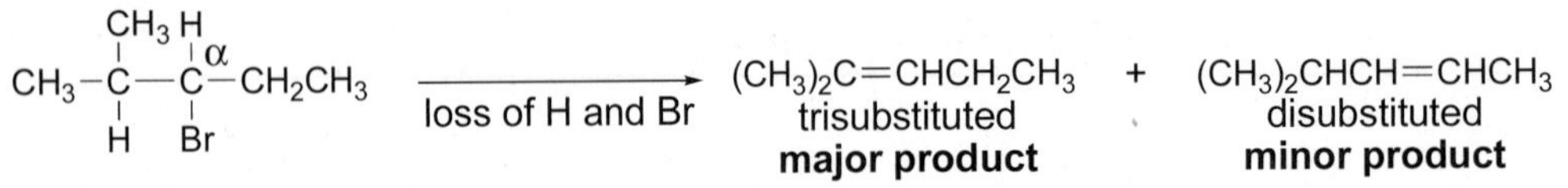

b. 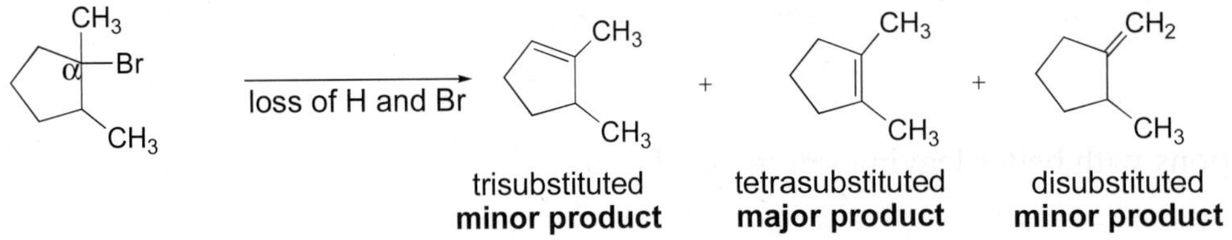

c. 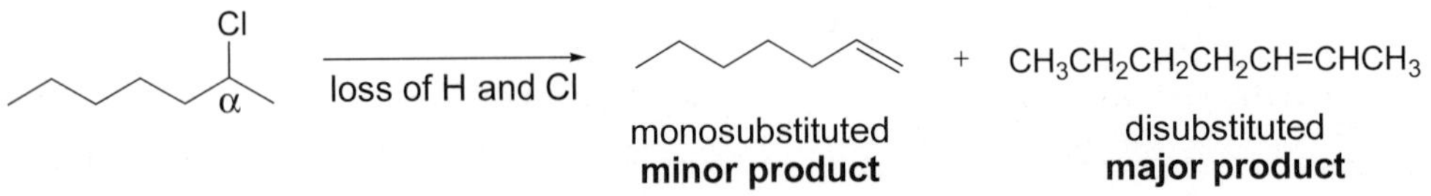

d. 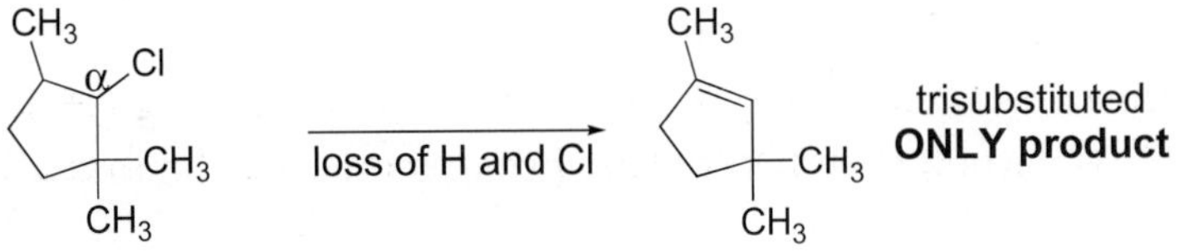

8.13 An E1 mechanism has two steps:
[1] The leaving group comes off, creating a carbocation.
[2] A base pulls off a proton from a β carbon, and a π bond forms.

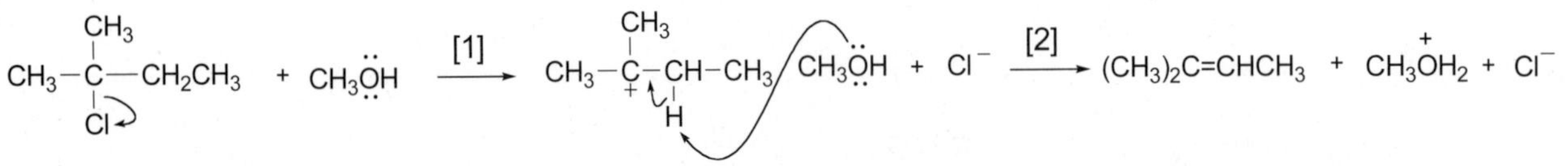

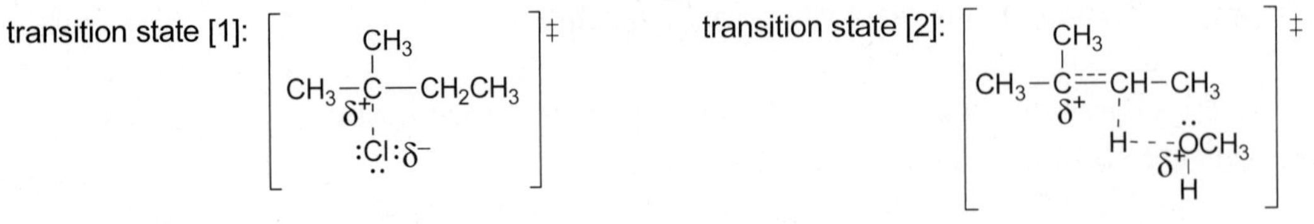

8.14 The Zaitsev rule states: In a β-elimination reaction, the major product has the more substituted double bond.

a.
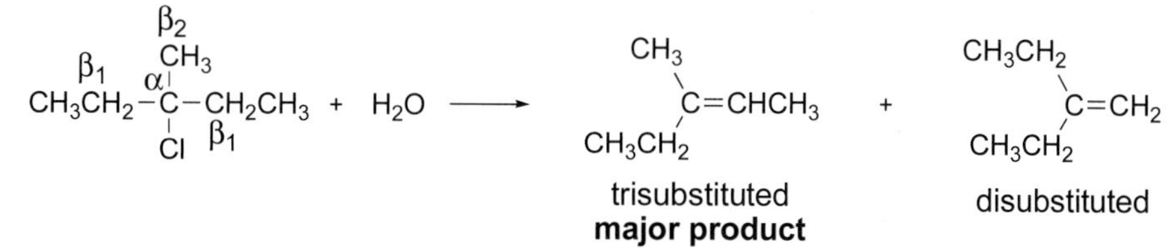

b.
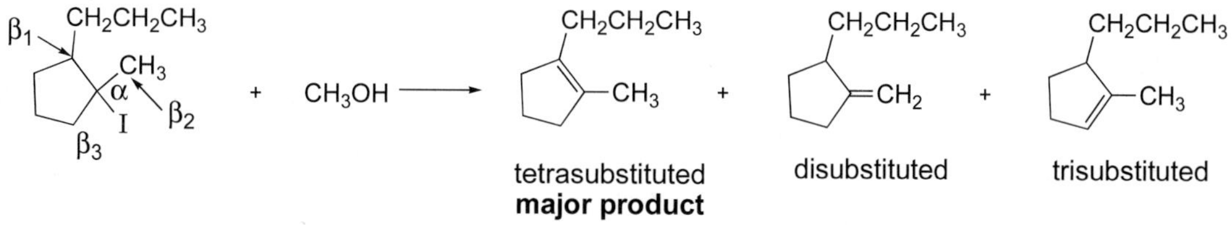

8.15 Use the following characteristics of an **E1 reaction** to answer the questions:
[1] E1 reactions are first order and two steps.
[2] More substituted halides react faster.
[3] Weaker bases are preferred.
[4] Reactions with better leaving groups are faster.
[5] Reactions in polar protic solvents are faster.

Rate equation: rate = *k*[RX]. The base doesn't affect rate.
a. doubling the concentration of the alkyl halide = **rate doubles**
b. doubling the concentration of the base = **no change** (Base is not in the rate equation.)
c. changing the alkyl halide from $(CH_3)_3CBr$ to $CH_3CH_2CH_2Br$ = **rate decreases** (More substituted halides react faster.)
d. changing the leaving group from Cl^- to Br^- = **rate increases** (better leaving group)
e. changing the solvent from DMSO to CH_3OH = **rate increases** (Polar protic solvent favors E1.)

8.16 Both S_N1 and E1 reactions occur by forming a carbocation. To draw the products:
[1] **For the S_N1 reaction,** substitute the nucleophile for the leaving group.

[2] **For the E1 reaction,** remove a proton from a β carbon and create a new π bond.

a.
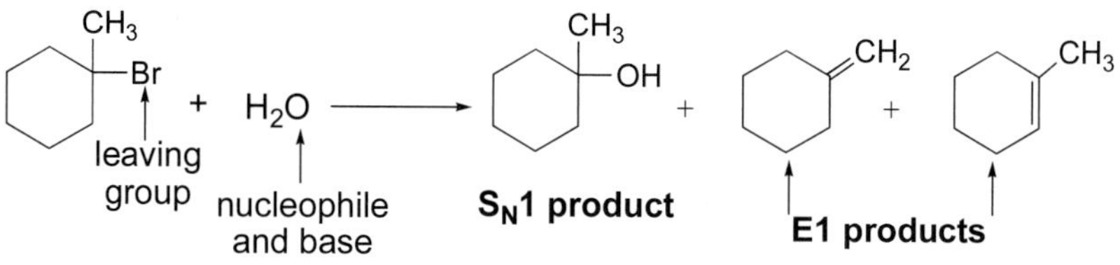

b.
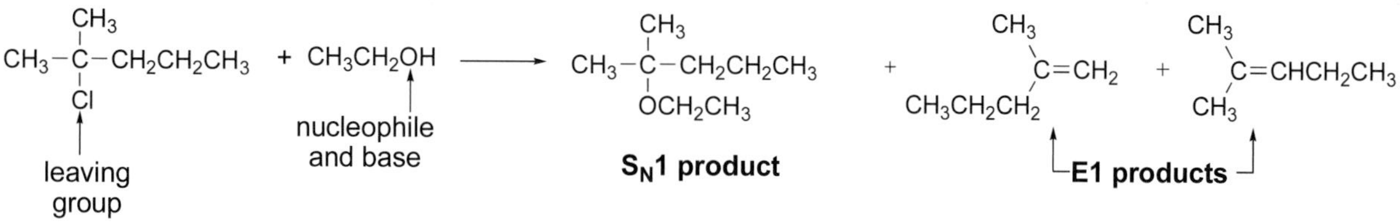

8.17 E2 reactions occur with anti periplanar geometry. **The anti periplanar arrangement uses a *staggered* conformation and has the H and X on *opposite sides* of the C–C bond.**

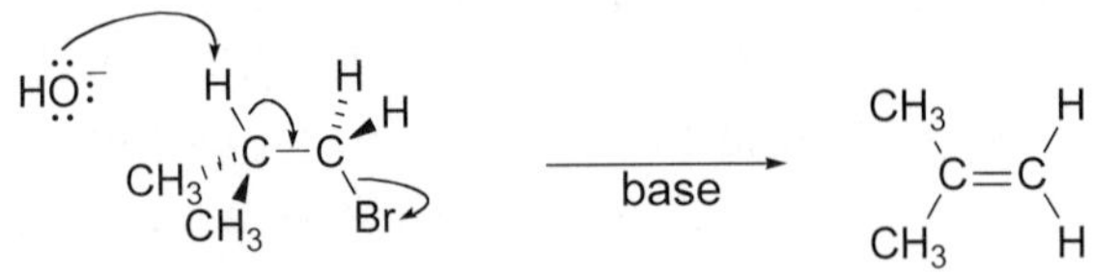

H and Br are on opposite sides =
anti periplanar

8.18 The E2 elimination reactions will occur in the anti periplanar orientation as drawn. To draw the product of elimination, maintain the orientation of the remaining groups around the C=C.

a.

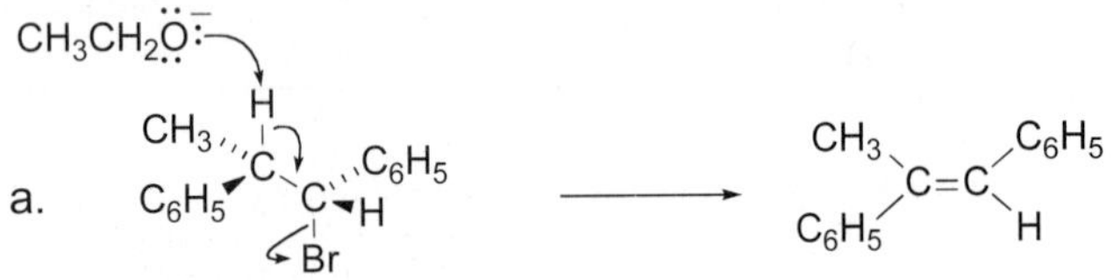

The two benzene rings remain on opposite sides of the newly formed C=C. This makes them **trans.**

The two benzene rings are anti in this conformation (one wedge, one dash).

diastereomers

b.

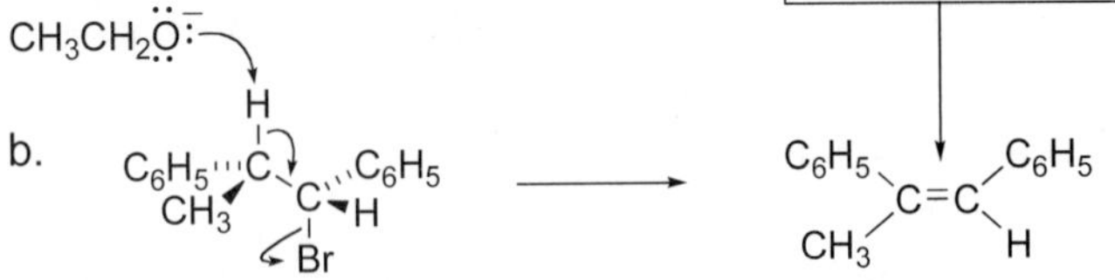

The two benzene rings remain on the same side of the newly formed C=C. This makes them **cis.**

The two benzene rings are gauche in this conformation (both drawn on dashes, behind the plane).

8.19 Note: The Zaitsev products predominate in E2 elimination *except* when substituents on a cyclohexane ring prevent a **trans diaxial** arrangement of H and X.

a.

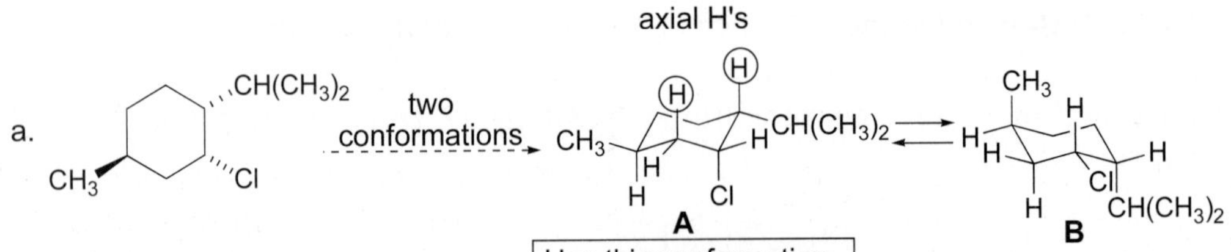

Use this conformation.
It has Cl axial and
two axial H's.

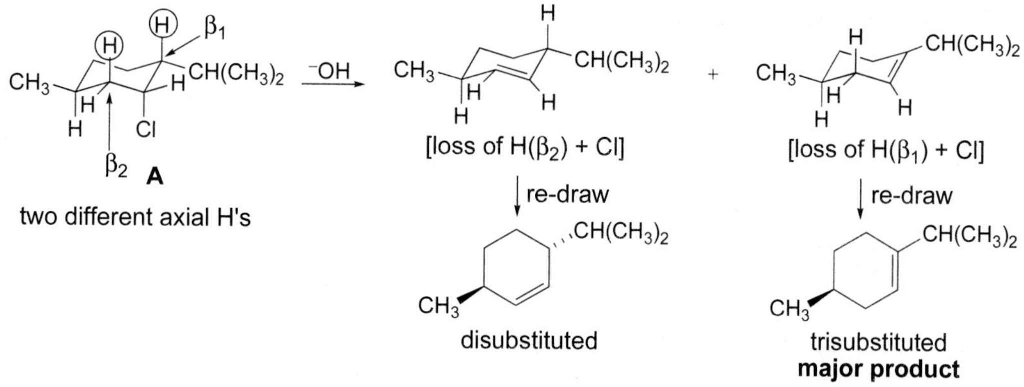
β1
CH(CH3)2
−OH
CH3
Cl
β2
A
two different axial H's
[loss of H(β2) + Cl]
re-draw
disubstituted
[loss of H(β1) + Cl]
re-draw
trisubstituted
major product

b.

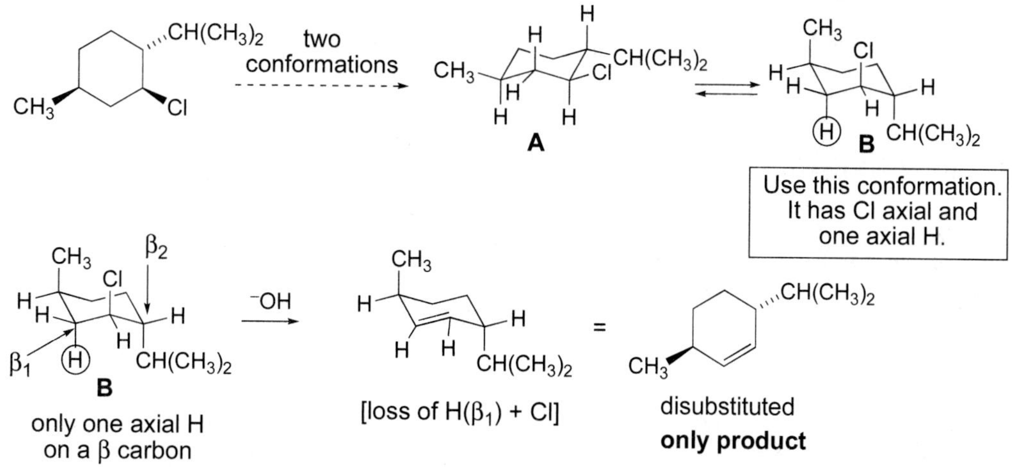
CH(CH3)2
CH3
Cl
two
conformations
A
B
Use this conformation.
It has Cl axial and
one axial H.
β2
β1
−OH
B
only one axial H
on a β carbon
[loss of H(β1) + Cl]
=
disubstituted
only product

8.20 Draw the chair conformations of *cis*-1-chloro-2-methylcyclohexane and its trans isomer. For E2 elimination reactions to occur, **there must be a H and X trans diaxial to each other.**

Two conformations of the cis isomer:

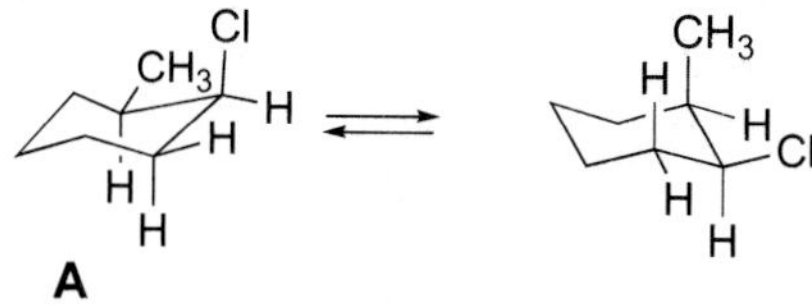
Cl
CH3
H

A

reacting conformation (axial Cl)

This reacting conformation has only one group axial, making it more stable and present in a higher concentration than **B.** This makes a **faster elimination reaction with the cis isomer.**

Two conformations of the trans isomer:

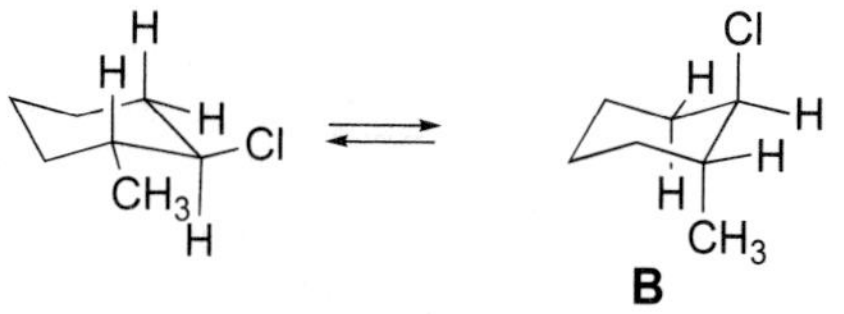
H
Cl
CH3

B

reacting conformation (axial Cl)

This conformation is less stable than **A**, since both CH_3 and Cl are axial. **This slows the rate of elimination from the trans isomer.**

8.21 E2 reactions are favored by strong negatively charged bases and occur with 1°, 2°, and 3° halides, with 3° being the most reactive.
E1 reactions are favored by weaker neutral bases and do not occur with 1° halides since they would have to form highly unstable carbocations.

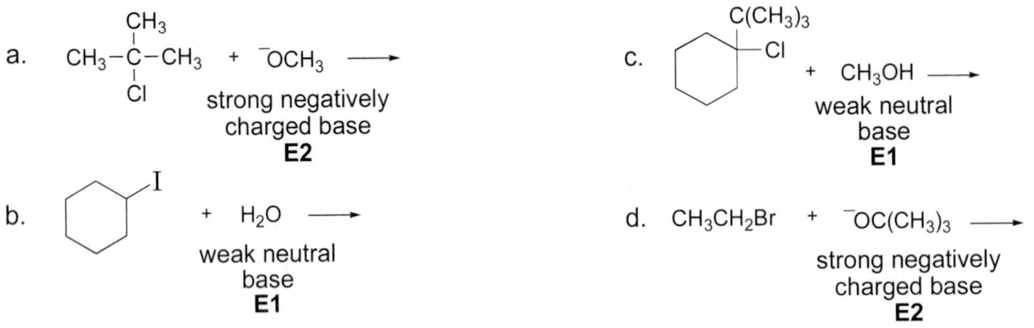
a.
CH_3
CH_3-C-CH_3
Cl
+ $^-OCH_3$
strong negatively charged base
E2
b.
I
+ H_2O
weak neutral base
E1
c.
$C(CH_3)_3$
Cl
+ CH_3OH
weak neutral base
E1
d. CH_3CH_2Br + $^-OC(CH_3)_3$
strong negatively charged base
E2

8.22 Draw the alkynes that result from removal of two equivalents of HX.

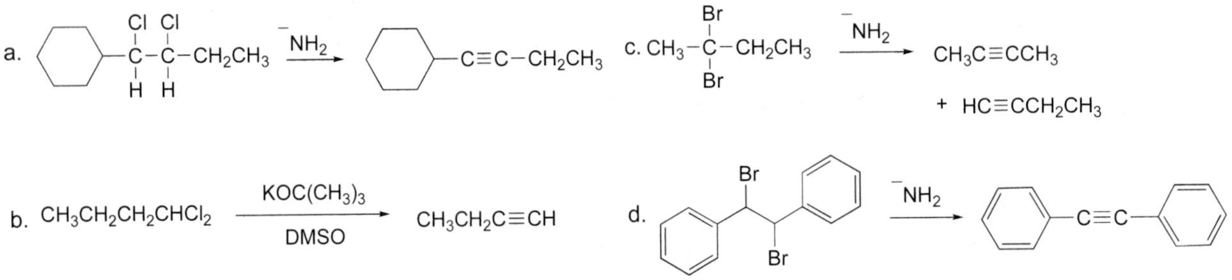
a.
Cl Cl
C−C−CH_2CH_3
H H
$^-NH_2$
C≡C−CH_2CH_3
c. $CH_3-C-CH_2CH_3$
Br
Br
$^-NH_2$
$CH_3C≡CCH_3$
+ $HC≡CCH_2CH_3$
b. $CH_3CH_2CH_2CHCl_2$
$KOC(CH_3)_3$
DMSO
$CH_3CH_2C≡CH$
d.
Br
Br
$^-NH_2$
C≡C

8.23

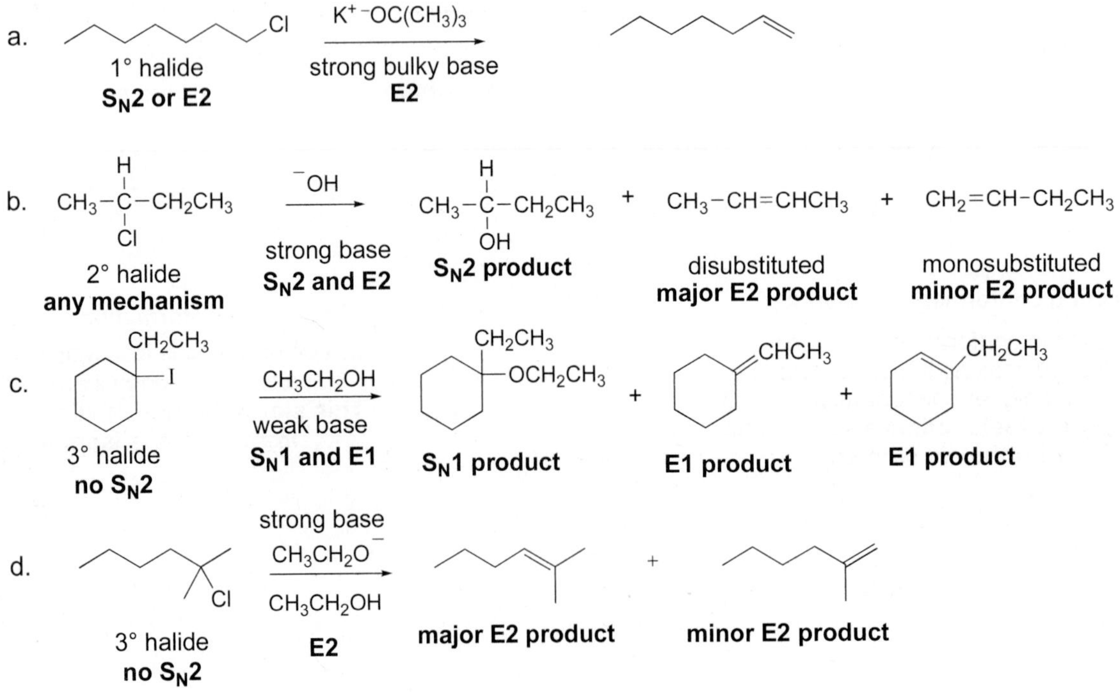
a.
Cl
1° halide
S_N2 or E2
$K^+ {}^-OC(CH_3)_3$
strong bulky base
E2
b.
H
$CH_3-C-CH_2CH_3$
Cl
2° halide
any mechanism
^-OH
strong base
S_N2 and E2
H
$CH_3-C-CH_2CH_3$
OH
S_N2 product
+ $CH_3-CH=CHCH_3$
disubstituted
major E2 product
+ $CH_2=CH-CH_2CH_3$
monosubstituted
minor E2 product
c.
CH_2CH_3
I
3° halide
no S_N2
CH_3CH_2OH
weak base
S_N1 and E1
CH_2CH_3
OCH_2CH_3
S_N1 product
+
$CHCH_3$
E1 product
+
CH_2CH_3
E1 product
d.
Cl
3° halide
no S_N2
strong base
$CH_3CH_2O^-$
CH_3CH_2OH
E2
major E2 product
+
minor E2 product

8.24

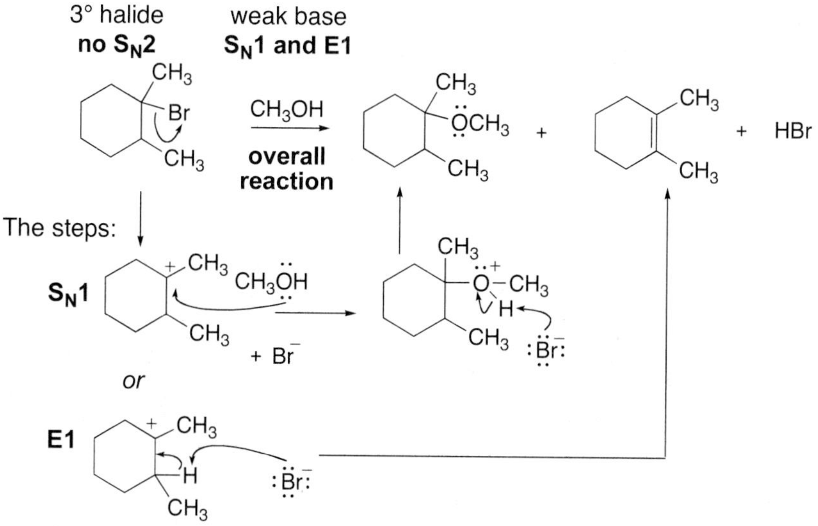

8.25 More substituted alkenes are more stable. Trans alkenes are generally more stable than cis alkenes. Order of stability:

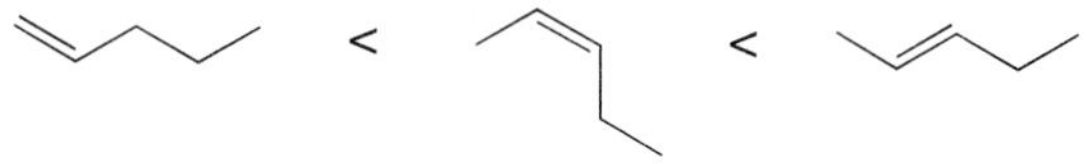

B least stable < C < A most stable

8.26 The trans isomer reacts faster. During elimination, Br must be axial to give trans diaxial elimination. In the trans isomer, the more stable conformation has the bulky *tert*-butyl group in the more roomy equatorial position. In the cis isomer, elimination can occur only when both the *tert*-butyl and Br groups are axial, a conformation that is not energetically favorable.

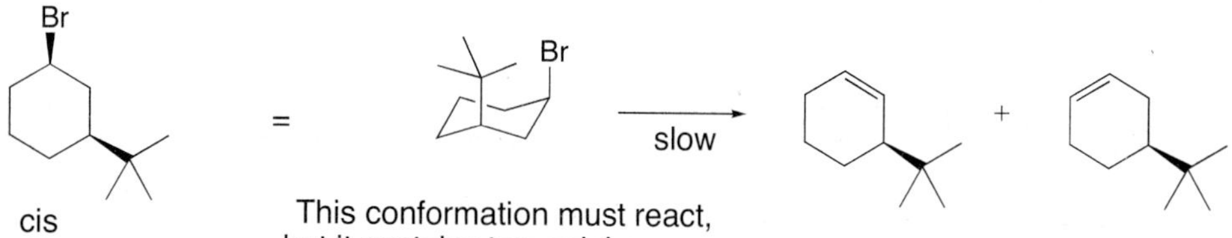

cis
D
cis-1-bromo-3-*tert*-butylcyclohexane

This conformation must react, but it contains two axial groups.

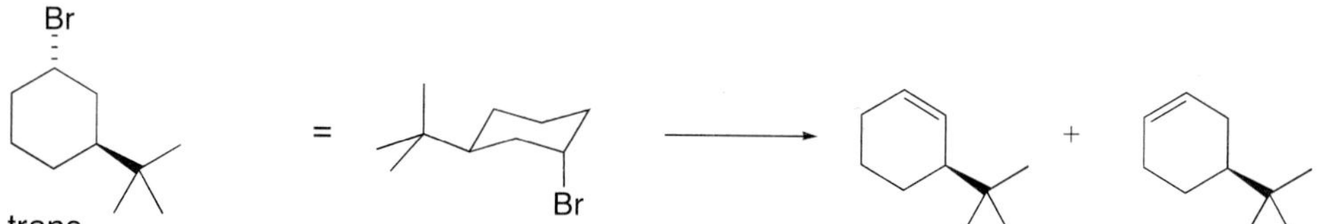

trans
E
trans-1-bromo-3-*tert*-butylcyclohexane

preferred conformation

8.27 Translate each model to a structure and arrange H and Br to be anti periplanar.

a.

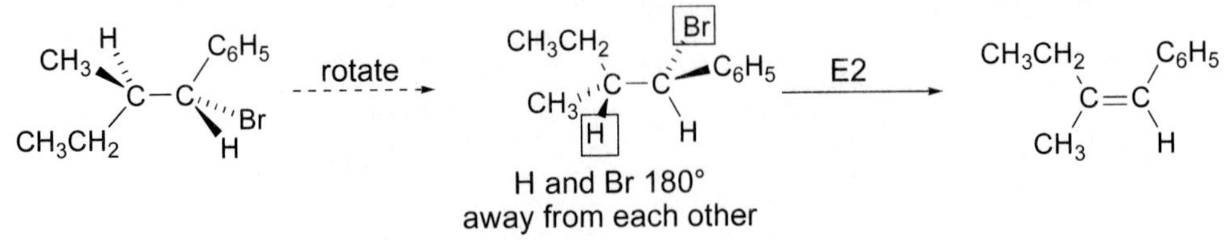
rotate
E2
H and Br 180°
away from each other

b.

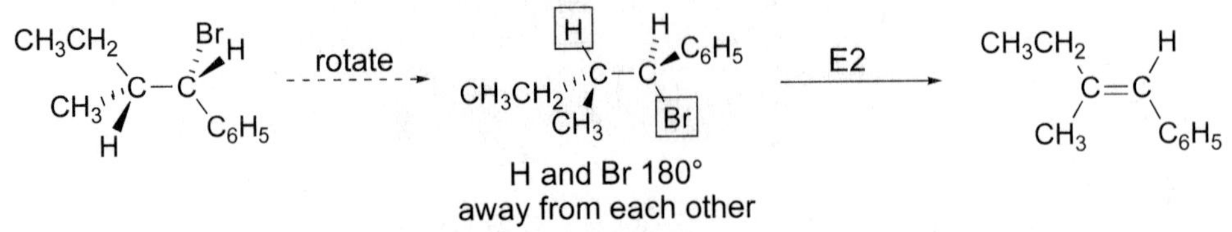
rotate
E2
H and Br 180°
away from each other

8.28

a. $CH_3CH_2CH_2CH_2CH_2CH_2Br$ ⟶ $CH_3CH_2CH_2CH_2CH{=}CH_2$

b. 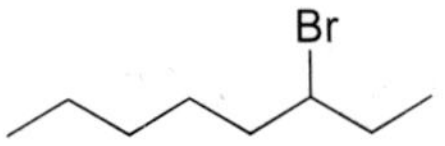 ⟶ $CH_3CH_2CH_2CH_2CH{=}CHCH_2CH_3$ + $CH_3CH_2CH_2CH_2CH_2CH{=}CHCH_3$

c. $CH_3CH_2CH(Cl)CH(CH_3)CH_3$ ⟶ $CH_3CH_2CH{=}C(CH_3)_2$ + $CH_3CH{=}CHCH(CH_3)_2$

d. 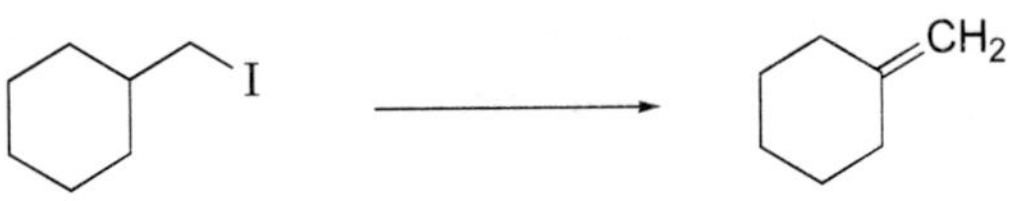

8.29 To give only one product in an elimination reaction, **the starting alkyl halide must have only one type of β carbon with H's.**

a. $CH_2{=}CHCH_2CH_2CH_3$ ⟵ $CH_2(Cl)$–$CH_2CH_2CH_2CH_3$ (α = CH_2Cl, β = adjacent CH_2)

b. $(CH_3)_2CHCH{=}CH_2$ ⟵ $(CH_3)_2CHCH_2$–CH_2Cl (β = CH_2, α = CH_2Cl)

c. 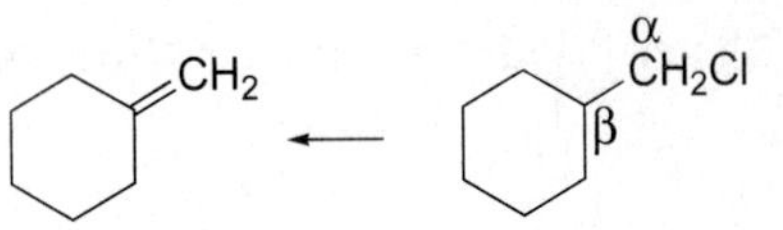

d. 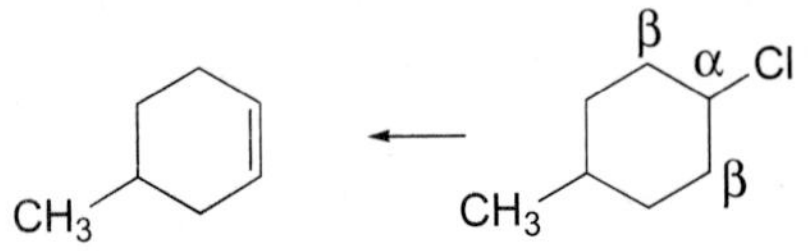

Two β carbons are identical.

e. 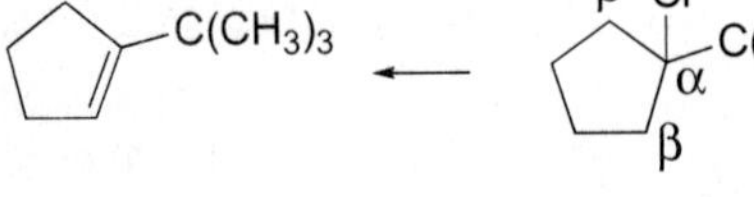

Two β carbons are identical.

8.30 To have stereoisomers, the two groups on each end of the double bond must be different from each other.

a. 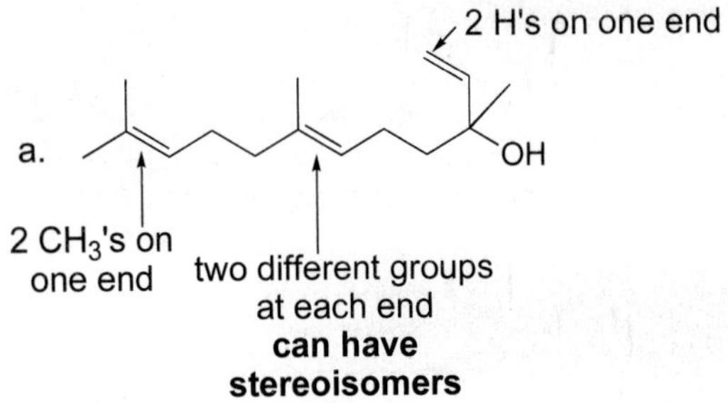
2 H's on one end
2 CH3's on one end
two different groups at each end
can have stereoisomers

b. 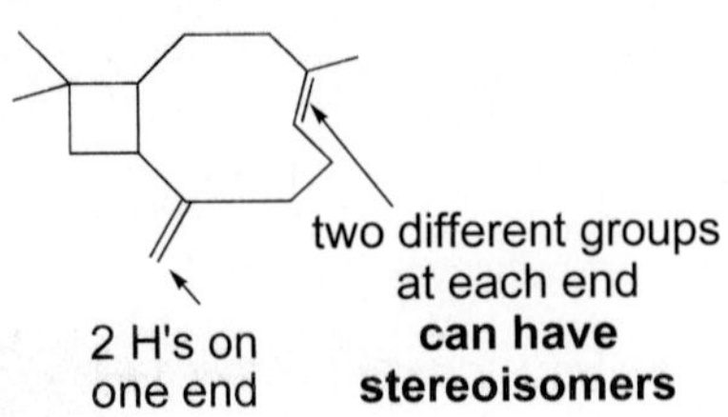
2 H's on one end
two different groups at each end
can have stereoisomers

8.31 Use the definitions in Answer 8.5.

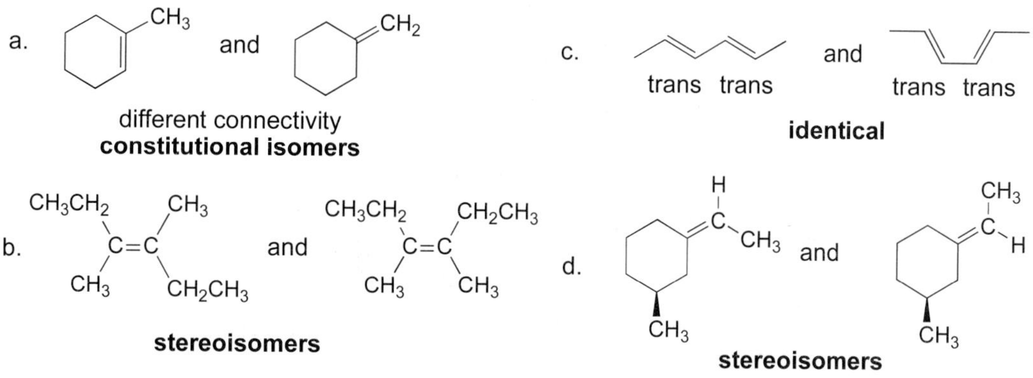
a.
and
different connectivity
constitutional isomers
b.
and
stereoisomers
c.
and
trans trans
trans trans
identical
d.
and
stereoisomers

8.32

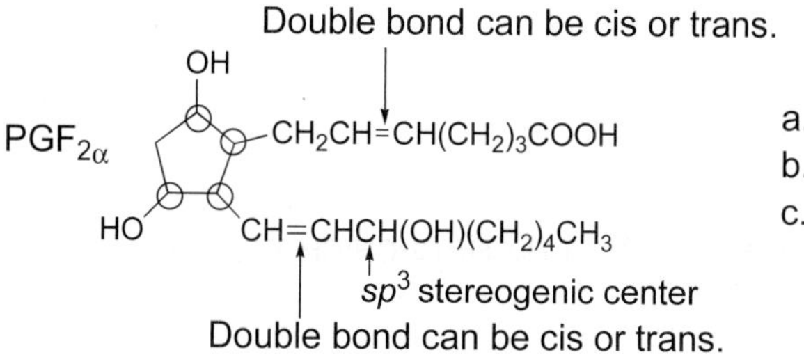
Double bond can be cis or trans.
OH
PGF2α
CH2CH=CH(CH2)3COOH
HO
CH=CHCH(OH)(CH2)4CH3
sp3 stereogenic center
Double bond can be cis or trans.

a. five sp^3 stereogenic centers (four circled, one labeled)
b. Two double bonds can both be cis or trans.
c. 2^7 = 128 stereoisomers possible

8.33 Use the rules from Answer 8.6 to rank the alkenes.

$CH_2=CHCH(CH_3)_2$	$CH_2=C(CH_3)CH_2CH_3$	$(CH_3)_2C=CHCH_3$
monosubstituted	disubstituted	trisubstituted
least stable	**intermediate stability**	**most stable**

8.34 A larger negative value for $\Delta H°$ means the reaction is more exothermic. Since both 1-butene and *cis*-2-butene form the same product (butane), these data show that 1-butene was higher in energy to begin with, **since more energy is released in the hydrogenation reaction.**

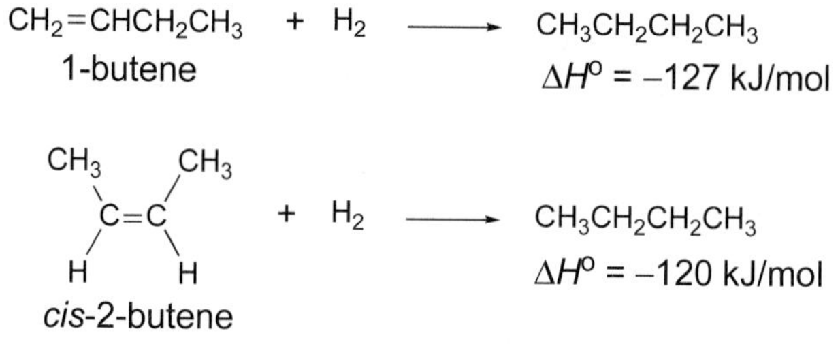
CH2=CHCH2CH3 + H2 → CH3CH2CH2CH3
1-butene
ΔH° = –127 kJ/mol
+ H2 → CH3CH2CH2CH3
ΔH° = –120 kJ/mol
cis-2-butene

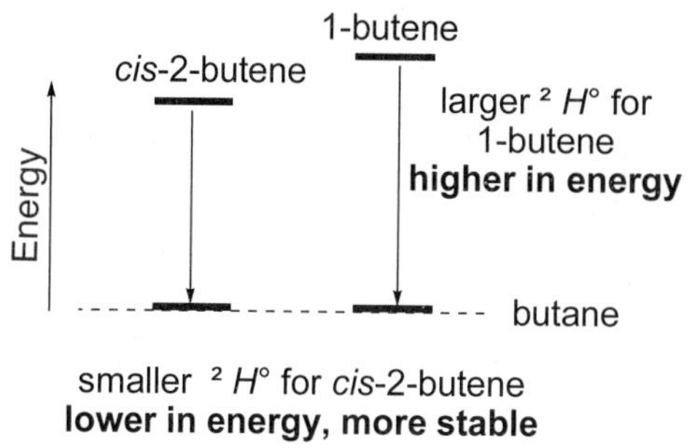
1-butene
cis-2-butene
Energy
larger ² H° for
1-butene
higher in energy
butane
smaller ² H° for cis-2-butene
lower in energy, more stable

8.35

a. 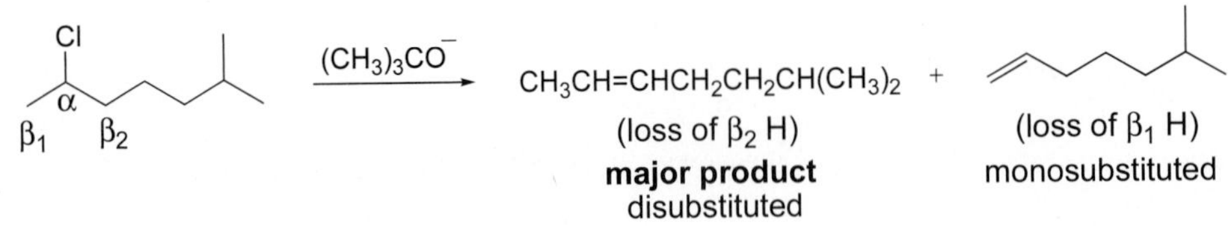
Cl
α
β1 β2
(CH3)3CO−
CH3CH=CHCH2CH2CH(CH3)2 +
(loss of β2 H)
major product
disubstituted
(loss of β1 H)
monosubstituted

b. 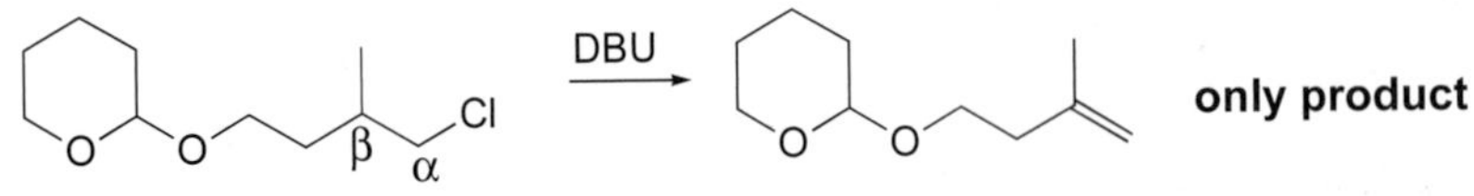
O O
β α Cl
DBU
O O
only product

c. 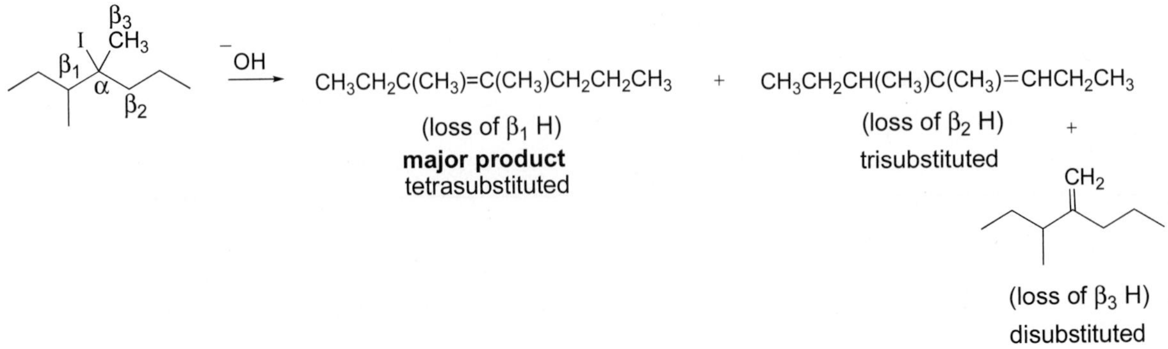
β3
I CH3
β1
α
β2
−OH
CH3CH2C(CH3)=C(CH3)CH2CH2CH3 +
CH3CH2CH(CH3)C(CH3)=CHCH2CH3
(loss of β1 H)
major product
tetrasubstituted
(loss of β2 H)
trisubstituted
+
CH2
(loss of β3 H)
disubstituted

d. 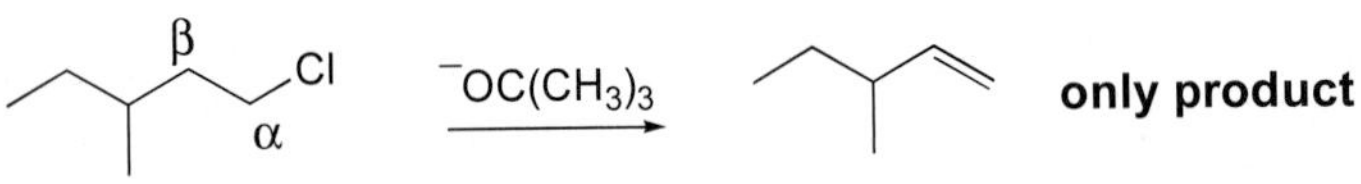
β
Cl
α
−OC(CH3)3
only product

e. 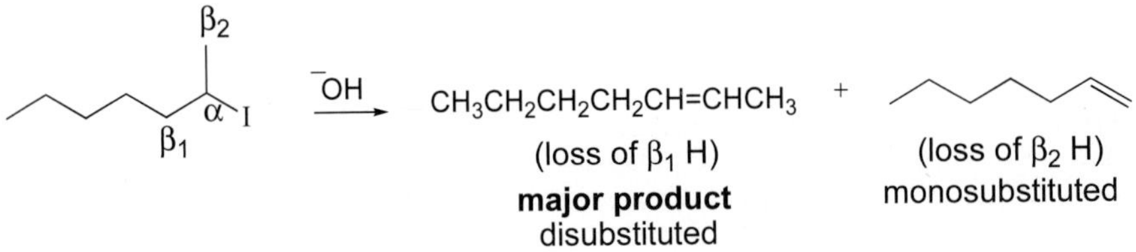
β2
α I
β1
−OH
CH3CH2CH2CH2CH=CHCH3 +
(loss of β1 H)
major product
disubstituted
(loss of β2 H)
monosubstituted

f. 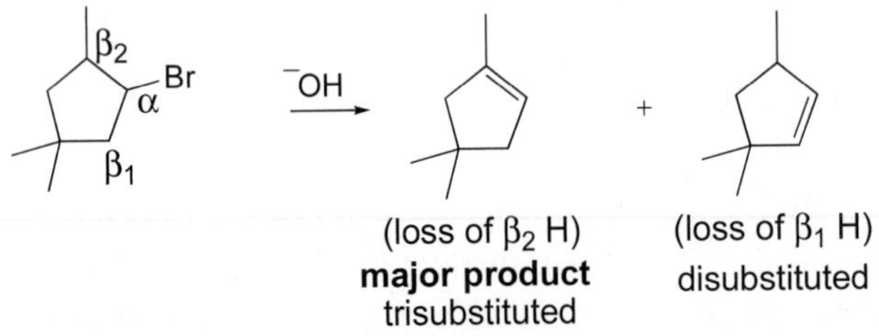
β2
Br
α
β1
−OH
+
(loss of β2 H)
major product
trisubstituted
(loss of β1 H)
disubstituted

8.36 To give only one alkene as the product of elimination, the alkyl halide must have either:

- only one β carbon with a hydrogen atom
- all identical β carbons, so the resulting elimination products are identical

a. 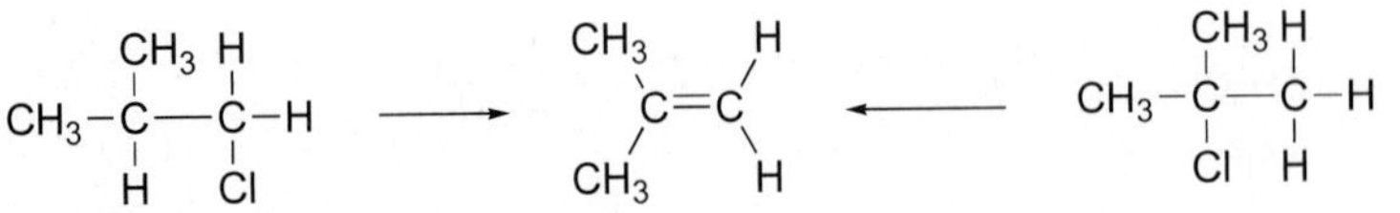
CH3 H
CH3–C–C–H
H Cl
CH3 H
C=C
CH3 H
CH3 H
CH3–C–C–H
Cl H

b. 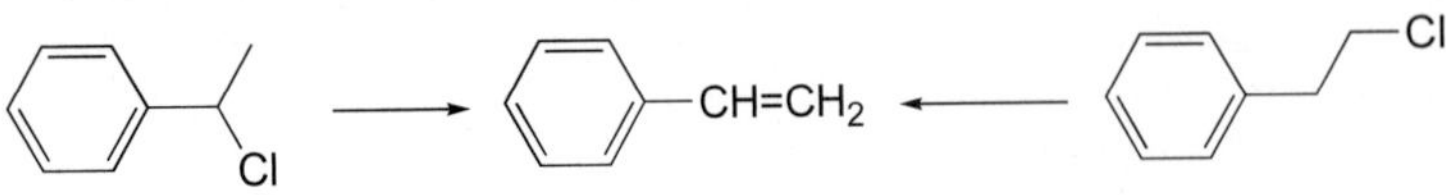
Cl
CH=CH2
Cl

c.

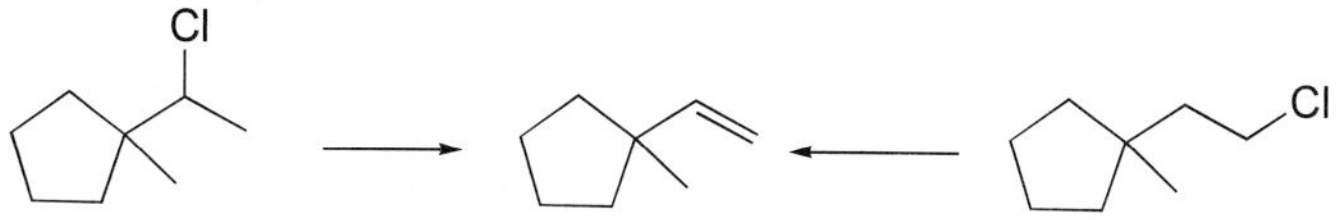

8.37 Draw the products of the E2 reaction and compare the number of C's bonded to the C=C.

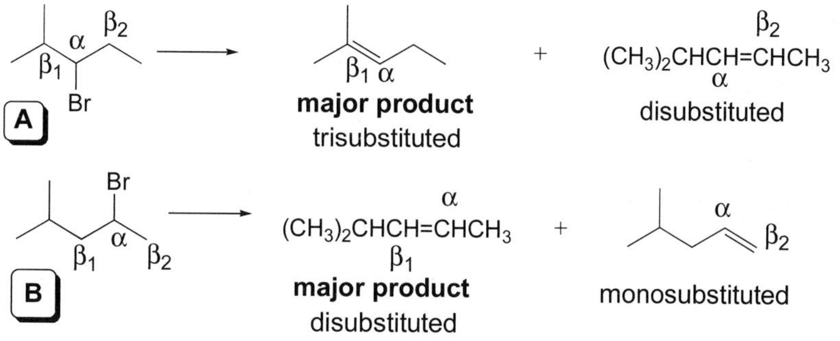

A yields a trisubstituted alkene as the major product and a disubstituted alkene as minor product. **B** yields a disubstituted alkene as the major product and a monosubstituted alkene as minor product. Since the major and minor products formed from **A** have more alkyl groups on the C=C (making them more stable) than those formed from **B, A** reacts faster in an elimination reaction.

8.38

a. Mechanism:

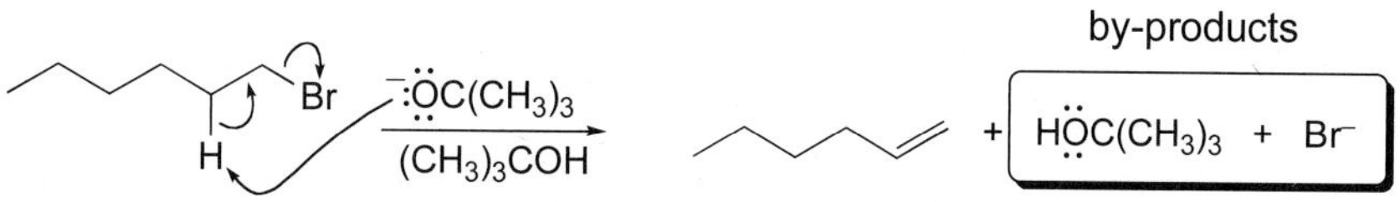

b. Rate = k[R–Br][$^{-}$OC(CH$_3$)$_3$]

[1] Solvent changed to DMF (polar aprotic) = **rate increases**

[2] [$^{-}$OC(CH$_3$)$_3$] decreased = **rate decreases**

[3] Base changed to $^{-}$OH = **rate decreases** (weaker base)

[4] Halide changed to 2° = **rate increases** (More substituted RX reacts faster.)

[5] Leaving group changed to I^{-} = **rate increases** (better leaving group)

8.39

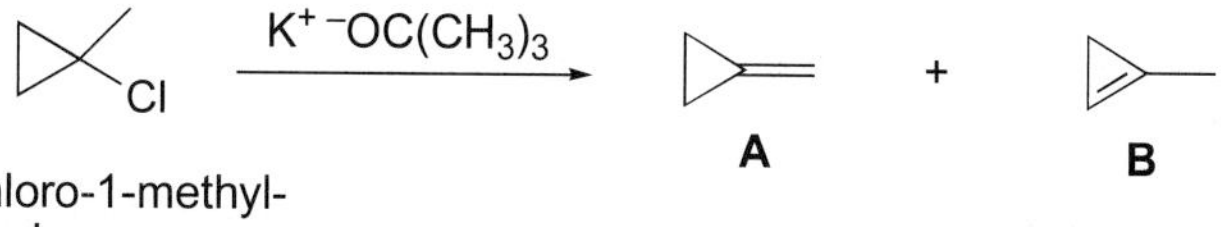

1-chloro-1-methyl-
cyclopropane

The dehydrohalogenation of an alkyl halide usually forms the more stable alkene. In this case, **A** is more stable than **B** even though **A** contains a disubstituted C=C whereas **B** contains a trisubstituted C=C. The double bond in **B** is part of a three-membered ring, and is less stable than **A** because of severe angle strain around both C's of the double bond.

8.40

a. 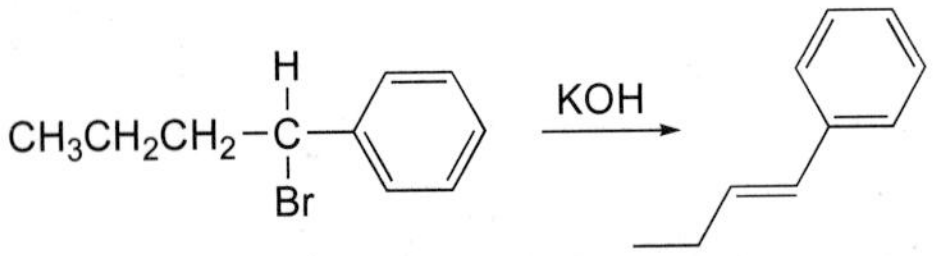
H
$CH_3CH_2CH_2$–C–
Br
KOH

trans isomer more stable
major product

b. 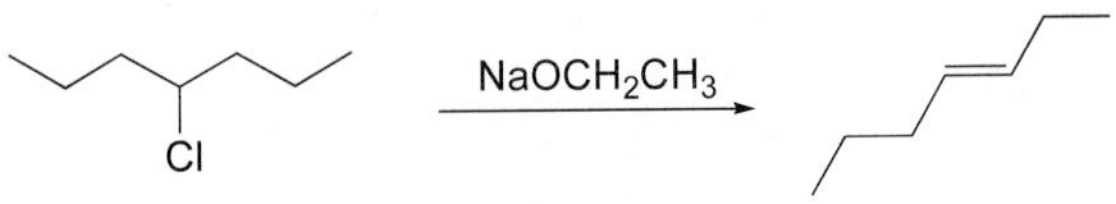
Cl
$NaOCH_2CH_3$

trans isomer more stable
major product

8.41

a. 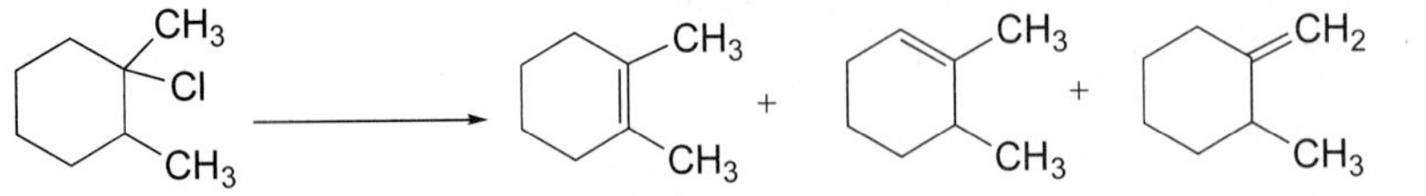
CH_3
Cl
CH_3
CH_3
CH_3
+
CH_3
CH_3
+
CH_2
CH_3

tetrasubstituted — **major product**; trisubstituted; disubstituted

b. 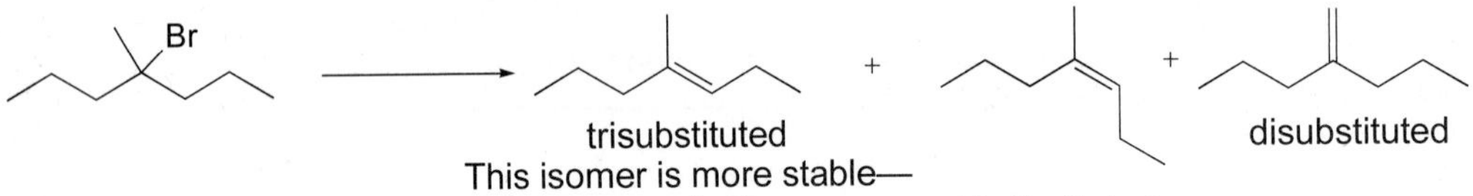
Br
+
+

trisubstituted
This isomer is more stable—
large groups farther away.
major product

trisubstituted

disubstituted

c. 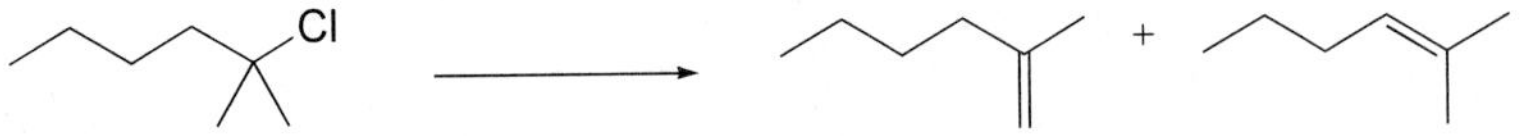
Cl
+

disubstituted

trisubstituted
major product

8.42 Use the rules from Answer 8.21.

a. 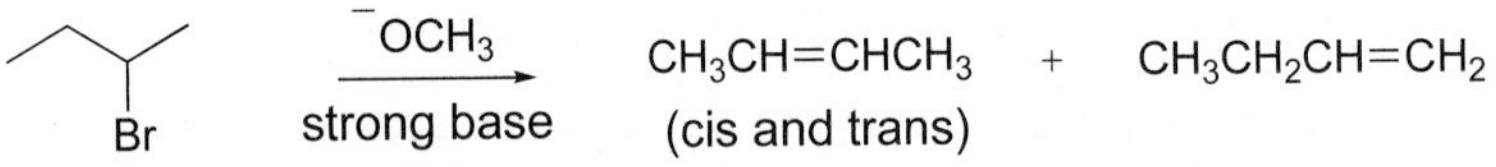
Br
$^-OCH_3$

2° halide; strong base, **E2**

$CH_3CH{=}CHCH_3$ (cis and trans) + $CH_3CH_2CH{=}CH_2$

b. 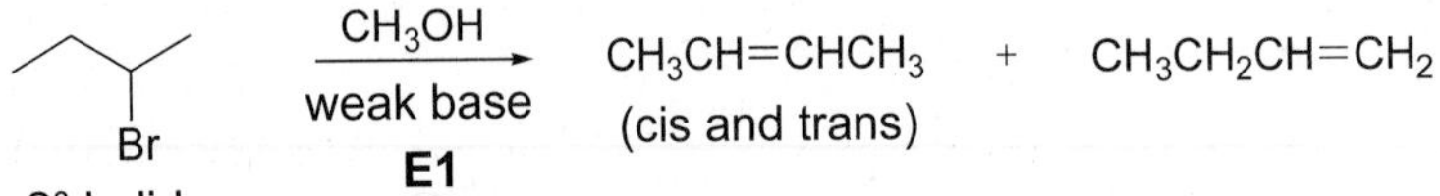
Br
CH_3OH

2° halide; weak base, **E1**

$CH_3CH{=}CHCH_3$ (cis and trans) + $CH_3CH_2CH{=}CH_2$

c. 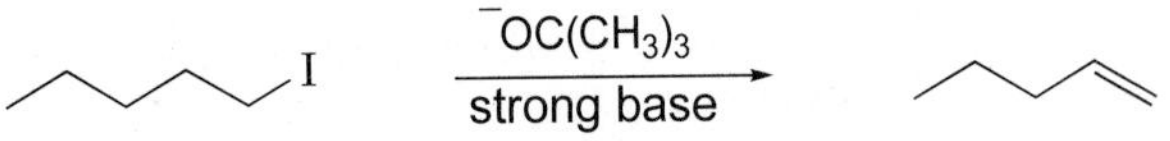
I
$^-OC(CH_3)_3$

1° halide; strong base, **E2**

d. 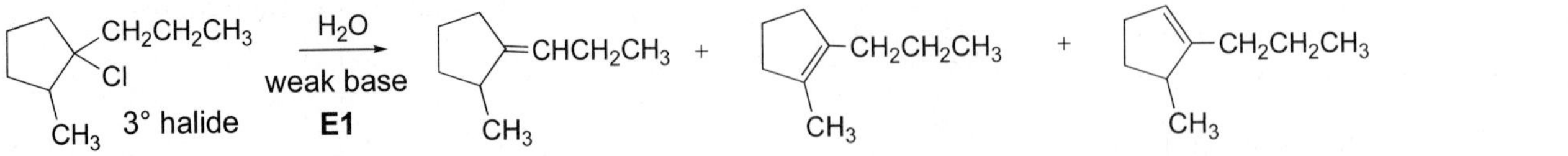
$CH_2CH_2CH_3$
Cl
CH_3
H_2O
$=CHCH_2CH_3$
CH_3
+
$-CH_2CH_2CH_3$
CH_3
+
$-CH_2CH_2CH_3$
CH_3

3° halide; weak base, **E1**

e. 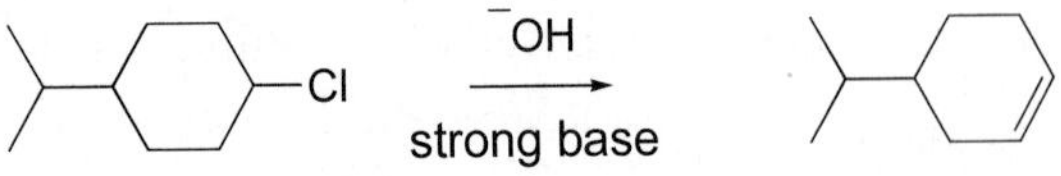
Cl
^-OH

2° halide; strong base, **E2**

f. 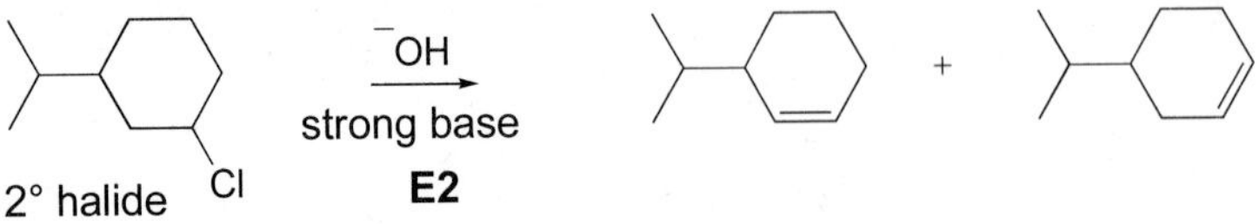
Cl
^-OH
+

2° halide; strong base, **E2**

8.43 The order of reactivity is the same for both E2 and E1: 1° < 2° < 3°.

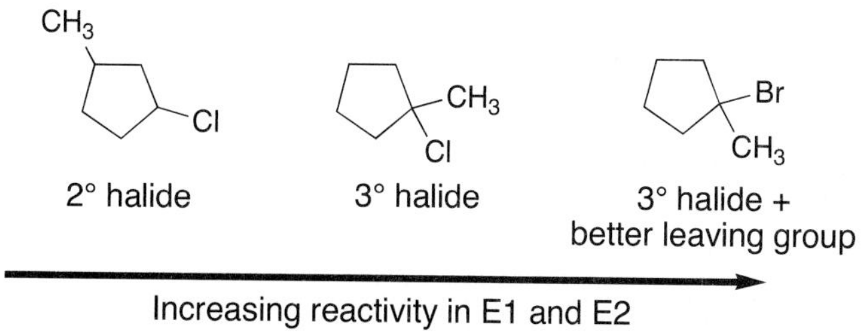

8.44

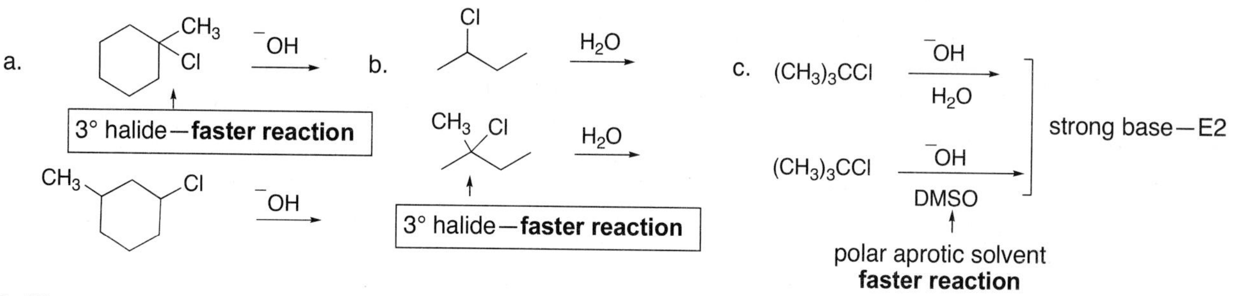

8.45

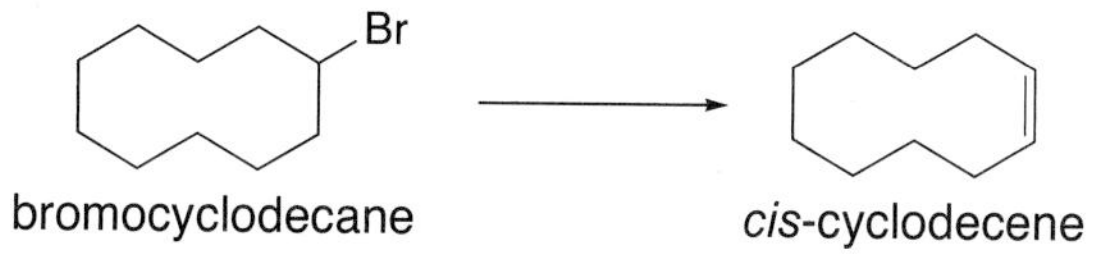

In a ten-membered ring, the cis isomer is more stable and, therefore, the preferred elimination product. The trans isomer is less stable because strain is introduced when two ends of the double bond are connected in a trans arrangement in this medium-sized ring.

8.46 With the strong base $^{-}OCH_2CH_3$, the mechanism is E2, whereas with dilute base, the mechanism is E1. E2 elimination proceeds with anti periplanar arrangement of H and X. In the E1 mechanism there is no requirement for elimination to proceed with anti periplanar geometry. In this case the major product is always the most stable, more substituted alkene. Thus, **C** is the major product under E1 conditions. (In Chapter 9, we will learn that additional elimination products may form in the E1 reaction due to carbocation rearrangement.)

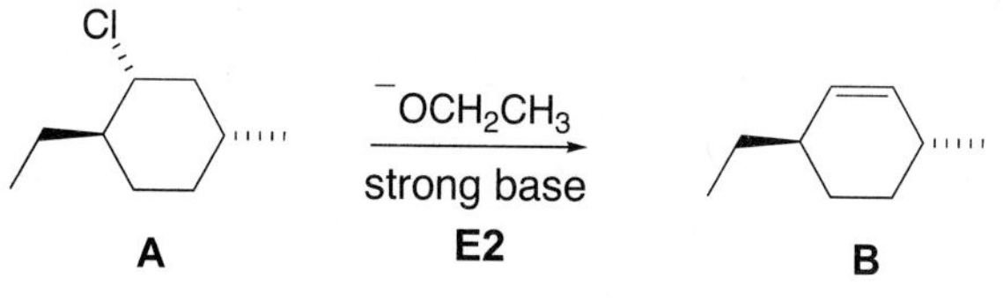

Since this is an E2 mechanism, dehydrohalogenation needs an anti periplanar H to form the double bond. There is only one H trans to Cl, so the disubstituted alkene **B** must form.

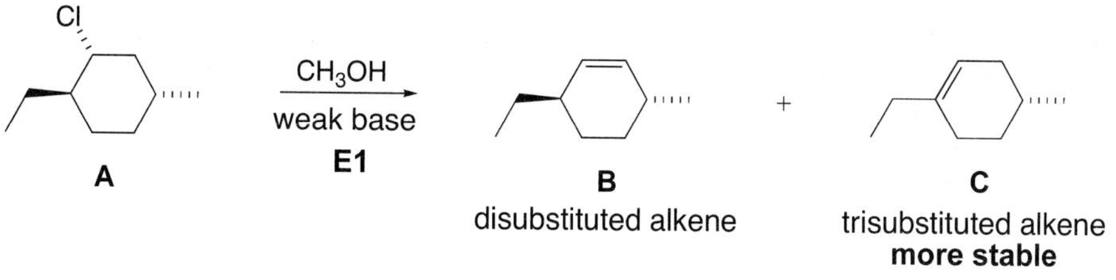

8.47

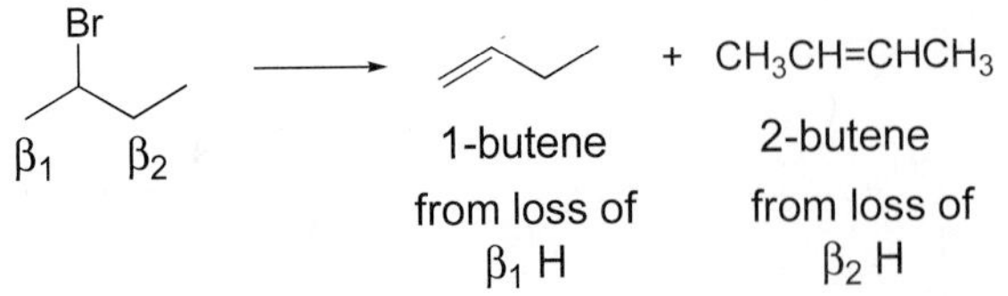

	1-butene	2-butene
Na^+ $^-OCH_2CH_3$	19%	81%
K^+ $^-OC(CH_3)_3$	33%	67%

The H's on the CH_2 group of the β_2 carbon are more sterically hindered than the H's on the CH_3 group of the β_1 carbon. Since K^{+} $^{-}OC(CH_3)_3$ is a much bulkier base than Na^{+} $^{-}OCH_2CH_3$, it is easier to remove the more accessible H on β_1, giving it a higher percentage of 1-butene.

8.48 H and Br must be anti during the E2 elimination. Rotate if necessary to make them anti; then eliminate.

a.

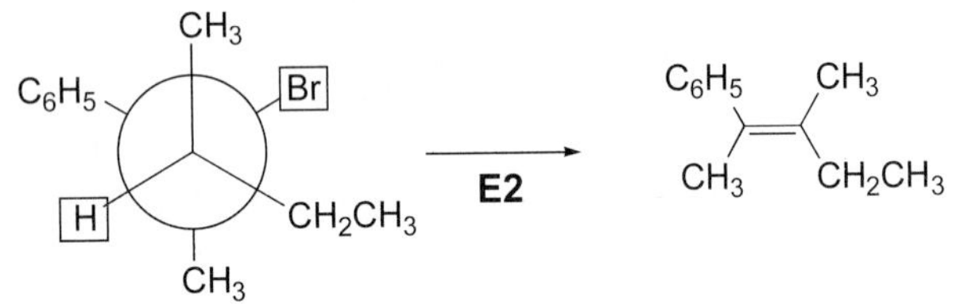

b.

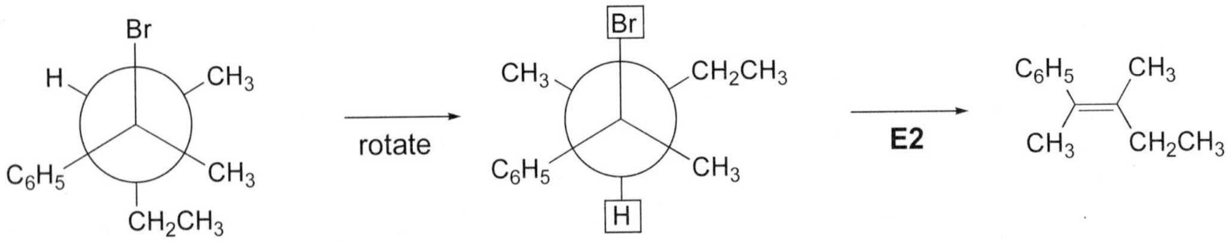

c.

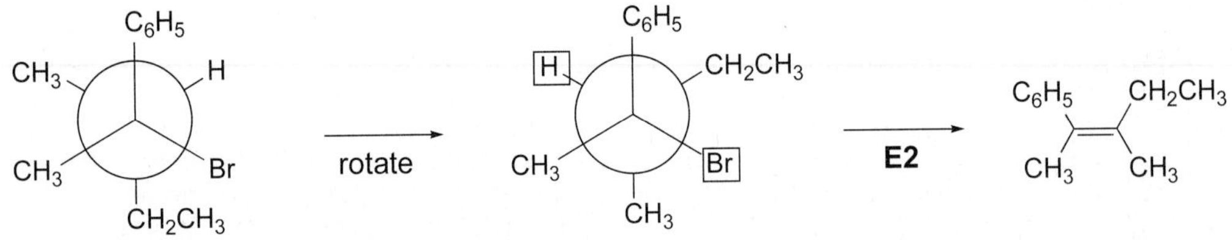

8.49

a.

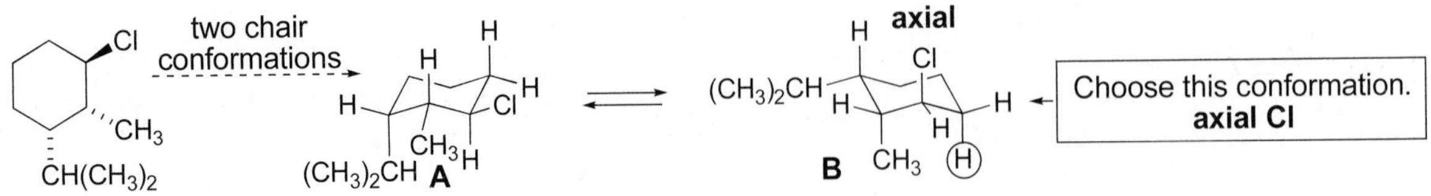

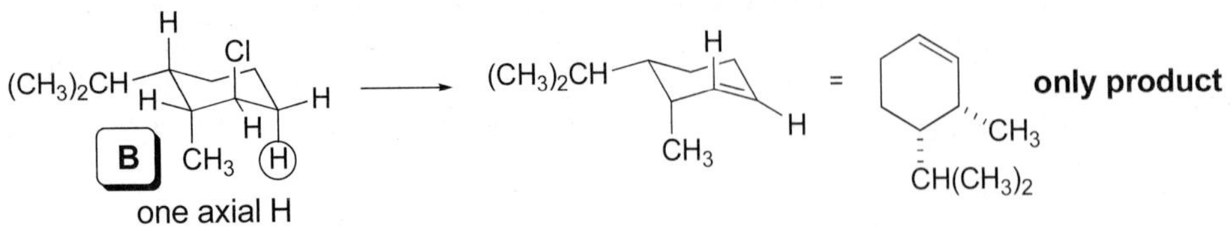

b.

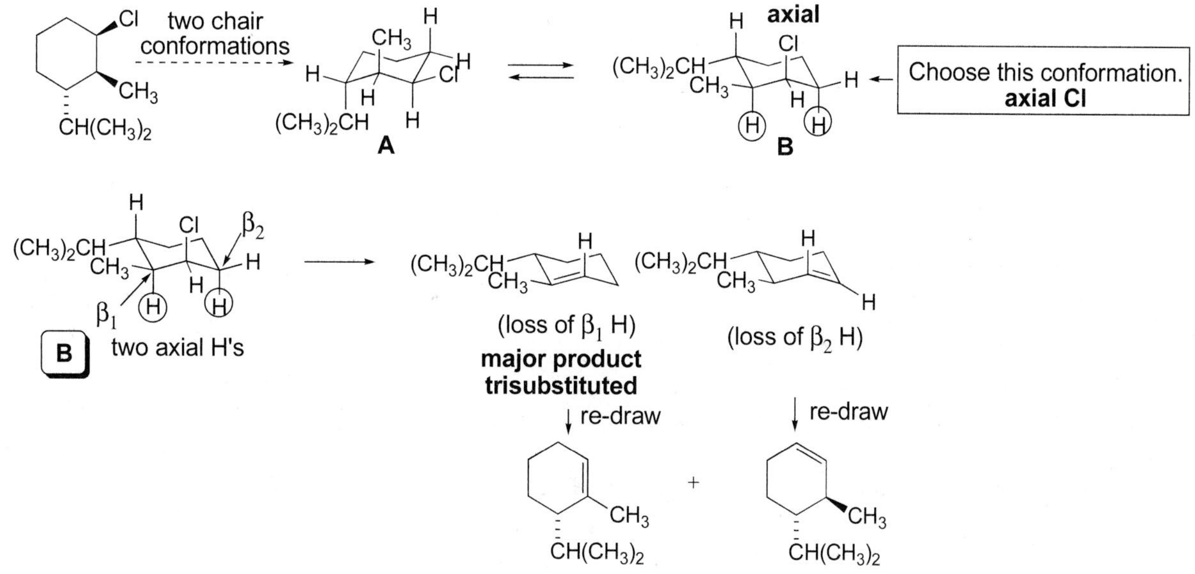
two chair conformations
A
axial
B
Choose this conformation. axial Cl
two axial H's
(loss of β1 H)
major product
trisubstituted
(loss of β2 H)
re-draw
re-draw

c.

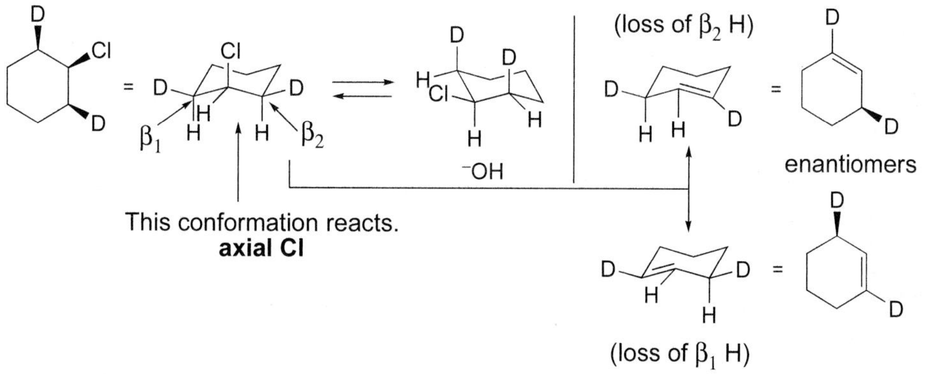
This conformation reacts.
axial Cl
(loss of β2 H)
enantiomers
(loss of β1 H)

d.

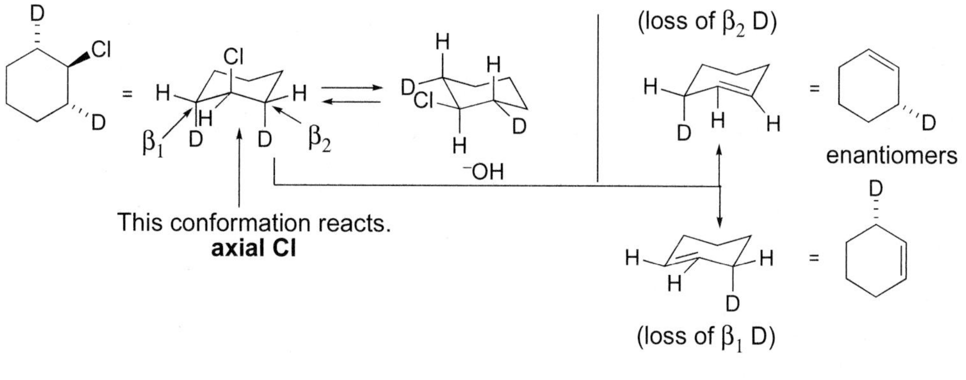
This conformation reacts.
axial Cl
(loss of β2 D)
enantiomers
(loss of β1 D)

8.50

a.

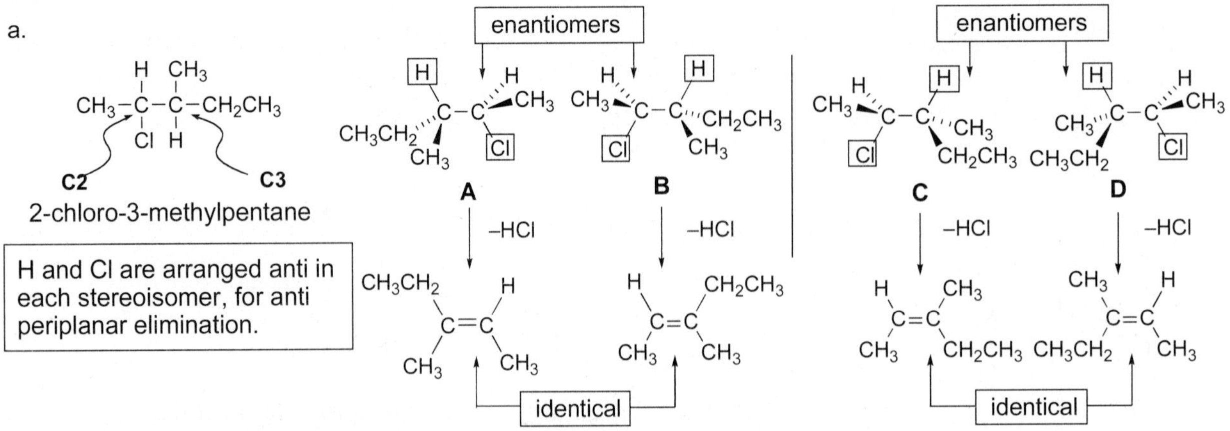
enantiomers
enantiomers
2-chloro-3-methylpentane
C2
C3
A
B
C
D
–HCl
–HCl
–HCl
–HCl
H and Cl are arranged anti in each stereoisomer, for anti periplanar elimination.
identical
identical

b. Two different alkenes are formed as products.

c. The products are diastereomers: Two enantiomers (**A** and **B**) give identical products. **A** and **B** are diastereomers of **C** and **D.** Each pair of enantiomers gives a single alkene. Thus, diastereomers give diastereomeric products.

8.51

a.

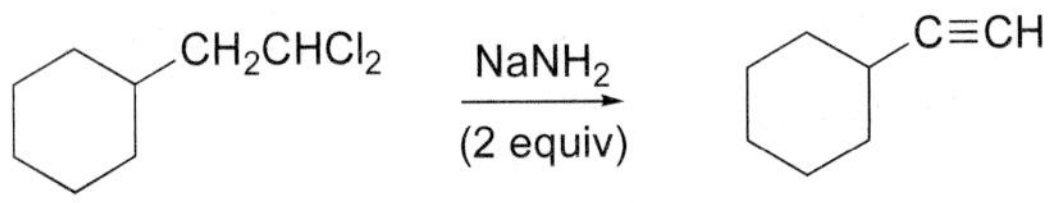
NaNH2
(2 equiv)

b.

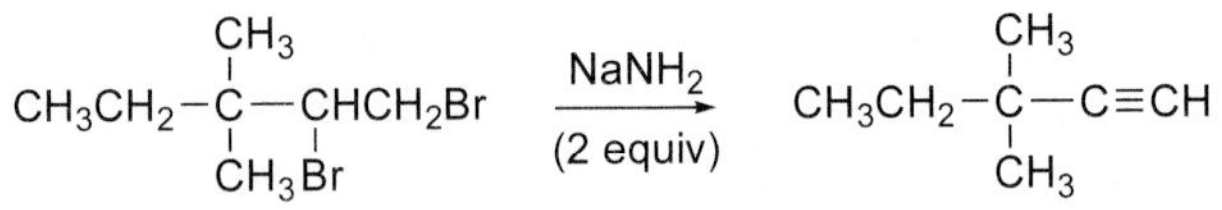
NaNH2
(2 equiv)

c.

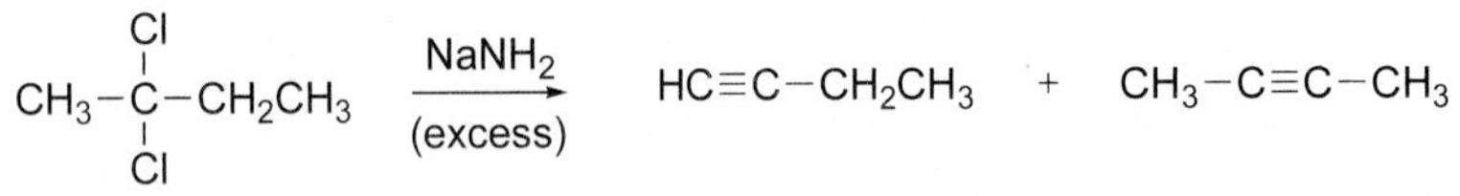
NaNH2
(excess)

d.

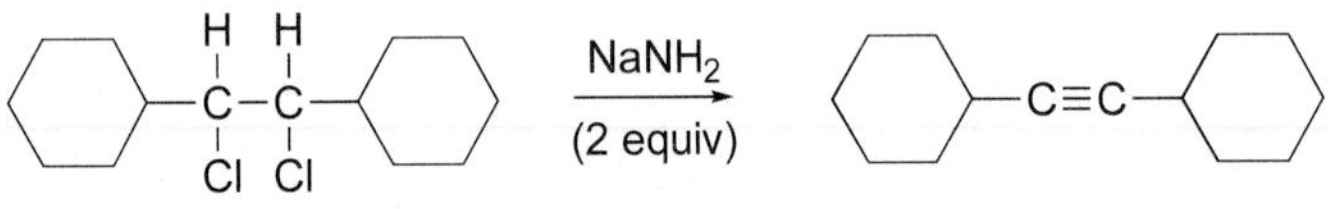
NaNH2
(2 equiv)

8.52

a.

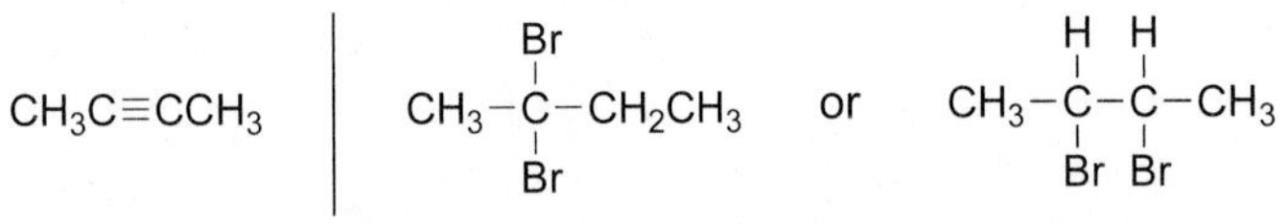
or

b.

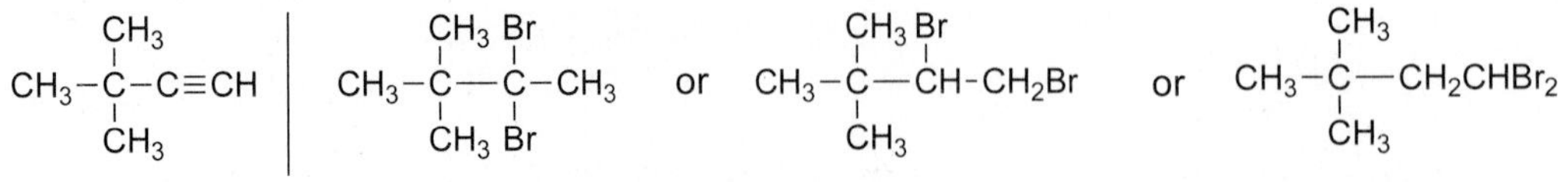
or
or

c.

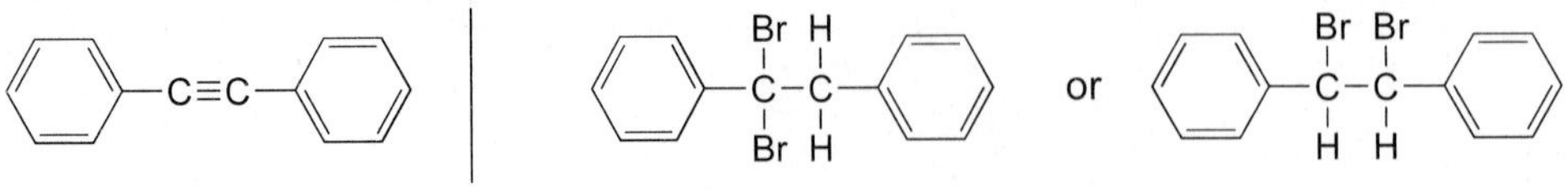
or

8.53

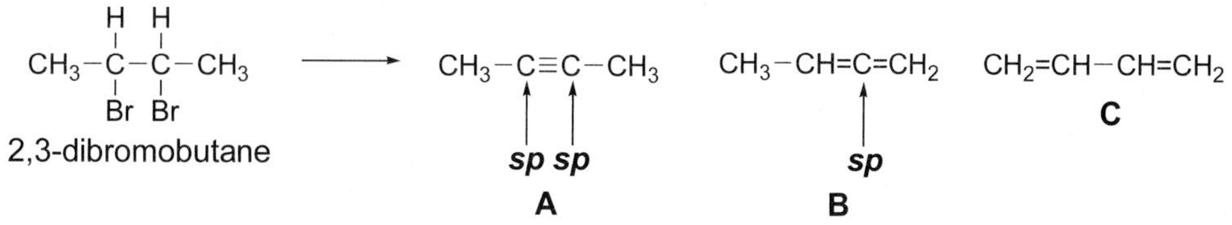
2,3-dibromobutane
sp sp
A
sp
B
C

8.54 Use the "Summary chart on the four mechanisms: S_N1, S_N2, E1, or E2" on p. 8–2 to answer the questions.

a. Both S_N1 and E1 involve carbocation intermediates.
b. Both S_N1 and E1 have two steps.
c. S_N1, S_N2, E1, and E2 all have increased reaction rates with better leaving groups.
d. Both S_N2 and E2 have increased rates when changing from CH_3OH (a protic solvent) to $(CH_3)_2SO$ (an aprotic solvent).
e. In S_N1 and E1 reactions, the rate depends on only the alkyl halide concentration.
f. Both S_N2 and E2 are concerted reactions.
g. CH_3CH_2Br and NaOH react by an S_N2 mechanism.
h. Racemization occurs in S_N1 reactions.
i. In S_N1, E1, and E2 mechanisms, 3° alkyl halides react faster than 1° or 2° halides.
j. E2 and S_N2 reactions follow second-order rate equations.

8.55

a. 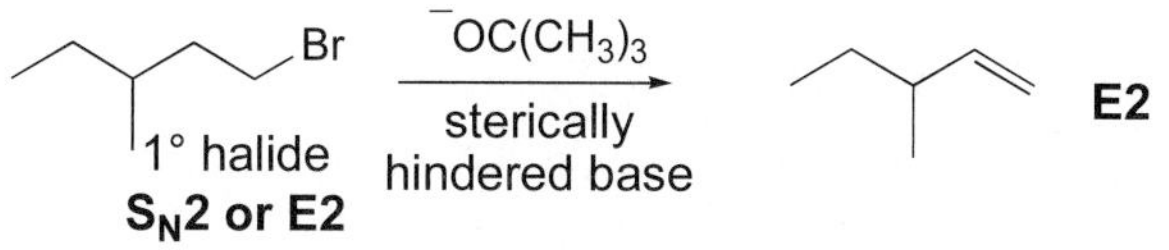
Br
⁻OC(CH3)3
sterically hindered base
1° halide
SN2 or E2
E2

b. 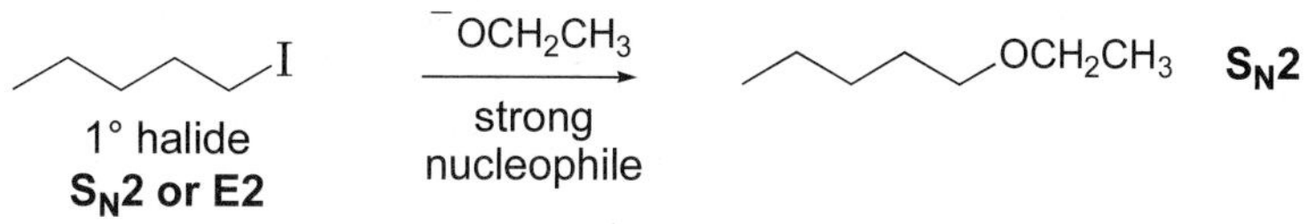
I
⁻OCH2CH3
strong nucleophile
1° halide
SN2 or E2
OCH2CH3
SN2

c. 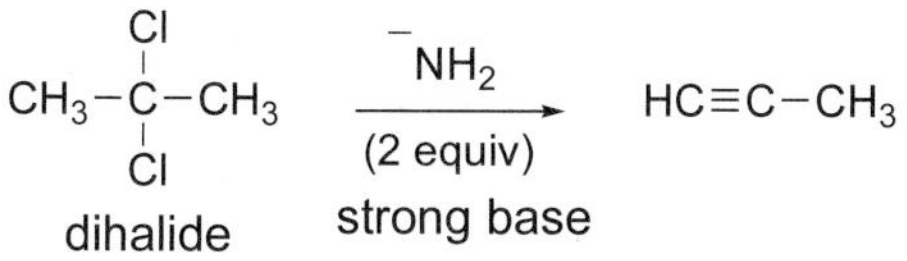
CH3–C(Cl)(Cl)–CH3
⁻NH2
(2 equiv)
dihalide
strong base
HC≡C–CH3

d. 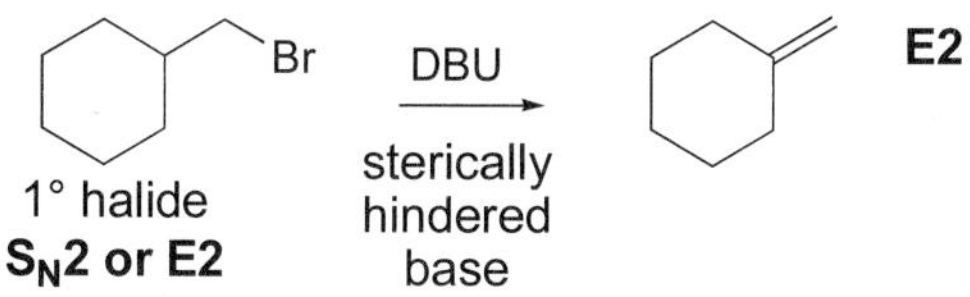
Br
DBU
sterically hindered base
1° halide
SN2 or E2
E2

e. 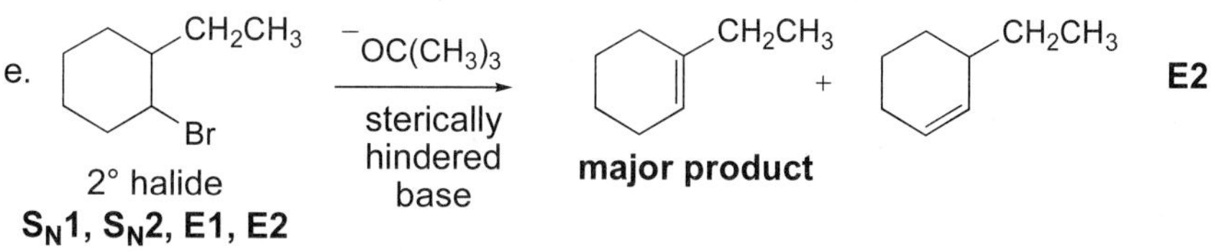
CH2CH3
Br
⁻OC(CH3)3
sterically hindered base
2° halide
SN1, SN2, E1, E2
CH2CH3
major product
CH2CH3
E2

f.
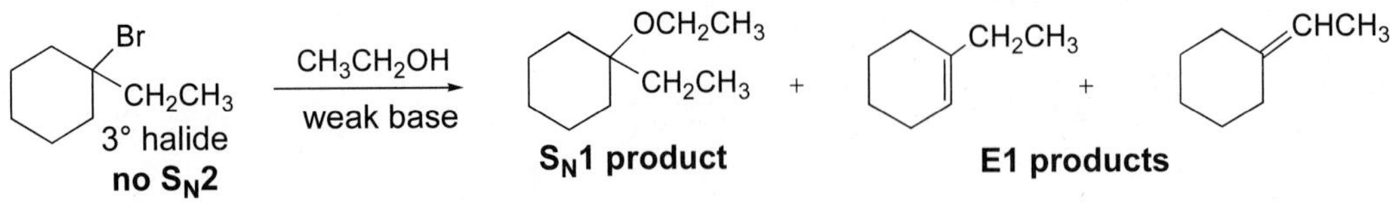
Br
CH₂CH₃
3° halide
no SN2
CH₃CH₂OH
weak base
OCH₂CH₃
CH₂CH₃
SN1 product
CH₂CH₃
CHCH₃
E1 products

g. $(CH_3)_2CH-CHCH_2Br$ (with Br on CH) $\xrightarrow{2\ NaNH_2}$ $(CH_3)_2CH-C\equiv CH$

dihalide

h.
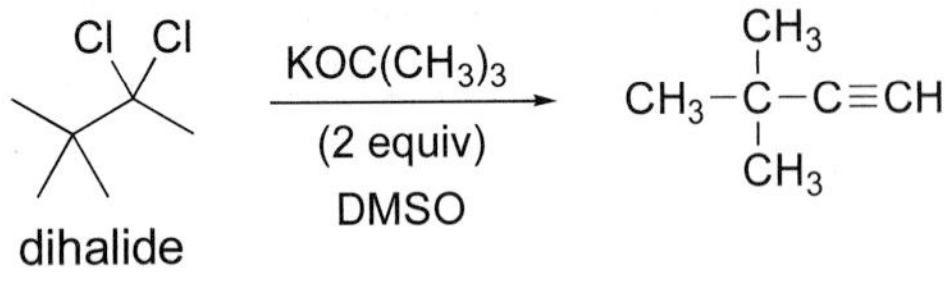
Cl Cl
dihalide
KOC(CH₃)₃
(2 equiv)
DMSO
CH₃
CH₃–C–C≡CH
CH₃

i.
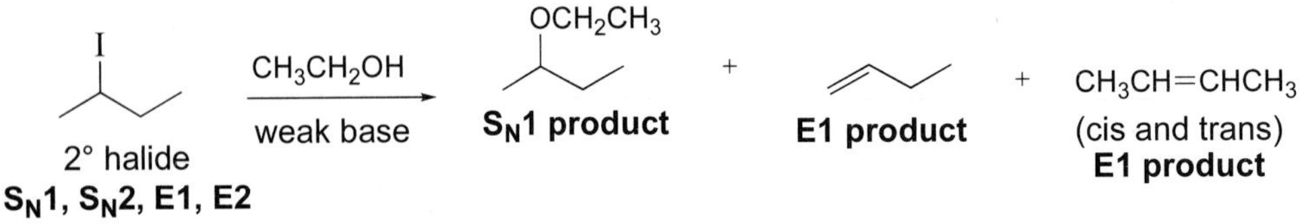
I
2° halide
SN1, SN2, E1, E2
CH₃CH₂OH
weak base
OCH₂CH₃
SN1 product
E1 product
CH₃CH=CHCH₃
(cis and trans)
E1 product

j.
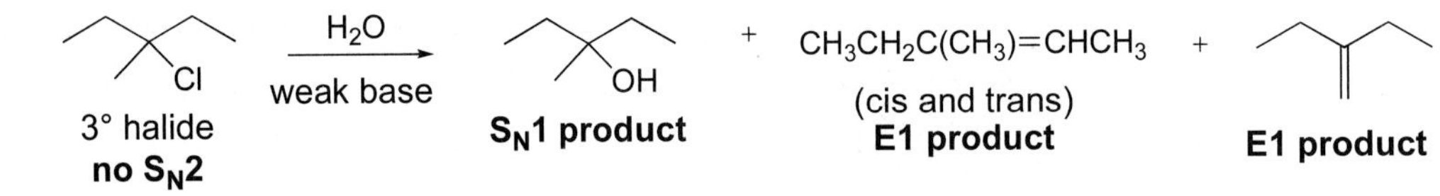
Cl
3° halide
no SN2
H₂O
weak base
OH
SN1 product
CH₃CH₂C(CH₃)=CHCH₃
(cis and trans)
E1 product
E1 product

8.56 [1] $NaOCOCH_3$ is a good nucleophile and weak base, and substitution is favored. [3] $KOC(CH_3)_3$ is a strong, bulky base that reacts by E2 elimination when there is a β hydrogen in the alkyl halide.

a. CH_3Cl

$\xrightarrow{[1]\ NaOCOCH_3}$ CH_3OCOCH_3

$\xrightarrow{[2]\ NaOCH_3}$ CH_3OCH_3

$\xrightarrow{[3]\ KOC(CH_3)_3}$ $CH_3OC(CH_3)_3$

b.
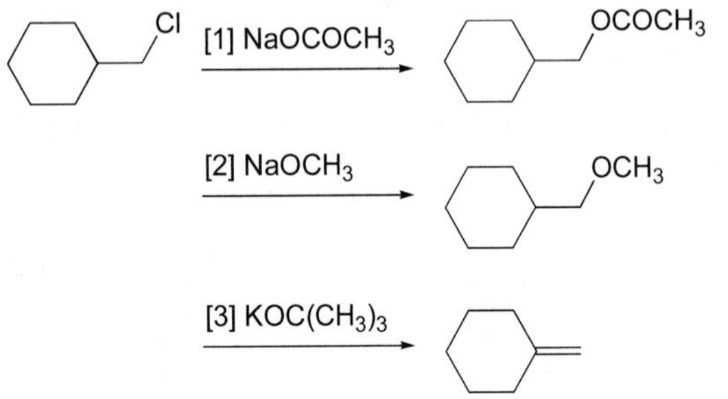
Cl
[1] NaOCOCH₃
OCOCH₃
[2] NaOCH₃
OCH₃
[3] KOC(CH₃)₃

c.
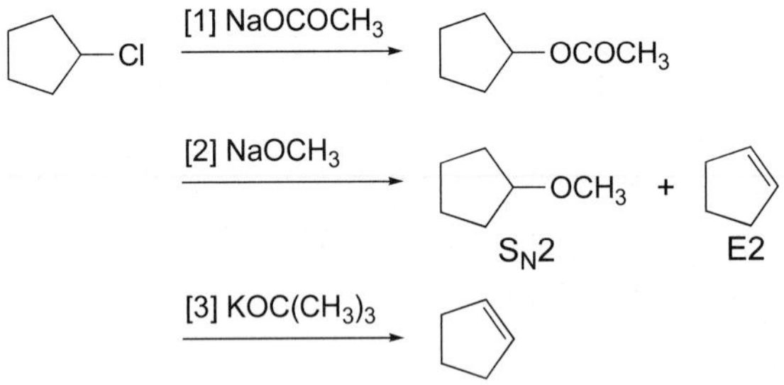
Cl
[1] NaOCOCH₃
OCOCH₃
[2] NaOCH₃
OCH₃
SN2
E2
[3] KOC(CH₃)₃

d.
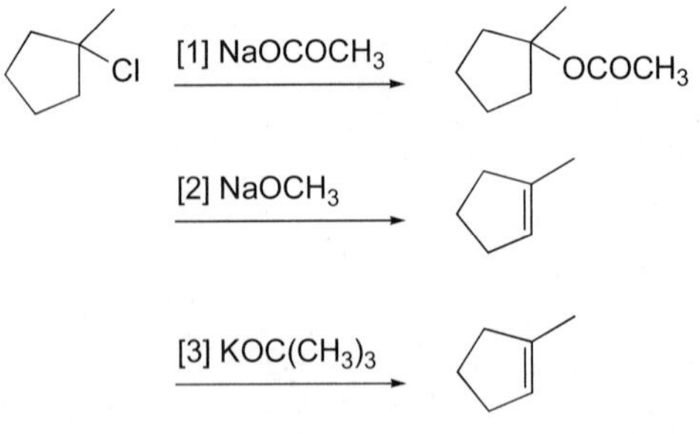
Cl
[1] NaOCOCH₃
OCOCH₃
[2] NaOCH₃
[3] KOC(CH₃)₃

8.57

a. two enantiomers:

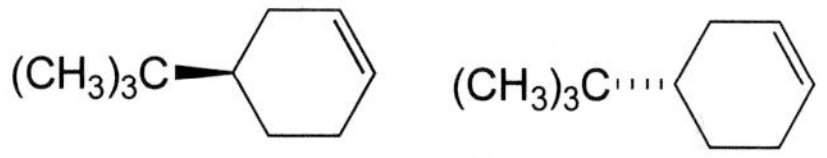
(CH3)3C
(CH3)3C

A B

b. The bulky *tert*-butyl group anchors the cyclohexane ring and occupies the more roomy equatorial position. The cis isomer has the Br atom axial, while the trans isomer has the Br atom equatorial. For dehydrohalogenation to occur on a halo cyclohexane, the halogen must be axial to afford trans diaxial elimination of H and X. The cis isomer readily reacts since the Br atom is axial. The only way for the trans isomer to react is for the six-membered ring to flip into a highly unstable conformation having both $(CH_3)_3C$ and Br axial. Thus, the trans isomer reacts much more slowly.

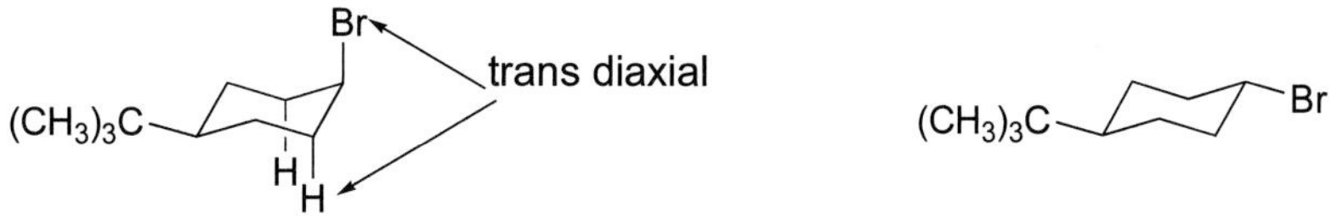
Br
trans diaxial
(CH3)3C
H
H
(CH3)3C
Br

cis-1-bromo-4-*tert*-butylcyclohexane *trans*-1-bromo-4-*tert*-butylcyclohexane

c. two products:

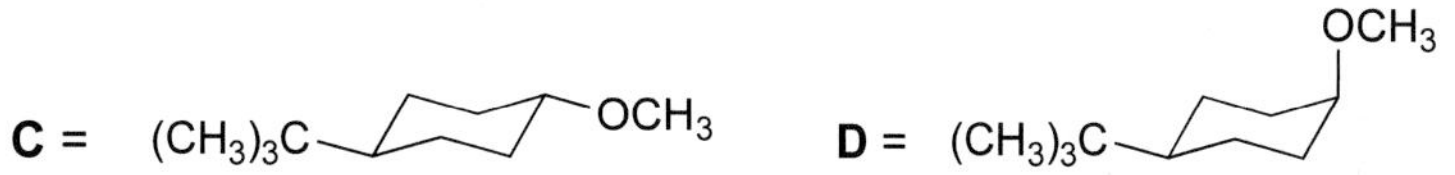
C = (CH3)3C
OCH3
D = (CH3)3C
OCH3

d. *cis*-1-Bromo-4-*tert*-butylcyclohexane reacts faster. With the strong nucleophile $^{-}OCH_3$, backside attack occurs by an S_N2 reaction, and with the cis isomer, the nucleophile can approach from the equatorial direction, avoiding 1,3-diaxial interactions.

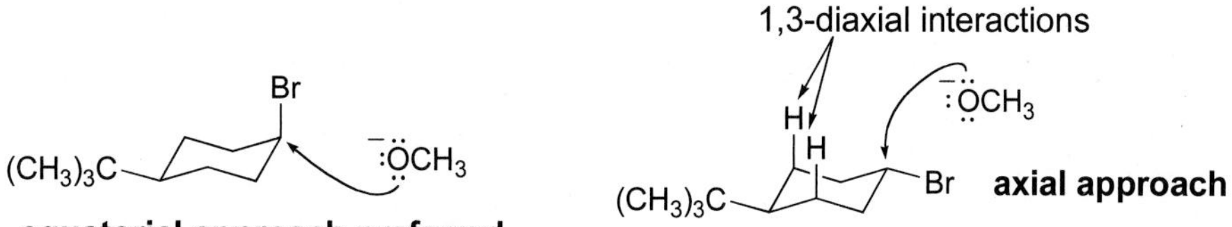
Br
(CH3)3C
:ÖCH3
1,3-diaxial interactions
H
H
:ÖCH3
(CH3)3C
Br
axial approach

equatorial approach preferred

cis-1-bromo-4-*tert*-butylcyclohexane *trans*-1-bromo-4-*tert*-butylcyclohexane

e. The bulky base $^{-}OC(CH_3)_3$ favors elimination by an E2 mechanism, affording a mixture of two enantiomers, **A** and **B.** The strong nucleophile $^{-}OCH_3$ favors nucleophilic substitution by an S_N2 mechanism. Inversion of configuration results from backside attack of the nucleophile.

8.58

a.

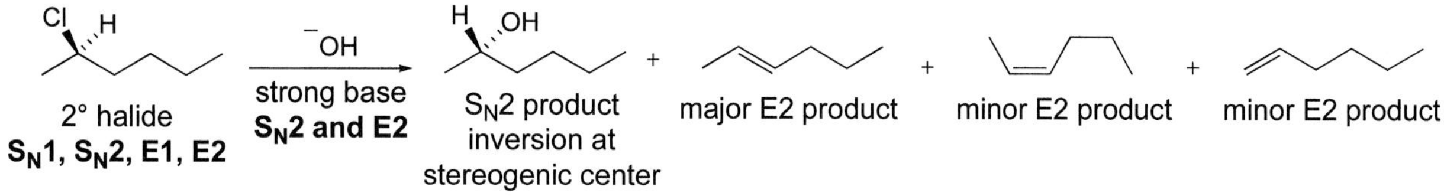
Cl H
2° halide
SN1, SN2, E1, E2
−OH
strong base
SN2 and E2
H OH
SN2 product
inversion at
stereogenic center
+
major E2 product
+
minor E2 product
+
minor E2 product

b.

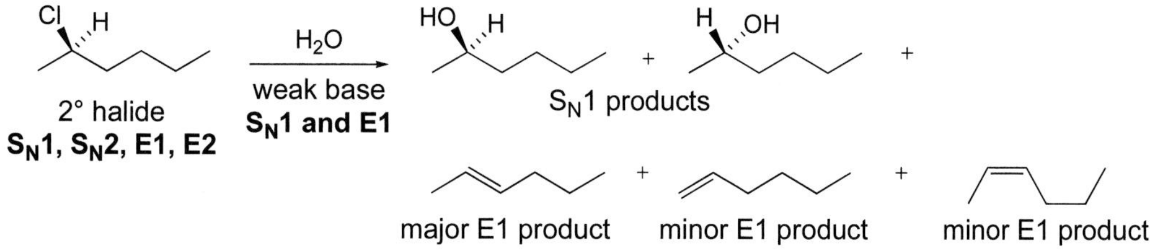
Cl H
2° halide
SN1, SN2, E1, E2
H2O
weak base
SN1 and E1
HO H
+
H OH
+
SN1 products
+
+
major E1 product
minor E1 product
minor E1 product

c.

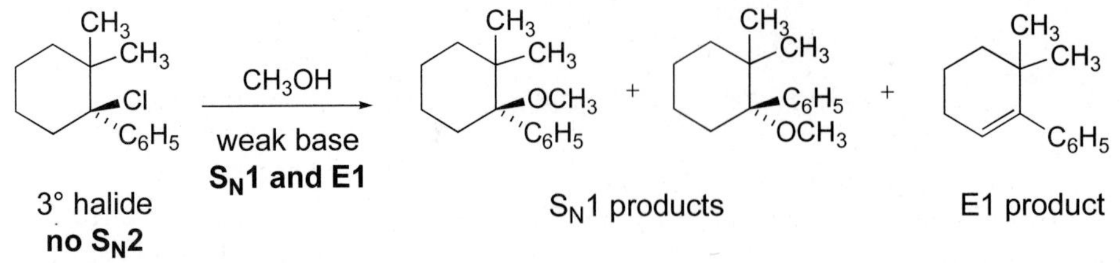
CH3
CH3
Cl
C6H5
CH3OH
weak base
SN1 and E1
3° halide
no SN2
OCH3
SN1 products
E1 product

d.

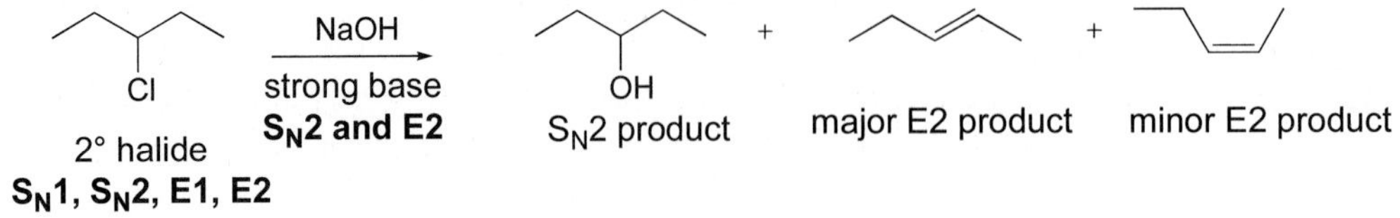
Cl
NaOH
strong base
SN2 and E2
2° halide
SN1, SN2, E1, E2
OH
SN2 product
major E2 product
minor E2 product

e.

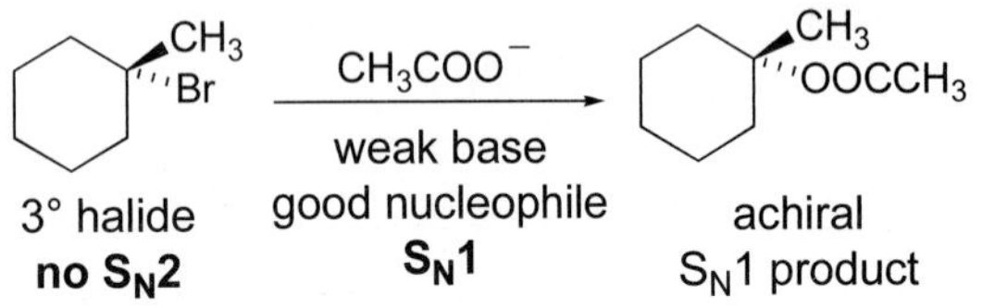
CH3
Br
CH3COO−
weak base
good nucleophile
SN1
3° halide
no SN2
OOCCH3
achiral
SN1 product

f.

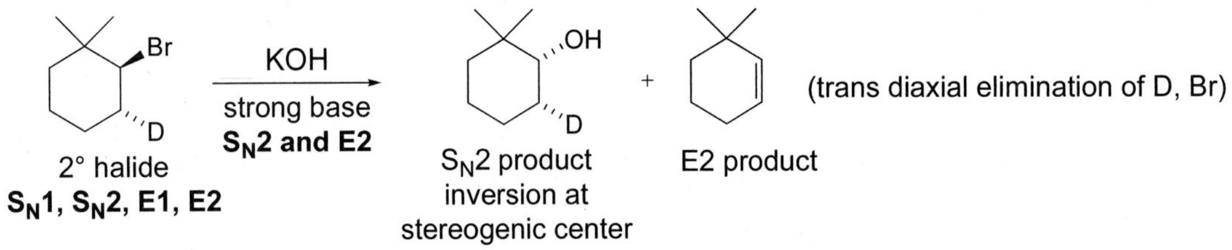
Br
D
KOH
strong base
SN2 and E2
2° halide
SN1, SN2, E1, E2
OH
SN2 product
inversion at
stereogenic center
E2 product
(trans diaxial elimination of D, Br)

8.59

a.

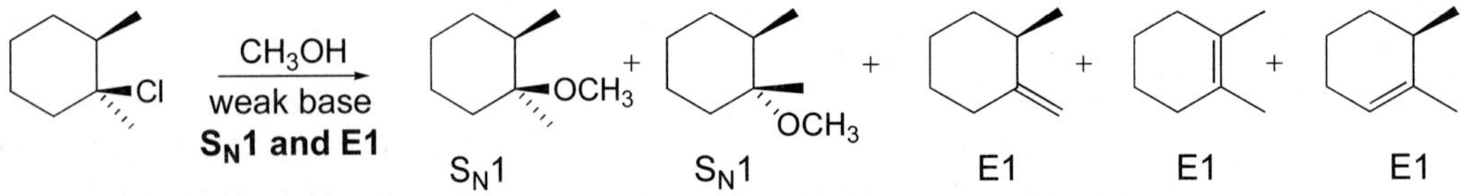
Cl
CH3OH
weak base
SN1 and E1
OCH3
SN1
SN1
E1
E1
E1

b.

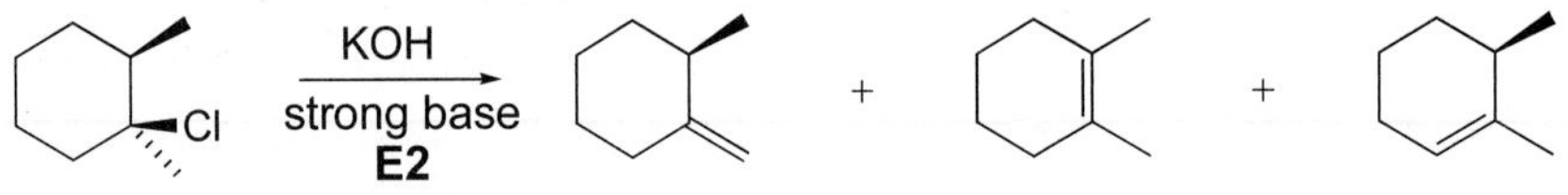
Cl
KOH
strong base
E2

8.60

a.

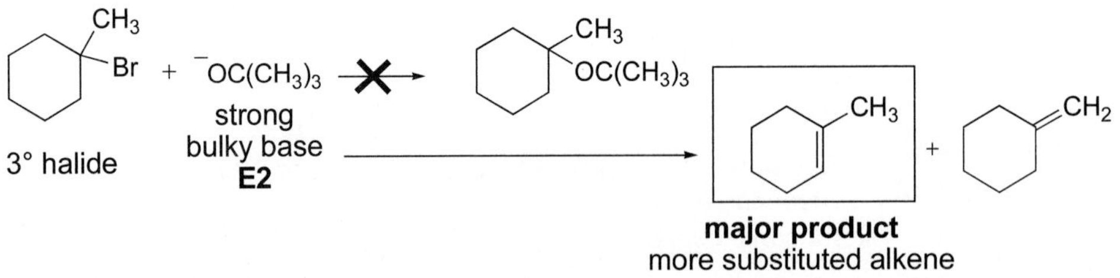
CH3
Br
−OC(CH3)3
3° halide
strong
bulky base
E2
OC(CH3)3
CH3
CH2
major product
more substituted alkene

No substitution occurs with a strong bulky base and a 3° RX. The C with the leaving group is too crowded for an S_N2 substitution to occur. Elimination occurs instead by an E2 mechanism.

b. 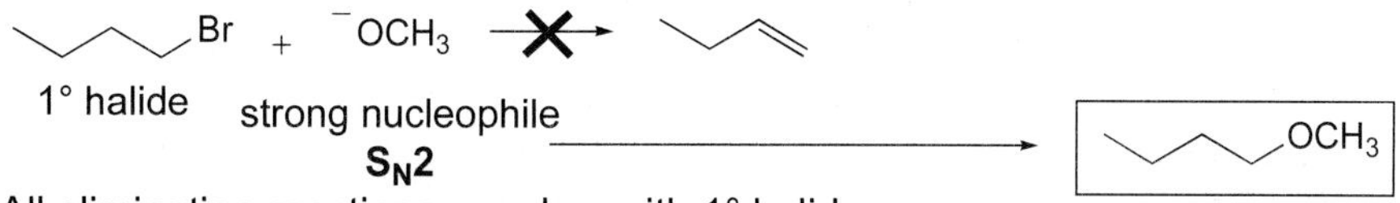
Br
+
$^-OCH_3$
1° halide
strong nucleophile
S_N2
OCH_3

All elimination reactions are slow with 1° halides.
The strong nucleophile reacts by an S_N2 mechanism instead.

c. 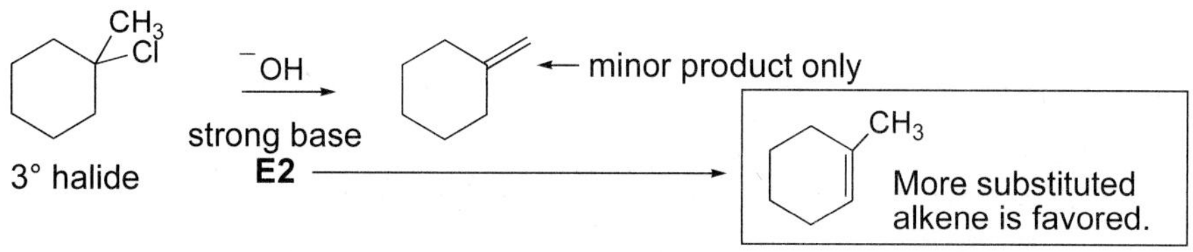
CH_3
Cl
3° halide
^-OH
strong base
E2
← minor product only
CH_3
More substituted
alkene is favored.

d. 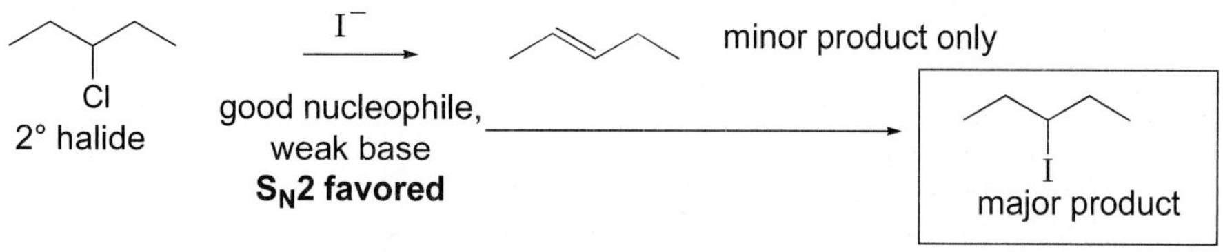
Cl
2° halide
I^-
good nucleophile,
weak base
S_N2 favored
minor product only
I
major product

The 2° halide can react by an E2 or S_N2 reaction with a negatively charged nucleophile or base. Since I^- is a weak base, substitution by an S_N2 mechanism is favored.

8.61

3° halide, weak base:
S_N1 and E1

a. 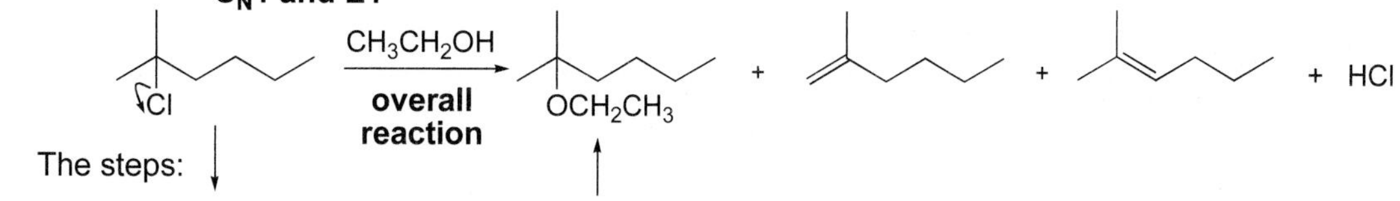
Cl
CH_3CH_2OH
overall
reaction
OCH_2CH_3
+
+
+ HCl
The steps:

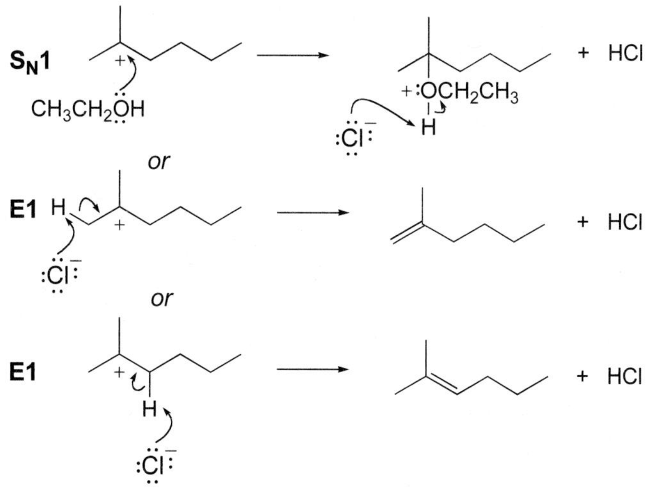
S_N1
+
$CH_3CH_2\ddot{O}H$
+ HCl
$+:OCH_2CH_3$
H
:Cl:
or
E1 H
+
:Cl:
+ HCl
or
E1
+
H
:Cl:
+ HCl

Any base (such as CH_3CH_2OH or Cl^-) can be used to remove a proton to form an alkene. If Cl^- is used, HCl is formed as a reaction by-product. If CH_3CH_2OH is used, $(CH_3CH_2OH_2)^+$ is formed instead.

b.

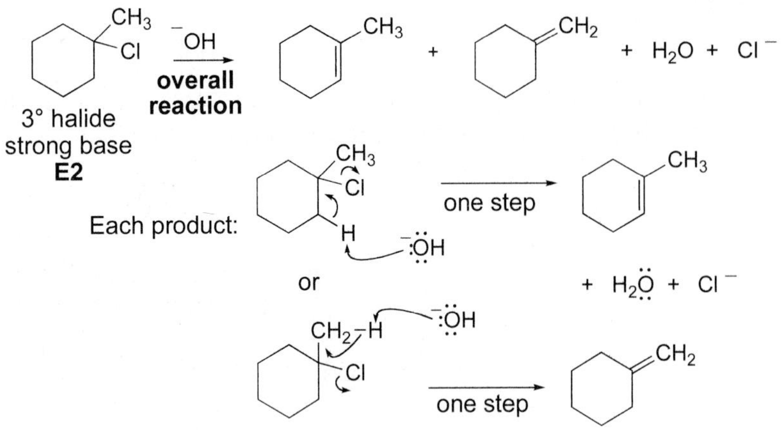

8.62 Draw the products of each reaction with the 1° alkyl halide.

a.

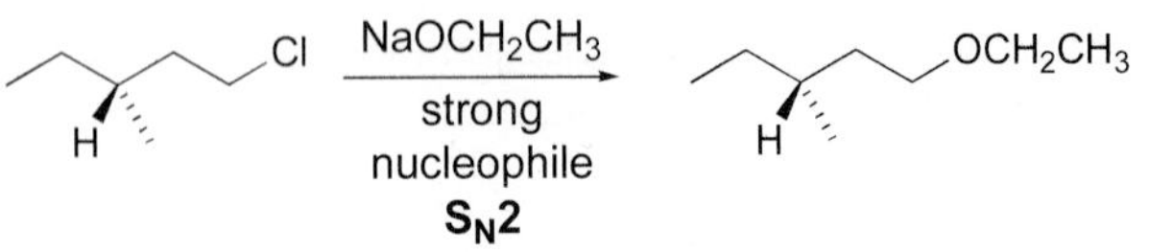

c.

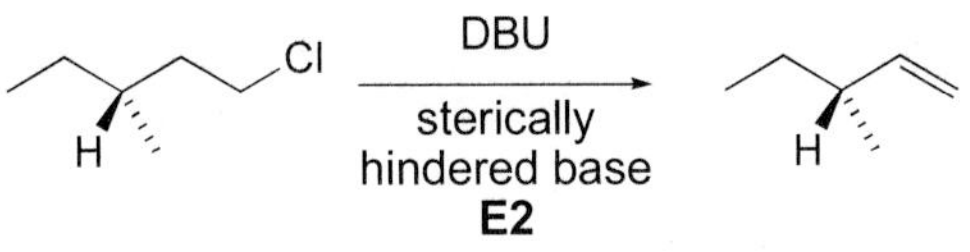

b.

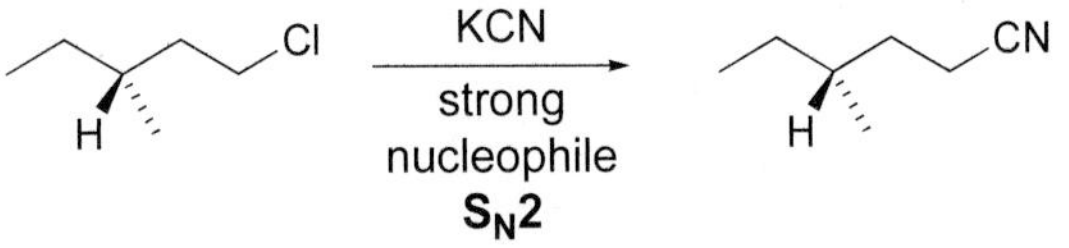

8.63

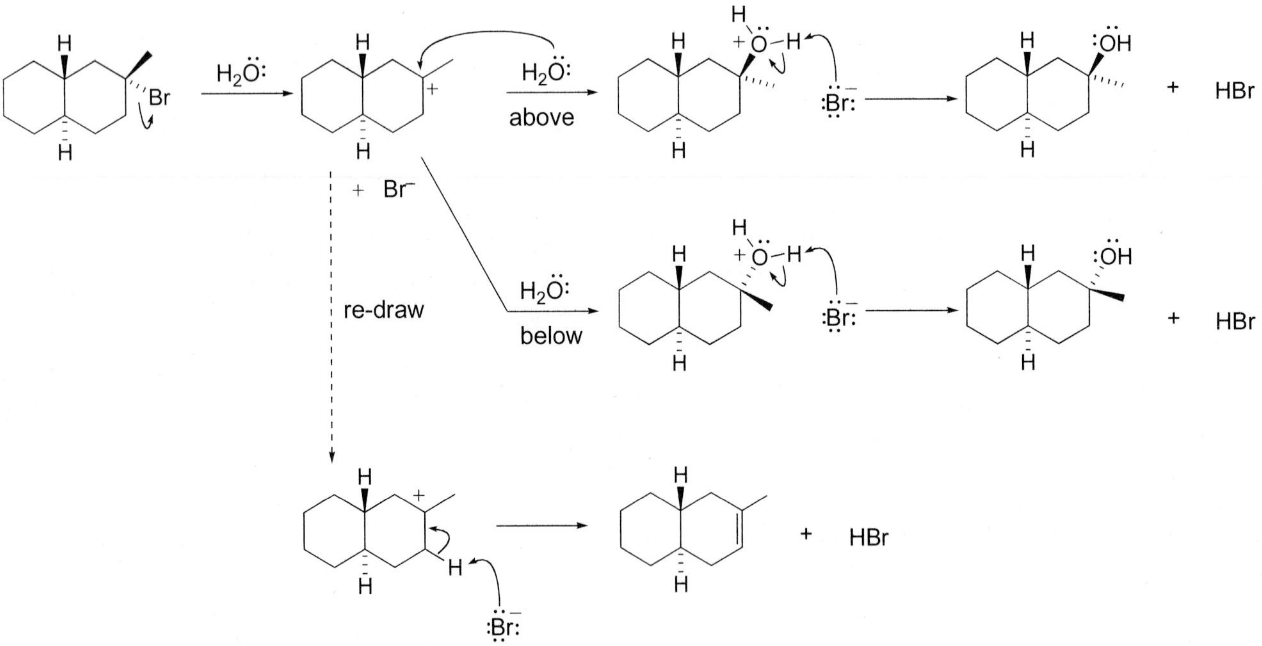

8.64

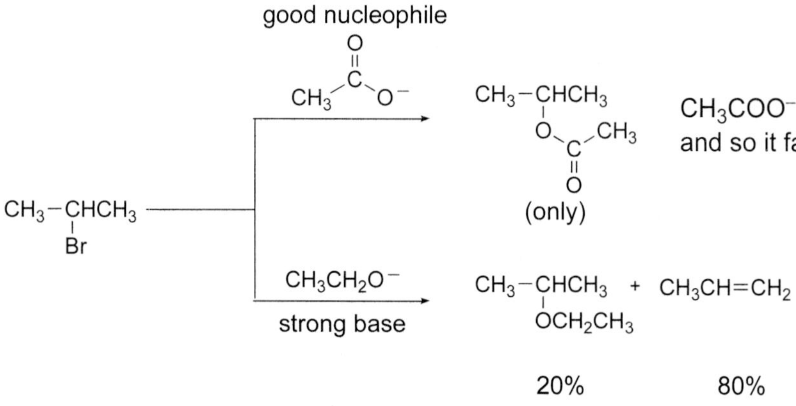

CH_3COO^- is a good nucleophile and a weak base and so it favors substitution by S_N2.

The strong base gives both S_N2 and E2 products, but since the 2° RX is somewhat hindered to substitution, the E2 product is favored.

8.65

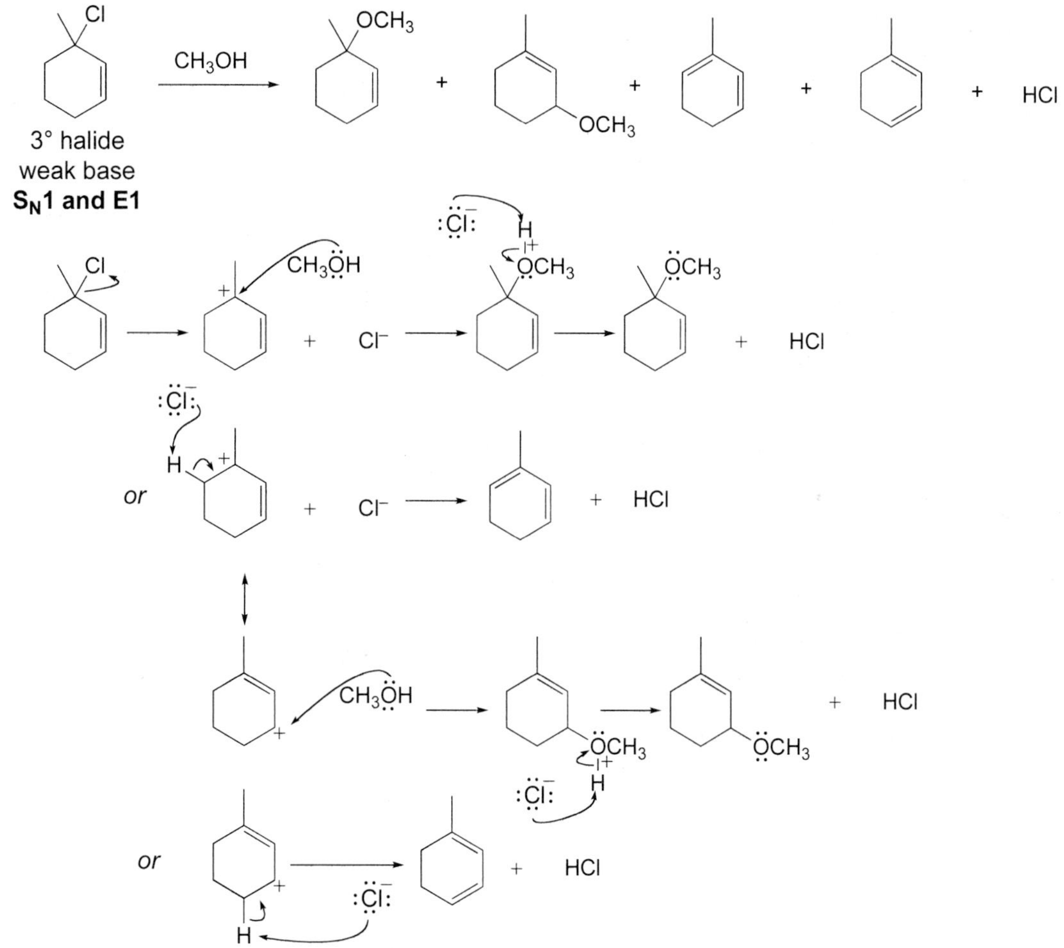

8.66 E2 elimination needs a leaving group and a hydrogen in the **trans diaxial** position.

Two different conformations:

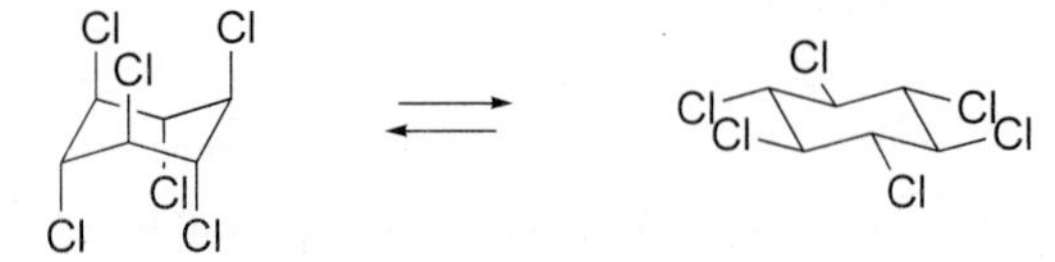

This conformation has Cl's axial, but no H's axial. This conformation has no Cl's axial.

For elimination to occur, a cyclohexane must have a H and Cl in the trans diaxial arrangement. Neither conformation of this isomer has both atoms—H and Cl—axial; thus, this isomer only slowly loses HCl by elimination.

8.67

H and Br are ***anti periplanar.***
Elimination can occur.

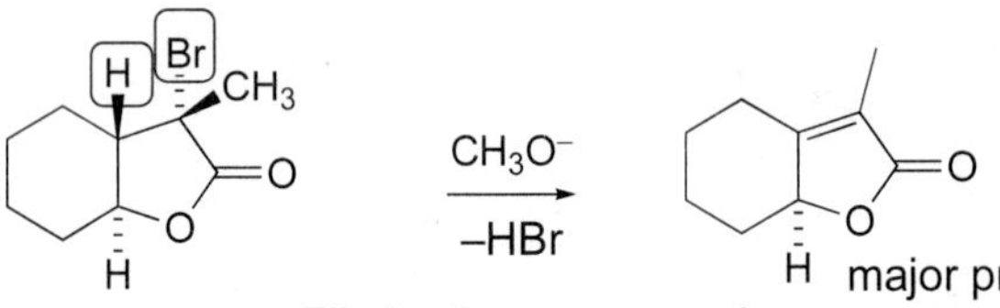
CH_3O^-
–HBr

major product

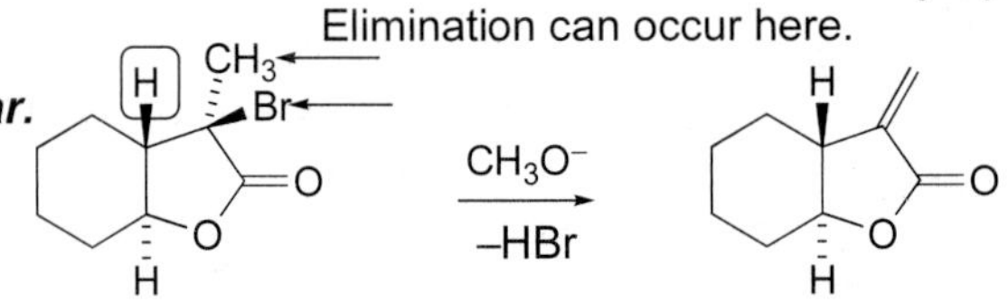
Elimination can occur here.
CH_3O^-
–HBr

H (in the ring) and Br are **NOT *anti periplanar.***
Elimination can**not** occur using this H.
Instead elimination must occur with the H on the CH_3 group.

Elimination cannot occur in the ring because the required anti periplanar geometry is not present.

8.68

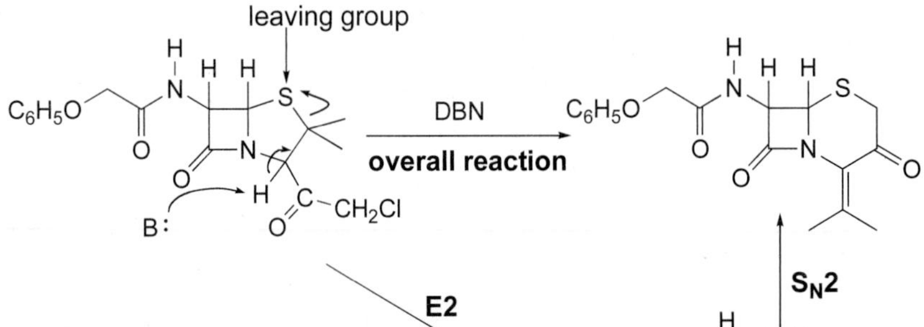
leaving group
DBN
overall reaction
E2

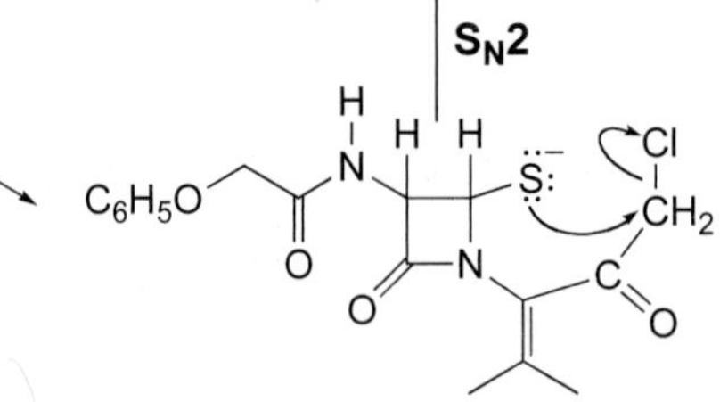
S_N2

A sequence of two reactions forms the final product: E2 elimination opens the five-membered ring. Then the sulfur nucleophile displaces the Cl^- leaving group to form the six-membered ring.

8.69

a.

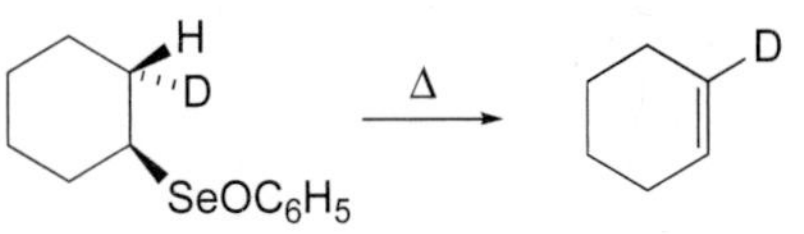

$SeOC_6H_5$ and H are on the same side of the ring.
syn elimination

b.

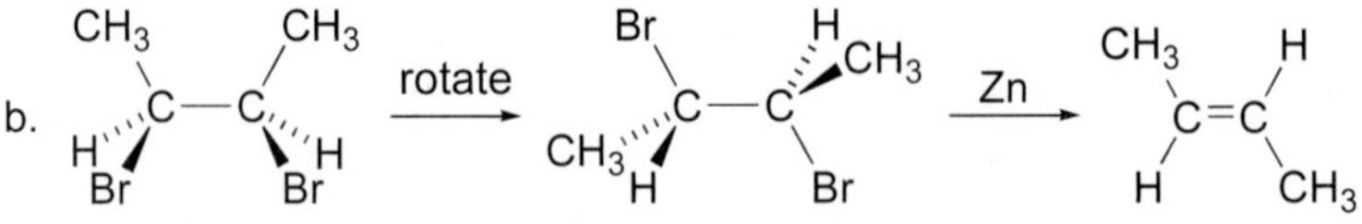
rotate
Zn

Both Br atoms are on the opposite sides of the C–C bond.
anti elimination

8.70 One equivalent of $NaNH_2$ removes one mole of HBr in an anti periplanar fashion from each dibromide. Two modes of elimination are possible for each compound.

a.

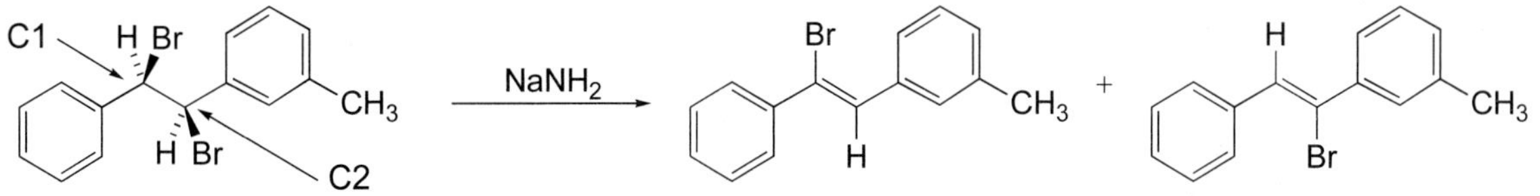

A

H and Br are anti periplanar on C1 and C2 as drawn.

loss of H from C1
loss of Br from C2
C

loss of H from C2
loss of Br from C1
D

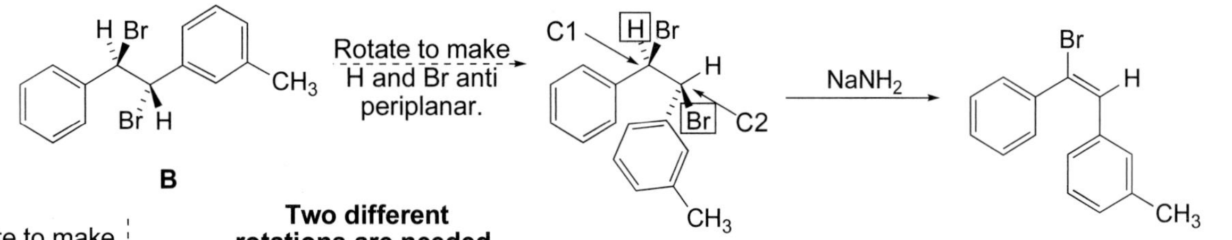

B

Two different rotations are needed.

loss of H from C1
loss of Br from C2
F

Rotate to make H and Br anti periplanar.

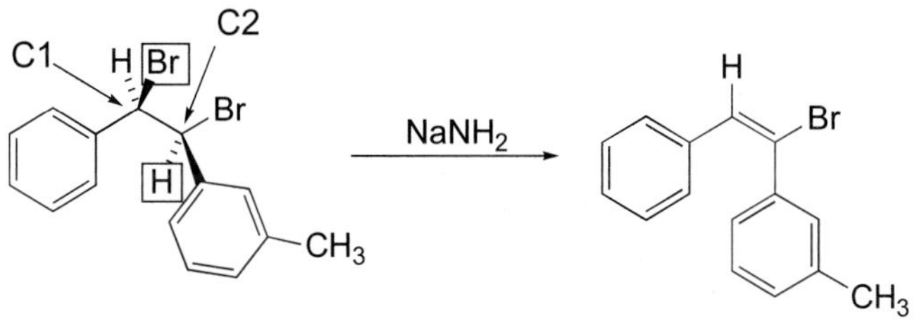

loss of H from C2
loss of Br from C1
E

b. **C** and **F** are diastereomers.
D and **E** are diastereomers.
C and **D** are constitutional isomers.
E and **F** are constitutional isomers.

Chapter 9 Alcohols, Ethers, and Epoxides

Chapter Review

General facts about ROH, ROR, and epoxides

- All three compounds contain an O atom that is sp^3 hybridized and tetrahedral (9.2).

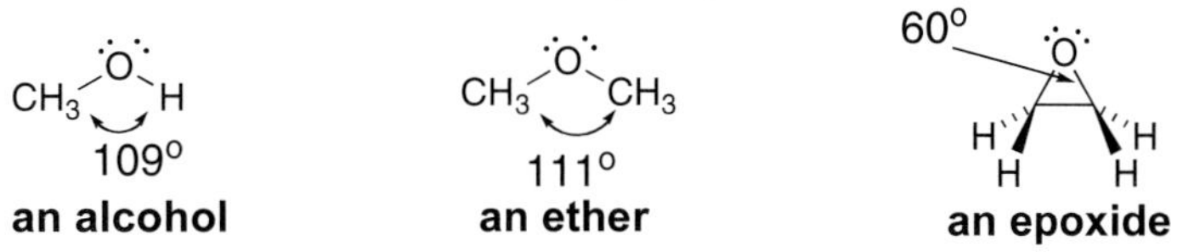

- All three compounds have polar C–O bonds, but only alcohols have an O–H bond for intermolecular hydrogen bonding (9.4).

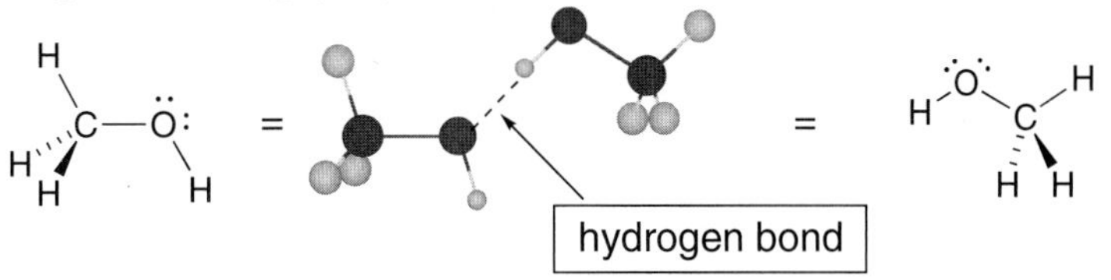

- Alcohols and ethers do not contain a good leaving group. Nucleophilic substitution can occur only after the OH (or OR) group is converted to a better leaving group (9.7A).

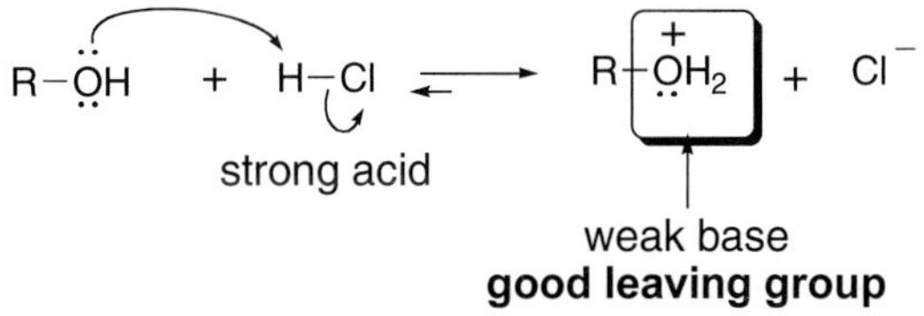

- Epoxides have a leaving group located in a strained three-membered ring, making them reactive to strong nucleophiles and acids HZ that contain a nucleophilic atom Z (9.15).

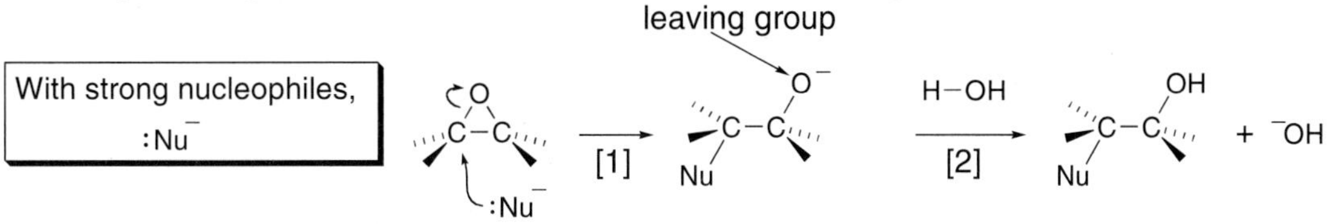

A new reaction of carbocations (9.9)

- Less stable carbocations rearrange to more stable carbocations by shift of a hydrogen atom or an alkyl group. Besides rearrangement, carbocations also react with nucleophiles (7.13) and bases (8.6).

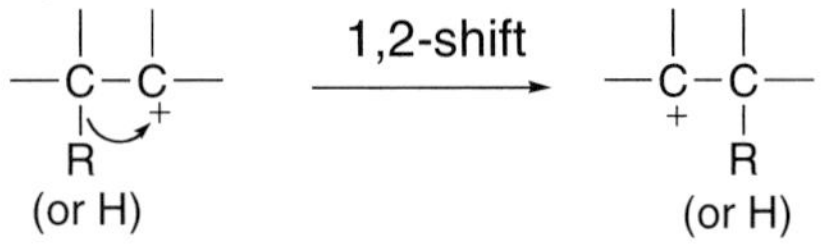

Preparation of alcohols, ethers, and epoxides (9.6)

[1] Preparation of alcohols

- The mechanism is S_N2.
- The reaction works best for CH_3X and 1° RX.

[2] Preparation of alkoxides (a Brønsted–Lowry acid–base reaction)

[3] Preparation of ethers (Williamson ether synthesis)

- The mechanism is S_N2.
- The reaction works best for CH_3X and 1° RX.

[4] Preparation of epoxides (intramolecular S_N2 reaction)

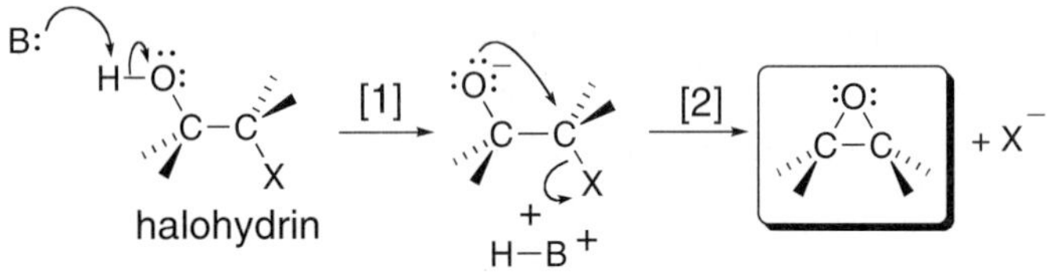

- A two-step reaction sequence:
  [1] Removal of a proton with base forms an alkoxide.
  [2] Intramolecular **S_N2** reaction forms the epoxide.

Reactions of alcohols

[1] Dehydration to form alkenes

[a] Using strong acid (9.8, 9.9)

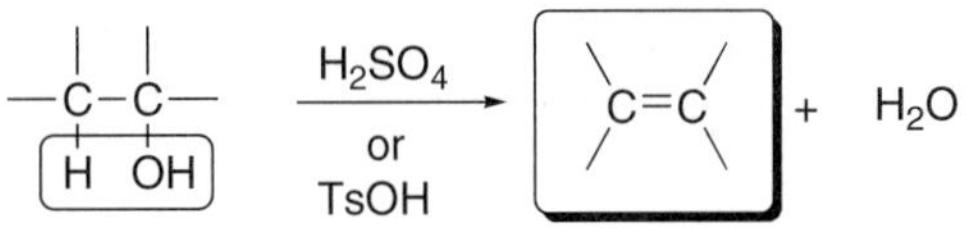

- Order of reactivity: $R_3COH > R_2CHOH > RCH_2OH$.
- The mechanism for 2° and 3° ROH is E1; carbocations are intermediates and rearrangements occur.
- The mechanism for 1° ROH is E2.
- The Zaitsev rule is followed.

[b] Using $POCl_3$ and pyridine (9.10)

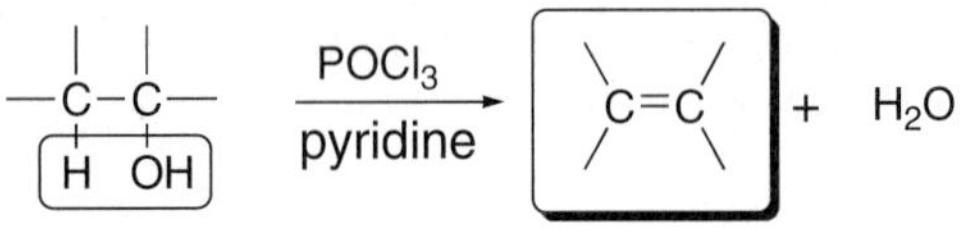

- The mechanism is E2.
- No carbocation rearrangements occur.

[2] Reaction with HX to form RX (9.11)

- Order of reactivity: $R_3COH > R_2CHOH > RCH_2OH$.
- The mechanism for 2° and 3° ROH is S_N1; carbocations are intermediates and rearrangements occur.
- The mechanism for CH_3OH and 1° ROH is S_N2.

[3] Reaction with other reagents to form RX (9.12)

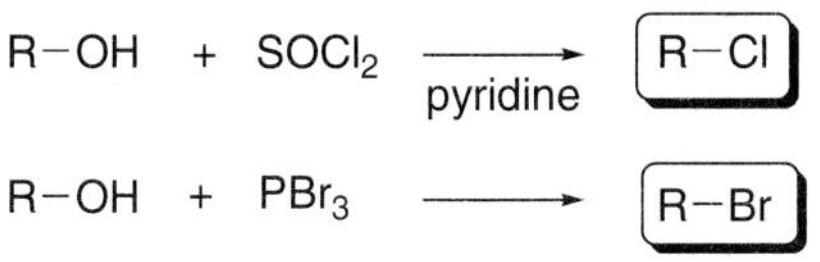
R–OH + SOCl2
pyridine
R–Cl
R–OH + PBr3
R–Br

- Reactions occur with CH_3OH and 1° and 2° ROH.
- The reactions follow an S_N2 mechanism.

[4] Reaction with tosyl chloride to form alkyl tosylates (9.13A)

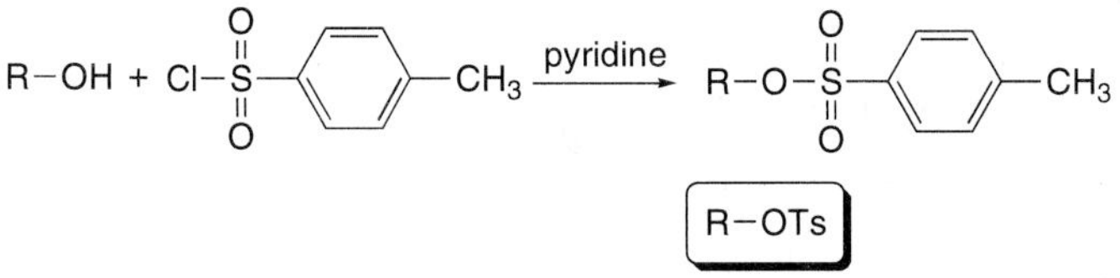
pyridine
R–OTs

- The C–O bond is not broken so the configuration at a stereogenic center is retained.

Reactions of alkyl tosylates

Alkyl tosylates undergo either substitution or elimination depending on the reagent (9.13B).

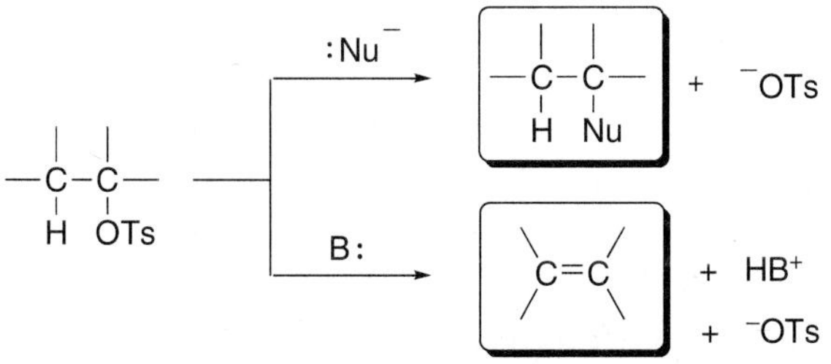
:Nu⁻
+ ⁻OTs
B:
+ HB⁺
+ ⁻OTs

- Substitution is carried out with strong :Nu⁻, so the mechanism is S_N2.
- Elimination is carried out with strong bases, so the mechanism is E2.

Reactions of ethers

Only one reaction is useful: Cleavage with strong acids (9.14)

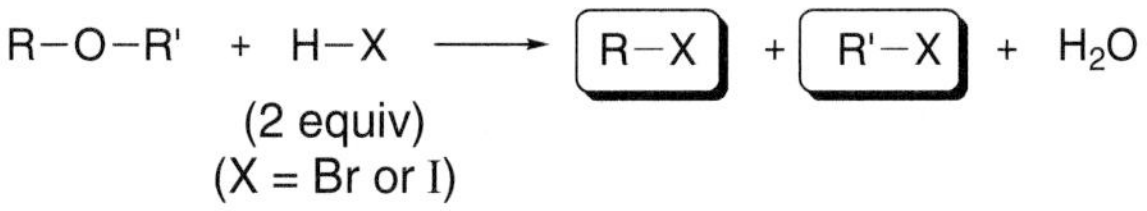
R–O–R' + H–X
(2 equiv)
(X = Br or I)
R–X + R'–X + H2O

- With 2° and 3° R groups, the mechanism is S_N1.
- With CH_3 and 1° R groups the mechanism is S_N2.

Reactions of epoxides

Epoxide rings are opened with nucleophiles :Nu⁻ and acids HZ (9.15).

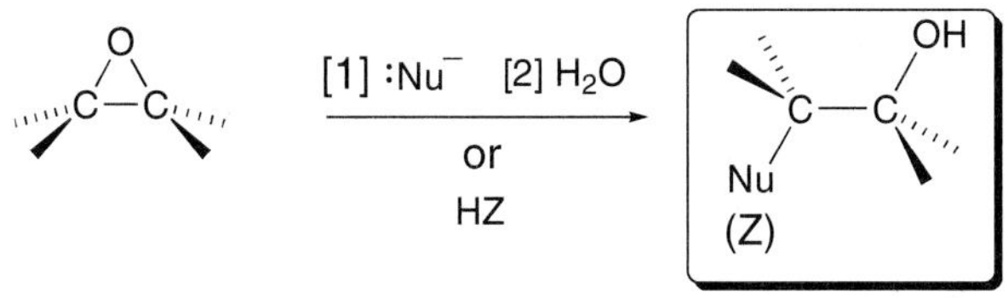
[1] :Nu⁻ [2] H2O
or
HZ
OH
Nu
(Z)

- The reaction occurs with backside attack, resulting in trans or anti products.
- With :Nu⁻, the mechanism is S_N2, and nucleophilic attack occurs at the less substituted C.
- With HZ, the mechanism is between S_N1 and S_N2, and attack of Z^- occurs at the more substituted C.

Practice Test on Chapter Review

1. Give the IUPAC name for each of the following compounds.

a. 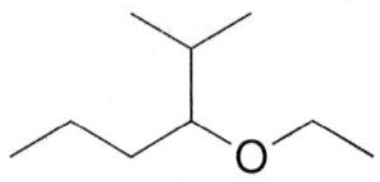

b. 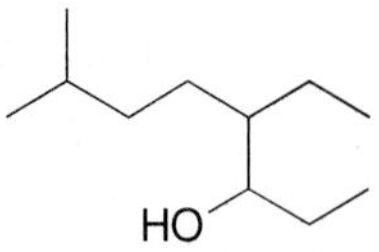
HO

2. Draw the organic products formed in each reaction. Draw all stereogenic centers using wedges and dashes.

a. 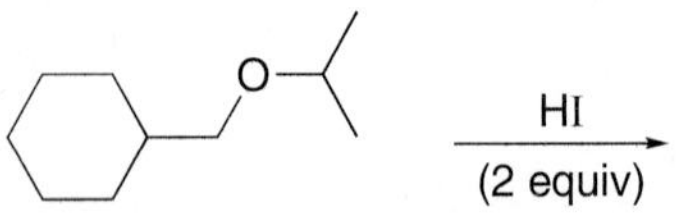
O
HI
(2 equiv)

b. 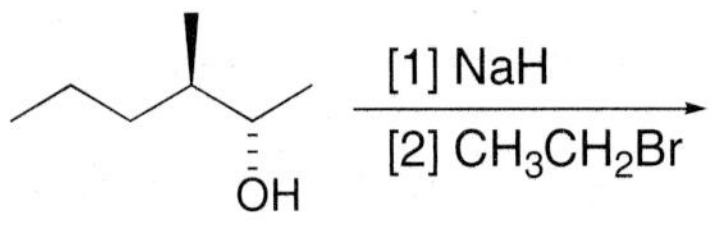
OH
[1] NaH
[2] CH3CH2Br

c. 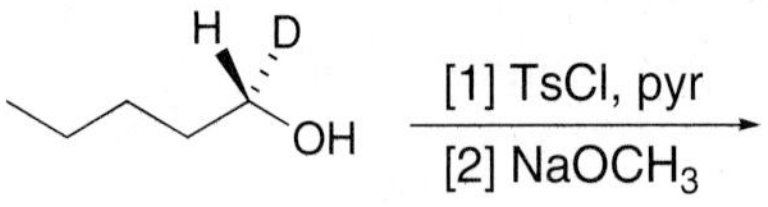
H D
OH
[1] TsCl, pyr
[2] NaOCH3

d. 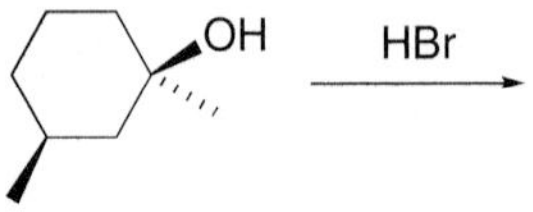
OH
HBr

e. 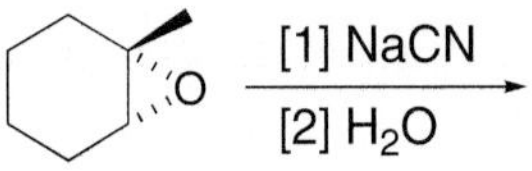
O
[1] NaCN
[2] H2O

f. 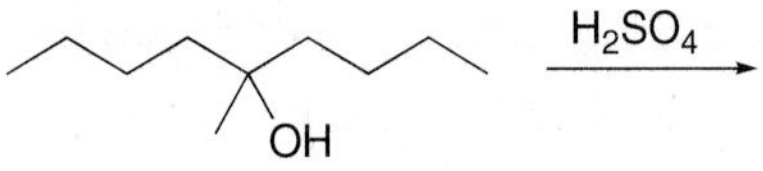
OH
H2SO4

3. What starting material is needed for the following reaction?

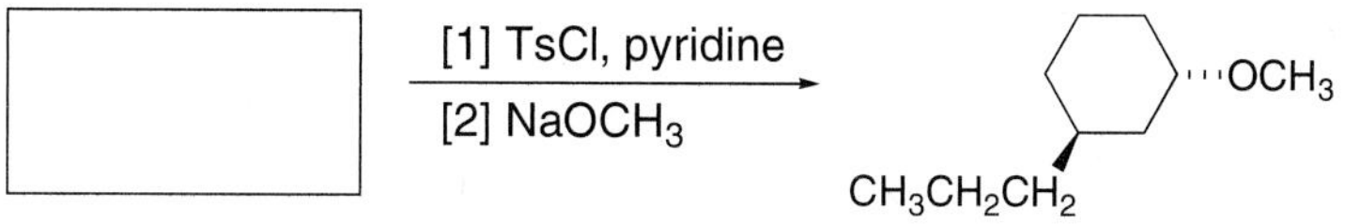
[1] TsCl, pyridine
[2] NaOCH$_3$
OCH$_3$
CH$_3$CH$_2$CH$_2$

4. What alkoxide and alkyl halide are needed to make the following ether?

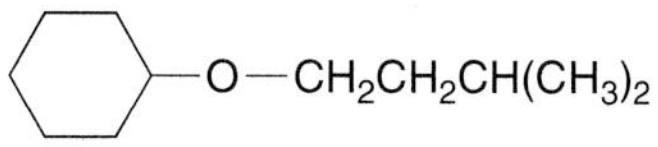
O—CH$_2$CH$_2$CH(CH$_3$)$_2$

Answers to Practice Test

1. a. 3-ethoxy-2-methylhexane

b. 4-ethyl-7-methyl-3-octanol

2.

a. 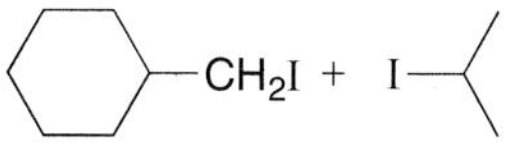
CH$_2$I + I

b. 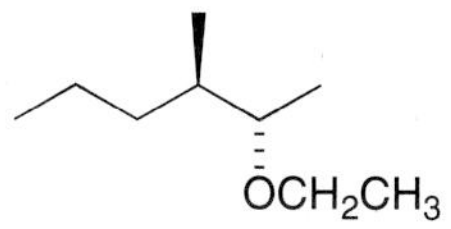
OCH$_2$CH$_3$

c. 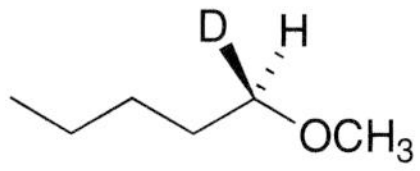
D H
OCH$_3$

d. 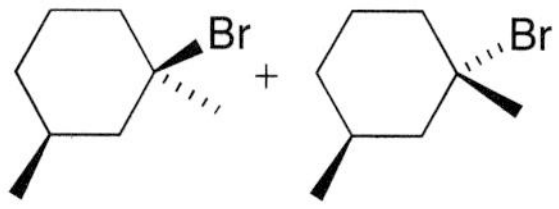
Br
+
Br

e. 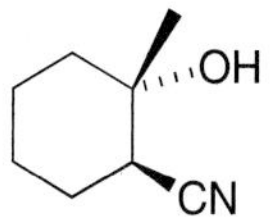
OH
CN

f. 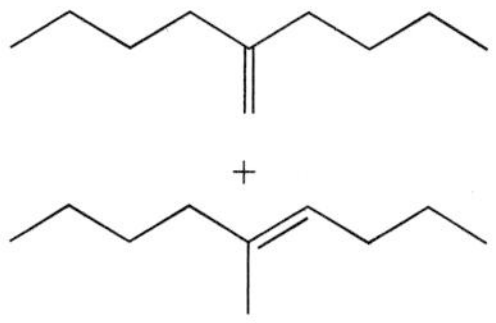
+

3. 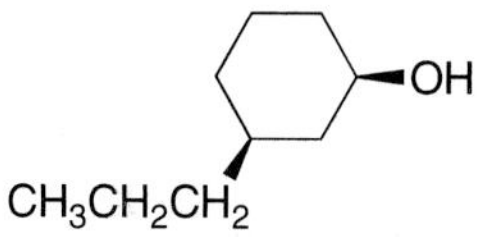
OH
CH$_3$CH$_2$CH$_2$

4. 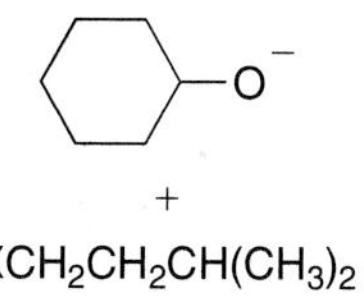
O$^-$
+
XCH$_2$CH$_2$CH(CH$_3$)$_2$

Answers to Problems

9.1 • **Alcohols** are classified as 1°, 2°, or 3°, depending on the number of carbon atoms bonded to the carbon with the OH group.

• **Symmetrical ethers** have two identical R groups, and **unsymmetrical ethers** have R groups that are different.

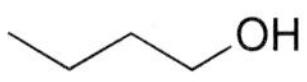
OH

1° alcohol

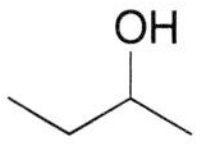
OH

2° alcohol

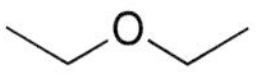
O

symmetrical ether

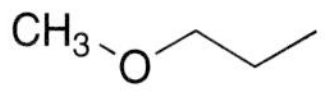
CH$_3$
O

unsymmetrical ether

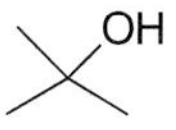
OH

3° alcohol

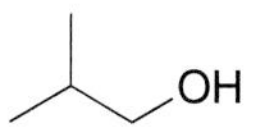
OH

1° alcohol

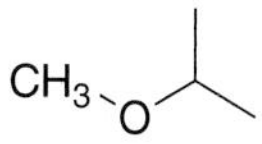
CH$_3$
O

unsymmetrical ether

9.2 Use the definitions in Answer 9.1.

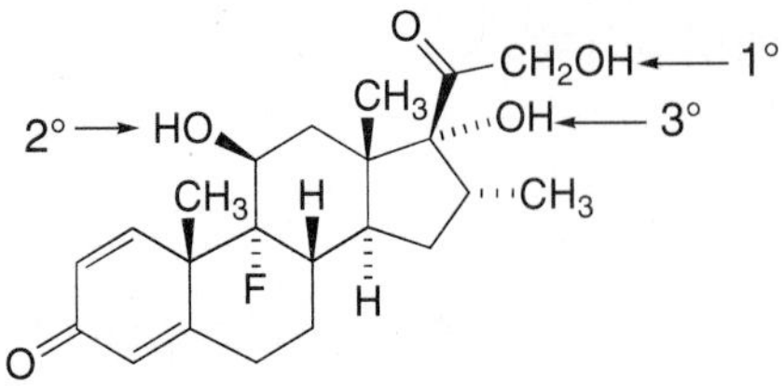

9.3 To name an alcohol:

[1] **Find the longest chain that has the OH group as a substituent.** Name the molecule as a derivative of that number of carbons by changing the ***-e*** ending of the alkane to the suffix ***-ol.***

[2] **Number the carbon chain to give the OH group the lower number.** When the OH group is bonded to a ring, the ring is numbered beginning with the OH group, and the "1" is usually omitted.

[3] Apply the other rules of nomenclature to complete the name.

a. [1] 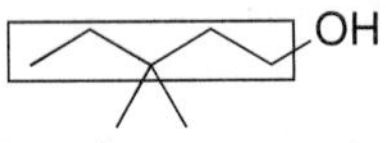

5 carbons = **pentanol**

[2] 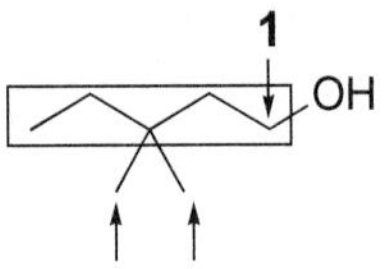

[3] **3,3-dimethyl-1-pentanol**

b. [1] 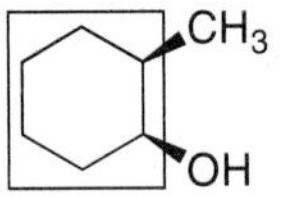

6 carbon ring = **cyclohexanol**

[2] 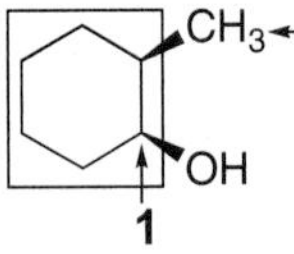

2-methyl

[3] ***cis*-2-methylcyclohexanol**

c. [1] 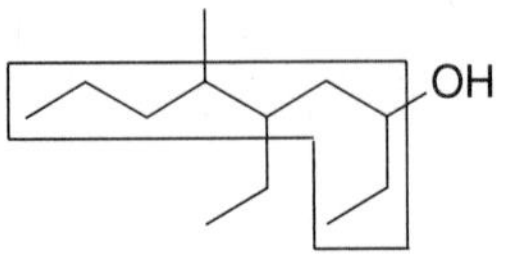

9 carbons = **nonanol**

[2] 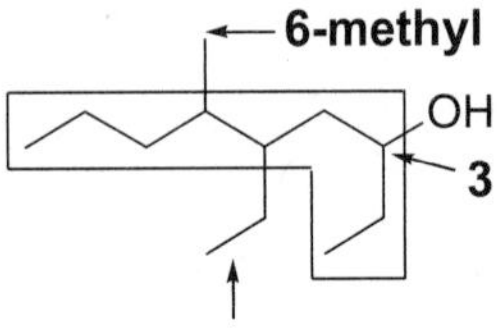

6-methyl

5-ethyl

[3] **5-ethyl-6-methyl-3-nonanol**

9.4 To work backwards from a name to a structure:

[1] Find the parent name and draw its structure.

[2] Add the substituents to the long chain.

a. 7,7-dimethyl-4-**octanol**

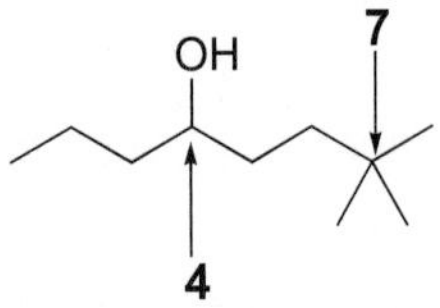

c. 2-*tert*-butyl-3-methyl**cyclohexanol**

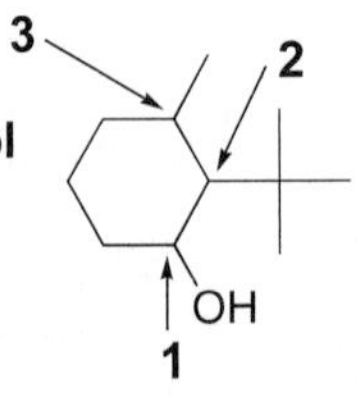

b. 5-methyl-4-propyl-3-**heptanol**

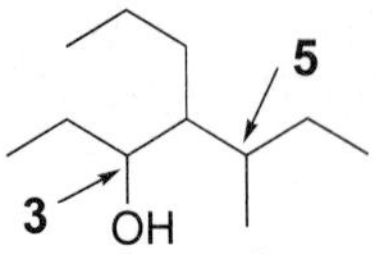

d. *trans*-1,2-**cyclohexanediol**

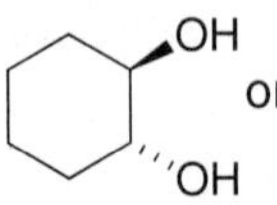

or

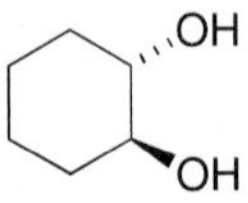

9.5 To name simple ethers:

[1] Name both alkyl groups bonded to the oxygen.

[2] Arrange these names alphabetically and add the word ***ether.*** For symmetrical ethers, name the alkyl group and add the prefix ***di.***

To name ethers using the IUPAC system:

[1] Find the two alkyl groups bonded to the ether oxygen. The smaller chain becomes the substituent, named as an alkoxy group.

[2] Number the chain to give the lower number to the first substituent.

a. **common name:**

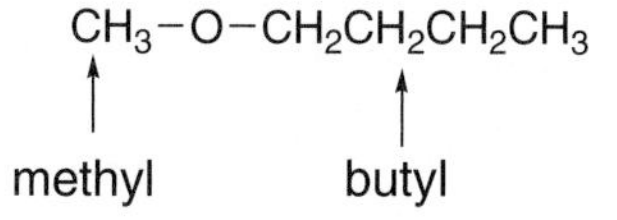
$CH_3-O-CH_2CH_2CH_2CH_3$
methyl
butyl

butyl methyl ether

IUPAC name:

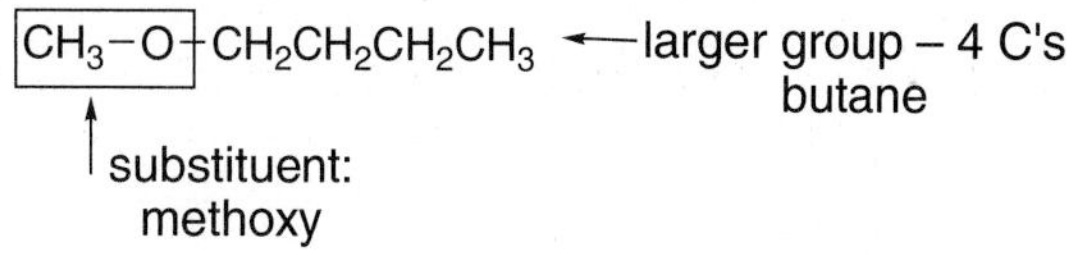
$CH_3-O-CH_2CH_2CH_2CH_3$
larger group – 4 C's
butane
substituent:
methoxy

1-methoxybutane

b. **common name:**

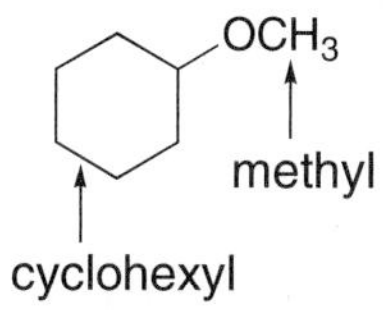
OCH_3
methyl
cyclohexyl

cyclohexyl methyl ether

IUPAC name:

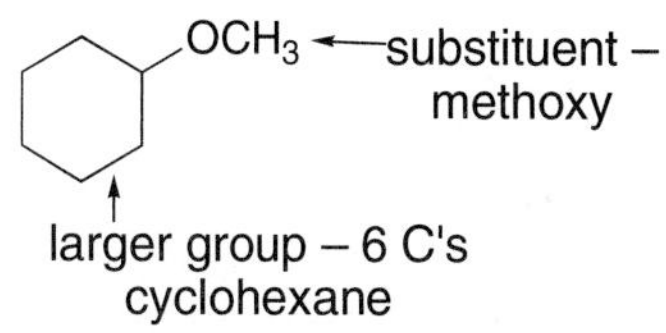
OCH_3
substituent –
methoxy
larger group – 6 C's
cyclohexane

methoxycyclohexane

c. **common name:**

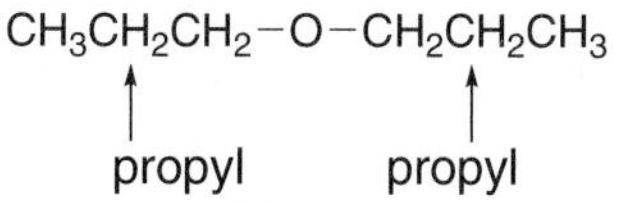
$CH_3CH_2CH_2-O-CH_2CH_2CH_3$
propyl
propyl

dipropyl ether

IUPAC name:

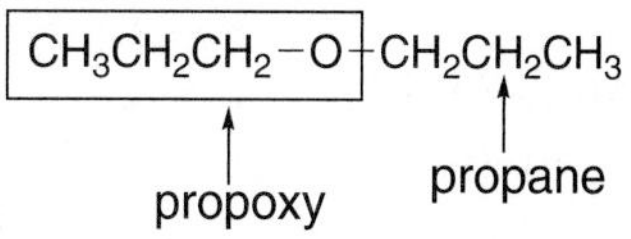
$CH_3CH_2CH_2-O-CH_2CH_2CH_3$
propoxy
propane

1-propoxypropane

9.6 Name the ether using the rules from Answer 9.5.

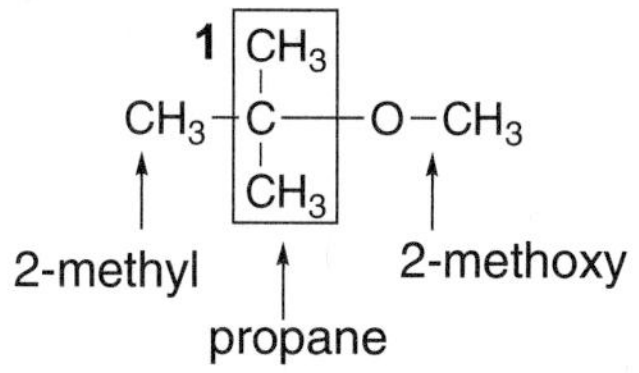
1
CH_3
CH_3
C
$O-CH_3$
CH_3
2-methyl
2-methoxy
propane

2-methoxy-2-methylpropane

9.7 Three ways to name epoxides:

[1] Epoxides are named as derivatives of oxirane, the simplest epoxide.

[2] Epoxides can be named by considering the oxygen as a substituent called an **epoxy** group, bonded to a hydrocarbon chain or ring. Use two numbers to designate which two atoms the oxygen is bonded to.

[3] Epoxides can be named as **alkene oxides** by mentally replacing the epoxide oxygen by a double bond. Name the alkene (Chapter 10) and add the word ***oxide.***

a. 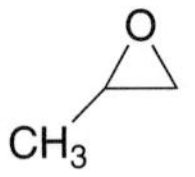

Three possibilities:
[1] **methyloxirane**
[2] **1,2-epoxypropane**
[3] **propene oxide**

c. 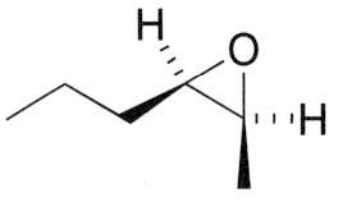

Three possibilities:
[1] ***cis*-2-methyl-3-propyloxirane**
[2] ***cis*-2,3-epoxyhexane**
[3] ***cis*-2-hexene oxide**

b. 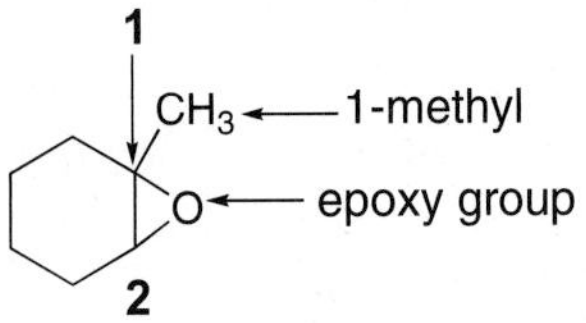

Two possibilities:
[1] 6 carbons = cyclohexane
1,2-epoxy-1-methylcyclohexane
[2] **1-methylcyclohexene oxide**

9.8 Two rules for boiling point:

[1] **The stronger the forces the higher the bp.**

[2] **Bp increases as the extent of the hydrogen bonding increases.** For alcohols with the same number of carbon atoms: hydrogen bonding and bp's increase: 3° ROH < 2° ROH < 1° ROH.

a. 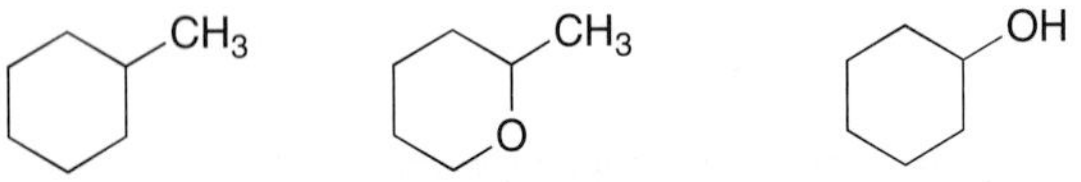

VDW **lowest bp**	VDW DD **intermediate bp**	VDW DD hydrogen bonding **highest bp**

b. 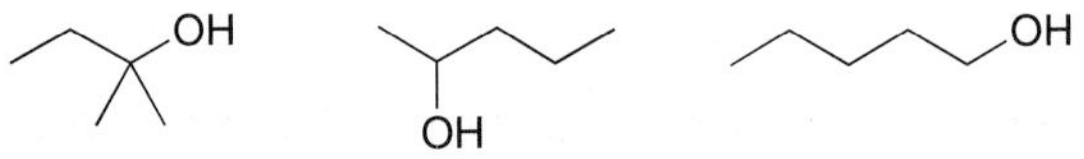

3° ROH **lowest bp**	2° ROH **intermediate bp**	1° ROH **highest bp**

9.9 Strong nucleophiles (like ^-CN) favor S_N2 reactions. The use of crown ethers in nonpolar solvents increases the nucleophilicity of the anion, and this increases the rate of the S_N2 reaction. The nucleophile does not appear in the rate equation for the S_N1 reaction. Nonpolar solvents cannot solvate carbocations, so this disfavors S_N1 reactions as well.

9.10 Draw the products of substitution in the following reactions by substituting OH or OR for X in the starting material.

a. $CH_3CH_2CH_2CH_2{-}Br + {}^-OH \longrightarrow CH_3CH_2CH_2CH_2{-}OH + Br^-$ **alcohol**

b. 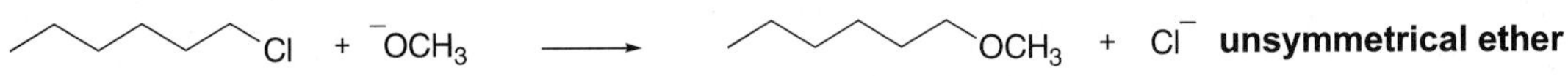

c. 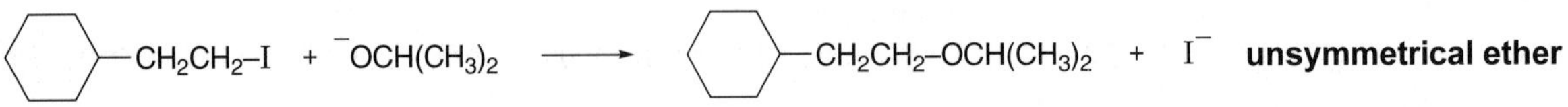

d. 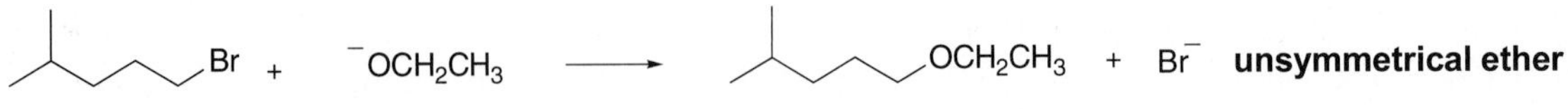

9.11 Two possible routes to **X** are shown. Path [2] with a 1° alkyl halide is preferred. Path [1] cannot occur because the leaving group would be bonded to an sp^2 hybridized C, making it an unreactive aryl halide.

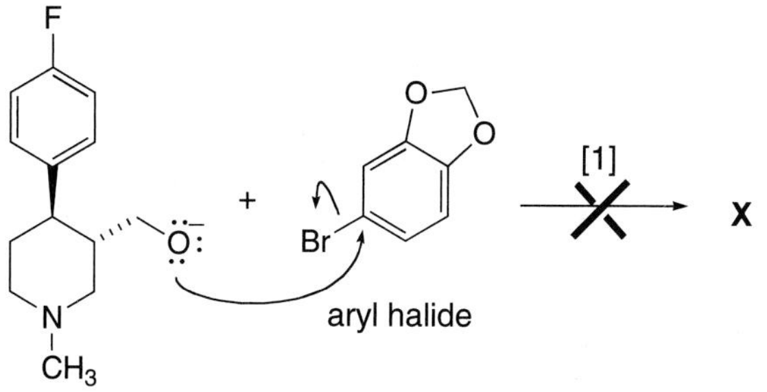

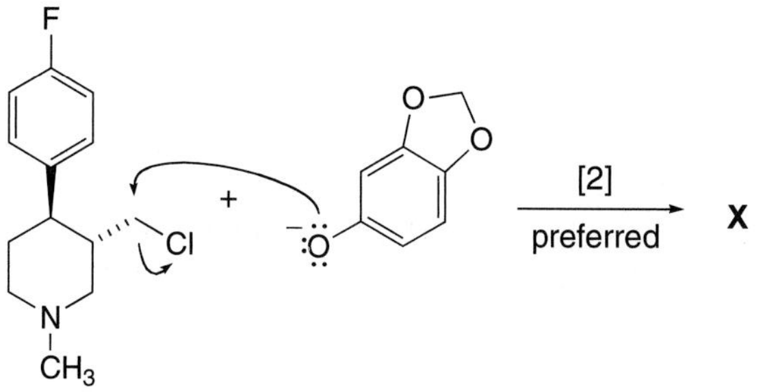

1° alkyl halide

9.12 NaH and NaNH₂ are strong bases that will remove a proton from an alcohol, creating a nucleophile.

a. 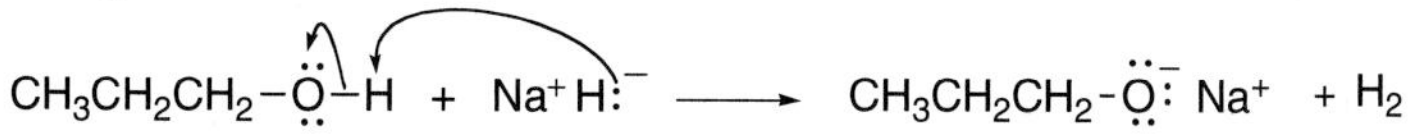

b. 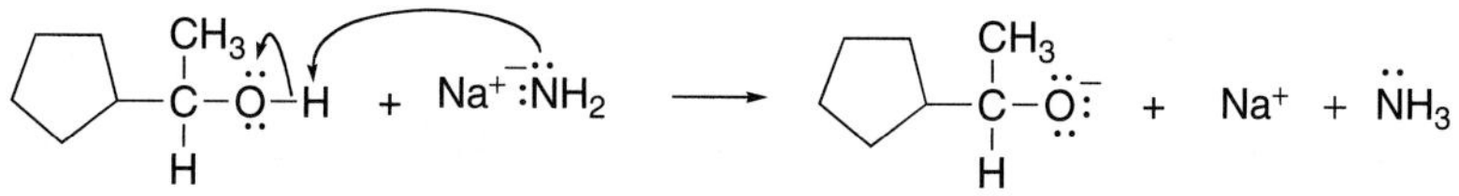

c. 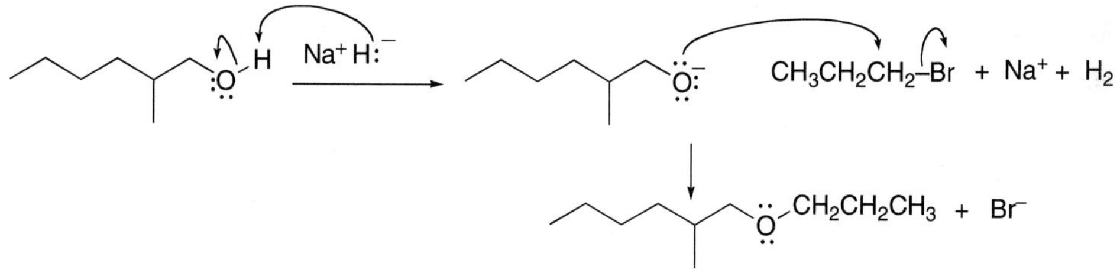

d. 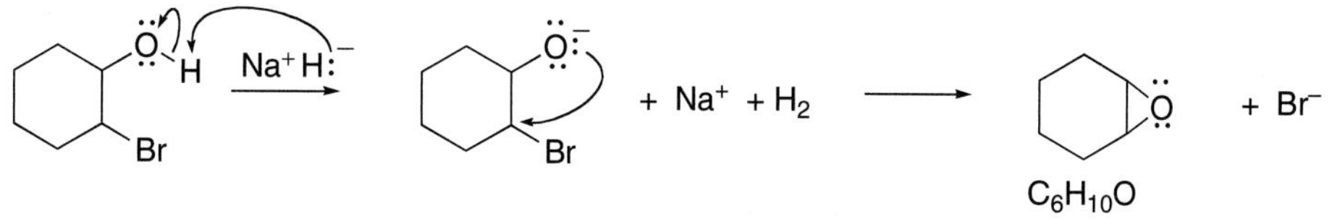

9.13 Dehydration follows the Zaitsev rule, so the more stable, more substituted alkene is the major product.

a. 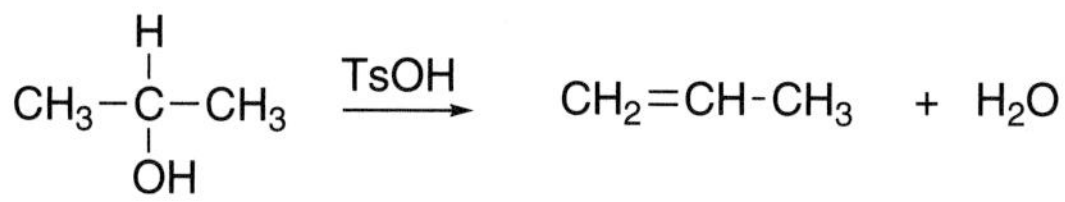

b. 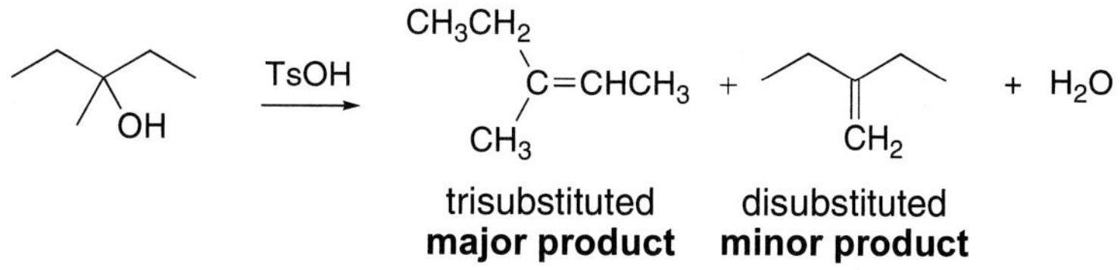

c. 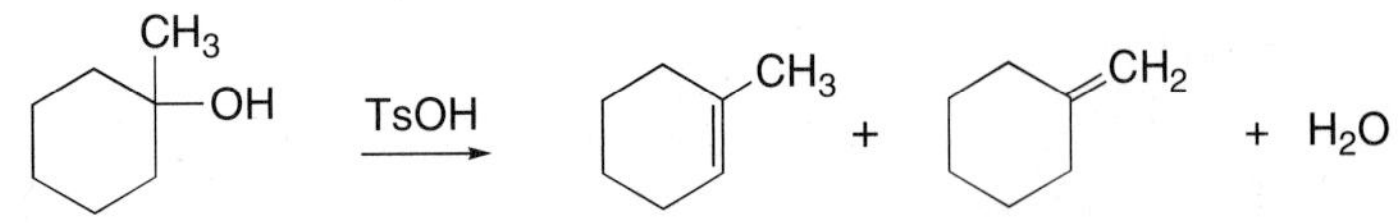
CH3
OH
TsOH
CH3
+
CH2
+ H2O

trisubstituted **major product** disubstituted **minor product**

9.14 The rate of dehydration increases as the number of R groups increases.

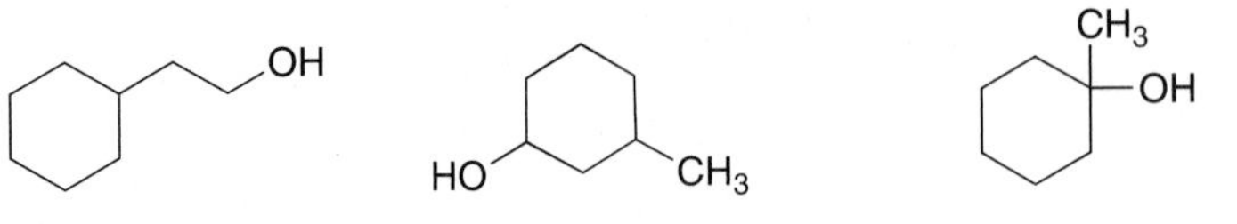
OH
HO
CH3
CH3
OH

1° alcohol	2° alcohol	3° alcohol
slowest reaction	**intermediate reactivity**	**fastest reaction**

9.15

transition state [1]:

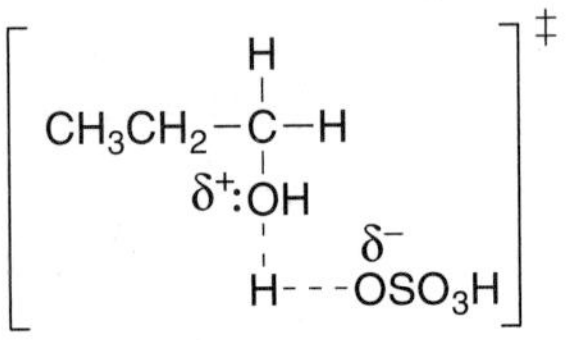
H
CH3CH2–C–H
δ+:OH
δ–
H---OSO3H
‡

transition state [2]:

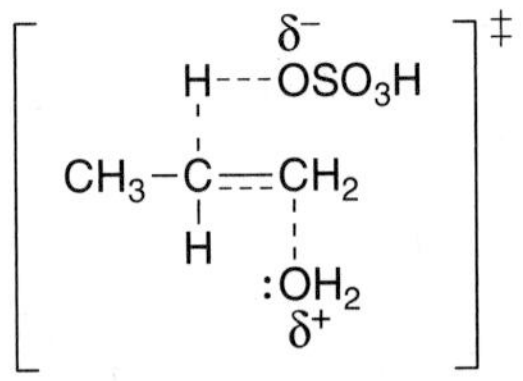
δ–
H---OSO3H
CH3–C---CH2
H
:OH2
δ+
‡

9.16

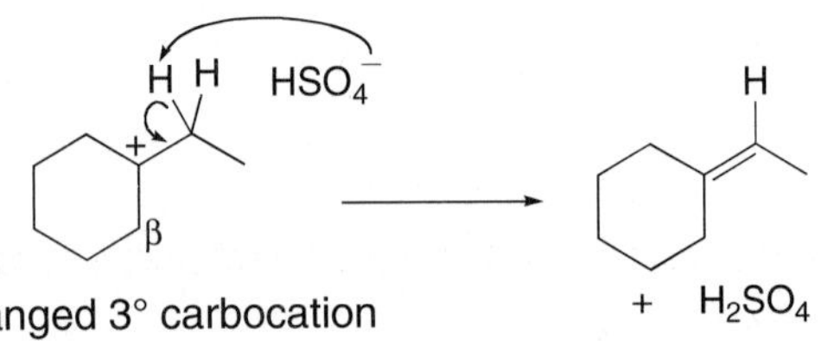
H H HSO4–
+
β
H
+ H2SO4

rearranged 3° carbocation

This alkene is also formed in addition to **Y** from the rearranged carbocation.

The initially formed 2° carbocation gives two alkenes:

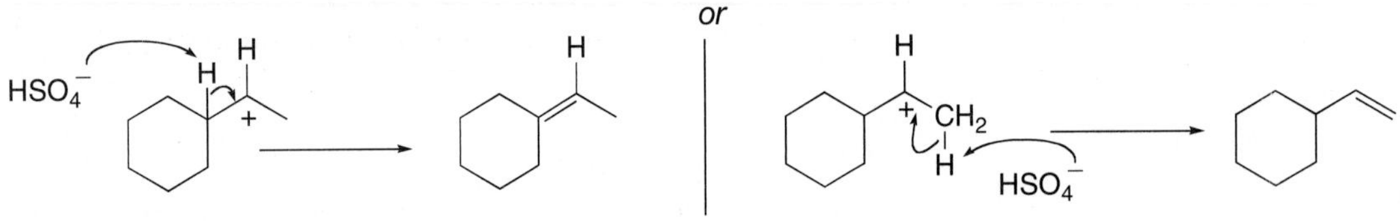
HSO4–
H
H
+
H
or
H
+ CH2
H
HSO4–

9.17

a. 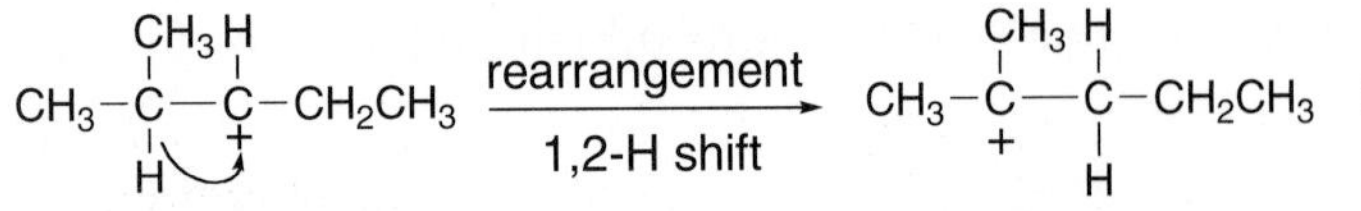
CH3 H
CH3–C–C–CH2CH3
H +
rearrangement
1,2-H shift
CH3 H
CH3–C–C–CH2CH3
+ H

2° carbocation

3° carbocation **more stable**

c. 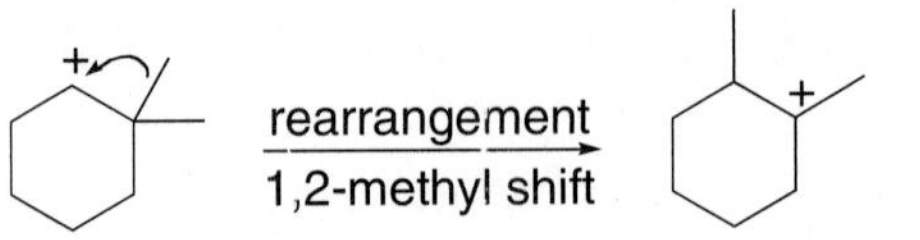
+
rearrangement
1,2-methyl shift
+

2° carbocation

3° carbocation **more stable**

b. 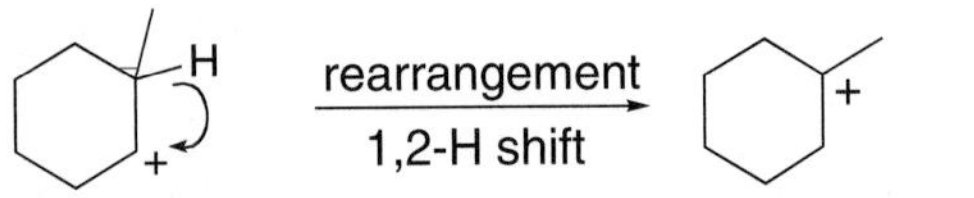
H
+
rearrangement
1,2-H shift
+

2° carbocation

3° carbocation **more stable**

9.18

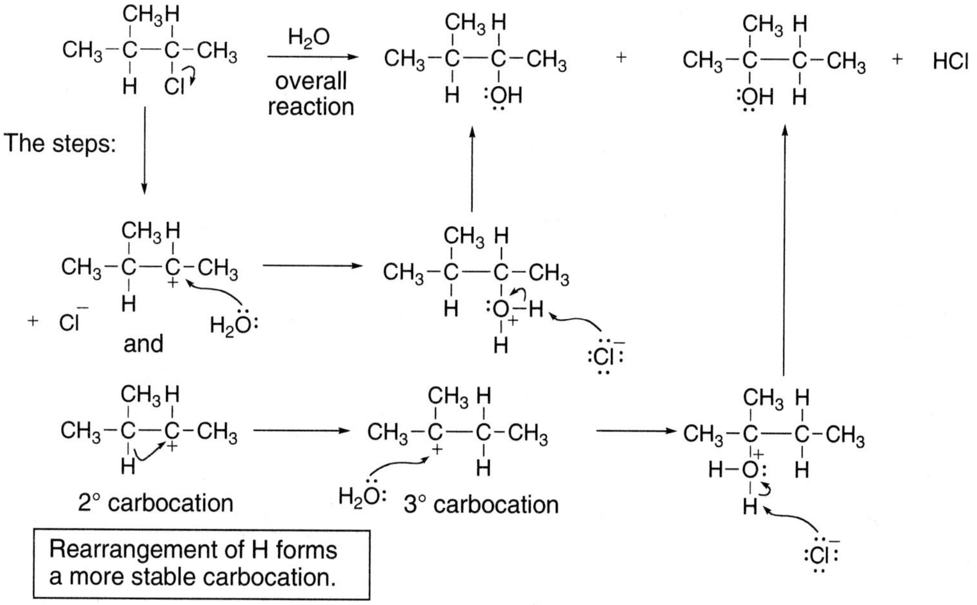
H2O
overall reaction
The steps:
and
2° carbocation
3° carbocation
Rearrangement of H forms a more stable carbocation.
+ HCl

9.19

a. 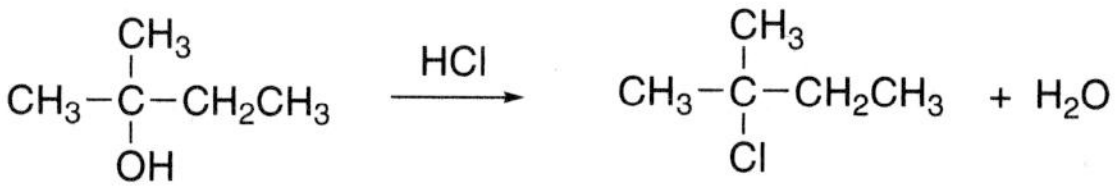

c. 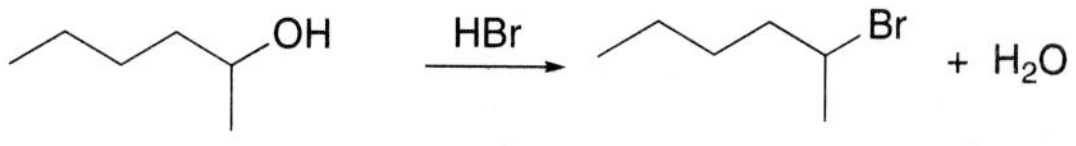

b. 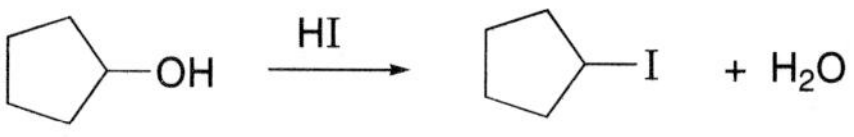

9.20 • **CH_3OH and 1° alcohols** follow an S_N2 mechanism, which results in inversion of configuration.

• **Secondary (2°) and 3° alcohols** follow an S_N1 mechanism, which results in racemization at a stereogenic center.

a. 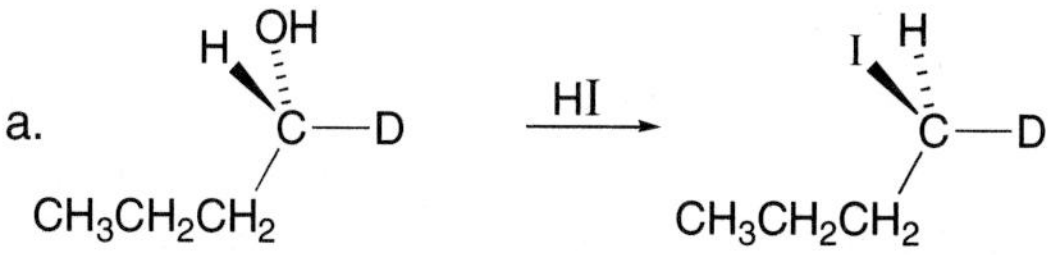

1° alcohol so **inversion of configuration**

b. 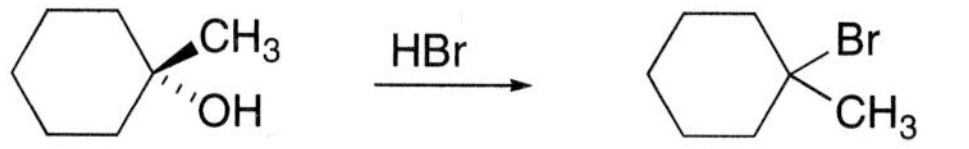

achiral starting material achiral product

3° alcohol, so Br^- attacks from above and below. The product is achiral.

c. 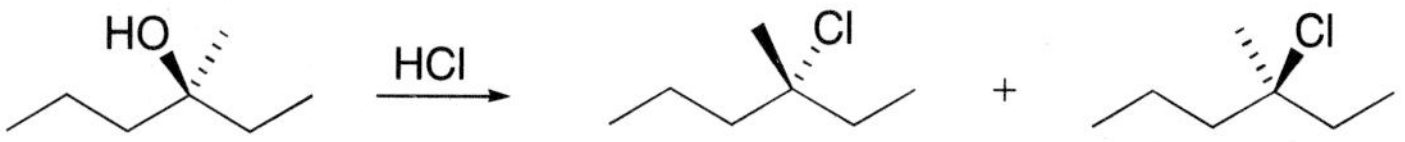

3° alcohol = **racemization**

9.21

a.

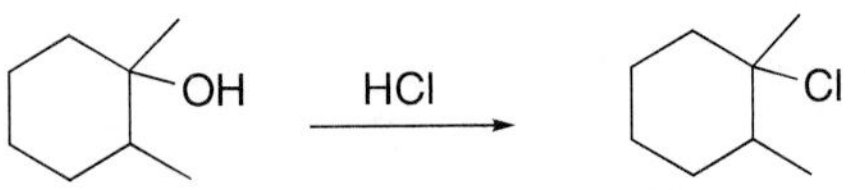
OH
HCl
Cl

c.

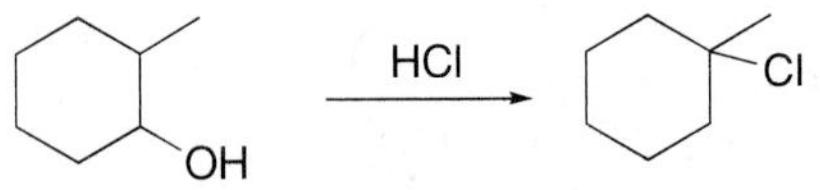
OH
HCl
Cl

(product formed after a 1,2-H shift)

b.

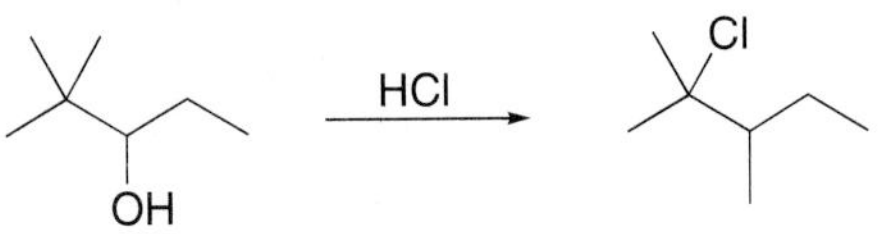
OH
HCl
Cl

(product formed after a 1,2-CH_3 shift)

9.22 Substitution reactions of alcohols using $SOCl_2$ proceed by an S_N2 mechanism. Therefore, there is **inversion of configuration** at a stereogenic center.

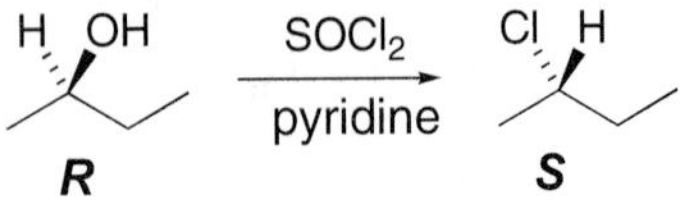
H OH
$SOCl_2$
pyridine
Cl H
R
S

Reactions using $SOCl_2$ proceed by an S_N2 mechanism = **inversion of configuration.**

9.23 Substitution reactions of alcohols using PBr_3 proceed by an S_N2 mechanism. Therefore, there is inversion of configuration at a stereogenic center.

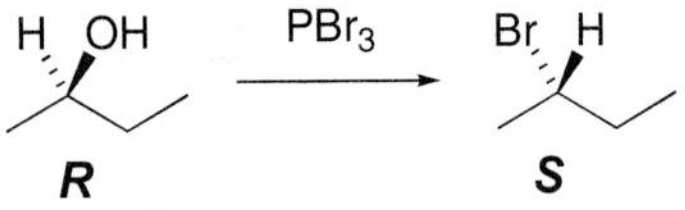
H OH
PBr_3
Br H
R
S

Reactions using PBr_3 proceed by an S_N2 mechanism = **inversion of configuration.**

9.24 Stereochemistry for conversion of ROH to RX by reagent:

[1] **HX**—with 1°, S_N2, so inversion of configuration; with 2° and 3°, S_N1, so racemization.

[2] **$SOCl_2$**—S_N2, so inversion of configuration.

[3] **PBr_3**—S_N2, so inversion of configuration.

a.

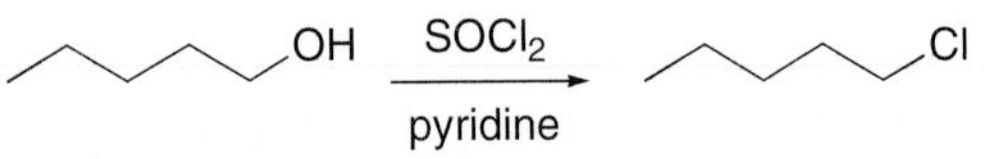
OH
$SOCl_2$
pyridine
Cl

c.

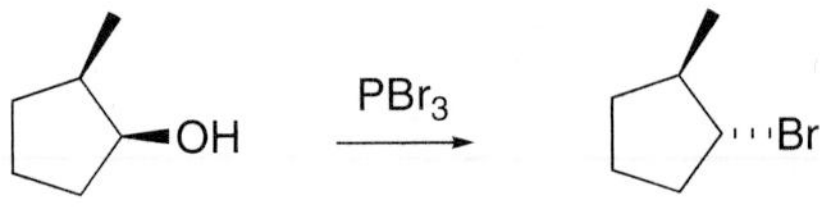
OH
PBr_3
Br

S_N2 = **inversion**

b.

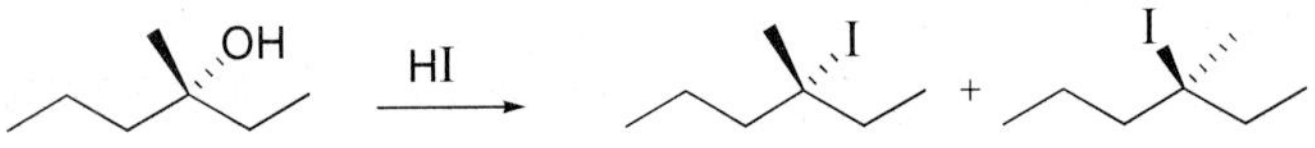
OH
HI
I
+
I

3° alcohol, S_N1 = **racemization**

9.25 To do a two-step synthesis with this starting material:

[1] Convert the OH group into a good leaving group (by using either PBr_3 or $SOCl_2$).

[2] Add the nucleophile for the S_N2 reaction.

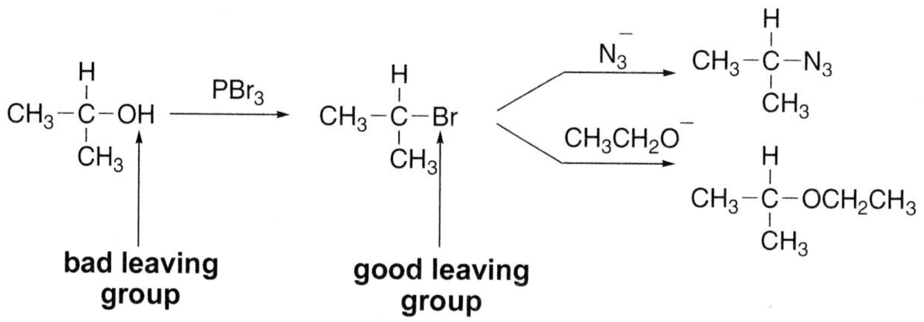

9.26

a. 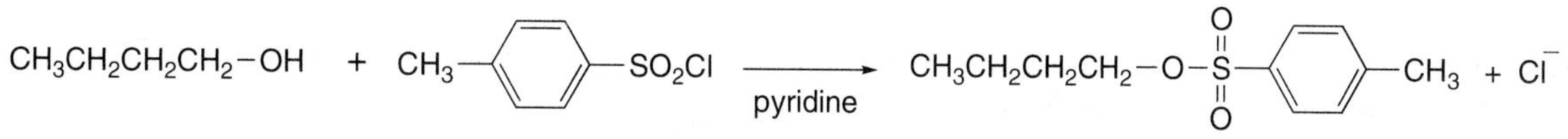

b. 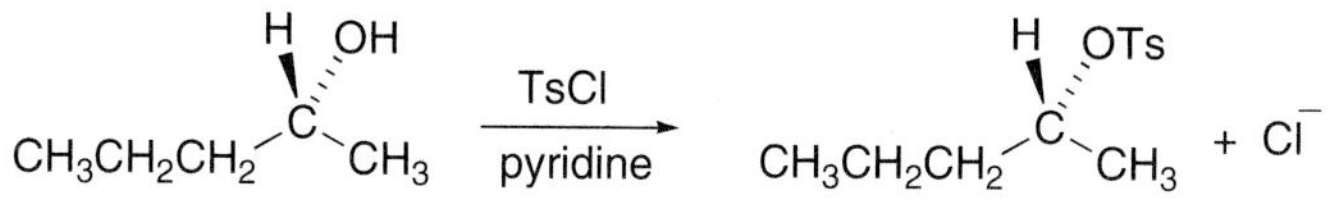

9.27

a. 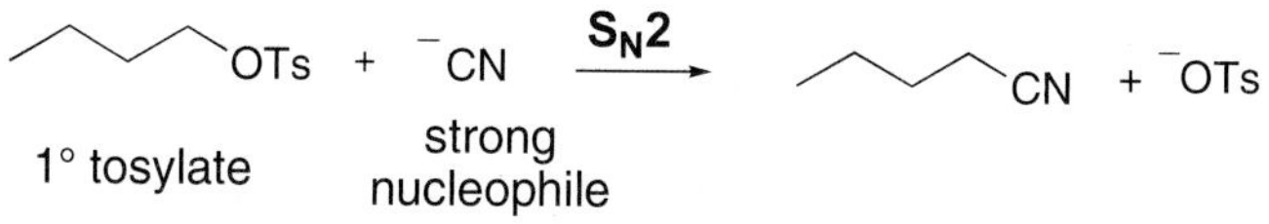

b. 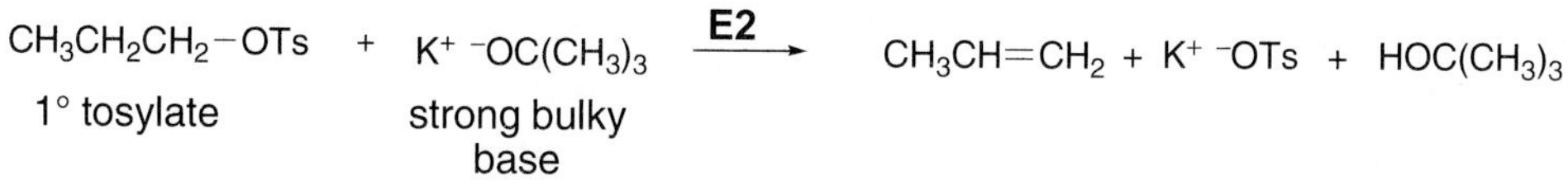

c. 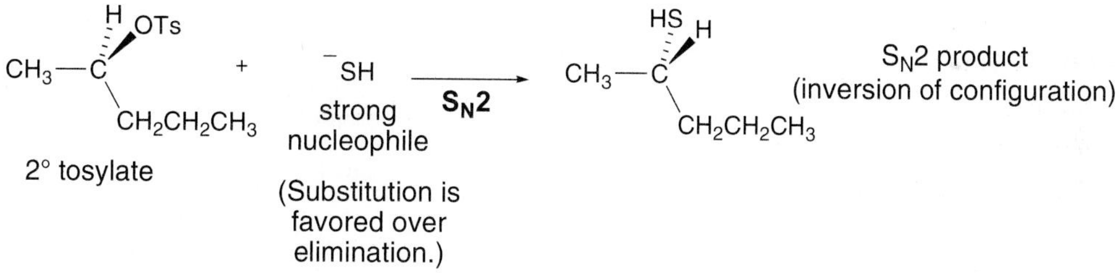

9.28

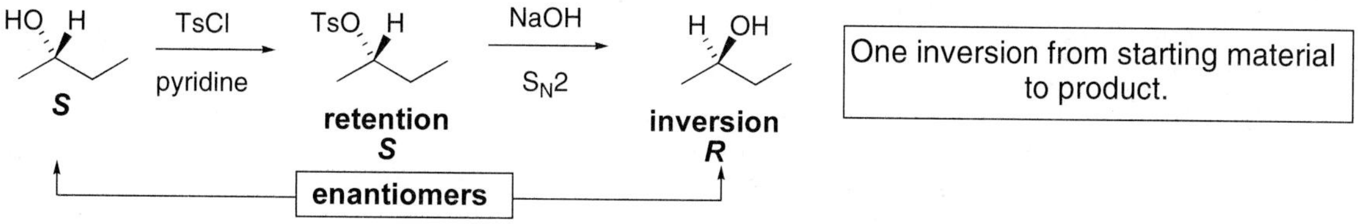

9.29 These reagents can be classified as:

[1] $SOCl_2$, PBr_3, HCl, and HBr replace OH with X by a substitution reaction.

[2] Tosyl chloride (TsCl) makes OH a better leaving group by converting it to OTs.

[3] Strong acids (H_2SO_4) and $POCl_3$ (pyridine) result in elimination by dehydration.

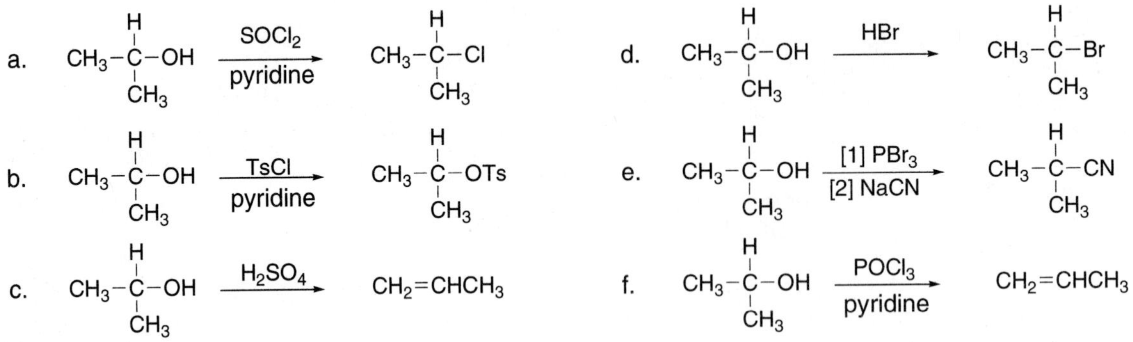
a.
SOCl2
pyridine
b.
TsCl
pyridine
c.
H2SO4
CH2=CHCH3
d.
HBr
e.
[1] PBr3
[2] NaCN
f.
POCl3
pyridine
CH2=CHCH3

9.30

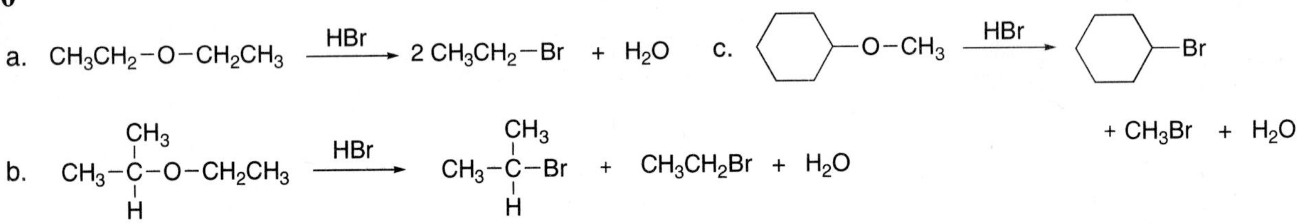
a. CH3CH2–O–CH2CH3
HBr
2 CH3CH2–Br + H2O
c.
HBr
+ CH3Br + H2O
b.
HBr
+ CH3CH2Br + H2O

9.31 Ether cleavage can occur by either an S_N1 or S_N2 mechanism, but neither mechanism can occur when the ether O atom is bonded to an aromatic ring. An S_N1 reaction would require formation of a highly unstable carbocation on a benzene ring, a process that does not occur. An S_N2 reaction would require backside attack through the plane of the aromatic ring, which is also not possible. Thus, cleavage of the Ph–OCH_3 bond does not occur.

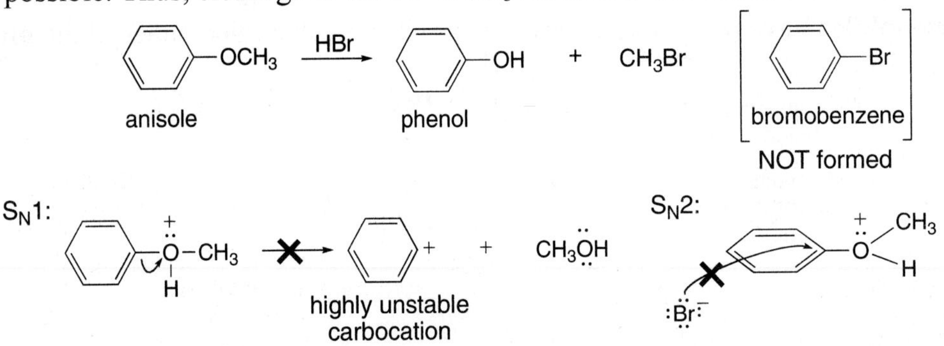
HBr
+ CH3Br
anisole
phenol
bromobenzene
NOT formed
SN1:
+
CH3OH
highly unstable
carbocation
SN2:

9.32 Two rules for reaction of an epoxide:

[1] Nucleophiles attack from the **back side** of the epoxide.

[2] Negatively charged nucleophiles attack at the **less substituted carbon.**

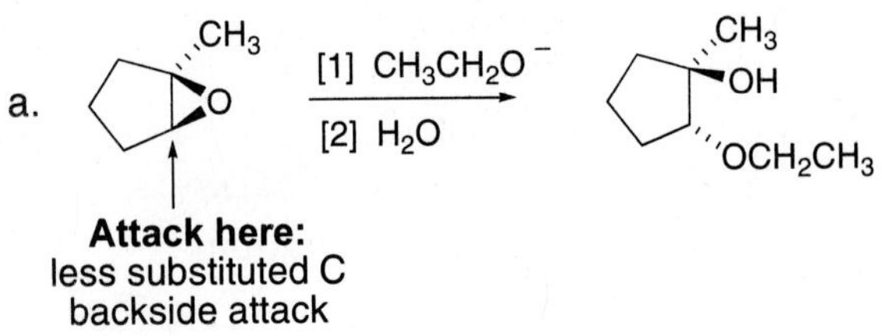
a.
[1] CH3CH2O−
[2] H2O
Attack here:
less substituted C
backside attack

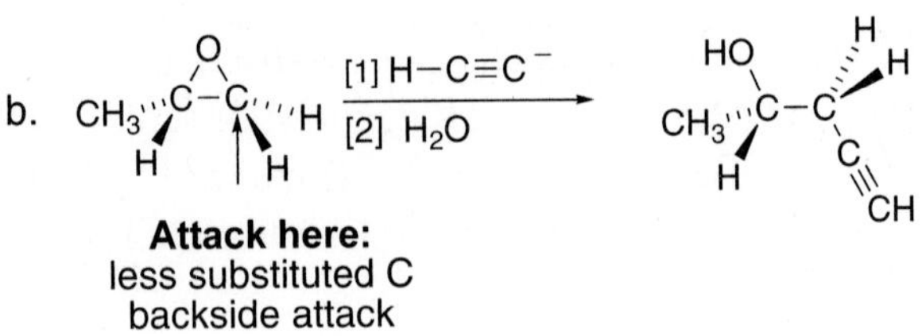
b.
[1] H–C≡C−
[2] H2O
Attack here:
less substituted C
backside attack

9.33 In both isomers, $^{-}$OH attacks from the back side at either C–O bond.

cis-2,3-dimethyloxirane

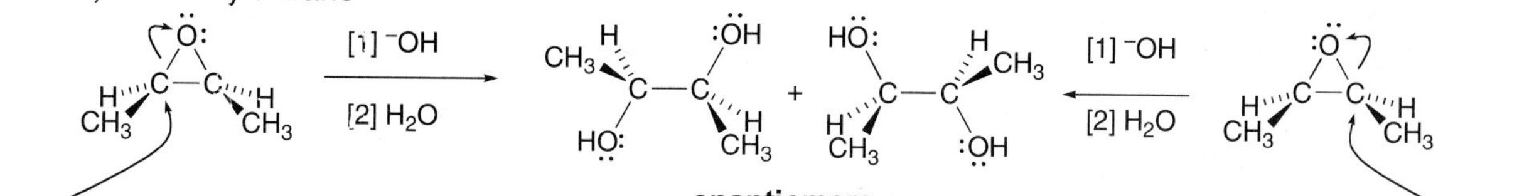

enantiomers

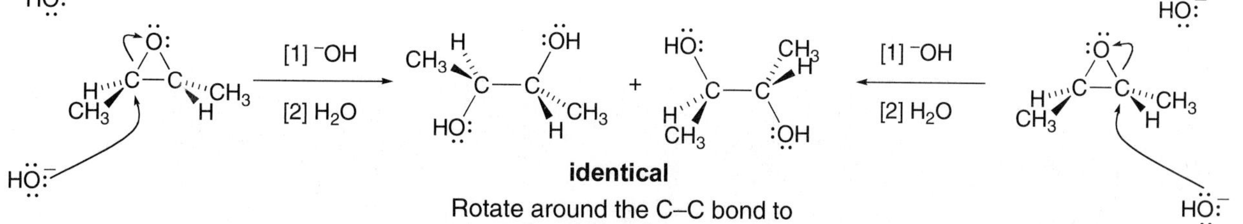

identical

Rotate around the C–C bond to see the plane of symmetry.

trans-2,3-dimethyloxirane

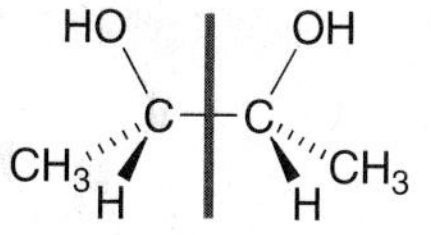

meso compound

9.34 Remember the difference between negatively charged nucleophiles and neutral nucleophiles:

- **Negatively charged nucleophiles attack first,** followed by protonation, and the nucleophile attacks at the **less substituted carbon.**
- **Neutral nucleophiles have protonation first,** followed by nucleophilic attack at the **more substituted carbon.**

But, trans or anti products are always formed regardless of the nucleophile.

a.

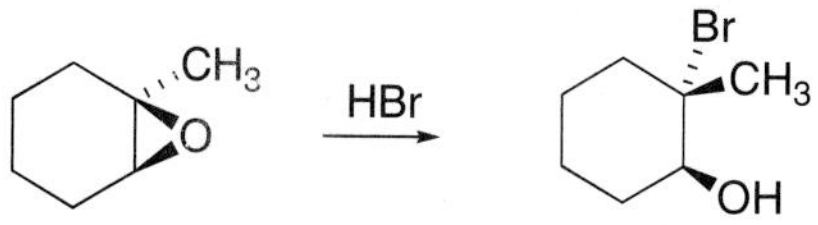

neutral nucleophile: attack at **more** substituted C

c.

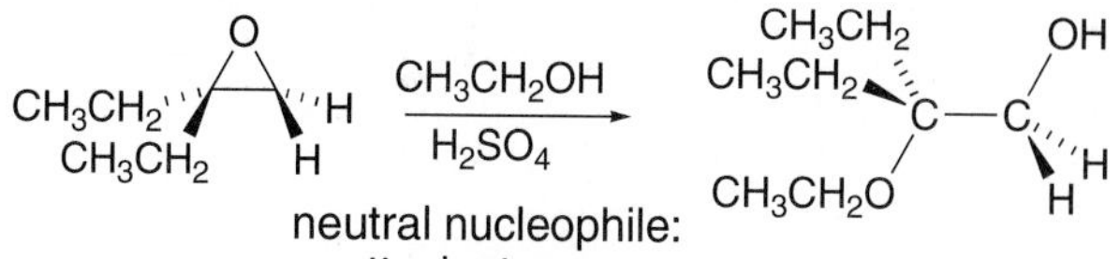

neutral nucleophile: attack at **more** substituted C

b.

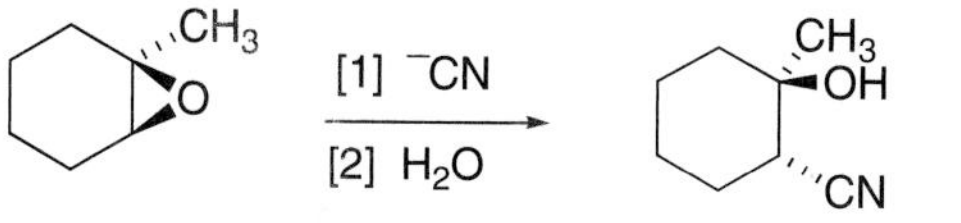

negatively charged nucleophile: attack at **less** substituted C

d.

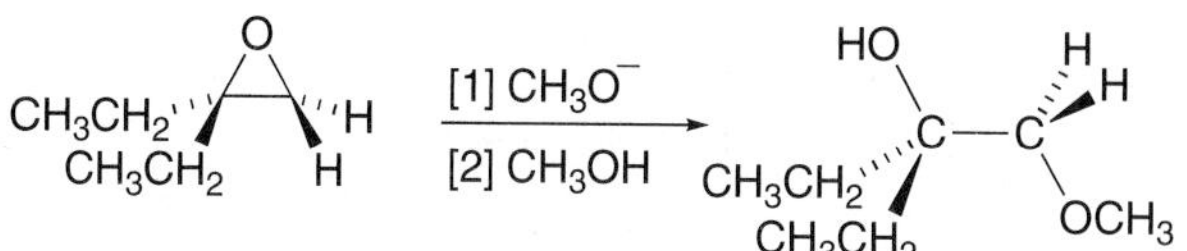

negatively charged nucleophile: attack at **less** substituted C

9.35

a.
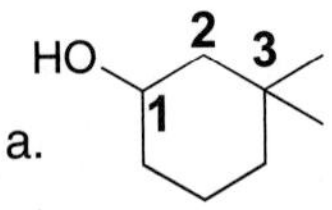

6 C ring ⟶ cyclohexanol
2 CH_3's at C3
3,3-dimethylcyclohexanol

c.
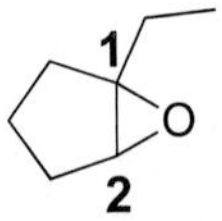

1,2-epoxy-1-ethylcyclopentane
or
1-ethylcyclopentene oxide

b.
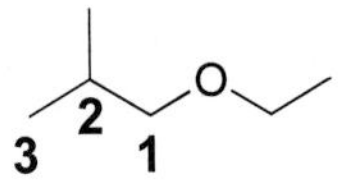

ethyl isobutyl ether
or
1-ethoxy-2-methylpropane

9.36

a. (1*R*,2*R*)-2-isobutylcyclopentanol

b. 2° alcohol

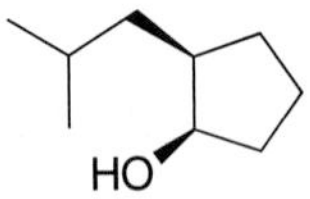

A

c. stereoisomer

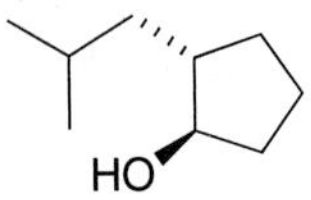

(1*R*,2*S*)-2-isobutylcyclopentanol

d. constitutional isomer

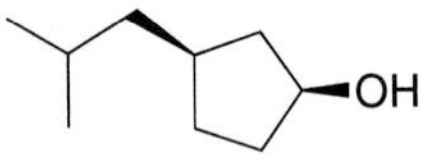

(1*S*,3*S*)-3-isobutylcyclopentanol

e. constitutional isomer with an ether

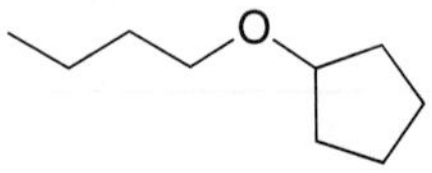

butoxycyclopentane

f.

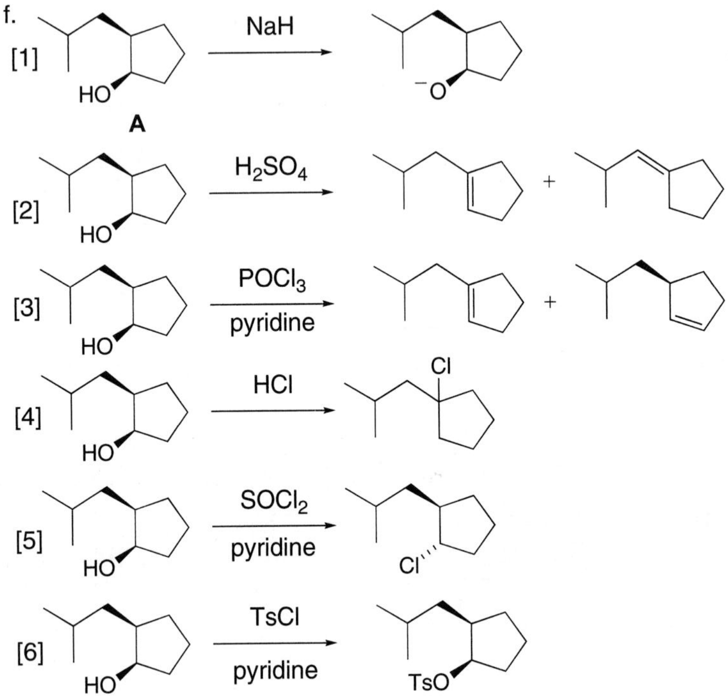

9.37

a.
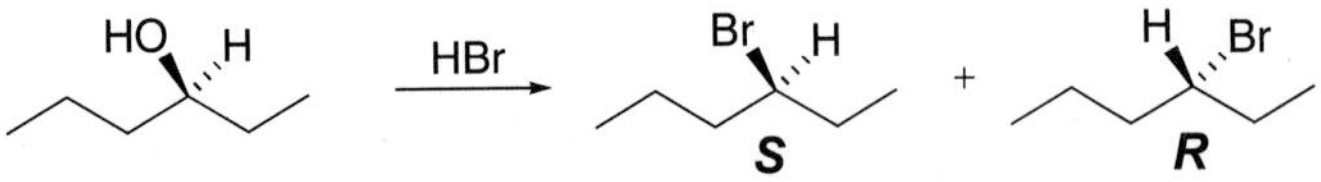

2° alcohol
S_N1 = racemization

b.
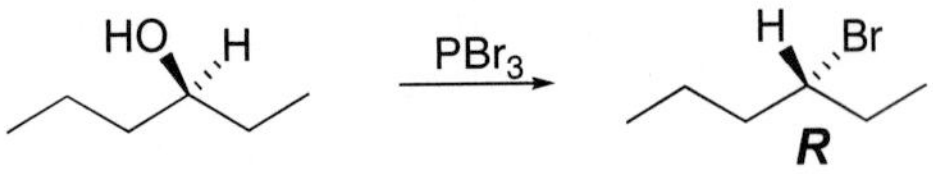

PBr_3 follows
S_N2 = inversion.

c.
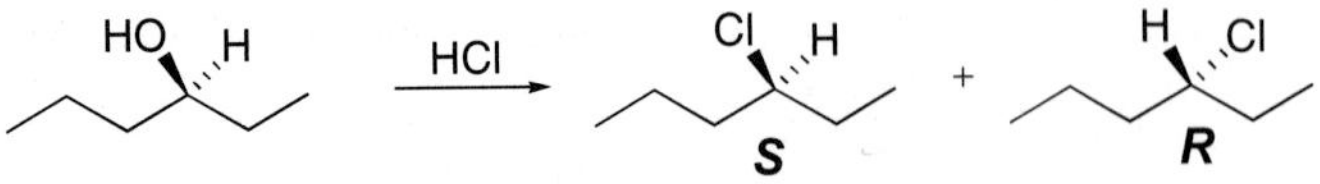

2° alcohol
S_N1 = racemization

d. 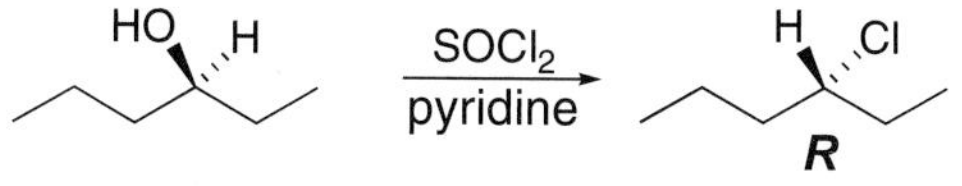
HO
H
$SOCl_2$
pyridine
H
Cl
R

$SOCl_2$ follows **S_N2 = inversion.**

9.38 Draw the structure of each alcohol, using the definitions in Answer 9.1.

a. 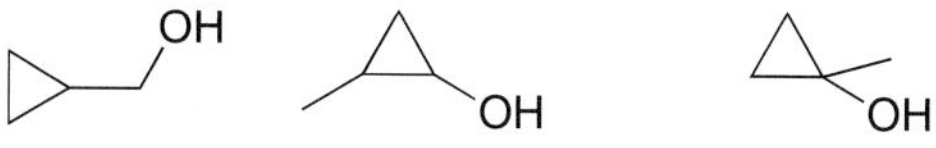
OH
OH
OH

1° 2° 3°

b. 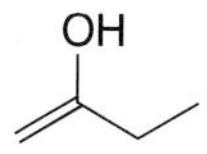
OH

enol

9.39 Use the directions from Answer 9.3.

a. $(CH_3)_2CHCH_2CH_2CH_2OH$

[1] 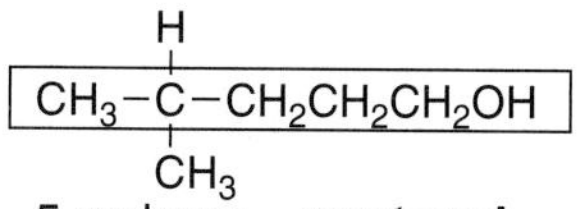
H
CH3–C–CH2CH2CH2OH
CH3

5 carbons = **pentanol**

[2] 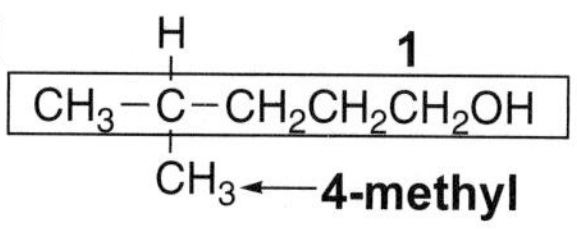
H
1
CH3–C–CH2CH2CH2OH
CH3
4-methyl

[3] **4-methyl-1-pentanol**

b. $(CH_3)_2CHCH_2CH(CH_2CH_3)CH(OH)CH_2CH_3$

[1] 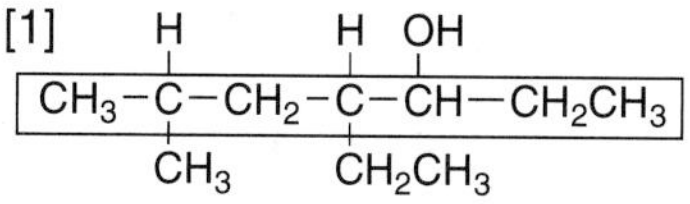
H
H OH
CH3–C–CH2–C–CH–CH2CH3
CH3
CH2CH3

7 carbons = **heptanol**

[2] 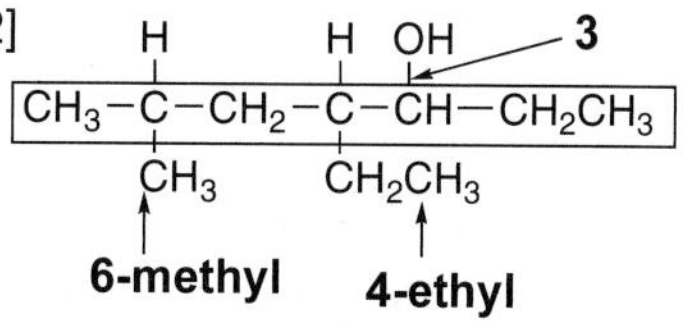
H
H OH
3
CH3–C–CH2–C–CH–CH2CH3
CH3
CH2CH3
6-methyl
4-ethyl

[3] **4-ethyl-6-methyl-3-heptanol**

c.

[1] 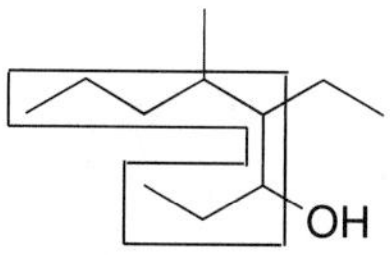
OH

8 carbons = **octanol**

[2] 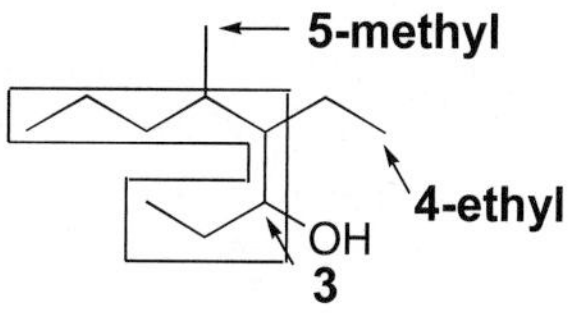
5-methyl
4-ethyl
OH
3

[3] **4-ethyl-5-methyl-3-octanol**

d.

[1] 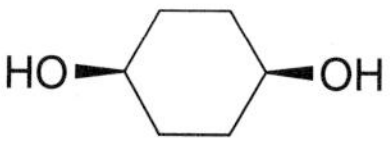
HO
OH

cyclohexanediol

[2] 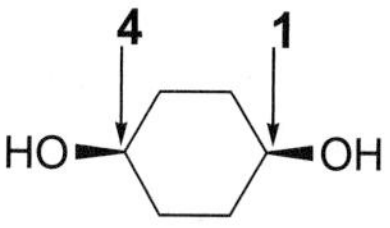
4
1
HO
OH

cis

[3] ***cis*-1,4-cyclohexanediol**

e.

[1] 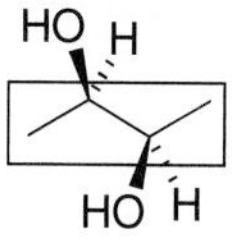
HO H
HO H

4 carbons = **butanediol**

[2] 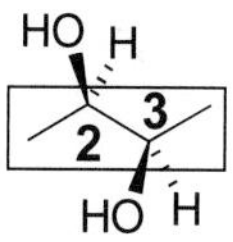
HO H
3
2
HO H

2*R*,3*R*

[3] **(2*R*,3*R*)-2,3-butanediol**

f.

[1] 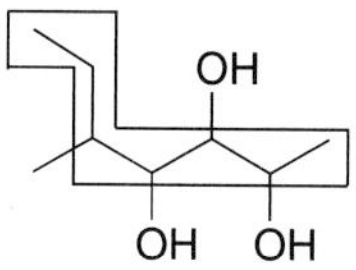
OH
OH OH

7 carbons = **heptanetriol**

[2] 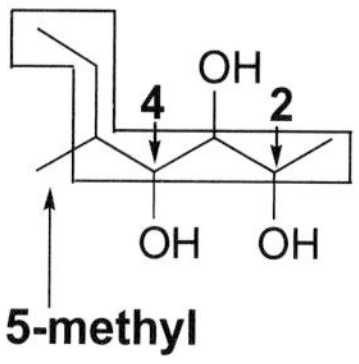
OH
4
2
OH OH
5-methyl

[3] **5-methyl-2,3,4-heptanetriol**

g.

[1] 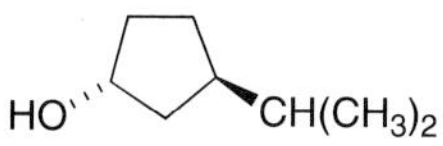
HO
CH(CH3)2

5 carbons = **cyclopentanol**

[2] 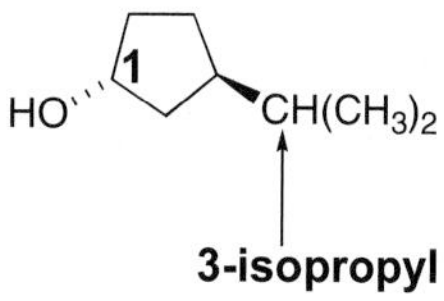
1
HO
CH(CH3)2
3-isopropyl

[3] ***trans*-3-isopropylcyclopentanol**

9.40 Use the rules from Answers 9.5 and 9.7.

a. 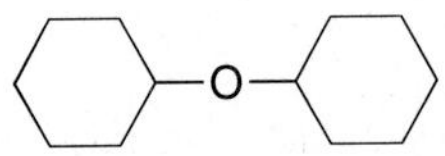
O

dicyclohexyl ether

b. 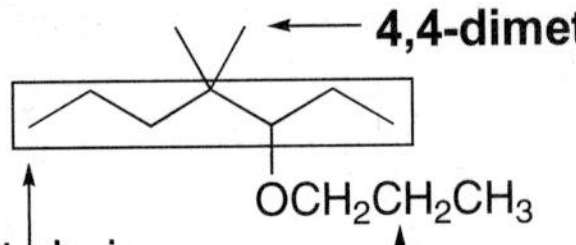
4,4-dimethyl
OCH2CH2CH3

longest chain = **heptane**

substituent = **3-propoxy**

4,4-dimethyl-3-propoxyheptane

c. 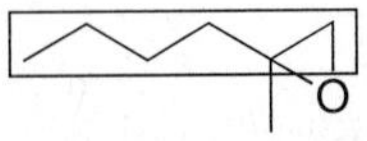
O

1,2-epoxy-2-methylhexane
or **2-butyl-2-methyloxirane**
or **2-methylhexene oxide**

d. 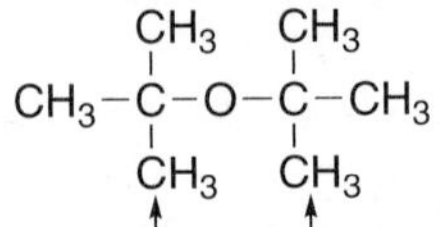
CH3 CH3
CH3–C–O–C–CH3
CH3 CH3

***tert*-butyl** ***tert*-butyl**
di-*tert*-butyl ether

9.41 Use the directions from Answer 9.4.

a. 4-ethyl-3-**heptanol** 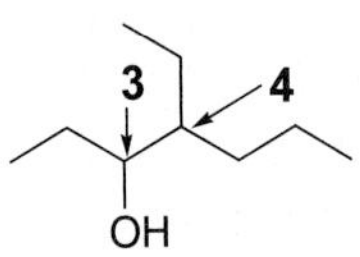
3
4
OH

b. *trans*-2-methyl**cyclohexanol** 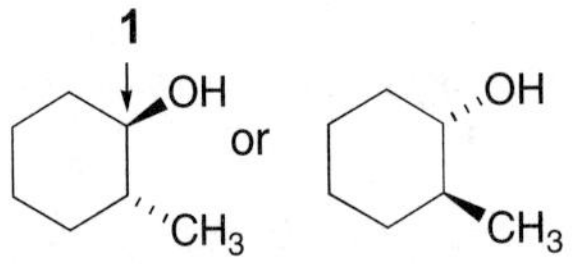
1
OH
or
CH3
OH
CH3

c. 2,3,3-trimethyl-2-**butanol** 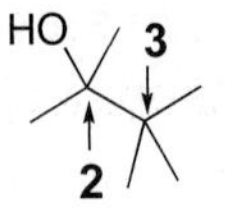
HO
3
2

d. 6-*sec*-butyl-7,7-diethyl-4-**decanol** 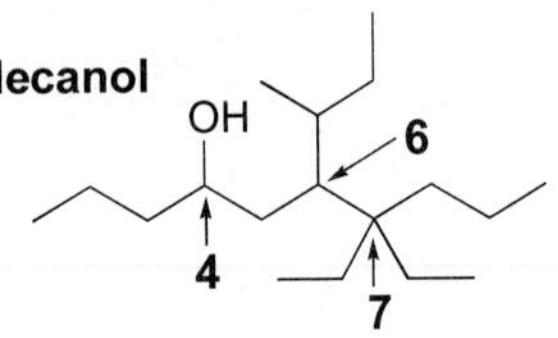
OH
6
4
7

e. 3-chloro-1,2-**propanediol** 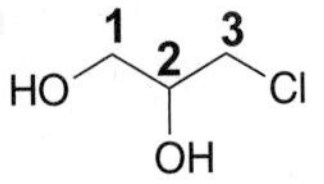
1
2
3
HO
Cl
OH

f. diisobutyl ether 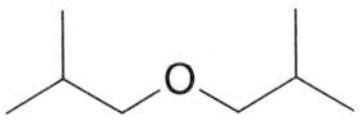
O

g. 1,2-epoxy-1,3,3-trimethyl**cyclohexane** 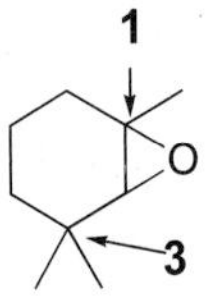
1
O
3

h. 1-ethoxy-3-ethyl**heptane** 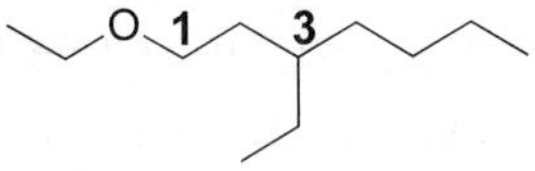
O
1
3

i. (2*R*,3*S*)-3-isopropyl-2-**hexanol** 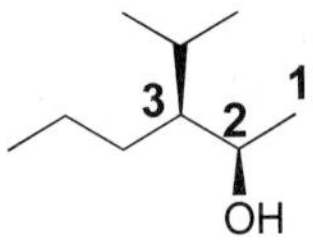
3
2
1
OH

j. (2*S*)-2-ethoxy-1,1-dimethyl**cyclopentane** 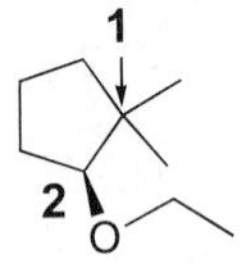
1
2
O

9.42

Eight constitutional isomers of molecular formula $C_5H_{12}O$ containing an OH group:

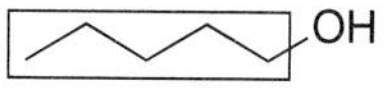

1-pentanol
1° alcohol

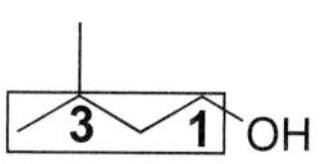

3-methyl-1-butanol
1° alcohol

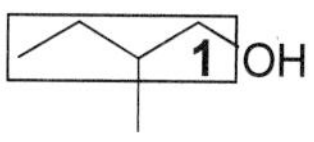

2-methyl-1-butanol
1° alcohol

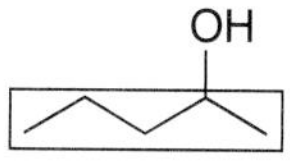

2-pentanol
2° alcohol

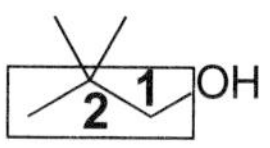

2,2-dimethyl-1-propanol
1° alcohol

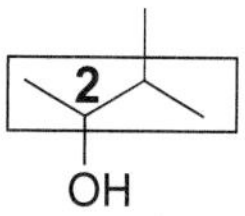

3-methyl-2-butanol
2° alcohol

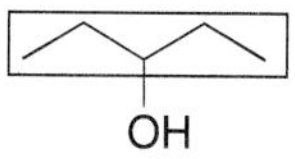

3-pentanol
2° alcohol

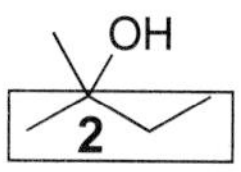

2-methyl-2-butanol
3° alcohol

9.43 Use the boiling point rules from Answer 9.8.

a.

$CH_3CH_2OCH_3$	$(CH_3)_2CHOH$	$CH_3CH_2CH_2OH$
↑	↑	↑
ether	2° alcohol	1° alcohol
no hydrogen bonding	hydrogen bonding	hydrogen bonding
lowest bp	**intermediate bp**	**highest bp**

b.

$CH_3CH_2CH_2CH_2CH_2CH_3$	$CH_3CH_2CH_2CH_2CH_2CH_2OH$	$HOCH_2CH_2CH_2CH_2CH_2CH_2OH$
no OH group	one OH group	two OH groups
lowest water solubility	**intermediate water solubility**	**highest water solubility**

9.44 Melting points depend on intermolecular forces and symmetry. $(CH_3)_2CHCH_2OH$ has a lower melting point than $CH_3CH_2CH_2CH_2OH$ because branching decreases surface area and makes $(CH_3)_2CHCH_2OH$ less symmetrical so it packs less well. Although $(CH_3)_3COH$ has the most branching and least surface area, it is the most symmetrical, so it packs best in a crystalline lattice, giving it the highest melting point.

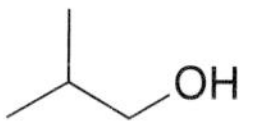

–108 °C
lowest melting point

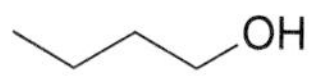

–90 °C
intermediate melting point

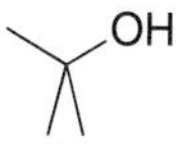

26 °C
highest melting point

9.45 Stronger intermolecular forces increase boiling point. All of the compounds can hydrogen bond, but both diols have more opportunity for hydrogen bonding since they have two OH groups, making their bp's higher than the bp of 1-butanol. 1,2-Propanediol can also intramolecularly hydrogen bond. Intramolecular hydrogen bonding decreases the amount of intermolecular hydrogen bonding, so the bp of 1,2-propanediol is somewhat lower.

Increasing boiling point →

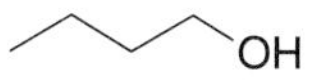

1-butanol
118 °C

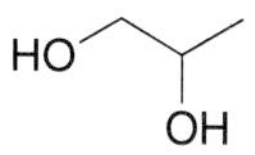

1,2-propanediol
187 °C

1,3-propanediol
215 °C

9.46

a. $CH_3CH_2CH_2OH \xrightarrow{H_2SO_4} CH_3CH{=}CH_2 + H_2O$

b. $CH_3CH_2CH_2OH \xrightarrow{NaH} CH_3CH_2CH_2O^- \; Na^+ + H_2$

c. $CH_3CH_2CH_2OH \xrightarrow[ZnCl_2]{HCl} CH_3CH_2CH_2Cl + H_2O$

d. $CH_3CH_2CH_2OH \xrightarrow{HBr} CH_3CH_2CH_2Br + H_2O$

e. $CH_3CH_2CH_2OH \xrightarrow[pyridine]{SOCl_2} CH_3CH_2CH_2Cl$

f. $CH_3CH_2CH_2OH \xrightarrow{PBr_3} CH_3CH_2CH_2Br$

g. $CH_3CH_2CH_2OH \xrightarrow[pyridine]{TsCl} CH_3CH_2CH_2OTs$

h. $CH_3CH_2CH_2OH \xrightarrow{[1]\ NaH} CH_3CH_2CH_2O^- \; Na^+ \xrightarrow{[2]\ CH_3CH_2Br} CH_3CH_2CH_2OCH_2CH_3$

i. $CH_3CH_2CH_2OH \xrightarrow{[1]\ TsCl} CH_3CH_2CH_2OTs \xrightarrow{[2]\ NaSH} CH_3CH_2CH_2SH$

9.47

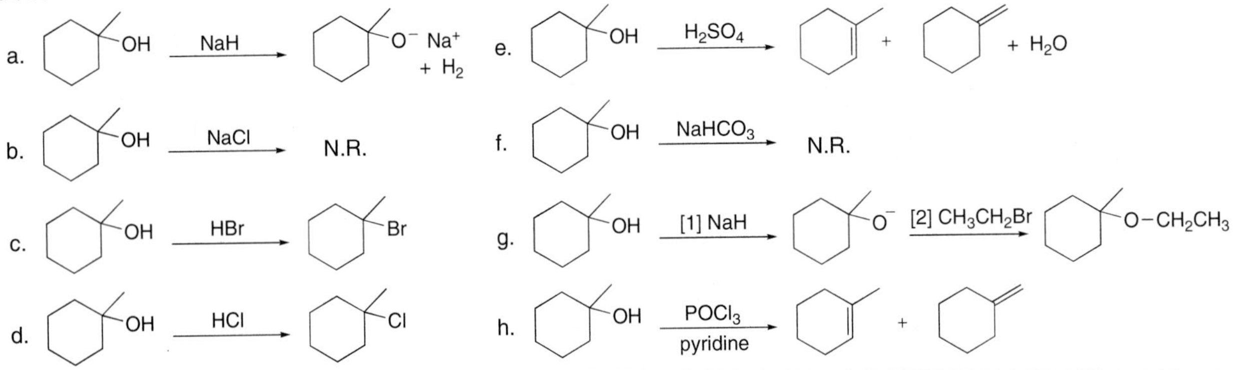

9.48 Dehydration follows the Zaitsev rule, so the more stable, more substituted alkene is the major product.

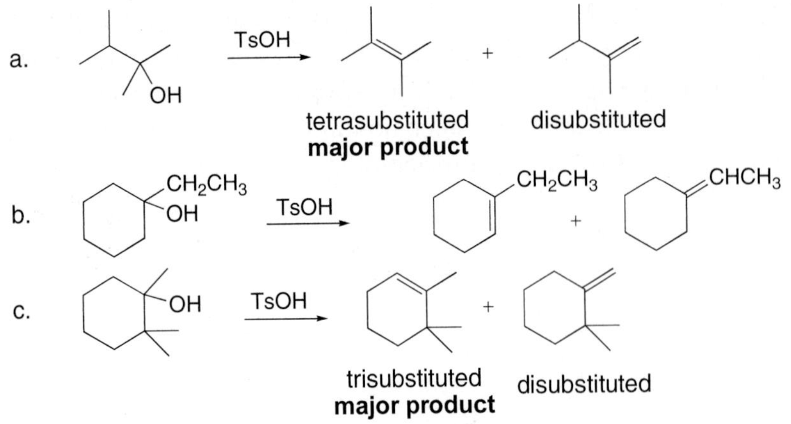

d. $CH_3CH_2CH_2CH_2OH \xrightarrow{\text{TsOH}} CH_3CH_2CH{=}CH_2$

e.

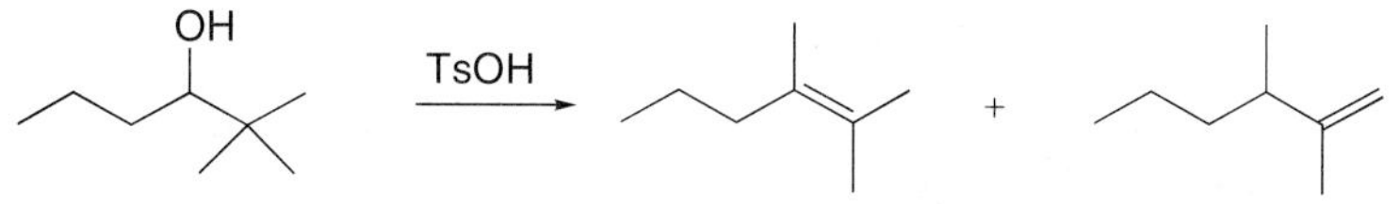

tetrasubstituted
major product

disubstituted

Two products formed
by carbocation rearrangement

9.49 The most stable alkene is the major product.

trans and disubstituted
major product

monosubstituted

cis and disubstituted

9.50 OTs is a good leaving group and will easily be replaced by a nucleophile. Draw the products by substituting the nucleophile in the reagent for OTs in the starting material.

a. $CH_3CH_2CH_2CH_2{-}OTs \xrightarrow[\mathbf{S_N2}]{CH_3SH} CH_3CH_2CH_2CH_2{-}SCH_3 + HOTs$

b. $CH_3CH_2CH_2CH_2{-}OTs \xrightarrow[\mathbf{S_N2}]{NaOCH_2CH_3} CH_3CH_2CH_2CH_2{-}OCH_2CH_3 + Na^+ \ {}^-OTs$

c. $CH_3CH_2CH_2CH_2{-}OTs \xrightarrow[\mathbf{S_N2}]{NaOH} CH_3CH_2CH_2CH_2{-}OH + Na^+ \ {}^-OTs$

d. $CH_3CH_2CH_2CH_2{-}OTs \xrightarrow[\mathbf{E2}]{K^+ \ {}^-OC(CH_3)_3} CH_3CH_2CH{=}CH_2 + (CH_3)_3COH + K^+ \ {}^-OTs$

9.51

a.

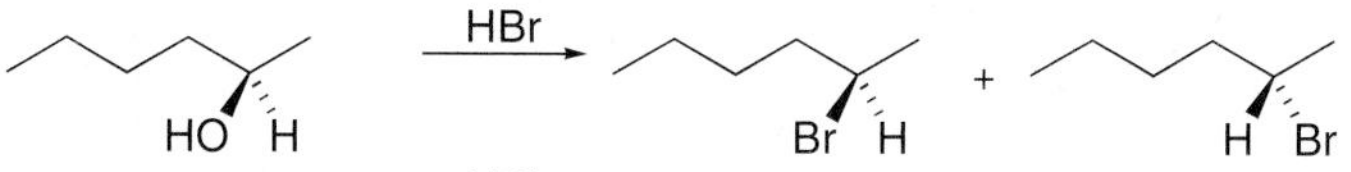

2° Alcohol will undergo S_N1.
racemization

b.

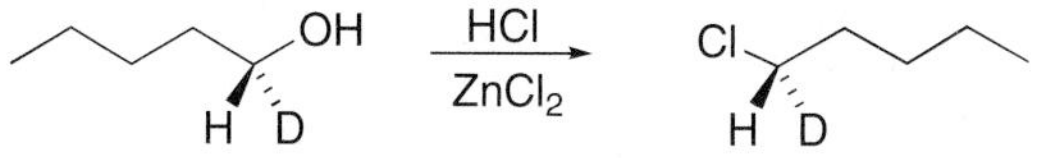

1° Alcohol will undergo S_N2.
inversion

c.

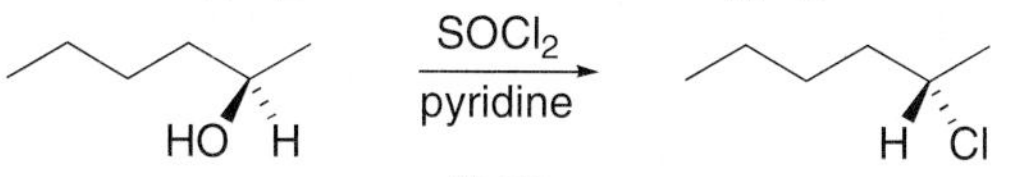

$SOCl_2$ always implies S_N2.
inversion

d.

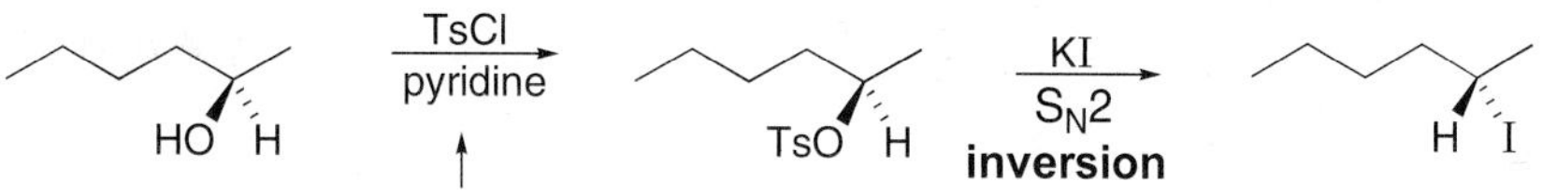

inversion

Configuration is maintained.
C–O bond is not broken.

9.52

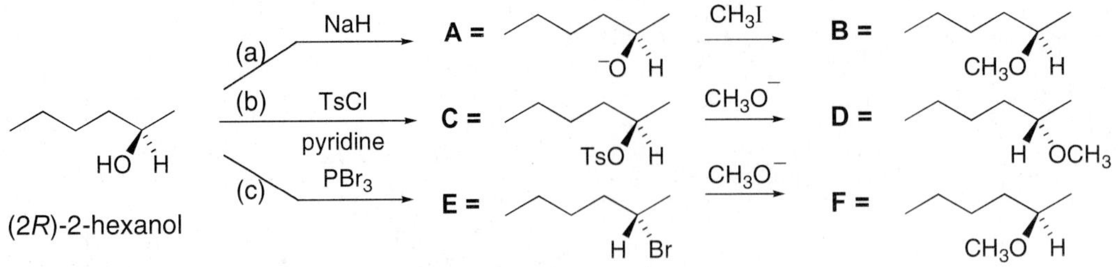

Routes (a) and (c) given identical products, labeled **B** and **F**.

9.53 Acid-catalyzed dehydration follows an E1 mechanism for 2° and 3° ROH with an added step to make a good leaving group. The three steps are:

[1] Protonate the oxygen to make a good leaving group.
[2] Break the C–O bond to form a carbocation.
[3] Remove a β hydrogen to form the π bond.

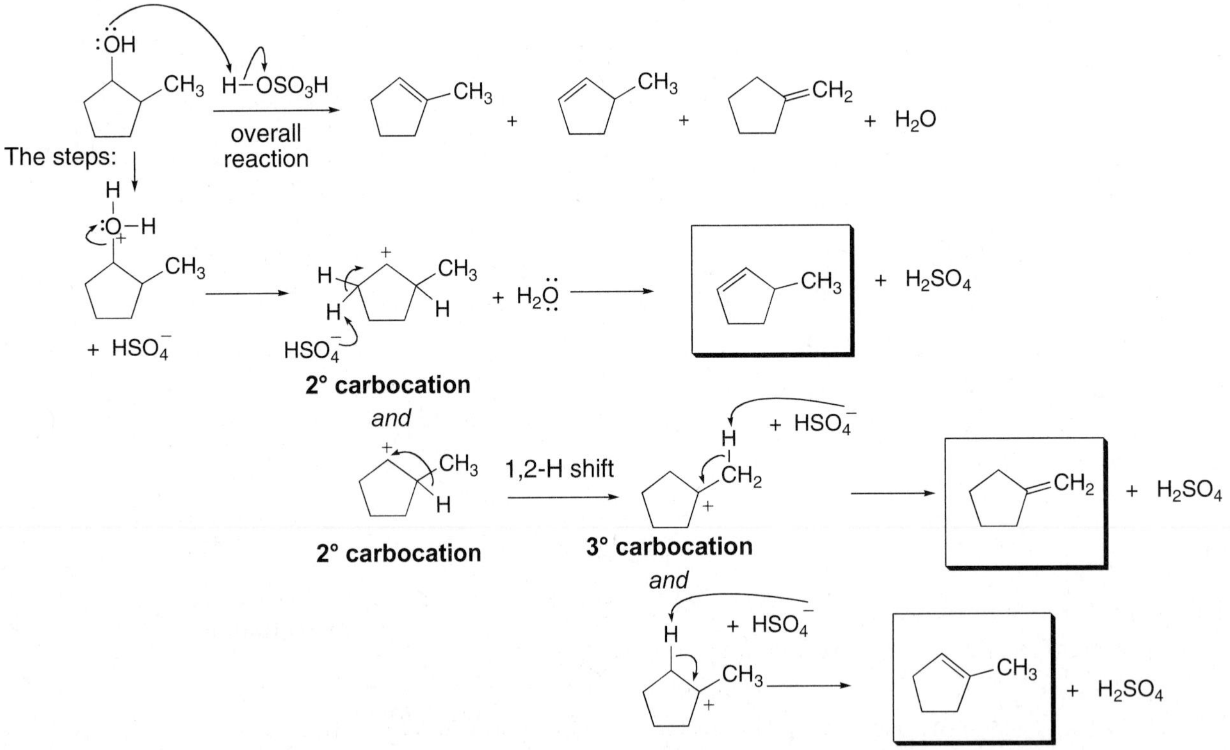

9.54 With $POCl_3$ (pyridine), elimination occurs by an E2 mechanism. Since only one carbon has a β hydrogen, only one product is formed. With H_2SO_4, the mechanism of elimination is E1. A 2° carbocation rearranges to a 3° carbocation, which has three pathways for elimination.

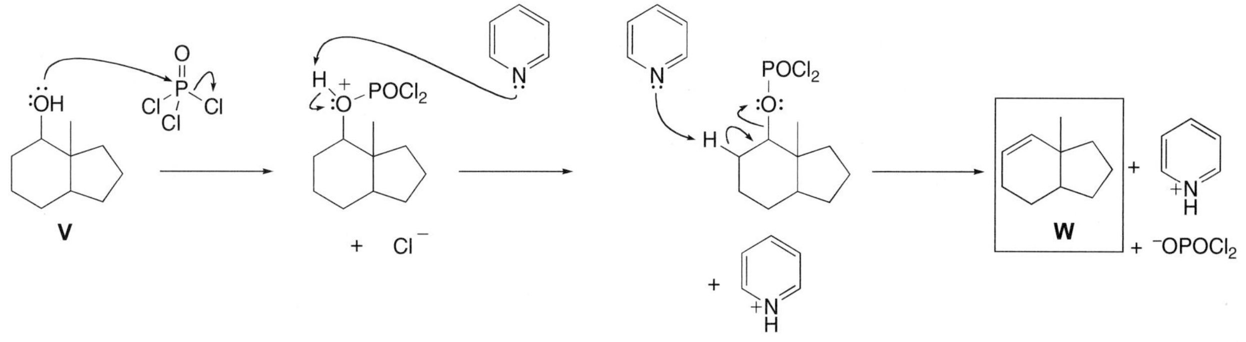

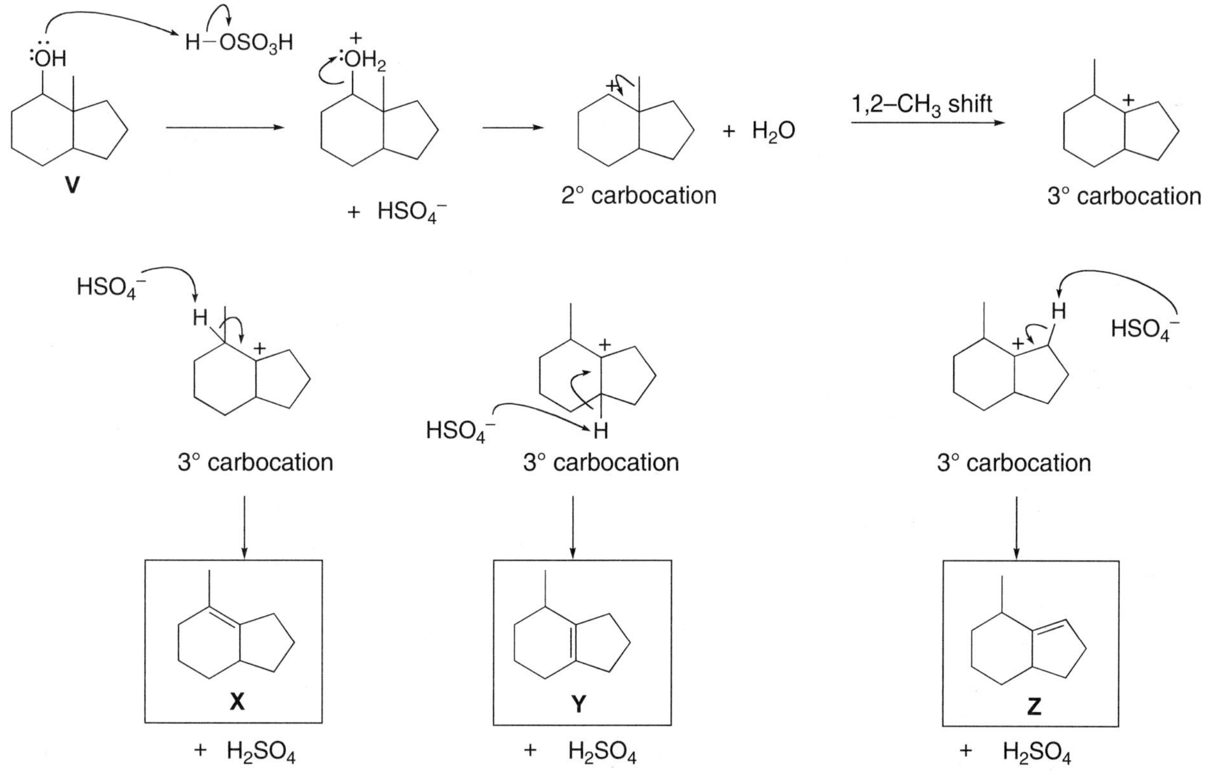

9.55 To draw the mechanism:

[1] Protonate the oxygen to make a good leaving group.
[2] Break the C–O bond to form a carbocation.
[3] Look for possible rearrangements to make a more stable carbocation.
[4] Remove a β hydrogen to form the π bond.

Dark and light circles are meant to show where the carbons in the starting material appear in the product.

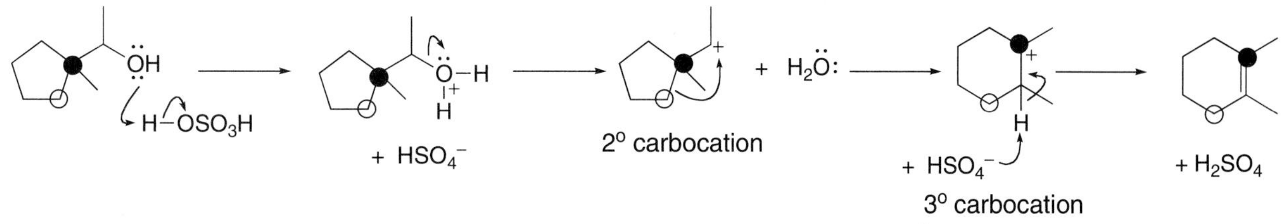

9.56

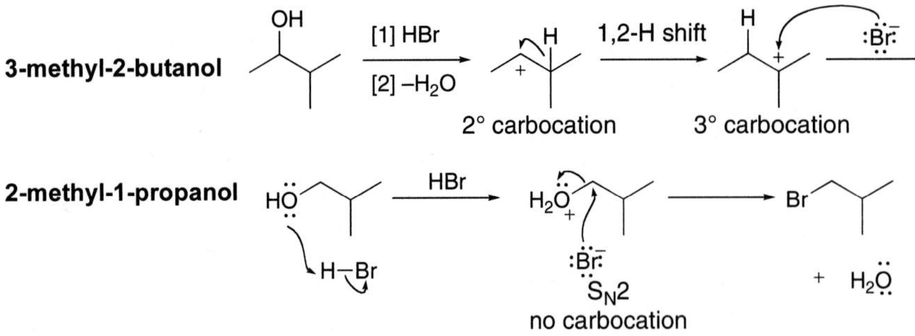
3-methyl-2-butanol
OH
[1] HBr
[2] –H2O
2° carbocation
1,2-H shift
3° carbocation
:Br:⁻
Br
2-methyl-1-propanol
HBr
H–Br
H2O
:Br:⁻
SN2
no carbocation
Br
+ H2O

The 2° alcohol reacts by an S_N1 mechanism to form a carbocation that rearranges.

The 1° alcohol reacts with HBr by an S_N2 mechanism.
no carbocation intermediate = no rearrangement possible

9.57

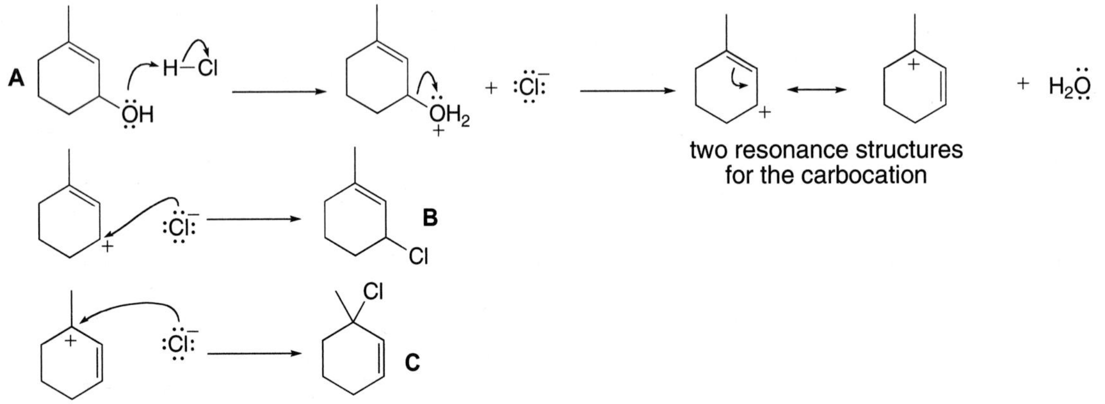
A
H–Cl
OH
OH2
+ :Cl:⁻
+ H2O
two resonance structures for the carbocation
:Cl:⁻
B
Cl
C

9.58

$$CH_3CH_2CH_2CH_2OH \xrightarrow[\text{overall reaction}]{H_2SO_4,\ NaBr} CH_3CH_2CH_2CH_2Br + CH_3CH_2CH{=}CH_2 + CH_3CH_2CH_2CH_2OCH_2CH_2CH_2CH_3$$

Step [1] for all products: Formation of a good leaving group

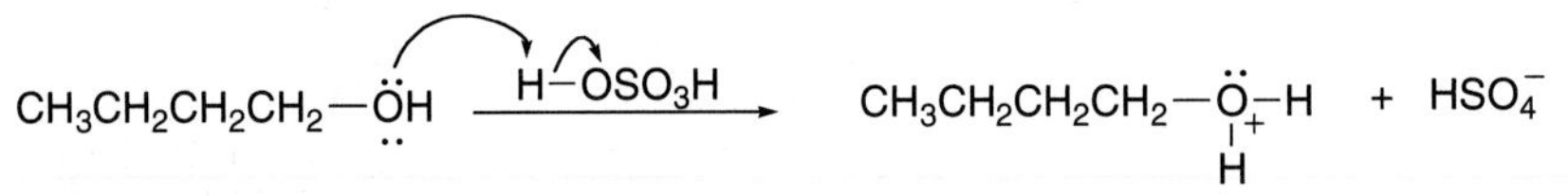
CH3CH2CH2CH2—OH
H–OSO3H
CH3CH2CH2CH2—O–H
H
+ HSO4⁻

Formation of $CH_3CH_2CH_2CH_2Br$:

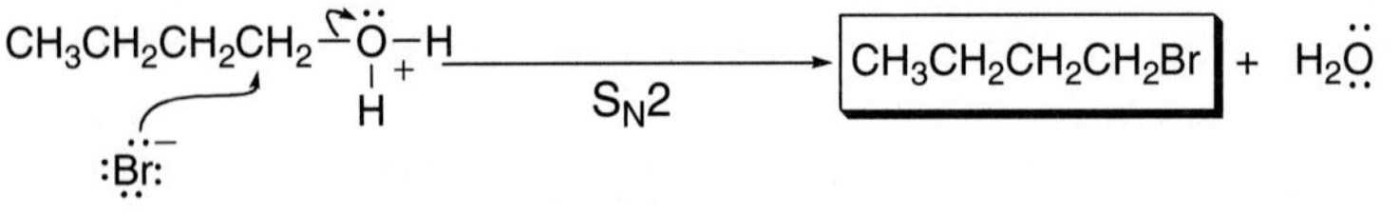
CH3CH2CH2CH2–O–H
H
:Br:⁻
SN2
CH3CH2CH2CH2Br
+ H2O

Formation of $CH_3CH_2CH{=}CH_2$:

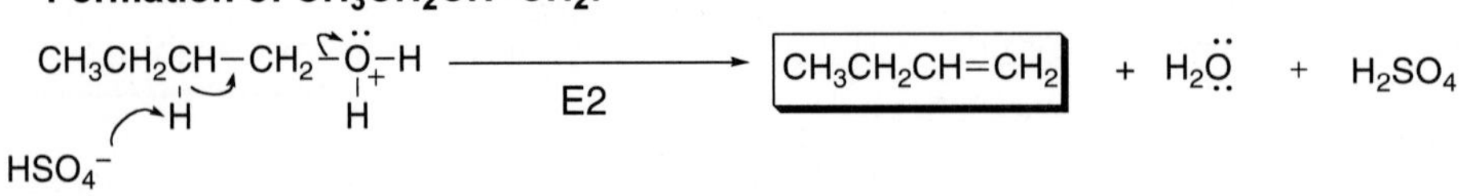
CH3CH2CH–CH2–O–H
H
H
HSO4⁻
E2
CH3CH2CH=CH2
+ H2O
+ H2SO4

Ether formation (from the protonated alcohol):

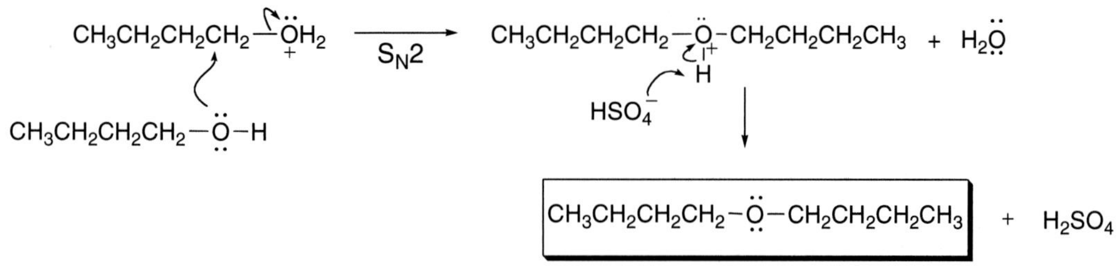

CH3CH2CH2CH2–OH2 +
CH3CH2CH2CH2–O–H
SN2
CH3CH2CH2CH2–O–CH2CH2CH2CH3 + H2O
H
HSO4−
CH3CH2CH2CH2–O–CH2CH2CH2CH3
+ H2SO4

9.59

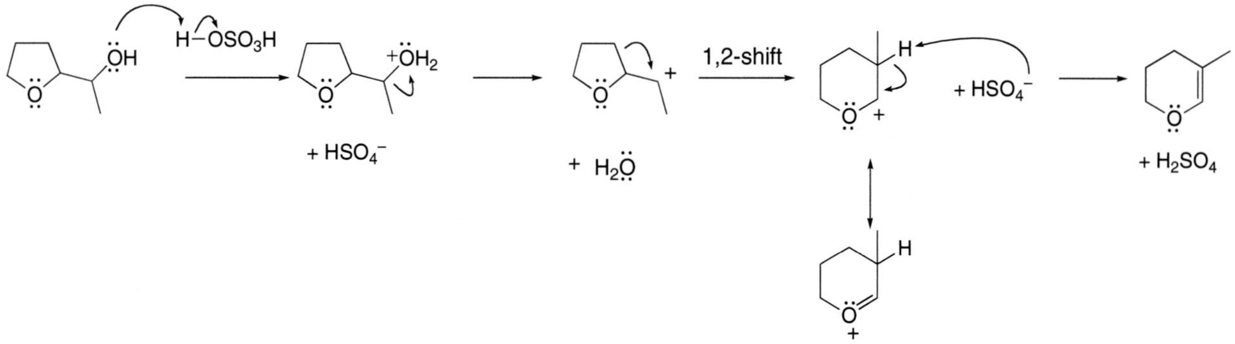

OH
H–OSO3H
O
+OH2
+ HSO4−
+ H2O
1,2-shift
H
+ HSO4−
+ H2SO4

9.60

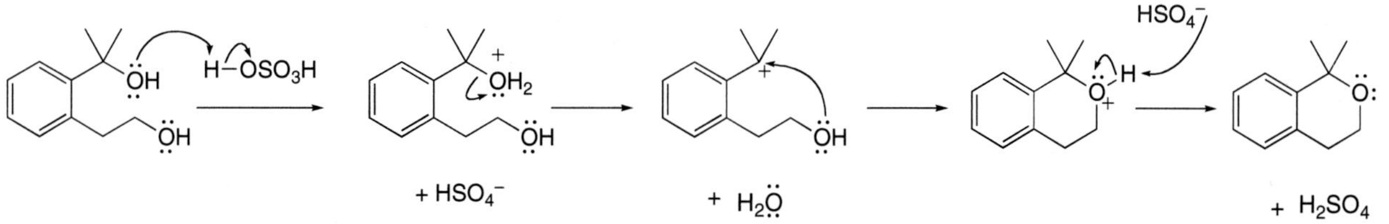

OH
H–OSO3H
OH
+ OH2
+ HSO4−
+ H2O
HSO4−
H
O
+ H2SO4

9.61

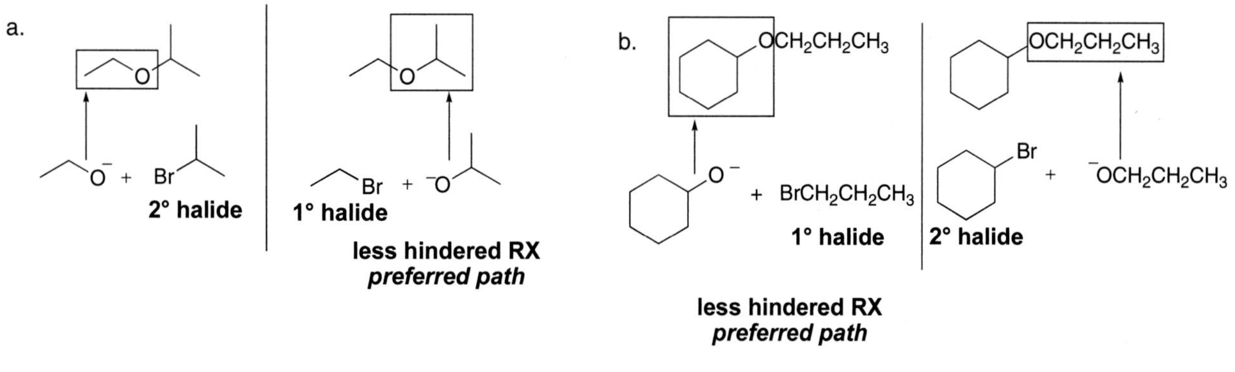

a.
O
O− + Br
2° halide
Br + −O
1° halide
less hindered RX
preferred path
b.
OCH2CH2CH3
O−
+ BrCH2CH2CH3
1° halide
OCH2CH2CH3
Br
+ −OCH2CH2CH3
2° halide
less hindered RX
preferred path

c.

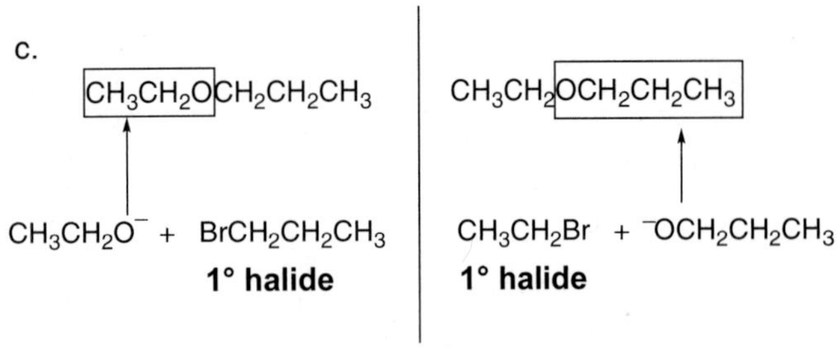
CH3CH2OCH2CH2CH3
CH3CH2OCH2CH2CH3
CH3CH2O⁻ + BrCH2CH2CH3
1° halide
CH3CH2Br + ⁻OCH2CH2CH3
1° halide

Neither path preferred.

9.62 A tertiary halide is too hindered and an aryl halide too unreactive to undergo a Williamson ether synthesis.

Two possible sets of starting materials:

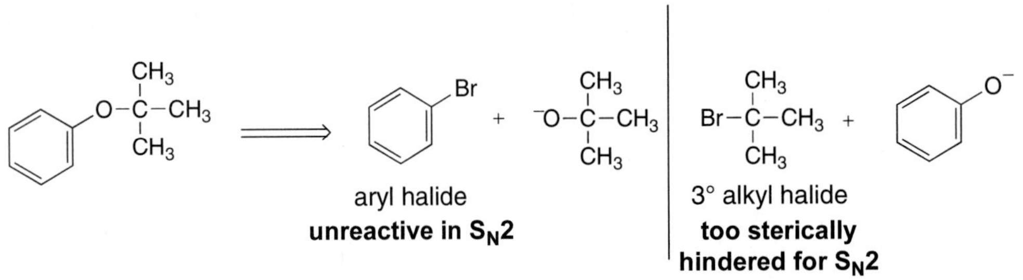
aryl halide
unreactive in SN2
3° alkyl halide
too sterically
hindered for SN2

9.63

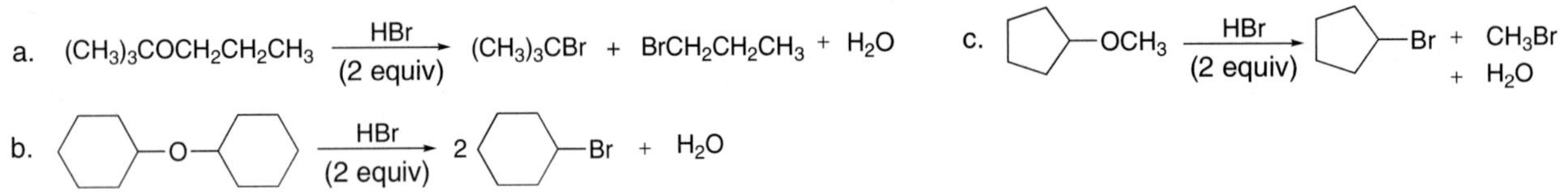
a. (CH3)3COCH2CH2CH3
HBr
(2 equiv)
(CH3)3CBr + BrCH2CH2CH3 + H2O
b.
HBr
(2 equiv)
2
c.
OCH3
HBr
(2 equiv)
Br + CH3Br
+ H2O

9.64

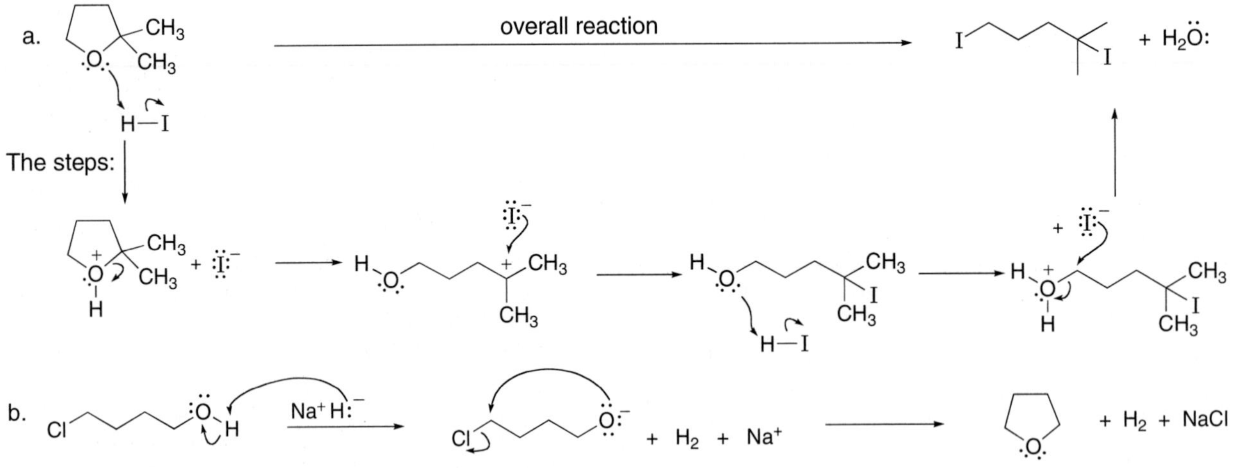
a.
overall reaction
+ H2O:
The steps:
b.
Na⁺ H:⁻
+ H2 + Na⁺
+ H2 + NaCl

9.65

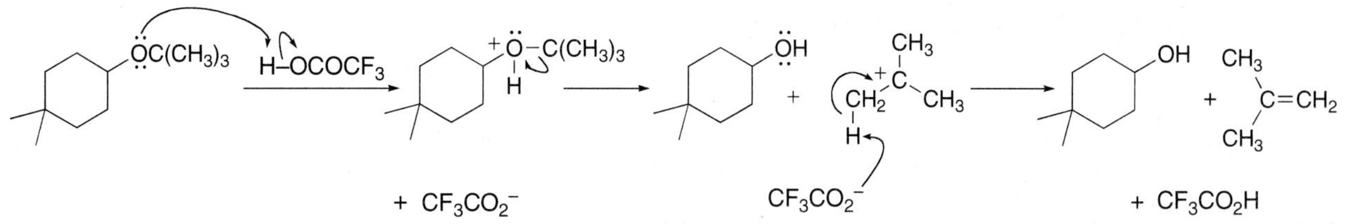
H–OCOCF₃
+ CF₃CO₂⁻
CF₃CO₂⁻
+ CF₃CO₂H

9.66

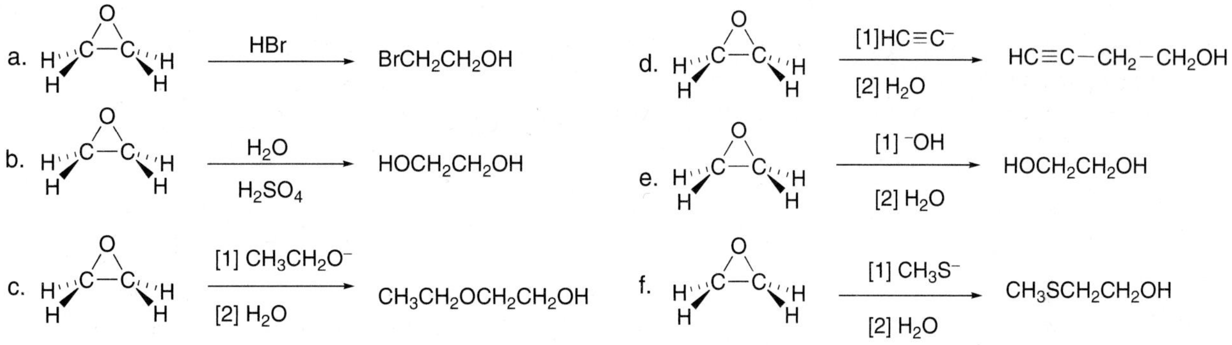
a.
HBr
BrCH₂CH₂OH
b.
H₂O
H₂SO₄
HOCH₂CH₂OH
c.
[1] CH₃CH₂O⁻
[2] H₂O
CH₃CH₂OCH₂CH₂OH
d.
[1]HC≡C⁻
[2] H₂O
HC≡C–CH₂–CH₂OH
e.
[1] ⁻OH
[2] H₂O
HOCH₂CH₂OH
f.
[1] CH₃S⁻
[2] H₂O
CH₃SCH₂CH₂OH

9.67

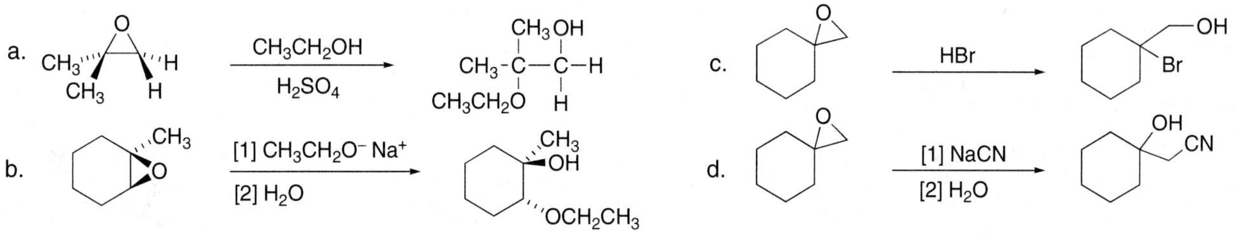
a.
CH₃CH₂OH
H₂SO₄
b.
[1] CH₃CH₂O⁻ Na⁺
[2] H₂O
c.
HBr
d.
[1] NaCN
[2] H₂O

9.68

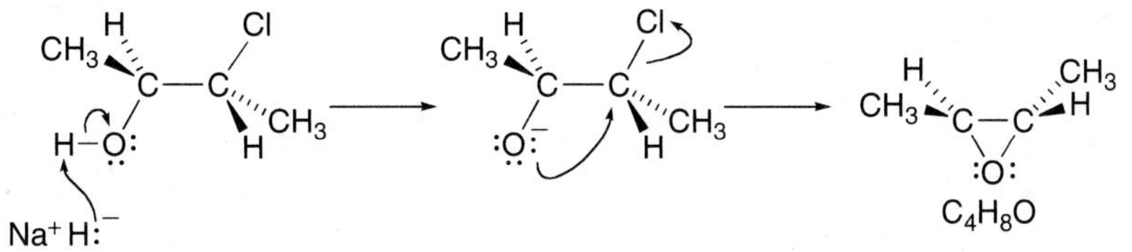
a.
Na⁺ H:⁻
C₄H₈O

The 2 CH_3 groups are anti in the starting material, making them trans in the product.

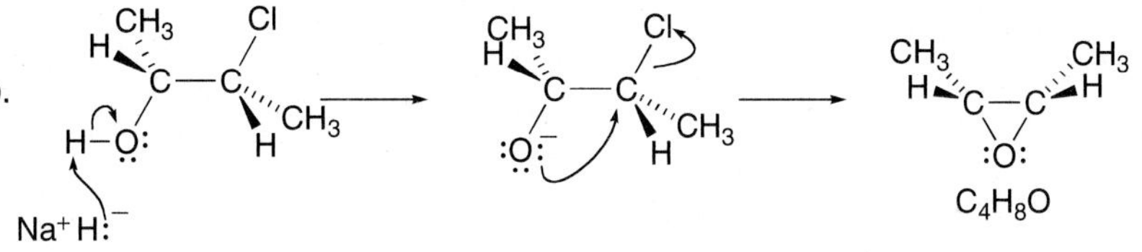
b.
Na⁺ H:⁻
C₄H₈O

The 2 CH_3 groups are gauche in the starting material, making them cis in the product.

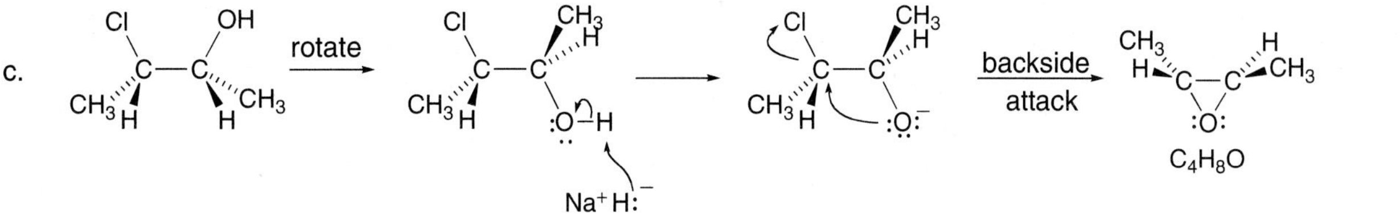
c.
rotate
Na⁺ H:⁻
backside
attack
C₄H₈O

9.69 First, use the names to draw the structures of the starting material and both products. Because the product has two OH groups, one OH must come from the epoxide oxygen, and one must come from the nucleophile, either ^{-}OH or H_2O.

With ^{-}OH, the nucleophile attacks at the less substituted end of the epoxide to form the *R* isomer of the product.

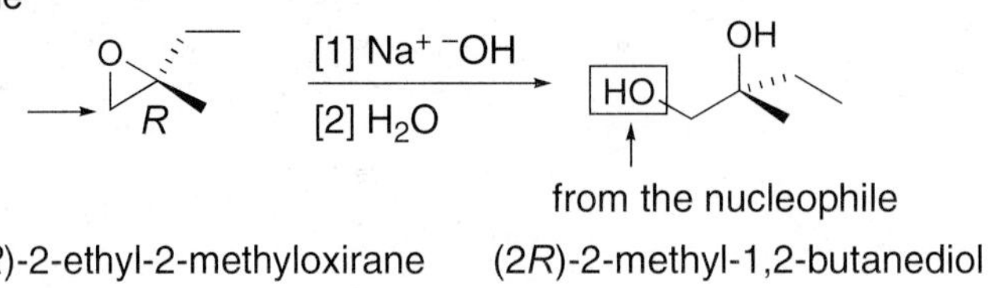
R
[1] Na+ −OH
[2] H2O
OH
HO
from the nucleophile
(2R)-2-ethyl-2-methyloxirane
(2R)-2-methyl-1,2-butanediol

With H_2O and H_2SO_4, H_2O attacks at the stereogenic center, from the back side, and the *S* isomer is formed.

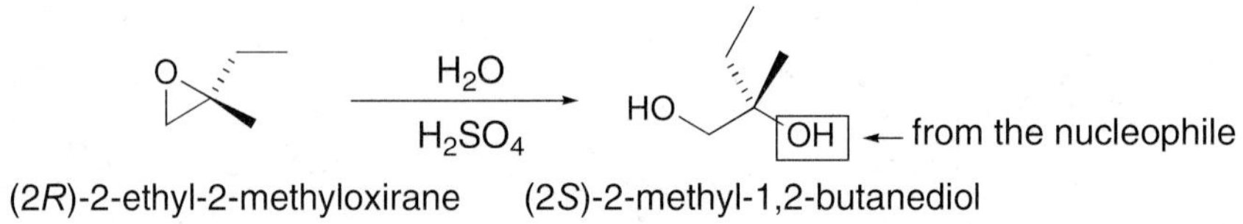
H2O
H2SO4
HO
OH
from the nucleophile
(2R)-2-ethyl-2-methyloxirane
(2S)-2-methyl-1,2-butanediol

9.70

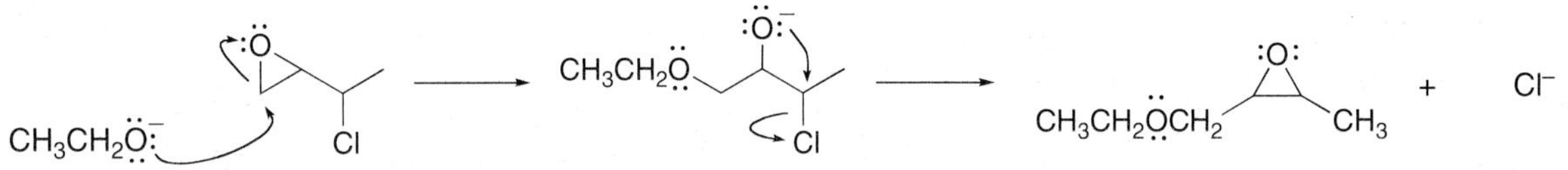
CH3CH2O:−
Cl
CH3CH2O
Cl
CH3CH2OCH2
CH3
+
Cl−

9.71

a.

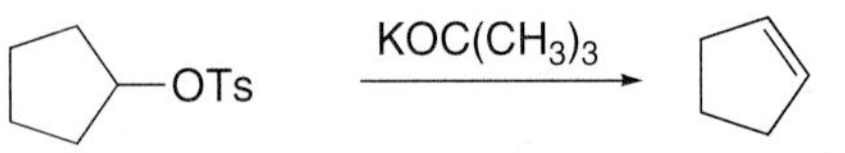
OTs
KOC(CH3)3

Bulky base favors E2.

b.

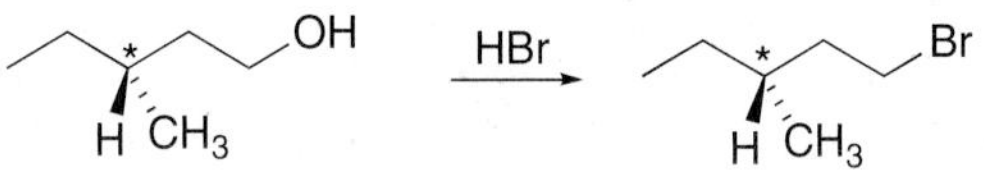
OH
H CH3
HBr
Br
H CH3

Keep the stereochemistry at the stereogenic center [*] the same here since no bond is broken to it.

c.

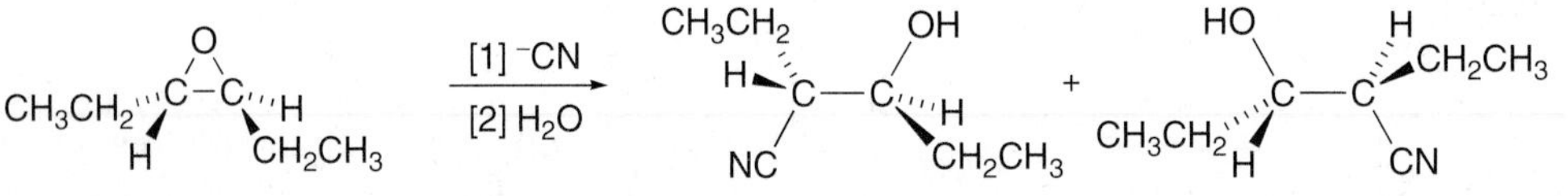
CH3CH2
H
CH2CH3
[1] −CN
[2] H2O
OH
NC
CH2CH3
+
HO
CN

identical

d.

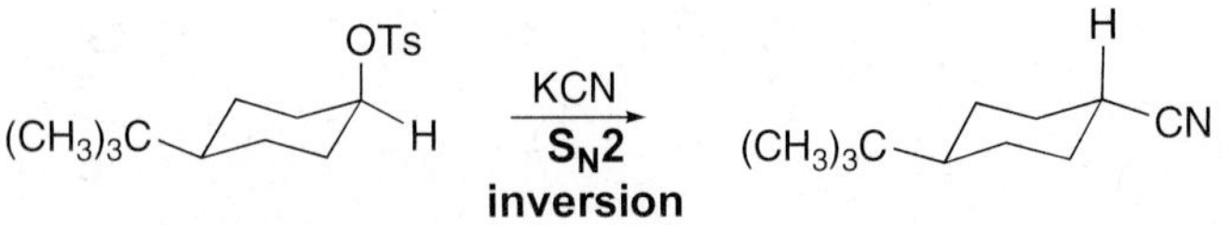
OTs
(CH3)3C
H
KCN
SN2
inversion
(CH3)3C
CN

e.

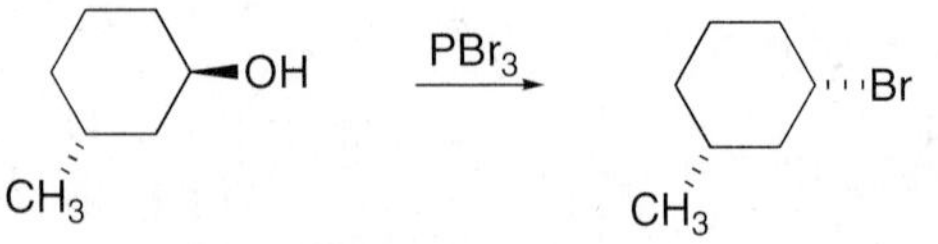
OH
CH3
PBr3
Br
CH3

S_N2 inversion

f.

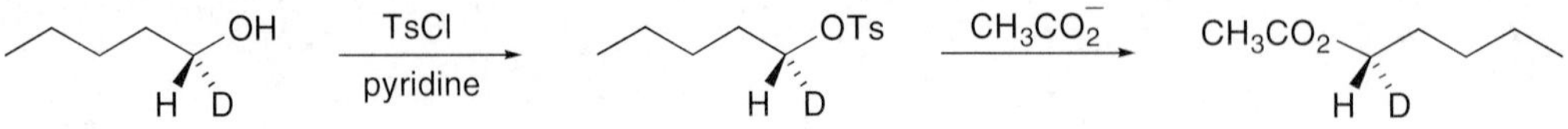
OH
H D
TsCl
pyridine
OTs
CH3CO2−
CH3CO2

g. 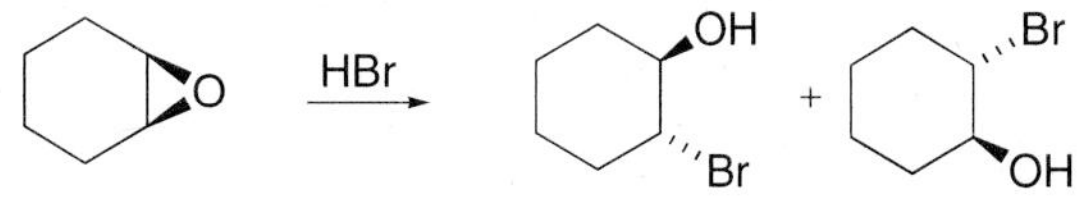
O
HBr
OH
Br
+
Br
OH

h. 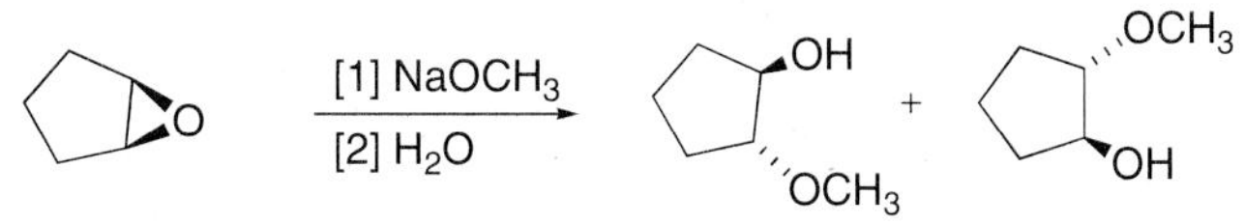
O
[1] NaOCH3
[2] H2O
OH
OCH3
+
OCH3
OH

i. 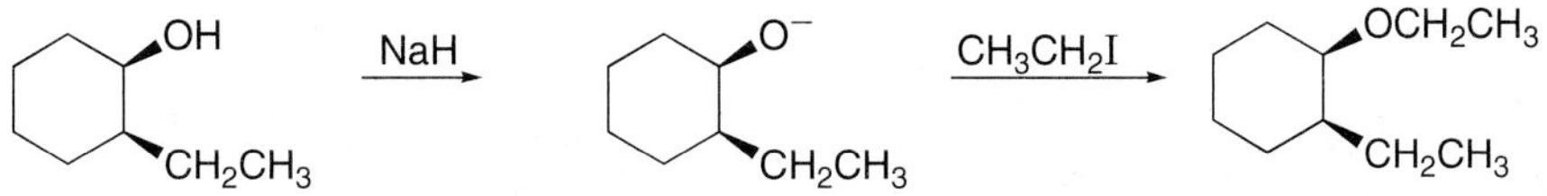
OH
CH2CH3
NaH
O−
CH2CH3
CH3CH2I
OCH2CH3
CH2CH3

j. 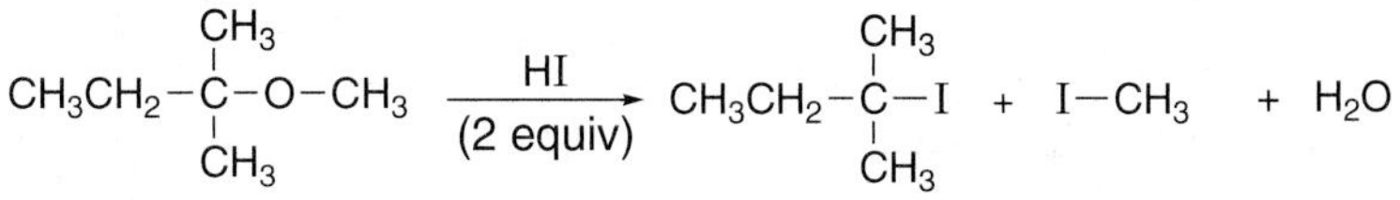
CH3
CH3CH2–C–O–CH3
CH3
HI
(2 equiv)
CH3
CH3CH2–C–I
CH3
+ I–CH3
+ H2O

9.72

a. 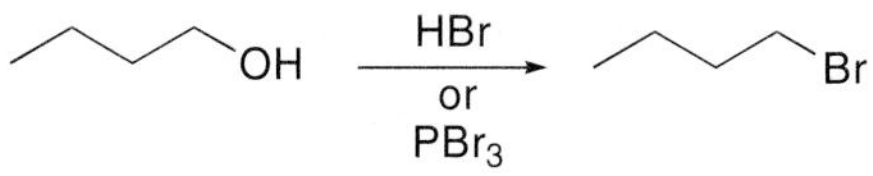
OH
HBr
or
PBr3
Br

b. 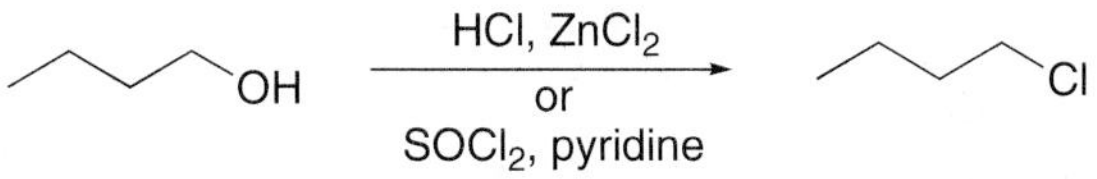
OH
HCl, ZnCl2
or
SOCl2, pyridine
Cl

c. 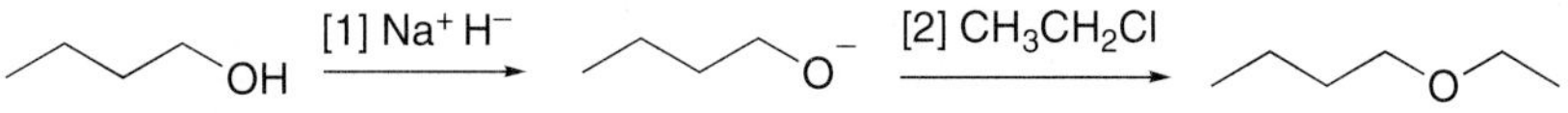
OH
[1] Na+ H−
O−
[2] CH3CH2Cl
O

d. 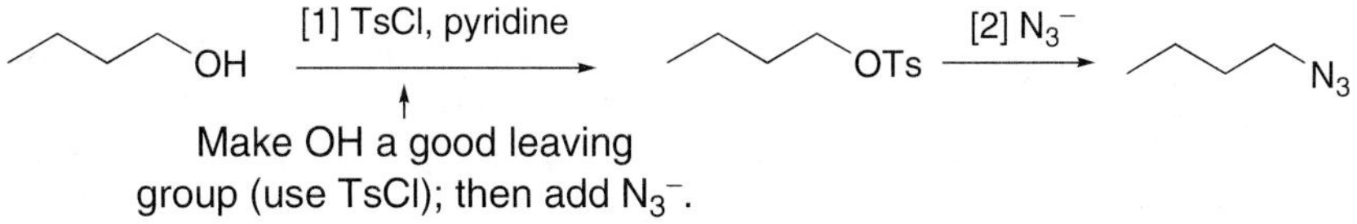
OH
[1] TsCl, pyridine
OTs
[2] N3−
N3
Make OH a good leaving
group (use TsCl); then add N3−.

9.73

a. 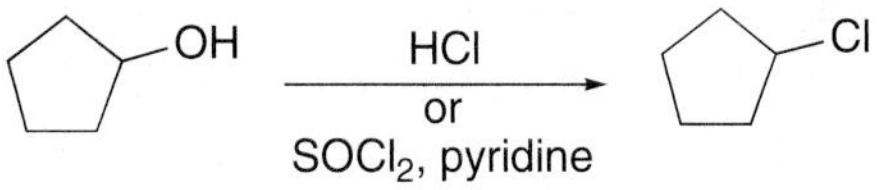
OH
HCl
or
SOCl2, pyridine
Cl

b. 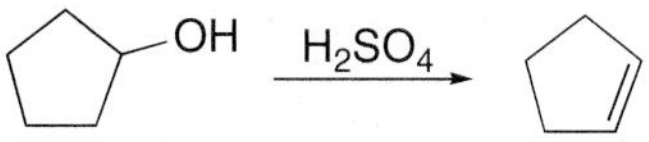
OH
H2SO4

c. 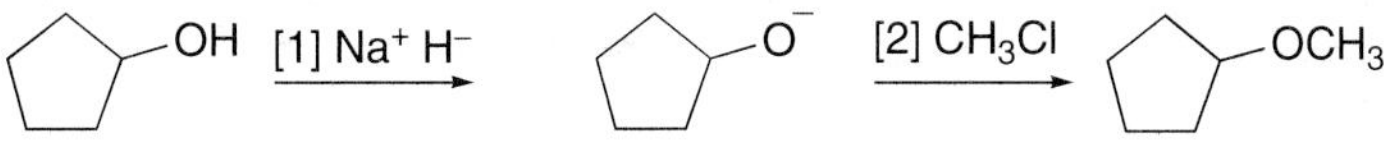
OH
[1] Na+ H−
O−
[2] CH3Cl
OCH3

d. 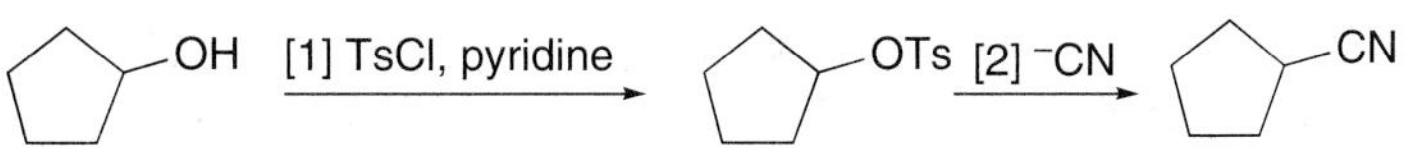
OH
[1] TsCl, pyridine
OTs
[2] −CN
CN

Make OH a good leaving group (use TsCl); then add $^{-}$CN.

9.74

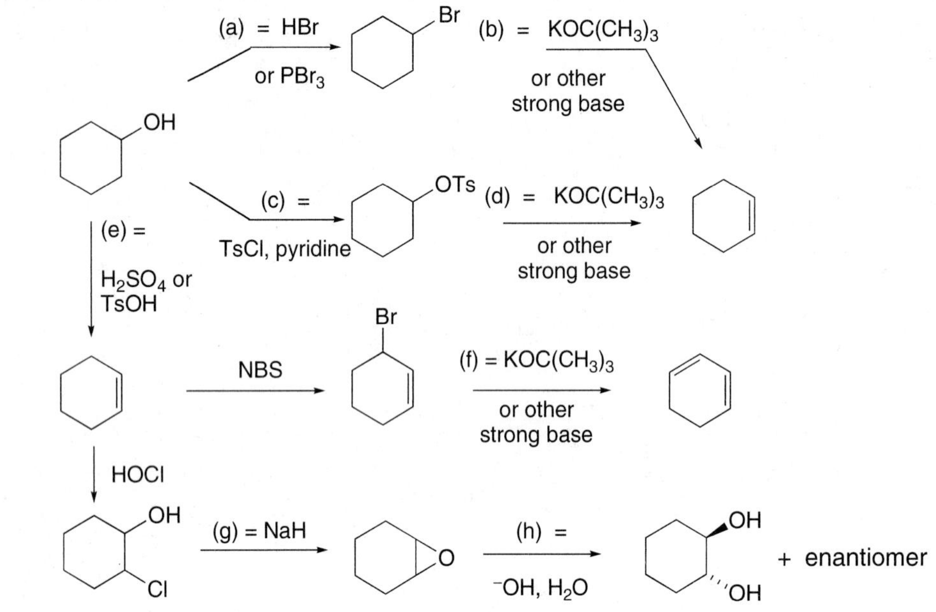

9.75

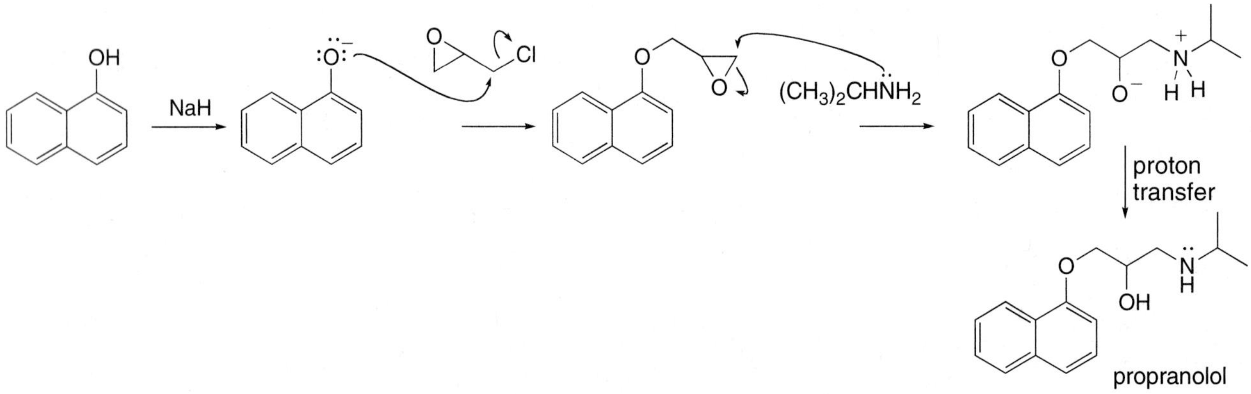

9.76 With the cis isomer, ^-OH acts as a nucleophile to displace Br^- from the back side, forming a trans diol (**A**). With the trans isomer, the two functional groups are arranged in a manner that allows an intramolecular S_N2. ^-OH removes a proton to form an alkoxide, which can then displace Br^- by intramolecular backside attack to afford an ether (**B**). Such a reaction is not possible with the cis isomer because the nucleophile and leaving group are on the same side.

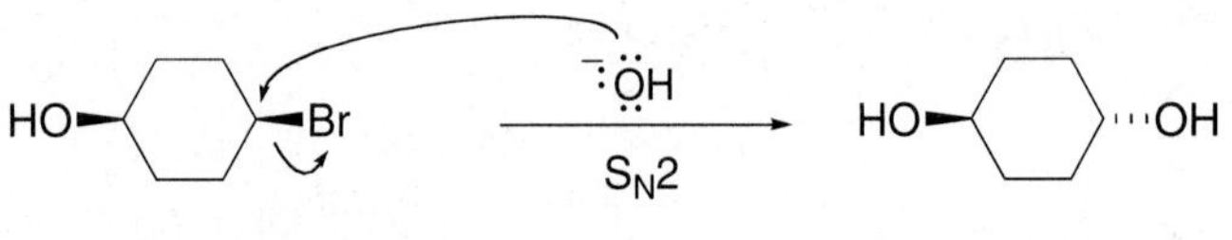

cis-4-bromocyclohexanol

A

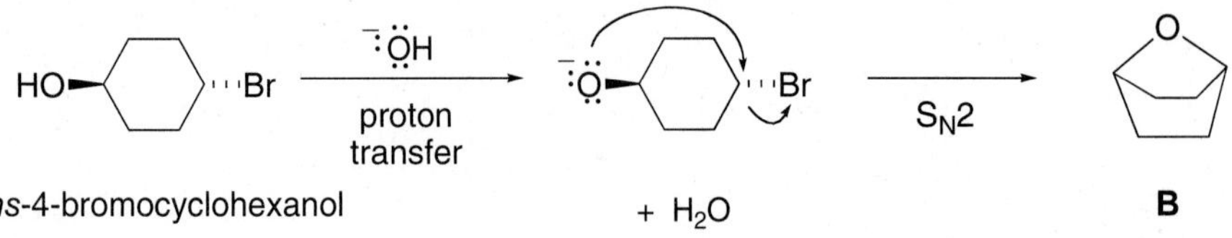

trans-4-bromocyclohexanol

B

9.77 If the base is not bulky, it can react as a nucleophile and open the epoxide ring. The bulky base cannot act as a nucleophile, and will only remove the proton.

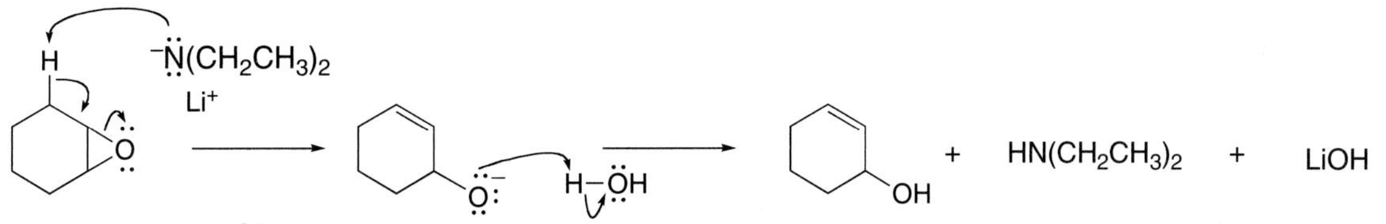

9.78 First form the 2° carbocation. Then lose a proton to form each product.

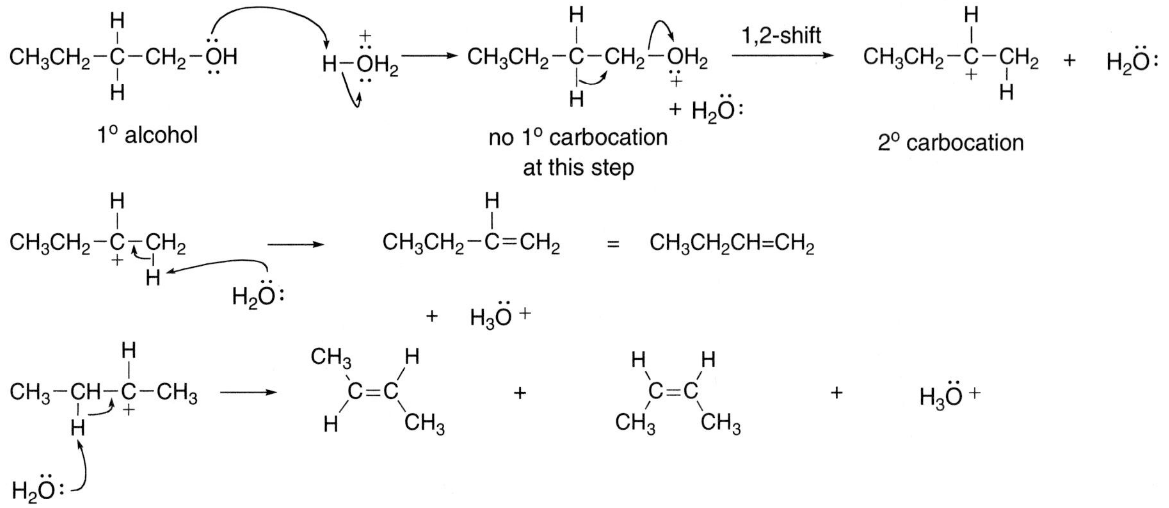

9.79

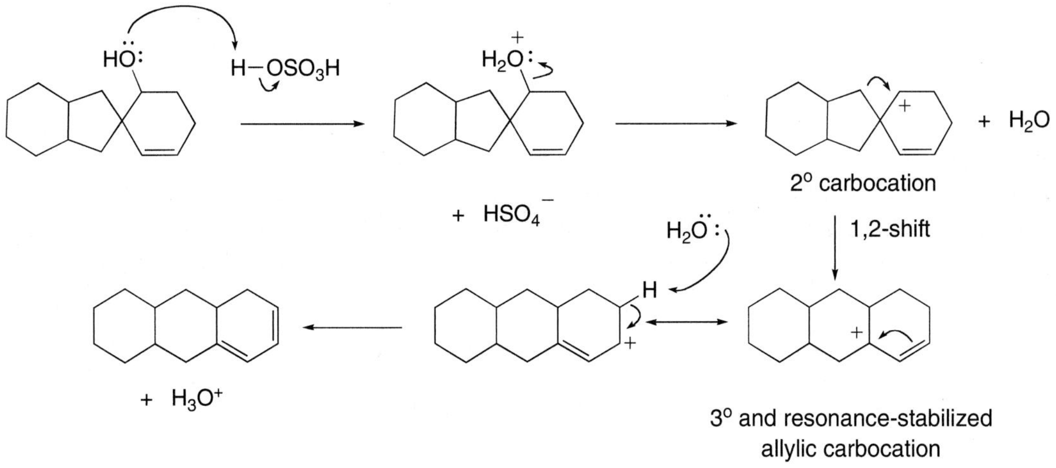

9.80

a.

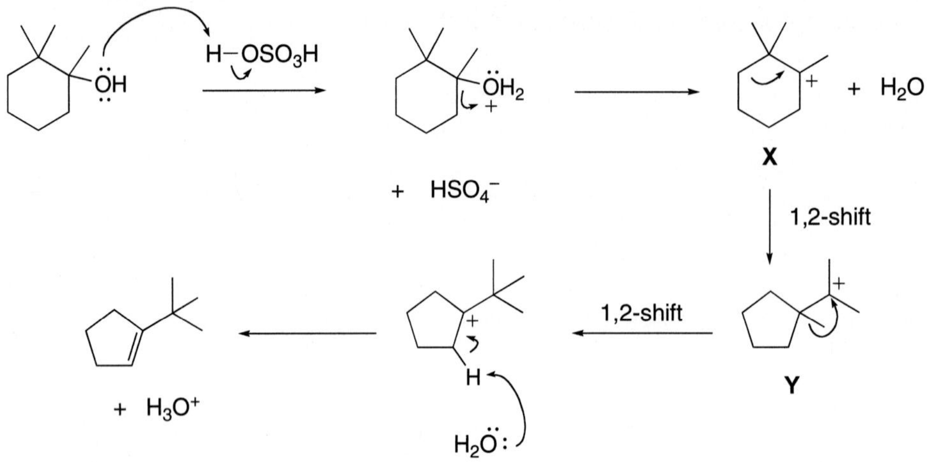

b. Other elimination products can form from carbocations **X** and **Y.**

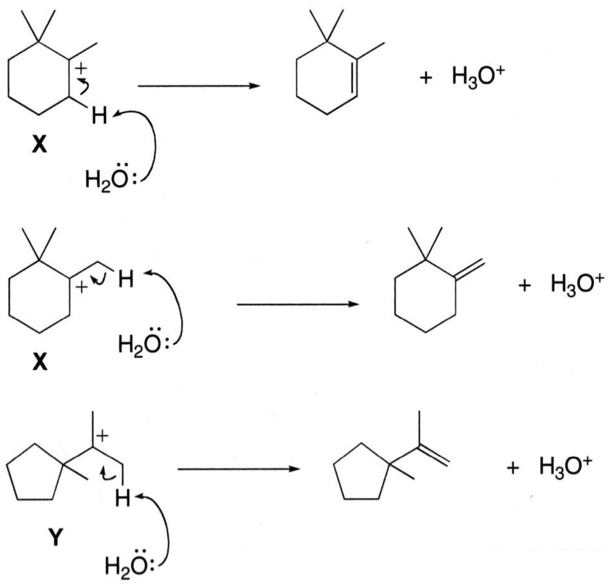

9.81

a.

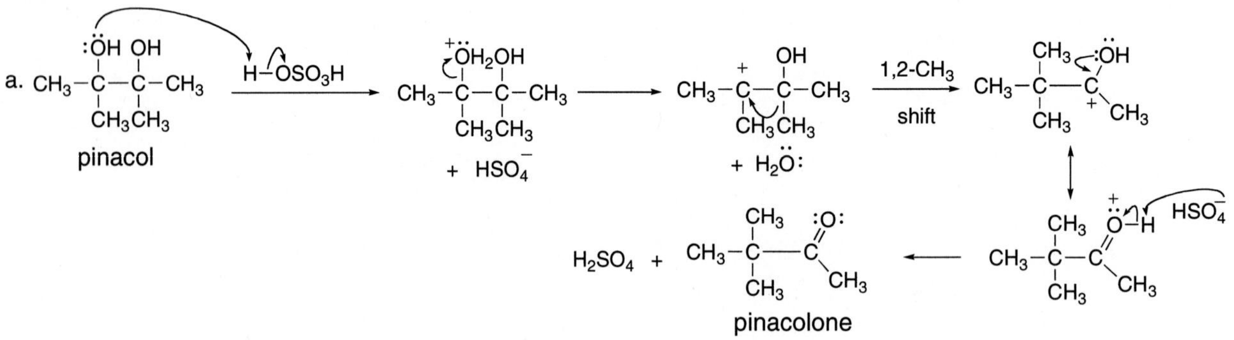

b. Two different carbocations can form. The carbocation with the (+) charge adjacent to the benzene rings (**A**) is more stable, so it is preferred.

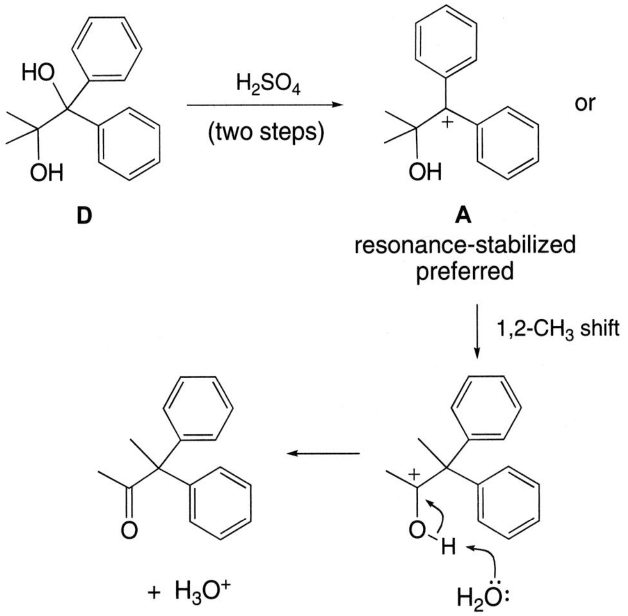

9.82

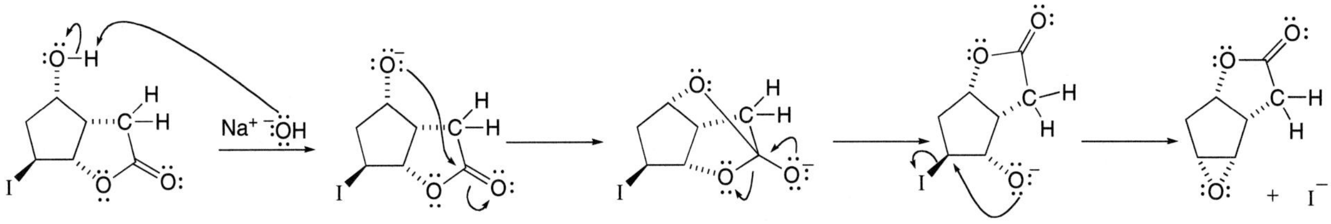

9.83 The conversion of **X** to **Y** requires two operations. **X** contains both a nucleophile (NH_2) and a leaving group (OSO_2CH_3), so an intramolecular S_N2 reaction forms an aziridine. Since the aziridine is strained, the amine nucleophile ($CH_2{=}CHCH_2NH_2$) opens the ring by backside attack, resulting in the trans stereochemistry of the two N's on the six-membered ring.

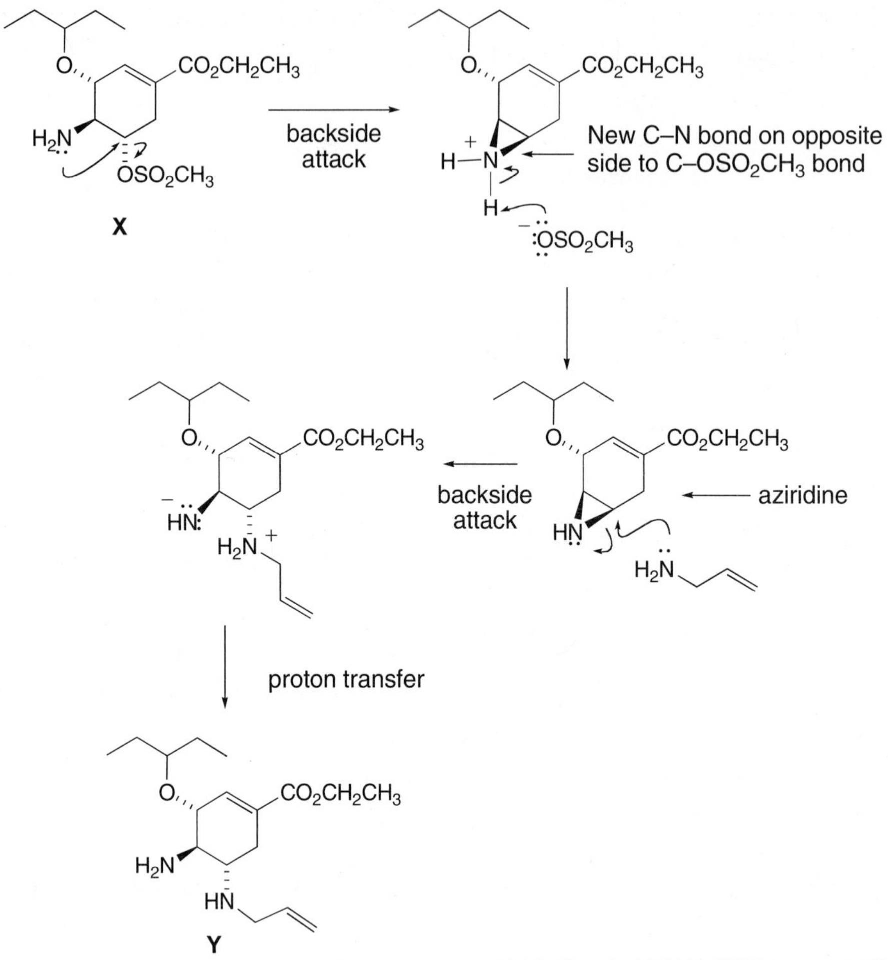

Chapter 10 Alkenes

Chapter Review

General facts about alkenes

- Alkenes contain a carbon–carbon double bond consisting of a stronger σ bond and a weaker π bond. Each carbon is sp^2 hybridized and trigonal planar (10.1).
- Alkenes are named using the suffix *-ene* (10.3).
- Alkenes with different groups on each end of the double bond exist as a pair of diastereomers, identified by the prefixes *E* and *Z* (10.3B).

Two higher priority groups on **opposite** sides

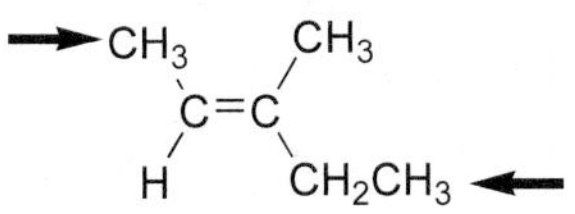

***E* isomer**
(2*E*)-3-methyl-2-pentene

Two higher priority groups on the **same** side

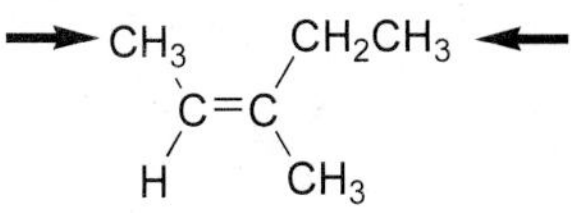

***Z* isomer**
(2*Z*)-3-methyl-2-pentene

- Alkenes have weak intermolecular forces, giving them low mp's and bp's, and making them water insoluble. A cis alkene is more polar than a trans alkene, giving it a slightly higher boiling point (10.4).

cis-2-butene

more polar isomer →

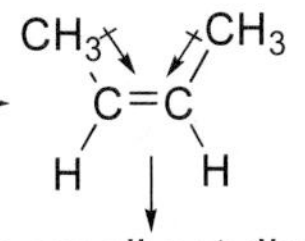

a small net dipole
higher bp

trans-2-butene

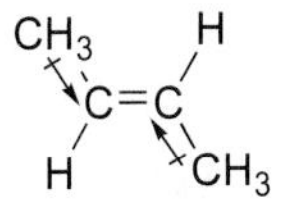

← **less polar isomer**

no net dipole
lower bp

- Since a π bond is electron rich and much weaker than a σ bond, alkenes undergo addition reactions with electrophiles (10.8).

Stereochemistry of alkene addition reactions (10.8)

A reagent XY adds to a double bond in one of three different ways:

- **Syn addition**—X and Y add from the same side.

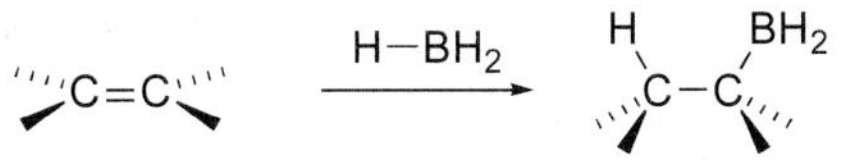

- Syn addition occurs in **hydroboration.**

- **Anti addition**—X and Y add from opposite sides.

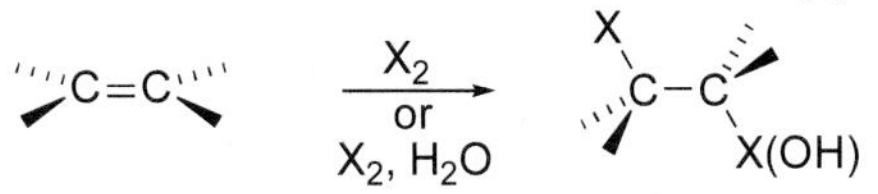

- Anti addition occurs in **halogenation** and **halohydrin formation.**

- **Both syn and anti addition** occur when carbocations are intermediates.

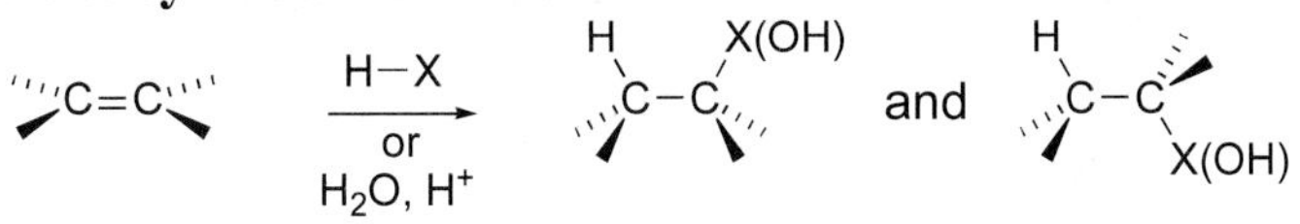

- Syn and anti addition occur in **hydrohalogenation** and **hydration.**

Addition reactions of alkenes

[1] **Hydrohalogenation**—Addition of HX (X = Cl, Br, I) (10.9–10.11)

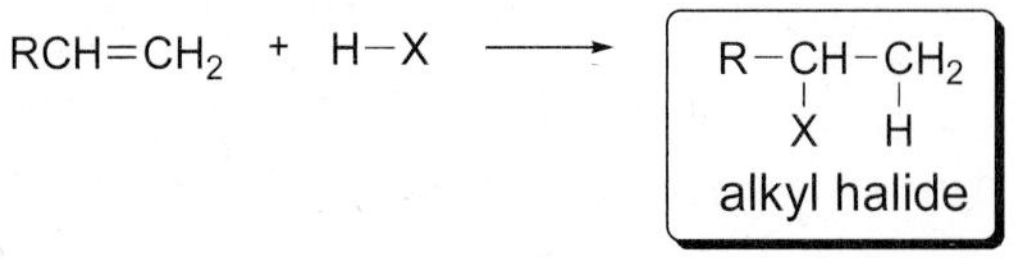
RCH=CH2 + H–X
R–CH–CH2
X H
alkyl halide

- The mechanism has two steps.
- Carbocations are formed as intermediates.
- Carbocation rearrangements are possible.
- Markovnikov's rule is followed. H bonds to the less substituted C to form the more stable carbocation.
- Syn and anti addition occur.

[2] **Hydration** and related reactions—Addition of H_2O or ROH (10.12)

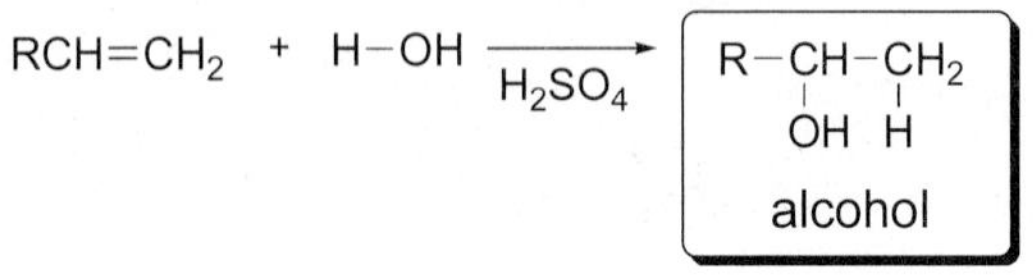
RCH=CH2 + H–OH
H2SO4
R–CH–CH2
OH H
alcohol

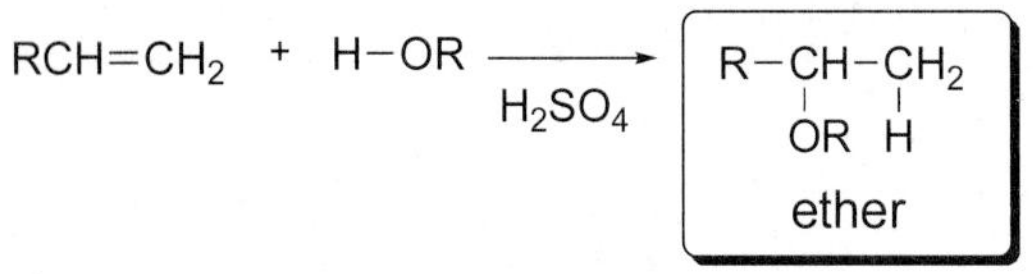
RCH=CH2 + H–OR
H2SO4
R–CH–CH2
OR H
ether

For both reactions:

- The mechanism has three steps.
- Carbocations are formed as intermediates.
- Carbocation rearrangements are possible.
- Markovnikov's rule is followed. H bonds to the less substituted C to form the more stable carbocation.
- Syn and anti addition occur.

[3] **Halogenation**—Addition of X_2 (X = Cl or Br) (10.13–10.14)

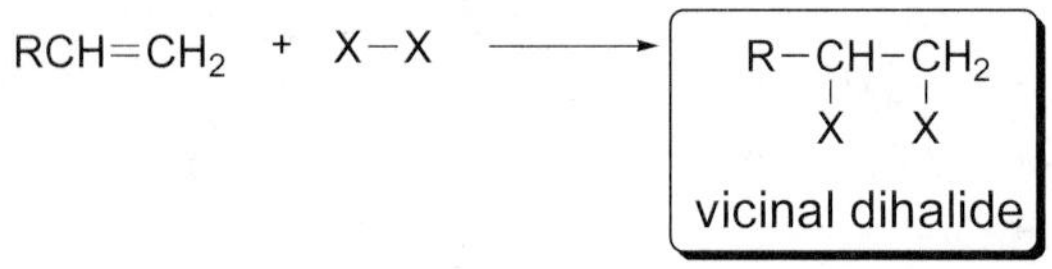
RCH=CH2 + X–X
R–CH–CH2
X X
vicinal dihalide

- The mechanism has two steps.
- Bridged halonium ions are formed as intermediates.
- No rearrangements occur.
- Anti addition occurs.

[4] **Halohydrin formation**—Addition of OH and X (X = Cl, Br) (10.15)

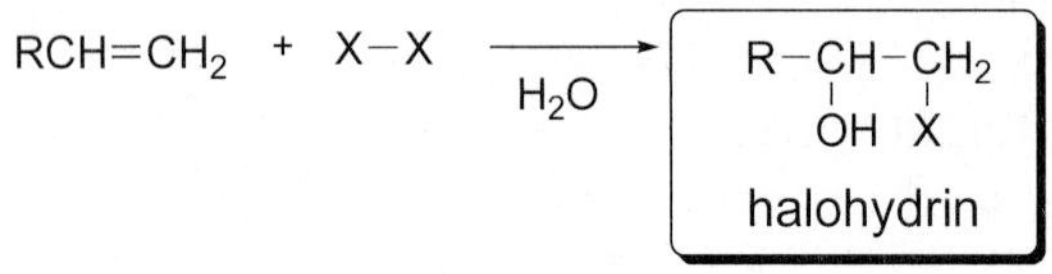
RCH=CH2 + X–X
H2O
R–CH–CH2
OH X
halohydrin

- The mechanism has three steps.
- Bridged halonium ions are formed as intermediates.
- No rearrangements occur.
- X bonds to the less substituted C.
- Anti addition occurs.
- NBS in DMSO and H_2O adds Br and OH in the same fashion.

[5] **Hydroboration–oxidation**—Addition of H_2O (10.16)

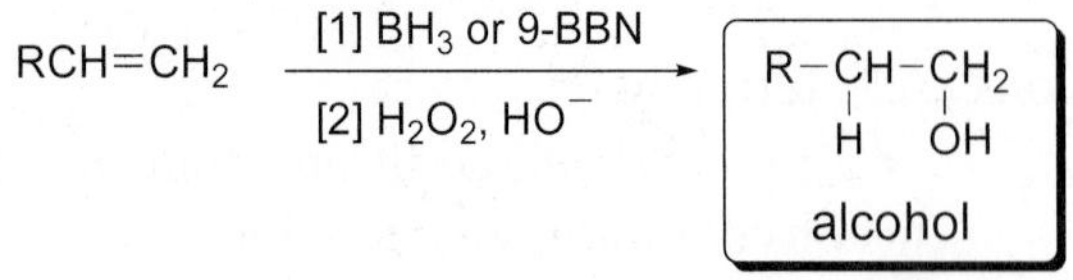
RCH=CH2
[1] BH3 or 9-BBN
[2] H2O2, HO−
R–CH–CH2
H OH
alcohol

- Hydroboration has a one-step mechanism.
- No rearrangements occur.
- OH bonds to the less substituted C.
- Syn addition of H_2O results.

Practice Test on Chapter Review

1. Give the IUPAC name for the following compounds.

a. 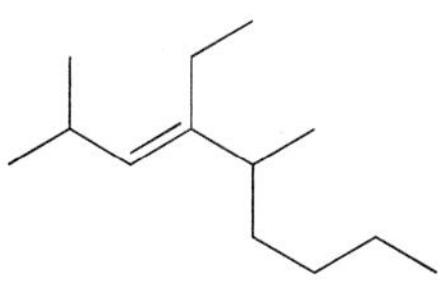

b. 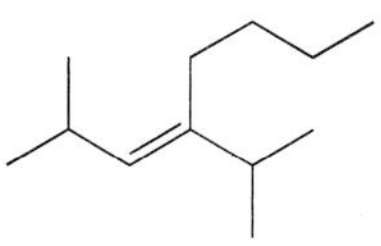

2. Draw the organic products formed in the following reactions. Draw all stereogenic centers using wedges and dashes.

a. 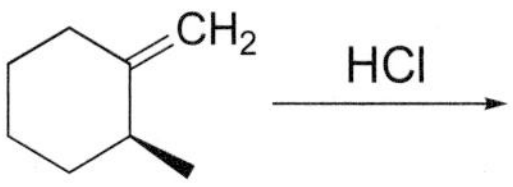

b. 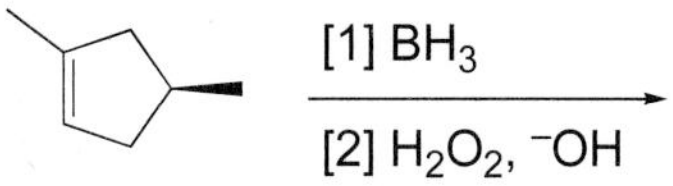

c. 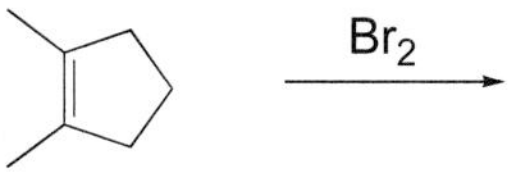

d. 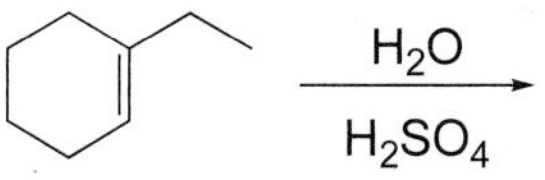

3. Fill in the table with the stereochemistry observed in the reaction of an alkene with each reagent. Choose from syn, anti, or both syn and anti.

Reagent	Stereochemistry
a. [1] 9-BBN; [2] H_2O_2, ^{-}OH	
b. H_2O, H_2SO_4	
c. Cl_2, H_2O	
d. HI	
e. Br_2	

4. a. In which of the following reactions are carbocation rearrangements are observed?
   1. hydrohalogenation
   2. halohydrin formation
   3. hydroboration–oxidation
   4. Carbocation rearrangements are observed in reactions (1) and (2).
   5. Carbocation rearrangements are observed in reactions (1), (2), and (3).

   b. Which of the following products are formed when HCl is added to 3-methyl-1-pentene?
   1. 2-chloro-2-methylpentane
   2. 3-chloro-3-methylpentane
   3. 1-chloro-3-methylpentane
   4. Both (1) and (2) are formed.
   5. Products (1), (2), and (3) are all formed.

Answers to Practice Test

1. a. (3*E*)-4-ethyl-2,5-dimethyl-3-nonene
   b. (3*E*)-4-isopropyl-2-methyl-3-octene

2.

a. 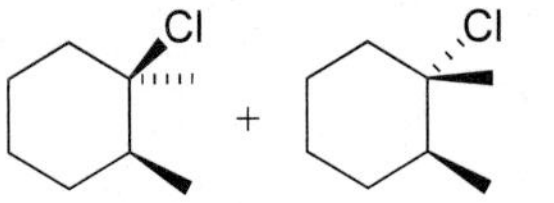

b. 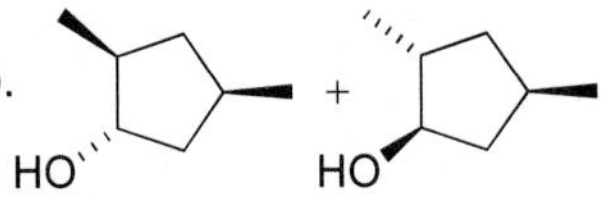

c. 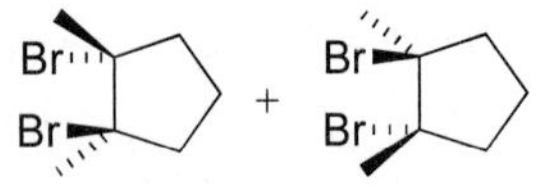

d. 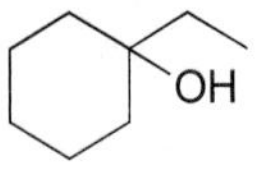

3. a. syn
   b. both
   c. anti
   d. both
   e. anti

4. a. 1
   b. 2

Answers to Problems

10.1

Six alkenes of molecular formula C_5H_{10}:

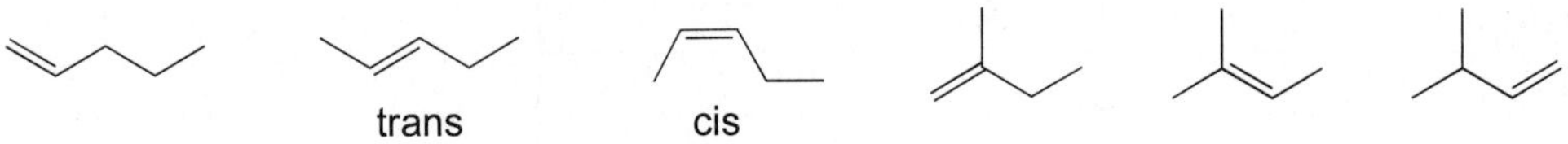

trans cis
diastereomers

10.2 To determine the number of degrees of unsaturation:

[1] Calculate the maximum number of H's ($2n + 2$).
[2] Subtract the actual number of H's from the maximum number.
[3] Divide by two.

a. C_2H_2
[1] maximum number of H's = 2*n* + 2 = 2(2) + 2 = 6
[2] subtract actual from maximum = 6 – 2 = 4
[3] divide by two = 4/2 = **2 degrees of unsaturation**

b. C_6H_6
[1] maximum number of H's = 2*n* + 2 = 2(6) + 2 = 14
[2] subtract actual from maximum = 14 – 6 = 8
[3] divide by two = 8/2 = **4 degrees of unsaturation**

c. C_8H_{18}
[1] maximum number of H's = 2*n* + 2 = 2(8) + 2 = 18
[2] subtract actual from maximum = 18 – 18 = 0
[3] divide by two = 0/2 = **0 degrees of unsaturation**

d. C_7H_8O
Ignore the O.
[1] maximum number of H's = 2*n* + 2 = 2(7) + 2 = 16
[2] subtract actual from maximum = 16 – 8 = 8
[3] divide by two = 8/2 = **4 degrees of unsaturation**

e. $C_7H_{11}Br$
Because of Br, add one more H (11 + 1 H = 12 H's).
[1] maximum number of H's = 2*n* + 2 = 2(7) + 2 = 16
[2] subtract actual from maximum = 16 – 12 = 4
[3] divide by two = 4/2 = **2 degrees of unsaturation**

f. C_5H_9N
Because of N, subtract one H (9 – 1 H = 8 H's).
[1] maximum number of H's = 2*n* + 2 = 2(5) + 2 = 12
[2] subtract actual from maximum = 12 – 8 = 4
[3] divide by two = 4/2 = **2 degrees of unsaturation**

10.3

One possibility for C_6H_{10}:

a. a compound that has 2 π bonds 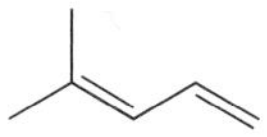

b. a compound that has 1 ring and 1 π bond 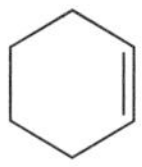

c. a compound with 2 rings 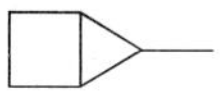

d. a compound with 1 triple bond 

10.4 To name an alkene:

[1] Find the longest chain that contains the double bond. Change the ending from ***-ane*** to ***-ene.***
[2] Number the chain to give the double bond the lower number. The alkene is named by the first number.
[3] Apply all other rules of nomenclature.

To name a cycloalkene:

[1] When a double bond is located in a ring, it is always located between C1 and C2. Omit the "1" in the name. Change the ending from ***-ane*** to ***-ene.***
[2] Number the ring clockwise or counterclockwise to give the first substituent the lower number.
[3] Apply all other rules of nomenclature.

a. [1] $CH_2{=}CHCH(CH_3)CH_2CH_3$
5 C chain with double bond
pentene

[2] $CH_2{=}CHCHCH_2CH_3$ with CH_3 on C3 (**1** → C1; **3-methyl** → CH_3; **1-pentene** → double bond)

[3] **3-methyl-1-pentene**

b. [1] $(CH_3CH_2)_2C{=}CHCH_2CH_2CH_3$
7 C chain with double bond
heptene

[2] $(CH_3CH_2)(CH_3CH_2)C{=}CHCH_2CH_2CH_3$ (**3** → C3; **3-ethyl** → CH_3CH_2; **3-heptene** → double bond)

[3] **3-ethyl-3-heptene**

c. [1]

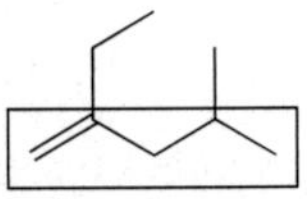

5 C chain with double bond
pentene

[2]

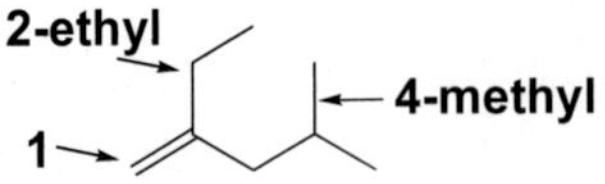

1-pentene

[3] **2-ethyl-4-methyl-1-pentene**

d. [1]

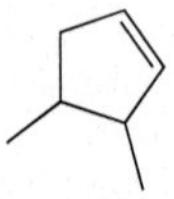

5 C ring with a double bond
cyclopentene

[2]

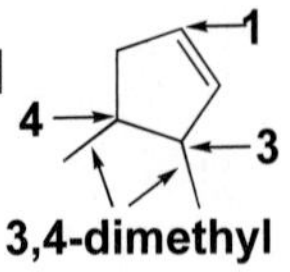

[3] **3,4-dimethylcyclopentene**

e. [1]

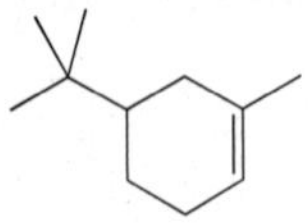

6 C ring with a double bond
cyclohexene

[2]

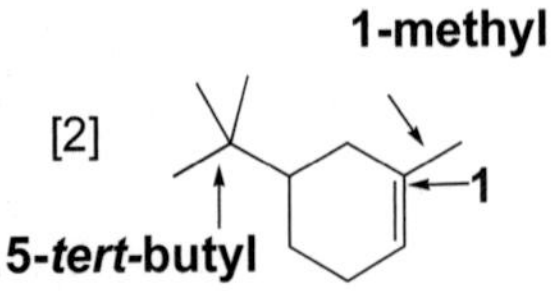

[3] **5-*tert*-butyl-1-methylcyclohexene**

10.5 Use the rules from Answer 10.4 to name the compounds. Enols are named to give the OH the lower number. Compounds with two C=C's are named with the suffix ***-adiene.***

a. [1]

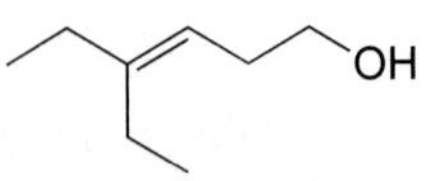

6 C chain with double bond
hexene

[2]

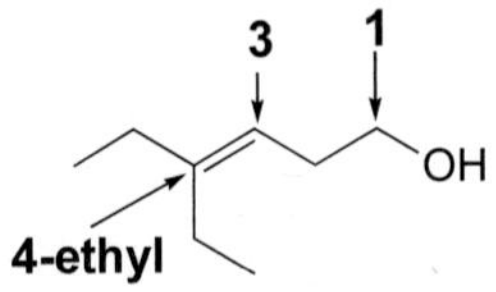

[3] **4-ethyl-3-hexen-1-ol**

b. [1]

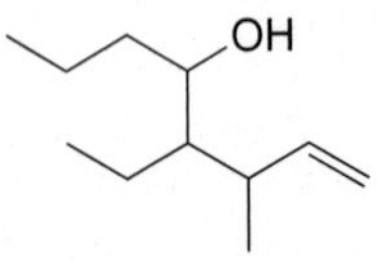

8 C chain with double bond
octene

[2]

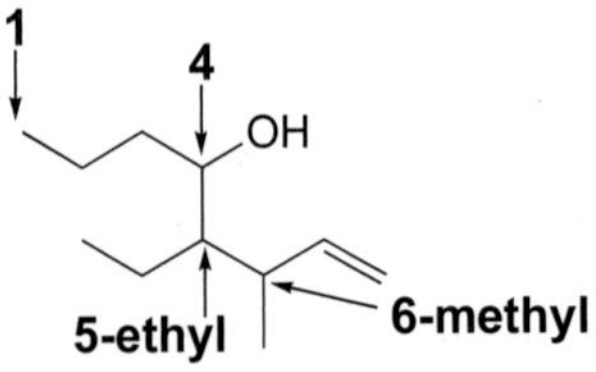

[3] **5-ethyl-6-methyl-7-octen-4-ol**

c. [1]

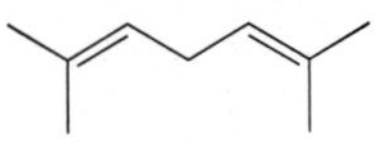

7 C chain with two double bonds
heptadiene

[2]

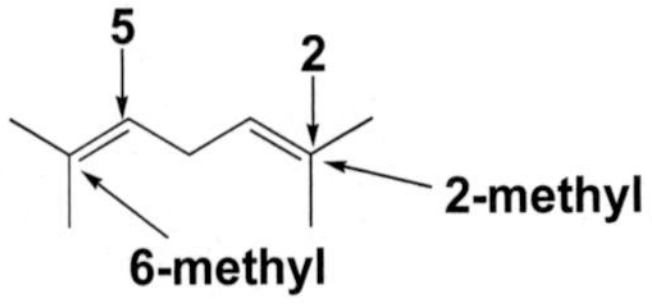

[3] **2,6-dimethyl-2,5-heptadiene**

10.6 To label an alkene as *E* or *Z*:

[1] **Assign priorities** to the two substituents ***on each end*** using the rules for *R,S* nomenclature.

[2] **Assign *E* or *Z*** depending on the location of the two higher priority groups.

- The ***E*** prefix is used when the two higher priority groups are on **opposite sides.**
- The ***Z*** prefix is used when the two higher priority groups are on the **same side** of the double bond.

a.

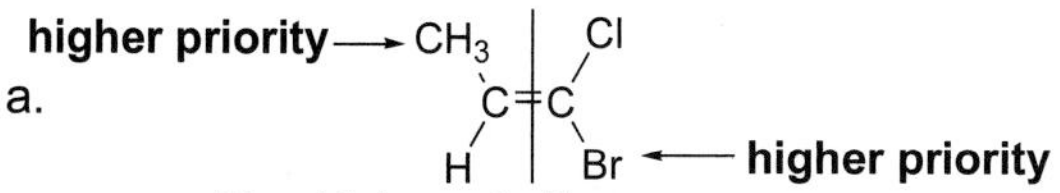

Two higher priority groups are on opposite sides: ***E* isomer.**

b.

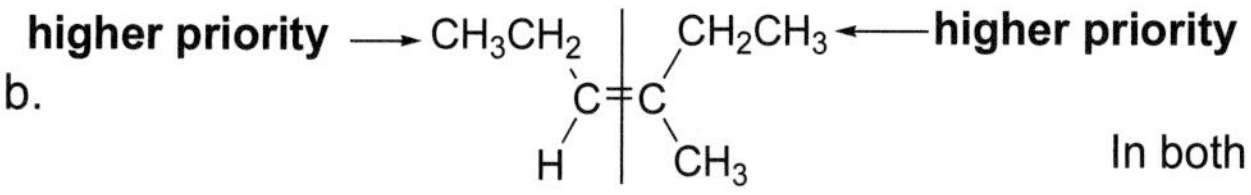

Two higher priority groups are on the same side: ***Z* isomer.**

c.

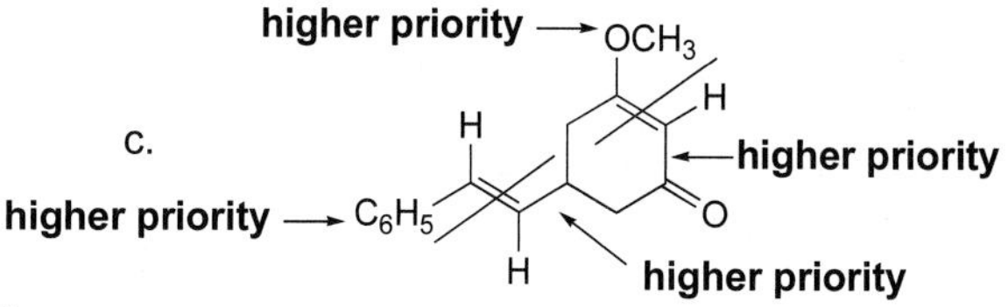

kavain

In both double bonds, the two higher priority groups are on opposite sides: ***E* isomers.**

10.7

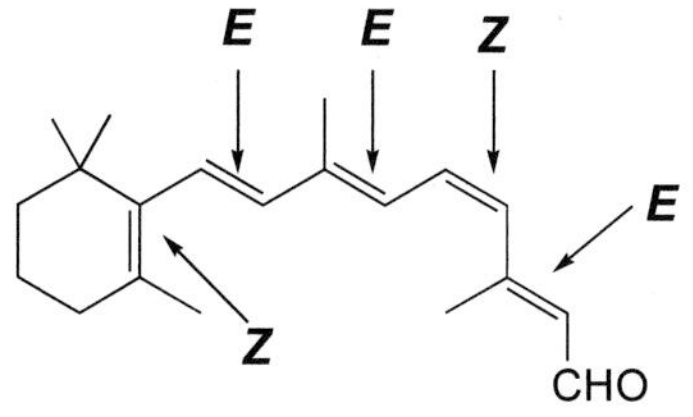

skeletal structure of 11-*cis*-retinal

10.8 To work backwards from a name to a structure:

[1] Find the parent name and functional group and draw, remembering that the double bond is between C1 and C2 for cycloalkenes.

[2] Add the substituents to the appropriate carbons.

a. (3*Z*)-4-ethyl-3-heptene

7 carbons

The higher priority groups are on the same side = ***Z*.**

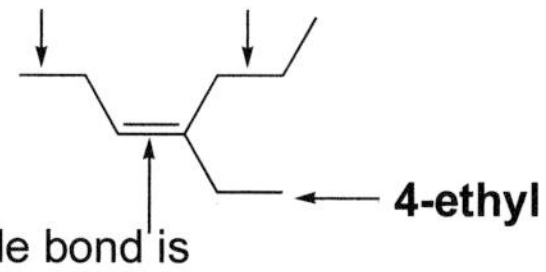

The double bond is between C3 and C4.

b. (2*E*)-3,5,6-trimethyl-2-octene

8 carbons

The double bond is between C2 and C3.

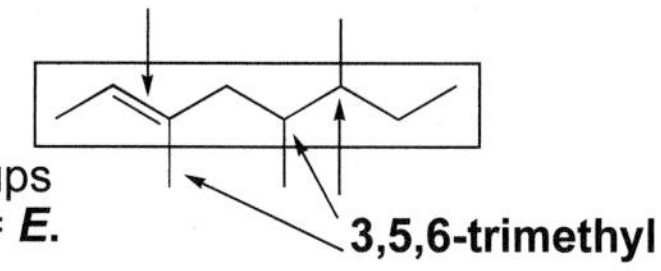

The higher priority groups are on opposite sides = ***E*.**

3,5,6-trimethyl

c. (1*Z*)-2-bromo-1-iodo-1-hexene

6 carbons

The double bond is between C1 and C2.

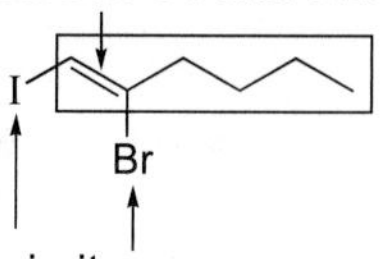

The higher priority groups are on the same side = ***Z*.**

10.9 Draw all of the stereoisomers and then use the rules from Answer 10.6 to name each diene.

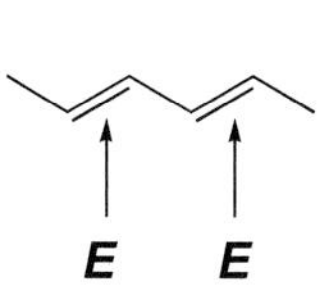

(2*E*,4*E*)-2,4-hexadiene

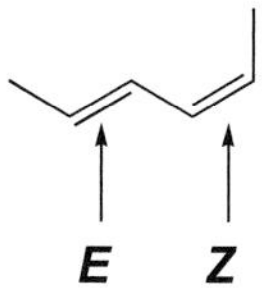

(2*E*,4*Z*)-2,4-hexadiene

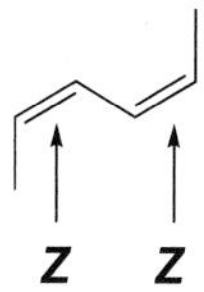

(2*Z*,4*Z*)-2,4-hexadiene

10.10 To rank the isomers by increasing boiling point:
Look for polarity differences: *small net dipoles* make an alkene more polar, giving it a higher boiling point than an alkene with *no net dipole*. Cis isomers have a higher boiling point than their trans isomers.

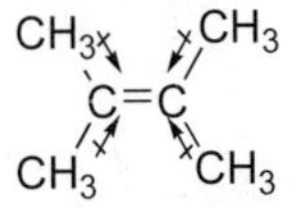

All dipoles cancel.
smallest surface area
no net dipole
lowest bp

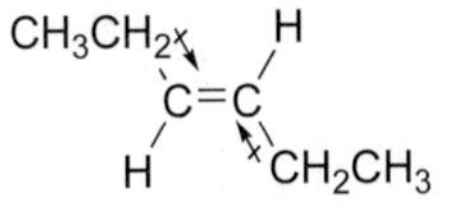

Two dipoles cancel.
no net dipole
trans isomer
intermediate bp

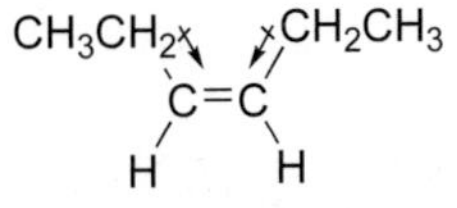

Two dipoles reinforce.
net dipole
cis isomer
highest bp

10.11 Increasing number of double bonds = decreasing melting point.

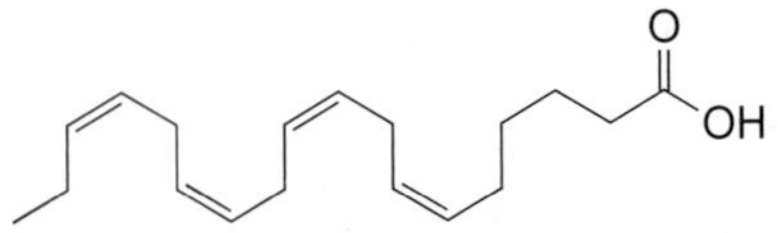

stearidonic acid
4 double bonds
lowest melting point

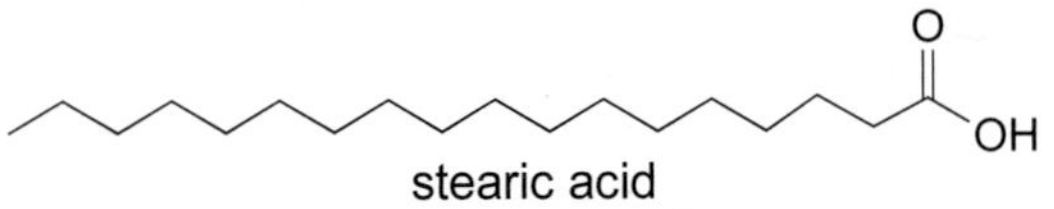

stearic acid
no double bonds
highest melting point

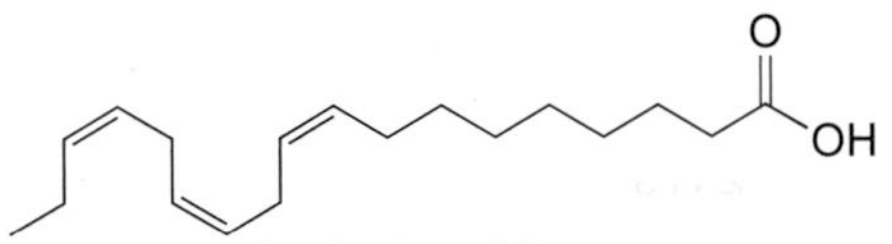

linolenic acid
3 double bonds
intermediate melting point

10.12

a. 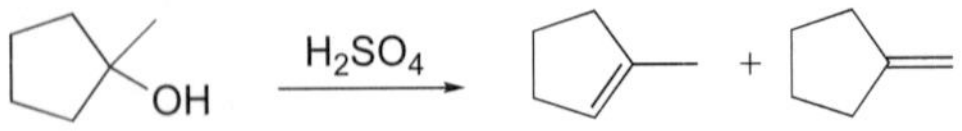

b. 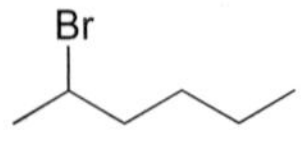 $\xrightarrow{NaOCH_2CH_3}$ $CH_2{=}CHCH_2CH_2CH_2CH_3$ + $CH_3CH{=}CHCH_2CH_2CH_3$

10.13 To draw the products of an addition reaction:
[1] Locate the two bonds that will be broken in the reaction. Always break the π bond.
[2] Draw the product by forming two new σ bonds.

a. 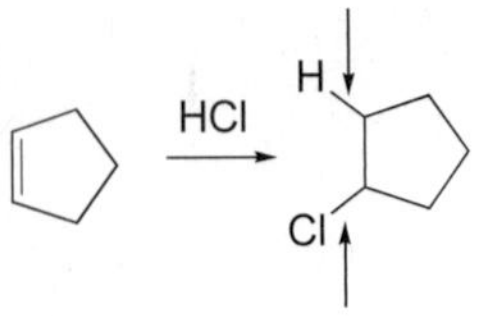 two new σ bonds

c. 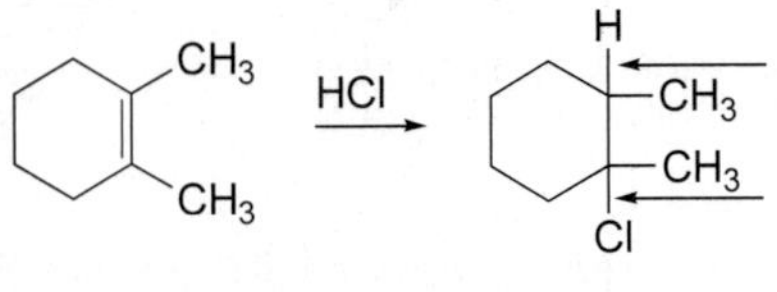 two new σ bonds

b. $CH_3CH_2CH_2CH{=}CHCH_2CH_2CH_3$ $\xrightarrow{HCl}$ 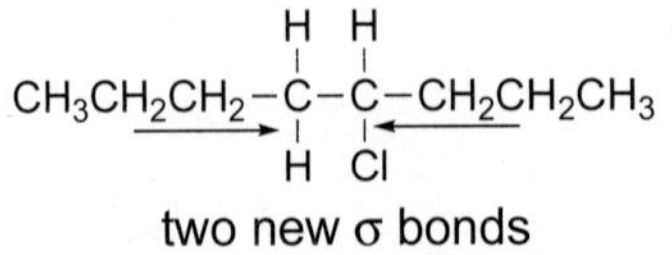

two new σ bonds

10.14 Addition reactions of HX occur in two steps:
[1] The double bond attacks the H atom of HX to form a carbocation.
[2] X^- attacks the carbocation to form a C–X bond.

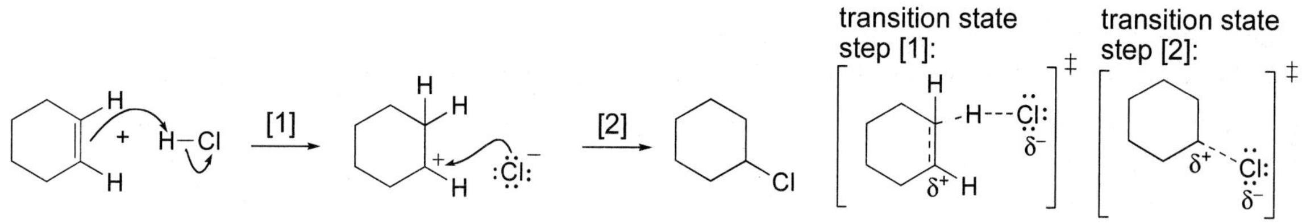

10.15 Addition to alkenes follows Markovnikov's rule: When HX adds to an unsymmetrical alkene, the H bonds to the C that has more H's to begin with.

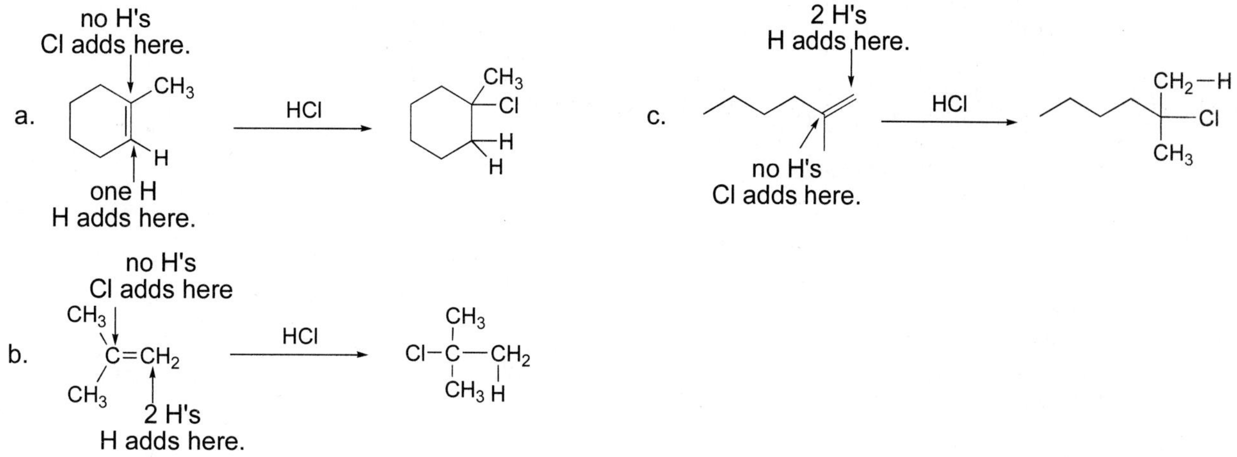

10.16 To determine which alkene will react faster, draw the carbocation that forms in the rate-determining step. The more stable, more substituted the carbocation, the lower the E_a to form it and the faster the reaction.

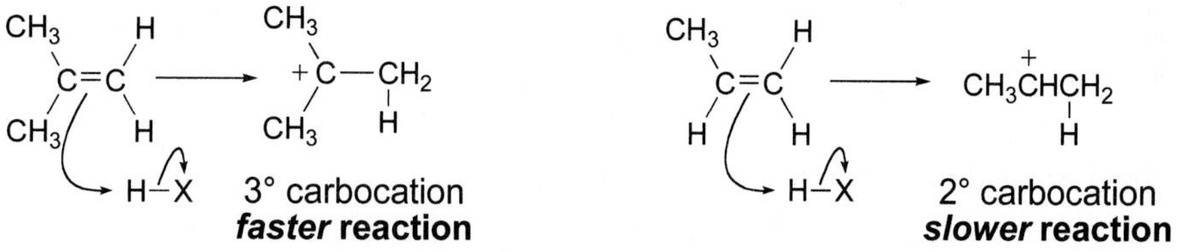

10.17 Look for rearrangements of a carbocation intermediate to explain these results.

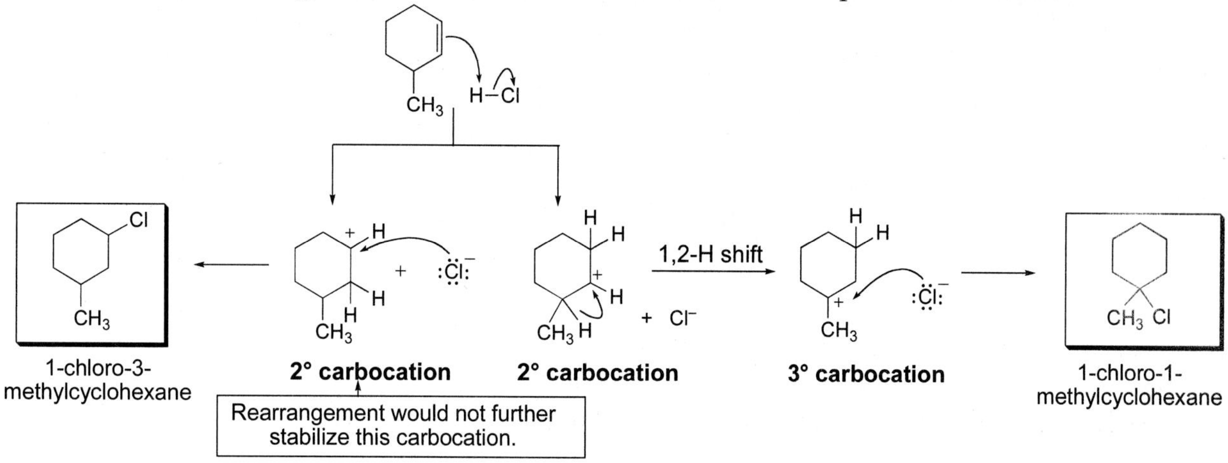

10.18 Addition of HX to alkenes involves the formation of carbocation intermediates. Rearrangement of the carbocation will occur if it forms a more stable carbocation.

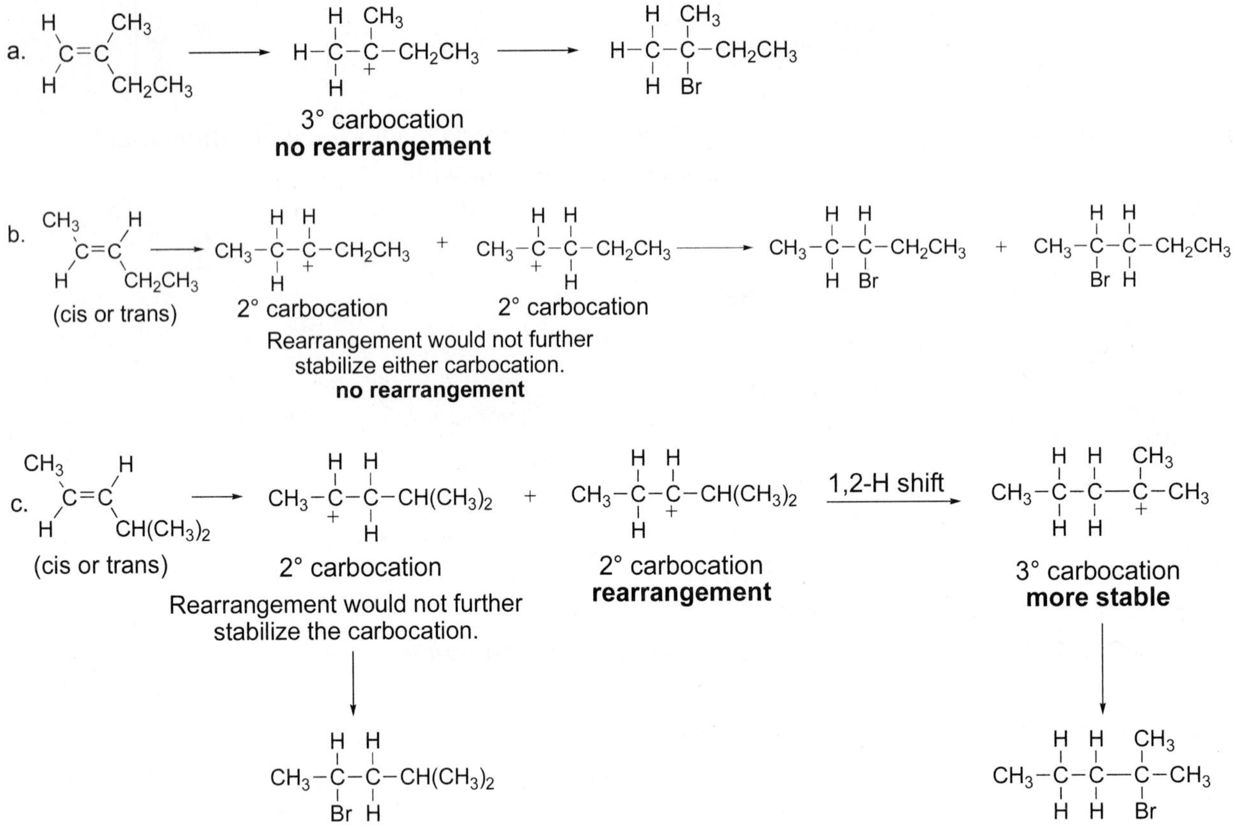

10.19 To draw the products, remember that addition of HX proceeds via a carbocation intermediate.

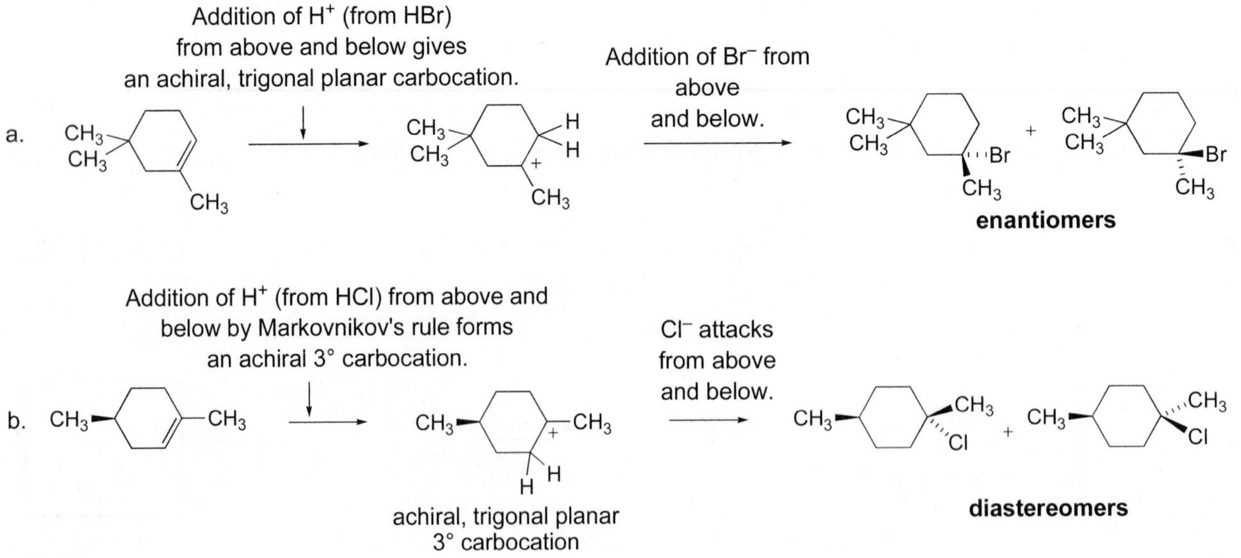

10.20 The product of syn addition will have H and Cl both up or down (both on wedges or both dashes), while the product of anti addition will have one up and one down (one wedge, one dash).

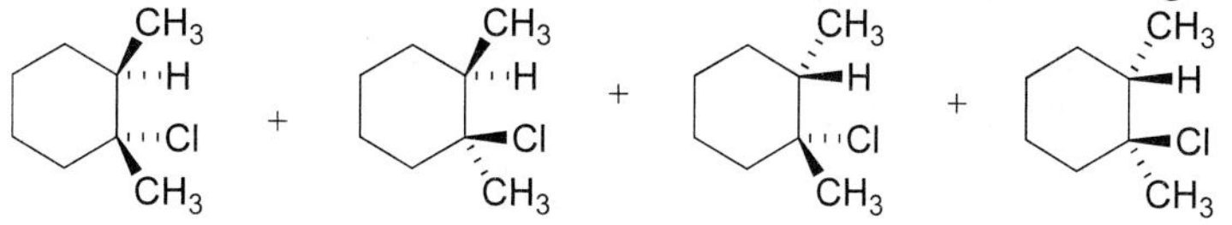
CH3
H
Cl
CH3
+

A	**B**	**C**	**D**
syn addition	anti addition	anti addition	syn addition

10.21

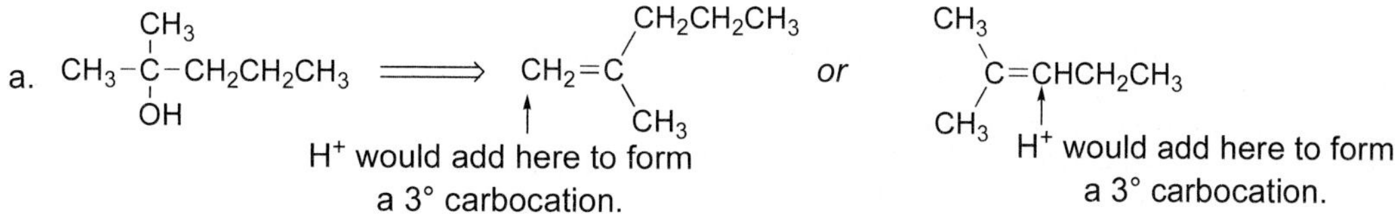
a.
CH3
CH3–C–CH2CH2CH3
OH
CH2=C
CH2CH2CH3
CH3
H+ would add here to form
a 3° carbocation.
or
CH3
C=CHCH2CH3
CH3
H+ would add here to form
a 3° carbocation.

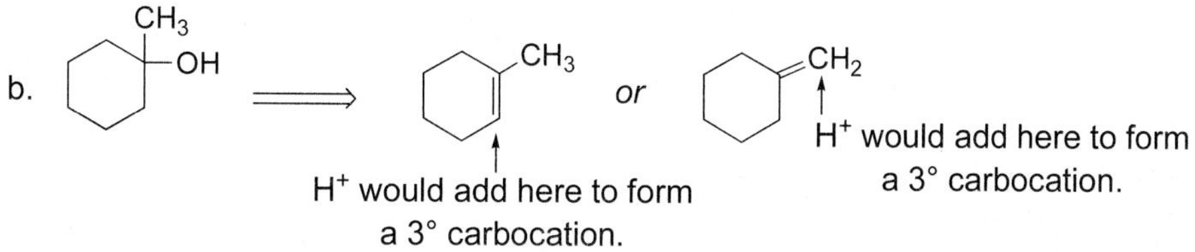
b.
CH3
OH
CH3
or
CH2
H+ would add here to form
a 3° carbocation.
H+ would add here to form
a 3° carbocation.

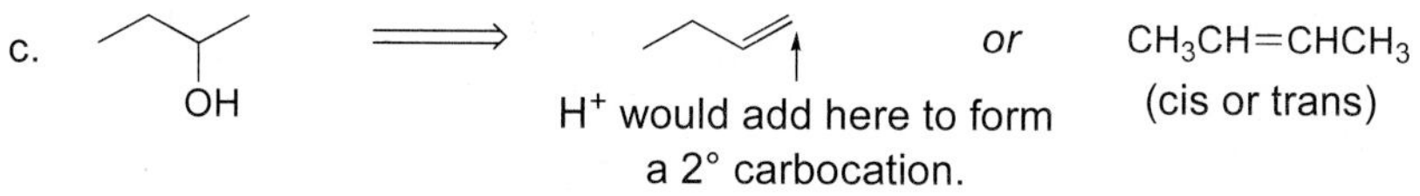
c.
OH
or
CH3CH=CHCH3
(cis or trans)
H+ would add here to form
a 2° carbocation.

10.22

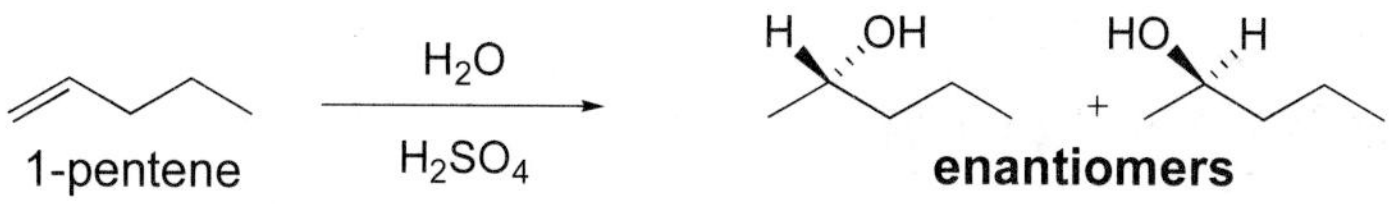
H2O
H2SO4
1-pentene
H
OH
HO
H
+
enantiomers

10.23 Halogenation of an alkene adds two elements of X in an anti fashion.

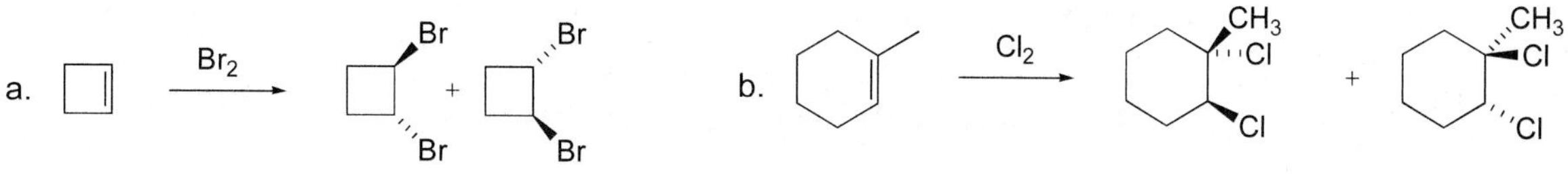
a.
Br2
Br
Br
+
b.
Cl2
CH3
Cl
Cl
+

10.24 To draw the products of halogenation of an alkene, remember that the halogen adds to both ends of the double bond but only anti addition occurs.

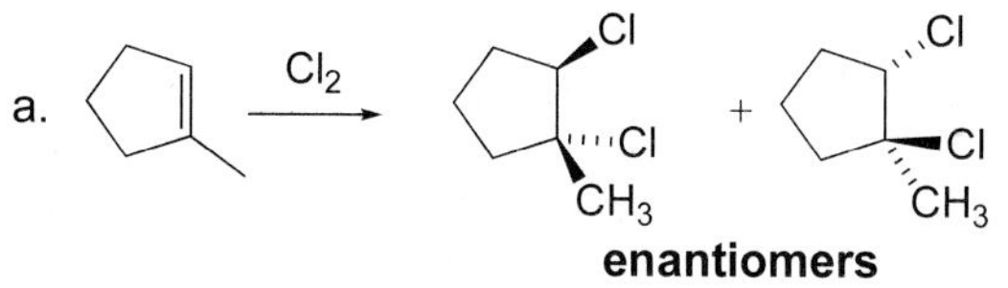
a.
Cl2
Cl
Cl
CH3
+
enantiomers

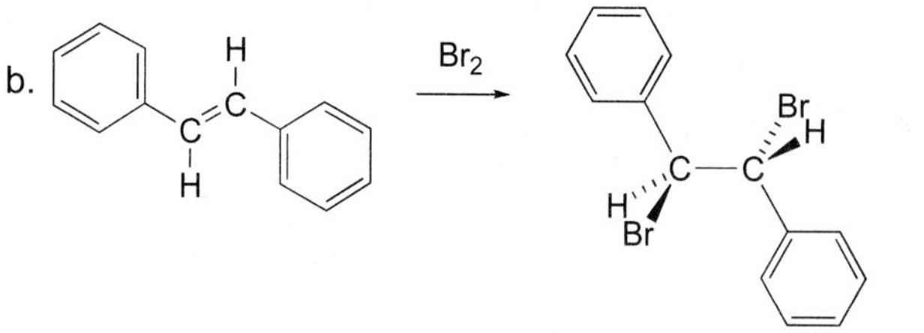
b.
H
C=C
H
Br2
Br
H
C
C
H
Br

achiral meso compound

c. 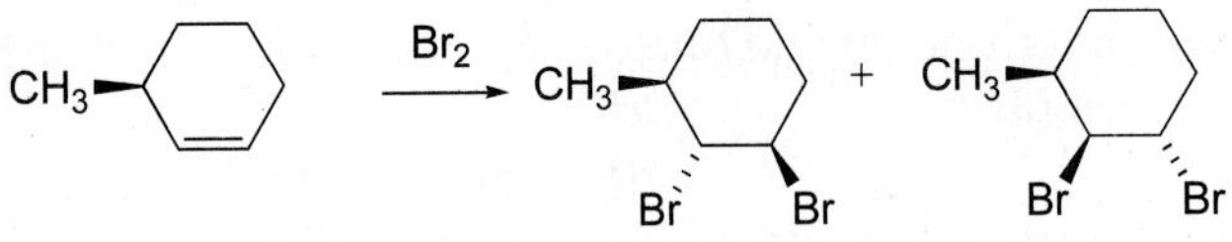

diastereomers

10.25 The two steps in the mechanism for the halogenation of an alkene are:
[1] Addition of X^+ to the alkene to form a bridged halonium ion
[2] Nucleophilic attack by X^-

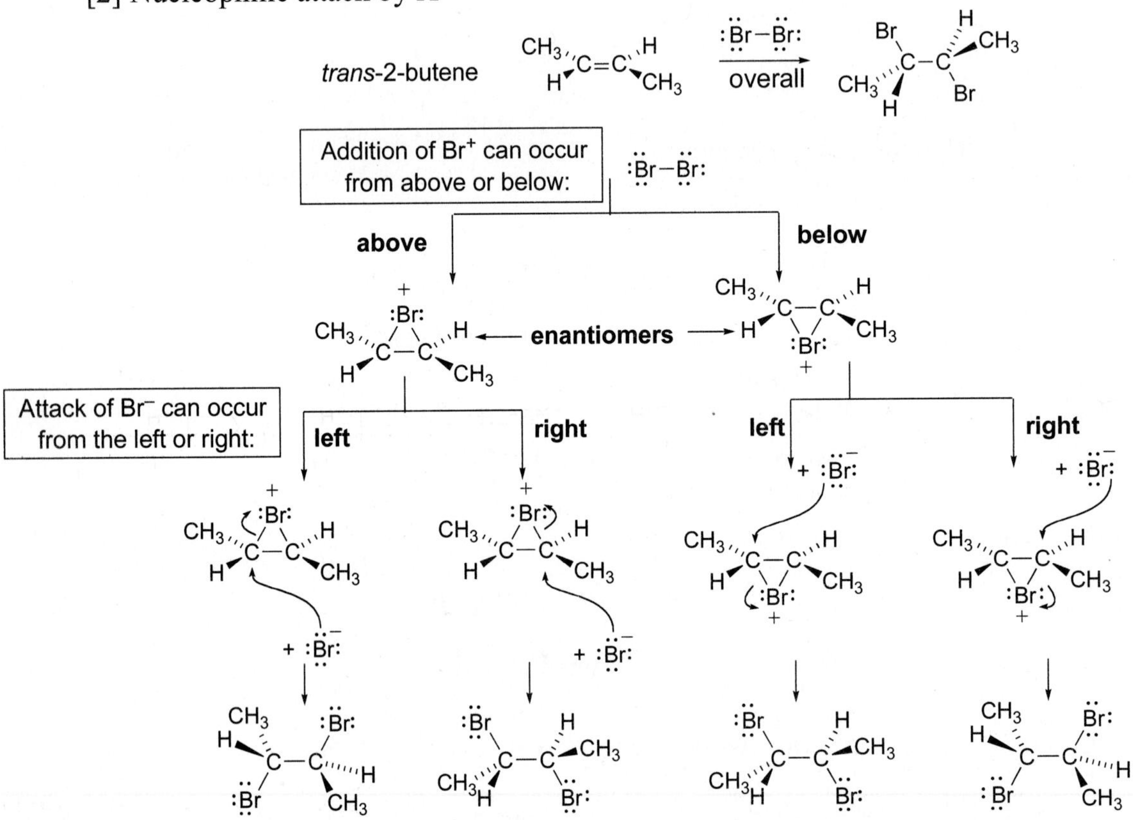

All four compounds are identical—an achiral meso compound.

10.26 Halohydrin formation adds the elements of X and OH across the double bond in an anti fashion. The reaction is regioselective so X ends up on the carbon that had more H's to begin with.

a. 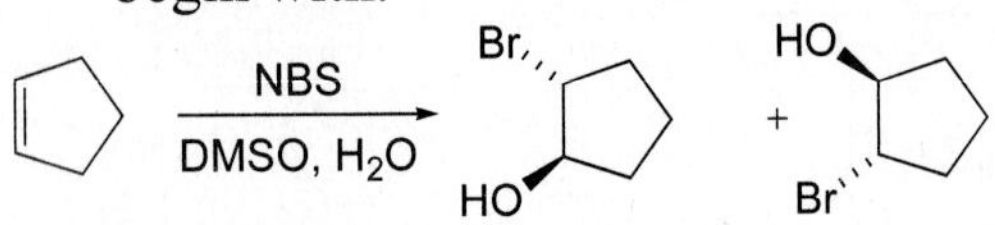

b. 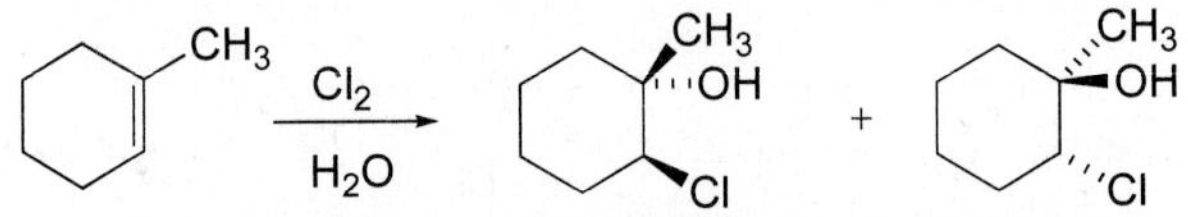

Cl bonds to the carbon with more H's to begin with.

10.27

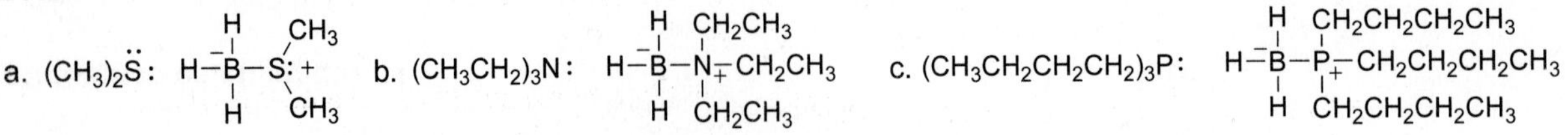

10.28 In hydroboration the boron atom is the electrophile and becomes bonded to the carbon atom that had more H's to begin with.

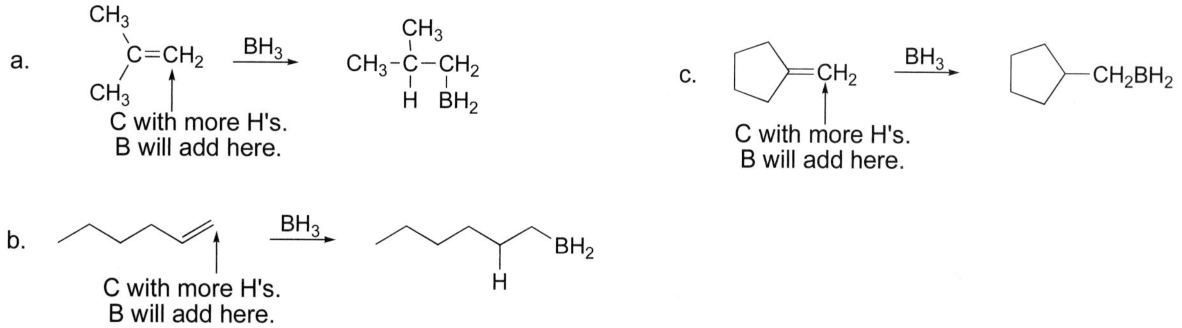
a.
C with more H's.
B will add here.
c.
C with more H's.
B will add here.
b.
C with more H's.
B will add here.

10.29 The hydroboration–oxidation reaction occurs in two steps:
[1] Syn addition of BH_3, with the boron on the less substituted carbon atom
[2] OH replaces the BH_2 with retention of configuration.

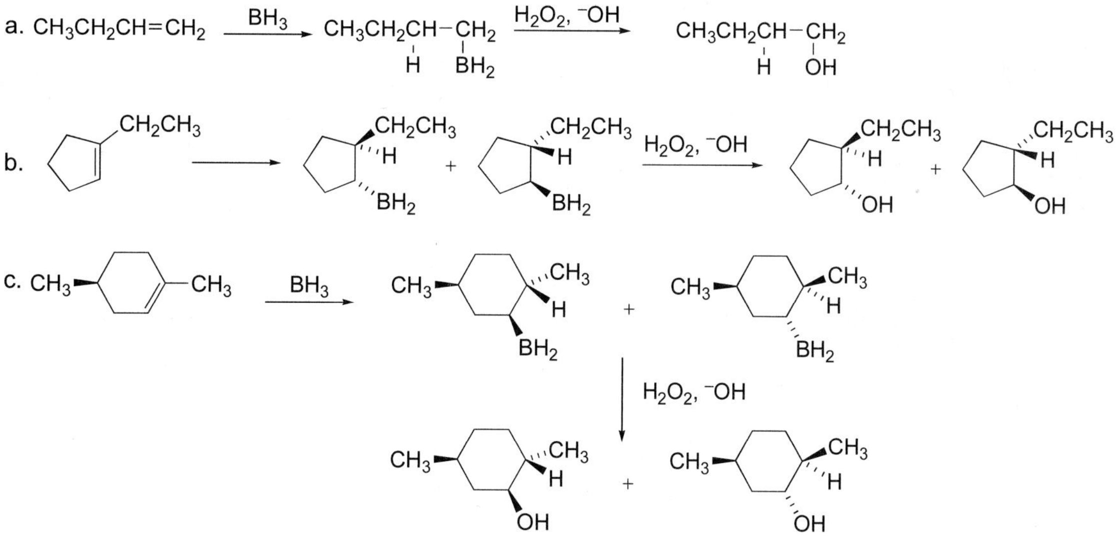

10.30 Remember that hydroboration results in addition of OH on the less substituted C.

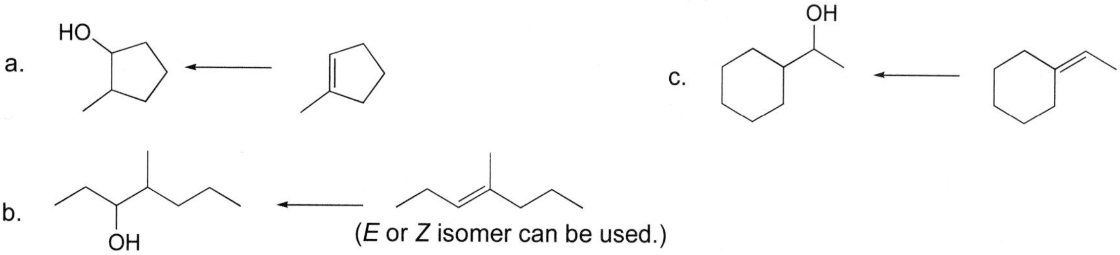
(E or Z isomer can be used.)

10.31

a.

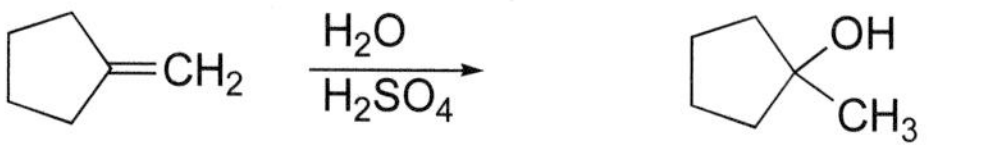

Hydration places the OH on the more substituted carbon.

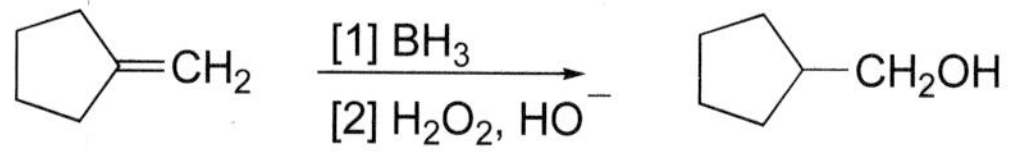

Hydroboration–oxidation places the OH on the less substituted carbon.

b.

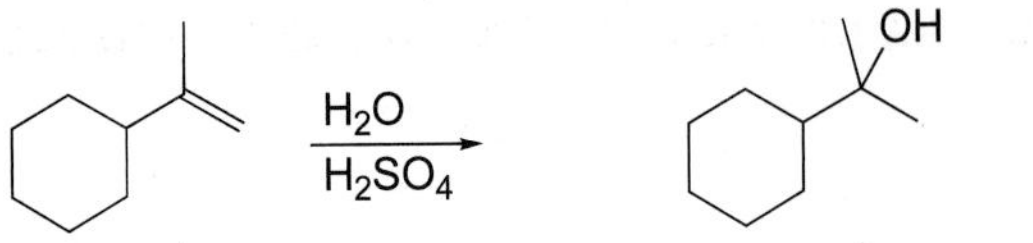

H_2O
H_2SO_4
OH

Hydration places the OH on the more substituted carbon.

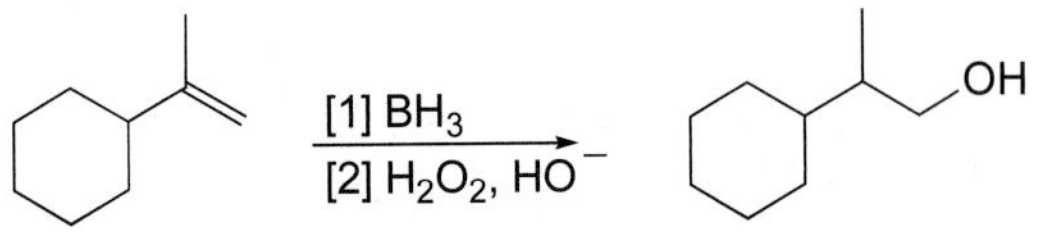

[1] BH_3
[2] H_2O_2, HO^-
OH

Hydroboration–oxidation places the OH on the less substituted carbon.

c.

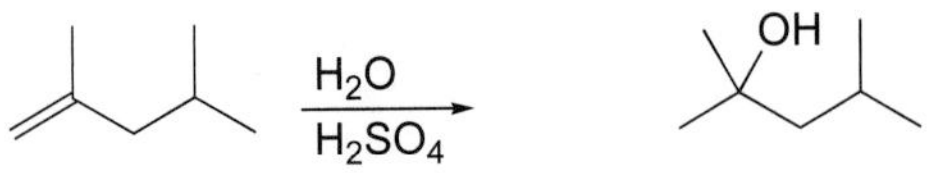

H_2O
H_2SO_4
OH

Hydration places the OH on the more substituted carbon.

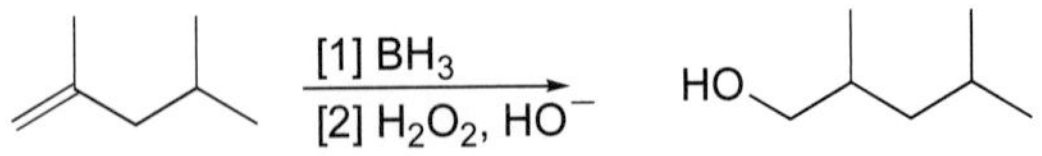

[1] BH_3
[2] H_2O_2, HO^-
HO

Hydroboration–oxidation places the OH on the less substituted carbon.

10.32 There are always two steps in this kind of question:
[1] **Identify the functional group and decide what types of reactions it undergoes** (e.g., substitution, elimination, or addition).
[2] **Look at the reagent and determine if it is an electrophile, nucleophile, acid, or base.**

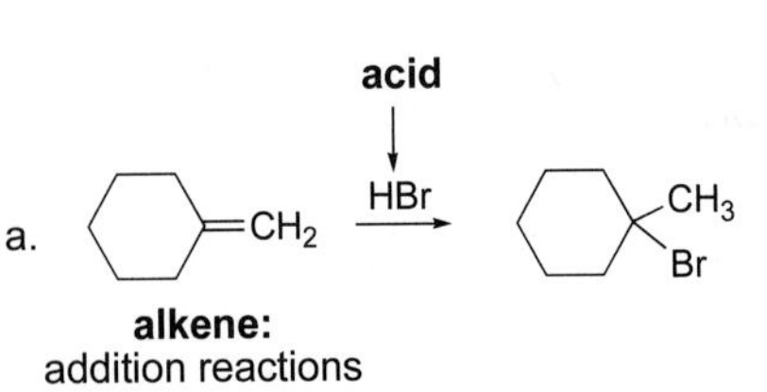

acid
a.
$=CH_2$
HBr
CH_3
Br
alkene:
addition reactions

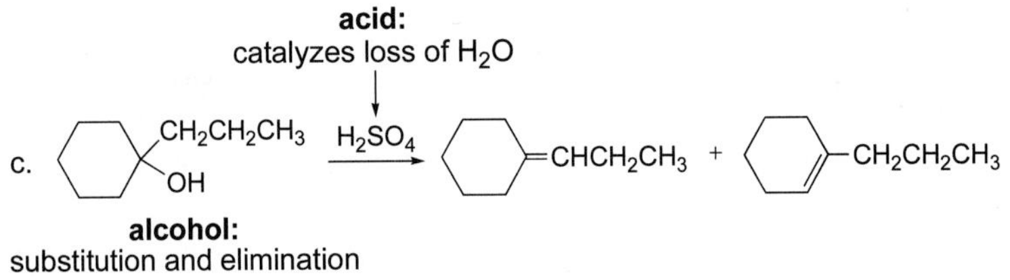

acid:
catalyzes loss of H_2O
c.
$CH_2CH_2CH_3$
OH
H_2SO_4
$=CHCH_2CH_3$
+
$-CH_2CH_2CH_3$
alcohol:
substitution and elimination

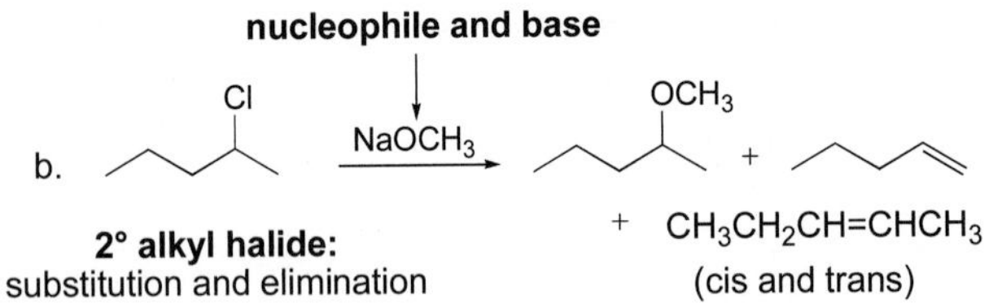

nucleophile and base
b.
Cl
$NaOCH_3$
OCH_3
+
+ $CH_3CH_2CH=CHCH_3$
(cis and trans)
2° alkyl halide:
substitution and elimination

10.33 To devise a synthesis:
[1] Look at the starting material and decide what reactions it can undergo.
[2] Look at the product and decide what reactions could make it.

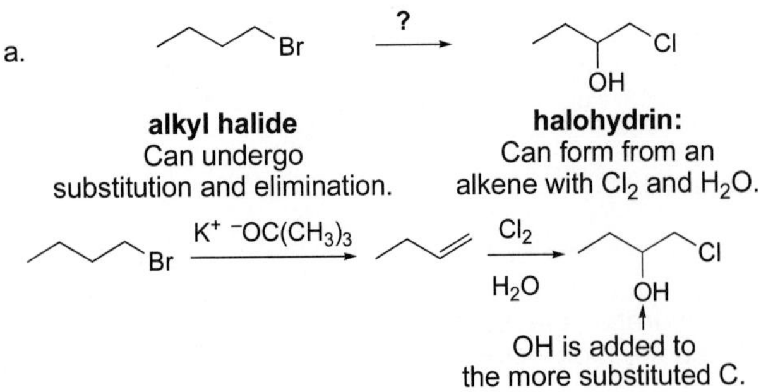

a.
Br
?
Cl
OH
alkyl halide
Can undergo
substitution and elimination.
halohydrin:
Can form from an
alkene with Cl_2 and H_2O.
Br
K^+ $^-OC(CH_3)_3$
Cl_2
H_2O
Cl
OH
OH is added to
the more substituted C.

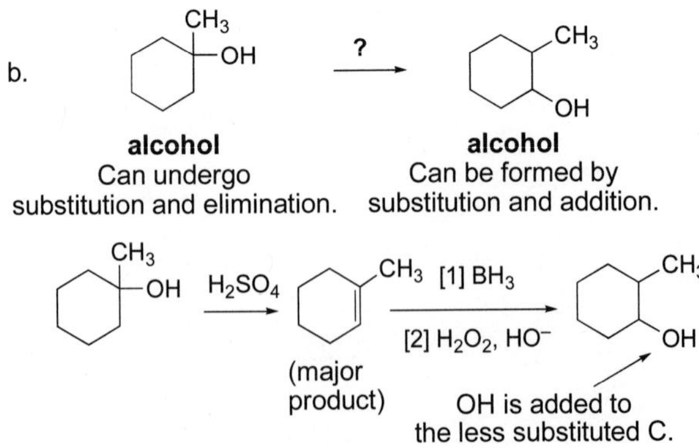

b.
CH_3
OH
?
CH_3
OH
alcohol
Can undergo
substitution and elimination.
alcohol
Can be formed by
substitution and addition.
CH_3
OH
H_2SO_4
CH_3
(major
product)
[1] BH_3
[2] H_2O_2, HO^-
CH_3
OH
OH is added to
the less substituted C.

10.34 Convert each ball-and-stick model to a skeletal structure and then name the molecule.

a. 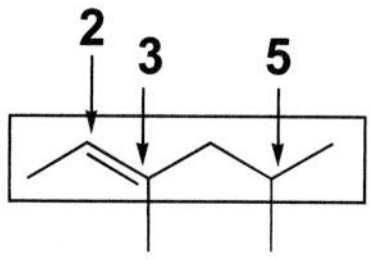
2
3
5

6 C chain with a C=C → hexene
C=C at C2 → 2-hexene
2 CH_3's at C3 and C5
two higher priority groups on opposite sides → *E* isomer
Answer: **(2*E*)-3,5-dimethyl-2-hexene**

b. 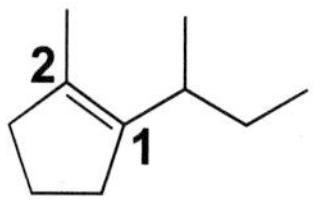
2
1

5 C ring with a C=C → cyclopentene
sec-butyl at C1
methyl at C2
Answer: **1-*sec*-butyl-2-methylcyclopentene**

10.35

a. 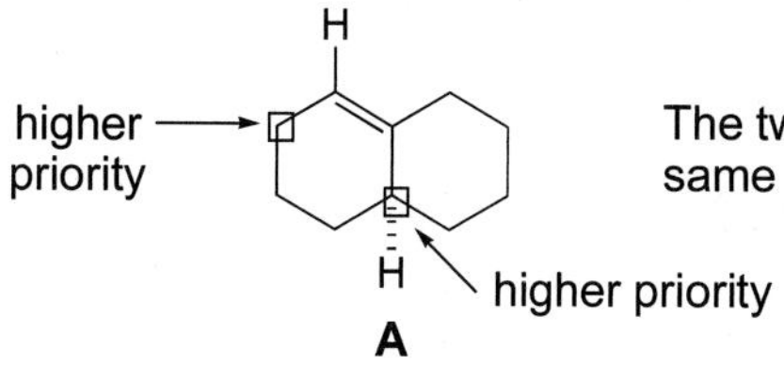
H
higher priority
H
higher priority
A

The two higher priority groups are on the same side of the C=C, making it a ***Z*** alkene.

b. Add H_2O in a Markovnikov fashion to form two products.

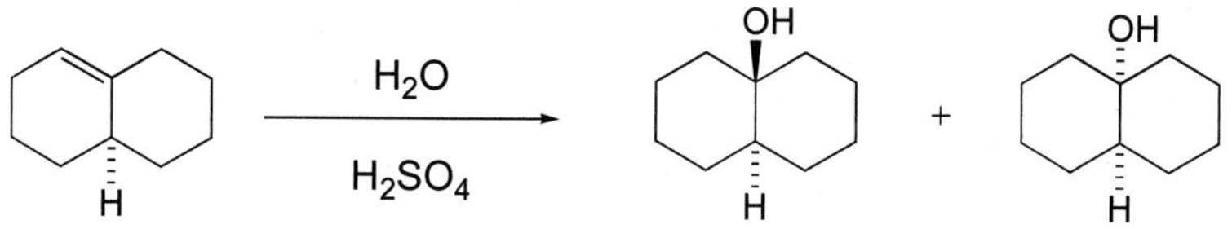
H
H2O
H2SO4
OH
H
+
OH
H

10.36

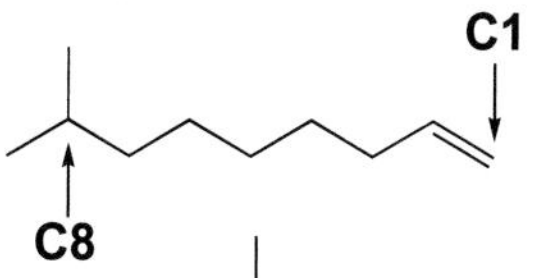
C1
C8

8-methyl-1-nonene

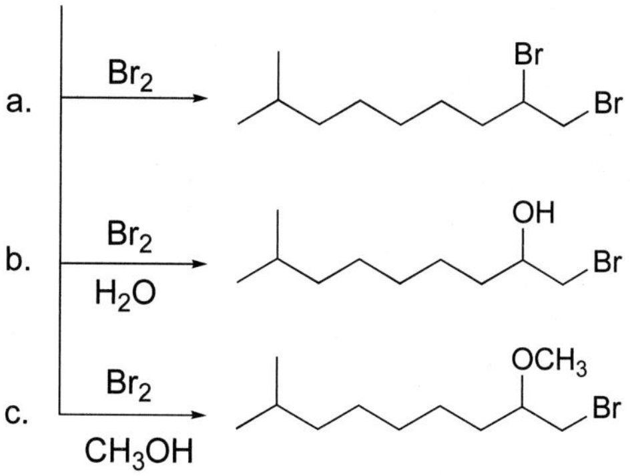
a.
Br2
Br
Br
b.
Br2
H2O
OH
Br
c.
Br2
CH3OH
OCH3
Br

10.37 Use the directions from Answer 10.2 to calculate degrees of unsaturation.

a. C_3H_4
[1] maximum number of H's = 2*n* + 2 = 2(3) + 2 = 8
[2] subtract actual from maximum = 8 – 4 = 4
[3] divide by 2 = 4/2 = **2 degrees of unsaturation**

b. C_6H_8
[1] maximum number of H's = 2*n* + 2 = 2(6) + 2 = 14
[2] subtract actual from maximum = 14 – 8 = 6
[3] divide by 2 = 6/2 = **3 degrees of unsaturation**

c. $C_{40}H_{56}$
[1] maximum number of H's = 2*n* + 2 = 2(40) + 2 = 82
[2] subtract actual from maximum = 82 – 56 = 26
[3] divide by 2 = 26/2 = **13 degrees of unsaturation**

d. C_8H_8O
Ignore the O.
[1] maximum number of H's = 2*n* + 2 = 2(8) + 2 = 18
[2] subtract actual from maximum = 18 – 8 = 10
[3] divide by 2 = 10/2 = **5 degrees of unsaturation**

e. $C_{10}H_{16}O_2$
Ignore both O's.
[1] maximum number of H's = 2*n* + 2 = 2(10) + 2 = 22
[2] subtract actual from maximum = 22 – 16 = 6
[3] divide by 2 = 6/2 = **3 degrees of unsaturation**

f. C_8H_9Br
Because of Br, add one H (9 + 1 = 10 H's).
[1] maximum number of H's = 2*n* + 2 = 2(8) + 2 = 18
[2] subtract actual from maximum = 18 – 10 = 8
[3] divide by 2 = 8/2 = **4 degrees of unsaturation**

g. C_8H_9ClO
Ignore the O; count Cl as one more H (9 + 1 = 10 H's).
[1] maximum number of H's = 2*n* + 2 = 2(8) + 2 = 18
[2] subtract actual from maximum = 18 – 10 = 8
[3] divide by 2 = 8/2 = **4 degrees of unsaturation**

h. C_7H_9Br
Because of Br, add one H (9 + 1 = 10 H's).
[1] maximum number of H's = 2*n* + 2 = 2(7) + 2 = 16
[2] subtract actual from maximum = 16 –10 = 6
[3] divide by 2 = 6/2 = **3 degrees of unsaturation**

i. $C_7H_{11}N$
Because of N, subtract one H (11 – 1 = 10 H's).
[1] maximum number of H's = 2*n* + 2 = 2(7) + 2 = 16
[2] subtract actual from maximum = 16 – 10 = 6
[3] divide by 2 = 6/2 = **3 degrees of unsaturation**

j. C_4H_8BrN
Because of Br, add one H, but subtract one for N (8 + 1 – 1 = 8 H's).
[1] maximum number of H's = 2*n* + 2 = 2(4) + 2 = 10
[2] subtract actual from maximum = 10 – 8 = 2
[3] divide by 2 = 2/2 = **1 degree of unsaturation**

10.38 First determine the number of degrees of unsaturation in the compound. Then decide which combinations of rings and π bonds could exist.

$C_{10}H_{14}$
[1] maximum number of H's = 2*n* + 2 = 2(10) + 2 = 22
[2] subtract actual from maximum = 22 – 14 = 8
[3] divide by two = 8/2 = **4 degrees of unsaturation**

possibilities:
4 π bonds
3 π bonds + 1 ring
2 π bonds + 2 rings
1 π bond + 3 rings
4 rings

10.39 The statement is incorrect because when naming isomers with more than two groups on a double bond, one must use an *E*,*Z* label, rather than a cis, trans label.

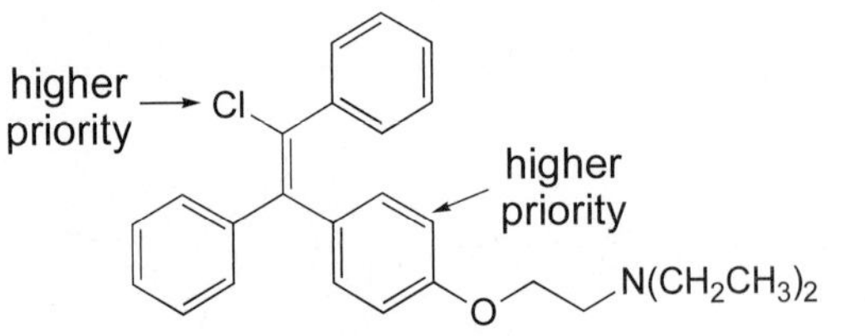
higher priority
Cl
higher priority
O
$N(CH_2CH_3)_2$
enclomiphene
***E* isomer**

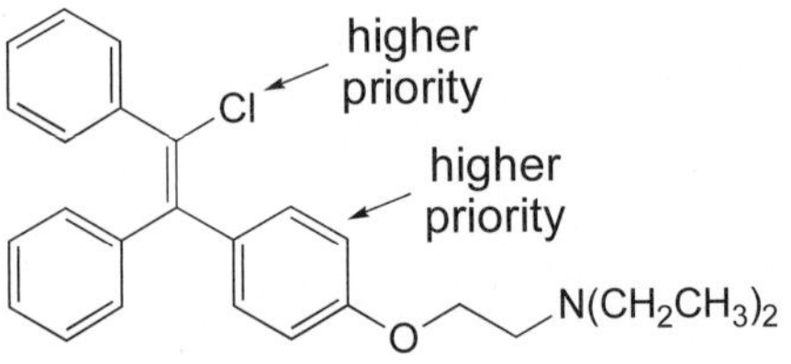
higher priority
Cl
higher priority
O
$N(CH_2CH_3)_2$
zuclomiphene
***Z* isomer**

10.40 Name the alkenes using the rules in Answers 10.4 and 10.6.

a. $CH_2{=}CHCH_2CH(CH_3)CH_2CH_3$

6 C chain with a double bond = **hexene**

CH_3
$CH_2{=}CHCH_2CHCH_2CH_3$
1-hexene **4-methyl**

4-methyl-1-hexene

b. 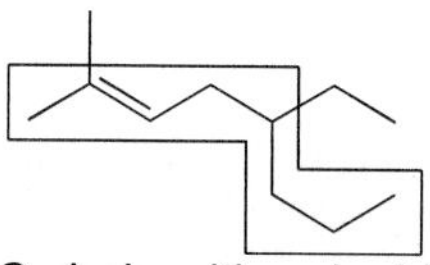

8 C chain with a double bond = **octene**

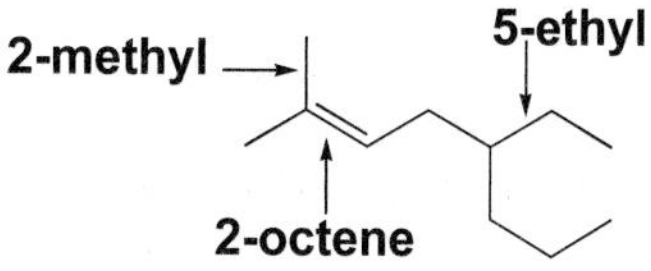

5-ethyl-2-methyl-2-octene

c. 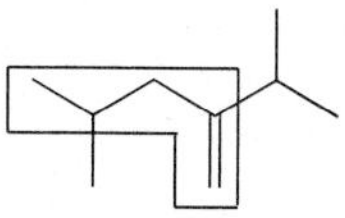

5 C chain with a double bond = **pentene**

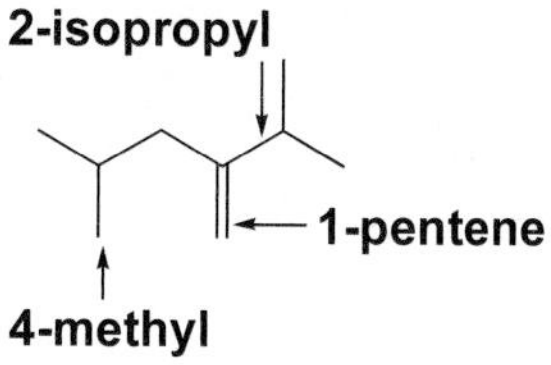

2-isopropyl-4-methyl-1-pentene

d. 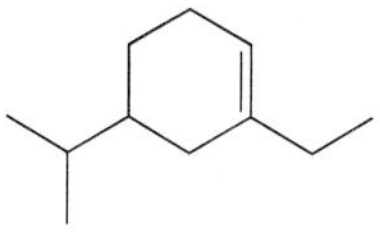

6 C ring with a double bond = **cyclohexene**

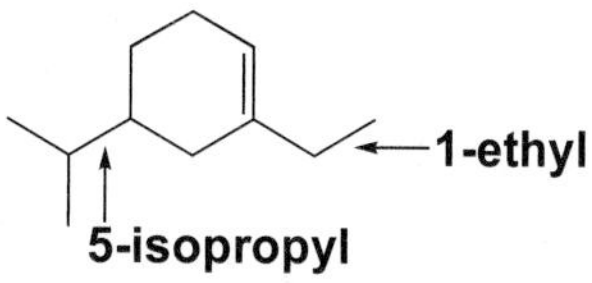

1-ethyl-5-isopropylcyclohexene

e. 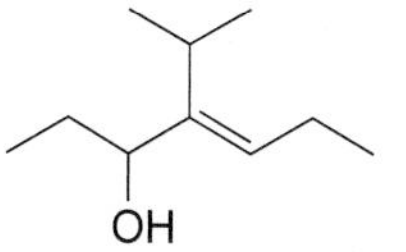

7 C chain with a double bond = **heptene**

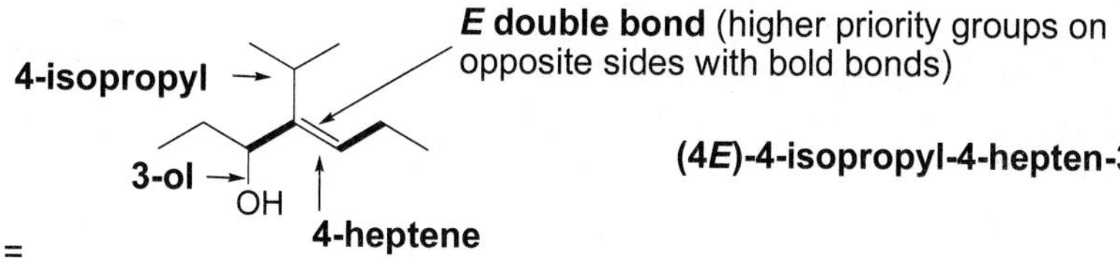

(4*E*)-4-isopropyl-4-hepten-3-ol

f. 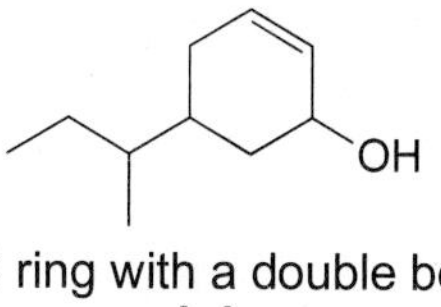

6 C ring with a double bond = **cyclohexene**

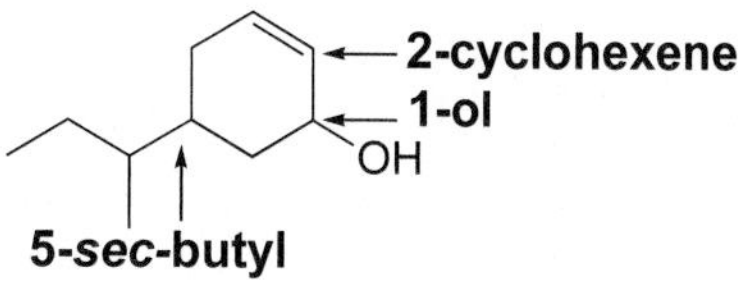

5-*sec*-butyl-2-cyclohexenol

10.41 Use the directions from Answer 10.8.

a. (3*E*)-4-ethyl-3-**heptene**

7 carbons

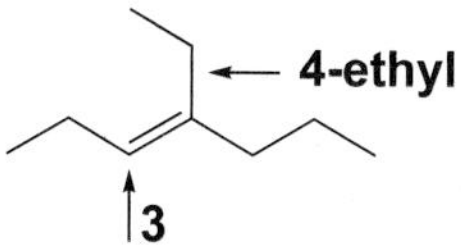

Higher priority groups on opposite sides = *E*.

b. 3,3-dimethyl**cyclopentene**

5 carbon ring

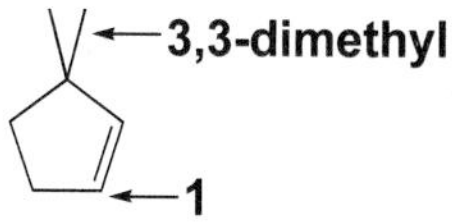

c. *cis*-4-**octene**

8 carbons

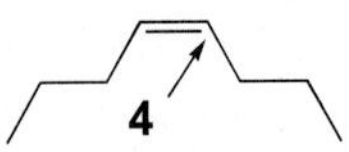

Higher priority groups on the same side = cis.

d. 4-vinyl**cyclopentene**

5 carbon ring

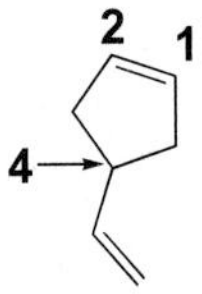

e. (2*Z*)-3-isopropyl-2-**heptene**

7 carbons

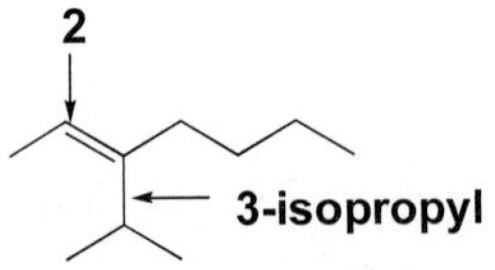

Higher priority groups on the same side = *Z*.

f. *cis*-3,4-dimethyl**cyclopentene**

5 carbon ring

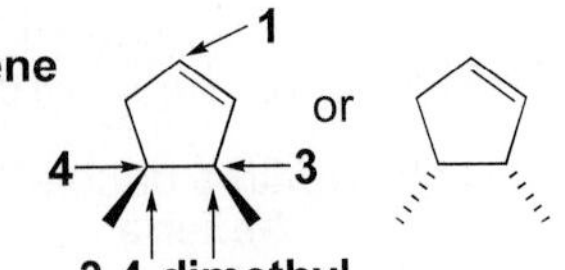

g. *trans*-2-**heptene**

7 carbons

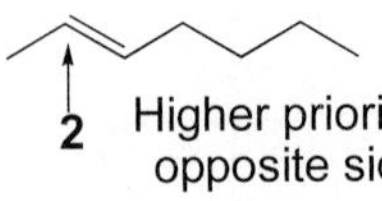

Higher priority groups on opposite sides = trans.

h. 1-isopropyl-4-propyl**cyclohexene**

6 carbon ring

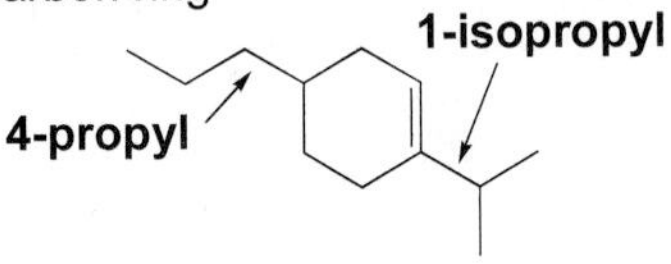

10.42

a.

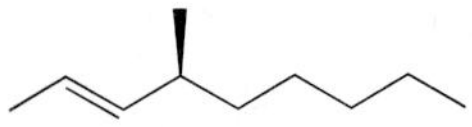

(2*E*,4*S*)-4-methyl-2-nonene
A

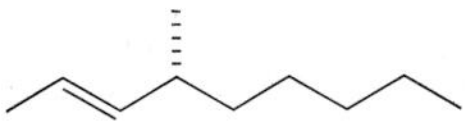

(2*E*,4*R*)-4-methyl-2-nonene
B

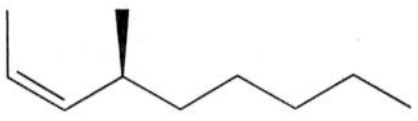

(2*Z*,4*S*)-4-methyl-2-nonene
C

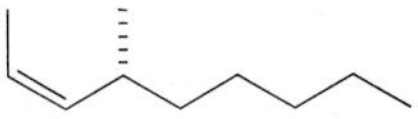

(2*Z*,4*R*)-4-methyl-2-nonene
D

b. **A** and **B** are enantiomers. **C** and **D** are enantiomers.

c. Pairs of diastereomers: **A** and **C, A** and **D, B** and **C, B** and **D.**

10.43

a.

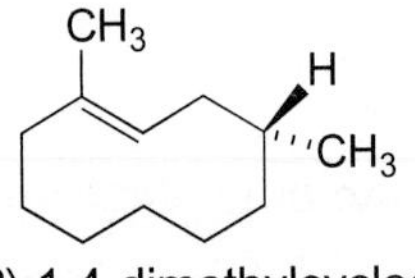

(1*E*,4*R*)-1,4-dimethylcyclodecene

b.

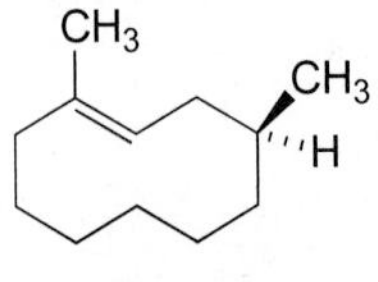

(1*E*,4*S*)-1,4-dimethylcyclodecene
enantiomer

c.

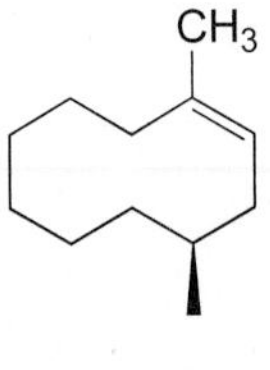

(1*Z*,4*S*)-1,4-dimethylcyclodecene
diastereomer

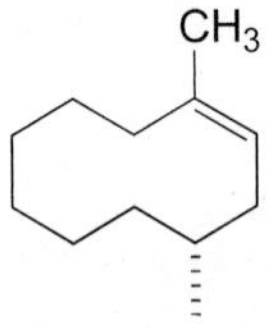

(1*Z*,4*R*)-1,4-dimethylcyclodecene
diastereomer

10.44 Name the alkene from which the epoxide can be derived and add the word *oxide.*

a.

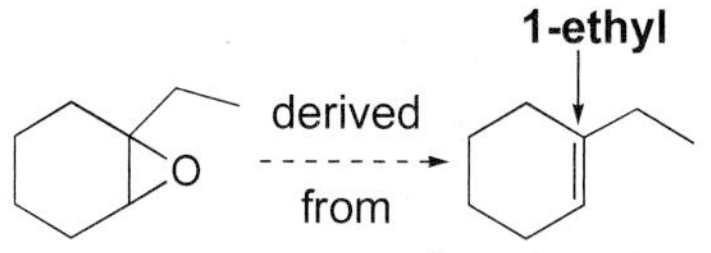
1-ethyl
O
derived
from

6 carbon ring
cyclohexene
1-ethylcyclohexene

1-ethylcyclohexene oxide

b.

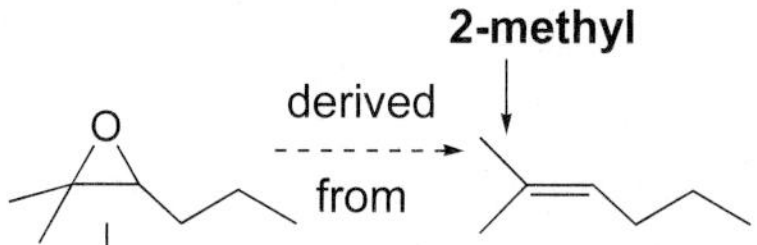
2-methyl
O
derived
from

6 carbon chain
hexene
2-methyl-2-hexene

2-methyl-2-hexene oxide

c.

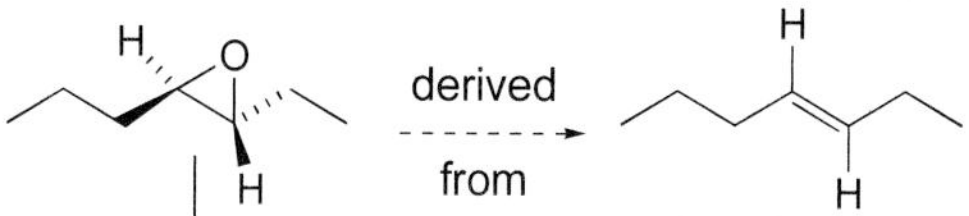
H
O
H
derived
from
H
H

7 carbon chain
heptene
(3*E*)- 3-heptene
or
***trans*-3-heptene**

(3*E*)- 3-heptene oxide
or
***trans*-3-heptene oxide**

d.

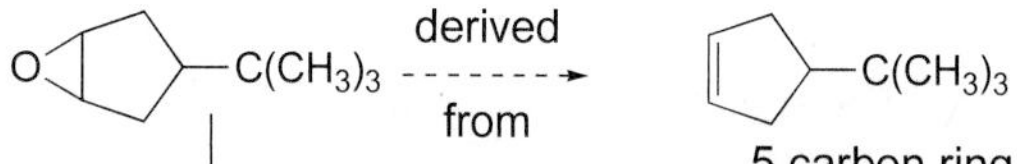
O
C(CH3)3
derived
from
C(CH3)3

5 carbon ring
cyclopentene
4-*tert*-butylcyclopentene

4-*tert*-butylcyclopentene oxide

10.45

a. 2-butyl-3-methyl-1-pentene

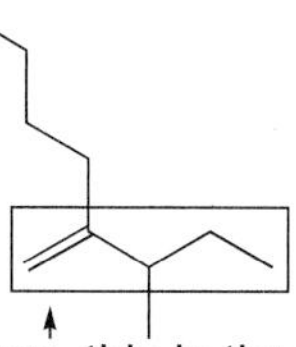

As written, this is the parent chain, but there is another longer chain containing the double bond.

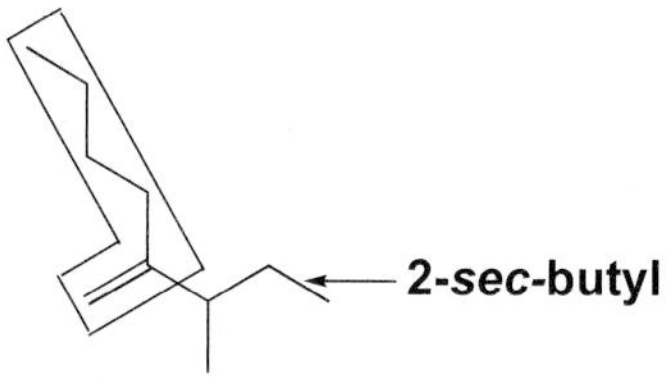
2-sec-butyl

new name:
2-*sec*-butyl-1-hexene

b. (*Z*)-2-methyl-2-hexene

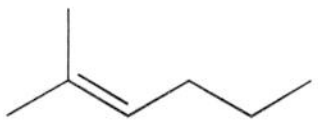

Two groups on one end of the C=C are the same (2 CH_3's), so no *E* and *Z* isomers are possible.

new name:
2-methyl-2-hexene

c. (*E*)-1-isopropyl-1-butene

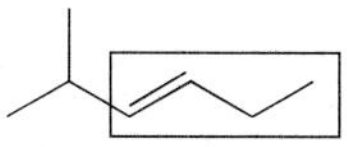

As written, this is the parent chain, but there is another longer chain containing the double bond.

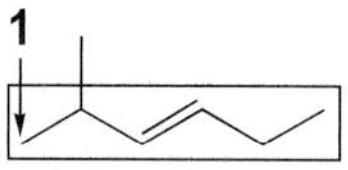
1

new name:
(3*E*)-2-methyl-3-hexene

d. 5-methylcyclohexene

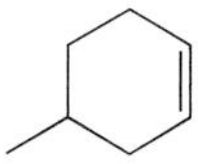

As written the methyl is at C5. Re-number to put it at C4.

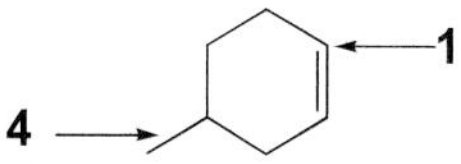
1
4

new name:
4-methylcyclohexene

e. 4-isobutyl-2-methylcylohexene

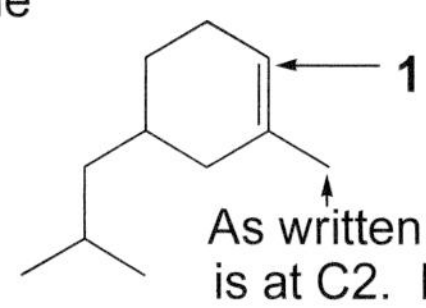
1

As written this methyl is at C2. Re-number to put it at C1.

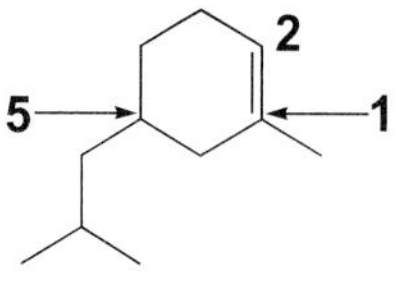
2
5
1

new name:
5-isobutyl-1-methylcyclohexene

f. 1-*sec*-butyl-2-cyclopentene

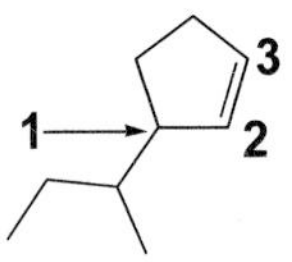

This has the double bond between C2 and C3. Cycloalkenes must have the double bond between C1 and C2. Re-number.

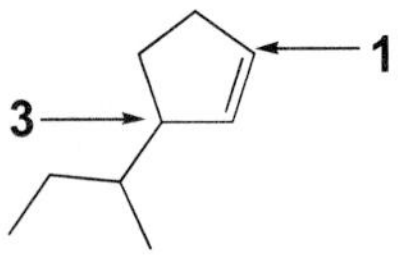

new name:
3-*sec*-butylcyclopentene

g. 1-cyclohexen-4-ol

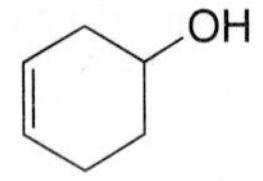

The numbering is incorrect. When a compound contains both a double bond and an OH group, number the C skeleton to give the OH group the lower number.

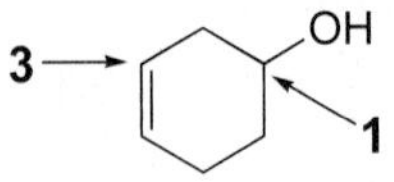

3-cyclohexenol (The "1" can be omitted.)

h. 3-ethyl-3-octen-5-ol

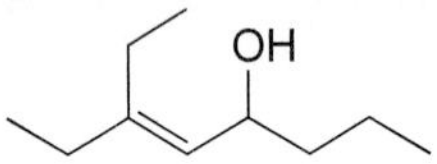

The numbering is incorrect. When a compound contains both a double bond and an OH group, number the C skeleton to give the OH group the lower number.

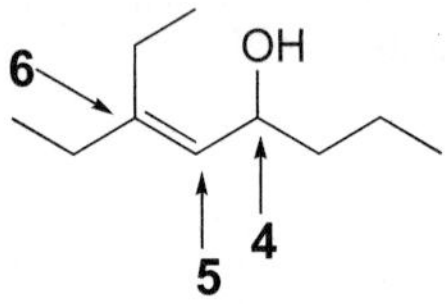

6-ethyl-5-octen-4-ol

10.46 a, b. *E*,*Z*, and *R*,*S* designations are shown.

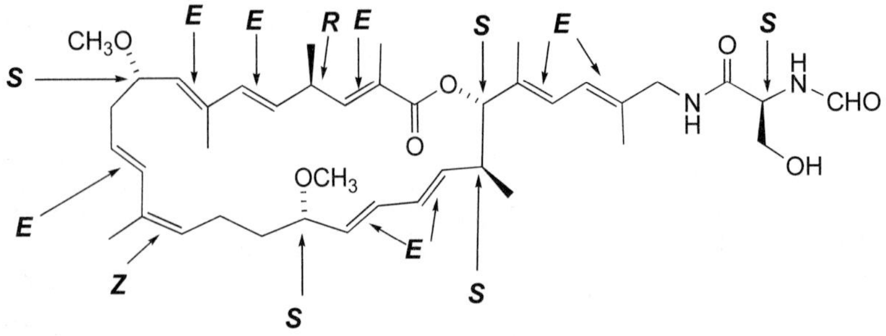

c. Nine double bonds that can be *E* or *Z*
Six tetrahedral stereogenic centers
Maximum possible number of stereoisomers = 2^{15}

10.47

stearic acid

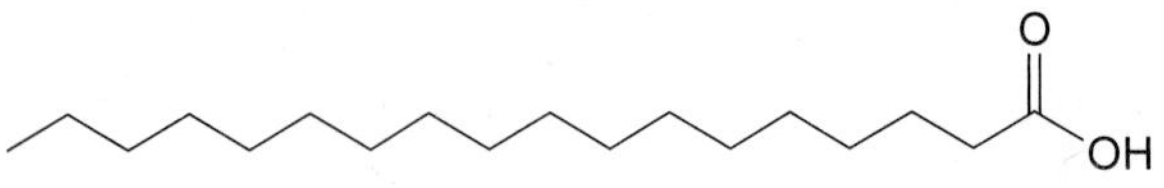

hlghest melting point
no double bonds

elaidic acid

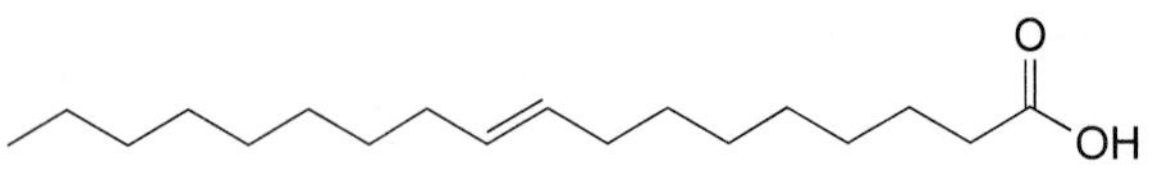

intermediate melting point
one *E* double bond

oleic acid

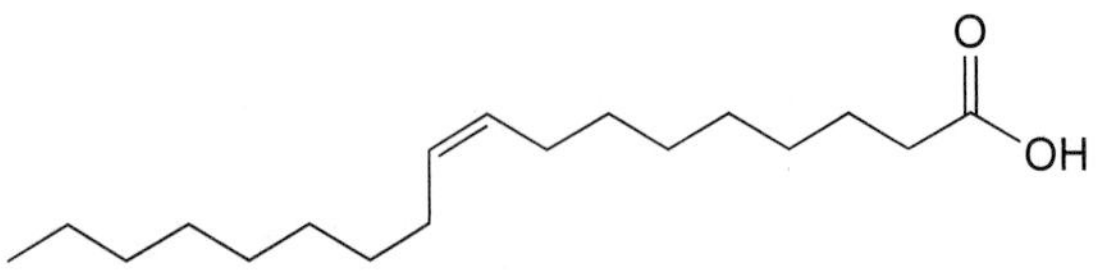

lowest melting point
one *Z* double bond

10.48

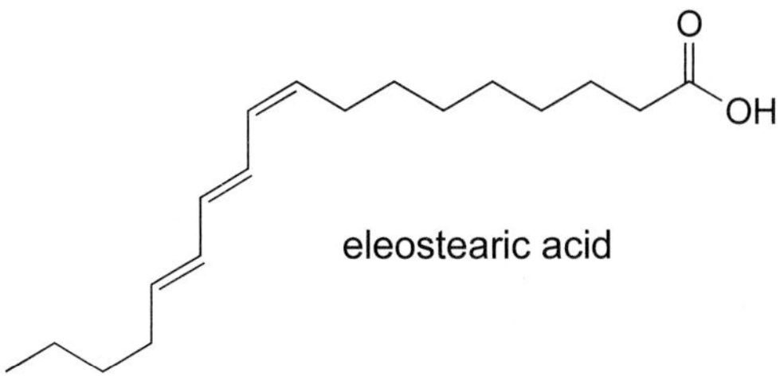

eleostearic acid

a. 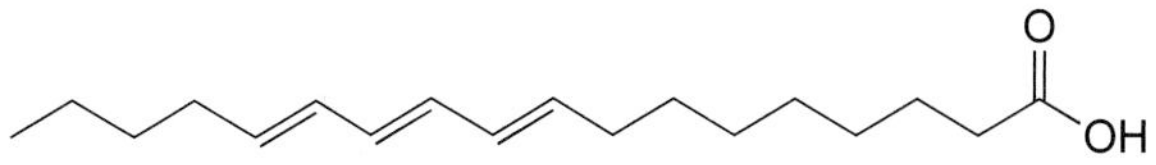

all trans double bonds
higher melting point

b. 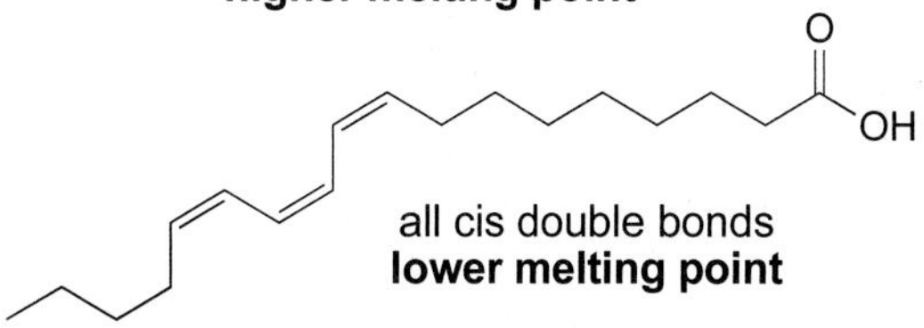

all cis double bonds
lower melting point

10.49 The more negative the $\Delta H°$, the larger the K_{eq} assuming entropy changes are comparable. Calculate the $\Delta H°$ for each reaction and compare.

$CH_2{=}CH_2$ + HI ⟶ $CH_3CH_2{-}I$

[1] Bonds broken

	$\Delta H°$ (kJ/mol)
C–C π bond	+ 267
H–I	+ 297
Total	+ 564 kJ/mol

[2] Bonds formed

	$\Delta H°$ (kJ/mol)
$CH_2ICH_2{-}H$	– 410
C–I	– 222
Total	– 632 kJ/mol

[3] Overall $\Delta H°$ =

sum in Step [1]
+
sum in Step [2]

+ 564 kJ/mol
– 632 kJ/mol

– 68 kJ/mol

$CH_2{=}CH_2$ + HCl ⟶ $CH_3CH_2{-}Cl$

[1] Bonds broken

	$\Delta H°$ (kJ/mol)
C–C π bond	+ 267
H–Cl	+ 431
Total	+ 698 kJ/mol

[2] Bonds formed

	$\Delta H°$ (kJ/mol)
$CH_2ClCH_2{-}H$	– 410
C–Cl	– 339
Total	– 749 kJ/mol

[3] Overall $\Delta H°$ =

sum in Step [1]
+
sum in Step [2]

+ 698 kJ/mol
– 749 kJ/mol

– 51 kJ/mol

Compare the $\Delta H°$:
Addition of HI: **–68 kJ/mol** = more negative $\Delta H°$, larger K_{eq}
Addition of HCl: **–51 kJ/mol**

10.50

a. 
HBr

f. 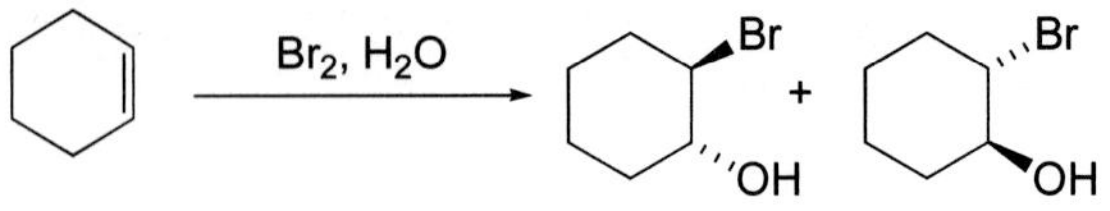
Br2, H2O

b. 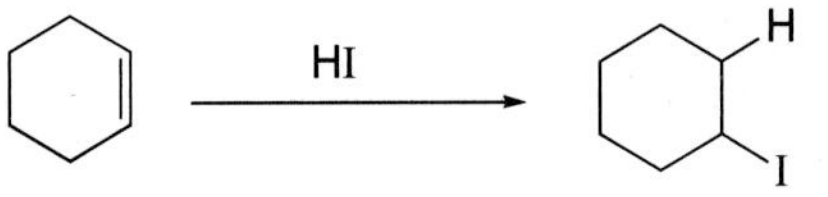
HI

g. 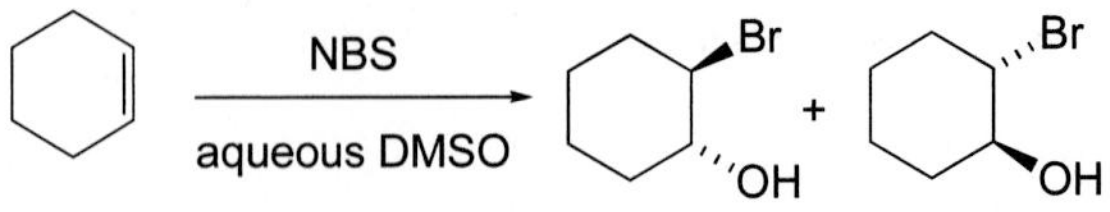
NBS
aqueous DMSO

c. 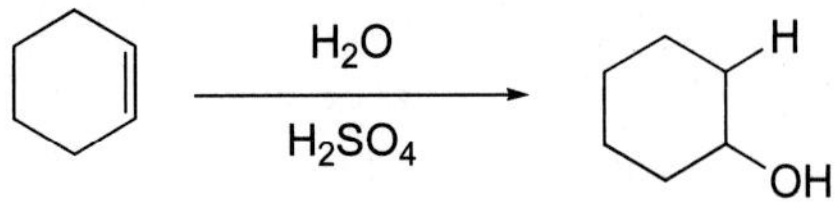
H2O
H2SO4

h. 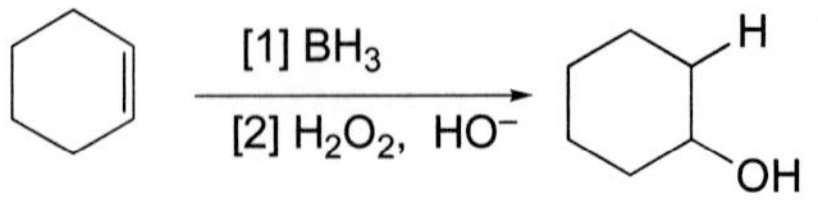
[1] BH3
[2] H2O2, HO−

d. 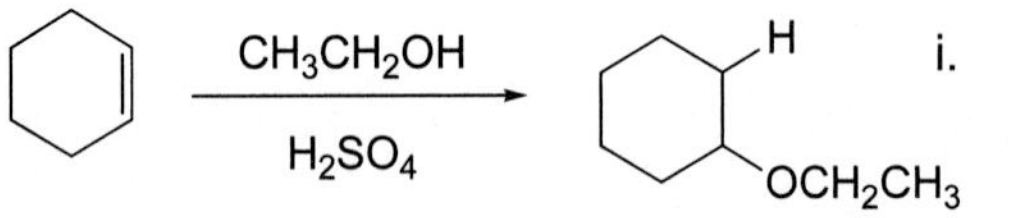
CH3CH2OH
H2SO4

i. 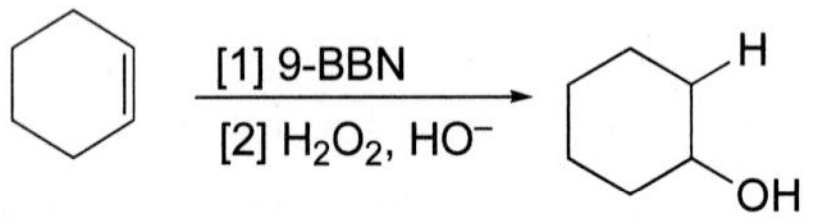
[1] 9-BBN
[2] H2O2, HO−

e. 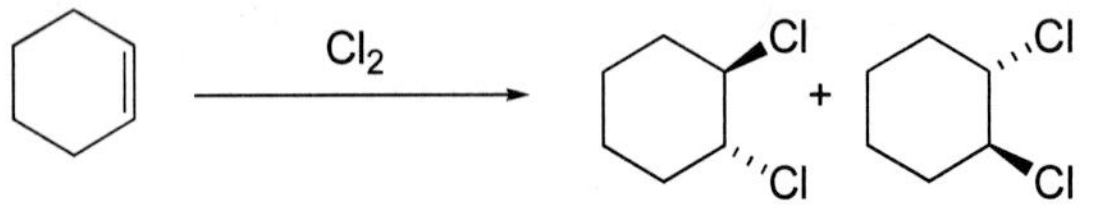
Cl2

10.51

a. 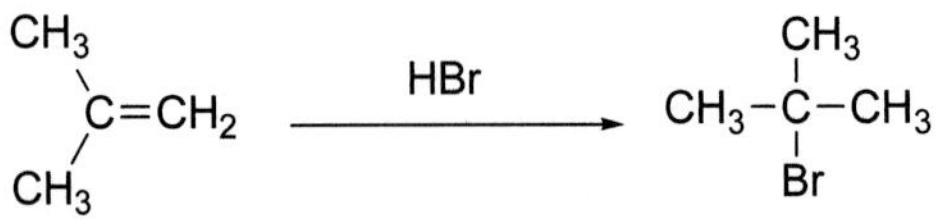
HBr

f. 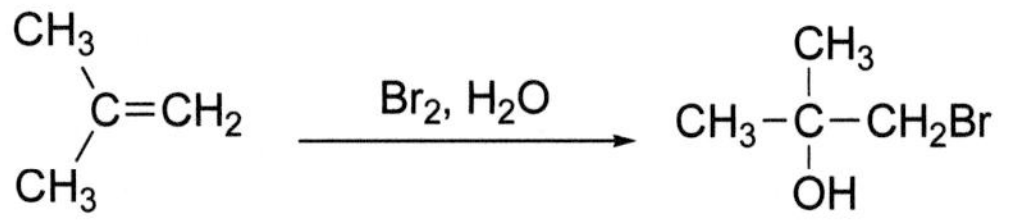
Br2, H2O

b. 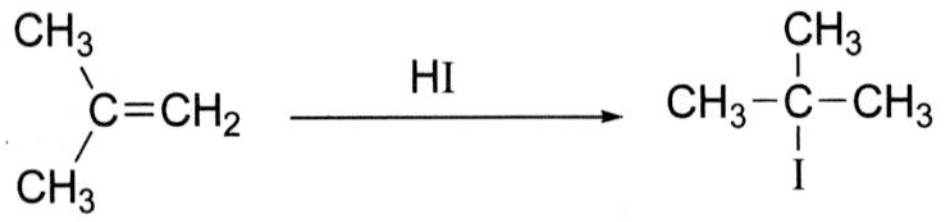
HI

g. 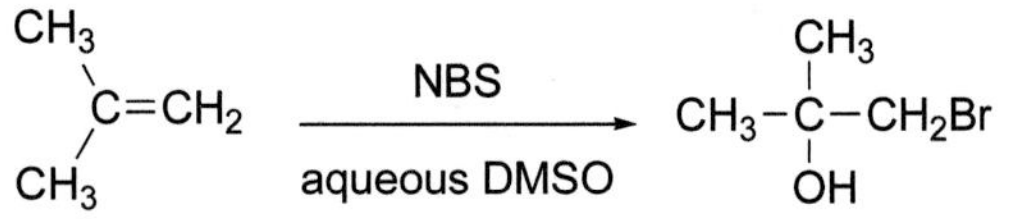
NBS
aqueous DMSO

c. 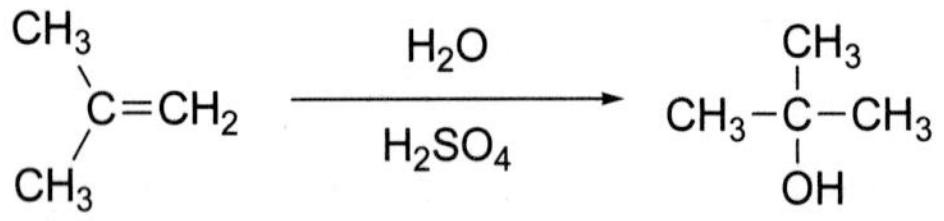
H2O
H2SO4

h. 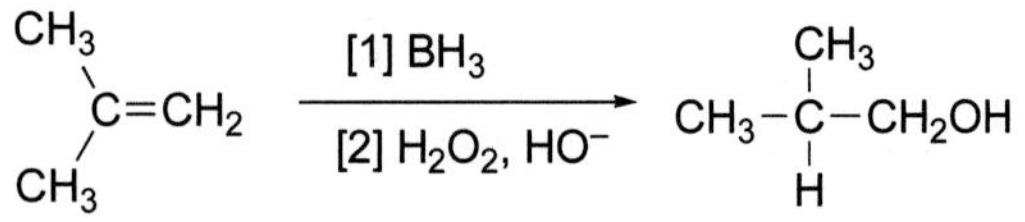
[1] BH3
[2] H2O2, HO−

d. 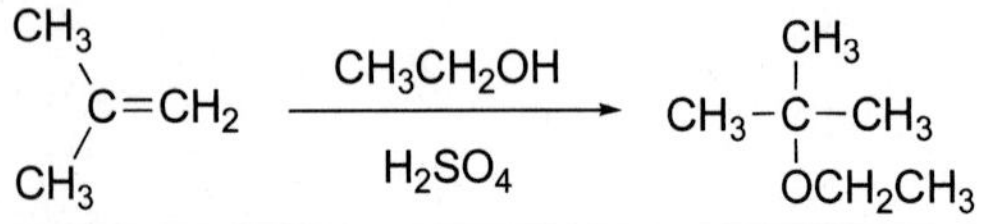
CH3CH2OH
H2SO4

i. 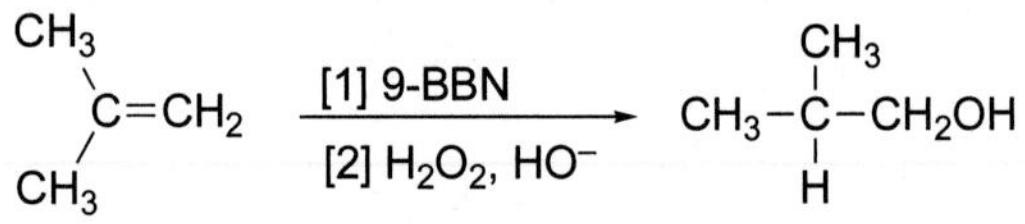
[1] 9-BBN
[2] H2O2, HO−

e. 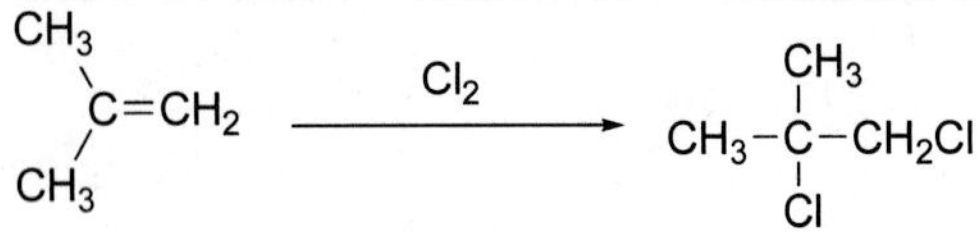
Cl2

10.52

a. 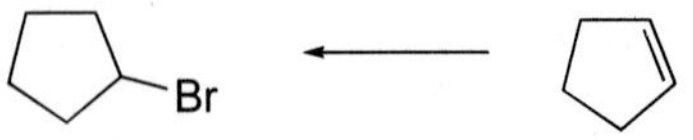

d. 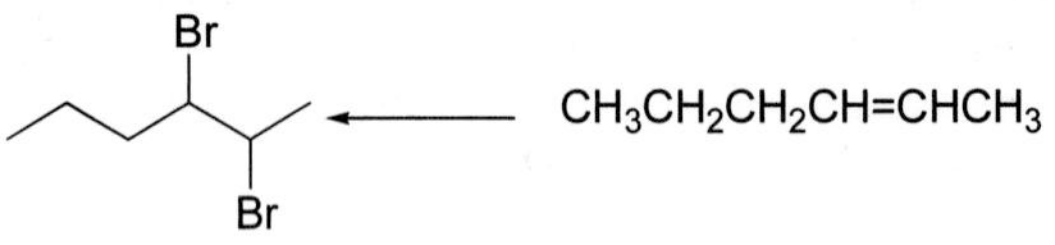
CH3CH2CH2CH=CHCH3

b. 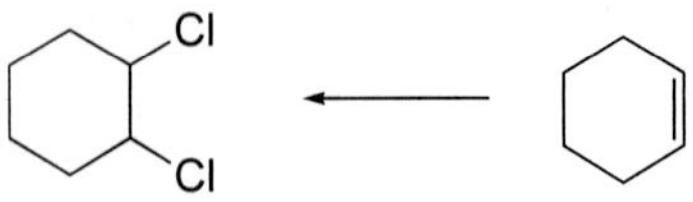

e. 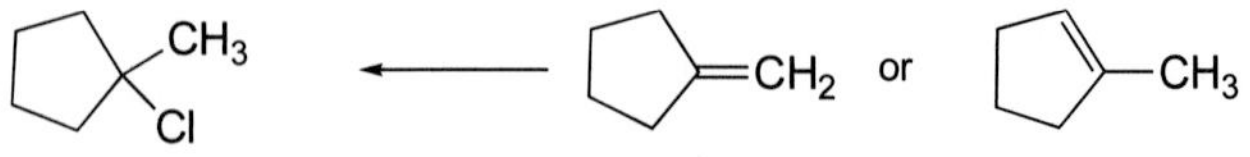
or

c. 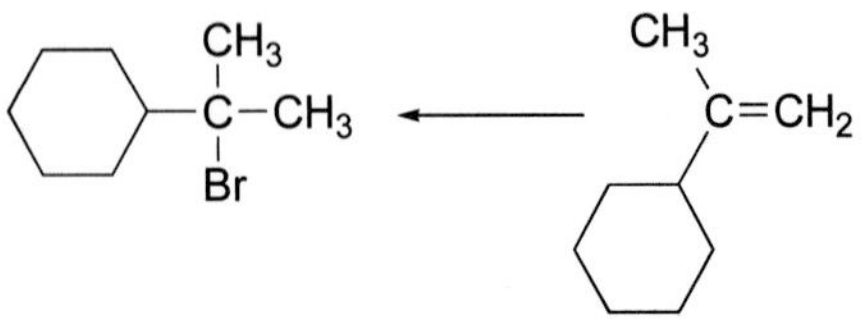

f. 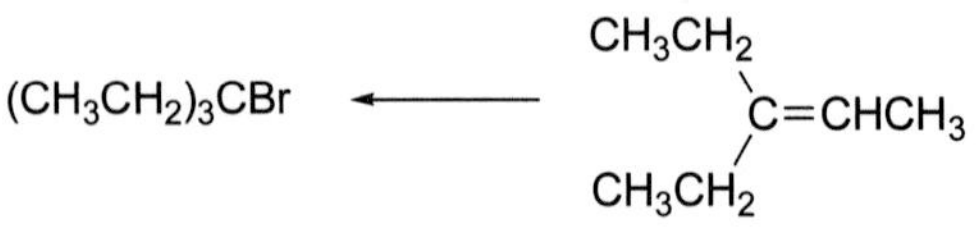
(CH3CH2)3CBr

10.53 Hydroboration–oxidation results in addition of an OH group on the less substituted carbon, whereas acid-catalyzed addition of H_2O results in the addition of an OH group on the more substituted carbon.

a. 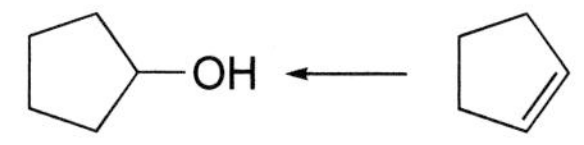
OH

hydroboration–oxidation
and
acid-catalyzed addition

c. 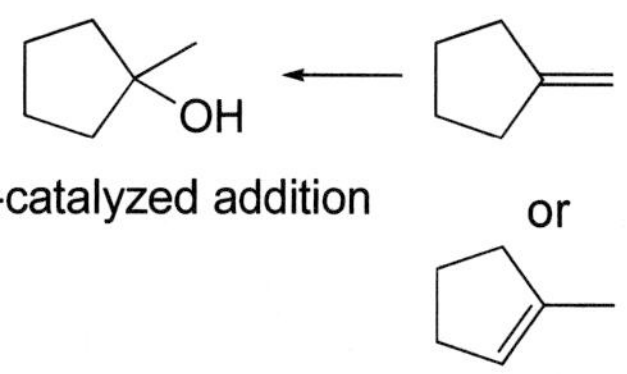
OH
or

acid-catalyzed addition

e. 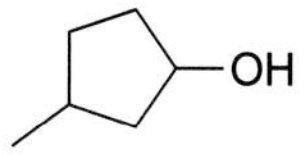
OH

Both methods would give product mixtures.

b. 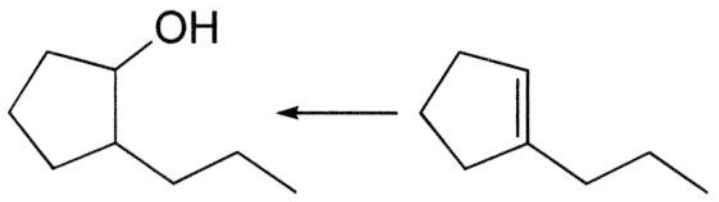
OH

hydroboration–oxidation

d. 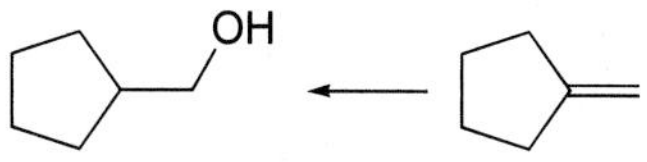
OH

hydroboration–oxidation

10.54

a. $(CH_3CH_2)_2C{=}CHCH_2CH_3$

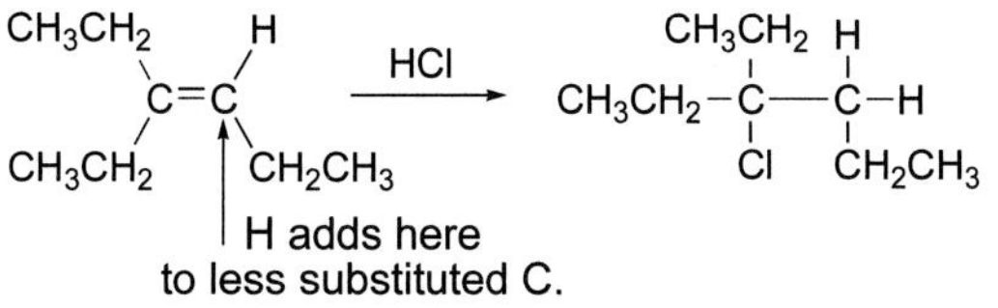
CH3CH2
H
C=C
CH3CH2
CH2CH3
HCl
CH3CH2 H
CH3CH2–C–C–H
Cl CH2CH3
H adds here
to less substituted C.

b. $(CH_3CH_2)_2C{=}CH_2$

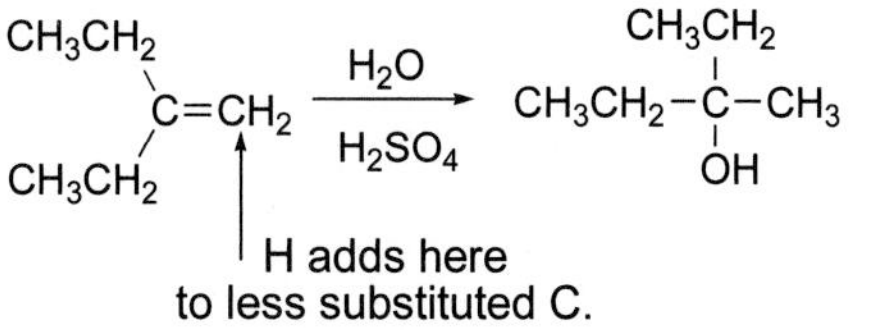
CH3CH2
C=CH2
CH3CH2
H2O
H2SO4
CH3CH2
CH3CH2–C–CH3
OH
H adds here
to less substituted C.

c. 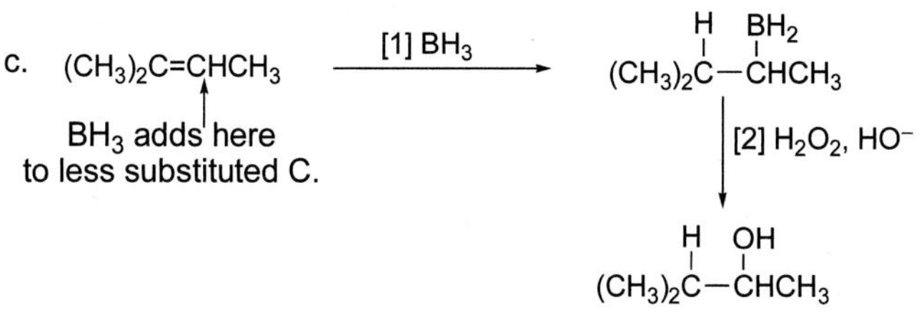
(CH3)2C=CHCH3
BH3 adds here
to less substituted C.
[1] BH3
H BH2
(CH3)2C–CHCH3
[2] H2O2, HO–
H OH
(CH3)2C–CHCH3

d. 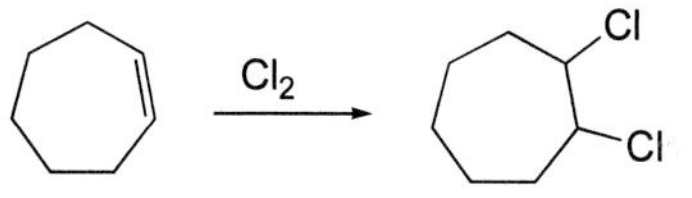
Cl2
Cl
Cl

e. 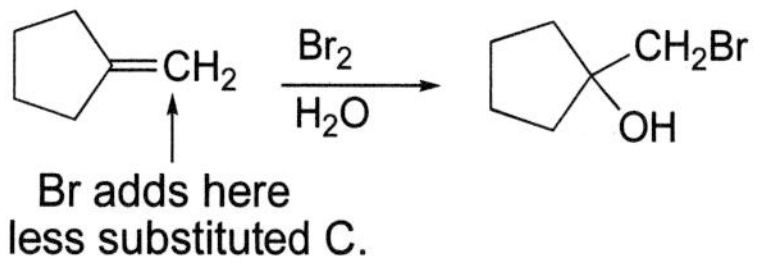
CH2
Br2
H2O
CH2Br
OH
Br adds here
to less substituted C.

f. 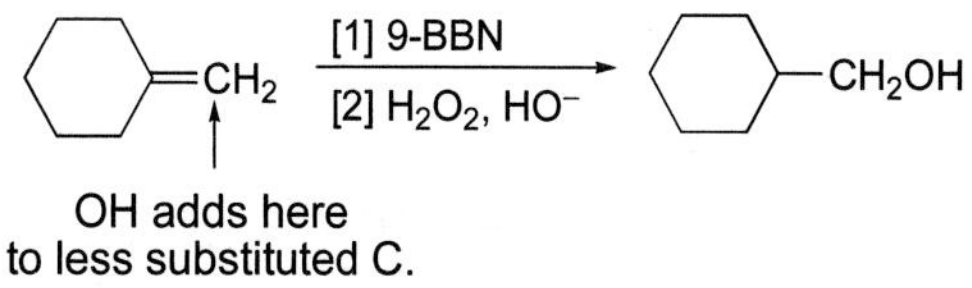
CH2
[1] 9-BBN
[2] H2O2, HO–
CH2OH
OH adds here
to less substituted C.

g. 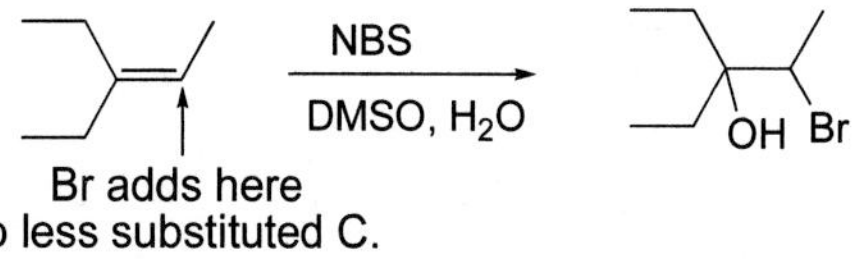
NBS
DMSO, H2O
OH Br
Br adds here
to less substituted C.

h. 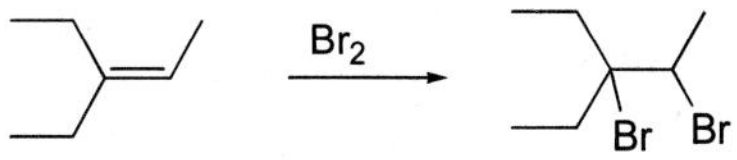
Br2
Br Br

10.55

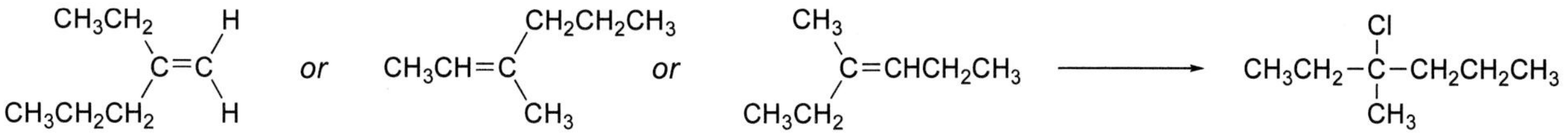
CH3CH2
H
C=C
CH3CH2CH2
H
or
CH3CH=C
CH2CH2CH3
CH3
or
CH3
C=CHCH2CH3
CH3CH2
Cl
CH3CH2–C–CH2CH2CH3
CH3

10.56

a. 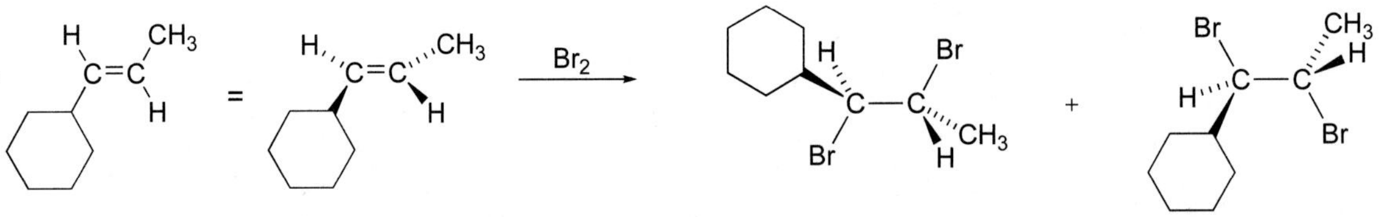

b. 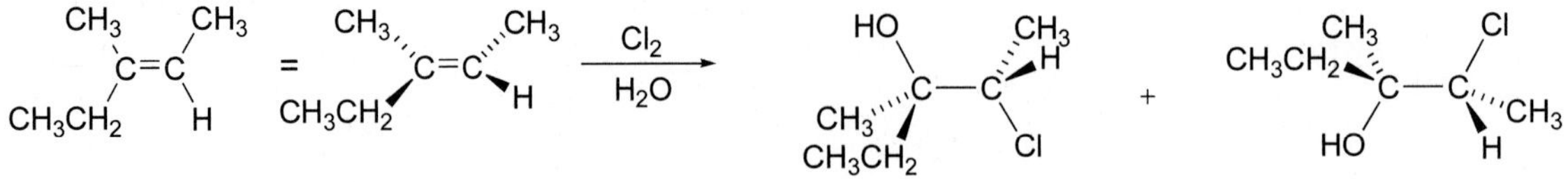

c. 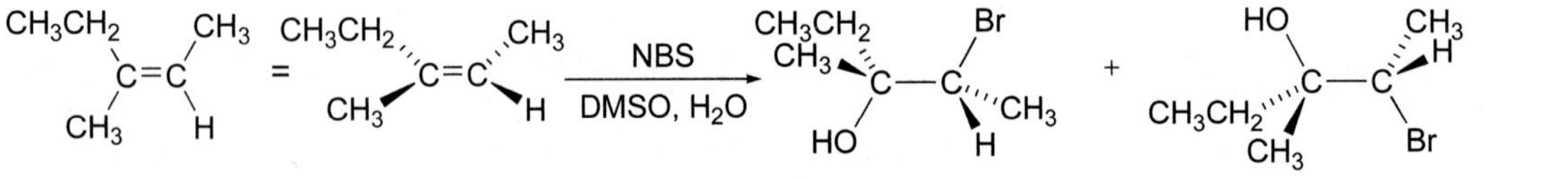

10.57

a. 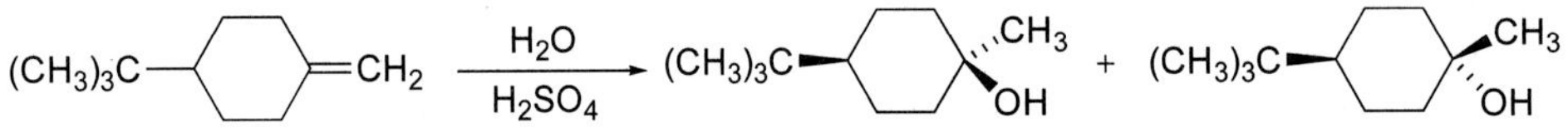

b. 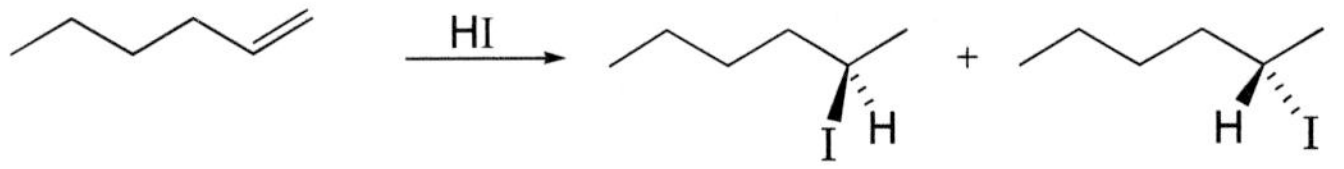

c. 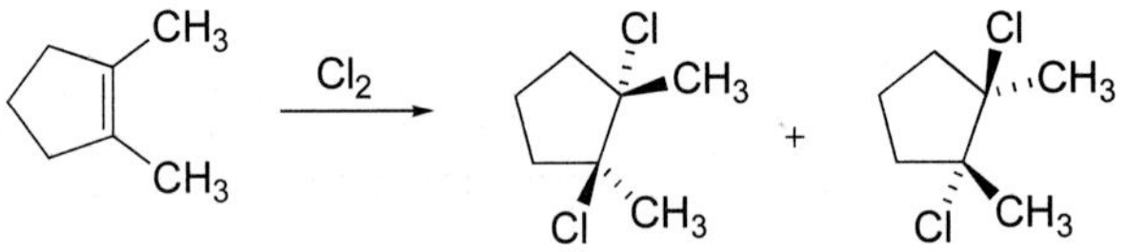 only anti addition

d. 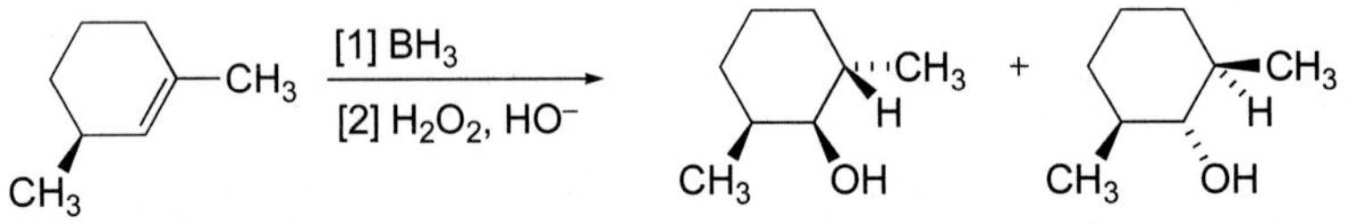 only syn addition

e. 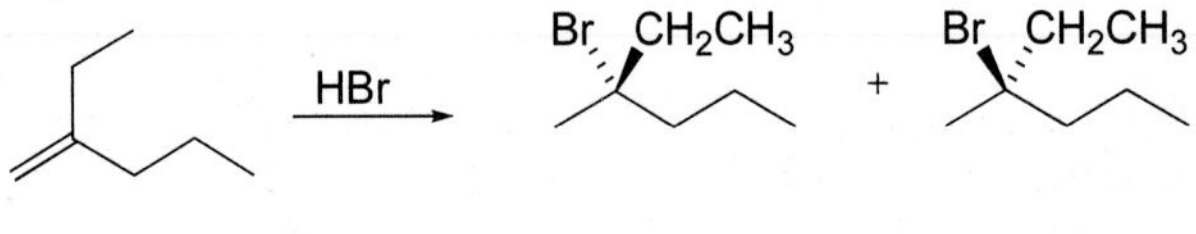

f. 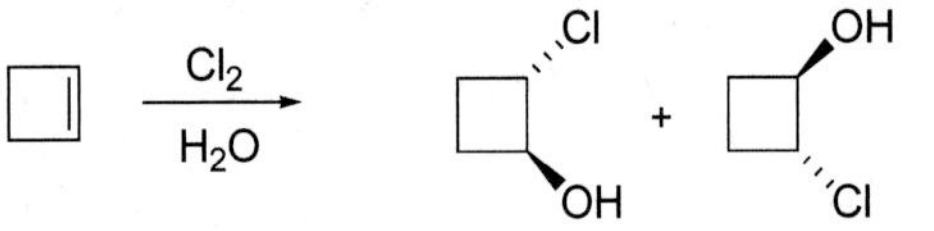 only anti addition

g. 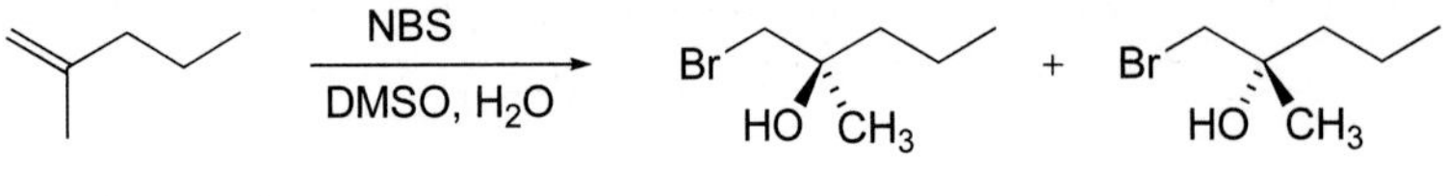

h. 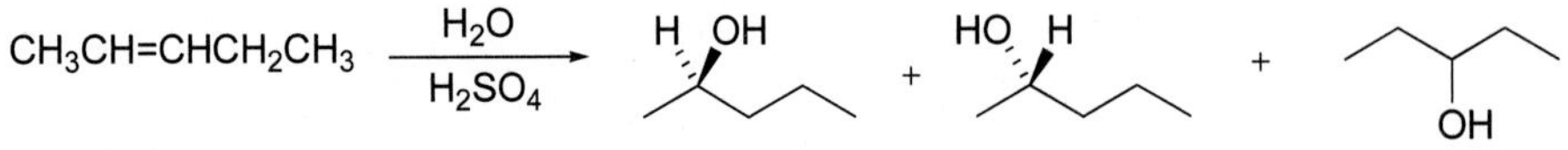

10.58 Draw each reaction. (a) The cis isomer of 4-octene gives two enantiomers on addition of Br_2. (b) The trans isomer gives a meso compound.

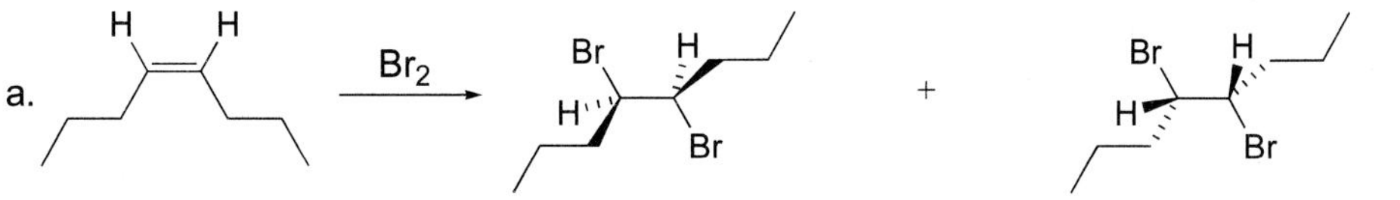
a.
Br_2

***cis*-4-octene** (4*R*,5*R*)-4,5-dibromooctane (4*S*,5*S*)-4,5-dibromooctane

enantiomers

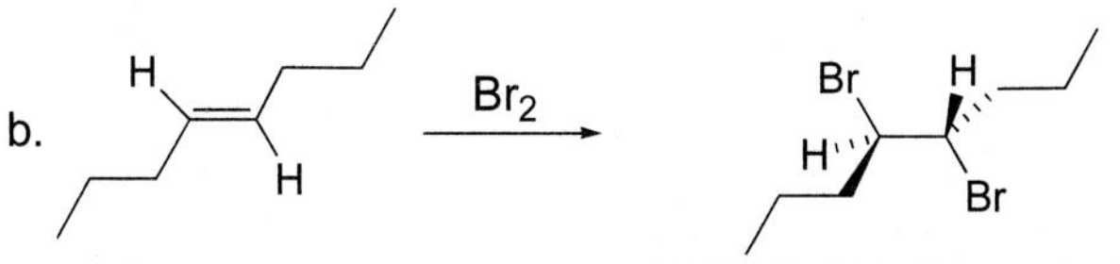
b.
Br_2

***trans*-4-octene** (4*R*,5*S*)-4,5-dibromooctane

meso compound

10.59

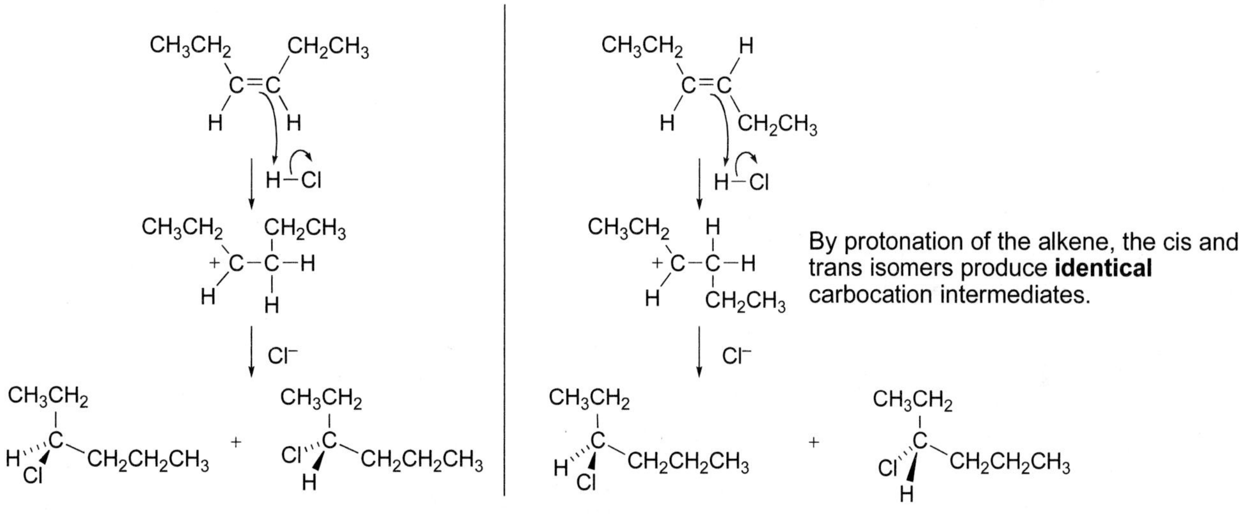
By protonation of the alkene, the cis and trans isomers produce **identical** carbocation intermediates.

Both *cis*- and *trans*-3-hexene give the same racemic mixture of products, so the reaction is not stereospecific.

10.60

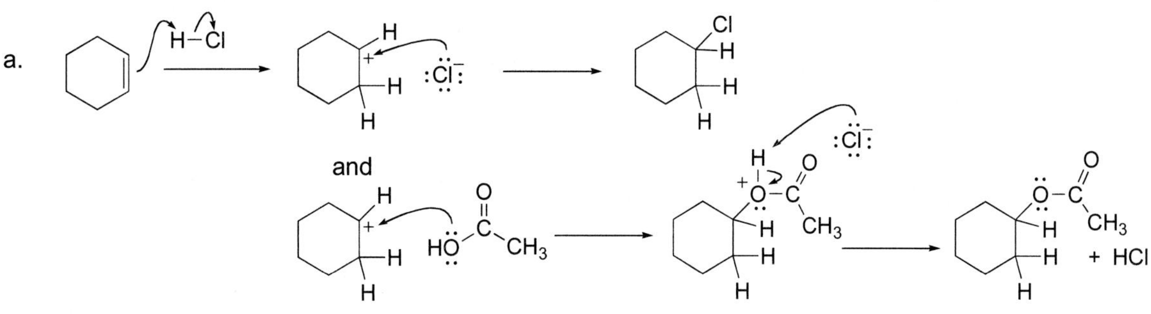
a.
and
+ HCl

b.

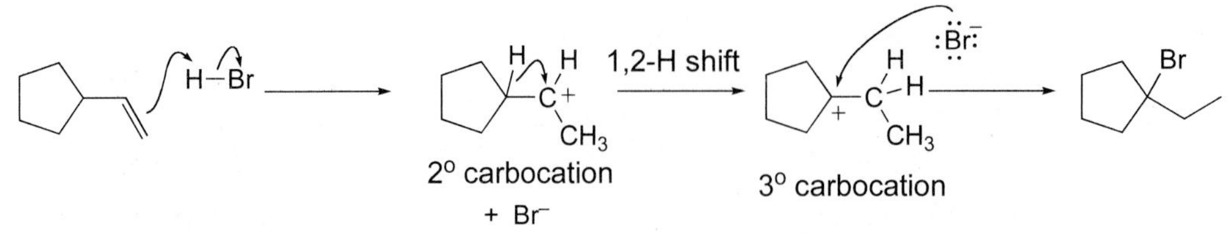
H–Br
1,2-H shift
2° carbocation
+ Br⁻
3° carbocation
Br

10.61

a.

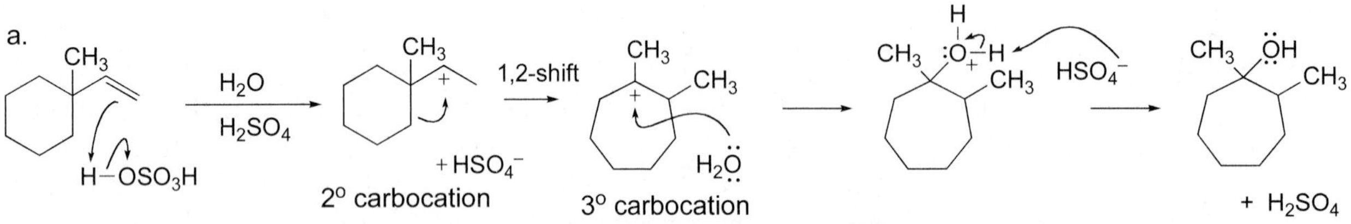
H–OSO3H
H2O
H2SO4
2° carbocation
+ HSO4⁻
1,2-shift
3° carbocation
H2O
HSO4⁻
+ H2SO4

b.

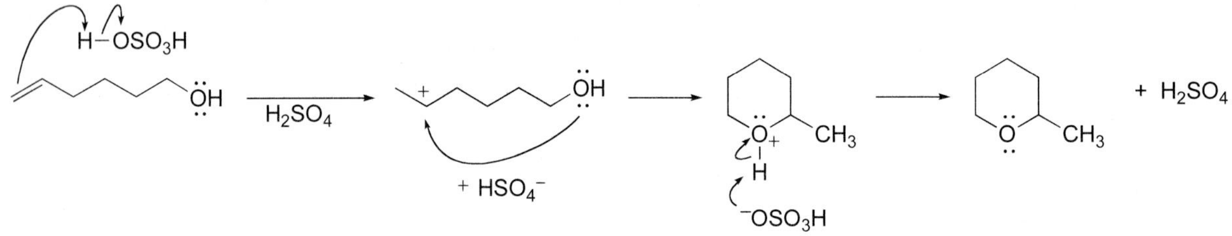
H–OSO3H
OH
H2SO4
+ HSO4⁻
CH3
⁻OSO3H
+ H2SO4

10.62

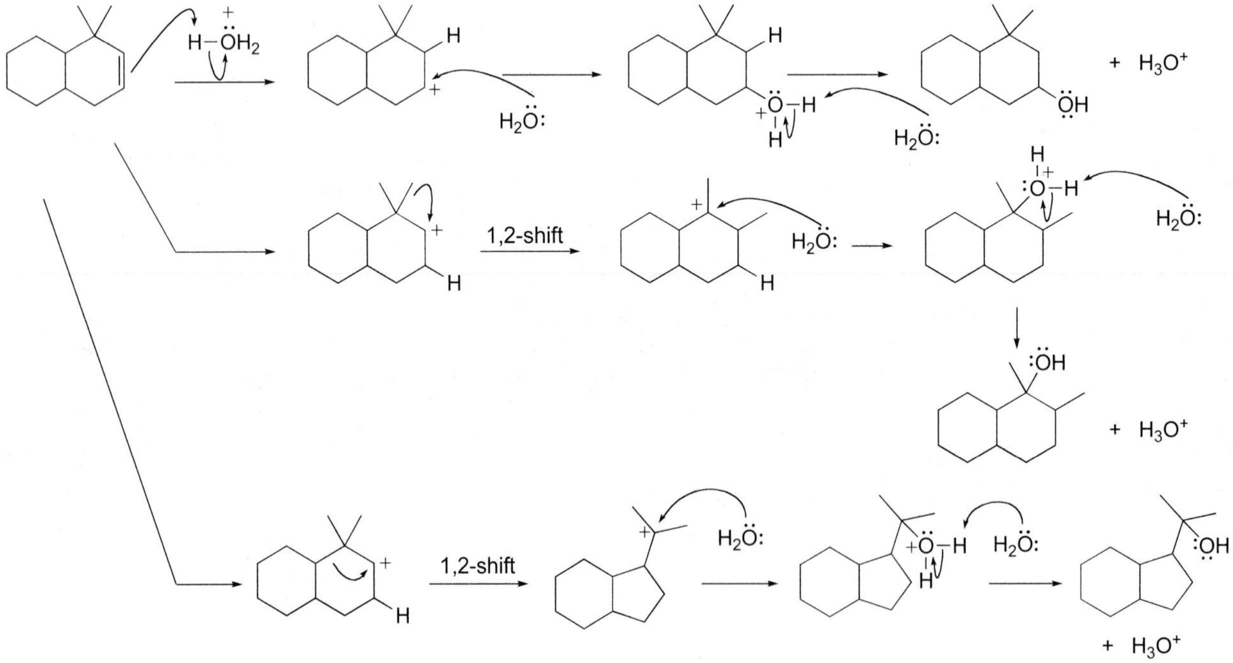
H–OH2
H2O:
+ H3O⁺
1,2-shift
:OH
H2O:
+ H3O⁺
1,2-shift
H2O:
:OH
+ H3O⁺

10.63 The isomerization reaction occurs by protonation and deprotonation.

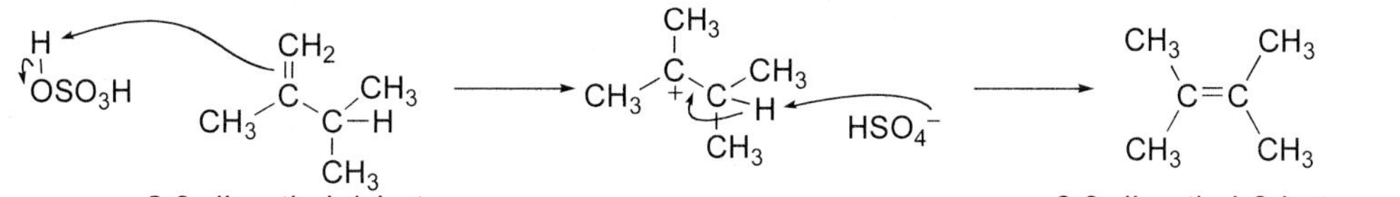
H
OSO3H
CH2
CH3
CH3
C–H
CH3
CH3
C
CH3
CH3
C
H
CH3
HSO4–
CH3
CH3
C=C
CH3
CH3

2,3-dimethyl-1-butene — 2,3-dimethyl-2-butene

10.64

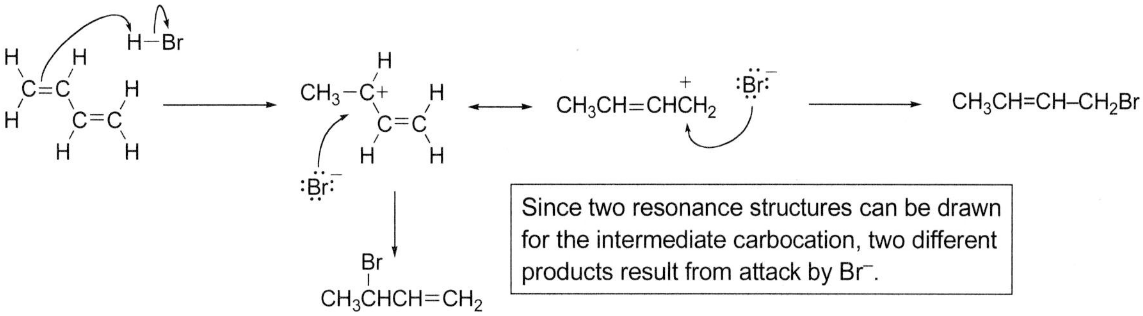
H–Br
CH3–C+
:Br:–
Br
CH3CHCH=CH2
CH3CH=CHCH2
CH3CH=CH–CH2Br

Since two resonance structures can be drawn for the intermediate carbocation, two different products result from attack by Br^-.

10.65

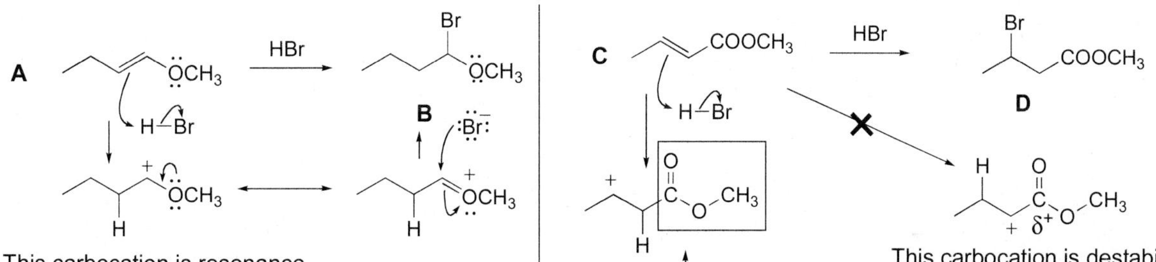
A
ÖCH3
HBr
Br
ÖCH3
H–Br
B
:Br:–
ÖCH3
H
H
C
COOCH3
HBr
Br
COOCH3
D
H–Br
O
C
O
CH3
H
O
C
O
CH3
δ+

This carbocation is resonance stabilized by the O atom, and therefore preferentially forms and results in **B.**

This carbocation is formed preferentially and results in product **D.** It is not destabilized by an adjacent electron-withdrawing $COOCH_3$ group.

This carbocation is destabilized by the δ^+ on the adjacent C, so it does not form.

10.66

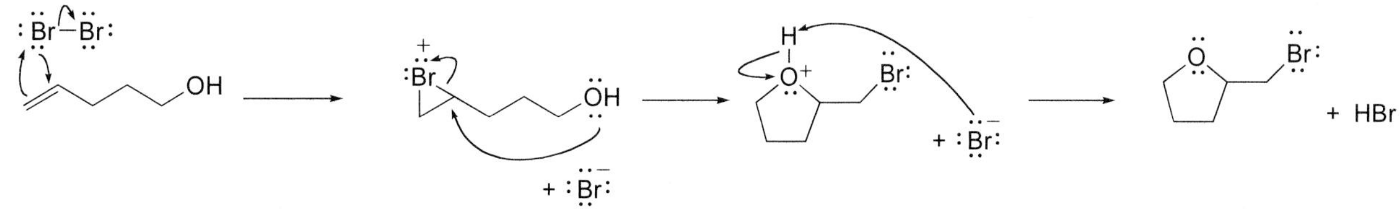
:Br–Br:
OH
:Br
OH
+ :Br:–
H
O+
Br:
+ :Br:–
O
Br:
+ HBr

10.67

a.

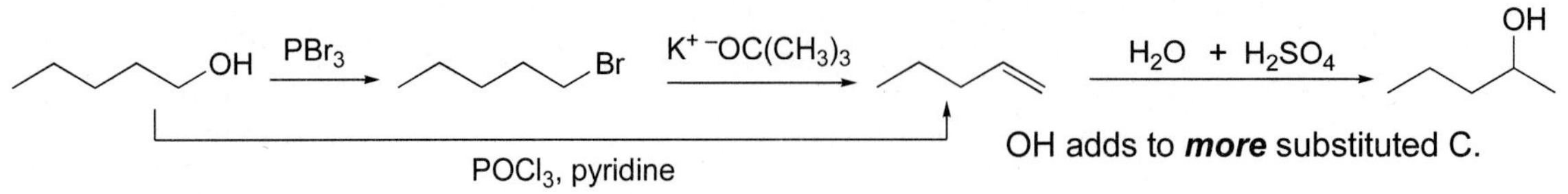
OH
PBr3
Br
K+ −OC(CH3)3
H2O + H2SO4
OH
POCl3, pyridine
OH adds to *more* substituted C.

b.

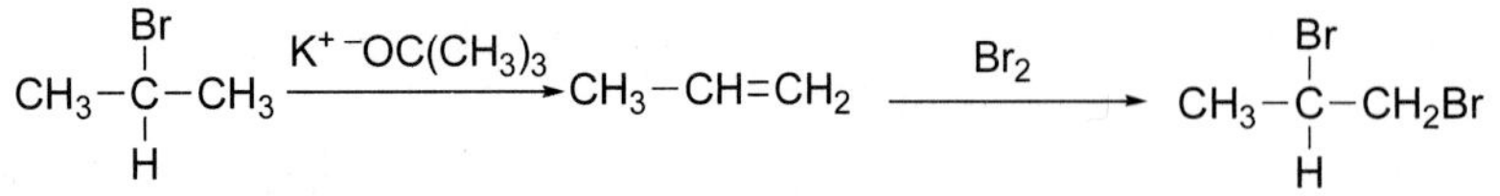
Br
CH3−C−CH3
H
K+ −OC(CH3)3
CH3−CH=CH2
Br2
Br
CH3−C−CH2Br
H

c.

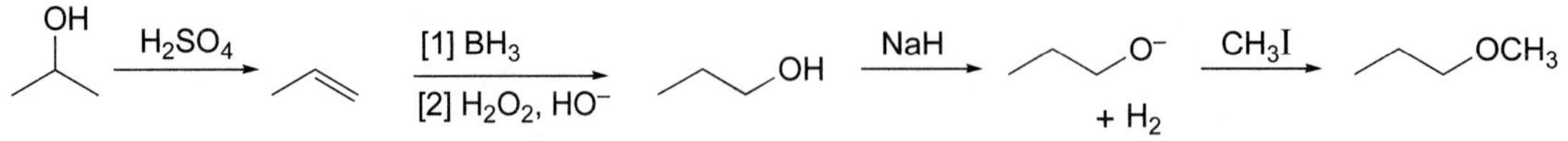
OH
H2SO4
[1] BH3
[2] H2O2, HO−
OH
NaH
O−
+ H2
CH3I
OCH3

d.

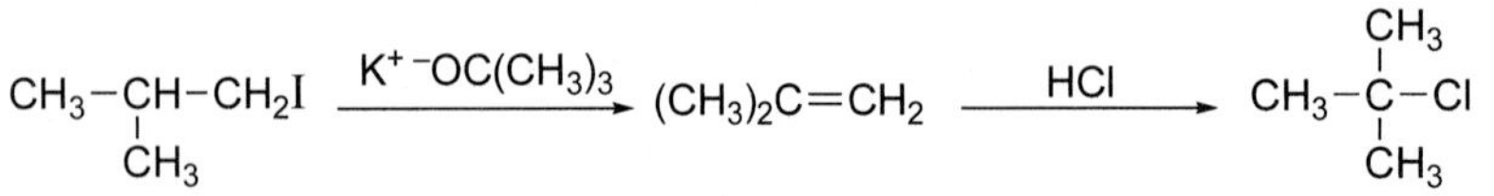
CH3−CH−CH2I
CH3
K+ −OC(CH3)3
(CH3)2C=CH2
HCl
CH3
CH3−C−Cl
CH3

e.

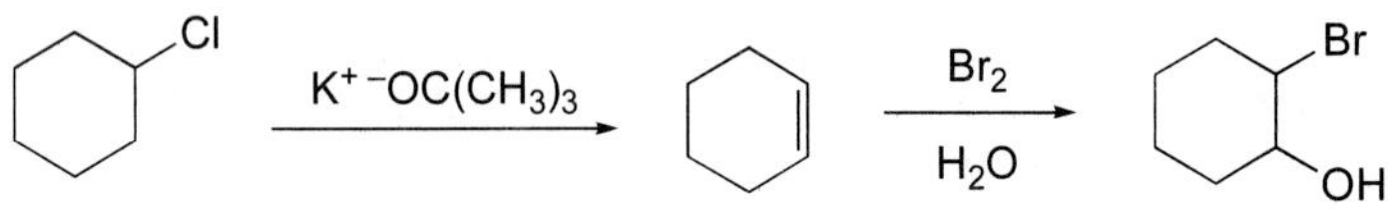
Cl
K+ −OC(CH3)3
Br2
H2O
Br
OH

f.

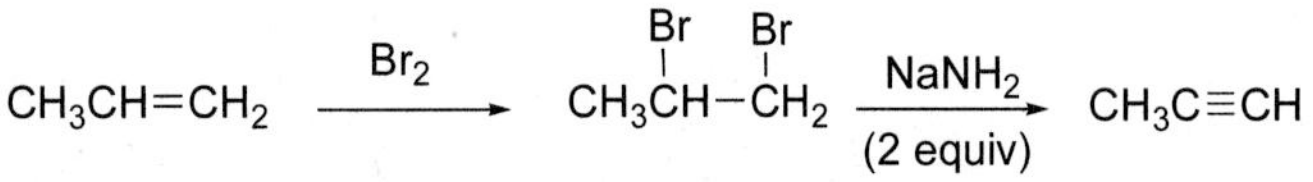
CH3CH=CH2
Br2
Br Br
CH3CH−CH2
NaNH2
(2 equiv)
CH3C≡CH

10.68

a.

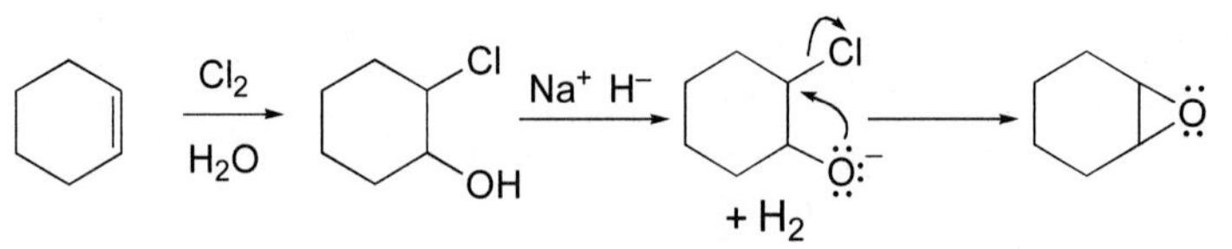
Cl2
H2O
Cl
OH
Na+ H−
Cl
O:−
+ H2
O

b.

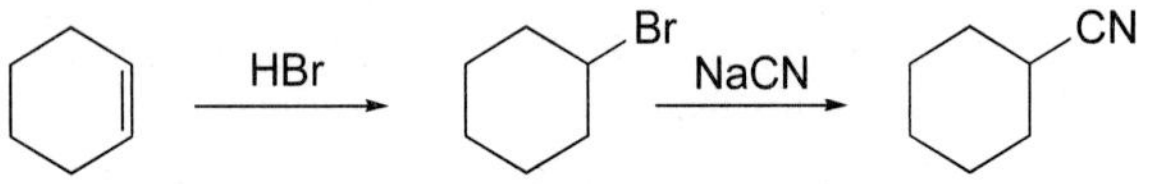
HBr
Br
NaCN
CN

c.

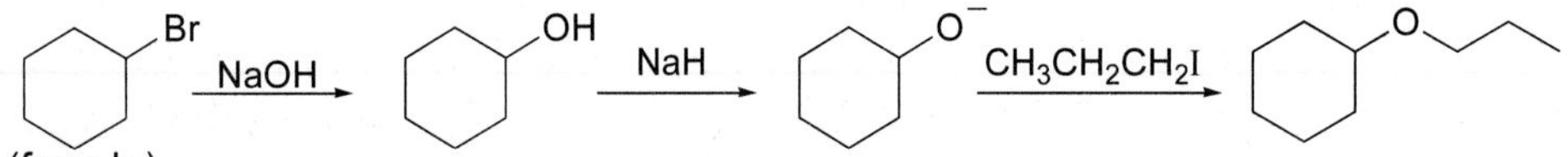
Br
NaOH
OH
NaH
O−
CH3CH2CH2I
O

(from b.)

d.

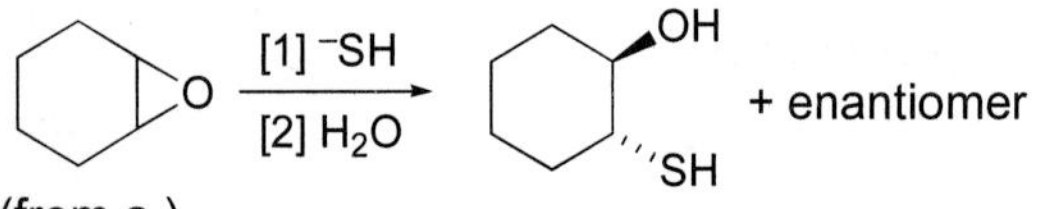
O
[1] −SH
[2] H2O
OH
SH
+ enantiomer

(from a.)

e.

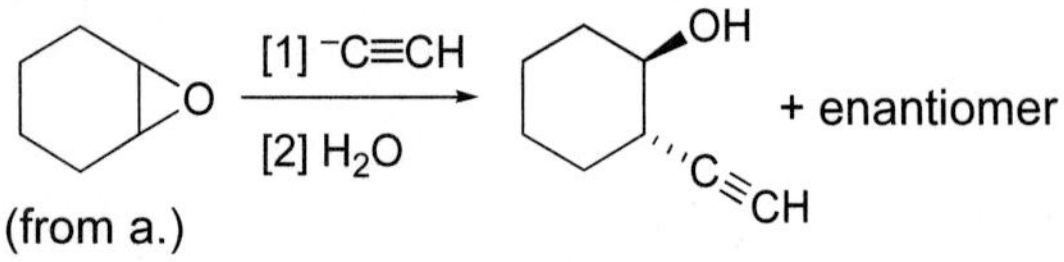
O
[1] −C≡CH
[2] H2O
OH
C≡CH
+ enantiomer

(from a.)

10.69

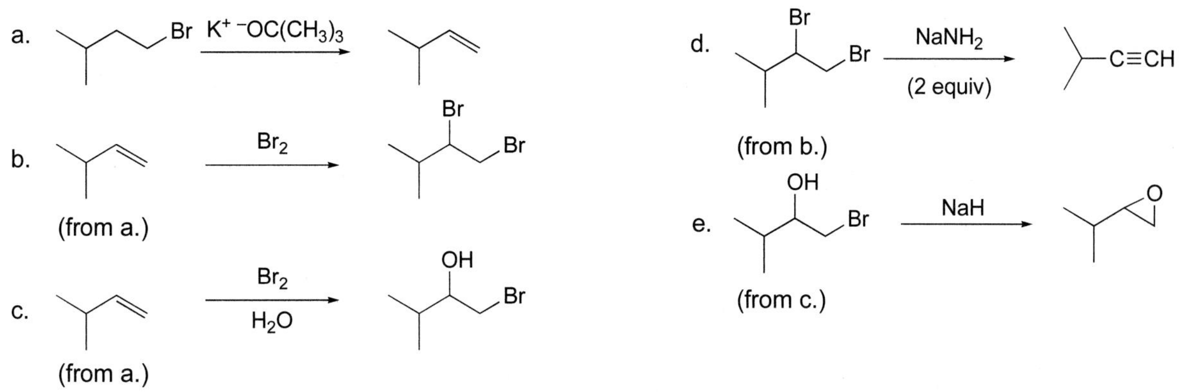
a.
Br
K+ −OC(CH3)3
b.
Br2
Br
Br
(from a.)
c.
Br2
H2O
OH
Br
(from a.)
d.
Br
Br
NaNH2
(2 equiv)
C≡CH
(from b.)
e.
OH
Br
NaH
O
(from c.)

10.70

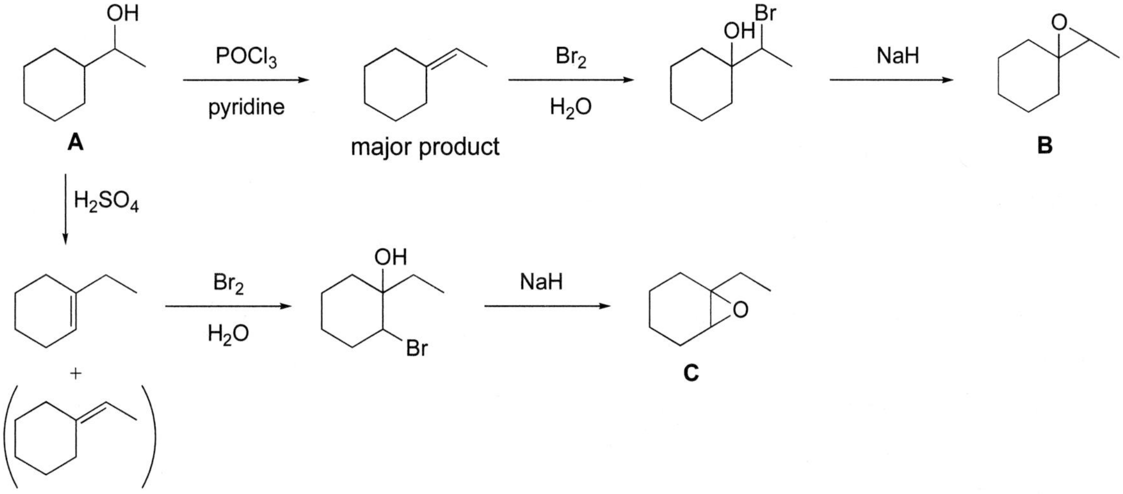
OH
A
POCl3
pyridine
major product
Br2
H2O
Br
OH
NaH
O
B
H2SO4
+
Br2
H2O
OH
Br
NaH
O
C

10.71 Having two rings joined together as in **A** and **B** creates a very rigid ring system and constrains bond angles. Evidently the bond angles around the C=C in **A** are close enough to the trigonal planar bond angle of 120° so that **A** is stable. With **B,** however, the C=C is located at a carbon shared by both rings and the bond angles around the C=C deviate greatly from the desired angle, so that **B** is not a stable compound.

10.72 a. Br_2 adds in an anti fashion to form a meso dibromide. Rotate around the C–C bond to place H and Br anti periplanar in the second step. HBr can be eliminated in two ways, but both give the same product.

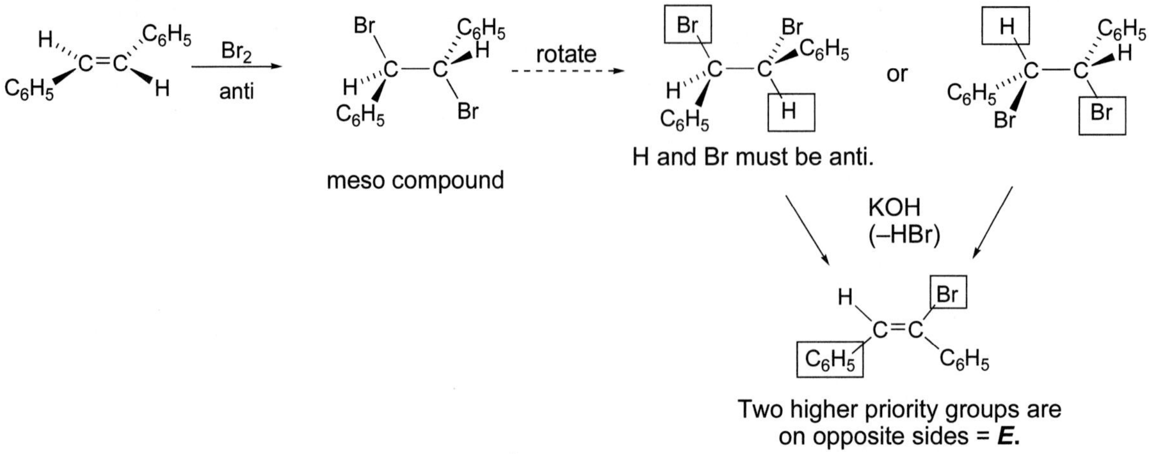
Br2
anti
rotate
or
meso compound
H and Br must be anti.
KOH
(–HBr)
Two higher priority groups are
on opposite sides = E.

b. Br_2 addition forms two enantiomers. Anti periplanar elimination of H and Br gives the same alkene from both compounds.

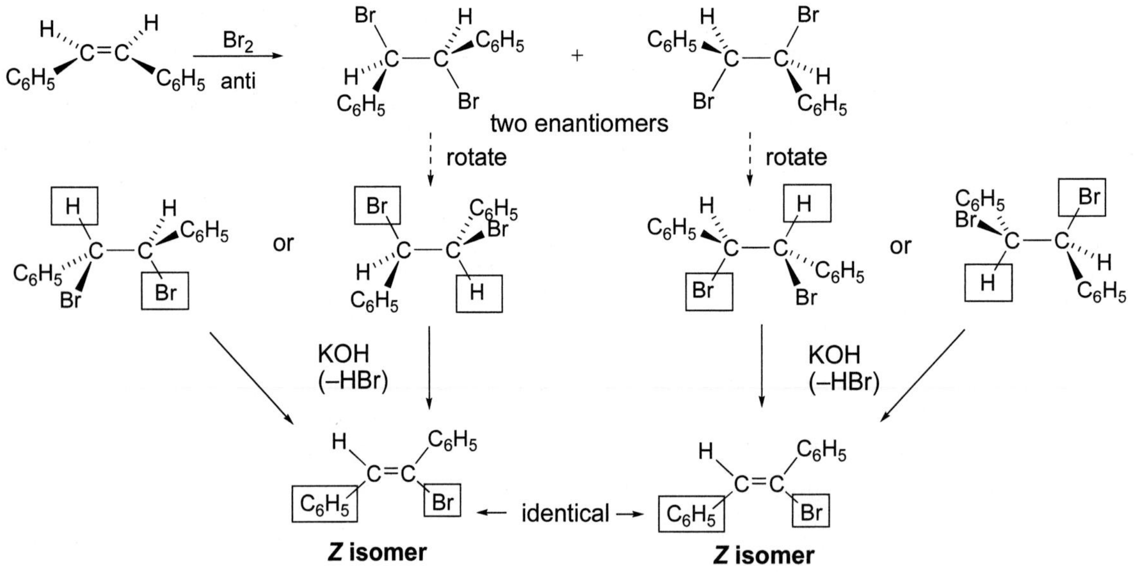
Br2
anti
two enantiomers
rotate
rotate
or
or
KOH
(–HBr)
KOH
(–HBr)
identical
Z isomer
Z isomer

c. The products in (a) and (b) are diastereomers.

10.73

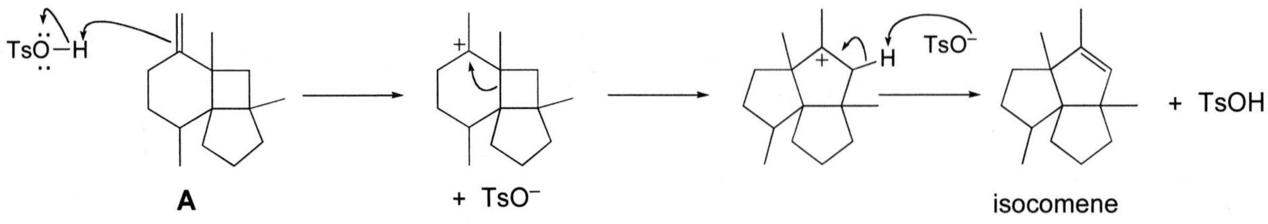
TsO–H
+ TsO⁻
TsO⁻
+ TsOH
A
isocomene

10.74

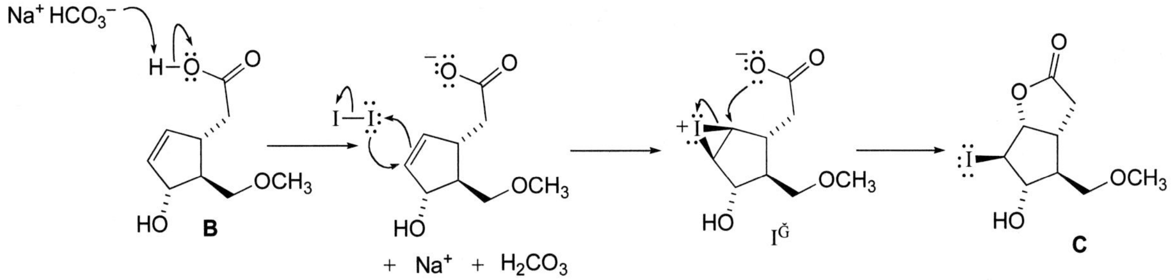

10.75

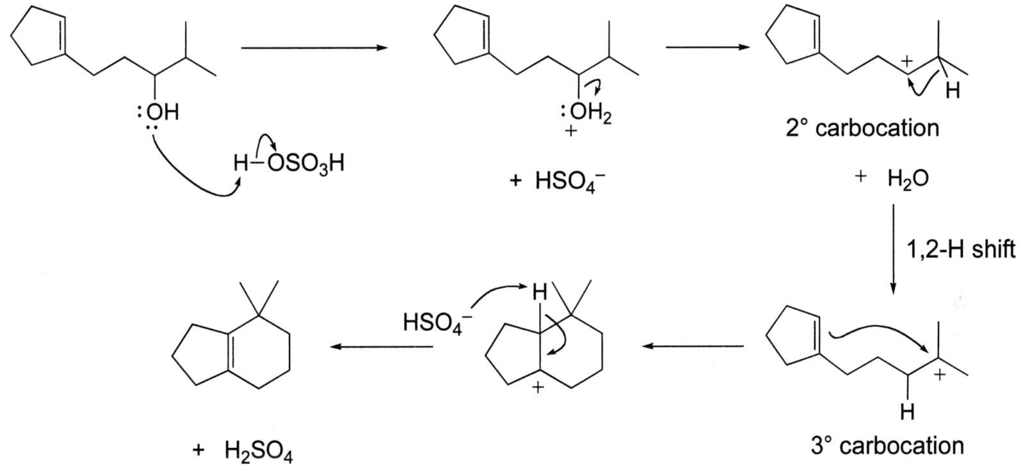

10.76

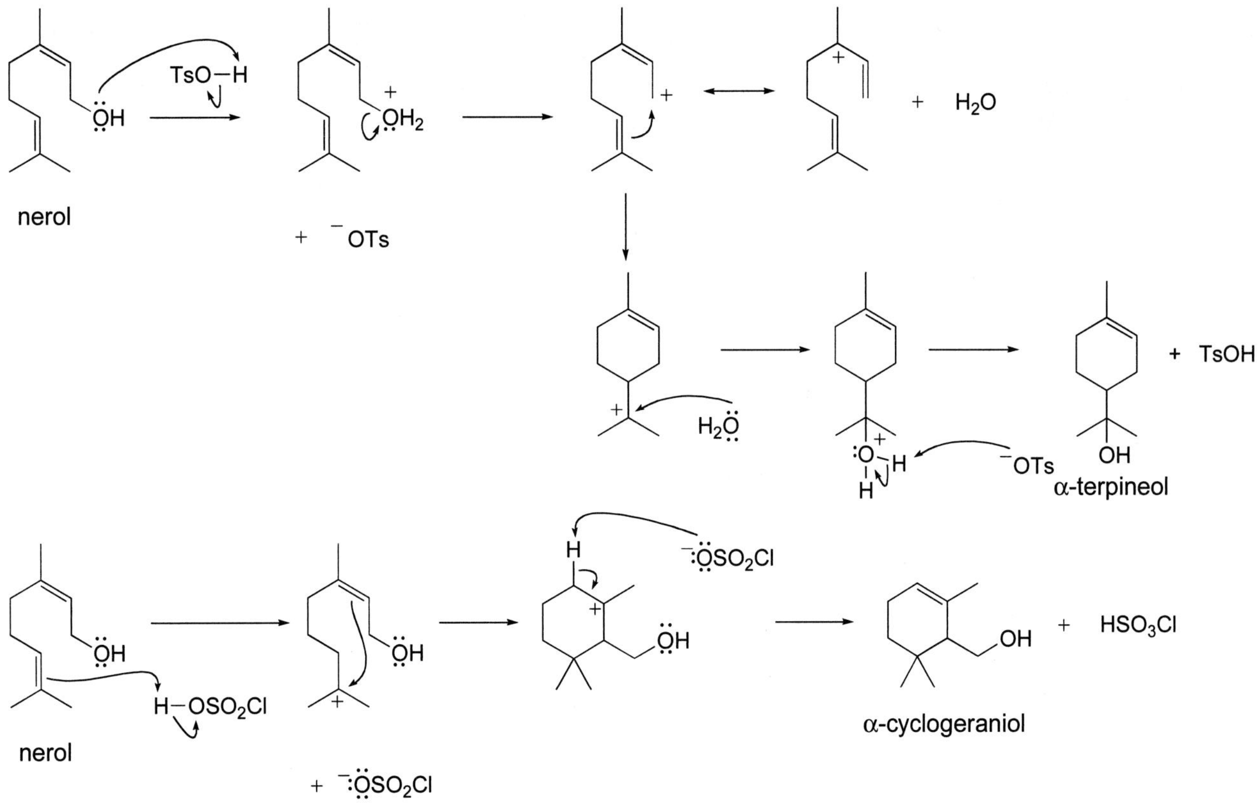

10.77

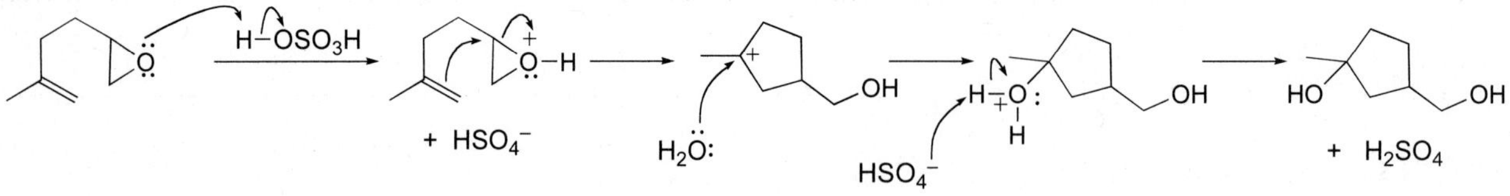

Chapter 11 Alkynes

Chapter Review

General facts about alkynes

- Alkynes contain a carbon–carbon triple bond consisting of a strong σ bond and two weak π bonds. Each carbon is *sp* hybridized and linear (11.1).

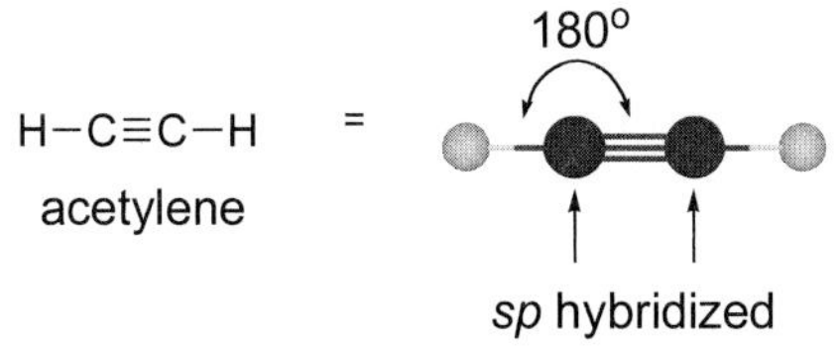
180°
H−C≡C−H
acetylene
=
sp hybridized

- Alkynes are named using the suffix ***-yne*** (11.2).
- Alkynes have weak intermolecular forces, giving them low mp's and low bp's, and making them water insoluble (11.3).
- Since its weaker π bonds make an alkyne electron rich, alkynes undergo addition reactions with electrophiles (11.6).

Addition reactions of alkynes

[1] Hydrohalogenation—Addition of HX (X = Cl, Br, or I) (11.7)

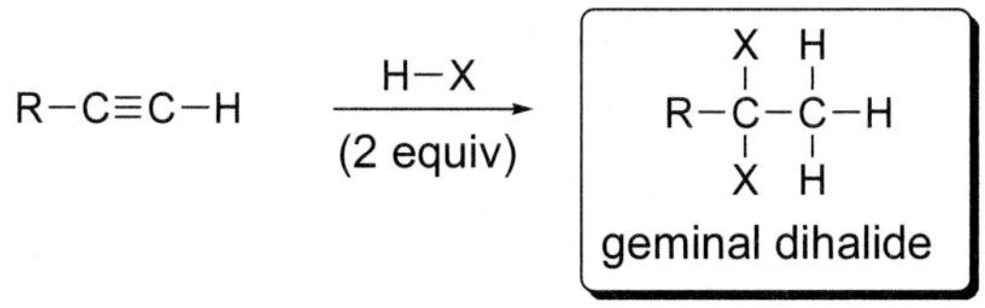
R−C≡C−H
H−X
(2 equiv)
geminal dihalide

- Markovnikov's rule is followed. H bonds to the less substituted C in order to form the more stable carbocation.

[2] Halogenation—Addition of X_2 (X = Cl or Br) (11.8)

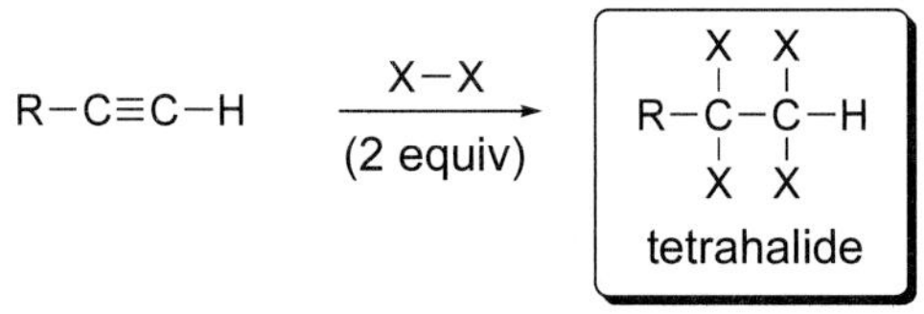
R−C≡C−H
X−X
(2 equiv)
tetrahalide

- Bridged halonium ions are formed as intermediates.
- Anti addition of X_2 occurs.

[3] Hydration—Addition of H_2O (11.9)

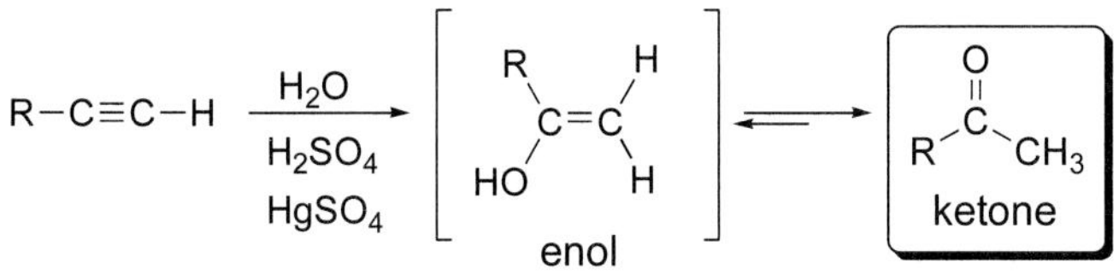
R−C≡C−H
H2O
H2SO4
HgSO4
enol
ketone

- Markovnikov's rule is followed. H bonds to the less substituted C in order to form the more stable carbocation.
- The unstable enol that is first formed rearranges to a carbonyl group.

[4] Hydroboration–oxidation—Addition of H_2O (11.10)

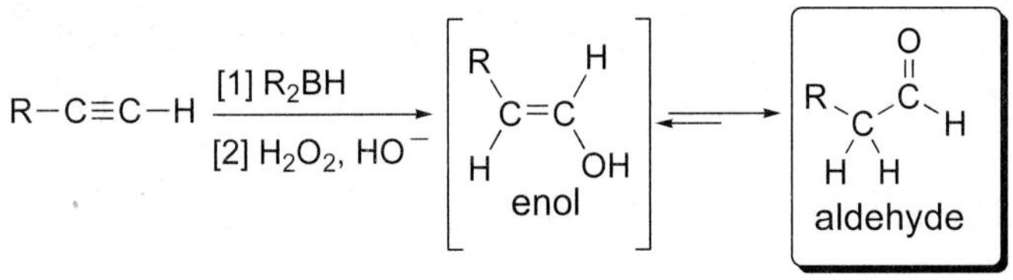
R−C≡C−H
[1] R2BH
[2] H2O2, HO−
R
H
C=C
H
OH
enol
O
R
C
C
H
H H
aldehyde

- The unstable enol, first formed after oxidation, rearranges to a carbonyl group.

Reactions involving acetylide anions

[1] Formation of acetylide anions from terminal alkynes (11.6B)

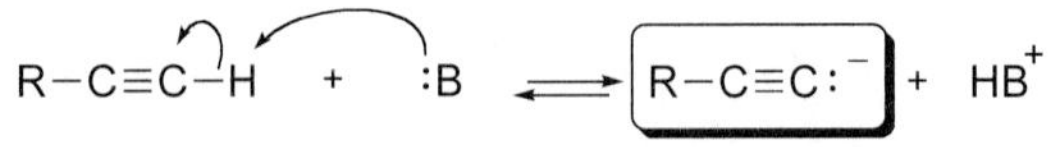
R−C≡C−H
+
:B
R−C≡C:−
+
HB+

- Typical bases used for the reaction are $NaNH_2$ and NaH.

[2] Reaction of acetylide anions with alkyl halides (11.11A)

H−C≡C:−
+
R−X
H−C≡C−R
+
X−

- The reaction follows an S_N2 mechanism.
- The reaction works best with CH_3X and RCH_2X.

[3] Reaction of acetylide anions with epoxides (11.11B)

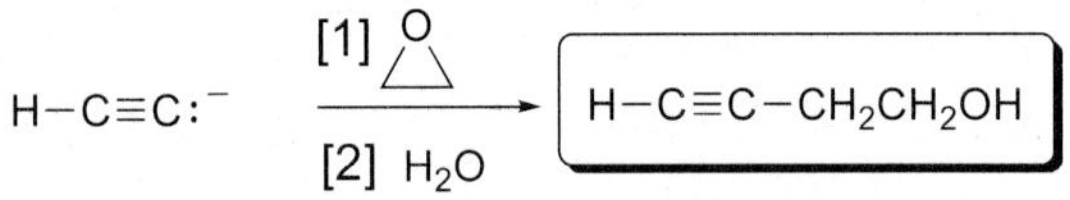
H−C≡C:−
[1]
[2] H2O
H−C≡C−CH2CH2OH

- The reaction follows an S_N2 mechanism.
- Ring opening occurs from the back side at the less substituted end of the epoxide.

Practice Test on Chapter Review

1. Draw the structure for the compound with the following IUPAC name: 5-*tert*-butyl-6,6-dimethyl-3-nonyne.

2. a. Which of the following compounds is an enol tautomer of compound **A?**

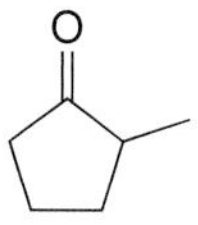
O

A

1. 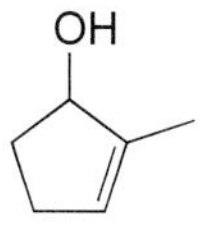
OH

2. 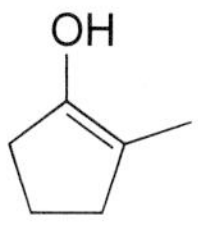
OH

3. 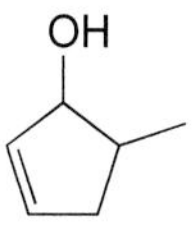
OH

4. **A** can be a tautomer of both compounds (1) and (2).
5. **A** can be a tautomer of compounds (1), (2), and (3).

b. Which of the following bases is strong enough to deprotonate $CH_3C{\equiv}CH$ (propyne, pK_a = 25)? The pK_a's of the conjugate acids of the bases are given in parentheses.

1. CH_3Li (pK_a = 50)
2. $NaOCH_3$ (pK_a = 15.5)
3. $NaOCOCH_3$ (pK_a = 4.8)
4. The bases in (1) and (2) are both strong enough.
5. The bases in (1), (2), and (3) are all strong enough.

3. Draw the organic products formed in the following reactions.

a. 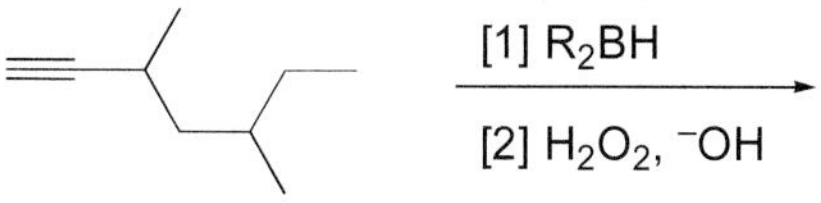
[1] R2BH
[2] H2O2, −OH

b. 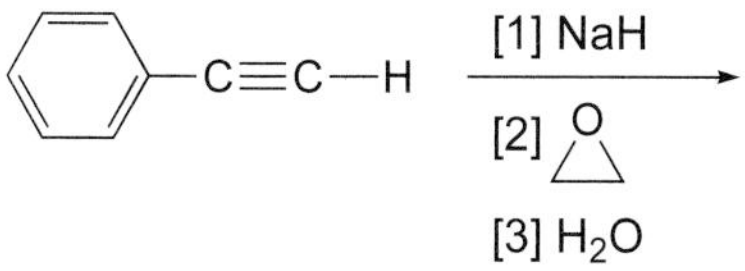
C≡C—H
[1] NaH
[2] O
[3] H2O

c. 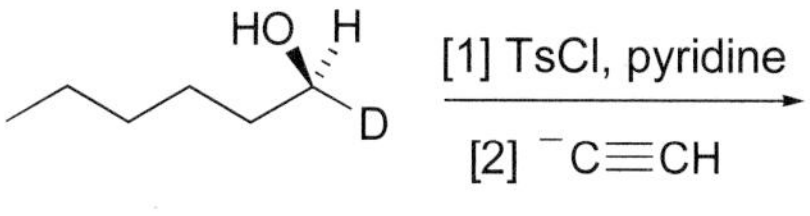
HO H
D
[1] TsCl, pyridine
[2] −C≡CH

d. 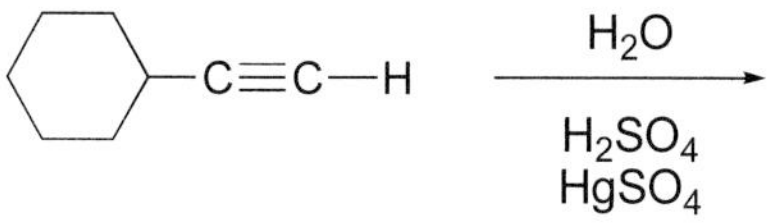
C≡C—H
H2O
H2SO4
HgSO4

e. 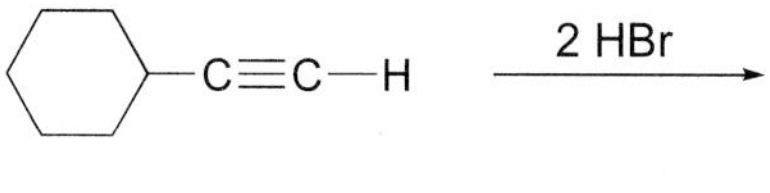
C≡C—H
2 HBr

4. Draw two different enol tautomers for the following compound.

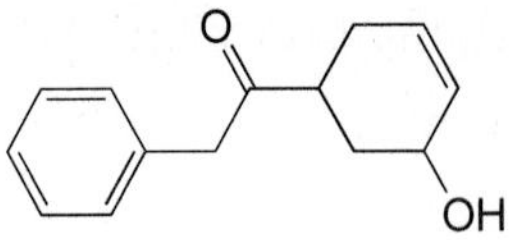

5. What acetylide anion and alkyl halide are needed to make the following alkyne?

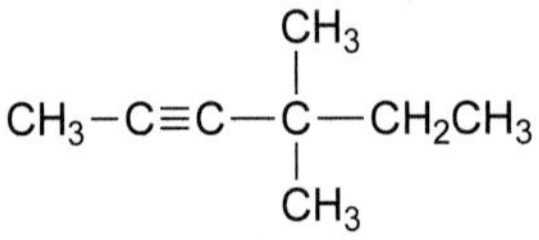

Answers to Practice Test

1.

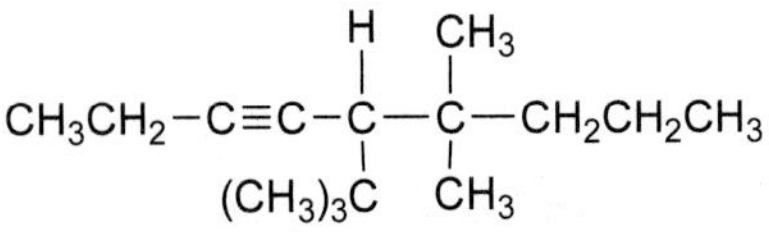

2. a. 2
   b. 1

3.

a.

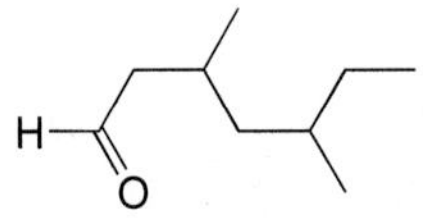

b.

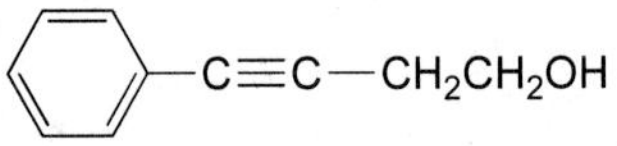

c.

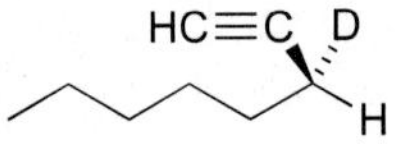

d.

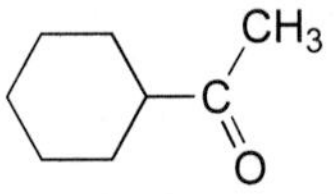

e.

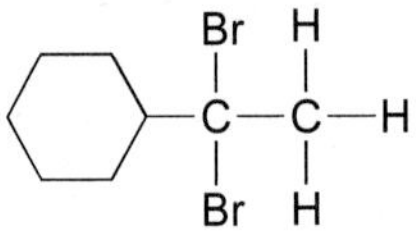

4.

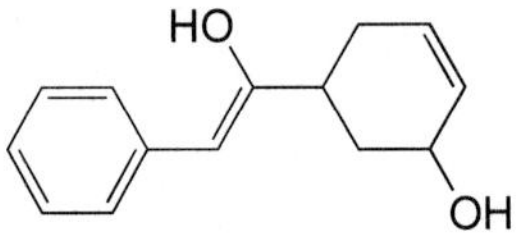

(*E* + *Z*)

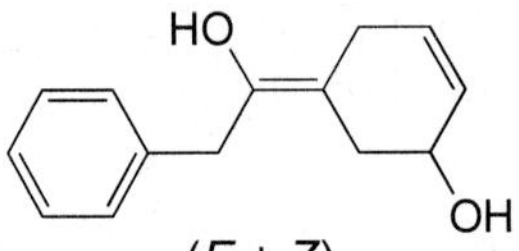

(*E* + *Z*)

5.

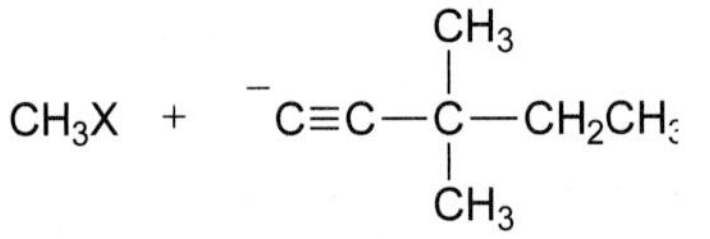

Answers to Problems

11.1 • An ***internal alkyne*** has the triple bond somewhere in the *middle* of the carbon chain.
• A ***terminal alkyne*** has the triple bond at the *end* of the carbon chain.

$HC\equiv C-CH_2CH_2CH_3$	$CH_3-C\equiv C-CH_2CH_3$	$HC\equiv C-CH(CH_3)-CH_3$
terminal alkyne	internal alkyne	terminal alkyne

11.2

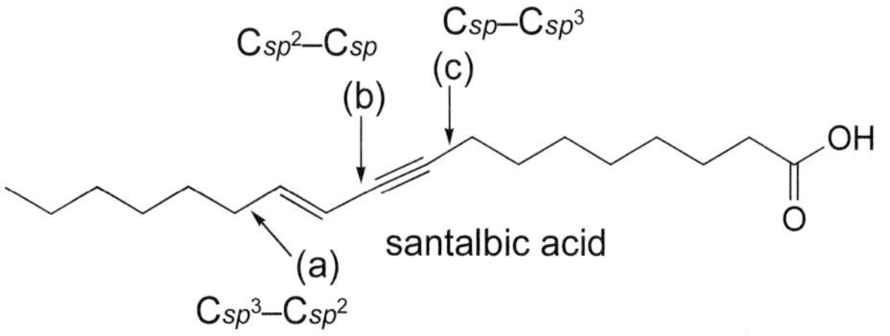
Csp²–Csp
(b)
Csp–Csp³
(c)
OH
O
santalbic acid
(a)
Csp³–Csp²

Increasing bond strength: a < c < b

11.3 To name an alkyne:
[1] Find the longest chain that contains both atoms of the triple bond, change the *-ane* ending of the parent name to *-yne*, and number the chain to give the first carbon of the triple bond the lower number.
[2] Name all substituents following the other rules of nomenclature.

a. $H-C\equiv C-CH_2C(CH_2CH_2CH_3)_2CH_2CH_2CH_3$

4,4-dipropyl-1-heptyne

b. $CH_3C\equiv CCCl(CH_3)CH_2CH_3$

4-chloro-4-methyl-2-hexyne

c. $CH_2{=}CHCH_2CH(CH_2CH_3)C\equiv CC(CH_3)_2CH_2CH_2CH_3$ (Number to give the lower number to the first site of unsaturation.)

4-ethyl-7,7-dimethyl-1-decen-5-yne

d.

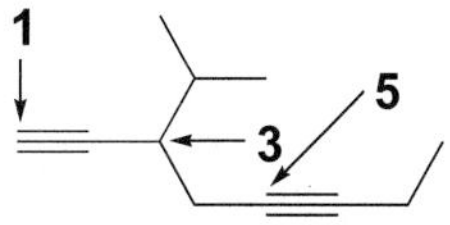
1
5
3

(The longest chain must contain both functional groups.)

3-isopropyl-1,5-octadiyne

11.4 **To work backwards from a name to a structure:**
[1] Find the parent name and the functional group.
[2] Add the substituents to the appropriate carbon.

a. *trans*-2-ethynyl**cyclopentanol**
5 C ring with OH at C1

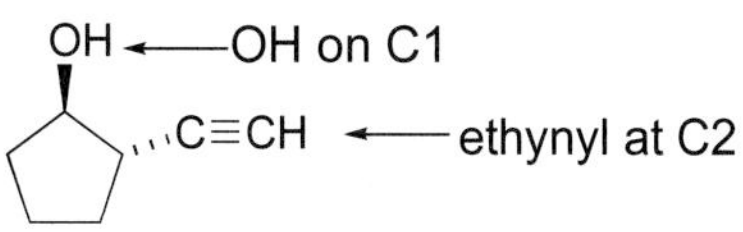
OH
OH on C1
C≡CH
ethynyl at C2

or

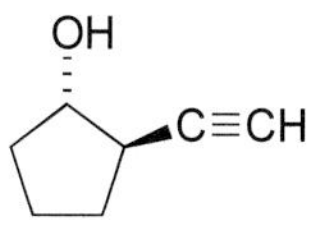
OH
C≡CH

b. 4-*tert*-butyl-5-**decyne**
10 C chain with a triple bond

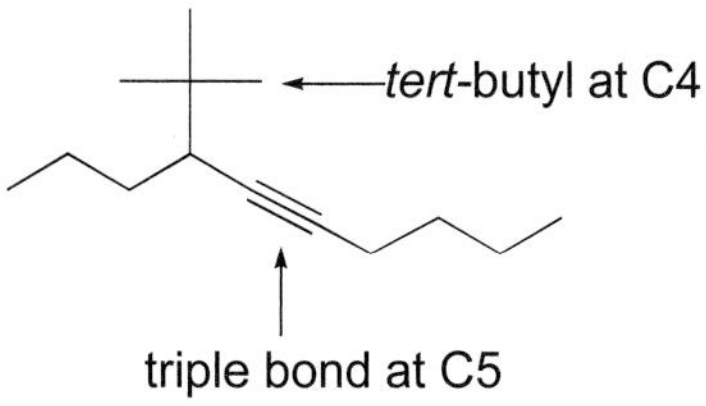
tert-butyl at C4
triple bond at C5

c. 3-methyl**cyclononyne**

9 C ring with a triple bond at C1

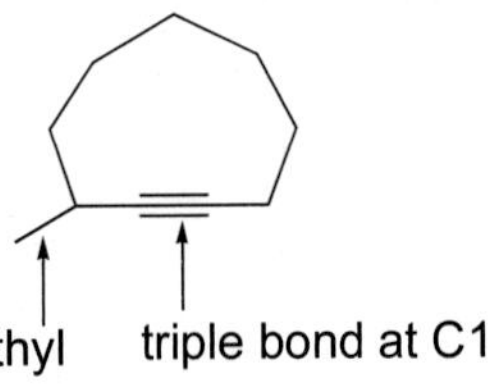
3-methyl
triple bond at C1

11.5 Two factors cause the boiling point increase. The linear *sp* hybridized C's of the alkyne allow for more van der Waals attraction between alkyne molecules. Also, since a triple bond is more polarizable than a double bond, this increases the van der Waals forces between two molecules as well.

11.6 **To convert an alkene to an alkyne:**
[1] Make a vicinal dihalide from the alkene by addition of X_2.
[2] Add base to remove two equivalents of HX and form the alkyne.

a. $Br_2CH(CH_2)_4CH_3 \xrightarrow{Na^+ \, ^-NH_2} [BrCH{=}CHCH_2CH_2CH_2CH_3] \xrightarrow{Na^+ \, ^-NH_2} HC{\equiv}CCH_2CH_2CH_2CH_3$

(bracketed intermediate: not isolated)

b. $CH_2{=}CCl(CH_2)_3CH_3 \xrightarrow{Na^+ \, ^-NH_2} HC{\equiv}CCH_2CH_2CH_2CH_3$

c. $CH_2{=}CH(CH_2)_3CH_3 \xrightarrow{Cl_2} CH_2(Cl)CH(Cl)CH_2CH_2CH_2CH_3 \xrightarrow[\text{(2 equiv)}]{Na^+ \, ^-NH_2} HC{\equiv}CCH_2CH_2CH_2CH_3$

11.7 Acetylene has a pK_a of 25, so **bases having a conjugate acid with a pK_a *above* 25** will be able to deprotonate it.

a. CH_3NH^- [pK_a (CH_3NH_2) = 40]
pK_a > 25 = **Can deprotonate acetylene.**

b. CO_3^{2-} [pK_a (HCO_3^-) = 10.2]
pK_a < 25 = **Cannot deprotonate acetylene.**

c. $CH_2{=}CH^-$ [pK_a ($CH_2{=}CH_2$) = 44]
pK_a > 25 = **Can deprotonate acetylene.**

d. $(CH_3)_3CO^-$ {pK_a [$(CH_3)_3COH$] = 18}
pK_a < 25 = **Cannot deprotonate acetylene.**

11.8 To draw the products of reactions with HX:
- Add two moles of HX to the triple bond, following Markovnikov's rule.
- Both X's end up on the more substituted C.

a. $CH_3CH_2CH_2CH_2{-}C{\equiv}C{-}H \xrightarrow{2\ HBr} CH_3CH_2CH_2CH_2{-}CBr_2{-}CH_3$

b. $CH_3{-}C{\equiv}C{-}CH_2CH_3 \xrightarrow{2\ HBr} CH_3{-}CH_2{-}CBr_2{-}CH_2CH_3 + CH_3{-}CBr_2{-}CH_2{-}CH_2CH_3$

c.

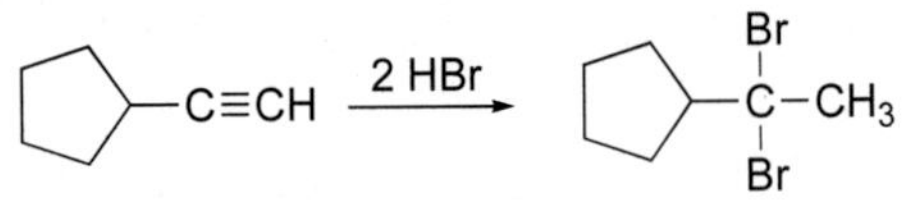
C≡CH
2 HBr
Br
C−CH3
Br

11.9

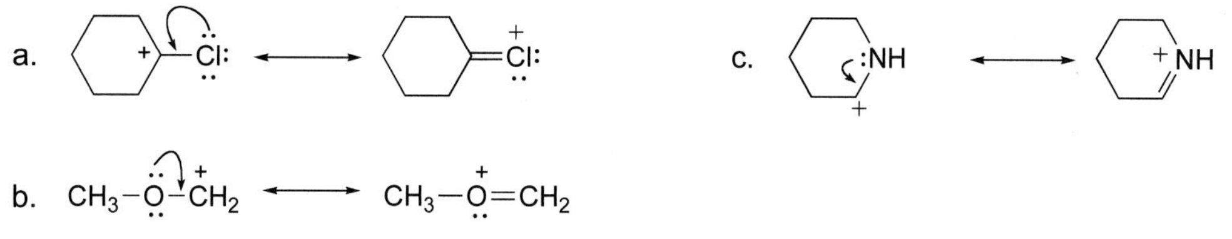

a.
b.
c.

11.10 Addition of one equivalent of X_2 to alkynes forms trans dihalides.
Addition of two equivalents of X_2 to alkynes forms tetrahalides.

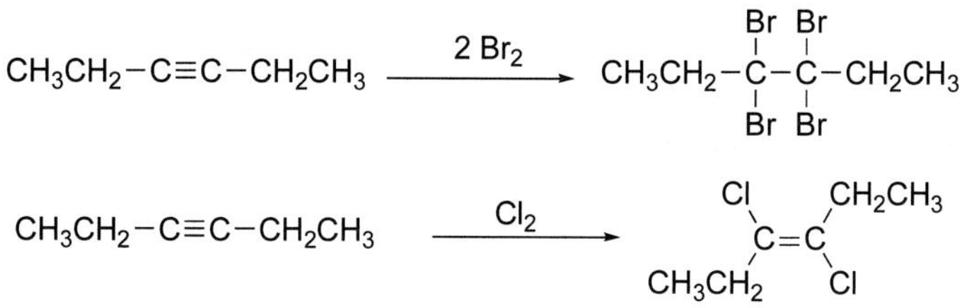

trans dihalide

11.11

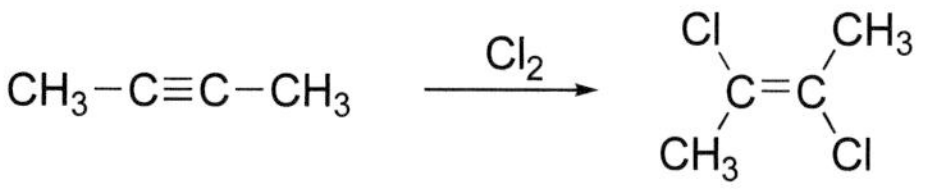

The two Cl atoms are electron withdrawing, making the π bond less electron rich and therefore less reactive with an electrophile.

11.12 To draw the keto form of each enol:

[1] Change the C–OH to a C=O at one end of the double bond.

[2] At the other end of the double bond, add a proton.

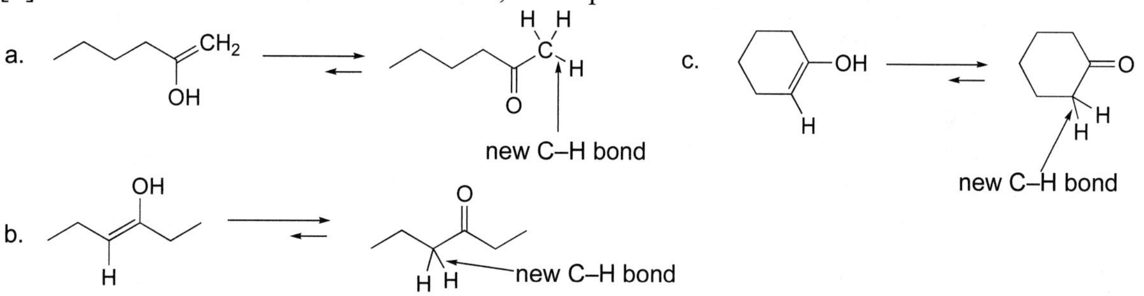

a.
b.
c.
new C–H bond
new C–H bond
new C–H bond

11.13 The treatment of alkynes with H_2O, H_2SO_4, and $HgSO_4$ yields ketones.

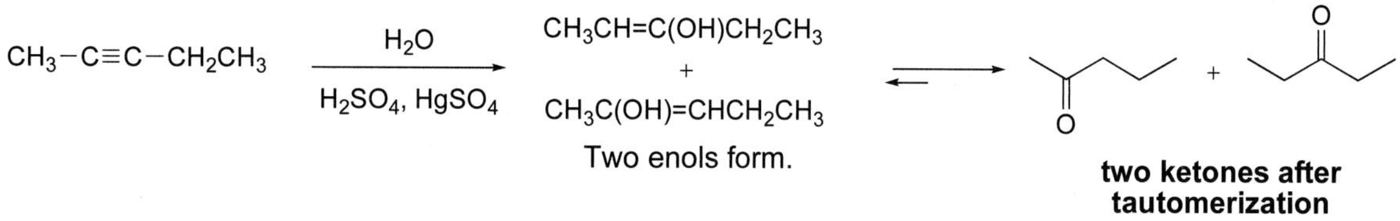

Two enols form.
two ketones after tautomerization

11.14

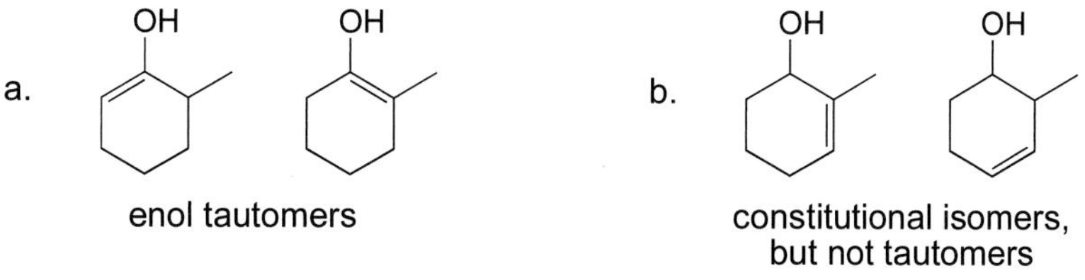

a.
b.
enol tautomers
constitutional isomers, but not tautomers

11.15 Reaction with H_2O, H_2SO_4, and $HgSO_4$ adds the oxygen to the *more* substituted carbon. Reaction with [1] R_2BH, [2] H_2O_2, ^-OH adds the oxygen to the *less* substituted carbon.

a. 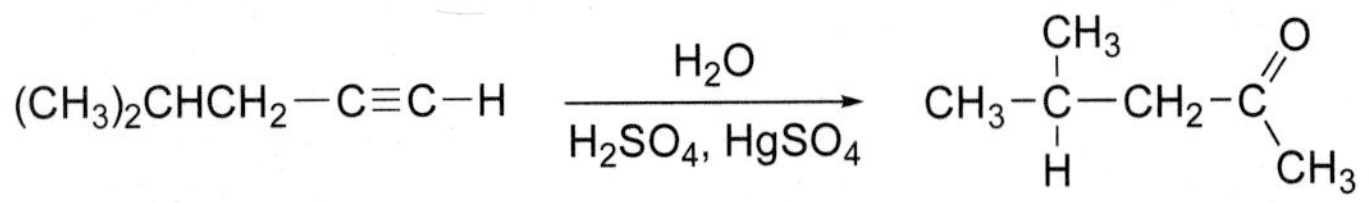

Forms a **ketone.** H_2O is added with the O atom on the *more* substituted carbon.

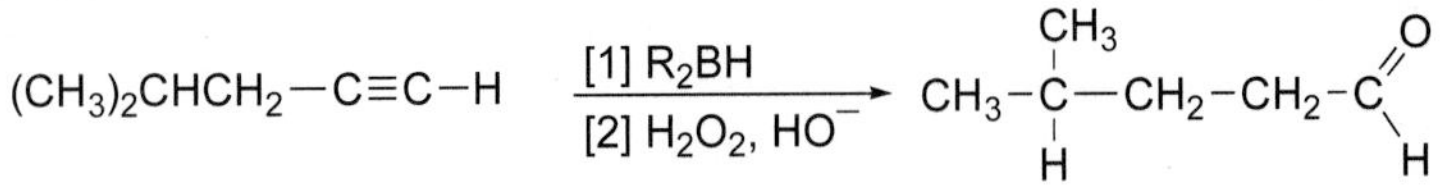

Forms an **aldehyde.** H_2O is added with the O atom on the *less* substituted carbon.

b. 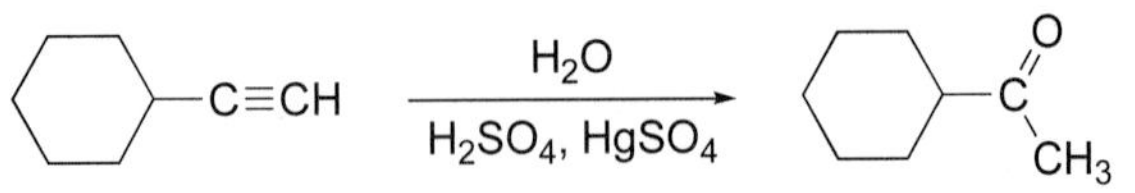

Forms a **ketone.** H_2O is added with the O atom on the *more* substituted carbon.

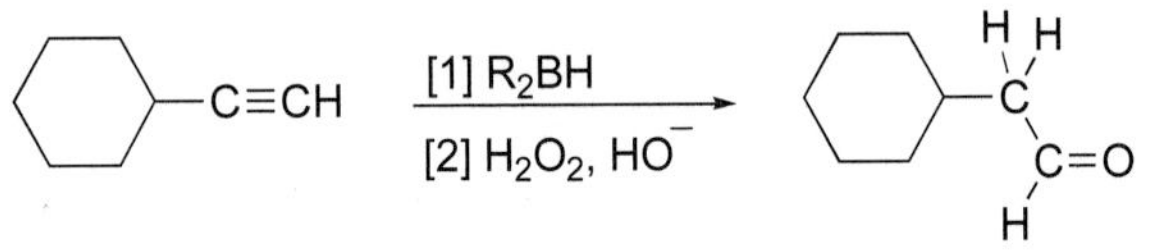

Forms an **aldehyde.** H_2O is added with the O atom on the *less* substituted carbon.

11.16

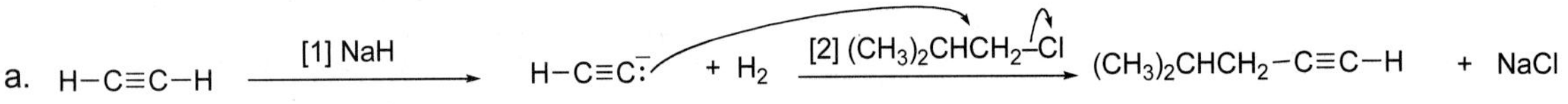

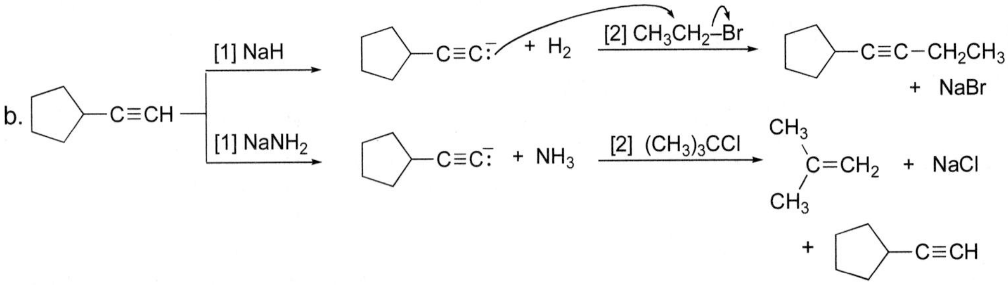

1° alkyl halide **substitution product**

3° alkyl halide **elimination product**

11.17

a. 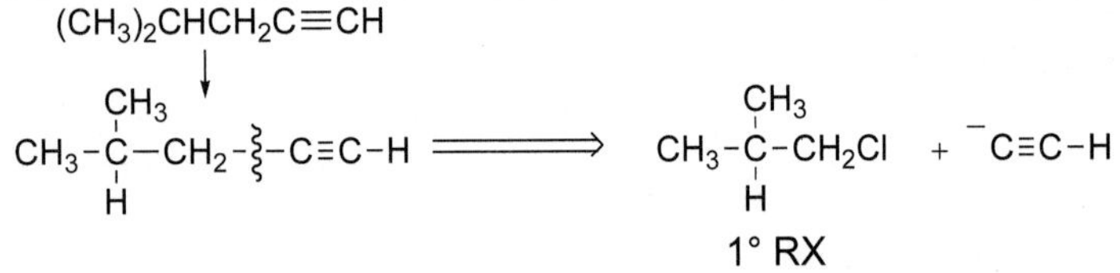

terminal alkyne only one possibility

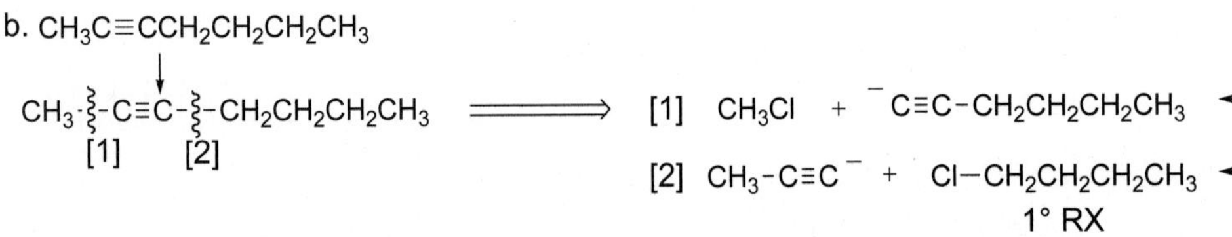

internal alkyne two possibilities

c. $(CH_3)_3CC{\equiv}CCH_2CH_3$

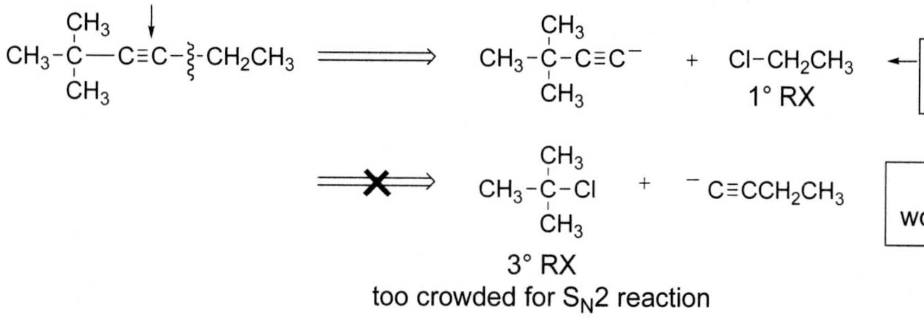

3° RX
too crowded for S_N2 reaction
1° RX

internal alkyne
only one possibility

The 3° alkyl halide would undergo elimination.

11.18

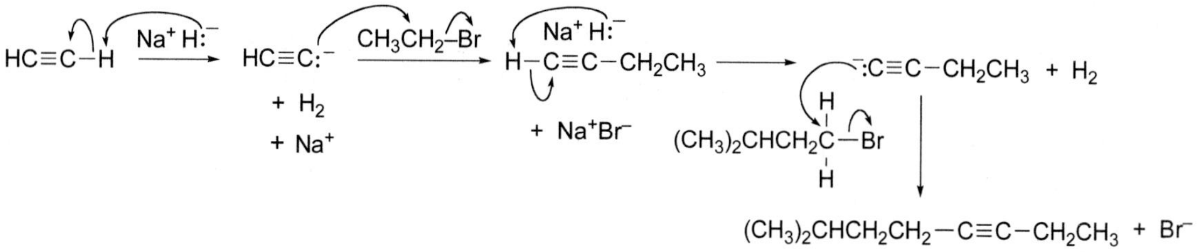

11.19

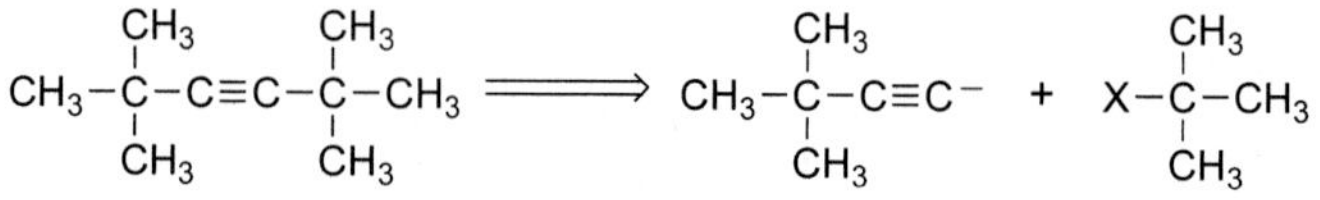

2,2,5,5-tetramethyl-3-hexyne

The 3° alkyl halide is too crowded for nucleophilic substitution. Instead, it would undergo elimination with the acetylide anion.

11.20

a.

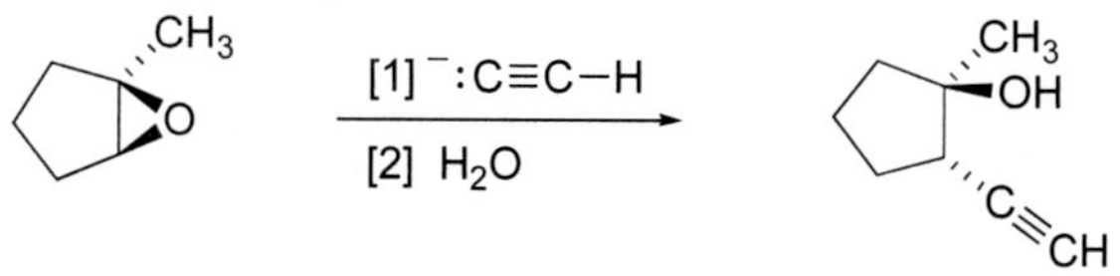

Epoxide is drawn up, so the **acetylide anion attacks from *below* at *less* substituted C.**

b.

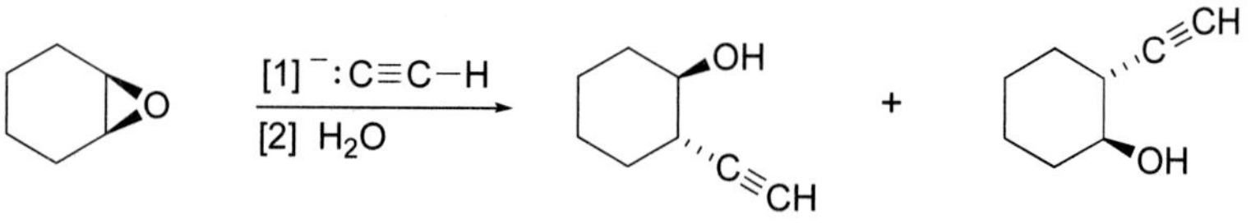

enantiomers

Backside attack of the nucleophile ($^-C{\equiv}CH$) at either C since both ends are equally substituted

11.21

a. $CH_3CH_2CH_2Br \xrightarrow{CH_3CH_2C{\equiv}C^-Na^+} CH_3CH_2CH_2C{\equiv}CCH_2CH_3$

b. $(CH_3)_2CHCH_2CH_2Cl \xrightarrow{CH_3CH_2C{\equiv}C^-Na^+} (CH_3)_2CHCH_2CH_2C{\equiv}CCH_2CH_3$

c. $(CH_3CH_2)_3CCl \xrightarrow{CH_3CH_2C{\equiv}C^-Na^+} (CH_3CH_2)_2C{=}CHCH_3 + CH_3CH_2C{\equiv}CH$

d. $BrCH_2CH_2CH_2CH_2OH \xrightarrow{CH_3CH_2C{\equiv}C^-Na^+} CH_3CH_2C{\equiv}CH + BrCH_2CH_2CH_2CH_2O^-Na^+$

e.
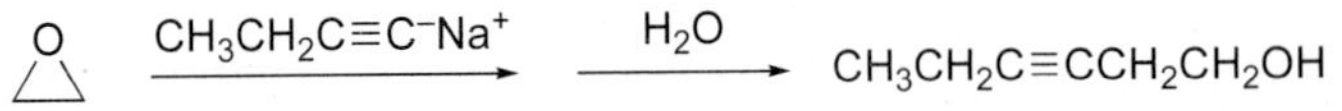

f.
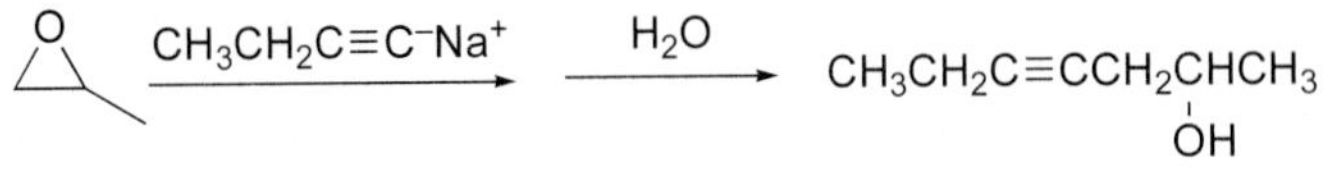

11.22 To use a retrosynthetic analysis:

[1] **Count the number of carbon atoms** in the starting material and product.

[2] **Look at the functional groups** in the starting material and product.

- Determine what types of reactions can form the product.
- Determine what types of reactions the starting material can undergo.

[3] **Work backwards** from the product to make the starting material.

[4] Write out the synthesis in the synthetic direction.

$$\underset{\text{6 C's}}{CH_3CH_2C{\equiv}CCH_2CH_3} \overset{?}{\Longrightarrow} \underset{\text{2 C's}}{HC{\equiv}CH}$$

$$CH_3CH_2C{\equiv}CCH_2CH_3 \Longrightarrow CH_3CH_2C{\equiv}C^- + CH_3CH_2Br \Longrightarrow HC{\equiv}C^- + CH_3CH_2Br$$

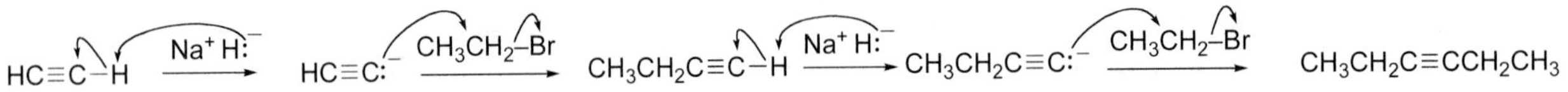

11.23

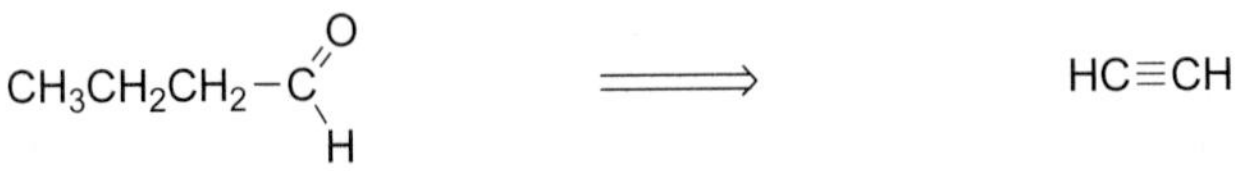

product:
4 carbons, aldehyde functional group
(can be made by hydroboration–oxidation of a terminal alkyne)

starting material:
2 carbons, C≡C functional group
(can form an acetylide anion by reaction with NaH)

Retrosynthetic analysis:

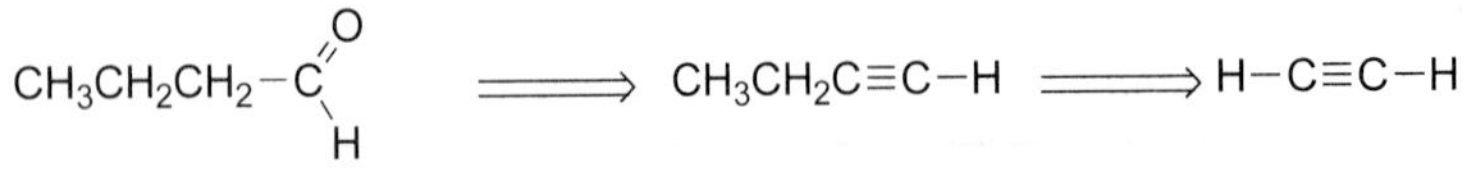

Forward direction:

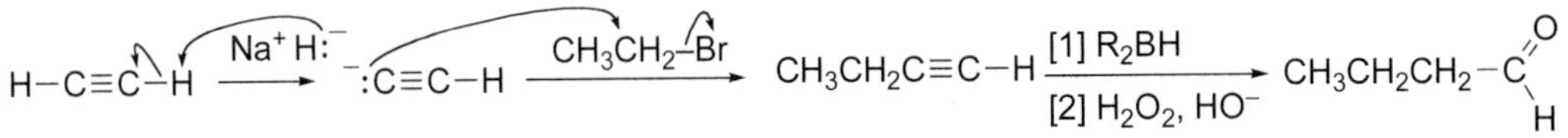

11.24

a.
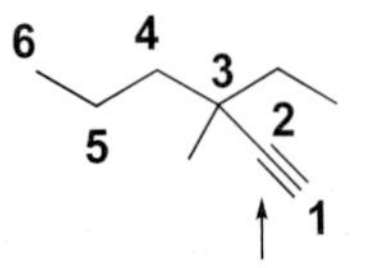

1-hexyne

6 C alkyne → hexyne
C≡C at C1 → 1-hexyne
CH_3 and CH_2CH_3 at C3
3-ethyl-3-methyl-1-hexyne

b.
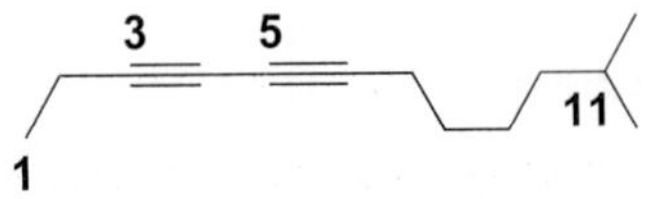

12 C chain with 2 C≡C's → dodecadiyne
C≡C's at C3 and C5 → 3,5-dodecadiyne
CH_3 at C11
11-methyl-3,5-dodecadiyne

11.25

a.

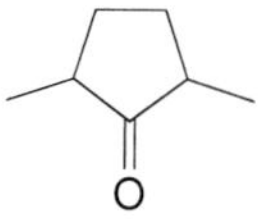

keto form

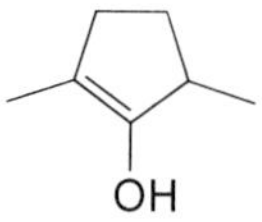

enol form

b.

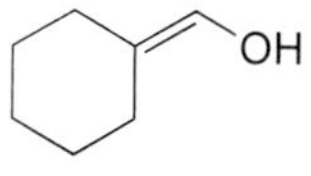

enol form

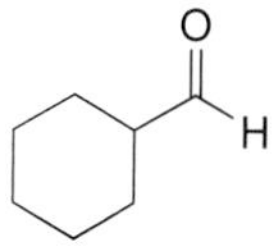

keto form

11.26

a, b.

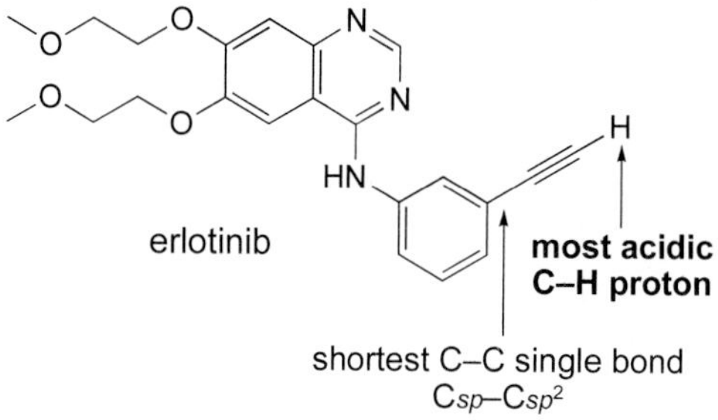
most acidic
C–H proton
shortest C–C single bond
Csp–Csp²

erlotinib

c.
d. * = *sp* hybridized C
e. 3 < 1 < 2

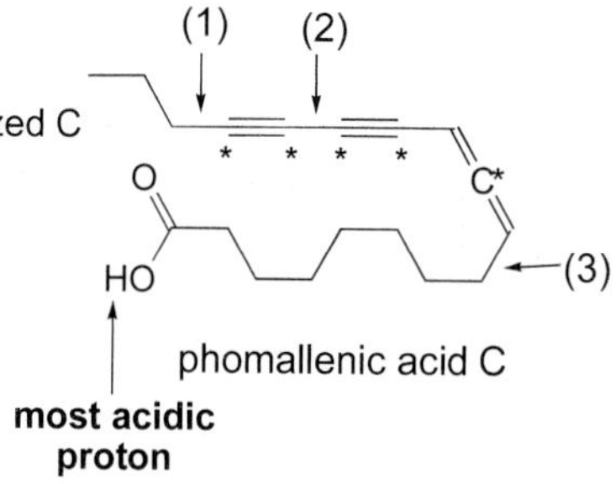
(1)
(2)
(3)
most acidic
proton

phomallenic acid C

11.27 Use the rules from Answer 11.3 to name the alkynes.

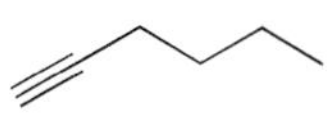

1-hexyne

3-hexyne

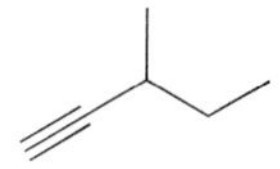

3-methyl-1-pentyne

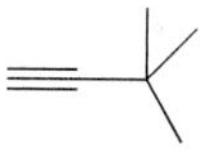

3,3-dimethyl-1-butyne

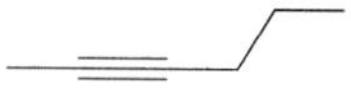

2-hexyne

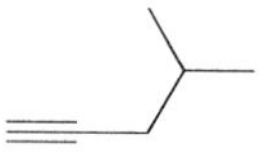

4-methyl-1-pentyne

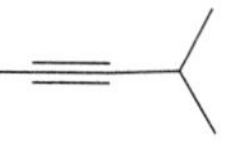

4-methyl-2-pentyne

11.28 Use the rules from Answer 11.3 to name the alkynes.

a. $CH_3CH_2CH(CH_3)C{\equiv}CCH_2CH_3$ **5-methyl-3-heptyne**
(5 = 5-methyl; 3 = 3-heptyne)

b. $CH_3CH(CH_3)C{\equiv}CCH(CH_3)CH_3$ **2,5-dimethyl-3-hexyne**
(3-hexyne; 2,5-dimethyl)

c. $CH_3CH_2CH(CH_2CH_3)C{\equiv}CCH(CH_2CH_3)CH(CH_3)CH_2CH_3$ **3,6-diethyl-7-methyl-4-nonyne**
(4-nonyne; 7-methyl; 3,6-diethyl)

d. $HC{\equiv}C{-}CH(CH_2CH_3)CH_2CH_2CH_3$ **3-ethyl-1-hexyne**
(1-hexyne; 3-ethyl)

e. $CH_3CH_2C{\equiv}CCH_2C{\equiv}CCH_3$ **2,5-octadiyne**
(5; 2)

f.

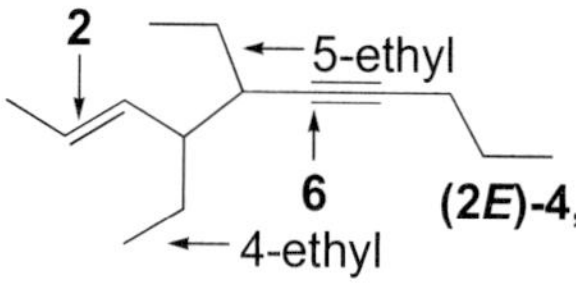
2
5-ethyl
6
4-ethyl

(2*E*)-4,5-diethyl-2-decen-6-yne

g.

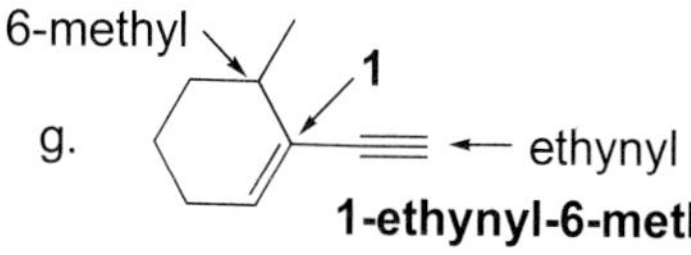
6-methyl
1
ethynyl

1-ethynyl-6-methylcyclohexene

11.29 Use the directions from Answer 11.4 to draw each structure.

a. 5,6-dimethyl-2-**heptyne**

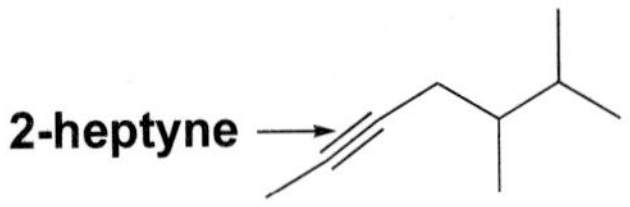
2-heptyne

b. 5-*tert*-butyl-6,6-dimethyl-3-**nonyne**

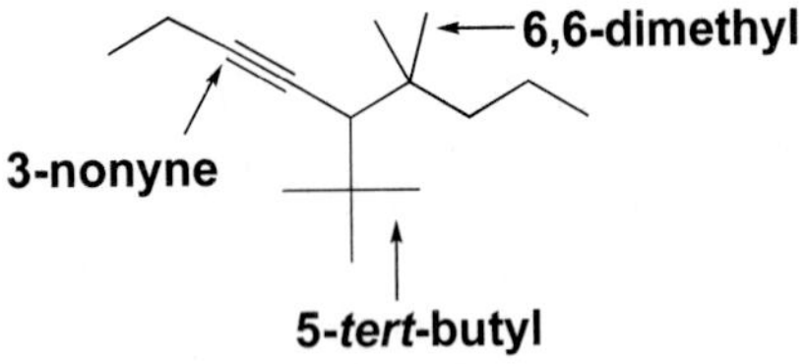
6,6-dimethyl
3-nonyne
5-*tert*-butyl

c. (4*S*)-4-chloro-2-**pentyne**

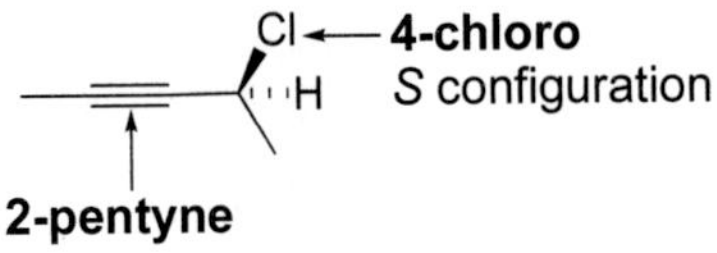
Cl
4-chloro
H
S configuration
2-pentyne

d. *cis*-1-ethynyl-2-methyl**cyclopentane**

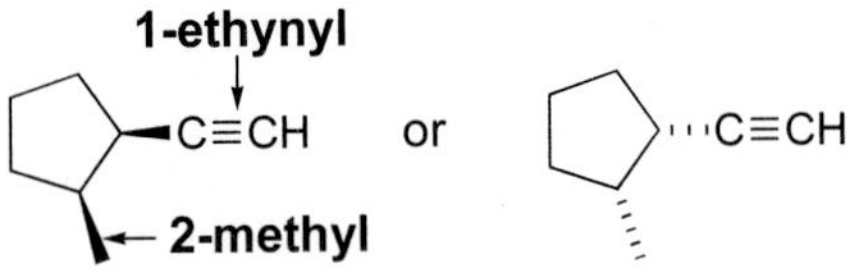
1-ethynyl
C≡CH
or
C≡CH
2-methyl

e. 3,4-dimethyl-1,5-**octadiyne**

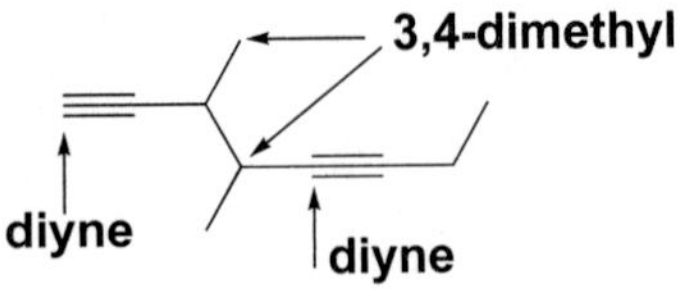
3,4-dimethyl
diyne
diyne

f. (6*Z*)-6-methyl-6-**octen-1-yne**

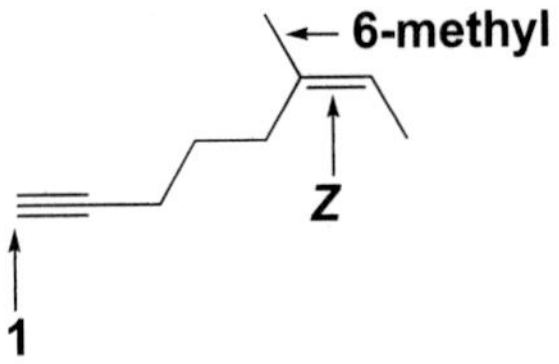
6-methyl
Z
1

11.30 Keto–enol tautomers are constitutional isomers in equilibrium that differ in the location of a double bond and a hydrogen. The OH in an enol must be bonded to a C=C.

a.

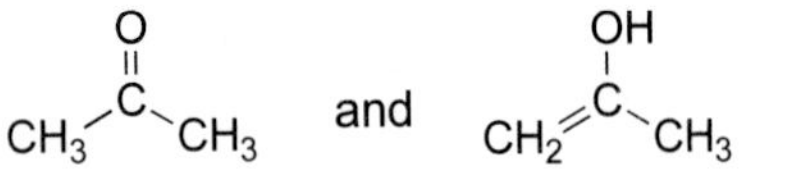
O
C
CH3
CH3
and
OH
C
CH2
CH3

- C=O
- one more CH bond

- C=C
- OH on C=C

keto–enol tautomers

c.

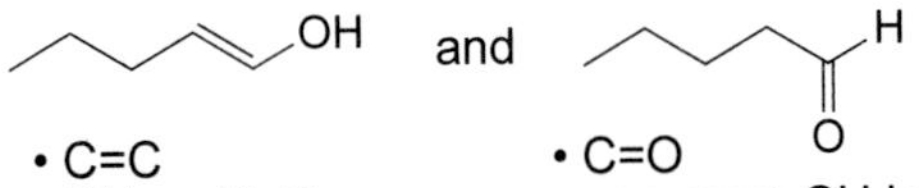
OH
and
H
O

- C=C
- OH on C=C

- C=O
- one more CH bond

keto–enol tautomers

b.

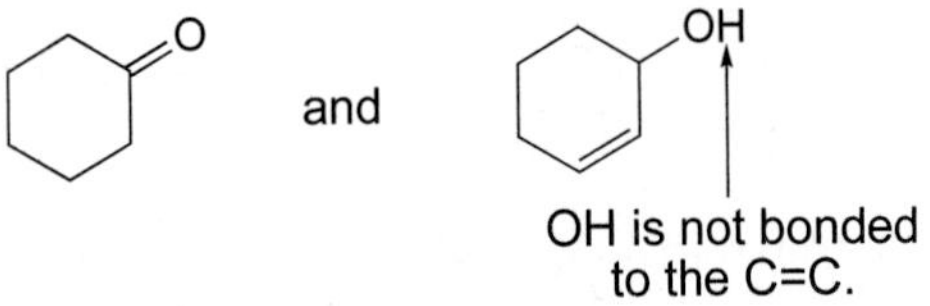
O
and
OH
OH is not bonded to the C=C.

NOT keto–enol tautomers

d.

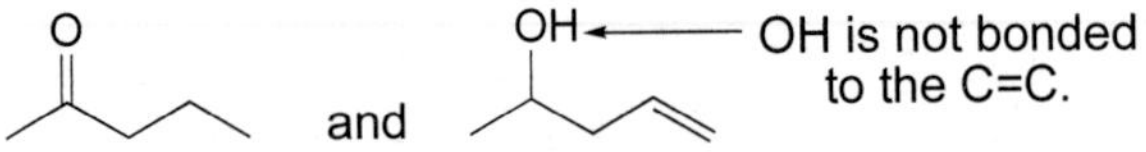
O
and
OH
OH is not bonded to the C=C.

NOT keto–enol tautomers

11.31 **To draw the enol form of each keto form:** [1] Change the C=O to a C–OH. [2] Change one single C–C bond to a double bond, making sure the OH group is bonded to the C=C. Use the directions from Answer 11.12 to draw each keto form.

a. CH_3CH_2CHO =

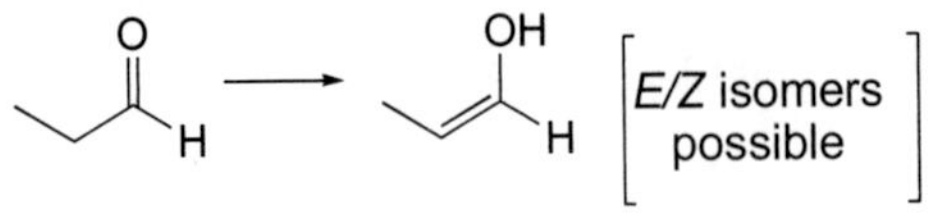
O
H
OH
H
E/Z isomers possible

c.

OH
O
H

b.

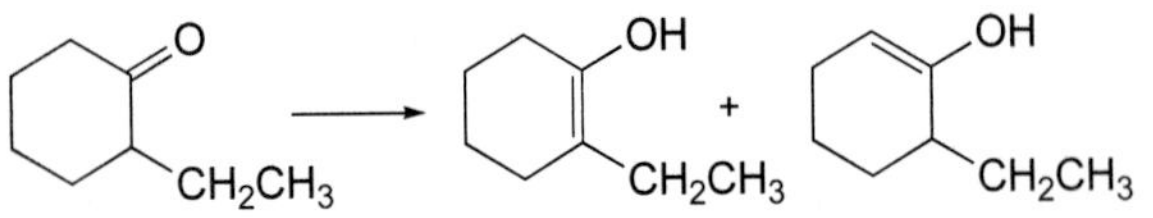
O
CH2CH3
OH
CH2CH3
+
OH
CH2CH3

d.

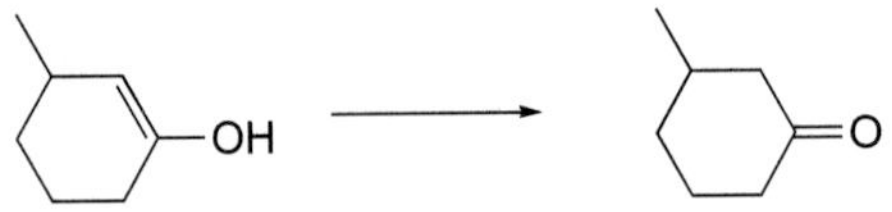
OH
O

11.32 Tautomers are constitutional isomers that are in equilibrium and differ in the location of a double bond and a hydrogen atom.

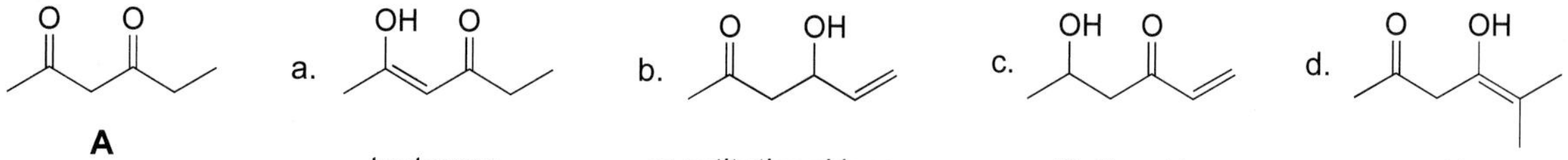

A
a.
b.
c.
d.

A	a.	b.	c.	d.
	tautomer	constitutional isomer	constitutional isomer	neither

11.33

(*E* and *Z*)

2-butanone

C=C has one C bonded to it.

C=C has two C's bonded to it. The more substituted double bond is **more stable.**

11.34

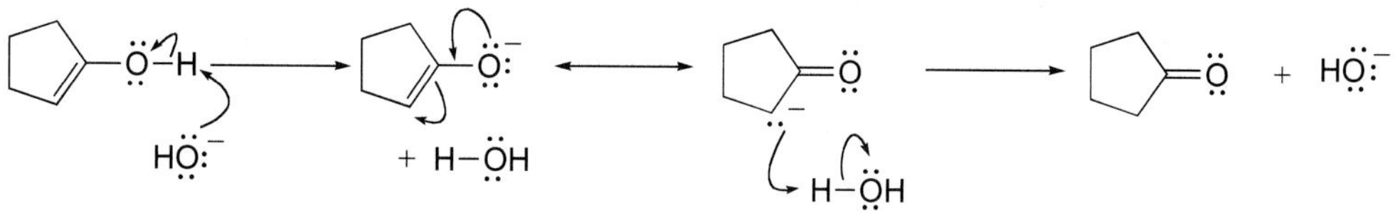

11.35

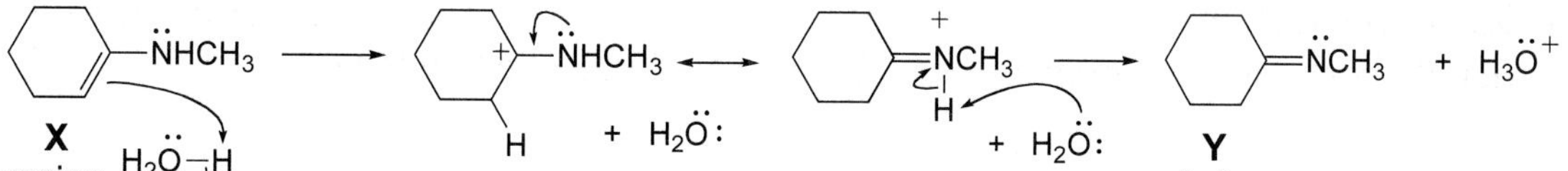

X
enamine
Y
imine

11.36

$HC{\equiv}CCH_2CH_2CH_2CH_3$

a. HCl (2 equiv) → $CH_3{-}CCl_2{-}CH_2CH_2CH_2CH_3$

b. HBr (2 equiv) → $CH_3{-}CBr_2CH_2CH_2CH_2CH_3$

c. Cl_2 (2 equiv) → $HCCl_2{-}CCl_2CH_2CH_2CH_2CH_3$

d. H_2O, H_2SO_4, $HgSO_4$ → $CH_3C(=O)CH_2CH_2CH_2CH_3$

e. [1] R_2BH; [2] H_2O_2, HO^- → $HC(=O)CH_2CH_2CH_2CH_2CH_3$

f. NaH → $Na^{+}\,{}^{-}C{\equiv}CCH_2CH_2CH_2CH_3$

g. [1] $^-NH_2$; [2] CH_3CH_2Br → $CH_3CH_2C{\equiv}CCH_2CH_2CH_2CH_3$

h. [1] $^-NH_2$; [2] ; [3] H_2O → $HOCH_2CH_2{-}C{\equiv}CCH_2CH_2CH_2CH_3$

11.37

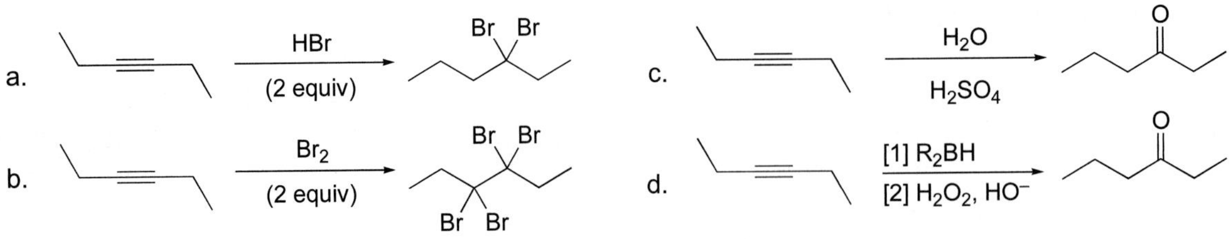
a.
HBr
(2 equiv)
Br Br
b.
Br2
(2 equiv)
Br Br
Br Br
c.
H2O
H2SO4
O
d.
[1] R2BH
[2] H2O2, HO–
O

11.38

a. 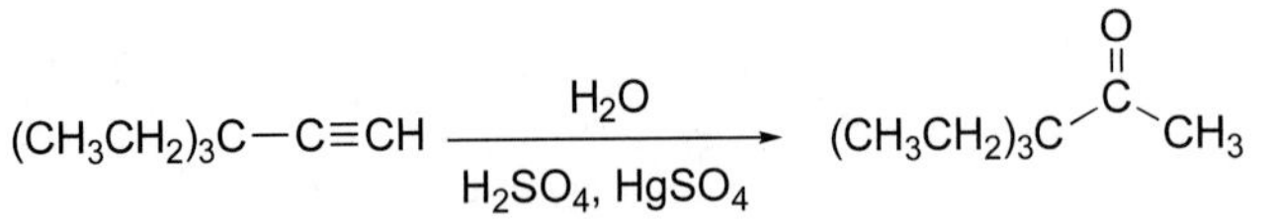
(CH3CH2)3C—C≡CH
H2O
H2SO4, HgSO4
O
C
(CH3CH2)3C
CH3

b. $(CH_3CH_2)_3C{-}C{\equiv}CH \xrightarrow[\text{[2] } H_2O_2,\ HO^-]{\text{[1] } R_2BH} (CH_3CH_2)_3C{-}CH_2CHO$

c. $(CH_3CH_2)_3C{-}C{\equiv}CH \xrightarrow[\text{(2 equiv)}]{HCl} (CH_3CH_2)_3CCCl_2CH_3$

d. $(CH_3CH_2)_3C{-}C{\equiv}CH \xrightarrow[\text{[2] } CH_3CH_2Br]{\text{[1] NaH}} (CH_3CH_2)_3C{-}C{\equiv}CCH_2CH_3$

11.39 Reaction rate (which is determined by E_a) and enthalpy ($\Delta H°$) are not related. More exothermic reactions are not necessarily faster. Since the addition of HX to an alkene forms a more stable carbocation in an endothermic, rate-determining step, this carbocation is formed faster by the Hammond postulate.

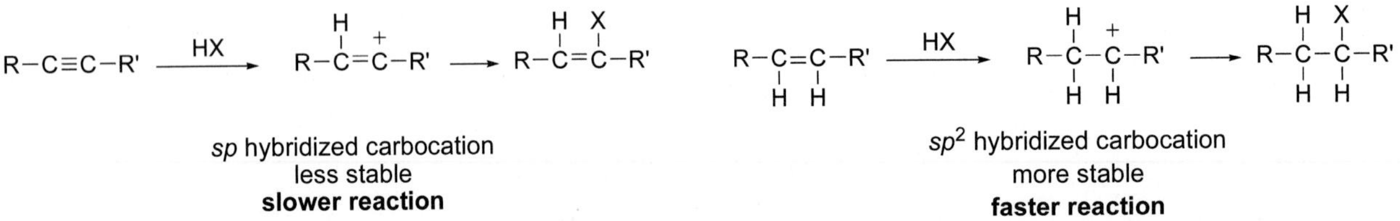
R–C≡C–R'
HX
R–C=C–R'
R–C=C–R'
R–C=C–R'
HX
R–C–C–R'
R–C–C–R'
sp hybridized carbocation
less stable
slower reaction
*sp*2 hybridized carbocation
more stable
faster reaction

11.40

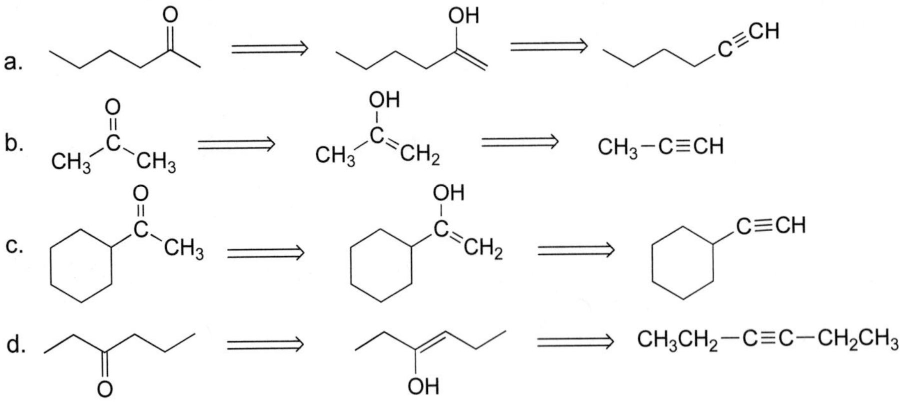
a.
O
OH
C≡CH
b.
O
C
CH3
CH3
OH
C
CH3
CH2
CH3–C≡CH
c.
O
C
CH3
OH
C
CH2
C≡CH
d.
O
OH
CH3CH2–C≡C–CH2CH3

11.41 To determine what two alkynes could yield the given ketone, work backwards by drawing the enols and then the alkynes.

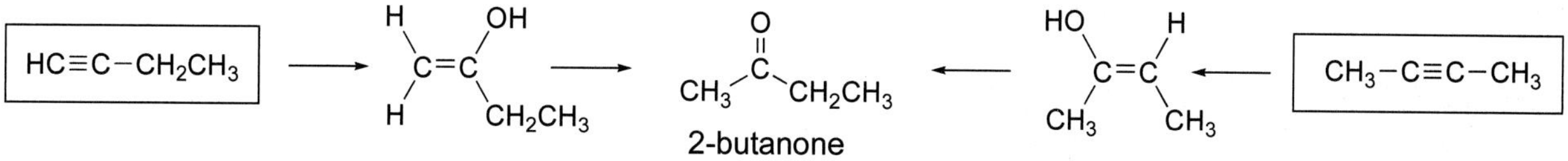

11.42

a. 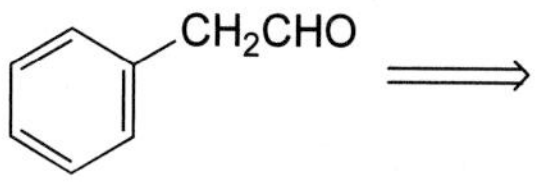

b. 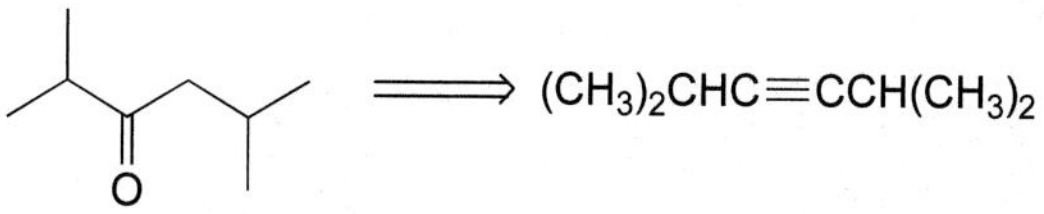

11.43

a. 

b. 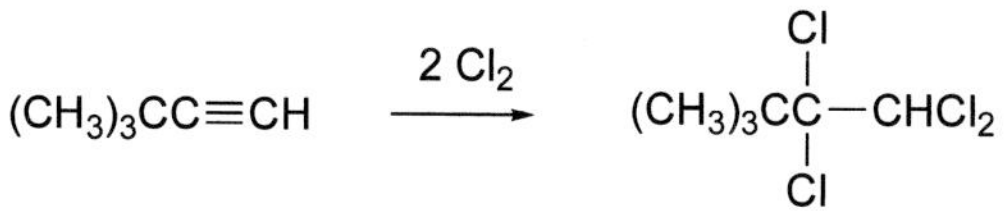

c. 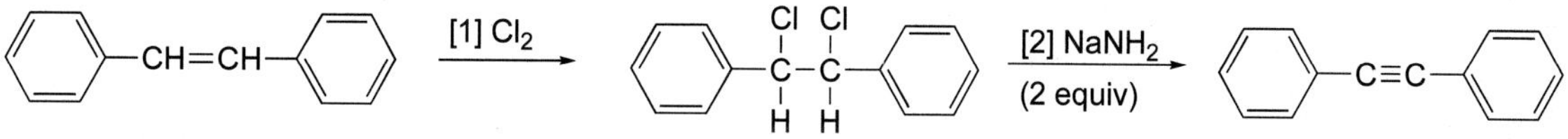

d. 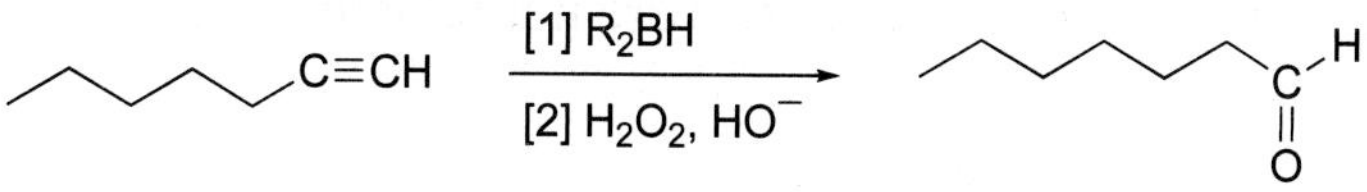

e. $HC\equiv C^- + D_2O \longrightarrow HC\equiv CD + DO^-$

f. 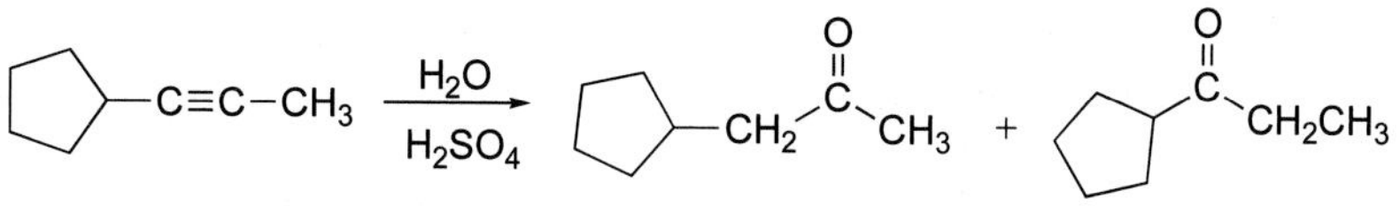

g. $CH_3CH_2C\equiv C^- + CH_3CH_2CH_2\text{–}OTs \longrightarrow CH_3CH_2C\equiv CCH_2CH_2CH_3 + {}^-OTs$

h. 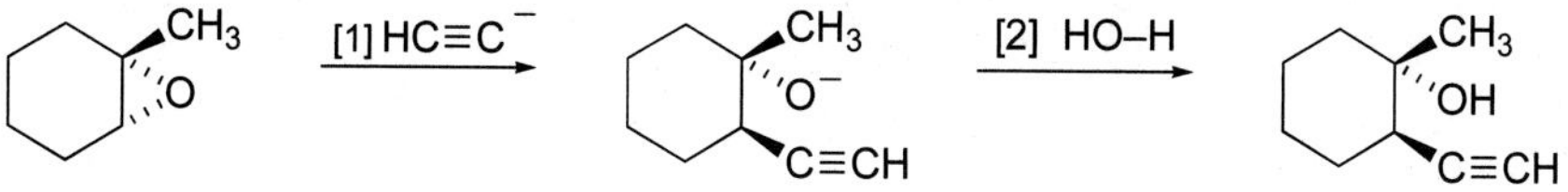

i. 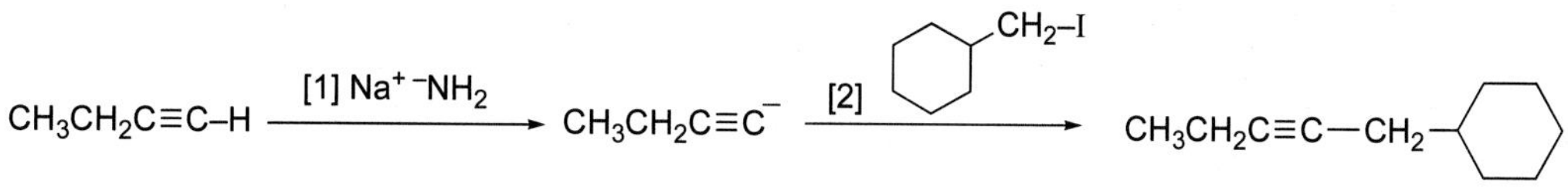

j. 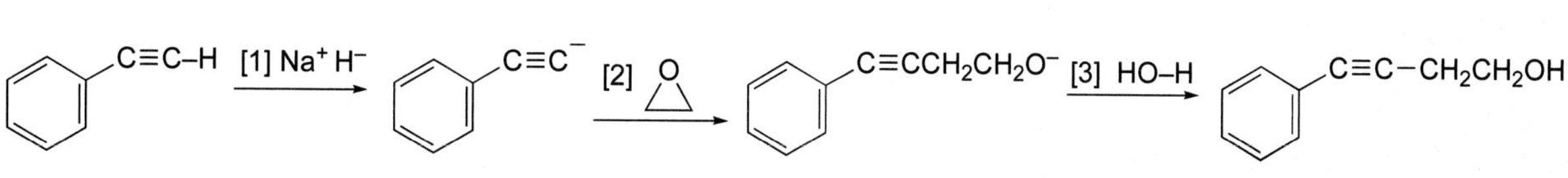

11.44

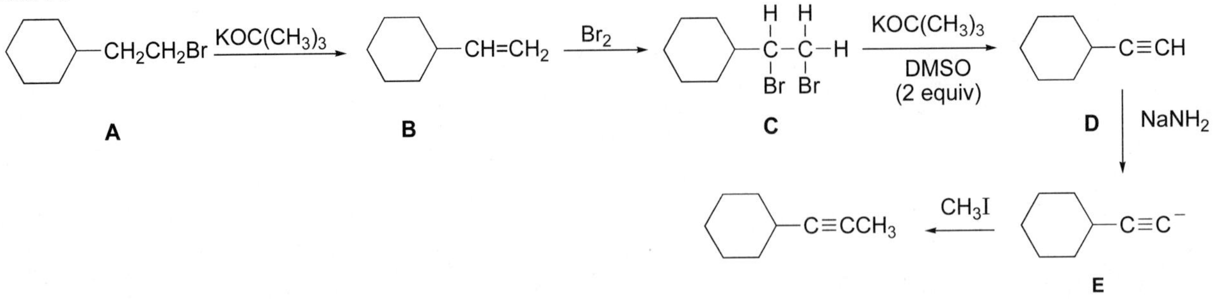

11.45

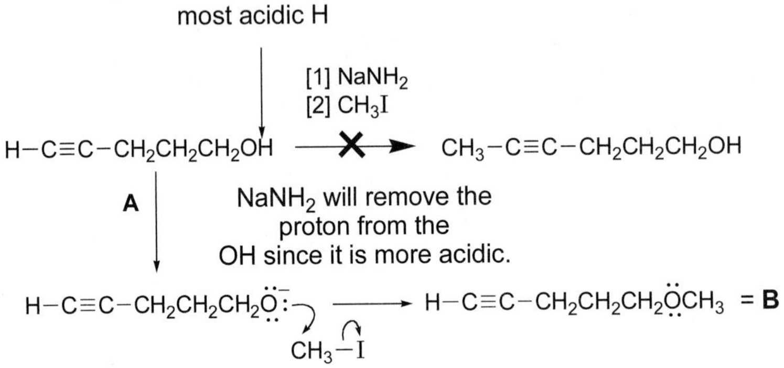

11.46

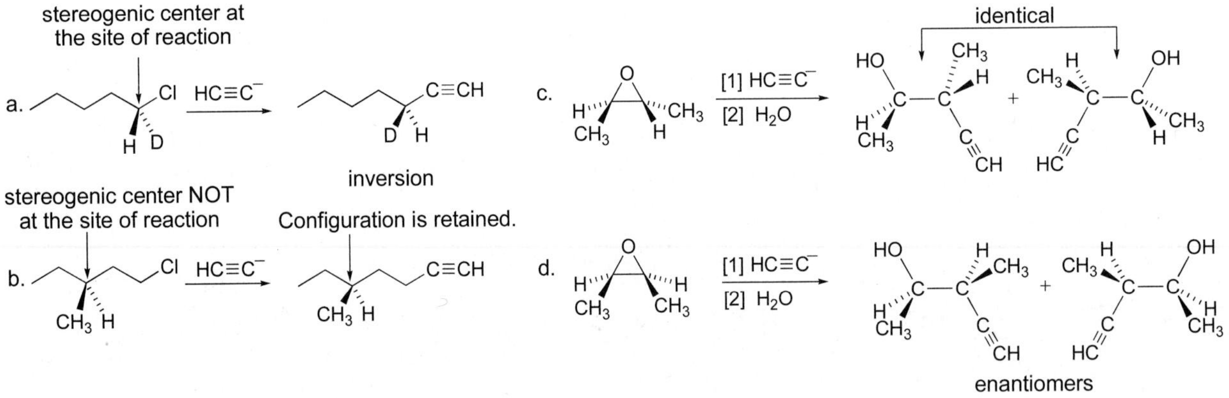

11.47

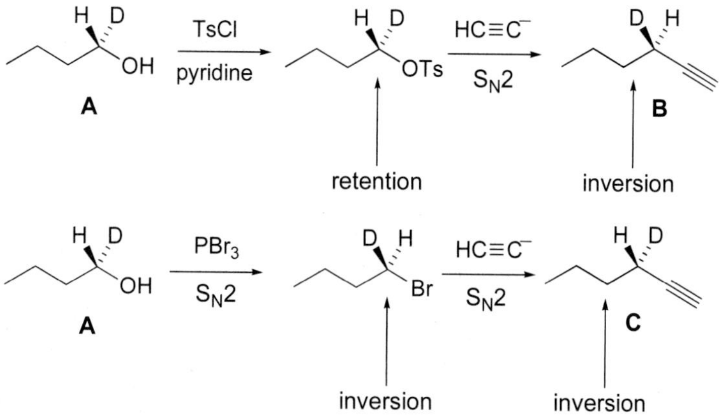
TsCl
pyridine
OTs
HC≡C⁻
SN2
A
B
retention
inversion
PBr3
SN2
Br
C
inversion
inversion

11.48

a.

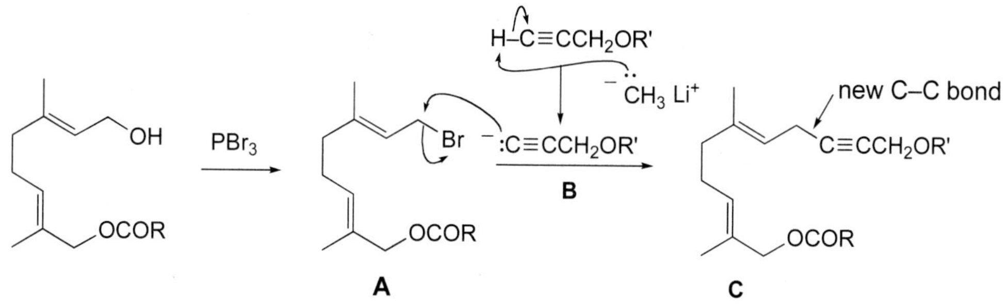
OH
OCOR
PBr3
H–C≡CCH2OR'
CH3 Li+
Br
⁻:C≡CCH2OR'
B
new C–C bond
C≡CCH2OR'
A
C

b.

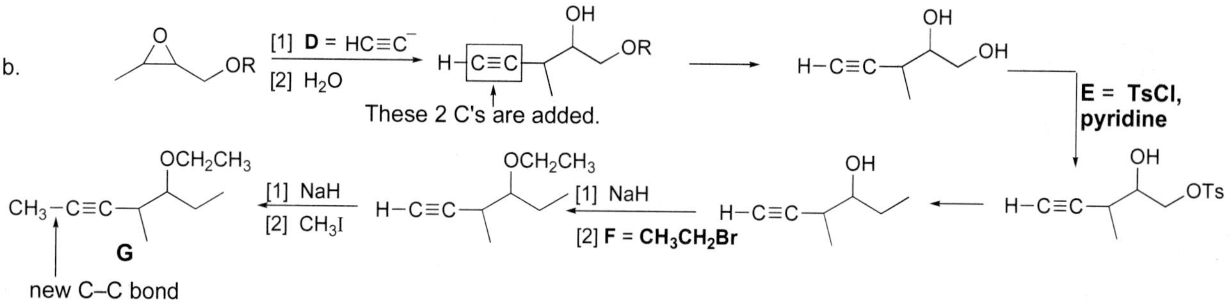
OR
[1] D = HC≡C⁻
[2] H2O
These 2 C's are added.
E = TsCl, pyridine
OTs
[1] NaH
[2] F = CH3CH2Br
OCH2CH3
[1] NaH
[2] CH3I
G
new C–C bond

11.49

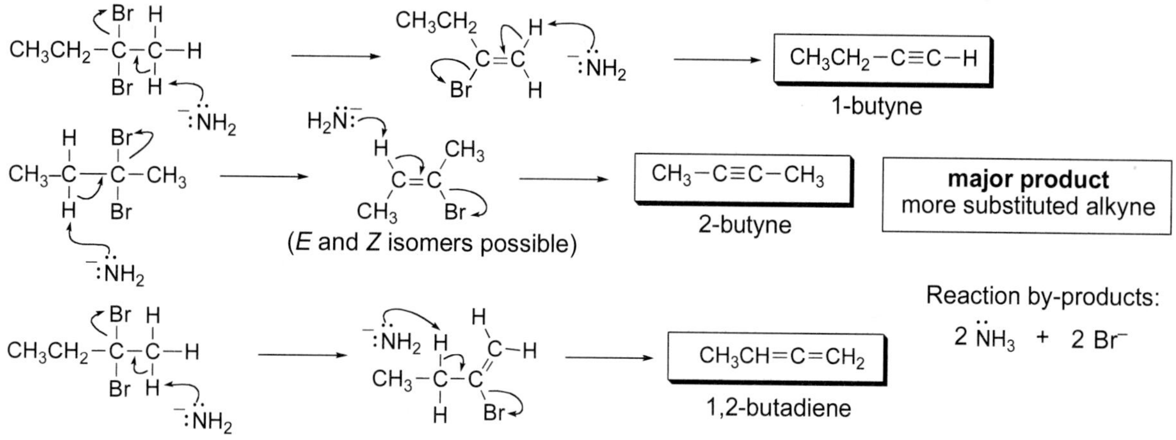
CH3CH2–C≡C–H
1-butyne
CH3–C≡C–CH3
2-butyne
major product
more substituted alkyne
(E and Z isomers possible)
Reaction by-products:
2 NH3 + 2 Br⁻
CH3CH=C=CH2
1,2-butadiene

11.50 A carbanion is more stable when its lone pair is in an orbital with a higher percentage of the smaller *s* orbital. A carbocation is more stable when its positive charge is due to a vacant orbital with a lower percentage of the smaller *s* orbital. In $HC{\equiv}C^+$, the positively charged C uses two *p* orbitals to form two π bonds. If the σ bond is formed using an *sp* hybrid orbital, the second hybrid orbital would have to remain vacant, a highly unstable situation.

$HC{\equiv}C^-$	$CH_2{=}CH^-$	$HC{\equiv}C^+$	$CH_2{=}CH^+$
sp hybridized higher % *s*-character **more stable**	*sp*[2] hybridized lower % *s*-character **less stable**	*sp* hybridized Vacant orbital has 50% *s*-character. **less stable**	*sp* hybridized Vacant orbital is a *p* orbital. **more stable**

11.51

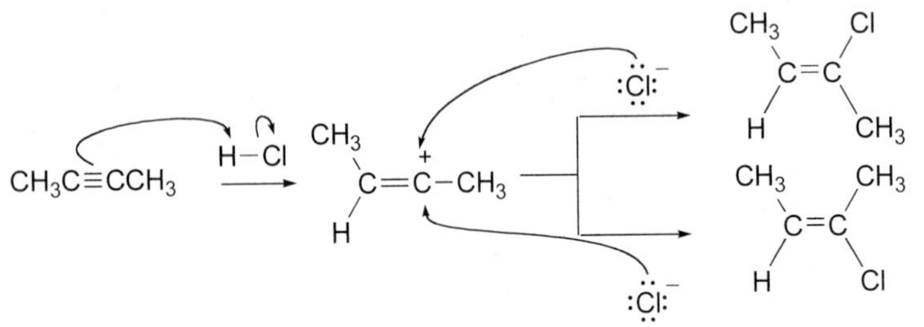

Cl^- attack on the opposite side to the H yields the ***Z*** isomer.

Cl^- attack on the same side as the H yields the ***E*** isomer.

11.52

a.

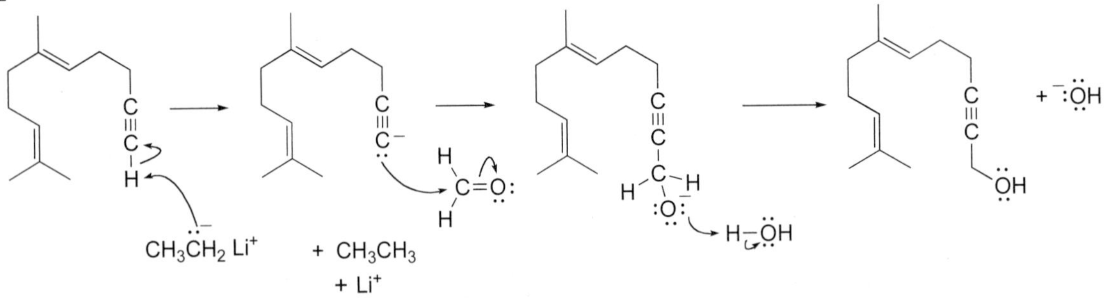

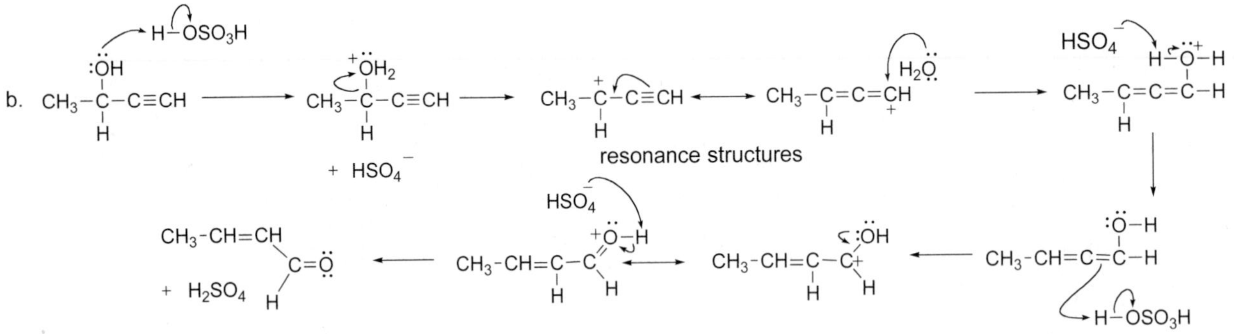

11.53

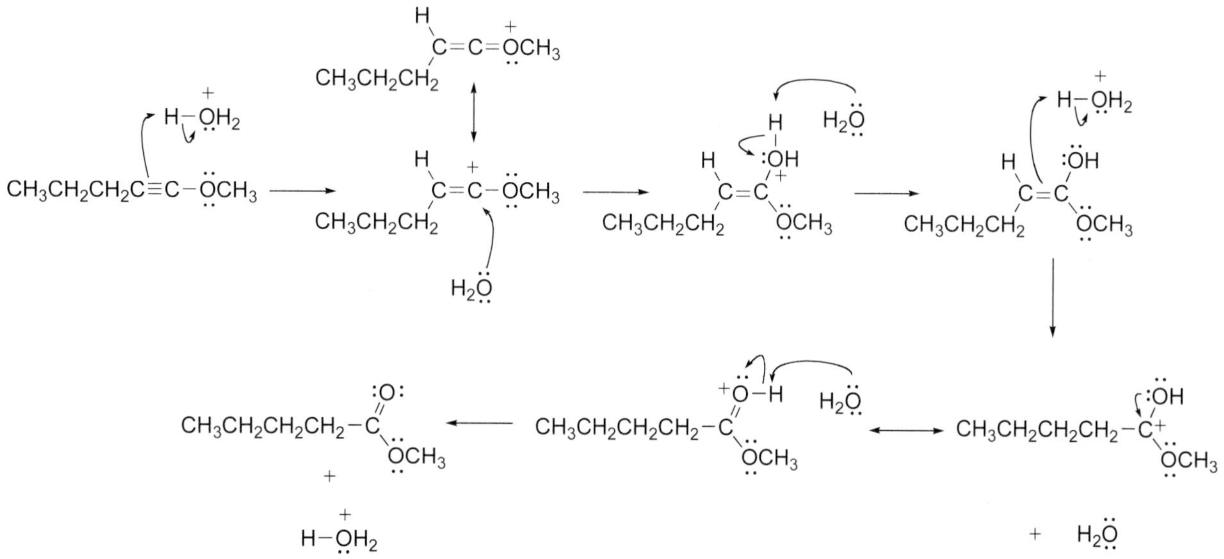

11.54

a. $C_6H_5CH_2CHBr_2 \xrightarrow[\text{(2 equiv)}\ \text{DMSO}]{KOC(CH_3)_3} C_6H_5C\equiv CH$

b. $C_6H_5CHBrCH_3 \xrightarrow{KOC(CH_3)_3} C_6H_5CH{=}CH_2 \xrightarrow{Br_2} C_6H_5CHBrCH_2Br \xrightarrow[\text{excess}]{NaNH_2} C_6H_5C\equiv CH$

c. $C_6H_5CH_2CH_2OH \xrightarrow{H_2SO_4} C_6H_5CH{=}CH_2 \xrightarrow{Br_2} C_6H_5CHBrCH_2Br \xrightarrow[\text{excess}]{NaNH_2} C_6H_5C\equiv CH$

11.55 The alkyl halides must be methyl or 1°.

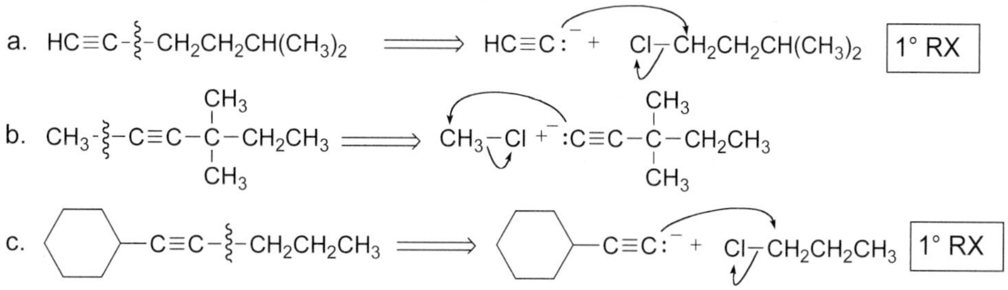

11.56

a. $HC\equiv C\text{–}H \xrightarrow{Na^+ H^-} HC\equiv C^- \xrightarrow{(CH_3)_2CHCH_2\text{–}Cl} (CH_3)_2CHCH_2C\equiv CH$

b. $HC\equiv C\text{–}H \xrightarrow{Na^+ H^-} HC\equiv C^- \xrightarrow{CH_3CH_2CH_2\text{–}Cl} \boxed{CH_3CH_2CH_2C\equiv CH} \xrightarrow{NaH} CH_3CH_2CH_2C\equiv C^-$

$CH_3CH_2CH_2C\equiv C^- \xrightarrow{CH_3CH_2CH_2\text{–}Cl} CH_3CH_2CH_2C\equiv CCH_2CH_2CH_3$

c. $CH_3CH_2CH_2C{\equiv}CH \xrightarrow[\text{[2] } H_2O_2,\ HO^-]{\text{[1] } R_2BH} CH_3CH_2CH_2CH_2CHO$
(from b.)

d. 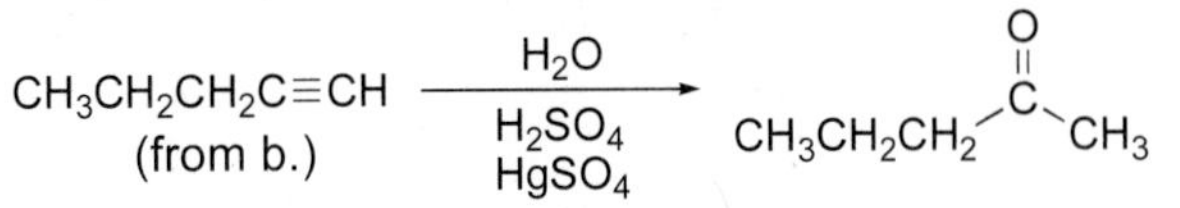

e. $CH_3CH_2CH_2C{\equiv}CH \xrightarrow{2\ HCl} CH_3CH_2CH_2CCl_2CH_3$
(from b.)

f. 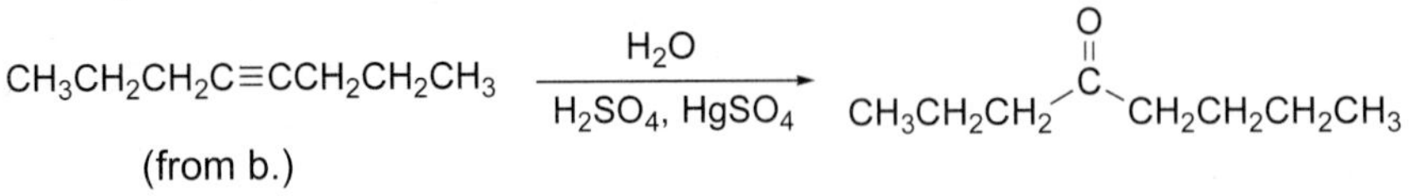

11.57

a. $CH_3CH_2CH{=}CH_2 \xrightarrow{Cl_2} CH_3CH_2CHCl{-}CH_2Cl \xrightarrow{2\ ^-NH_2} CH_3CH_2C{\equiv}CH$

b. $CH_3CH_2C{\equiv}CH \xrightarrow[\text{(2 equiv)}]{HBr} CH_3CH_2CBr_2CH_3$
(from a.)

c. $CH_3CH_2C{\equiv}CH \xrightarrow[\text{(2 equiv)}]{Cl_2} CH_3CH_2CCl_2CHCl_2$
(from a.)

d. $CH_3CH_2CH{=}CH_2 \xrightarrow{Br_2} CH_3CH_2CHBrCH_2Br$

e. $CH_3CH_2C{\equiv}CH \xrightarrow{NaH} CH_3CH_2C{\equiv}C^- \xrightarrow{CH_3CH_2CH_2{-}Br} CH_3CH_2C{\equiv}C{-}CH_2CH_2CH_3$
(from a.)

f. 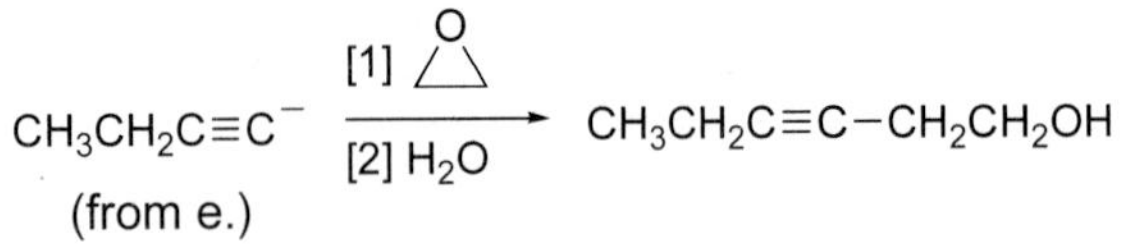

g. 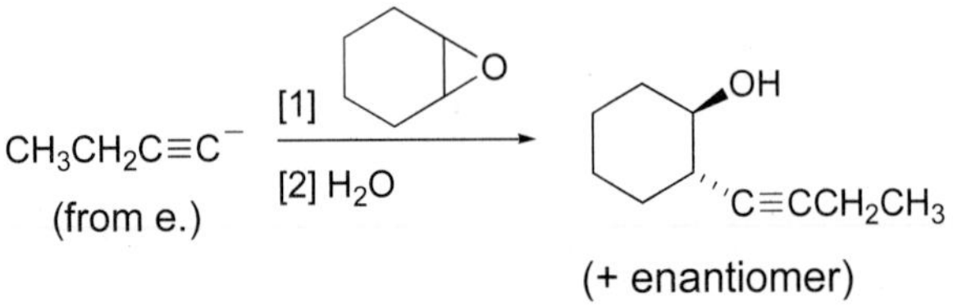

11.58

a. $HC{\equiv}CH \xrightarrow{NaH} HC{\equiv}C^- \xrightarrow{CH_3CH_2CH_2CH_2CH_2CH_2Br} CH_3CH_2CH_2CH_2CH_2CH_2C{\equiv}CH$

b. $CH_3CH_2CH_2CH_2CH_2CH_2C{\equiv}CH \xrightarrow{NaH} CH_3CH_2CH_2CH_2CH_2CH_2C{\equiv}C^- \xrightarrow{CH_3CH_2Br} CH_3CH_2CH_2CH_2CH_2CH_2C{\equiv}CCH_2CH_3$
(from a.)

c. 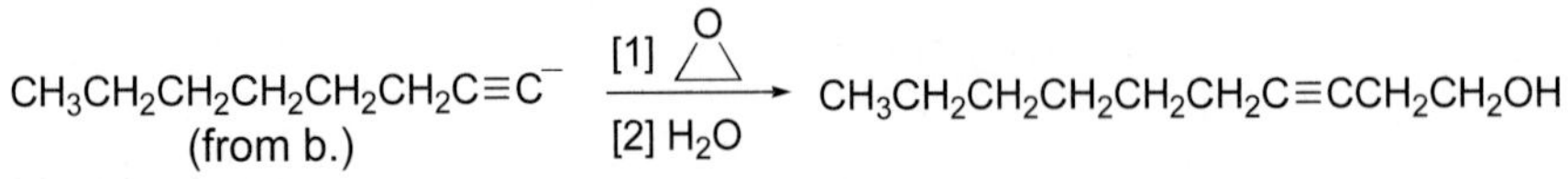

d. $CH_3CH_2CH_2CH_2CH_2CH_2C{\equiv}CCH_2CH_2OH \xrightarrow[\text{[2] } CH_3CH_2Br]{\text{[1] NaH}} CH_3CH_2CH_2CH_2CH_2CH_2C{\equiv}CCH_2CH_2OCH_2CH_3$
(from c.)

11.59

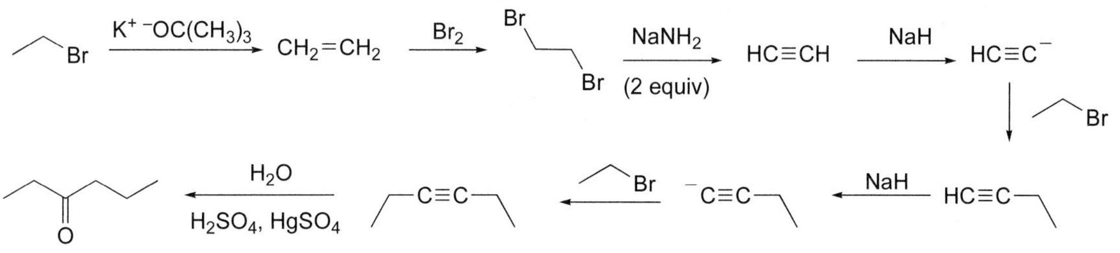

11.60

a.

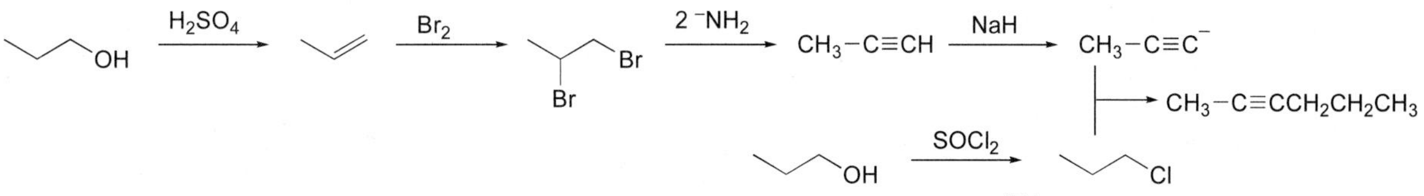

b.

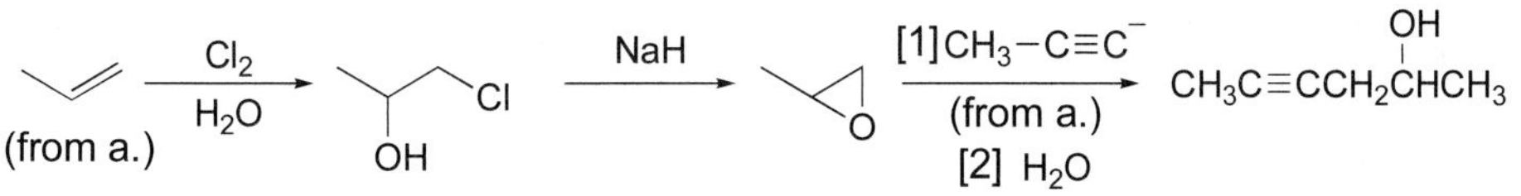

11.61

a.

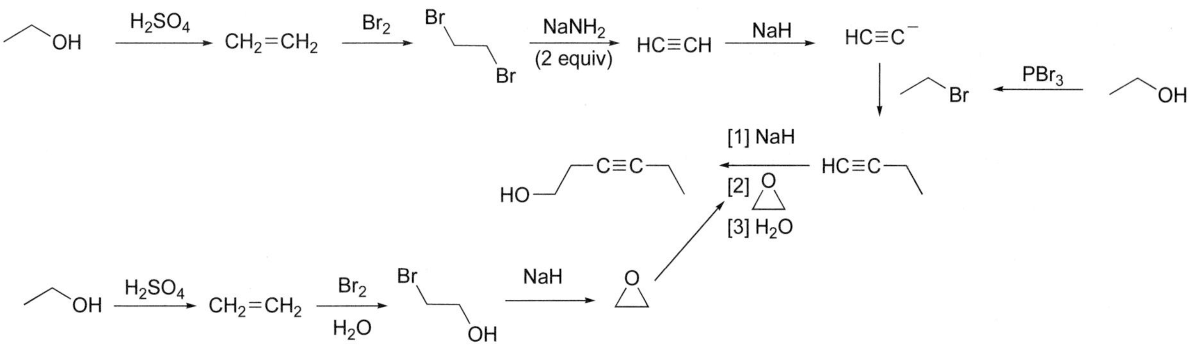

b.

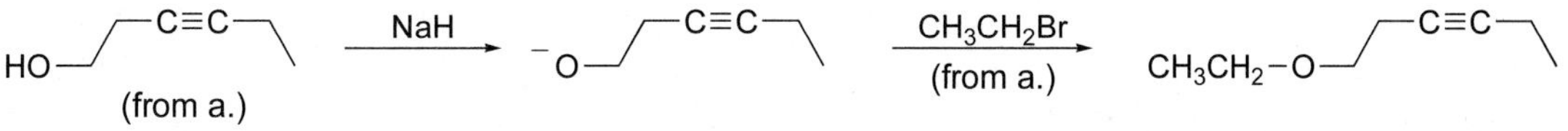

11.62 Two resonance structures can be drawn for an enol.

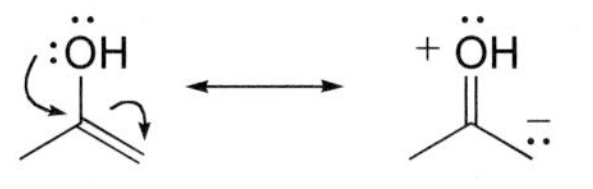
negative charge on C that
is part of the enol C=C

Since the second resonance structure places an electron pair (and therefore a negative charge) on an enol carbon, this makes the C=C more nucleophilic than the C=C of an alkene for which no additional resonance forms can be drawn. Thus, the OH group donates electron density to the C=C by a resonance effect.

11.63

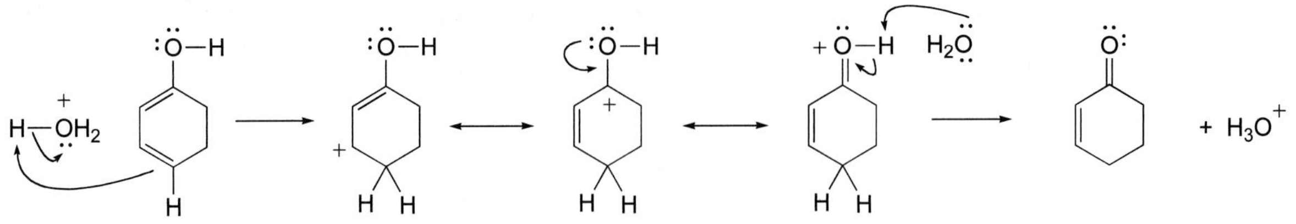

11.64

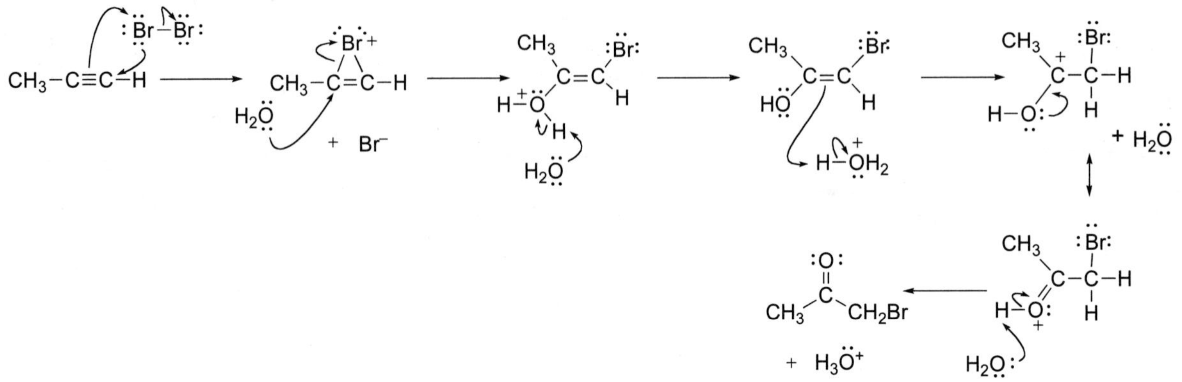

11.65

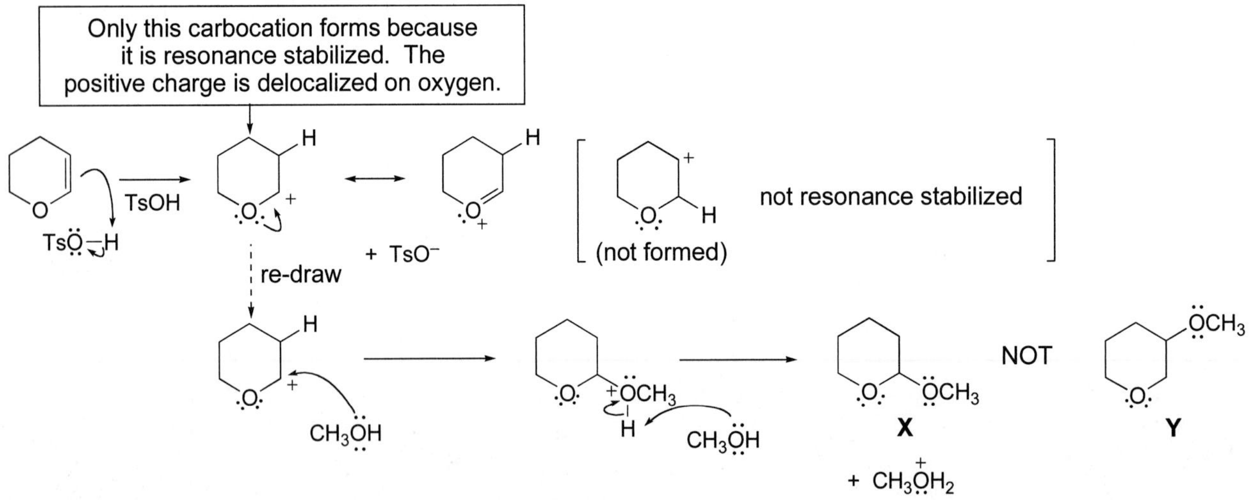
Only this carbocation forms because it is resonance stabilized. The positive charge is delocalized on oxygen.
TsOH
re-draw
+ TsO⁻
(not formed)
not resonance stabilized
NOT
X
Y

11.66 A more stable internal alkyne can be isomerized to a less stable terminal alkyne under these reaction conditions because when $CH_3CH_2C{\equiv}CH$ is first formed, it contains an *sp* hybridized C–H bond, which is more acidic than any proton in $CH_3{-}C{\equiv}C{-}CH_3$. Under the reaction conditions, this proton is removed with base. Formation of the resulting acetylide anion drives the equilibrium to favor its formation. Protonation of this acetylide anion gives the less stable terminal alkyne.

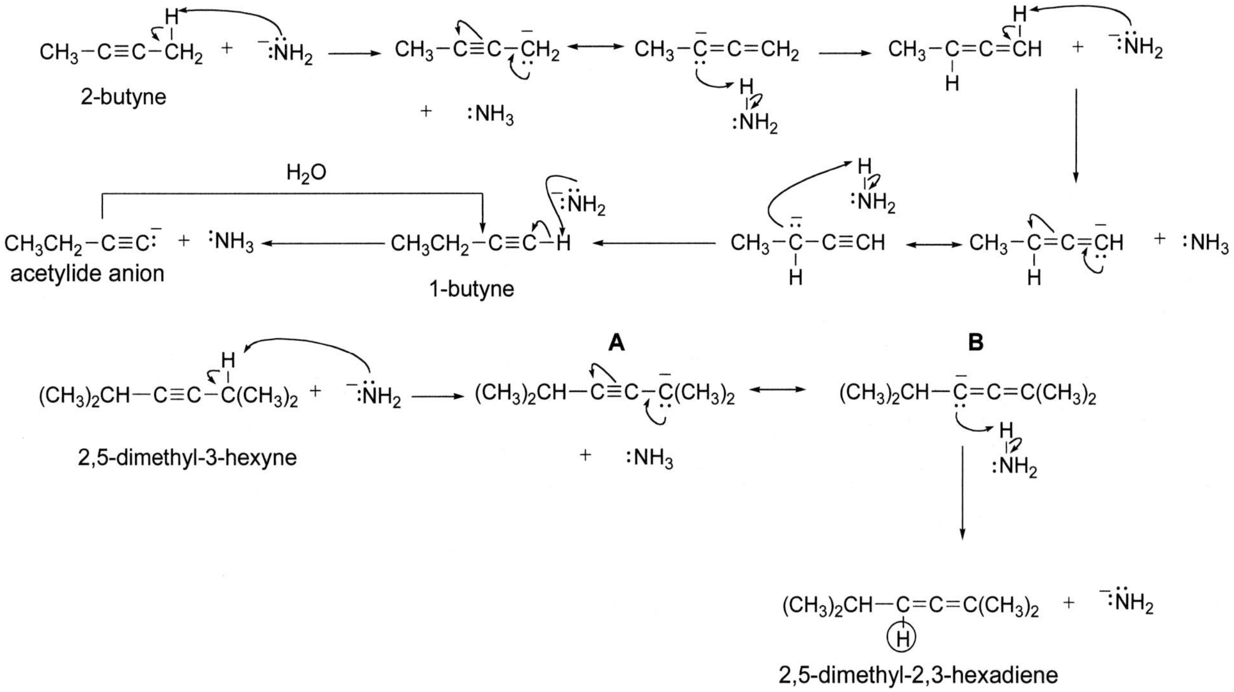

In this case the reaction stops with formation of 2,5-dimethyl-2,3-hexadiene because a terminal alkyne (with an acidic *sp* hybridized C–H bond) is not formed. Removal of the circled H in the diene re-forms the anion shown in resonance structures **A** and **B.**

11.67

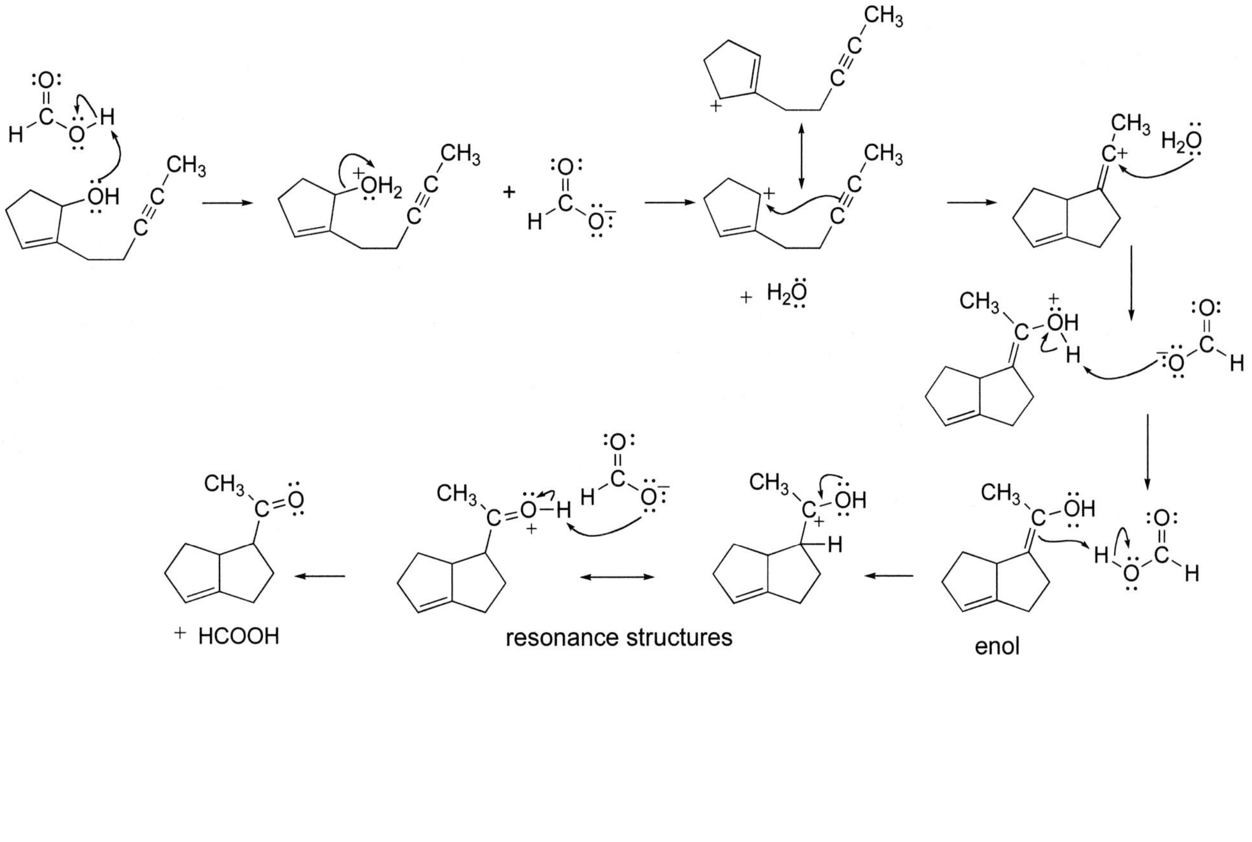

11.68 In the presence of acid, (*R*)-α-methylbutyrophenone enolizes to form an achiral enol.

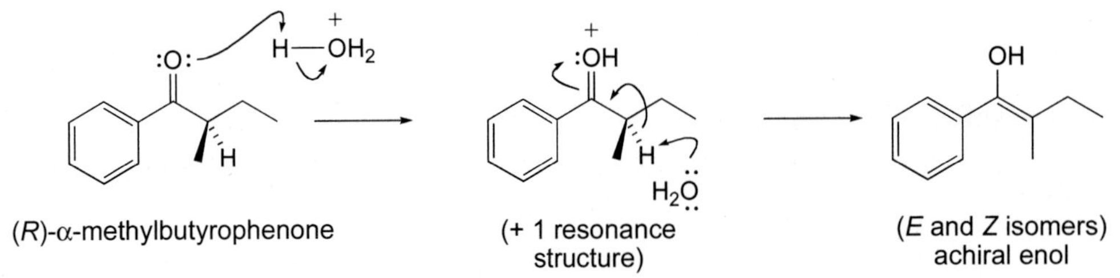
:O:
H—OH2
+
:OH
H
H2O
OH
(R)-α-methylbutyrophenone
(+ 1 resonance structure)
(E and Z isomers) achiral enol

The achiral enol can then be protonated from above or below the plane to form a racemic mixture that is optically inactive.

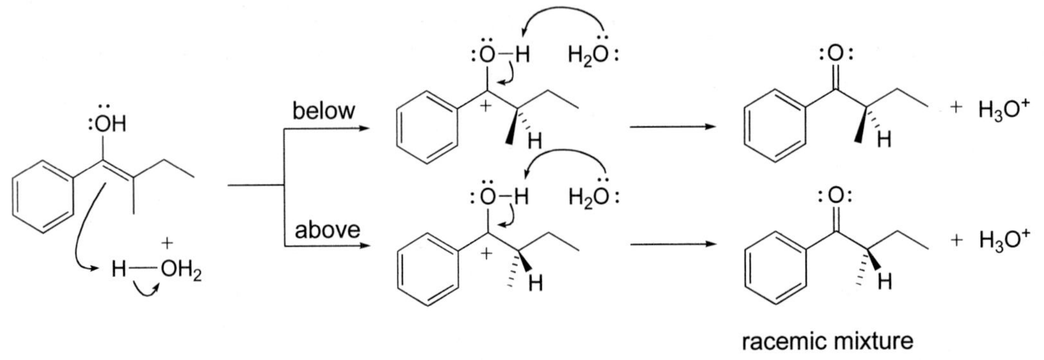
:OH
H—OH2
below
above
:O–H
H2O:
H
:O:
+ H3O+
racemic mixture

Chapter 12 Oxidation and Reduction

Chapter Review

Summary: Terms that describe reaction selectivity

- A **regioselective reaction** forms predominately or exclusively one constitutional isomer (Section 8.5).

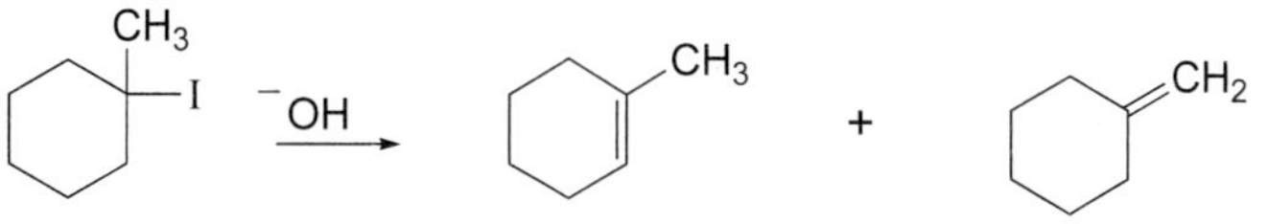

CH_3
I
^-OH
CH_3
+
CH_2

major product trisubstituted alkene — **minor product** disubstituted alkene

- A **stereoselective reaction** forms predominately or exclusively one stereoisomer (Section 8.5).

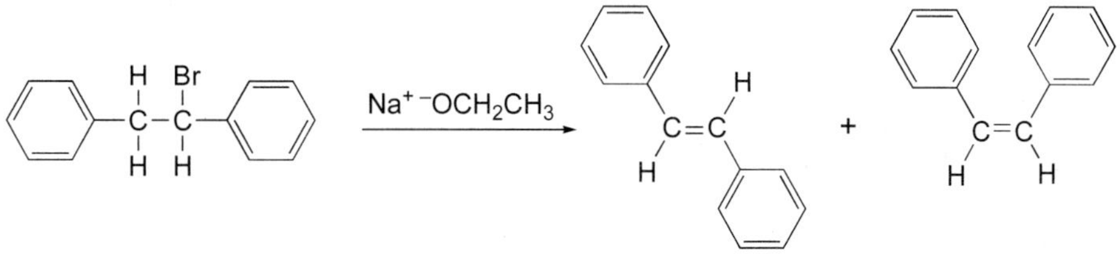

H Br
H H
$Na^+ \, ^-OCH_2CH_3$
H
C=C
H
+
C=C
H H

trans alkene **major product** — cis alkene **minor product**

- An **enantioselective reaction** forms predominately or exclusively one enantiomer (Section 12.15).

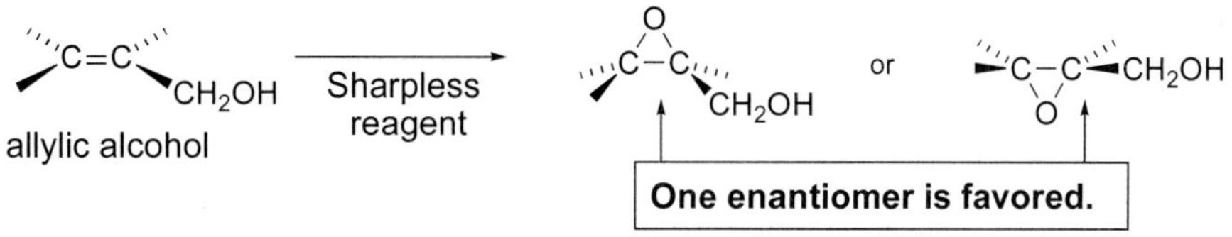

C=C
CH_2OH
allylic alcohol
Sharpless reagent
O
C–C
CH_2OH
or
C–C
CH_2OH
O
One enantiomer is favored.

Definitions of oxidation and reduction

Oxidation reactions result in:

- an increase in the number of C–Z bonds, *or*
- a decrease in the number of C–H bonds.

Reduction reactions result in:

- a decrease in the number of C–Z bonds, *or*
- an increase in the number of C–H bonds.

[Z = an element more electronegative than C]

Reduction reactions

[1] Reduction of alkenes—Catalytic hydrogenation (12.3)

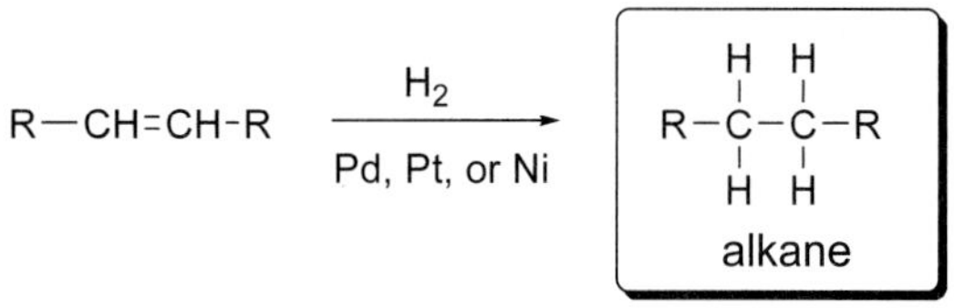

R–CH=CH-R
H_2
Pd, Pt, or Ni
H H
R–C–C–R
H H
alkane

- **Syn addition** of H_2 occurs.
- Increasing alkyl substitution on the C=C decreases the rate of reaction.

[2] Reduction of alkynes

[a]

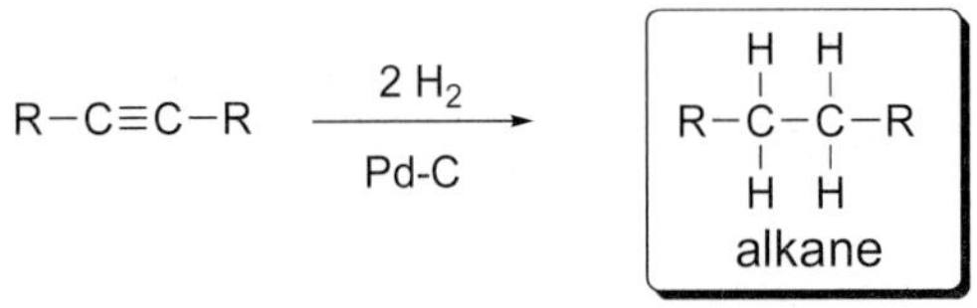

- Two equivalents of H_2 are added and four new C–H bonds are formed (12.5A).

[b]

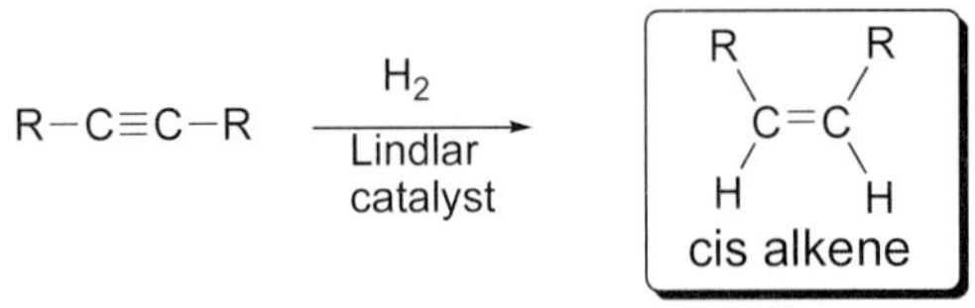

- **Syn addition** of H_2 occurs, forming a **cis** alkene (12.5B).
- The Lindlar catalyst is deactivated so that reaction stops after one equivalent of H_2 has been added.

[c]

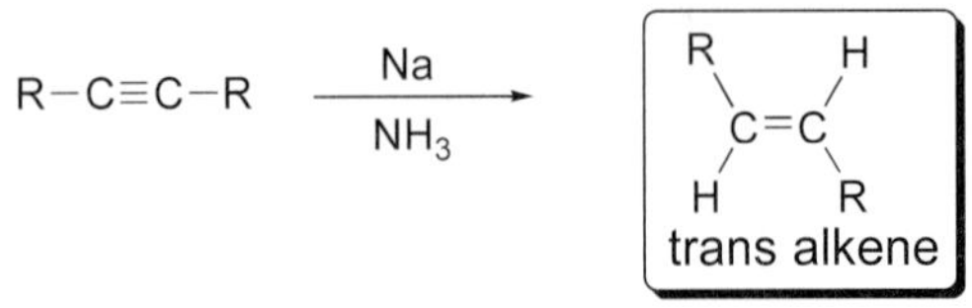

- **Anti addition** of H_2 occurs, forming a **trans** alkene (12.5C).

[3] Reduction of alkyl halides (12.6)

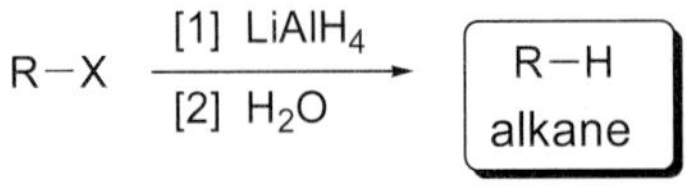

- The reaction follows an S_N2 mechanism.
- CH_3X and RCH_2X react faster than more substituted RX.

[4] Reduction of epoxides (12.6)

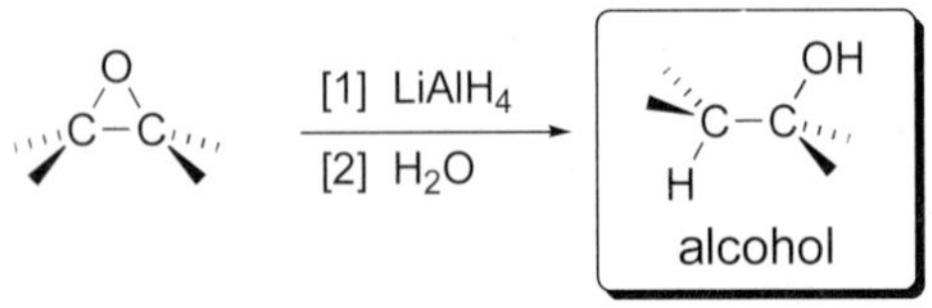

- The reaction follows an S_N2 mechanism.
- In unsymmetrical epoxides, H^- (from $LiAlH_4$) attacks at the less substituted carbon.

Oxidation reactions

[1] Oxidation of alkenes

[a] Epoxidation (12.8)

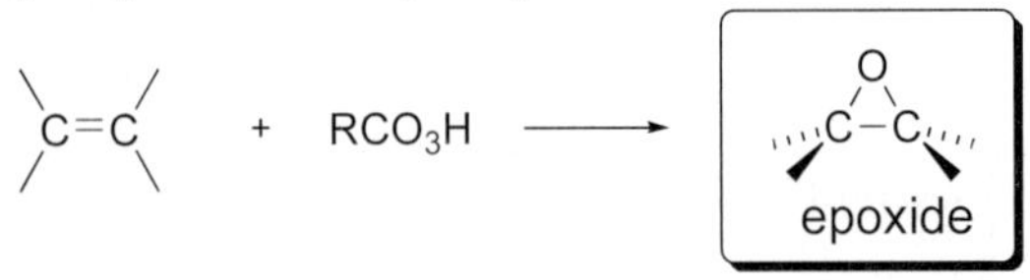

- The mechanism has **one step.**
- **Syn addition** of an O atom occurs.
- The reaction is stereospecific.

[b] Anti dihydroxylation (12.9A)

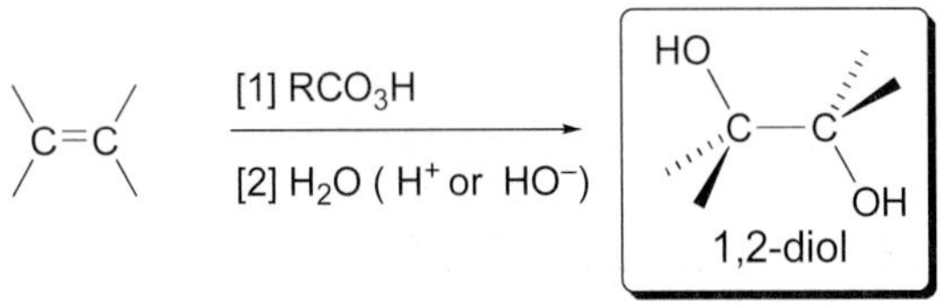

- Ring opening of an epoxide intermediate with ^-OH or H_2O forms a 1,2-diol with two OH groups added in an **anti** fashion.

[c] Syn dihydroxylation (12.9B)

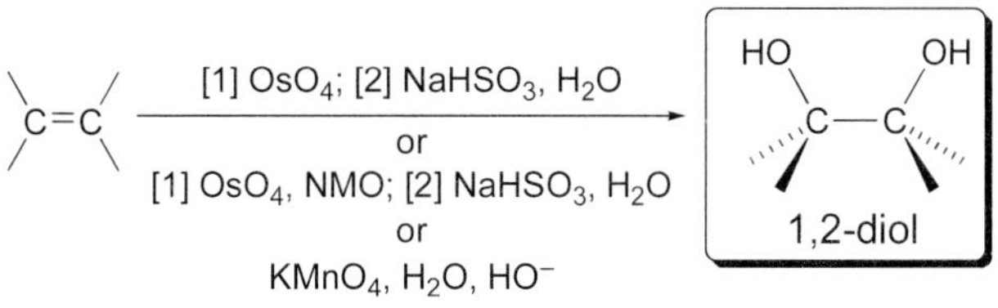

- Each reagent adds two new C–O bonds to the C=C in a **syn** fashion.

[d] Oxidative cleavage (12.10)

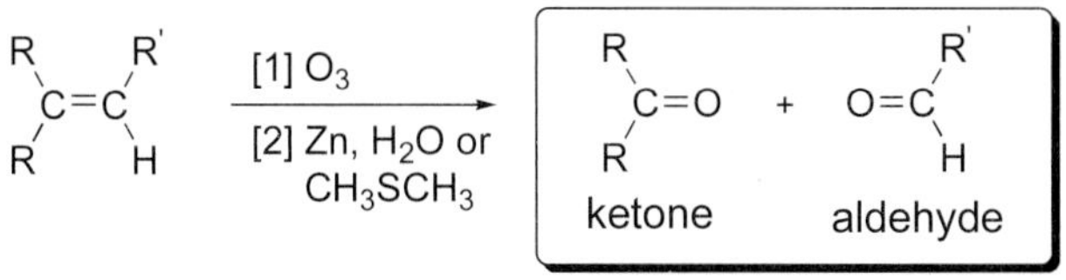

- Both the σ and π bonds of the alkene are cleaved to form two carbonyl groups.

[2] Oxidative cleavage of alkynes (12.11)

[a]

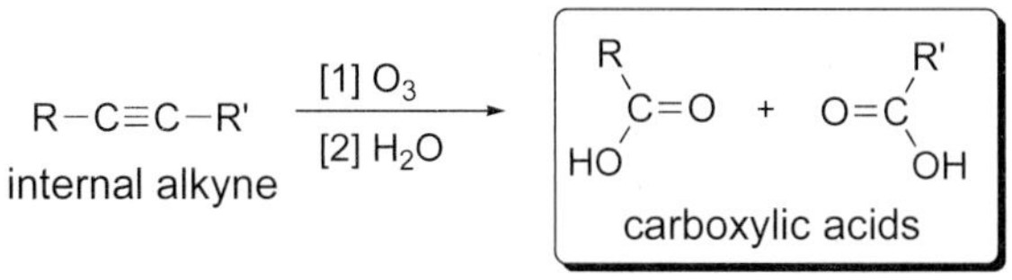

- The σ bond and both π bonds of the alkyne are cleaved.

[b]

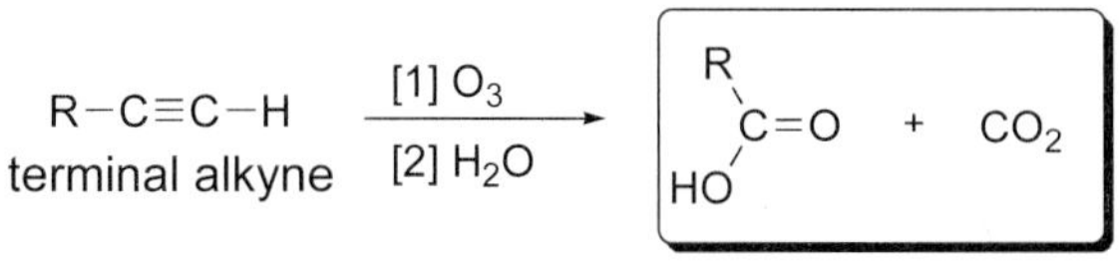

[3] Oxidation of alcohols (12.12, 12.13)

[a]

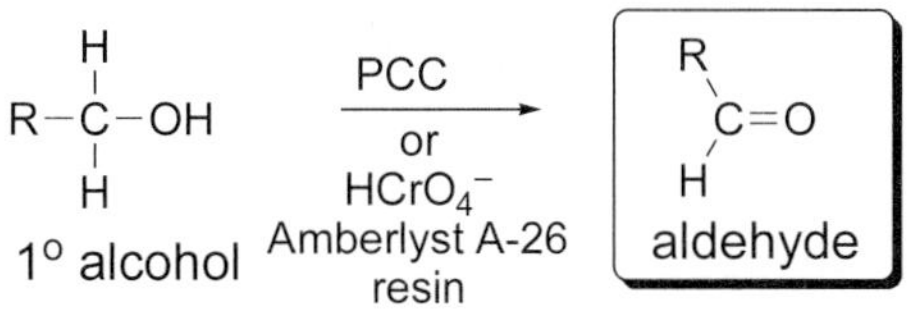

- Oxidation of a 1° alcohol with PCC or $HCrO_4^-$ (Amberlyst A-26 resin) stops at the aldehyde stage. Only one C–H bond is replaced by a C–O bond.

[b]

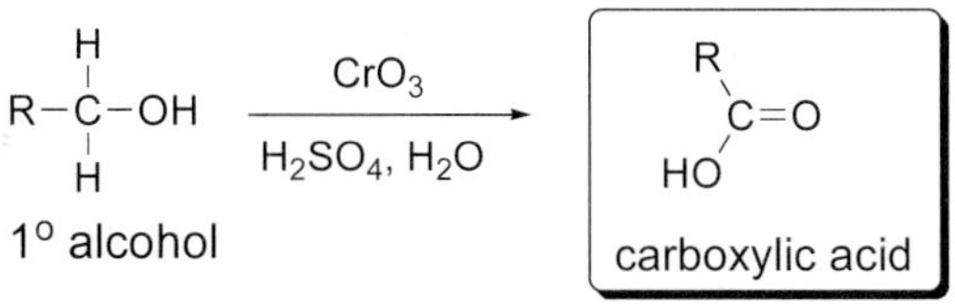

- Oxidation of a 1° alcohol under harsher reaction conditions—CrO_3 (or $Na_2Cr_2O_7$ or $K_2Cr_2O_7$) + H_2O + H_2SO_4—affords a RCOOH. Two C–H bonds are replaced by two C–O bonds.

[c]

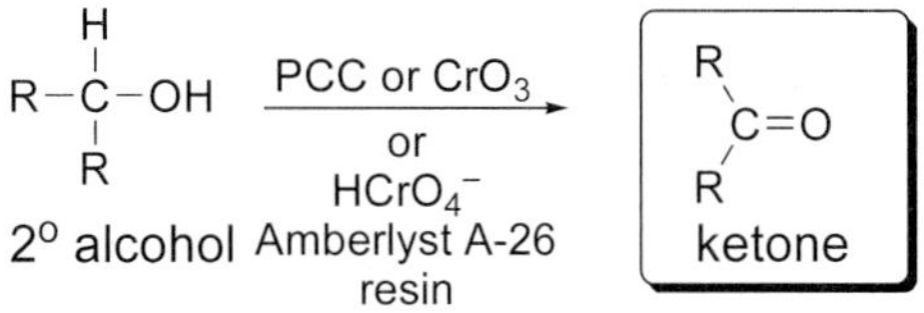

- Since a 2° alcohol has only one C–H bond on the carbon bearing the OH group, all Cr^{6+} reagents—PCC, CrO_3, $Na_2Cr_2O_7$, $K_2Cr_2O_7$, or $HCrO_4^-$ (Amberlyst A-26 resin)—oxidize a 2° alcohol to a ketone.

[4] Asymmetric epoxidation of allylic alcohols (12.15)

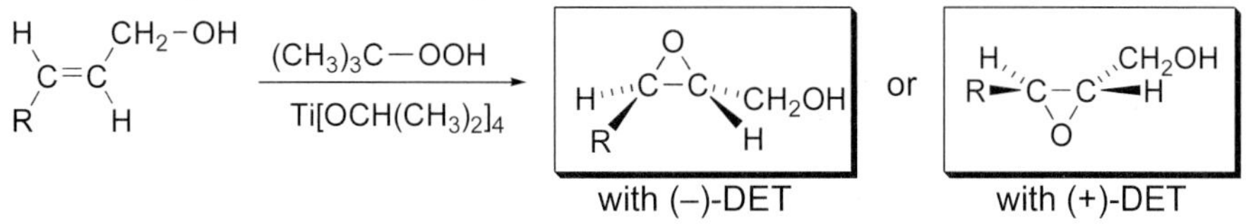

Practice Test on Chapter Review

1.a. Compound **X** has a molecular formula of C_9H_{12} and contains no triple bonds. **X** is hydrogenated to a compound of molecular formula C_9H_{14} with excess H_2 and a palladium catalyst. What can be said about **X?**

1. **X** has four rings.
2. **X** has three rings and one double bond.
3. **X** has two rings and two double bonds.
4. **X** has one ring and three double bonds.
5. **X** has four double bonds.

b. Syn addition to an alkene occurs exclusively with which reagents?

1. OsO_4
2. $KMnO_4$, H_2O, ^{-}OH
3. mCPBA, then H_2O, ^{-}OH
4. Both reagents (1) and (2) give syn addition exclusively.
5. Reagents (1), (2), and (3) give syn addition exclusively.

c. Which of the following reagents adds to an alkene exclusively in an anti fashion?

1. Br_2
2. H_2, Pd-C
3. BH_3, then H_2O_2, ^{-}OH
4. Reagents (1) and (2) both add in an anti fashion.
5. Reagents (1), (2), and (3) all add in an anti fashion.

2. Label each statement as True (T) or False (F).

a. PCC oxidizes 1° alcohols to aldehydes.
b. CrO_3 oxidizes 2° alcohols to ketones.
c. Treatment of 2-hexyne with Na in NH_3 forms *cis*-2-hexene.
d. Reduction of propene oxide with $LiAlH_4$ forms 1-propanol.
e. Ozonolysis of 2-methyl-2-octene forms one ketone and one aldehyde.
f. mCPBA is an oxidizing agent that converts alkenes to trans diols.
g. 1-Octen-5-yne reacts with H_2 and Pd-C, but does not react with H_2 and Lindlar catalyst.
h. Treatment of cyclohexene with OsO_4 affords an optically inactive product mixture that contains two enantiomers.

3. Label each reagent as an oxidizing agent, reducing agent, or neither.

a. O_3
b. $LiAlH_4$
c. mCPBA
d. H_2O, H_2SO_4
e. PCC
f. Na, NH_3

4. Draw the organic products formed in each reaction and indicate stereochemistry when necessary.

a.

b.

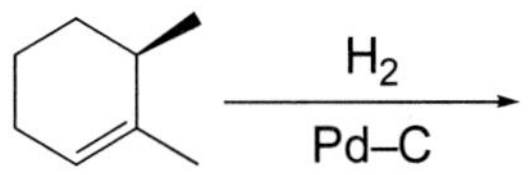

c.

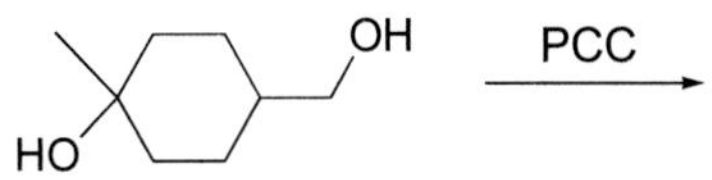

d.

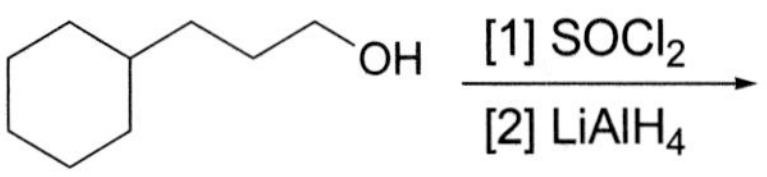

5. a. Fill in the appropriate starting material (including any needed stereochemistry) in the following reaction.

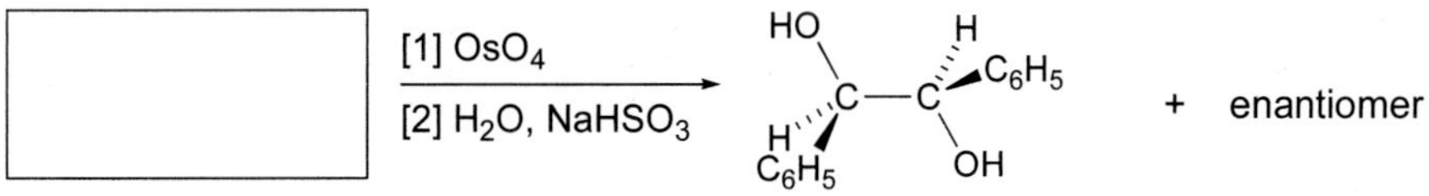

b. Fill in the appropriate reagent in the following reaction.

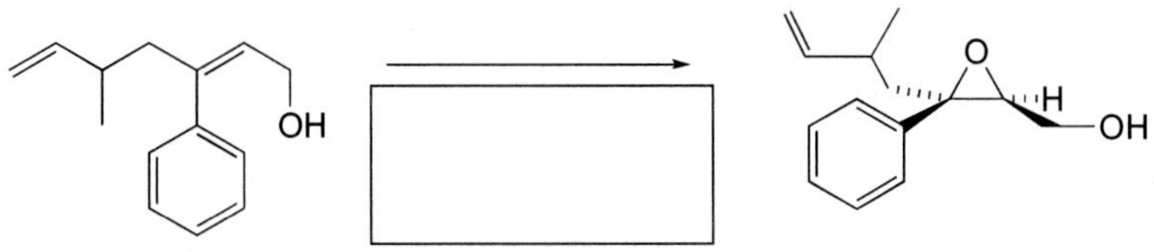

c. What starting material is needed for the following reaction?

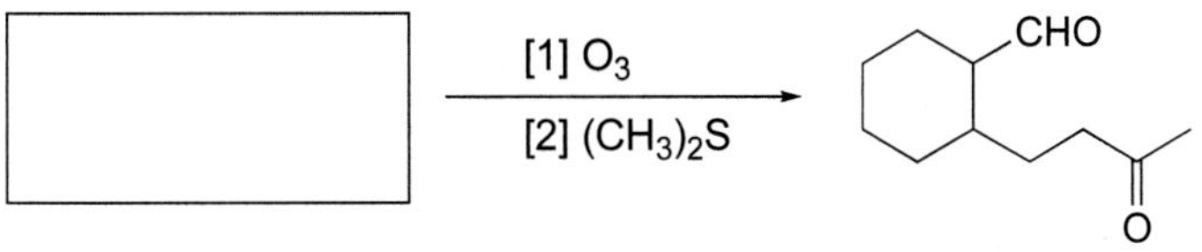

Answers to Practice Test

1.a. 2
b. 4
c. 1

2.a. T
b. T
c. F
d. F
e. T
f. F
g. F
h. F

3.a. oxidizing
b. reducing
c. oxidizing
d. neither
e. oxidizing
f. reducing

4.

a. 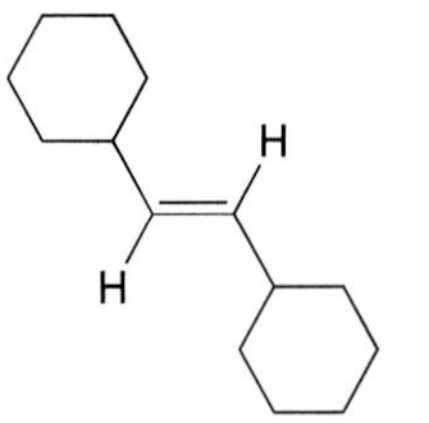

b. 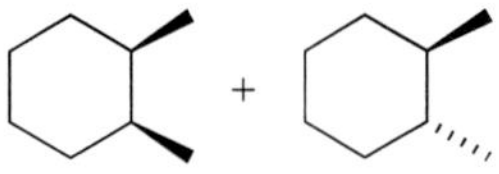

c. 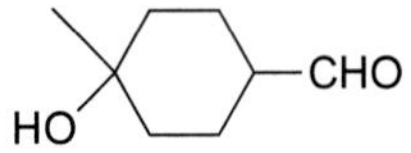

d. 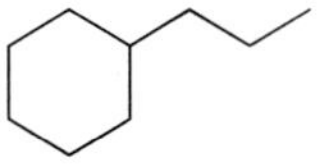

5.

a. 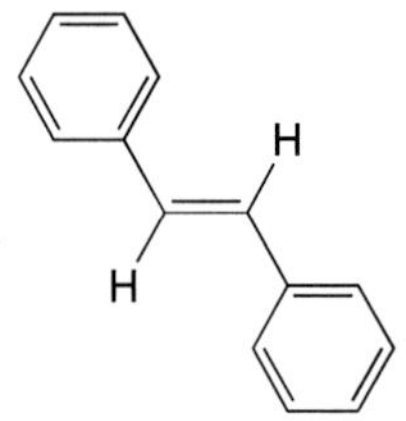

b. Sharpless reagent
(+)-DET

c. 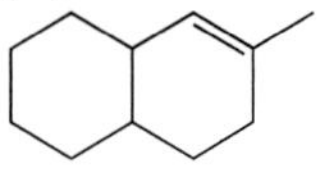

Chapter 12: Answers to Problems

12.1 *Oxidation* results in an *increase* in the number of C–Z bonds (usually C–O bonds) *or* a *decrease* in the number of C–H bonds.
Reduction results in a *decrease* in the number of C–Z bonds (usually C–O bonds) *or* an *increase* in the number of C–H bonds.

a.  **oxidation**

b. 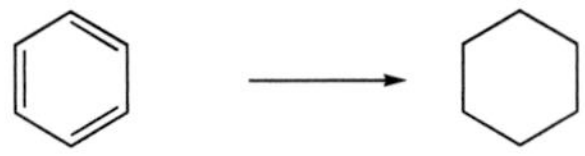 **reduction**

c. 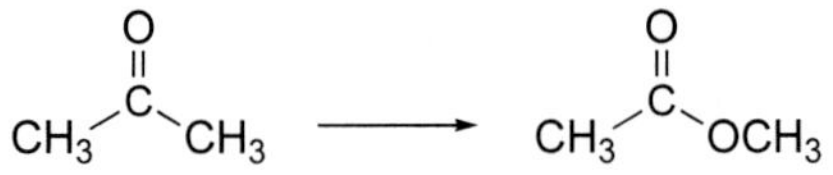 **oxidation**

d. $CH_2{=}CH_2$ ⟶ CH_3CH_2Cl **neither**
1 new C–H bond
and 1 new C–Cl bond

12.2 **Hydrogenation** is the addition of hydrogen. When alkenes are hydrogenated, they are *reduced* by the addition of H_2 to the π bond. To draw the alkane product, add a H to each C of the double bond.

a. 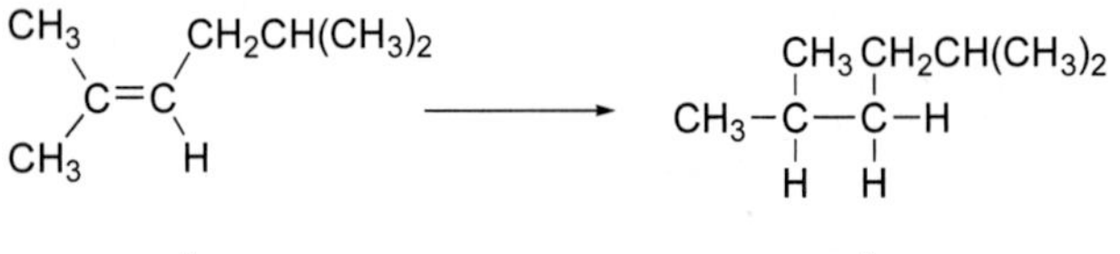

c. 

b. 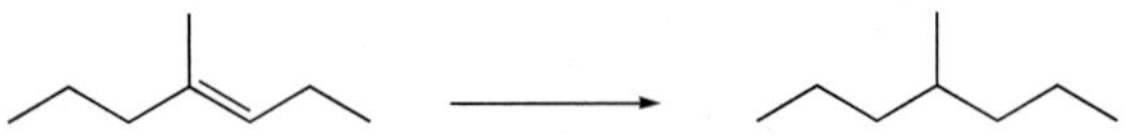

12.3 Draw the alkenes that form each alkane when hydrogenated.

a. 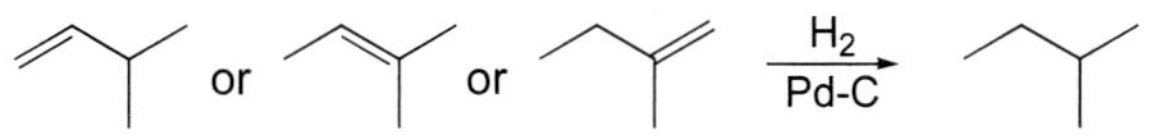

c. 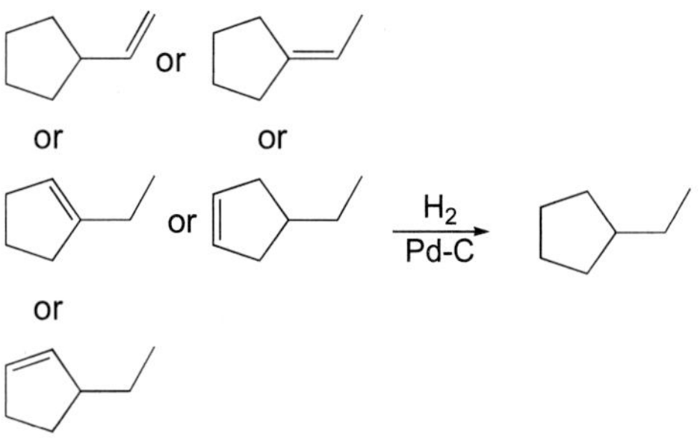

b. 

12.4 Cis alkenes are less stable than trans alkenes, so they have larger heats of hydrogenation. Increasing alkyl substitution increases the stability of a C=C, thus decreasing the heat of hydrogenation.

a. 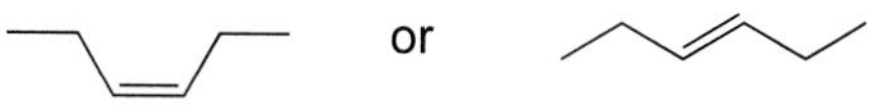

cis alkane
less stable
***larger* heat of hydrogenation**

trans alkane

b. 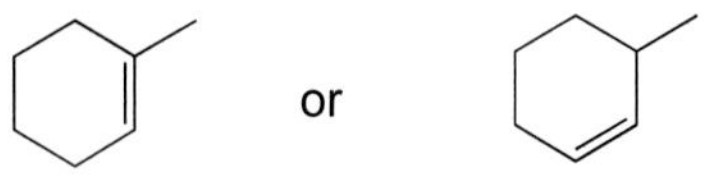

trisubstituted

disubstituted
less stable
***larger* heat of hydrogenation**

12.5 Hydrogenation products must be identical to use hydrogenation data to evaluate the relative stability of the starting materials.

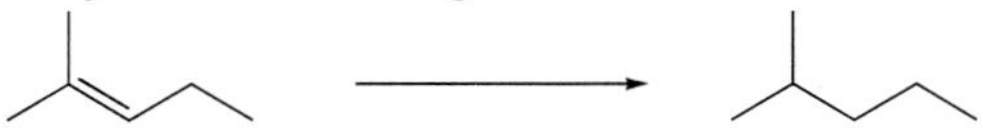

2-methyl-2-pentene

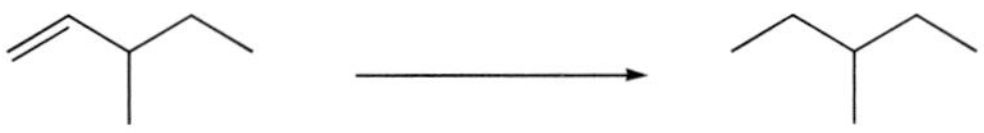

3-methyl-1-pentene

Different products are formed. Hydrogenation data can't be used to determine the relative stability of the starting materials.

12.6

new stereogenic center

Two enantiomers are formed in equal amounts:

a. 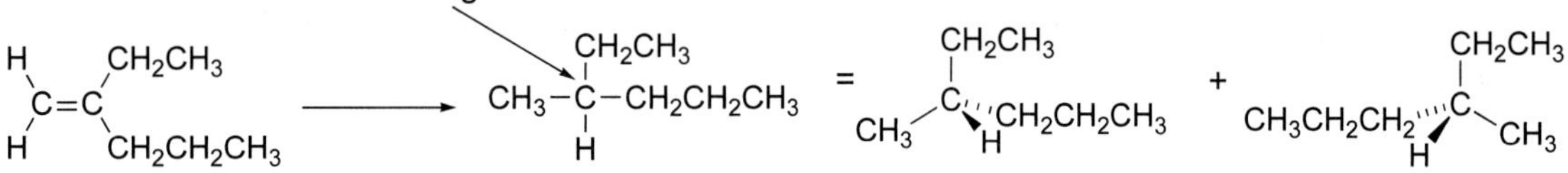

b. 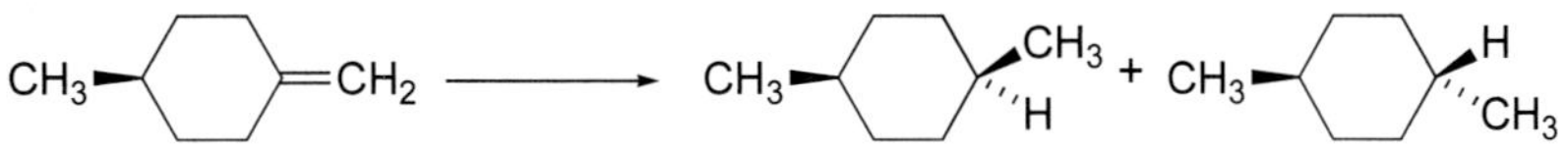

diastereomers

c. 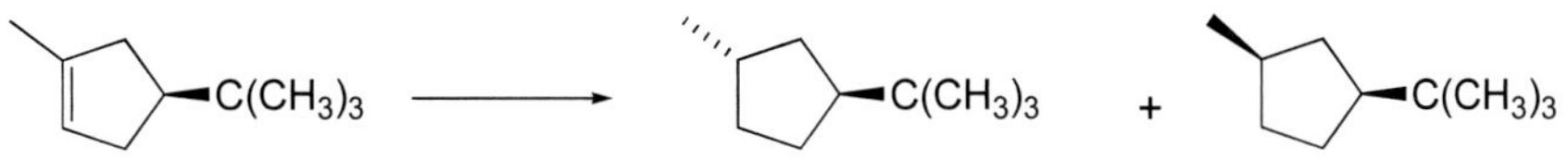

diastereomers

12.7

Compound	Molecular formula before hydrogenation	Molecular formula after hydrogenation	Number of rings	Number of π bonds
A	$C_{10}H_{12}$	$C_{10}H_{16}$	3	2
B	C_4H_8	C_4H_{10}	0	1
C	C_6H_8	C_6H_{12}	1	2

12.8

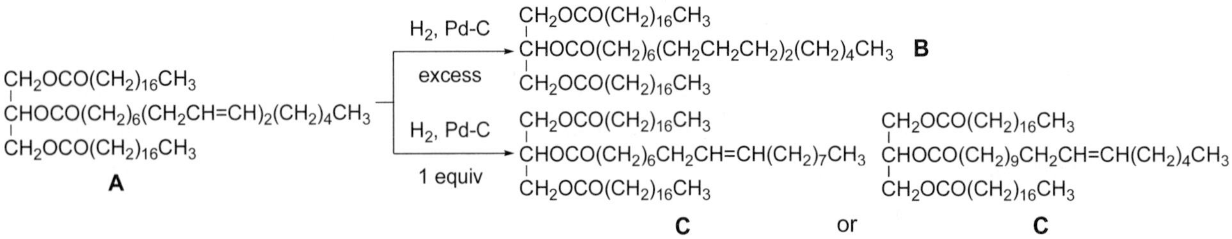

A has 2 double bonds. **lowest melting point**

C has 1 double bond. **intermediate melting point**

B has 0 double bonds. **highest melting point**

12.9 Hydrogenation of $HC{\equiv}CCH_2CH_2CH_3$ and $CH_3C{\equiv}CCH_2CH_3$ yields the same compound. The heat of hydrogenation is larger for $HC{\equiv}CCH_2CH_2CH_3$ than for $CH_3C{\equiv}CCH_2CH_3$ because internal alkynes are more stable (lower in energy) than terminal alkynes.

12.10

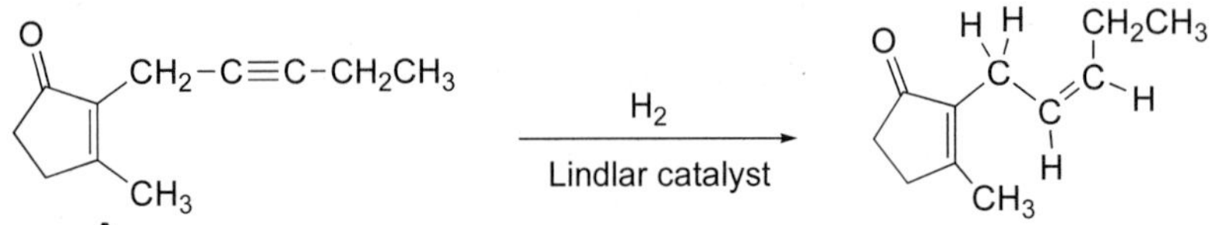

A

***cis*-jasmone**

(perfume component isolated from jasmine flowers)

12.11 In the presence of Pd-C, H_2 adds to alkenes and alkynes to form alkanes. In the presence of the Lindlar catalyst, only alkynes react with H_2 to form cis alkenes.

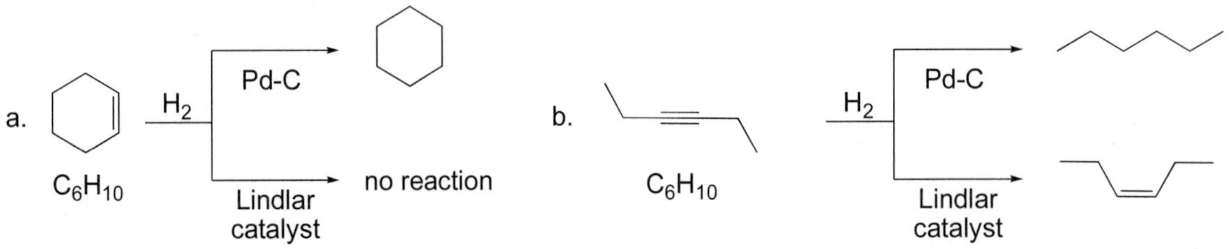

12.12 Use the directions from Answer 12.11.

a. $CH_3OCH_2CH_2C{\equiv}CCH_2CH(CH_3)_2 \xrightarrow[\text{Pd-C}]{H_2\text{ (excess)}} CH_3OCH_2CH_2CH_2CH_2CH_2CH(CH_3)_2$

b. 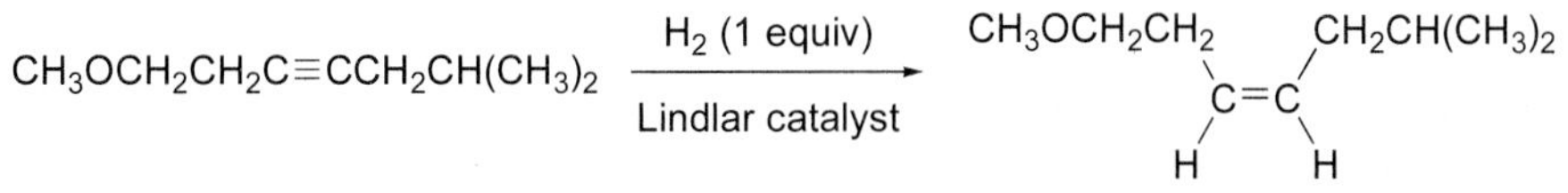
$CH_3OCH_2CH_2C{\equiv}CCH_2CH(CH_3)_2$
H_2 (1 equiv)
Lindlar catalyst

c. 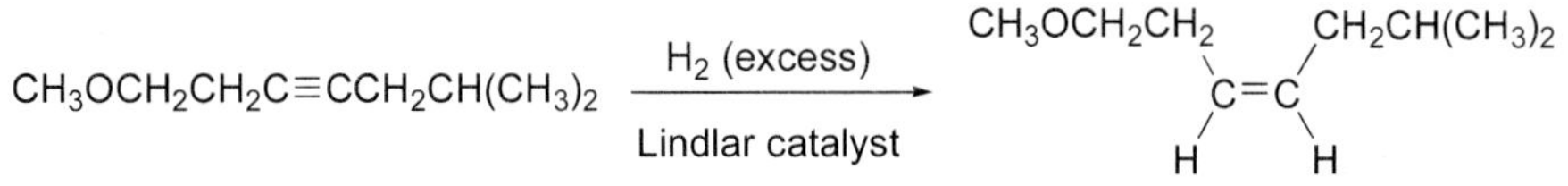
$CH_3OCH_2CH_2C{\equiv}CCH_2CH(CH_3)_2$
H_2 (excess)
Lindlar catalyst

d. 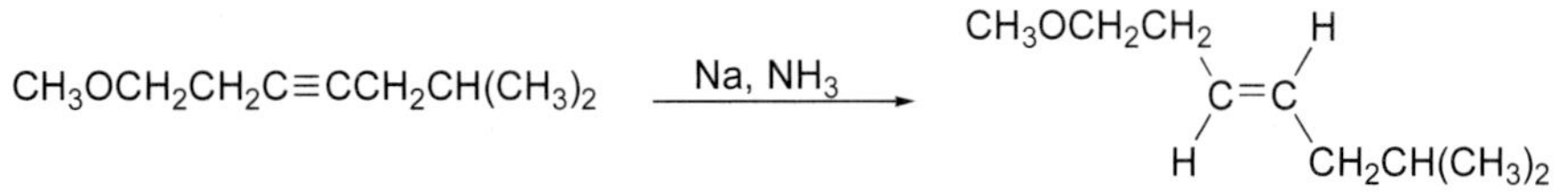
$CH_3OCH_2CH_2C{\equiv}CCH_2CH(CH_3)_2$
Na, NH_3

12.13

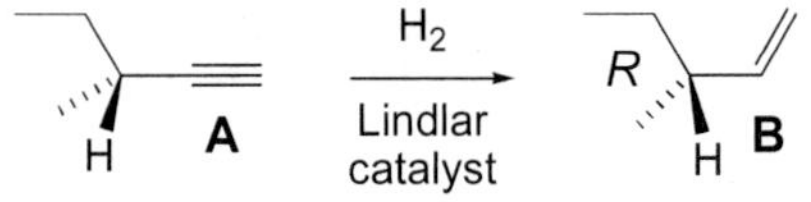
A
H_2
Lindlar catalyst
B

12.14 $LiAlH_4$ reduces alkyl halides to alkanes and epoxides to alcohols.

a. 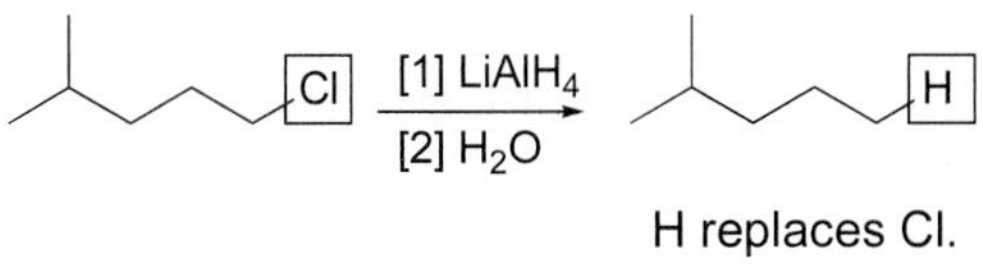
[1] $LiAlH_4$
[2] H_2O
H replaces Cl.

b. 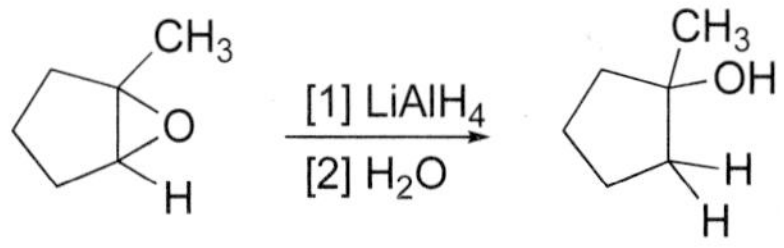
[1] $LiAlH_4$
[2] H_2O

12.15 To draw the product, add an O atom across the π bond of the C=C.

a. 
$(CH_3)_2C{=}CH_2$
mCPBA

c. 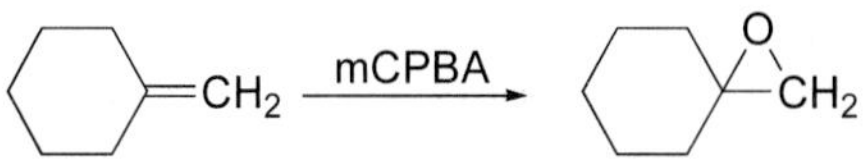
mCPBA

b. 
$(CH_3)_2C{=}C(CH_3)_2$
mCPBA

12.16 For epoxidation reactions:
- There are two possible products: O adds from above and below the double bond.
- Substituents on the C=C retain their original configuration in the products.

a. 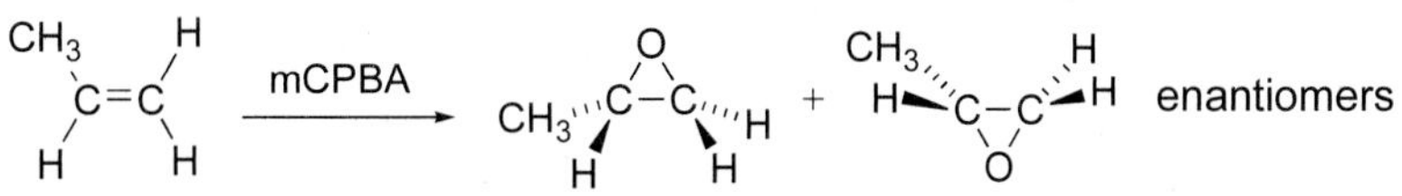
mCPBA
enantiomers

b. 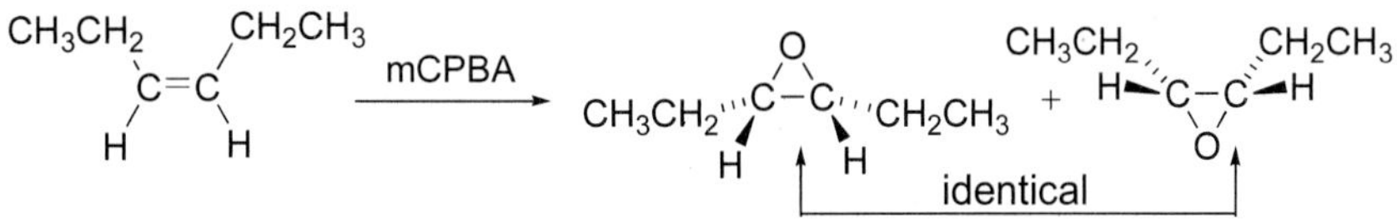
mCPBA
identical

c. 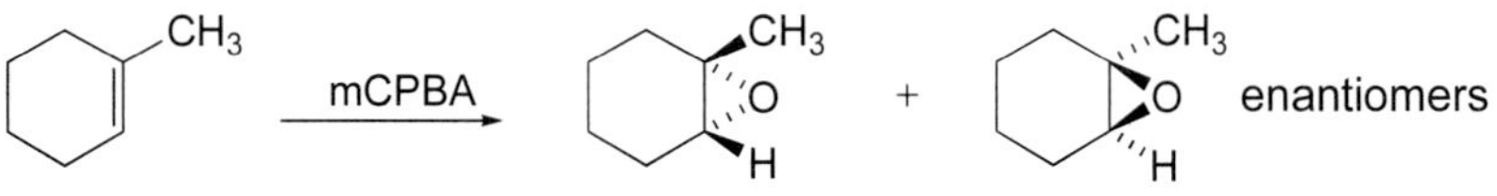
mCPBA
enantiomers

12.17 Treatment of an alkene with a peroxyacid followed by H_2O, HO^- adds two hydroxy groups in an **anti** fashion. *cis*-2-Butene and *trans*-2-butene yield different products of dihydroxylation. *cis*-2-Butene gives a mixture of two enantiomers and *trans*-2-butene gives a meso compound. The reaction is stereospecific because two stereoisomeric starting materials give different products that are also stereoisomers of each other.

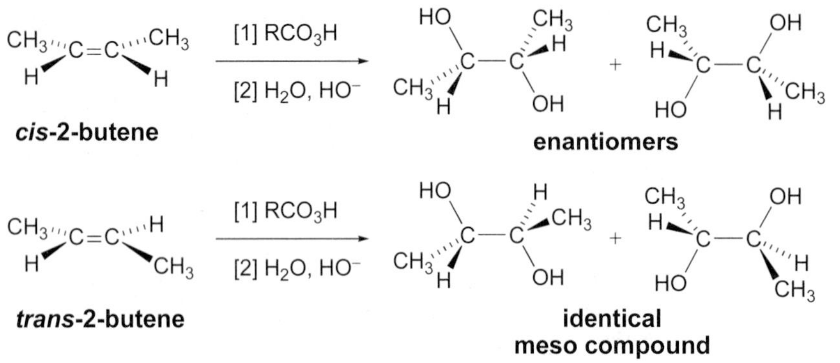

[1] RCO3H
[2] H2O, HO−
cis-2-butene
enantiomers
trans-2-butene
identical
meso compound

12.18 Treatment of an alkene with OsO_4 adds two hydroxy groups in a **syn** fashion. *cis*-2-Butene and *trans*-2-butene yield different stereoisomers in this dihydroxylation, so the reaction is stereospecific.

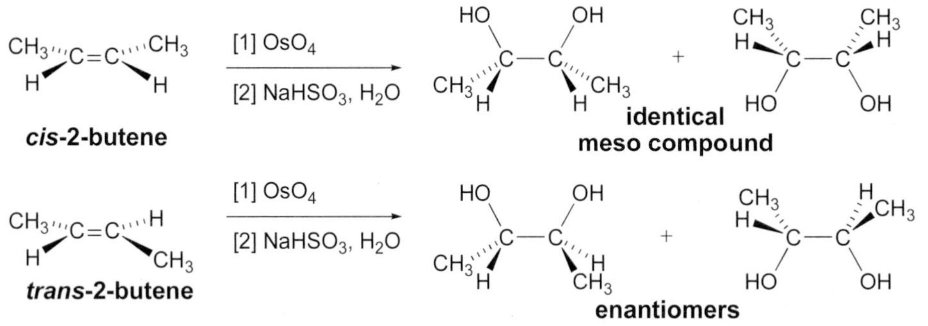

[1] OsO4
[2] NaHSO3, H2O
cis-2-butene
identical
meso compound
trans-2-butene
enantiomers

12.19 To draw the oxidative cleavage products:

- **Locate all the π bonds** in the molecule.
- **Replace all C=C's with *two* C=O's.**

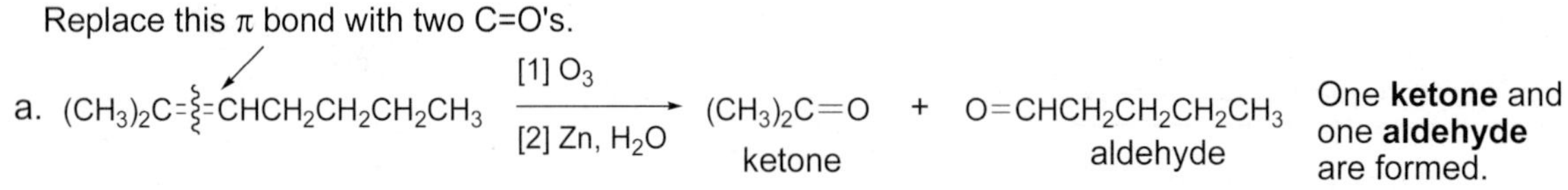

Replace this π bond with two C=O's.
a. (CH3)2C=CHCH2CH2CH2CH3
[1] O3
[2] Zn, H2O
(CH3)2C=O
ketone
O=CHCH2CH2CH2CH3
aldehyde
One ketone and one aldehyde are formed.

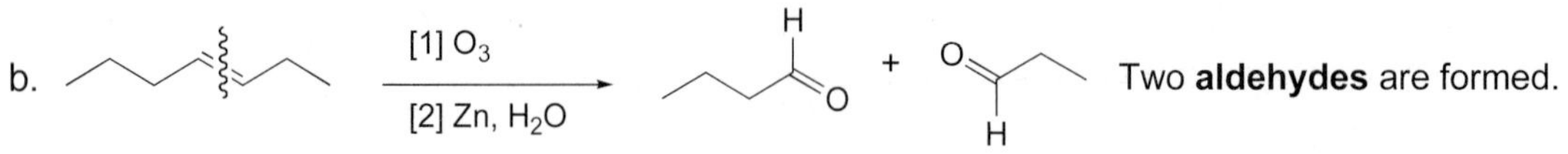

b.
[1] O3
[2] Zn, H2O
Two aldehydes are formed.

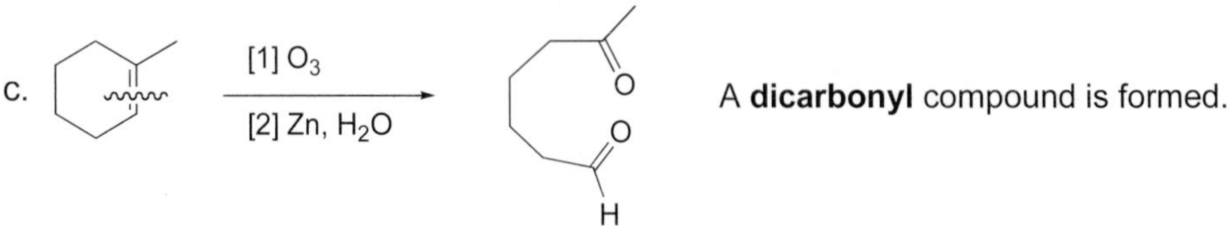

c.
[1] O3
[2] Zn, H2O
A dicarbonyl compound is formed.

12.20 To find the alkene that yields the oxidative cleavage products:

- **Find the two carbonyl groups** in the products.
- **Join the two carbonyl carbons** together with a double bond. This is the double bond that was broken during ozonolysis.

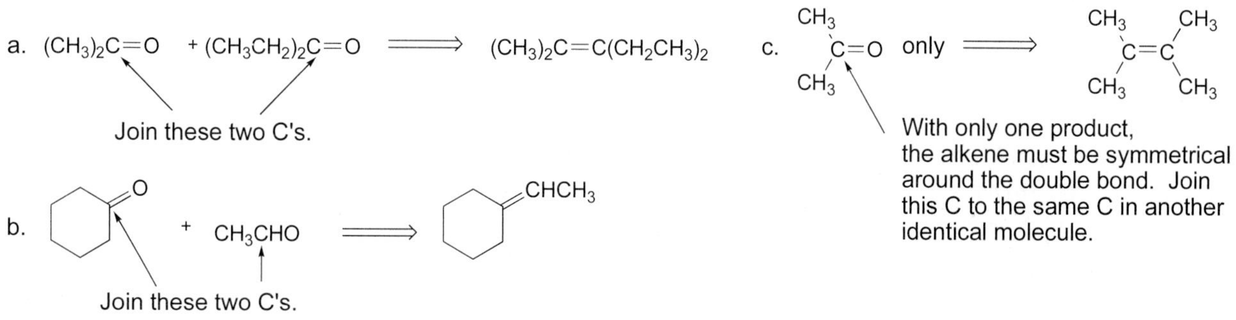
a. $(CH_3)_2C{=}O$ + $(CH_3CH_2)_2C{=}O$ ⟹ $(CH_3)_2C{=}C(CH_2CH_3)_2$
Join these two C's.
b. + CH_3CHO ⟹ CHCH3
Join these two C's.
c. only ⟹
With only one product, the alkene must be symmetrical around the double bond. Join this C to the same C in another identical molecule.

12.21

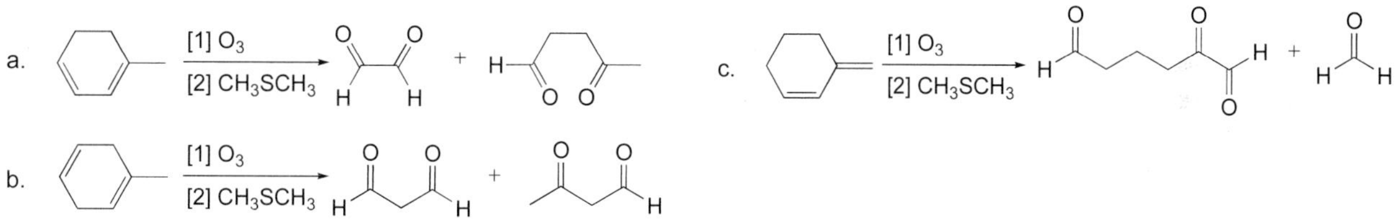
a. [1] O3 [2] CH3SCH3
b. [1] O3 [2] CH3SCH3
c. [1] O3 [2] CH3SCH3

12.22 To draw the products of oxidative cleavage of alkynes:

- **Locate the triple bond.**
- For internal alkynes, **convert the *sp* hybridized C to COOH.**
- For terminal alkynes, the ***sp* hybridized C–H becomes CO_2.**

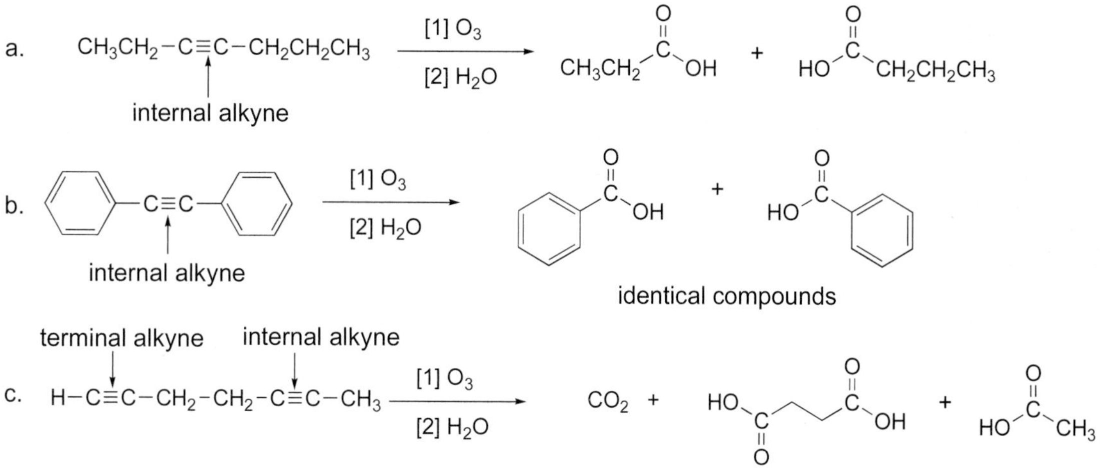
a. $CH_3CH_2{-}C{\equiv}C{-}CH_2CH_2CH_3$ [1] O3 [2] H2O
internal alkyne
b. [1] O3 [2] H2O
internal alkyne
identical compounds
terminal alkyne
internal alkyne
c. $H{-}C{\equiv}C{-}CH_2{-}CH_2{-}C{\equiv}C{-}CH_3$ [1] O3 [2] H2O CO_2 +

12.23

a. CO_2 + $CH_3(CH_2)_8CO_2H$

⇓

$CH_3(CH_2)_8-C\equiv CH$

b. $CH_3CH_2CH(CH_3)CO_2H$

⇓

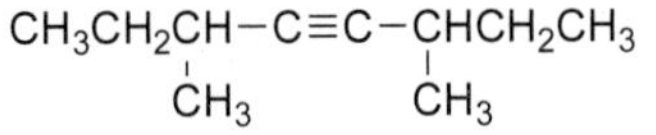

c. $CH_3CH_2CO_2H$, $HO_2CCH_2CO_2H$, CH_3CO_2H

⇓

$CH_3CH_2-C\equiv C-CH_2-C\equiv C-CH_3$

d. $HO_2C(CH_2)_{14}CO_2H$ ⇒ 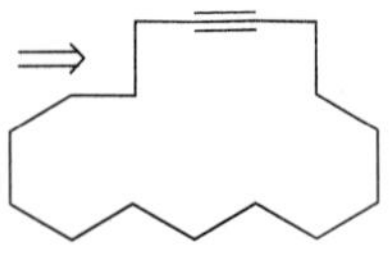

12.24 For the **oxidation of alcohols,** remember:

- **1° Alcohols** are oxidized to aldehydes with PCC.
- **1° Alcohols** are oxidized to carboxylic acids with oxidizing agents like CrO_3 or $Na_2Cr_2O_7$.
- **2° Alcohols** are oxidized to ketones with all Cr^{6+} reagents.

a. 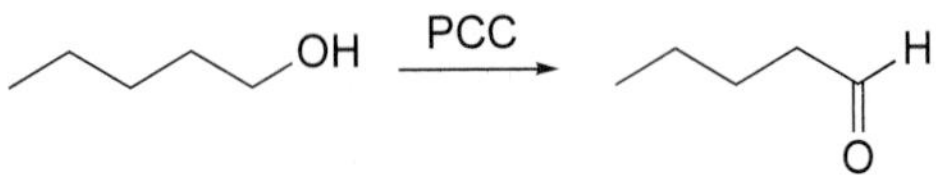

b. 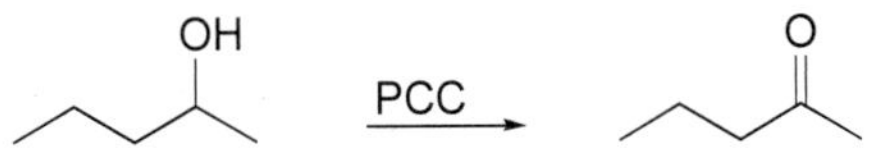

c. 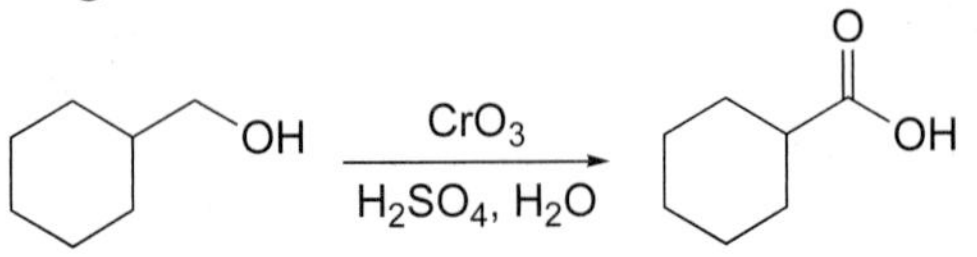

d. 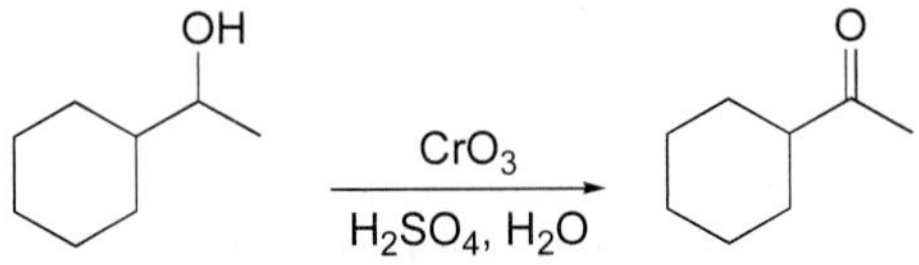

12.25 Upon treatment with $HCrO_4^-$–Amberlyst A-26 resin:

- **1° Alcohols** are oxidized to aldehydes.
- **2° Alcohols** are oxidized to ketones.

a. 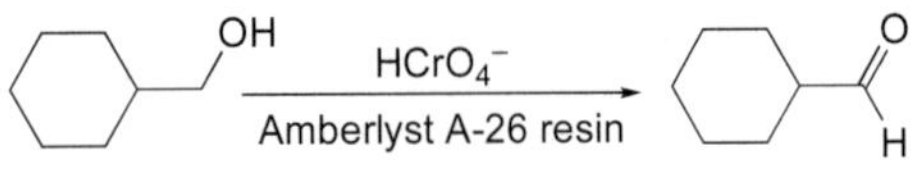

b. 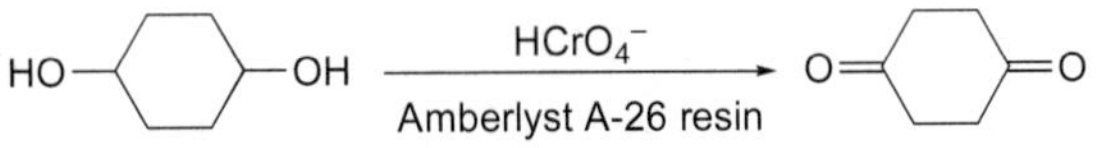

c. 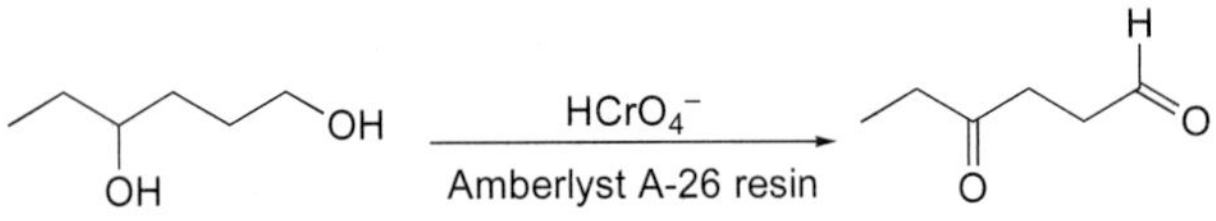

12.26

a. 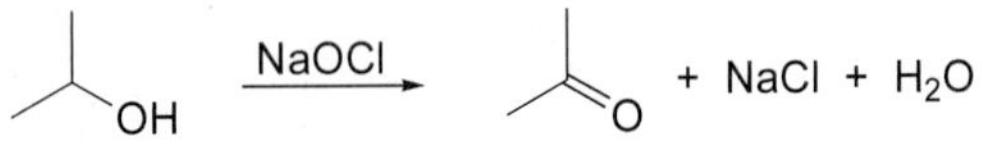

The by-products of the reaction with sodium hypochlorite are water and table salt (NaCl), as opposed to the by-products with $HCrO_4^-$–Amberlyst A-26 resin, which contain carcinogenic Cr^{3+} metal.

b. Oxidation with NaOCl has at least two advantages over oxidation with CrO_3, H_2SO_4 and H_2O. Since no Cr^{6+} is used as oxidant, there are no Cr by-products that must be disposed of. Also, CrO_3 oxidation is carried out in corrosive inorganic acids (H_2SO_4) and oxidation with NaOCl avoids this.

12.27 To draw the products of a **Sharpless epoxidation:**

- With the C=C horizontal, draw the allylic alcohol with the OH on the **top right** of the alkene.
- Add the new oxygen **above** the plane if (–)-DET is used and **below** the plane if (+)-DET is used.

a. 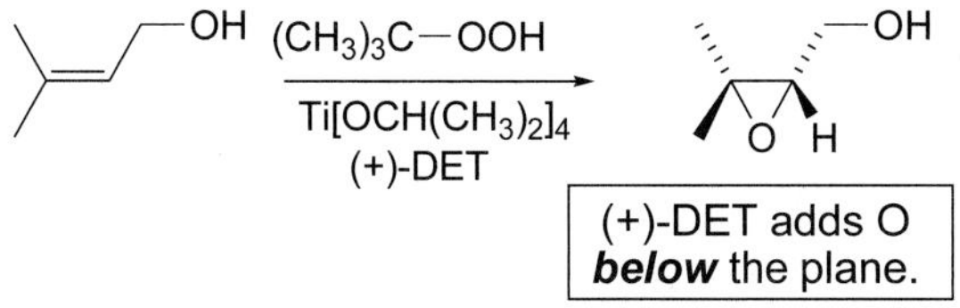
OH
(CH3)3C—OOH
Ti[OCH(CH3)2]4
(+)-DET
OH
O
H
(+)-DET adds O
below the plane.

b. 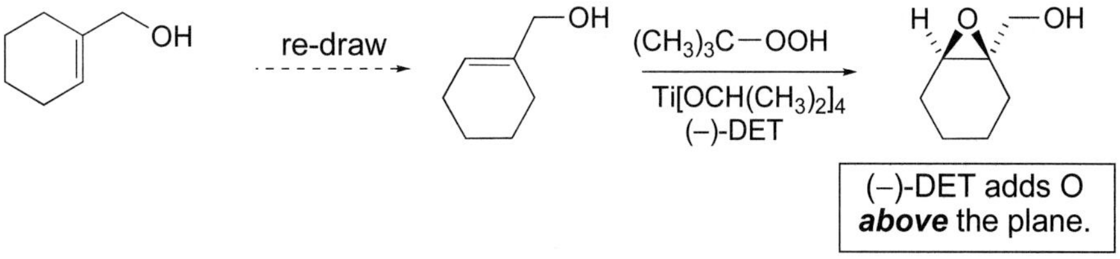
OH
re-draw
OH
(CH3)3C—OOH
Ti[OCH(CH3)2]4
(–)-DET
H
O
OH
(–)-DET adds O
above the plane.

12.28 Sharpless epoxidation needs an ***allylic alcohol*** as the starting material. Alkenes with no allylic OH group will not undergo reaction with the Sharpless reagent.

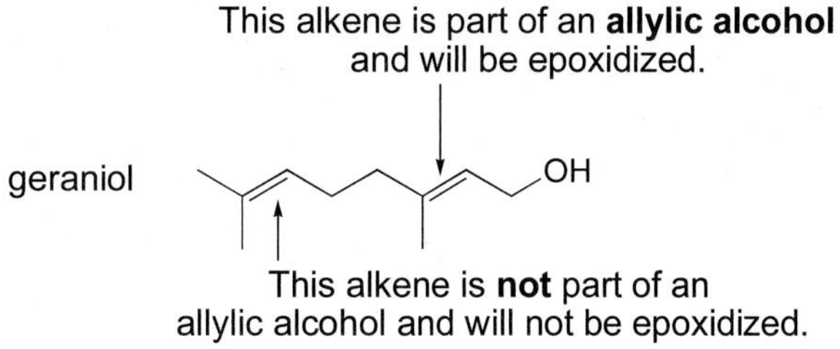
This alkene is part of an allylic alcohol
and will be epoxidized.
geraniol
OH
This alkene is not part of an
allylic alcohol and will not be epoxidized.

12.29

a. 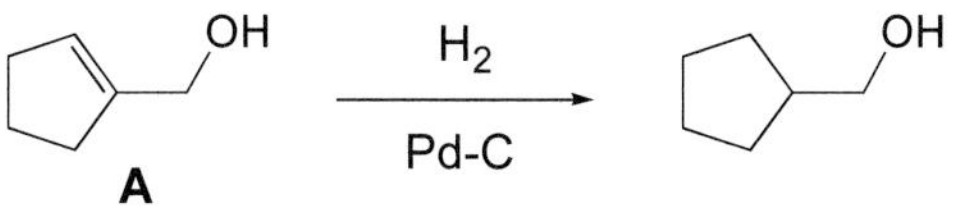
OH
A
H2
Pd-C
OH

b. 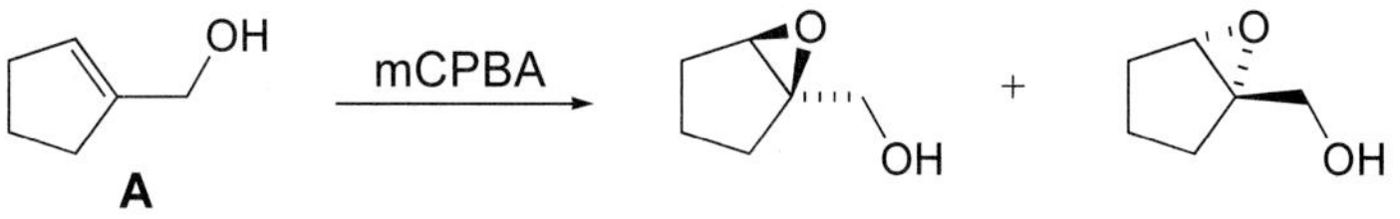
OH
A
mCPBA
O
OH
+
O
OH

c. 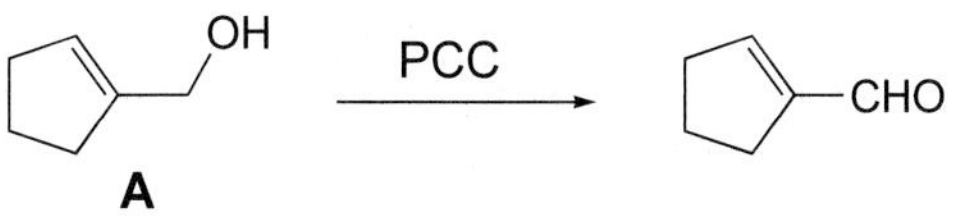
OH
A
PCC
CHO

d. 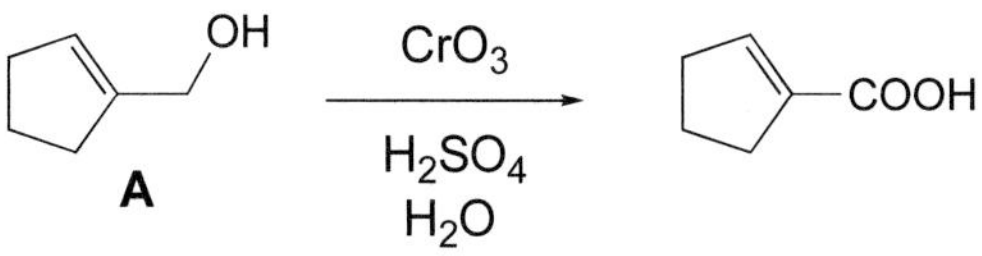
OH
A
CrO3
H2SO4
H2O
COOH

e. 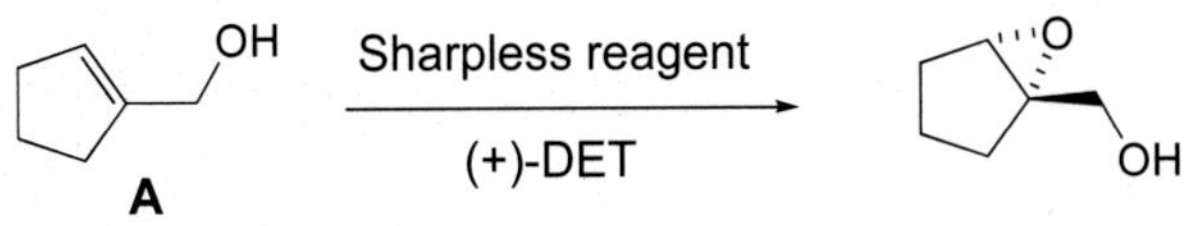
OH
Sharpless reagent
(+)-DET
A
O
OH

12.30

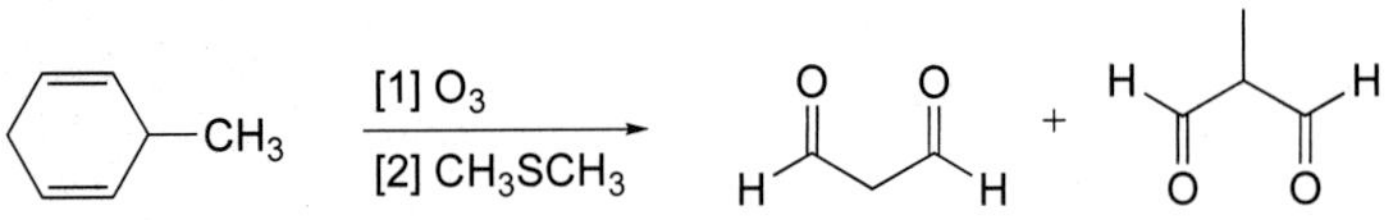
CH3
[1] O3
[2] CH3SCH3
O
O
H
H
+
H
H
O
O

12.31

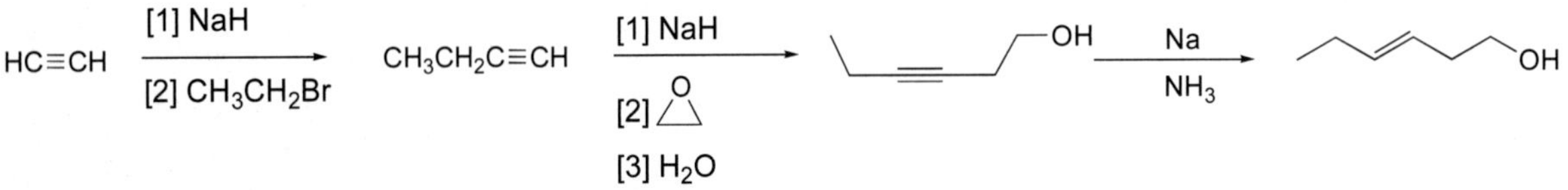
HC≡CH
[1] NaH
[2] CH3CH2Br
CH3CH2C≡CH
[1] NaH
[2]
O
[3] H2O
OH
Na
NH3
OH

12.32 Use the rules from Answer 12.1.

a. 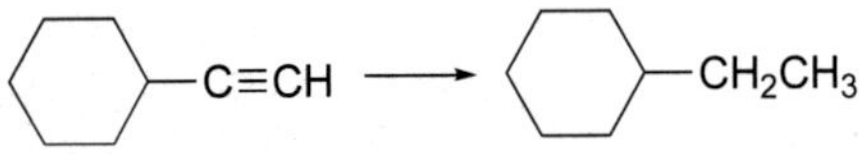
C≡CH
CH2CH3
reduction

c. 
O
OH
reduction

b. $CH_3CH_2Br \longrightarrow CH_2{=}CH_2$ **neither**

1 C–H and 1 C–Br bond are removed.

d. 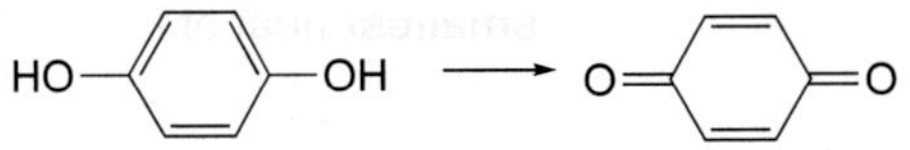
HO
OH
O
O
oxidation

12.33 Use the principles from Answer 12.2 and draw the products of syn addition of H_2 from above and below the C=C.

a. 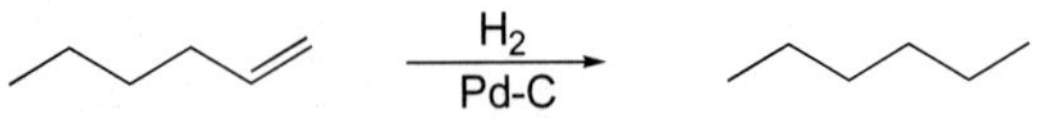
H2
Pd-C

b. 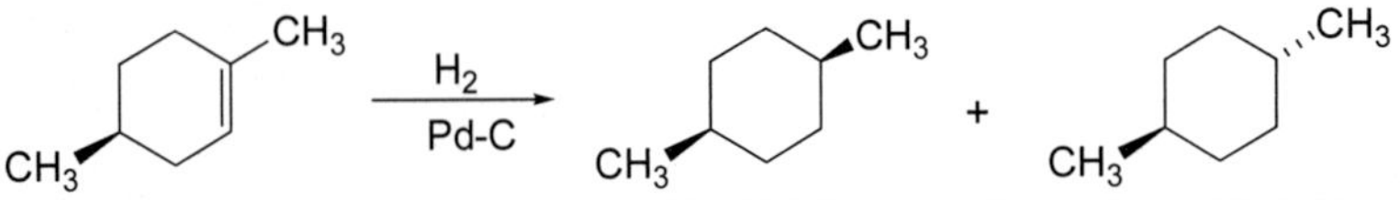
CH3
CH3
H2
Pd-C
CH3
CH3
+
CH3
CH3

c. 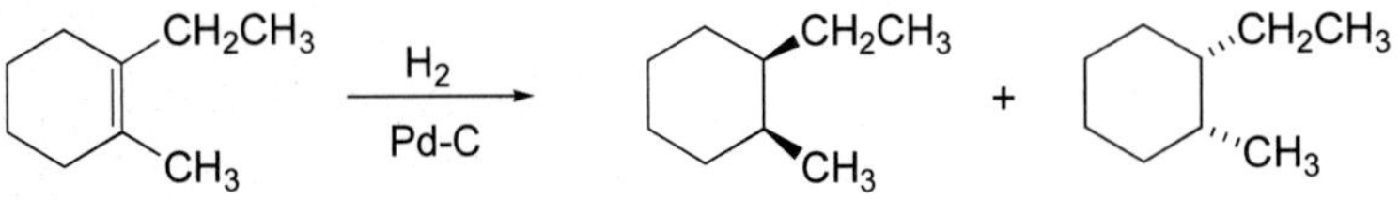
CH2CH3
CH3
H2
Pd-C
CH2CH3
CH3
+
CH2CH3
CH3

d. 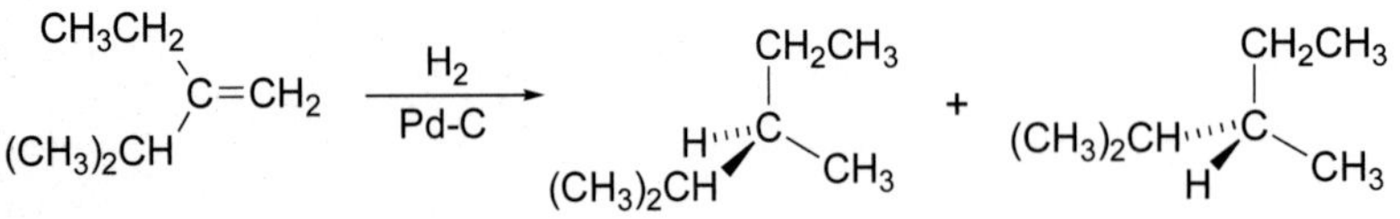
CH3CH2
C=CH2
(CH3)2CH
H2
Pd-C
CH2CH3
H
C
CH3
(CH3)2CH
+
CH2CH3
(CH3)2CH
C
H
CH3

12.34 Increasing alkyl substitution increases alkene stability, thus decreasing the heat of hydrogenation.

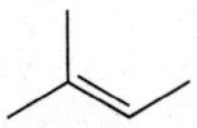

2-methyl-2-butene

trisubstituted

smallest $\Delta H°$ = –112 kJ/mol

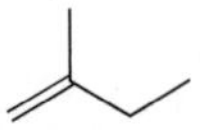

2-methyl-1-butene

disubstituted

intermediate $\Delta H°$ = –119 kJ/mol

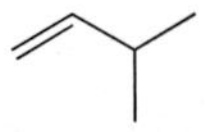

3-methyl-1-butene

monosubstituted

largest $\Delta H°$ = –127 kJ/mol

12.35

A possible structure:

a. Compound **A:** molecular formula C_5H_8: hydrogenated to C_5H_{10}.
2 degrees of unsaturation, 1 is hydrogenated.
1 ring and 1 π bond →

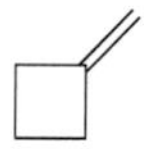

b. Compound **B:** molecular formula $C_{10}H_{16}$: hydrogenated to $C_{10}H_{18}$.
3 degrees of unsaturation, 1 is hydrogenated.
2 rings and 1 π bond →

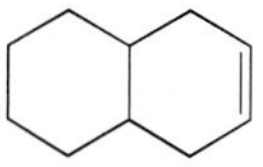

c. Compound **C:** molecular formula C_8H_8: hydrogenated to C_8H_{16}.
5 degrees of unsaturation, 4 are hydrogenated.
1 ring and 4 π bonds →

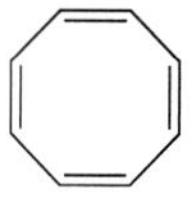

12.36

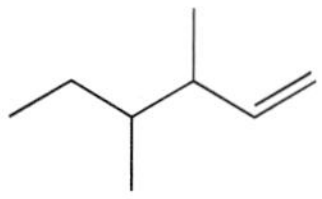

A

a. **mono**substituted
largest heat of hydrogenation
b. **fastest** reaction rate

c.

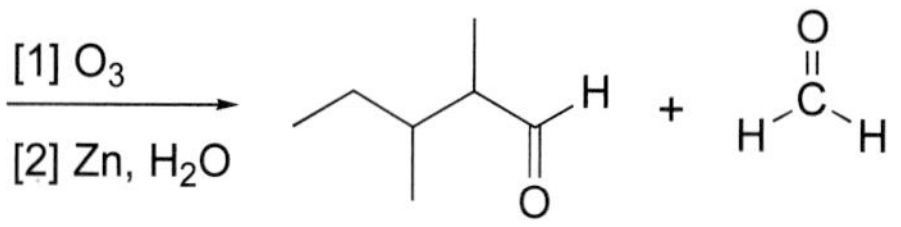
[1] O3
[2] Zn, H2O
H
+
O
H
C
H
O

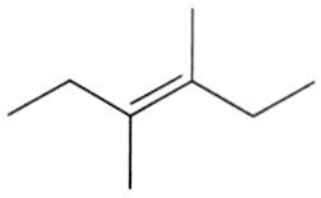

B

a. **tetra**substituted
smallest heat of hydrogenation
b. **slowest** reaction rate

c.

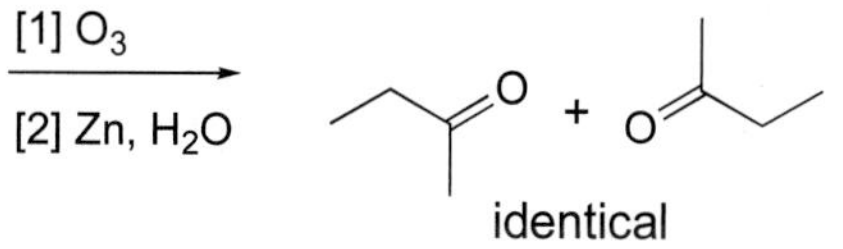
[1] O3
[2] Zn, H2O
O
+
O
identical

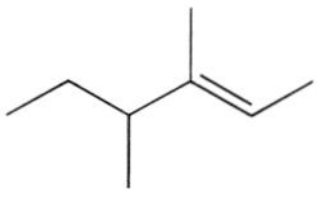

C

a. **tri**substituted
intermediate heat of hydrogenation
b. **intermediate** reaction rate

c.

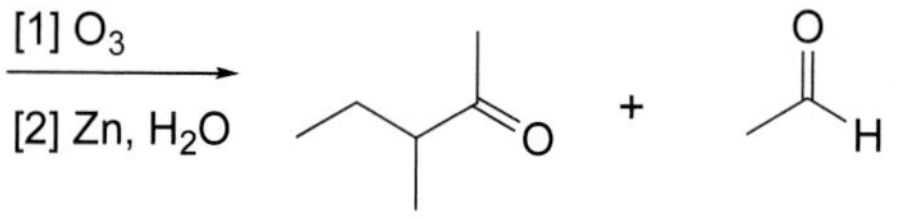
[1] O3
[2] Zn, H2O
O
+
O
H

12.37

a.

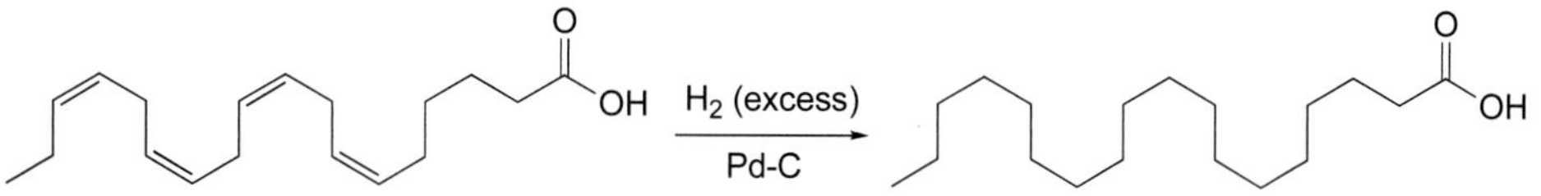
O
OH
H2 (excess)
Pd-C
O
OH

stearidonic acid   stearic acid

b.

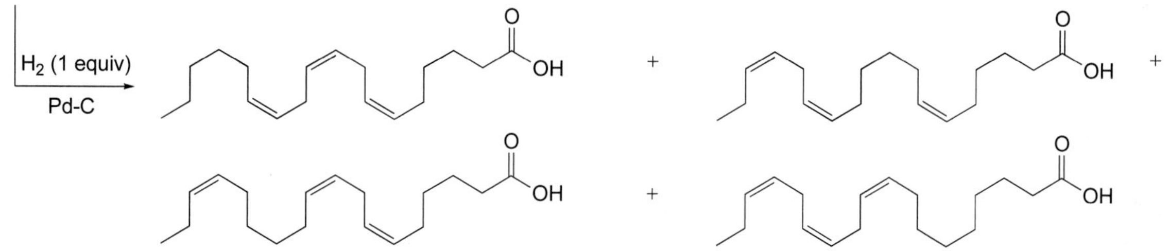
H2 (1 equiv)
Pd-C
O
OH
+
O
OH
+
O
OH
+
O
OH

c.

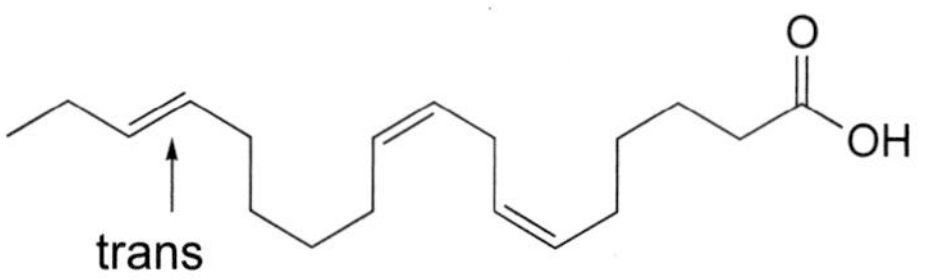
O
OH
trans

one possibility

d.

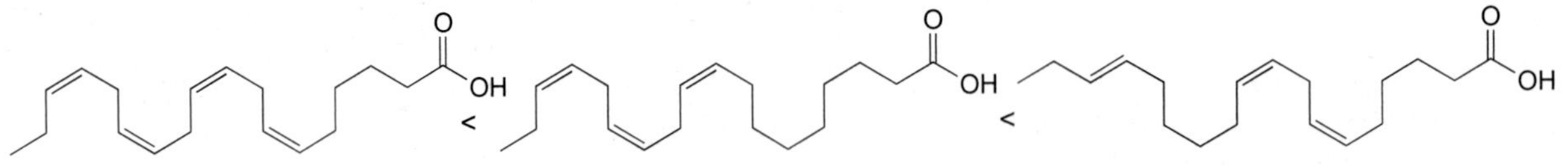

OH
<
OH
<
OH

stearidonic acid
4 cis C=C's

product in (b)
3 cis C=C's

product in (c)
2 cis and one trans C=C's

12.38

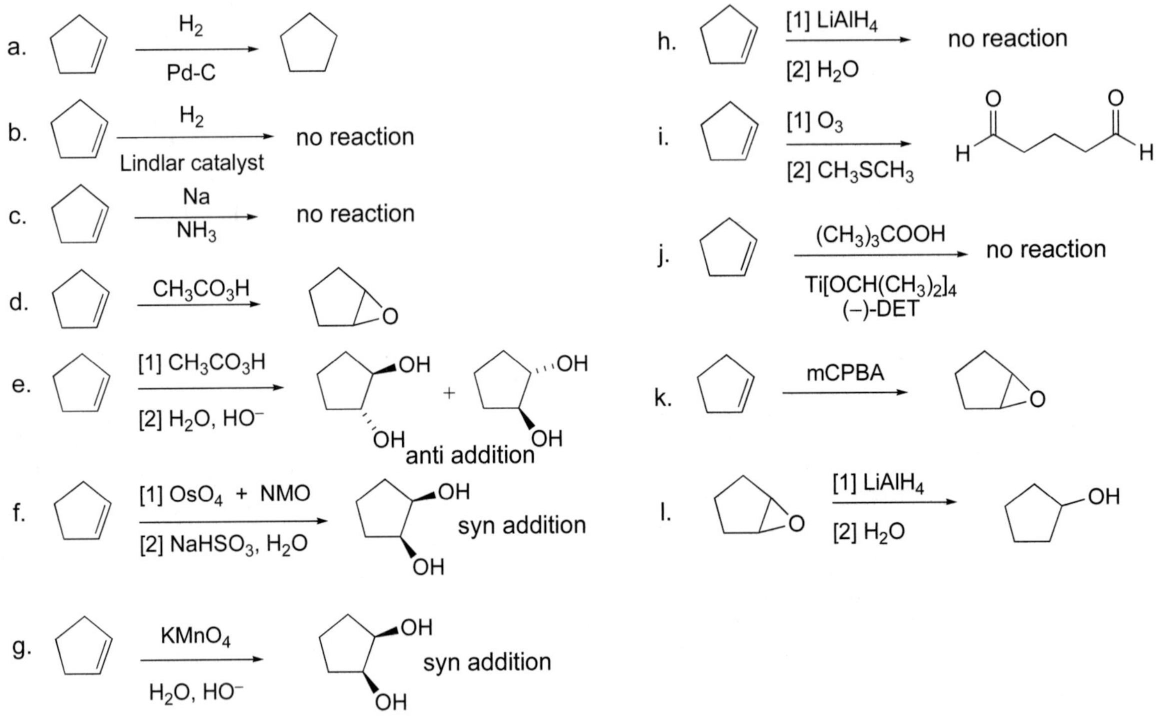

a.
H_2
Pd-C
b.
H_2
Lindlar catalyst
no reaction
c.
Na
NH_3
no reaction
d.
CH_3CO_3H
O
e.
[1] CH_3CO_3H
[2] H_2O, HO^-
OH
OH
+
OH
OH
anti addition
f.
[1] OsO_4 + NMO
[2] $NaHSO_3$, H_2O
OH
OH
syn addition
g.
$KMnO_4$
H_2O, HO^-
OH
OH
syn addition
h.
[1] $LiAlH_4$
[2] H_2O
no reaction
i.
[1] O_3
[2] CH_3SCH_3
O
O
H
H
j.
$(CH_3)_3COOH$
$Ti[OCH(CH_3)_2]_4$
(–)-DET
no reaction
k.
mCPBA
O
l.
O
[1] $LiAlH_4$
[2] H_2O
OH

12.39

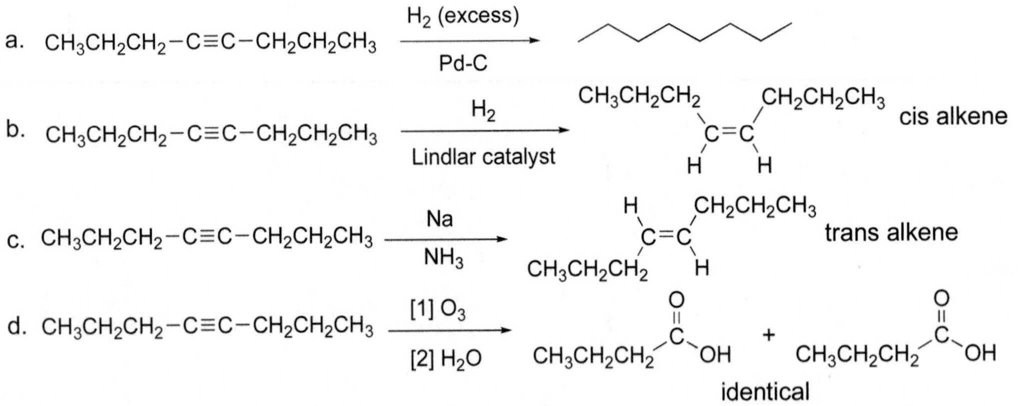

a. $CH_3CH_2CH_2-C{\equiv}C-CH_2CH_2CH_3$
H_2 (excess)
Pd-C
b. $CH_3CH_2CH_2-C{\equiv}C-CH_2CH_2CH_3$
H_2
Lindlar catalyst
$CH_3CH_2CH_2$
$CH_2CH_2CH_3$
C=C
H
H
cis alkene
c. $CH_3CH_2CH_2-C{\equiv}C-CH_2CH_2CH_3$
Na
NH_3
H
$CH_2CH_2CH_3$
C=C
$CH_3CH_2CH_2$
H
trans alkene
d. $CH_3CH_2CH_2-C{\equiv}C-CH_2CH_2CH_3$
[1] O_3
[2] H_2O
O
$CH_3CH_2CH_2$
C
OH
+
O
$CH_3CH_2CH_2$
C
OH
identical

12.40

a.

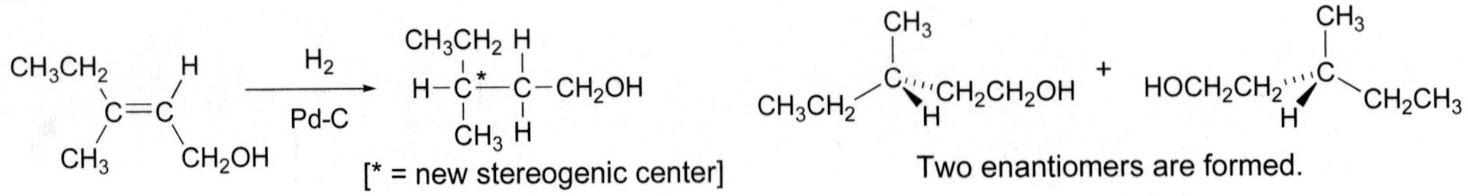

CH_3CH_2
H
C=C
CH_3
CH_2OH
H_2
Pd-C
CH_3CH_2 H
H–C*–C–CH_2OH
CH_3 H
[* = new stereogenic center]
CH_3
CH_3CH_2
C
CH_2CH_2OH
H
+
CH_3
$HOCH_2CH_2$
C
CH_2CH_3
H
Two enantiomers are formed.

b. 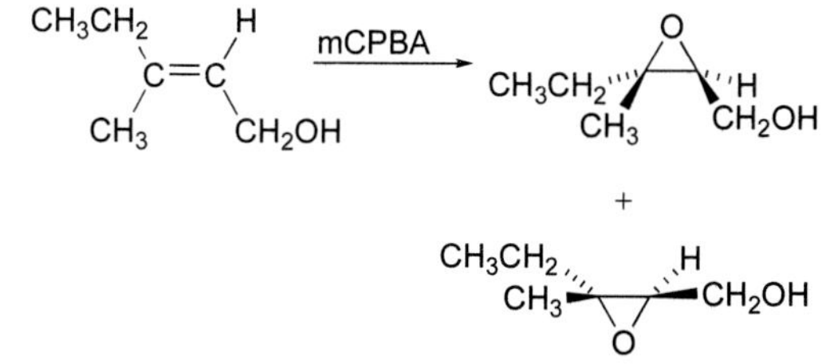

c. 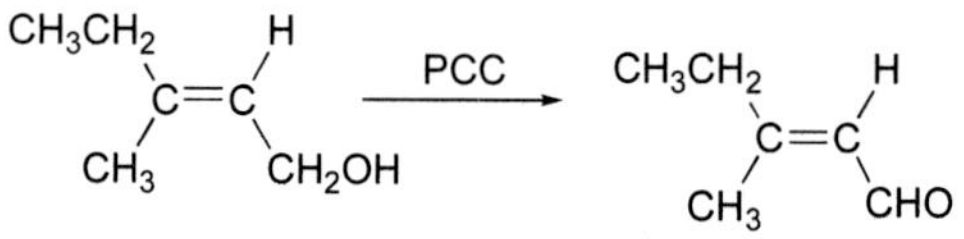

d. 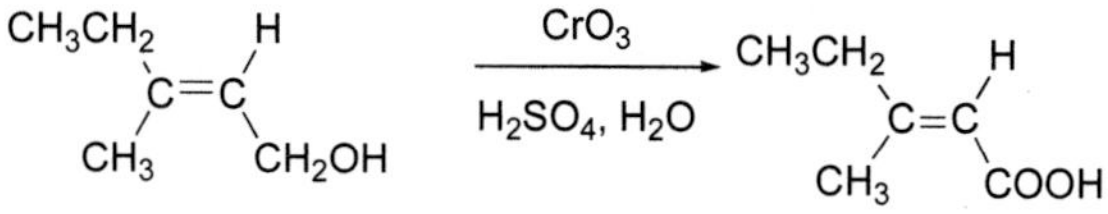

e. 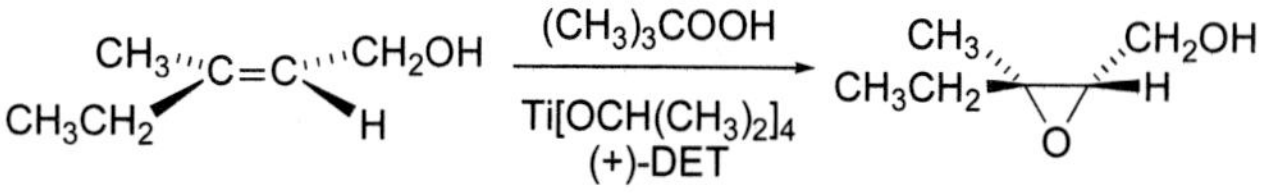

f. 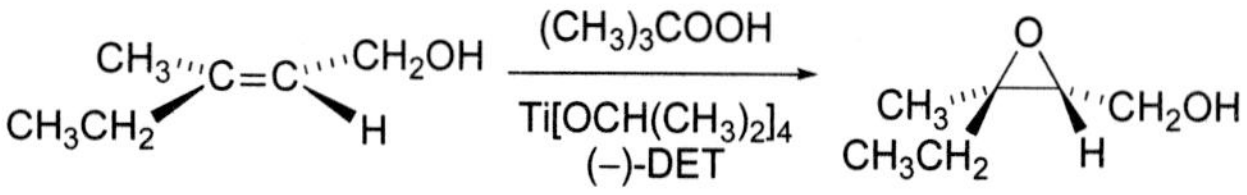

g. 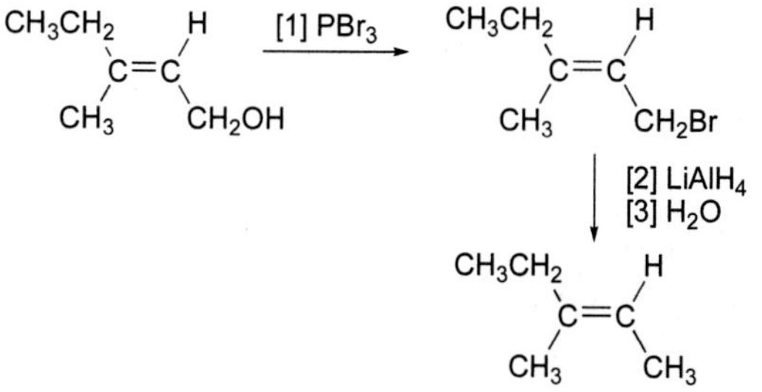

h. 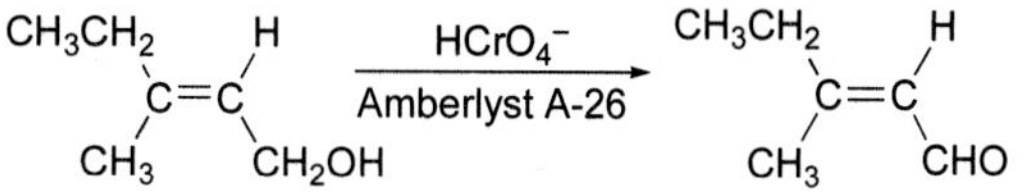

12.41

a. 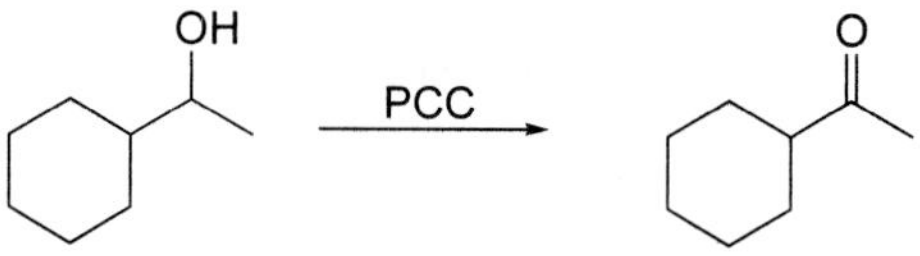

b. 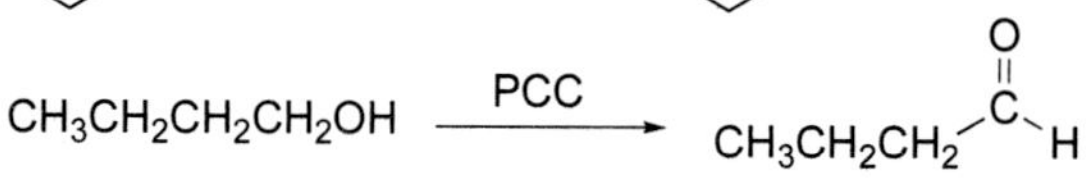

c. 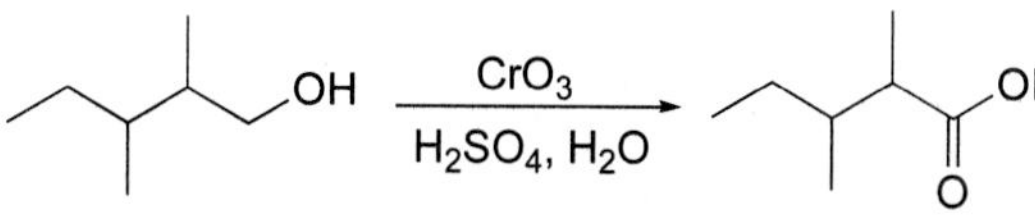

12.42

a. 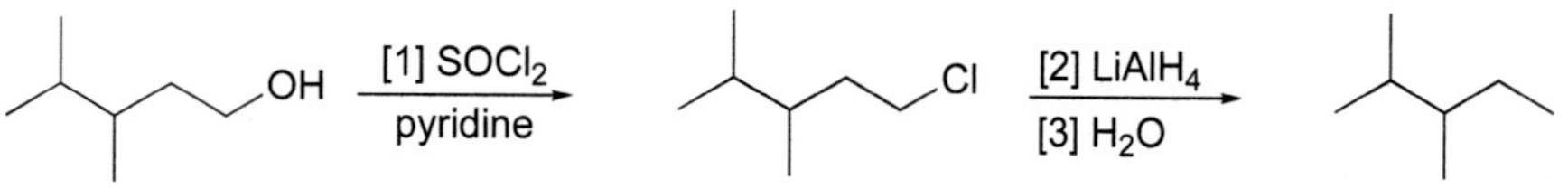

b. 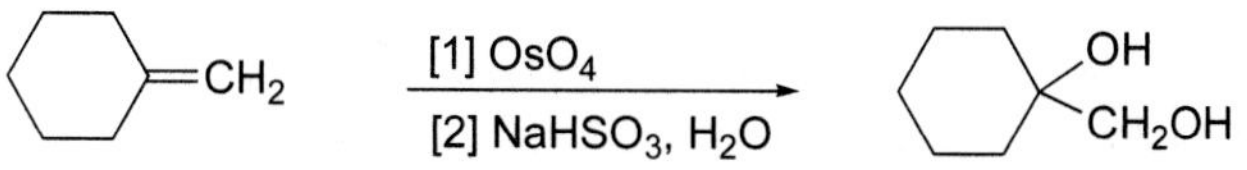

c. 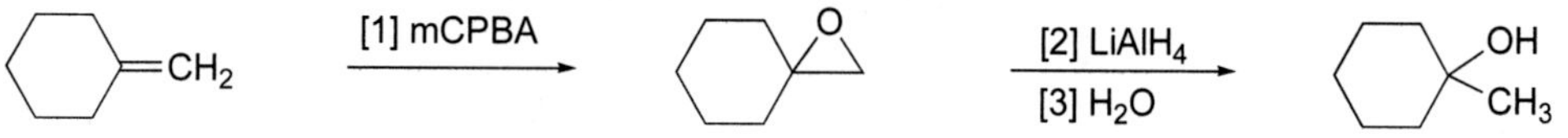

d. 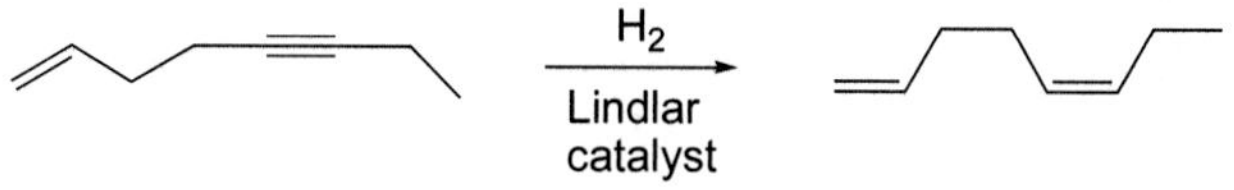

12.43

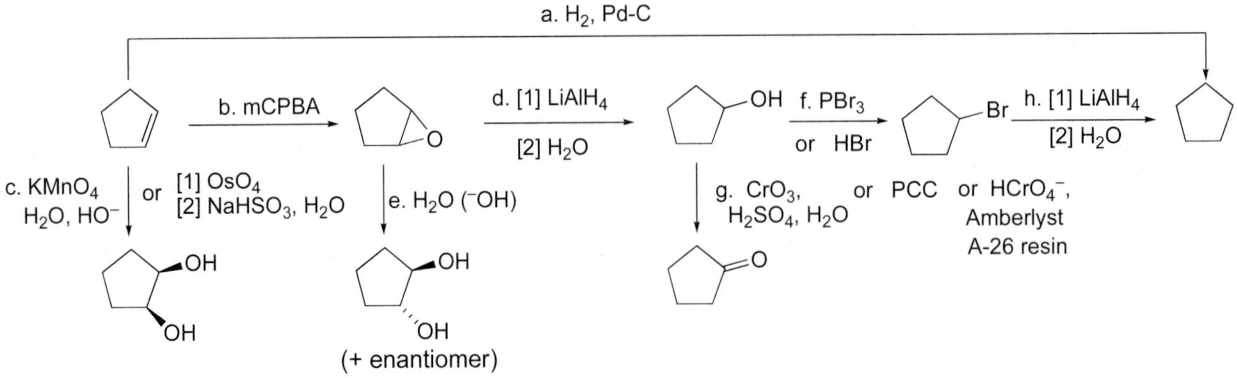
a. H_2, Pd-C
b. mCPBA
d. [1] $LiAlH_4$
[2] H_2O
OH
f. PBr_3
or HBr
Br
h. [1] $LiAlH_4$
[2] H_2O
O
c. $KMnO_4$
H_2O, HO^-
or
[1] OsO_4
[2] $NaHSO_3$, H_2O
e. H_2O (^-OH)
g. CrO_3,
H_2SO_4, H_2O
or PCC or $HCrO_4^-$,
Amberlyst
A-26 resin
OH
OH
OH
OH
(+ enantiomer)
O

12.44 $LiAlH_4$ attacks at the less substituted end of an unsymmetrical epoxide to form an alcohol with an OH on the more substituted carbon.

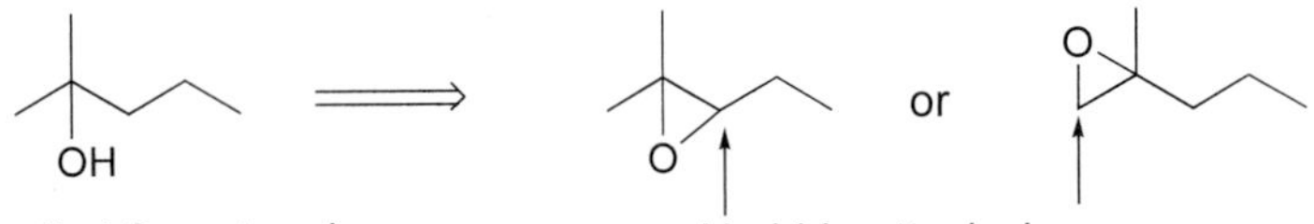
OH
or
O
O

2-methyl-2-pentanol

Hydride attacks here.

12.45 The two sides of the C=C of **A** are different. Since D_2 adds only from above, this must mean that this side is less sterically hindered. Other reagents will also add from the same side.

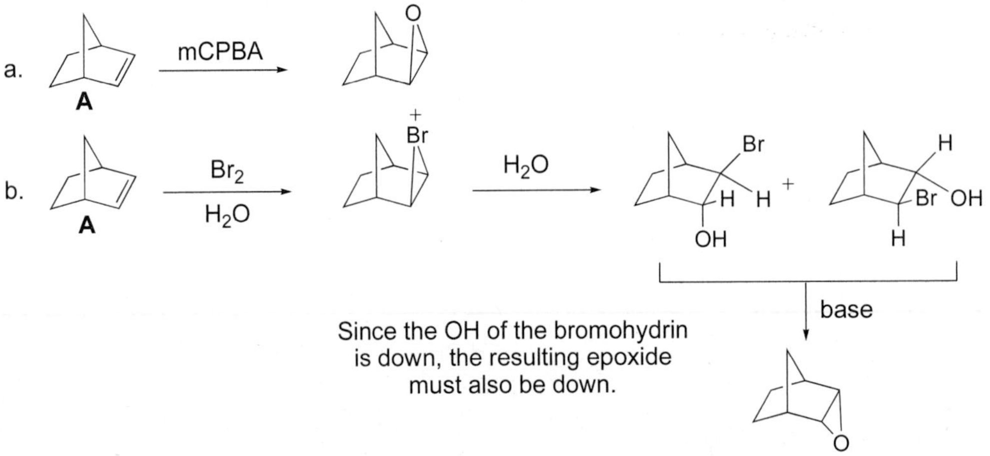
a.
A
mCPBA
O
b.
A
Br_2
H_2O
Br^+
H_2O
Br
H
H
OH
+
H
Br
OH
H
base
Since the OH of the bromohydrin
is down, the resulting epoxide
must also be down.
O

12.46 Alkenes treated with [1] OsO_4 followed by $NaHSO_3$ in H_2O will undergo syn addition, whereas alkenes treated with [2] CH_3CO_3H followed by ^-OH in H_2O will undergo anti addition.

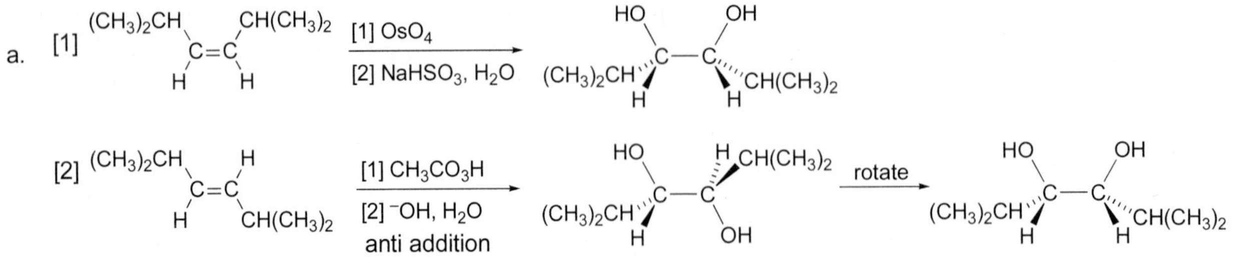
a. [1]
$(CH_3)_2CH$
$CH(CH_3)_2$
C=C
H
H
[1] OsO_4
[2] $NaHSO_3$, H_2O
HO
OH
$(CH_3)_2CH$
$CH(CH_3)_2$
H
H
[2]
$(CH_3)_2CH$
H
C=C
H
$CH(CH_3)_2$
[1] CH_3CO_3H
[2] ^-OH, H_2O
anti addition
HO
H
$CH(CH_3)_2$
$(CH_3)_2CH$
H
OH
rotate
HO
OH
$(CH_3)_2CH$
$CH(CH_3)_2$
H
H

b. [1]

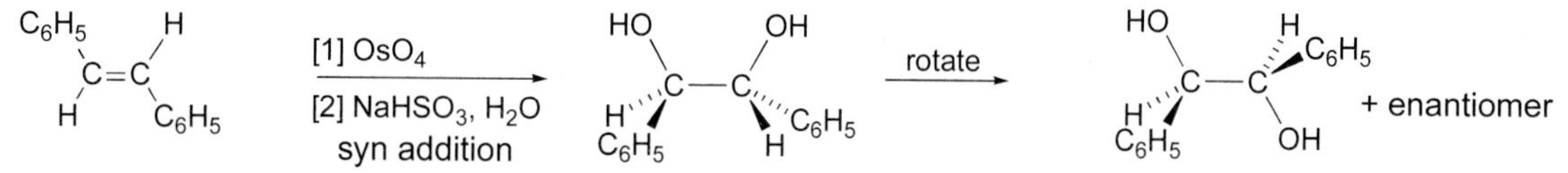
C6H5
H
C=C
H
C6H5
[1] OsO4
[2] NaHSO3, H2O
syn addition
HO
OH
H
C6H5
C6H5
H
rotate
HO
H
C6H5
H
C6H5
OH
+ enantiomer

[2]

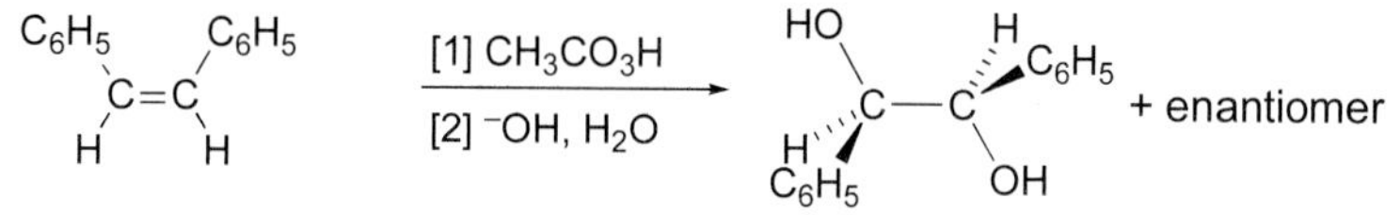
C6H5
C6H5
C=C
H
H
[1] CH3CO3H
[2] −OH, H2O
HO
H
C6H5
H
C6H5
OH
+ enantiomer

c. [1]

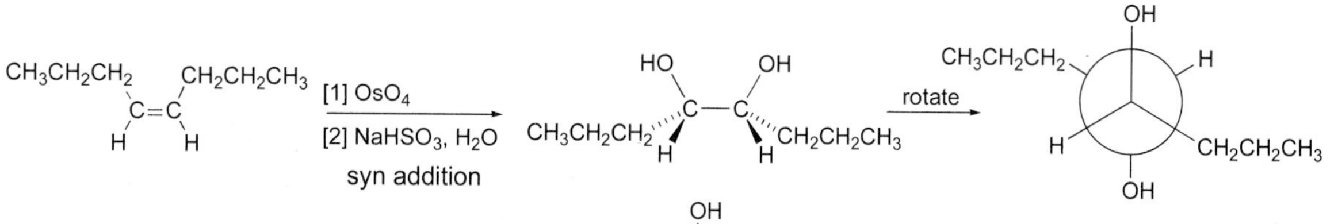
CH3CH2CH2
CH2CH2CH3
C=C
H
H
[1] OsO4
[2] NaHSO3, H2O
syn addition
HO
OH
CH3CH2CH2
H
H
CH2CH2CH3
rotate
OH
CH3CH2CH2
H
H
CH2CH2CH3
OH

[2]

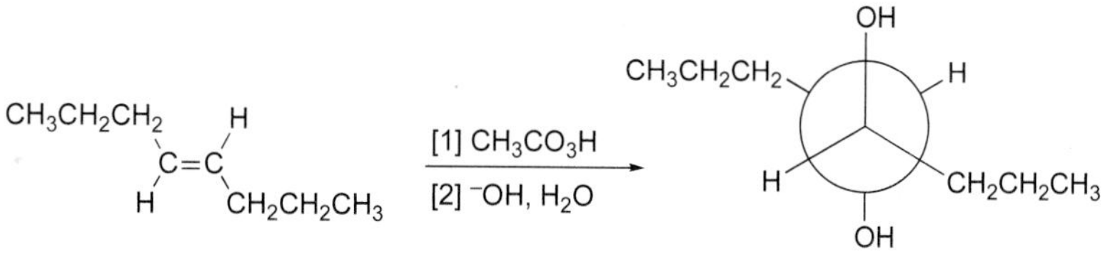
CH3CH2CH2
H
C=C
H
CH2CH2CH3
[1] CH3CO3H
[2] −OH, H2O
OH
CH3CH2CH2
H
H
CH2CH2CH3
OH

12.47

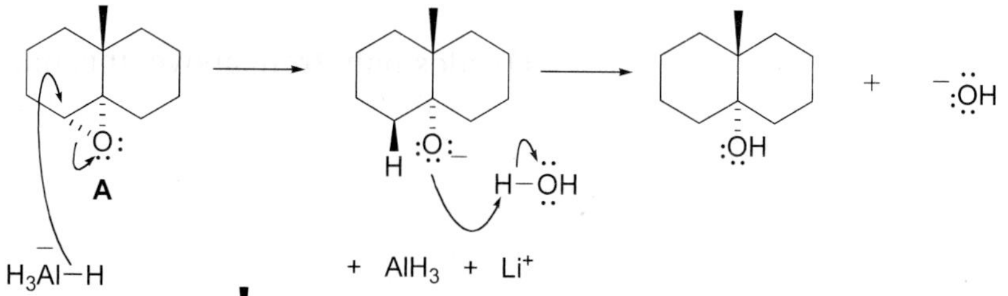
A
H3Al–H
Li+
H
H–OH
+ AlH3 + Li+
:OH
+
−:OH

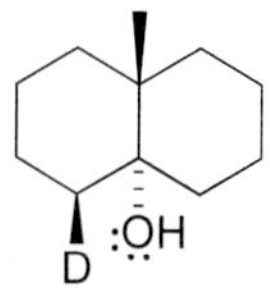
D
:OH

D^- (from $LiAlD_4$) opens the epoxide ring from the back side, so it is oriented on a wedge in the final product.

12.48

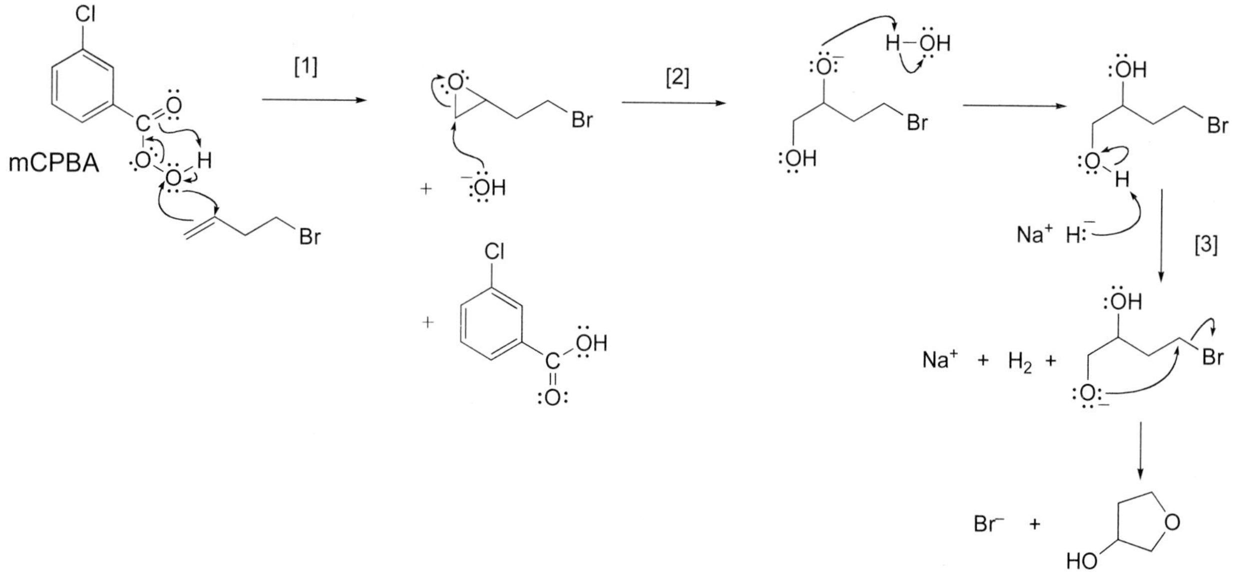
Cl
mCPBA
H
Br
[1]
Br
+
−:OH
Cl
+
OH
:O:
[2]
H–OH
Br
:OH
Br
:OH
H
Na+ H:−
[3]
:OH
Na+ + H2 +
Br
Br− +
O
HO

12.49 Use the directions from Answer 12.19.

a. $(CH_3CH_2)_2C{=}CHCH_2CH_3 \xrightarrow[\text{[2] } CH_3SCH_3]{\text{[1] } O_3} (CH_3CH_2)_2C{=}O + O{=}CHCH_2CH_3$

b. 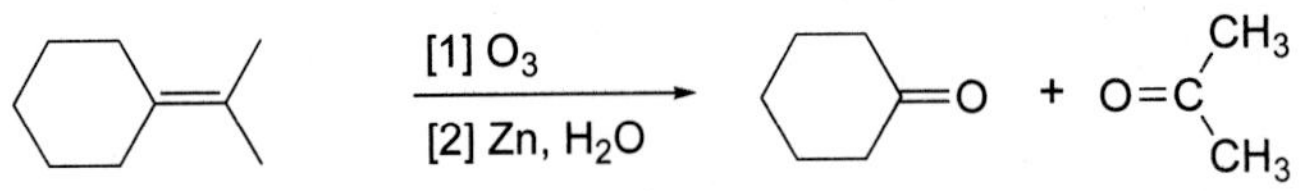
[1] O3
[2] Zn, H2O
=O
+ O=C
CH3
CH3

c. 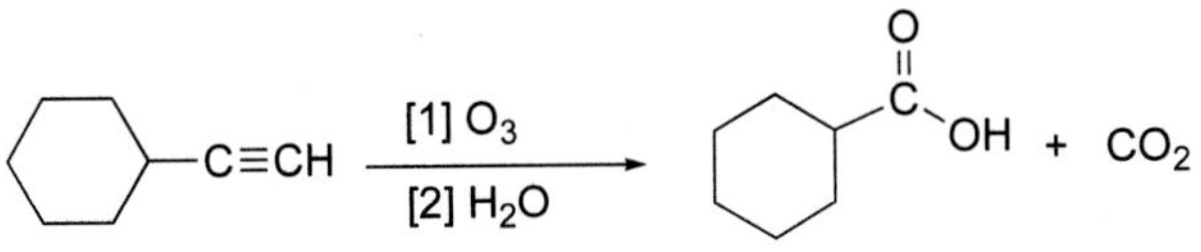
C≡CH
[1] O3
[2] H2O
O
C
OH
+ CO2

d. 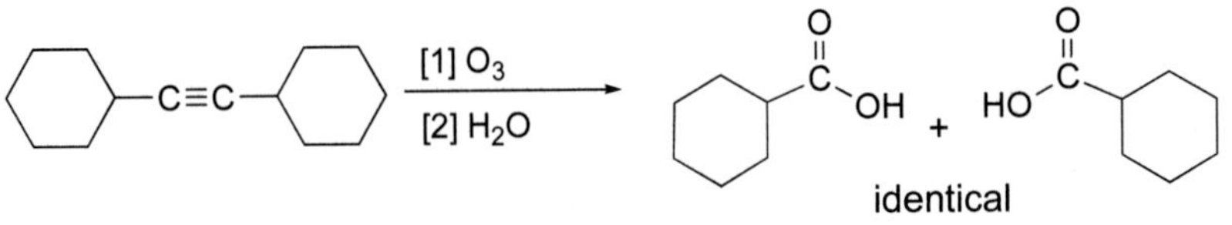
C≡C
[1] O3
[2] H2O
O
C
OH
+
HO
identical

12.50

a. $(CH_3)_2C{=}O$ and $CH_2{=}O \Longrightarrow (CH_3)_2C{=}CH_2$

b. 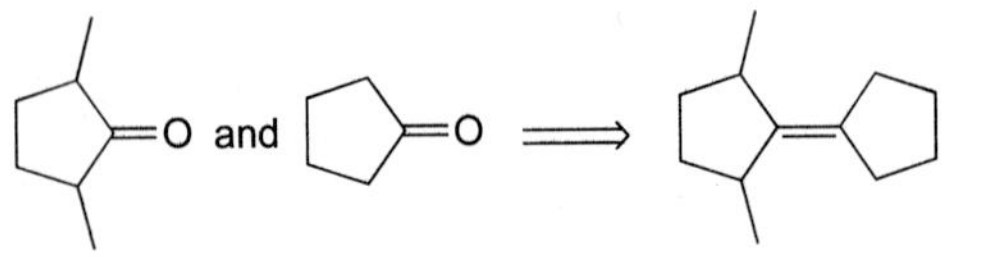
=O and
=O

c. $CH_3CH_2CH_2CHO$ only $\Longrightarrow CH_3CH_2CH_2CH{=}CHCH_2CH_2CH_3$

Join this C to the same C in another identical molecule.

d. 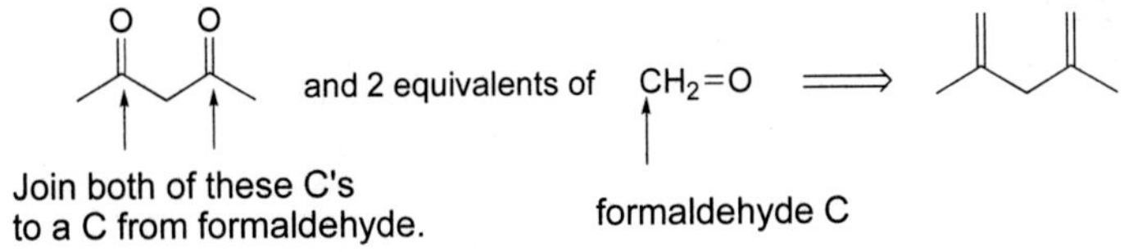
O
O
and 2 equivalents of CH2=O
Join both of these C's to a C from formaldehyde.
formaldehyde C

12.51 Use the directions from Answer 12.20.

a. 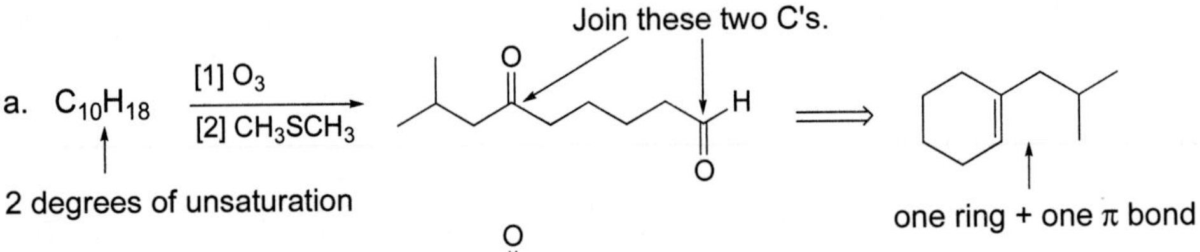
C10H18
[1] O3
[2] CH3SCH3
2 degrees of unsaturation
Join these two C's.
O
H
O
one ring + one π bond

b. 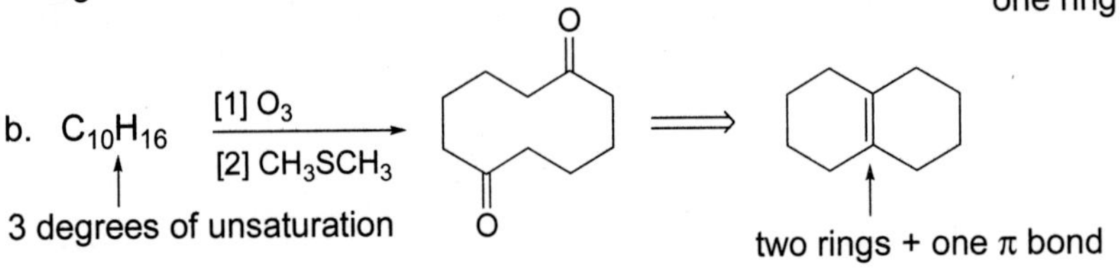
C10H16
[1] O3
[2] CH3SCH3
3 degrees of unsaturation
O
O
two rings + one π bond

12.52

a. $CH_3CH_2CH_2CH_2COOH$ and $CO_2 \Longrightarrow CH_3CH_2CH_2CH_2C{\equiv}CH$

(Join these two C's.)

b. CH_3CH_2COOH and $CH_3CH_2CH_2COOH \Longrightarrow CH_3CH_2C{\equiv}CCH_2CH_2CH_3$

(Join these two C's.)

c. 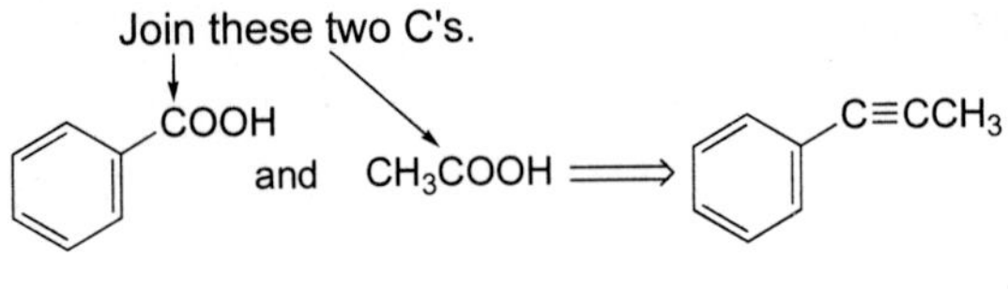
Join these two C's.
COOH
and CH3COOH
C≡CCH3

12.53

a.

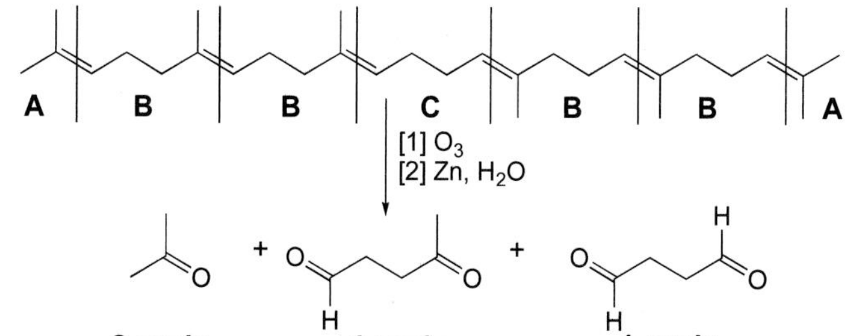
A
B
B
C
B
B
A
[1] O_3
[2] Zn, H_2O
H
H
H

squalene

2 equiv (from portion A) **4 equiv** (from portion B) **1 equiv** (from portion C)

b.

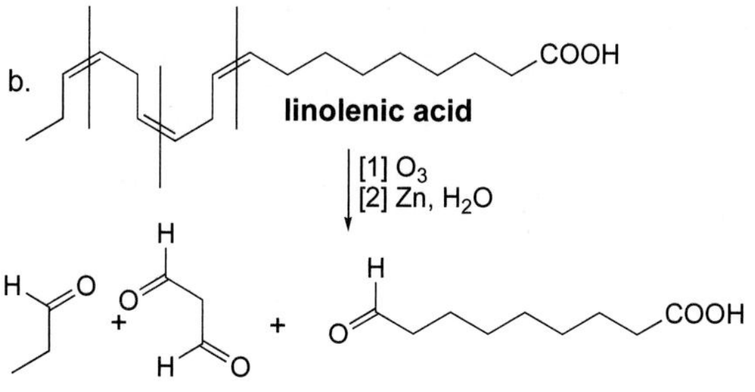
COOH
[1] O_3
[2] Zn, H_2O
H
H
H
H
COOH

linolenic acid

2 equiv

c.

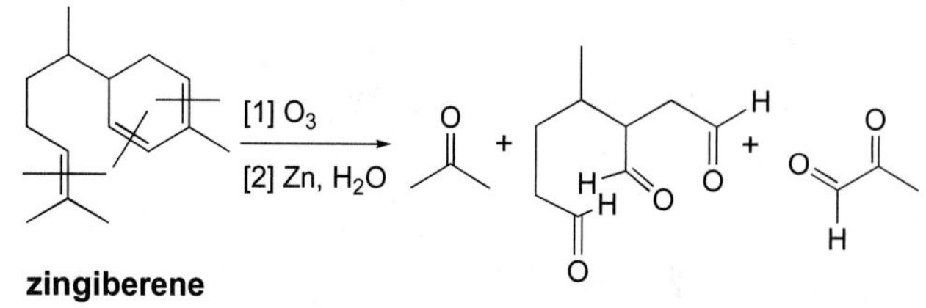
[1] O_3
[2] Zn, H_2O
H
H
H
H

zingiberene

12.54

a.

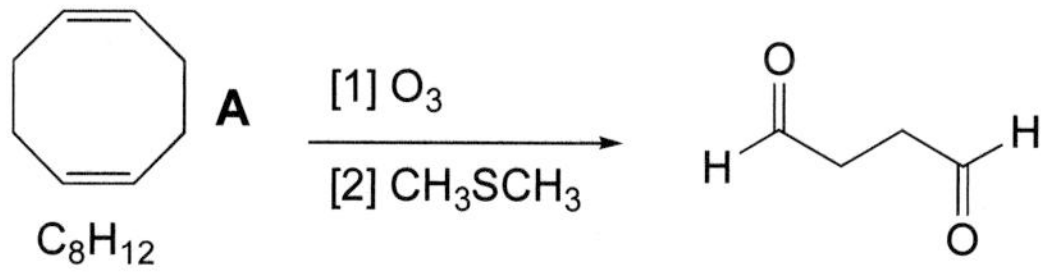
[1] O_3
[2] CH_3SCH_3
H
H

A C_8H_{12}

b.

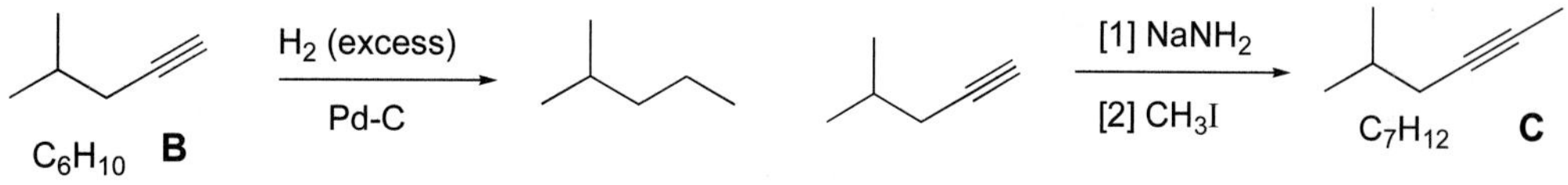
H_2 (excess)
Pd-C
[1] $NaNH_2$
[2] CH_3I

C_6H_{10} **B** C_7H_{12} **C**

12.55

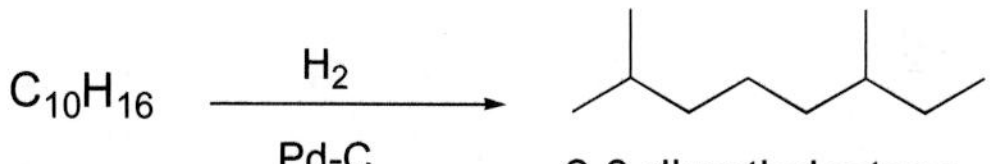
$C_{10}H_{16}$
H_2
Pd-C

3 degrees of unsaturation

2,6-dimethyloctane

The hydrogenation reaction tells you that both oximene and myrcene have 3 π bonds (and no rings). Use this carbon backbone and add in the double bonds based on the oxidative cleavage products.

Oximene: $(CH_3)_2C{=}O$ $CH_2{=}O$ $CH_2(CHO)_2$ $CH_3-C(=O)-CHO$ ⟹

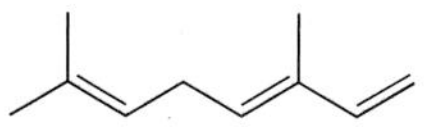

Myrcene: $(CH_3)_2C{=}O$ $CH_2{=}O$ (2 equiv) $H-C(=O)-CH_2CH_2-C(=O)-CHO$ ⟹

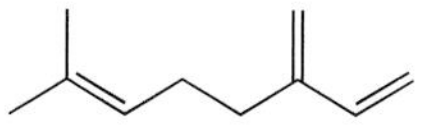

12.56

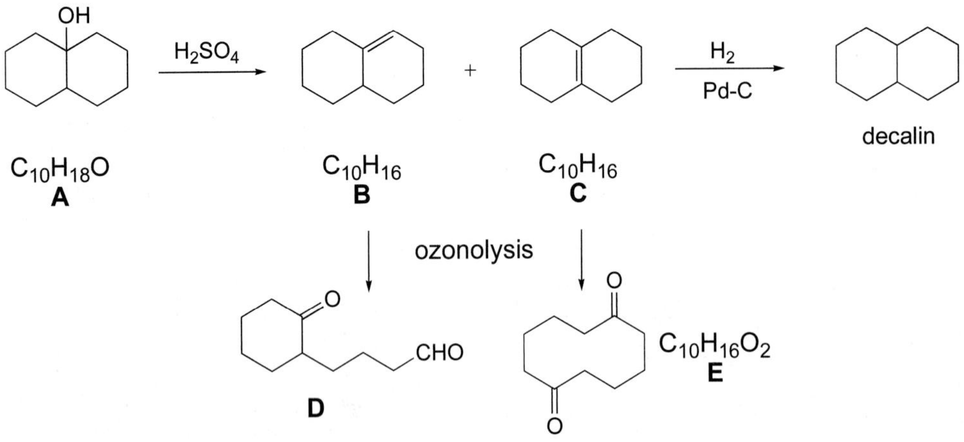
OH
H_2SO_4
+
H_2
Pd-C
decalin
$C_{10}H_{18}O$
A
$C_{10}H_{16}$
B
$C_{10}H_{16}$
C
ozonolysis
O
CHO
D
O
O
$C_{10}H_{16}O_2$
E

12.57 Since hydrogenation of DHA forms $CH_3(CH_2)_{20}COOH$, DHA is a 22-carbon fatty acid. The ozonolysis products show where the double bonds are located.

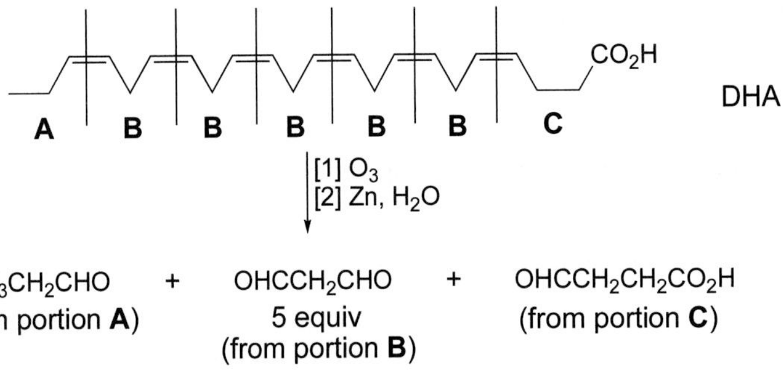
CO_2H
DHA
A B B B B B C
[1] O_3
[2] Zn, H_2O
CH_3CH_2CHO (from portion A)
+
$OHCCH_2CHO$ 5 equiv (from portion B)
+
$OHCCH_2CH_2CO_2H$ (from portion C)

12.58 The stereogenic center (labeled with *) in both structures can be *R* or *S*.

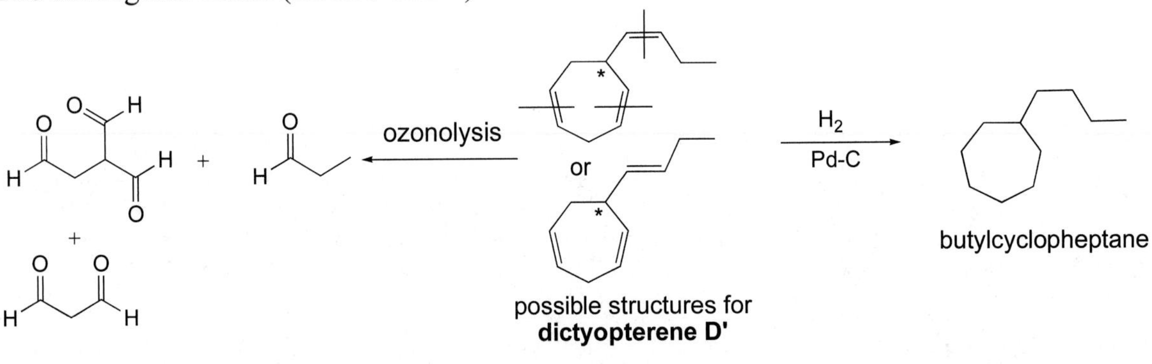
O
H
O
H
+
H
O
H
O
+
O
O
H
H
ozonolysis
*
or
*
H_2
Pd-C
butylcycloheptane
possible structures for
dictyopterene D'

12.59

a.

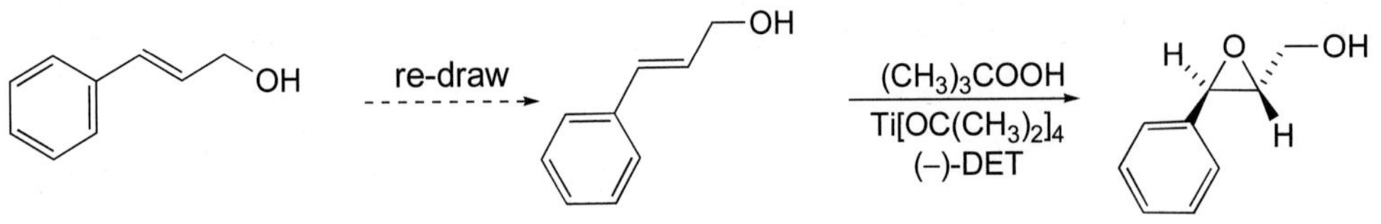
OH
re-draw
OH
$(CH_3)_3COOH$
$Ti[OC(CH_3)_2]_4$
(–)-DET
H
O
OH
H

b.

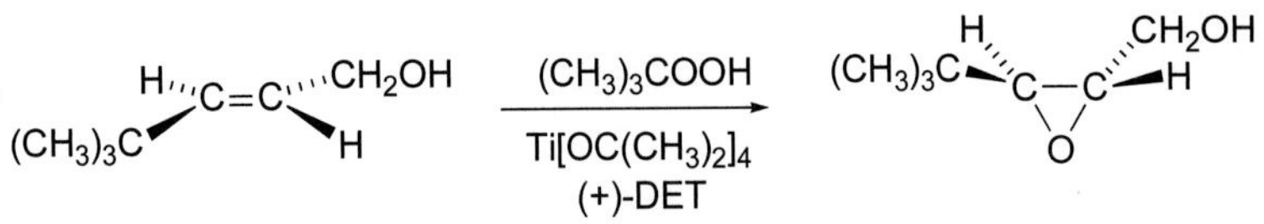
H
C=C
CH_2OH
$(CH_3)_3C$
H
$(CH_3)_3COOH$
$Ti[OC(CH_3)_2]_4$
(+)-DET
H
CH_2OH
$(CH_3)_3C$
C—C
H
O

12.60

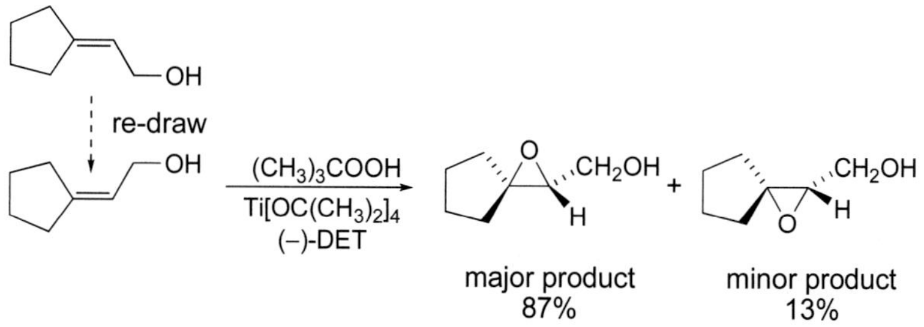

re-draw
OH
$(CH_3)_3COOH$
$Ti[OC(CH_3)_2]_4$
(–)-DET
CH_2OH
major product
87%
minor product
13%

enantiomeric excess = % one enantiomer – % second enantiomer

ee = 87% – 13% = **74%**

12.61

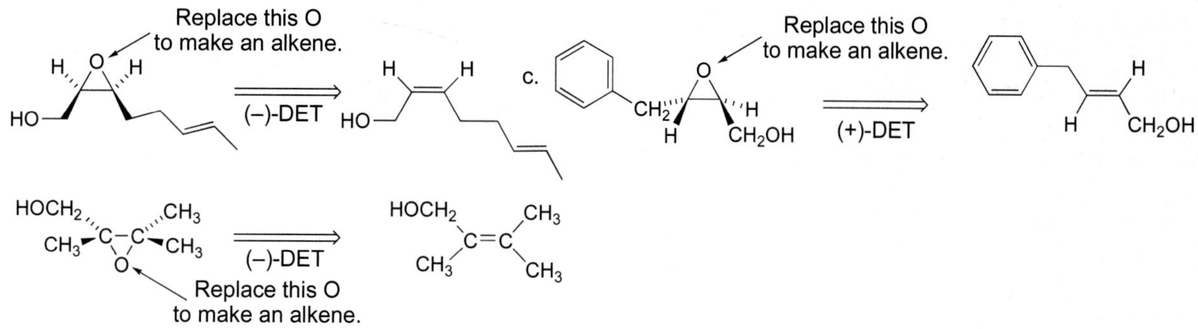

Replace this O to make an alkene.
(–)-DET
$HOCH_2$
CH_3
(+)-DET
CH_2OH

12.62 Use retrosynthetic analysis to devise a synthesis of each hydrocarbon from acetylene.

a. $CH_3CH_2CH{=}CH_2 \Longrightarrow CH_3CH_2CH{\equiv}CH \Longrightarrow {}^{-}C{\equiv}CH \Longrightarrow HC{\equiv}CH$

$$HC{\equiv}CH \xrightarrow{NaH} {}^{-}C{\equiv}CH \xrightarrow{CH_3CH_2Cl} CH_3CH_2C{\equiv}CH \xrightarrow[\text{Lindlar catalyst}]{H_2} CH_3CH_2CH{=}CH_2$$

b.

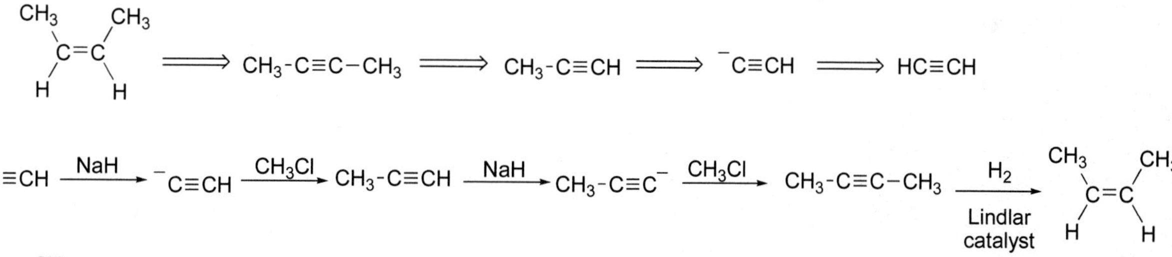

$CH_3\text{-}C{\equiv}C{-}CH_3$
$CH_3\text{-}C{\equiv}CH$
$^{-}C{\equiv}CH$
$HC{\equiv}CH$
NaH
CH_3Cl
H_2
Lindlar catalyst

c.

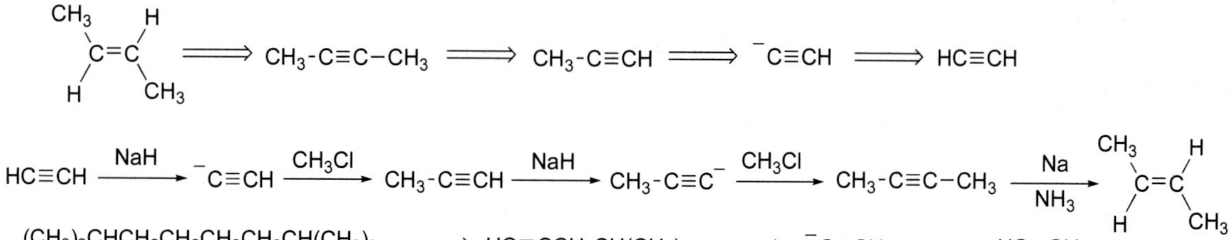

$CH_3\text{-}C{\equiv}C{-}CH_3$
$CH_3\text{-}C{\equiv}CH$
$^{-}C{\equiv}CH$
$HC{\equiv}CH$
NaH
CH_3Cl
Na
NH_3

d. $(CH_3)_2CHCH_2CH_2CH_2CH_2CH(CH_3)_2 \Longrightarrow HC{\equiv}CCH_2CH(CH_3)_2 \Longrightarrow {}^{-}C{\equiv}CH \Longrightarrow HC{\equiv}CH$

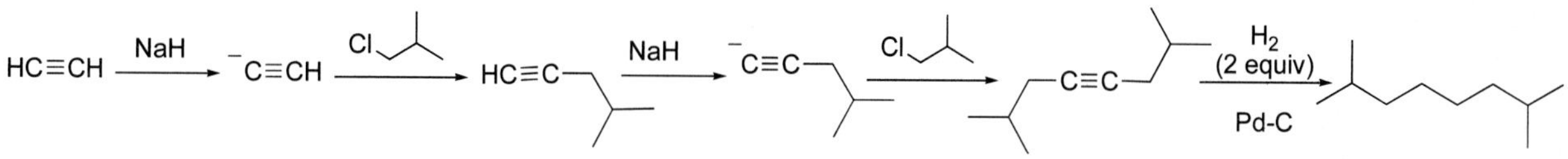

$HC{\equiv}CH$
NaH
$^{-}C{\equiv}CH$
Cl
H_2
(2 equiv)
Pd-C

12.63

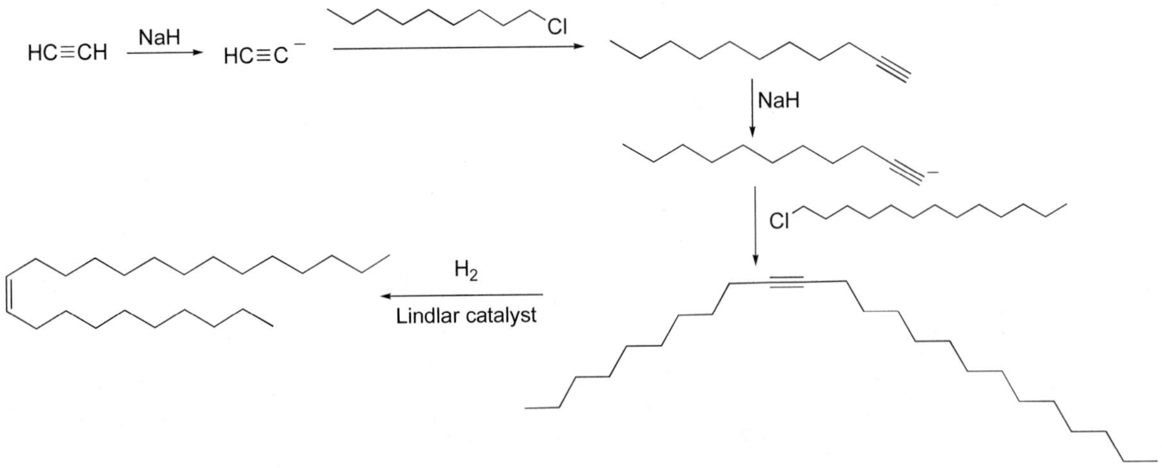

12.64

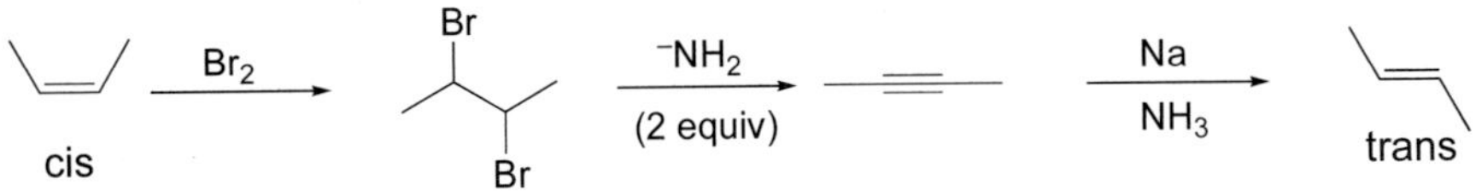

12.65

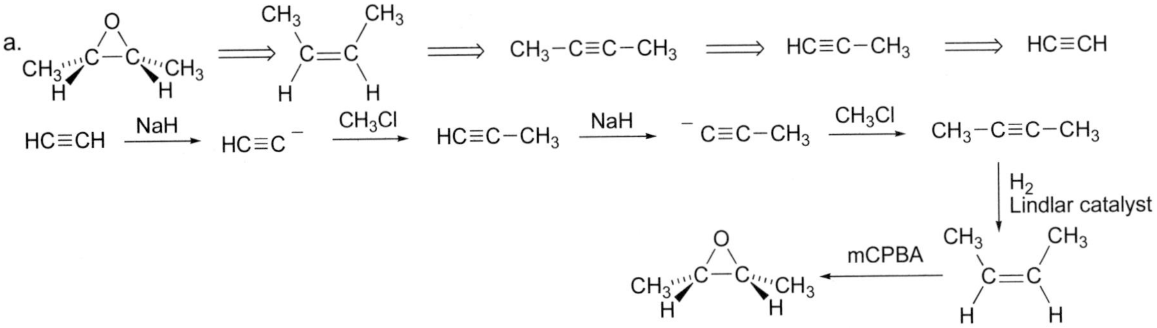

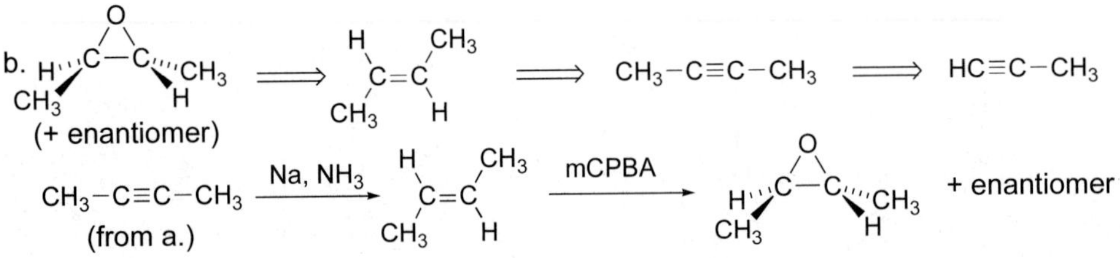

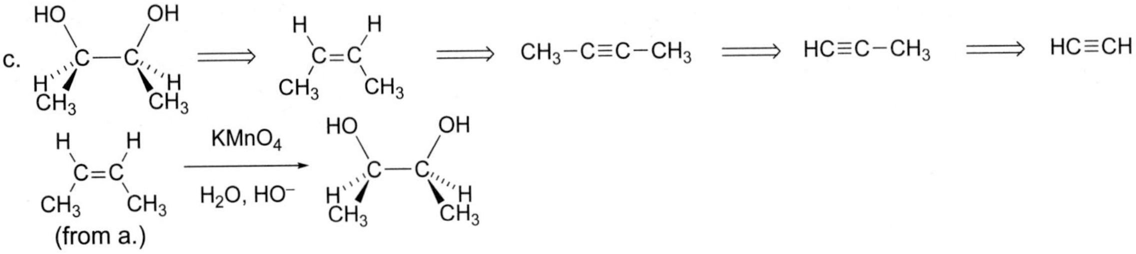

d. 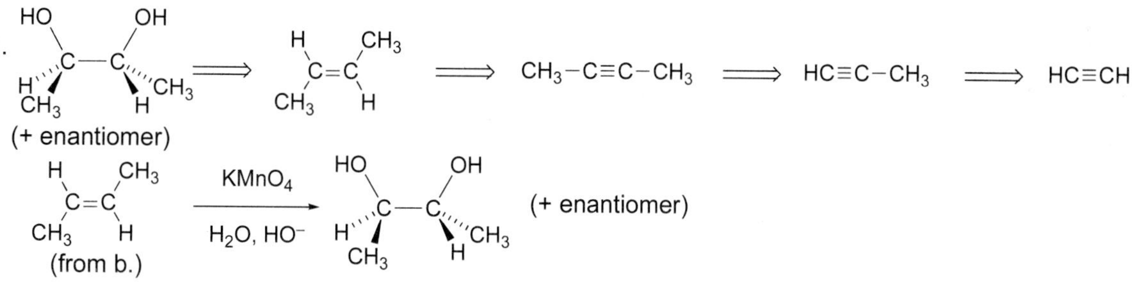

12.66

a. 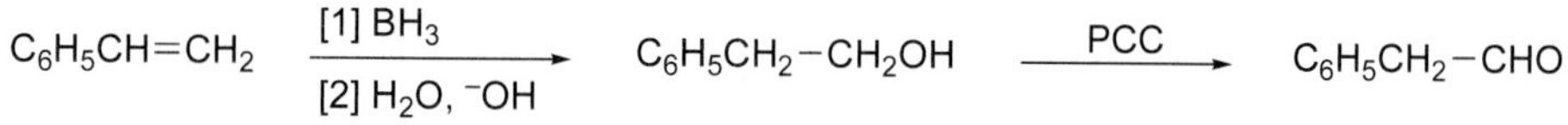

b. 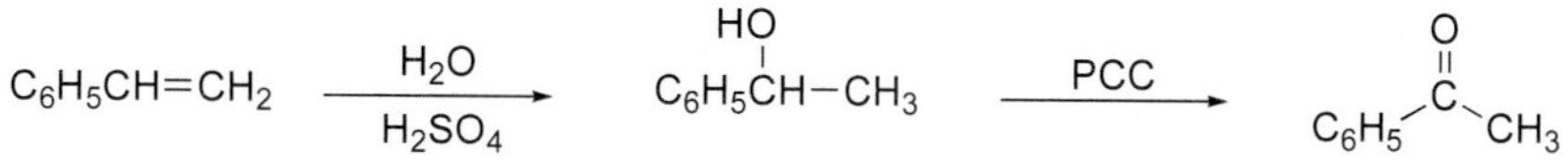

c. 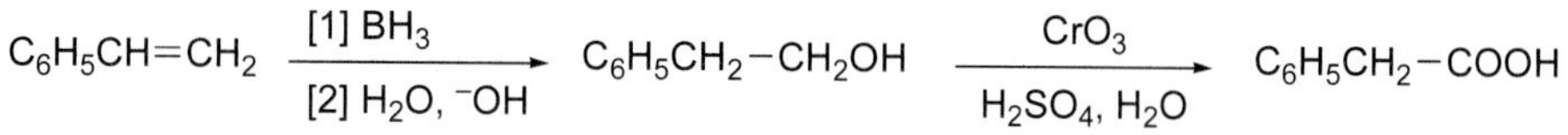

d. 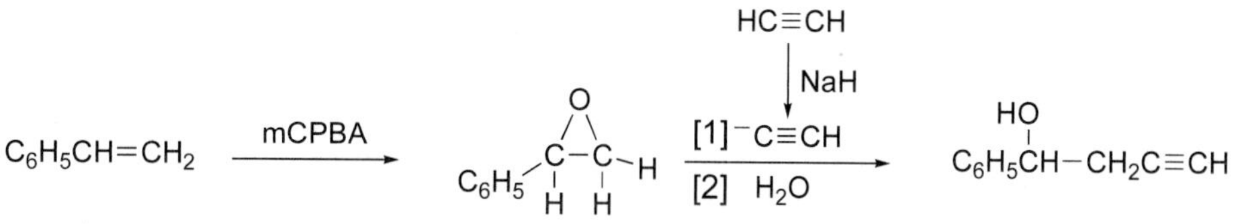

12.67

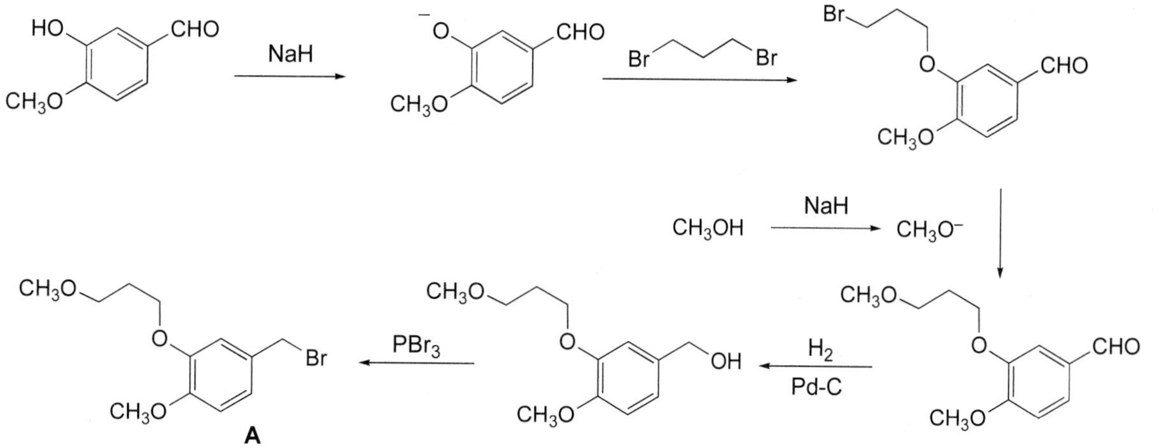

12.68

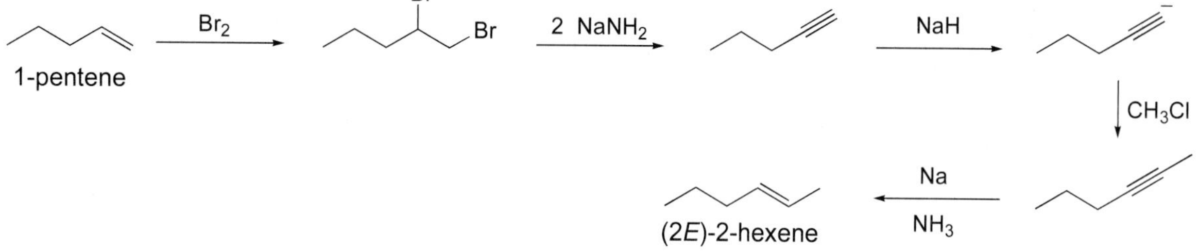

12.69

a. 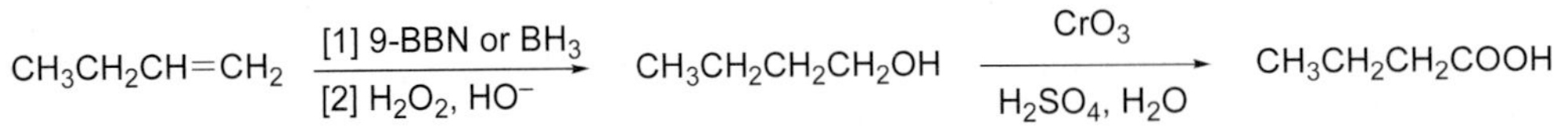

b. 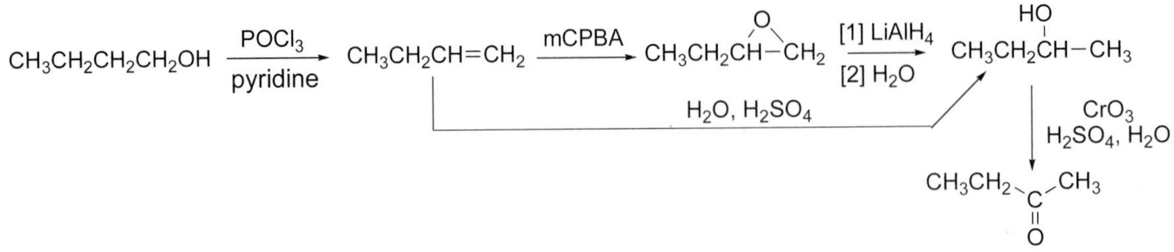

c. 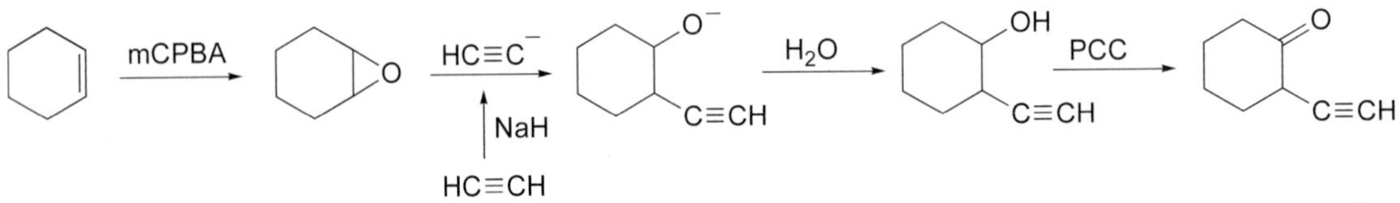

d. 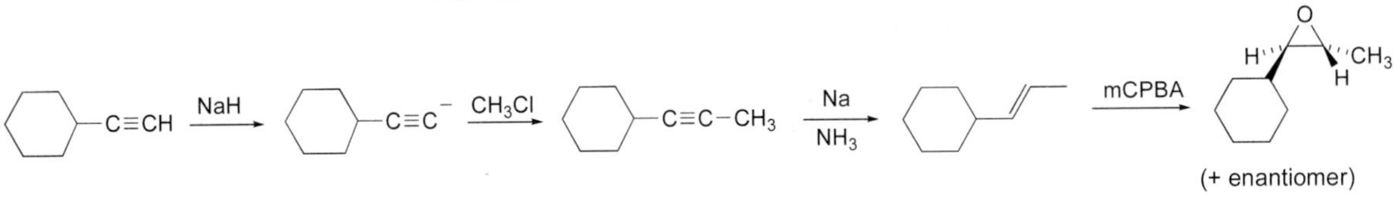

12.70

a. 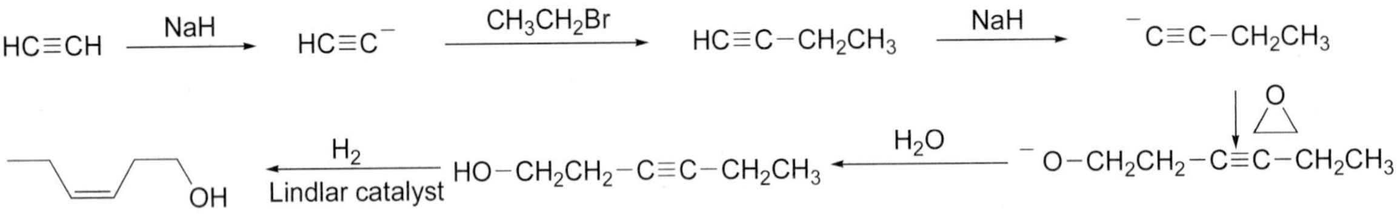

b. 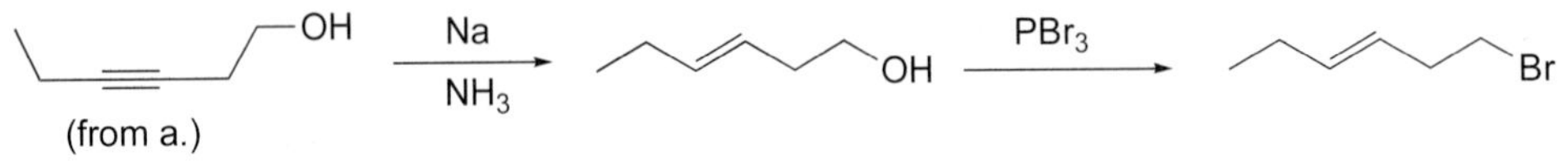

c. 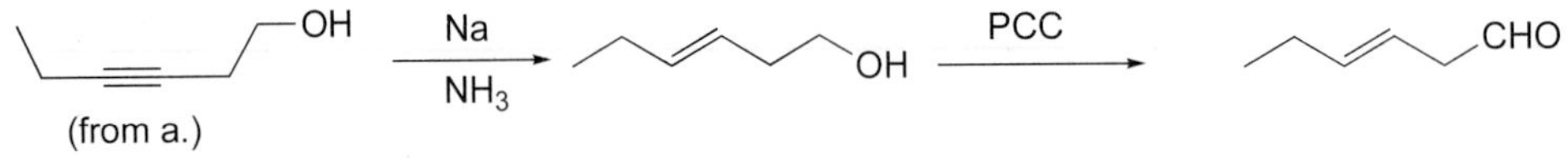

12.71 Determine which 2 C's can come from HC≡CH and two alkyl halides that are unhindered (1° or CH_3X).

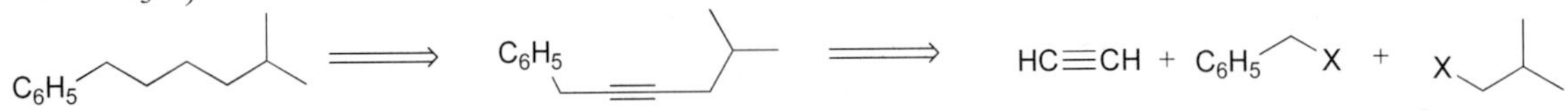

1-phenyl-5-methylhexane

In synthetic direction:

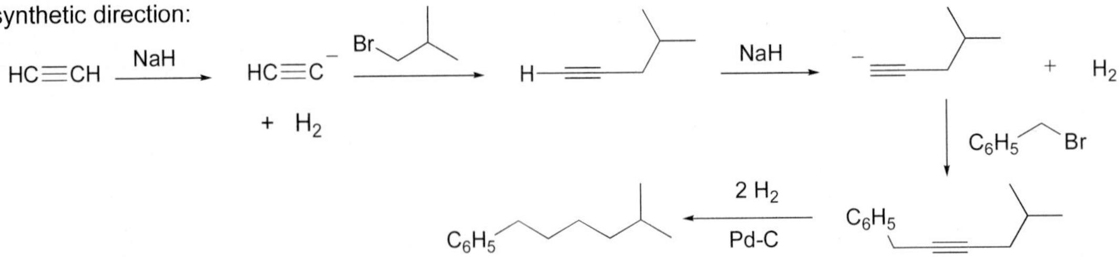

12.72

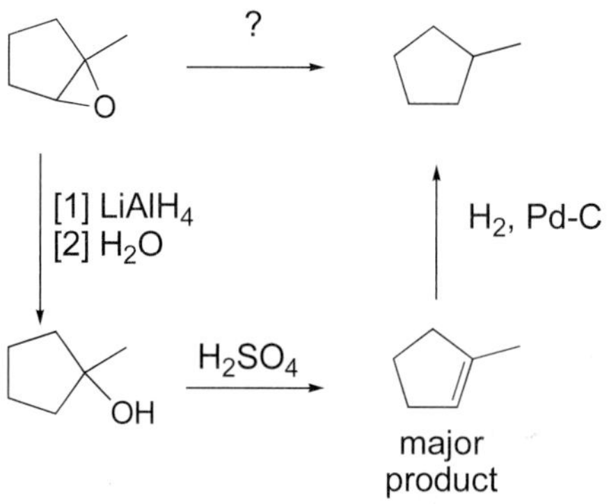

12.73

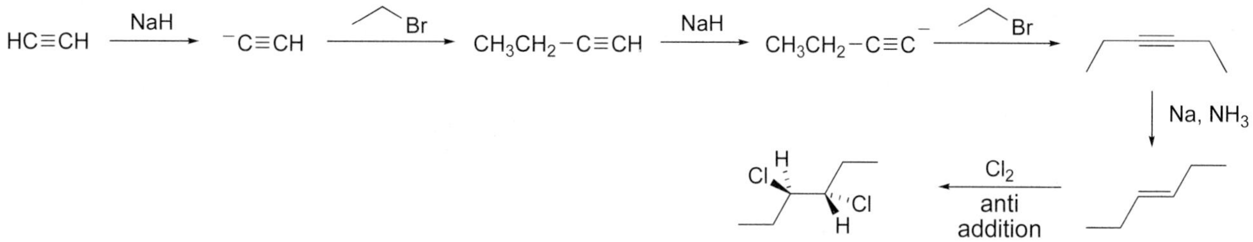

(3*R*,4*S*)-3,4-dichlorohexane

12.74

a.

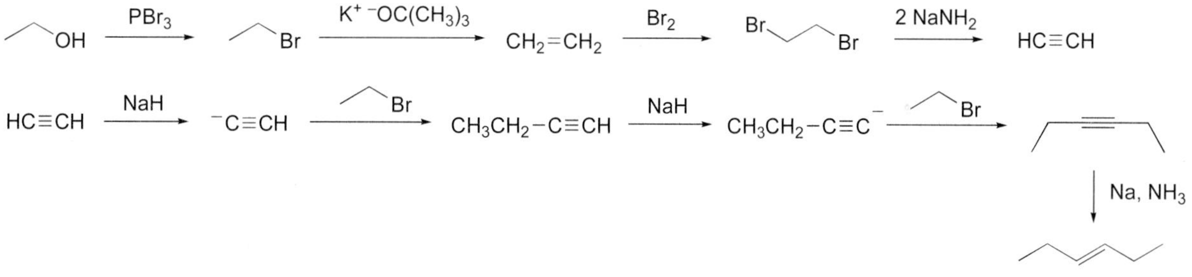

b.

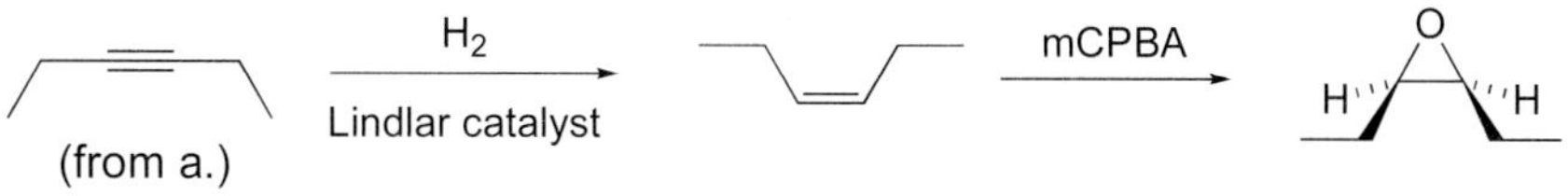

c.

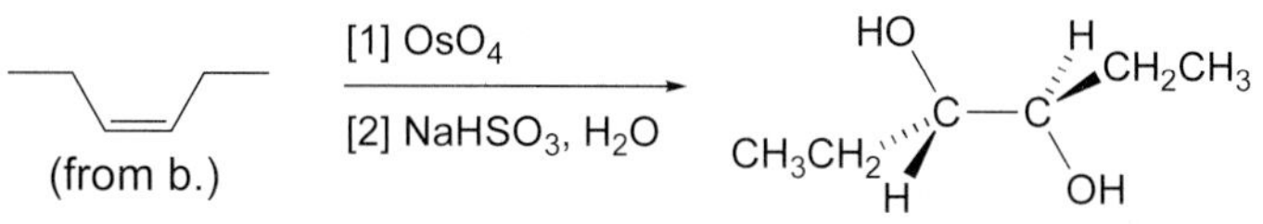

12.75

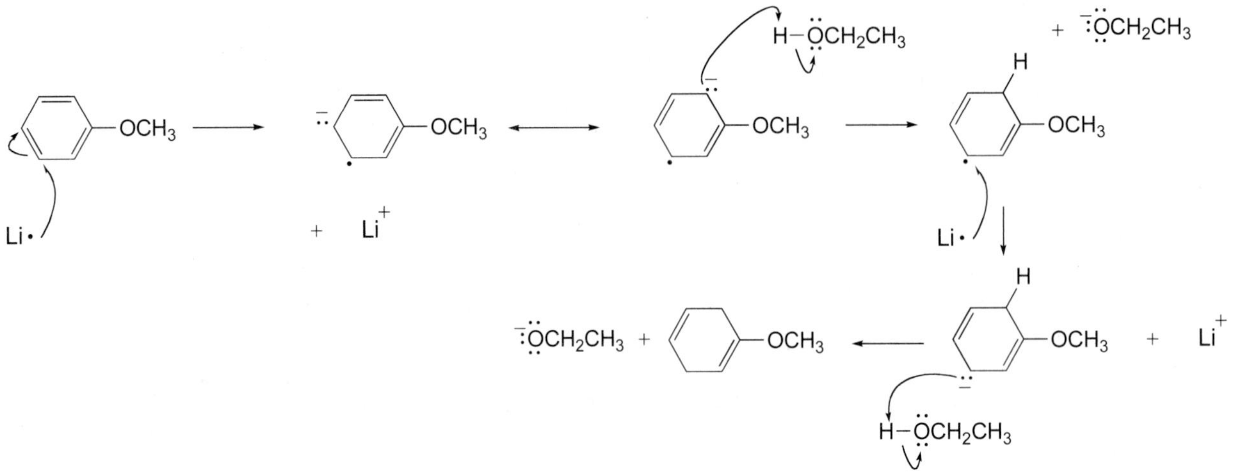

12.76

The favored conformation
for both molecules places
the *tert*-butyl group equatorial.

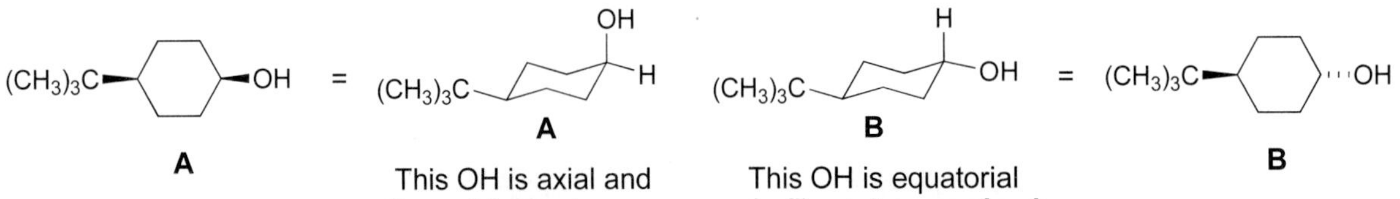

This OH is axial and will react **faster** because the OH group is more hindered.

This OH is equatorial and will react **more slowly** because the OH group is less hindered.

12.77

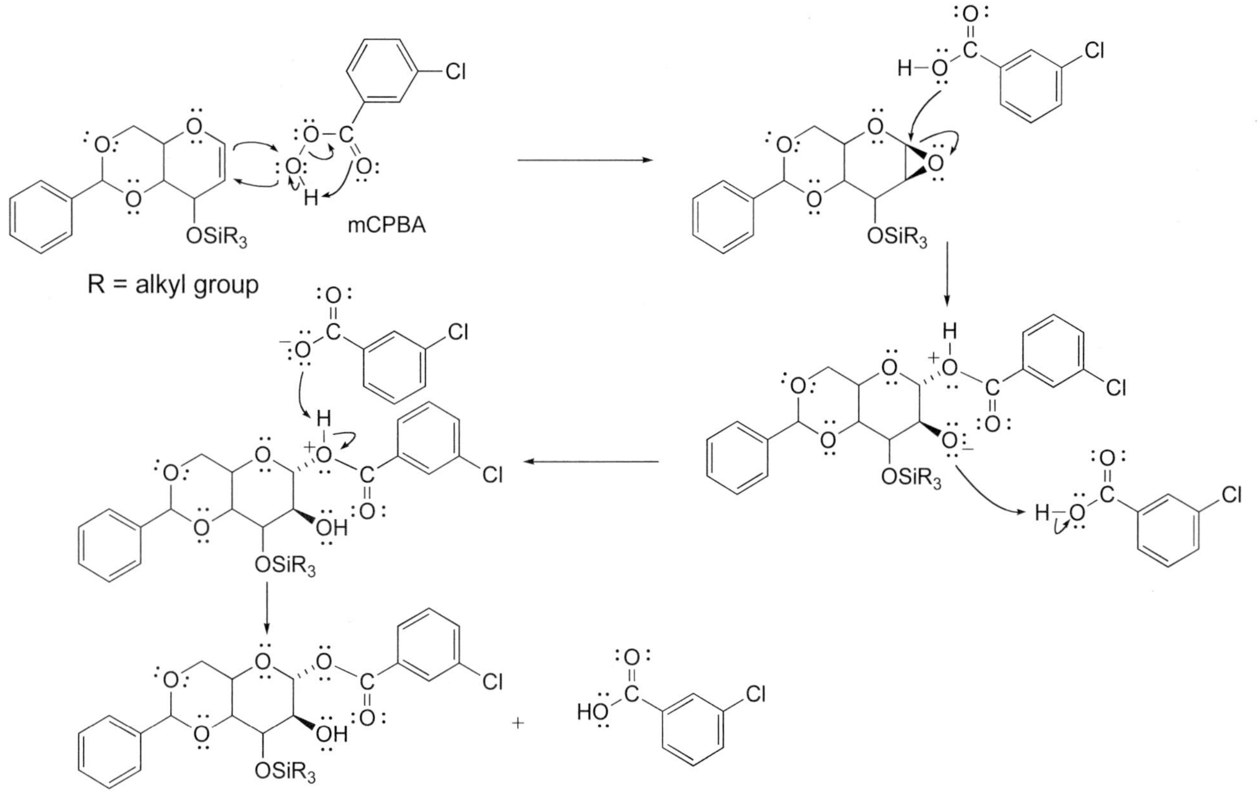
mCPBA
OSiR3
R = alkyl group

12.78

a.

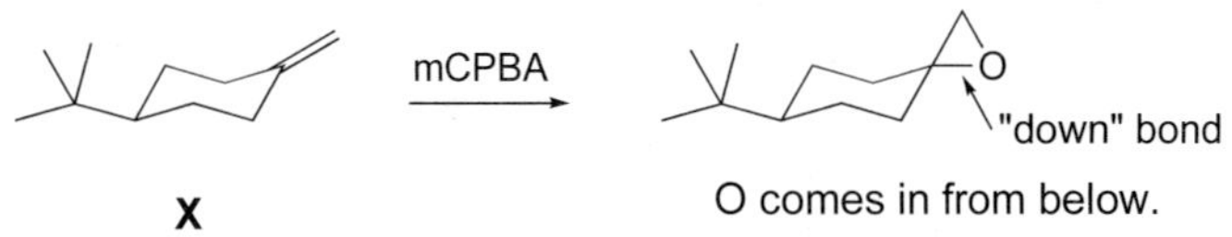
mCPBA
"down" bond
X
O comes in from below.

b.

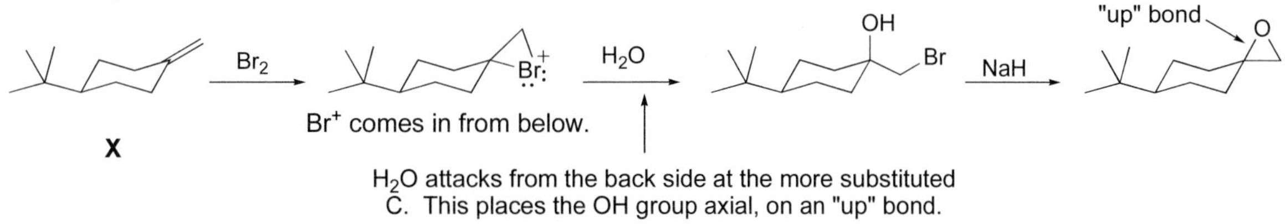
Br2
H2O
OH
Br
NaH
"up" bond
X
Br+ comes in from below.
H2O attacks from the back side at the more substituted C. This places the OH group axial, on an "up" bond.

12.79 The two OH's are added to opposite faces of the C=C, so anti addition occurs.

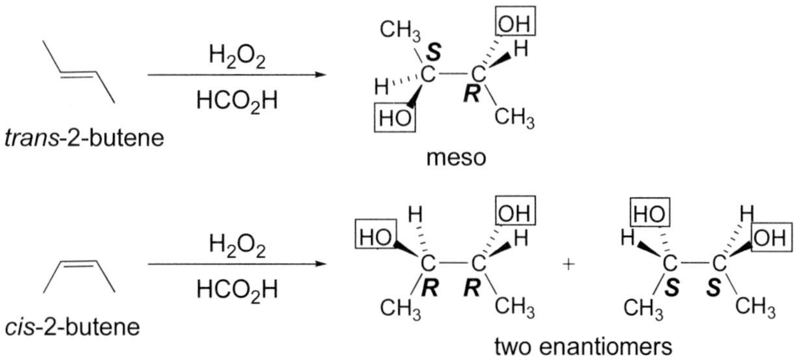
H2O2
HCO2H
trans-2-butene
meso
cis-2-butene
two enantiomers

12.80

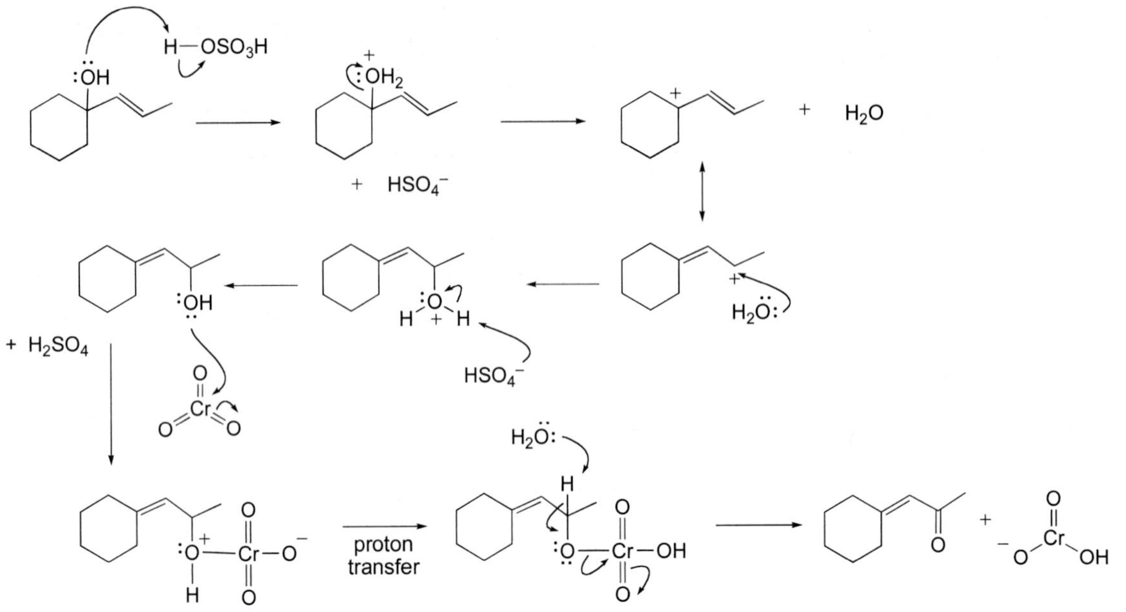

:ÖH
H—OSO$_3$H
$\overset{+}{\text{O}}$H$_2$
+ HSO$_4^-$
+ H$_2$O
H$_2$Ö:
HSO$_4^-$
:ÖH
+ H$_2$SO$_4$
proton transfer
Cr
OH

12.81

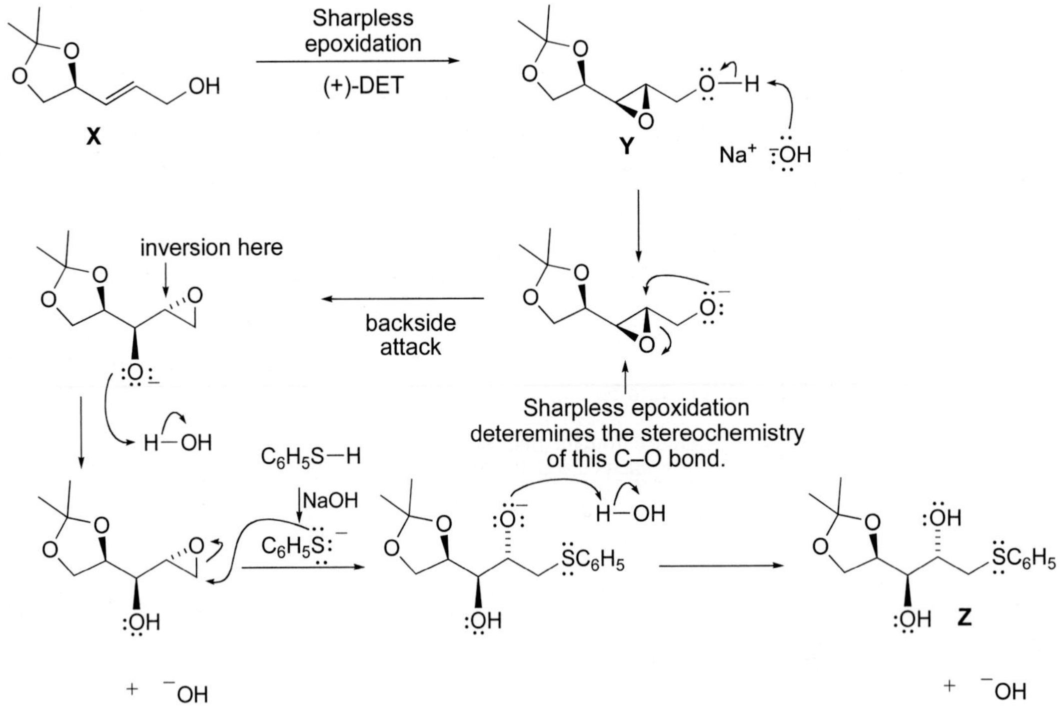

OH
X
Sharpless epoxidation
(+)-DET
Y
Na$^+$:ÖH
inversion here
backside attack
Sharpless epoxidation deteremines the stereochemistry of this C–O bond.
H—OH
C$_6$H$_5$S—H
NaOH
C$_6$H$_5$S:$^-$
SC$_6$H$_5$
:ÖH
Z
+ $^-$OH

Chapter 13 Mass Spectrometry and Infrared Spectroscopy

Chapter Review

Mass spectrometry (MS)

- Mass spectrometry measures the molecular weight of a compound (13.1A).
- The mass of the molecular ion (**M**) = the molecular weight of a compound. Except for isotope peaks at M + 1 and M + 2, the molecular ion has the highest mass in a mass spectrum (13.1A).
- The base peak is the tallest peak in a mass spectrum (13.1A).
- A compound with an odd number of N atoms gives an odd molecular ion. A compound with an even number of N atoms (including zero) gives an even molecular ion (13.1B).
- Organic chlorides show two peaks for the molecular ion (M and M + 2) in a 3:1 ratio (13.2).
- Organic bromides show two peaks for the molecular ion (M and M + 2) in a 1:1 ratio (13.2).
- The fragmentation of radical cations formed in a mass spectrometer gives lower molecular weight fragments, often characteristic of a functional group (13.3).
- High-resolution mass spectrometry gives the molecular formula of a compound (13.4A).

Electromagnetic radiation

- The wavelength and frequency of electromagnetic radiation are *inversely* related by the following equations: $\lambda = c/\nu$ or $\nu = c/\lambda$ (13.5).
- The energy of a photon is proportional to its frequency; the higher the frequency the higher the energy: $E = h\nu$ (13.5).

Infrared spectroscopy (IR, 13.6 and 13.7)

- Infrared spectroscopy identifies functional groups.
- IR absorptions are reported in wavenumbers:

$$\textbf{wavenumber} = \tilde{\nu} = 1/\lambda$$

- The functional group region from **4000–1500 cm^{-1}** is the most useful region of an IR spectrum.
- C–H, O–H, and N–H bonds absorb at high frequency, ≥ 2500 cm^{-1}.
- As bond strength increases, the wavenumber of an absorption increases; thus triple bonds absorb at higher wavenumber than double bonds.

C=C	C≡C
~1650 cm^{-1}	~2250 cm^{-1}

→ **Increasing bond strength**
Increasing $\tilde{\nu}$

- The higher the percent *s*-character, the stronger the bond, and the higher the wavenumber of an IR absorption.

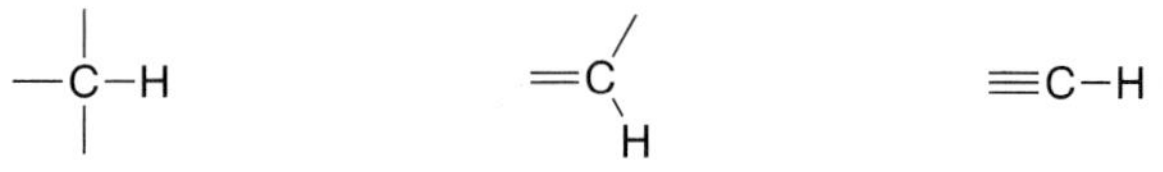

C_{sp^3}–H	C_{sp^2}–H	C_{sp}–H
25% *s*-character	33% *s*-character	50% *s*-character
3000–2850 cm^{-1}	3150–3000 cm^{-1}	3300 cm^{-1}

→ **Increasing percent *s*-character**
Increasing $\tilde{\nu}$

Practice Test on Chapter Review

1. a. Which compound has a molecular ion at 112 and a peak at 1720 cm^{-1} in its IR spectrum?

1. 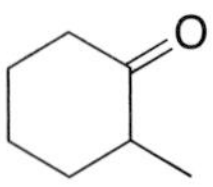

2. 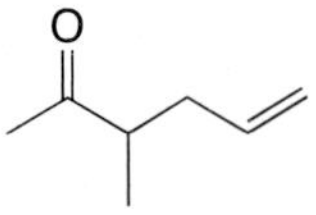

3. 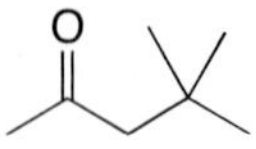

4. Compounds (1) and (2) both fit these criteria.
5. Compounds (1), (2), and (3) all fit these criteria.

b. Which of the following compounds has peaks at 3300, 3000, and 2250 cm^{-1} in its IR spectrum?

1. 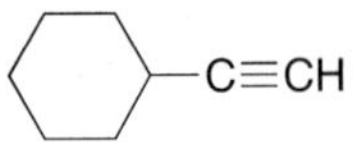

2. 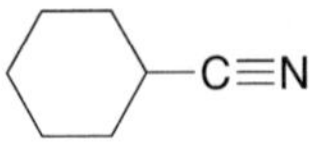

3. 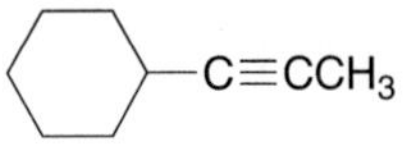

4. Compounds (1) and (2) have these peaks in their IR spectra.
5. Compounds (1), (2), and (3) all contain these peaks in their IR spectra.

c. What is the base peak in a mass spectrum?
1. the peak due to the radical cation formed when a molecule loses an electron
2. the tallest peak in the mass spectrum
3. the peak due to the fragment with the largest *m*/*z* ratio
4. Both (1) and (2) describe the base peak.
5. Statements (1), (2), and (3) describe the base peak.

d. Which compounds are possible structures for a molecule that has a molecular ion at 150 in its mass spectrum?

1. 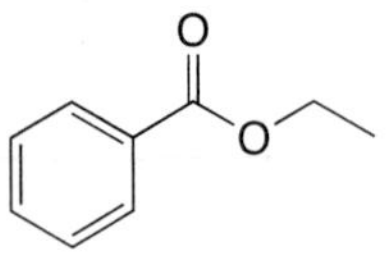

2. 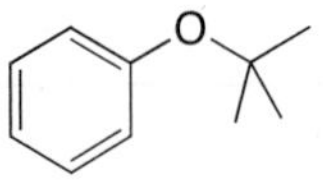

3. 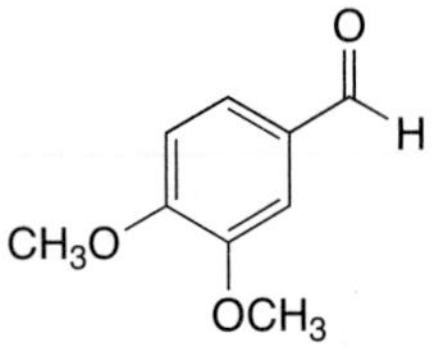

4. Both (1) and (2) are possible structures.
5. Compounds (1), (2), and (3) are all possible structures.

e. Which compounds exhibit prominent M+2 peaks in their mass spectra?

1. 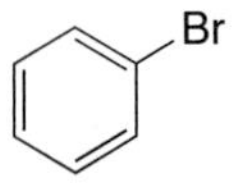

2. 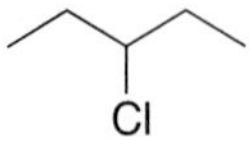

3. 

4. Both (1) and (2) show M + 2 peaks.
5. Compounds (1), (2), and (3) all show M + 2 peaks.

2. Answer each question with the number that corresponds to one of the following regions of an IR spectrum.

   1. 4000–2500 cm^{-1}
   2. 2500–2000 cm^{-1}
   3. 2000–1500 cm^{-1}
   4. < 1500 cm^{-1}

   a. This region is called the fingerprint region of an IR spectrum.
   b. The OH group of 1-propanol absorbs in this region.
   c. The C=N of $C_6H_5CH_2CH{=}NCH_3$ absorbs in this region.
   d. An unsymmetrical C≡C absorbs in this region.
   e. An *sp* hybridized C–H bond absorbs in this region.
   f. Ethyl benzoate ($C_6H_5CO_2CH_2CH_3$) absorbs in all regions of the IR except this one.

3. Answer True (T) or False (F).
   a. IR spectroscopy is useful for determining the molecular weight of a compound.
   b. A C–H bond that absorbs at 3140 cm^{-1} is stronger than a C–H bond that absorbs at 2950 cm^{-1}.
   c. A compound with a molecular ion at 109 contains a N atom.
   d. A compound with a base peak at 57 must contain a N atom.
   e. 2-Butyne shows an IR absorption at 2250 cm^{-1}.
   f. 1-Propanol shows an IR absorption at 3200–3600 cm^{-1}.
   g. An ether shows no IR absorptions at 3200–3600 or 1700 cm^{-1}.
   h. In its mass spectrum, a compound that has a molecular ion with two peaks of approximately equal intensity at 124 and 126 contains chlorine.

Answers to Practice Test

1.a. 4	2.a. 4	3.a. F	e. F
b. 1	b. 1	b. T	f. T
c. 2	c. 3	c. T	g. T
d. 4	d. 2	d. F	h. F
e. 4	e. 1		
	f. 2		

Answers to Problems

13.1 The molecular ion formed from each compound is equal to its molecular weight.

a. C_3H_6O	b. $C_{10}H_{20}$	c. $C_8H_8O_2$	d. $C_{10}H_{15}N$
molecular weight = **58**	molecular weight = **140**	molecular weight = **136**	molecular weight = **149**
molecular ion (*m/z*) = **58**	molecular ion (*m/z*) = **140**	molecular ion (*m/z*) = **136**	molecular ion (*m/z*) = **149**

13.2 Some possible formulas for each molecular ion:

a. Molecular ion at 72: C_5H_{12}, C_4H_8O, $C_3H_4O_2$

b. Molecular ion at 100: C_8H_4, C_7H_{16}, $C_6H_{12}O$, $C_5H_8O_2$

c. Molecular ion at 73: $C_4H_{11}N$, $C_2H_7N_3$

13.3 To calculate the molecular ions you would expect for compounds with Cl, calculate the molecular weight using each of the two most common isotopes of Cl (^{35}Cl and ^{37}Cl).

a. $C_4H_9{}^{35}Cl$ = **92**
$C_4H_9{}^{37}Cl$ = **94**
Two peaks in 3:1 ratio at *m/z* 92 and 94

c. $C_4H_{11}N$ = **73**
One peak at *m/z* 73

b. C_3H_7F = **62**
One peak at *m/z* 62

d. $C_4H_4N_2$ = **80**
One peak at *m/z* 80

13.4 Convert the ball-and-stick model to a skeletal structure and determine the molecular formula. Calculate the molecular weight using each of the two common isotopes for Br (^{79}Br and ^{81}Br).

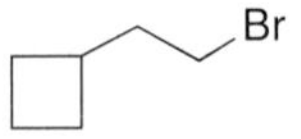
Br

$C_6H_{11}Br$

$C_6H_{11}{}^{79}Br$ = **162**
$C_6H_{11}{}^{81}Br$ = **164**
Two peaks in a 1:1 ratio at *m/z* 162 and 164

13.5 After calculating the mass of the molecular ion, draw the structure and determine which C–C bond is broken to form fragments of the appropriate mass-to-charge ratio.

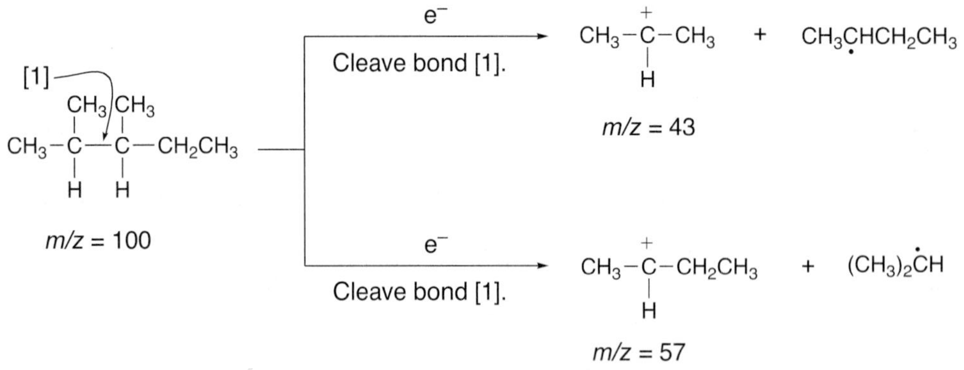
[1]
CH3 CH3
CH3–C–C–CH2CH3
H H
m/z = 100
e⁻
Cleave bond [1].
CH3–C–CH3
H
+
CH3CHCH2CH3
m/z = 43
e⁻
Cleave bond [1].
CH3–C–CH2CH3
H
+
(CH3)2CH
m/z = 57

13.6

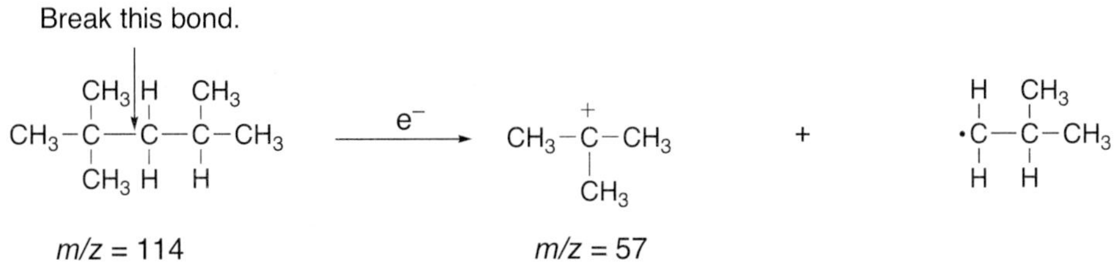
Break this bond.
e⁻
m/z = 114
m/z = 57

This 3° carbocation is more stable than others that can form, and is therefore the most abundant fragment.

13.7

a.

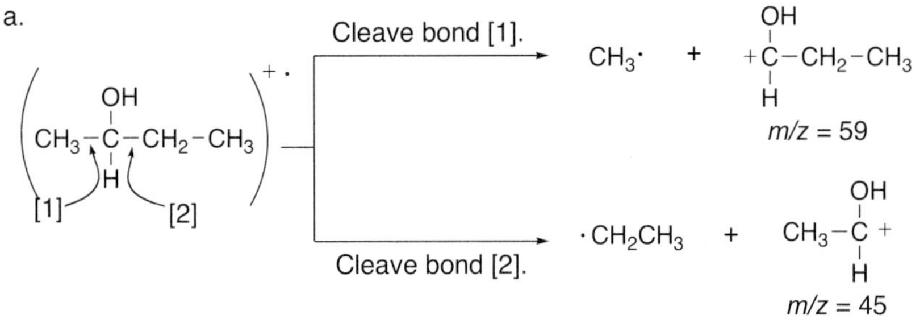
Cleave bond [1].
Cleave bond [2].
[1]
[2]
m/z = 59
m/z = 45

b.

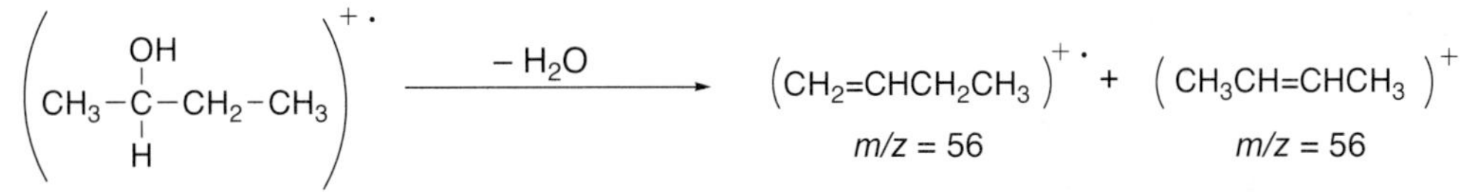
– H2O
m/z = 56
m/z = 56

13.8

a.

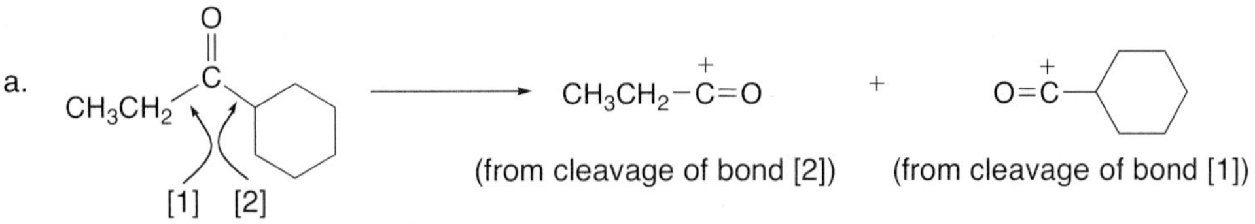
[1] [2]
(from cleavage of bond [2])
(from cleavage of bond [1])

b. $CH_3CH_2CH_2CH_2CH_2CH_2OH \longrightarrow {}^{+}CH_2OH$

c. $CH_3CH_2CH_2CHO \longrightarrow CH_3CH_2CH_2\overset{+}{C}{=}O + H\overset{+}{C}{=}O$

13.9 Use the exact mass values given in Table 13.1 to calculate the exact mass of each compound.

$C_7H_5NO_3$	$C_8H_9NO_2$	$C_{10}H_{17}N$
mass: 151.0270	mass: 151.0634 compound **X**	mass: 151.1362

13.10

benzene
C_6H_6 *m/z* = 78

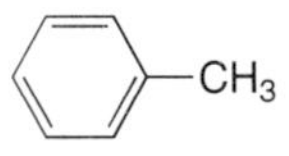

toluene
C_7H_8 *m/z* = 92

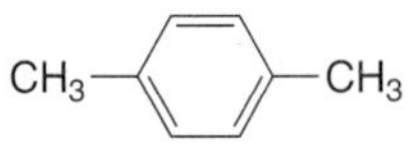

p-xylene
C_8H_{10} *m/z* = 106

GC–MS analysis:
Three peaks in the gas chromatogram.
Order of peaks: benzene, toluene, *p*-xylene, in order of increasing bp.
Molecular ions observed in the three mass spectra: 78, 92, 106.

13.11 **Wavelength and frequency are inversely proportional.** The higher frequency light will have a shorter wavelength.

a. Light having $\lambda = 10^2$ nm has a higher ν than light with $\lambda = 10^4$ nm.
b. Light having $\lambda = 100$ nm has a higher ν than light with $\lambda = 100$ μm.
c. Blue light has a higher ν than red light.

13.12 The **energy of a photon** is *proportional* to its **frequency,** and inversely proportional to its wavelength.

a. Light having $\nu = 10^8$ Hz is of higher energy than light having $\nu = 10^4$ Hz.
b. Light having $\lambda = 10$ nm is of higher energy than light having $\lambda = 1000$ nm.
c. Blue light is of higher energy than red light.

13.13 Higher wavenumbers are proportional to higher frequencies and higher energies.

a. IR light with a wavenumber of 3000 cm^{-1} is higher in energy than IR light with a wavenumber of 1500 cm^{-1}.
b. IR light having $\lambda = 10$ μm is higher in energy than IR light having $\lambda = 20$ μm.

13.14 Stronger bonds absorb at a higher wavenumber. Bonds to lighter atoms (H versus D) absorb at higher wavenumber.

a. $CH_3-C\equiv C-CH_2CH_3$ or $CH_2=C(CH_3)_2$
↑ stronger bond, higher wavenumber

b. CH_3-H or CH_3-D
↑ lighter atom H, higher wavenumber

13.15 Cyclopentane and 1-pentene are both composed of C–C and C–H bonds, but 1-pentene also has a C=C bond. This difference will give the IR of 1-pentene an additional peak at 1650 cm^{-1} (for the C=C). 1-Pentene will also show C–H absorptions for sp^2 hybridized C–H bonds at 3150–3000 cm^{-1}.

13.16 Look at the functional groups in each compound below to explain how each IR is different.

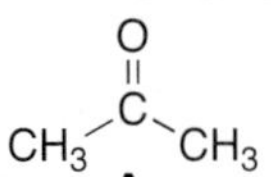

A

$CH_3OCH=CH_2$

B

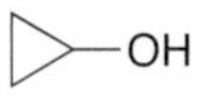

C

C=O peak at ~1700 cm^{-1} | C=C peak at 1650 cm^{-1}, C_{sp^2}–H at 3150–3000 cm^{-1} | O–H peak at 3200–3600 cm^{-1}

13.17 a. Compound **A** has peaks at ~3150 (sp^2 hybridized C–H), 3000–2850 (sp^3 hybridized C–H), and 1650 (C=C) cm^{-1}.

b. Compound **B** has a peak at 3000–2850 (sp^3 hybridized C–H) cm^{-1}.

13.18 All compounds show an absorption at 3000–2850 cm^{-1} due to the sp^3 hybridized C–H bonds. Additional peaks in the functional group region for each compound are shown.

a.

no additional peaks

b.
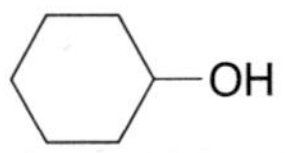

O–H bond at 3600–3200 cm^{-1}

c.
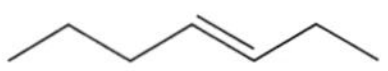

Csp^2–H at 3150–3000 cm^{-1}
C=C bond at 1650 cm^{-1}

d.
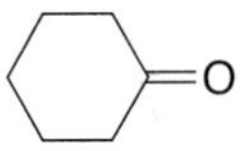

C=O bond at ~1700 cm^{-1}

e.
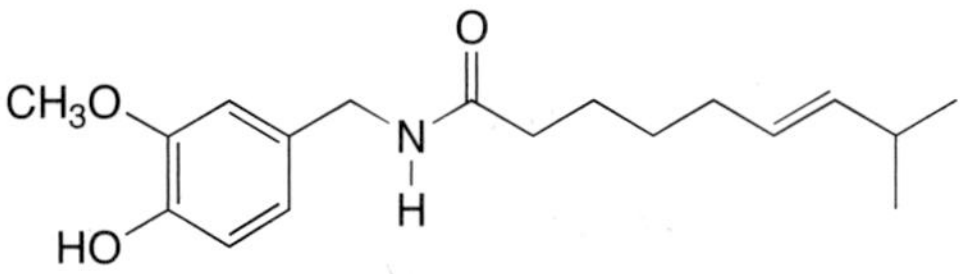

O–H at 3600–3200 cm^{-1}
N–H at 3500–3200 cm^{-1}
Csp^2–H at 3150–3000 cm^{-1}
C=O at ~1700 cm^{-1}
C=C at 1650 cm^{-1}
aromatic ring at 1600, 1500 cm^{-1}

13.19

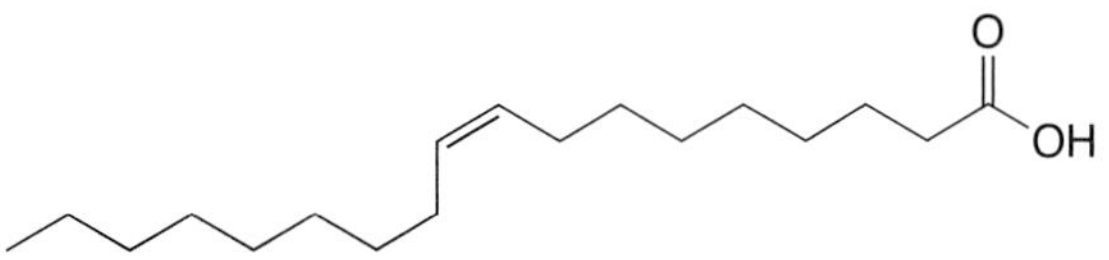

Csp^2–H at 3150–3000 cm^{-1}
Csp^3–H at 3000–2850 cm^{-1}
C=O at ~1700 cm^{-1}
C=C at 1650 cm^{-1}
O–H above 3000 cm^{-1}

[The OH of a COOH is much broader than the OH of an alcohol and occurs at 3500–2500 cm^{-1} (see Chapter 19).]

13.20 Possible structures are (a) $CH_3COOCH_2CH_3$ and (c) $CH_3CH_2COOCH_3$. Compounds (b) and (d) also have an OH group that would give a strong absorption at ~3600–3200 cm^{-1}, which is absent in the IR spectrum of **X,** thus excluding them as possibilities.

13.21

a. Hydrocarbon with a molecular ion at $m/z = 68$
IR absorptions at 3310 cm^{-1} = Csp–H bond
3000–2850 cm^{-1} = Csp^3–H bonds
2120 cm^{-1} = C≡C bond
Molecular formula: C_5H_8

$H-C{\equiv}C-CH_2CH_2CH_3$ or $H-C{\equiv}C-CH(CH_3)CH_3$

b. Compound with C, H, and O with a molecular ion at $m/z = 60$
IR absorptions at 3600–3200 cm^{-1} = O–H bond
3000–2850 cm^{-1} = Csp^3–H bonds
Molecular formula: C_3H_8O

$CH_3CH_2CH_2-O-H$ or $CH_3CH(CH_3)-O-H$

13.22

a. 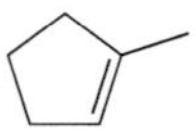

Csp^2–H at 3000–3150 cm^{-1}
Csp^3–H at 2850–3000 cm^{-1}
C=C at 1650 cm^{-1}

b. 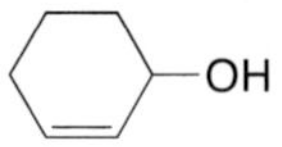

O–H at 3200–3600 cm^{-1}
Csp^2–H at 3000–3150 cm^{-1}
Csp^3–H at 2850–3000 cm^{-1}
C=C at 1650 cm^{-1}

13.23

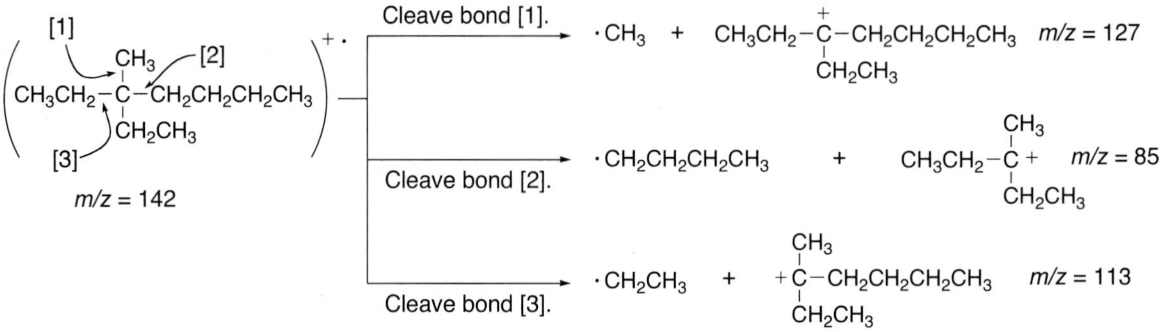
[1]
[2]
[3]
CH3
CH3CH2–C–CH2CH2CH2CH3
CH2CH3
m/z = 142
Cleave bond [1].
·CH3 + CH3CH2–C–CH2CH2CH2CH3 m/z = 127
CH2CH3
Cleave bond [2].
·CH2CH2CH2CH3 + CH3CH2–C+ m/z = 85
CH3
CH2CH3
Cleave bond [3].
·CH2CH3 + +C–CH2CH2CH2CH3 m/z = 113
CH3
CH2CH3

13.24

a. 

molecular formula: C_6H_6
molecular ion (*m/z*): **78**

c. 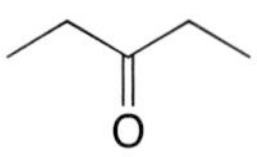

molecular formula: $C_5H_{10}O$
molecular ion (*m/z*): **86**

e. $(CH_3)_3CCH(Br)CH(CH_3)_2$

molecular formula: $C_8H_{17}Br$
molecular ions (*m/z*): **192, 194**

b. 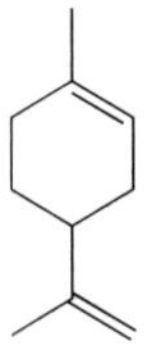

molecular formula: $C_{10}H_{16}$
molecular ion (*m/z*): **136**

d. 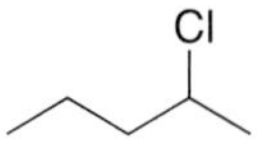
Cl

molecular formula: $C_5H_{11}Cl$
molecular ions (*m/z*): **106, 108**

13.25

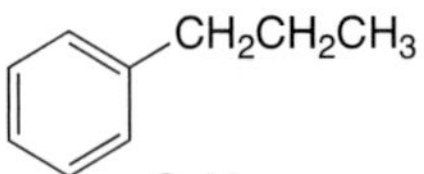
CH2CH2CH3

C_9H_{12}
molecular weight = 120

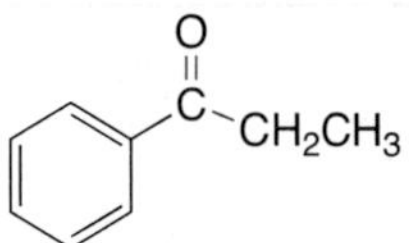
O
C
CH2CH3

$C_9H_{10}O$
molecular weight = 134

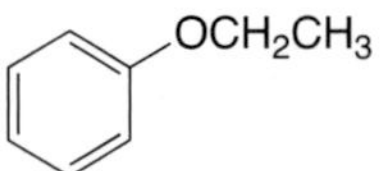
OCH2CH3

$C_8H_{10}O$
molecular weight = 122

13.26 Examples are given for each molecular ion.

a. molecular ion 102: C_8H_6, $C_6H_{14}O$, $C_5H_{10}O_2$, $C_5H_{14}N_2$
b. molecular ion 98: C_8H_2, C_7H_{14}, $C_6H_{10}O$, $C_5H_6O_2$
c. molecular ion 119: C_8H_9N, $C_6H_5N_3$
d. molecular ion 74: C_6H_2, $C_4H_{10}O$, $C_3H_6O_2$

13.27 Likely molecular formula, C_8H_{16} (one degree of unsaturation—one ring or one π bond).

Four structures with m/z = 112

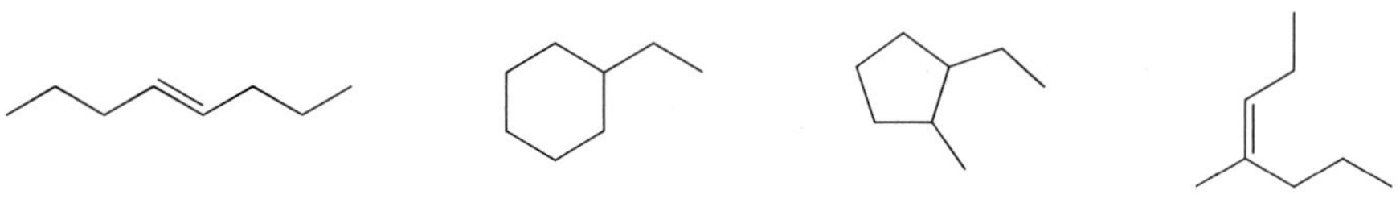

13.28

CH_3-CH-CO_2CH_3
Cl
B
$C_4H_7O_2Cl$
molecular weight: **122, 124**
should show 2 peaks for the molecular ion with a **3:1 ratio**

Mass spectrum [1]

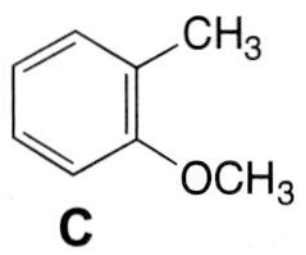

C
$C_8H_{10}O$
molecular weight: **122**

Mass spectrum [2]

$CH_3CH_2CH_2Br$
A
C_3H_7Br
molecular weight: **122, 124**
should show 2 peaks for the molecular ion with a **1:1 ratio**

Mass spectrum [3]

13.29

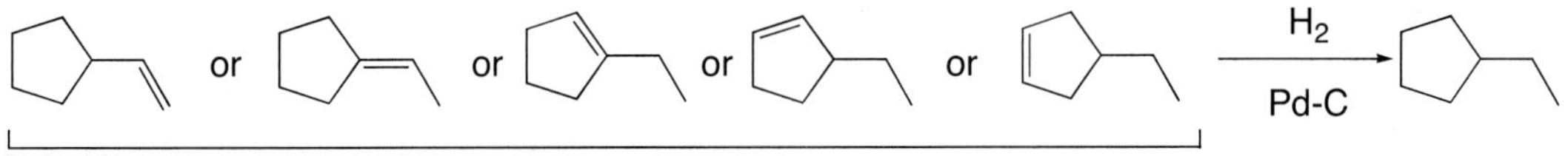

Possible structures
C_7H_{12}
(exact mass 96.0940)

13.30

a.

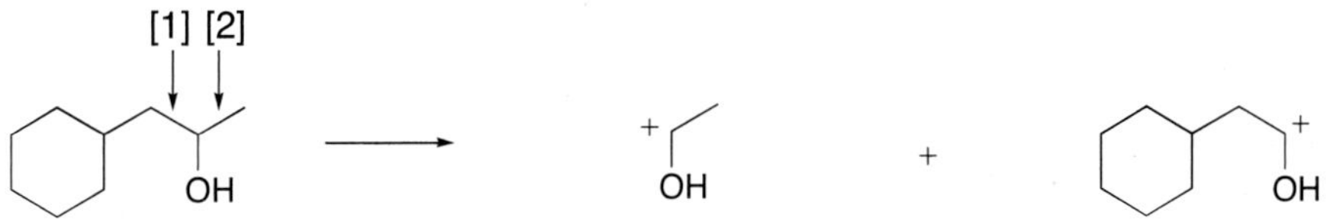

(from cleavage of bond [1]) (from cleavage of bond [2])

b.

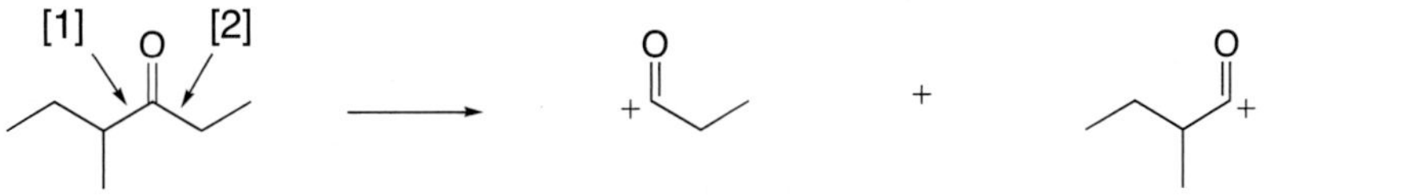

(from cleavage of bond [1]) (from cleavage of bond [2])

c.

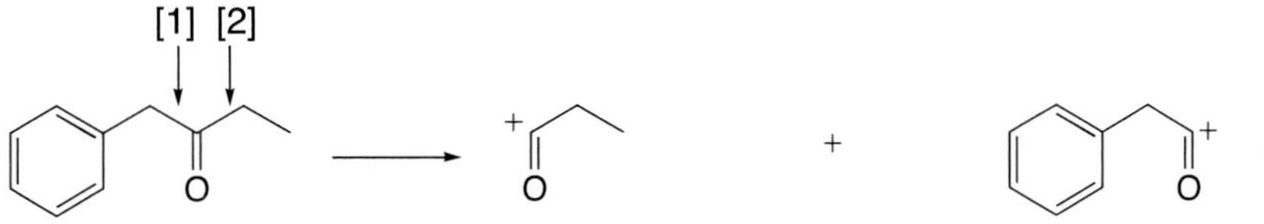

(from cleavage of bond [1]) (from cleavage of bond [2])

13.31

a.
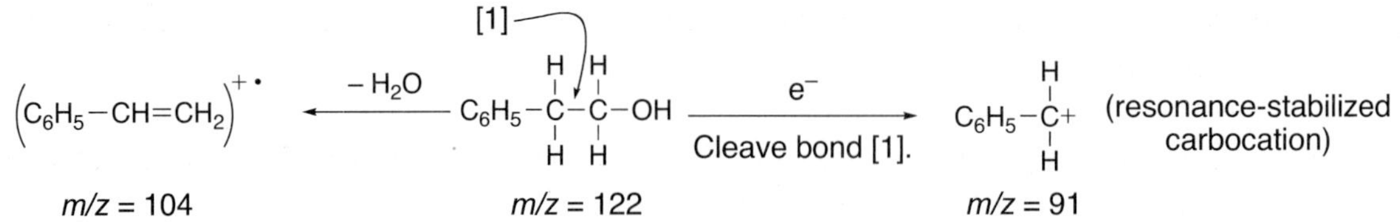

b.
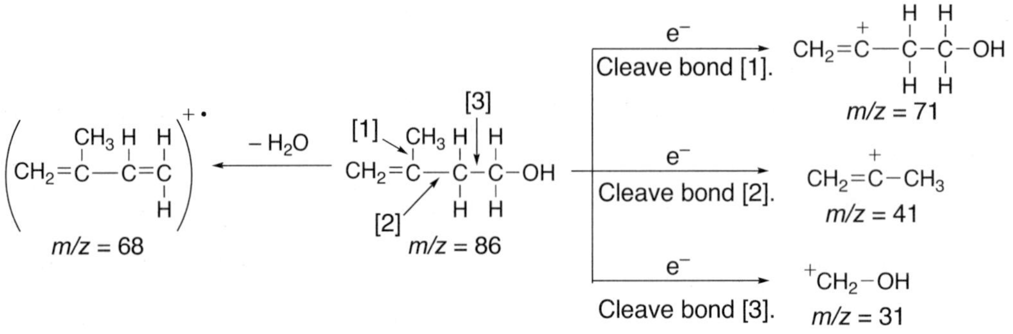

13.32

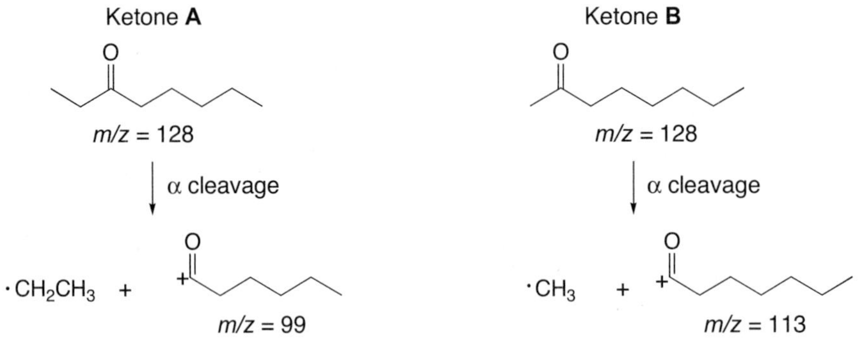

This is ketone **A** since α cleavage gives a fragment with *m/z* of 99.

This is ketone **B** since α cleavage gives a fragment with *m/z* of 113.

13.33 One possible structure is drawn for each set of data:

a. A compound that contains a benzene ring and has a molecular ion at *m/z* = 107

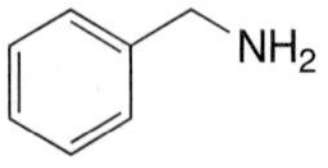

C_7H_9N

b. A hydrocarbon that contains only sp^3 hybridized carbons and a molecular ion at *m/z* = 84

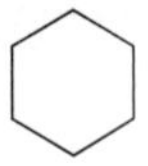

C_6H_{12}

c. A compound that contains a carbonyl group and gives a molecular ion at *m/z* = 114

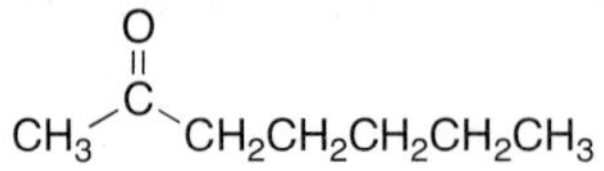

$C_7H_{14}O$

d. A compound that contains C, H, N, and O and has an exact mass for the molecular ion at 101.0841

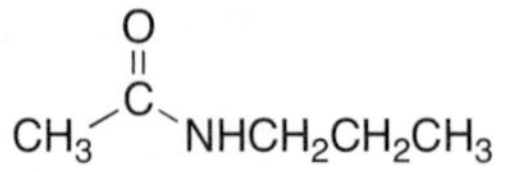

$C_5H_{11}NO$

13.34 Use the values given in Table 13.1 to calculate the exact mass of each compound. $C_8H_{11}NO_2$ (exact mass 153.0790) is the correct molecular formula.

13.35 Two isomers such as $CH_2{=}CHCH_2CH_2CH_2CH_3$ and $(CH_3)_2C{=}CHCH_2CH_3$ have the same molecular formulas and therefore give the same exact mass, so they are not distinguishable by their exact mass spectra.

13.36 Alpha cleavage of a 1° alcohol (RCH_2OH) forms an alkyl radical (R•) and a resonance-stabilized carbocation with $m/z = 31$.

$$^{+}CH_2OH \longleftrightarrow CH_2{=}\overset{+}{O}H \qquad m/z = 31$$

resonance-stabilized carbocation

13.37 An ether fragments by α cleavage because the resulting carbocation is resonance stabilized.

$(CH_3)_2CH \overset{[1]}{-} CH_2{-}O{-}CH_2 \overset{[2]}{-} CH_3$

Cleave bond [1]. → $(CH_3)_2\dot{C}H$ + $\overset{+}{C}H_2{-}\ddot{O}{-}CH_2{-}CH_3 \longleftrightarrow CH_2{=}\overset{+}{O}{-}CH_2{-}CH_3$

resonance-stabilized carbocations

Cleave bond [2]. → $\cdot CH_3$ + $(CH_3)_2CH{-}CH_2{-}\ddot{O}{-}\overset{+}{C}H_2 \longleftrightarrow (CH_3)_2CH{-}CH_2{-}\overset{+}{O}{=}CH_2$

13.38

a. $(CH_3)_2C{=}O$ or $(CH_3)_2CH{-}OH$
stronger bond (C=O)
higher $\tilde{\nu}$ absorption

b. $(CH_3)_2C{=}NCH_3$ or $(CH_3)_2CH{-}NCH_3$
stronger bond (C=N)
higher $\tilde{\nu}$ absorption

c. 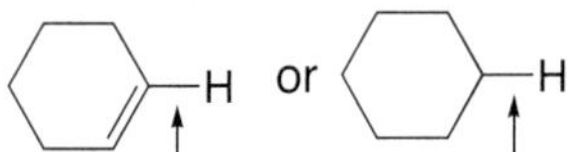
stronger bond
higher $\tilde{\nu}$ absorption

13.39 Locate the functional groups in each compound. Use Table 13.2 to determine what IR absorptions each would have.

a. 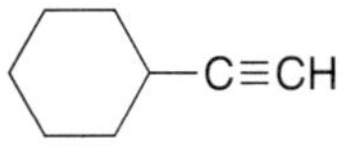
Csp–H at 3300 cm^{-1}
Csp^3–H at 2850–3000 cm^{-1}
C–C triple bond at 2250 cm^{-1}

b. 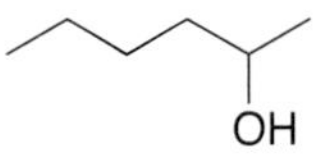
O–H at 3200–3600 cm^{-1}
Csp^3–H at 2850–3000 cm^{-1}

c. 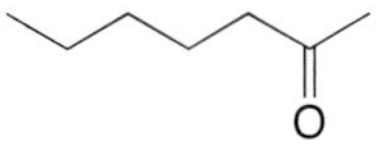
Csp^3–H at 2850–3000 cm^{-1}
C=O at 1700 cm^{-1}

d. 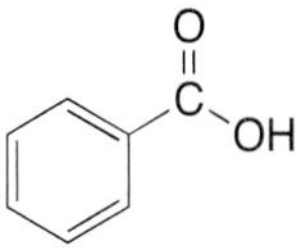
O–H at > 3000 cm^{-1}
Csp^2–H at 3000–3150 cm^{-1}
C=O at ~1700 cm^{-1}
phenyl group at 1600, 1500 cm^{-1}
[The OH of the RCOOH is even broader than the OH of an alcohol (3500–2500 cm^{-1}), as we will learn in Chapter 19.]

13.40

a.  and $HC{\equiv}CCH_2CH_2CH_3$

C=C bond, 1650 cm^{-1}, Csp^2–H at 3150–3000 cm^{-1}

C≡C bond, 2250 cm^{-1}, Csp–H at 3300 cm^{-1}

b. 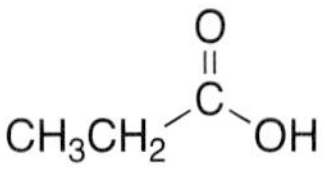 and 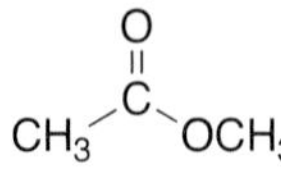

O–H bond, > 3000 cm^{-1}
[See note on OH in Answer 13.39d.]

no O–H bond

c. 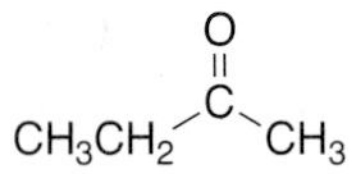

C=O bond
1700 cm^{-1}

and $CH_3CH{=}CHCH_2OH$
O–H bond
3200–3600 cm^{-1}
Csp^2–H at 3150–3000 cm^{-1}
C=C bond at 1650 cm^{-1}

d. 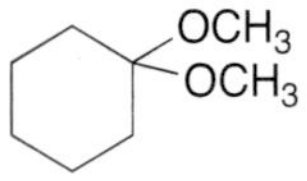

no C=O bond

and 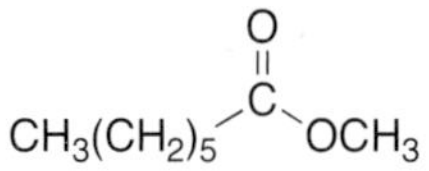

C=O bond
~1700 cm^{-1}

e. $CH_3C{\equiv}CCH_3$ and $CH_3CH_2C{\equiv}CH$

no C≡C absorption due to symmetry

Csp–H bond
3300 cm^{-1}
C≡C bond at ~2250 cm^{-1}

f. $HC{\equiv}CCH_2N(CH_2CH_3)_2$ and $CH_3(CH_2)_5C{\equiv}N$

Csp–H bond
3300 cm^{-1}

13.41 The IR absorptions above 1500 cm^{-1} are different for each of the narcotics.

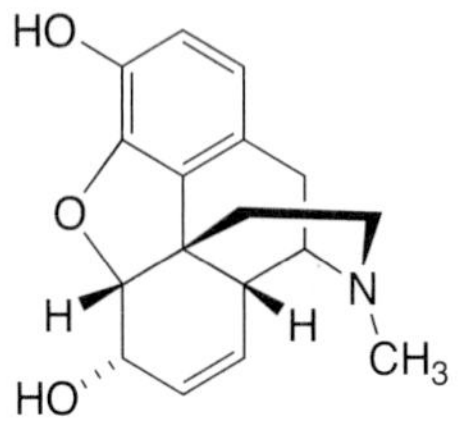

morphine

- O–H bond at ~3200–3600 cm^{-1}
- no C=O bond

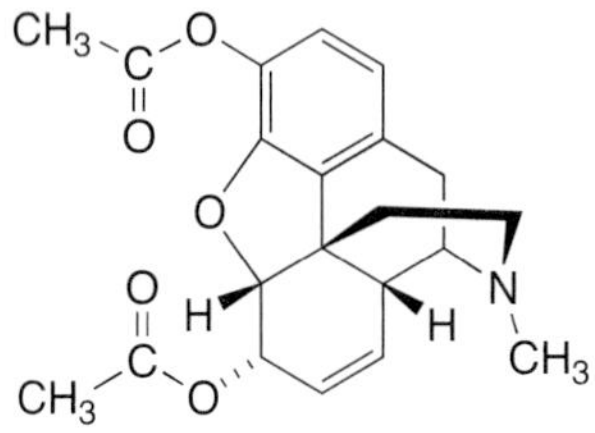

heroin

- C=O bond at ~1700 cm^{-1}
- no O–H bond

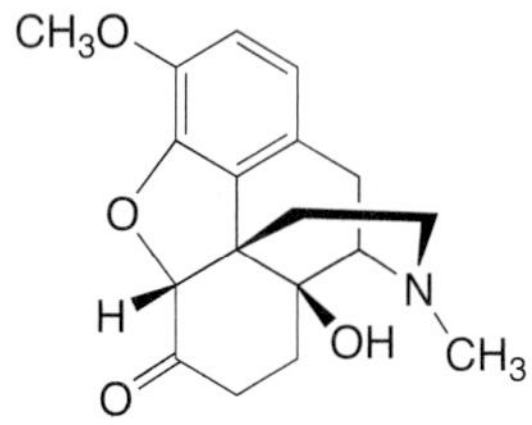

oxycodone

- C=O bond at ~1700 cm^{-1}
- O–H bond at ~3200–3600 cm^{-1}

13.42 Look for a **change in functional groups** from starting material to product to see how IR could be used to determine when the reaction is complete.

a. 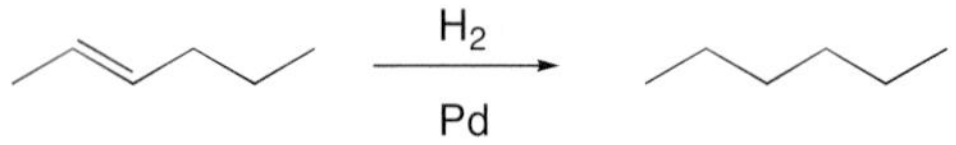

Loss of the C=C will be visible in the IR by disappearance of the peak at 1650 cm^{-1}.

b. 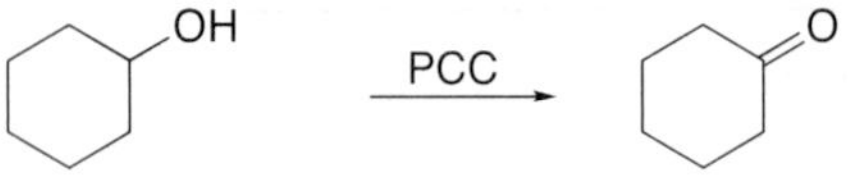

Loss of the O–H group will be visible in the IR by disappearance of the peak at 3200–3600 cm^{-1} and appearance of the C=O at ~1700 cm^{-1}.

c. 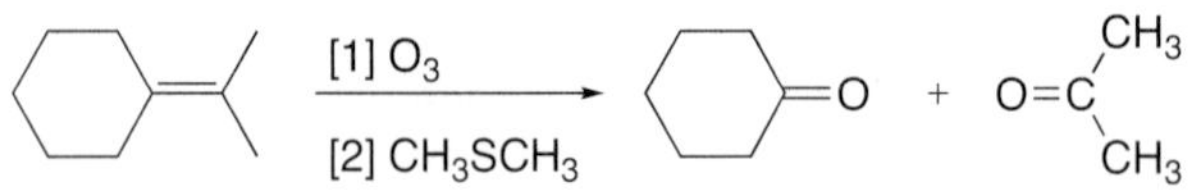

Loss of the C=C will be visible in the IR by disappearance of the peak at 1650 cm^{-1} and appearance of the C=O at ~1700 cm^{-1}.

d. 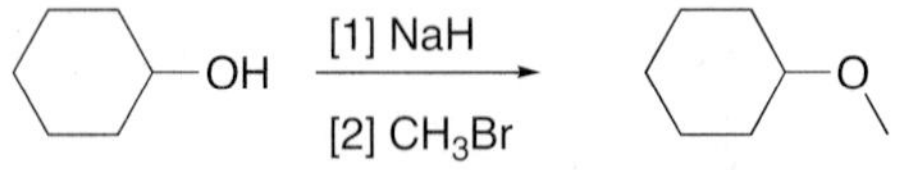

Loss of the O–H will be visible in the IR by disappearance of the peak at 3200–3600 cm^{-1}.

13.43 In addition to Csp^3–H at ~3000–2850 cm^{-1}:

Spectrum [1]:

CH_2=C(CH_3)$CH_2CH_2CH_2CH_3$ (**B**)
C=C peak at 1650 cm^{-1}
Csp^2–H at ~3150 cm^{-1}

Spectrum [2]:

$(CH_3CH_2)_3$COH (**F**)
OH at 3600–3200 cm^{-1}

Spectrum [3]:

$(CH_3)_2$CHOCH$(CH_3)_2$ (**D**)
No other peaks above 1500 cm^{-1}

Spectrum [4]:

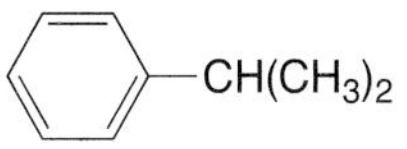

(**C**)
Csp^2–H at ~3150 cm^{-1}
Phenyl peaks at 1600 and 1500 cm^{-1}

Spectrum [5]:

$CH_3CH_2CH_2CH_2$COOH (**A**)
OH at ~3500–2500 cm^{-1}
C=O at ~1700 cm^{-1}

Spectrum [6]:

CH_3COOC$(CH_3)_3$ (**E**)
C=O at ~1700 cm^{-1}

13.44

a. Compound with a molecular ion at m/z = 72
IR absorption at 1725 cm^{-1} = C=O bond
Molecular formula: C_4H_8O

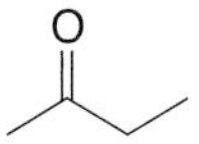

b. Compound with a molecular ion at m/z = 55
The odd molecular ion means an odd number of N's present. Molecular formula: C_3H_5N
IR absorption at 2250 cm^{-1} = C≡N bond
$CH_3CH_2C \equiv N$

c. Compound with a molecular ion at m/z = 74
IR absorption at 3600–3200 cm^{-1} = O–H bond
Molecular formula: $C_4H_{10}O$

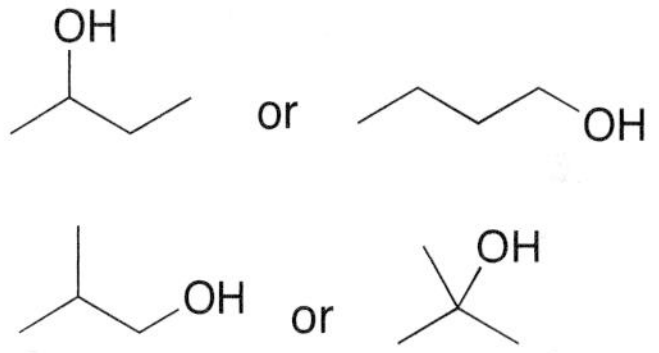

13.45

Chiral hydrocarbon with a molecular ion at m/z = 82
Molecular formula: C_6H_{10}
IR absorptions at 3300 cm^{-1} = Csp–H bond
3000–2850 cm^{-1} = Csp^3–H bonds
2250 cm^{-1} = C≡C bond

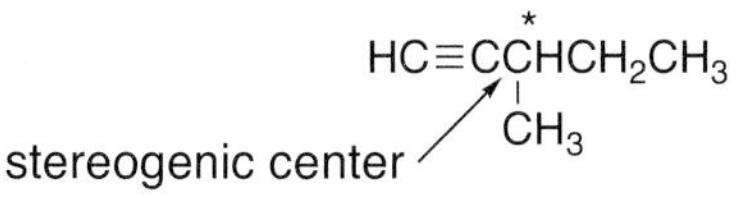

Two possible enantiomers:

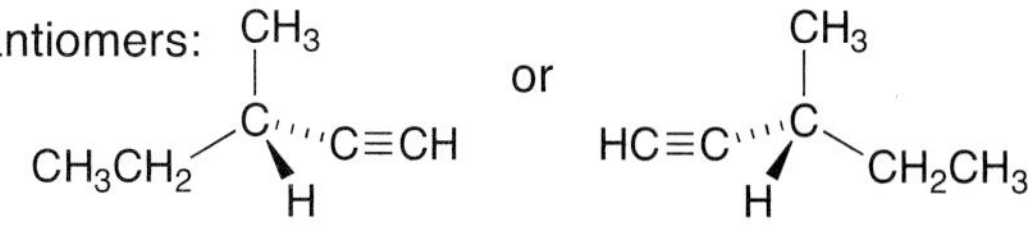

13.46 The chiral compound **Y** has a strong absorption at 2970–2840 cm^{-1} in its IR spectrum due to sp^3 hybridized C–H bonds. The two peaks of equal intensity at 136 and 138 indicate the presence of a Br atom. The molecular formula is C_4H_9Br. Only one constitutional isomer of this molecular formula has a stereogenic center:

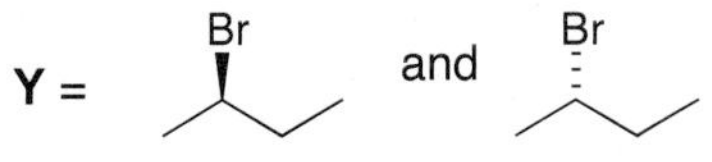

two possible enantiomers

13.47 The molecular ion of 192 suggests $C_{12}H_{16}O_2$ as a possible molecular formula. IR absorption at 1721 cm^{-1} is due to a C=O, and the absorptions around 3000 cm^{-1} are due to C_{sp^2}–H and C_{sp^3}–H. The compound is an ester, formed in the following manner.

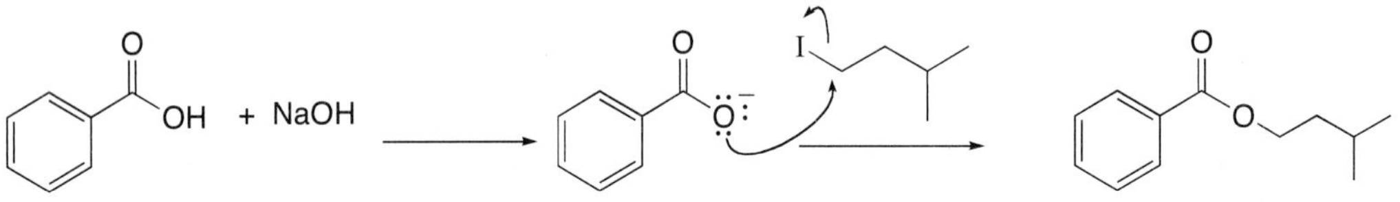

H

$C_{12}H_{16}O_2$

13.48

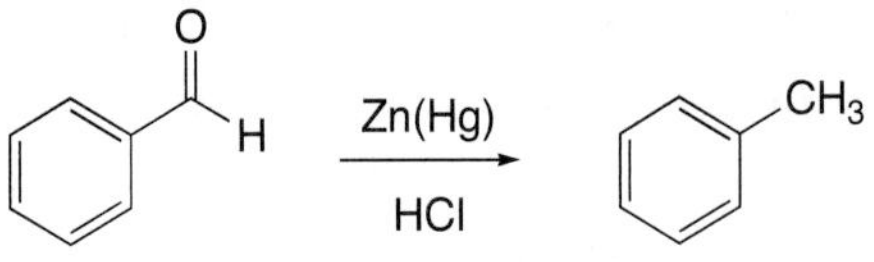

Z

m/z = 92; molecular formula C_7H_8
IR absorptions at:
3150–2950 cm^{-1} = C_{sp^3}–H and C_{sp^2}–H bonds
1605 cm^{-1} and 1496 cm^{-1} due to phenyl group

13.49

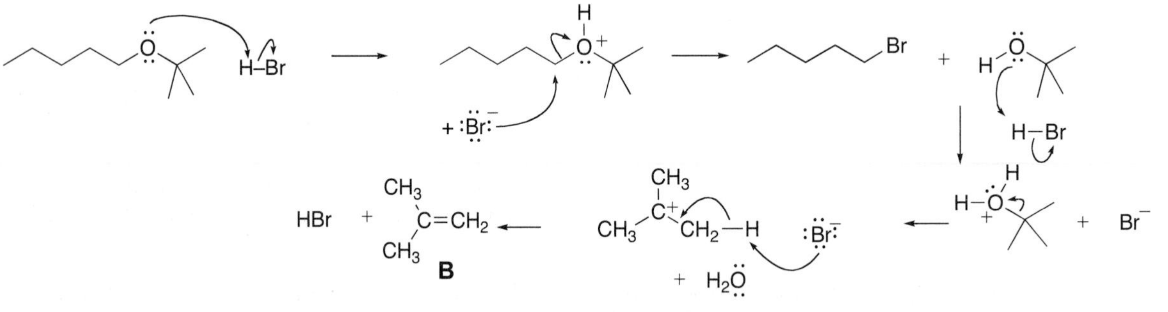

13.50 The molecular ion of 144 suggests $C_8H_{16}O_2$ as a possible molecular formula for **X.** The IR absorption at 1739 cm^{-1} is due to a C=O, and the absorptions at less than 3000 cm^{-1} are due to C_{sp^3}–H.

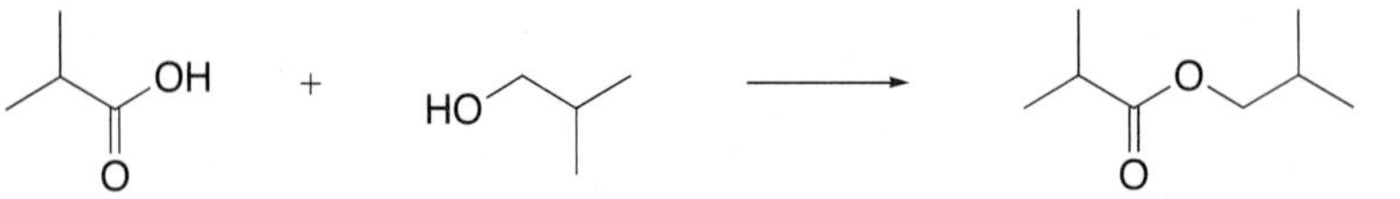

2-methyl-1-propanol

$C_8H_{16}O_2$
X
possible structure

13.51

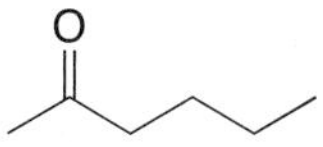

fragments:

J

$C_6H_{12}O$
m/z = 100
IR absorption at 2962 cm^{-1} = Csp^3–H bonds
1718 cm^{-1} = C=O bond

α cleavage product *m/z* = 43 α cleavage product *m/z* = 85

The fragment at *m/z* = 57 could be due to $(C_4H_9)^+$ or $(C_3H_5O)^+$.

13.52

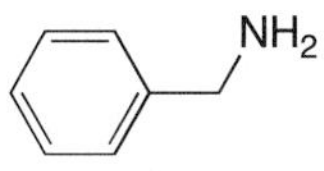

K

C_7H_9N
m/z = 107
IR absorptions at 3373 and 3290 cm^{-1} = N–H
3062 cm^{-1} = Csp^2–H bonds
2920 cm^{-1} = Csp^3–H bonds
1600 cm^{-1} = benzene ring

The odd molecular ion indicates the presence of a N atom.

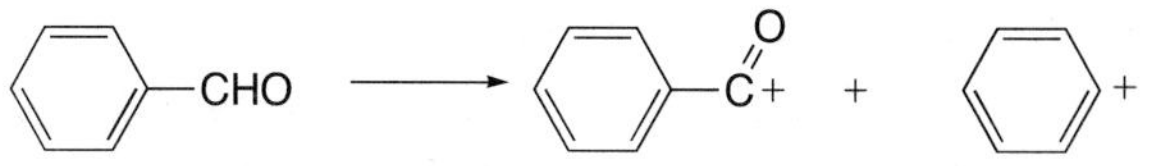

L
C_7H_6O
m/z = 106

m/z = 105 *m/z* = 77

IR absorption at 3068 cm^{-1} = Csp^2–H bonds on ring
2850 cm^{-1} = Csp^3–H bond
2820 cm^{-1} and 2736 cm^{-1} = C–H of RCHO (Appendix E)
1703 cm^{-1} = C=O bond
1600 cm^{-1} = aromatic ring

13.53

Possible structures of **P**:

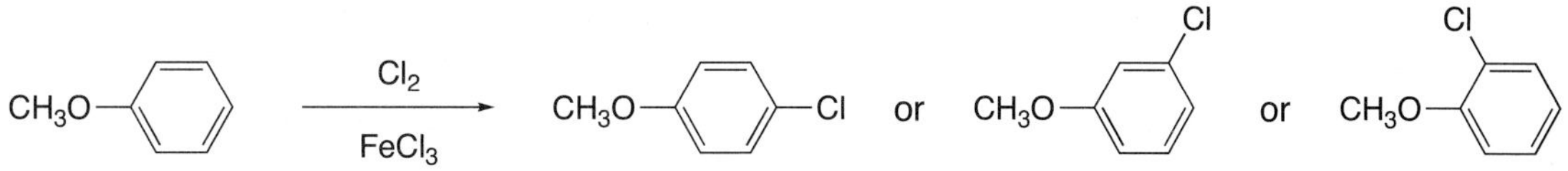

C_7H_7ClO

m/z = 142, 144
IR absorption at 3096–2837 cm^{-1} = Csp^3–H bonds and Csp^2–H bonds
1582 cm^{-1} and 1494 cm^{-1} = benzene ring

The peak at M + 2 shows the presence of Cl or Br. Since Cl_2 is a reactant, the compound presumably contains Cl.

13.54 The mass spectrum has a molecular ion at 71. The odd mass suggests the presence of an odd number of N atoms; likely formula, C_4H_9N. The IR absorption at ~3300 cm^{-1} is due to N–H and the 3000–2850 cm^{-1} is due to sp^3 hybridized C–H bonds.

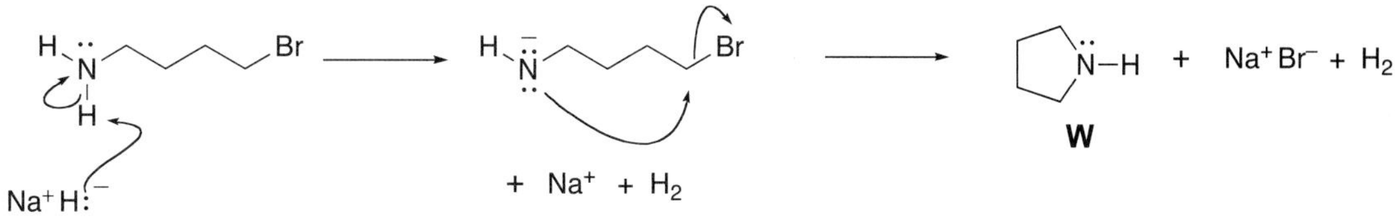

W

13.55 Because the carbonyl absorption of an amide is at lower wavenumber than the carbonyl absorption of an ester, the C=O of the amide must be weaker and have more single bond character. This can be explained by resonance. Although both an ester and amide are resonance stabilized, the N atom of the amide is more basic, making it more willing to donate its electron pair.

This form contributes more to the hybrid, so there is more single bond character.

This form contributes less to the hybrid.

Since the amide carbonyl has more single bond character, the bond is weaker and it absorbs at lower wavenumber.

13.56 The α,β-unsaturated carbonyl compound has three resonance structures, two of which place a single bond between the C and O atoms. This means that the C–O bond has partial single bond character, making it weaker than a regular C=O bond, and moving the absorption to lower wavenumber.

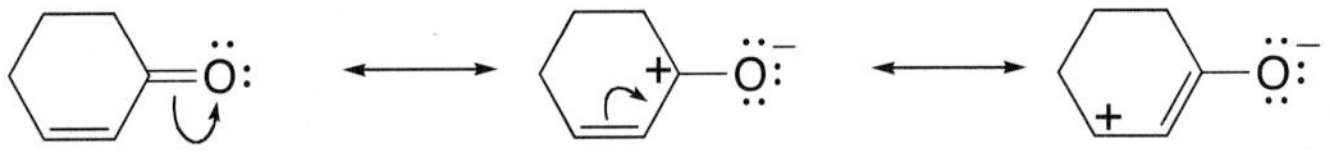

three resonance structures for 2-cyclohexenone

13.57 If a ketone carbonyl absorbs at lower wavenumber than an aldehyde carbonyl, the ketone carbonyl is weaker and has more single bond character. This can be explained by the fact that R groups are electron donating and stabilize an adjacent (+) charge.

The two R groups stabilize the (+) charge, so this form contributes more to the hybrid than the charge-separated resonance form of an aldehyde.

One R group stabilizes the (+) charge less.

As a result, the charge-separated resonance form of a ketone, which contains a C–O single bond, contributes more to the hybrid of a ketone, making the C=O weaker and shifting the absorption to lower wavenumber.

13.58

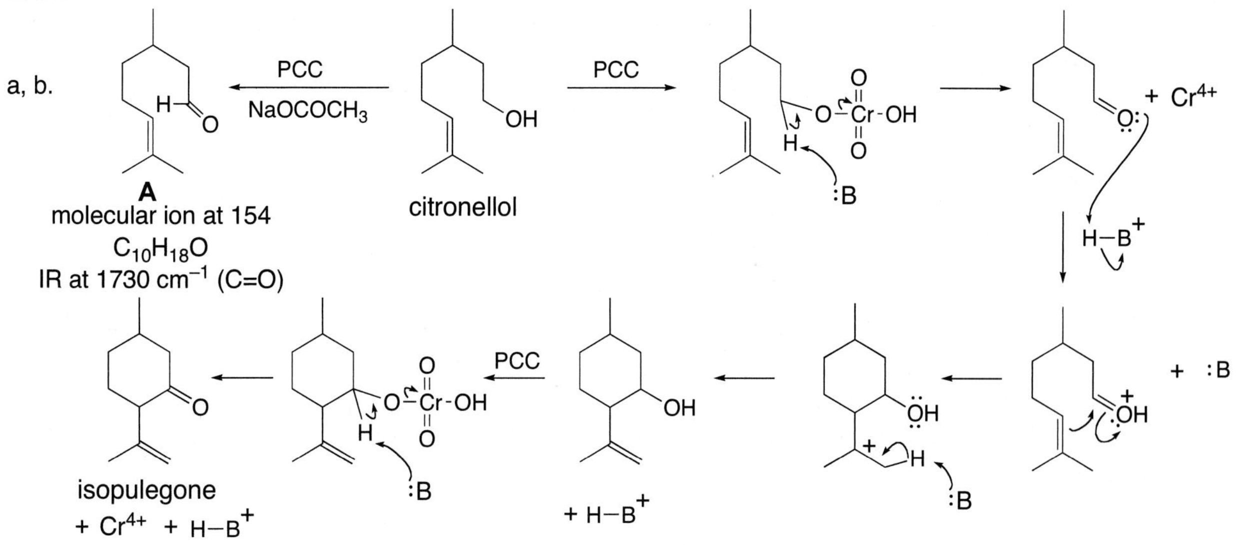
a, b.
PCC
NaOCOCH3
PCC
OH
A
molecular ion at 154
C10H18O
IR at 1730 cm−1 (C=O)
citronellol
O–Cr–OH
:B
+ Cr4+
H–B+
+ :B
PCC
OH
isopulegone
+ Cr4+ + H–B+
+ H–B+

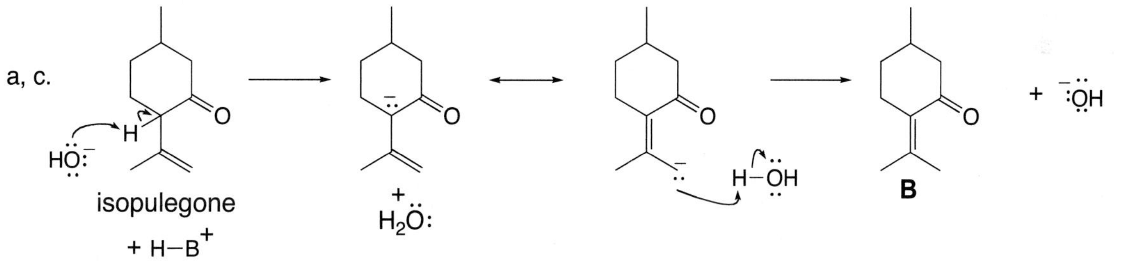
a, c.
HO:−
isopulegone
+ H–B+
H2O:
H–OH
B
+ :OH

Chapter 14 Nuclear Magnetic Resonance Spectroscopy

Chapter Review

^{1}H NMR spectroscopy

[1] The **number of signals** equals the number of different types of protons (14.2).

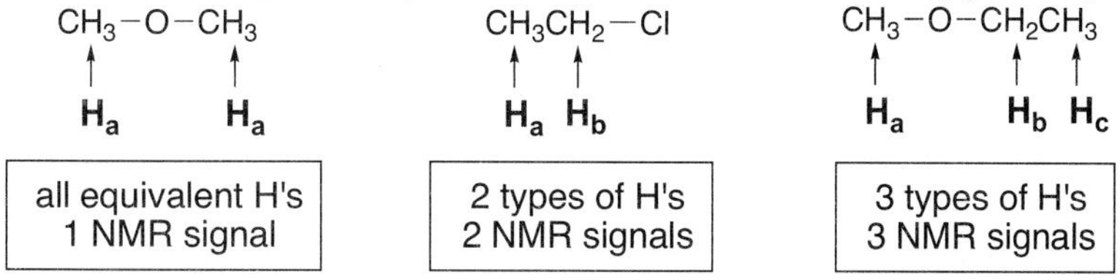
CH3–O–CH3
Ha Ha
all equivalent H's 1 NMR signal
CH3CH2–Cl
Ha Hb
2 types of H's 2 NMR signals
CH3–O–CH2CH3
Ha Hb Hc
3 types of H's 3 NMR signals

[2] The **position of a signal** (its chemical shift) is determined by shielding and deshielding effects.

- Shielding shifts an absorption upfield; deshielding shifts an absorption downfield.
- Electronegative atoms withdraw electron density, deshield a nucleus, and shift an absorption downfield (14.3).

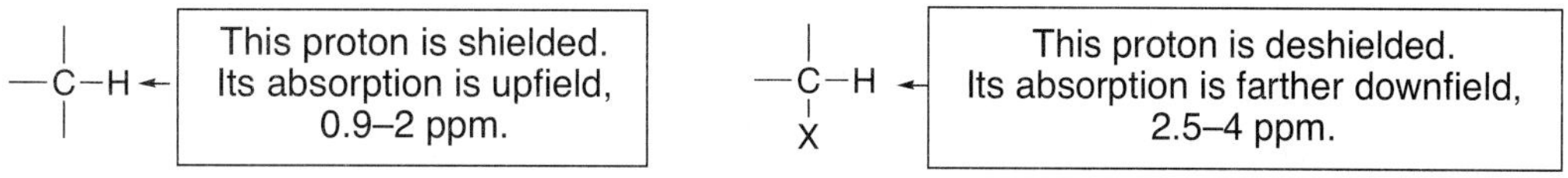
This proton is shielded. Its absorption is upfield, 0.9–2 ppm.
X
This proton is deshielded. Its absorption is farther downfield, 2.5–4 ppm.

- Loosely held π electrons can either shield or deshield a nucleus. Protons on benzene rings and double bonds are deshielded and absorb downfield, whereas protons on triple bonds are shielded and absorb upfield (14.4).

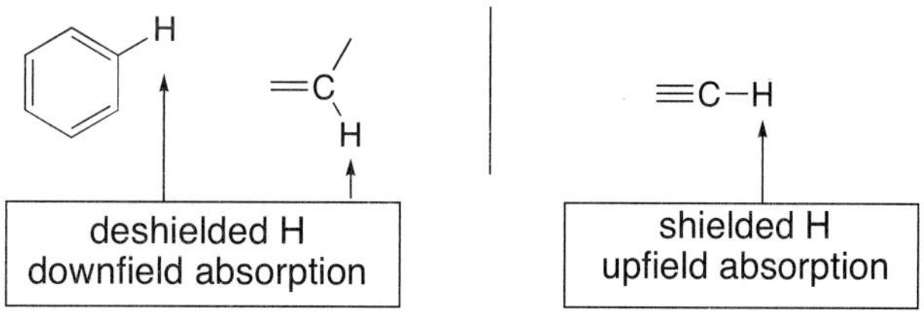
deshielded H downfield absorption
shielded H upfield absorption

[3] The **area under an NMR signal** is proportional to the number of absorbing protons (14.5).

[4] **Spin–spin splitting** tells about nearby nonequivalent protons (14.6–14.8).

- Equivalent protons do not split each other's signals.
- A set of n nonequivalent protons on the same carbon or adjacent carbons split an NMR signal into $n + 1$ peaks.
- OH and NH protons do not cause splitting (14.9).
- When an absorbing proton has two sets of nearby nonequivalent protons that are equivalent to each other, use the $n + 1$ rule to determine splitting.
- When an absorbing proton has two sets of nearby nonequivalent protons that are not equivalent to each other, the number of peaks in the NMR signal = $(n + 1)(m + 1)$. In flexible alkyl chains, peak overlap often occurs, resulting in $n + m + 1$ peaks in an NMR signal.

^{13}C NMR spectroscopy (14.11)

[1] The number of signals equals the number of different types of carbon atoms. All signals are single lines.

[2] The relative position of ^{13}C signals is determined by shielding and deshielding effects.

- Carbons that are sp^3 hybridized are shielded and absorb upfield.
- Electronegative elements (N, O, and X) shift absorptions downfield.
- The carbons of alkenes and benzene rings absorb downfield.
- Carbonyl carbons are highly deshielded, and absorb farther downfield than other carbon types.

Practice Test on Chapter Review

1. a. Which of the following statements is true about ¹H NMR absorptions?
   1. A signal that occurs at 1800 Hz on a 300 MHz NMR spectrometer occurs at 3000 Hz on a 500 MHz NMR spectrometer.
   2. A signal that occurs at 3.3 ppm on a 60 MHz NMR absorbs at 198 Hz upfield from TMS.
   3. A signal that occurs at 600 Hz is downfield from a signal that occurs at 800 Hz.
   4. Statements (1) and (2) are both true.
   5. Statements (1), (2), and (3) are all true.

   b. Which of the following statements is true about ¹H NMR spectroscopy?
   1. Electronegative elements shield a nucleus so an absorption shifts downfield.
   2. A triplet is due to a proton that has four adjacent nonequivalent protons.
   3. Circulating π electrons create a magnetic field that reinforces the applied field in the vicinity of the protons in benzene.
   4. Statements (1) and (2) are both true.
   5. Statements (1), (2), and (3) are all true.

2. How many different types of protons does each of the following molecules contain?

a. 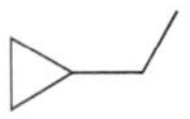

c. $(CH_3)_2C{=}CHCH_3$

e. 

g. 

b. 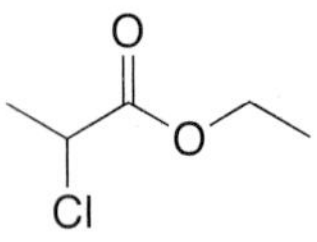

d. 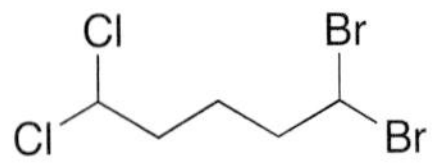

f. 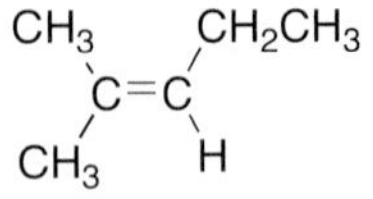

h. 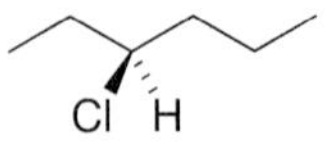

3. Into how many peaks will each of the circled protons be split in a proton NMR spectrum?

a. 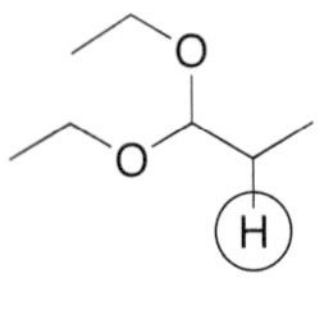

c. 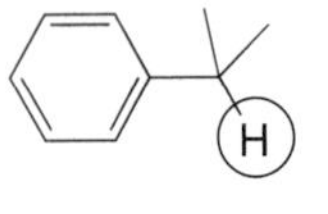

e. 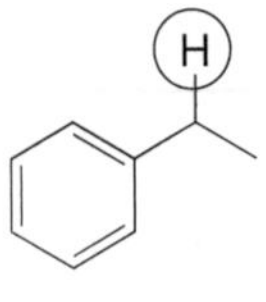

g. 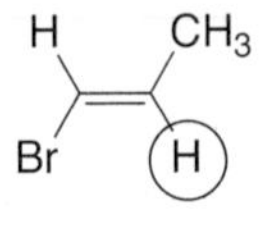

b. 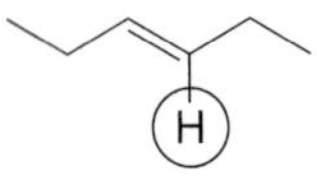

d. 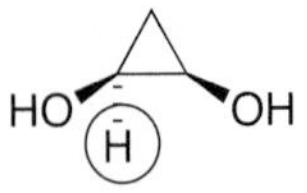

f. 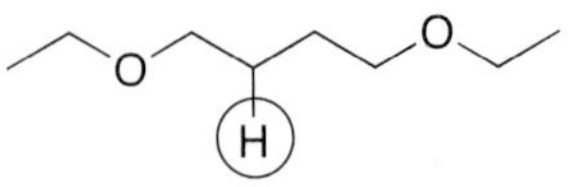

4. How many lines are presents in the ^{13}C NMR spectrum of each compound?

a. 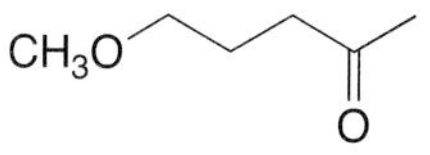

c. 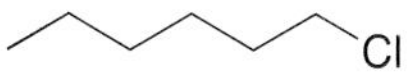

e. 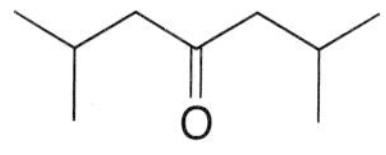

b. $CH_3CH_2CH_2CH_2CH_2CH_2CH_2CH_3$

d. 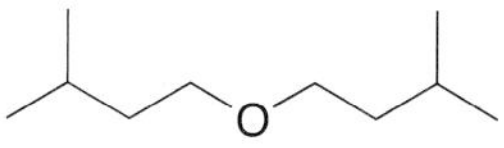

f. 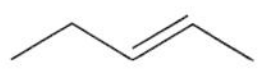

5. With reference to the ^1H NMR absorptions in the following compound, (a) which proton absorbs farthest upfield; (b) which proton absorbs farthest downfield?

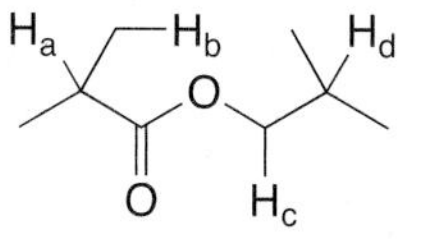

6. With reference to the ^{13}C NMR absorptions in the following compound, (a) which carbon absorbs farthest downfield; (b) which carbon absorbs farthest upfield?

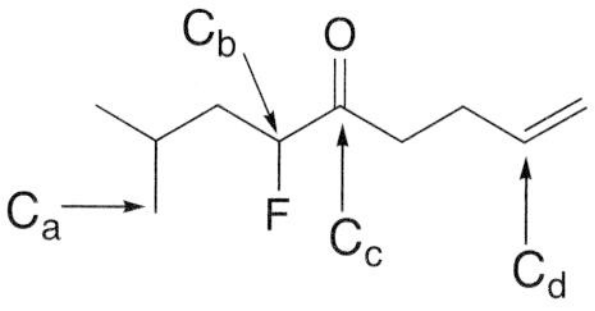

Answers to Practice Test

1. a. 1	2. a. 5	3. a. 8	4. a. 6	5. a. H_b	6. a. C_c
b. 3	b. 5	b. 3	b. 4	b. H_c	b. C_a
	c. 4	c. 7	c. 6		
	d. 5	d. 4	d. 4		
	e. 4	e. 4	e. 4		
	f. 5	f. 3	f. 5		
	g. 3	g. 8			
	h. 9				

Answers to Problems

14.1 Use the formula δ = [observed chemical shift (Hz)/ν of the NMR (MHz)] to calculate the chemical shifts.

a. **CH_3 protons:**
δ = [1715 Hz] / [500 MHz]
= **3.43 ppm**

OH proton:
δ = [1830 Hz] / [500 MHz]
= **3.66 ppm**

b. The positive direction of the δ scale is downfield from TMS. The CH_3 protons absorb upfield from the OH proton.

14.2 Calculate the chemical shifts as in Answer 14.1.

a. one signal:
δ = [1017 Hz] / [300 MHz]
= **3.39 ppm**

second signal:
δ = [1065 Hz] / [300 MHz]
= **3.55 ppm**

b. one signal:
3.39 = [*x* Hz] / [500 MHz]
x = **1695 Hz**

second signal:
3.55 = [*x* Hz] / [500 MHz]
x = **1775 Hz**

14.3 To determine if two H's are equivalent replace each by an atom X. If this yields the same compound or mirror images, the two H's are equivalent. Each kind of H will give one NMR signal.

a. CH_3CH_3
1 kind of H
1 NMR signal

b. $CH_3CH_2CH_3$
2 kinds of H's
2 NMR signals

c. $CH_3CH_2CH_2CH_3$
2 kinds of H's
2 NMR signals

d. $(CH_3)_2CHCH(CH_3)_2$
2 kinds of H's
2 NMR signals

e. $CH_3CH_2CO_2CH_2CH_3$
4 kinds of H's
4 NMR signals

f. $CH_3OCH_2CH(CH_3)_2$
4 kinds of H's
4 NMR signals

g. $CH_3(CH_2)_7Cl$
8 kinds of H's
8 NMR signals

h. $CH_3CH_2CH_2OH$
4 kinds of H's
4 NMR signals

14.4 Draw in all of the H's and compare them. If two H's are cis and trans to the same group, they are equivalent.

a. 4 identical H's
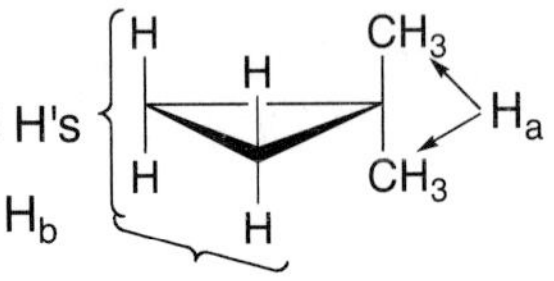

2 NMR signals

b.
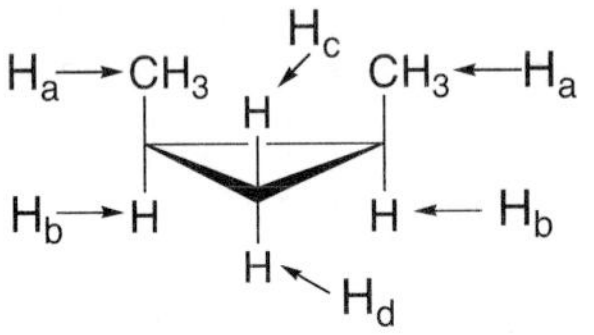

4 NMR signals

c.
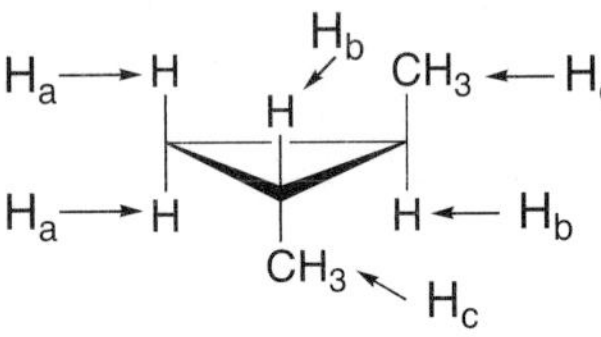

3 NMR signals

14.5 If replacement of H with X yields enantiomers, the protons are **enantiotopic.**
If replacement of H with X yields diastereomers, the protons are **diastereotopic.** In general, if the compound has **one stereogenic center,** the protons in a CH_2 group are **diastereotopic.**

a. $CH_3CH_2CH_2CH_2CH_2CH_3$

↓ replacement of H with X

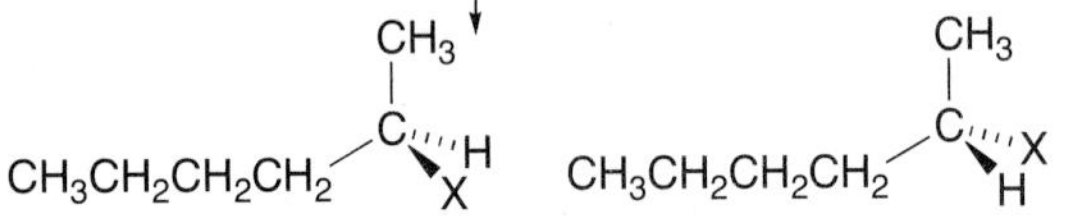

enantiomers =
enantiotopic H's

b. $CH_3CH_2CH_2CH_2CH_3$

↓ replacement of H with X

$CH_3CH_2CHCH_2CH_3$ (with X on the central C) no stereogenic center
neither enantiotopic nor diastereotopic

c. $CH_3CH(OH)CH_2CH_2CH_3$

Pick one configuration at the existing stereogenic center.

replacement of H with X

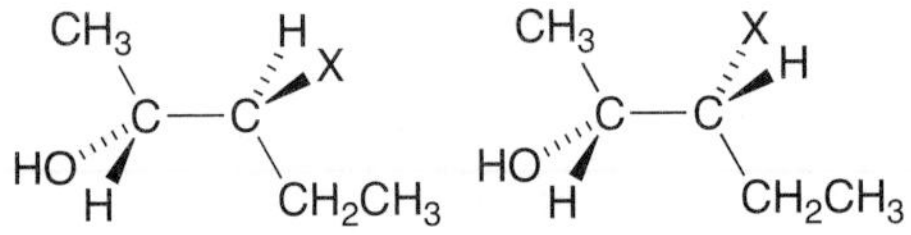

diastereomers =
diastereotopic H's

14.6 The two protons of a CH_2 group are different from each other if the compound has one stereogenic center. Replace one proton with X and compare the products.

a. The stereogenic center makes the H's in the CH_2 group diastereotopic and therefore different from each other.

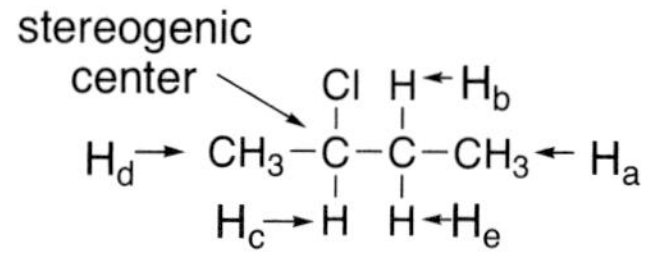

5 NMR signals

b.

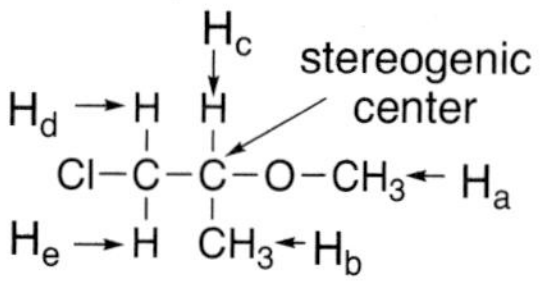

5 NMR signals

c.

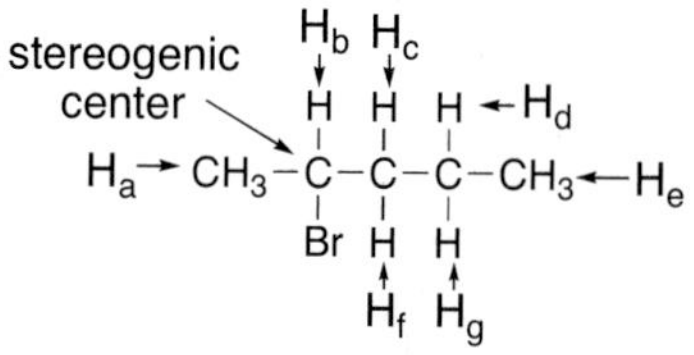

7 NMR signals

14.7 Decreased electron density deshields a nucleus and the absorption goes downfield. Absorption also shifts downfield with increasing alkyl substitution.

a. FC**H₂**CH₂CH₂Cl

F is more electronegative than Cl. The CH_2 group adjacent to the F is more deshielded and the H's will absorb farther downfield.

b. CH₃CH₂CH₂C**H₂**OCH₃

The CH_2 group adjacent to the O will absorb farther downfield because it is closer to the electronegative O atom.

c. C**H₃**OC(CH₃)₃

The CH_3 group bonded to the O atom will absorb farther downfield.

14.8

a. 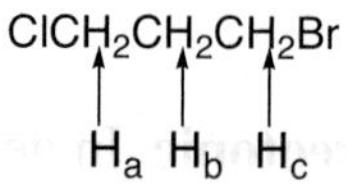

3 types of protons:
$H_b < H_c < H_a$

b. 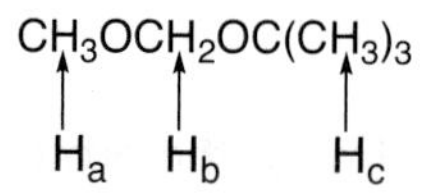

3 types of protons:
$H_c < H_a < H_b$

c. 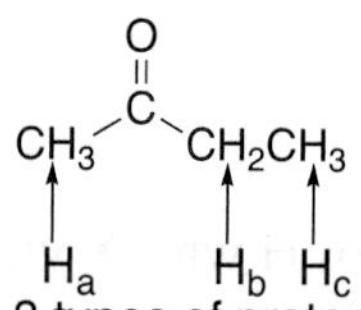

3 types of protons:
$H_c < H_a < H_b$

14.9

a. 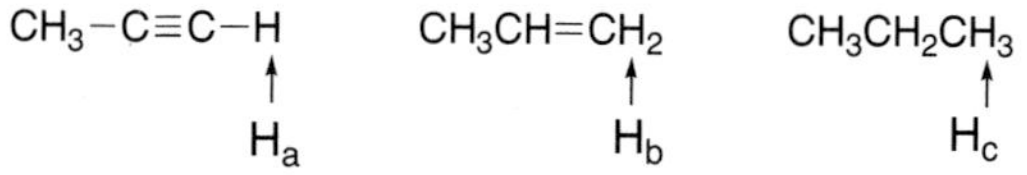

H_c protons are shielded because they are bonded to an *sp*³ C.
H_a is shielded because it is bonded to an *sp* C.
H_b protons are deshielded because they are bonded to an *sp*² C.

$H_c < H_a < H_b$

b. 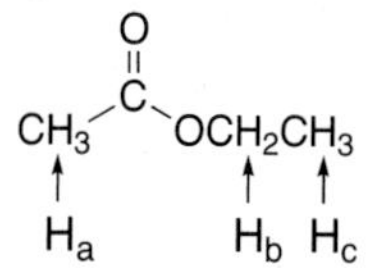

H_c protons are shielded because they are bonded to an *sp*³ C.
H_a protons are deshielded slightly because the CH_3 group is bonded to a C=O.
H_b protons are deshielded because the CH_2 group is bonded to an O atom.

$H_c < H_a < H_b$

14.10 An integration ratio of 2:3 means that there are two types of hydrogens in the compound, and that the ratio of one type to another type is 2:3.

a. CH_3CH_2Cl
2 types of H's
3:2 - YES

b. $CH_3CH_2CH_3$
2 types of H's
6:2 or 3:1 - no

c. $CH_3CH_2OCH_2CH_3$
2 types of H's
6:4 or 3:2 - YES

d. $CH_3OCH_2CH_2OCH_3$
2 types of H's
6:4 or 3:2 - YES

14.11 To determine how many protons give rise to each signal:

- Divide the total number of integration units by the total number of protons to find the number of units per H.
- Divide each integration value by this value and round to the nearest whole number.

$C_8H_{14}O_2$

total number of integration units = 14 + 12 + 44 = 70 units
total number of protons = 14 H's
70 units/14 H's = **5 units per H**

Signal [A] = 14/5 = **3 H**
Signal [B] = 12/5 = **2 H**
Signal [C] = 44/5 = **9 H**

14.12

downfield absorption closer to O

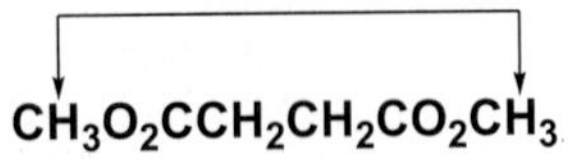

A

ratio of absorbing signals 2:3

Signal [1] = **4 H = 2.64**
Signal [2] = **6 H = 3.69** ← 6 H's with downfield absorption

downfield absorption closer to O

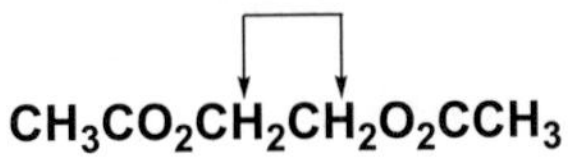

B

ratio of absorbing signals 3:2

Signal [1] = **6 H = 2.09**
Signal [2] = **4 H = 4.27** ← 4 H's with downfield absorption

14.13 To determine the **splitting pattern** for a molecule:

- Determine the number of different kinds of protons.
- Nonequivalent protons on the same C or adjacent C's split each other.
- Apply the $n + 1$ rule.

a.

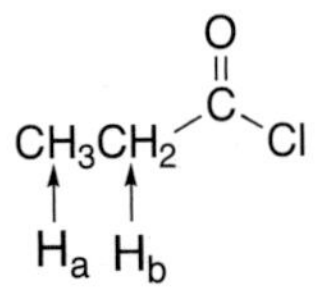

H_a: 3 peaks - triplet
H_b: 4 peaks - quartet

b.

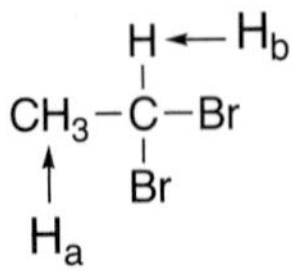

H_a: 2 peaks - doublet
H_b: 4 peaks - quartet

c.

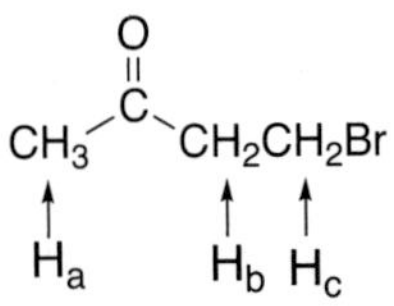

H_a: 1 peak - singlet
H_b: 3 peaks - triplet
H_c: 3 peaks - triplet

d.

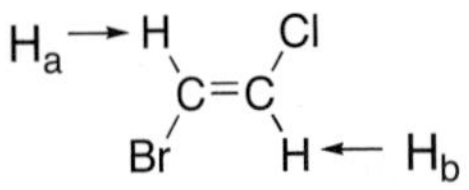

H_a: 2 peaks - doublet
H_b: 2 peaks - doublet

e.

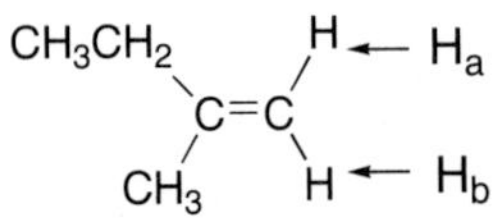

H_a: 2 peaks - doublet
H_b: 2 peaks - doublet

f.

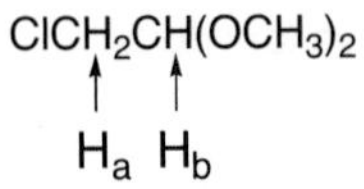

H_a: 2 peaks - doublet
H_b: 3 peaks - triplet

14.14 Use the directions from Answer 14.13.

a.

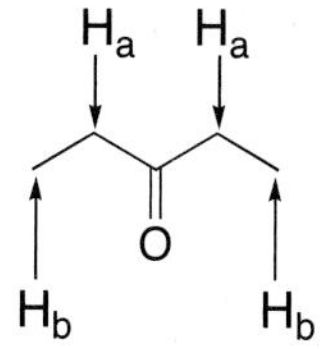

H_a: quartet
H_b: triplet
2 NMR signals

c.

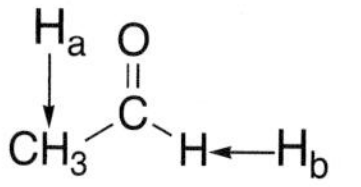

H_a: doublet
H_b: quartet
2 NMR signals

b.

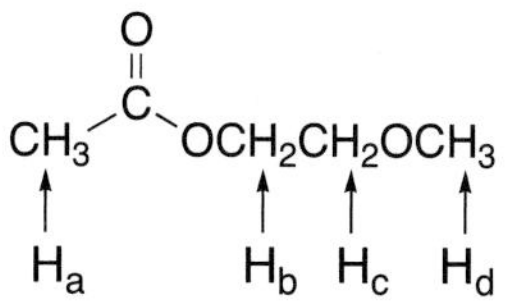

H_a and H_d are both singlets.
H_b: triplet
H_c: triplet
4 NMR signals

d. $Cl_2CHCH_2CO_2CH_3$

H_a H_b H_c

H_a: triplet
H_b: doublet
H_c: singlet
3 NMR signals

14.15 CH_3CH_2Cl

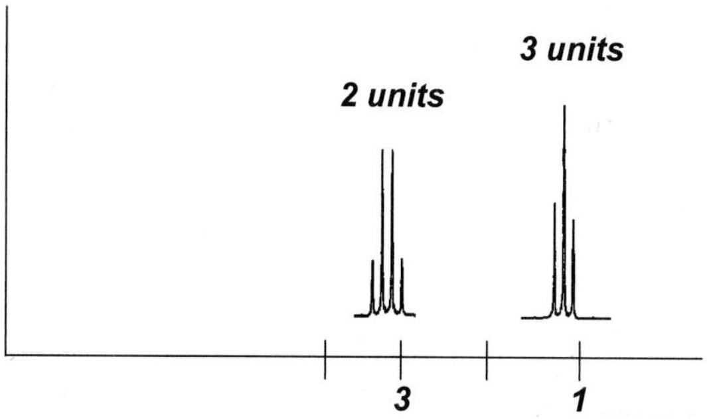

3 units
2 units
3
1
chemical shift (ppm)

There are two kinds of protons, and they can split each other. The CH_3 signal will be split by the CH_2 protons into 2 + 1 = 3 peaks. It will be upfield from the CH_2 protons since it is farther from the Cl. The CH_2 signal will be split by the CH_3 protons into 3 + 1 = 4 peaks. It will be downfield from the CH_3 protons since the CH_2 protons are closer to the Cl. The ratio of integration units will be 3:2.

14.16

a. $(CH_3)_2CHCO_2CH_3$

split by 6 equivalent H's
6 + 1 = **7 peaks**

b. $CH_3CH_2CH_2CH_2CH_3$

H_a H_b H_c

H_a: split by 2 H's
3 peaks
H_c: split by 4 equivalent H's
5 peaks
H_b: split by 2 sets of H's
(3 + 1)(2 + 1) = **12 peaks (maximum)**
Since this is a flexible alkyl chain, the signal due to H_b will have peak overlap, and 3 + 2 + 1 = **6 peaks** will likely be visible.

c.

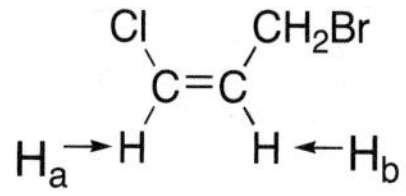

H_a: split by 1 H
2 peaks
H_b: split by 2 sets of H's
(1 + 1)(2 + 1) = **6 peaks**

d.

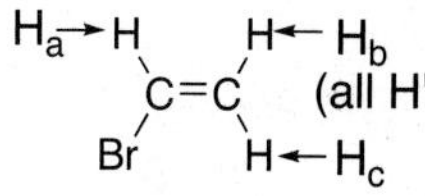

(all H's)

H_a: split by 2 different H's
(1+1)(1+1) = **4 peaks**
H_b: split by 2 different H's
(1+1)(1+1) = **4 peaks**
H_c: split by 2 different H's
(1+1)(1+1) = **4 peaks**

14.17

a. $CH_3OCH_2CH_3$

H_a H_b H_c

H_a: singlet at ~3 ppm
H_b: quartet at ~3.5 ppm
H_c: triplet at ~1 ppm

b.

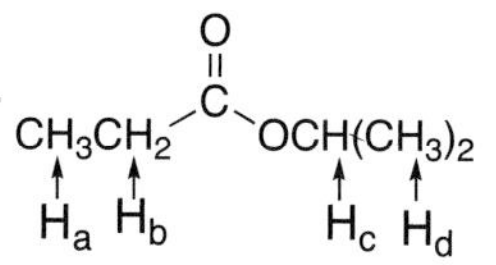

H_a: triplet at ~1 ppm
H_b: quartet at ~2 ppm
H_c: septet at ~3.5 ppm
H_d: doublet at ~1 ppm

c. $CH_3OCH_2CH_2CH_2OCH_3$

H_a H_b H_c H_b H_a

H_a: singlet at ~3 ppm
H_b: triplet at ~3.5 ppm
H_c: quintet at ~1.5 ppm

d.

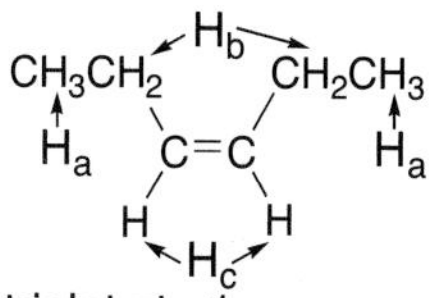

H_a: triplet at ~1 ppm
H_b: multiplet (8 peaks) at ~2.5 ppm
H_c: triplet at ~5 ppm

14.18

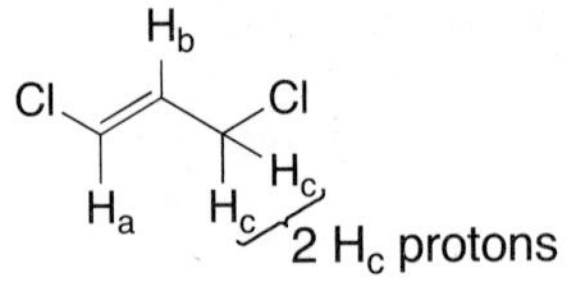
H$_b$
Cl
Cl
H$_c$
H$_a$
H$_c$
2 H$_c$ protons

trans-1,3-dichloropropene

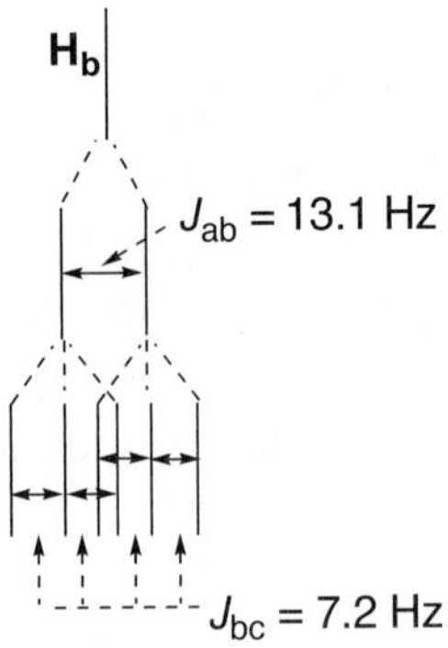
H$_b$
J_{ab} = 13.1 Hz
J_{bc} = 7.2 Hz

Splitting diagram for H$_b$

1 **trans** H$_a$ proton splits H$_b$ into
1 + 1 = 2 peaks
a doublet

2 H$_c$ protons split H$_b$ into
2 + 1 = 3 peaks
Now it's a doublet of triplets.

14.19

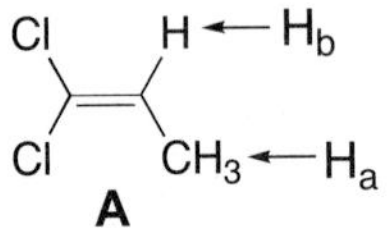
Cl
H ← H$_b$
Cl
CH$_3$ ← H$_a$

A

H$_a$: 1.75 ppm, doublet, 3 H, J = 6.9 Hz
H$_b$: 5.89 ppm, quartet, 1 H, J = 6.9 Hz

$C_3H_4Cl_2$

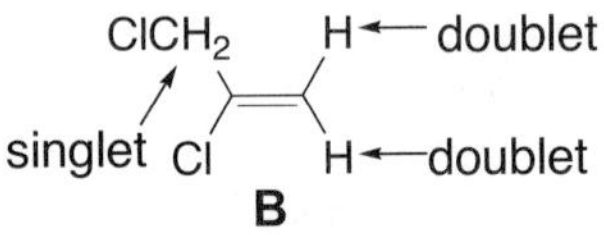
ClCH$_2$
H ← doublet
singlet
Cl
H ← doublet

B

signal at 4.16 ppm, singlet, 2 H
signal at 5.42 ppm, doublet, 1 H, J = 1.9 Hz
signal at 5.59 ppm, doublet, 1 H, J = 1.9 Hz

14.20 Remember that OH (or NH) protons do not split other signals, and are not split by adjacent protons.

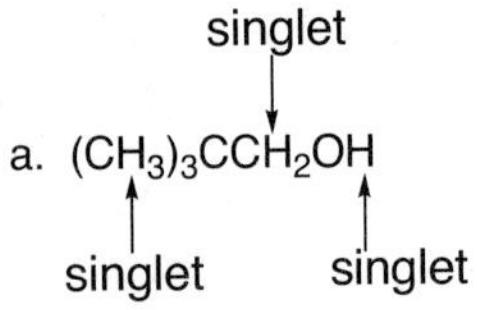
singlet
a. (CH$_3$)$_3$CCH$_2$OH
singlet
singlet

3 NMR signals

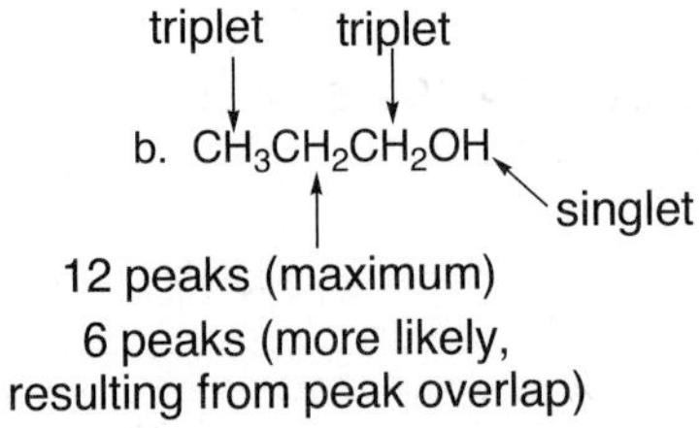
triplet
triplet
b. CH$_3$CH$_2$CH$_2$OH
singlet
12 peaks (maximum)
6 peaks (more likely,
resulting from peak overlap)

4 NMR signals

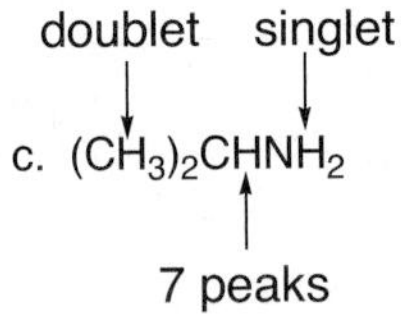
doublet
singlet
c. (CH$_3$)$_2$CHNH$_2$
7 peaks

3 NMR signals

14.21

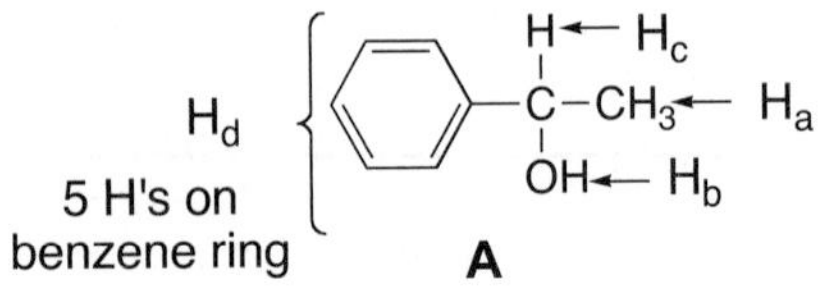
H$_d$
5 H's on
benzene ring
H ← H$_c$
C–CH$_3$ ← H$_a$
OH ← H$_b$

A

H$_a$: doublet at ~1.4 due to the CH_3 group, split into two peaks by one adjacent nonequivalent H (H$_c$).
H$_b$: singlet at ~2.7 due to the OH group. OH protons are not split by nor do they split adjacent protons.
H$_c$: quartet at ~4.7 due to the CH group, split into four peaks by the adjacent CH_3 group.
H$_d$: Five protons on the benzene ring.

14.22

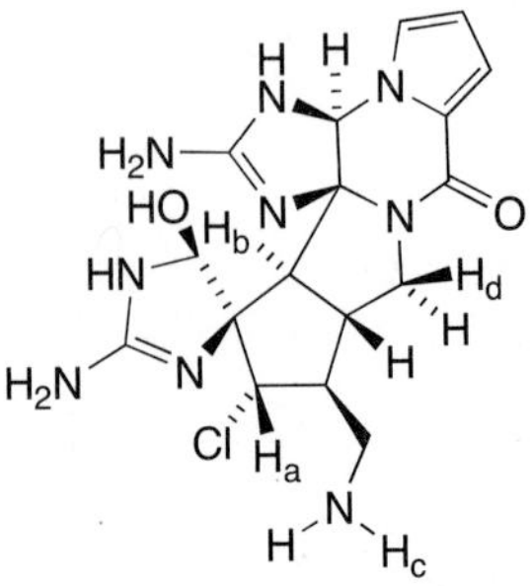
H
H
N
N
H$_2$N
HO
H$_b$
N
N
O
HN
H$_d$
H
H
H$_2$N
N
Cl
H$_a$
N
H
H$_c$

palau'amine

H$_a$: one adjacent nonequivalent H, so two peaks
H$_b$: one adjacent nonequivalent H, so two peaks
H$_c$: H$_c$ is located on a N atom so there is no splitting and it appears as one peak.
H$_d$: H$_d$ has one nonequivalent H on the same carbon and one on an adjacent carbon, so it is split into (1 + 1)(1 + 1) = 4 peaks (a doublet of doublets).

14.23 Use these steps to propose a structure consistent with the molecular formula, IR, and NMR data.

- Calculate the **degrees of unsaturation.**
- Use the IR data to determine what types of **functional groups** are present.
- Determine the number of different **types of protons.**
- Calculate the **number of H's** giving rise to each signal.
- Analyze the **splitting pattern** and put the molecule together.
- Use the **chemical shift** information to check the structure.

- Molecular formula $C_7H_{14}O_2$

  $2n + 2 = 2(7) + 2 = 16$
  $16 - 14 = 2/2 =$ **1 degree of unsaturation**
  1 π bond or 1 ring

- IR peak at 1740 cm^{-1}

  C=O absorption is around 1700 cm^{-1} (causes the degree of unsaturation).
  No signal at 3200–3600 cm^{-1} means there is no O–H bond.

- NMR data:

absorption	**ppm**	**integration**	
singlet	1.2	26	→ 26 units/3 units per H = **9 H's**
triplet	1.3	10	→ 10 units/3 units per H = **3 H's** (probably a CH_3 group)
quartet	4.1	6	→ 6 units/3 units per H = **2 H's** (probably a CH_2 group)

  - 3 kinds of H's
  - number of H's per signal
    total integration units: 26 + 10 + 6 = 42 units
    42 units / 14 H's = 3 units per H
  - look at the splitting pattern
    The singlet (9 H) is likely from a *tert*-butyl group:

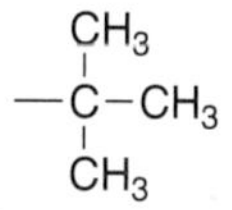

    The CH_3 and CH_2 groups split each other: CH_3-CH_2—

- Join the pieces together.

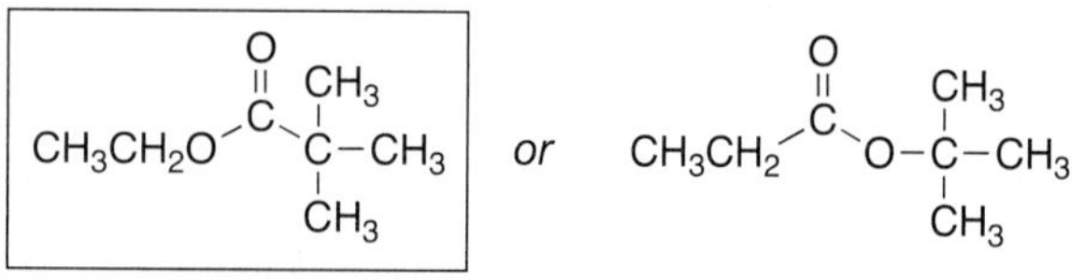

Pick this structure due to the chemical shift data.
The CH_2 group is shifted downfield (4 ppm), so it is close to the electron-withdrawing O.

14.24

- Molecular formula: C_3H_8O
  - ➢ Calculate degrees of unsaturation
    $2n + 2 = 2(3) + 2 = 8$
    $8 - 8 =$ **0 degrees of unsaturation**
- IR peak at 3200–3600 cm^{-1}
  - ➢ Peak at 3200–3600 cm^{-1} is due to an **O–H bond.**
- NMR data:
  - doublet at ~1.2 (6 H)
  - singlet at ~2.2 (1 H)
  - septet at ~4 (1 H)

3 types of H's
septet from 1 H ← split by 6 H's
singlet from 1 H ← from the O–H proton
doublet from 6 H's ← split by 1 H

➢ Put information together:

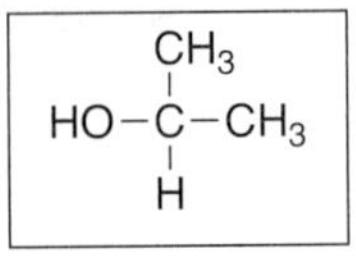

CH3
HO–C–CH3
H

14.25 Identify each compound from the ^{1}H NMR data.

a.

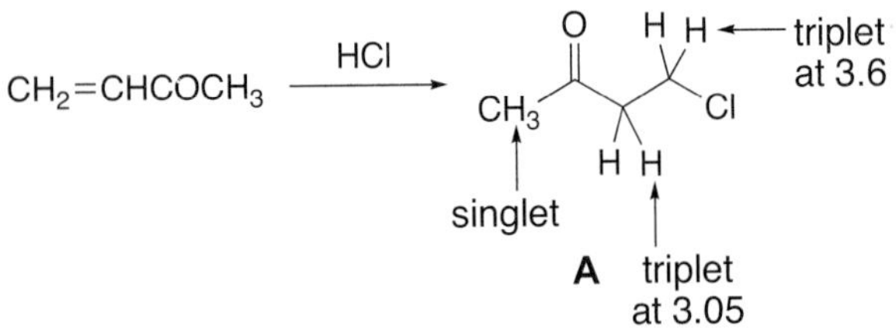

CH2=CHCOCH3
HCl
O
H H
triplet at 3.6
CH3
Cl
H H
singlet
A
triplet at 3.05

b.

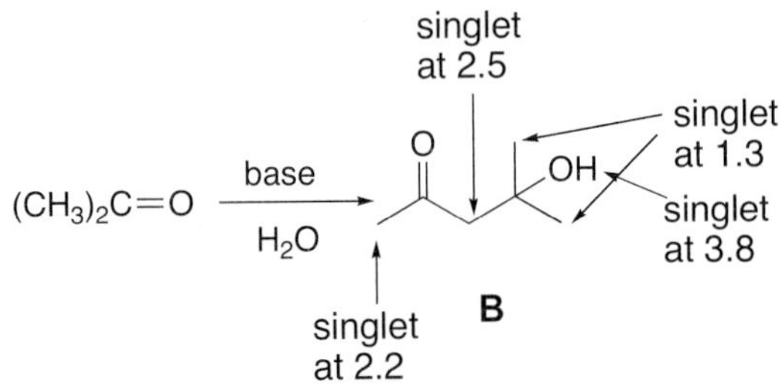

(CH3)2C=O
base
H2O
singlet at 2.5
O
OH
singlet at 1.3
singlet at 3.8
singlet at 2.2
B

14.26 Each different kind of carbon atom will give a different ^{13}C NMR signal.

a. $CH_3CH_2CH_2CH_3$
C_a C_b C_b C_a
2 kinds of C's
2 ^{13}C NMR signals

b.

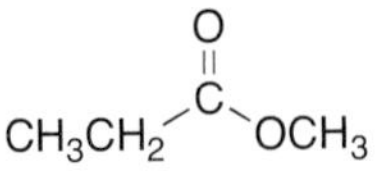

O
C
CH3CH2
OCH3

Each C is different.
4 kinds of C's
4 ^{13}C NMR signals

c. $CH_3CH_2CH_2{-}O{-}CH_2CH_2CH_3$
C_a C_b C_c C_c C_b C_a
same groups on both sides of O
3 kinds of C's
3 ^{13}C NMR signals

d.

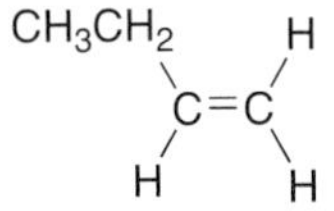

CH3CH2
H
C=C
H
H

Each C is different.
4 kinds of C's
4 ^{13}C NMR signals

14.27

a.

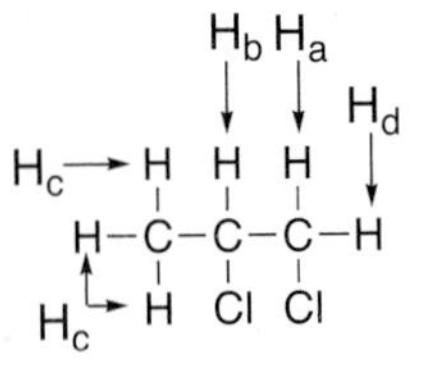

Hb Ha
Hd
Hc
H H H
H–C–C–C–H
H Cl Cl
Hc

4 ^{1}H NMR signals

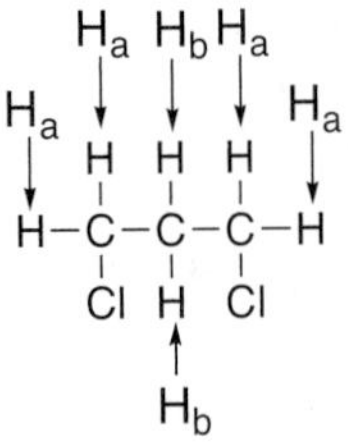

Ha Hb Ha
Ha
Ha
H H H
H–C–C–C–H
Cl H Cl
Hb

2 ^{1}H NMR signals

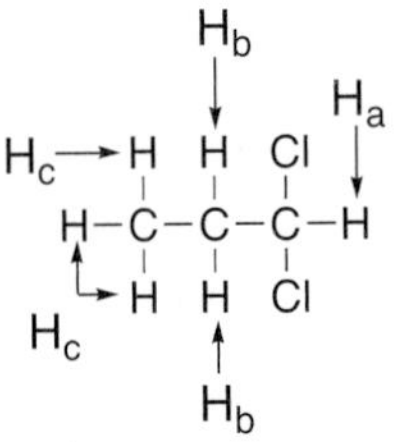

Hb
Ha
Hc
H H Cl
H–C–C–C–H
H H Cl
Hc
Hb

3 ^{1}H NMR signals

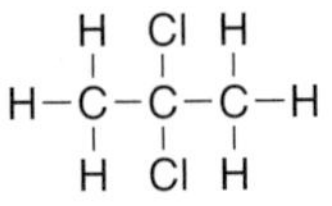

H Cl H
H–C–C–C–H
H Cl H

all H's identical
1 ^{1}H NMR signal

b.

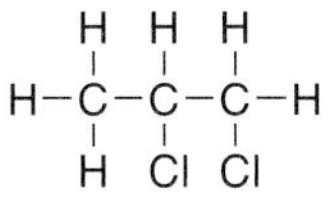

Each C is different.
3 kinds of C's
3 ^{13}C NMR signals

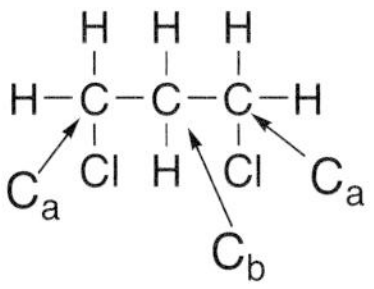

2 kinds of C's
2 ^{13}C NMR signals

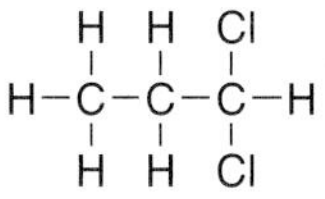

Each C is different.
3 kinds of C's
3 ^{13}C NMR signals

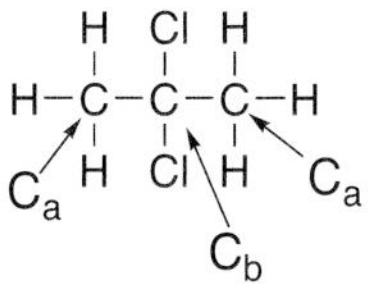

2 kinds of C's
2 ^{13}C NMR signals

c. Although the number of ^{13}C signals cannot be used to distinguish these isomers, each isomer exhibits a different number of signals in its ^{1}H NMR spectrum. As a result, the isomers are distinguishable by ^{1}H NMR spectroscopy.

14.28

These 2 C's are different because they are cis and trans to different groups.

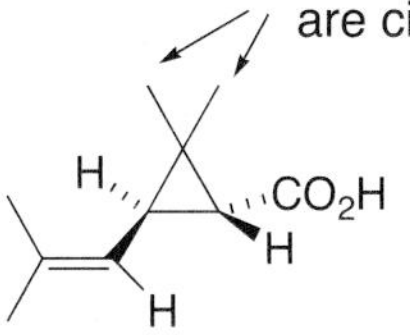
H
CO2H
H
H

chrysanthemic acid

Every carbon is different so there are 10 lines for the 10 C atoms.

14.29 Electronegative elements shift absorptions downfield. The carbons of alkenes and benzene rings, and carbonyl carbons are also shifted downfield.

a. 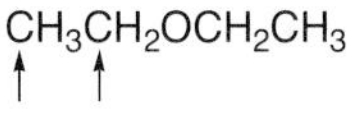
CH3CH2OCH2CH3

The CH_2 group is closer to the electronegative O and will be farther downfield.

b. 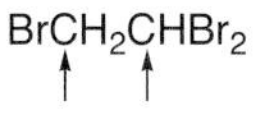
BrCH2CHBr2

The C of the $CHBr_2$ group has two bonds to electronegative Br atoms and will be farther downfield.

c. 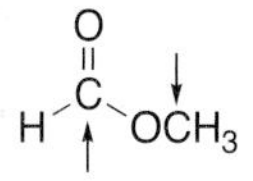
O
C
H
OCH3

The carbonyl carbon is highly deshielded and will be farther downfield.

d. 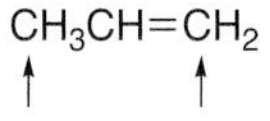
CH3CH=CH2

The CH_2 group is part of a double bond and will be farther downfield.

14.30

a. In order of lowest to highest chemical shift:

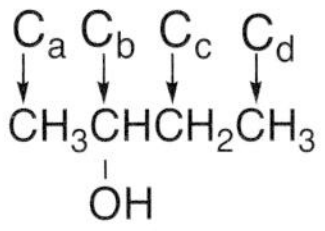
Ca Cb Cc Cd
CH3CHCH2CH3
OH

$C_d < C_a < C_c < C_b$

b. In order of lowest to highest chemical shift:

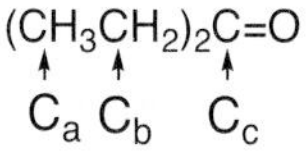
(CH3CH2)2C=O
Ca Cb Cc

$C_a < C_b < C_c$

14.31

- molecular formula $C_4H_8O_2$
  $2n + 2 = 2(4) + 2 = 10$
  $10 - 8 = 2/2 =$ **1 degree of unsaturation**
- no IR peaks at 3200–3600 or 1700 cm^{-1}
  no O–H or C=O
- ^{1}H NMR spectrum at 3.69 ppm
  only one kind of proton
- ^{13}C NMR spectrum at 67 ppm
  only one kind of carbon

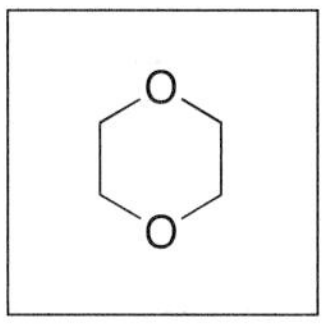
O
O

This structure satisifies all the data. One ring is one degree of unsaturation. All carbons and protons are identical.

14.32

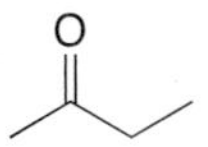

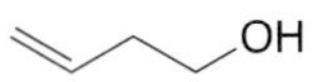

- molecular formula C_4H_8O
  $2n + 2 = 2(4) + 2 = 10$
  $10 - 8 = 2/2 =$ **1 degree of unsaturation**
- ^{13}C NMR signal at > 160 ppm due to C=O

- molecular formula C_4H_8O
  $2n + 2 = 2(4) + 2 = 10$
  $10 - 8 = 2/2 =$ **1 degree of unsaturation**
- all ^{13}C NMR signals at < 160 ppm
  NO C=O

14.33

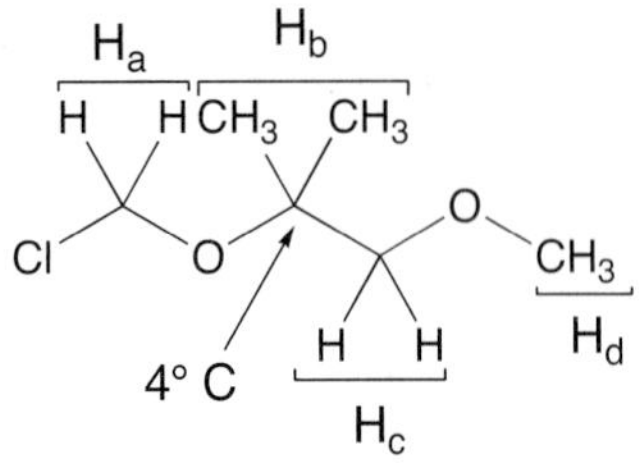

A

a. 4 ^1H NMR signals
b. 5 ^{13}C NMR signals (including the 4° C)

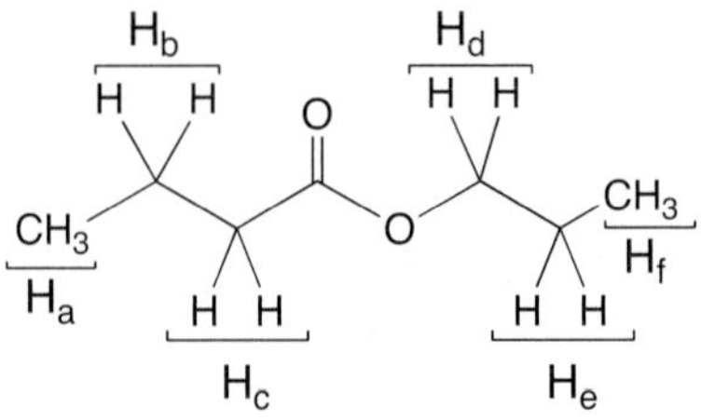

B

a. 6 ^1H NMR signals
b. 7 ^{13}C NMR signals (including the carbonyl C)

14.34

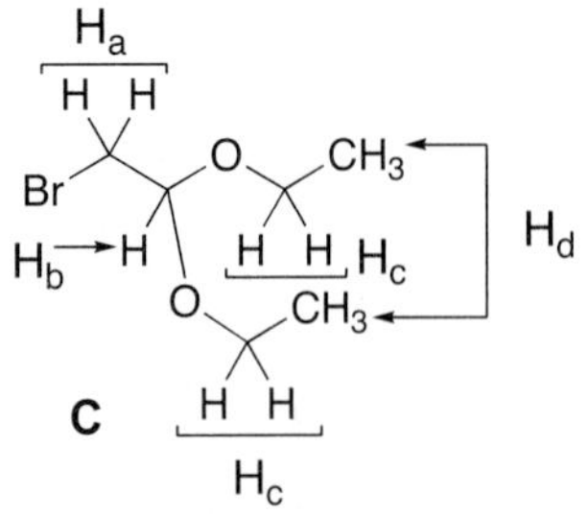

C

a. 4 ^1H NMR signals
b. H_a: 1 adjacent H, so 2 peaks
   H_b: 2 adjacent H's, so 3 peaks
   H_c: 3 adjacent H's, so 4 peaks
   H_d: 2 adjacent H's, so 3 peaks

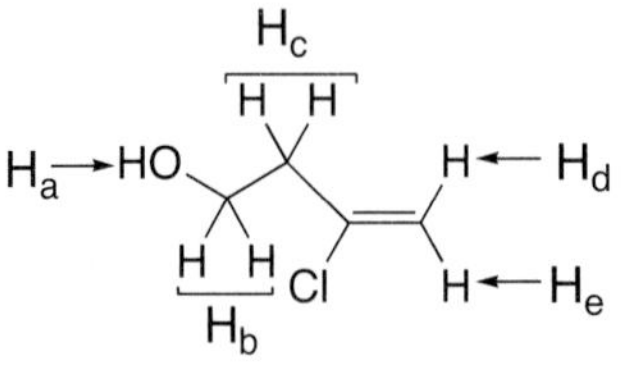

D

a. 5 ^1H NMR signals
b. H_a: singlet
   H_b: 2 adjacent H's, so 3 peaks
   H_c: 2 adjacent H's, so 3 peaks
   H_d: 1 nonequivalent H on the same C, so 2 peaks
   H_e: 1 nonequivalent H on the same C, so 2 peaks

14.35 Use the directions from Answer 14.3.

a. $(CH_3)_3CH$
2 kinds of H's

b. $(CH_3)_3CC(CH_3)_3$
1 kind of H

c. $CH_3CH_2OCH_2CH_2CH_2CH_2CH_3$
7 kinds of H's

d.
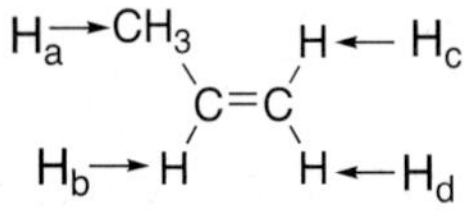

4 kinds of H's

e.
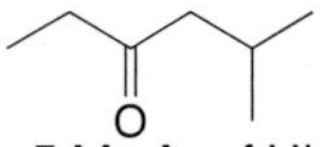

5 kinds of H's

f.
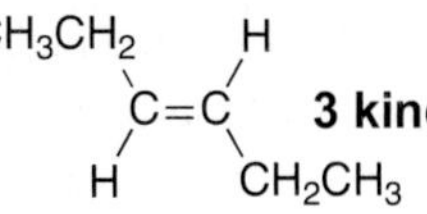

3 kinds of H's

g. $CH_3CH_2CH_2OCH_2CH_2CH_3$
3 kinds of H's

h.
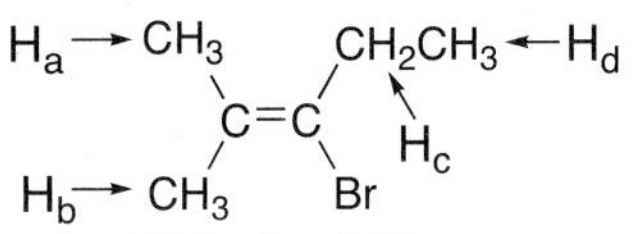

4 kinds of H's

i.
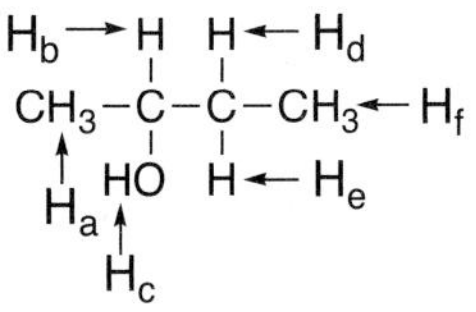

6 kinds of H's

j.
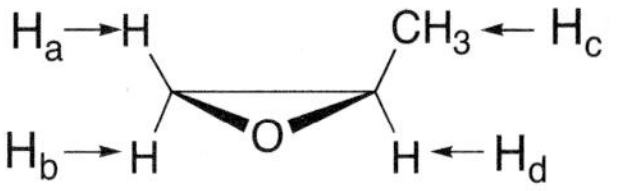

4 kinds of H's

14.36

a.
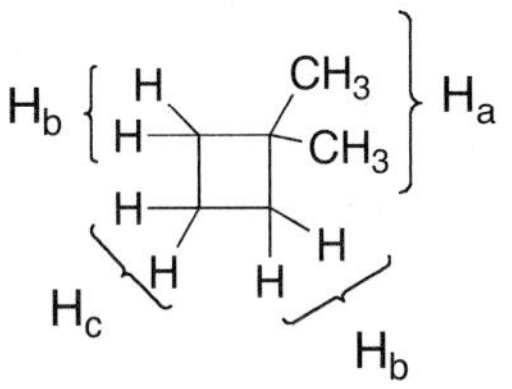

3 kinds of protons

c.
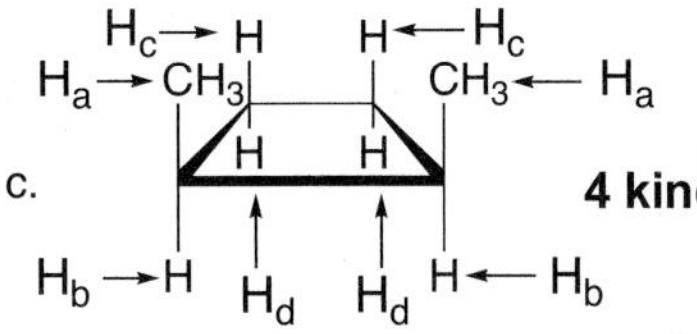

4 kinds of protons

b.
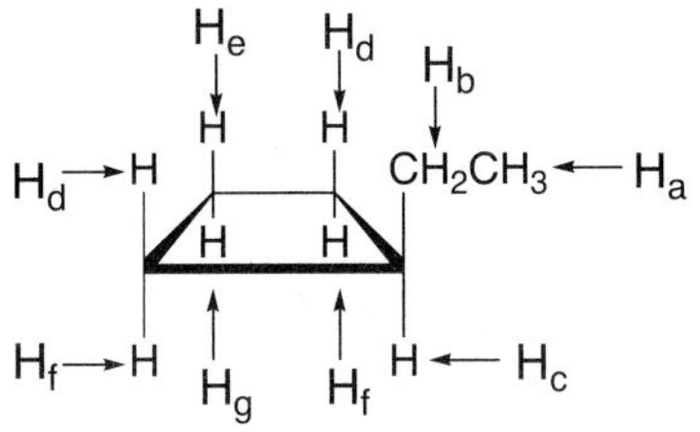

7 kinds of protons

d.
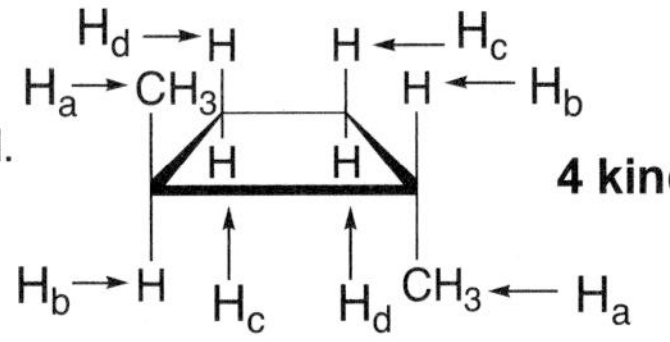

4 kinds of protons

14.37

a.
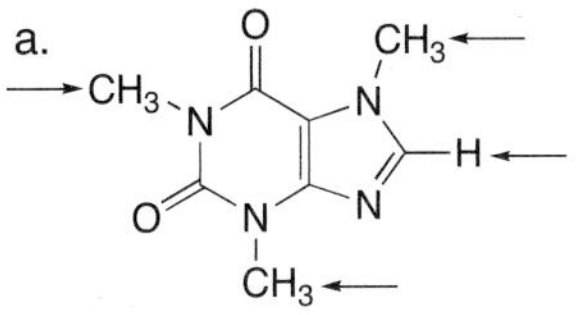

caffeine
4 NMR signals

b.
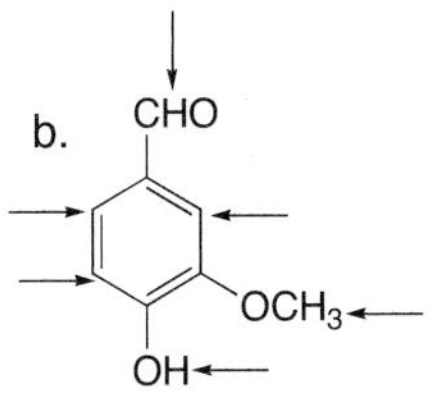

vanillin
6 NMR signals

c.
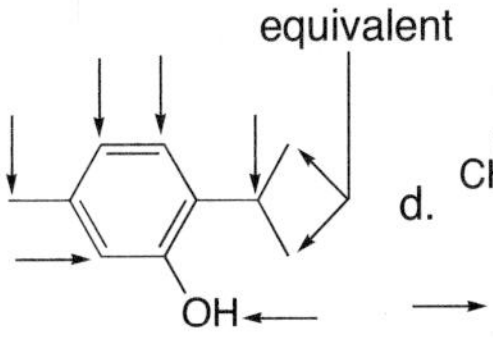

thymol
7 NMR signals

d.
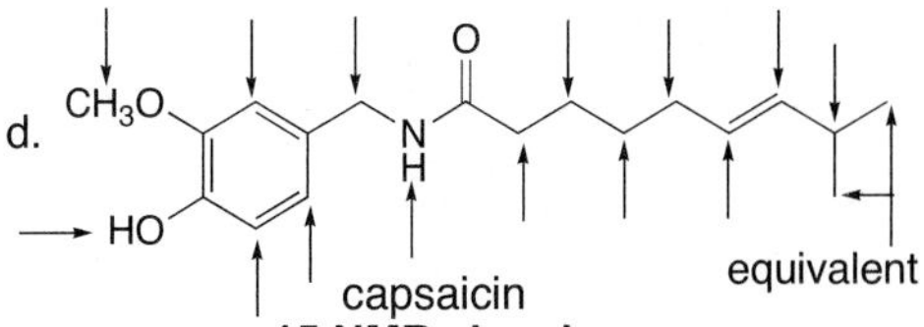

capsaicin
15 NMR signals

14.38

δ (in ppm) = [observed chemical shift (Hz)] / ν of the NMR (MHz)]

a. 2.5 = x Hz/300 MHz
x = **750 Hz**

b. ppm = 1200 Hz/300 MHz
= **4 ppm**

c. 2.0 = x Hz/300 MHz
x = **600 Hz**

14.39

2.16 = x Hz/500 MHz
x = 1080 Hz (chemical shift of acetone in Hz)
1080 Hz + 1570 Hz = **2650 Hz**
2650 Hz/500 MHz = **5.3 ppm** (chemical shift of the CH_2Cl_2 signal)

14.40 Use the directions from Answer 14.7.

a. $CH_3CH_2CH_2CH_2CH_3$ or $CH_3CH_2CH_2OCH_3$ (arrow at OCH_3)
Adjacent O deshields the H's.
farther downfield

b. $CH_3CH_2CH_2I$ or $CH_3CH_2CH_2F$ (arrow at CH_2F)
More electronegative F deshields the H's.
farther downfield

c. $CH_3OCH_2CH_3$ (CH_3 or CH_2)
Increasing alkyl substitution
farther downfield

d. $CH_3CH_2CHBr_2$ or $CH_3CH_2CH_2Br$ (arrow at $CHBr_2$)
Two electronegative Br's deshield the H.
farther downfield

14.41 Use the directions from Answer 14.11.

[total number of integration units] / [total number of protons]
[13 + 33 + 73] / 10 = ~12 units per proton

Signal of 13 units is from **1 H.**
Signal of 33 units is from **3 H's.**
Signal of 73 units is from **6 H's.**

14.42

a. $CH_3CO_2C(CH_3)_3$ and $CH_3CO_2CH_3$
(H_a, H_b; H_a, H_b)
$H_a : H_b = 1:3$ $H_a : H_b = 1:1$
different ratio of peak areas
H_b in $CH_3CO_2CH_3$ is farther downfield than all H's in $CH_3CO_2C(CH_3)_3$.

b. $CH_3OCH_2CH_2OCH_3$ and $CH_3OCH_2OCH_3$
(H_a H_b H_b H_a; H_a H_b H_a)
$H_a : H_b = 3:2$ $H_a : H_b = 3:1$
different ratio of peak areas

c.

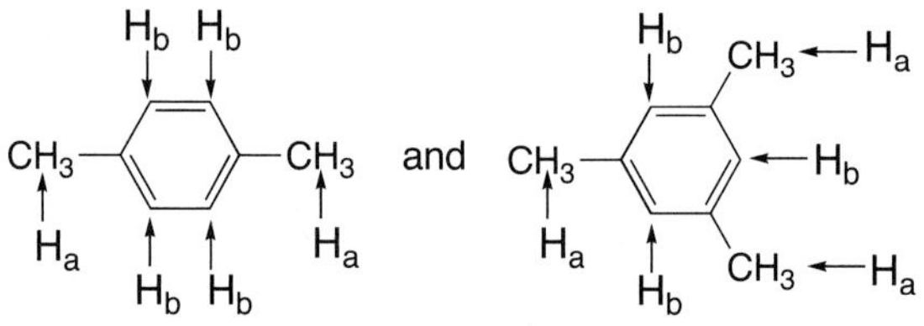

$H_a : H_b = 3:2$ $H_a : H_b = 3:1$
different ratio of peak areas

14.43 The following compounds give one singlet in a ^{1}H NMR spectrum:

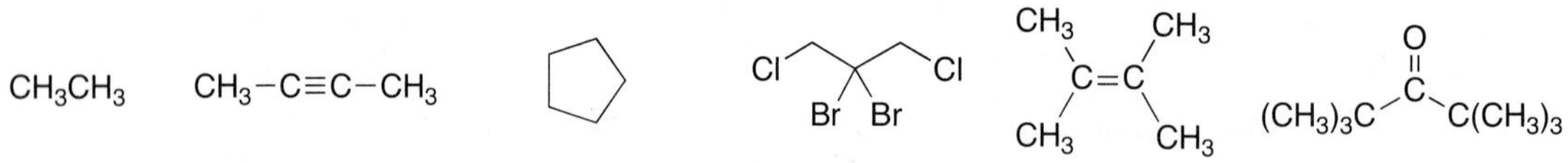

14.44

a. $CH_3CH(OCH_3)_2$
CH_3 protons split by 1 H = **doublet**
CH proton split by 3 H's = **quartet**

b.

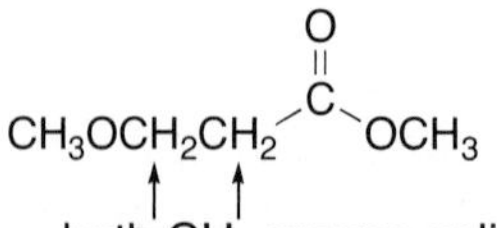

both CH_2 groups split each other = **triplets**

c.

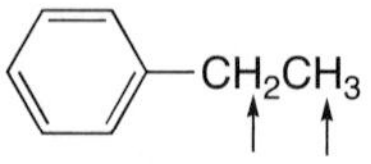

CH_3 protons split by 2 H's = **triplet**
CH_2 protons split by 3 H's = **quartet**

d. $CH_3OCH_2CHCl_2$

CH_2 protons split by 1 H = **doublet**
CH proton split by 2 H's = **triplet**

e. 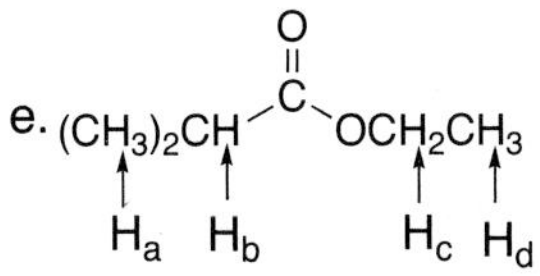

H_a protons split by 1 H = **doublet**
H_b proton split by 6 H's = **septet**
H_c protons split by 3 H's = **quartet**
H_d protons split by 2 H's = **triplet**

f. $HOCH_2CH_2CH_2OH$ (H_a, H_b)

H_a protons split by 2 CH_2 groups = **quintet**
H_b protons split by 2 H's = **triplet**

g. $CH_3CH_2CH_2CH_2OH$ (H_a H_b H_c H_d)

H_a protons split by 2 H's = **triplet**
H_b protons split by CH_3 + CH_2 protons = **12 peaks** (maximum)
H_c protons split by 2 different CH_2 groups = **9 peaks** (maximum)
H_d protons split by 2 H's = **triplet**
Since H_b and H_c are located in a flexible alkyl chain, it is likely that peak overlap occurs, so that the following is observed: H_b (3 + 2 + 1 = 6 peaks), H_c (2 + 2 + 1 = 5 peaks).

h. 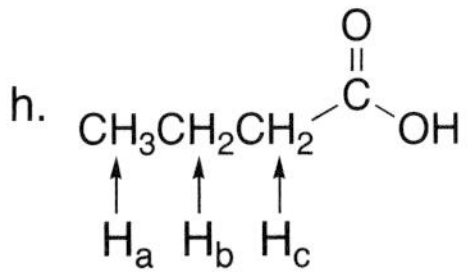

H_a protons split by 2 H's = **triplet**
H_c protons split by 2 H's = **triplet**
H_b protons split by CH_3 + CH_2 protons = **12 peaks** (maximum)
Since H_b is located in a flexible alkyl chain, it is likely that peak overlap occurs, so that only 3 + 2 + 1 = 6 peaks will be observed.

i. 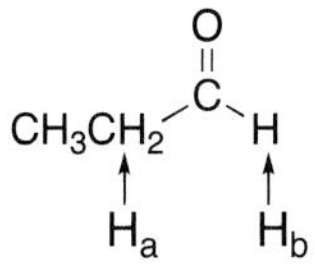

H_a: split by CH_3 group + H_b = **8 peaks** (maximum)
H_b: split by 2 H's = **triplet**

j. 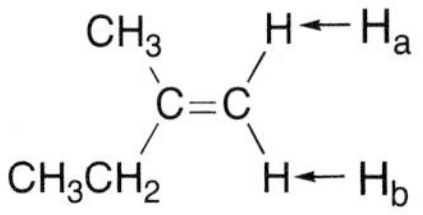

H_a: split by 1 H = **doublet**
H_b: split by 1 H = **doublet**

k. 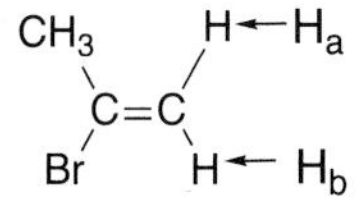

H_a: split by 1 H = **doublet**
H_b: split by 1 H = **doublet**

l. 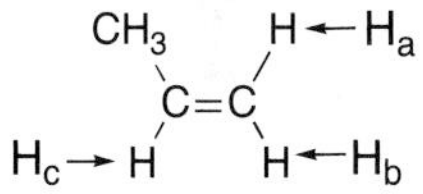

H_a: split by H_b + H_c - **doublet of doublets** (4 peaks)
H_b: split by H_a + H_c - **doublet of doublets** (4 peaks)
H_c: split by CH_3, H_a + H_b - **16 peaks**

14.45

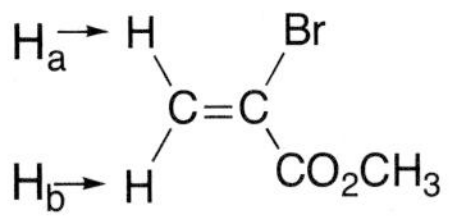

H_a: split by 1 H = **doublet**
H_b: split by 1 H = **doublet**
H_a and H_b are geminal.

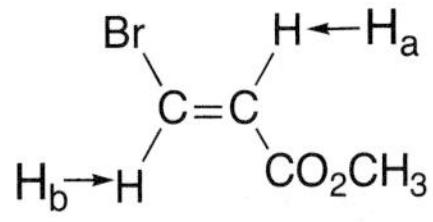

H_a: split by 1 H = **doublet**
H_b: split by 1 H = **doublet**
H_a and H_b are trans.

Both compounds exhibit two doublets for the H's on the C=C, but the coupling constants ($J_{geminal}$ and J_{trans}) are different. $J_{geminal}$ is much smaller than J_{trans} (0–3 Hz versus 11–18 Hz).

14.46

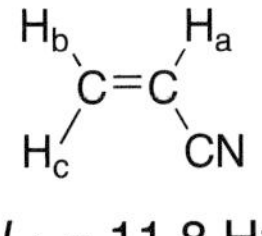

J_{ab} = 11.8 Hz
J_{bc} = 0.9 Hz
J_{ac} = 18 Hz

H_a: doublet of doublets at 5.7 ppm. Two large J values are seen for the H's cis (J_{ab} = 11.8 Hz) and trans (J_{ac} = 18 Hz) to H_a.
H_b: doublet of doublets at ~6.2 ppm. One large J value is seen for the cis H (J_{ab} = 11.8 Hz). The geminal coupling (J_{bc} = 0.9 Hz) is hard to see.
H_c: doublet of doublets at ~6.6 ppm. One large J value is seen for the trans H (J_{ac} = 18 Hz). The geminal coupling (J_{bc} = 0.9 Hz) is hard to see.

Splitting diagram for H_a

1 **trans** H_c proton splits H_a into
1 + 1 = 2 peaks
a doublet

1 **cis** H_b proton splits H_a into
1 + 1 = 2 peaks
Now it's a doublet of doublets.

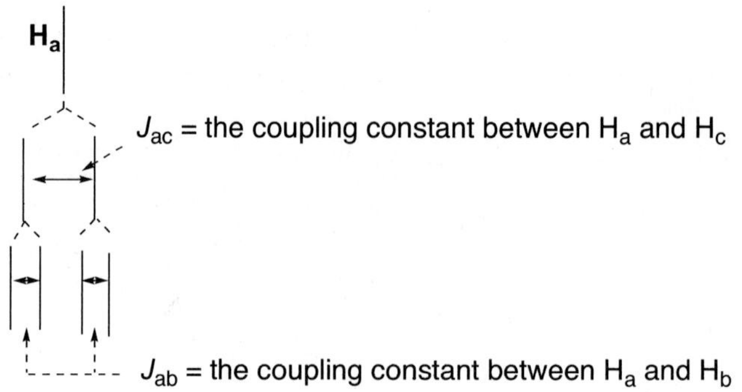
Ha
Jac = the coupling constant between Ha and Hc
Jab = the coupling constant between Ha and Hb

14.47

Four constitutional isomers of C_4H_9Br:

Br
Br
Br
Br

4 different C's   4 different C's   2 different C's   3 different C's

14.48 Only two compounds in Problem 14.43 give one signal in their ^{13}C NMR spectrum:

CH_3CH_3

14.49

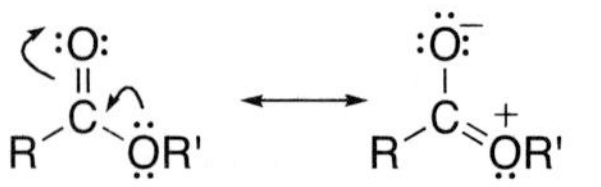
:O:
R
C
OR'
:O:
R
C
+
OR'

The O atom of an ester donates electron density, so the carbonyl carbon has less δ^+, making it less deshielded than the carbonyl carbon of an aldyhyde or ketone. Therefore, the carbonyl carbon of an aldehyde or ketone is more deshielded and absorbs farther downfield.

14.50

a. $HC(CH_3)_3$
2 signals

d. 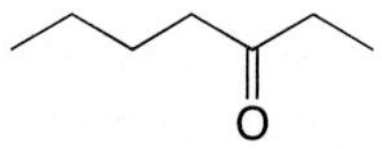
O
7 signals

g. 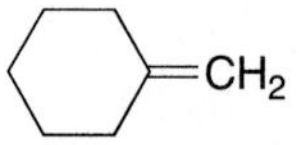
CH2
5 signals

b. 
5 signals

e. 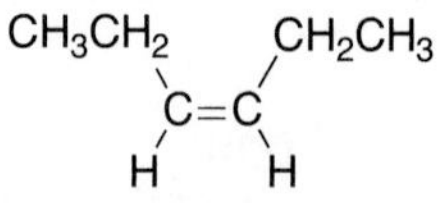
CH3CH2
CH2CH3
C=C
H
H
3 signals

h. 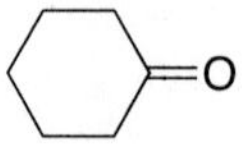
O
4 signals

c. $CH_3OCH(CH_3)_2$
3 signals

f. 
OH
7 signals

i. 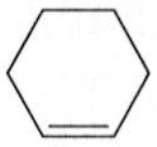
3 signals

14.51

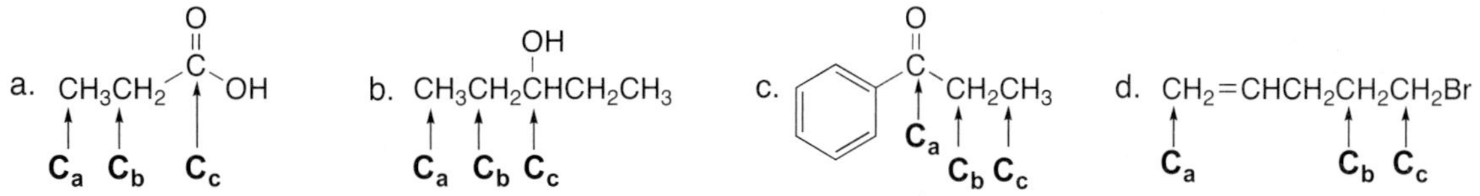
a. CH3CH2 C OH
Ca Cb Cc
b. CH3CH2CHCH2CH3
OH
Ca Cb Cc
c. CH2CH3
Ca Cb Cc
d. CH2=CHCH2CH2CH2Br
Ca Cb Cc

a. $C_a < C_b < C_c$ b. $C_a < C_b < C_c$ c. $C_c < C_b < C_a$ d. $C_b < C_c < C_a$

14.52

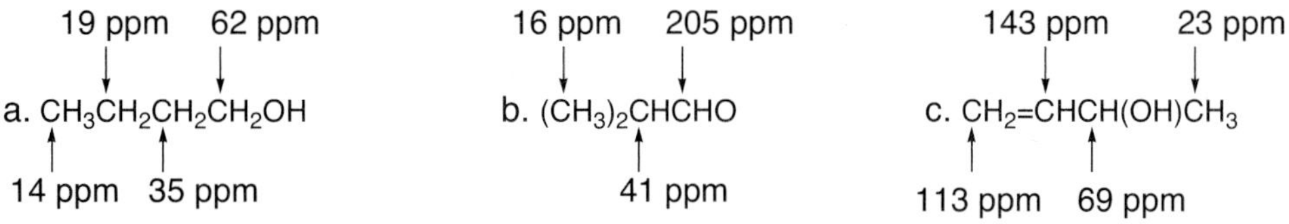
19 ppm 62 ppm
a. CH3CH2CH2CH2OH
14 ppm 35 ppm
16 ppm 205 ppm
b. (CH3)2CHCHO
41 ppm
143 ppm 23 ppm
c. CH2=CHCH(OH)CH3
113 ppm 69 ppm

14.53

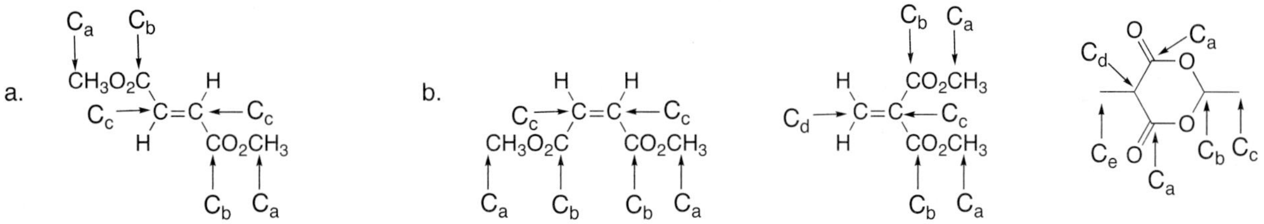
a.
b.
Ca Cb Cc Cd Ce

a. 3 different C's
3 signals

b. **3 signals**

4 signals

5 signals

14.54 Use the directions from Answer 14.23.

a. **$C_4H_8Br_2$:** 0 degrees of unsaturation
IR peak at 3000–2850 cm^{-1}: **Csp^3–H bonds**
NMR: singlet at 1.87 ppm (6 H) (2 CH_3 groups)
singlet at 3.86 ppm (2 H) (CH_2 group)

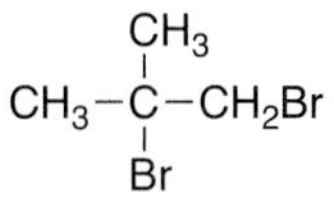
CH3
CH3–C–CH2Br
Br

b. **$C_3H_6Br_2$:** 0 degrees of unsaturation
IR peak at 3000–2850 cm^{-1}: **Csp^3–H bonds**
NMR: quintet at 2.4 ppm (split by 2 CH_2 groups)
triplet at 3.5 ppm (split by 2 H's)

Br
Br

c. **$C_5H_{10}O_2$: 1 degree of unsaturation**
IR peak at 1740 cm^{-1}: **C=O**
NMR: triplet at 1.15 ppm (3 H) (CH_3 split by 2 H's)
triplet at 1.25 ppm (3 H) (CH_3 split by 2 H's)
quartet at 2.30 ppm (2 H) (CH_2 split by 3 H's)
quartet at 4.72 ppm (2 H) (CH_2 split by 3 H's)

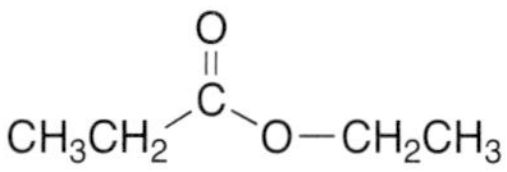
O
CH3CH2 C O–CH2CH3

d. **$C_6H_{14}O$:** 0 degrees of unsaturation
IR peak at 3600–3200 cm^{-1}: **O–H**
NMR: triplet at 0.8 ppm (6 H) (2 CH_3 groups split by CH_2 groups)
singlet at 1.0 ppm (3 H) (CH_3)
quartet at 1.5 ppm (4 H) (2 CH_2 groups split by CH_3 groups)
singlet at 1.6 ppm (1 H) (O–H proton)

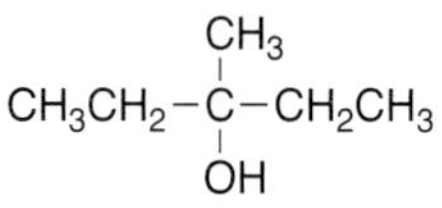
CH3
CH3CH2–C–CH2CH3
OH

e. **$C_6H_{14}O$:** 0 degrees of unsaturation
IR peak at 3000–2850 cm^{-1}: **C_{sp^3}–H bonds**
NMR: doublet at 1.10 ppm (integration = 30 units) (from 12 H's)
septet at 3.60 ppm (integration = 5 units) (from 2 H's)

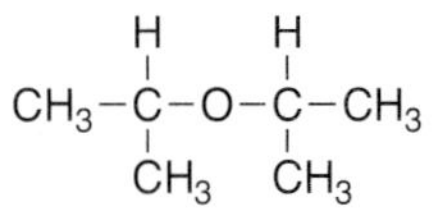

f. **C_3H_6O: 1 degree of unsaturation**
IR peak at 1730 cm^{-1}: **C=O**
NMR: triplet at 1.11 ppm
multiplet at 2.46 ppm
triplet at 9.79 ppm

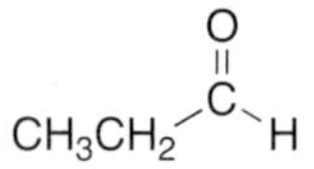

14.55

Two isomers of $C_9H_{10}O$: 5 degrees of unsaturation (benzene ring likely)

Compound A:
IR absorption at 1742 cm^{-1}: **C=O**
NMR data:
Absorptions:
singlet at 2.15 (3 H) (CH_3 group)
singlet at 3.70 (2 H) (CH_2 group)
broad singlet at 7.20 (5 H)
(likely a monosubstituted benzene ring)

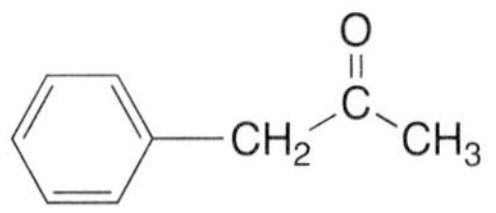

Compound B:
IR absorption at 1688 cm^{-1}: **C=O**
NMR data:
Absorptions:
triplet at 1.22 (3 H) (CH_3 group split by 2 H's)
quartet at 2.98 (2 H) (CH_2 group split by 3 H's)
multiplet at 7.28–7.95 (5 H)
(likely a monosubstituted benzene ring)

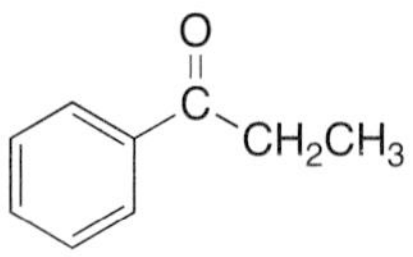

14.56 IR absorptions:
3088–2897 cm^{-1}: *sp*^{2} and *sp*^{3} hybridized C–H
1740 cm^{-1}: C=O
1606 cm^{-1}: benzene ring

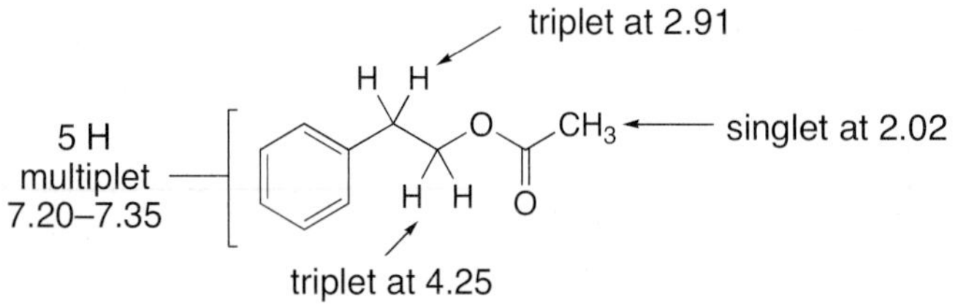
triplet at 2.91
5 H
multiplet
7.20–7.35
singlet at 2.02
triplet at 4.25

$C_{10}H_{12}O_2$
W

14.57 IR absorption at 1713 cm^{-1} is due to C=O.

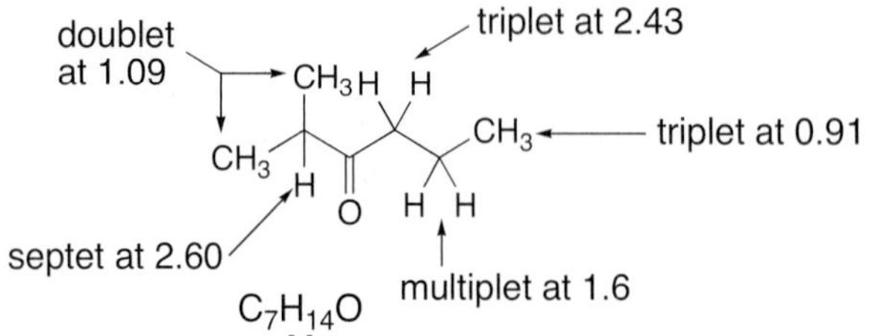
doublet
at 1.09
triplet at 2.43
triplet at 0.91
septet at 2.60
multiplet at 1.6

$C_7H_{14}O$
V

14.58

Compound C:

molecular ion 146 (molecular formula $C_6H_{10}O_4$)
IR absorption at 1762 cm^{-1}: **C=O**
^{1}**H NMR** data:

Absorptions:
H_a: doublet at 1.47 (3 H) (CH_3 group adjacent to CH)
H_b: singlet at 2.07 (6 H) (2 CH_3 groups)
H_c: quartet at 6.84 (1 H adjacent to CH_3)

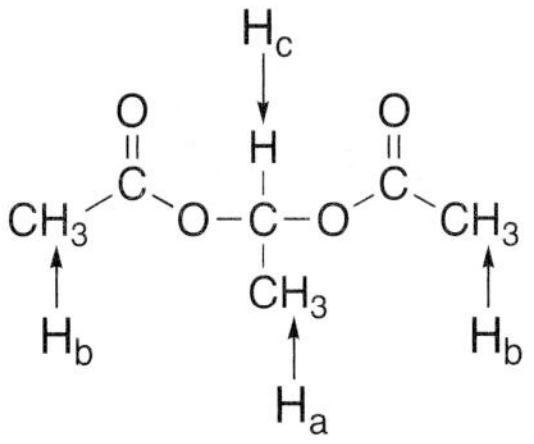

14.59

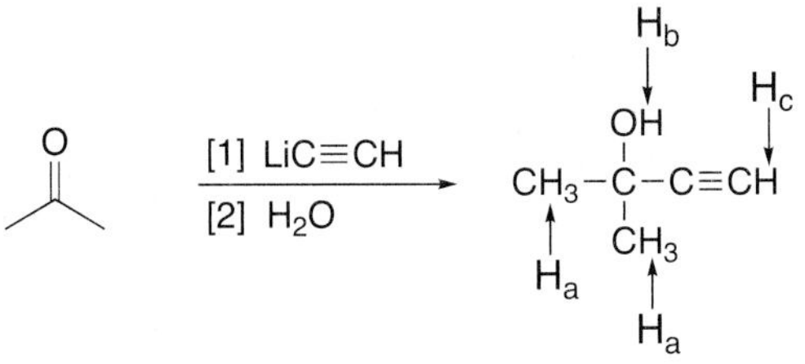

D

Compound D:

molecular ion 84 (molecular formula C_5H_8O)
IR absorptions at 3600–3200 cm^{-1}: OH
3303 cm^{-1}: C_{sp}–H
2938 cm^{-1}: C_{sp^3}–H
2120 cm^{-1}: C≡C

^{1}**H NMR** data:

Absorptions:
H_a: singlet at 1.53 (6 H) (2 CH_3 groups)
H_b: singlet at 2.37 (1 H)
H_c: singlet at 2.43 (1 H)
(H_b, H_c): alkynyl CH and OH

14.60

Compound E:
$C_4H_8O_2$:
1 degree of unsaturation
IR absorption at 1743 cm^{-1}: **C=O**
NMR data:

total integration units/# H's
(23 + 29 + 30)/8 = ~10 units per H

H_a: quartet at 4.1 (23 units - **2 H**)
H_b: singlet at 2.0 (29 units - **3 H**)
H_c: triplet at 1.4 (30 units - **3 H**)

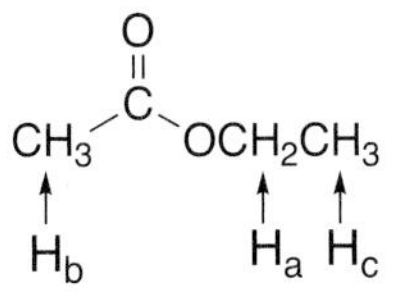

Compound F:
$C_4H_8O_2$:
1 degree of unsaturation
IR absorption at 1730 cm^{-1}: **C=O**
NMR data:

total integration units/# H's
(18 + 30 + 31)/8 = ~10 units per H

H_a: singlet at 4.1 (18 units - **2 H**)
H_b: singlet at 3.4 (30 units - **3 H**)
H_c: singlet at 2.1 (31 units - **3 H**)

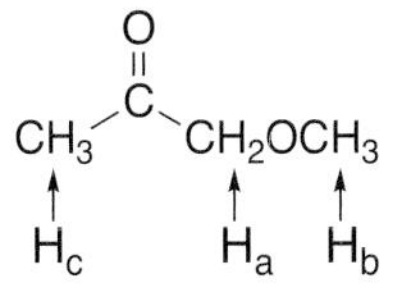

14.61

Compound H:

$C_8H_{11}N$:

4 degrees of unsaturation

IR absorptions at 3365 cm^{-1}: N–H
3284 cm^{-1}: N–H
3026 cm^{-1}: C_{sp^2}–H
2932 cm^{-1}: C_{sp^3}–H
1603 cm^{-1}: due to benzene
1497 cm^{-1}: due to benzene

NMR data:

multiplet at 7.2–7.4 ppm, **5 H** on a benzene ring
H_a: triplet at 2.9 ppm, **2 H,** split by 2 H's
H_b: triplet at 2.8 ppm, **2 H,** split by 2 H's
H_c: singlet at 1.1 ppm, **2 H,** no splitting (on NH_2)

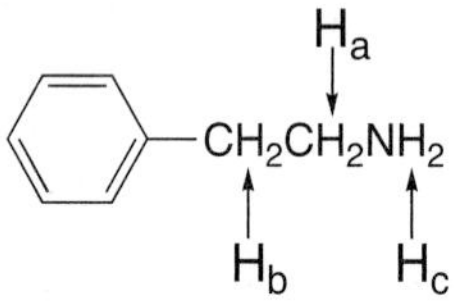

Compound I:

$C_8H_{11}N$:

4 degrees of unsaturation

IR absorptions at 3367 cm^{-1}: N–H
3286 cm^{-1}: N–H
3027 cm^{-1}: C_{sp^2}–H
2962 cm^{-1}: C_{sp^3}–H
1604 cm^{-1}: due to benzene
1492 cm^{-1}: due to benzene

NMR data:

multiplet at 7.2–7.4 ppm, **5 H** on a benzene ring
H_a: quartet at 4.1 ppm, **1 H,** split by 3H's
H_b: singlet at 1.45 ppm, **2 H,** no splitting (NH_2)
H_c: doublet at 1.4 ppm, **3 H,** split by 1 H

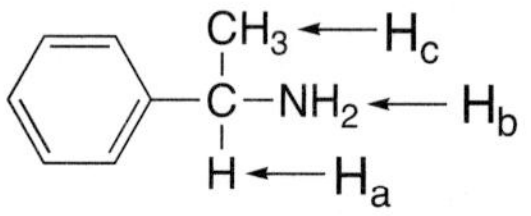

14.62

a. **$C_9H_{10}O_2$:**

5 degrees of unsaturation

IR absorption at 1718 cm^{-1}: **C=O**

NMR data:

multiplet at 7.4–8.1 ppm, **5 H** on a benzene ring
quartet at 4.4 ppm, **2 H,** split by 3 H's
triplet at 1.3 ppm, **3 H,** split by 2 H's

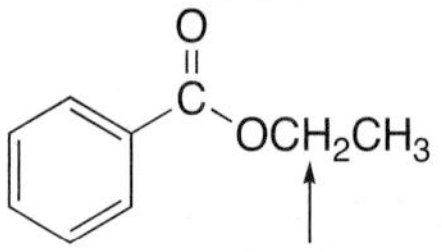

downfield due to the O atom

b. **C_9H_{12}:**

4 degrees of unsaturation

IR absorption at 2850–3150 cm^{-1}:

C–H bonds

NMR data:

singlet at 7.1–7.4 ppm, **5 H,** benzene
septet at 2.8 ppm, **1 H,** split by 6 H's
doublet at 1.3 ppm, **6 H,** split by 1 H

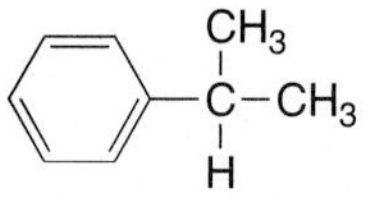

14.63 IR absorption at 1717 cm^{-1} is due to a C=O.

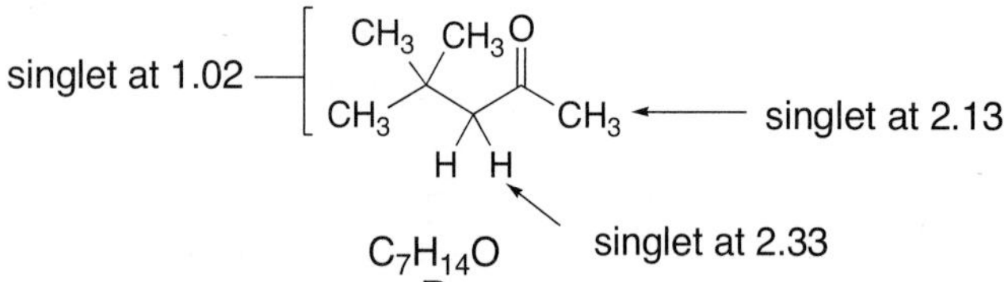

$C_7H_{14}O$
R

14.64 IR absorption at 1730 cm^{-1} is due to a C=O. Eight lines in the ^{13}C NMR spectrum means there are eight different types of C.

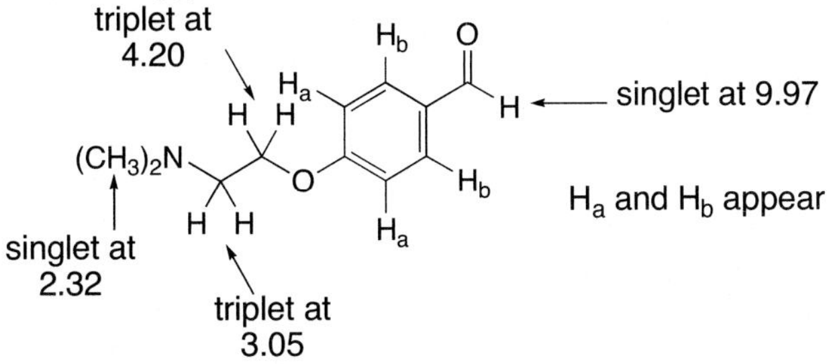

H_a and H_b appear as two doublets.

14.65

a. Compound **J** has a molecular ion at 72: molecular formula $\mathbf{C_4H_8O}$

1 degree of unsaturation

IR spectrum at 1710 cm^{-1}: **C=O**

^1H NMR data (ppm):

1.0 (triplet, 3 H), split by 2 H's
2.1 (singlet, 3 H)
2.4 (quartet, 2 H), split by 3 H's

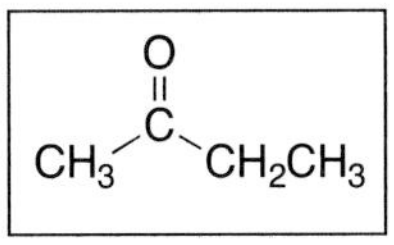

b. Compound **K** has a molecular ion at 88: molecular formula $\mathbf{C_5H_{12}O}$

0 degrees of unsaturation

IR spectrum at 3600–3200 cm^{-1}: **O–H bond**

^1H NMR data (ppm):

0.9 (triplet, 3 H), split by 2 H's
1.2 (singlet, 6 H), due to 2 CH_3 groups
1.5 (quartet, 2 H), split by 3 H's
1.6 (singlet, 1 H), due to the OH proton

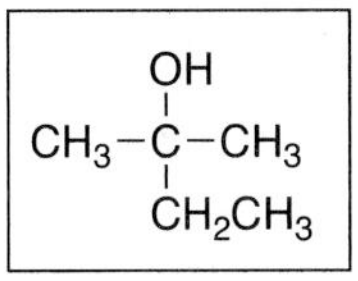

14.66

Compound **L** has a molecular ion at 90: molecular formula $\mathbf{C_4H_{10}O_2}$

0 degrees of unsaturation

IR absorptions at 2992 and 2941 cm^{-1}: C_{sp^3}–H

^1H NMR data (ppm):

H_a: 1.2 (doublet, 3 H), split by 1 H
H_b: 3.3 (singlet, 6 H), due to 2 CH_3 groups
H_c: 4.8 (quartet, 1 H), split by 3 adjacent H's

total integration units/# H's
(25 + 46 + 7)/10 = ~8 units per H

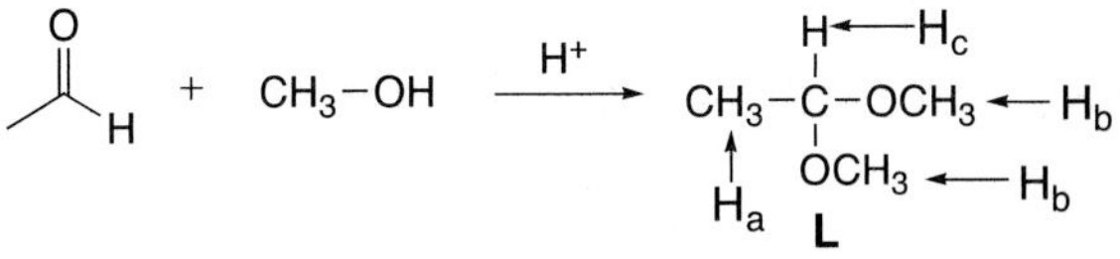

14.67

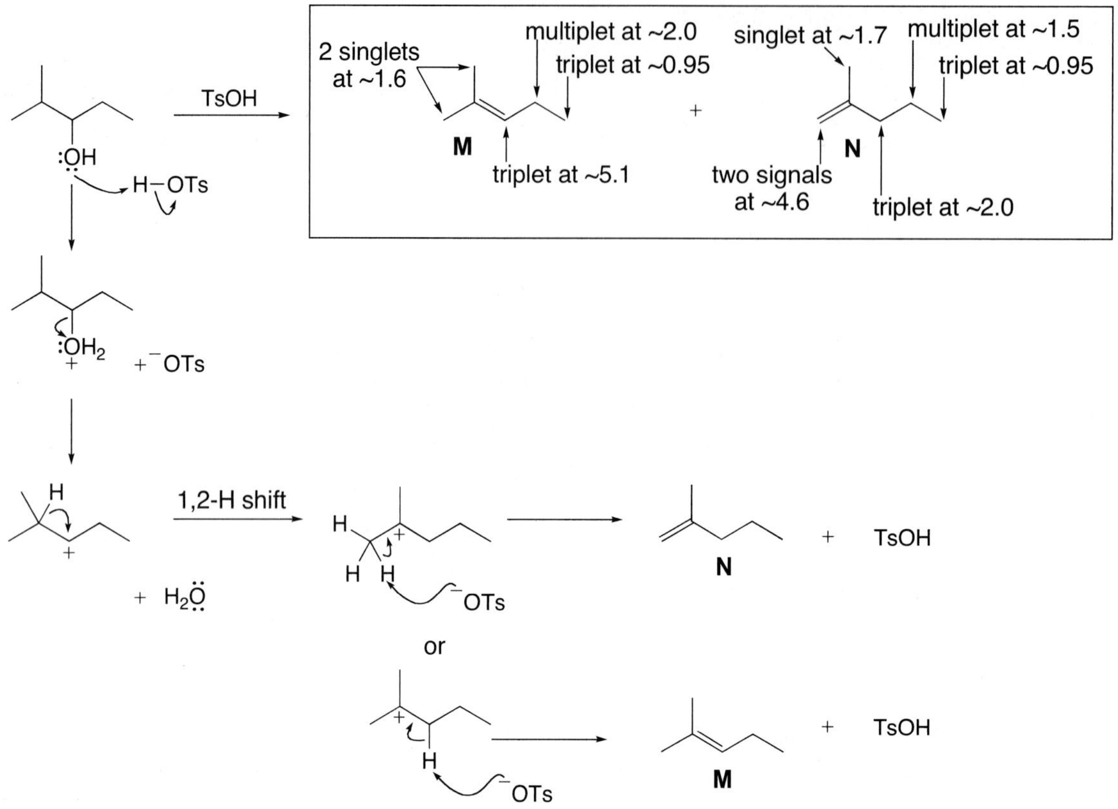

14.68

Compound **O** has a molecular formula **$C_{10}H_{12}O$.**

5 degrees of unsaturation

IR absorption at 1687 cm^{-1}

^{1}H NMR data (ppm):

H_a: 1.0 (triplet, 3 H), due to CH_3 group, split by 2 adjacent H's

H_b: 1.7 (sextet, 2 H), split by CH_3 and CH_2 groups

H_c: 2.9 (triplet, 2 H), split by 2 H's

7.4–8.0 (multiplet, 5 H), benzene ring

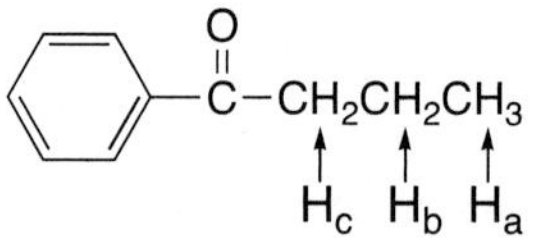

O

14.69

Compound **P** has a molecular formula **$C_5H_9ClO_2$.**

1 degree of unsaturation

^{13}C NMR shows 5 different C's, including a C=O.

^{1}H NMR data (ppm):

H_a: 1.3 (triplet, 3 H), split by 2 H's

H_b: 2.8 (triplet, 2 H), split by 2 H's

H_c: 3.7 (triplet, 2 H), split by 2 H's

H_d: 4.2 (quartet, 2 H), split by CH_3 group

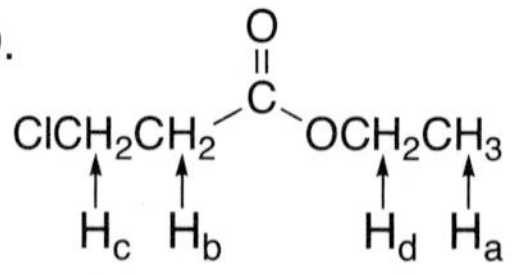

P

14.70

Compound Q: Molecular ion at 86.
Molecular formula: **$C_5H_{10}O$:**
1 degree of unsaturation
IR absorption at ~1700 cm^{-1}: **C=O**
NMR data:
H_a: doublet at 1.1 ppm, 2 CH_3 groups split by 1 H
H_b: singlet at 2.1 ppm, CH_3 group
H_c: septet at 2.6 ppm, 1 H split by 6 H's

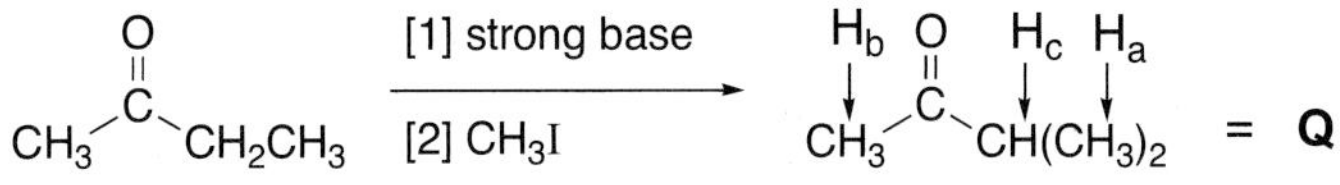

MW = 86

14.71

a. Compound **R,** the odor of banana: $C_7H_{14}O_2$
1 degree of unsaturation
^{1}H NMR (ppm):
H_a: 0.93 (doublet, 6 H)
H_b: 1.52 (multiplet, 2 H)
H_c: 1.69 (multiplet, 1 H)
H_d: 2.04 (singlet, 3 H)
H_e: 4.10 (triplet, 2 H)

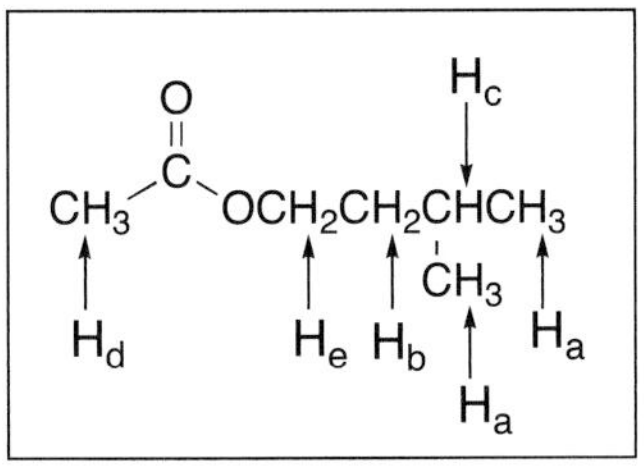

b. Compound **S,** the odor of rum: $C_7H_{14}O_2$
1 degree of unsaturation
^{1}H NMR (ppm):
H_a: 0.94 (doublet, 6 H)
H_b: 1.15 (triplet, 3 H)
H_c: 1.91 (multiplet, 1 H)
H_d: 2.33 (quartet, 2 H)
H_e: 3.86 (doublet, 2 H)

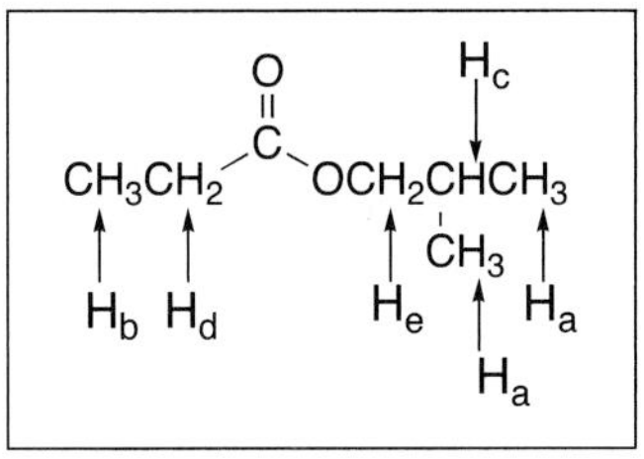

14.72

C_6H_{12}:
1 degree of unsaturation

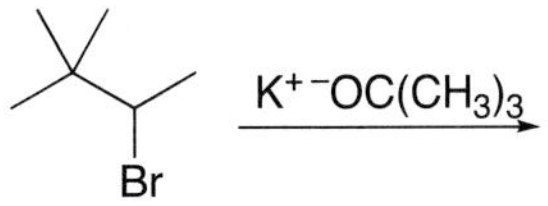

T ^{1}H NMR of **T** (ppm):
H_a: 1.01 (singlet, 9 H)
H_b: 4.82 (doublet of doublets, 1 H, J = 10, 1.7 Hz)
H_c: 4.93 (doublet of doublets, 1 H, J = 18, 1.7 Hz)
H_d: 5.83 (doublet of doublets, 1 H, J = 18, 10 Hz)

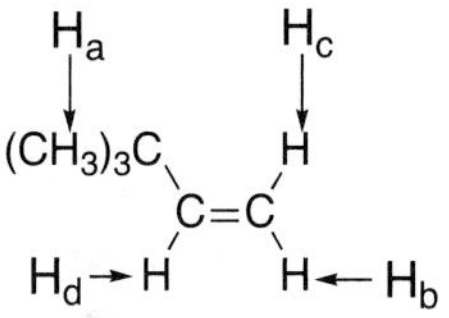

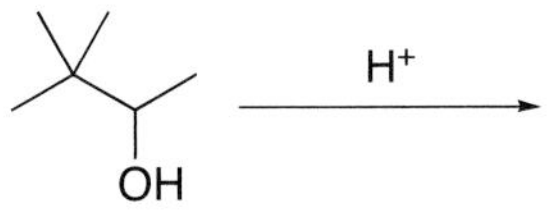

U ^{1}H NMR of **U**: 1.60 (singlet) ppm.

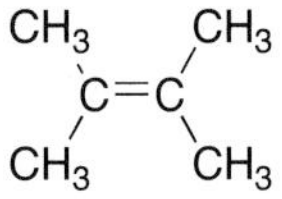

All H's are identical, so there is only one singlet in the NMR.

14.73

a.

$C_6H_{12}O_2$:
1 degree of unsaturation
IR peak at 1740 cm^{-1}: **C=O**
^{1}H NMR 2 signals: 2 types of H's
^{13}C NMR: 4 signals: 4 kinds of C's, including one at ~170 ppm due a C=O

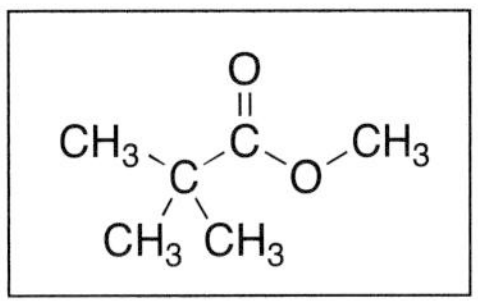

b.

C_6H_{10}:
2 degrees of unsaturation
IR peak at 3000 cm^{-1}: **Csp^3–H bonds**
peak at 3300 cm^{-1}: **C_{sp}–H bond**
peak at ~2150 cm^{-1}: **C≡C bond**
^{13}C NMR: 4 signals: 4 kinds of C's

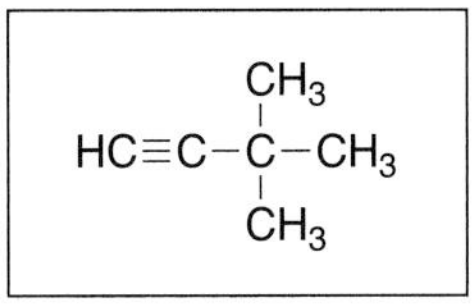

14.74 a. Since **A** has no absorptions at 1700 cm^{-1} or 3600–3200 cm^{-1}, it has no C=O or OH. An oxygen-containing compound without these functional groups is an ether (or an epoxide). Since **B** is formed from a reaction with HCl, **A** must contain an epoxide, because ethers are unreactive with HCl.

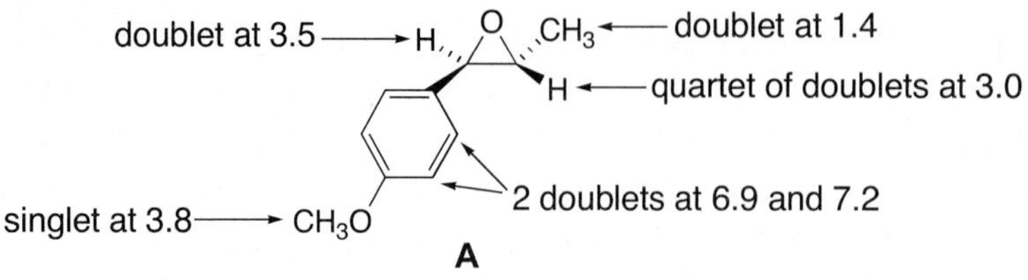

b. Epoxide **A** is equally substituted by R groups on both C's. With HCl, the epoxide is protonated first and then backside attack by Cl^- forms the chlorohydrin. Attack at the C adjacent to the benzene ring is preferred because the δ^+ in the transition state at this carbon can be delocalized on the benzene ring.

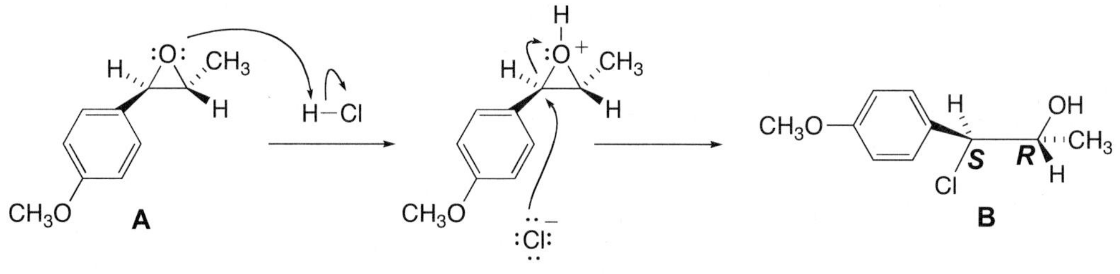

The benzene ring and CH_3 group must be trans in the epoxide to give the correct configuration at the two stereogenic centers in the product.

14.75

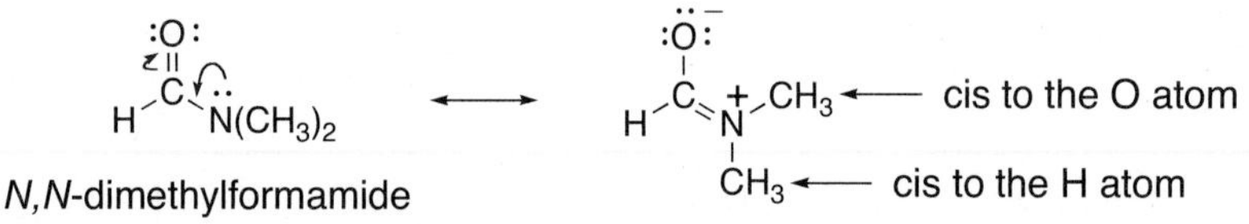

A second resonance structure for *N,N*-dimethylformamide places the two CH_3 groups in different environments. One CH_3 group is cis to the O atom, and one is cis to the H atom. This gives rise to two different absorptions for the CH_3 groups.

14.76

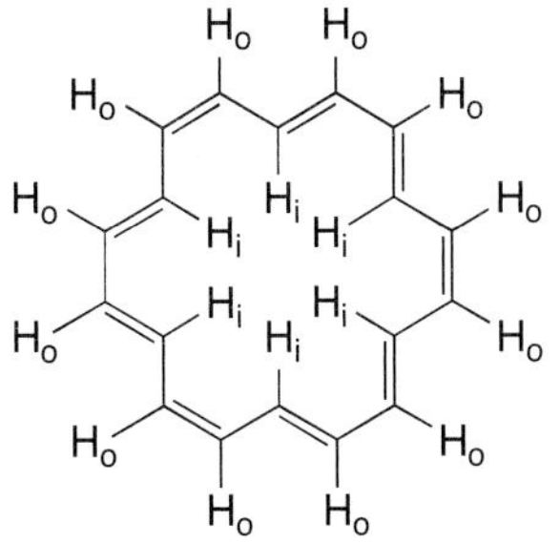

18-Annulene has 18 π electrons that create an **induced magnetic field** similar to the 6 π electrons of benzene. 18-Annulene has 12 protons that are oriented on the outside of the ring (labeled H_o), and 6 protons that are oriented inside the ring (labeled H_i). The induced magnetic field reinforces the external field in the vicinity of the protons on the outside of the ring. These H_o protons are deshielded and so they absorb downfield (8.9 ppm). In contrast, the induced magnetic field is opposite in direction to the applied magnetic field in the vicinity of the protons on the inside of the ring. This shields the H_i protons and the absorption is therefore very far upfield, even higher than TMS (–1.8 ppm).

14.77

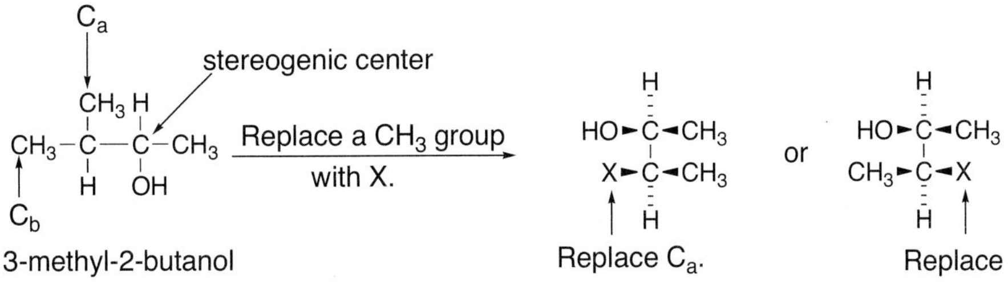

3-methyl-2-butanol

The CH_3 groups are not equivalent to each other, since replacement of each by X forms two diastereomers.

Thus, every C in this compound is different and there are five ^{13}C signals.

14.78

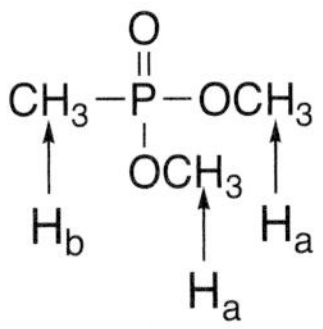

All 6 H_a protons are equivalent.

One P atom splits each nearby CH_3 into a doublet by the $n + 1$ rule, making two doublets.

14.79 a. Splitting pattern:

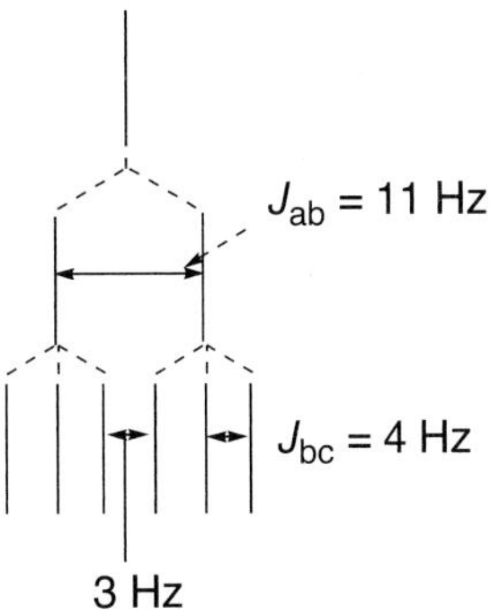

b. Three resonance structures can be drawn for 2-cyclohexenone.

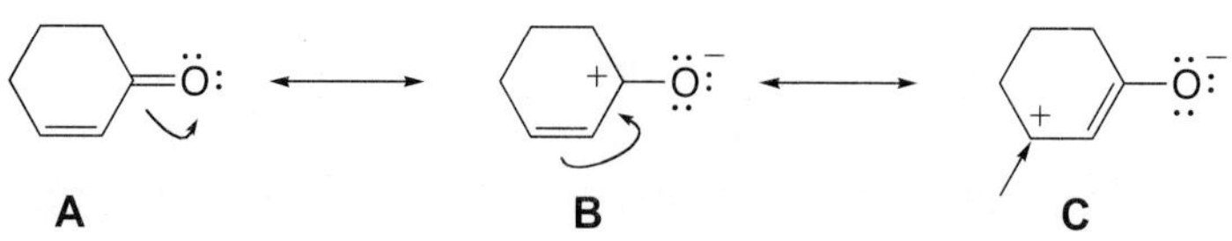

Resonance structure **C** places a (+) charge on one C of the C=C, deshielding the H attached to it and shifting the absorption downfield.

Chapter 15 Radical Reactions

Chapter Review

General features of radicals

- A radical is a reactive intermediate with an unpaired electron (15.1).
- A carbon radical is *sp*^{2} hybridized and trigonal planar (15.1).
- The stability of a radical increases as the number of C's bonded to the radical carbon increases (15.1).

least stable			most stable
$\dot{C}H_3$	$R\dot{C}H_2$	$R_2\dot{C}H$	$R_3\dot{C}$
	1°	2°	3°

→ **Increasing alkyl substitution**
Increasing radical stability

- Allylic radicals are stabilized by resonance, making them more stable than 3° radicals (15.10).

CH2=CH–CH2 ⟷ CH2–CH=CH2

two resonance structures for the allyl radical

Radical reactions

[1] Halogenation of alkanes (15.4)

$$R{-}H \xrightarrow[h\nu \text{ or } \Delta]{X_2} R{-}X$$

X = Cl or Br — R–X: alkyl halide

- The reaction follows a radical chain mechanism.
- The weaker the C–H bond, the more readily the H is replaced by X.
- Chlorination is faster and less selective than bromination (15.6).
- Radical substitution results in racemization at a stereogenic center (15.8).

[2] Allylic halogenation (15.10)

$$CH_2{=}CH{-}CH_3 \xrightarrow[h\nu \text{ or ROOR}]{NBS} CH_2{=}CHCH_2Br$$

allylic halide

- The reaction follows a radical chain mechanism.

[3] Radical addition of HBr to an alkene (15.13)

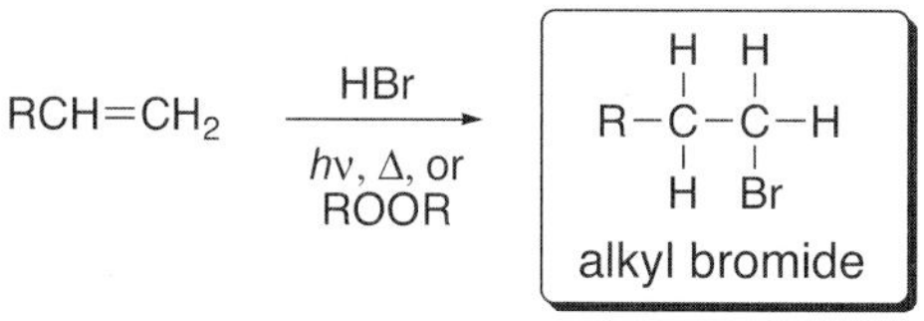
RCH=CH2
HBr
hν, Δ, or ROOR
alkyl bromide

- A radical addition mechanism is followed.
- Br bonds to the less substituted carbon atom to form the more substituted, more stable radical.

[4] Radical polymerization of alkenes (15.14)

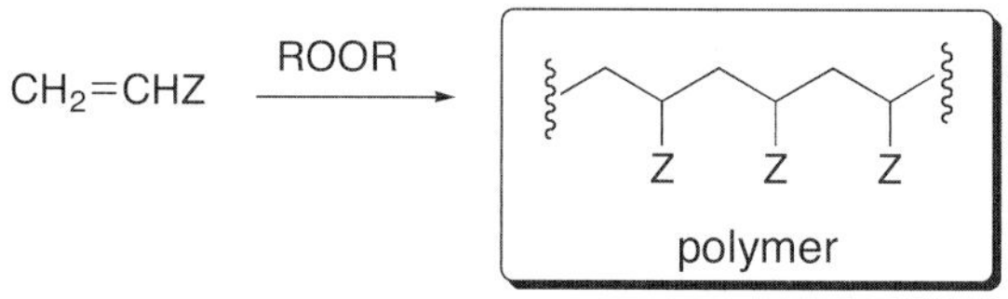
CH2=CHZ
ROOR
Z
Z
Z
polymer

- A radical addition mechanism is followed.

Practice Test on Chapter Review

1. a. Which alkyl halide(s) can be made in good yield by radical halogenation of an alkane?

1. 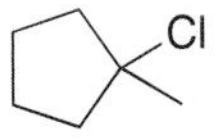

2. 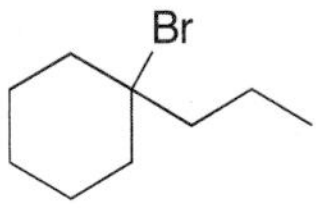

3. 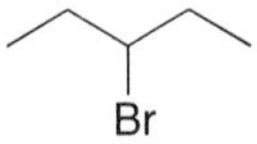

4. Both (1) and (2) can be made in good yield.
5. Compounds (1), (2), and (3) can all be made in good yield.

b. In which of the following reactions will rearrangement ***not*** occur?
1. halogenation of an alkane with Cl_2 and heat
2. addition of Cl_2 to an alkene
3. addition of HCl to an alkene
4. Rearrangements do not occur in reactions (1) and (2).
5. Rearrangements do not occur in reactions (1), (2), and (3).

c. Which labeled H is most easily abstracted in a radical halogenation reaction?

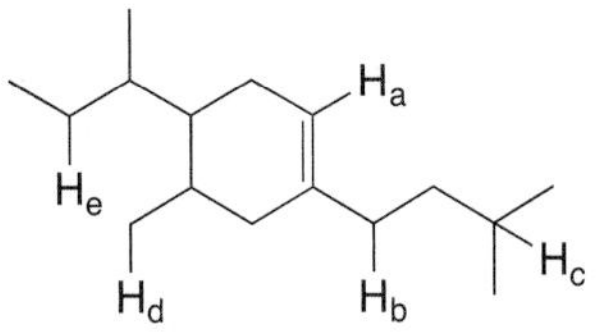

1. H_a
2. H_b
3. H_c
4. H_d
5. H_e

d. Which of the labeled C–H bonds in the following compound has the smallest bond dissociation energy?

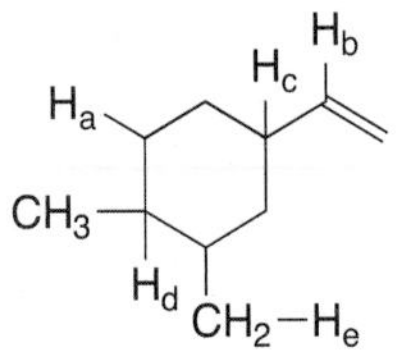

1. C–H_a
2. C–H_b
3. C–H_c
4. C–H_d
5. C–H_e

2. (a) Which radical is the most stable? (b) Which radical is the least stable?

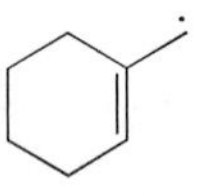

A

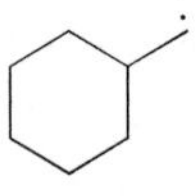

B

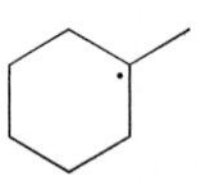

C

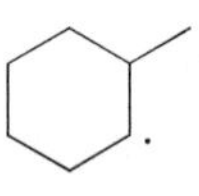

D

3. Draw all of the organic products formed in each reaction. Indicate stereochemistry in part (c).

a. 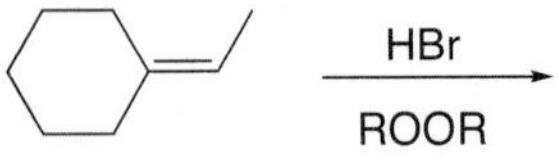

b. 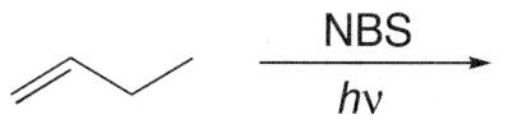

c. 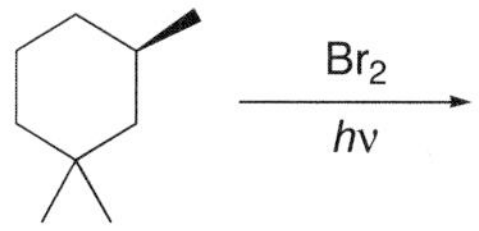

4. What monomer is needed to make the following polymer?

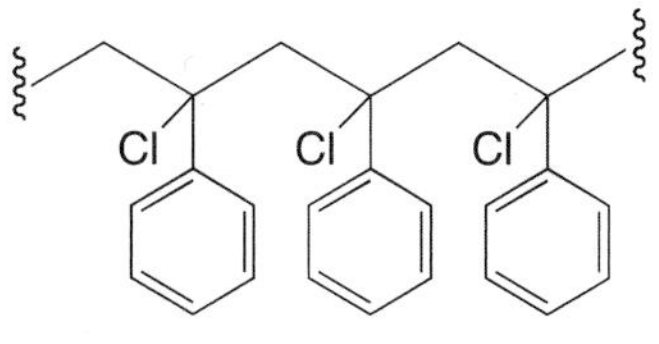

5. In each box, fill in the appropriate reagents needed to carry out the given reaction. This question involves reactions from Chapter 15, as well as previous chapters.

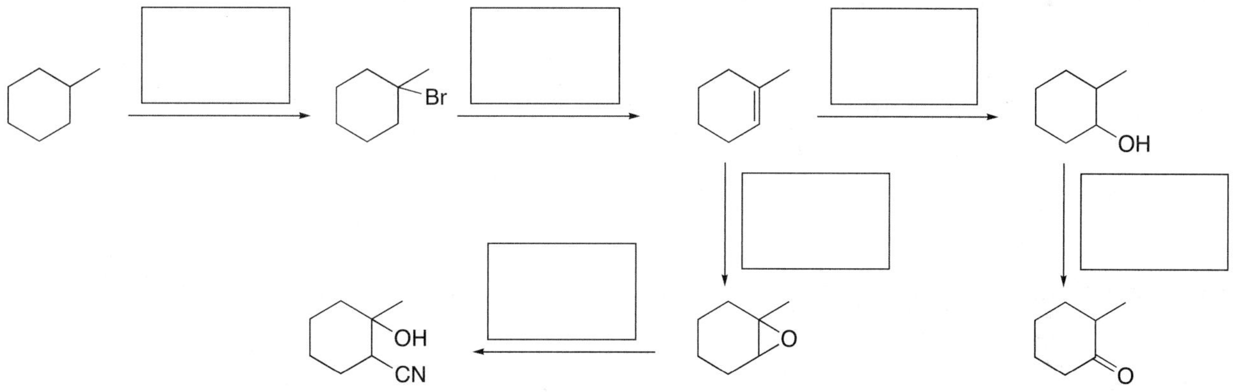

Answers to Practice Test

1.a. 2
b. 4
c. 2
d. 3

2.a. **A**
b. **B**

3.a. 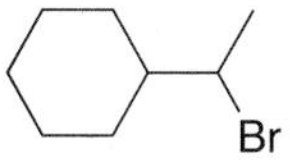

3.b. 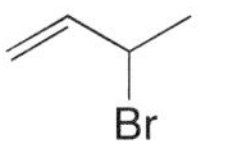 + $BrCH_2CH{=}CHCH_3$ (cis and trans)

3.c. 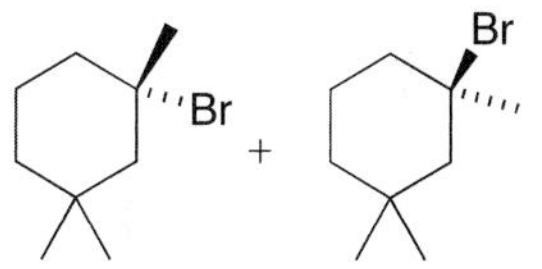

4. 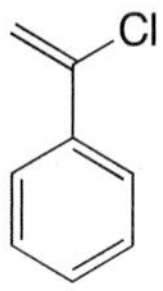

5.

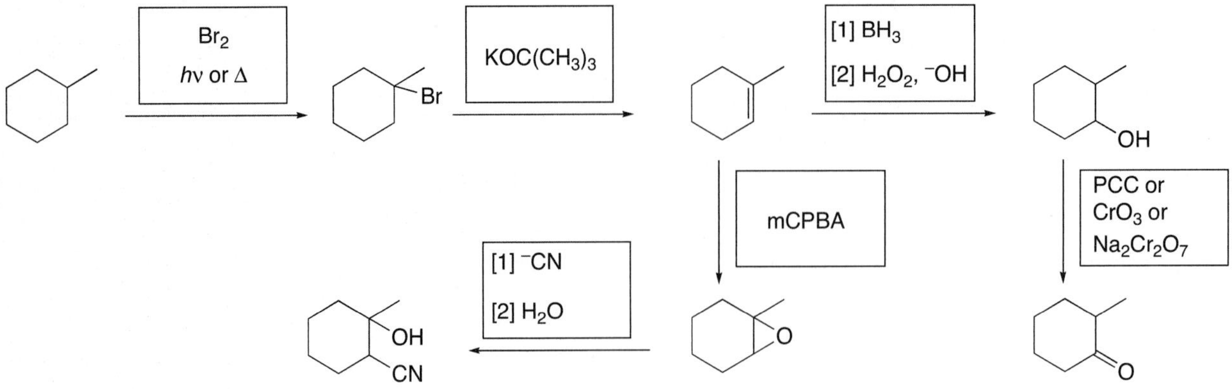

Answers to Problems

15.1 1° Radicals are on C's bonded to one other C; 2° radicals are on C's bonded to two other C's; 3° radicals are on C's bonded to three other C's.

a. $CH_3CH_2{-}\dot{C}HCH_2CH_3$ — **2° radical**

b. 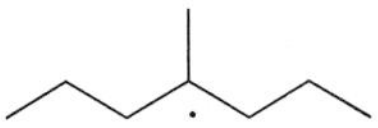 — **3° radical**

c. 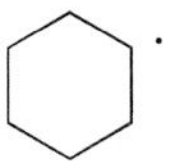 — **2° radical**

d. 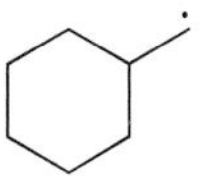 — **1° radical**

15.2 The stability of a radical increases as the number of alkyl groups bonded to the radical carbon increases. Draw the most stable radical.

a. $(CH_3)_2\dot{C}CH_2CH_3$ b. $(CH_3)_3C\dot{C}HCH_3$ c. $(CH_3)_3C\dot{C}H_2$ d. 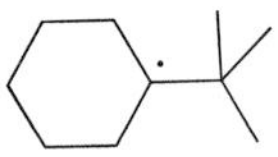

15.3 Reaction of a radical with:

- an alkane abstracts a hydrogen atom and creates a new carbon radical.
- an alkene generates a new bond to one carbon and a new carbon radical.
- another radical forms a bond.

a. $CH_3{-}CH_3 \xrightarrow{:\ddot{Cl}\cdot} CH_3{-}\dot{C}H_2 + H{-}\ddot{Cl}:$

b. $CH_2{=}CH_2 \xrightarrow{:\ddot{Cl}\cdot} \dot{C}H_2{-}CH_2(:\ddot{Cl}:)$

c. $:\ddot{Cl}\cdot \xrightarrow{:\ddot{Cl}\cdot} :\ddot{Cl}{-}\ddot{Cl}:$

d. $:\ddot{Cl}\cdot + \cdot\ddot{O}{-}\ddot{O}\cdot \longrightarrow :\ddot{Cl}{-}\ddot{O}{-}\ddot{O}\cdot$

15.4 **Monochlorination** is a radical substitution reaction in which a Cl replaces a H, thus generating an alkyl halide.

a. 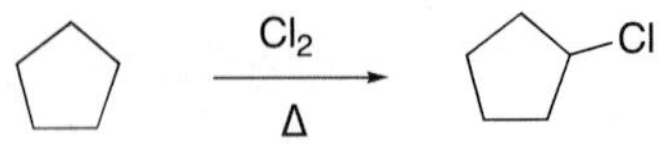

b. $CH_3CH_2CH_2CH_2CH_2CH_3 \xrightarrow[\Delta]{Cl_2} ClCH_2CH_2CH_2CH_2CH_2CH_3 + CH_3{-}CH(Cl){-}CH_2CH_2CH_2CH_3 + CH_3CH_2{-}CH(Cl){-}CH_2CH_2CH_3$

c. $(CH_3)_3CH \xrightarrow[\Delta]{Cl_2} CH_3{-}C(Cl)(CH_3){-}CH_3 + CH_3{-}C(H)(CH_3){-}CH_2Cl$

15.5

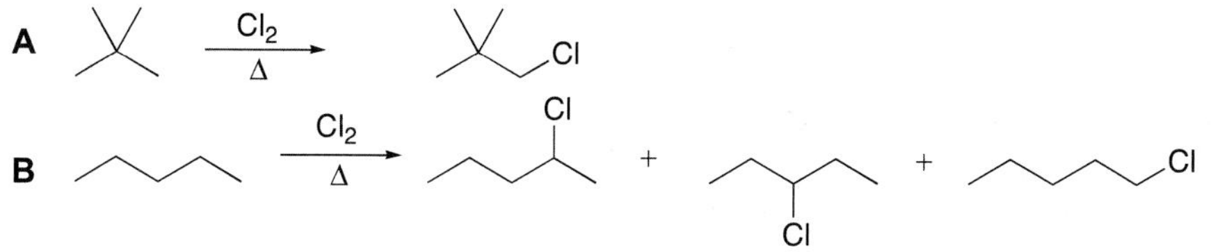

15.6

Initiation:

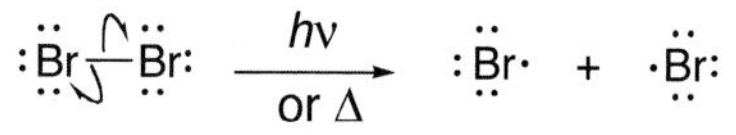

Propagation:

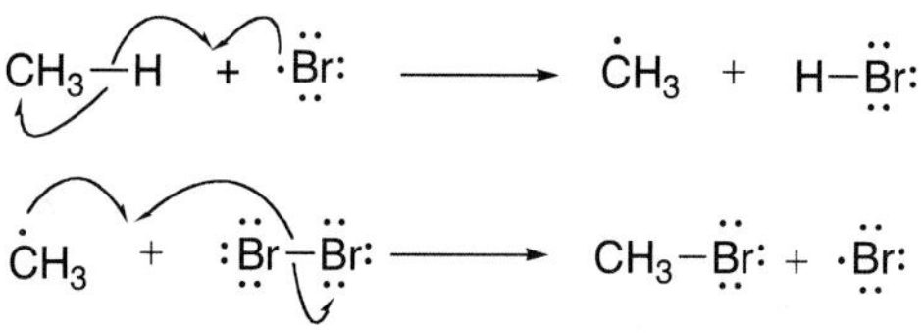

Termination:

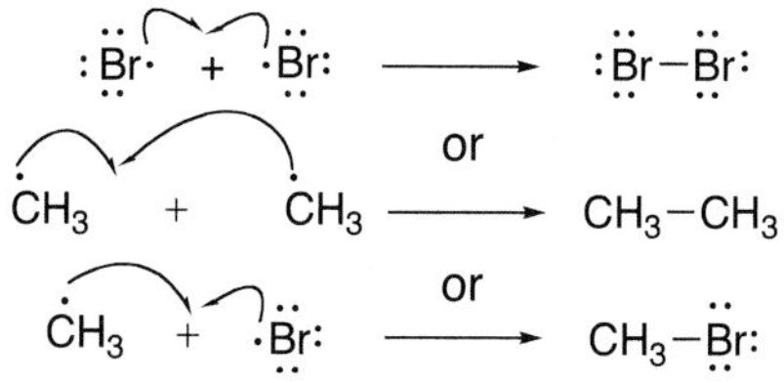

15.7

Step 1:

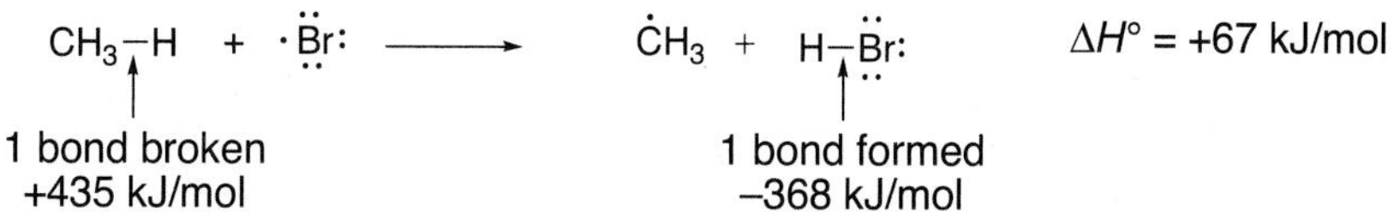

Step 2:

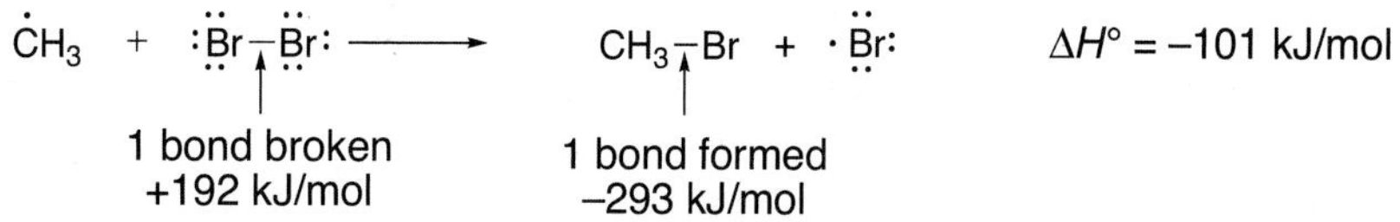

15.8 The rate-determining step for halogenation reactions is formation of $CH_3\cdot + HX$.

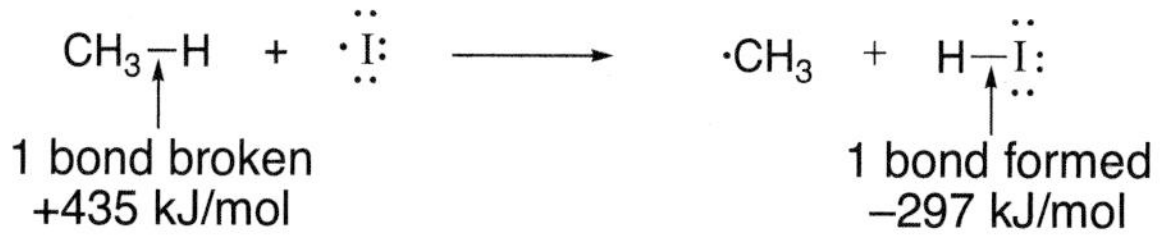

$\Delta H° = +138$ kJ/mol

This reaction is more endothermic and has a higher E_a than a similar reaction with Cl_2 or Br_2.

15.9 The **weakest C–H bond** in each alkane is the **most readily cleaved** during radical halogenation.

a.

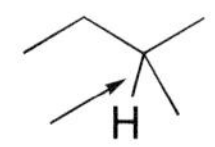

3°
most reactive

b.

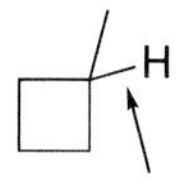

3°
most reactive

c.

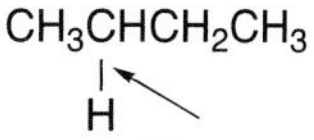

2°
most reactive

15.10 To draw the product of bromination:

- Draw out the starting material and find the most reactive C–H bond (on the most substituted C).
- The major product is formed by **cleavage of the *weakest* C–H bond.**

a. 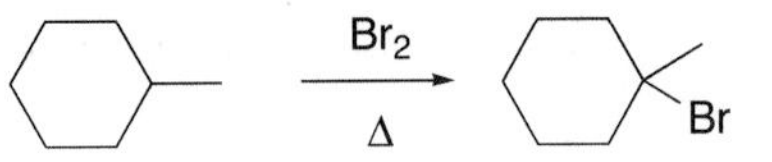

c. 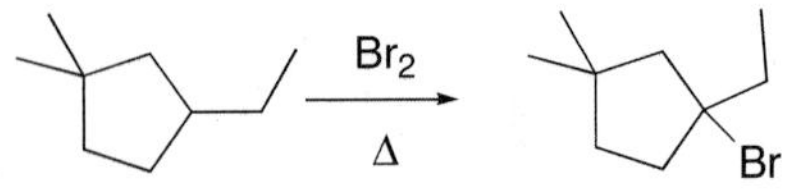

b. 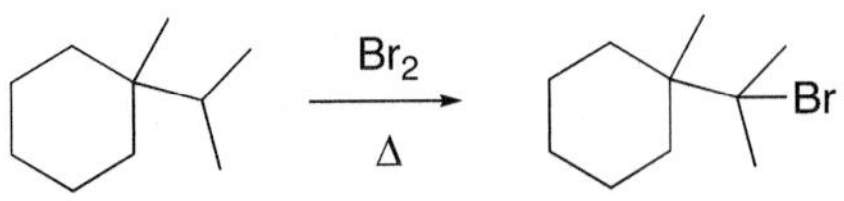

d. 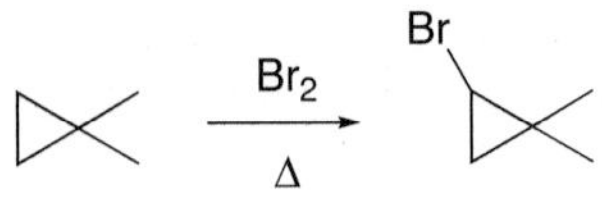

15.11 If 1° C–H and 3° C–H bonds were equally reactive there would be nine times as much $(CH_3)_2CHCH_2Cl$ as $(CH_3)_3CCl$ since the ratio of 1° to 3° H's is 9:1. The fact that the ratio is only 63:37 shows that the 1° C–H bond is less reactive than the 3° C–H bond. $(CH_3)_2CHCH_2Cl$ is still the major product, though, because there are nine 1° C–H bonds and only one 3° C–H bond.

15.12

a. 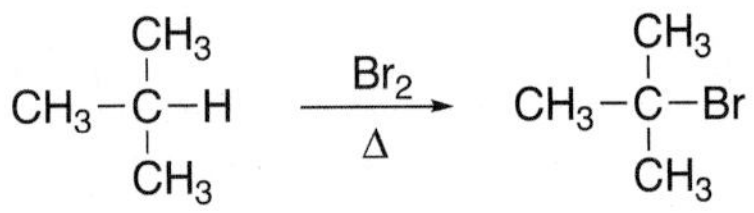

c. 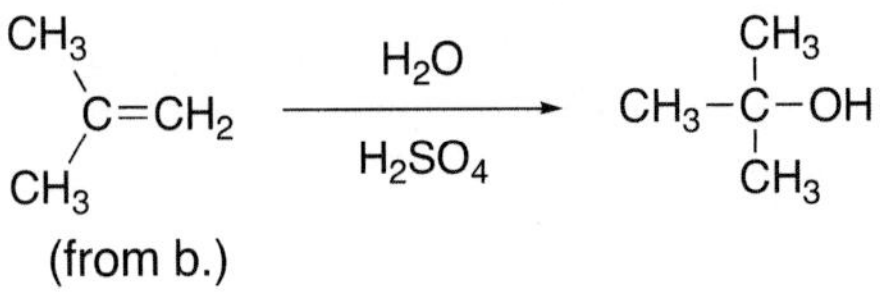

b. 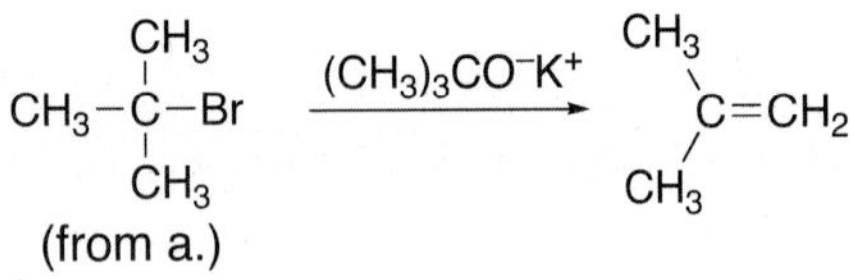

d. 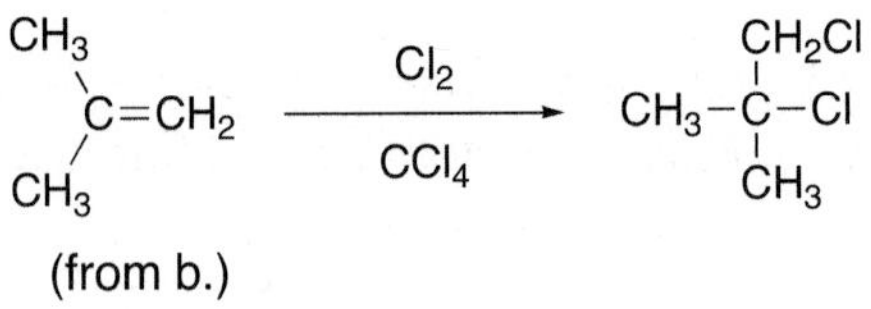

15.13

a. 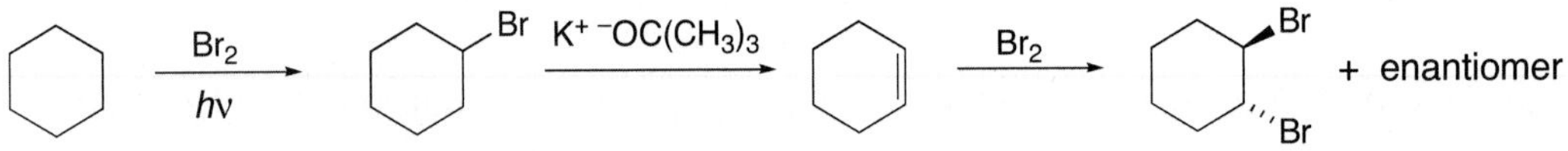

b. 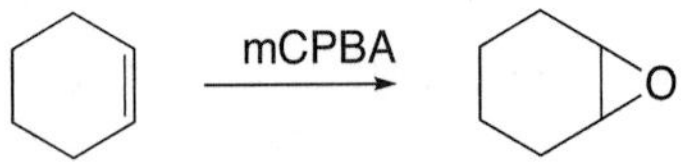

(from a.)

15.14 Since the reaction does not occur at the stereogenic center, leave it as is.

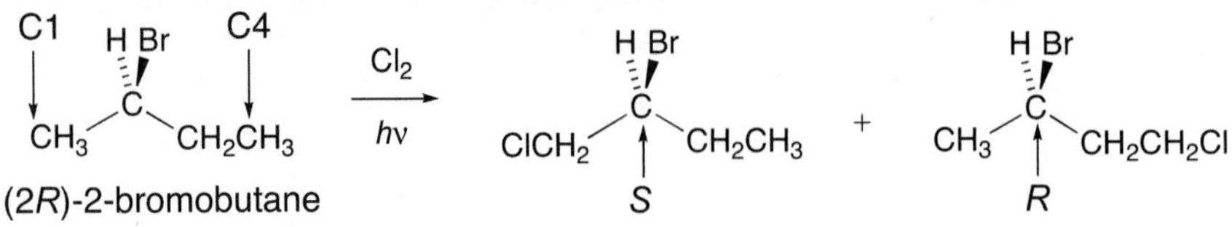
C1
C4
H Br
Cl2
hν
(2R)-2-bromobutane
ClCH2
CH2CH3
S
CH3
CH2CH2Cl
R

15.15

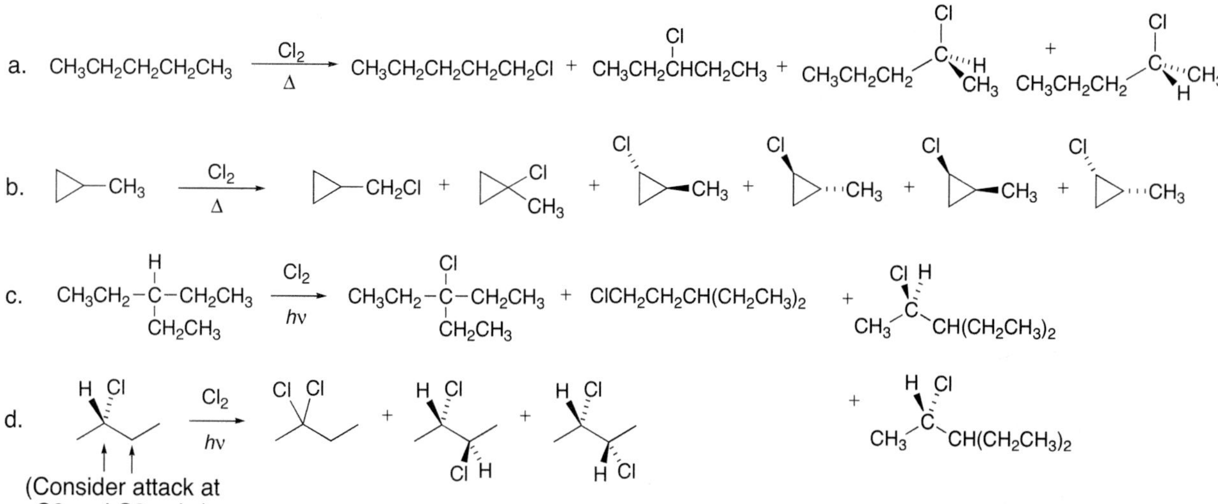

(Consider attack at C2 and C3 only.)

15.16

Chain propagation:

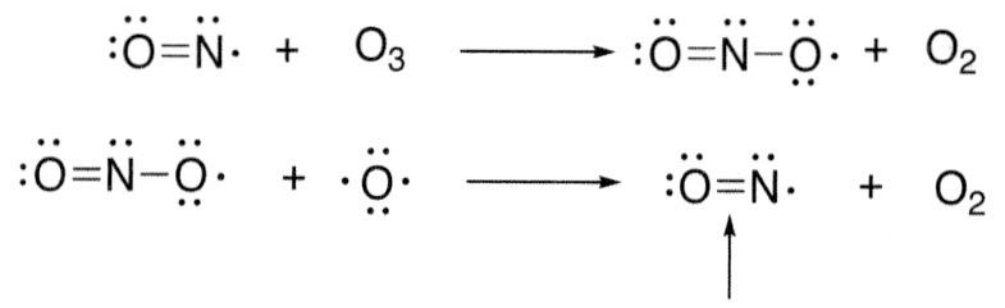

The radical is re-formed.

15.17 Draw the resonance structure by moving the π bond and the unpaired electron. The hybrid is drawn with dashed lines for bonds that are in one resonance structure but not another. The symbol $\delta^{\bullet}$ is used on any atom that has an unpaired electron in any resonance structure.

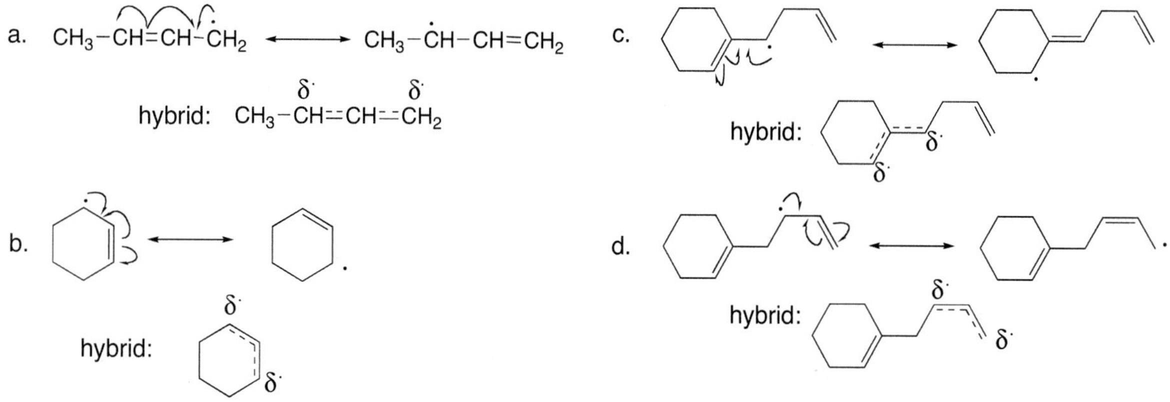

15.18 Reaction of an alkene with NBS or $Br_2 + h\nu$ yields allylic substitution products.

a.

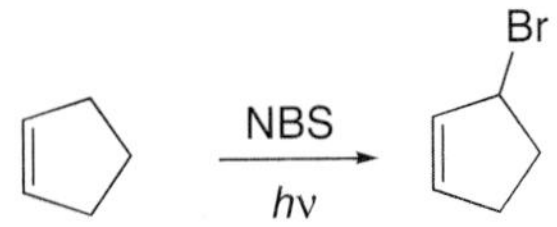

b. $CH_2{=}CH{-}CH_3 \xrightarrow[h\nu]{NBS} CH_2{=}CH{-}CH_2Br$

c. $CH_2{=}CH{-}CH_3 \xrightarrow{Br_2} \underset{Br\ \ Br}{CH_2CHCH_3}$

15.19

a. $CH_3{-}CH{=}CH{-}CH_3 \xrightarrow[h\nu]{NBS} CH_3{-}CH{=}CH{-}CH_2Br + CH_3CH(Br)CH{=}CH_2$

b.

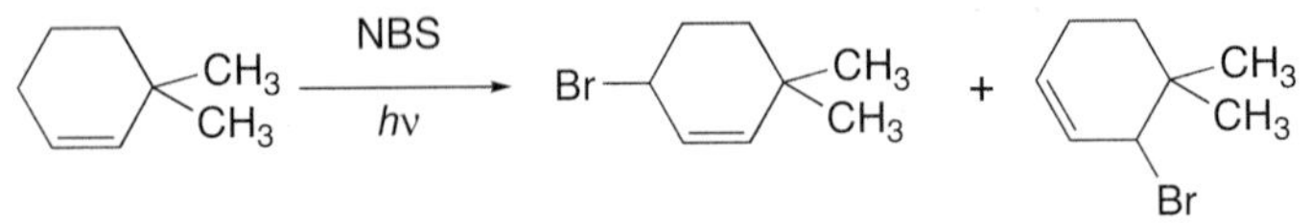

c. $CH_2{=}C(CH_2CH_3)_2 \xrightarrow[h\nu]{NBS} CH_2{=}C(CHBrCH_3)(CH_2CH_3) + BrCH_2C(CH_2CH_3){=}CHCH_3$

15.20

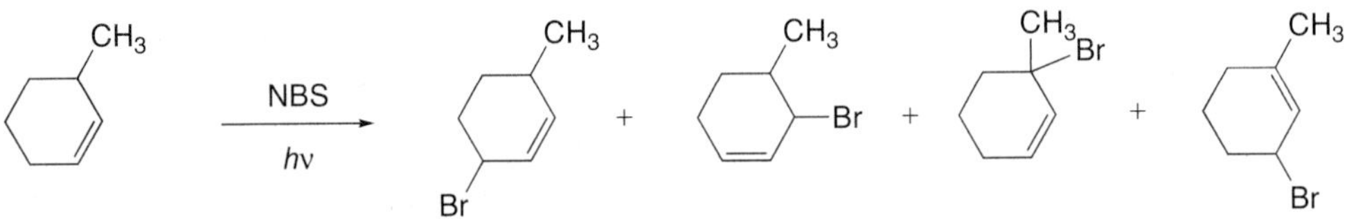

15.21 Reaction of an alkene with NBS + $h\nu$ yields allylic substitution products.

a.

one possible product: **high yield**

b. $CH_3CH_2CH{=}CHCH_2Br$

c.

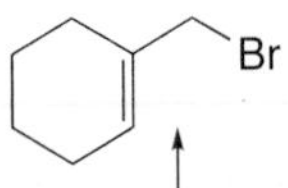

Cannot be made in high yield by allylic halogenation.
Any alkene starting material would yield a mixture of allylic halides.

15.22 The weakest C–H bond is most readily cleaved. To draw the hydroperoxide products, add OOH to each carbon that bears a radical in one of the resonance structures.

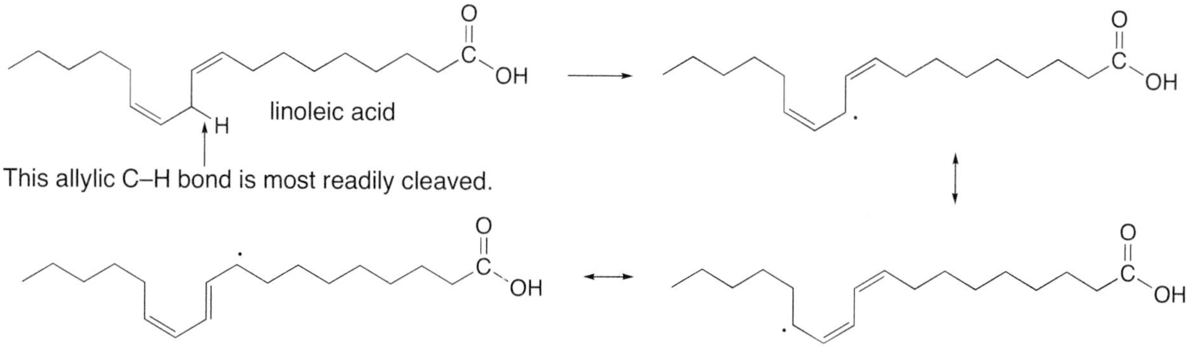
linoleic acid
This allylic C–H bond is most readily cleaved.

hydroperoxide products:

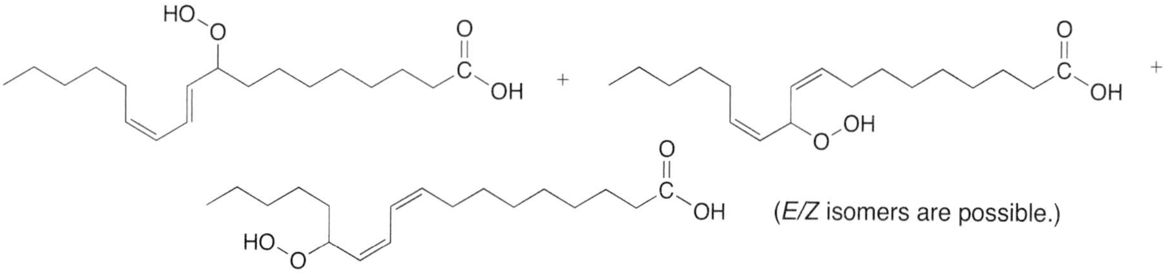
(E/Z isomers are possible.)

15.23 Only (b) has an OH on a benzene ring, so it may be an antioxidant.

b.

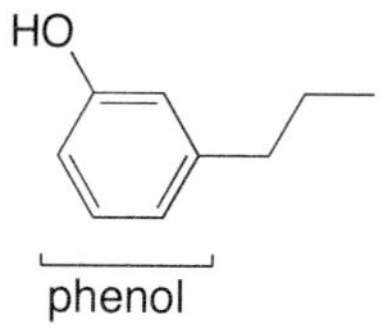
phenol

15.24

a. $CH_2{=}CHCH_2CH_2CH_2CH_3 \xrightarrow{HBr} CH_3CH(Br)CH_2CH_2CH_2CH_3$

$CH_2{=}CHCH_2CH_2CH_2CH_3 \xrightarrow[ROOR]{HBr} CH_2BrCH_2CH_2CH_2CH_2CH_3$

b.

c. $CH_3CH{=}CHCH_2CH_2CH_3 \xrightarrow[\text{or HBr, ROOR}]{HBr} CH_3CH(Br){-}CH_2CH_2CH_2CH_3 + CH_3CH_2{-}CH(Br)CH_2CH_2CH_3$

15.25 In addition of HBr under radical conditions:

- Br· adds first to form the more stable radical.
- Then H· is added to the carbon radical.

2 radical possibilities:

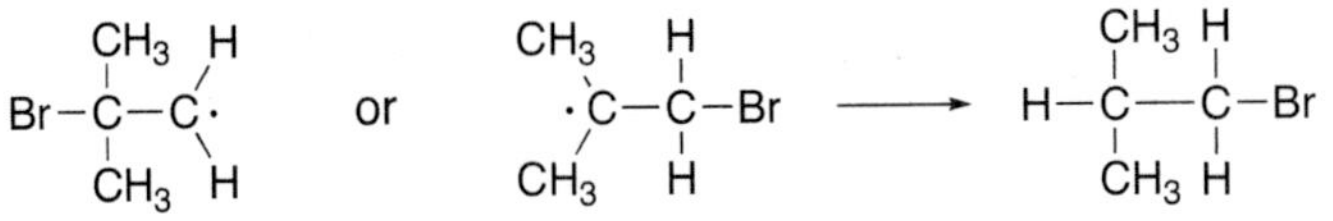
CH3 H
Br-C-C·
CH3 H
or
CH3 H
·C-C-Br
CH3 H
CH3 H
H-C-C-Br
CH3 H

1° radical *less* stable

3° radical ***more* stable** This radical forms.

15.26

a.

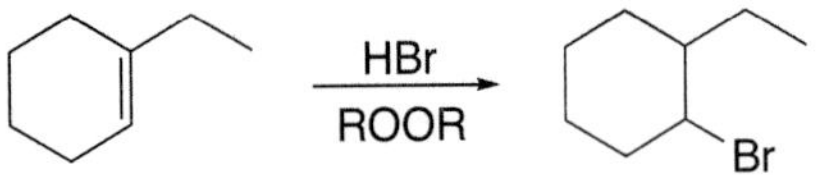
HBr
ROOR
Br

b.

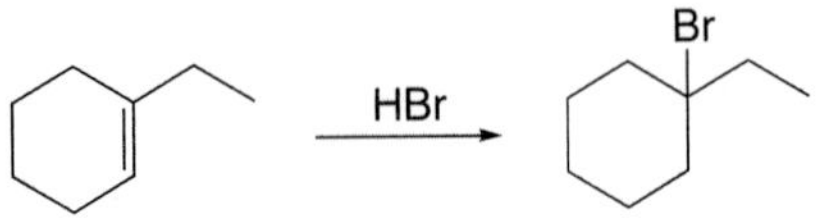
HBr
Br

c.

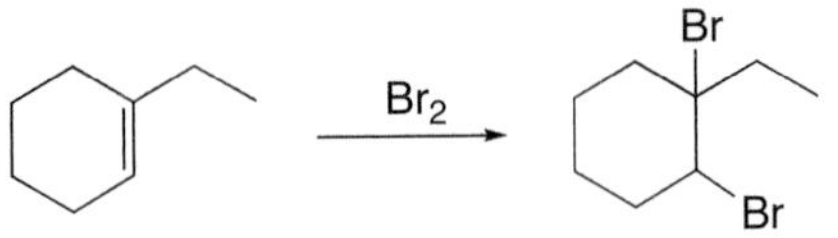
Br2
Br
Br

15.27

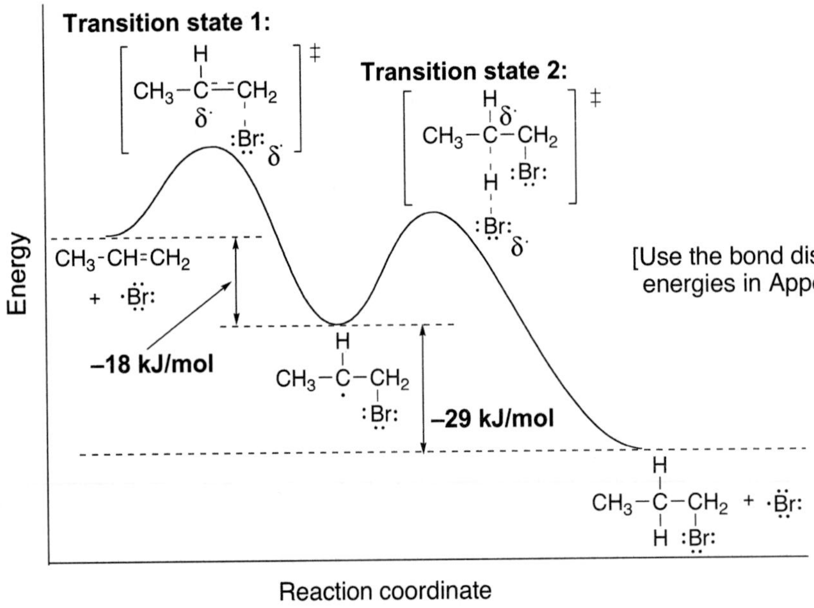
Transition state 1:
Transition state 2:
Energy
CH3-CH=CH2
+ ·Br:
–18 kJ/mol
–29 kJ/mol
Reaction coordinate

[Use the bond dissociation energies in Appendix C.]

15.28

a.

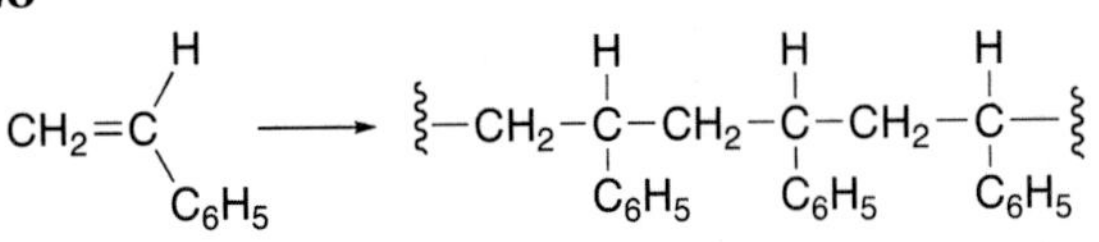
CH2=C
H
C6H5

polystyrene

b.

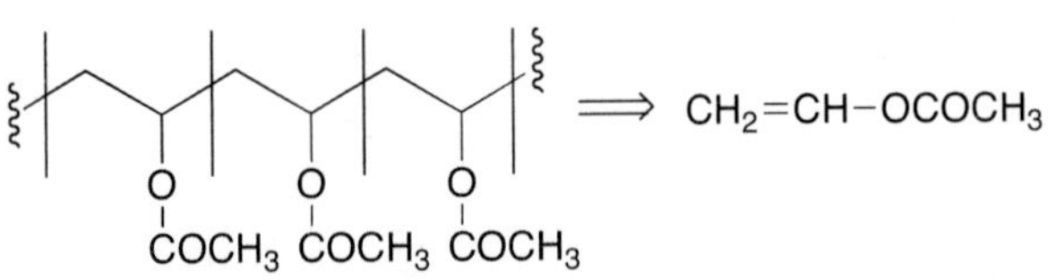
COCH3 COCH3 COCH3
CH2=CH-OCOCH3

poly(vinyl acetate)

15.29

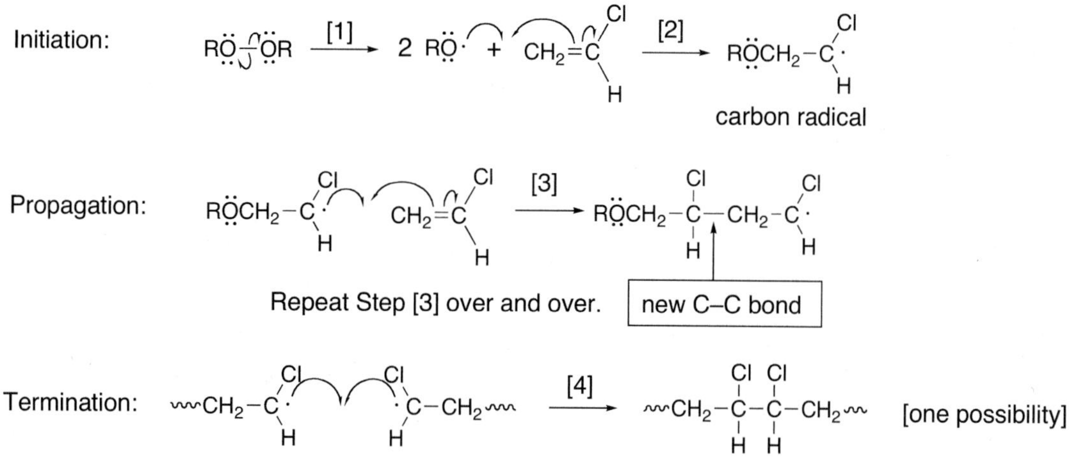
Initiation:
[1]
2 RȮ·
carbon radical
[2]
Propagation:
[3]
Repeat Step [3] over and over.
new C–C bond
Termination:
[4]
[one possibility]

15.30 With Cl_2, each H of the starting material can be replaced by Cl. With Br_2, cleavage of the weakest C–H bond is preferred.

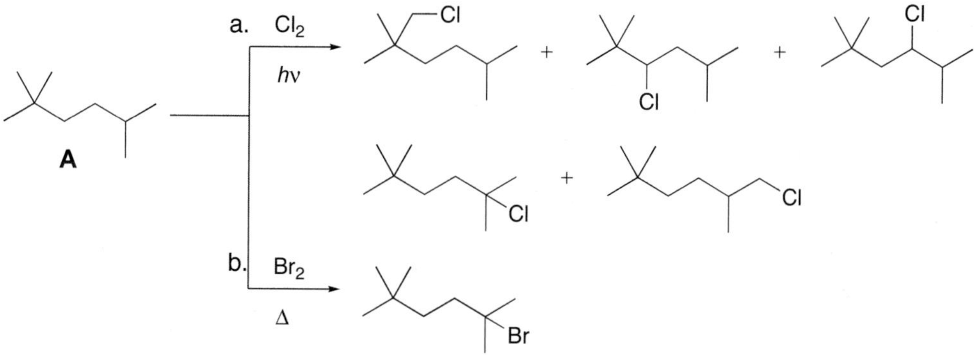
A
a. Cl2
hν
b. Br2
Δ
Cl
Br

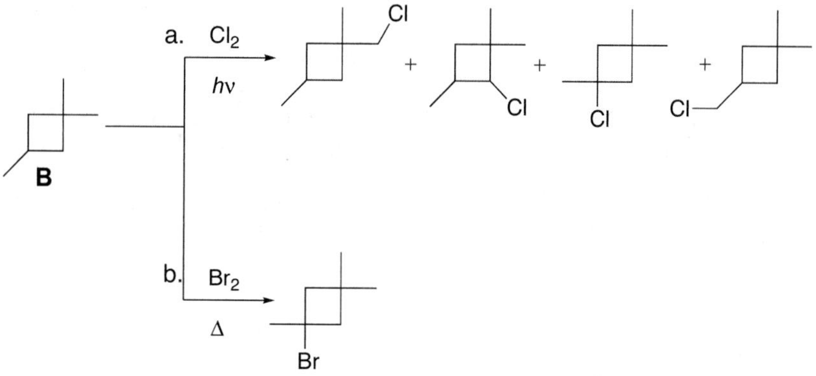
B
a. Cl2
hν
b. Br2
Δ
Cl
Br

15.31

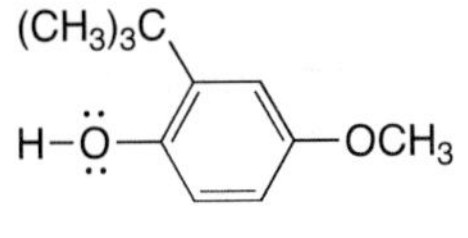

(CH3)3C
H–Ö
OCH3

Abstraction of the phenol H produces a resonance-stabilized radical.

BHA

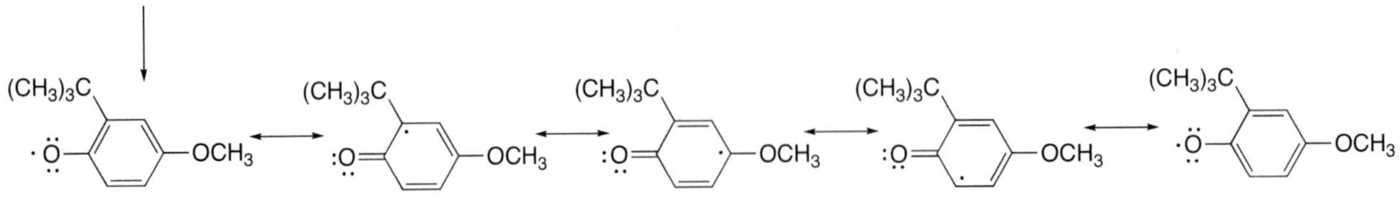

(CH3)3C
OCH3

15.32

a. increasing bond strength: 2 < 3 < 1

b. and c.

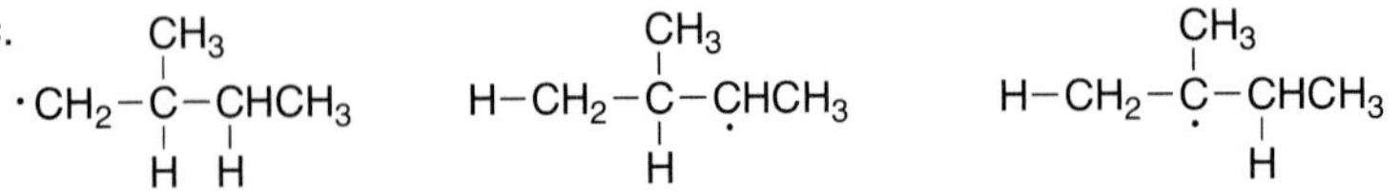

CH3
·CH2–C–CHCH3
H H
H–CH2–C–CHCH3
H

1° radical	2° radical	3° radical
least stable	**intermediate stability**	**most stable**

d. increasing ease of H abstraction: 1 < 3 < 2

15.33 Use the directions from Answer 15.2 to rank the radicals.

a.

$(CH_3)_2CHCH_2CH(CH_3)\dot{C}H_2$	$(CH_3)_2CH\dot{C}HCH(CH_3)_2$	$(CH_3)_2\dot{C}CH_2CH(CH_3)_2$
1° radical	2° radical	3° radical
least stable	**intermediate stability**	**most stable**

b.

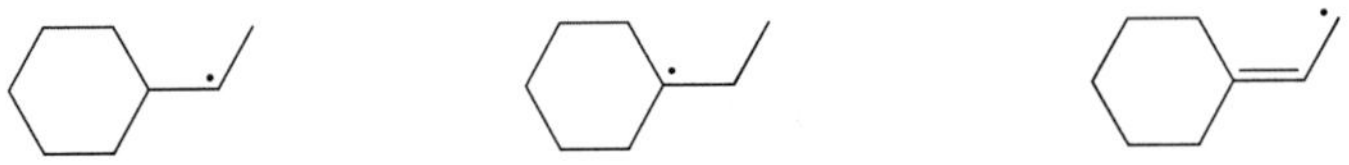

2° radical	3° radical	allylic radical
least stable	**intermediate stability**	**most stable**

15.34 Draw the radical formed by cleavage of the benzylic C–H bond. Then draw all of the resonance structures. Having more resonance structures (five in this case) makes the radical more stable, and the benzylic C–H bond weaker.

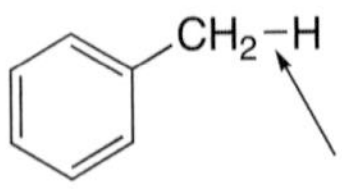

CH2–H

benzylic C–H bond
bond dissociation energy = 356 kJ/mol

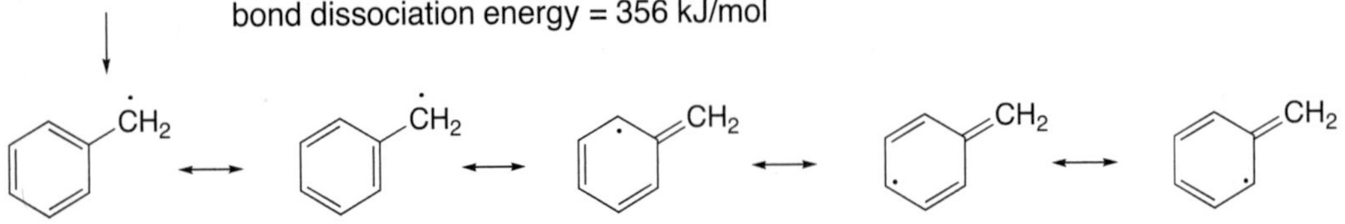

CH2

15.35

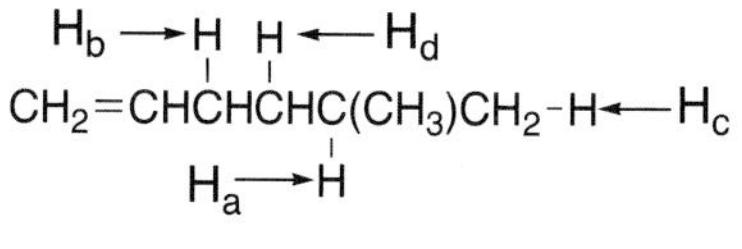

H_a = bonded to an *sp*^{3} 3° carbon
H_b = bonded to an allylic carbon
H_c = bonded to an *sp*^{3} 1° carbon
H_d = bonded to an *sp*^{3} 2° carbon

Increasing ease of abstraction:
$H_c < H_d < H_a < H_b$

15.36

a. 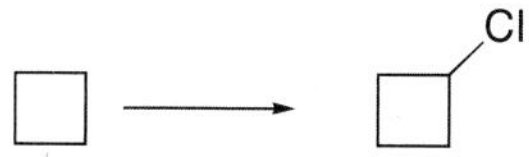

b. 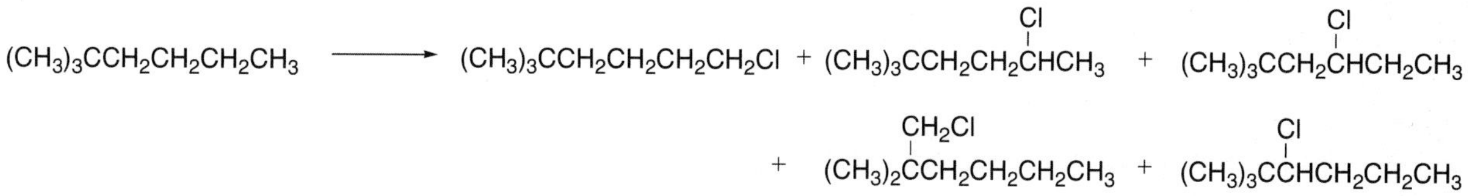

c. 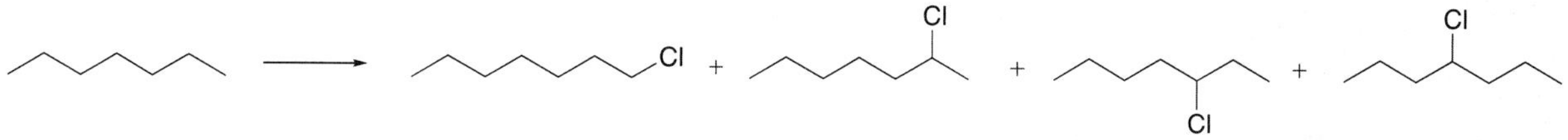

d. 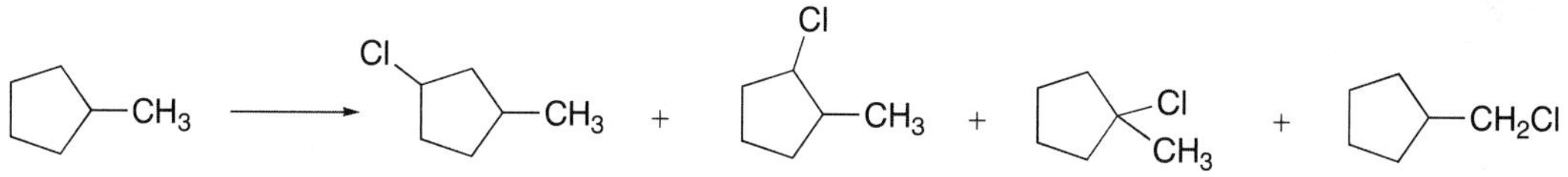

15.37 To draw the product of bromination:

- Draw out the starting material and find the most reactive C–H bond (on the most substituted C).
- The major product is formed by **cleavage of the *weakest* C–H bond.**

a. 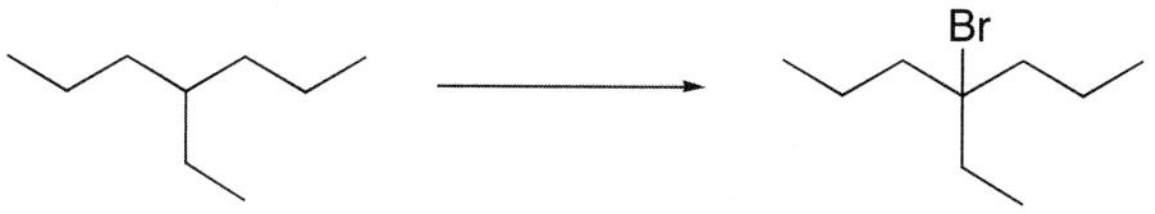

c. 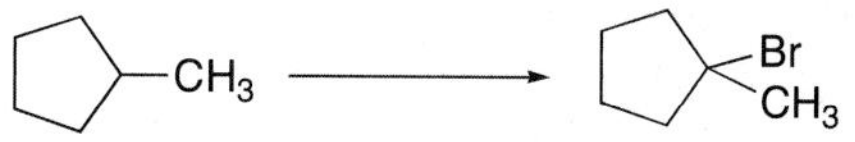

b. 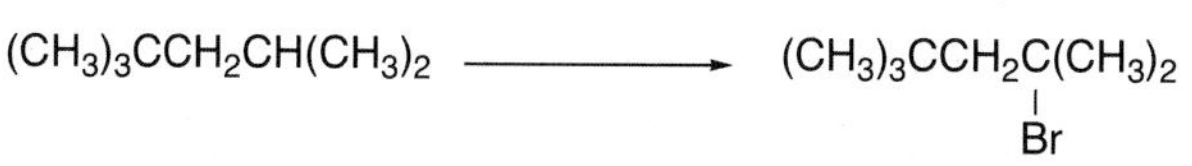

d. 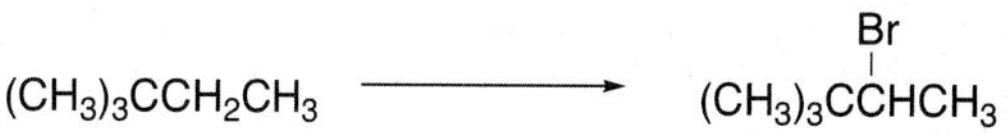

15.38 Draw all of the alkane isomers of C_6H_{14} and their products on chlorination. Then determine which letter corresponds to which alkane.

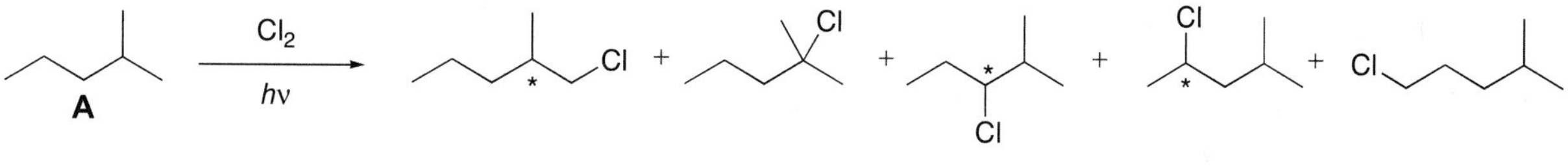

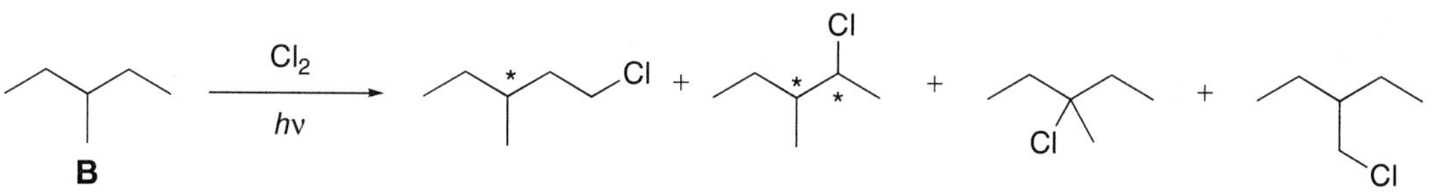

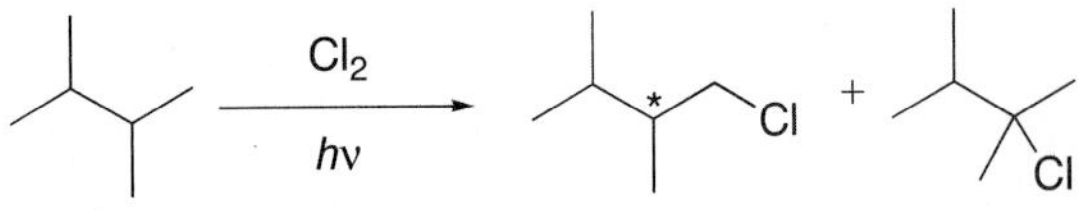

C

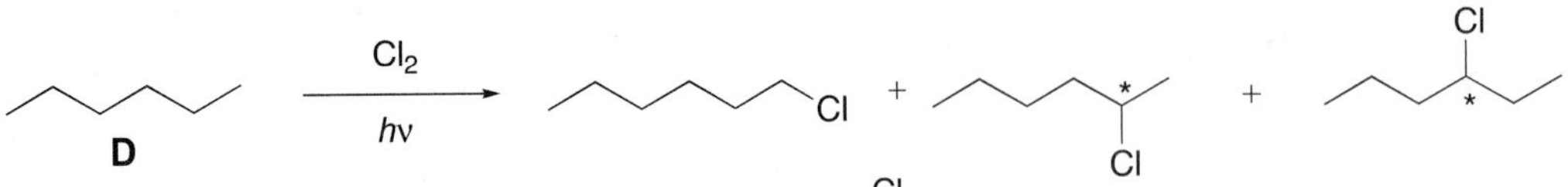

D

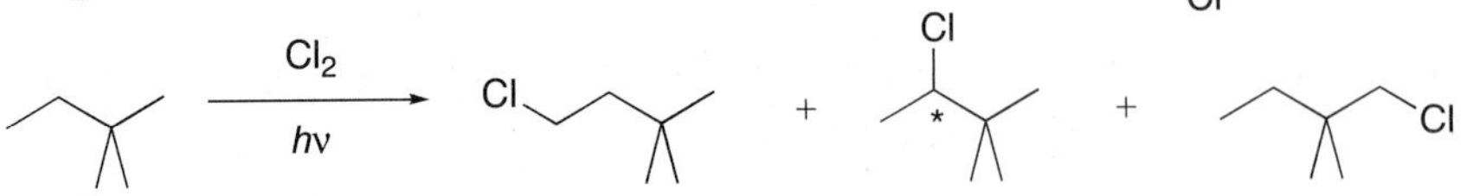

E

[* = stereogenic center]

15.39 Halogenation replaces a C–H bond with a C–X bond. To find the alkane needed to make each of the alkyl halides, replace the X with an H.

a. 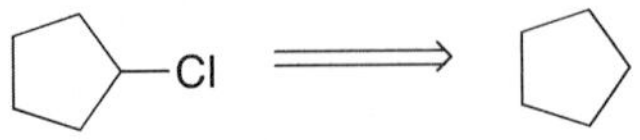

b. 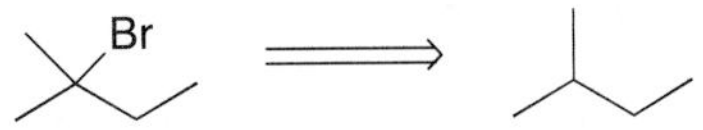

c. 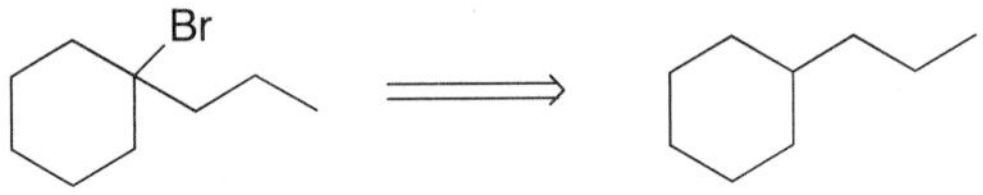

d. $(CH_3)_3CCH_2Cl$ ⟹ $(CH_3)_3CCH_3$

15.40 For an alkane to yield one major product on monohalogenation with Cl_2, all of the hydrogens must be identical in the starting material. For an alkane to yield one major product on bromination, it must have a more substituted carbon in the starting material.

a. 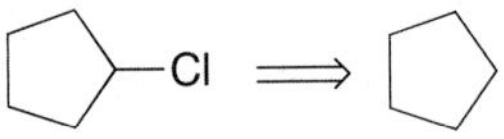

b. 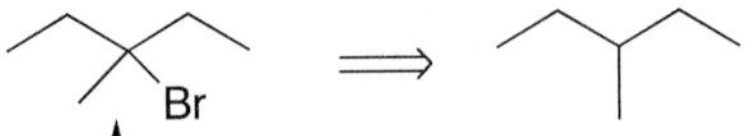

These two compounds can be formed in high yield from an alkane.

c. 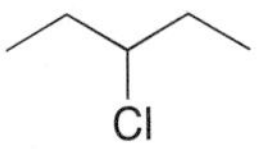

three different C–H bonds

d. 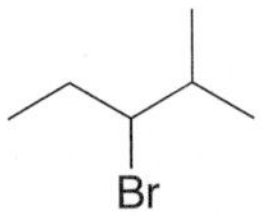

Br on 2° carbon
The product with Br on 3° carbon will form predominantly.

These two compounds cannot be formed in high yield from an alkane.

15.41 A single constitutional isomer is formed in both halogenations in (a), (c), and (d). Bromination often forms a single product by cleavage of the weakest C–H bond. For chlorination to form a single product, the starting material must have only one kind of H that reacts. In (c), a single chlorination product is formed because there is only one type of sp^3 hybridized C–H bond.

a. 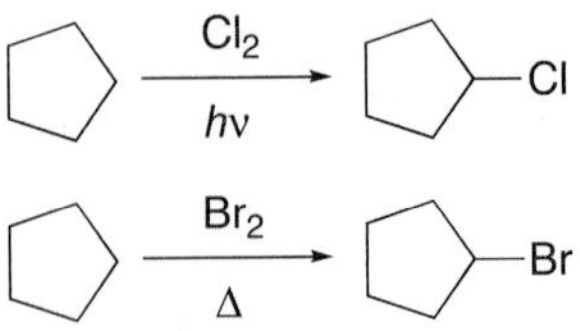

b. 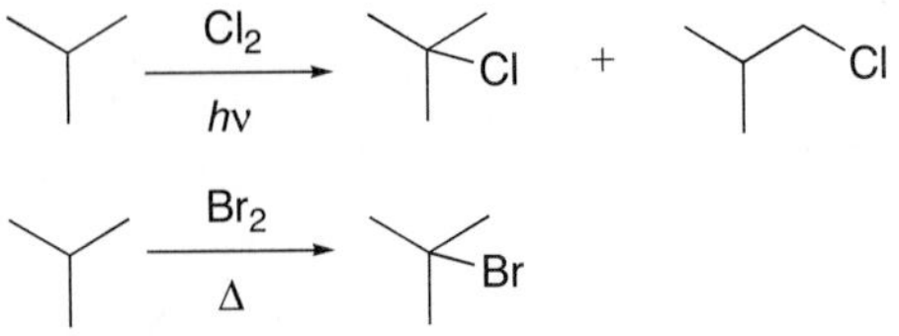

c. 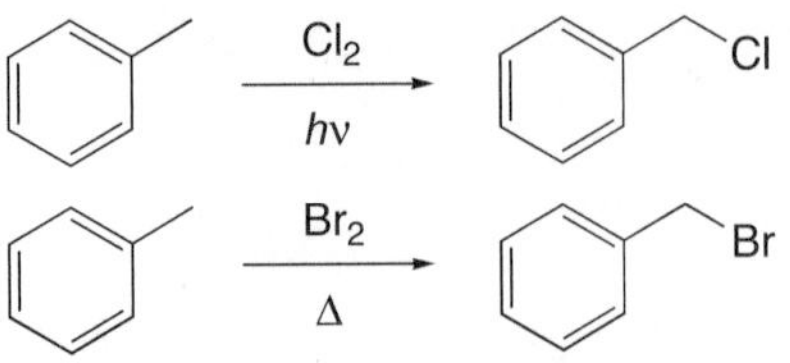

d. 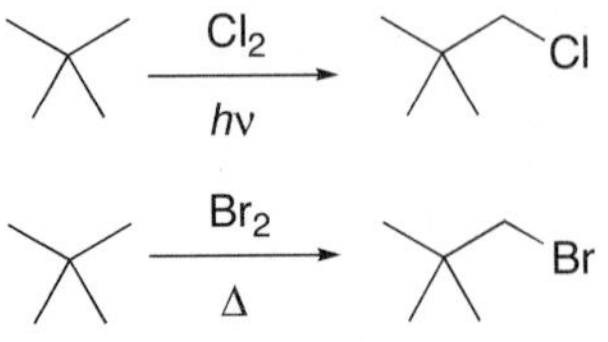

e. 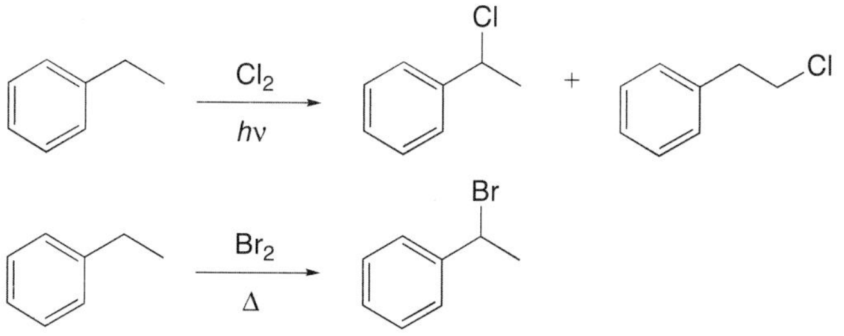
Cl
Cl2
hv
+
Cl
Br
Br2
Δ

15.42 In bromination, the predominant (or exclusive) product is formed by cleavage of the weaker C–H bond to form the more stable radical intermediate.

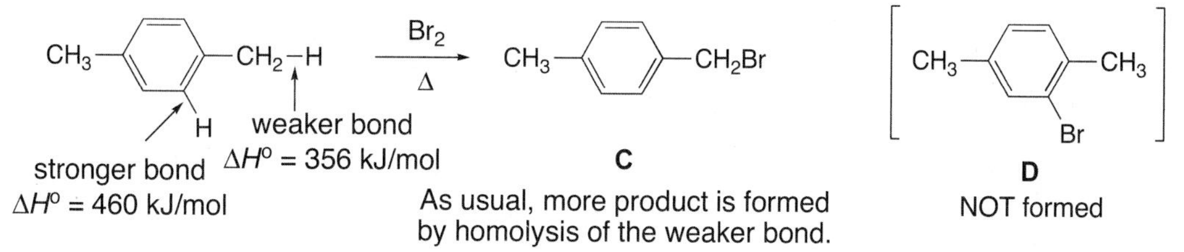
CH3
CH2–H
Br2
Δ
CH3
CH2Br
CH3
CH3
H
weaker bond
Br
stronger bond
ΔH° = 356 kJ/mol
C
D
ΔH° = 460 kJ/mol
As usual, more product is formed
by homolysis of the weaker bond.
NOT formed

15.43 Chlorination is not selective so a mixture of products results. Bromination is selective, and the major product is formed by cleavage of the weakest C–H bond.

a. 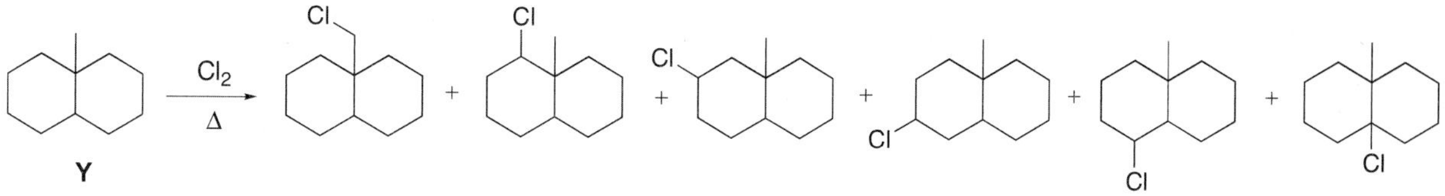
Y
Cl2
Δ
Cl
Cl
Cl
Cl
Cl
Cl

b. 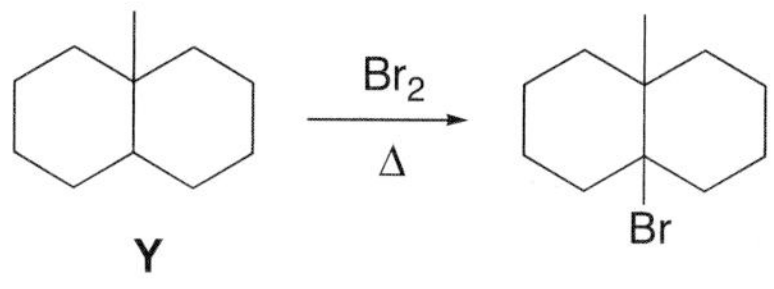
Y
Br2
Δ
Br

c. 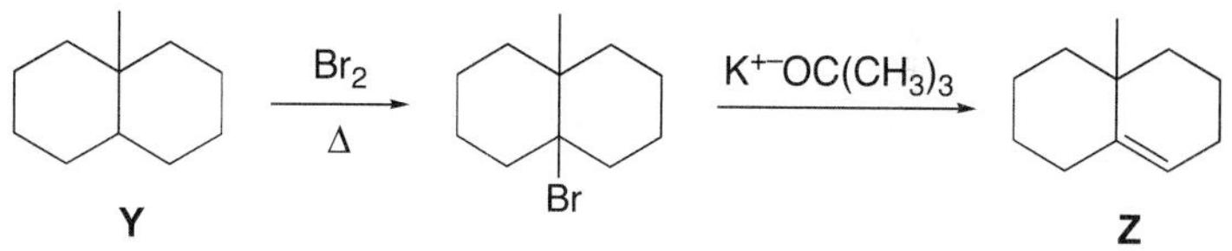
Y
Br2
Δ
Br
K+ −OC(CH3)3
Z

15.44 Draw the resonance structures by moving the π bonds and the radical.

a. 
CH2
CH2

b. 

c. 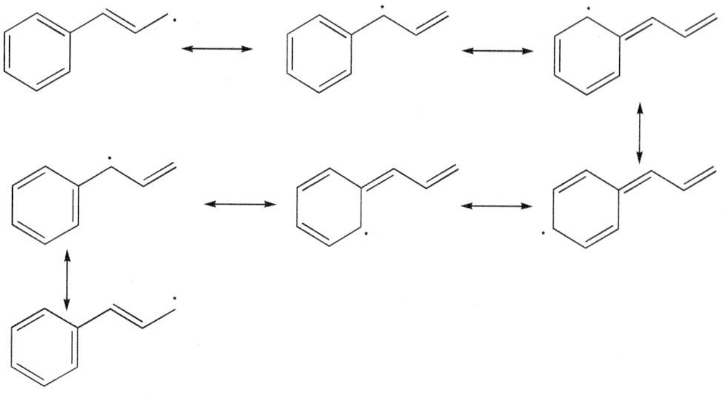

15.45 Reaction of an alkene with NBS + *hν* yields allylic substitution products.

a. 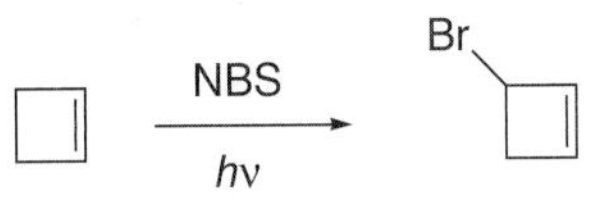

b. $CH_3CH_2CH{=}CHCH_2CH_3 \xrightarrow[h\nu]{NBS} CH_3CH_2CH{=}CHCH(Br)CH_3 + CH_3CH_2CH(Br)CH{=}CHCH_3$

c. $(CH_3)_2C{=}CHCH_3 \xrightarrow[h\nu]{NBS} (CH_3)_2C{=}CHCH_2Br + BrCH_2C(CH_3){=}CHCH_3 + CH_2{=}C(CH_3)CH(Br)CH_3 + (CH_3)_2C(Br)CH{=}CH_2$

d. 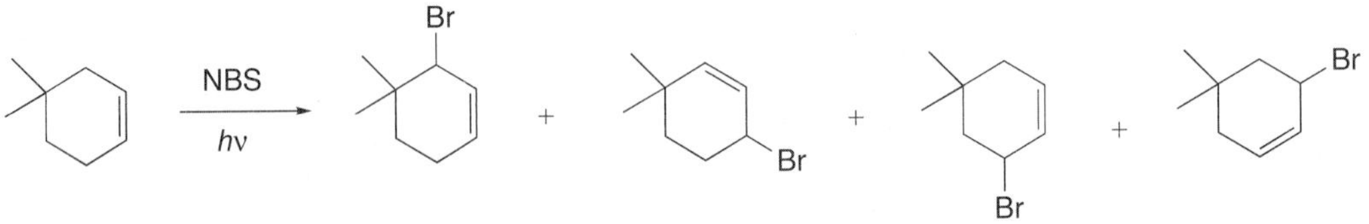

15.46 It is not possible to form 5-bromo-1-methylcyclopentene in good yield by allylic bromination because several other products are formed. 1-Methylcyclopentene has three different types of allylic hydrogens (labeled with *), all of which can be removed during radical bromination.

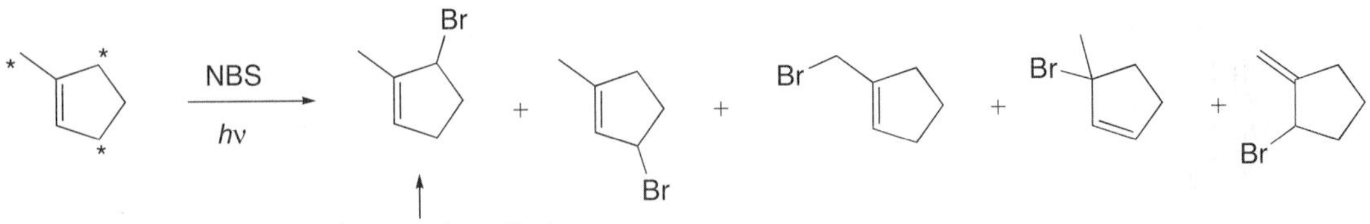

5-bromo-1-methyl-
cyclopentene

15.47

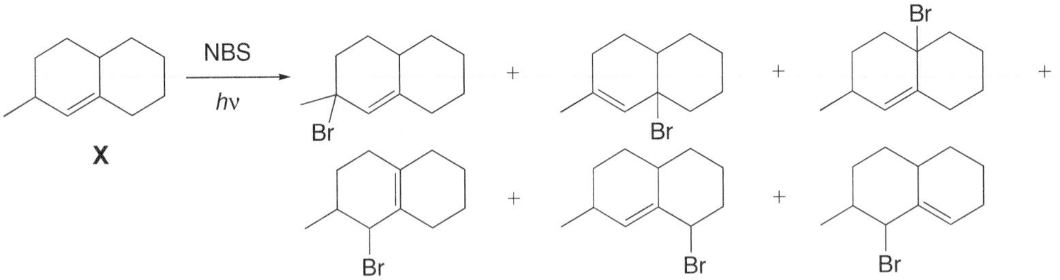

15.48

a. 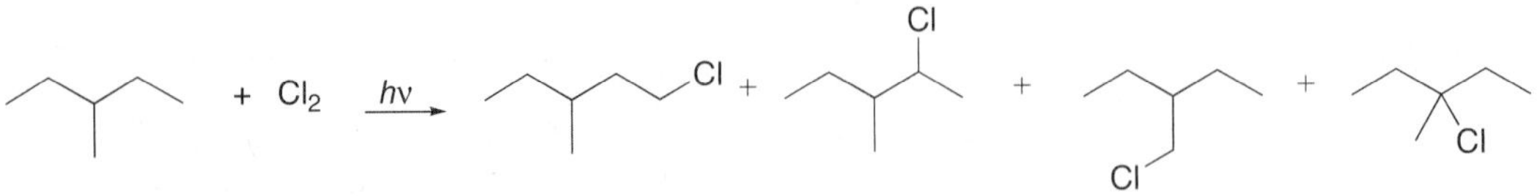

b. 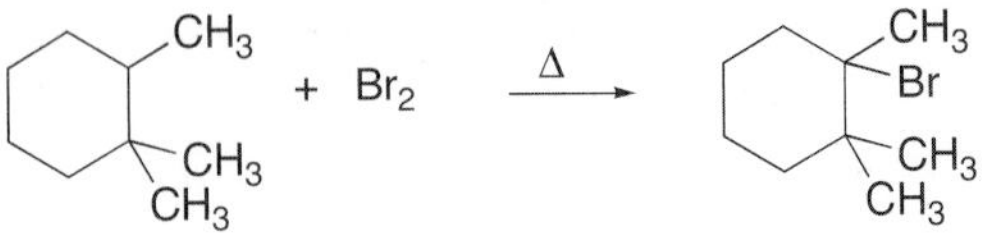

(major product)

c. 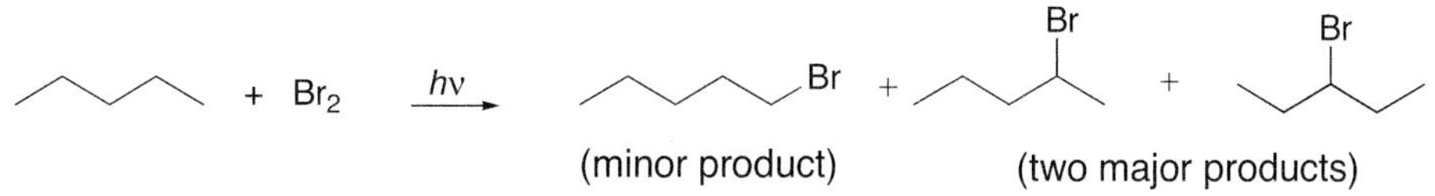

d. 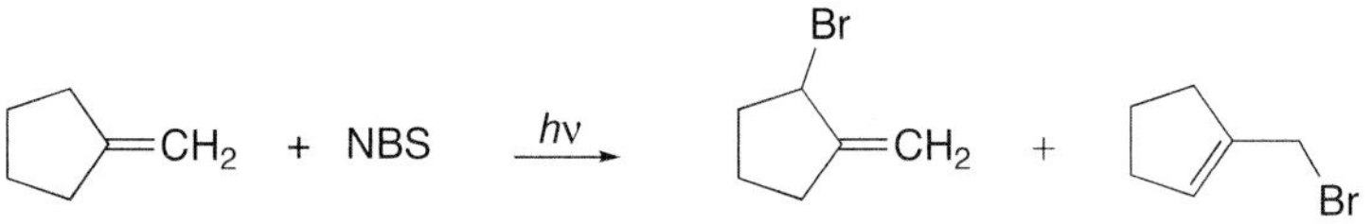

e. 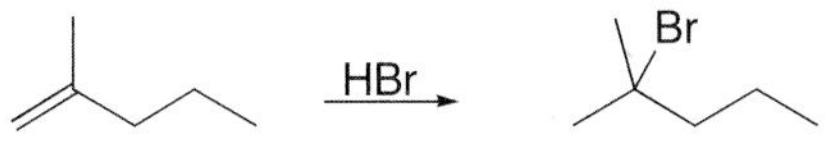

f. 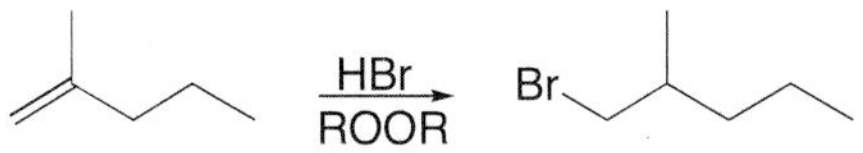

g. 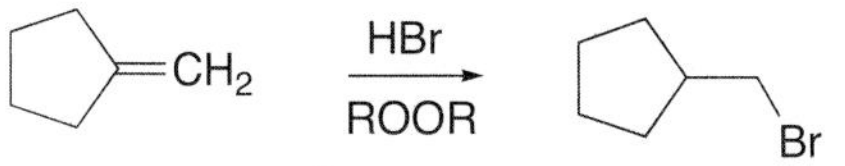

h. 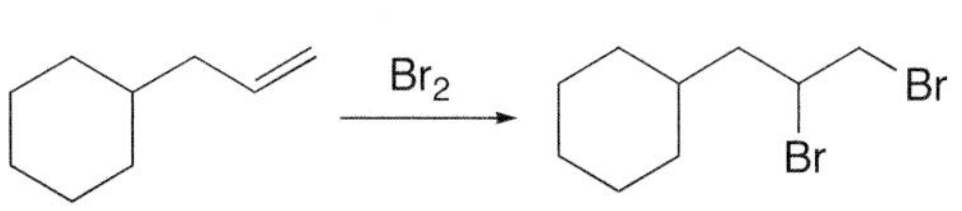

i. 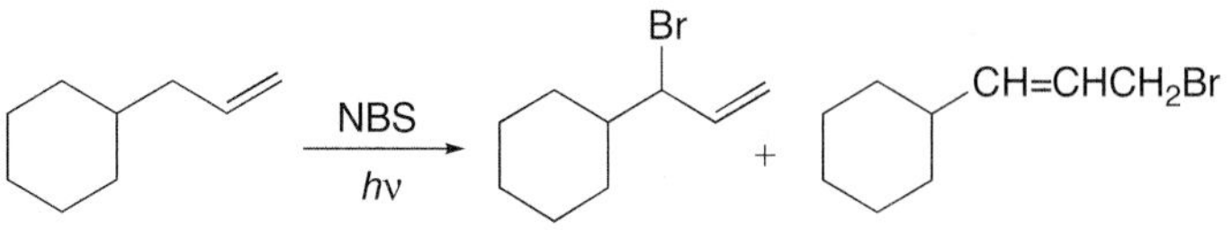

15.49

a. 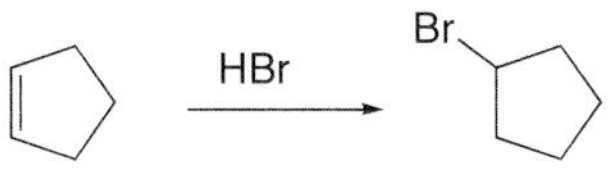

b. 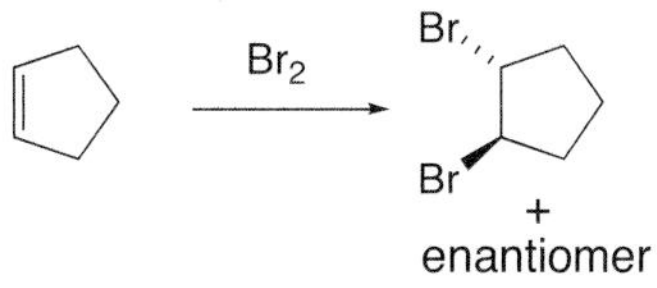

c. 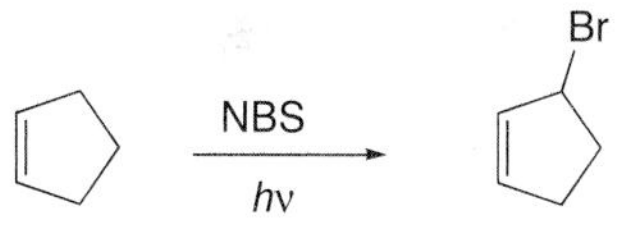

15.50

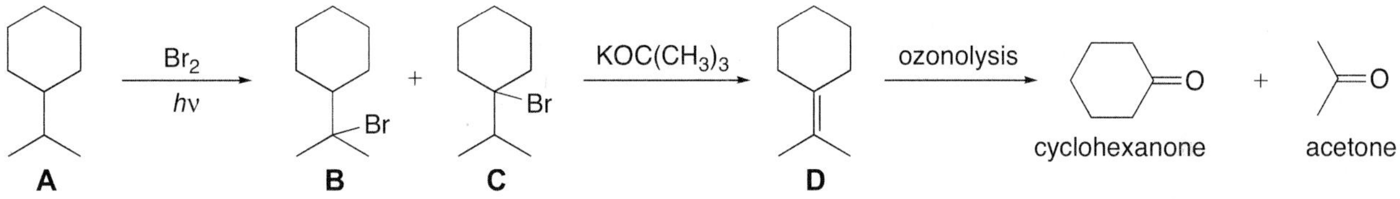

15.51

a. 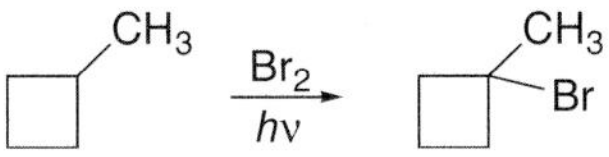

b. 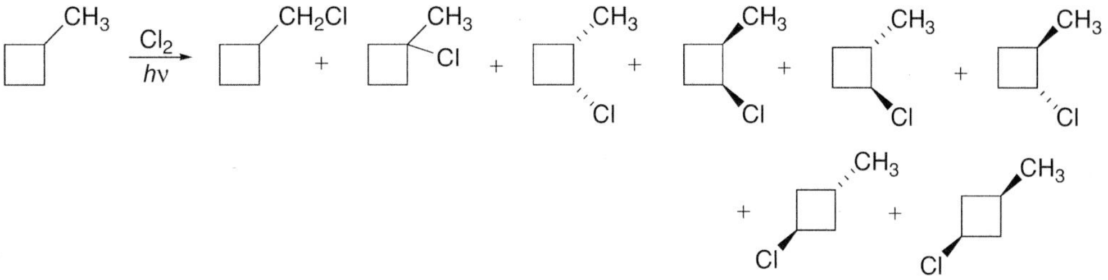

c. 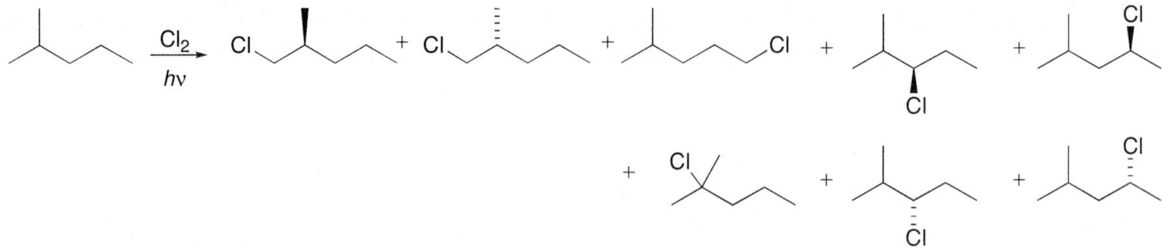

d. 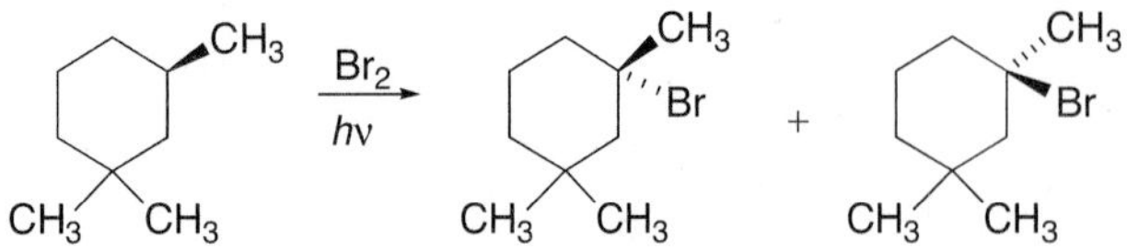

e. 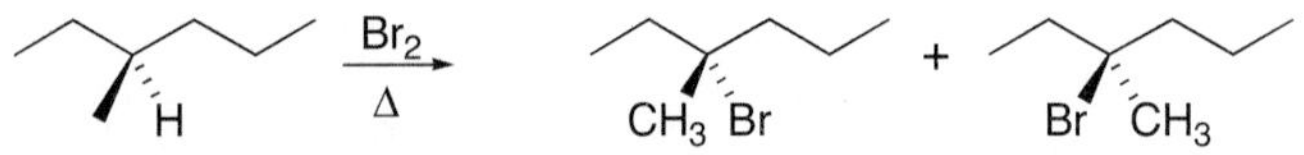

f. 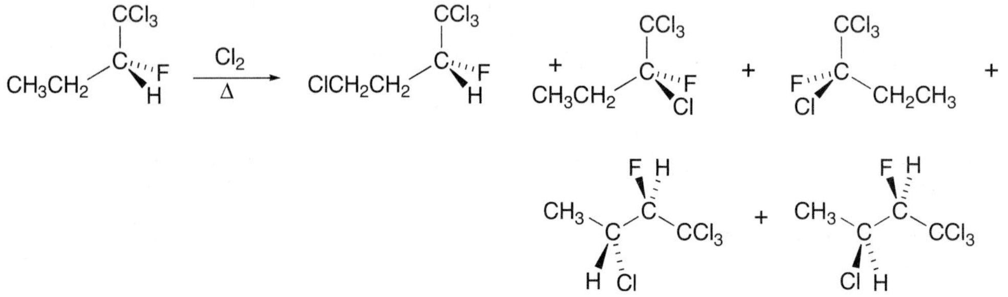

15.52

a. 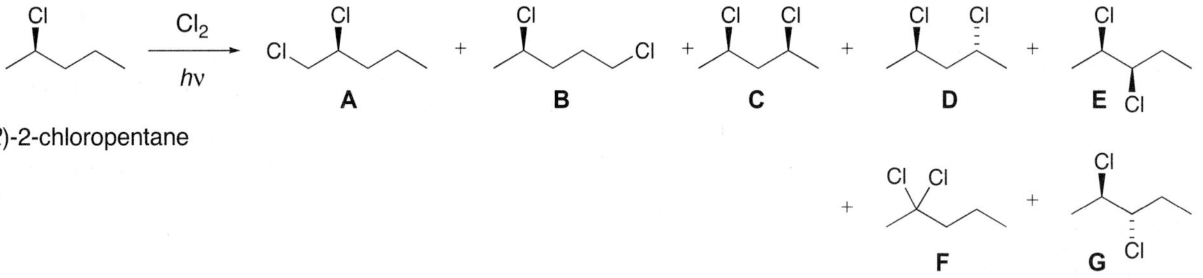

(2*R*)-2-chloropentane

b. There would be seven fractions, since each molecule drawn has different physical properties.

c. Fractions **A, B, D, E,** and **G** would show optical activity.

15.53

a. 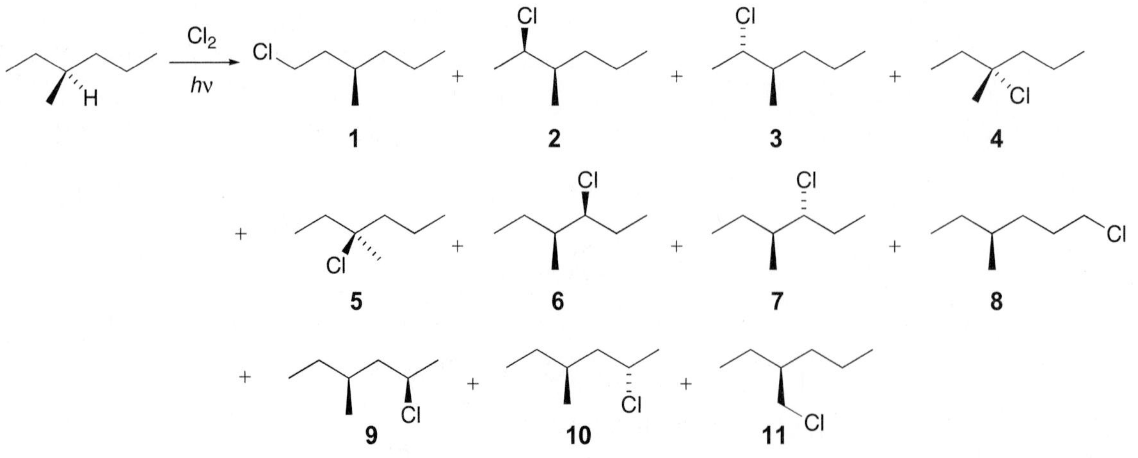

a. There would be 10 fractions, since **4** and **5** (two enantiomers) would be in the same fraction.
b. All fractions except the one that contains **4** and **5** would be optically active.

15.54

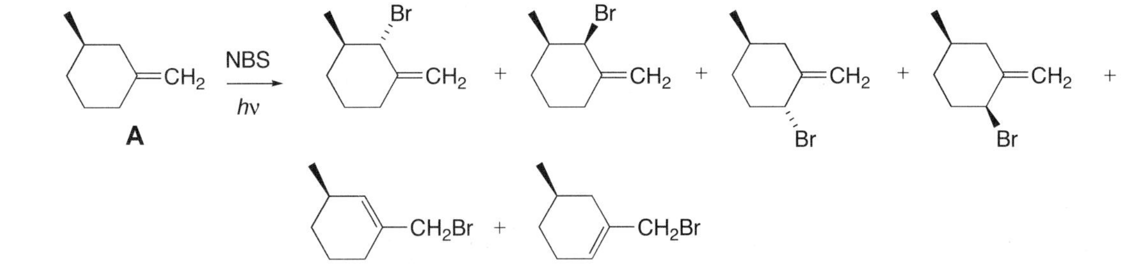

NBS
hν
A
Br
CH2
CH2Br

15.55

a.

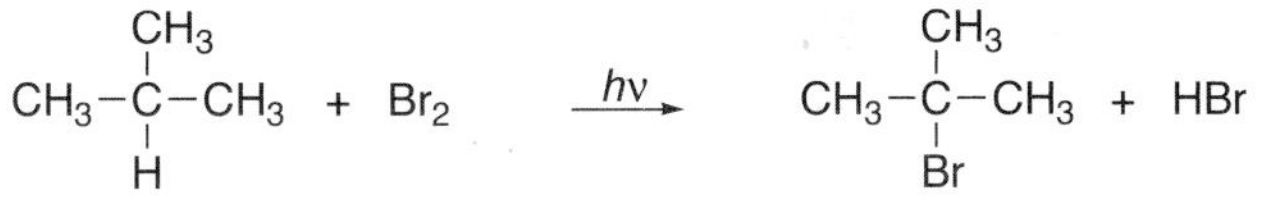

CH3
CH3–C–CH3 + Br2
H
hν
CH3–C–CH3 + HBr
Br

C–H bond broken	Br–Br bond broken	C–Br bond formed	H–Br bond formed
+381 kJ/mol	+192 kJ/mol	–272 kJ/mol	–368 kJ/mol

total bonds broken = +573 kJ/mol total bonds formed = –640 kJ/mol $\Delta H° = –67$ kJ/mol

b. Initiation: :Br–Br: $\xrightarrow[\text{or } \Delta]{h\nu}$:Br· + ·Br:

Propagation: $(CH_3)_3C$–H + ·Br: ⟶ $(CH_3)_3C$· + H–Br:

$(CH_3)_3C$· + :Br–Br: ⟶ $(CH_3)_3C$–Br + ·Br:

Termination: (one possibility) :Br· + ·Br: ⟶ :Br–Br:

c. $\Delta H°$ = (bonds broken) – (bonds formed)
= (+381 kJ/mol) + (–368 kJ/mol)
= +13 kJ/mol

$\Delta H°$ = (bonds broken) – (bonds formed)
= (+192 kJ/mol) + (–272 kJ/mol)
= –80 kJ/mol

d, e.

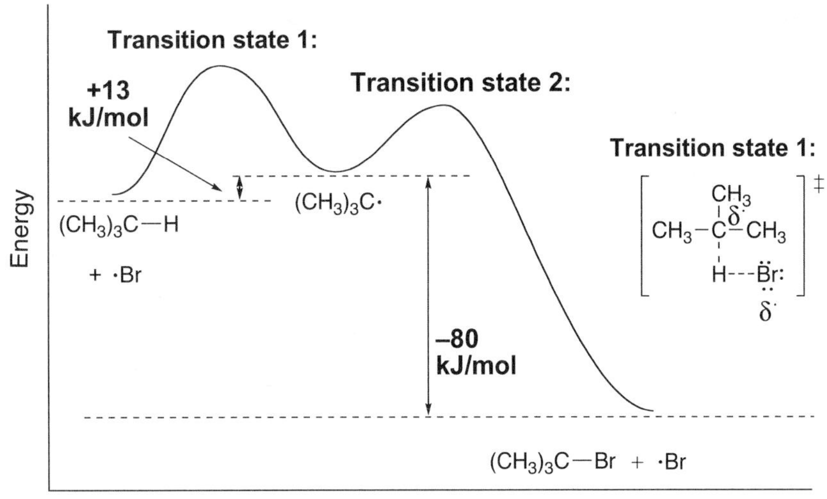

Transition state 1:
Transition state 2:
+13
kJ/mol
(CH3)3C—H
+ ·Br
(CH3)3C·
–80
kJ/mol
(CH3)3C—Br + ·Br
Energy
Reaction coordinate

Transition state 1: **Transition state 2:**

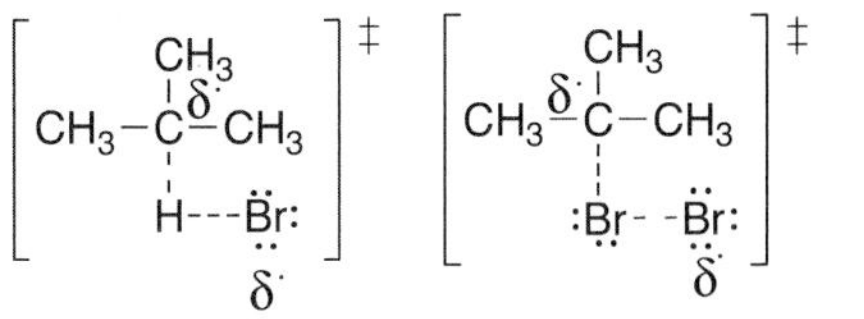

CH3
CH3–C–CH3
H---Br:
δ·
CH3
CH3–C–CH3
:Br- -Br:
δ·
‡

15.56

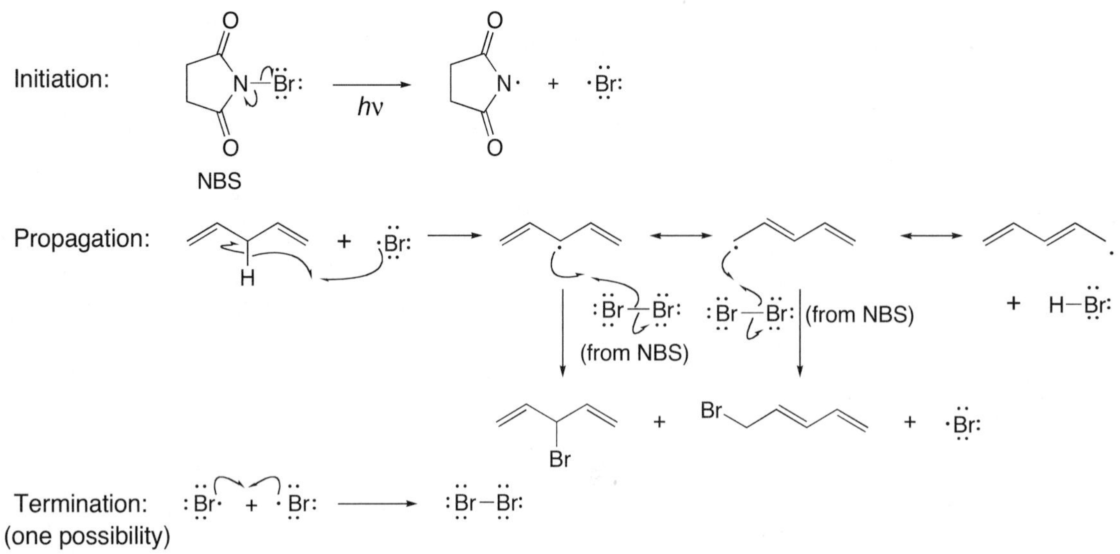

15.57 Calculate the $\Delta H°$ for the propagation steps of the reaction of CH_4 with I_2 to show why it does not occur at an appreciable rate.

$$CH_3{-}H \ (+435 \text{ kJ/mol}) + \cdot I: \longrightarrow \cdot CH_3 + H{-}I \ (-297 \text{ kJ/mol}) \qquad \Delta H° = +138 \text{ kJ/mol}$$

This step is highly endothermic, making it difficult for chain propagation to occur over and over again.

$$\cdot CH_3 + I{-}I \ (+151 \text{ kJ/mol}) \longrightarrow CH_3{-}I \ (-234 \text{ kJ/mol}) + \cdot I: \qquad \Delta H° = -83 \text{ kJ/mol}$$

15.58 Calculate $\Delta H°$ for each of these steps, and use these values to explain why this alternate mechanism is unlikely.

[1] $CH_4 + :Cl\cdot \longrightarrow CH_3Cl + H\cdot$

C–H bond broken +435 kJ/mol; C–Cl bond formed –351 kJ/mol; $\Delta H° = +84$ kJ/mol

The $\Delta H°$ for Step [1] is very endothermic, making this mechanism unlikely.

[2] $H\cdot + Cl_2 \longrightarrow HCl + :Cl\cdot$

Cl–Cl bond broken +242 kJ/mol; H–Cl bond formed –431 kJ/mol; $\Delta H° = -189$ kJ/mol

15.59

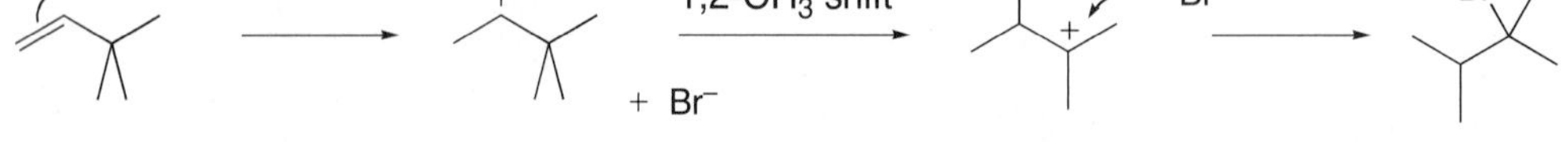

3,3-dimethyl-1-butene → $2°$ carbocation → $3°$ carbocation → 2-bromo-2,3-dimethylbutane

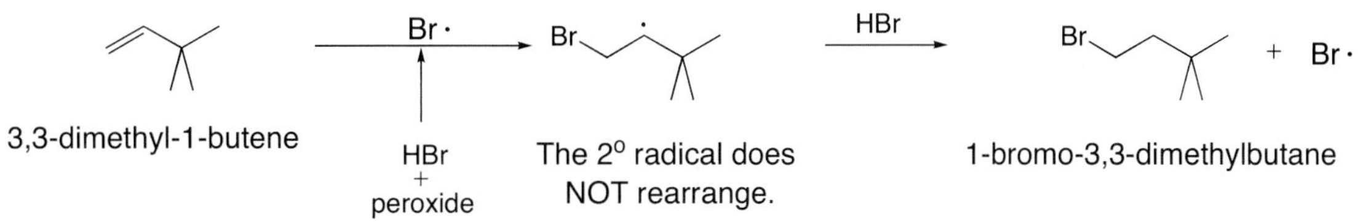
Br·
HBr
Br
HBr
Br
+ Br·
3,3-dimethyl-1-butene
HBr
+
peroxide
The 2° radical does
NOT rearrange.
1-bromo-3,3-dimethylbutane

Addition of HBr without added peroxide occurs by an ionic mechanism and forms a 2° carbocation, which rearranges to a more stable 3° carbocation. The addition of H^+ occurs first, followed by Br^-. Addition of HBr with added peroxide occurs by a radical mechanism and forms a 2° radical that does not rearrange. In the radical mechanism Br• adds first, followed by H•.

15.60

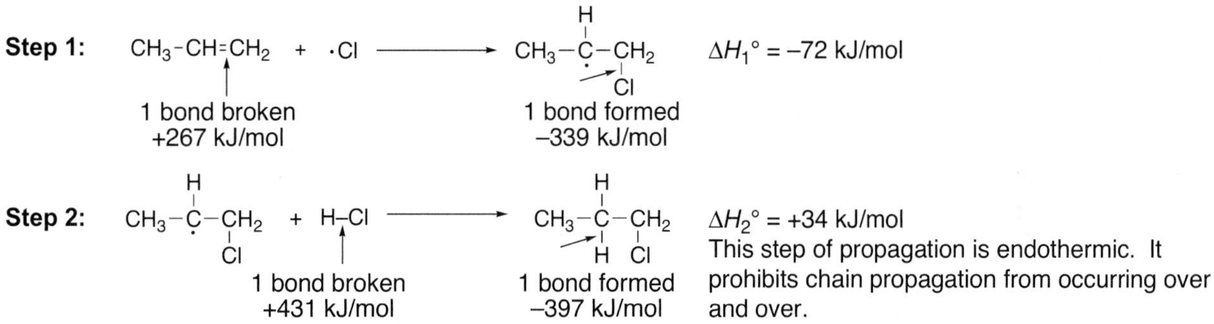
Step 1:
1 bond broken
+267 kJ/mol
1 bond formed
–339 kJ/mol
ΔH1° = –72 kJ/mol
Step 2:
1 bond broken
+431 kJ/mol
1 bond formed
–397 kJ/mol
ΔH2° = +34 kJ/mol
This step of propagation is endothermic. It prohibits chain propagation from occurring over and over.

15.61

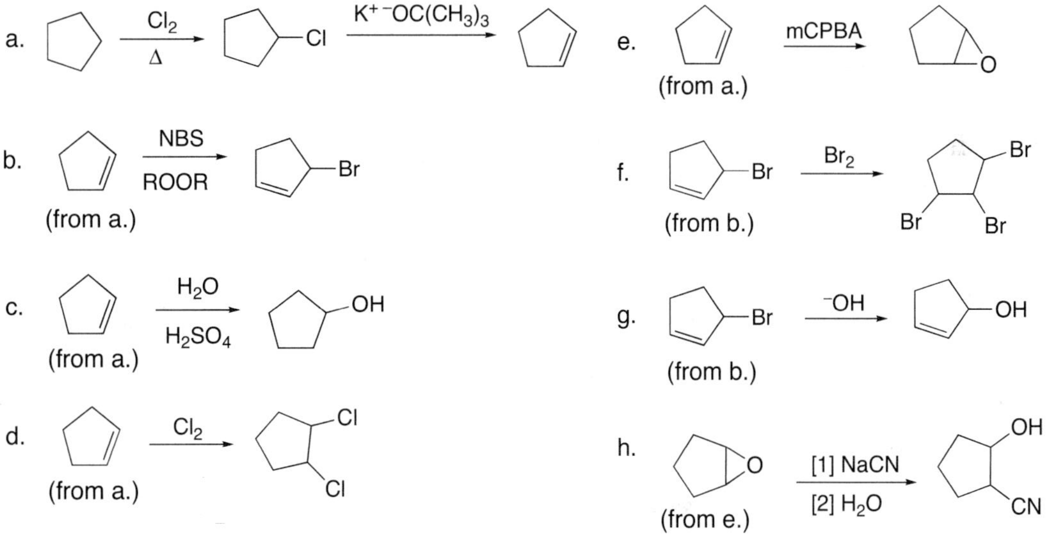
a.
Cl2
Δ
Cl
K+ –OC(CH3)3
b.
NBS
ROOR
Br
(from a.)
c.
H2O
H2SO4
OH
(from a.)
d.
Cl2
Cl
Cl
(from a.)
e.
mCPBA
O
(from a.)
f.
Br
Br2
Br
Br
Br
(from b.)
g.
Br
–OH
OH
(from b.)
h.
O
[1] NaCN
[2] H2O
OH
CN
(from e.)

15.62

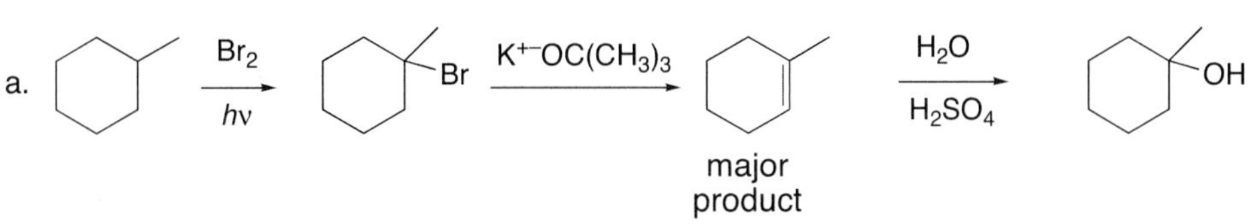
a.
Br2
hν
Br
K+ –OC(CH3)3
major
product
H2O
H2SO4
OH

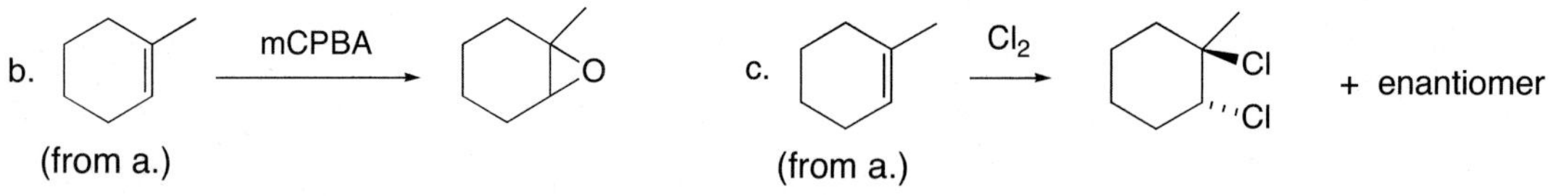
b.
mCPBA
O
(from a.)
c.
Cl2
Cl
Cl
+ enantiomer
(from a.)

15.63

a.

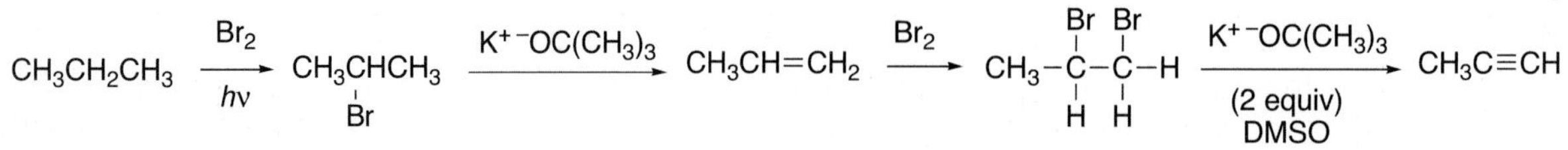
CH3CH2CH3
Br2
hν
CH3CHCH3
Br
K+ −OC(CH3)3
CH3CH=CH2
Br2
Br Br
CH3–C–C–H
H H
K+ −OC(CH3)3
(2 equiv)
DMSO
CH3C≡CH

b.

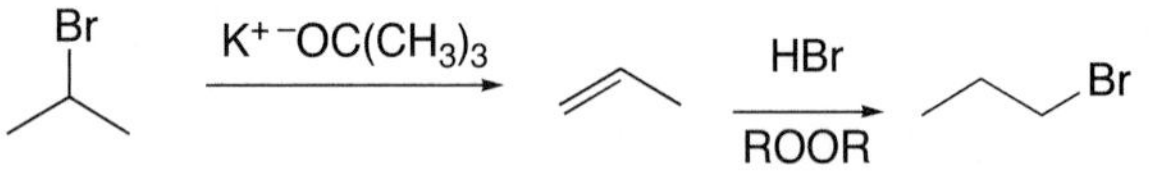
Br
K+ −OC(CH3)3
HBr
ROOR
Br

c.

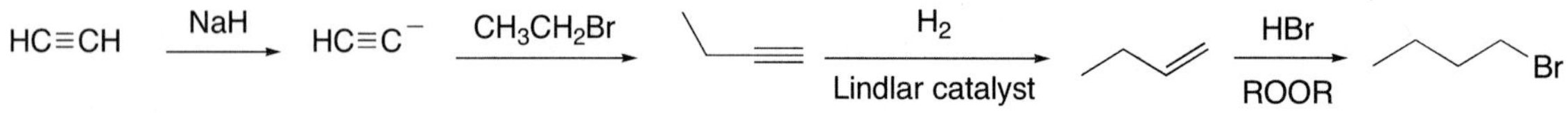
HC≡CH
NaH
HC≡C−
CH3CH2Br
H2
Lindlar catalyst
HBr
ROOR
Br

15.64

a. $$CH_3-CH_3 \xrightarrow[h\nu]{Br_2} CH_3-CH_2Br \xrightarrow{K^+\,^-OC(CH_3)_3} CH_2=CH_2 \xrightarrow{Br_2} BrCH_2-CH_2Br \xrightarrow{2\ NaNH_2} HC\equiv CH$$

b. $$HC\equiv CH \xrightarrow{NaH} HC\equiv C^- \xrightarrow[\text{(from a.)}]{CH_3-CH_2Br} HC\equiv CCH_2CH_3$$
(from a.)

c.

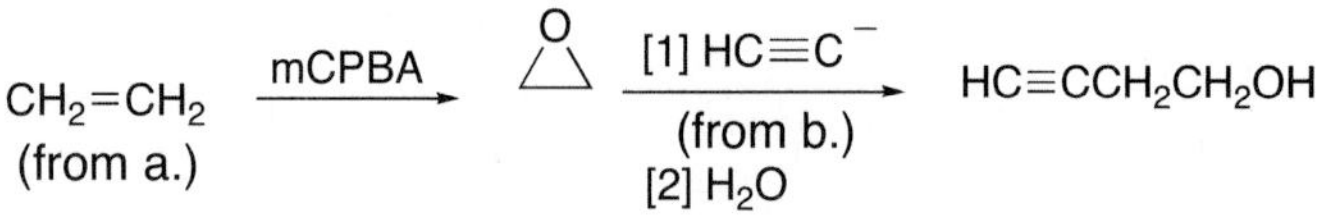
CH2=CH2
(from a.)
mCPBA
O
[1] HC≡C−
(from b.)
[2] H2O
HC≡CCH2CH2OH

d.

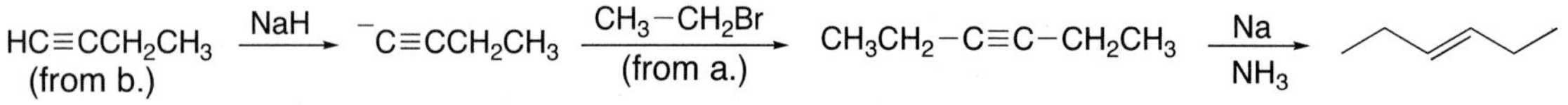
HC≡CCH2CH3
(from b.)
NaH
−C≡CCH2CH3
CH3–CH2Br
(from a.)
CH3CH2–C≡C–CH2CH3
Na
NH3

e.

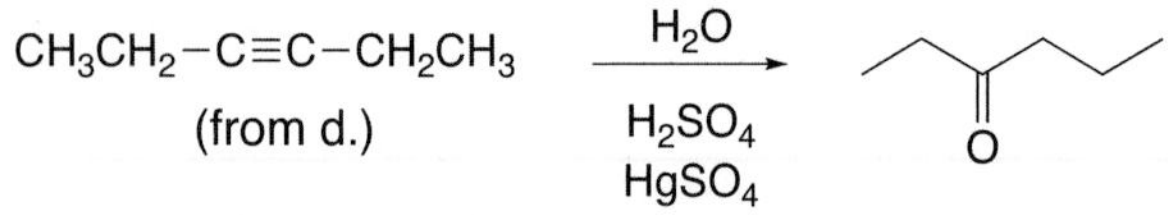
CH3CH2–C≡C–CH2CH3
(from d.)
H2O
H2SO4
HgSO4
O

15.65

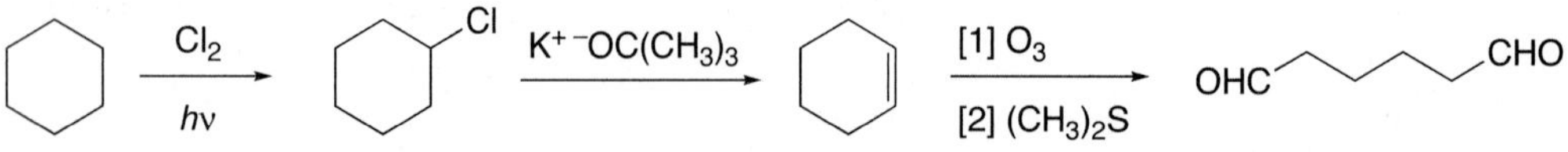
Cl2
hν
Cl
K+ −OC(CH3)3
[1] O3
[2] (CH3)2S
OHC
CHO

15.66

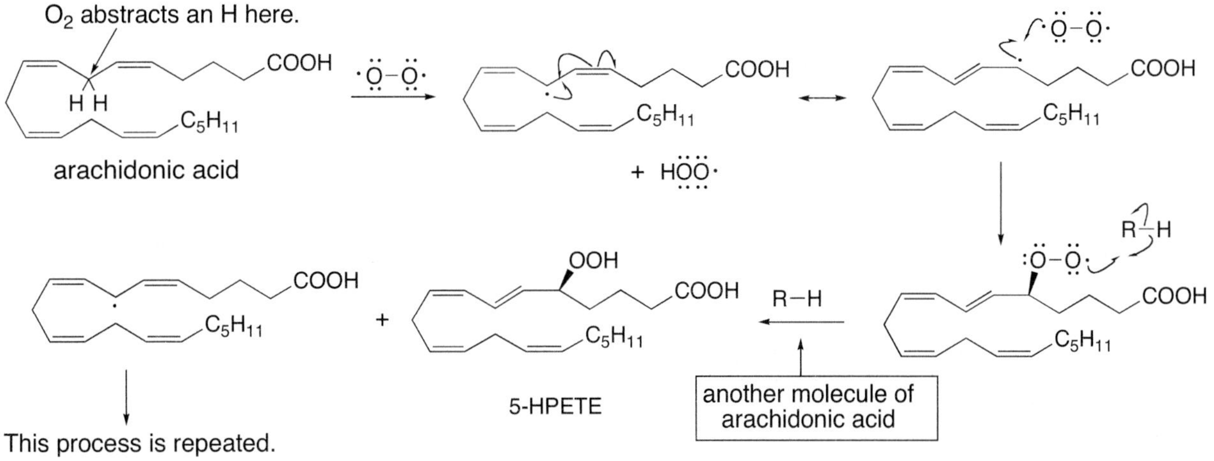
O2 abstracts an H here.
COOH
H H
C5H11
arachidonic acid
+ HOO·
5-HPETE
R–H
another molecule of arachidonic acid
This process is repeated.

15.67

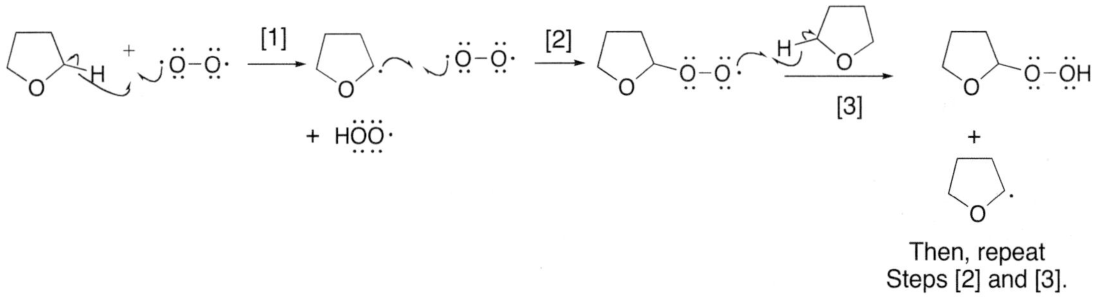
[1]
[2]
[3]
+ HOO·
Then, repeat Steps [2] and [3].

15.68

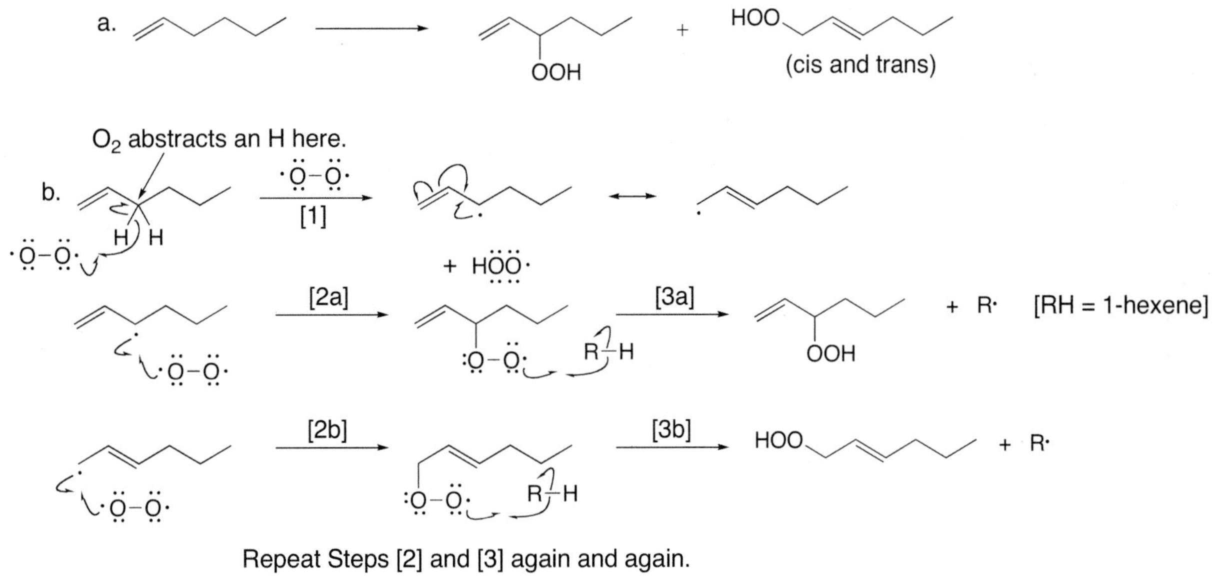
a.
OOH
HOO
(cis and trans)
O2 abstracts an H here.
b.
[1]
+ HOO·
[2a]
[3a]
+ R·
[RH = 1-hexene]
[2b]
[3b]
Repeat Steps [2] and [3] again and again.

15.69 For resonance structures **A–F,** an additional resonance form can be drawn that moves the position of the three π bonds in the ring bonded to two OH groups.

a. 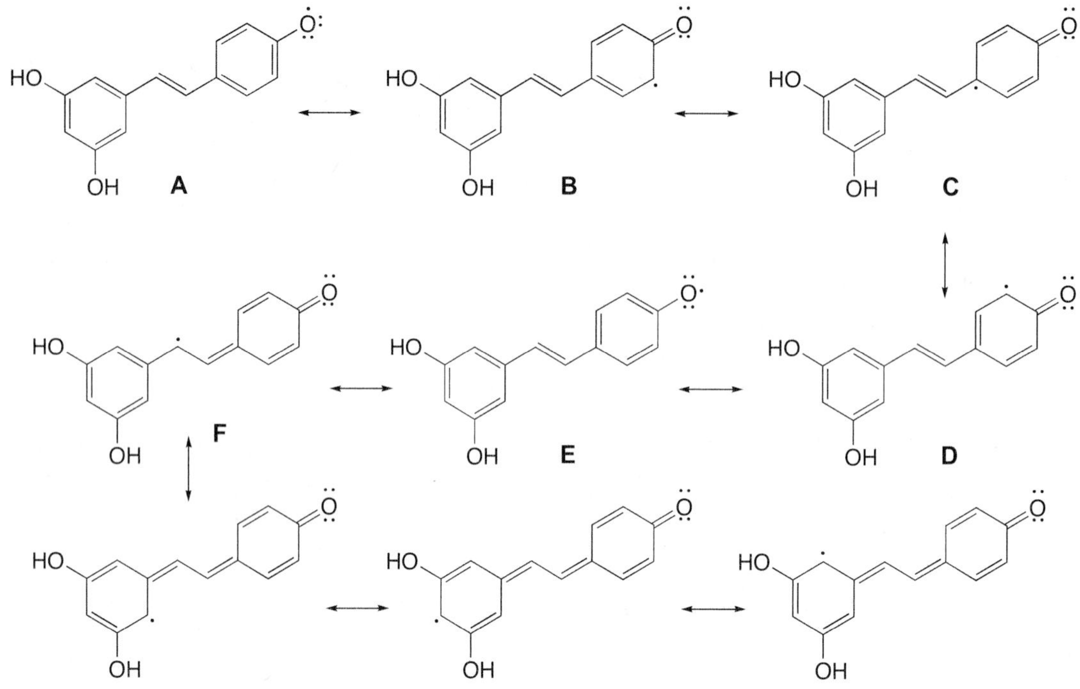

b. Homolysis of the indicated OH bond is preferred because it allows the resulting radical to delocalize over both benzene rings. Cleavage of one of the other OH bonds gives a radical that delocalizes over only one of the benzene rings.

15.70 Abstraction of the labeled H forms a highly resonance-stabilized radical. Four of the possible resonance structures are drawn.

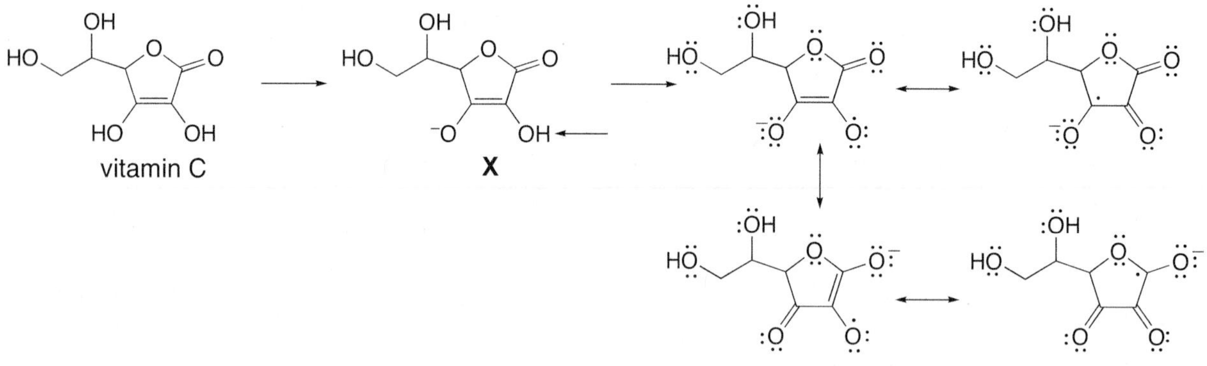

15.71 The monomers used in radical polymerization always contain double bonds.

a. 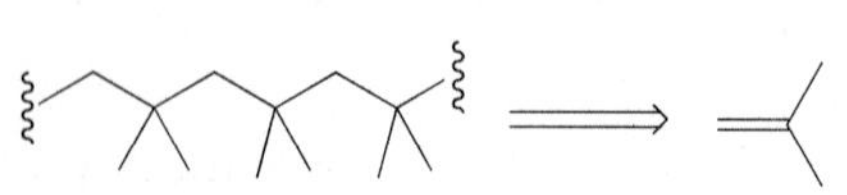

polyisobutylene

b. 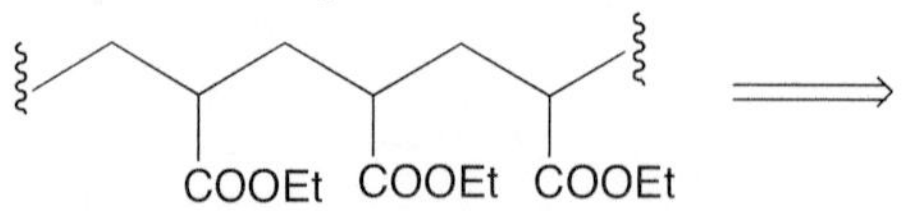 $CH_2{=}CHCO_2Et$

poly(ethyl acrylate)
(used in Latex paints)

Et = CH_2CH_3

15.72

a.

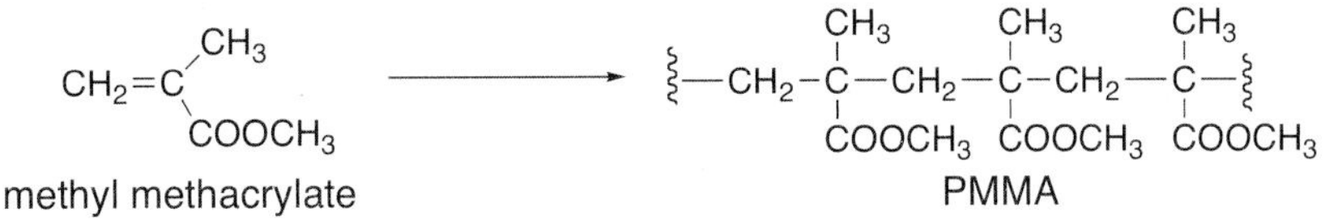

b.

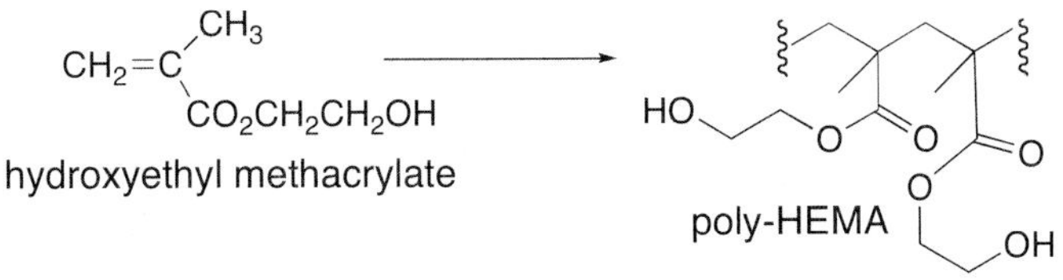

15.73 Polystyrene has H atoms bonded to benzylic carbons, carbons bonded directly to a benzene ring. These C–H bonds are unusually weak because the radical that results from homolysis is resonance stabilized.

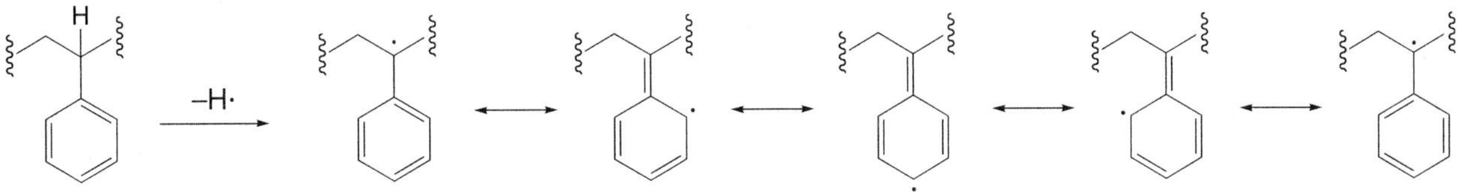

No such resonance stabilization is possible for the radical that results from C–H bond cleavage in polyethylene.

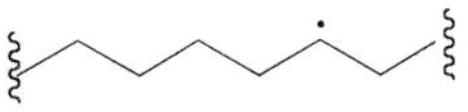

15.74

Overall reaction:

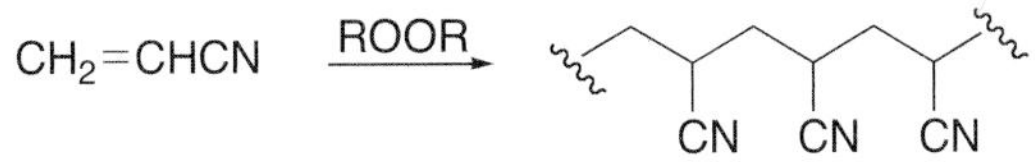

Initiation:

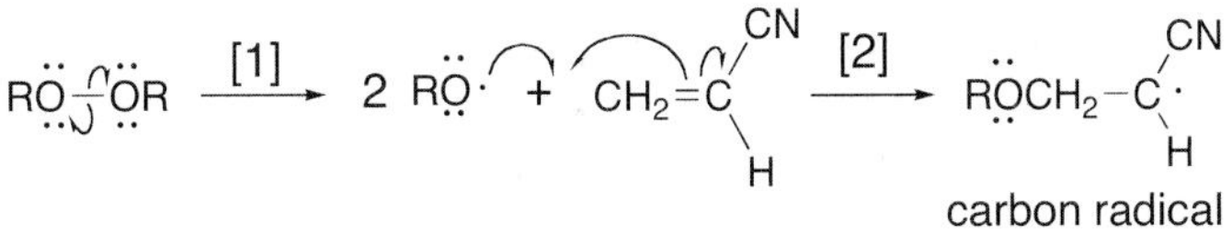

Propagation:

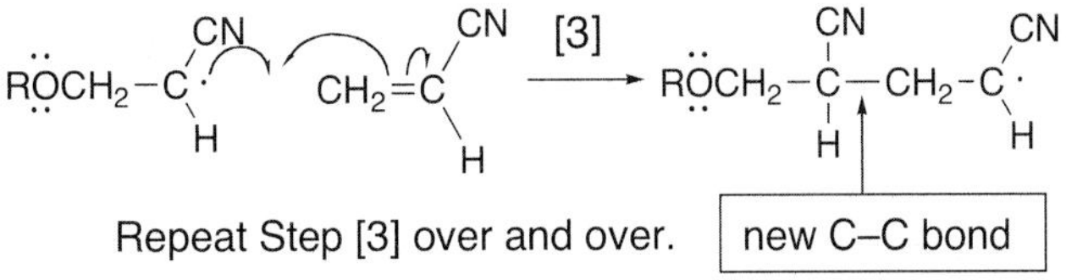

Repeat Step [3] over and over.

Termination:

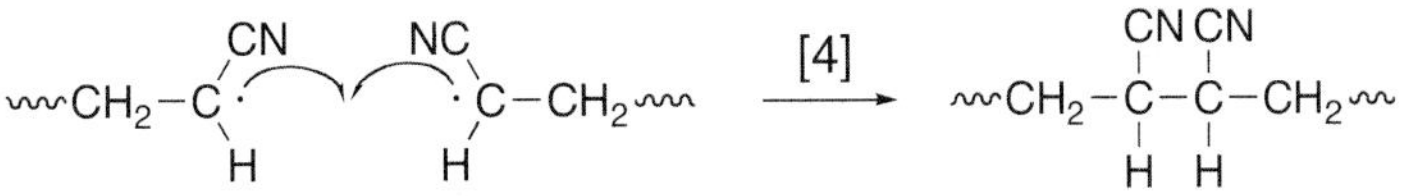

[one possibility]

15.75

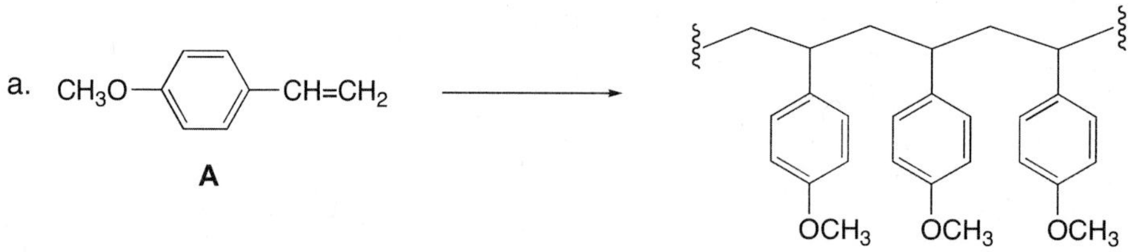
a. CH_3O—⟨⟩—CH=CH_2
A
OCH_3
OCH_3
OCH_3

b. The OCH_3 group stabilizes an intermediate carbocation by resonance. This makes **A** react faster than styrene in cationic polymerization.

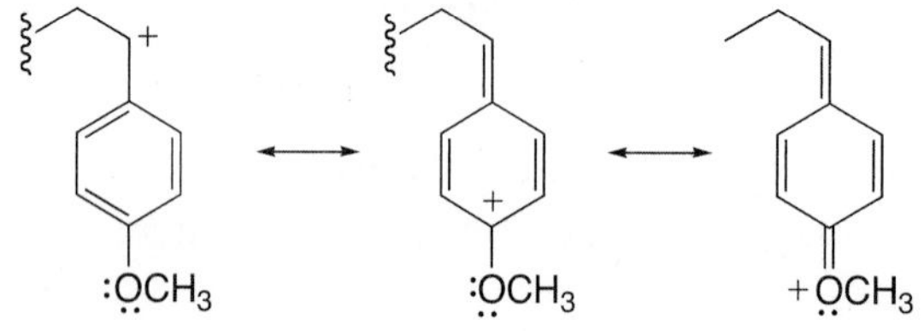
:$\ddot{O}CH_3$
:$\ddot{O}CH_3$
+$\ddot{O}CH_3$

three of the possible resonance structures

15.76

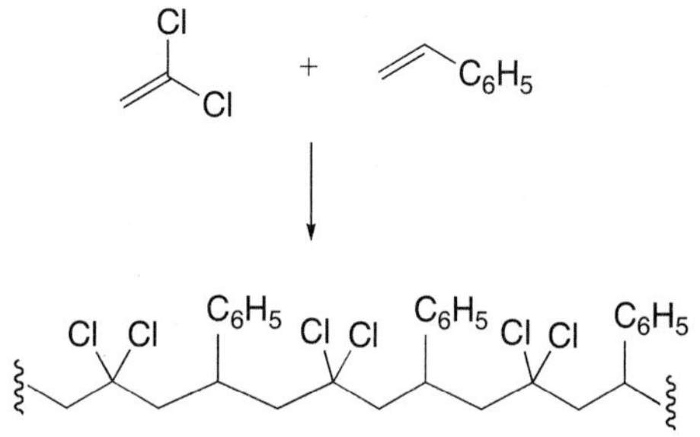
Cl
Cl
+
C_6H_5
Cl Cl
C_6H_5
Cl Cl
C_6H_5
Cl Cl
C_6H_5

alternating copolymer

15.77

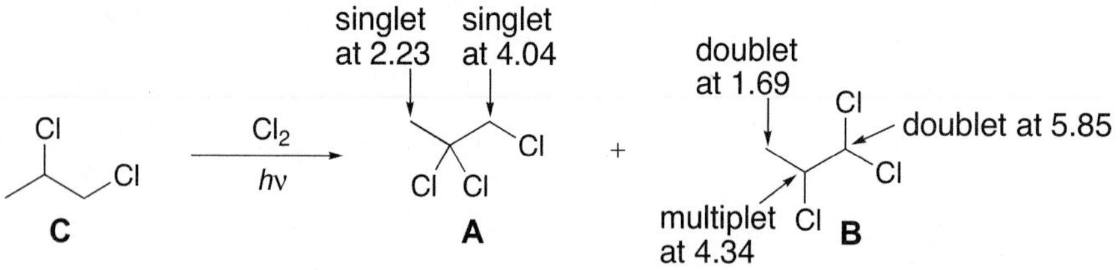
Cl
Cl
C
Cl_2
hν
singlet at 2.23
singlet at 4.04
Cl
Cl Cl
A
+
doublet at 1.69
Cl
doublet at 5.85
Cl
multiplet at 4.34
Cl
B

15.78

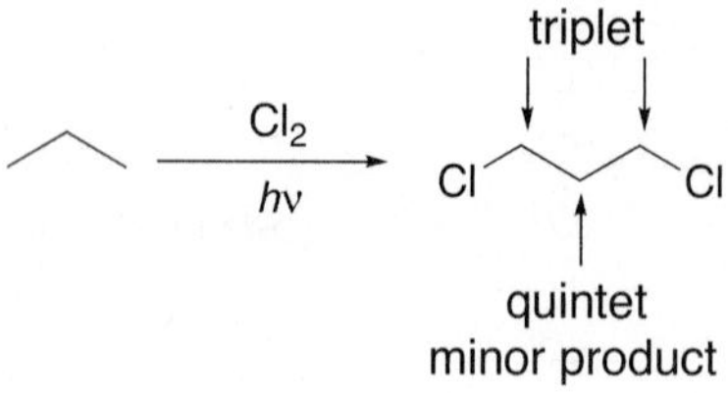
Cl_2
hν
triplet
Cl
Cl
quintet
minor product

molecular formula $C_3H_6Cl_2$

Integration:

(57 units + 29 units)/6 H's = 14 units per H

one signal is 57 units/14 units per H = 4 H's

second signal is 29 units/14 units per H = 2 H's

^{1}H NMR data:

quintet at 2.2 (2 H's) split by 4 H's

triplet at 3.7 (4 H's) split by 2 H's

15.79

a. 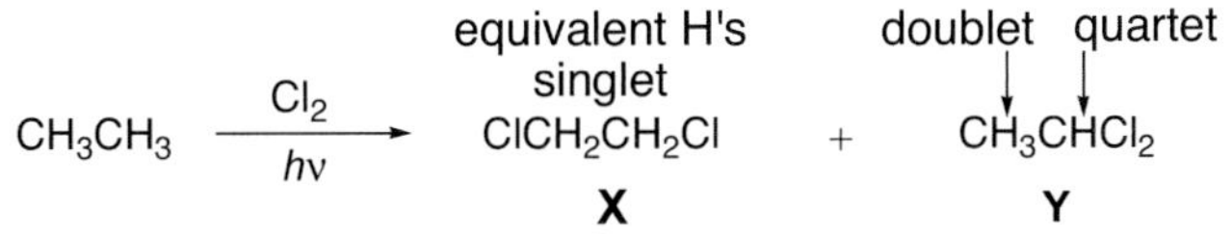

Cl2
hν
equivalent H's
singlet
ClCH2CH2Cl
X
doublet
quartet
CH3CHCl2
Y

b. 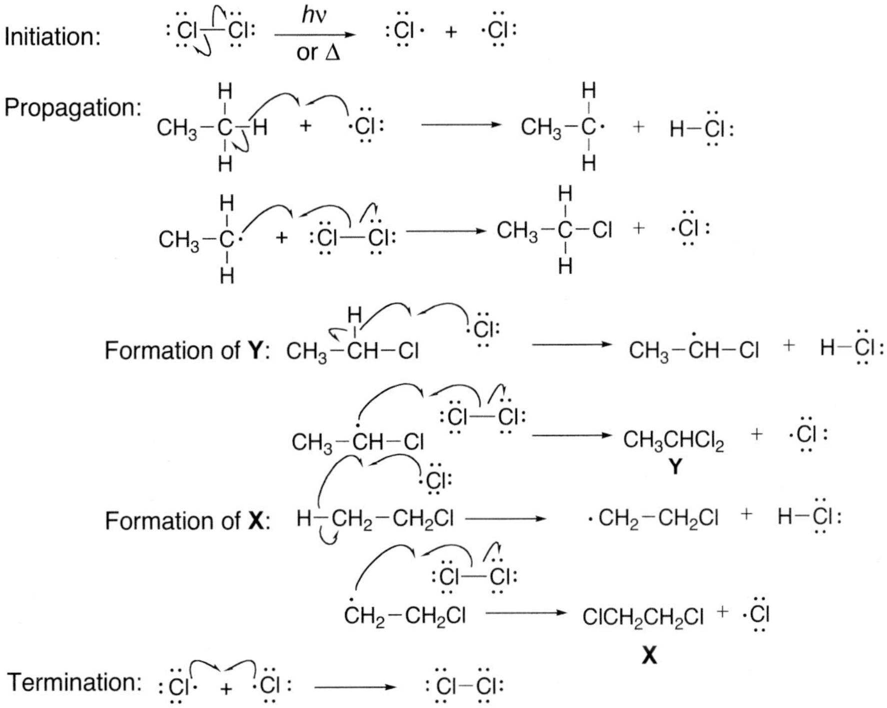

Initiation:
hν
or Δ
Propagation:
Formation of Y:
Formation of X:
Termination:

15.80

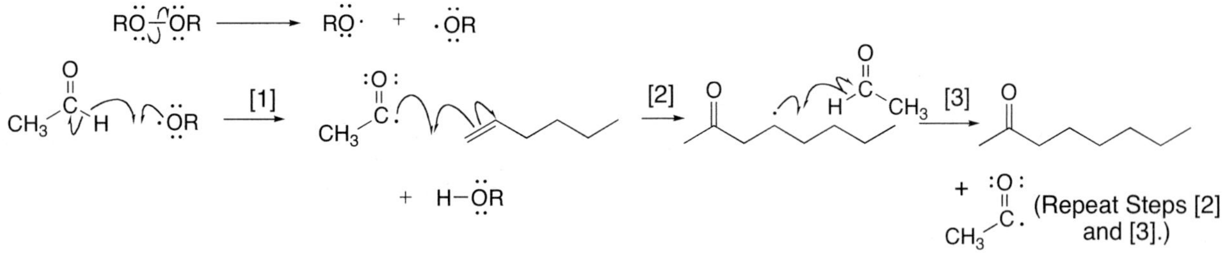

[1]
[2]
[3]
(Repeat Steps [2] and [3].)

15.81 a. The triphenylmethyl radical is highly resonance stabilized, because the radical can be delocalized on each of the benzene rings. As an example using one ring:

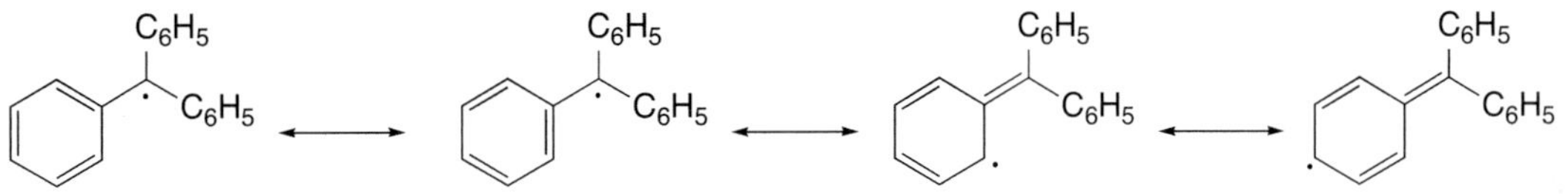

In addition, the radical is very sterically hindered, making it difficult to undergo reactions.

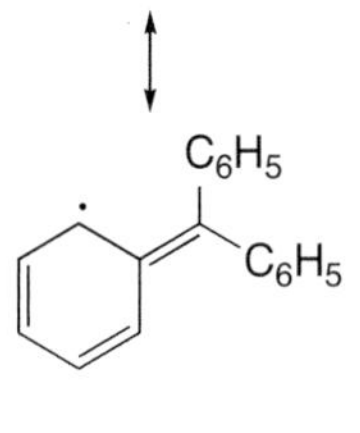

b. First, draw the resonance form of the radical that places the unpaired electron on the C that forms the new C–C bond.

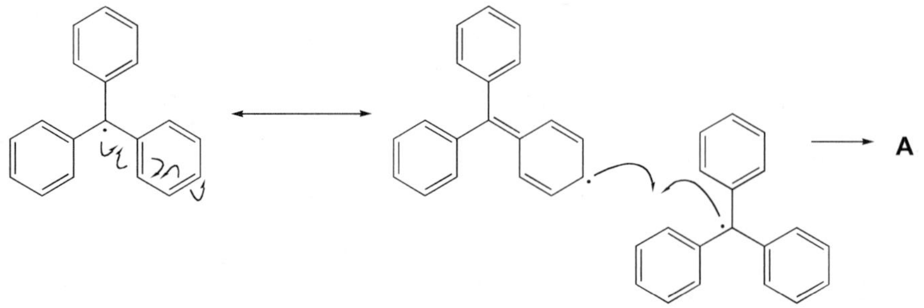
A

c. Hexaphenylethane formation would require two very crowded 3° radicals to combine. The formation of **A** results from a radical on one of the six-membered rings, which is much more accessible for reaction.

d. The ^{1}H NMR spectrum of hexaphenylethane should show signals only in the aromatic region (7–8 ppm), whereas the ^{1}H NMR spectrum of **A** will also have signals for the *sp*^{2} hybridized C–H bonds (4.5–6.0 ppm) of the alkenes, as well as the single H on the *sp*^{3} hybridized carbon. The ^{13}C NMR spectrum of hexaphenylethane should consist of lines due to the 4° C's and the aromatic C's. For **A,** the ^{13}C NMR spectrum will also have lines for the *sp*^{3} and *sp*^{2} hybridized C's that are not contained in the aromatic rings.

15.82

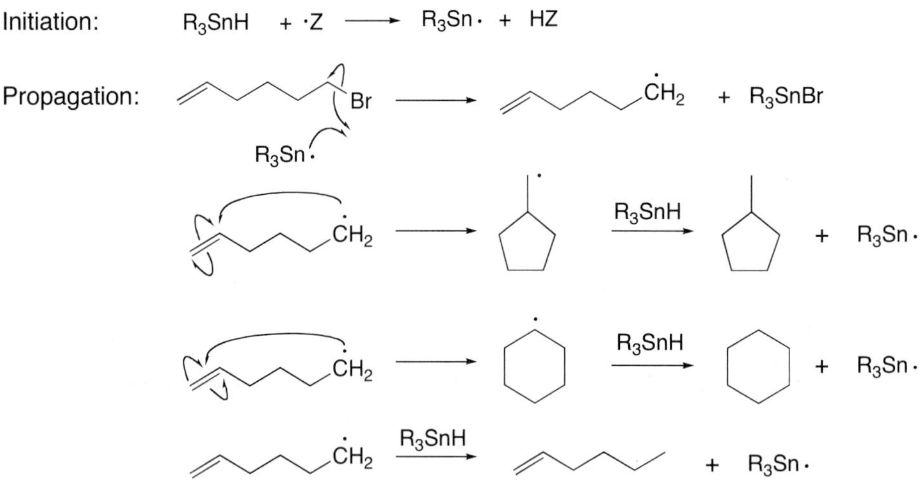
Initiation:
R3SnH + ·Z → R3Sn· + HZ
Propagation:
Br
CH2
+ R3SnBr
R3Sn·
CH2
R3SnH
+ R3Sn·
CH2
R3SnH
+ R3Sn·
CH2
R3SnH
+ R3Sn·

15.83

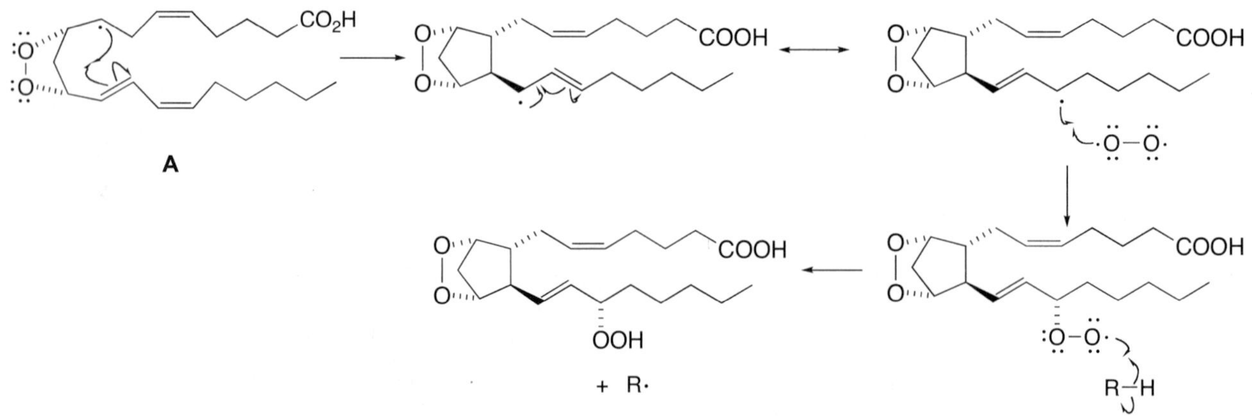
CO2H
A
COOH
COOH
COOH
COOH
OOH
+ R·
R–H

Chapter 16 Conjugation, Resonance, and Dienes

Chapter Review

Conjugation and delocalization of electron density

- The overlap of *p* orbitals on three or more adjacent atoms allows electron density to delocalize, thus adding stability (16.1).
- An allyl carbocation ($CH_2{=}CHCH_2^+$) is more stable than a 1° carbocation because of *p* orbital overlap (16.2).
- In a system X=Y–Z:, Z is generally sp^2 hybridized to allow the lone pair to occupy a *p* orbital, making the system conjugated (16.5).

Four common examples of resonance (16.3)

[1] The three atom "allyl" system:

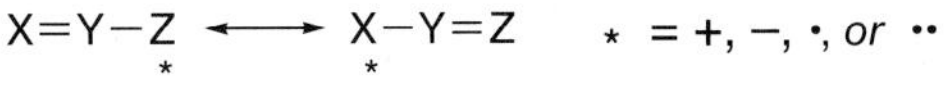
X=Y–Z
X–Y=Z
* = +, –, •, or ••

[2] Conjugated double bonds:

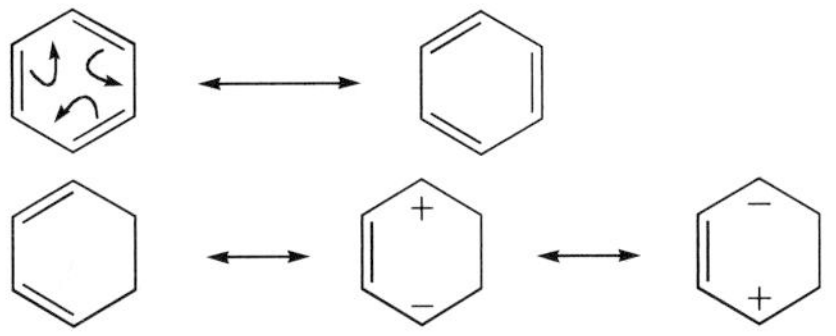

[3] Cations having a positive charge adjacent to a lone pair:

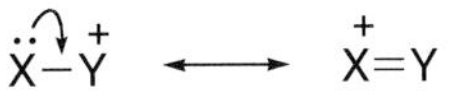
X–Y
X=Y

[4] Double bonds having one atom more electronegative than the other:

X=Y
X–Y:
Electronegativity of Y > X

Rules on evaluating the relative "stability" of resonance structures (16.4)

[1] Structures with more bonds and fewer charges are more stable.

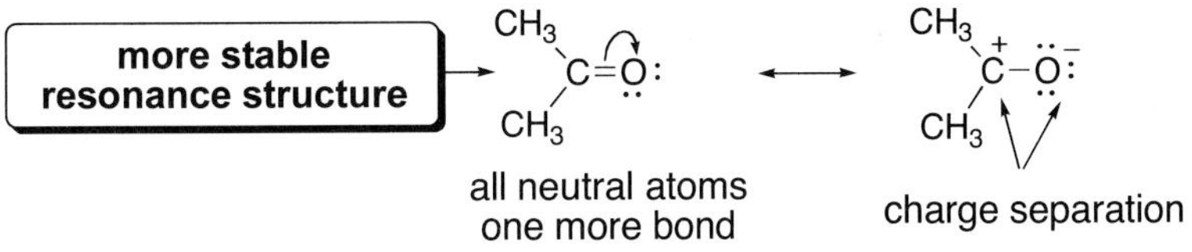
more stable
resonance structure
all neutral atoms
one more bond
charge separation

[2] Structures in which every atom has an octet are more stable.

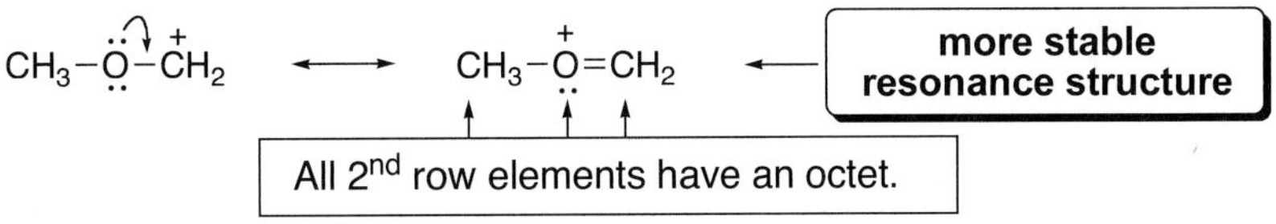
more stable
resonance structure
All 2nd row elements have an octet.

[3] Structures that place a negative charge on a more electronegative element are more stable.

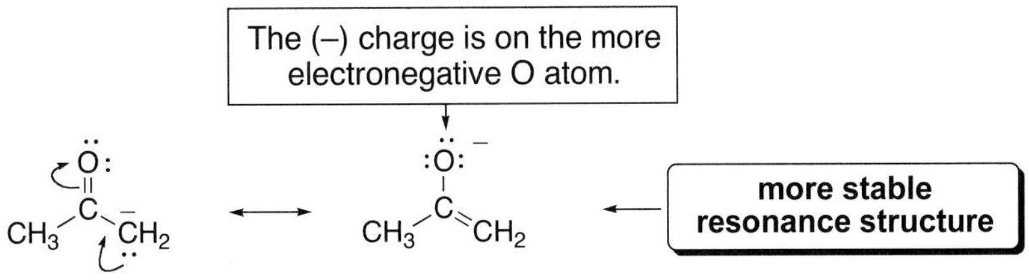
The (–) charge is on the more
electronegative O atom.
more stable
resonance structure

The unusual properties of conjugated dienes

[1] The C–C σ bond joining the two double bonds is unusually short (16.8).

[2] Conjugated dienes are more stable than similar isolated dienes. ΔH° of hydrogenation is smaller for a conjugated diene than for an isolated diene converted to the same product (16.9).

[3] The reactions are unusual:

- Electrophilic addition affords products of 1,2-addition and 1,4-addition (16.10, 16.11).
- Conjugated dienes undergo the Diels–Alder reaction, a reaction that does not occur with isolated dienes (16.12–16.14).

[4] Conjugated dienes absorb UV light in the 200–400 nm region. As the number of conjugated π bonds increases, the absorption shifts to longer wavelength (16.15).

Reactions of conjugated dienes

[1] Electrophilic addition of HX (X = halogen) (16.10, 16.11)

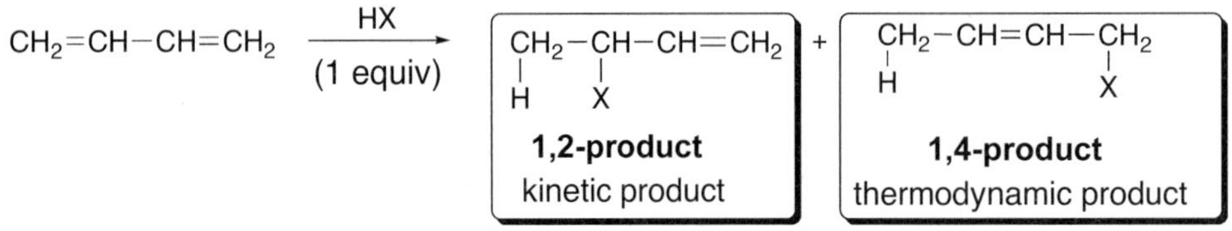

- The mechanism has two steps.
- Markovnikov's rule is followed. Addition of H^+ forms the more stable allylic carbocation.
- The 1,2-product is the kinetic product. When H^+ adds to the double bond, X^- adds to the end of the allylic carbocation to which it is closer (C2 not C4). The kinetic product is formed faster at low temperature.
- The thermodynamic product has the more substituted, more stable double bond. The thermodynamic product predominates at equilibrium. With 1,3-butadiene, the thermodynamic product is the 1,4-product.

---

[2] Diels–Alder reaction (16.12–16.14)

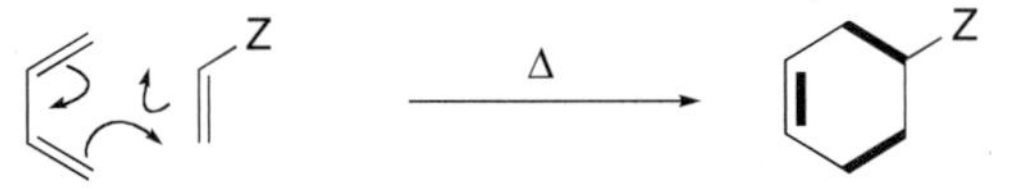

1,3-diene **dienophile**

[The three new bonds are labeled in **bold**.]

- The reaction forms two σ and one π bond in a six-membered ring.
- The reaction is initiated by heat.
- The mechanism is concerted: all bonds are broken and formed in a single step.
- The diene must react in the *s*-cis conformation (16.13A).
- Electron-withdrawing groups in the dienophile increase the reaction rate (16.13B).
- The stereochemistry of the dienophile is retained in the product (16.13C).
- Endo products are preferred (16.13D).

Practice Test on Chapter Review

1. a. Which of the following statements is true about the Diels–Alder reaction?
   1. The reaction is faster with electron-donating groups in the dienophile.
   2. The reaction is endothermic.
   3. The diene must adopt the *s*-cis conformation.
   4. Statements (1) and (2) are true.
   5. Statements (1), (2), and (3) are all true.

   b. Which of the following statements is true about the absorption of ultraviolet light by unsaturated systems?
   1. 1,4-Pentadiene requires light having a wavelength < 200 nm for electron promotion.
   2. 1,3-Cyclohexadiene absorbs ultraviolet light with a wavelength > 200 nm.
   3. As the number of conjugated π bonds increases, the energy difference between the excited state and ground state decreases.
   4. Statements (1) and (2) are true.
   5. Statements (1), (2), and (3) are all true.

   c. Which of the following compounds contains a labeled carbon atom that is sp^2 hybridized?

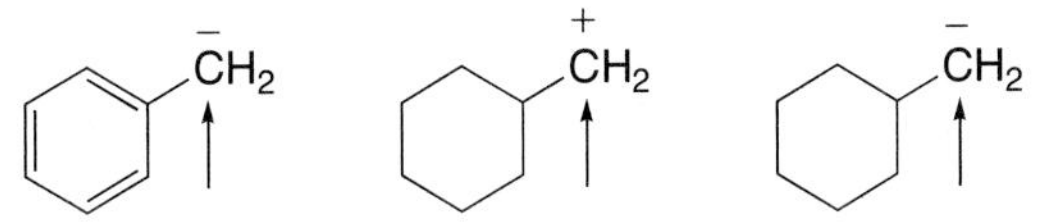

   1. **A** only
   2. **B** only
   3. **C** only
   4. **A** and **B**
   5. **A, B,** and **C**

   d. Which of the following represent valid resonance structures for **A?**

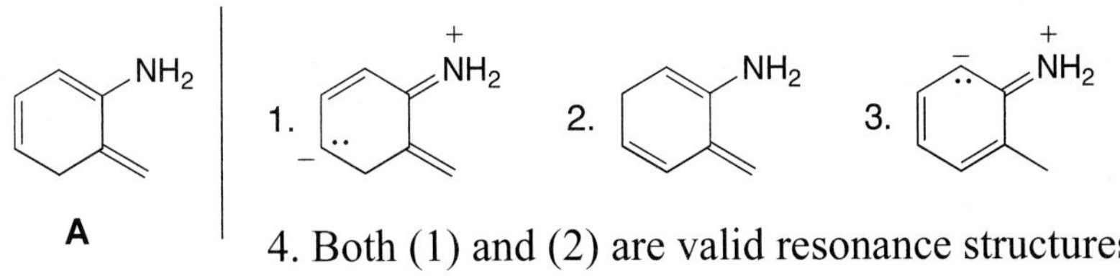

   4. Both (1) and (2) are valid resonance structures.
   5. Structures (1), (2), and (3) are all valid.

2. Name the following compounds and indicate the conformation around the σ bond that joins the two double bonds.

a. 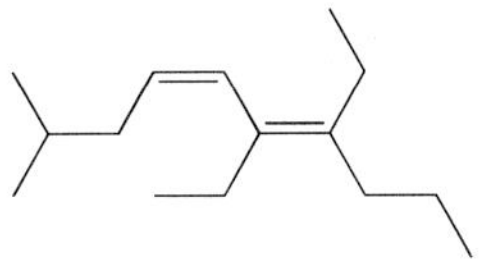

b. 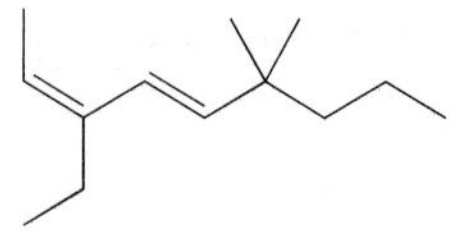

3. a. Consider the four hydrocarbons (**A–D**) drawn below. [1] Which compound absorbs the *shortest* wavelength of ultraviolet light? [2] Which compound absorbs the *longest* wavelength of ultraviolet light?

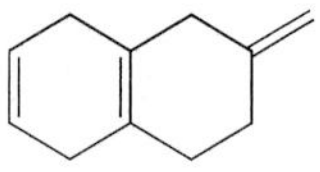
A

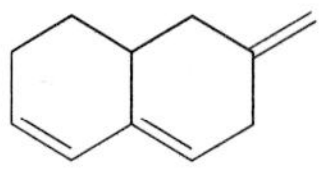
B

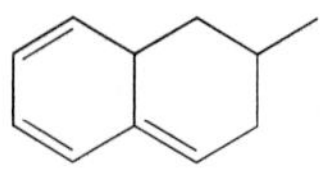
C

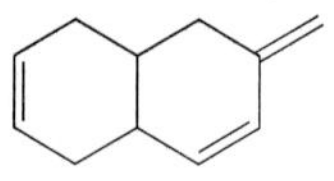
D

b. Consider the four dienes (**A–D**) drawn below. [1] Which diene is *most* reactive in the Diels–Alder reaction? [2] Which diene is the *least* reactive in the Diels–Alder reaction?

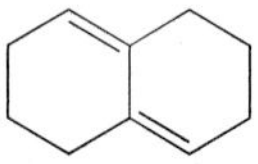
A

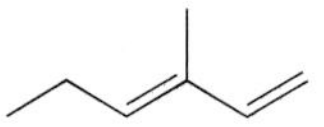
B

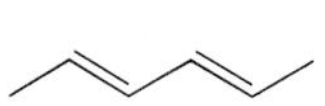
C

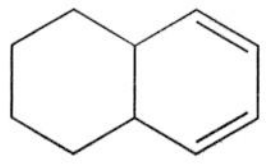
D

4. Draw the organic products formed in each reaction. In part (b), label the kinetic and thermodynamic products.

a. 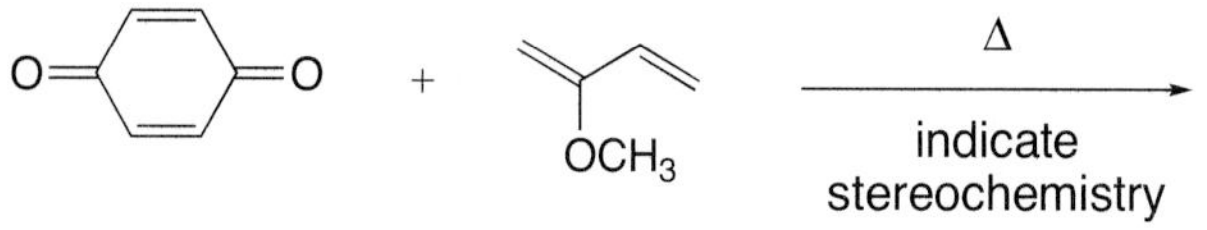
O
O
+
OCH3
Δ
indicate
stereochemistry

b. 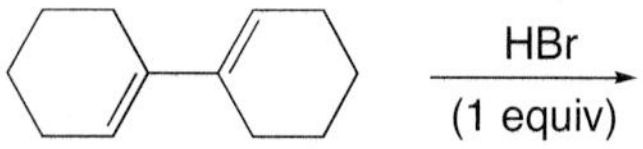
HBr
(1 equiv)

c. 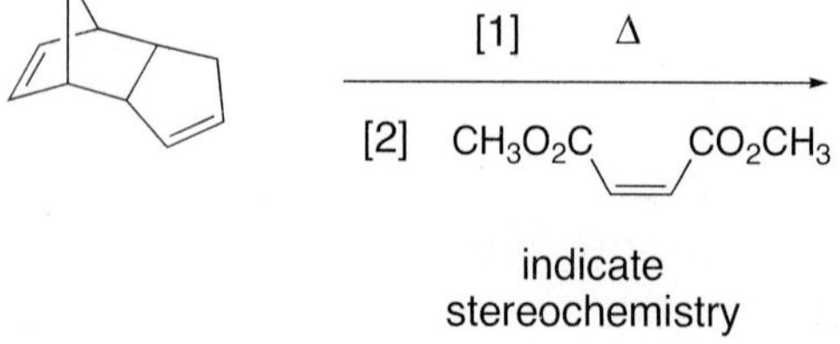
[1] Δ
[2] CH3O2C CO2CH3
indicate
stereochemistry

5. What diene and dienophile are needed to synthesize the following Diels–Alder adducts?

a.

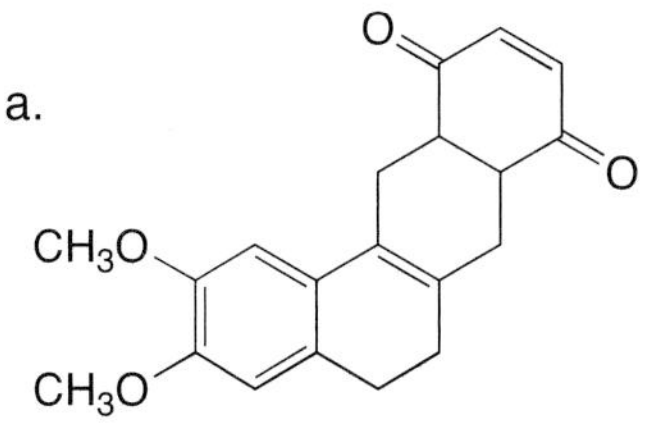

b.

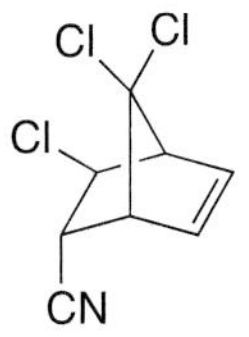

Answers to Practice Test

1.a. 3
b. 5
c. 4
d. 1

2.a. (4*Z*,6*E*)-6,7-diethyl-2-methyl-4,6-decadiene, *s*-trans

b. (2*Z*,4*E*)-3-ethyl-6,6-dimethyl-2,4-nonadiene, *s*-trans

3.a. [1] **A;** [2] **C**
b. [1] **D;** [2] **A**

4.a.

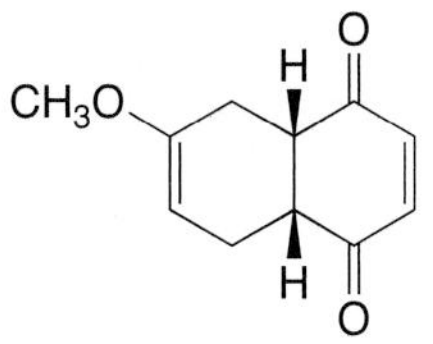

(both H's up or both H's down)

b.

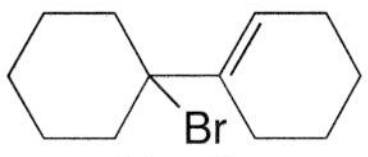

kinetic

+

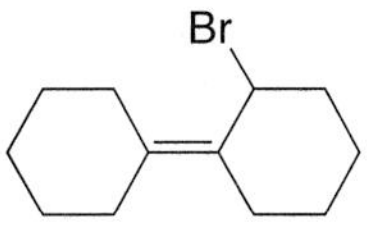

thermodynamic

c.

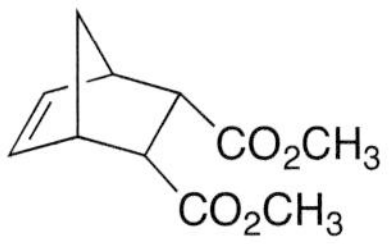

5.a.

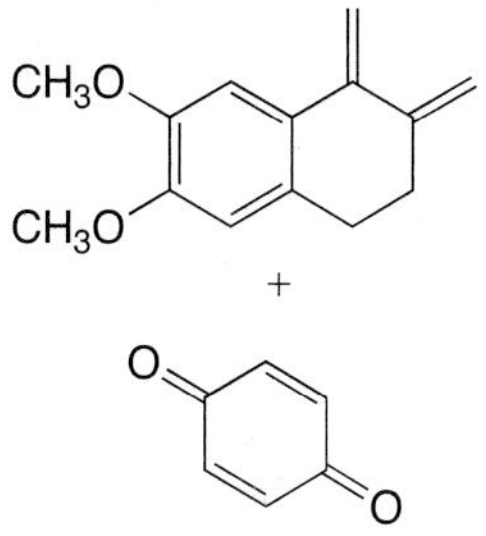

b.

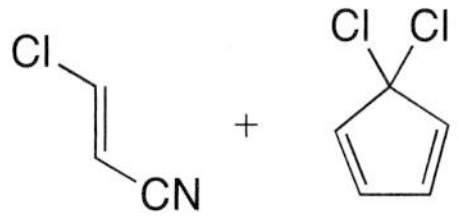

Answers to Problems

16.1 **Isolated dienes** have two double bonds separated by two or more σ bonds.
Conjugated dienes have two double bonds separated by only one σ bond.

a. 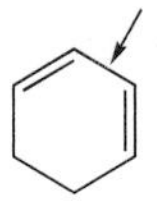

One σ bond separates two double bonds = **conjugated diene**

b. 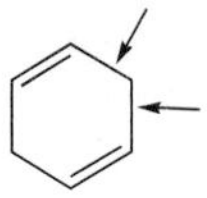

Two σ bonds separate two double bonds = **isolated diene**

c. 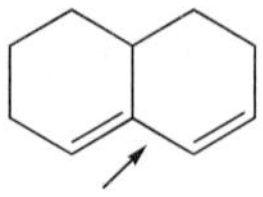

One σ bond separates two double bonds = **conjugated diene**

d. 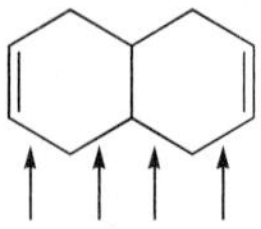

Four σ bonds separate two double bonds = **isolated diene**

16.2 **Conjugation** occurs when there are overlapping *p* orbitals on three or more adjacent atoms. Double bonds separated by two σ bonds are not conjugated.

a. $CH_2{=}CH{-}CH{=}CH{-}CH{=}CH_2$

All of the carbon atoms are sp^2 hybridized. Each π bond is separated by only one σ bond.
conjugated

b. 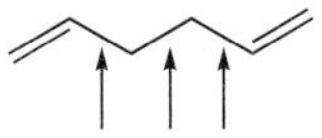

The two π bonds are separated by three σ bonds.
NOT conjugated

c. 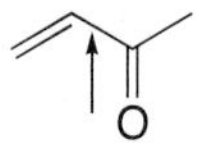

The two π bonds are separated by only one σ bond.
conjugated

d. 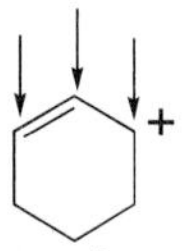

Three adjacent carbon atoms are sp^2 hybridized and have an unhybridized *p* orbital.
conjugated

e. 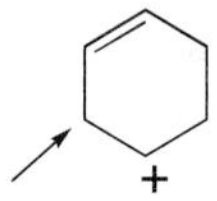

This carbon is not sp^2 hybridized.
NOT conjugated

16.3 Two resonance structures differ only in the placement of electrons. All σ bonds stay in the same place. Nonbonded electrons and π bonds can be moved. To draw the hybrid:

- Use a dashed line between atoms that have a π bond in one resonance structure and not the other.
- Use a δ symbol for atoms with a charge or radical in one structure but not the other.

a. 

resonance hybrid: 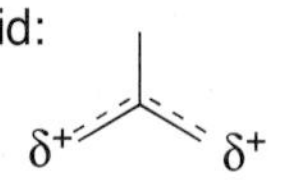

The + charge is delocalized on two carbons.

b. 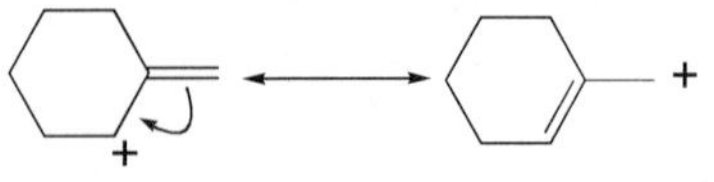

resonance hybrid: 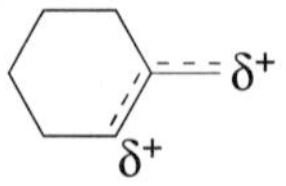

The + charge is delocalized on two carbons.

c. 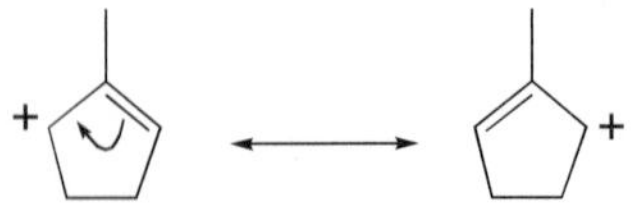

resonance hybrid: 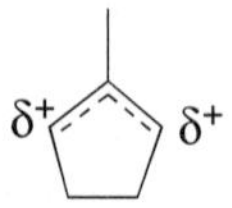

The + charge is delocalized on two carbons.

16.4 S_N1 reactions proceed via a carbocation intermediate. Draw the carbocation formed on loss of Cl and compare. The more stable the carbocation, the faster the S_N1 reaction.

3-chloro-1-propene
more reactive

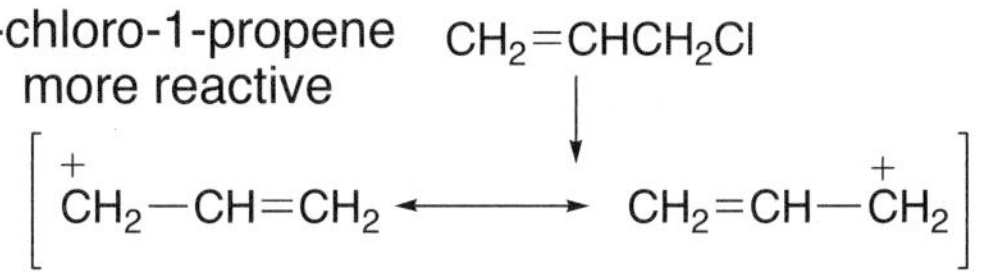
CH2=CHCH2Cl
CH2—CH=CH2
CH2=CH—CH2

resonance-stabilized carbocation

Two resonance structures delocalize the positive charge on 2 C's making 3-chloro-1-propene more reactive.

$CH_3CH_2CH_2Cl$ is a 1° halide, which does not react by an S_N1 reaction because cleavage of the C–Cl bond forms a highly unstable 1° carbocation.

1-chloropropane
less reactive

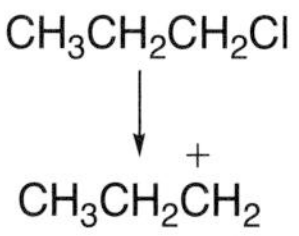
CH3CH2CH2Cl
CH3CH2CH2

only one Lewis structure
very unstable

16.5

a. 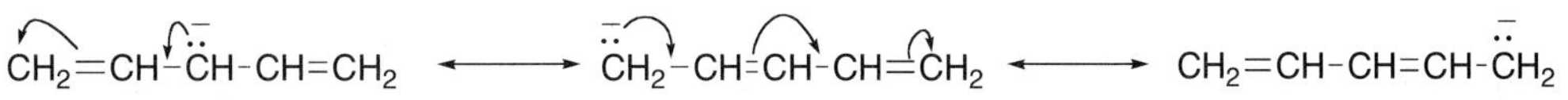
CH2=CH-CH-CH=CH2
CH2-CH=CH-CH=CH2
CH2=CH-CH=CH-CH2

Move the charge and the double bond.

b. 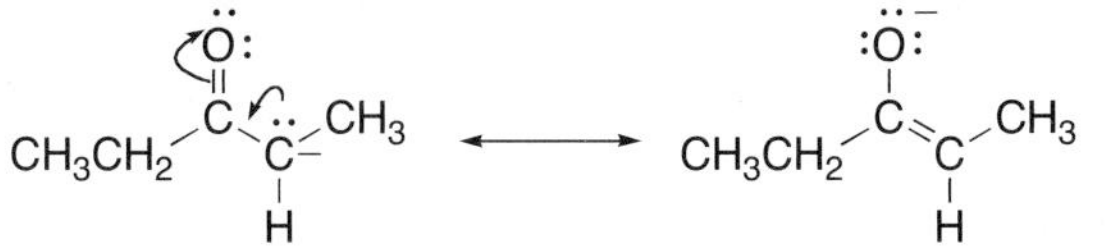
O:
CH3CH2
CH3
H
:O:
CH3CH2
CH3
H

Move the charge and the double bond.

c. 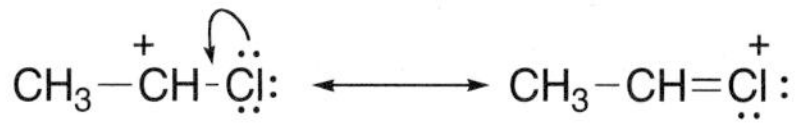
CH3—CH-Cl:
CH3-CH=Cl:

Move the lone pair.

d. 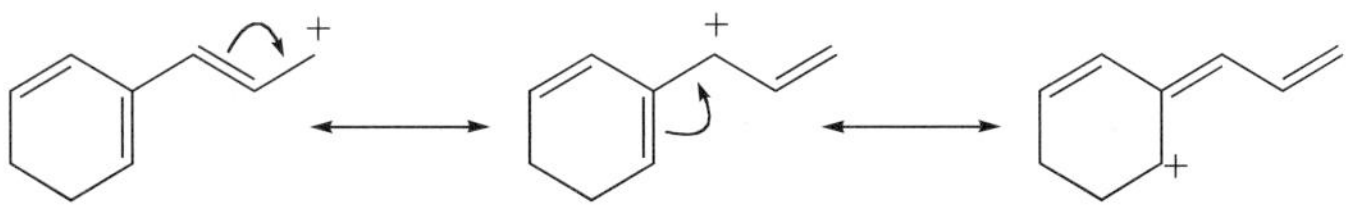

Move the charge and the double bond.

16.6 To compare the resonance structures remember:

- Resonance structures with **more bonds** are better.
- Resonance structures in which **every atom has an octet** are better.
- Resonance structures with **neutral atoms** are better than those with charge separation.
- Resonance structures that place a **negative charge on a more electronegative atom** are better.

a. 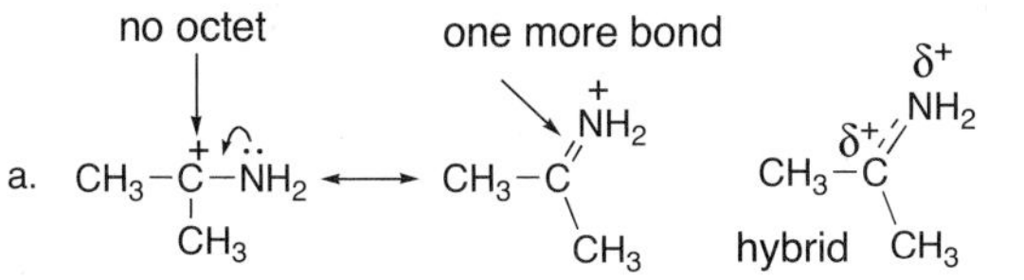
no octet
one more bond
CH3-C-NH2
CH3
CH3-C
NH2
CH3
δ+
NH2
δ+
CH3-C
hybrid
CH3

least stable | one more bond All atoms have an octet. better resonance structure **intermediate stability** | **most stable**

c. 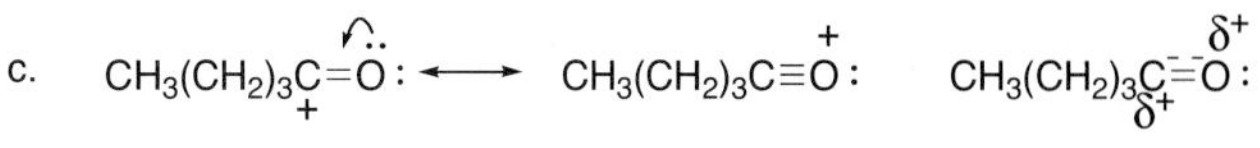
CH3(CH2)3C=O:
CH3(CH2)3C≡O:
δ+
CH3(CH2)3C=O:
δ+

least stable | one more bond better resonance structure **intermediate stability** | **most stable**

b. 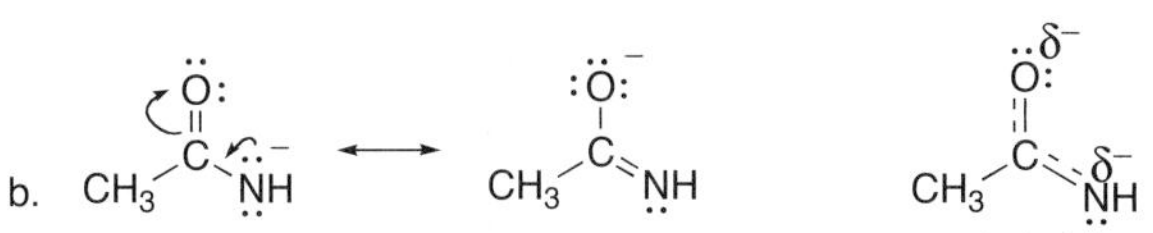
O:
CH3
NH
:O:
CH3
NH
δ−
O:
CH3
δ−
NH

least stable | negative charge on the more electronegative atom better resonance structure **intermediate stability** | hybrid **most stable**

d. 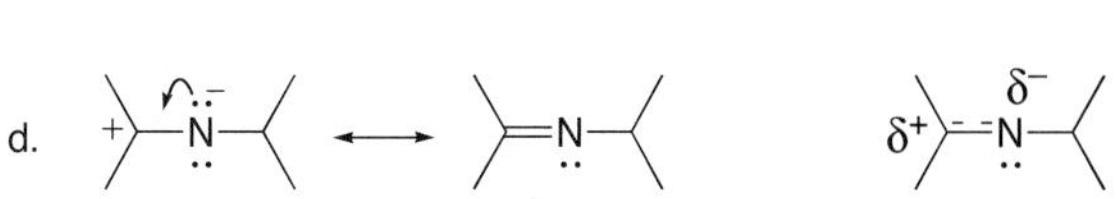
N
N
δ−
δ+
N

least stable | one more bond better resonance structure **intermediate stability** | **most stable**

16.7

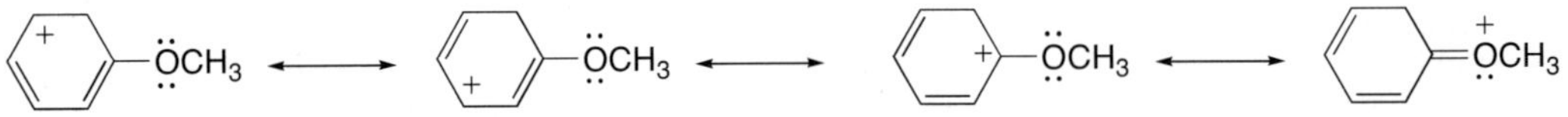
ÖCH3
ÖCH3
ÖCH3
OCH3

largest contribution
more bonds and all
atoms have octets

16.8 Remember that in any allyl system, there must be *p* orbitals to delocalize the lone pair.

a. 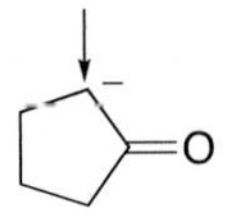

*sp*² hybridized
trigonal planar geometry

b. 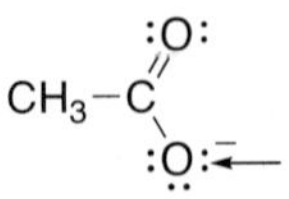
:O:
CH3–C
:O:

*sp*² hybridized
trigonal planar geometry

c. 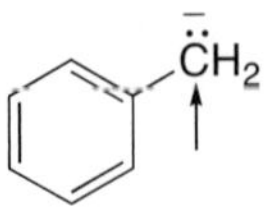
CH2

*sp*² hybridized
trigonal planar geometry

16.9 The **s-cis** conformation has two double bonds on the **same side** of the single bond. The **s-trans** conformation has two double bonds on **opposite sides** of the single bond.

a. (2*E*,4*E*)-2,4-**octadiene** in the *s*-trans conformation

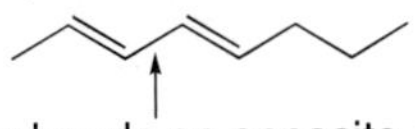

double bonds on opposite sides
s-trans

b. (3*E*,5*Z*)- 3,5-**nonadiene** in the *s*-cis conformation

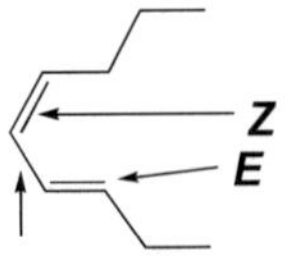
Z
E

double bonds on the same side
s-cis

c. (3*Z*,5*Z*)-4,5-dimethyl-3,5-**decadiene** in both the *s*-cis and *s*-trans conformations

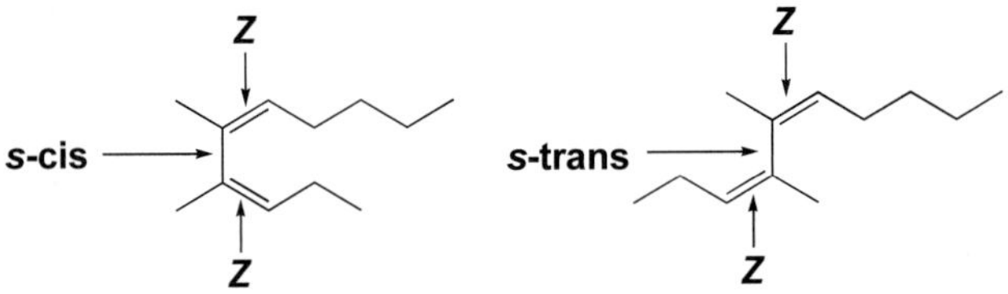
Z
s-cis
Z
Z
s-trans
Z

16.10

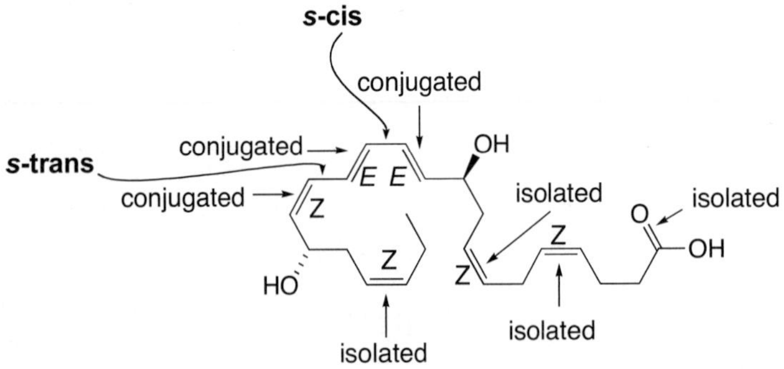
s-cis
conjugated
s-trans
conjugated
conjugated
E E
Z
OH
isolated
isolated
O
Z
OH
Z
Z
HO
isolated
isolated

16.11 Bond length depends on hybridization and percent *s*-character. Bonds with a higher percent *s*-character have smaller orbitals and are shorter.

HC≡C–C≡CH

sp hybridized carbons
50% *s*-character
shortest bond

CH_2=CH–CH=CH_2

*sp*² hybridized carbons
33% *s*-character
intermediate length

CH_3–CH_3

*sp*³ hybridized carbons
25% *s*-character
longest bond

16.12 Two equivalent resonance structures delocalize the π bond and the negative charge.

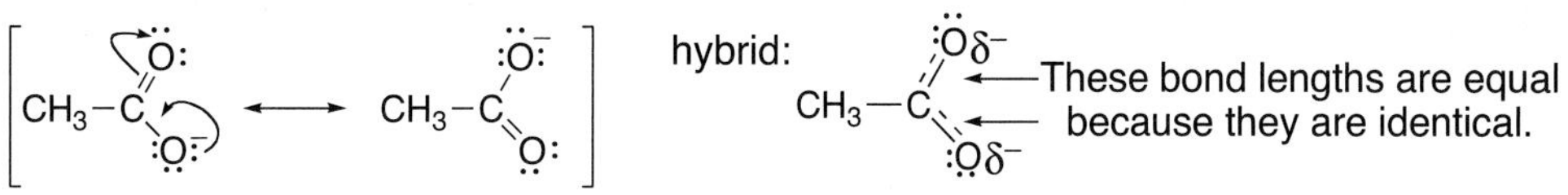

16.13 The **less stable** (higher energy) **diene** has the **larger heat of hydrogenation.** Isolated dienes are higher in energy than conjugated dienes, so they will have a larger heat of hydrogenation.

a. 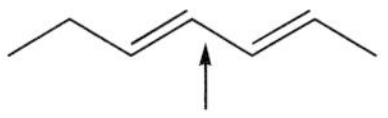 or 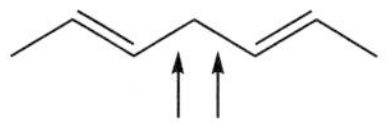

Double bonds separated by one σ bond = **conjugated diene**
smaller heat of hydrogenation

Double bonds separated by two σ bonds = **isolated diene**
larger heat of hydrogenation

b.  or 

Double bonds separated by one σ bond = **conjugated diene**
smaller heat of hydrogenation

Double bonds separated by two σ bonds = **isolated diene**
larger heat of hydrogenation

16.14 Isolated dienes are higher in energy than conjugated dienes. Compare the location of the double bonds in the compounds below.

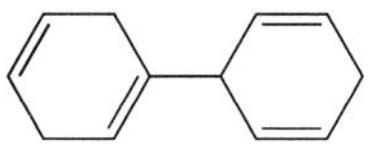

0 conjugated double bonds
least stable

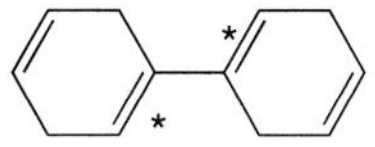

2 conjugated double bonds
intermediate stability

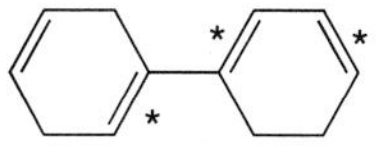

3 conjugated double bonds
most stable

16.15 Conjugated dienes react with HX to form 1,2- and 1,4-products.

a. $CH_3-CH=CH-CH=CH-CH_3 \xrightarrow{HCl} CH_3-CH(H)-CH(Cl)-CH=CH-CH_3 + CH_3-CH(H)-CH=CH-CH(Cl)-CH_3$

1,2-product **1,4-product**

b. 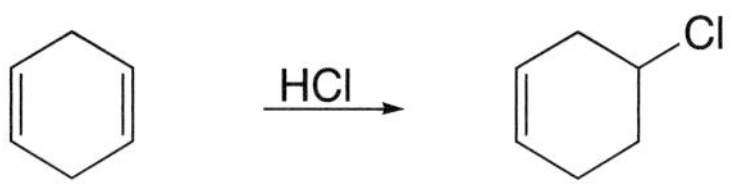

isolated diene

c. 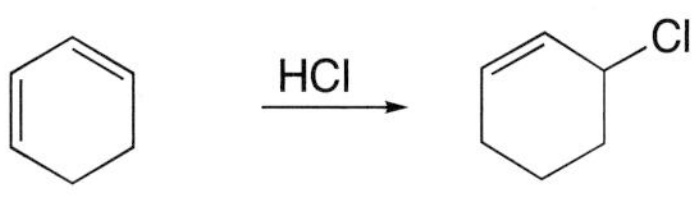

d. 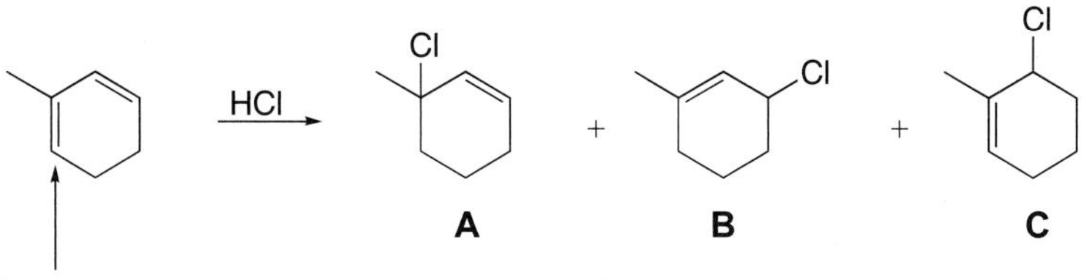

This double bond is more reactive, so **C** is probably a minor product because it results from HCl addition to the less reactive double bond.

16.16 The mechanism for addition of DCl has two steps:

[1] **Addition of D^+** forms a resonance-stabilized carbocation.

[2] **Nucleophilic attack of Cl^-** forms 1,2- and 1,4-products.

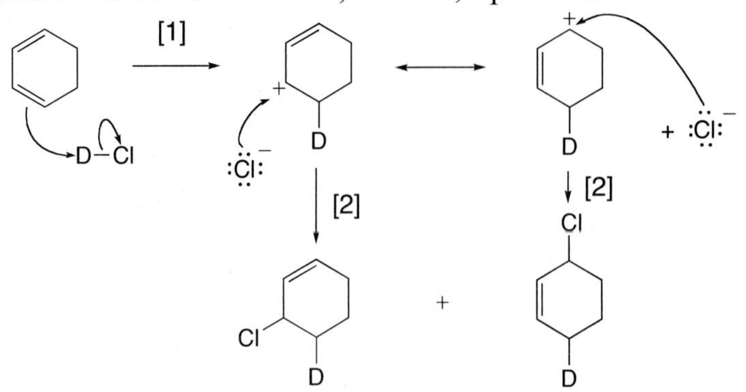

16.17 Label the products as 1,2- or 1,4-products. The 1,2-product is the kinetic product, and the 1,4-product, which has the more substituted double bond, is the thermodynamic product.

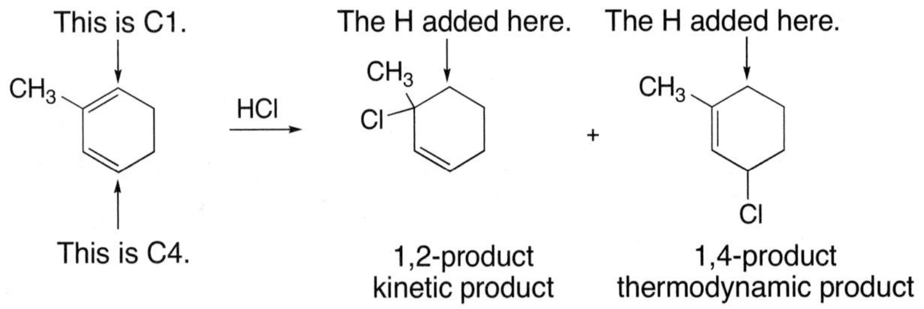

16.18 To draw the products of a Diels–Alder reaction:

[1] Find the 1,3-diene and the dienophile.

[2] Arrange them so the diene is on the left and the dienophile is on the right.

[3] Cleave three bonds and use arrows to show where the new bonds will be formed.

a.
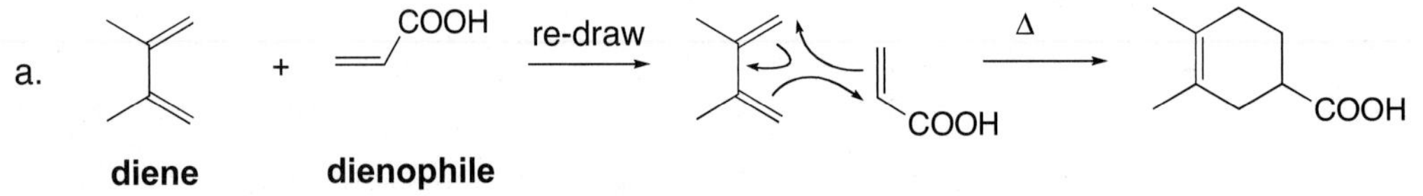

b.
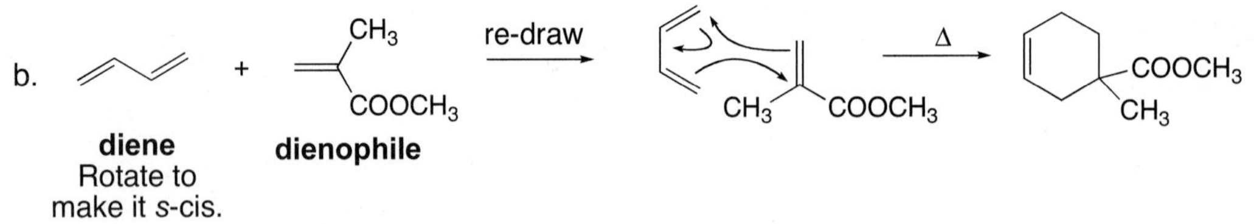

c.
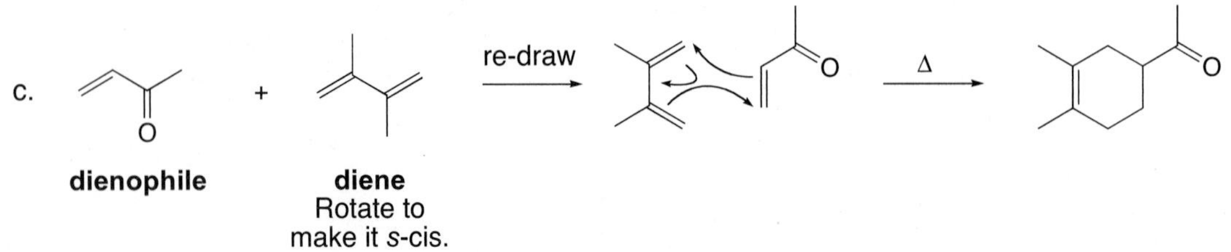

16.19 For a diene to be reactive in a Diels–Alder reaction, **a diene must be able to adopt an *s*-cis conformation.**

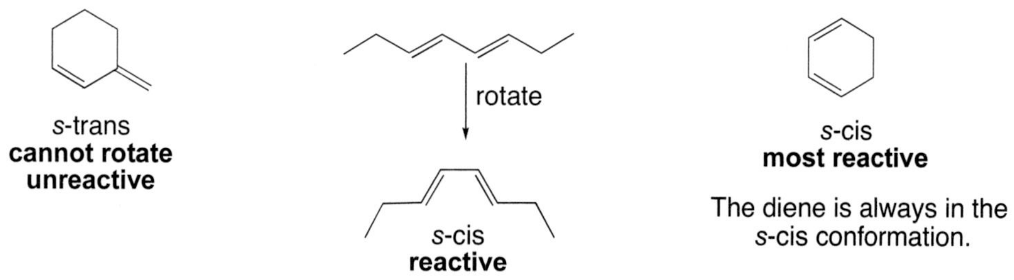
s-trans
cannot rotate
unreactive
rotate
s-cis
reactive
s-cis
most reactive
The diene is always in the s-cis conformation.

16.20 Zingiberene reacts much faster than β-sesquiphellandrene as a Diels–Alder diene because its diene is constrained in the *s*-cis conformation. The diene in β-sesquiphellandrene is constrained in the *s*-trans conformation, so it is unreactive in the Diels–Alder.

16.21 Electron-withdrawing substituents in the dienophile increase the reaction rate.

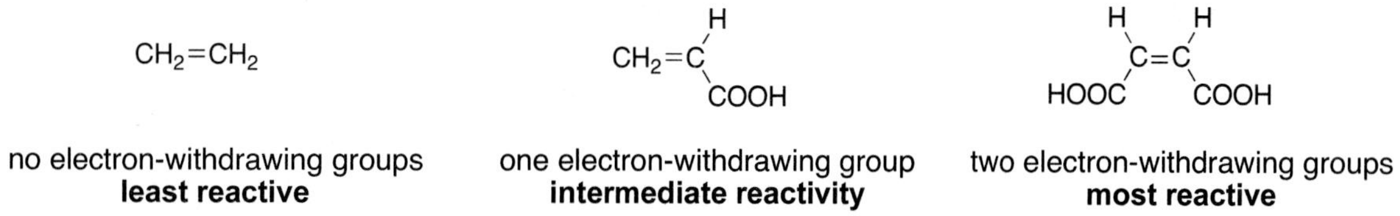
CH2=CH2
no electron-withdrawing groups
least reactive
CH2=C(H)COOH
one electron-withdrawing group
intermediate reactivity
HOOC(H)C=C(H)COOH
two electron-withdrawing groups
most reactive

16.22 A cis dienophile forms a cis-substituted cyclohexene.
A trans dienophile forms a trans-substituted cyclohexene.

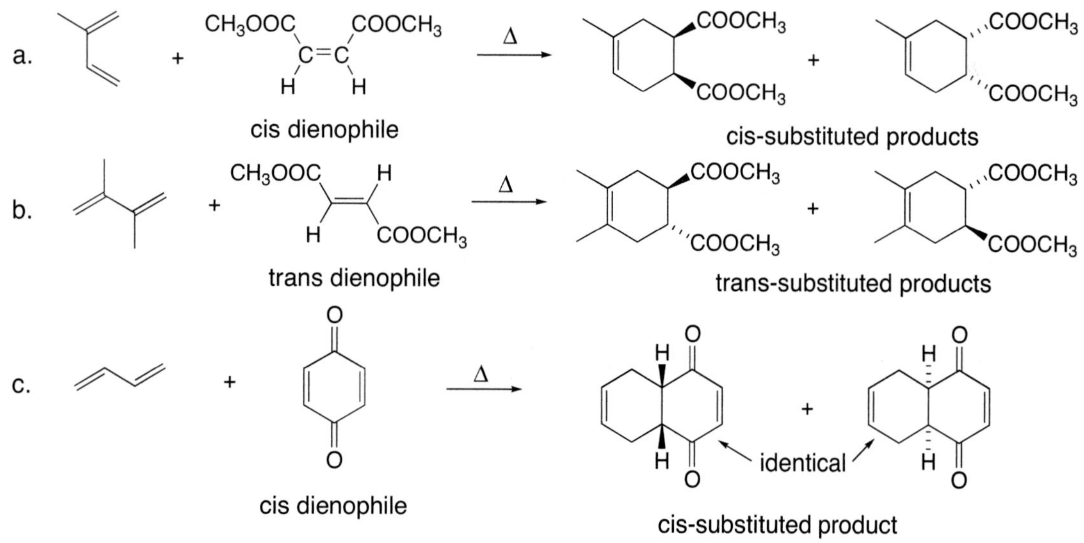
a.
CH3OOC COOCH3
C=C
H H
cis dienophile
Δ
COOCH3
COOCH3
cis-substituted products
b.
CH3OOC H
H COOCH3
trans dienophile
Δ
trans-substituted products
c.
O
cis dienophile
H
identical
cis-substituted product

16.23 The **endo product** (with the substituents under the plane of the new six-membered ring) is the preferred product.

a. 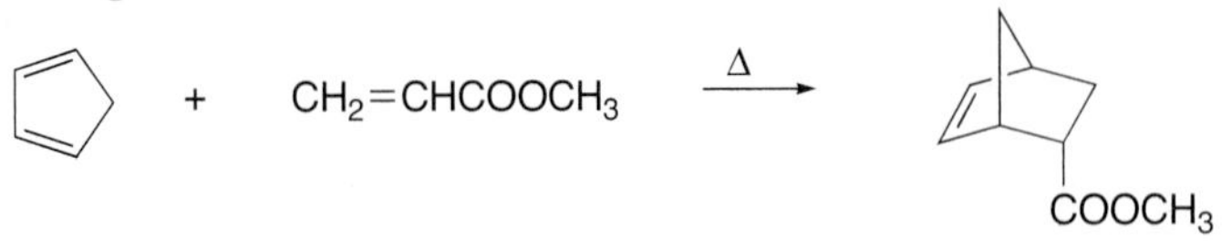

$CH_2{=}CHCOOCH_3$
Δ
$COOCH_3$

endo substituent

b. 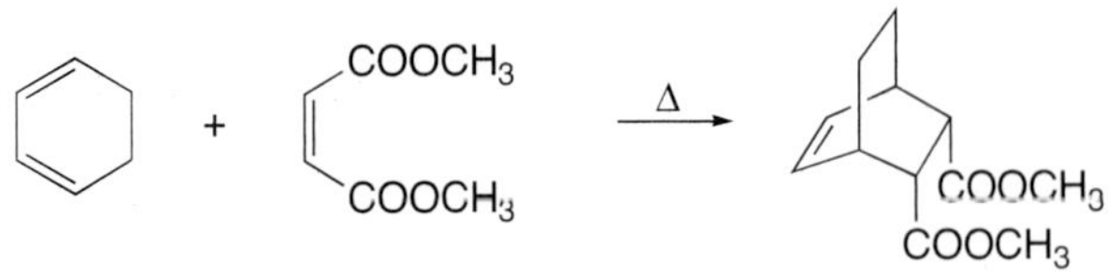

$COOCH_3$
$COOCH_3$
Δ
$COOCH_3$
$COOCH_3$

both groups **endo**

16.24 To find the diene and dienophile needed to make each of the products:
[1] Find the six-membered ring with a C–C double bond.
[2] Draw three arrows to work backwards.
[3] Follow the arrows to show the diene and dienophile.

a. 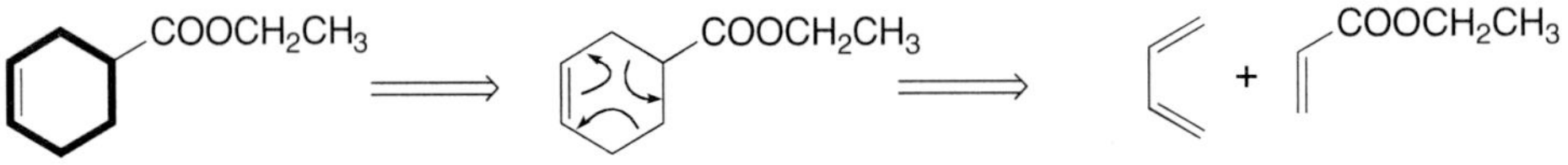

$COOCH_2CH_3$
$COOCH_2CH_3$
$COOCH_2CH_3$

b. 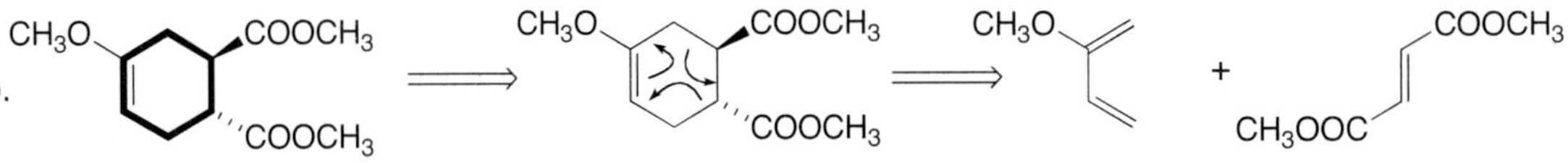

CH_3O
$COOCH_3$
$COOCH_3$
CH_3OOC

c. 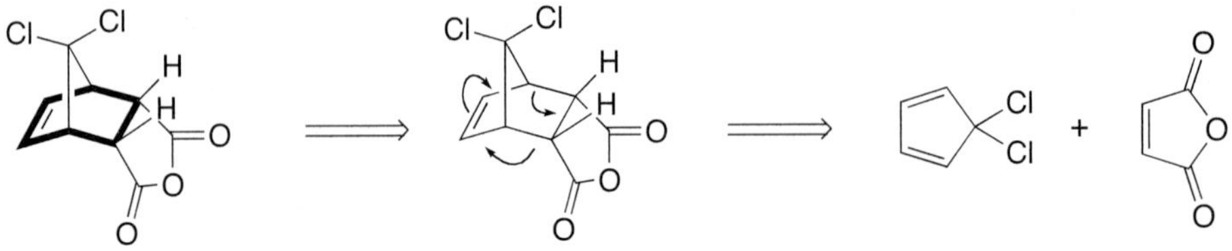

Cl
Cl
H
H
O

16.25

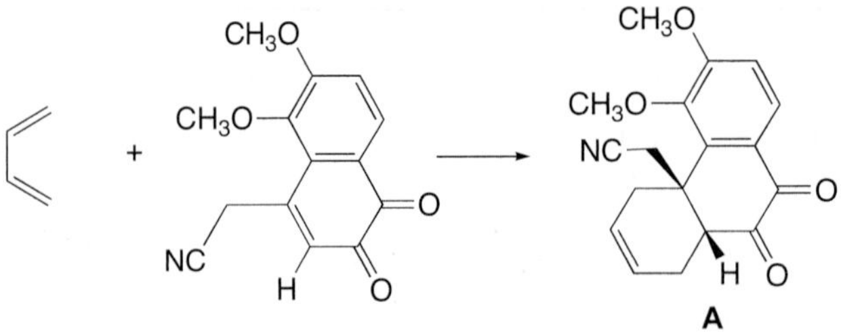

CH_3O
NC
H
O

A

(+ enantiomer)

16.26 Conjugated molecules absorb light at a longer wavelength than molecules that are not conjugated.

a. 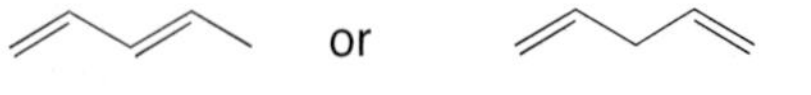

conjugated longer wavelength | or | not conjugated

b. 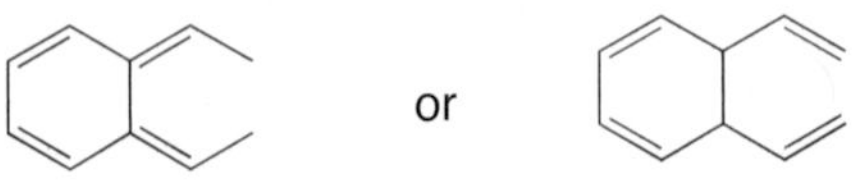

all double bonds conjugated longer wavelength | or | one set of conjugated dienes

16.27 Sunscreens contain conjugated systems to absorb UV radiation from sunlight. Look for conjugated systems in the compounds below.

a.

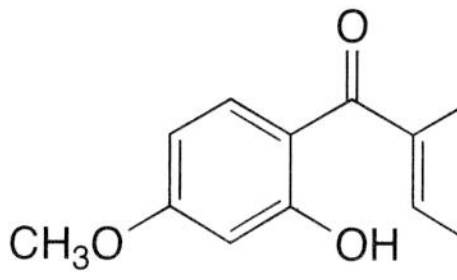

O
CH_3O
OH

conjugated system
could be a sunscreen

b.

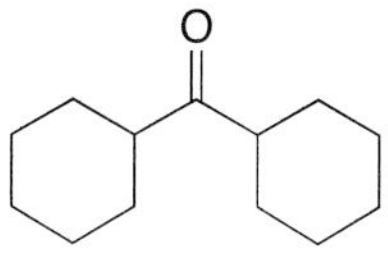

O

not a conjugated system

c.

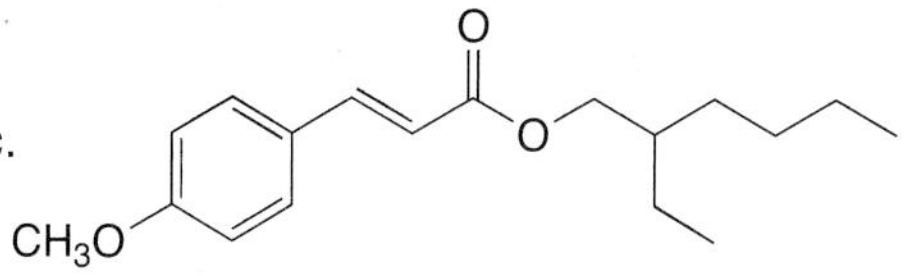

O
O
CH_3O

conjugated system
could be a sunscreen

16.28

a.

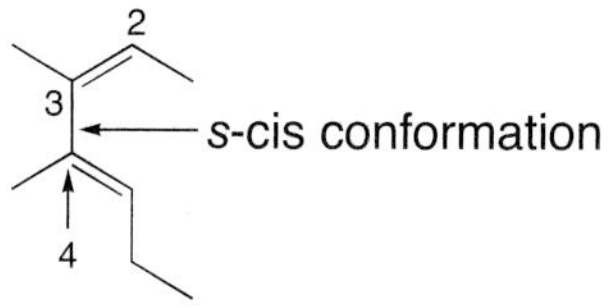

2
3
4
s-cis conformation

(2*Z*,4*E*)-3,4-dimethyl-2,4-heptadiene

b.

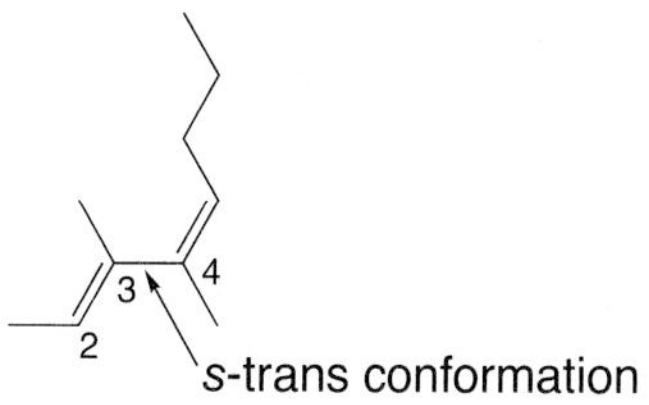

2
3
4
s-trans conformation

(2*E*,4*Z*)-3,4-dimethyl-2,4-octadiene

16.29

a.

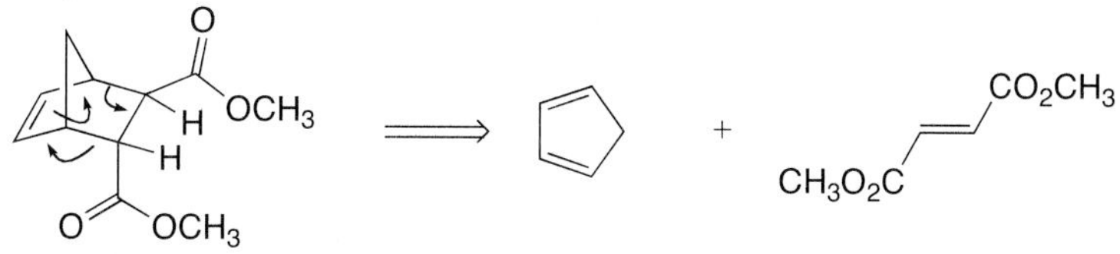

O
H
OCH_3
H
O
OCH_3
+
CO_2CH_3
CH_3O_2C

b.

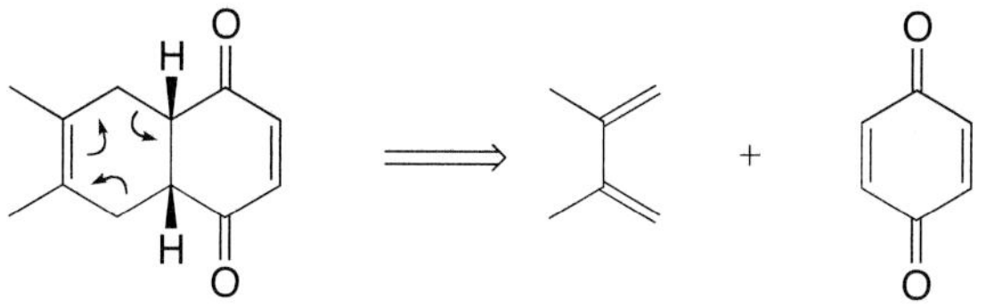

H
O
H
O
+
O
O

16.30 Use the definition from Answer 16.1.

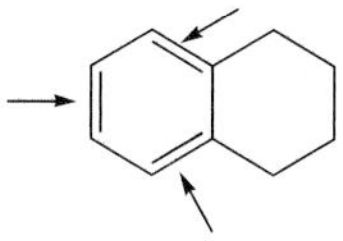

3 π bonds with only
1 σ bond between
conjugated

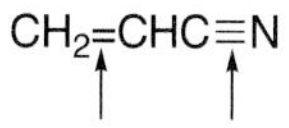

$CH_2{=}CHC{\equiv}N$

2 multiple bonds with only
1 σ bond between
conjugated

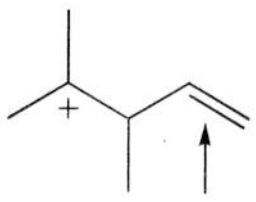

+

1 π bond with
no adjacent sp^2 hybridized atoms
NOT conjugated

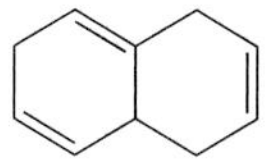

3 π bonds with 2 or
more σ bonds between
NOT conjugated

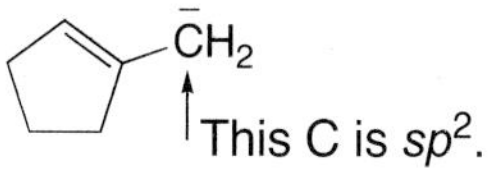

$\bar{C}H_2$
This C is sp^2.

1 π bond with
an adjacent sp^2 hybridized atom

The lone pair occupies a *p* orbital,
so there are *p* orbitals on
three adjacent atoms.

conjugated

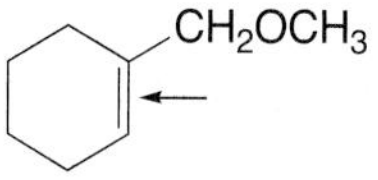

CH_2OCH_3

1 π bond with
no adjacent sp^2 hybridized atoms
NOT conjugated

16.31

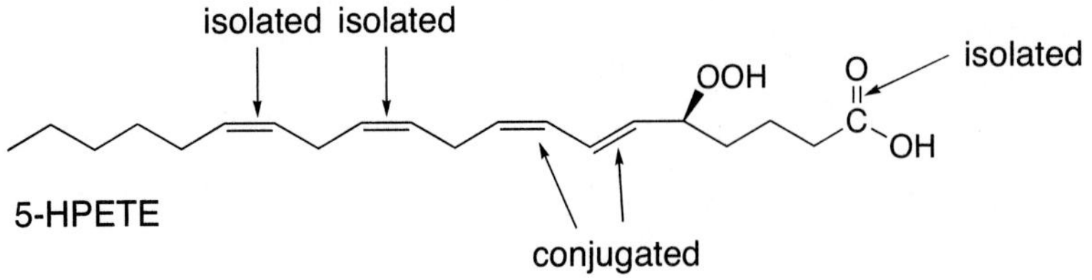

16.32

a.

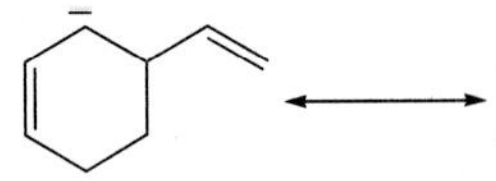

b.

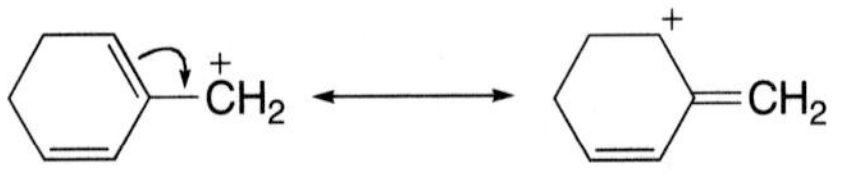

c.

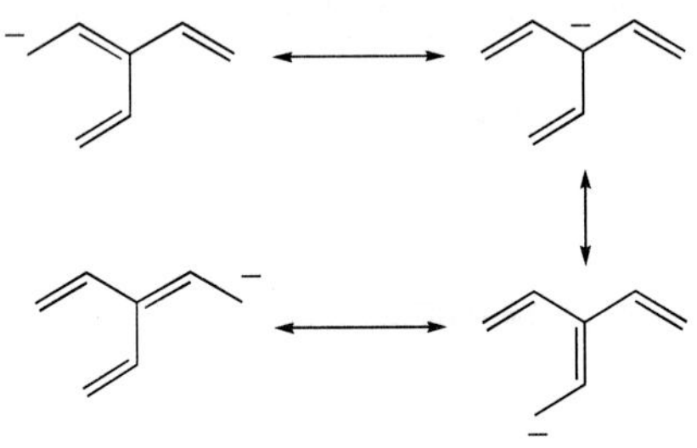

d.

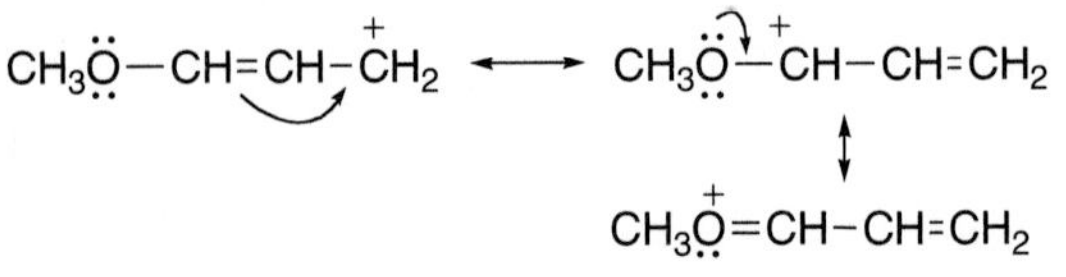

e.

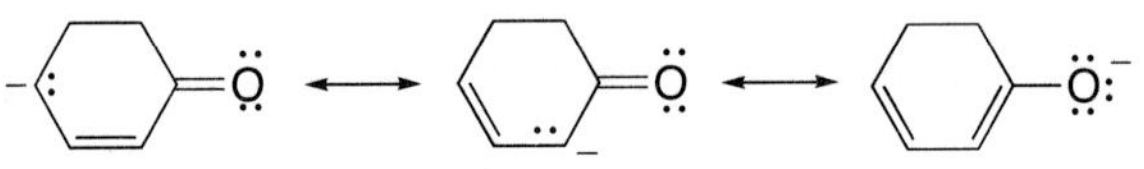

f.

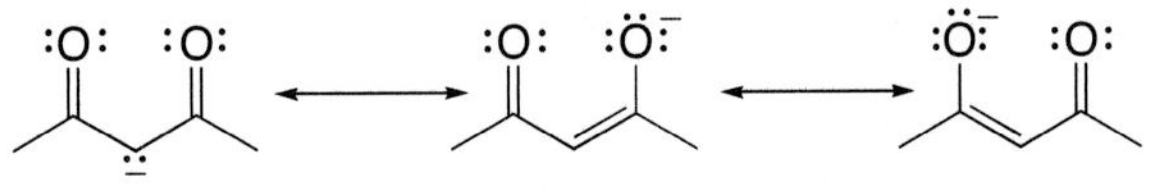

16.33

a.

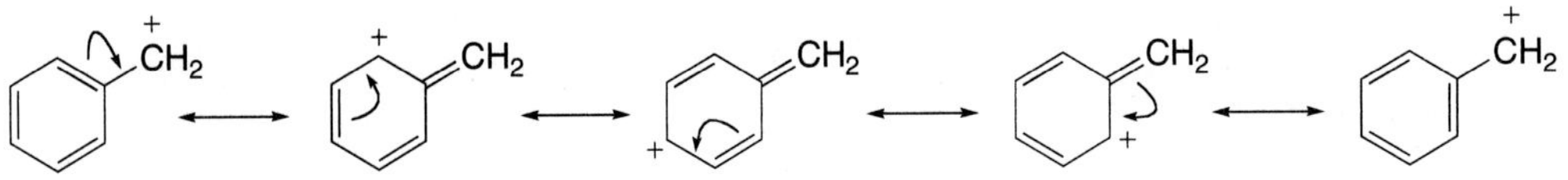

b.

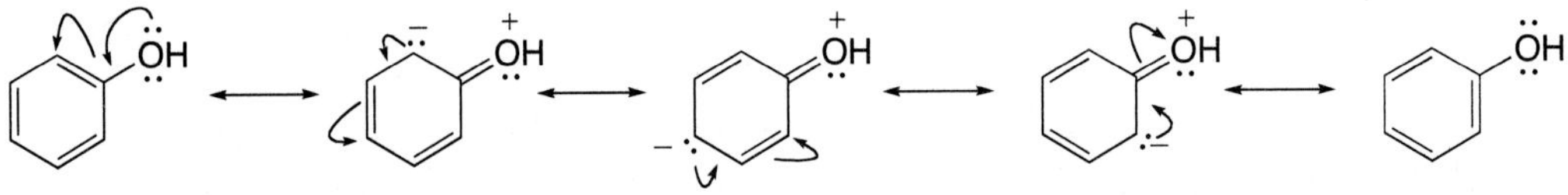

c.

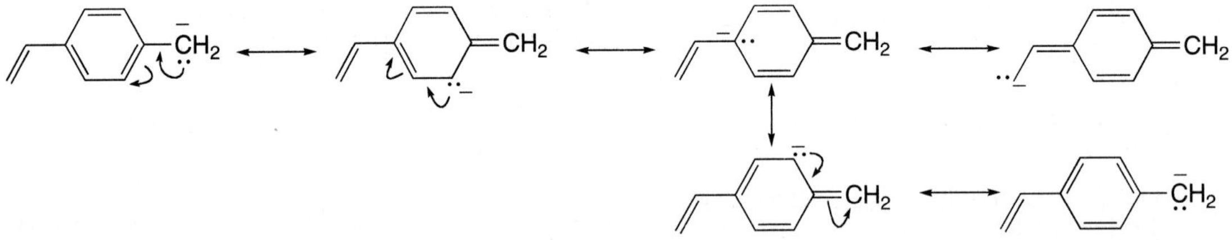

d.

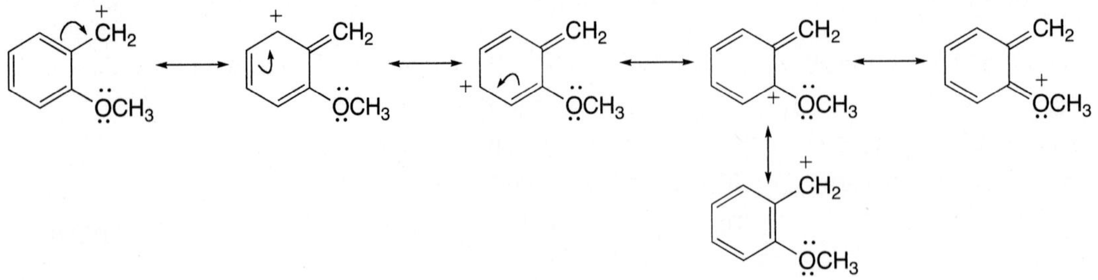

16.34 No additional resonance structures can be drawn for compounds (a) and (d).

b. 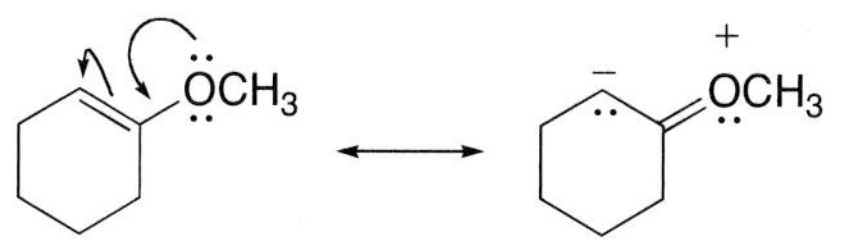

c. 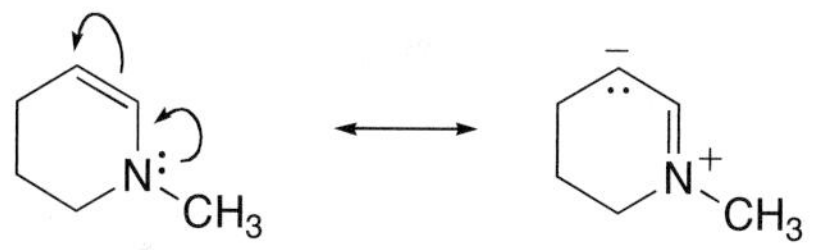

16.35

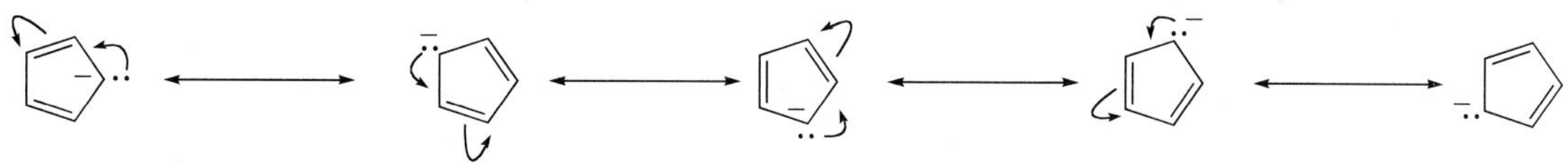

resonance hybrid:

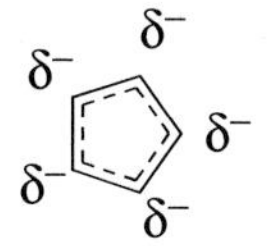

Five resonance structures delocalize the negative charge on five C's, making them all equivalent.

All of the carbons are identical in the anion.

16.36

a. $CH_2{=}CH{-}CH_2{-}H$ (more acidic)

↓

$\overset{-}{\ddot{C}}H_2{-}CH{=}CH_2$ ⟷ $CH_2{=}CH{-}\overset{-}{\ddot{C}}H_2$

Resonance stabilization delocalizes the negative charge on 2 C's after loss of a proton. This makes propene more acidic than propane.

$CH_3CH_2CH_2{-}H$ (less acidic)

↓

$CH_3CH_2\overset{-}{\ddot{C}}H_2$

only one Lewis structure

b. Draw the products of cleavage of the bond.

ethane $CH_3{-}CH_3$

↓

$\cdot CH_3$ + $\cdot CH_3$

Two unstable radicals form.

1-butene $CH_3{-}CH_2CH{=}CH_2$

↓

$\cdot CH_3$ + $\dot{C}H_2{-}CH{=}CH_2$ ⟷ $CH_2{=}CH{-}\dot{C}H_2$

One resonance-stabilized radical forms. This makes the bond dissociation energy lower because a more stable radical is formed.

16.37 Use the directions from Answer 16.9.

a. (3*Z*)-1,3-pentadiene in the *s*-trans conformation

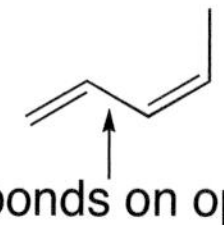

double bonds on opposite sides
s-trans

b. (2*E*,4*Z*)-1-bromo-3-methyl-2,4-hexadiene

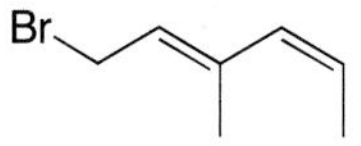

c. (2*E*,4*E*,6*E*)-2,4,6-octatriene

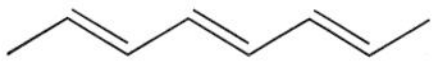

d. (2*E*,4*E*)-3-methyl-2,4-hexadiene in the *s*-cis conformation

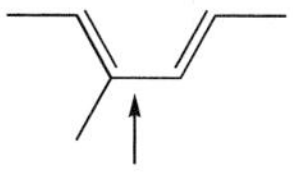

s-cis

16.38

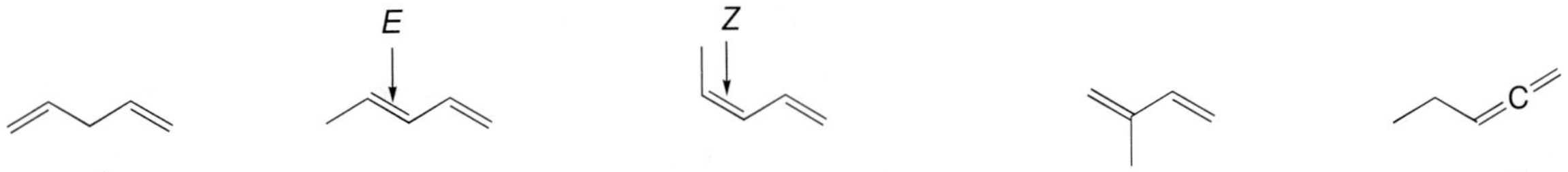
E
Z

1,4-pentadiene (3*E*)-1,3-pentadiene (3*Z*)-1,3-pentadiene 2-methyl-1,3-butadiene 1,2-pentadiene

3-methyl-1,2-butadiene 2,3-pentadiene

16.39

2*E*,4*E* 2*E*,4*Z* 2*Z*,4*E* 2*Z*,4*Z*

16.40

a. 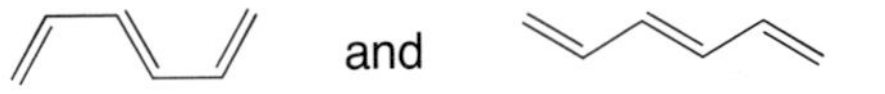

(3*E*)-1,3,5-hexatriene both *s*-cis and (3*E*)-1,3,5-hexatriene both *s*-trans

different conformations

c. 
E
Z

(3*E*)-1,3,5-hexatriene and (3*Z*)-1,3,5-hexatriene

different stereoisomers

b. 

(3*Z*)-1,3,5-hexatriene both *s*-cis and (3*Z*)-1,3,5-hexatriene both *s*-trans

different conformations

16.41 Use the directions from Answer 16.13 and recall that more substituted double bonds are more stable.

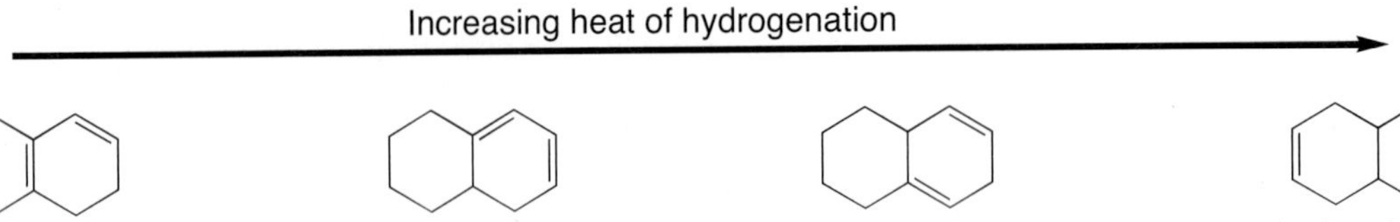
Increasing heat of hydrogenation

conjugated diene one tetra-, one disubstituted double bond **smallest** heat of hydrogenation	conjugated diene one di-, one trisubstituted double bond **smaller intermediate** heat of hydrogenation	isolated diene one di-, one trisubstituted double bond **larger intermediate** heat of hydrogenation	isolated diene both disubstituted double bonds **largest** heat of hydrogenation

16.42 Conjugated dienes react with HX to form 1,2- and 1,4-products.

a. 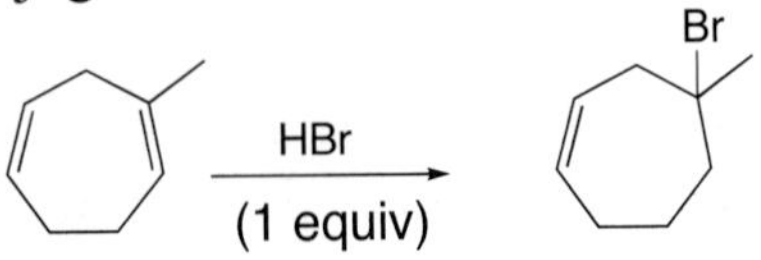
HBr
(1 equiv)
Br

isolated diene

major product, formed by addition of HBr to the more substituted C=C

b. 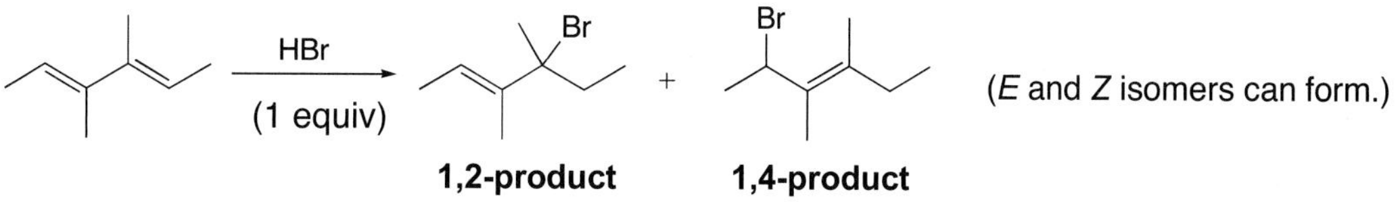

c. 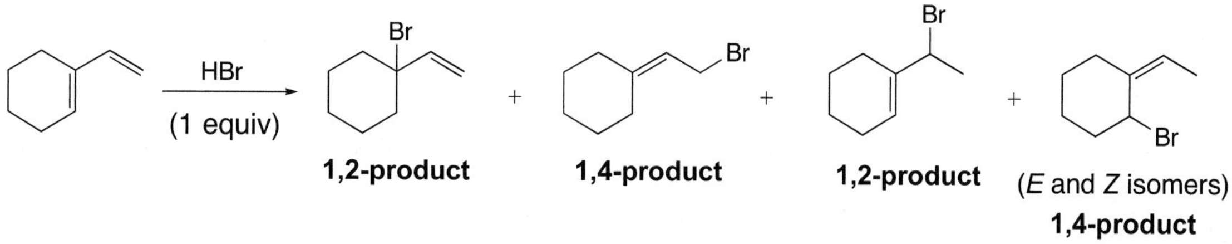

16.43

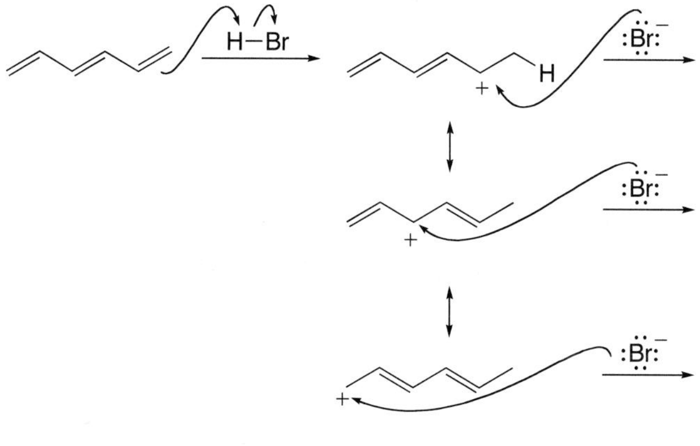

16.44

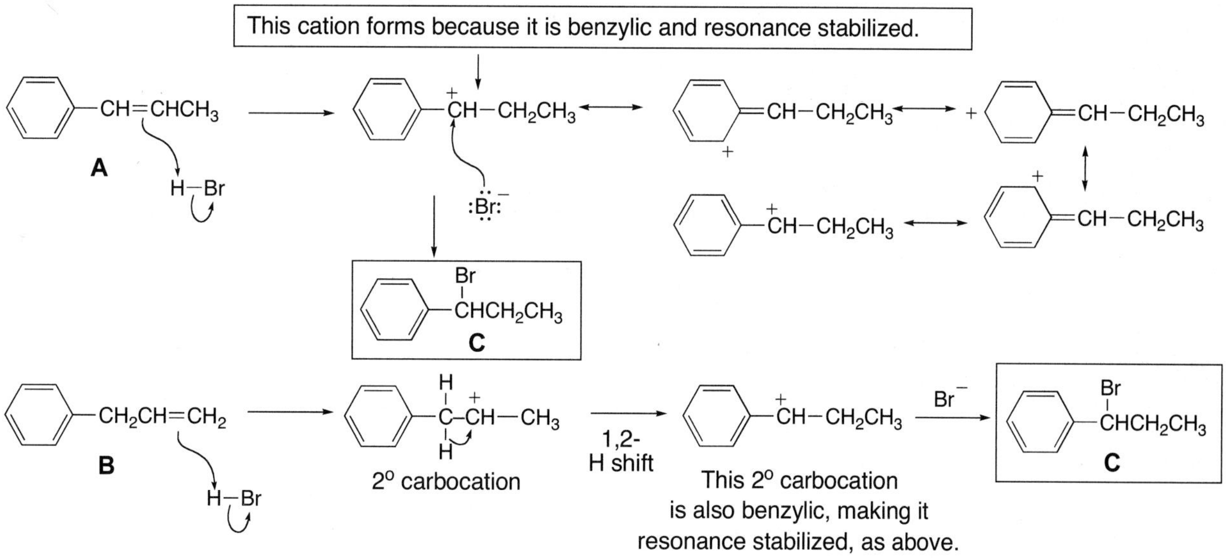

16.45 To draw the mechanism for reaction of a diene with HBr and ROOR, recall from Chapter 15 that when an alkene is treated with HBr under these radical conditions, the Br ends up on the carbon with more H's to begin with.

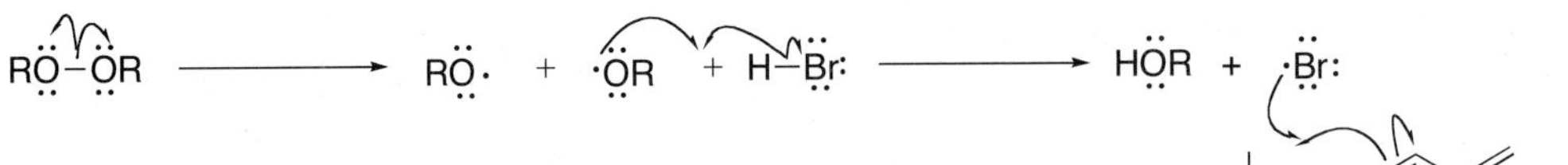

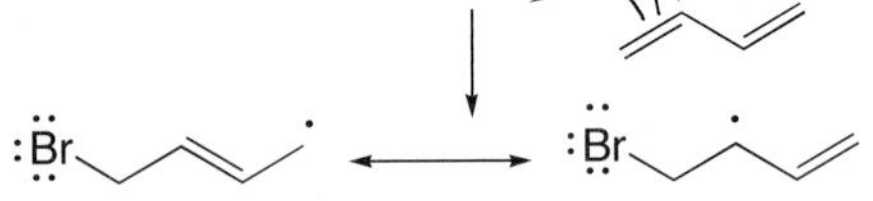

Use each resonance structure to react with HBr.

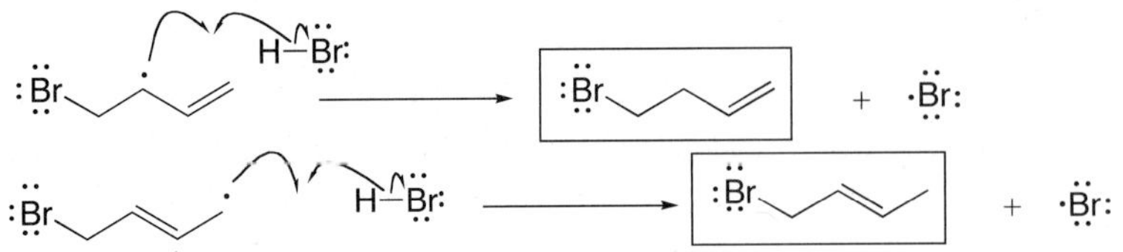

16.46

a, b.

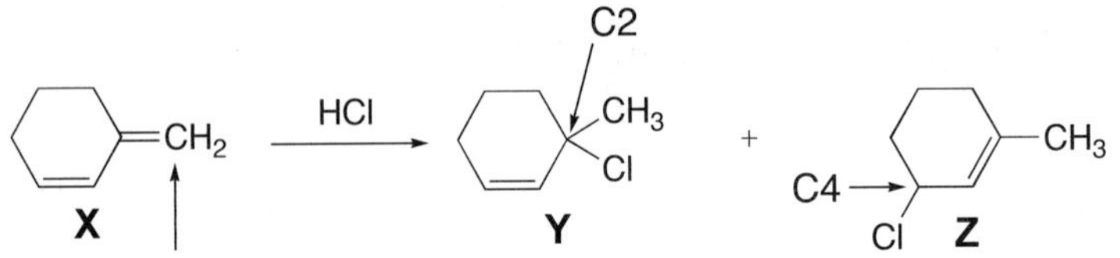

H adds here at C1.

Cl added at C2.
1,2-product
kinetic product

Cl added at C4.
1,4-product
thermodynamic product

Y is the kinetic product because of the proximity effect. H and Cl add across two adjacent atoms.
Z is the thermodynamic product because it has a more stable trisubstituted double bond.

Addition occurs at the labeled double bond due to the stability of the carbocation intermediate.

c.

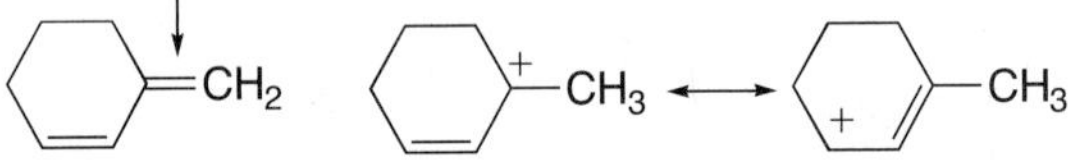

The two resonance structures for this allylic cation are 3° and 2° carbocations.

more stable intermediate
Addition occurs here.

If addition occurred at the other C=C, the following allylic carbocation would form:

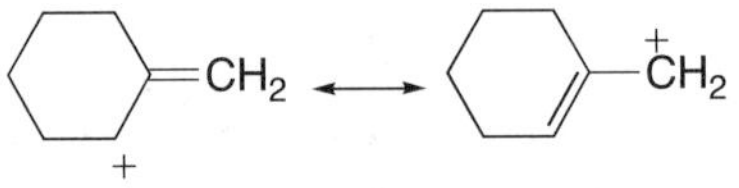

The two resonance structures for this allylic cation are 1° and 2° carbocations.

less stable

16.47 Addition of HCl at the terminal double bond forms a carbocation that is highly resonance stabilized since it is both allylic and benzylic. Such stabilization does not occur when HCl is added to the other double bond. This gives rise to two products of electrophilic addition.

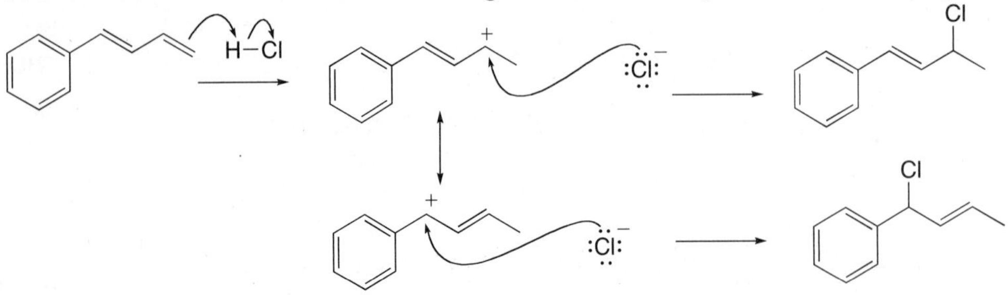

1,2-product

1,4-product

(+ three more resonance structures that delocalize the positive charge onto the benzene ring)

16.48 There are two possible products:

disubstituted C=C

trisubstituted C=C

1,2-product **1,4-product**

The 1,2-product is always the kinetic product because of the proximity effect. In this case, it is also the thermodynamic (more stable) product because it contains a more highly substituted C=C (trisubstituted) than the 1,4-product (disubstituted). Thus, the 1,2-product is the major product at high and low temperature.

16.49 The electron pairs on O can be donated to the double bond through resonance. This increases the electron density of the double bond, making it less electrophilic and therefore less reactive in a Diels–Alder reaction.

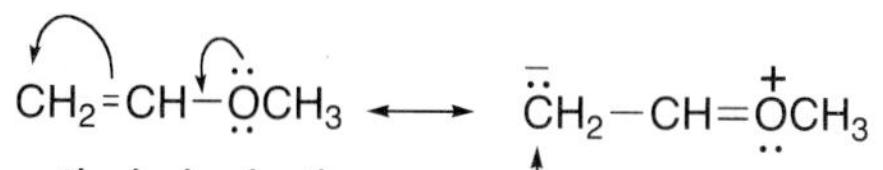

methyl vinyl ether

This C now bears a net negative charge.

16.50 Use the directions from Answer 16.18.

a.

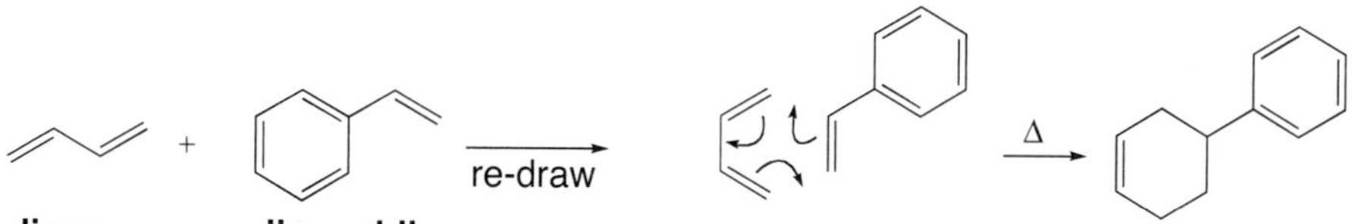

diene **dienophile**

b.

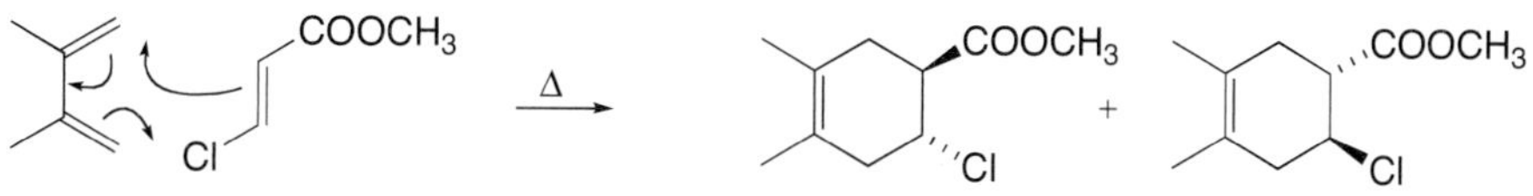

diene **trans dienophile** **trans-substituted products**

c.

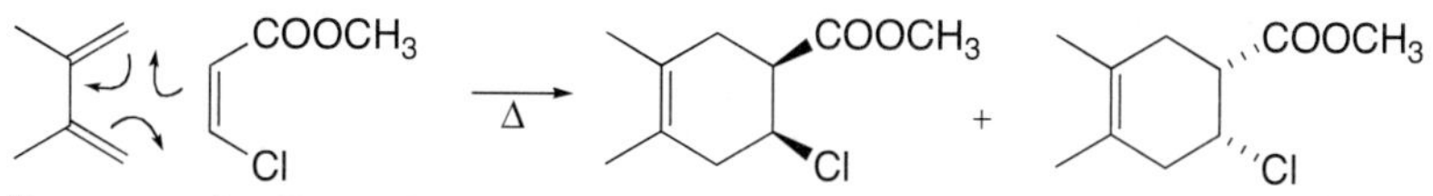

diene **cis dienophile** **cis-substituted products**

d.

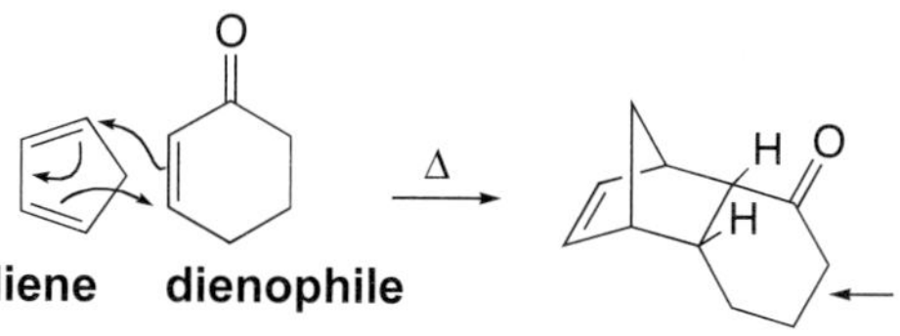

diene **dienophile** ← **endo ring**

e.

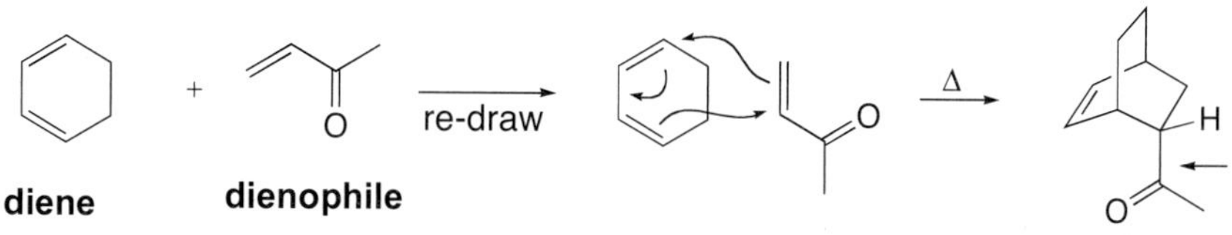

diene **dienophile** ← **endo substituent**

f.

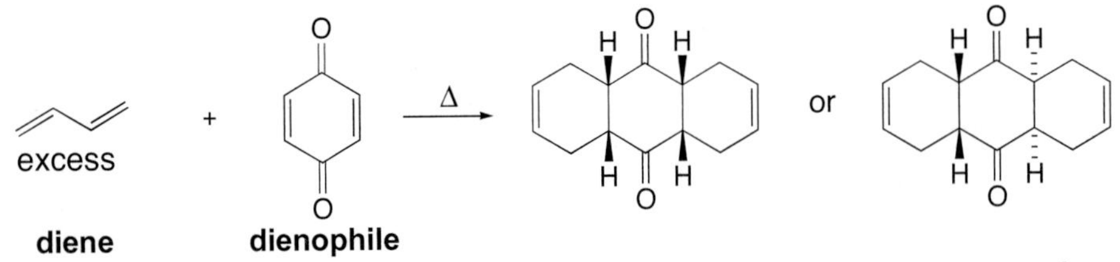

Both C=C's of the dienophile react so two Diels–Alder reactions take place.

16.51 Use the directions from Answer 16.24.

a.

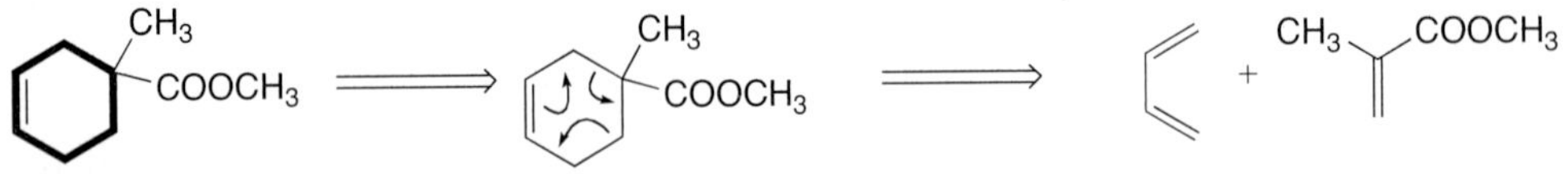

b.

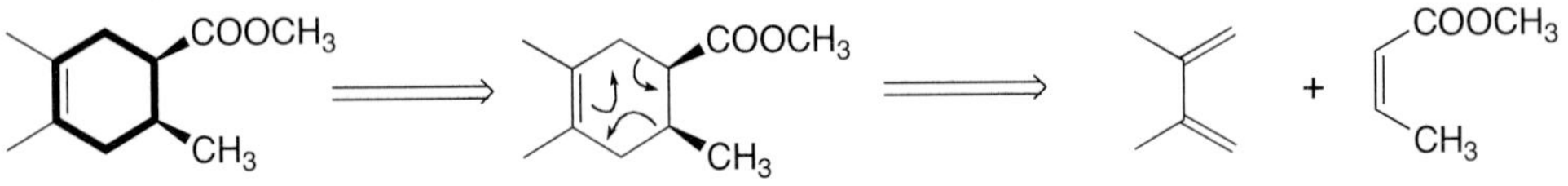

c.

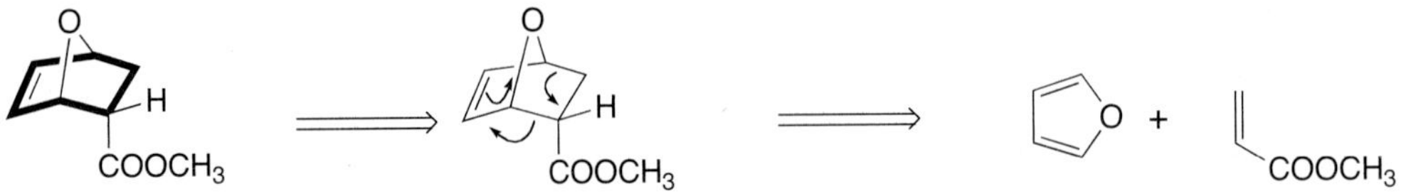

d.

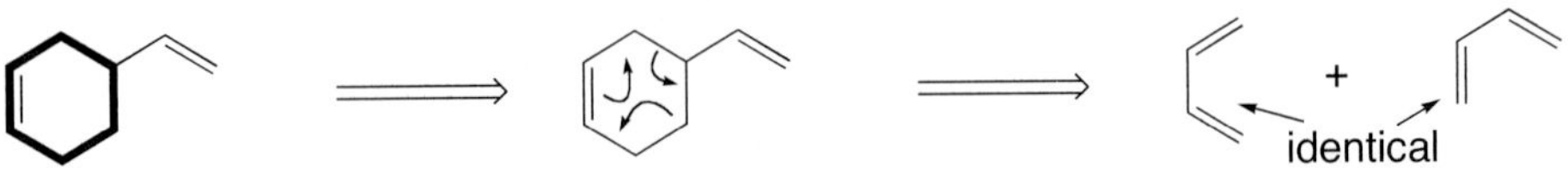

e.

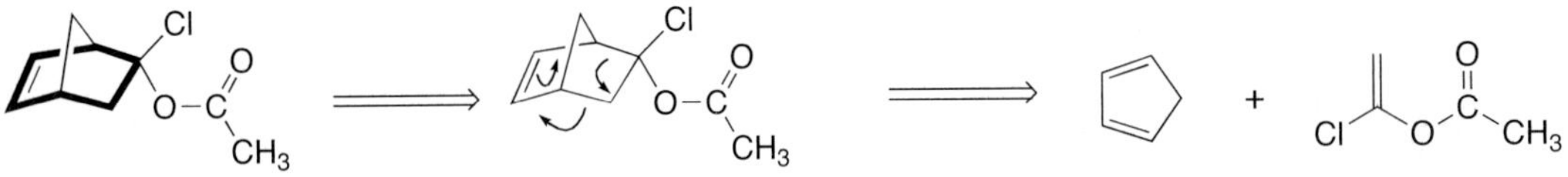

f.

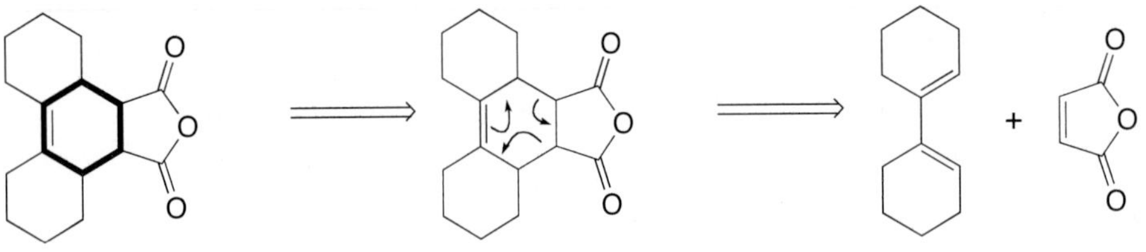

16.52

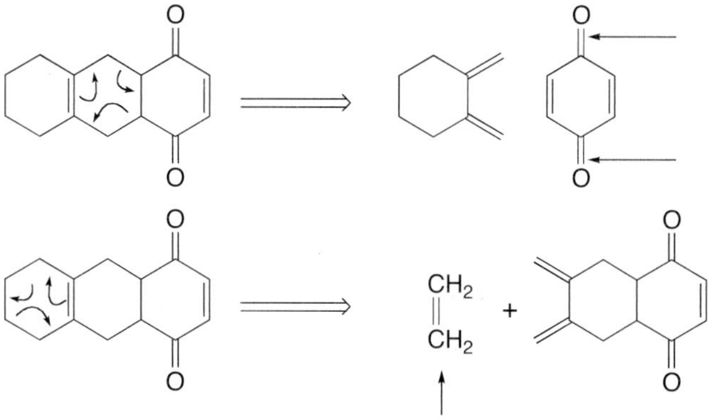
O
O
O
O
O
O
O
O
CH_2
CH_2
+

This pathway is **preferred** because the dienophile has electron-withdrawing C=O groups that make it more reactive.

no electron-withdrawing groups
less reactive

16.53

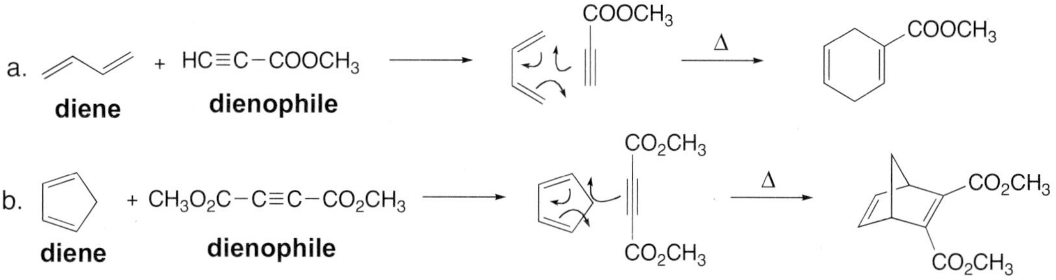
a.
+ HC≡C−COOCH₃
diene
dienophile
$COOCH_3$
Δ
$COOCH_3$
b.
+ $CH_3O_2C-C\equiv C-CO_2CH_3$
diene
dienophile
CO_2CH_3
CO_2CH_3
Δ
CO_2CH_3
CO_2CH_3

16.54

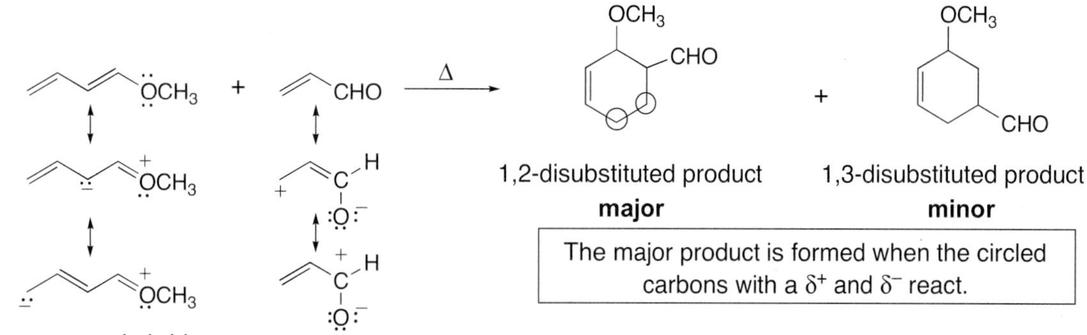
OCH_3
+
CHO
Δ
OCH_3
CHO
+
OCH_3
CHO
OCH_3
H
C
:O:
OCH_3
H
C
:O:
1,2-disubstituted product
major
1,3-disubstituted product
minor
The major product is formed when the circled carbons with a δ+ and δ− react.

resonance hybrids:

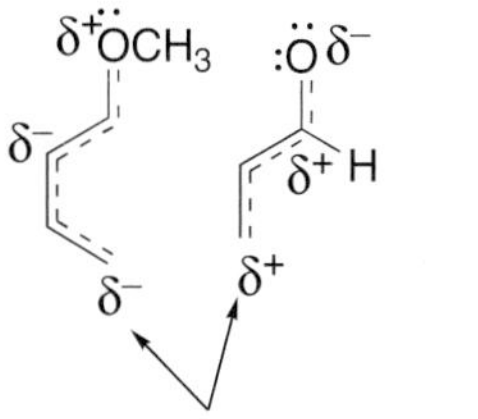
δ+ OCH_3
:O δ−
δ−
δ+ H
δ−
δ+

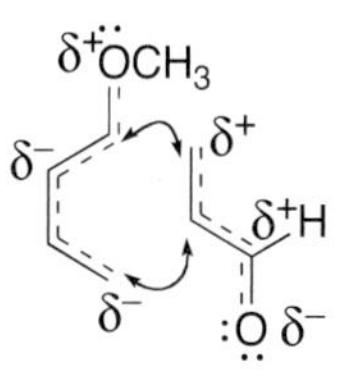
δ+ OCH_3
δ−
δ+
δ+H
δ−
:O δ−

For the 1,2-product, carbons with unlike charges would react. This is favored because the electron-rich and the electron-poor C's can bond.

For the 1,3-product, there are no partial charges of opposite sign on reacting carbons. This arrangement is less attractive.

16.55

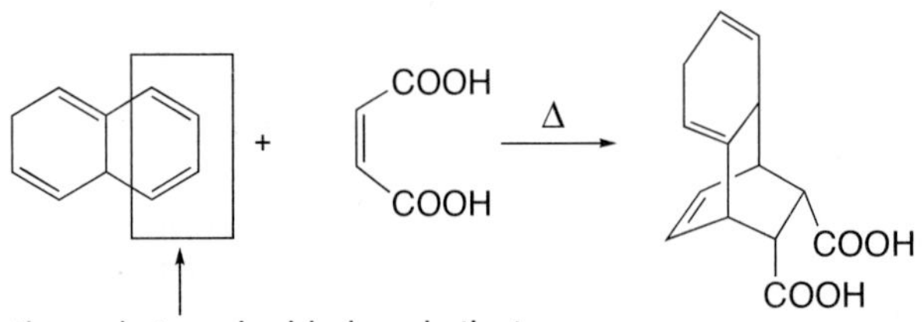
COOH
COOH
Δ
COOH
COOH

These are the only two double bonds that are conjugated and have the *s*-cis conformation needed for a Diels–Alder reaction.

16.56

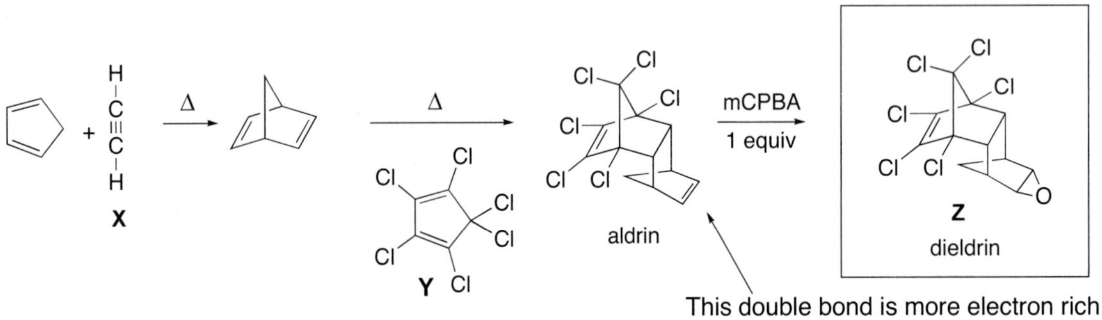
H–C≡C–H
X
Δ
Δ
Y
aldrin
mCPBA
1 equiv
Z
dieldrin

This double bond is more electron rich, so it is epoxidized more readily.

16.57

In each problem, the synthesis must begin with the preparation of cyclopentadiene from dicyclopentadiene.

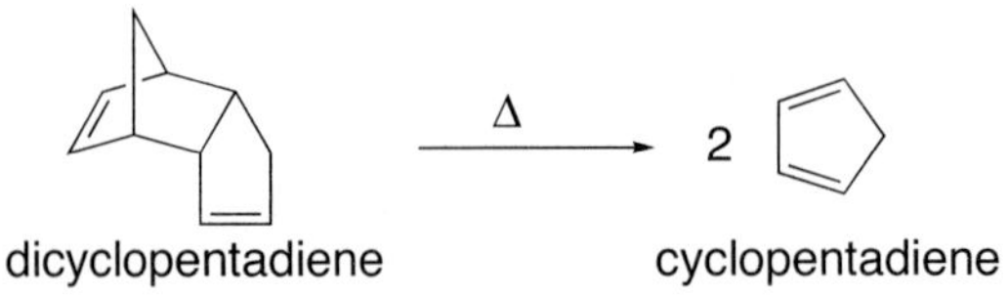
Δ
2
dicyclopentadiene
cyclopentadiene

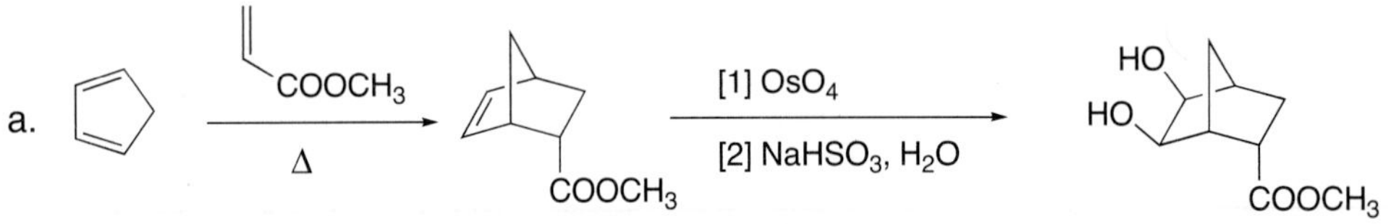
a.
COOCH3
Δ
[1] OsO4
[2] NaHSO3, H2O
HO
HO
COOCH3

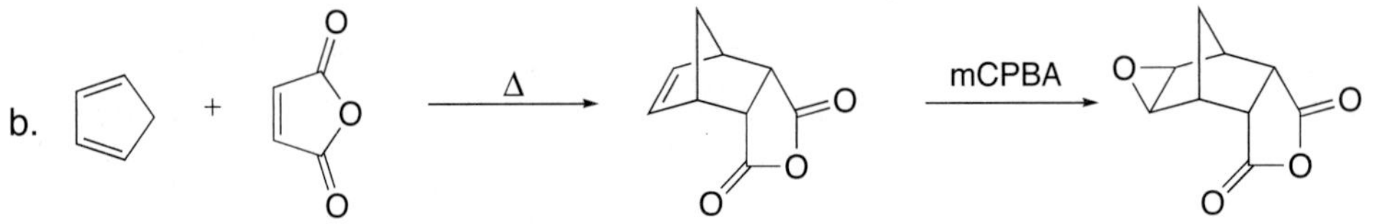
b.
Δ
mCPBA

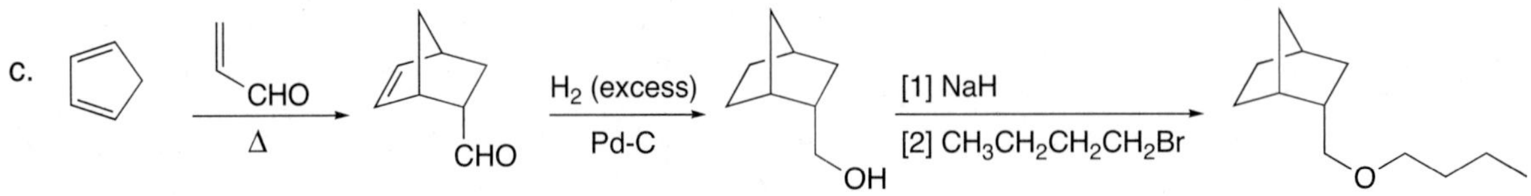
c.
CHO
Δ
H2 (excess)
Pd-C
OH
[1] NaH
[2] CH3CH2CH2CH2Br

16.58

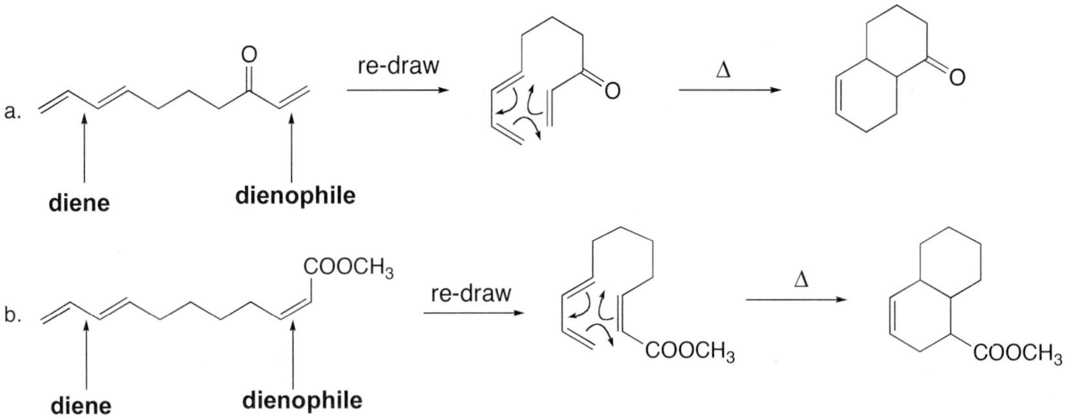
a.
O
re-draw
Δ
O
O
diene
dienophile
b.
COOCH3
re-draw
Δ
COOCH3
COOCH3
diene
dienophile

16.59 A transannular Diels–Alder reaction forms a tricyclic product from a monocyclic starting material.

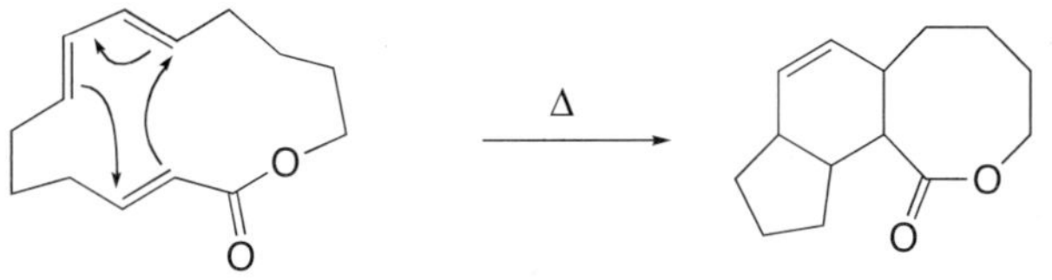
O
O
Δ
O
O

16.60

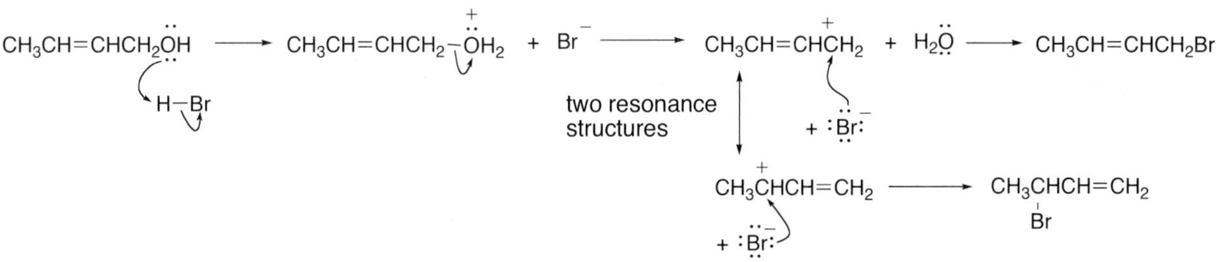
CH3CH=CHCH2OH
H–Br
CH3CH=CHCH2–OH2
+ Br−
CH3CH=CHCH2
+ H2O
CH3CH=CHCH2Br
two resonance structures
+ :Br:−
CH3CHCH=CH2
+ :Br:−
CH3CHCH=CH2
Br

16.61

a. $(CH_3)_2C{=}CHCH_2CH_2CH{=}CH_2$ $\xrightarrow{HCl}$ $(CH_3)_2C(Cl)CH_2CH_2CH_2CH{=}CH_2$ + $(CH_3)_2C{=}CHCH_2CH_2CHClCH_3$

isolated diene — **major product** — **minor product**

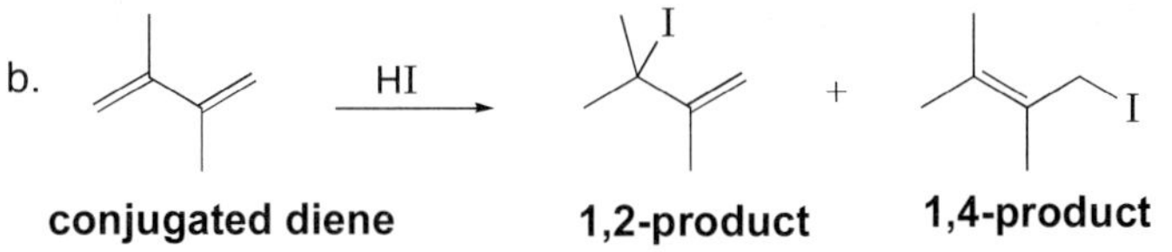
b.
HI
I
+
I
conjugated diene
1,2-product
1,4-product

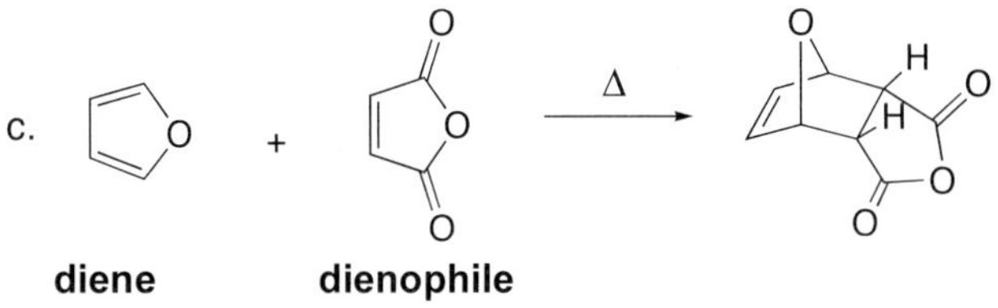
c.
O
+
O
O
O
Δ
O
H
H
O
O
O
diene
dienophile

d. 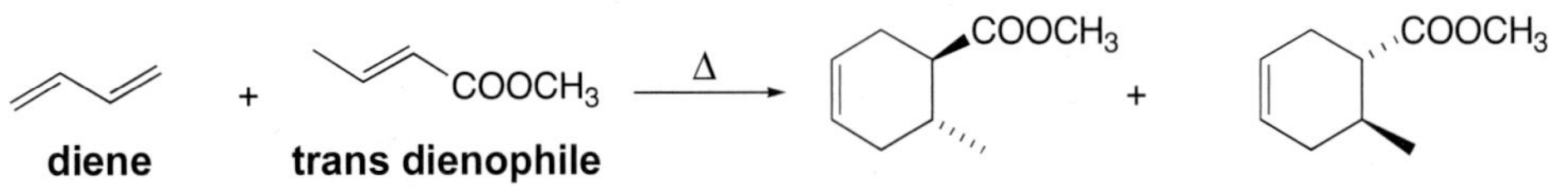
COOCH3
Δ
COOCH3
COOCH3

diene trans dienophile

e. 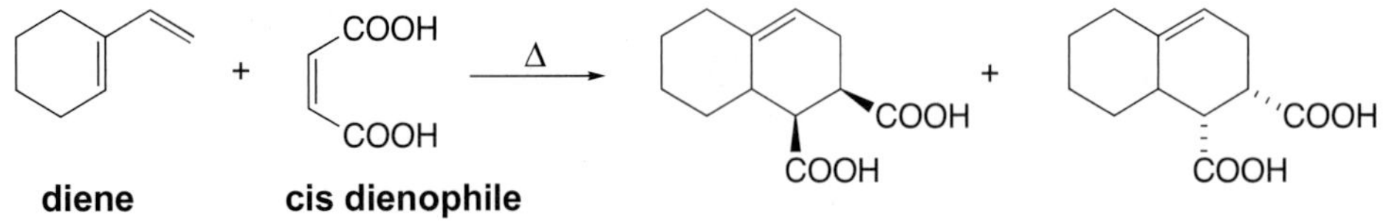
COOH
COOH
Δ
COOH
COOH
COOH
COOH

diene cis dienophile

f. 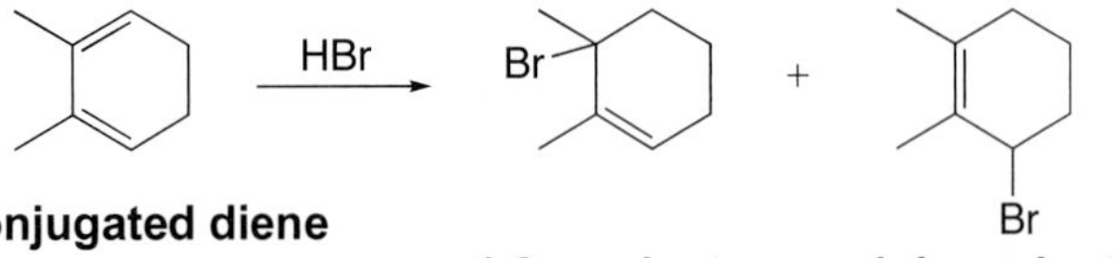
HBr
Br
Br

conjugated diene 1,2-product 1,4-product

16.62 The more stable the carbocation, the faster the S_N1 reaction. The carbocation from **A** is more stable because the lone pairs on the O atom of the OCH_3 afford additional resonance stabilization.

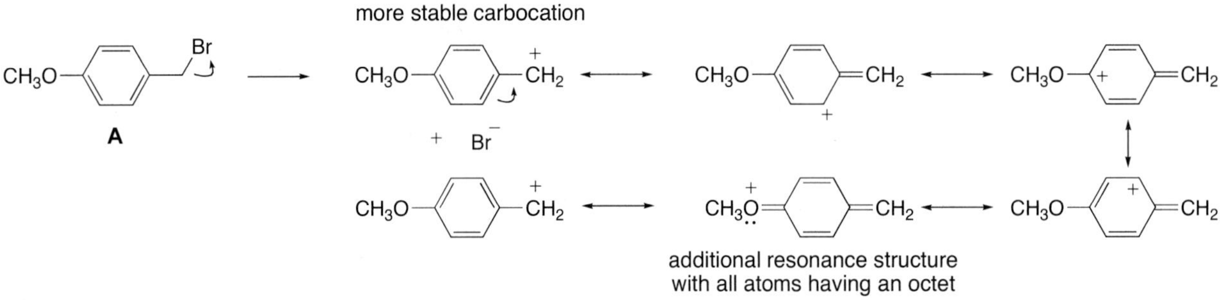
more stable carbocation
A
Br
CH3O
CH2
Br
additional resonance structure
with all atoms having an octet

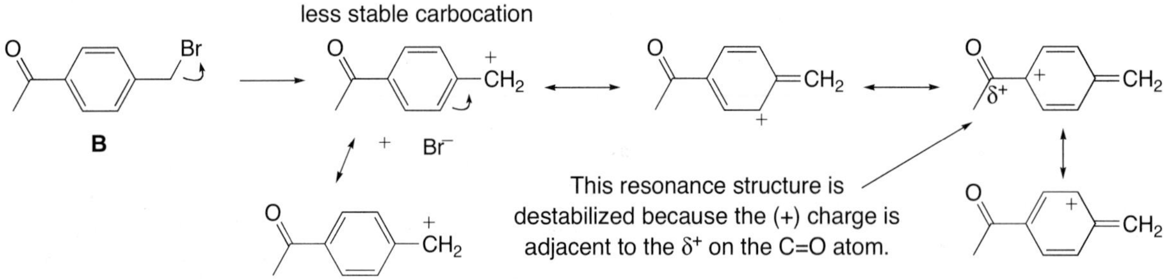
less stable carbocation
B
Br
CH2
Br
δ+
This resonance structure is
destabilized because the (+) charge is
adjacent to the δ+ on the C=O atom.

16.63 The mechanism is E1, with formation of a resonance-stabilized carbocation.

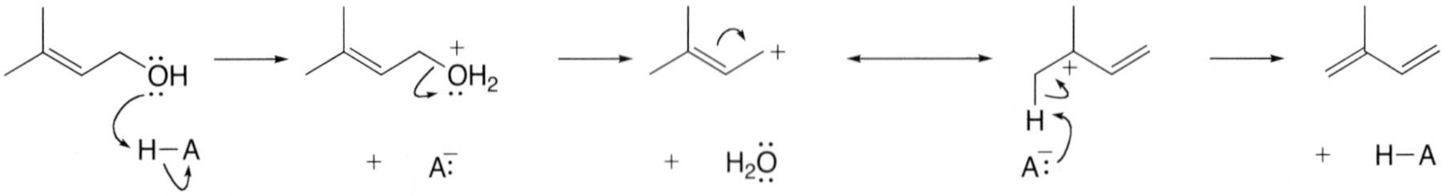
OH
H–A
OH2
A:
H2O
H
A:
H–A

16.64

a.

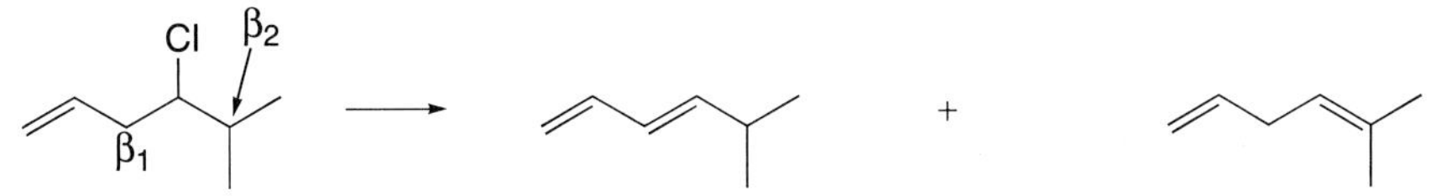
Cl
β_2
β_1
+

loss of H (from β_1 C) + Cl
conjugated
more stable
major product

loss of H (from β_2 C) + Cl
more substituted

b. Dehydrohalogentaion generally forms the more stable product. In this reaction, loss of H from the β_1 carbon forms a more stable conjugated diene, so this product is preferred even though it does not contain the more substituted C=C.

16.65

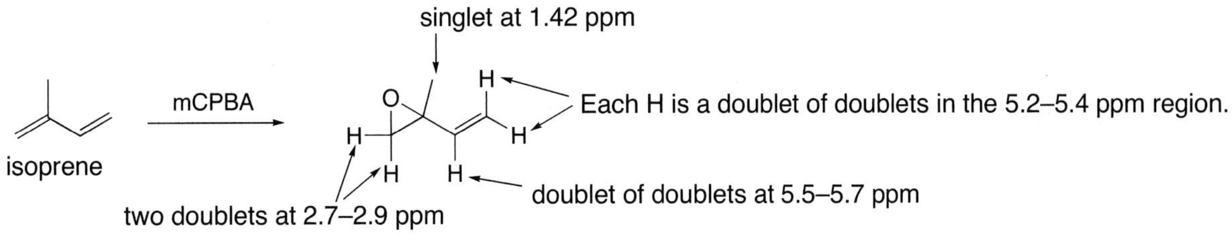
singlet at 1.42 ppm
isoprene
mCPBA
O
H
H
H
H
H
Each H is a doublet of doublets in the 5.2–5.4 ppm region.
doublet of doublets at 5.5–5.7 ppm
two doublets at 2.7–2.9 ppm

16.66

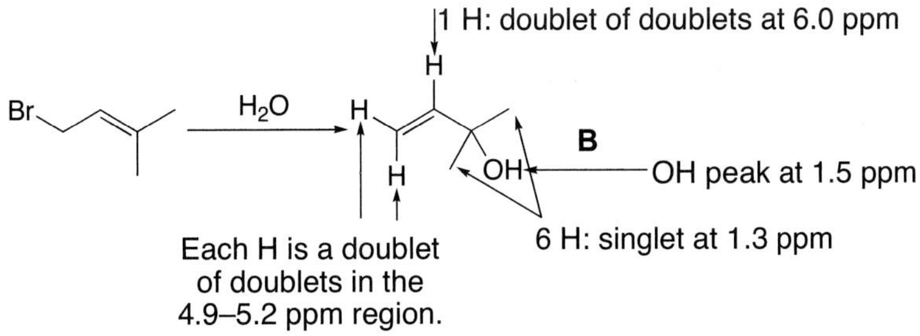
1 H: doublet of doublets at 6.0 ppm
Br
H_2O
H
H
H
B
OH
OH peak at 1.5 ppm
6 H: singlet at 1.3 ppm
Each H is a doublet
of doublets in the
4.9–5.2 ppm region.

The IR shows an OH absorption at 3200–3600 cm^{-1}.

16.67

isolated diene
shortest wavelength
1

2 conjugated bonds
intermediate wavelength
2

3 conjugated bonds
intermediate wavelength
3

4 conjugated bonds
longest wavelength
4

16.68

The phenol makes ferulic acid an antioxidant. Loss of H forms a highly stabilized phenoxy radical that inhibits radical formation during oxidation. →

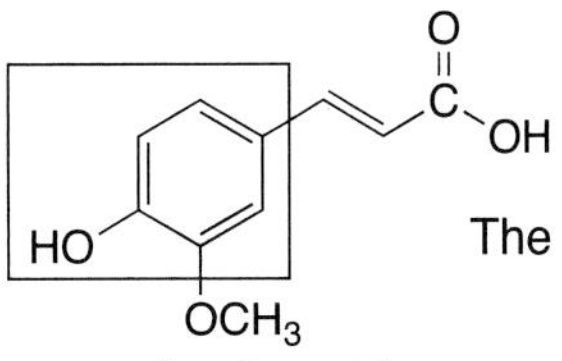
O
C
OH
HO
OCH_3

ferulic acid

The highly conjugated π system makes it a sunscreen.

16.69 There are two possible modes of addition of HBr to allene. When H^+ adds to the terminal carbon, a 2° vinyl carbocation is formed, which affords 2-bromo-1-propene after nucleophilic attack.

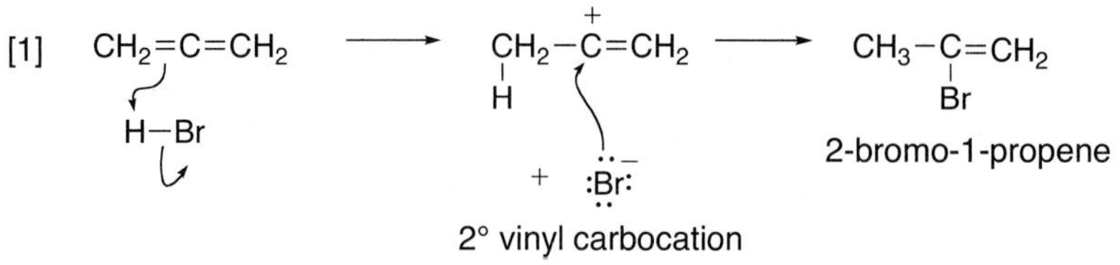
[1]
$CH_2=C=CH_2$
H–Br
$CH_2-\overset{+}{C}=CH_2$
H
:Br:
2° vinyl carbocation
$CH_3-C=CH_2$
Br
2-bromo-1-propene

When H^+ adds to the middle carbon, an intermediate carbocation with a (+) charge adjacent to the C=C is formed. This carbocation is not resonance stabilized (at least initially), because the two C=C's of allene are oriented 90° to each other, a geometry that does not allow for overlap of the C=C with the empty *p* orbital of the carbocation.

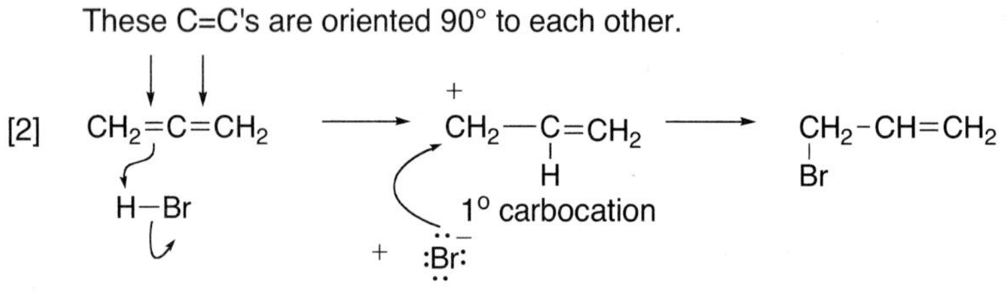
These C=C's are oriented 90° to each other.
[2]
$CH_2=C=CH_2$
H–Br
$\overset{+}{C}H_2-C=CH_2$
H
1° carbocation
:Br:
$CH_2-CH=CH_2$
Br

As a result, path [1] forms a more stable carbocation and is preferred.

16.70

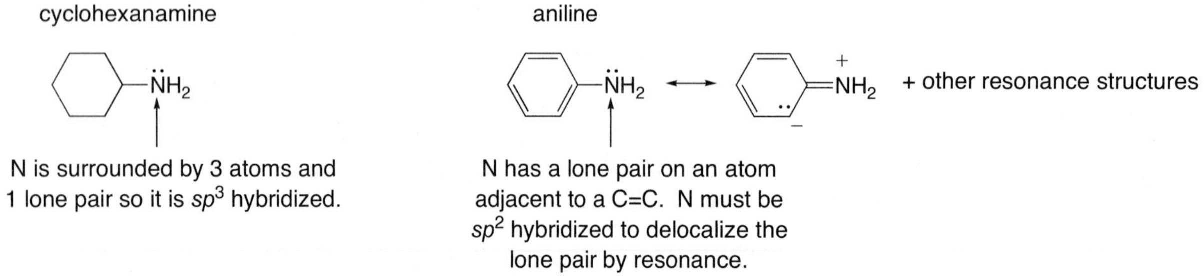
cyclohexanamine
NH_2
N is surrounded by 3 atoms and
1 lone pair so it is sp^3 hybridized.
aniline
NH_2
NH_2
+ other resonance structures
N has a lone pair on an atom
adjacent to a C=C. N must be
sp^2 hybridized to delocalize the
lone pair by resonance.

Basicity is a measure of how willing an atom is to donate an electron pair. Since the lone pair on the N in aniline is delocalized on the benzene ring, it is less available for donation to a proton. This makes aniline much less basic.

16.71

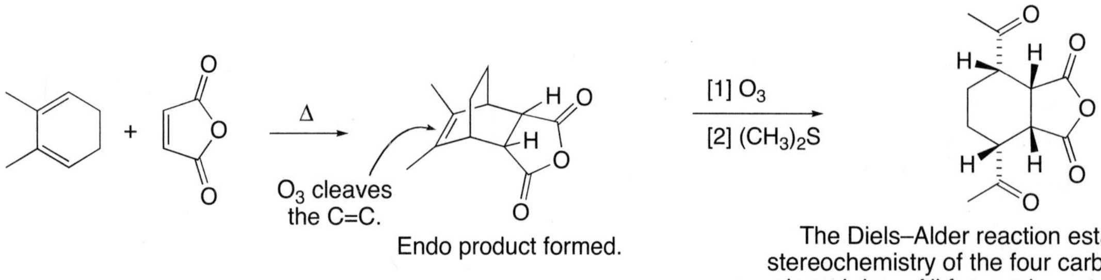
Δ
O₃ cleaves
the C=C.
Endo product formed.
[1] O_3
[2] $(CH_3)_2S$

The Diels–Alder reaction establishes the stereochemistry of the four carbons on the six-membered ring. All four carbon atoms bonded to the six-membered ring are on the same side.

16.72

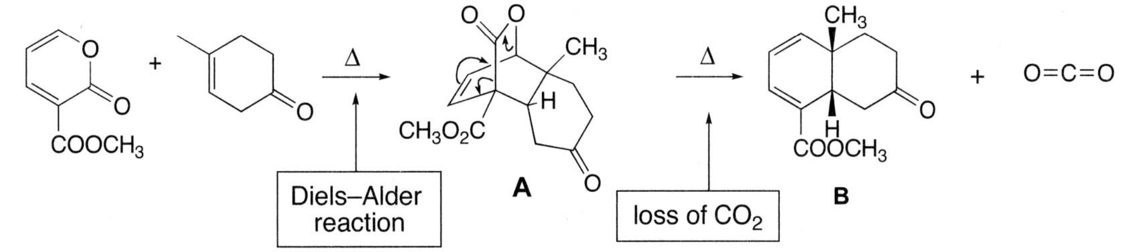

16.73

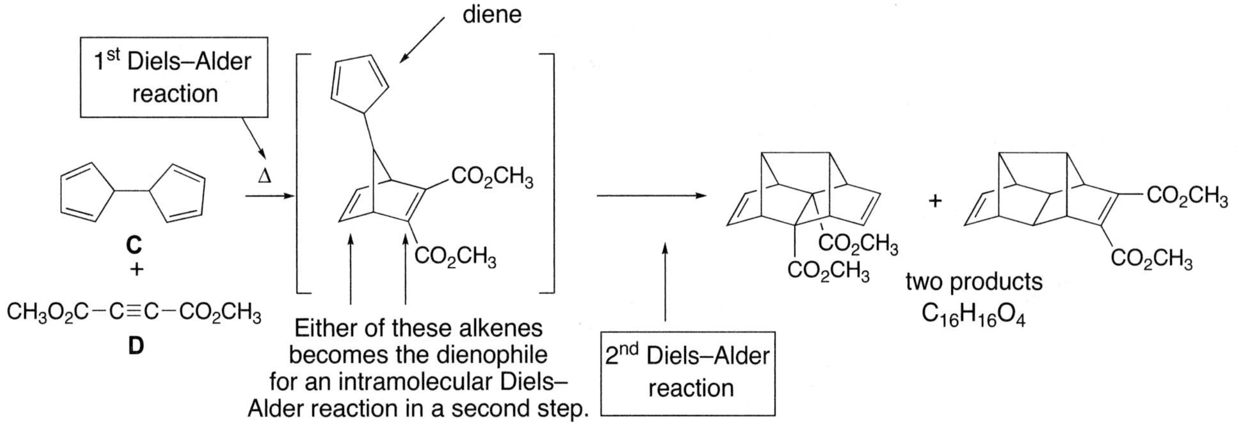

16.74 Retro Diels–Alder reaction forms a conjugated diene. Intramolecular Diels–Alder reaction then forms **N.**

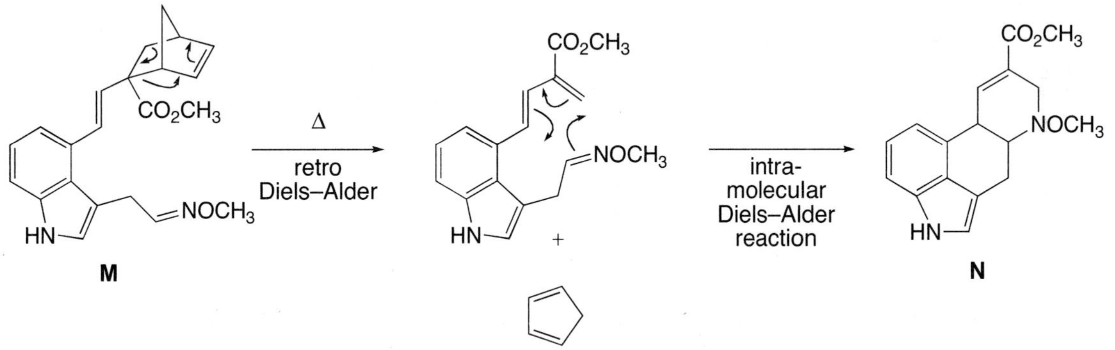

Chapter 17 Benzene and Aromatic Compounds

Chapter Review

Comparing aromatic, antiaromatic, and nonaromatic compounds (17.7)

• **Aromatic compound**	• A cyclic, planar, completely conjugated compound that contains $4n + 2$ π electrons ($n = 0, 1, 2, 3$, and so forth). • An aromatic compound is more stable than a similar acyclic compound having the same number of π electrons.
• **Antiaromatic compound**	• A cyclic, planar, completely conjugated compound that contains $4n$ π electrons ($n = 0, 1, 2, 3$, and so forth). • An antiaromatic compound is less stable than a similar acyclic compound having the same number of π electrons.
• **A compound that is not aromatic**	• A compound that lacks one (or more) of the requirements to be aromatic or antiaromatic.

Properties of aromatic compounds

- Every carbon has a *p* orbital to delocalize electron density (17.2).
- They are unusually stable. ΔH° for hydrogenation is much less than expected, given the number of degrees of unsaturation (17.6).
- They do not undergo the usual addition reactions of alkenes (17.6).
- ^{1}H NMR spectra show highly deshielded protons because of ring currents (17.4).

Examples of aromatic compounds with 6 π electrons (17.8)

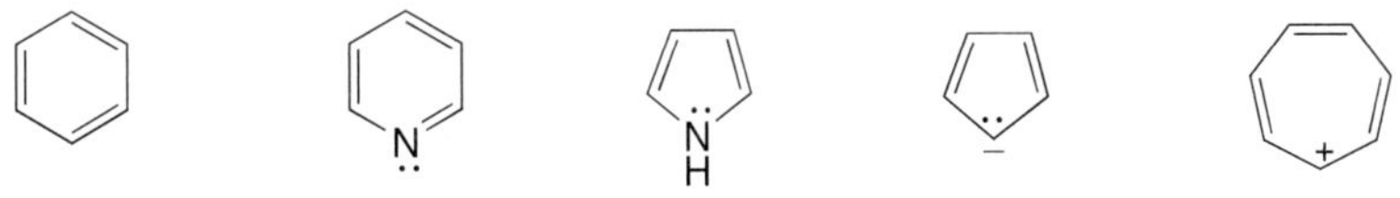

benzene　pyridine　pyrrole　cyclopentadienyl anion　tropylium cation

Examples of compounds that are not aromatic (17.8)

not cyclic　not planar　not completely conjugated

Practice Test on Chapter Review

1. Give the IUPAC name for each of the following compounds.

a. 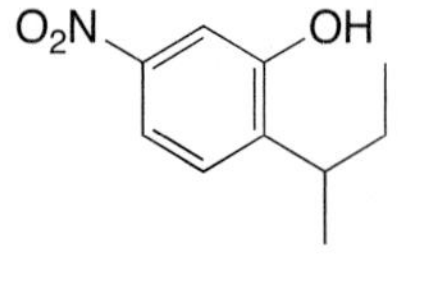

b. 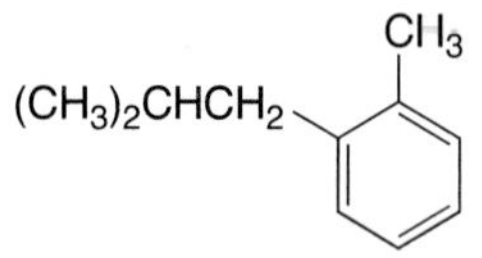

c. 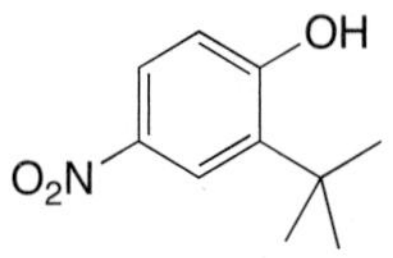

2. Label each compound as aromatic, nonaromatic, or antiaromatic. Choose only **one** possibility. Assume all completely conjugated rings are planar.

a. 

b. 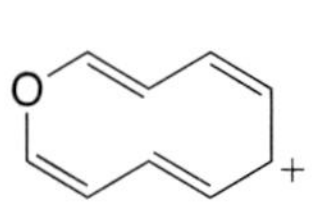

c. 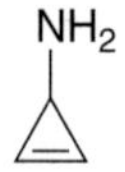

d. 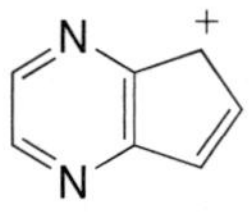

e. 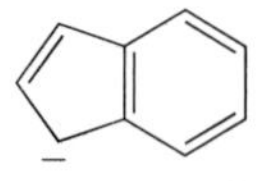

f. 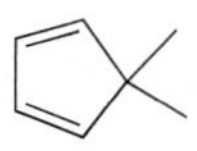

g. 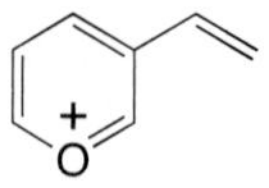

h. 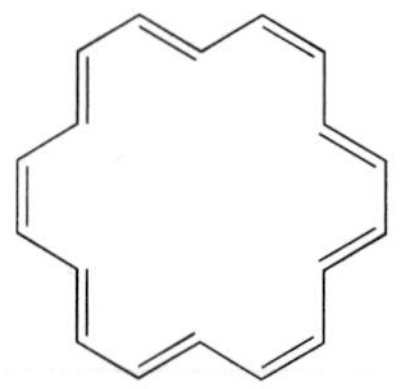

i. 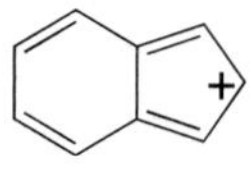

j. 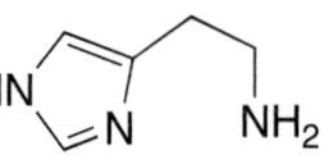

3. Answer the following questions about compounds **A–E** drawn below.

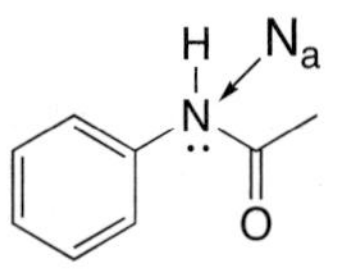

A

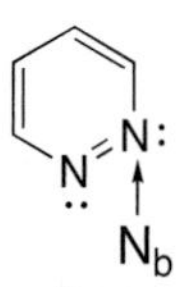

B

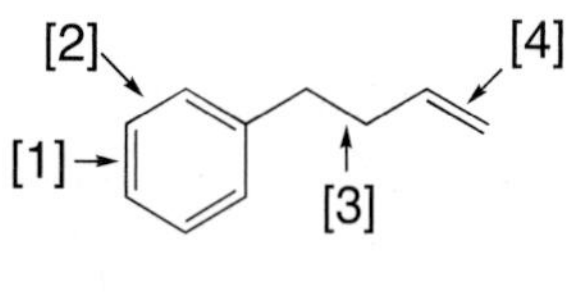

C

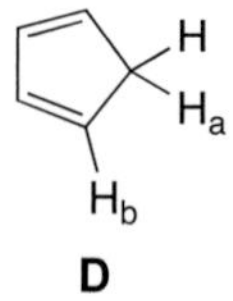

D

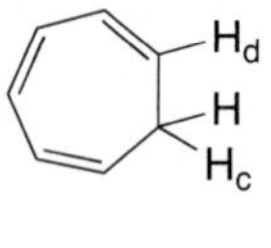

E

a. How is nitrogen N_a in compound **A** hybridized?
b. In what type of orbital does the lone pair on N_a reside?
c. How is nitrogen N_b in compound **B** hybridized?
d. In what type of orbital does the lone pair on N_b reside?
e. Which of the labeled bonds in compound **C** is the shortest?
f. Which of the labeled bonds in compound **C** is the longest?
g. When considering both compounds **D** and **E,** which of the labeled hydrogen atoms (H_a, H_b, H_c, or H_d) is the most acidic? Give only **one** answer.
h. When considering both compounds **D** and **E,** which of the labeled hydrogen atoms (H_a, H_b, H_c, or H_d) is the least acidic? Give only **one** answer.

Answers to Practice Test

1.a. 2-*sec*-butyl-5-nitrophenol
b. *o*-isobutyltoluene
c. 2-*tert*-butyl-4-nitrophenol

2.a. nonaromatic
b. aromatic
c. nonaromatic
d. antiaromatic
e. aromatic
f. nonaromatic
g. aromatic
h. aromatic
i. antiaromatic
j. aromatic

3.a. sp^2
b. p
c. sp^2
d. sp^2
e. 4
f. 3
g. H_a
h. H_c

Answers to Problems

17.1 Move the electrons in the π bonds to draw all major resonance structures.

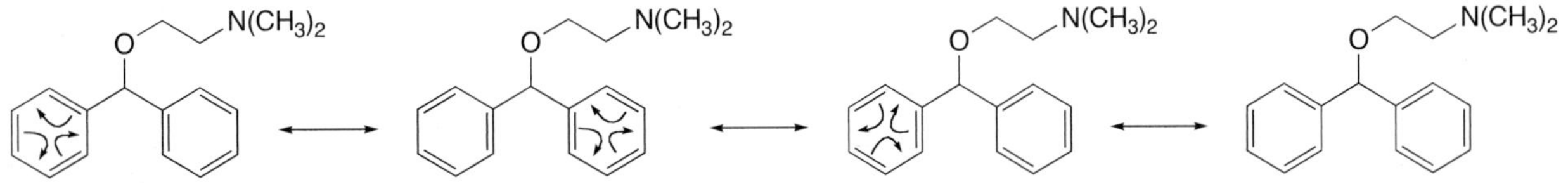
N(CH3)2
O

diphenhydramine

17.2 Look at the hybridization of the atoms involved in each bond. Carbons in a benzene ring are surrounded by three groups and are sp^2 hybridized.

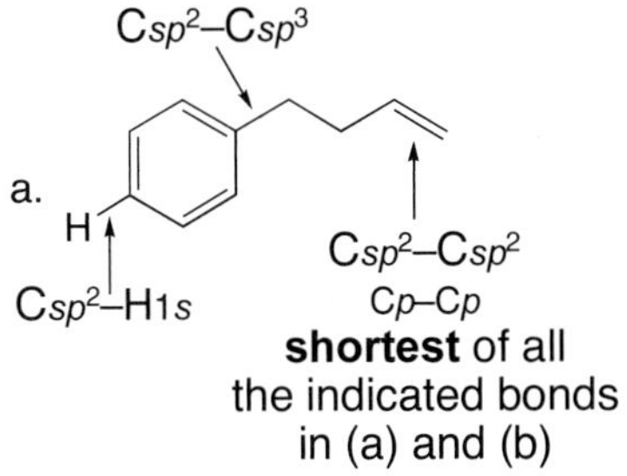
Csp2–Csp3
a.
H
Csp2–H1s
Csp2–Csp2
Cp–Cp
shortest of all
the indicated bonds
in (a) and (b)

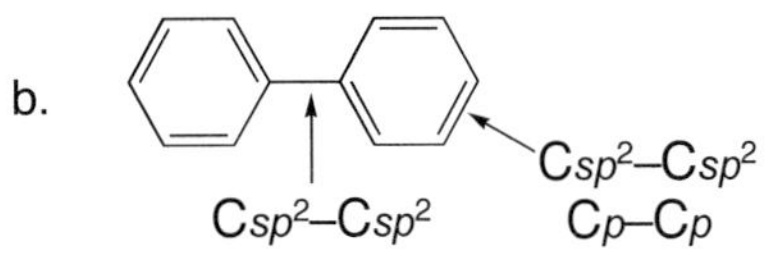
b.
Csp2–Csp2
Csp2–Csp2
Cp–Cp

17.3

- To name a benzene ring with **one substituent,** name the substituent and add the word *benzene.*
- To name a **disubstituted ring,** select the correct prefix (ortho = 1,2; meta = 1,3; para = 1,4) and alphabetize the substituents. Use a common name if it is a derivative of that monosubstituted benzene.
- To name a **polysubstituted ring,** number the ring to give the lowest possible numbers and then follow other rules of nomenclature.

a. isopropyl group → $PhCH(CH_3)_2$

isopropylbenzene

c. Two groups are 1,3 = meta.

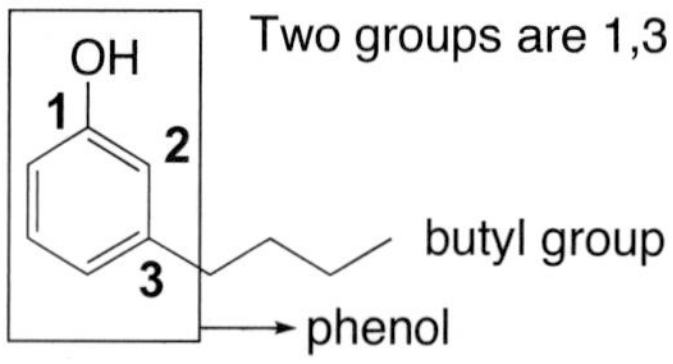
OH
1
2
3
butyl group
phenol

***m*-butylphenol**

b.

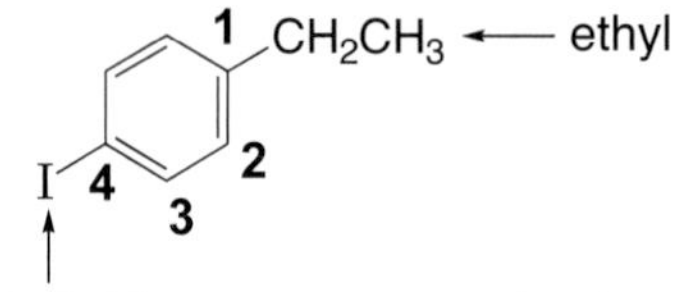
1
CH2CH3
ethyl
2
3
4
I
iodo

Two groups are 1,4 = para.

***p*-ethyliodobenzene**

d.

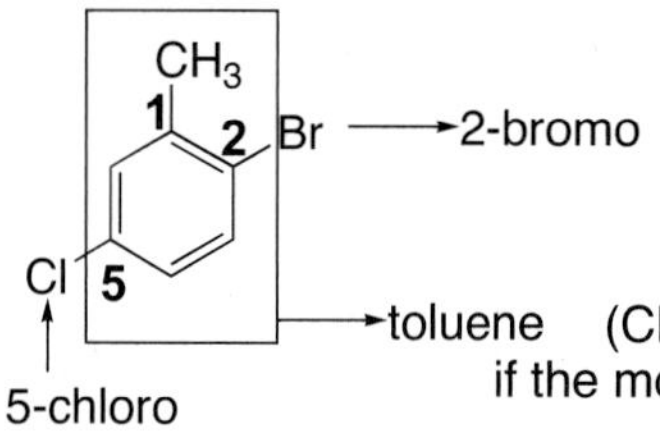
CH3
1
2
Br
2-bromo
Cl
5
toluene
5-chloro

(CH_3 group must be at the "1" position, if the molecule is named as a toluene derivative.)

2-bromo-5-chlorotoluene

17.4 Work backwards to draw the structures from the names.

a. isobutylbenzene

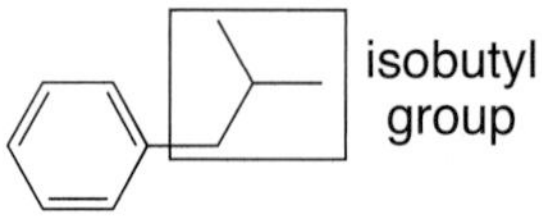
isobutyl
group

c. *cis*-1,2-diphenylcyclohexane

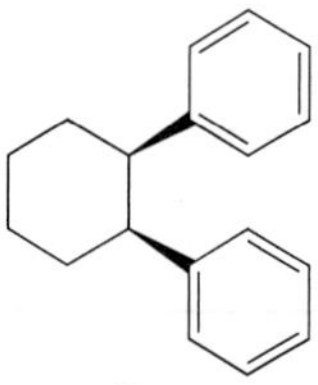

e. 4-chloro-1,2-diethylbenzene

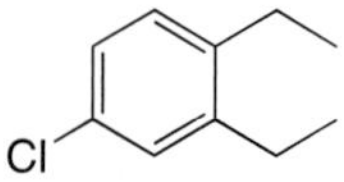
Cl

b. *o*-dichlorobenzene

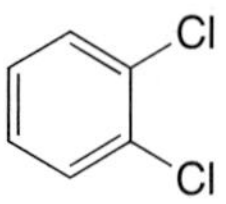
Cl
Cl

d. *m*-bromoaniline

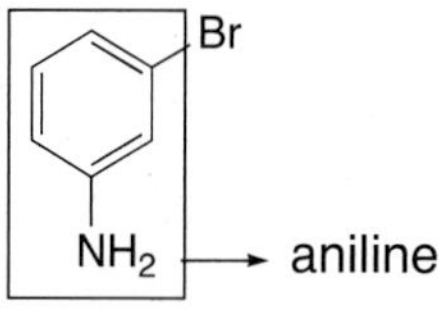
Br
NH2
aniline

f. 3-*tert*-butyl-2-ethyltoluene

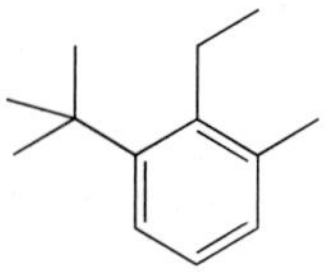

17.5

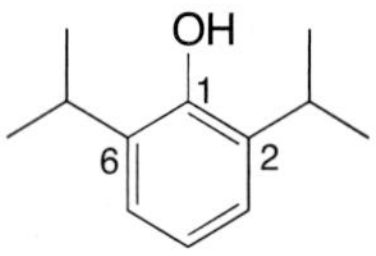
OH
1
2
6

propofol

17.6

Molecular formula $C_{10}H_{14}O_2$: 4 degrees of unsaturation
IR absorption at 3150–2850 cm^{-1}: sp^2 and sp^3 hybridized C–H bonds
NMR absorptions (ppm):
- 1.4 (triplet, 6 H)
- 4.0 (quartet, 4 H)
- 6.8 (singlet, 4 H)

17.7 Count the different types of carbons to determine the number of ^{13}C NMR signals.

a.

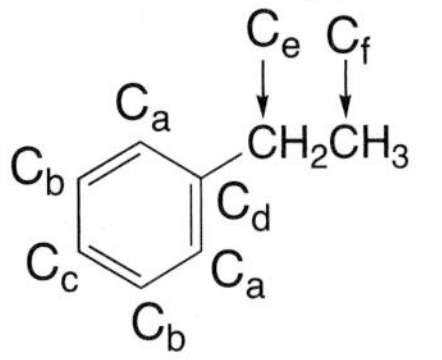

4 types of C's in the benzene ring
6 signals

b.

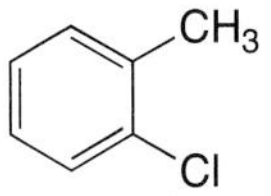

All C's are different.
7 signals

c.

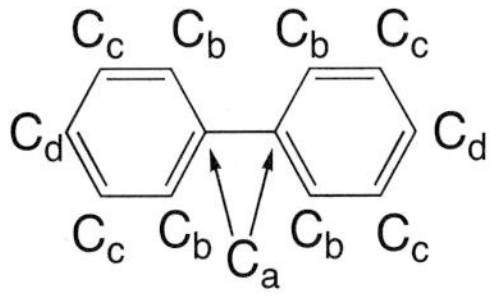

4 signals

17.8 The less stable compound has a larger heat of hydrogenation.

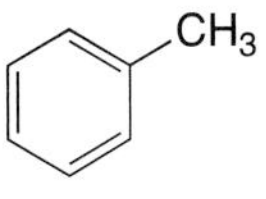

A

benzene ring, more stable
smaller $\Delta H°$

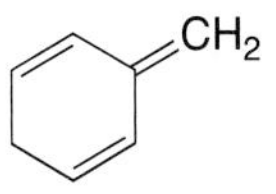

B

no benzene ring, less stable
larger $\Delta H°$

17.9 The protons on sp^2 hybridized carbons in aromatic hydrocarbons are highly deshielded and absorb at 6.5–8 ppm whereas hydrocarbons that are not aromatic show an absorption at 4.5–6 ppm, typical of protons bonded to the C=C of an alkene.

a.

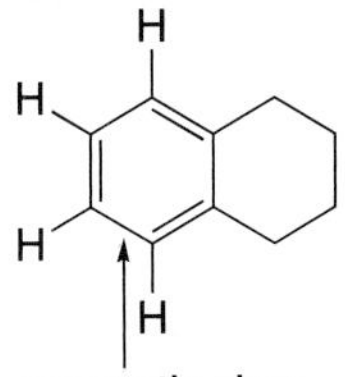

aromatic ring
H's ~6.5–8 ppm

b.

not aromatic
alkene H's ~4.5–6 ppm

c.

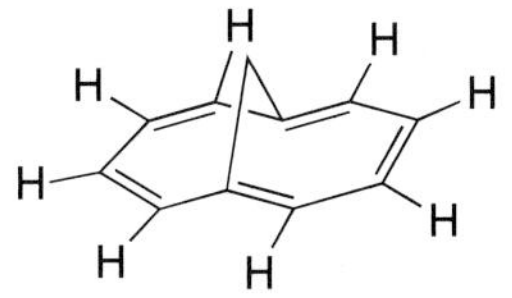

aromatic ring
H's ~6.5–8 ppm

17.10 To be aromatic, a ring must have $4n + 2$ π electrons.

16 π e^-	20 π e^-	22 π e^-
$4n$	$4n$	$4n + 2$
$4(4) = 16$	$4(5) = 20$	$4(5) + 2 = 22$
antiaromatic	**antiaromatic**	**aromatic**

17.11

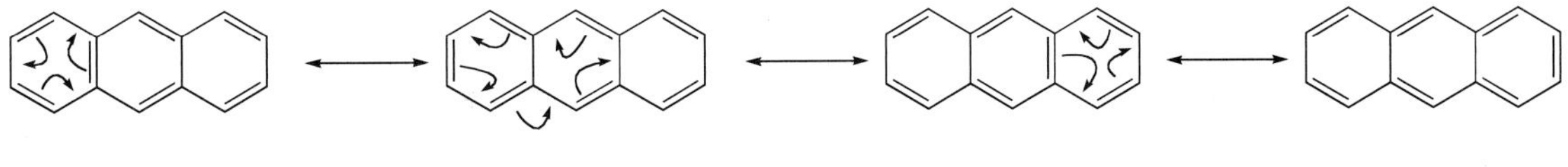

17.12 In determining if a heterocycle is aromatic, count a nonbonded electron pair if it makes the ring aromatic in calculating $4n + 2$. Lone pairs on atoms already part of a multiple bond cannot be delocalized in a ring, and so they are never counted in determining aromaticity.

a. 

Count one lone pair from O.
$4n + 2 = 4(1) + 2 = 6$
aromatic

b. 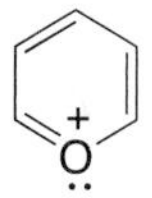

no lone pair from O
$4n + 2 = 4(1) + 2 = 6$
aromatic

c. 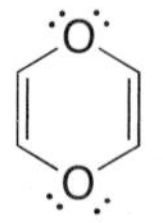

With one lone pair from each O there would be 8 electrons. If O's are sp^3 hybridized, the ring is not completely conjugated.
not aromatic

d. 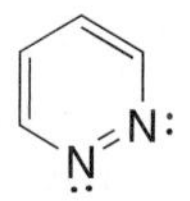

Both N atoms are part of a double bond, so the lone pairs cannot be counted: there are 6 electrons.
$4n + 2 = 4(1) + 2 = 6$
aromatic

17.13

quinine
(antimalarial drug)

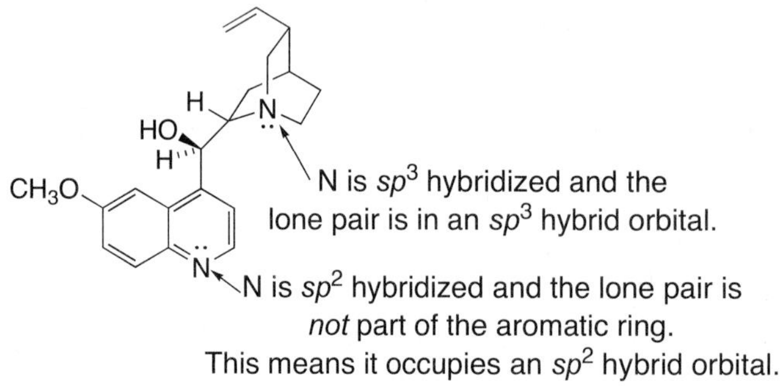
HO
H
CH3O
N
N
N is sp3 hybridized and the lone pair is in an sp3 hybrid orbital.
N is sp2 hybridized and the lone pair is not part of the aromatic ring.
This means it occupies an sp2 hybrid orbital.

17.14

a. The five-membered ring is aromatic because it has 6 π electrons, two from each π bond and two from the N atom that is not part of a double bond.

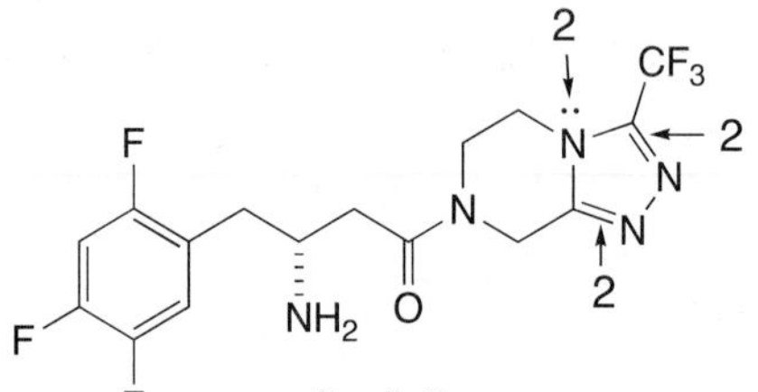
2
CF3
2
2
F
F
F
N
N
N
N
NH2
O

sitagliptin

b, c.

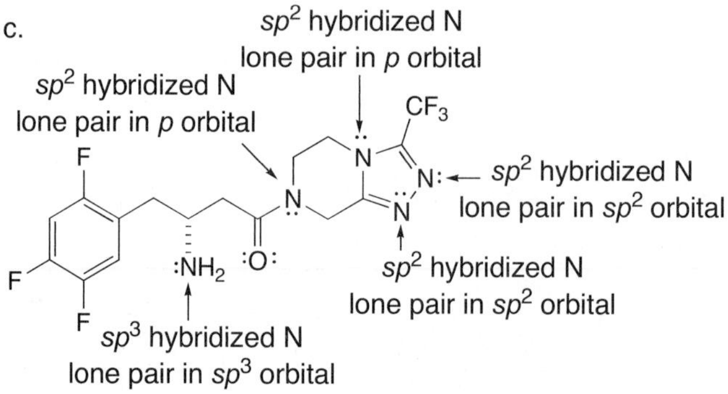
sp2 hybridized N
lone pair in p orbital
sp2 hybridized N
lone pair in p orbital
CF3
F
N
N:
sp2 hybridized N
lone pair in sp2 orbital
N
N
F
:NH2
:O:
sp2 hybridized N
lone pair in sp2 orbital
F
sp3 hybridized N
lone pair in sp3 orbital

17.15 Since a neutral oxygen atom forms only two bonds, it must always donate its electron pair to a delocalized π electron system (like the N atom of pyrrole). It can never be part of a double bond, because it would carry a net (+) charge. With nitrogen, however, a N atom can either donate an electron pair or be part of a double bond, since N forms three bonds. In a neutral five-membered aromatic ring, there are two π bonds (where the O atom cannot be located), and only one atom that can donate its electron pair (where the O atom may reside).

17.16 Compare the conjugate base of 1,3,5-cycloheptatriene with the conjugate base of cyclopentadiene. Remember that the compound with the more stable conjugate base will have a lower pK_a.

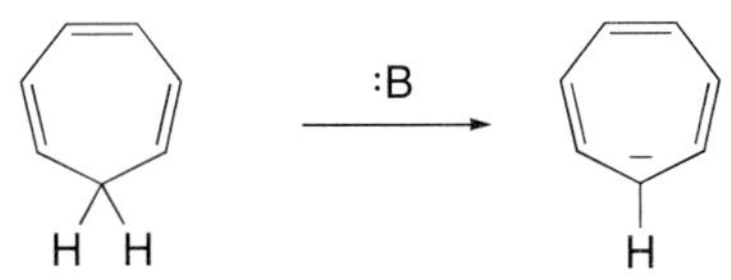
:B
H H
H

1,3,5-cycloheptatriene
pK_a = 39

8 π Electrons make this conjugate base especially unstable (**antiaromatic**).

Since the conjugate base is unstable, the pK_a of 1,3,5-cycloheptatriene is **high**.

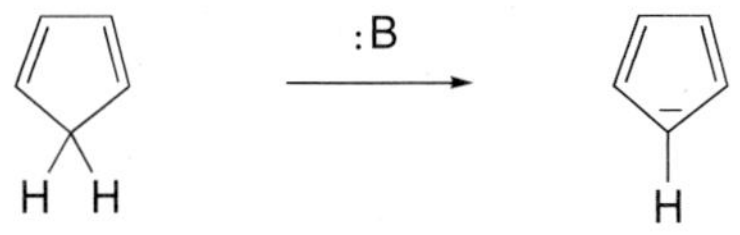
:B
H H
H

cyclopentadiene

6 π electrons
aromatic conjugate base
very stable anion

Since the conjugate base is very stable, the pK_a of cyclopentadiene is much **lower**.

17.17 The compound with the most stable conjugate base is the most acidic.

Conjugate bases:

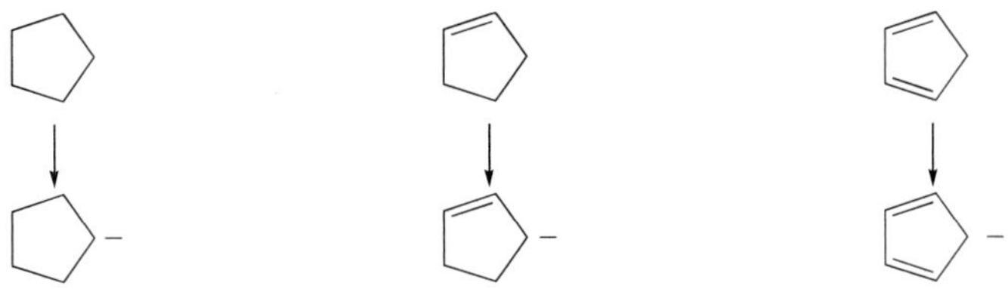

no resonance delocalization	2 resonance structures	**aromatic conjugate base** most stable
most unstable base so **least acidic acid**	The acid is **intermediate in acidity.**	The acid is the **most acidic.**

17.18

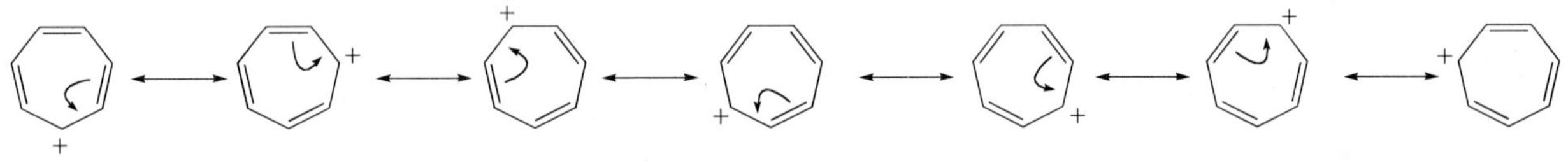

17.19 To be aromatic, the ions must have $4n + 2$ π electrons. Ions in (b) and (c) do not have the right number of π electrons to be aromatic.

a. 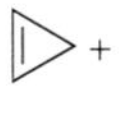
2 π electrons
4(0) + 2 = 2
aromatic

d. 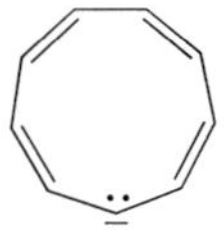
10 π electrons
4(2) + 2 = 10
aromatic

17.20

A =

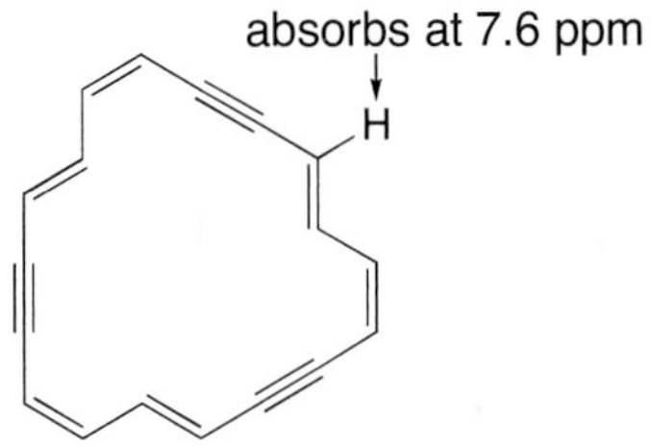
absorbs at 7.6 ppm
H

The NMR indicates that **A** is aromatic. The C's of the triple bond are *sp* hybridized. Each triple bond has one set of electrons in *p* orbitals that overlap with other *p* orbitals on adjacent atoms in the ring. This overlap allows electrons to delocalize. Each C of the triple bonds also has a *p* orbital in the plane of the ring. The electrons in these *p* orbitals are localized between the C's of the triple bond, not delocalized in the ring. Although **A** has 24 π e^- total, only 18 e^- are delocalized around the ring.

17.21 In using the inscribed polygon method, always draw the vertex pointing down.

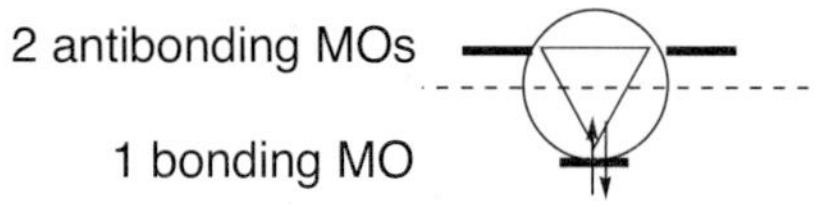
2 antibonding MOs
1 bonding MO

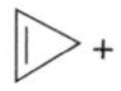
+

2 π electrons
All bonding MOs are filled.
aromatic

17.22 Draw the inscribed pentagons with the vertex pointing down. Then draw the molecular orbitals (MOs) and add the electrons.

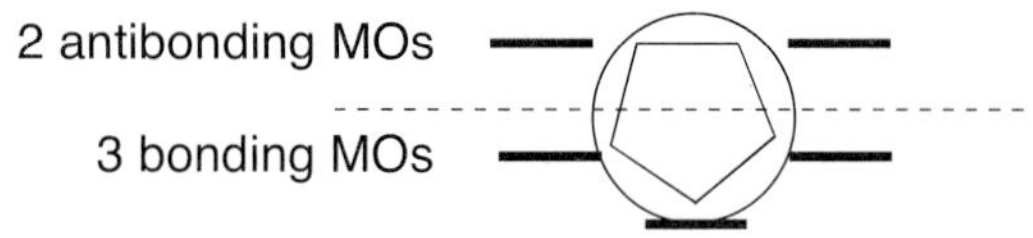
2 antibonding MOs
3 bonding MOs

Cation:

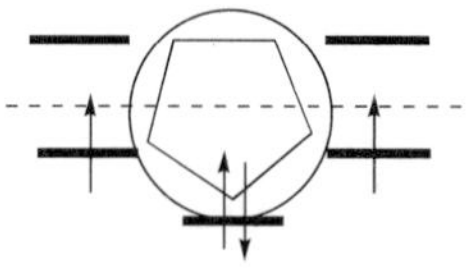

4 π electrons
Not all bonding MOs are filled.
not aromatic

Radical:

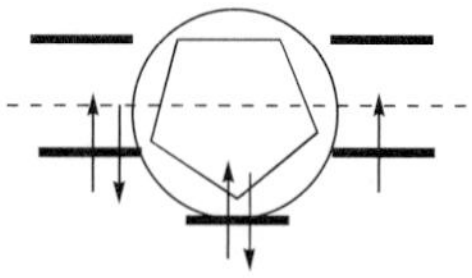

5 π electrons
Not all bonding MOs are filled.
not aromatic

17.23 C_{60} would exhibit only one ^{13}C NMR signal because all the carbons are identical.

17.24

a. 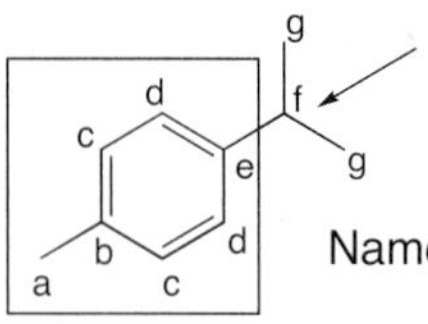
g
f
g
d
c
e
b
d
a
c
isopropyl group

Name as a derivative of toluene.

Answer: *p*-isopropyltoluene
seven lines in ^{13}C NMR (lettered C_a–C_g)

b. 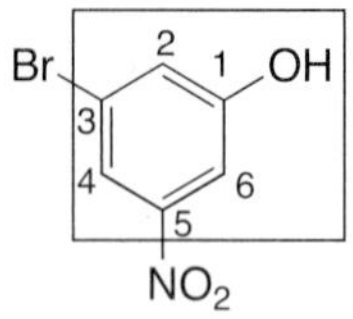
Br
OH
NO2
1
2
3
4
5
6

Name as a derivative of phenol.

Answer: 3-bromo-5-nitrophenol
All C's are different, so there are six lines in the ^{13}C NMR.

17.25

a. 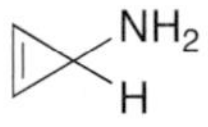
NH2
H

not completely conjugated
not aromatic

b. 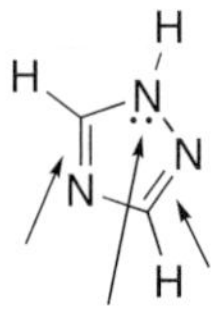
H
H
N
N
N
H

6 π electrons
aromatic

c. 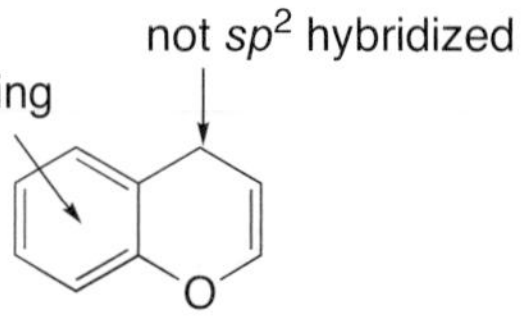
not sp2 hybridized
aromatic ring
O

The six-membered ring is aromatic. The bicyclic ring system with the O atom is not completely conjugated, so it is nonaromatic.

17.26

a. If the Kekulé description of benzene was accurate, only one product would form in Reaction [1], but there would be four (not three) dibromobenzenes (**A–D**), because adjacent C–C bonds are different—one is single and one is double. Thus, compounds **A** and **B** would *not* be identical. **A** has two Br's bonded to the same double bond, but **B** has two Br's on different double bonds.

b. In the resonance description, only one product would form in Reaction [1], since all C's are identical, but only three dibromobenzenes (ortho, meta, and para isomers) are possible.

A and **B** are identical because each C–C bond is identical and intermediate in bond length between a C–C single and C–C double bond.

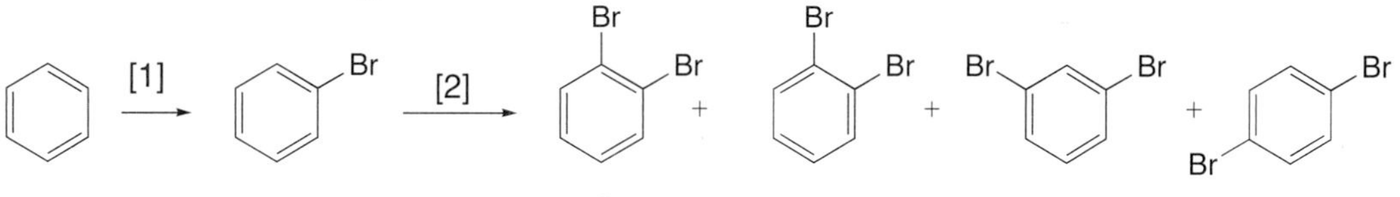

A **B** **C** **D**

17.27

C_8H_{10}:

C_8H_9Br:

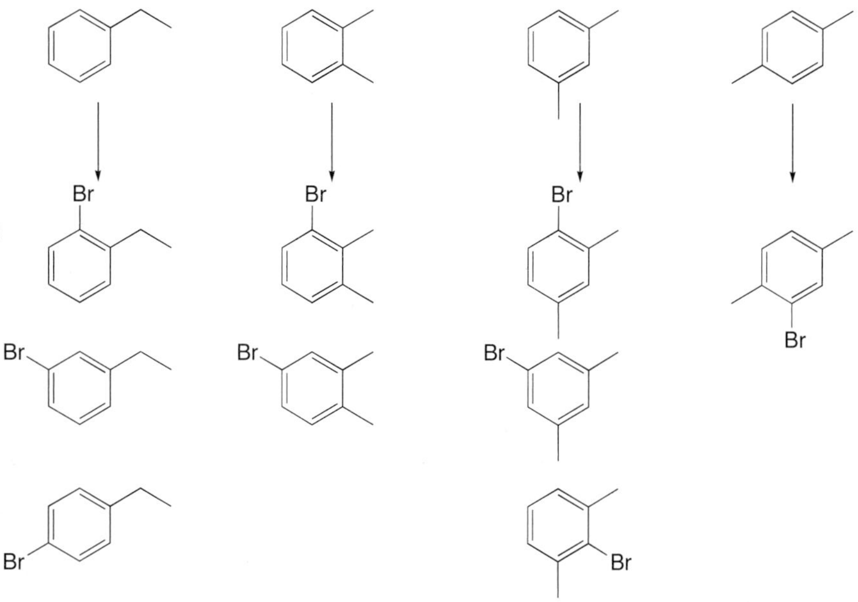

3 isomers **2 isomers** **3 isomers** **1 isomer**

17.28 To name the compounds use the directions from Answer 17.3.

a. 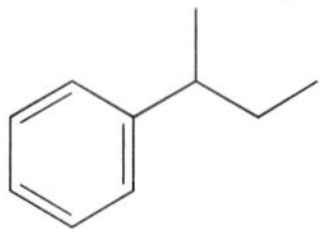

sec-butylbenzene

b. 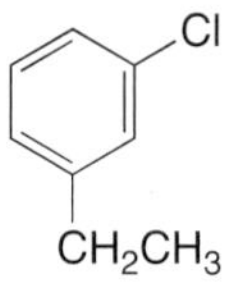

m-chloroethylbenzene

c. 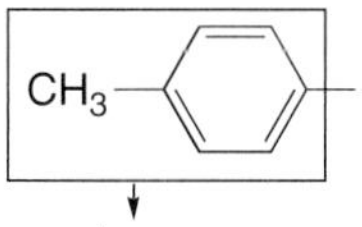

toluene

p-chlorotoluene

d. 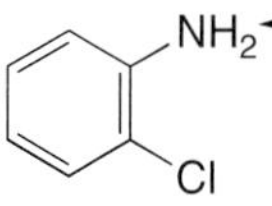

← aniline

o-chloroaniline

e. 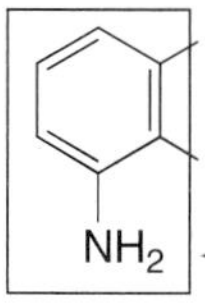

← aniline

2,3-dibromoaniline

f. 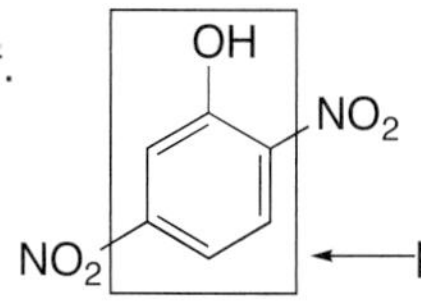

← phenol (OH at C1)

2,5-dinitrophenol

g. 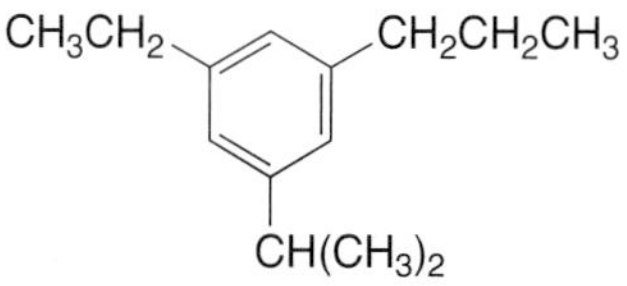

1-ethyl-3-isopropyl-5-propylbenzene

h. 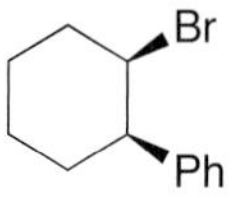

cis-1-bromo-2-phenylcyclohexane

17.29

a. *p*-dichlorobenzene

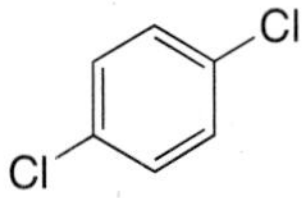

b. *m*-chlorophenol

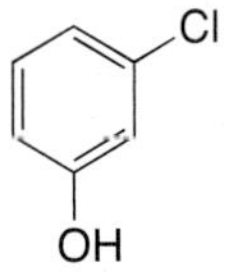

c. *p*-iodoaniline

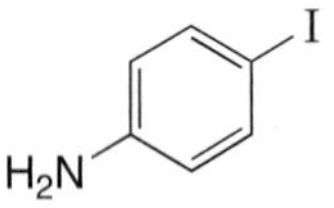

d. *o*-bromonitrobenzene

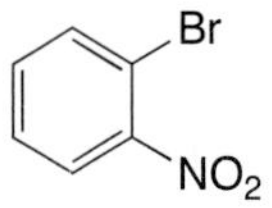

e. 2,6-dimethoxytoluene

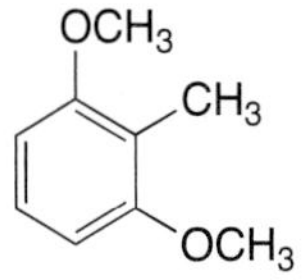

f. 2-phenyl-1-butene

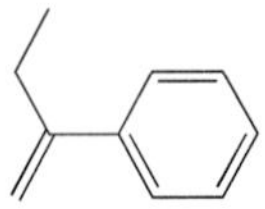

g. 2-phenyl-2-propen-1-ol

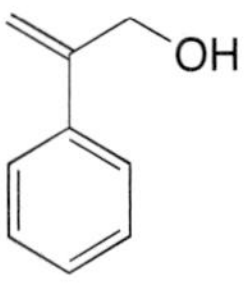

h. *trans*-1-benzyl-3-phenylcyclopentane

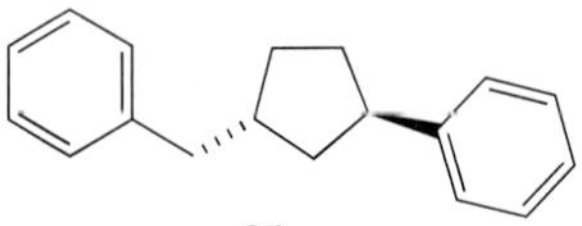

or

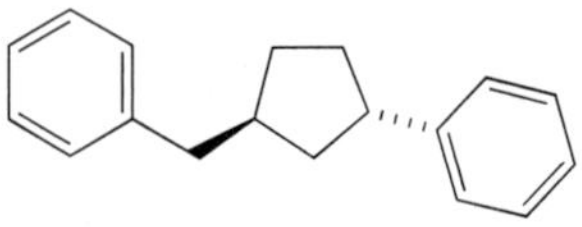

17.30

a, b. constitutional isomers of molecular formula $\mathbf{C_8H_9Cl}$ and names of the trisubstituted benzenes

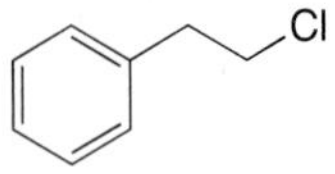

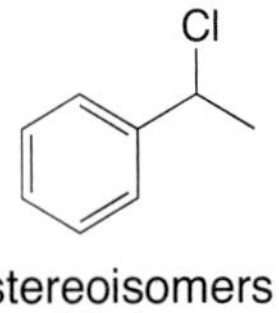

stereoisomers for this isomer

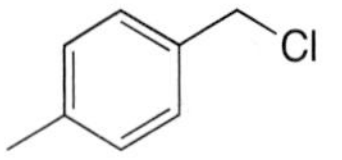

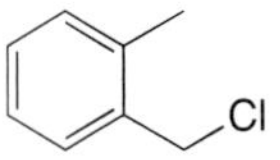

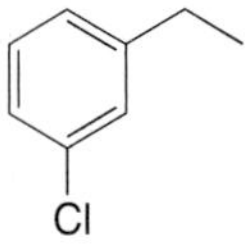

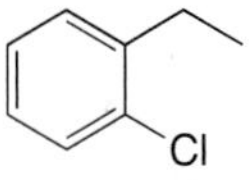

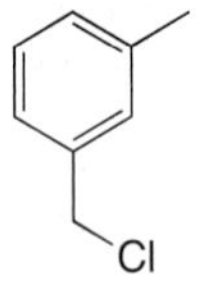

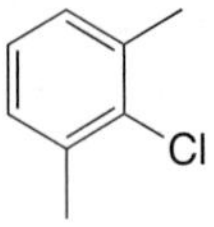

2-chloro-1,3-dimethylbenzene

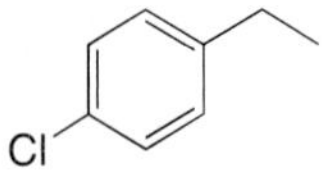

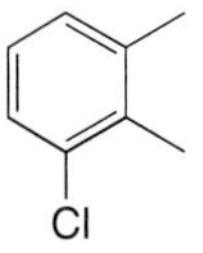

1-chloro-2,3-dimethylbenzene

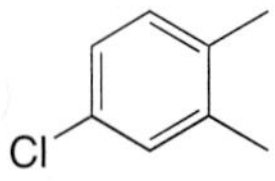

4-chloro-1,2-dimethylbenzene

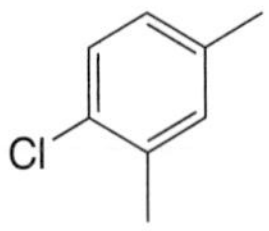

1-chloro-2,4-dimethylbenzene

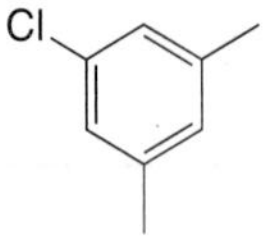

1-chloro-3,5-dimethylbenzene

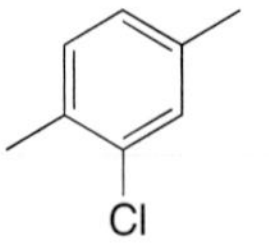

2-chloro-1,4-dimethylbenzene

c. stereoisomers

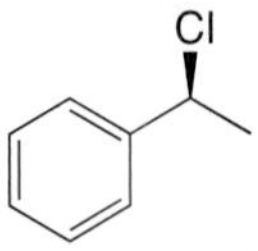

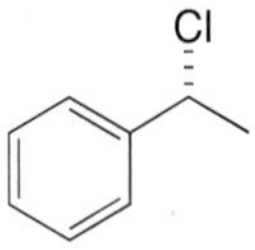

17.31 Count the electrons in the π bonds. Each π bond holds two electrons.

a.

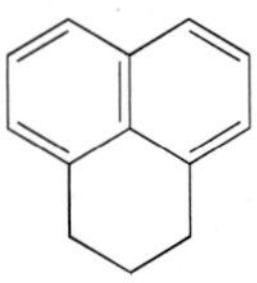

10 π electrons

b.

7 π electrons

c.

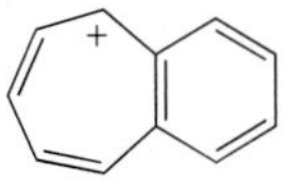

10 π electrons

d.

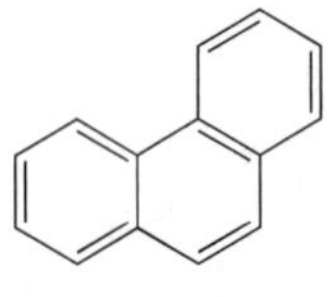

14 π electrons

e.

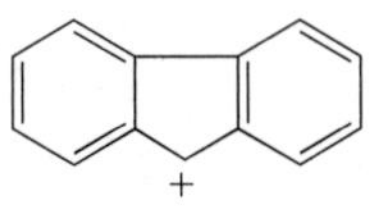

12 π electrons

17.32 To be aromatic, the compounds must be cyclic, planar, completely conjugated, and have $4n + 2$ π electrons.

a. 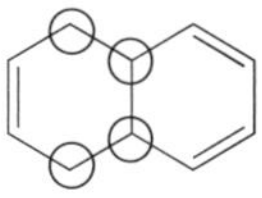

Circled C's are not sp^2.
not completely conjugated
not aromatic

b. 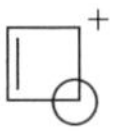

Circled C is not sp^2.
not completely conjugated
not aromatic

c. 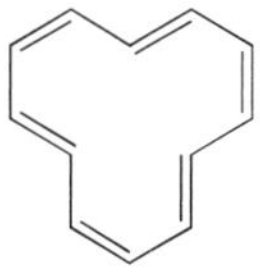

12 π electrons
does **not** have $4n + 2$
π electrons
not aromatic

d. 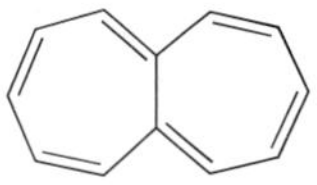

12 π electrons
does **not** have $4n + 2$
π electrons
not aromatic

17.33 In determining if a heterocycle is aromatic, count a nonbonded electron pair if it makes the ring aromatic in calculating $4n + 2$. Lone pairs on atoms already part of a multiple bond cannot be delocalized in a ring, and so they are never counted in determining aromaticity.

a. 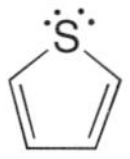

6 π electrons
counting a lone pair from S
4(1) + 2 = 6
aromatic

b. 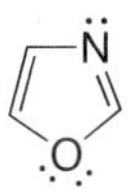

6 π electrons
counting a lone pair from O
4(1) + 2 = 6
aromatic

c. 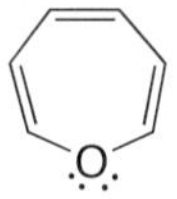

not aromatic

d. 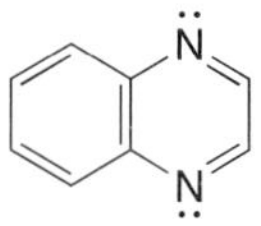

10 π electrons
4(2) + 2 = 10
aromatic

e. 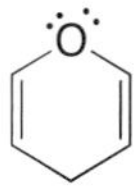

not aromatic

f. 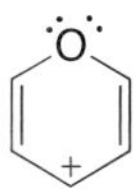

6 π electrons,
counting a lone pair from O
4(1) + 2 = 6
aromatic

g. 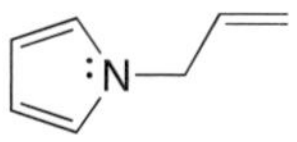

6 π electrons
counting the lone
pair from N
4(1) + 2 = 6
aromatic

h. 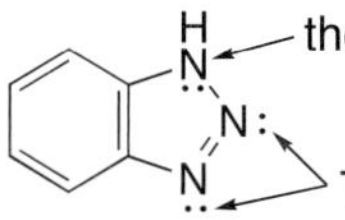

Count these $2e^-$.

These lone pairs are on doubly bonded N atoms, so they can't be counted.

10 π electrons
4(2) + 2 = 10
aromatic

17.34

a. 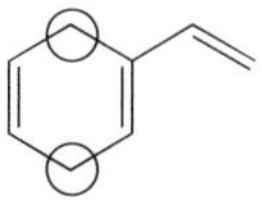

Circled C's are
not sp^2.
not aromatic

b. 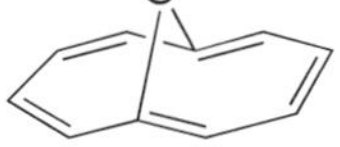

10 π electrons
in 10-membered ring
4(2) + 2 = 10
aromatic

c. 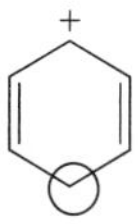

Circled C is
not sp^2.
not aromatic

d. 

4 π electrons
4(1) = 4
antiaromatic

17.35

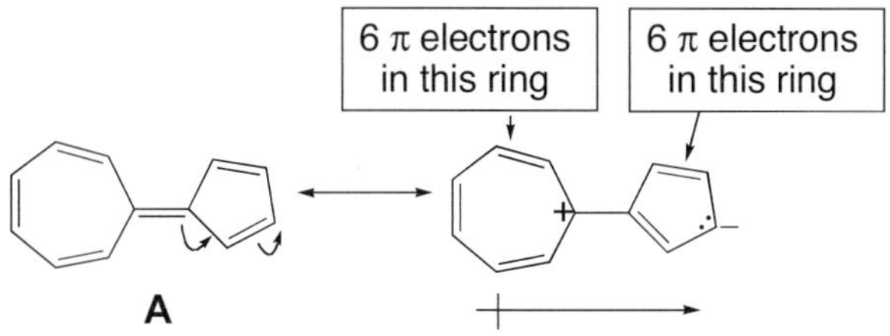
6 π electrons in this ring
6 π electrons in this ring
A

A resonance structure can be drawn for **A** that places a negative charge in the five-membered ring and a positive charge in the seven-membered ring. This resonance structure shows that each ring has six π electrons, making it aromatic. The molecule possesses a dipole such that the seven-membered ring is electron deficient and the five-membered ring is electron rich.

17.36 Each compound is completely conjugated. A compound with $4n + 2$ π electrons is especially stable, while a compound with $4n$ π electrons is especially unstable.

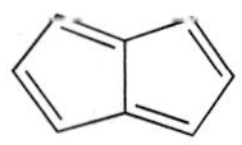

pentalene

8 π electrons
4(2) = 8
antiaromatic
unstable

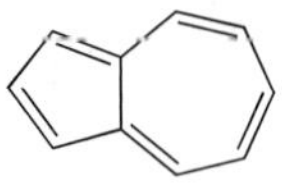

azulene

10 π electrons
4(2) + 2 = 10
aromatic
very stable

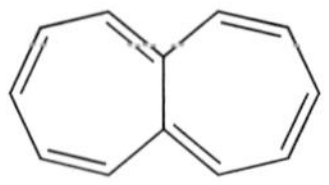

heptalene

12 π electrons
6(2) = 12
antiaromatic
unstable

17.37

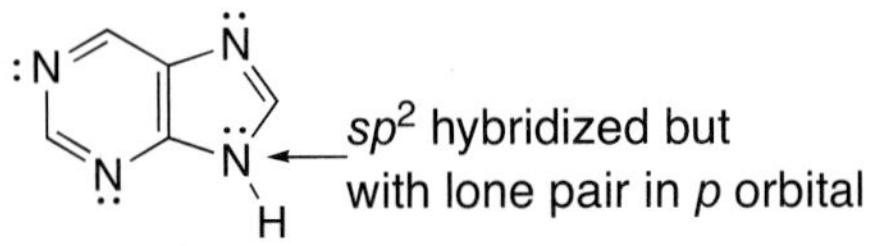

purine

a. Each N atom is sp^2 hybridized.
b. The three unlabeled N atoms are sp^2 hybridized with lone pairs in one of the sp^2 hybrid orbitals. The labeled N has its lone pair in a *p* orbital.
c. 10 π electrons
d. Purine is cyclic, planar, completely conjugated, and has 10 π electrons [4(2) + 2] so it is aromatic.

17.38

C

a. 16 total π electrons
b. 14 π electrons delocalized in the ring. [Note: Two of the electrons in the triple bond are localized between two C's, perpendicular to the π electrons delocalized in the ring.]
c. By having two of the *p* orbitals of the C–C triple bond co-planar with the *p* orbitals of all the C=C's, the total number of π electrons delocalized in the ring is 14. 4(3) + 2 = 14, so the ring is **aromatic.**

17.39 A second resonance structure can be drawn for the six-membered ring that gives it three π bonds, thus making it aromatic with six π electrons.

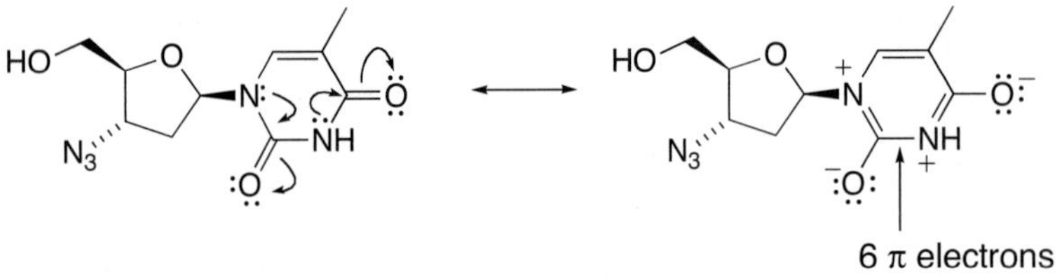

17.40 The rate of an S_N1 reaction increases with increasing stability of the intermediate carbocation.

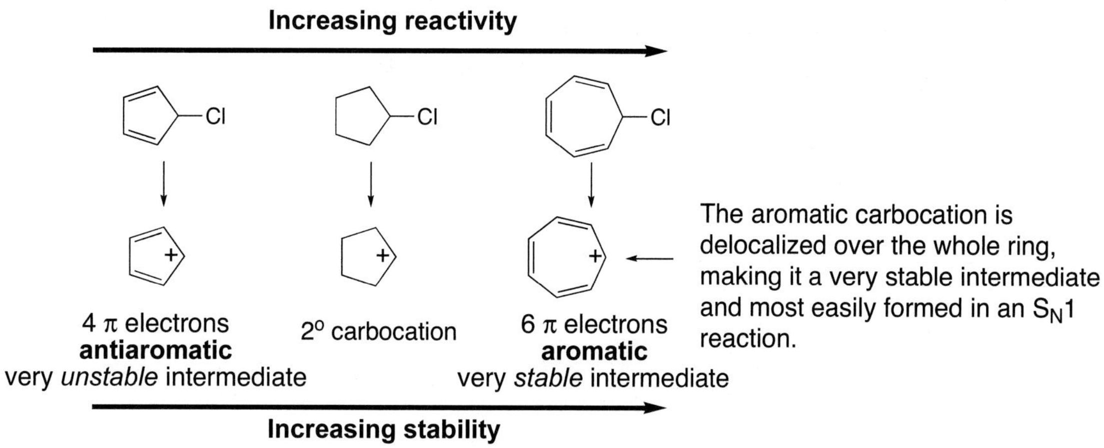
Increasing reactivity
Cl
Cl
Cl
The aromatic carbocation is delocalized over the whole ring, making it a very stable intermediate and most easily formed in an S_N1 reaction.
4 π electrons
antiaromatic
very unstable intermediate
2° carbocation
6 π electrons
aromatic
very stable intermediate
Increasing stability

17.41

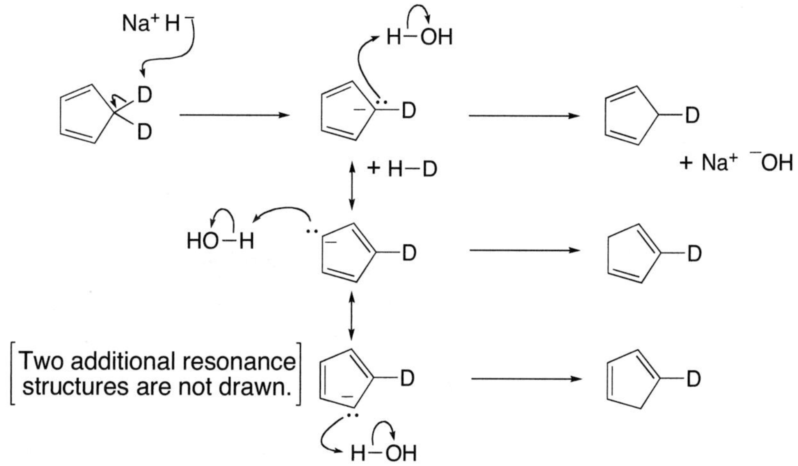
Na+ H
D
D
H–OH
D
+ H–D
D
+ Na+ −OH
HO–H
D
D
Two additional resonance structures are not drawn.
D
D
H–OH

17.42 α-Pyrone reacts like benzene because it is aromatic. A second resonance structure can be drawn showing how the ring has six π electrons. Thus, α-pyrone undergoes reactions characteristic of aromatic compounds—that is, substitution rather than addition.

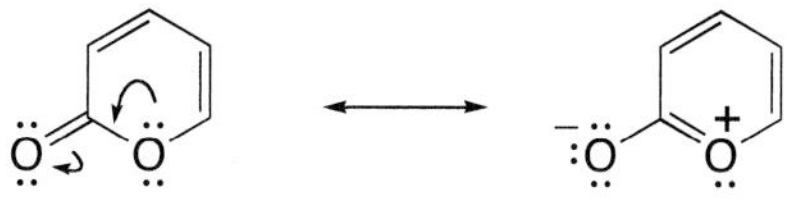

α-pyrone   6 π electrons

17.43

a. 

cyclopropenyl radical

b. 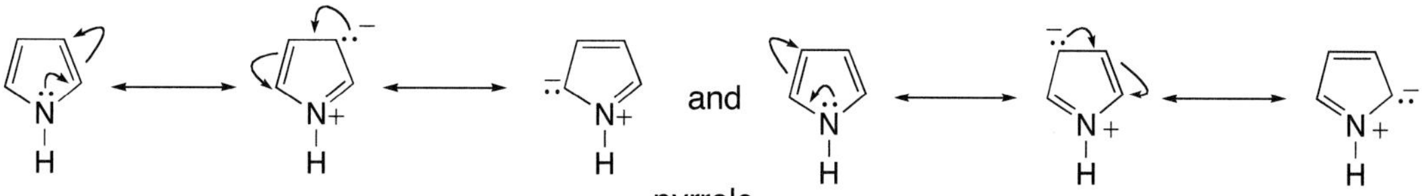
N
H
N+
H
N+
H
and
N
H
N+
H
N+
H

pyrrole

c. 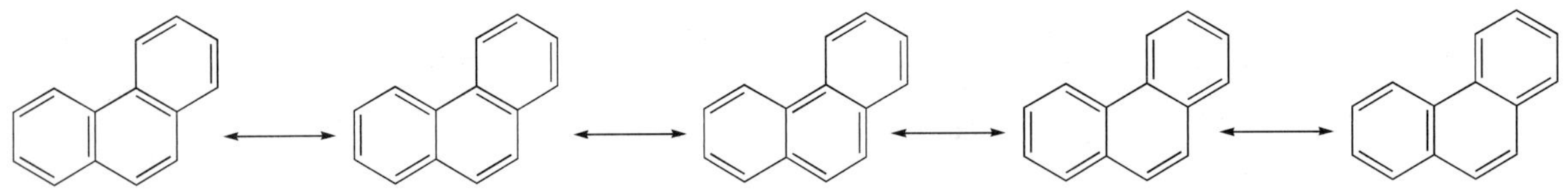

phenanthrene

17.44

Naphthalene can be drawn as three resonance structures:

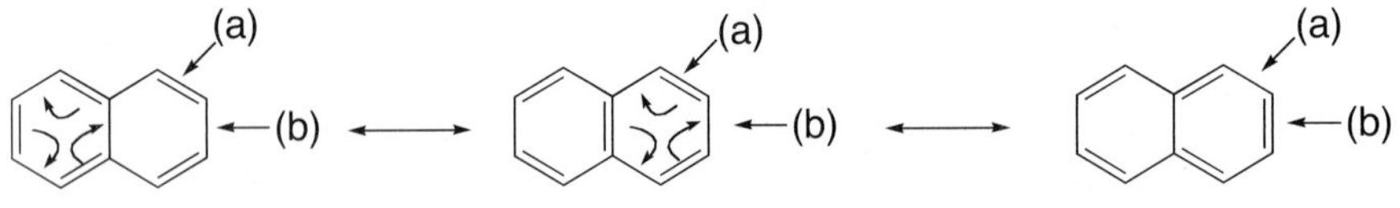

In two of the resonance structures bond (a) is a double bond, and bond (b) is a single bond. Therefore, bond (b) has more single bond character, making it longer.

17.45

a. 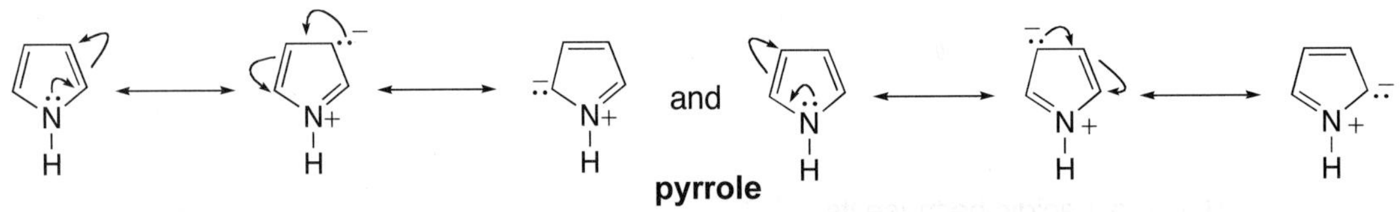

pyrrole

Pyrrole is less resonance stabilized than benzene because four of the resonance structures have charges, making them less good.

b. 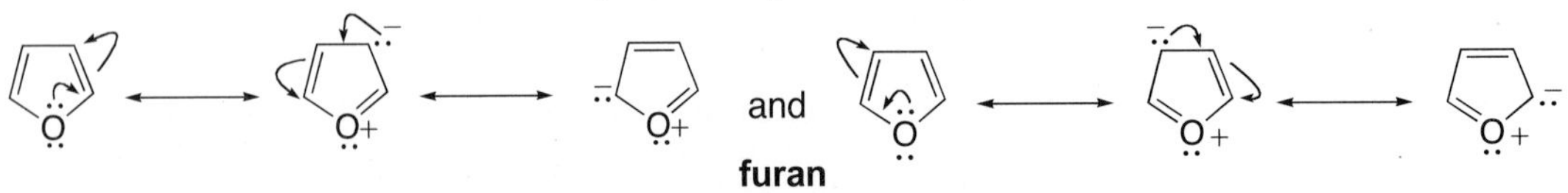

furan

Furan is less resonance stabilized than pyrrole because its O atom is less basic, so it donates electron density less "willingly." Thus, charge-separated resonance forms are more minor contributors to the hybrid than the charge-separated resonance forms of pyrrole.

17.46 The compound with the more stable conjugate base is the stronger acid. Draw and compare the conjugate bases of each pair of compounds.

conjugate bases

a. 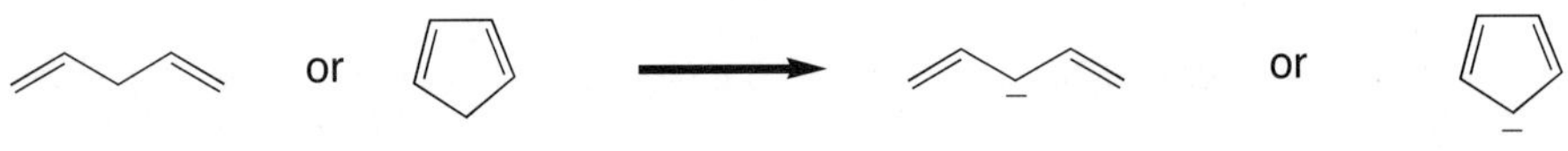

more acidic

resonance-stabilized but not aromatic

6 π electrons, aromatic
more stable conjugate base
Its acid is more acidic.

b. 

more acidic

6 π electrons, aromatic
more stable conjugate base
Its acid is more acidic.

antiaromatic
highly destabilized
conjugate base

17.47

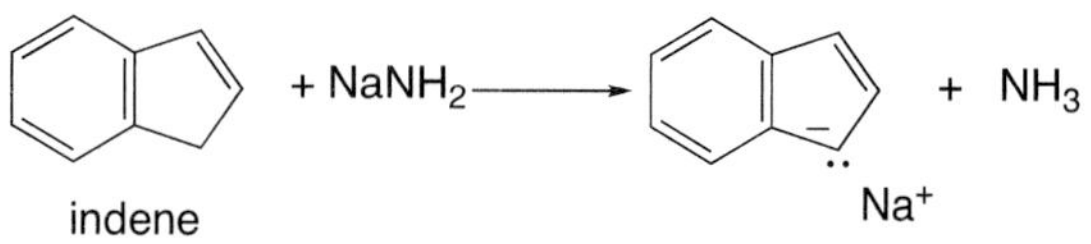

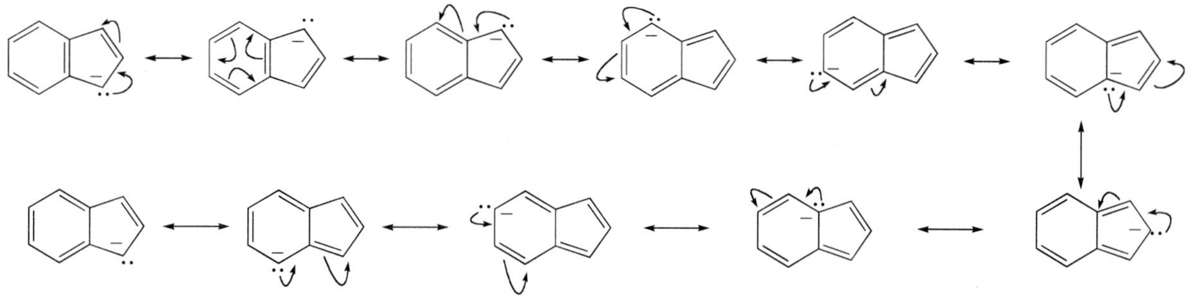

The conjugate base of indene has 10 π electrons, making it aromatic and very stable. Therefore, indene is more acidic than many hydrocarbons.

17.48

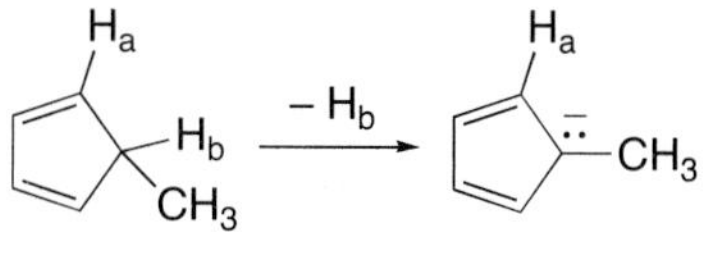

A

H_b is most acidic because its conjugate base is aromatic (6 π electrons).

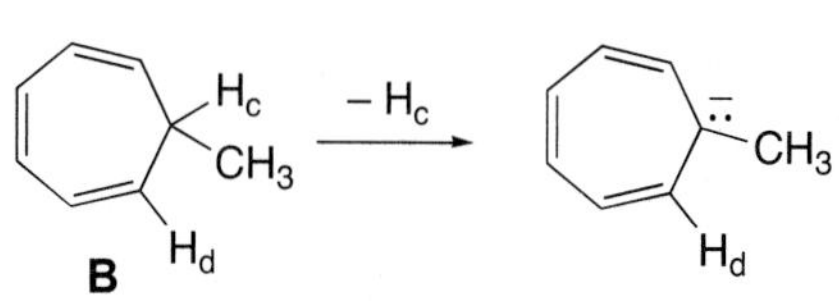

B

H_c is least acidic because its conjugate base has 8 π electrons, making it antiaromatic.

17.49

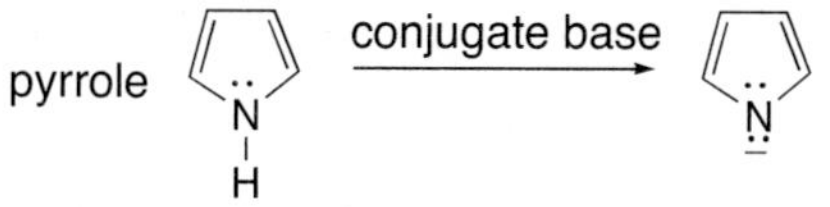

Both pyrrole and the conjugate base of pyrrole have 6 π electrons in the ring, making them both aromatic. Thus, deprotonation of pyrrole does not result in a gain of aromaticity since the starting material is aromatic to begin with.

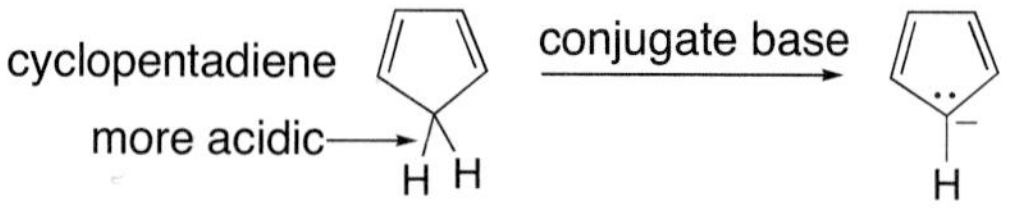

Cyclopentadiene is not aromatic, but the conjugate base has 6 π electrons and is therefore aromatic. This makes the C–H bond in cyclopentadiene more acidic than the N–H bond in pyrrole, since deprotonation of cyclopentadiene forms an aromatic conjugate base.

17.50

a.

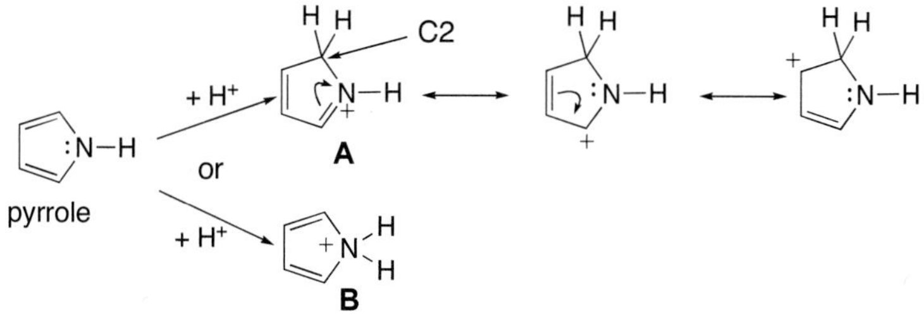

Protonation at C2 forms conjugate acid **A** because the positive charge can be delocalized by resonance. There is no resonance stabilization of the positive charge in **B**.

b. 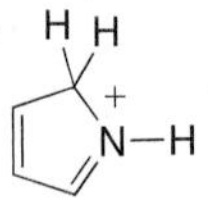
H H
N–H

A
$pK_a = 0.4$

Loss of a proton from **A** (which is not aromatic) gives two electrons to N, and forms pyrrole, which has six π electrons that can then delocalize in the five-membered ring, making it aromatic. This makes deprotonation a highly favorable process, and **A** more acidic.

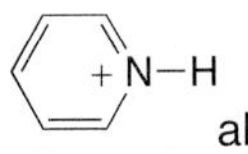
N–H

$pK_a = 5.2$
C

Both **C** and its conjugate base pyridine are aromatic. Since **C** has six π electrons, it is already aromatic to begin with, so there is less to be gained by deprotonation, and **C** is thus less acidic than **A**.

17.51

a.

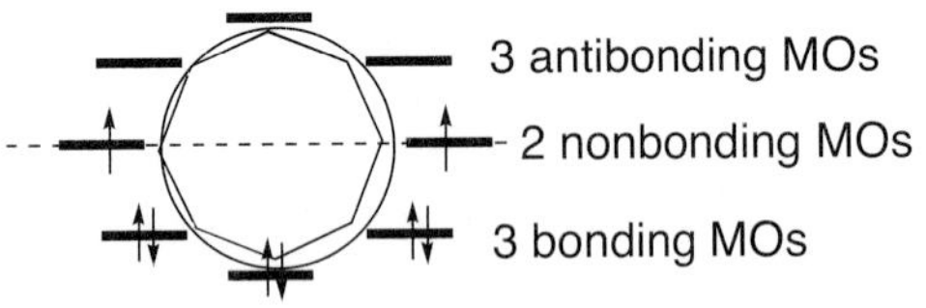
3 antibonding MOs
2 nonbonding MOs
3 bonding MOs

cyclooctatetraene and its 8 π electrons

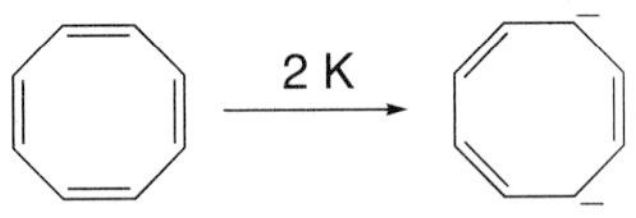
2 K

cyclooctatetraene → dianion of cyclooctatetraene

b. Even if cyclooctatetraene were flat, it has two unpaired electrons in its HOMOs (nonbonding MOs) so it cannot be aromatic.
c. The dianion has 10 π electrons.
d. The two additional electrons fill the nonbonding MOs; that is, all the bonding and nonbonding MOs are filled with electrons in the dianion.
e. The dianion is aromatic since its HOMOs are completely filled, and it has no electrons in antibonding MOs.

17.52

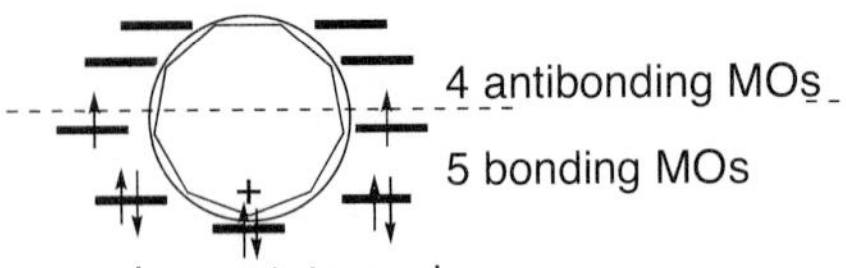
4 antibonding MOs
5 bonding MOs

cyclononatetraenyl cation

8 π electrons
antiaromatic

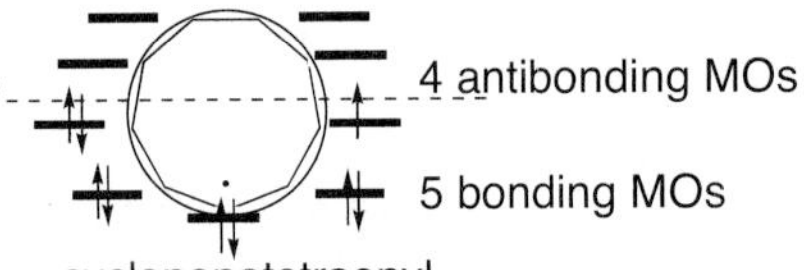
4 antibonding MOs
5 bonding MOs

cyclononatetraenyl radical

9 π electrons
not aromatic

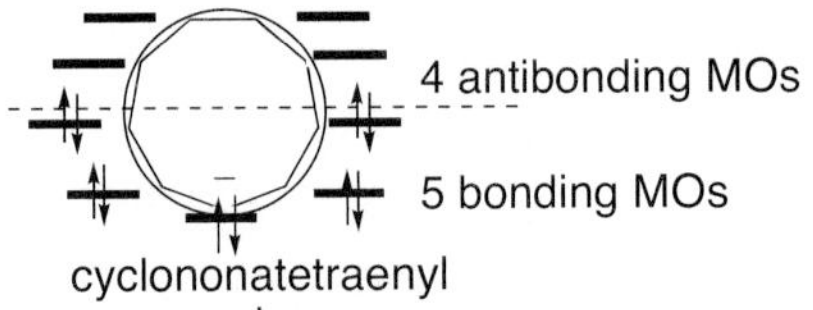
4 antibonding MOs
5 bonding MOs

cyclononatetraenyl anion

10 π electrons
aromatic

All bonding MOs are filled.

17.53 The number of different types of C's = the number of signals.

a. 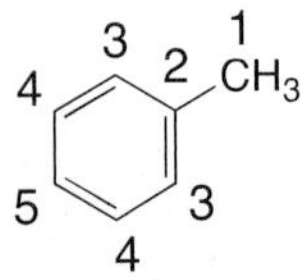
1
2
3
4
5
3
4
CH3

5 different C's

b. 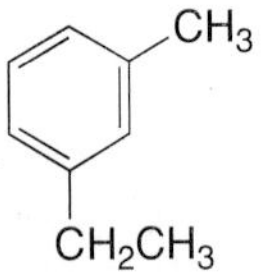
CH3
CH2CH3

all unique
9 different C's

c. 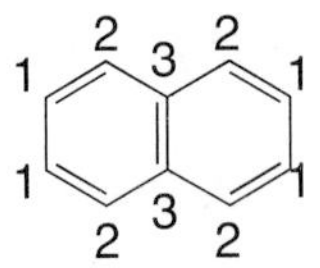
2 3 2
1 1
1 1
2 3 2

3 different C's

d. 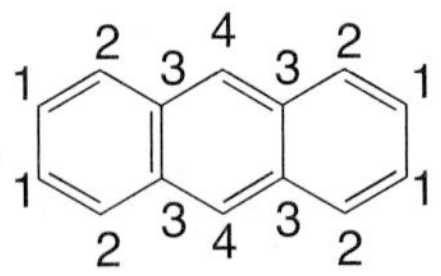
2 3 4 3 2
1 1
1 1
2 3 4 3 2

4 different C's

17.54 Draw the three isomers and count the different types of carbons in each. Then match the structures with the data.

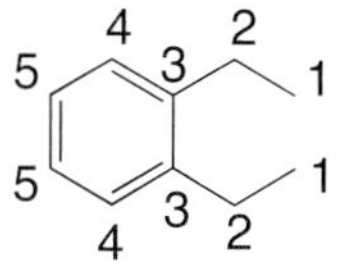

ortho isomer
5 types of C
5 lines in spectrum
Spectrum [B]

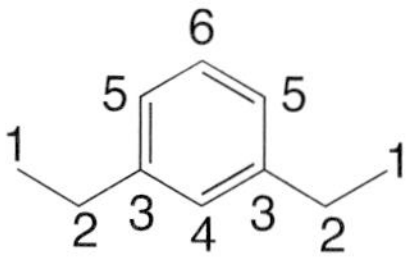

meta isomer
6 types of C
6 lines in spectrum
Spectrum [A]

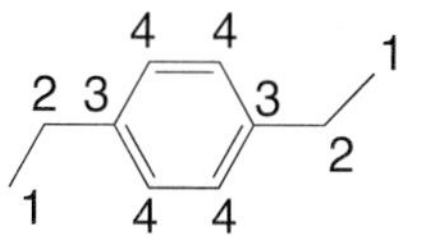

para isomer
4 types of C
4 lines in spectrum
Spectrum [C]

17.55

a. $C_{10}H_{14}$: IR absorptions at 3150–2850 (*sp*^{2} and *sp*^{3} hybridized C–H), 1600, and 1500 (due to a benzene ring) cm^{-1}

^{1}H NMR data:

Absorption	ppm	# of H's	Explanation
doublet	1.2	6	6 H's adjacent to 1 H
singlet	2.3	3	CH_3
septet	3.1	1	1 H adjacent to 6 H's
multiplet	7–7.4	4	a disubstituted benzene ring

(doublet and septet:) $(CH_3)_2CH$ group

You can't tell from these data where the two groups are on the benzene ring. They are not para, since the para arrangement usually gives two sets of distinct peaks (resembling two doublets) so there are two possible structures—ortho and meta isomers.

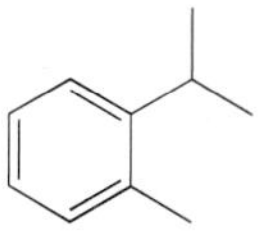

or

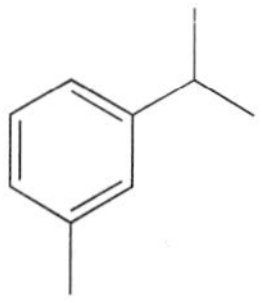

b. C_9H_{12}: ^{13}C NMR signals at 21, 127, and 138 ppm → means three different types of C's.
^{1}H NMR shows two types of H's: 9 H's probably means 3 CH_3 groups; the other 3 H's are very deshielded so they are bonded to a benzene ring.
Only one possible structure fits:

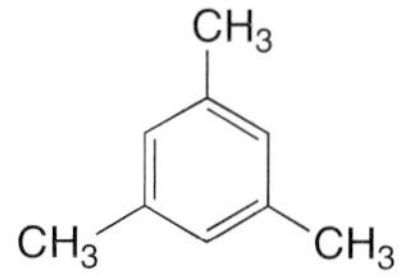
CH3
CH3
CH3

c. C_8H_{10}: IR absorptions at 3108–2875 (*sp*^{2} and *sp*^{3} hybridized C–H), 1606, and 1496 (due to a benzene ring) cm^{-1}

^{1}H NMR data:

Absorption	ppm	# of H's	Explanation
triplet	1.3	3	3 H's adjacent to 2 H's
quartet	2.7	2	2 H's adjacent to 3 H's
multiplet	7.3	5	a monosubstituted benzene ring

Structure:

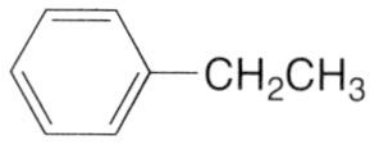
CH2CH3

17.56

a. Compound **A:** Molecular formula $C_8H_{10}O$
IR absorption at 3150–2850 (*sp*^{2} and *sp*^{3} hybridized C–H) cm^{-1}
^{1}H NMR data:

Absorption	ppm	# of H's	Explanation
triplet	1.4	3	3 H's adjacent to 2 H's
quartet	3.95	2	2 H's adjacent to 3 H's
multiplet	6.8–7.3	5	a monosubstituted benzene ring

Structure:

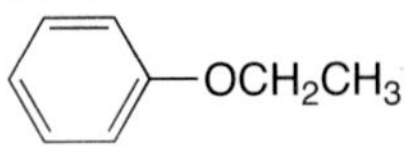
OCH2CH3

b. Compound **B:** Molecular formula $C_9H_{10}O_2$
IR absorption at 1669 (C=O) cm^{-1}
^{1}H NMR data:

Absorption	ppm	# of H's	Explanation
singlet	2.5	3	CH_3 group
singlet	3.8	3	CH_3 group
doublet	6.9	2	2 H's on a benzene ring
doublet	7.9	2	2 H's on a benzene ring

Structure:

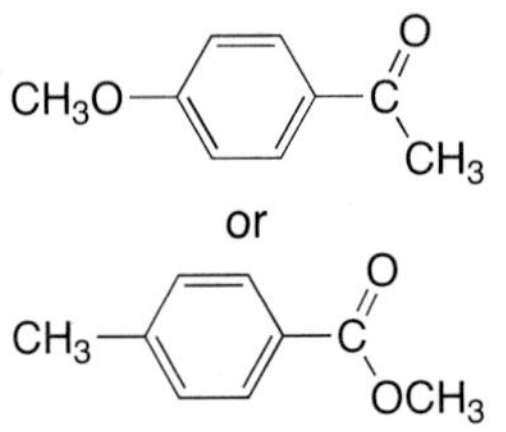
CH3O
O
C
CH3
or
CH3
O
C
OCH3

It would be hard to distinguish these two compounds with the given data.

17.57

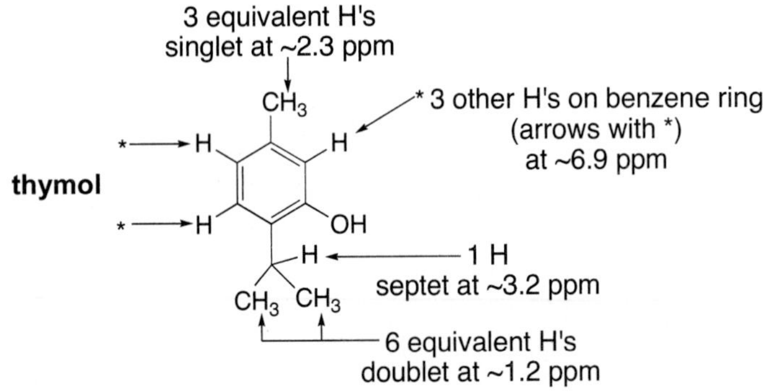
3 equivalent H's
singlet at ~2.3 ppm
CH3
H
H
H
H
OH
* 3 other H's on benzene ring
(arrows with *)
at ~6.9 ppm
thymol
1 H
septet at ~3.2 ppm
CH3
CH3
6 equivalent H's
doublet at ~1.2 ppm

IR absorptions:
3500–3200 cm^{-1} (O–H)
3150–2850 cm^{-1} (C–H bonds)
1621 and 1585 cm^{-1} (benzene ring)

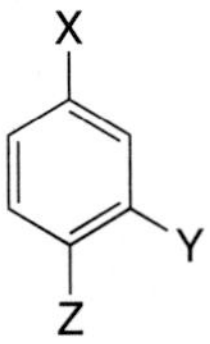
X
Y
Z

basic structure of thymol

Thymol must have this basic structure, given the NMR and IR data since it is a trisubstituted benzene ring with one singlet and two doublets in the NMR at ~6.9 ppm. However, which group [OH, CH_3, or $CH(CH_3)_2$] corresponds to X, Y, and Z is not readily distinguished with the given data. The correct structure for thymol is given.

17.58

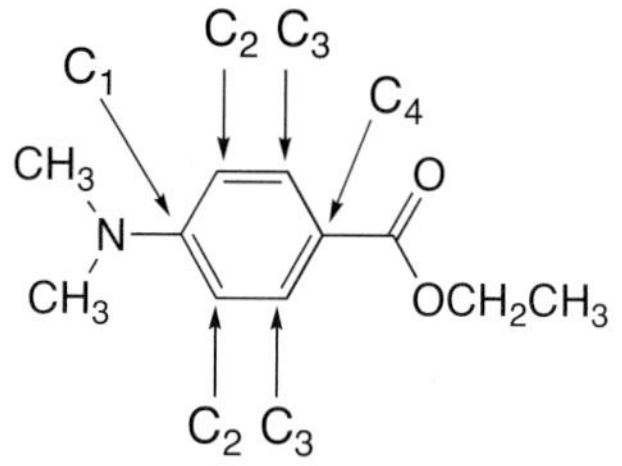
C1
C2 C3
C4
CH3
N
CH3
O
OCH2CH3
C2 C3

^{13}C NMR has four lines that are located in the aromatic region (~110–155 ppm), corresponding to the four different types of carbons in the aromatic ring of the para isomer. The ortho and meta isomers have six different C's, and so six lines would be expected for each of them.

17.59 Because tetrahydrofuran has a higher boiling point and is more water soluble, it must be more polar and have stronger intermolecular forces than furan. There are two contributing factors. One lone pair on furan's O atom is delocalized on the five-membered ring to make it aromatic. This makes it less available for H-bonding with water and other intermolecular interactions. Also, the C–O bonds in furan are less polar than the C–O bonds in tetrahydrofuran because of hybridization. The sp^2 hybridized C's of furan pull a little more electron density towards them than do the sp^3 hybridized C's of tetrahydrofuran. This counteracts the higher electronegativity of O compared to C to a small extent.

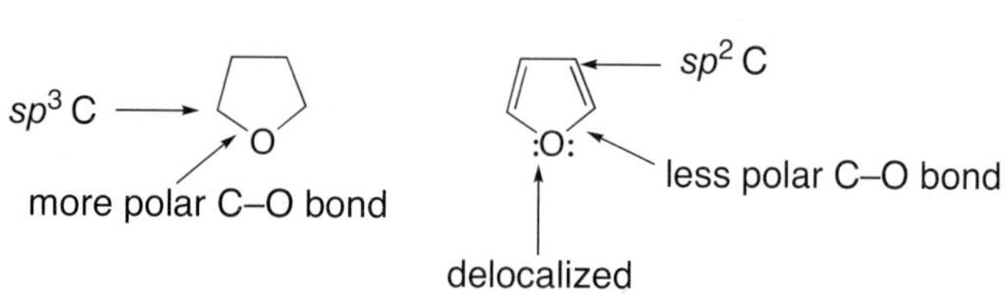
sp3 C
O
more polar C–O bond
sp2 C
:O:
less polar C–O bond
delocalized

17.60

a, b.

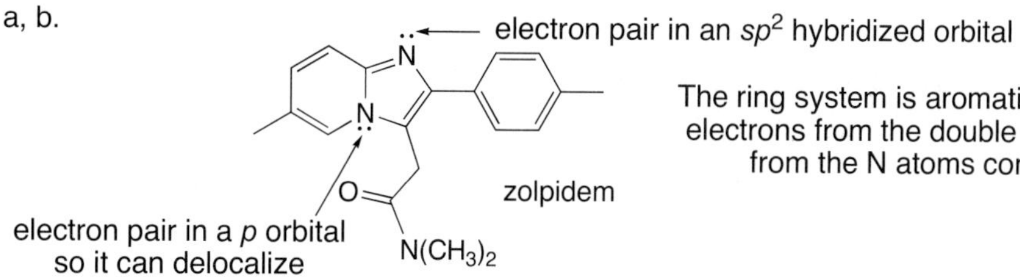
electron pair in an sp2 hybridized orbital
N
N
O
N(CH3)2
zolpidem
electron pair in a p orbital
so it can delocalize

The ring system is aromatic with 10 π electrons, 8 π electrons from the double bonds and 2 π electrons from the N atoms common to both rings.

c.

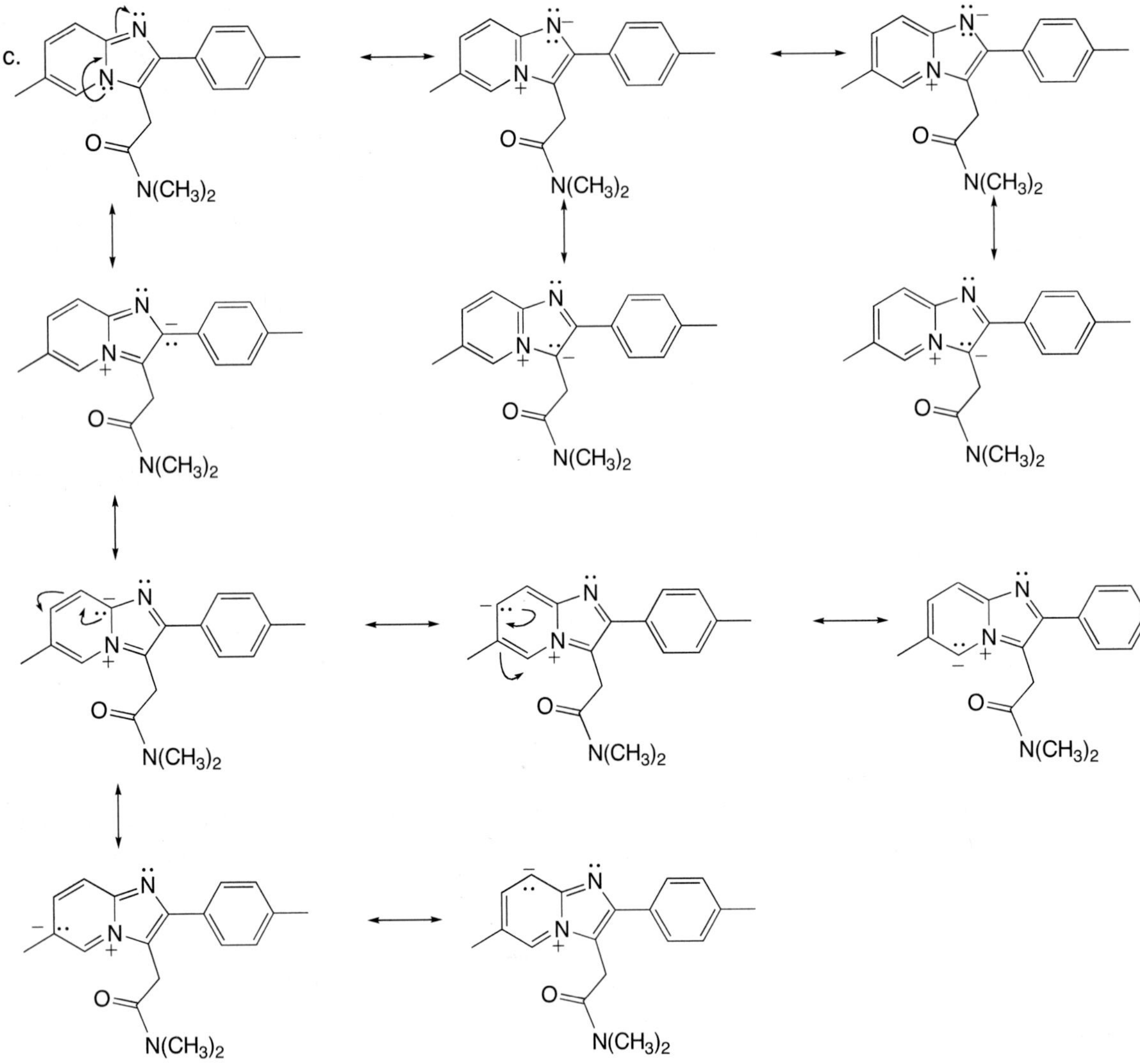

17.61

a.

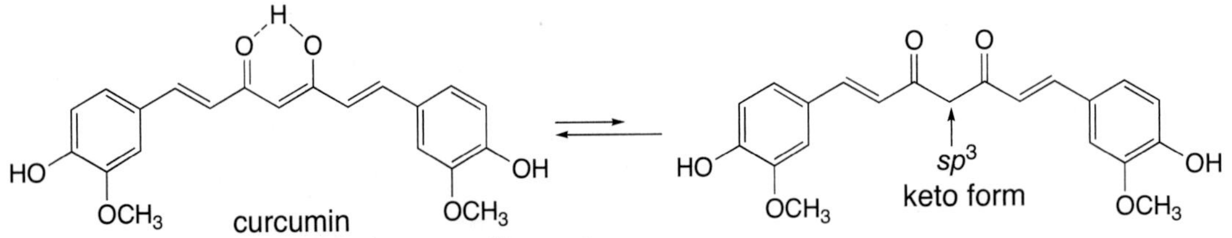

The enol form is more stable because the enol double bond makes a highly conjugated system. The enol OH can also intramolecularly hydrogen bond to the nearby carbonyl O atom.

b.

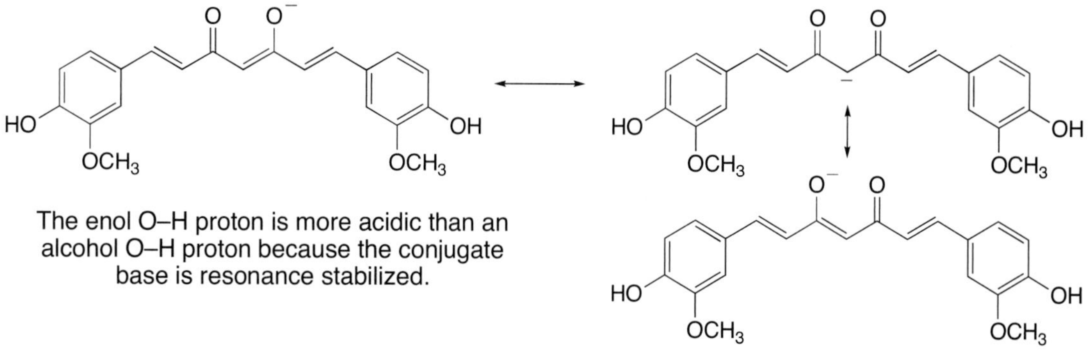

The enol O–H proton is more acidic than an alcohol O–H proton because the conjugate base is resonance stabilized.

c. Curcumin is colored because it has many conjugated π electrons, which shift absorption of light from the UV to the visible region.

d. Curcumin is an antioxidant because it contains a phenol. Homolytic cleavage affords a resonance-stabilized phenoxy radical, which can inhibit oxidation from occurring, much like vitamin E and BHT in Chapter 15.

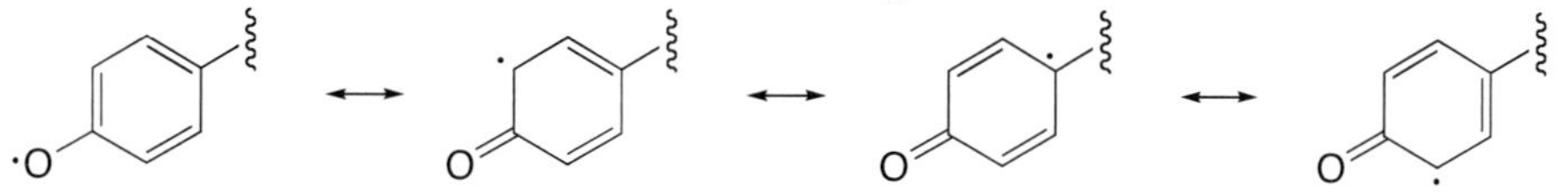

(+ other resonance structures)

phenoxy radical

Resonance delocalizes the radical on the ring and C chain of curcumin.

17.62 a. Pyrazole rings are aromatic because they have six π electrons—two from the lone pair on the N atom that is not part of the double bond and four from the double bonds.

b.

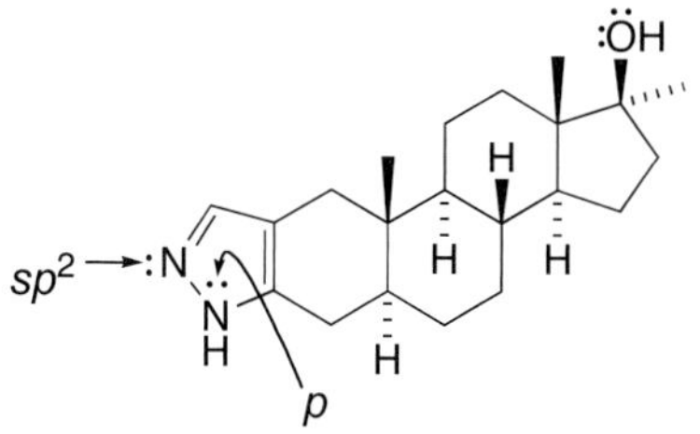

c.

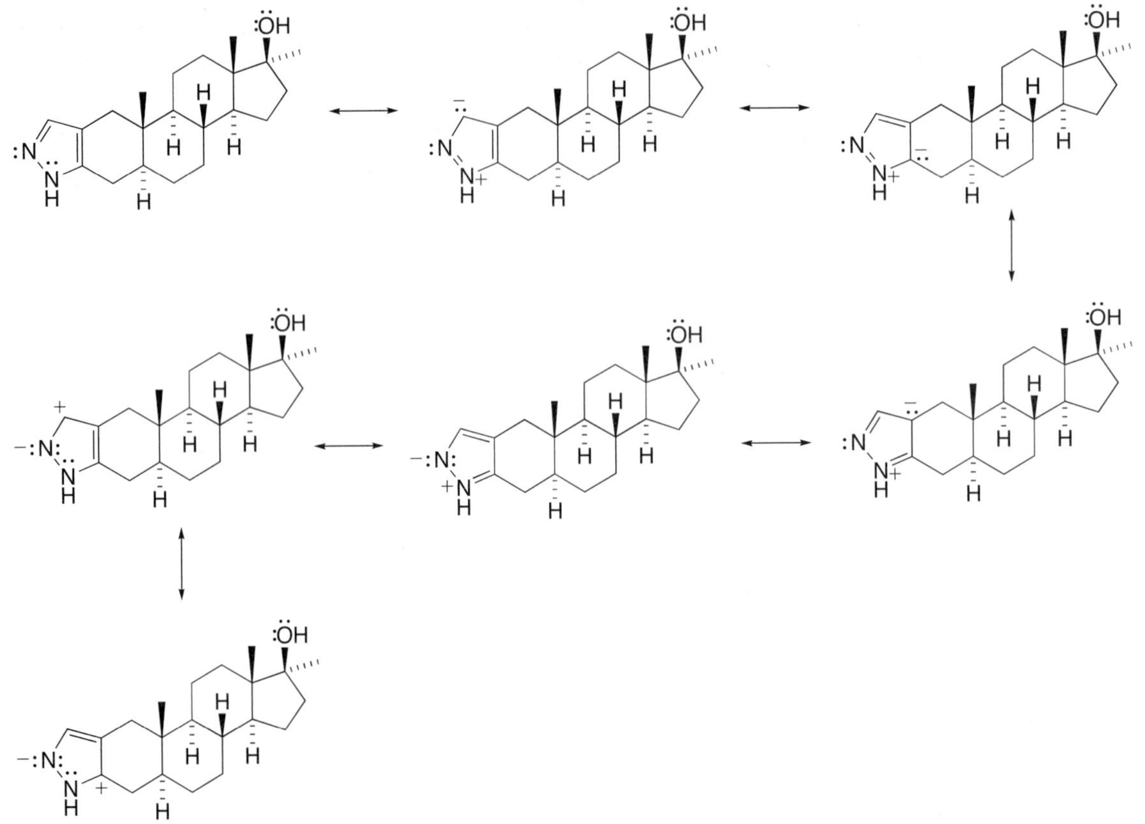

d. The N atom in the NH bond in the pyrazole ring is sp^2 hybridized with 33% *s*-character, increasing the acidity of the N–H bond. The N–H bond of CH_3NH_2 contains an sp^3 hybridized N atom.

17.63 Both **A** and **B** are cyclic, and if the lone pair of electrons on N is in a *p* orbital, they are completely conjugated with 10 π electrons, a number that satisfies Hückel's rule. To be aromatic, **A** and **B** must be planar, and the internal bond angles of **A** and **B** would be much larger than 120°, the theoretical bond angle of sp^2 hybridized C's. The fact that **A** is aromatic means that the lone pair on N occupies a *p* orbital, so it can delocalize on the nine-membered ring. The stabilization gained by being aromatic is greater than any angle strain. With **B,** the lone pair on N is also delocalized on the C=O, making it less available for donation to the ring, so the ring is not aromatic.

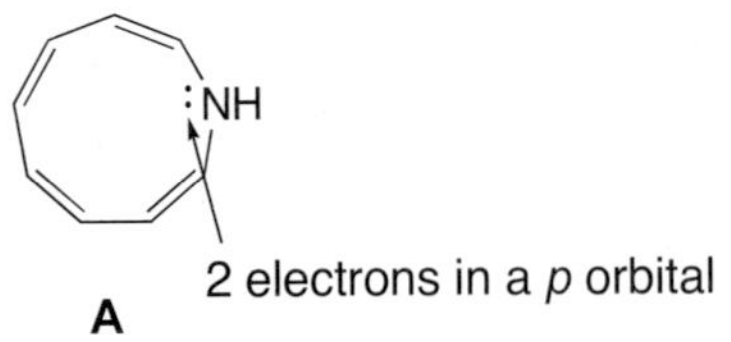
2 electrons in a p orbital

A

10 π electrons

B

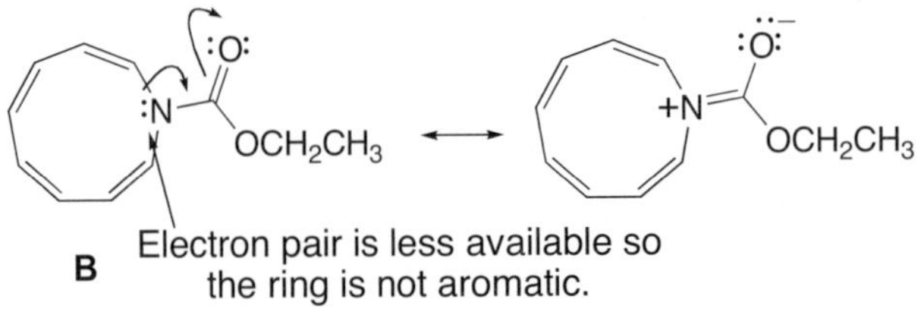
Electron pair is less available so
the ring is not aromatic.

17.64 With 14 π electrons in the double bonds, the system is aromatic [4(3) + 2 = 14 π electrons]. The ring current generated by the circulating π electrons deshields the protons on the C=C's, so they absorb downfield (8.14–8.67 ppm). The CH_3 groups, however, are very shielded since they lie above and below the plane, so they absorb far upfield (–4.25 ppm). The dianion of **C** now has 16 π electrons, making it antiaromatic, so the position of the absorptions reverses. The C=C protons are now shielded (–3 ppm), and the CH_3 protons are now deshielded (21 ppm).

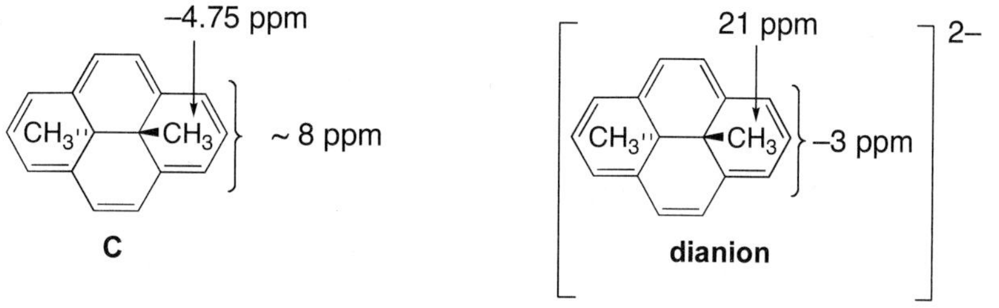

17.65 A second resonance structure for **A** shows that the ring is completely conjugated and has six π electrons, making it aromatic and especially stable. A similar charge-separated resonance structure for **B** makes the ring completely conjugated, but gives the ring four π electrons, making it antiaromatic and especially unstable.

17.66 The conversion of carvone to carvacrol involves acid-catalyzed isomerization of two double bonds and tautomerization of a ketone to an enol tautomer. In this case the enol form is part of an aromatic phenol. Each isomerization of a C=C involves Markovnikov addition of a proton, followed by deprotonation.

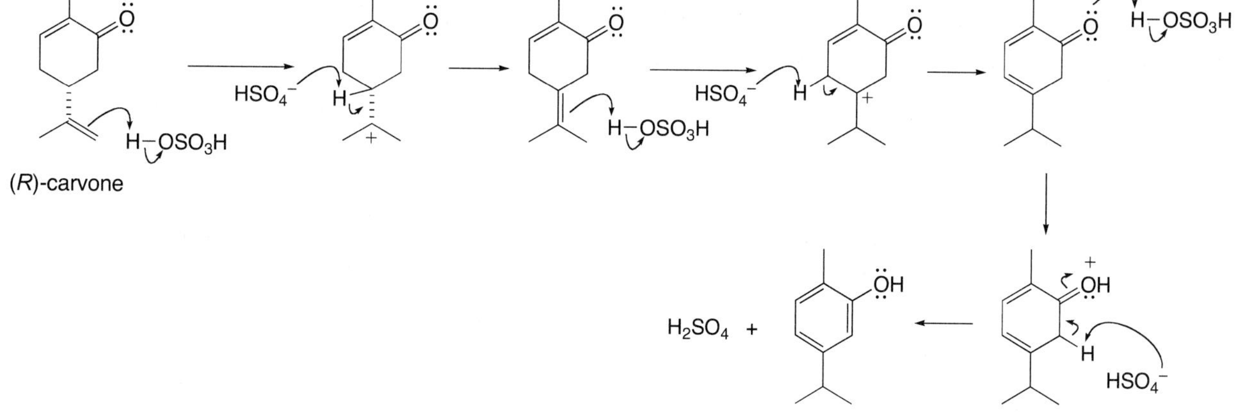

17.67 Resonance structures for triphenylene:

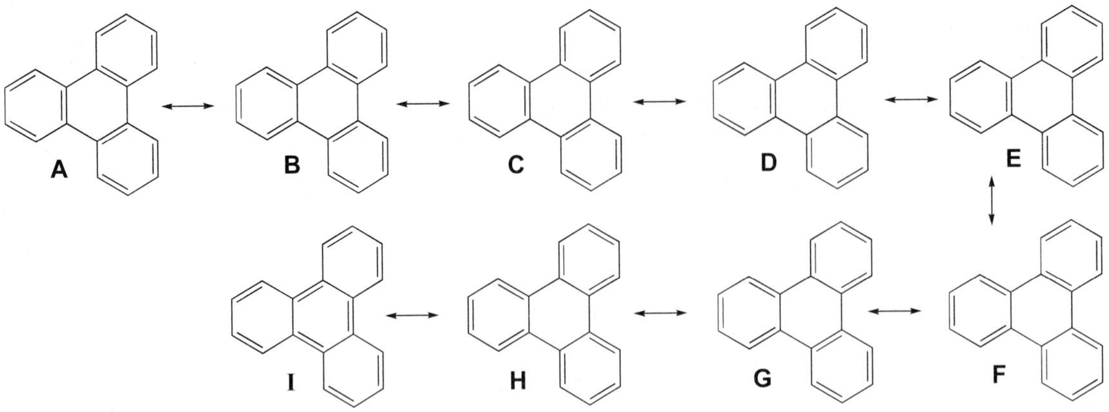
A
B
C
D
E
F
G
H
I

Resonance structures **A–H** all keep three double and three single bonds in the three six-membered rings on the periphery of the molecule. This means that each ring behaves like an isolated benzene ring undergoing substitution rather than addition because the π electron density is delocalized within each six-membered ring. Only resonance structure **I** does not have this form. Each C–C bond of triphenylene has four (or five) resonance structures in which it is a single bond and four (or five) resonance structures in which it is a double bond.

Resonance structures for phenanthrene:

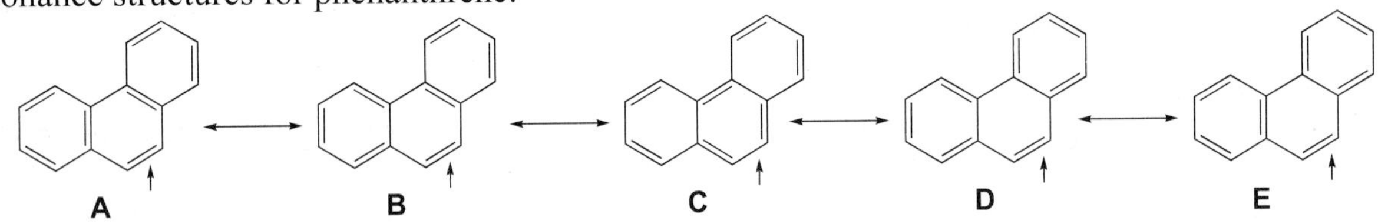
A
B
C
D
E

With phenanthrene, however, four of the five resonance structures keep a double bond at the labeled C's. (Only **C** does not.) This means that these two C's have more double bond character than other C–C bonds in phenanthrene, making them more susceptible to addition rather than substitution.

17.68

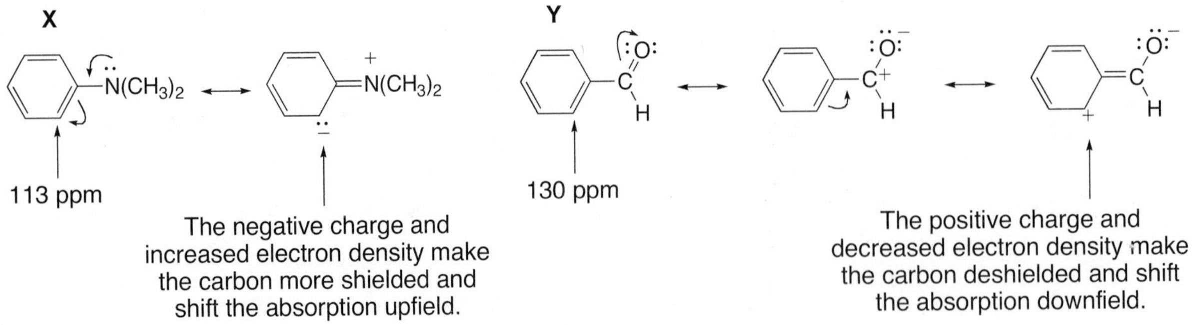
X
N(CH3)2
N(CH3)2
113 ppm
The negative charge and increased electron density make the carbon more shielded and shift the absorption upfield.
Y
130 ppm
The positive charge and decreased electron density make the carbon deshielded and shift the absorption downfield.

Chapter 18 Reactions of Aromatic Compounds

Chapter Review

Mechanism of electrophilic aromatic substitution (18.2)

- Electrophilic aromatic substitution follows a two-step mechanism. Reaction of the aromatic ring with an electrophile forms a carbocation, and loss of a proton regenerates the aromatic ring.
- The first step is rate-determining.
- The intermediate carbocation is stabilized by resonance; a minimum of three resonance structures can be drawn. The positive charge is always located ortho or para to the new C–E bond.

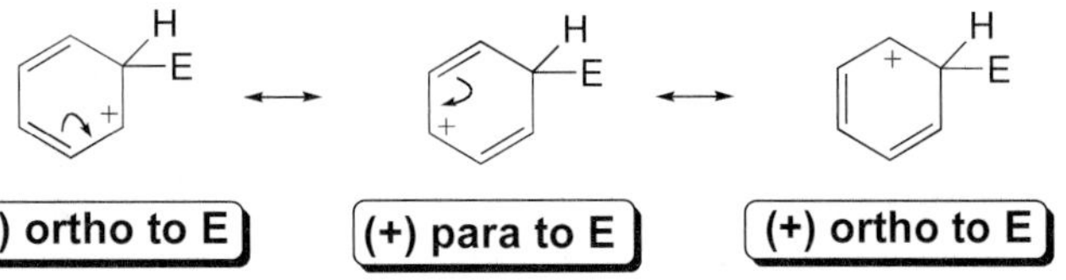

Three rules describing the reactivity and directing effects of common substituents (18.7–18.9)

[1] All ortho, para directors except the halogens activate the benzene ring.
[2] All meta directors deactivate the benzene ring.
[3] The halogens deactivate the benzene ring.

Summary of substituent effects in electrophilic aromatic substitution (18.6–18.9)

	Substituent	Inductive effect	Resonance effect	Reactivity	Directing effect
[1]	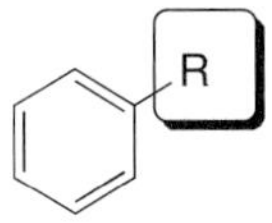 R = alkyl	donating	none	activating	ortho, para
[2]	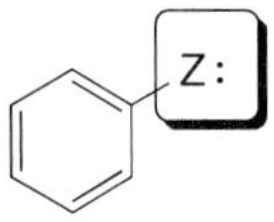 Z = N or O	withdrawing	donating	activating	ortho, para
[3]	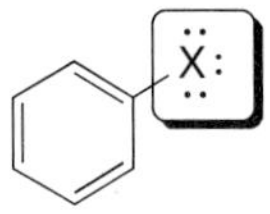 X = halogen	withdrawing	donating	deactivating	ortho, para
[4]	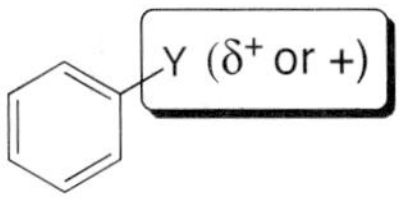	withdrawing	withdrawing	deactivating	meta

Five examples of electrophilic aromatic substitution

[1] Halogenation—Replacement of H by Cl or Br (18.3)

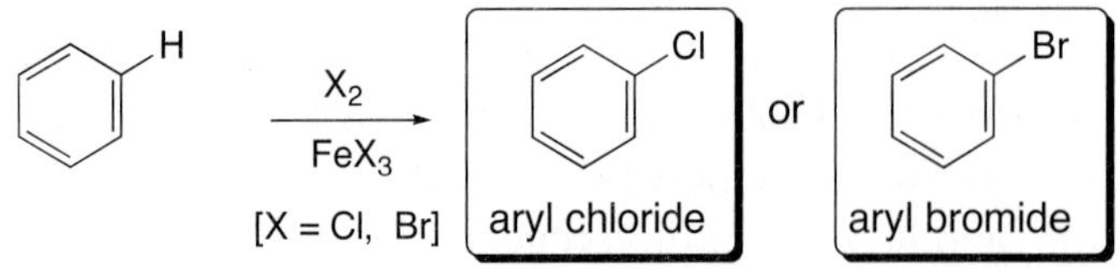
H
X_2
FeX_3
[X = Cl, Br]
Cl
aryl chloride
or
Br
aryl bromide

- Polyhalogenation occurs on benzene rings substituted by OH and NH_2 (and related substituents) (18.10A).

[2] Nitration—Replacement of H by NO_2 (18.4)

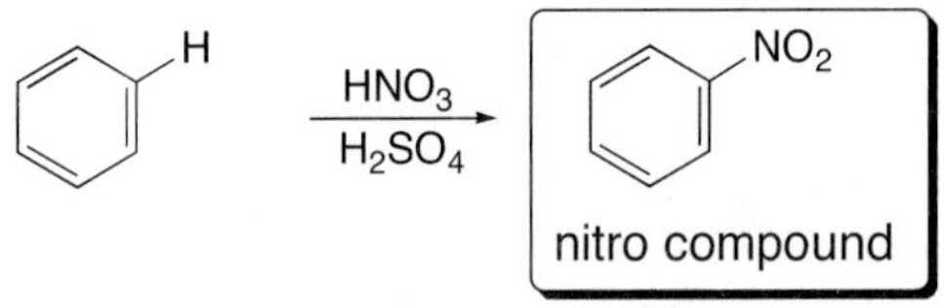
H
HNO_3
H_2SO_4
NO_2
nitro compound

[3] Sulfonation—Replacement of H by SO_3H (18.4)

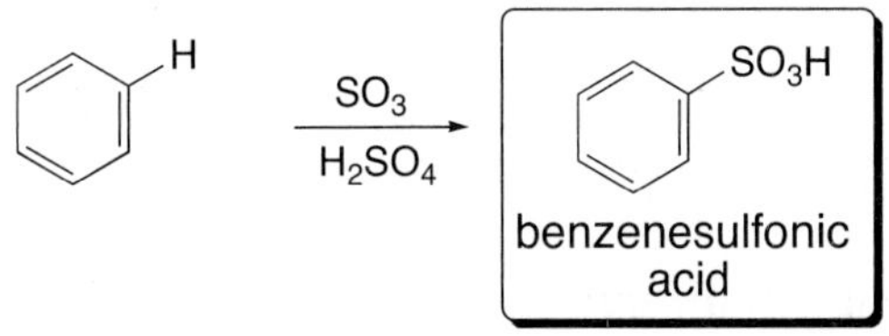
H
SO_3
H_2SO_4
SO_3H
benzenesulfonic acid

[4] Friedel–Crafts alkylation—Replacement of H by R (18.5)

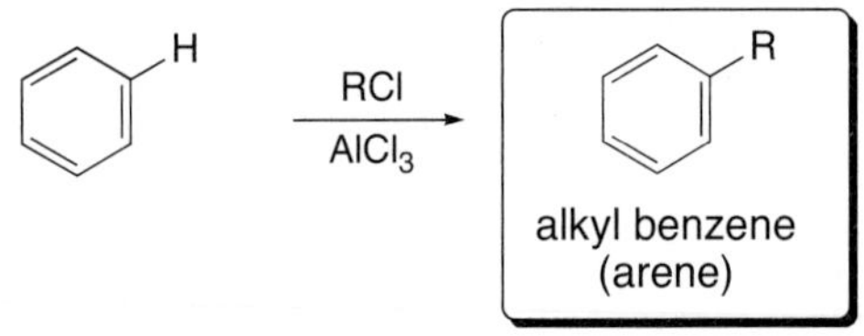
H
RCl
$AlCl_3$
R
alkyl benzene (arene)

- Rearrangements can occur.
- Vinyl halides and aryl halides are unreactive.
- The reaction does not occur on benzene rings substituted by meta deactivating groups or NH_2 groups (18.10B).
- Polyalkylation can occur.

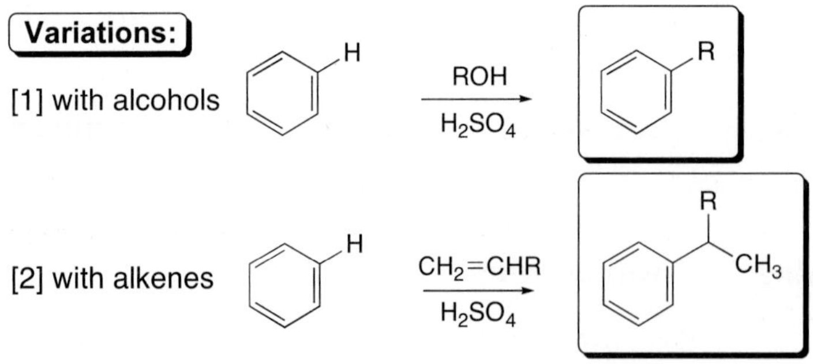
Variations:
[1] with alcohols
H
ROH
H_2SO_4
R
[2] with alkenes
H
$CH_2{=}CHR$
H_2SO_4
R
CH_3

[5] Friedel–Crafts acylation—Replacement of H by RCO (18.5)

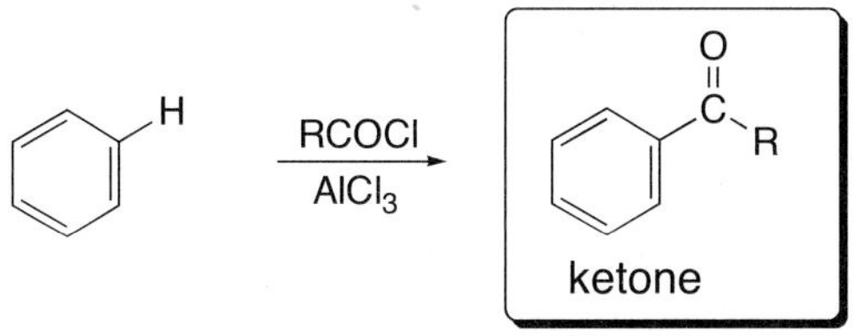

- The reaction does not occur on benzene rings substituted by meta deactivating groups or NH_2 groups (18.10B).

Nucleophilic aromatic substitution (18.13)

[1] Nucleophilic substitution by an addition–elimination mechanism

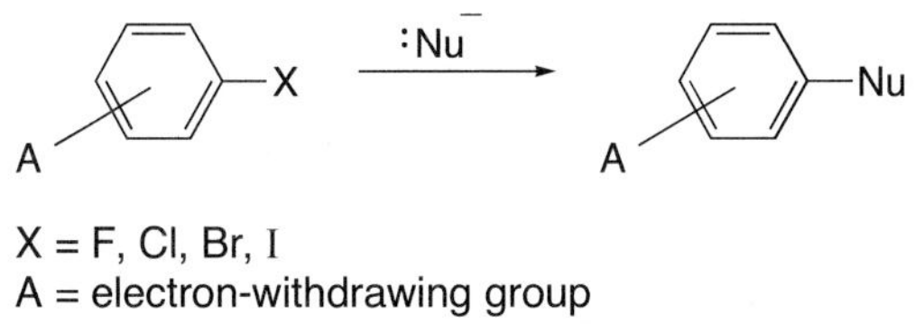

- The mechanism has two steps.
- Strong electron-withdrawing groups at the ortho or para position are required.
- Increasing the number of electron-withdrawing groups increases the rate.
- Increasing the electronegativity of the halogen increases the rate.

[2] Nucleophilic substitution by an elimination–addition mechanism

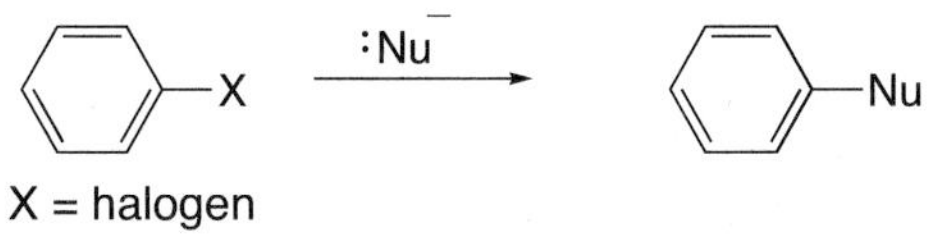

- Reaction conditions are harsh.
- Benzyne is formed as an intermediate.
- Product mixtures may result.

Other reactions of benzene derivatives

[1] Benzylic halogenation (18.14)

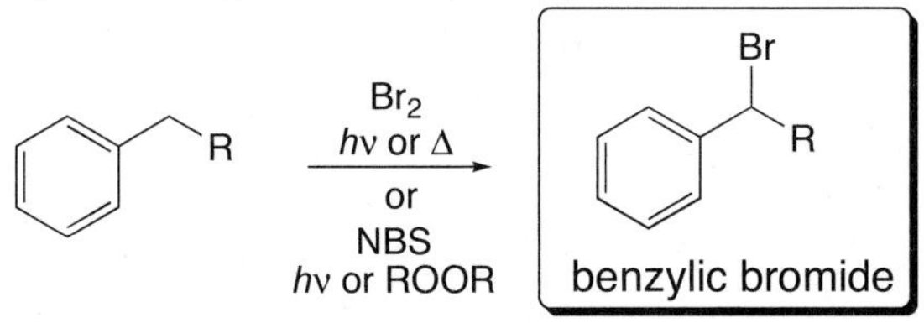

[2] Oxidation of alkyl benzenes (18.15A)

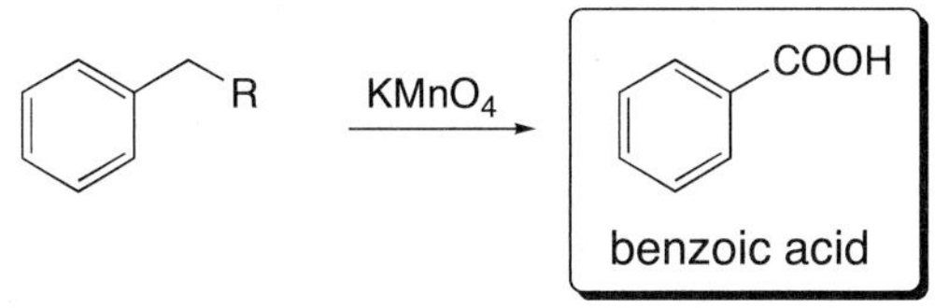

- A benzylic C–H bond is needed for reaction.

[3] Reduction of ketones to alkyl benzenes (18.15B)

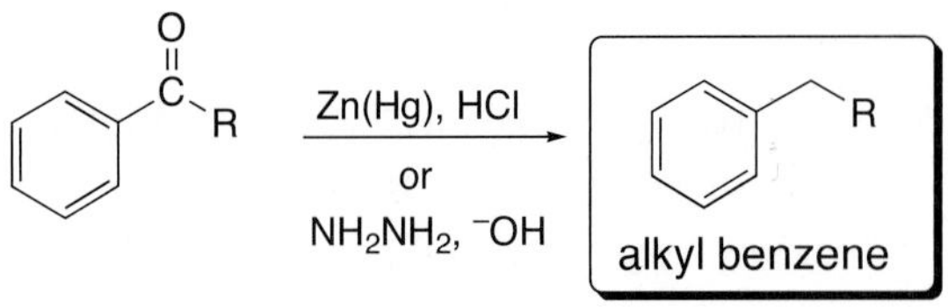

[4] Reduction of nitro groups to amino groups (18.15C)

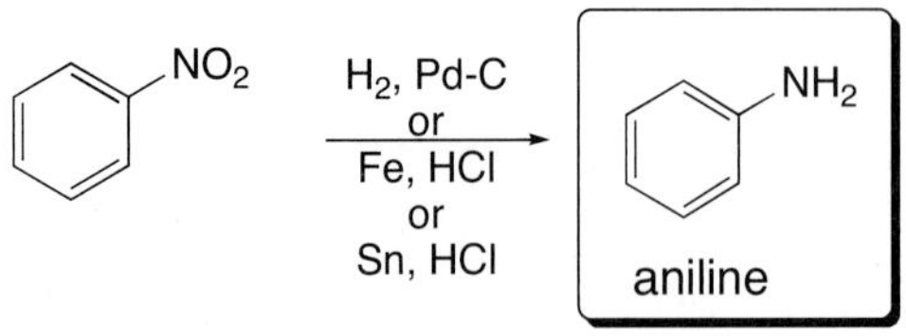

Practice Test on Chapter Review

1. a. Which of the following statements is true about an ethoxy substituent (–OCH_2CH_3) on a benzene ring?
   1. OCH_2CH_3 increases the rates of both electrophilic substitution and nucleophilic substitution.
   2. OCH_2CH_3 decreases the rates of both electrophilic substitution and nucleophilic substitution.
   3. OCH_2CH_3 increases the rate of electrophilic substitution and decreases the rate of nucleophilic substitution.
   4. OCH_2CH_3 decreases the rate of electrophilic substitution and increases the rate of nucleophilic substitution.
   5. None of these statements is true.

   b. Which of the following statements is true about a –CO_2CH_3 group on a benzene ring?
   1. CO_2CH_3 increases the rates of both electrophilic substitution and nucleophilic substitution.
   2. CO_2CH_3 decreases the rates of both electrophilic substitution and nucleophilic substitution.
   3. CO_2CH_3 increases the rate of electrophilic substitution and decreases the rate of nucleophilic substitution.
   4. CO_2CH_3 decreases the rate of electrophilic substitution and increases the rate of nucleophilic substitution.
   5. None of these statements is true.

c. Which of the following is *not* a valid resonance structure for the carbocation that results from ortho attack of an electrophile on $C_6H_5C(CH_3){=}CH_2$?

1. 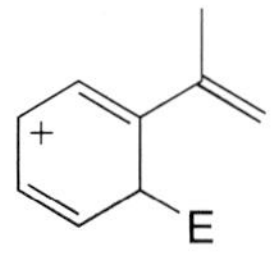
+
E

3. 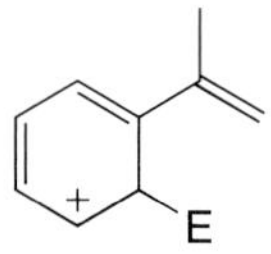
+
E

5. 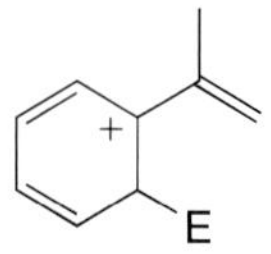
+
E

2. 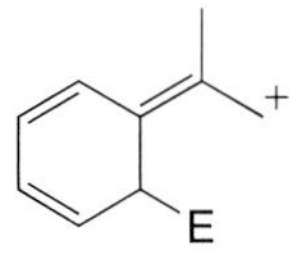
+
E

4. 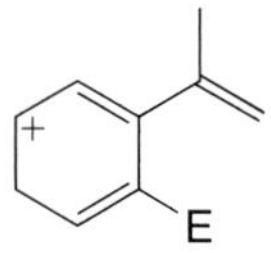
+
E

2. Draw the organic products formed in the following reactions.

a. 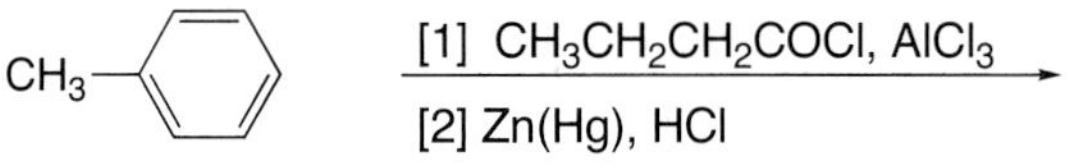
CH3
[1] CH3CH2CH2COCl, AlCl3
[2] Zn(Hg), HCl

e. 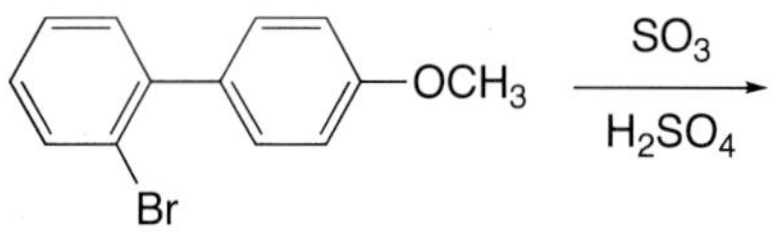
OCH3
Br
SO3
H2SO4

b. 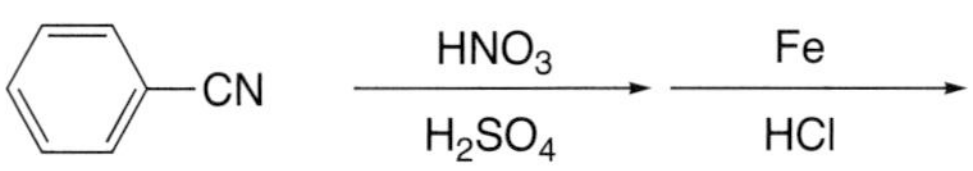
CN
HNO3
H2SO4
Fe
HCl

f. 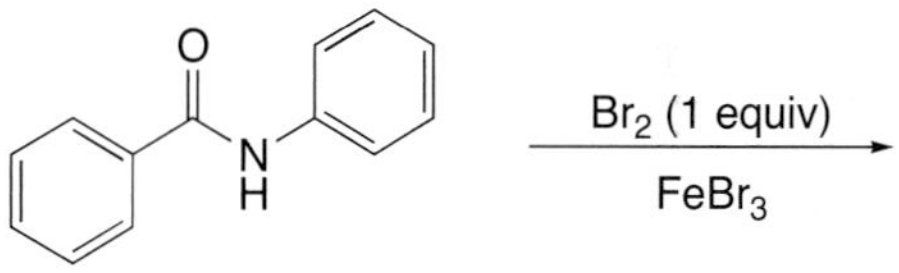
O
N
H
Br2 (1 equiv)
FeBr3

c. 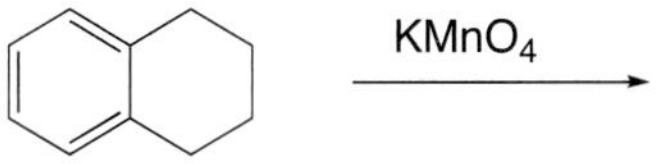
KMnO4

g. 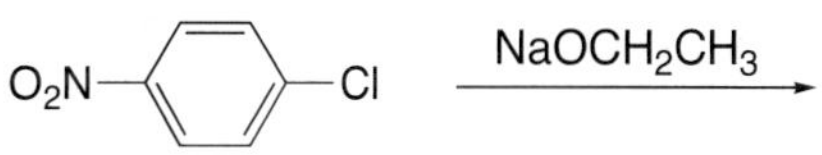
O2N
Cl
NaOCH2CH3

d. 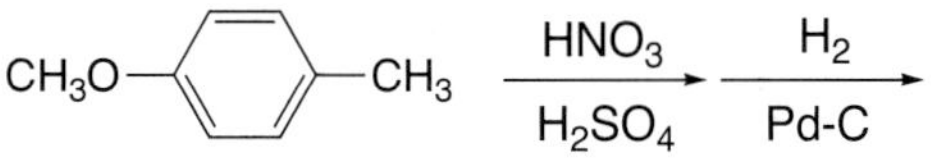
CH3O
CH3
HNO3
H2SO4
H2
Pd-C

h. 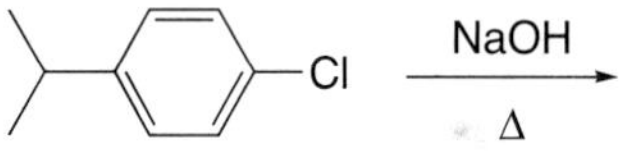
Cl
NaOH
Δ

3. (a) Considering the compound drawn below, which ring is most reactive in electrophilic aromatic substitution? Which ring is the least reactive in electrophilic aromatic substitution?

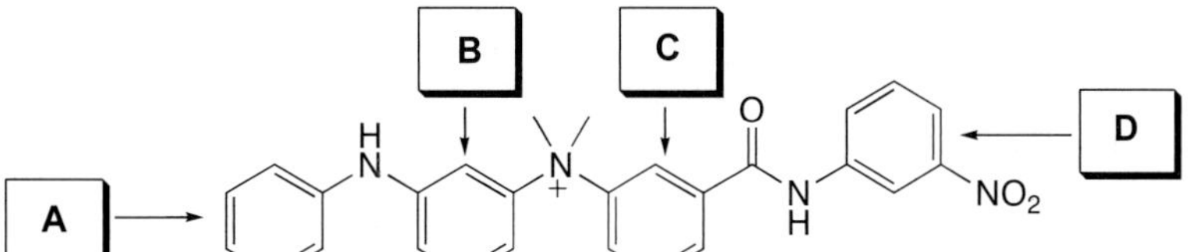
A
B
C
D
H
N
N
+
O
N
H
NO2

4. Classify each substituent as [1] ortho, para activating, [2] ortho, para deactivating, or [3] meta deactivating.

a. –Br
b. $–CH_2CH_2CH_2Br$
c. –COOH
d. $–NHCOCH_2CH_3$
e. $–N(CH_2)_6COCH_3$
f. $–CCl_3$

5. What reagents are needed to convert toluene ($C_6H_5CH_3$) to each compound?

a. C_6H_5COOH
b. $C_6H_5CH_2Br$
c. *p*-bromotoluene
d. *o*-nitrotoluene
e. *p*-ethyltoluene
f. 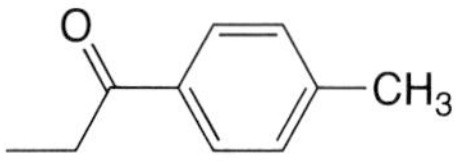
O
CH3

Answers to Practice Test

1. a. 3
   b. 4
   c. 4

2.

a. 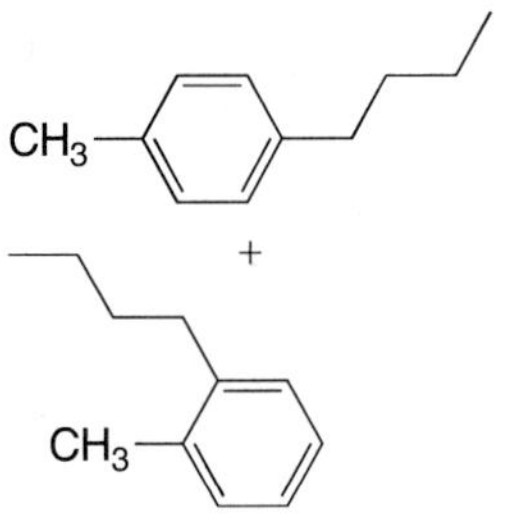

b. 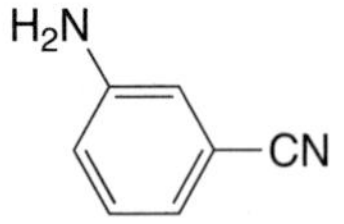

c. 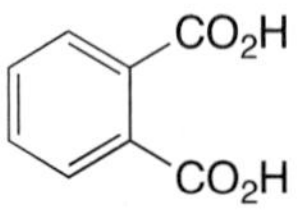

d. 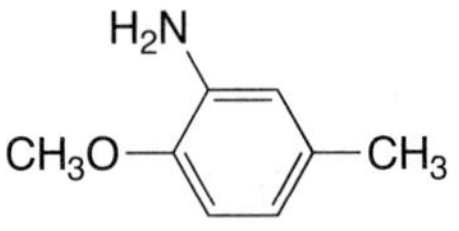

e. 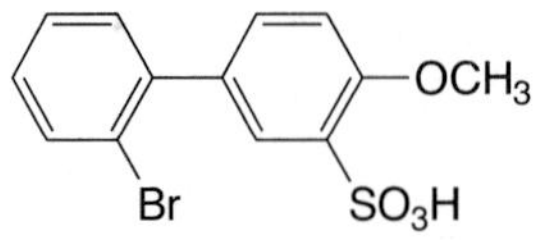

f. 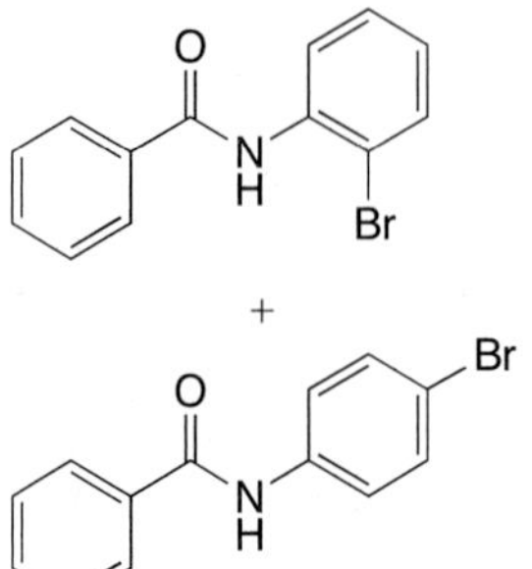

g. 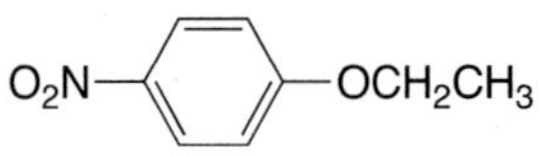

h. 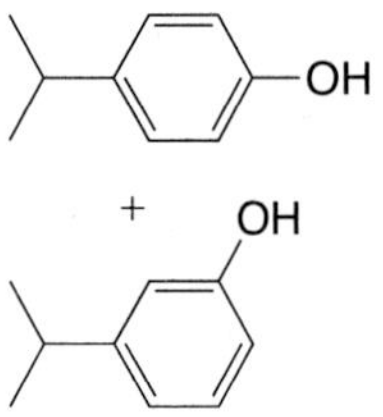

3. a. **A**
   b. **C**

4. a. 2
   b. 1
   c. 3
   d. 1
   e. 1
   f. 3

5. a. $KMnO_4$
   b. Br_2, *hν*
   c. Br_2, $FeBr_3$
   d. HNO_3, H_2SO_4
   e. CH_3CH_2Cl, $AlCl_3$
   f. CH_3CH_2COCl, $AlCl_3$

Answers to Problems

18.1 The π electrons of benzene are delocalized over the six atoms of the ring, increasing benzene's stability and making them less available for electron donation. With an alkene, the two π electrons are localized between the two C's, making them more nucleophilic and thus more reactive with an electrophile than the delocalized electrons in benzene.

18.2

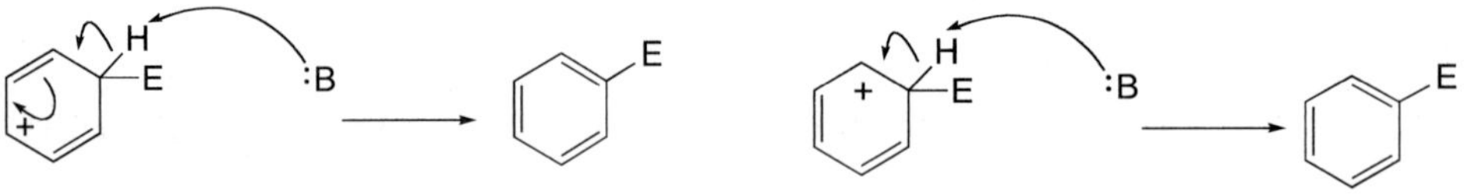

18.3 Reaction with Cl_2 and $FeCl_3$ as the catalyst occurs in two parts. First is the formation of an electrophile, followed by a two-step substitution reaction.

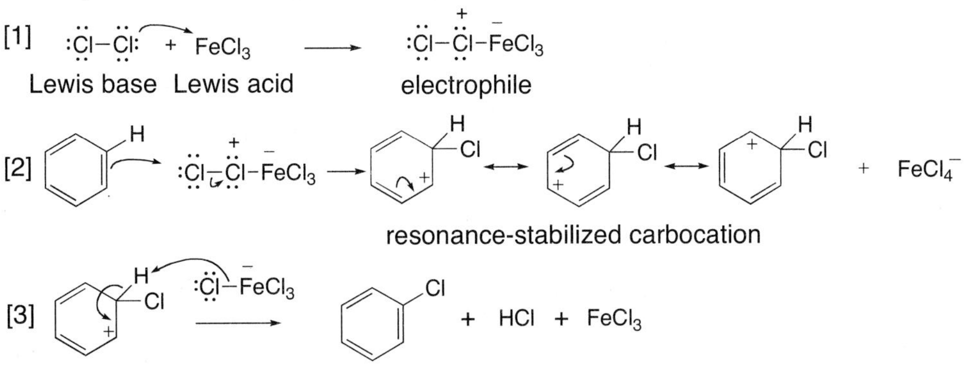
[1]
Lewis base Lewis acid
electrophile
[2]
+ FeCl4–
resonance-stabilized carbocation
[3]
+ HCl + FeCl3

18.4 There are two parts in the mechanism. The first part is formation of an electrophile. The second part is a two-step substitution reaction.

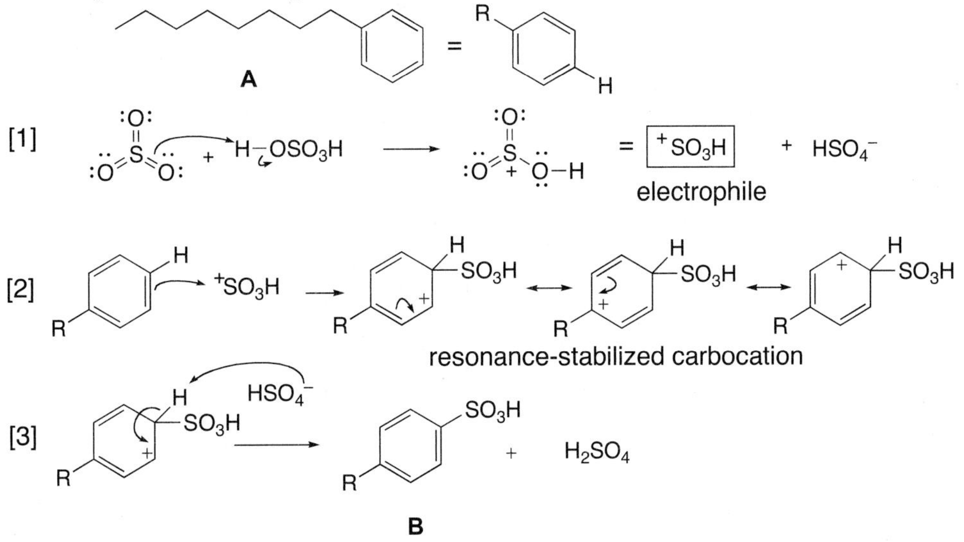
A
[1]
+SO3H
+ HSO4–
electrophile
[2]
resonance-stabilized carbocation
[3]
+ H2SO4
B

18.5 Friedel–Crafts alkylation results in the transfer of an alkyl group from a halogen to a benzene ring. In Friedel–Crafts acylation an acyl group is transferred from a halogen to a benzene ring.

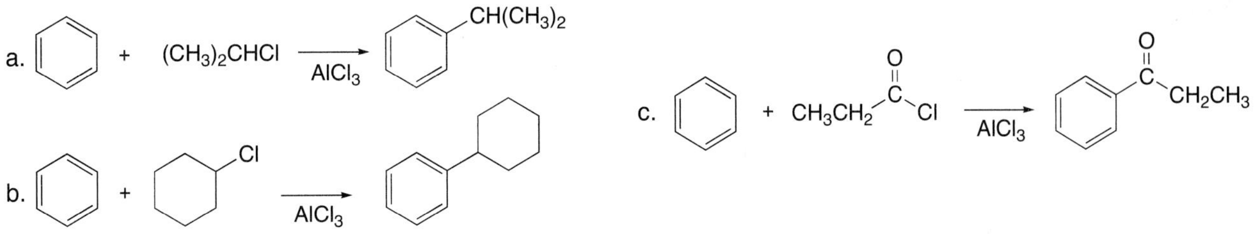
a.
(CH3)2CHCl
AlCl3
CH(CH3)2
b.
AlCl3
c.
CH3CH2
AlCl3
CH2CH3

18.6 Remember that an acyl group is transferred from a Cl atom to a benzene ring. To draw the acid chloride, substitute a Cl for the benzene ring.

a. 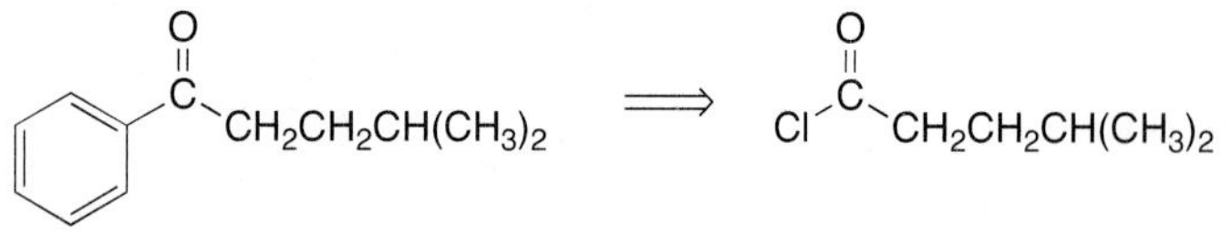

c. 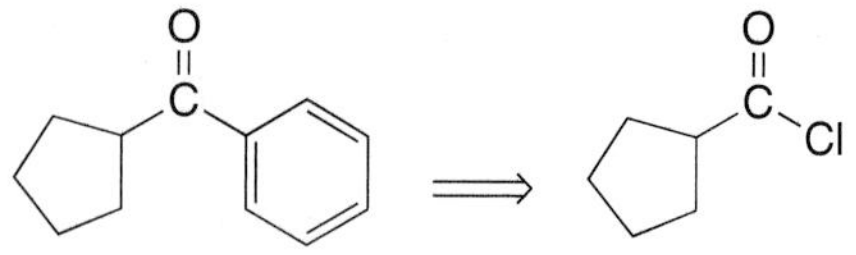

b. 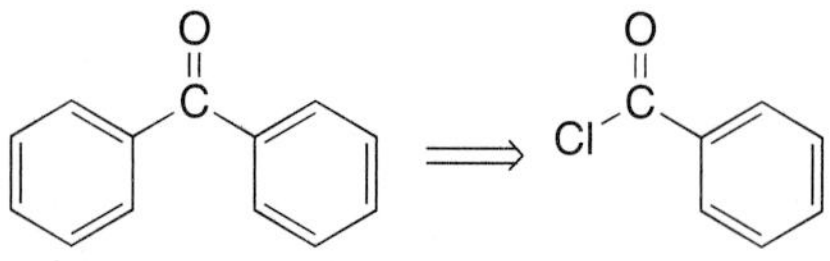

18.7 To be reactive in a Friedel–Crafts alkylation reaction, the X must be bonded to an sp^3 hybridized carbon atom.

a. 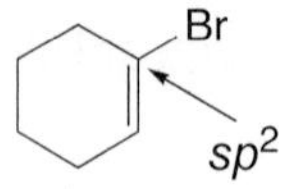

unreactive

b. 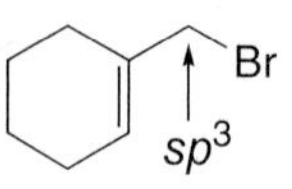

reactive

c. 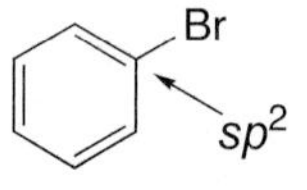

unreactive

d. 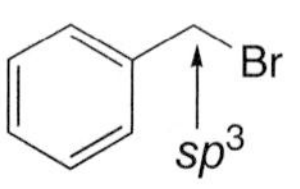

reactive

18.8 The product has an "unexpected" carbon skeleton, so rearrangement must have occurred.

[1] 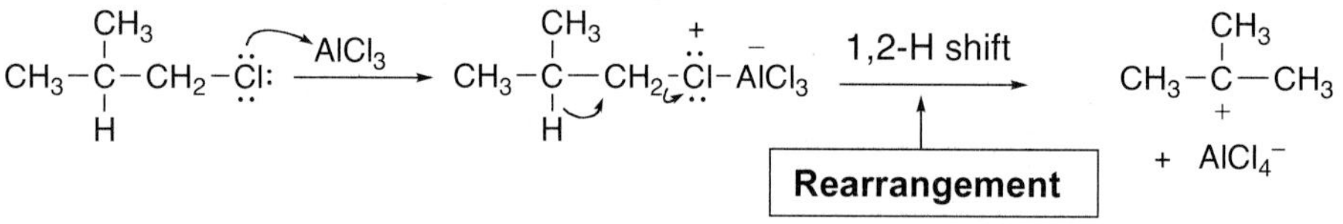

[2] 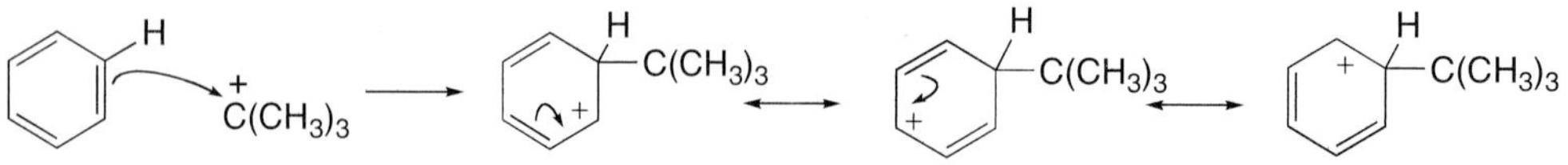

[3] 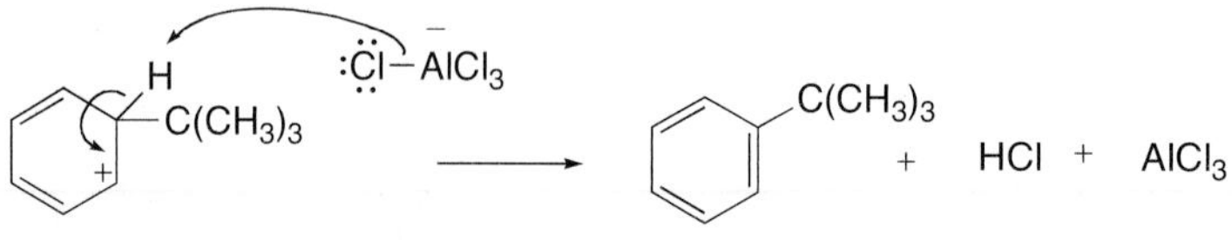

18.9 Both alkenes and alcohols can form carbocations for Friedel–Crafts alkylation reactions.

a. 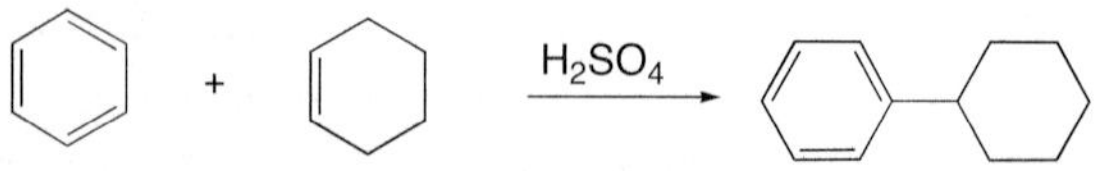

c. 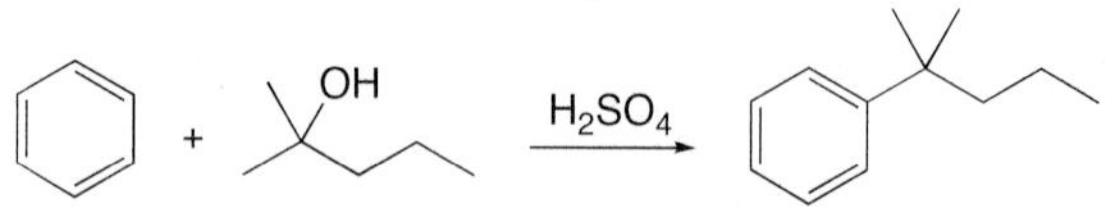

b. 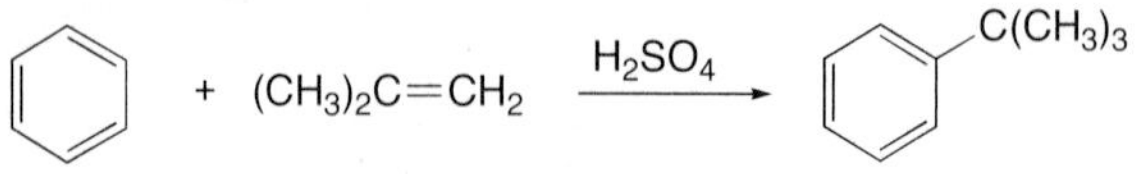

d. 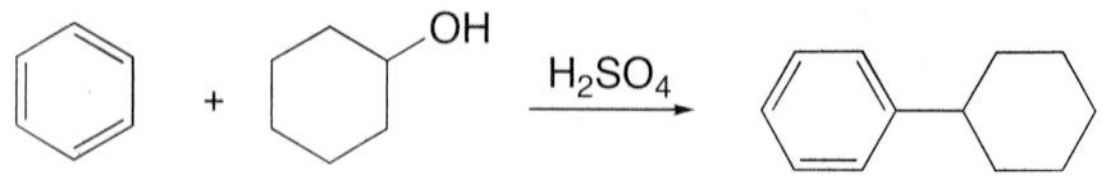

18.10

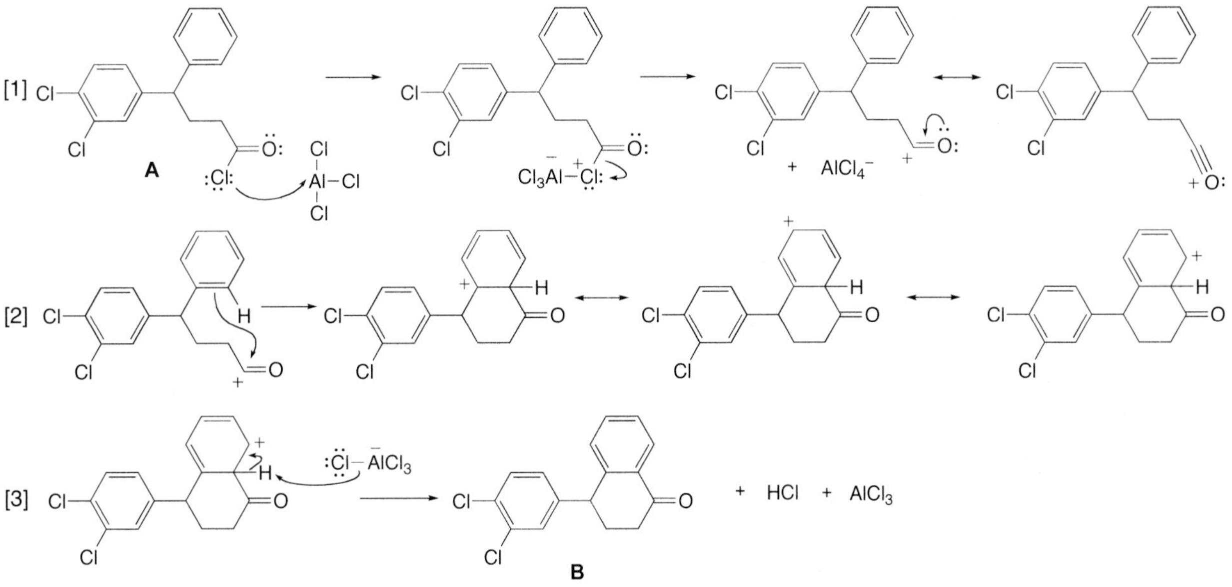

18.11 In parts (b) and (c), a 1,2-shift occurs to afford a rearrangement product.

a.

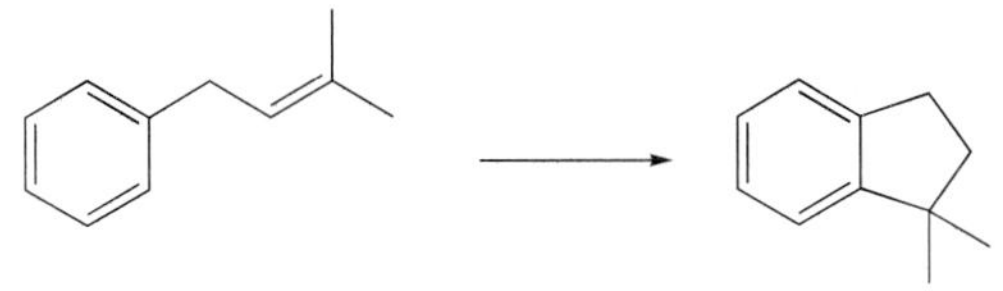

c.

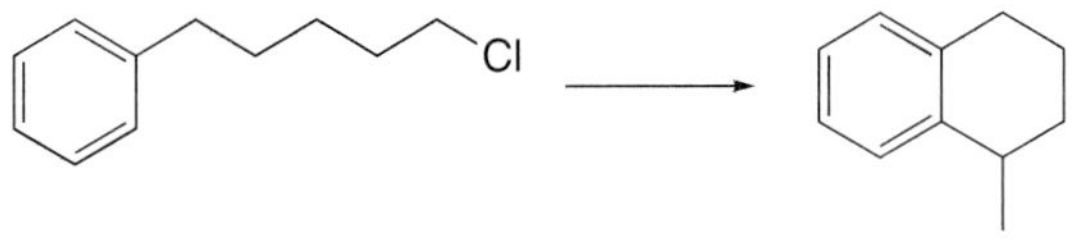

b.

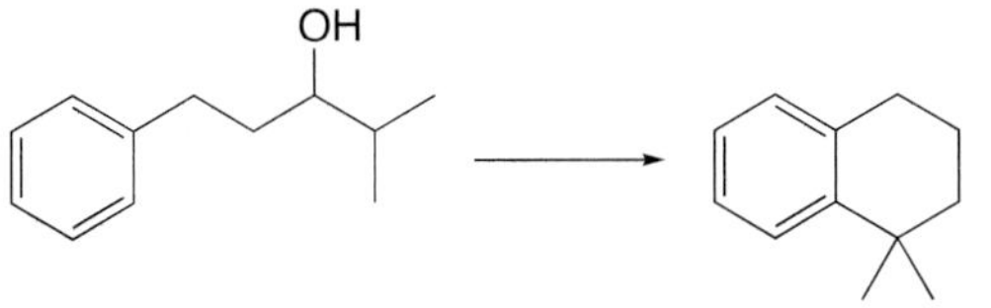

18.12

a. $-CH_2CH_2CH_2CH_3$
alkyl group
electron donating

b. $-Br$
halide
electron withdrawing

c. $-OCH_2CH_3$
electronegative O
electron withdrawing

18.13 Electron-donating groups place a negative charge in the benzene ring. Draw the resonance structures to show how $-OCH_3$ puts a negative charge in the ring. Electron-withdrawing groups place a positive charge in the benzene ring. Draw the resonance structures to show how $-COCH_3$ puts a positive charge in the ring.

a.

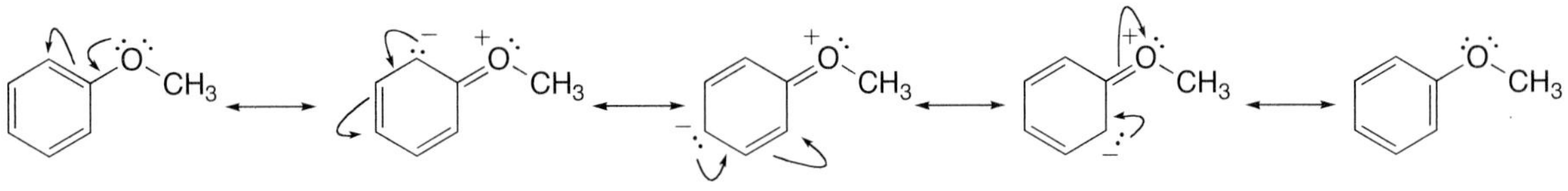

b.

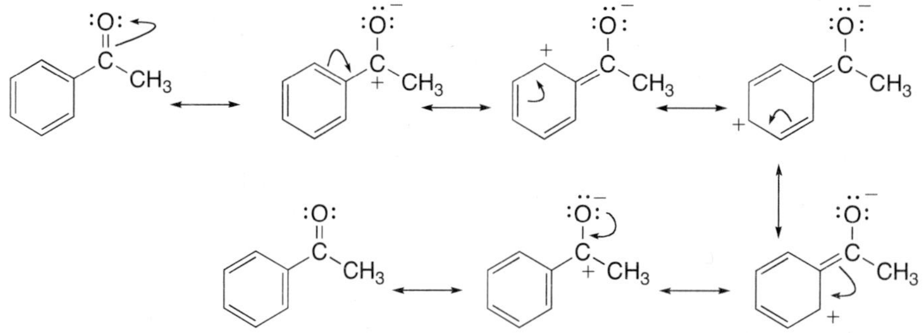

18.14 To classify each substituent, look at the atom bonded directly to the benzene ring. All R groups and Z groups (except halogens) are electron donating. All groups with a positive charge, δ^+, or halogens are electron withdrawing.

a.

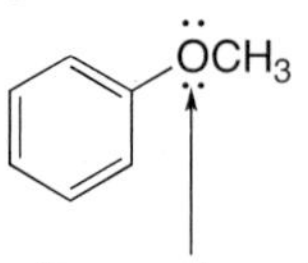

lone pair on O
electron donating

b.

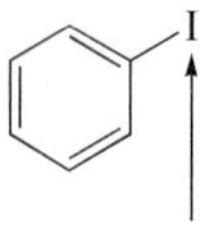

halogen
electron withdrawing

c.

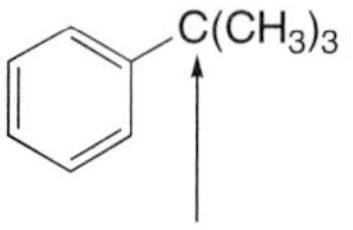

R group
electron donating

18.15 **Electron-donating groups** make the compound ***react faster*** than benzene in electrophilic aromatic substitution. **Electron-withdrawing groups** make the compound ***react more slowly*** than benzene in electrophilic aromatic substitution.

a.

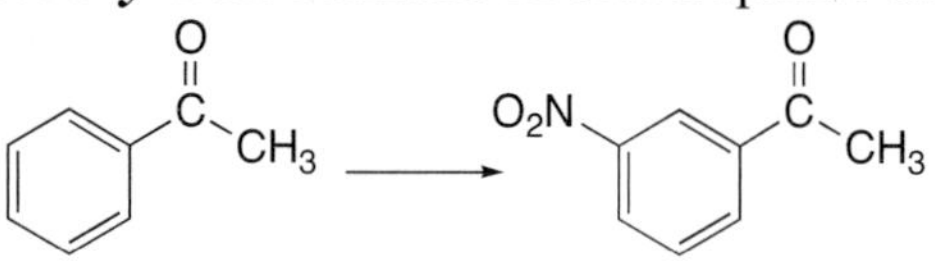

electron withdrawing
reacts slower

b.

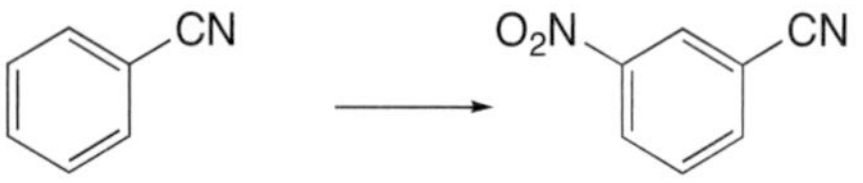

electron withdrawing
reacts slower

c.

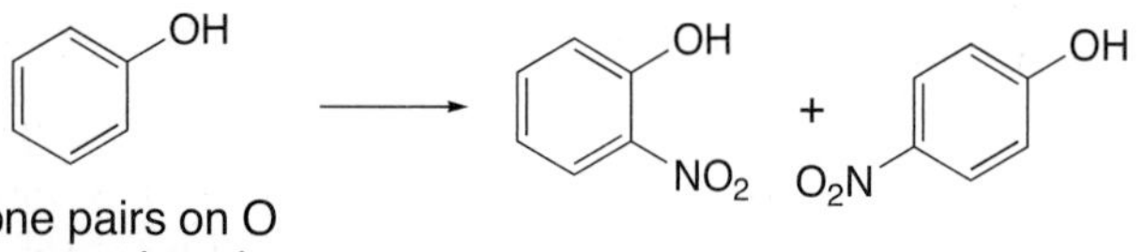

lone pairs on O
electron donating
reacts faster

d.

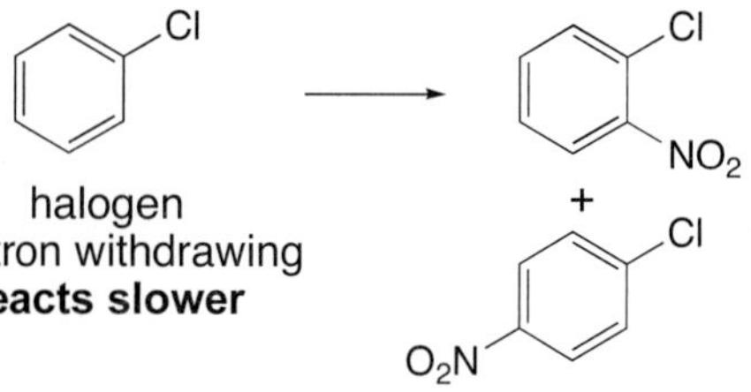

halogen
electron withdrawing
reacts slower

e.

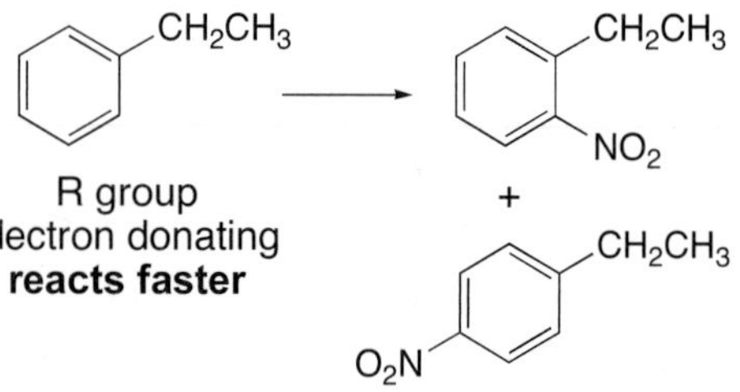

R group
electron donating
reacts faster

18.16 **Electron-donating groups** make the compound ***more reactive*** than benzene in electrophilic aromatic substitution. **Electron-withdrawing groups** make the compound ***less reactive*** than benzene in electrophilic aromatic substitution.

a.

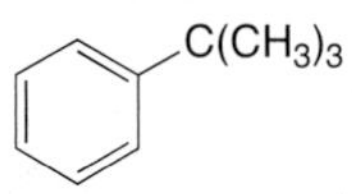

R group
electron donating
more reactive

b.

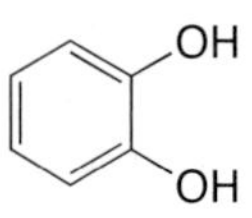

two OH's
electron donating
more reactive

c.

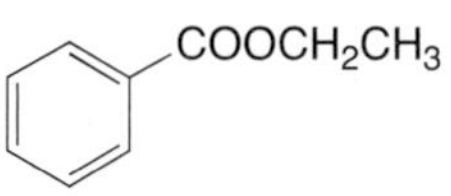

C with 2 electronegative O's
electron withdrawing
less reactive

d.

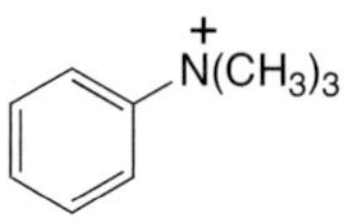

electron withdrawing
less reactive

18.17

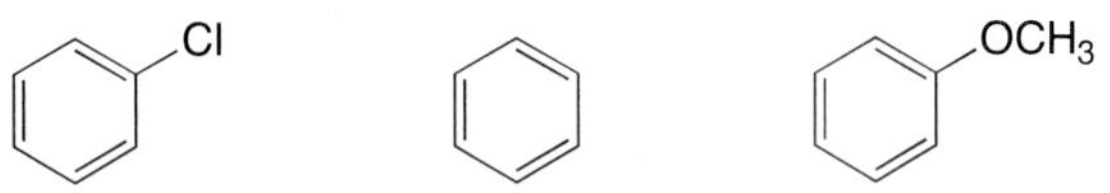

halogen electron withdrawing **least reactive** | **intermediate reactivity** | lone pairs on O electron donating **most reactive**

18.18 Chlorine inductively withdraws electron density and decreases the rate of electrophilic aromatic substitution. The closer the Cl is to the ring, the larger the effect it has. The larger the number of Cl's, the larger the effect.

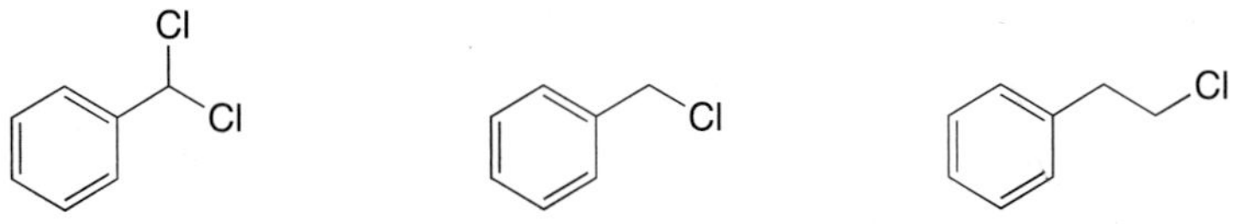

least reactive | **intermediate reactivity** | **most reactive**

18.19 Especially stable resonance structures have all atoms with an octet. Carbocations with additional electron donor R groups are also more stable structures. Especially unstable resonance structures have adjacent like charges.

a.

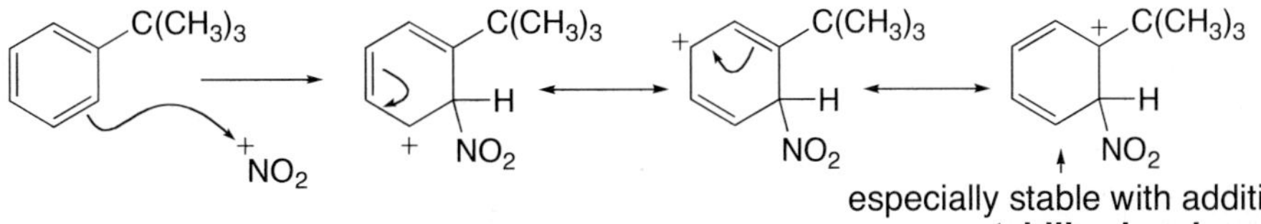

especially stable with additional R group
stabilized carbocation

b.

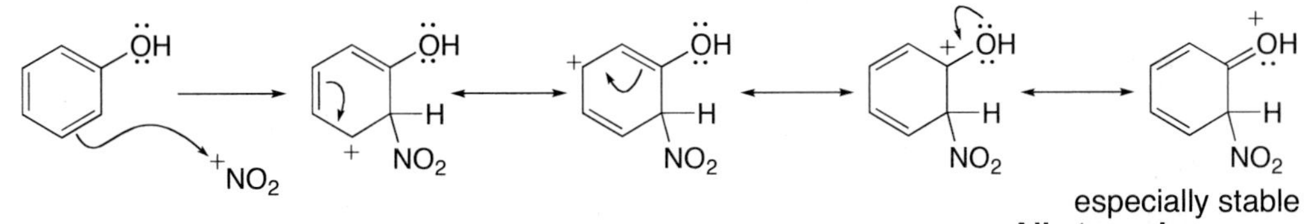

especially stable
All atoms have an octet.

c.

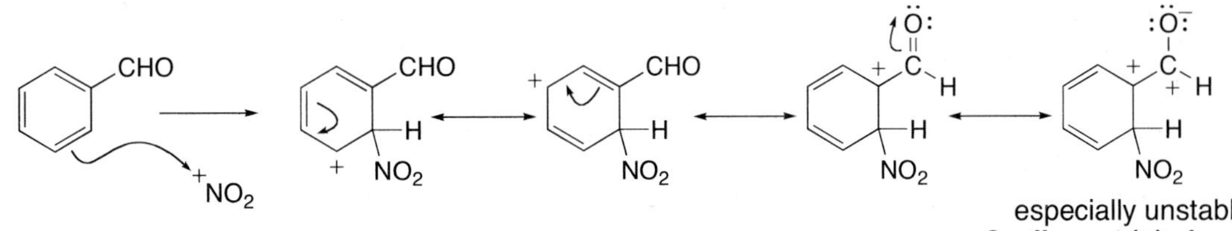

especially unstable
2 adjacent (+) charges

18.20 Polyhalogenation occurs with highly activated benzene rings containing OH, NH_2, and related groups with a catalyst.

a.

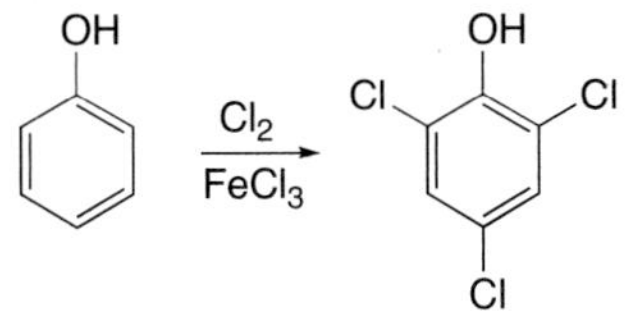

b.

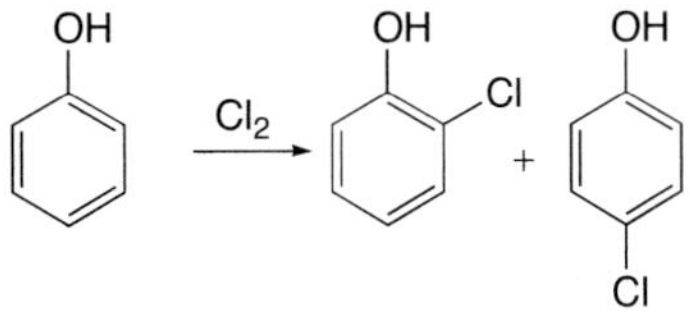

c.

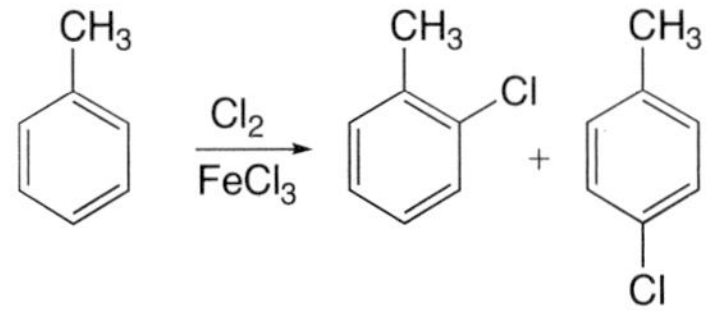

18.21 Friedel–Crafts reactions do not occur with strongly deactivating substituents including NO_2, or with NH_2, NR_2, or NHR groups.

a.
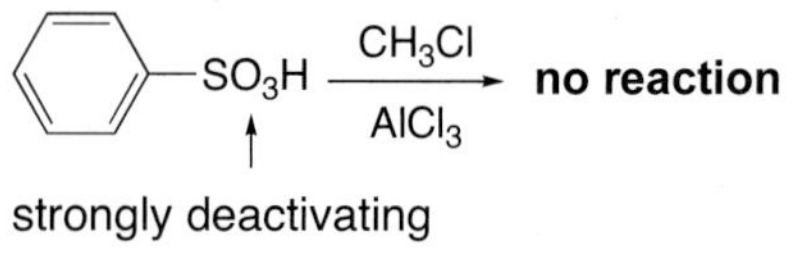

c.
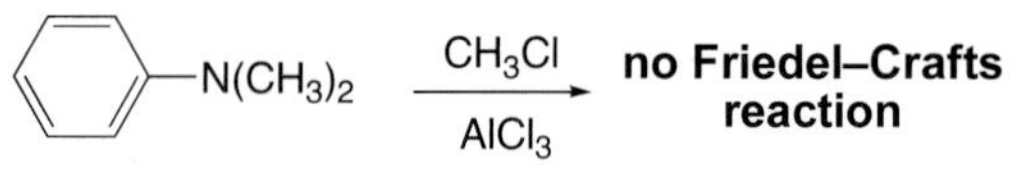

b.
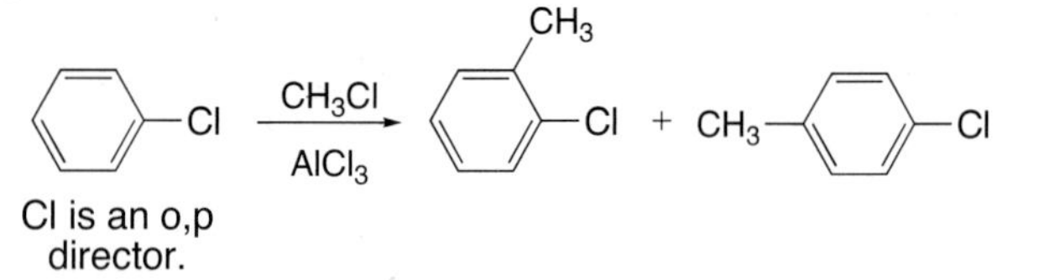

d.
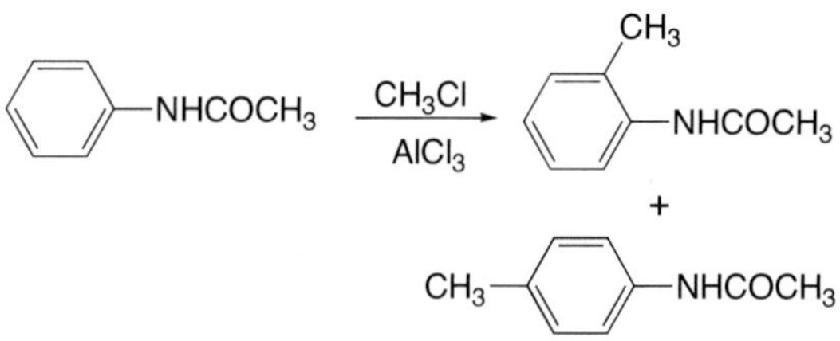

18.22 To draw the product of reaction with these disubstituted benzene derivatives and HNO_3, H_2SO_4 remember:

- If the two directing effects reinforce each other, the new substituent will be on the position reinforced by both.
- If the directing effects oppose each other, the stronger activator wins.
- No substitution occurs between two meta substituents.

a.
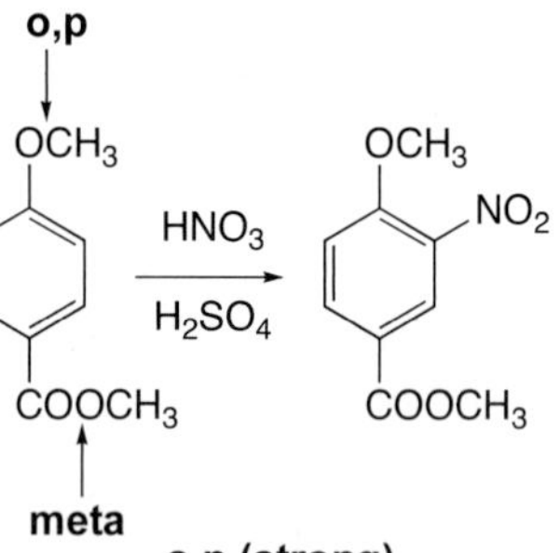

c.
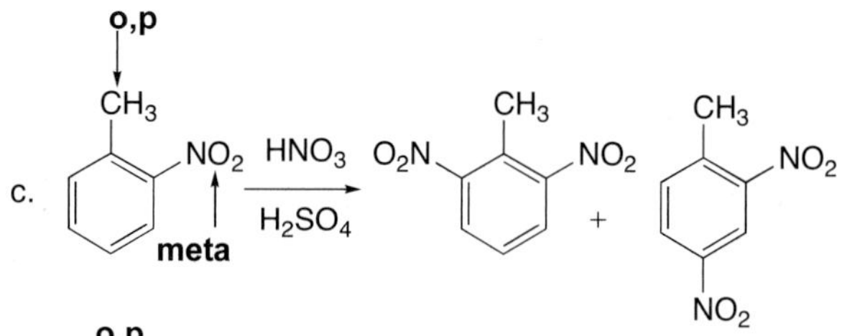

b.
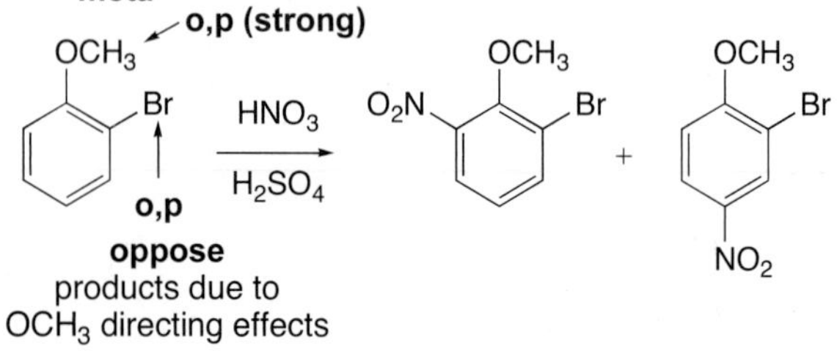

d.
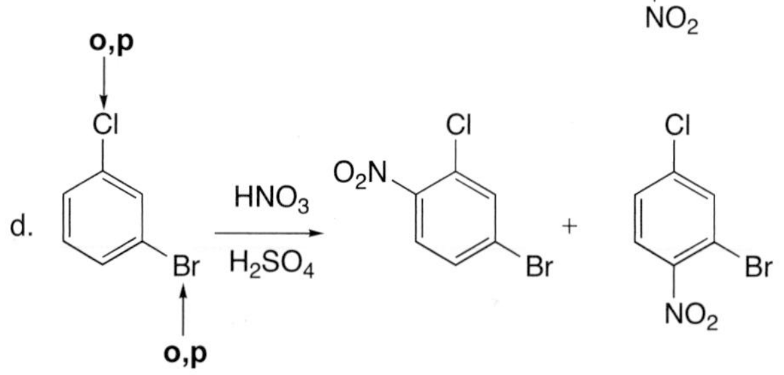

18.23

a.
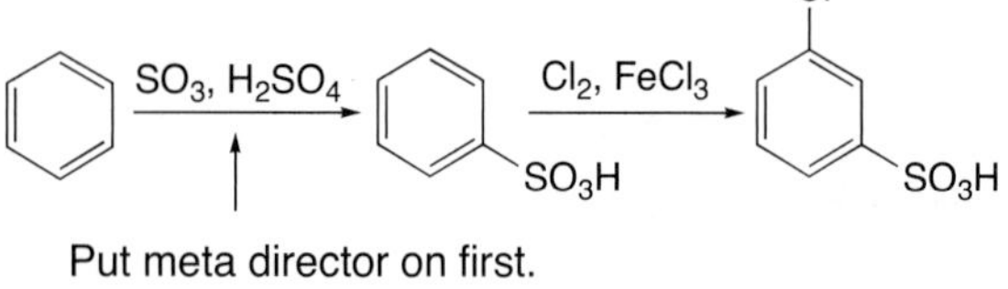

c.
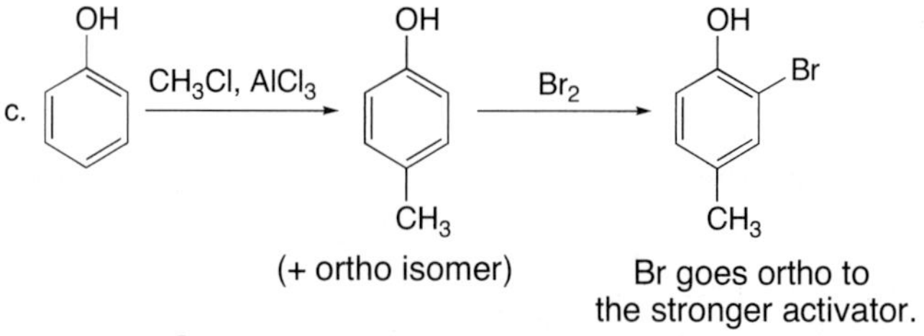

b.
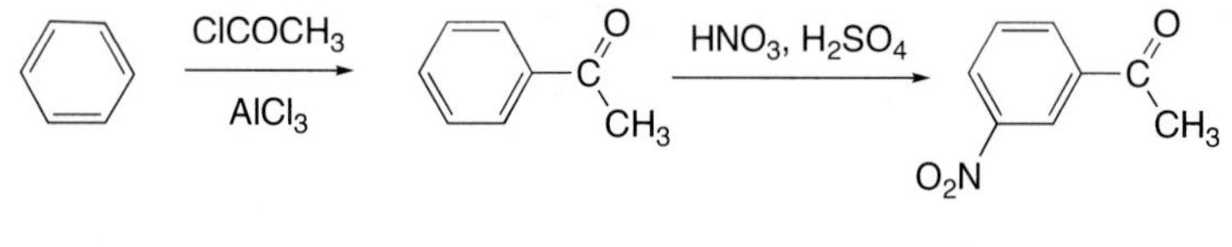

18.24

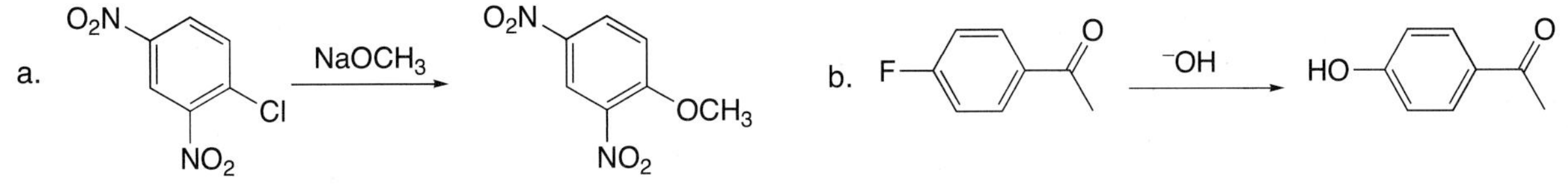

18.25

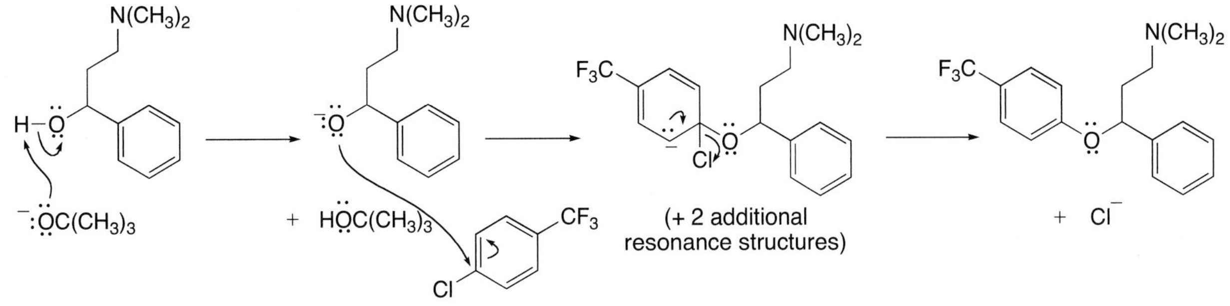

18.26

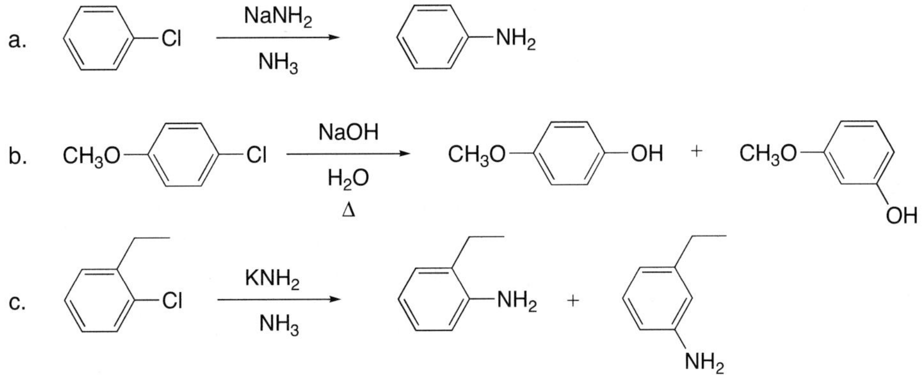

18.27

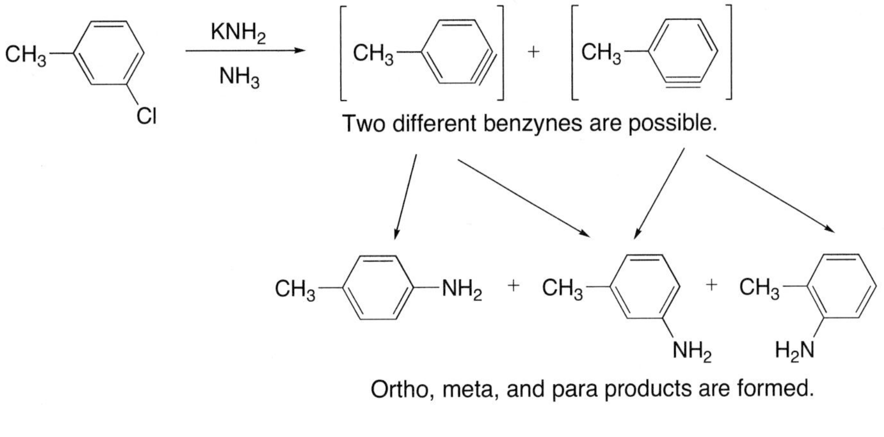

18.28 This reaction proceeds via a radical bromination mechanism and two radicals are possible: **A** (2° and benzylic) and **B** (1°). Since **B** (which leads to $C_6H_5CH_2CH_2Br$) is much less stable, this radical is not formed so only $C_6H_5CH(Br)CH_3$ is formed as product.

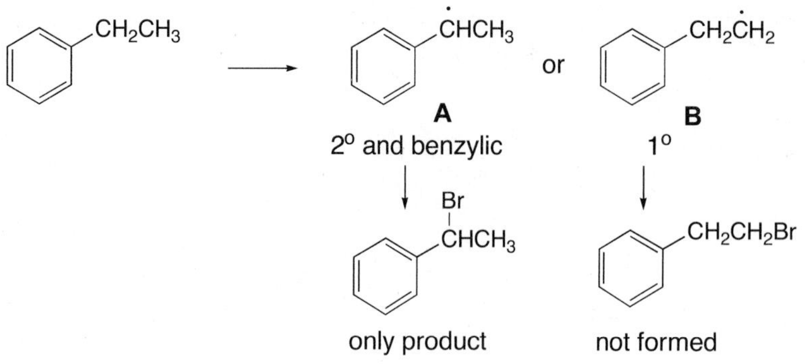

18.29

a.
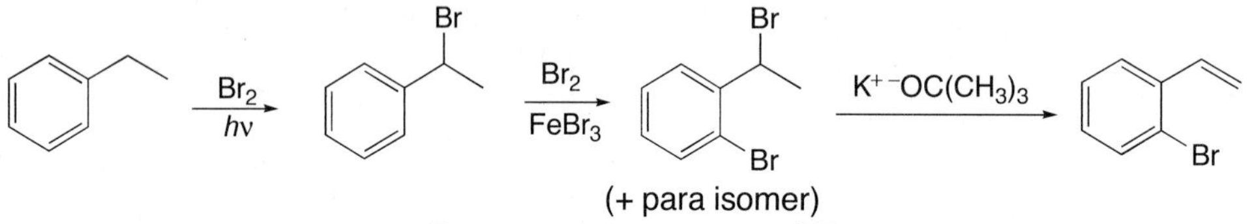

b.
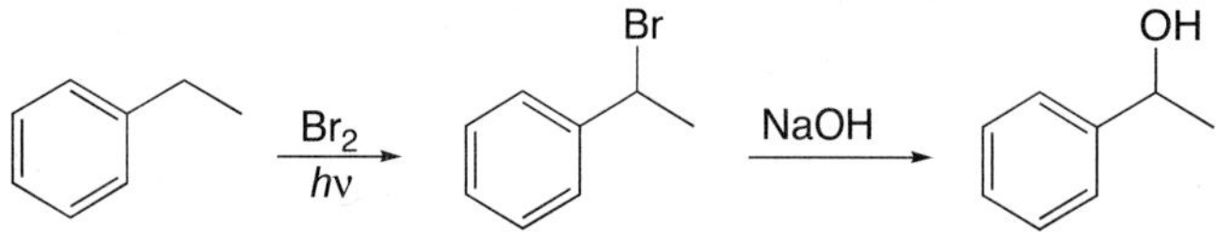

c.
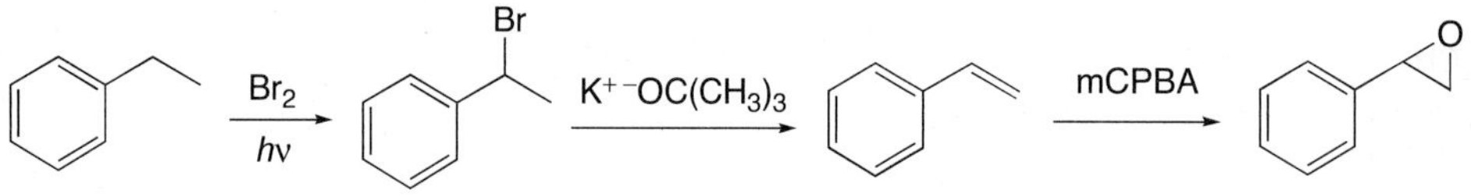

d.
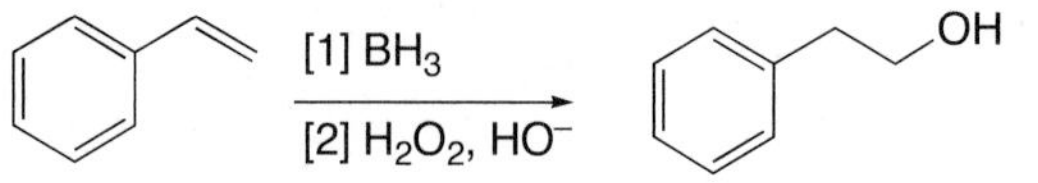

(from c.)

18.30 First use an acylation reaction, and then reduce the carbonyl group to form the alkyl benzenes.

a.
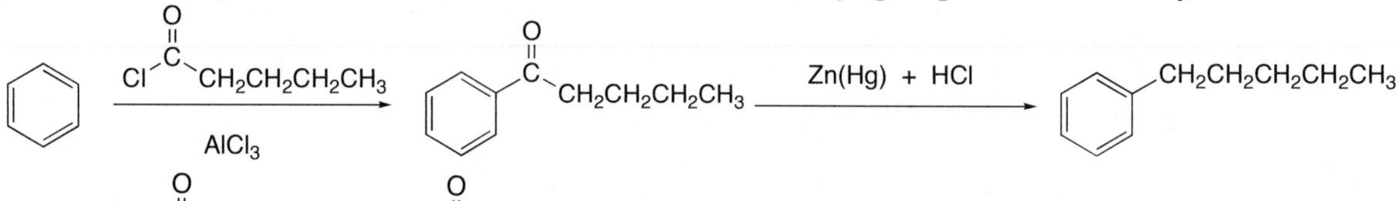

b.
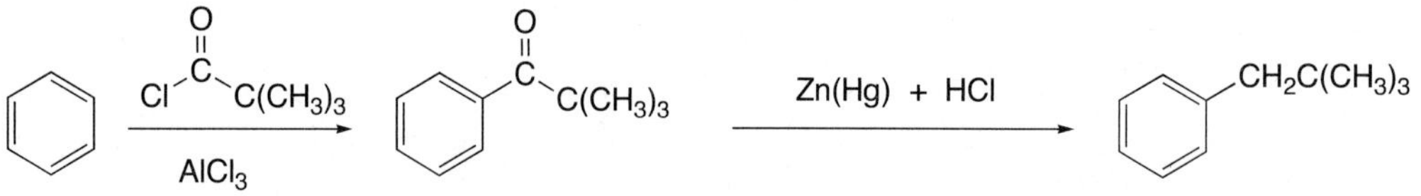

18.31

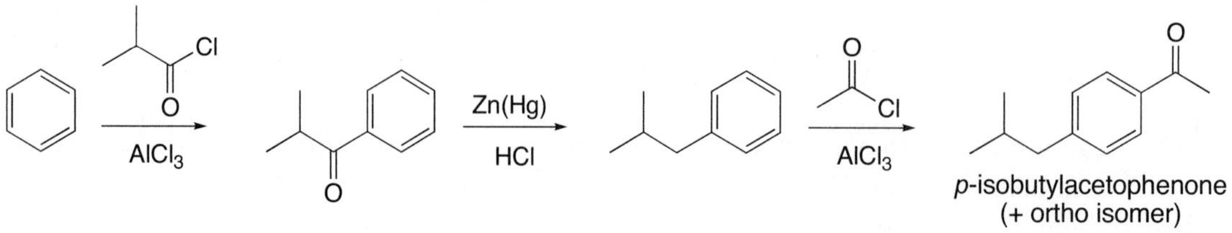

p-isobutylacetophenone
(+ ortho isomer)

18.32

a. 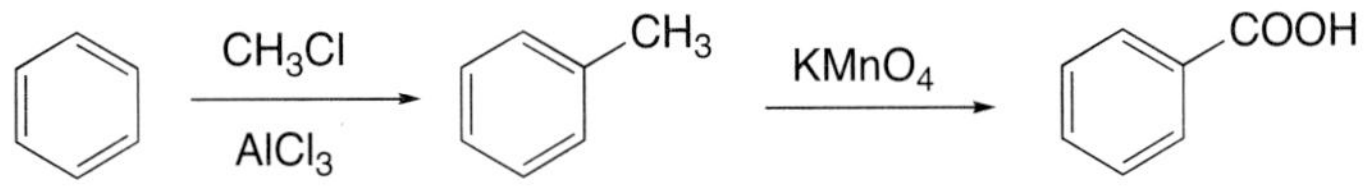

b. 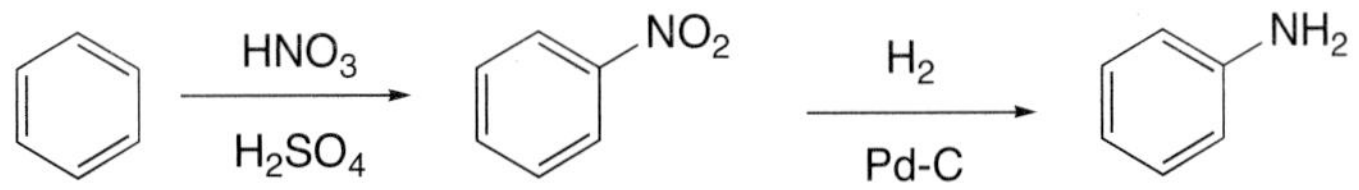

c. 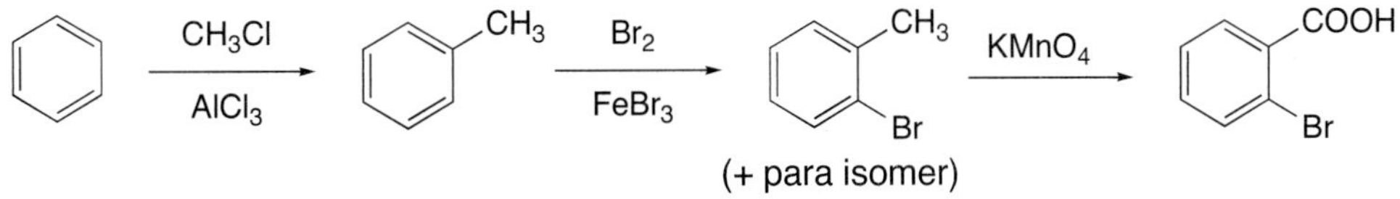

18.33

a. 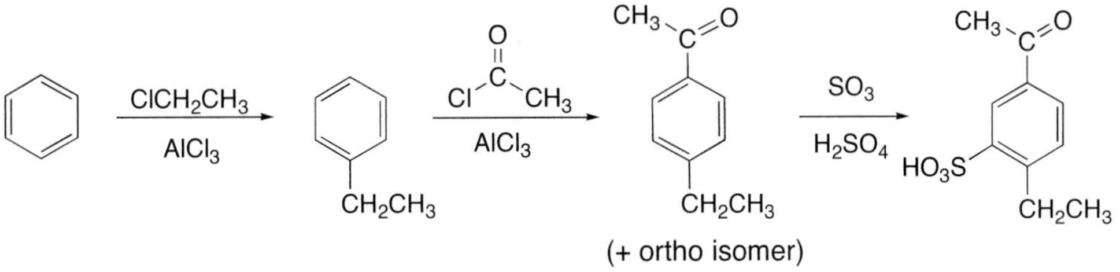

b. 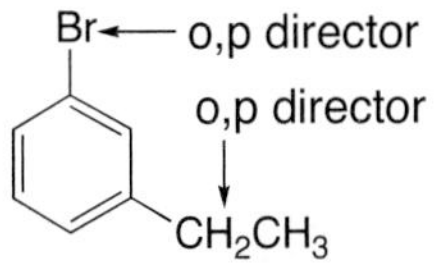

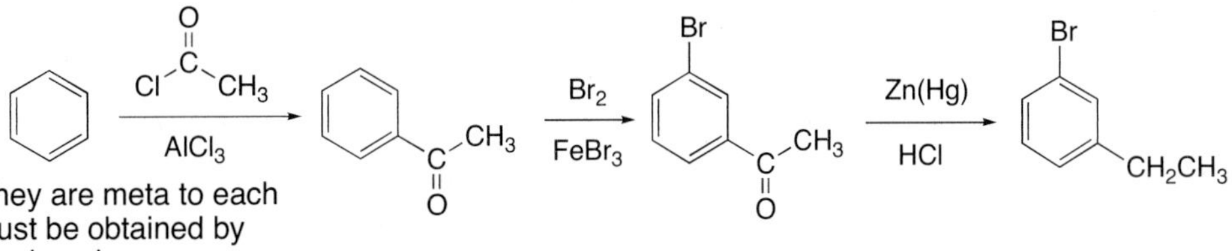

Both are o,p directors, but they are meta to each other. The alkyl group must be obtained by reduction of a carbonyl.

c. 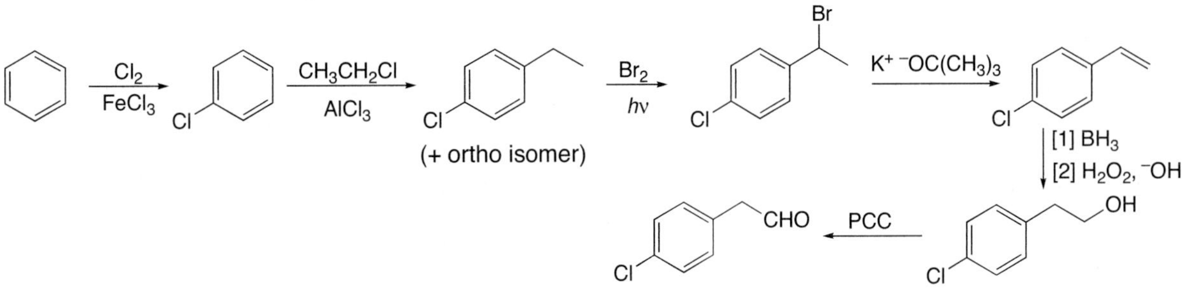

18.34

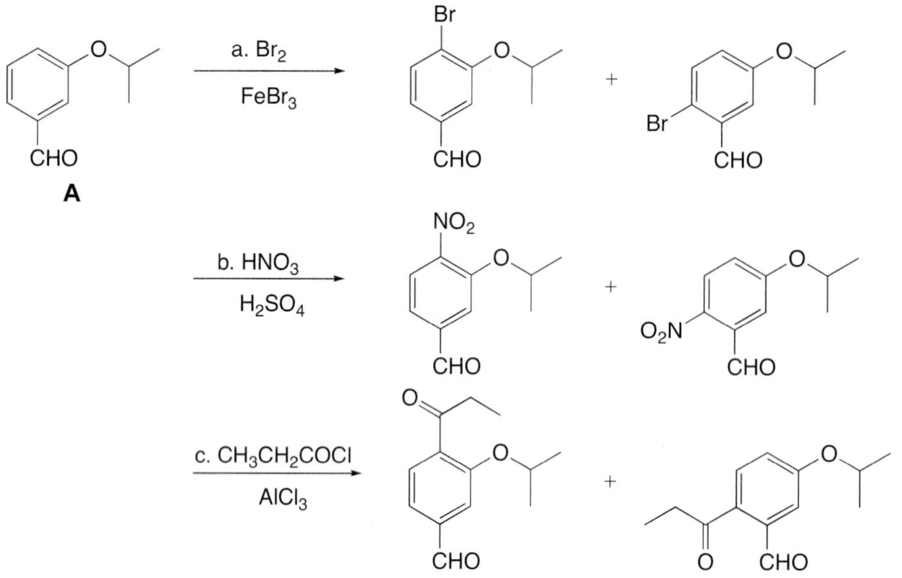

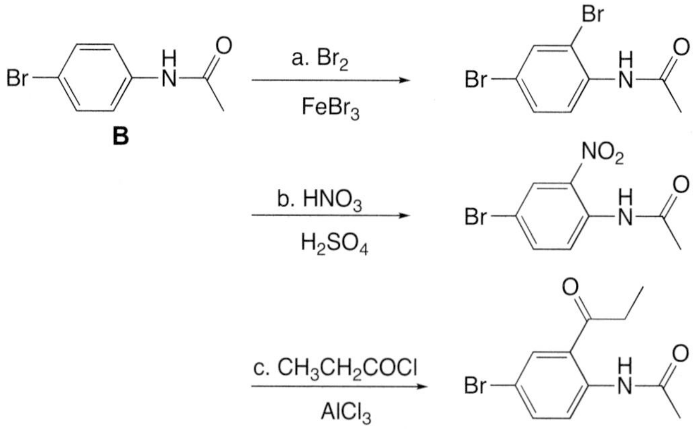

18.35 Intramolecular Friedel–Crafts acylation occurs on the more activated aromatic ring.

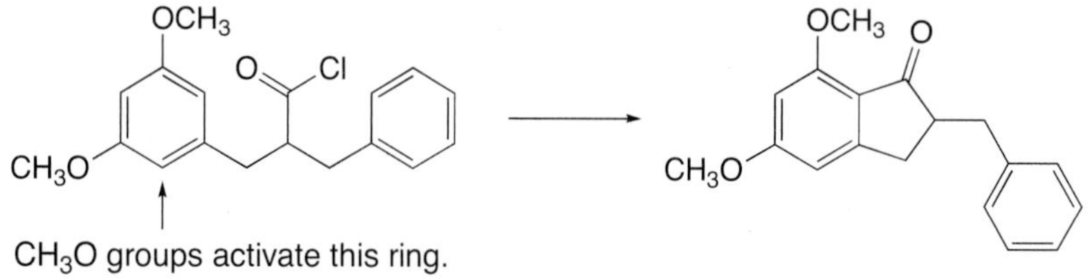

18.36 OH is an ortho, para director.

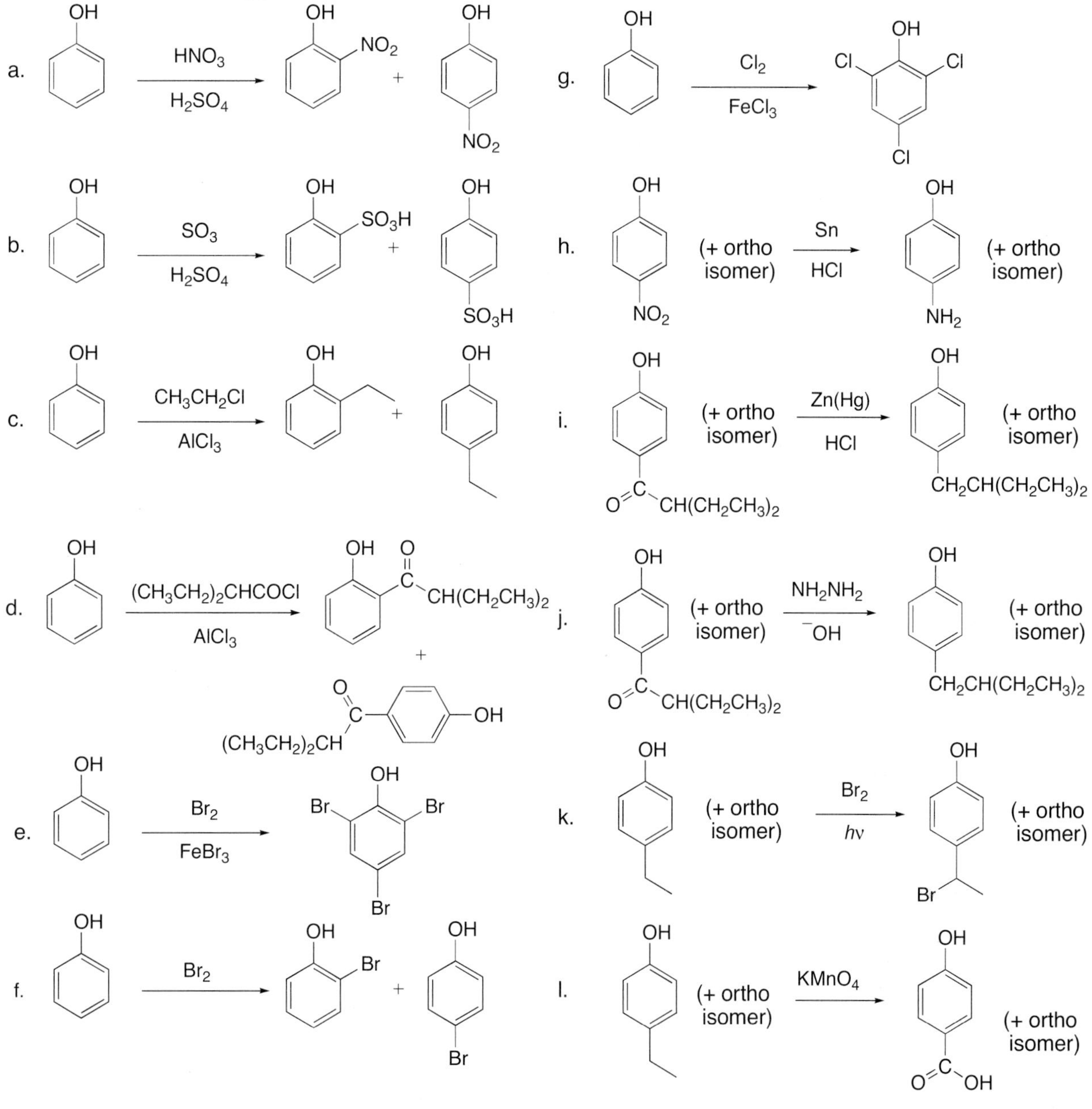

18.37

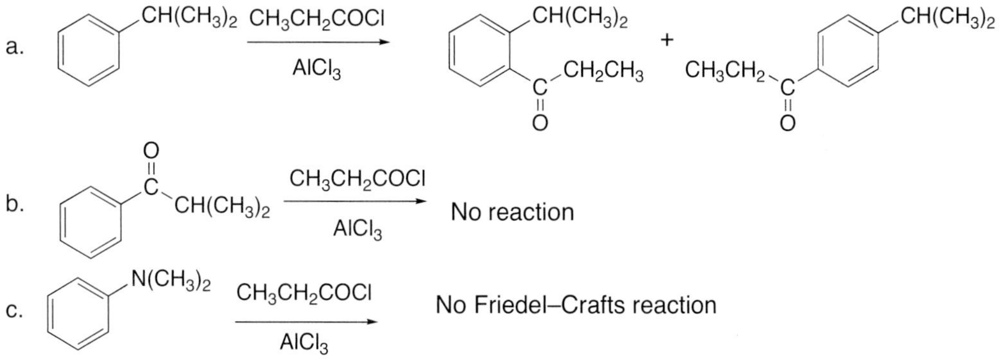

d. 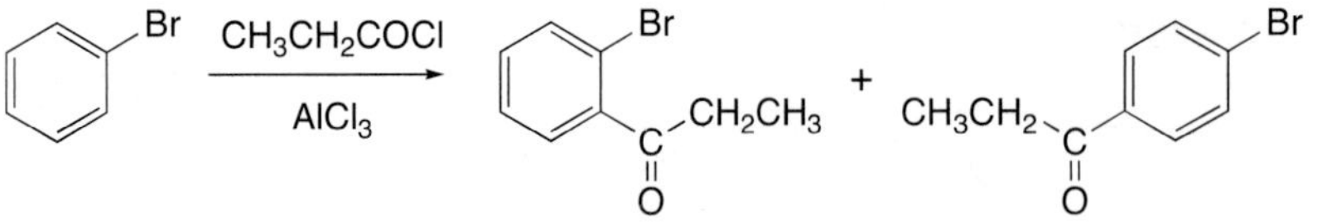

e. 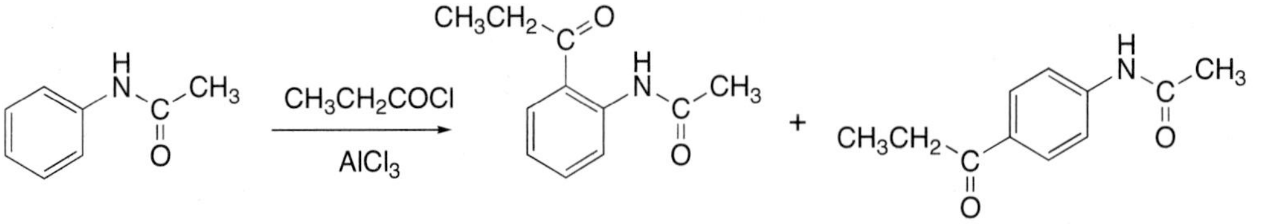

18.38

a. 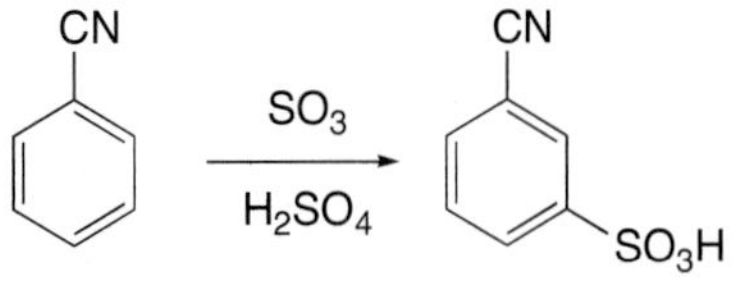

b. 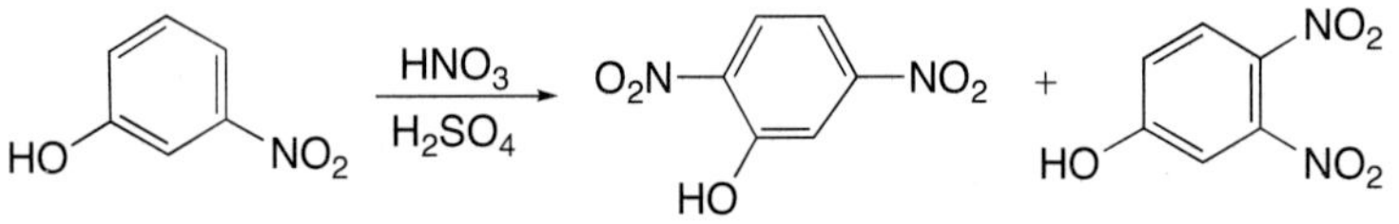

c. 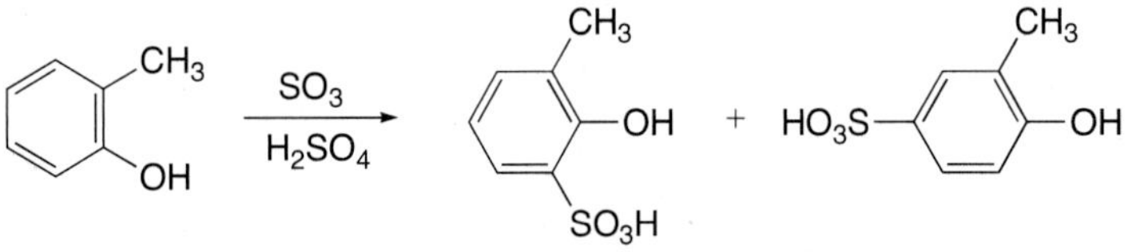

d. 

e. 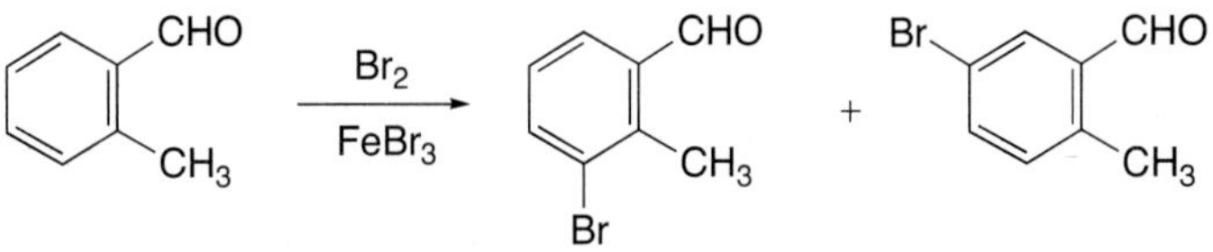

f. 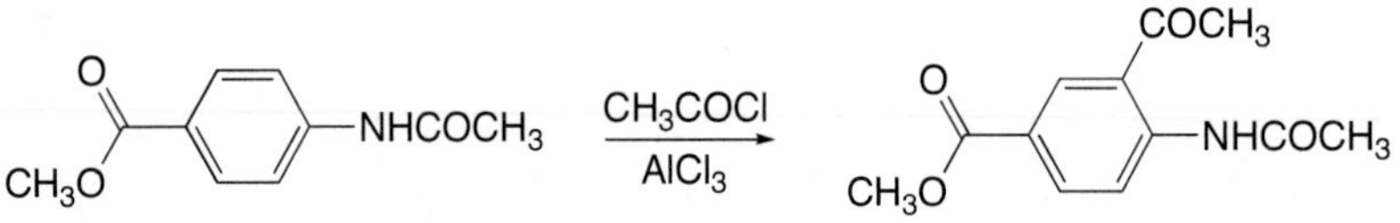

g. 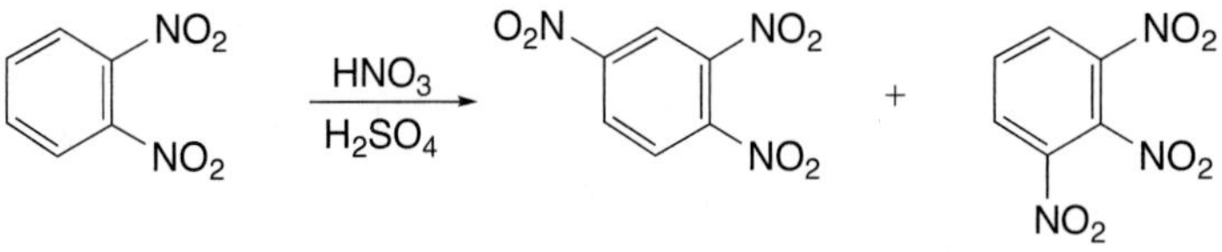

h. 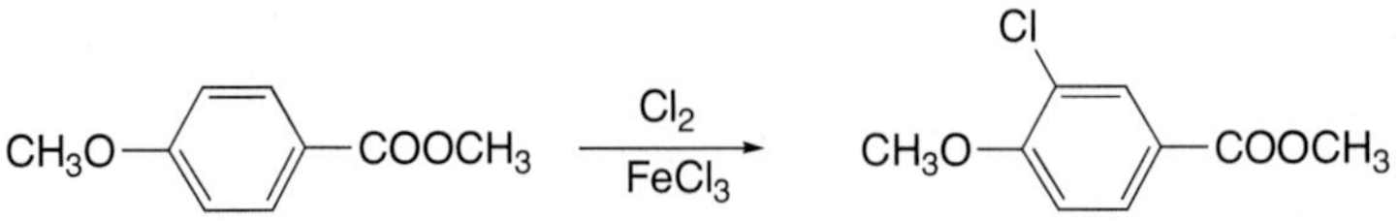

i. 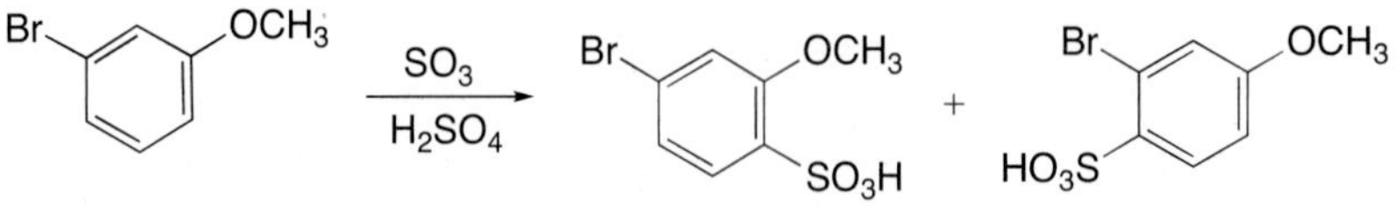

j. 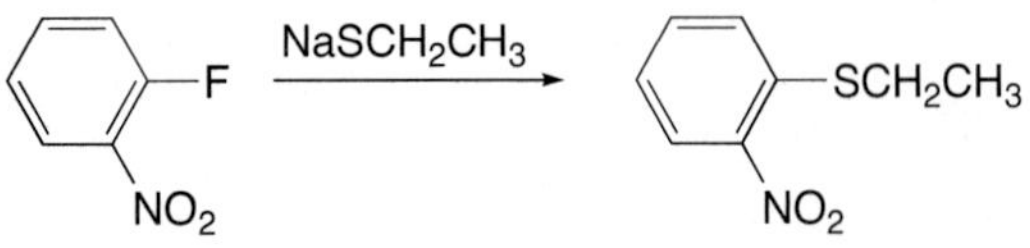

18.39 Watch out for rearrangements.

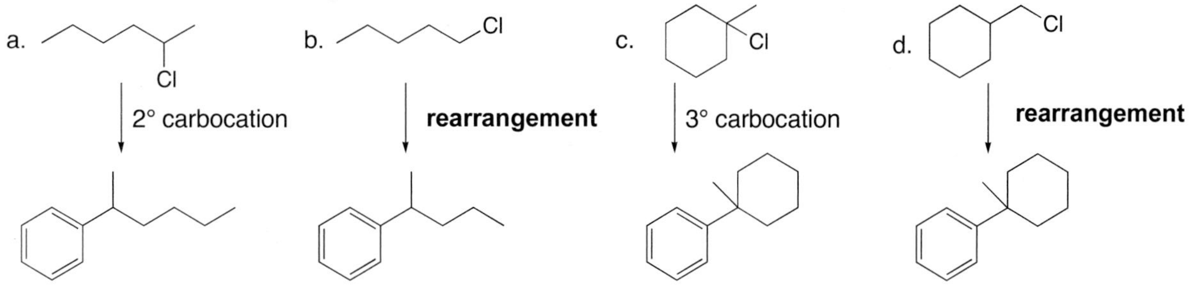
a.
Cl
2° carbocation
b.
Cl
rearrangement
c.
Cl
3° carbocation
d.
Cl
rearrangement

18.40

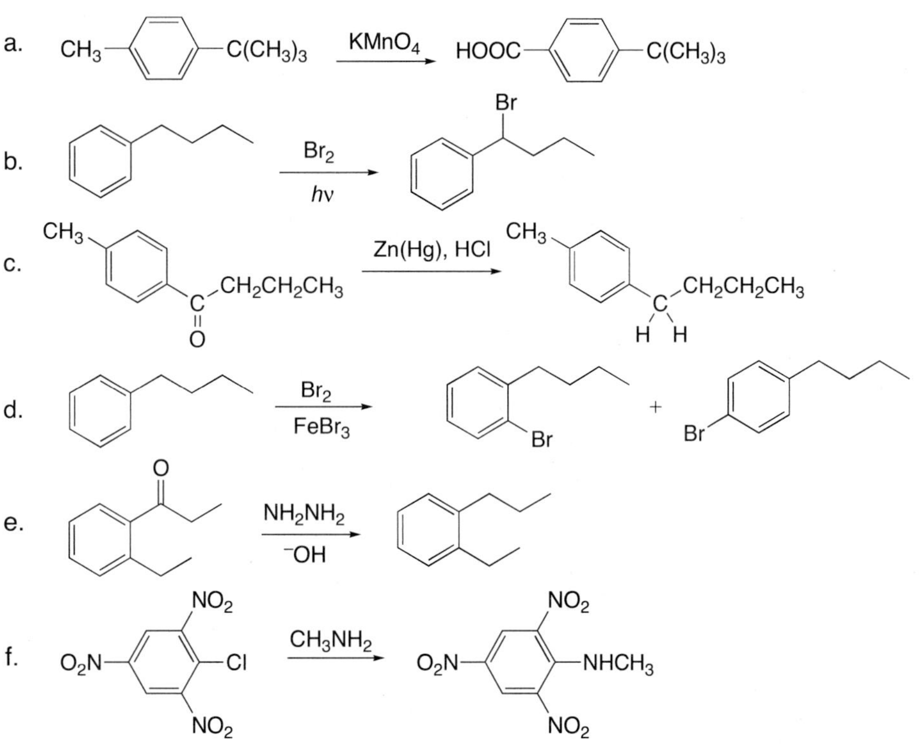
a.
CH3
C(CH3)3
KMnO4
HOOC
C(CH3)3
b.
Br2
hν
Br
c.
CH3
C
O
CH2CH2CH3
Zn(Hg), HCl
CH3
C
H H
CH2CH2CH3
d.
Br2
FeBr3
Br
+
Br
e.
O
NH2NH2
-OH
f.
NO2
O2N
Cl
NO2
CH3NH2
NO2
O2N
NHCH3
NO2

18.41

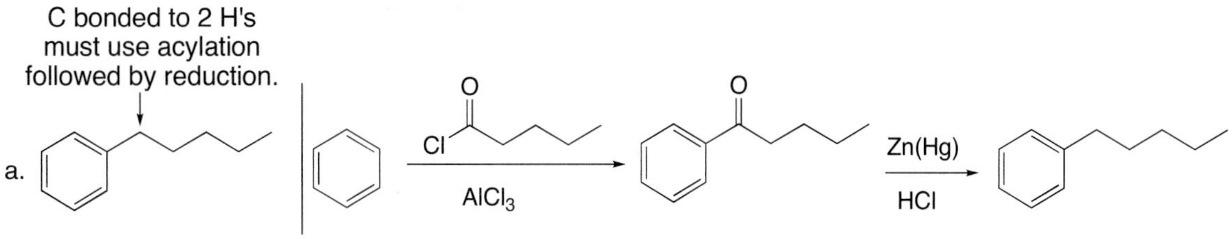
C bonded to 2 H's
must use acylation
followed by reduction.
a.
O
Cl
AlCl3
O
Zn(Hg)
HCl

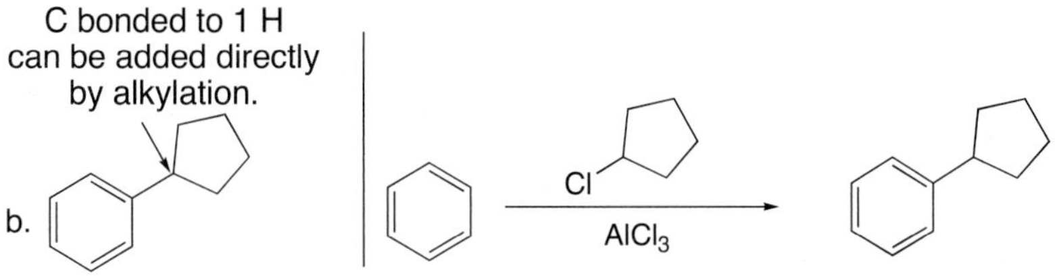
C bonded to 1 H
can be added directly
by alkylation.
b.
Cl
AlCl3

c. 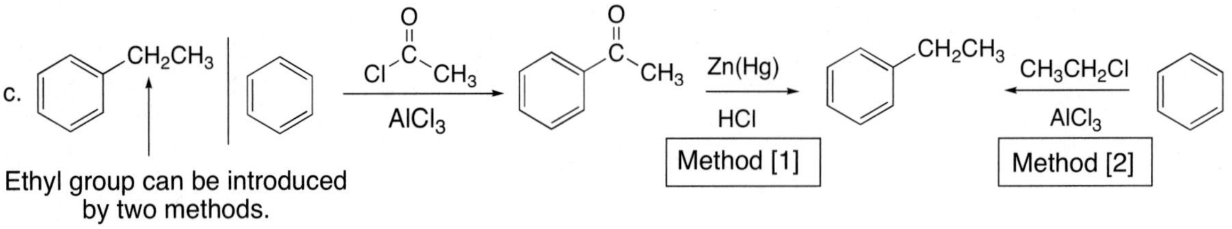
CH2CH3
Ethyl group can be introduced by two methods.
O
Cl C CH3
AlCl3
CH3
Zn(Hg)
HCl
Method [1]
CH2CH3
CH3CH2Cl
AlCl3
Method [2]

d. 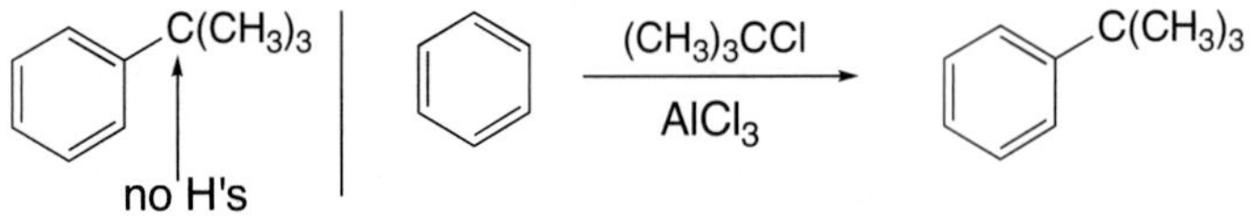
C(CH3)3
no H's
(CH3)3CCl
AlCl3
C(CH3)3

18.42

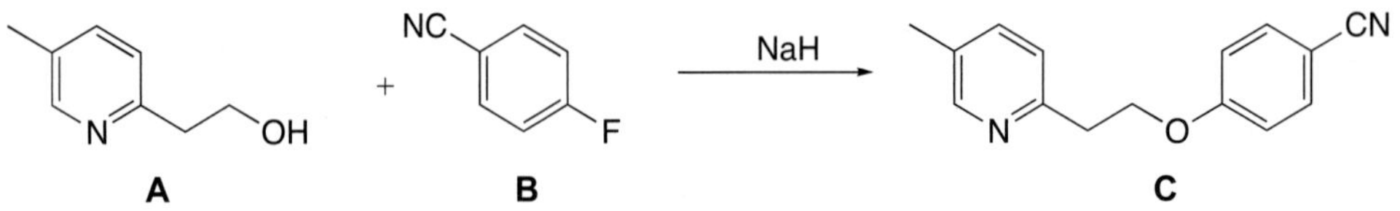
N
OH
A
NC
F
B
NaH
CN
N
O
C

18.43

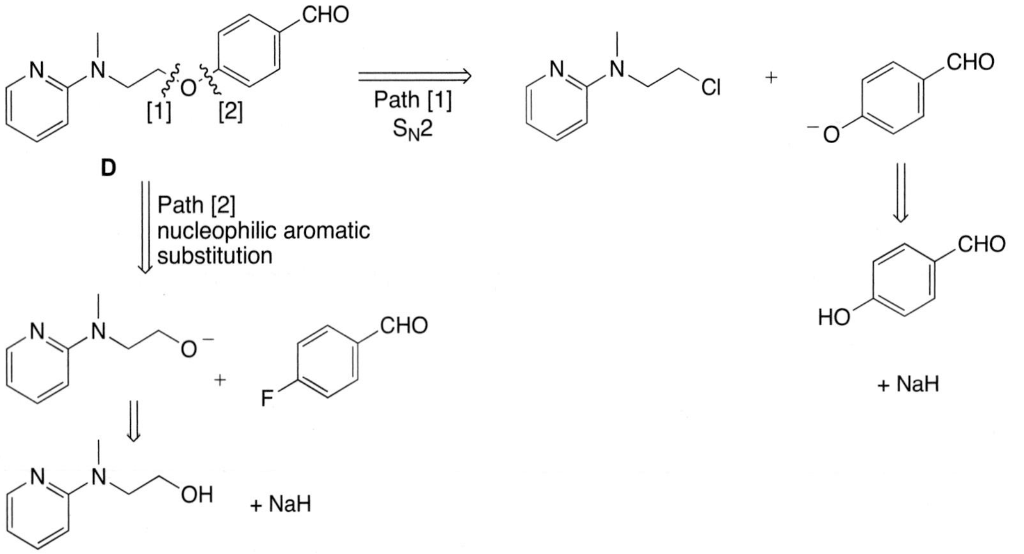
CHO
N
N
O
[1]
[2]
D
Path [1]
SN2
Cl
CHO
−O
CHO
HO
+ NaH
Path [2]
nucleophilic aromatic
substitution
O−
CHO
F
OH
+ NaH

18.44

a. 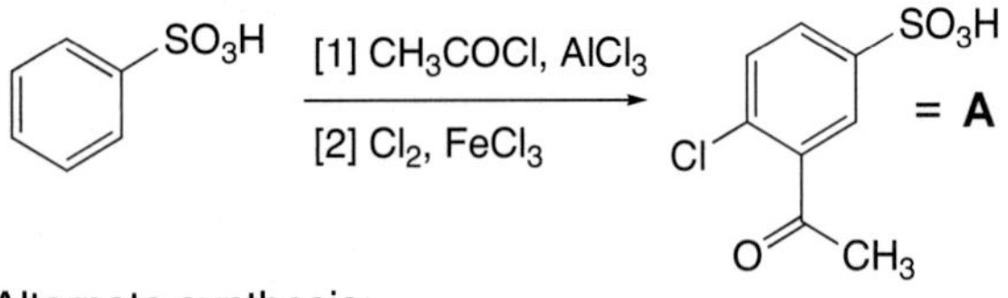
SO3H
[1] CH3COCl, AlCl3
[2] Cl2, FeCl3
SO3H
Cl
O
CH3
= A

Step [1] won't work because a Friedel–Crafts reaction can't be done on a deactivated benzene ring, as is the case with the SO_3H substituent. Even if Step [1] did work, the second step would introduce Cl meta to SO_3H, not para as drawn.

Alternate synthesis:

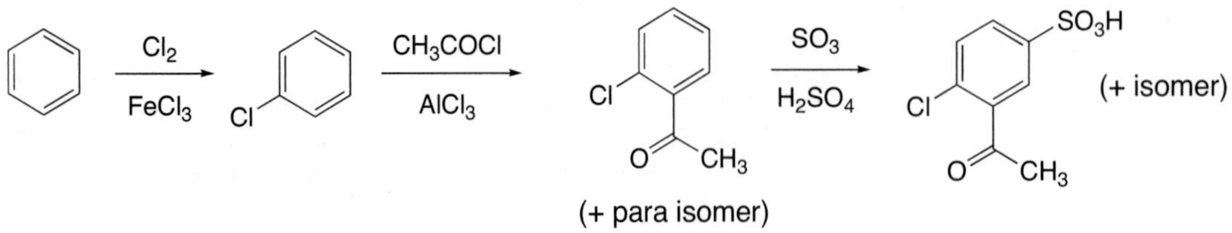
Cl2
FeCl3
Cl
CH3COCl
AlCl3
Cl
O
CH3
(+ para isomer)
SO3
H2SO4
SO3H
Cl
O
CH3
(+ isomer)

b. 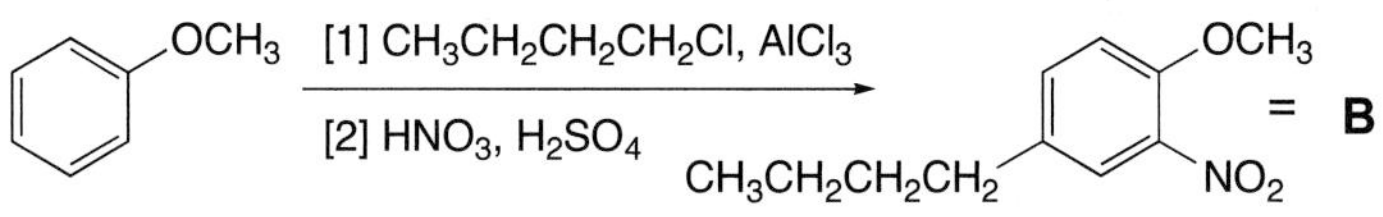

Step [1] involves a Friedel–Crafts alkylation using a 1° alkyl halide that will undergo rearrangement, so that a butyl group will not be introduced as a side chain.

Alternate synthesis:

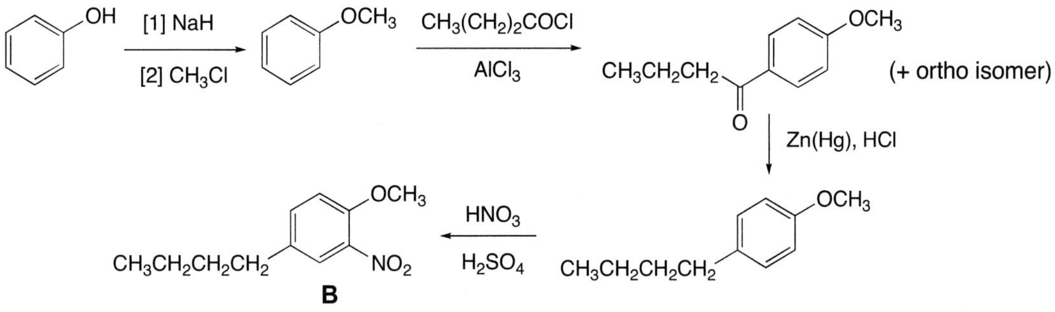

18.45 Use the directions from Answer 18.16 to rank the compounds.

a. 

least reactive | **intermediate reactivity** | **most reactive**

b. 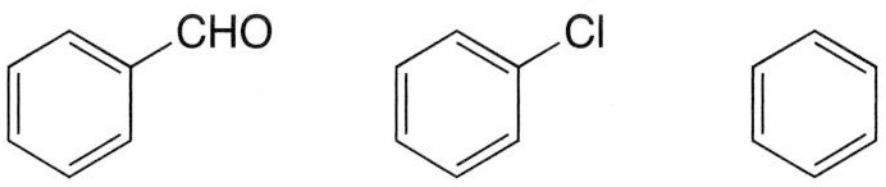

least reactive | **intermediate reactivity** | **most reactive**

c. 

least reactive | **intermediate reactivity** | **most reactive**

d. 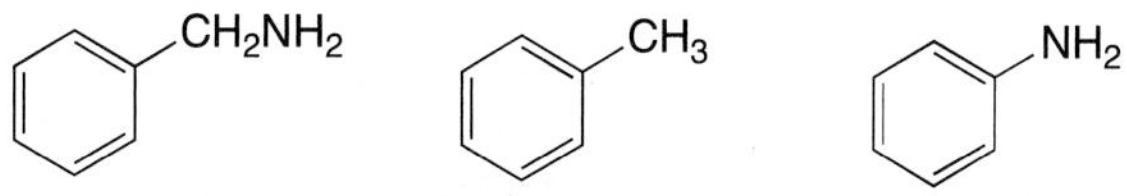

least reactive | **intermediate reactivity** | **most reactive**

18.46

[1] 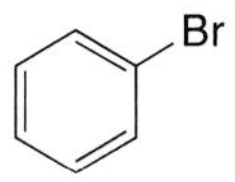

a. withdraw
b. donate
c. less
d. deactivate

[2] 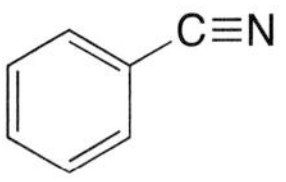

a. withdraw
b. withdraw
c. less
d. deactivate

[3] 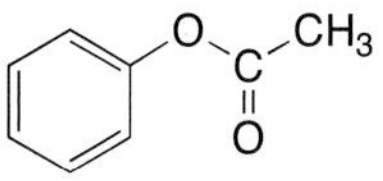

a. withdraw
b. donate
c. more
d. activate

18.47

a. 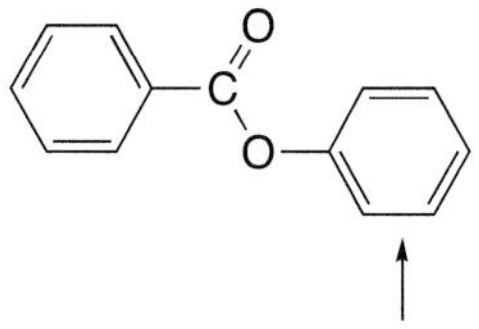

more electron rich
due to O atom
more reactive

b. 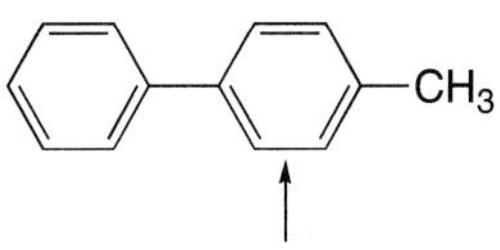

more electron rich
due to CH_3 group
more reactive

c. 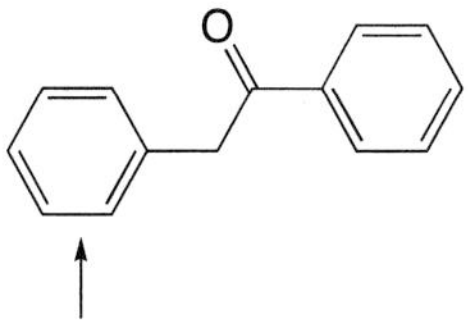

more electron rich
due to C atom
more reactive

18.48

a.

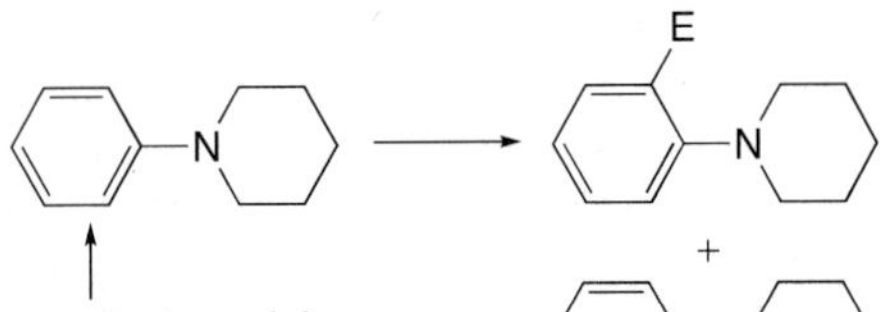

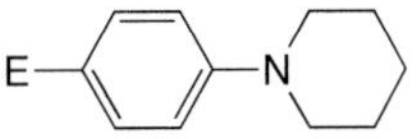

more electron rich
due to N atom
faster

c. electron withdrawing

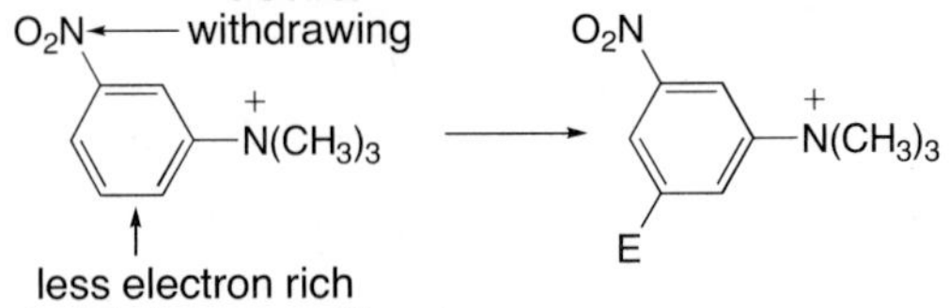

less electron rich
due to (+) charge on N and
electron-withdrawing NO_2 group
slower

b.

less electron rich
due to (+) charge on N
slower

d.

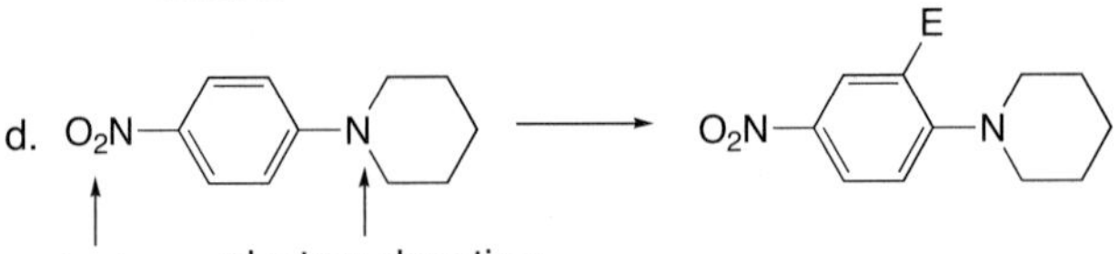

electron withdrawing   electron donating

Effects cancel out.
similar in reactivity to benzene

18.49

a.

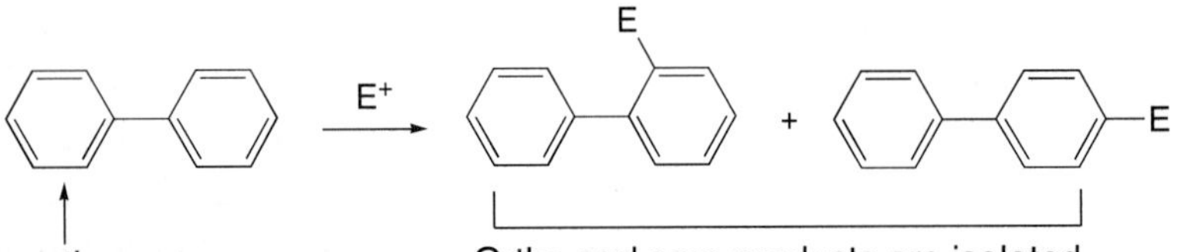

ortho, para
director

Ortho and para products are isolated.

A benzene ring is an electron-rich substituent that stabilizes an intermediate positive charge by an electron-donating resonance effect. As a result, it activates a benzene ring toward reaction with electrophiles.

With ortho and para attack there is additional resonance stabilization that delocalizes the positive charge onto the second benzene ring. Such additional stabilization is not possible with meta attack.

Ortho attack:

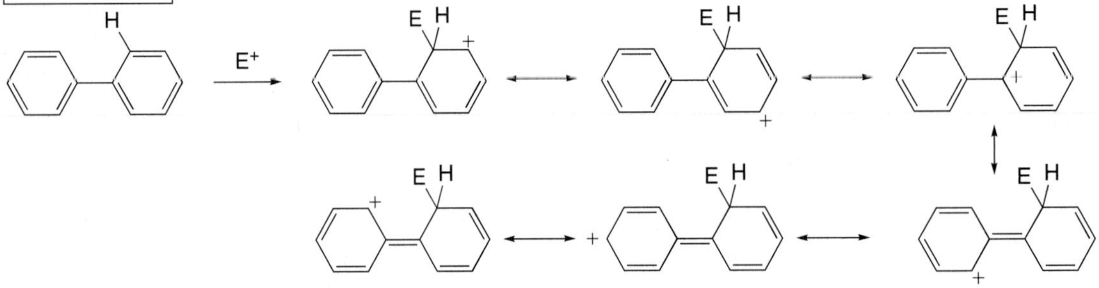

Meta attack:

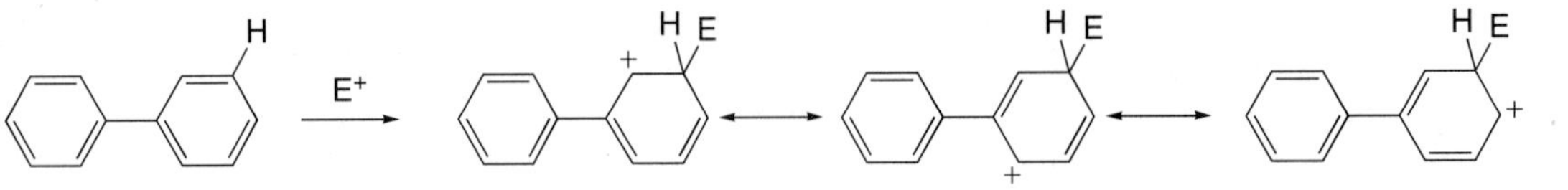

Para attack:

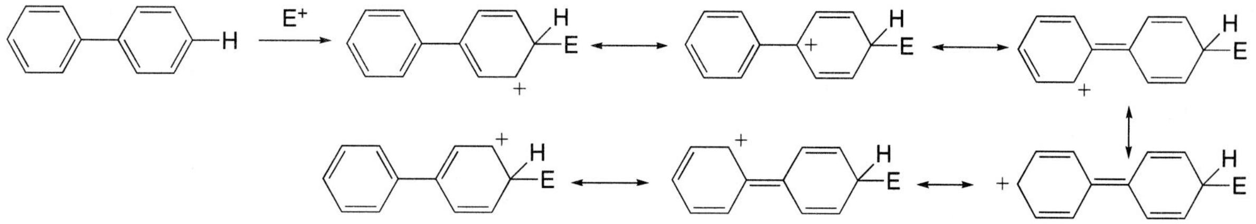

b.

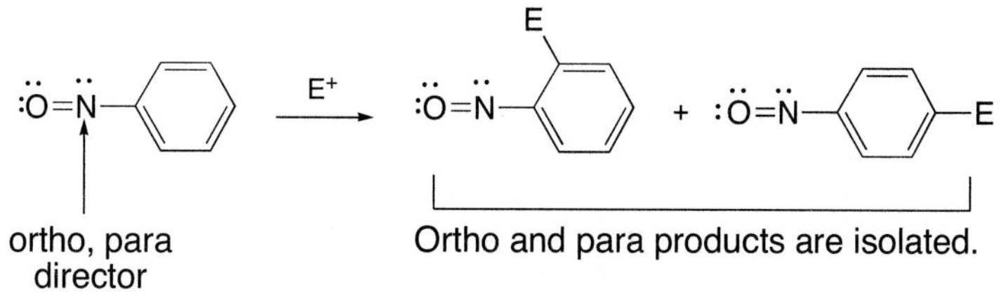

With ortho and para attack there is additional resonance stabilization that delocalizes the positive charge onto the nitroso group. Such additional stabilization is not possible with meta attack. This makes –NO an ortho, para director. Since the N atom bears a partial (+) charge (because it is bonded to a more electronegative O atom), the –NO group inductively withdraws electron density, thus deactivating the benzene ring towards electrophilic attack. In this way, the –NO group resembles the halogens. Thus, the electron-donating resonance effect makes –NO an o,p director, but the electron-withdrawing inductive effect makes it a deactivator.

Ortho attack:

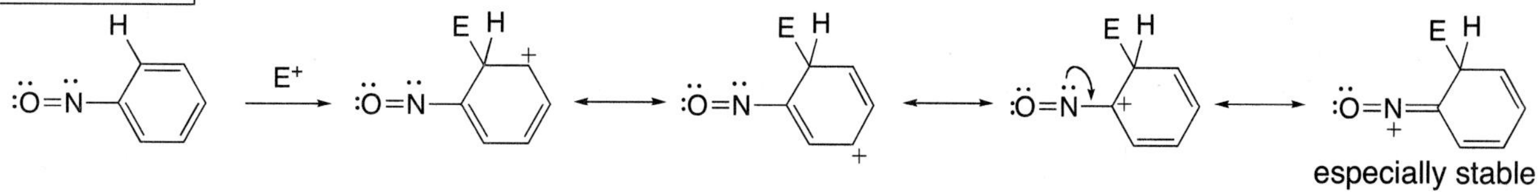

Meta attack:

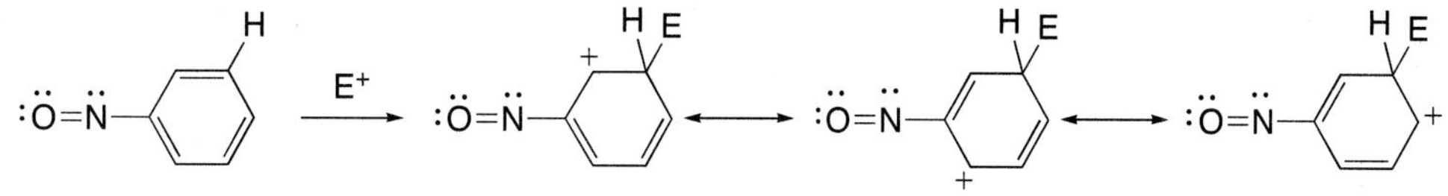

Para attack:

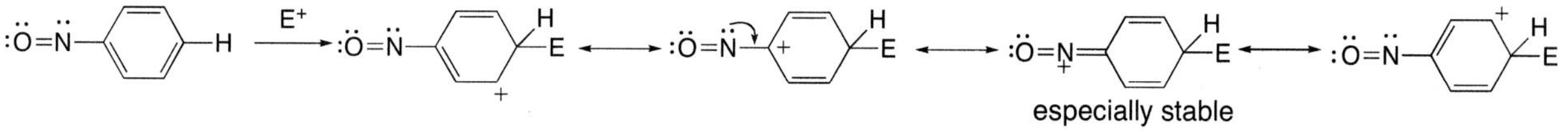

18.50

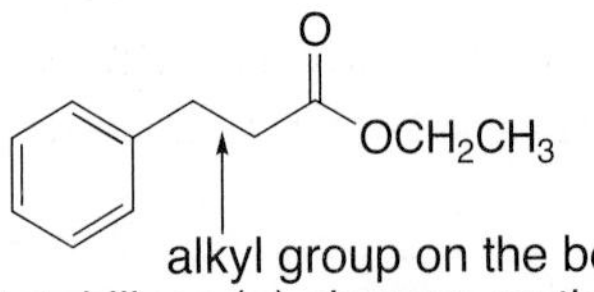

alkyl group on the benzene ring
R stabilizes (+) charges on the o,p positions by an electron-donating inductive effect. This group behaves like any other R group so that ortho and para products are formed in electrophilic aromatic substitution.

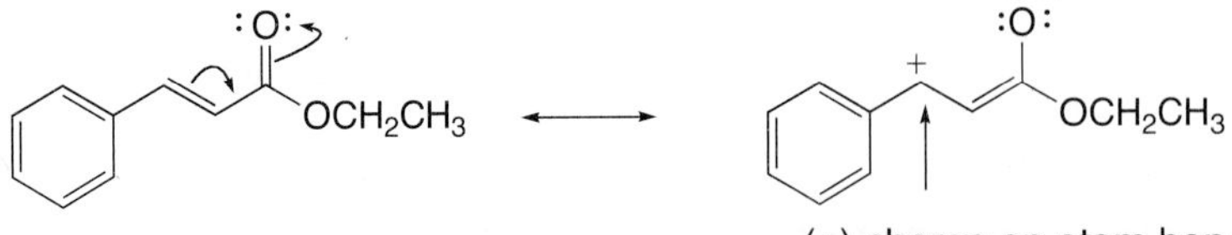

(+) charge on atom bonded to the benzene ring
Drawing resonance structures in electrophilic aromatic substitution results in especially unstable structures for attack at the o,p positions—two (+) charges on adjacent atoms. This doesn't happen with meta attack, so meta attack is preferred. This is identical to the situation observed with all meta directors.

18.51 Under the acidic conditions of nitration, the N atom of the starting material gets protonated, so the atom directly bonded to the benzene ring bears a (+) charge. This makes it a meta director, so the new NO_2 group is introduced meta to it.

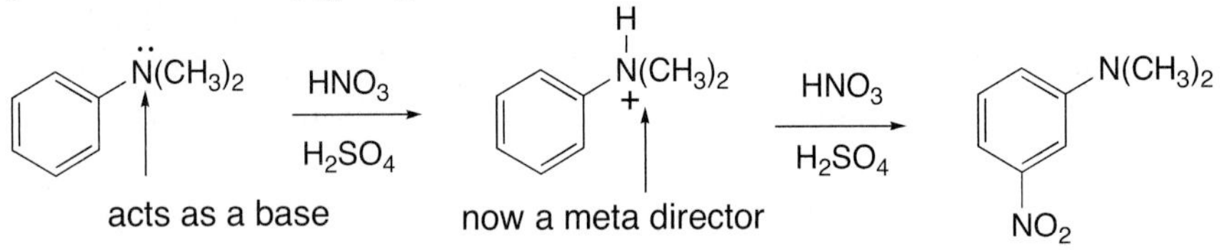

18.52 Increasing the number of electron-withdrawing groups (especially at the ortho and para positions to the leaving group) increases the rate of nucleophilic aromatic substitution. Increasing the electronegativity of the halogen increases the rate.

a.

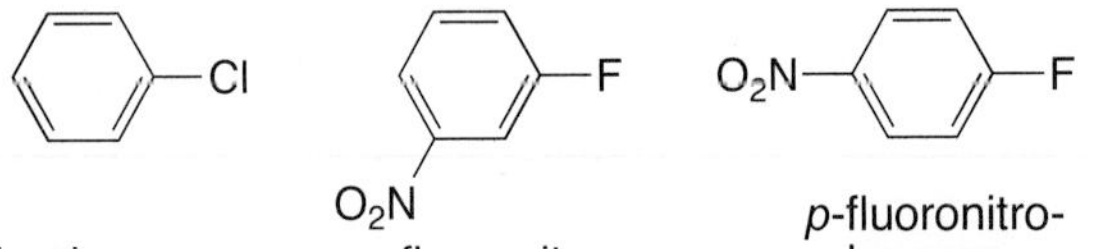

chlorobenzene **least reactive** — *m*-fluoronitrobenzene — *p*-fluoronitrobenzene **most reactive**

b.

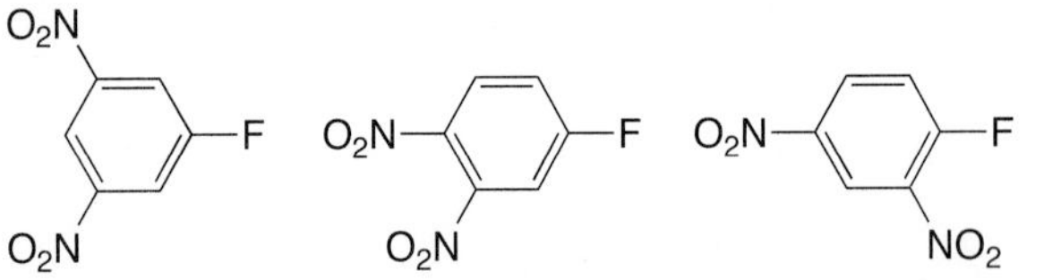

1-fluoro-3,5-dinitrobenzene **least reactive** — 1-fluoro-3,4-dinitrobenzene — 1-fluoro-2,4-dinitrobenzene **most reactive**

c.

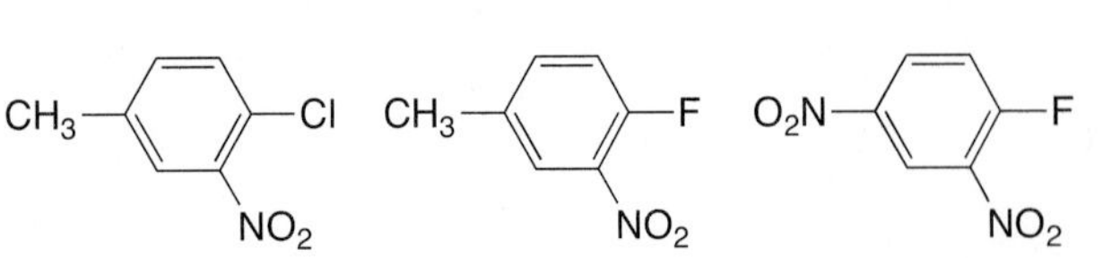

4-chloro-3-nitrotoluene **least reactive** — 4-fluoro-3-nitrotoluene — 1-fluoro-2,4-dinitrobenzene **most reactive**

18.53 A CH_3O group has an electron-donating resonance effect. This stabilizes a (+) charge, so it increases stability of the carbocation intermediate in electrophilic aromatic substitution. This destabilizes a (–) charge, so it decreases the stability of the carbanion intermediate in nucleophilic aromatic substitution.

18.54

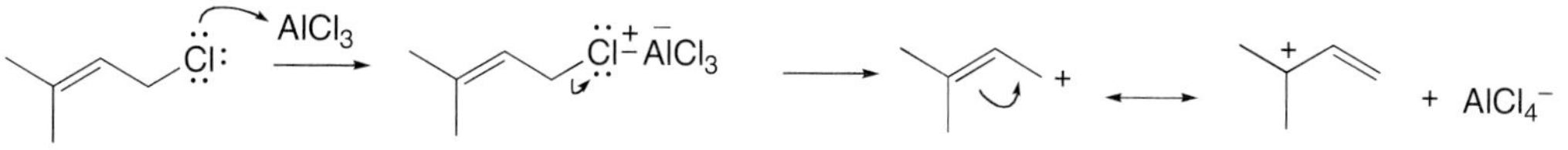

resonance-stabilized carbocation

Use both resonance forms to show how two products are formed.

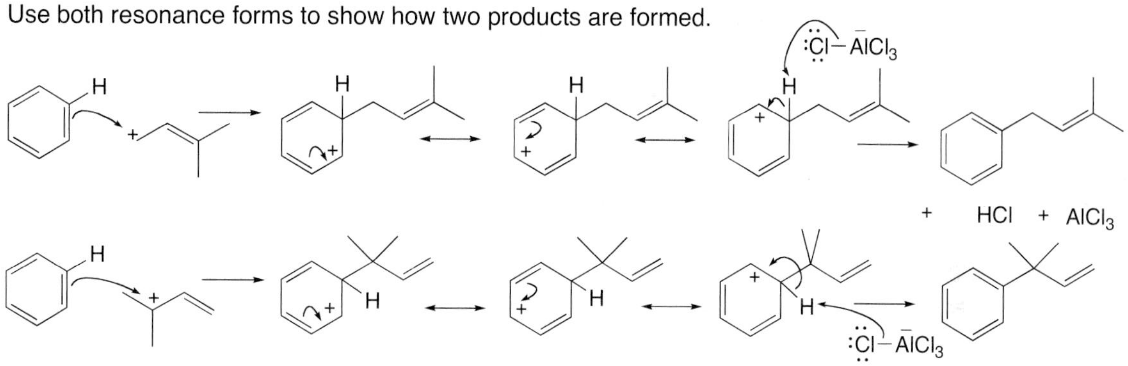

18.55

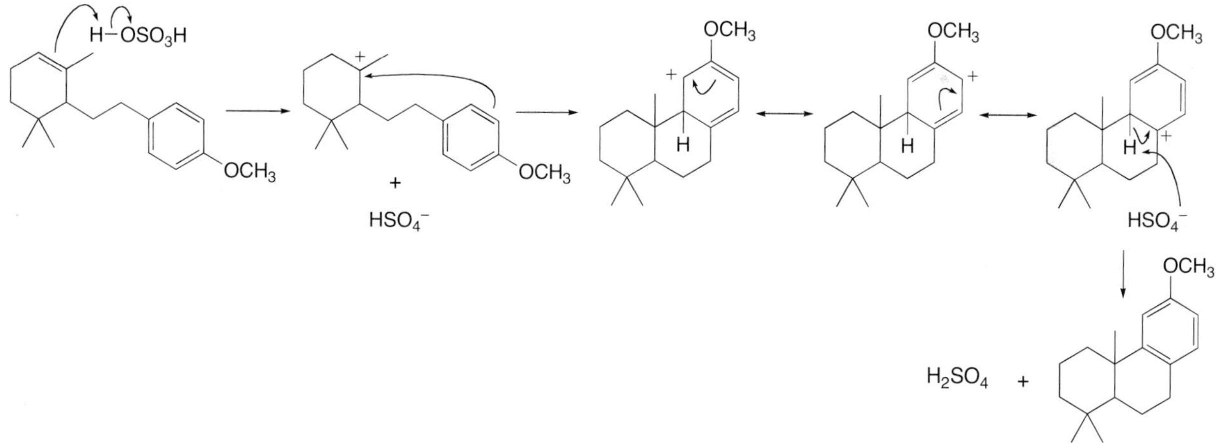

18.56

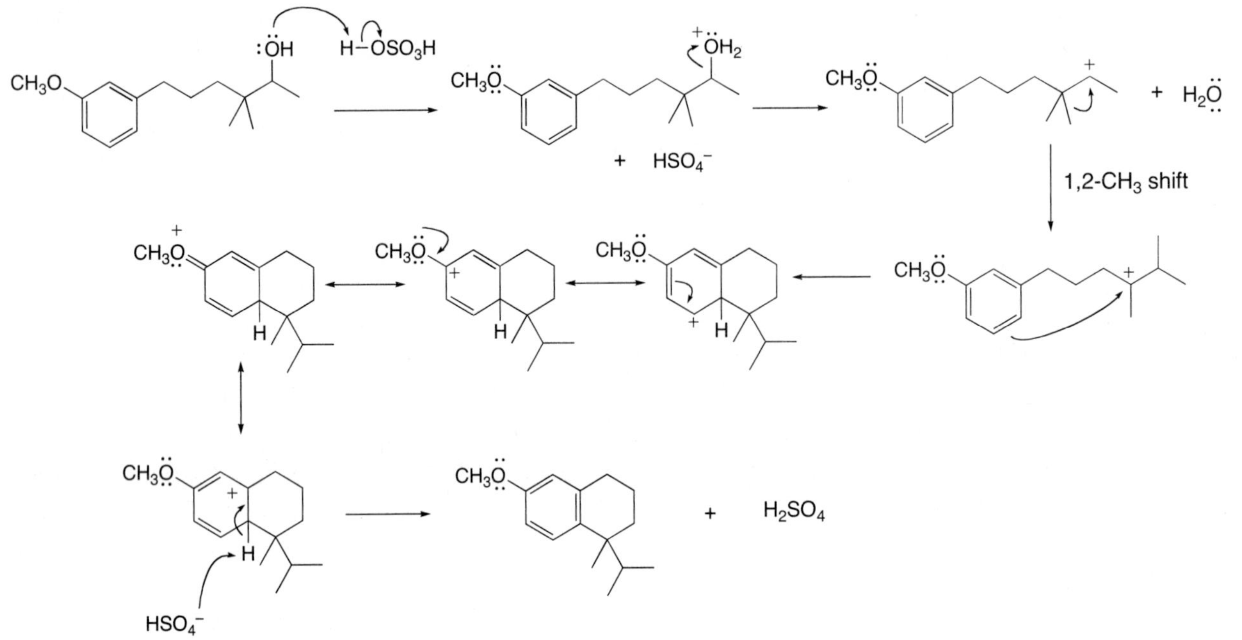

18.57

a. The product has one stereogenic center.

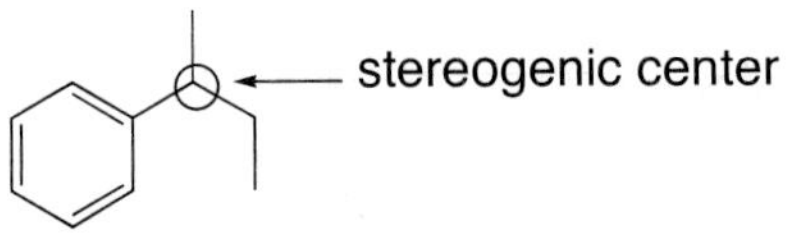

b. The mechanism for Friedel–Crafts alkylation with this 2° halide involves formation of a trigonal planar carbocation. Since the carbocation is achiral, it reacts with benzene with equal probability from two possible directions (above and below) to afford an optically inactive, racemic mixture of two products.

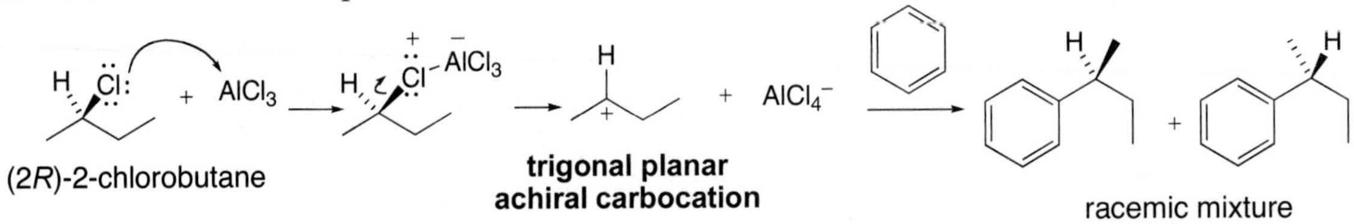

18.58 The reaction follows the two-step addition–elimination mechanism for nucleophilic aromatic substitution.

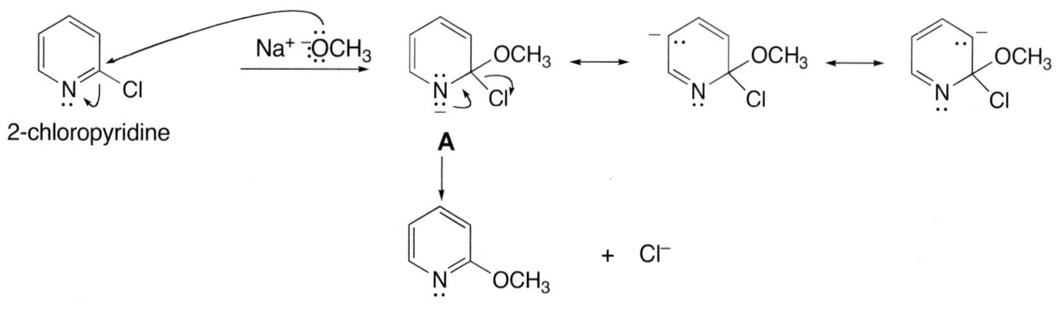

Resonance structure **A** is stabilized because the negative charge is located on an electronegative N. This makes nucleophilic aromatic substitution on 2-chloropyridine faster than a similar reaction with chlorobenzene, which has no N atom to stabilize the intermediate negative charge.

18.59 Since there is no electron-withdrawing group on the benzene ring, the mechanism likely proceeds via elimination–addition.

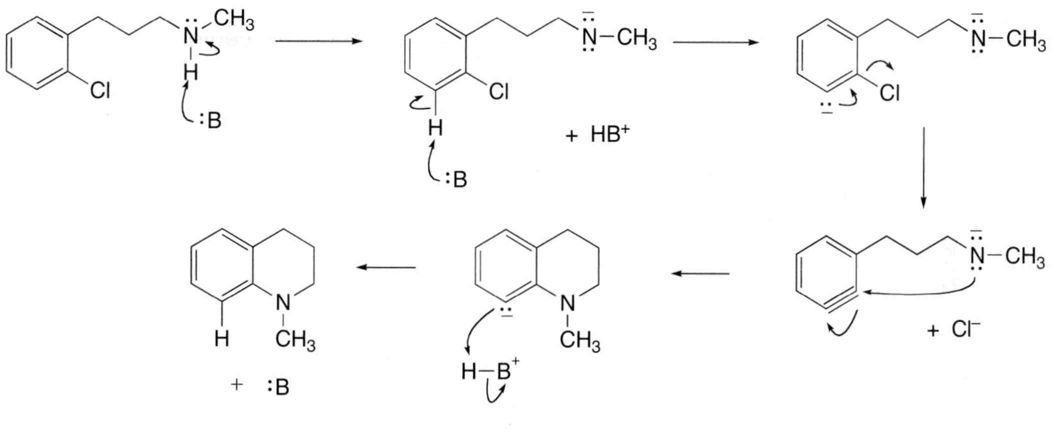

18.60

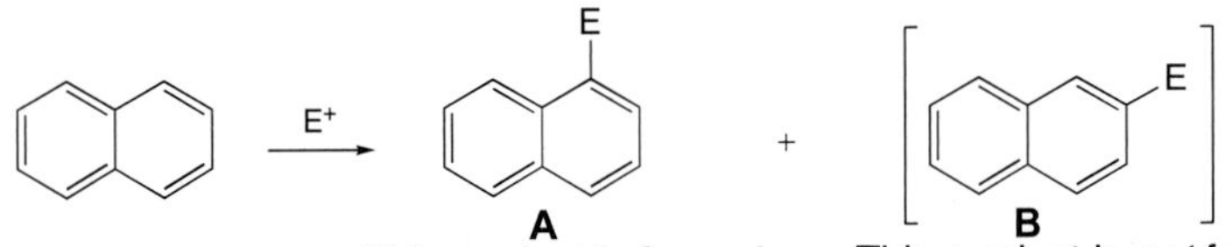

E⁺
E
E
A
B

This product is formed. This product is *not* formed.

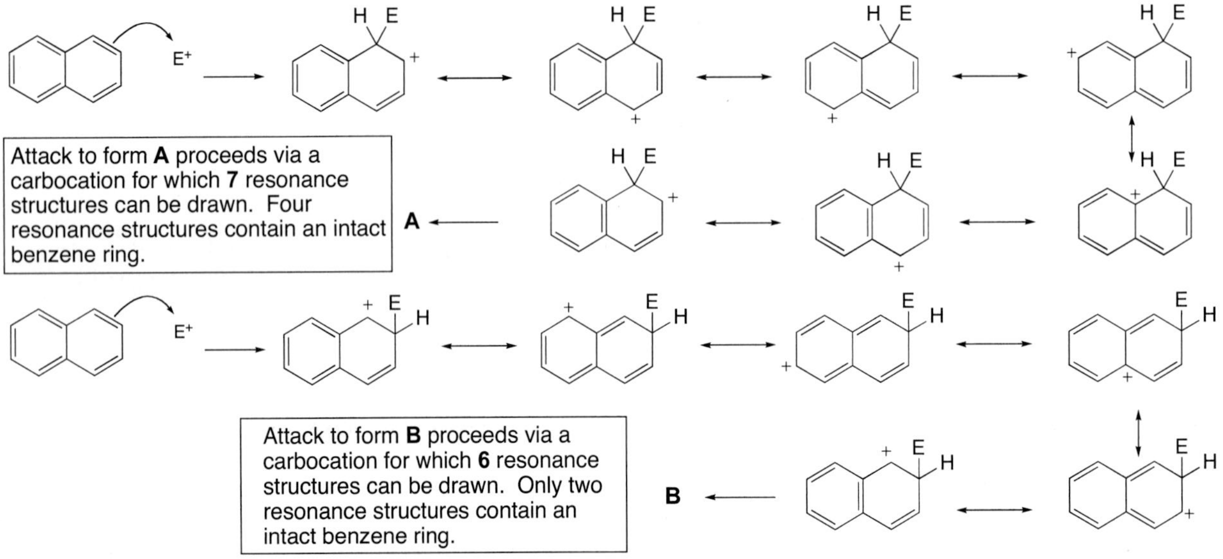

E⁺
H E
A
E⁺
E H
B

Attack to form **A** proceeds via a carbocation for which **7** resonance structures can be drawn. Four resonance structures contain an intact benzene ring.

Attack to form **B** proceeds via a carbocation for which **6** resonance structures can be drawn. Only two resonance structures contain an intact benzene ring.

A reaction that occurs by way of the more stable carbocation is preferred, so product **A** is formed.

18.61

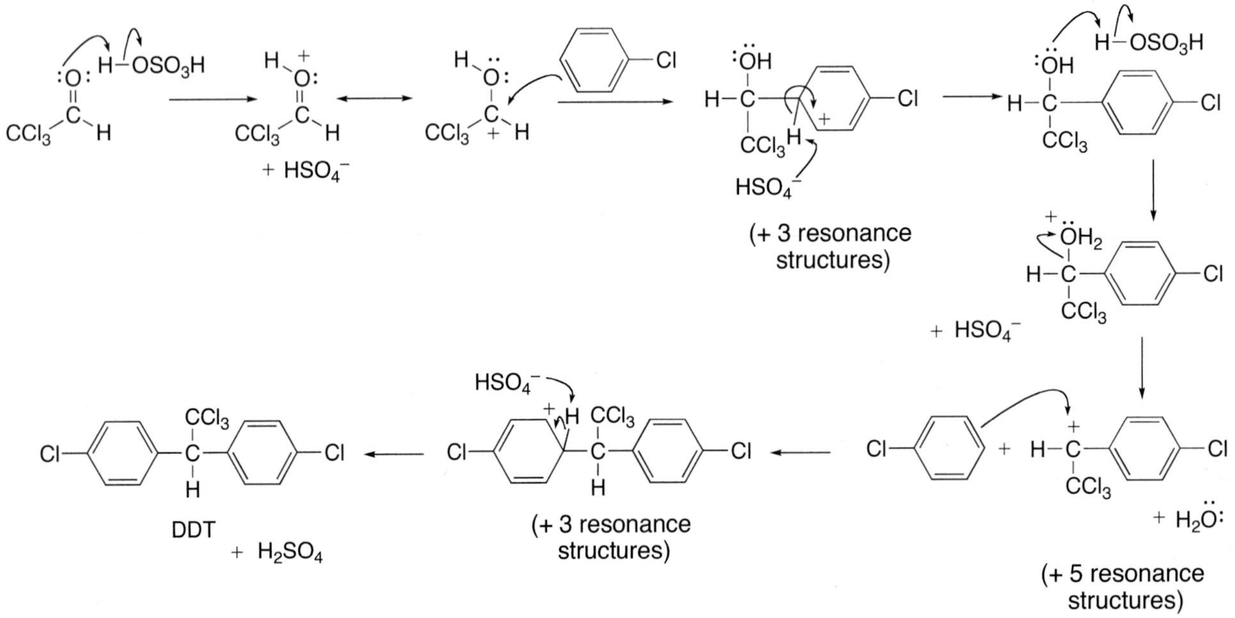

H–OSO₃H
CCl₃
+ HSO₄⁻
Cl
HSO₄⁻
(+ 3 resonance structures)
+ HSO₄⁻
+ H₂O:
(+ 5 resonance structures)
DDT
+ H₂SO₄

18.62

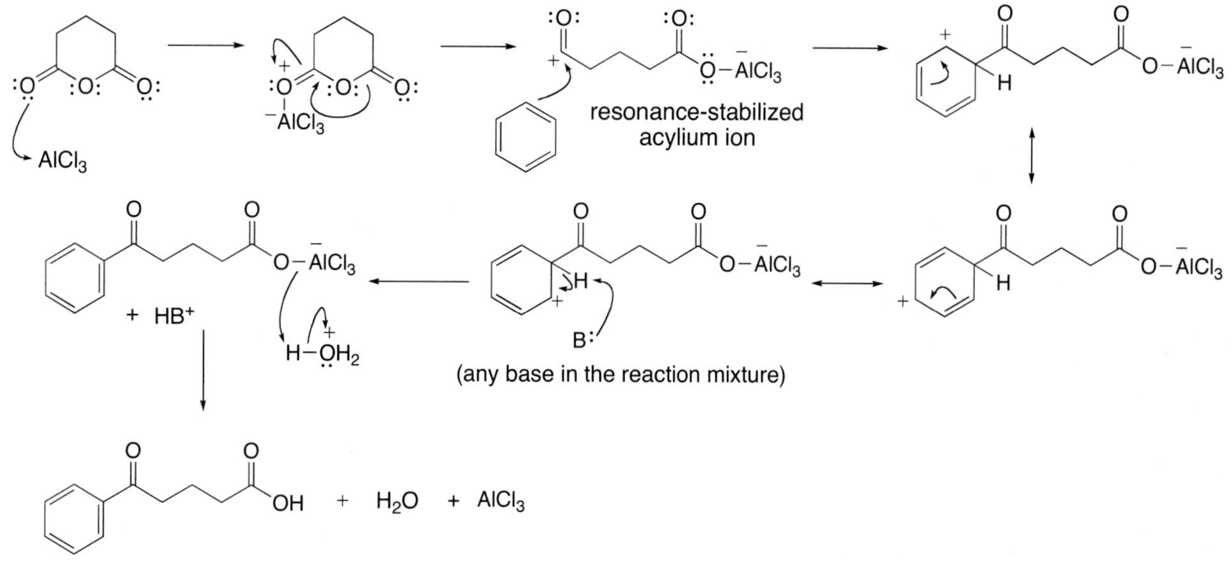

AlCl3
resonance-stabilized
acylium ion
B:
(any base in the reaction mixture)
+ HB+
OH + H2O + AlCl3

18.63 Benzyl bromide forms a resonance-stabilized intermediate that allows it to react rapidly under S_N1 conditions.

Formation of a resonance-stabilized carbocation:

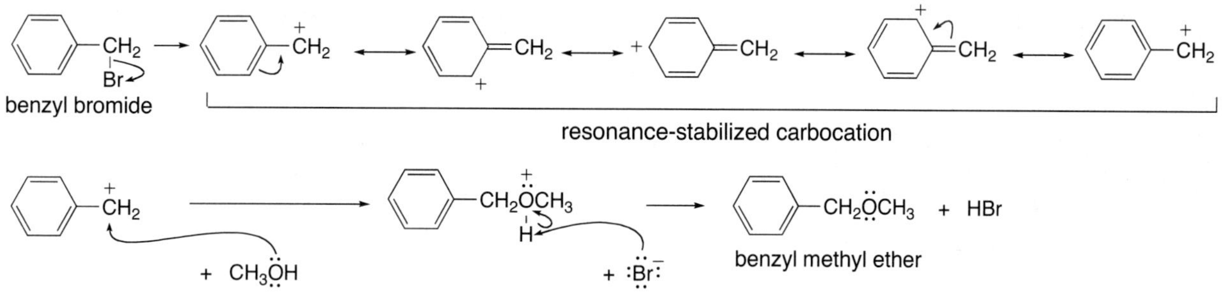

benzyl bromide
resonance-stabilized carbocation
benzyl methyl ether

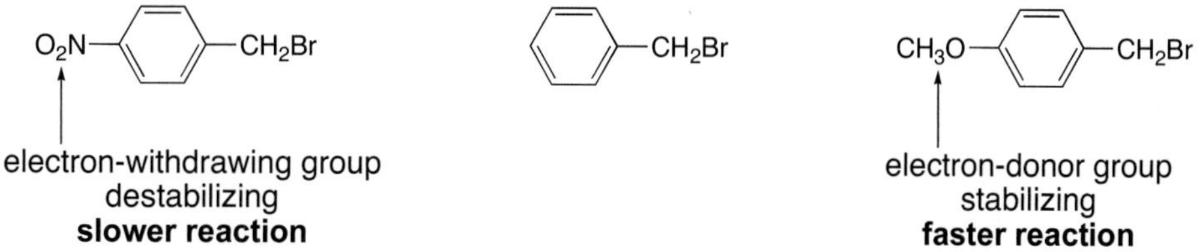

electron-withdrawing group
destabilizing
slower reaction
electron-donor group
stabilizing
faster reaction

The electron-withdrawing NO_2 group will destabilize the carbocation so the benzylic halide will be less reactive, while the electron-donating OCH_3 group will stabilize the carbocation, so the benzylic halide will be more reactive.

18.64

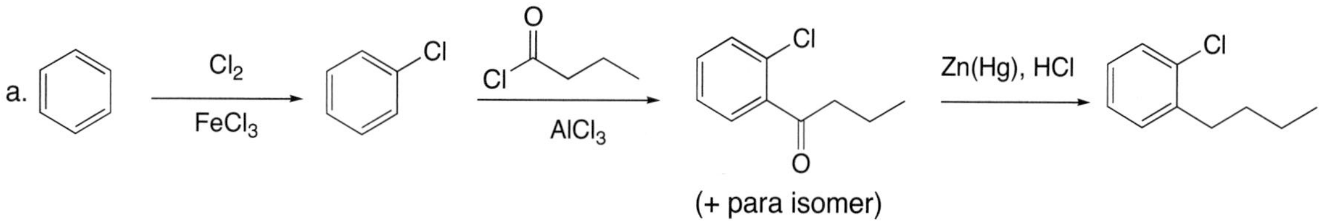

a.
Cl2
FeCl3
AlCl3
(+ para isomer)
Zn(Hg), HCl

b. 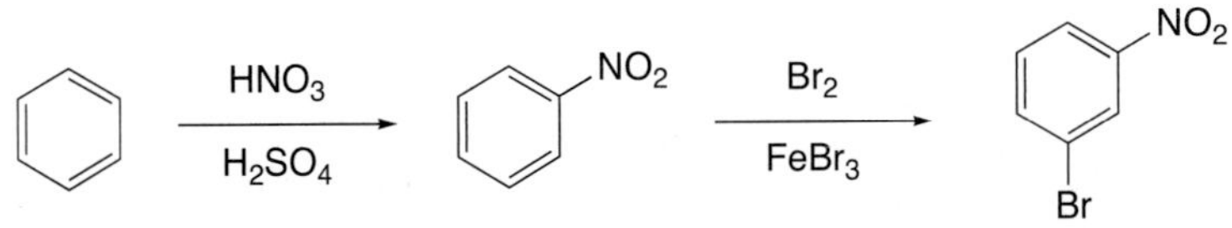

c. 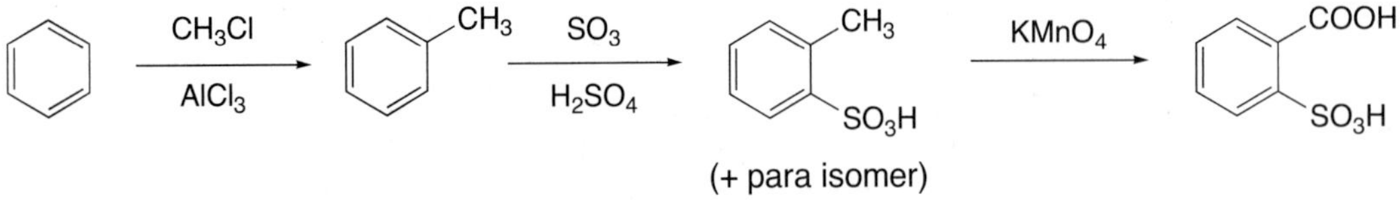

d. 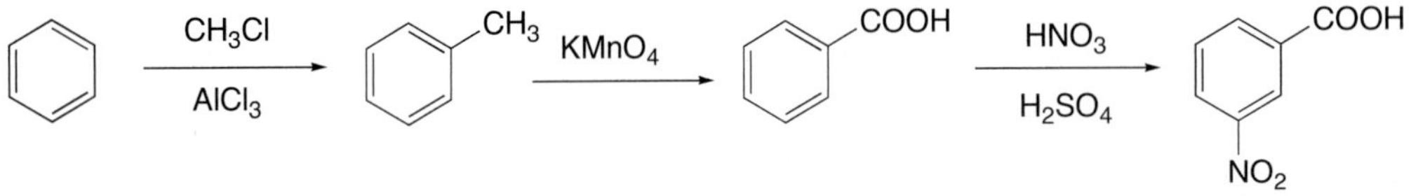

e. 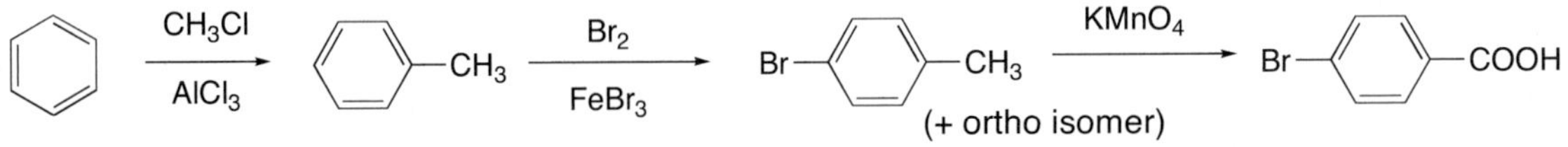

f. 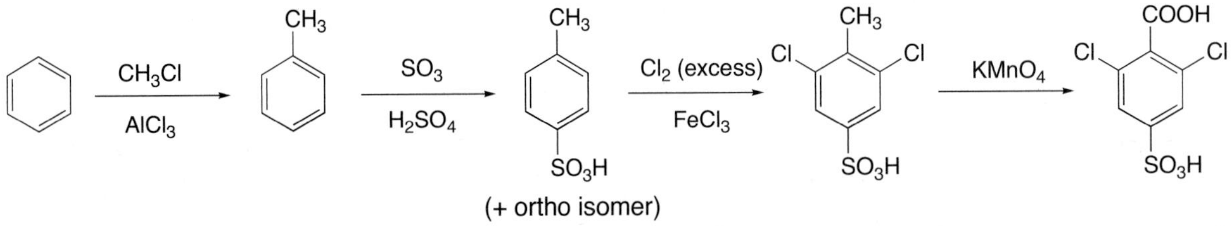

g. 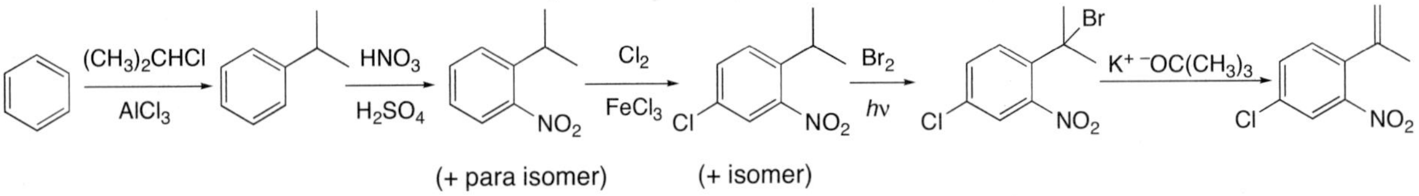

18.65

a. 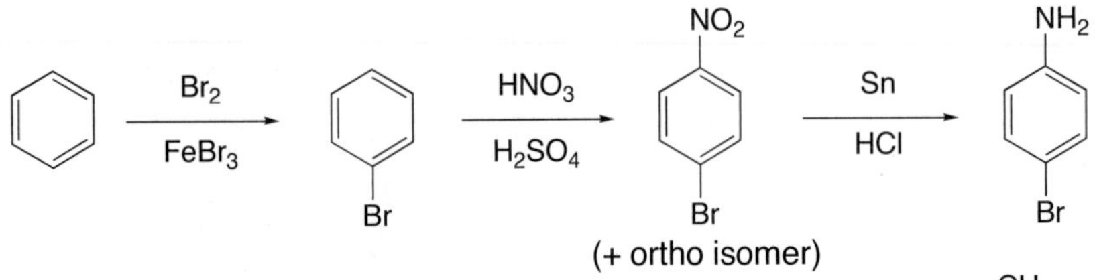

b. 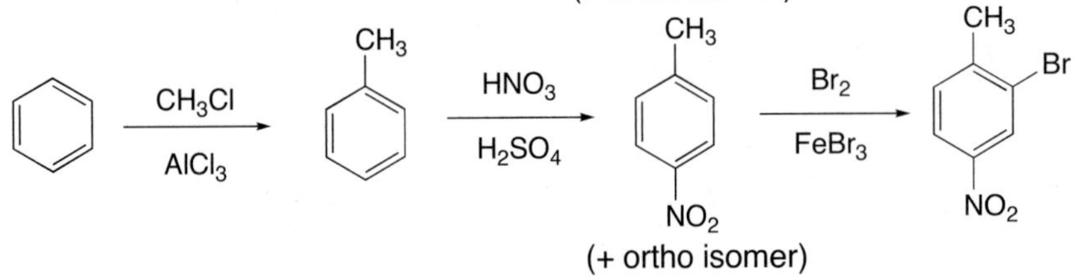

c.

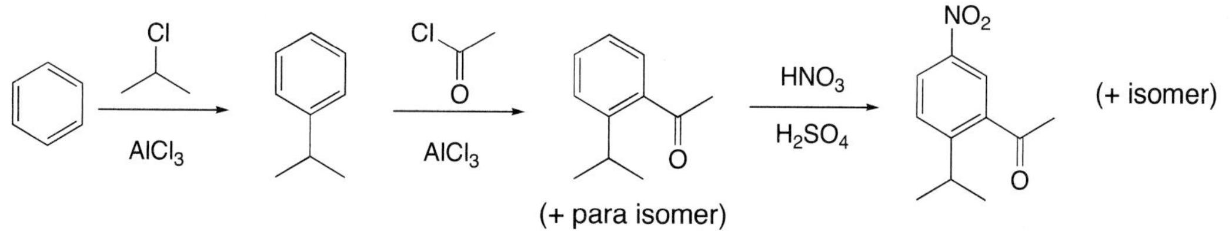

d.

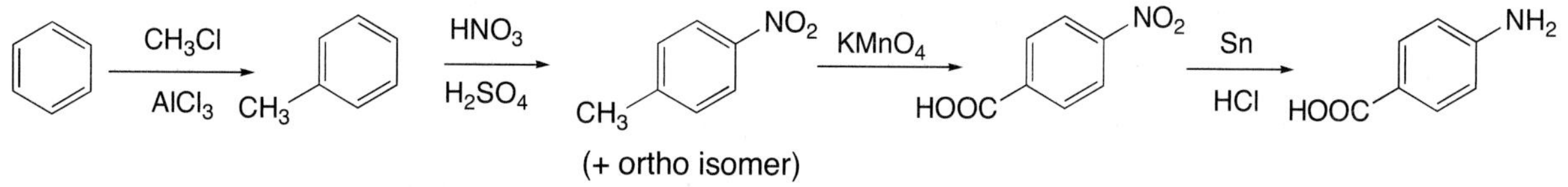

e.

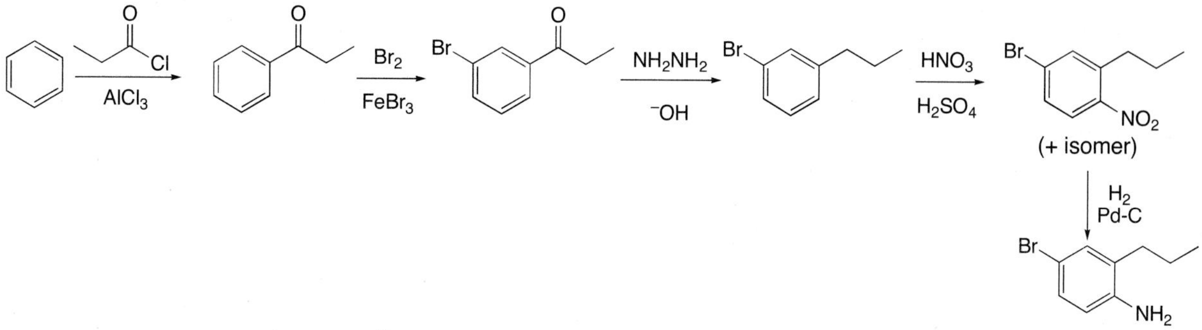

f.

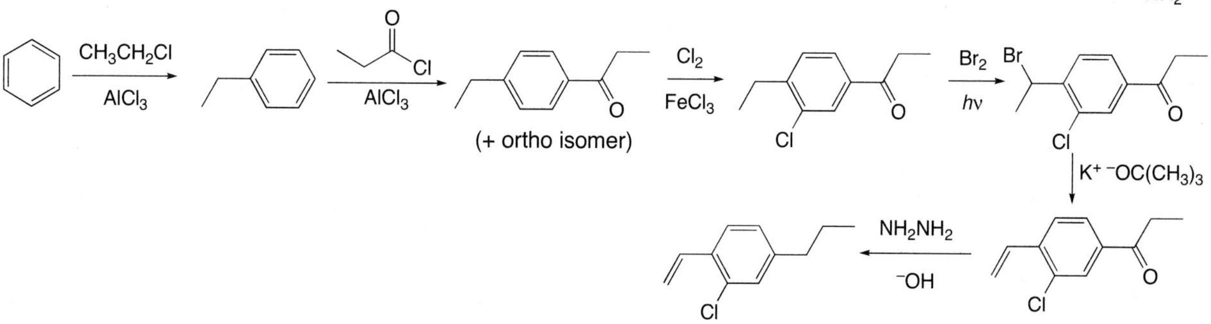

18.66

a.

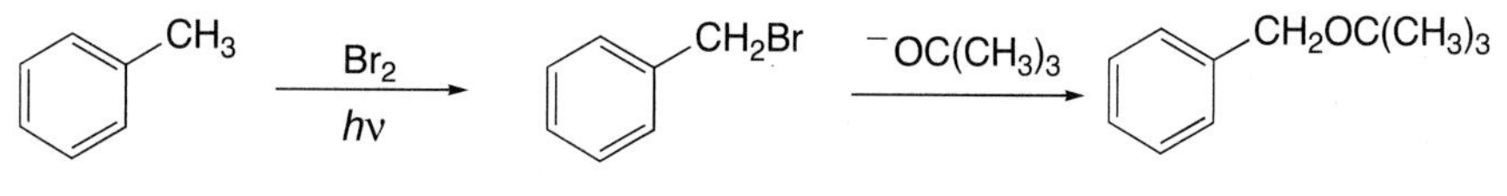

b.

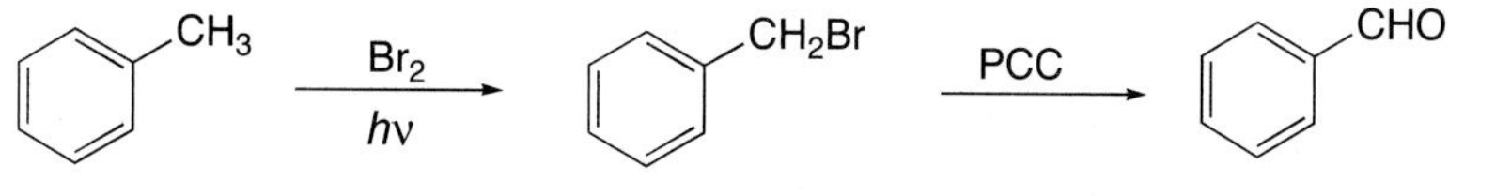

c.

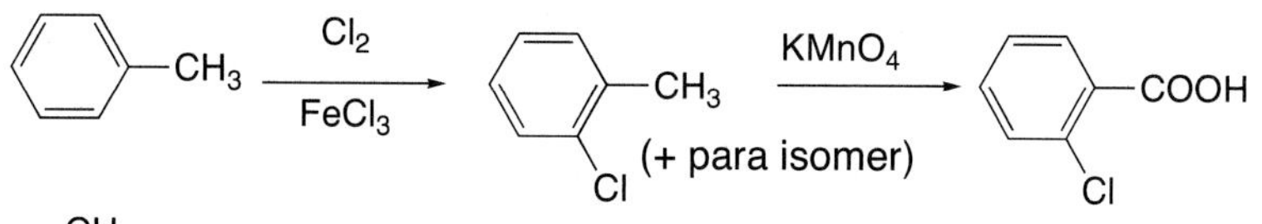

d.

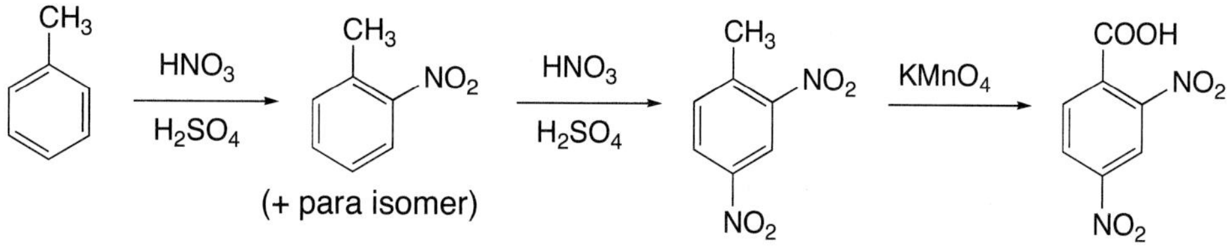

e. 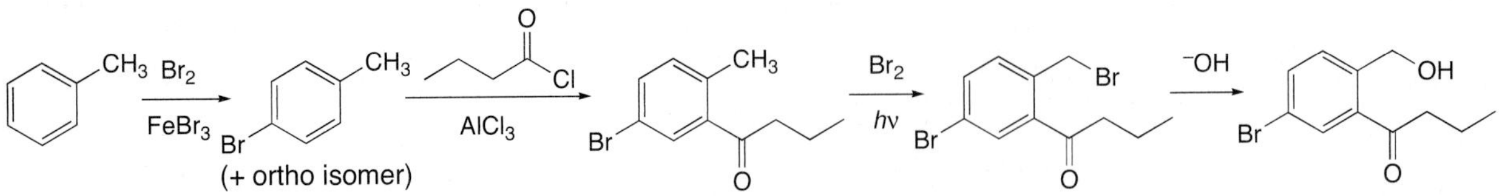

f. 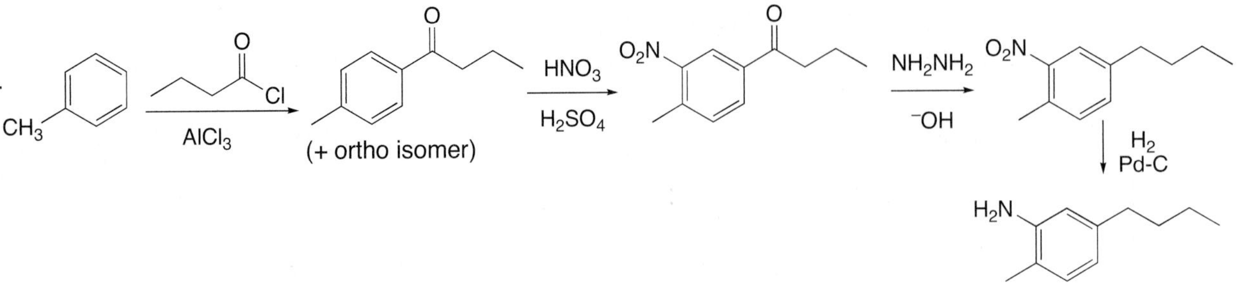

g. 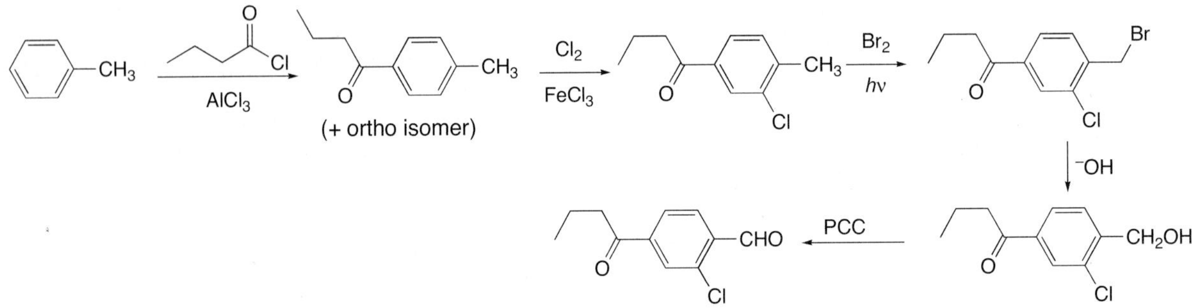

18.67

a. 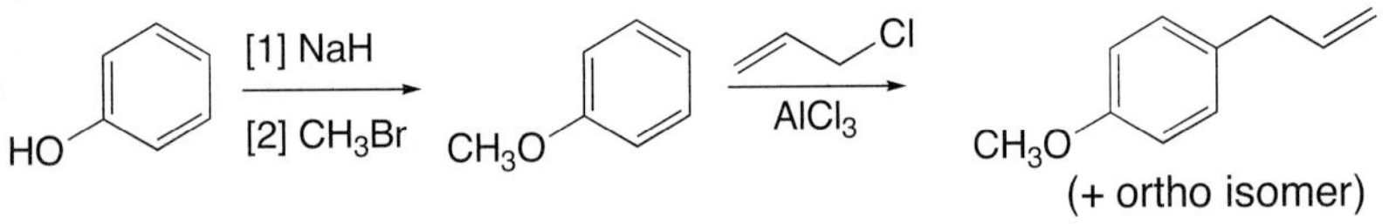

b. 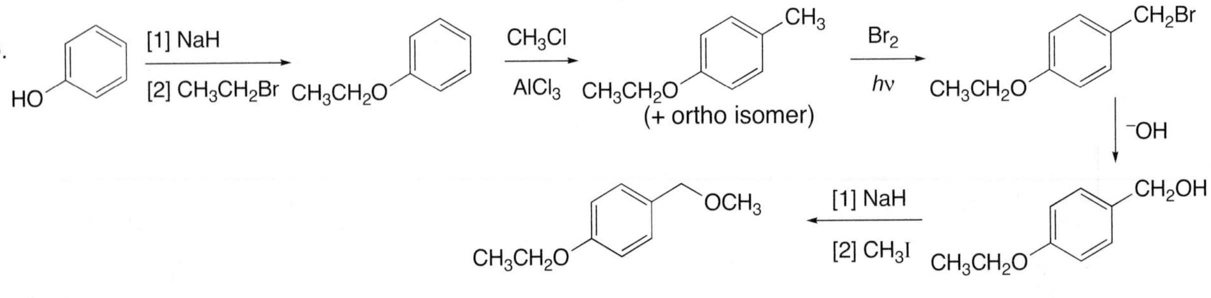

c. 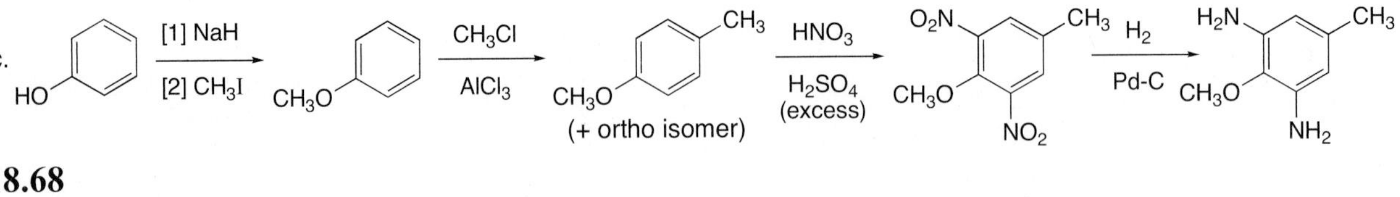

18.68

a. 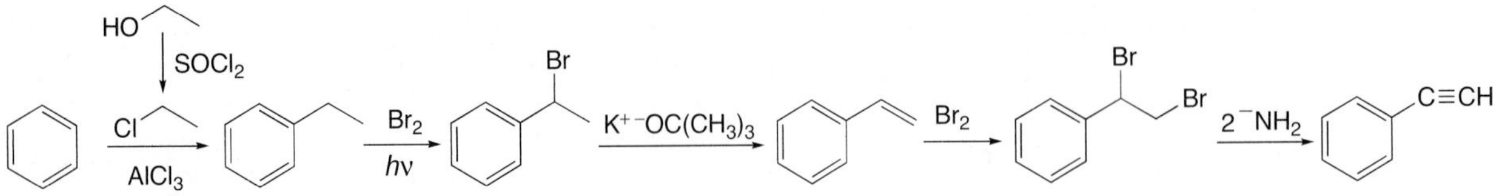

b. 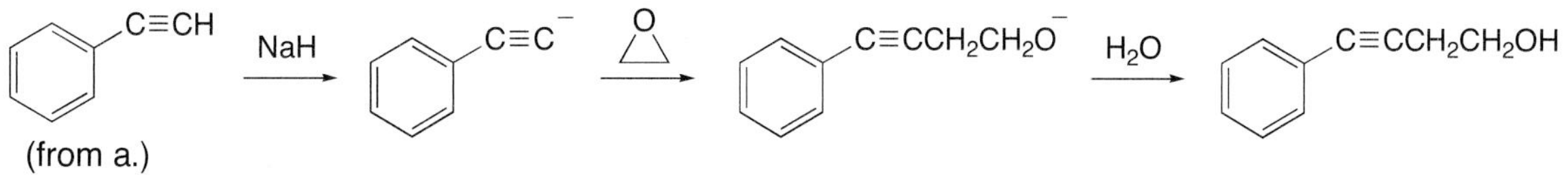

c. 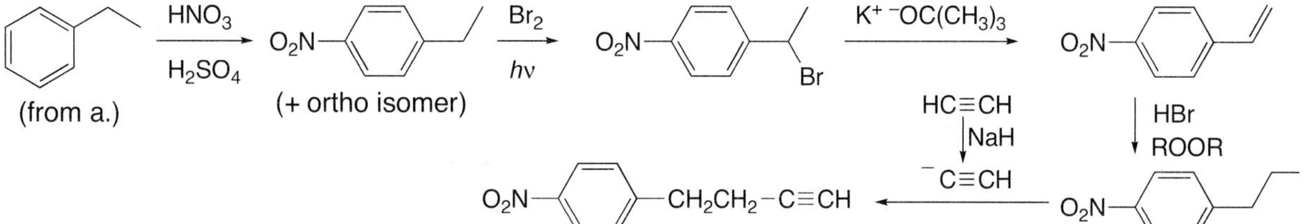

d. 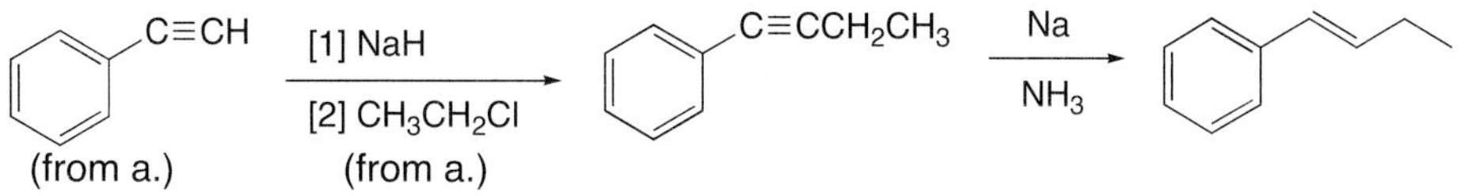

e. 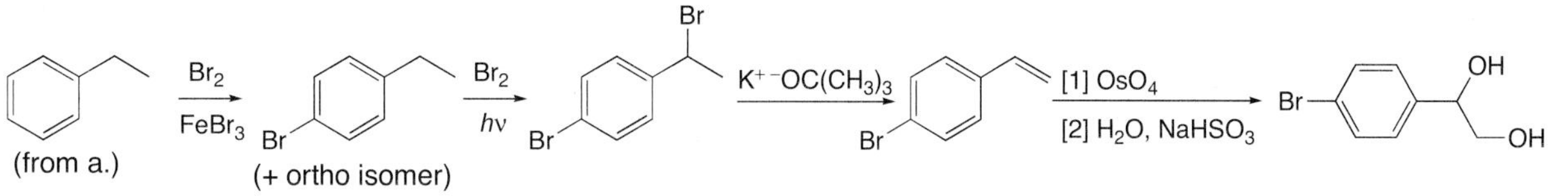

f. 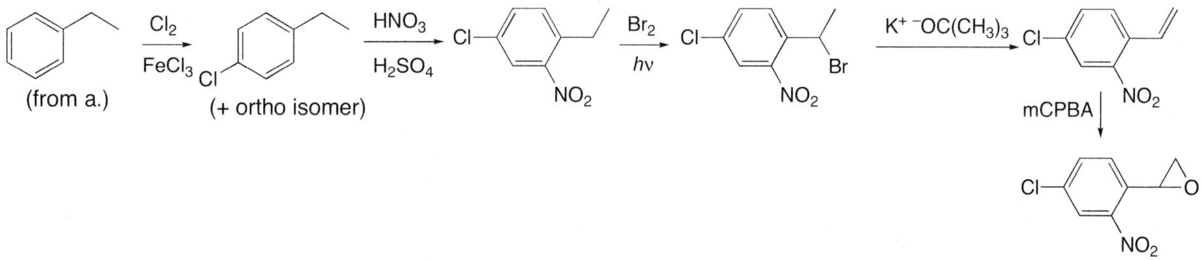

18.69 One possibility:

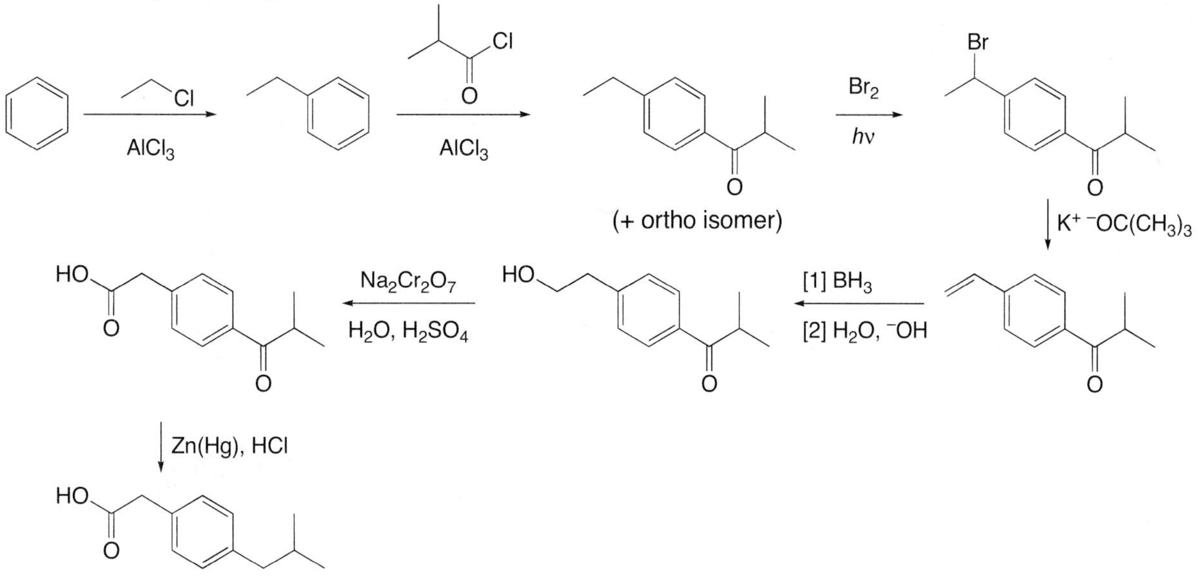

ibufenac

18.70

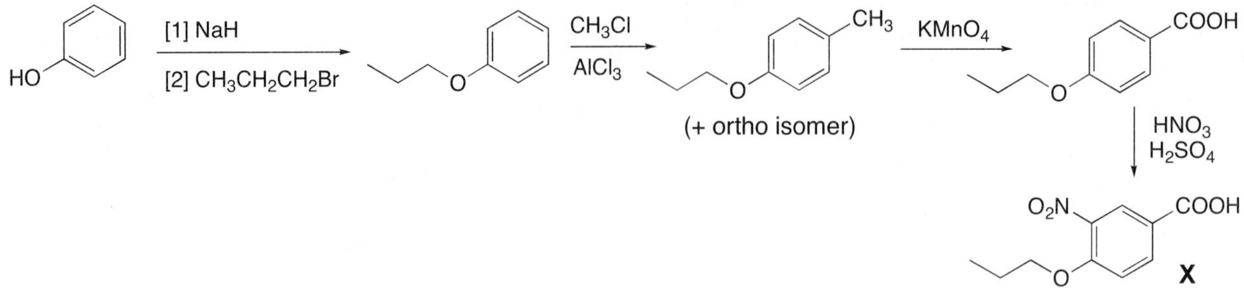

18.71 Use integration data and the molecular formula to determine the number of H's that give rise to each signal (Section 14.5, *How To*).

^{1}H NMR data of compound **A** (C_8H_9Br):

Absorption	**ppm**	**# of H's**	**Explanation**
triplet	1.2	3	3 H's adjacent to 2 H's
quartet	2.6	2	2 H's adjacent to 3 H's
two signals	7.1 and 7.4	2 + 2	para disubstituted benzene

Structure:

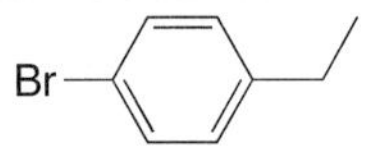

^{1}H NMR data of compound **B** (C_8H_9Br):

Absorption	**ppm**	**# of H's**	**Explanation**
triplet	3.1	2	2 H's adjacent to 2 H's
triplet	3.5	2	2 H's adjacent to 2 H's
multiplet	7.1–7.4	5	monosubstituted benzene

Structure:

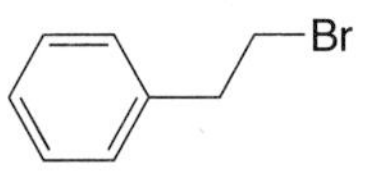

18.72 IR absorption at 1717 cm^{-1} means compound **C** has a C=O.

^{1}H NMR data of compound **C** ($C_{10}H_{12}O$):

Absorption	**ppm**	**# of H's**	**Explanation**
singlet	2.1	3	3 H's
triplet	2.8	2	2 H's adjacent to 2 H's
triplet	2.9	2	2 H's adjacent to 2 H's
multiplet	7.1–7.4	5	monosubstituted benzene

Structure:

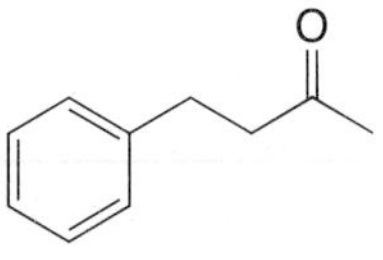

18.73

^{1}H NMR data of compound **X** ($C_{10}H_{12}O$):

Absorption	**ppm**	**# of H's**	**Explanation**
doublet	1.3	6	6 H's adjacent to 1 H
septet	3.5	1	1 H adjacent to 6 H's
multiplet	7.4–8.1	5	monosubstituted benzene

Structure:

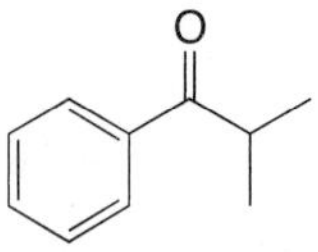

^{1}H NMR data of compound **Y** ($C_{10}H_{14}$):

Absorption	**ppm**	**# of H's**	**Explanation**
doublet	0.9	6	6 H's adjacent to 1 H
multiplet	1.8	1	1 H adjacent to many H's
doublet	2.5	2	2 H's adjacent to 1 H
multiplet	7.1–7.3	5	monosubstituted benzene

Structure:

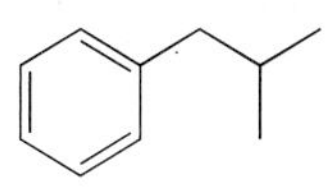

18.74

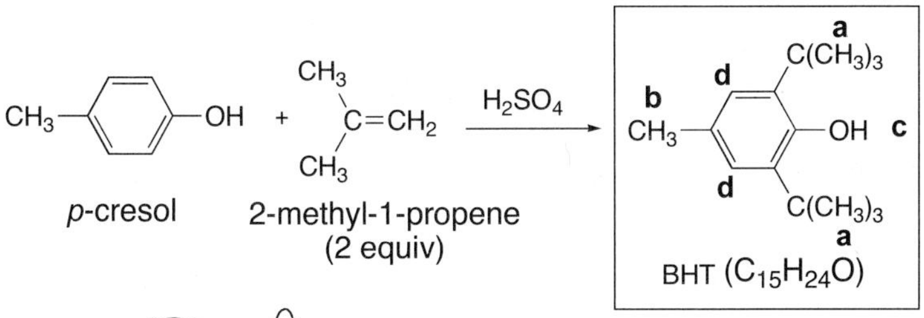

^{1}H NMR spectral data:
1.4 (singlet, 18 H) (a)
2.27 (singlet, 3 H) (b)
5.0 (singlet, 1 H) (c)
7.0 (singlet, 2 H) (d) ppm

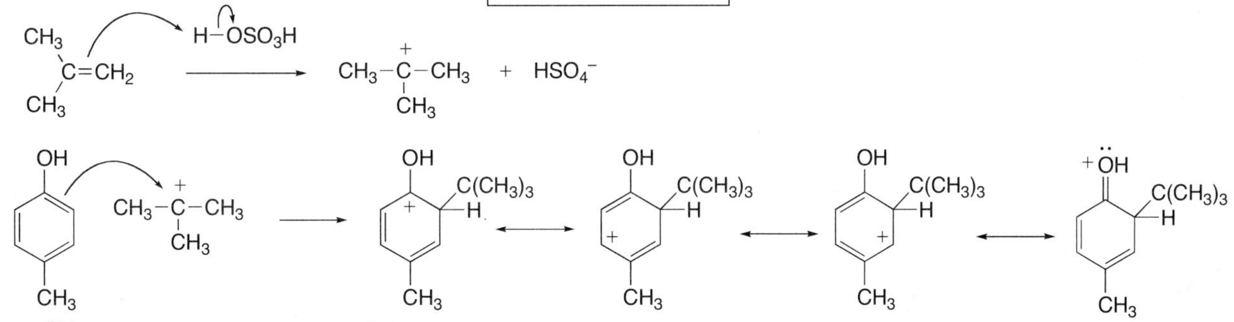

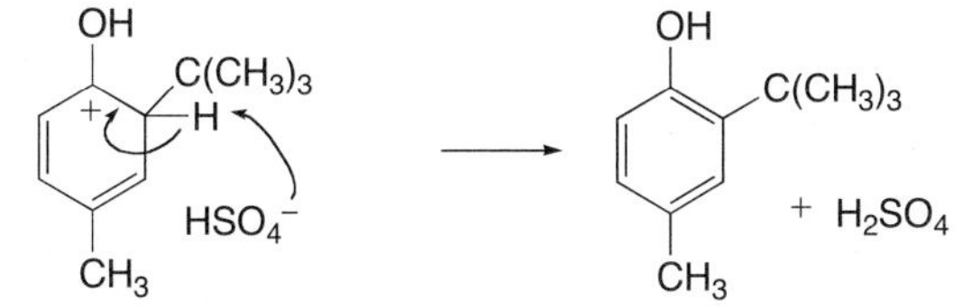

Repeat to add the second $C(CH_3)_3$ group.

18.75 Five resonance structures can be drawn for phenol, three of which place a negative charge on the ortho and para carbons. These illustrate that the electron density at these positions is increased, thus shielding the protons at these positions and shifting the absorptions to lower chemical shift. Similar resonance structures cannot be drawn with a negative charge at the meta position, so it is more deshielded and absorbs farther downfield, at higher chemical shift.

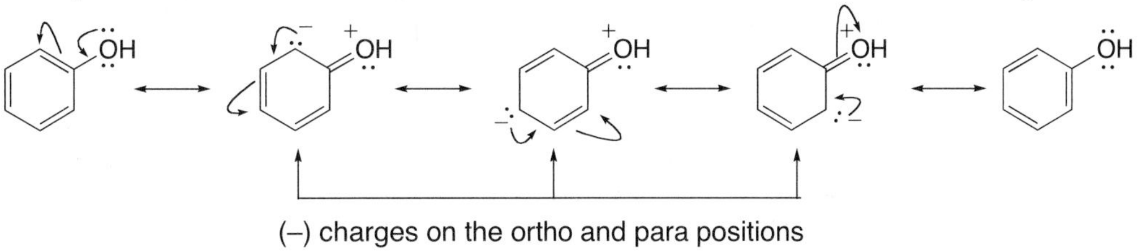

18.76 a. Pyridine: The electron-withdrawing inductive effect of N makes the ring electron poor. Also, electrophiles E^+ can react with N, putting a positive charge on the ring. This makes the ring less reactive with another positively charged species.

To understand why substitution occurs at C3, compare the stability of the carbocation formed by attack at C2 and C3.

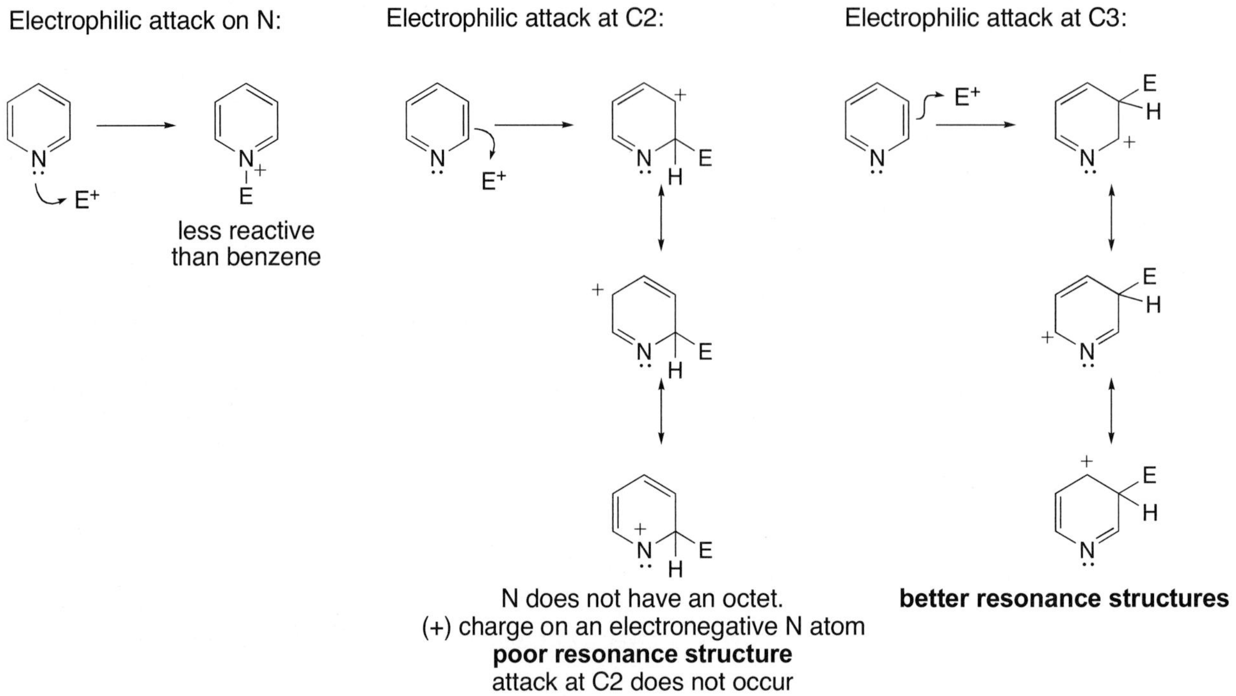
Electrophilic attack on N:
E+
E
less reactive
than benzene
Electrophilic attack at C2:
E+
N does not have an octet.
(+) charge on an electronegative N atom
poor resonance structure
attack at C2 does not occur
Electrophilic attack at C3:
E+
better resonance structures

Since attack at C3 forms a more stable carbocation, attack at C3 occurs. Attack at C4 generates a carbocation of similar stability to attack at C2, so attack at C4 does not occur.

b. Pyrrole is more reactive than benzene because the C's are more electron rich. The lone pair on N has an electron-donating resonance effect.

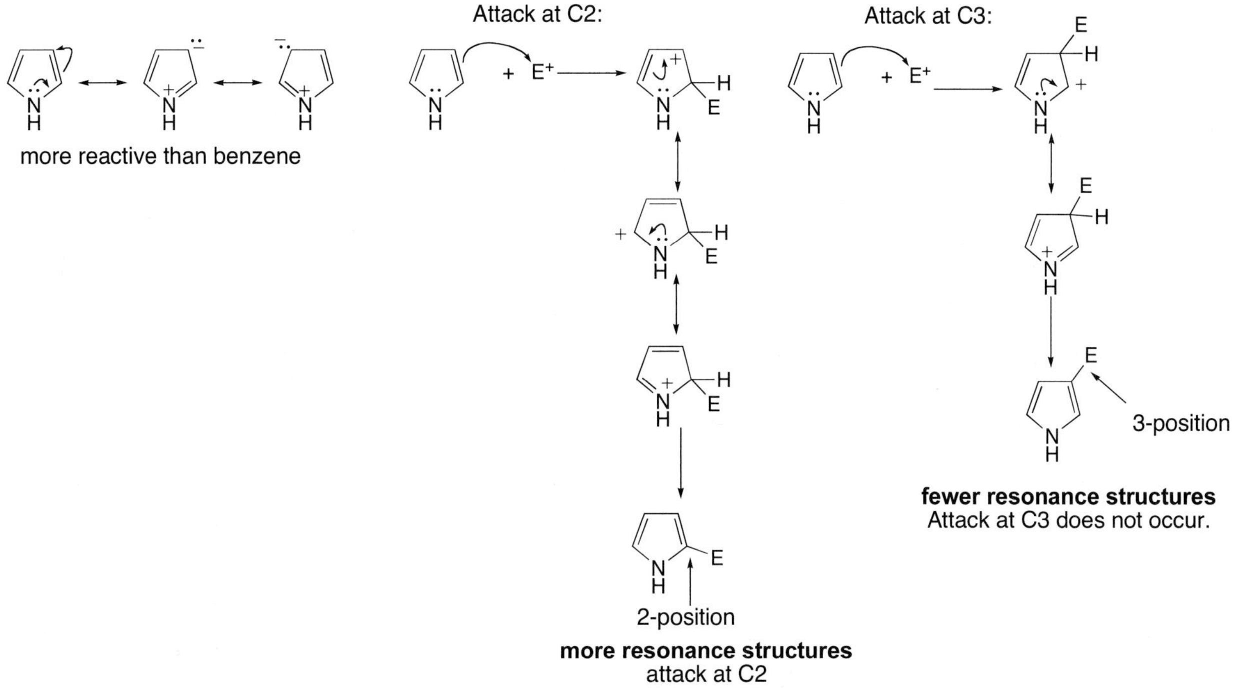

Since attack at C2 forms a more stable carbocation, electrophilic substitution occurs at C2.

18.77

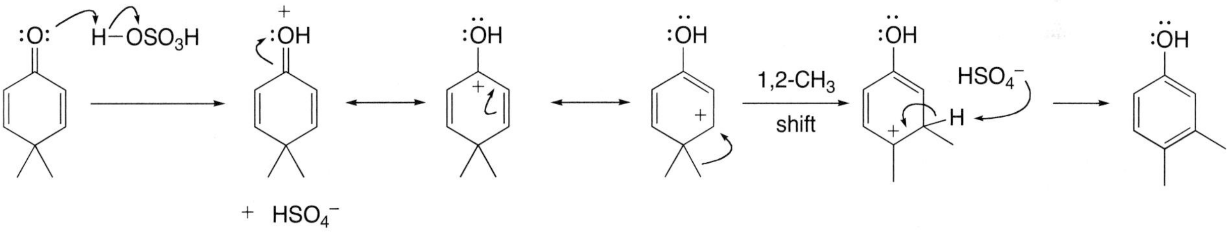

18.78 Draw a stepwise mechanism for the following intramolecular reaction, which was used in the synthesis of the female sex hormone estrone.

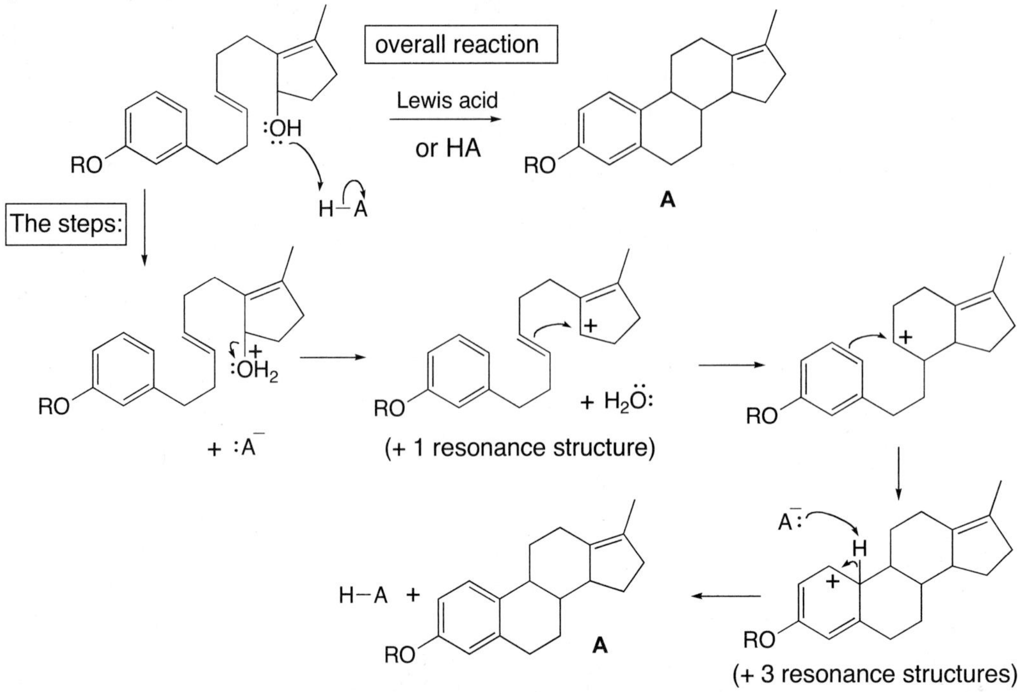

18.79 a. In quinoline the lone pair on N occupies an sp^2 hybrid orbital, so it can never be donated to the ring by resonance. The N atom decreases the electron density of the ring in which it is located by an electron-withdrawing inductive effect, so substitution occurs on the other ring. In indole, the N atom donates its electron pair (which is contained in a *p* orbital) to the five-membered ring, increasing its electron density, so substitution occurs on the five-membered ring with the N atom.

b. In the presence of acid, the N atom is protonated prior to electrophilic attack. For substitution to occur at C8 rather than C7, the carbocation that results from electrophilic addition at C8 must be more stable. Attack at C8 generates a carbocation with more resonance structures and four structures keep one ring aromatic (**1–4**). Attack at C7 generates a carbocation with fewer resonance structures and only two have an intact aromatic ring (**5** and **6**).

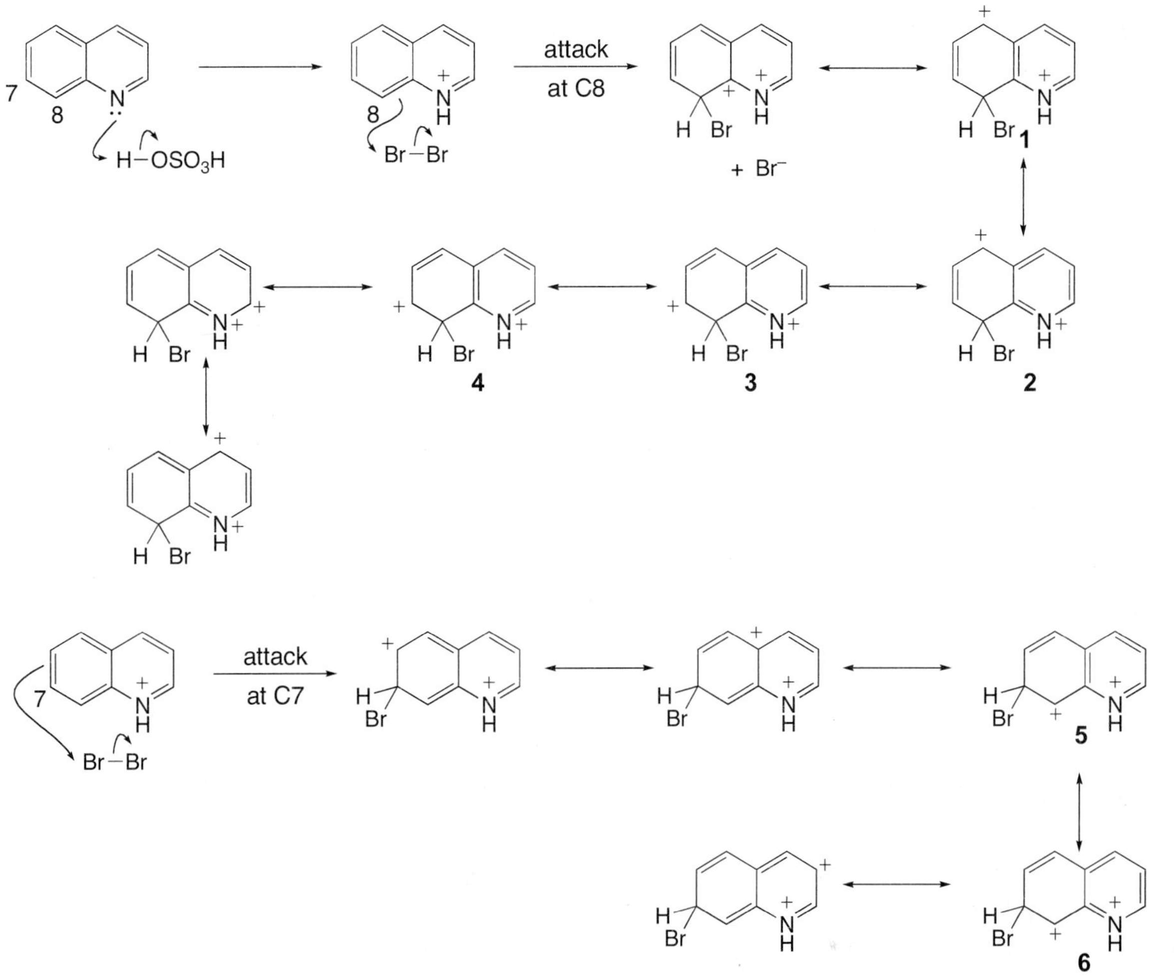

c. With indole, attack at C3 forms the more highly resonance-stabilized carbocation.

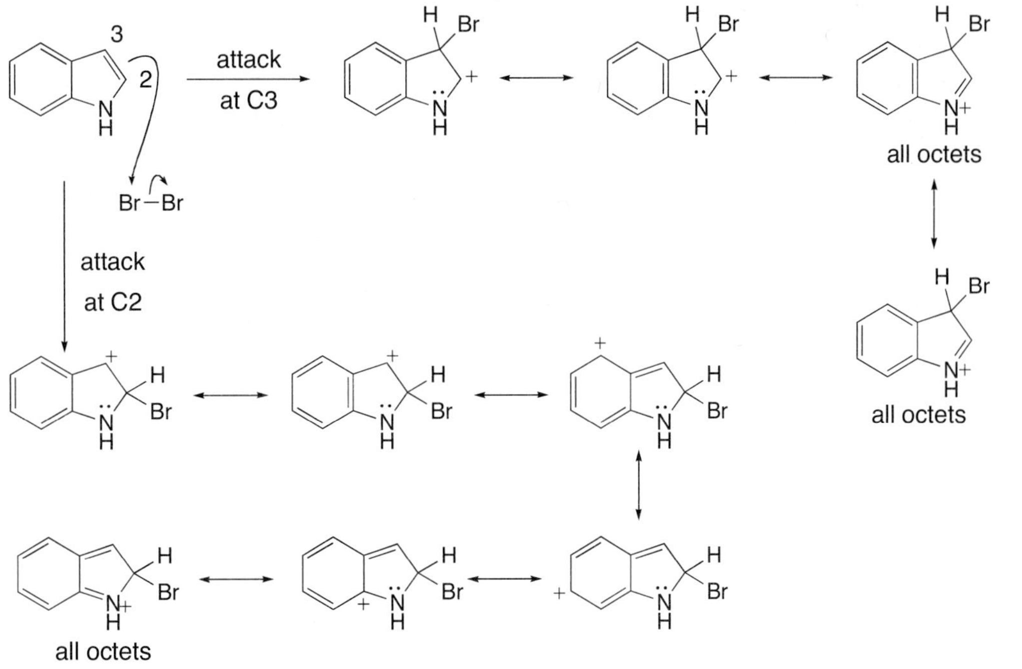

Attack at C3 forms resonance structures, all of which have an intact aromatic ring, and two of which have all atoms with octets. Attack at C2 forms a cation with more resonance structures, but only two have an intact aromatic ring, and only one has complete octets.

18.80

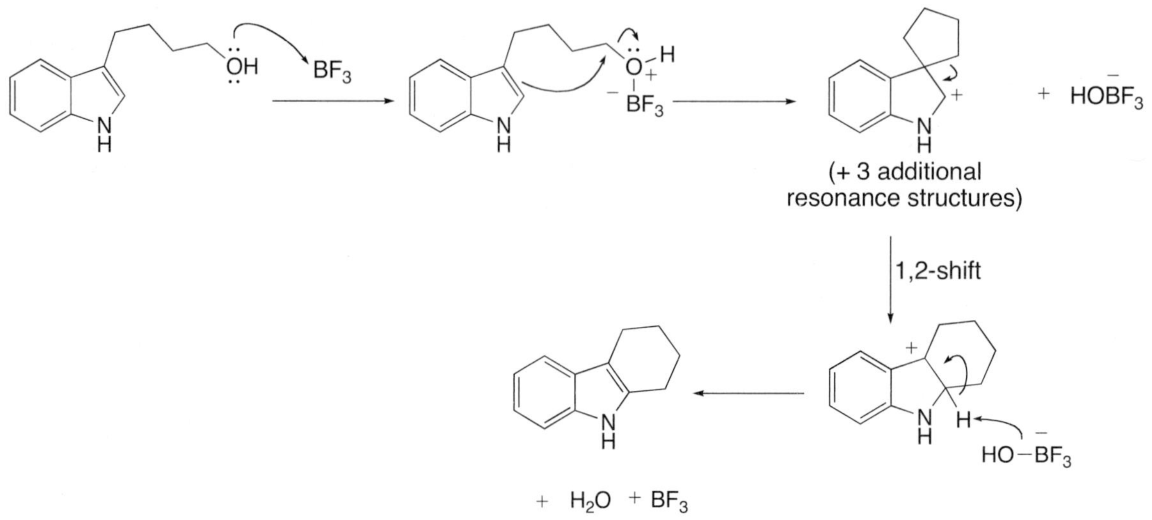

ÖH
BF3
O
H
BF3
+ HOBF3
(+ 3 additional resonance structures)
1,2-shift
H
HO−BF3
N
H
+ H2O + BF3

Chapter 19 Carboxylic Acids and the Acidity of the O–H Bond

Chapter Review

General facts

- Carboxylic acids contain a carboxy group (COOH). The central carbon is sp^2 hybridized and trigonal planar (19.1).
- Carboxylic acids are identified by the suffixes *-oic acid*, *carboxylic acid*, or *-ic acid* (19.2).
- Carboxylic acids are polar compounds that exhibit hydrogen bonding interactions (19.3).

Summary of spectroscopic absorptions (19.4)

IR absorptions	C=O	~1710 cm^{-1}
	O–H	3500–2500 cm^{-1} (very broad and strong)
^{1}H NMR absorptions	O–H	10–12 ppm (highly deshielded proton)
	C–H α to COOH	2–2.5 ppm (somewhat deshielded Csp^3–H)
^{13}C NMR absorption	C=O	170–210 ppm (highly deshielded carbon)

General acid–base reaction of carboxylic acids (19.9)

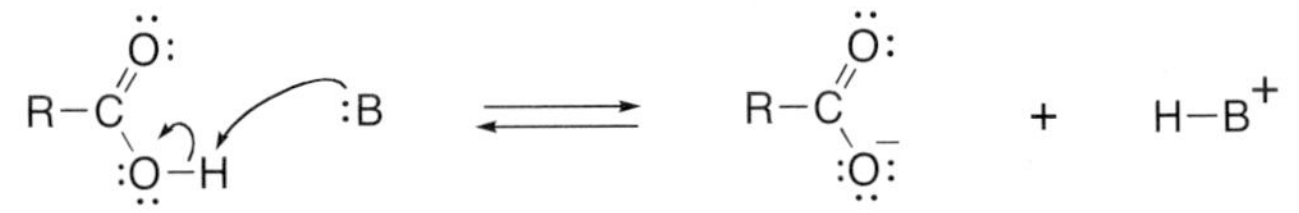

R–C
:B
R–C
+
H–B+

p$K_a \approx 5$ carboxylate anion

- Carboxylic acids are especially acidic because carboxylate anions are resonance stabilized.
- For equilibrium to favor the products, the base must have a conjugate acid with a pK_a > 5. Common bases are listed in Table 19.3.

Factors that affect acidity

Resonance effects. A carboxylic acid is more acidic than an alcohol or phenol because its conjugate base is more effectively stabilized by resonance (19.9).

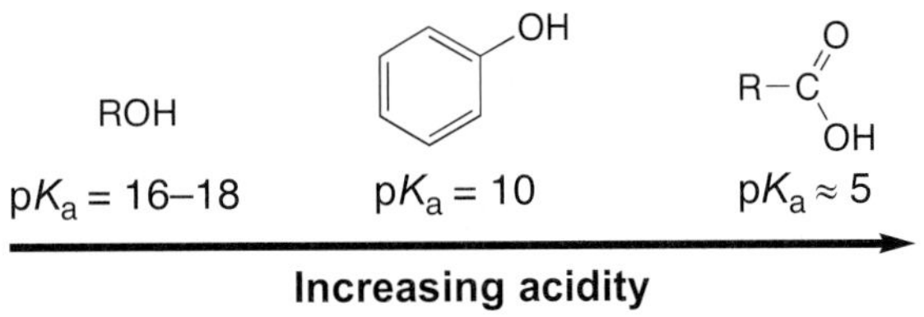

ROH
OH
R–C
OH
pK_a = 16–18
pK_a = 10
p$K_a \approx$ 5
Increasing acidity

Inductive effects. Acidity increases with the presence of electron-withdrawing groups (like the electronegative halogens) and decreases with the presence of electron-donating groups (like polarizable alkyl groups) (19.10).

Substituted benzoic acids.

- Electron-donor groups (D) make a substituted benzoic acid less acidic than benzoic acid.
- Electron-withdrawing groups (W) make a substituted benzoic acid more acidic than benzoic acid.

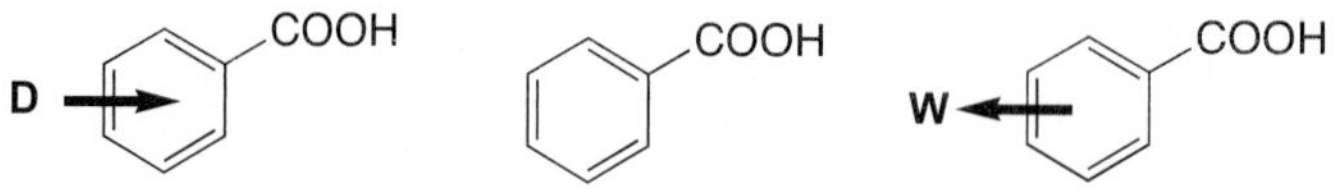

less acidic higher pK_a $pK_a > 4.2$	$pK_a = 4.2$	more acidic lower pK_a $pK_a < 4.2$

Increasing acidity →

Other facts

- Extraction is a useful technique for separating compounds having different solubility properties. Carboxylic acids can be separated from other organic compounds by extraction, because aqueous base converts a carboxylic acid into a water-soluble carboxylate anion (19.12).
- A sulfonic acid (RSO_3H) is a strong acid because it forms a weak, resonance-stabilized conjugate base on deprotonation (19.13).
- Amino acids have an amino group on the α carbon to the carboxy group [$RCH(NH_2)COOH$]. Amino acids exist as zwitterions at pH ≈ 6. Adding acid forms a species with a net (+1) charge $[RCH(NH_3)COOH]^+$. Adding base forms a species with a net (–1) charge $[RCH(NH_2)COO]^-$ (19.14).

Practice Test on Chapter Review

1. a. Give the IUPAC name for the following compound.

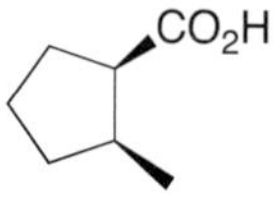

b. Draw the structure corresponding to the following name: sodium *m*-bromobenzoate.

2. a. Which of the labeled atoms is least acidic?

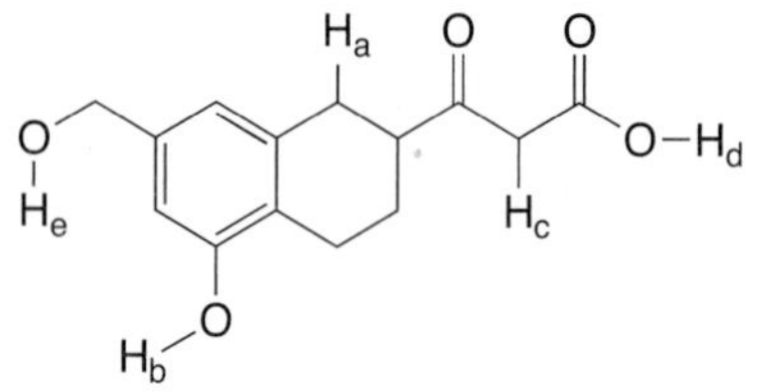

1. H_a 2. H_b 3. H_c 4. H_d 5. H_e

b. Which of the following carboxylic acids has the lowest pK_a?

1. 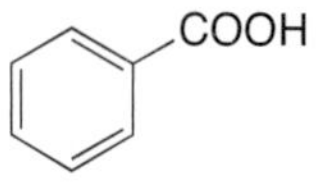

2. 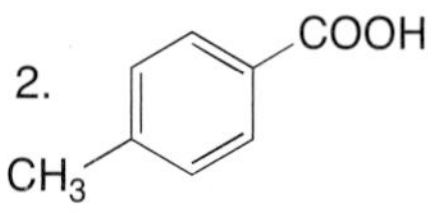

3. 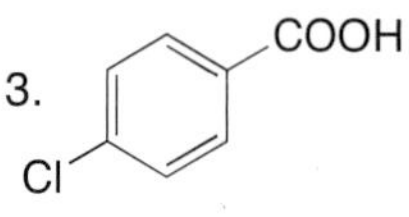

4. 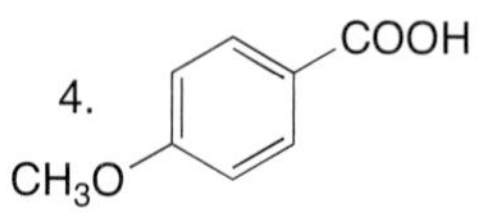

5. 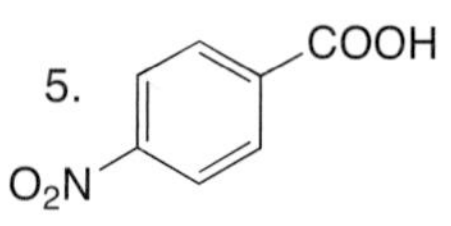

c. Which compound(s) can be converted to **A** by an oxidation reaction?

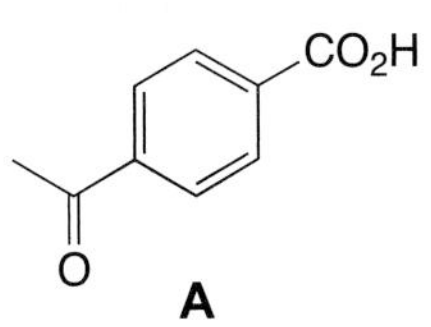
CO2H

A

1. 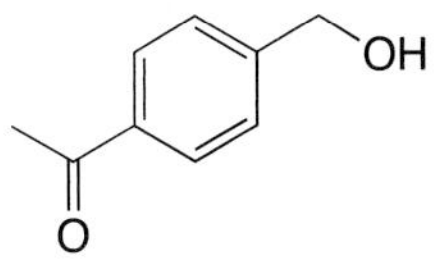
OH
O

2. 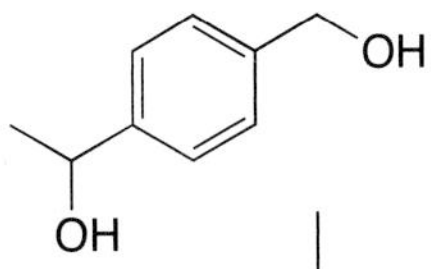
OH
OH

3. 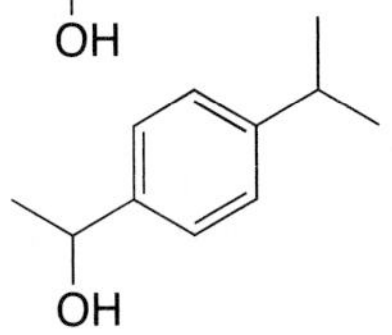
OH

4. Both [1] and [2] can be converted to **A.**

5. Compounds [1], [2], and [3] can all be converted to **A.**

3. Rank the following compounds in order of increasing basicity. Label the ***least*** basic compound as **1,** the ***most*** basic compound as **3,** and the compound of ***intermediate*** basicity as **2.**

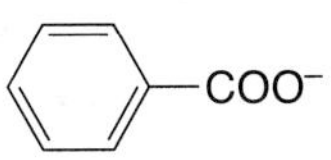
COO⁻

A

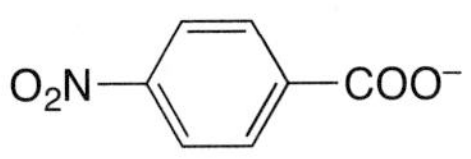
O2N
COO⁻

B

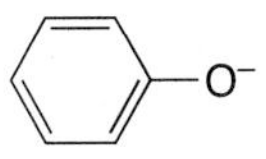
O⁻

C

4. Draw the organic products formed in each of the following reactions.

a. 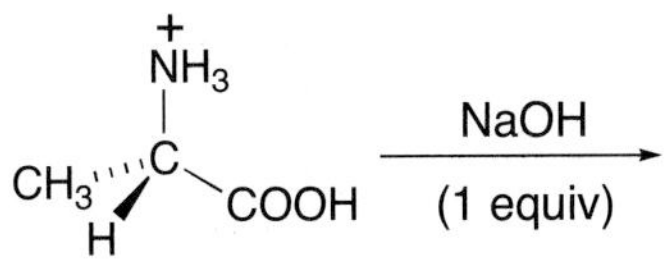
NH3
CH3
C
H
COOH
NaOH
(1 equiv)

b. 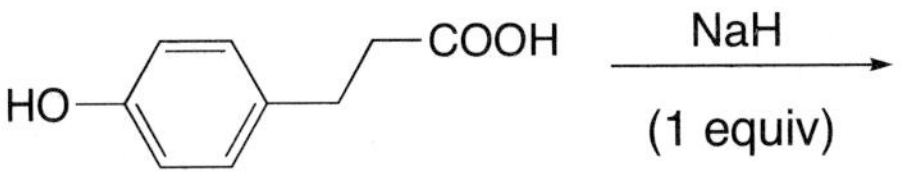
HO
COOH
NaH
(1 equiv)

c. 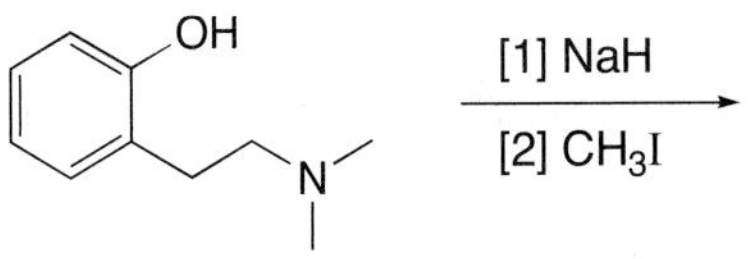
OH
N
[1] NaH
[2] CH3I

Answers to Practice Test

1.a. *cis*-2-methylcyclopentanecarboxylic acid

b. 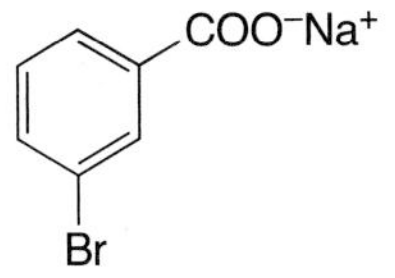
COO⁻Na⁺
Br

2.a. 1
b. 5
c. 5

3. **A**–2
B–1
C–3

4.a. 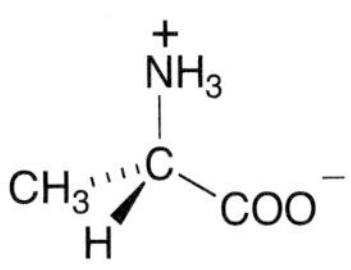
NH3
CH3
C
H
COO⁻

b. 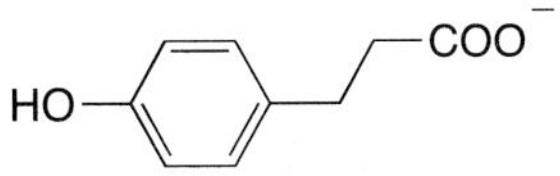
HO
COO⁻

c. 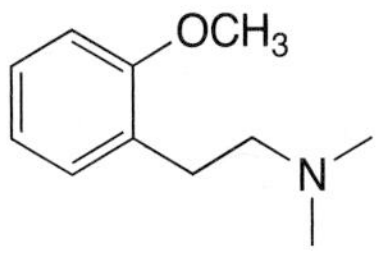
OCH3
N

Answers to Problems

19.1 To name a carboxylic acid:

[1] Find the longest chain containing the COOH group and change the *-e* ending to *-oic acid.*
[2] Number the chain to put the COOH carbon at C1, but omit the number from the name.
[3] Follow all other rules of nomenclature.

a. 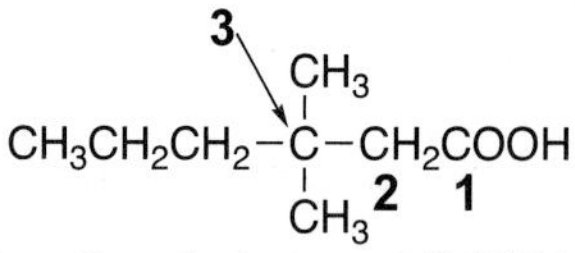
3
CH3
CH3CH2CH2–C–CH2COOH
CH3 2 1

Number the chain to put COOH at C1.
6 carbon chain = **hexanoic acid**
3,3-dimethylhexanoic acid

c. 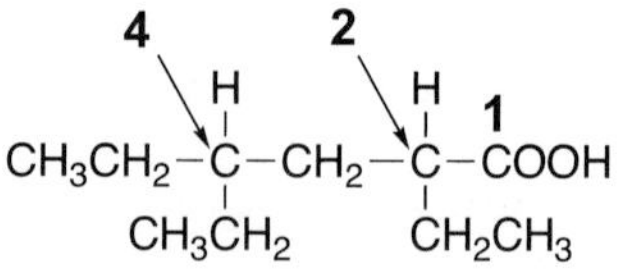
4 2
H H 1
CH3CH2–C–CH2–C–COOH
CH3CH2 CH2CH3

Number the chain to put COOH at C1.
6 carbon chain = **hexanoic acid**
2,4-diethylhexanoic acid

b. 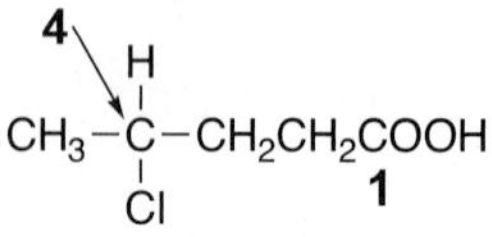
4
H
CH3–C–CH2CH2COOH
Cl 1

Number the chain to put COOH at C1.
5 carbon chain = **pentanoic acid**
4-chloropentanoic acid

d. 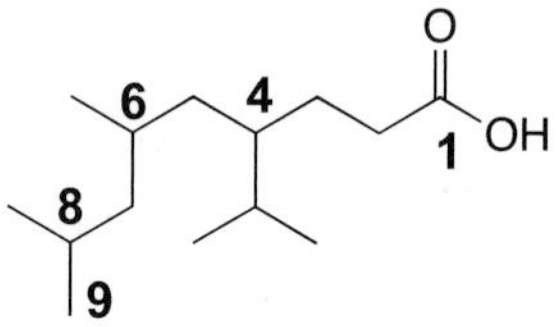
O
6 4
1 OH
8
9

Number the chain to put COOH at C1.
9 carbon chain = **nonanoic acid**
4-isopropyl-6,8-dimethylnonanoic acid

19.2

a. 2-bromo**butanoic acid**

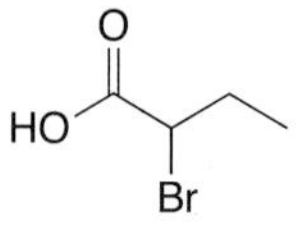

c. 3,3,4-trimethyl**heptanoic acid**

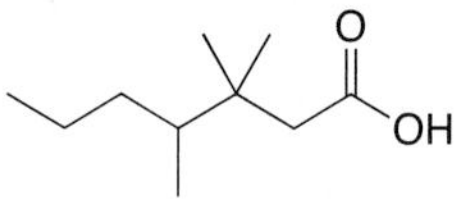

e. 3,4-diethyl**cyclohexanecarboxylic acid**

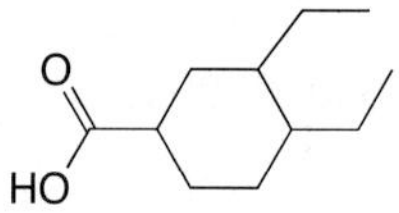

b. 2,3-dimethyl**pentanoic acid**

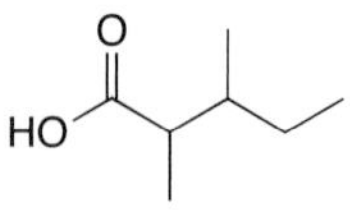

d. 2-*sec*-butyl-4,4-diethyl**nonanoic acid**

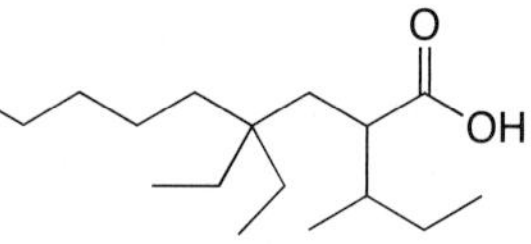

f. 1-isopropyl**cyclobutane-carboxylic acid**

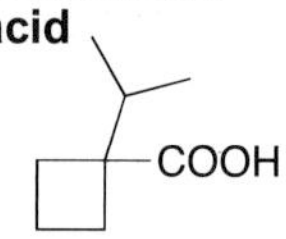

19.3

a. α-methoxy**valeric acid**

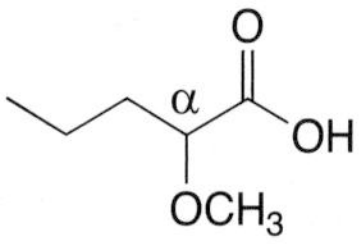

c. α,β-dimethyl**caproic acid**

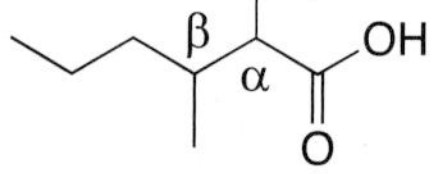

b. β-phenyl**propionic acid**

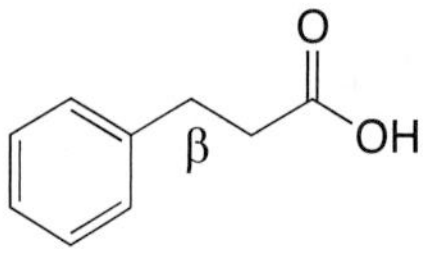

d. α-chloro-β-methyl**butyric acid**

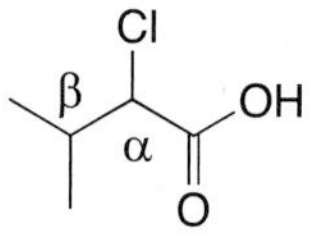

19.4

a. 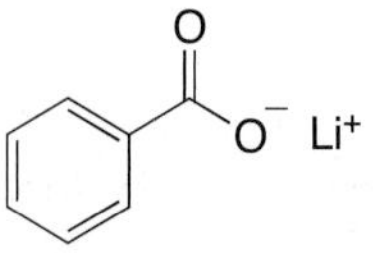

lithium benzoate

b. 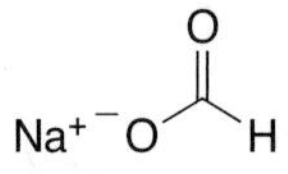

sodium formate
or
sodium methanoate

c. 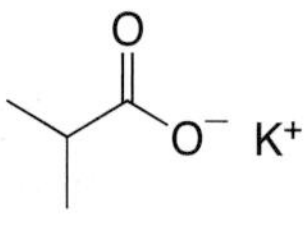

potassium 2-methylpropanoate

d. 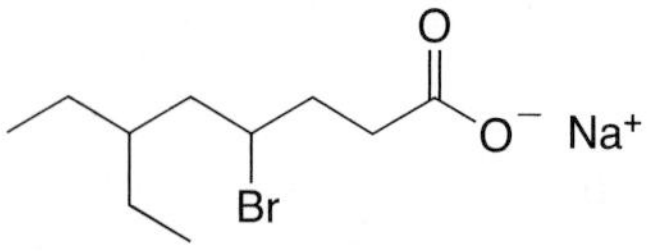

sodium 4-bromo-6-ethyl-octanoate

19.5

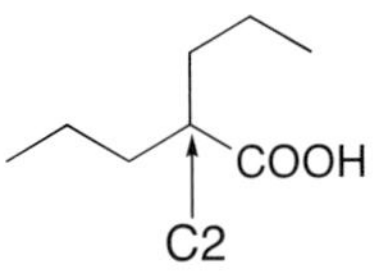
COOH
C2

2-propyl**pentanoic acid**

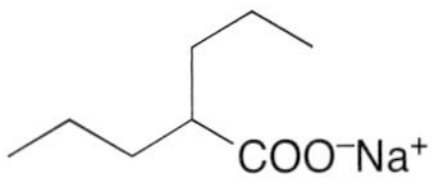
COO⁻Na⁺

sodium 2-propyl**pentanoate**

19.6 More polar molecules have a higher boiling point and are more water soluble.

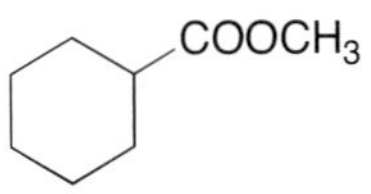
$COOCH_3$

least polar
lowest boiling point
least H_2O soluble

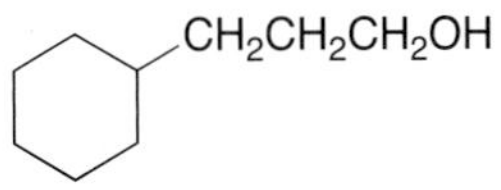
$CH_2CH_2CH_2OH$

intermediate polarity
intermediate boiling point

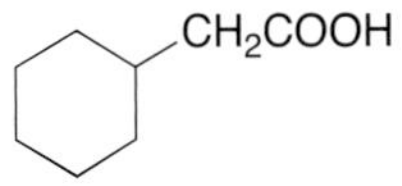
CH_2COOH

most polar
highest boiling point
most H_2O soluble

19.7 Look for functional group differences to distinguish the compounds by IR. Besides *sp*^{3} hybridized C–H bonds at 3000–2850 cm^{-1} (which all three compounds have), the following functional group absorptions are seen:

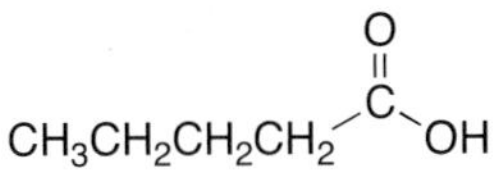
$CH_3CH_2CH_2CH_2$
O
C
OH

carboxylic acid
2 strong absorptions
~1710 (C=O)
~2500–3500 (OH) cm^{-1}

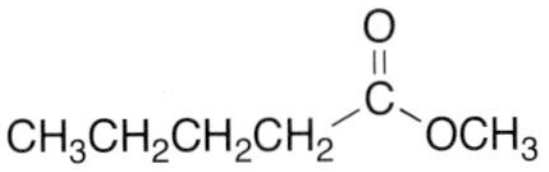
$CH_3CH_2CH_2CH_2$
O
C
OCH_3

ester
1 strong absorption
~1700 (C=O) cm^{-1}

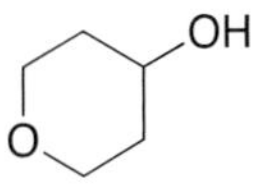
OH
O

alcohol
1 strong absorption
~3600–3200 (OH) cm^{-1}

19.8

Molecular formula: $C_4H_8O_2$
one degree of unsaturation

^{1}H NMR data (ppm):
0.95 (triplet, 3 H)
1.65 (multiplet, 2 H)
2.30 (triplet, 2 H)
11.8 (singlet, 1 H)

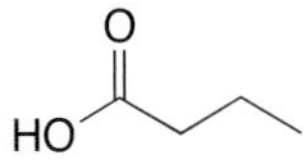
O
HO

19.9

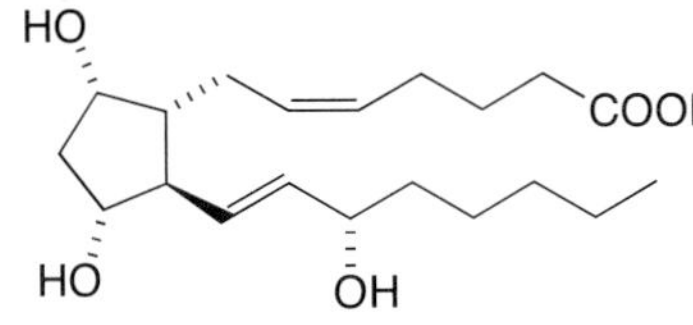
HO
COOH
HO
OH

$PGF_{2\alpha}$
a prostaglandin

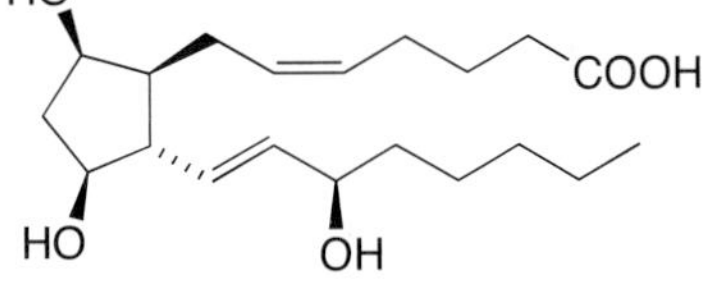
HO
COOH
HO
OH

enantiomer

There are five tetrahedral stereogenic centers. Both double bonds can exhibit cis–trans isomerism. Therefore, there are 2^7 = 128 stereoisomers.

19.10 1° Alcohols are converted to carboxylic acids by oxidation reactions.

a. 
O
OH
OH

c. 
COOH
CH_2OH

b. 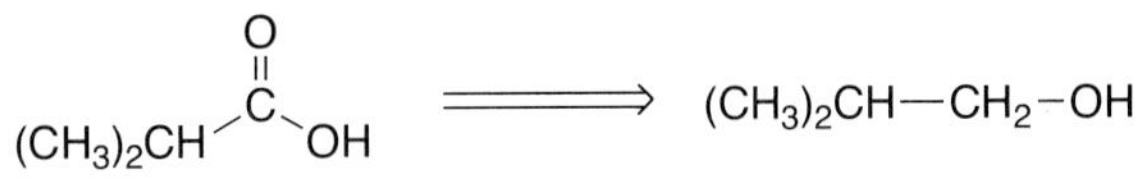
O
C
$(CH_3)_2CH$
OH
$(CH_3)_2CH—CH_2–OH$

19.11

a.

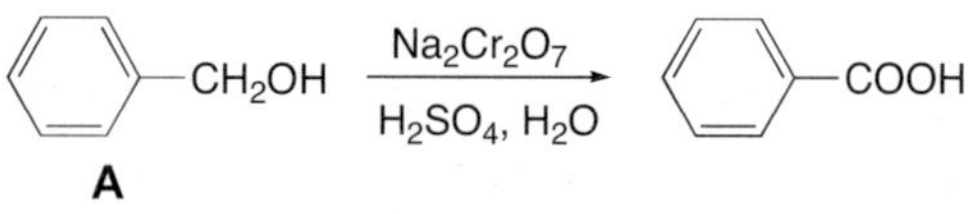

c.

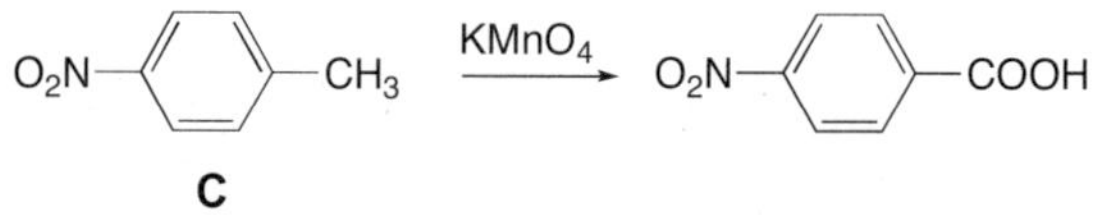

(Any R group with benzylic H's can be present para to NO_2.)

b. $CH_3C{\equiv}CCH_3$ (**B**) $\xrightarrow[\text{[2] } H_2O]{\text{[1] } O_3}$ CH_3COOH (2 equiv)

d.

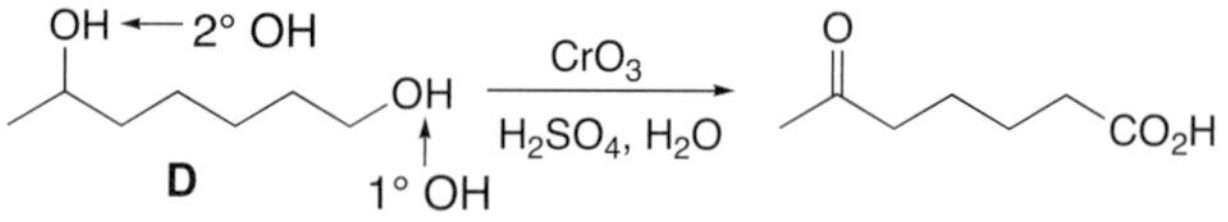

19.12

a.

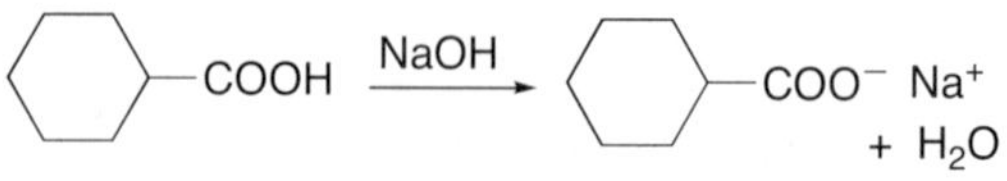

c. $CH_3-C(CH_3)_2-OH \xrightarrow{NaH} CH_3-C(CH_3)_2-O^- \ Na^+ + H_2$

b.

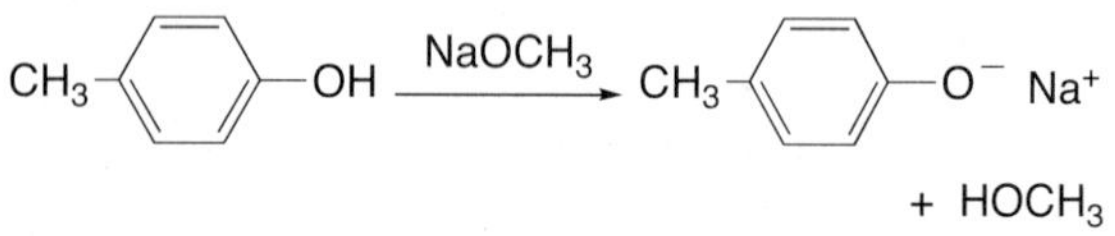

d.

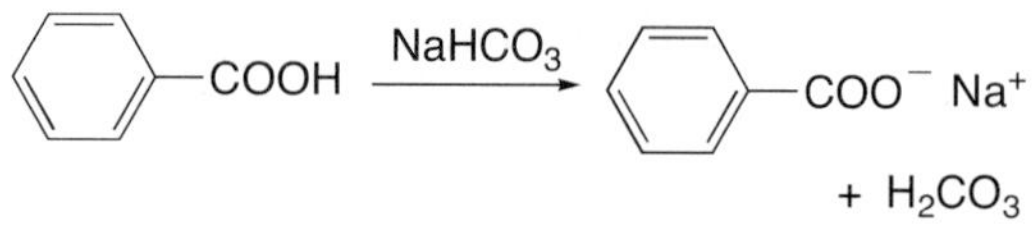

19.13 CH_3COOH has a pK_a of 4.8. Any base having a conjugate acid with a pK_a higher than 4.8 can deprotonate it.

a. F^- pK_a (HF) = 3.2 **not strong enough**
b. $(CH_3)_3CO^-$ pK_a [$(CH_3)_3COH$]= 18 **strong enough**
c. CH_3^- pK_a (CH_4) = 50 **strong enough**
d. $^-NH_2$ pK_a (NH_3) = 38 **strong enough**
e. Cl^- pK_a (HCl) = –7.0 **not strong enough**

19.14

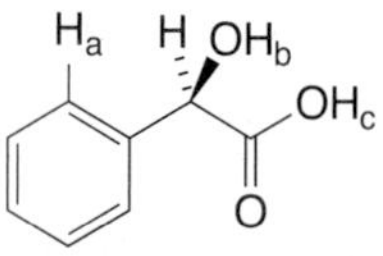

mandelic acid

Increasing acidity: $H_a < H_b < H_c$

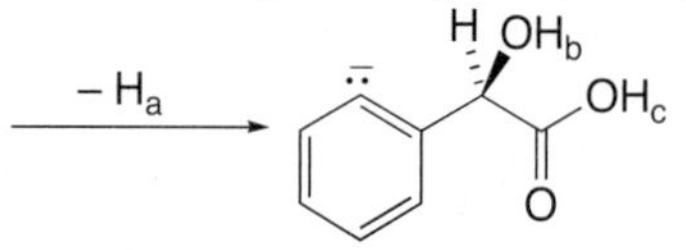

negative charge on C
unstable conjugate base

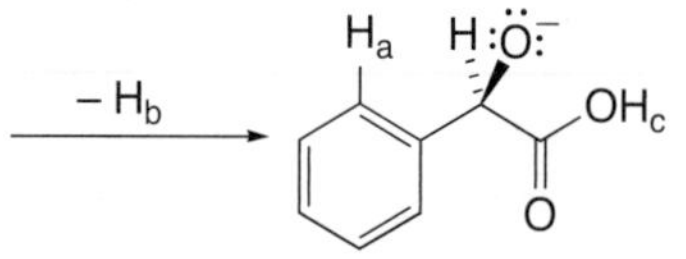

negative charge on O
more stable conjugate base

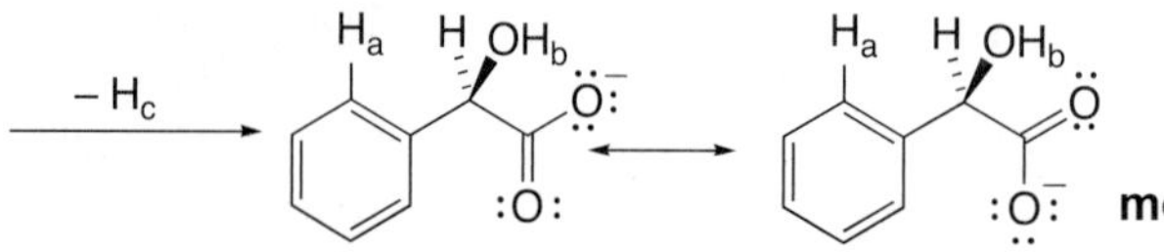

negative charge on O, resonance stabilized
most stable conjugate base

19.15 Electron-withdrawing groups make an acid more acidic, lowering its pK_a.

CH_3CH_2-COOH	ICH_2-COOH	CF_3-COOH
least acidic	one electron-withdrawing group	three electron-withdrawing F's
pK_a = 4.9	intermediate acidity	most acidic
	pK_a = 3.2	pK_a = 0.2

19.16

a. CH_3COOH — **least acidic**; $HSCH_2COOH$ — **intermediate acidity**; $HOCH_2COOH$ — **most acidic**

b. ICH_2CH_2COOH — **least acidic**; ICH_2COOH — **intermediate acidity**; $I_2CHCOOH$ — **most acidic**

19.17

a.

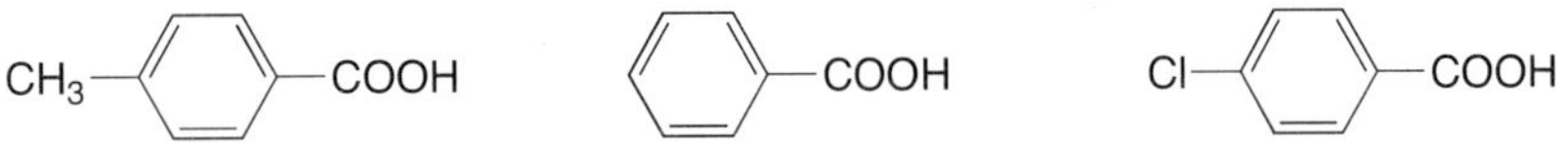
CH3
COOH
COOH
Cl
COOH

least acidic — **intermediate acidity** — **most acidic**

b.

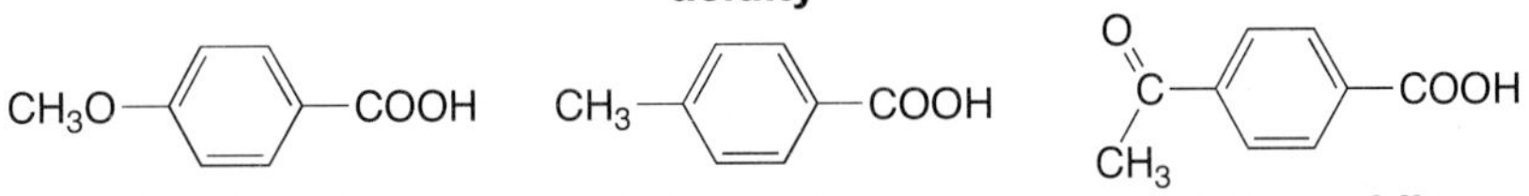
CH3O
COOH
CH3
COOH
O
C
CH3
COOH

least acidic — **intermediate acidity** — **most acidic**

19.18

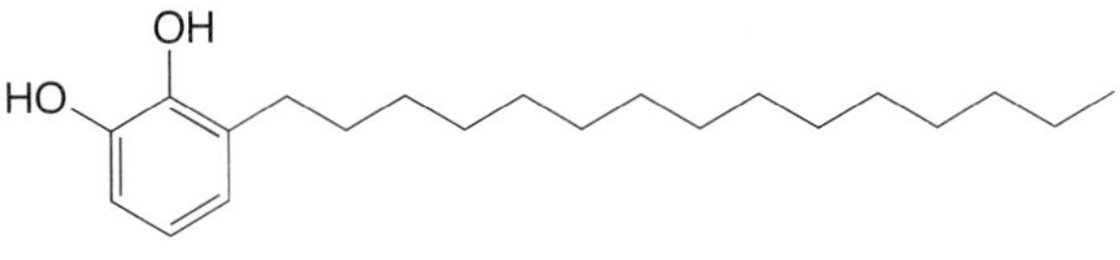
OH
HO

A

Phenol **A** has a higher pK_a than phenol because of its substituents. Both the OH and CH_3 are electron-donating groups, which make the conjugate base less stable. Therefore, the acid is **less acidic.**

19.19 To separate compounds by an extraction procedure, they must have different solubility properties.

a. $CH_3(CH_2)_6COOH$ and $CH_3CH_2CH_2CH_2CH{=}CH_2$: **YES.** The acid can be extracted into aqueous base, while the alkene will remain in an organic layer.

b. $CH_3CH_2CH_2CH_2CH{=}CH_2$ and $(CH_3CH_2CH_2)_2O$: **NO.** Both compounds are soluble in organic solvents and insoluble in water. Neither is acidic enough to be extracted into aqueous base.

c. $CH_3(CH_2)_6COOH$ and NaCl: one carboxylic acid, one salt: **YES.** The carboxylic acid is soluble in an organic solvent while the salt is soluble in water.

d. NaCl and KCl: two salts: **NO.**

19.20

$CF_3SO_3H \longrightarrow CF_3SO_3^-$ (weaker conjugate base, better leaving group)

CF_3 is electron *withdrawing.*
stronger acid
lower pK_a

$CH_3SO_3H \longrightarrow CH_3SO_3^-$ (stronger conjugate base, worse leaving group)

CH_3 is electron *donating.*
weaker acid
higher pK_a

19.21

phenylalanine

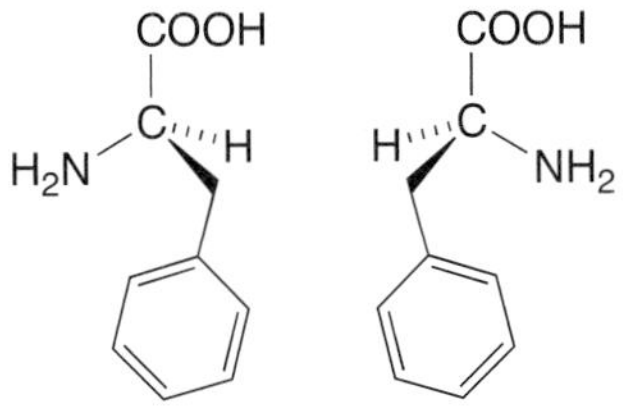
COOH
C
H
H2N
COOH
H
C
NH2

R — *S*

methionine

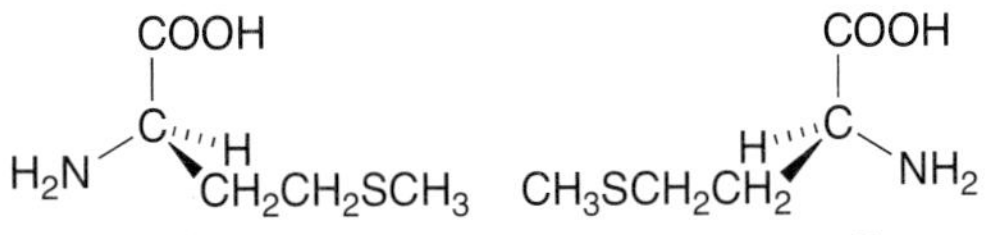
COOH
C
H
H2N
CH2CH2SCH3
COOH
H
C
NH2
CH3SCH2CH2

R — *S*

19.22 Since amino acids exist as zwitterions (i.e., salts), they are too polar to be soluble in organic solvents like diethyl ether. Thus, they are soluble in water.

19.23

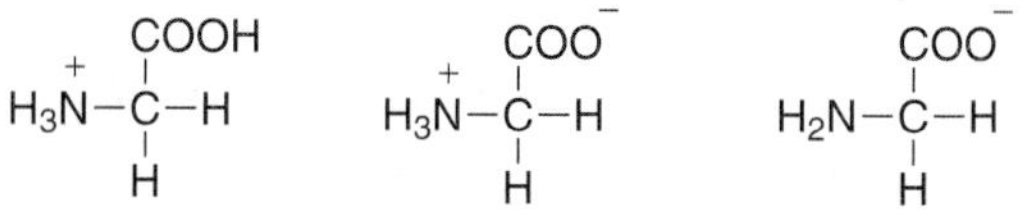

pH = 1 | glycine neutral form | pH = 11

19.24

$$pI = \frac{pK_a(COOH) + pK_a(NH_3^+)}{2} = \frac{(2.58) + (9.24)}{2} = 5.91$$

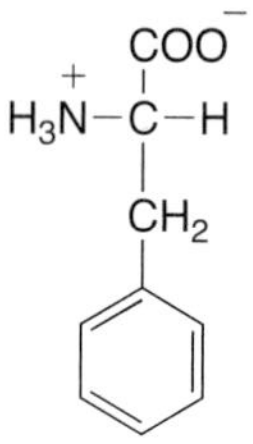

19.25

electron-withdrawing group

The nearby (+) stabilizes the conjugate base by an electron-withdrawing inductive effect, thus making the starting acid more acidic.

19.26

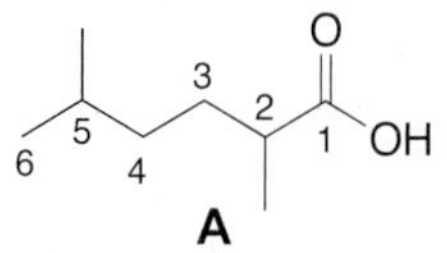

A

a. 2,5-dimethylhexanoic acid

b.

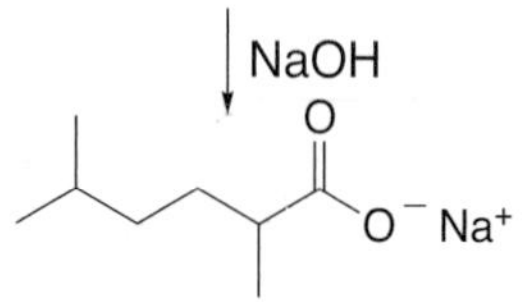

c. sodium 2,5-dimethylhexanoate

d. An alcohol or ether would have a much higher pK_a than a carboxylic acid.

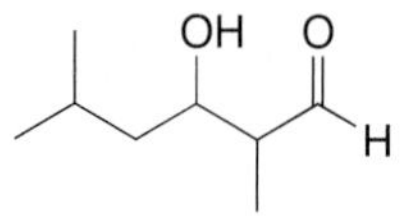

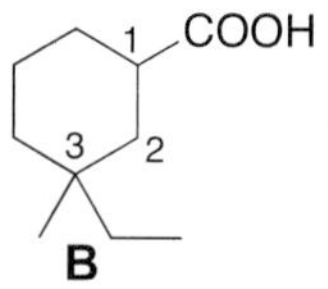

B

a. 3-ethyl-3-methylcyclohexanecarboxylic acid

b.

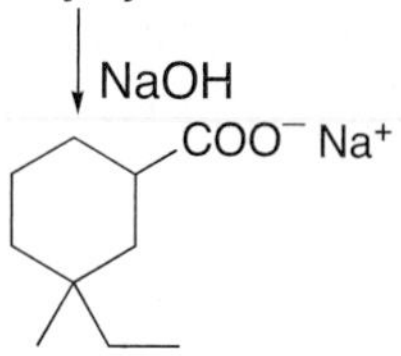

c. sodium 3-ethyl-3-methylcyclohexanecarboxylate

d.

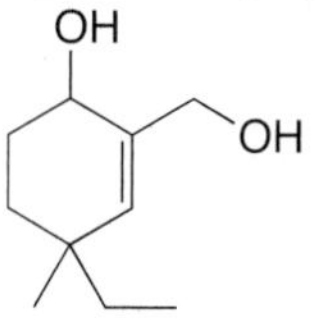

19.27

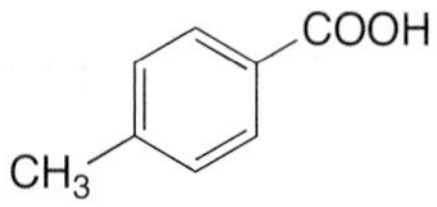

least acidic

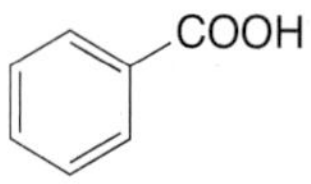

intermediate acidity

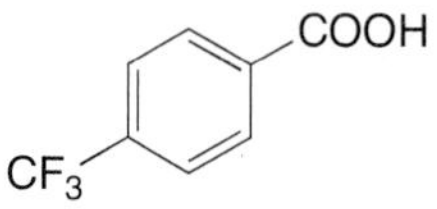

most acidic

19.28 Use the directions from Answer 19.1 to name the compounds.

a. $(CH_3)_2CHCH_2CH_2CO_2H$ 4-methylpentanoic acid

b. $BrCH_2COOH$ 2-bromoacetic acid or 2-bromoethanoic acid

c. 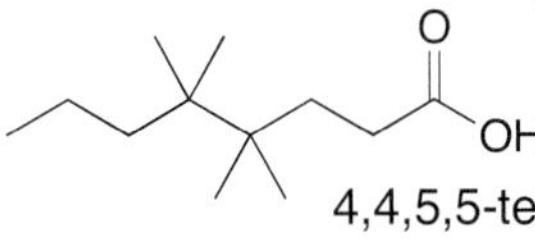
4,4,5,5-tetramethyloctanoic acid

d. $CH_3CH_2CH_2COO^{-}Li^{+}$ lithium butanoate

e. 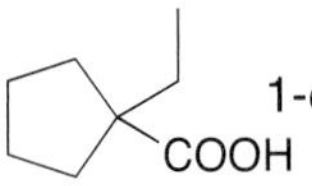
1-ethylcyclopentanecarboxylic acid

f. 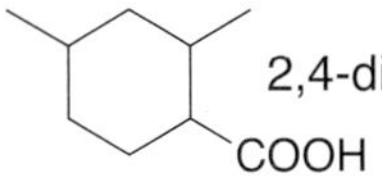
2,4-dimethylcyclohexanecarboxylic acid

g. 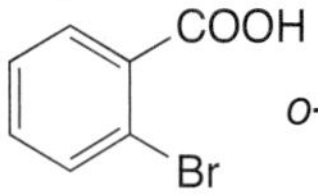
o-bromobenzoic acid

h. 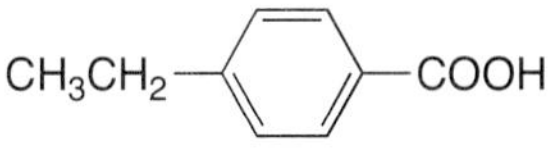
p-ethylbenzoic acid

i. 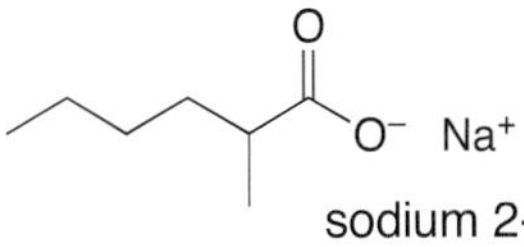
sodium 2-methylhexanoate

j. 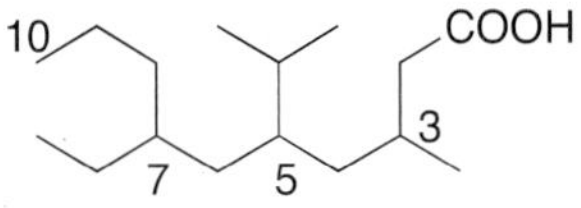
7-ethyl-5-isopropyl-3-methyldecanoic acid

19.29

a. 3,3-dimethylpentanoic acid 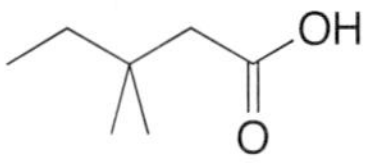

b. 4-chloro-3-phenylheptanoic acid 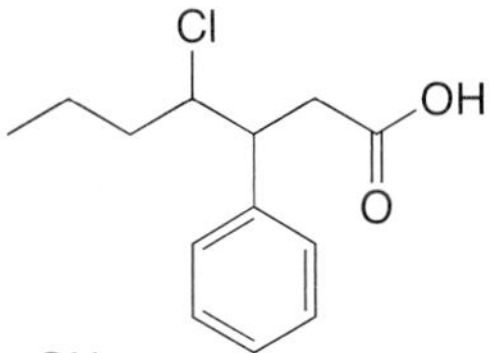

c. (2*R*)-2-chloropropanoic acid 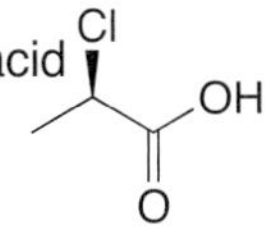

d. β,β-dichloropropionic acid 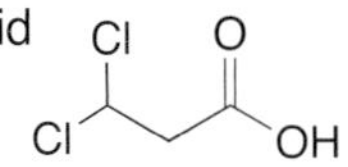

e. *m*-hydroxybenzoic acid 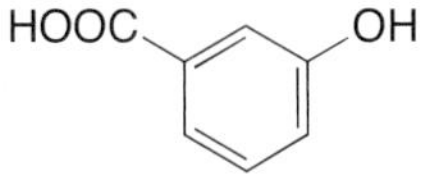

f. *o*-chlorobenzoic acid 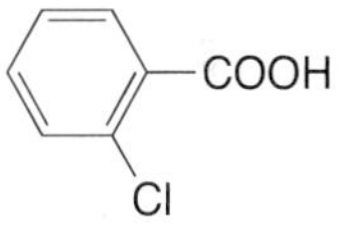

g. potassium acetate 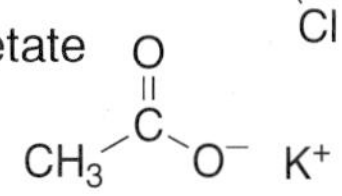

h. sodium α-bromobutyrate 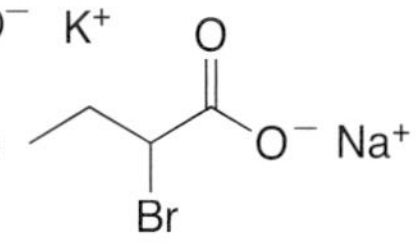

i. 2,2-dichloropentanedioic acid 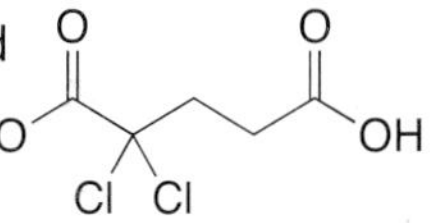

j. 4-isopropyl-2-methyloctanedioic acid 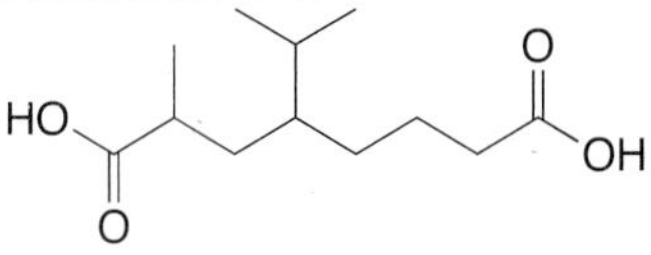

19.30

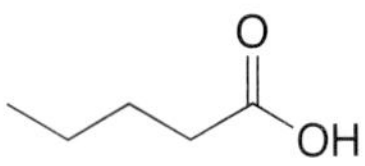
pentanoic acid

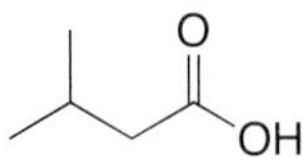
3-methylbutanoic acid

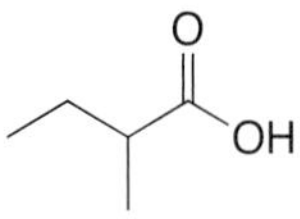
2-methylbutanoic acid

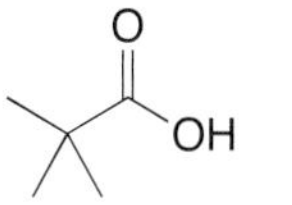
2,2-dimethylpropanoic acid

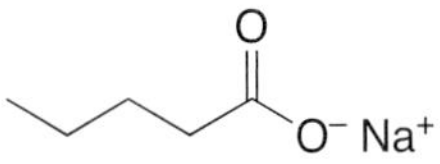
sodium pentanoate

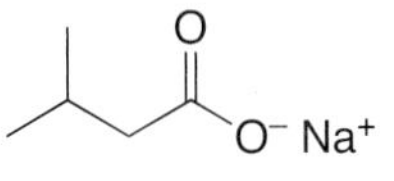
sodium 3-methylbutanoate

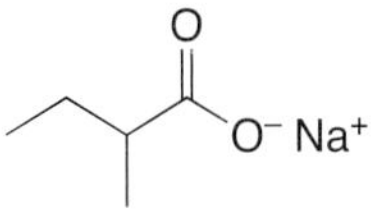
sodium 2-methylbutanoate

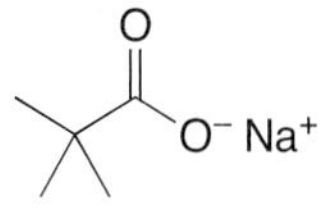
sodium 2,2-dimethylpropanoate

19.31

a. 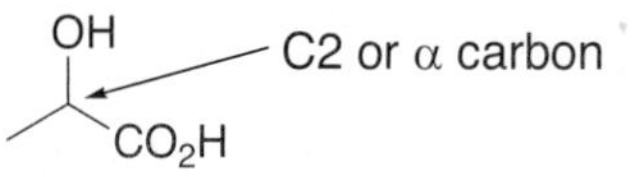
OH
C2 or α carbon
CO_2H

IUPAC: 2-hydroxy**propanoic acid**
common: α-hydroxy**propionic acid**

b. 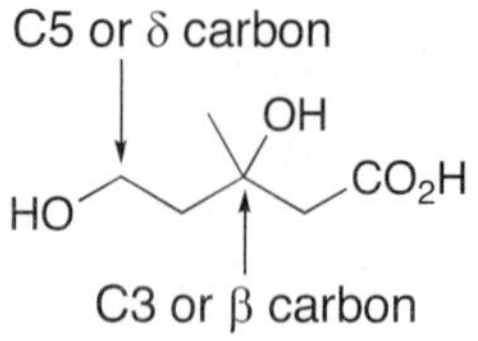
C5 or δ carbon
OH
HO
CO_2H
C3 or β carbon

IUPAC: 3,5-dihydroxy-3-methyl**pentanoic acid**
common: β,δ-dihydroxy-β-methyl**valeric acid**

19.32

a. 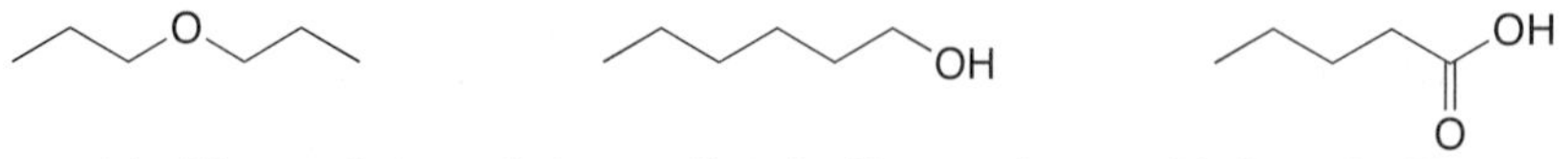
O
OH
OH
O

lowest boiling point | **intermediate boiling point** | **highest boiling point**

b. 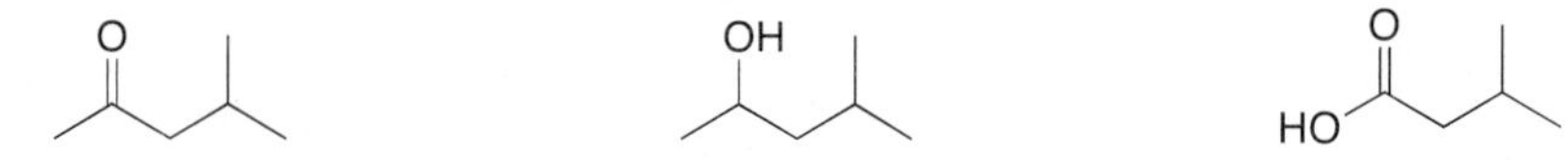
O
OH
O
HO

lowest boiling point | **intermediate boiling point** | **highest boiling point**

19.33

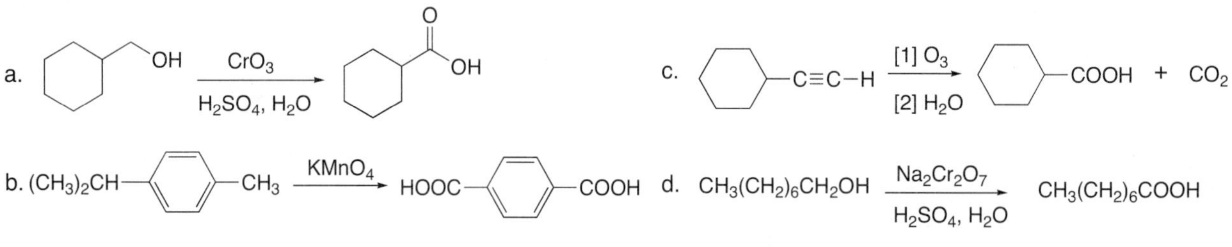
a.
OH
CrO_3
H_2SO_4, H_2O
O
OH
c.
C≡C–H
[1] O_3
[2] H_2O
COOH + CO_2
b. $(CH_3)_2CH$
CH_3
$KMnO_4$
HOOC
COOH

d. $CH_3(CH_2)_6CH_2OH \xrightarrow[H_2SO_4,\ H_2O]{Na_2Cr_2O_7} CH_3(CH_2)_6COOH$

19.34

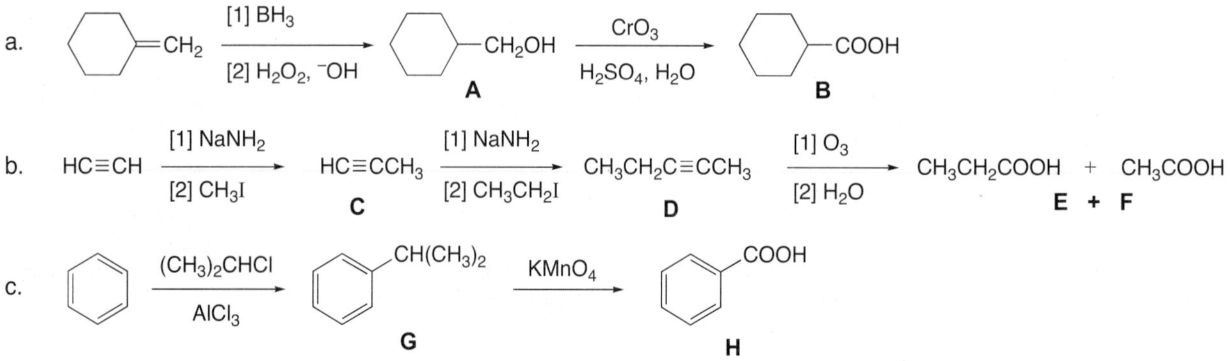
a.
$=CH_2$
[1] BH_3
[2] H_2O_2, ^-OH
CH_2OH
A
CrO_3
H_2SO_4, H_2O
COOH
B
b.
HC≡CH
[1] $NaNH_2$
[2] CH_3I
HC≡CCH_3
C
[1] $NaNH_2$
[2] CH_3CH_2I
$CH_3CH_2C{\equiv}CCH_3$
D
[1] O_3
[2] H_2O
CH_3CH_2COOH + CH_3COOH
E + F
c.
$(CH_3)_2CHCl$
$AlCl_3$
$CH(CH_3)_2$
G
$KMnO_4$
COOH
H

19.35

Bases: [1] ^-OH pK_a (H_2O) = 15.7; [2] $CH_3CH_2^-$ pK_a (CH_3CH_3) = 50; [3] $^-NH_2$ pK_a (NH_3) = 38; [4] NH_3 pK_a (NH_4^+) = 9.4; [5] HC≡C$^-$ pK_a (HC≡CH) = 25.

a. 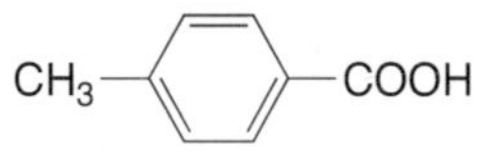
CH_3
COOH

pK_a = 4.3
All of the bases can deprotonate this.

b. 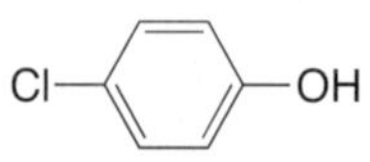
Cl
OH

pK_a = 9.4
^-OH, $CH_3CH_2^-$, $^-NH_2$, and HC≡C$^-$ can deprotonate this.

c. $(CH_3)_3COH$

pK_a = 18
$CH_3CH_2^-$, $^-NH_2$, and HC≡C$^-$ can deprotonate this.

19.36

a. 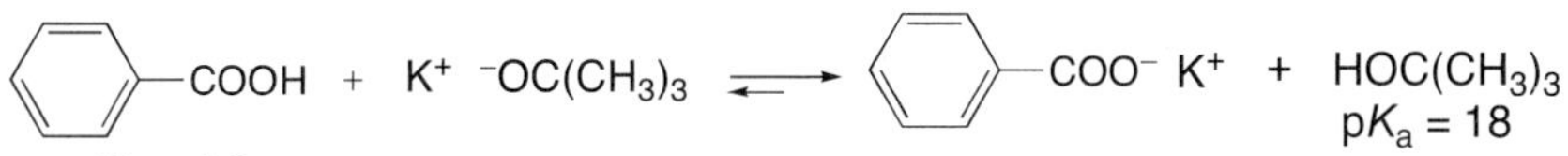
COOH
+ K+ −OC(CH3)3
COO− K+
+ HOC(CH3)3

pK_a = 4.2; pK_a = 18

Reaction favors products.

b. 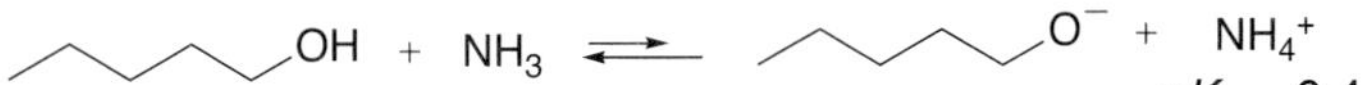
OH
+ NH3
O−
+ NH4+

pK_a ≈ 16; pK_a = 9.4

Reaction favors reactants.

c. 
OH
+ Na+NH2−
O−
+ NH3 + Na+

pK_a = 10; pK_a = 38

Reaction favors products.

d. 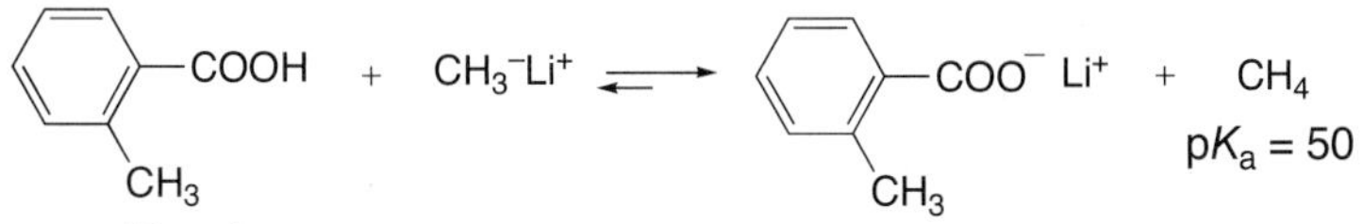
COOH
CH3
+ CH3−Li+
COO− Li+
CH3
+ CH4

pK_a ≈ 4; pK_a = 50

Reaction favors products.

e. 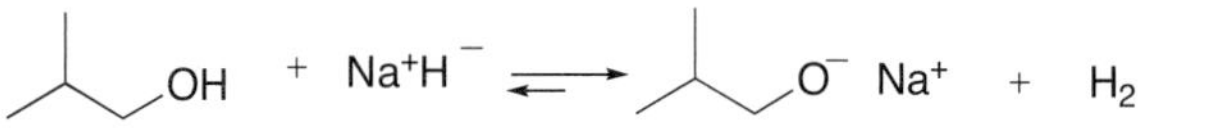
OH
+ Na+H−
O− Na+
+ H2

pK_a ≈ 16; pK_a = 35

Reaction favors products.

f. 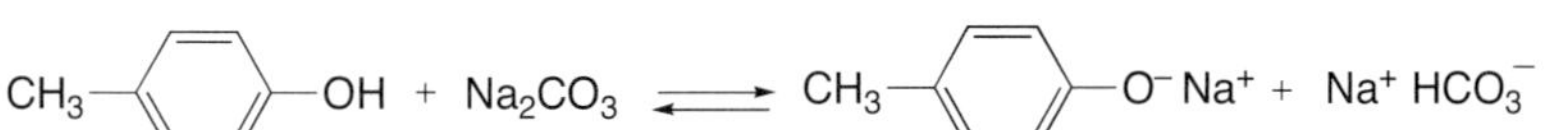
CH3
OH
+ Na2CO3
CH3
O− Na+
+ Na+ HCO3−

pK_a = 10.2; pK_a = 10.2

With the same pK_a for the starting acid and the conjugate acid, an equal amount of starting materials and products is present.

19.37 The stronger acid has a lower pK_a and a weaker conjugate base.

a. 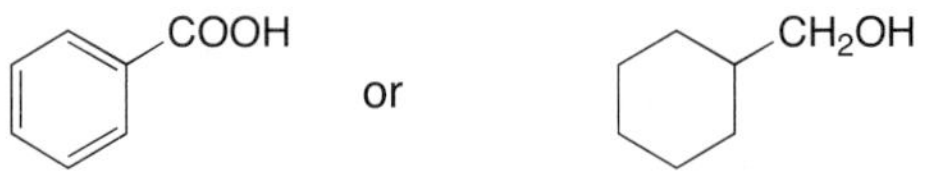
COOH
or
CH2OH

carboxylic acid	alcohol
stronger acid	weaker acid
lower pK_a	higher pK_a
weaker conjugate base	**stronger conjugate base**

b. $ClCH_2COOH$ or FCH_2COOH

$ClCH_2COOH$	FCH_2COOH
	F is more electronegative.
weaker acid	stronger acid
higher pK_a	**lower pK_a**
stronger conjugate base	weaker conjugate base

c. 
CH3
COOH
or
Cl
COOH

CH3 is electron donating.	Cl is electron withdrawing.
weaker acid	stronger acid
higher pK_a	**lower pK_a**
stronger conjugate base	weaker conjugate base

d. $NCCH_2COOH$ or CH_3COOH

$NCCH_2COOH$	CH_3COOH
CN is electron withdrawing.	
stronger acid	weaker acid
lower pK_a	higher pK_a
weaker conjugate base	**stronger conjugate base**

19.38

a. 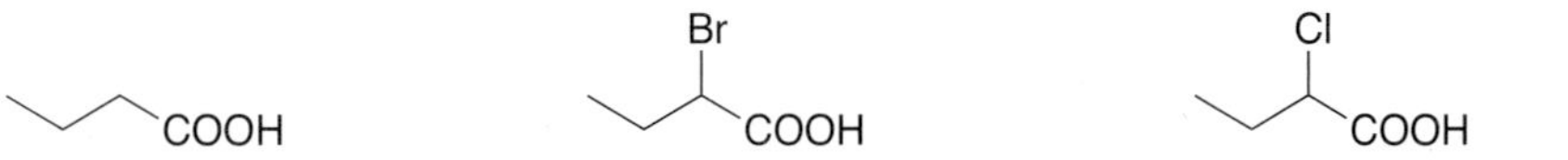
COOH
Br
COOH
Cl
COOH

least acidic | Br is electronegative **intermediate acidity** | Cl more electronegative **most acidic**

b. 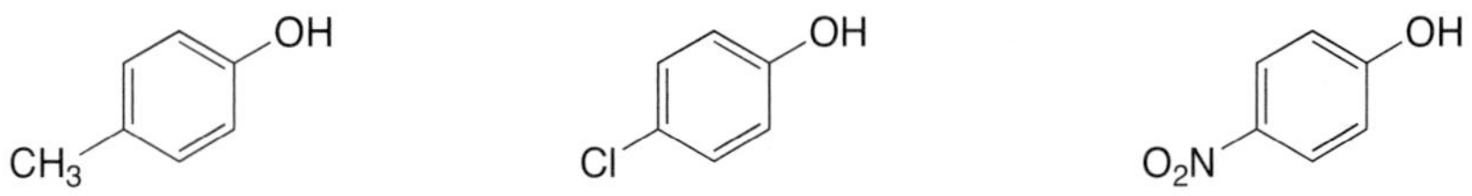
OH
CH3
OH
Cl
OH
O2N

least acidic | **intermediate acidity** | **most acidic**

19.39

a. $BrCH_2COO^-$ — **weakest base**; $BrCH_2CH_2COO^-$ — **intermediate basicity**; $(CH_3)_3CCOO^-$ — **strongest base**

b.

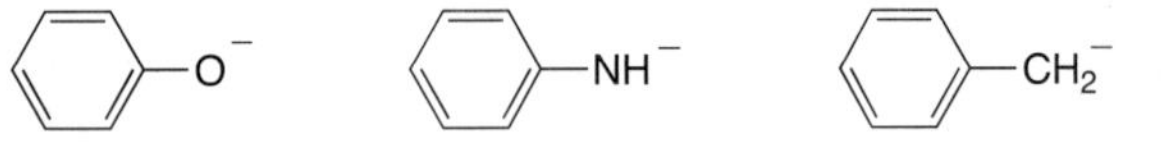

weakest base **intermediate basicity** **strongest base**

c.

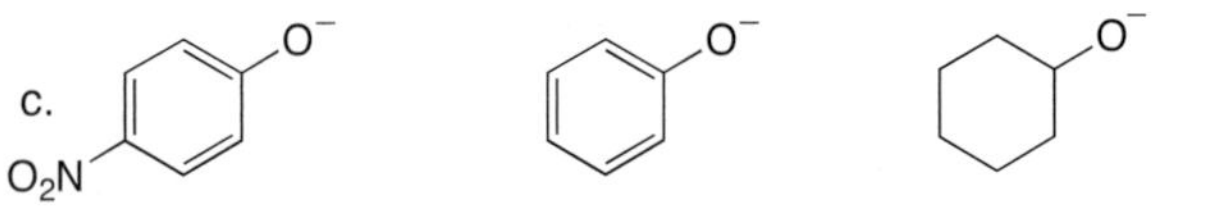
O₂N

weakest base **intermediate basicity** **strongest base**

19.40

Increasing acidity →

	ICH_2COOH	$BrCH_2COOH$	FCH_2COOH	$F_2CHCOOH$	F_3CCOOH
pK_a values	least acidic 3.12	2.86	2.66	1.24	most acidic 0.28

19.41 The OH of the phenol group in morphine is more acidic than the OH of the alcohol (p$K_a \approx 10$ versus p$K_a \approx 16$). KOH is basic enough to remove the phenolic OH, the most acidic proton.

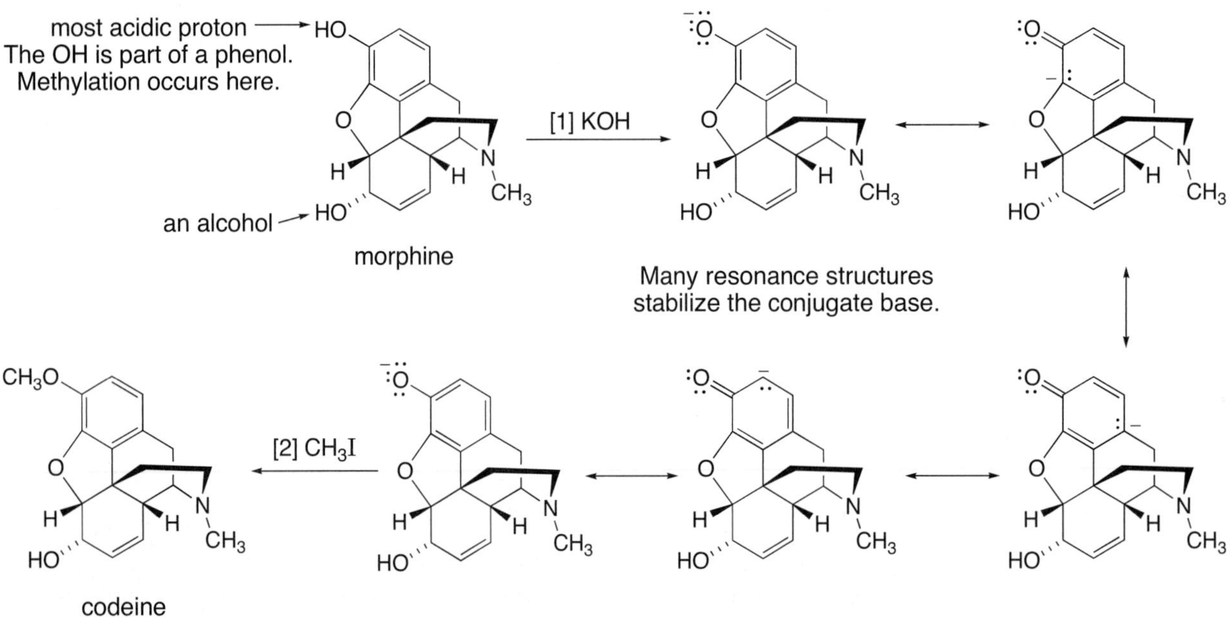
most acidic proton
The OH is part of a phenol.
Methylation occurs here.
an alcohol
morphine
[1] KOH
Many resonance structures stabilize the conjugate base.
[2] CH₃I
codeine

19.42 The closer the electron-withdrawing $CH_3CO–$ group is to the carboxylic acid, the more it will stabilize the conjugate base, making the acid stronger.

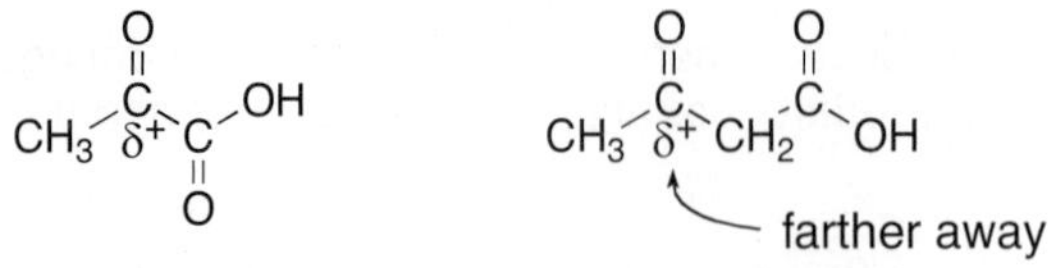
farther away

pyruvic acid
stronger acid

acetoacetic acid
weaker acid

19.43

a. The negative charge on the conjugate base of *p*-nitrophenol is delocalized on the NO_2 group, stabilizing the conjugate base, and making *p*-nitrophenol more acidic than phenol (where the negative charge is delocalized only around the benzene ring).

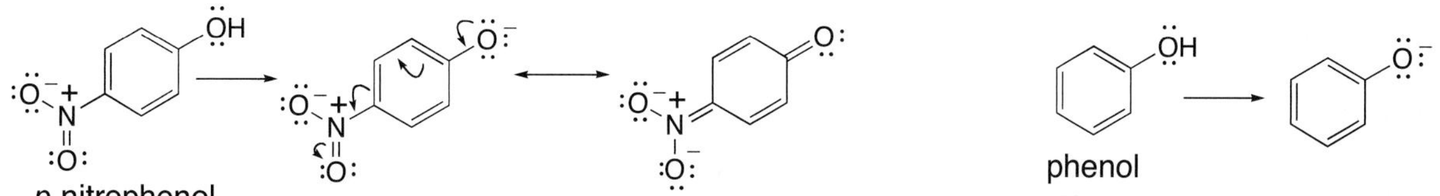

p-nitrophenol
pK_a = 7.2

two of the possible resonance structures for the conjugate base [See part (b) for all the possible resonance structures.]

phenol
pK_a = 10

b. In the para isomer, the negative charge of the conjugate base is delocalized over both the benzene ring and onto the NO_2 group, whereas in the meta isomer it cannot be delocalized onto the NO_2 group. This makes the conjugate base from the para isomer more highly resonance stabilized, and the para substituted phenol more acidic than its meta isomer.

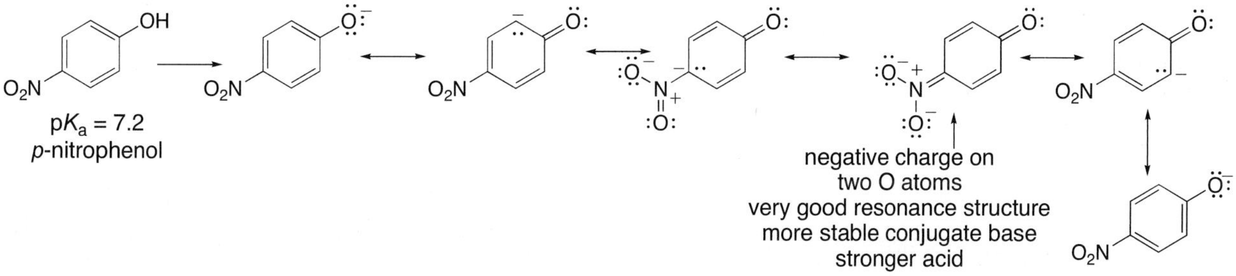
negative charge on
two O atoms
very good resonance structure
more stable conjugate base
stronger acid

pK_a = 7.2
p-nitrophenol

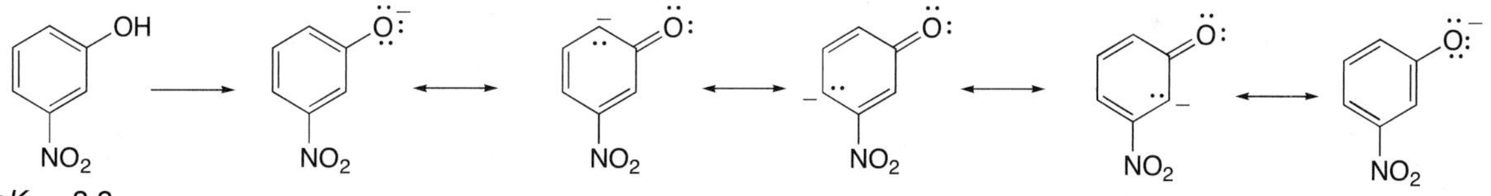

pK_a = 8.3
m-nitrophenol

19.44 A CH_3O group has an electron-withdrawing inductive effect and an electron-donating resonance effect. In 2-methoxyacetic acid, the OCH_3 group is bonded to an sp^3 hybridized C, so there is no way to donate electron density by resonance. The CH_3O group withdraws electron density because of the electronegative O atom, stabilizing the conjugate base, and making CH_3OCH_2COOH a stronger acid than CH_3COOH.

more acidic acid

more stable conjugate base

In *p*-methoxybenzoic acid, the CH_3O group is bonded to an sp^2 hybridized C, so it can donate electron density by a resonance effect. This destabilizes the conjugate base, making the starting material less acidic than C_6H_5COOH.

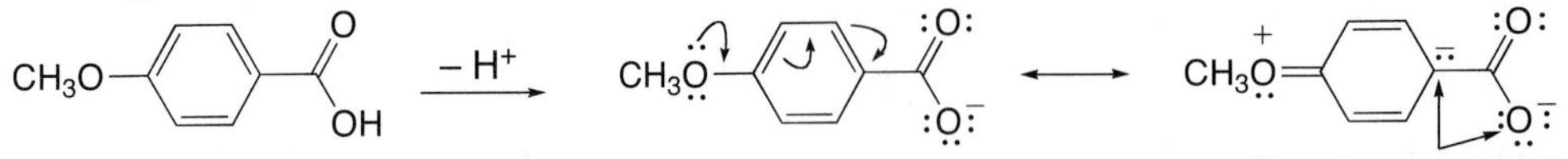

less acidic acid

like charges nearby
less stable conjugate base

19.45 Phenol has a pK_a of 10, making *p*-methylthiophenol (pK_a = 9.53) the stronger acid. A substituent that increases the acidity of a phenol must withdraw electron density to stabilize the negative charge of the conjugate base. An electron-withdrawing substituent deactivates a benzene ring towards electrophilic aromatic substitution, making *p*-methylthiophenol less reactive than phenol.

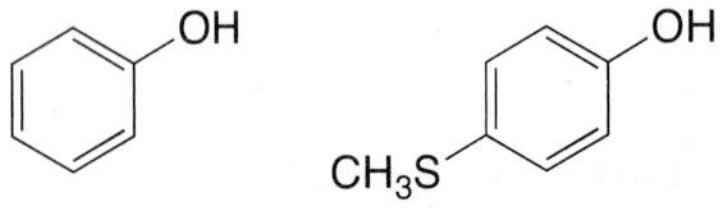

stronger acid
less reactive in
electrophilic substitution

19.46

The O in **A** is more electronegative than the N in **C** so there is a stronger electron-withdrawing inductive effect. This stabilizes the conjugate base of **A**, making **A** more acidic than **C**.

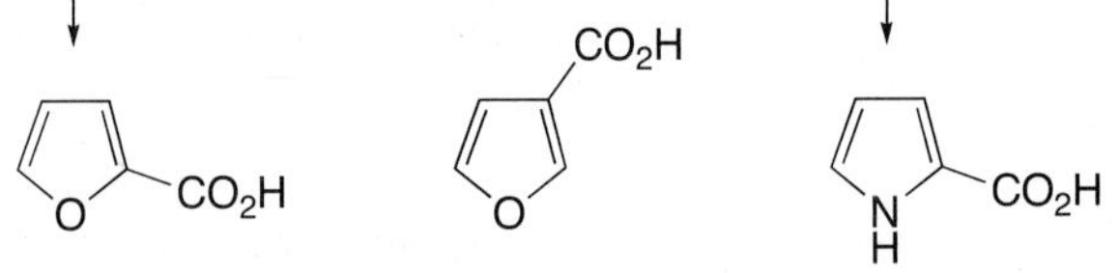

A	**B**	**C**
pK_a = 3.2	pK_a = 3.9	pK_a = 4.4

Since the O in **A** is closer to the COOH group than the O atom in **B**, there is a stronger electron-withdrawing inductive effect. This makes **A** more acidic than **B**.

19.47

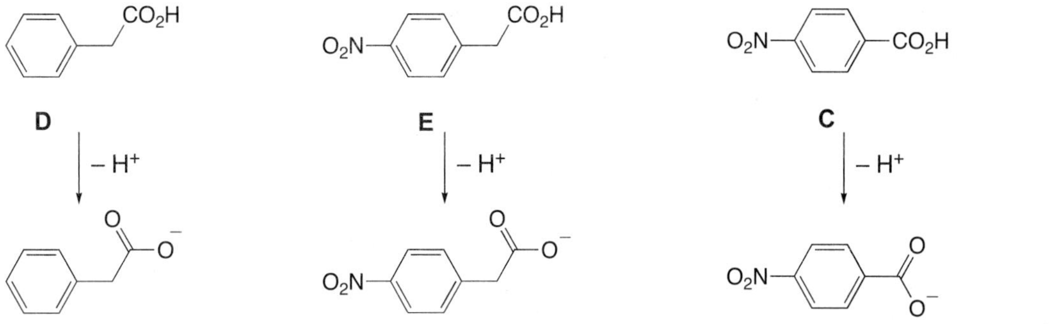

Since the benzene ring is bonded to the α carbon (not the carbonyl carbon), this compound is not much different than any alkyl-substituted carboxylic acid.
least acidic

The electron-withdrawing inductive effect of the NO_2 group helps stabilize the COO^- group.
intermediate acidity

Since the NO_2 group is bonded to a benzene ring that is bonded directly to the carbonyl group, inductive effects and resonance effects stabilize the conjugate base. For example, a resonance structure can be drawn that places a (+) charge close to the COO^- group.
most acidic

Two of the resonance structures for the conjugate base of **C**:

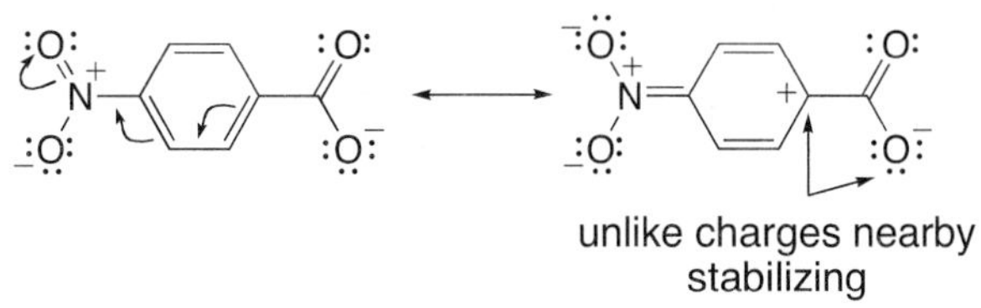

19.48

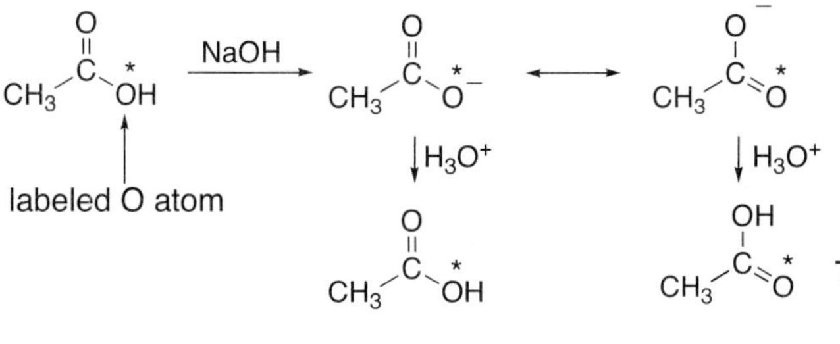

The resonance-stabilized carboxylate anion can now be protonated on either O atom, the one with the label and the one without the label.

The label is now in two different locations.

19.49

a.

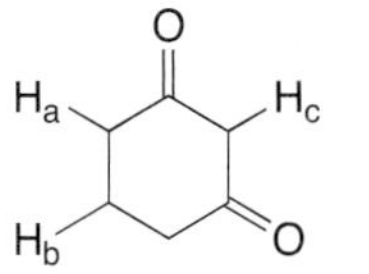

1,3-cyclohexanedione
increasing acidity: H_b < H_a < H_c

loss of H_b:

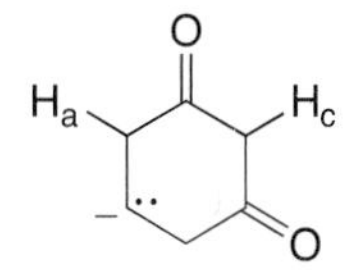

one Lewis structure
least stable conjugate base

The most acidic proton forms the most stable conjugate base.

loss of H_a:

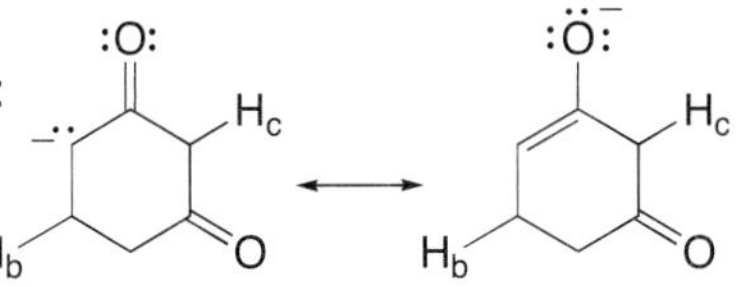

2 resonance structures
intermediate stability

loss of H_c:

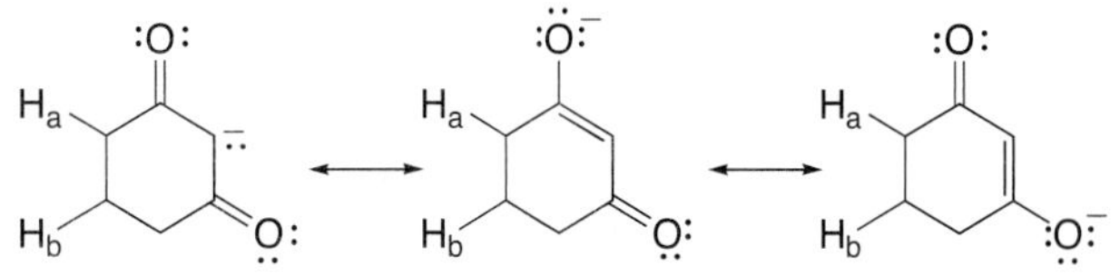

3 resonance structures
most stable conjugate base

b.

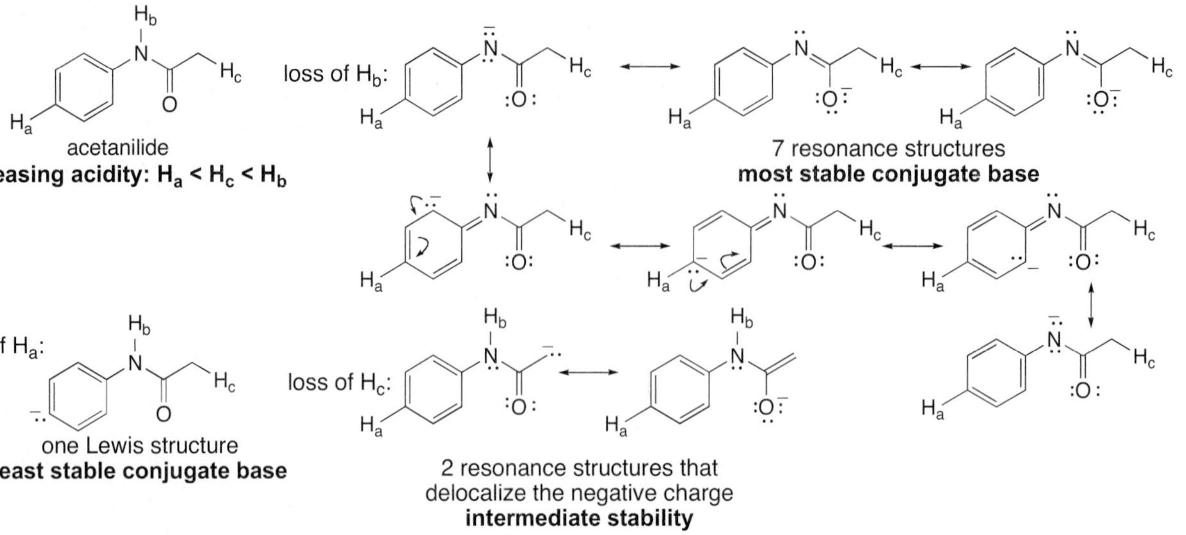
acetanilide
increasing acidity: $H_a < H_c < H_b$
loss of H_b:
7 resonance structures
most stable conjugate base
loss of H_a:
one Lewis structure
least stable conjugate base
loss of H_c:
2 resonance structures that delocalize the negative charge
intermediate stability

19.50

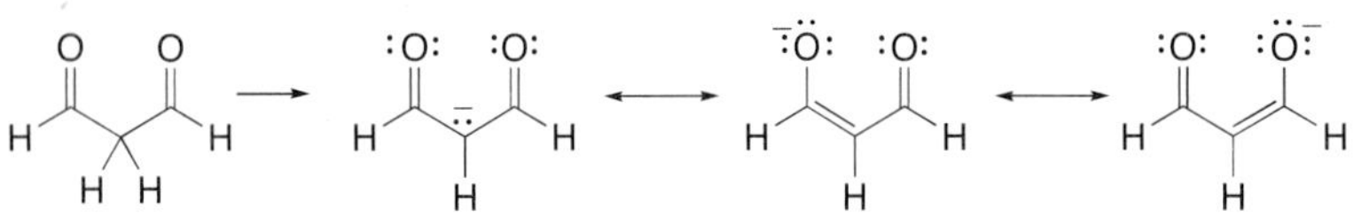

The conjugate base is resonance stabilized. Two of the structures place a negative charge on an O atom.
weaker conjugate base
stronger acid

The conjugate base has only one Lewis structure.
stronger conjugate base
weaker acid

19.51

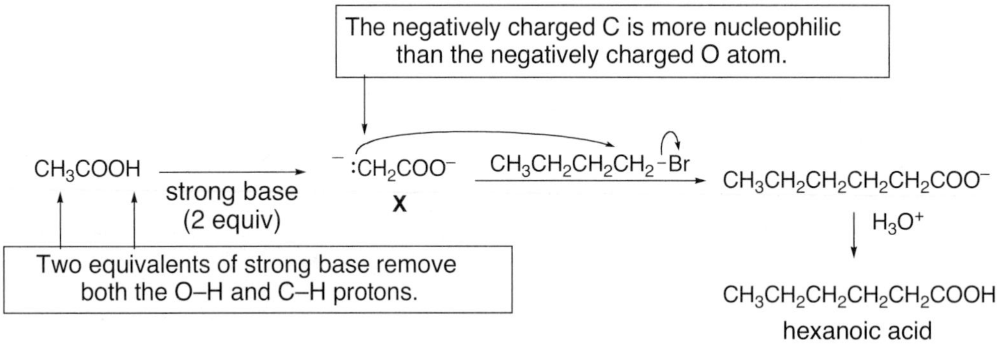
The negatively charged C is more nucleophilic than the negatively charged O atom.
CH3COOH
strong base
(2 equiv)
:CH2COO–
X
CH3CH2CH2CH2–Br
CH3CH2CH2CH2CH2COO–
H3O+
CH3CH2CH2CH2CH2COOH
hexanoic acid
Two equivalents of strong base remove both the O–H and C–H protons.

19.52

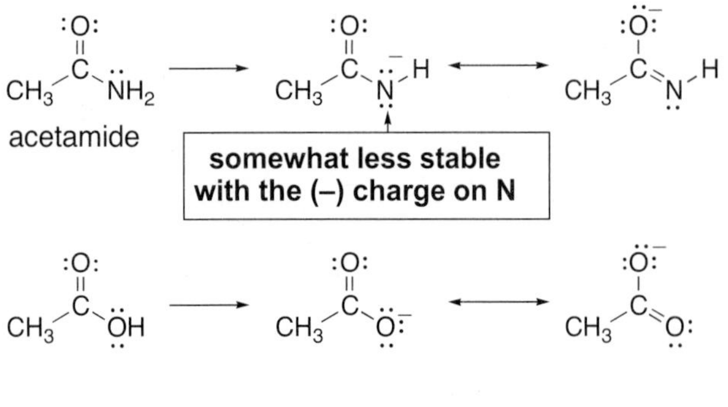
acetamide
somewhat less stable with the (–) charge on N

O is more electronegative than N, making the conjugate base of CH_3COOH more stable than the conjugate base of acetamide. Therefore, acetamide is less acidic.

19.53

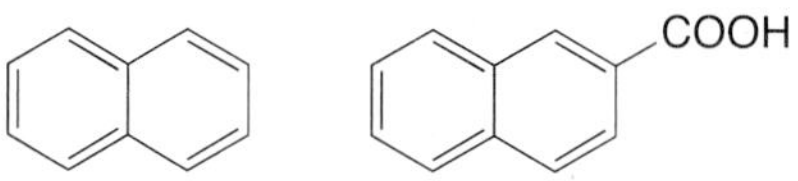
COOH

A B

- Dissolve both compounds in CH_2Cl_2.
- Add 10% $NaHCO_3$ solution. This makes a carboxylate anion ($C_{10}H_7COO^-$) from **B,** which dissolves in the aqueous layer. The other compound (**A**) remains in the CH_2Cl_2.
- Separate the layers.

19.54

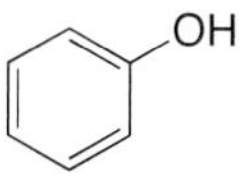
OH

and

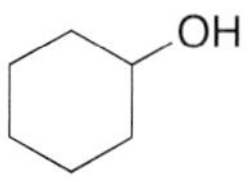
OH

- Dissolve both compounds in CH_2Cl_2.
- Add 10% NaOH solution. This converts C_6H_5OH into a phenoxide anion, $C_6H_5O^-$, which dissolves in the aqueous solution. The alcohol remains in the organic layer (neutral) since it is not acidic enough to be deprotonated to any significant extent by NaOH.
- Separate the layers.

19.55 To separate two compounds in an aqueous extraction, one must be water soluble (or be able to be converted into a water-soluble ionic compound by an acid–base reaction), and the other insoluble. 1-Octanol has greater than 5 C's, making it insoluble in water. Octane is an alkane, also insoluble in water. Neither compound is acidic enough to be deprotonated by a base in aqueous solution. Since their solubility properties are similar, they cannot be separated by an extraction procedure.

19.56

a. Molecular formula: $C_3H_5ClO_2$ → one double bond or ring
IR: 3500–2500 cm^{-1}, 1714 cm^{-1} → C=O and O–H
NMR data: 2.87 (triplet, 2 H), 3.76 (triplet, 2 H), and 11.8 (singlet, 1 H) ppm

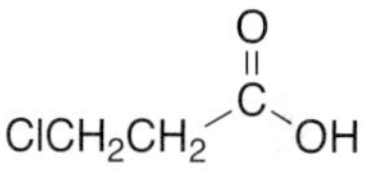
O
ClCH2CH2
C
OH

b. Molecular formula: $C_8H_8O_3$ → 5 double bonds or rings
IR: 3500–2500 cm^{-1}, 1688 cm^{-1} → C=O and O–H
NMR data: 3.8 (singlet, 3 H), 7.0 (doublet, 2 H), 7.9 (doublet, 2 H), and 12.7 (singlet, 1 H) ppm
↑ (7.0 and 7.9 doublets) para disubstituted benzene ring

CH3O
COOH

c. Molecular formula: $C_8H_8O_3$ → 5 double bonds or rings
IR: 3500–2500 cm^{-1}, 1710 cm^{-1} → C=O and O–H
NMR data: 4.7 (singlet, 2 H), 6.9–7.3 (multiplet, 5 H), and 11.3 (singlet, 1 H) ppm
↑ (6.9–7.3 multiplet) monosubstituted benzene ring

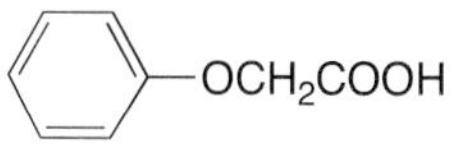
OCH2COOH

19.57

Compound **A:** Molecular formula $C_4H_8O_2$ (one degree of unsaturation)
IR absorptions at 3600–3200 (O–H), 3000–2800 (C–H), and 1700 (C=O) cm^{-1}
^1H NMR data:

Absorption	ppm	# of H's	Explanation
singlet	2.2	3	a CH_3 group
singlet	2.55	1	1 H adjacent to none or OH
triplet	2.7	2	2 H's adjacent to 2 H's
triplet	3.9	2	2 H's adjacent to 2 H's

Structure:

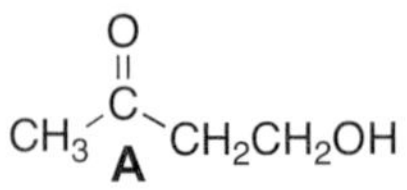

Compound **B:** Molecular formula $C_4H_8O_2$ (one degree of unsaturation)
IR absorptions at 3500–2500 (O–H) and 1700 (C=O) cm^{-1}
^1H NMR data:

Absorption	ppm	# of H's	Explanation
doublet	1.6	6	6 H's adjacent to 1 H
septet	2.3	1	1 H adjacent to 6 H's
singlet (very broad)	10.7	1	OH of RCOOH

Structure:

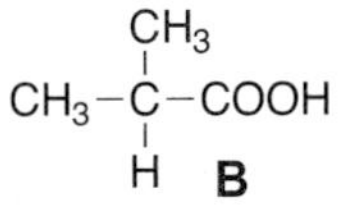

19.58

Compound **C:** Molecular formula $C_4H_8O_3$ (one degree of unsaturation)
IR absorptions at 3600–2500 (O–H) and 1734 (C=O) cm^{-1}
^1H NMR data:

Absorption	ppm	# of H's	Explanation
triplet	1.2	3	a CH_3 group adjacent to 2 H's
quartet	3.6	2	2 H's adjacent to 3 H's
singlet	4.1	2	2 H's
singlet	11.3	1	OH of COOH

Structure:

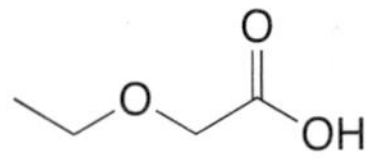

19.59

Compound **D:** Molecular formula $C_9H_9ClO_2$ (five degrees of unsaturation)
^{13}C NMR data: 30, 36, 128, 130, 133, 139, 179 = 7 different types of C's
^1H NMR data:

Absorption	ppm	# of H's	Explanation
triplet	2.7	2	2 H's adjacent to 2 H's
triplet	2.9	2	2 H's adjacent to 2 H's
two signals	7.2	4	on benzene ring
singlet	11.7	1	OH of COOH

Structure:

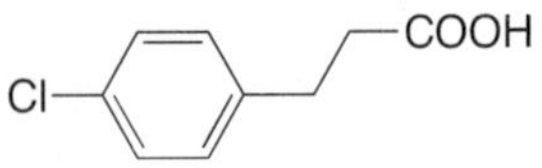

19.60

Molecular formula: $C_8H_6O_4$: 6 degrees of unsaturation
IR 1692 cm^{-1} (C=O)
^1H NMR 8.2 and 10.0 ppm (singlets)

↑ aromatic H ↑ COOH

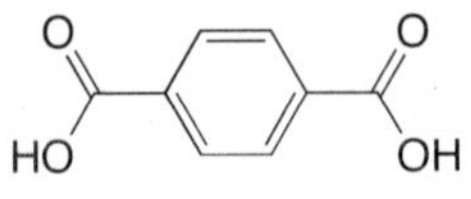

19.61

A 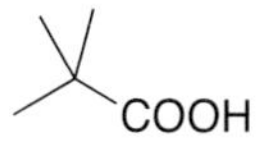 3 different C's
Spectrum [2]: peaks at 27, 39, 186 ppm

B  5 different C's
Spectrum [1]: peaks at 14, 22, 27, 34, 181 ppm

C 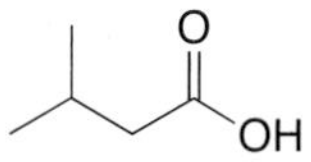 4 different C's
Spectrum [3]: peaks at 22, 26, 43, 180 ppm

19.62

GBL: Molecular formula $C_4H_6O_2$ (two degrees of unsaturation)
IR absorption at 1770 (C=O) cm^{-1}
^{1}H NMR data:

Absorption	**ppm**	**# of H's**	**Explanation**
multiplet	2.28	2	2 H's adjacent to several H's
triplet	2.48	2	2 H's adjacent to 2 H's
triplet	4.35	2	2 H's adjacent to 2 H's

Structure:

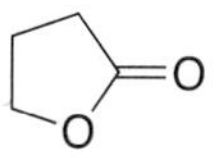

GBL

19.63

threonine

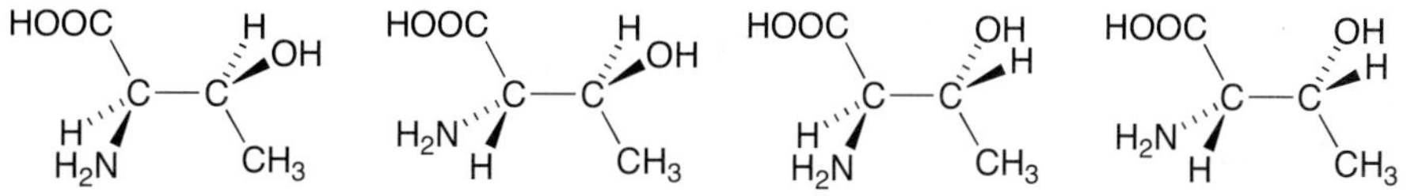

2*R*,3*S* — 2*S*,3*S* — 2*R*,3*R* — 2*S*,3*R* naturally occurring

19.64

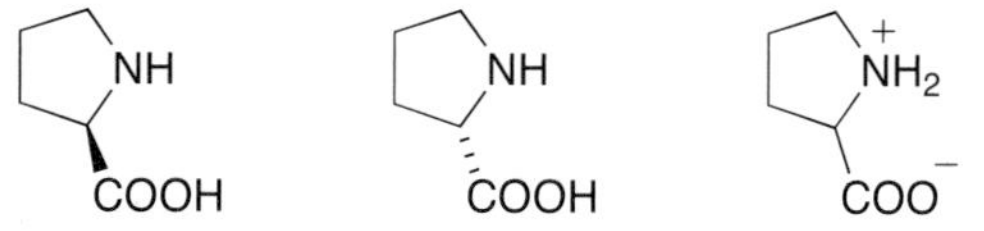

proline — enantiomer — zwitterion

19.65

a. methionine

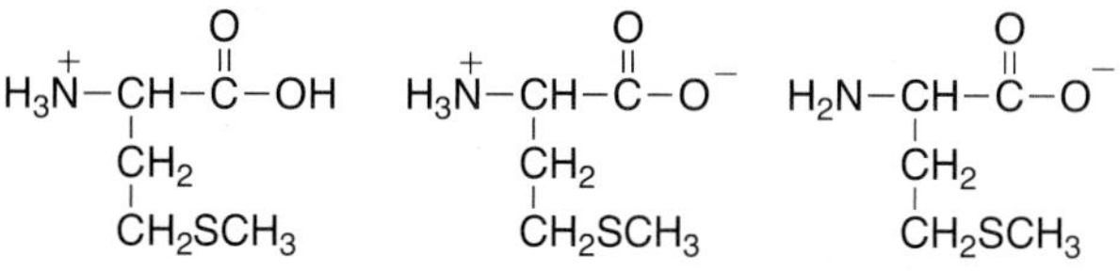

pH = 1 — pH = 6 form at isoelectric point — pH = 11

b. serine

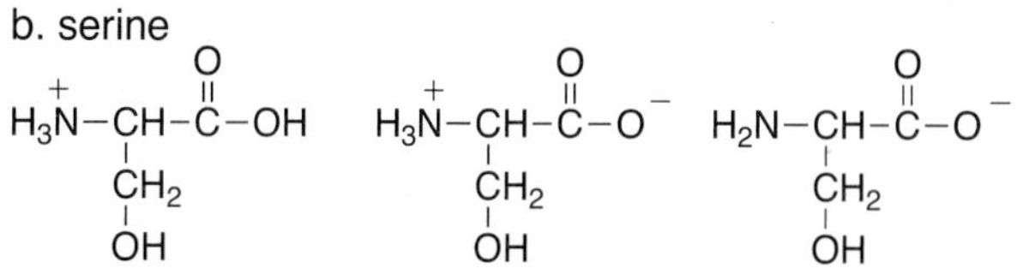

pH = 1 — pH = 6 form at isoelectric point — pH = 11

19.66

a. cysteine $pI = \dfrac{pK_a(COOH) + pK_a(NH_3^+)}{2}$ = (2.05) + (10.25) / 2 = **6.15**

b. methionine $pI = \dfrac{pK_a(COOH) + pK_a(NH_3^+)}{2}$ = (2.28) + (9.21) / 2 = **5.75**

19.67

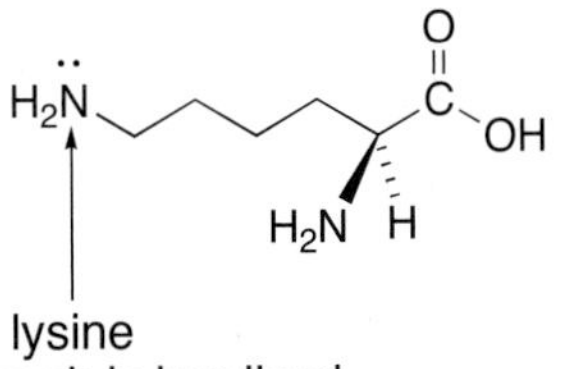

lysine
This lone pair is localized on the N atom, making it a base.

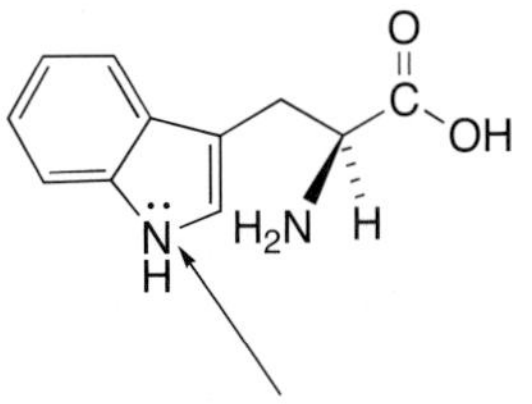

tryptophan
This lone pair is delocalized in the π system to give 10 π electrons, making it aromatic. This is similar to pyrrole (Chapter 17). Since these electrons are delocalized in the aromatic system, this N atom in tryptophan is not basic.

19.68 The first equivalent of NH_3 acts as a base to remove a proton from the carboxylic acid. A second equivalent then acts as a nucleophile to displace X to form the ammonium salt of the amino acid.

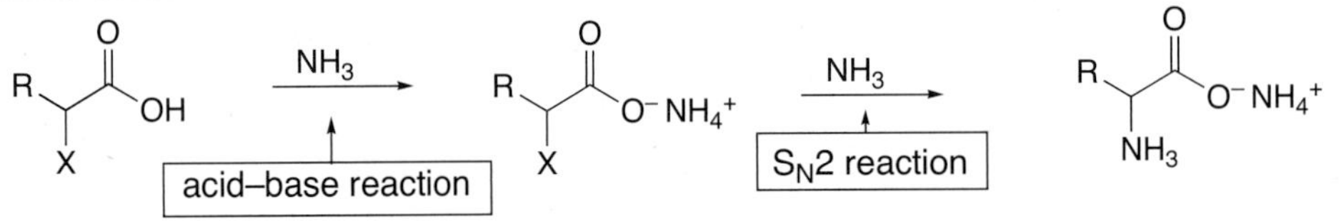

19.69

a. At pH = 1, the net charge is (+1).

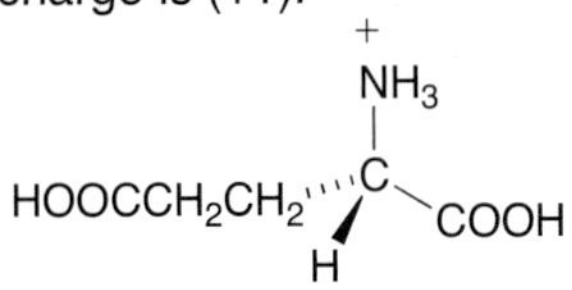

b. increasing pH: As base is added, the most acidic proton is removed first, then the next most acidic proton, and so forth.

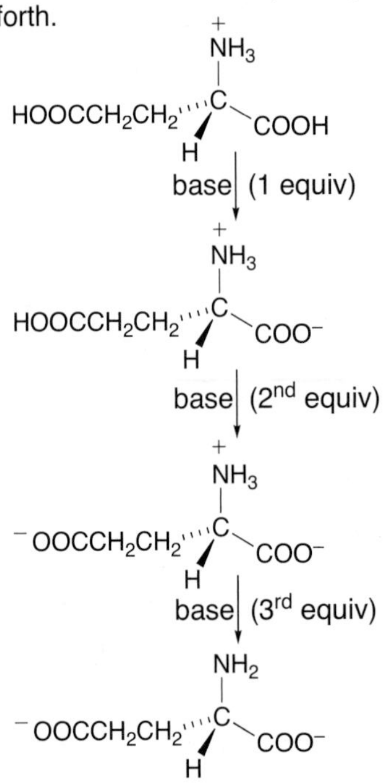

c. monosodium glutamate

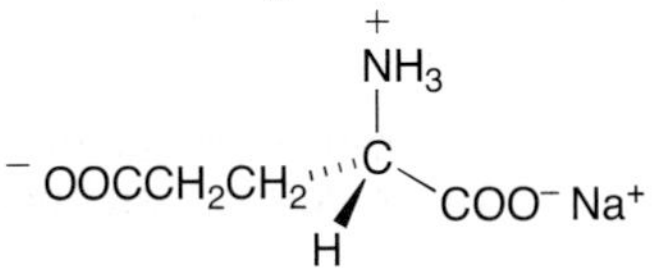

19.70 The first equivalent of NaH removes the most acidic proton—that is, the OH proton on the phenol. The resulting phenoxide can then act as a nucleophile to displace I to form a substitution product. With two equivalents, both OH protons are removed. In this case the more nucleophilic O atom is the stronger base—that is, the alkoxide derived from the alcohol (not the phenoxide), so this negatively charged O atom reacts first in a nucleophilic substitution reaction.

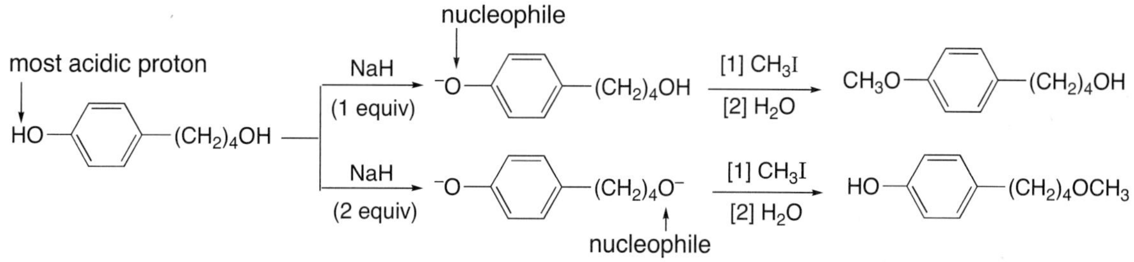

19.71

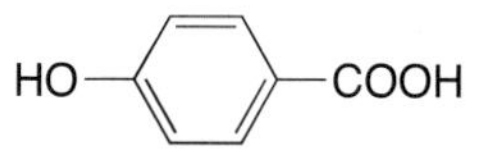

p-hydroxybenzoic acid
less acidic than benzoic acid

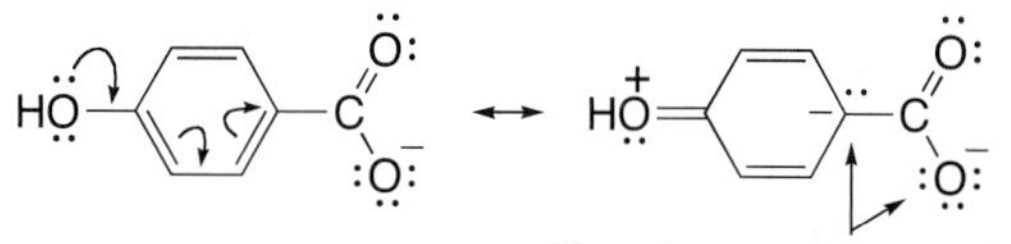

like charges on nearby atoms
destabilizing

The OH group donates electron density by its resonance effect and this destabilizes the conjugate base, making the acid less acidic than benzoic acid.

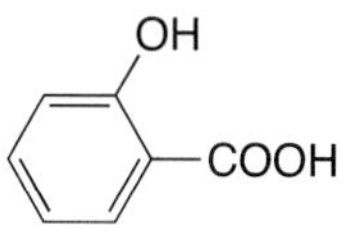

o-hydroxybenzoic acid
more acidic than benzoic acid

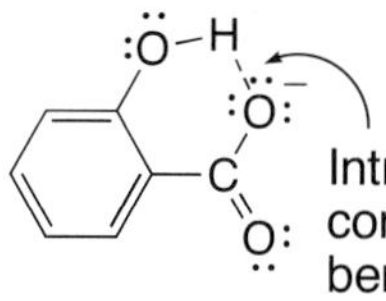

Intramolecular hydrogen bonding stabilizes the conjugate base, making the acid more acidic than benzoic acid.

19.72

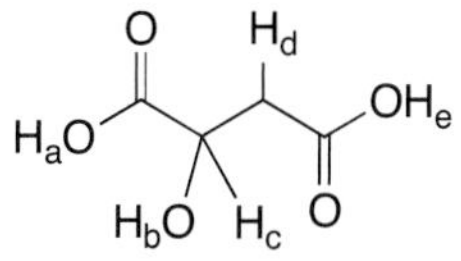

2-hydroxybutanedioic acid
increasing acidity:
$H_d < H_c < H_b < H_e < H_a$

H_a and H_e must be the two most acidic protons since they are part of carboxylic acids. Loss of a proton forms a resonance-stabilized carboxylate anion that has the negative charge delocalized on two O atoms. H_a is more acidic than H_e because the nearby OH group on the α carbon increases acidity by an electron-withdrawing inductive effect. H_b is the next most acidic proton because the conjugate base places a negative charge on the electronegative O atom, but it is not resonance stabilized.

The least acidic H's are H_c and H_d since these H's are bonded to C atoms. The electronegative O atom further acidifies H_c by an electron-withdrawing inductive effect.

19.73

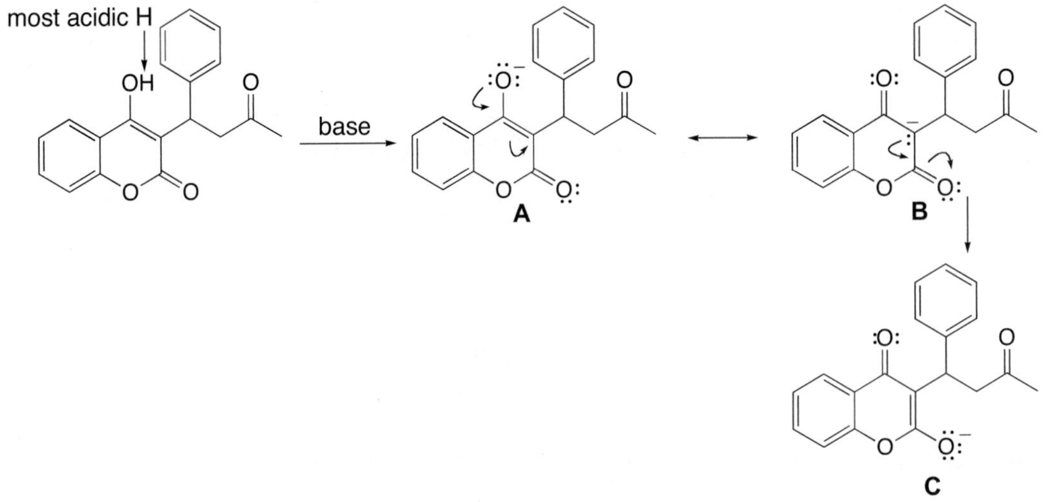

The conjugate base has three resonance structures, two of which place a negative charge on the oxygens. In this way the conjugate base resembles a carboxylate anion. In addition, the C=C's in **A** and **C** are conjugated.

Chapter 20 Introduction to Carbonyl Chemistry

Chapter Review

Reduction reactions

[1] Reduction of aldehydes and ketones to 1° and 2° alcohols (20.4)

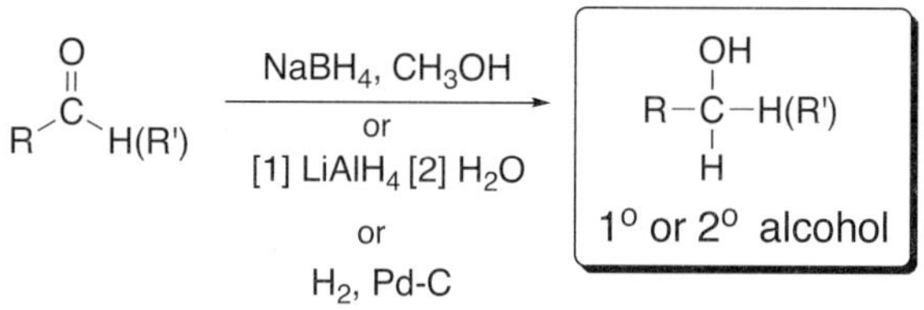

[2] Reduction of α,β-unsaturated aldehydes and ketones (20.4C)

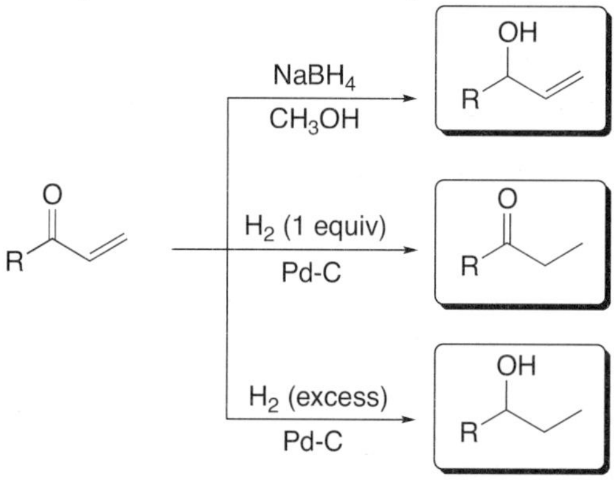

- reduction of the C=O only
- reduction of the C=C only
- reduction of both π bonds

[3] Enantioselective ketone reduction (20.6)

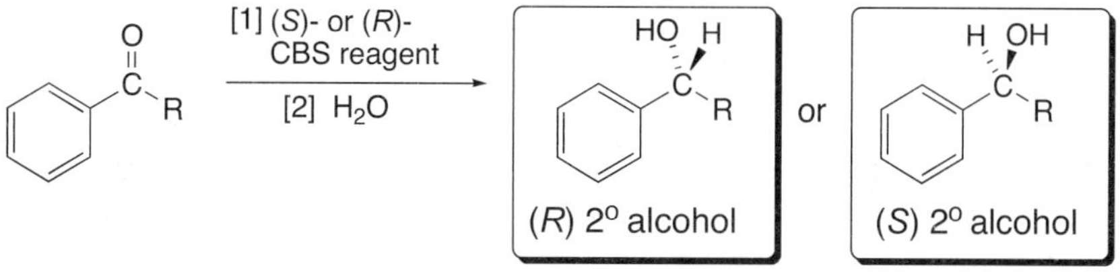

- A single enantiomer is formed.

[4] Reduction of acid chlorides (20.7A)

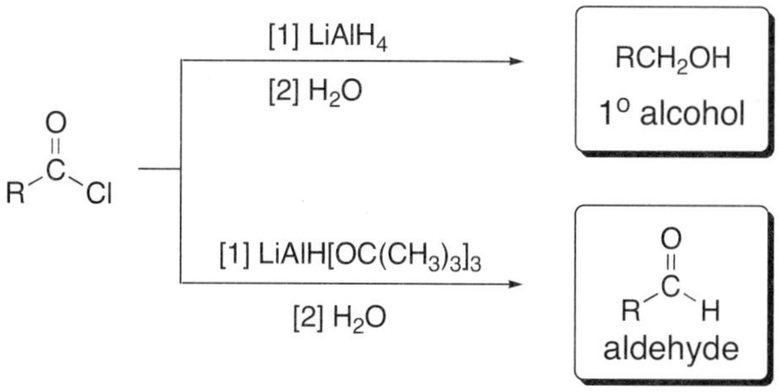

- $LiAlH_4$, a strong reducing agent, reduces an acid chloride to a 1° alcohol.
- With $LiAlH[OC(CH_3)_3]_3$, a milder reducing agent, reduction stops at the aldehyde stage.

[5] Reduction of esters (20.7A)

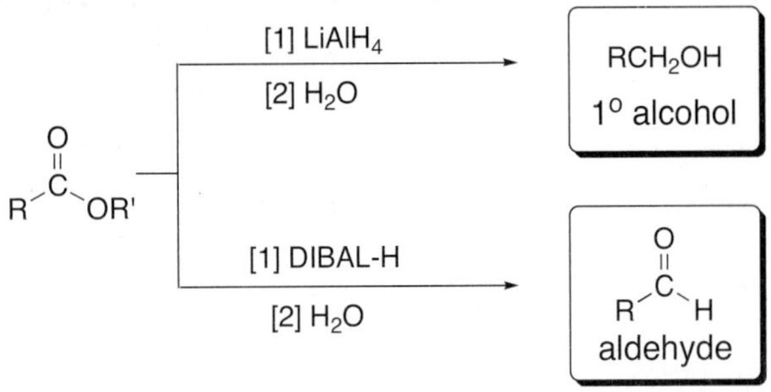

- $LiAlH_4$, a strong reducing agent, reduces an ester to a 1° alcohol.
- With DIBAL-H, a milder reducing agent, reduction stops at the aldehyde stage.

[6] Reduction of carboxylic acids to 1° alcohols (20.7B)

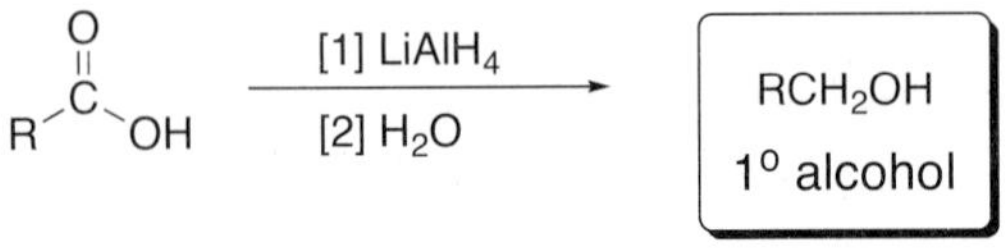

[7] Reduction of amides to amines (20.7B)

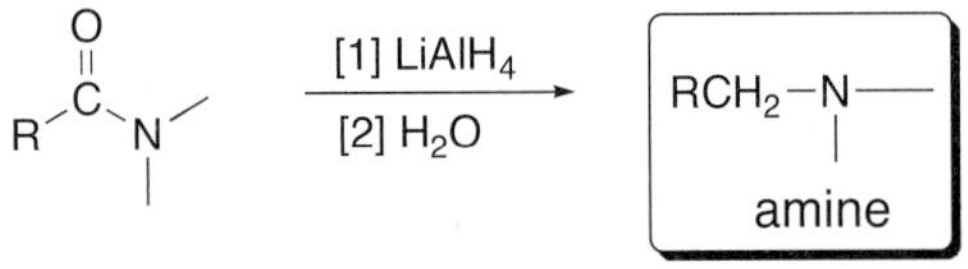

Oxidation reactions

Oxidation of aldehydes to carboxylic acids (20.8)

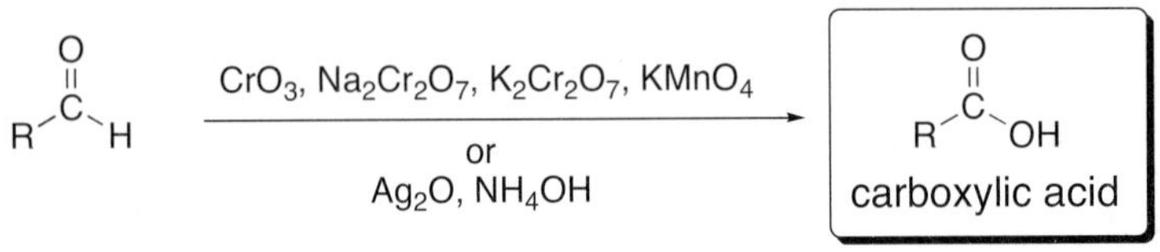

- All Cr^{6+} reagents except PCC oxidize RCHO to RCOOH.
- Tollens reagent (Ag_2O + NH_4OH) oxidizes RCHO only. Primary (1°) and secondary (2°) alcohols do not react with Tollens reagent.

Preparation of organometallic reagents (20.9)

[1] Organolithium reagents:

$$R{-}X + 2\,Li \longrightarrow \boxed{R{-}Li} + LiX$$

[2] Grignard reagents:

$$R{-}X + Mg \xrightarrow[(CH_3CH_2)_2O]{} \boxed{R{-}Mg{-}X}$$

[3] Organocuprate reagents:

$$R{-}X + 2\,Li \longrightarrow R{-}Li + LiX$$

$$2\,R{-}Li + CuI \longrightarrow \boxed{R_2Cu^{-}\ Li^{+}} + LiI$$

[4] Lithium and sodium acetylides:

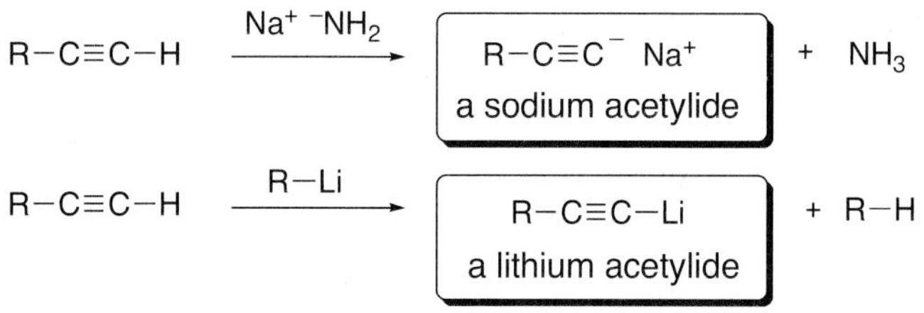
R−C≡C−H
Na+ −NH2
R−C≡C− Na+
a sodium acetylide
+ NH3
R−C≡C−H
R−Li
R−C≡C−Li
a lithium acetylide
+ R−H

Reactions with organometallic reagents

[1] Reaction as a base (20.9C)

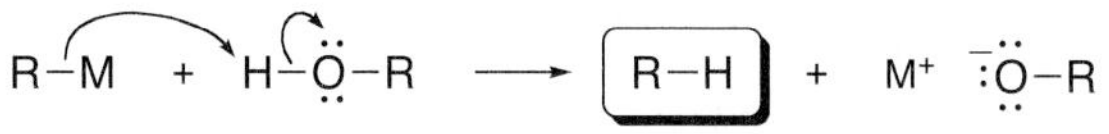
R−M
+
H−Ö−R
R−H
+
M+
:Ö−R

- RM = RLi, RMgX, R_2CuLi
- This acid–base reaction occurs with H_2O, ROH, RNH_2, R_2NH, RSH, RCOOH, $RCONH_2$, and RCONHR.

[2] Reaction with aldehydes and ketones to form 1°, 2°, and 3° alcohols (20.10)

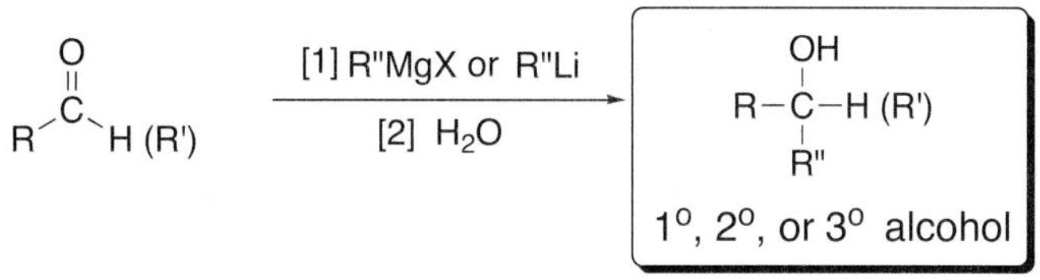
[1] R"MgX or R"Li
[2] H2O
1°, 2°, or 3° alcohol

[3] Reaction with esters to form 3° alcohols (20.13A)

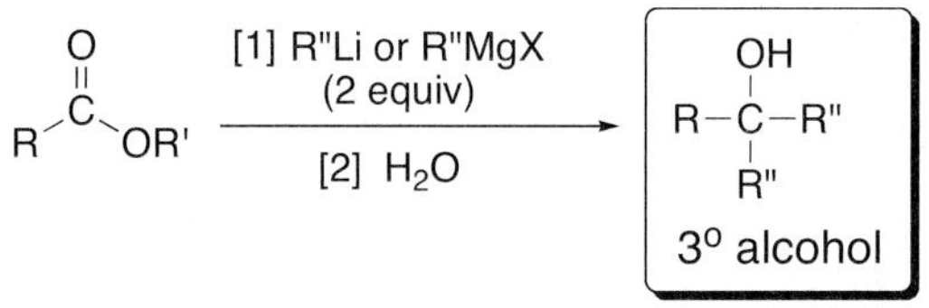
[1] R"Li or R"MgX
(2 equiv)
[2] H2O
3° alcohol

[4] Reaction with acid chlorides (20.13)

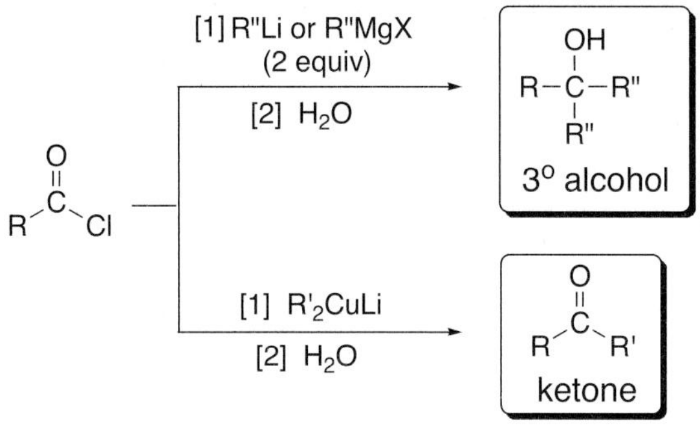
[1] R"Li or R"MgX
(2 equiv)
[2] H2O
3° alcohol
[1] R'2CuLi
[2] H2O
ketone

- More reactive organometallic reagents—R"Li and R"MgX—add two equivalents of R" to an acid chloride to form a 3° alcohol with two identical R" groups.
- Less reactive organometallic reagents—R'_2CuLi—add only one equivalent of R' to an acid chloride to form a ketone.

[5] Reaction with carbon dioxide—Carboxylation (20.14A)

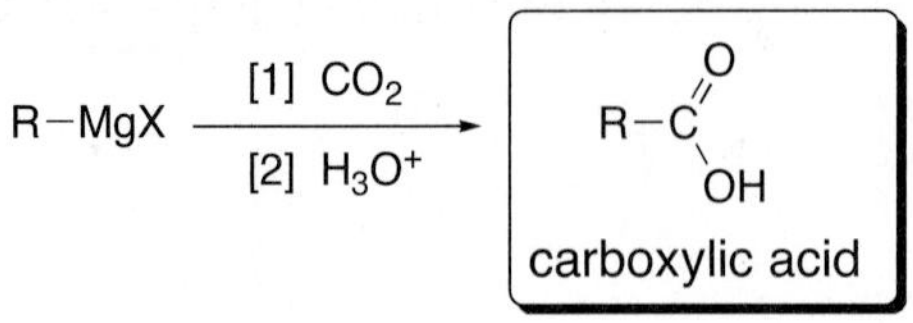
R–MgX
[1] CO2
[2] H3O+
R–C(=O)OH
carboxylic acid

[6] Reaction with epoxides (20.14B)

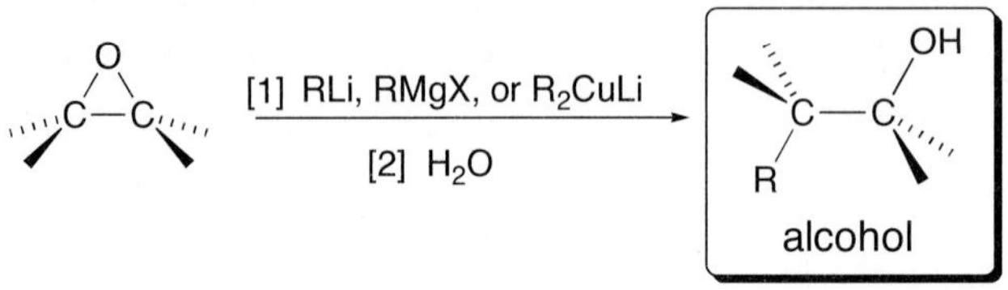
[1] RLi, RMgX, or R2CuLi
[2] H2O
OH
R
alcohol

[7] Reaction with α,β-unsaturated aldehydes and ketones (20.15B)

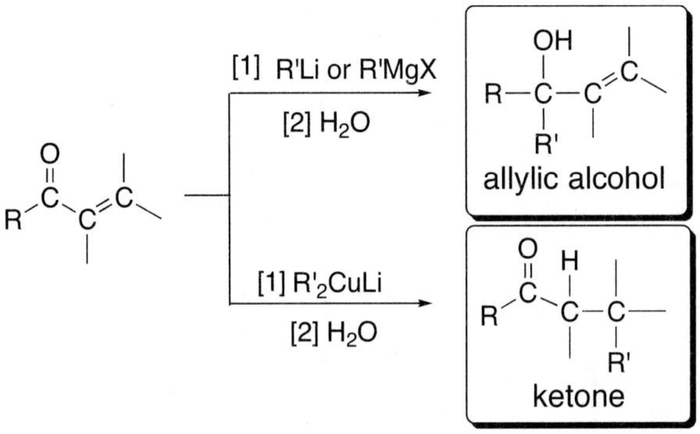
[1] R'Li or R'MgX
[2] H2O
allylic alcohol
[1] R'2CuLi
[2] H2O
ketone

- More reactive organometallic reagents—R'Li and R'MgX—react with α,β-unsaturated carbonyls by 1,2-addition.
- Less reactive organometallic reagents—R'_2CuLi— react with α,β-unsaturated carbonyls by 1,4-addition.

Protecting groups (20.12)

[1] Protecting an alcohol as a *tert*-butyldimethylsilyl ether

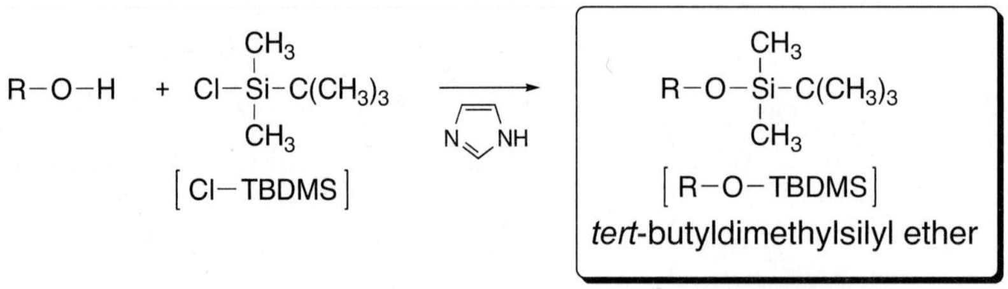
R–O–H
[Cl–TBDMS]
[R–O–TBDMS]
tert-butyldimethylsilyl ether

[2] Deprotecting a *tert*-butyldimethylsilyl ether to re-form an alcohol

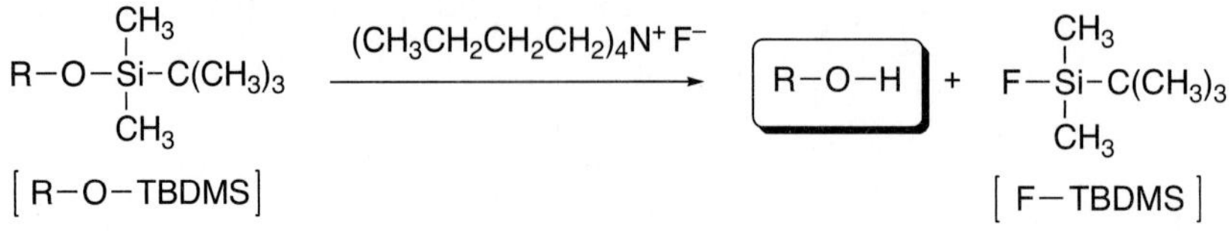
(CH3CH2CH2CH2)4N+ F−
[R–O–TBDMS]
R–O–H
[F–TBDMS]

Practice Test on Chapter Review

1. Which compounds undergo nucleophilic addition and which undergo substitution?

a. 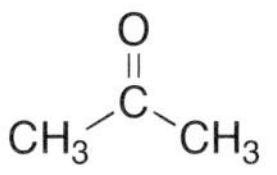
b. 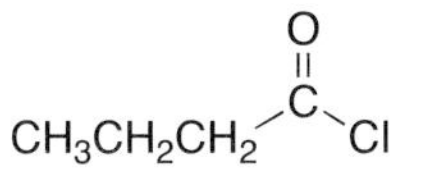
c. 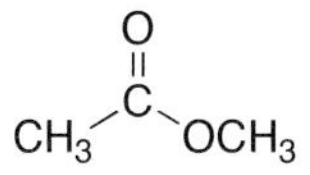
d. 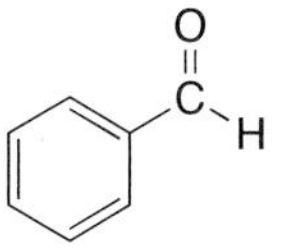

2. What product is formed when $CH_3CH_2CH_2Li$ reacts with each compound, followed by quenching with water and acid?

a. CH_3CH_2CHO
b. $(CH_3)_2CO$
c. $CH_3CH_2CO_2CH_3$
d. CH_3CH_2COCl
e. CO_2
f. $CH_2{=}CHCOCH_3$
g. ethylene oxide
h. CH_3COOH

3. What product is formed when $HO(CH_2)_4CHO$ is treated with each reagent?

a. $NaBH_4$, CH_3OH
b. PCC
c. Ag_2O, NH_4OH
d. $Na_2Cr_2O_7$, H_2SO_4, H_2O

4. What reagent is needed to convert $(CH_3CH_2)_2CHCOCl$ into each compound?

a. $(CH_3CH_2)_2CHCOCH_2CH_3$
b. $(CH_3CH_2)_2CHCHO$
c. $(CH_3CH_2)_2CHC(OH)(CH_2CH_3)_2$
d. $(CH_3CH_2)_2CHCH_2OH$

5. Draw the organic products formed in the following reactions.

a. 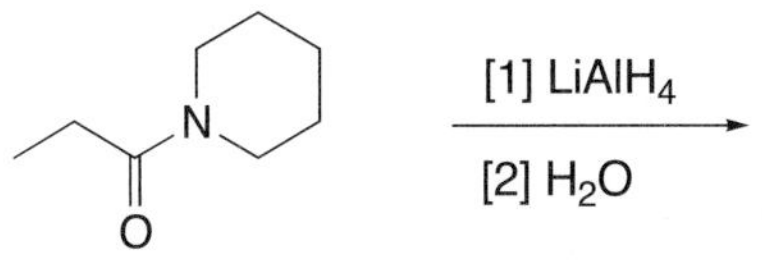
[1] LiAlH4
[2] H2O

b. 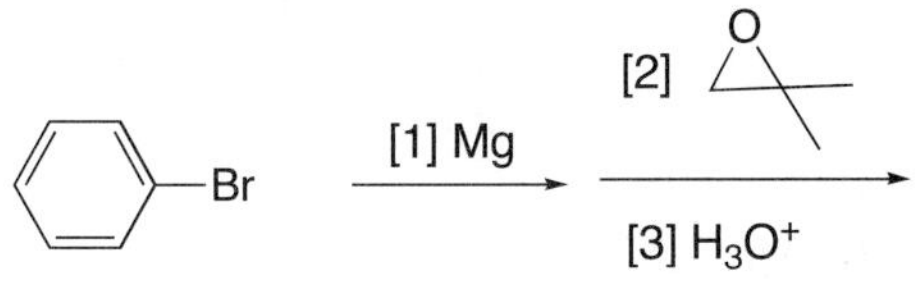
[1] Mg
[2]
[3] H3O+

c. 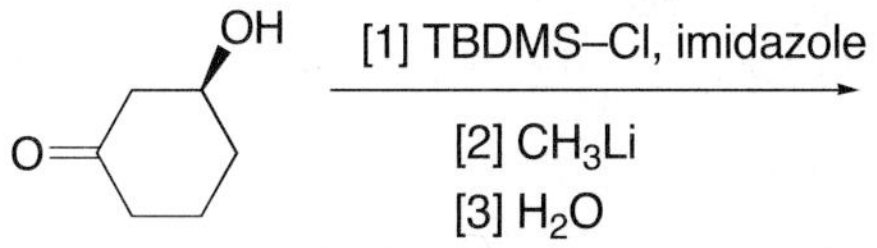
[1] TBDMS–Cl, imidazole
[2] CH3Li
[3] H2O
[Indicate stereochemistry.]

d. 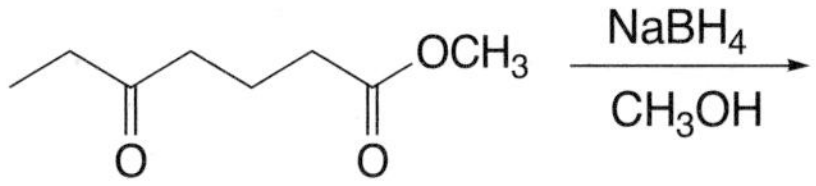
NaBH4
CH3OH

6. What starting materials are needed to synthesize each compound using the indicated reagent or functional group?

a. Synthesize: 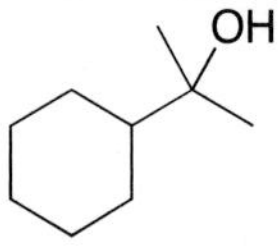
OH

from an ester

c. Synthesize: 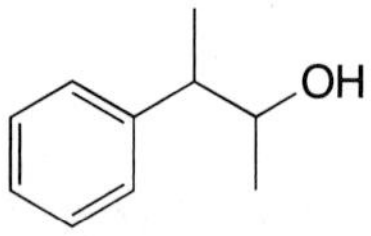
OH

using a Grignard reagent

b. Synthesize: 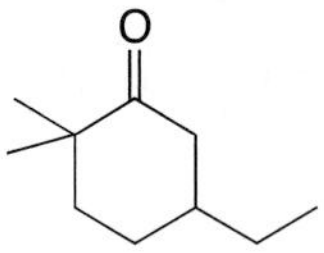
O

using an organocuprate reagent

Answers to Practice Test

1. a. addition
   b. substitution
   c. substitution
   d. addition

2. a. $CH_3CH_2CH(OH)CH_2CH_2CH_3$
   b. $(CH_3)_2C(OH)CH_2CH_2CH_3$
   c. $(CH_3CH_2)_3COH$
   d. $(CH_3CH_2)_3COH$
   e. $CH_3CH_2CH_2CO_2H$
   f. $CH_2{=}CHC(OH)(CH_3)CH_2CH_2CH_3$
   g. $CH_3(CH_2)_4OH$
   h. $CH_3CH_2CH_3$ + CH_3CO_2H

3. a. $HO(CH_2)_5OH$
   b. $OHC(CH_2)_3CHO$
   c. $HO(CH_2)_4CO_2H$
   d. $HO_2C(CH_2)_3CO_2H$

4. a. $(CH_3CH_2)_2CuLi$
   b. DIBAL-H
   c. CH_3CH_2MgBr
   d. $LiAlH_4$

5.

a. 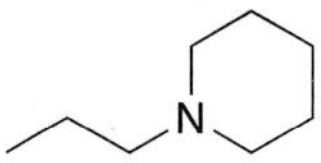
N

b. 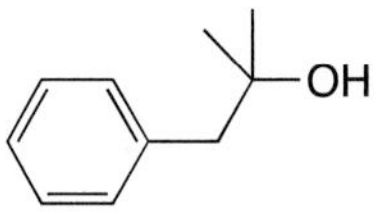
OH

c. 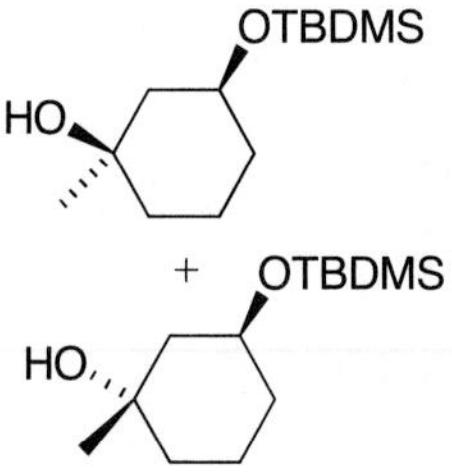
OTBDMS
HO
+
OTBDMS
HO

d. 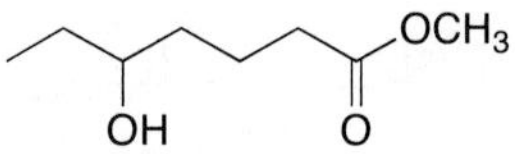
OCH3
OH
O

6.

a. 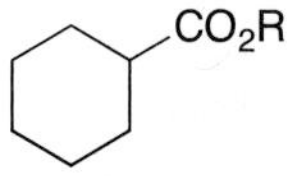
CO2R

+ CH_3MgBr

b. 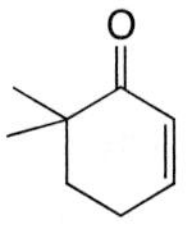
O

+ 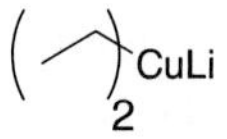
CuLi
2

c. 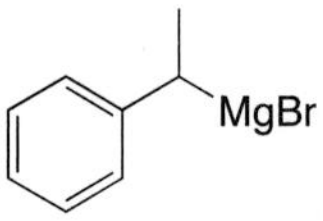
MgBr

+ CH_3CHO

Answers to Problems

20.1

a. 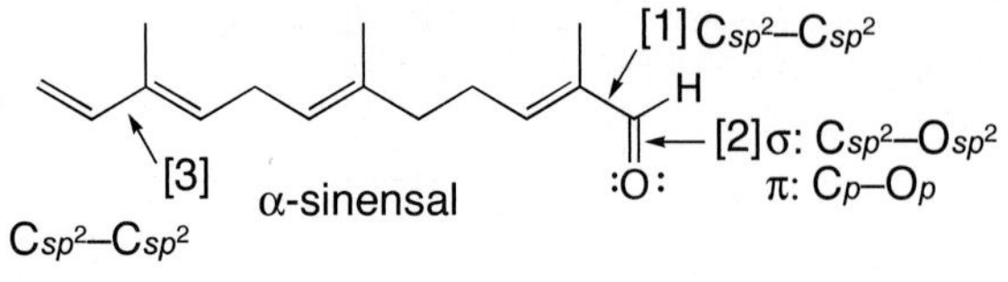
[1] Csp2–Csp2
H
[2]σ: Csp2–Osp2
π: Cp–Op
:O:
[3]
Csp2–Csp2
α-sinensal

b. The O is sp^2 hybridized.
Both lone pairs occupy sp^2 hybrid orbitals.

20.2 A carbonyl compound with a reasonable leaving group (NR_2 or OR bonded to the C=O) undergoes substitution reactions. Those without good leaving groups undergo addition.

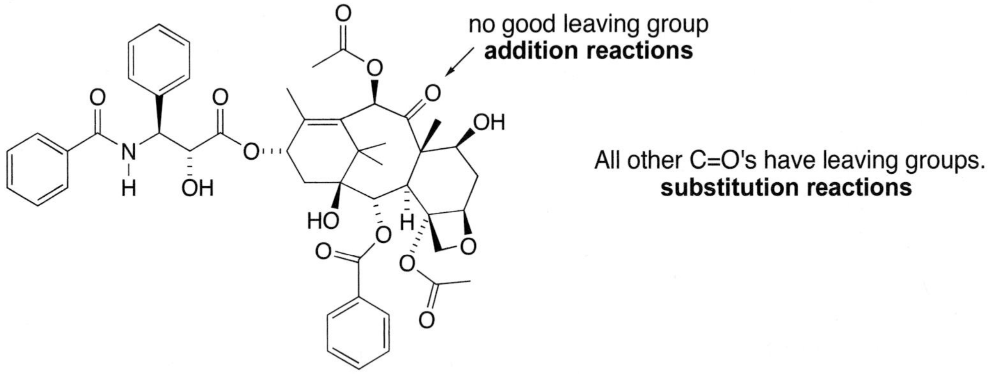
no good leaving group
addition reactions
All other C=O's have leaving groups.
substitution reactions

20.3 Aldehydes are more reactive than ketones. In carbonyl compounds with leaving groups, the better the leaving group, the more reactive the carbonyl compound.

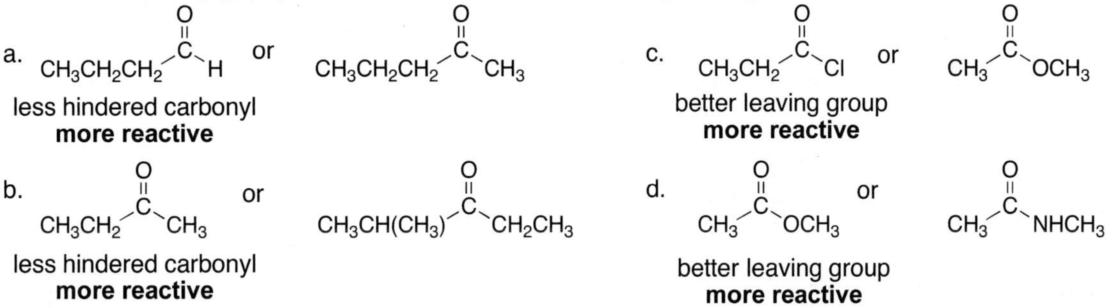
a.
or
less hindered carbonyl
more reactive
c.
or
better leaving group
more reactive
b.
or
less hindered carbonyl
more reactive
d.
or
better leaving group
more reactive

20.4 $NaBH_4$ reduces aldehydes to 1° alcohols and ketones to 2° alcohols.

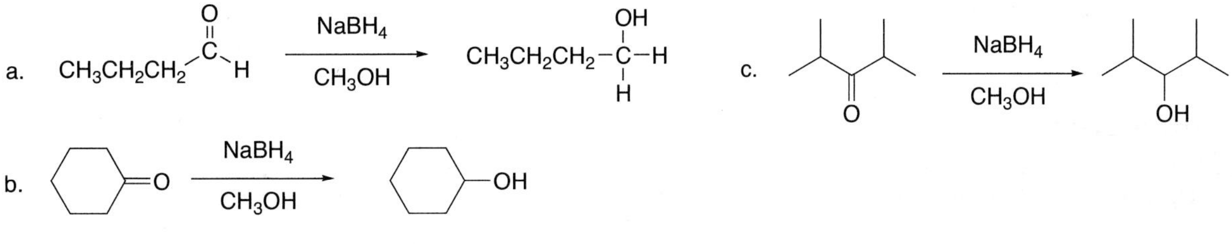
a.
NaBH4
CH3OH
b.
NaBH4
CH3OH
c.
NaBH4
CH3OH

20.5 1° Alcohols are prepared from aldehydes and 2° alcohols are from ketones.

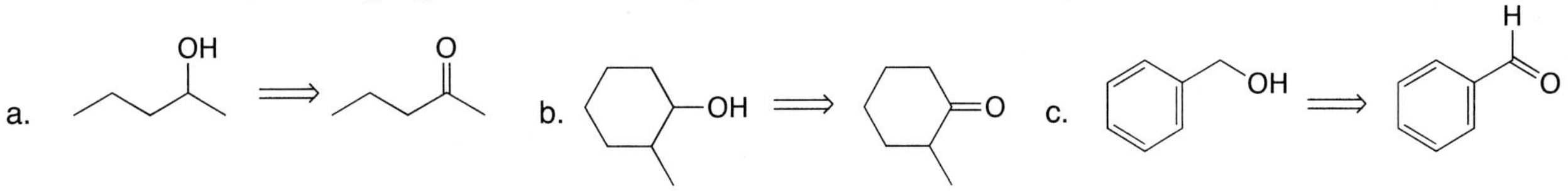
a.
b.
c.

20.6

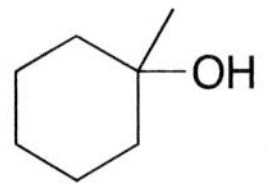

1-methylcyclohexanol

3° Alcohols cannot be made by reduction of a carbonyl group, because they do not contain a H on the C with the OH.

20.7

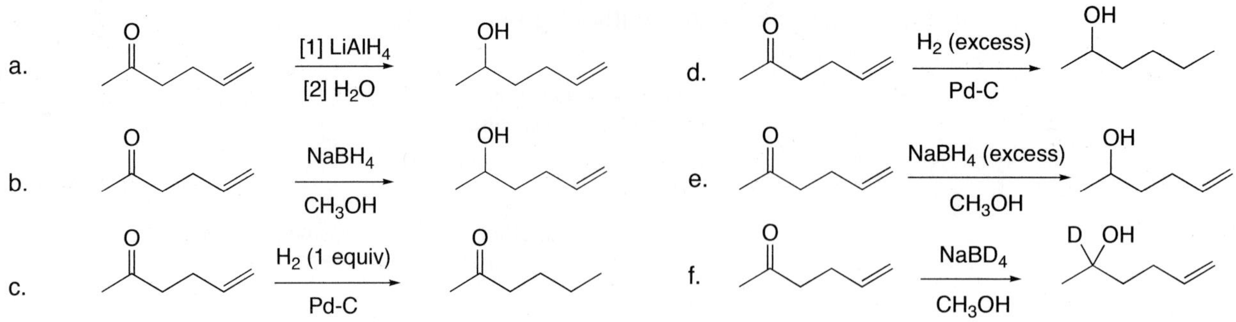
a.
[1] LiAlH4
[2] H2O
b.
NaBH4
CH3OH
c.
H2 (1 equiv)
Pd-C
d.
H2 (excess)
Pd-C
e.
NaBH4 (excess)
CH3OH
f.
NaBD4
CH3OH
D OH

20.8

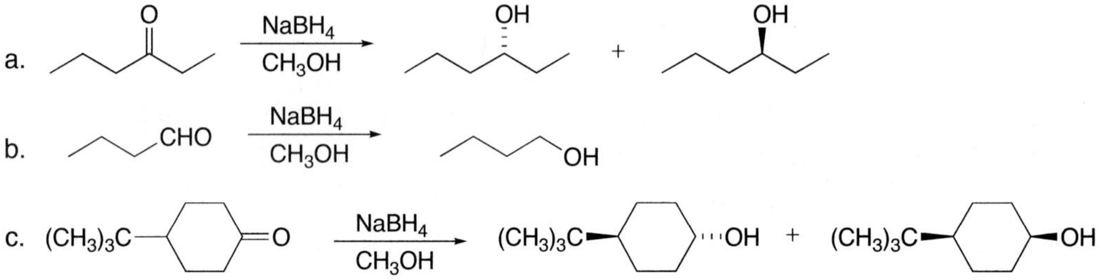
a.
NaBH4
CH3OH
b.
CHO
NaBH4
CH3OH
OH
c. (CH3)3C
NaBH4
CH3OH
(CH3)3C
OH
(CH3)3C
OH

20.9 The 2° alcohol comes from a carbonyl group. Since hydride was delivered from the back side, the (*R*)-CBS reagent must be used.

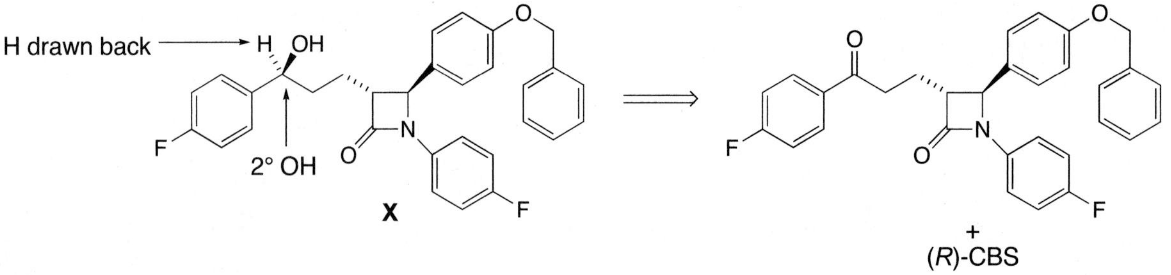
H drawn back
H OH
2° OH
X
+
(R)-CBS

20.10

Part [1]: Nucleophilic substitution of H for Cl

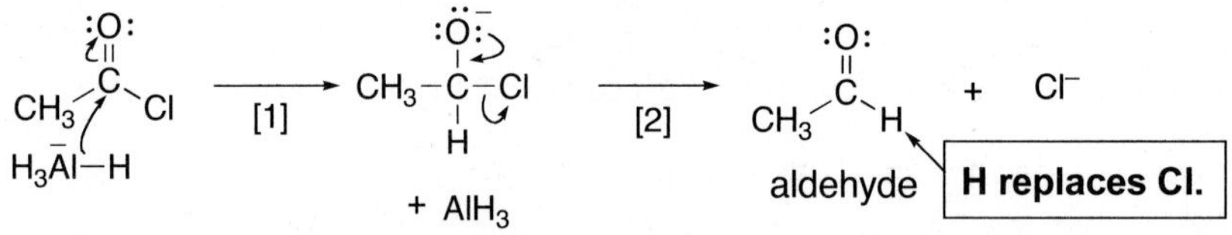
[1]
[2]
+ AlH3
+ Cl⁻
aldehyde
H replaces Cl.

Part [2]: Nucleophilic addition of H⁻ to form an alcohol

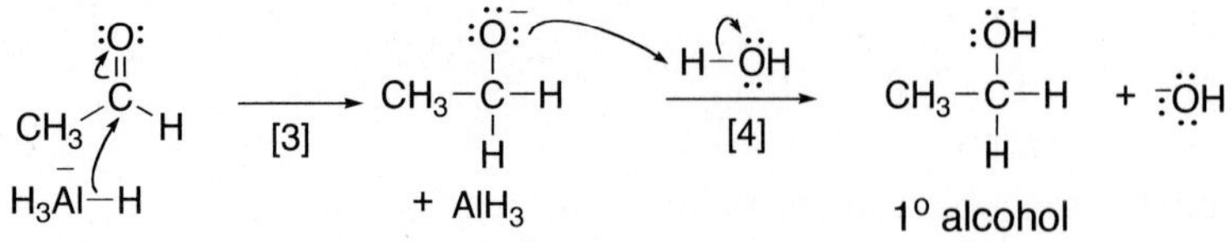
[3]
[4]
+ AlH3
1° alcohol

20.11 Acid chlorides and esters can be reduced to 1° alcohols. Keep the carbon skeleton the same in drawing an ester and acid chloride precursor.

a. 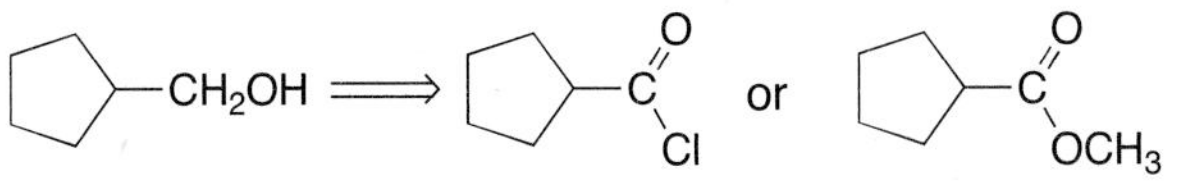

b. 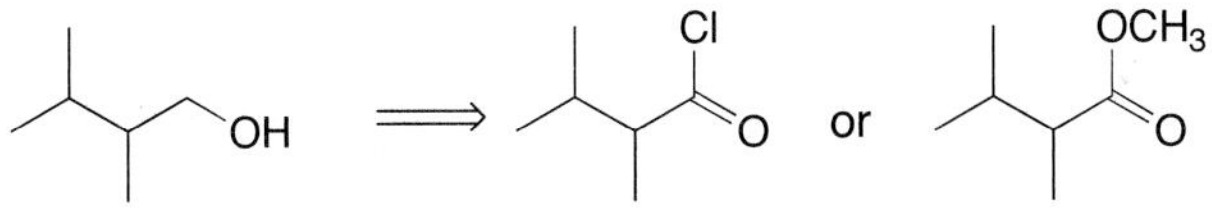

c. 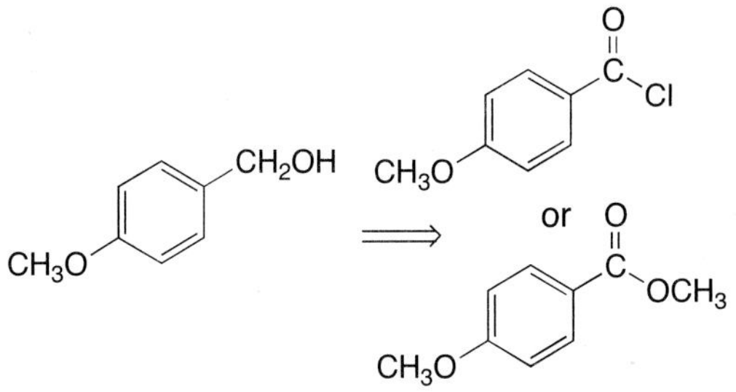

20.12

a. 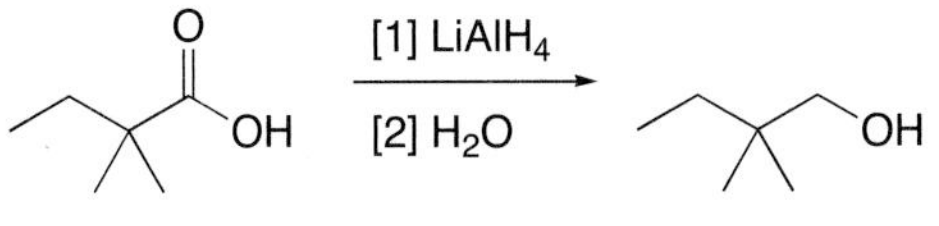

c. 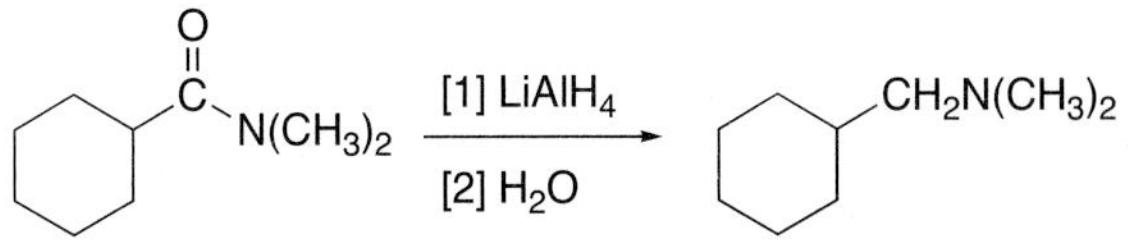

b. 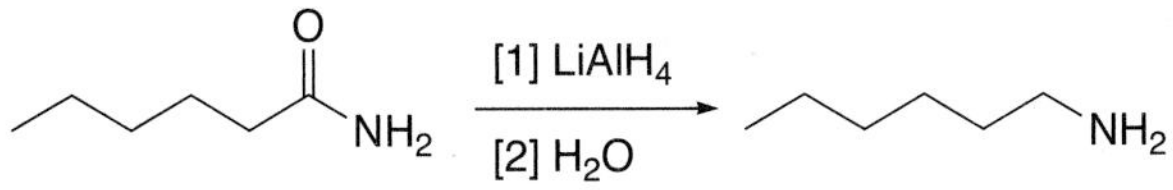

d. 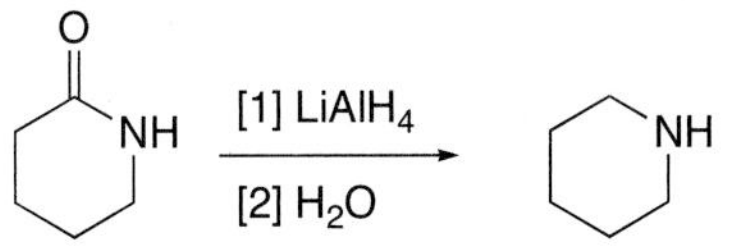

20.13

a. 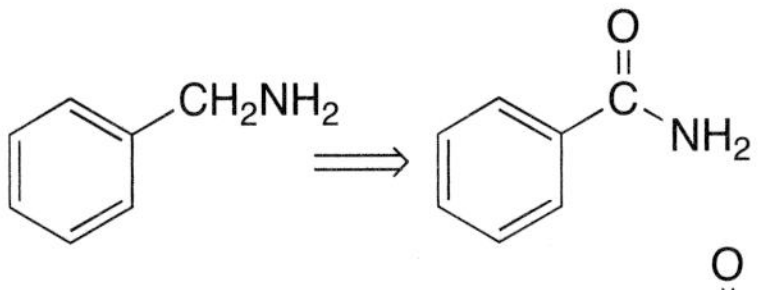

c. 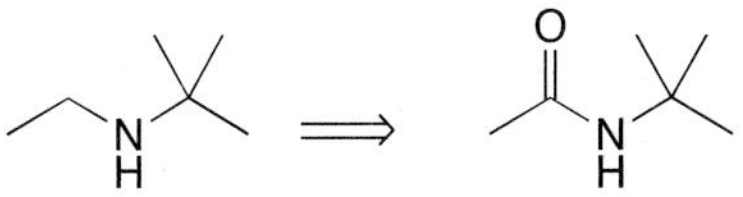

b. 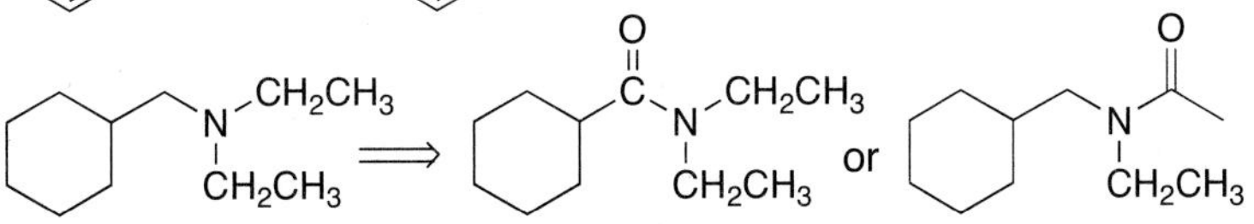

20.14

a. 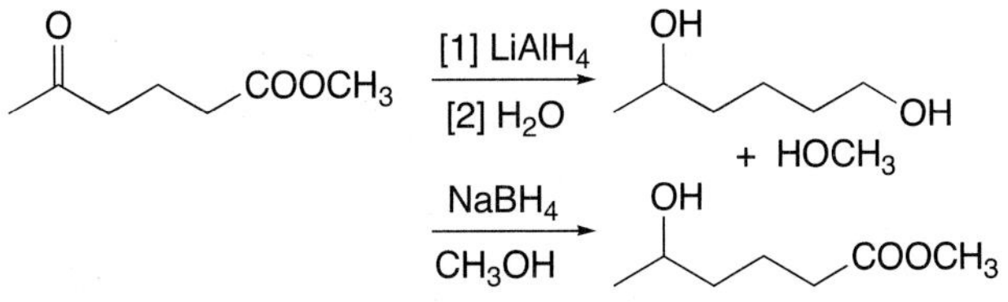

c. 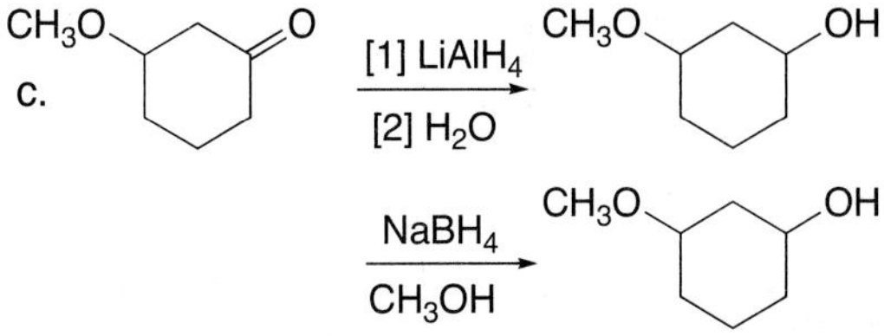

b. 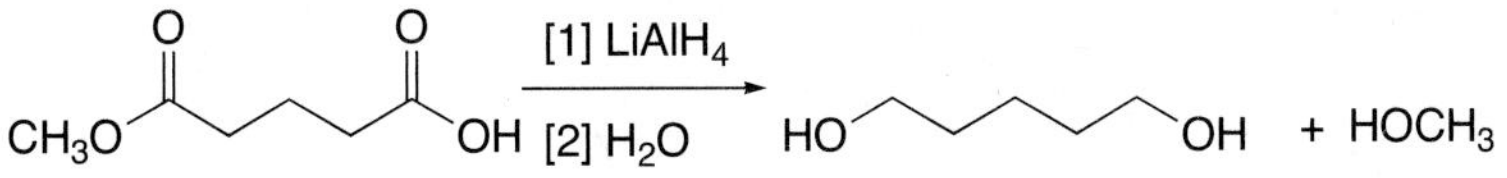

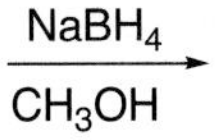 **Neither functional group reduced**

20.15

a. 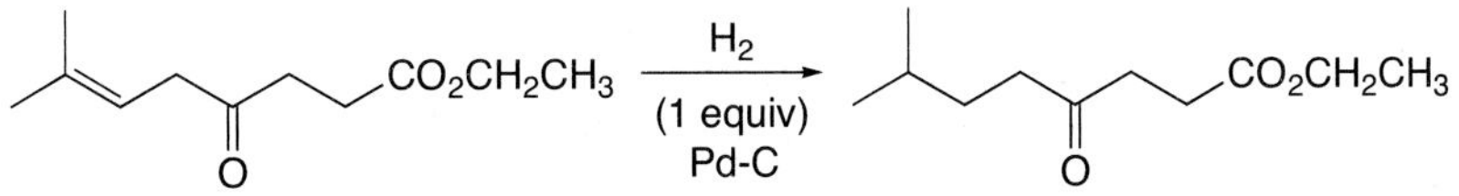

b. 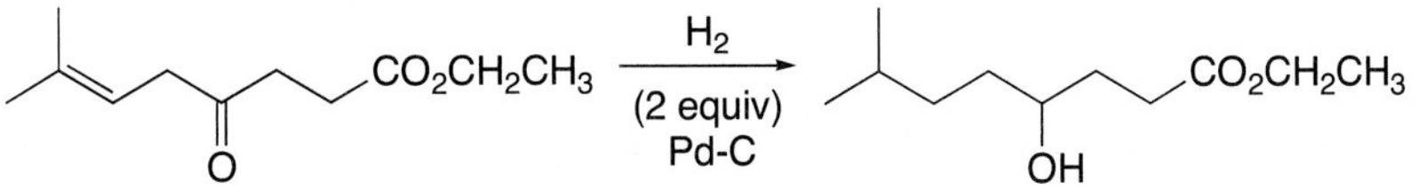

c. 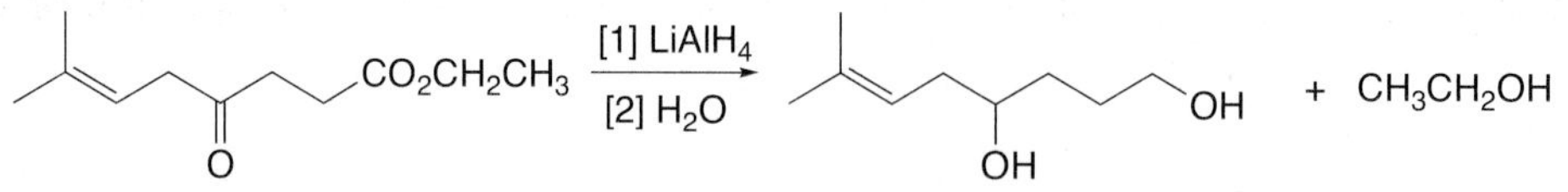

d. 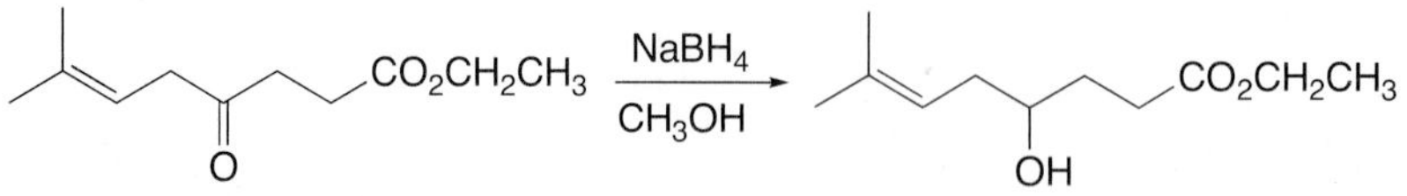

20.16 Tollens reagent reacts only with aldehydes.

a. 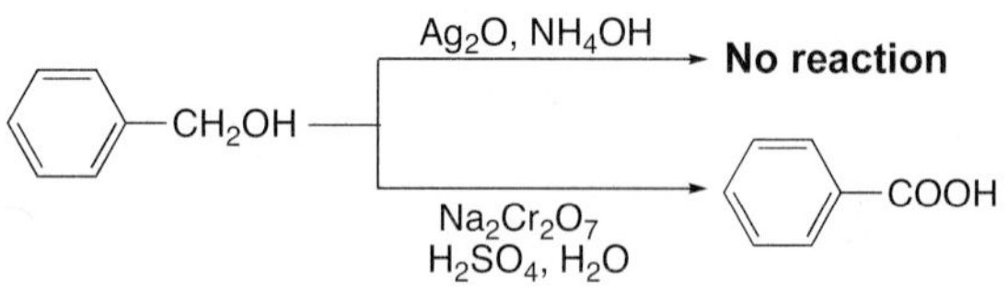

b. 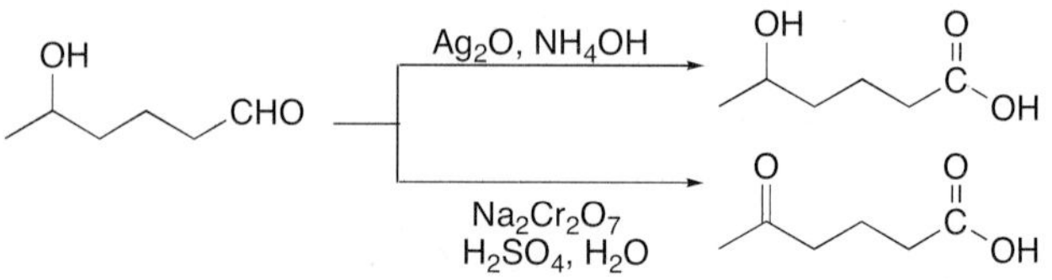

20.17

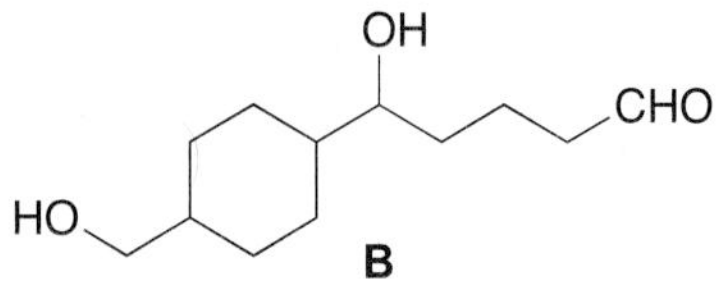

c. 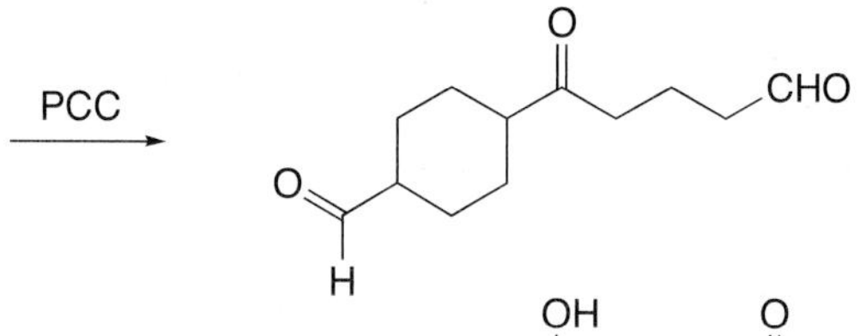

a. 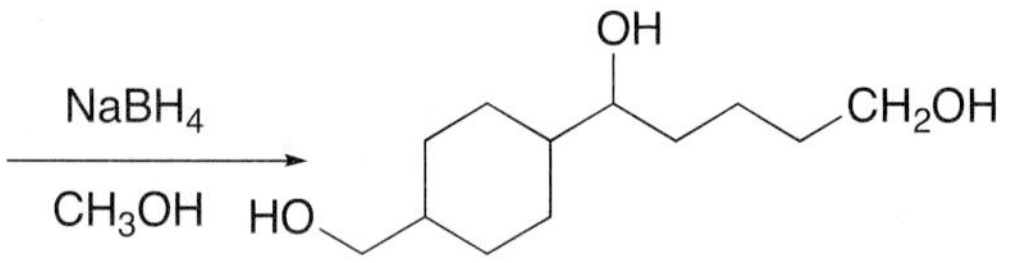

d. 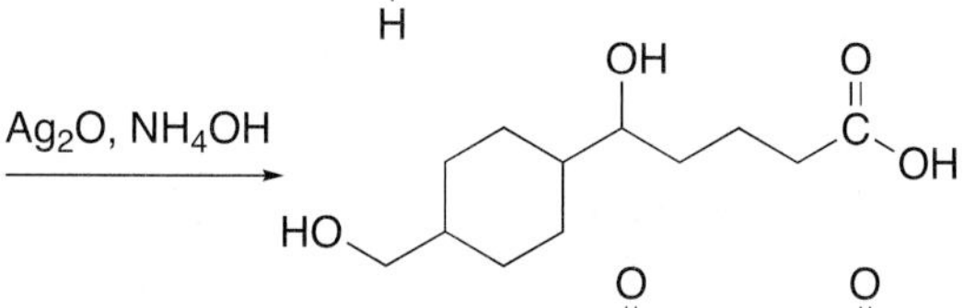

b. 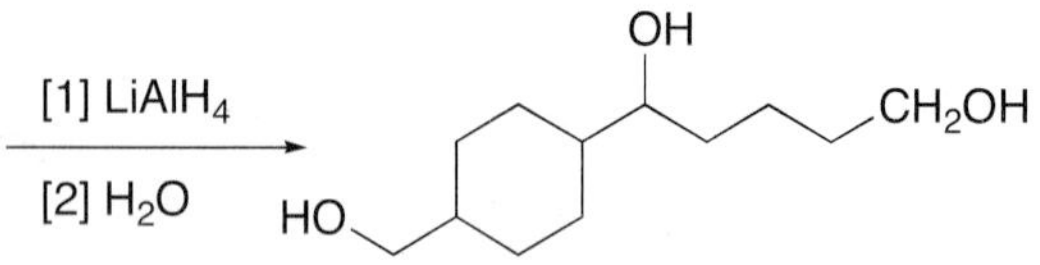

e. 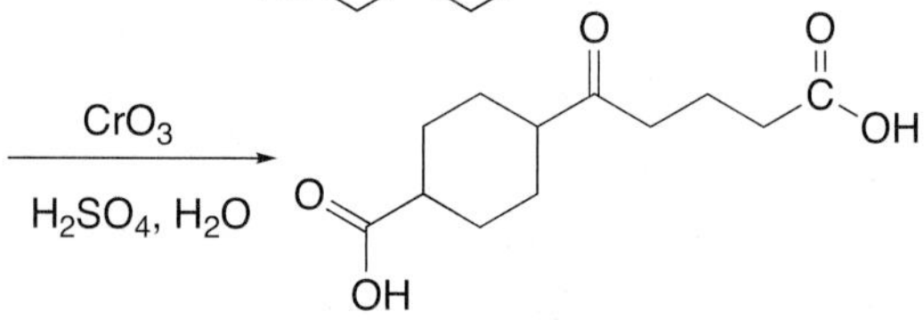

20.18

a. $CH_3CH_2Br + 2\ Li \longrightarrow CH_3CH_2Li + LiBr$

b. $CH_3CH_2Br + Mg \longrightarrow CH_3CH_2MgBr$

c. $CH_3CH_2Br + 2\ Li \longrightarrow CH_3CH_2Li + LiBr$

$2\ CH_3CH_2Li + CuI \longrightarrow LiCu(CH_2CH_3)_2 + LiI$

20.19

$HC{\equiv}CCH_2CH_2CH_2CH_2CH_2CH_3 + NaH \longrightarrow Na^{+}\ {}^{-}C{\equiv}CCH_2CH_2CH_2CH_2CH_2CH_3 + H_2$ ← hydrogen gas

$HC{\equiv}CCH_2CH_2CH_2CH_2CH_2CH_3 + CH_3MgBr \longrightarrow BrMgC{\equiv}CCH_2CH_2CH_2CH_2CH_2CH_3 + CH_4$ ← methane gas

20.20

a. 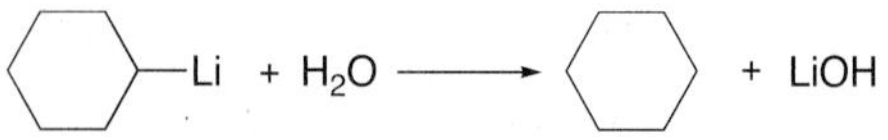

b. 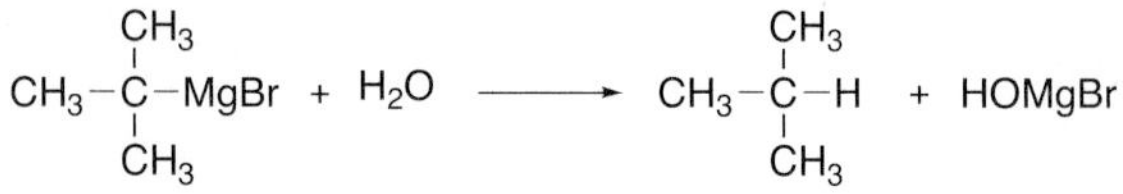

c. 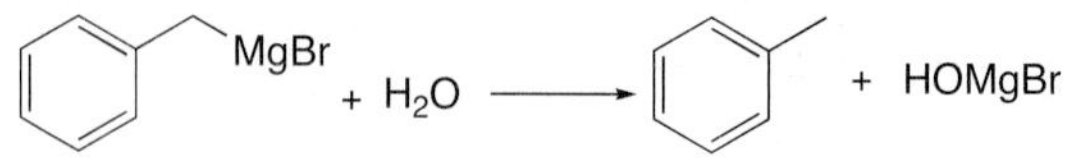

d. $CH_3CH_2C{\equiv}C{-}Li + H_2O \longrightarrow CH_3CH_2C{\equiv}CH + LiOH$

20.21 To draw the products, add the alkyl or phenyl group to the carbonyl carbon and protonate the oxygen.

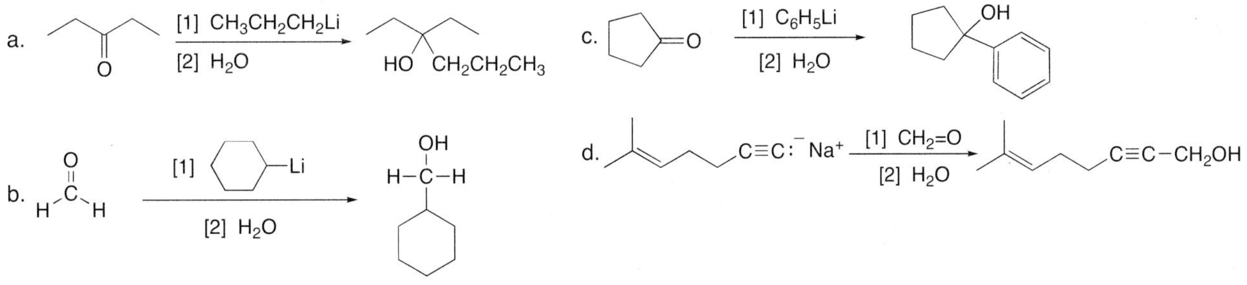
a.
[1] CH3CH2CH2Li
[2] H2O
HO CH2CH2CH3
b.
[1] Li
[2] H2O
OH
H–C–H
c.
[1] C6H5Li
[2] H2O
OH
d.
C≡C:⁻ Na+
[1] CH2=O
[2] H2O
C≡C–CH2OH

20.22 Addition of RM always occurs from above and below the plane of the molecule.

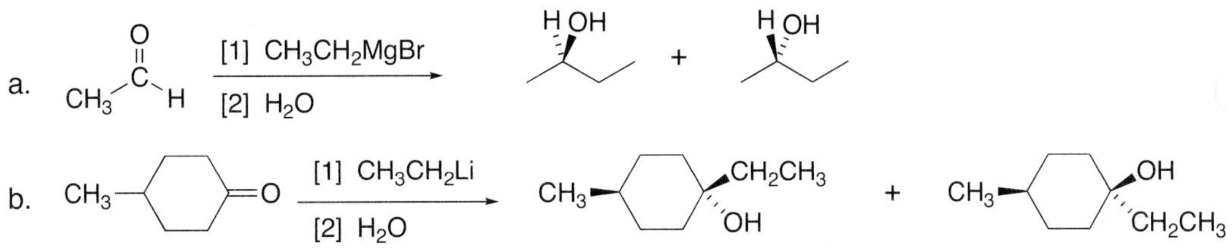
a.
CH3 C H
[1] CH3CH2MgBr
[2] H2O
H OH
+
H OH
b.
CH3
[1] CH3CH2Li
[2] H2O
CH3
CH2CH3
OH
+
CH3
OH
CH2CH3

20.23

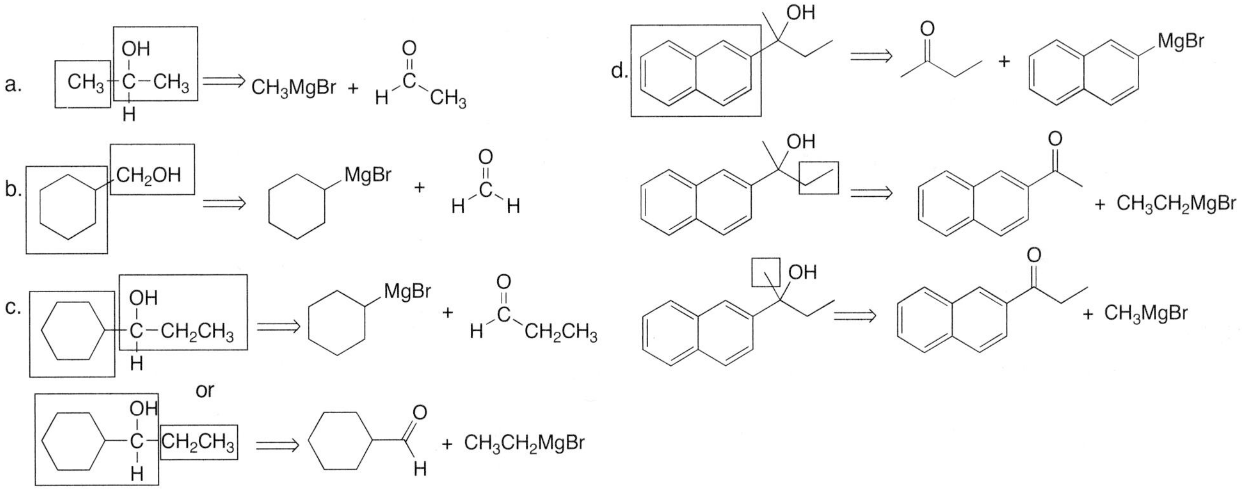
a.
CH3 OH C–CH3 H
CH3MgBr +
H C CH3
b.
CH2OH
MgBr
+
H C H
c.
OH C–CH2CH3 H
MgBr
+
H C CH2CH3
or
OH C CH2CH3 H
+ CH3CH2MgBr
d.
OH
MgBr
+
OH
+ CH3CH2MgBr
OH
+ CH3MgBr

20.24

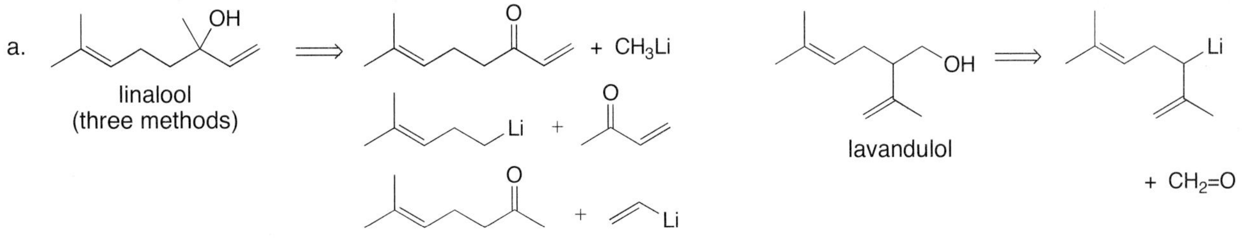
a.
OH
linalool
(three methods)
+ CH3Li
Li
+
+
Li
OH
lavandulol
Li
+ CH2=O

b.

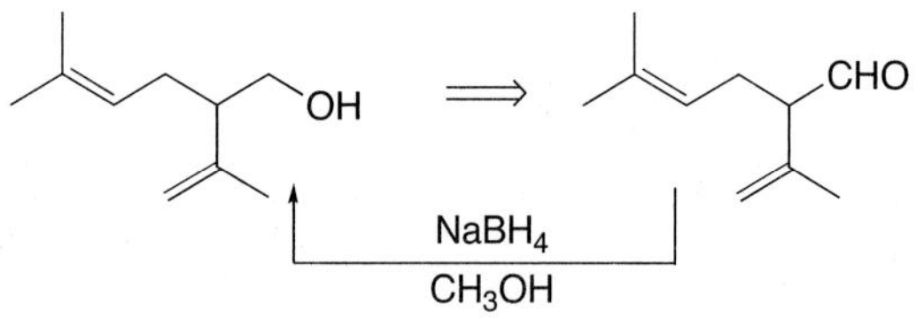
OH
CHO
NaBH4
CH3OH

c. Linalool is a 3° ROH. Therefore, it has no H on the carbon with the OH group, and cannot be prepared by reduction of a carbonyl compound.

20.25

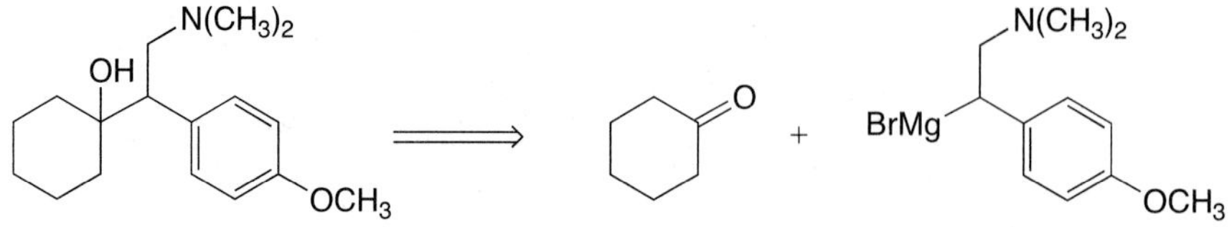
N(CH3)2
OH
OCH3
O
+
BrMg
N(CH3)2
OCH3

venlafaxine

20.26

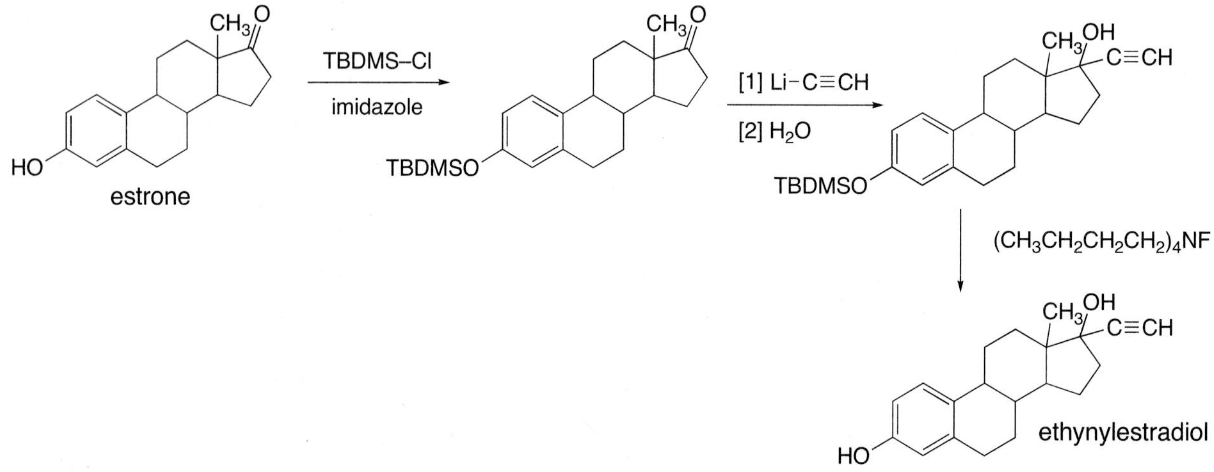
CH3 O
HO
estrone
TBDMS–Cl
imidazole
CH3 O
TBDMSO
[1] Li−C≡CH
[2] H2O
CH3 OH
C≡CH
TBDMSO
(CH3CH2CH2CH2)4NF
CH3 OH
C≡CH
HO
ethynylestradiol

20.27

a.

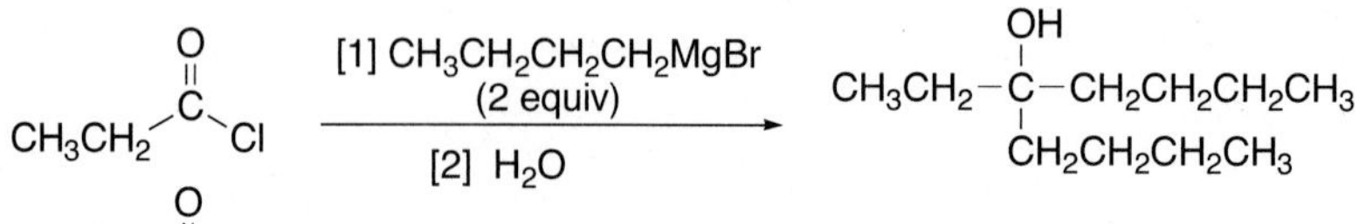
O
CH3CH2 C Cl
[1] CH3CH2CH2CH2MgBr
(2 equiv)
[2] H2O
OH
CH3CH2−C−CH2CH2CH2CH3
CH2CH2CH2CH3

b.

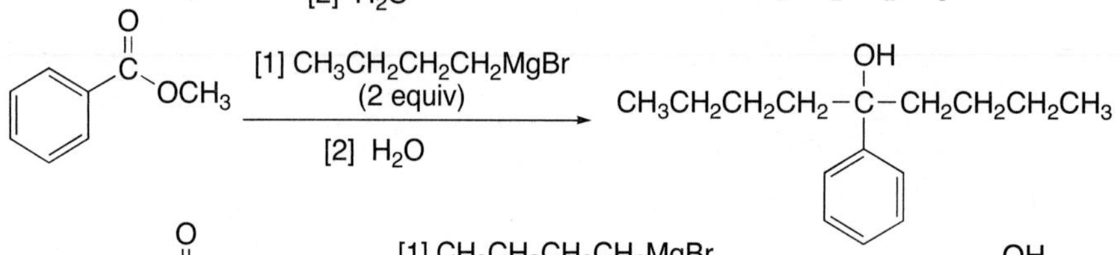
O
C
OCH3
[1] CH3CH2CH2CH2MgBr
(2 equiv)
[2] H2O
OH
CH3CH2CH2CH2−C−CH2CH2CH2CH3

c.

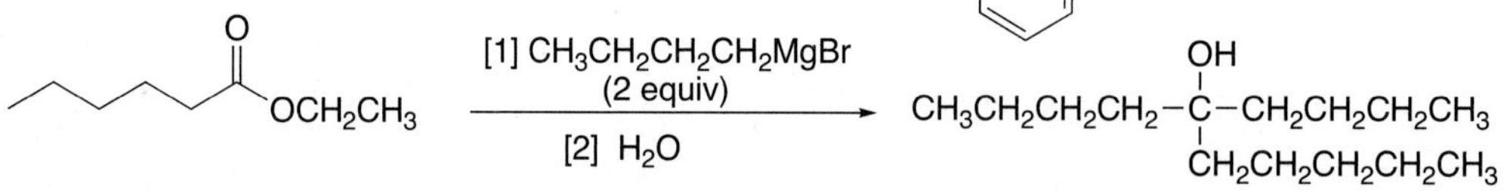
O
OCH2CH3
[1] CH3CH2CH2CH2MgBr
(2 equiv)
[2] H2O
OH
CH3CH2CH2CH2−C−CH2CH2CH2CH3
CH2CH2CH2CH2CH3

20.28

a.

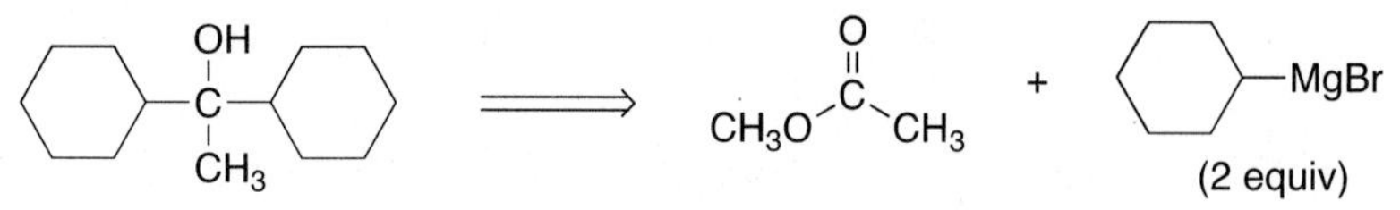
OH
C
CH3
O
CH3O C CH3
+
MgBr
(2 equiv)

b.

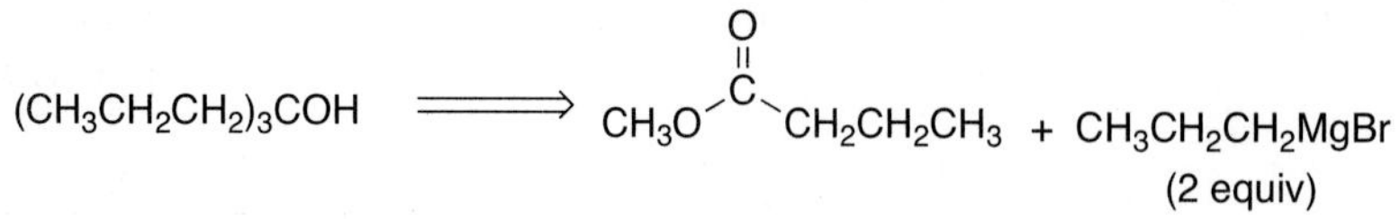
(CH3CH2CH2)3COH
O
CH3O C CH2CH2CH3
+ CH3CH2CH2MgBr
(2 equiv)

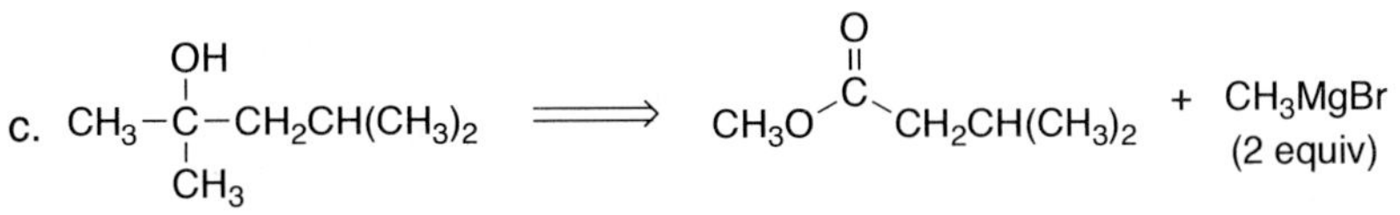

20.29 The R group of the organocuprate has replaced the Cl on the acid chloride.

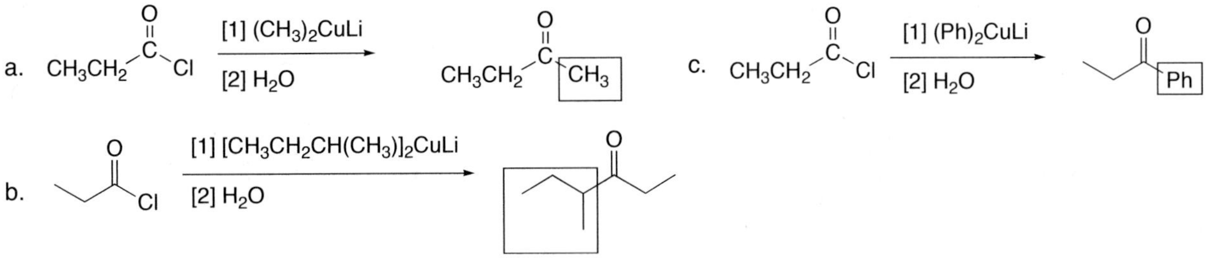

20.30

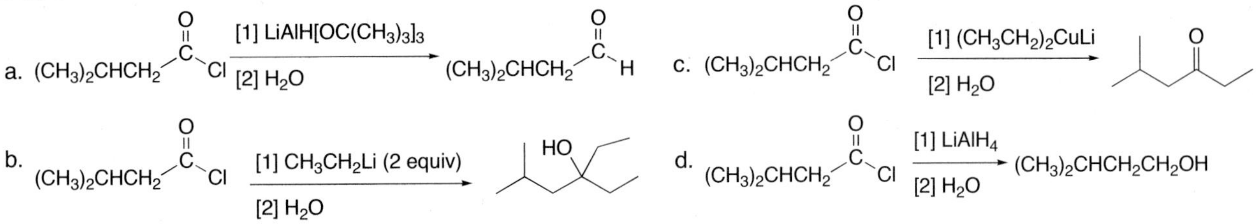

20.31

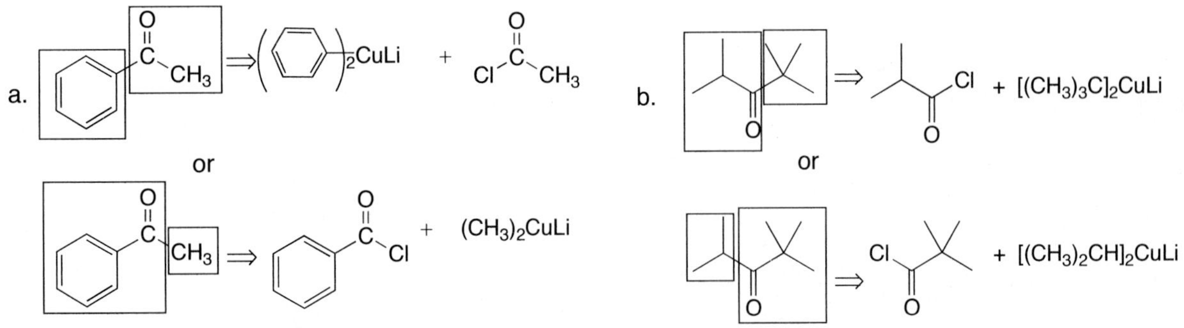

20.32

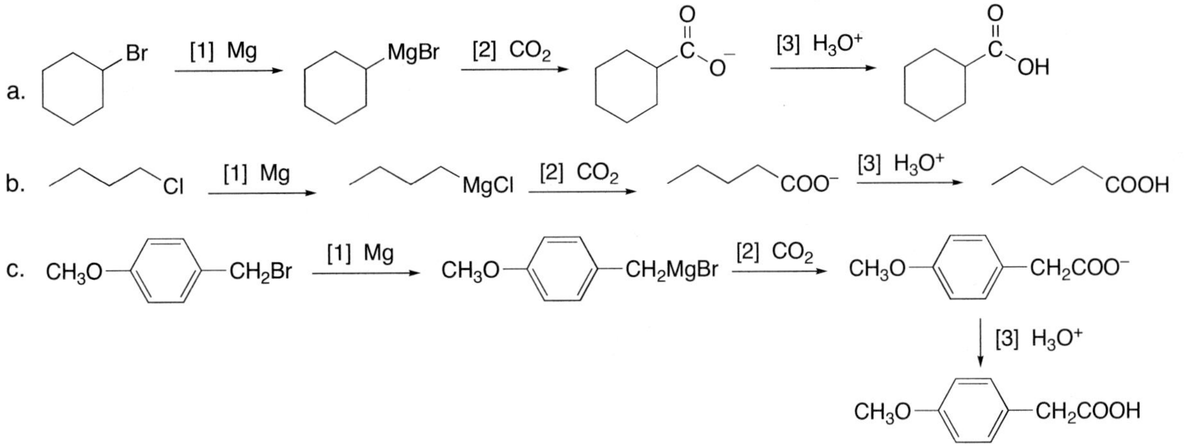

20.33

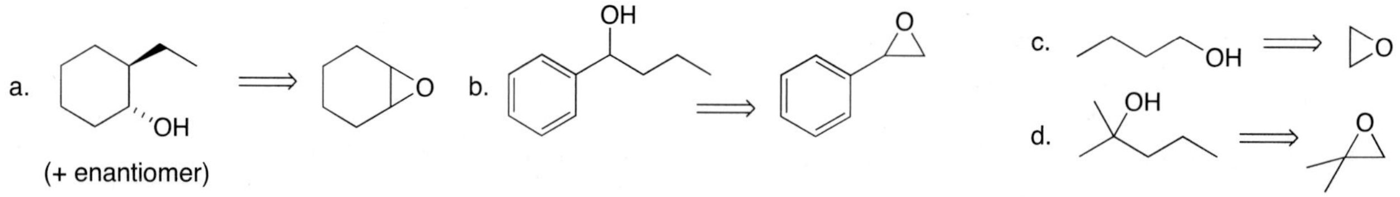
a.
OH
(+ enantiomer)
O
b.
OH
O
c.
OH
O
d.
OH
O

20.34 The characteristic reaction of α,β-unsaturated carbonyl compounds is nucleophilic addition. Grignard and organolithium reagents react by 1,2-addition and organocuprate reagents react by 1,4-addition.

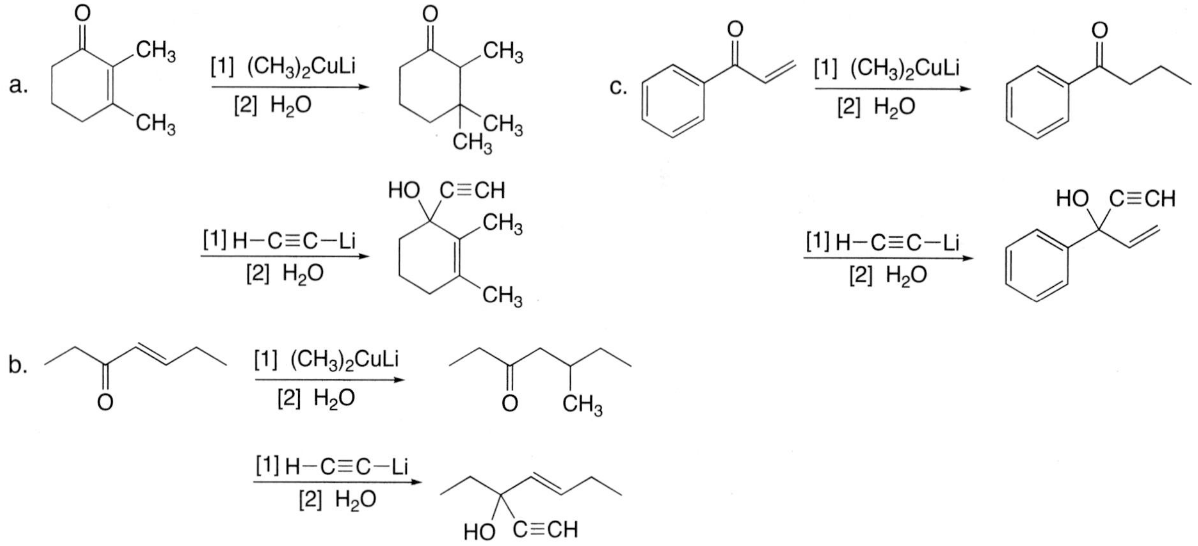
a.
CH3
CH3
[1] (CH3)2CuLi
[2] H2O
[1] H–C≡C–Li
[2] H2O
HO C≡CH
b.
c.
CH3
HO C≡CH

20.35

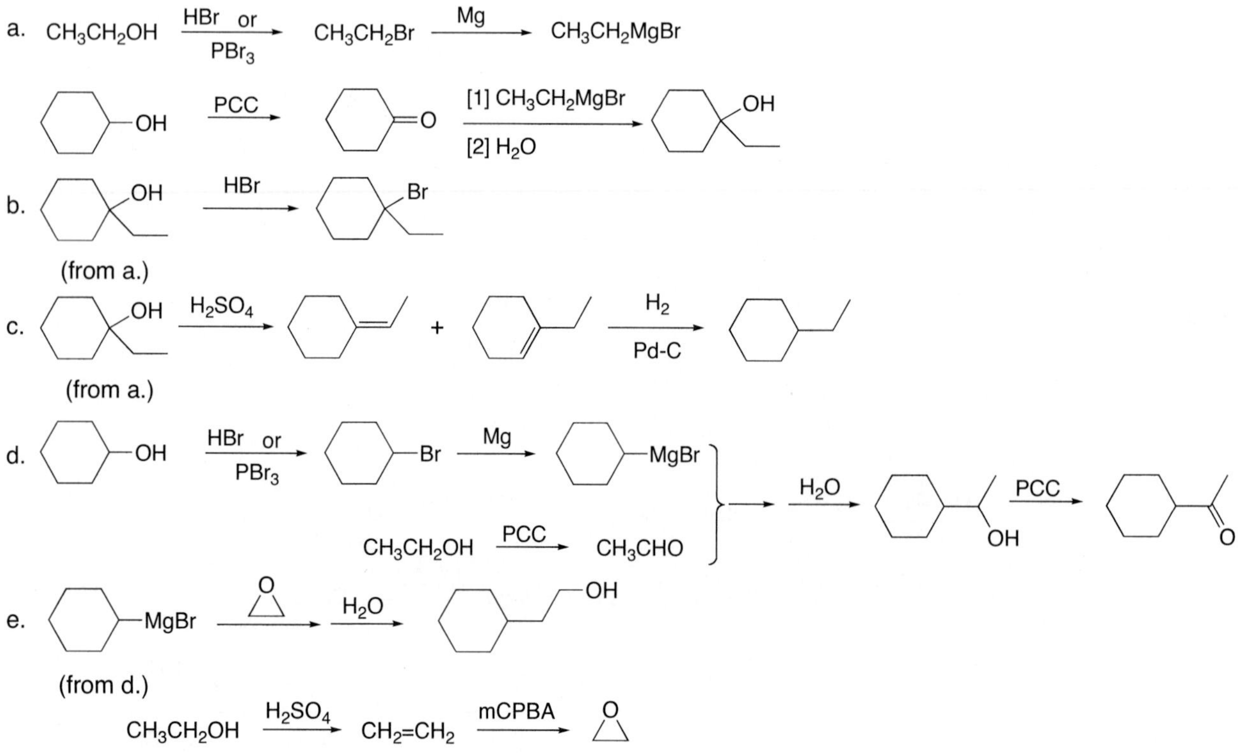
a. CH3CH2OH
HBr or PBr3
CH3CH2Br
Mg
CH3CH2MgBr
PCC
[1] CH3CH2MgBr
[2] H2O
OH
b.
HBr
Br
(from a.)
c.
H2SO4
H2
Pd-C
(from a.)
d.
HBr or PBr3
Br
Mg
MgBr
H2O
PCC
CH3CH2OH
CH3CHO
e.
MgBr
(from d.)
CH3CH2OH
H2SO4
CH2=CH2
mCPBA

20.36

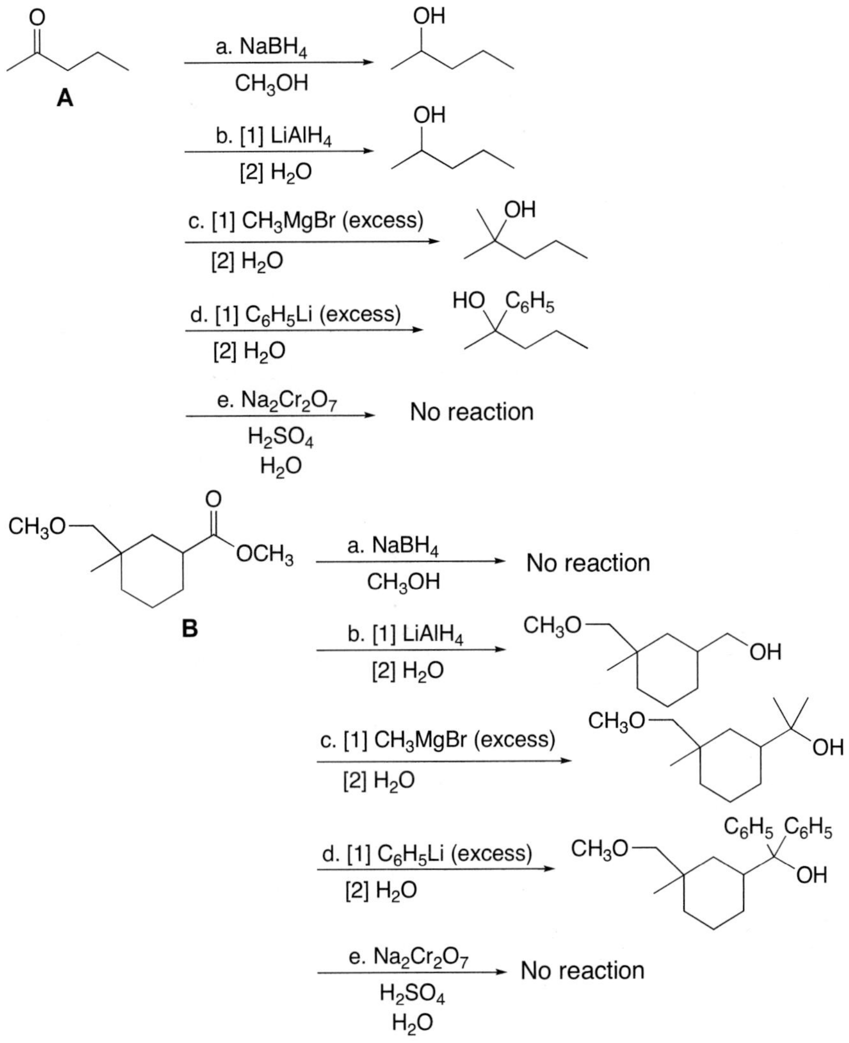
O
A
a. NaBH4
CH3OH
OH
b. [1] LiAlH4
[2] H2O
OH
c. [1] CH3MgBr (excess)
[2] H2O
OH
d. [1] C6H5Li (excess)
[2] H2O
HO C6H5
e. Na2Cr2O7
H2SO4
H2O
No reaction
CH3O
O
OCH3
B
a. NaBH4
CH3OH
No reaction
b. [1] LiAlH4
[2] H2O
CH3O
OH
c. [1] CH3MgBr (excess)
[2] H2O
CH3O
OH
d. [1] C6H5Li (excess)
[2] H2O
C6H5 C6H5
CH3O
OH
e. Na2Cr2O7
H2SO4
H2O
No reaction

20.37

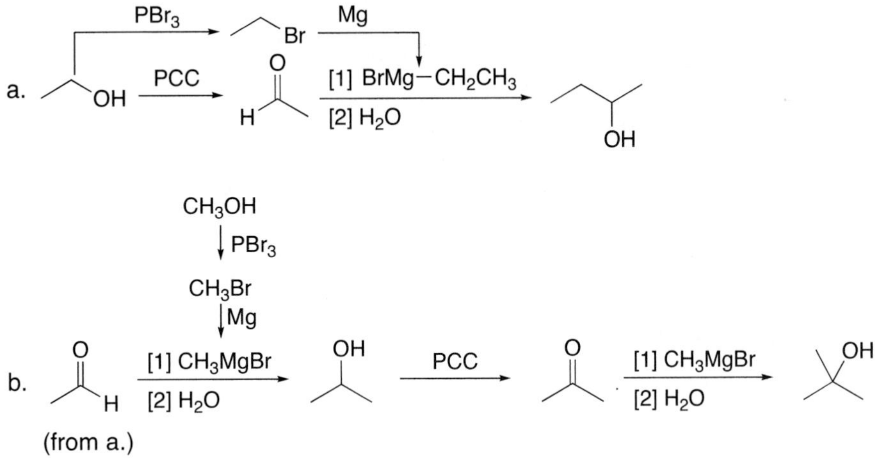
a.
PBr3
Br
Mg
OH
PCC
O
H
[1] BrMg−CH2CH3
[2] H2O
OH
CH3OH
PBr3
CH3Br
Mg
b.
O
H
(from a.)
[1] CH3MgBr
[2] H2O
OH
PCC
O
[1] CH3MgBr
[2] H2O
OH

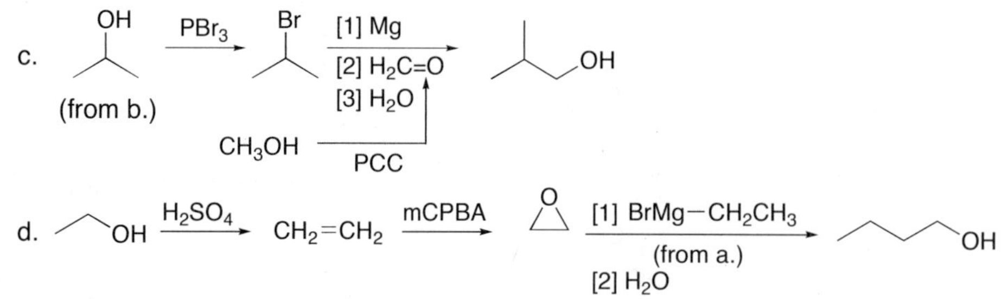
c.
OH
PBr3
Br
[1] Mg
[2] H2C=O
[3] H2O
OH
(from b.)
CH3OH
PCC
d.
OH
H2SO4
CH2=CH2
mCPBA
O
[1] BrMg−CH2CH3
(from a.)
[2] H2O
OH

20.38

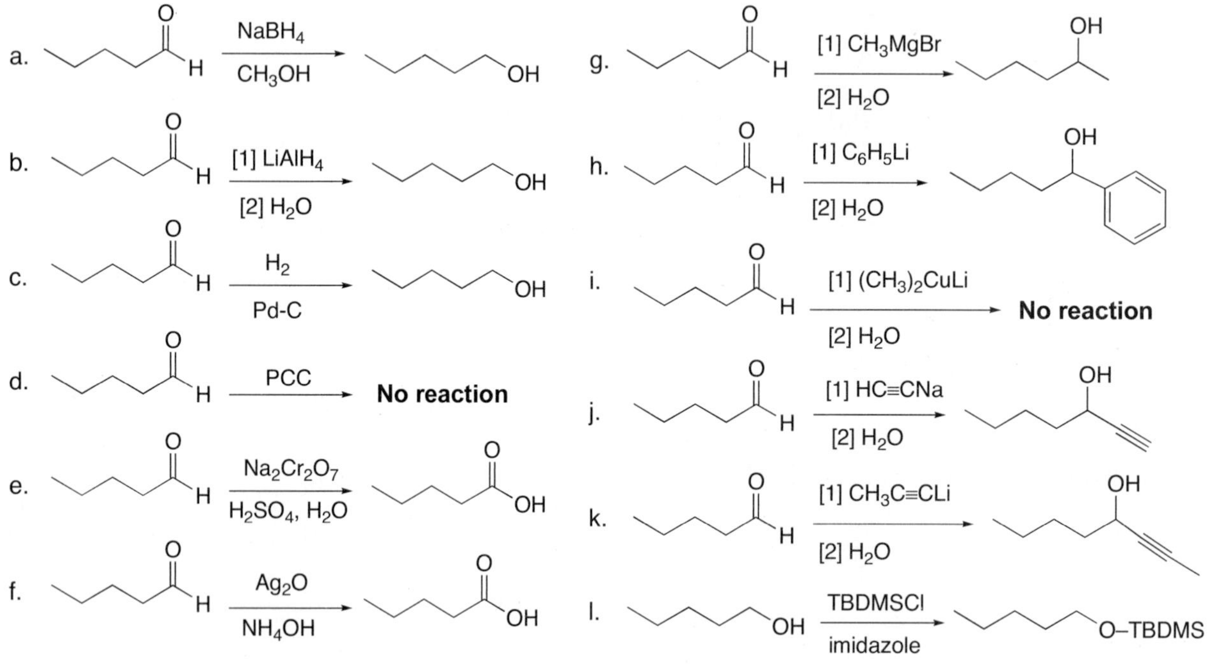
a.
NaBH4
CH3OH
b.
[1] LiAlH4
[2] H2O
c.
H2
Pd-C
d.
PCC
No reaction
e.
Na2Cr2O7
H2SO4, H2O
f.
Ag2O
NH4OH
g.
[1] CH3MgBr
[2] H2O
h.
[1] C6H5Li
[2] H2O
i.
[1] (CH3)2CuLi
[2] H2O
No reaction
j.
[1] HC≡CNa
[2] H2O
k.
[1] CH3C≡CLi
[2] H2O
l.
TBDMSCl
imidazole
O–TBDMS

20.39

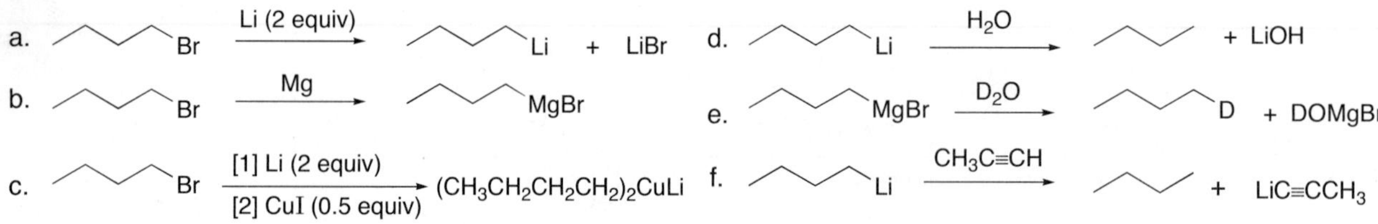
a.
Br
Li (2 equiv)
Li + LiBr
b.
Mg
MgBr
c.
[1] Li (2 equiv)
[2] CuI (0.5 equiv)
(CH3CH2CH2CH2)2CuLi
d.
H2O
+ LiOH
e.
D2O
+ DOMgBr
f.
CH3C≡CH
+ LiC≡CCH3

20.40

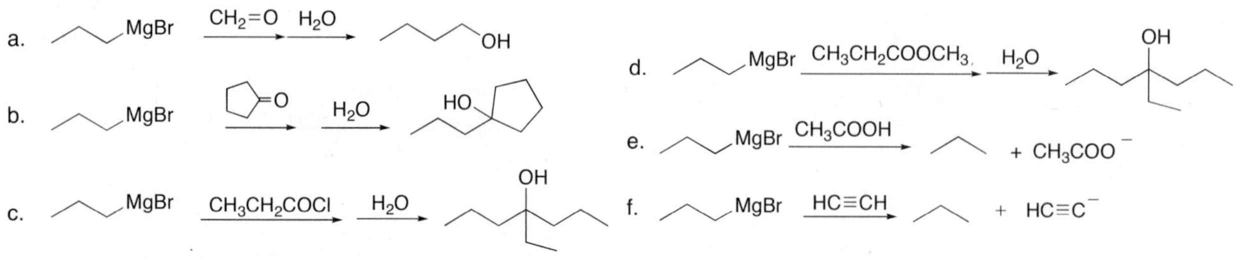
a.
MgBr
CH2=O
H2O
OH
b.
H2O
HO
c.
CH3CH2COCl
d.
CH3CH2COOCH3
e.
CH3COOH
+ CH3COO−
f.
HC≡CH
+ HC≡C−

g. 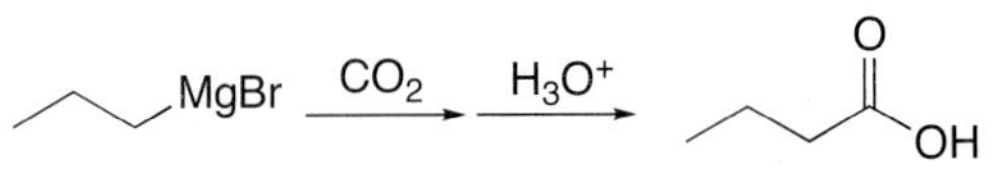
MgBr
CO2
H3O+
O
OH

i. 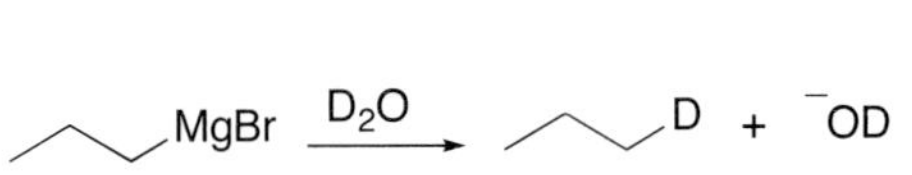
MgBr
D2O
D
+
OD

h. 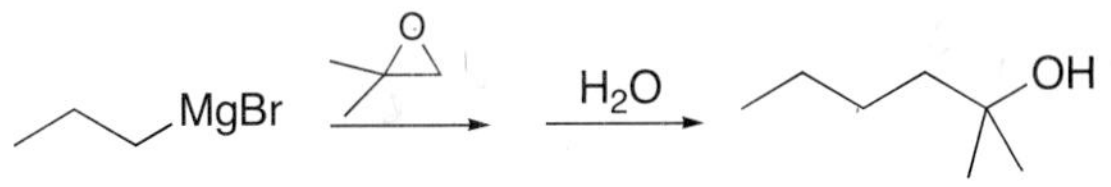
MgBr
O
H2O
OH

j. 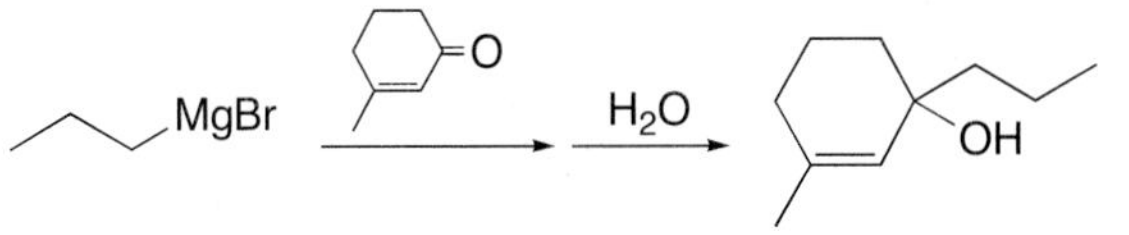
MgBr
O
H2O
OH

20.41

a. 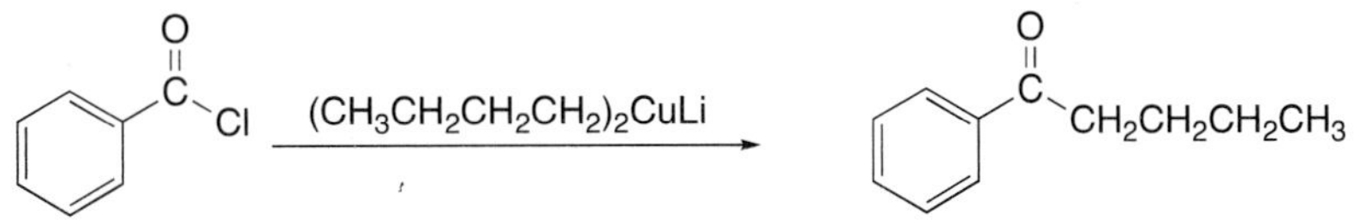
O
C
Cl
(CH3CH2CH2CH2)2CuLi
O
C
CH2CH2CH2CH3

b. 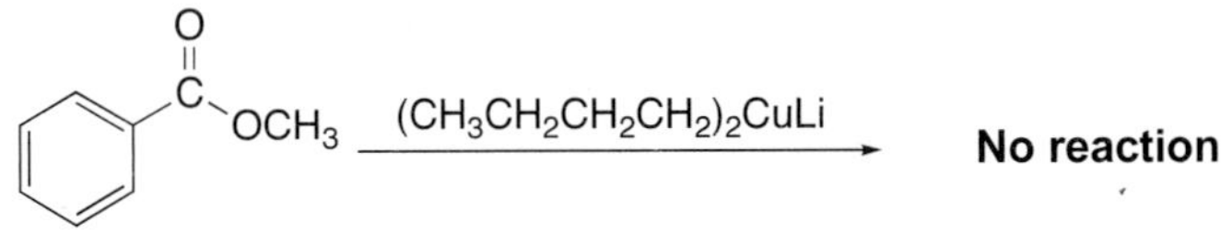
O
C
OCH3
(CH3CH2CH2CH2)2CuLi
No reaction

c. 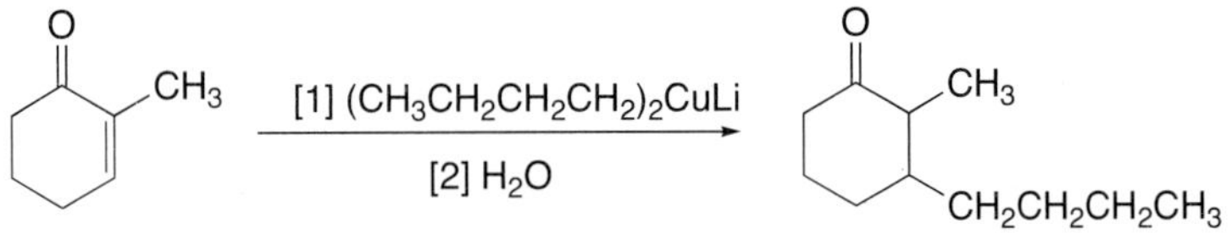
O
CH3
[1] (CH3CH2CH2CH2)2CuLi
[2] H2O
O
CH3
CH2CH2CH2CH3

d. 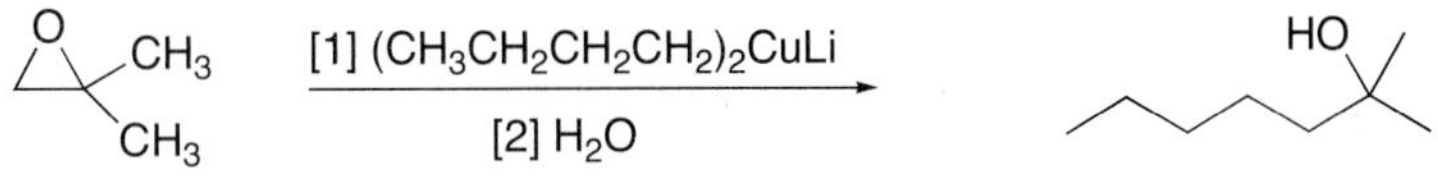
O
CH3
CH3
[1] (CH3CH2CH2CH2)2CuLi
[2] H2O
HO

20.42 Arrange the larger group [$(CH_3)_3C$–] on the left side of the carbonyl.

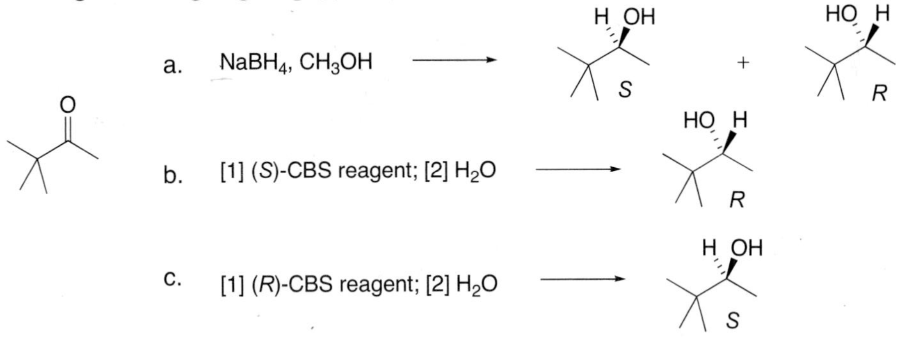
O
a.
NaBH4, CH3OH
H OH
S
+
HO H
R
b.
[1] (S)-CBS reagent; [2] H2O
HO H
R
c.
[1] (R)-CBS reagent; [2] H2O
H OH
S

20.43

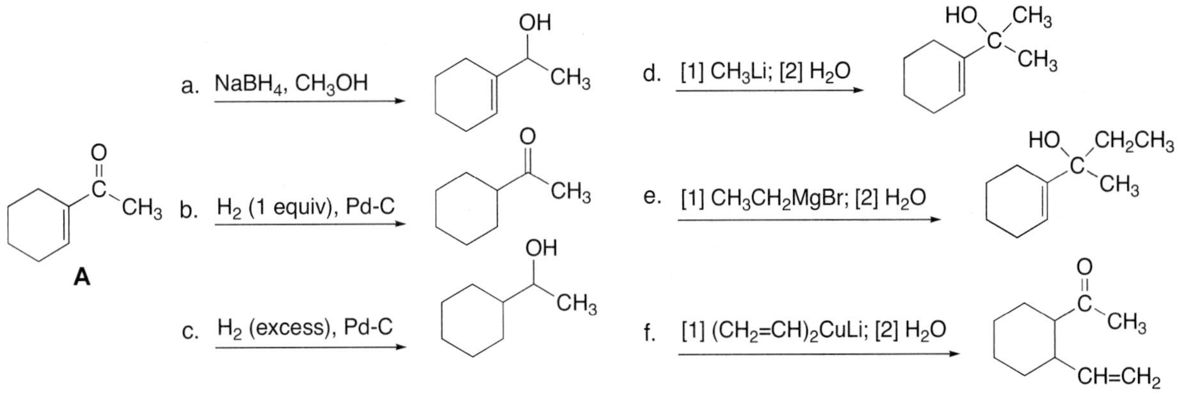
O
C
CH3
A
a. NaBH4, CH3OH
OH
CH3
b. H2 (1 equiv), Pd-C
O
CH3
c. H2 (excess), Pd-C
OH
CH3
d. [1] CH3Li; [2] H2O
HO
CH3
C
CH3
e. [1] CH3CH2MgBr; [2] H2O
HO
CH2CH3
C
CH3
f. [1] (CH2=CH)2CuLi; [2] H2O
O
C
CH3
CH=CH2

20.44

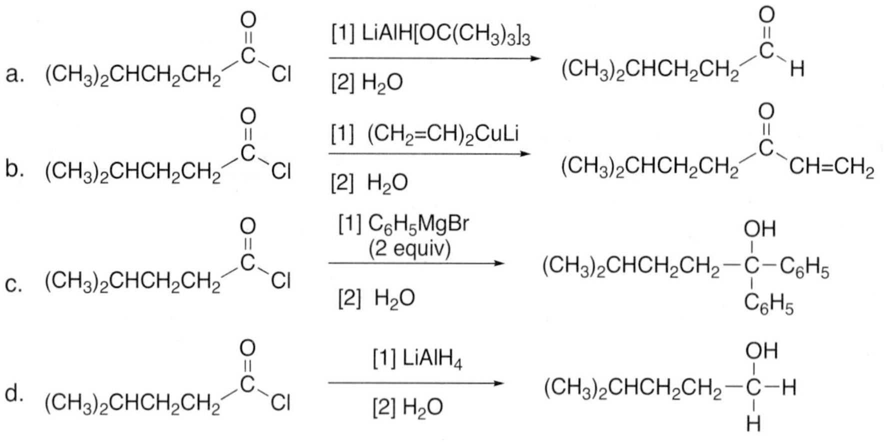

20.45

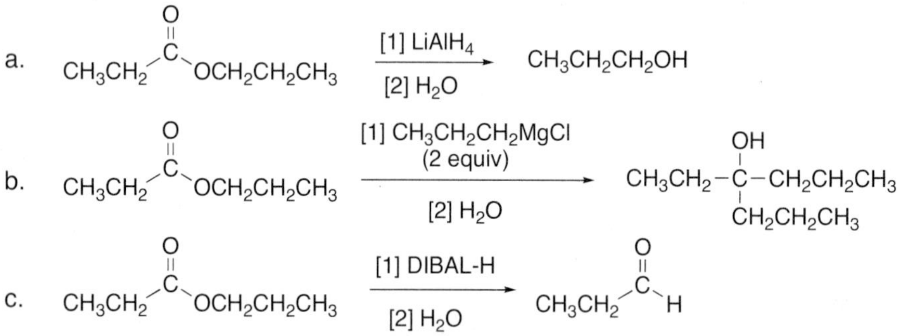

20.46

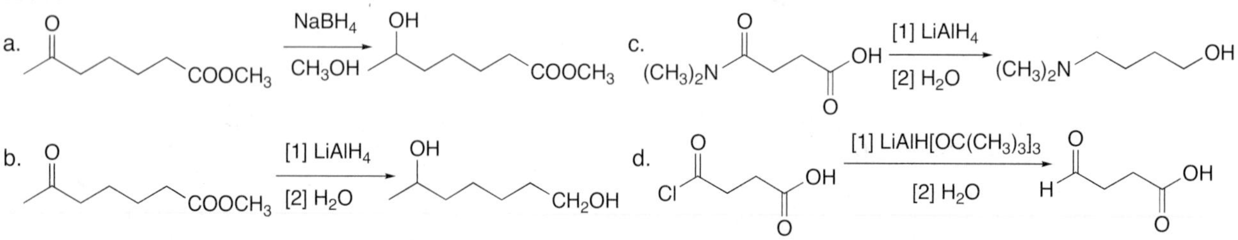

20.47

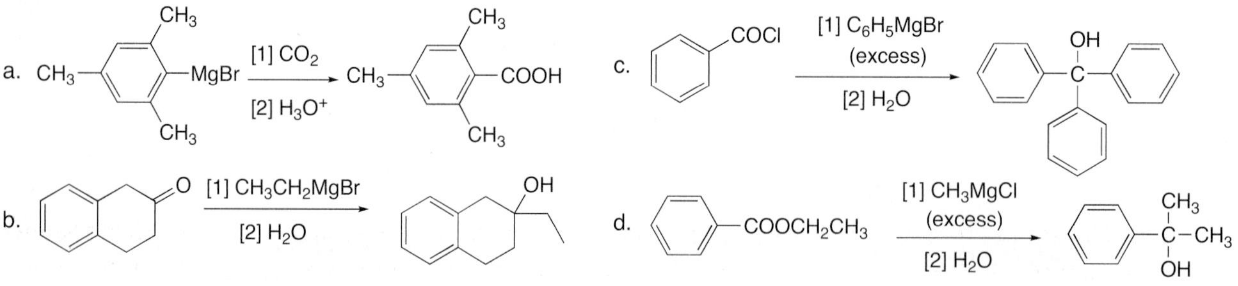

e. 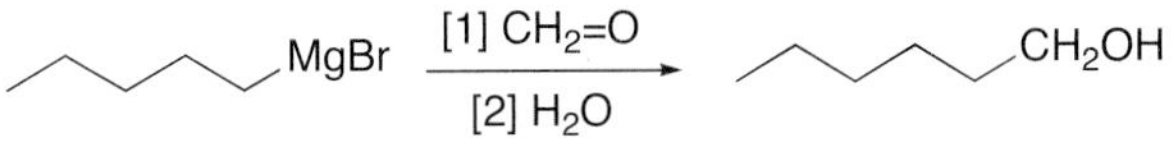
MgBr
[1] CH2=O
[2] H2O
CH2OH

g. 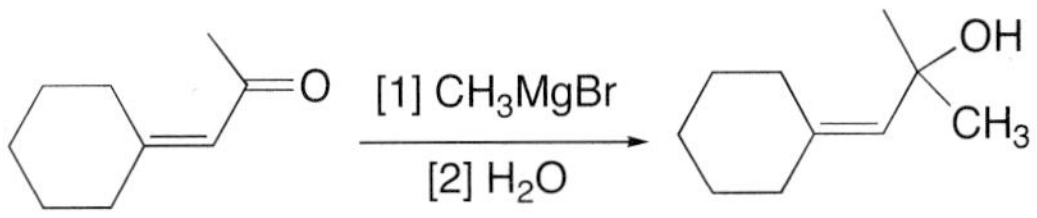
O
[1] CH3MgBr
[2] H2O
OH
CH3

f. 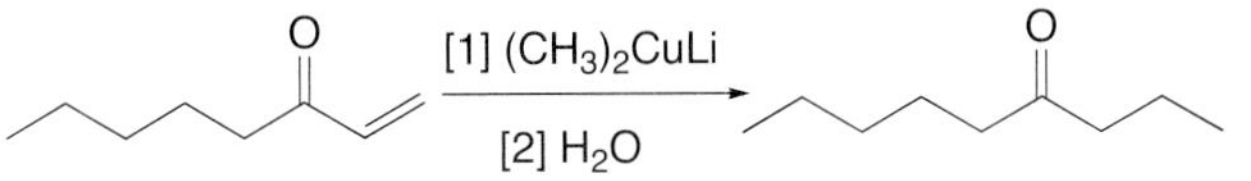
O
[1] (CH3)2CuLi
[2] H2O
O

h. 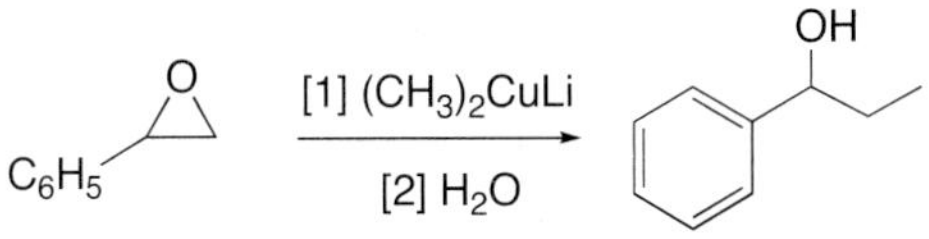
O
C6H5
[1] (CH3)2CuLi
[2] H2O
OH

20.48

a. 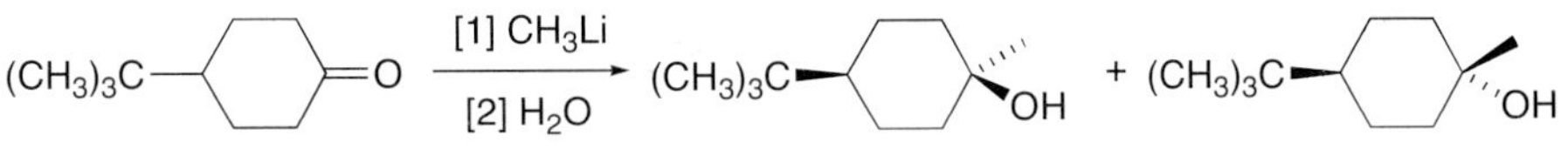
(CH3)3C
O
[1] CH3Li
[2] H2O
(CH3)3C
OH
+ (CH3)3C
OH

b. 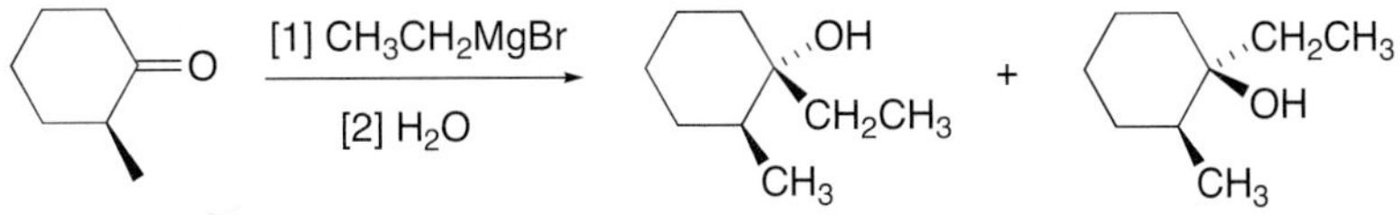
O
[1] CH3CH2MgBr
[2] H2O
OH
CH2CH3
CH3
+
CH2CH3
OH
CH3

c. 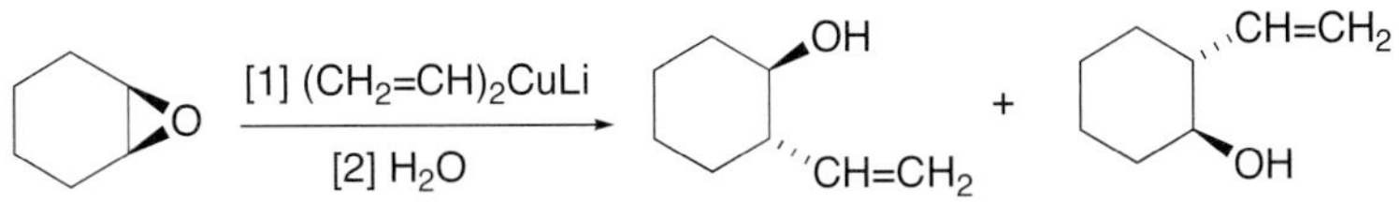
O
[1] (CH2=CH)2CuLi
[2] H2O
OH
CH=CH2
+
CH=CH2
OH

d. 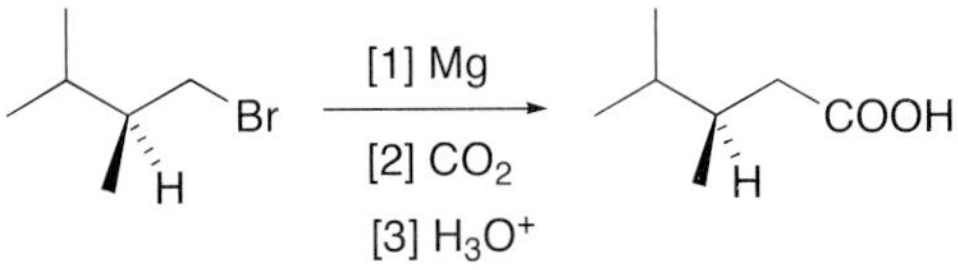
Br
H
[1] Mg
[2] CO2
[3] H3O+
COOH
H

e. 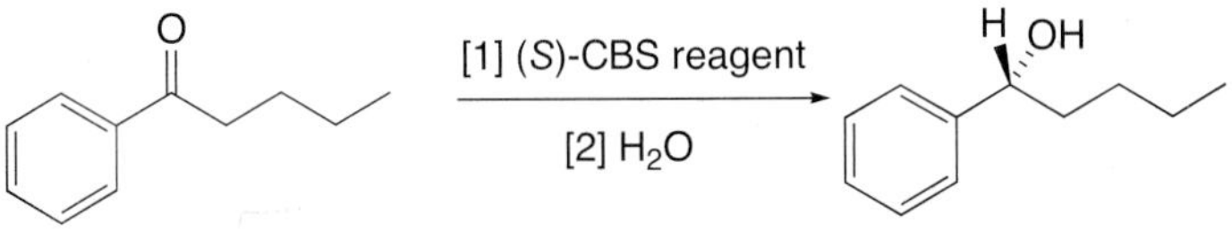
O
[1] (S)-CBS reagent
[2] H2O
H OH

f. 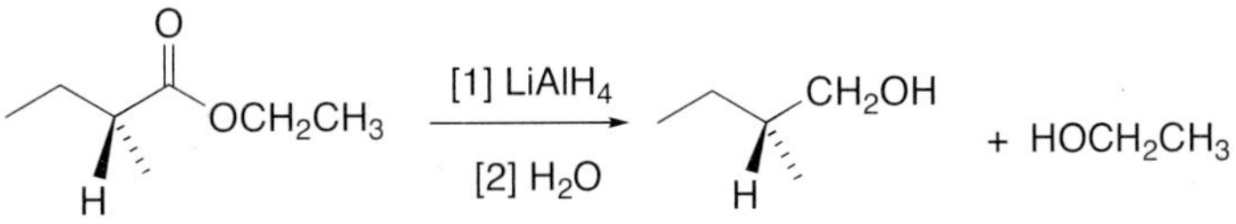
O
OCH2CH3
H
[1] LiAlH4
[2] H2O
CH2OH
H
+ HOCH2CH3

20.49 Three carbons bear a δ^+ because they are bonded to electronegative O atoms.

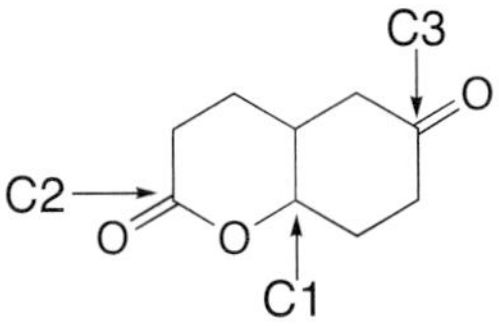
C3
O
C2
O
O
C1

C1 is an sp^3 hybridized C bonded to an O so it bears a δ^+. There are no additional resonance structures that affect C1. C2 is part of a carbonyl that has three resonance structures, only one of which places a (+) charge on C. The O atom of the ester donates its electron pair, making the carbonyl C less electrophilic than C3. C3 is most electrophilic. Its carbonyl is stabilized by two resonance structures, one of which places a (+) charge on carbon.

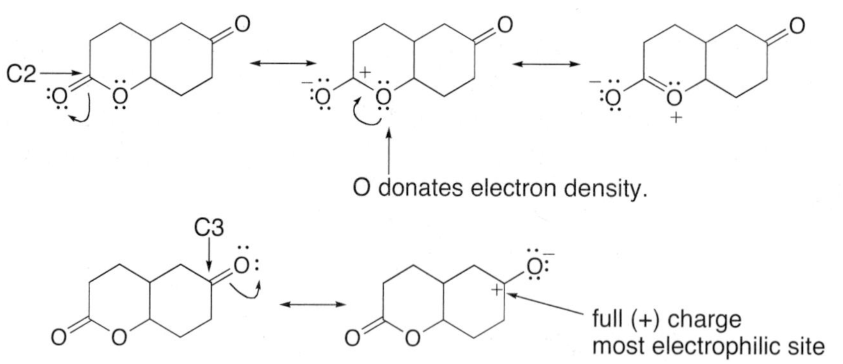
C2
O donates electron density.
C3
full (+) charge
most electrophilic site

20.50 The organolithium reagent is a nucleophile and a base. As a base it can remove the most acidic proton (between the benzene ring and C=O) to form an enolate that is protonated by D_3O^+.

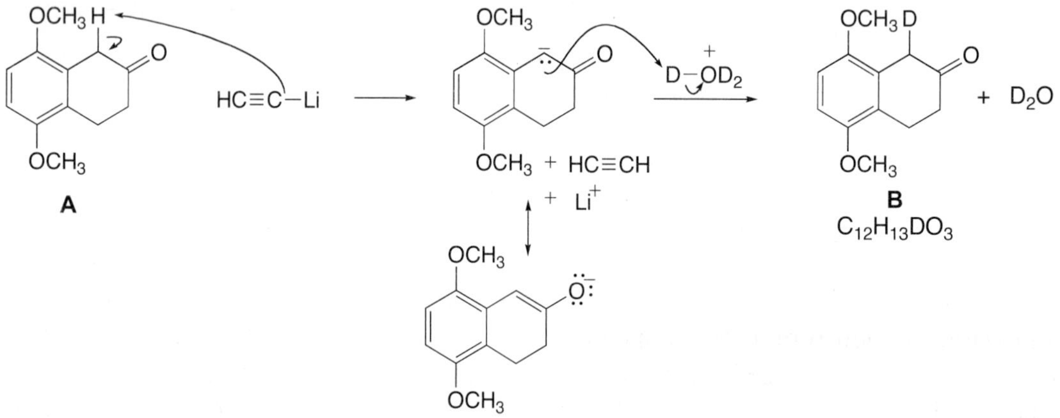
OCH3 H
O
OCH3
A
HC≡C–Li
OCH3
OCH3 + HC≡CH
+ Li+
D–OD2
OCH3 D
OCH3
B
C12H13DO3
+ D2O

20.51 Both ketones are chiral molecules with carbonyl groups that have one side more sterically hindered than the other. In both reductions, hydride approaches from the less hindered side.

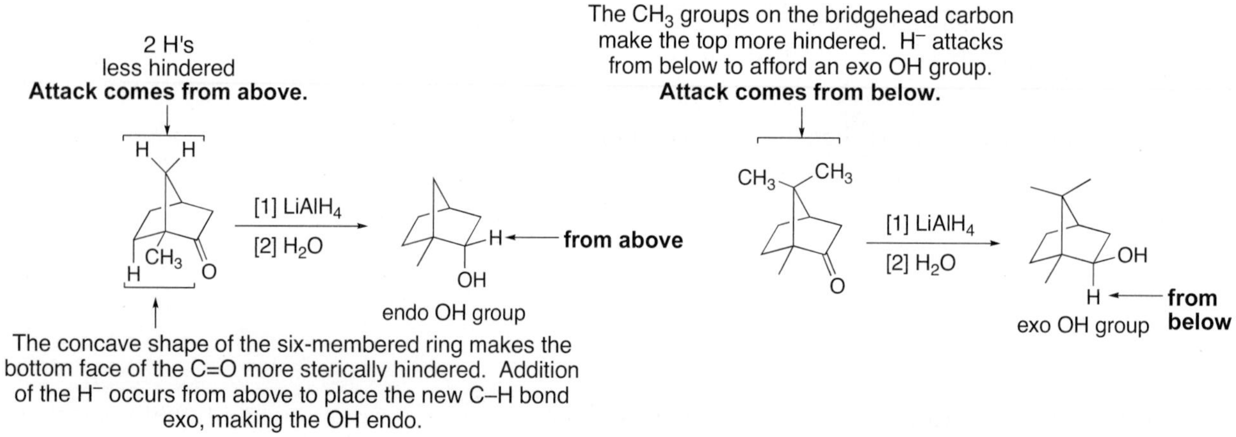
2 H's
less hindered
Attack comes from above.
H H
CH3
H
O
[1] LiAlH4
[2] H2O
H
from above
OH
endo OH group
The concave shape of the six-membered ring makes the bottom face of the C=O more sterically hindered. Addition of the H⁻ occurs from above to place the new C–H bond exo, making the OH endo.
The CH3 groups on the bridgehead carbon make the top more hindered. H⁻ attacks from below to afford an exo OH group.
Attack comes from below.
CH3 CH3
O
[1] LiAlH4
[2] H2O
OH
H
from below
exo OH group

20.52 Since a Grignard reagent contains a carbon atom with a partial negative charge, it acts as a base and reacts with the OH of the starting halide, $BrCH_2CH_2CH_2CH_2OH$. This acid–base reaction destroys the Grignard reagent so that addition cannot occur. To get around this problem, the OH group can be protected as a *tert*-butyldimethylsilyl ether, from which a Grignard reagent can be made.

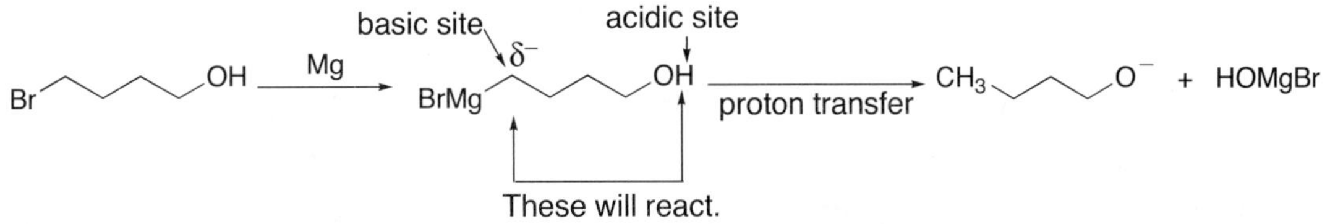

INSTEAD: Use a protecting group.

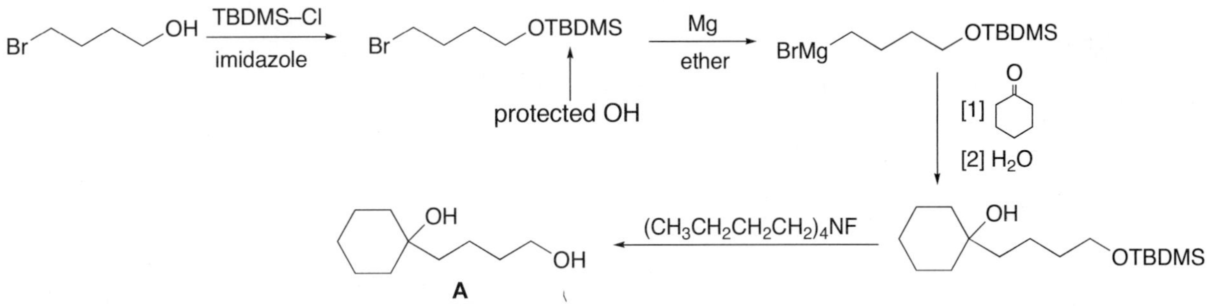

20.53 Compounds **F, G,** and **K** are all alcohols with aromatic rings so there will be many similarities in their proton NMR spectra. These compounds will, however, show differences in absorptions due to the CH protons on the carbon bearing the OH group. **F** has a CH_2OH group, which will give a singlet in the 3–4 ppm region of the spectrum. **G** is a 3° alcohol that has no protons on the C bonded to the OH group so it will have no peak in the 3–4 ppm region of the spectrum. **K** is a 2° alcohol that will give a doublet in the 3–4 ppm region of the spectrum for the CH proton on the carbon with the OH group.

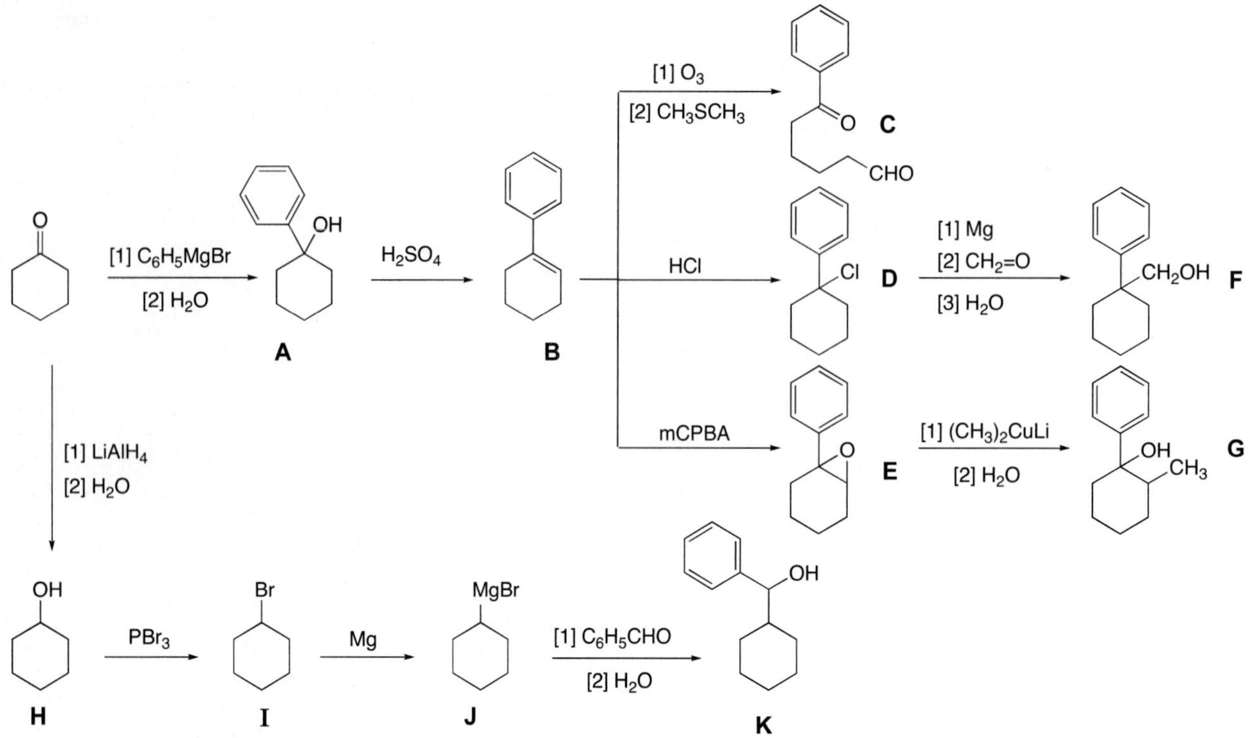
[1] C6H5MgBr
[2] H2O
A
H2SO4
B
[1] O3
[2] CH3SCH3
C
CHO
HCl
D
[1] Mg
[2] CH2=O
[3] H2O
CH2OH
F
mCPBA
E
[1] (CH3)2CuLi
[2] H2O
G
OH
CH3
[1] LiAlH4
[2] H2O
H
PBr3
Br
I
Mg
MgBr
J
[1] C6H5CHO
[2] H2O
K

20.54

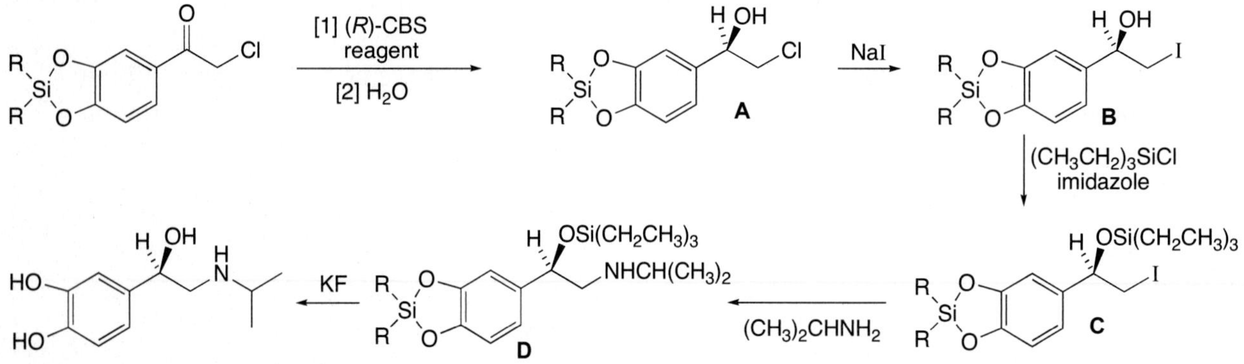
[1] (R)-CBS reagent
[2] H2O
A
NaI
B
(CH3CH2)3SiCl
imidazole
C
(CH3)2CHNH2
D
NHCH(CH3)2
OSi(CH2CH3)3
KF

20.55

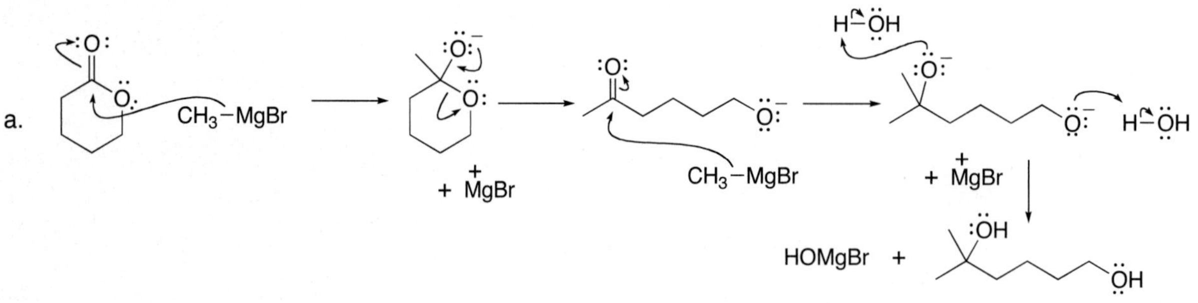
a.
CH3–MgBr
+ MgBr
CH3–MgBr
+ MgBr
HOMgBr +

b.

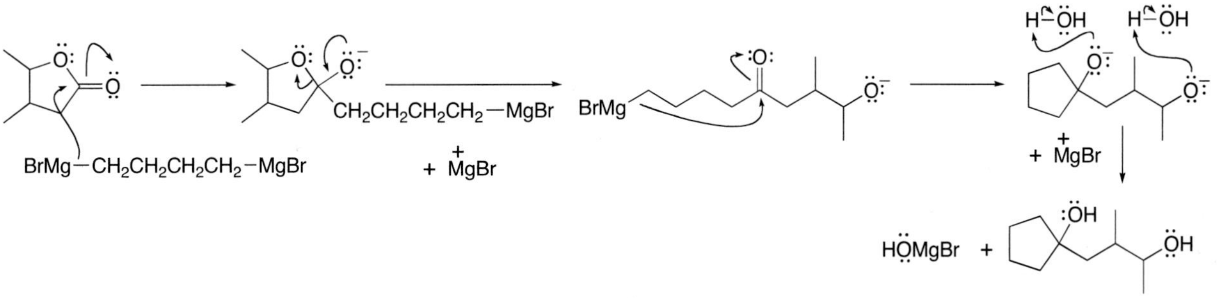

20.56

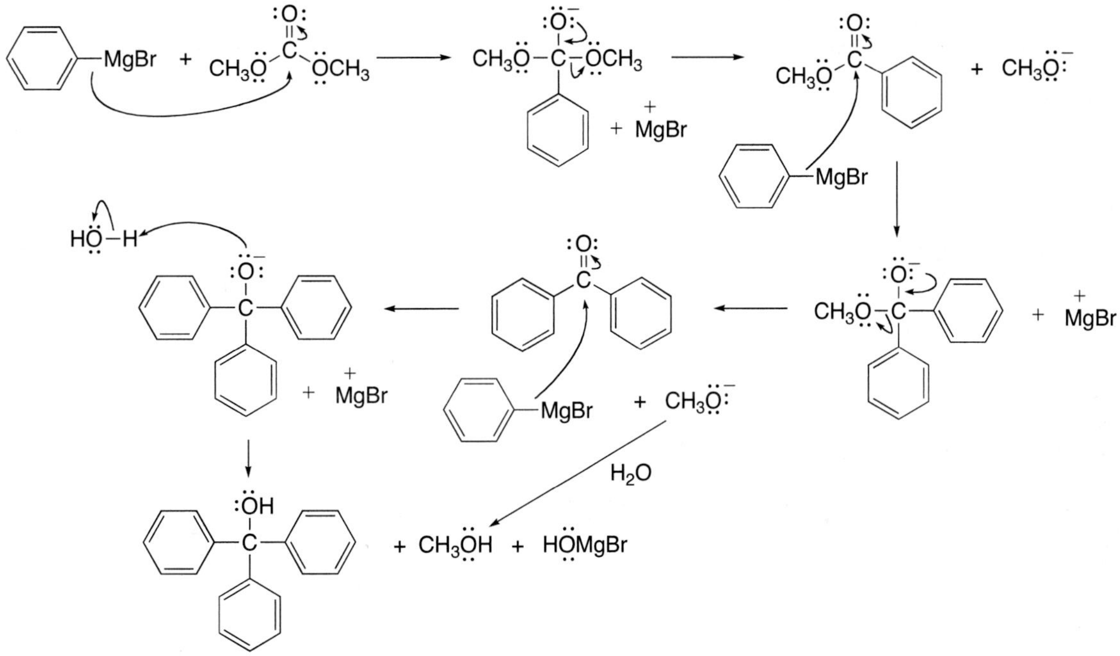

20.57

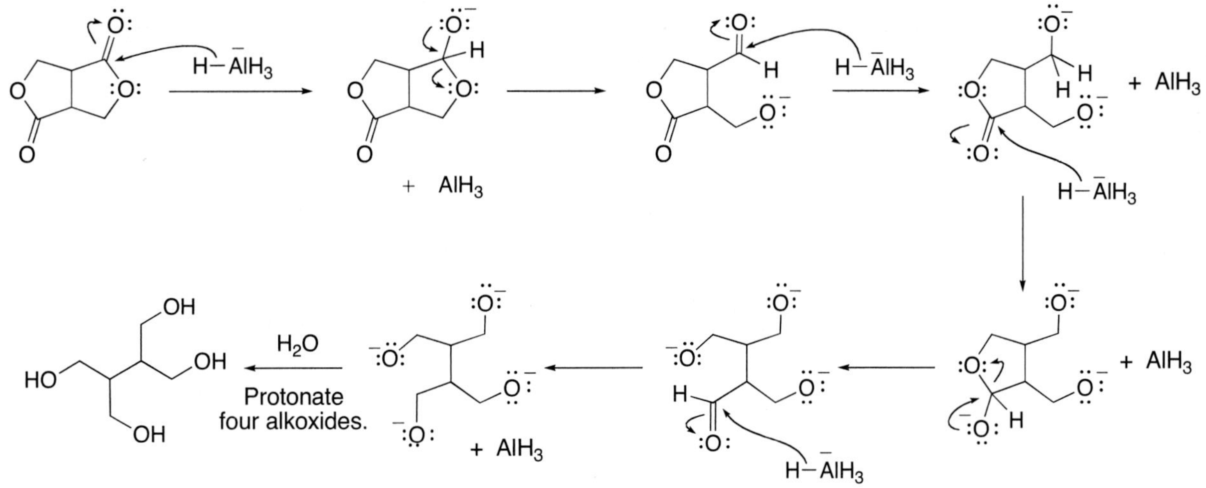

20.58

a. 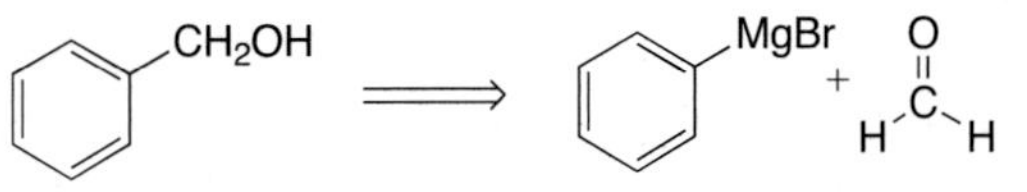

b. 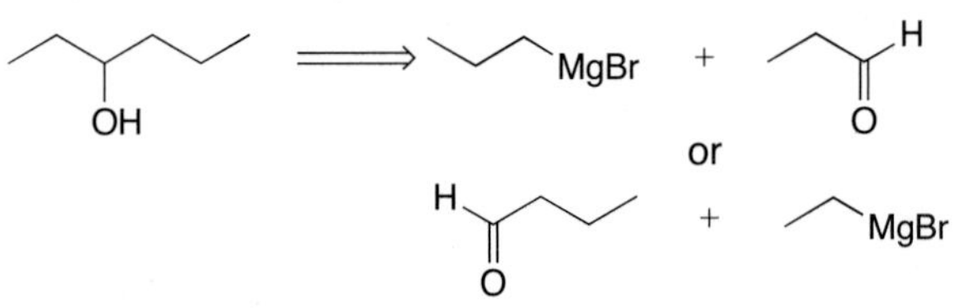

c. 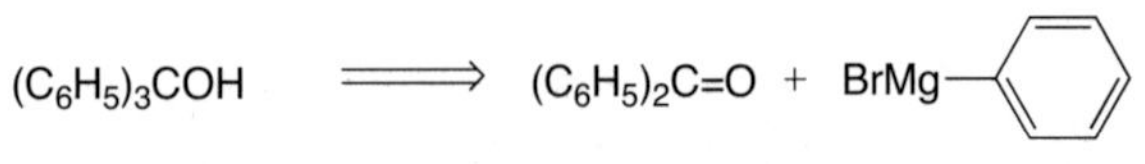

d. 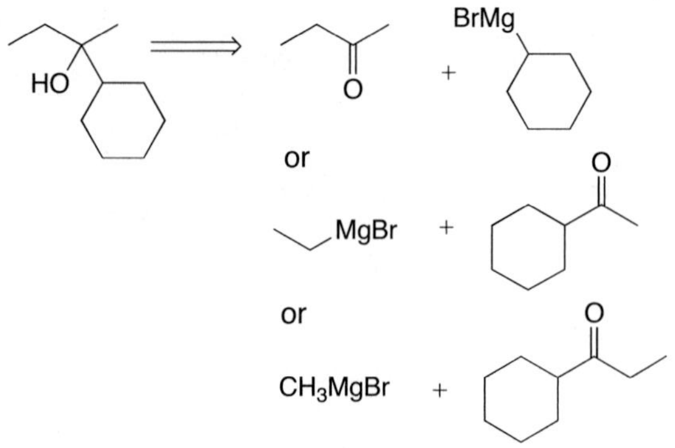

e. 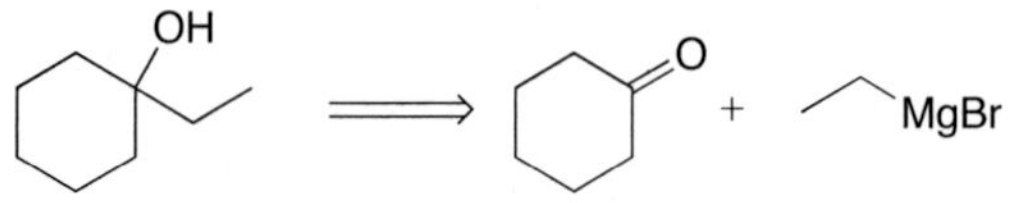

20.59

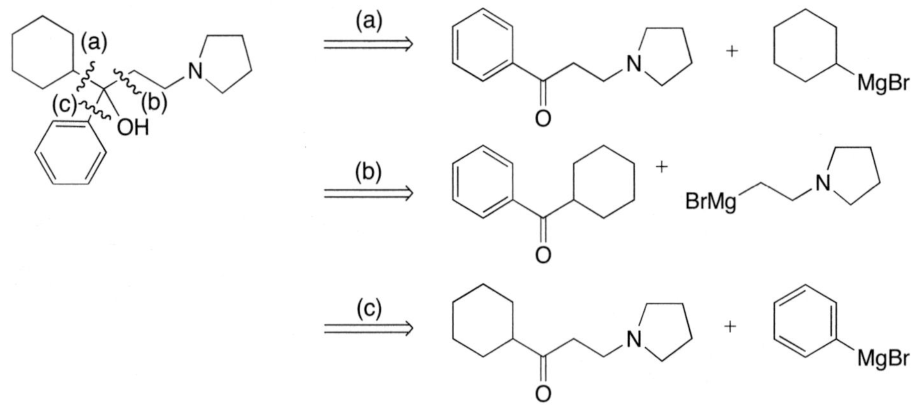

20.60

a. 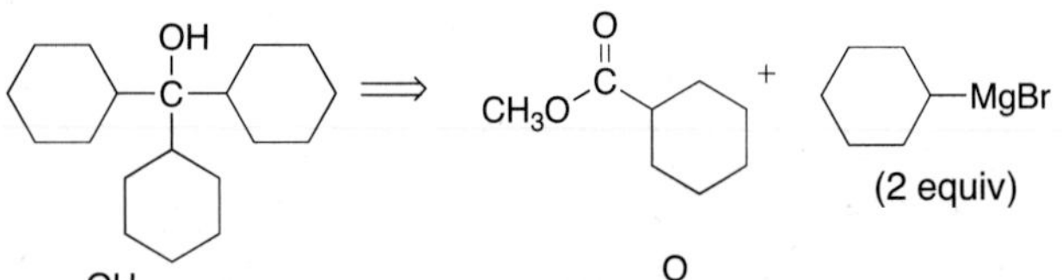

b. 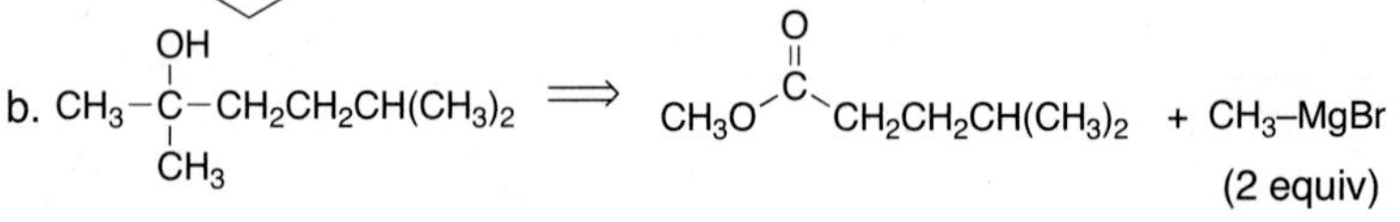

c. 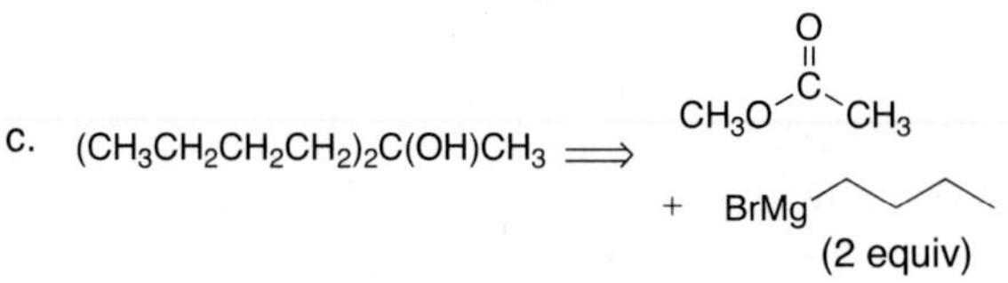

20.61

a.

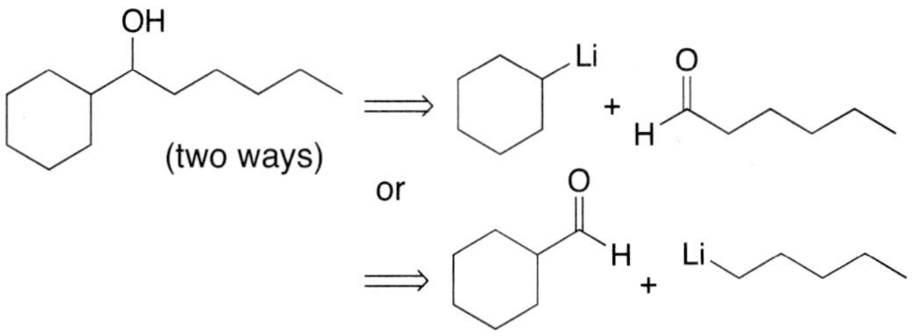
(two ways)
or

b.

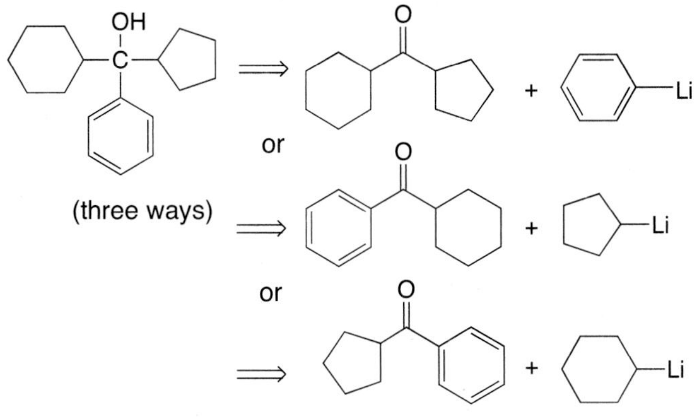
(three ways)
or
or

c.

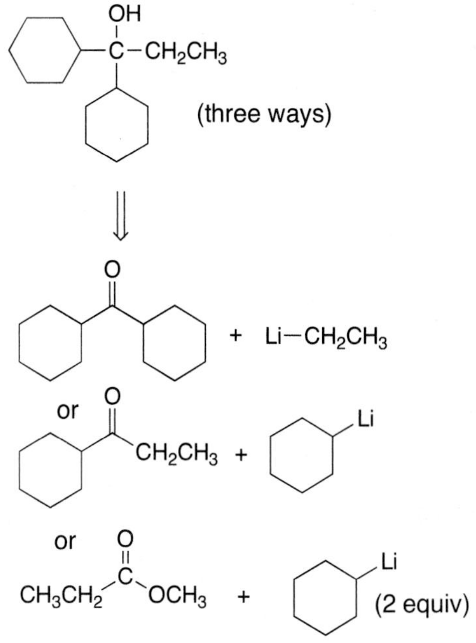
(three ways)
or
or
(2 equiv)

20.62

a.

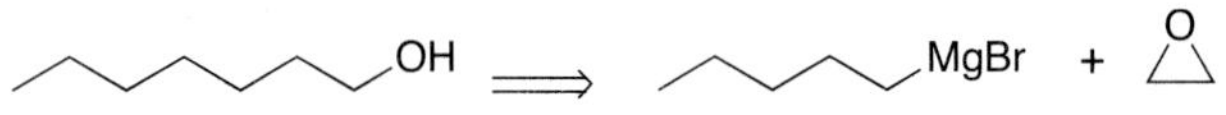

b.

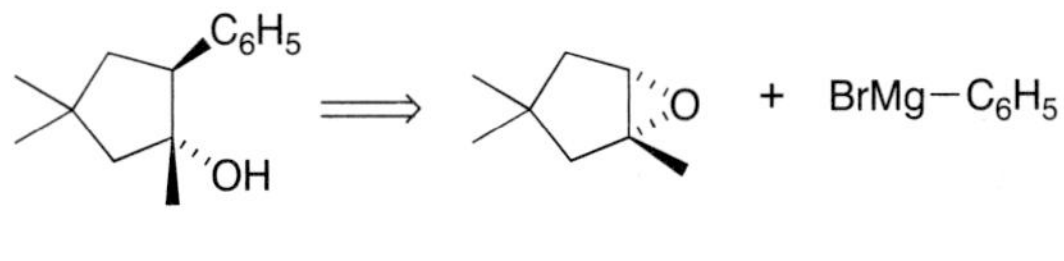

c.

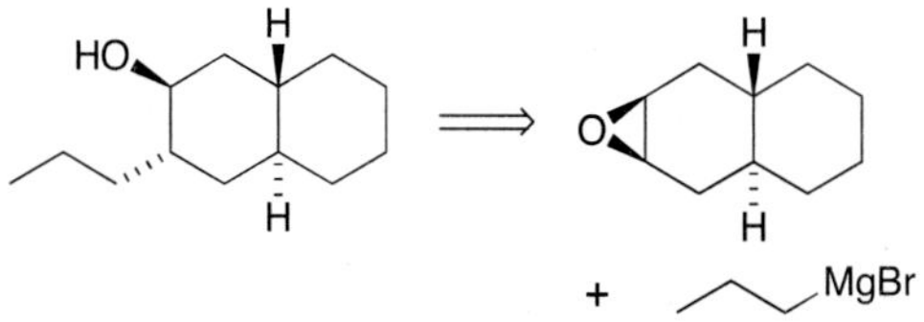

20.63

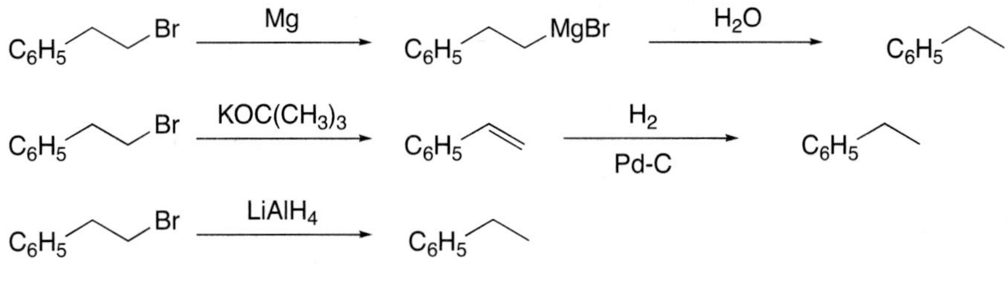
Mg
H_2O
$KOC(CH_3)_3$
H_2
Pd-C
$LiAlH_4$

20.64

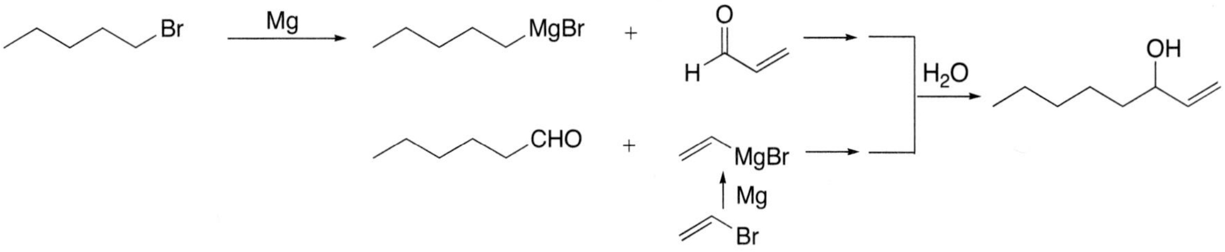
Mg
H_2O
Mg

20.65

a. 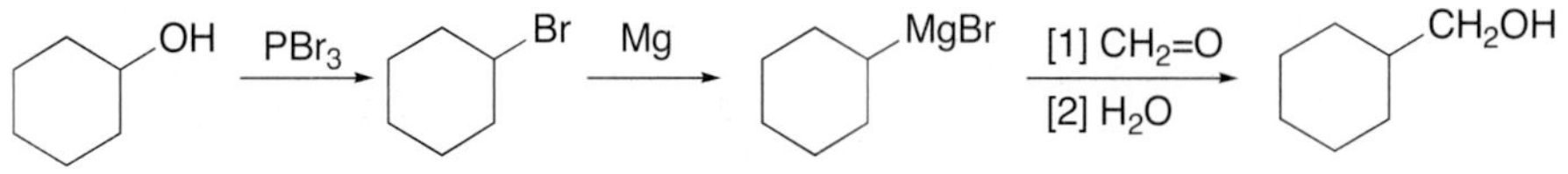

b. 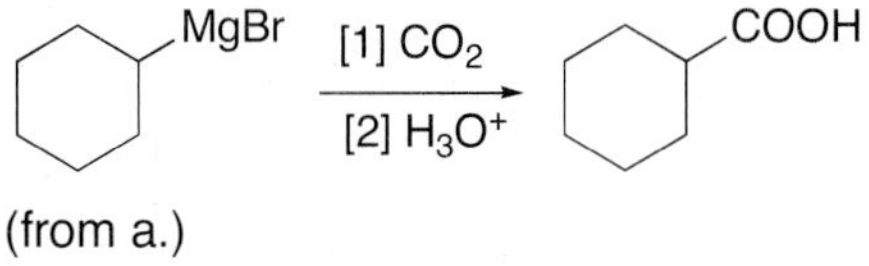

c. 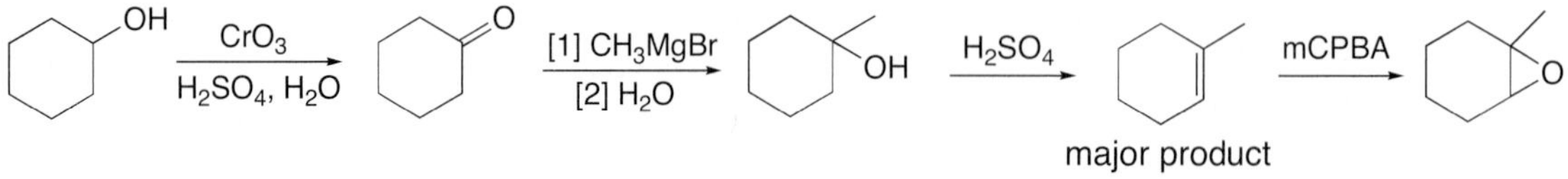

d. 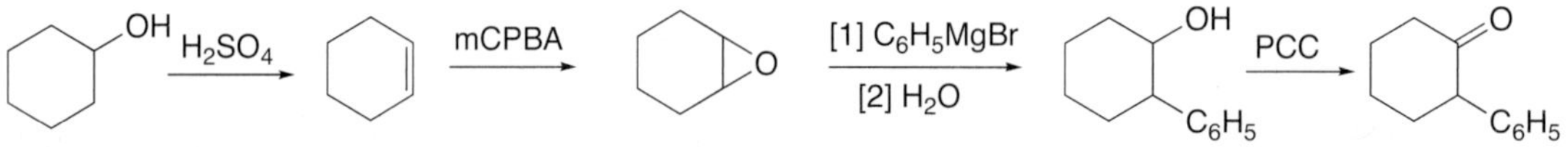

e. 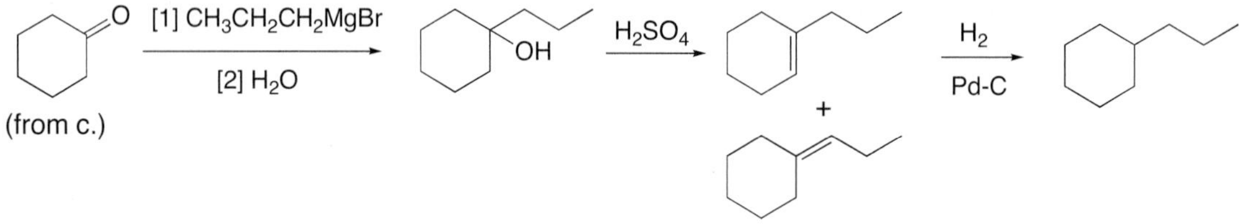

f. 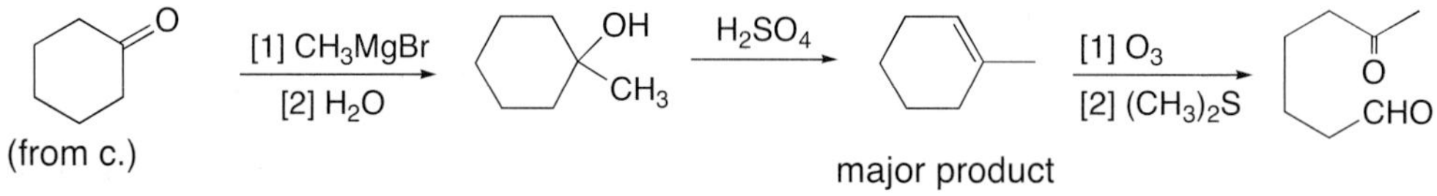

g. 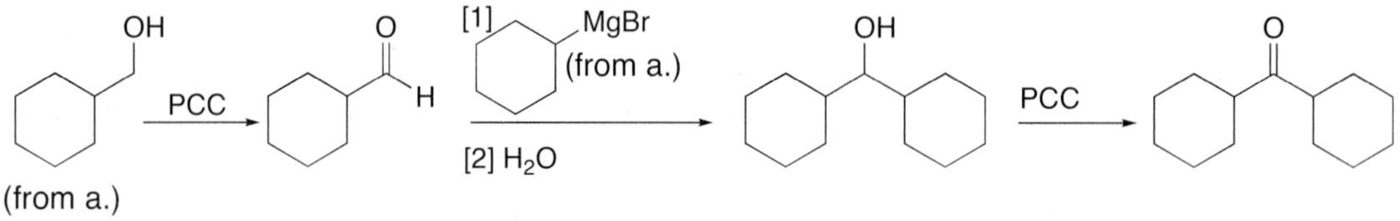

h. 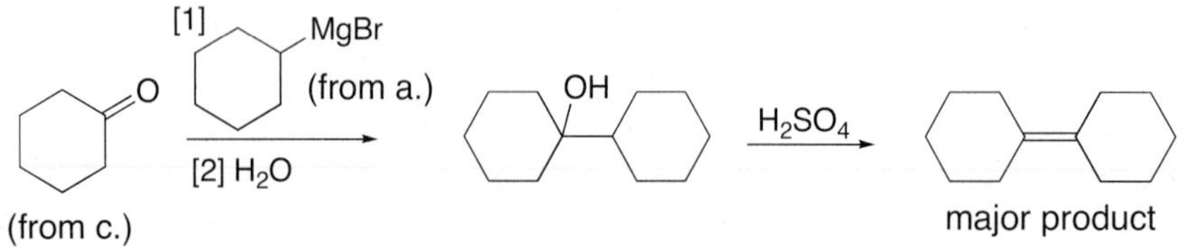

20.66

a. 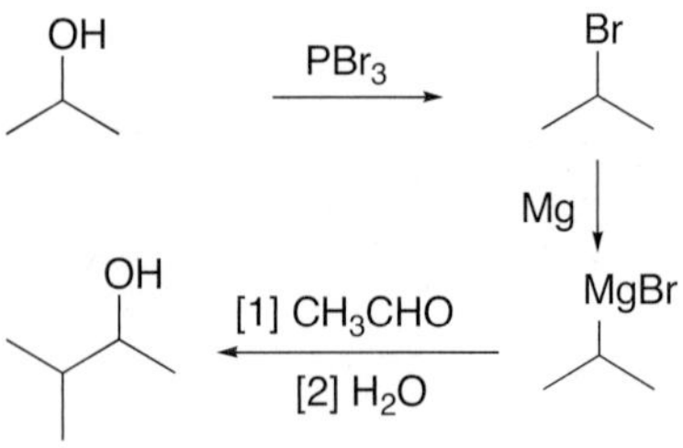

b. 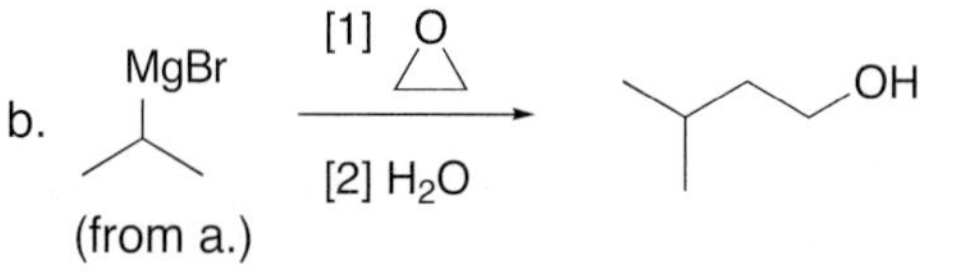

c. 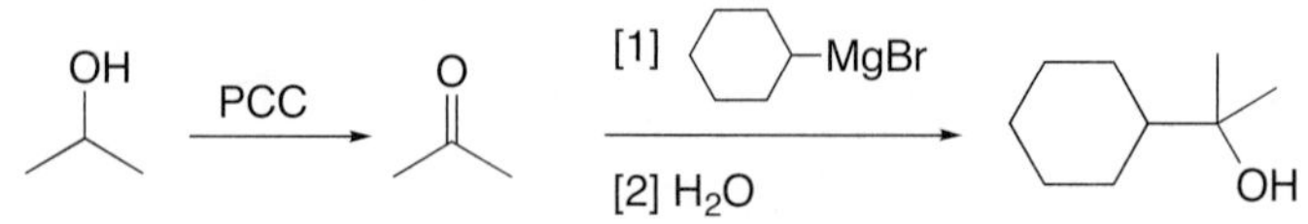

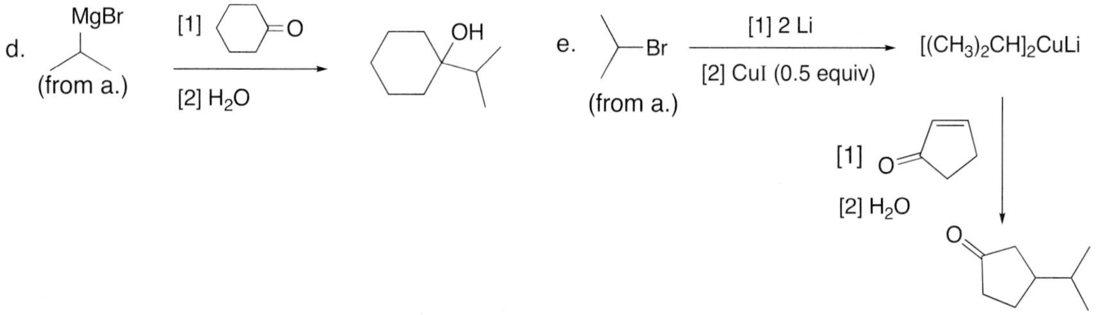
d.
MgBr
(from a.)
[1]
[2] H2O
OH
e.
Br
(from a.)
[1] 2 Li
[2] CuI (0.5 equiv)
[(CH3)2CH]2CuLi
[1]
[2] H2O
O

20.67

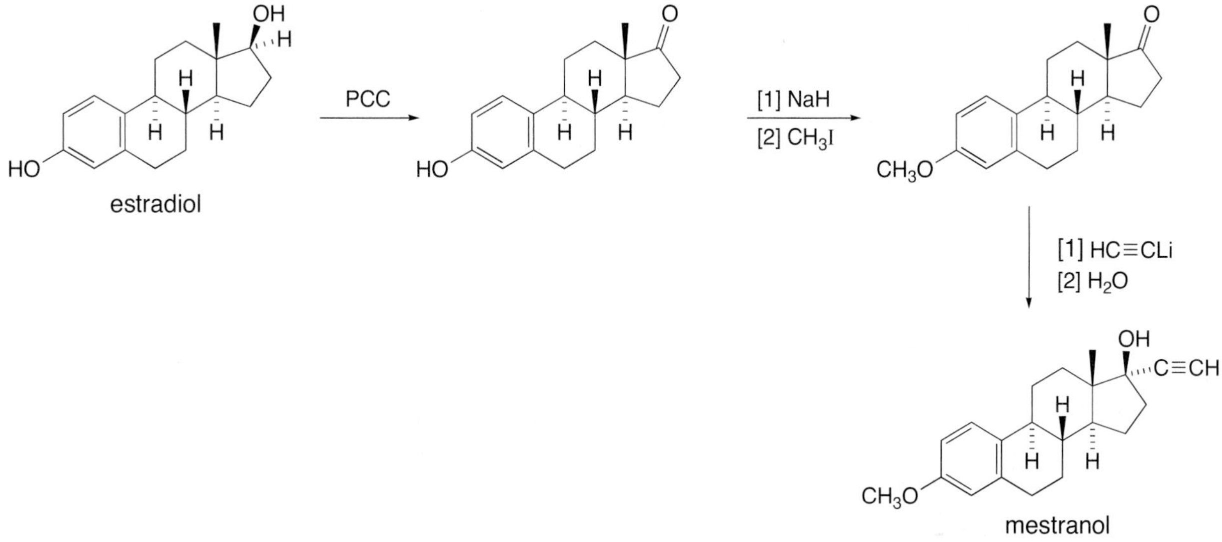
OH
H
HO
estradiol
PCC
O
[1] NaH
[2] CH3I
CH3O
[1] HC≡CLi
[2] H2O
C≡CH
mestranol

20.68

a.

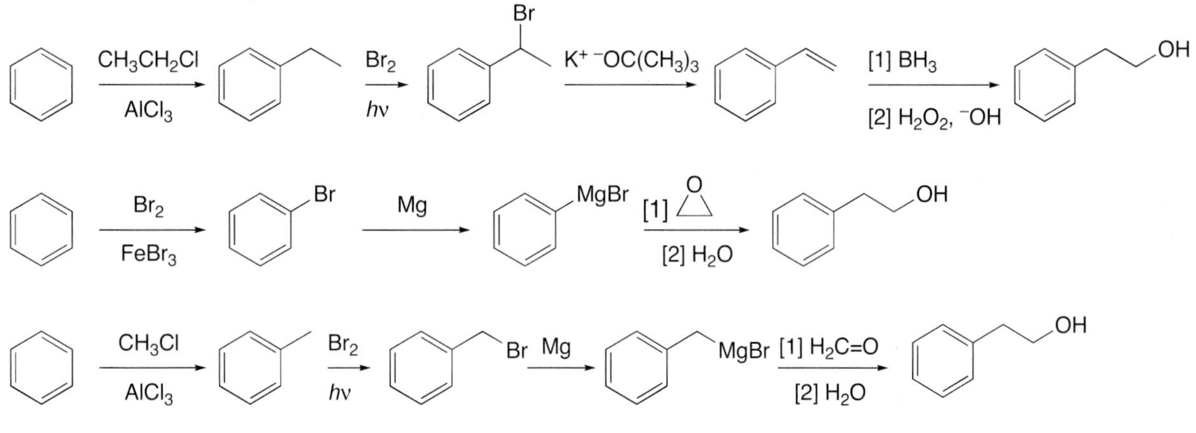
CH3CH2Cl
AlCl3
Br2
hν
Br
K+ −OC(CH3)3
[1] BH3
[2] H2O2, −OH
OH
Br2
FeBr3
Mg
MgBr
[1]
[2] H2O
CH3Cl
AlCl3
[1] H2C=O

b.

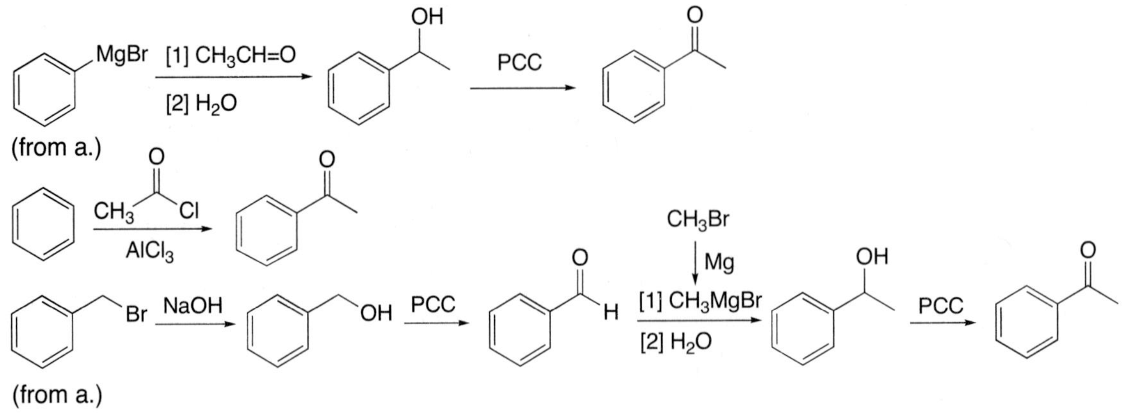
MgBr
[1] $CH_3CH{=}O$
[2] H_2O
OH
PCC
O
(from a.)
CH_3
Cl
$AlCl_3$
CH_3Br
Mg
Br
NaOH
OH
PCC
H
[1] CH_3MgBr
[2] H_2O
OH
PCC
(from a.)

20.69

a.

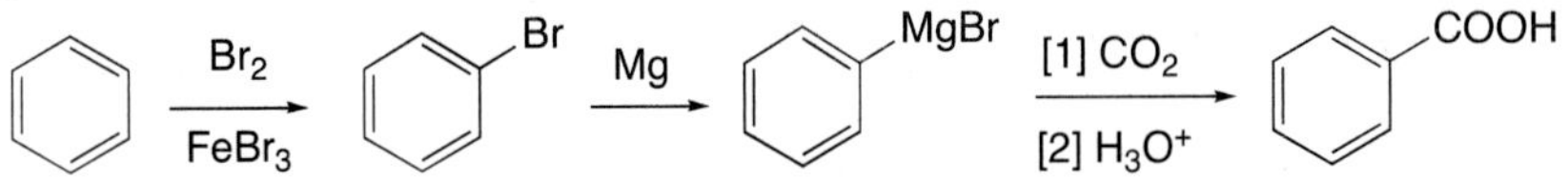
Br_2
$FeBr_3$
Br
Mg
MgBr
[1] CO_2
[2] H_3O^+
COOH

b.

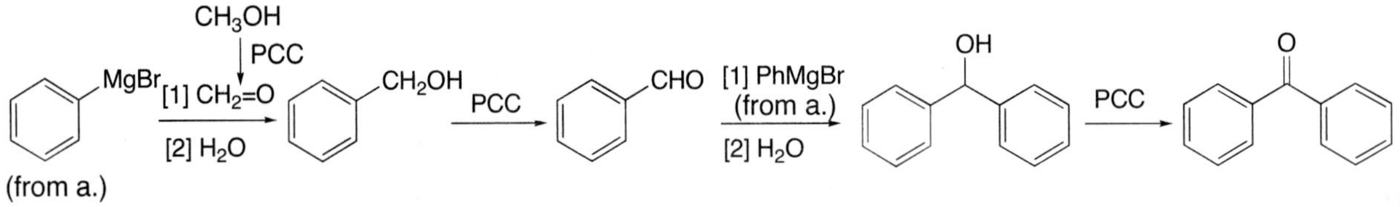
CH_3OH
PCC
MgBr
[1] $CH_2{=}O$
[2] H_2O
(from a.)
CH_2OH
PCC
CHO
[1] PhMgBr
(from a.)
[2] H_2O
OH
PCC
O

c.

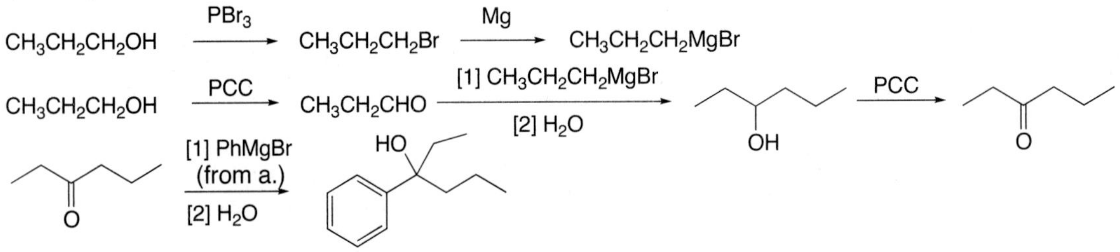
$CH_3CH_2CH_2OH$
PBr_3
$CH_3CH_2CH_2Br$
Mg
$CH_3CH_2CH_2MgBr$
$CH_3CH_2CH_2OH$
PCC
CH_3CH_2CHO
[1] $CH_3CH_2CH_2MgBr$
[2] H_2O
OH
PCC
O
[1] PhMgBr
(from a.)
[2] H_2O
HO

d.

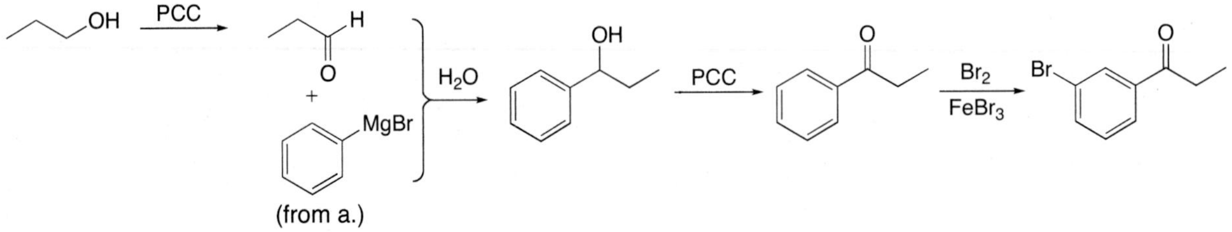
OH
PCC
H
O
+
MgBr
(from a.)
H_2O
OH
PCC
O
Br_2
$FeBr_3$
Br

20.70

a.

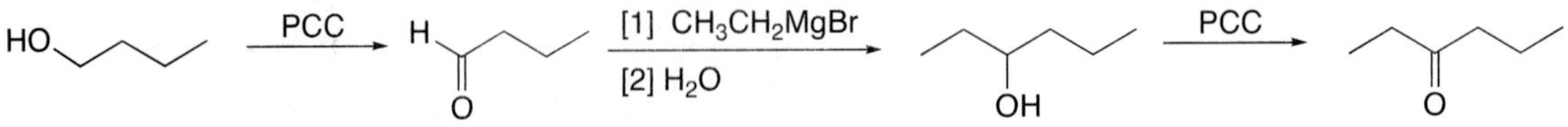
HO
PCC
H
O
[1] CH_3CH_2MgBr
[2] H_2O
OH
PCC
O

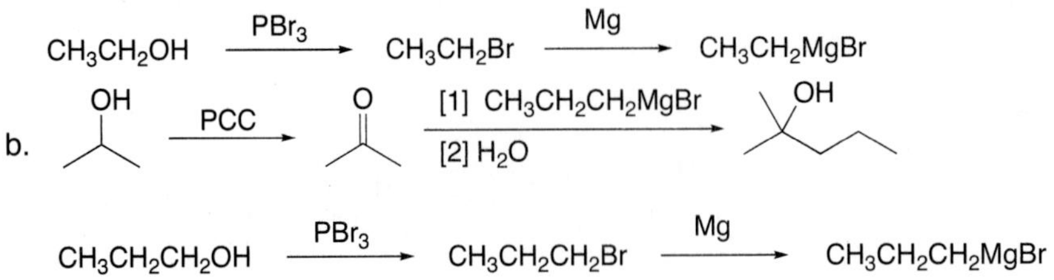
CH_3CH_2OH
PBr_3
CH_3CH_2Br
Mg
CH_3CH_2MgBr
b.
OH
PCC
O
[1] $CH_3CH_2CH_2MgBr$
[2] H_2O
OH
$CH_3CH_2CH_2OH$
PBr_3
$CH_3CH_2CH_2Br$
Mg
$CH_3CH_2CH_2MgBr$

c. 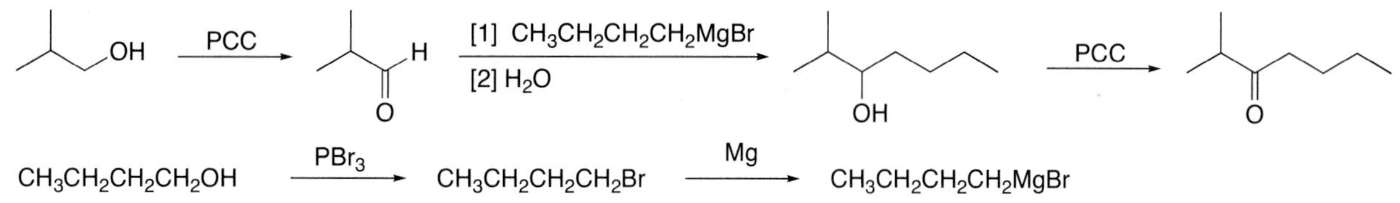
PCC
[1] CH3CH2CH2CH2MgBr
[2] H2O
OH
PCC
CH3CH2CH2CH2OH
PBr3
CH3CH2CH2CH2Br
Mg
CH3CH2CH2CH2MgBr

d. 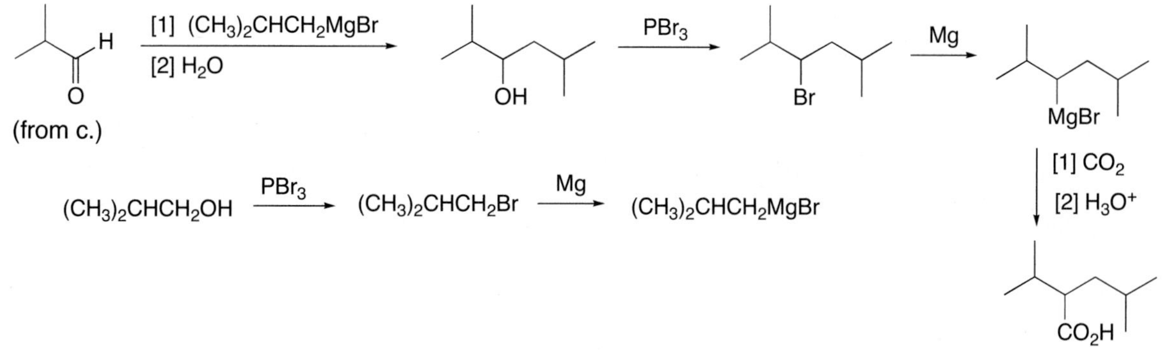
(from c.)
[1] (CH3)2CHCH2MgBr
[2] H2O
OH
PBr3
Br
Mg
MgBr
[1] CO2
[2] H3O+
CO2H
(CH3)2CHCH2OH
PBr3
(CH3)2CHCH2Br
Mg
(CH3)2CHCH2MgBr

e. 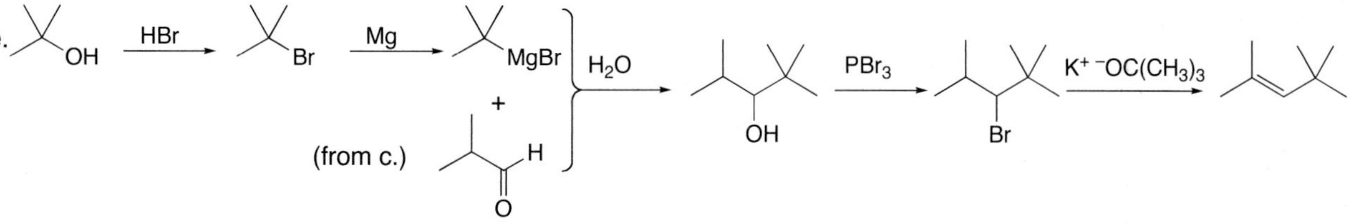
OH
HBr
Br
Mg
MgBr
H2O
(from c.)
OH
PBr3
Br
K+ −OC(CH3)3

20.71

a. 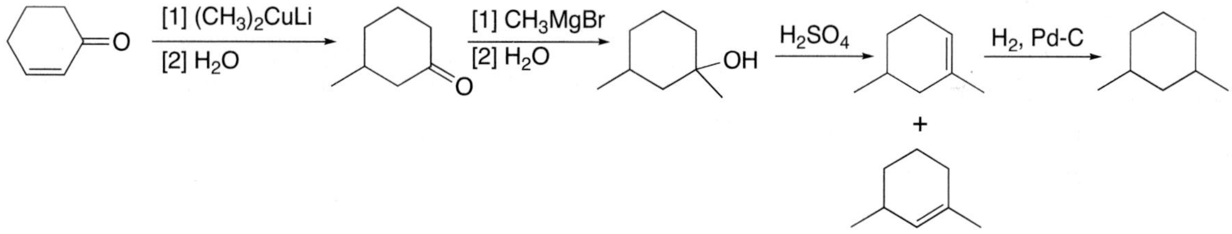
[1] (CH3)2CuLi
[2] H2O
[1] CH3MgBr
[2] H2O
OH
H2SO4
H2, Pd-C

b. 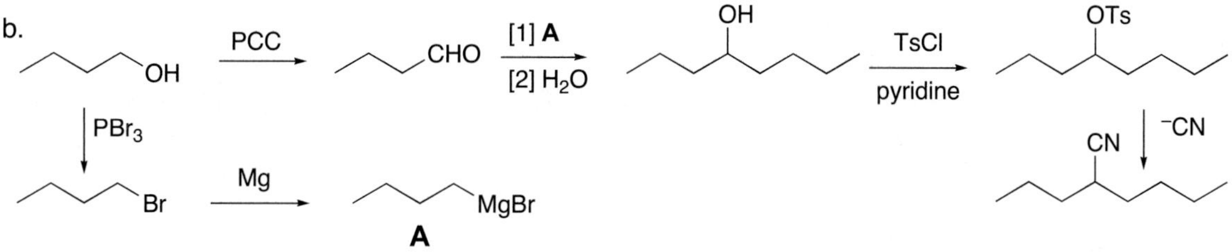
OH
PCC
CHO
[1] A
[2] H2O
OH
TsCl
pyridine
OTs
−CN
CN
PBr3
Br
Mg
MgBr
A

c. 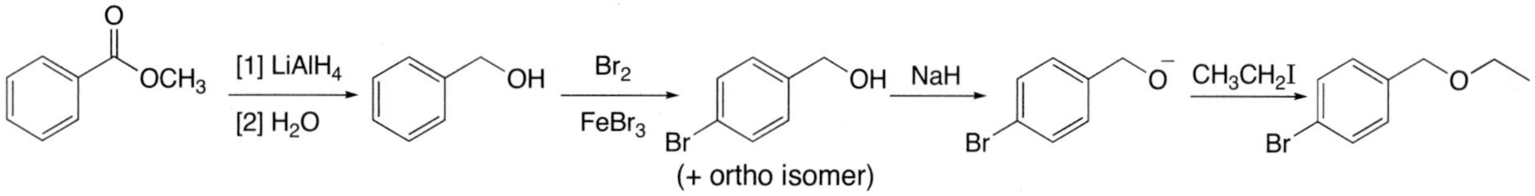
OCH3
[1] LiAlH4
[2] H2O
OH
Br2
FeBr3
Br
OH
(+ ortho isomer)
NaH
Br
CH3CH2I
Br

d. 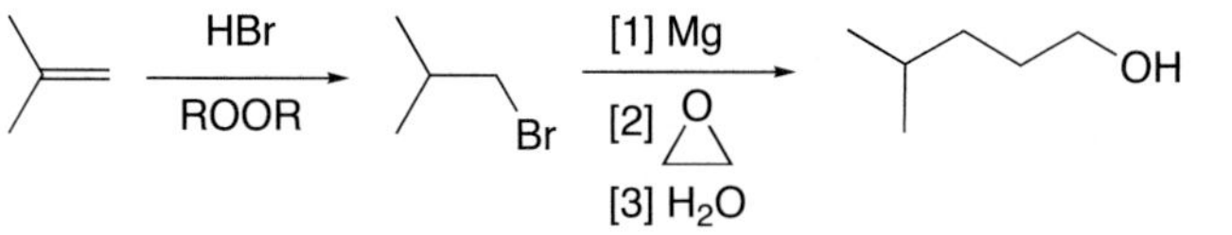
HBr
ROOR
Br
[1] Mg
[2]
[3] H2O
OH

e. 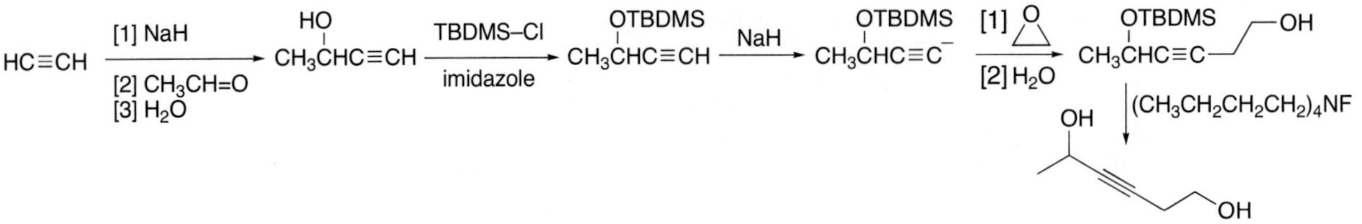

20.72

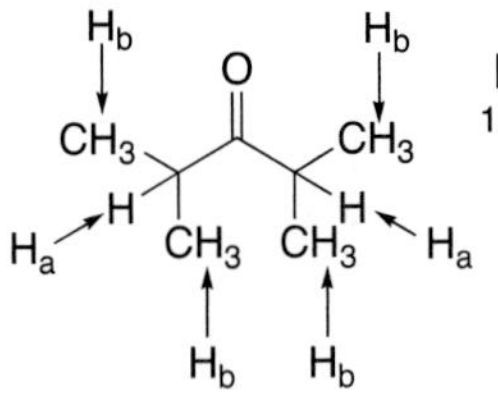

$C_7H_{14}O$

A

IR peak: 1716 cm^{-1} (C=O)
^1H NMR: 2 signals (ppm)
doublet 1.2 (H_b)
septet 2.7 (H_a)

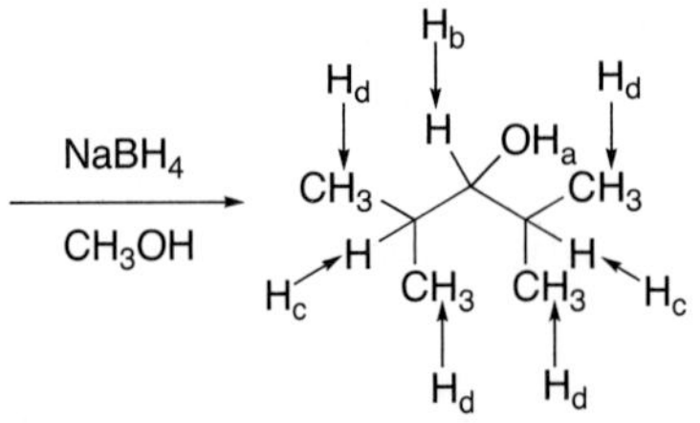

$C_7H_{16}O$

B

IR peak: 3600–3200 cm^{-1} (OH)
^1H NMR: 4 signals (ppm)
doublet 0.9 (H_d)
singlet 1.5 (H_a)
multiplet 1.7 (H_c)
triplet 3.0 (H_b)

20.73

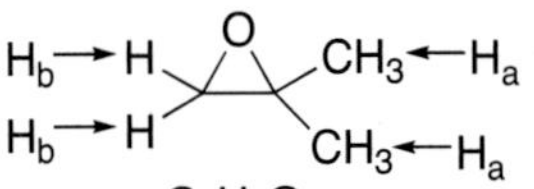

C_4H_8O

C

^1H NMR: 2 signals (ppm)
singlet (6 H) 1.3 (H_a)
singlet (2 H) 2.4 (H_b)

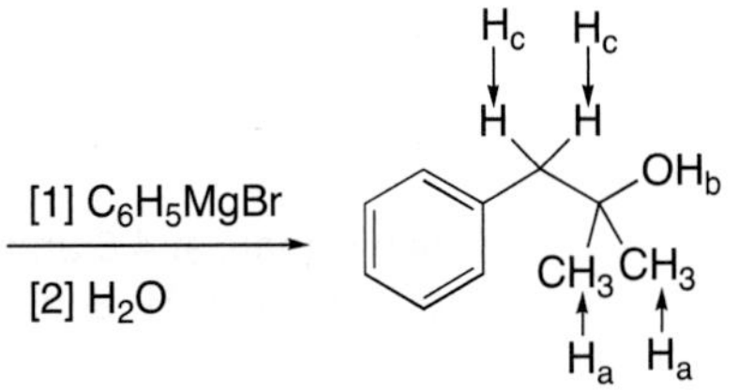

$C_{10}H_{14}O$

D

IR peak 3600–3200 cm^{-1} (OH)
^1H NMR: 4 signals (ppm)
singlet (6 H) 1.2 (H_a)
singlet (1 H) 1.6 (H_b)
singlet (2 H) 2.7 (H_c)
multiplet (5 H) 7.2 (benzene ring)

20.74

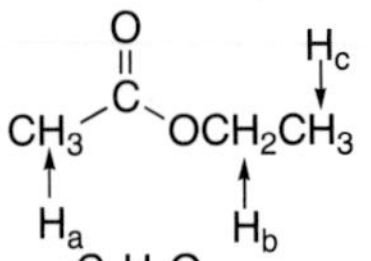

$C_4H_8O_2$

E

IR peak 1743 cm^{-1} (C=O)
^1H NMR: 2 signals (ppm)
triplet (3 H) 1.2 (H_c)
singlet (3 H) 2.0 (H_a)
quartet (2 H) 4.1 (H_b)

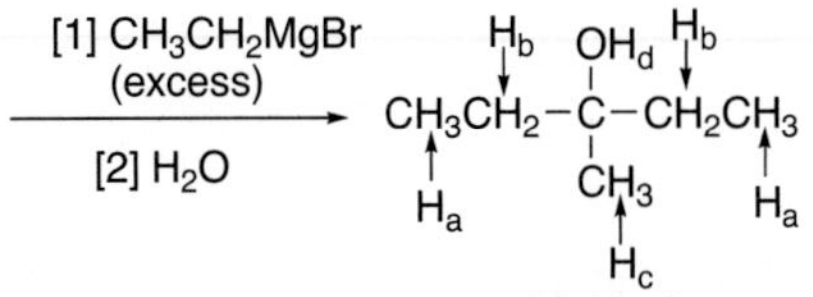

$C_6H_{14}O$

F

IR peak 3600–3200 cm^{-1} (OH)
^1H NMR: 4 signals (ppm)
triplet (6 H) 0.9 (H_a)
singlet (3 H) 1.1 (H_c)
quartet (4 H) 1.5 (H_b)
singlet (1 H) 1.55 (H_d)

20.75 Molecular ion at $m/z = 86$: $C_5H_{10}O$ (possible molecular formula).

Determine the number of integration units per H:

Total number of integration units: 25 + 17 + 24 + 17 = 83

83 units/10 H's = 8.3 units per H

Divide each integration value by 8.3 to determine the number of H's per signal:

25 units/ 8.3 = 3 H's

24 units/ 8.3 = 3 H's

17 units/ 8.3 = 2 H's

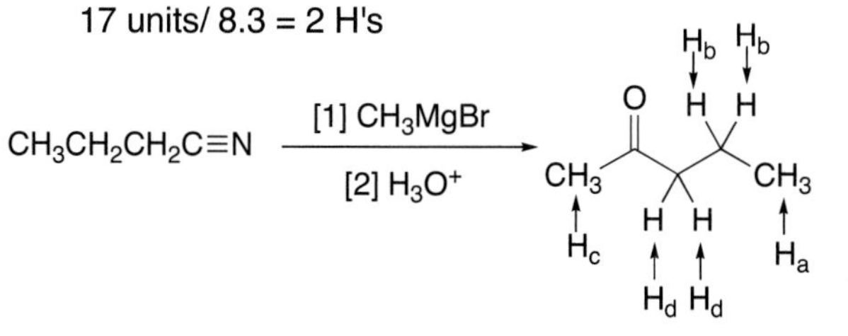

$CH_3CH_2CH_2C{\equiv}N$
[1] CH_3MgBr
[2] H_3O^+

G

IR peak 1721 cm^{-1} (C=O)

^{1}H NMR: 4 signals (ppm)

triplet (3 H) 0.9 (H_a)

sextet (2 H) 1.6 (H_b)

singlet (3 H) 2.1 (H_c)

triplet (2 H) 2.4 (H_d)

20.76 Molecular ion at $m/z = 86$: $C_5H_{10}O$ (possible molecular formula).

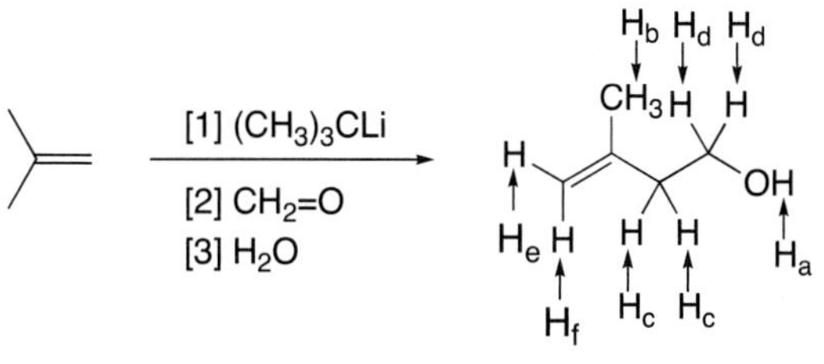

[1] $(CH_3)_3CLi$
[2] $CH_2{=}O$
[3] H_2O

H

IR peaks: 3600–3200 cm^{-1} (OH)

1651 cm^{-1} (C=C)

^{1}H NMR: 6 signals (ppm)

singlet (1 H) 1.7 (H_a)

singlet (3 H) 1.8 (H_b)

triplet (2 H) 2.2 (H_c)

triplet (2 H) 3.8 (H_d)

two signals at 4.8 and 4.9 due to 2 H's: H_e and H_f

20.77

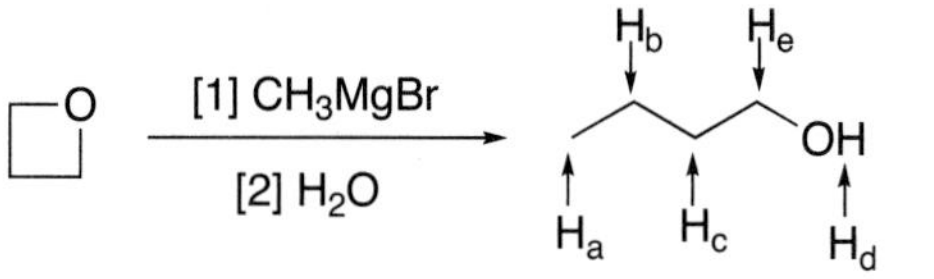

[1] CH_3MgBr
[2] H_2O

IR peak 3600–3200 cm^{-1} (OH)

^{1}H NMR: 5 signals (ppm)

triplet (3 H) 0.94 (H_a)

multiplet (2 H) 1.39 (H_b)

multiplet (2 H) 1.53 (H_c)

singlet (1 H) 2.24 (H_d)

triplet (2 H) 3.63 (H_e)

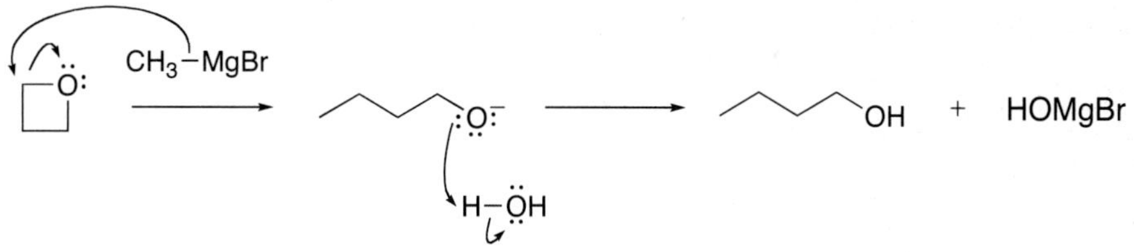

CH_3–MgBr
+
HOMgBr

20.78

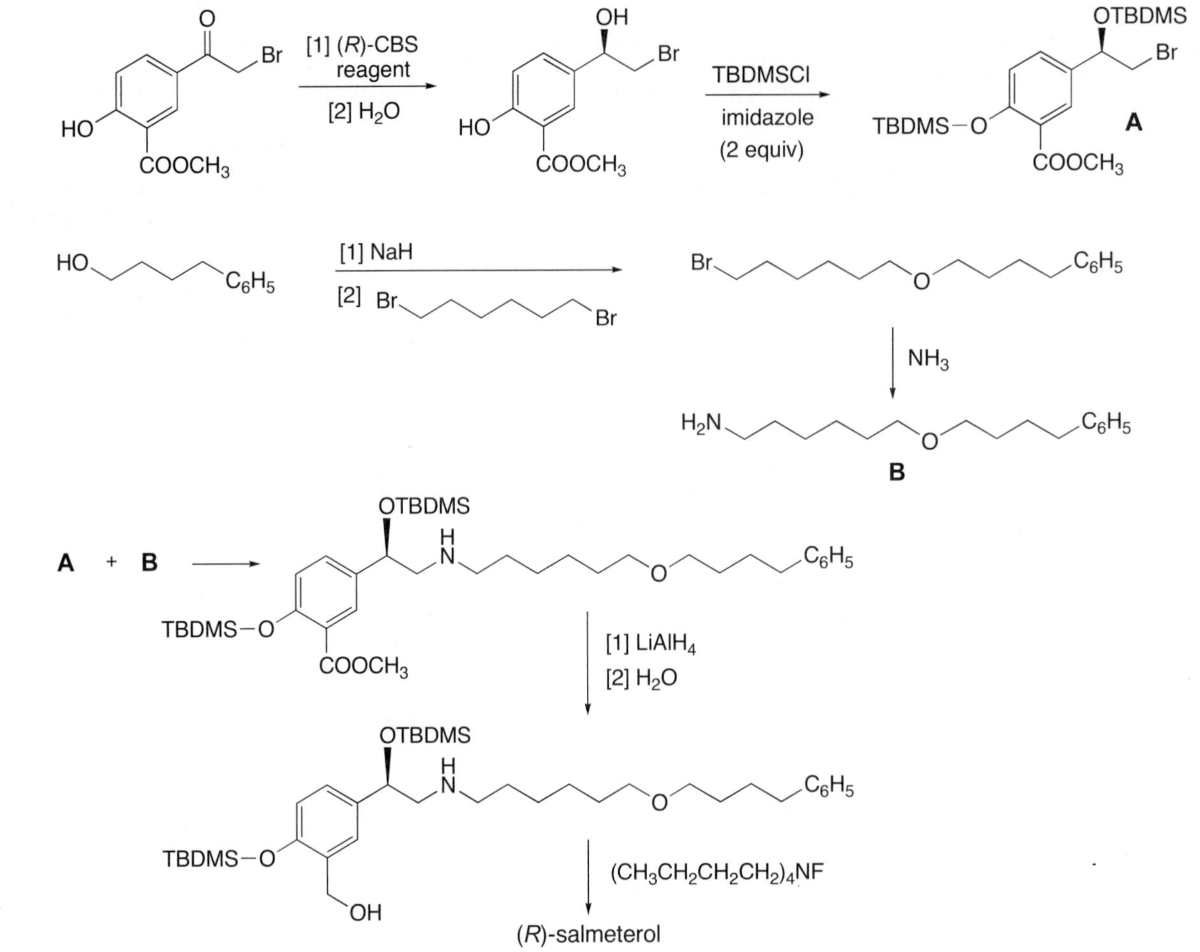

20.79

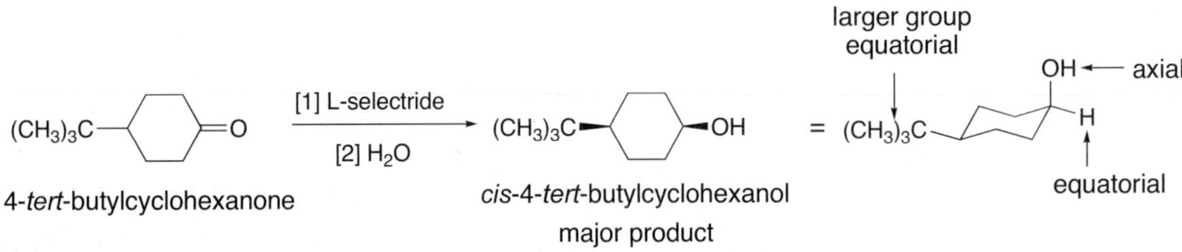

L-Selectride adds H^- to a C=O group. There are two possible reduction products—cis and trans isomers—but the cis isomer is favored. The key element is that the three *sec*-butyl groups make L-selectride a large, bulky reducing agent that attacks the carbonyl group from the less hindered direction.

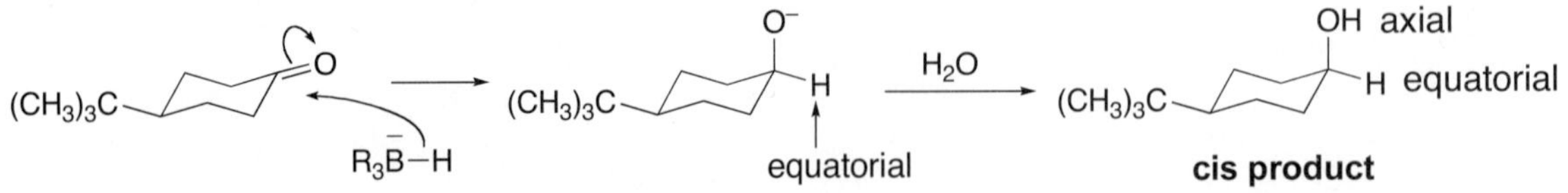

When H^- adds from the equatorial direction, the product has an axial OH and a new equatorial H. Since the equatorial direction is less hindered, this mode of attack is favored with large bulky reducing agents like L-selectride. In this case, the product is cis.

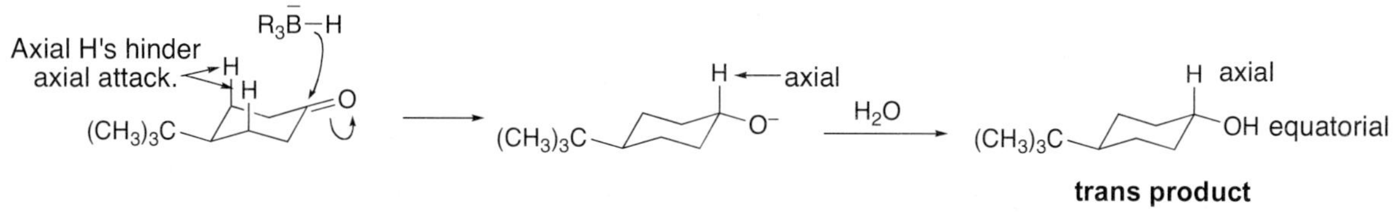

The axial H's hinder H^- attack from the axial direction. As a result, this mode of attack is more difficult with larger reducing agents. In this case the product is trans. This product is not formed to any appreciable extent.

20.80 The β carbon of an α,β-unsaturated carbonyl compound absorbs farther downfield in the ^{13}C NMR spectrum than the α carbon, because the β carbon is deshielded and bears a partial positive charge as a result of resonance. Since three resonance structures can be drawn for an α,β-unsaturated carbonyl compound, one of which places a positive charge on the β carbon, the decrease of electron density at this carbon deshields it, shifting the ^{13}C absorption downfield. This is not the case for the α carbon.

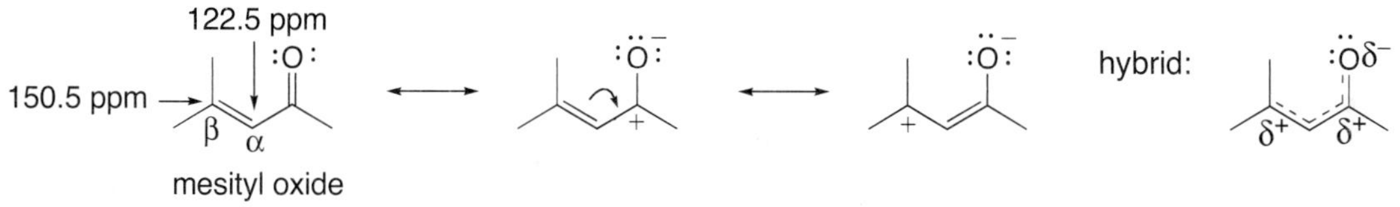

20.81

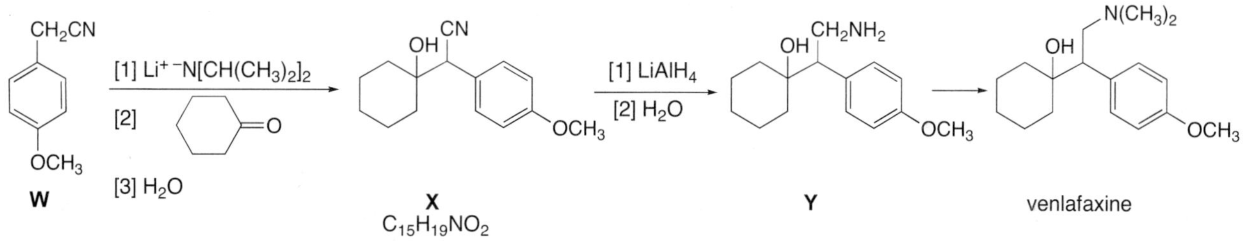

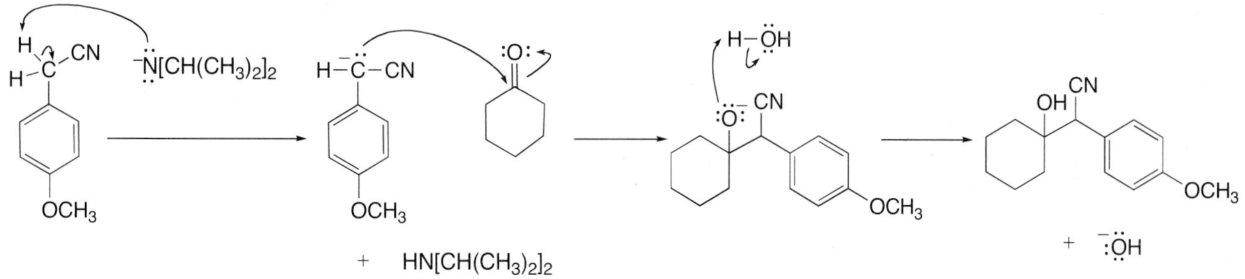

20.82

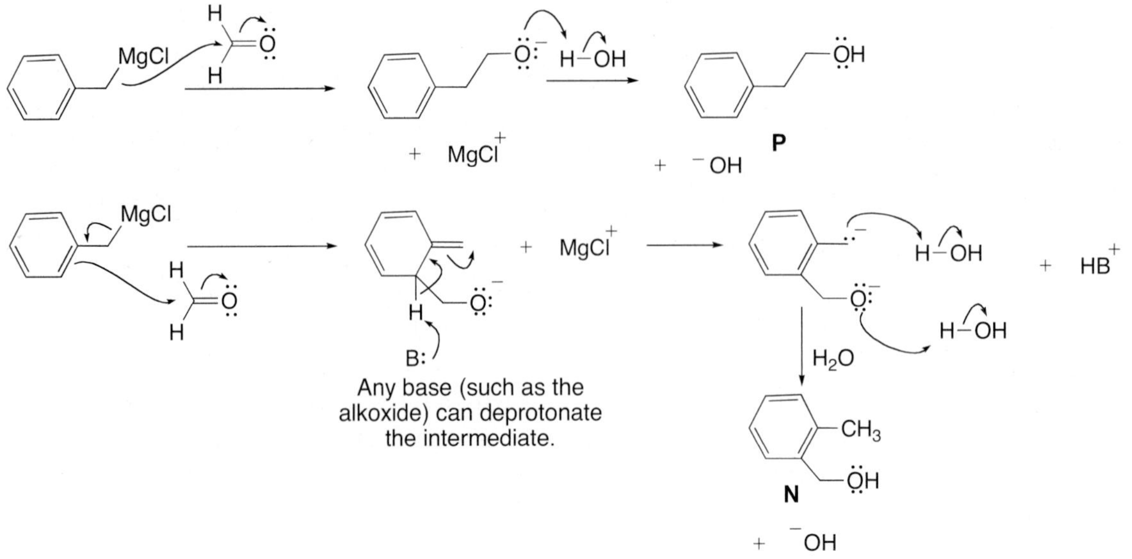

20.83

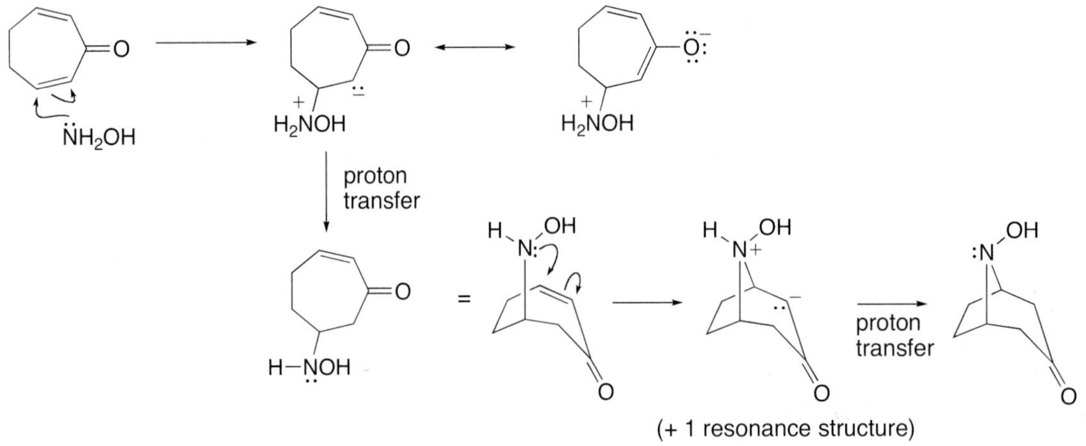

20.84

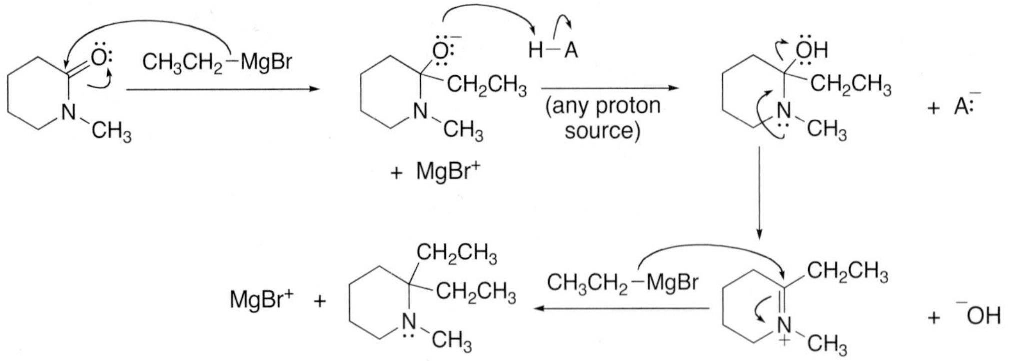

Chapter 21 Aldehydes and Ketones—Nucleophilic Addition

Chapter Review

General facts

- Aldehydes and ketones contain a carbonyl group bonded to only H atoms or R groups. The carbonyl carbon is sp^2 hybridized and trigonal planar (21.1).
- Aldehydes are identified by the suffix *-al,* while ketones are identified by the suffix *-one* (21.2).
- Aldehydes and ketones are polar compounds that exhibit dipole–dipole interactions (21.3).

Summary of spectroscopic absorptions of RCHO and R_2CO (21.4)

IR absorptions	C=O	~1715 cm^{-1} for ketones • increasing frequency with decreasing ring size ~1730 cm^{-1} for aldehydes • For both RCHO and R_2CO, the frequency decreases with conjugation.
	C_{sp^2}–H of CHO	~2700–2830 cm^{-1} (one or two peaks)
^{1}H NMR absorptions	CHO	9–10 ppm (highly deshielded proton)
	C–H α to C=O	2–2.5 ppm (somewhat deshielded C_{sp^3}–H)
^{13}C NMR absorption	C=O	190–215 ppm

Nucleophilic addition reactions

[1] Addition of hydride (H^-) (21.8)

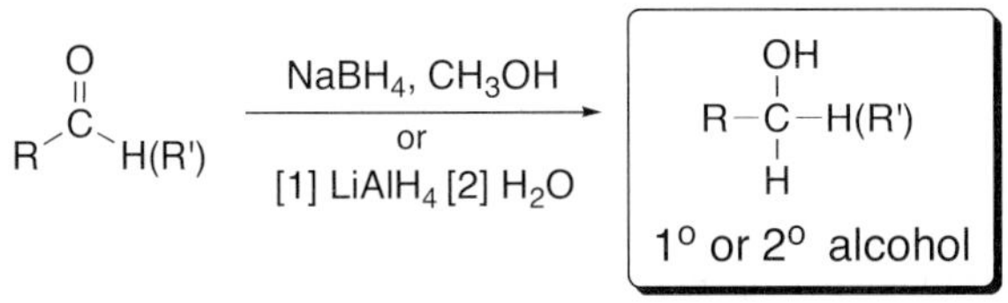

- The mechanism has two steps.
- $H:^-$ adds to the planar C=O from both sides.

[2] Addition of organometallic reagents (R^-) (21.8)

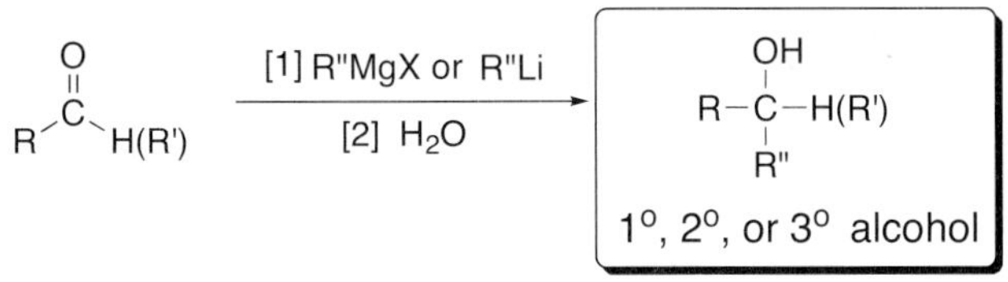

- The mechanism has two steps.
- $R:^-$ adds to the planar C=O from both sides.

[3] Addition of cyanide (^-CN) (21.9)

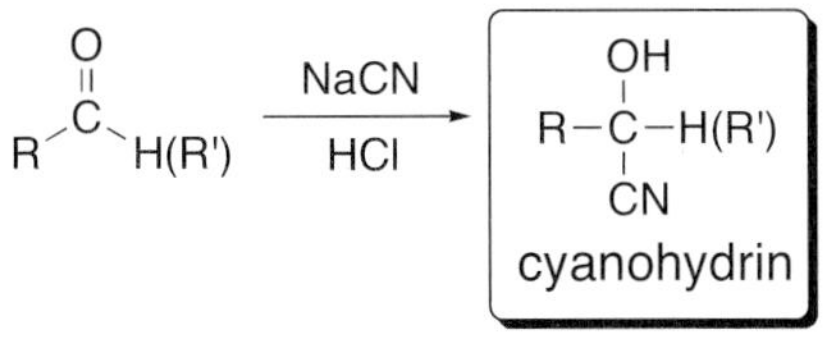

- The mechanism has two steps.
- ^-CN adds to the planar C=O from both sides.

[4] Wittig reaction (21.10)

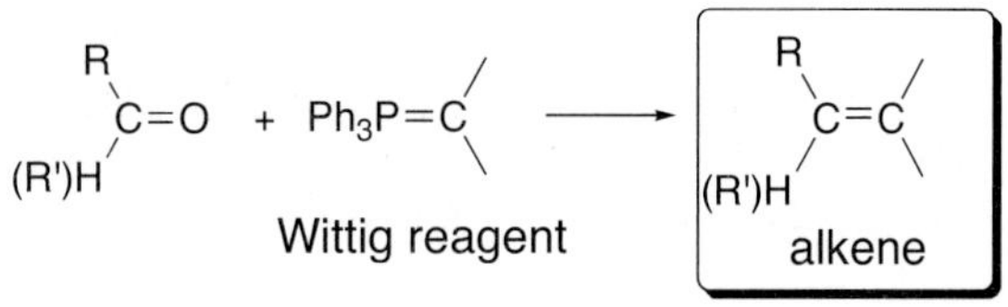

- The reaction forms a new C–C σ bond and a new C–C π bond.
- $Ph_3P{=}O$ is formed as by-product.

[5] Addition of 1° amines (21.11)

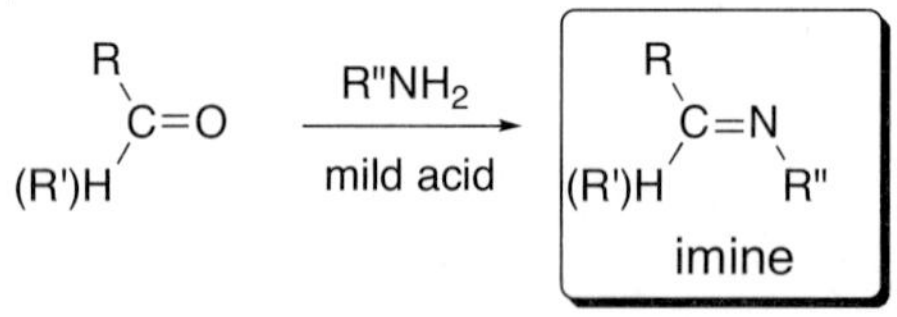

- The reaction is fastest at pH 4–5.
- The intermediate carbinolamine is unstable, and loses H_2O to form the C=N.

[6] Addition of 2° amines (21.12)

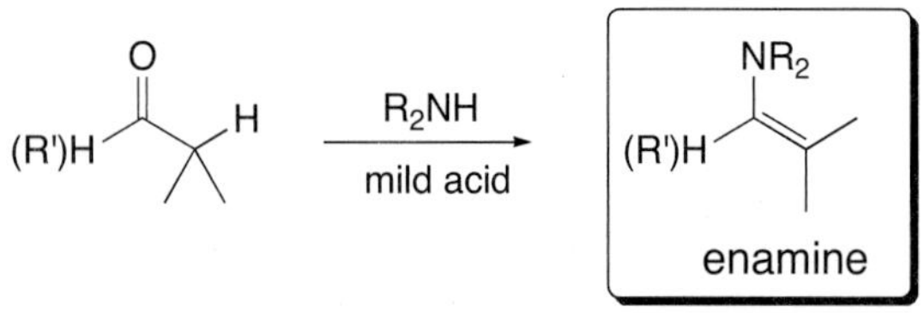

- The reaction is fastest at pH 4–5.
- The intermediate carbinolamine is unstable, and loses H_2O to form the C=C.

[7] Addition of H_2O—Hydration (21.13)

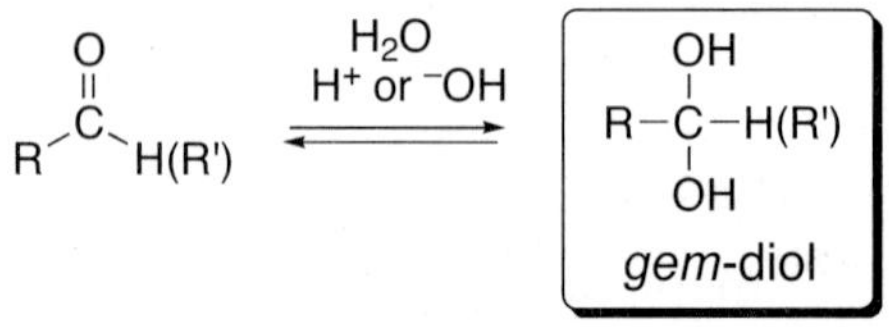

- The reaction is reversible. Equilibrium favors the product only with less stable carbonyl compounds (e.g., H_2CO and Cl_3CCHO).
- The reaction is catalyzed with either H^+ or ^-OH.

[8] Addition of alcohols (21.14)

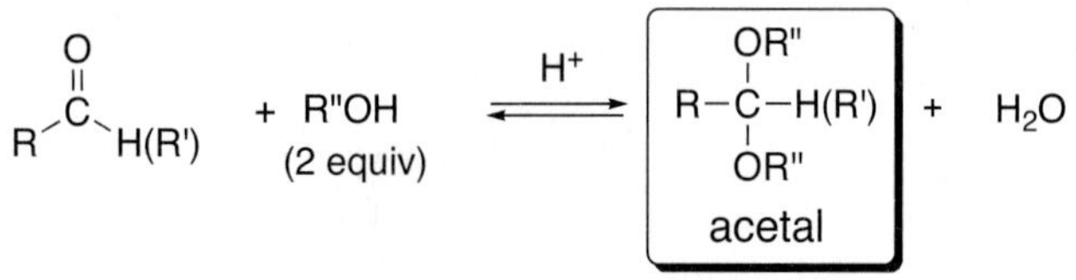

- The reaction is reversible.
- The reaction is catalyzed with acid.
- Removal of H_2O drives the equilibrium to favor the products.

Other reactions

[1] Synthesis of Wittig reagents (21.10A)

$$RCH_2X \xrightarrow[\text{[2] Bu–Li}]{\text{[1] } Ph_3P:} Ph_3P{=}CHR$$

- Step [1] is best with CH_3X and RCH_2X since the reaction follows an S_N2 mechanism.
- A strong base is needed for proton removal in Step [2].

[2] Conversion of cyanohydrins to aldehydes and ketones (21.9)

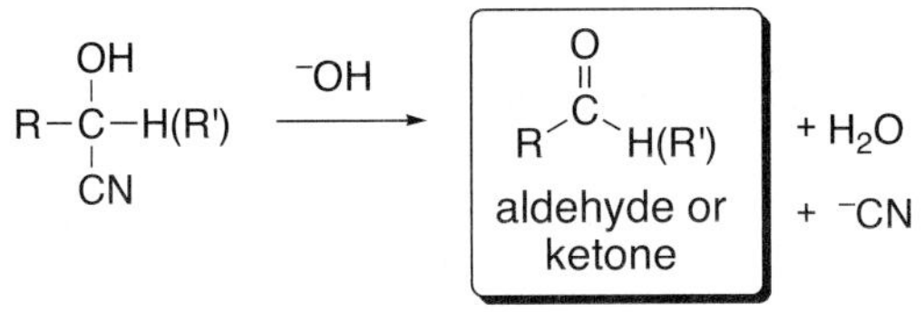

- This reaction is the reverse of cyanohydrin formation.

[3] Hydrolysis of nitriles (21.9)

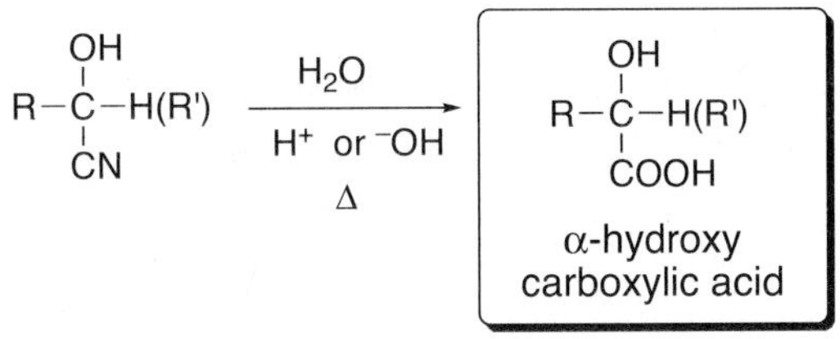

[4] Hydrolysis of imines and enamines (21.12)

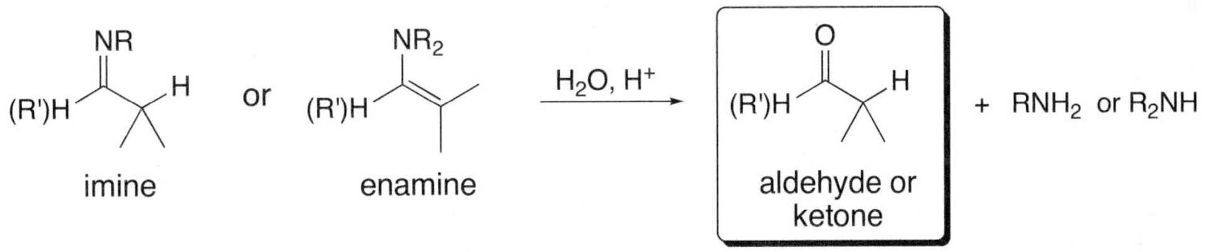

[5] Hydrolysis of acetals (21.14)

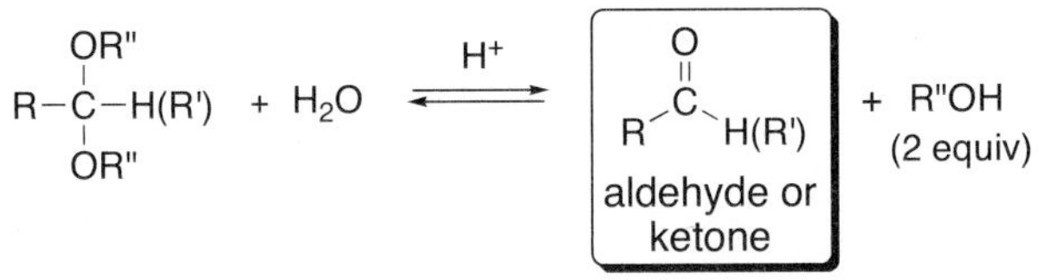

- The reaction is acid catalyzed and is the reverse of acetal synthesis.
- A large excess of H_2O drives the equilibrium to favor the products.

Practice Test on Chapter Review

1. Give the IUPAC name for the following compounds.

a. 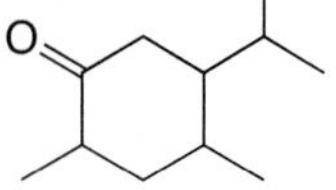

b. 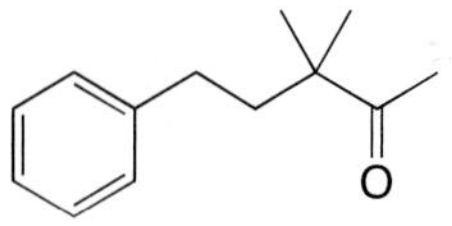

c. 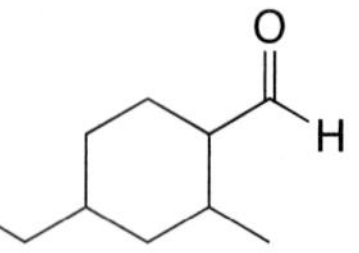

2. (a) Considering compounds **A–D,** which compound forms the smallest amount of hydrate? (b) Which compound forms the largest amount of hydrate?

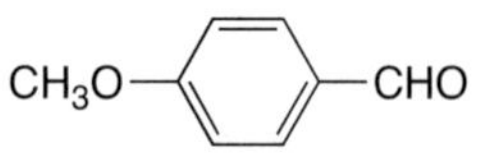

A

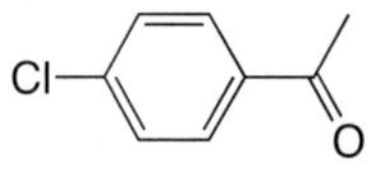

B

C

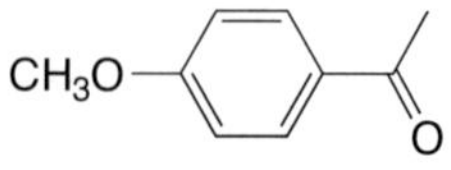

D

3. (a) Considering compounds **A–D,** which compound absorbs at the ***lowest*** wavenumber in its IR spectrum? (b) Which compound absorbs at the ***highest*** wavenumber in its IR spectrum?

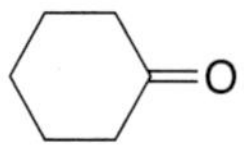

A

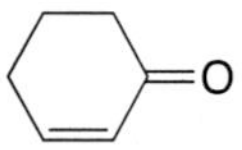

B

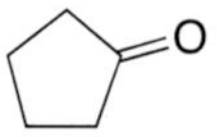

C

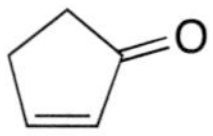

D

4. Fill in the lettered reagents (**A–G**) in the following reaction scheme.

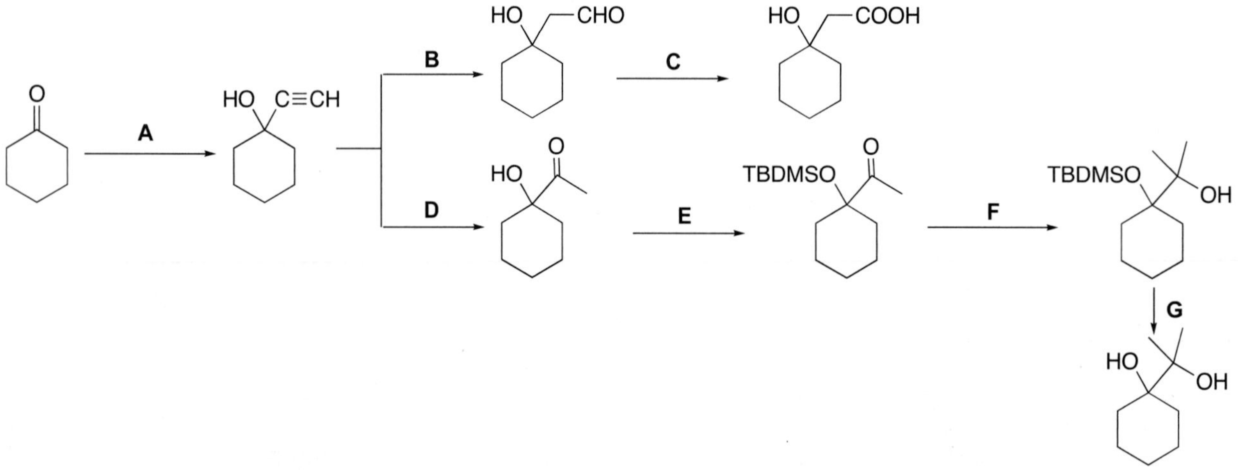

5. Draw the organic products formed in the following reactions.

a. 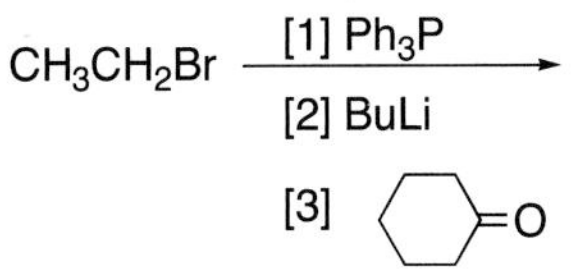
CH3CH2Br
[1] Ph3P
[2] BuLi
[3]
O

b. 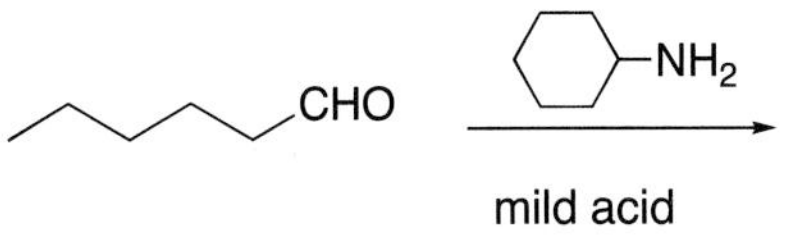
CHO
NH2
mild acid

c. 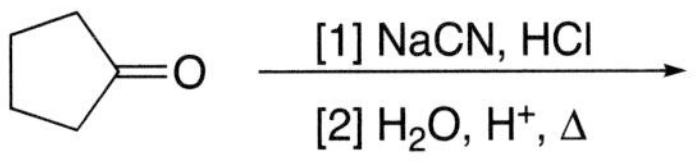
O
[1] NaCN, HCl
[2] H2O, H+, Δ

d. 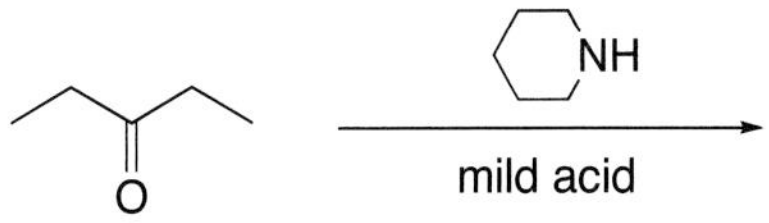
O
NH
mild acid

e. 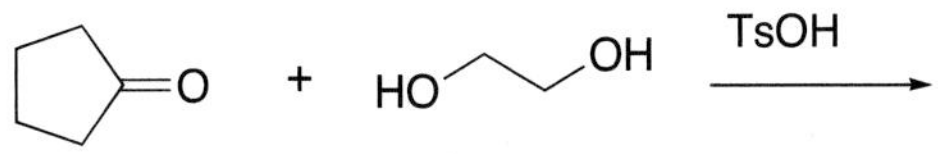
O
+
HO
OH
TsOH

f. 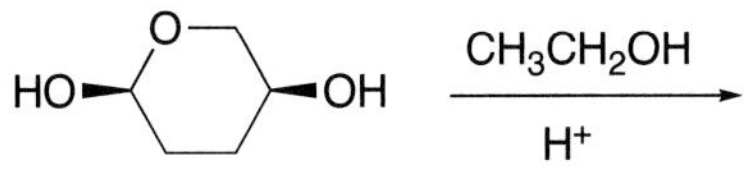
HO
O
OH
CH3CH2OH
H+
[Indicate stereochemistry.]

Answers to Practice Test

1.a. 5-isopropyl-2,4-dimethylcyclohexanone
b. 3,3-dimethyl-5-phenyl-2-pentanone
c. 4-ethyl-2-methylcyclohexanecarbaldehyde

2. a. **D**
b. **C**

3. a. **B**
b. **C**

4.
A = [1] LiC≡CH; [2] H_2O
B = [1] R_2BH; [2] H_2O_2, ^{-}OH
C = Ag_2O, NH_4OH
D = H_2O, H_2SO_4, $HgSO_4$
E = TBDMS–Cl, pyridine
F = [1] CH_3Li; [2] H_2O
G = $(CH_3CH_2CH_2CH_2)_4N^{+}F^{-}$

5.
a. 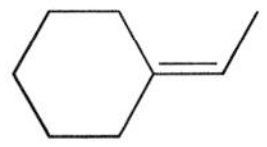

b. 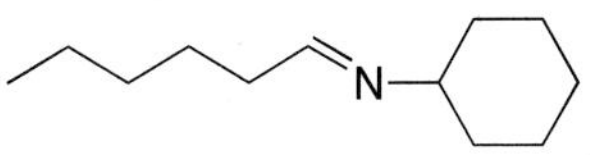
N

c. 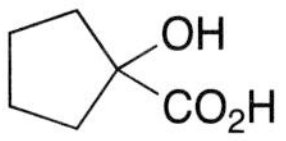
OH
CO2H

d. 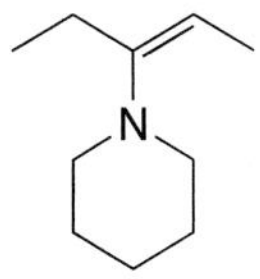
N
(*E* + *Z*)

e. 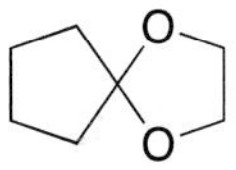
O
O

f. 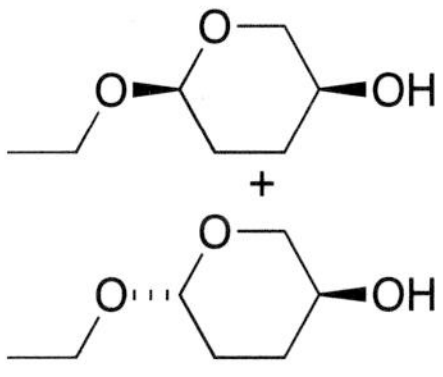
O
O
OH
+
O
O
OH

Answers to Problems

21.1 As the number of R groups bonded to the carbonyl C increases, reactivity towards nucleophilic attack decreases. Steric hindrance decreases reactivity as well.

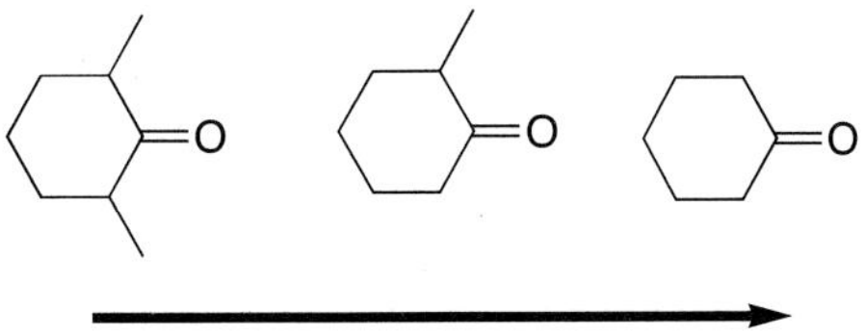
O
O
O

Increasing reactivity
decreasing steric hindrance

21.2 More stable aldehydes are less reactive towards nucleophilic attack.

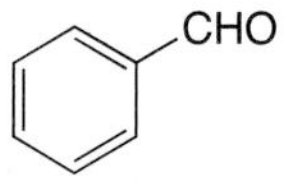

benzaldehyde
Several resonance structures delocalize the partial positive charge on the carbonyl carbon, making it more stable and less reactive towards nucleophilic attack.

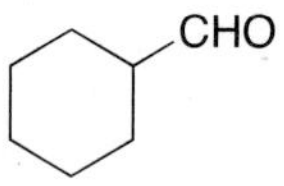

cyclohexanecarbaldehyde
This aldehyde has no added resonance stabilization.

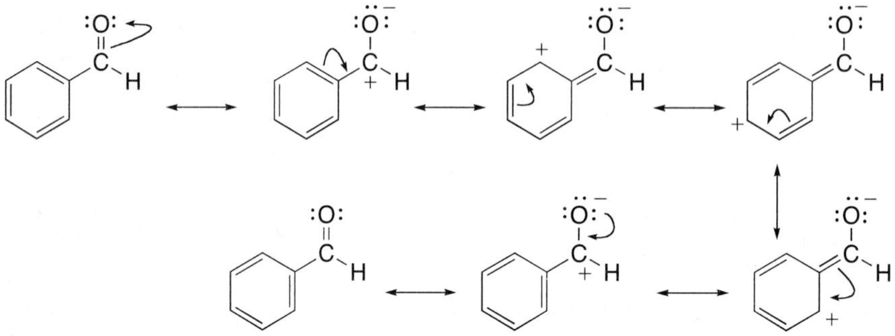

21.3 • To name an aldehyde with a chain of atoms: [1] Find the longest chain with the CHO group and change the *-e* ending to *-al*. [2] Number the carbon chain to put the CHO at C1, but omit this number from the name. Apply all other nomenclature rules.

• To name an aldehyde with the CHO bonded to a ring: [1] Name the ring and add the suffix-*carbaldehyde*. [2] Number the ring to put the CHO group at C1, but omit this number from the name. Apply all other nomenclature rules.

a. $(CH_3)_3CC(CH_3)_2CH_2CHO$

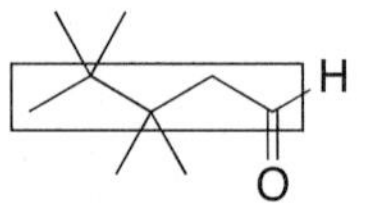

5 C chain = pentanal

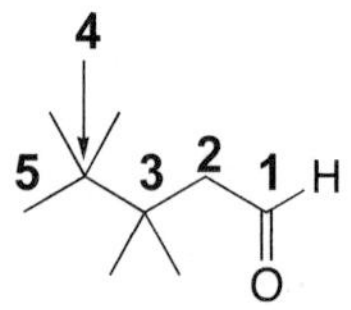

3,3,4,4-tetramethylpentanal

b.

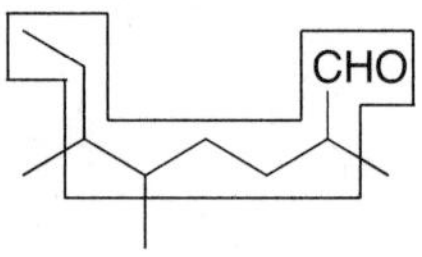

8 C chain = octanal

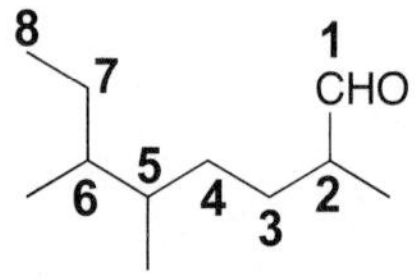

2,5,6-trimethyloctanal

c.

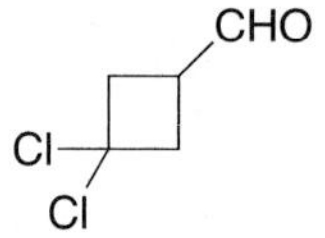

4 C ring = cyclobutanecarbaldehyde

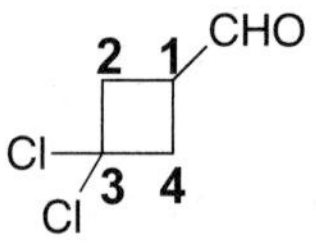

3,3-dichlorocyclobutane-carbaldehyde

21.4 Work backwards from the name to the structure, referring to the nomenclature rules in Answer 21.3.

a. 2-isobutyl-3-isopropyl**hexanal**

6 C chain

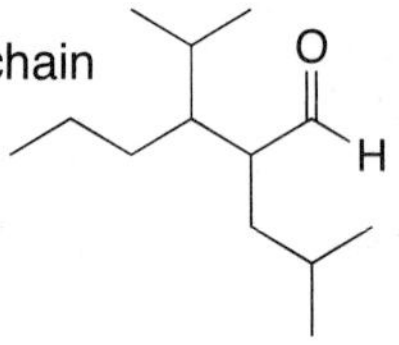

b. *trans*-3-methyl**cyclopentanecarbaldehyde**

5 carbon ring

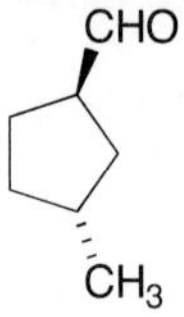

or

c. 1-methyl**cyclopropanecarbaldehyde**

3 carbon ring

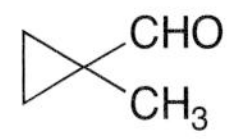

d. 3,6-diethyl**nonanal**

9 C chain

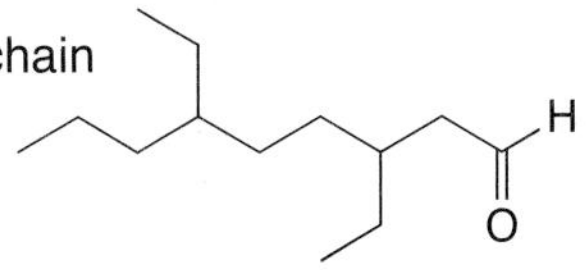

21.5 • To name an acyclic ketone: [1] Find the longest chain with the carbonyl group and change the *-e* ending to *-one*. [2] Number the carbon chain to give the carbonyl C the lower number. Apply all other nomenclature rules.

• To name a cyclic ketone: [1] Name the ring and change the *-e* ending to *-one*. [2] Number the C's to put the carbonyl C at C1 and give the next substituent the lower number. Apply all other nomenclature rules.

a.

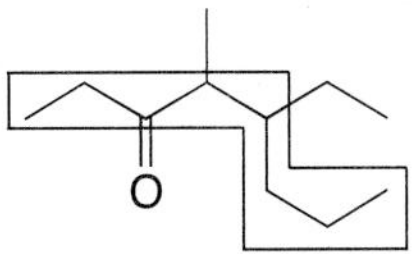

8 C chain = octanone

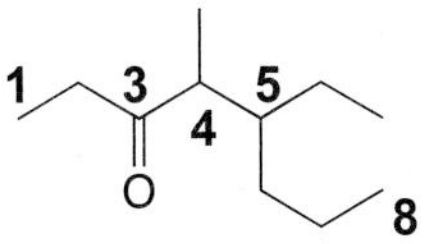

5-ethyl-4-methyl-3-octanone

c. $(CH_3)_3CCOC(CH_3)_3$

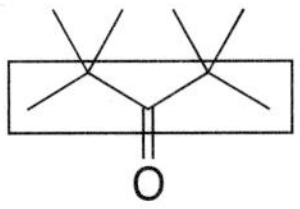

5 C chain = pentanone

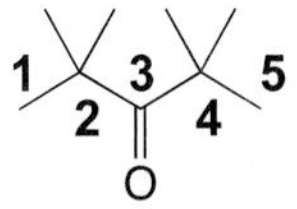

2,2,4,4-tetramethyl-3-pentanone

b.

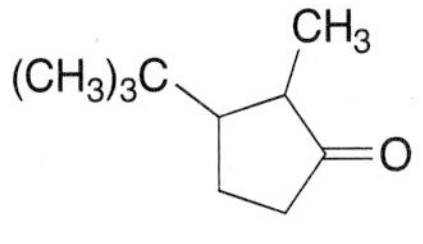

5 C ring = cyclopentanone

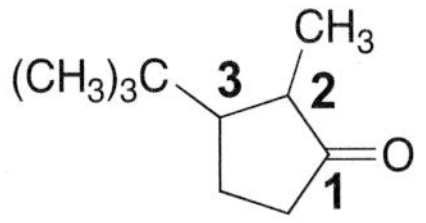

3-*tert*-butyl-2-methylcyclopentanone

21.6 Most common names are formed by naming both alkyl groups on the carbonyl C, arranging them alphabetically, and adding the word ketone.

a. *sec*-butyl ethyl ketone

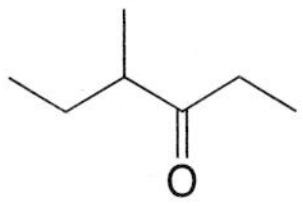

b. methyl vinyl ketone

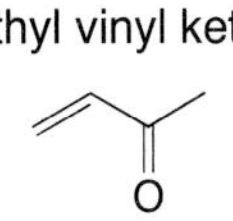

c. *p*-ethylacetophenone

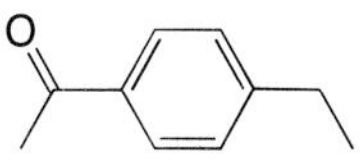

d. 3-benzoyl-2-benzylcyclopentanone

5 C ketone

benzyl group:

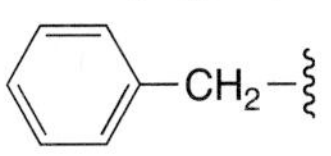

benzoyl group:

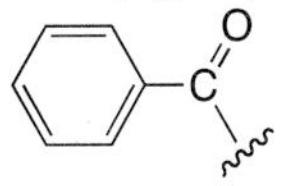

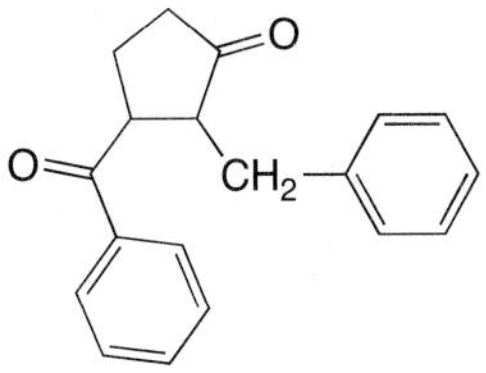

e. 6,6-dimethyl-2-cyclohexenone

6 C ketone

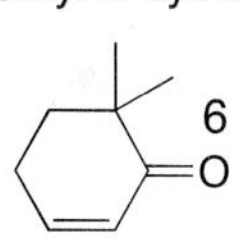

f. 3-ethyl-5-hexenal

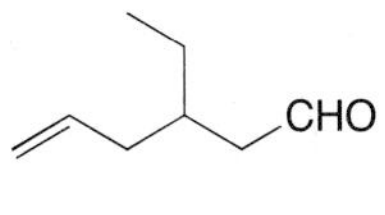

21.7 Compounds with both a C–C double bond and an aldehyde are named as enals.

a. (2*Z*)-3,7-dimethyl-2,6-octadienal

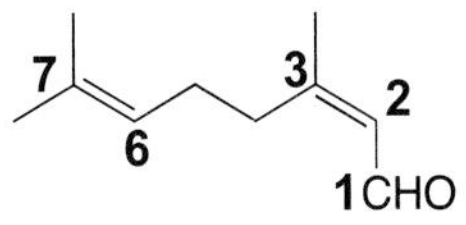

neral

b. (2*E*,6*Z*)-2,6-nonadienal

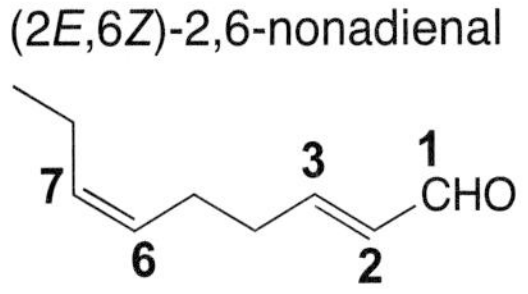

cucumber aldehyde

21.8 Even though both compounds have polar C–O bonds, the electron pairs around the sp^3 hybridized O atom of diethyl ether are more crowded and less able to interact with electron-deficient sites in other diethyl ether molecules. The O atom of the carbonyl group of 2-butanone extends out from the carbon chain, making it less crowded. The lone pairs of electrons on the O atom can more readily interact with the electron-deficient sites in the other molecules, resulting in stronger forces and a higher boiling point.

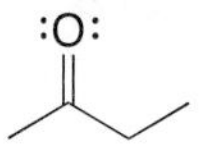
2-butanone

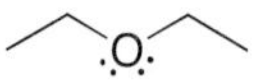
diethyl ether

21.9 For cyclic ketones, the carbonyl absorption shifts to higher wavenumber as the size of the ring decreases and the ring strain increases. Conjugation of the carbonyl group with a C=C or a benzene ring shifts the absorption to lower wavenumber.

a. 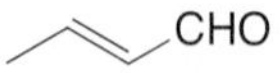 or 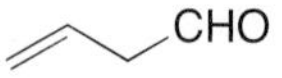

conjugated C=O
lower wavenumber

higher wavenumber

b. 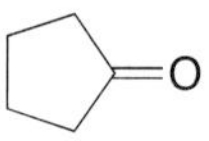 or 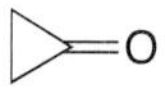

smaller ring
higher wavenumber

21.10 The number of lines in their ^{13}C NMR spectra can distinguish the constitutional isomers.

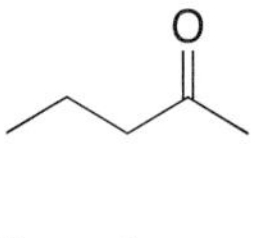
2-pentanone
5 lines

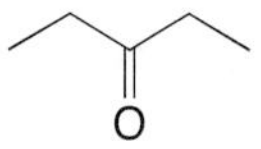
3-pentanone
3 lines

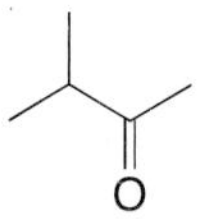
3-methyl-2-butanone
4 lines

21.11

a. $CH_3CH_2CH_2COOCH_3 \xrightarrow[\text{[2] } H_2O]{\text{[1] DIBAL-H}} CH_3CH_2CH_2CHO$

b. $CH_3CH_2CH_2CH_2OH \xrightarrow{\text{PCC}} CH_3CH_2CH_2CHO$

c. $HC{\equiv}CCH_2CH_3 \xrightarrow[\text{[2] } H_2O_2,\ HO^-]{\text{[1] } R_2BH} CH_3CH_2CH_2CHO$

d. $CH_3CH_2CH_2CH{=}CHCH_2CH_2CH_3 \xrightarrow[\text{[2] Zn, } H_2O]{\text{[1] } O_3} CH_3CH_2CH_2CHO$

21.12

a. 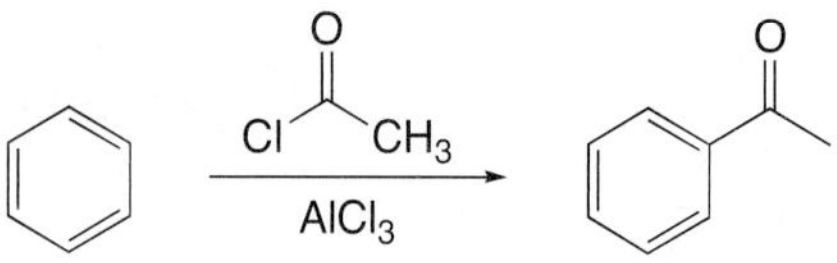

c. 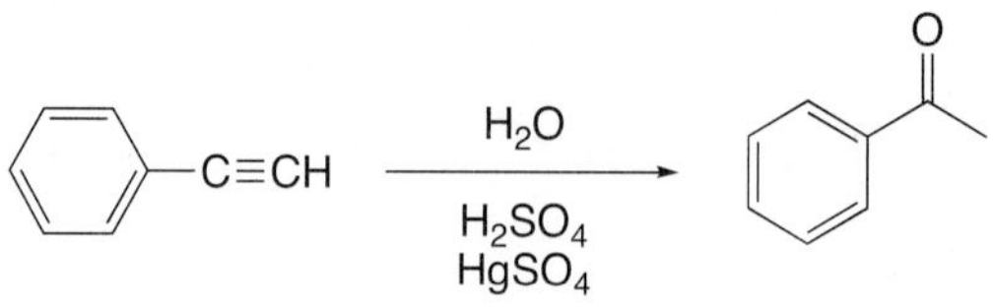

b. 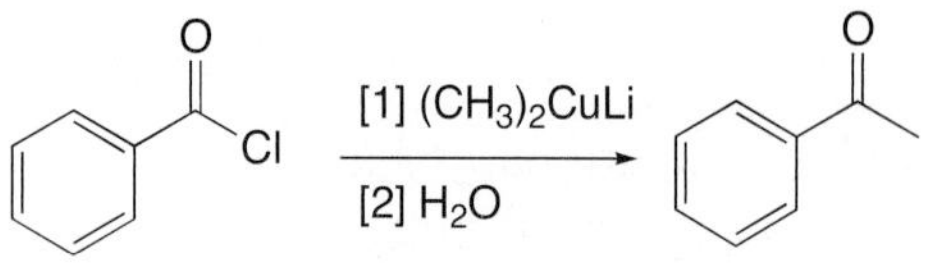

21.13

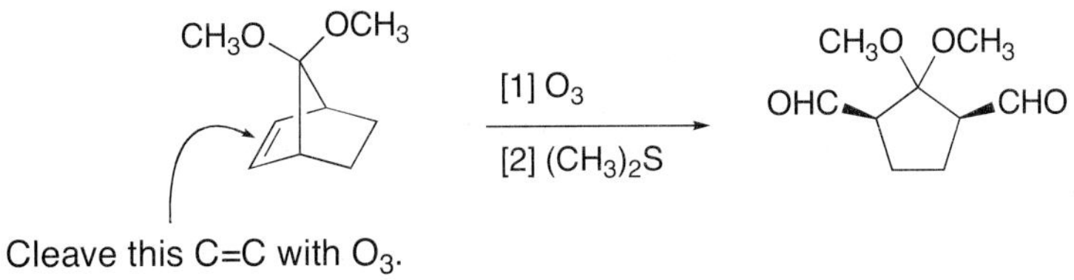

21.14 Addition of hydride or R–M occurs at a planar carbonyl C, so two different configurations at a new stereogenic center are possible.

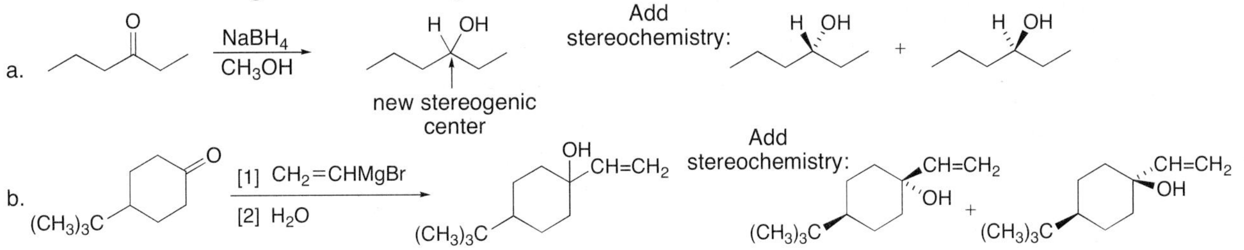

21.15 Treatment of an aldehyde or ketone with NaCN, HCl adds HCN across the double bond. Cyano groups are hydrolyzed by H_3O^+ to replace the three C–N bonds with three C–O bonds.

21.16

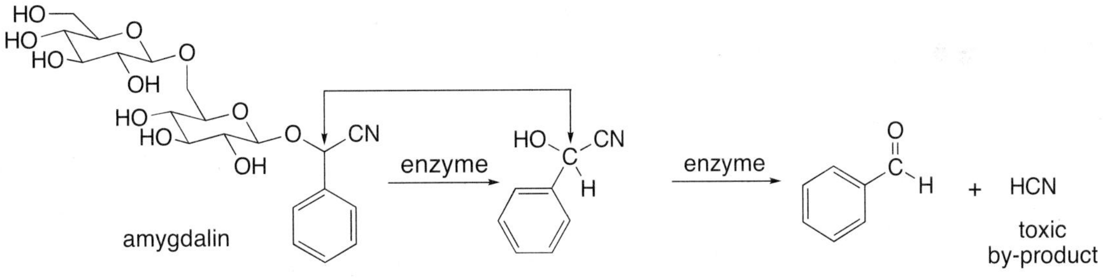

21.17

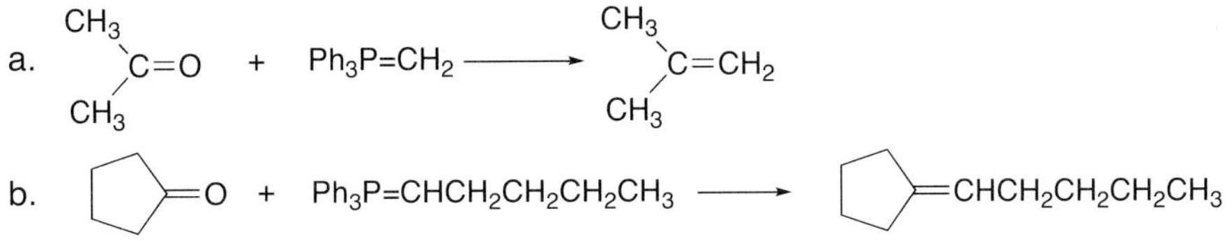

21.18

a. $Ph_3P{:} + Br{-}CH_2CH_3 \longrightarrow Ph_3\overset{+}{P}{-}CH_2CH_3\ Br^- \xrightarrow{\text{BuLi}} Ph_3P{=}CHCH_3$

b. $Ph_3P{:} + Br{-}CH(CH_3)_2 \longrightarrow Ph_3\overset{+}{P}{-}CH(CH_3)_2\ Br^- \xrightarrow{\text{BuLi}} Ph_3P{=}C(CH_3)_2$

c. $Ph_3P{:} + Br{-}CH_2C_6H_5 \longrightarrow Ph_3\overset{+}{P}{-}CH_2C_6H_5\ Br^- \xrightarrow{\text{BuLi}} Ph_3P{=}CHC_6H_5$

21.19

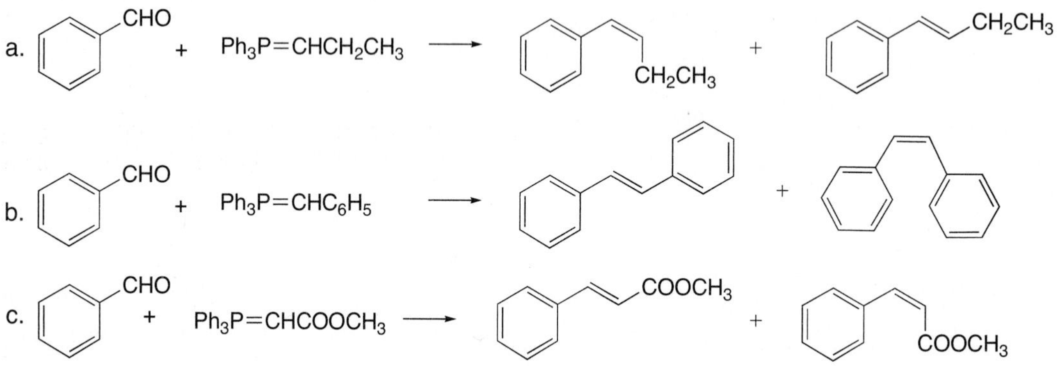
a.
CHO
+ Ph3P=CHCH2CH3
CH2CH3
+
CH2CH3
b.
CHO
+ Ph3P=CHC6H5
+
c.
CHO
+ Ph3P=CHCOOCH3
COOCH3
+
COOCH3

21.20

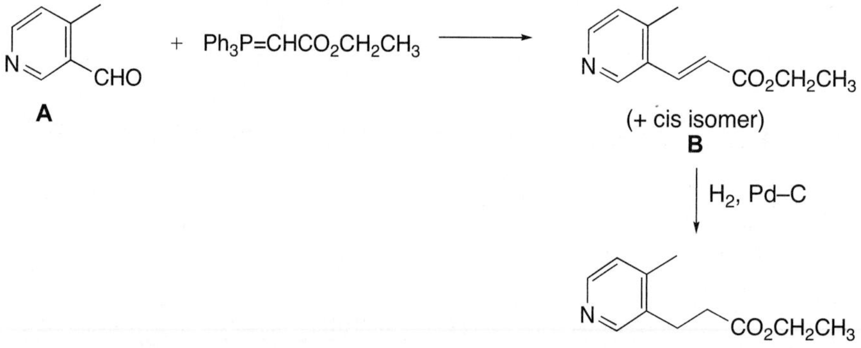
N
CHO
+ Ph3P=CHCO2CH2CH3
N
CO2CH2CH3
(+ cis isomer)
H2, Pd–C
N
CO2CH2CH3

A B C

21.21 To draw the starting materials of the Wittig reactions, find the C=C and cleave it. Replace it with a C=O in one half of the molecule and a C=PPh_3 in the other half. The preferred pathway uses a Wittig reagent derived from a less hindered alkyl halide.

a.

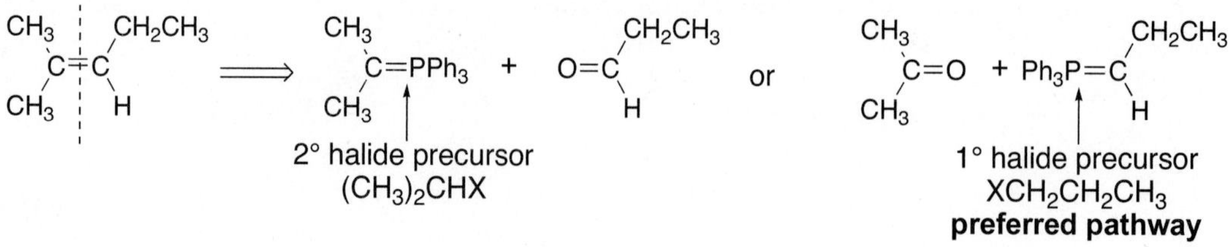
CH3
CH2CH3
C=C
CH3
H
CH3
C=PPh3
+ O=C
CH2CH3
H
CH3
or
CH3
C=O
+ Ph3P=C
CH2CH3
H
CH3
2° halide precursor
(CH3)2CHX
1° halide precursor
XCH2CH2CH3
preferred pathway

b.

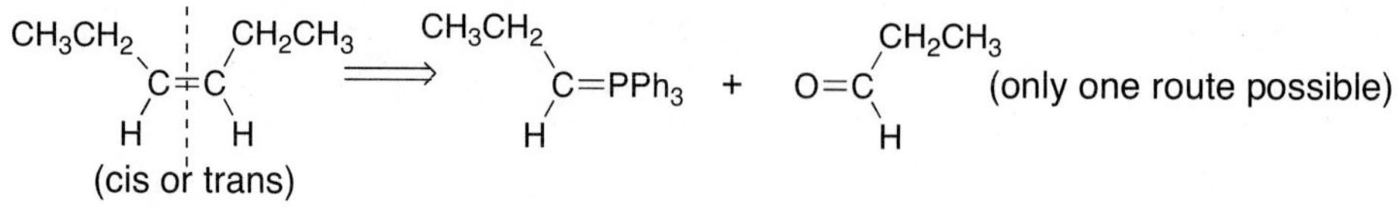
CH3CH2
CH2CH3
C=C
H
H
(cis or trans)
CH3CH2
C=PPh3
H
+ O=C
CH2CH3
H
(only one route possible)

c.
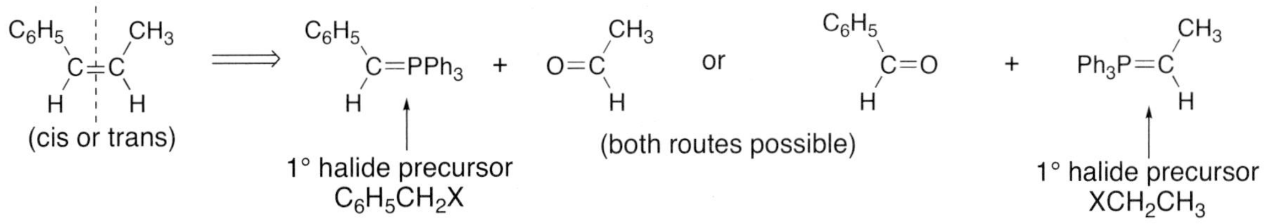
(cis or trans)
1° halide precursor
$C_6H_5CH_2X$
(both routes possible)
or
1° halide precursor
XCH_2CH_3

21.22

a. Two-step sequence:

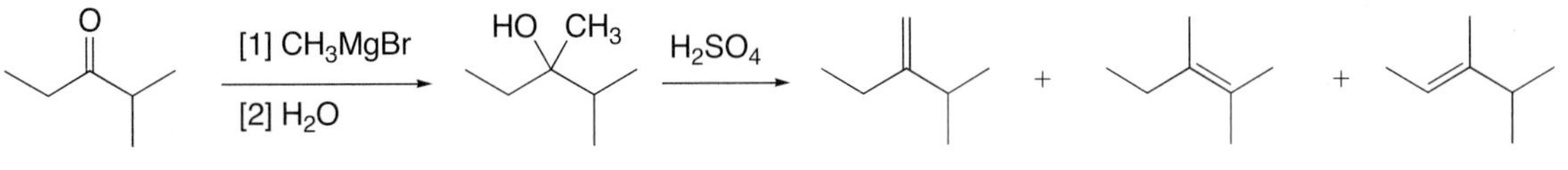
[1] CH_3MgBr
[2] H_2O
H_2SO_4
minor product
tetrasubstituted
major product
(E and Z isomers)

One-step sequence:

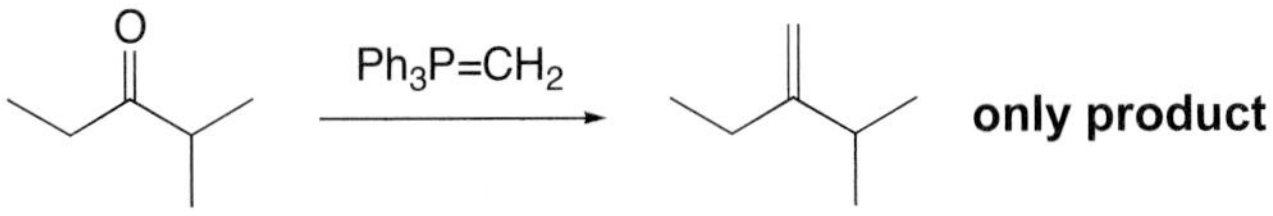
$Ph_3P{=}CH_2$
only product

b. Two-step sequence:

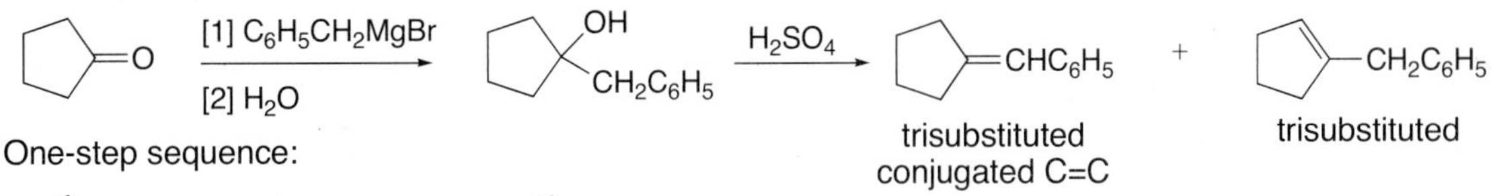
[1] $C_6H_5CH_2MgBr$
[2] H_2O
H_2SO_4
trisubstituted
conjugated C=C
trisubstituted

One-step sequence:

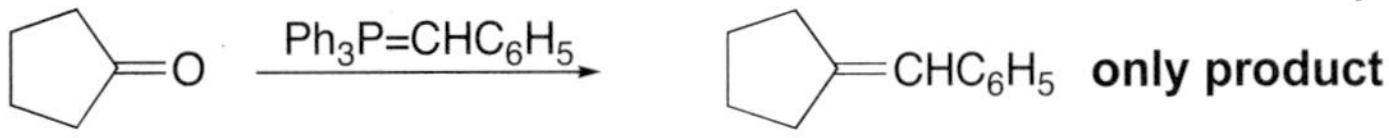
$Ph_3P{=}CHC_6H_5$
CHC_6H_5
only product

21.23 When a 1° amine reacts with an aldehyde or ketone, the C=O is replaced by C=NR.

a.
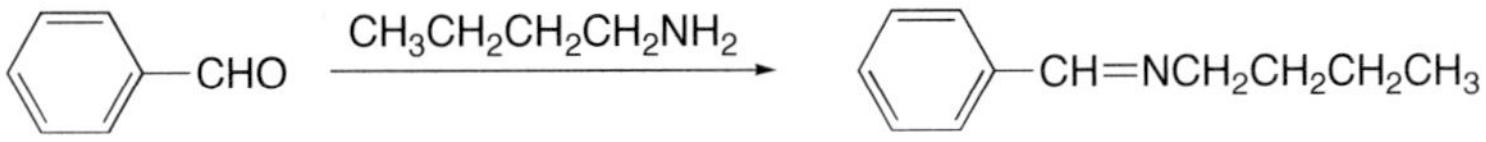

b.
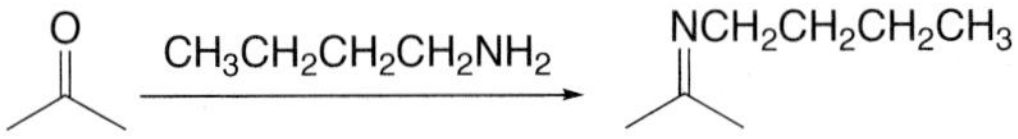

c.
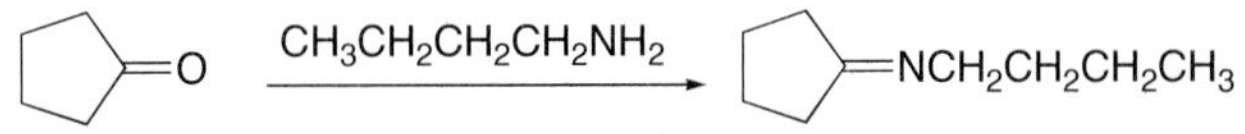

21.24 Remember that the C=NR is formed from a C=O and an NH_2 group of a 1° amine.

a.
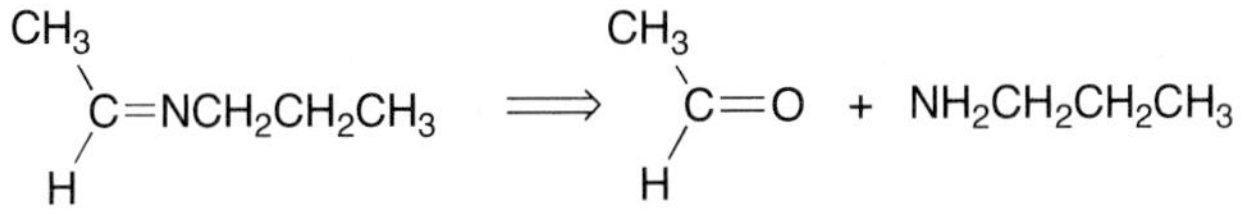

b.
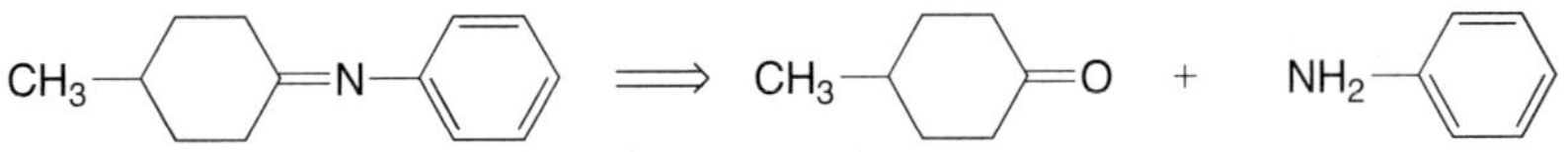

21.25

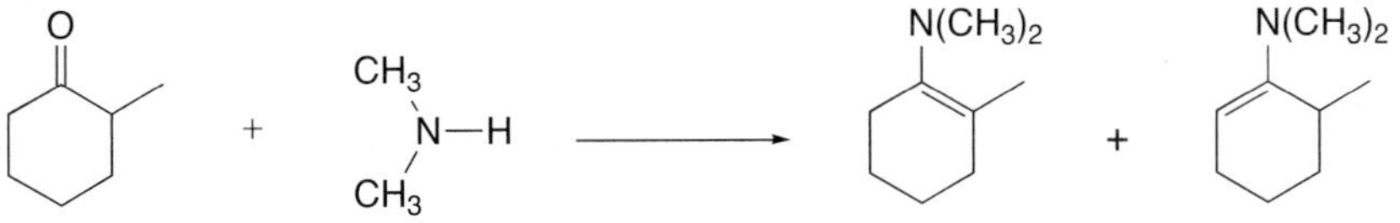

21.26 • Imines are hydrolyzed to 1° amines and a carbonyl compound.
• Enamines are hydrolyzed to 2° amines and a carbonyl compound.

a.
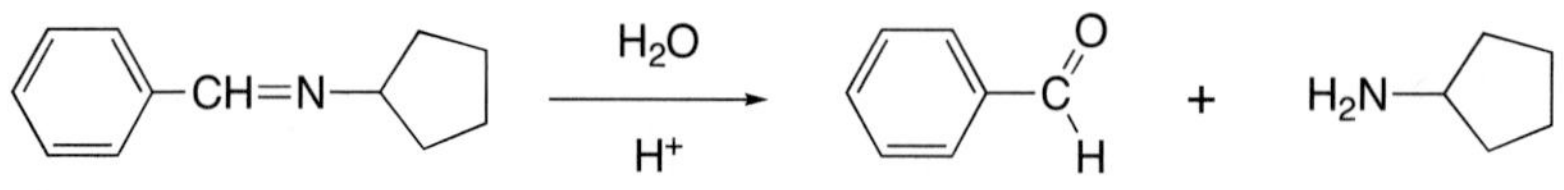
CH=N
H_2O
H^+
O
C
H
+
H_2N

imine — 1° amine

b.
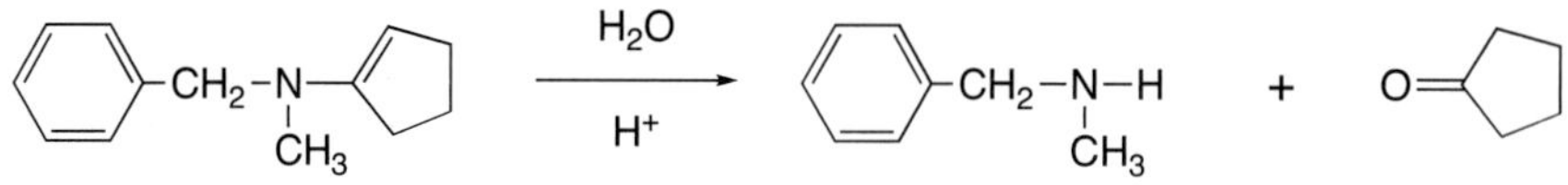
CH_2–N
CH_3
H_2O
H^+
CH_2–N–H
CH_3
+
O

enamine — 2° amine

c.
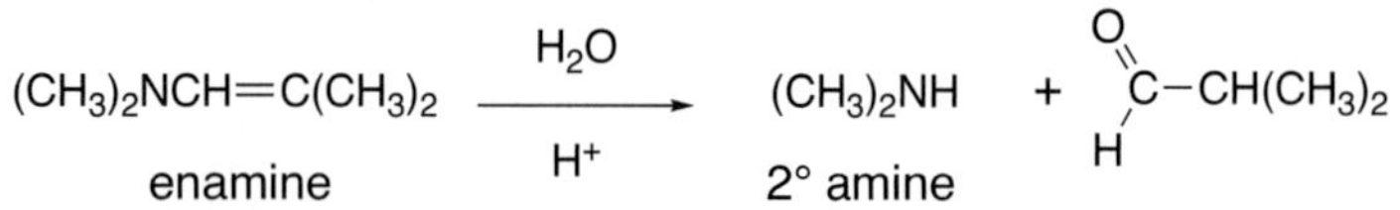
$(CH_3)_2NCH{=}C(CH_3)_2$
H_2O
H^+
$(CH_3)_2NH$
+
O
C–$CH(CH_3)_2$
H

enamine — 2° amine

21.27 • A substituent that **donates** electron density to the carbonyl C stabilizes it, **decreasing** the percentage of hydrate at equilibrium.
• A substituent that **withdraws** electron density from the carbonyl C destabilizes it, **increasing** the percentage of hydrate at equilibrium.

a. $CH_3CH_2CH_2CHO$ or $CH_3CH_2COCH_3$

one R group on C=O
higher percentage of hydrate

2 R groups
on C=O

b. CH_3CF_2CHO or CH_3CH_2CHO

F atoms are electron withdrawing.
higher percentage of hydrate

21.28

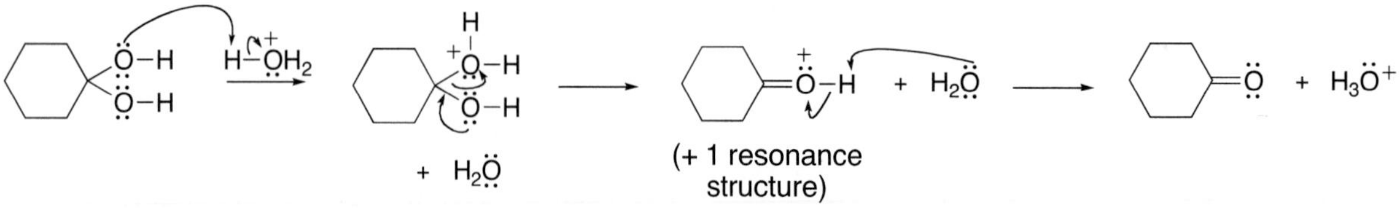
O–H
O–H
$H–OH_2$
H
O–H
O–H
+ H_2O
O–H
+ H_2O
(+ 1 resonance
structure)
O
+ H_3O^+

21.29 Treatment of an aldehyde or ketone with two equivalents of alcohol results in the formation of an acetal (a C bonded to two OR groups).

a.
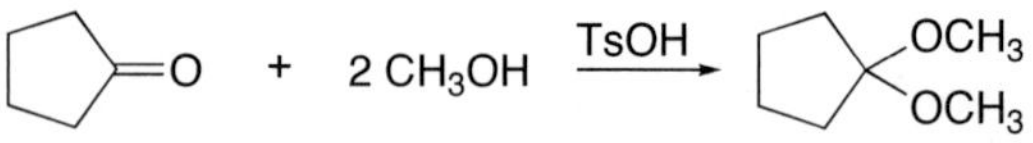
O
+
2 CH_3OH
TsOH
OCH_3
OCH_3

b.
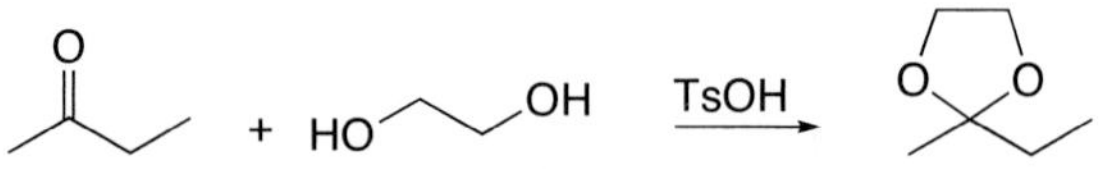
O
+ HO
OH
TsOH
O
O

21.30

a.
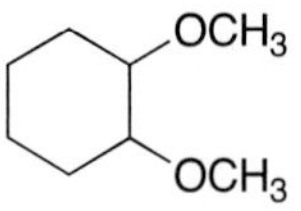
OCH_3
OCH_3

2 OR groups
on different C's
2 ethers

b.
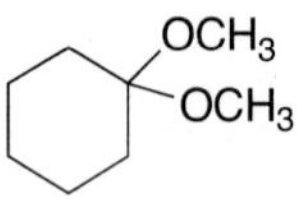
OCH_3
OCH_3

2 OR groups
on same C
acetal

c.
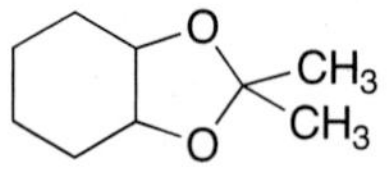
O
O
CH_3
CH_3

2 OR groups
on same C
acetal

d.
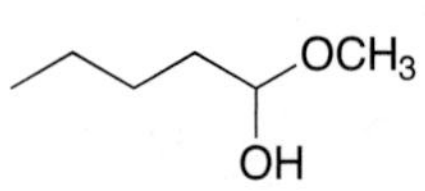
OCH_3
OH

1 OR group and
1 OH group
on same C
hemiacetal

21.31 The mechanism has two parts: [1] nucleophilic addition of ROH to form a hemiacetal; [2] conversion of the hemiacetal to an acetal.

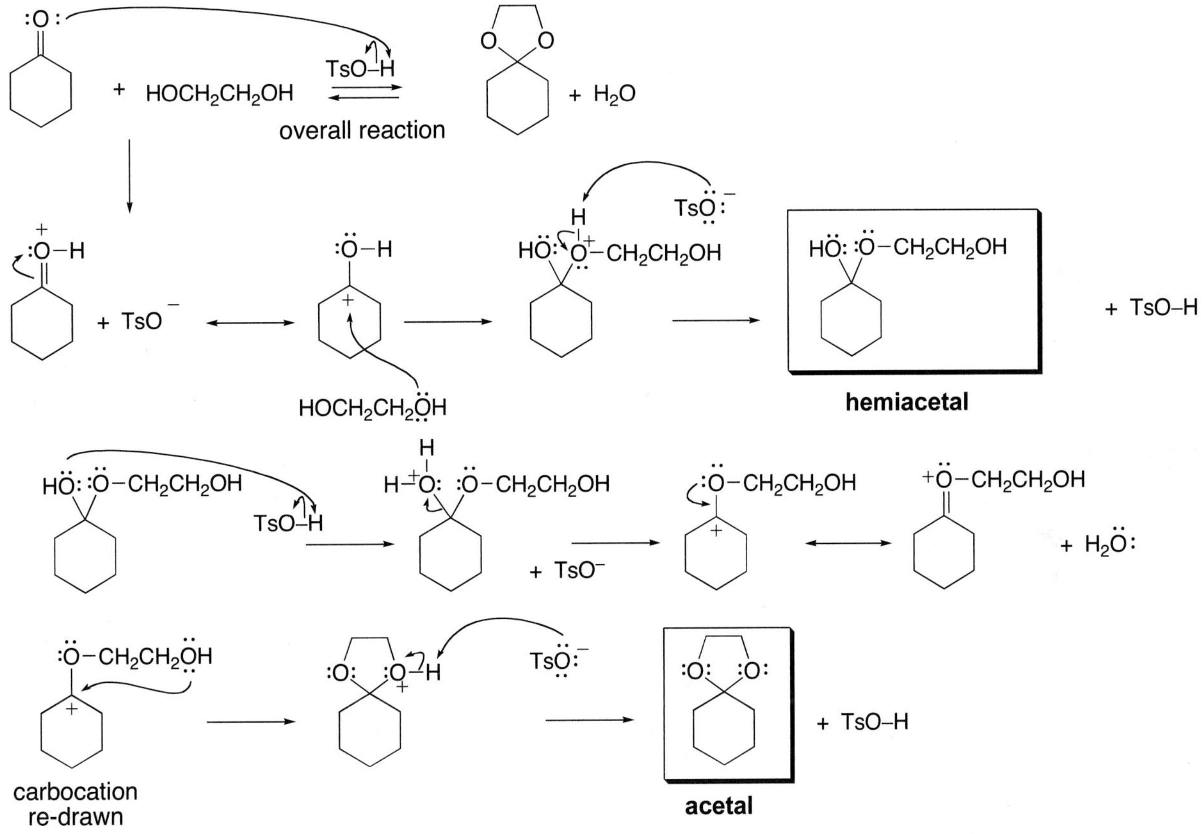

overall reaction
hemiacetal
carbocation re-drawn
acetal

21.32

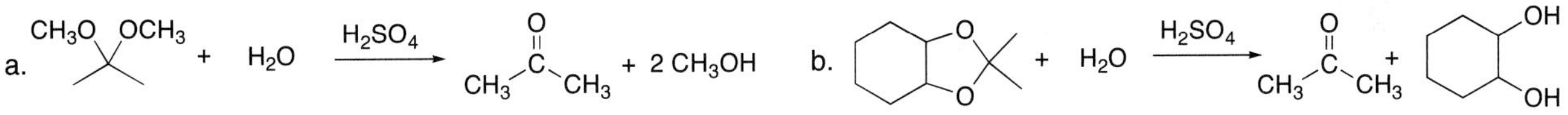

21.33

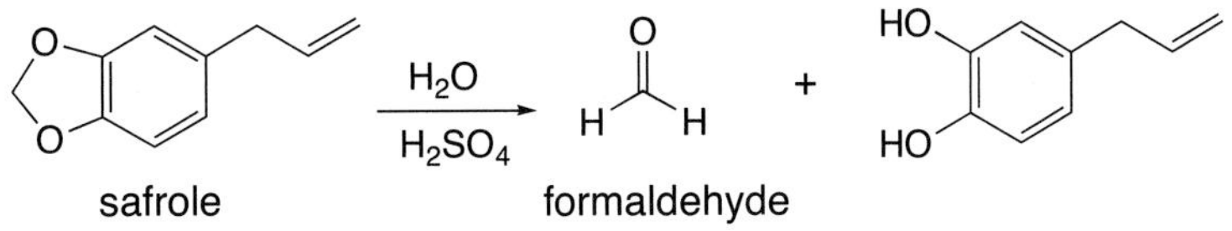

safrole
formaldehyde

21.34 Use an acetal protecting group to carry out the reaction.

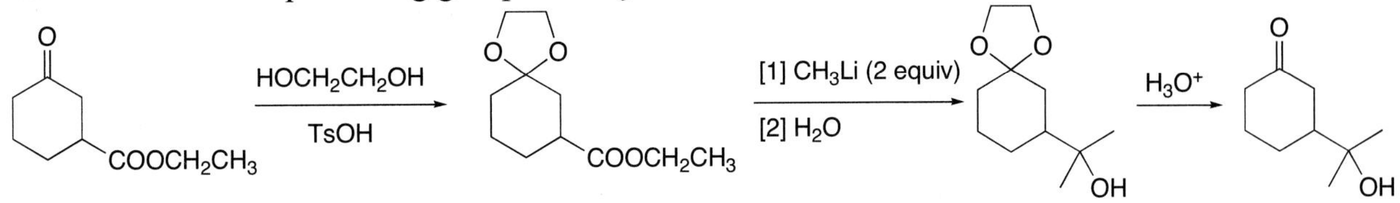

21.35

a. 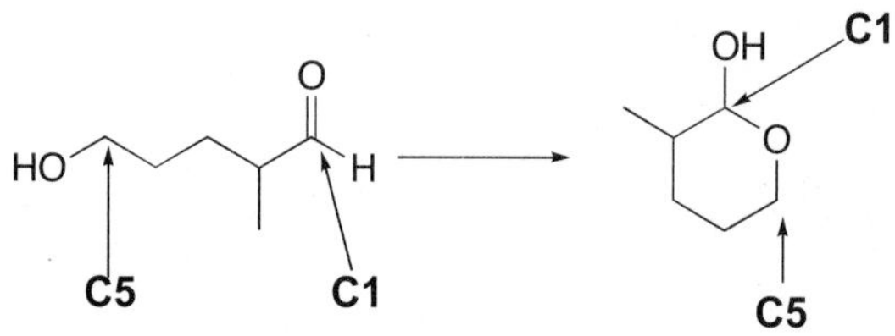

b. 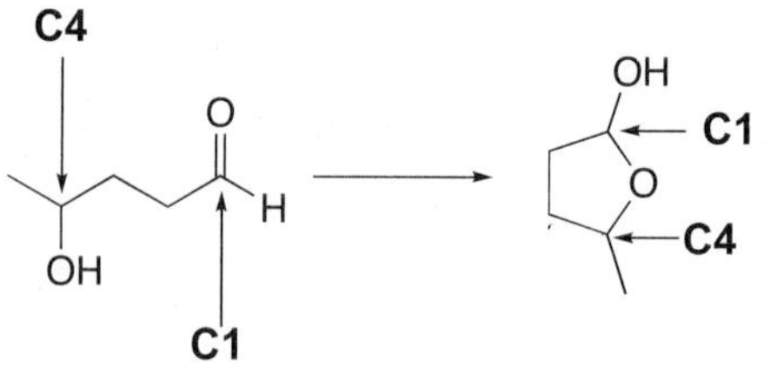

21.36

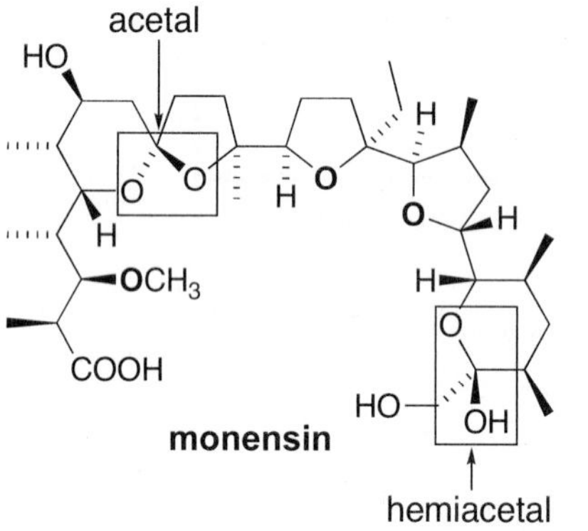

monensin

Ether **O** atoms are indicated in **bold.**

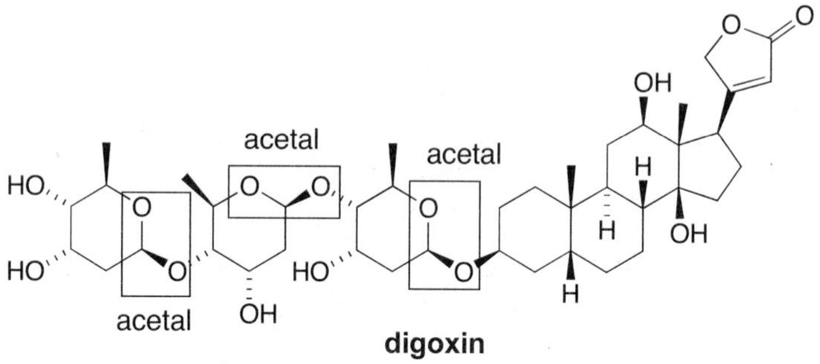

digoxin

21.37 The hemiacetal OH is replaced by an OR group to form an acetal.

a. 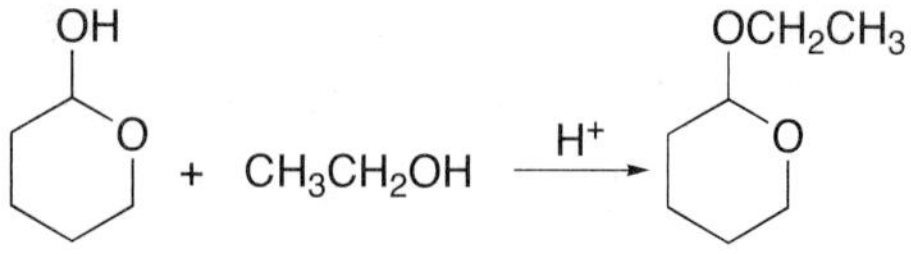

b. 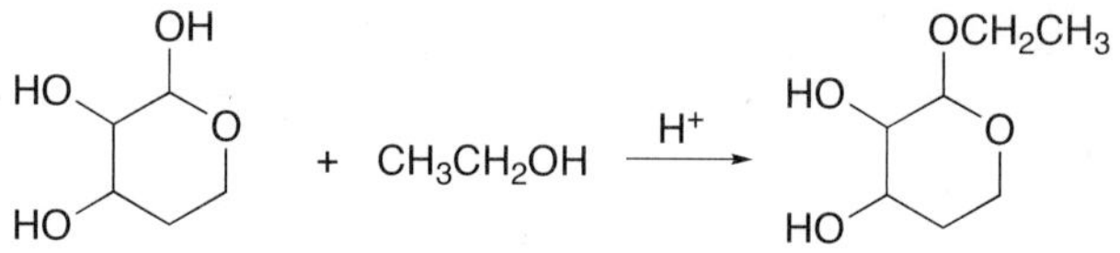

21.38

a. 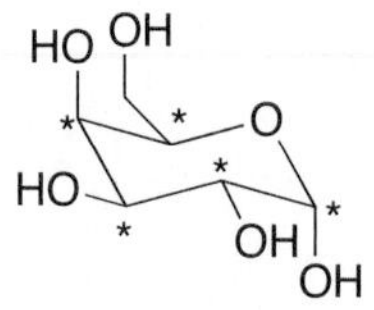

5 stereogenic centers (labeled with *)

d. 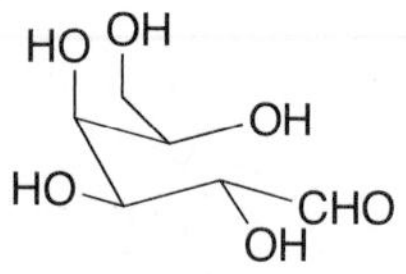

b. 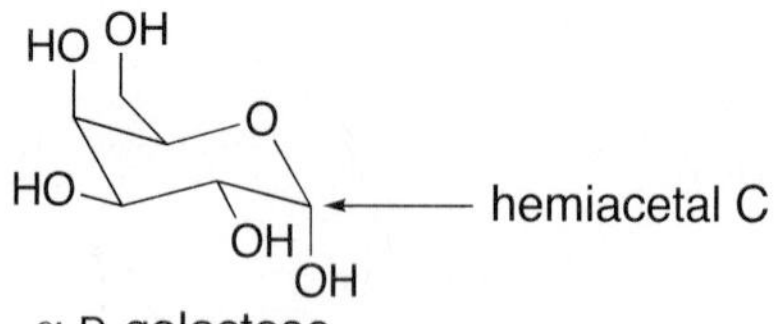

α-D-galactose

e. 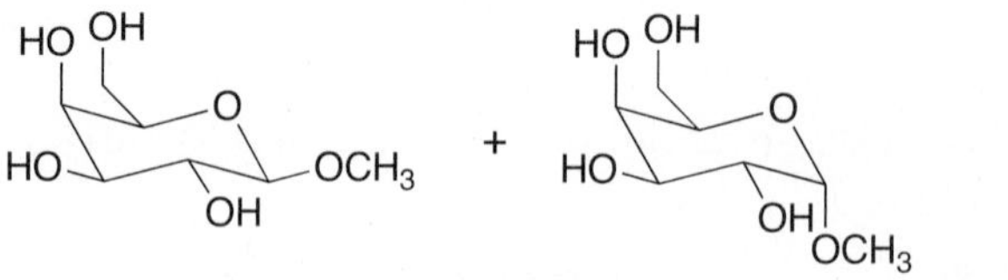

c. 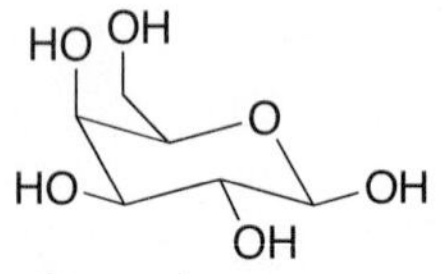

β-D-galactose

21.39

a.

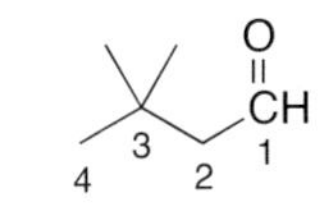
O
CH
4
3
2
1

3,3-dimethylbutanal
A

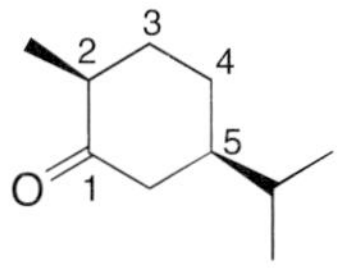
2
3
4
5
O
1

cis-5-isopropyl-2-methylcyclohexanone
B

b.

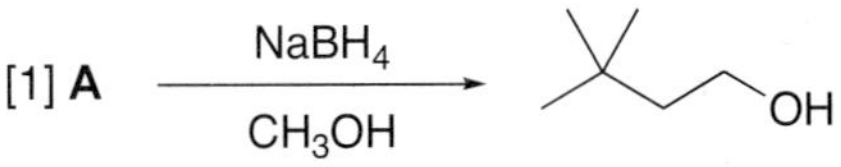
[1] A
NaBH4
CH3OH
OH

[2] A
CH3MgBr
H2O
H
OH
+
H
OH

[3] A
Ph3P=CHOCH3
OCH3
(+ cis isomer)

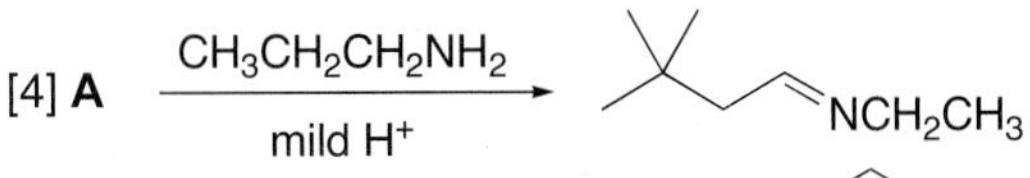
[4] A
CH3CH2CH2NH2
mild H+
NCH2CH3

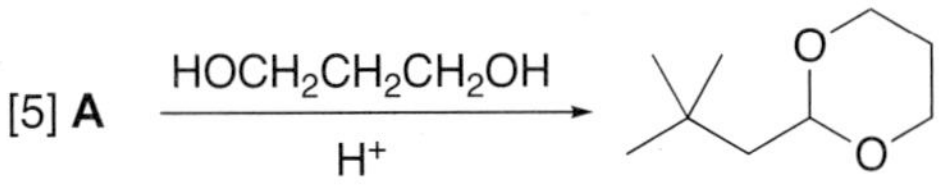
[5] A
HOCH2CH2CH2OH
H+
O
O

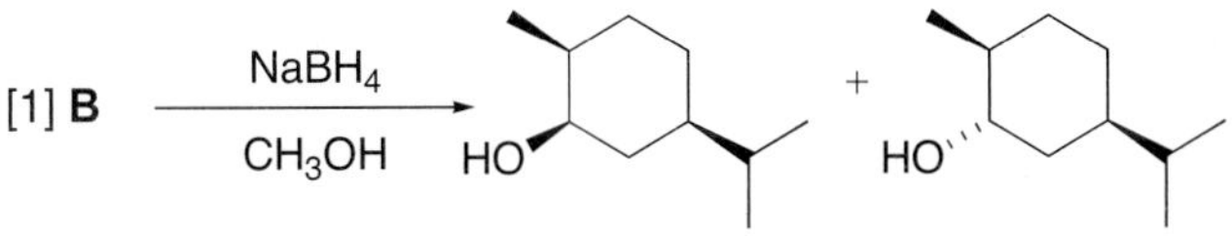
[1] B
NaBH4
CH3OH
HO
+
HO

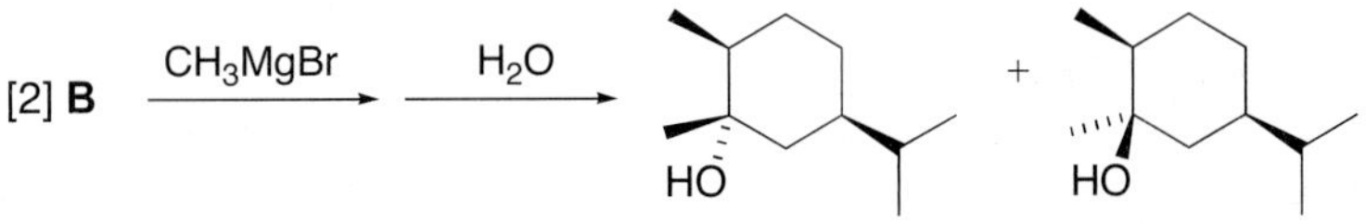
[2] B
CH3MgBr
H2O
HO
+
HO

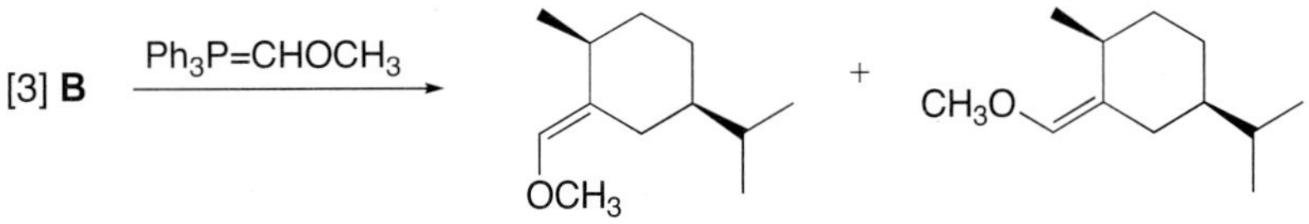
[3] B
Ph3P=CHOCH3
OCH3
+
CH3O

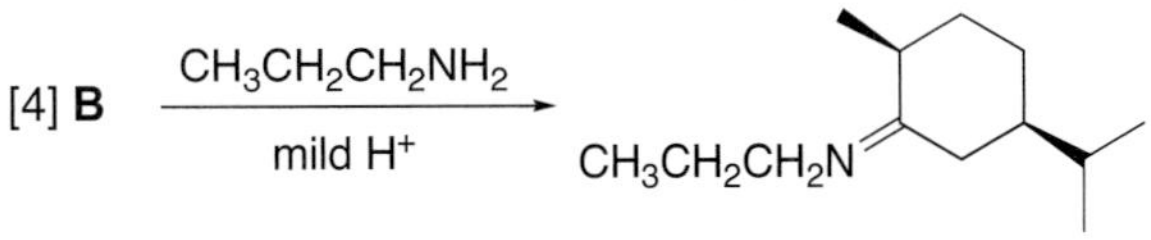
[4] B
CH3CH2CH2NH2
mild H+
CH3CH2CH2N

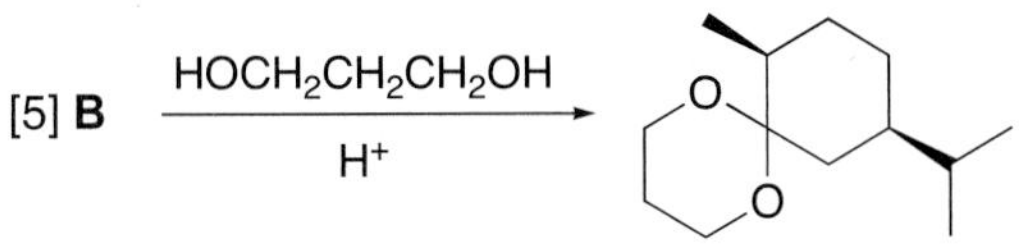
[5] B
HOCH2CH2CH2OH
H+
O
O

21.40 The least hindered carbonyl group is the most reactive.

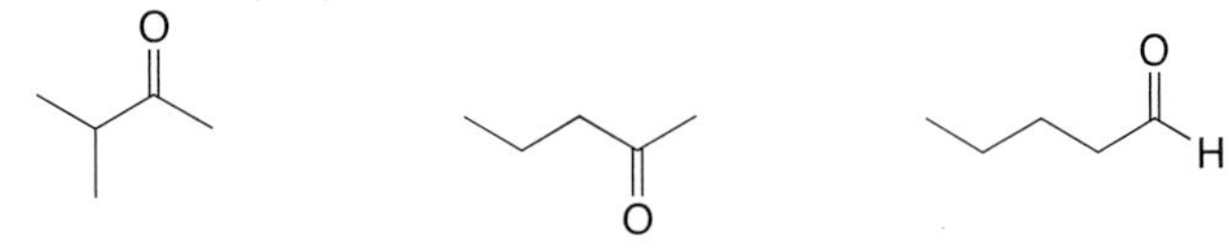
O
O
O
H

least reactive | intermediate reactivity | most reactive

21.41

a. 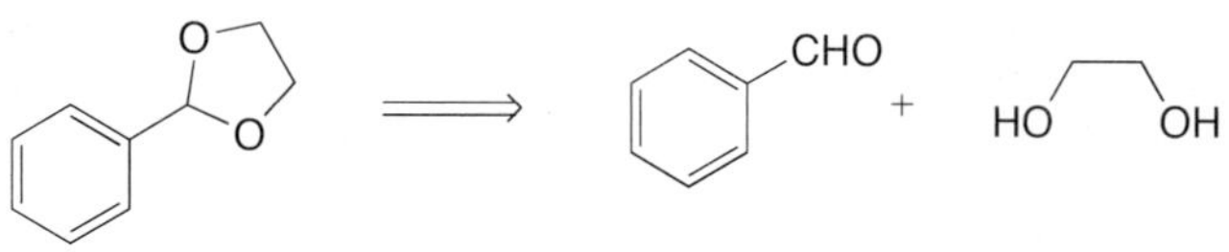

b. 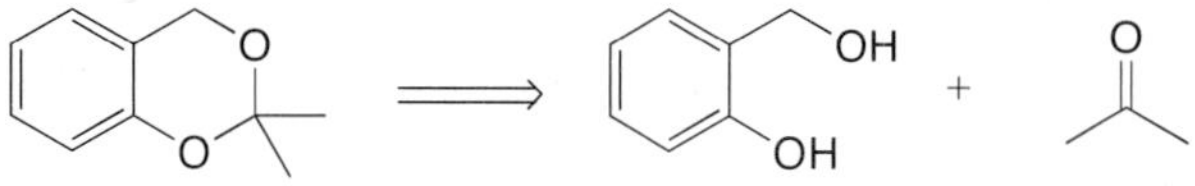

21.42 Use the rules from Answers 21.3 and 21.5 to name the aldehydes and ketones.

a. 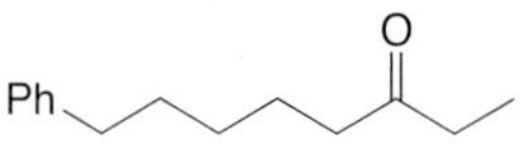
8 C = octanone
8-phenyl-3-octanone

b. 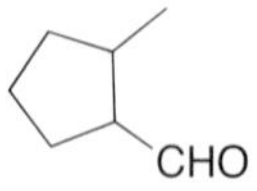
5 C ring
2-methyl-cyclopentanecarbaldehyde

c. 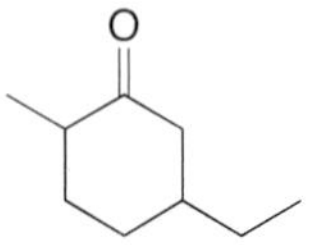
6 C ring = cyclohexanone
5-ethyl-2-methyl-cyclohexanone

d. 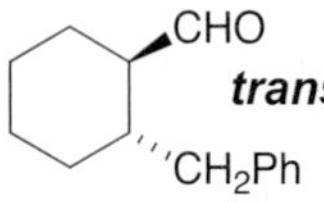
***trans*-2-benzylcyclohexanecarbaldehyde**

e. 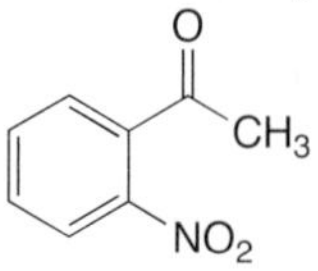
***o*-nitroacetophenone**

f. 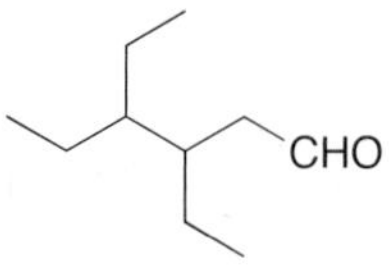
6 C = hexanal
3,4-diethylhexanal

g. 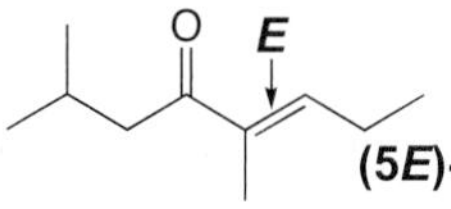
8 C = octenone
(5*E*)-2,5-dimethyl-5-octen-4-one

h. 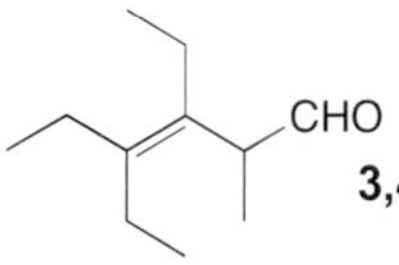
6 C = hexenal
3,4-diethyl-2-methyl-3-hexenal

21.43

a. 2-methyl-3-phenylbutanal

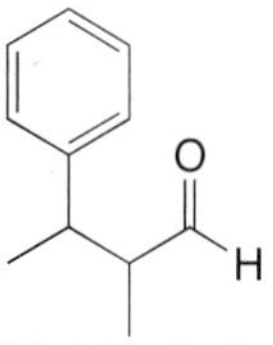

b. dipropyl ketone

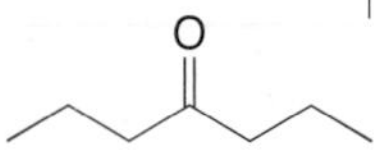

c. 3,3-dimethylcyclohexanecarbaldehyde

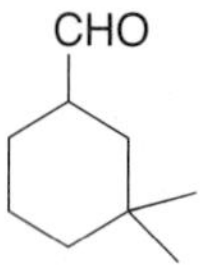

d. α-methoxypropionaldehyde

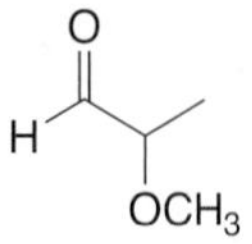

e. 3-benzoylcyclopentanone

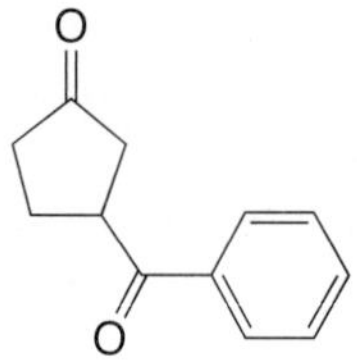

f. 2-formylcyclopentanone

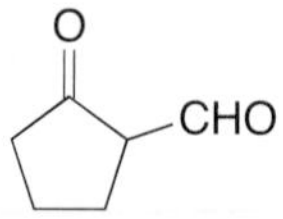

g. (3*R*)-3-methyl-2-heptanone

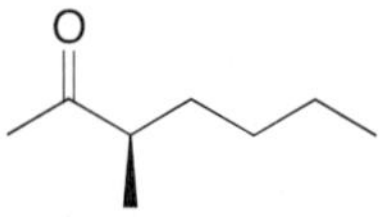

h. *m*-acetylbenzaldehyde

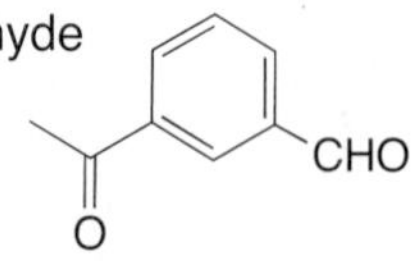

i. 2-*sec*-butyl-3-cyclopentenone

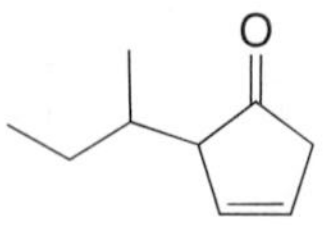

j. 5,6-dimethyl-1-cyclohexenecarbaldehyde

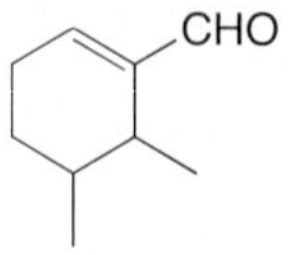

21.44

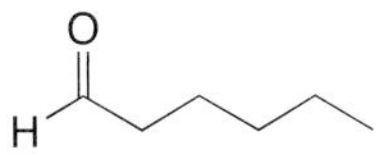

hexanal

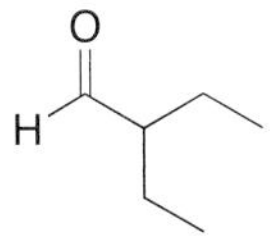

2-ethylbutanal

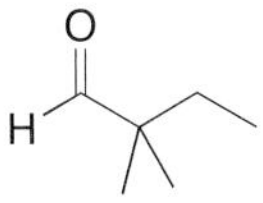

2,2-dimethylbutanal

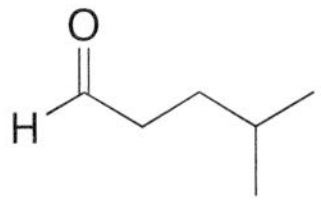

4-methylpentanal

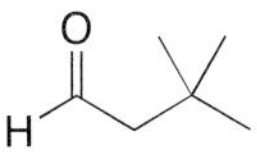

3,3-dimethylbutanal

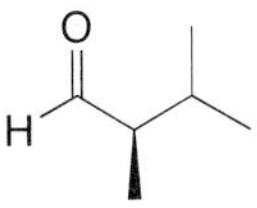

(2*R*)-2,3-dimethylbutanal

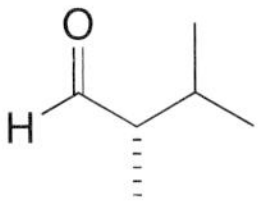

(2*S*)-2,3-dimethylbutanal

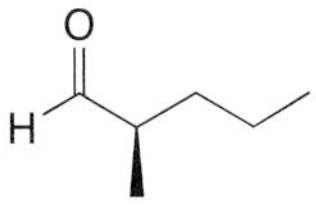

(2*R*)-2-methylpentanal

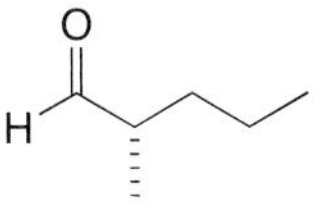

(2*S*)-2-methylpentanal

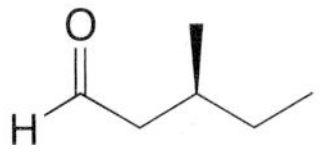

(3*S*)-3-methylpentanal

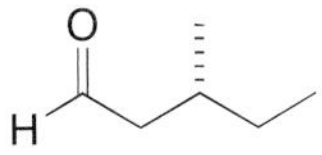

(3*R*)-3-methylpentanal

21.45

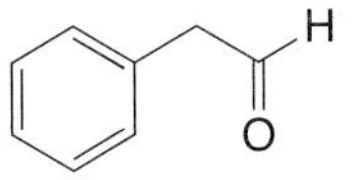

= $C_6H_5CH_2CHO$ phenylacetaldehyde

a. $NaBH_4$, CH_3OH → $C_6H_5CH_2CH_2OH$

b. [1] $LiAlH_4$; [2] H_2O → $C_6H_5CH_2CH_2OH$

c. [1] CH_3MgBr; [2] H_2O → $C_6H_5CH_2CH(OH)CH_3$

d. NaCN, HCl → $C_6H_5CH_2CH(OH)CN$

e. $Ph_3P{=}CHCH_3$ → $C_6H_5CH_2CH{=}CHCH_3$ (*E* and *Z* isomers)

f. $(CH_3)_2CHNH_2$, mild acid →

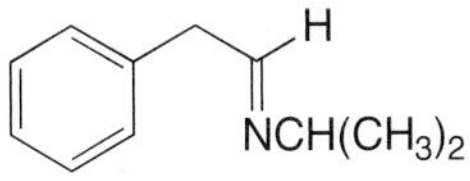

g. $(CH_3CH_2)_2NH$, mild acid →

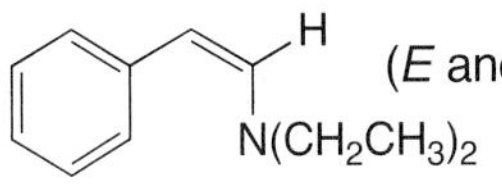

(*E* and *Z* isomers)

h. CH_3CH_2OH (excess), H^+ →

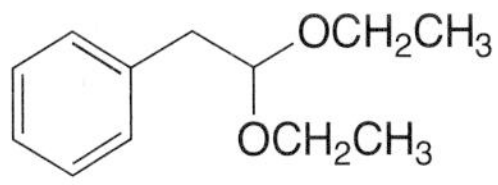

i.

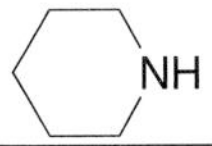

mild acid →

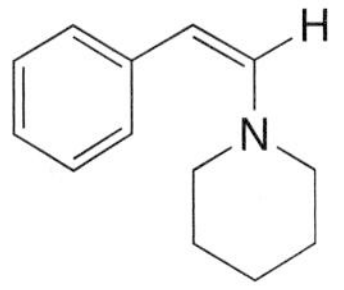

(*E* and *Z* isomers)

j.

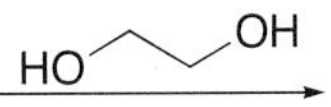

H^+ →

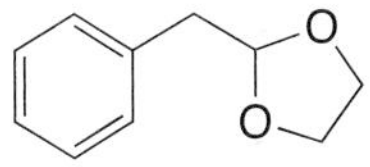

21.46

a. CH_3CH_2Cl → [1] Ph_3P; [2] BuLi; [3] $(CH_3)_2C{=}O$ → $CH_3CH{=}C(CH_3)_2$

b.

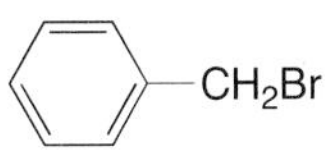

[1] Ph_3P; [2] BuLi; [3] $C_6H_5CH_2CH_2CHO$ →

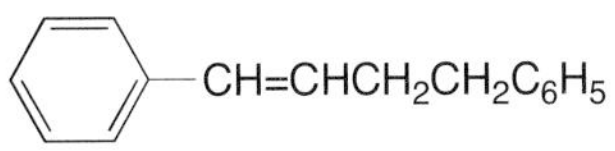

(*E* and *Z* isomers)

c.

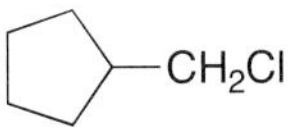

[1] Ph_3P; [2] BuLi; [3] $CH_3CH_2CH_2CHO$ →

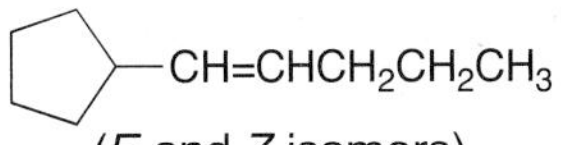

(*E* and *Z* isomers)

21.47

a. $Ph_3P{=}CHCH_2CH_2CH_3 \Longrightarrow BrCH_2CH_2CH_2CH_3$

b. $Ph_3P{=}C(CH_2CH_2CH_3)_2 \Longrightarrow BrCH(CH_2CH_2CH_3)_2$

c. $Ph_3P{=}CHCH{=}CH_2 \Longrightarrow BrCH_2CH{=}CH_2$

21.48

a. 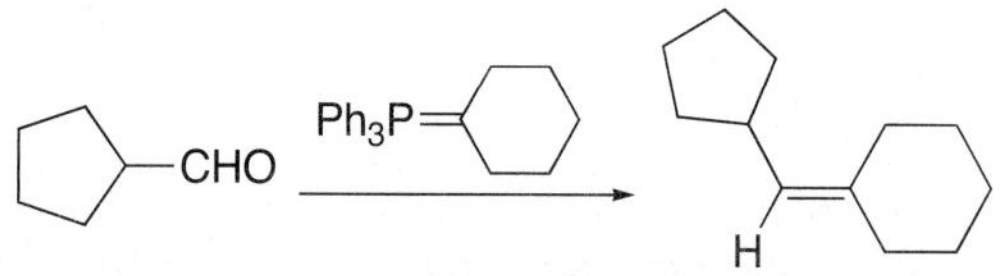

b. 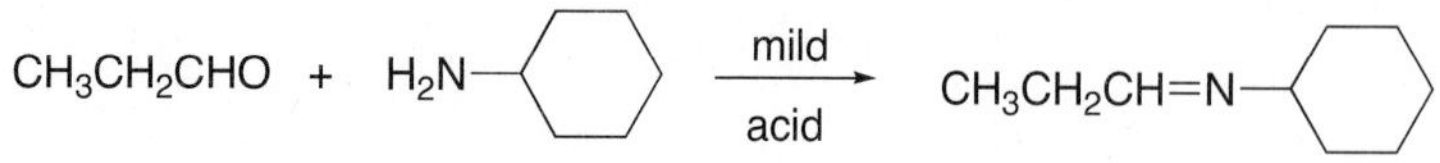

c. 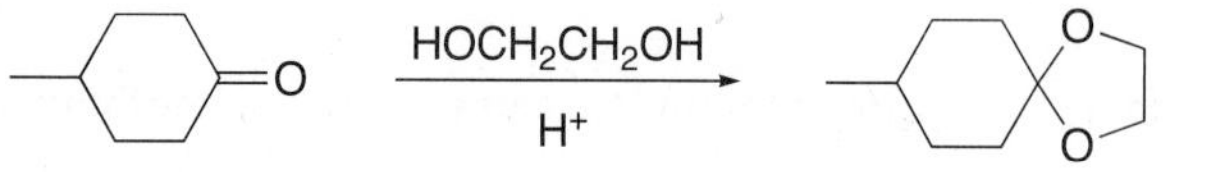

d. 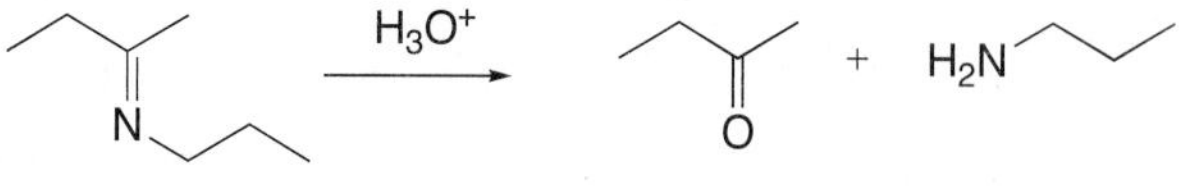

e. 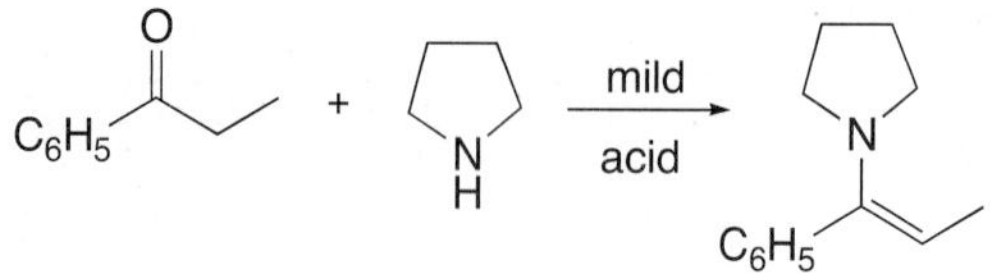

(*E* and *Z* isomers)

f. 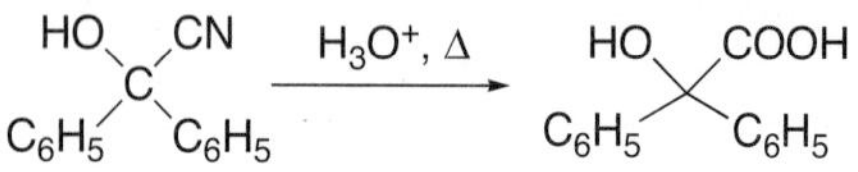

g. 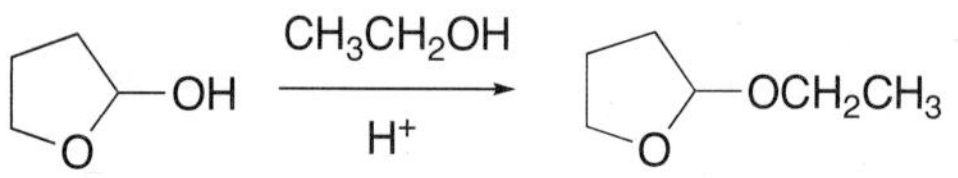

h. 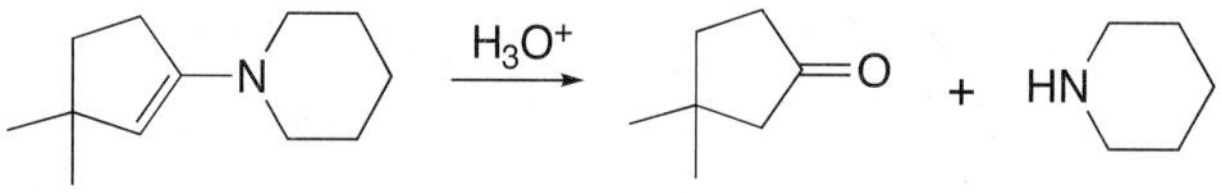

i. 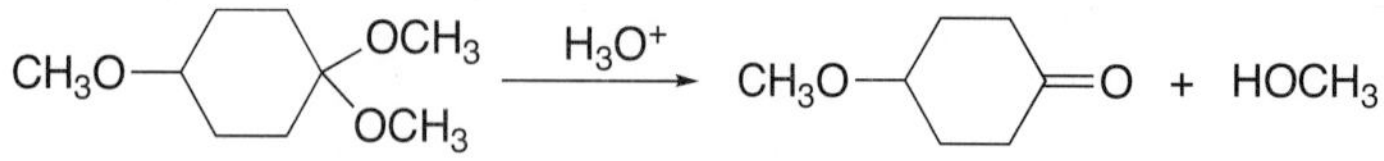

j. 

21.49

a. 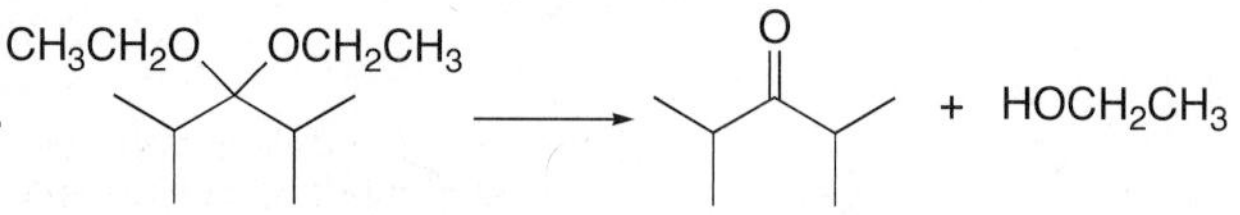

b. 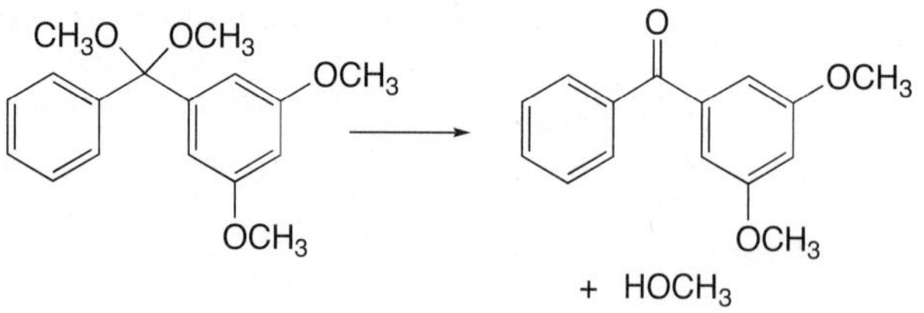

c. 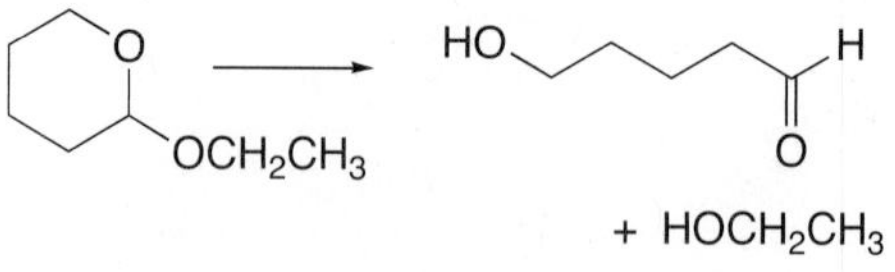

21.50 Consider para product only, when an ortho, para mixture can result.

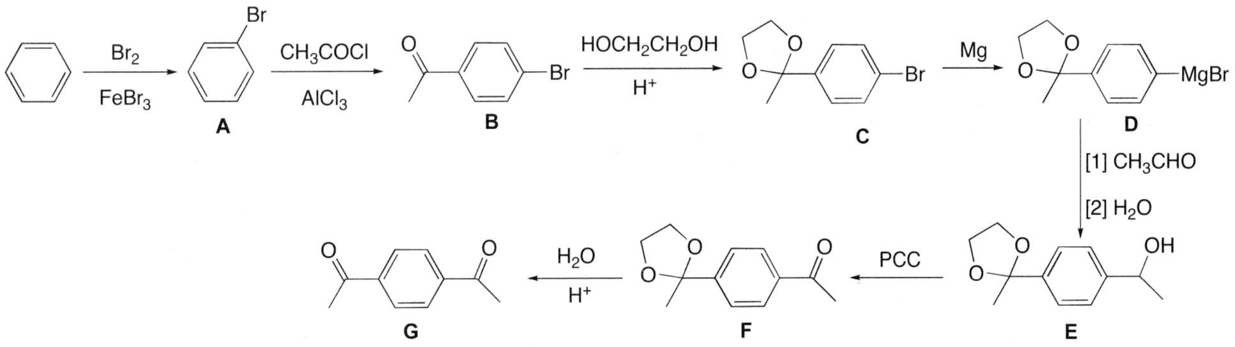
Br2
FeBr3
A
CH3COCl
AlCl3
B
HOCH2CH2OH
H+
C
Mg
D
[1] CH3CHO
[2] H2O
E
PCC
F
H2O
H+
G

21.51

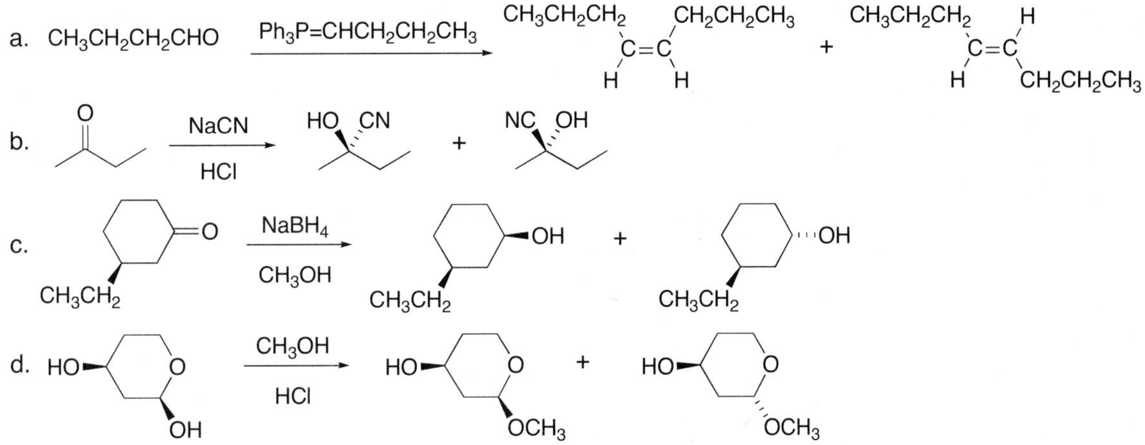
a. CH3CH2CH2CHO
Ph3P=CHCH2CH2CH3
b.
NaCN
HCl
c.
NaBH4
CH3OH
d.
CH3OH
HCl

21.52

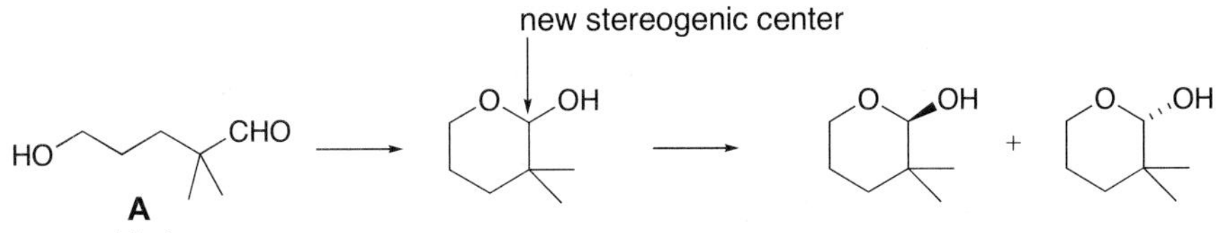
new stereogenic center
A
achiral

An equal mixture of enantiomers results, so the product is optically inactive.

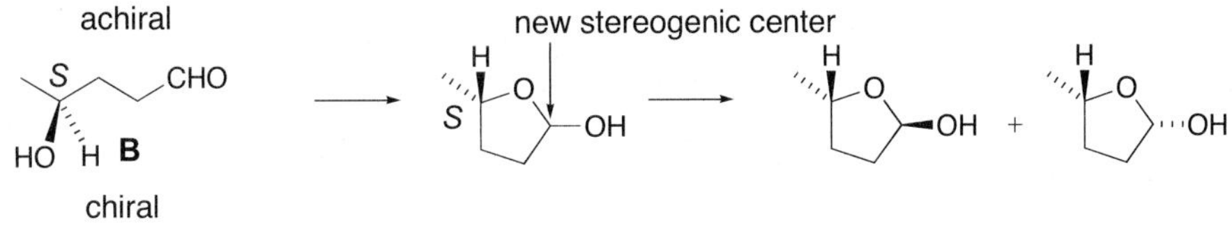
new stereogenic center
B
chiral

A mixture of diastereomers results. Both compounds are chiral and they are not enantiomers, so the mixture is optically active.

21.53

a.

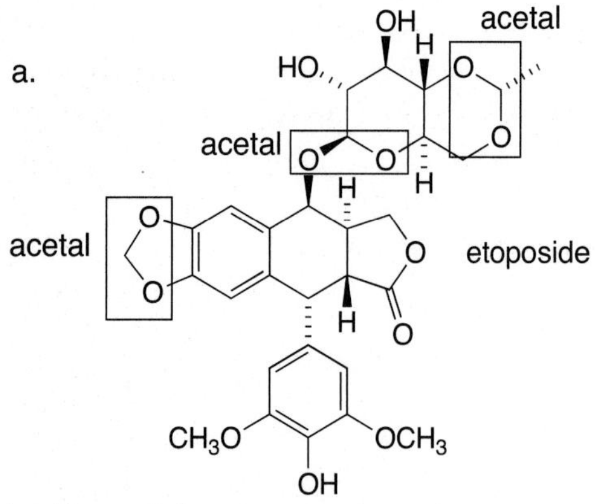
acetal
acetal
acetal
HO
OH
H
O
etoposide
CH3O
OCH3
OH

b. Lines of cleavage are drawn in.

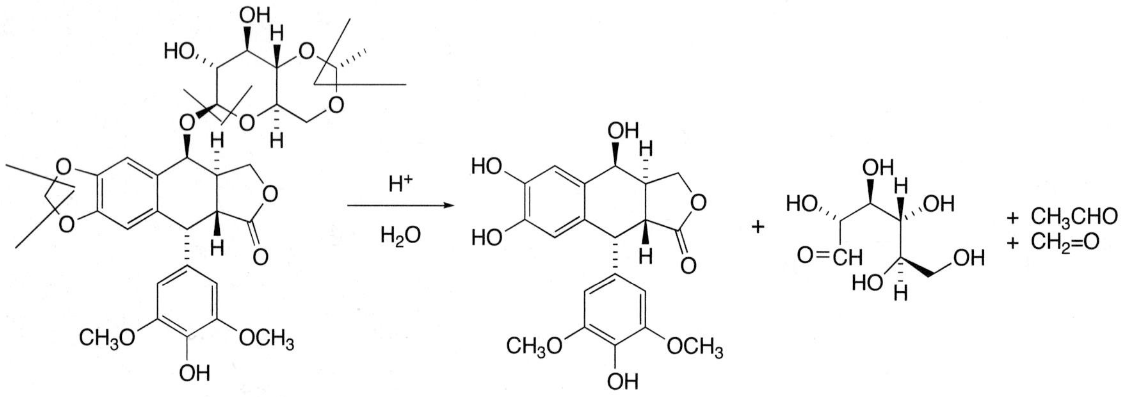
H+
H2O
+ CH3CHO
+ CH2=O
O=CH

21.54 Use the rules from Answer 21.1.

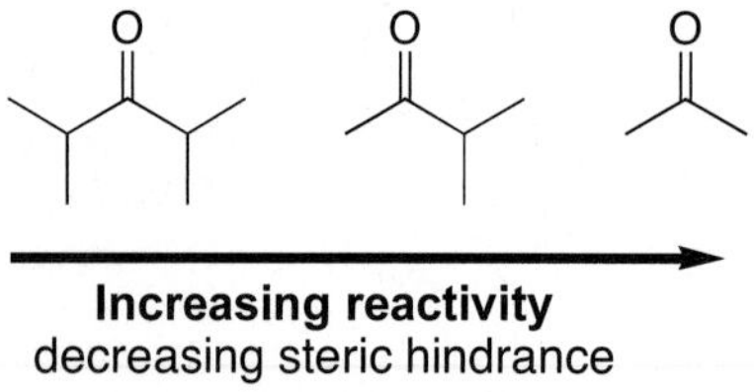
Increasing reactivity
decreasing steric hindrance

21.55 The less stable carbonyl compound forms the higher percentage of hydrate.

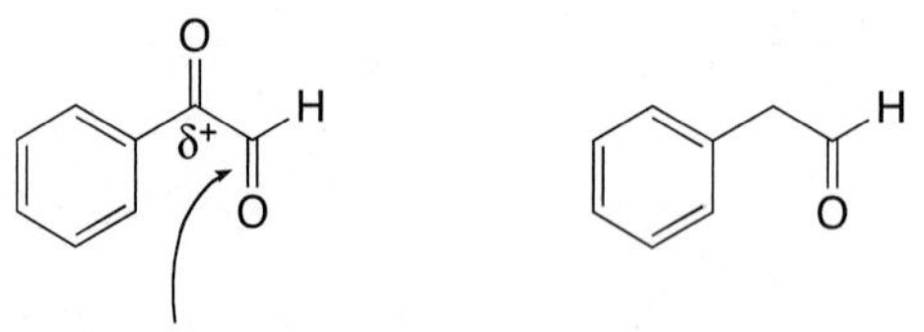
δ+

The aldehyde is destabilized since there is a δ^+ on its adjacent carbon, which is part of a C=O. Thus, PhCOCHO has the higher concentration of hydrate.

21.56 Electron-donating groups decrease the amount of hydrate at equilibrium by stabilizing the carbonyl starting material. Electron-withdrawing groups increase the amount of hydrate at equilibrium by destabilizing the carbonyl starting material. Electron-donating groups make the IR absorption of the C=O shift to lower wavenumber because they stabilize the charge-separated resonance form, giving the C=O more single bond character.

O_2N
$COCH_3$
CH_3O
$COCH_3$

	p-nitroacetophenone	*p*-methoxyacetophenone
a.	NO_2 withdrawing group **less stable**	CH_3O donating group **more stable**
b.	**higher percentage of hydrate**	**lower percentage of hydrate**
c.	**higher wavenumber**	**lower wavenumber**

21.57 Use the principles from Answer 21.21.

a.

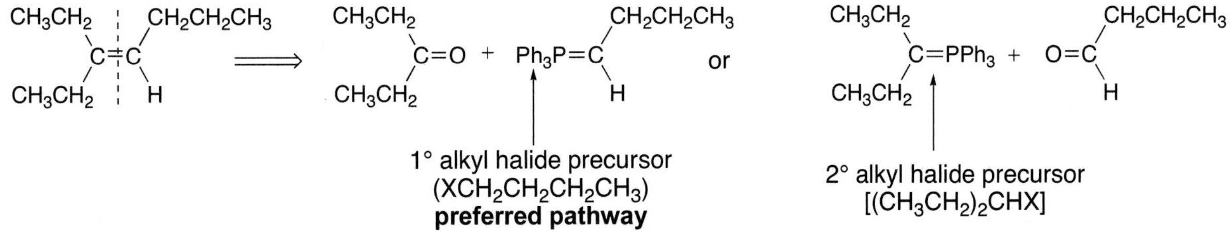

or
1° alkyl halide precursor
($XCH_2CH_2CH_2CH_3$)
preferred pathway
2° alkyl halide precursor
[$(CH_3CH_2)_2CHX$]

b.

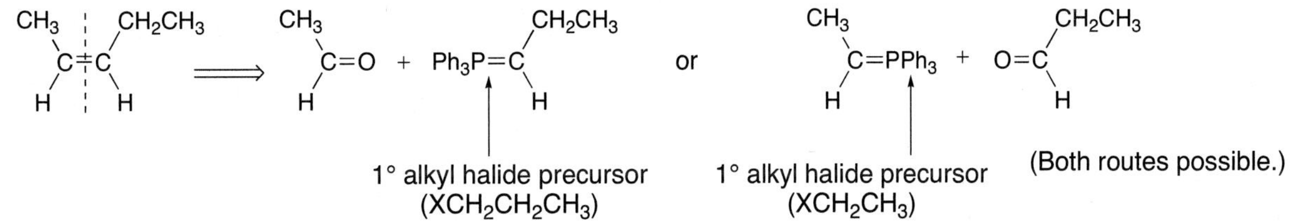

or
1° alkyl halide precursor
($XCH_2CH_2CH_3$)
1° alkyl halide precursor
(XCH_2CH_3)
(Both routes possible.)

c.

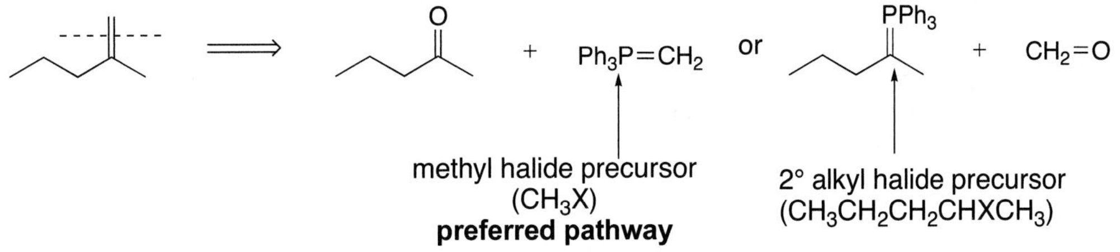

or
methyl halide precursor
(CH_3X)
preferred pathway
2° alkyl halide precursor
($CH_3CH_2CH_2CHXCH_3$)

d.

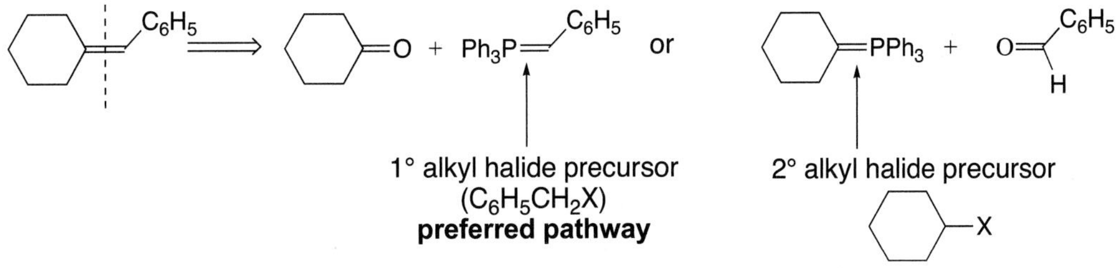

or
1° alkyl halide precursor
($C_6H_5CH_2X$)
preferred pathway
2° alkyl halide precursor

21.58

a.

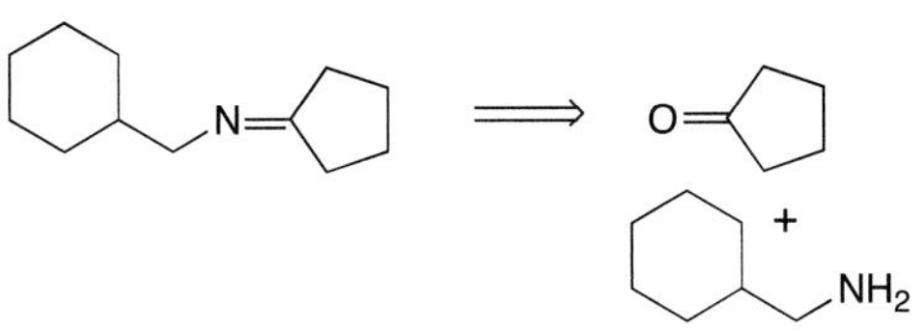

b.

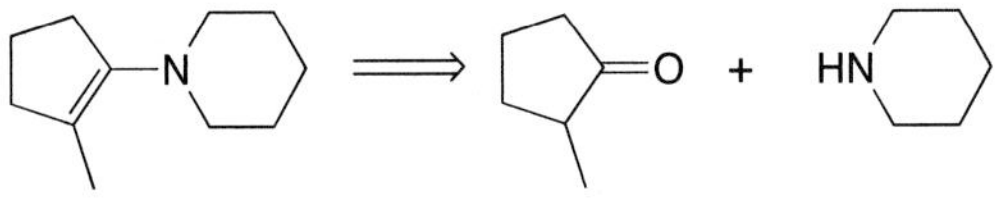

c.

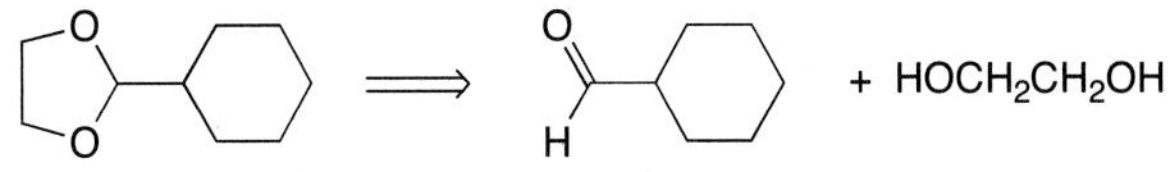

+ $HOCH_2CH_2OH$

d.

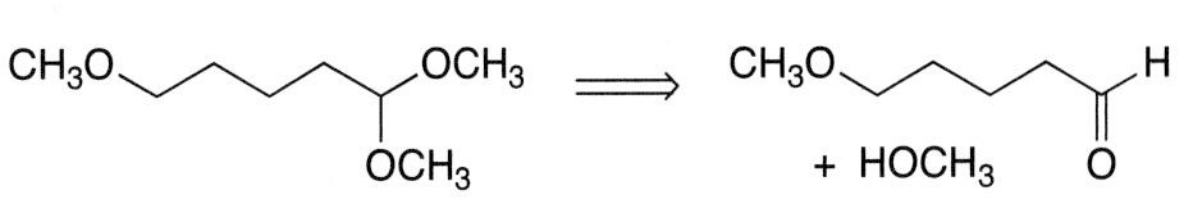

+ $HOCH_3$

21.59

a. $C_6H_5–CH_2OH \xrightarrow{\text{PCC}} C_6H_5–CHO$

b. $C_6H_5–COCl \xrightarrow[\text{[2] } H_2O]{\text{[1] LiAlH[OC(CH}_3)_3]_3} C_6H_5–CHO$

c. $C_6H_5–COOCH_3 \xrightarrow[\text{[2] } H_2O]{\text{[1] DIBAL-H}} C_6H_5–CHO$

d. $C_6H_5–COOH \xrightarrow[\text{[2] } H_2O]{\text{[1] LiAlH}_4} C_6H_5–CH_2OH \xrightarrow{\text{PCC}} C_6H_5–CHO$

e. $C_6H_5–CH_3 \xrightarrow{\text{KMnO}_4} C_6H_5–COOH \xrightarrow[\text{[2] } H_2O]{\text{[1] LiAlH}_4} C_6H_5–CH_2OH \xrightarrow{\text{PCC}} C_6H_5–CHO$

f. $C_6H_5–CH{=}CH_2 \xrightarrow[\text{[2] Zn, } H_2O]{\text{[1] } O_3} C_6H_5–CHO$

g. $C_6H_5–CH{=}NCH_2CH_2CH_3 \xrightarrow[H^+]{H_2O} C_6H_5–CHO$

h. $C_6H_5–CH(OCH_2CH_3)_2 \xrightarrow[H^+]{H_2O} C_6H_5–CHO$

21.60

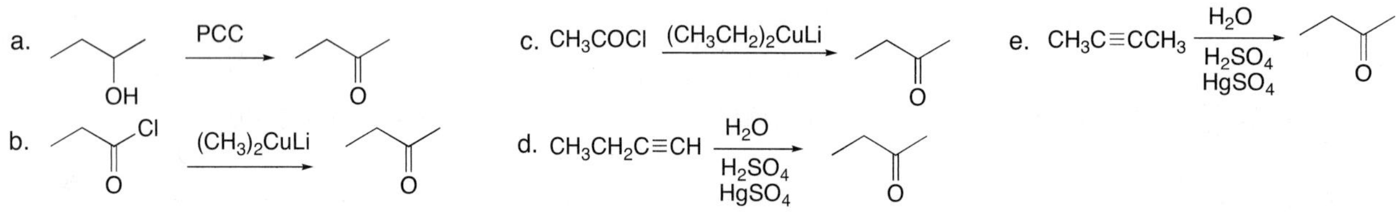
a.
PCC
OH
O
b.
Cl
(CH3)2CuLi
c. CH3COCl
(CH3CH2)2CuLi
d. CH3CH2C≡CH
H2O
H2SO4
HgSO4
e. CH3C≡CCH3

21.61

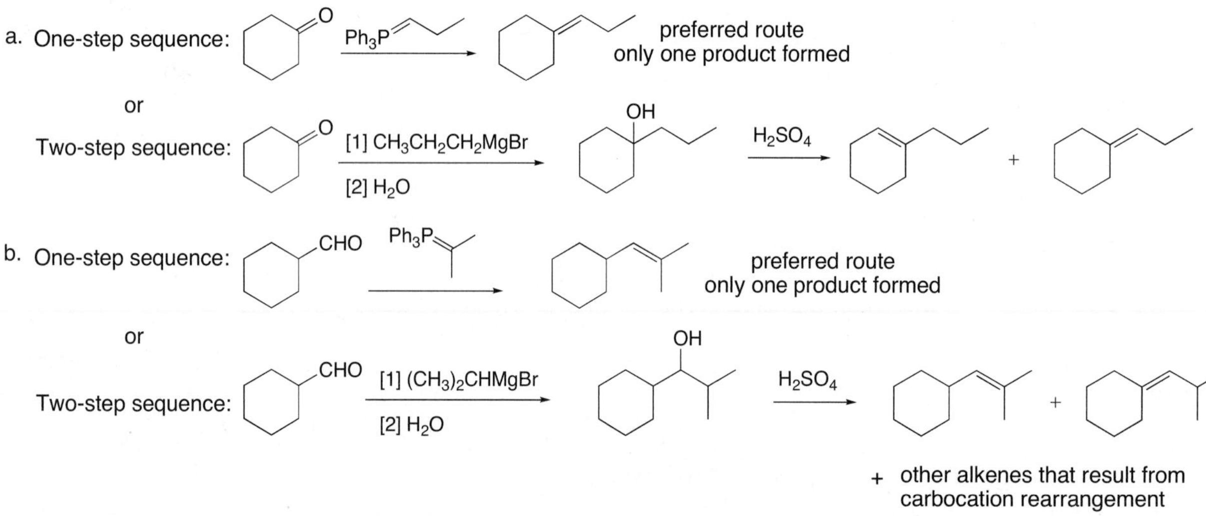
a. One-step sequence:
Ph3P
preferred route
only one product formed
or
Two-step sequence:
[1] CH3CH2CH2MgBr
[2] H2O
OH
H2SO4
+
b. One-step sequence:
CHO
Ph3P
preferred route
only one product formed
or
Two-step sequence:
[1] (CH3)2CHMgBr
[2] H2O
+ other alkenes that result from
carbocation rearrangement

21.62

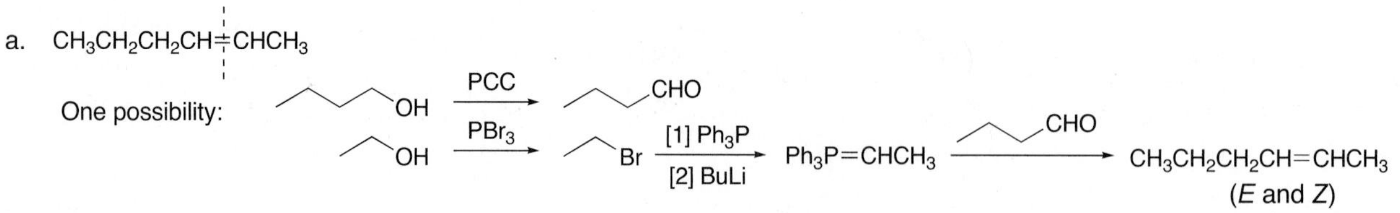
a. CH3CH2CH2CH=CHCH3
One possibility:
OH
PCC
CHO
PBr3
Br
[1] Ph3P
[2] BuLi
Ph3P=CHCH3
CH3CH2CH2CH=CHCH3
(E and Z)

b.

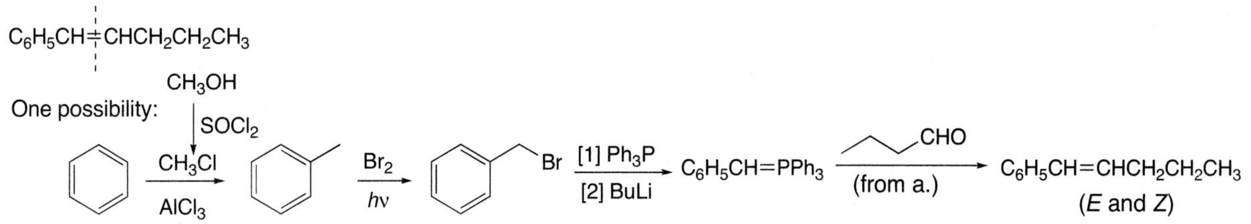
C6H5CH=CHCH2CH2CH3
One possibility:
CH3OH
SOCl2
CH3Cl
AlCl3
Br2
hν
Br
[1] Ph3P
[2] BuLi
C6H5CH=PPh3
CHO
(from a.)
C6H5CH=CHCH2CH2CH3
(E and Z)

c.

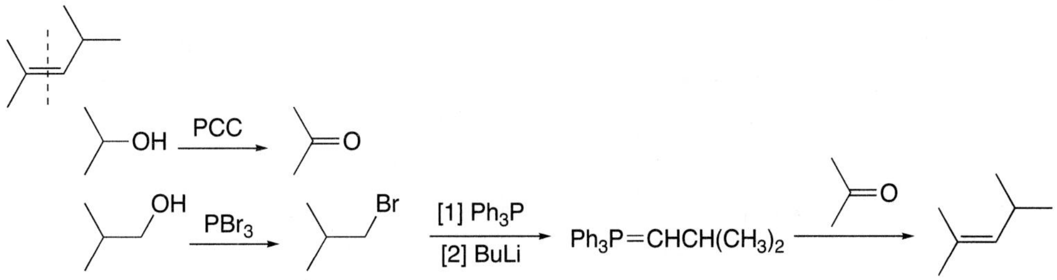
OH
PCC
O
OH
PBr3
Br
[1] Ph3P
[2] BuLi
Ph3P=CHCH(CH3)2
O

21.63

a.

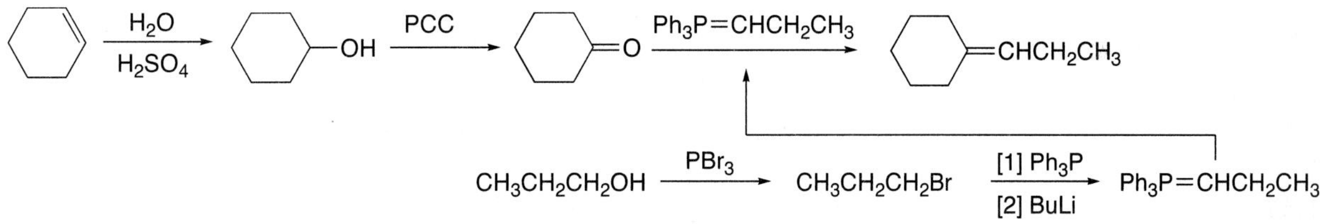
H2O
H2SO4
OH
PCC
O
Ph3P=CHCH2CH3
CHCH2CH3
CH3CH2CH2OH
PBr3
CH3CH2CH2Br
[1] Ph3P
[2] BuLi
Ph3P=CHCH2CH3

b.

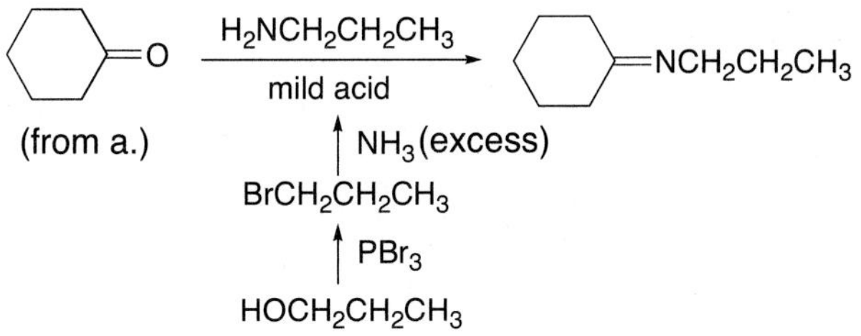
O
(from a.)
H2NCH2CH2CH3
mild acid
NCH2CH2CH3
NH3 (excess)
BrCH2CH2CH3
PBr3
HOCH2CH2CH3

c.

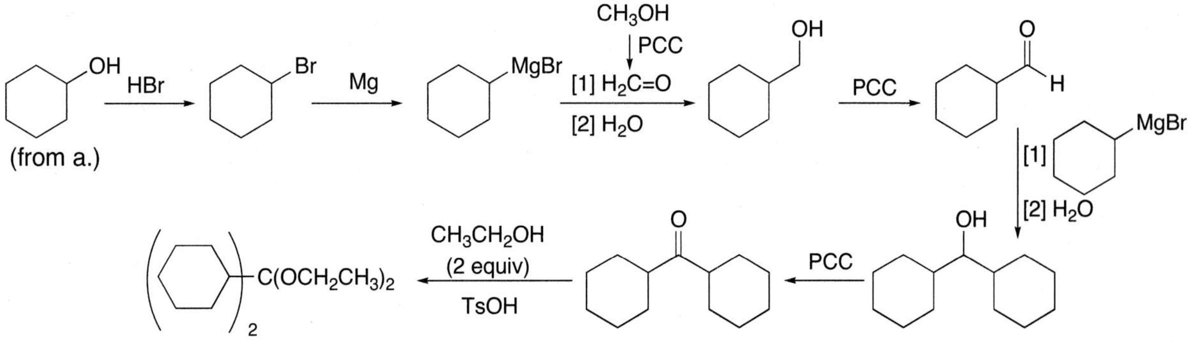
OH
(from a.)
HBr
Br
Mg
MgBr
CH3OH
PCC
[1] H2C=O
[2] H2O
OH
PCC
O
H
[1]
MgBr
[2] H2O
OH
PCC
O
CH3CH2OH
(2 equiv)
TsOH
C(OCH2CH3)2
2

d.

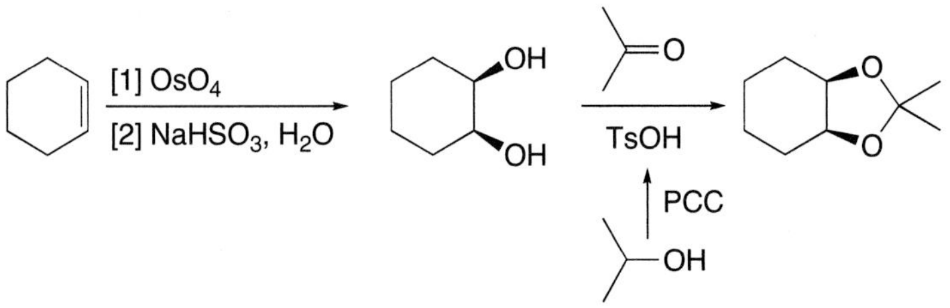
[1] OsO4
[2] NaHSO3, H2O
OH
OH
O
TsOH
PCC
OH
O
O

21.64

a.

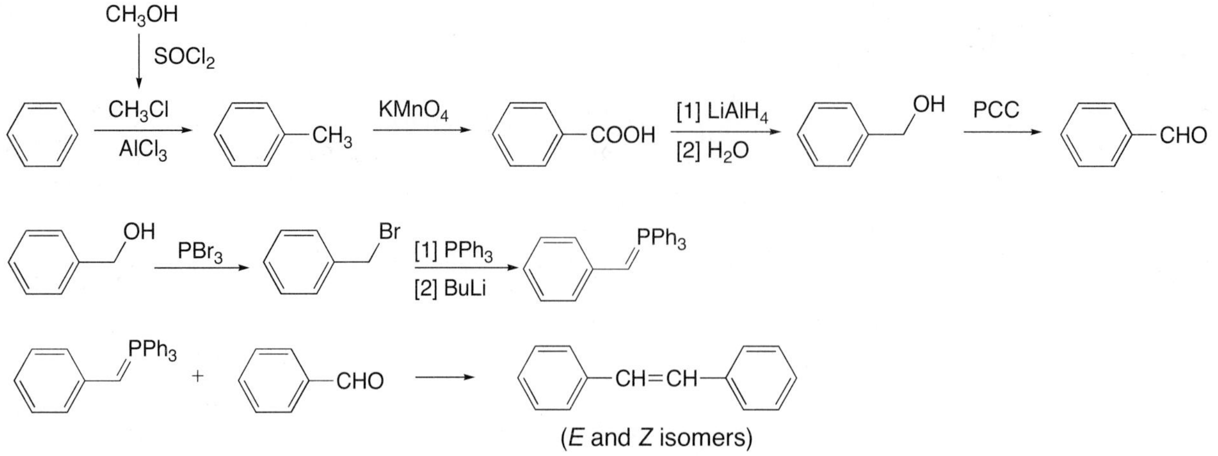

b.

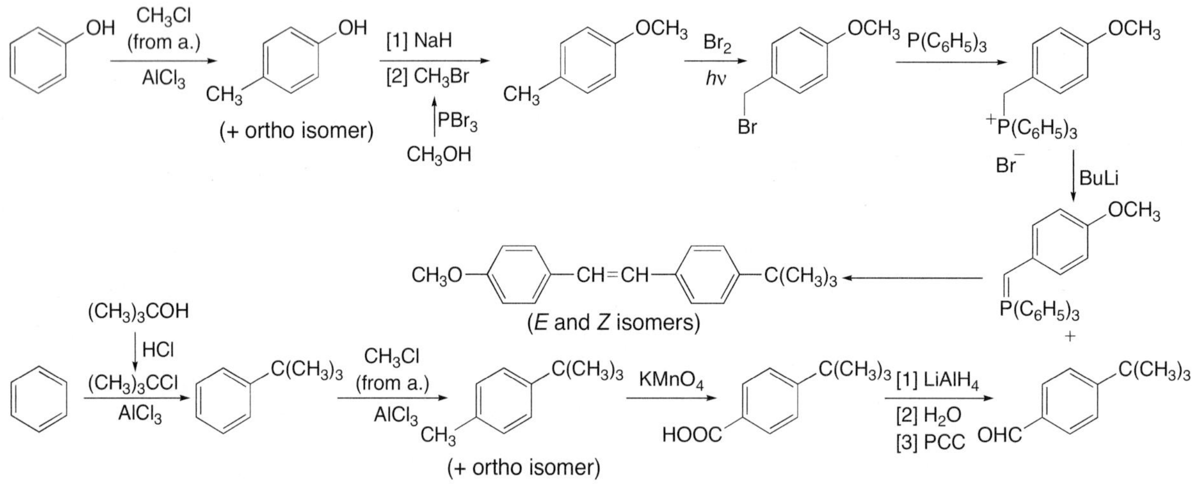

21.65

a.

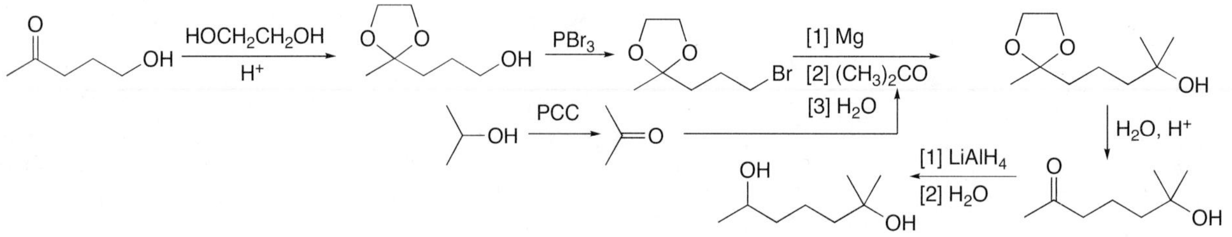

b.

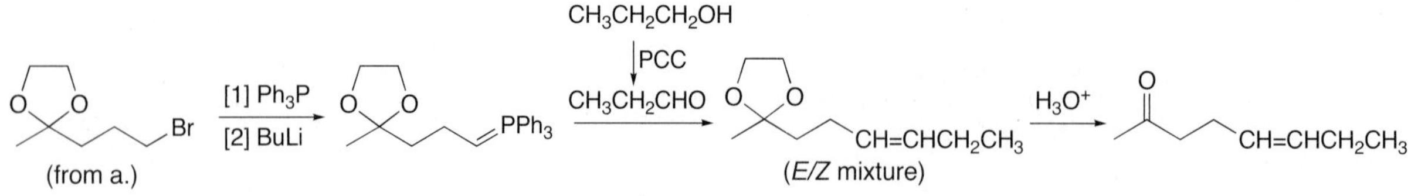

21.66

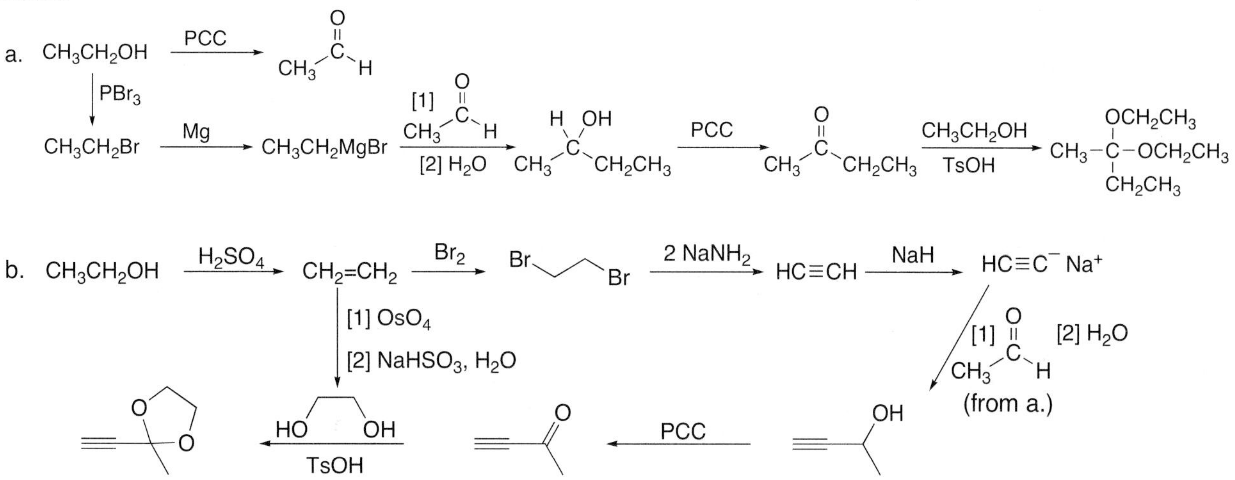

21.67

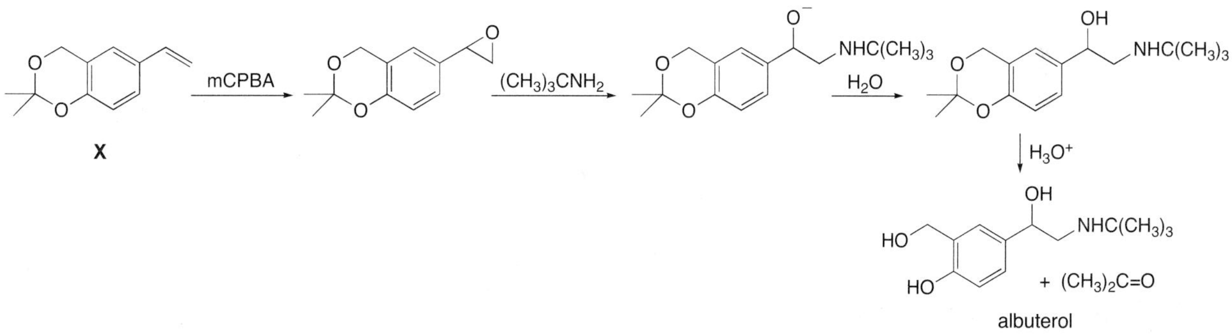

21.68

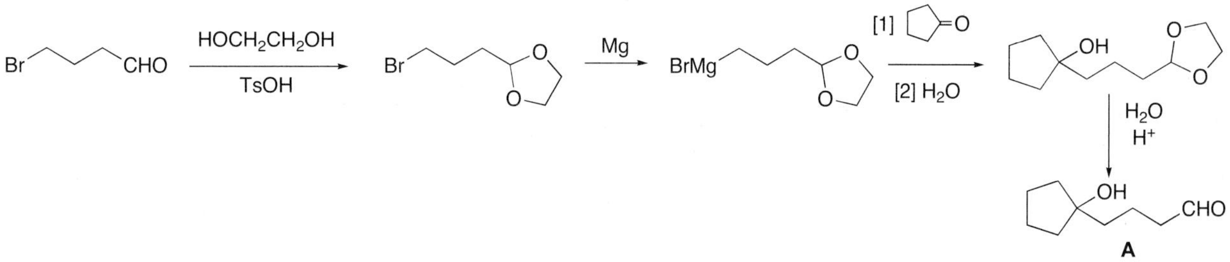

21.69

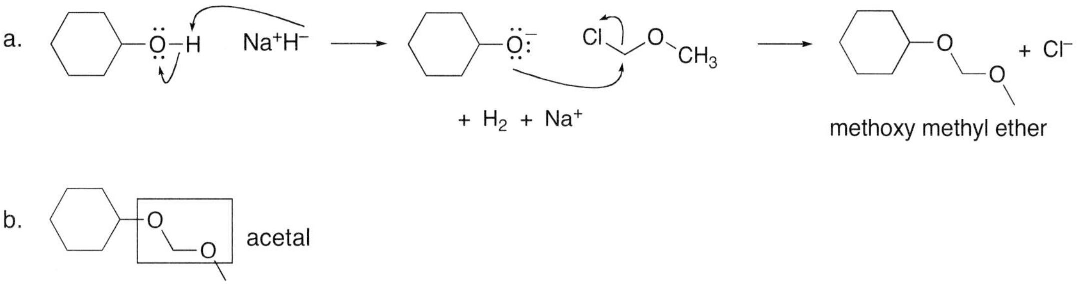

c.

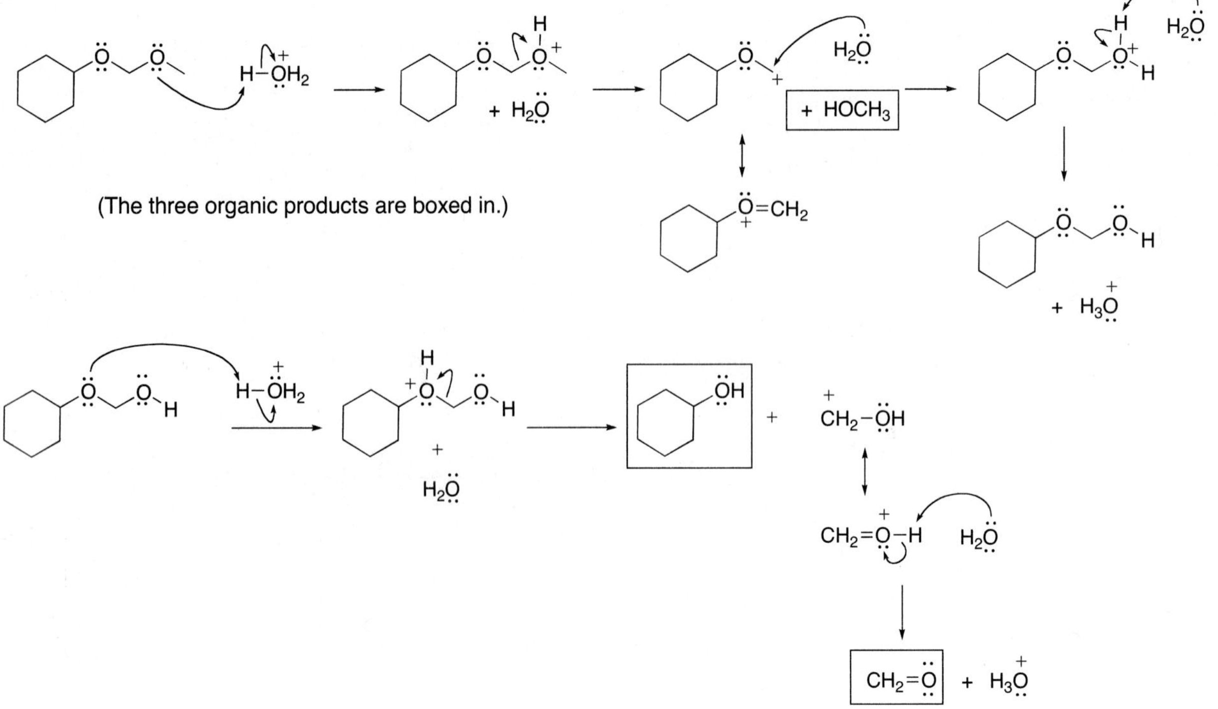
+ HOCH3
(The three organic products are boxed in.)

21.70

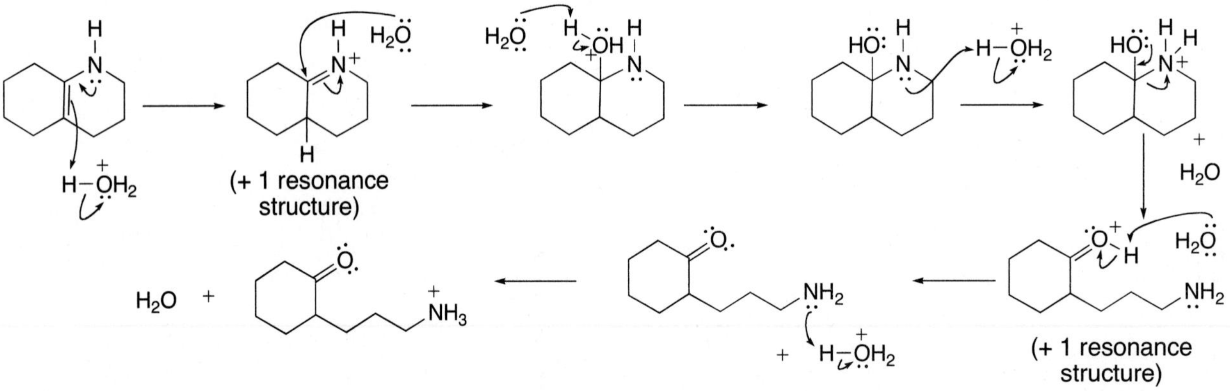
(+ 1 resonance structure)
(+ 1 resonance structure)

21.71

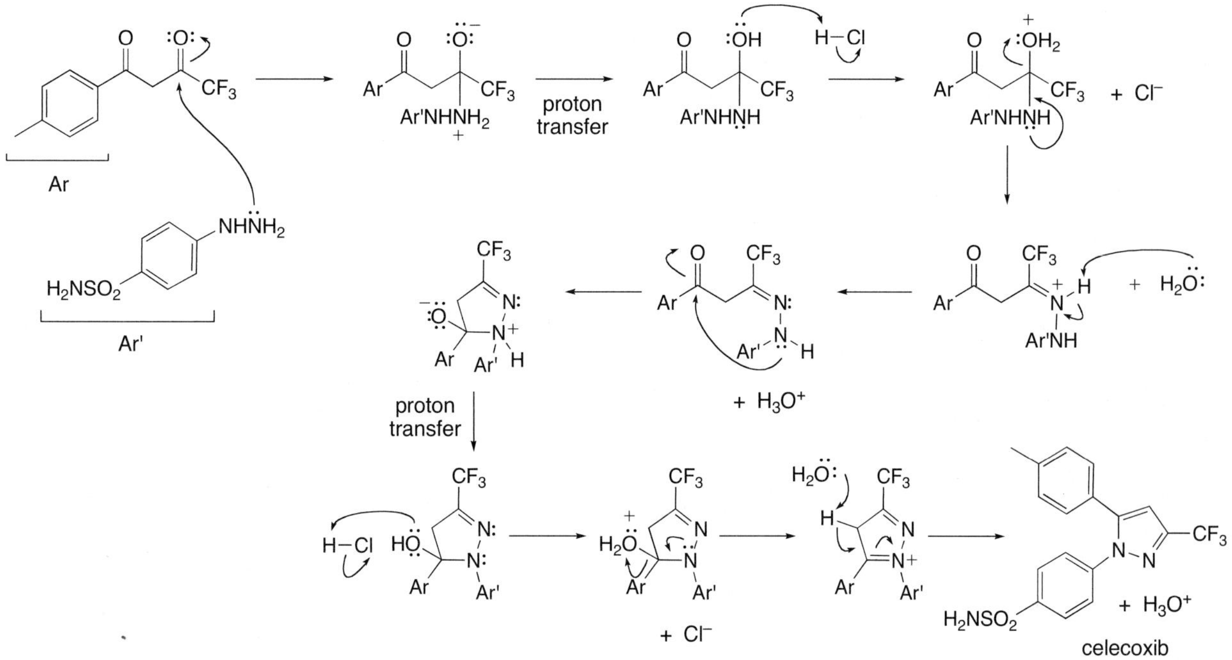
Ar
Ar'
proton
transfer
+ Cl⁻
+ H₃O⁺
+ Cl⁻
celecoxib

21.72 The OH groups react with the C=O in an intramolecular reaction, first to form a hemiacetal, and then to form an acetal.

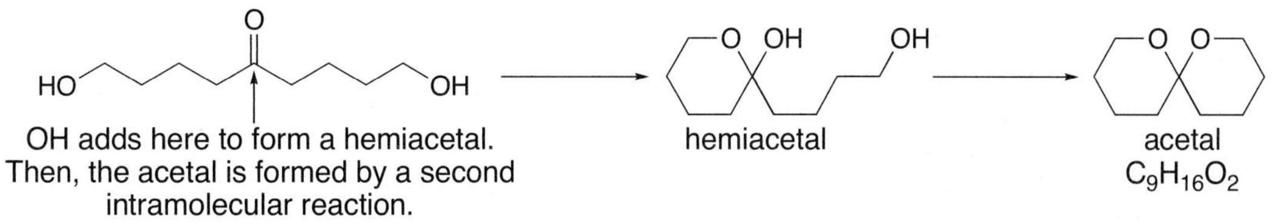
OH adds here to form a hemiacetal.
Then, the acetal is formed by a second intramolecular reaction.
hemiacetal
acetal
C9H16O2

21.73

a.

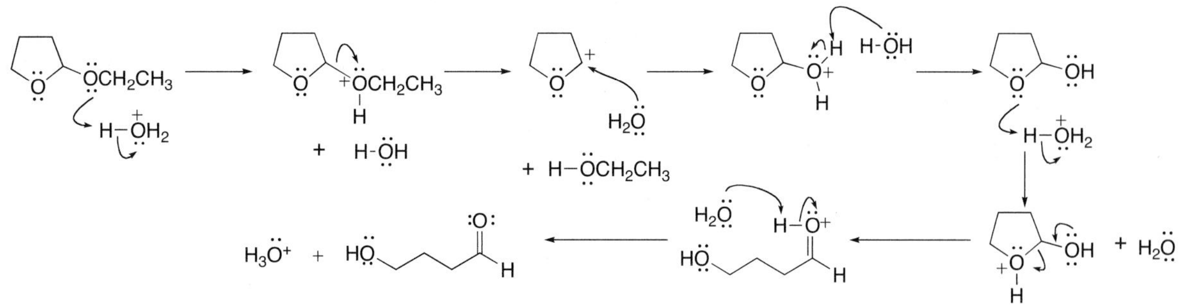

b.

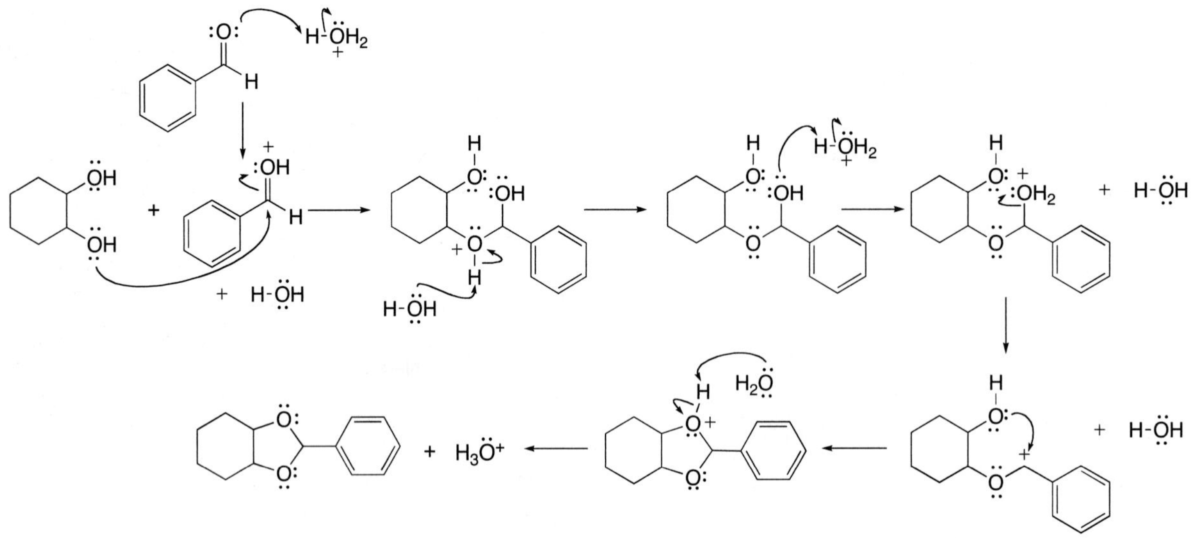

21.74

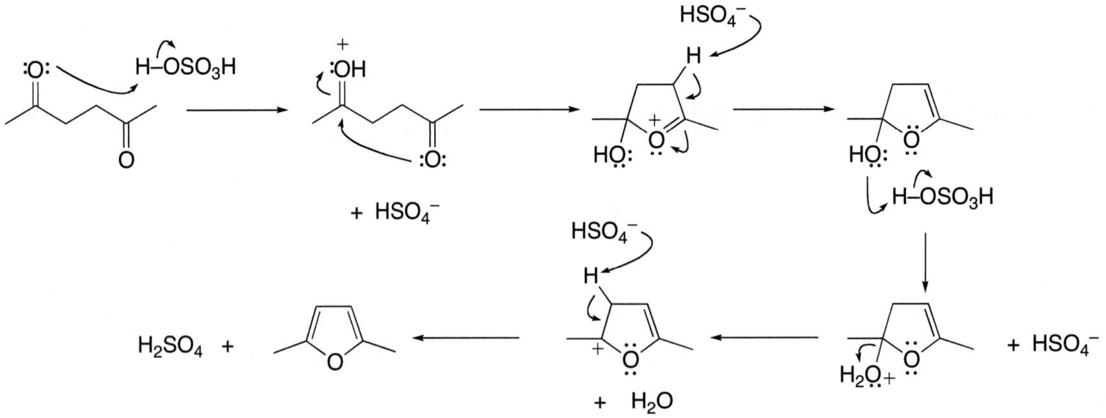

21.75

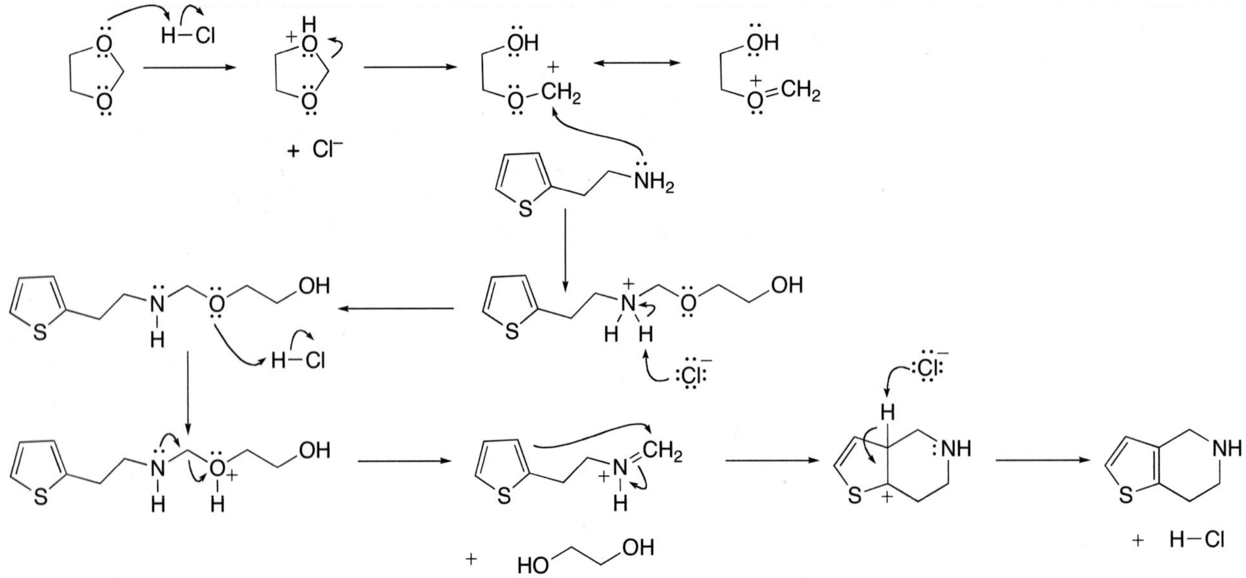

21.76

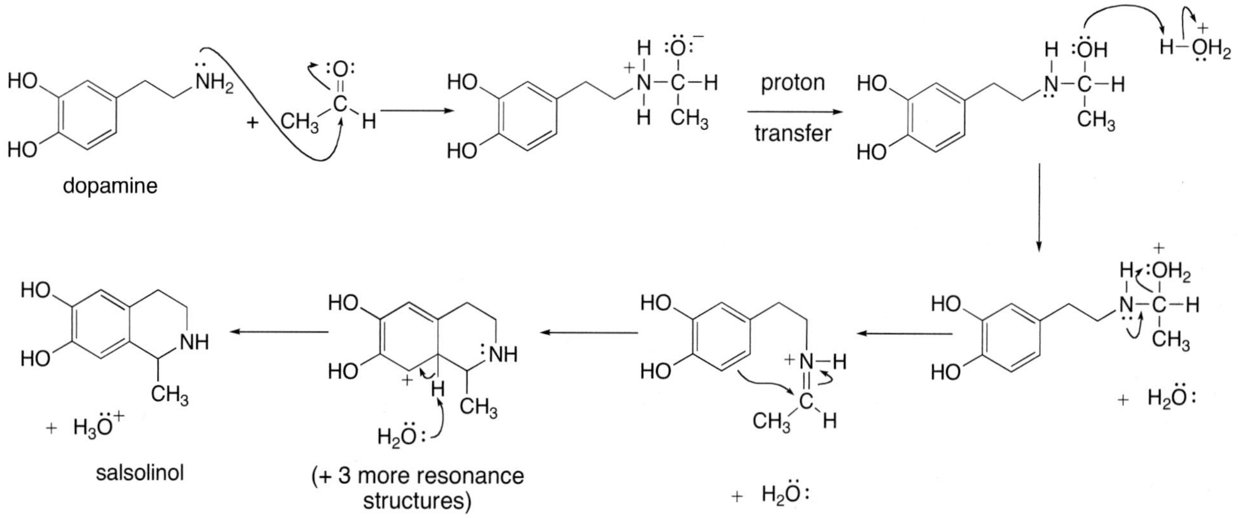
dopamine
proton
transfer
salsolinol
(+ 3 more resonance structures)

21.77

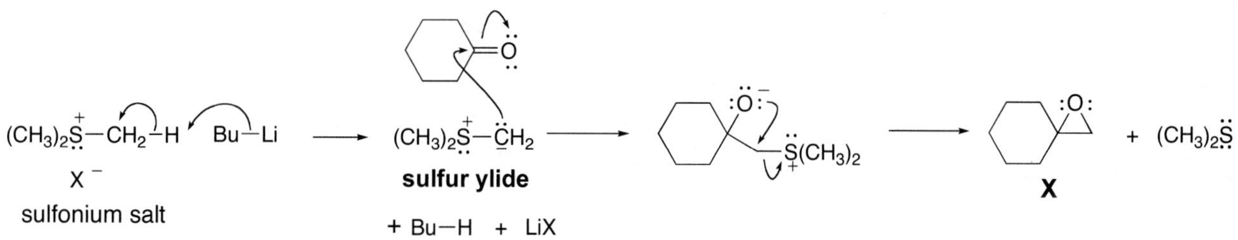
sulfonium salt
sulfur ylide
+ Bu—H + LiX
X

21.78 Hemiacetal **A** is in equilibrium with its acyclic hydroxy aldehyde. The aldehyde can undergo hydride reduction to form 1,4-butanediol and a Wittig reaction to form an alkene.

a.

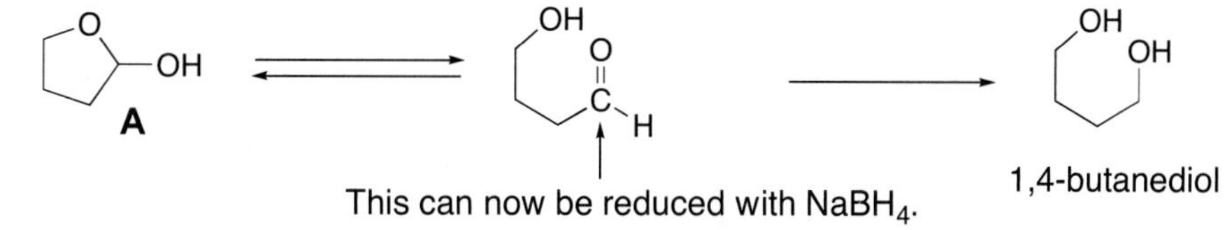
A
This can now be reduced with NaBH4.
1,4-butanediol

b.

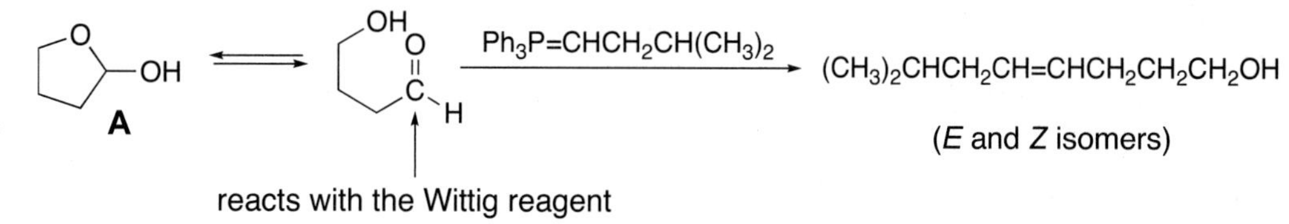
A
Ph3P=CHCH2CH(CH3)2
(CH3)2CHCH2CH=CHCH2CH2CH2OH
(E and Z isomers)
reacts with the Wittig reagent

c.

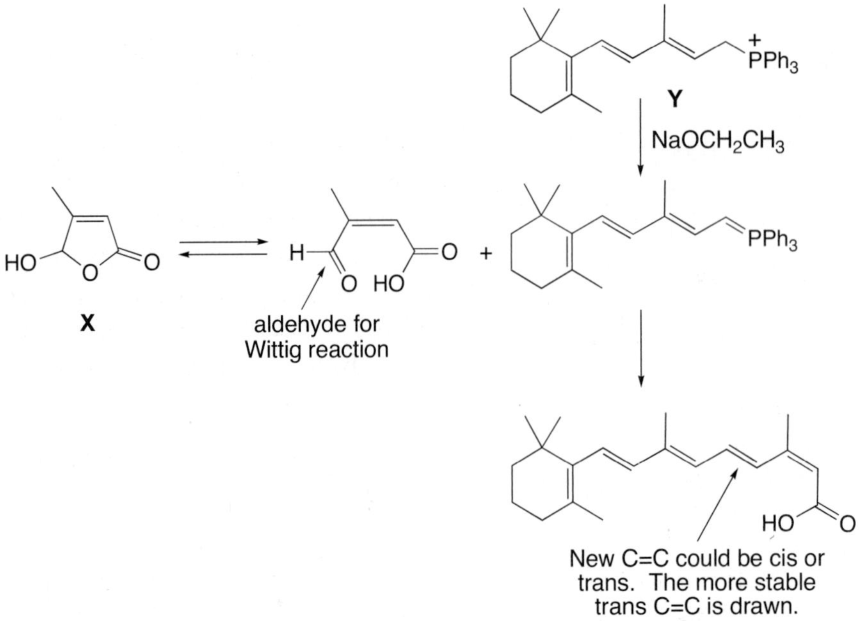

PPh3
Y
NaOCH2CH3
HO
O
X
H
O HO
aldehyde for
Wittig reaction
PPh3
HO
O
New C=C could be cis or
trans. The more stable
trans C=C is drawn.

isotretinoin

21.79

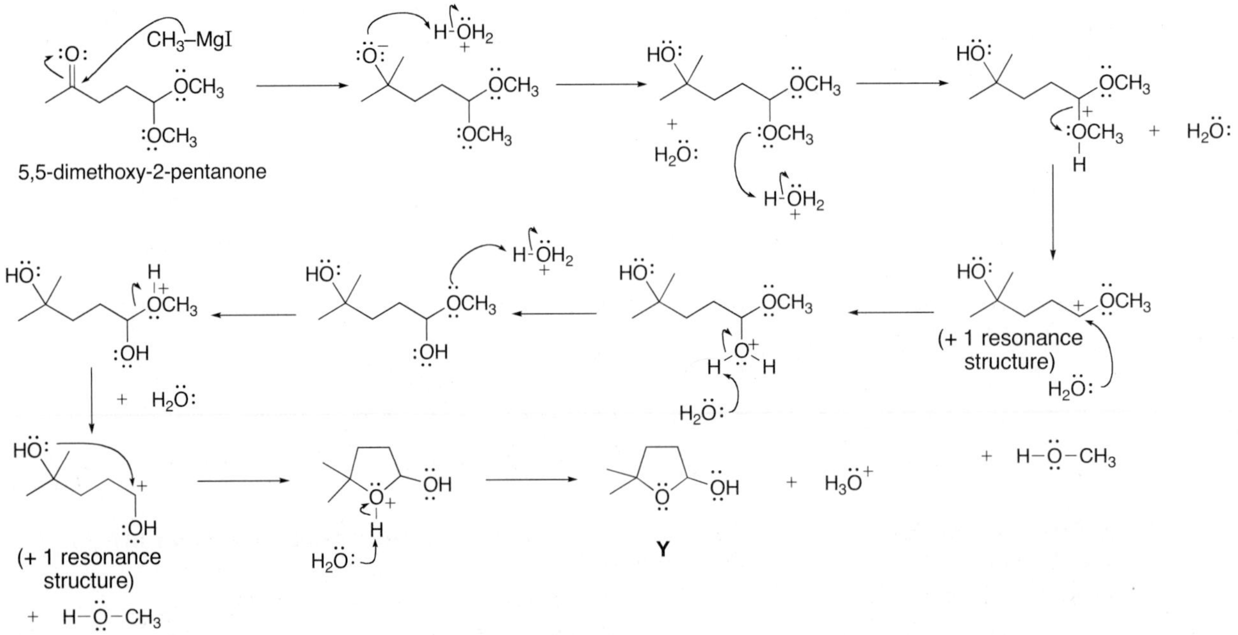

CH3–MgI
5,5-dimethoxy-2-pentanone
(+ 1 resonance structure)
(+ 1 resonance structure)
+ H–O–CH3
Y
+ H3O+

21.80

cyclopropenone ($1640\ cm^{-1}$)

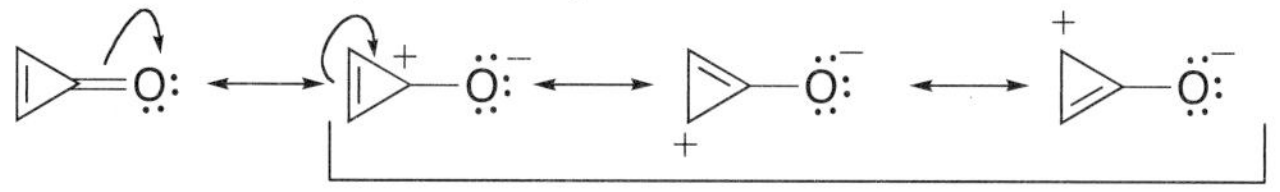

2-cyclohexenone ($1685\ cm^{-1}$)

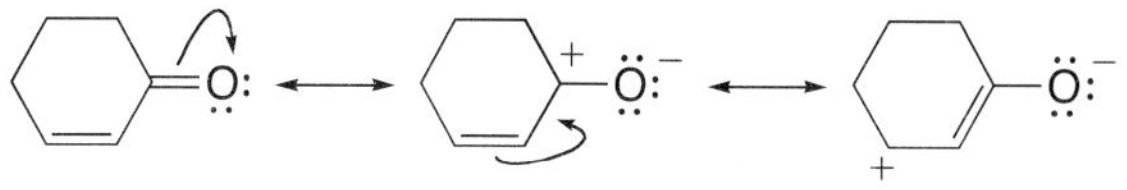

These three resonance structures include an aromatic ring; $4n + 2 = 2\ \pi$ electrons. Although they are charge separated, the stabilized aromatic ring makes these three structures contribute to the hybrid more than usual. Since these three resonance contributors have a C–O single bond, the absorption is shifted to a lower wavenumber.

There are three resonance structures for 2-cyclohexenone, but the charge-separated resonance structures are not aromatic so they contribute less to the resonance hybrid. The C=O absorbs in the usual region for a conjugated carbonyl.

21.81

A. Molecular formula $C_5H_{10}O$ → 1 degree of unsaturation
IR absorptions at 1728, 2791, 2700 cm^{-1} → C=O, CHO
NMR data: singlet at 1.08 (9 H) → 3 CH_3 groups
singlet at 9.48 (1 H) ppm → CHO

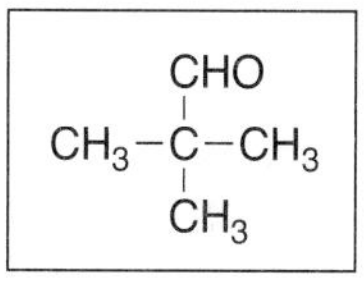
CHO
CH3–C–CH3
CH3

B. Molecular formula $C_5H_{10}O$ → 1 degree of unsaturation
IR absorption at 1718 cm^{-1} → C=O
NMR data: doublet at 1.10 (6 H) → 2 CH_3's adjacent to H
singlet at 2.14 (3 H) → CH_3
septet at 2.58 (1 H) ppm → CH adjacent to 2 CH_3's

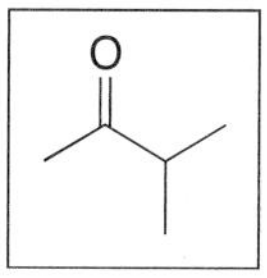
O

C. Molecular formula $C_{10}H_{12}O$ → 5 degrees of unsaturation (4 due to a benzene ring)
IR absorption at 1686 cm^{-1} → C=O
NMR data: triplet at 1.21 (3 H) → CH_3 adjacent to 2 H's
singlet at 2.39 (3 H) → CH_3
quartet at 2.95 (2 H) → CH_2 adjacent to 3 H's
doublet at 7.24 (2 H) → 2 H's on benzene ring
doublet at 7.85 (2 H) ppm → 2 H's on benzene ring

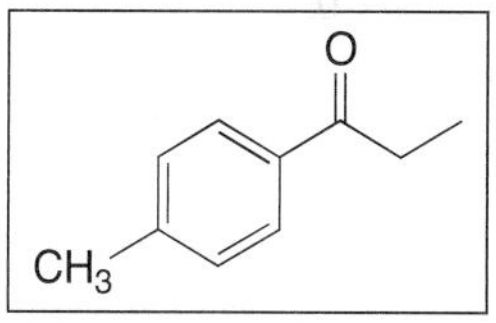
O
CH3

D. Molecular formula $C_{10}H_{12}O$ → 5 degrees of unsaturation (4 due to a benzene ring)
IR absorption at 1719 cm^{-1} → C=O
NMR data: triplet at 1.02 (3 H) → CH_3 adjacent 2 H's
quartet at 2.45 (2 H) → 2 H's adjacent to 3 H's
singlet at 3.67 (2 H) → CH_2
multiplet at 7.06–7.48 (5 H) ppm → a monosubstituted benzene ring

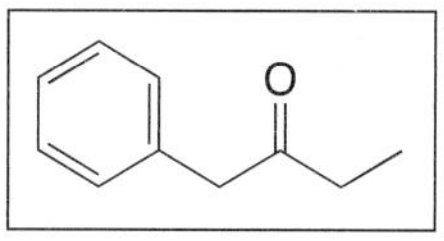
O

21.82

$C_7H_{16}O_2$: 0 degrees of unsaturation
IR: 3000 cm^{-1}: **C–H bonds**
NMR data (ppm):
H_a: quartet at 3.5 (**4 H**), split by 3 H's
H_b: singlet at 1.4 (**6 H**)
H_c: triplet at 1.2 (**6 H**), split by 2 H's

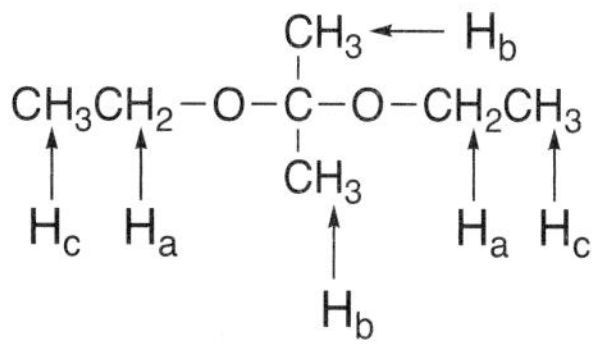
CH3 ← Hb
CH3CH2–O–C–O–CH2CH3
CH3
Hc Ha
Ha Hc
Hb

21.83

A. Molecular formula $C_9H_{10}O$
5 degrees of unsaturation
IR absorption at 1700 cm^{-1} → C=O
IR absorption at ~2700 cm^{-1} → CH of RCHO
NMR data (ppm):
triplet at 1.2 (2 H's adjacent)
quartet at 2.7 (3 H's adjacent)
doublet at 7.3 (2 H's on benzene)
doublet at 7.7 (2 H's on benzene)
singlet at 9.9 (CHO)

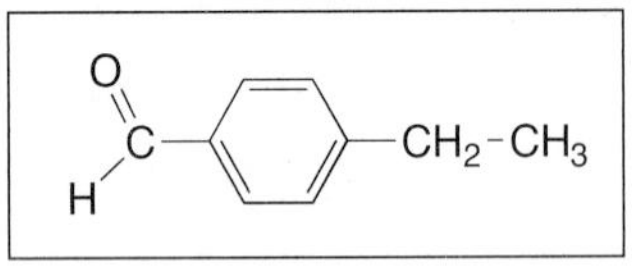

B. Molecular formula $C_9H_{10}O$
5 degrees of unsaturation
IR absorption at 1720 cm^{-1} → C=O
IR absorption at ~2700 cm^{-1} → CH of RCHO
NMR data (ppm):
2 triplets at 2.85 and 2.95 (suggests $–CH_2CH_2–$)
multiplet at 7.2 (benzene H's)
signal at 9.8 (CHO)

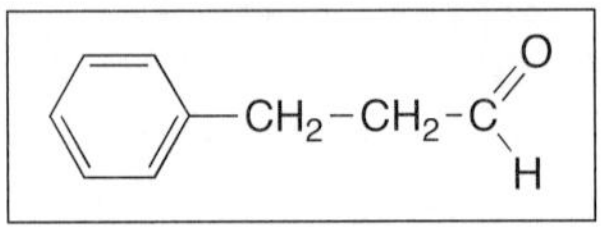

21.84

C. Molecular formula $C_6H_{12}O_3$
1 degree of unsaturation
IR absorption at 1718 cm^{-1} → C=O
To determine the number of H's that give rise to each signal, first find the number of integration units per H by dividing the total number of integration units (7 + 40 + 14 + 21 = 82) by the number of H's (12); 82/12 = 6.8. Then divide each integration unit by this number (6.8).
NMR data (ppm):
singlet at 2.2 (3 H's)
doublet at 2.7 (2 H's)
singlet at 3.2 (6 H's – 2 OCH_3 groups)
triplet at 4.8 (1 H)

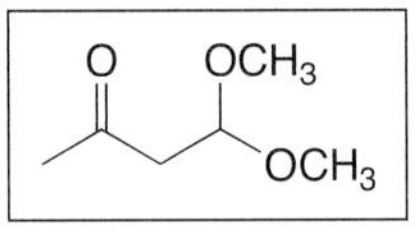

21.85

D. Molecular ion at m/z = 150: $C_9H_{10}O_2$ (possible molecular formula)
5 degrees of unsaturation
IR absorption at 1692 cm^{-1} → C=O
NMR data (ppm):
triplet at 1.5 (3 H's – CH_3CH_2)
quartet at 4.1 (2 H's – CH_3CH_2)
doublet at 7.0 (2 H's – on benzene ring)
doublet at 7.8 (2 H's – on benzene ring)
singlet at 9.9 (1 H – on aldehyde)

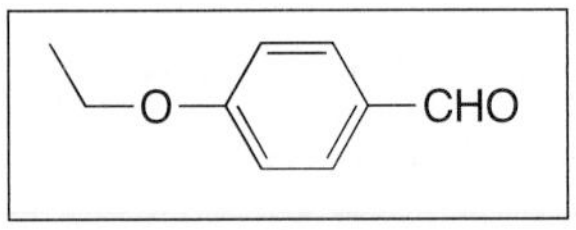

21.86

a. 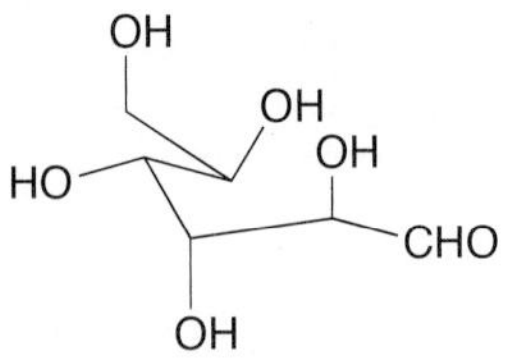

b. 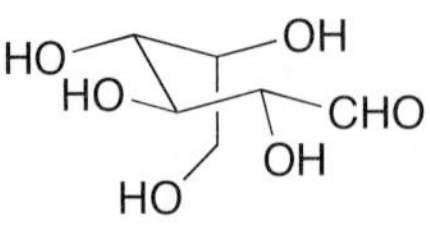

21.87

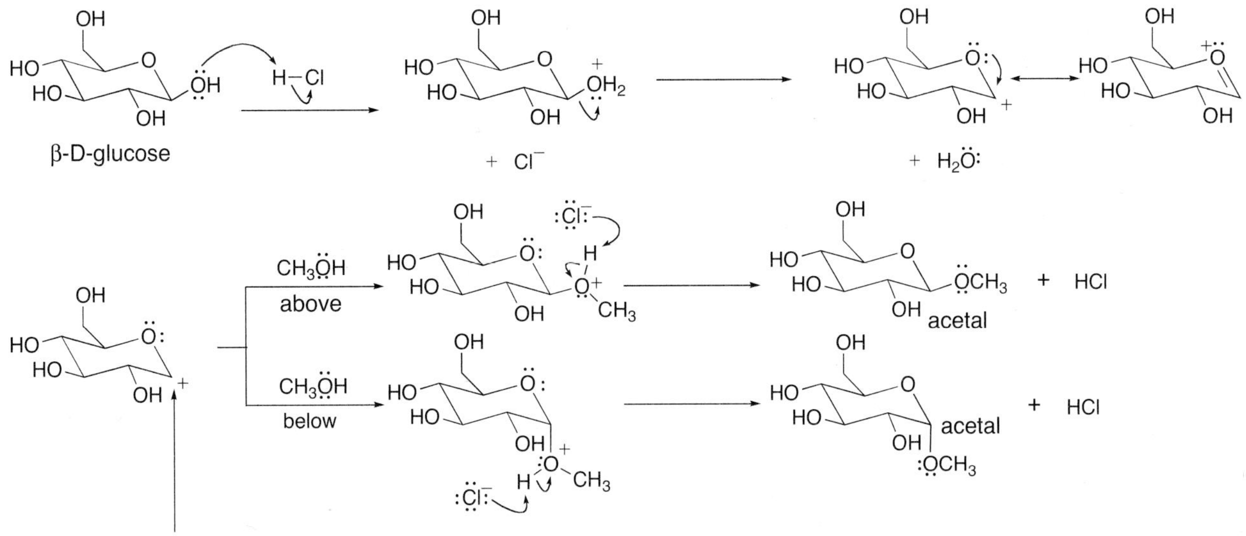

The carbocation is trigonal planar, so CH_3OH attacks from two different directions, and two different acetals are formed.

21.88

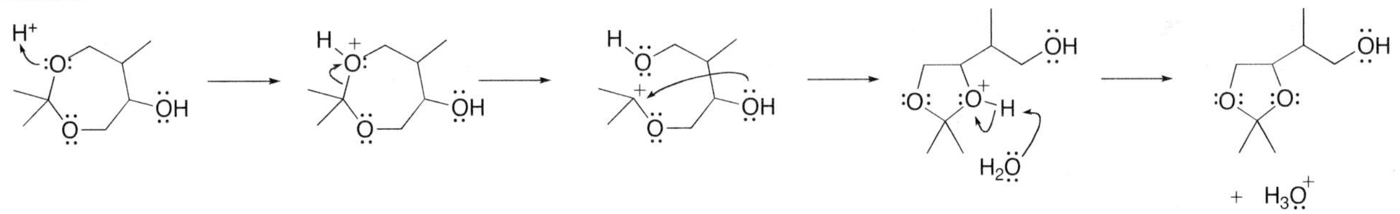

21.89

a. 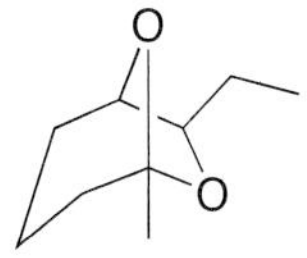

brevicomin

b. 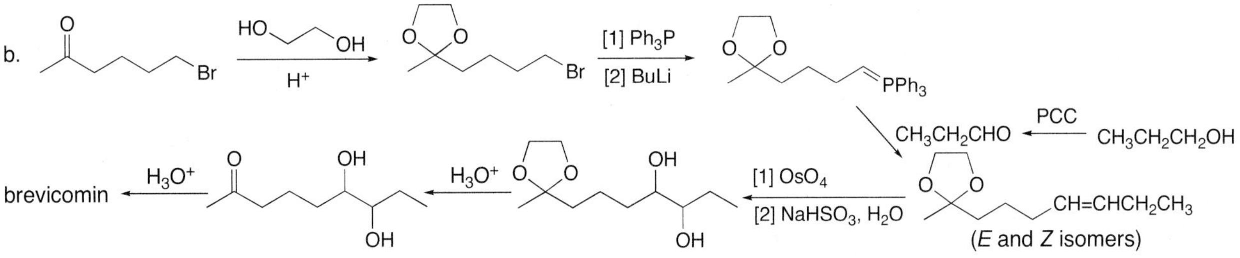

21.90

a. 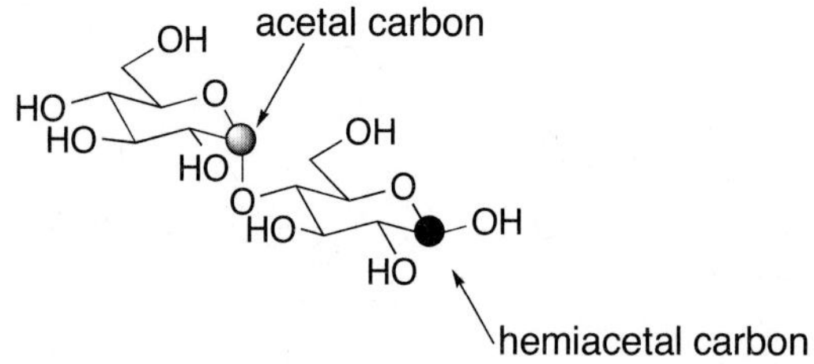
acetal carbon
hemiacetal carbon

c. 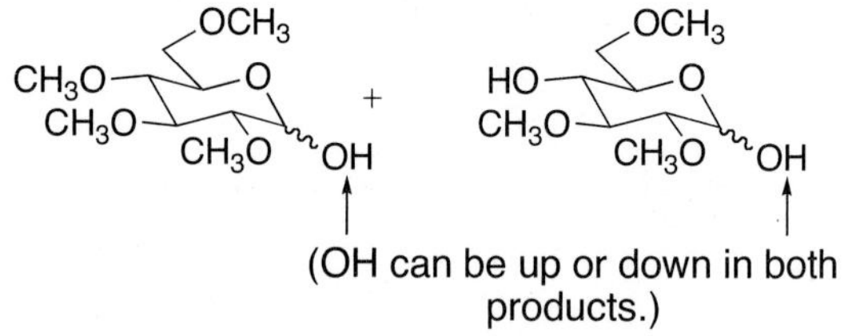
(OH can be up or down in both products.)

b. 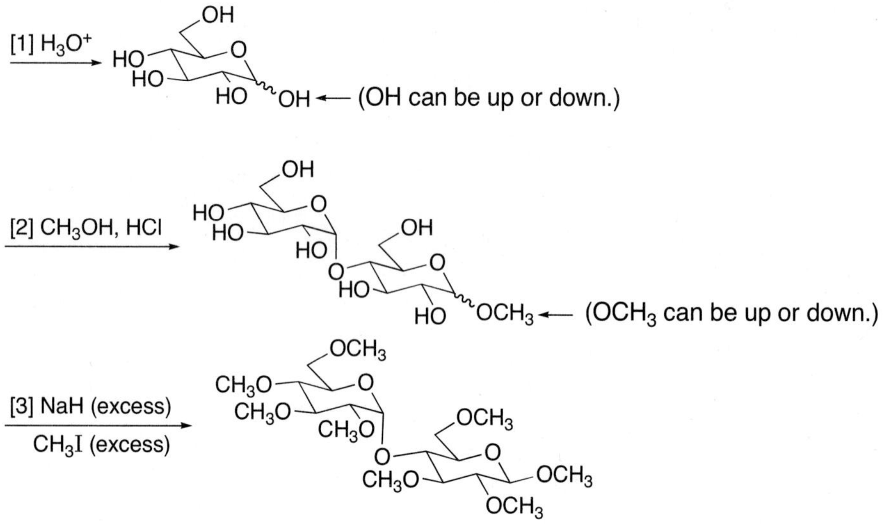
[1] H3O+
(OH can be up or down.)
[2] CH3OH, HCl
(OCH3 can be up or down.)
[3] NaH (excess)
CH3I (excess)

21.91

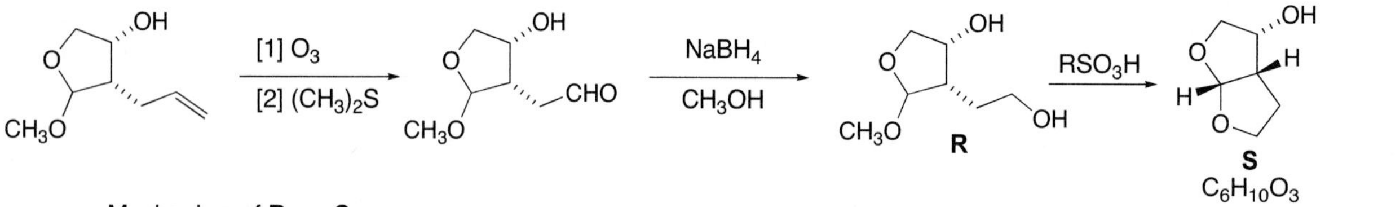
[1] O3
[2] (CH3)2S
NaBH4
CH3OH
R
RSO3H
S
C6H10O3

Mechanism of **R** → **S**:

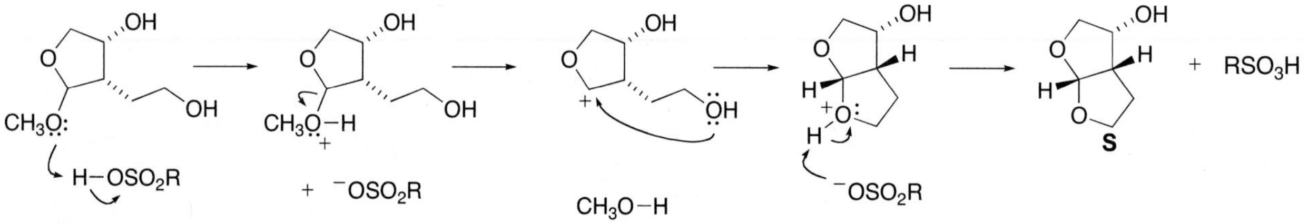
+ RSO3H
S

21.92 The mechanism involves S_N2 displacement of Br, followed by intramolecular enamine formation.

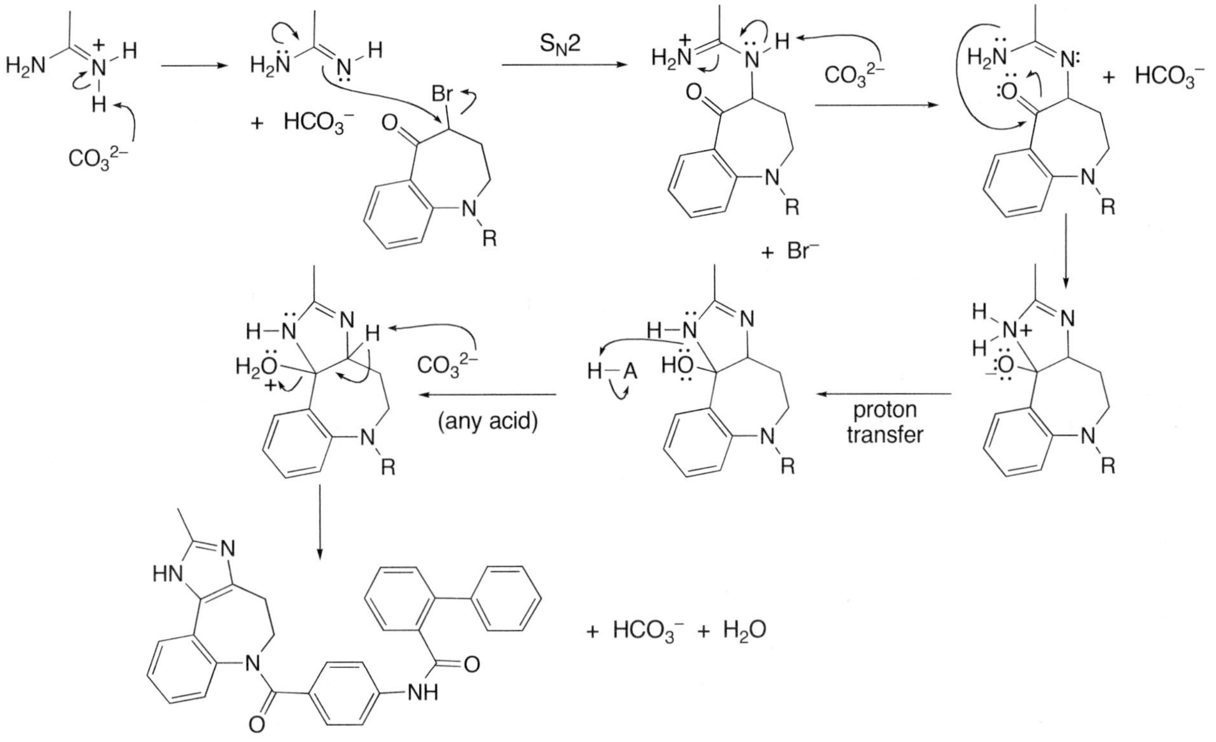

conivaptan

Chapter 22 Carboxylic Acids and Their Derivatives—Nucleophilic Acyl Substitution

Chapter Review

Summary of spectroscopic absorptions of RCOZ (22.5)

IR absorptions
- All RCOZ compounds have a C=O absorption in the region 1600–1850 cm^{-1}.
  - RCOCl: 1800 cm^{-1}
  - $(RCO)_2O$: 1820 and 1760 cm^{-1} (two peaks)
  - RCOOR': 1735–1745 cm^{-1}
  - $RCONR'_2$: 1630–1680 cm^{-1}
- Additional amide absorptions occur at 3200–3400 cm^{-1} (N–H stretch) and 1640 cm^{-1} (N–H bending).
- Decreasing the ring size of a cyclic lactone, lactam, or anhydride increases the frequency of the C=O absorption.
- Conjugation shifts the C=O to lower wavenumber.

^1H NMR absorptions
- C–H α to the C=O absorbs at 2–2.5 ppm.
- N–H of an amide absorbs at 7.5–8.5 ppm.

^{13}C NMR absorption
- C=O absorbs at 160–180 ppm.

Summary of spectroscopic absorptions of RCN (22.5)

IR absorption
- C≡N absorption at 2250 cm^{-1}

^{13}C NMR absorption
- C≡N absorbs at 115–120 ppm.

Summary: The relationship between the basicity of Z^- and the properties of RCOZ

- **Increasing basicity of the leaving group** (22.2)
- **Increasing resonance stabilization** (22.2)

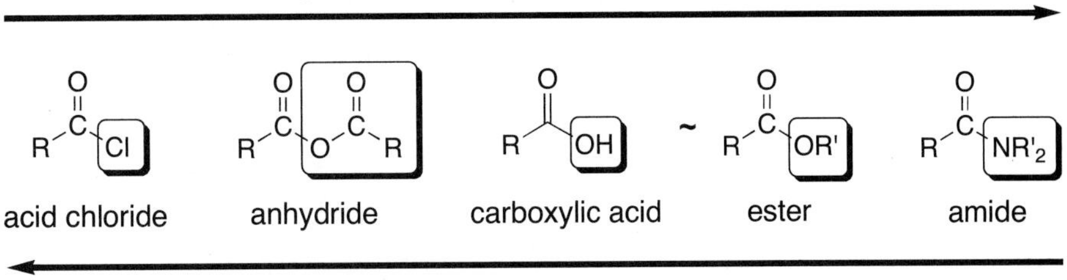
Cl
OH
OR'
NR'2
acid chloride
anhydride
carboxylic acid
ester
amide

- **Increasing leaving group ability** (22.7B)
- **Increasing reactivity** (22.7B)
- **Increasing frequency of the C=O absorption in the IR** (22.5)

General features of nucleophilic acyl substitution

- The characteristic reaction of compounds having the general structure RCOZ is nucleophilic acyl substitution (22.1).
- The mechanism consists of two steps (22.7A):
  [1] Addition of a nucleophile to form a tetrahedral intermediate
  [2] Elimination of a leaving group
- More reactive acyl compounds can be used to prepare less reactive acyl compounds. The reverse is not necessarily true (22.7B).

Nucleophilic acyl substitution reactions

[1] Reaction that synthesizes acid chlorides (RCOCl)

From RCOOH (22.10A):

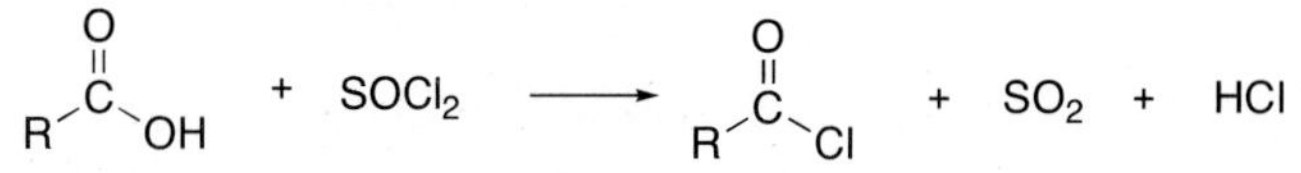
+ $SOCl_2$
+ SO_2 + HCl

[2] Reactions that synthesize anhydrides [$(RCO)_2O$]

[a] From RCOCl (22.8):

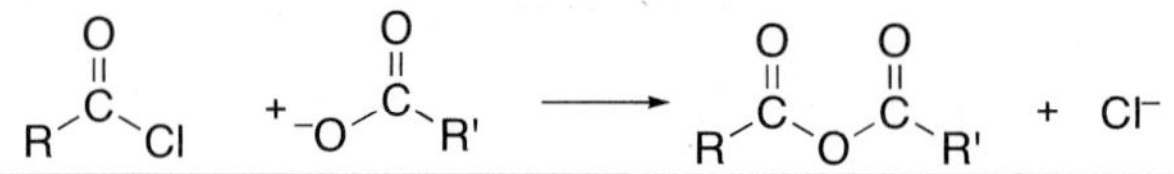
+ Cl^-

[b] From dicarboxylic acids (22.10B):

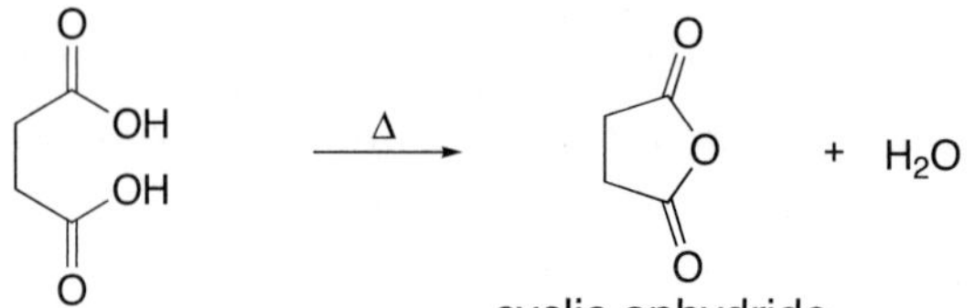
Δ
+ H_2O

cyclic anhydride

[3] Reactions that synthesize carboxylic acids (RCOOH)

[a] From RCOCl (22.8):

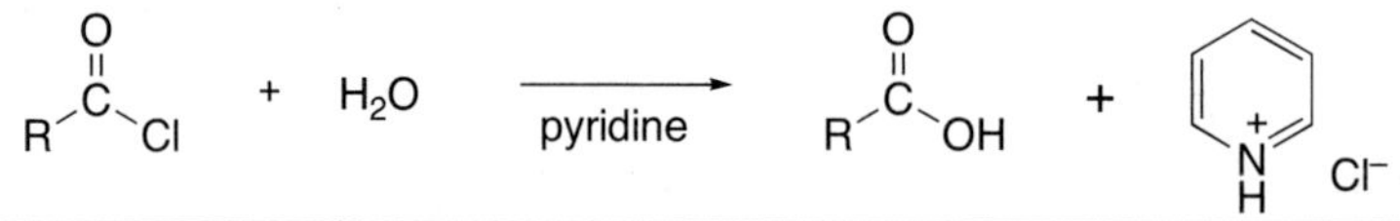
+ H_2O
pyridine
Cl^-

[b] From $(RCO)_2O$ (22.9):

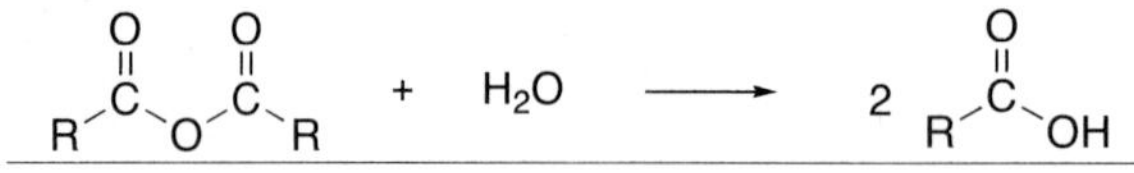
+ H_2O
2

[c] From RCOOR' (22.11):

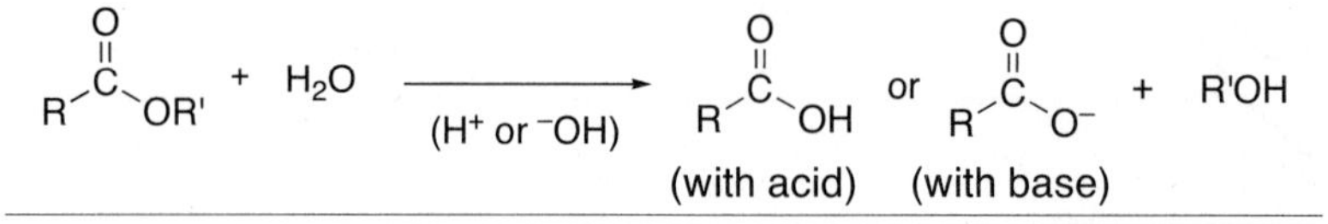
+ H_2O
(H^+ or ^-OH)
or
+ R'OH
(with acid)
(with base)

[d] From $RCONR'_2$ (R' = H or alkyl, 22.13):

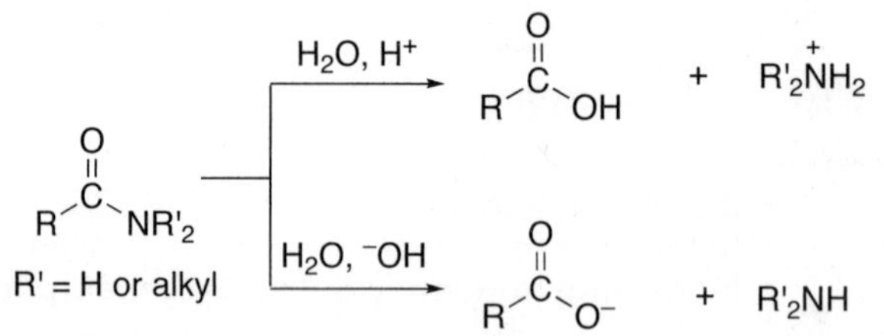
H_2O, H^+
+ $R'_2\overset{+}{N}H_2$
R' = H or alkyl
H_2O, ^-OH
+ R'_2NH

[4] Reactions that synthesize esters (RCOOR')

[a] From RCOCl (22.8):

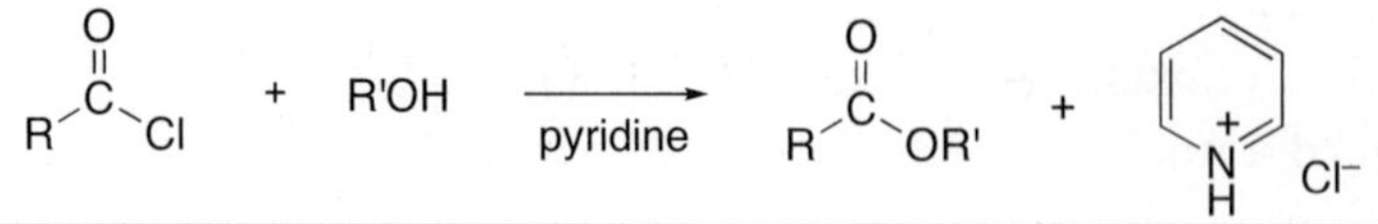
+ R'OH
pyridine
Cl^-

[b] From $(RCO)_2O$ (22.9):

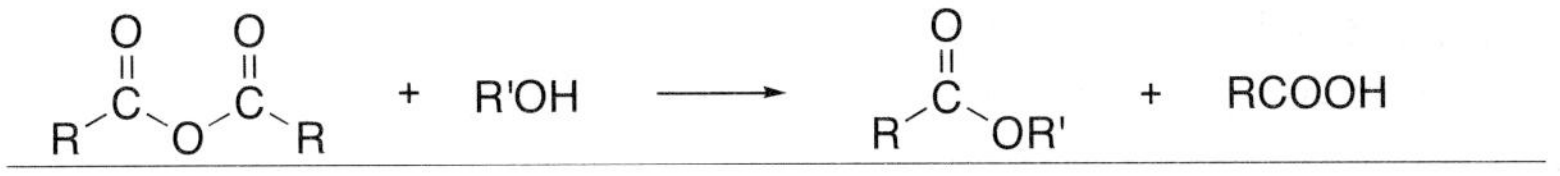

[c] From RCOOH (22.10C):

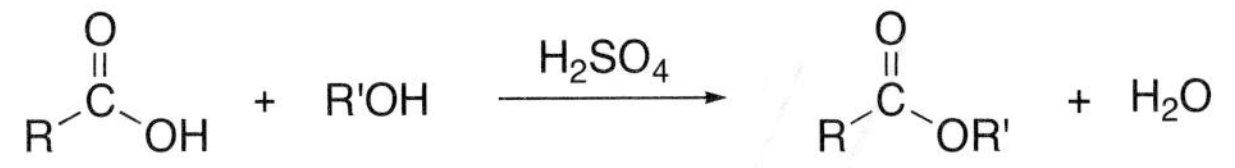

[5] Reactions that synthesize amides ($RCONH_2$) [The reactions are written with NH_3 as the nucleophile to form $RCONH_2$. Similar reactions occur with $R'NH_2$ to form RCONHR', and with R'_2NH to form $RCONR'_2$.]

[a] From RCOCl (22.8):

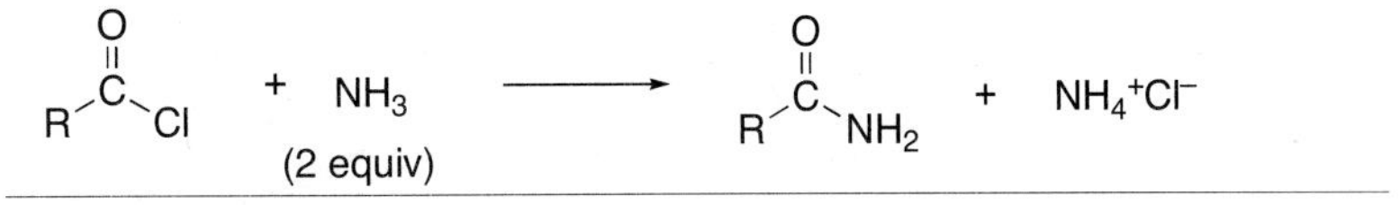

[b] From $(RCO)_2O$ (22.9):

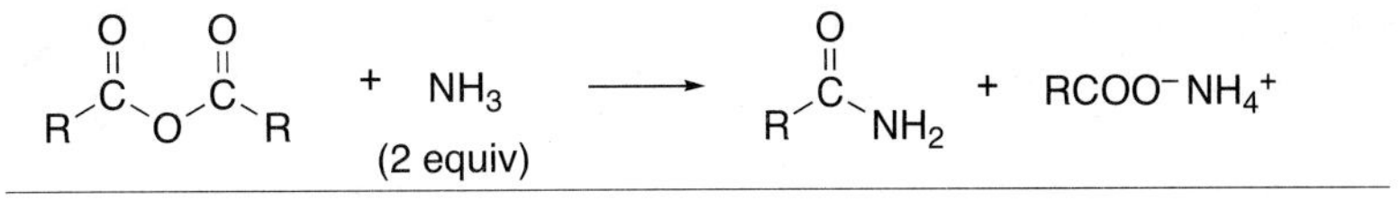

[c] From RCOOH (22.10D):

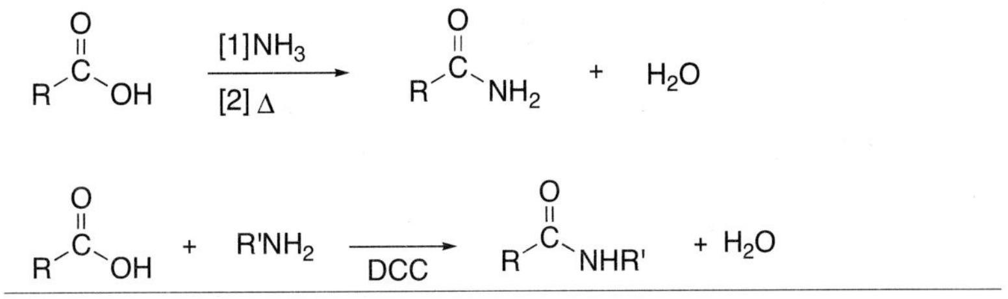

[d] From RCOOR' (22.11):

Nitrile synthesis (22.18)

Nitriles are prepared by S_N2 substitution using unhindered alkyl halides as starting materials.

$$R{-}X \;+\; {}^{-}CN \xrightarrow{S_N2} R{-}C{\equiv}N \;+\; X^{-}$$

$R = CH_3$, 1°

Reactions of nitriles

[1] Hydrolysis (22.18A)

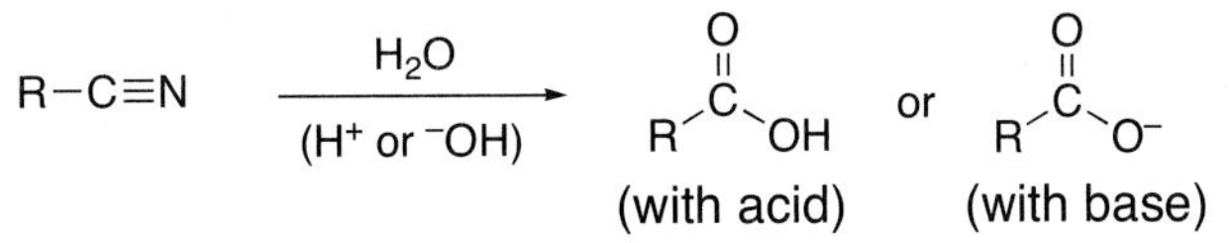

[2] Reduction (22.18B)

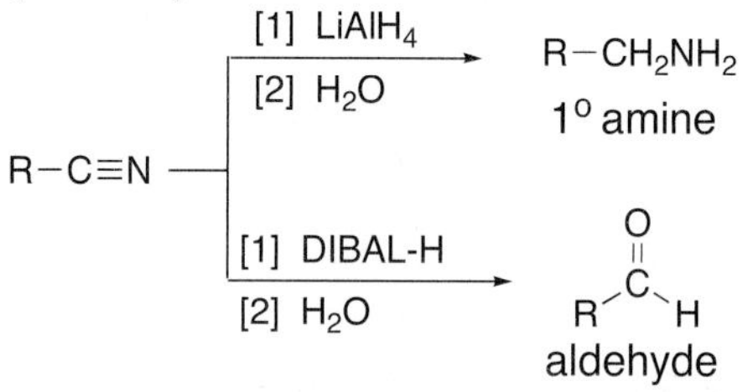

[3] Reaction with organometallic reagents (22.18C)

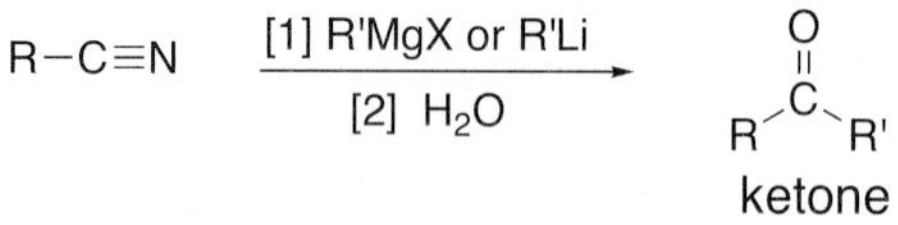

Practice Test on Chapter Review

1. Give the IUPAC name for each of the following compounds.

a. 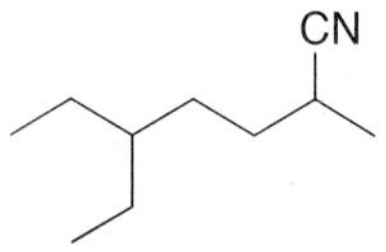

b. 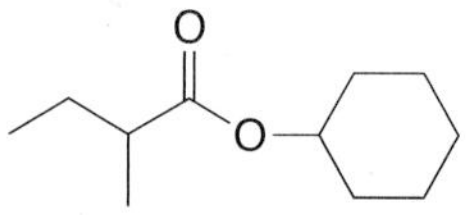

c. 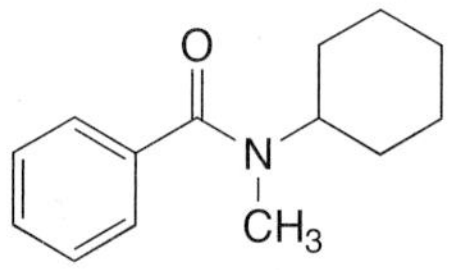

2. (a) Which compound absorbs at the *lowest* wavenumber in the IR? (b) Which compound absorbs at the *highest* wavenumber?

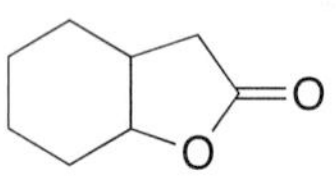

A

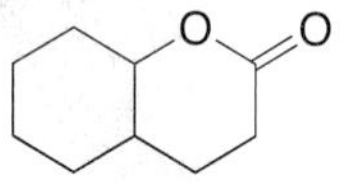

B

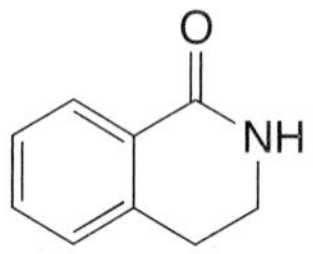

C

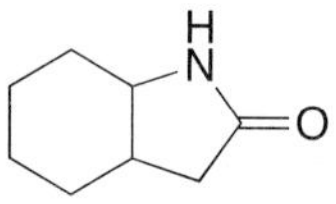

D

3. a. Which of the following reaction conditions can be used to synthesize an ester?

   1. RCOCl + R'OH + pyridine
   2. RCOOH + R'OH + H_2SO_4
   3. RCOOH + R'OH + NaOH
   4. Both methods [1] and [2] can be used to synthesize an ester.
   5. Methods [1], [2], and [3] can all be used to synthesize an ester.

   b. Which of the following compounds is most reactive in nucleophilic acyl substitution?

   1. CH_3COCl
   2. CH_3COOCH_3
   3. $CH_3CON(CH_3)_2$
   4. $(CH_3CO)_2O$
   5. CH_3COOH

4. What reagent is needed to convert $(CH_3CH_2)_2CHCOOH$ into each compound?
   a. $(CH_3CH_2)_2CHCOO^-Na^+$
   b. $(CH_3CH_2)_2CHCOCl$
   c. $(CH_3CH_2)_2CHCON(CH_3)_2$
   d. $(CH_3CH_2)_2CHCO_2CH_2CH_3$
   e. $[(CH_3CH_2)_2CHCO]_2O$

5. What reagent is needed to convert $CH_3CH_2CH_2CN$ to each compound?
   a. $CH_3CH_2CH_2COOH$
   b. $CH_3CH_2CH_2CH_2NH_2$
   c. $CH_3CH_2CH_2COCH_2CH_3$
   d. $CH_3CH_2CH_2CHO$

6. Draw the organic products formed in the following reactions.

a.
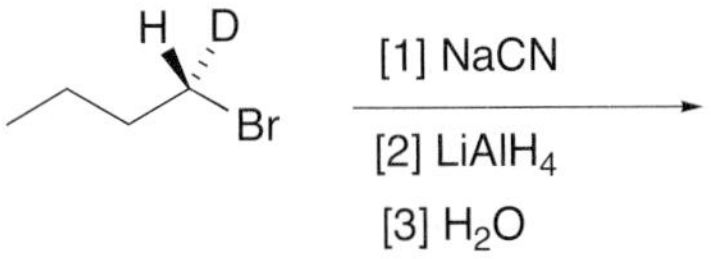

[Indicate stereochemistry.]

d.
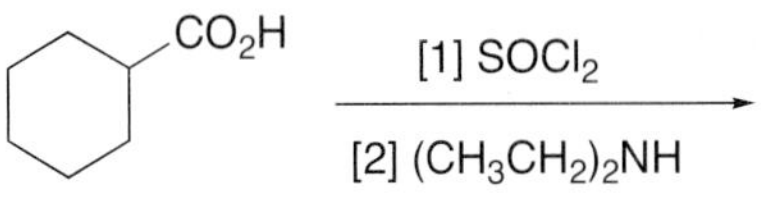

b.
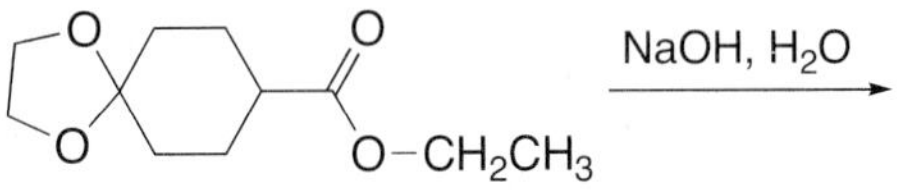

e.
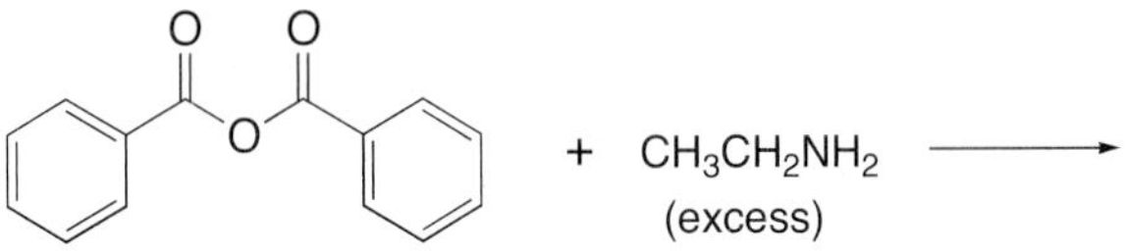

c.
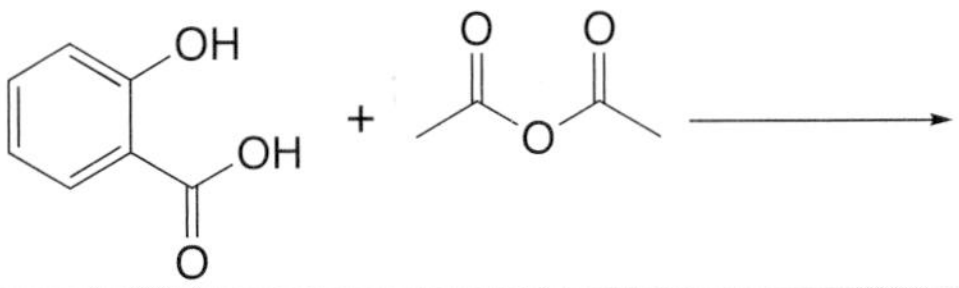

f.
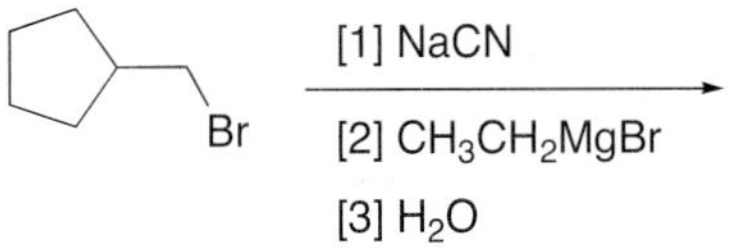

Answers to Practice Test

1. a. 5-ethyl-2-methyl-heptanenitrile
   b. cyclohexyl 2-methylbutanoate
   c. *N*-cyclohexyl-*N*-methylbenzamide
2. a. **C**
   b. **A**
3. a. 4
   b. 1
4. a. NaOH
   b. $SOCl_2$
   c. $HN(CH_3)_2$, DCC
   d. CH_3CH_2OH, H_2SO_4
   e. heat
5. a. H_3O^+
   b. [1] $LiAlH_4$; [2] H_2O
   c. [1] CH_3CH_2Li; [2] H_2O
   d. [1] DIBAL-H; [2] H_2O
6.

a.
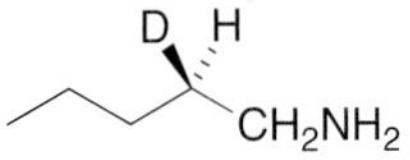

b.
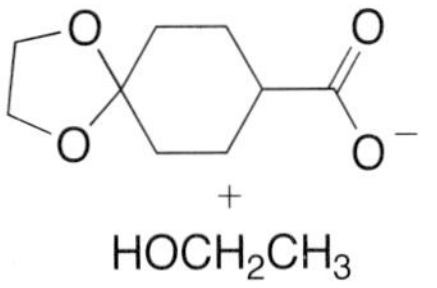

c.
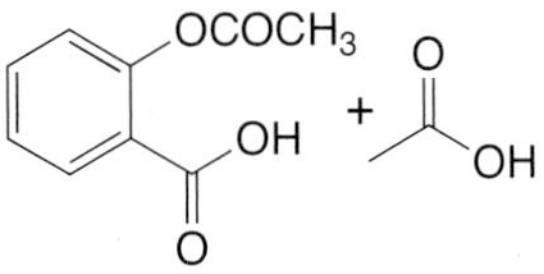

d.
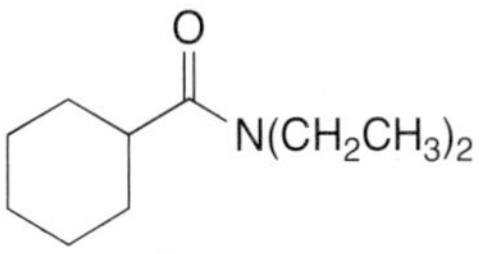

e.
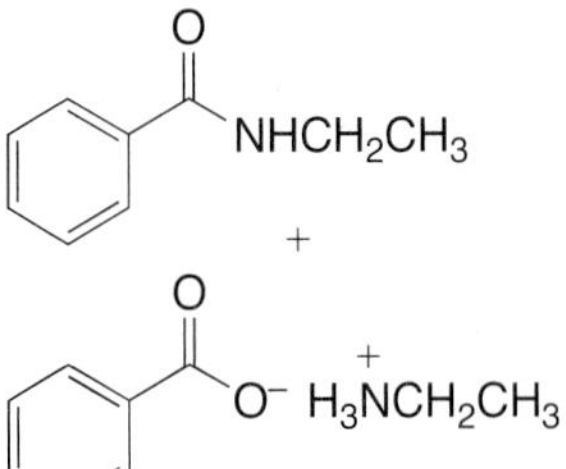

f.
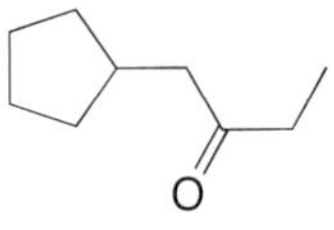

Answers to Problems

22.1 The number of C–N bonds determines the classification as a 1°, 2°, or 3° amide.

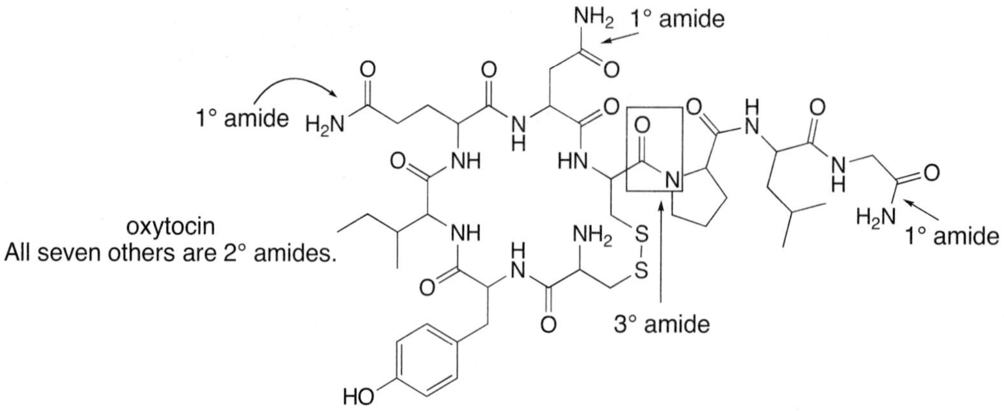
NH2 1° amide
1° amide H2N
oxytocin
All seven others are 2° amides.
H2N 1° amide
3° amide
HO

22.2 As the basicity of Z increases, the stability of RCOZ increases because of added resonance stabilization.

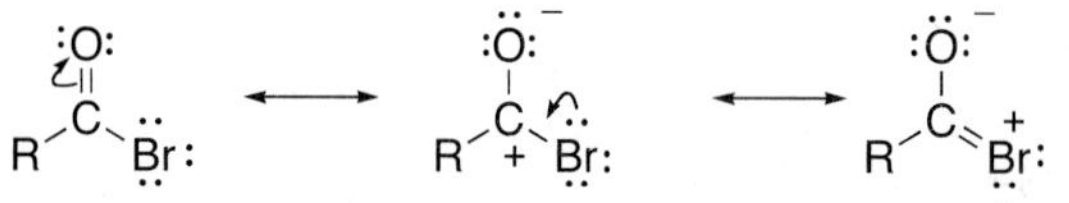

The **basicity of Z** determines how much this structure contributes to the hybrid. Br^- is less basic than ^-OH, so RCOBr is less stable than RCOOH.

22.3

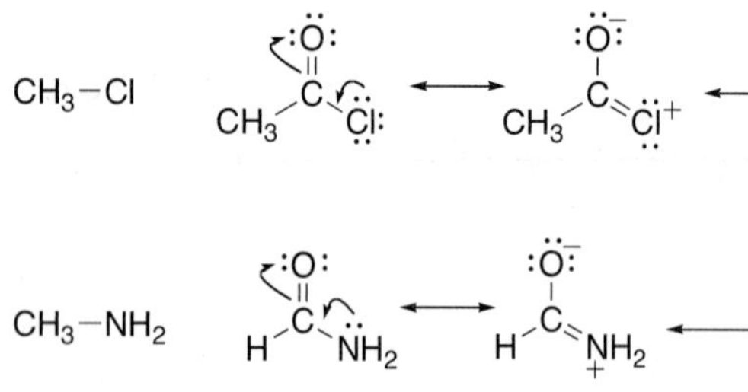

This resonance structure contributes little to the hybrid since Cl^- is a weak base. Thus, the C–Cl bond has little double bond character, making it similar in length to the C–Cl bond in CH_3Cl.

This resonance structure contributes more to the hybrid since $^-NH_2$ is more basic. Thus, the C–N bond in $HCONH_2$ has more double bond character, making it shorter than the C–N bond in CH_3NH_2.

22.4

a. $(CH_3CH_2)_2CH{-}COCl$

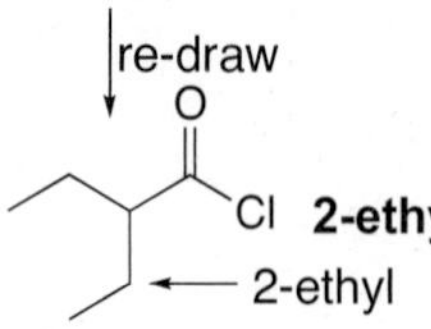
re-draw
Cl
2-ethyl

2-ethylbutanoyl chloride

b. $C_6H_5COOCH_3$

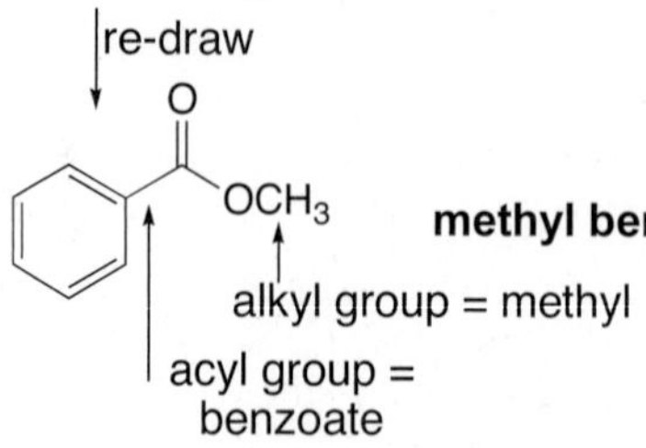
re-draw
OCH3
alkyl group = methyl
acyl group = benzoate

methyl benzoate

c. $CH_3CH_2CON(CH_3)CH_2CH_3$

re-draw

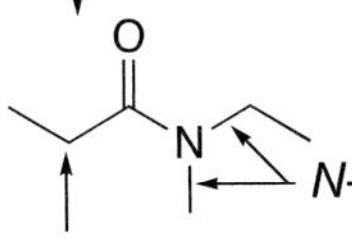

N-ethyl-*N*-methyl

acyl group = propanamide

***N*-ethyl-*N*-methylpropanamide**

d.

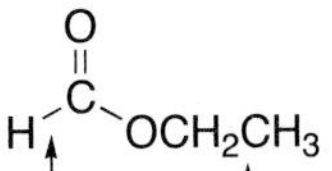

alkyl group = ethyl

acyl group = formate

ethyl formate

e.

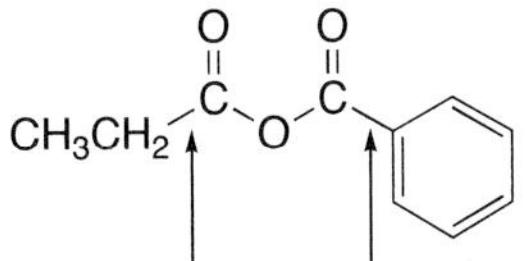

benzoic propanoic anhydride

acyl group = propanoic

acyl group = benzoic

f.

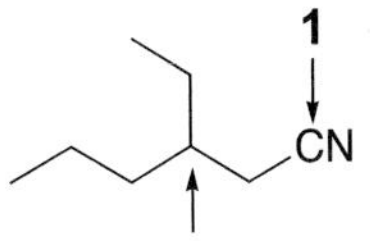

1

3

3-ethylhexanenitrile

6 carbon chain = hexanenitrile

22.5

a. 5-methylheptanoyl chloride

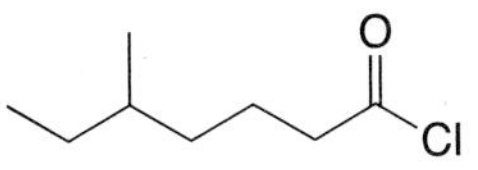

b. isopropyl propanoate

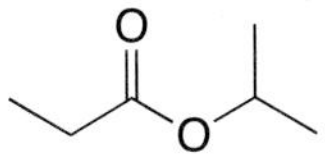

c. acetic formic anhydride

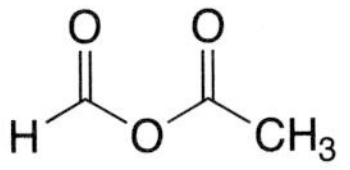

d. *N*-isobutyl-*N*-methylbutanamide

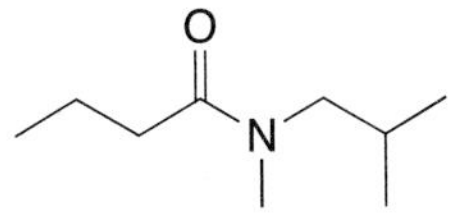

e. 3-methylpentanenitrile

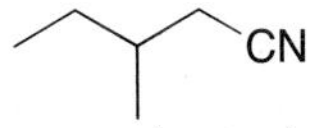

f. *o*-cyanobenzoic acid

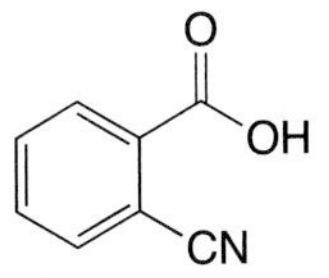

g. *sec*-butyl 2-methylhexanoate

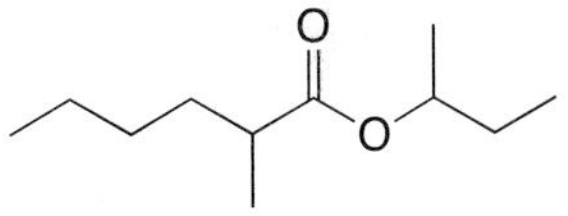

h. *N*-ethylhexanamide

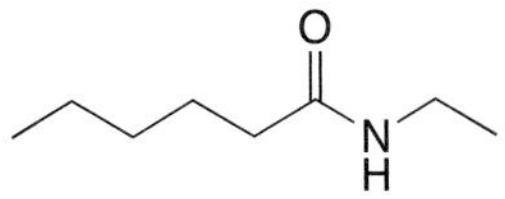

22.6 CH_3CONH_2 has two H's bonded to N that can hydrogen bond. $CH_3CON(CH_3)_2$ does not have any H's capable of hydrogen bonding. This means CH_3CONH_2 has much stronger intermolecular forces, which leads to a higher boiling point.

22.7

a. 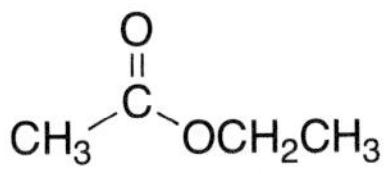 and 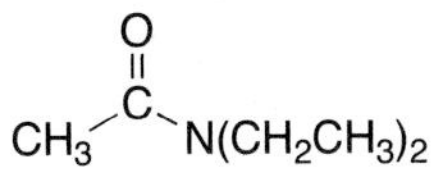

amide: C=O at lower wavenumber

c. 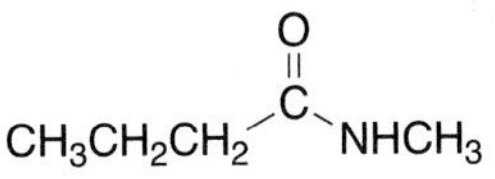 and 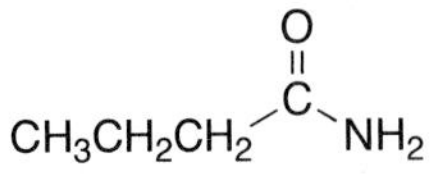

2° amide: 1 N–H absorption at 3200–3400 cm^{-1}

1° amide: 2 N–H absorptions

b. 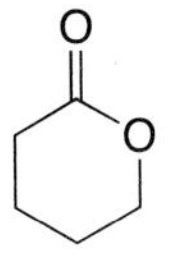 and 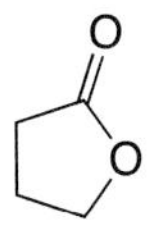

smaller ring: C=O at a higher wavenumber

d. 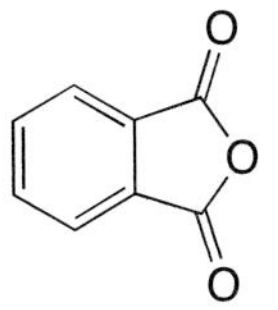 and 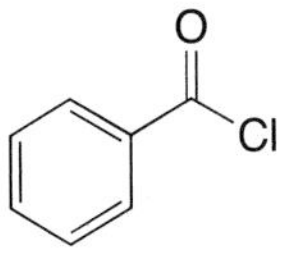

anhydride: 2 C=O peaks

22.8

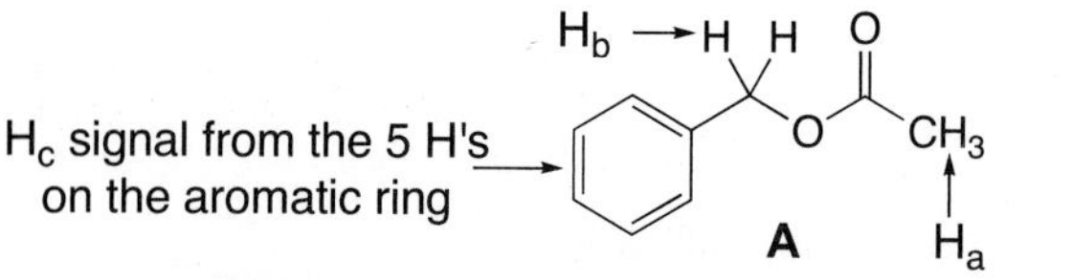
Hb
H H O
Hc signal from the 5 H's on the aromatic ring
O
CH3
A
Ha

Molecular formula $C_9H_{10}O_2$
5 degrees of unsaturation
IR: 1743 cm^{-1} from ester C=O
3091–2895 cm^{-1} from *sp*^{2} and *sp*^{3} C–H
^{1}H NMR: H_a = 2.06 ppm (singlet, 3 H) – CH_3
H_b = 5.08 ppm (singlet, 2 H) – CH_2
H_c = 7.33 ppm (broad singlet, 5 H)

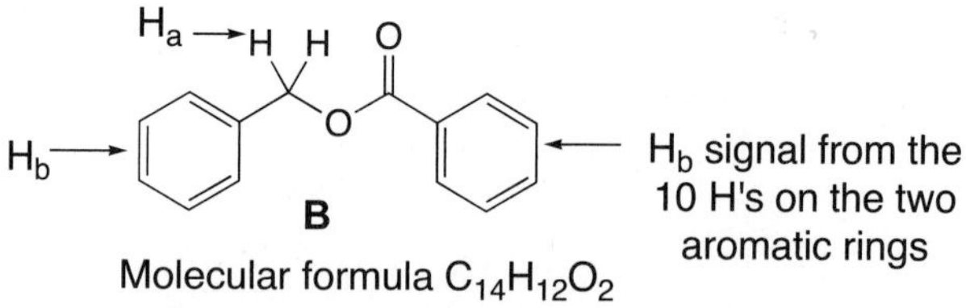
Ha
H H O
Hb
O
B
Hb signal from the 10 H's on the two aromatic rings

Molecular formula $C_{14}H_{12}O_2$
9 degrees of unsaturation
IR: 1718 cm^{-1} from conjugated ester C=O
3091–2953 cm^{-1} from *sp*^{2} and *sp*^{3} C–H
^{1}H NMR: H_a = 5.35 ppm (singlet, 2 H)
H_b = 7.26–8.15 ppm (multiplets, 10 H)

22.9 More reactive acyl compounds can be converted to less reactive acyl compounds.

a. CH_3COCl (more reactive) → **YES** → CH_3COOH (less reactive)

b. $CH_3CONHCH_3$ (less reactive) → **NO** → CH_3COOCH_3 (more reactive)

c. CH_3COOCH_3 (less reactive) → **NO** → CH_3COCl (more reactive)

d. $(CH_3CO)_2O$ (more reactive) → **YES** → CH_3CONH_2 (less reactive)

22.10 The better the leaving group is, the more reactive the carboxylic acid derivative. The weakest base is the best leaving group.

a.

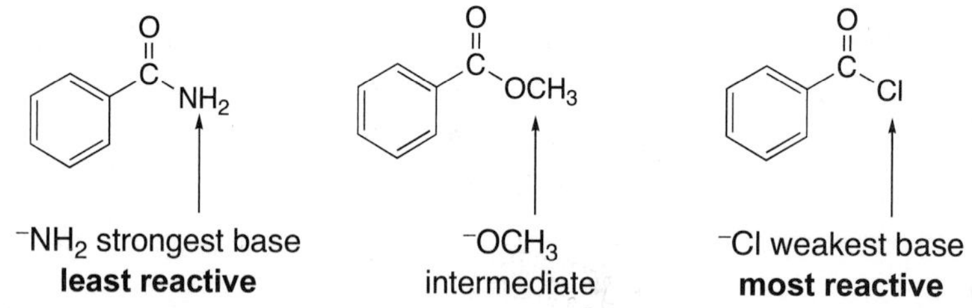
NH2
OCH3
Cl
⁻NH2 strongest base
least reactive
⁻OCH3
intermediate
⁻Cl weakest base
most reactive

b.

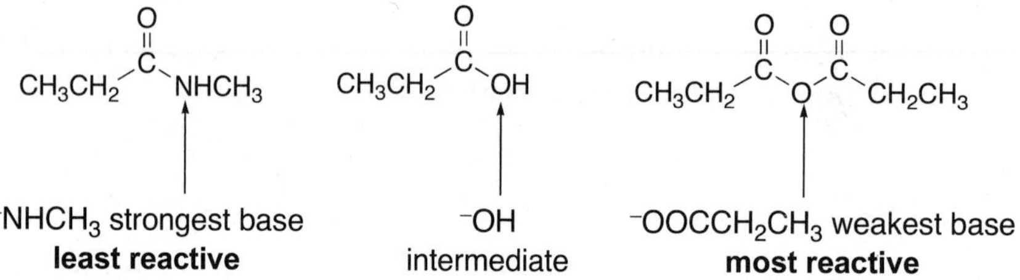
CH3CH2 NHCH3
CH3CH2 OH
CH3CH2 O CH2CH3
⁻NHCH3 strongest base
least reactive
⁻OH
intermediate
⁻OOCCH2CH3 weakest base
most reactive

22.11

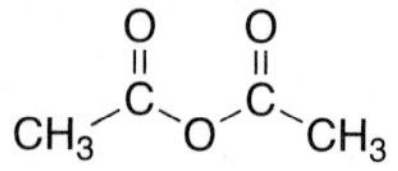

acetic anhydride

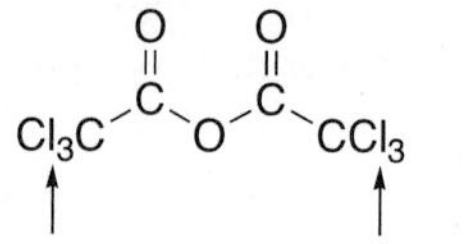

trichloroacetic anhydride

The Cl atoms are electron withdrawing, which makes the conjugate base (the leaving group, CCl_3COO^-) weaker and more stable.

22.12

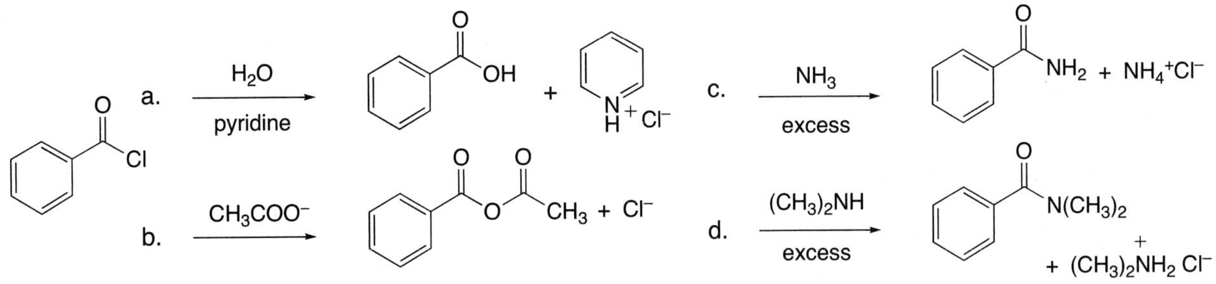

22.13 The mechanism has three steps: [1] nucleophilic attack by O; [2] proton transfer; [3] elimination of the Cl^- leaving group to form the product.

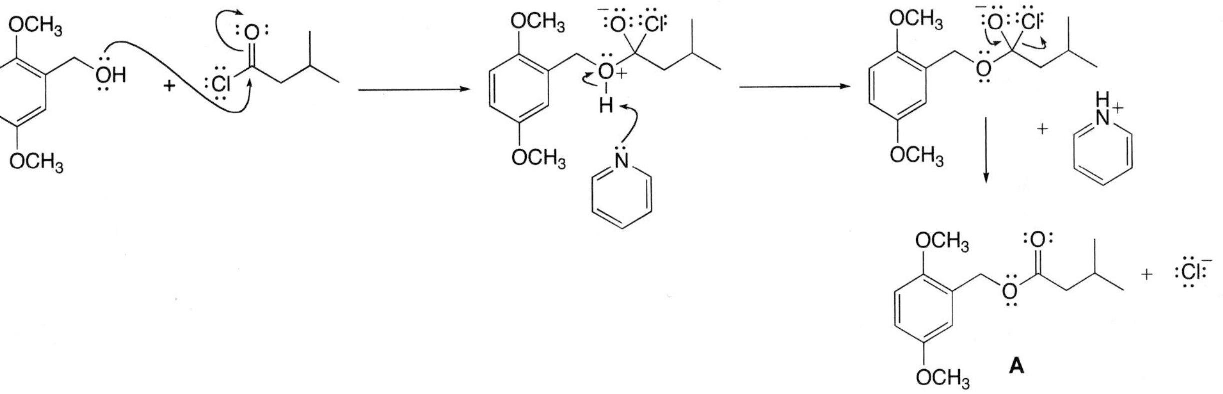

22.14

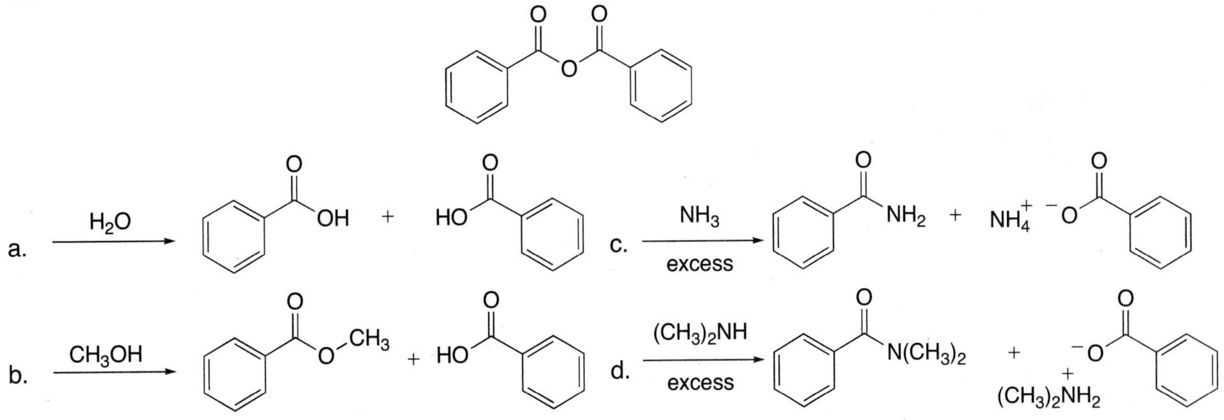

22.15 Reaction of a carboxylic acid with thionyl chloride converts it to an acid chloride.

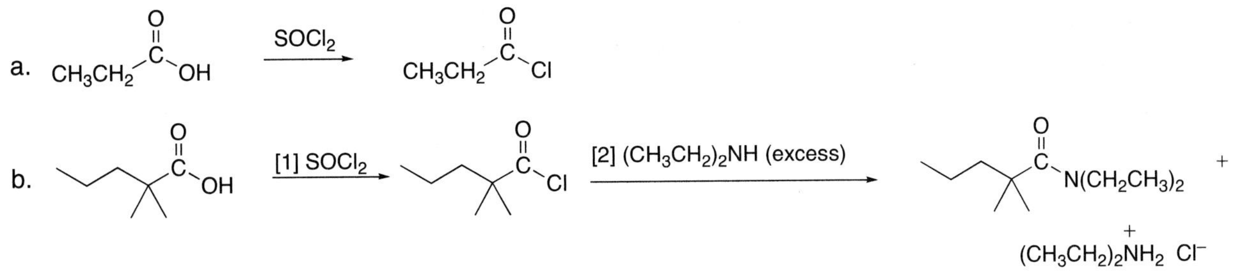

22.16

a.
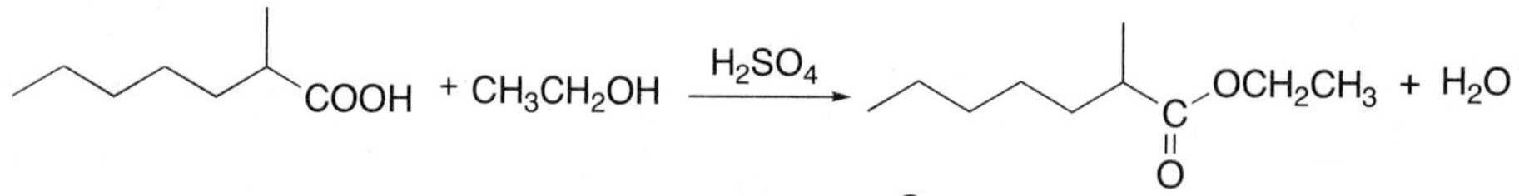

b.
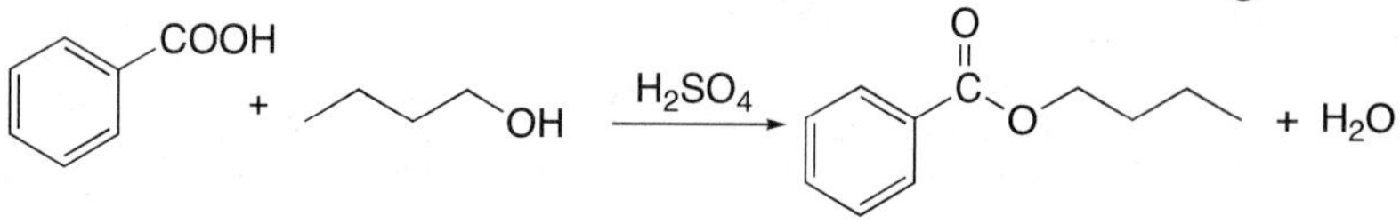

c.
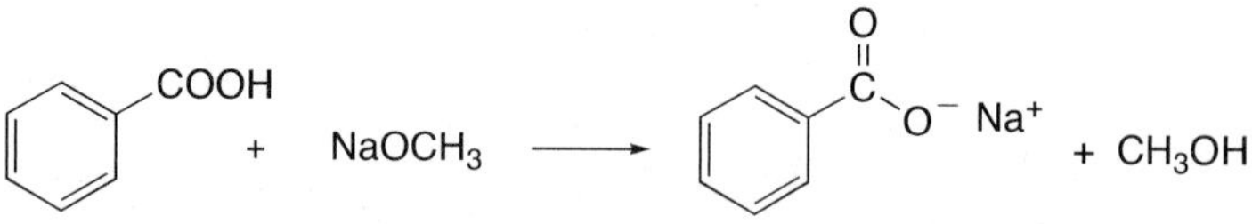

d.
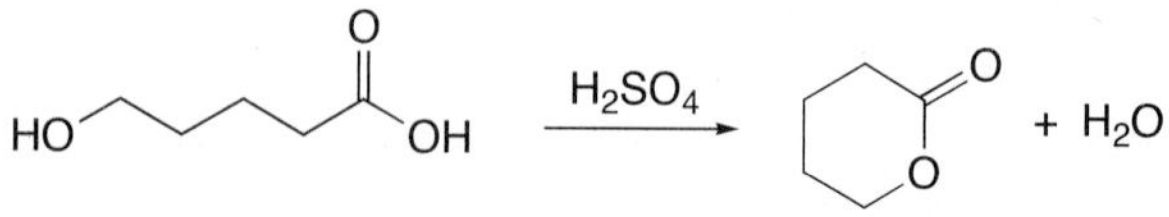

22.17

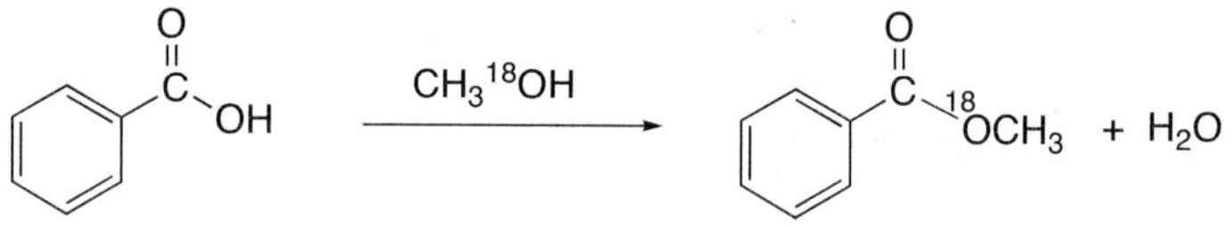

22.18

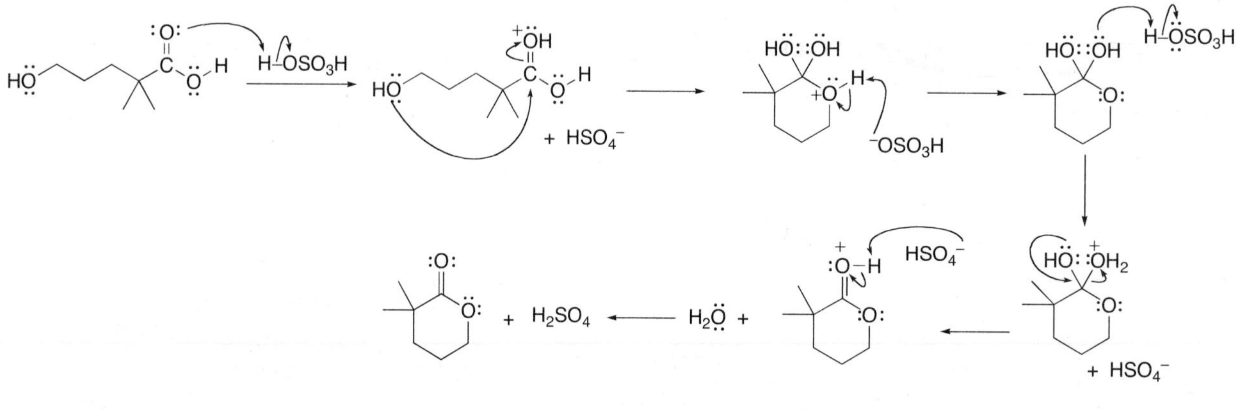

22.19

a.
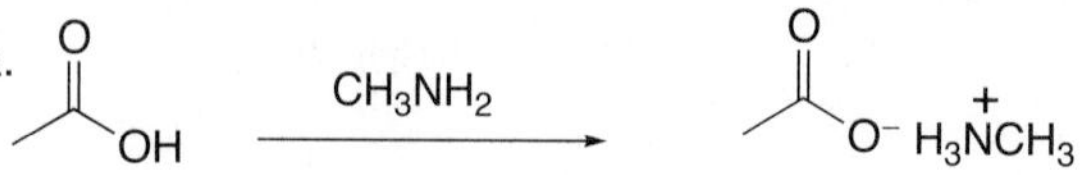

c.
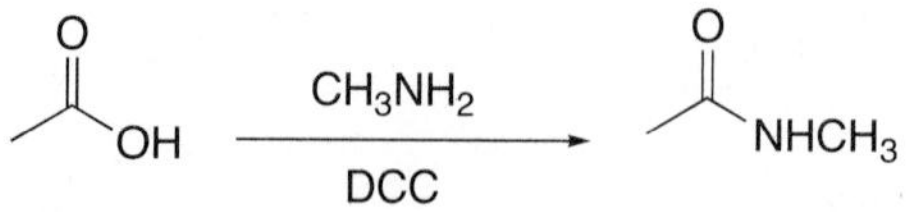

b.
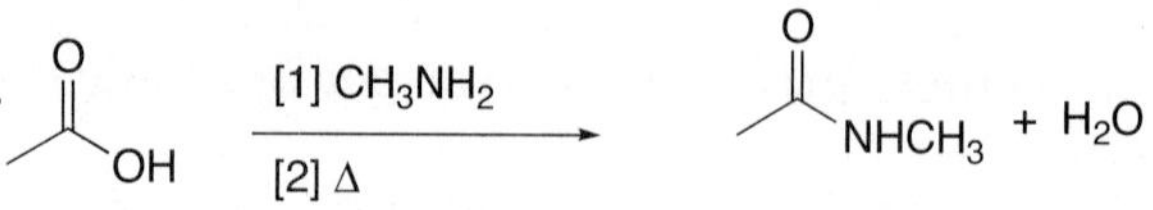

22.20

a.

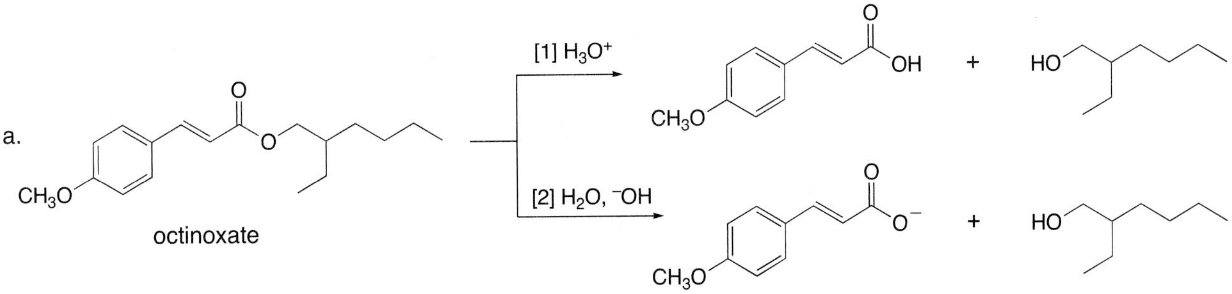

octinoxate
[1] H_3O^+
[2] H_2O, ^-OH
CH_3O
OH
HO
O^-

b.

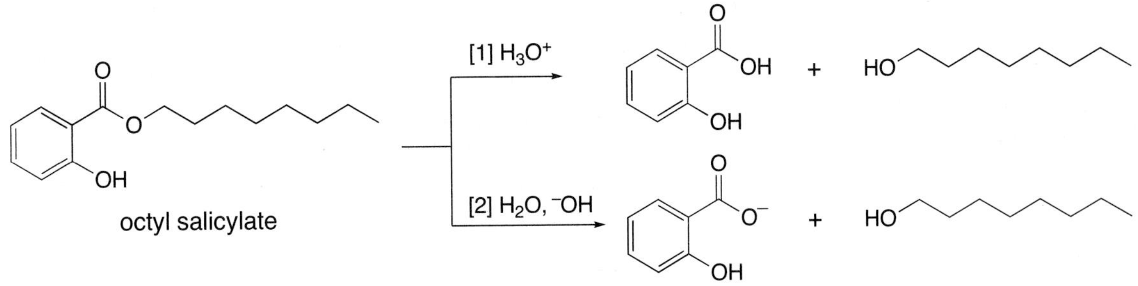

octyl salicylate
[1] H_3O^+
[2] H_2O, ^-OH
OH
HO
O^-

22.21 Bonds broken during hydrolysis are indicated.

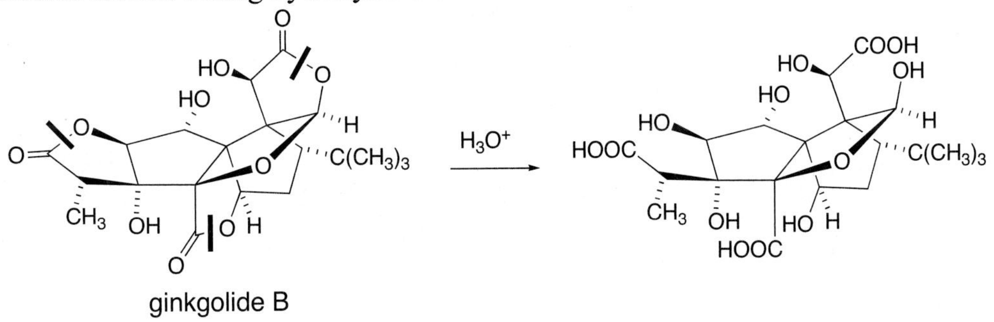

ginkgolide B
H_3O^+
$C(CH_3)_3$
CH_3
HOOC
COOH

22.22

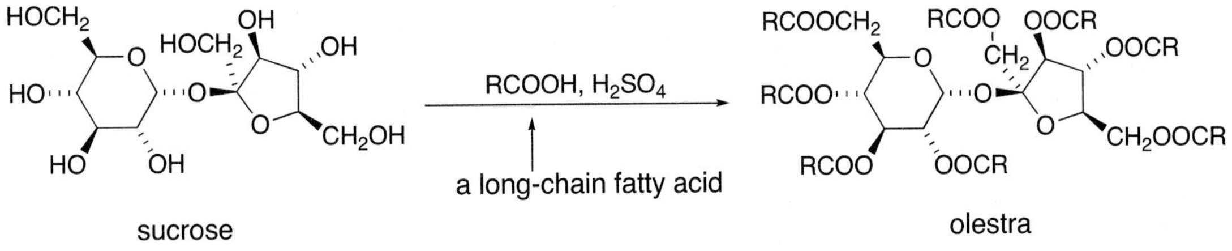

sucrose
RCOOH, H_2SO_4
a long-chain fatty acid
olestra

22.23

$CH_2OCO(CH_2)_{15}CH_3$
$CHOCO(CH_2)_{15}CH_3$
$CH_2OCO(CH_2)_7CH{=}CH(CH_2)_7CH_3$ (cis)

$\xrightarrow{\text{hydrolysis}}$

$CH_2\text{-}OH$
$CH\text{-}OH$
$CH_2\text{-}OH$
glycerol

\+

$Na^+ \ ^-OOC(CH_2)_{15}CH_3$
$Na^+ \ ^-OOC(CH_2)_{15}CH_3$
$Na^+ \ ^-OOC(CH_2)_7CH{=}CH(CH_2)_7CH_3$ (cis)
soap

22.24

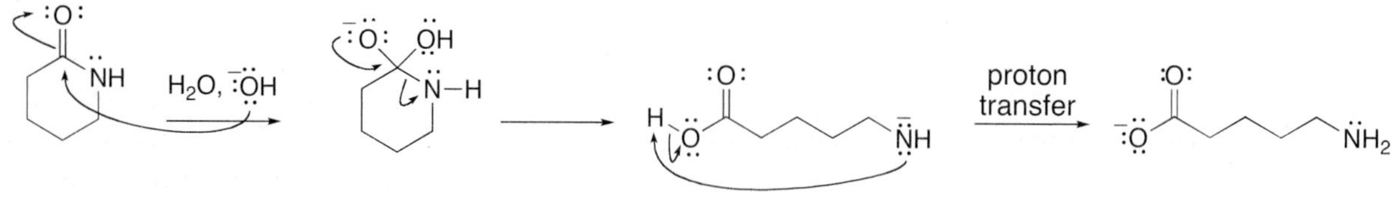

22.25 Aspirin has an ester, a more reactive acyl group, whereas acetaminophen has an amide, a less reactive acyl group.

a. The ester makes aspirin more easily hydrolyzed with water from the air than acetaminophen. Therefore, Tylenol can be kept for many years, whereas aspirin decomposes.

b. Similarly, aspirin will be hydrolyzed and decompose in the aqueous medium of a liquid medication, but acetaminophen is stable due to the less reactive amide group, allowing it to remain unchanged while dissolved in H_2O.

acetylsalicylic acid

acetaminophen

22.26

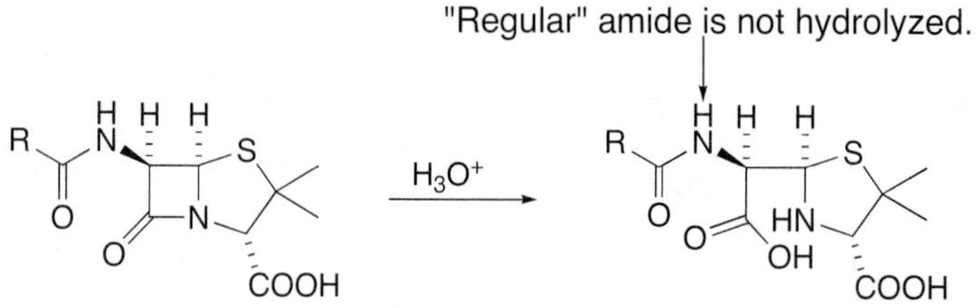

22.27

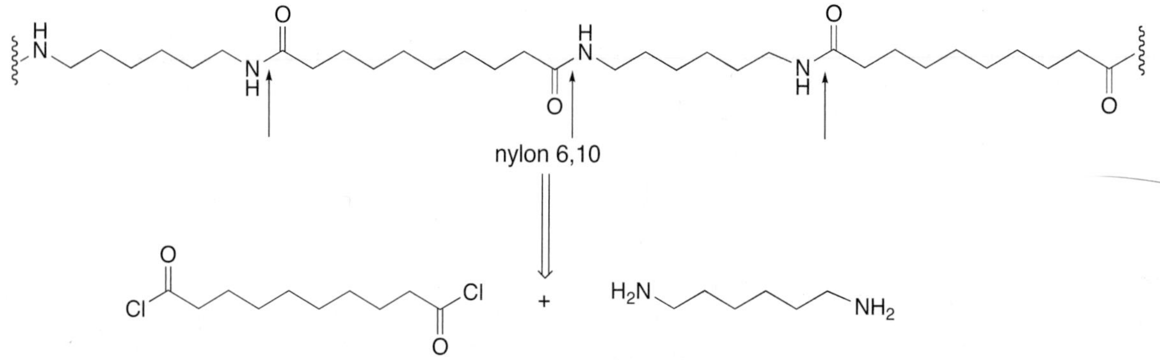

22.28

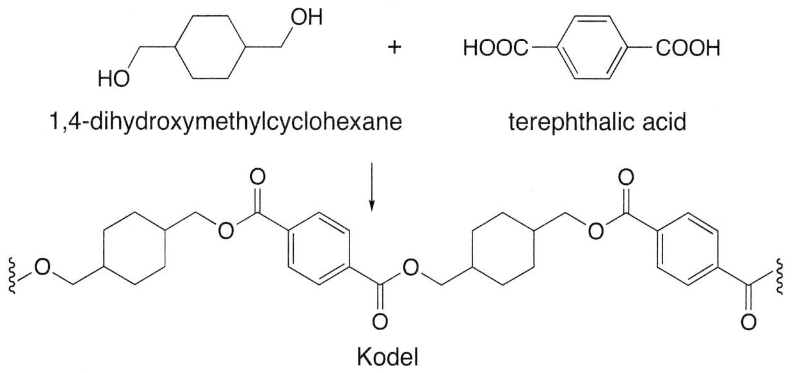
OH
HO
+
HOOC
COOH
1,4-dihydroxymethylcyclohexane
terephthalic acid
O
Kodel

In the polyester Kodel, most of the bonds in the polymer backbone are part of a ring, so there are fewer degrees of freedom. Fabrics made from Kodel are stiff and crease resistant, due to these less flexible polyester fibers.

22.29

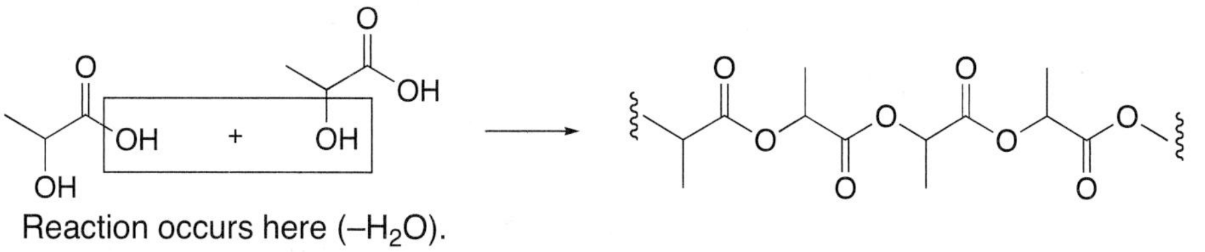
O
OH
+
OH
Reaction occurs here (–H2O).

PLA
polyl(lactic acid)

22.30 Acetyl CoA acetylates the NH_2 group of glucosamine, since the NH_2 group is the most nucleophilic site.

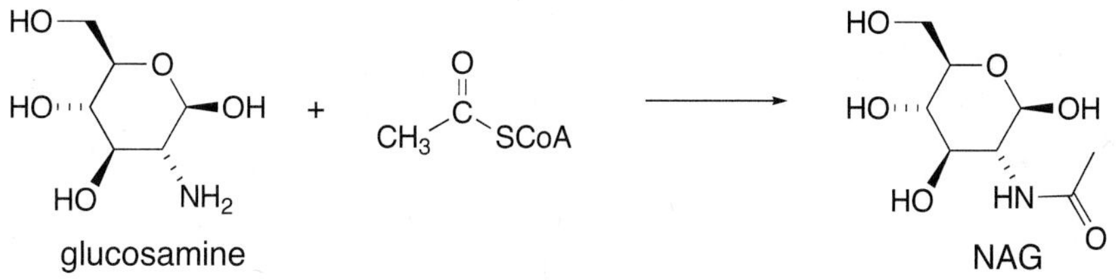
HO
O
OH
+
CH3
C
SCoA
NH2
glucosamine
HN
NAG

22.31

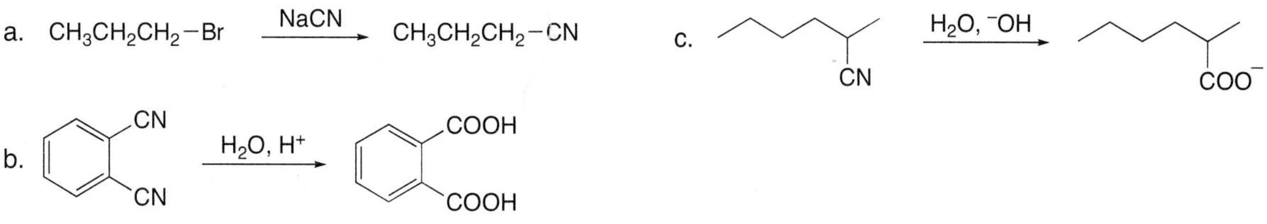
a. CH3CH2CH2–Br
NaCN
CH3CH2CH2–CN
c.
CN
H2O, –OH
COO–
b.
CN
H2O, H+
COOH

22.32

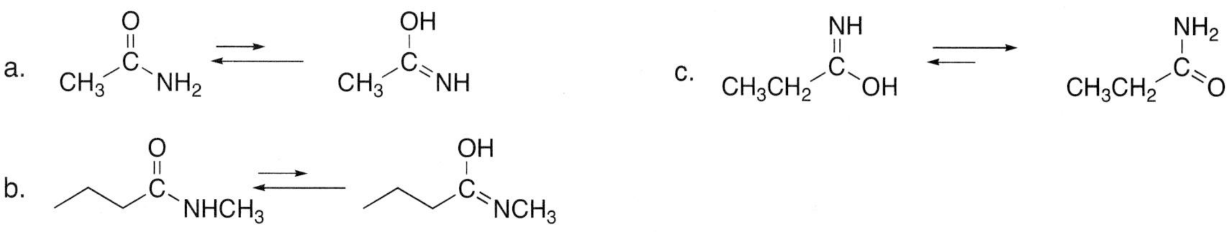
a.
CH3
NH2
OH
NH
b.
NHCH3
NCH3
c.
CH3CH2
OH
NH2
O

22.33

a. 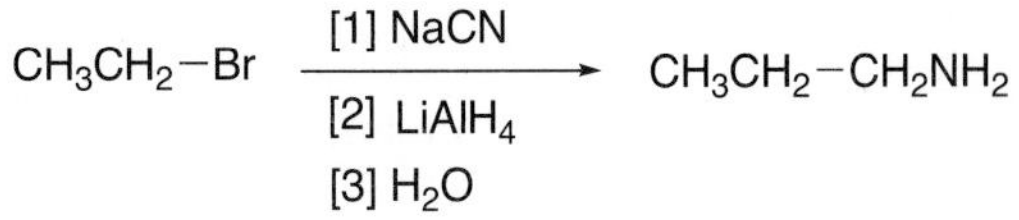

b. 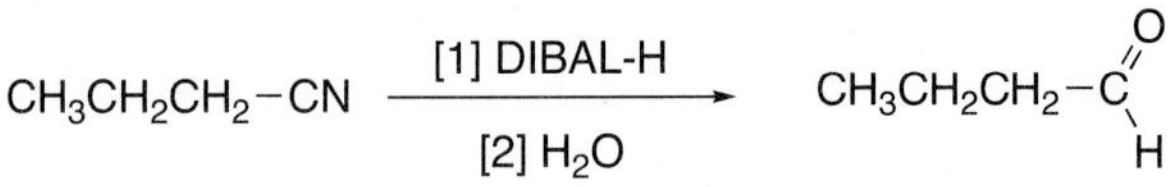

22.34

a. 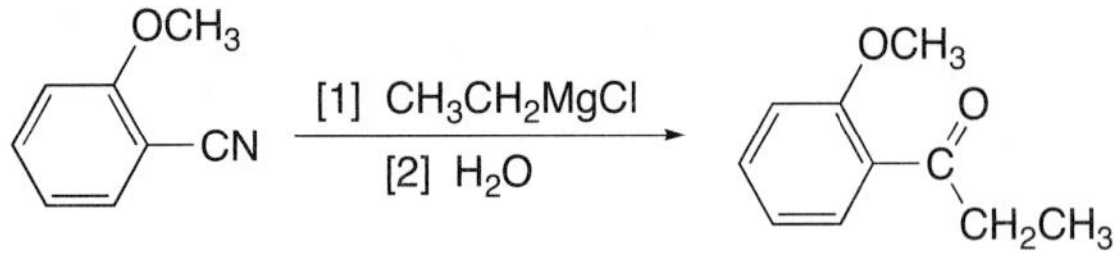

b. 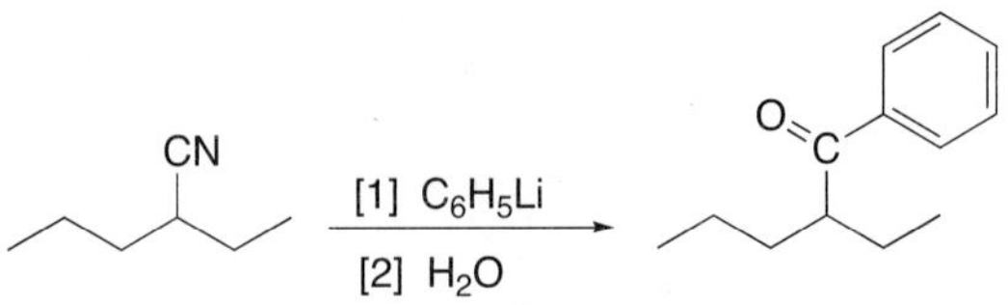

22.35

a. 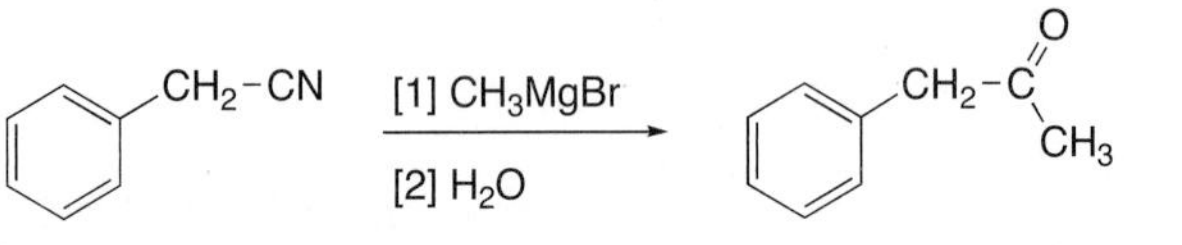

c. 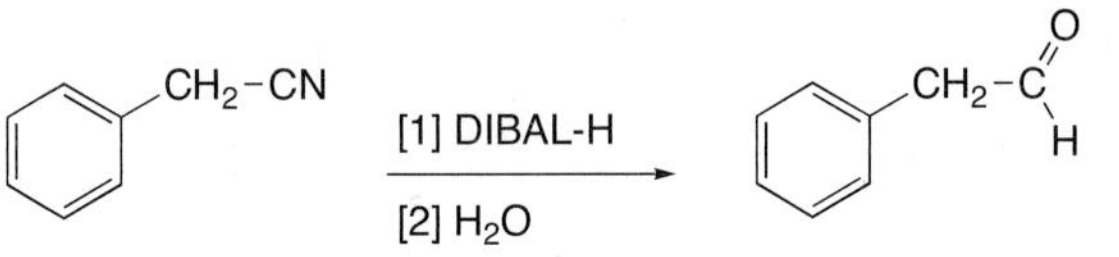

b. 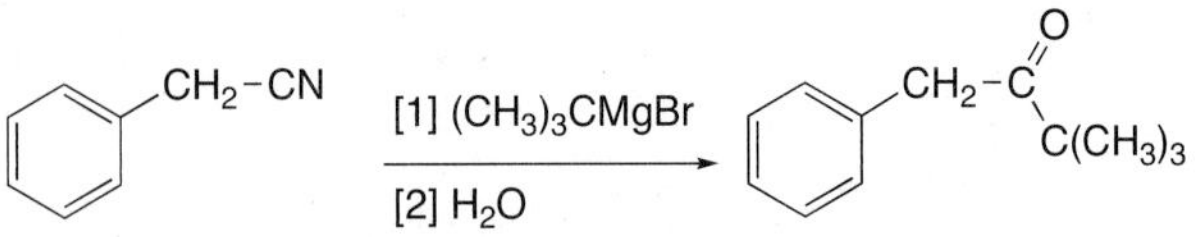

d. 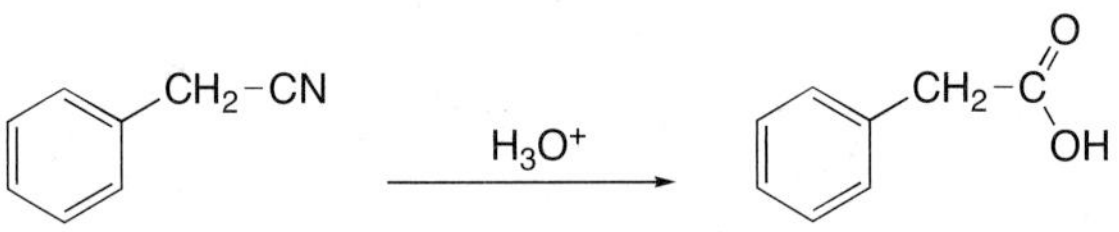

22.36

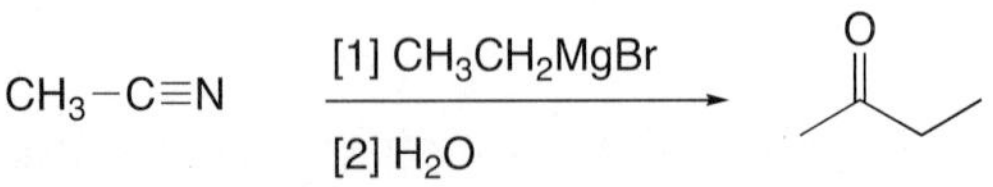

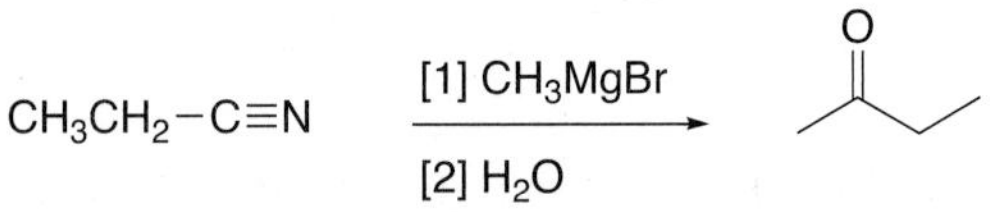

22.37 The better the leaving group, the more reactive the acyl compound.

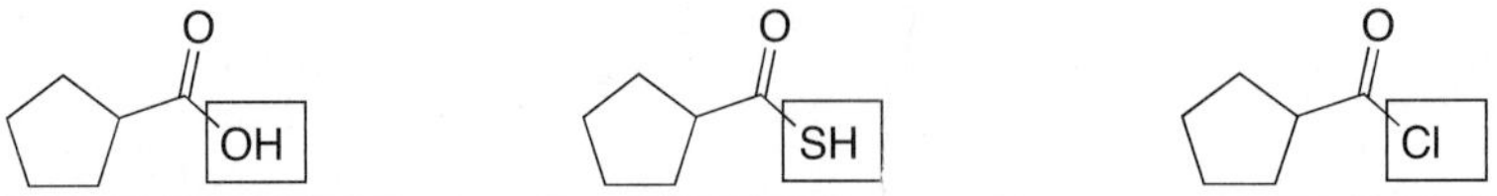

worst leaving group **least reactive** | **intermediate reactivity** | best leaving group **most reactive**

22.38

a. 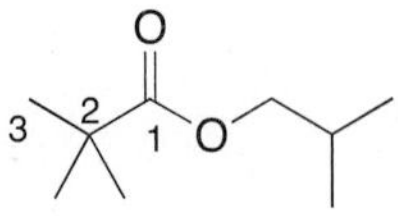

A
isobutyl 2,2-dimethyl-propanoate

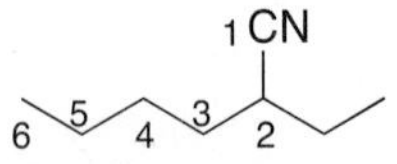

B
2-ethylhexanenitrile

b.

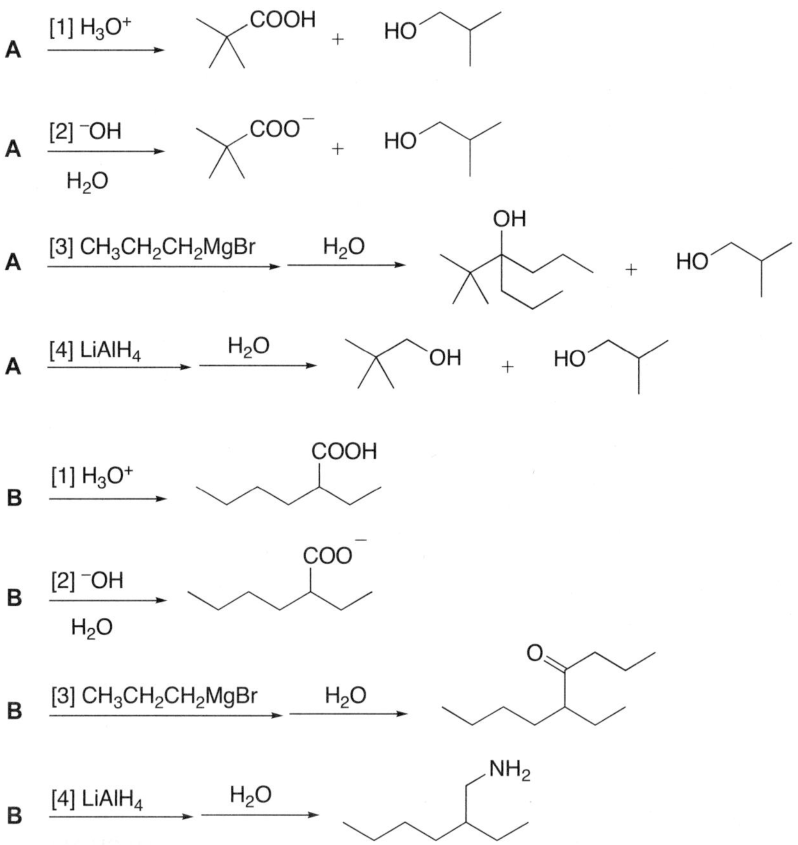
A
[1] H_3O^+
COOH
HO
A
[2] ^-OH
H_2O
COO^-
HO
A
[3] $CH_3CH_2CH_2MgBr$
H_2O
OH
HO
A
[4] $LiAlH_4$
H_2O
OH
HO
B
[1] H_3O^+
COOH
B
[2] ^-OH
H_2O
COO^-
B
[3] $CH_3CH_2CH_2MgBr$
H_2O
O
B
[4] $LiAlH_4$
H_2O
NH_2

22.39 Better leaving groups make acyl compounds more reactive. **C** has an electron-withdrawing NO_2 group, which stabilizes the negative charge of the leaving group, whereas **D** has an electron-donating OCH_3 group, which destabilizes the leaving group.

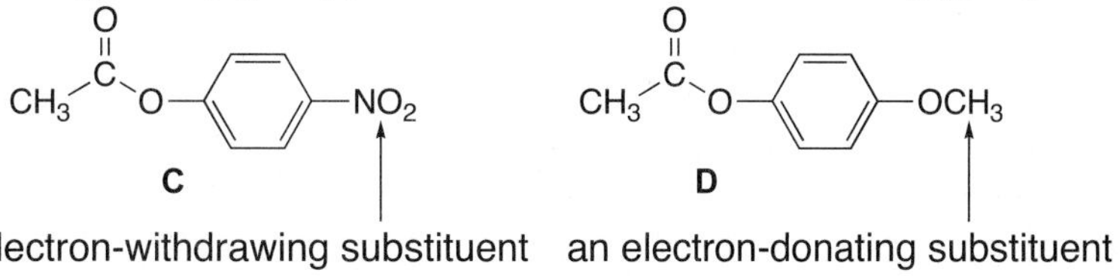
CH_3
NO_2
C
CH_3
OCH_3
D
an electron-withdrawing substituent
an electron-donating substituent

N+
N+
OCH_3
OCH_3

leaving group from **C** — one possible resonance structure

Delocalizing the negative charge on the NO_2 stabilizes the leaving group, making **C** more reactive than **D**.

leaving group from **D** — one possible resonance structure

Adjacent negative charges destabilize the leaving group.

22.40

a. 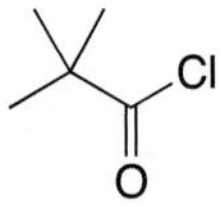 **2,2-dimethylpropanoyl chloride**

b. 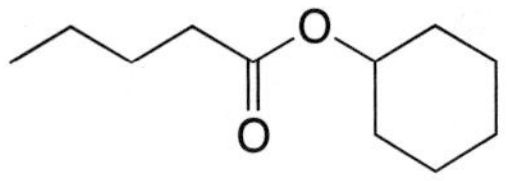 **cyclohexyl pentanoate**

c. 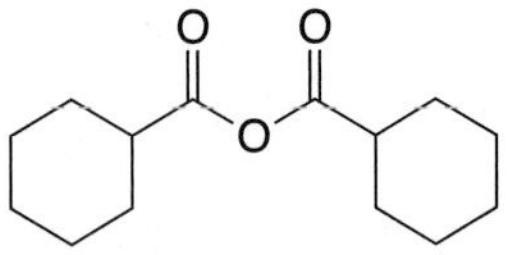

cyclohexanecarboxylic anhydride

d. 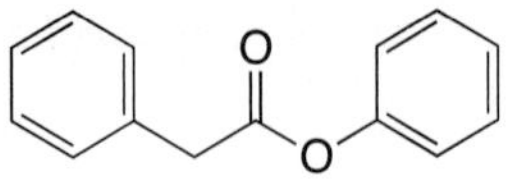 **phenyl phenylacetate**

e. 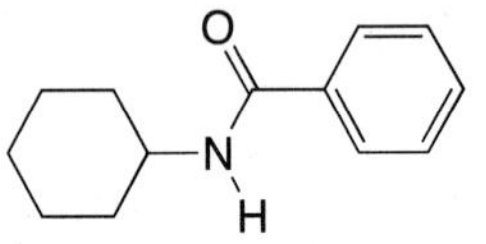 ***N*-cyclohexylbenzamide**

f. 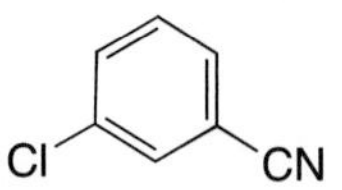 ***m*-chlorobenzonitrile**

g. 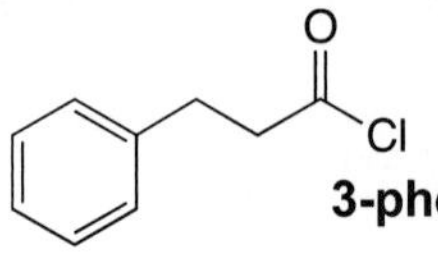 **3-phenylpropanoyl chloride**

h. 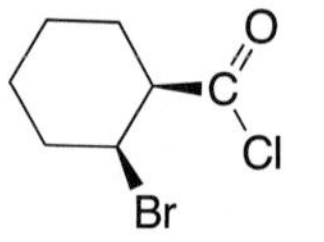 ***cis*-2-bromocyclohexane-carbonyl chloride**

i. 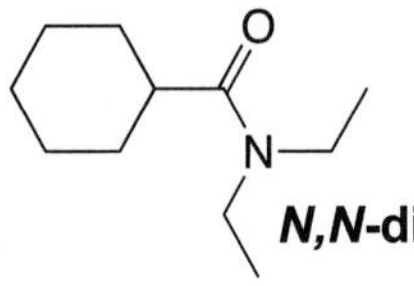 ***N,N*-diethylcyclohexanecarboxamide**

j. 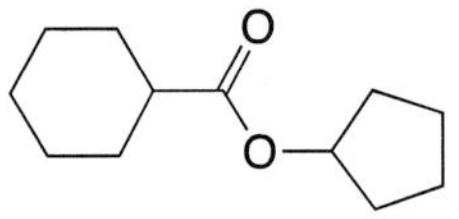 **cyclopentyl cyclohexanecarboxylate**

22.41

a. propanoic anhydride

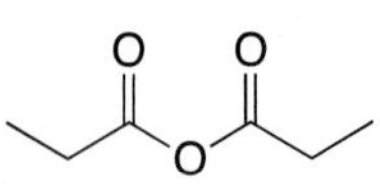

b. α-chlorobutyryl chloride

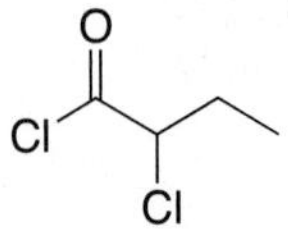

c. cyclohexyl propanoate

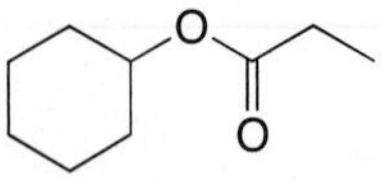

d. cyclohexanecarboxamide

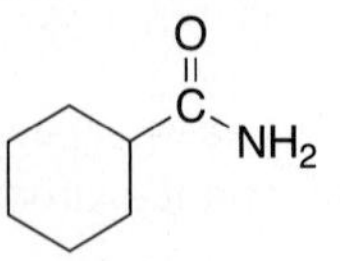

e. isopropyl formate

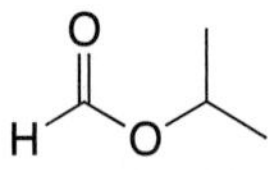

f. *N*-cyclopentylpentanamide

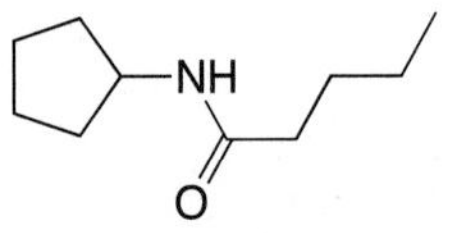

g. 4-methylheptanenitrile

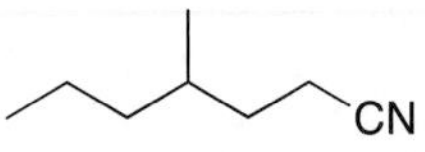

h. vinyl acetate

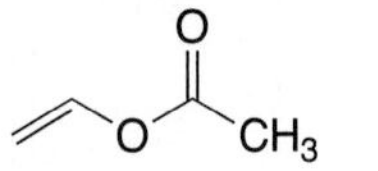

i. benzoic propanoic anhydride

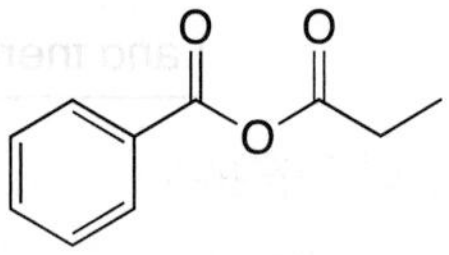

j. 3-methylhexanoyl chloride

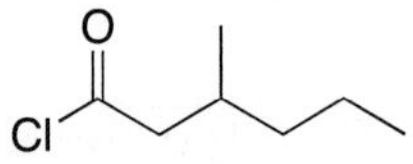

k. octyl butanoate

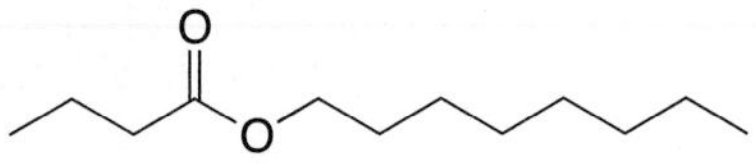

l. *N,N*-dibenzylformamide

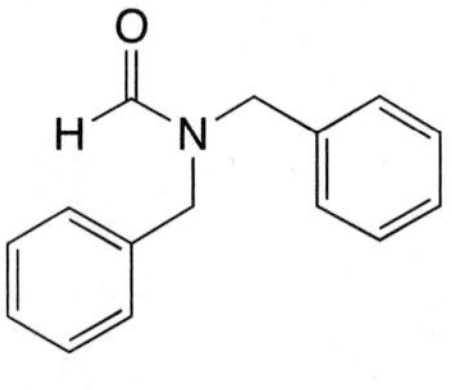

22.42 Rank the compounds using the rules from Answer 22.10.

a. 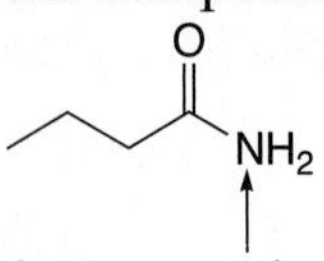

$^{-}NH_2$ strongest base
least reactive

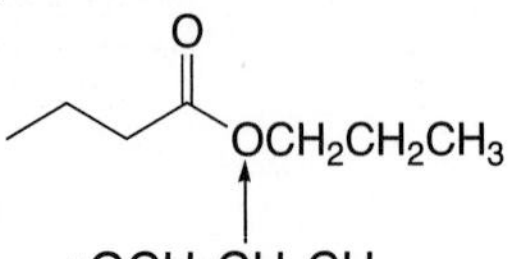

$^{-}OCH_2CH_2CH_3$
intermediate

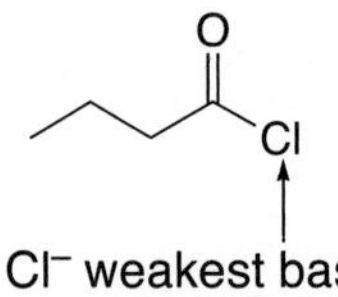

Cl^{-} weakest base
most reactive

b.

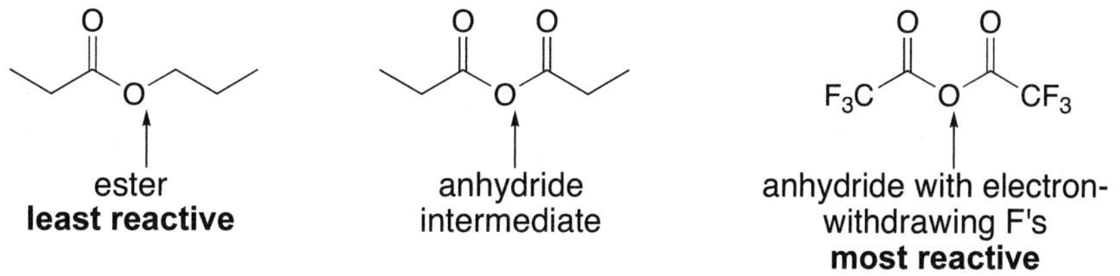
F3C
CF3
ester
least reactive
anhydride
intermediate
anhydride with electron-withdrawing F's
most reactive

22.43

resonance structures for the leaving group

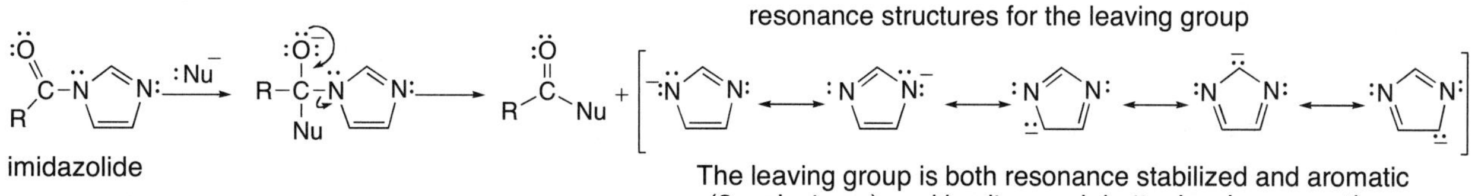
:Nu⁻
Nu
imidazolide

The leaving group is both resonance stabilized and aromatic (6 π electrons), making it a much better leaving group than exists in a regular amide.

22.44

Reaction as an acid:

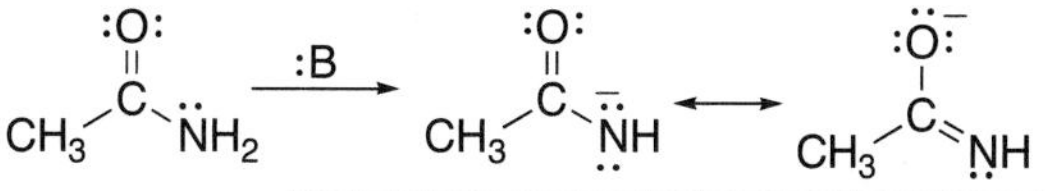
:B
CH3
NH2
NH

These two resonance structures make the conjugate base more stable, and therefore CH_3CONH_2 a stronger acid.

$CH_3CH_2{-}\ddot{N}H_2 \xrightarrow{:B} CH_3CH_2{-}\ddot{N}H^-$

no resonance stabilization of the conjugate base

Reaction as a base:

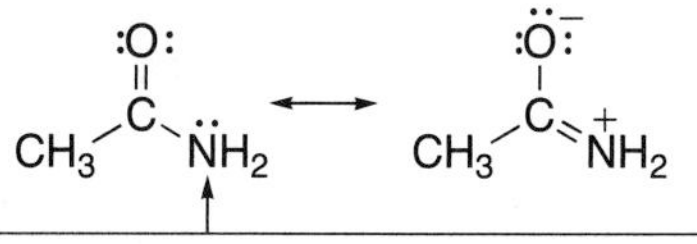
CH3
NH2

This electron pair is delocalized by resonance, making it less available for electron donation. Thus, CH_3CONH_2 is a much weaker base.

$CH_3CH_2{-}\ddot{N}H_2$ ← This electron pair is localized on N.

22.45

$CH_3CH_2CH_2CH_2COCl$

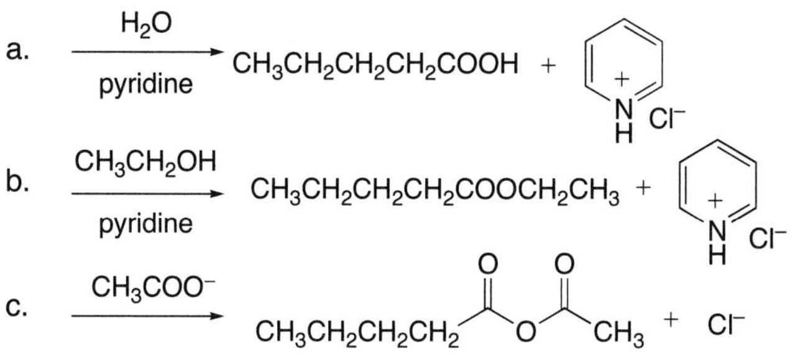
a.
H2O
pyridine
CH3CH2CH2CH2COOH +
Cl⁻
b.
CH3CH2OH
pyridine
CH3CH2CH2CH2COOCH2CH3 +
Cl⁻
c.
CH3COO⁻
CH3CH2CH2CH2
CH3
+ Cl⁻

d. $\xrightarrow[\text{excess}]{NH_3}$ $CH_3CH_2CH_2CH_2CONH_2$ + $\overset{+}{N}H_4$ Cl^-

e. $\xrightarrow[\text{excess}]{(CH_3CH_2)_2NH}$ $CH_3CH_2CH_2CH_2CON(CH_2CH_3)_2$ + $(CH_3CH_2)_2\overset{+}{N}H_2$ Cl^-

f. $\xrightarrow[\text{excess}]{C_6H_5NH_2}$ $CH_3CH_2CH_2CH_2CONHC_6H_5$ + $C_6H_5\overset{+}{N}H_3$ Cl^-

22.46

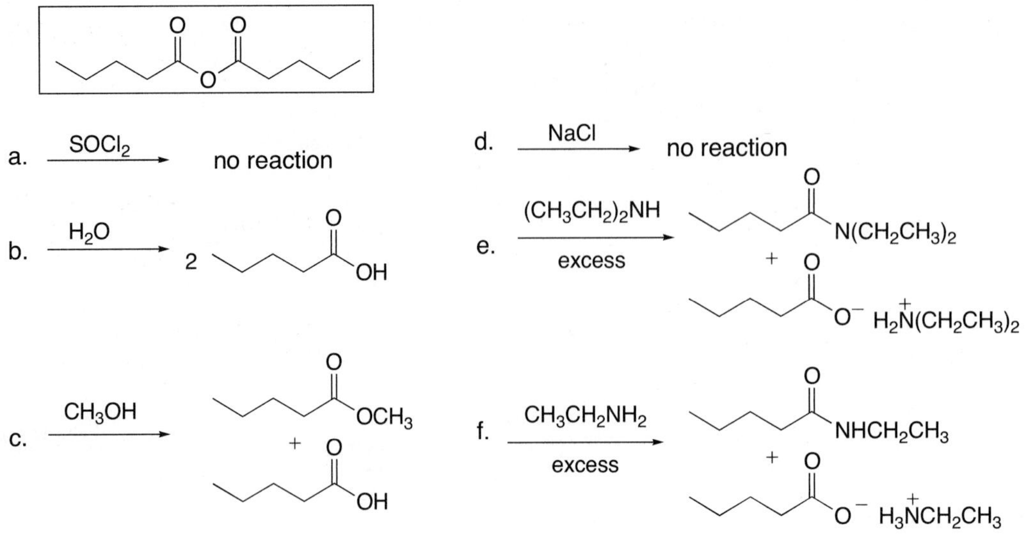
a.
SOCl2
no reaction
b.
H2O
2
OH
c.
CH3OH
OCH3
+
OH
d.
NaCl
no reaction
e.
(CH3CH2)2NH
excess
N(CH2CH3)2
+
O− H2N(CH2CH3)2
f.
CH3CH2NH2
excess
NHCH2CH3
+
O− H3NCH2CH3

22.47

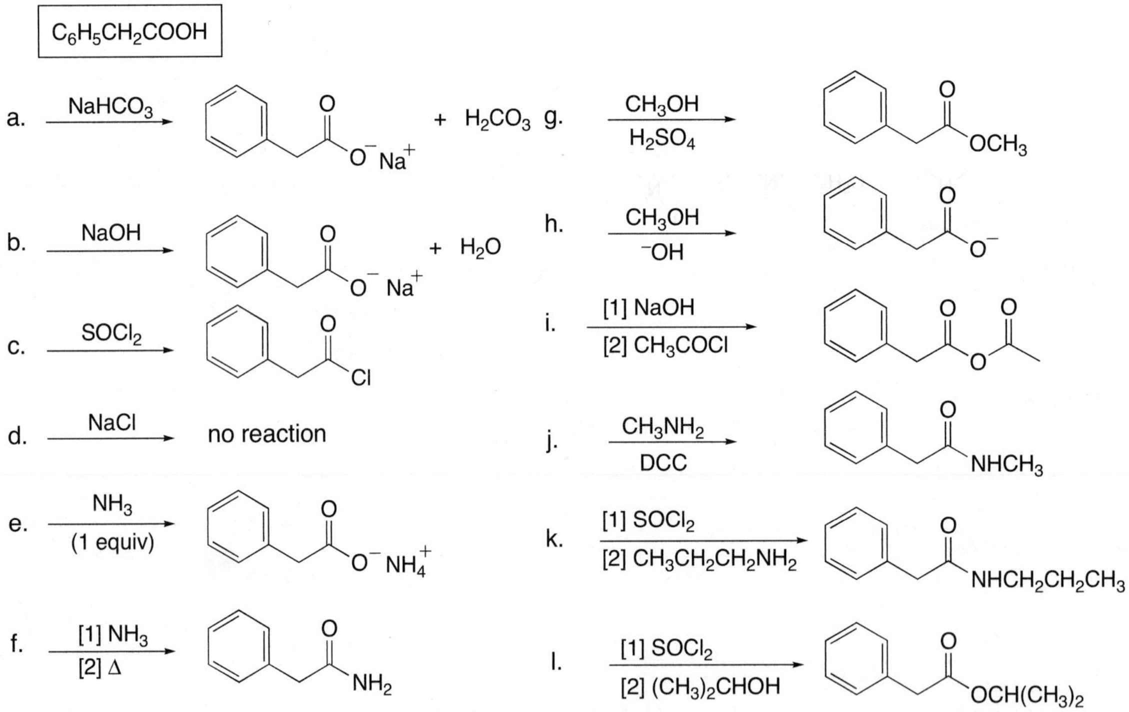
C6H5CH2COOH
a.
NaHCO3
O− Na+
+ H2CO3
b.
NaOH
O− Na+
+ H2O
c.
SOCl2
Cl
d.
NaCl
no reaction
e.
NH3
(1 equiv)
O− NH4+
f.
[1] NH3
[2] Δ
NH2
g.
CH3OH
H2SO4
OCH3
h.
CH3OH
−OH
O−
i.
[1] NaOH
[2] CH3COCl
j.
CH3NH2
DCC
NHCH3
k.
[1] SOCl2
[2] CH3CH2CH2NH2
NHCH2CH2CH3
l.
[1] SOCl2
[2] (CH3)2CHOH
OCH(CH3)2

22.48

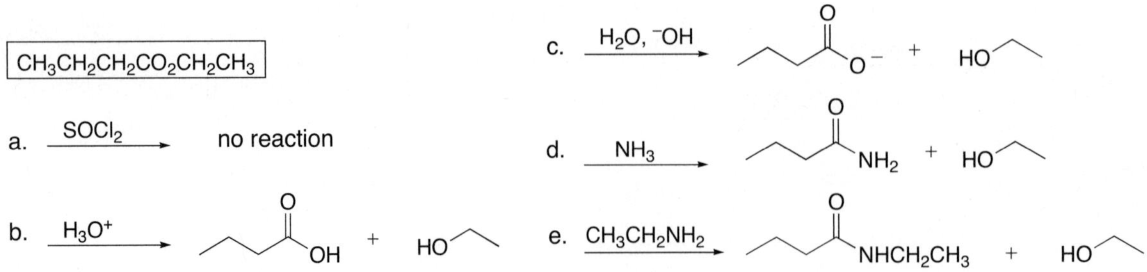
CH3CH2CH2CO2CH2CH3
a.
SOCl2
no reaction
b.
H3O+
OH
+
HO
c.
H2O, −OH
O−
+
HO
d.
NH3
NH2
+
HO
e.
CH3CH2NH2
NHCH2CH3
+
HO

22.49

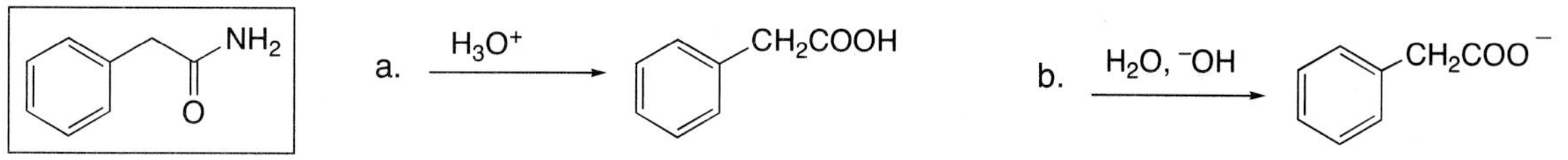

22.50

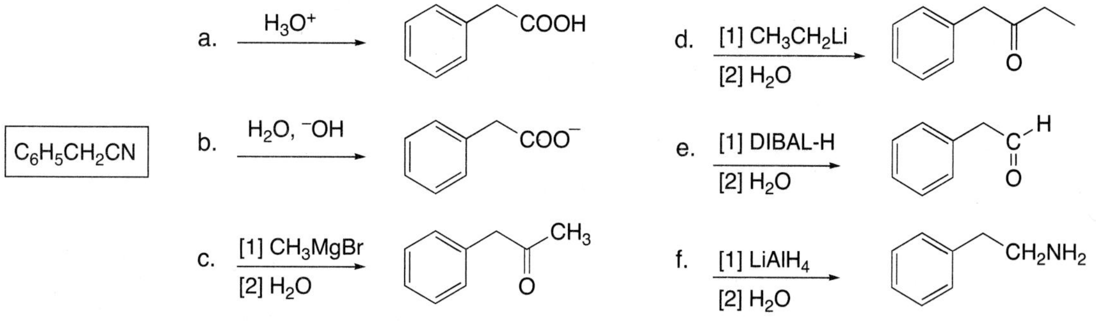

22.51

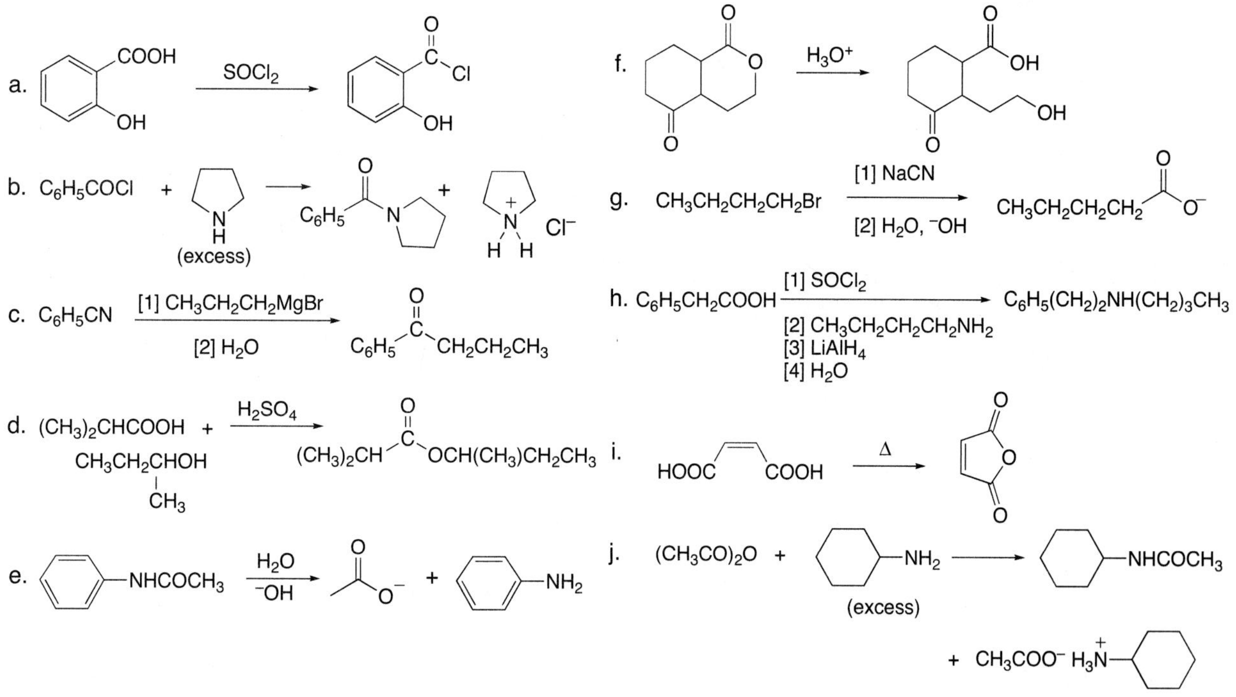

22.52 Both lactones and acetals are hydrolyzed with aqueous acid, but only lactones react with aqueous base.

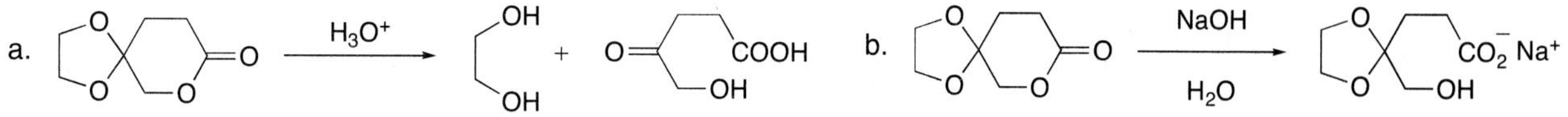

X X

22.53

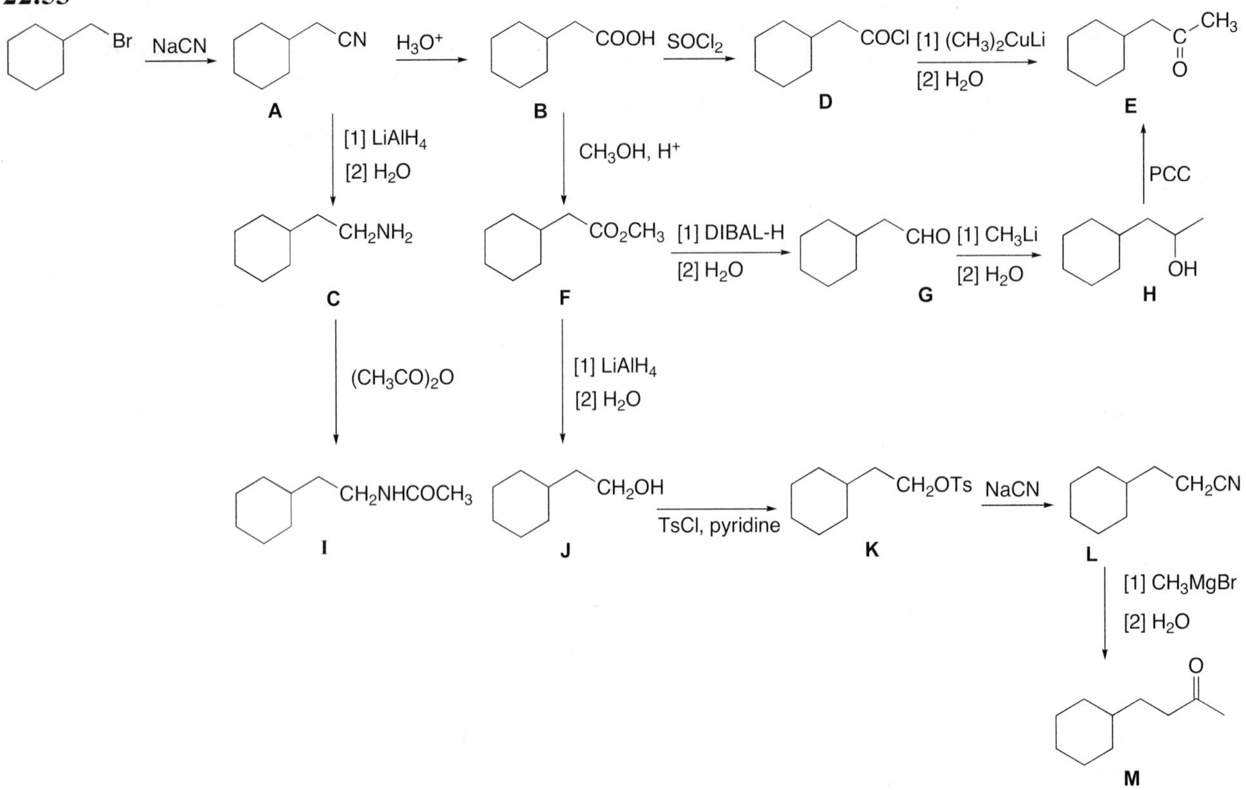

22.54

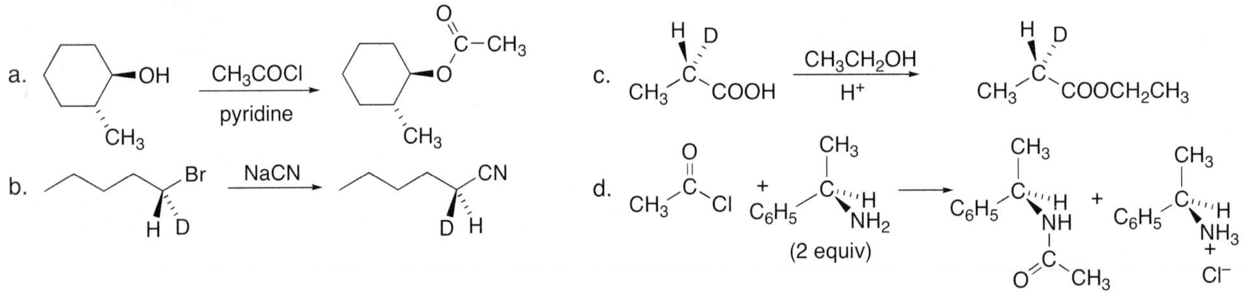

22.55 Hydrolyze the amide and ester bonds in both starting materials to draw the products.

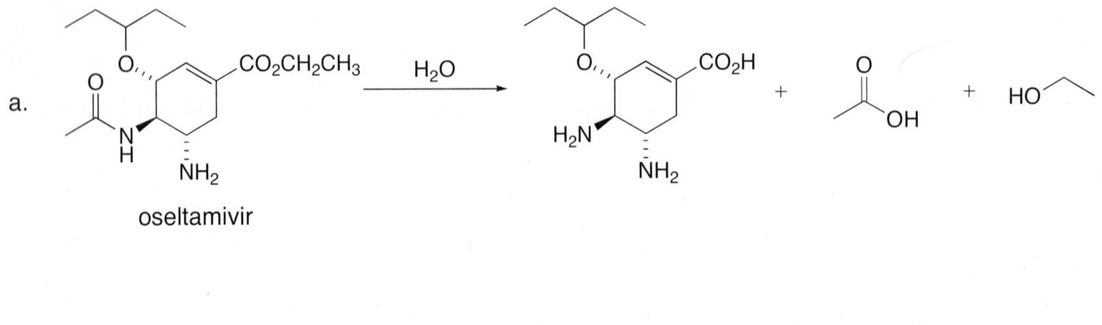

b.

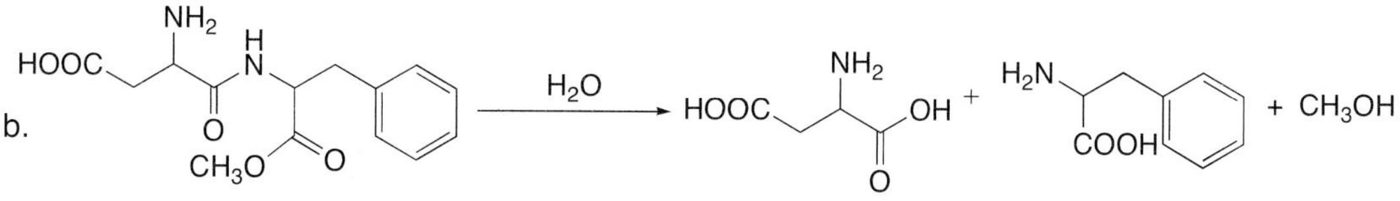

aspartame
phenylalanine

22.56

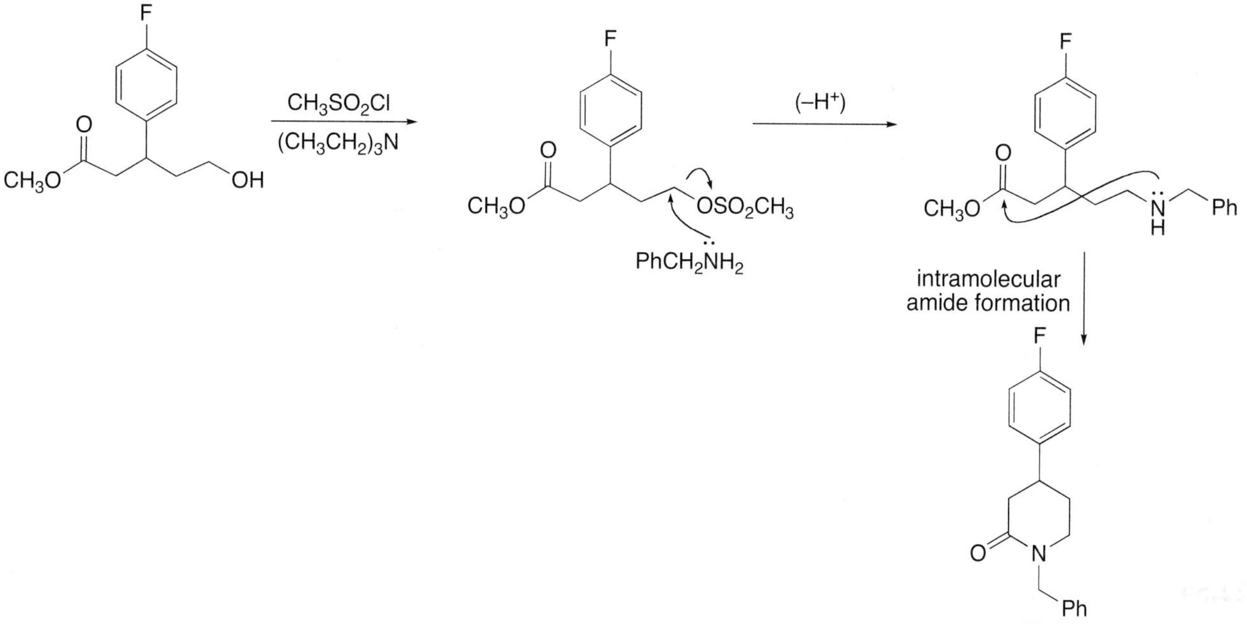

intramolecular amide formation
F

F

$C_{18}H_{18}FNO$

22.57

a.

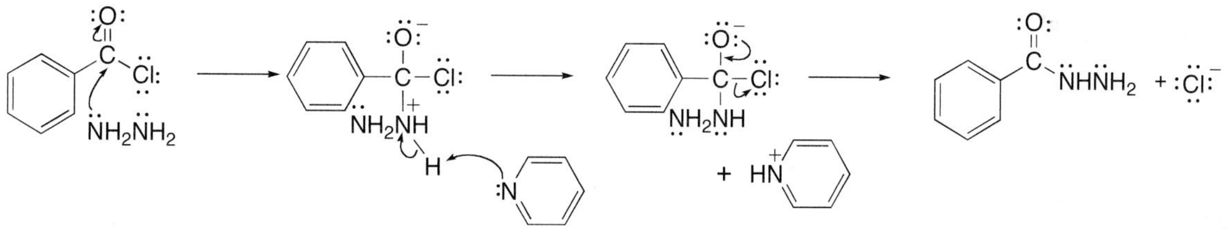

b.

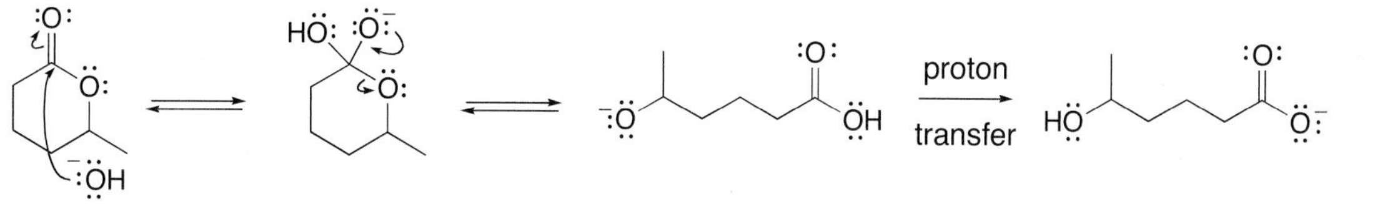

proton transfer

22.58

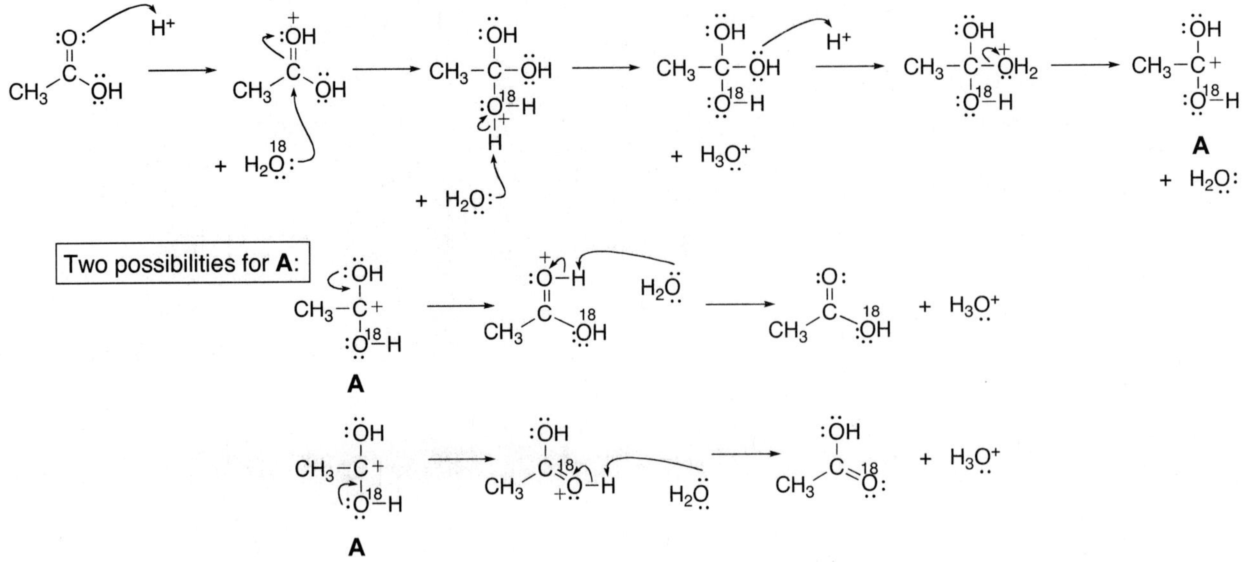
H+
+ H2O:
+ H3O+
A
+ H2O:
Two possibilities for A:
A
+ H3O+
A
+ H3O+

22.59

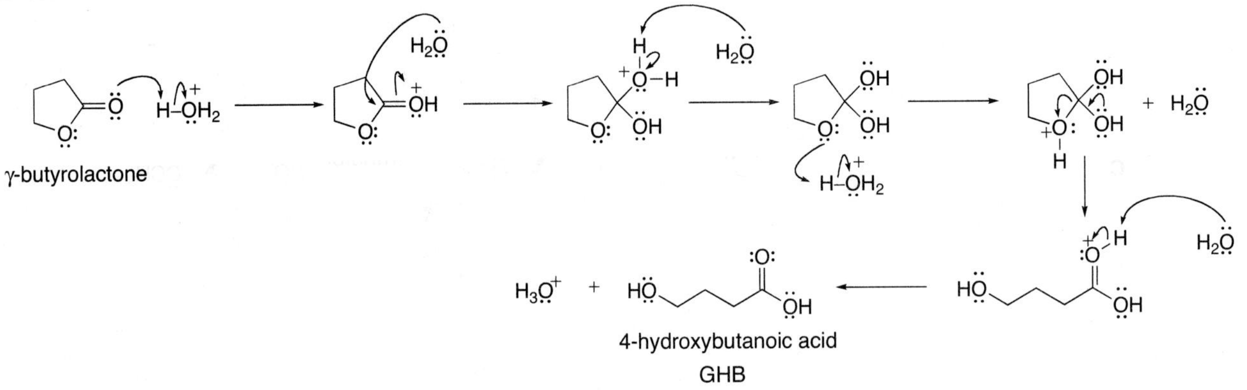
γ-butyrolactone
+ H2O
H3O+
4-hydroxybutanoic acid
GHB

22.60

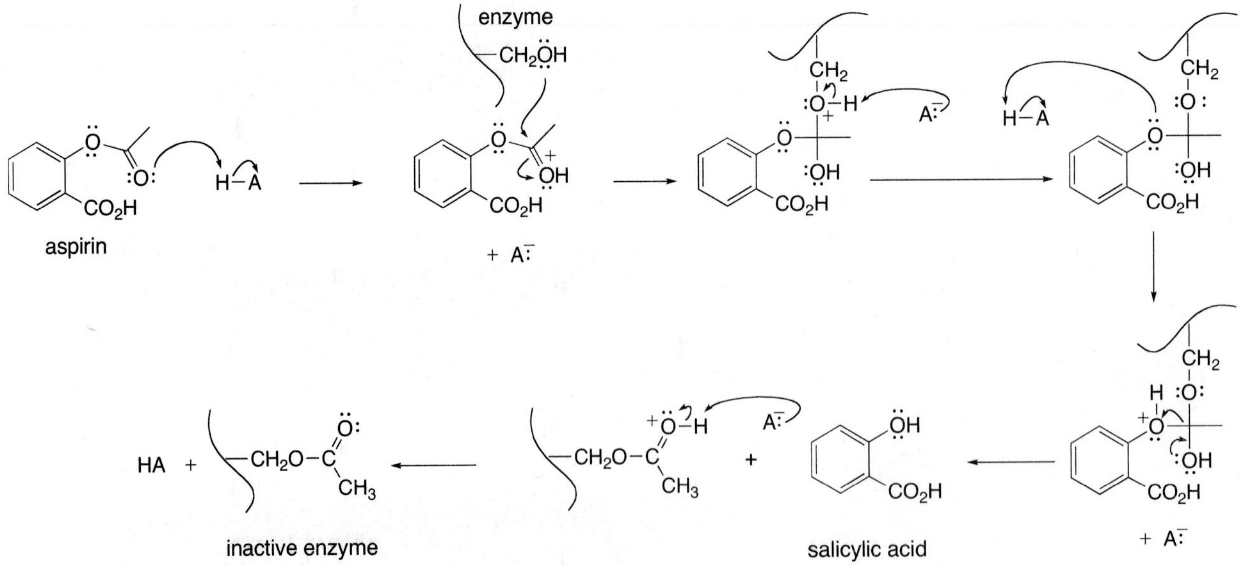
aspirin
enzyme
+ A:
HA
inactive enzyme
salicylic acid
+ A:

22.61

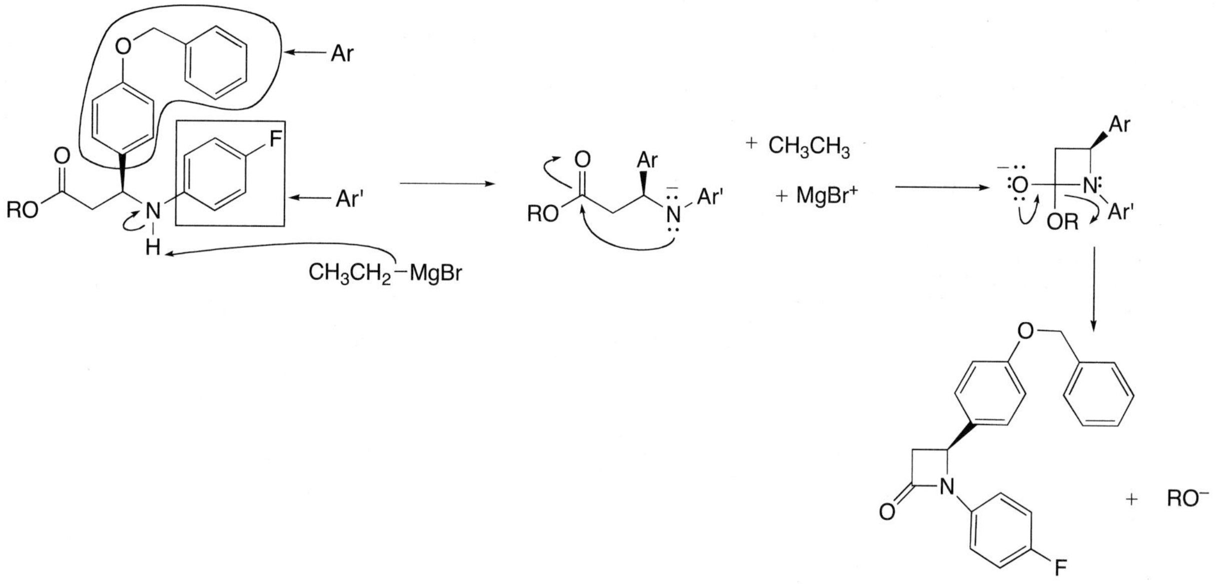
Ar
Ar'
RO
CH3CH2–MgBr
+ CH3CH3
+ MgBr+
OR
+ RO–
F

22.62

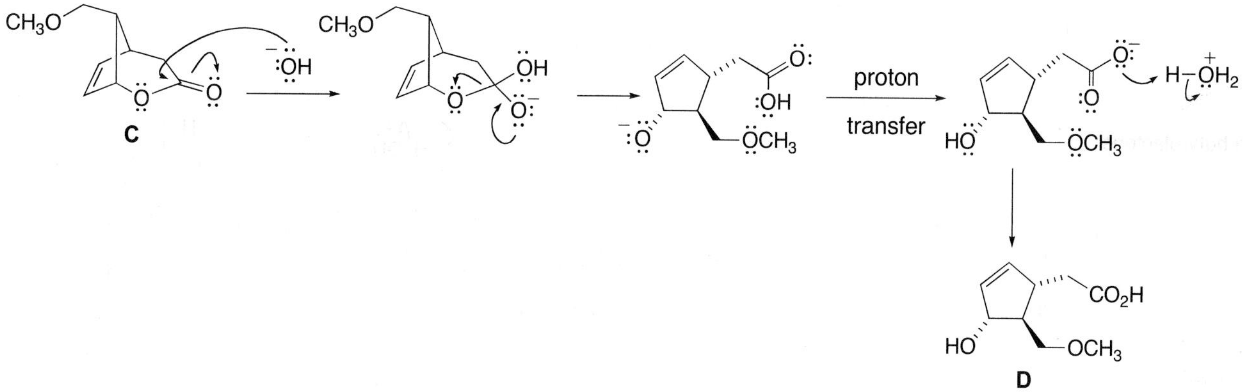
CH3O
C
:OH
proton
transfer
OCH3
CO2H
HO
D

22.63

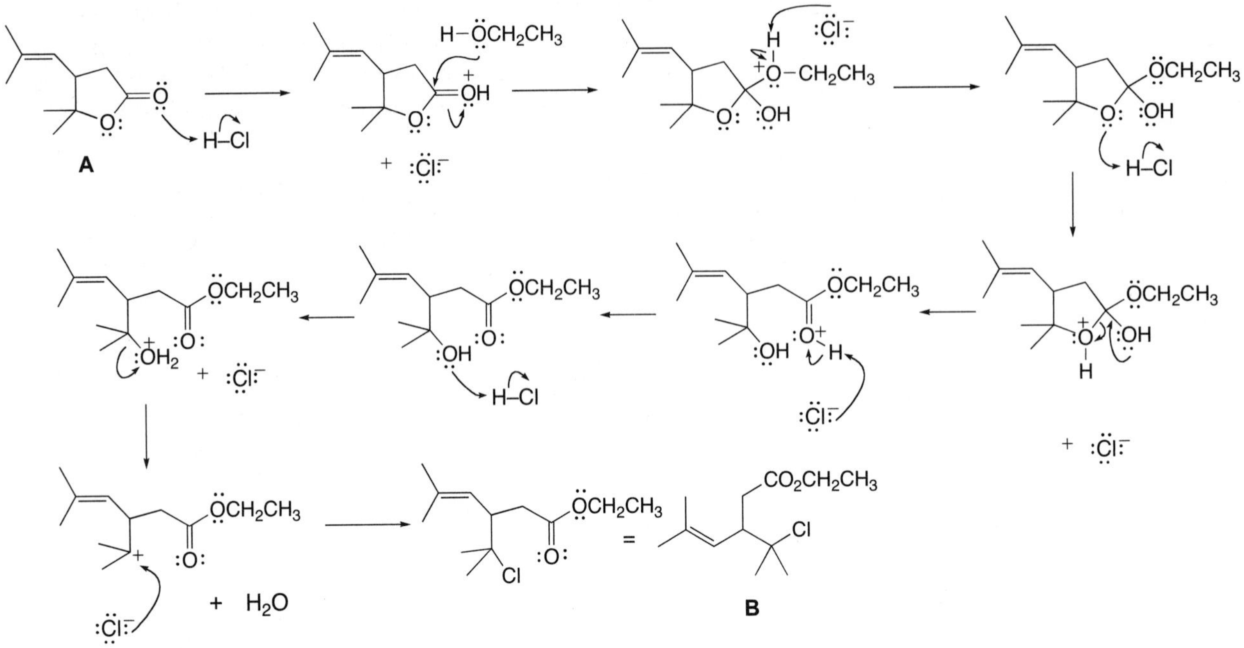

22.64 The mechanism is composed of two parts: hydrolysis of the acetal and intramolecular Fischer esterification of the hydroxy carboxylic acid.

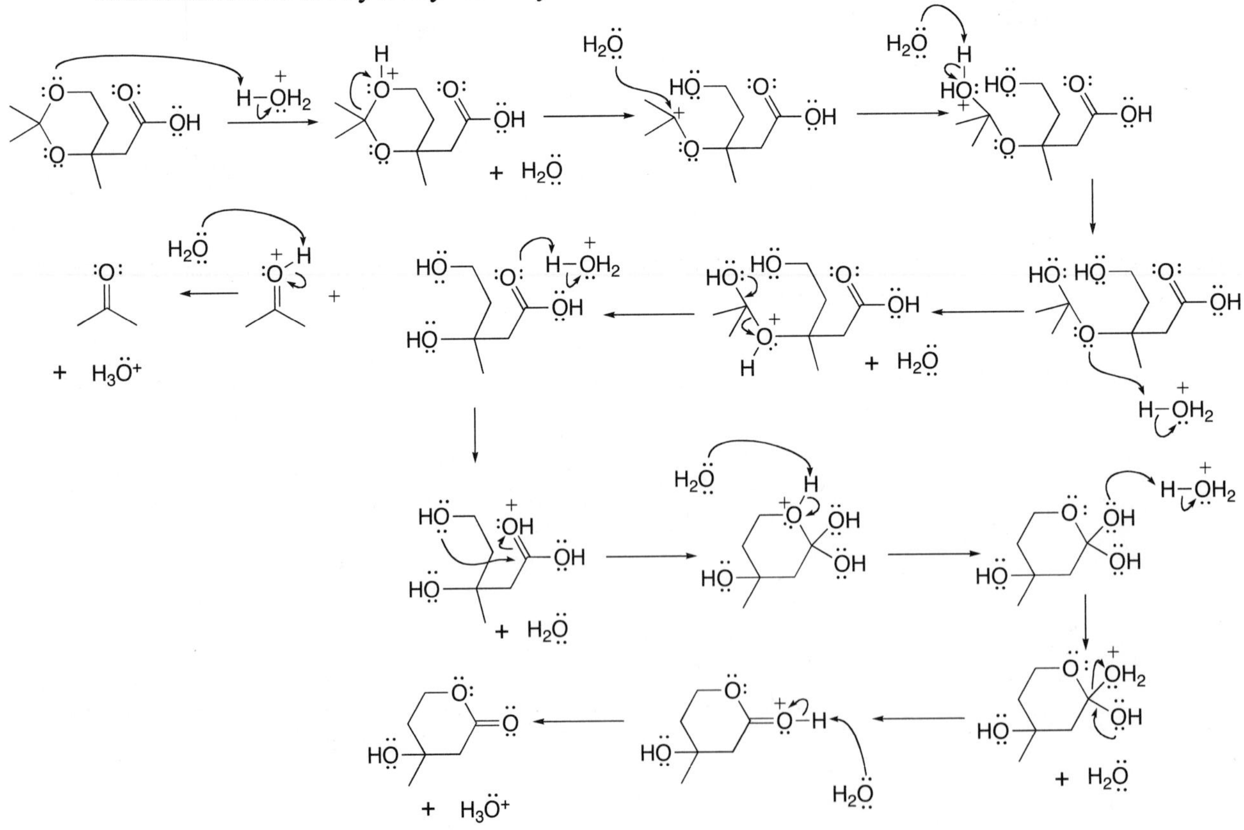

22.65

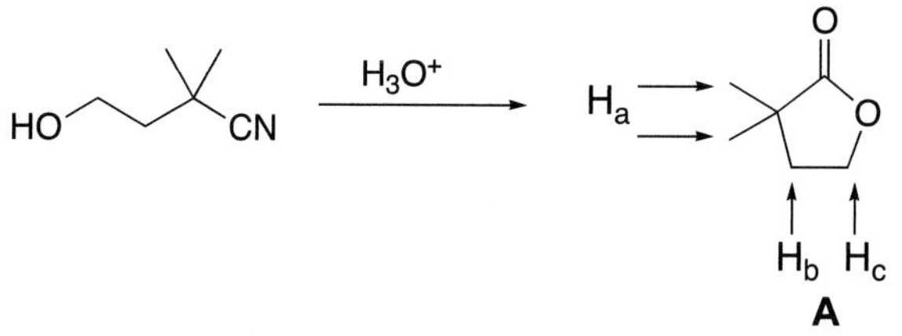

A

$C_6H_{10}O_2$: 2 degrees of unsaturation

IR: 1770 cm^{-1} from ester C=O in a five-membered ring

^{1}H NMR: H_a = 1.27 ppm (singlet, 6 H) – 2 CH_3 groups

H_b = 2.12 ppm (triplet, 2 H) – CH_2 bonded to CH_2

H_c = 4.26 ppm (triplet, 2 H) – CH_2 bonded to CH_2

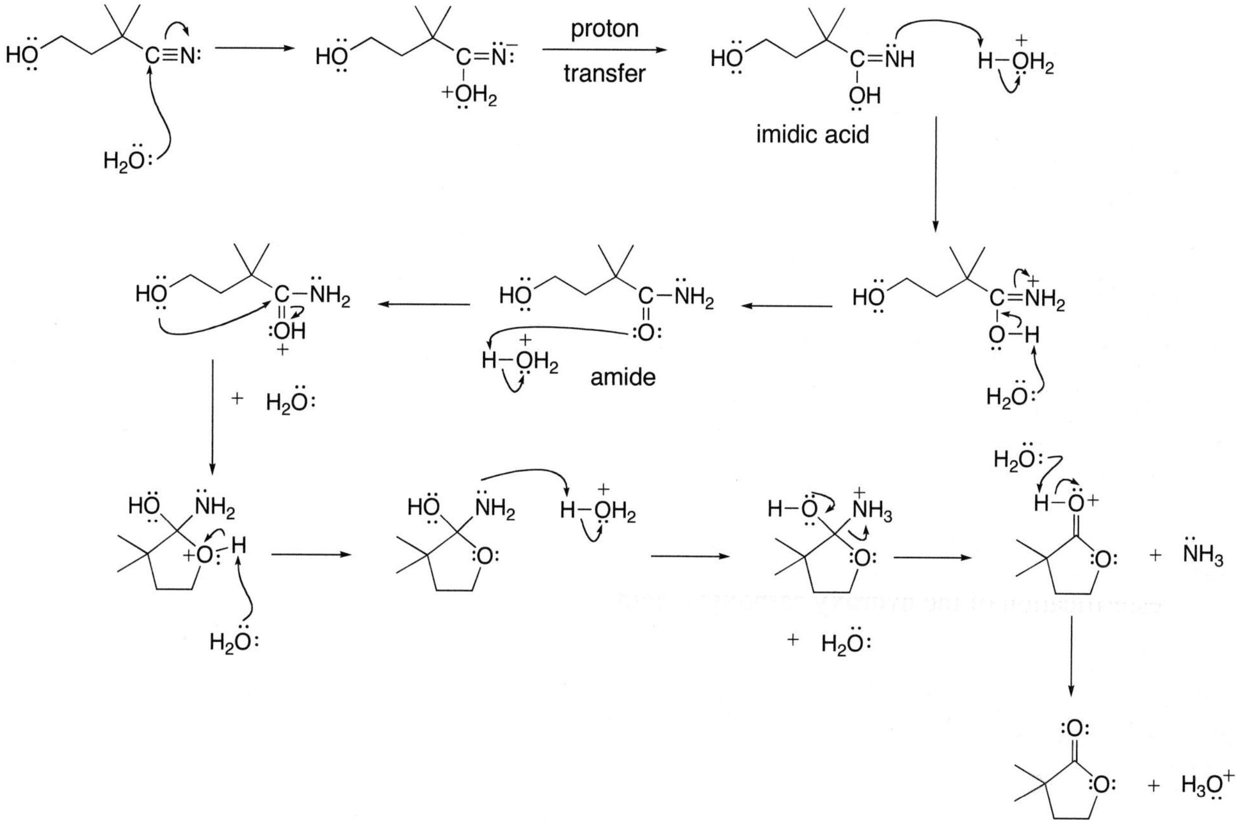

22.66 Fischer esterification is the treatment of a carboxylic acid with an alcohol in the presence of an acid catalyst to form an ester.

a. $(CH_3)_3CCO_2CH_2CH_3$ ⟹ $(CH_3)_3CCOOH$ + $HOCH_2CH_3$

c. 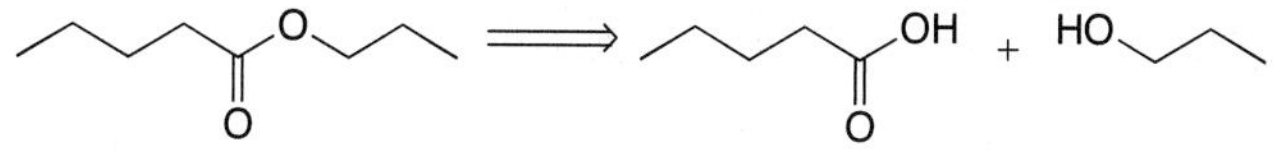

b. 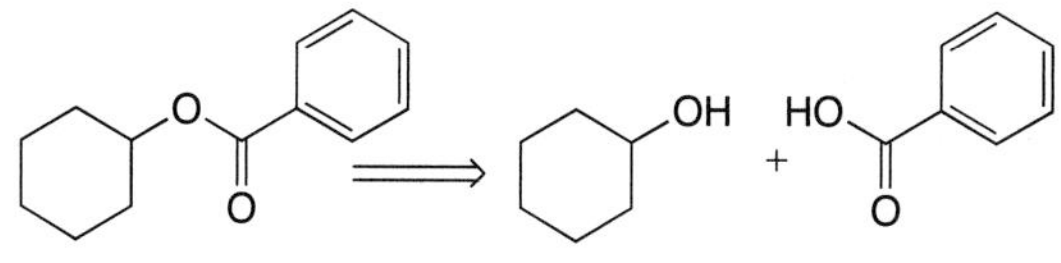

d. 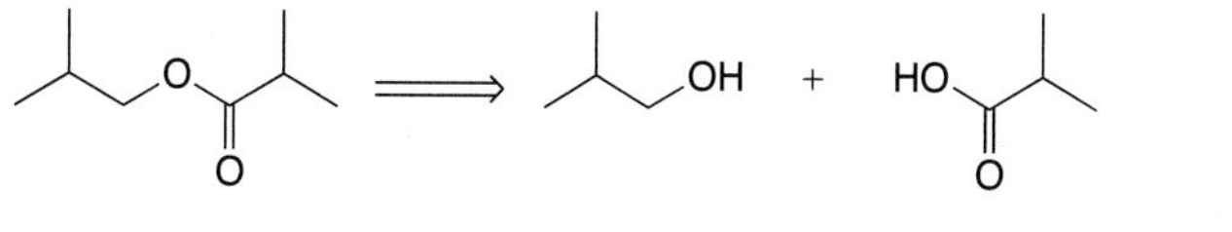

22.67

a. 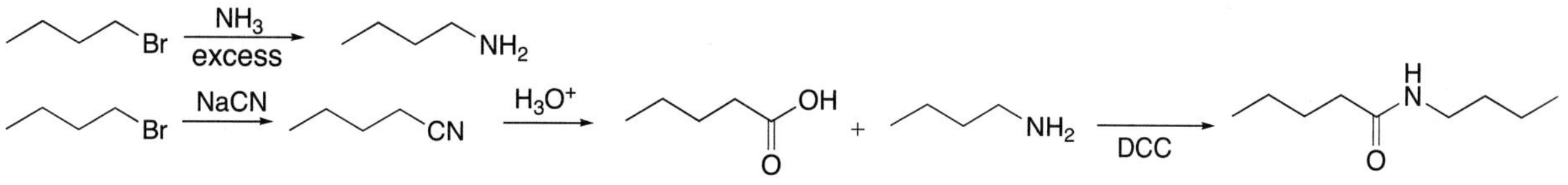

b.
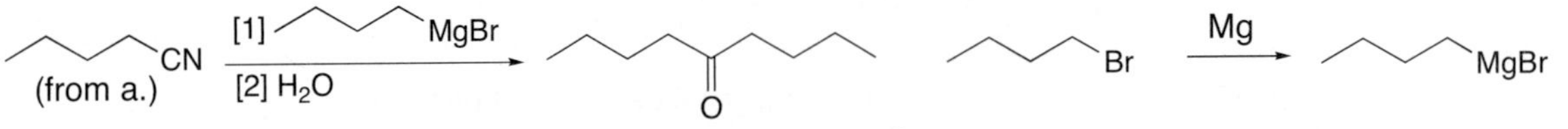
[1] MgBr
[2] H2O
CN
(from a.)
O
Br
Mg
MgBr

c.
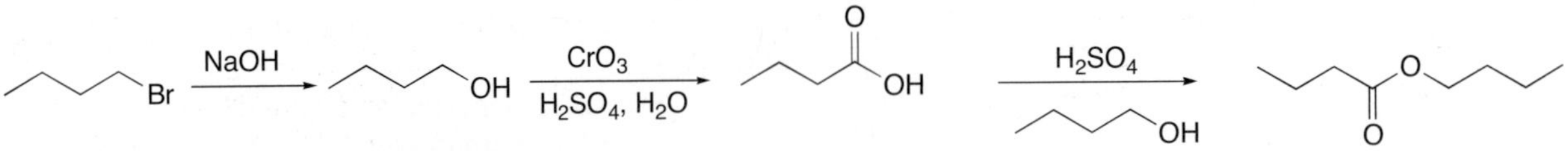
NaOH
Br
OH
CrO3
H2SO4, H2O
O
OH
H2SO4
OH
O
O

d.
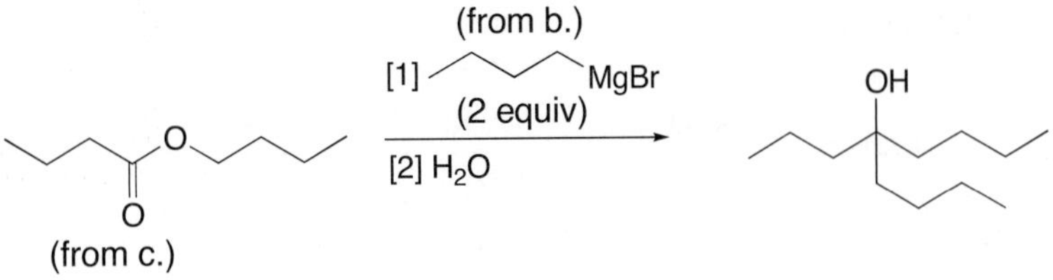
(from b.)
[1] MgBr
(2 equiv)
[2] H2O
O
O
(from c.)
OH

22.68

a.
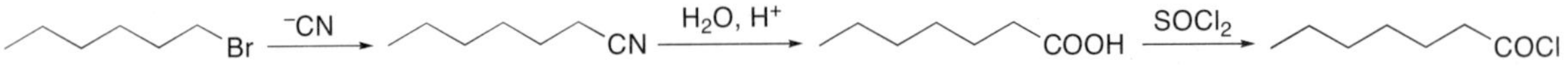
Br
−CN
CN
H2O, H+
COOH
SOCl2
COCl

b.
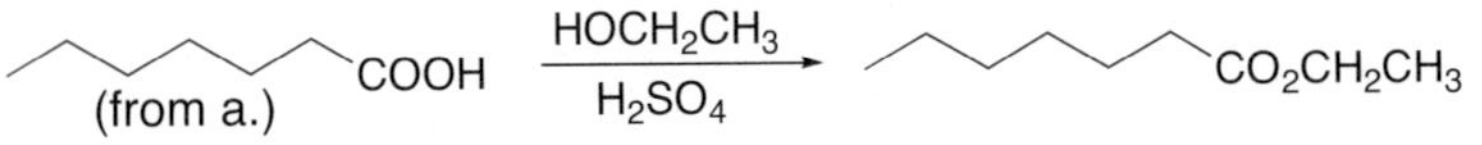
COOH
(from a.)
HOCH2CH3
H2SO4
CO2CH2CH3

c.
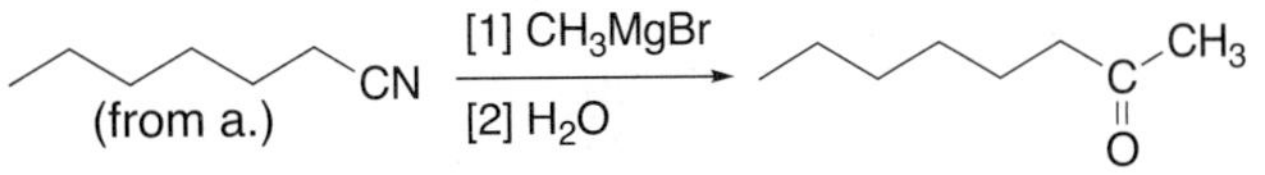
CN
(from a.)
[1] CH3MgBr
[2] H2O
C
CH3
O

d.
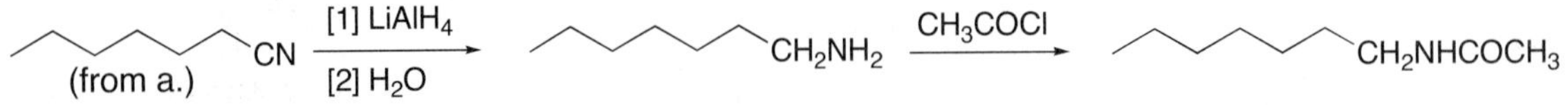
CN
(from a.)
[1] LiAlH4
[2] H2O
CH2NH2
CH3COCl
CH2NHCOCH3

22.69

a. $CH_3Cl + NaCN \longrightarrow CH_3{-}CN \xrightarrow{H_3O^+} CH_3{-}COOH$

$CH_3{-}Cl + Mg \longrightarrow CH_3{-}MgCl \xrightarrow[\text{[2] } H_3O^+]{\text{[1] } CO_2} CH_3{-}COOH$

b.
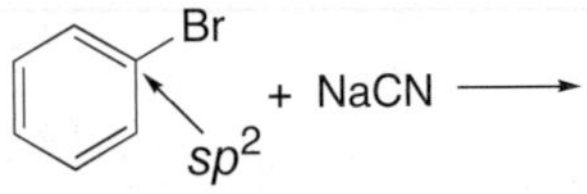
Br
sp2
+ NaCN

This method can't be used because an S_N2 reaction can't be done on an *sp*^{2} hybridized C.

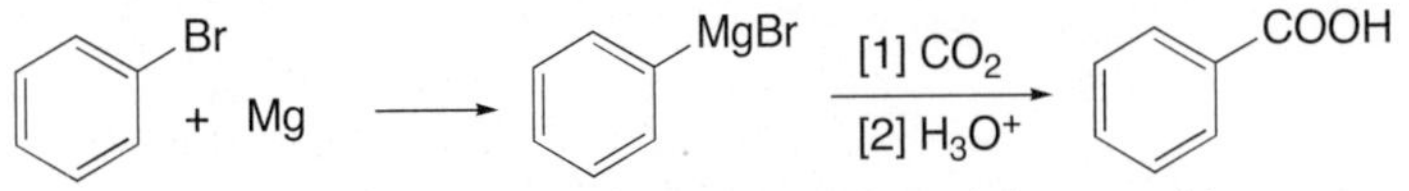
Br
+ Mg
MgBr
[1] CO2
[2] H3O+
COOH

c. $(CH_3)_3CCl + NaCN \longrightarrow$ This method can't be used because an S_N2 reaction can't be done on a 3° C.

$(CH_3)_3C{-}Cl + Mg \longrightarrow (CH_3)_3C{-}MgCl \xrightarrow[\text{[2] } H_3O^+]{\text{[1] } CO_2} (CH_3)_3C{-}COOH$

d. $HOCH_2CH_2CH_2CH_2Br + NaCN \longrightarrow HOCH_2CH_2CH_2CH_2{-}CN \xrightarrow{H_3O^+} HOCH_2CH_2CH_2CH_2{-}COOH$

$HOCH_2CH_2CH_2CH_2{-}Br + Mg \longrightarrow$ This method can't be used because you can't make a Grignard reagent with an acidic OH group.

22.70

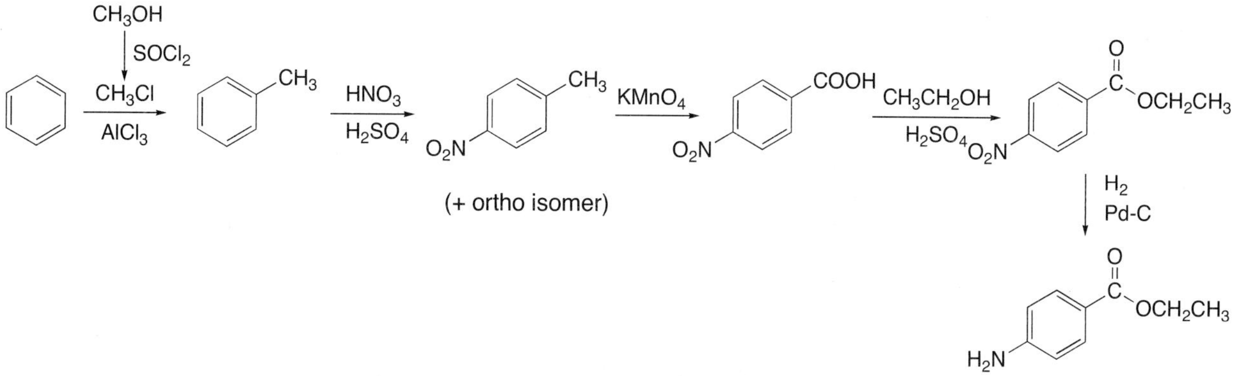
CH3OH
SOCl2
CH3Cl
AlCl3
CH3
HNO3
H2SO4
O2N
(+ ortho isomer)
KMnO4
COOH
CH3CH2OH
H2SO4
OCH2CH3
H2
Pd-C
H2N

22.71

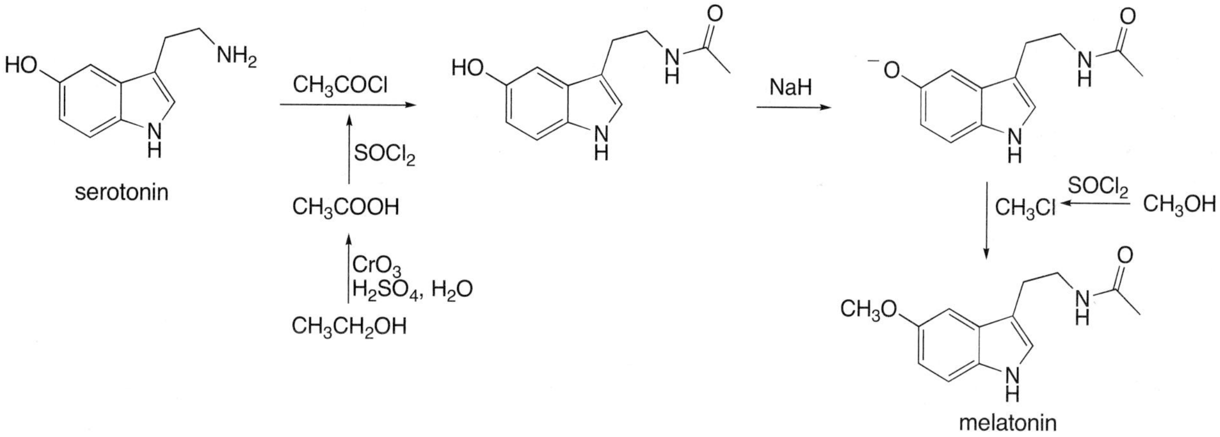
HO
NH2
serotonin
CH3COCl
SOCl2
CH3COOH
CrO3
H2SO4, H2O
CH3CH2OH
NaH
SOCl2
CH3Cl
CH3OH
CH3O
melatonin

22.72

a. 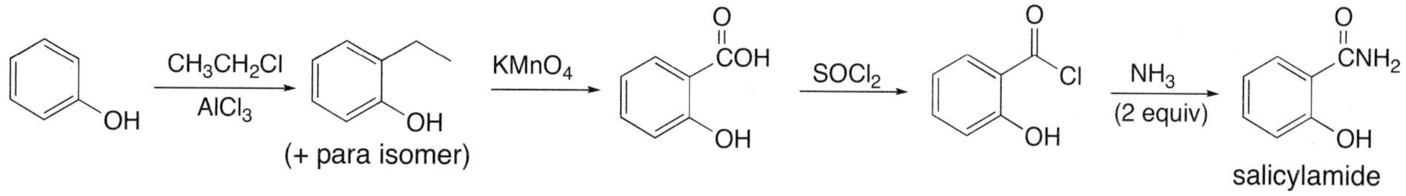
OH
CH3CH2Cl
AlCl3
(+ para isomer)
KMnO4
COH
SOCl2
Cl
NH3
(2 equiv)
CNH2
salicylamide

b. 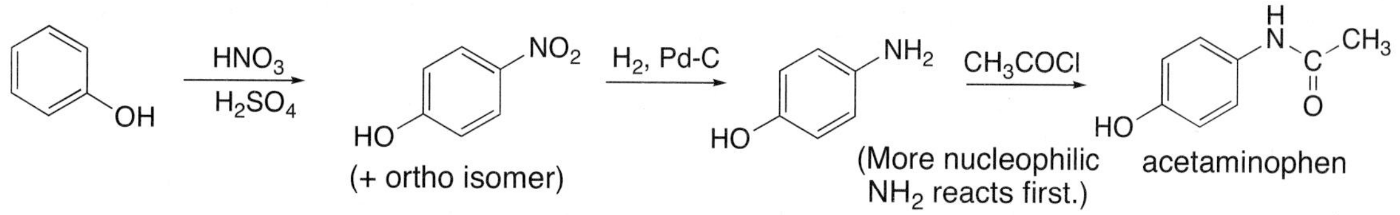
OH
HNO3
H2SO4
NO2
HO
(+ ortho isomer)
H2, Pd-C
NH2
CH3COCl
(More nucleophilic
NH2 reacts first.)
acetaminophen

c. 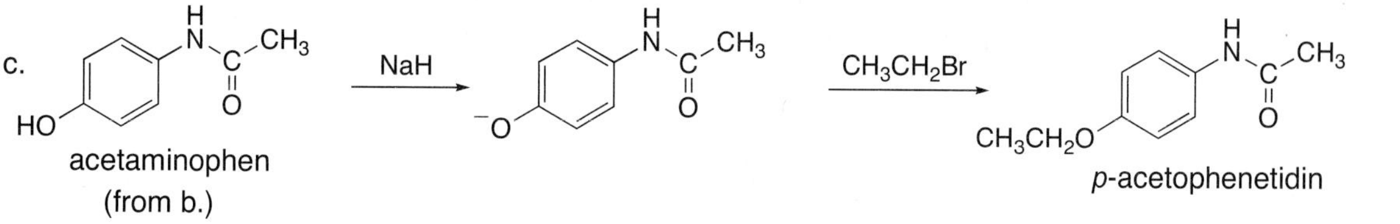
HO
acetaminophen
(from b.)
NaH
CH3CH2Br
CH3CH2O
p-acetophenetidin

22.73

a.

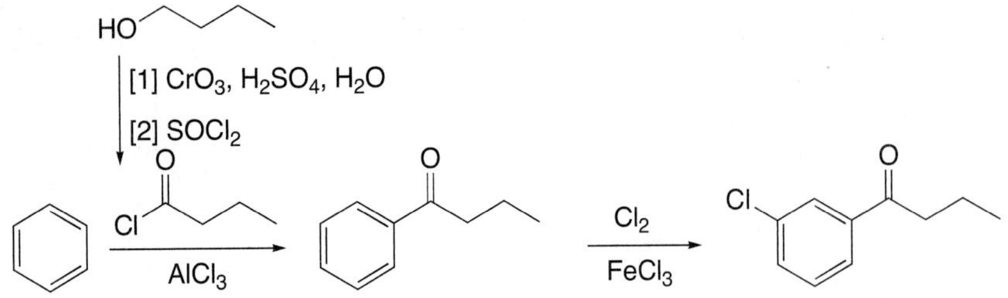
HO
[1] CrO3, H2SO4, H2O
[2] SOCl2
O
Cl
AlCl3
O
Cl2
FeCl3
Cl
O

b.

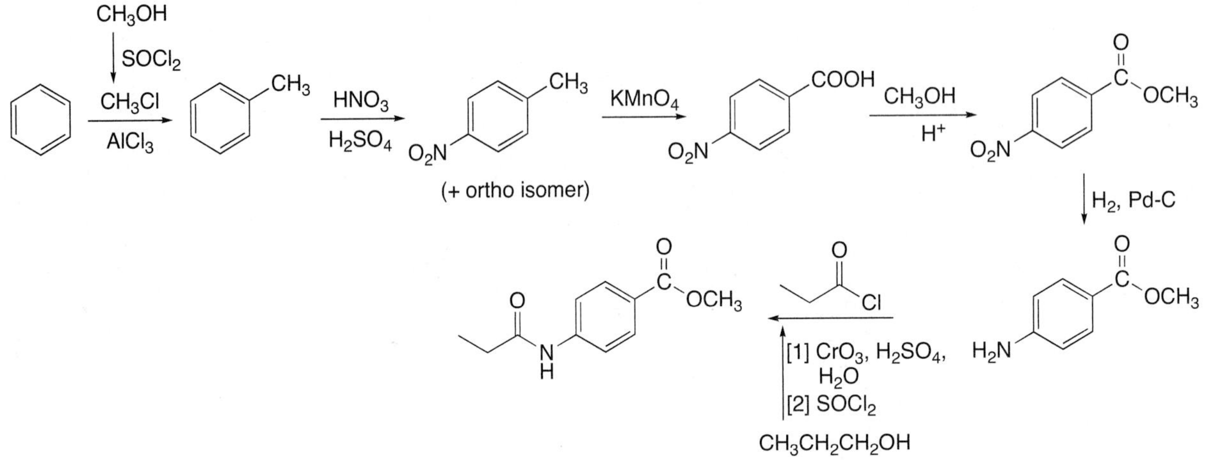
CH3OH
SOCl2
CH3Cl
AlCl3
CH3
HNO3
H2SO4
O2N
CH3
(+ ortho isomer)
KMnO4
COOH
O2N
CH3OH
H+
O
C
OCH3
O2N
H2, Pd-C
O
C
OCH3
H2N
O
Cl
[1] CrO3, H2SO4, H2O
[2] SOCl2
CH3CH2CH2OH
O
N
H
O
C
OCH3

c.

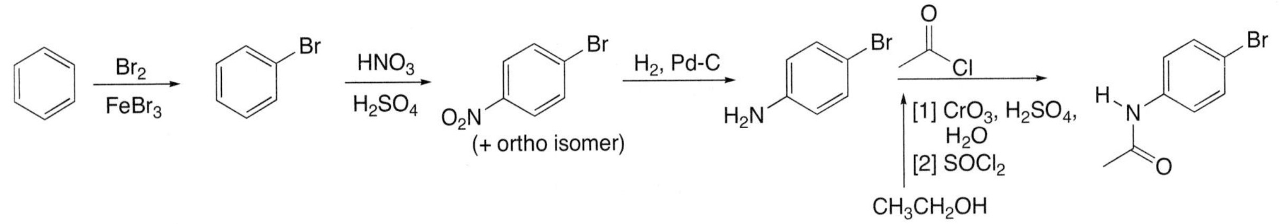
Br2
FeBr3
Br
HNO3
H2SO4
Br
O2N
(+ ortho isomer)
H2, Pd-C
Br
H2N
O
Cl
[1] CrO3, H2SO4, H2O
[2] SOCl2
CH3CH2OH
Br
H
N
O

d.

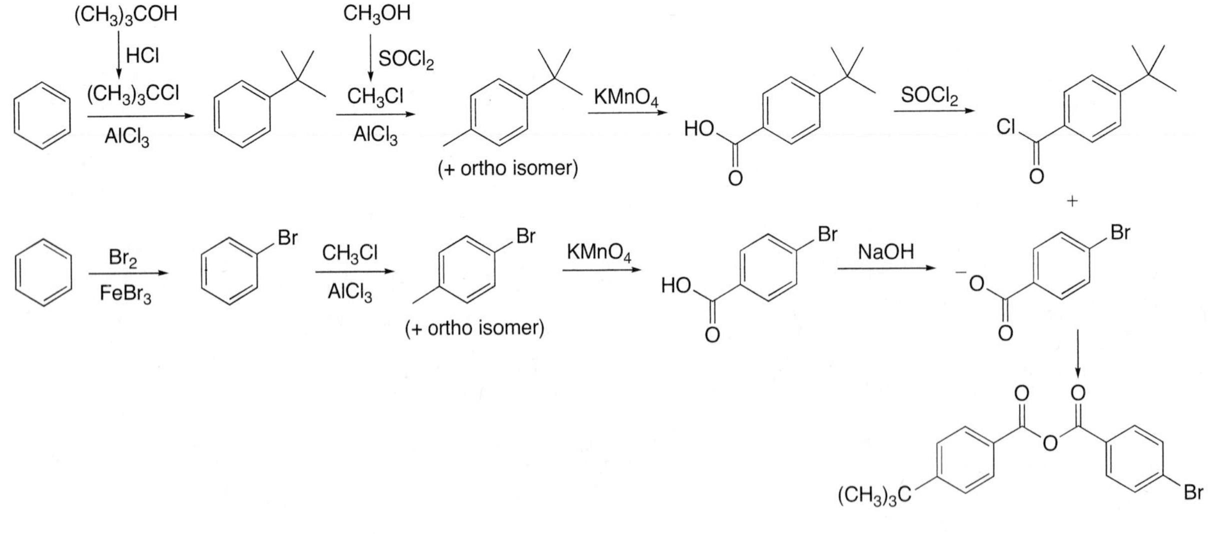
(CH3)3COH
HCl
(CH3)3CCl
AlCl3
CH3OH
SOCl2
CH3Cl
AlCl3
(+ ortho isomer)
KMnO4
HO
O
SOCl2
Cl
O
+
Br2
FeBr3
Br
CH3Cl
AlCl3
Br
(+ ortho isomer)
KMnO4
Br
HO
O
NaOH
Br
−O
O
O
O
O
(CH3)3C
Br

22.74

a. 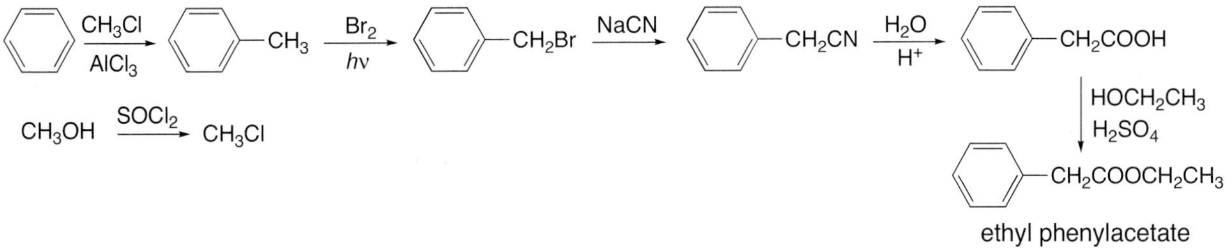
CH3Cl
AlCl3
CH3
Br2
hν
CH2Br
NaCN
CH2CN
H2O
H+
CH2COOH
HOCH2CH3
H2SO4
CH2COOCH2CH3
ethyl phenylacetate
CH3OH
SOCl2
CH3Cl

b. 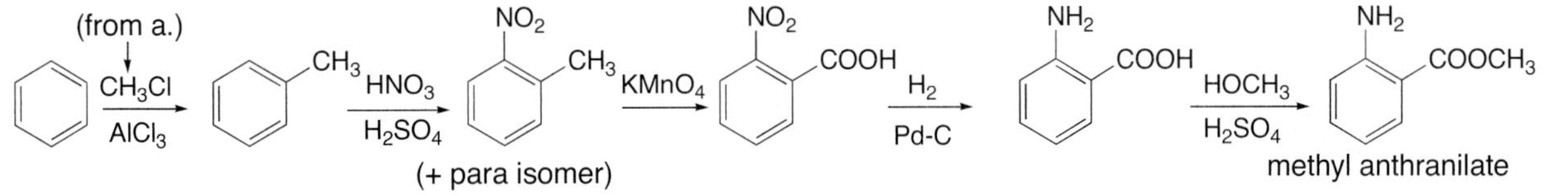
(from a.)
CH3Cl
AlCl3
CH3
HNO3
H2SO4
NO2
(+ para isomer)
KMnO4
COOH
H2
Pd-C
NH2
HOCH3
H2SO4
COOCH3
methyl anthranilate

c. 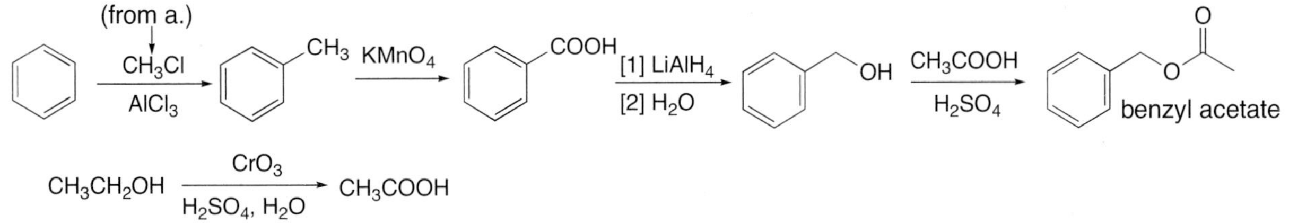
(from a.)
CH3Cl
AlCl3
CH3
KMnO4
COOH
[1] LiAlH4
[2] H2O
OH
CH3COOH
H2SO4
benzyl acetate
CH3CH2OH
CrO3
H2SO4, H2O
CH3COOH

22.75

a. 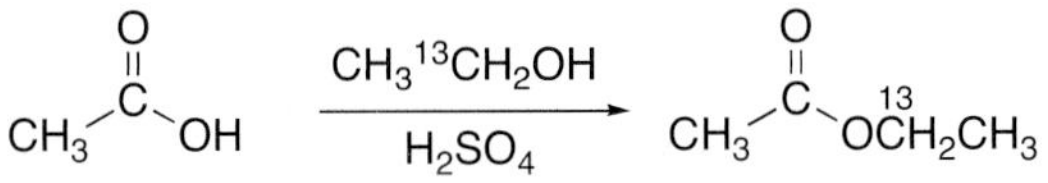
CH3
OH
CH3 13CH2OH
H2SO4
OCH2CH3

b. 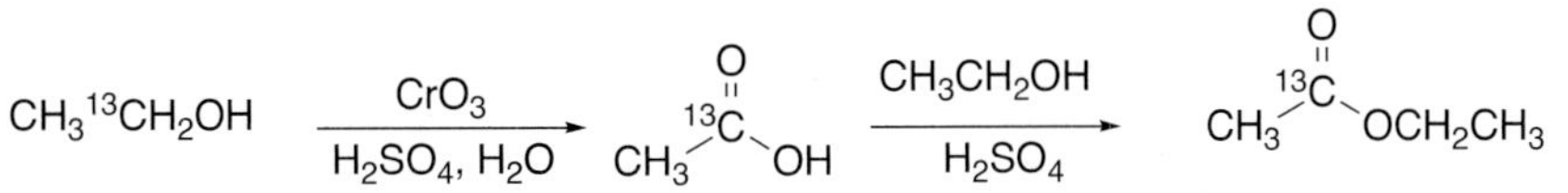
CH3 13CH2OH
CrO3
H2SO4, H2O
CH3CH2OH
H2SO4
OCH2CH3

c. 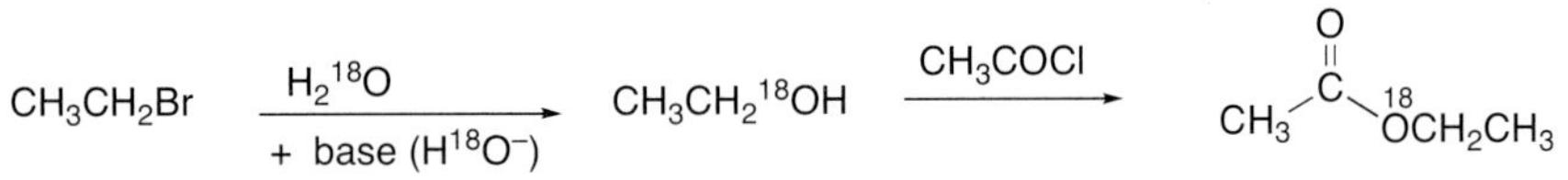
CH3CH2Br
H2 18O
+ base (H18O−)
CH3CH2 18OH
CH3COCl
OCH2CH3

d. 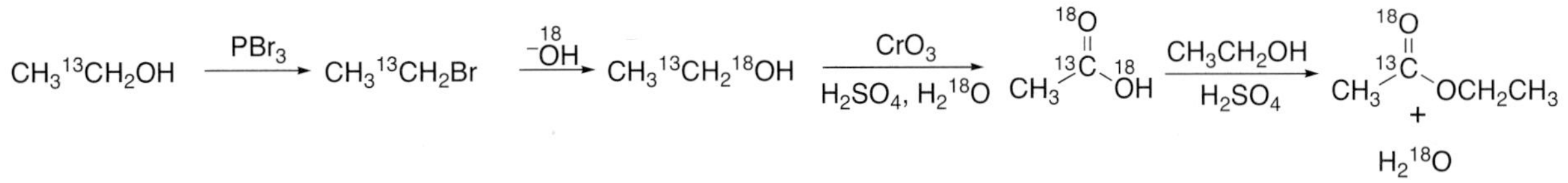
CH3 13CH2OH
PBr3
CH3 13CH2Br
−18OH
CH3 13CH2 18OH
CrO3
H2SO4, H2 18O
CH3CH2OH
H2SO4
OCH2CH3
+
H2 18O

22.76

a. 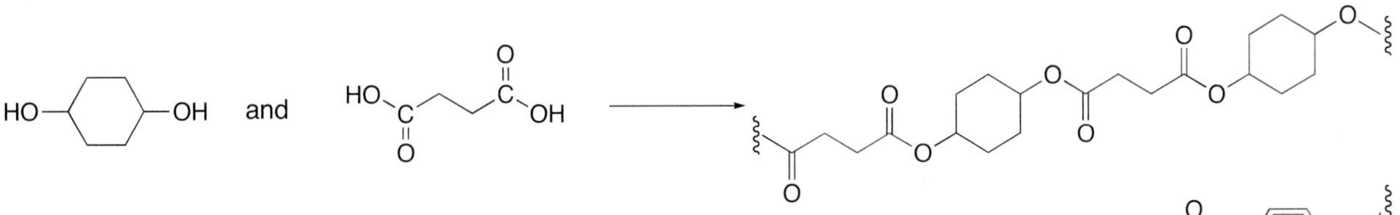
HO
OH
and

b. 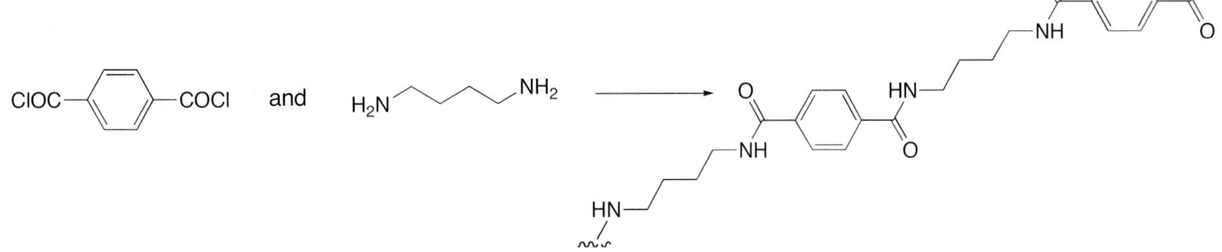
ClOC
COCl
and
H2N
NH2
NH
HN

22.77

a. 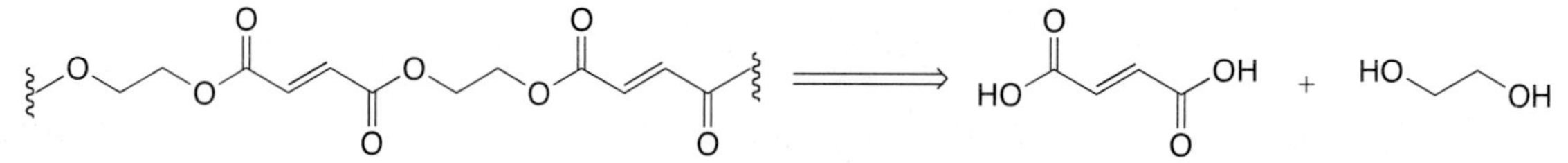

b. 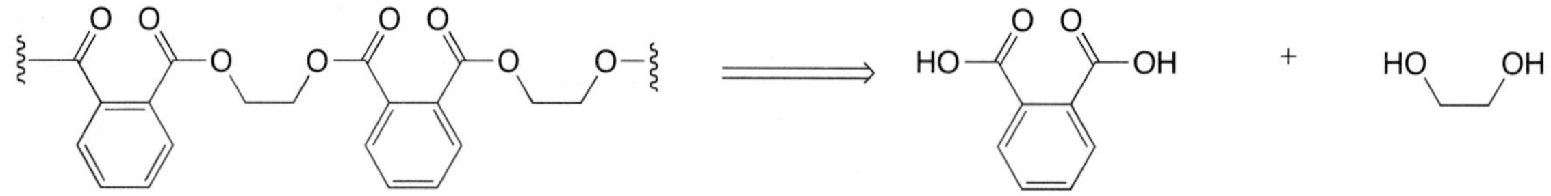

22.78

a. Docetaxel has fewer C's and one more OH group than taxol. This makes docetaxel more water soluble than taxol.

b. 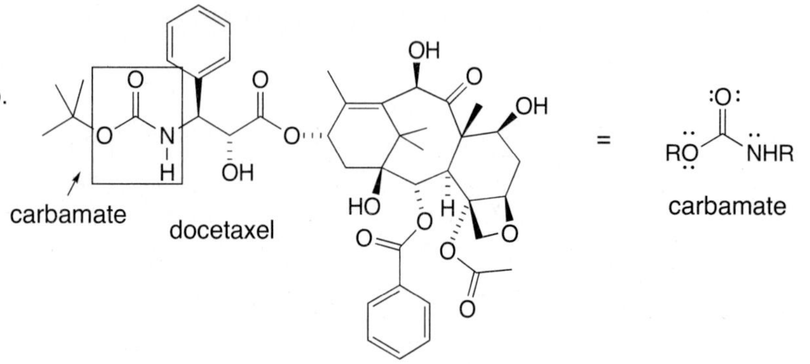
carbamate
docetaxel
carbamate

1	**4**	**3**	**2**
most stable	least stable		More basic N atom allows N to donate electron density more than O, so this structure contributes more than **3** to the hybrid.

Increasing stability: 4 < 3 < 2 < 1

c. 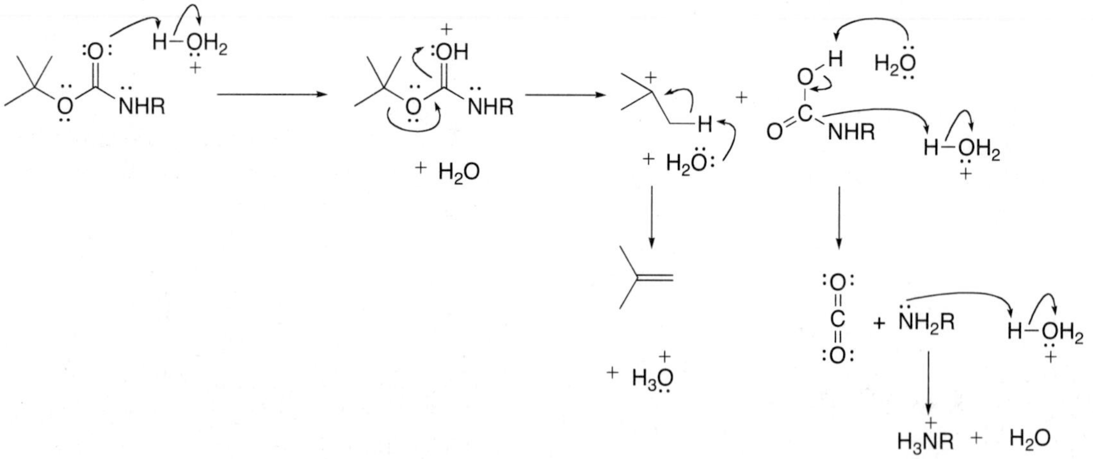

d.

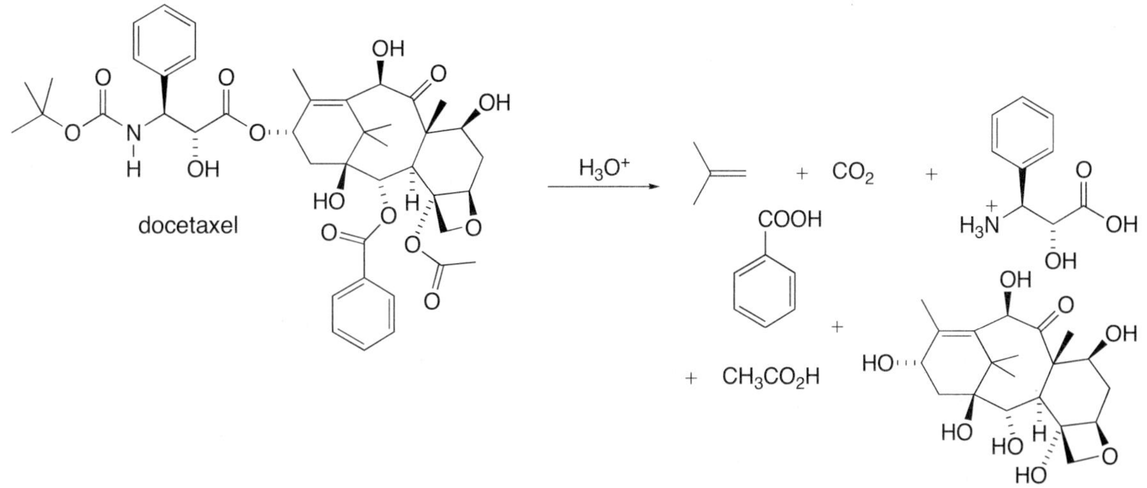
docetaxel
H_3O^+
CO_2
COOH
CH_3CO_2H

22.79

a. 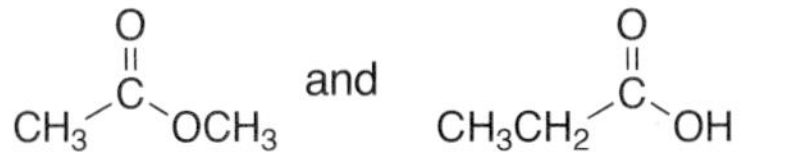

contains a broad, strong OH absorption at 3500–2500 cm^{-1}

c. 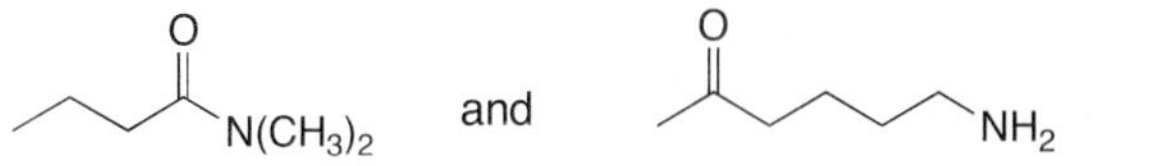

C=O at < 1700 cm^{-1} due to the stabilized amide

2 NH absorptions at 3200–3400 cm^{-1} C=O absorption at higher wavenumber

b. 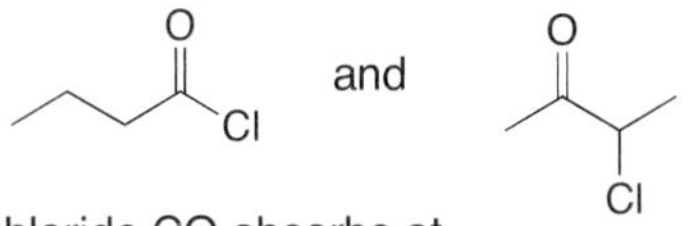

Acid chloride CO absorbs at much higher wavenumber.

ketone

d. 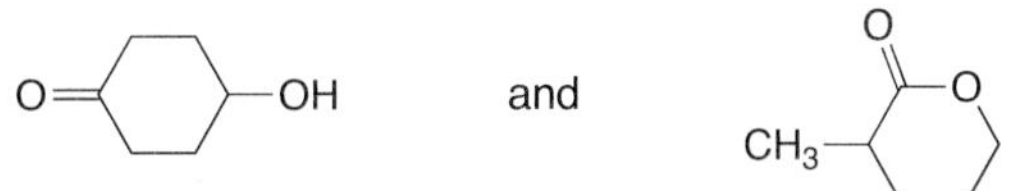

OH absorption at 3500–3200 cm^{-1} + C=O

only C=O

22.80

a. $C_6H_5COOCH_2CH_3$ $CH_3CH_2COOCH_2CH_3$ 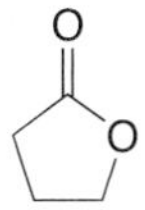

Increasing wavenumber →

b. most resonance stabilized — least resonance stabilized

CH_3CONH_2 CH_3COOCH_3 CH_3COCl

Increasing wavenumber →

22.81

a. $C_6H_{12}O_2$ → one degree of unsaturation
IR: 1738 cm^{-1} → C=O
NMR: 1.12 (triplet, 3 H), 1.23 (doublet, 6 H), 2.28 (quartet, 2 H), 5.00 (septet, 1 H) ppm

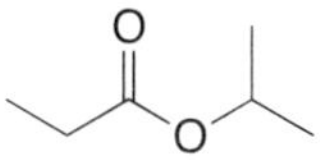

b. C_4H_7N
IR: 2250 cm^{-1} → triple bond
NMR: 1.08 (triplet, 3 H), 1.70 (multiplet, 2 H), 2.34 (triplet, 2 H) ppm

$CH_3CH_2CH_2C{\equiv}N$

c. C_8H_9NO
IR: 3328 (NH), 1639 (conjugated amide C=O) cm^{-1}
NMR: 2.95 (singlet, 3 H), 6.95 (singlet, 1 H), 7.3–7.7 (multiplet, 5 H) ppm

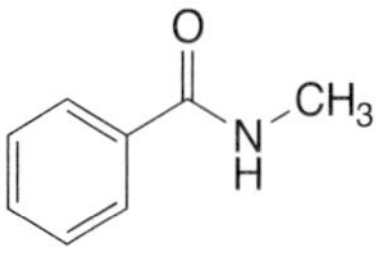

d. C_4H_7ClO → one degree of unsaturation
IR: 1802 cm^{-1} → C=O (high wavenumber, RCOCl)
NMR: 0.95 (triplet, 3 H), 1.07 (multiplet, 2 H), 2.90 (triplet, 2 H) ppm

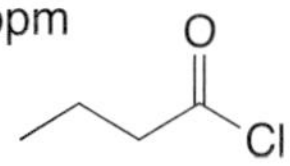

e. $C_5H_{10}O_2 \rightarrow$ one degree of unsaturation
IR: 1750 $cm^{-1} \rightarrow$ C=O
NMR: 1.20 (doublet, 6 H), 2.00 (singlet, 3 H), 4.95 (septet, 1 H) ppm

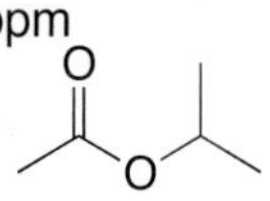

f. $C_{10}H_{12}O_2 \rightarrow$ five degrees of unsaturation
IR: 1740 $cm^{-1} \rightarrow$ C=O
NMR: 1.2 (triplet, 3 H), 2.4 (quartet, 2 H), 5.1 (singlet, 2 H), 7.1–7.5 (multiplet, 5 H) ppm

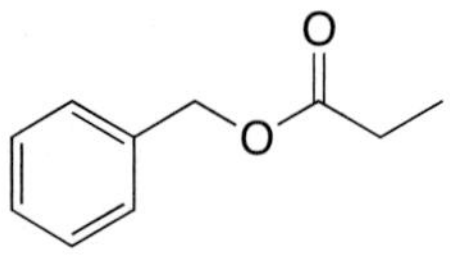

g. $C_8H_{14}O_3 \rightarrow$ two degrees of unsaturation
IR: 1810, 1770 $cm^{-1} \rightarrow$ 2 absorptions due to C=O (anhydride)
NMR: 1.25 (doublet, 12 H), 2.65 (septet, 2 H) ppm

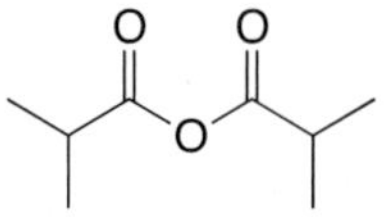

22.82

A. Molecular formula $C_{10}H_{12}O_2 \rightarrow$ five degrees of unsaturation
IR absorption at 1718 $cm^{-1} \rightarrow$ C=O
NMR data (ppm):
triplet at 1.4 (CH_3 adjacent to 2 H's)
singlet at 2.4 (CH_3)
quartet at 4.4 (CH_2 adjacent to CH_3)
doublet at 7.2 (2 H's on benzene ring)
doublet at 7.9 (2 H's on benzene ring)

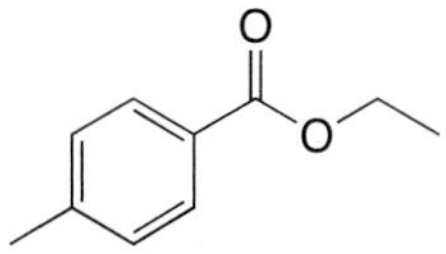

B. IR absorption at 1740 $cm^{-1} \rightarrow$ C=O
NMR data (ppm):
singlet at 2.0 (CH_3)
triplet at 2.9 (CH_2 adjacent to CH_2)
triplet at 4.4 (CH_2 adjacent to CH_2)
multiplet at 7.3 (5 H's, monosubstituted benzene)

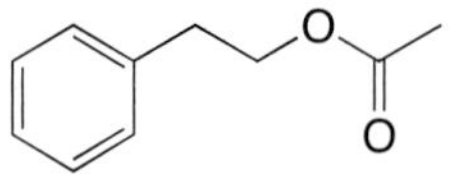

22.83

Molecular formula $C_{10}H_{13}NO_2 \rightarrow$ five degrees of unsaturation
IR absorptions at 3300 (NH) and 1680 (C=O, amide or conjugated) cm^{-1}
NMR data (ppm):
triplet at 1.4 (CH_3 adjacent to CH_2)
singlet at 2.2 (CH_3C=O)
quartet at 3.9 (CH_2 adjacent to CH_3)
doublet at 6.8 (2 H's on benzene ring)
singlet at 7.2 (NH)
doublet at 7.4 (2 H's on benzene ring)

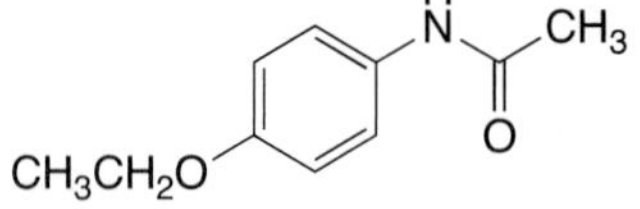

phenacetin

22.84

Molecular formula $C_{11}H_{15}NO_2 \rightarrow$ five degrees of unsaturation
IR absorption 1699 (C=O, amide or conjugated) cm^{-1}
NMR data (ppm):
triplet at 1.3 (3 H) (CH_3 adjacent to CH_2)
singlet at 3.0 (6 H) (2 CH_3 groups on N)
quartet at 4.3 (2 H) (CH_2 adjacent to CH_3)
doublet at 6.6 (2 H) (2 H's on benzene ring)
doublet at 7.9 (2 H) (2 H's on benzene ring)

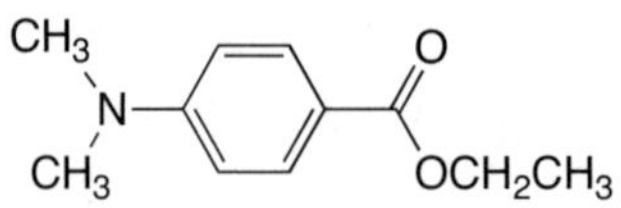

C

22.85

a. Molecular formula $C_6H_{12}O_2$ → one degree of unsaturation
IR absorption at 1743 cm^{-1} → C=O
^1H NMR data (ppm):
triplet at 0.9 (3 H) – CH_3 adjacent to CH_2
multiplet at 1.35 (2 H) – CH_2
multiplet at 1.60 (2 H) – CH_2
singlet at 2.1 (3 H – from CH_3 bonded to C=O)
triplet at 4.1 (2 H) – CH_2 adjacent to the electronegative O atom and another CH_2

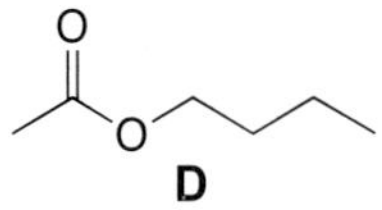
D

b. Molecular formula $C_6H_{12}O_2$ → one degree of unsaturation
IR absorption at 1746 cm^{-1} → C=O
^1H NMR data (ppm):
doublet at 0.9 (6 H) – 2 CH_3's adjacent to CH
multiplet at 1.9 (1 H)
singlet at 2.1 (3 H) – CH_3 bonded to C=O
doublet at 3.85 (2 H) – CH_2 bonded to electronegative O and CH

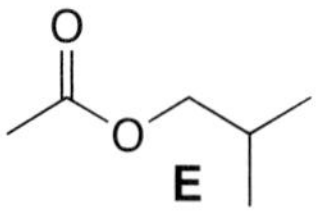
E

22.86 The extent of resonance stabilization affects the position of the C=O absorption in the IR of an amide.

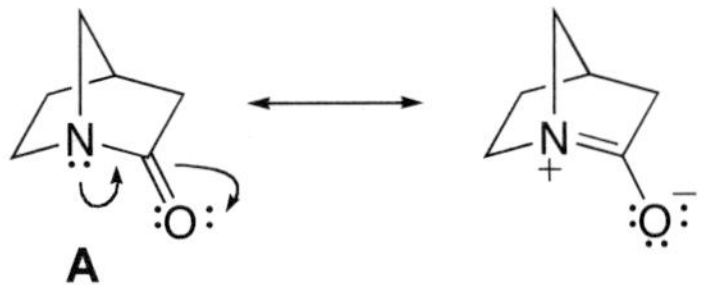
A

This resonance structure does not contribute significantly to the hybrid because it places a double bond at the bridgehead N, an impossible geometry in small rings. The C=O has more double bond character, so the absorption is at a higher wavenumber.

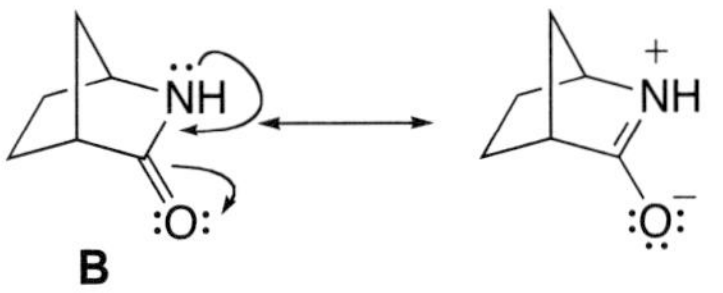
B

This resonance structure contributes significantly to the hybrid, so the C=O has more single bond character. The absorption shifts to a lower wavenumber.

22.87

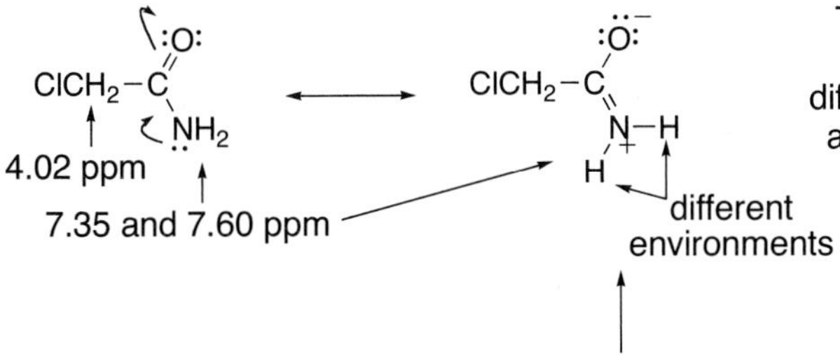
4.02 ppm
7.35 and 7.60 ppm
different environments

There is restricted rotation around the amide C–N bond. The 2 H's are in different environments (one is cis to an O atom, and one is cis to CH_2Cl), so they give different NMR signals.

This resonance structure makes a significant contribution to the resonance hybrid.

22.88

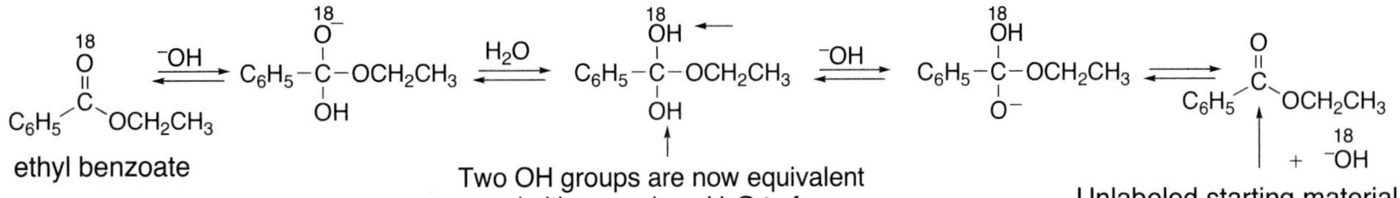
ethyl benzoate

Two OH groups are now equivalent and either can lose H_2O to form labeled or unlabeled ethyl benzoate.

Unlabeled starting material was recovered.

22.89

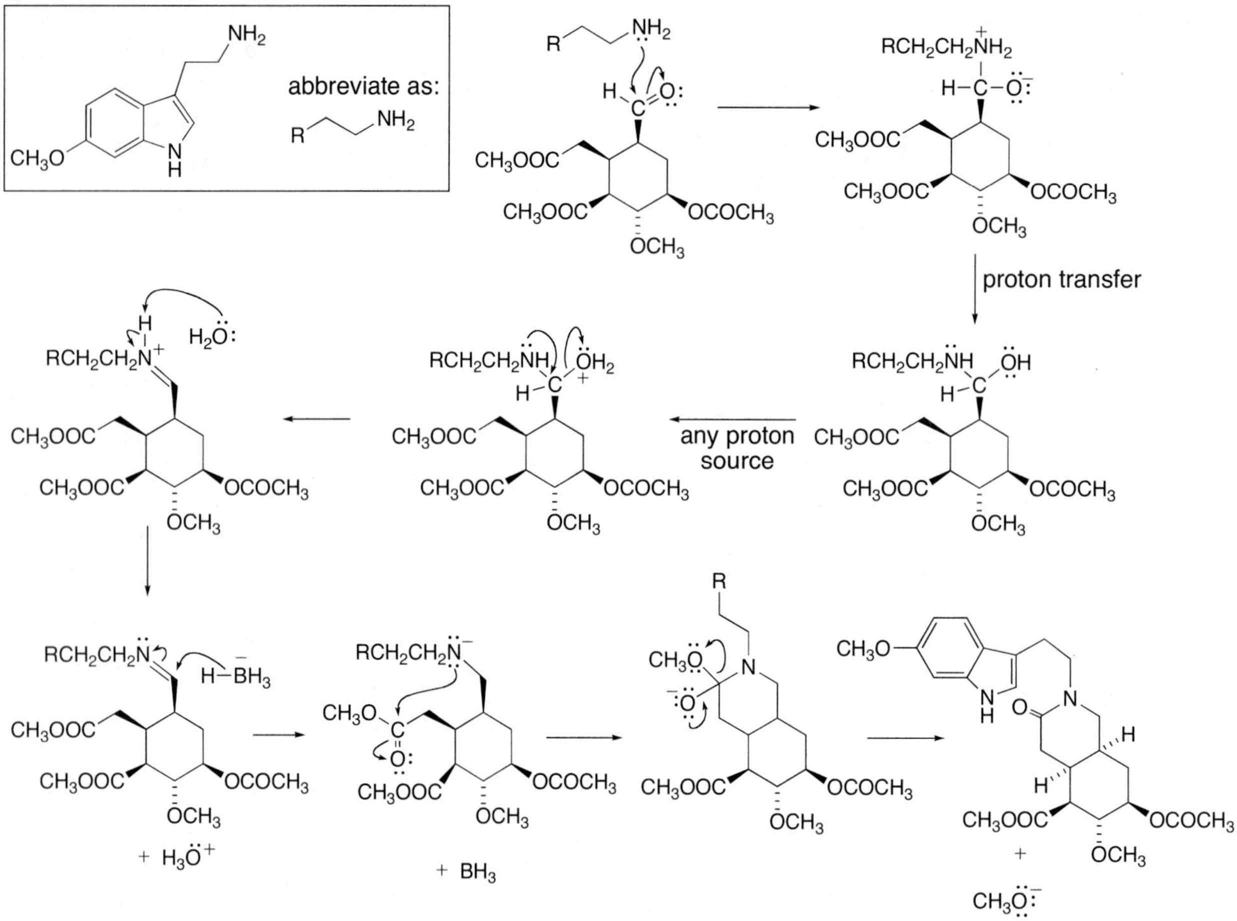

22.90 Both acetals are hydrolyzed by the usual mechanism for acetal hydrolysis (Steps [1 –[6]), forming four new OH groups. Intramolecular esterification forms a lactone (Steps [10]–[15]), followed by conversion of a carbonyl tautomer to an enol (Steps [16]–[17]). Both acetals are hydrolyzed at once in the given mechanism.

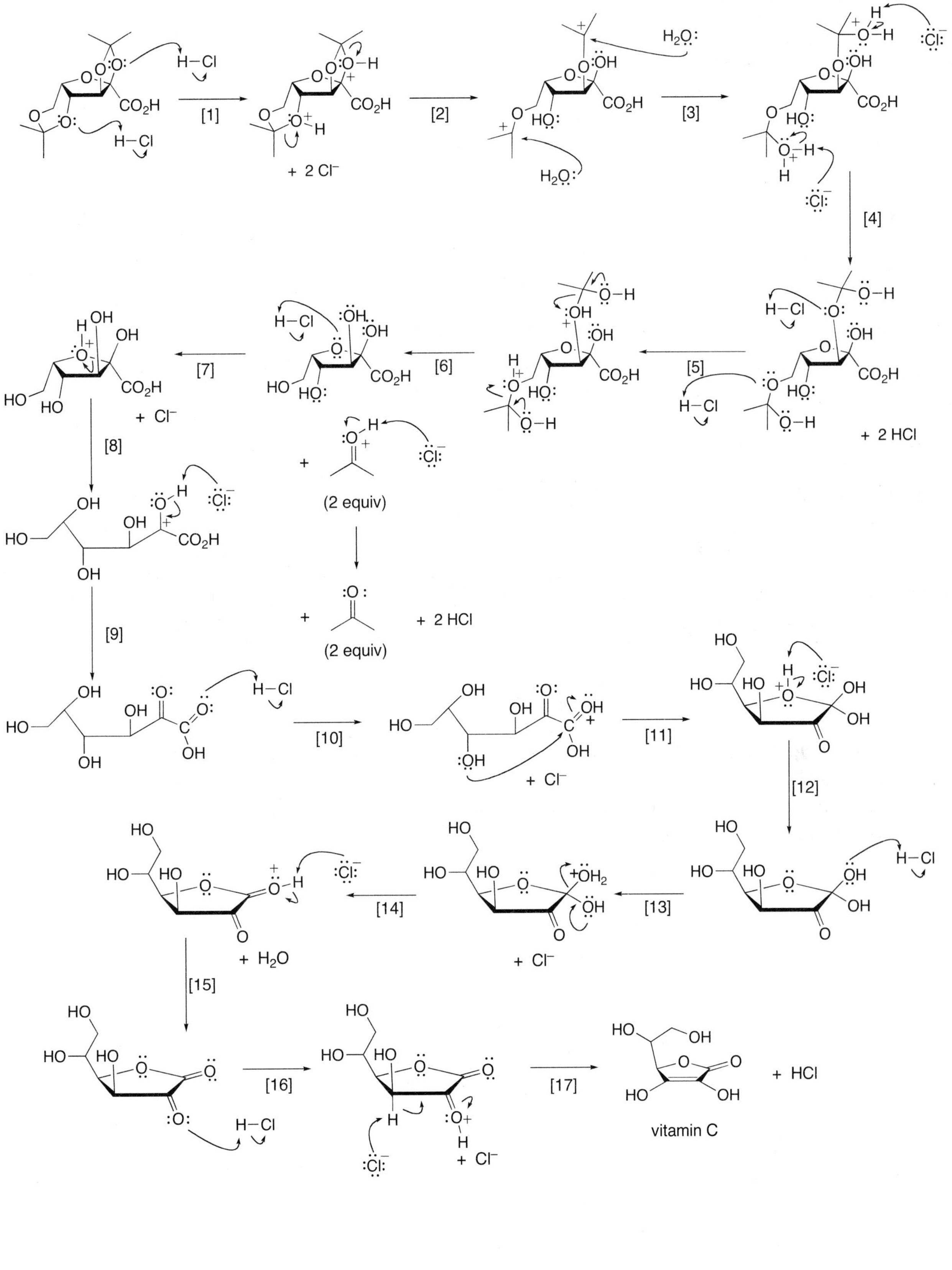

H–Cl
[1]
+ 2 Cl⁻
[2]
H₂O:
[3]
:Cl:⁻
[4]
+ 2 HCl
[5]
[6]
[7]
+ Cl⁻
[8]
(2 equiv)
+ 2 HCl
[9]
[10]
[11]
[12]
[13]
[14]
+ H₂O
[15]
[16]
[17]
vitamin C
+ HCl

22.91

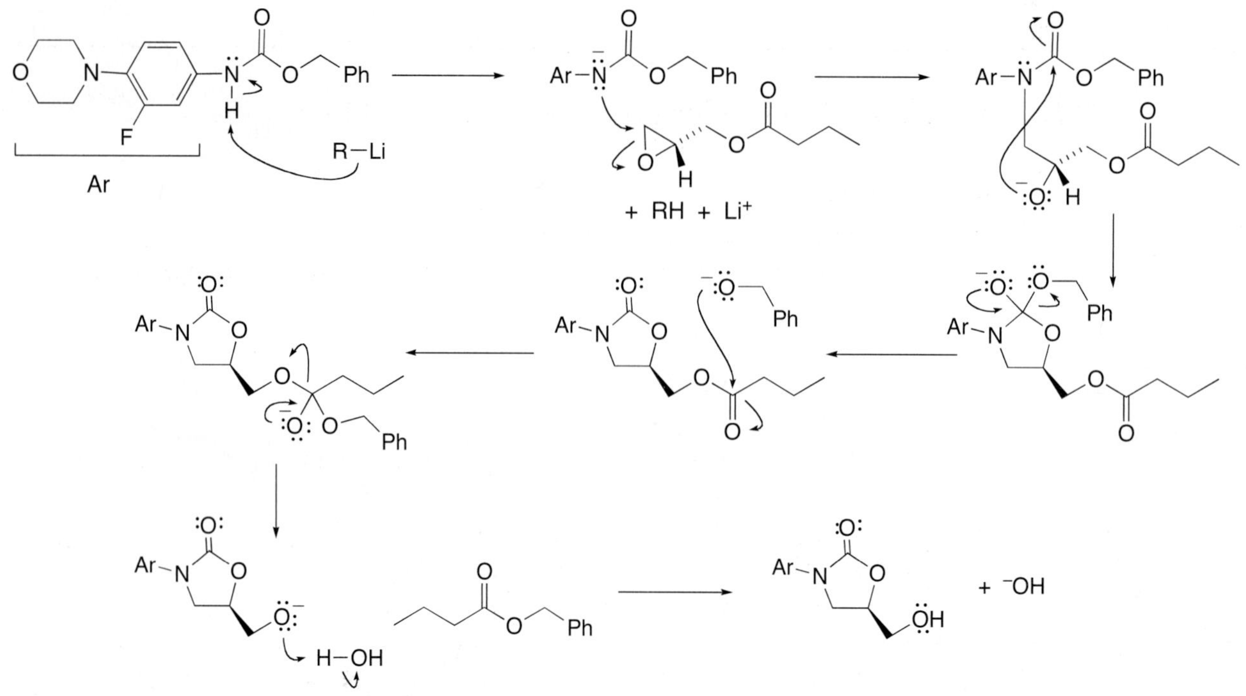
O
N
F
Ar
N
H
O
O
Ph
R—Li
Ar—N
O
O
Ph
O
O
O
H
+ RH + Li+
Ar—N
O
O
Ph
O
O
O
H
Ph
Ar—N
O
O
O
O
Ar—N
O
O
O
Ph
O
O
Ar—N
O
O
O
O
O
Ph
Ar—N
O
O
O
O
O
Ph
H—OH
Ar—N
O
O
OH
+ −OH

Chapter 23 Substitution Reactions of Carbonyl Compounds at the α Carbon

Chapter Review

Kinetic versus thermodynamic enolates (23.4)

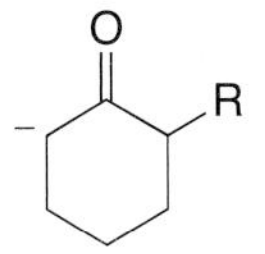

kinetic enolate

Kinetic enolate

- The less substituted enolate
- Favored by strong base, polar aprotic solvent, low temperature: LDA, THF, –78 °C

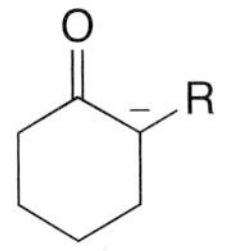

thermodynamic enolate

Thermodynamic enolate

- The more substituted enolate
- Favored by strong base, protic solvent, higher temperature: $NaOCH_2CH_3$, CH_3CH_2OH, room temperature

Halogenation at the α carbon

[1] Halogenation in acid (23.7A)

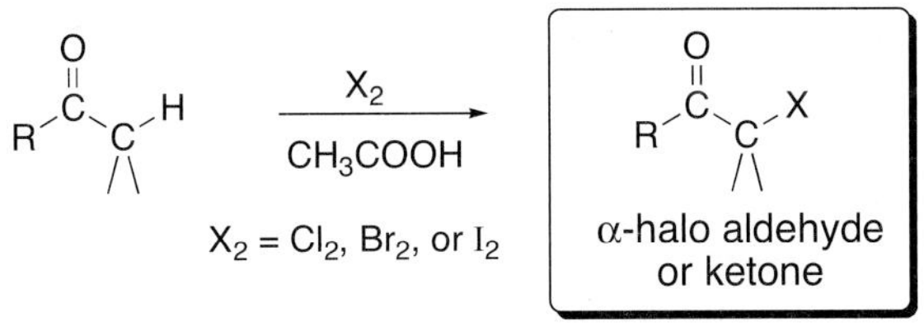
X2
CH3COOH
X2 = Cl2, Br2, or I2
α-halo aldehyde or ketone

- The reaction occurs via enol intermediates.
- Monosubstitution of X for H occurs on the α carbon.

[2] Halogenation in base (23.7B)

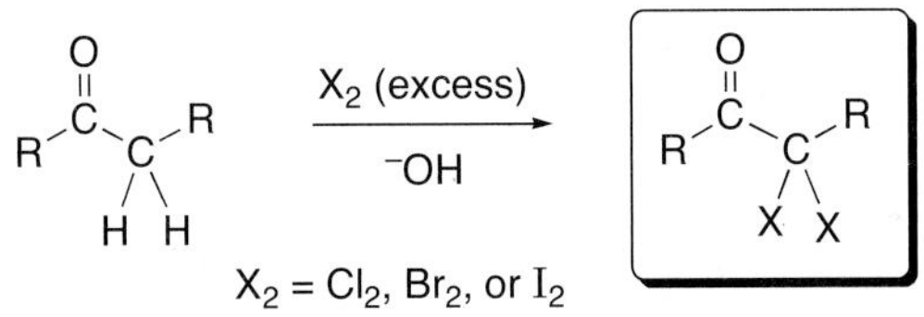
X2 (excess)
−OH
X2 = Cl2, Br2, or I2

- The reaction occurs via enolate intermediates.
- Polysubstitution of X for H occurs on the α carbon.

[3] Halogenation of *methyl* ketones in base—The haloform reaction (23.7B)

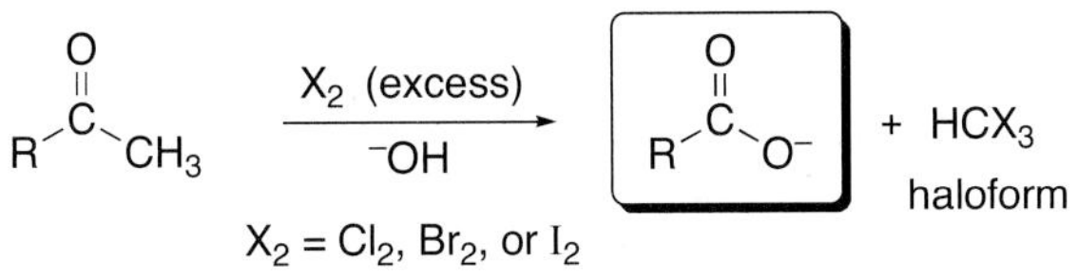
X2 (excess)
−OH
X2 = Cl2, Br2, or I2
+ HCX3
haloform

- The reaction occurs with methyl ketones and results in cleavage of a carbon–carbon σ bond.

Reactions of α-halo carbonyl compounds (23.7C)

[1] Elimination to form α,β-unsaturated carbonyl compounds

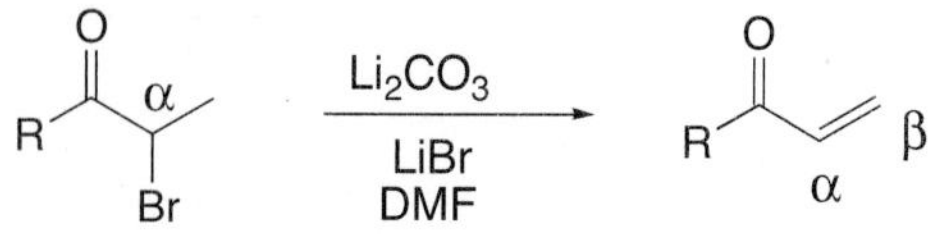
Li_2CO_3
LiBr
DMF

- Elimination of the elements of Br and H forms a new π bond, giving an α,β-unsaturated carbonyl compound.

[2] Nucleophilic substitution

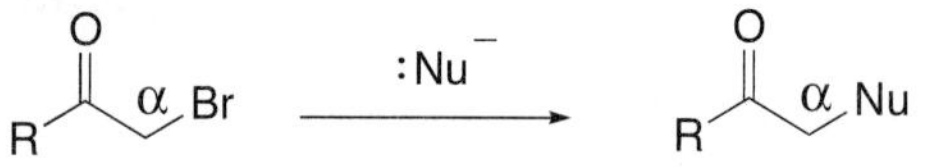
:Nu⁻

- The reaction follows an S_N2 mechanism, generating an α-substituted carbonyl compound.

Alkylation reactions at the α carbon

[1] Direct alkylation at the α carbon (23.8)

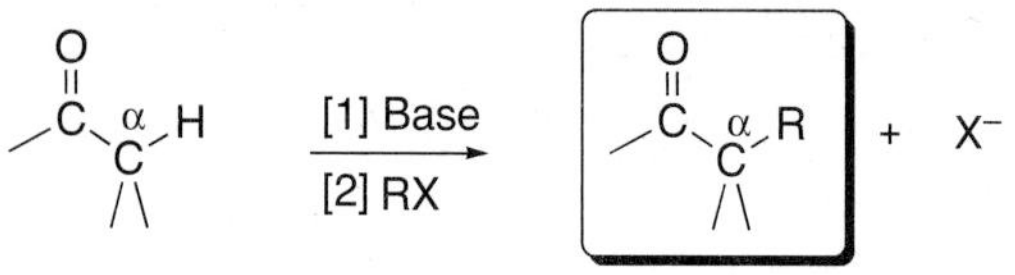
[1] Base
[2] RX
+ X⁻

- The reaction forms a new C–C bond to the α carbon.
- LDA is a common base used to form an intermediate enolate.
- The alkylation in Step [2] follows an S_N2 mechanism.

[2] Malonic ester synthesis (23.9)

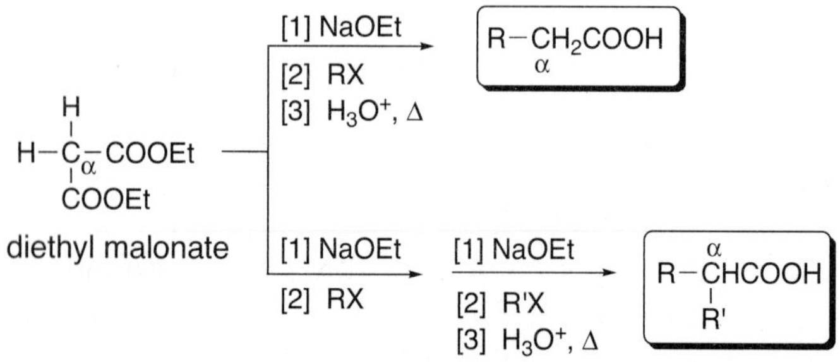
[1] NaOEt
[2] RX
[3] H_3O^+, Δ
R–CH_2COOH
diethyl malonate
[1] NaOEt
[2] R'X
[3] H_3O^+, Δ
R–CHCOOH
R'

- The reaction is used to prepare carboxylic acids with one or two alkyl groups on the α carbon.
- The alkylation in Step [2] follows an S_N2 mechanism.

[3] Acetoacetic ester synthesis (23.10)

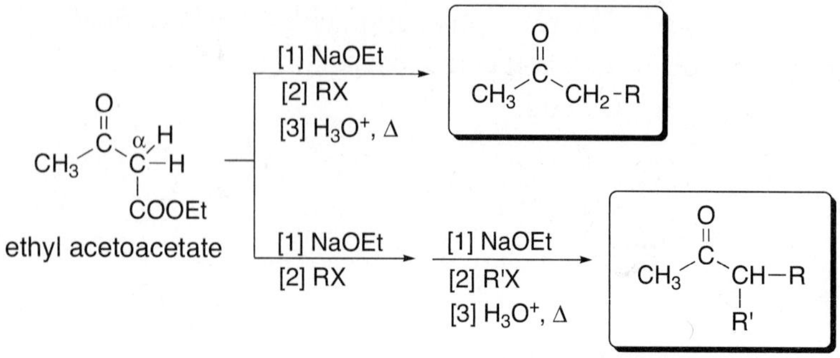
[1] NaOEt
[2] RX
[3] H_3O^+, Δ
ethyl acetoacetate
[1] NaOEt
[2] R'X
[3] H_3O^+, Δ

- The reaction is used to prepare ketones with one or two alkyl groups on the α carbon.
- The alkylation in Step [2] follows an S_N2 mechanism.

Practice Test on Chapter Review

1. a. Which of the following compounds can be prepared using either the acetoacetic ester or malonic ester syntheses?

1. 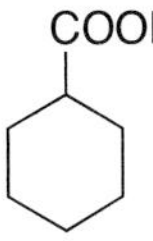

2. 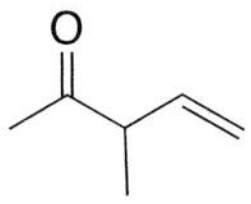

3. 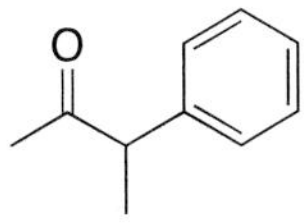

4. Both [1] and [2] can be prepared by one of these routes.
5. Compounds [1], [2], and [3] can all be prepared by these routes.

b. Which of the following compounds is ***not*** an enol form of dicarbonyl compound **A?**

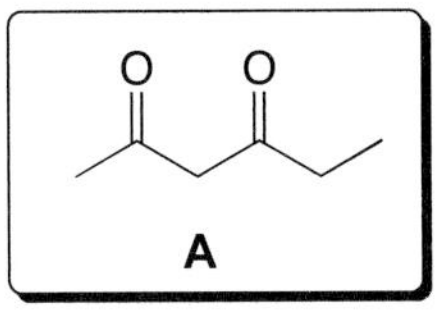

1. 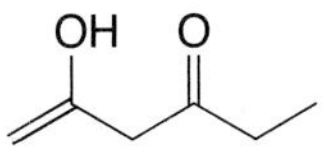

2. 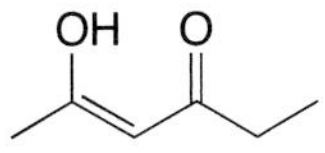

3. 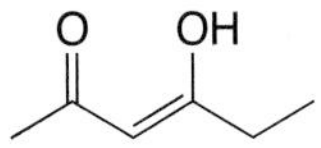

4. 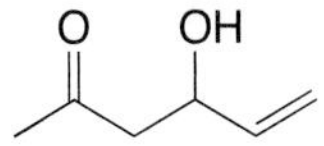

5. Compounds [1]Ǧ4] are all enols of **A.**

2. a. Which proton in compound **A** has the *lowest* pK_a?
b. Which proton in compound **A** has the *highest* pK_a?

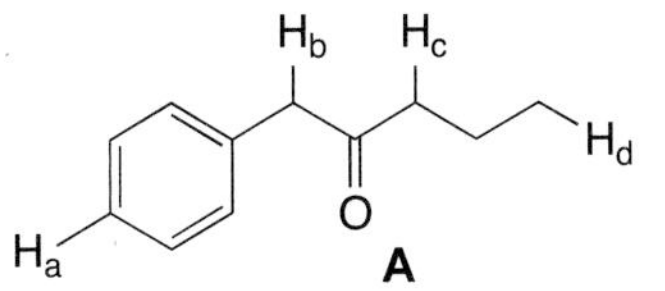

A

c. What proton in compound **B** is the least acidic?
d. What proton in compound **B** is the most acidic?

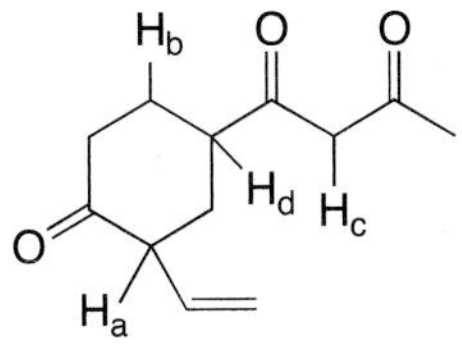

B

3. What reagents are needed to convert 4-heptanone to each compound?
a. 3-bromo-4-heptanone
b. 3-methyl-4-heptanone
c. 3,5-dimethyl-4-heptanone
d. 2-hepten-4-one
e. 2-methyl-4-heptanone

4. Draw the organic products formed in each of the following reactions.

a. 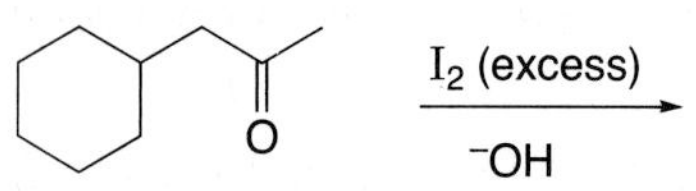
O
I_2 (excess)
^{-}OH

d. 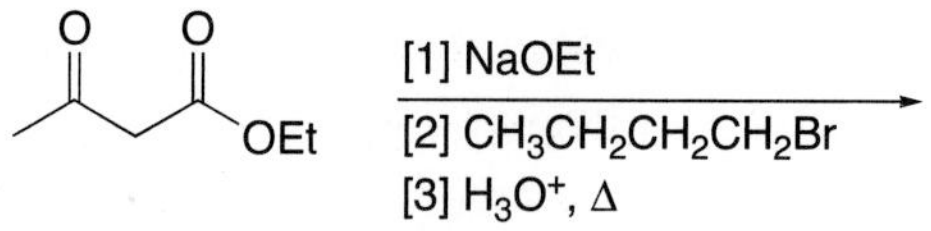
O
O
OEt
[1] NaOEt
[2] $CH_3CH_2CH_2CH_2Br$
[3] H_3O^+, Δ

b. 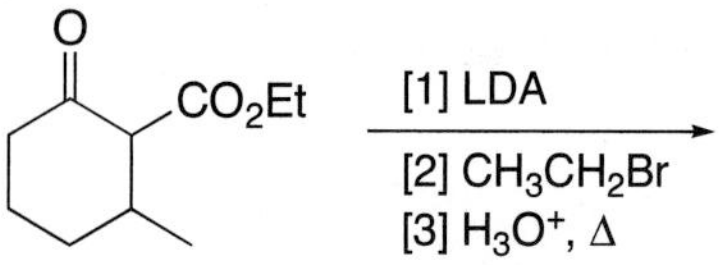
O
CO_2Et
[1] LDA
[2] CH_3CH_2Br
[3] H_3O^+, Δ

e. 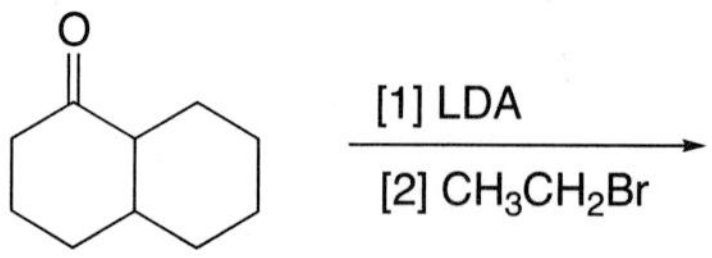
O
[1] LDA
[2] CH_3CH_2Br

c. $CH_2(CO_2Et)_2$ → [1] NaOEt; [2] CH_3CH_2Br → [1] NaOEt; [2] $C_6H_5CH_2Cl$; [3] H_3O^+, Δ

5. a. What starting materials are needed to synthesize carboxylic acid A by a malonic ester synthesis?

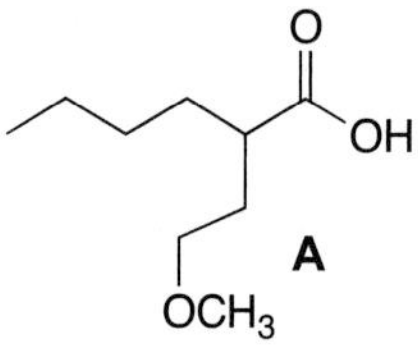
O
OH
OCH_3

A

b. What starting materials are needed to synthesize ketone **B** by the acetoacetic ester synthesis?

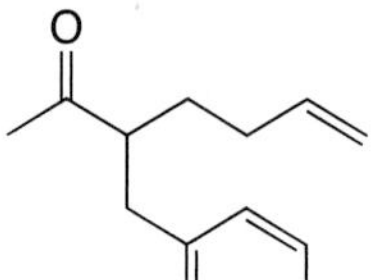
O

B

Answers to Practice Test

1. a. 1
   b. 4
2. a. H_b
   b. H_d
   c. H_b
   d. H_c
3. a. Br_2, CH_3CO_2H
   b. [1] LDA; [2] CH_3I
   c. []1 LDA; [2] CH_3I; [3] LDA; [4] CH_3I
   d. [1] Br_2, CH_3CO_2H; [2] Li_2CO_3, LiBr, DMF
   e. [1] Br_2, CH_3CO_2H; [2] Li_2CO_3, LiBr, DMF; [3] $(CH_3)_2CuLi$; [4] H_2O

4.

a. 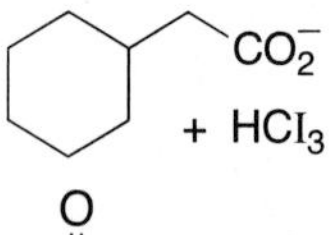
CO_2^-
+ HCI_3

b. 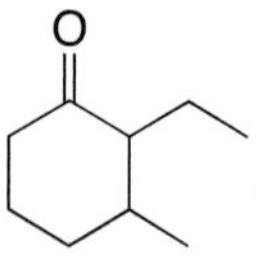
O

c. 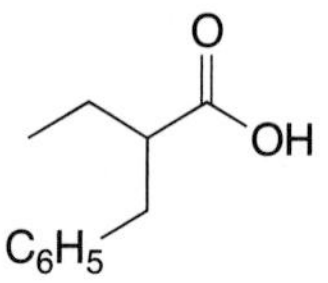
O
OH
C_6H_5

d. 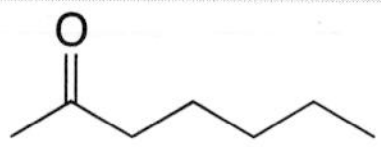
O

e. 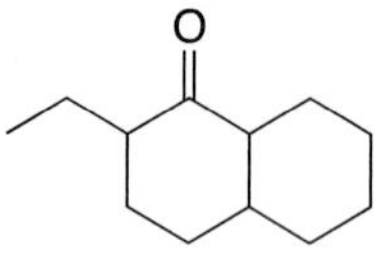
O

5.

a. 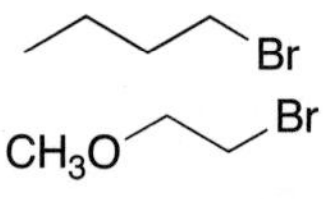
Br
CH_3O
Br

$CH_2(CO_2Et)_2$

b. 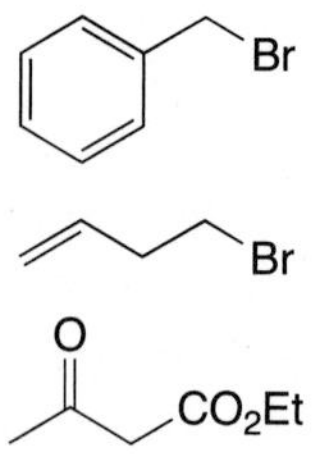
Br
Br
O
CO_2Et

Answers to Problems

23.1 • To convert a ketone to its enol tautomer, change the C=O to C–OH, make a new double bond to an α carbon, and remove a proton at the other end of the C=C.
• To convert an enol to its keto form, find the C=C bonded to the OH. Change the C–OH to a C=O, add a proton to the other end of the C=C, and delete the double bond.

[In cases where *E* and *Z* isomers are possible, only one stereoisomer is drawn.]

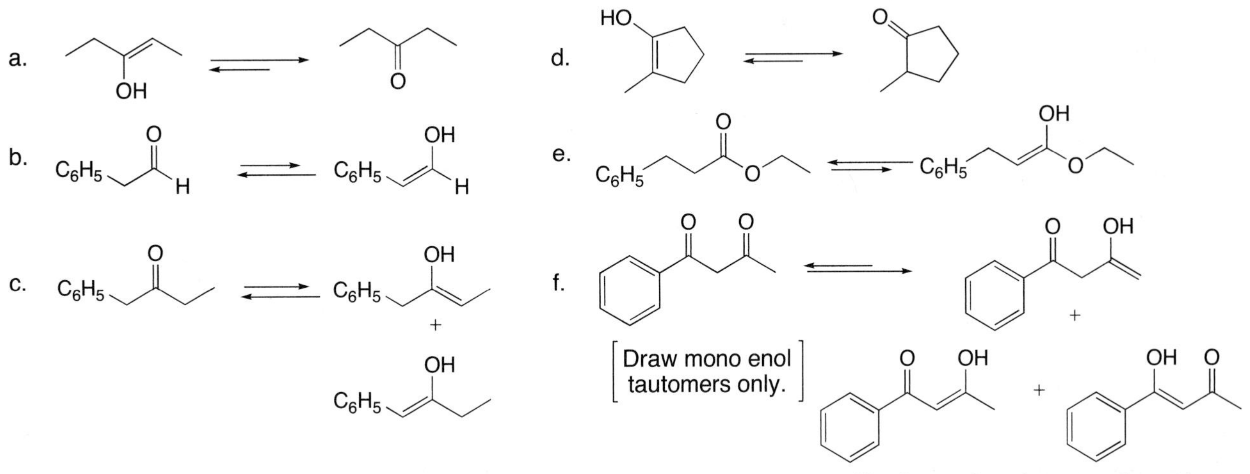
a.
b.
c.
d.
e.
f.
Draw mono enol tautomers only.

(Conjugated enols are preferred.)

23.2 The mechanism has two steps: protonation followed by deprotonation.

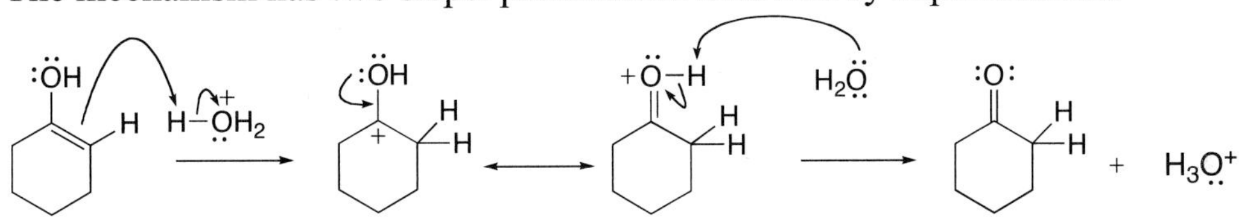

23.3

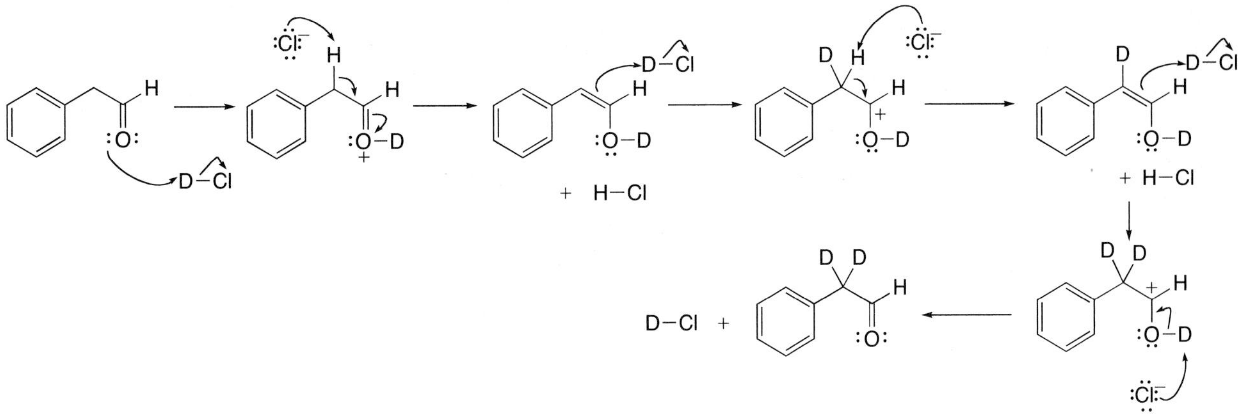

23.4

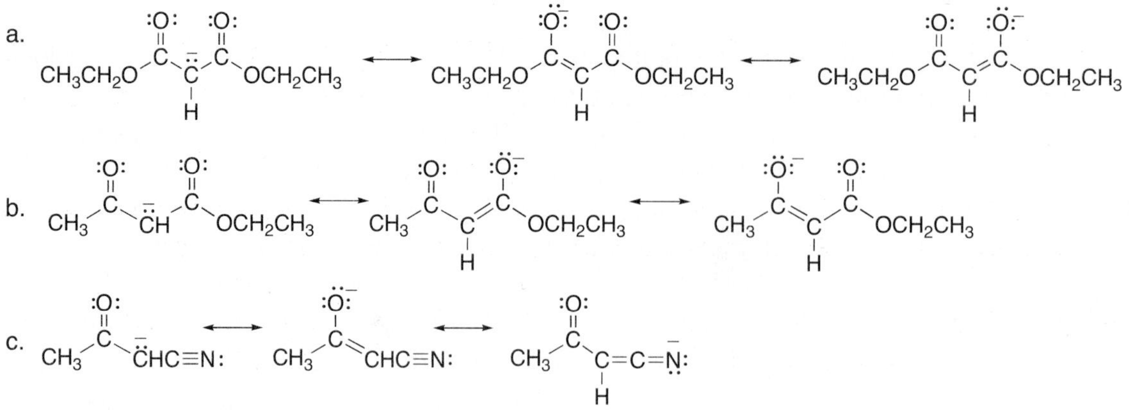

23.5 The indicated H's are α to a C=O or C≡N group, making them more acidic because their removal forms conjugate bases that are resonance stabilized.

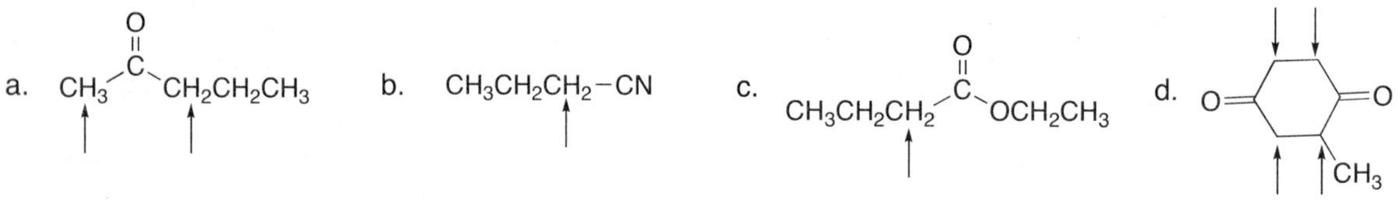

23.6

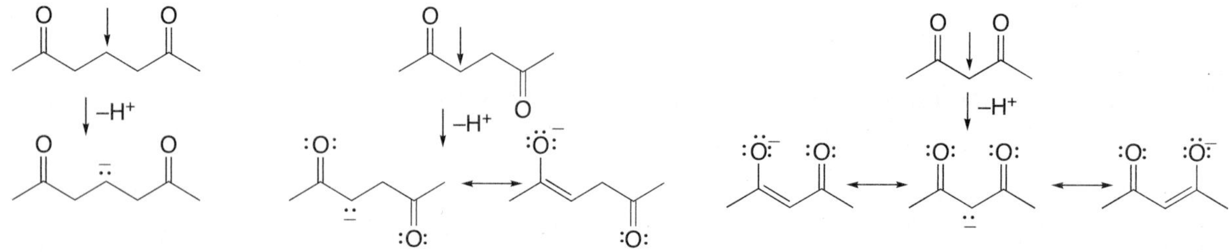

no resonance stabilization
least acidic

Two resonance structures stabilize the conjugate base.
intermediate acidity

Three resonance structures stabilize the conjugate base.
most acidic

23.7 In each of the reactions, the LDA pulls off the most acidic proton.

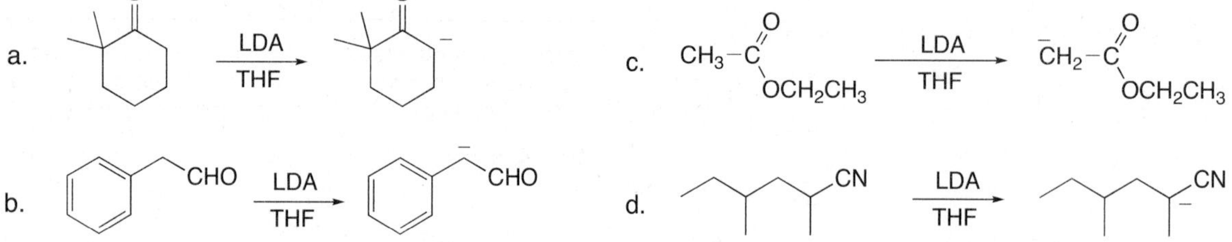

23.8

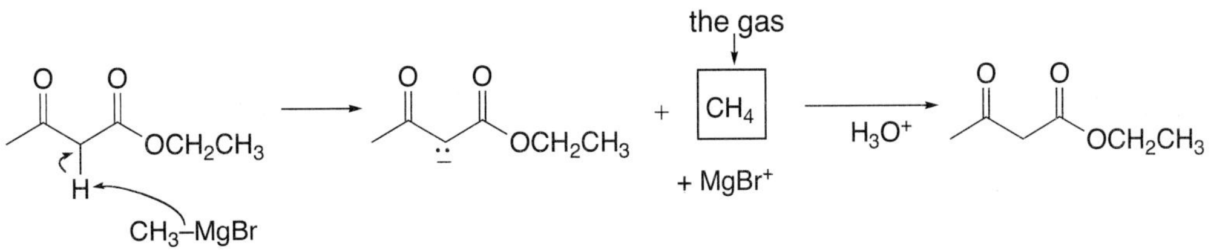

The CH_2 between the two C=O's contains acidic H's, so CH_3MgBr reacts as a base to remove a proton. Thus, proton transfer (not nucleophilic addition) occurs.

23.9 In addition to being strong bases, organolithiums are good nucleophiles that can add to a carbonyl group instead of pulling off a proton to generate an enolate.

23.10
- LDA, THF forms the kinetic enolate by removing a proton from the less substituted C.
- Treatment with $NaOCH_3$, CH_3OH forms the thermodynamic enolate by removing a proton from the more substituted C.

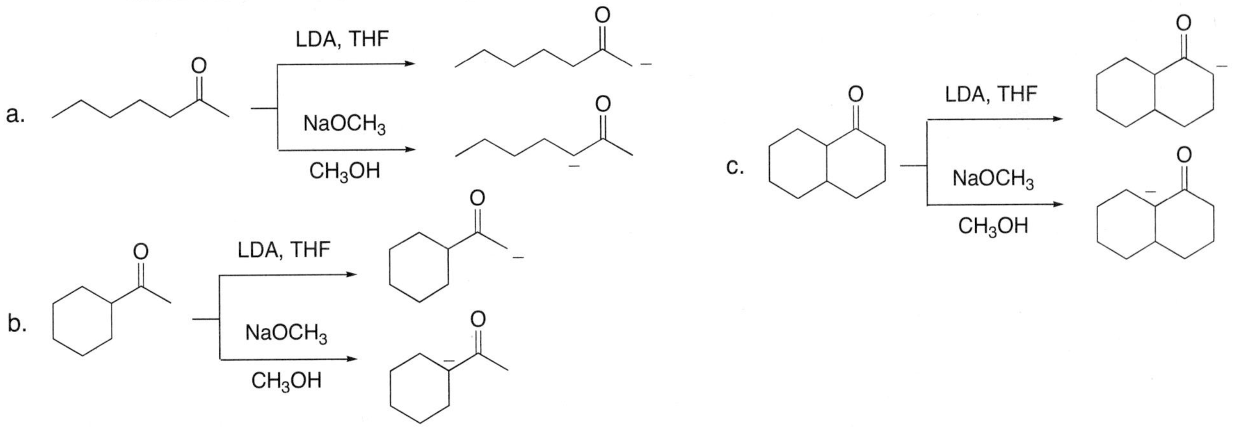

23.11

a. This acidic H is removed with base to form an achiral enolate.

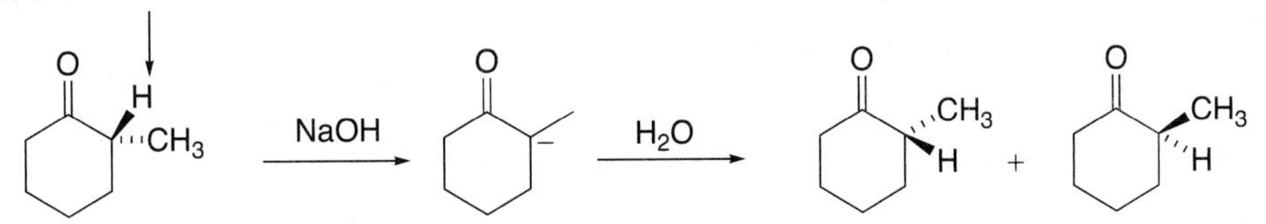

(2*R*)-2-methylcyclohexanone achiral

Protonation of the planar achiral enolate occurs with equal probability from two sides, so a racemic mixture is formed. The racemic mixture is optically inactive.

b.

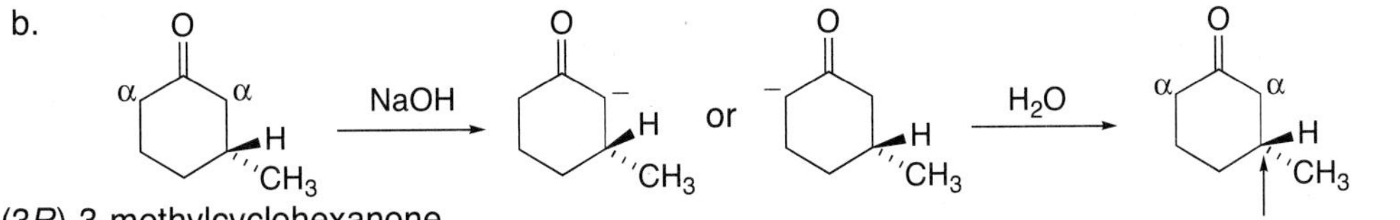

(3*R*)-3-methylcyclohexanone

This stereogenic center is not located at the α carbon, so it is not deprotonated with base. Its configuration is retained in the product, and the product remains optically active.

23.12

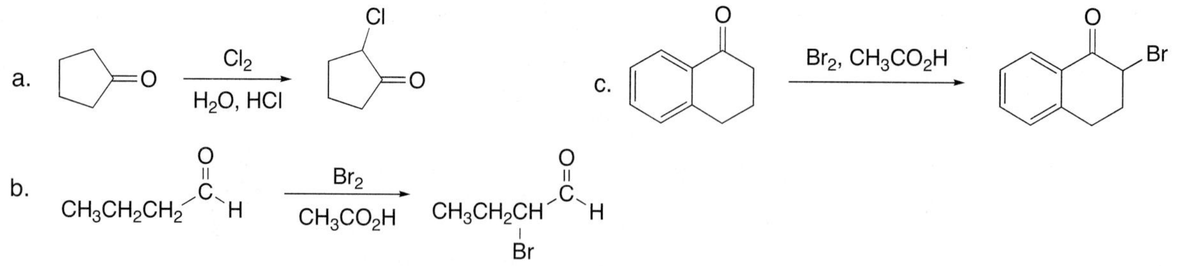
a.
Cl
Cl2
H2O, HCl
O
b.
CH3CH2CH2 C H
Br2
CH3CO2H
CH3CH2CH C H
Br
c.
Br2, CH3CO2H
Br

23.13

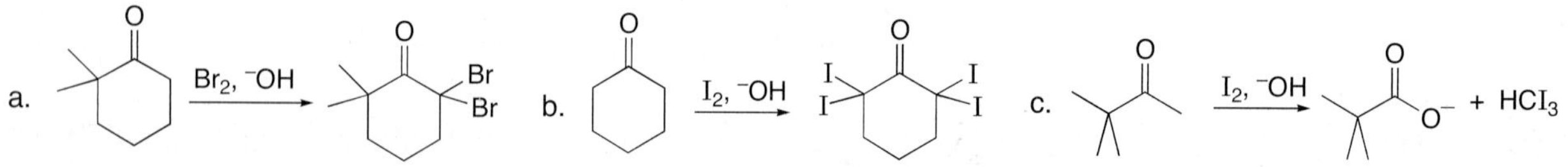
a.
Br2, −OH
Br
Br
b.
I2, −OH
I
c.
I2, −OH
O−
+ HCI3

23.14

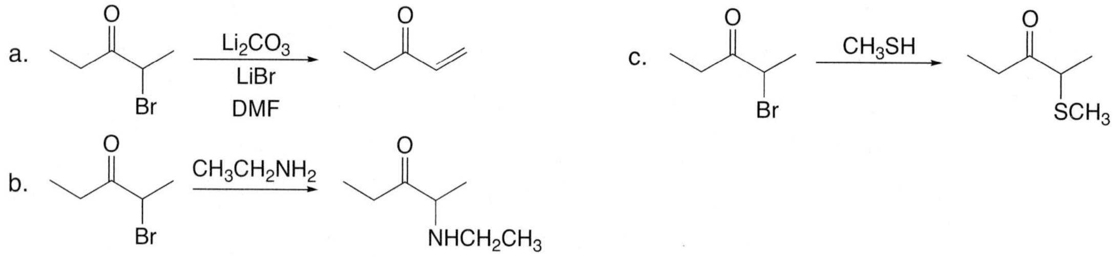
a.
Li2CO3
LiBr
DMF
Br
b.
CH3CH2NH2
NHCH2CH3
c.
CH3SH
SCH3

23.15 Bromination takes place on the α carbon to the carbonyl, followed by an S_N2 reaction with the nitrogen nucleophile.

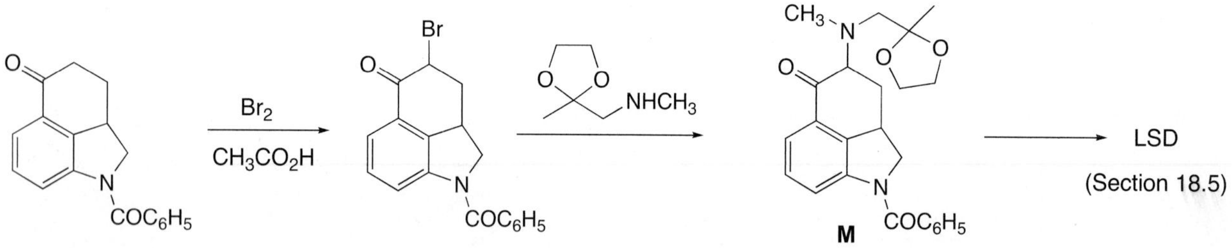
N
COC6H5
Br2
CH3CO2H
Br
NHCH3
CH3 N
M
LSD
(Section 18.5)

23.16

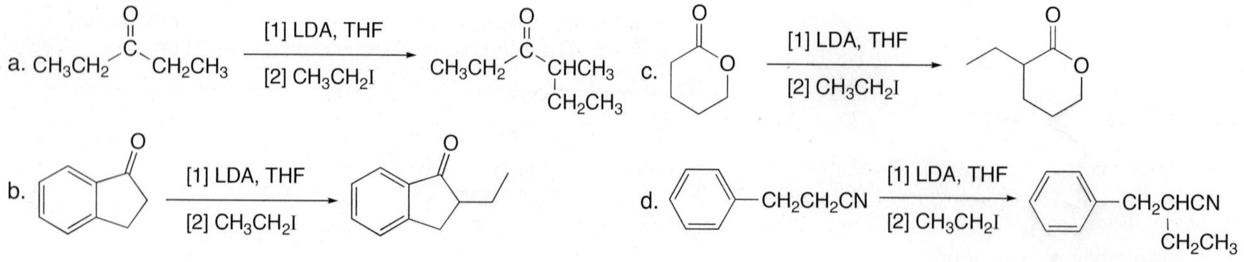
a. CH3CH2 C CH2CH3
[1] LDA, THF
[2] CH3CH2I
CH3CH2 C CHCH3
CH2CH3
b.
[1] LDA, THF
[2] CH3CH2I
c.
[1] LDA, THF
[2] CH3CH2I
d.
CH2CH2CN
[1] LDA, THF
[2] CH3CH2I
CH2CHCN
CH2CH3

23.17

a. 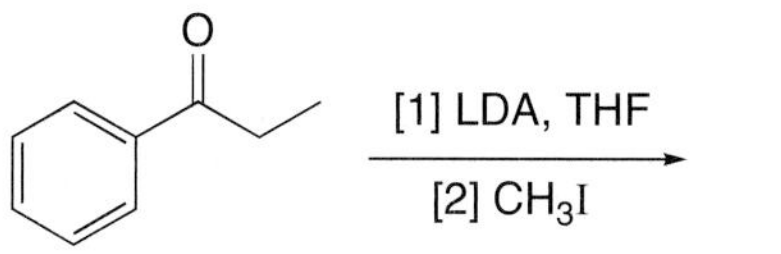
[1] LDA, THF
[2] CH_3I

b. 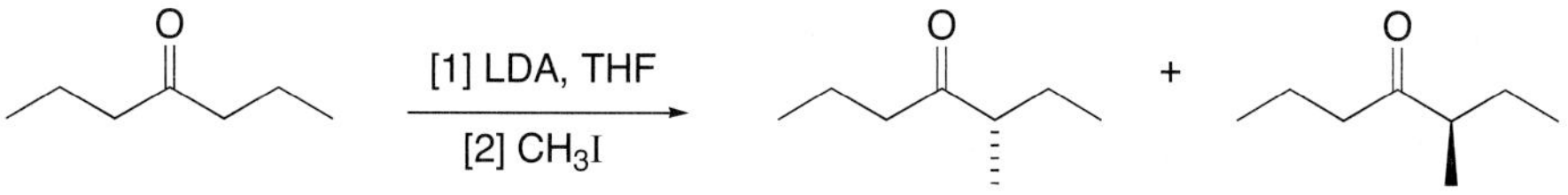
[1] LDA, THF
[2] CH_3I

c. 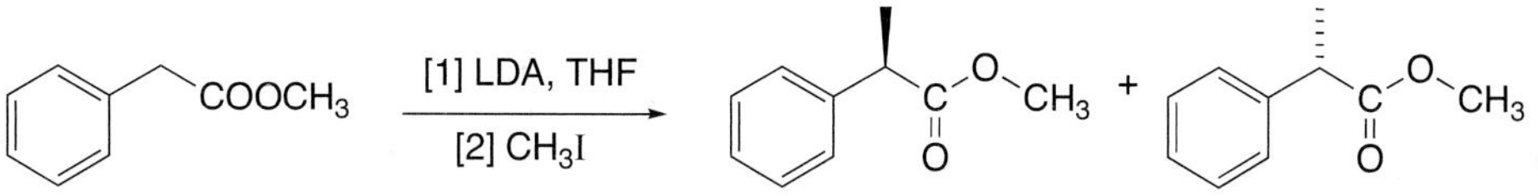
COOCH3
[1] LDA, THF
[2] CH_3I

23.18 Three steps are needed: [1] formation of an enolate; [2] alkylation; [3] hydrolysis of the ester.

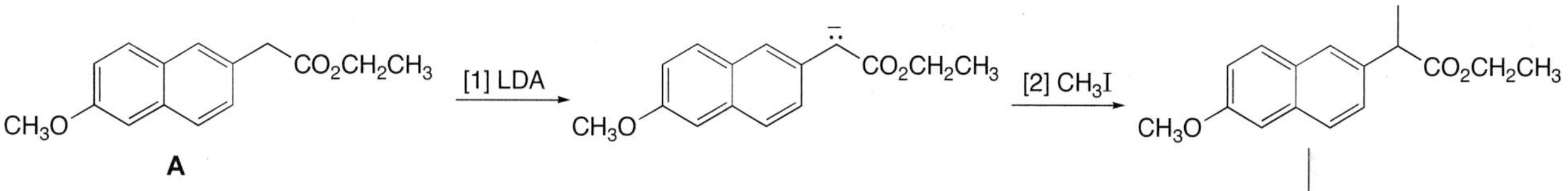
CO2CH2CH3
CH3O
A
[1] LDA
[2] CH_3I

The product is racemic because the new stereogenic center is formed by alkylation of a planar enolate with equal probability from above and below.

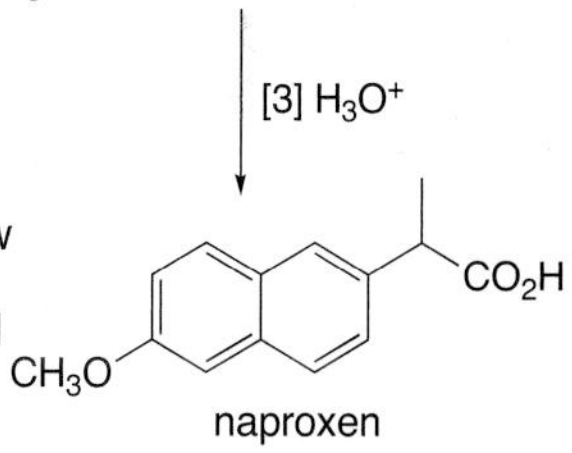
[3] H_3O^+
CO2H
CH3O
naproxen

23.19

a. 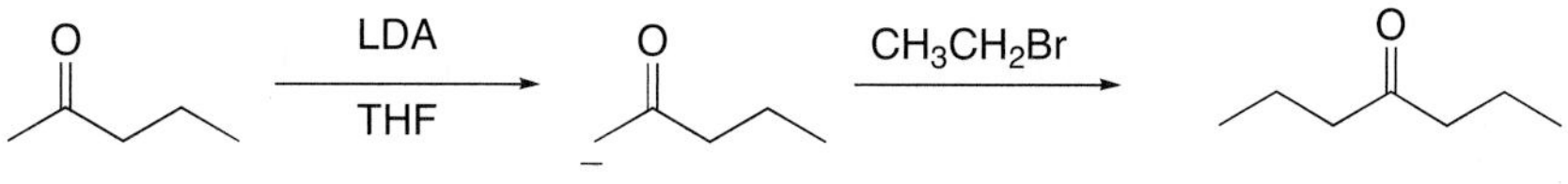
LDA
THF
CH_3CH_2Br

b. 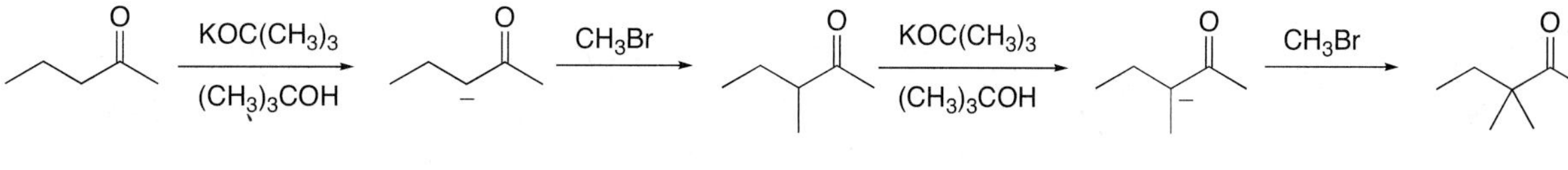
$KOC(CH_3)_3$
$(CH_3)_3COH$
CH_3Br

c. 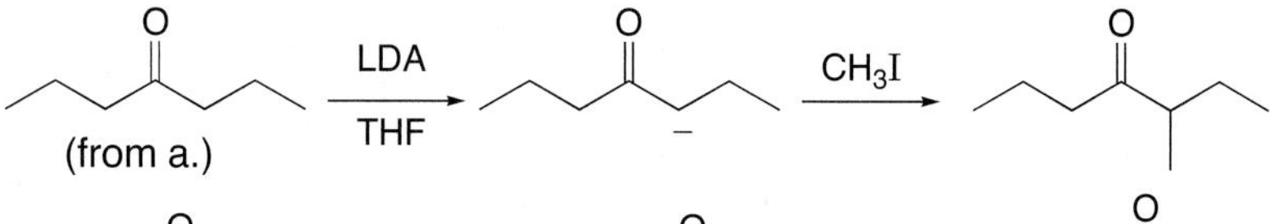
(from a.)
LDA
THF
CH_3I

d. 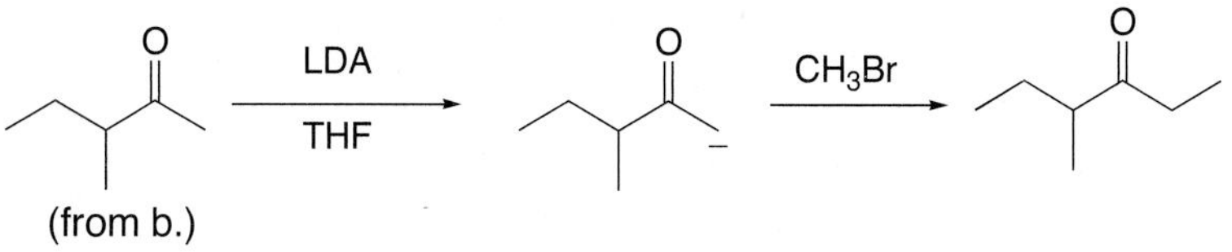
(from b.)
LDA
THF
CH_3Br

23.20

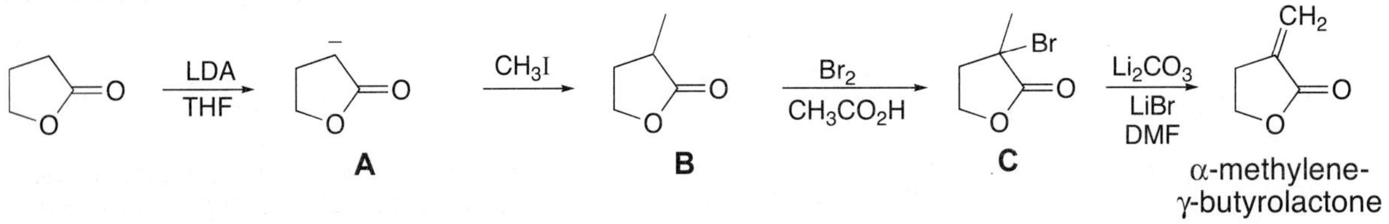

23.21 Decarboxylation occurs only when a carboxy group is bonded to the α C of another carbonyl group.

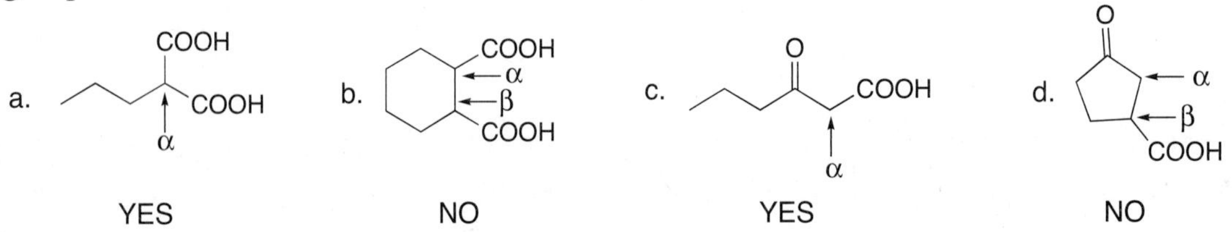

23.22

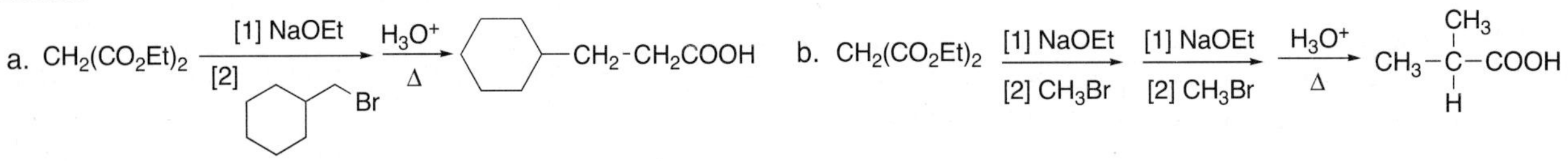

23.23

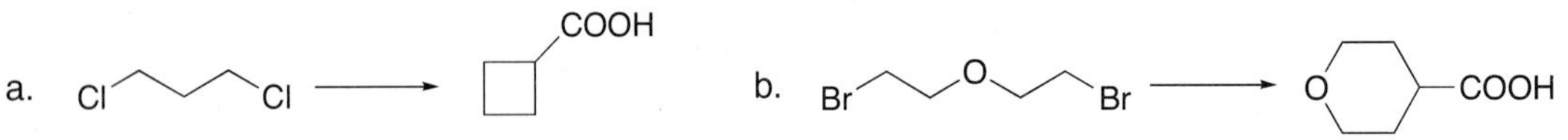

23.24 Locate the α C to the COOH group, and identify all of the alkyl groups bonded to it. These groups are from alkyl halides, and the remainder of the molecule is from diethyl malonate.

a. 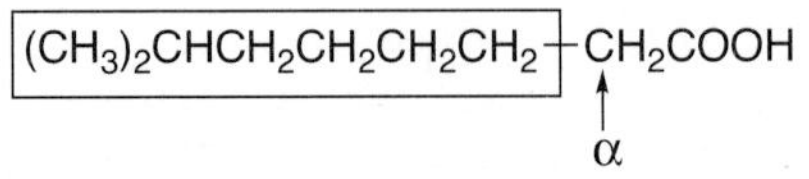

$$CH_2(CO_2Et)_2 \xrightarrow[\text{[2] }(CH_3)_2CHCH_2CH_2CH_2CH_2Br]{\text{[1] NaOEt}} \xrightarrow[\Delta]{H_3O^+} (CH_3)_2CHCH_2CH_2CH_2CH_2CH_2COOH$$

b. 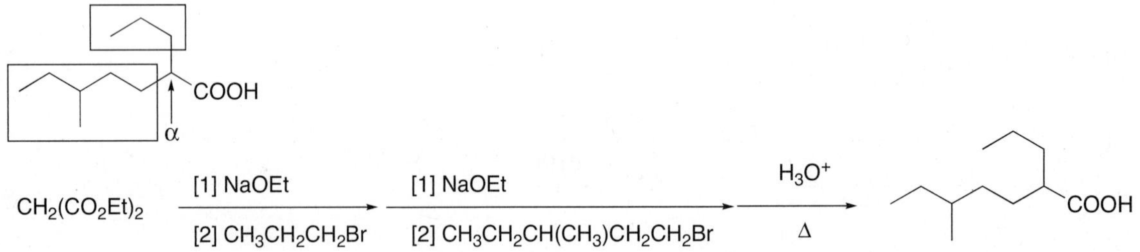

c. 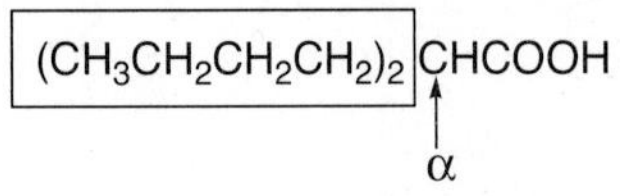

$$CH_2(CO_2Et)_2 \xrightarrow[\text{[2] }CH_3CH_2CH_2CH_2Br]{\text{[1] NaOEt}} \xrightarrow[\text{[2] }CH_3CH_2CH_2CH_2Br]{\text{[1] NaOEt}} \xrightarrow[\Delta]{H_3O^+} (CH_3CH_2CH_2CH_2)_2CHCOOH$$

23.25 The reaction works best when the alkyl halide is 1° or CH_3X, since this is an S_N2 reaction.

a. $(CH_3)_3C$–CH_2COOH

$(CH_3)_3CX$
3° alkyl halide
(too crowded)

b.

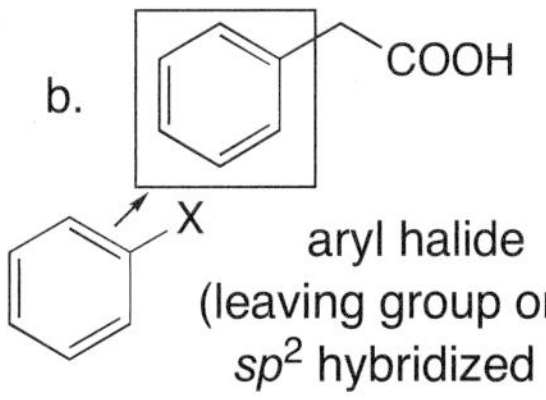

COOH
X

aryl halide
(leaving group on an
sp^2 hybridized C)

Aryl halides are unreactive
in S_N2 reactions.

c. $(CH_3)_3C$–COOH (α)

This compound has 3 CH_3 groups on the α carbon to the COOH. The malonic ester synthesis can be used to prepare mono- and disubstituted carboxylic acids only: RCH_2COOH and $R_2CHCOOH$, but not R_3CCOOH.

23.26

a.

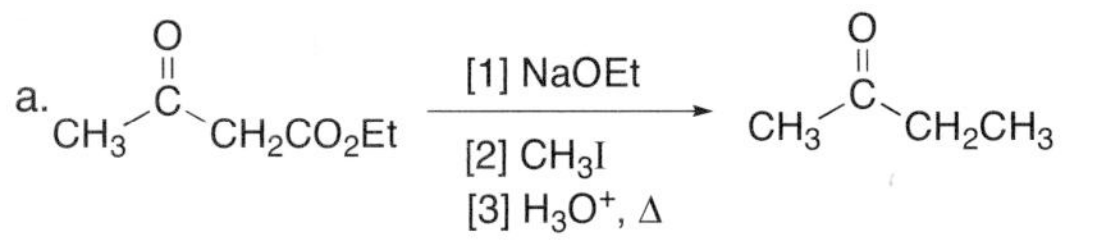

[1] NaOEt
[2] CH3I
[3] H3O+, Δ

b.

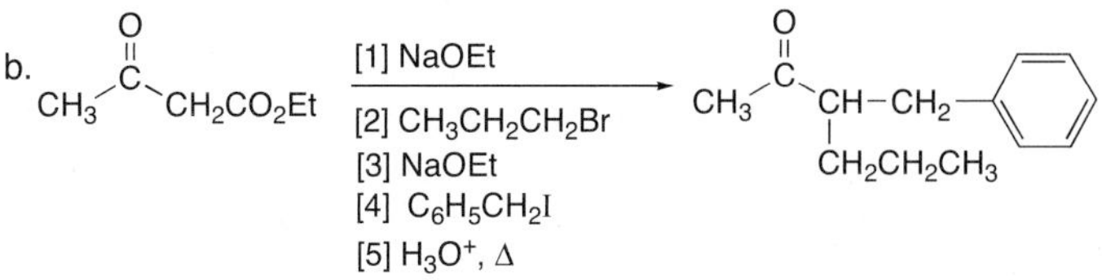

[1] NaOEt
[2] CH3CH2CH2Br
[3] NaOEt
[4] C6H5CH2I
[5] H3O+, Δ

23.27 Locate the α C. All alkyl groups on the α C come from alkyl halides, and the remainder of the molecule comes from ethyl acetoacetate.

a.

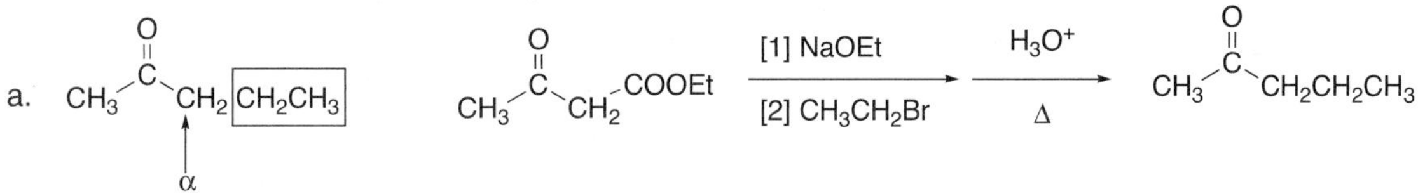

α
[1] NaOEt
[2] CH3CH2Br
H3O+
Δ

b.

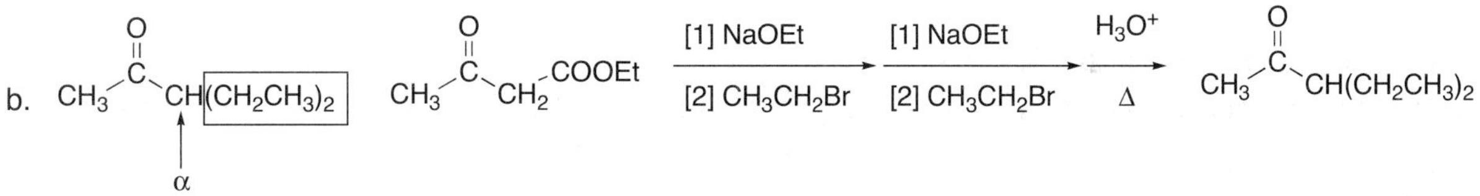

α
[1] NaOEt
[2] CH3CH2Br
[1] NaOEt
[2] CH3CH2Br
H3O+
Δ

c.

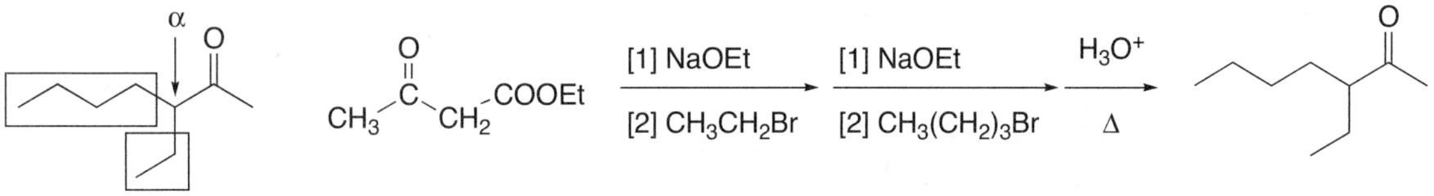

α
[1] NaOEt
[2] CH3CH2Br
[1] NaOEt
[2] CH3(CH2)3Br
H3O+
Δ

23.28

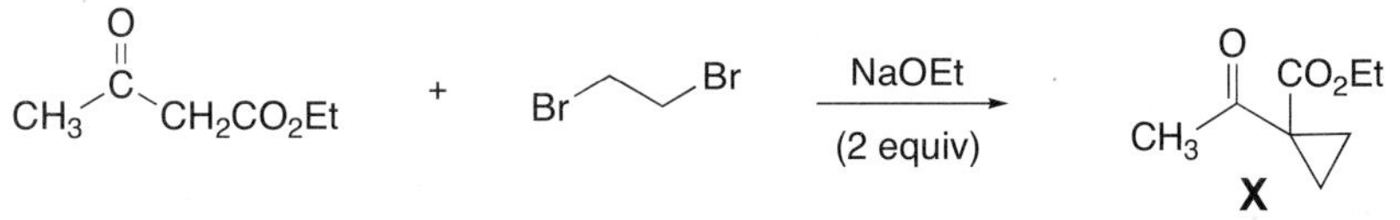

NaOEt
(2 equiv)
X

23.29

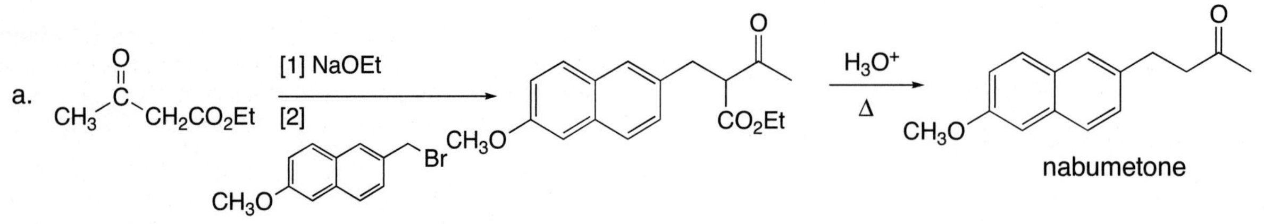
a.
[1] NaOEt
[2]
CH_3O
Br
CO_2Et
H_3O^+
Δ
nabumetone

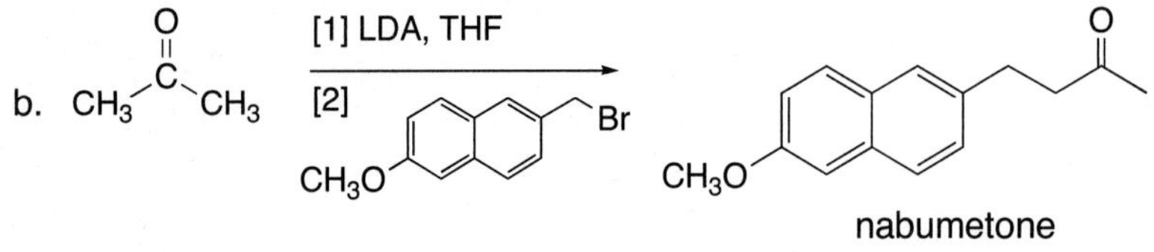
b.
[1] LDA, THF
[2]
CH_3O
Br
nabumetone

23.30 Use the directions from Answer 23.1 to draw the enol tautomer(s). In cases where *E* and *Z* isomers can form, only one isomer is drawn.

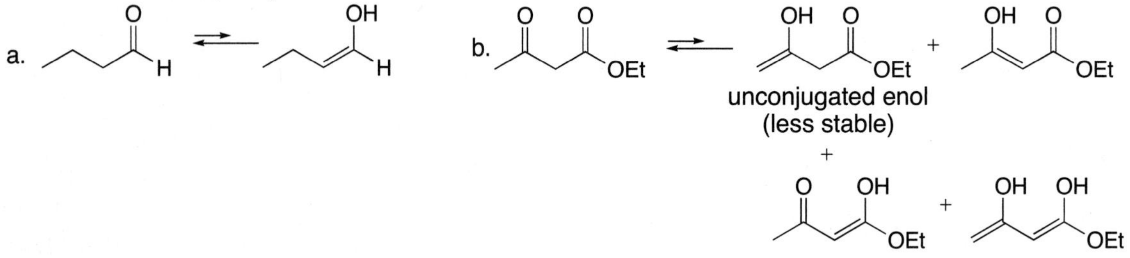
a.
b.
OEt
unconjugated enol
(less stable)

23.31

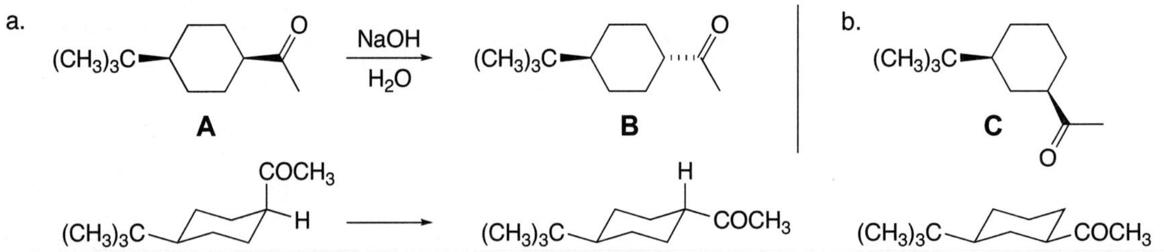
a.
NaOH
H_2O
A
B
b.
C
$(CH_3)_3C$
$COCH_3$

one axial and one equatorial group, **less stable**

Both groups are equatorial. **more stable**

This isomerization will occur since it makes a more stable compound.

Both groups are equatorial = cis.

Compound **C** will not isomerize since it already has the more stable arrangement of substituents.

23.32 Use the directions from Answer 23.1 to draw the enol tautomer(s). In cases where *E* and *Z* isomers can form, only one isomer is drawn.

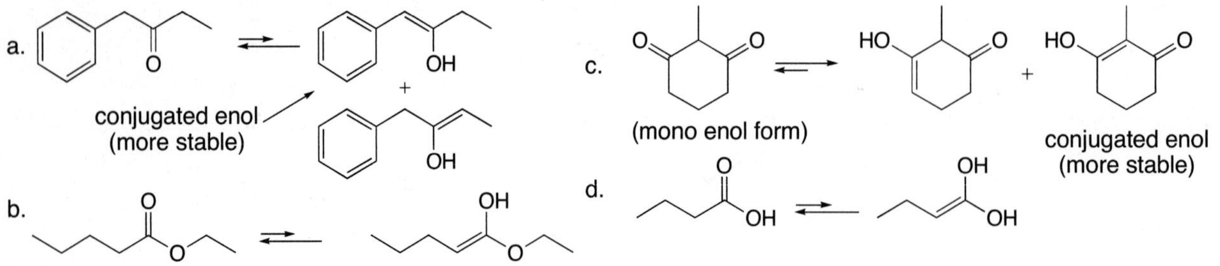
a.
conjugated enol
(more stable)
b.
c.
(mono enol form)
conjugated enol
(more stable)
d.

23.33

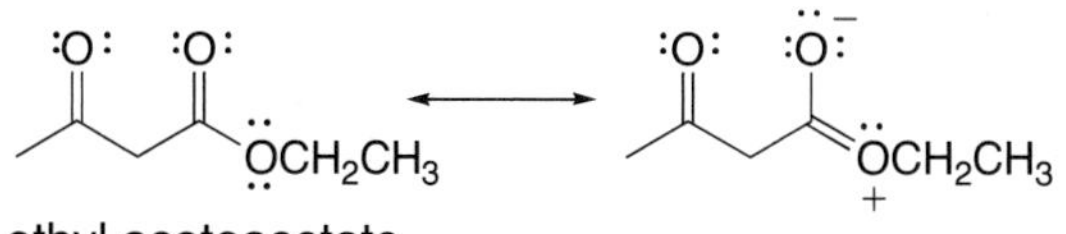

ethyl acetoacetate

The ester C=O is resonance stabilized, and is therefore less available for tautomerization. Since the carbonyl form of the ester group is stabilized by electron delocalization, less enol is present at equilibrium.

23.34

a. $CH_3CH_2CH_2CO_2CH(CH_3)_2$

b. 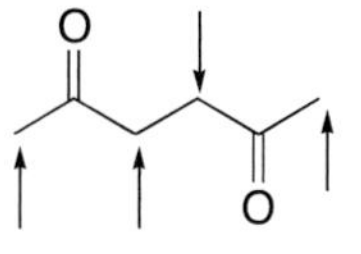

c. 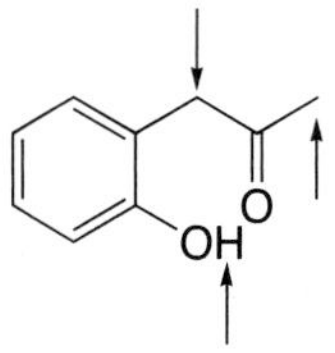

d. 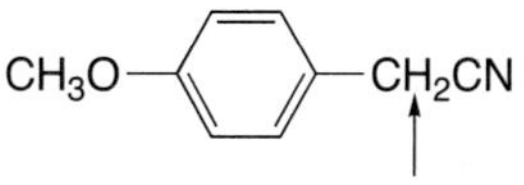

e. 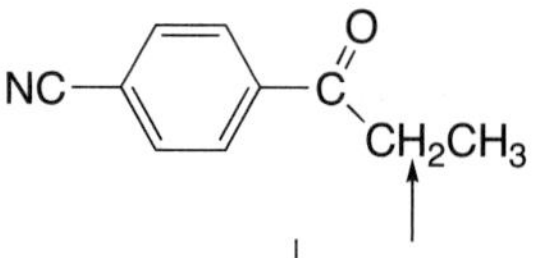

f. 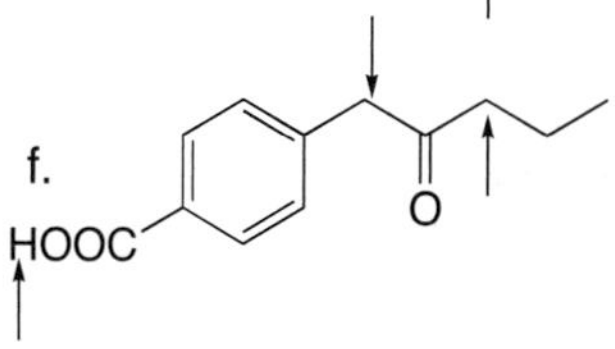

23.35

a. 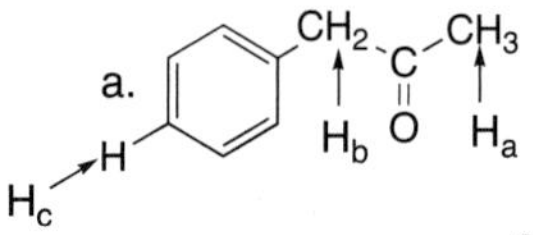

H_c is bonded to an *sp*^{2} hybridized C = **least acidic.**
H_a is bonded to an α C = **intermediate acidity.**
H_b is bonded to an α C, and is adjacent to a benzene ring = **most acidic.**

b. 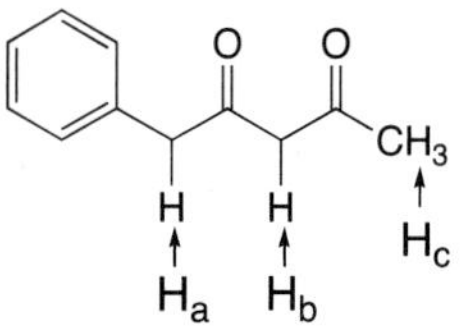

H_c is bonded to an α C = **least acidic.**
H_a is bonded to an α C, and is adjacent to a benzene ring = **intermediate acidity.**
H_b is bonded to an α C between two C=O groups = **most acidic.**

c. 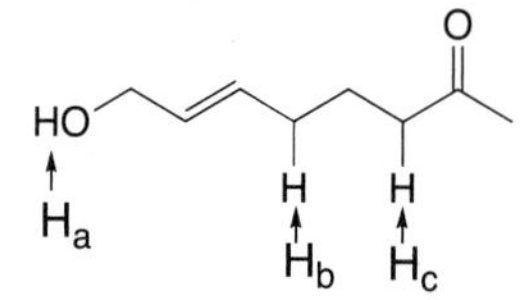

H_b is bonded to an *sp*^{3} hybridized C = **least acidic.**
H_c is bonded to an α C = **intermediate acidity.**
H_a is bonded to O = **most acidic.**

23.36

a. 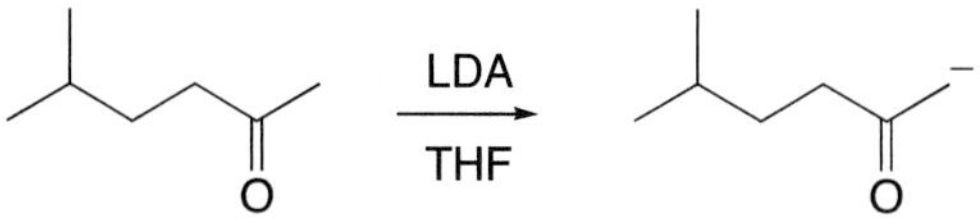

b. 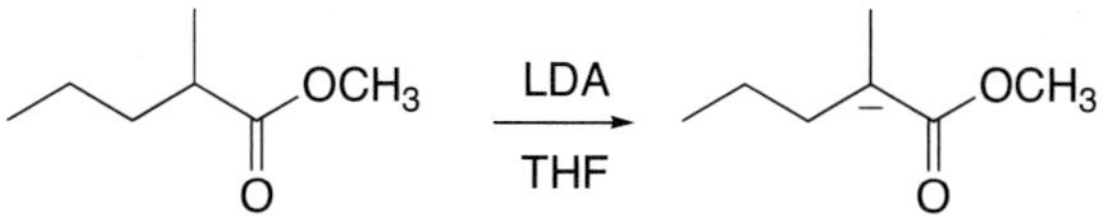

c. 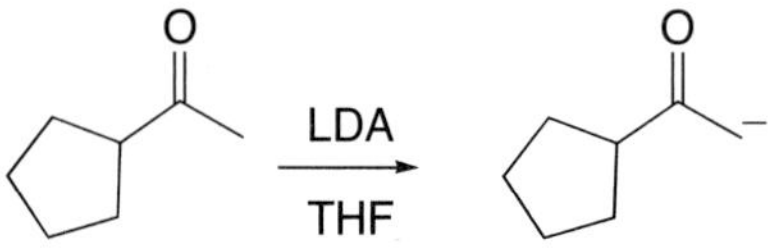

d. 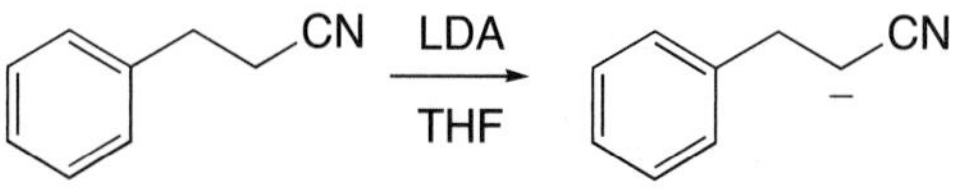

e. 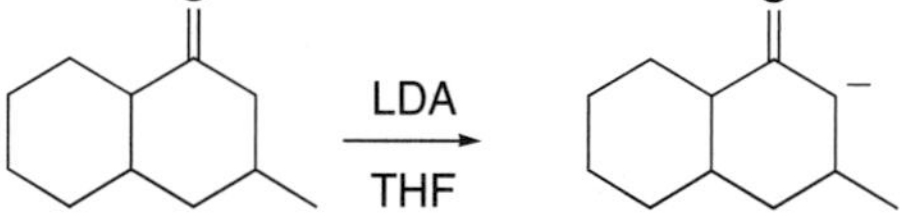

f. 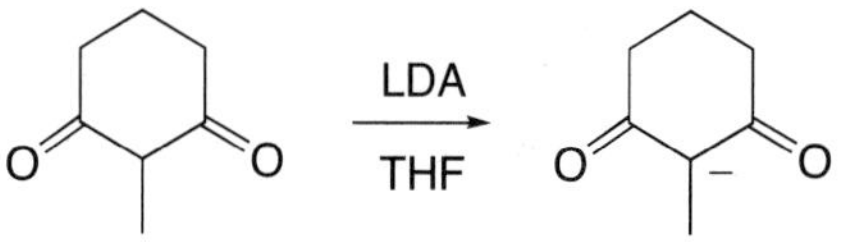

23.37 Enol tautomers have OH groups that give a broad OH absorption at 3600–3200 cm^{-1}, which could be detected readily in the IR.

23.38

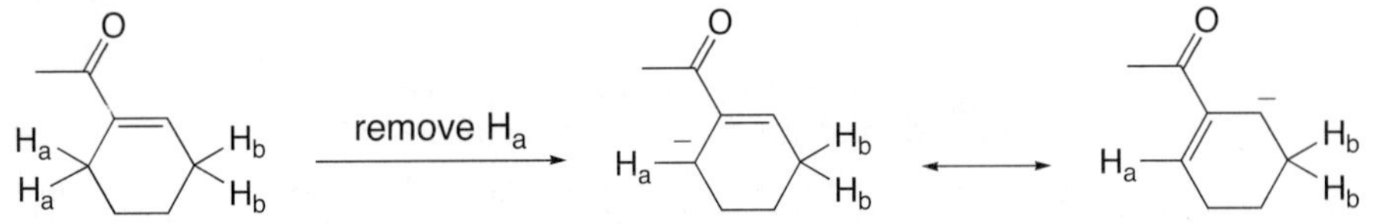

Removal of H_a gives two resonance structures. The negative charge is never on O.

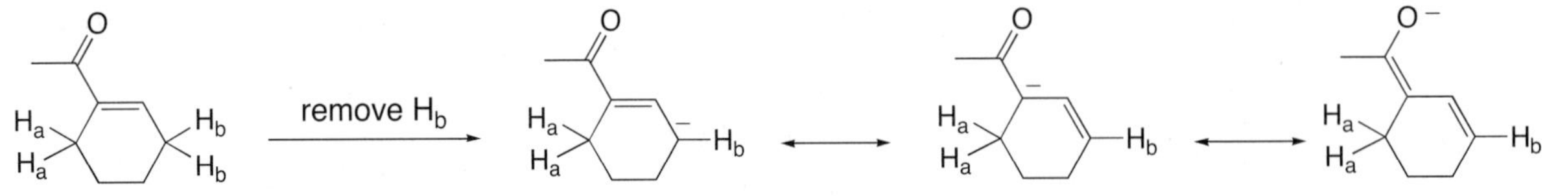

Removal of H_b gives three resonance structures. The negative charge is on O in one resonance structure, making the conjugate base more stable and H_b more acidic (lower pK_a).

23.39

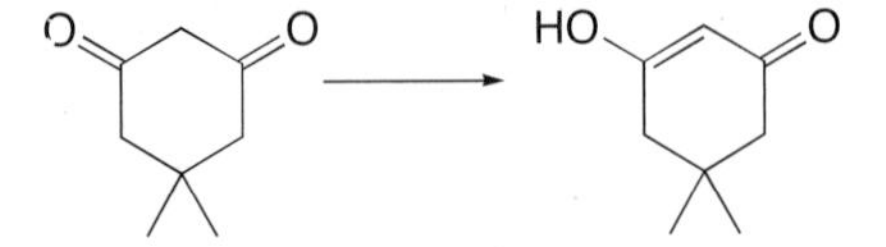

5,5-dimethyl-1,3-cyclohexanedione

5,5-Dimethyl-1,3-cyclohexanedione exists predominantly in its enol form because the C=C of the enol is conjugated with the other C=O of the dicarbonyl compound. Conjugation stabilizes this enol.

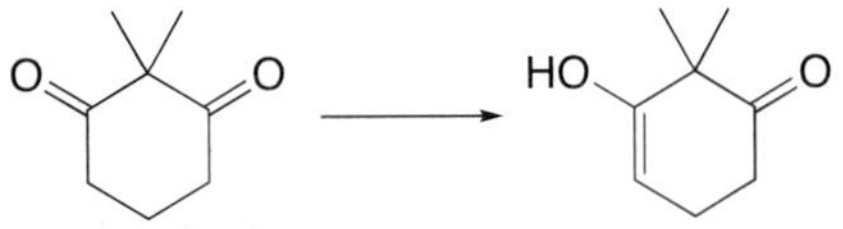

2,2-dimethyl-1,3-cyclohexanedione

The enol of 2,2-dimethyl-1,3-cyclohexanedione is not conjugated with the other carbonyl group. In this way it resembles the enol of any other carbonyl compound, and thus it is present in low concentration.

23.40 a.

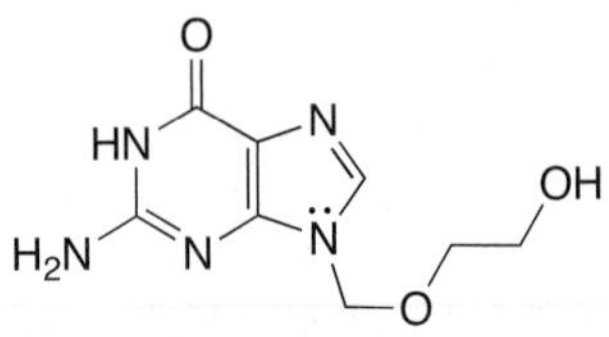

keto form
acyclovir

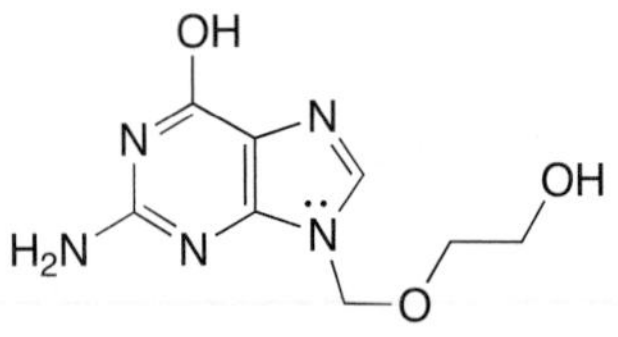

enol form

In the enol form, the bicyclic ring system has four π bonds (eight π electrons) and a lone pair on N, for a total of 10 π electrons. This makes it aromatic by Hückel's rule.

b. The keto form of acyclovir can also be drawn in a resonance form that gives it 10 π electrons, making it aromatic as well.

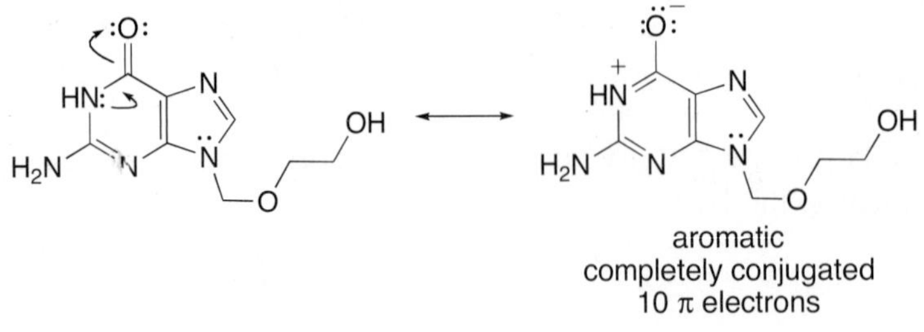

aromatic
completely conjugated
10 π electrons

23.41

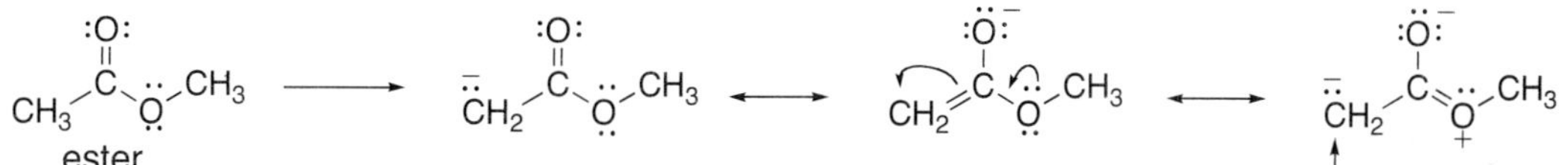

ester

The O atom of the ester OR group donates electron density by a resonance effect. The resulting resonance structure keeps a negative charge on the less electronegative C end of the enolate. This destabilizes the resonance hybrid of the conjugate base, and makes the α H's of the ester less acidic.

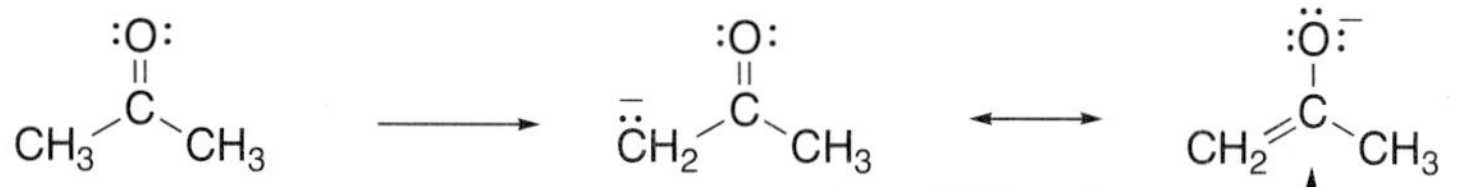

ketone

no additional resonance structures

This structure, which places a negative charge on the O atom, is the major contributor to the hybrid, stabilizing it, and making the α H's of the ketone more acidic.

23.42

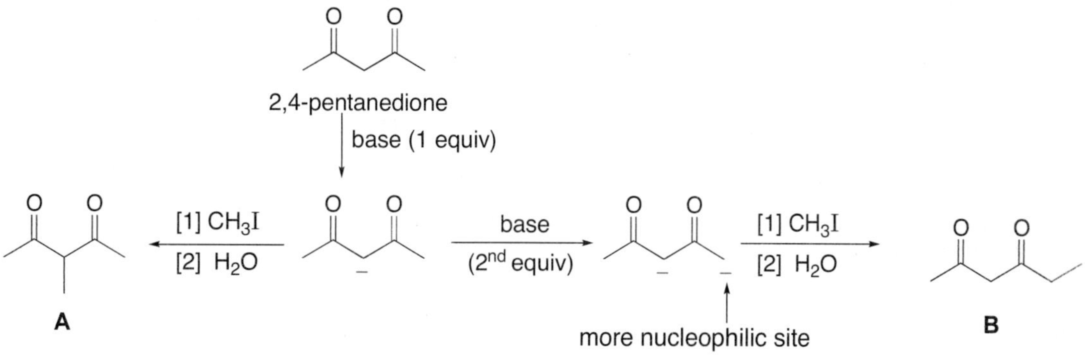
2,4-pentanedione
base (1 equiv)
[1] CH3I
[2] H2O
base
(2nd equiv)
[1] CH3I
[2] H2O
A
more nucleophilic site
B

One equivalent of base removes the most acidic proton between the two C=O's, to form **A** on alkylation with CH_3I.

With a second equivalent of base a dianion is formed. Since the second enolate is less resonance stabilized, it is more nucleophilic and reacts first in an alkylation with CH_3I, forming **B** after protonation with H_2O.

23.43 The mechanism of acid-catalyzed halogenation consists of two parts: **tautomerization** of the carbonyl compound to the enol form and **reaction of the enol with halogen.**

A higher percentage of the more stable enol is present.

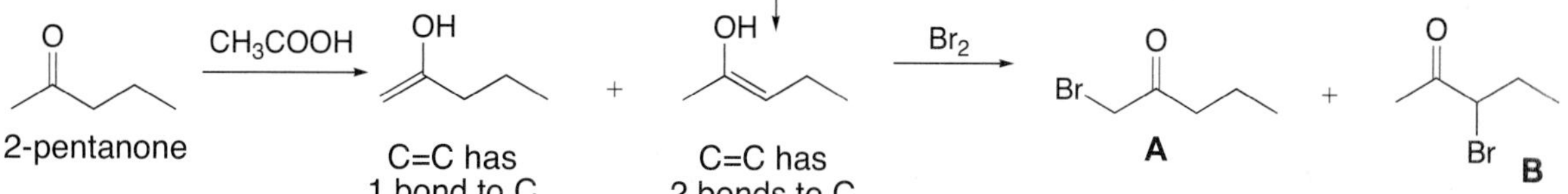
2-pentanone
CH3COOH
OH
OH
Br2
Br
A
Br
B

C=C has 1 bond to C

C=C has 2 bonds to C **more stable** (*E* and *Z* isomers)

major product formed from the more stable enol

23.44 • The mechanism of acid-catalyzed halogenation [Part (a)] consists of two parts: **tautomerization** of the carbonyl compound to the enol form and **reaction of the enol with halogen.**

• In the haloform reaction [Part (b)], the three H's of the CH_3 group are successively replaced by X, to form an intermediate that is oxidatively cleaved with base.

a.

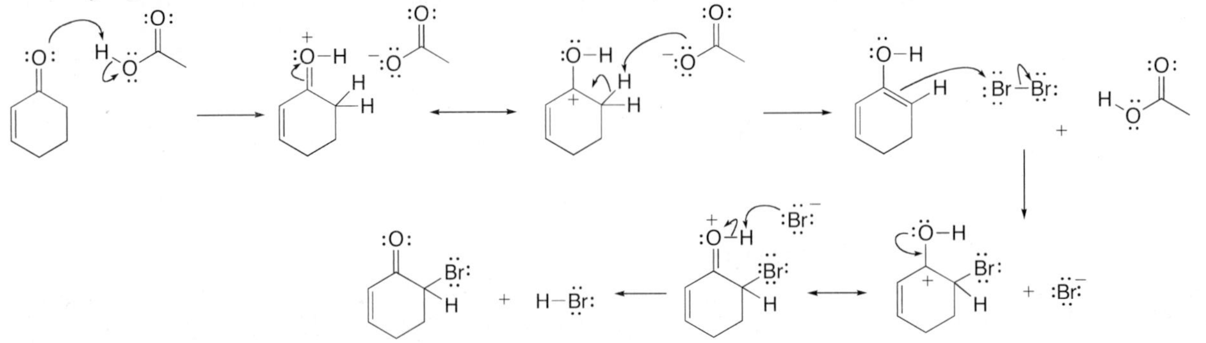

b.

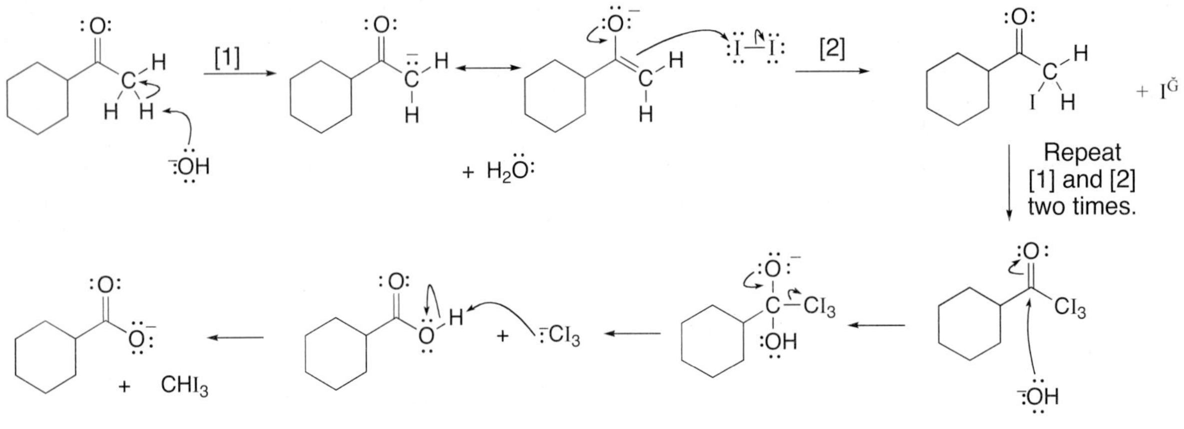
[1]
[2]
Repeat
[1] and [2]
two times.
+ CHI3

23.45 Use the directions from Answer 23.24.

a.

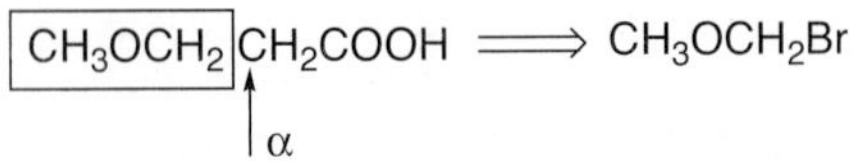
CH3OCH2CH2COOH ⟹ CH3OCH2Br
α

b.

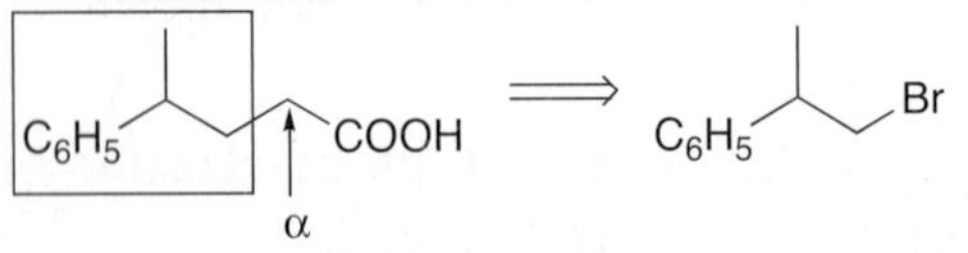
C6H5
COOH
α
C6H5
Br

c.

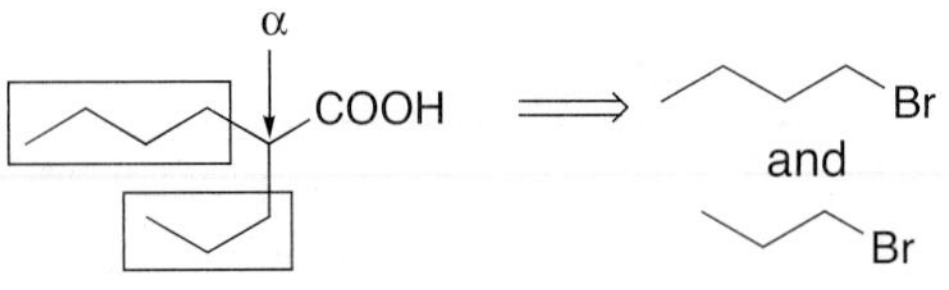
α
COOH
Br
and
Br

23.46

a.

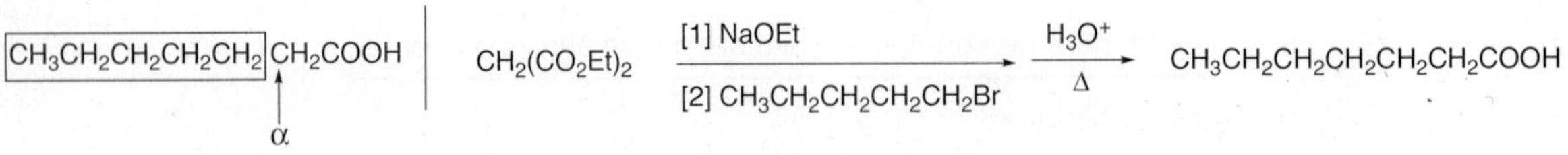
CH3CH2CH2CH2CH2CH2COOH
α
CH2(CO2Et)2
[1] NaOEt
[2] CH3CH2CH2CH2CH2Br
H3O+
Δ
CH3CH2CH2CH2CH2CH2COOH

b.

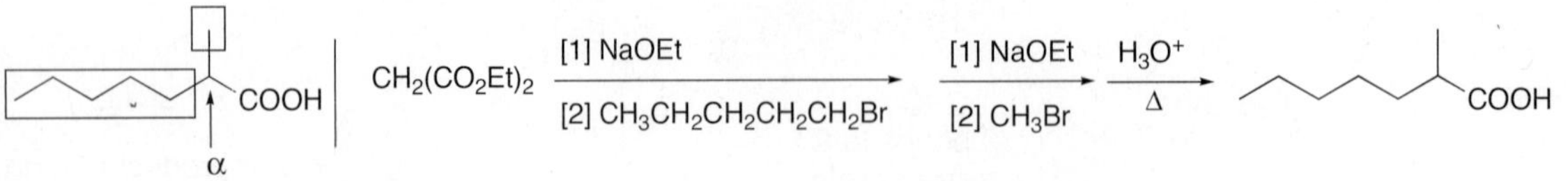
COOH
α
CH2(CO2Et)2
[1] NaOEt
[2] CH3CH2CH2CH2CH2Br
[1] NaOEt
[2] CH3Br
H3O+
Δ
COOH

c.

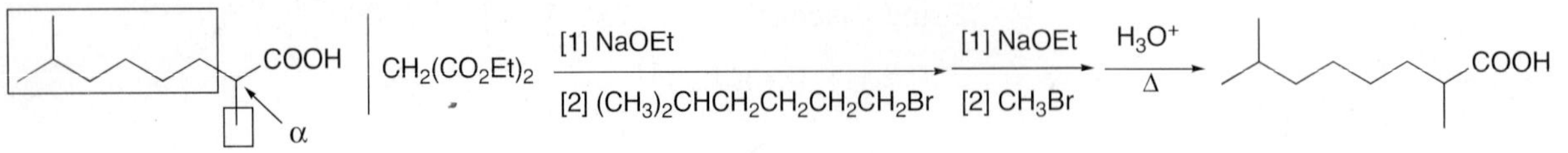
COOH
α
CH2(CO2Et)2
[1] NaOEt
[2] (CH3)2CHCH2CH2CH2CH2Br
[1] NaOEt
[2] CH3Br
H3O+
Δ
COOH

23.47

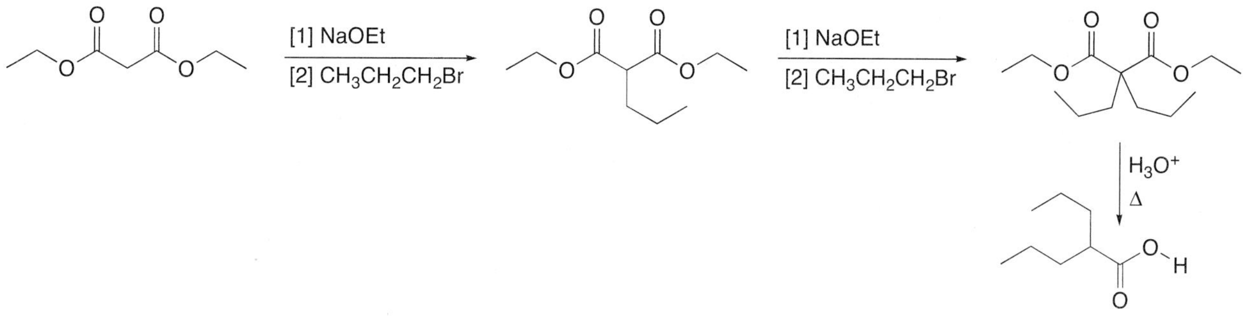

valproic acid

23.48

a. 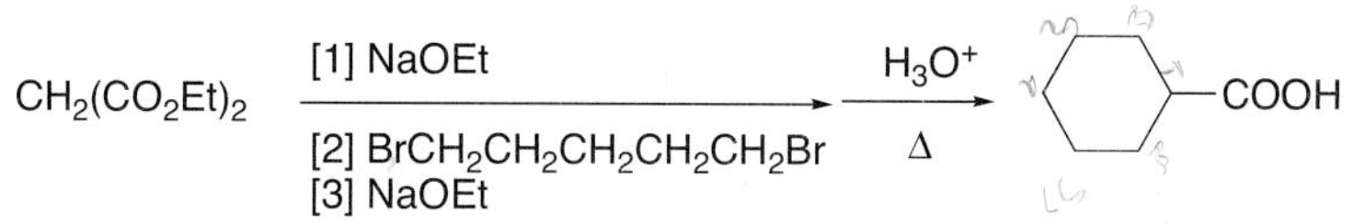

b. 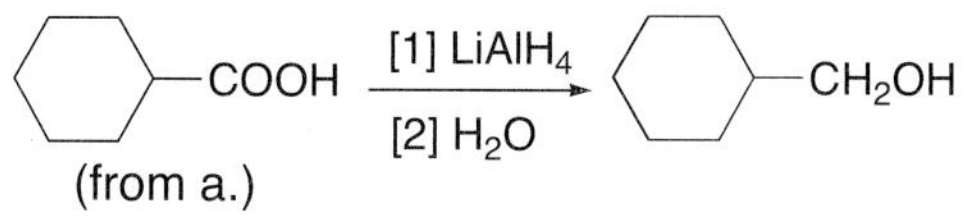

c. 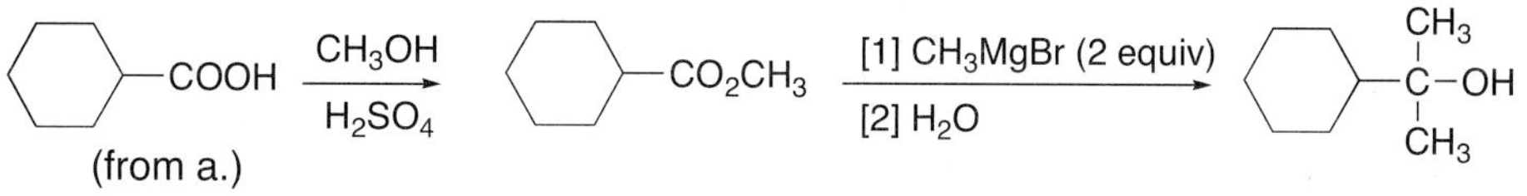

d. 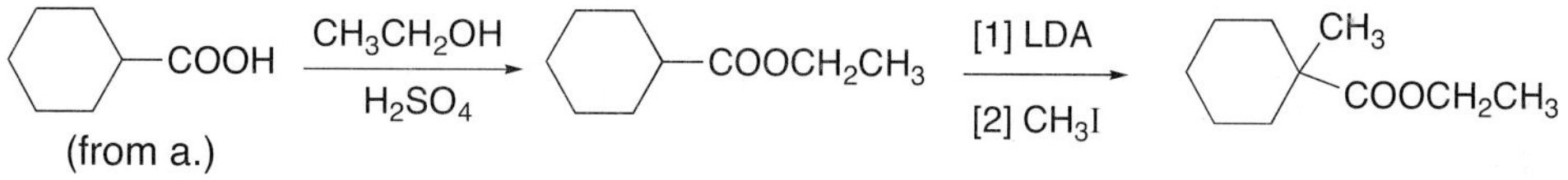

23.49

a. 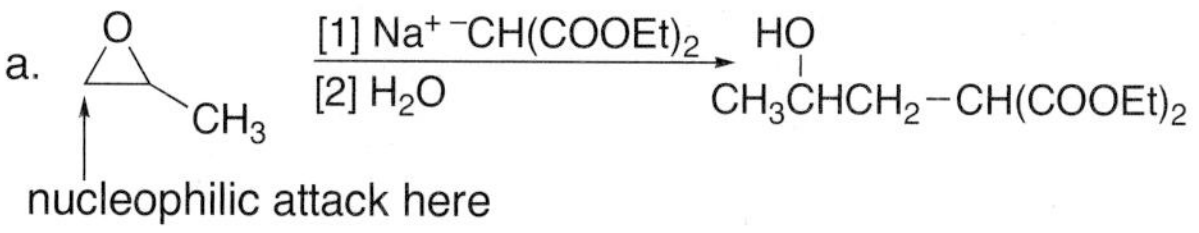

c. 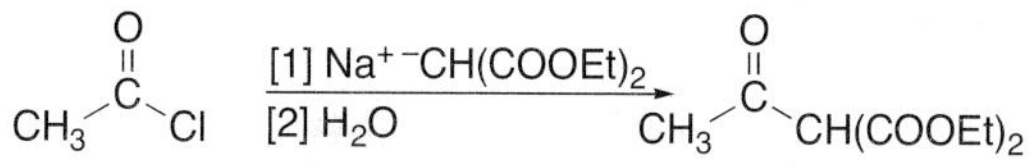

b. 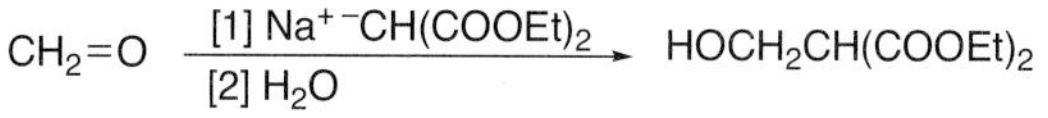

d. 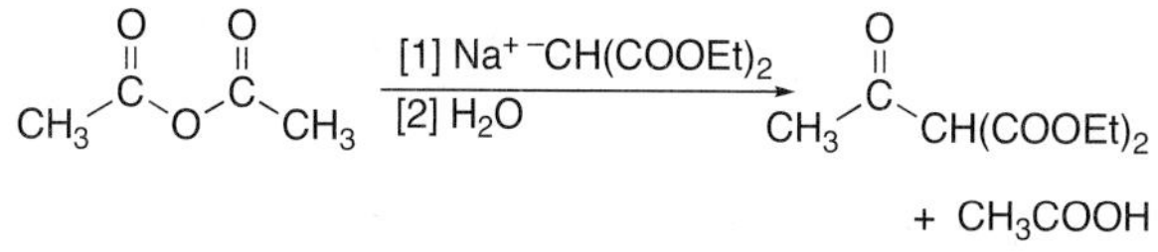

23.50 Use the directions from Answer 23.27.

a. 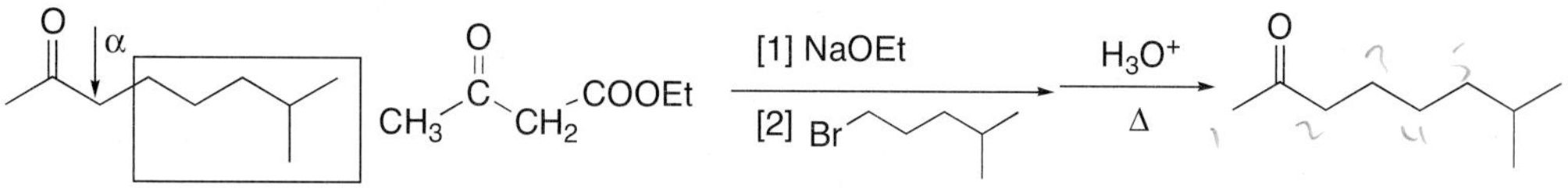

b. 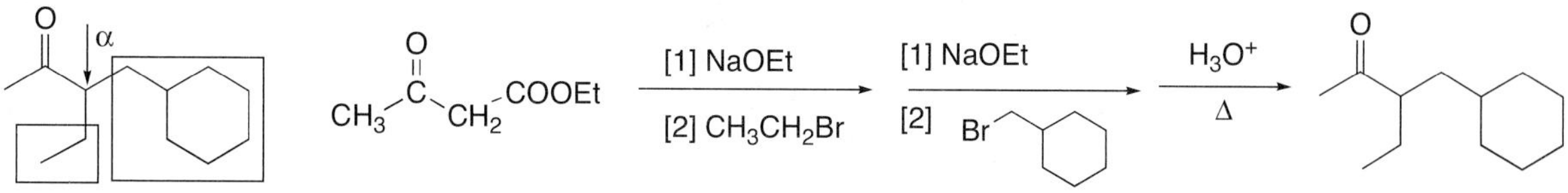

c. 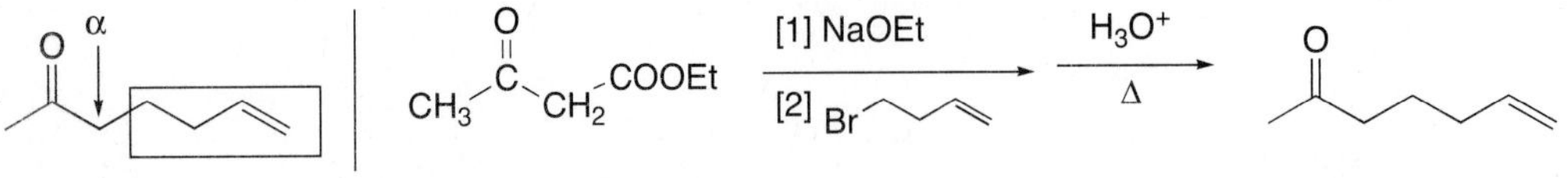

d. 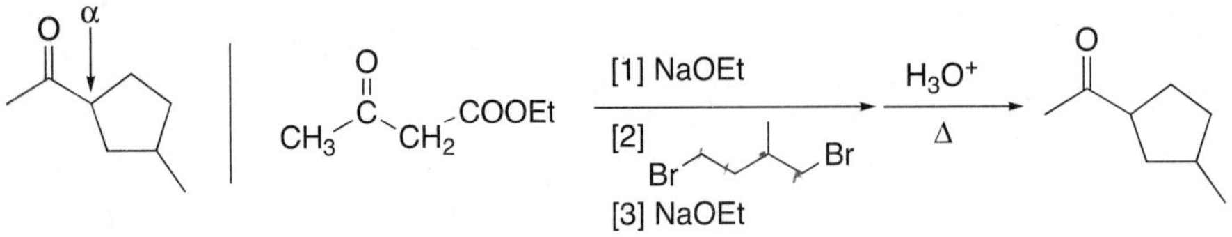

23.51

a. 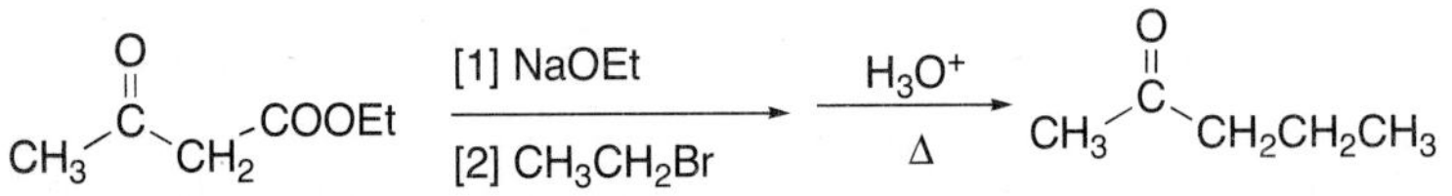

b. 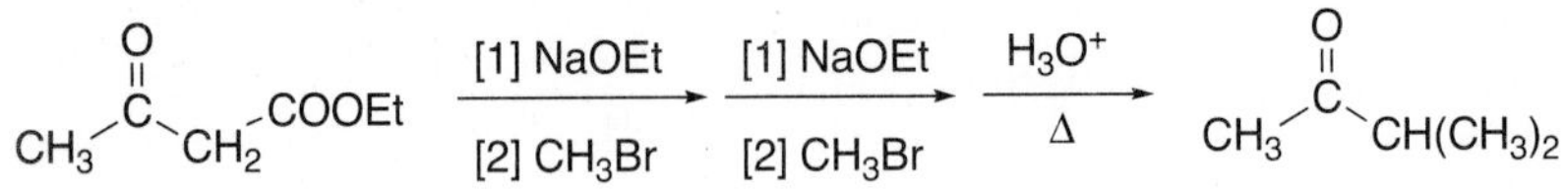

c. 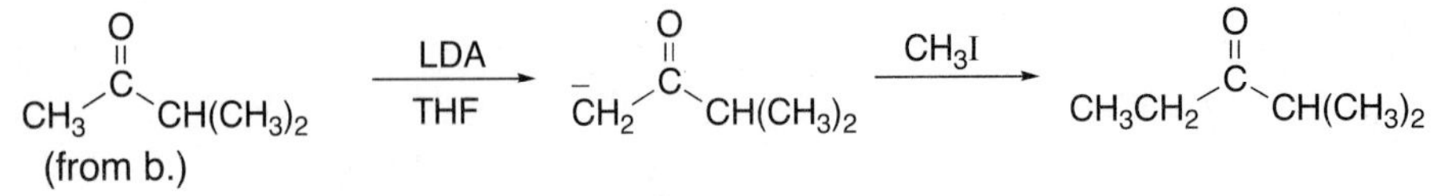

d. 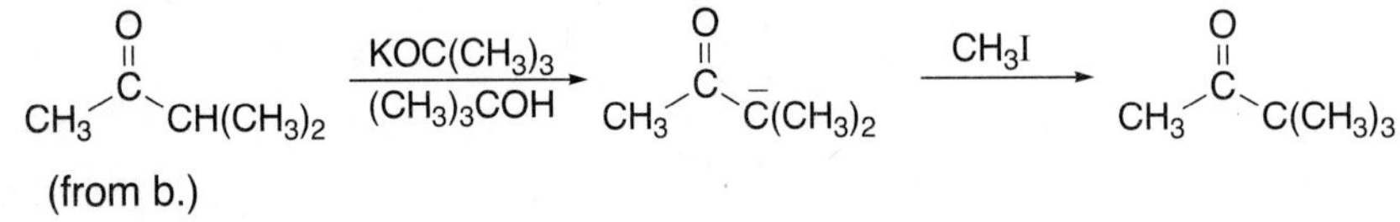

23.52

a. 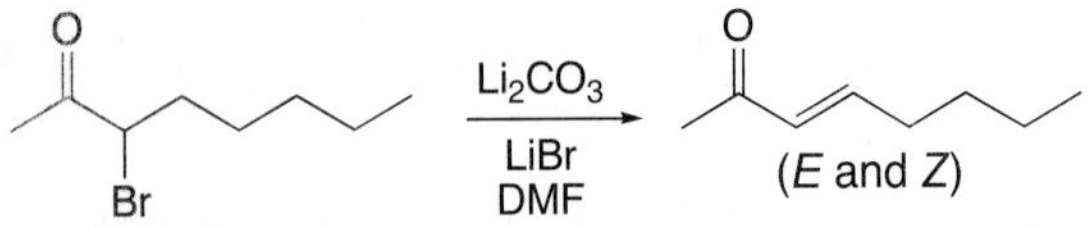

b. 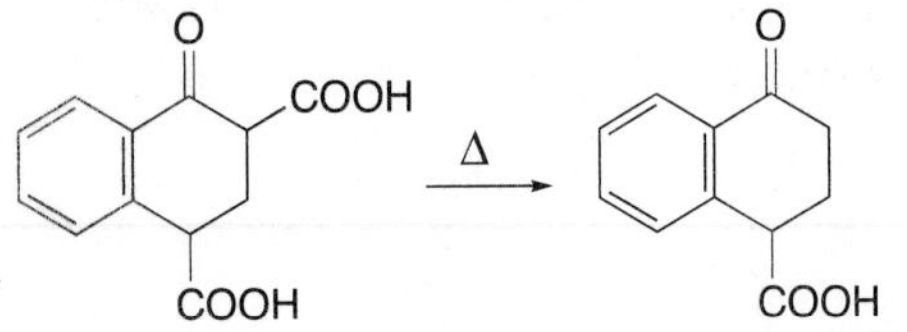

c. 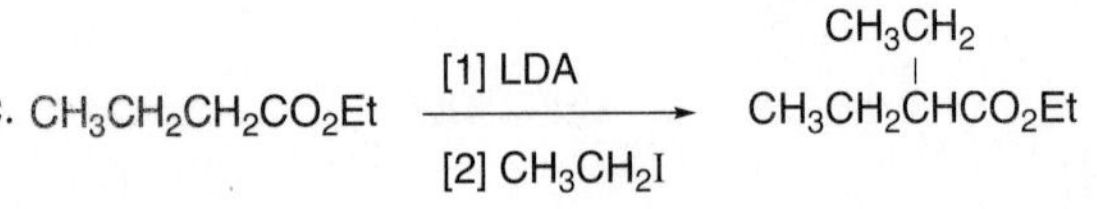

d. 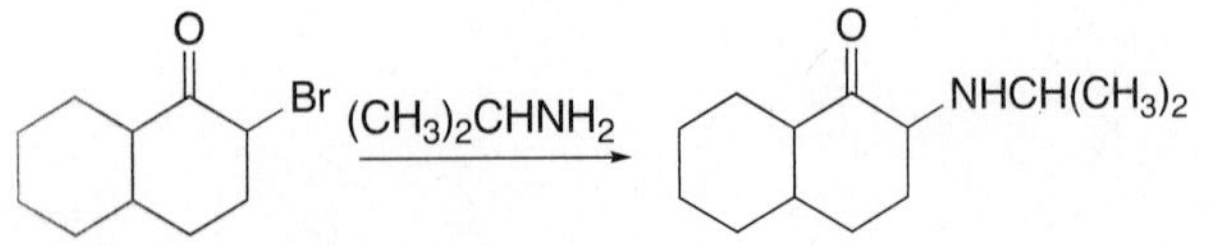

e. 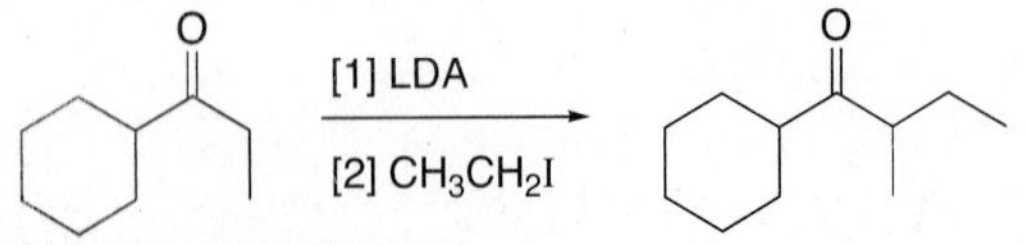

f. 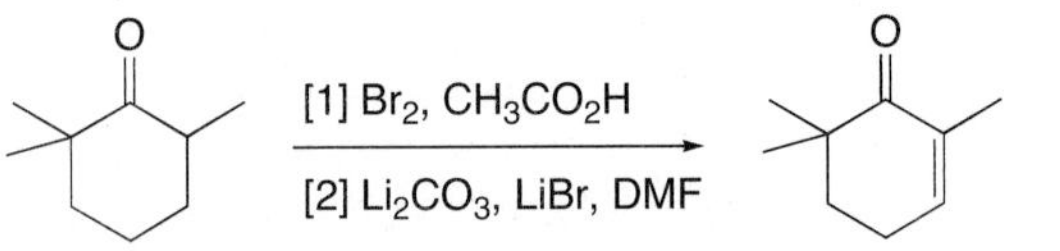

g. 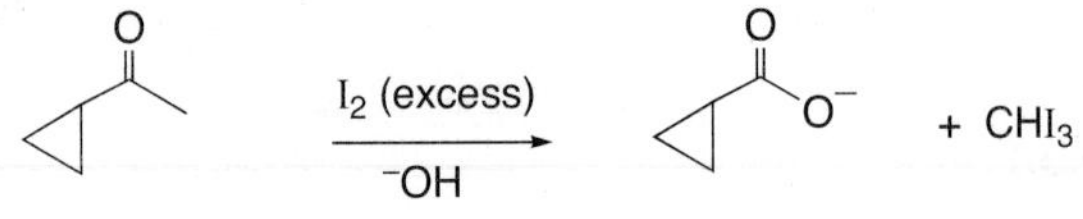

h. 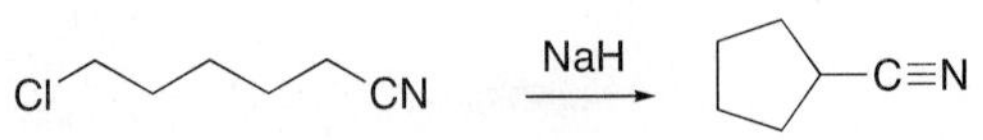

i. 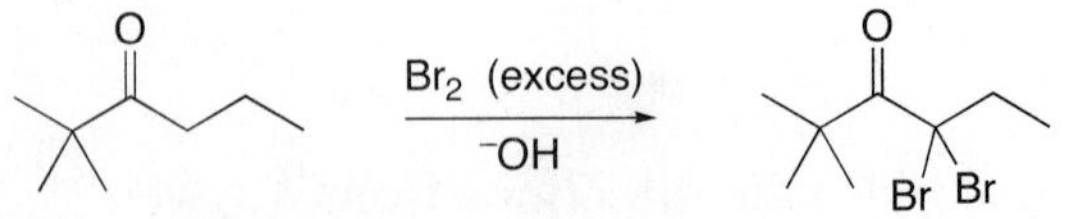

j. 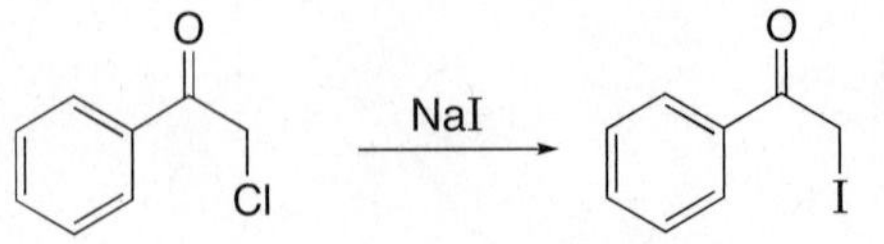

23.53

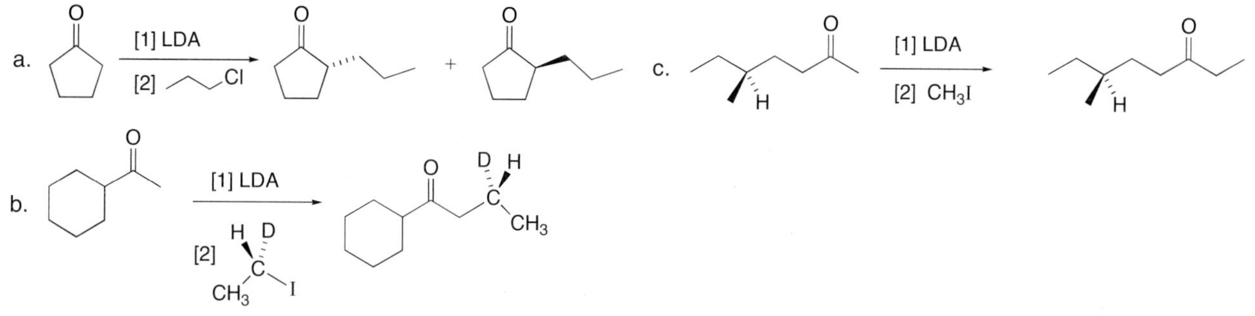

23.54

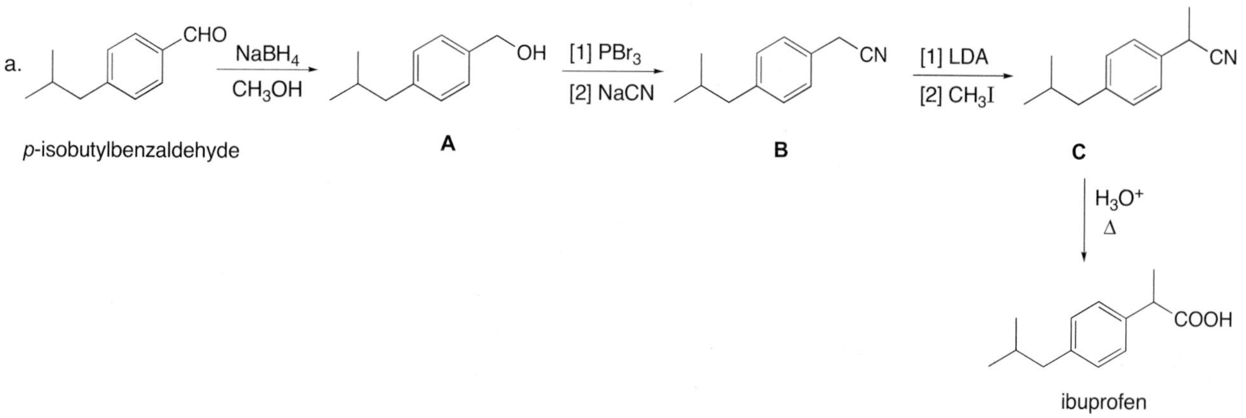

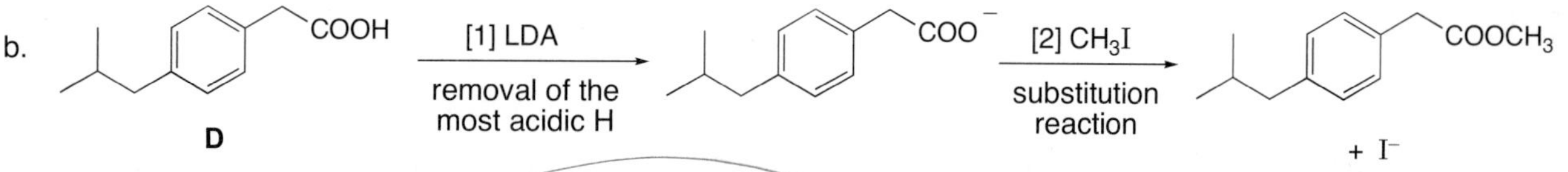

Removal of the most acidic proton with LDA forms a carboxylate anion that reacts as a nucleophile with CH_3I to form an ester as substitution product.

23.55

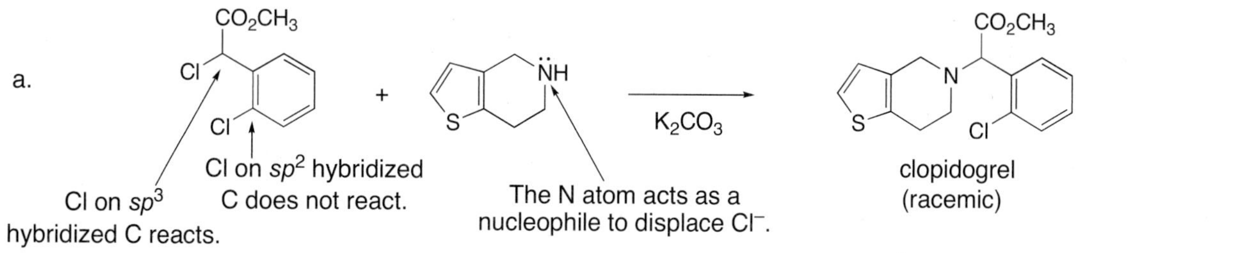

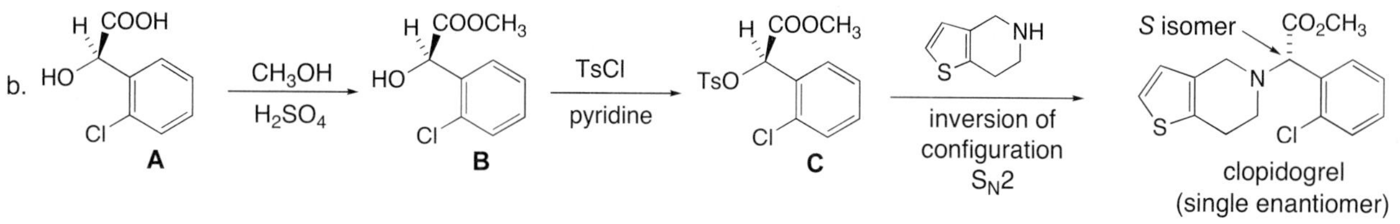

23.56

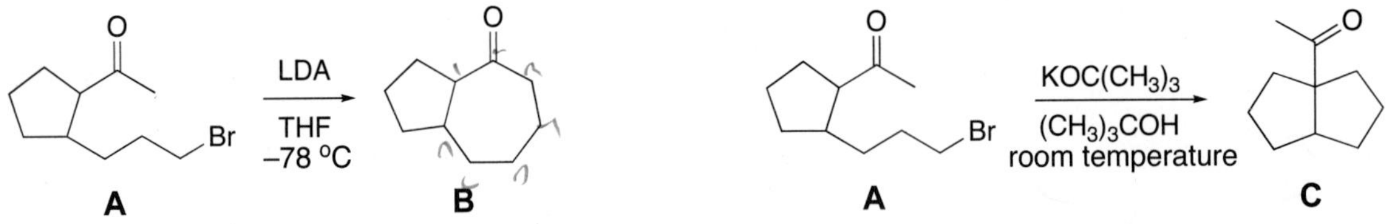

23.57

a.

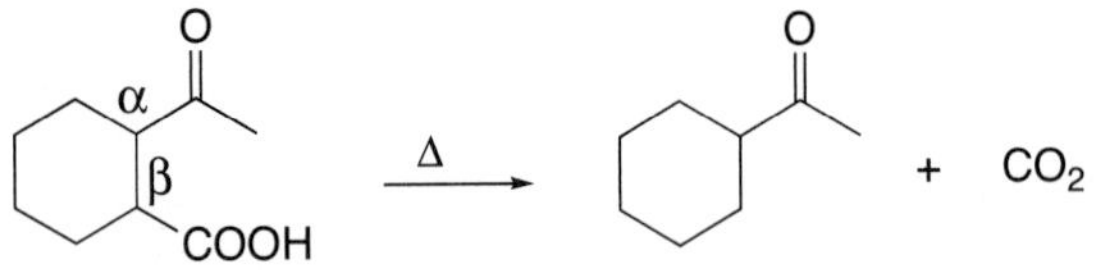

In order for decarboxylation to occur readily, the COOH group must be bonded to the α C of another carbonyl group. In this case, it is bonded to the β carbon.

b. $CH_2(CO_2Et)_2$ —[1] NaOEt; [2] $(CH_3CH_2)_3CBr$→ $(CH_3CH_2)_3CCH(CO_2Et)_2$

The 3° alkyl halide is too crowded to react with the strong nucleophile by an S_N2 mechanism.

c.

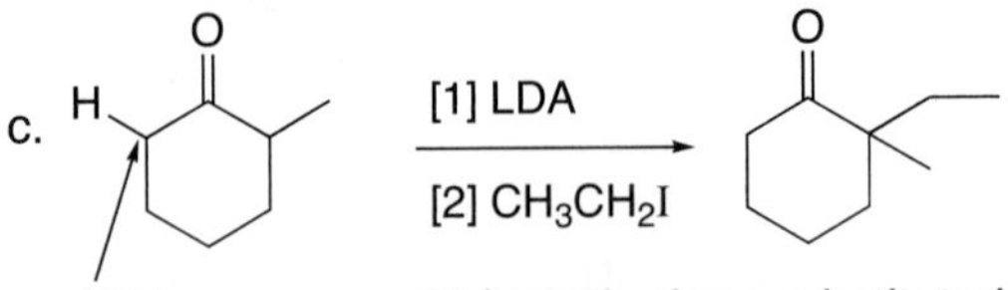

LDA removes a H from the less substituted C, forming the kinetic enolate. This product is from the thermodynamic enolate, which gives substitution on the more substituted α C.

23.58 Protonation in Step [3] can occur from below (to re-form the *R* isomer) or from above to form the *S* isomer as shown.

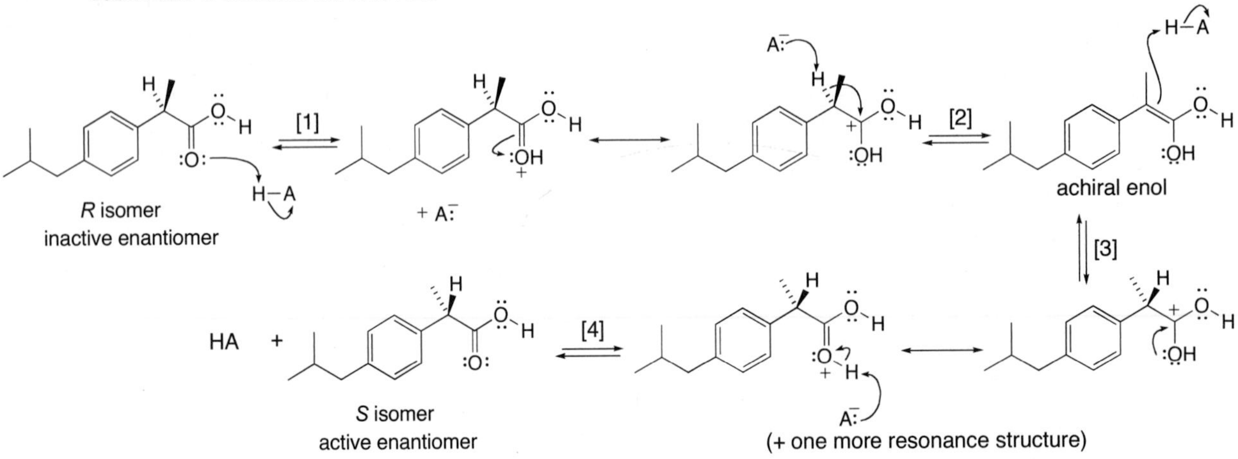

23.59

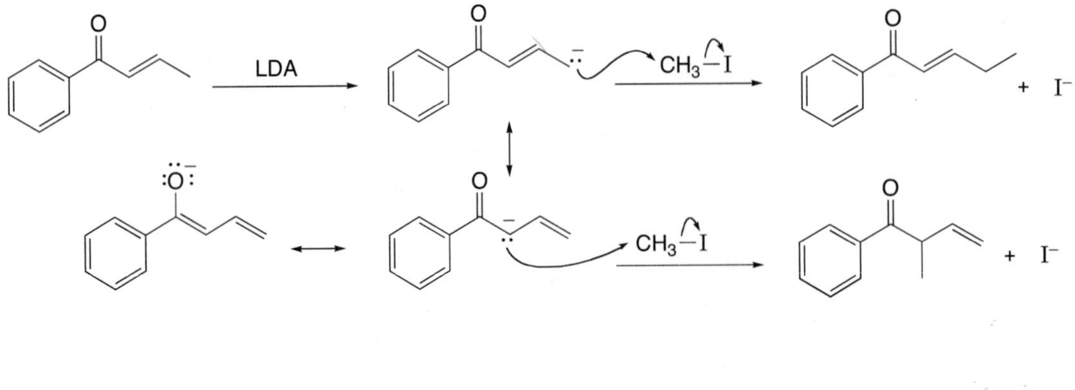

23.60

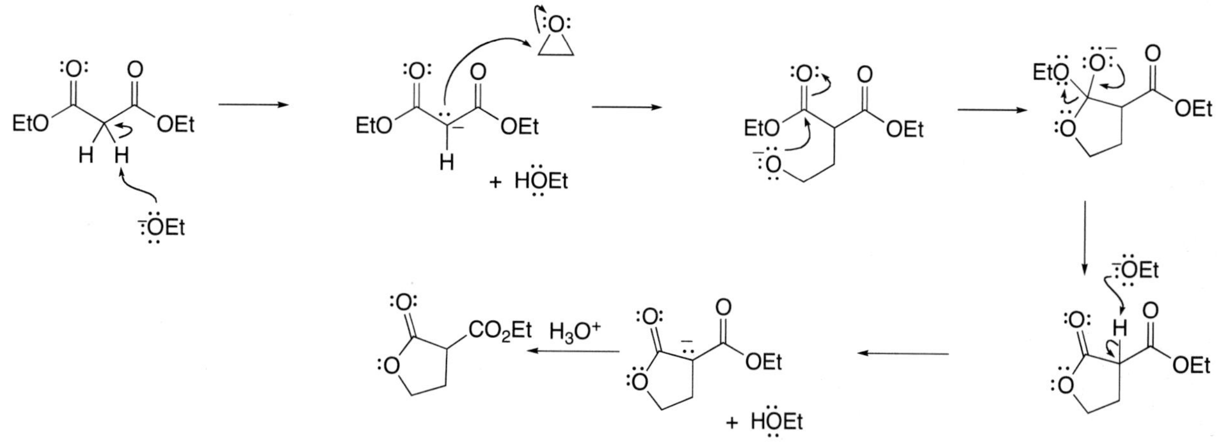

23.61 Protons on the γ carbon of an α,β-unsaturated carbonyl compound are acidic because of resonance.

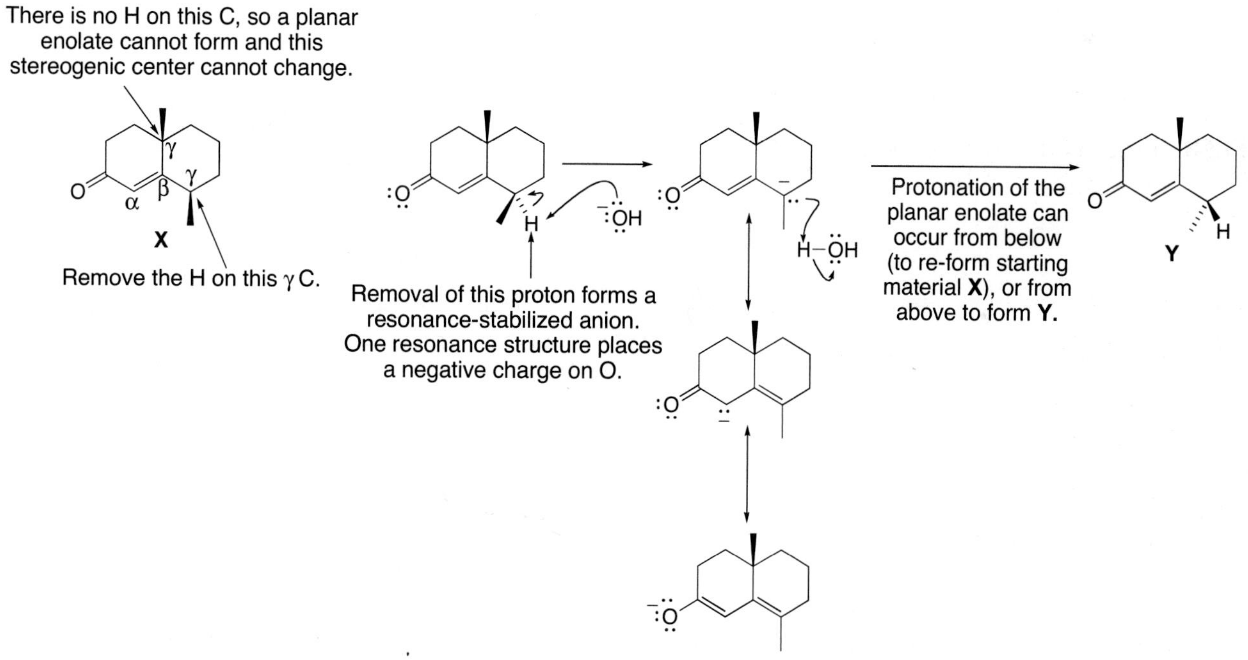

23.62

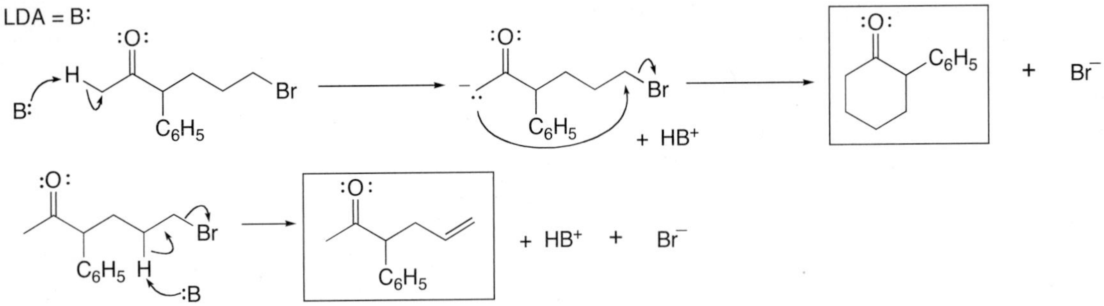

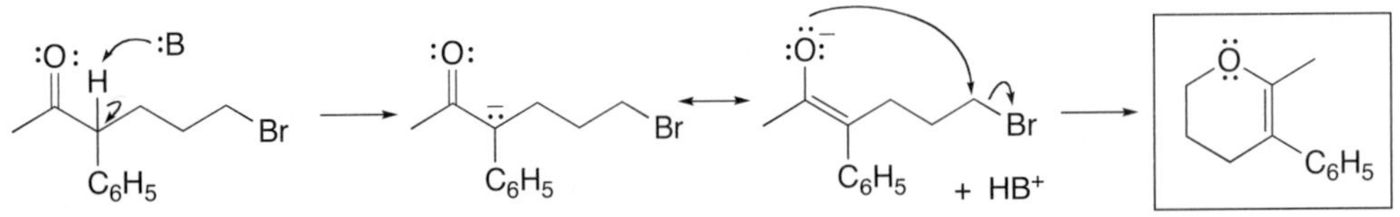

This reaction occurs with both bases [LDA and KOC(CH3)3].

+ Br−

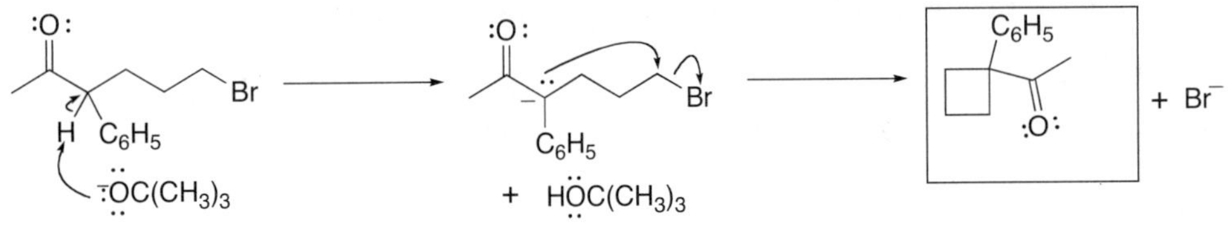

23.63

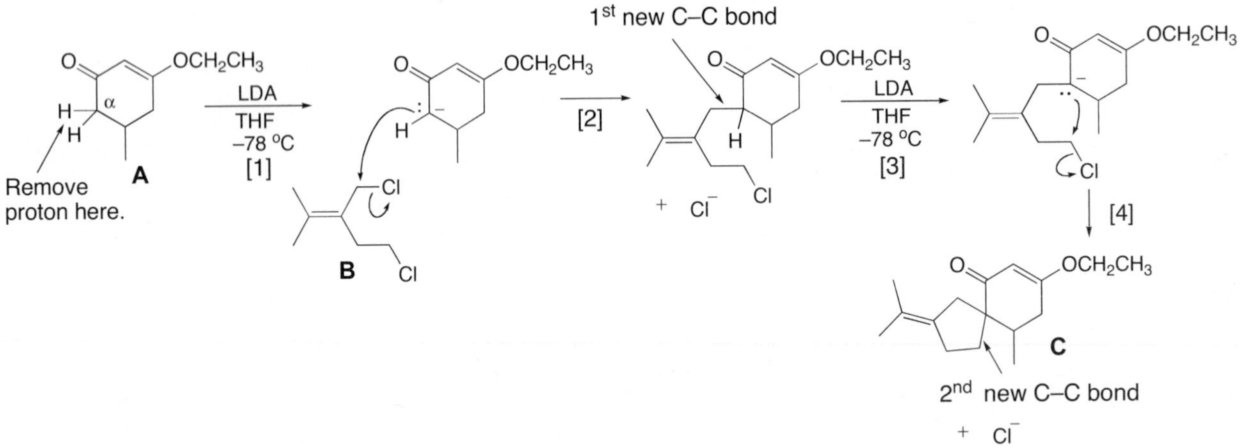

23.64 a. Since there are two C's bonded to the α carbon, there are two possible intramolecular alkylation reactions.

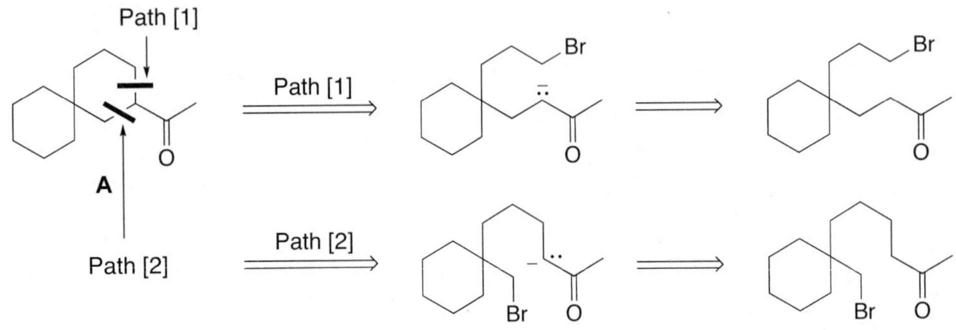

two different halo ketones possible

b.

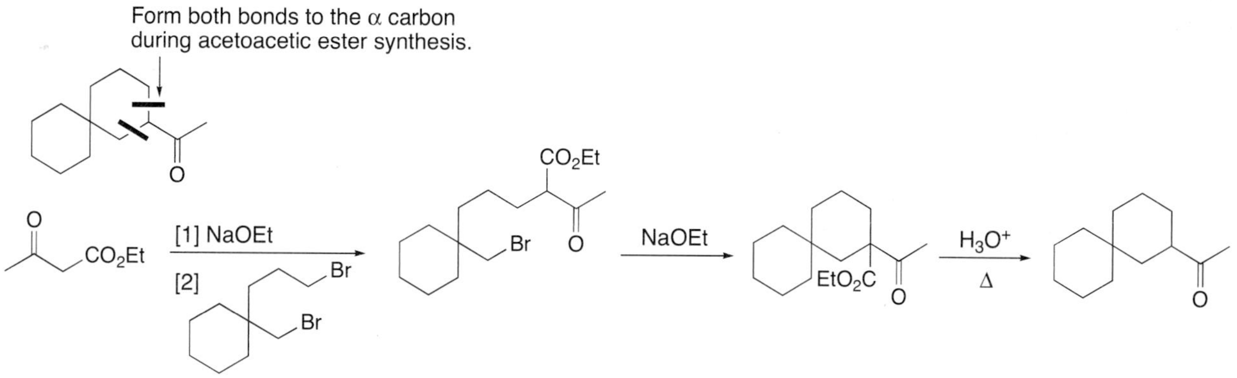

23.65

a.

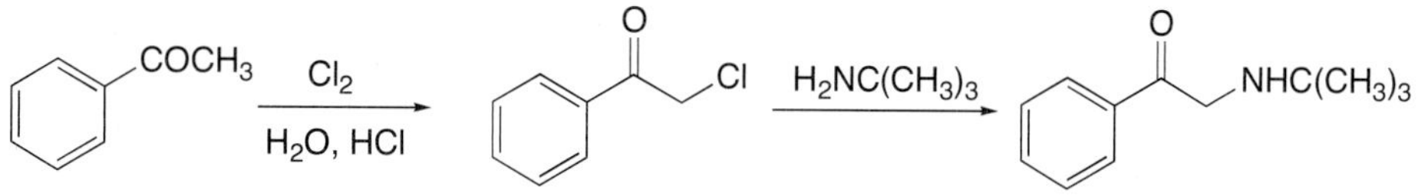

b.

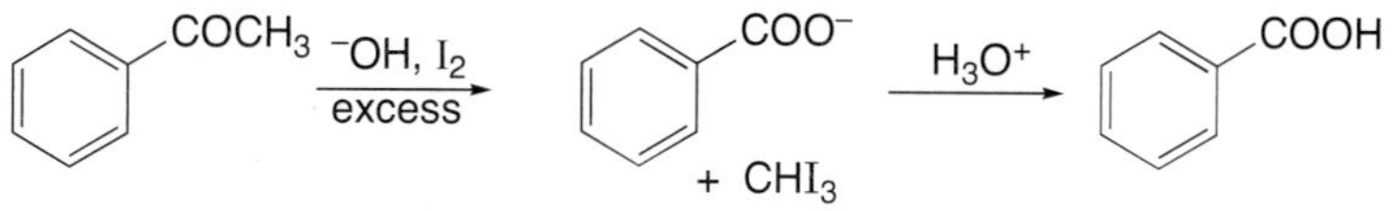

c.

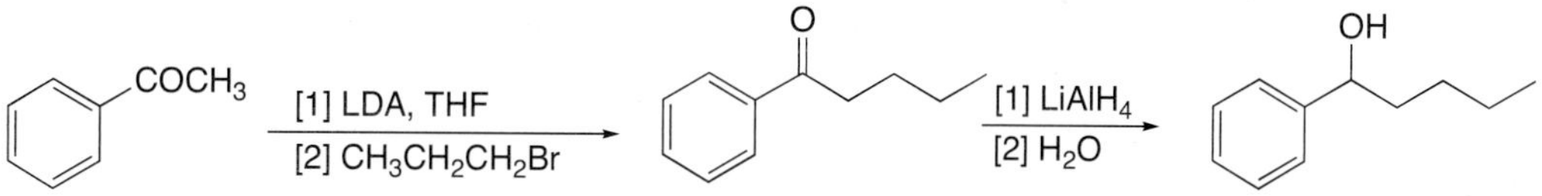

d.

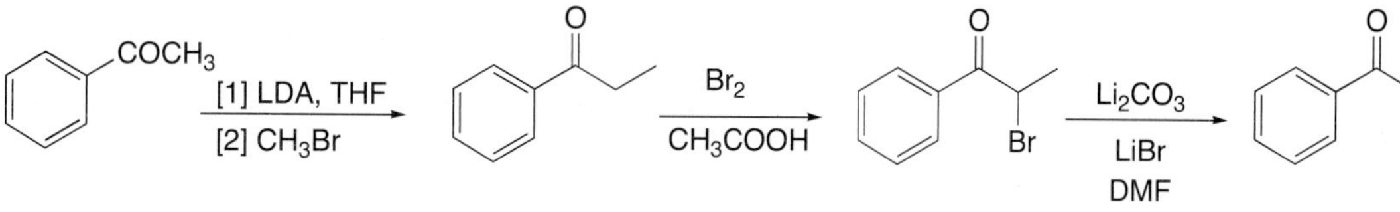

23.66

a.

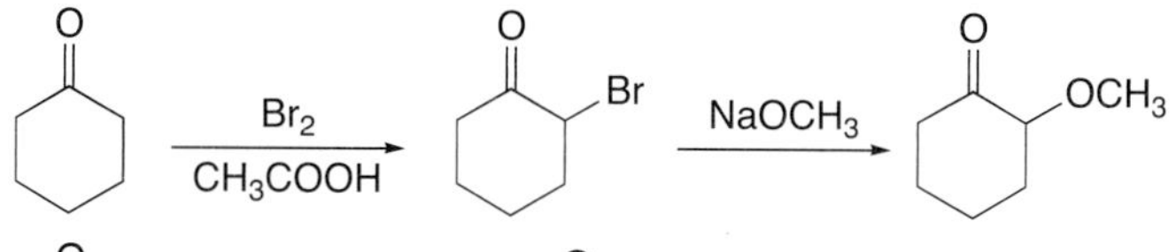

b.

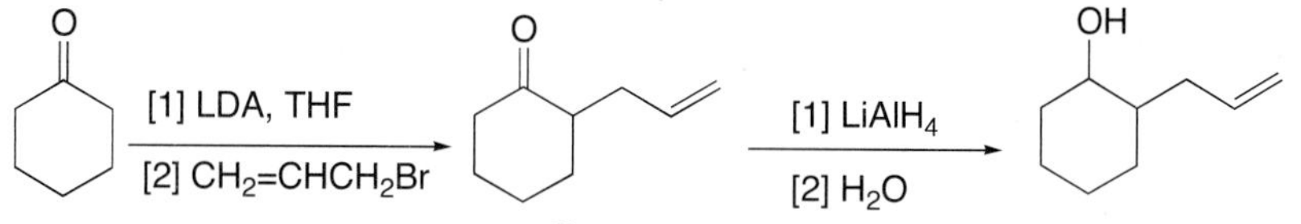

c.

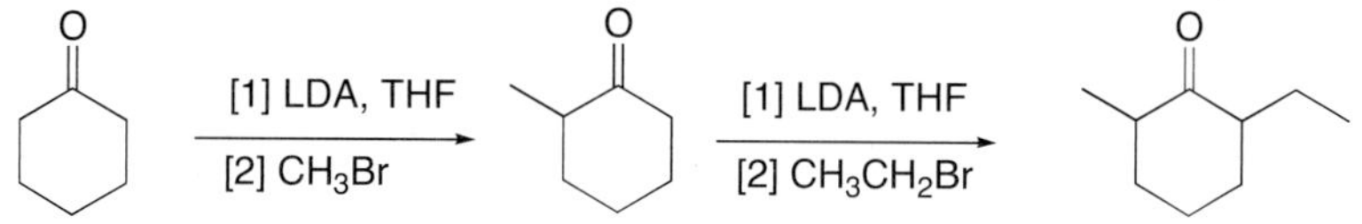

d.

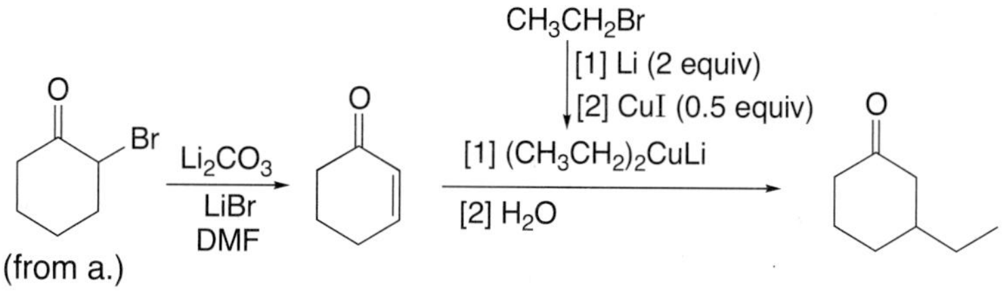

(from a.)

e.

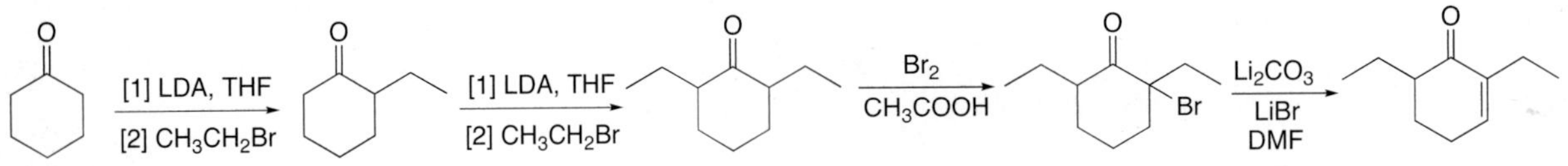

f.

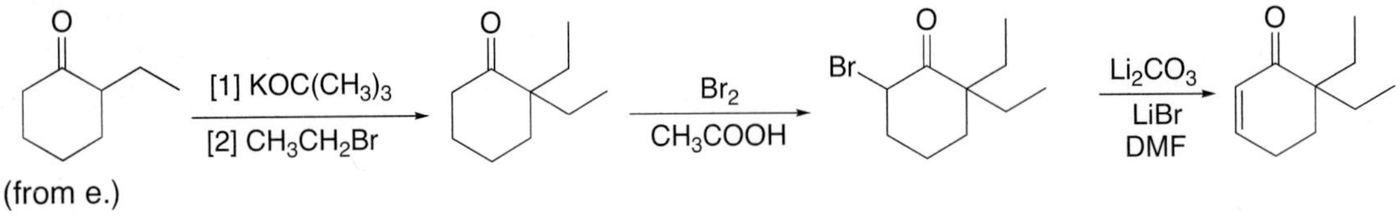

23.67

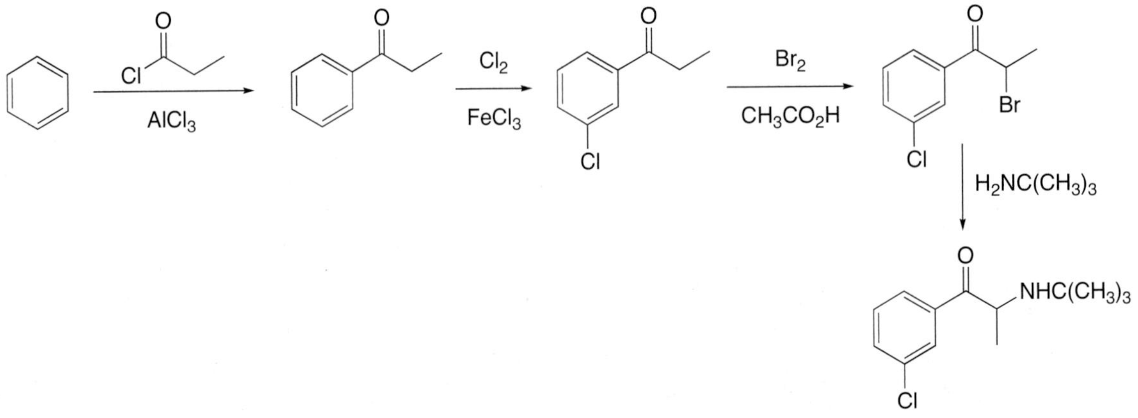

bupropion

23.68

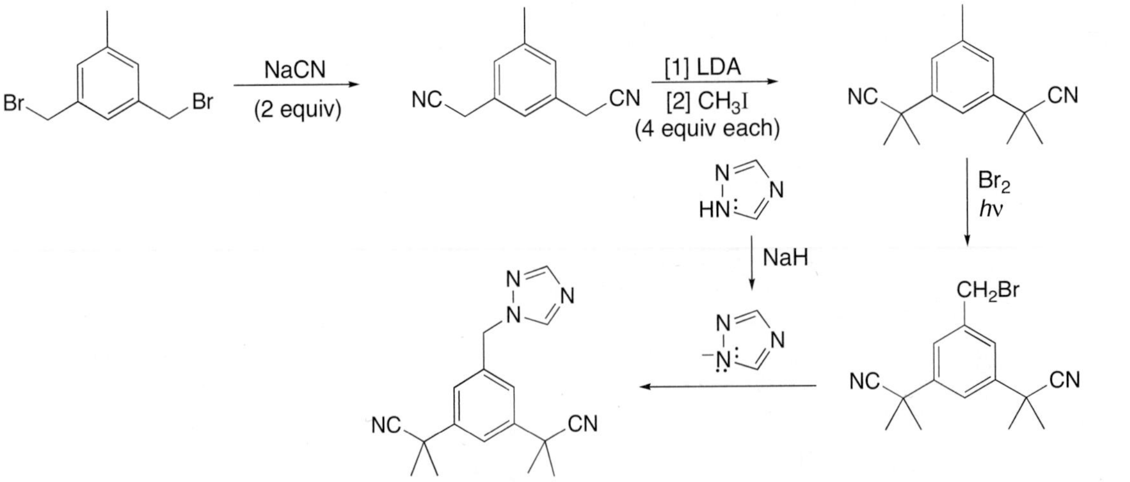

anastrozole

23.69

a.

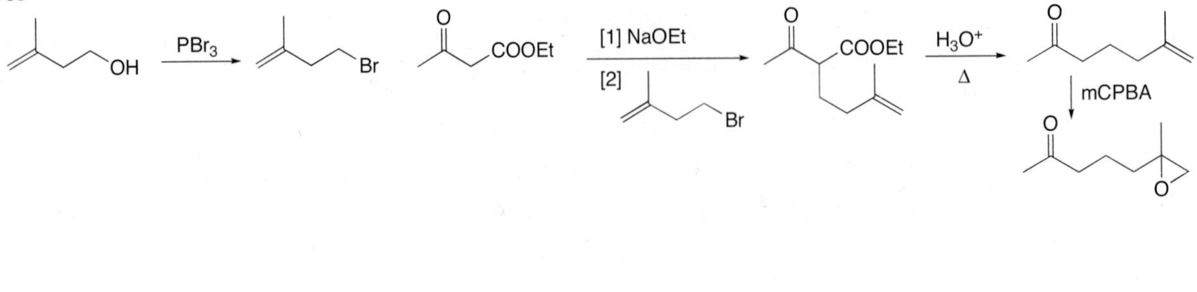

b. 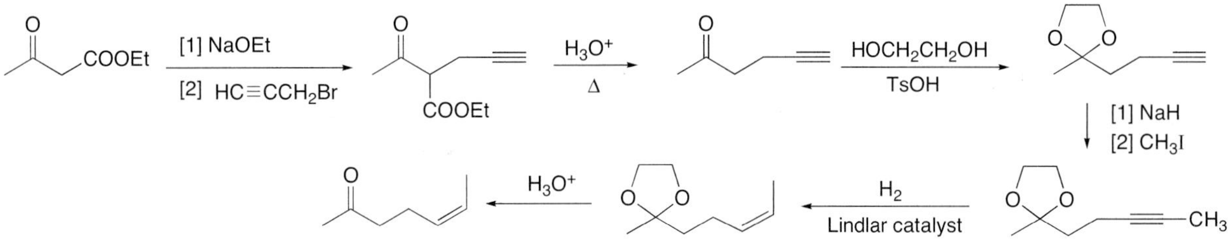
COOEt
[1] NaOEt
[2] HC≡CCH2Br
COOEt
H3O+
Δ
HOCH2CH2OH
TsOH
[1] NaH
[2] CH3I
CH3
H2
Lindlar catalyst
H3O+

23.70

a. 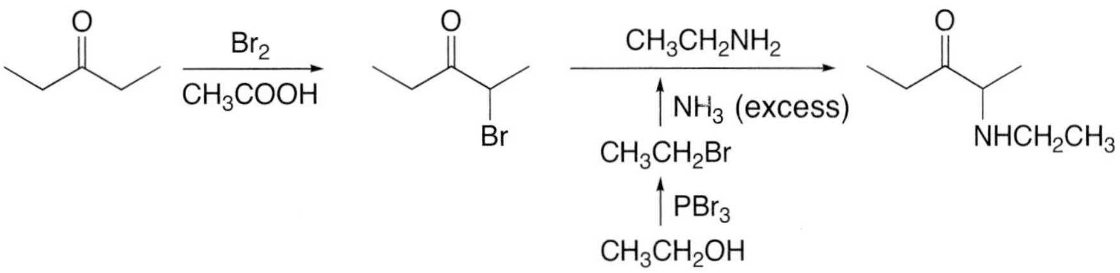
Br2
CH3COOH
Br
CH3CH2NH2
NH3 (excess)
CH3CH2Br
PBr3
CH3CH2OH
NHCH2CH3

b. 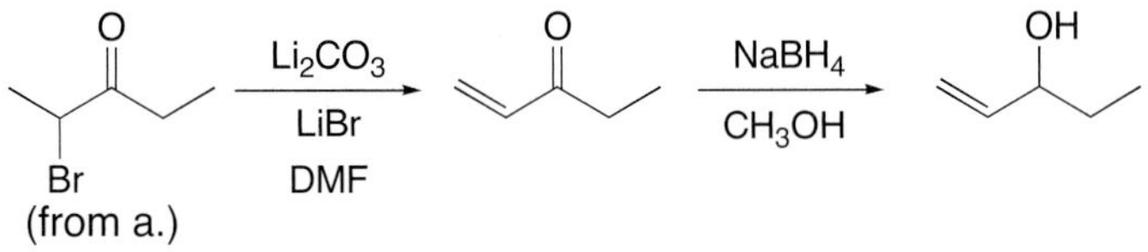
Br
(from a.)
Li2CO3
LiBr
DMF
NaBH4
CH3OH
OH

c. 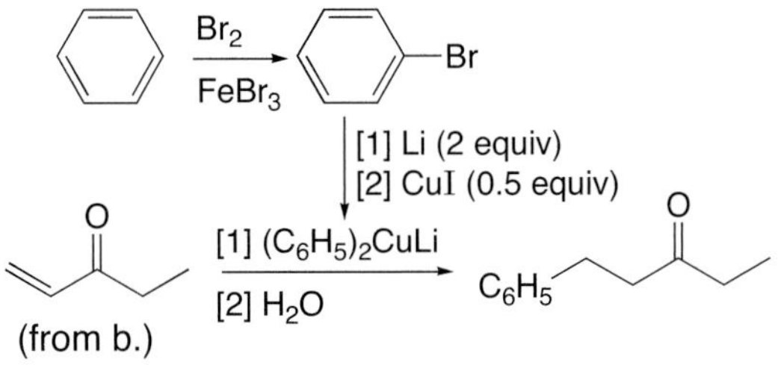
Br2
FeBr3
Br
[1] Li (2 equiv)
[2] CuI (0.5 equiv)
(from b.)
[1] (C6H5)2CuLi
[2] H2O
C6H5

d. 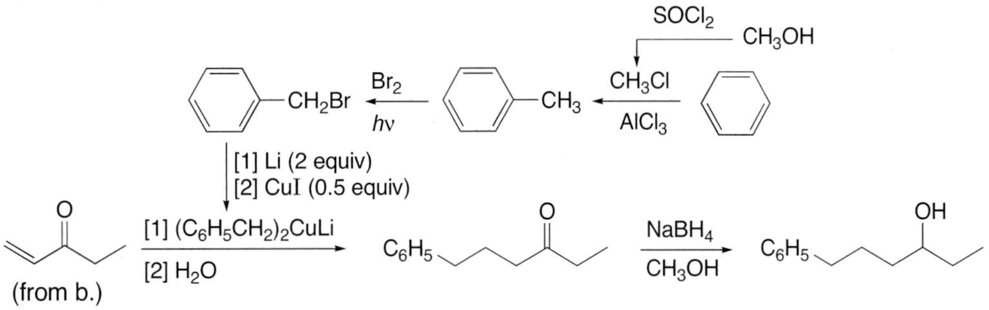
SOCl2
CH3OH
CH3Cl
AlCl3
CH3
Br2
hν
CH2Br
[1] Li (2 equiv)
[2] CuI (0.5 equiv)
(from b.)
[1] (C6H5CH2)2CuLi
[2] H2O
C6H5
NaBH4
CH3OH
OH

23.71

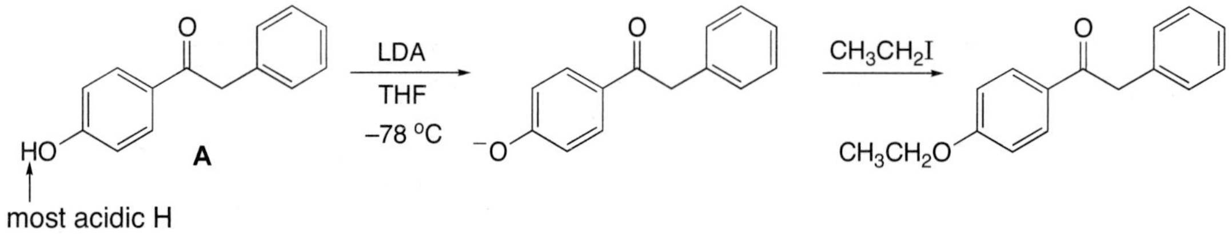

To synthesize the desired product, a protecting group is needed:

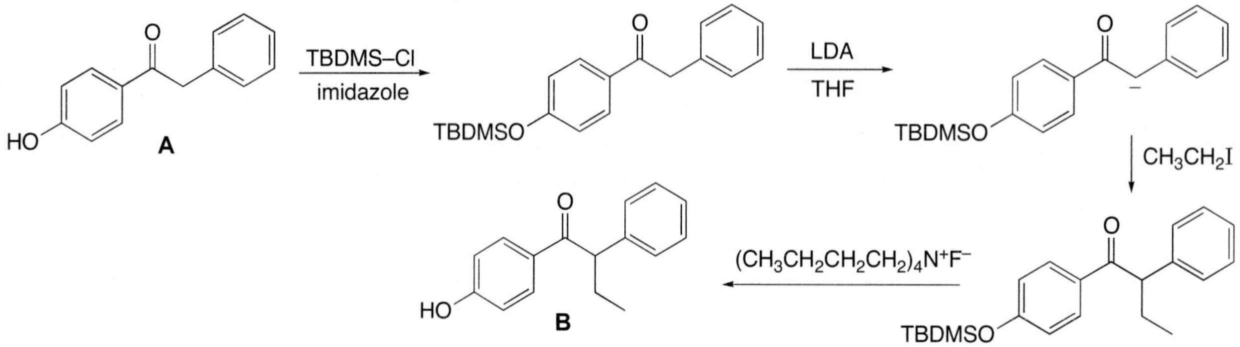

23.72

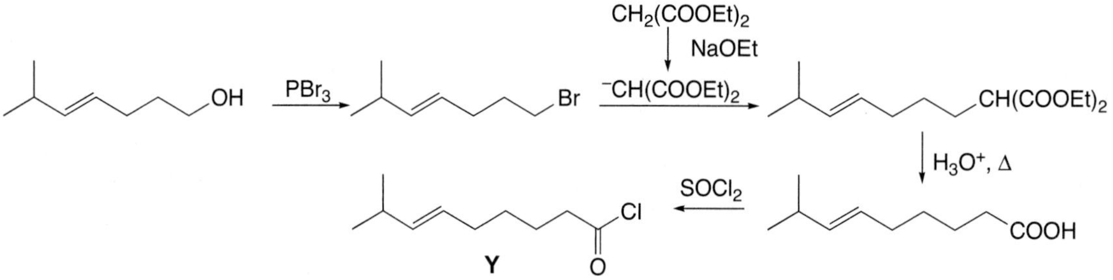

23.73

a.

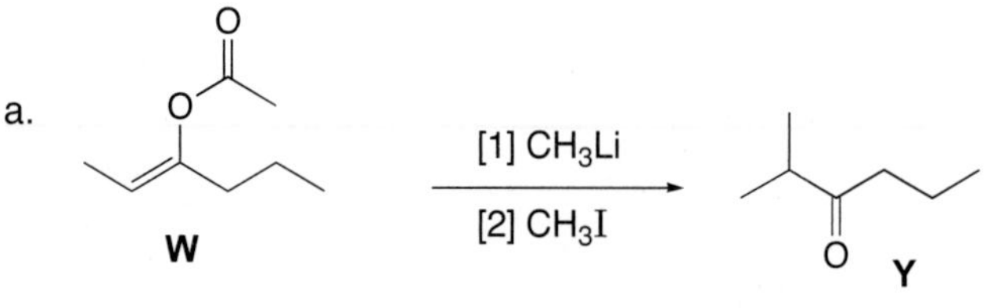

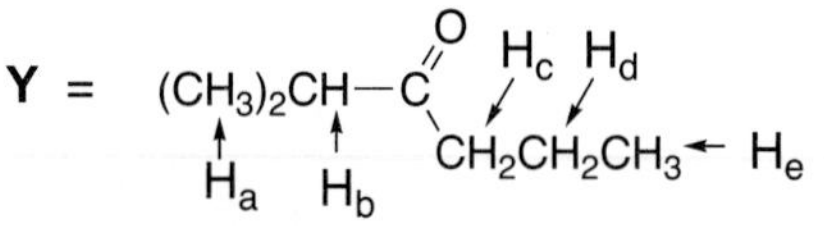

$C_7H_{14}O$ → one degree of unsaturation
IR peak at 1713 cm^{-1} → C=O
^1H NMR signals at (ppm)

- H_e: triplet at 0.8 (3 H)
- H_a: doublet at 0.9 (6 H)
- H_d: sextet at 1.4 (2 H)
- H_c: triplet at 1.9 (2 H)
- H_b: septet at 2.1 (1 H)

b.

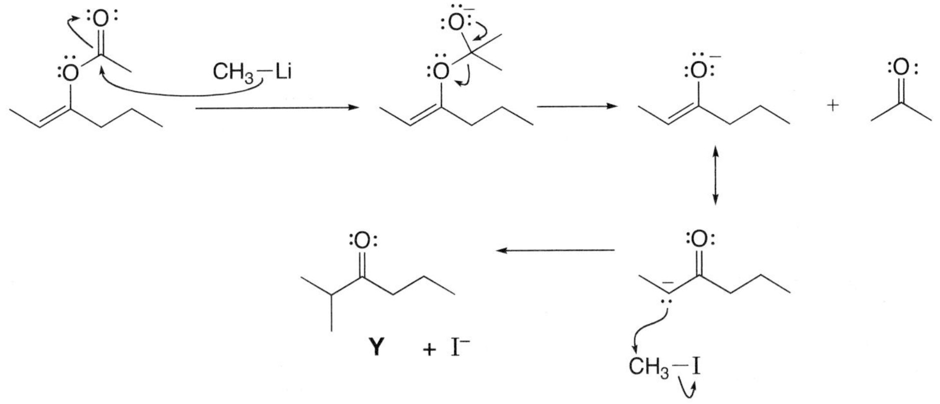

23.74 Removal of H_a with base does not generate an anion that can delocalize onto the carbonyl O atom, whereas removal of H_b generates an enolate that is delocalized on O.

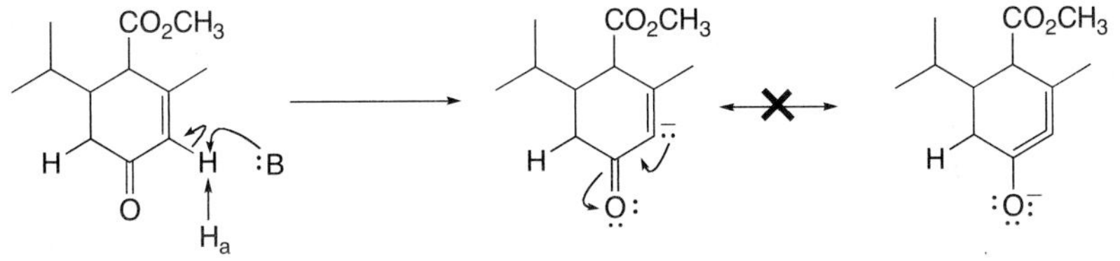

Delocalization of this sort can't occur by removal of H_a, making H_a less acidic.

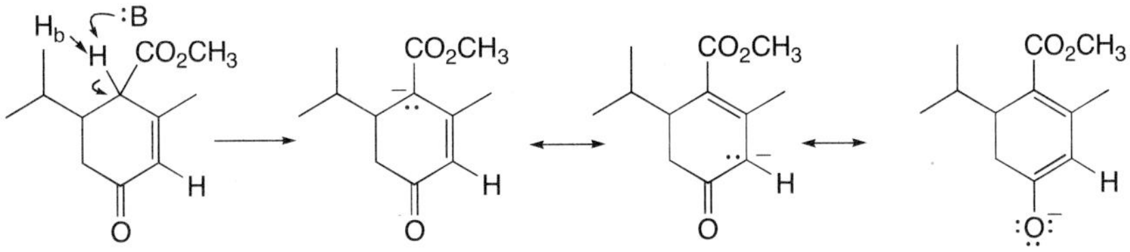

Removal of H_b gives an anion that is resonance stabilized so H_b is more acidic.

Mechanism:

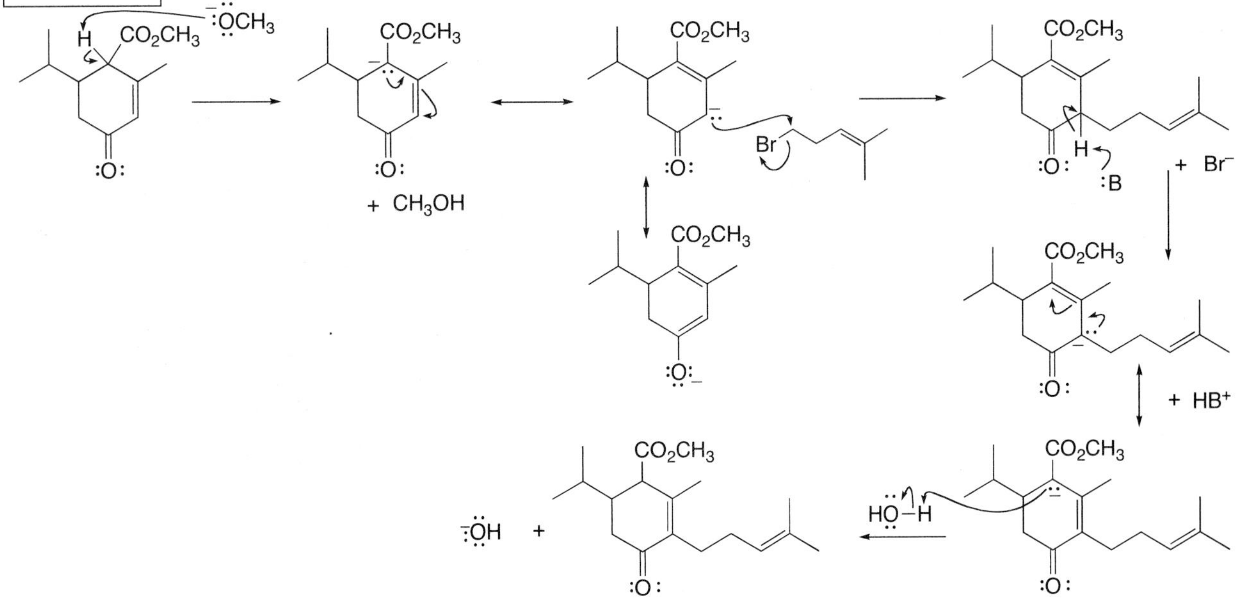

23.75

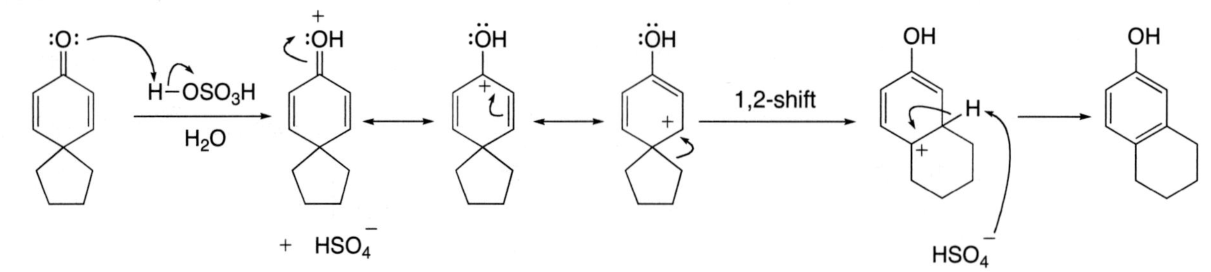

23.76

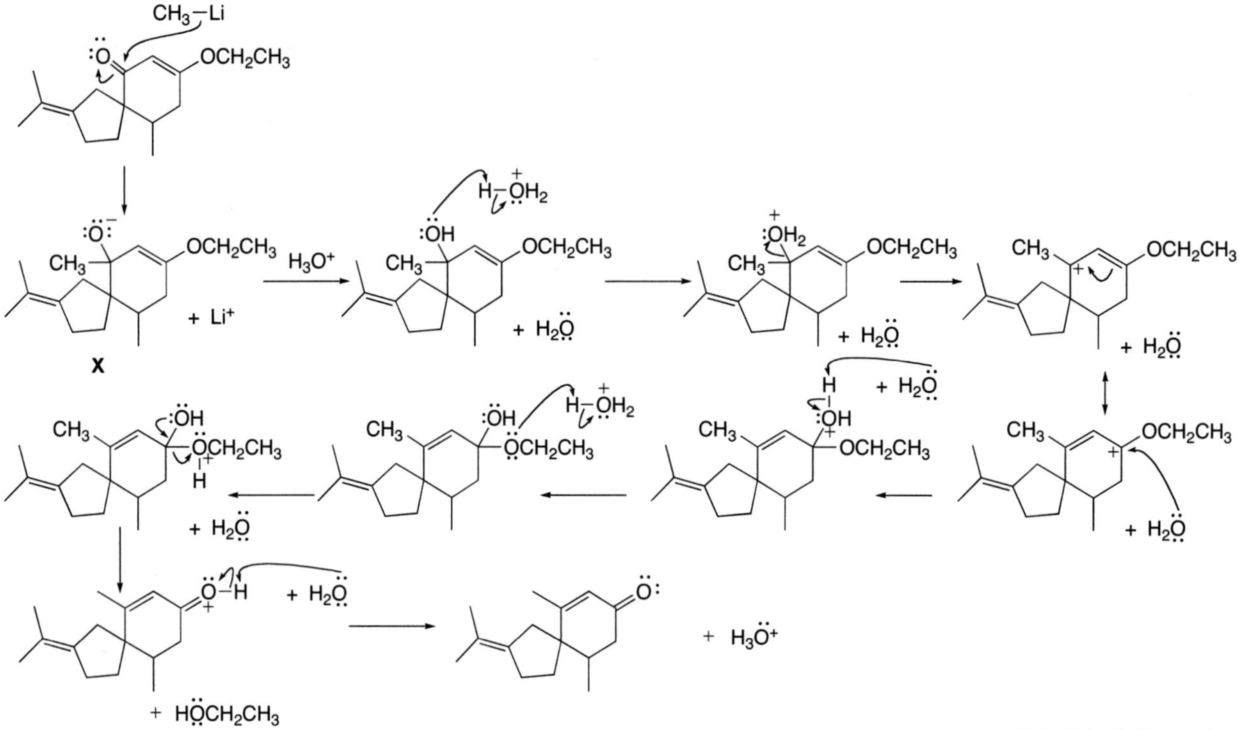

23.77

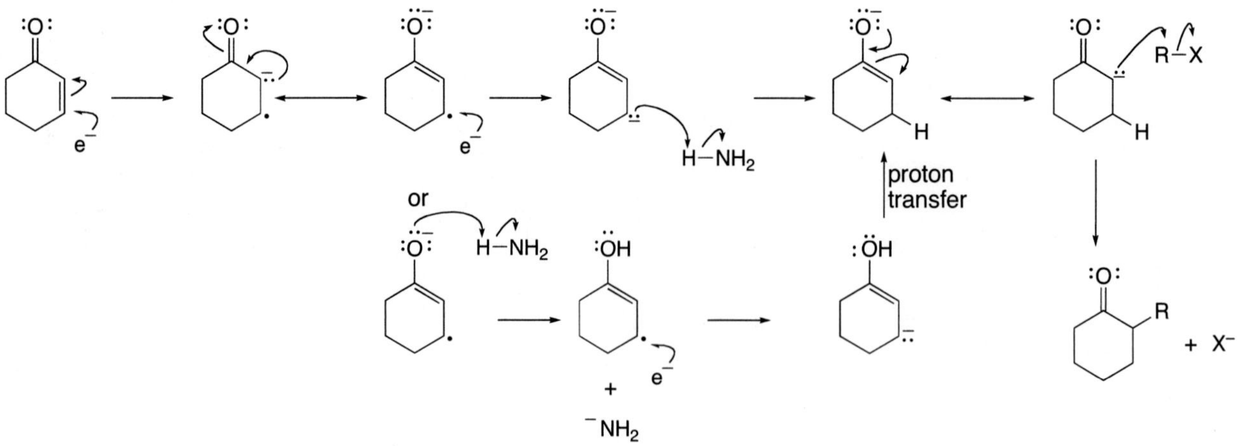

23.78 a. In the presence of base an achiral enolate that can be protonated from both sides is formed.

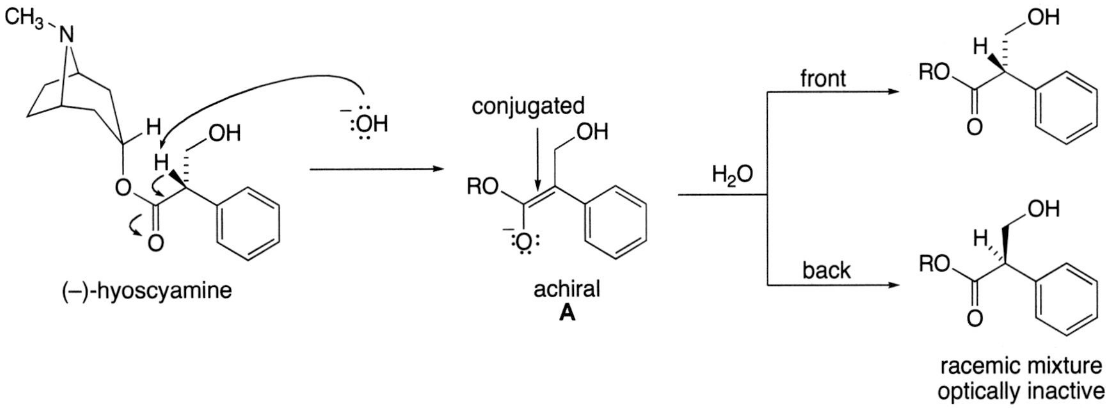

b. The enolate **A** formed from (–)-hyoscyamine is conjugated with the benzene ring, making it easier to form. The enolate **B** formed from (–)-littorine is not conjugated, so it is less readily formed.

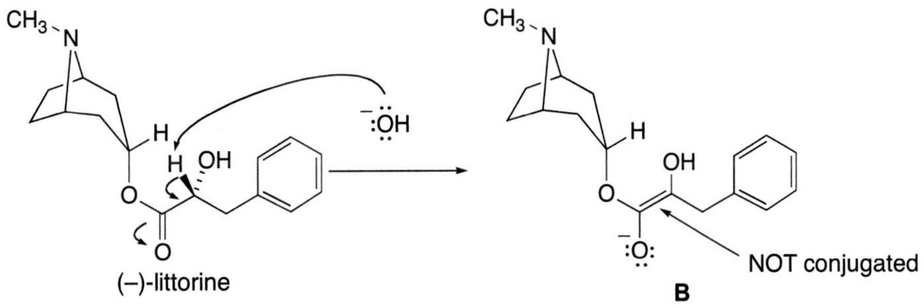

Chapter 24 Carbonyl Condensation Reactions

Chapter Review

The four major carbonyl condensation reactions

Reaction type — **Reaction**

[1] Aldol reaction (24.1)

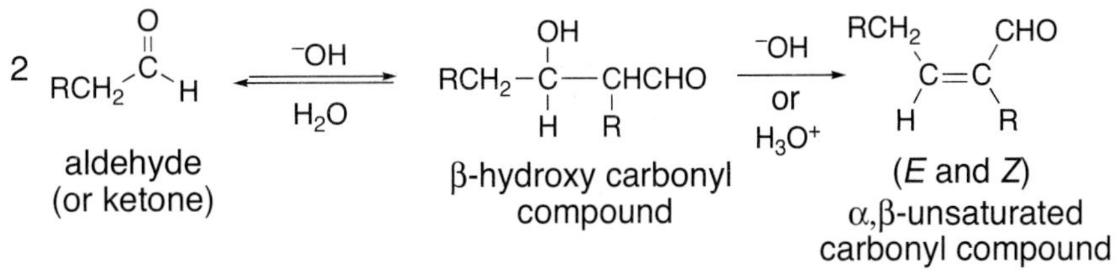

[2] Claisen reaction (24.5)

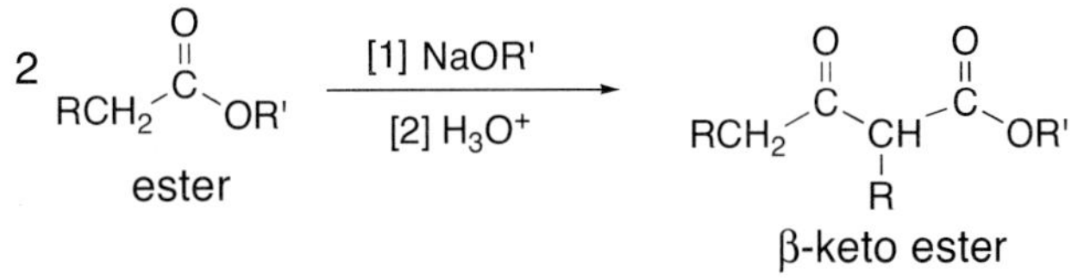

[3] Michael reaction (24.8)

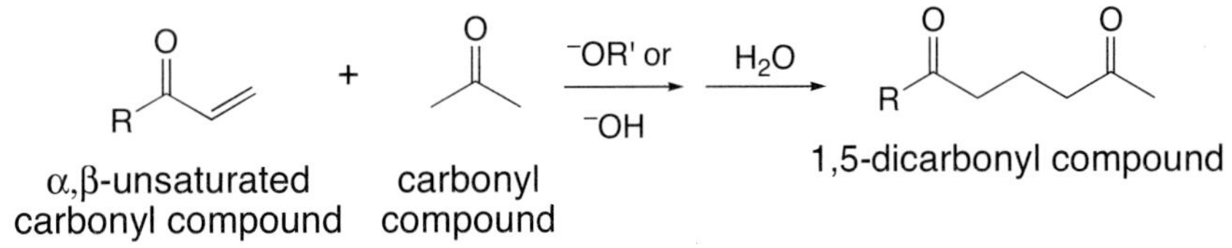

[4] Robinson annulation (24.9)

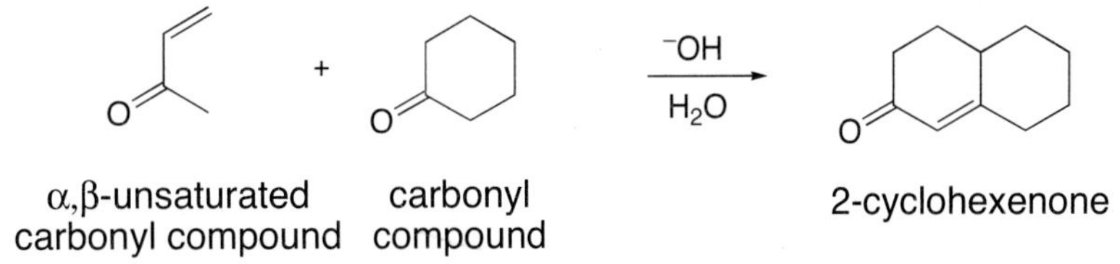

Useful variations

[1] Directed aldol reaction (24.3)

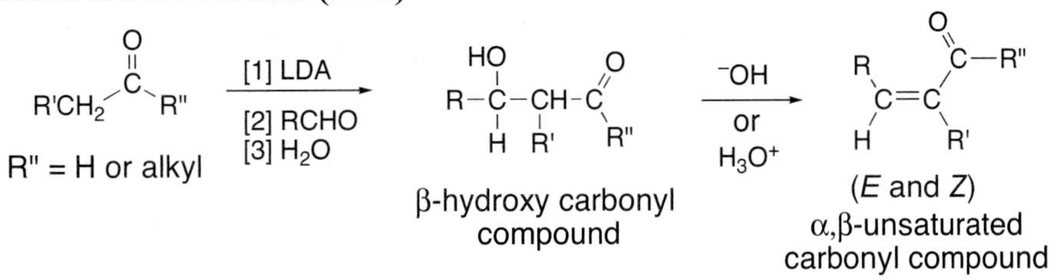

[2] Intramolecular aldol reaction (24.4)

[a] With 1,4-dicarbonyl compounds:

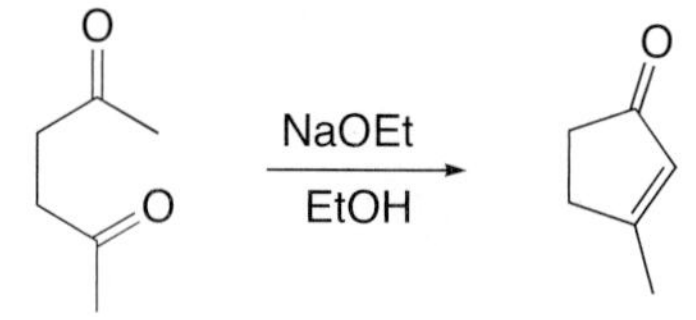

[b] With 1,5-dicarbonyl compounds:

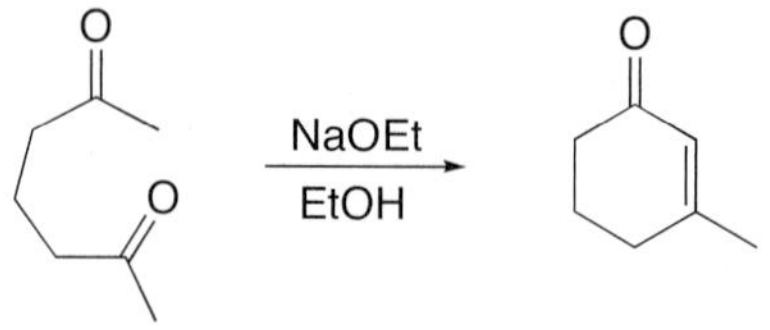

[3] Dieckmann reaction (24.7)

[a] With 1,6-diesters:

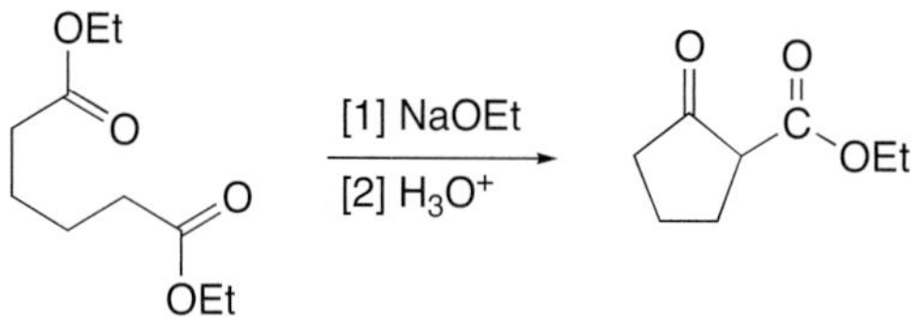

[b] With 1,7-diesters:

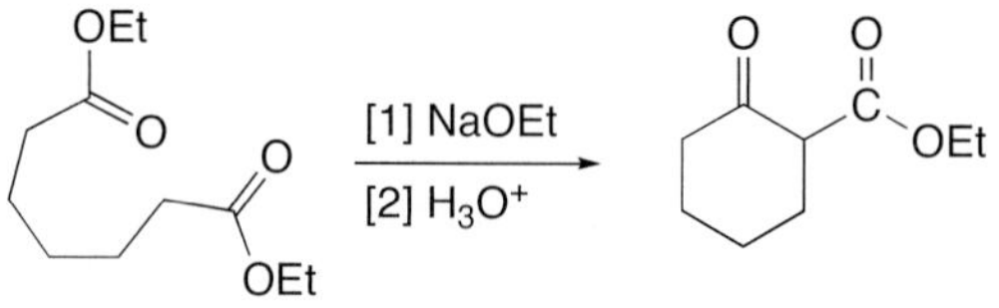

Practice Test on Chapter Review

1. a. Which compounds are possible Michael acceptors?

1. 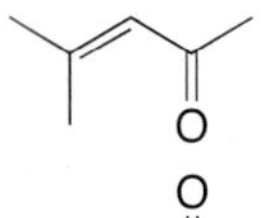

3. 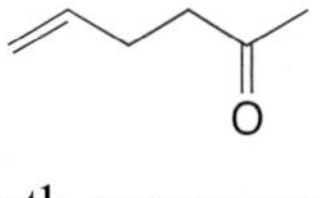

2. 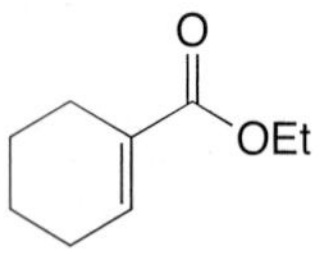

4. Both compounds [1] and [2] are Michael acceptors.

5. Compounds [1], [2], and [3] are all Michael acceptors.

b. Which of the following compounds can be formed by an aldol reaction?

1. 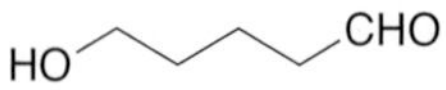

3. 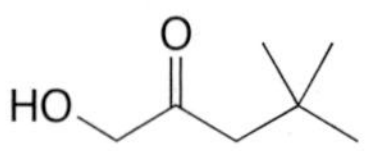

2. 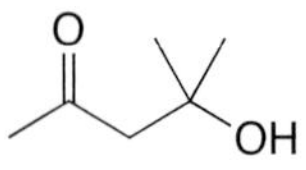

4. Both [1] and [2] can be formed by aldol reaction.

5. Compounds [1], [2], and [3] can all be formed by aldol reaction.

c. Which compounds can be formed in a Robinson annulation?

1. 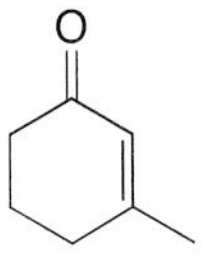

3. 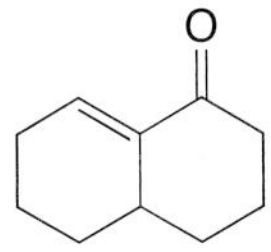

2. 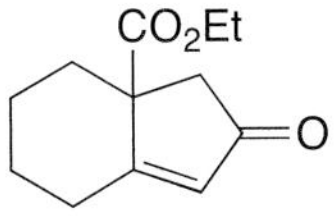

4. Compounds [1] and [2] can be formed by Robinson annulation.

5. Compounds [1], [2], and [3] can be formed by Robinson annulation.

d. What compounds can be used to form **A** by a condensation reaction?

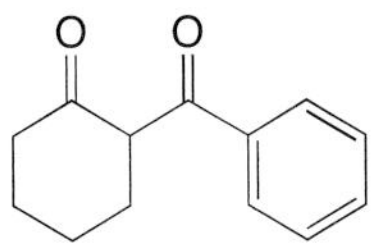

A

1. 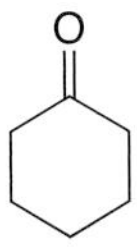 and 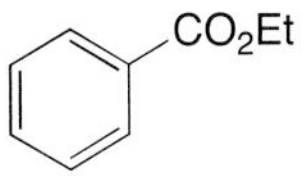

3. 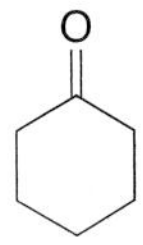 and 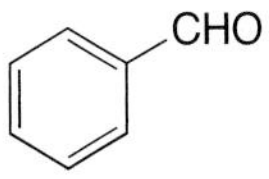

2. 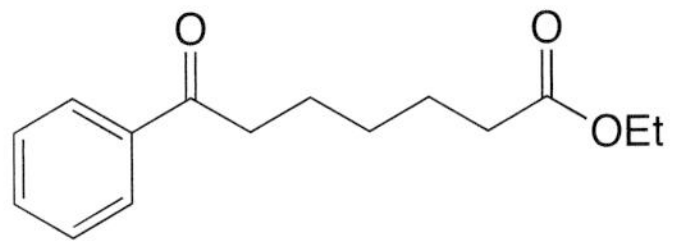

4. Compounds [1] and [2] can be used to form **A**.

5. Compounds [1], [2], and [3] can be used to form **A**.

2. Give the reagents required for each step.

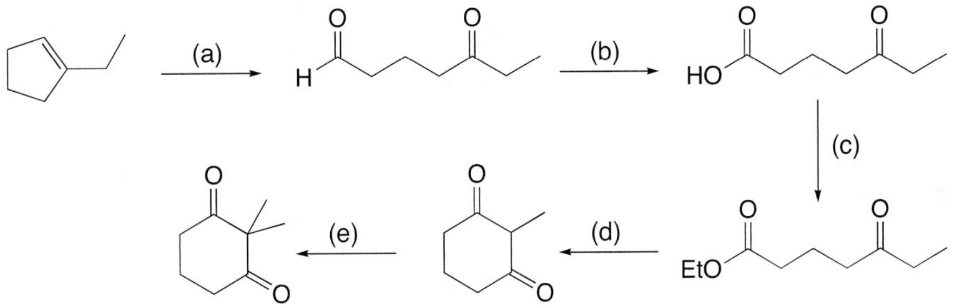

3. Draw the organic products formed in the following reactions.

a. 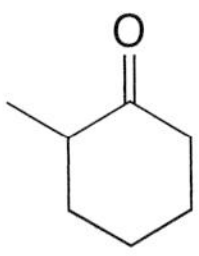 [1] LDA → [2] CH_3CH_2CHO [3] H_2O

c. 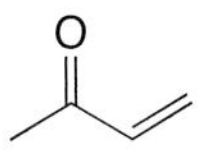 + 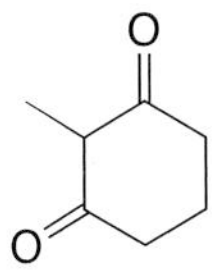 NaOEt, EtOH →

b. 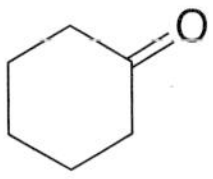 + HCO_2Et [1] NaOEt, EtOH → [2] H_3O^+

d. 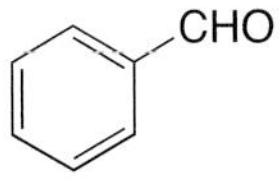 + 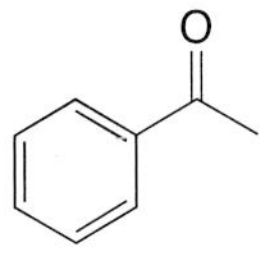 ^-OH, H_2O →

4. a. What organic starting materials are needed to synthesize **D** by a Robinson annulation reaction?

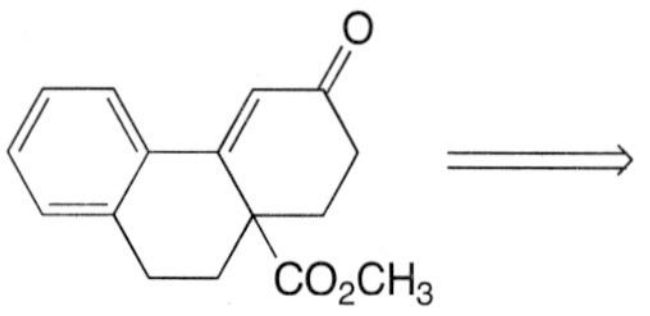

D

b. What organic starting materials are needed to synthesize β-keto ester **B** by a Dieckmann reaction?

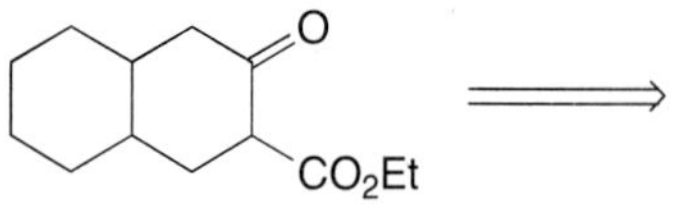

B

c. What starting materials are needed to synthesize **A** by an aldol reaction?

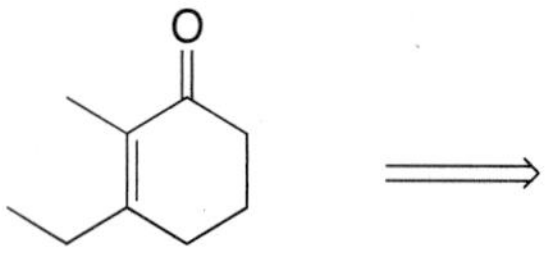

A

Answers to Practice Test

1.a. 4
  b. 2
  c. 1
  d. 4

2.a. [1] O_3; [2] $(CH_3)_2S$
  b. CrO_3, H_2SO_4, H_2O
  c. CH_3CH_2OH, H_2SO_4
  d. [1] NaOEt, EtOH; [2] H_3O^+
  e. [1] LDA; [2] CH_3I

3.

a. 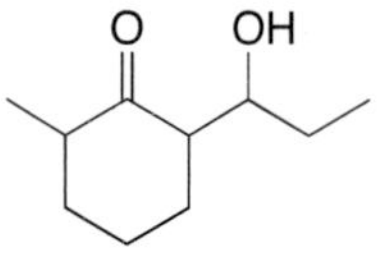

b. 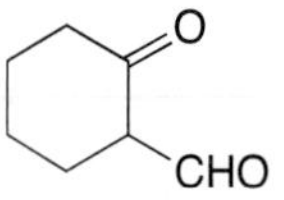

c. 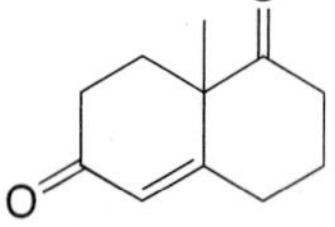

d. 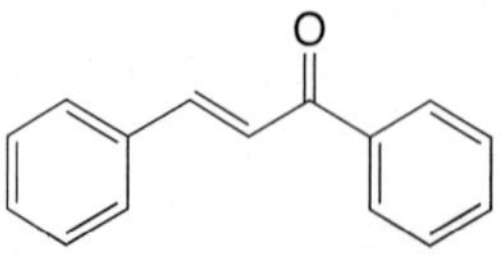

4.

a. 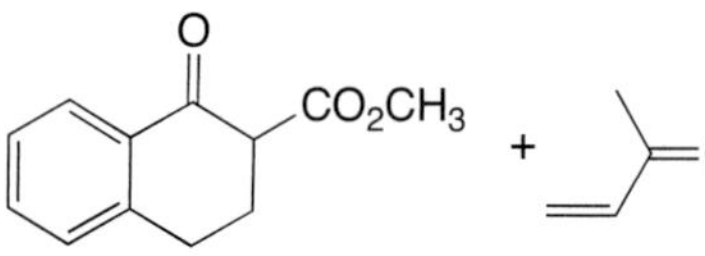

b. 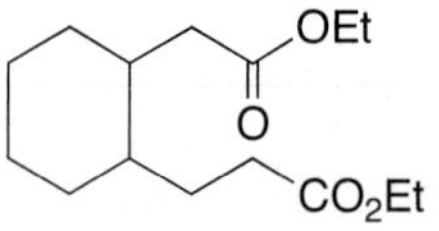

c. 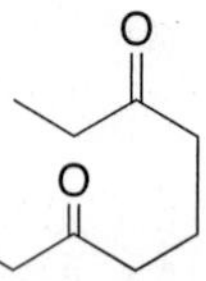

Chapter 24: Answers to Problems

24.1

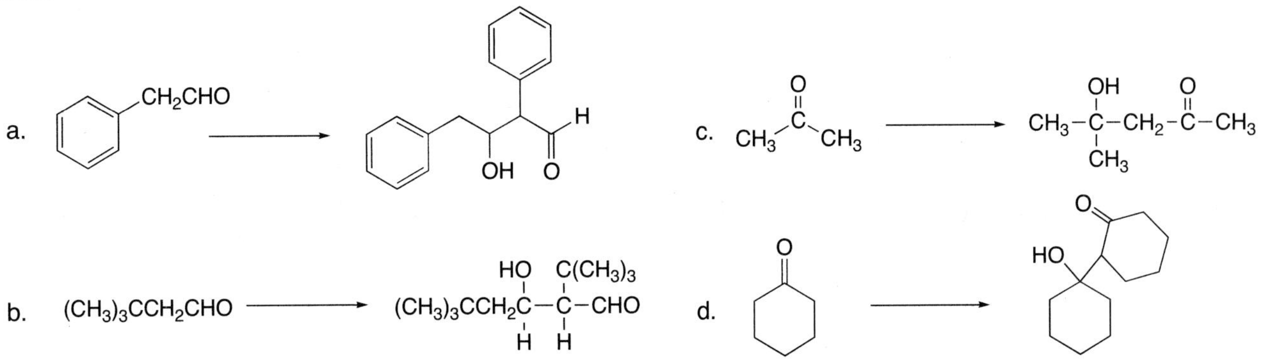
a.
CH_2CHO
OH
O
H
b. $(CH_3)_3CCH_2CHO$
HO C$(CH_3)_3$
$(CH_3)_3CCH_2C-C-CHO$
H H
c. CH_3 CH_3
OH O
$CH_3-C-CH_2-C-CH_3$
CH_3
d.
HO

24.2

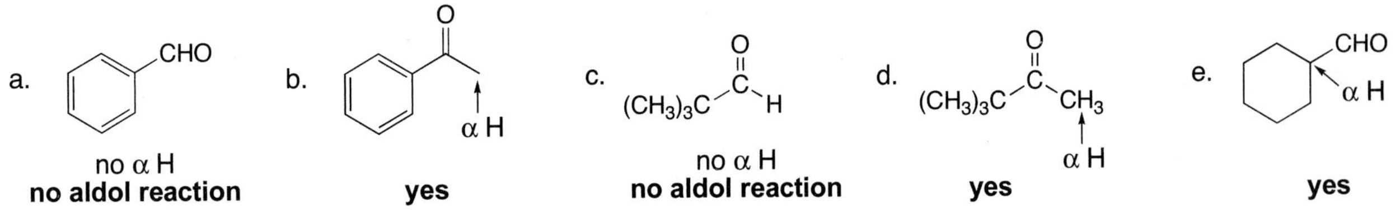
a. CHO
no α H
no aldol reaction
b. α H
yes
c. $(CH_3)_3C$ H
no α H
no aldol reaction
d. $(CH_3)_3C$ CH_3
α H
yes
e. CHO
α H
yes

24.3

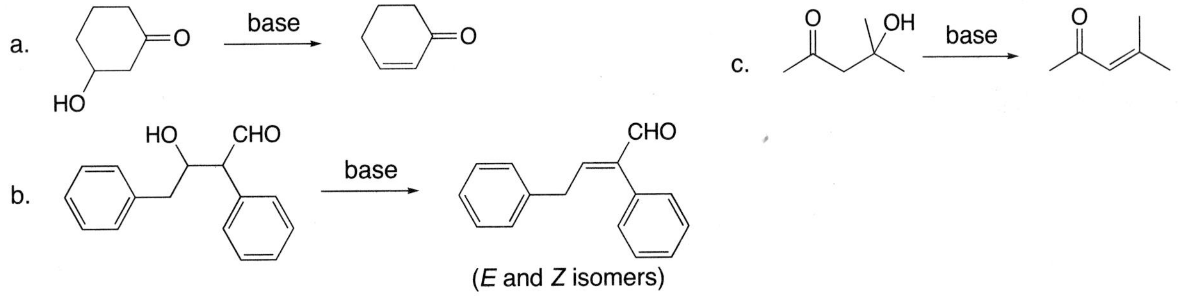
a.
HO
base
c.
OH
base
b.
HO CHO
base
CHO
(E and Z isomers)

24.4

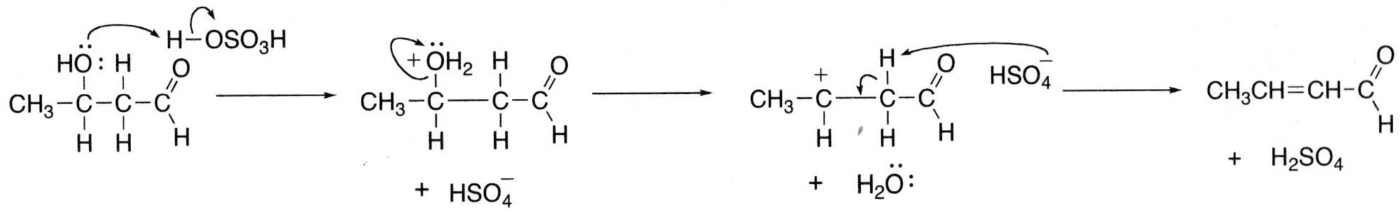
H–OSO_3H
$CH_3-C-C-C$
+ HSO_4^-
HSO_4^-
+ H_2O:
$CH_3CH=CH-C$
+ H_2SO_4

24.5 Locate the α and β C's to the carbonyl group, and break the molecule into two halves at this bond. The α C and all of the atoms bonded to it belong to one carbonyl component. The β C and all of the atoms bonded to it belong to the other carbonyl component.

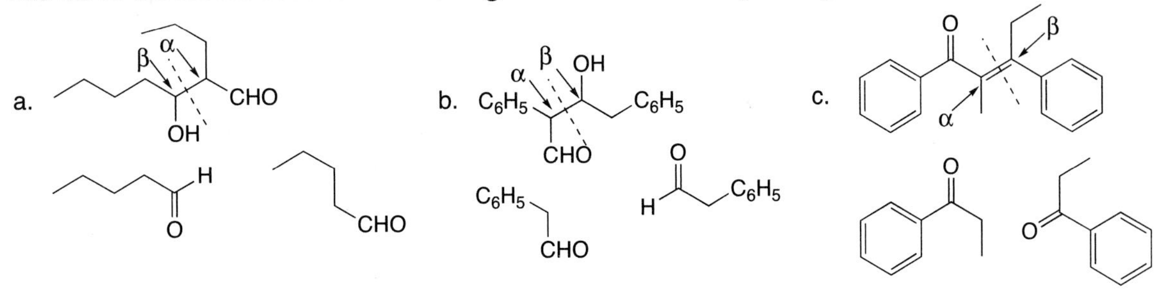
a.
β α
OH
CHO
H
O
CHO
b. C_6H_5
α β OH
C_6H_5
CHO
C_6H_5
CHO
H
C_6H_5
c.
β
α

24.6

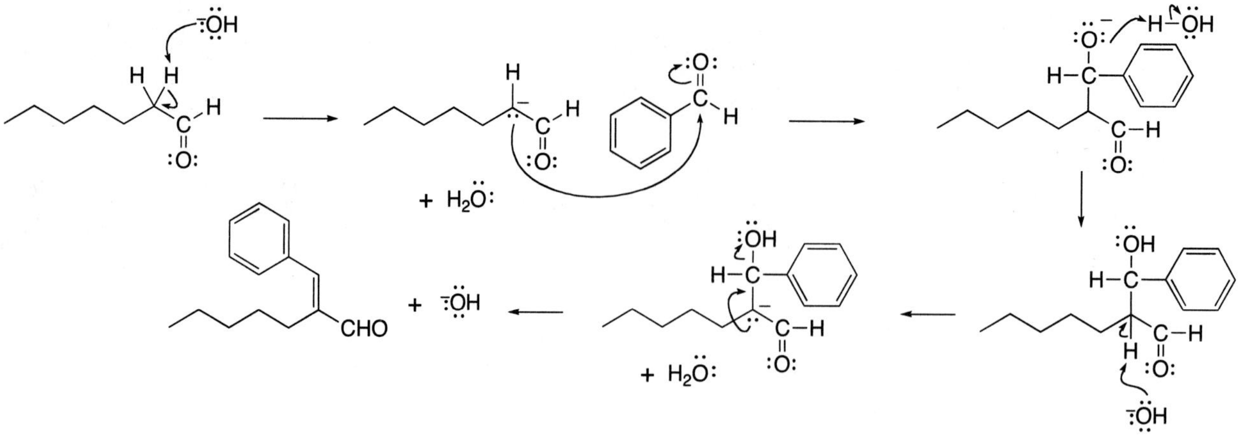
+ H_2O:
CHO
+ :OH
+ H_2O:

24.7

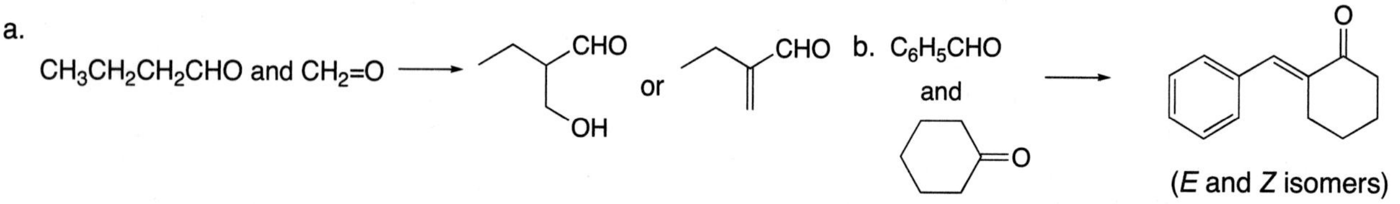
a.
$CH_3CH_2CH_2CHO$ and CH_2=O
CHO
OH
or
CHO
b. C_6H_5CHO
and
O
O
(*E* and *Z* isomers)

24.8

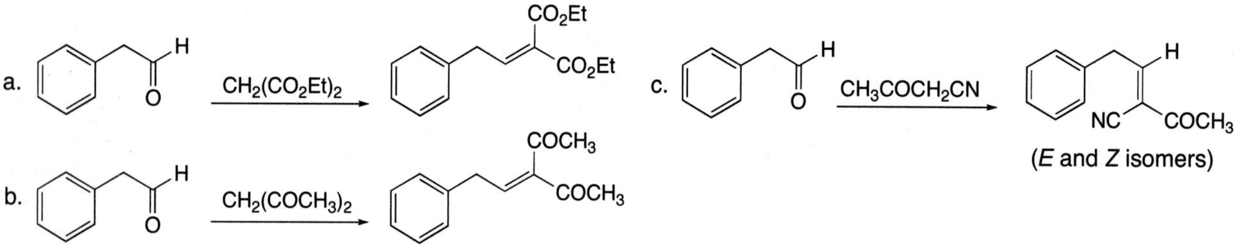
a.
$CH_2(CO_2Et)_2$
CO_2Et
CO_2Et
c.
CH_3COCH_2CN
NC
$COCH_3$
(*E* and *Z* isomers)
b.
$CH_2(COCH_3)_2$
$COCH_3$
$COCH_3$

24.9

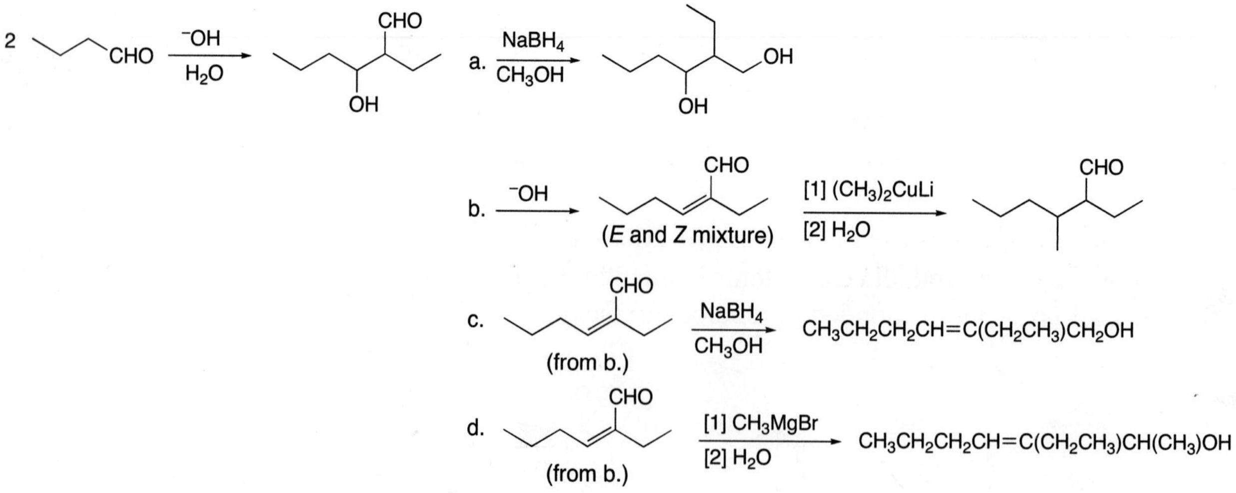
2
CHO
^-OH
H_2O
CHO
OH
a.
$NaBH_4$
CH_3OH
OH
OH
b.
^-OH
CHO
(*E* and *Z* mixture)
[1] $(CH_3)_2CuLi$
[2] H_2O
CHO
c.
CHO
(from b.)
$NaBH_4$
CH_3OH
$CH_3CH_2CH_2CH=C(CH_2CH_3)CH_2OH$
d.
CHO
(from b.)
[1] CH_3MgBr
[2] H_2O
$CH_3CH_2CH_2CH=C(CH_2CH_3)CH(CH_3)OH$

24.10 Find the α and β C's to the carbonyl group and break the bond between them.

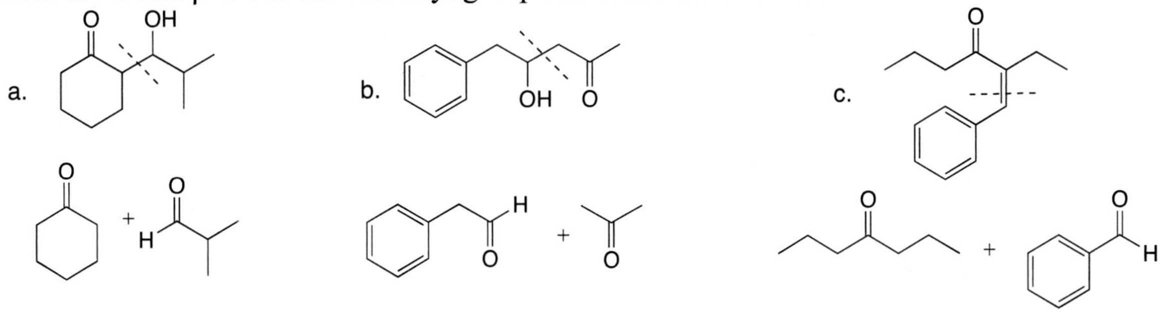

24.11

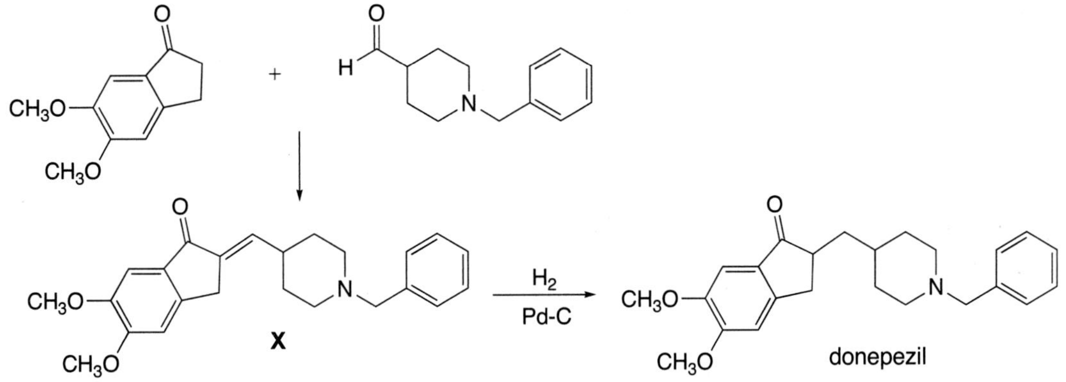

24.12 All enolates have a second resonance structure with a negative charge on O.

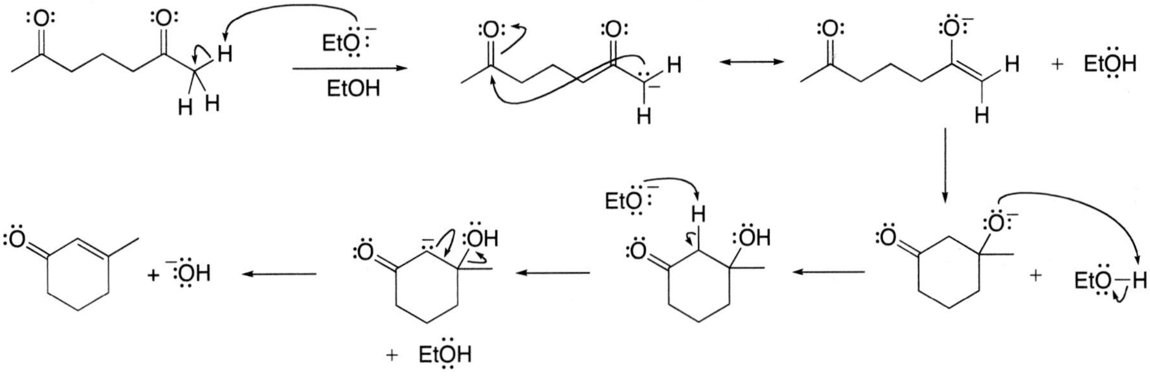

24.13

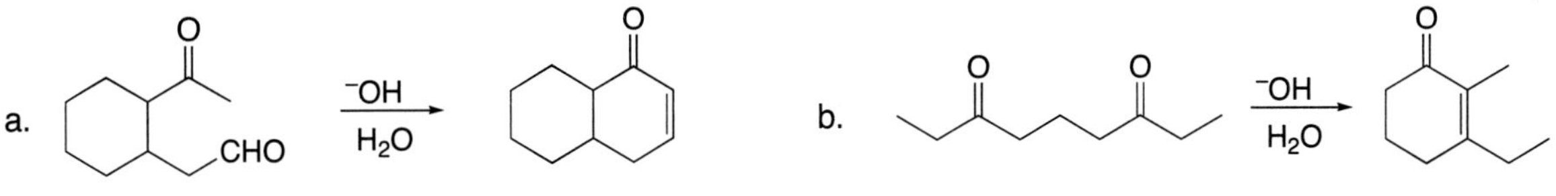

24.14

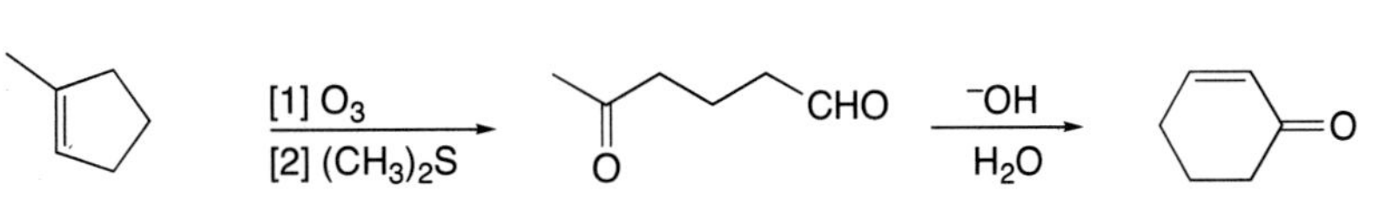

A B

24.15 Join the α C of one ester to the carbonyl C of the other ester to form the β-keto ester.

a.

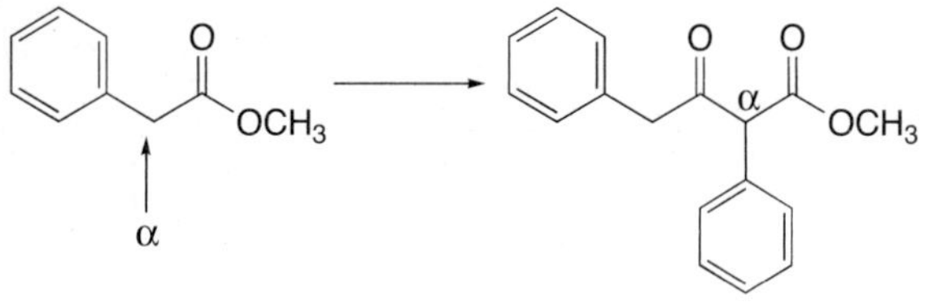

b.

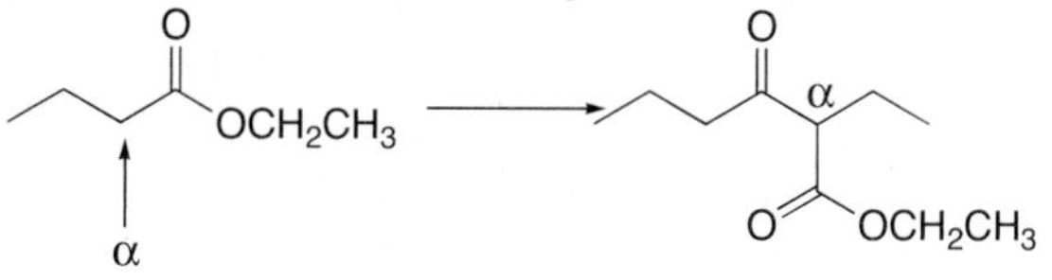

24.16 In a crossed Claisen reaction between an ester and a ketone, the enolate is formed from the ketone, and the product is a β-dicarbonyl compound.

a. $CH_3CH_2CO_2Et$ and HCO_2Et

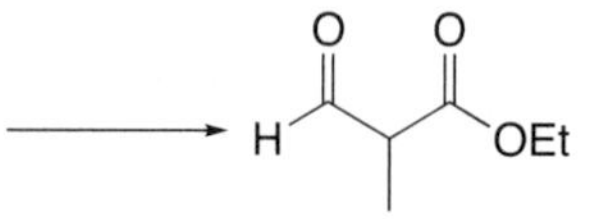

Only this compound can form an enolate.

b.

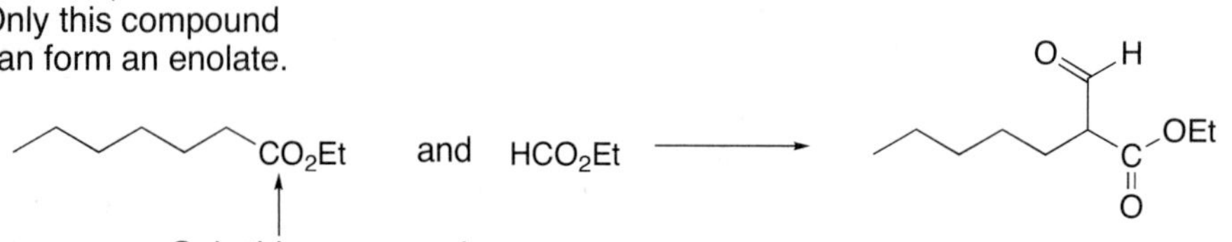

Only this compound can form an enolate.

c.

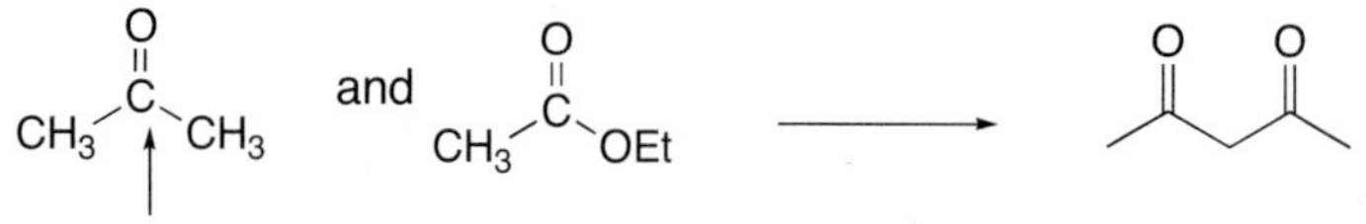

The ketone forms the enolate.

d.

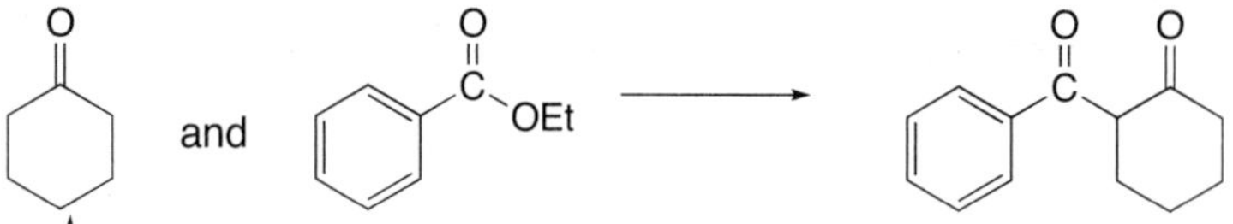

The ketone forms the enolate.

24.17 A β-dicarbonyl compound like avobenzone is prepared by a crossed Claisen reaction between a ketone and an ester.

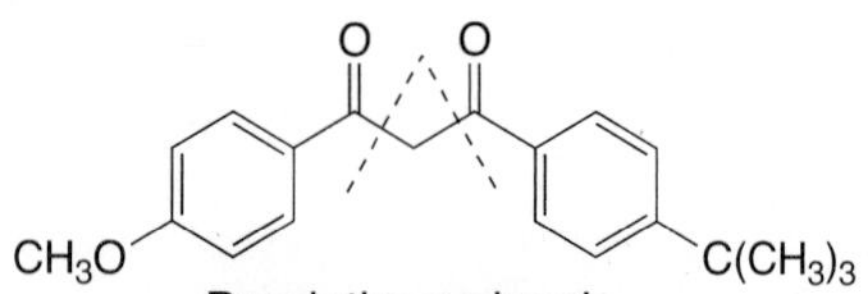

Break the molecule into two components at either dashed line.

avobenzone

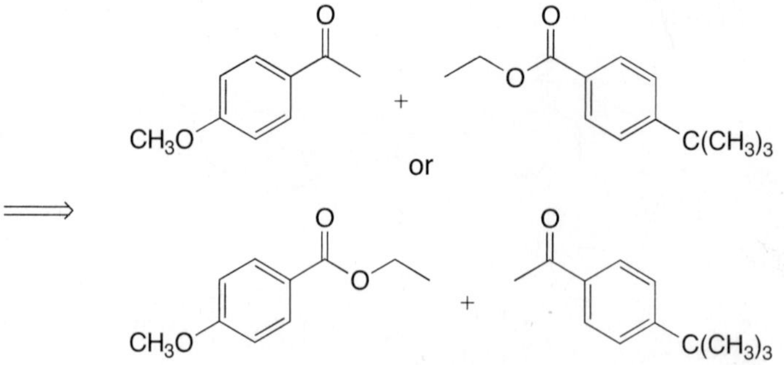

24.18

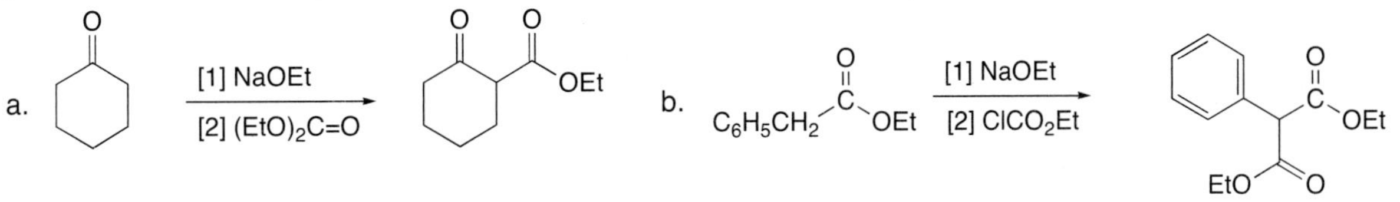
a.
[1] NaOEt
[2] $(EtO)_2C{=}O$
OEt
b.
$C_6H_5CH_2COEt$
[1] NaOEt
[2] $ClCO_2Et$
OEt
EtO

24.19

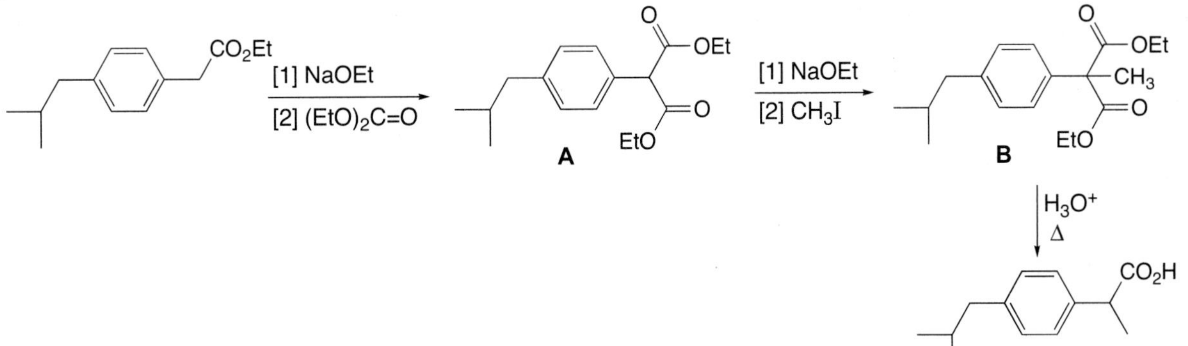
CO_2Et
[1] NaOEt
[2] $(EtO)_2C{=}O$
OEt
EtO
A
[1] NaOEt
[2] CH_3I
OEt
CH_3
EtO
B
H_3O^+
Δ
CO_2H

ibuprofen

24.20

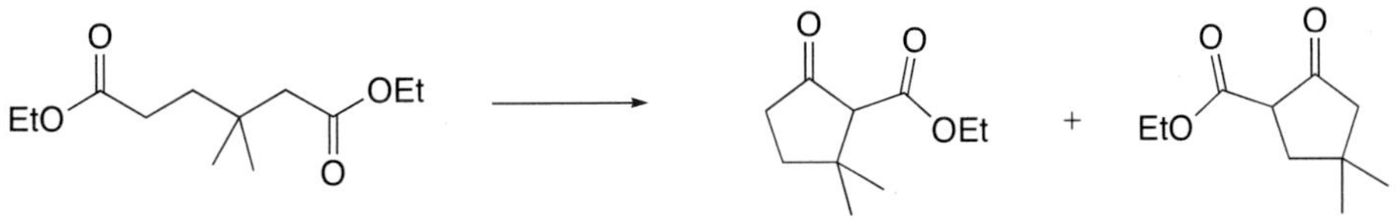
EtO
OEt
OEt
EtO

24.21 A Michael acceptor is an α,β-unsaturated carbonyl compound.

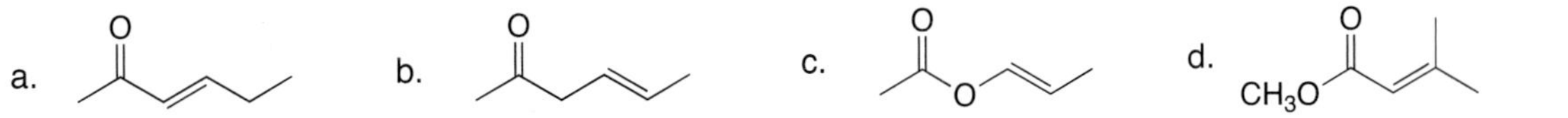
a.
b.
c.
d.
CH_3O

a. α,β-unsaturated **yes—Michael acceptor**

b. not α,β-unsaturated

c. not α,β-unsaturated

d. α,β-unsaturated **yes—Michael acceptor**

24.22

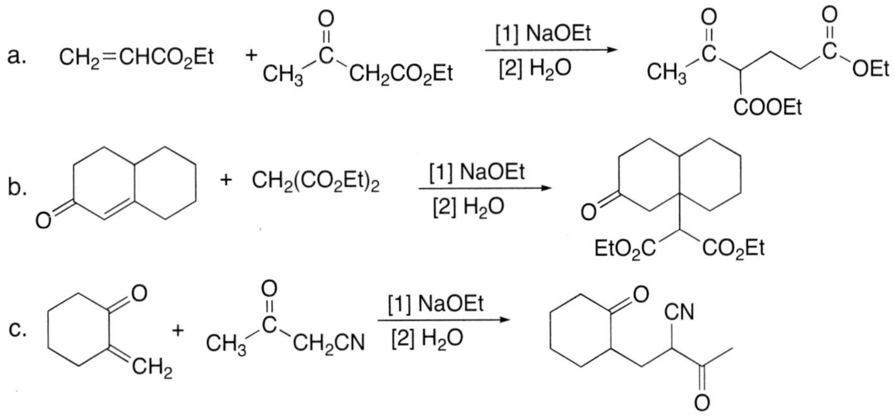
a. $CH_2{=}CHCO_2Et$ + $CH_3COCH_2CO_2Et$
[1] NaOEt
[2] H_2O
CH_3
OEt
COOEt
b.
+ $CH_2(CO_2Et)_2$
[1] NaOEt
[2] H_2O
EtO_2C
CO_2Et
c.
CH_2
+ CH_3COCH_2CN
[1] NaOEt
[2] H_2O
CN

24.23

a. 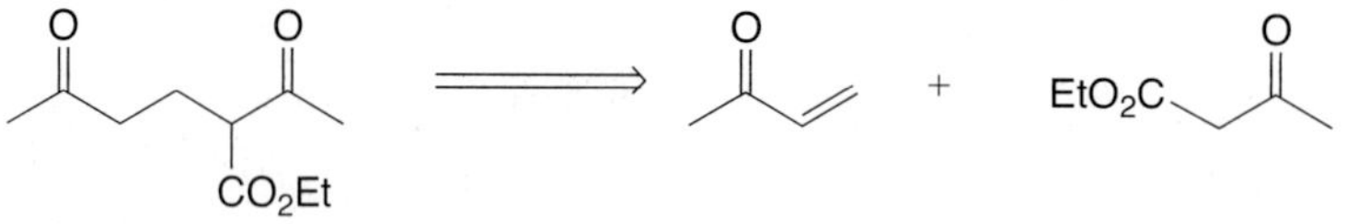
O
O
CO2Et
O
EtO2C
O

b. 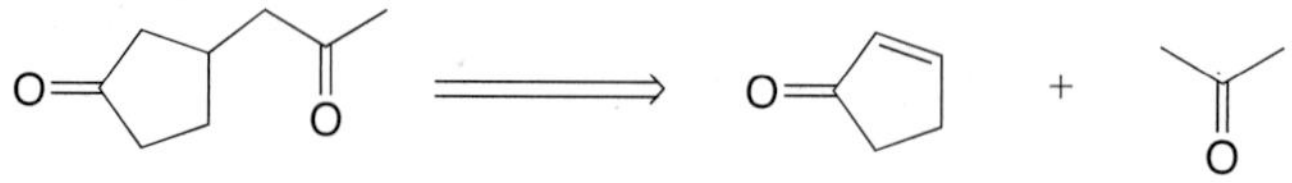
O
O
O
O

24.24 The Robinson annulation forms a six-membered ring and three new carbon–carbon bonds: two σ bonds and one π bond.

a. 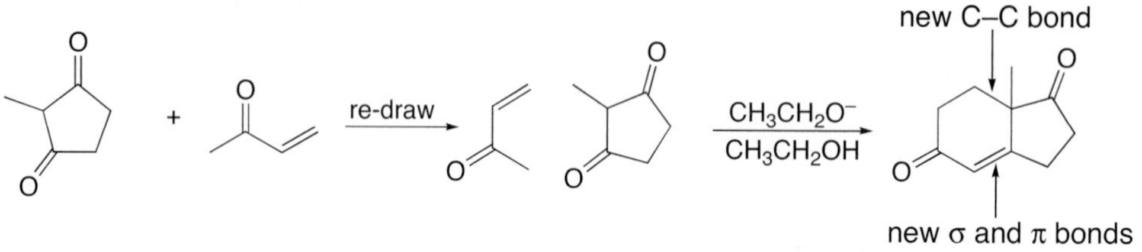
re-draw
CH3CH2O−
CH3CH2OH
new C–C bond
new σ and π bonds

b. 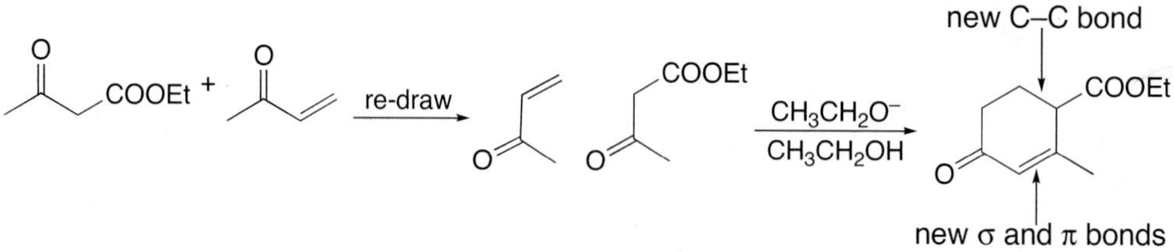
COOEt
re-draw
COOEt
CH3CH2O−
CH3CH2OH
new C–C bond
COOEt
new σ and π bonds

c. 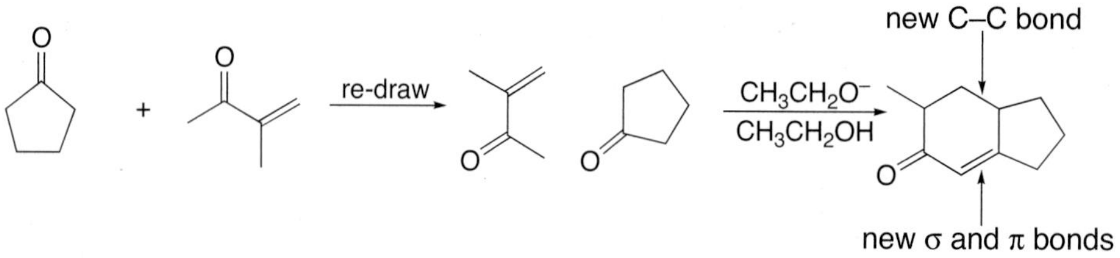
re-draw
CH3CH2O−
CH3CH2OH
new C–C bond
new σ and π bonds

d. 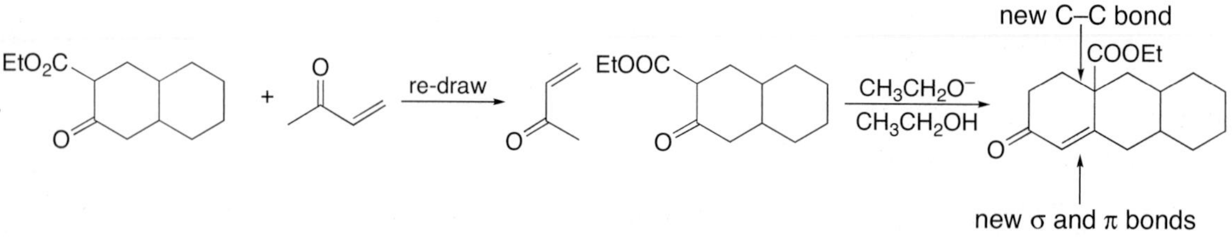
EtO2C
re-draw
EtOOC
CH3CH2O−
CH3CH2OH
new C–C bond
COOEt
new σ and π bonds

24.25

a. 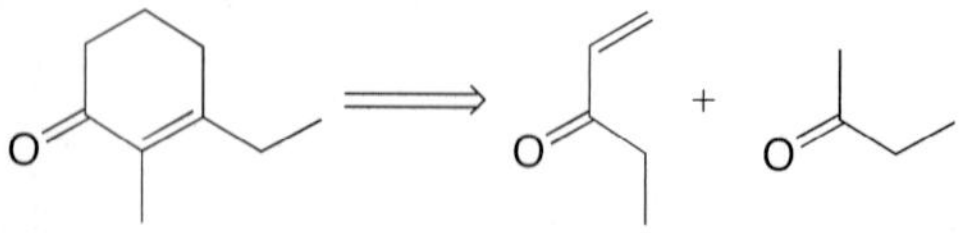

c. 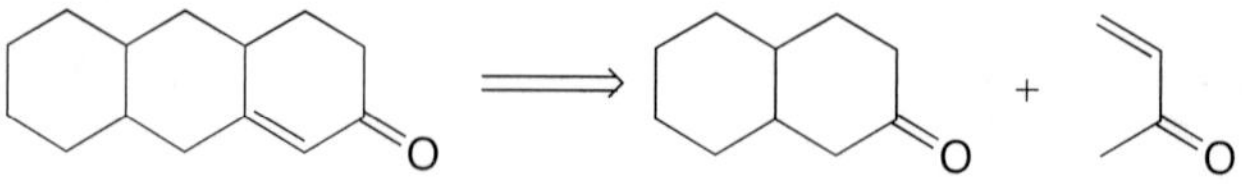

b. 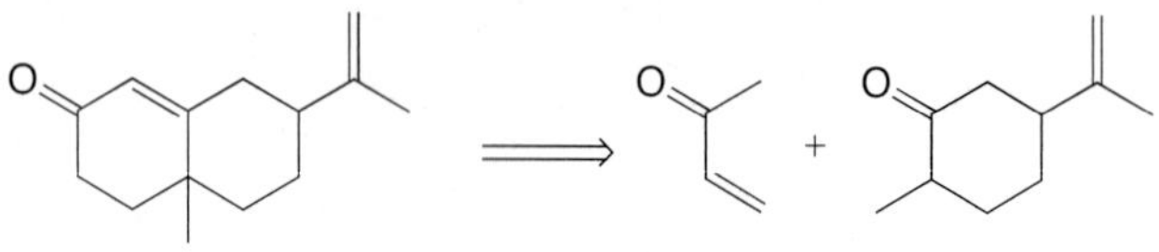

24.26

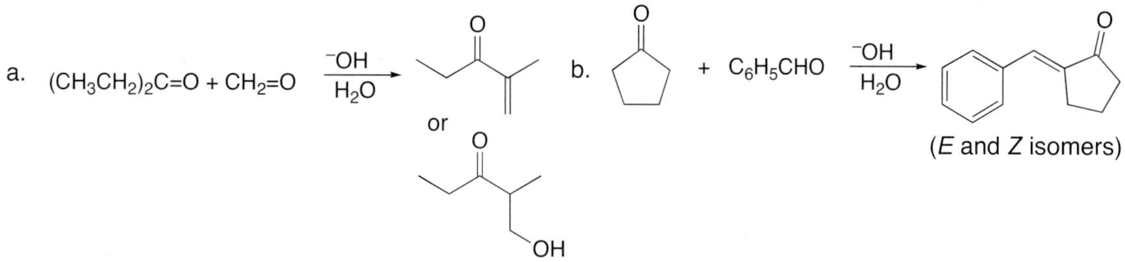
a. (CH3CH2)2C=O + CH2=O
⁻OH
H2O
or
OH
b.
+ C6H5CHO
⁻OH
H2O
(E and Z isomers)

24.27

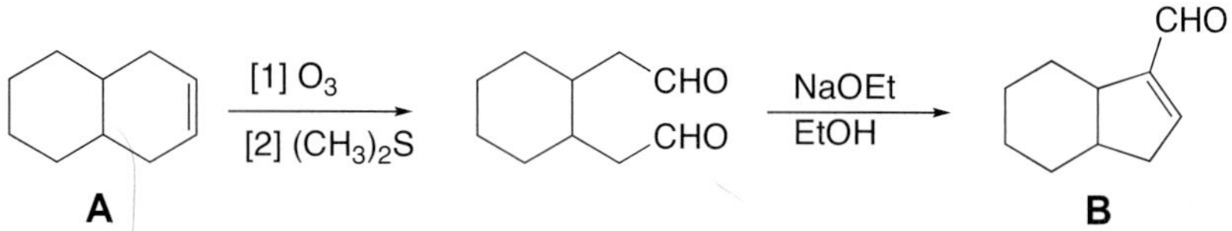
[1] O3
[2] (CH3)2S
CHO
CHO
NaOEt
EtOH
CHO
A
B

24.28 The product of an aldol reaction is a β-hydroxy carbonyl compound or an α,β-unsaturated carbonyl compound. The α,β-unsaturated carbonyl compound is drawn as product unless elimination of H_2O cannot form a conjugated system.

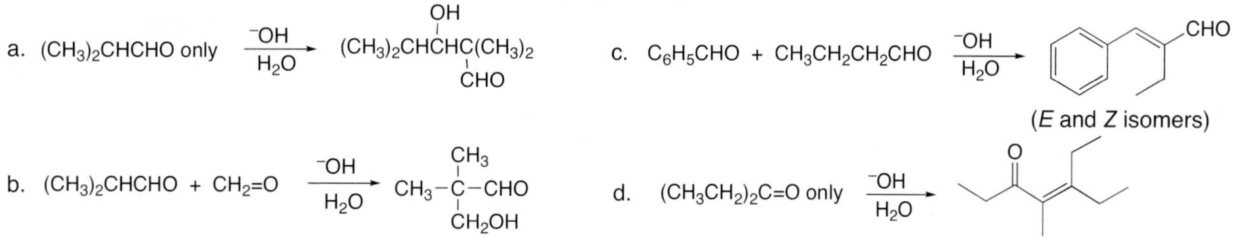
a. (CH3)2CHCHO only
⁻OH
H2O
OH
(CH3)2CHCHC(CH3)2
CHO
c. C6H5CHO + CH3CH2CH2CHO
⁻OH
H2O
CHO
(E and Z isomers)
b. (CH3)2CHCHO + CH2=O
⁻OH
H2O
CH3
CH3–C–CHO
CH2OH
d. (CH3CH2)2C=O only
⁻OH
H2O

24.29

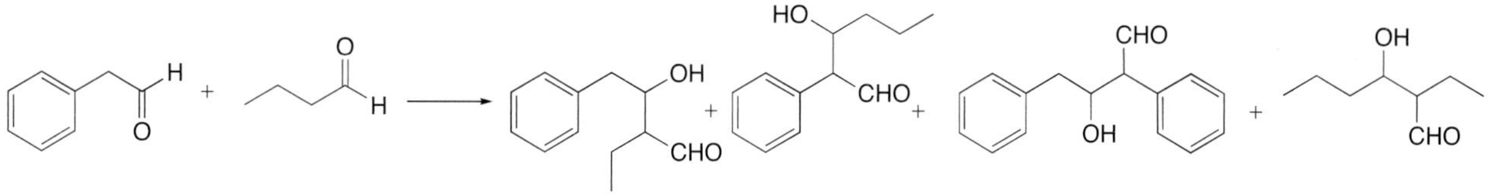
H
H
OH
CHO
HO
CHO
CHO
OH
OH
CHO

24.30

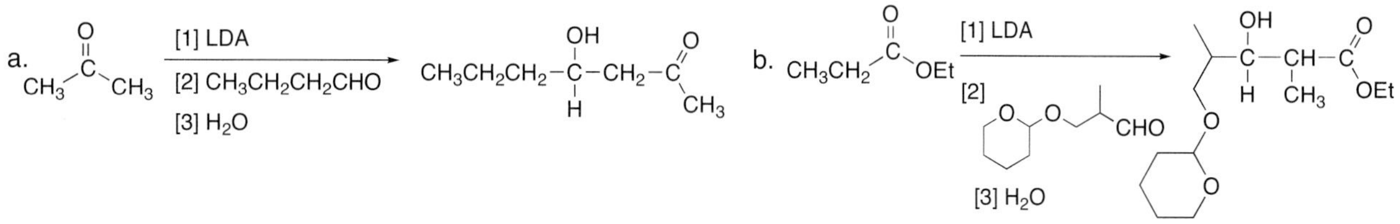
a.
[1] LDA
[2] CH3CH2CH2CHO
[3] H2O
OH
CH3CH2CH2–C–CH2–C
H
CH3
b. CH3CH2
OEt
[1] LDA
[2]
CHO
[3] H2O
OH
C–CH–C
H CH3
OEt

24.31

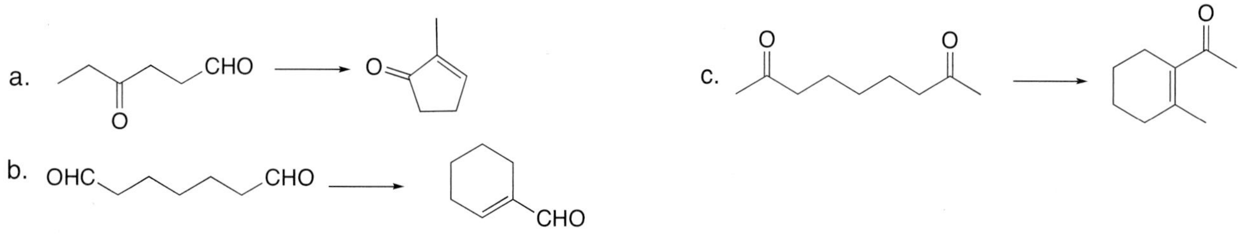
a.
CHO
c.
b. OHC
CHO
CHO

24.32 Locate the α and β C's to the carbonyl group, and break the molecule into two halves at this bond. The α C and all of the atoms bonded to it belong to one carbonyl component. The β C and all the atoms bonded to it belong to the other carbonyl component.

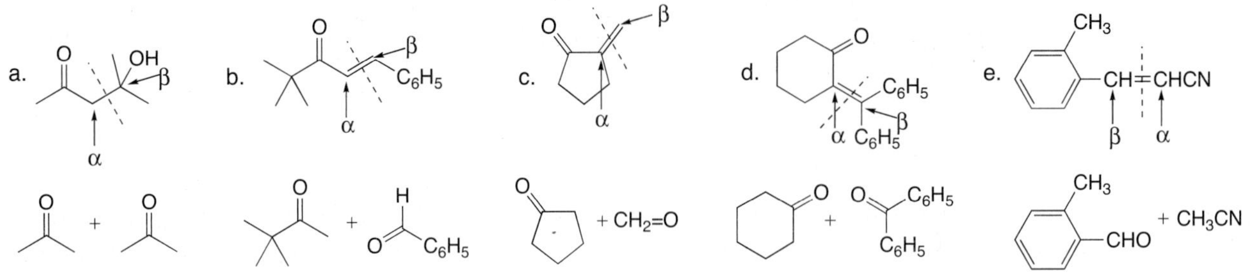
a.
b.
c.
d.
e.
OH
α
β
C_6H_5
CH_3
CH=CHCN
+ CH_2=O
CHO
+ CH_3CN

24.33

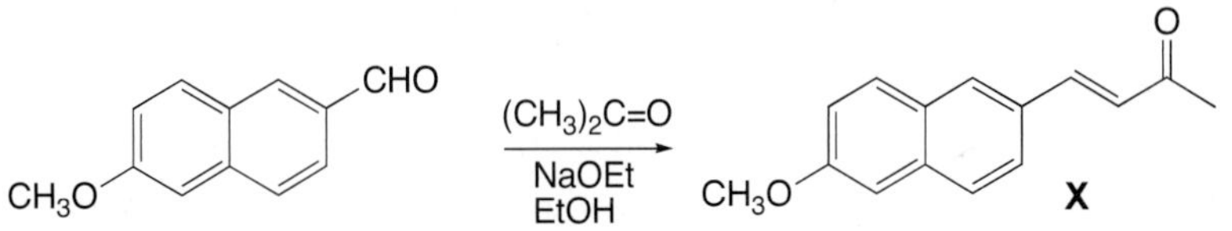
CHO
CH_3O
$(CH_3)_2C$=O
NaOEt
EtOH
X

24.34 Base removes the most acidic proton between the two C=O's in **B.** This enolate reacts with the aldehyde in **A** to form a product that loses H_2O.

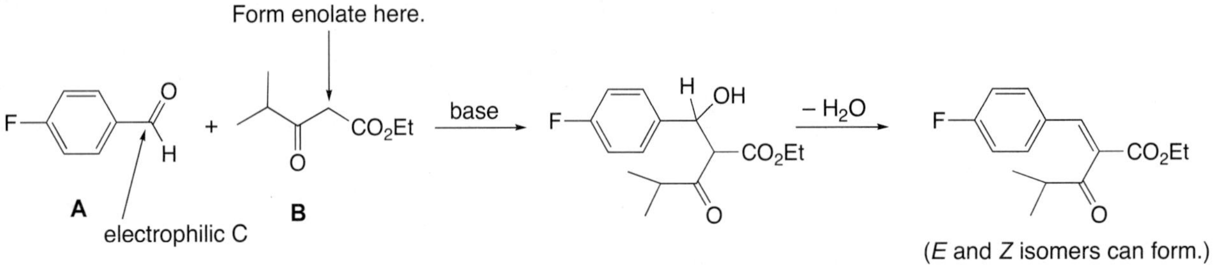
Form enolate here.
F
H
CO_2Et
base
OH
– H_2O
A
B
electrophilic C
(E and Z isomers can form.)

24.35

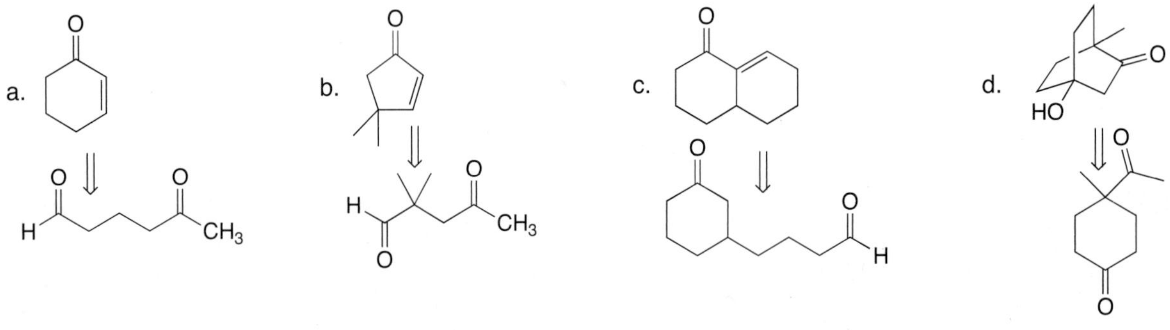
a.
b.
c.
d.
H
CH_3
HO

24.36 Ozonolysis cleaves the C=C, and base catalyzes an intramolecular aldol reaction.

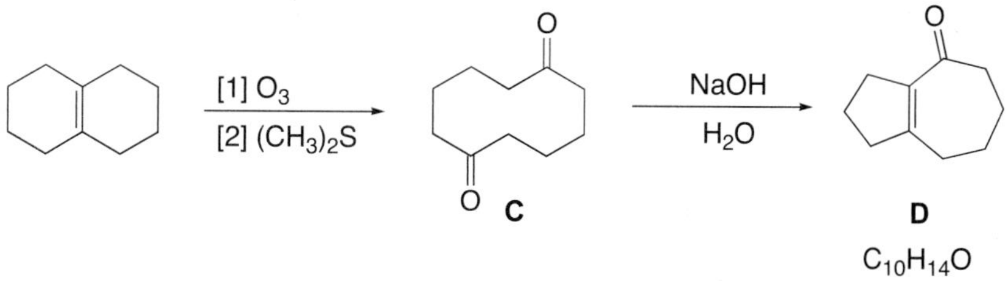
[1] O3
[2] (CH3)2S
C
NaOH
H2O
D
C10H14O

24.37 Aldol reactions proceed via resonance-stabilized enolates. **K** can form an enolate that allows for delocalization of the negative charge on O. Delocalization is not possible in **J,** because a double bond would be placed at a bridgehead carbon, which is geometrically impossible.

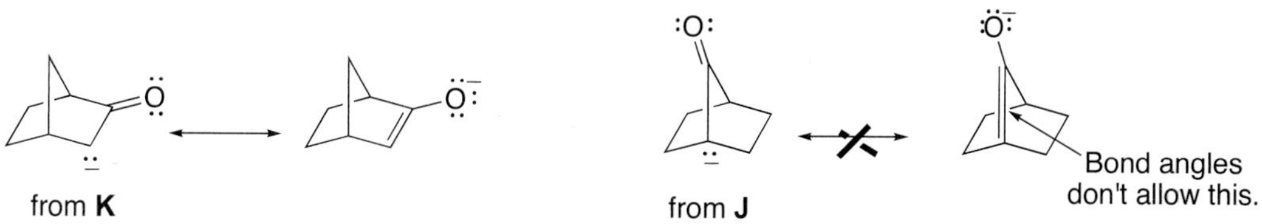
from K
from J
Bond angles
don't allow this.

24.38

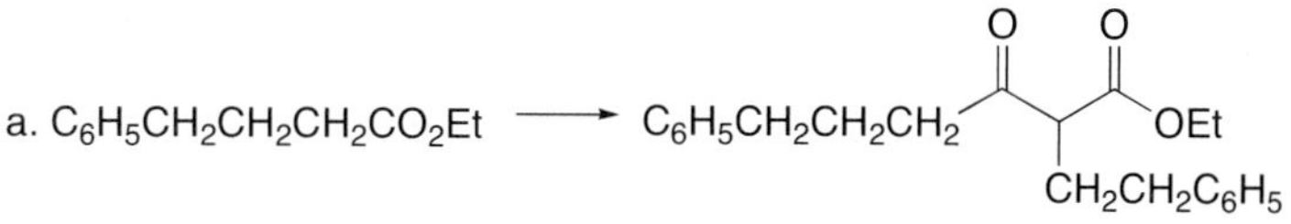
a. C6H5CH2CH2CH2CO2Et
C6H5CH2CH2CH2
OEt
CH2CH2C6H5

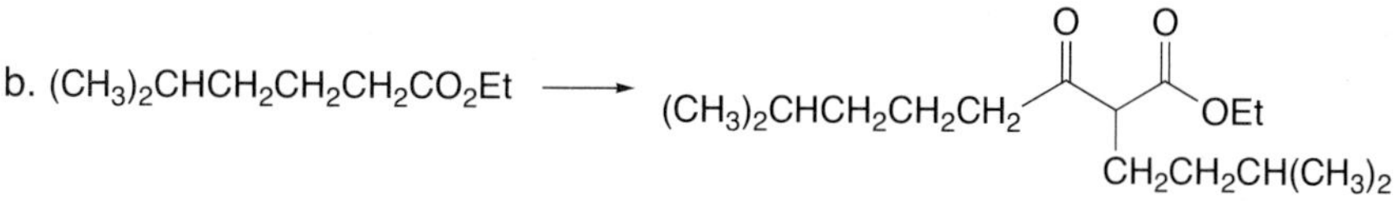
b. (CH3)2CHCH2CH2CH2CO2Et
(CH3)2CHCH2CH2CH2
OEt
CH2CH2CH(CH3)2

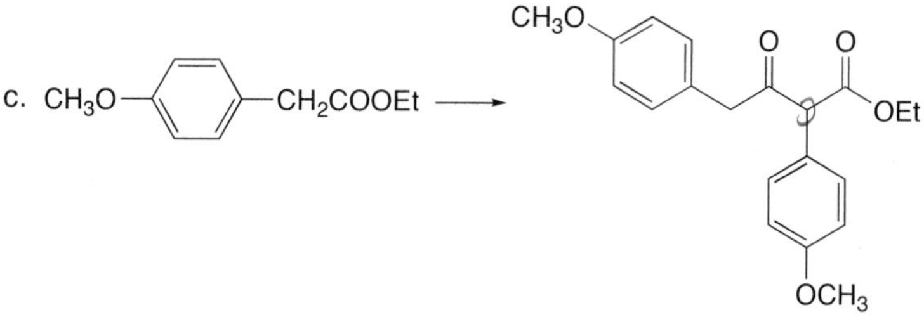
c. CH3O
CH2COOEt
CH3O
OEt
OCH3

24.39

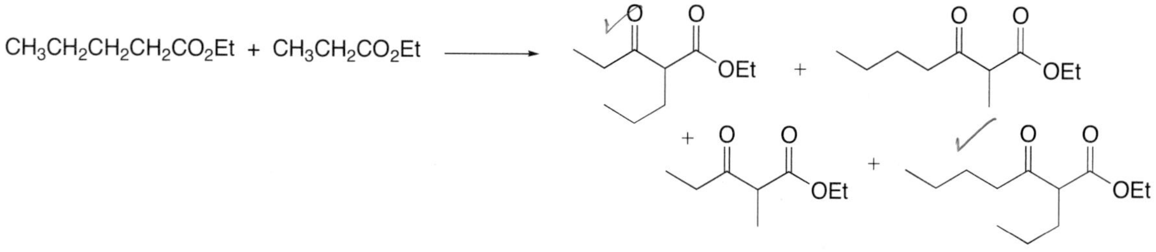
CH3CH2CH2CH2CO2Et + CH3CH2CO2Et
OEt
OEt
OEt
OEt

24.40

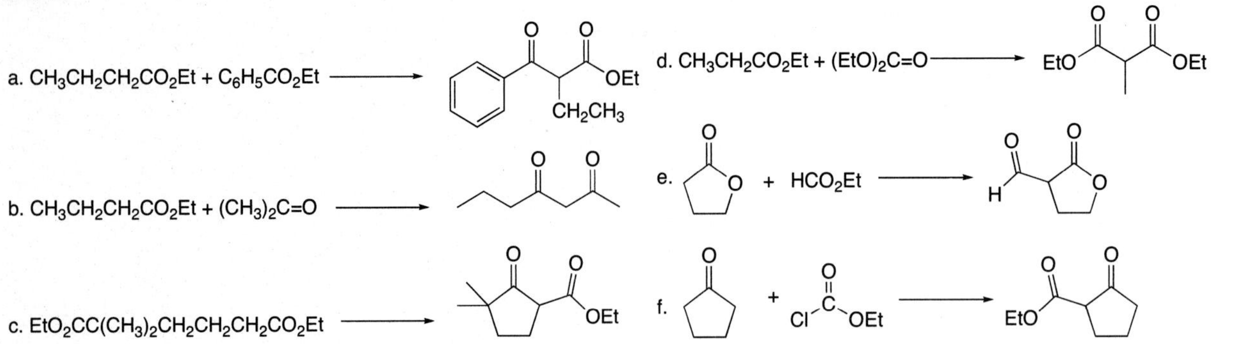
a. CH3CH2CH2CO2Et + C6H5CO2Et
OEt
CH2CH3
b. CH3CH2CH2CO2Et + (CH3)2C=O
c. EtO2CC(CH3)2CH2CH2CH2CO2Et
OEt
d. CH3CH2CO2Et + (EtO)2C=O
EtO
OEt
e.
+ HCO2Et
H
f.
Cl
OEt
EtO

24.41

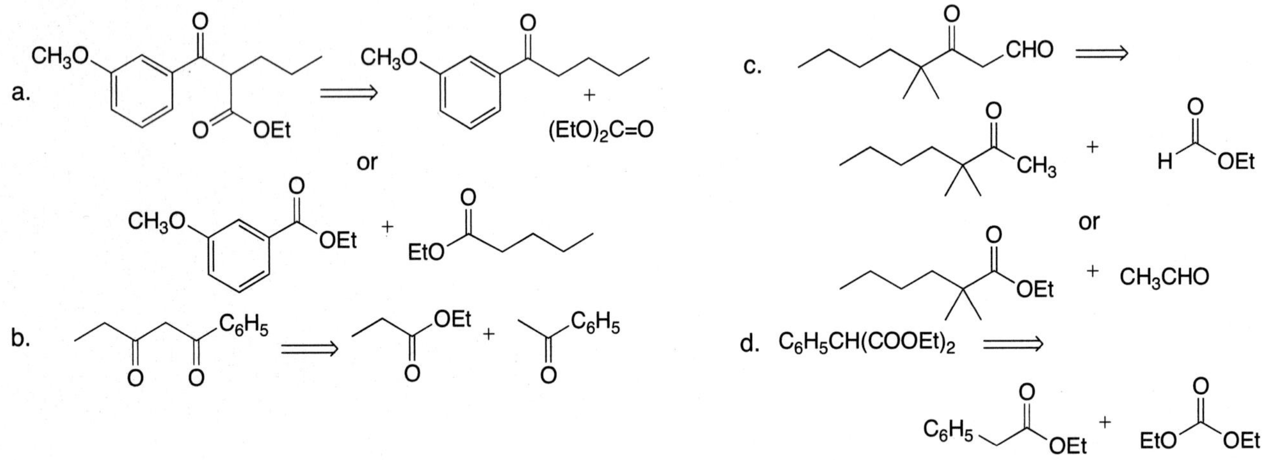
a.
CH3O
OEt
CH3O
(EtO)2C=O
or
CH3O
OEt
EtO
b.
C6H5
OEt
C6H5
c.
CHO
CH3
H
OEt
or
OEt
CH3CHO
d. C6H5CH(COOEt)2
C6H5
OEt
EtO
OEt

24.42 Only esters with two H's or three H's on the α carbon form enolates that undergo Claisen reaction to form resonance-stabilized enolates of the product β-keto ester. Thus, the enolate forms on the CH_2 α to one ester carbonyl, and cyclization yields a five-membered ring.

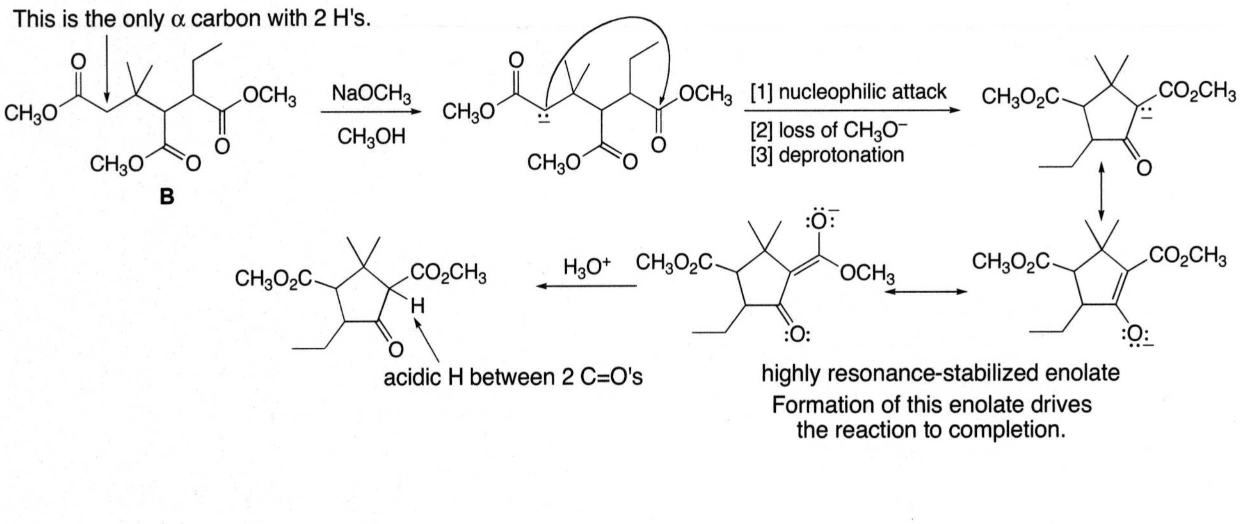
This is the only α carbon with 2 H's.
CH3O
OCH3
CH3O
B
NaOCH3
CH3OH
OCH3
[1] nucleophilic attack
[2] loss of CH3O−
[3] deprotonation
CH3O2C
CO2CH3
H3O+
acidic H between 2 C=O's
highly resonance-stabilized enolate
Formation of this enolate drives
the reaction to completion.

24.43

a. 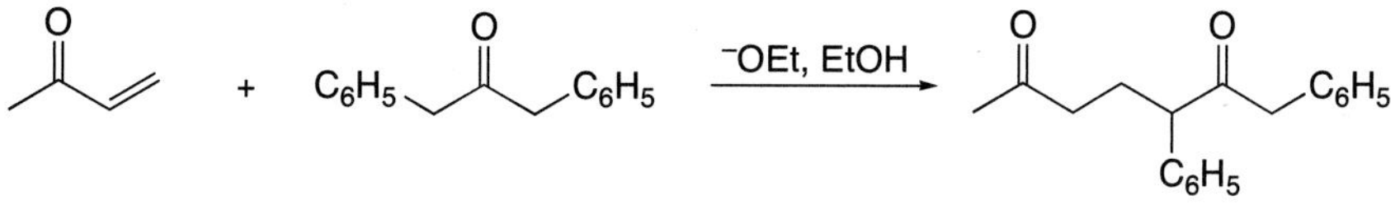
C6H5
C6H5
⁻OEt, EtOH
C6H5
C6H5

b. 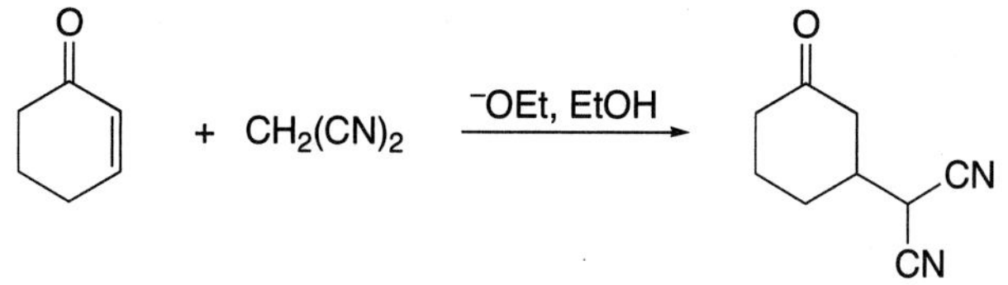
+ CH2(CN)2
⁻OEt, EtOH
CN
CN

24.44

a. 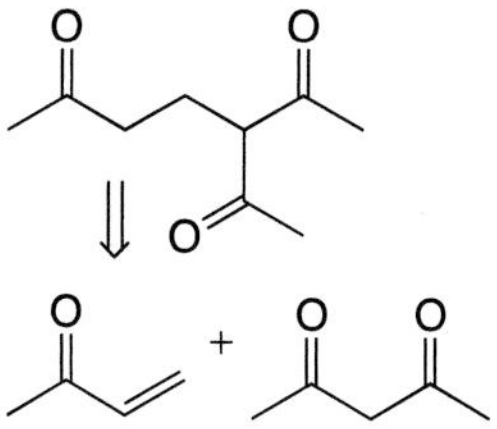

b. 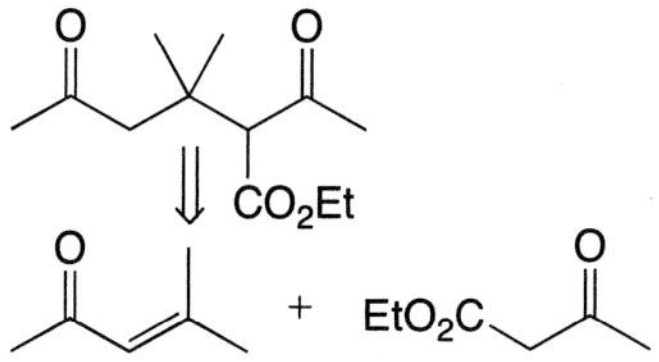
CO2Et
EtO2C

c. 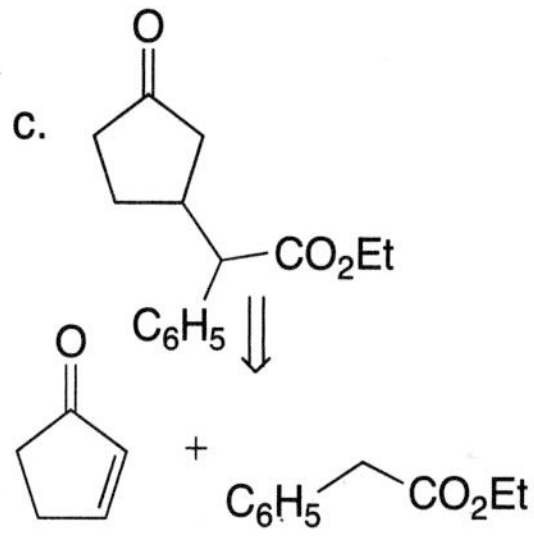
CO2Et
C6H5
C6H5
CO2Et

d. 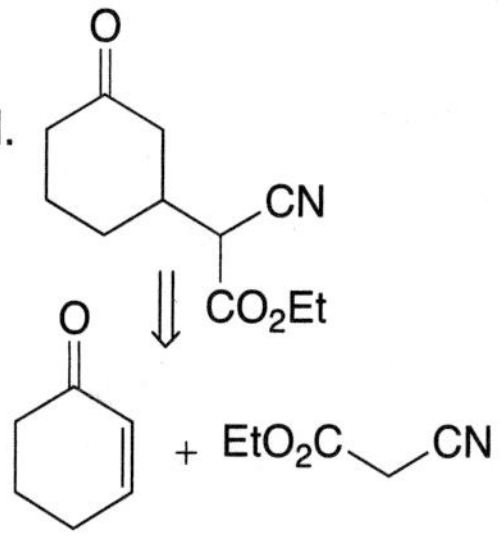
CN
CO2Et
EtO2C
CN

24.45

a. 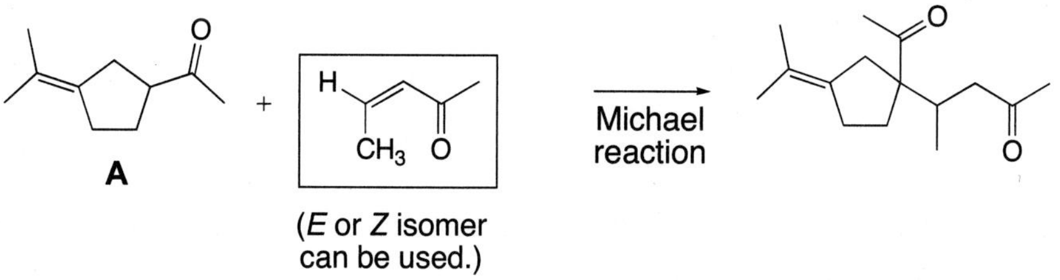
A
H
CH3
Michael
reaction
(E or Z isomer
can be used.)

b. 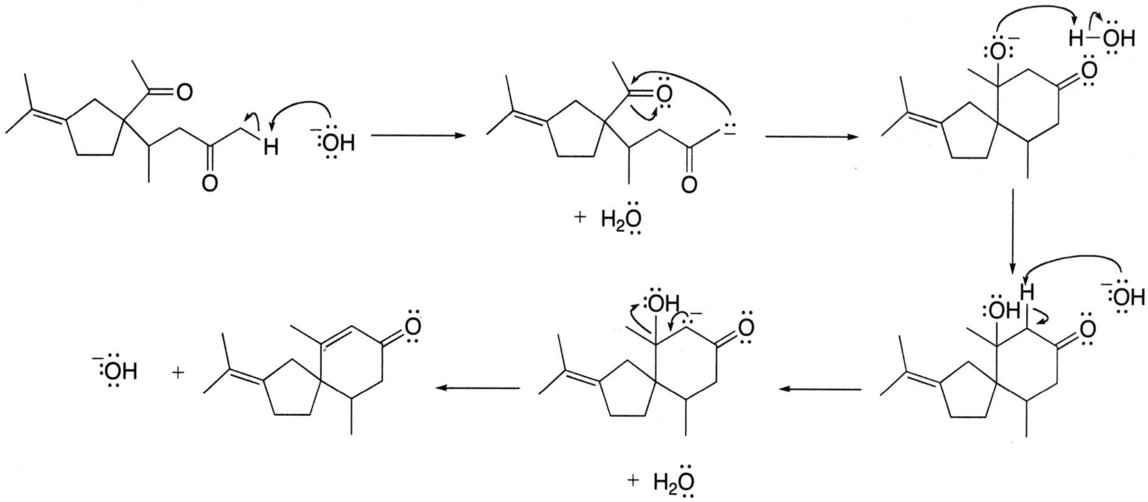
+ H2O
+ H2O

24.46

a. 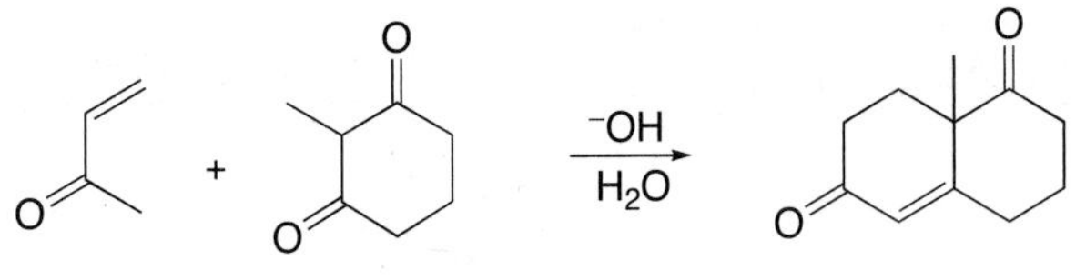
⁻OH
H2O

b. 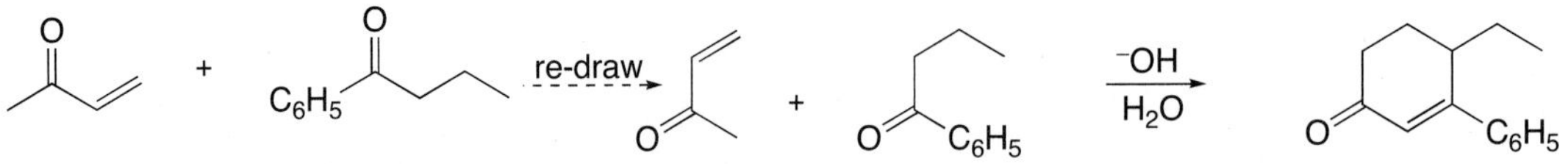
C6H5
re-draw
C6H5
⁻OH
H2O
C6H5

c. 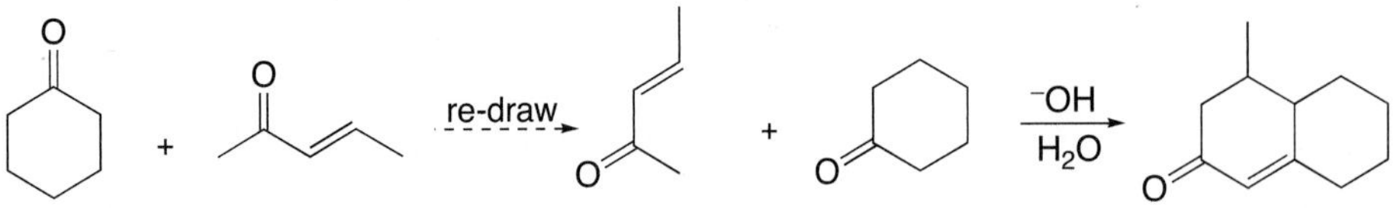
re-draw
⁻OH
H2O

d. 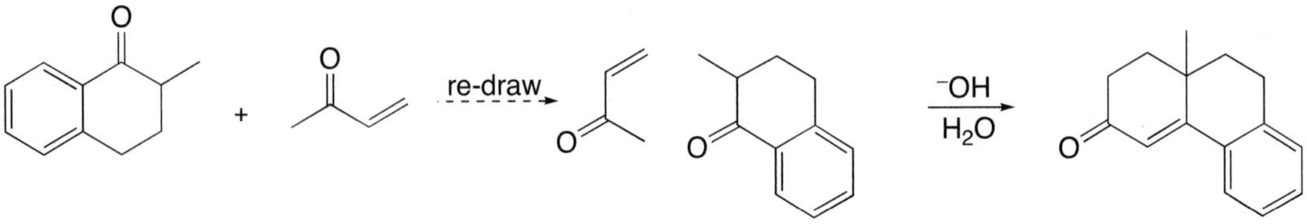
re-draw
⁻OH
H2O

24.47

a. 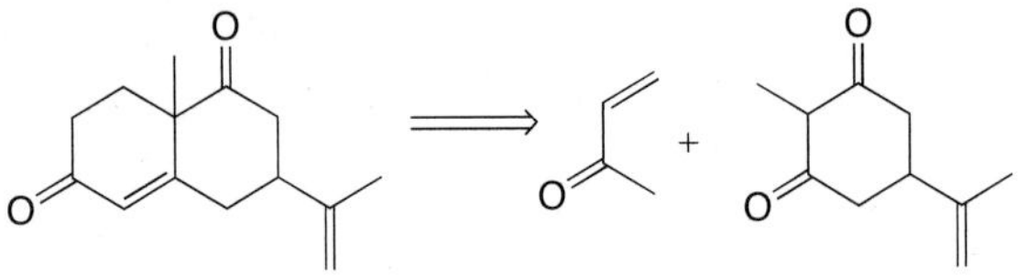

c. 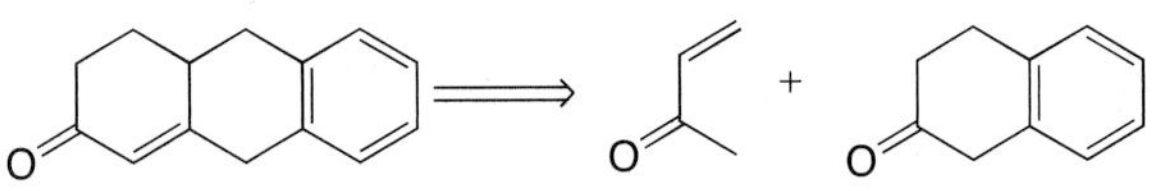

b. 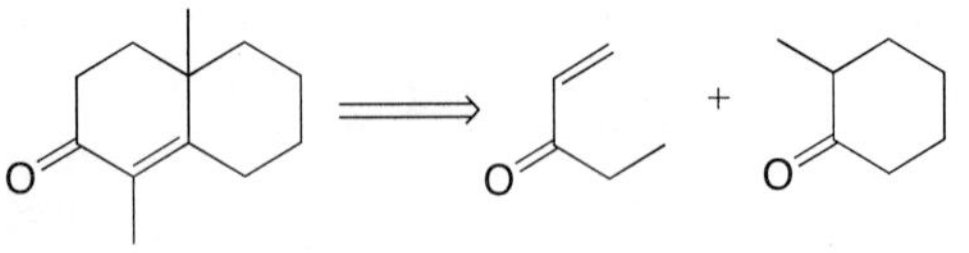

d. 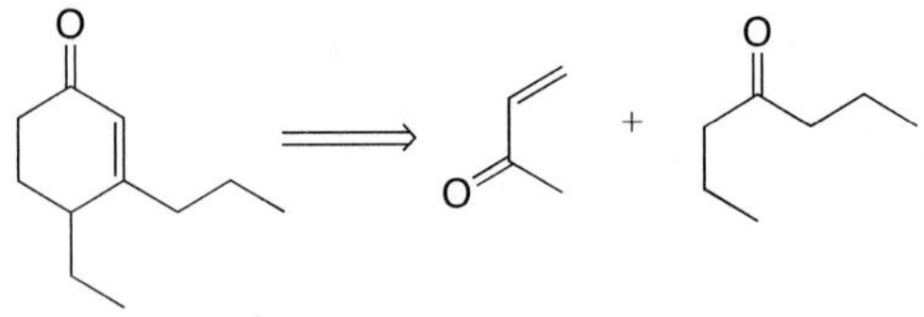

24.48

$CH_3CH_2CH_2CHO$

a. 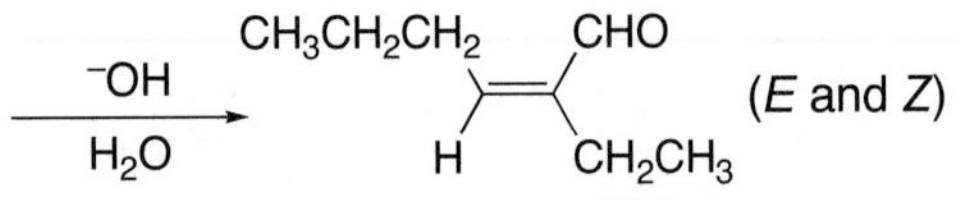
⁻OH
H2O
CH3CH2CH2
CHO
H
CH2CH3
(E and Z)

b. 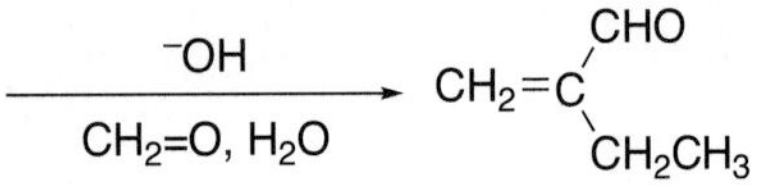
⁻OH
CH2=O, H2O
CHO
CH2=C
CH2CH3

c. 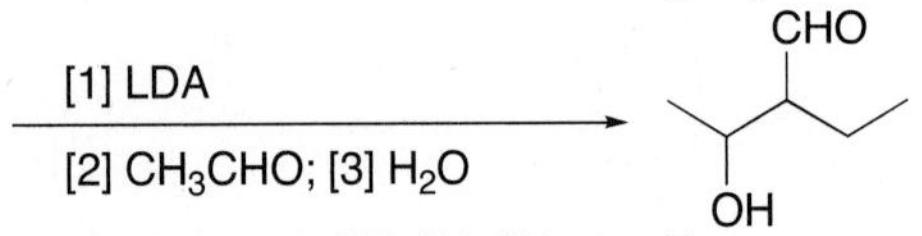
[1] LDA
[2] CH3CHO; [3] H2O
CHO
OH

d. 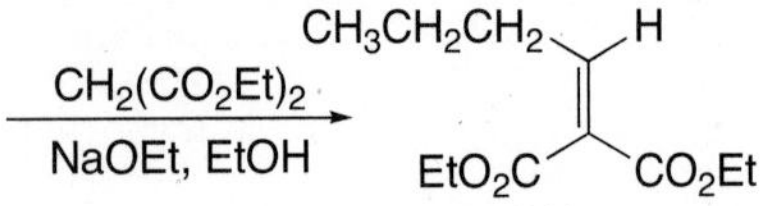
CH2(CO2Et)2
NaOEt, EtOH
CH3CH2CH2
H
EtO2C
CO2Et

e. 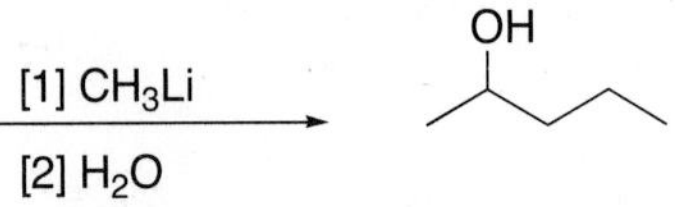
[1] CH3Li
[2] H2O
OH

f. $\xrightarrow[CH_3OH]{NaBH_4}$ $CH_3CH_2CH_2CH_2OH$

g. $\xrightarrow[Pd\text{-}C]{H_2}$ $CH_3CH_2CH_2CH_2OH$

h. 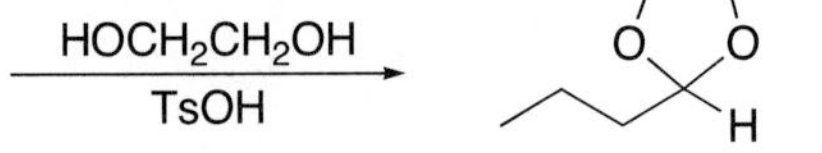
HOCH2CH2OH
TsOH
O
O
H

i. 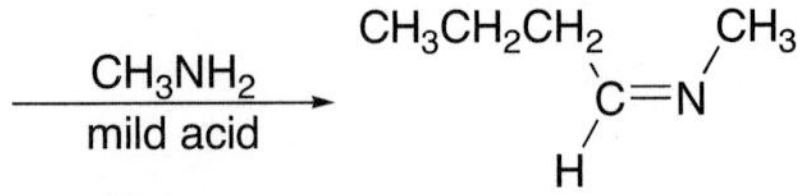
CH3NH2
mild acid
CH3CH2CH2
CH3
C=N
H

j. $\xrightarrow[\text{mild acid}]{(CH_3)_2NH}$ $CH_3CH_2CH{=}CHN(CH_3)_2$ (*E* and *Z*)

k. $\xrightarrow[H_2SO_4]{CrO_3}$ $CH_3CH_2CH_2COOH$

l. 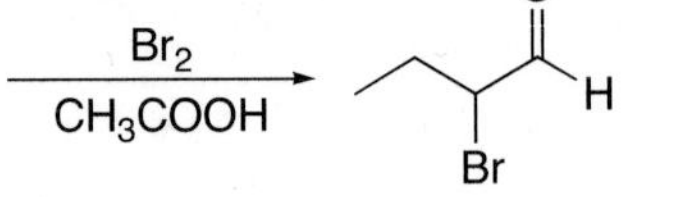
Br2
CH3COOH
O
H
Br

m. 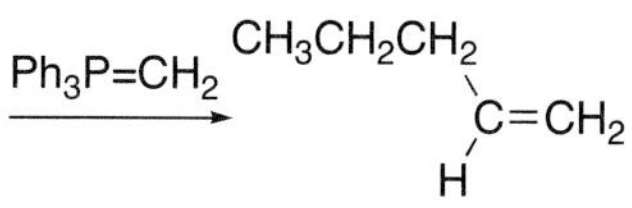
Ph3P=CH2
CH3CH2CH2
C=CH2
H

n. 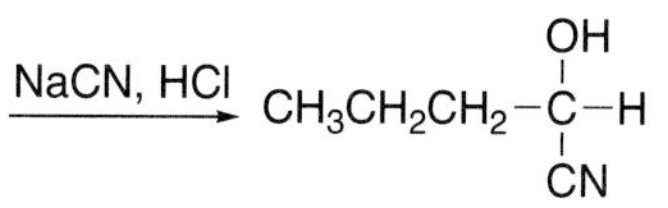
NaCN, HCl
OH
CH3CH2CH2–C–H
CN

o. 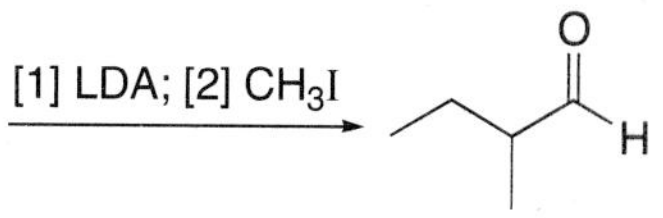
[1] LDA; [2] CH3I
O
H

24.49

a. 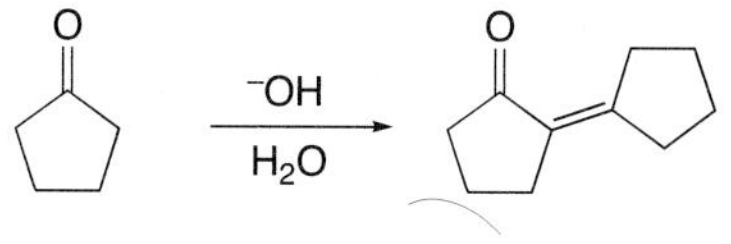
O
–OH
H2O
O

b. 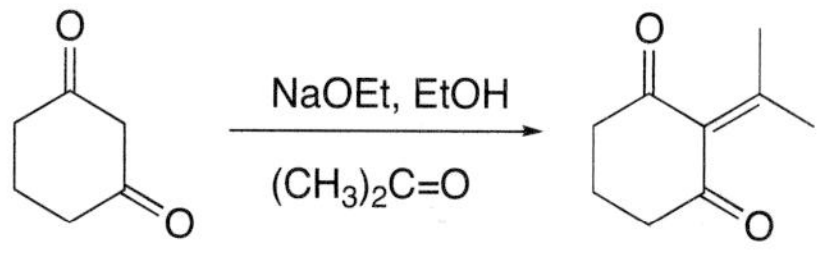
O
NaOEt, EtOH
(CH3)2C=O
O
O
O

c. 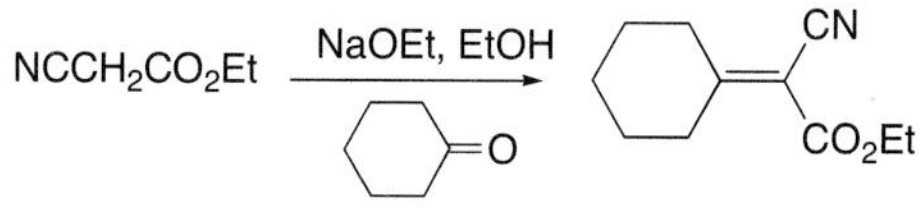
NCCH2CO2Et
NaOEt, EtOH
O
CN
CO2Et

d. 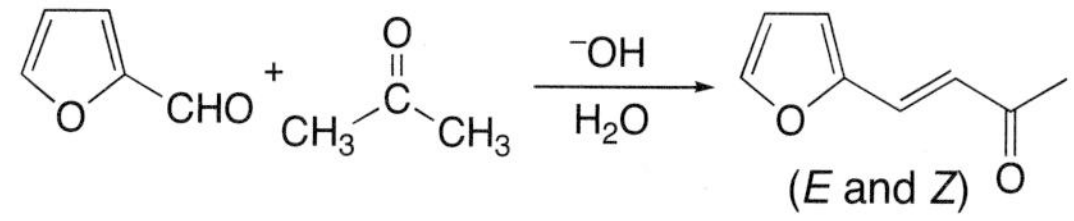
O
CHO
+
O
CH3
C
CH3
–OH
H2O
O
(E and Z)
O

e. 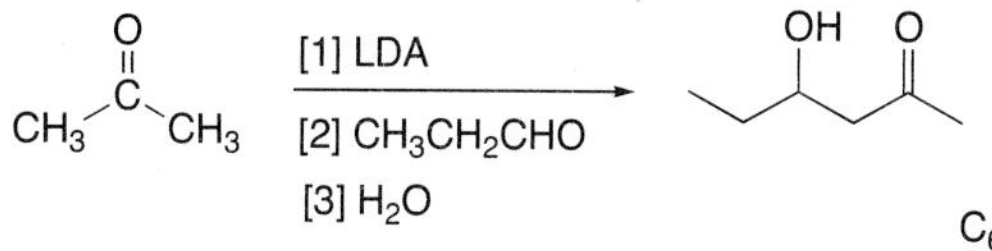
O
C
CH3
CH3
[1] LDA
[2] CH3CH2CHO
[3] H2O
OH
O

f. 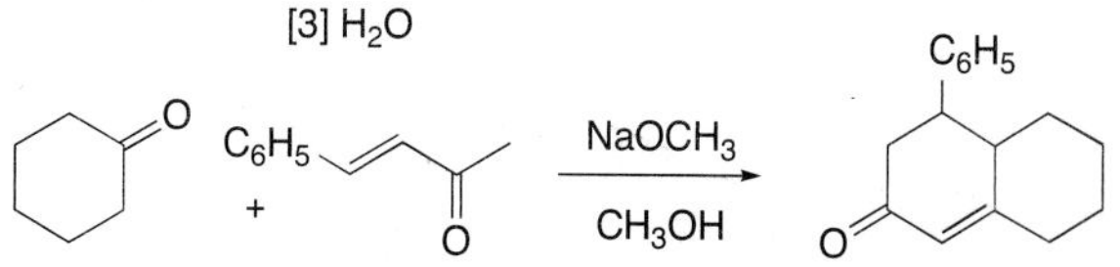
O
C6H5
+
O
NaOCH3
CH3OH
C6H5
O

g. 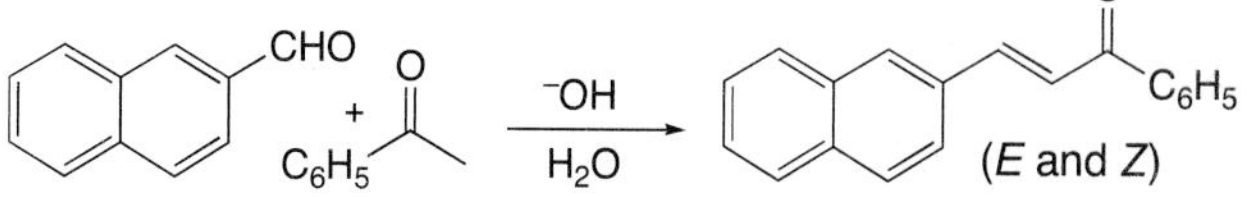
CHO
+
O
C6H5
–OH
H2O
O
C6H5
(E and Z)

h. 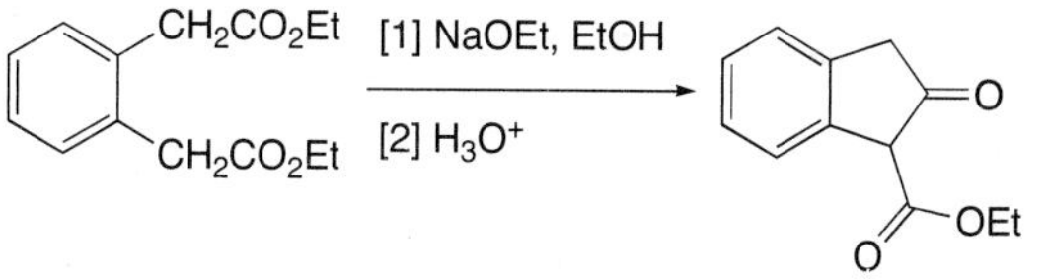
CH2CO2Et
CH2CO2Et
[1] NaOEt, EtOH
[2] H3O+
O
O
OEt

24.50

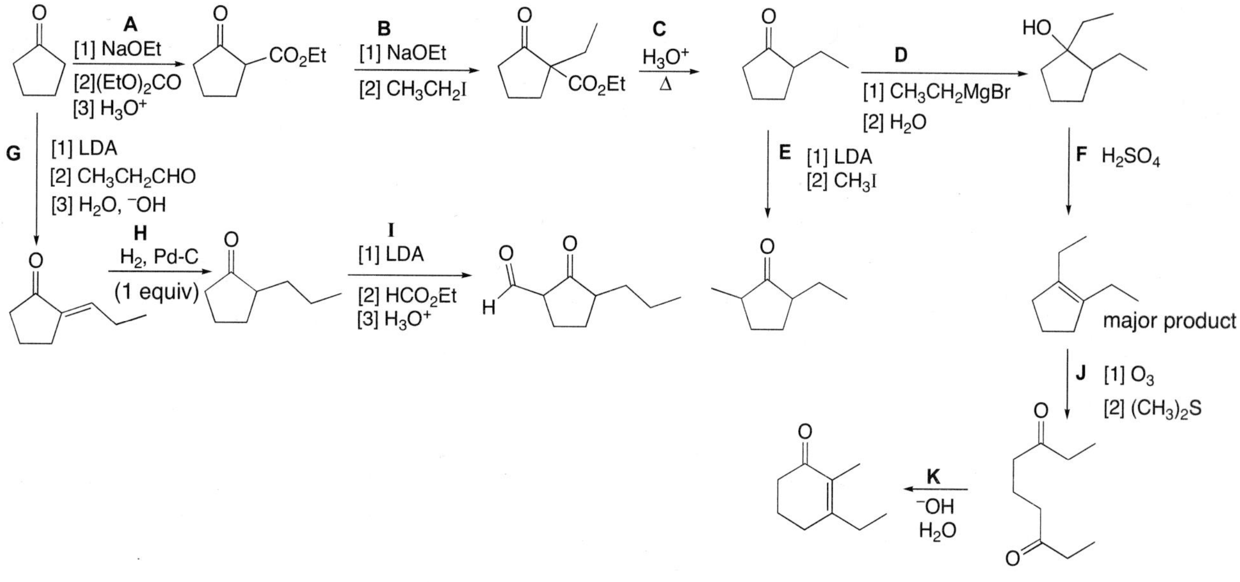
A
[1] NaOEt
[2](EtO)2CO
[3] H3O+
CO2Et
B
[1] NaOEt
[2] CH3CH2I
CO2Et
C
H3O+
Δ
D
[1] CH3CH2MgBr
[2] H2O
HO
G
[1] LDA
[2] CH3CH2CHO
[3] H2O, –OH
H
H2, Pd-C
(1 equiv)
I
[1] LDA
[2] HCO2Et
[3] H3O+
H
E
[1] LDA
[2] CH3I
F
H2SO4
major product
J
[1] O3
[2] (CH3)2S
K
–OH
H2O

24.51

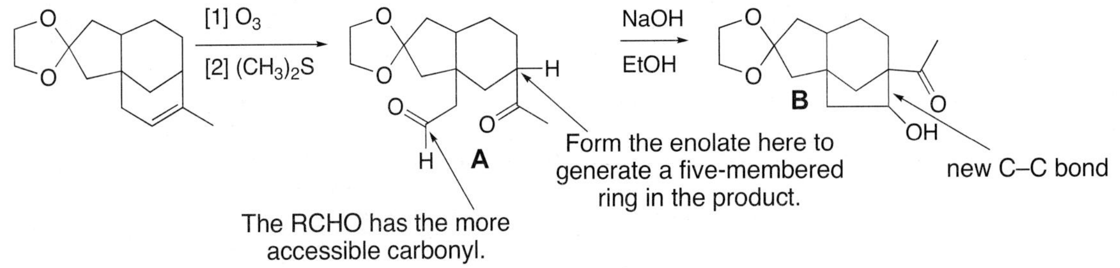
[1] O_3
[2] $(CH_3)_2S$
NaOH
EtOH
A
B
Form the enolate here to generate a five-membered ring in the product.
The RCHO has the more accessible carbonyl.
new C–C bond

24.52

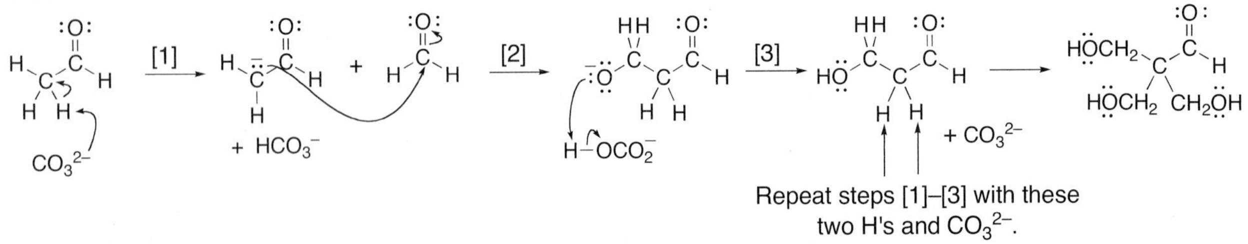
[1]
[2]
[3]
+ HCO_3^-
+ CO_3^{2-}
Repeat steps [1]–[3] with these two H's and CO_3^{2-}.

24.53 Enolate **A** is more substituted (and more stable) than either of the other two possible enolates and attacks an aldehyde carbonyl group, which is sterically less hindered than a ketone carbonyl. The resulting ring size (five-membered) is also quite stable. That is why 1-acetylcyclopentene is the major product.

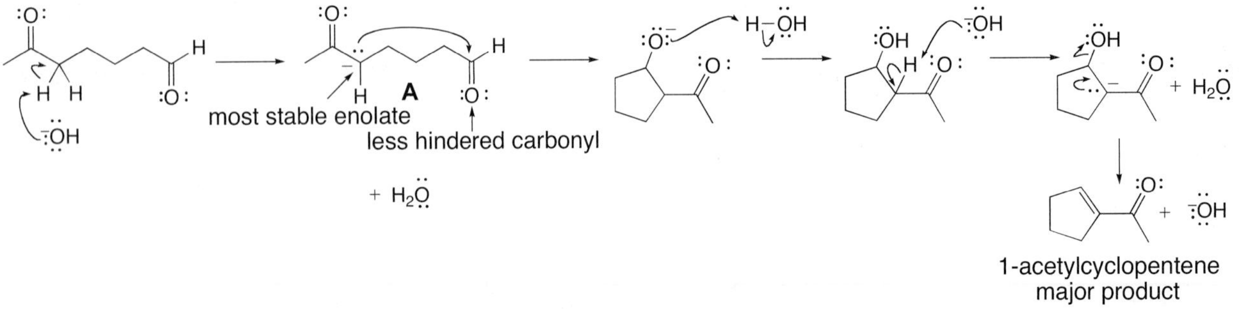
A
most stable enolate
less hindered carbonyl
+ H_2O
1-acetylcyclopentene
major product

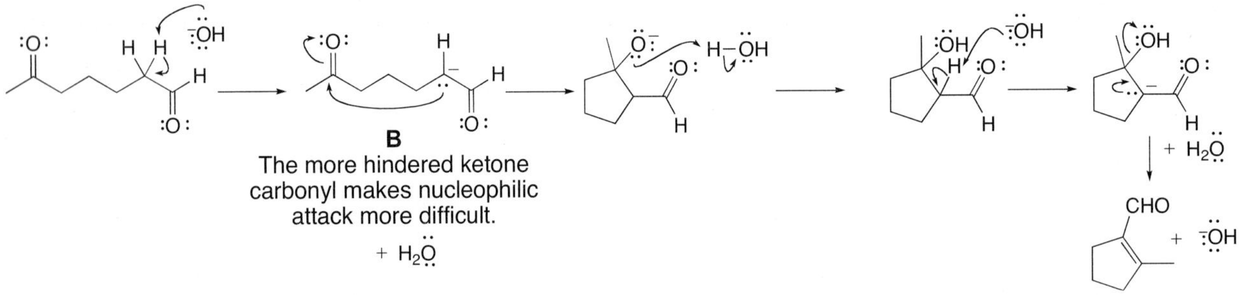
B
The more hindered ketone carbonyl makes nucleophilic attack more difficult.
+ H_2O
CHO

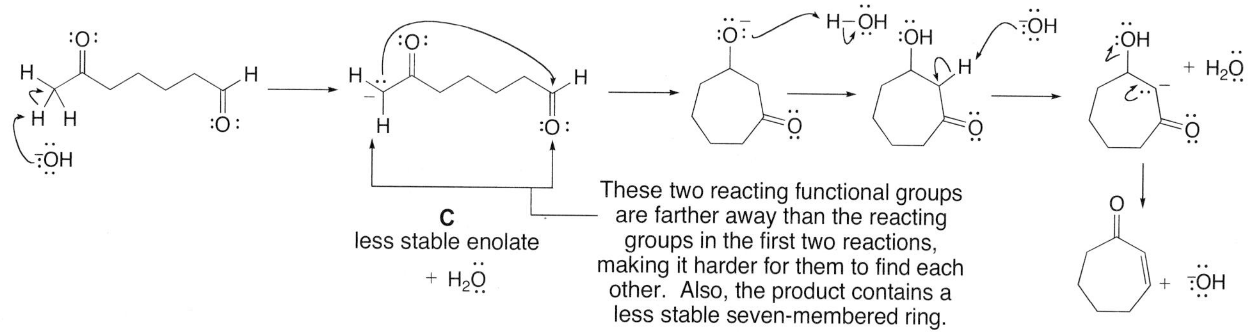
C
less stable enolate
+ H₂O
These two reacting functional groups are farther away than the reacting groups in the first two reactions, making it harder for them to find each other. Also, the product contains a less stable seven-membered ring.

24.54

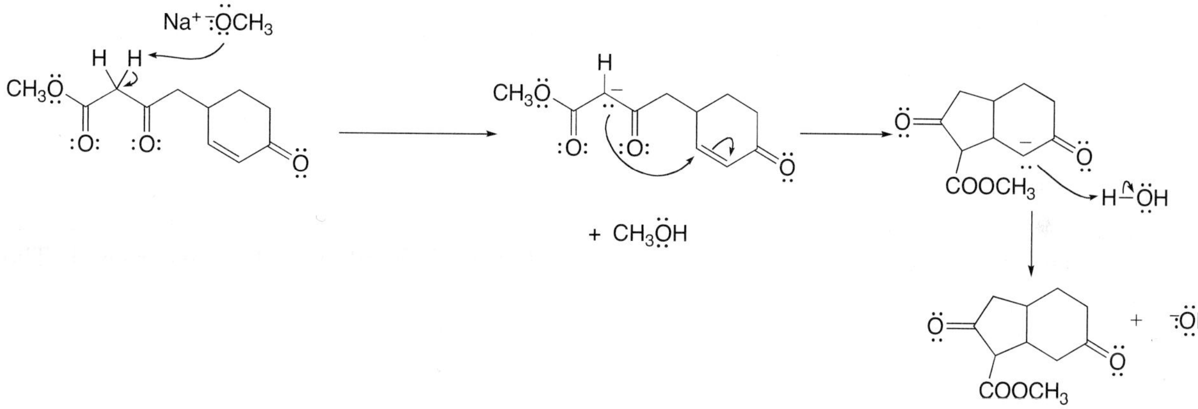

24.55 Removal of a proton from CH_3NO_2 forms an anion for which three resonance structures can be drawn.

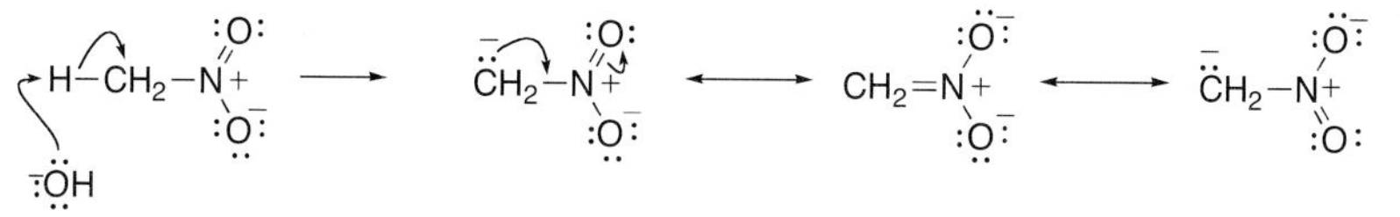

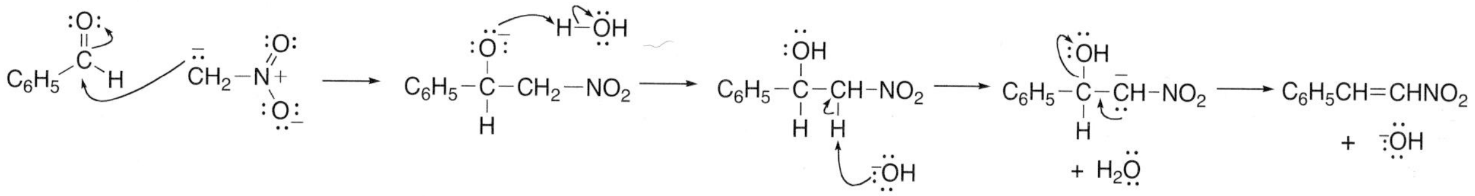

24.56 All enolates have a second resonance structure with a negative charge on O.

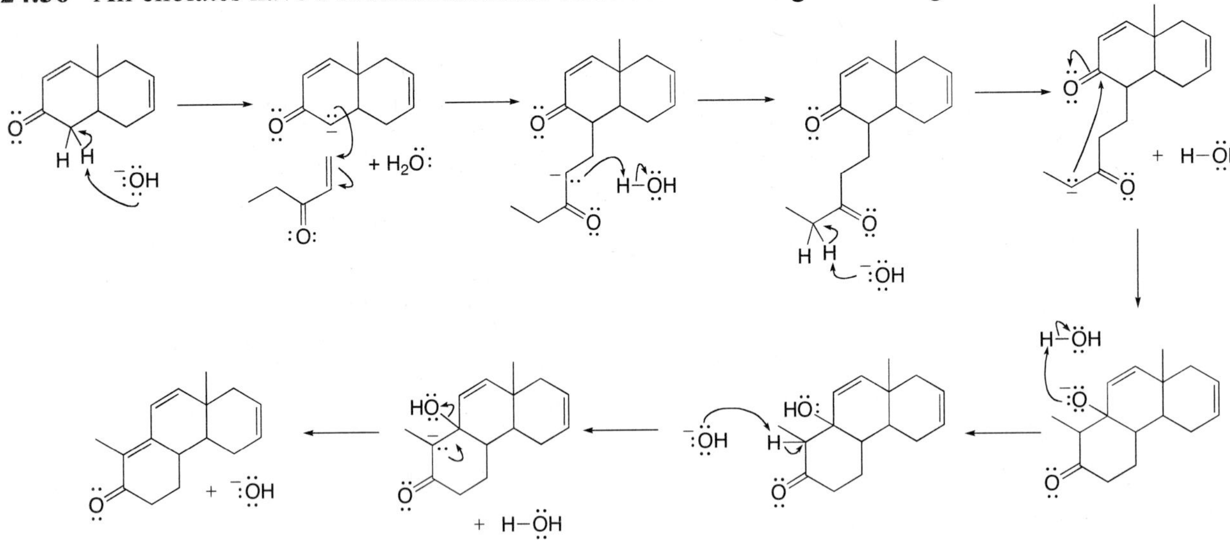

24.57 Et_3N reacts with phenylacetic acid to form a carboxylate anion that acts as a nucleophile to displace Br, forming **Y.** Then an intramolecular crossed-Claisen reaction yields rofecoxib.

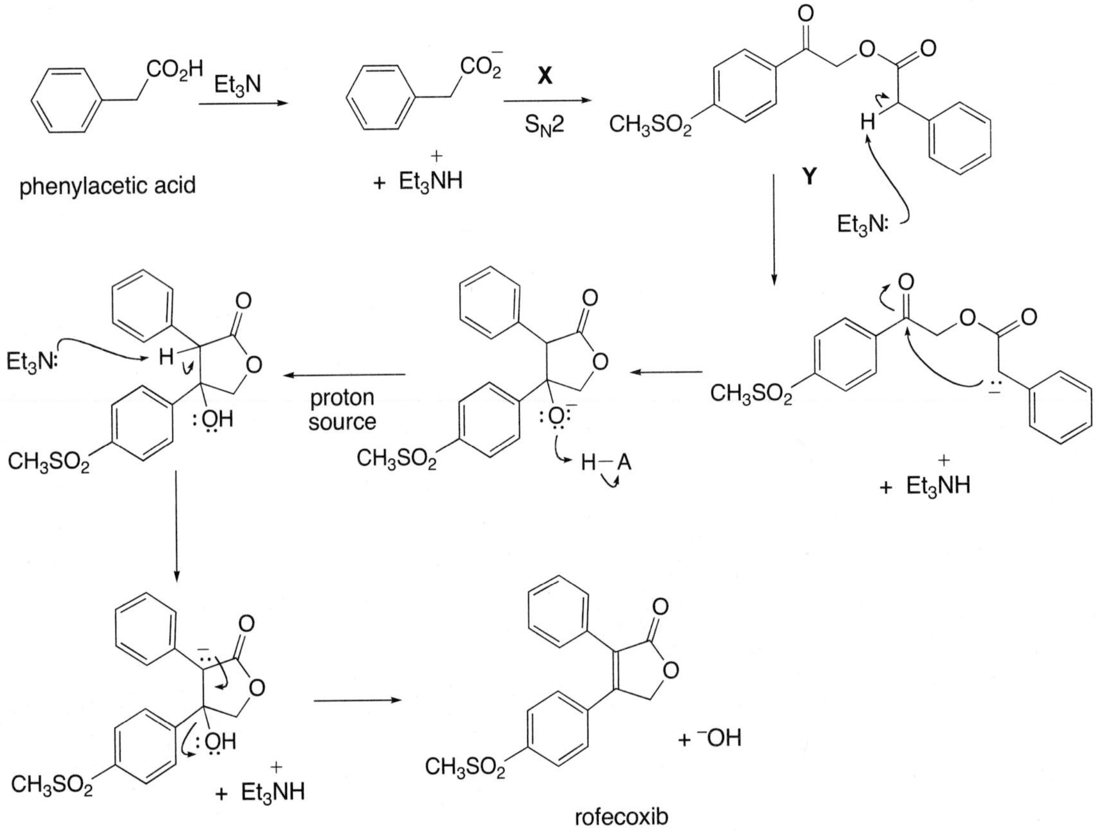

24.58 Polymerization occurs by repeated Michael reactions.

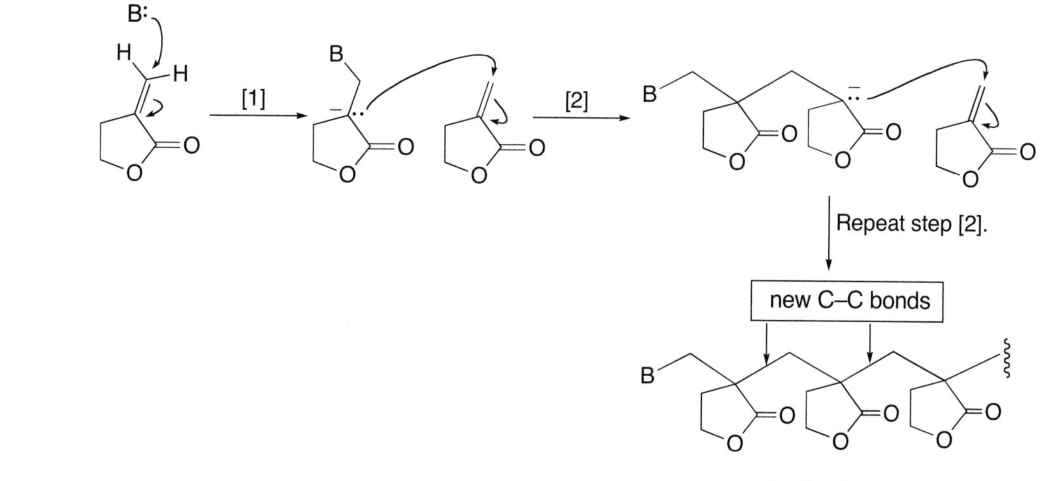

polytulipalin

24.59

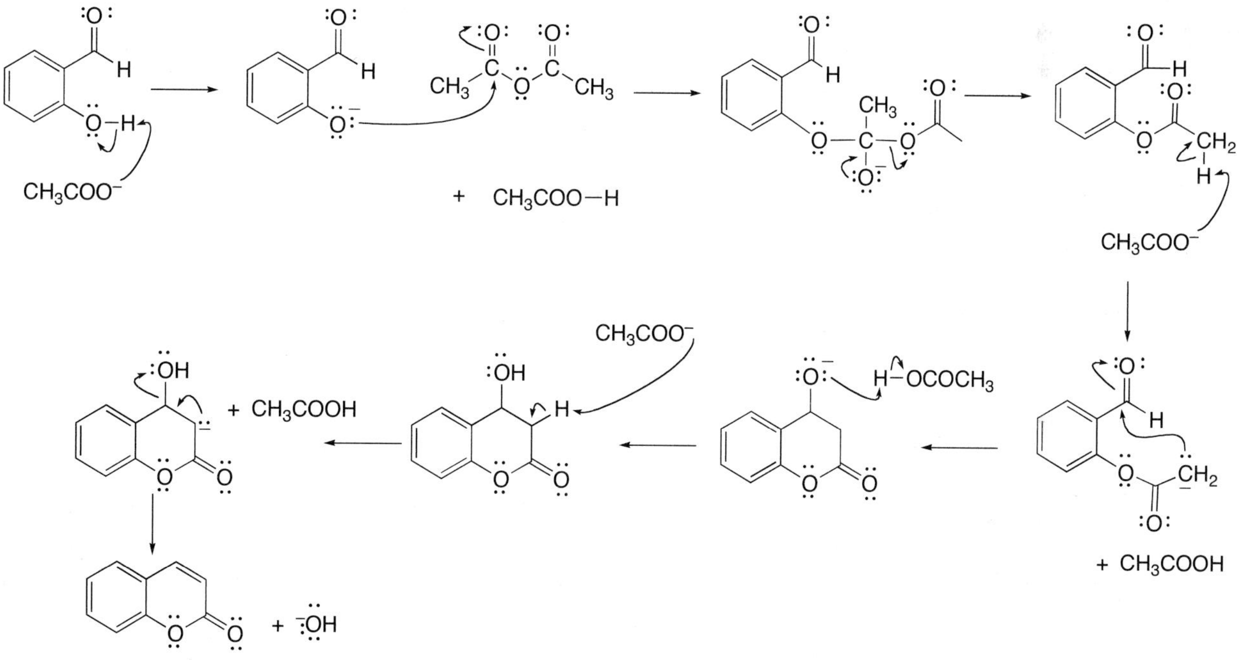

coumarin

24.60

a.

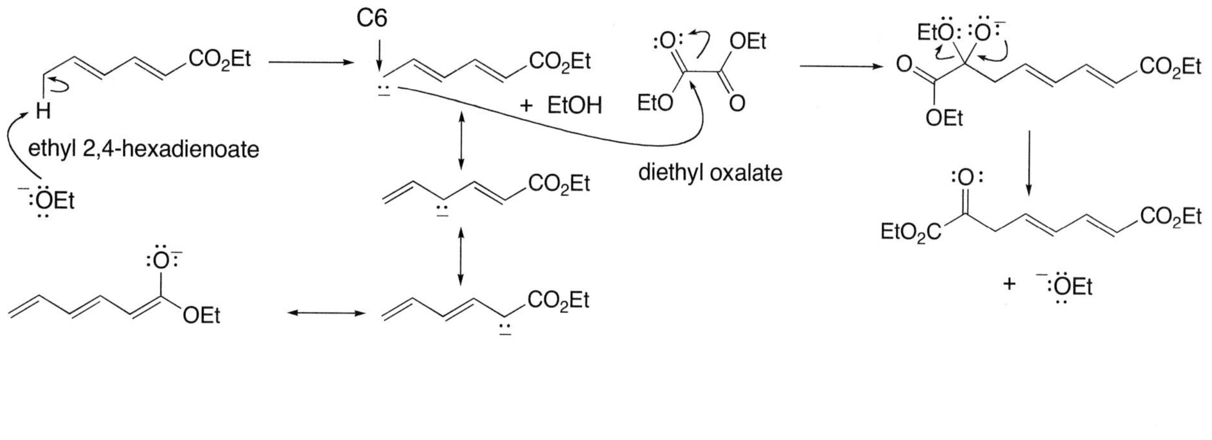

b. The protons on C6 are more acidic than other sp^3 hybridized C–H bonds because a highly resonance-stabilized carbanion is formed when a proton is removed. One resonance structure places a negative charge on the carbonyl O atom. This makes the protons on C6 similar in acidity to the α H's to a carbonyl.

c. This is a crossed Claisen because it involves the enolate of a conjugated ester reacting with the carbonyl group of a second ester.

24.61

a. 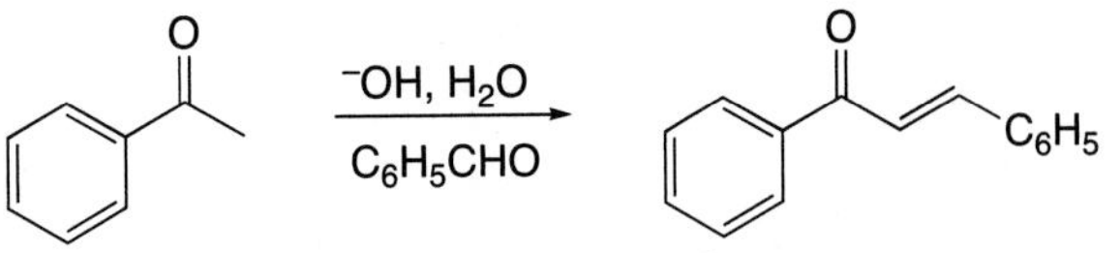
⁻OH, H₂O
C₆H₅CHO
C₆H₅

b. 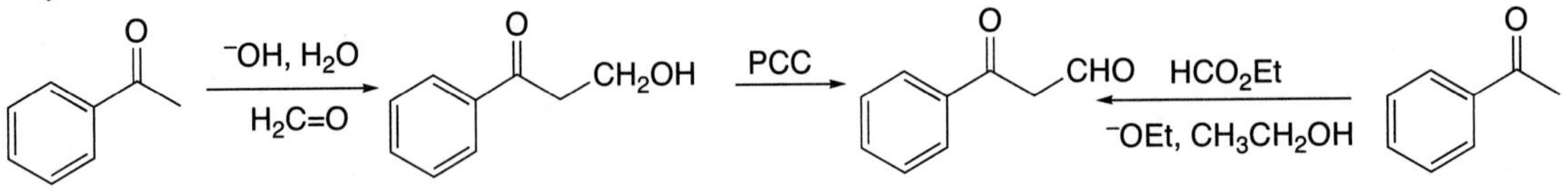
⁻OH, H₂O
H₂C=O
CH₂OH
PCC
CHO
HCO₂Et
⁻OEt, CH₃CH₂OH

c. 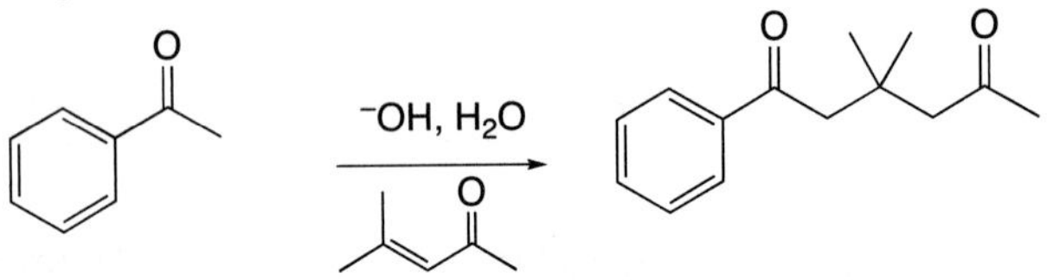
⁻OH, H₂O

d. 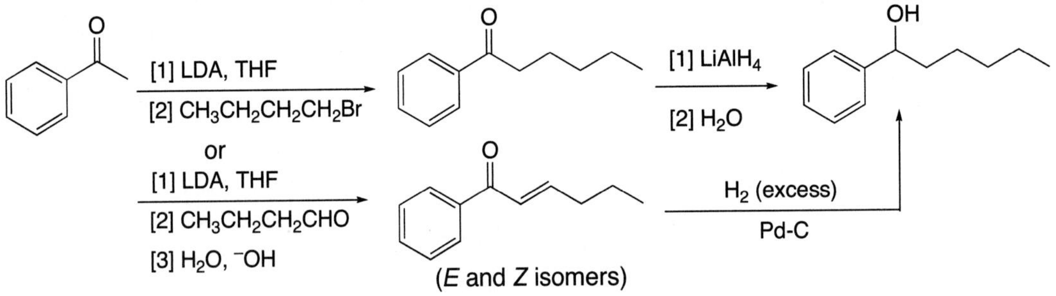
[1] LDA, THF
[2] CH₃CH₂CH₂CH₂Br
[1] LiAlH₄
[2] H₂O
OH
or
[1] LDA, THF
[2] CH₃CH₂CH₂CHO
[3] H₂O, ⁻OH
(E and Z isomers)
H₂ (excess)
Pd-C

e. 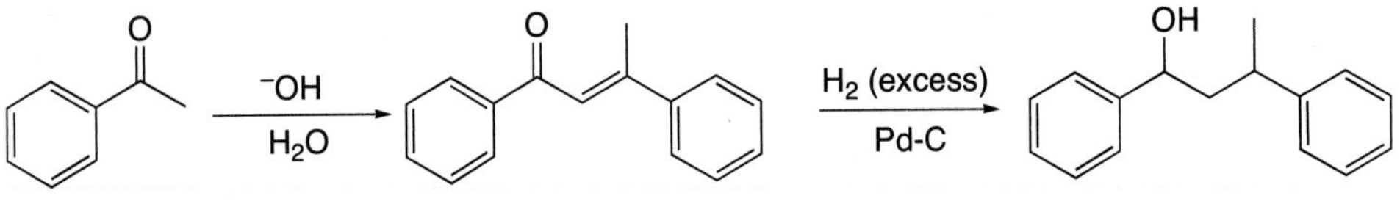
⁻OH
H₂O
H₂ (excess)
Pd-C
OH

24.62

a. 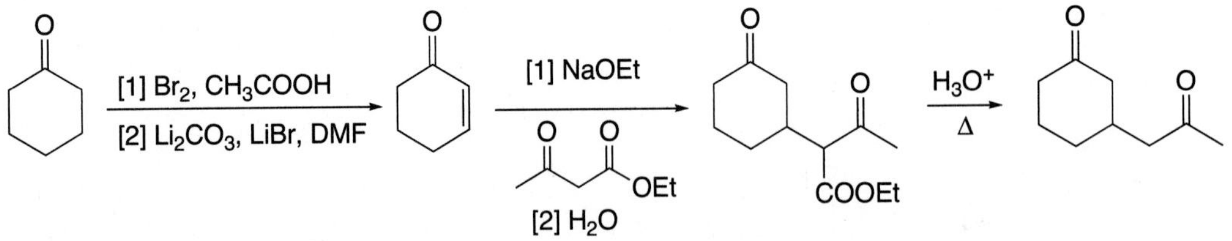
[1] Br₂, CH₃COOH
[2] Li₂CO₃, LiBr, DMF
[1] NaOEt
OEt
[2] H₂O
COOEt
H₃O⁺
Δ

b. 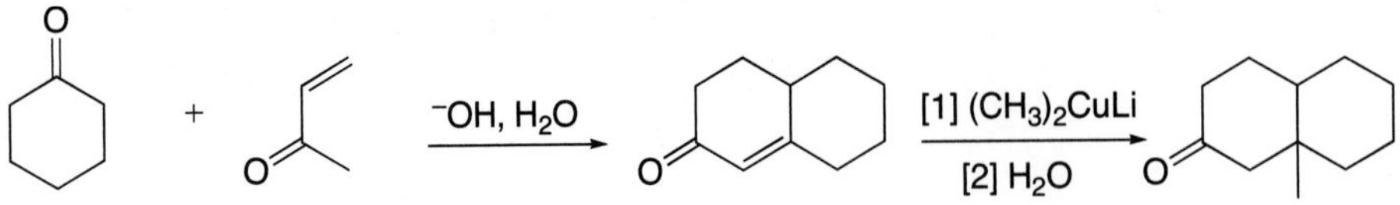
+
⁻OH, H₂O
[1] (CH₃)₂CuLi
[2] H₂O

24.63

a.
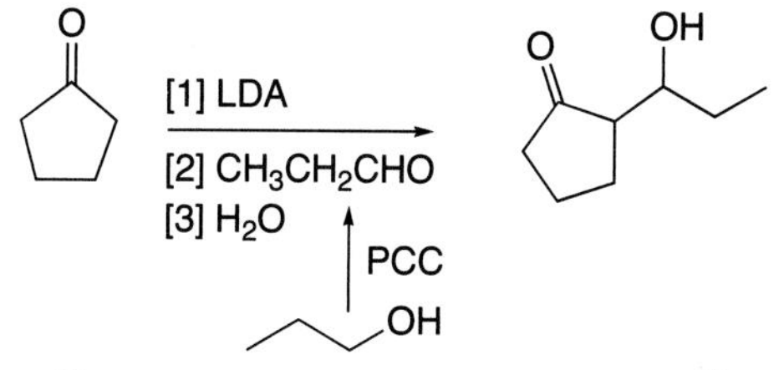
[1] LDA
[2] CH3CH2CHO
[3] H2O
PCC
OH
O
OH

b.
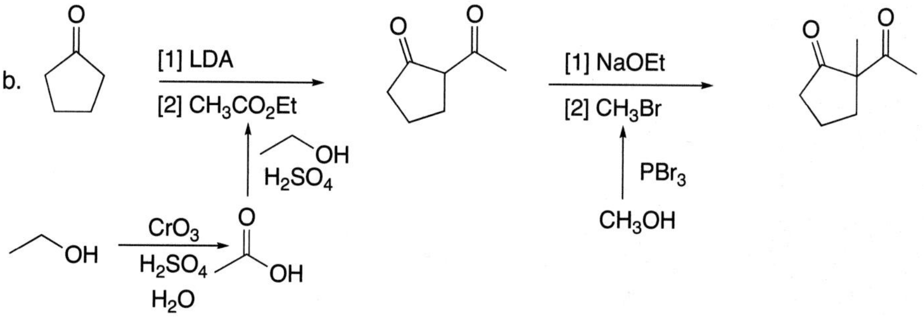
[1] LDA
[2] CH3CO2Et
OH
H2SO4
[1] NaOEt
[2] CH3Br
PBr3
CH3OH
OH
CrO3
H2SO4
H2O
OH

c.
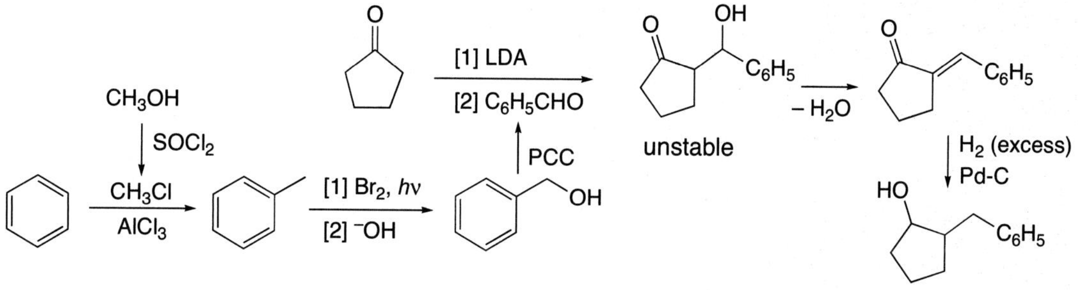
CH3OH
SOCl2
CH3Cl
AlCl3
[1] Br2, hν
[2] ⁻OH
OH
PCC
[1] LDA
[2] C6H5CHO
C6H5
unstable
– H2O
C6H5
H2 (excess)
Pd-C
HO
C6H5

d.
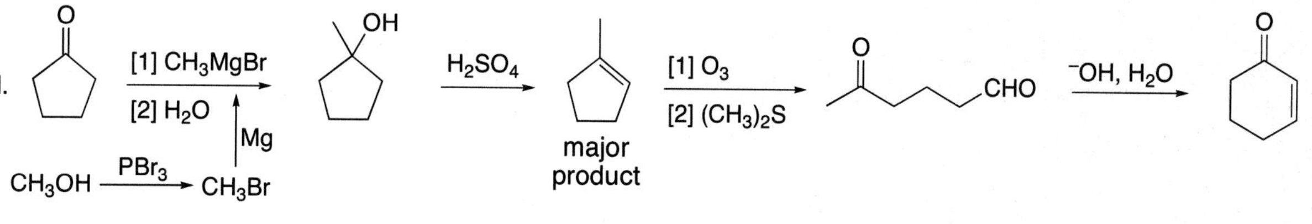
[1] CH3MgBr
[2] H2O
Mg
CH3OH
PBr3
CH3Br
OH
H2SO4
major product
[1] O3
[2] (CH3)2S
CHO
⁻OH, H2O

24.64

a.
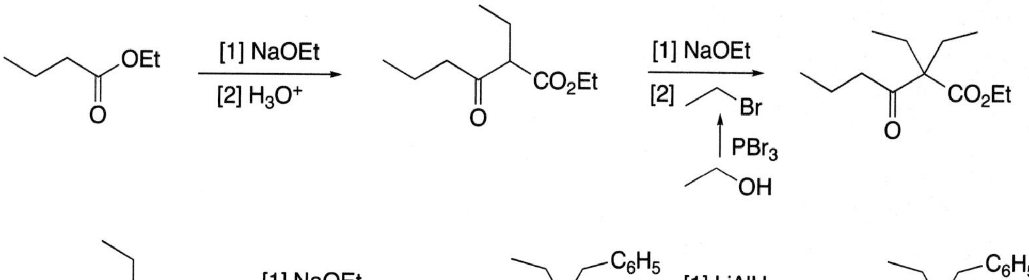
OEt
[1] NaOEt
[2] H3O+
CO2Et
[1] NaOEt
[2]
Br
PBr3
OH
CO2Et

b.
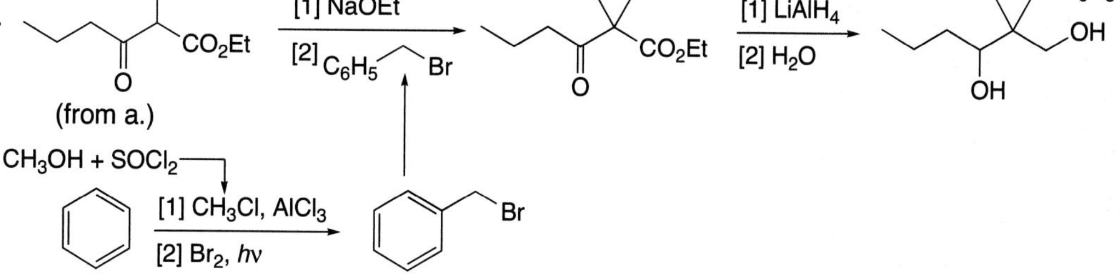
CO2Et
(from a.)
[1] NaOEt
[2] C6H5 Br
C6H5
CO2Et
[1] LiAlH4
[2] H2O
C6H5
OH
OH
CH3OH + SOCl2
[1] CH3Cl, AlCl3
[2] Br2, hν
Br

c.

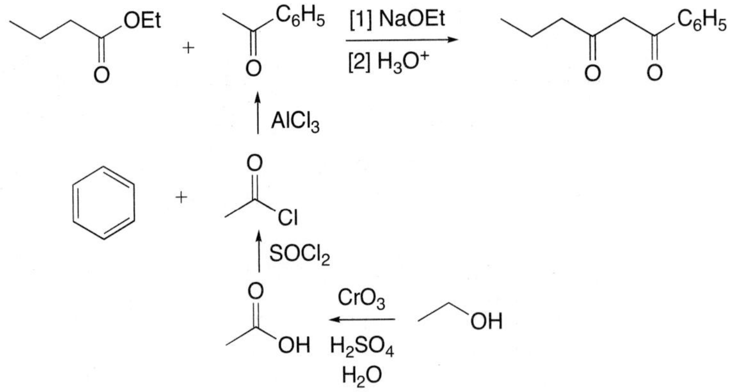
OEt
C_6H_5
[1] NaOEt
[2] H_3O^+
C_6H_5
$AlCl_3$
Cl
$SOCl_2$
CrO_3
OH
OH
H_2SO_4
H_2O

24.65

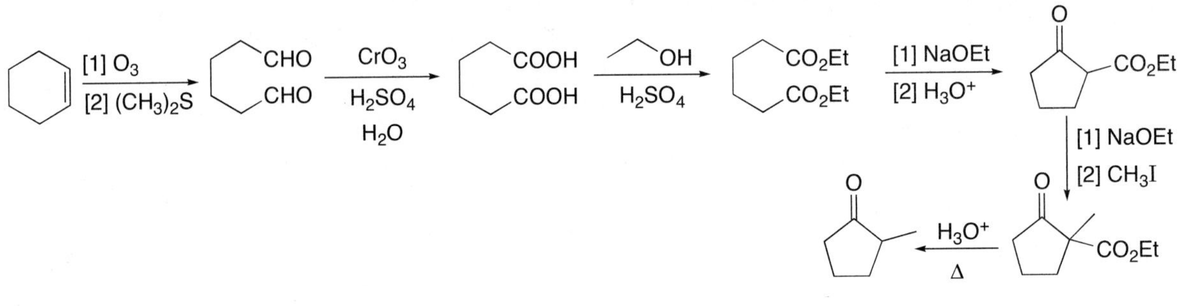
[1] O_3
[2] $(CH_3)_2S$
CHO
CHO
CrO_3
H_2SO_4
H_2O
COOH
COOH
OH
H_2SO_4
CO_2Et
CO_2Et
[1] NaOEt
[2] H_3O^+
CO_2Et
[1] NaOEt
[2] CH_3I
CO_2Et
H_3O^+
Δ

24.66

a.

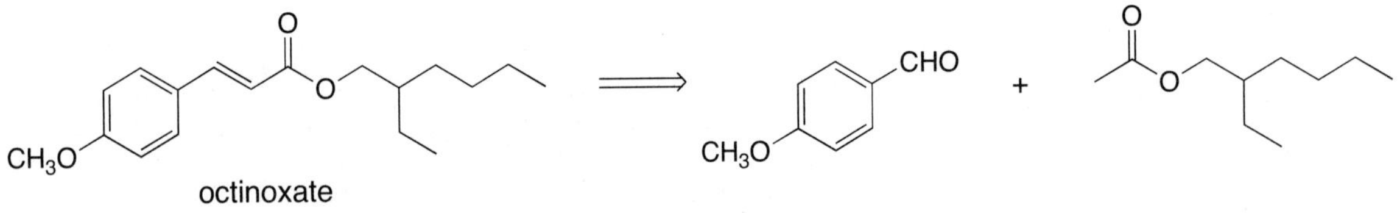
CH_3O
octinoxate
CHO
CH_3O

b.

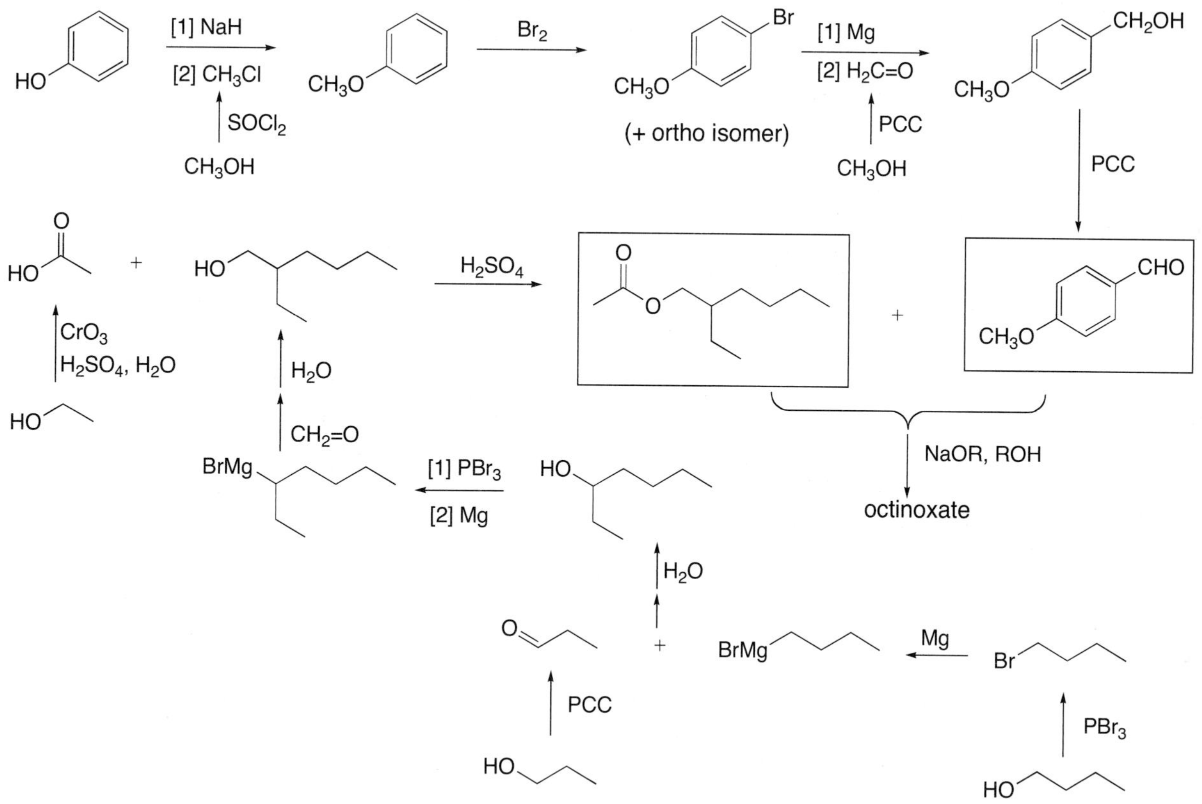

24.67

a.

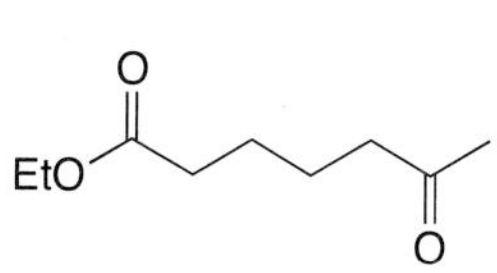

b.

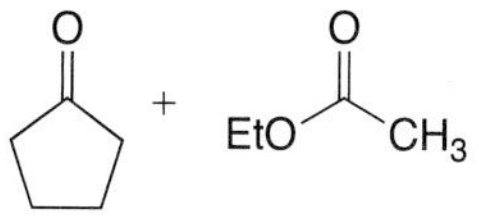

c.

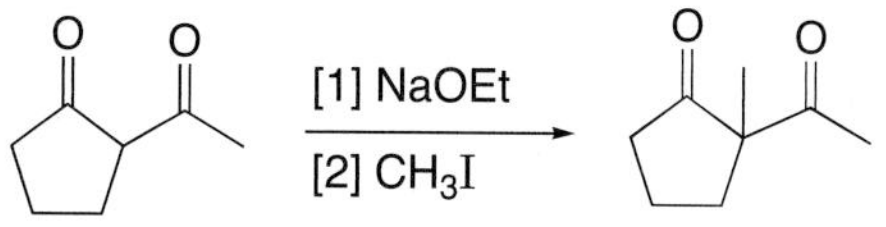

d.

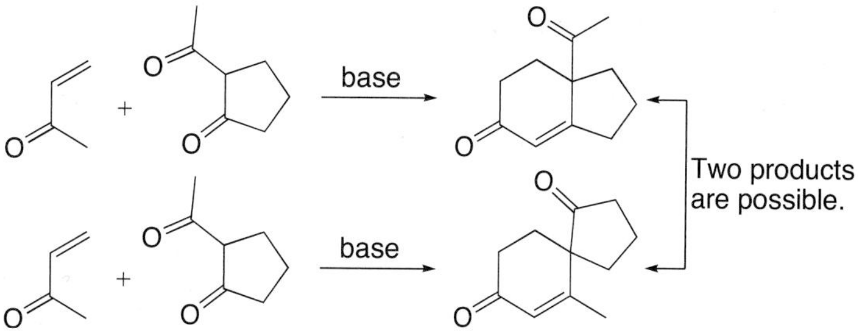

e.

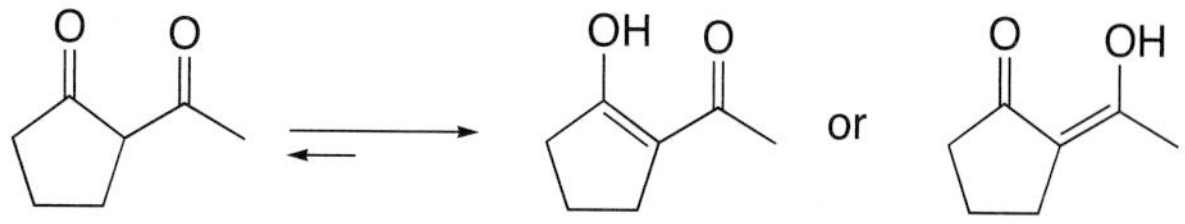

conjugated tautomers favored

24.68

a.

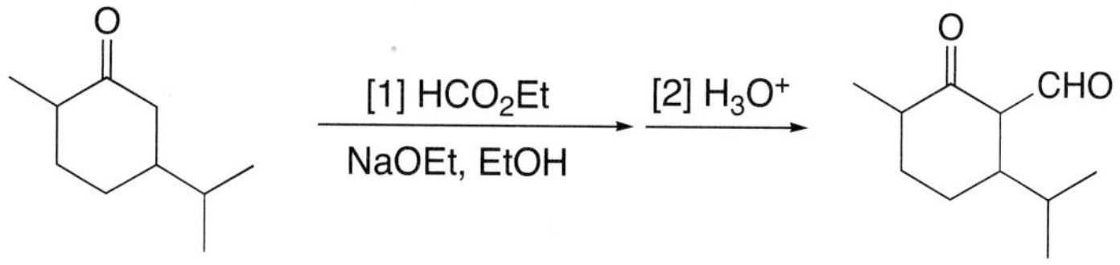

b.

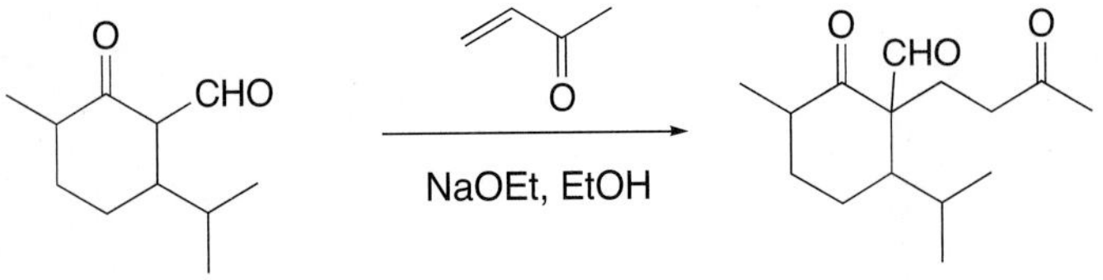

c.

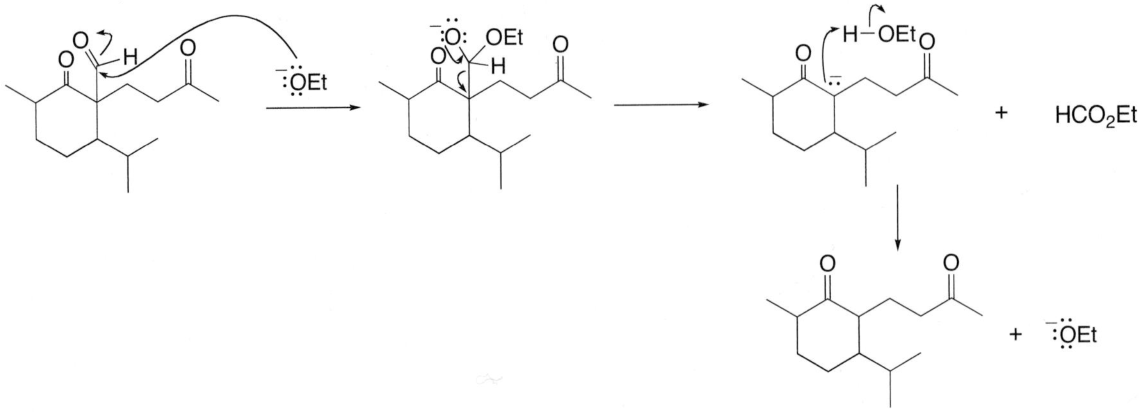

d.

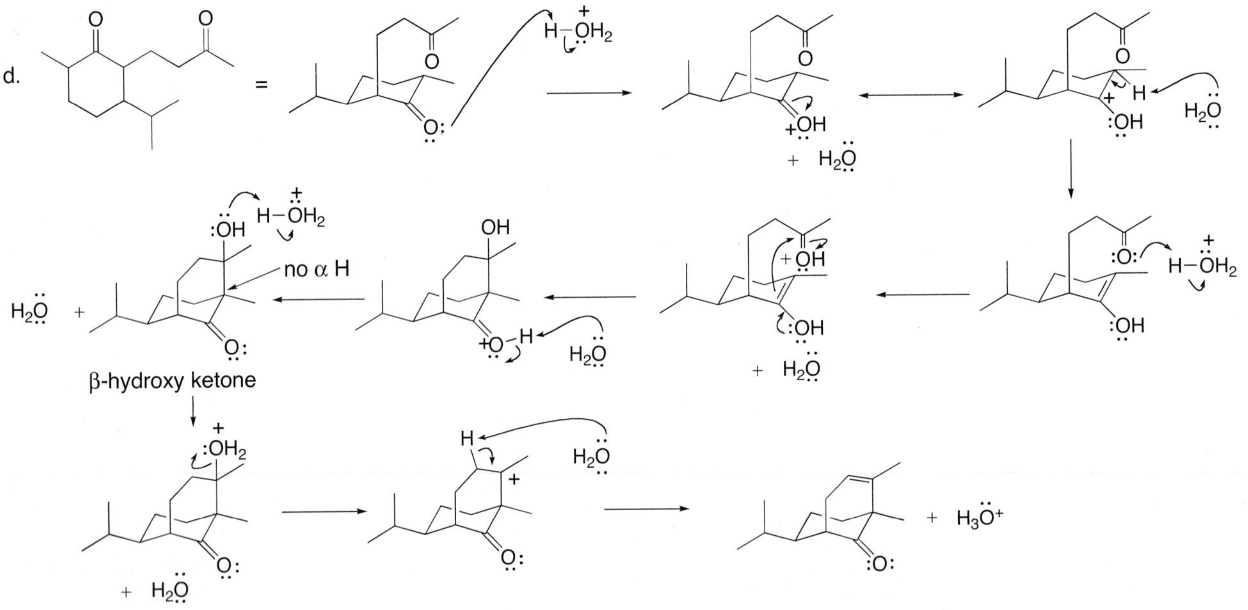

This reaction is an acid-catalyzed aldol that proceeds by way of enols not enolates. The β-hydroxy ketone initially formed cannot dehydrate to form an α,β-unsaturated carbonyl because there is no H on the α carbon. Thus, dehydration occurs, but the resulting C=C is not conjugated with the C=O.

e.

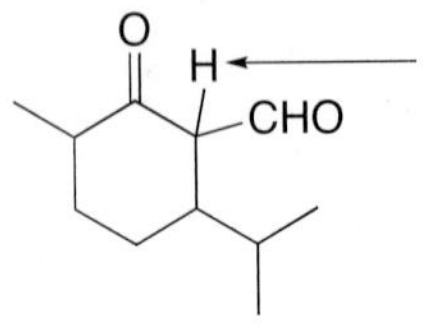

This H is now more acidic because it is located between two carbonyl groups. As a result, it is the most readily removed proton for the Michael reaction in the next step.

24.69

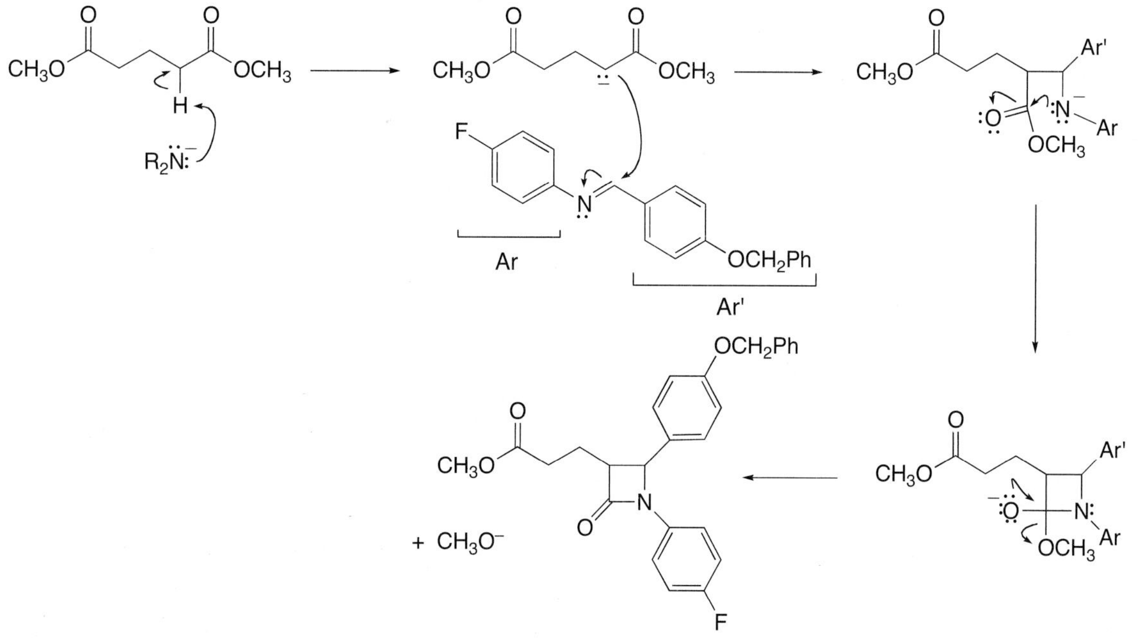

24.70 Rearrangement generates a highly resonance-stabilized enolate between two carbonyl groups.

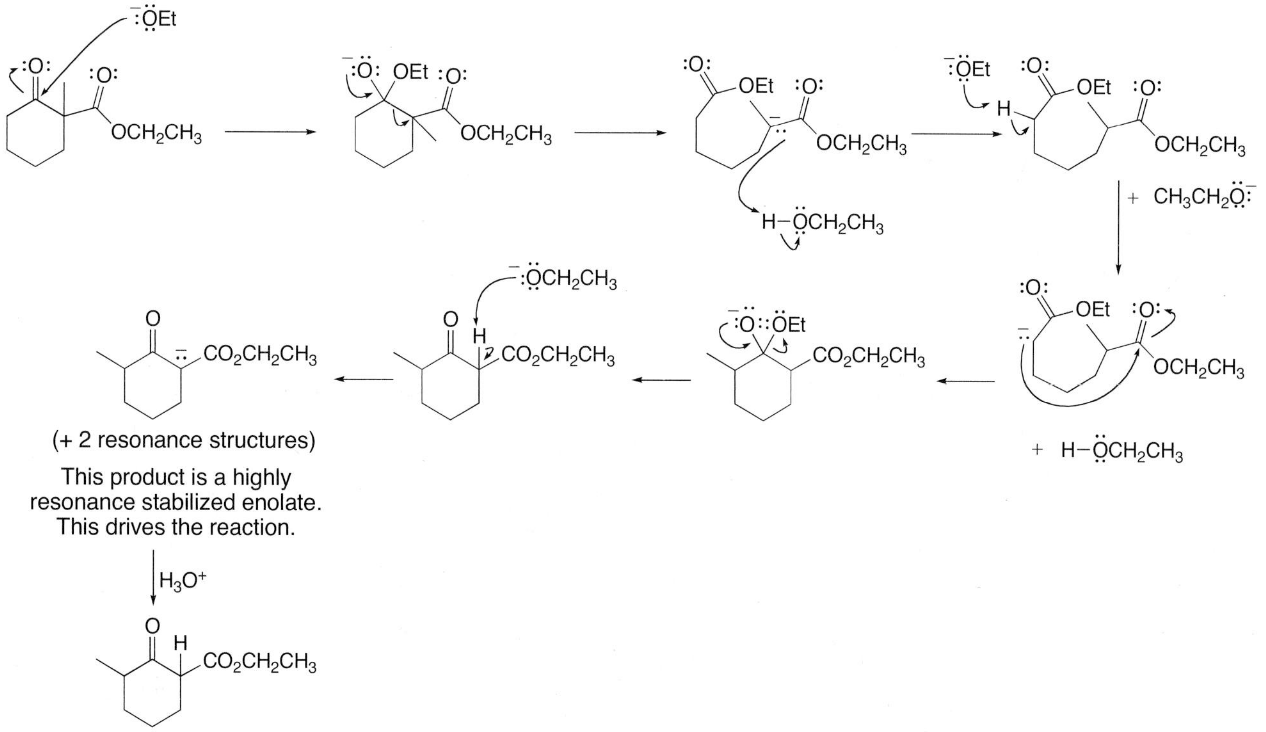
(+ 2 resonance structures)
This product is a highly resonance stabilized enolate. This drives the reaction.

24.71 All enolates have a second resonance structure with a negative charge on O.

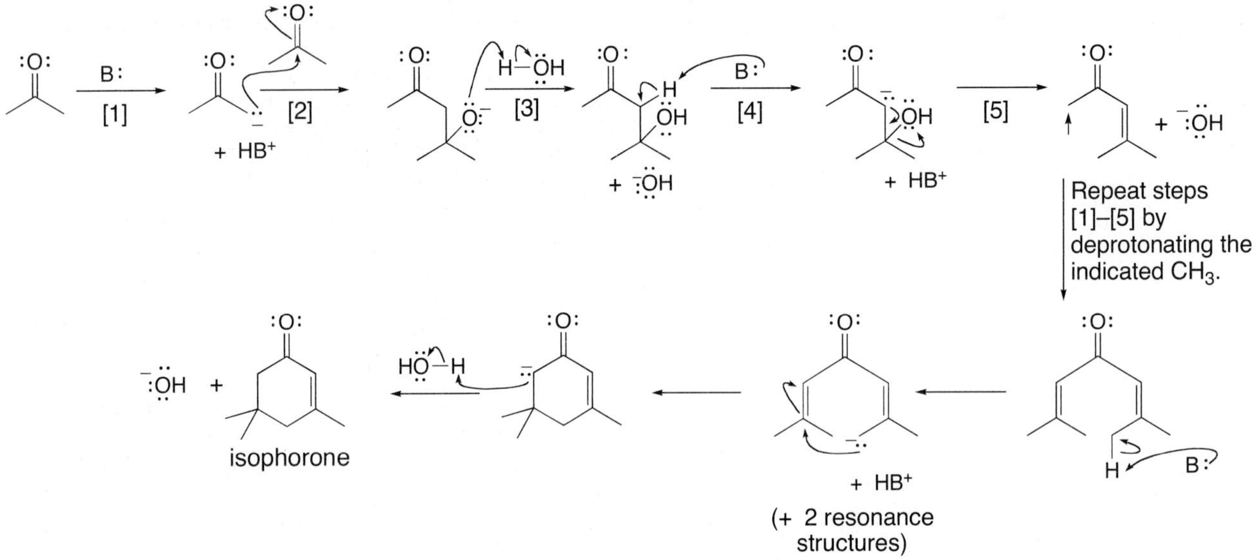

24.72 All enolates have a second resonance structure with a negative charge on O.

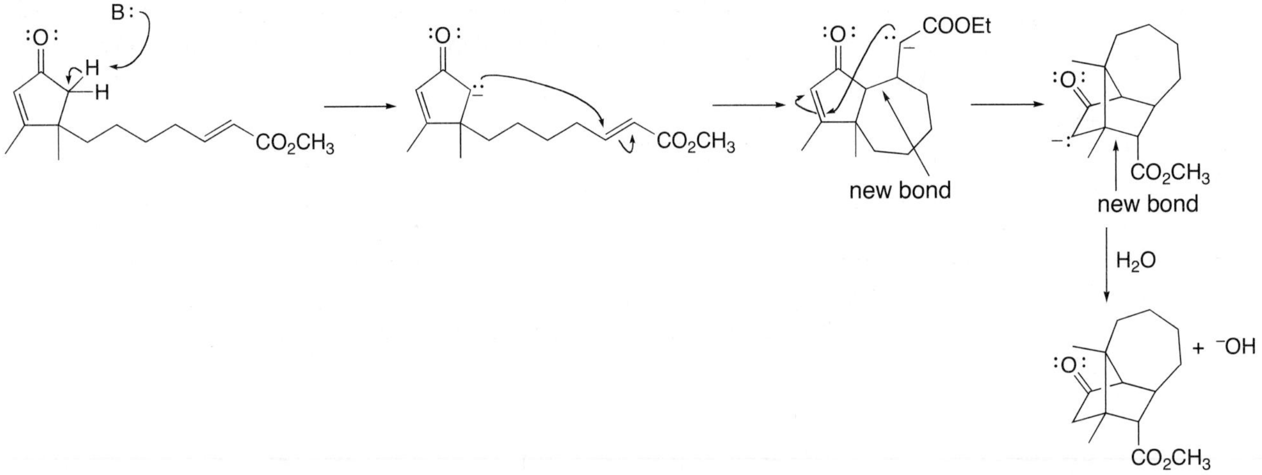

24.73

a.

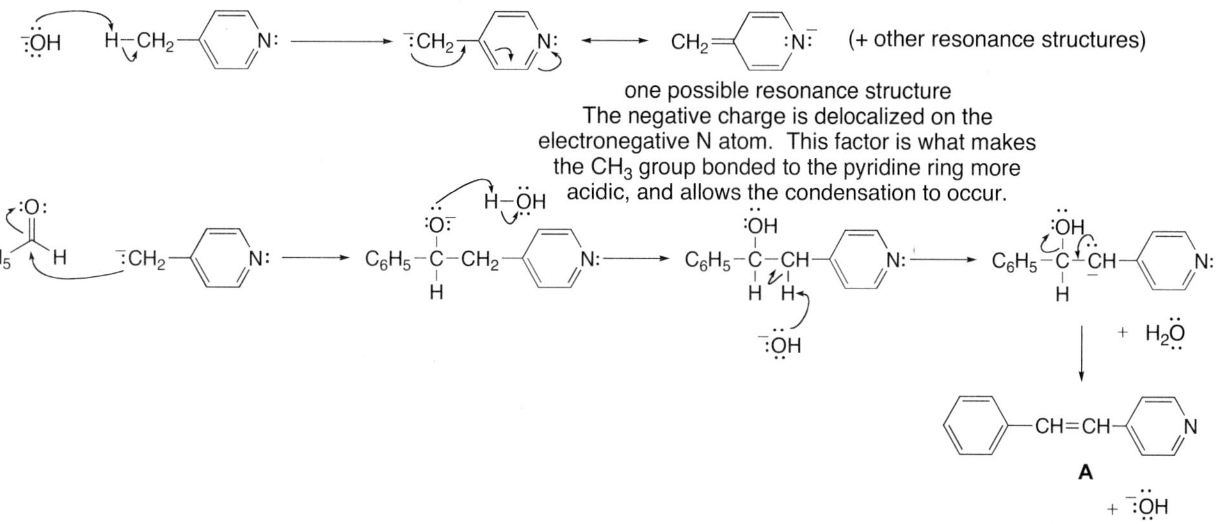
(+ other resonance structures)
one possible resonance structure
The negative charge is delocalized on the electronegative N atom. This factor is what makes the CH3 group bonded to the pyridine ring more acidic, and allows the condensation to occur.
A

b. The condensation reaction can occur only if the CH_3 group bonded to the pyridine ring has acidic hydrogens that can be removed with ^{-}OH.

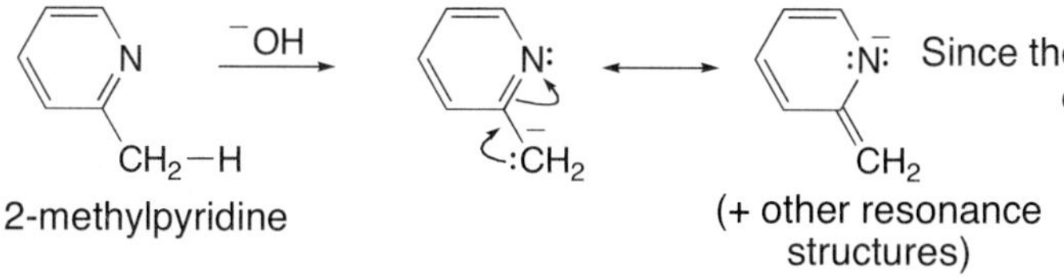
2-methylpyridine
(+ other resonance structures)

Since the negative charge is delocalized on the N, the CH_3 contains acidic H's and reaction will occur.

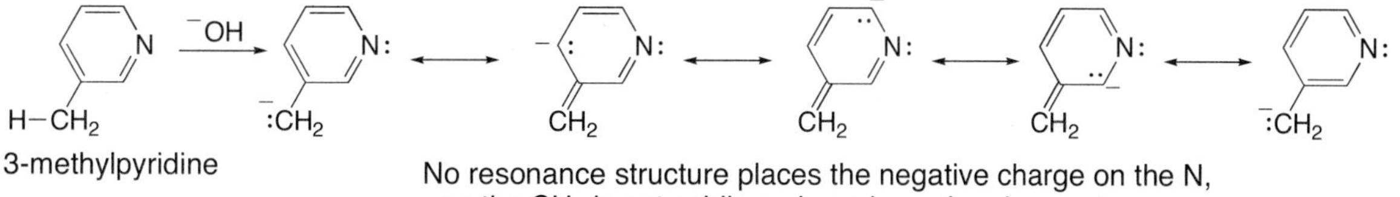
3-methylpyridine

No resonance structure places the negative charge on the N, so the CH_3 is not acidic and condensation does not occur.

24.74 Since the reaction takes place in acid, enols are involved. After the initial condensation reaction, the NH_2 and C=O groups form an imine by an intramolecular reaction.

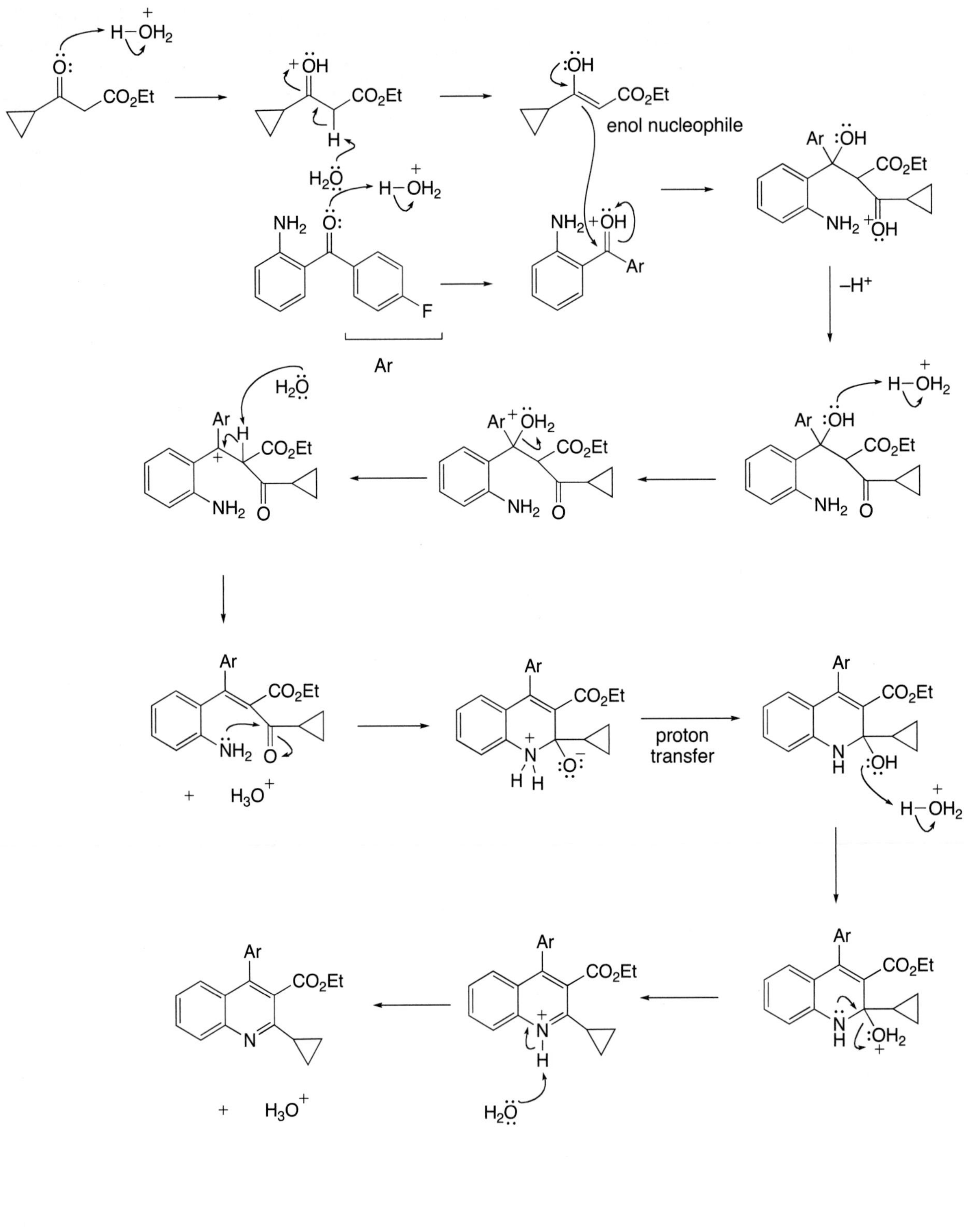

24.75

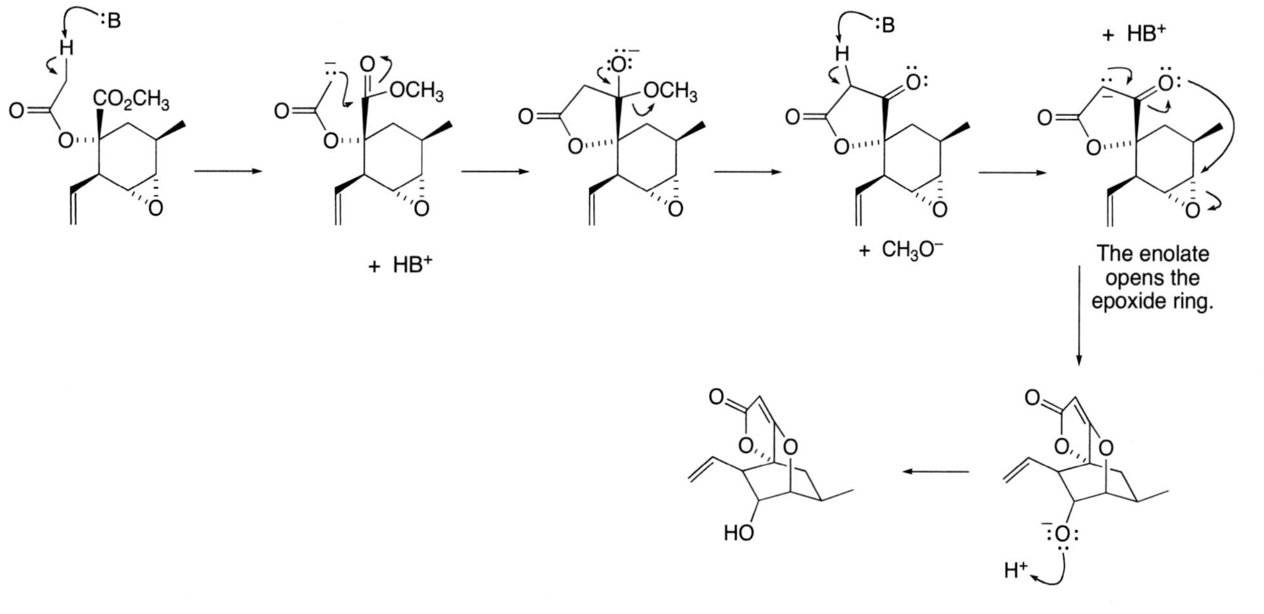
:B
H
CO_2CH_3
O
OCH₃
+ HB⁺
+ CH₃O⁻
+ HB⁺
The enolate opens the epoxide ring.
HO
H⁺

Chapter 25 Amines

Chapter Review

General facts

- Amines are organic nitrogen compounds having the general structure RNH_2, R_2NH, or R_3N, with a lone pair of electrons on N (25.1).
- Amines are named using the suffix *-amine* (25.3).
- All amines have polar C–N bonds. Primary (1°) and 2° amines have polar N–H bonds and are capable of intermolecular hydrogen bonding (25.4).
- The lone pair on N makes amines strong organic bases and nucleophiles (25.8).

Summary of spectroscopic absorptions (25.5)

Mass spectra	Molecular ion	Amines with an odd number of N atoms give an odd molecular ion.
IR absorptions	N–H	3300–3500 cm^{-1} (two peaks for RNH_2, one peak for R_2NH)
^{1}H NMR absorptions	NH	0.5–5 ppm (no splitting with adjacent protons)
	CH–N	2.3–3.0 ppm (deshielded C_{sp^3}–H)
^{13}C NMR absorption	C–N	30–50 ppm

Comparing the basicity of amines and other compounds (25.10)

- Alkylamines (RNH_2, R_2NH, and R_3N) are more basic than NH_3 because of the electron-donating R groups (25.10A).
- Alkylamines (RNH_2) are more basic than arylamines ($C_6H_5NH_2$), which have a delocalized lone pair from the N atom (25.10B).
- Arylamines with electron-donor groups are more basic than arylamines with electron-withdrawing groups (25.10B).
- Alkylamines (RNH_2) are more basic than amides ($RCONH_2$), which have a delocalized lone pair from the N atom (25.10C).
- Aromatic heterocycles with a localized electron pair on N are more basic than those with a delocalized lone pair from the N atom (25.10D).
- Alkylamines with a lone pair in an sp^3 hybrid orbital are more basic than those with a lone pair in an sp^2 hybrid orbital (25.10E).

Preparation of amines (25.7)

[1] Direct nucleophilic substitution with NH_3 and amines (25.7A)

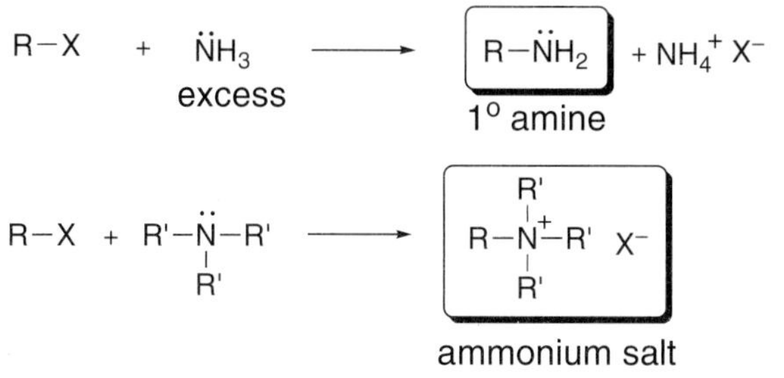

- The mechanism is S_N2.
- The reaction works best for CH_3X or RCH_2X.
- The reaction works best to prepare 1° amines and ammonium salts.

[2] Gabriel synthesis (25.7A)

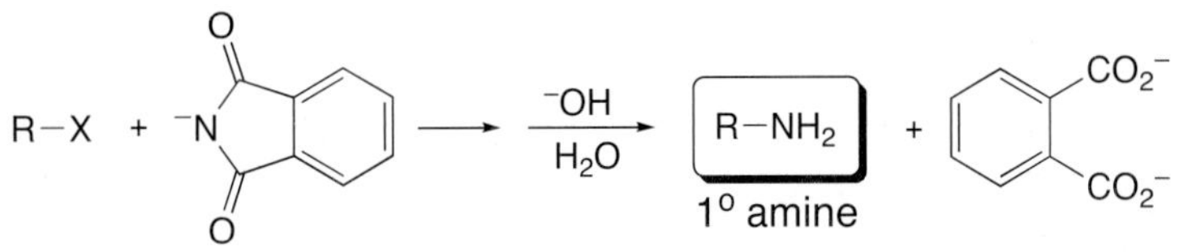

- The mechanism is S_N2.
- The reaction works best for CH_3X or RCH_2X.
- Only 1° amines can be prepared.

[3] Reduction methods (25.7B)

[a] From nitro compounds

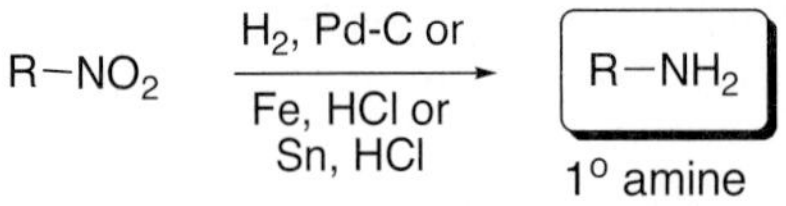

[b] From nitriles

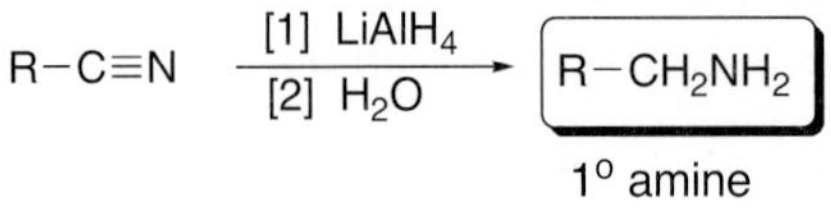

[c] From amides

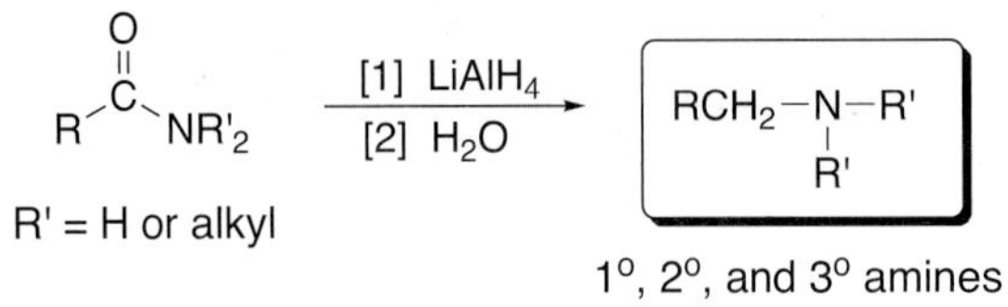

[4] Reductive amination (25.7C)

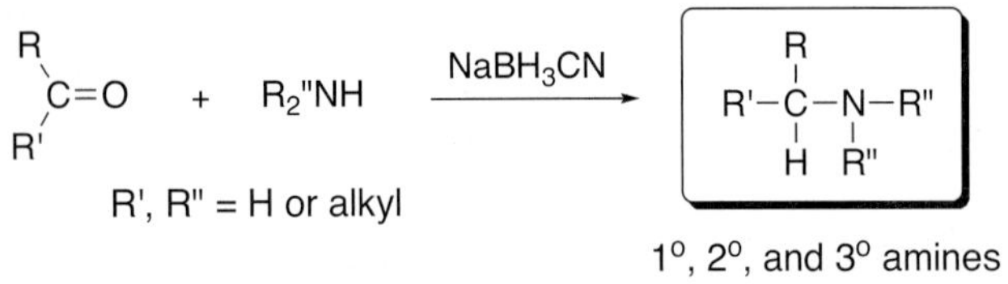

- Reductive amination adds one alkyl group (from an aldehyde or ketone) to a nitrogen nucleophile.
- Primary (1°), 2°, and 3° amines can be prepared.

Reactions of amines

[1] Reaction as a base (25.9)

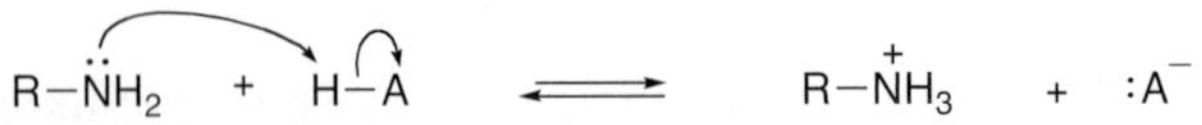

[2] Nucleophilic addition to aldehydes and ketones (25.11)

With 1° amines:

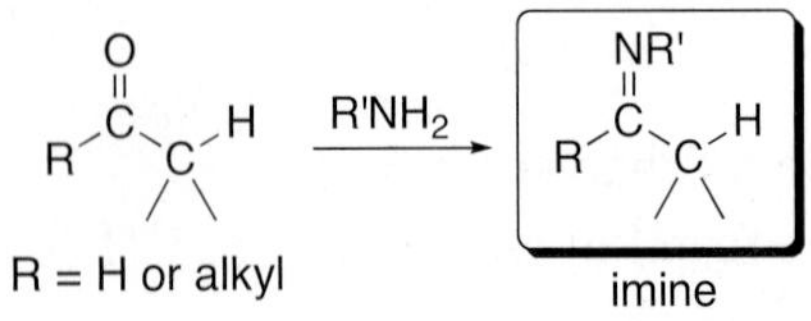

With 2° amines:

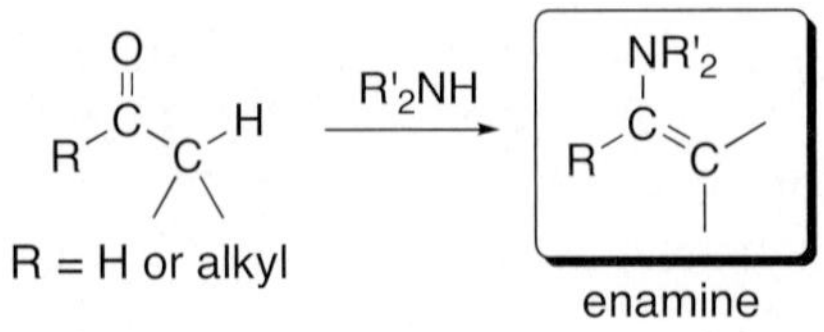

[3] Nucleophilic substitution with acid chlorides and anhydrides (25.11)

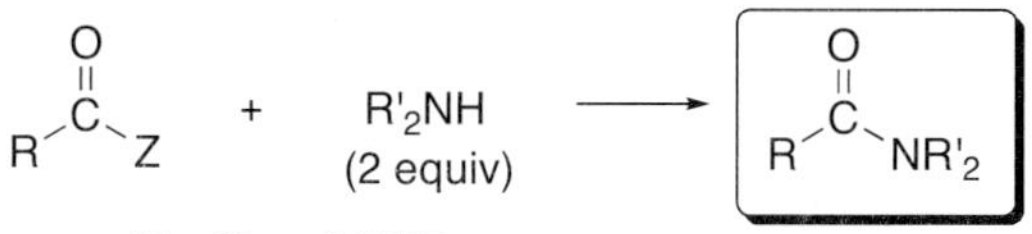
+
R'2NH
(2 equiv)
NR'2

Z = Cl or OCOR
R' = H or alkyl

1°, 2°, and 3° amides

[4] Hofmann elimination (25.12)

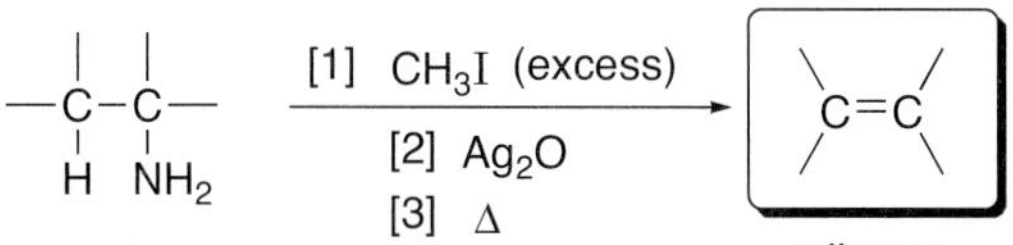
[1] CH3I (excess)
[2] Ag2O
[3] Δ

alkene

- The less substituted alkene is the major product.

[5] Reaction with nitrous acid (25.13)

With 1° amines:

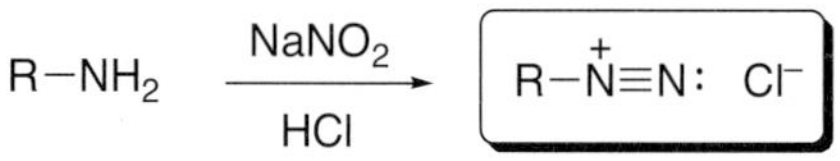
NaNO2
HCl

alkyl diazonium salt

With 2° amines:

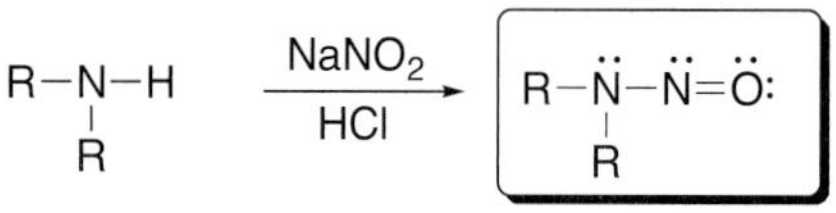
NaNO2
HCl

N-nitrosamine

Reactions of diazonium salts

[1] Substitution reactions (25.14)

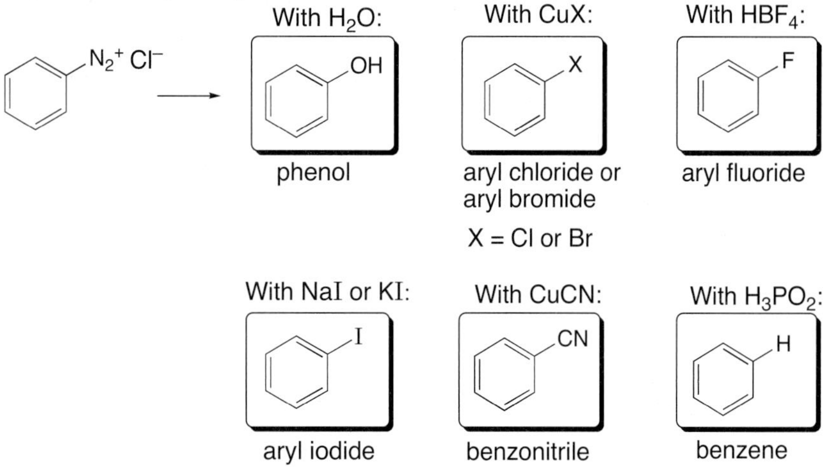
With H2O:
With CuX:
With HBF4:
phenol
aryl chloride or
aryl bromide
X = Cl or Br
aryl fluoride
With NaI or KI:
With CuCN:
With H3PO2:
aryl iodide
benzonitrile
benzene

[2] Coupling to form azo compounds (25.15)

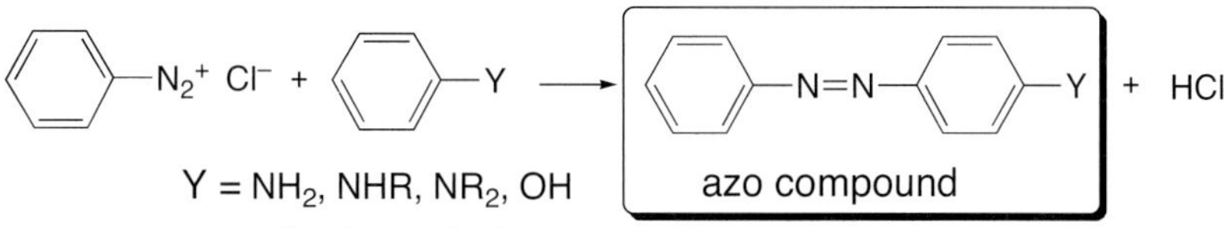
azo compound
+ HCl

Y = NH_2, NHR, NR_2, OH
(a strong electron-donor group)

Practice Test on Chapter Review

1. Give a systematic name for each of the following compounds.

a. 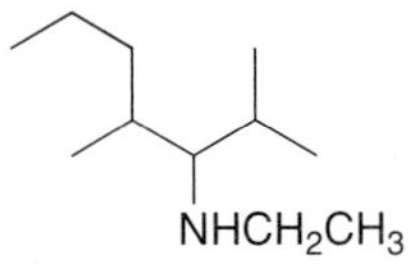
NHCH2CH3

b. 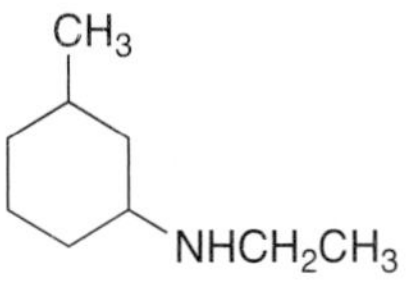
CH3
NHCH2CH3

2. (a) Which compound is the weakest base? (b) Which compound is the strongest base?

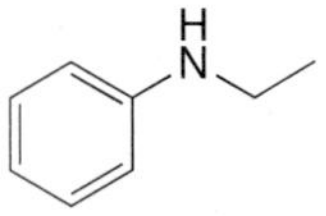
H
N
A

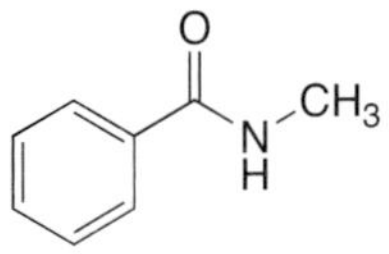
O
CH3
N
H
B

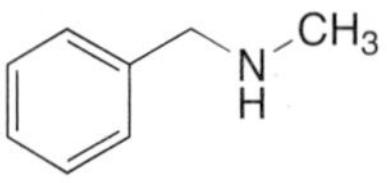
CH3
N
H
C

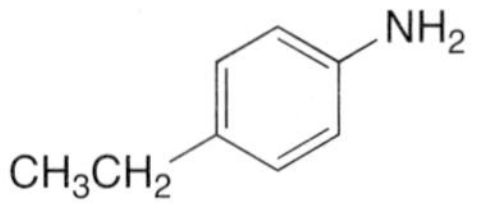
NH2
CH3CH2
D

3. (a) Which compound is the weakest base? (b) Which compound is the strongest base?

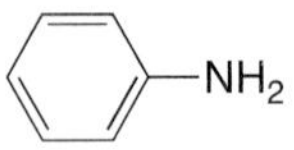
NH2
A

CH3
NH2
B

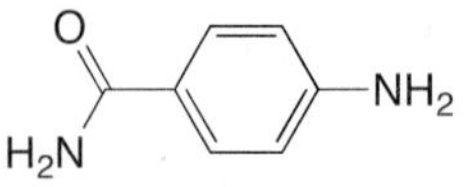
O
H2N
NH2
C

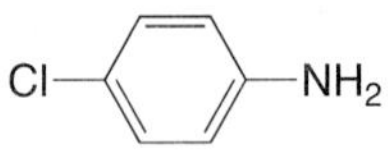
Cl
NH2
D

4. Draw the organic products formed in each of the following reactions.

a. 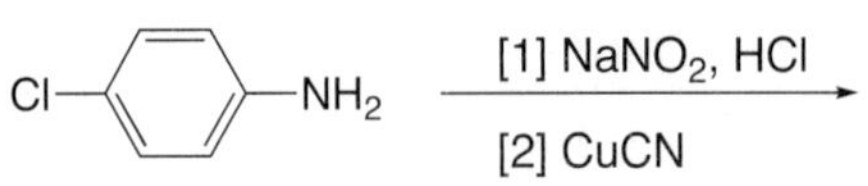
Cl
NH2
[1] NaNO2, HCl
[2] CuCN

b. 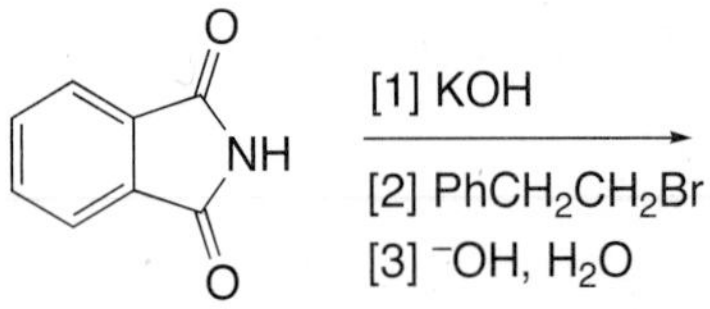
O
NH
O
[1] KOH
[2] PhCH2CH2Br
[3] ⁻OH, H2O

c. 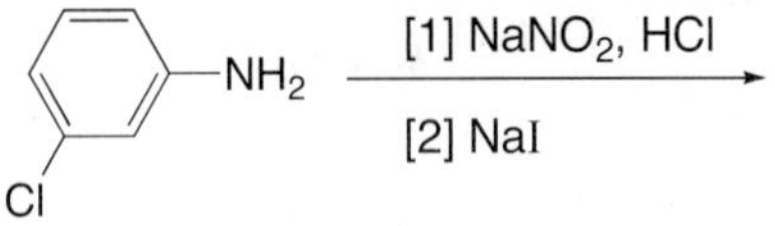
NH2
Cl
[1] NaNO2, HCl
[2] NaI

d. 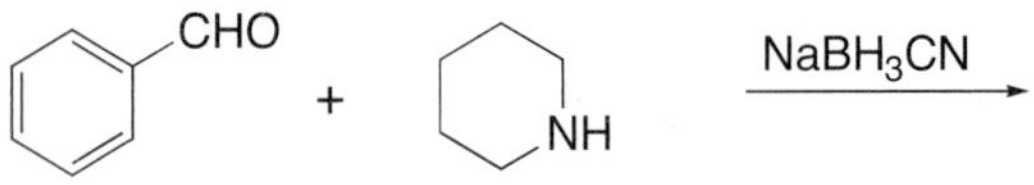
CHO
+
NH
NaBH3CN

e. 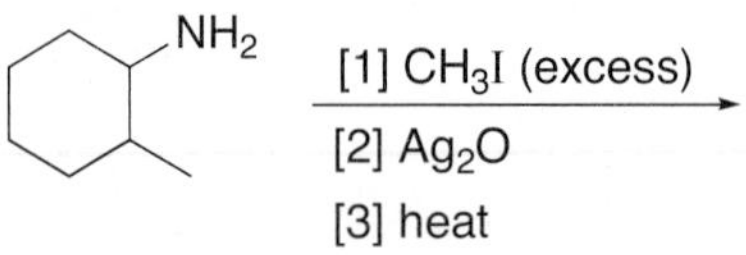
NH2
[1] CH3I (excess)
[2] Ag2O
[3] heat

5. Draw the products formed when the given amine is treated with [1] CH_3I (excess); [2] Ag_2O; [3] Δ, and indicate the major product. You need not consider any stereoisomers formed in the reaction.

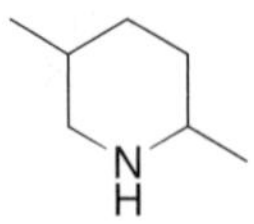
N
H

6. What organic starting materials are needed to synthesize **B** by reductive amination?

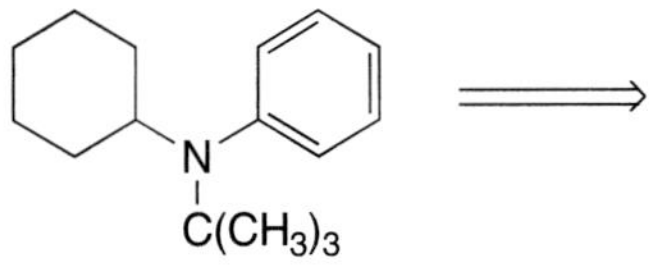

B

Answers to Practice Test

1.a. *N*-ethyl-2,4-dimethyl-3-heptanamine
b. *N*-ethyl-3-methylcyclohexanamine

2.a. **B**
b. **C**

3.a. **C**
b. **B**

4.

a. 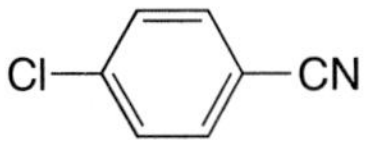

b. 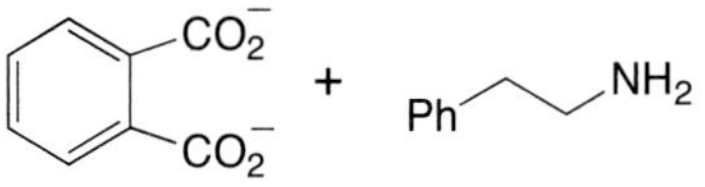

c. 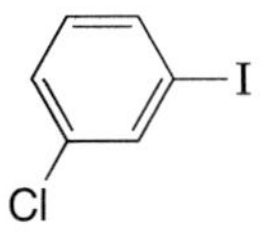

d. 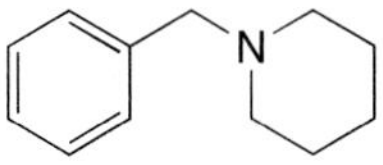

e. 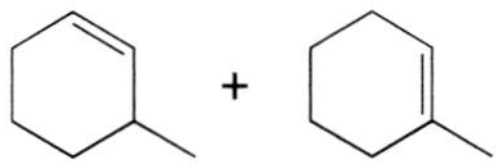

5.

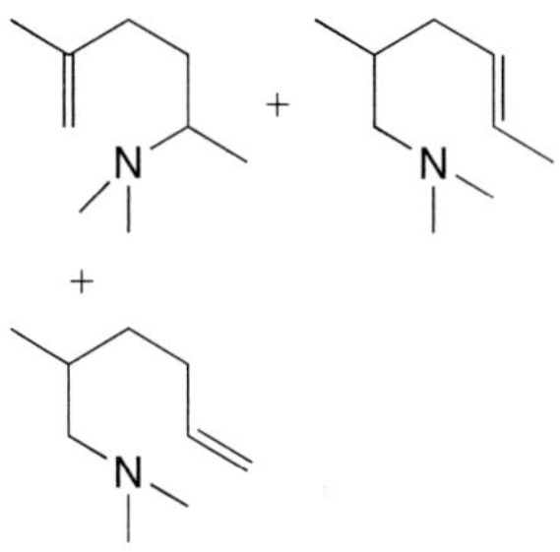

major

6.

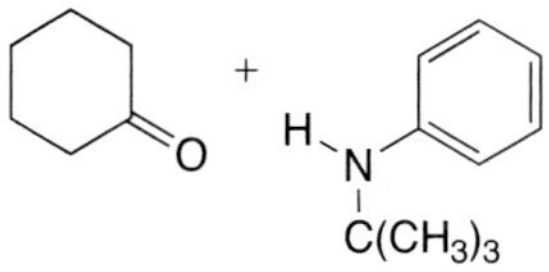

Answers to Problems

25.1 Amines are classified as 1°, 2°, or 3° by the number of alkyl groups bonded to the *nitrogen* atom.

a. 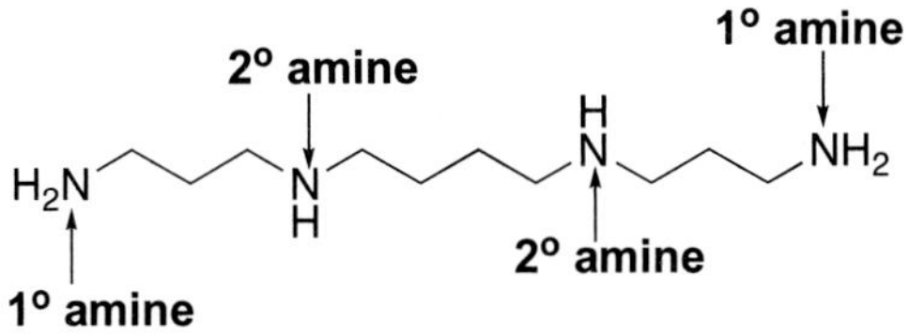

b. 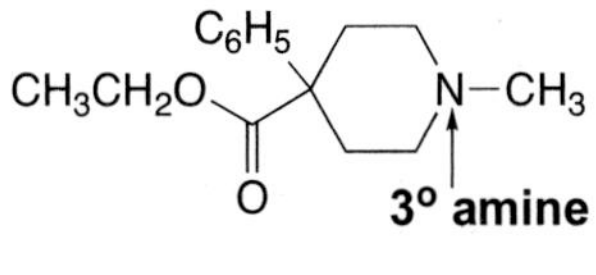

25.2

a. 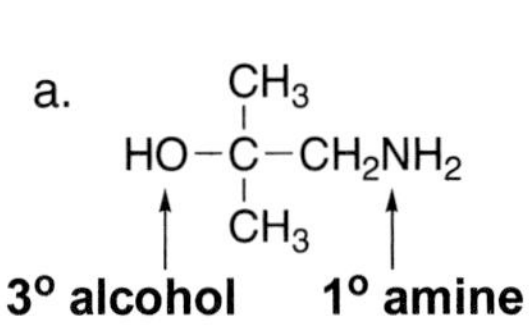

b. 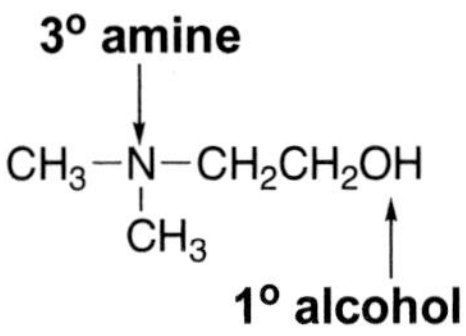

25.3 The N atom of a quaternary ammonium salt is a stereogenic center when the N is surrounded by four different groups. All stereogenic centers are circled.

a. 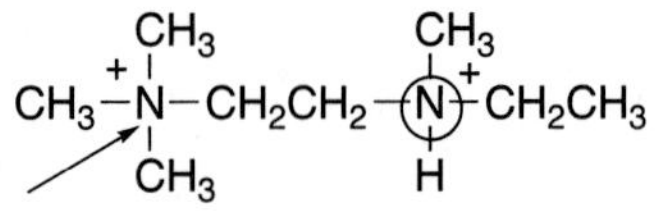

N has 3 similar groups.

b. 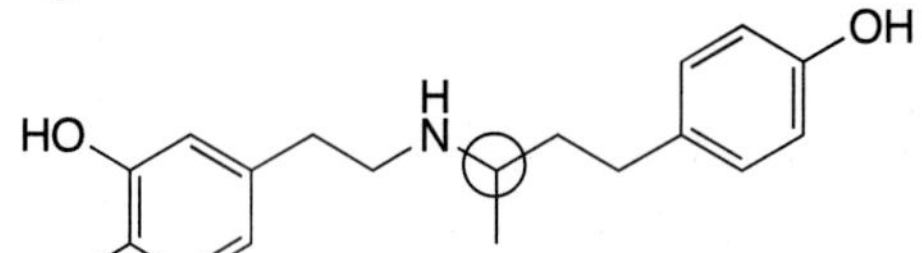

25.4

a. $CH_3CH_2CH(NH_2)CH_3$
2-butanamine
or
sec-butylamine

b. $(CH_3CH_2CH_2CH_2)_2NH$
dibutylamine

c. 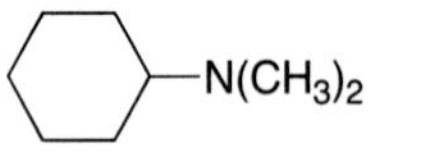
N,N-dimethylcyclohexanamine

d. 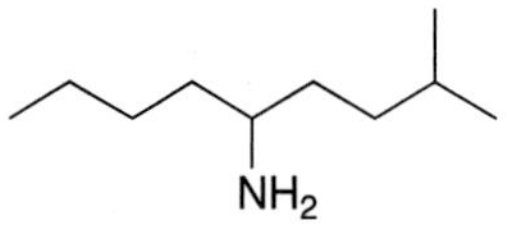
2-methyl-5-nonanamine

e. 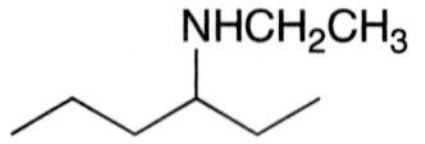
N-ethyl-3-hexanamine

f. 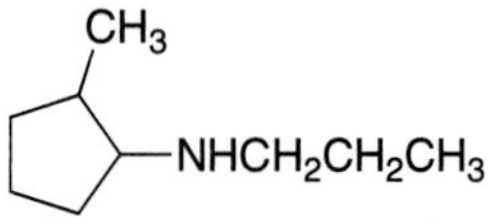
2-methyl-*N*-propylcyclopentanamine

25.5 An $\mathbf{NH_2}$ group named as a substituent is called an **amino group.**

a. 2,4-dimethyl-3-hexanamine
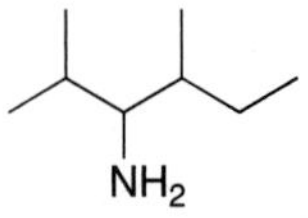

b. *N*-methylpentylamine
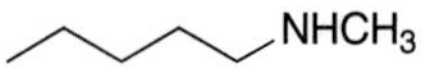

c. *N*-isopropyl-*p*-nitroaniline
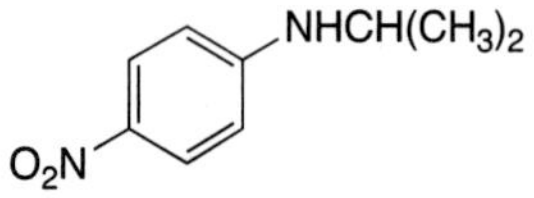

d. *N*-methylpiperidine
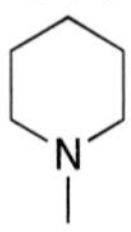

e. *N,N*-dimethylethylamine
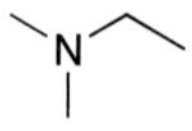

f. 2-aminocyclohexanone
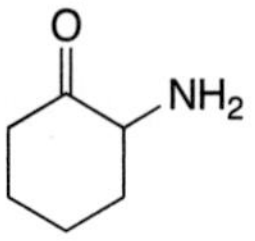

g. *N*-methylaniline
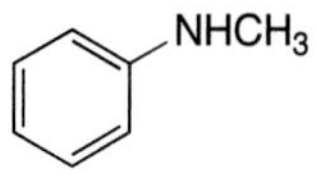

h. *m*-ethylaniline
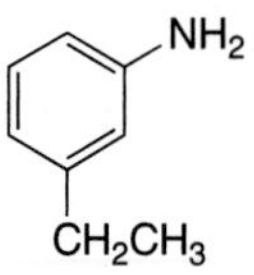

25.6 Primary (1°) and 2° amines have higher bp's than similar compounds (like ethers) incapable of hydrogen bonding, but lower bp's than alcohols that have stronger intermolecular hydrogen bonds. Tertiary amines (3°) have lower boiling points than 1° and 2° amines of comparable molecular weight because they have no N–H bonds.

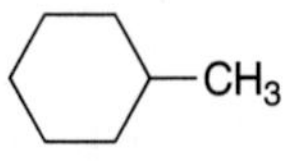
alkane
lowest
boiling point

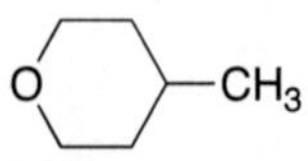
ether
intermediate
boiling point

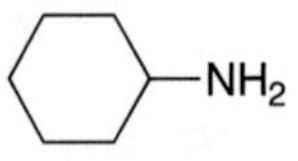
amine
N–H can hydrogen bond.
highest boiling point

25.7 **The NH signal occurs between 0.5 and 5.0 ppm.** The protons on the carbon bonded to the amine nitrogen are deshielded and typically absorb at 2.3–3.0 ppm. The NH protons are not split.

molecular formula $C_6H_{15}N$
^1H NMR absorptions (ppm):
0.9 (singlet, 1 H) → NH
1.10 (triplet, 3 H) → CH_3 adjacent to CH_2
1.15 (singlet, 9 H) → $(CH_3)_3C$
2.6 (quartet, 2 H) → CH_2 adjacent to CH_3

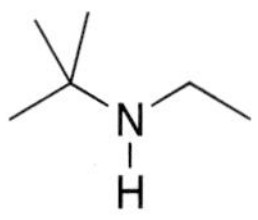

25.8 The atoms of 2-phenylethylamine are in bold.

a.

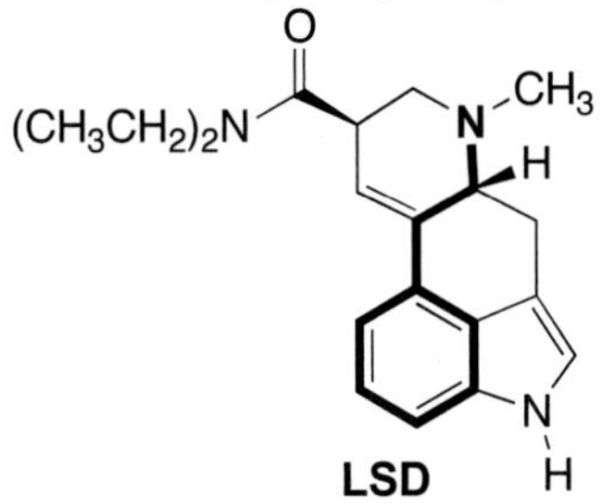

LSD
lysergic acid diethyl amide

b.

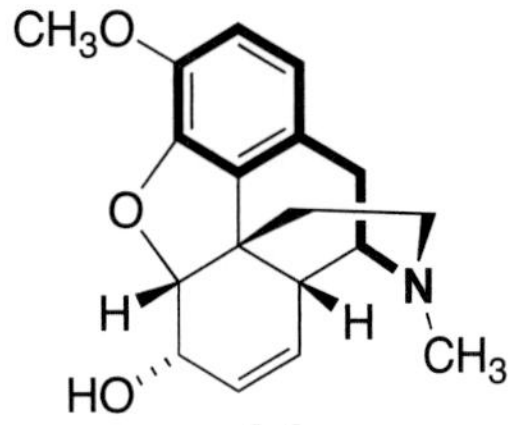

codeine

25.9 S_N2 reaction of an alkyl halide with NH_3 or an amine forms an amine or an ammonium salt.

a.

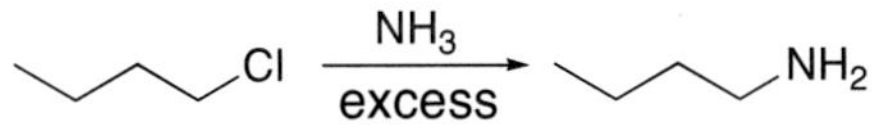

b.

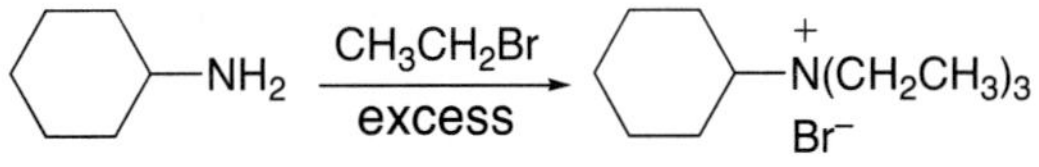

25.10 The Gabriel synthesis converts an alkyl halide into a 1° amine by a two-step process: nucleophilic substitution followed by hydrolysis.

a.

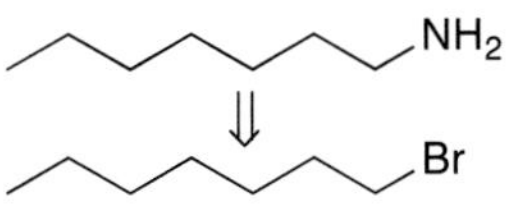

b. $(CH_3)_2CHCH_2CH_2NH_2$
⇓
$(CH_3)_2CHCH_2CH_2Br$

c.

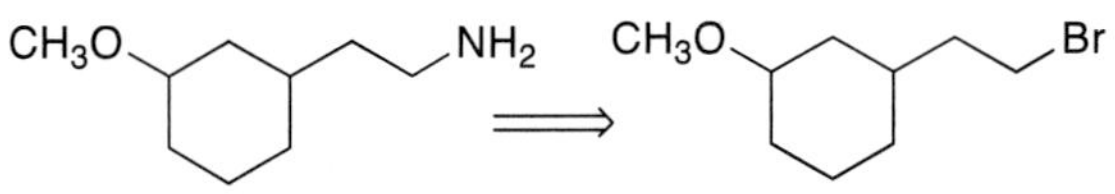

25.11 The Gabriel synthesis prepares 1° amines from alkyl halides. Since the reaction proceeds by an S_N2 mechanism, the halide must be CH_3 or 1°, and X can't be bonded to an *sp*² hybridized C.

a.

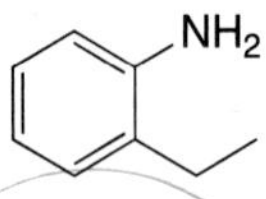

aromatic
An S_N2 does not occur on an aryl halide.
cannot be made by Gabriel synthesis

↑ too weak because to substitute

b.

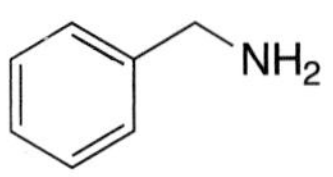

can be made by Gabriel synthesis

c.

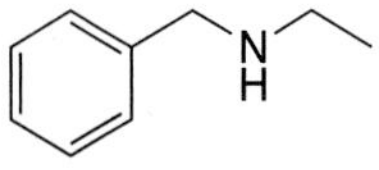

2° amine
cannot be made by Gabriel synthesis

d.

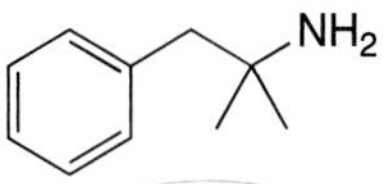

N on 3° C
An S_N2 does not occur on a 3° RX.
cannot be made by Gabriel synthesis

↑ SN2
block to substitute

25.12 Nitriles are reduced to 1° amines with $LiAlH_4$. Nitro groups are reduced to 1° amines using a variety of reducing agents. **Primary (1°), 2°, and 3° amides are reduced to 1°, 2°, and 3° amines** respectively, using $LiAlH_4$.

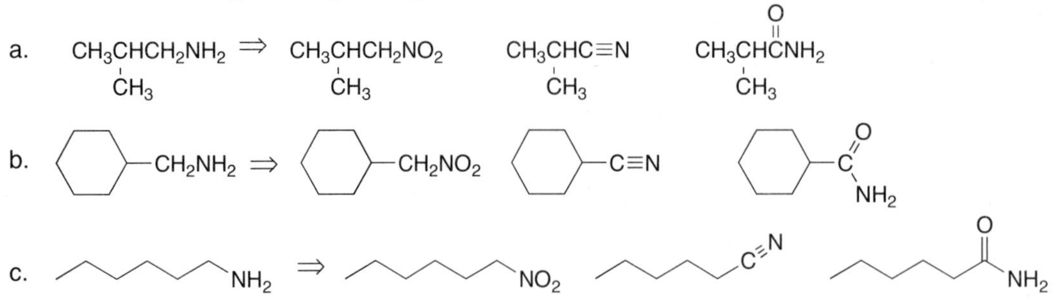

25.13 Primary (1°), 2°, and 3° amides are reduced to 1°, 2°, and 3° amines respectively, using $LiAlH_4$.

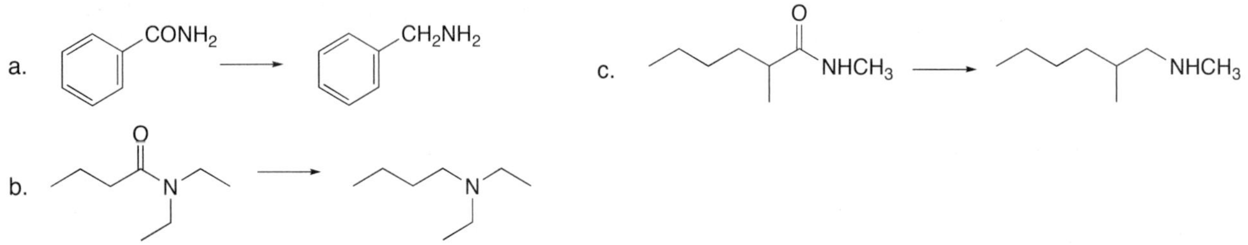

25.14 Only amines with a CH_2 or CH_3 bonded to the N can be made by reduction of an amide.

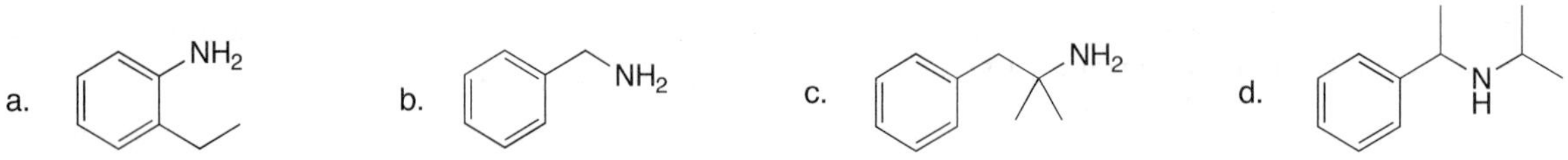

a. N bonded to benzene cannot be made by reduction of an amide

b. N bonded to CH_2 can be made by reduction of an amide

c. N bonded to a 3° C cannot be made by reduction of an amide

d. N on 2° C on both sides cannot be made by reduction of an amide

25.15 Reductive amination is a two-step method that converts aldehydes and ketones into 1°, 2°, and 3° amines. Reductive amination replaces a C=O by a C–H and C–N bond.

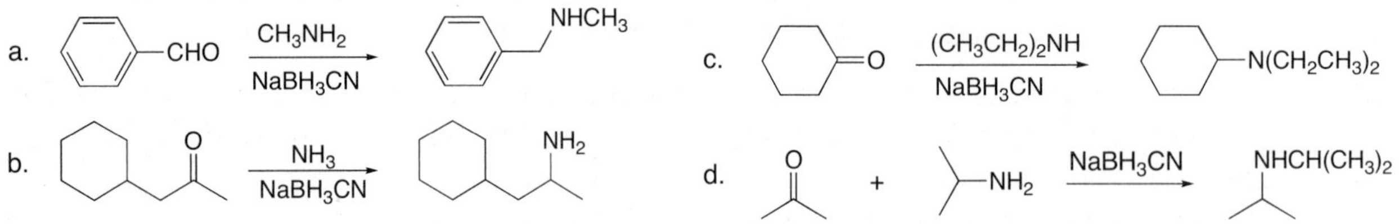

25.16 Reductive amination occurs using the ketone in **E** and the amine in **D.**

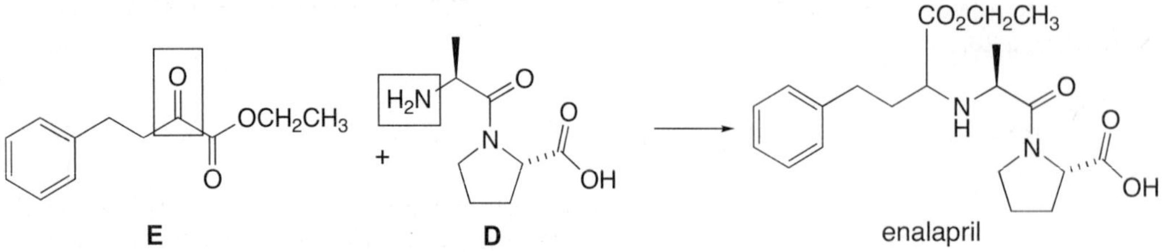

25.17

a. 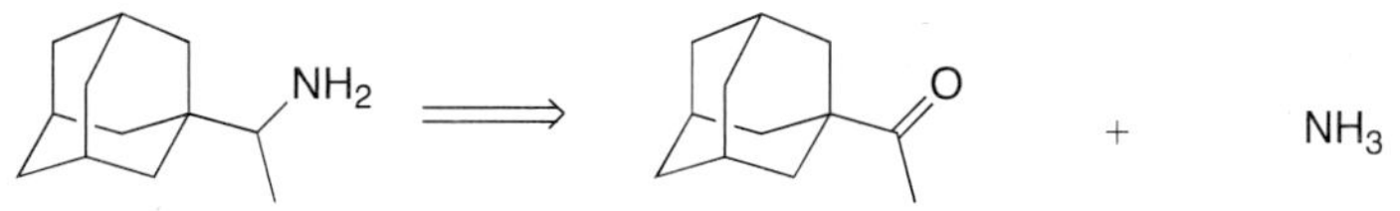

b. 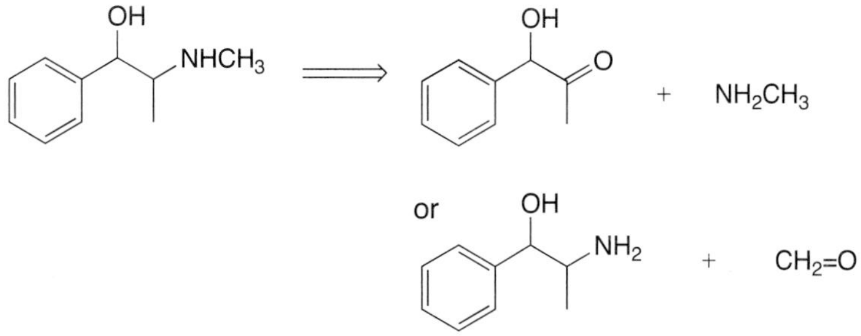

25.18

a. 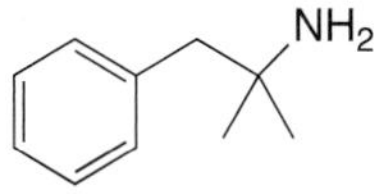

phentermine

Only amines that have a C bonded to a H and N atom can be made by reductive amination; that is, an amine must have the following structural feature:

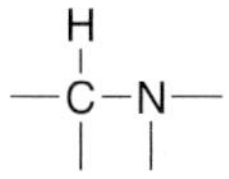

In phentermine, the C bonded to N is not bonded to a H, so it cannot be made by reductive amination.

b. systematic name: 2-methyl-1-phenyl-2-propanamine

25.19 The pK_a of many protonated amines is 10–11, so the pK_a of the starting acid must be **less than 10** for equilibrium to favor the products. Amines are thus readily protonated by strong inorganic acids (e.g., HCl and H_2SO_4) and by carboxylic acids.

a. $CH_3CH_2CH_2CH_2{-}NH_2 + HCl \rightleftharpoons CH_3CH_2CH_2CH_2{-}\overset{+}{N}H_3 + Cl^-$

HCl: pK_a = –7; product: pK_a ≈ 10, weaker acid, products favored

b. $C_6H_5COOH + (CH_3)_2NH \rightleftharpoons (CH_3)_2\overset{+}{N}H_2 + C_6H_5COO^-$

C_6H_5COOH: pK_a = 4.2; product: pK_a = 10.7, weaker acid, products favored

c. 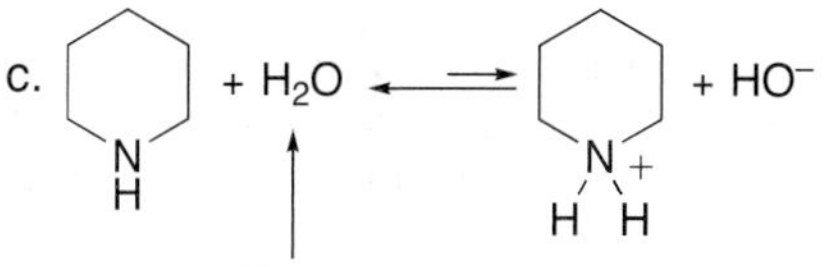

+ H2O
+ HO–
pKa = 15.7
weaker acid
reactants favored
pKa ≈ 10

25.20 An amine can be separated from other organic compounds by converting it to a water-soluble ammonium salt by an acid–base reaction. In each case, the extraction procedure would employ the following steps:

- Dissolve the amine and either **X** or **Y** in CH_2Cl_2.
- Add a solution of 10% HCl. The amine will be protonated and dissolve in the aqueous layer, while **X** or **Y** will remain in the organic layer as a neutral compound.
- Separate the layers.

a. 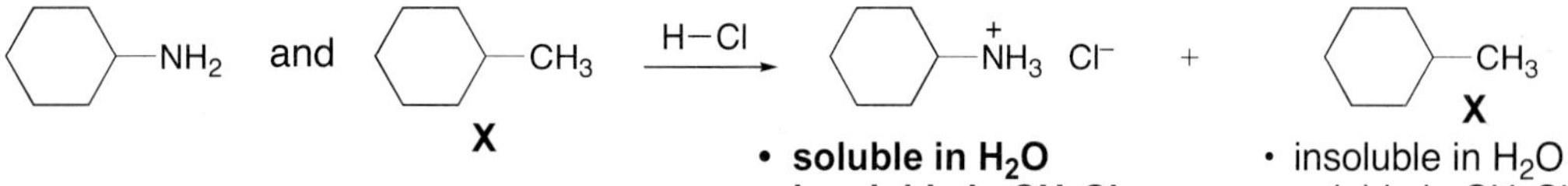

- **soluble in H_2O**
- **insoluble in CH_2Cl_2**

- insoluble in H_2O
- soluble in CH_2Cl_2

b. $(CH_3CH_2CH_2CH_2)_3N$ and $(CH_3CH_2CH_2CH_2)_2O$ **Y** $\xrightarrow{H-Cl}$ $(CH_3CH_2CH_2CH_2)_3\overset{+}{N}H\ Cl^-$ + $(CH_3CH_2CH_2CH_2)_2O$ **Y**

- **soluble in H_2O**
- **insoluble in CH_2Cl_2**

- insoluble in H_2O
- soluble in CH_2Cl_2

25.21 Primary (1°), 2°, and 3° alkylamines are more basic than NH_3 because of the electron-donating inductive effect of the R groups.

a. $(CH_3)_2NH$ and NH_3

2° alkylamine
CH_3 groups are electron donating.
stronger base

b. $CH_3CH_2NH_2$ and $ClCH_2CH_2NH_2$

1° alkylamine
stronger base

1° alkylamine
Cl is electron withdrawing.
weaker base

25.22 Arylamines are less basic than alkylamines because the electron pair on N is delocalized. Electron-donor groups add electron density to the benzene ring making the arylamine more basic than aniline. Electron-withdrawing groups remove electron density from the benzene ring, making the arylamine less basic than aniline.

a.

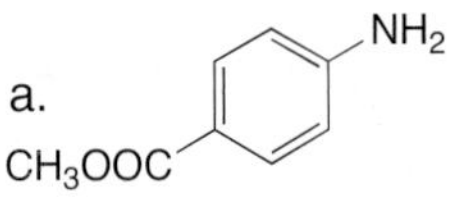

electron-withdrawing group
least basic

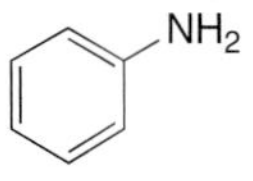

arylamine
intermediate basicity

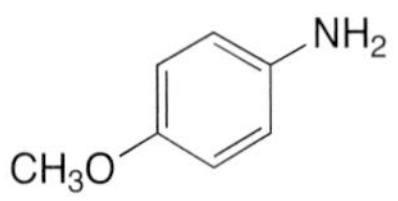

electron-donating group
most basic

b.

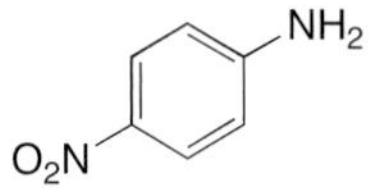

electron-withdrawing group
least basic

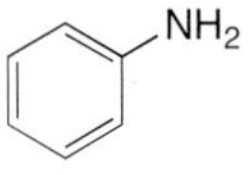

arylamine
intermediate basicity

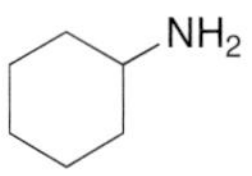

alkylamine
most basic

25.23 Amides are much less basic than amines because the electron pair on N is highly delocalized.

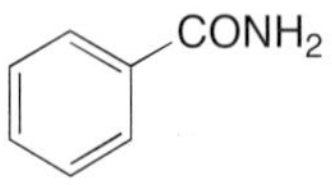

amide
least basic

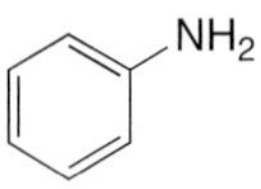

arylamine
intermediate basicity

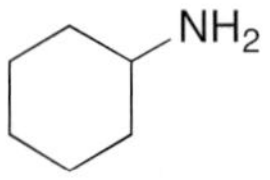

alkylamine
most basic

25.24

a. Electron pair on N occupies an *sp*² hybrid orbital.

*sp*² hybridized
more basic

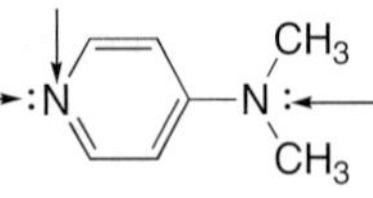

This N is also *sp*² hybridized but the electron pair occupies a *p* orbital, so it can delocalize onto the aromatic ring. Delocalization makes this N less basic.

DMAP
4-(*N*,*N*-dimethylamino)pyridine

b.

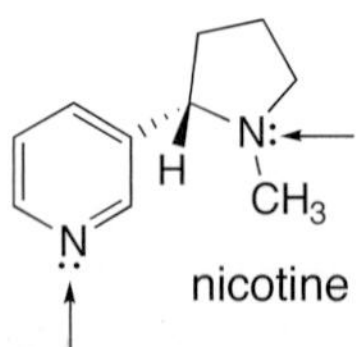

nicotine

*sp*³ hybridized N
stronger base

*sp*² hybridized N
higher percent *s*-character
weaker base

25.25

a.

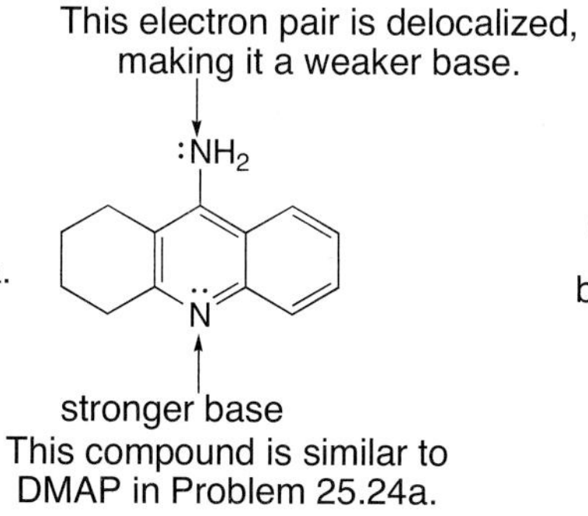
This electron pair is delocalized, making it a weaker base.
:NH2
N
stronger base
This compound is similar to DMAP in Problem 25.24a.

b.

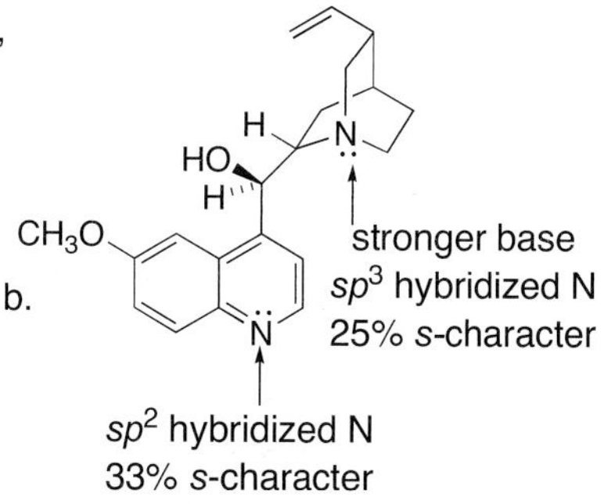
H
HO
H
N
CH3O
N
stronger base
sp3 hybridized N
25% s-character
sp2 hybridized N
33% s-character

c.

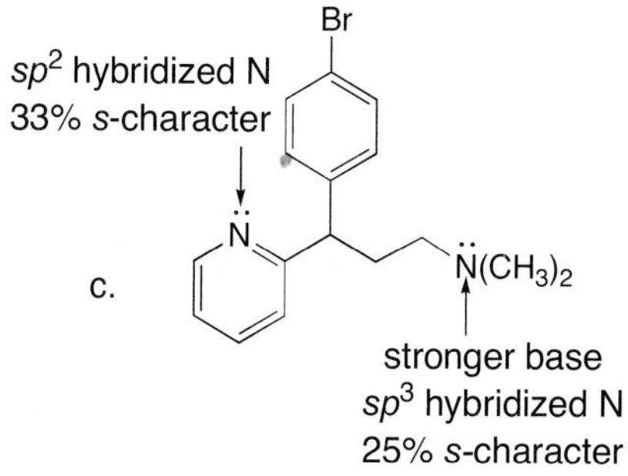
Br
sp2 hybridized N
33% s-character
N
N(CH3)2
stronger base
sp3 hybridized N
25% s-character

25.26 Amines attack carbonyl groups to form products of nucleophilic addition or substitution.

a.

O
CH3CH2CH2NH2
NCH2CH2CH3
O
(CH3CH2)2NH
N(CH2CH3)2

b.

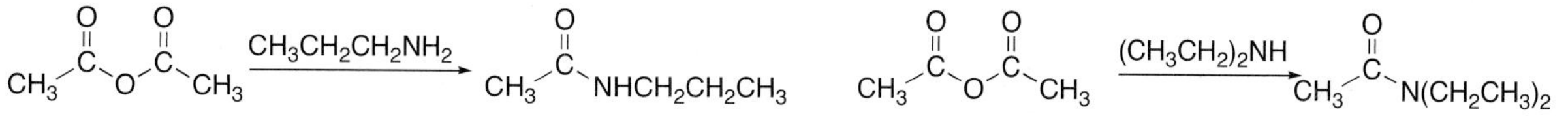
CH3
O
CH3
CH3CH2CH2NH2
CH3
NHCH2CH2CH3
(CH3CH2)2NH
N(CH2CH3)2

c.

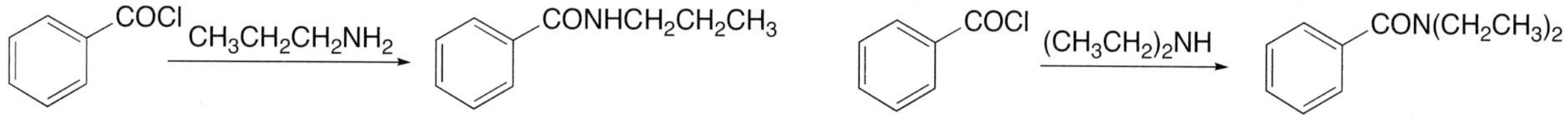
COCl
CH3CH2CH2NH2
CONHCH2CH2CH3
COCl
(CH3CH2)2NH
CON(CH2CH3)2

25.27 [1] Convert the amine (aniline) into an amide (acetanilide).
[2] **Carry out the Friedel–Crafts reaction.**
[3] **Hydrolyze the amide** to generate the free amino group.

a.

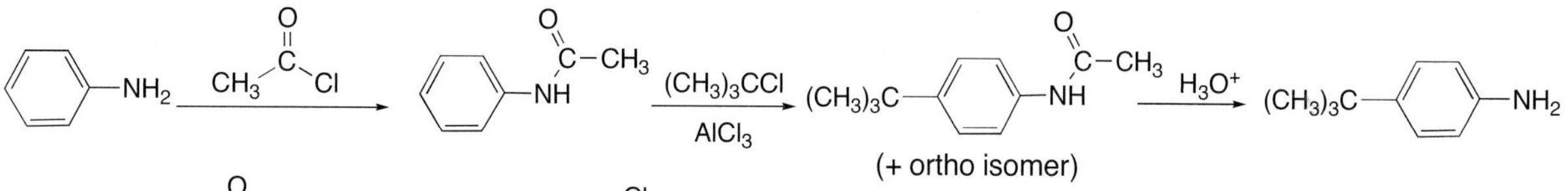
NH2
CH3
Cl
C–CH3
NH
(CH3)3CCl
AlCl3
(CH3)3C
NH
H3O+
(CH3)3C
NH2
(+ ortho isomer)

b.

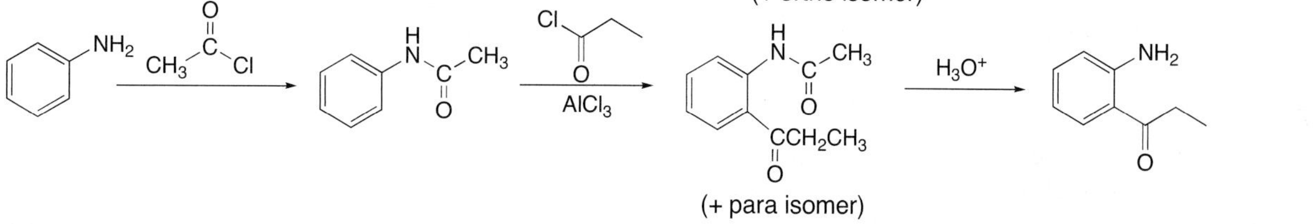
NH2
CH3
Cl
H
N
CH3
Cl
AlCl3
CCH2CH3
H3O+
NH2
(+ para isomer)

25.28

transition state:

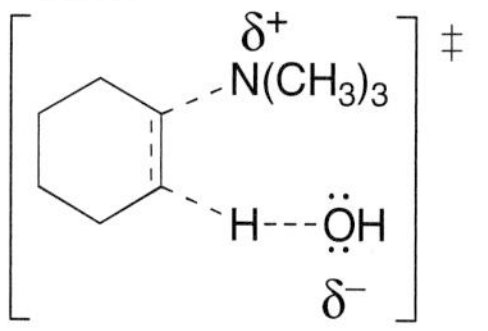
δ+
N(CH3)3
‡
H---ÖH
δ–

(no 3-D geometry shown here)

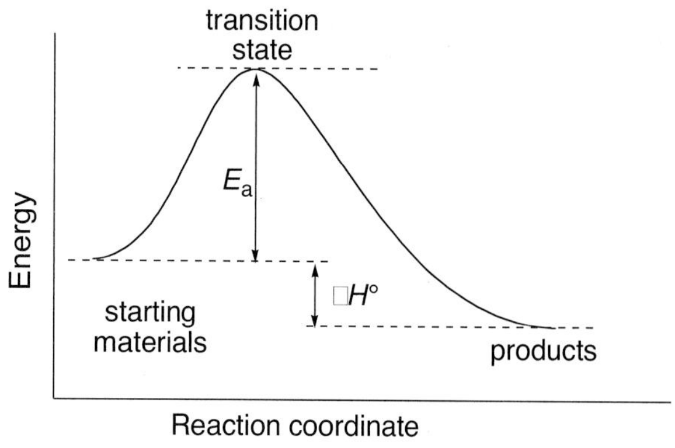
transition state
Ea
Energy
ΔH°
starting materials
products
Reaction coordinate

25.29

a. $CH_3CH_2CH_2CH_2{-}NH_2 \xrightarrow[\text{[2] } Ag_2O \text{ [3] } \Delta]{\text{[1] } CH_3I \text{ (excess)}} CH_3CH_2CH{=}CH_2$

c. 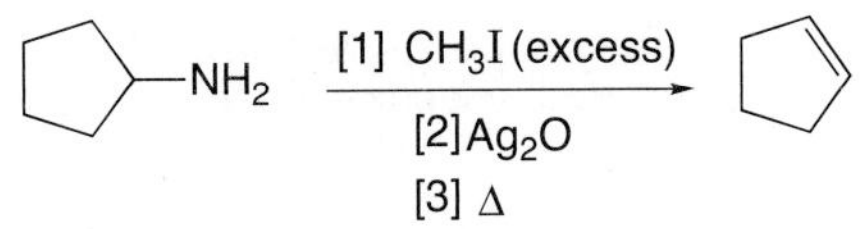

b. $(CH_3)_2CHNH_2 \xrightarrow[\text{[2] } Ag_2O \text{ [3] } \Delta]{\text{[1] } CH_3I \text{ (excess)}} CH_3CH{=}CH_2$

25.30 In a Hofmann elimination, the base removes a proton from the less substituted, more accessible β carbon atom, because of the bulky leaving group on the nearby α carbon.

a. 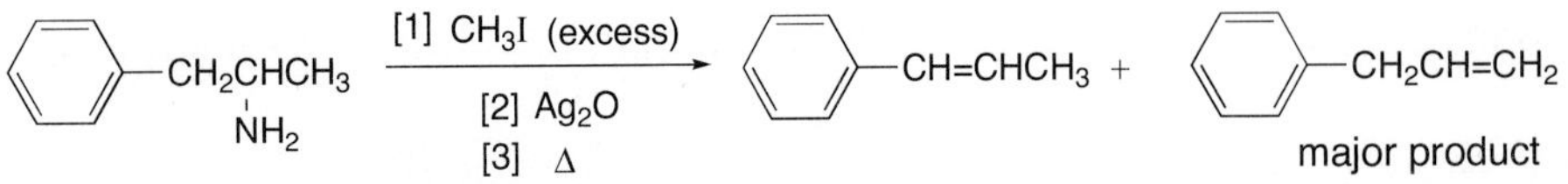

b. 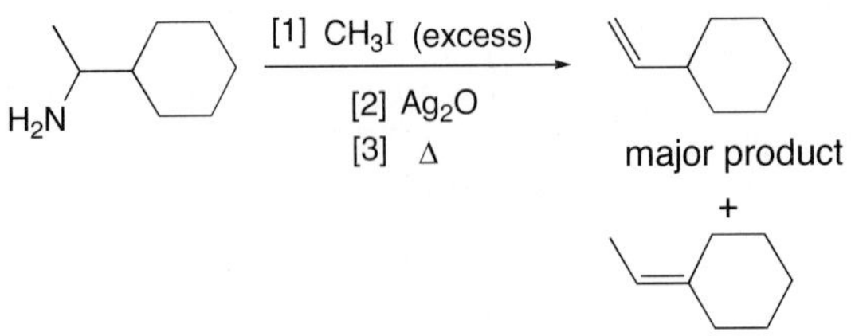

c. 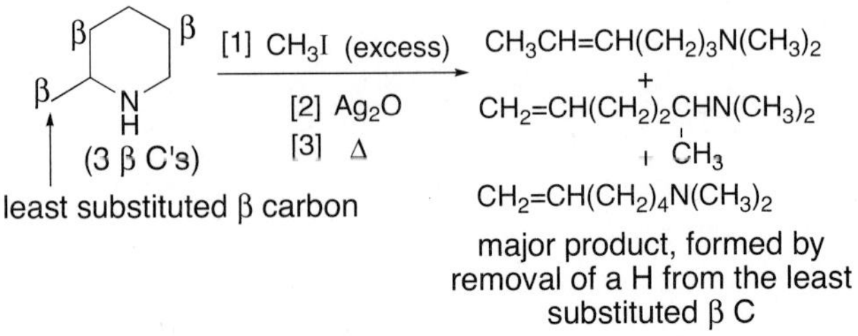

25.31

a. 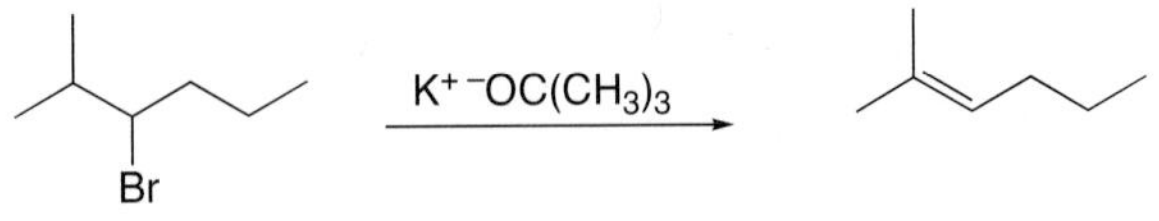

c. 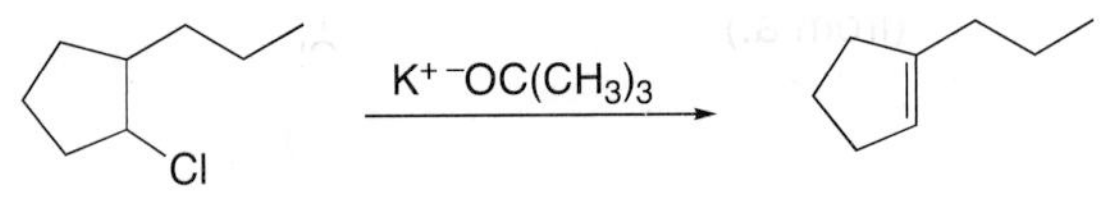

b. 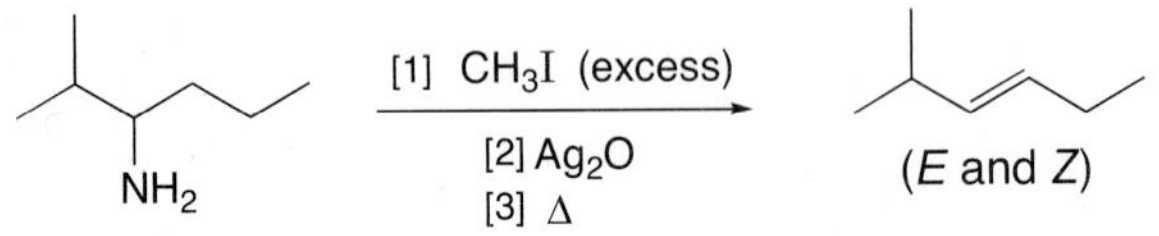

d. 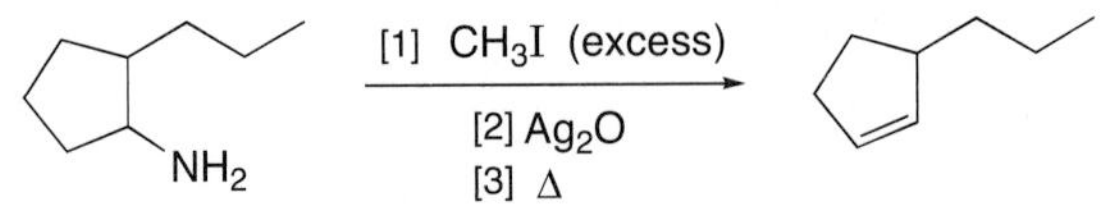

25.32

a. 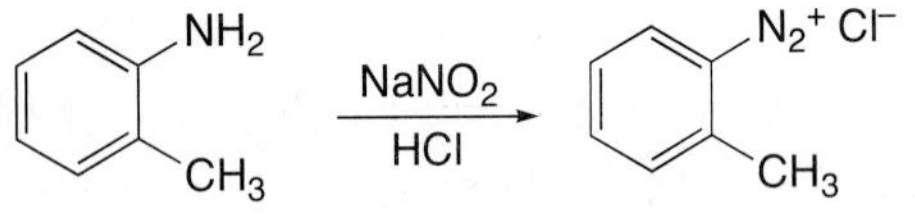

c. 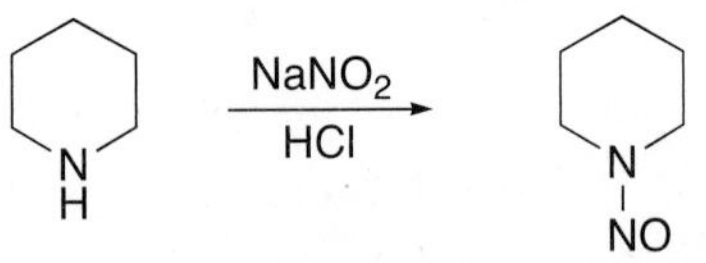

b. $CH_3CH_2{-}NH{-}CH_3 \xrightarrow[HCl]{NaNO_2} CH_3CH_2{-}N(NO){-}CH_3$

d. 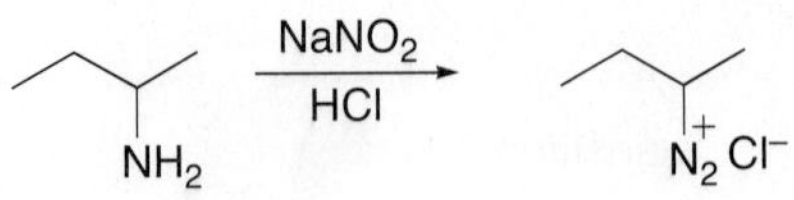

25.33

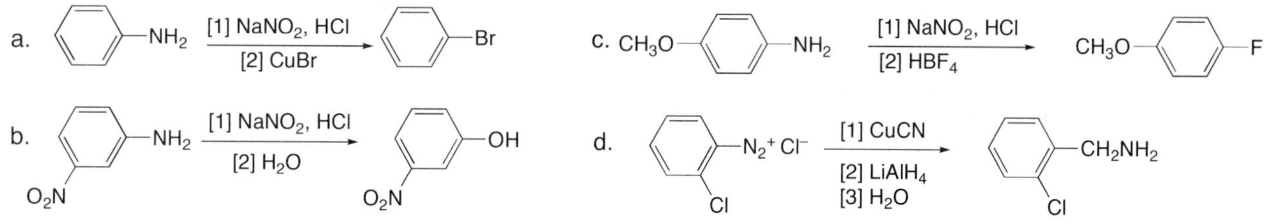

25.34

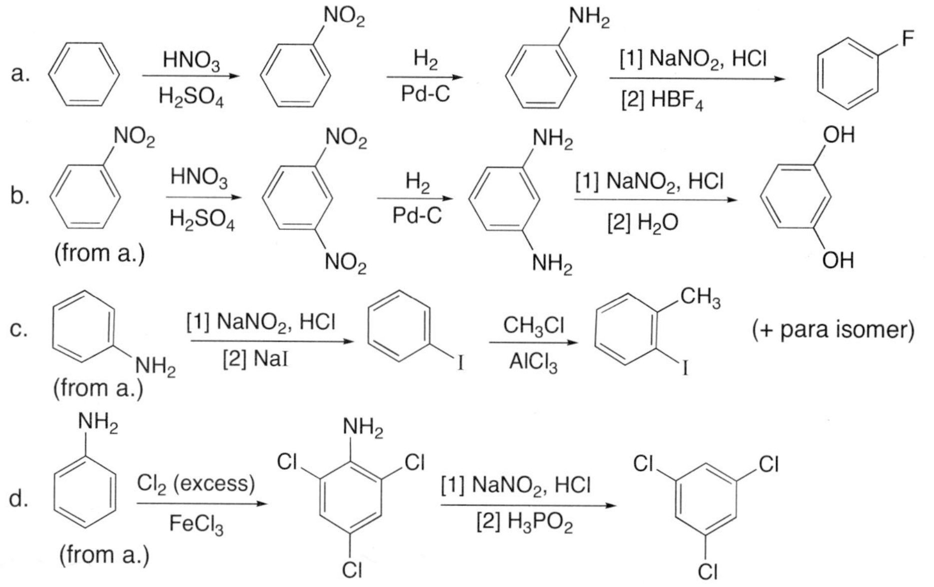

25.35

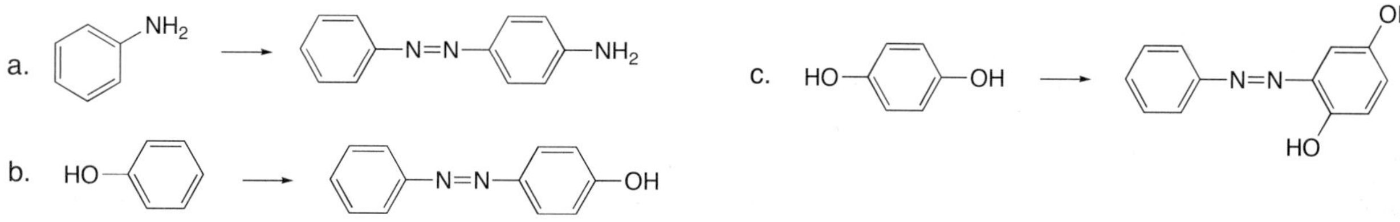

25.36 To determine what starting materials are needed to synthesize a particular azo compound, always divide the molecule into two components: **one has a benzene ring with a diazonium ion, and one has a benzene ring with a very strong electron-donor group.**

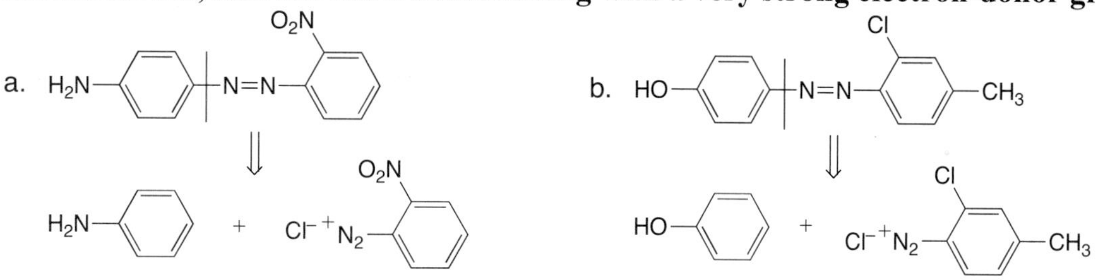

25.37

a.

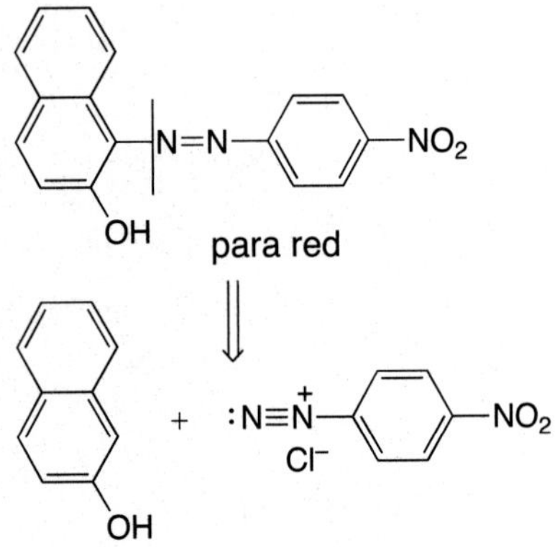

para red

b.

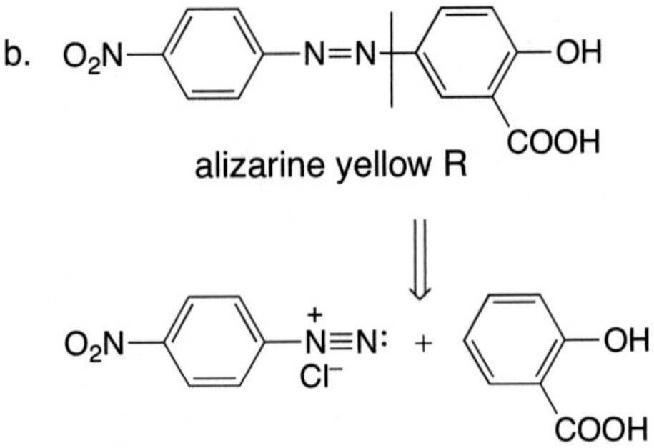

alizarine yellow R

25.38

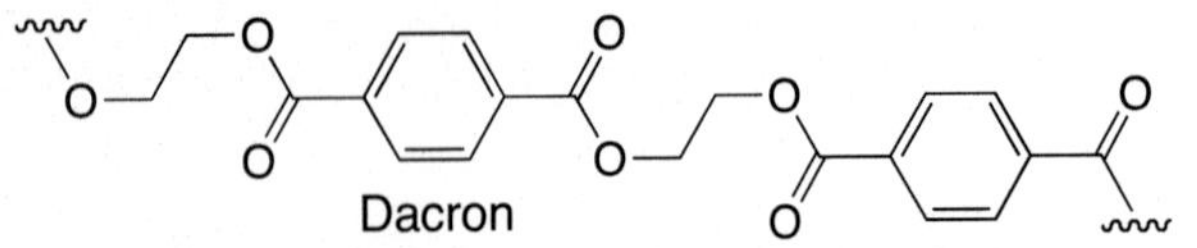

Dacron

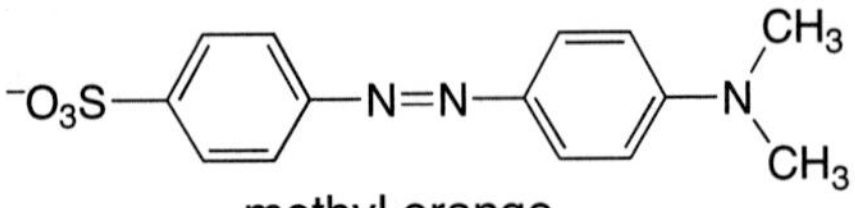

methyl orange

To bind to fabric, methyl orange (an anion) needs to interact with positively charged sites. Since Dacron is a neutral compound with no cationic sites on the chain, it does not bind methyl orange well.

25.39

a. 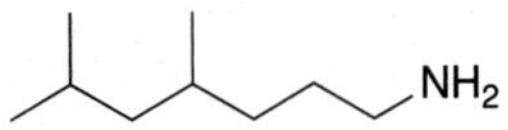

4,6-dimethyl-1-heptanamine

b. 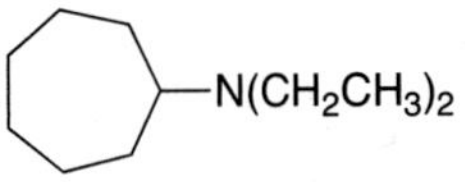

N,*N*-diethylcycloheptanamine

25.40

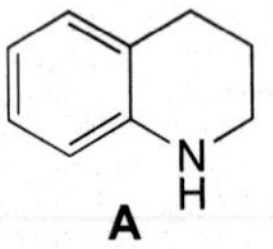

or

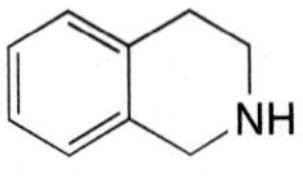

A
weaker base
(delocalized electron pair on N)

B
stronger base

25.41

a, b.

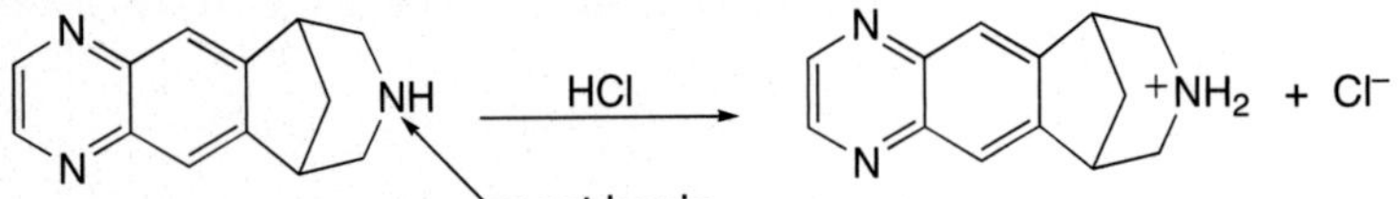

varenicline

most basic
only sp^3 hybridized N

25.42

a. $CH_3NHCH_2CH_2CH_2CH_3$
N-methyl-1-butanamine
(*N*-methylbutylamine)

b. 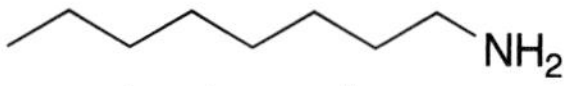
1-octanamine
(octylamine)

c. 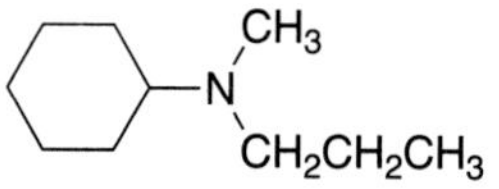
N-methyl-*N*-propylcyclohexanamine

d. $(CH_3CH_2CH_2)_3N$
tripropylamine

e. $(C_6H_5)_2NH$
diphenylamine

f. 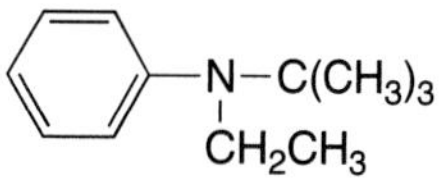
N-*tert*-butyl-*N*-ethylaniline

g. 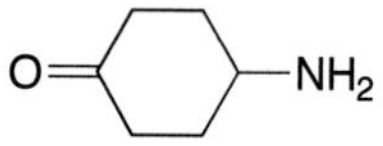
4-aminocyclohexanone

h. 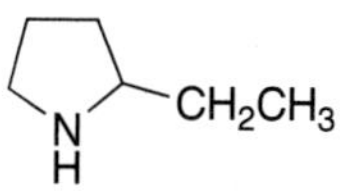
2-ethylpyrrolidine

i. $CH_3CH_2CH_2CH(NH_2)CH(CH_3)_2$
2-methyl-3-hexanamine

j. 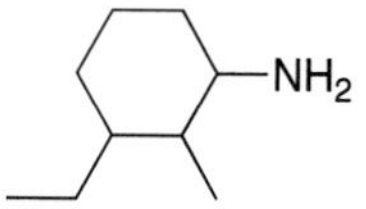
3-ethyl-2-methylcyclohexanamine

25.43

a. cyclobutylamine
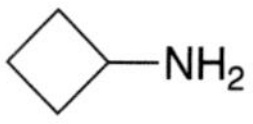

b. *N*-isobutylcyclopentylamine
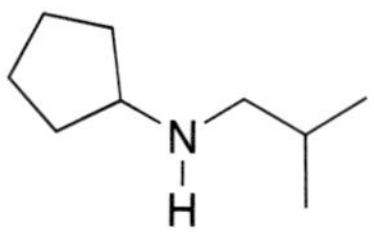

c. tri-*tert*-butylamine
$N[C(CH_3)_3]_3$

d. *N,N*-diisopropylaniline
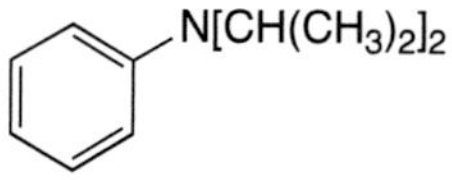

e. *N*-methylpyrrole
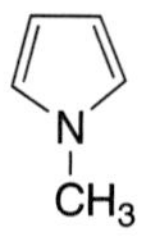

f. *N*-methylcyclopentylamine
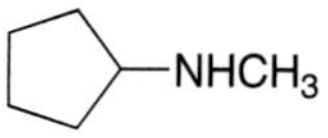

g. *cis*-2-aminocyclohexanol
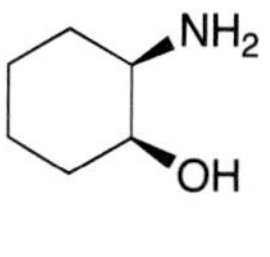 or 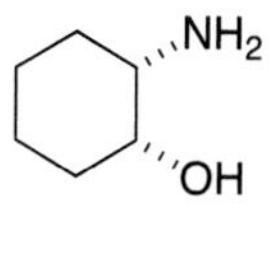

h. 3-methyl-2-hexanamine
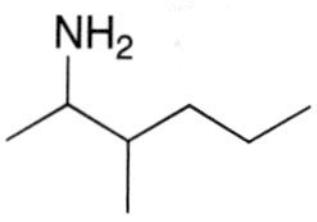

i. 2-*sec*-butylpiperidine
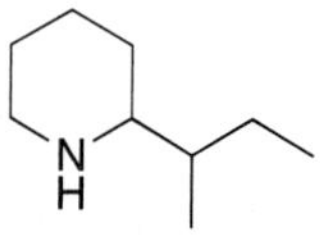

j. (2*S*)-2-heptanamine
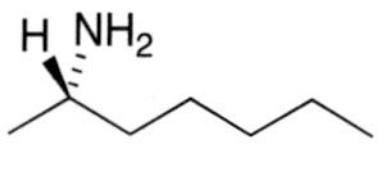

25.44

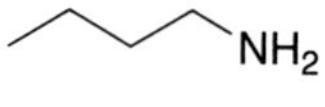
1-butanamine

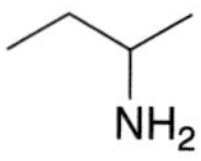
2-butanamine

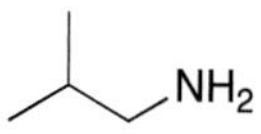
2-methyl-1-propanamine

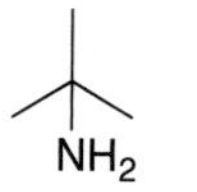
2-methyl-2-propanamine

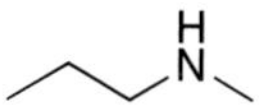
N-methyl-1-propanamine

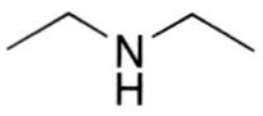
diethylamine

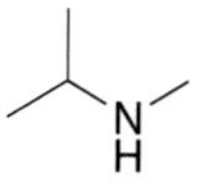
N-methyl-2-propanamine

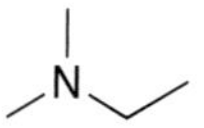
N,N-dimethylethanamine

25.45 [* denotes a stereogenic center.]

a. 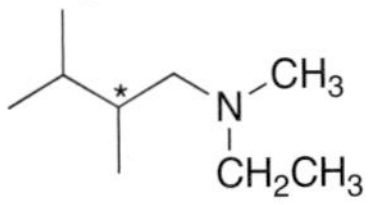

1 stereogenic center
2 stereoisomers

b. 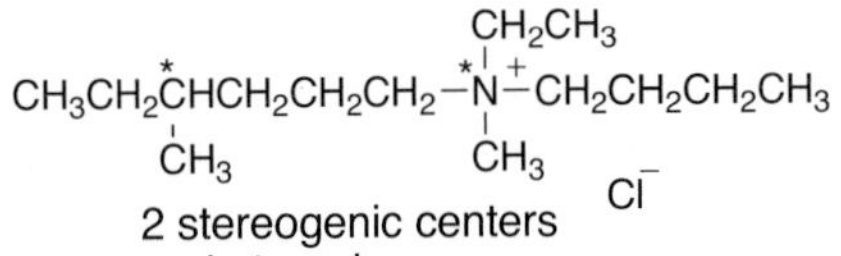

2 stereogenic centers
4 stereoisomers

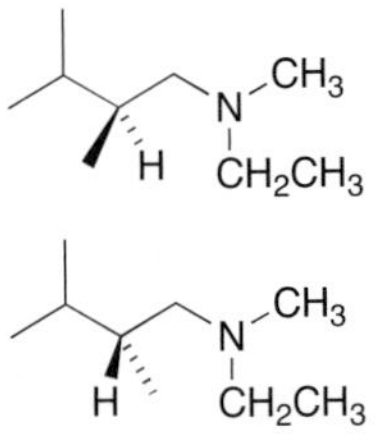

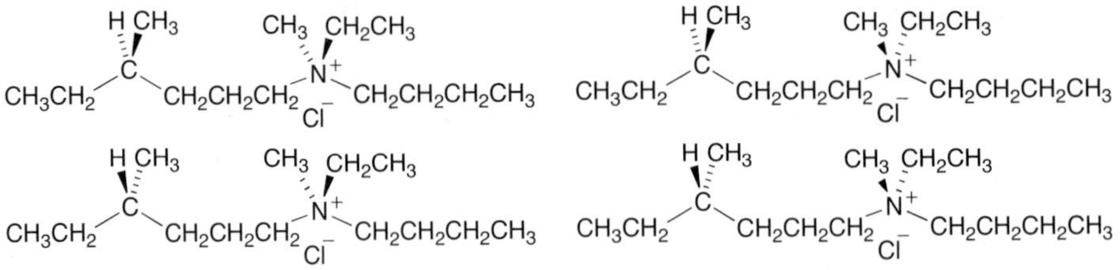

25.46

a. $(CH_3CH_2)_2NH$ or 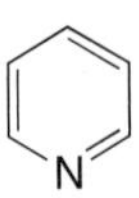

sp^3 hybridized N: **stronger base** | sp^2 hybridized N **weaker base**

b. $(CH_3CH_2)_2NH$ or $(ClCH_2CH_2)_2NH$

2° alkylamine **stronger base** | 2° alkylamine Cl is electron withdrawing. **weaker base**

25.47

a. 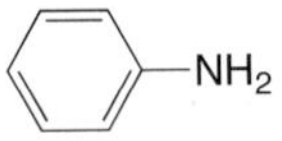 NH_3 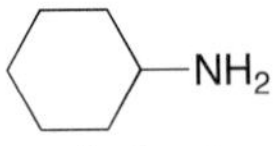

arylamine **least basic** | **intermediate basicity** | alkylamine **most basic**

b. 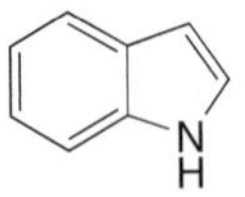 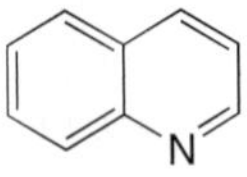 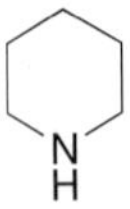

delocalized electron pair on N **least basic** | sp^2 hybridized N **intermediate basicity** | sp^3 hybridized N **most basic**

c. 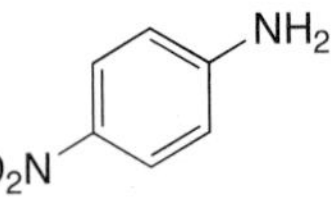 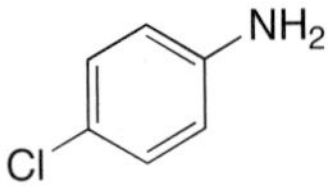 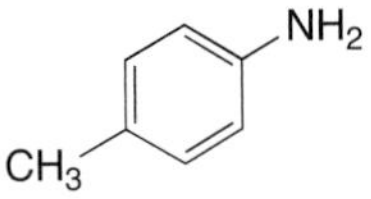

electron-withdrawing group **least basic** | **intermediate basicity** | electron-donating group **most basic**

d. $(C_6H_5)_2NH$ $C_6H_5NH_2$ 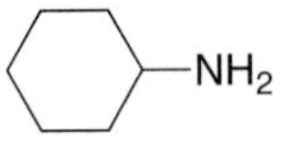

diarylamine **least basic** | arylamine **intermediate basicity** | alkylamine **most basic**

25.48 The electron-withdrawing inductive effect of the phenyl group stabilizes benzylamine, making its conjugate acid more acidic than the conjugate acid of cyclohexanamine. The conjugate acid of aniline is more acidic than the conjugate acid of benzylamine, since loss of a proton generates a resonance-stabilized amine, $C_6H_5NH_2$.

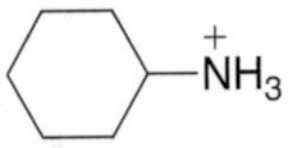 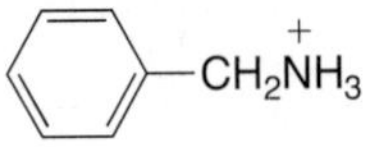 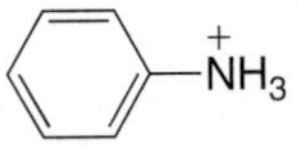

pK_a = 10.7 | pK_a intermediate | pK_a = 4.6

↓ ↓ ↓

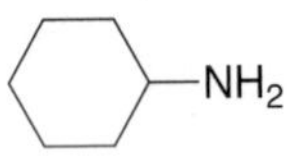 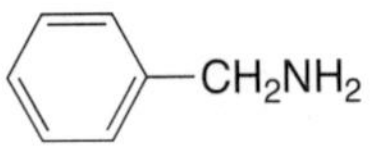 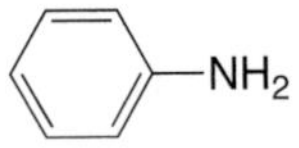

alkylamine cyclohexanamine | electron-withdrawing inductive effect of the sp^2 hybridized C's benzylamine | resonance-stabilized aromatic amine aniline

25.49 The most basic N atom is protonated on treatment with acid.

a.

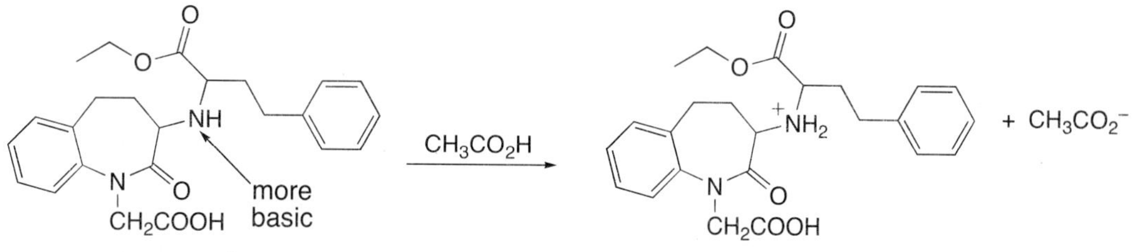

benazepril

b.

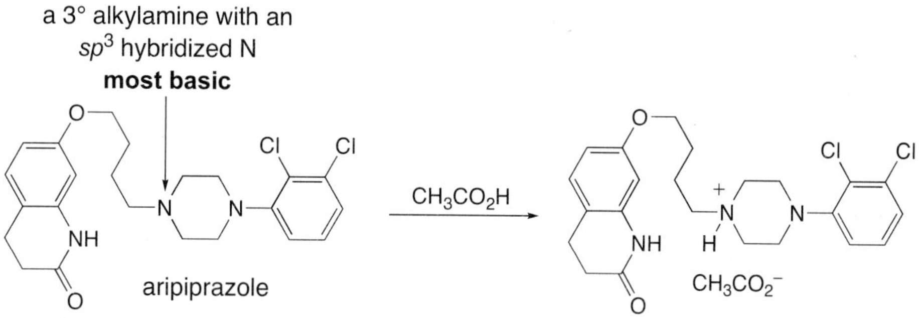

25.50

a.

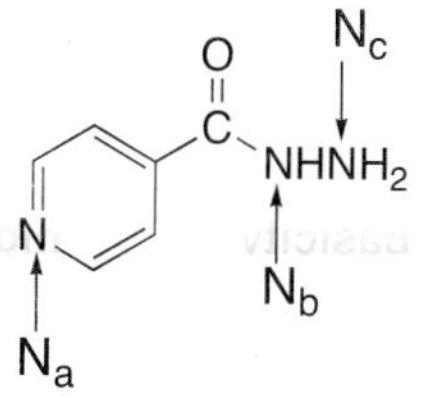

$N_b < N_a < N_c$

Order of basicity: $N_b < N_a < N_c$

N_b – The electron pair on this N atom is delocalized on the O atom; least basic.

N_a – The electron pair on this N atom is not delocalized, but is on an sp^2 hybridized atom.

N_c – The electron pair on this N atom is on an sp^3 hybridized N; most basic.

b.

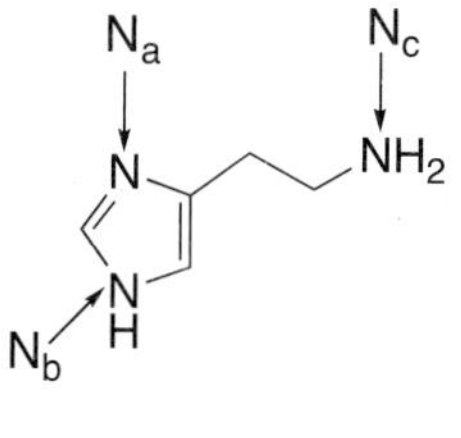

$N_b < N_a < N_c$

Order of basicity: $N_b < N_a < N_c$

N_b – The electron pair on this N atom is delocalized on the aromatic five-membered ring; least basic.

N_a – The electron pair on this N atom is not delocalized, but is on an sp^2 hybridized atom.

N_c – The electron pair on this N atom is on an sp^3 hybridized N; most basic.

25.51 The para isomer is the weaker base because the electron pair on its NH_2 group can be delocalized onto the NO_2 group. In the meta isomer, no resonance structure places the electron pair on the NO_2 group, and fewer resonance structures can be drawn:

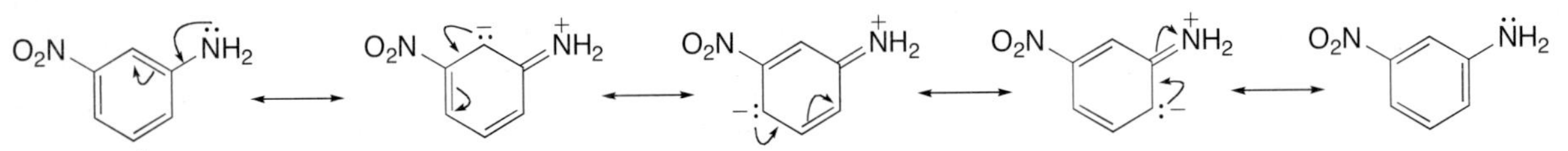

meta

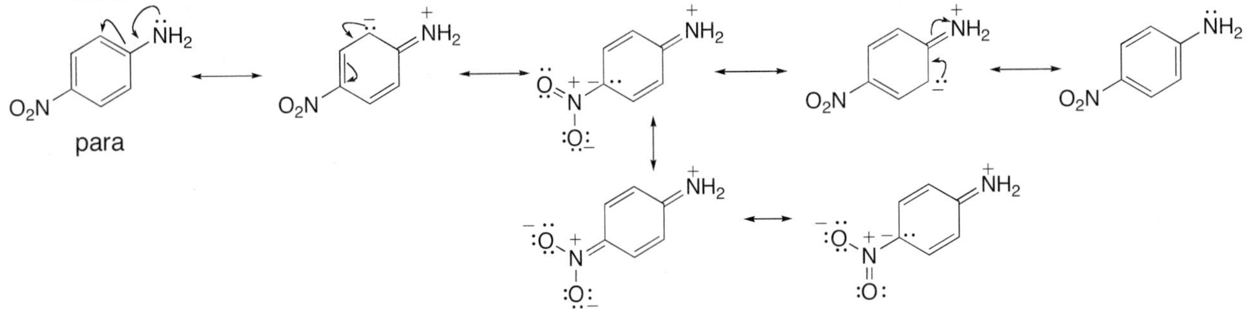

para

25.52

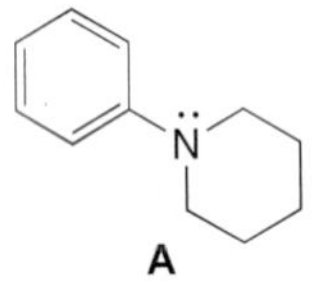

A

pK_a of the conjugate acid = 5.2
stronger conjugate acid
weaker base
The electron pair of this arylamine is delocalized on the benzene ring, decreasing its basicity.

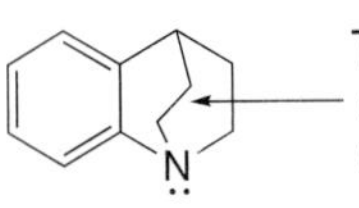

This two-carbon bridge makes it difficult for the lone pair on N to delocalize on the aromatic ring.

B

pK_a of the conjugate acid = 7.29
weaker conjugate acid
stronger base

Resonance structures that place a double bond between the N atom and the benzene ring are destabilized. Since the electron pair is more localized on N, compound **B** is more basic.

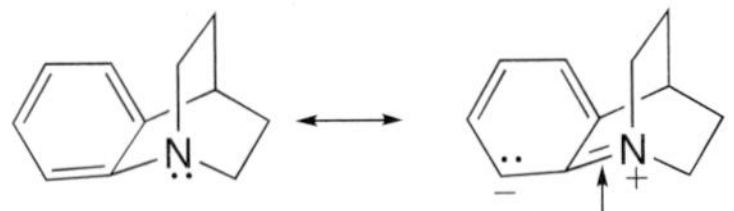

B

Geometry makes it difficult to have a double bond here.

25.53

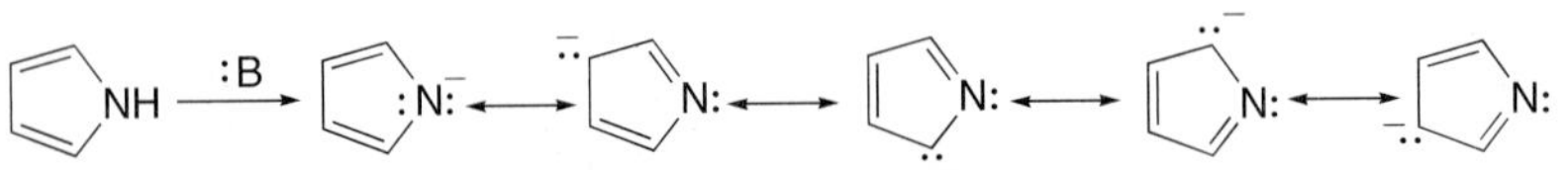

pyrrole
pK_a = 23
stronger acid

weaker conjugate base
The electron pair is delocalized, decreasing the basicity. The N atom is sp^2 hybridized.

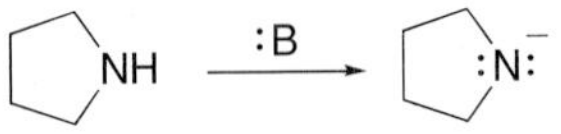

pyrrolidine
pK_a = 44
weaker acid

stronger conjugate base
The electron pair is not delocalized on the ring. The N atom is sp^3 hybridized.

25.54

a. $C_6H_5CH_2CH_2CH_2Br \xrightarrow[\text{excess}]{NH_3} C_6H_5CH_2CH_2CH_2NH_2$

b. $C_6H_5CH_2CH_2Br \xrightarrow{NaCN} C_6H_5CH_2CH_2CN \xrightarrow[\text{[2] } H_2O]{\text{[1] } LiAlH_4} C_6H_5CH_2CH_2CH_2NH_2$

c. $C_6H_5CH_2CH_2CH_2NO_2 \xrightarrow[\text{Pd-C}]{H_2} C_6H_5CH_2CH_2CH_2NH_2$

d. $C_6H_5CH_2CH_2CONH_2 \xrightarrow[\text{[2] } H_2O]{\text{[1] } LiAlH_4} C_6H_5CH_2CH_2CH_2NH_2$

e. $C_6H_5CH_2CH_2CHO \xrightarrow[NaBH_3CN]{NH_3} C_6H_5CH_2CH_2CH_2NH_2$

25.55

a. 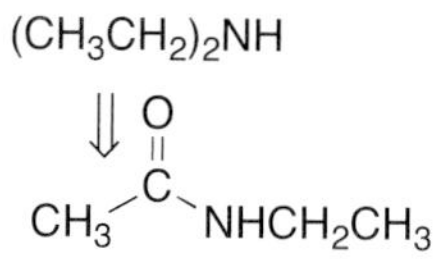

b. 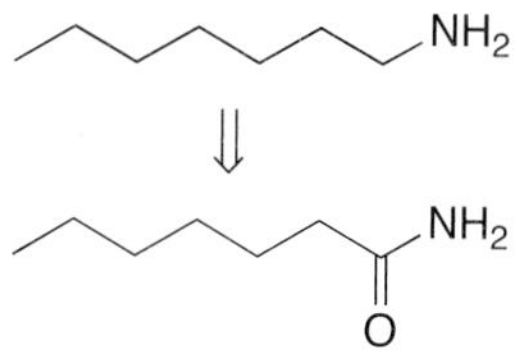

c. 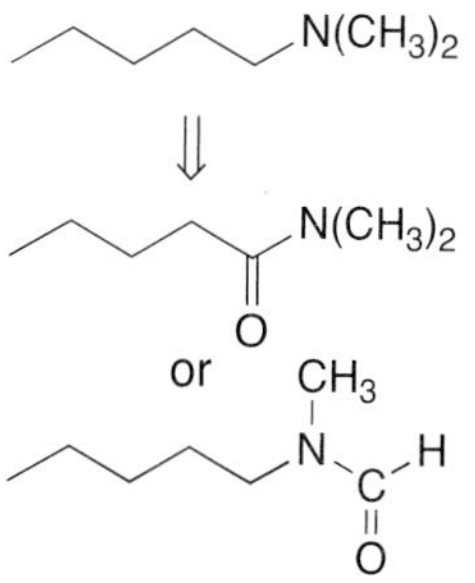

d. 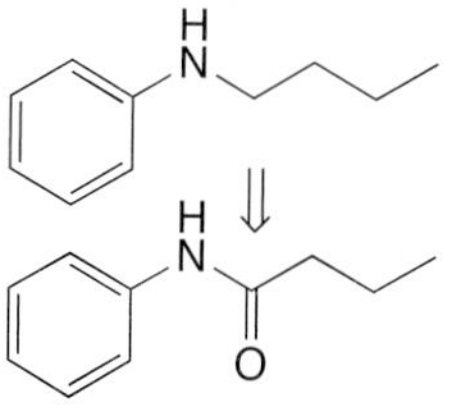

25.56 In reductive amination, one alkyl group on N comes from the carbonyl compound. The remainder of the molecule comes from NH_3 or an amine.

a. 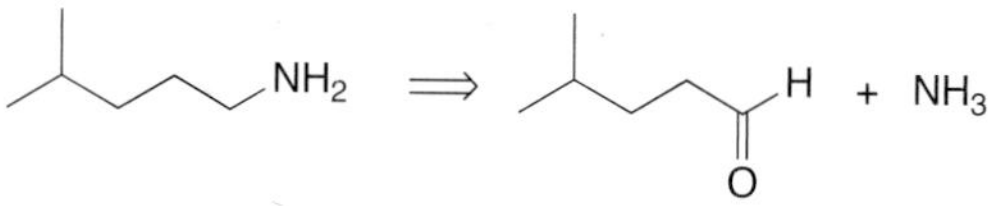

b. 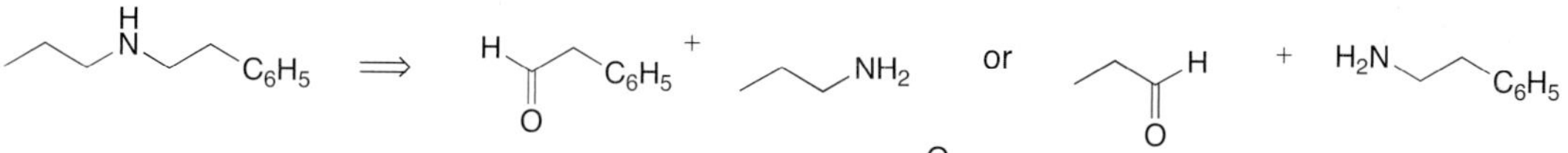

c. 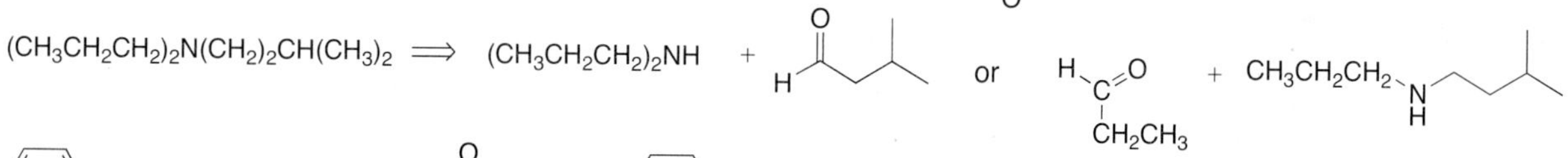

d. 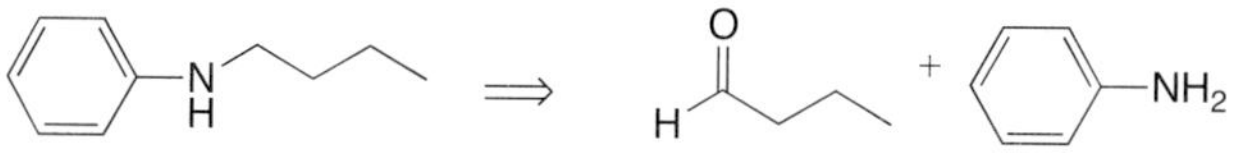

25.57

a. 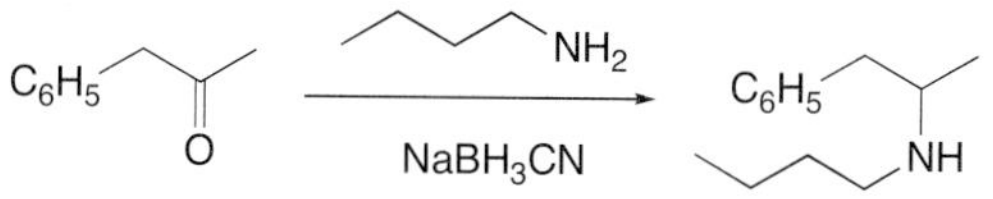

b. 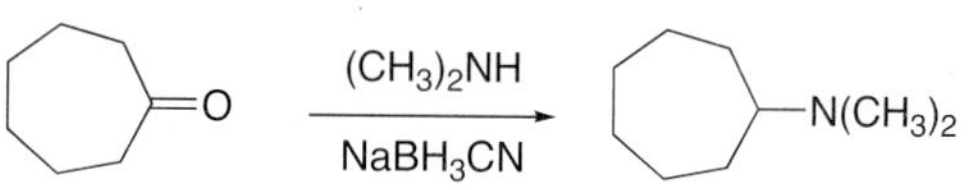

c. 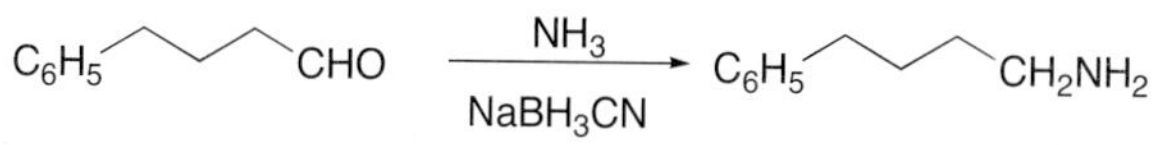

d. 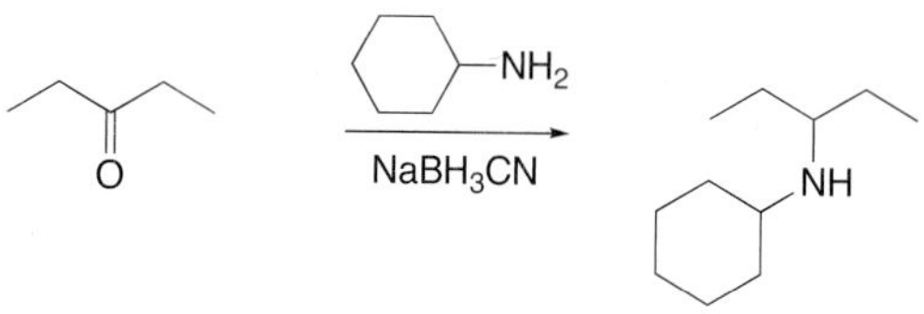

25.58

a. 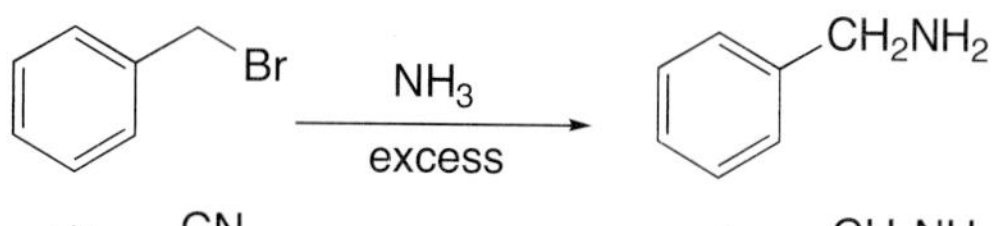

b. 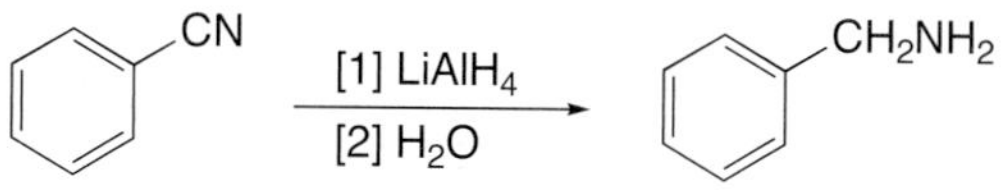

c. 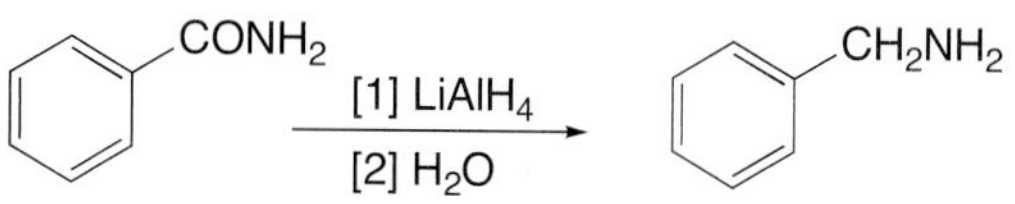

d. 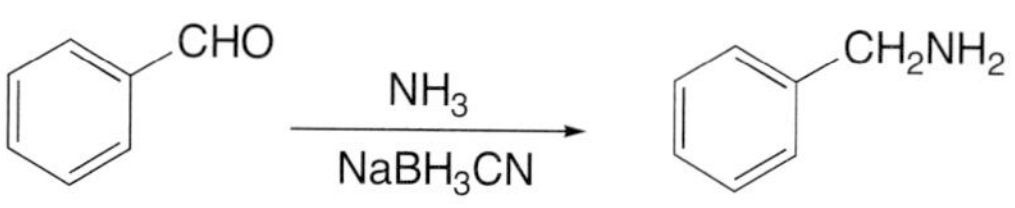

e. 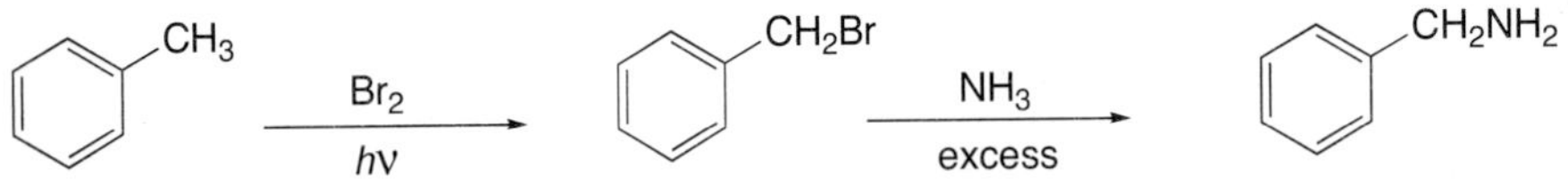
CH3
Br2
hν
CH2Br
NH3
excess
CH2NH2

f. 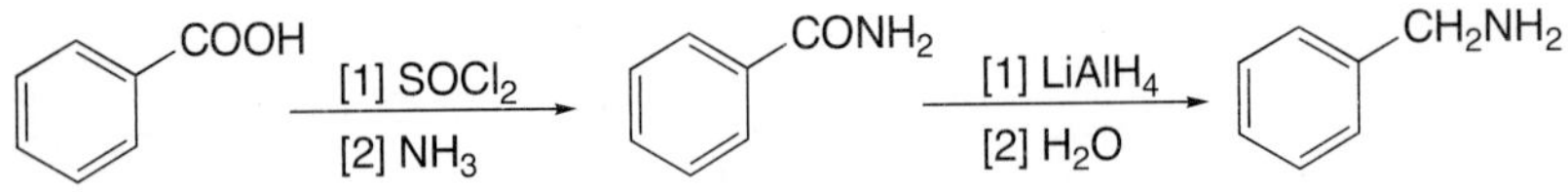
COOH
[1] SOCl2
[2] NH3
CONH2
[1] LiAlH4
[2] H2O
CH2NH2

g. 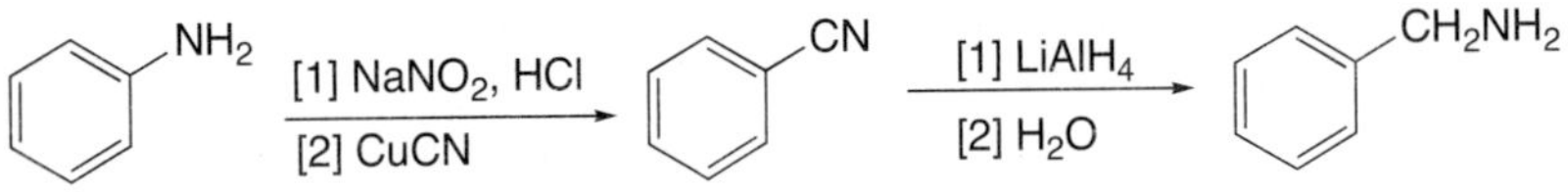
NH2
[1] NaNO2, HCl
[2] CuCN
CN
[1] LiAlH4
[2] H2O
CH2NH2

h. 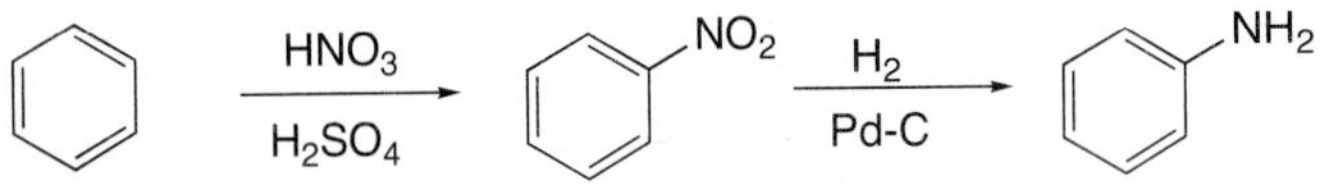
HNO3
H2SO4
NO2
H2
Pd-C
NH2
Then as in (g).

25.59 Use the directions from Answer 25.20. Separation can be achieved because benzoic acid reacts with aqueous base and aniline reacts with aqueous acid according to the following equations:

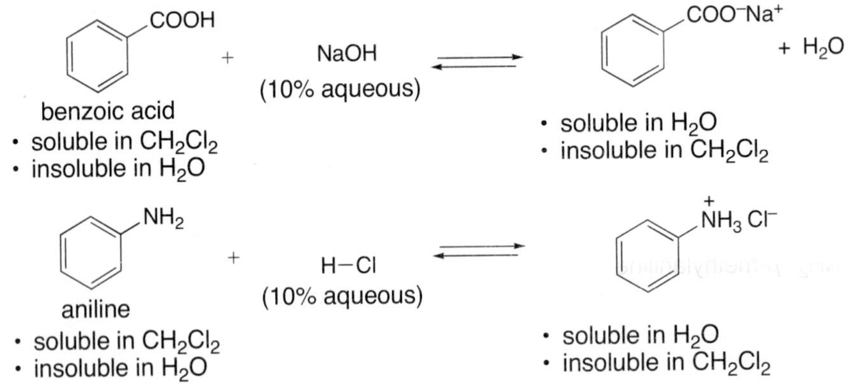
COOH
+
NaOH
(10% aqueous)
COO⁻Na⁺
+ H2O
benzoic acid
• soluble in CH2Cl2
• insoluble in H2O
• soluble in H2O
• insoluble in CH2Cl2
NH2
+
H–Cl
(10% aqueous)
NH3 Cl⁻
aniline
• soluble in CH2Cl2
• insoluble in H2O
• soluble in H2O
• insoluble in CH2Cl2

Toluene ($C_6H_5CH_3$), on the other hand, is not protonated or deprotonated in aqueous solution, so it is always soluble in CH_2Cl_2 and insoluble in H_2O. The following flow chart illustrates the process.

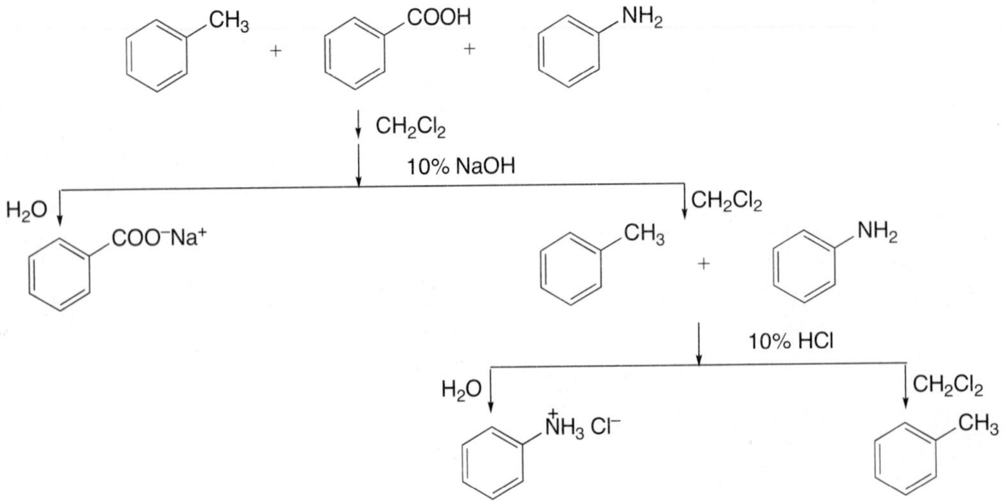
CH3
+
COOH
+
NH2
CH2Cl2
10% NaOH
H2O
COO⁻Na⁺
CH2Cl2
CH3
+
NH2
10% HCl
H2O
NH3 Cl⁻
CH2Cl2
CH3

25.60

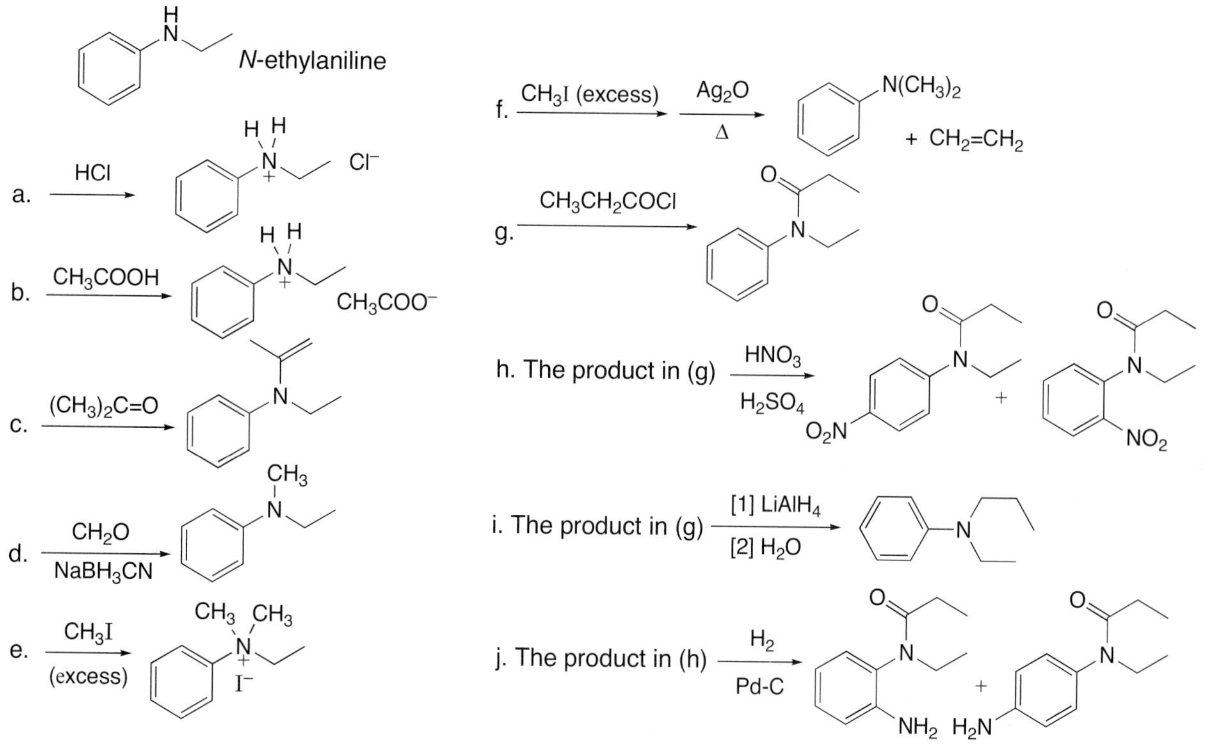
N-ethylaniline
a. HCl
Cl⁻
b. CH3COOH
CH3COO⁻
c. (CH3)2C=O
d. CH2O
NaBH3CN
e. CH3I
(excess)
I⁻
f. CH3I (excess)
Ag2O
Δ
N(CH3)2
+ CH2=CH2
g. CH3CH2COCl
h. The product in (g)
HNO3
H2SO4
O2N
NO2
i. The product in (g)
[1] LiAlH4
[2] H2O
j. The product in (h)
H2
Pd-C
NH2
H2N

25.61

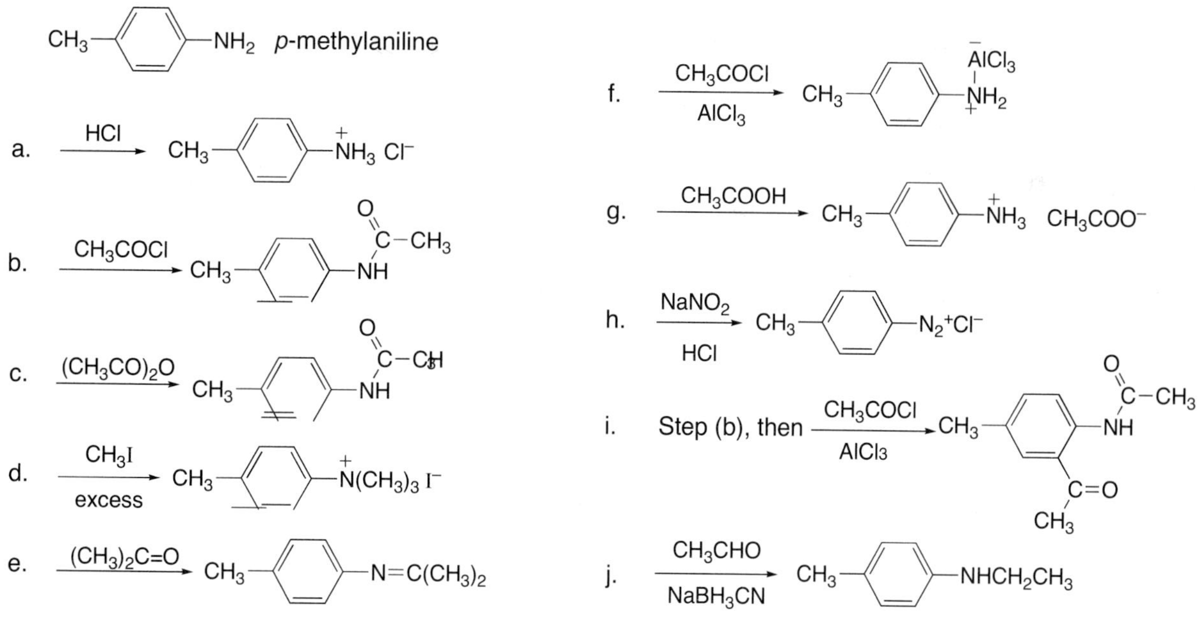
CH3
NH2
p-methylaniline
a. HCl
NH3 Cl⁻
b. CH3COCl
c. (CH3CO)2O
d. CH3I
excess
N(CH3)3 I⁻
e. (CH3)2C=O
N=C(CH3)2
f. CH3COCl
AlCl3
g. CH3COOH
NH3 CH3COO⁻
h. NaNO2
HCl
N2⁺Cl⁻
i. Step (b), then
CH3COCl
AlCl3
j. CH3CHO
NaBH3CN
NHCH2CH3

25.62

a. $CH_3(CH_2)_6NH_2 \xrightarrow[\text{[2] } Ag_2O \text{ [3] } \Delta]{\text{[1] } CH_3I \text{ (excess)}} CH_3(CH_2)_4CH{=}CH_2$

b.
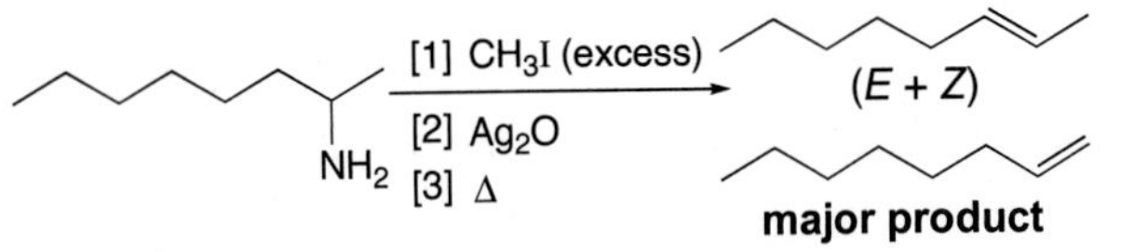
[1] CH_3I (excess)
[2] Ag_2O
[3] Δ
NH_2
(E + Z)
major product

c.
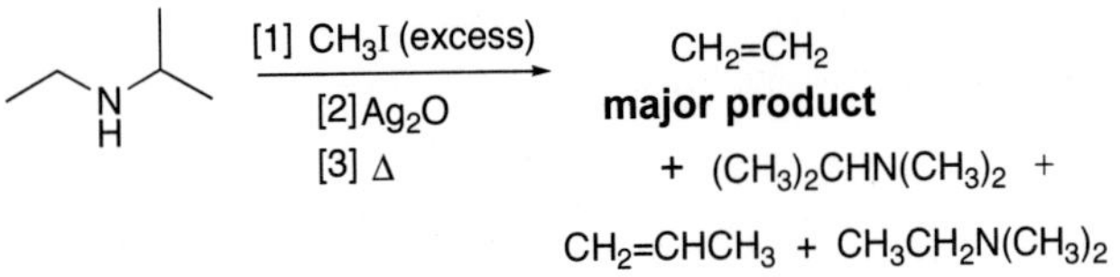
[1] CH_3I (excess)
[2] Ag_2O
[3] Δ
CH_2=CH_2
major product
+ $(CH_3)_2CHN(CH_3)_2$ +
CH_2=$CHCH_3$ + $CH_3CH_2N(CH_3)_2$

d.
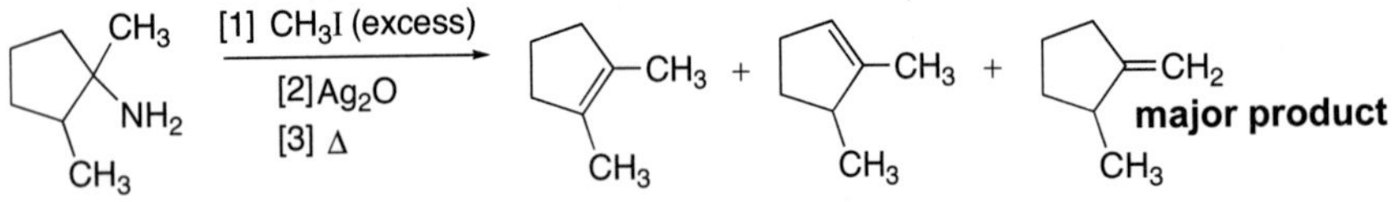
CH_3
NH_2
[1] CH_3I (excess)
[2] Ag_2O
[3] Δ
CH_2
major product

e.
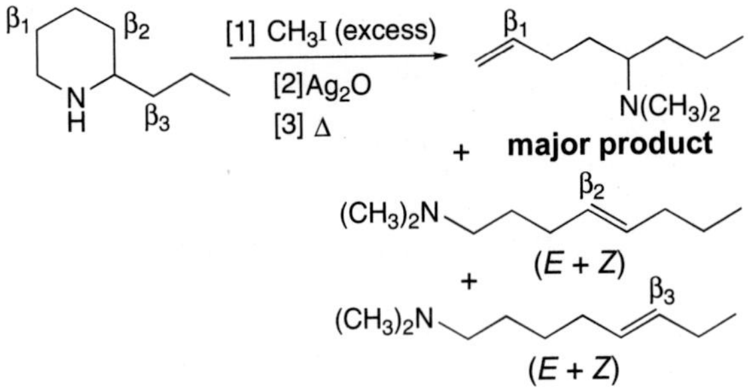
β1
β2
β3
[1] CH_3I (excess)
[2] Ag_2O
[3] Δ
$N(CH_3)_2$
major product
$(CH_3)_2N$
(E + Z)

25.63

a.
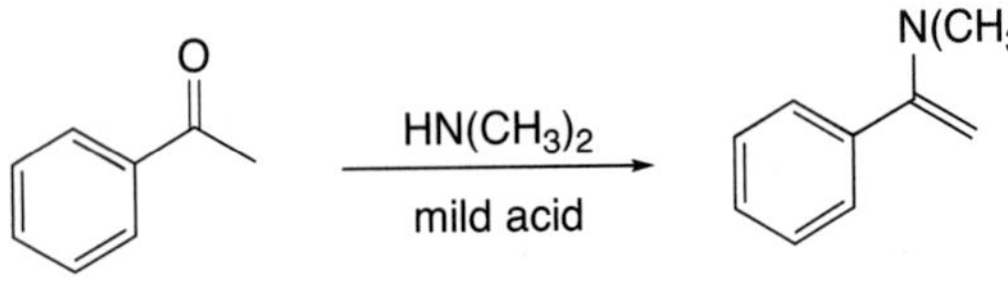
$HN(CH_3)_2$
mild acid
$N(CH_3)_2$

b.
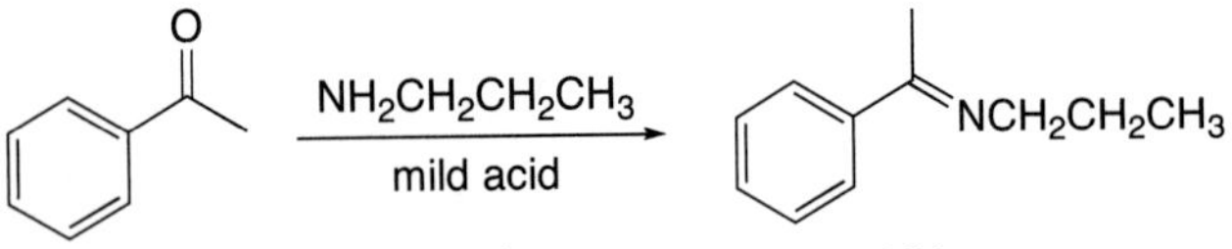
$NH_2CH_2CH_2CH_3$
mild acid
$NCH_2CH_2CH_3$

c.
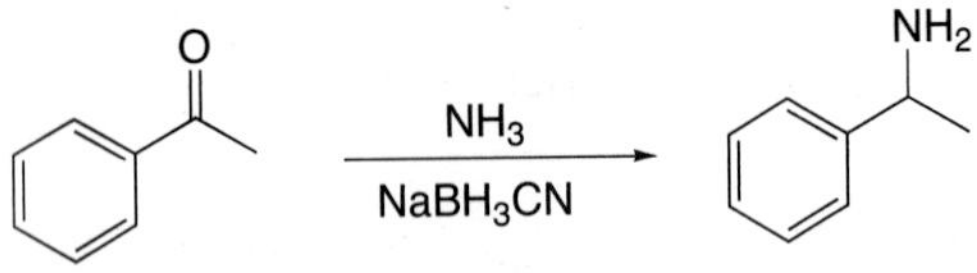
NH_3
$NaBH_3CN$
NH_2

d.
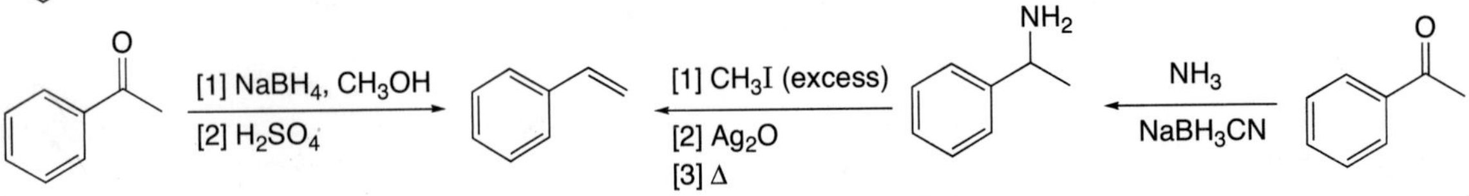
[1] $NaBH_4$, CH_3OH
[2] H_2SO_4
[1] CH_3I (excess)
[2] Ag_2O
[3] Δ
NH_2
NH_3
$NaBH_3CN$

e.
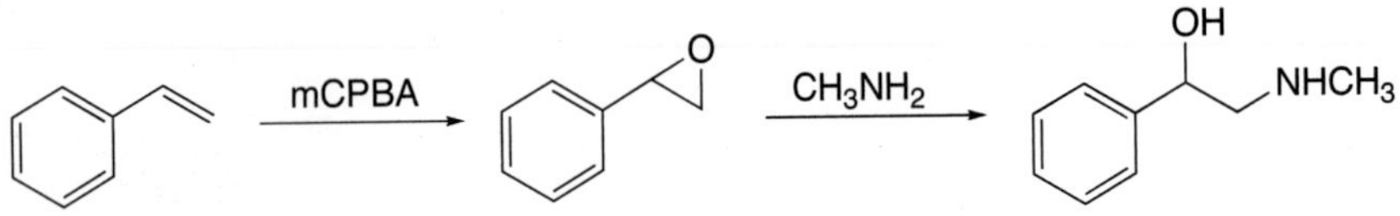
mCPBA
CH_3NH_2
OH
$NHCH_3$

(from d.)

f.
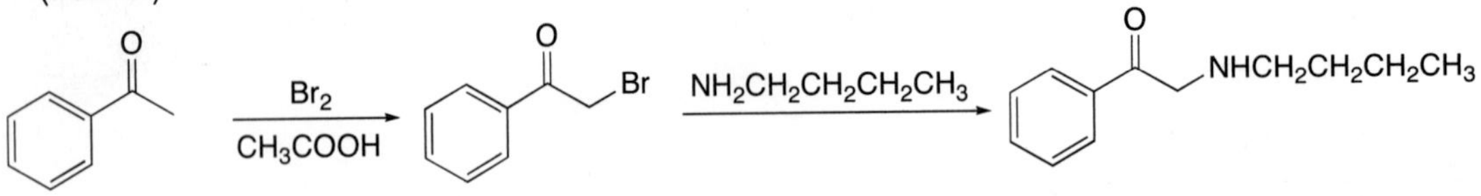
Br_2
CH_3COOH
Br
$NH_2CH_2CH_2CH_2CH_3$
$NHCH_2CH_2CH_2CH_3$

25.64

a.
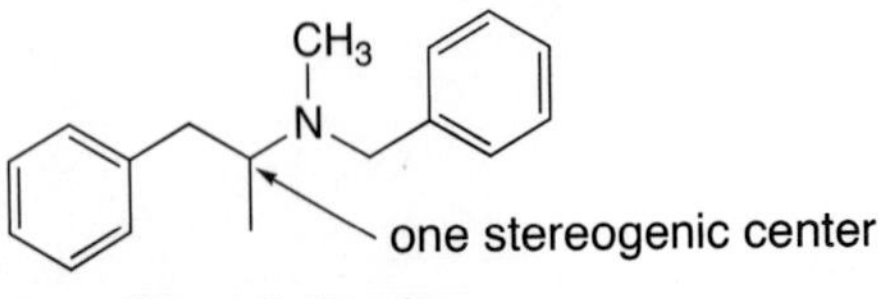
CH_3
N
one stereogenic center

benzphetamine

b. Amides that can be reduced to benzphetamine:

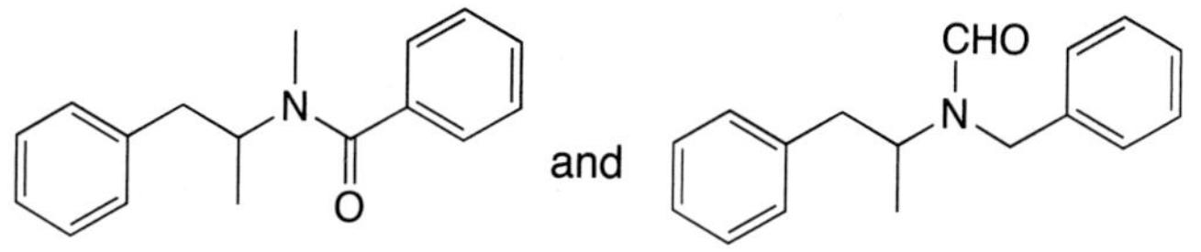
N
O
and
CHO
N

c. Amines + carbonyl compounds that form benzphetamine by reductive amination:

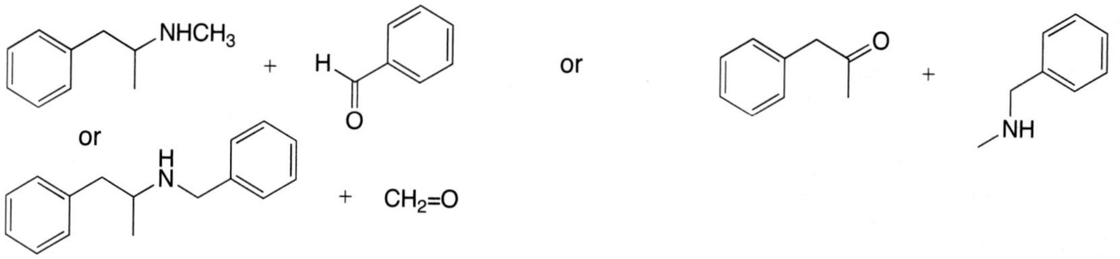
NHCH3
+
H
O
or
O
+
NH
or
H
N
+ CH2=O

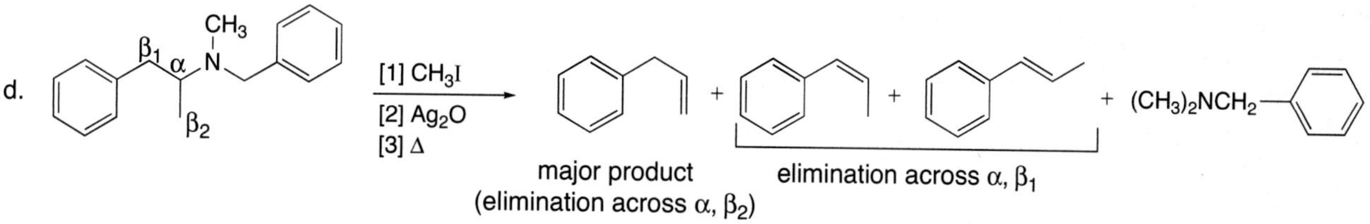
d.
CH3
β1
α
N
β2
[1] CH3I
[2] Ag2O
[3] Δ
+
+
+ (CH3)2NCH2
major product
(elimination across α, β2)
elimination across α, β1

25.65

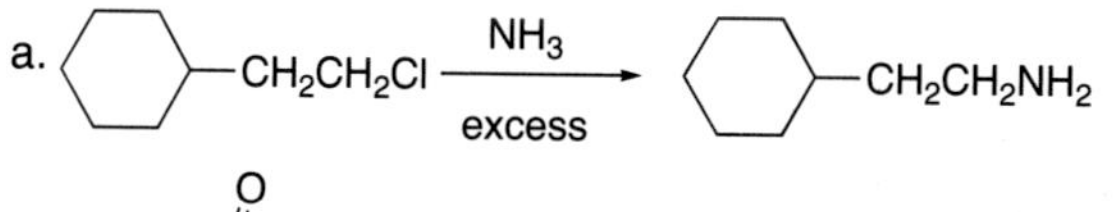
a.
CH2CH2Cl
NH3
excess
CH2CH2NH2

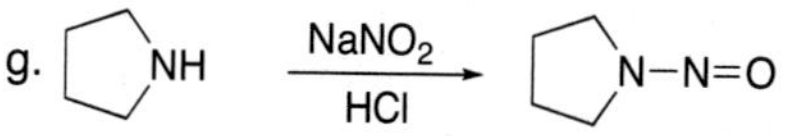
g.
NH
NaNO2
HCl
N–N=O

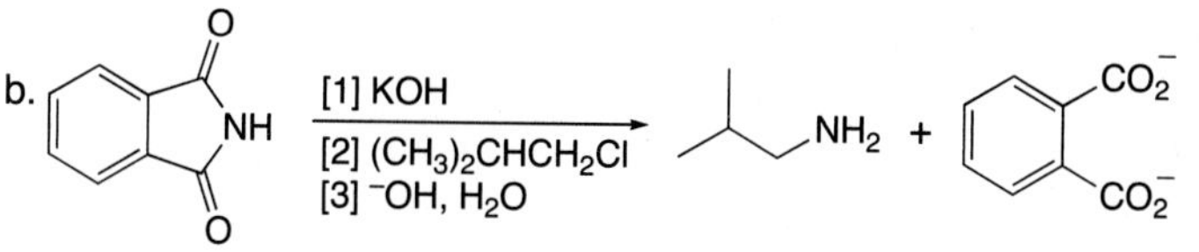
b.
O
NH
O
[1] KOH
[2] (CH3)2CHCH2Cl
[3] −OH, H2O
NH2 +
CO2−
CO2−

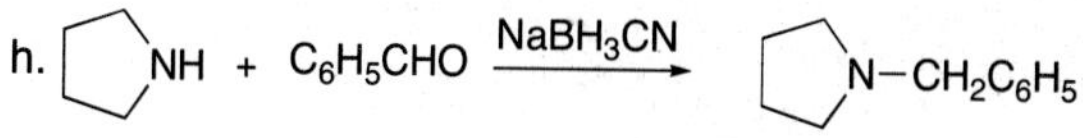
h.
NH
+ C6H5CHO
NaBH3CN
N–CH2C6H5

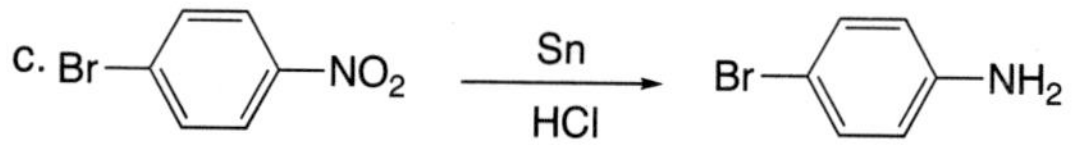
c. Br
NO2
Sn
HCl
Br
NH2

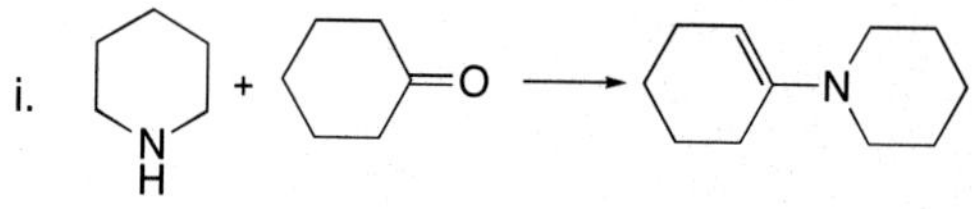
i.
N
H
+
O

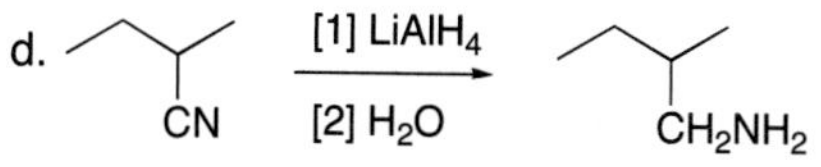
d.
CN
[1] LiAlH4
[2] H2O
CH2NH2

j. $CH_3CH_2CH_2{-}N{-}CH(CH_3)_2$ (N–H) $\xrightarrow{\text{[1] } CH_3I \text{ (excess)}}$ [2] Ag_2O [3] Δ

$CH_3CH{=}CH_2$ + $(CH_3)_2NCH(CH_3)_2$

$CH_3CH_2CH_2N(CH_3)_2$

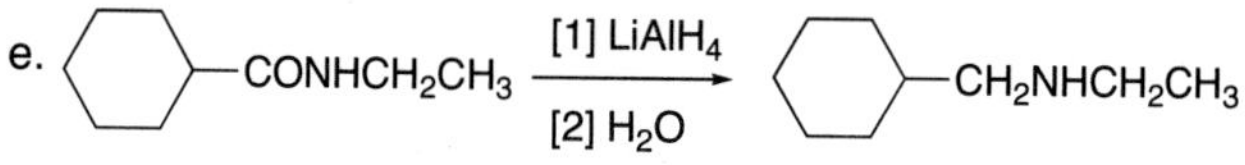
e.
CONHCH2CH3
[1] LiAlH4
[2] H2O
CH2NHCH2CH3

f. $C_6H_5CH_2CH_2NH_2$ + $(C_6H_5CO)_2O$ ⟶

$C_6H_5CH_2CH_2NHCOC_6H_5$ + $C_6H_5CH_2CH_2NH_3^+$ $C_6H_5COO^-$

25.66 NH_2 and H must be anti for the Hofmann elimination. Rotate around the C–C bond so the NH_2 and H are anti.

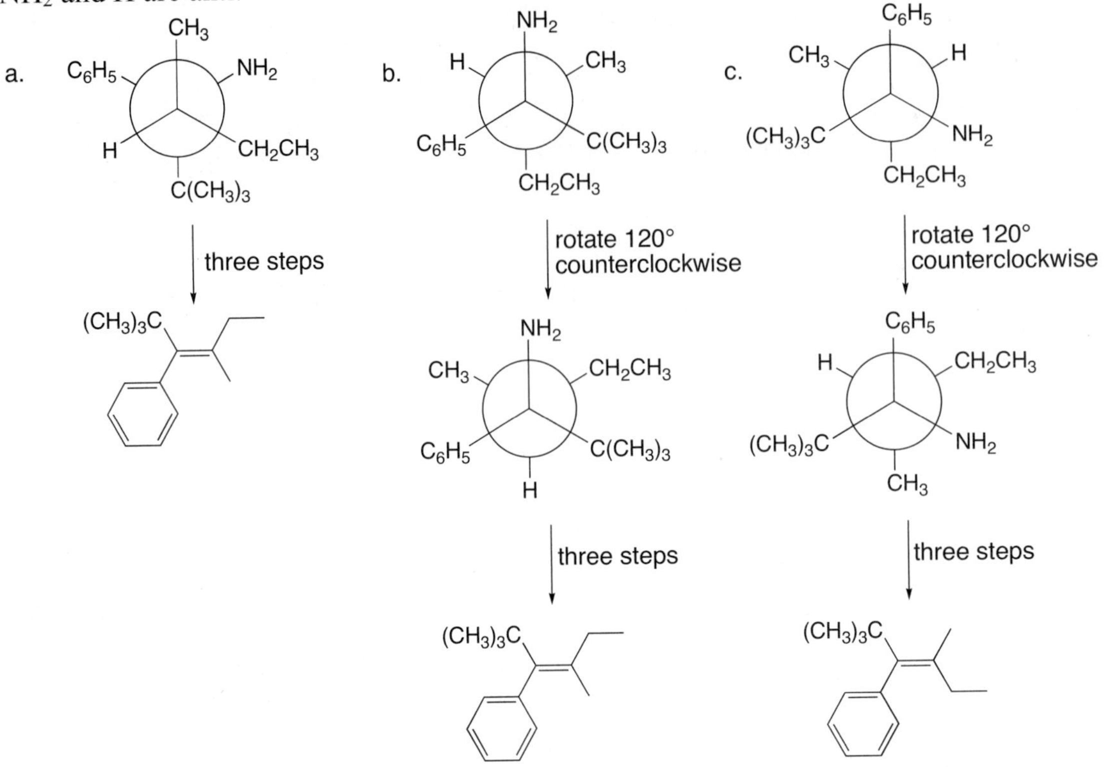
a.
CH3
C6H5
NH2
H
CH2CH3
C(CH3)3
three steps
(CH3)3C
b.
NH2
H
CH3
C6H5
C(CH3)3
CH2CH3
rotate 120°
counterclockwise
NH2
CH3
CH2CH3
C6H5
C(CH3)3
H
three steps
(CH3)3C
c.
C6H5
CH3
H
(CH3)3C
NH2
CH2CH3
rotate 120°
counterclockwise
C6H5
H
CH2CH3
(CH3)3C
NH2
CH3
three steps
(CH3)3C

25.67

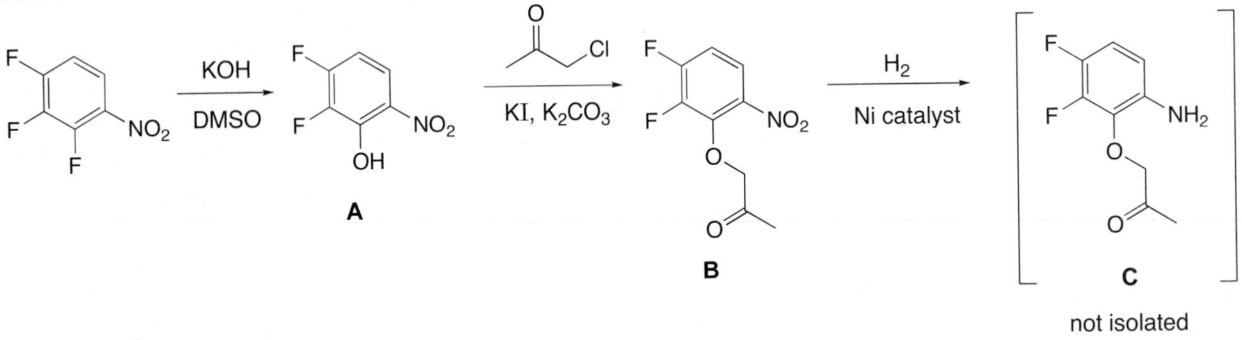
F
F
F
NO2
KOH
DMSO
F
F
NO2
OH
A
O
Cl
KI, K2CO3
F
F
NO2
O
O
B
H2
Ni catalyst
F
F
NH2
O
O
C
not isolated

25.68

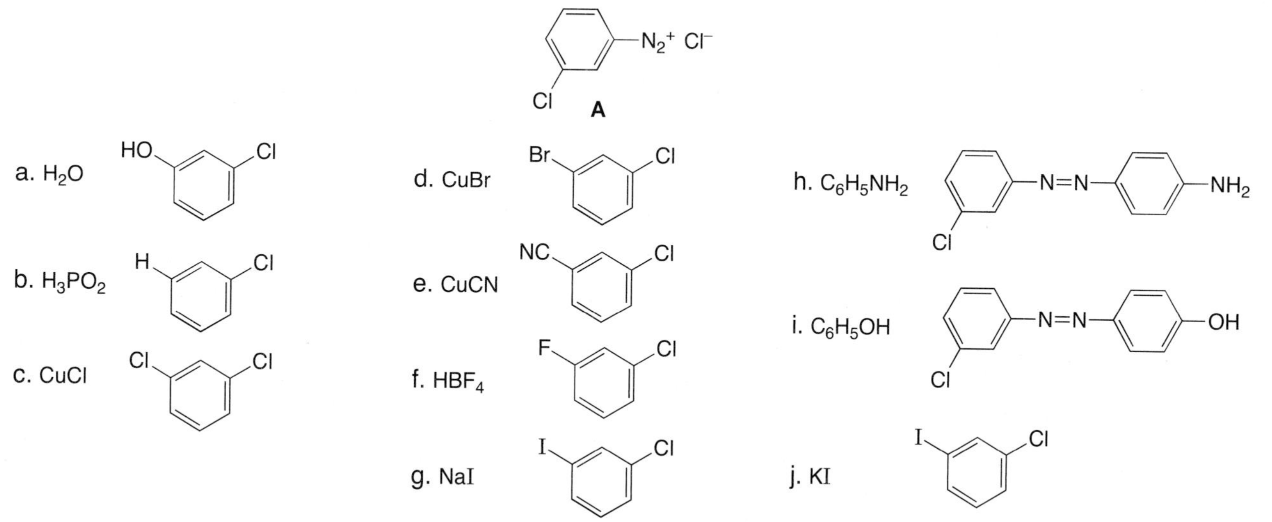

25.69

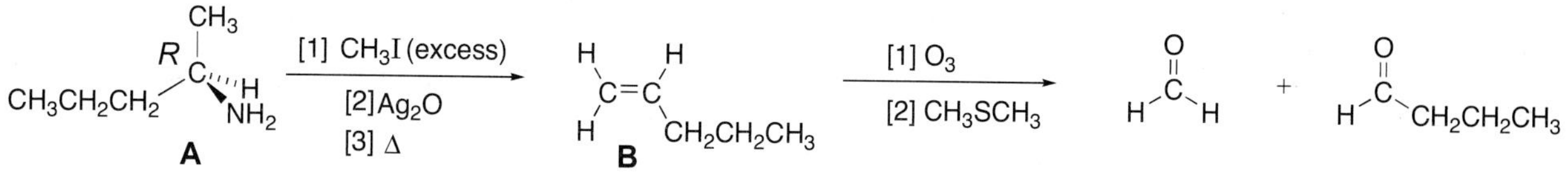

25.70

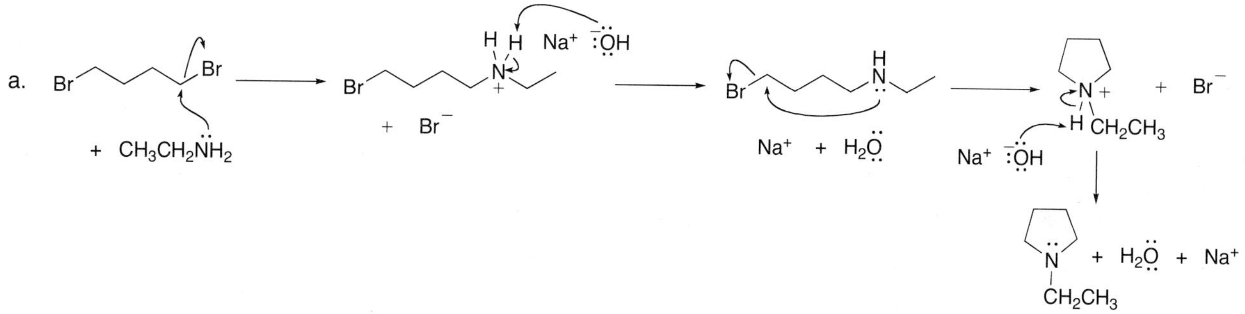

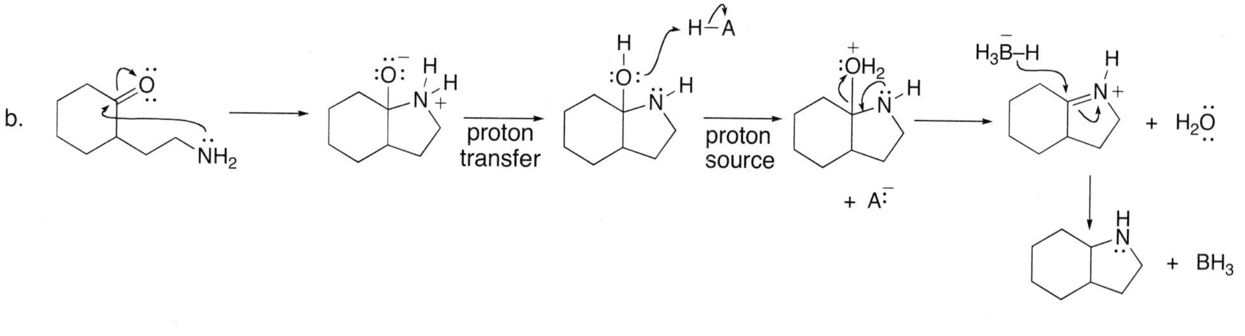

25.71

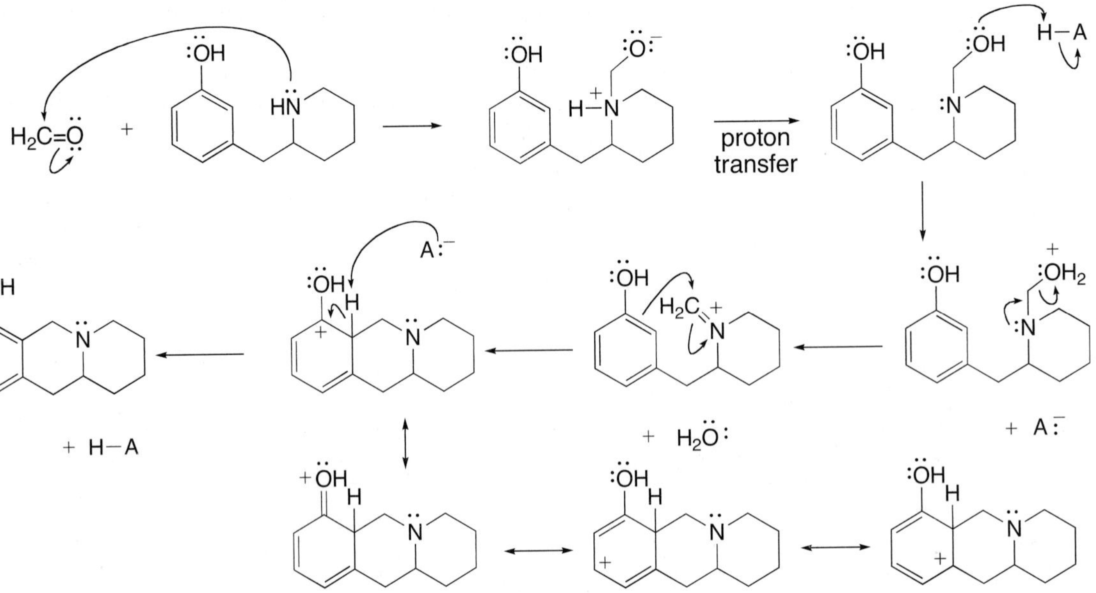

25.72

Overall reaction:

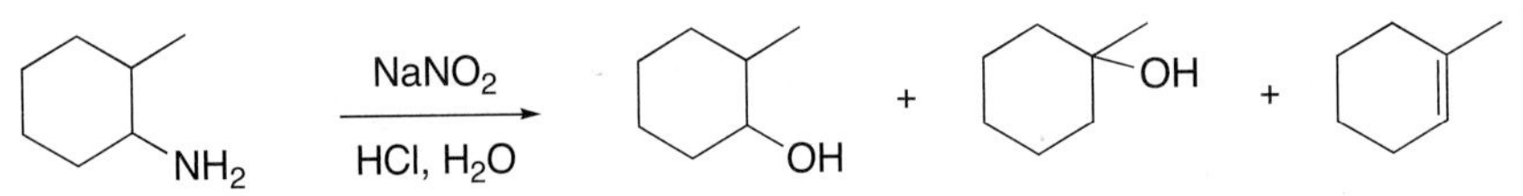

The steps:

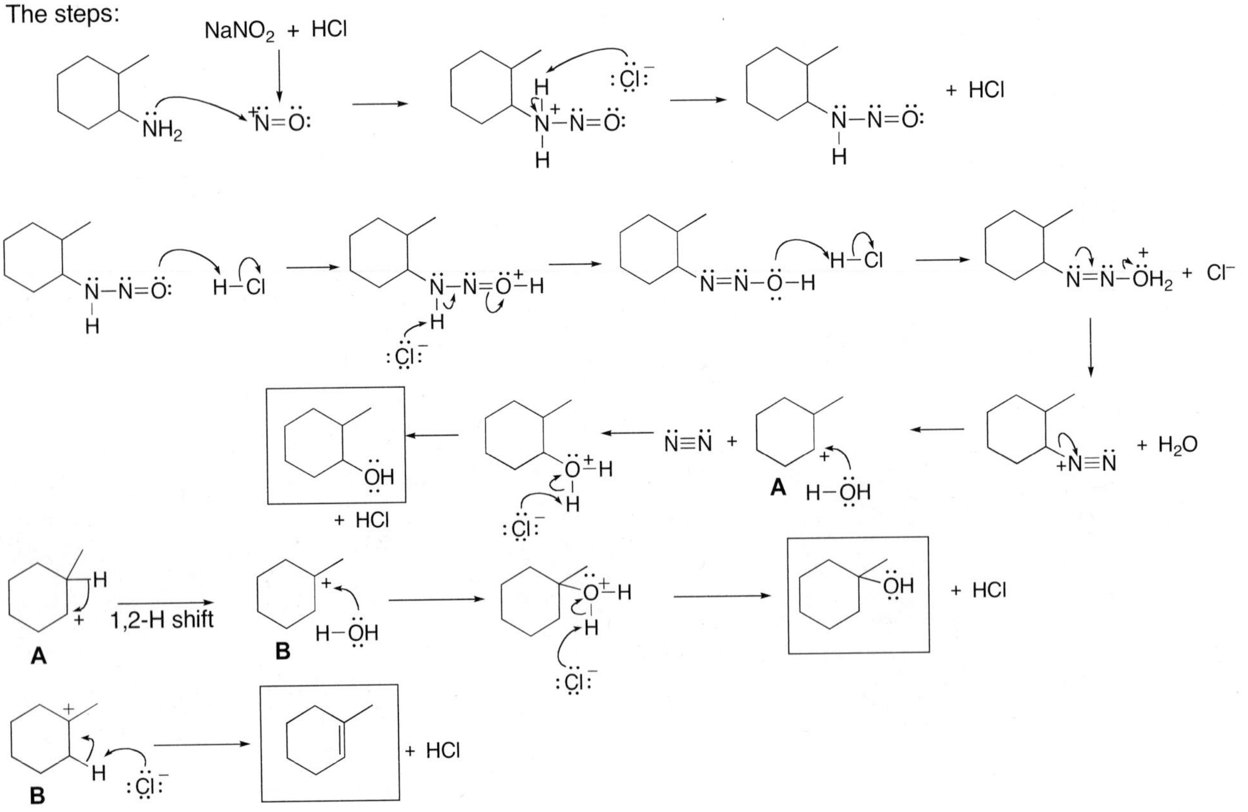

25.73 A nitrosonium ion (^+NO) is a weak electrophile so electrophilic aromatic substitution occurs only with a strong electron-donor group that stabilizes the intermediate carbocation.

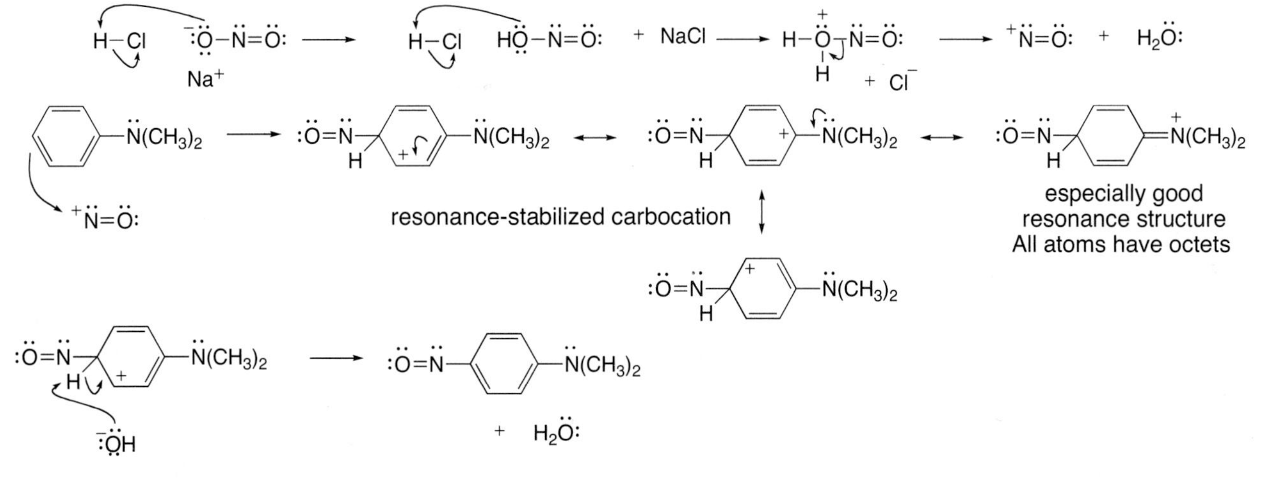
resonance-stabilized carbocation
especially good resonance structure
All atoms have octets

25.74

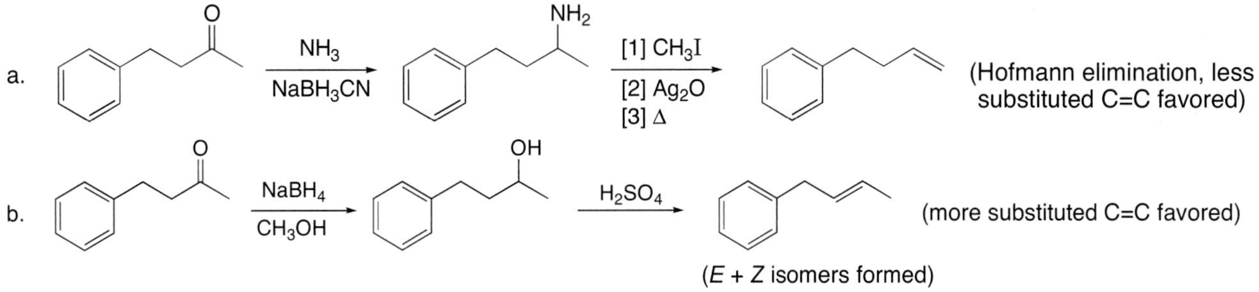
a.
NH3
NaBH3CN
[1] CH3I
[2] Ag2O
[3] Δ
(Hofmann elimination, less substituted C=C favored)
b.
NaBH4
CH3OH
H2SO4
(more substituted C=C favored)
(E + Z isomers formed)

25.75

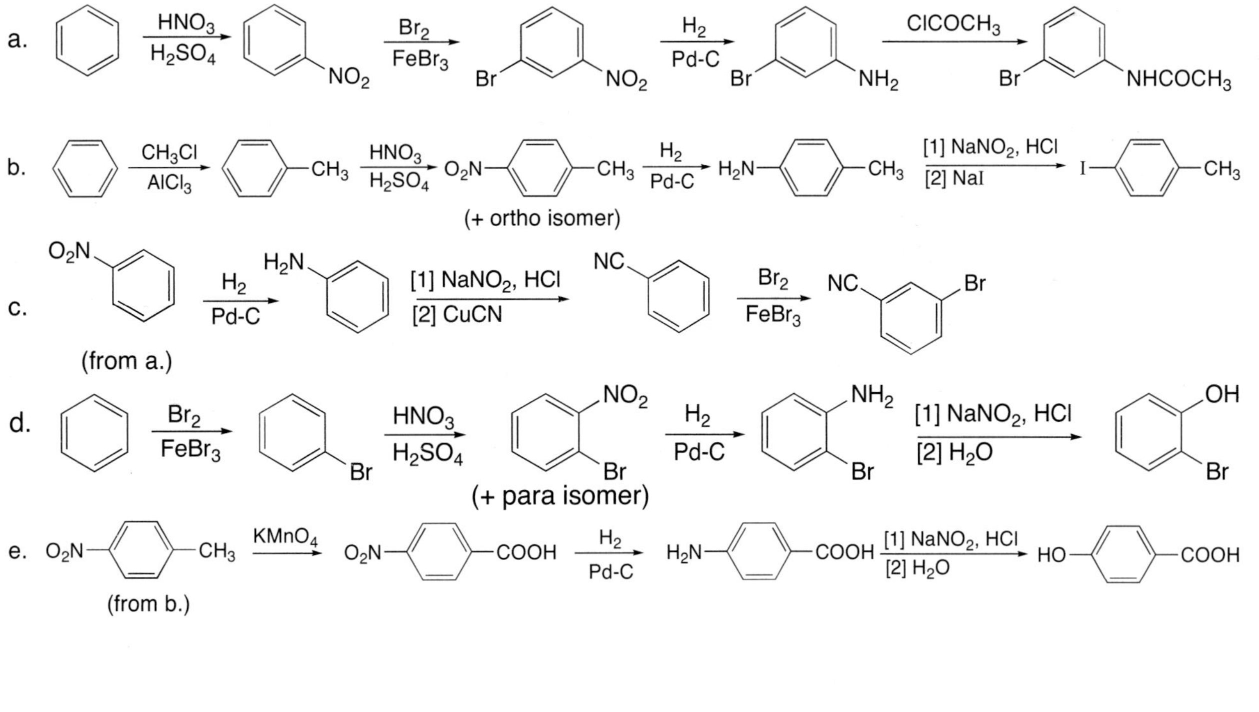
a.
HNO3
H2SO4
Br2
FeBr3
H2
Pd-C
ClCOCH3
b.
CH3Cl
AlCl3
(+ ortho isomer)
[1] NaNO2, HCl
[2] NaI
c.
(from a.)
[2] CuCN
d.
(+ para isomer)
[2] H2O
e.
KMnO4
(from b.)

f. 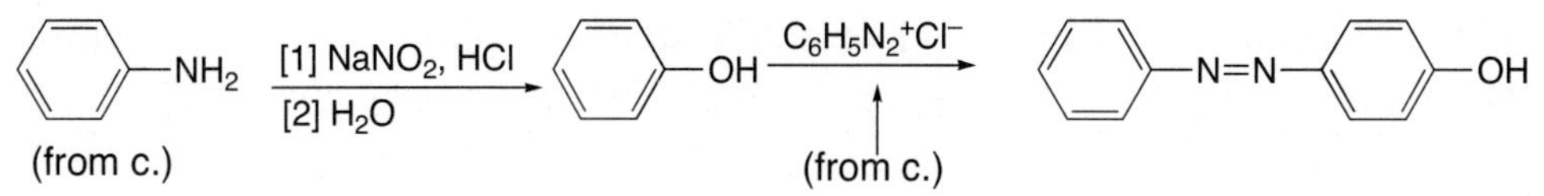

25.76

a. 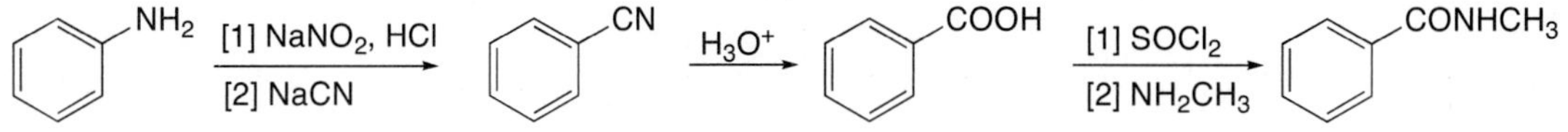

b. 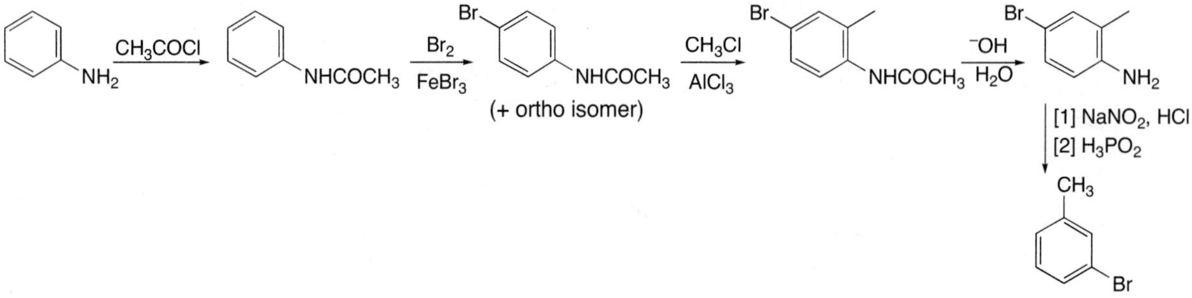

c. 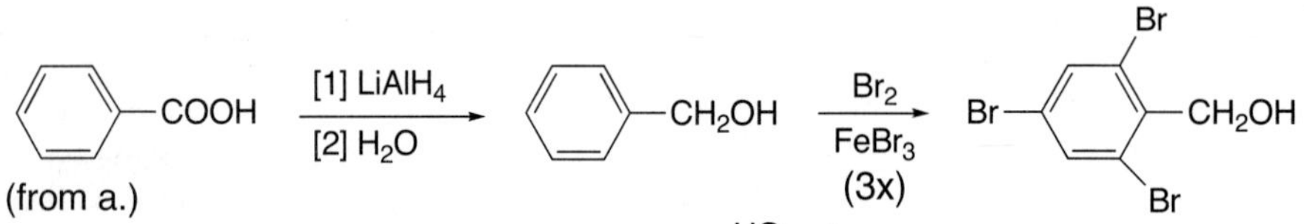

d. 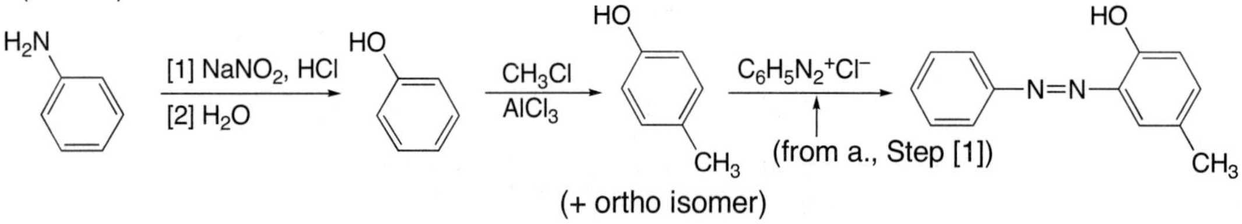

25.77

[1] 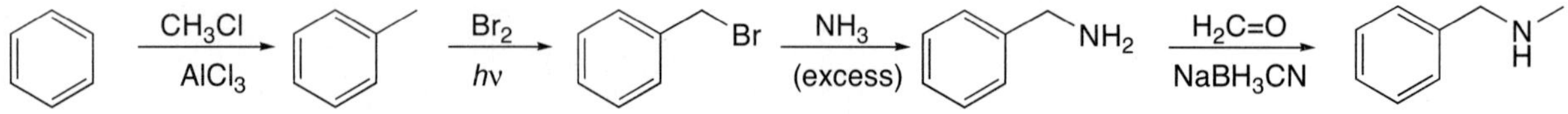

[2] 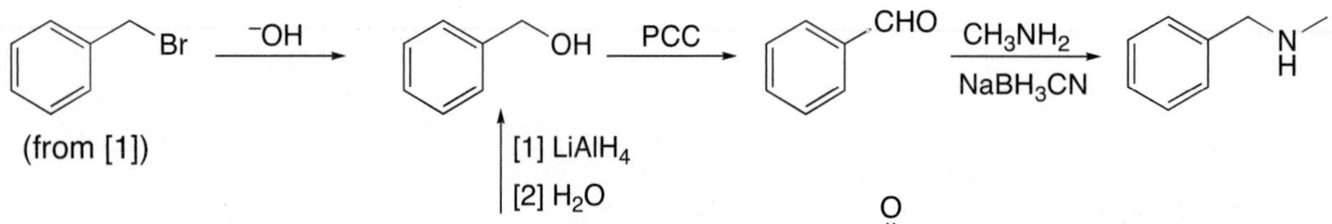

[3] 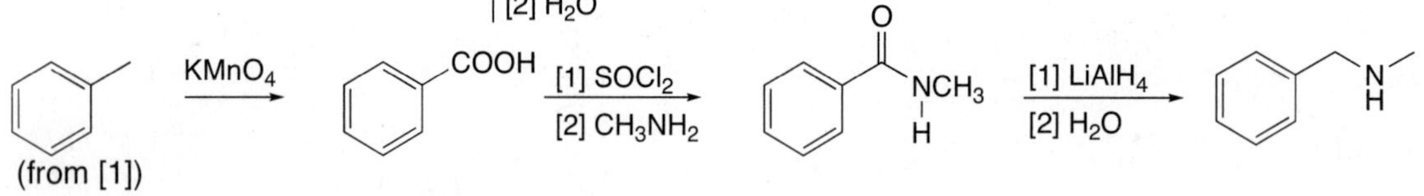

[4] 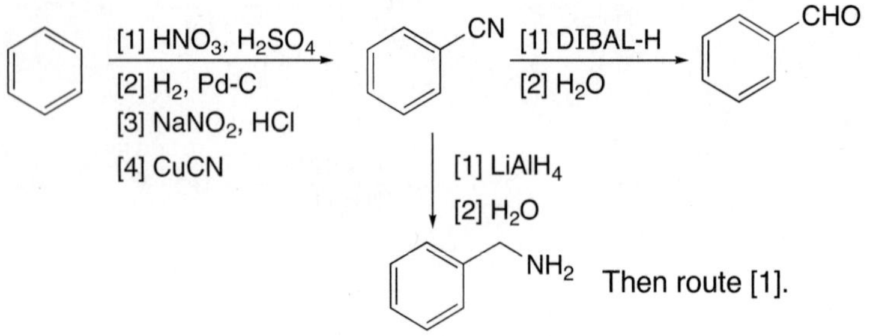

Then route [2].

Then route [1].

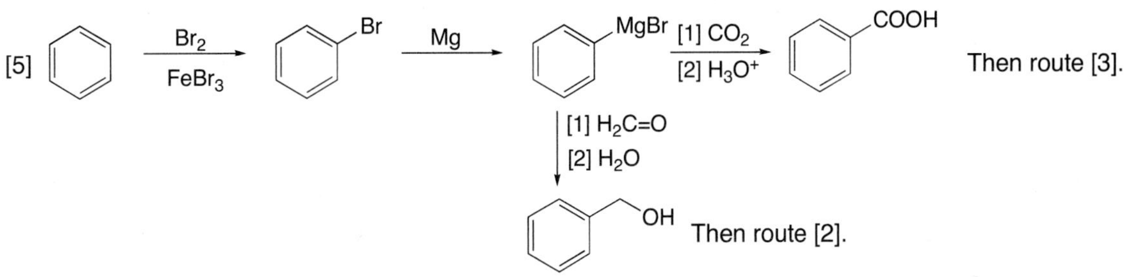
[5]
Br2
FeBr3
Br
Mg
MgBr
[1] CO2
[2] H3O+
COOH
Then route [3].
[1] H2C=O
[2] H2O
OH
Then route [2].

25.78

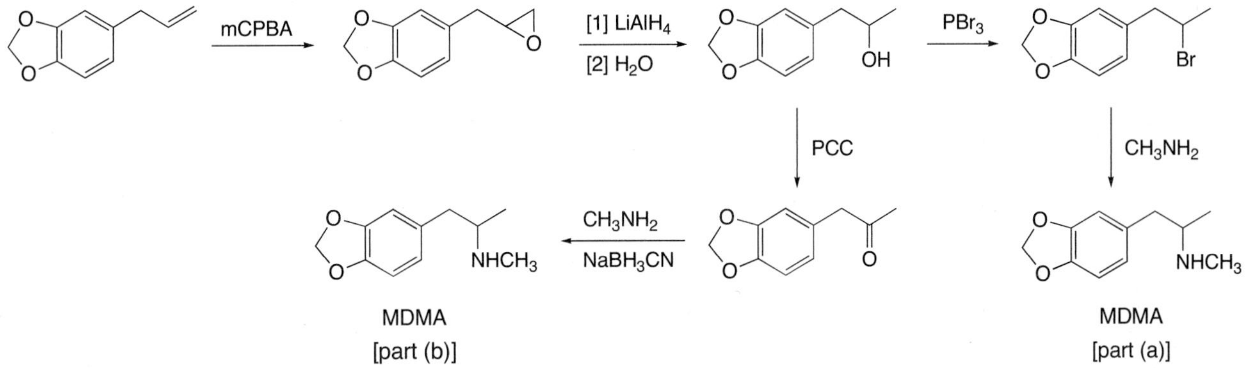
mCPBA
[1] LiAlH4
[2] H2O
OH
PBr3
Br
PCC
CH3NH2
CH3NH2
NaBH3CN
NHCH3
NHCH3
MDMA
[part (b)]
MDMA
[part (a)]

25.79

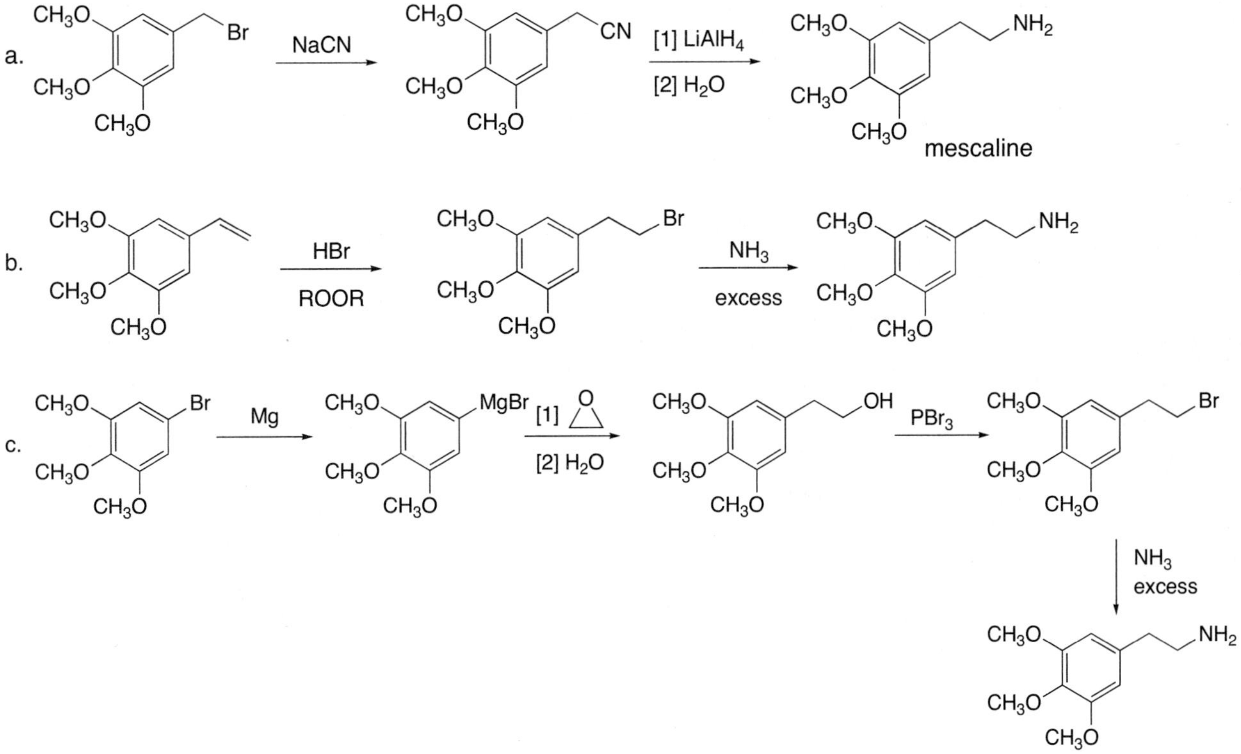
a.
CH3O
Br
NaCN
CN
[1] LiAlH4
[2] H2O
NH2
mescaline
b.
HBr
ROOR
NH3
excess
c.
Mg
MgBr
[1]
[2] H2O
OH
PBr3
NH3
excess

25.80

a. 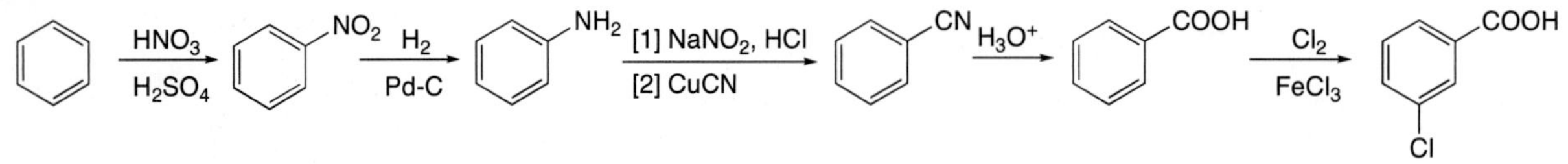

b. 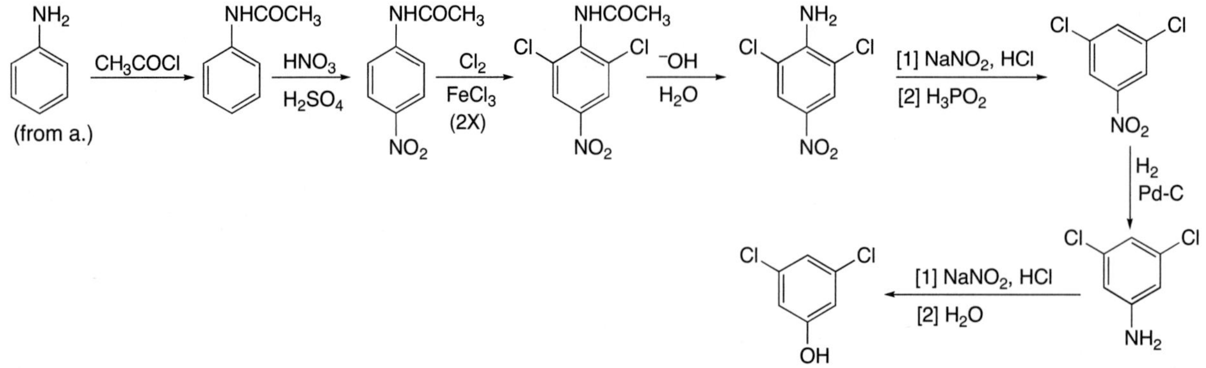

c. 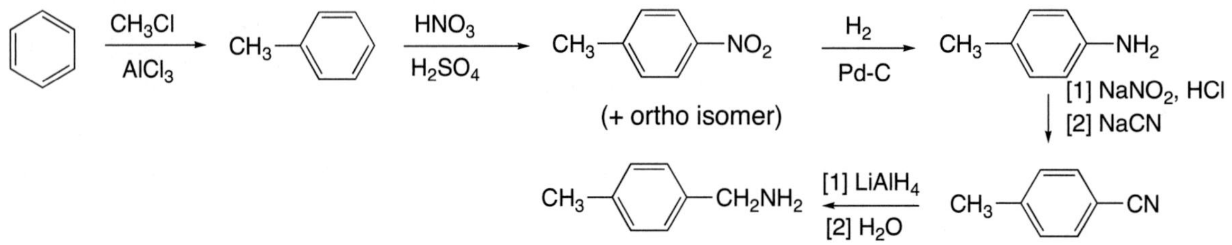

d. 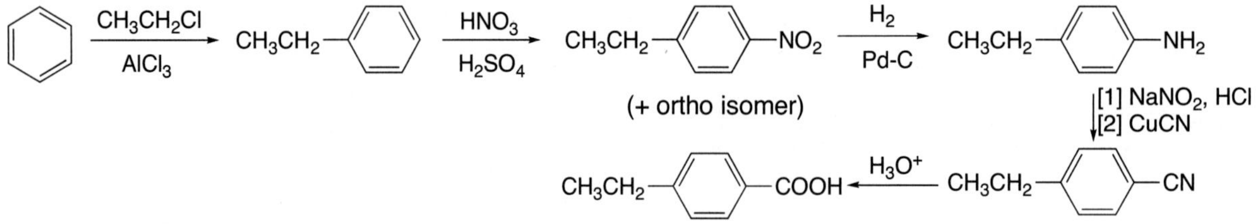

e. 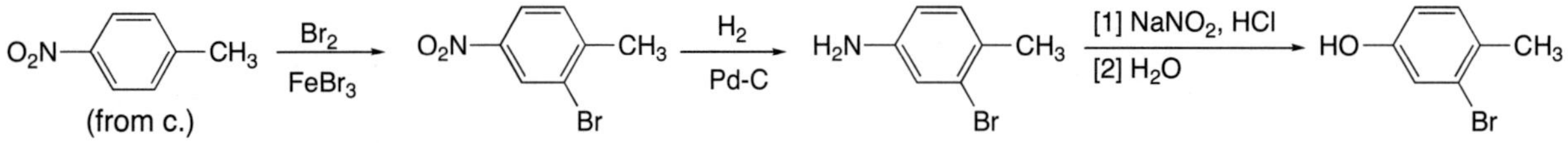

f. 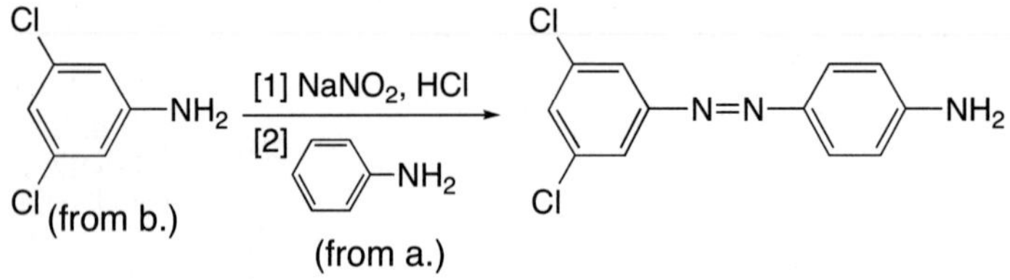

25.81

a. 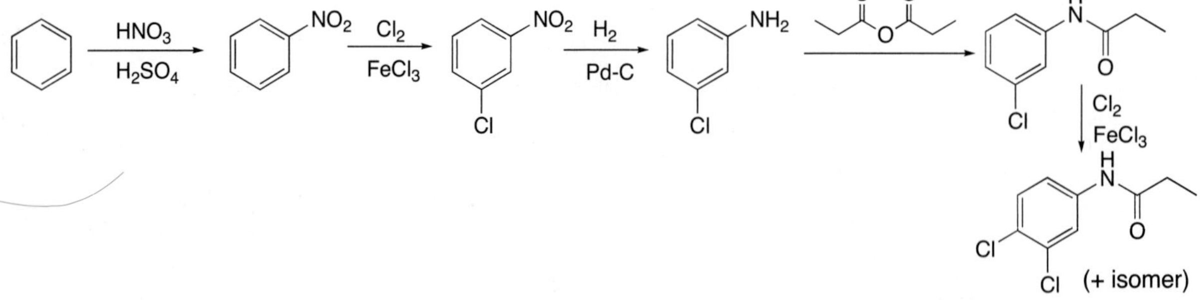

b.
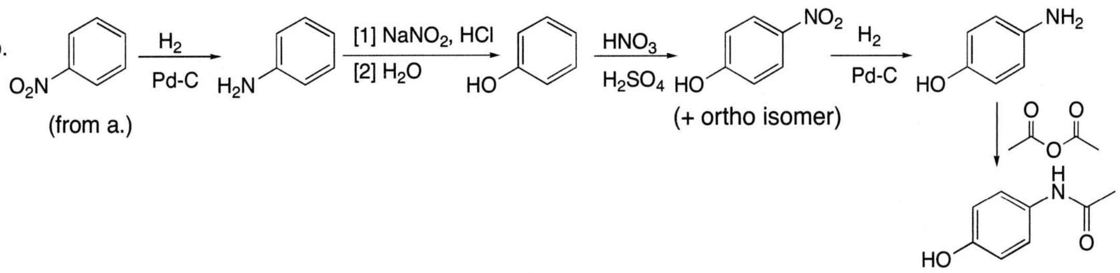
O2N
(from a.)
H2
Pd-C
H2N
[1] NaNO2, HCl
[2] H2O
HO
HNO3
H2SO4
NO2
(+ ortho isomer)
H2
Pd-C
NH2
H
N
O

c.
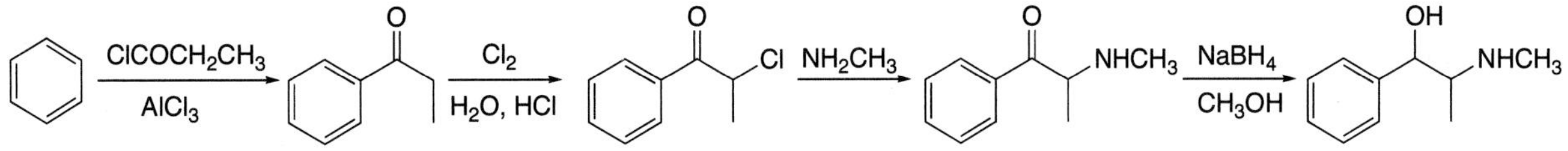
ClCOCH2CH3
AlCl3
O
Cl2
H2O, HCl
Cl
NH2CH3
NHCH3
NaBH4
CH3OH
OH

25.82

a.
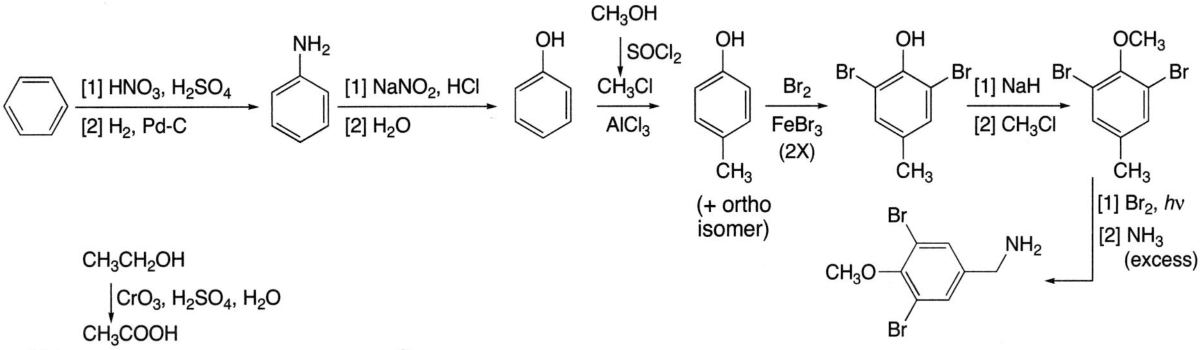
[1] HNO3, H2SO4
[2] H2, Pd-C
NH2
[1] NaNO2, HCl
[2] H2O
OH
CH3OH
SOCl2
CH3Cl
AlCl3
CH3
(+ ortho isomer)
Br2
FeBr3
(2X)
Br
[1] NaH
[2] CH3Cl
OCH3
[1] Br2, hν
[2] NH3 (excess)
CH3O
NH2

b.
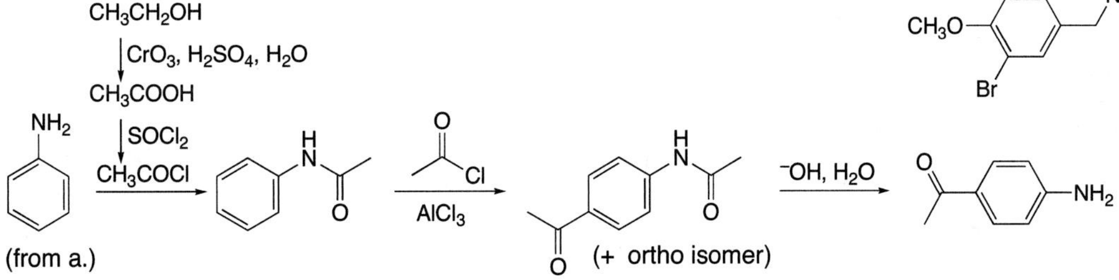
NH2
(from a.)
CH3CH2OH
CrO3, H2SO4, H2O
CH3COOH
SOCl2
CH3COCl
H
N
O
Cl
AlCl3
(+ ortho isomer)
−OH, H2O
NH2

c.
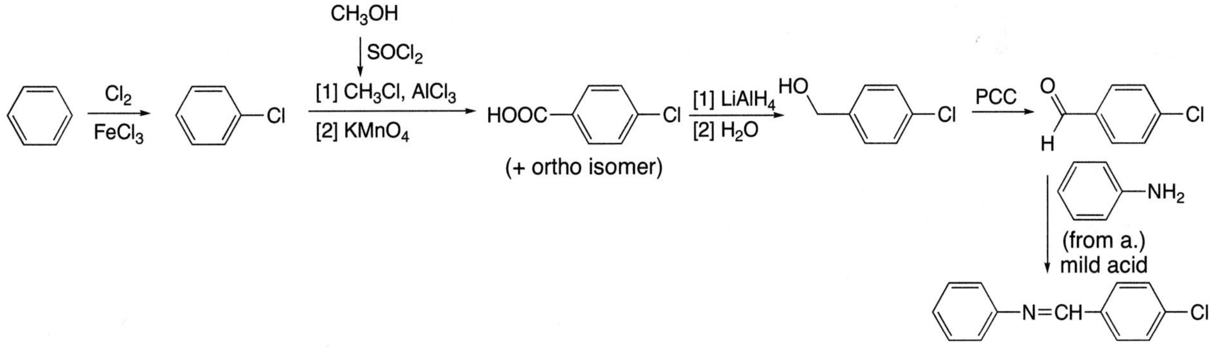
Cl2
FeCl3
Cl
CH3OH
SOCl2
[1] CH3Cl, AlCl3
[2] KMnO4
HOOC
(+ ortho isomer)
[1] LiAlH4
[2] H2O
HO
PCC
O
H
NH2
(from a.)
mild acid
N=CH

d.
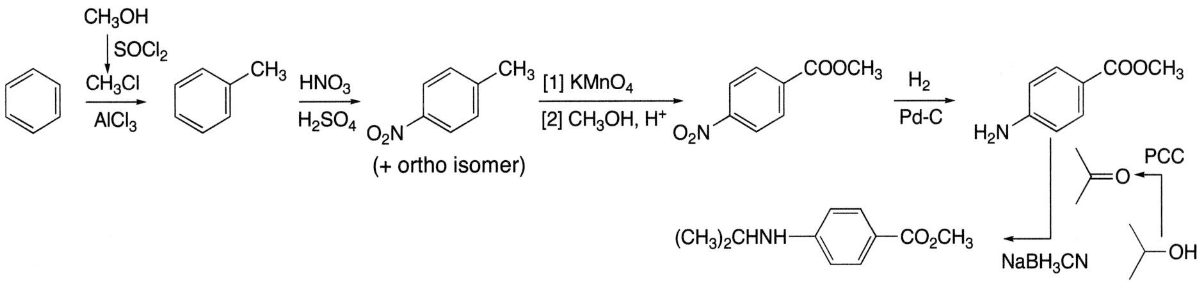
CH3OH
SOCl2
CH3Cl
AlCl3
CH3
HNO3
H2SO4
O2N
(+ ortho isomer)
[1] KMnO4
[2] CH3OH, H+
COOCH3
H2
Pd-C
H2N
PCC
O
OH
NaBH3CN
(CH3)2CHNH
CO2CH3

e. 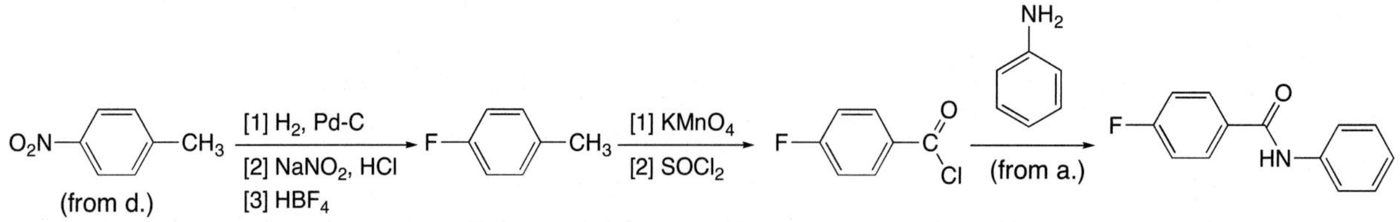

Probably a strong enough activator that the Friedel–Crafts reaction will still occur.

f. Make two parts:

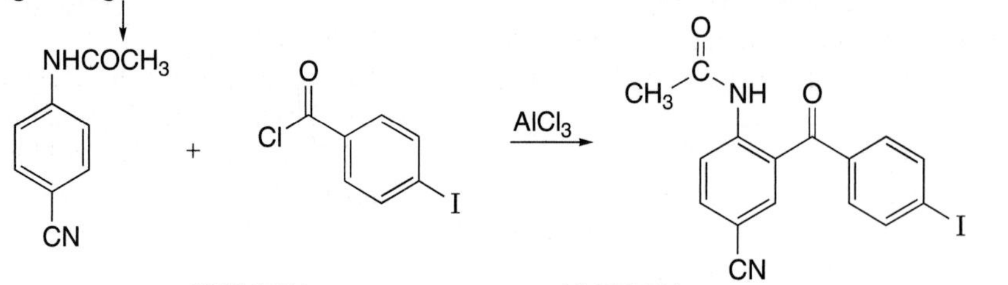

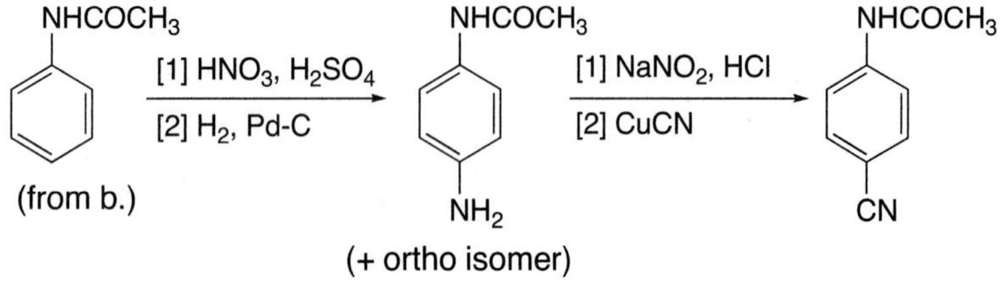

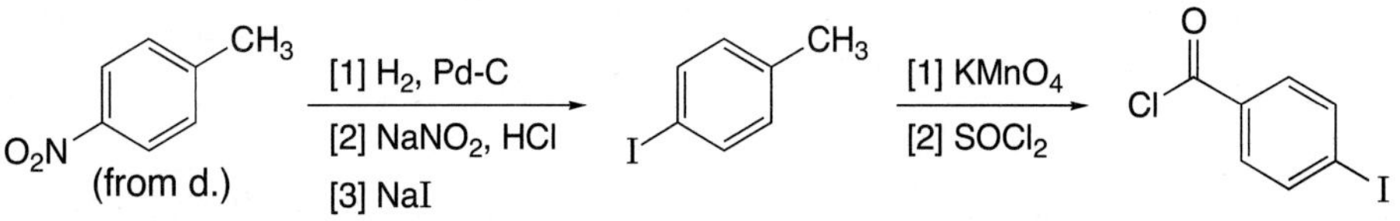

25.83

molecular weight = 87
$C_5H_{13}N$
two IR peaks = 1° amine

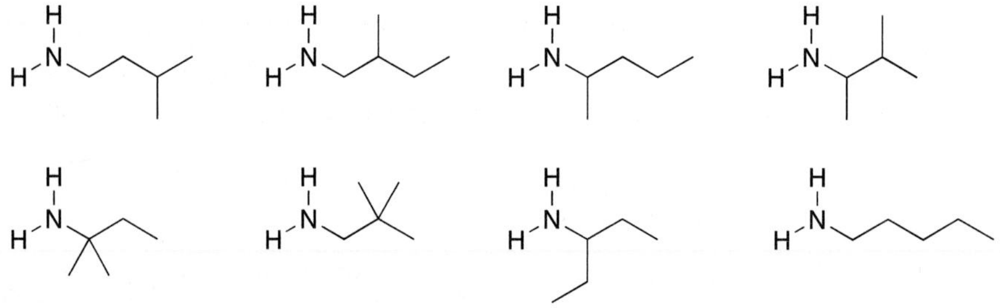

25.84

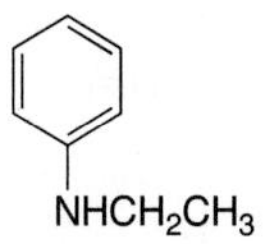

Compound **A:** $C_8H_{11}N$
IR absorption at 3400 cm^{-1}→ 2° amine
^{1}H NMR signals at (ppm):
1.3 (triplet, 3 H) CH_3 adjacent to 2 H's
3.1 (quartet, 2 H) CH_2 adjacent to 3 H's
3.6 (singlet, 1 H) amine H
6.8–7.2 (multiplet, 5 H) benzene ring

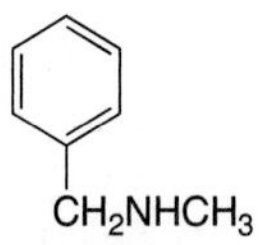

Compound **B:** $C_8H_{11}N$
IR absorption at 3310 cm^{-1} → 2° amine
^{1}H NMR signals at (ppm):
1.4 (singlet, 1 H) amine H
2.4 (singlet, 3 H) CH_3
3.8 (singlet, 2 H) CH_2
7.2 (multiplet, 5 H) benzene ring

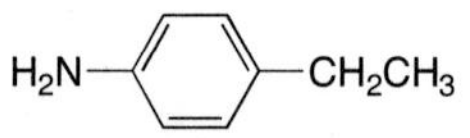

Compound **C:** $C_8H_{11}N$
IR absorption at 3430 and
3350 cm^{-1} → 1° amine
^{1}H NMR signals at (ppm):
1.3 (triplet, 3 H) CH_3 near CH_2
2.5 (quartet, 2 H) CH_2 near CH_3
3.6 (singlet, 2 H) amine H's
6.7 (doublet, 2 H) } para disubstituted
7.0 (doublet, 2 H) } benzene ring

25.85

Compound **D**:
Molecular ion at $m/z = 71$: C_3H_5NO (possible formula)
IR absorption at 3600–3200 $cm^{-1} \rightarrow$ OH
2263 $cm^{-1} \rightarrow$ CN
Use integration values and the molecular formula to determine the number of H's that give rise to each signal.
^1H NMR signals at (ppm):
2.6 (triplet, 2 H) CH_2 adjacent to 2 H's
3.2 (singlet, 1 H) OH
3.9 (triplet, 2 H) CH_2 adjacent to 2 H's

Compound **E**:
Molecular ion at $m/z = 75$: C_3H_9NO (possible formula)
IR absorption at 3600–3200 $cm^{-1} \rightarrow$ OH
3636 $cm^{-1} \rightarrow$ N–H of amine
^1H NMR signals at (ppm):
1.6 (quintet, 2 H) CH_2 split by 2 CH_2's
2.5 (singlet, 3 H) NH_2 and OH
2.8 (triplet, 2 H) CH_2 split by CH_2
3.7 (triplet, 2 H) CH_2 split by CH_2

25.86 Guanidine is a strong base because its conjugate acid is stabilized by resonance. This resonance delocalization makes guanidine easily donate its electron pair; thus it's a strong base.

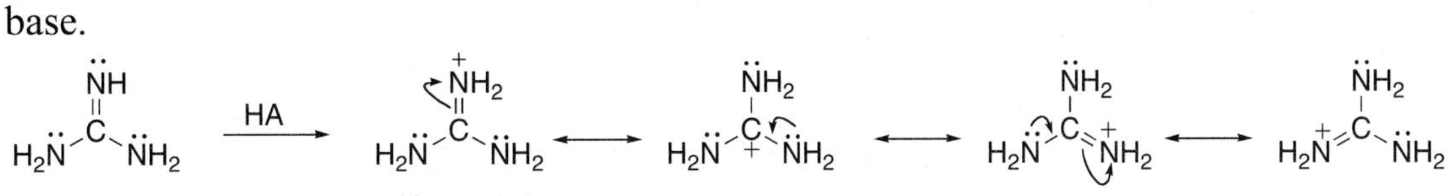

guanidine

$pK_a = 13.6$

25.87 The compound with the most available electron pair or the compound with the highest electron density on an atom (N in this case) is the strongest base. Pyrrole is the weakest base because its lone pair is delocalized on the five-membered ring to make it aromatic. Both imidazole and thiazole contain sp^2 hybridized N atoms with electron pairs that are localized on N. Imidazole is a stronger base than thiazole, because its second N atom is more basic than thiazole's S atom, so it places more electron density on N by a resonance effect.

imidazole — This N atom is the strongest base.

thiazole — This form contributes less to the hybrid than the equivalent resonance structure in imidazole.

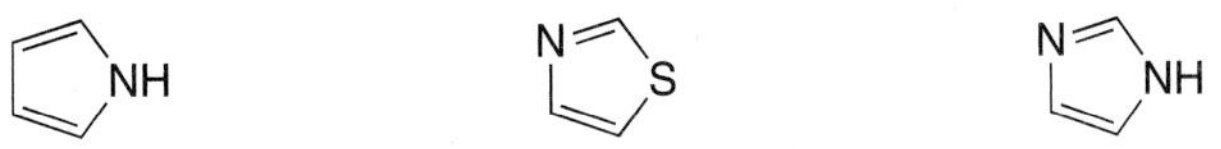

pyrrole **least basic**

thiazole **intermediate basicity**

imidazole **most basic**

25.88

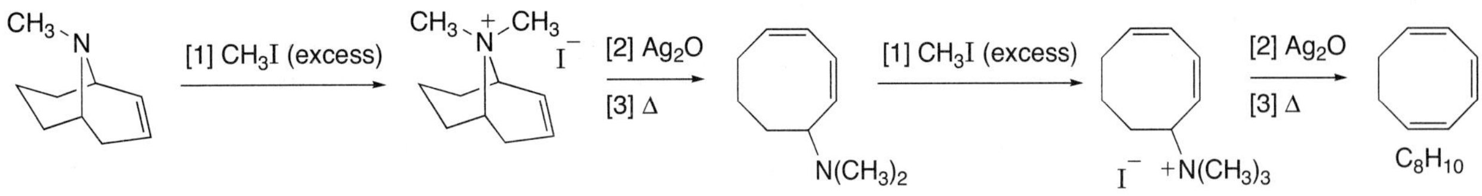

Y

25.89

One possibility:

a.

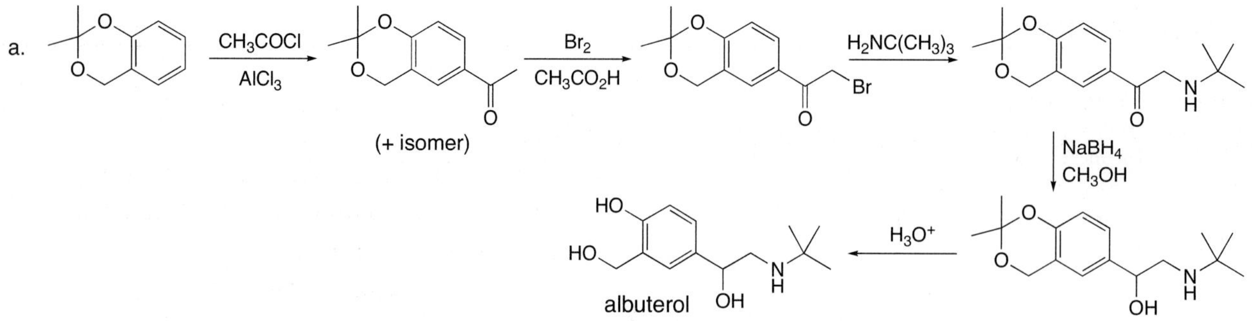

b.

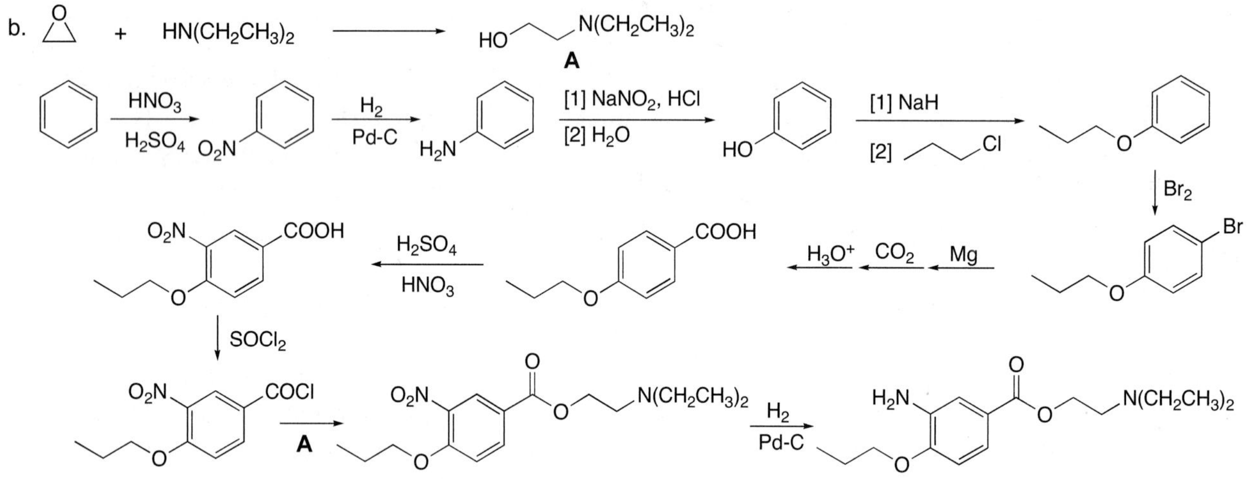

25.90 $CH_2=O$ reacts with the amine to form an intermediate imine, which undergoes an intramolecular Diels–Alder reaction.

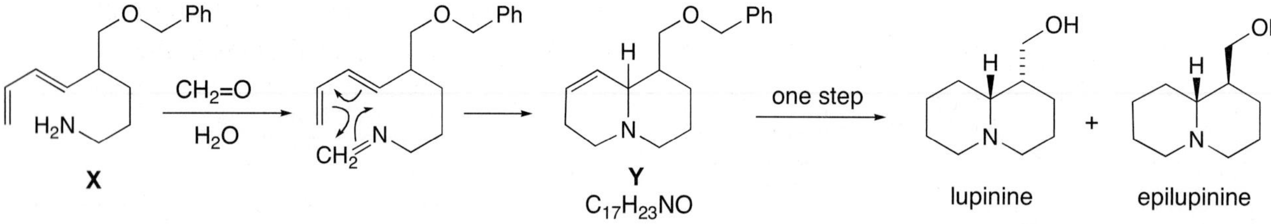

Chapter 26 Carbon–Carbon Bond-Forming Reactions in Organic Synthesis

Chapter Review

Coupling reactions

[1] Coupling reactions of organocuprate reagents (26.1)

$R'-X + R_2CuLi \longrightarrow$ **R'−R** + RCu + LiX

X = Cl, Br, I

- R'X can be CH_3X, RCH_2X, 2° cyclic halides, vinyl halides, and aryl halides.
- X may be Cl, Br, or I.
- With vinyl halides, coupling is stereospecific.

[2] Suzuki reaction (26.2)

$R'-X + R-BY_2 \xrightarrow[\text{NaOH}]{Pd(PPh_3)_4}$ **R'−R** + $HO-BY_2$ + NaX

X = Br, I

- R'X is most often a vinyl halide or aryl halide.
- With vinyl halides, coupling is stereospecific.

[3] Heck reaction (26.3)

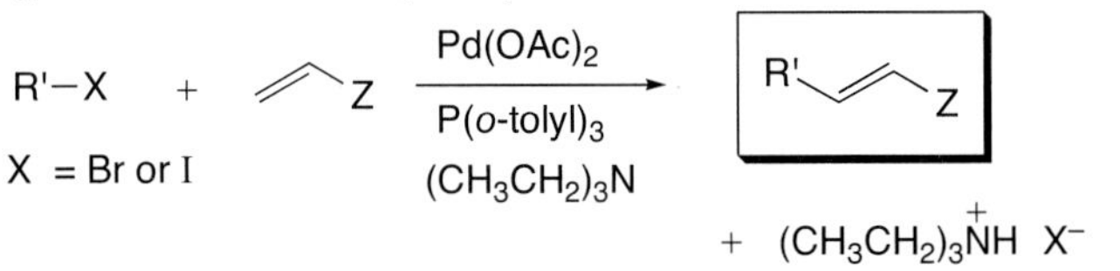

R'−X
+
Z
X = Br or I
Pd(OAc)2
P(o-tolyl)3
(CH3CH2)3N
R'
Z
+ (CH3CH2)3NH X−

- R'X is a vinyl halide or aryl halide.
- Z = H, Ph, COOR, or CN
- With vinyl halides, coupling is stereospecific.
- The reaction forms trans alkenes.

Cyclopropane synthesis

[1] Addition of dihalocarbenes to alkenes (26.4)

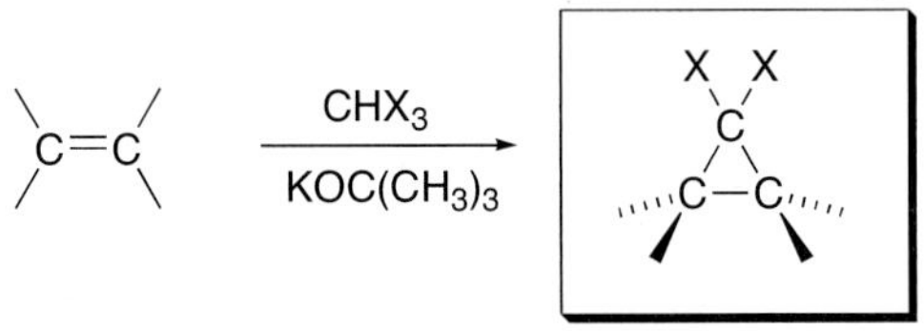

C=C
CHX3
KOC(CH3)3
X X
C
C−C

- The reaction occurs with syn addition.
- The position of substituents in the alkene is retained in the cyclopropane.

[2] Simmons–Smith reaction (26.5)

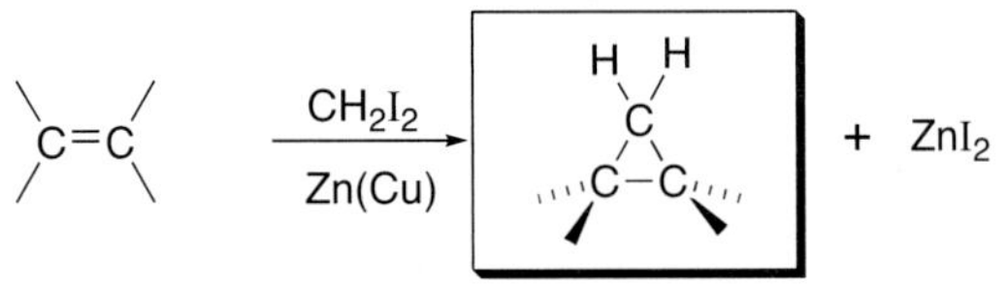

C=C
CH2I2
Zn(Cu)
H H
C
C−C
+ ZnI2

- The reaction occurs with syn addition.
- The position of substituents in the alkene is retained in the cyclopropane.

Metathesis (26.6)

$2\ RCH{=}CH_2 \xrightarrow[\text{catalyst}]{\text{Grubbs}}$ **RCH=CHR** + $CH_2{=}CH_2$

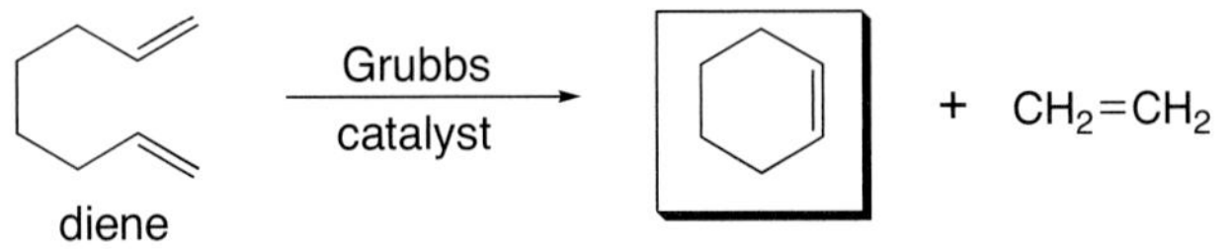

Grubbs
catalyst
+ CH2=CH2

diene

- Metathesis works best when $CH_2{=}CH_2$, a gas that escapes from the reaction mixture, is formed as one product.

Practice Test on Chapter Review

1. a. Which functional groups react with lithium dialkyl cuprates?
    1. epoxides
    2. vinyl halides
    3. acid chlorides
    4. Compounds [1] and [2] both react with R_2CuLi.
    5. Compounds [1], [2], and [3] all react with R_2CuLi.

   b. Which of the following statements is (are) true for the Suzuki reaction?
    1. Arylboranes can serve as one reactant.
    2. The reaction is stereospecific.
    3. The reaction occurs between a vinyl or aryl halide and an alkene in the presence of a palladium catalyst.
    4. Statements [1] and [2] are both true.
    5. Statements [1], [2], and [3] are all true.

   c. Which of the following compounds can react with $CH_2{=}CHCN$ in a Heck reaction?

    1. 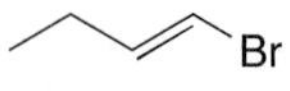
    2. 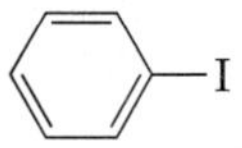
    3. $CH_2{=}CH_2$
    4. Both [1] and [2] can react.
    5. Compounds [1], [2], and [3] can all react.

   d. Which of the following compounds yields a pair of enantiomers on reaction with the Simmons–Smith reagent?

    1. 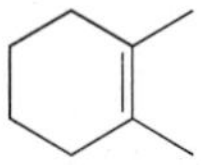
    2. 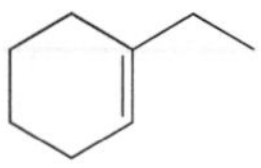
    3. 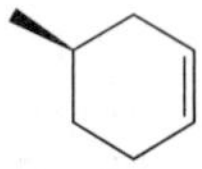
    4. Compounds [1] and [2] both yield a pair of enantiomers.
    5. Compounds [1], [2], and [3] all yield a pair of enantiomers.

   e. Which of the following compounds can be made by a ring-closing metathesis reaction?

    1. 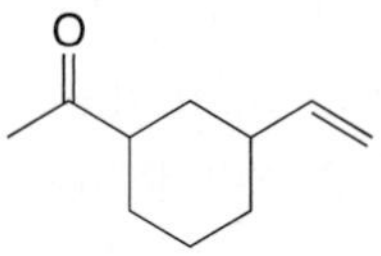
    2. 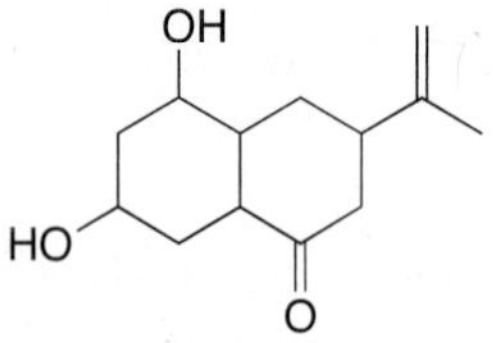
    3. 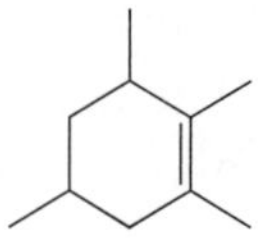
    4. Compounds [1] and [2] can both be prepared.
    5. Compounds [1], [2], and [3] can all be prepared.

f. Which of the following compounds can be prepared from $CH_3–C≡C–H$ by a Suzuki reaction? You may use other organic compounds or inorganic reagents.

1. 

2. 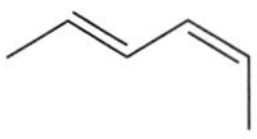

3. 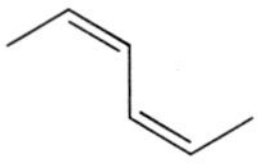

4. Compounds [1] and [2] can both be prepared.

5. Compounds [1], [2], and [3] can all be prepared.

2. Draw the product formed in each reaction. Indicate the stereochemistry around double bonds and stereogenic centers when necessary.

a. 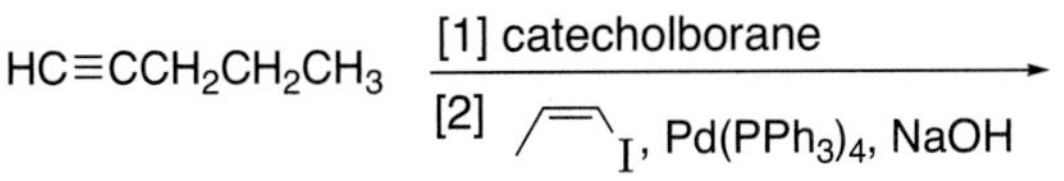
HC≡CCH2CH2CH3
[1] catecholborane
[2]
I, Pd(PPh3)4, NaOH

b. 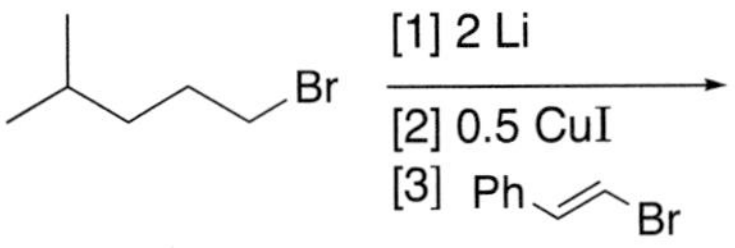
Br
[1] 2 Li
[2] 0.5 CuI
[3] Ph
Br

c. 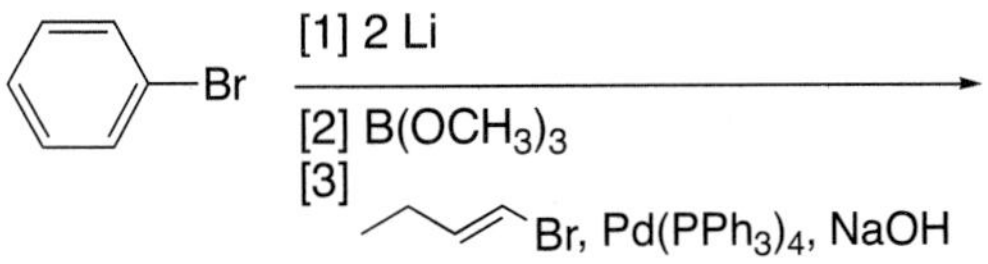
Br
[1] 2 Li
[2] B(OCH3)3
[3]
Br, Pd(PPh3)4, NaOH

d. 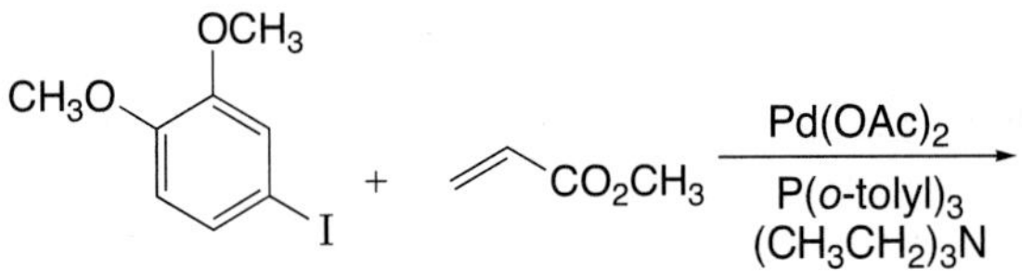
OCH3
CH3O
I
+
CO2CH3
Pd(OAc)2
P(o-tolyl)3
(CH3CH2)3N

e. 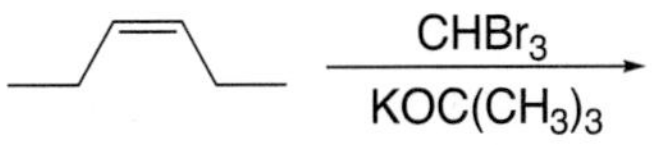
CHBr3
KOC(CH3)3

f. 
Grubbs
cataylst

g. 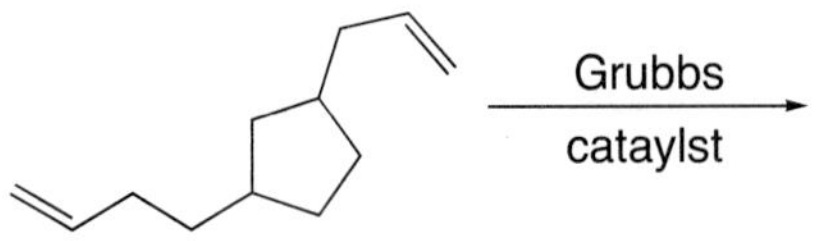
Grubbs
cataylst

3. What starting material is needed to synthesize each compound by ring-closure metathesis?

a. 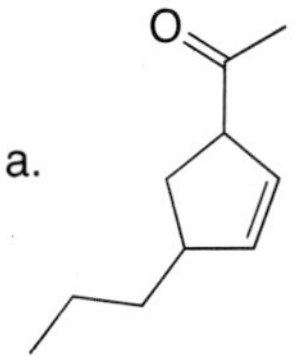
O

b. 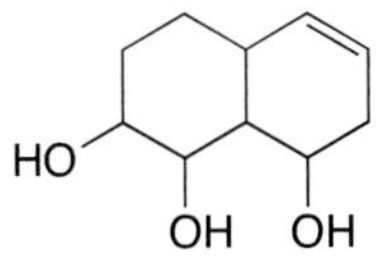
HO
OH
OH

c. 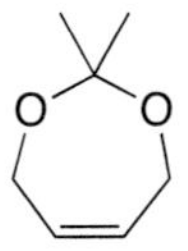
O
O

Answers to Practice Test

1.a. 5
b. 4
c. 4
d. 2
e. 3
f. 4

2.

a. 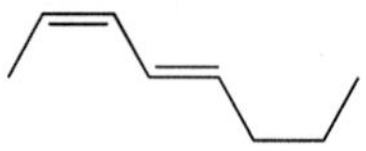

b. 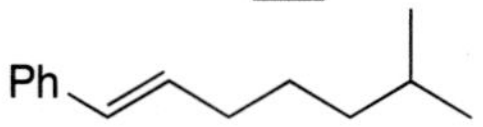

c. 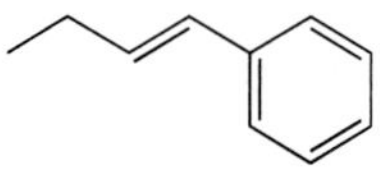

d. 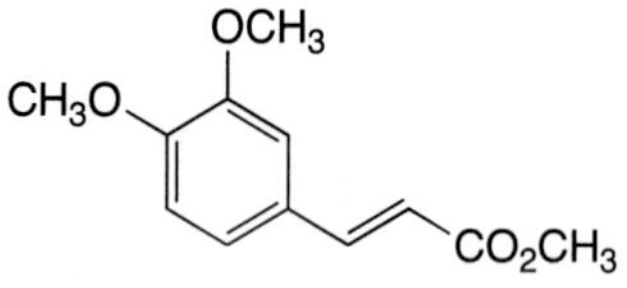
OCH3
CH3O
CO2CH3

e. 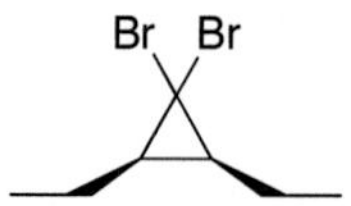
Br Br

f. 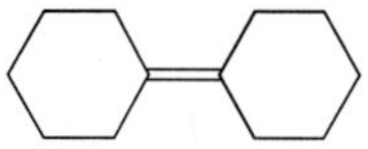

g. 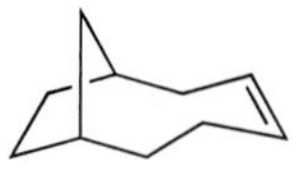

3.

a. 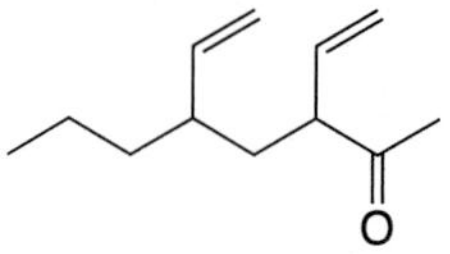
O

b. 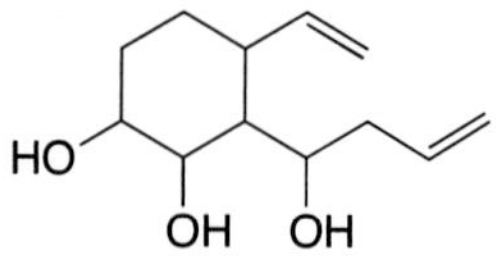
HO
OH OH

c. 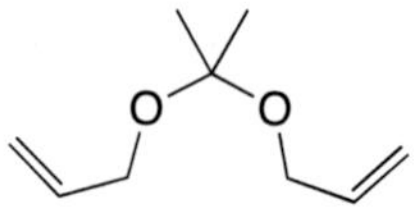
O
O

Answers to Problems

26.1 A new C–C bond is formed in each coupling reaction.

a. 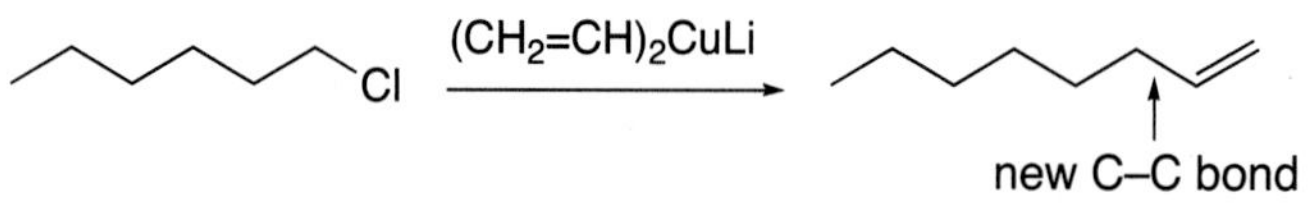
Cl
(CH2=CH)2CuLi
new C–C bond

b. 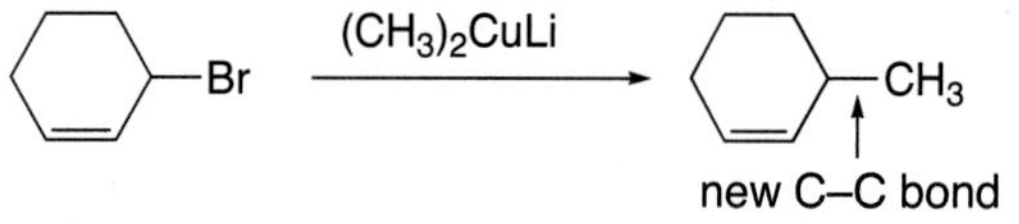
Br
(CH3)2CuLi
CH3
new C–C bond

c. 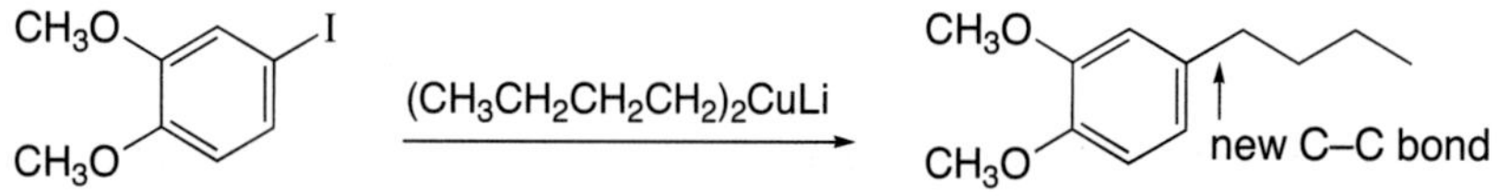
CH3O
CH3O
I
(CH3CH2CH2CH2)2CuLi
CH3O
CH3O
new C–C bond

d. 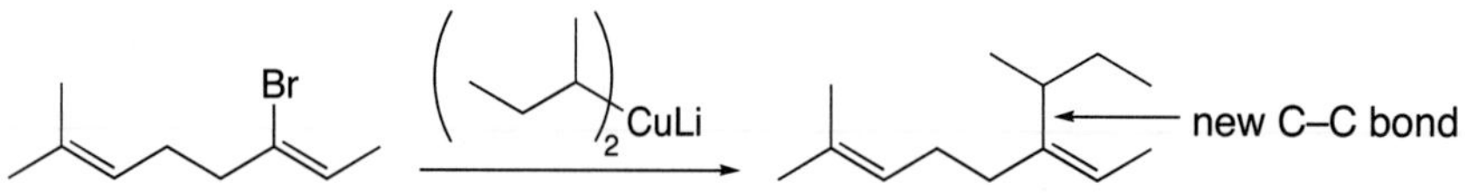
Br
CuLi
2
new C–C bond

26.2

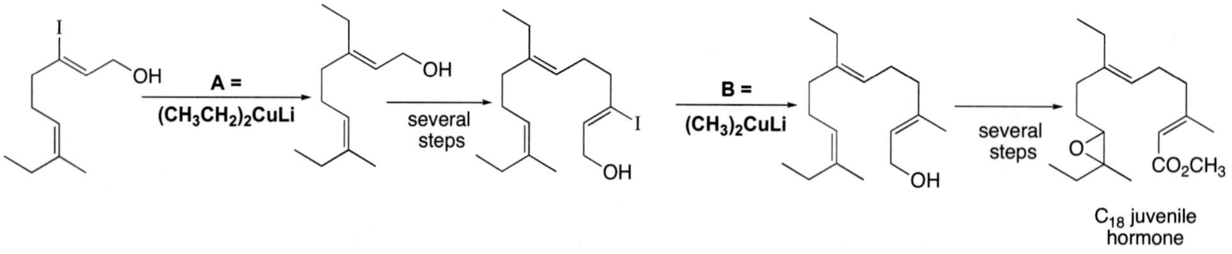
I
OH
A =
(CH3CH2)2CuLi
OH
several
steps
I
OH
B =
(CH3)2CuLi
OH
several
steps
O
CO2CH3
C18 juvenile
hormone

26.3

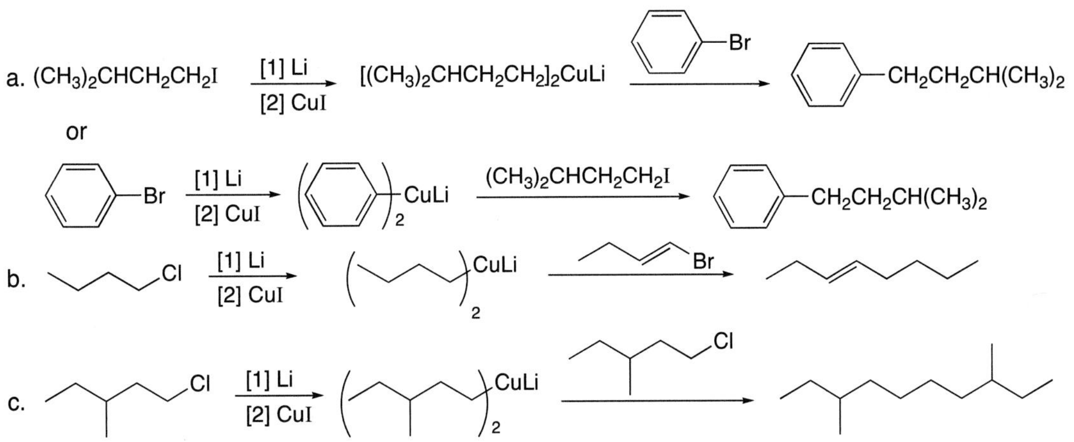
a. (CH3)2CHCH2CH2I
[1] Li
[2] CuI
[(CH3)2CHCH2CH2]2CuLi
Br
CH2CH2CH(CH3)2
or
Br
[1] Li
[2] CuI
CuLi
2
(CH3)2CHCH2CH2I
CH2CH2CH(CH3)2
b.
Cl
[1] Li
[2] CuI
CuLi
2
Br
c.
Cl
[1] Li
[2] CuI
CuLi
2
Cl

26.4

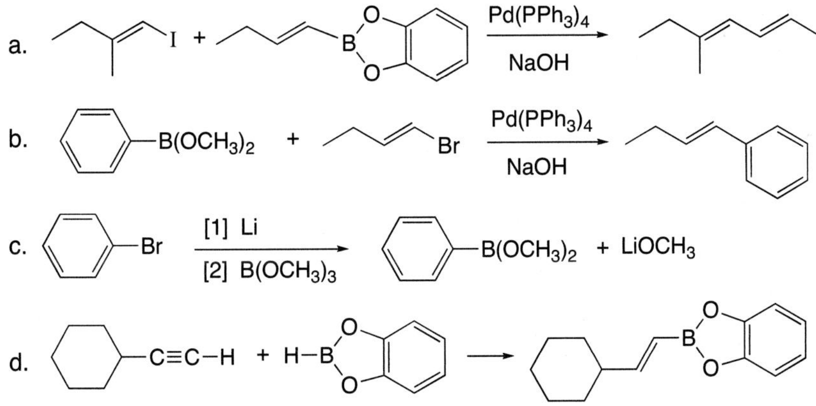
a.
I
+
O
B
O
Pd(PPh3)4
NaOH
b.
B(OCH3)2
+
Br
Pd(PPh3)4
NaOH
c.
Br
[1] Li
[2] B(OCH3)3
B(OCH3)2
+ LiOCH3
d.
C≡C–H
+ H–B
O
O
B
O
O

26.5 The Suzuki reaction forms a new carbon–carbon bond between a vinyl halide and an arylborane.

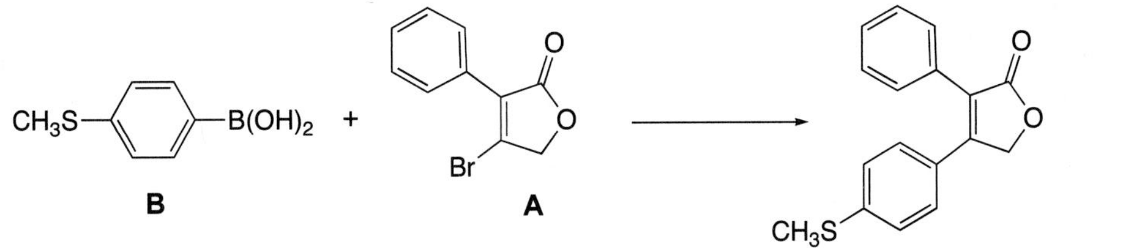
CH3S
B(OH)2
+
B
O
O
Br
A
O
O
CH3S

26.6

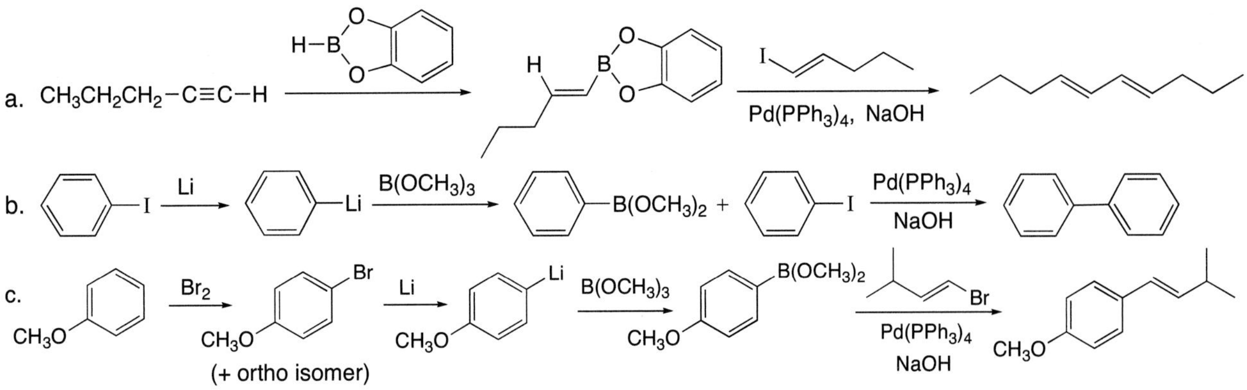
H–B
O
O
a. CH3CH2CH2–C≡C–H
H
B
O
O
I
Pd(PPh3)4, NaOH
b.
I
Li
Li
B(OCH3)3
B(OCH3)2 +
I
Pd(PPh3)4
NaOH
c.
CH3O
Br2
Br
CH3O
(+ ortho isomer)
Li
Li
CH3O
B(OCH3)3
B(OCH3)2
CH3O
Br
Pd(PPh3)4
NaOH
CH3O

26.7

a. 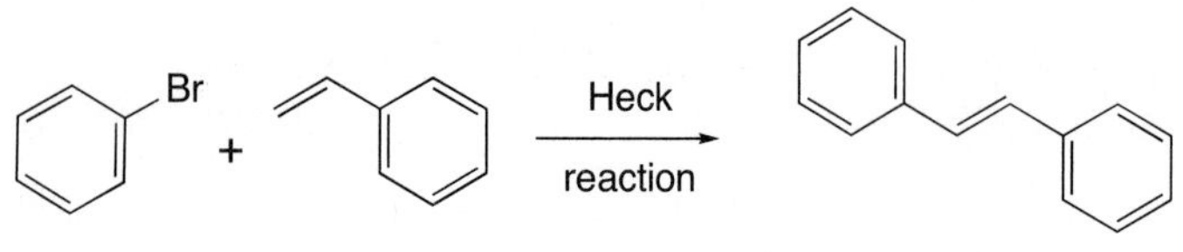

b. 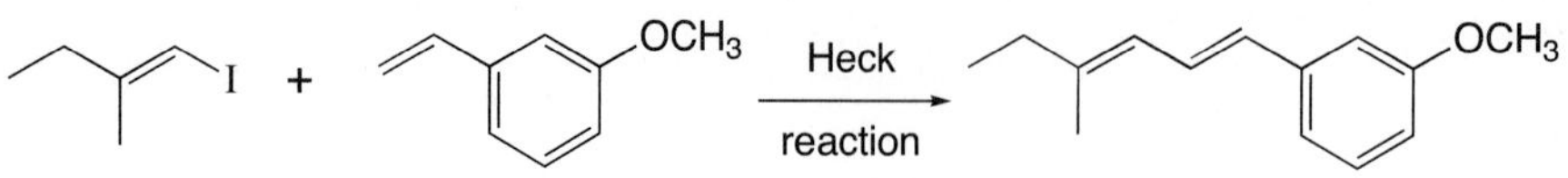

c. 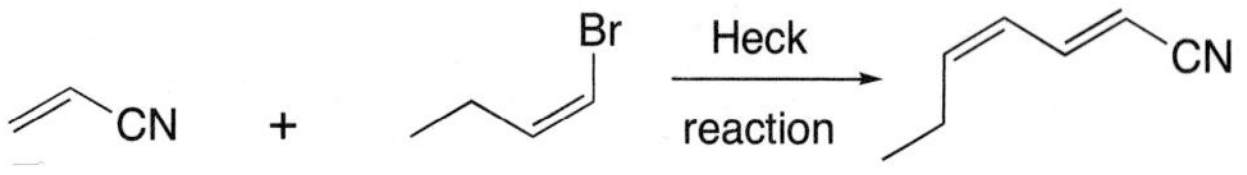

d. 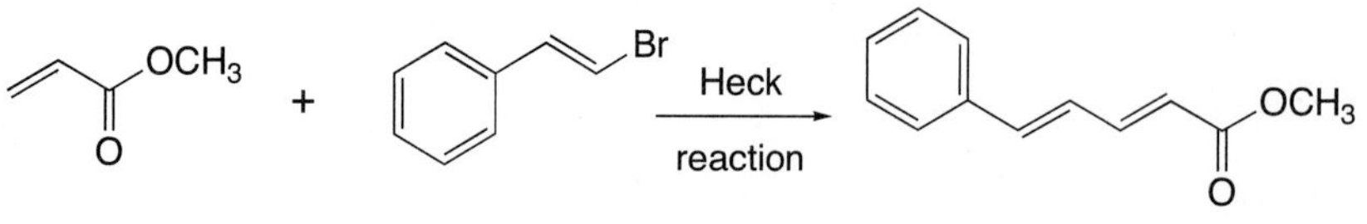

26.8 Locate the double bond with the aryl, COOR, or CN substituent, and break the molecule into two components at the end of the C=C not bonded to one of these substituents.

a. 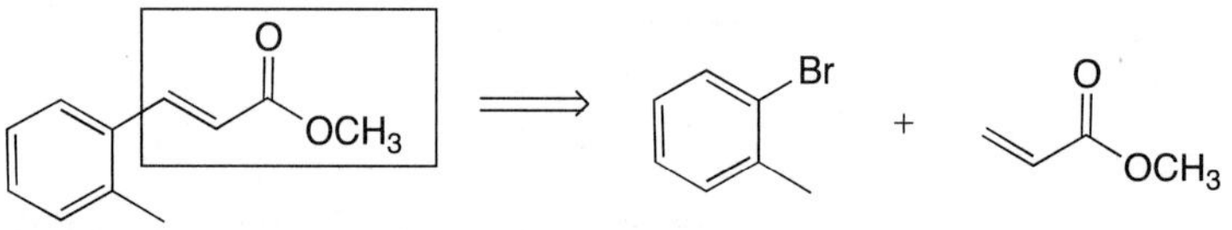

b. 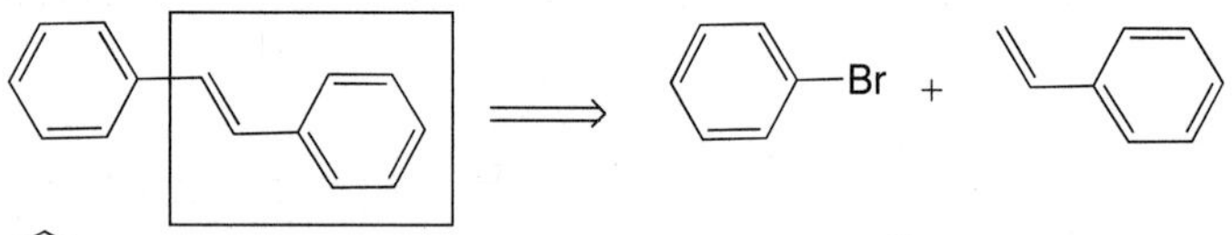

c. 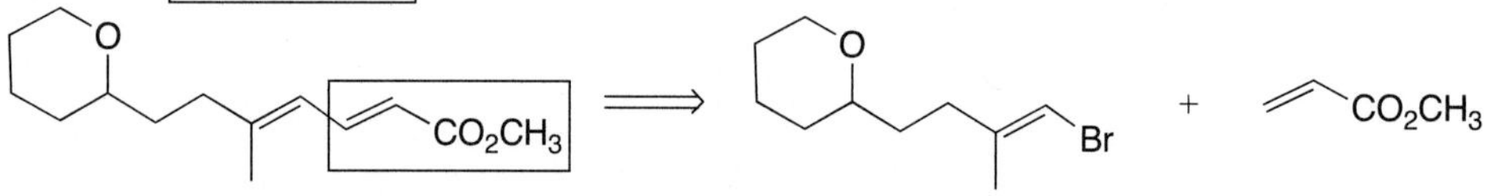

26.9 Add the carbene carbon from either side of the alkene.

a. 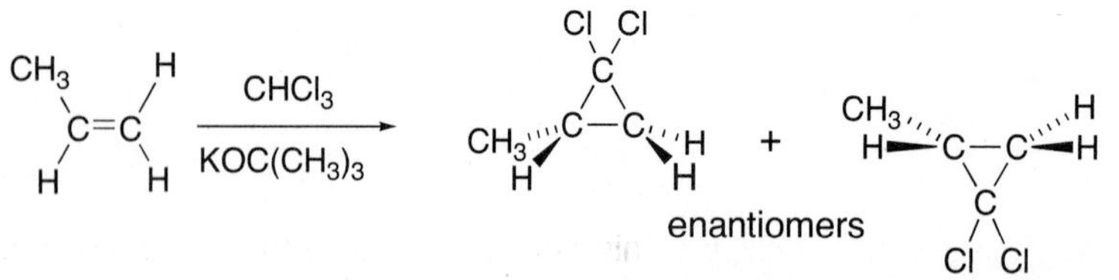

b. 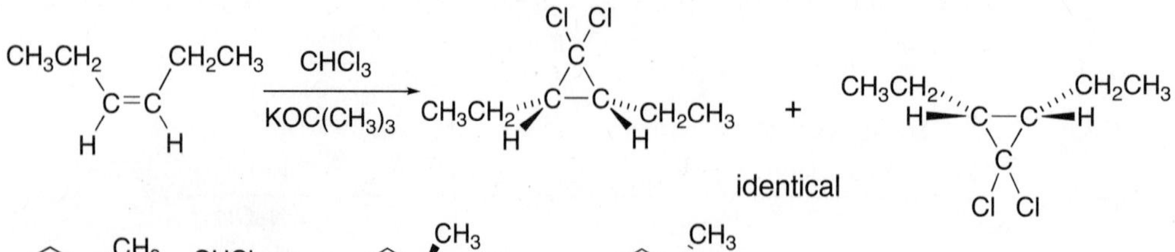

c. 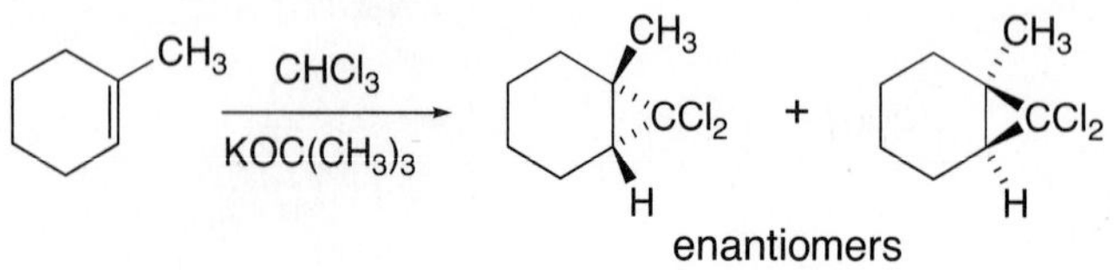

26.10

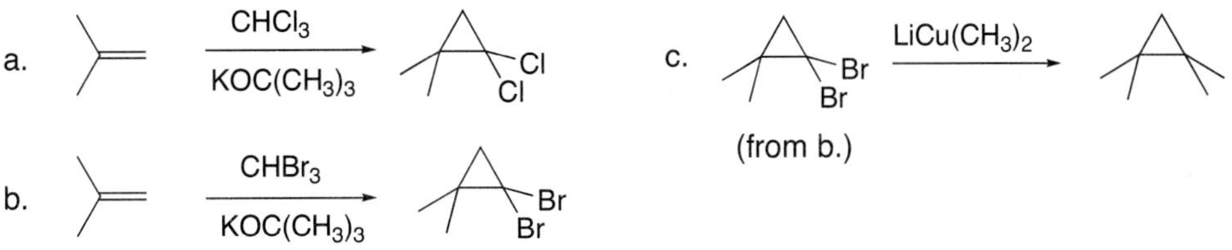

26.11

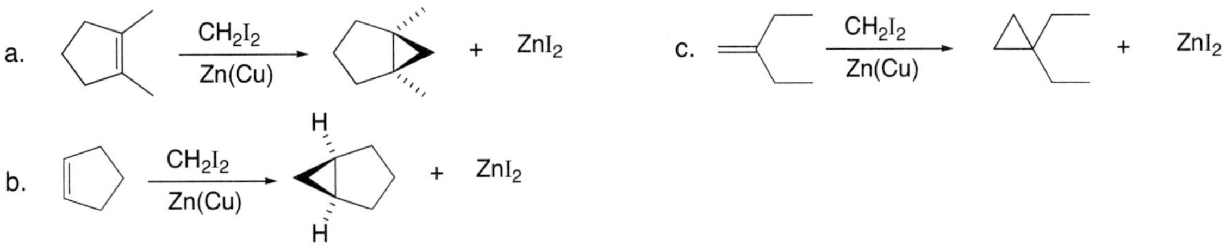

26.12 The relative position of substituents in the reactant is retained in the product.

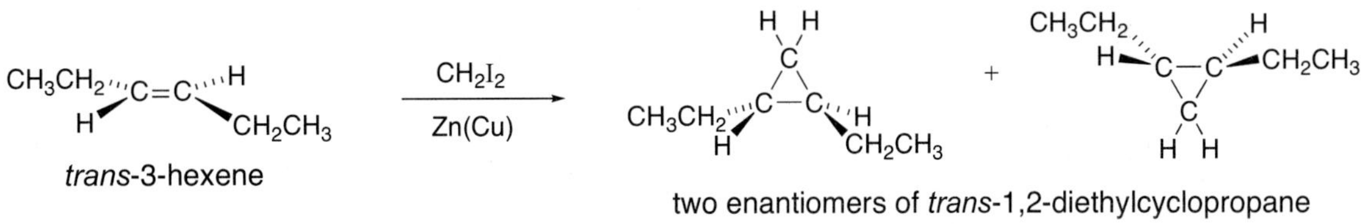

26.13

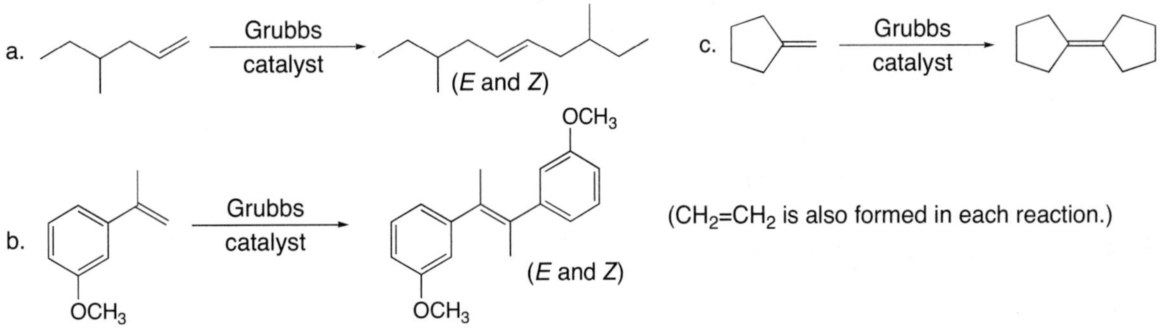

(CH_2=CH_2 is also formed in each reaction.)

26.14

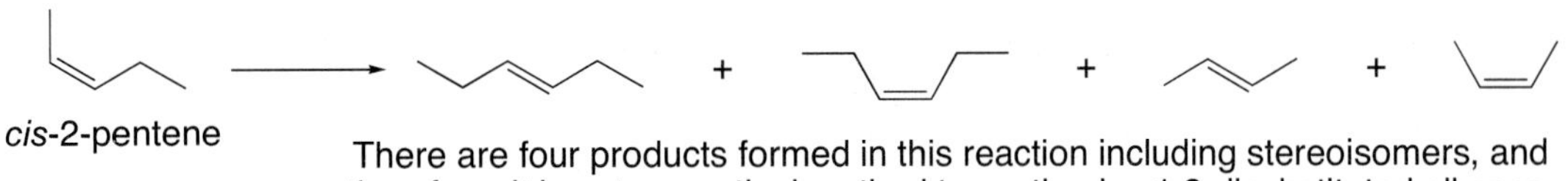

There are four products formed in this reaction including stereoisomers, and therefore, it is not a practical method to synthesize 1,2-disubstituted alkenes.

26.15

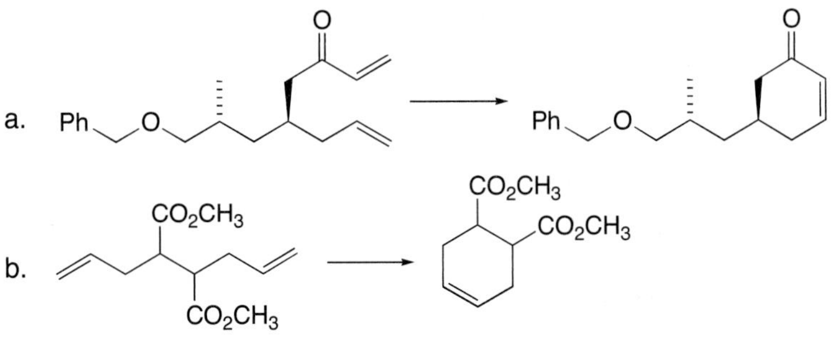

26.16

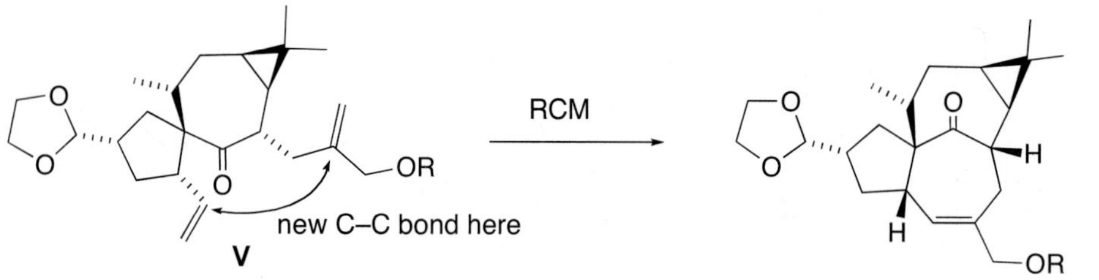

OR
new C–C bond here
V
RCM
H
H
OR

26.17 Cleave the C=C bond in the product, and then bond each carbon of the original alkene to a CH_2 group using a double bond.

a.

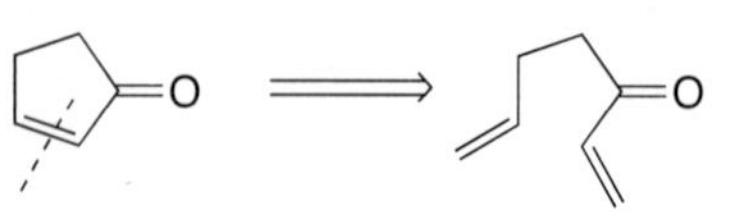

c.

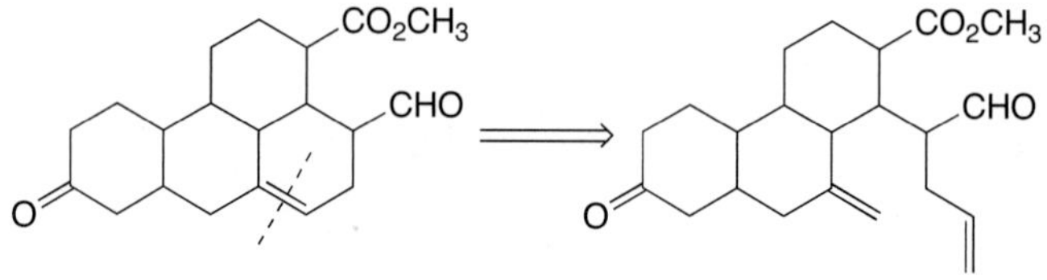

CO_2CH_3
CHO
CO_2CH_3
CHO

b.

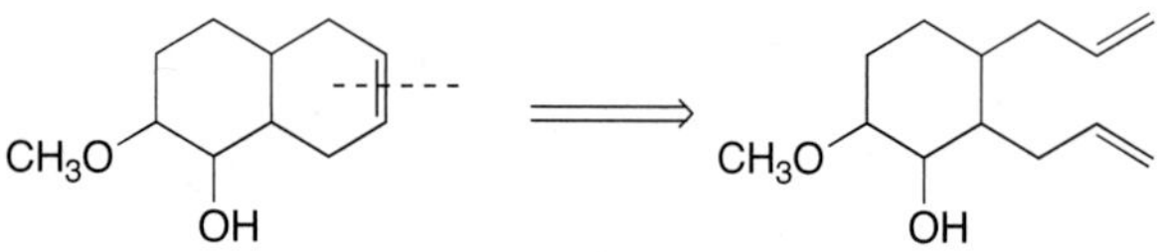

CH_3O
OH
CH_3O
OH

26.18 Inversion of configuration occurs with the substitution of the methyl group for the tosylate.

a.

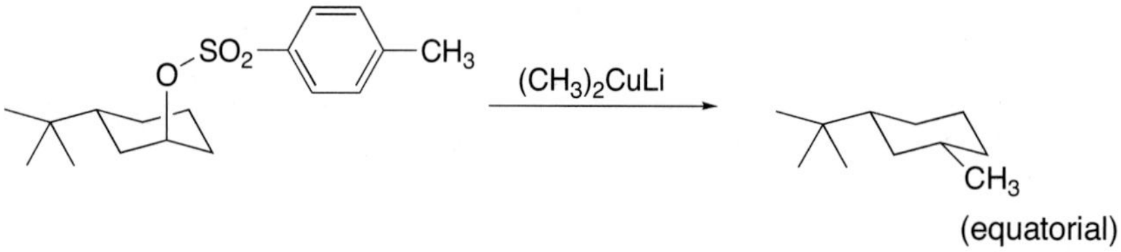

SO_2
CH_3
$(CH_3)_2CuLi$
CH_3
(equatorial)

b.

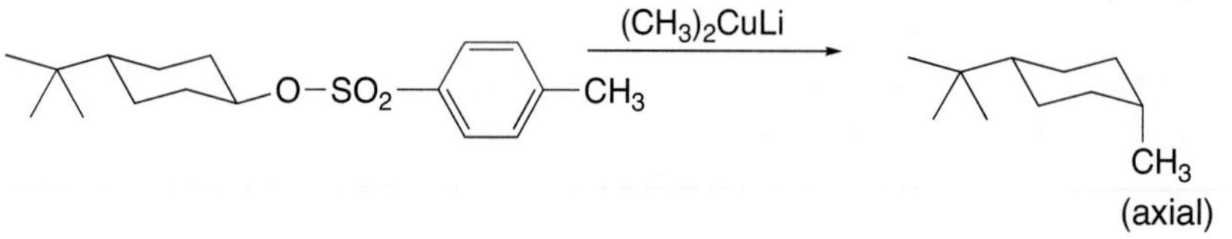

$O-SO_2$
CH_3
$(CH_3)_2CuLi$
CH_3
(axial)

26.19

a.

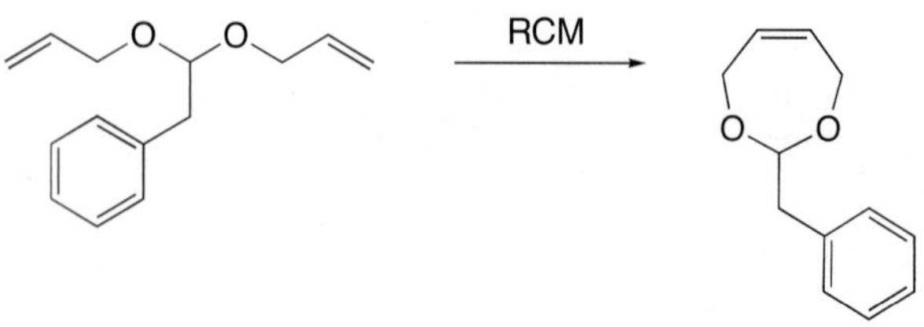

RCM

b.

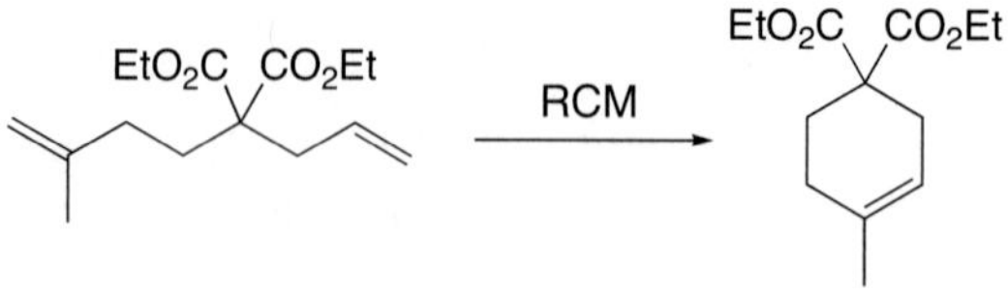

EtO_2C CO_2Et
RCM
EtO_2C CO_2Et

26.20

a. 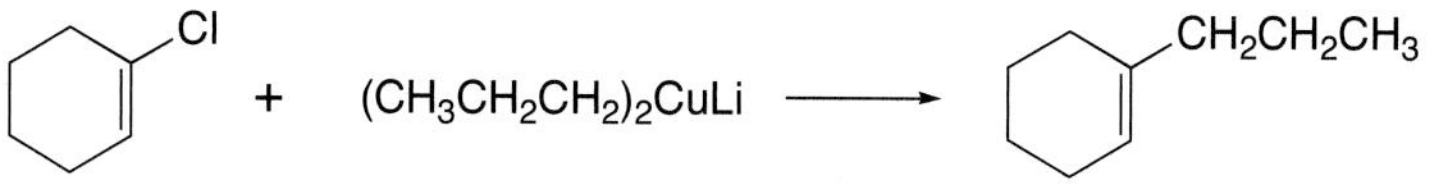
Cl
+
(CH3CH2CH2)2CuLi
CH2CH2CH3

b. 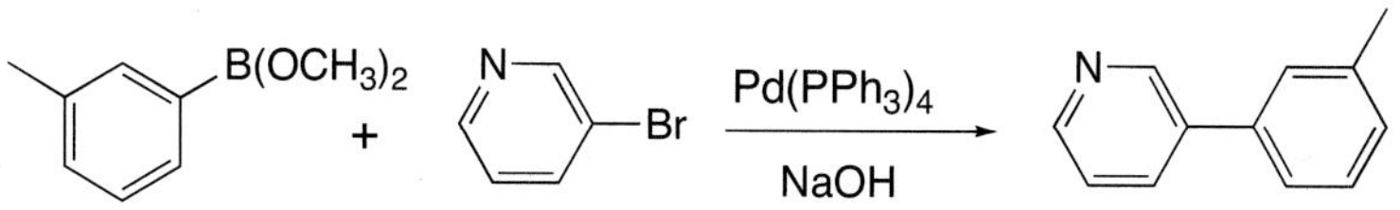
B(OCH3)2
+
N
Br
Pd(PPh3)4
NaOH
N

c. 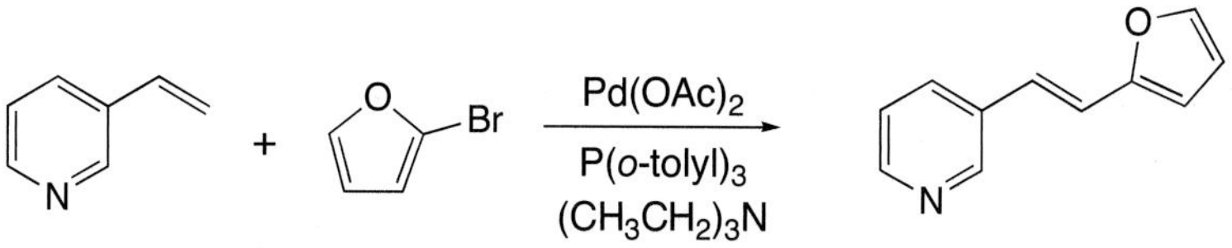
N
+
O
Br
Pd(OAc)2
P(o-tolyl)3
(CH3CH2)3N
O
N

d. 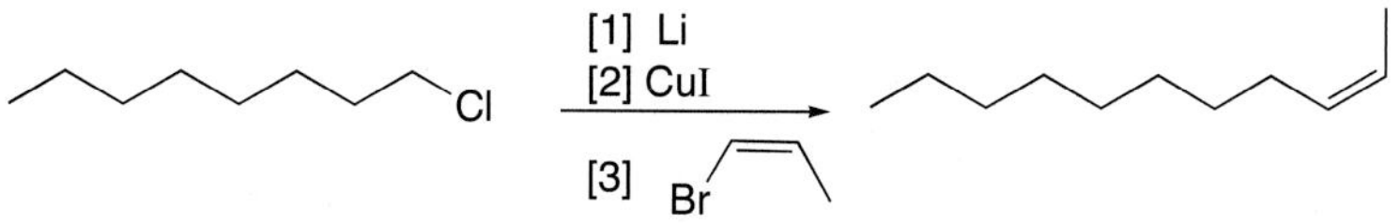
Cl
[1] Li
[2] CuI
[3] Br

e. 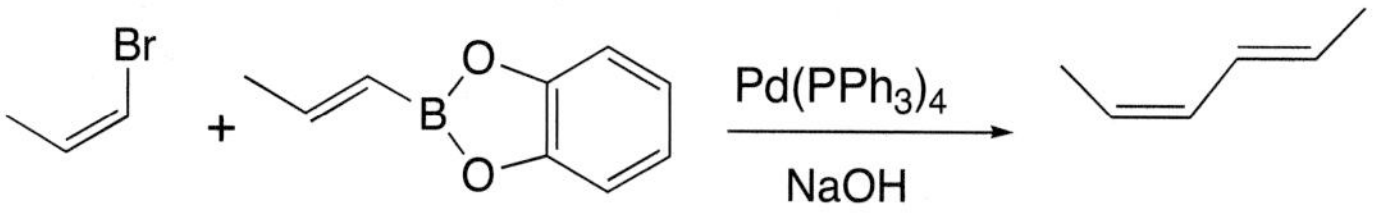
Br
+
O
B
O
Pd(PPh3)4
NaOH

f. 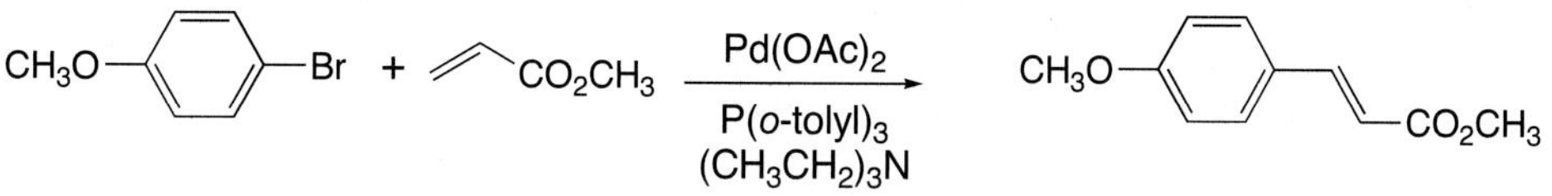
CH3O
Br
+
CO2CH3
Pd(OAc)2
P(o-tolyl)3
(CH3CH2)3N
CH3O
CO2CH3

g. 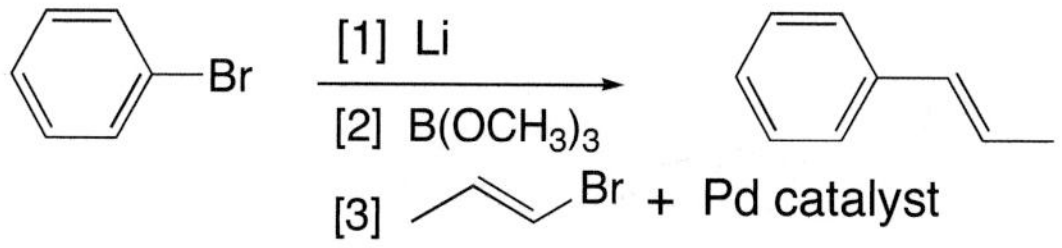
Br
[1] Li
[2] B(OCH3)3
[3] Br + Pd catalyst

h. 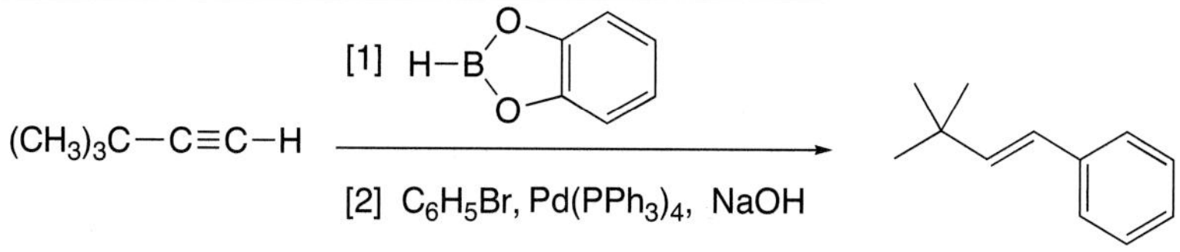
(CH3)3C–C≡C–H
[1] H–B
O
O
[2] C6H5Br, Pd(PPh3)4, NaOH

26.21

a. 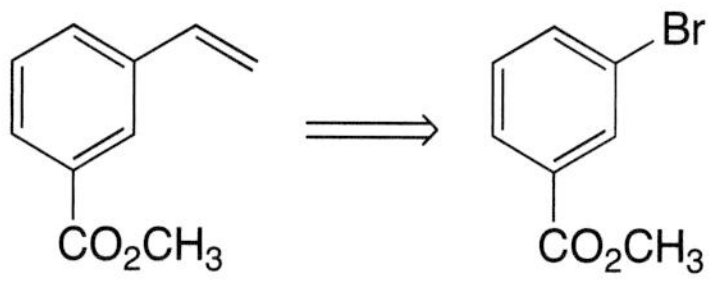
CO2CH3
Br
CO2CH3

b. 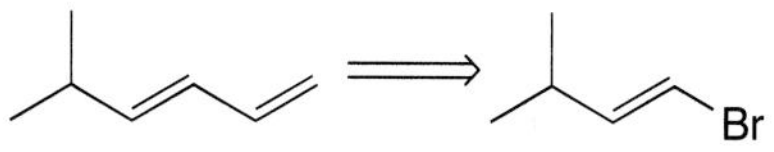
Br

c. 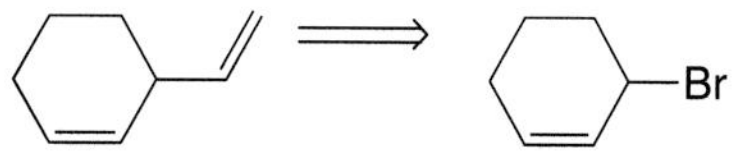
Br

d. 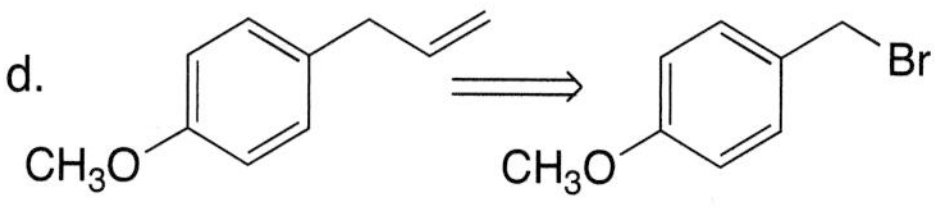
CH3O
Br
CH3O

26.22

Each coupling reaction uses $Pd(PPh_3)_4$ and NaOH to form the conjugated diene.

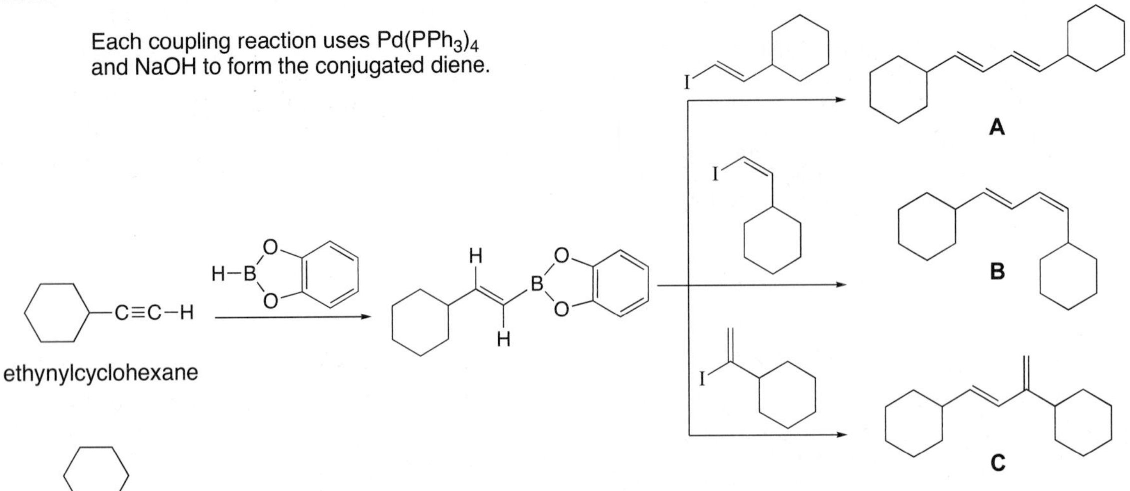

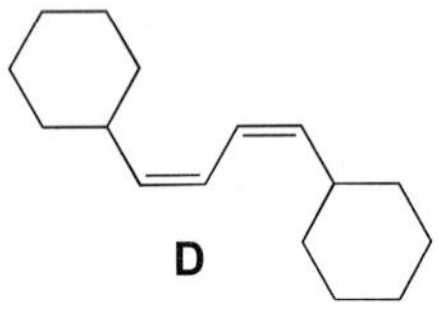

It is not possible to synthesize diene **D** using a Suzuki reaction with ethynylcyclohexane as starting material. Hydroboration of ethynylcyclohexane adds the elements of H and B in a syn fashion, affording a trans vinylborane. Since the Suzuki reaction is stereospecific, one of the double bonds in the product must be trans.

26.23 Locate the styrene part of the molecule, and break the molecule into two components. The second component in each reaction is styrene, $C_6H_5CH{=}CH_2$.

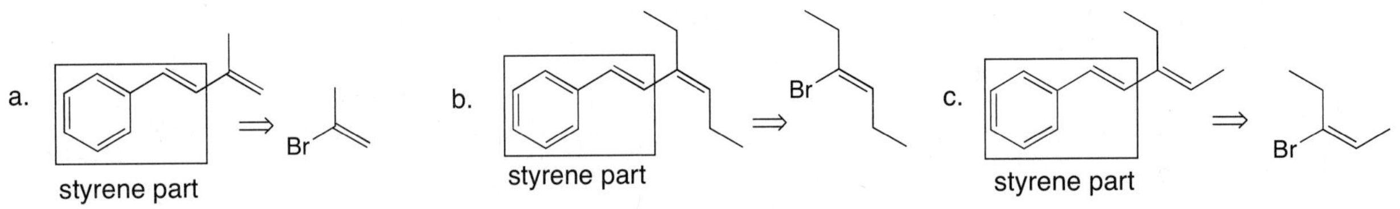

26.24

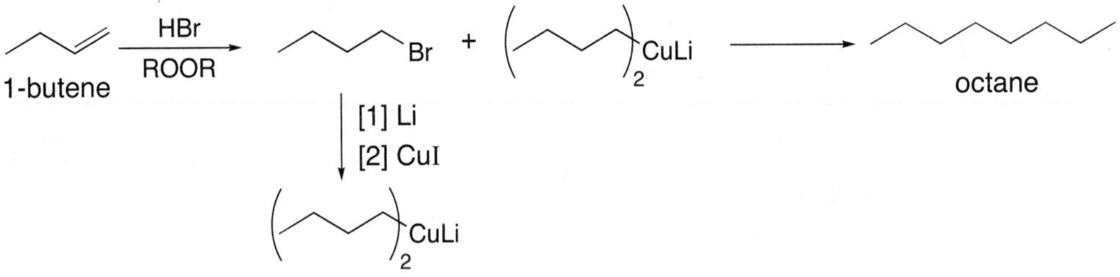

26.25 Add the carbene carbon from either side of the alkene.

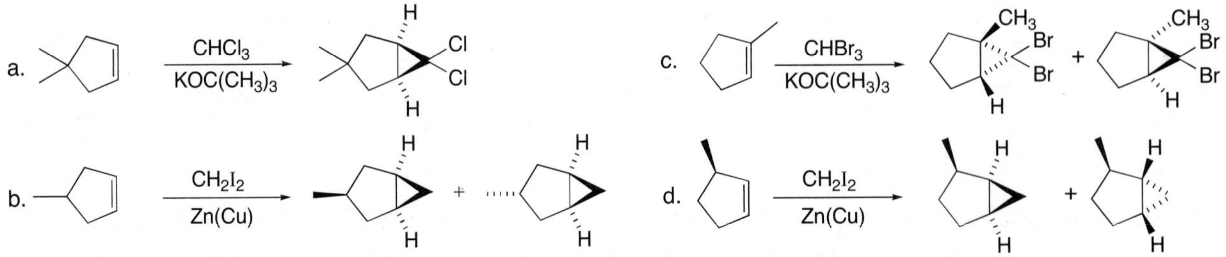

e.

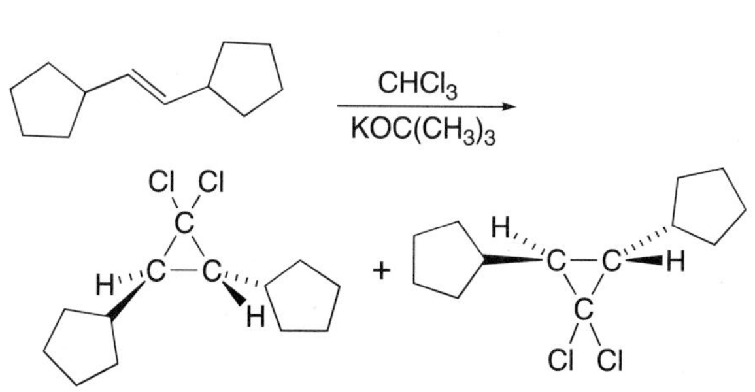

f.

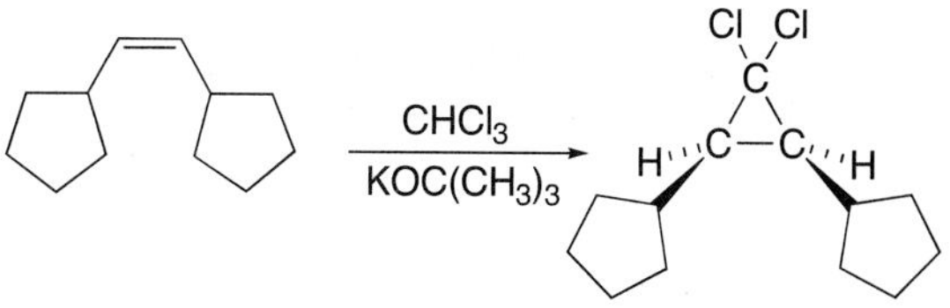

26.26 Since the new three-membered ring has a stereogenic center on the C bonded to the phenyl group, the phenyl group can be oriented in two different ways to afford two stereoisomers. These products are diastereomers of each other.

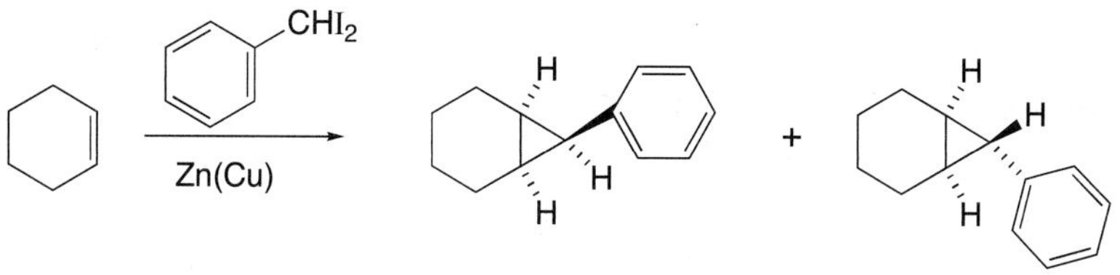

26.27 High dilution conditions favor intramolecular metathesis.

a.

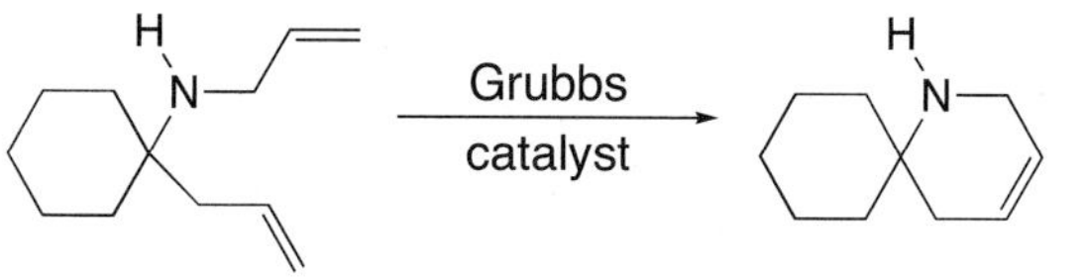

c.

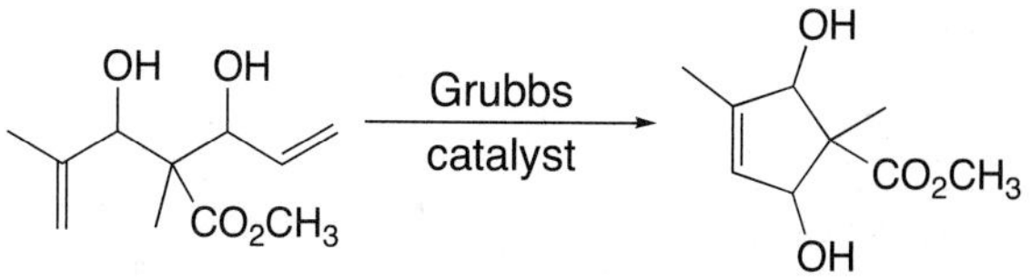

b.

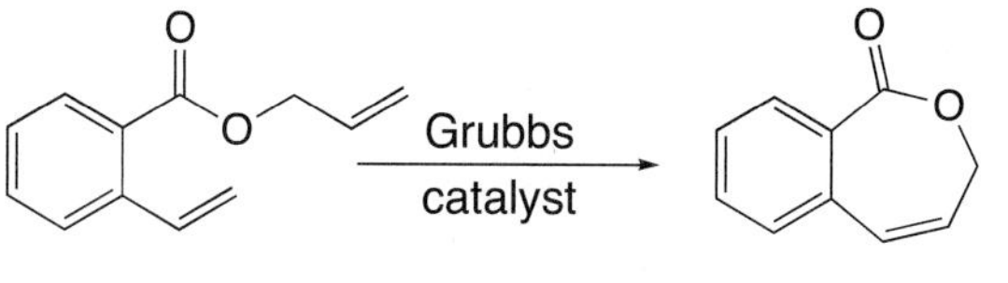

26.28 Retrosynthetically break the double bond in the cyclic compound and add a new $=CH_2$ at each end to find the starting material.

a.

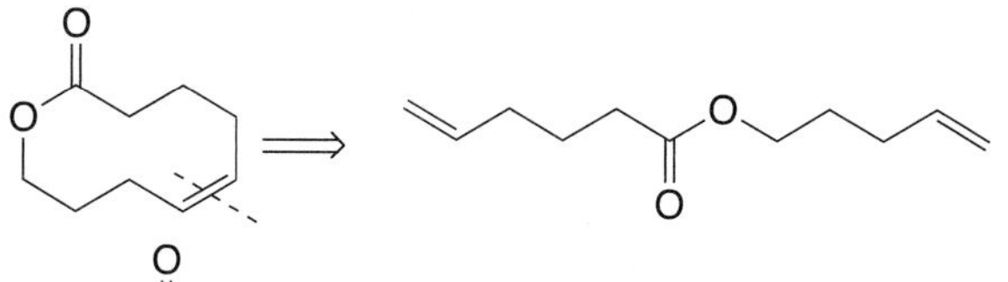

b.

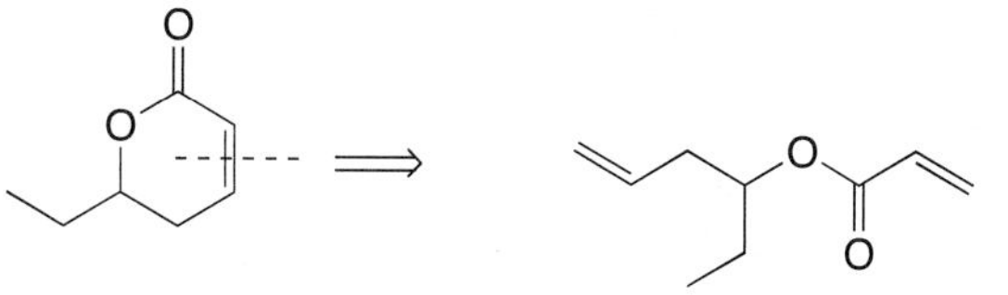

c.

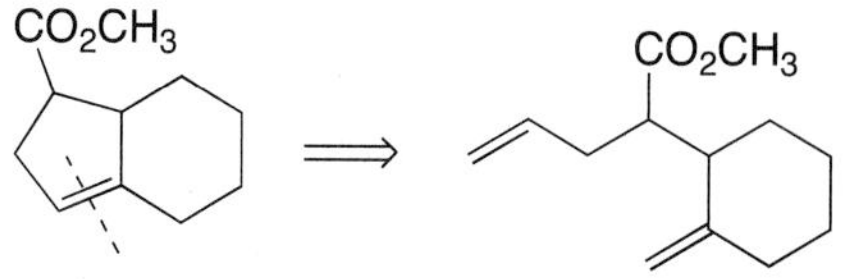

26.29 Alkene metathesis with two different alkenes is synthetically useful only when both alkenes are symmetrically substituted; that is, the two groups on each end of the double bond are identical to the two groups on the other end of the double bond.

a. $CH_3CH_2CH{=}CH_2$ + $CH_3CH_2CH_2CH{=}CH_2$ ⟶ $CH_3CH_2CH_2CH{=}CHCH_2CH_3$ (Z + E) + $CH_3CH_2CH{=}CHCH_2CH_3$ (Z + E) + $CH_3CH_2CH_2CH{=}CHCH_2CH_2CH_3$ (Z + E) + $CH_2{=}CH_2$

b. 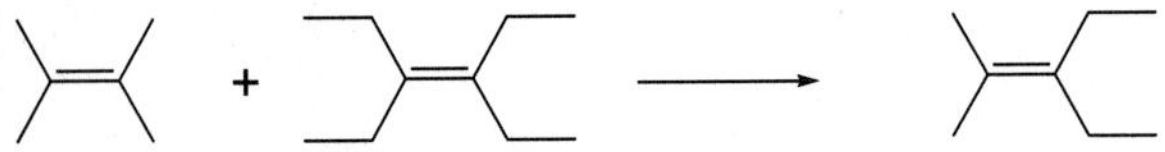
This reaction is synthetically useful since it yields only one product.

c. 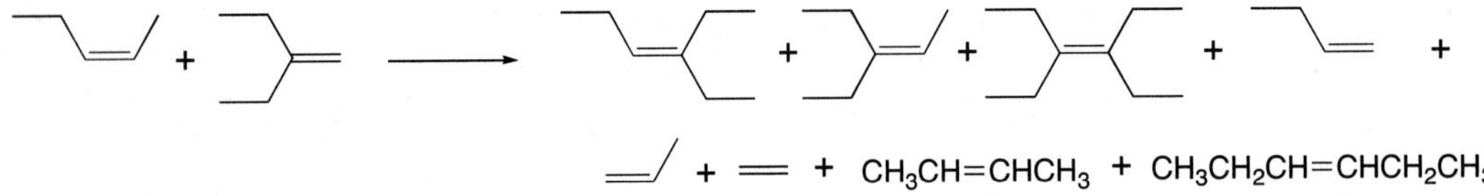
+ $CH_3CH{=}CHCH_3$ (Z + E) + $CH_3CH_2CH{=}CHCH_2CH_3$ (Z + E)

26.30

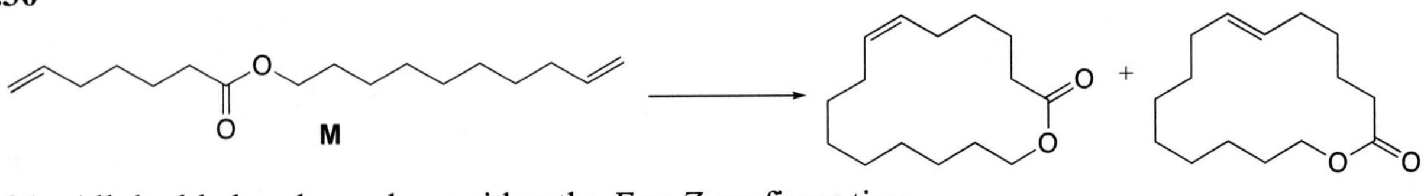
O
O
M
O
O
O
O

26.31 All double bonds can have either the *E* or *Z* configuration.

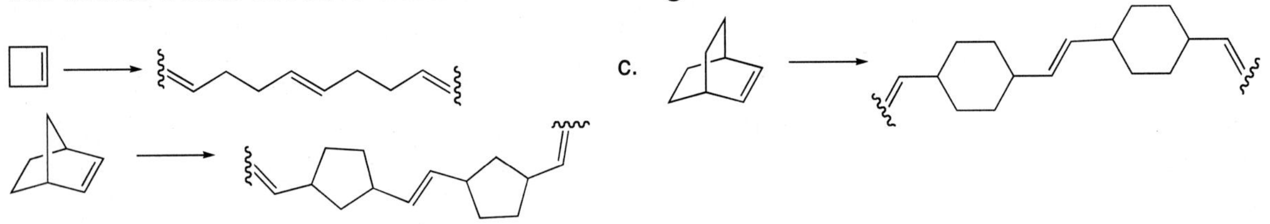
a.
b.
c.

26.32

a. 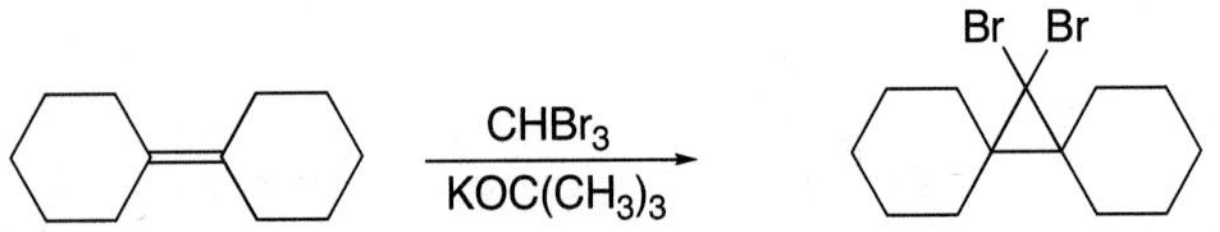
CHBr3
KOC(CH3)3
Br Br

b. 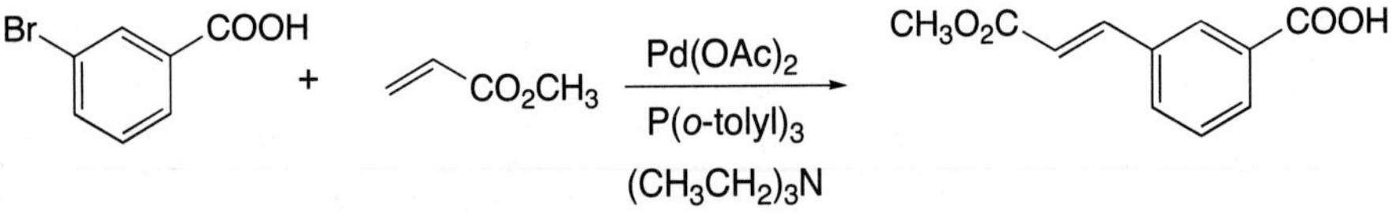
Br
COOH
CO2CH3
Pd(OAc)2
P(o-tolyl)3
(CH3CH2)3N
CH3O2C
COOH

c. 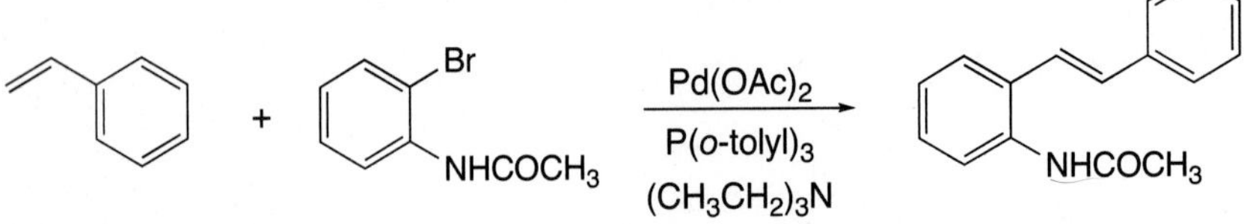
Br
NHCOCH3
Pd(OAc)2
P(o-tolyl)3
(CH3CH2)3N
NHCOCH3

d. 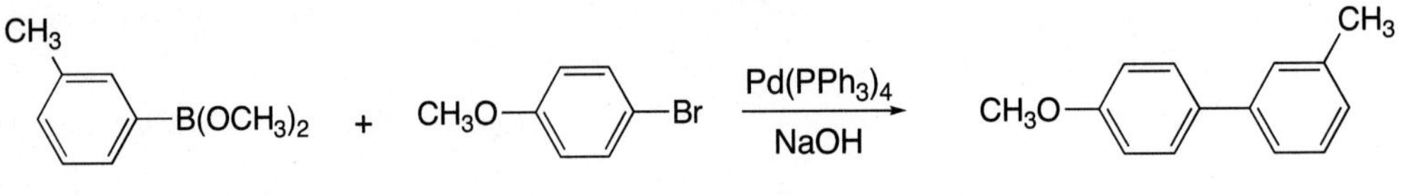
CH3
B(OCH3)2
CH3O
Br
Pd(PPh3)4
NaOH
CH3O
CH3

e. 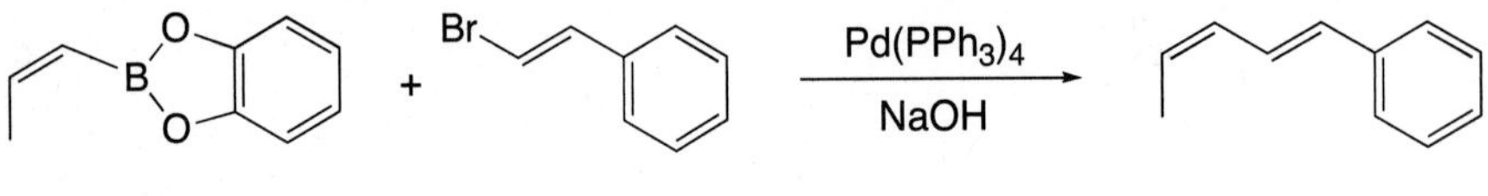
O
B
O
Br
Pd(PPh3)4
NaOH

f. 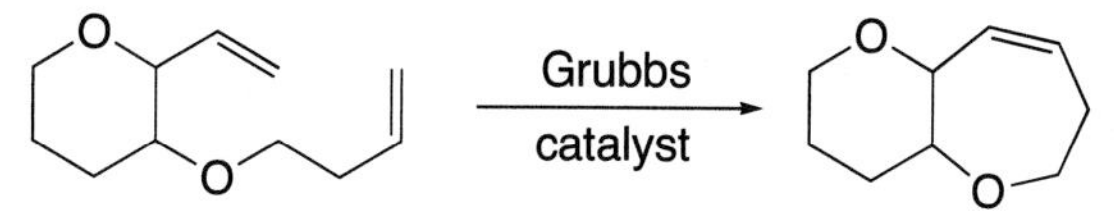
Grubbs
catalyst

g. 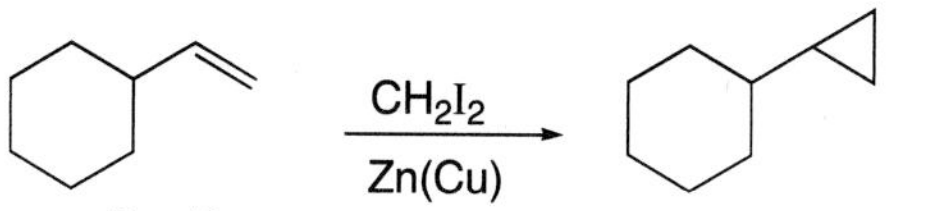
CH_2I_2
Zn(Cu)

h. 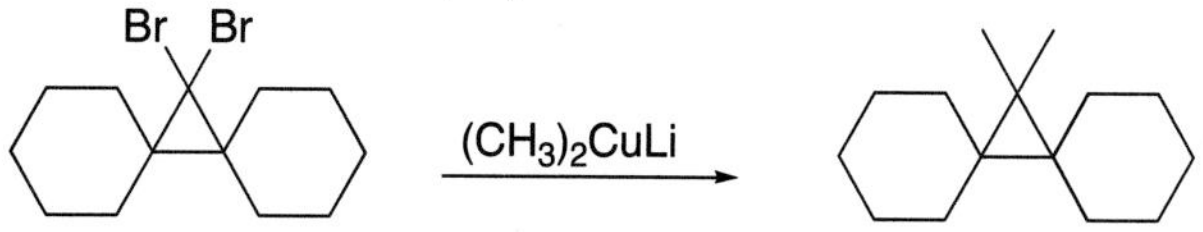
Br Br
$(CH_3)_2CuLi$

Product in (a)

i. 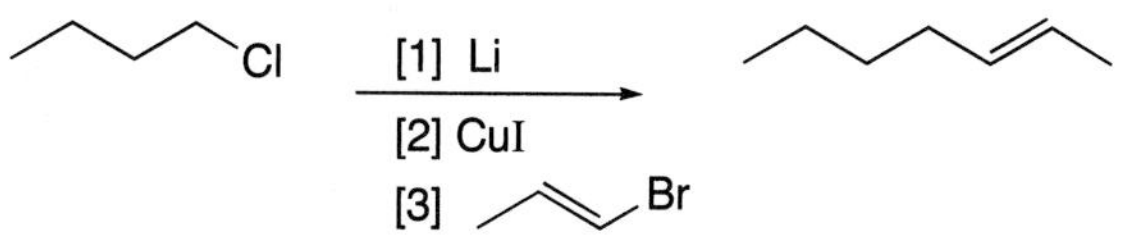
Cl
[1] Li
[2] CuI
[3] Br

j. 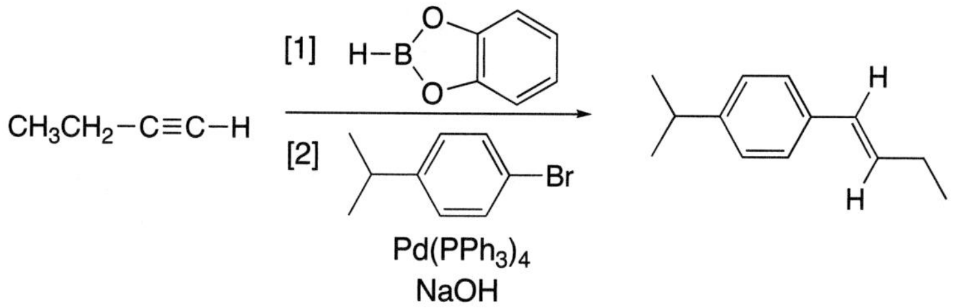
$CH_3CH_2-C\equiv C-H$
[1] H–B O O
[2] Br
$Pd(PPh_3)_4$
NaOH
H
H

26.33

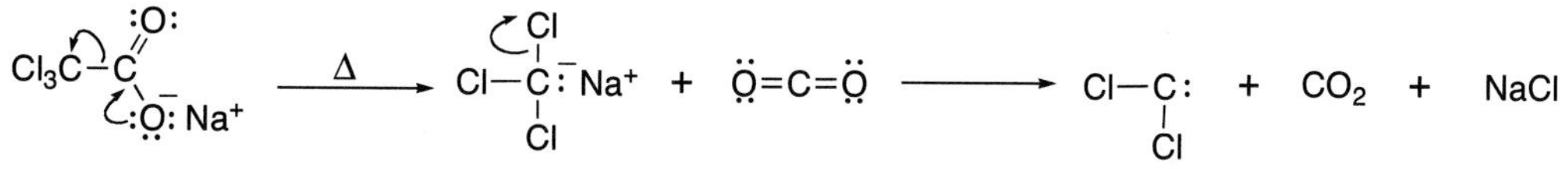
Cl_3C-C :O: :O: Na+
Δ
Cl–C: Na+ + O=C=O
Cl–C: + CO_2 + NaCl

26.34 This reaction follows the Simmons–Smith reaction mechanism illustrated in Mechanism 26.5.

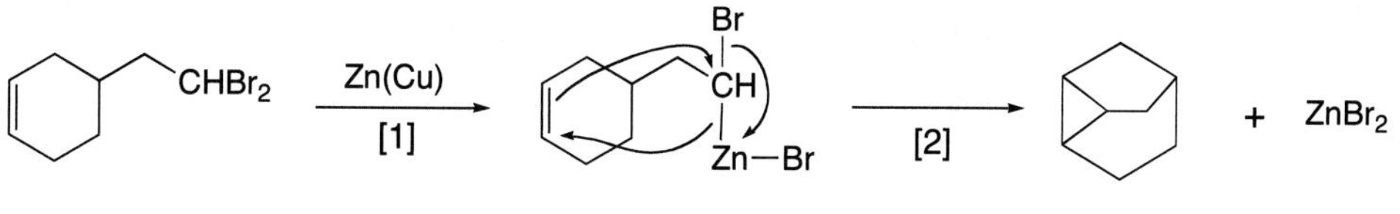
$CHBr_2$
Zn(Cu)
[1]
Br
CH
Zn—Br
[2]
+ $ZnBr_2$

26.35

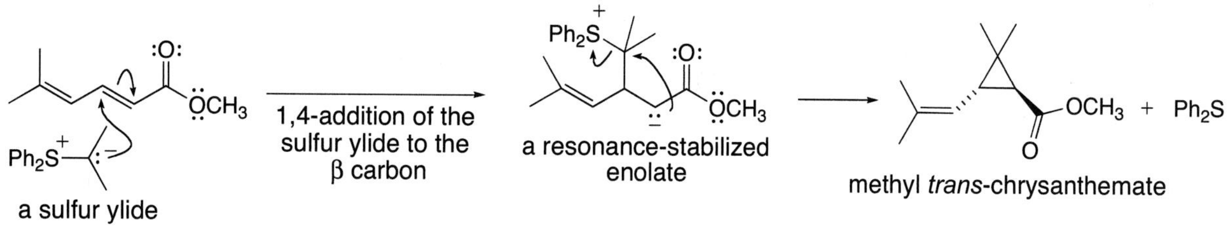
:O:
OCH_3
Ph_2S
a sulfur ylide
1,4-addition of the sulfur ylide to the β carbon
Ph_2S
:O:
OCH_3
a resonance-stabilized enolate
OCH_3 + Ph_2S
O
methyl trans-chrysanthemate

26.36

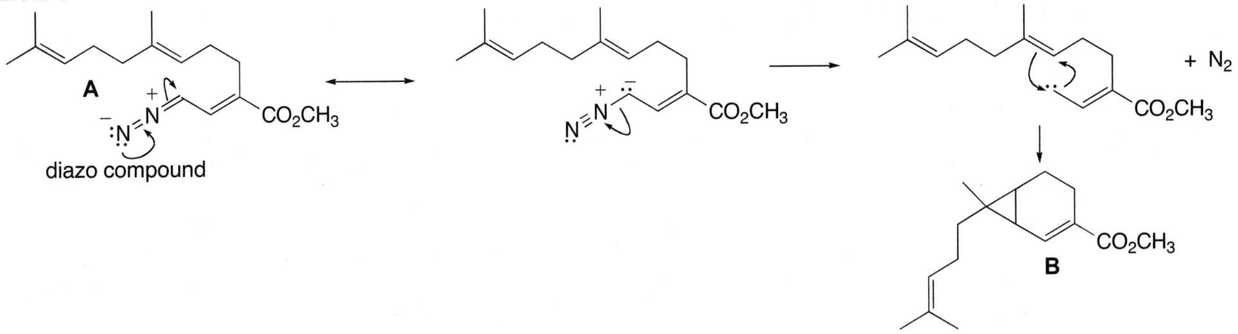
A
diazo compound
CO_2CH_3
+ N_2
B

26.37

a.

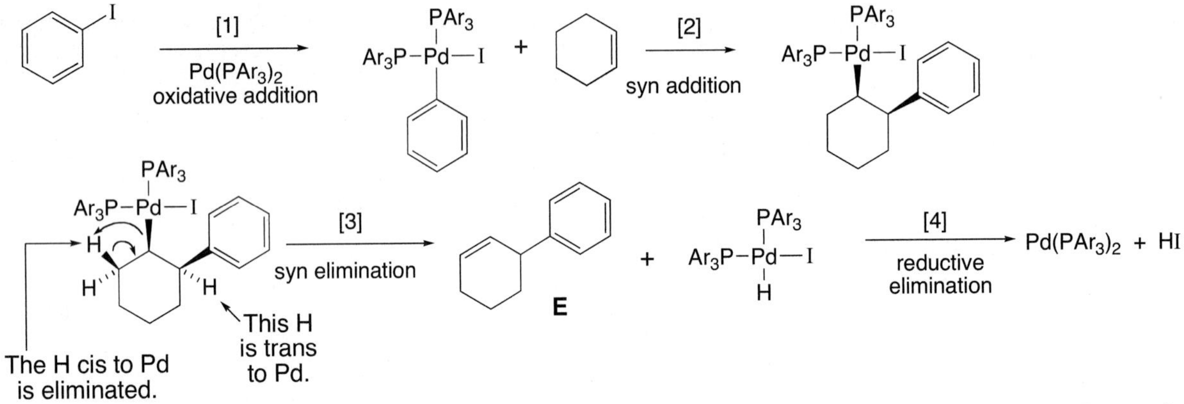
[1]
$Pd(PAr_3)_2$
oxidative addition
[2]
syn addition
[3]
syn elimination
E
[4]
reductive
elimination
$Pd(PAr_3)_2$ + HI
This H
is trans
to Pd.
The H cis to Pd
is eliminated.

b. This suggests that the stereochemistry in Step [3] must occur with syn elimination of H and Pd to form **E.** Product **F** cannot form because the only H on the C bonded to the benzene ring is trans to the Pd species, so it cannot be removed if elimination occurs in a syn fashion.

26.38

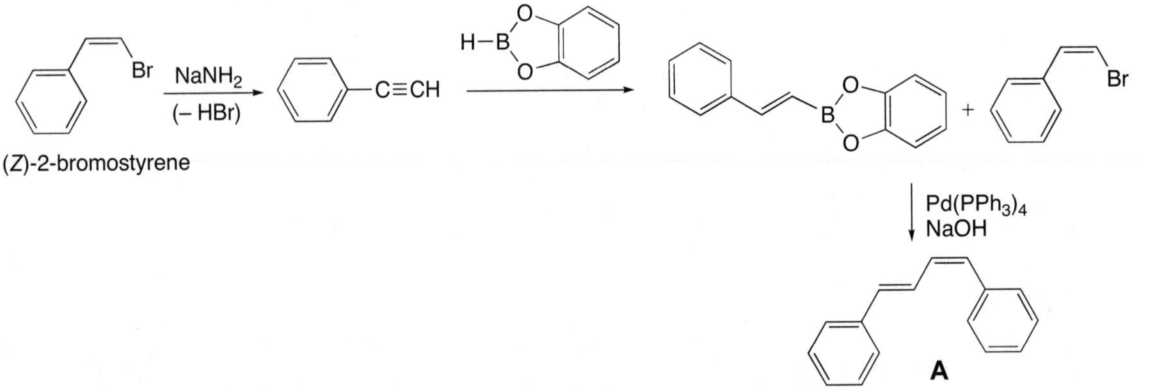
$NaNH_2$
(– HBr)
(Z)-2-bromostyrene
$Pd(PPh_3)_4$
NaOH
A

26.39

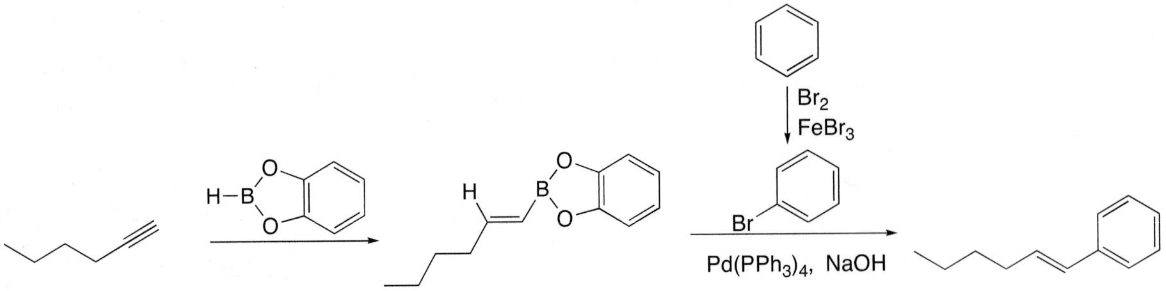
Br_2
$FeBr_3$
$Pd(PPh_3)_4$, NaOH

26.40

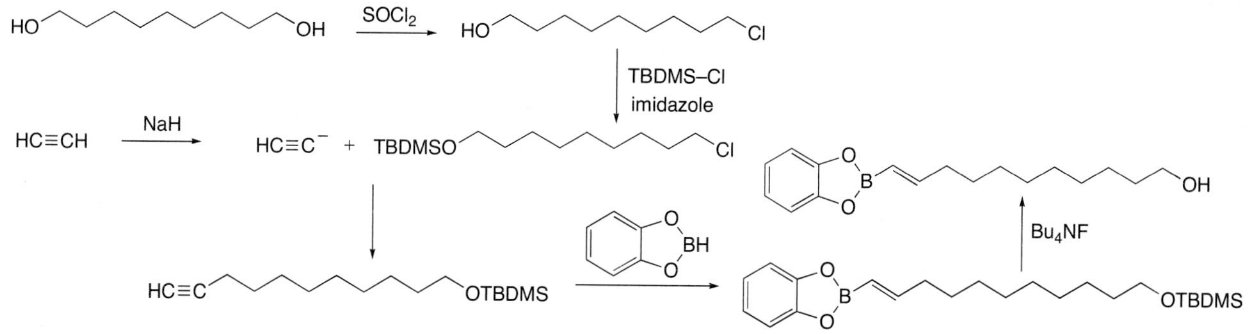

26.41

a. 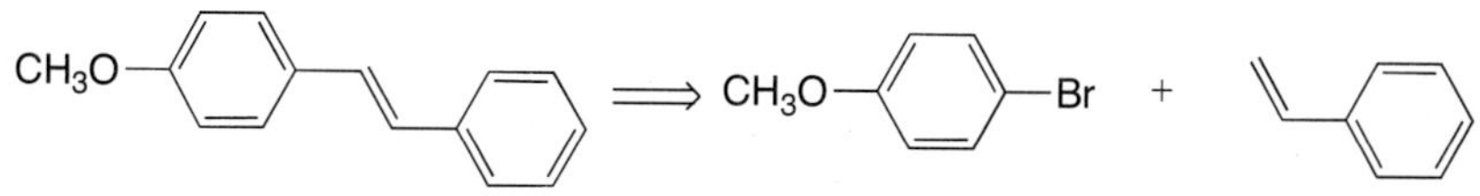

Synthesize these two components, and then use a Heck reaction to synthesize the product.

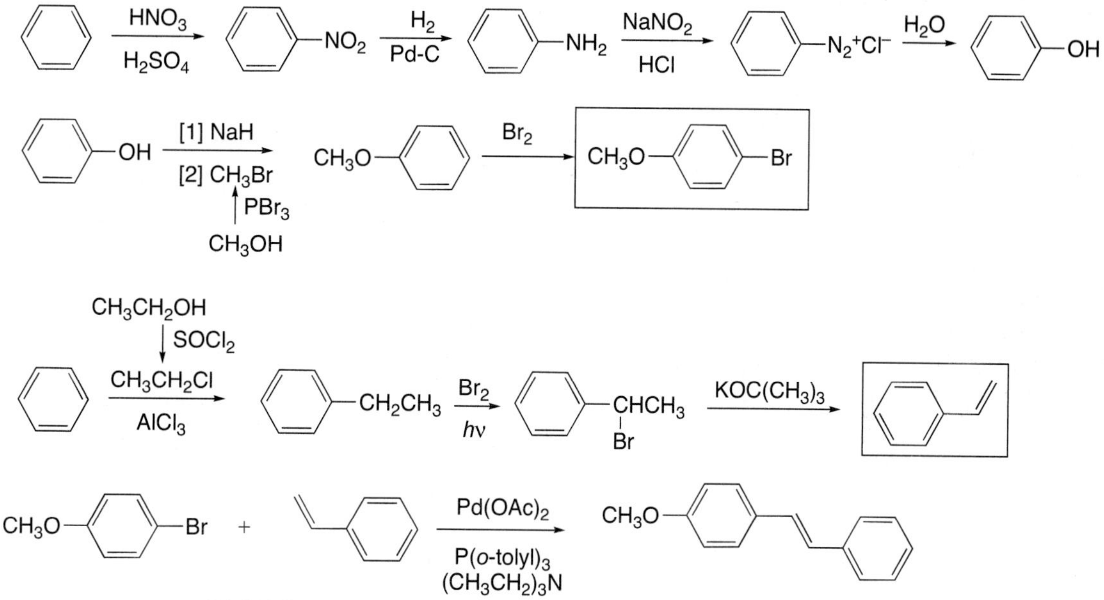

b. 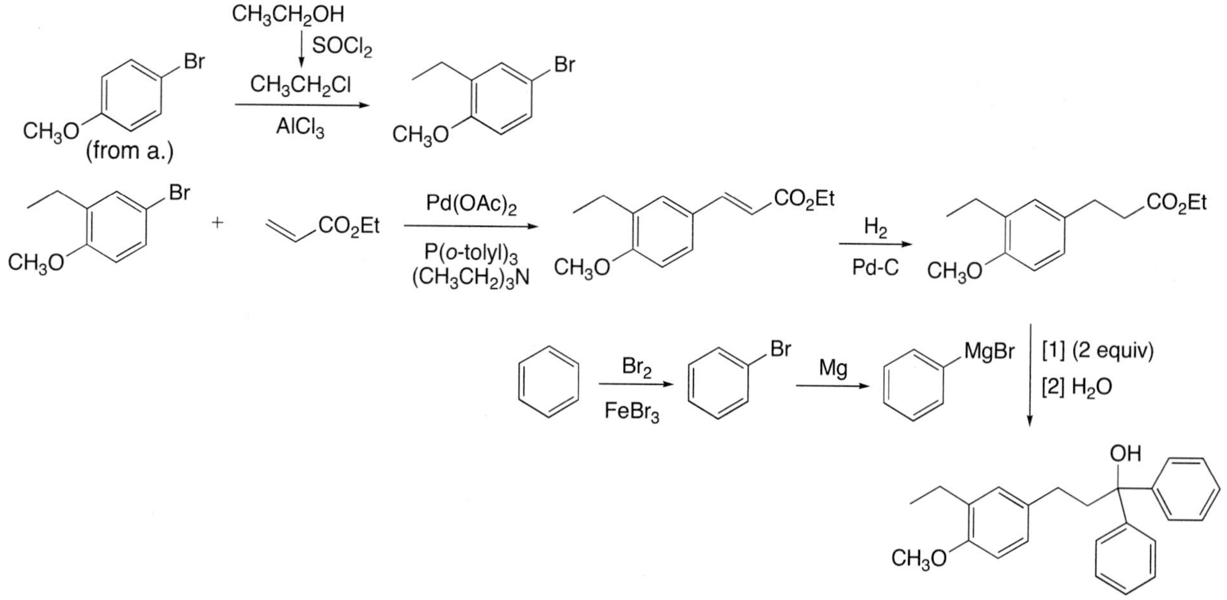

26.42

a.

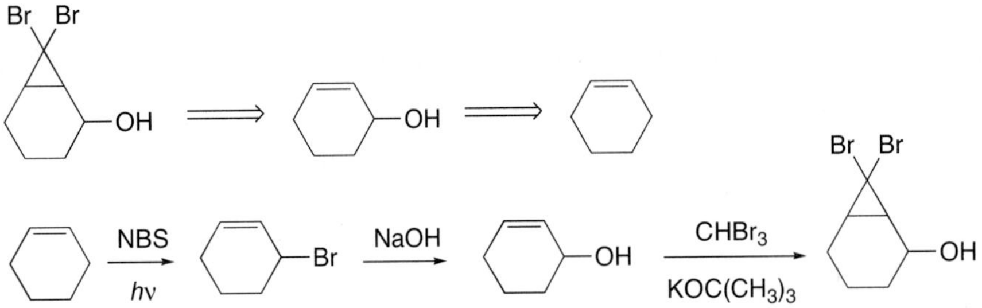

b.

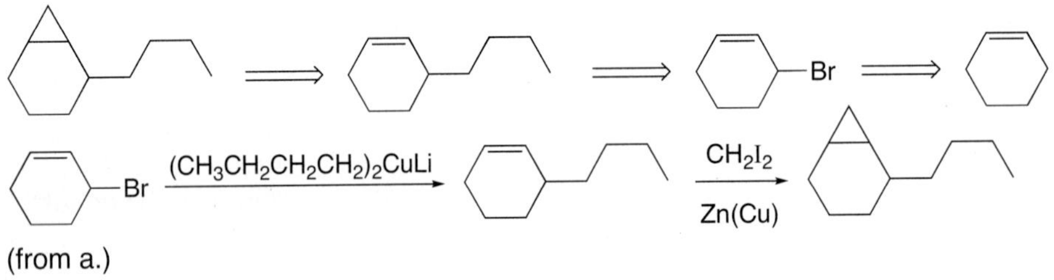

c.

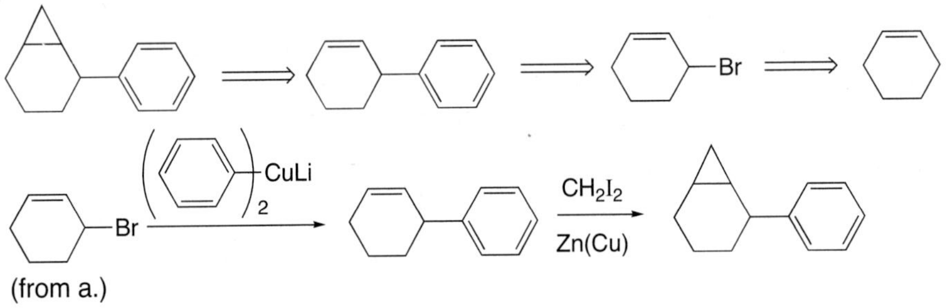

26.43

a.

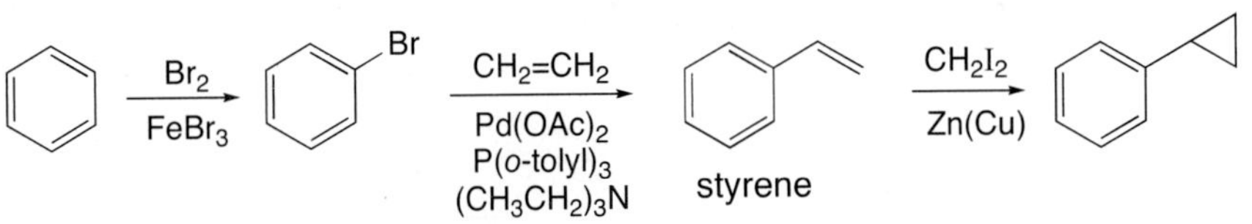

For an alternate synthesis of styrene, see Problem 26.41.

b.

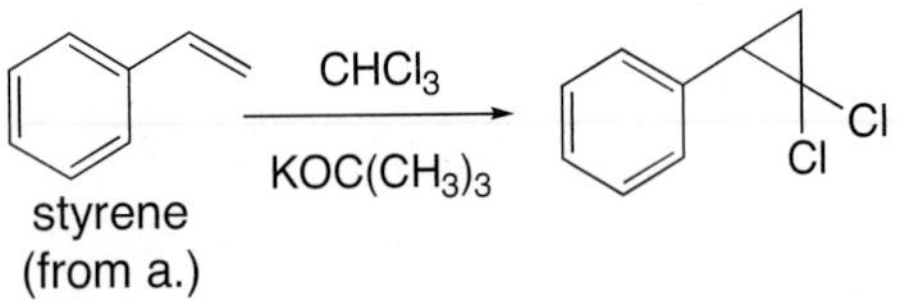

c.

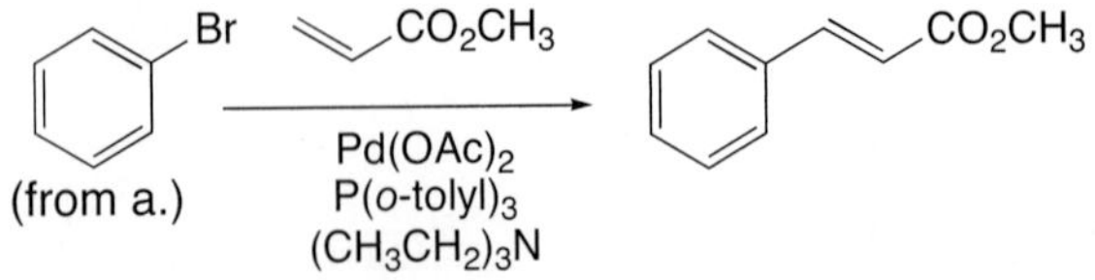

d.

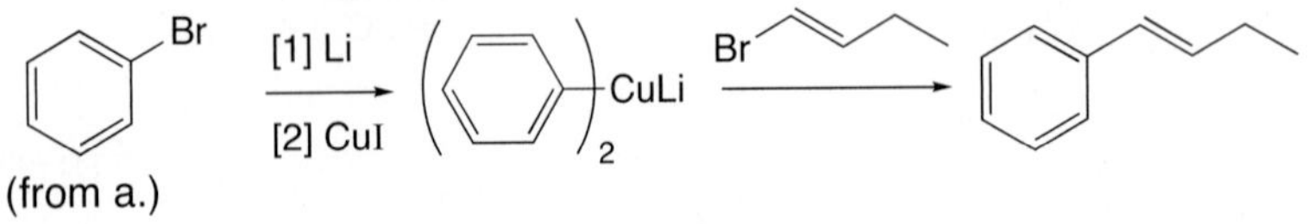

26.44

a.

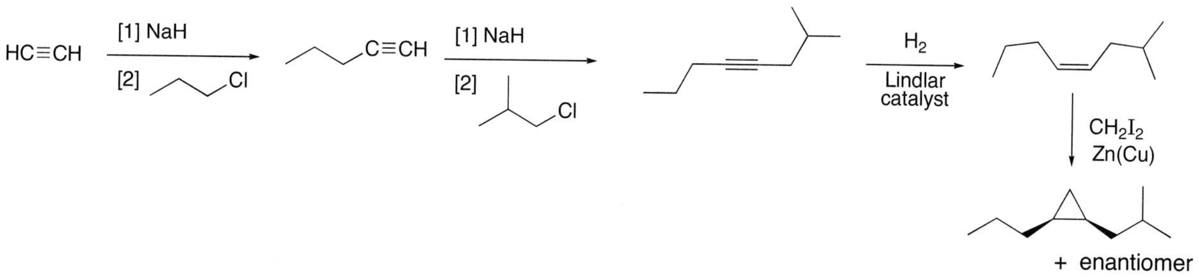
HC≡CH
[1] NaH
[2] Cl
C≡CH
[1] NaH
[2] Cl
H2
Lindlar catalyst
CH2I2
Zn(Cu)
+ enantiomer

b.

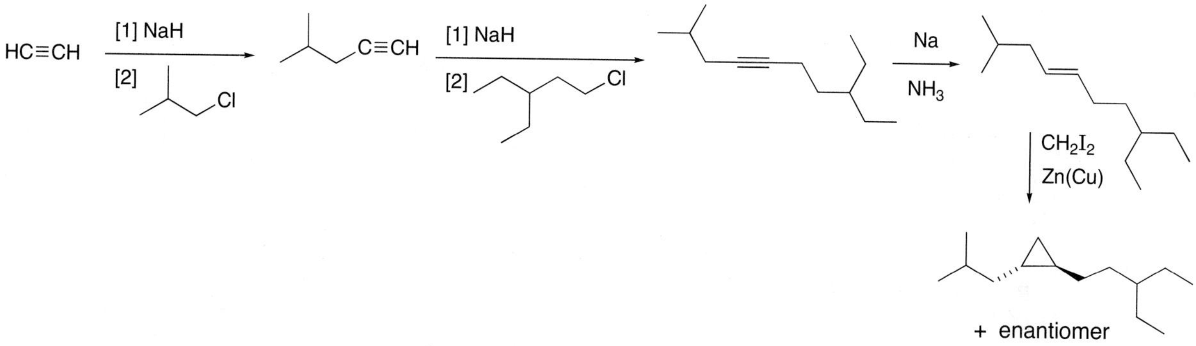
HC≡CH
[1] NaH
[2] Cl
C≡CH
[1] NaH
[2] Cl
Na
NH3
CH2I2
Zn(Cu)
+ enantiomer

c.

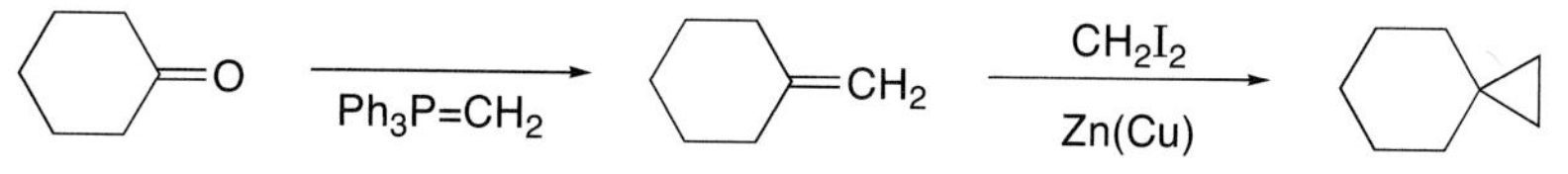
O
Ph3P=CH2
CH2
CH2I2
Zn(Cu)

d.

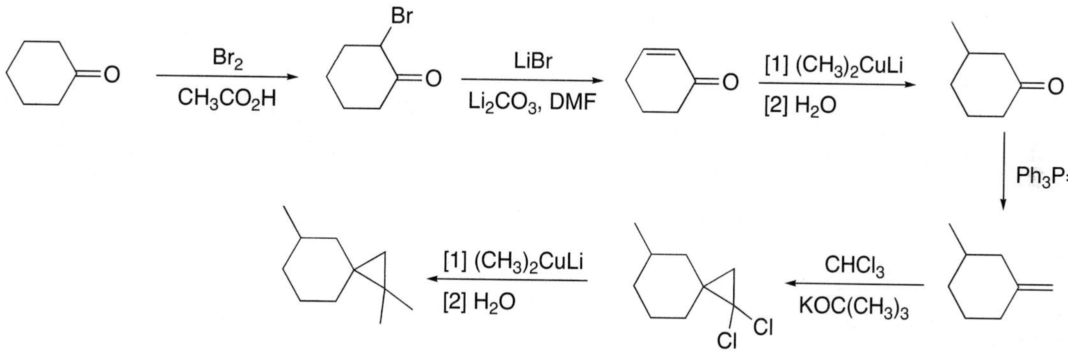
O
Br2
CH3CO2H
Br
O
LiBr
Li2CO3, DMF
O
[1] (CH3)2CuLi
[2] H2O
O
Ph3P=CH2
CHCl3
KOC(CH3)3
Cl
Cl
[1] (CH3)2CuLi
[2] H2O

26.45

a.

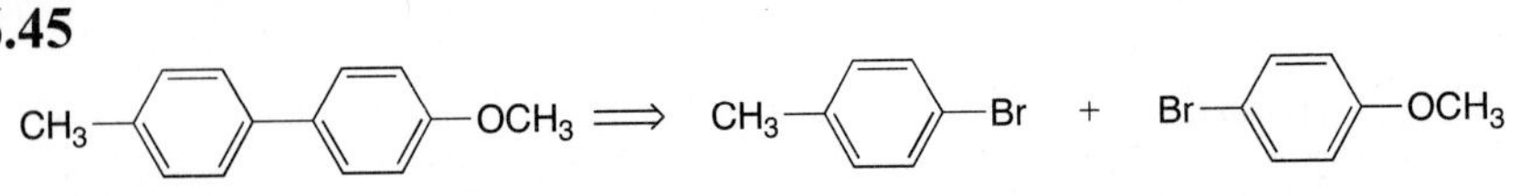
CH3
OCH3
CH3
Br
Br
OCH3

Either compound can be used to synthesize the organoborane, so two routes are possible.

Possibility [1]:

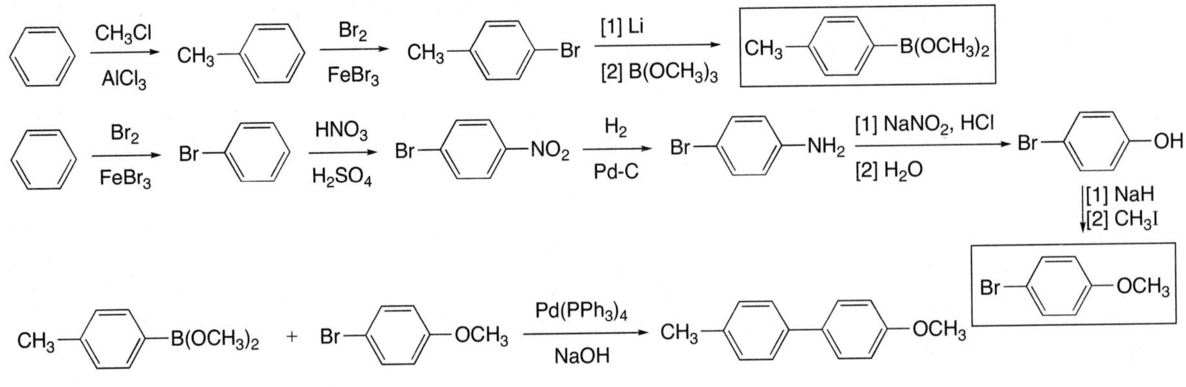
CH3Cl
AlCl3
CH3
Br2
FeBr3
CH3
Br
[1] Li
[2] B(OCH3)3
CH3
B(OCH3)2
Br2
FeBr3
Br
HNO3
H2SO4
Br
NO2
H2
Pd-C
Br
NH2
[1] NaNO2, HCl
[2] H2O
Br
OH
[1] NaH
[2] CH3I
Br
OCH3
CH3
B(OCH3)2
Br
OCH3
Pd(PPh3)4
NaOH
CH3
OCH3

Possibility [2]:

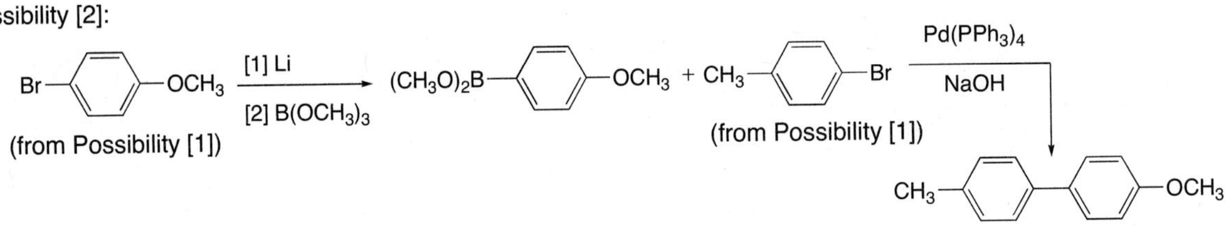
Br
OCH3
(from Possibility [1])
[1] Li
[2] B(OCH3)3
(CH3O)2B
OCH3
CH3
Br
(from Possibility [1])
Pd(PPh3)4
NaOH
CH3
OCH3

b.

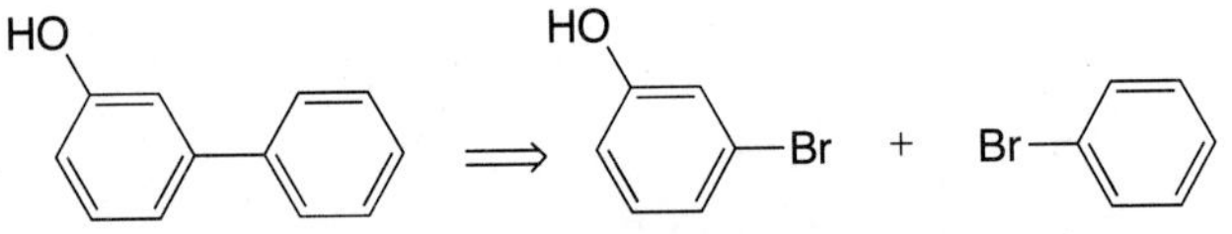
HO
HO
Br
Br

The acidic OH makes it impossible to prepare an organolithium reagent from this aryl halide, so this compound must be used as the aryl halide that couples with the organoborane from bromobenzene.

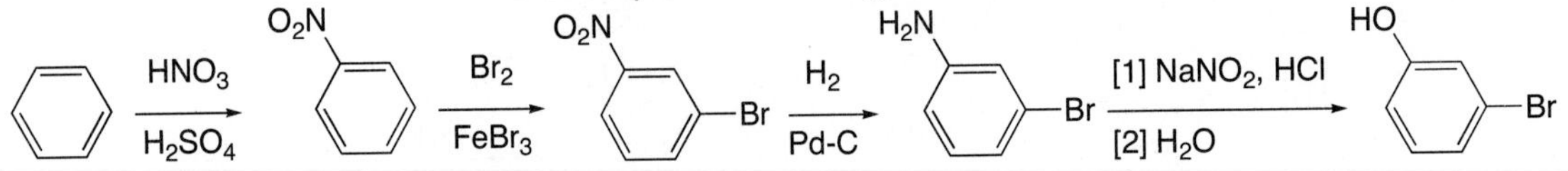
HNO3
H2SO4
O2N
Br2
FeBr3
O2N
Br
H2
Pd-C
H2N
Br
[1] NaNO2, HCl
[2] H2O
HO
Br

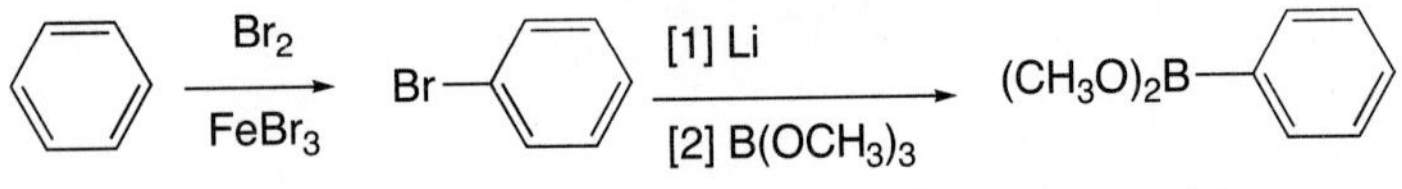
Br2
FeBr3
Br
[1] Li
[2] B(OCH3)3
(CH3O)2B

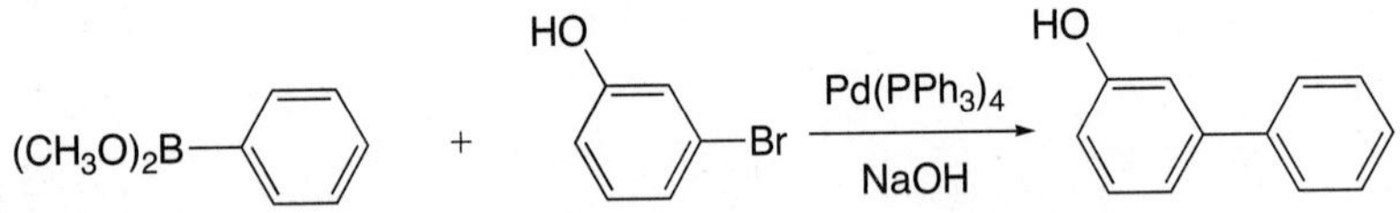
(CH3O)2B
HO
Br
Pd(PPh3)4
NaOH
HO

c.

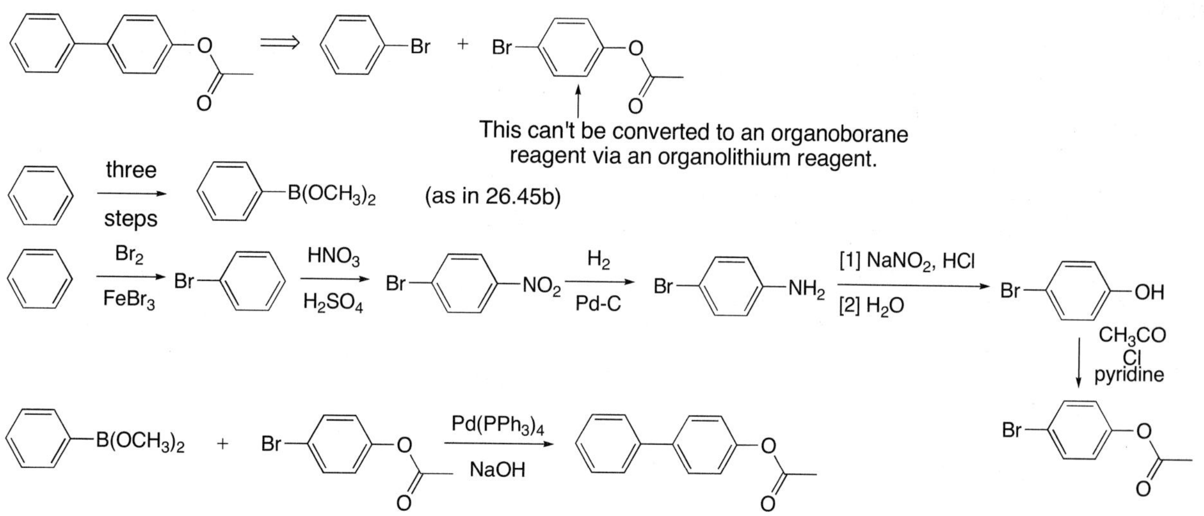
O
O
Br
Br
O
O
This can't be converted to an organoborane reagent via an organolithium reagent.
three
steps
B(OCH3)2
(as in 26.45b)
Br2
FeBr3
Br
HNO3
H2SO4
Br
NO2
H2
Pd-C
Br
NH2
[1] NaNO2, HCl
[2] H2O
Br
OH
CH3COCl
pyridine
Br
O
O
B(OCH3)2
Br
O
O
Pd(PPh3)4
NaOH
O
O

26.46

a.

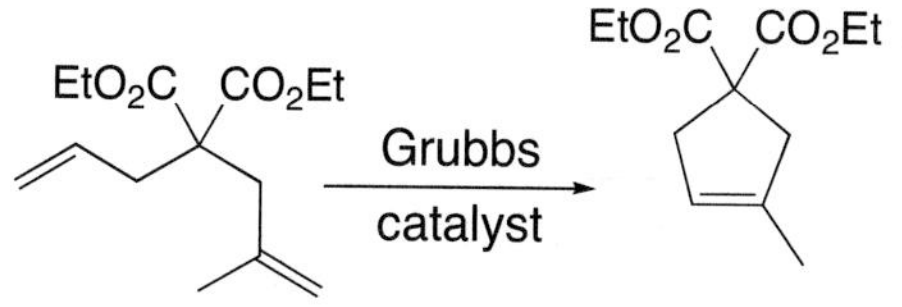
EtO2C CO2Et
Grubbs
catalyst
EtO2C CO2Et

Synthesis of starting material:

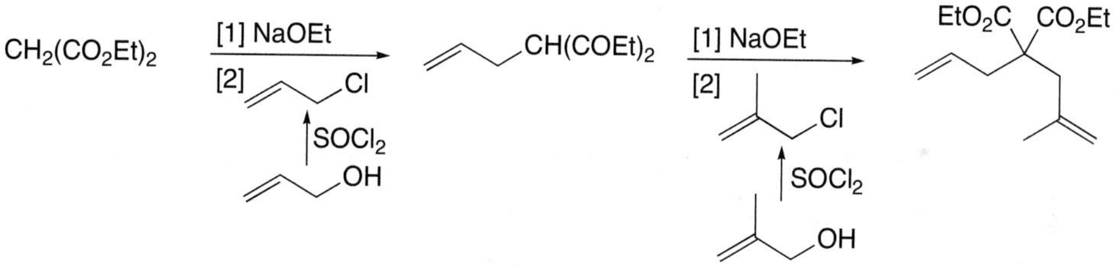
CH2(CO2Et)2
[1] NaOEt
[2]
Cl
SOCl2
OH
CH(COEt)2
[1] NaOEt
[2]
Cl
SOCl2
OH
EtO2C CO2Et

b.

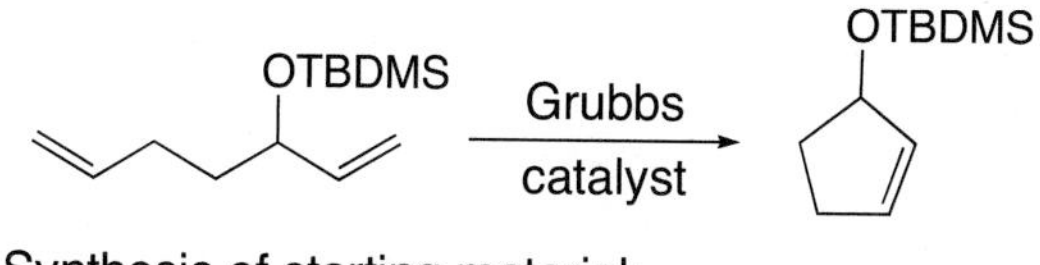
OTBDMS
Grubbs
catalyst
OTBDMS

Synthesis of starting material:

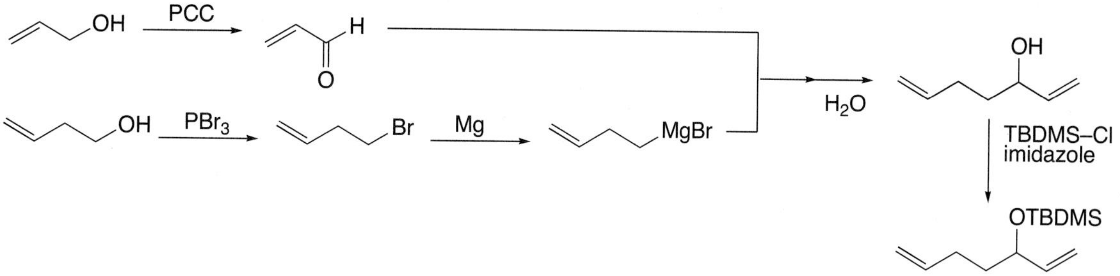
OH
PCC
H
O
OH
PBr3
Br
Mg
MgBr
H2O
OH
TBDMS–Cl
imidazole
OTBDMS

26.47

a. 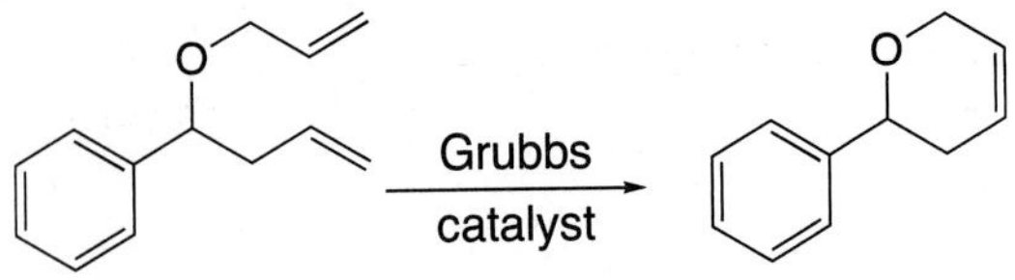

Synthesis of starting material:

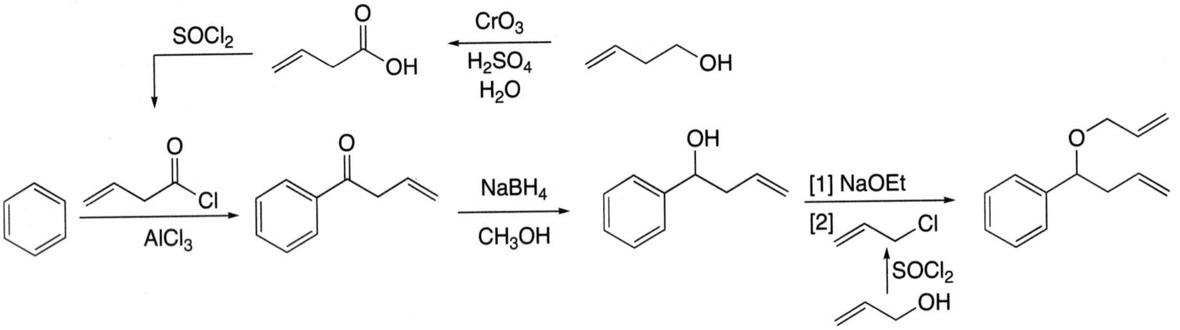

b. 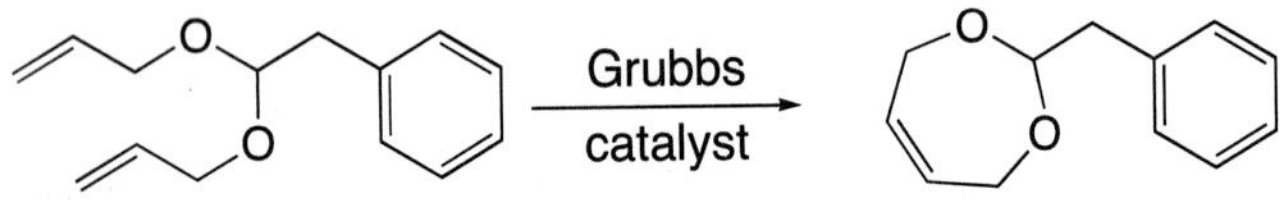

Synthesis of starting material:

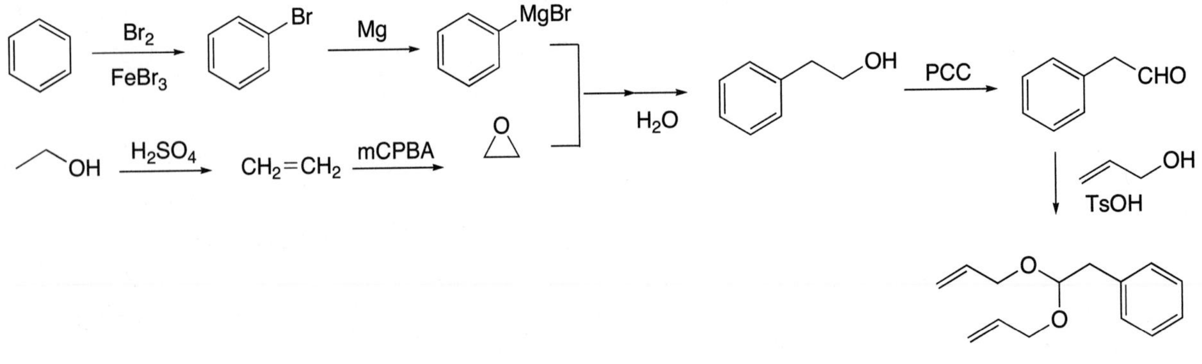

26.48

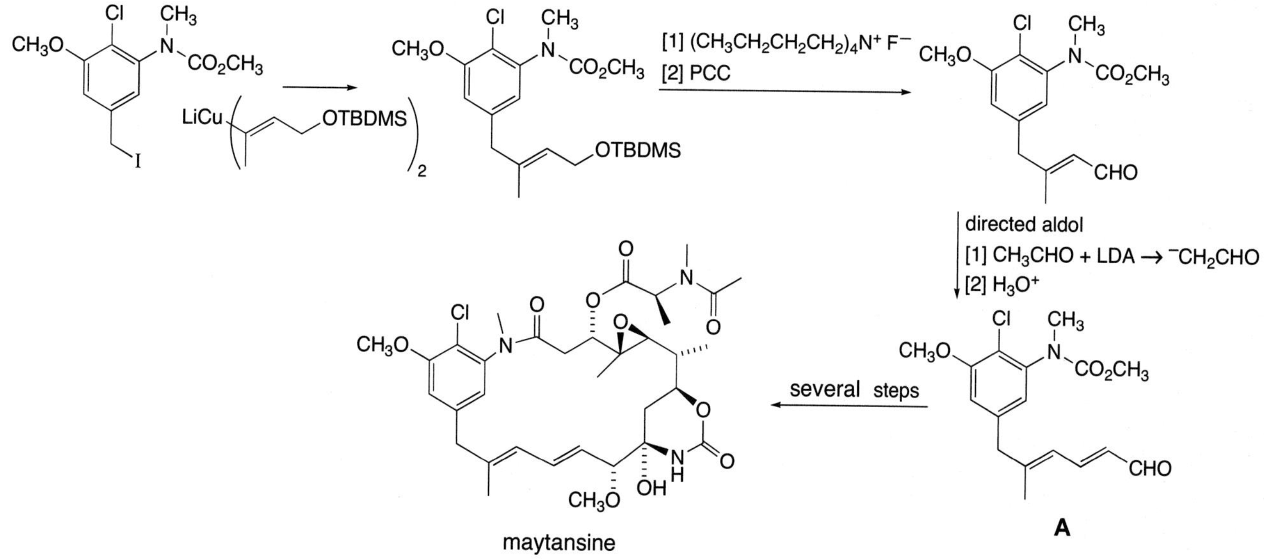

26.49

a.

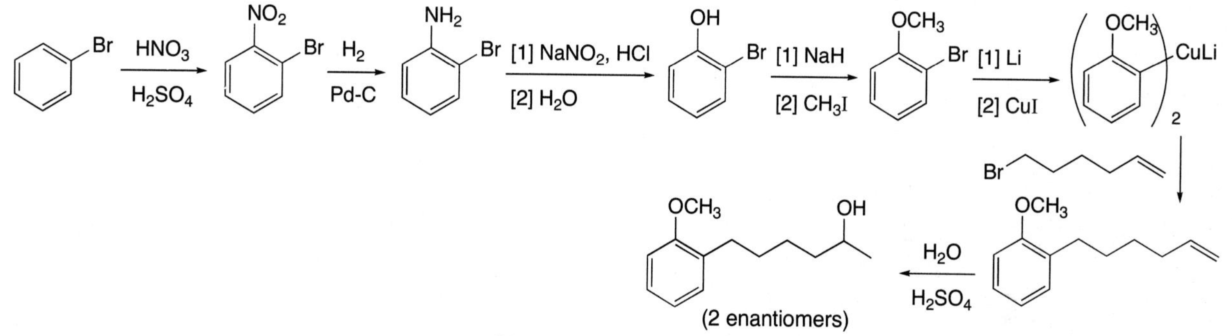

b.

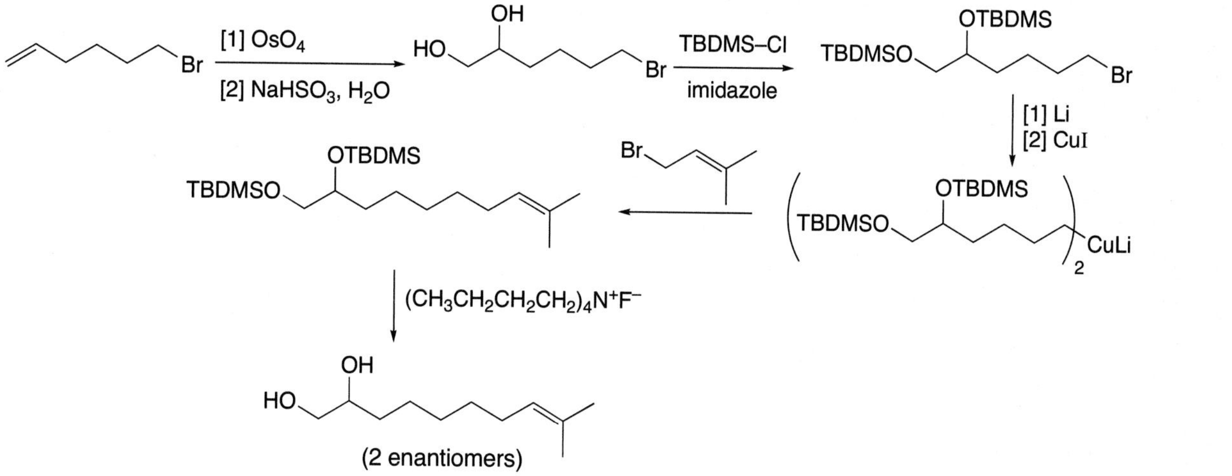

c.

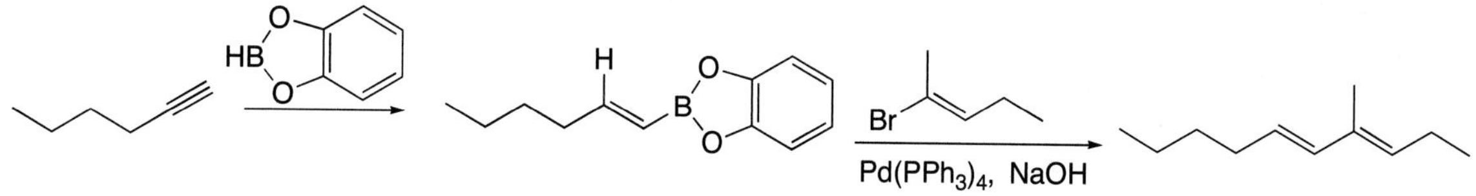

d.

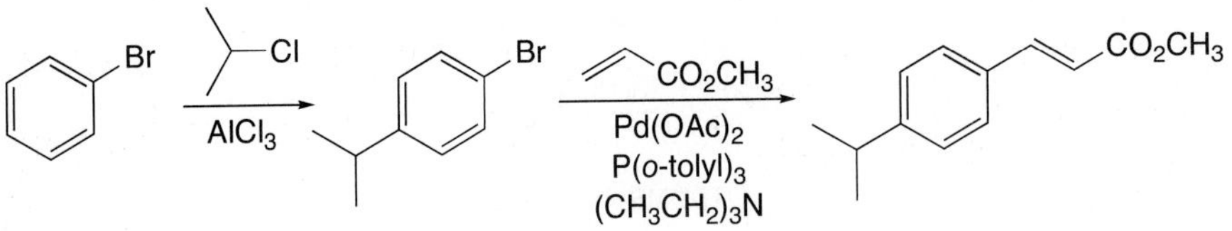

e.

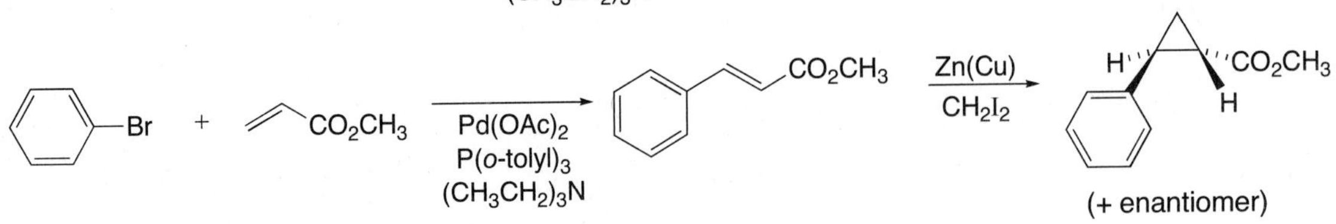

f.

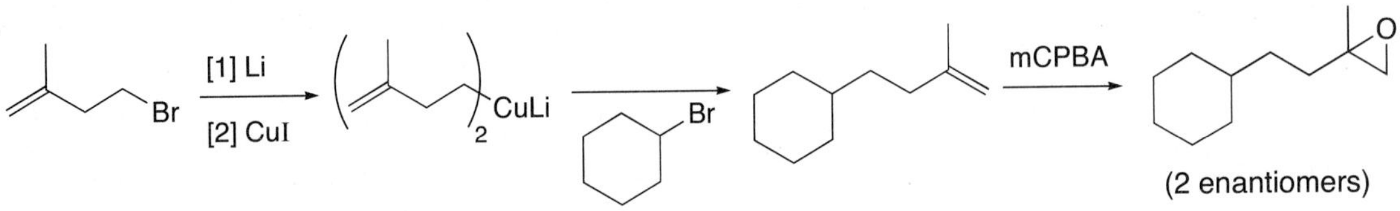

26.50

a.

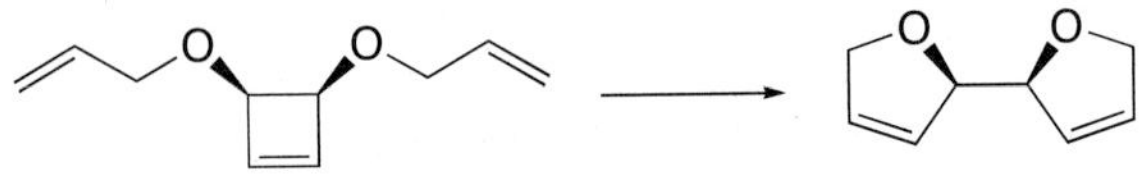

b.

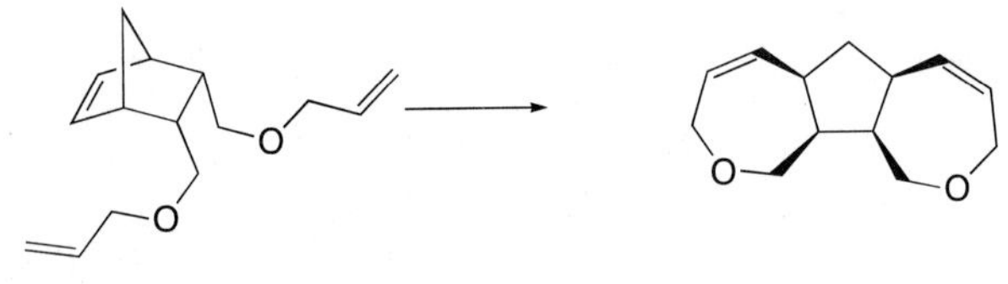

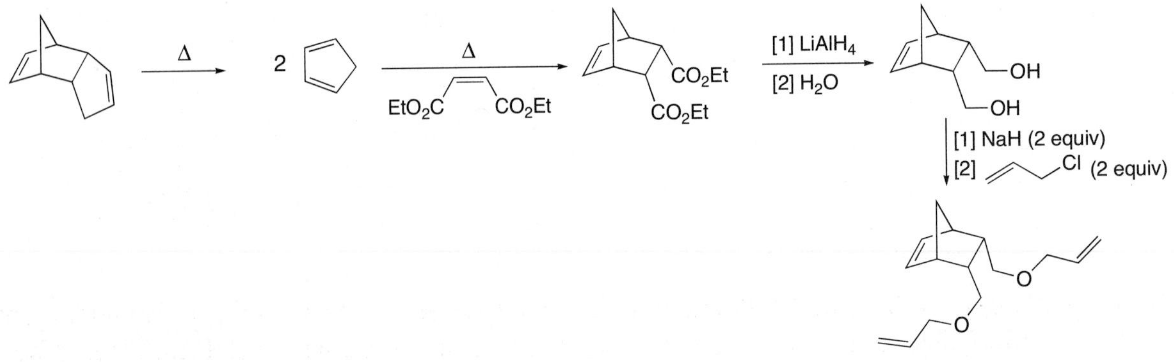

26.51 There is more than one way to form **Z** by metathesis reactions. One possibility involves ring opening of the bicyclic alkene followed by successive ring closures to generate the five- and seven-membered rings.

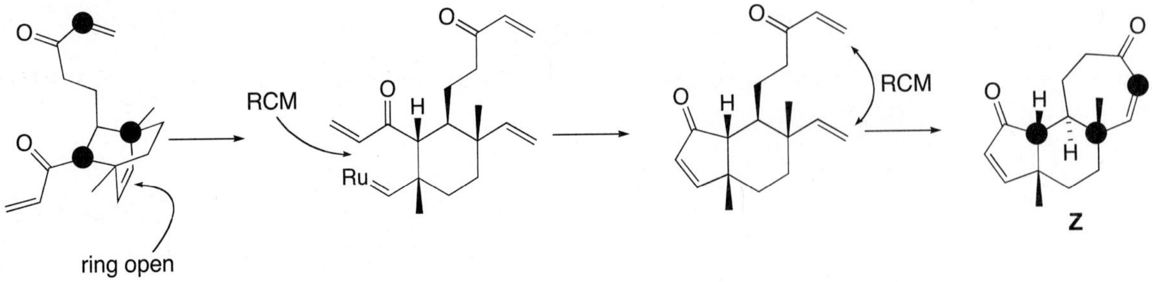

26.52

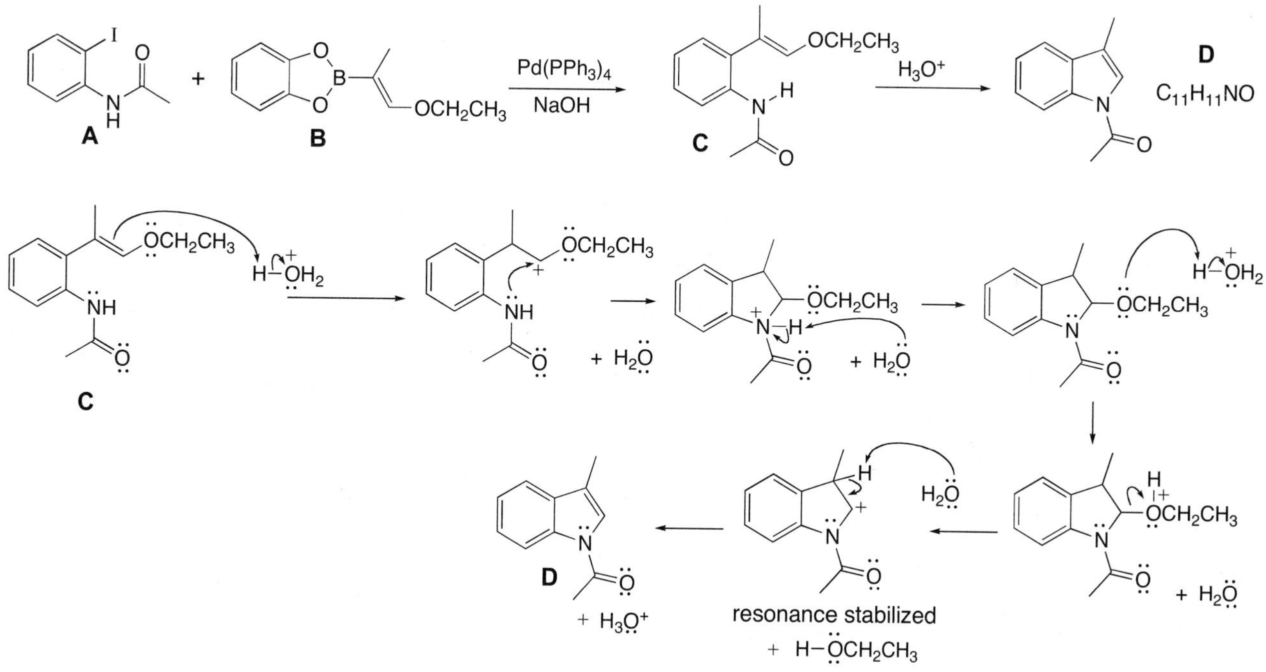

26.53

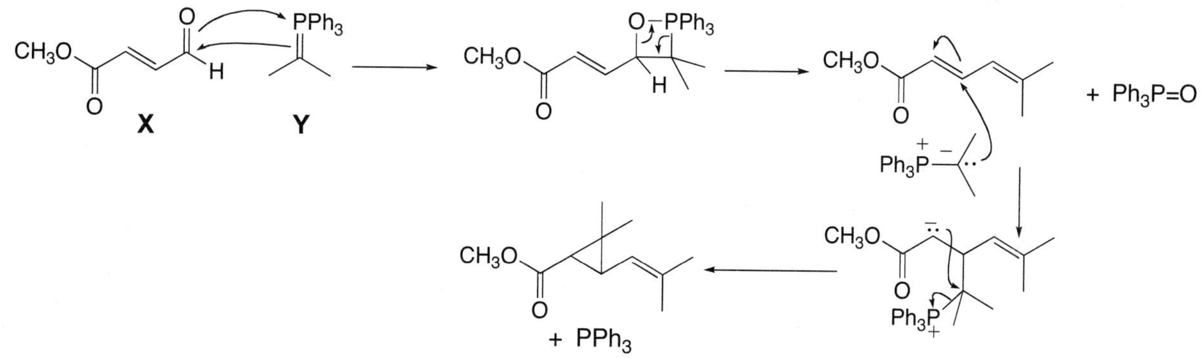

26.54 a. Reaction of a terminal alkene with the catalyst forms a metal–carbene that undergoes an intramolecular reaction with the triple bond, generating a new metal–carbene. A second intramolecular reaction forms the bicyclic product.

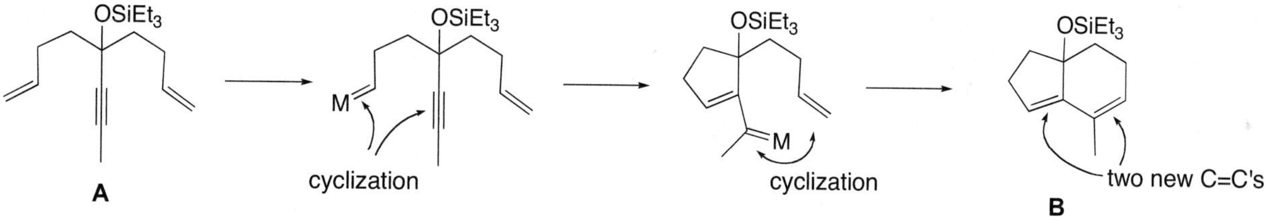

b. Two products are possible because the cascade of reactions can begin at two different double bonds.

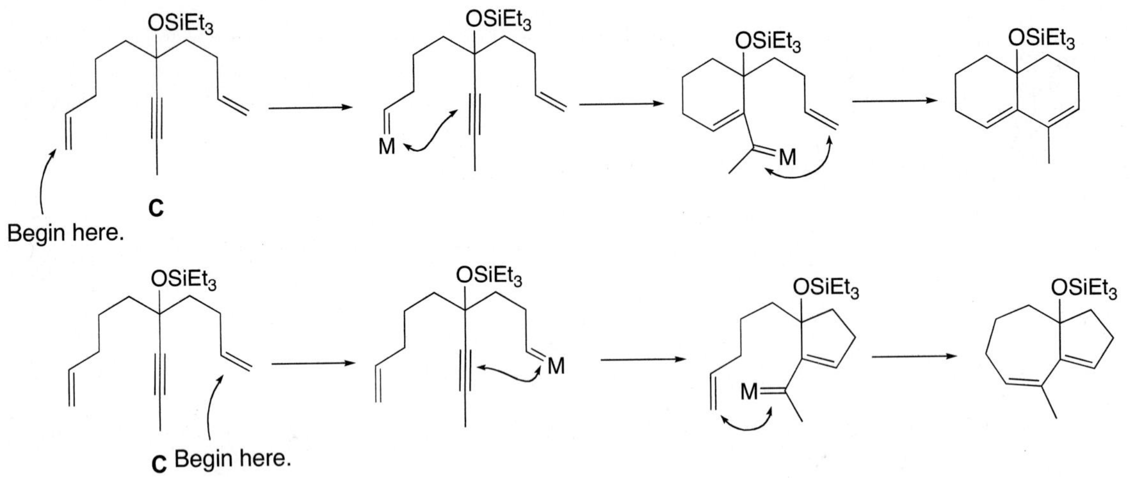

Chapter 27 Pericyclic Reactions

Chapter Review

Electrocyclic reactions (27.3)

Woodward–Hoffmann rules for electrocyclic reactions

Number of π bonds	Thermal reaction	Photochemical reaction
Even	Conrotatory	Disrotatory
Odd	Disrotatory	Conrotatory

Examples

The stereochemistry of a thermal electrocyclic reaction is opposite to that of a photochemical electrocyclic reaction.

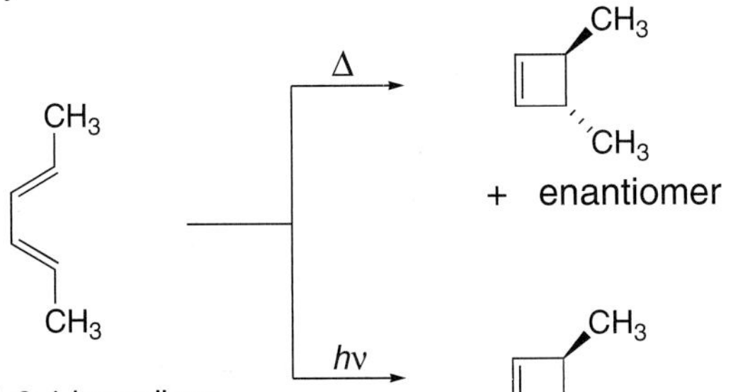
CH3
CH3
Δ
hv
CH3
CH3
+ enantiomer
CH3
CH3

(2*E*,4*E*)-2,4-hexadiene
2 π bonds

- A thermal electrocyclic reaction with an even number of π bonds occurs in a conrotatory fashion.
- A photochemical electrocyclic reaction with an even number of π bonds occurs in a disrotatory fashion.

Cycloaddition reactions (27.4)

Woodward–Hoffmann rules for cycloaddition reactions

Number of π bonds	Thermal reaction	Photochemical reaction
Even	Antarafacial	Suprafacial
Odd	Suprafacial	Antarafacial

Examples

[1] A thermal [4 + 2] cycloaddition takes place in a suprafacial fashion with an odd number of π bonds. An antarafacial photochemical [4 + 2] cycloaddition to form a six-membered ring cannot occur, because of the geometrical constraints of forming a six-membered ring.

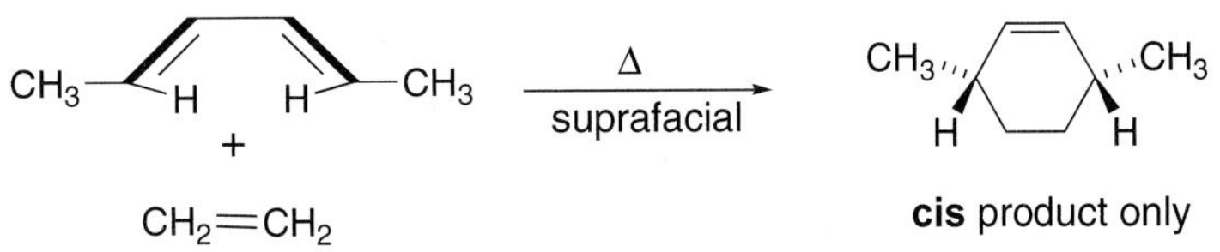
CH3
H
H
CH3
+
CH2=CH2
Δ
suprafacial
CH3
CH3
H
H

cis product only

[2] A photochemical [2 + 2] cycloaddition takes place in a suprafacial fashion with an even number of π bonds. An antarafacial thermal [2 + 2] cycloaddition to form a four-membered ring cannot occur, because of the geometrical constraints of forming a four-membered ring.

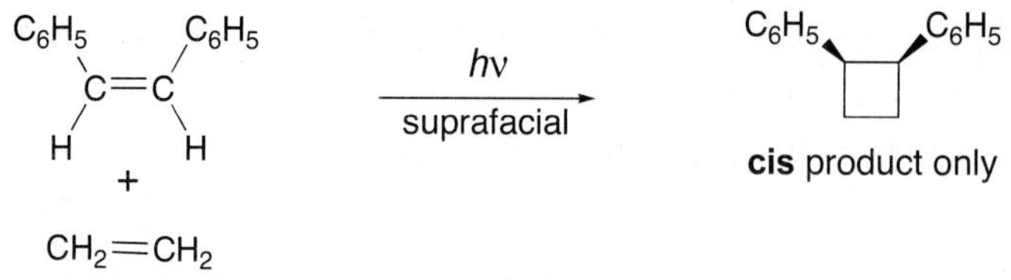

Sigmatropic rearrangements (27.5)

Woodward–Hoffmann rules for sigmatropic rearrangements

Number of electron pairs	Thermal reaction	Photochemical reaction
Even	Antarafacial	Suprafacial
Odd	Suprafacial	Antarafacial

Examples

[1] A **Cope rearrangement** is a thermal [3,3] sigmatropic rearrangement that converts a 1,5-diene into an isomeric 1,5-diene.

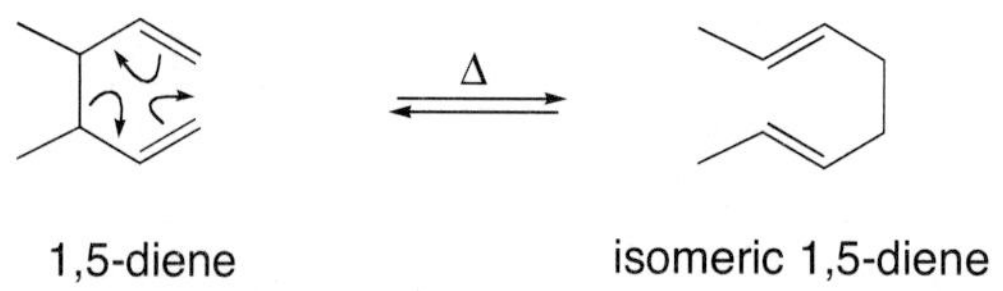

[2] An **oxy-Cope rearrangement** is a thermal [3,3] sigmatropic rearrangement that converts a 1,5-dien-3-ol into a δ, ε-unsaturated carbonyl compound, after tautomerization of an intermediate enol.

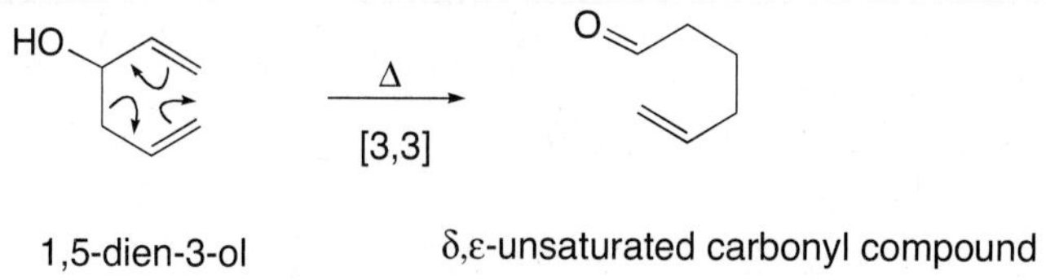

[3] A **Claisen rearrangement** is a thermal [3,3] sigmatropic rearrangement that converts an unsaturated ether into a γ,δ-unsaturated carbonyl compound.

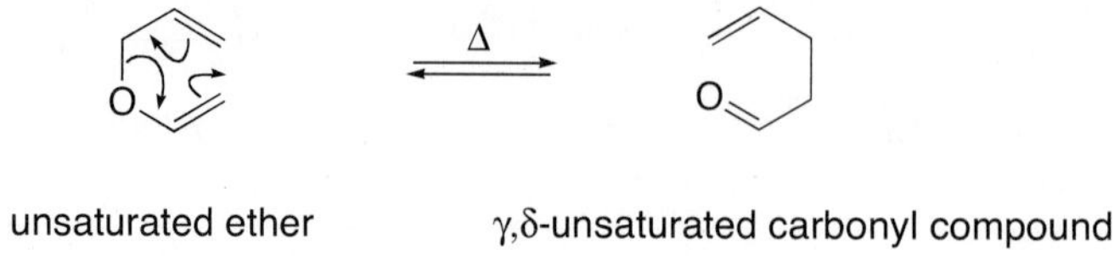

Practice Test on Chapter Review

1. a. Which of the following pericyclic reactions is symmetry allowed and readily occurs?
   1. a photochemical conrotatory electrocyclic ring closure of a conjugated triene
   2. a disrotatory thermal electrocyclic ring opening of a substituted cyclohexadiene
   3. a thermal [2 + 2] cycloaddition
   4. Reactions [1] and [2] will both occur.
   5. Reactions [1], [2], and [3] will all occur.

   b. Which of the following reactions requires suprafacial stereochemistry to be symmetry allowed?
   1. a photochemical [1,5] sigmatropic rearrangement
   2. a thermal [8 + 2] cycloaddition
   3. a photochemical [4 + 2] cycloaddition
   4. Reactions [1] and [2] are both suprafacial.
   5. Reactions [1], [2], and [3] are all suprafacial.

   c. What product(s) are formed from the photochemical [2 + 2] cycloaddition of (3*E*)-3-hexene?

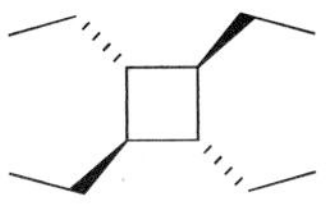
A

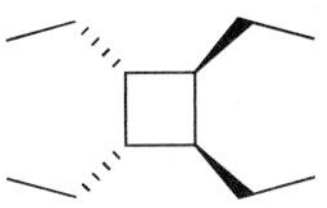
B

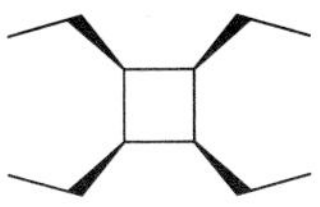
C

   1. **A** only
   2. **B** only
   3. **C** only
   4. **A** and **B**
   5. **A, B,** and **C**

   d. What product(s) are formed from the photochemical electrocyclic ring opening of *cis*-3,4-dimethylcyclobutene?

   1. (2*E*,4*E*)-2,4-hexadiene
   2. (2*E*,4*Z*)-2,4-hexadiene
   3. (3*Z*)-1,3,5-hexatriene
   4. Compounds [1] and [2] are both formed.
   5. Compounds [1], [2], and [3] are all formed.

e. What product(s) are formed by the [3,3] sigmatropic rearrangement of 1,5-cyclodecadien-3-ol?

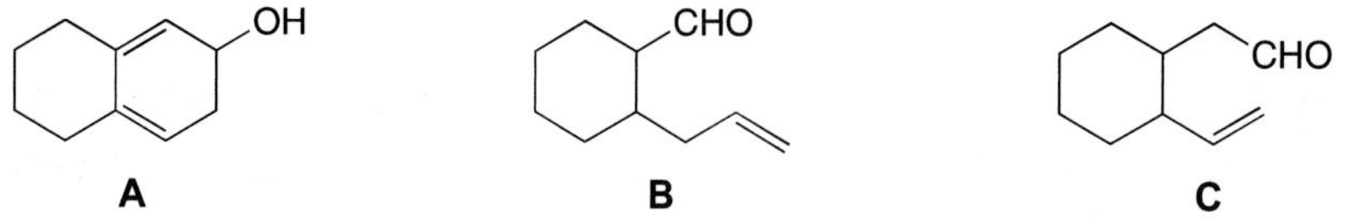

1. **A** only
2. **B** only
3. **C** only
4. **A** and **B**
5. **A, B,** and **C**

2. Consider the *p* orbitals of the terminal carbons of a conjugated polyene with like phases on the same side of the molecule (as in **A**) or opposite sides of the molecule (as in **B**), and answer each question.

a. Which drawing is consistent with the ground state HOMO of a conjugated triene?
b. Which drawing is consistent with the excited state LUMO of a conjugated diene?
c. Which drawing is consistent with the ground state LUMO for a conjugated tetraene?

3. What type of sigmatropic rearrangement is depicted in each reaction?

a.

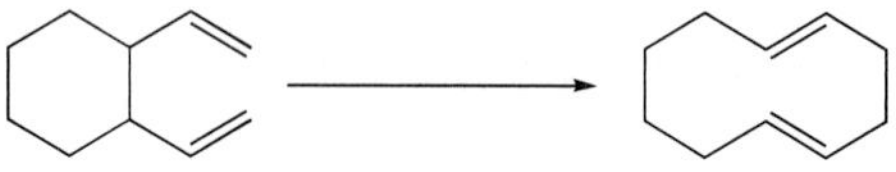

b.

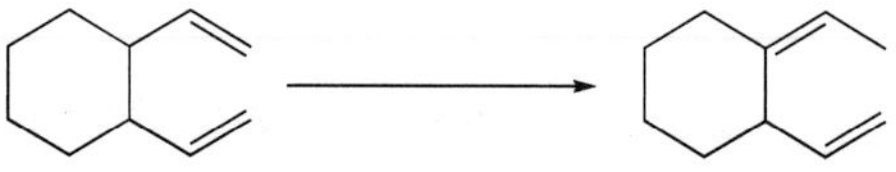

Answers to Practice Test

1. a. 4
   b. 2
   c. 4
   d. 1
   e. 3

2. a. **A**
   b. **B**
   c. **A**

3. a. [3,3]
   b. [1,3]

Answers to Problems

27.1 Use the following definitions:

- An **electrocyclic ring closure** is an intramolecular reaction that forms a cyclic product containing one more σ bond and one fewer π bond than the reactant. An **electrocyclic ring opening** is a reaction in which a σ bond of a cyclic reactant is cleaved to form a conjugated product with one more π bond.
- A **cycloaddition** is a reaction between two compounds with π bonds that forms a cyclic product with two new σ bonds.
- A **sigmatropic rearrangement** is a reaction in which a σ bond is broken in the reactant, the π bonds rearrange, and a σ bond is formed in the product.

a.

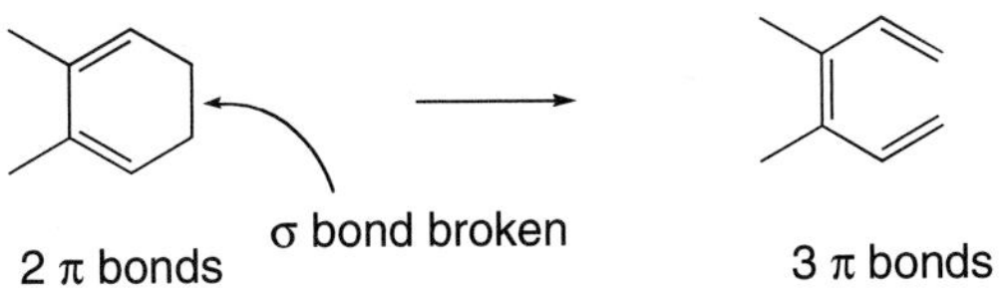
σ bond broken
2 π bonds
3 π bonds

electrocyclic reaction

b.

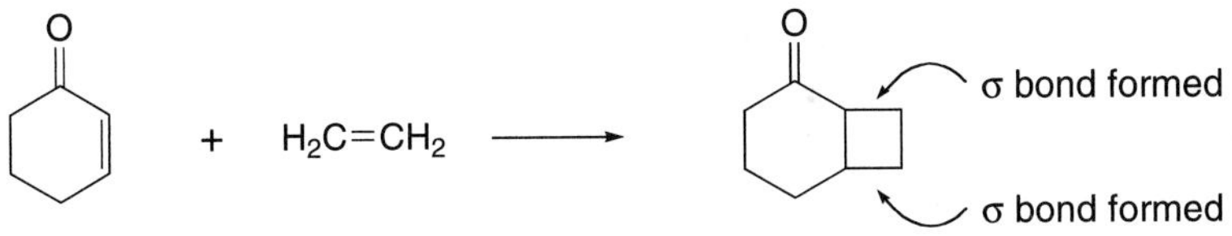
O
+
H2C=CH2
O
σ bond formed
σ bond formed

cycloaddition

c.

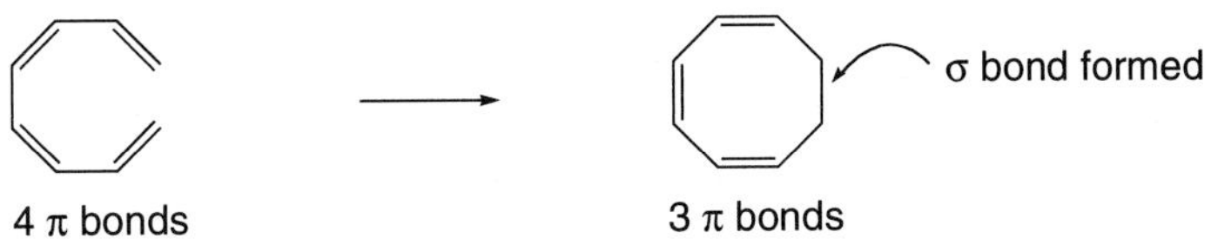
σ bond formed
4 π bonds
3 π bonds

electrocyclic reaction

d.

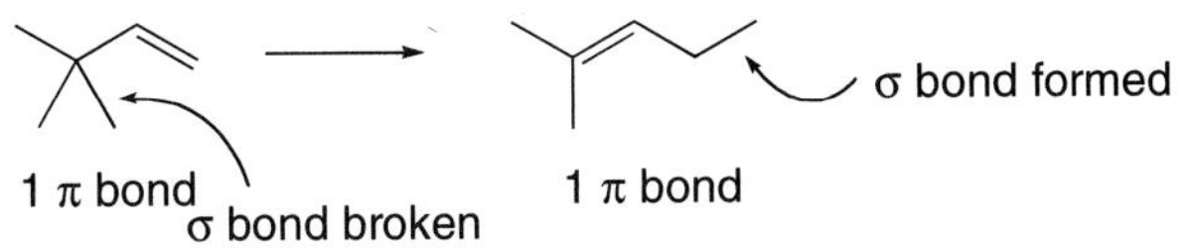
σ bond formed
1 π bond
σ bond broken
1 π bond

sigmatropic rearrangement

27.2 a. For a bonding molecular orbital, the number of bonding interactions is greater than the number of nodes.
b. For an antibonding molecular orbital, the number of bonding interactions is less than the number of nodes.

For 1,3-butadiene:

	Bonding	Nodes	Type of MO
ψ_1	3	0	bonding MO
ψ_2	2	1	bonding MO
ψ_3*	1	2	antibonding MO
ψ_4*	0	3	antibonding MO

27.3 The molecular orbitals of all conjugated dienes look similar.

a. b. Ground state c. Excited state

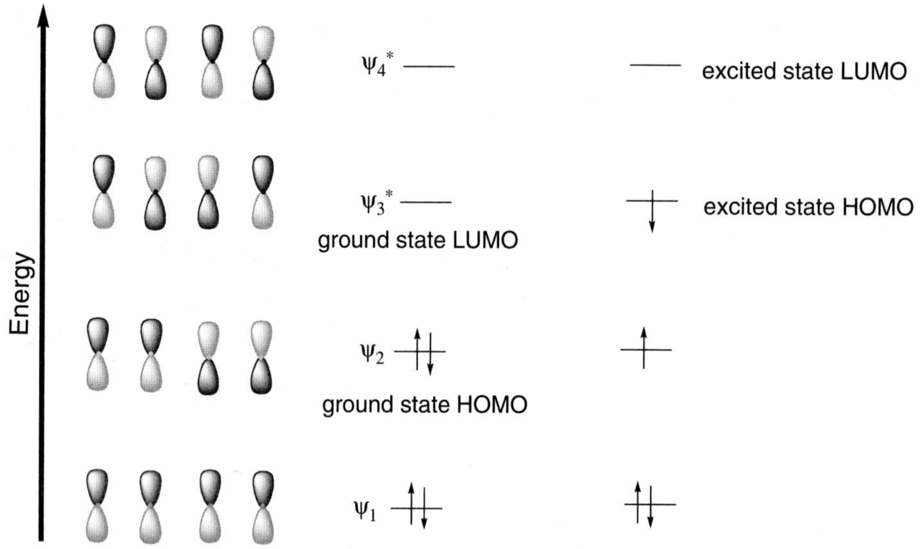
Energy
ψ_4^*
excited state LUMO
ψ_3^*
ground state LUMO
excited state HOMO
ψ_2
ground state HOMO
ψ_1

27.4 a. There are 10 molecular orbitals from the 10 *p* orbitals of the five π bonds.
b. Five molecular orbitals are bonding and five molecular orbitals are antibonding.
c. The lowest energy molecular orbital (ψ1) has zero nodes.

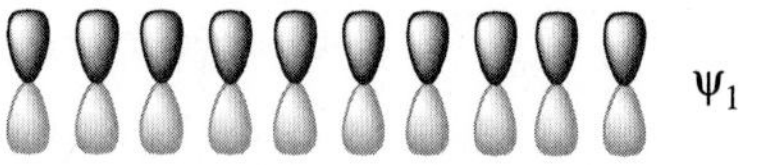
ψ_1

d. The highest energy molecular orbital (ψ_{10}*) has nine nodes.

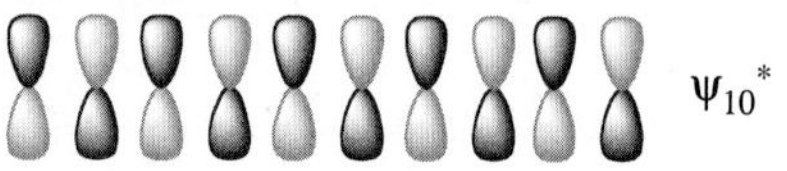
ψ_{10}^*

27.5 To draw the product of an electrocyclic reaction, use curved arrows and begin at a π bond. Move the π electrons to an adjacent carbon–carbon bond, and continue in a cyclic fashion.

a.

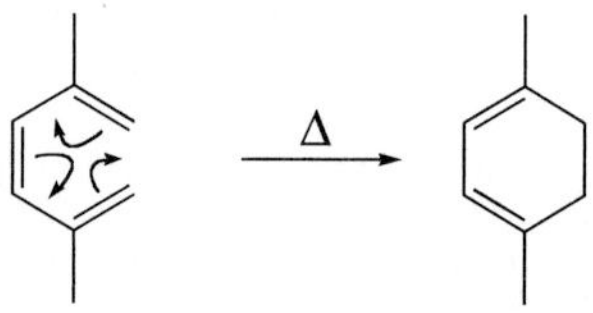
Δ

c.

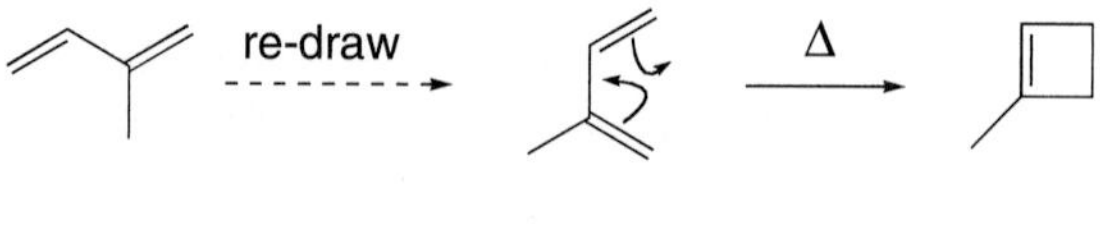
re-draw
Δ

b.

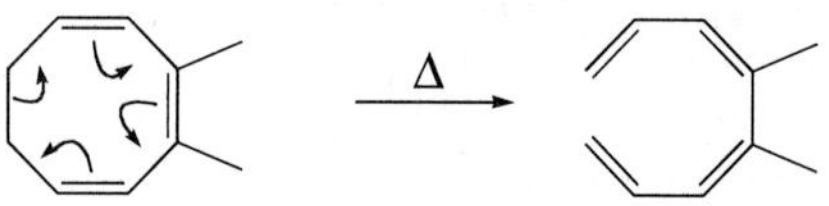
Δ

27.6 Thermal electrocyclic reactions occur in a *disrotatory* fashion for a conjugated polyene with an *odd* number of π bonds, and in a *conrotatory* fashion for a conjugated polyene with an *even* number of π bonds.

a.

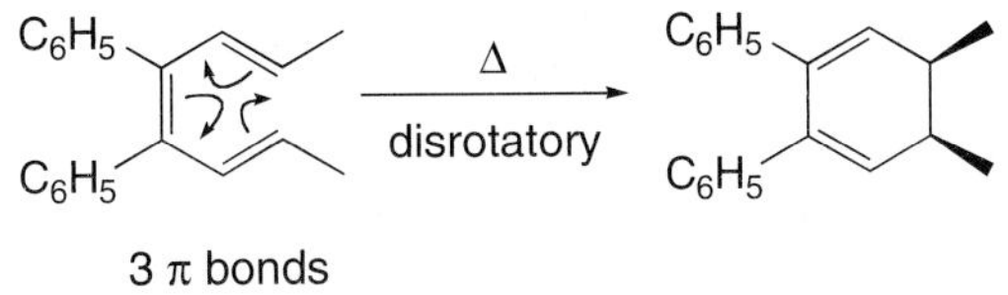

b.

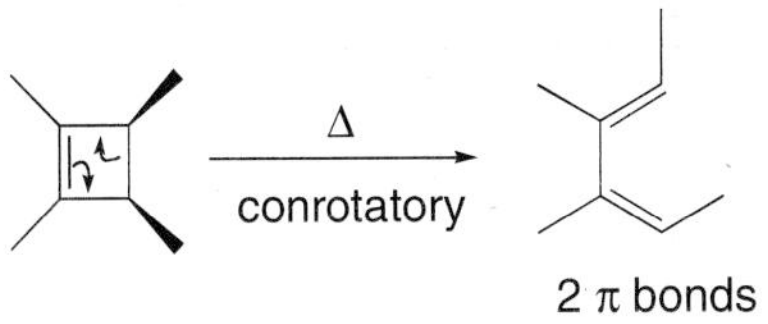

27.7 For an *even* number of π bonds, thermal electrocyclic reactions occur in a *conrotatory* fashion.

a.

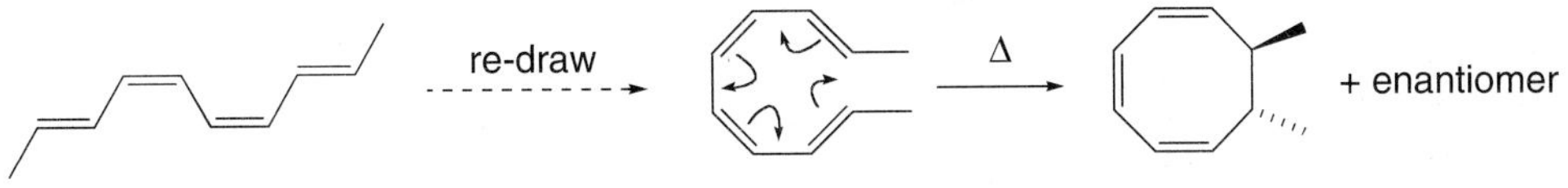

b.

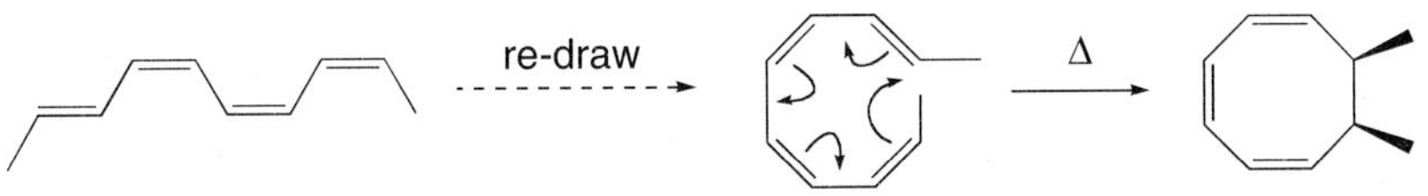

27.8 Photochemical electrocyclic reactions occur in a *conrotatory* fashion for a conjugated polyene with an *odd* number of π bonds, and in a *disrotatory* fashion for a conjugated polyene with an *even* number of π bonds.

a.

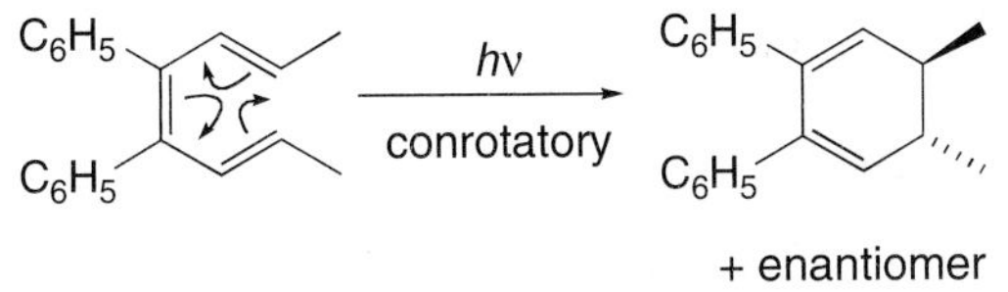

b.

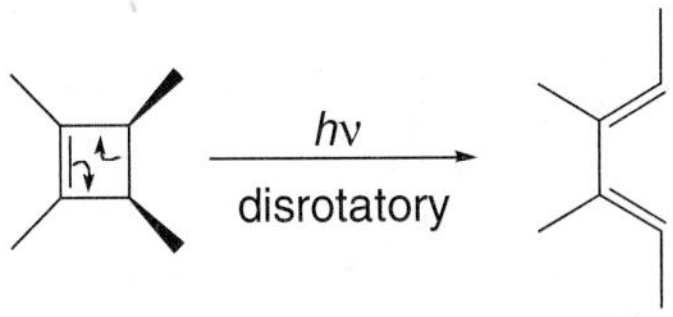

[The (*E*,*E*) diene is favored over the (*Z*,*Z*) diene.]

27.9 The photochemical electrocyclic reaction cleaves a six-membered ring to form a hexatriene.

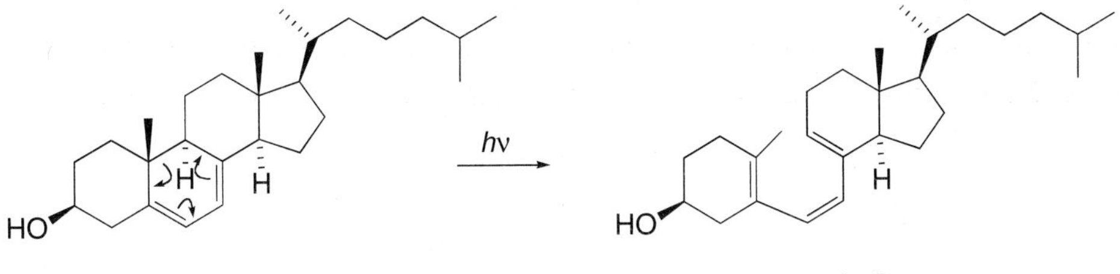

7-dehydrocholesterol provitamin D_3

27.10 Use the rules for electrocyclic reactions found in Answers 27.6 and 27.8.

a.

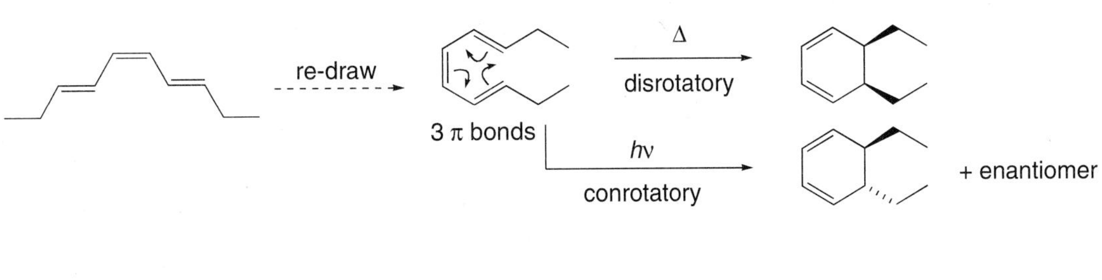

b.

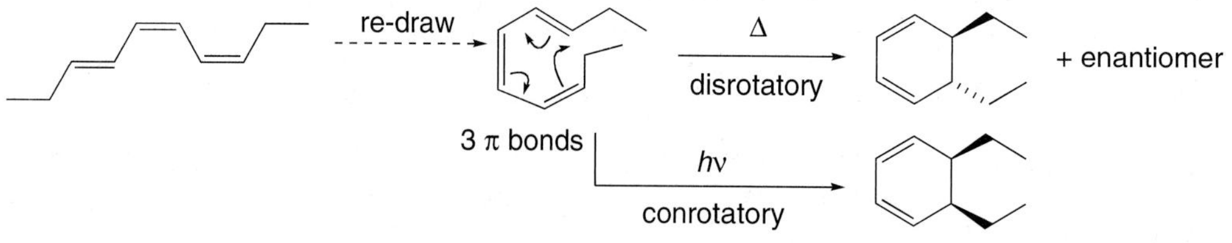

27.11 Use the rules for electrocyclic reactions found in Answer 27.6. A reaction with three π bonds and a disrotatory cyclization is thermal.

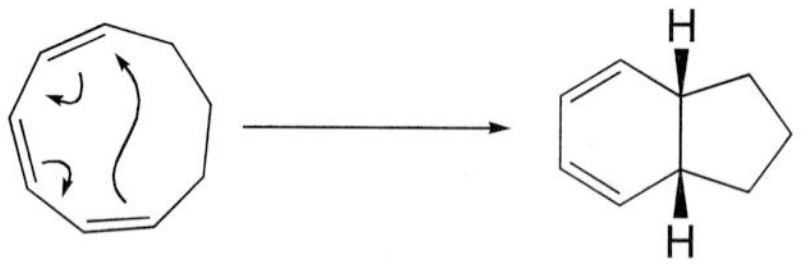

27.12 Count the number of π electrons in each reactant to classify the cycloaddition.

a.

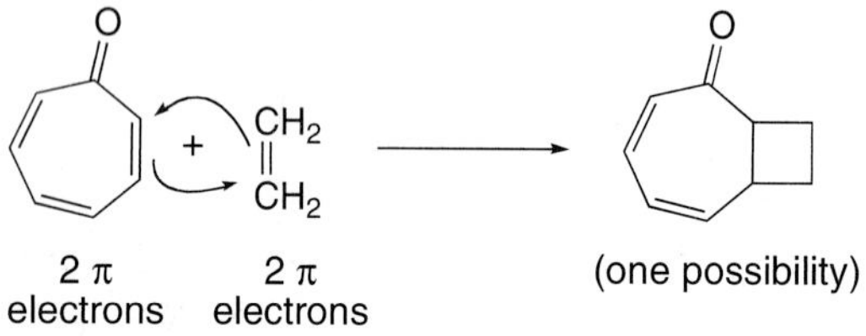

[2 + 2] cycloaddition

b.

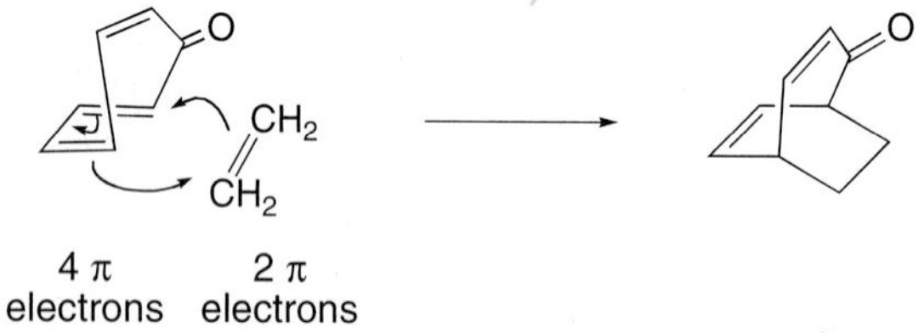

[4 + 2] cycloaddition

c.

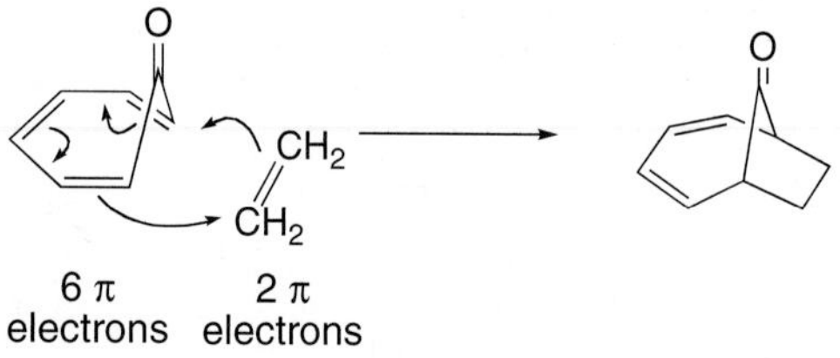

[6 + 2] cycloaddition

27.13 A thermal suprafacial addition is symmetry allowed in a [4 + 2] cycloaddition because like phases interact.

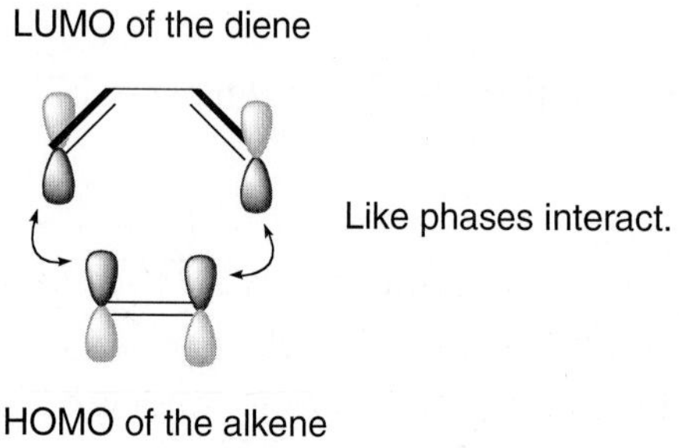

27.14 A thermal [4 + 2] cycloaddition is suprafacial.

a.
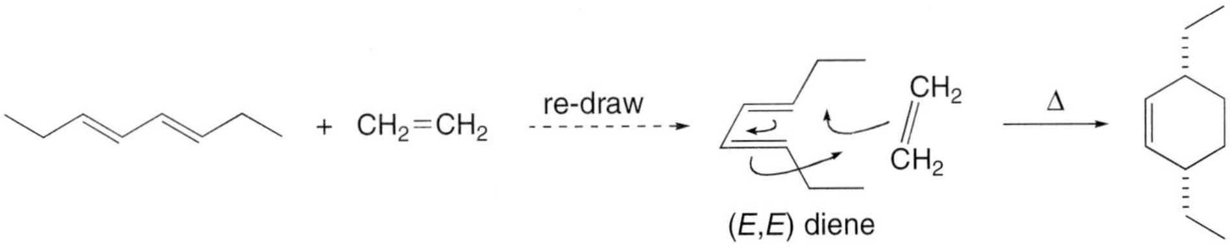

b.
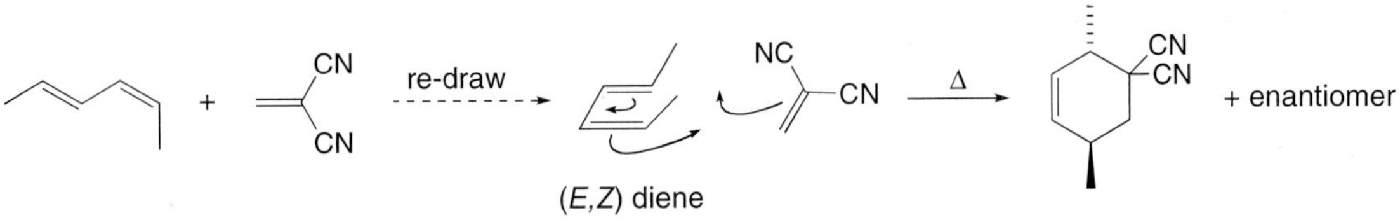

27.15

a.
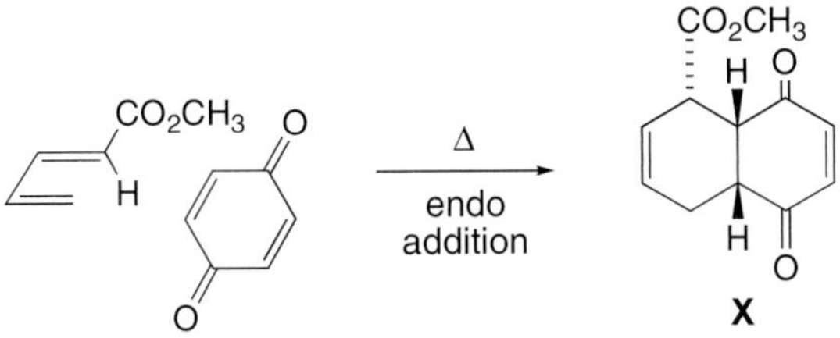

b.
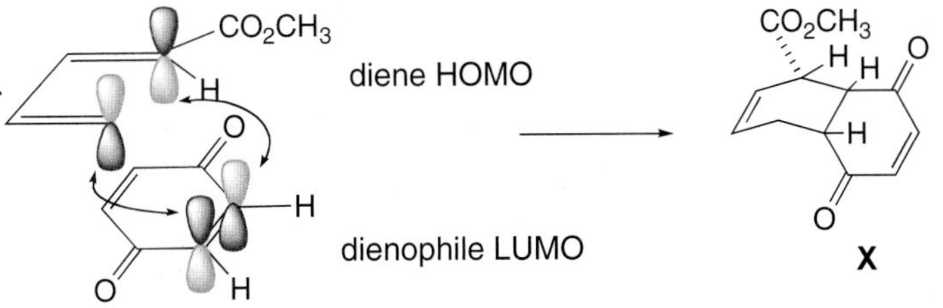

The dienophile is under the diene, by the rule of endo addition (Section 16.13).
The H's at the ring fusion are cis to each other, but trans to the CO_2CH_3 group.

27.16 A photochemical [2 + 2] cycloaddition is suprafacial.

a.
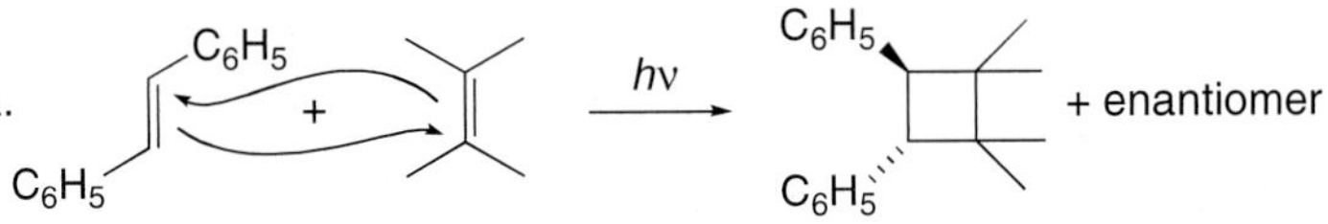

b.
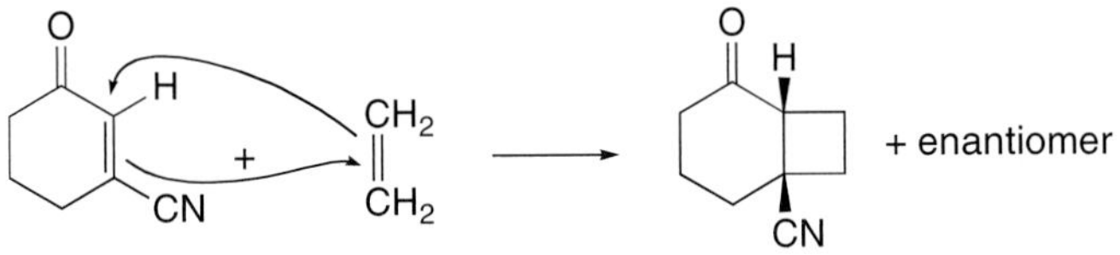

27.17 a. The photochemical [6 + 4] cycloaddition involves five π bonds (the total number of π electrons divided by two) and is antarafacial.

b. A thermal [8 + 2] cycloaddition involves five π bonds and is suprafacial.

27.18 A photochemical [4 + 2] cycloaddition like the Diels–Alder reaction must proceed by an antarafacial pathway. This would require either the 1,3-diene or the alkene component to twist 180° in order for the like phases of the *p* orbitals to overlap. Such a rotation is not possible in the formation of a six-membered ring.

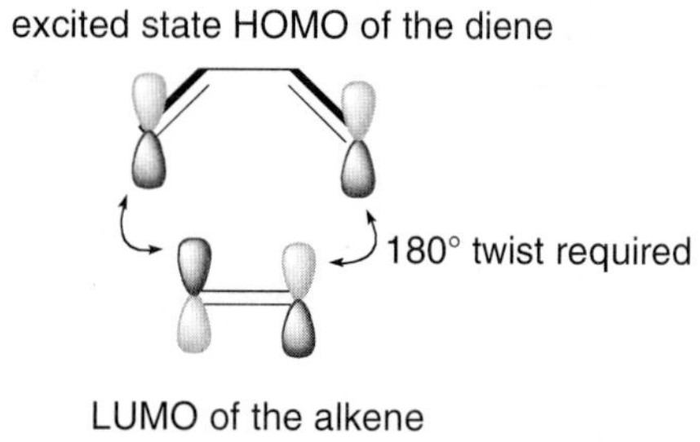
excited state HOMO of the diene
180° twist required
LUMO of the alkene

27.19 Locate the σ bonds broken and formed, and count the number of atoms that connects them.

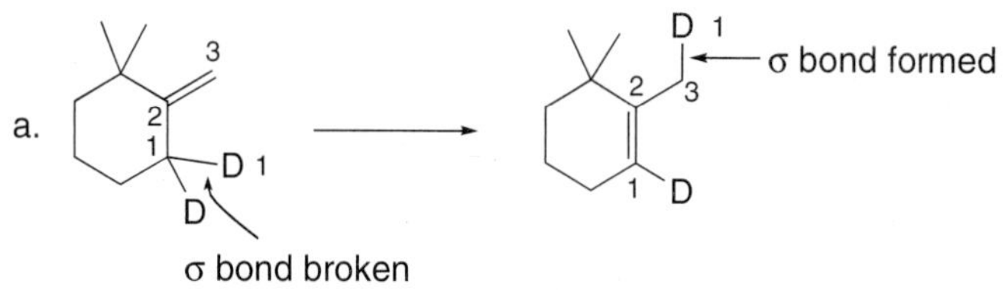
a.
σ bond broken
σ bond formed

[1,3] sigmatropic rearrangement

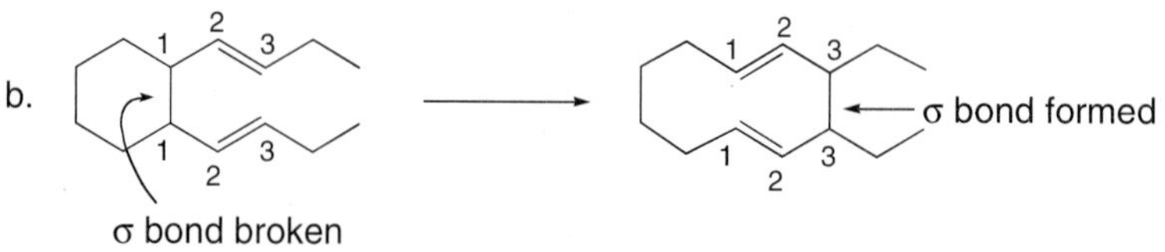
b.
σ bond broken
σ bond formed

[3,3] sigmatropic rearrangement

27.20

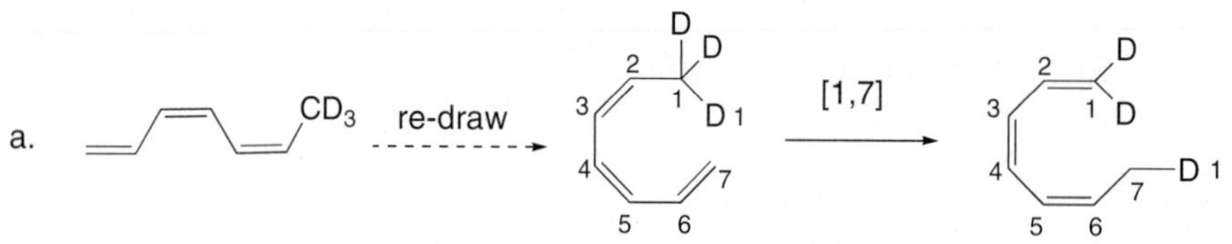
a.
CD_3
re-draw
[1,7]

b, c. The reaction involves four electron pairs (three π bonds and one σ bond), so it proceeds by an antarafacial pathway under thermal conditions, and by a suprafacial pathway under photochemical conditions.

27.21 Draw the products of each reaction.

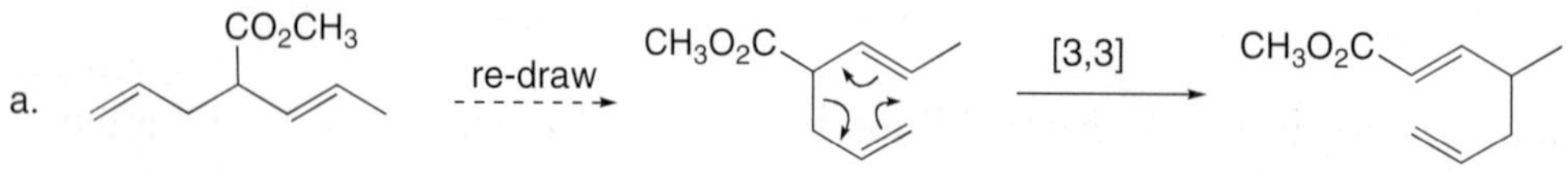
a.
CO_2CH_3
re-draw
CH_3O_2C
[3,3]
CH_3O_2C

b.
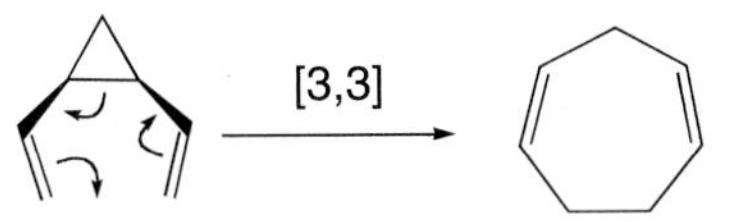

c.
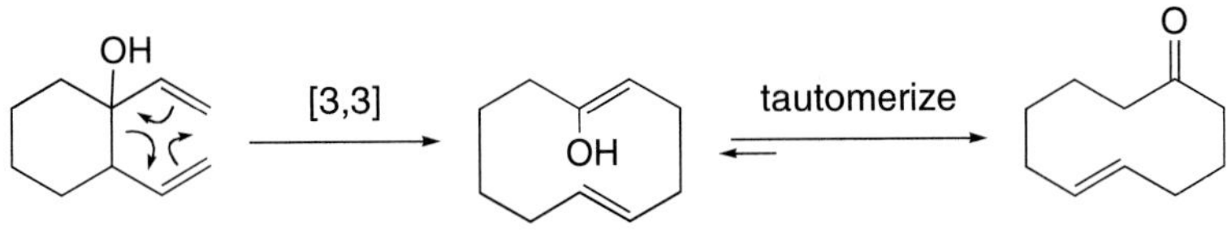

27.22 Draw the product after protonation.

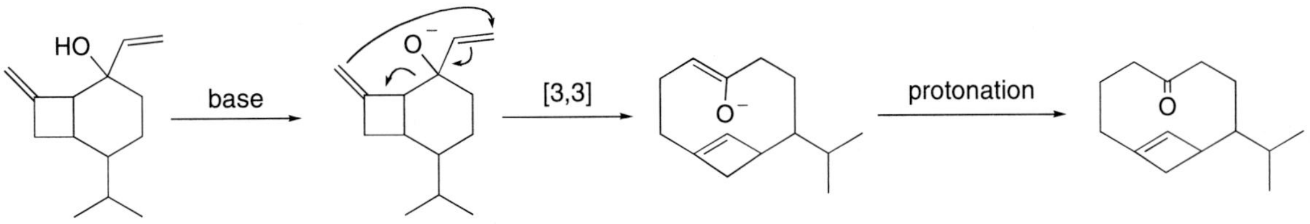

27.23 Draw the product of Claisen rearrangement.

a.
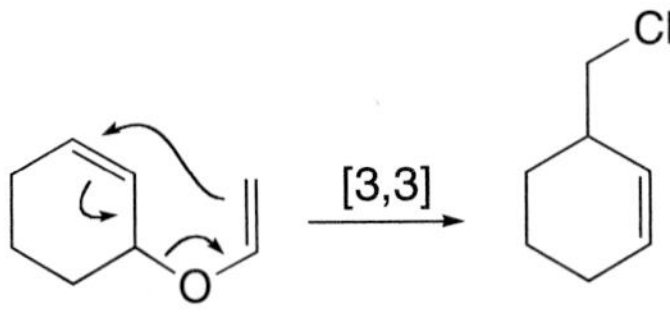

c.
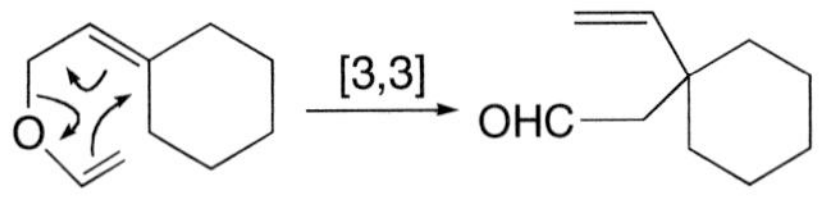

b.
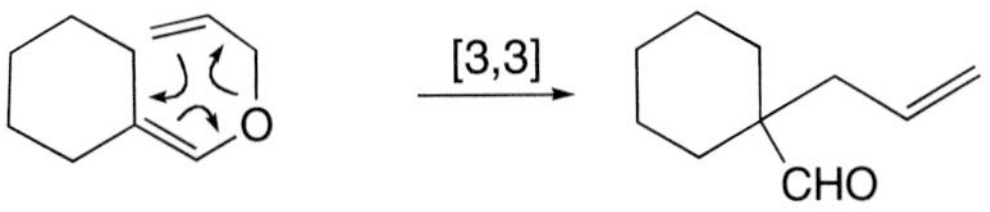

27.24

a.
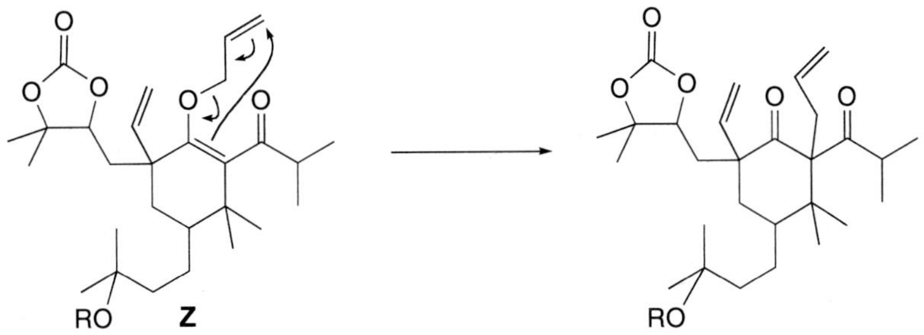

b.
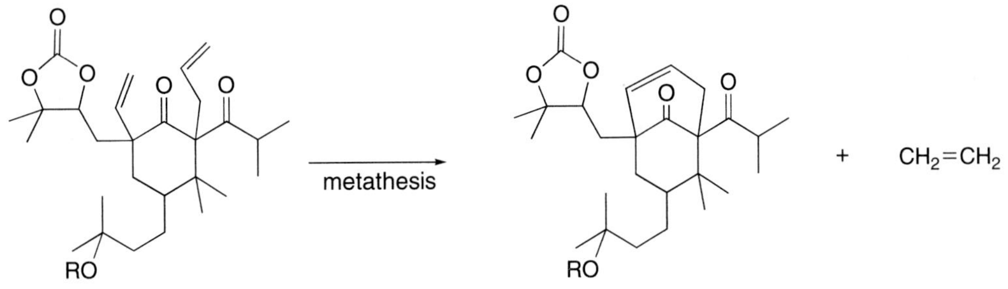

27.25 Predict the stereochemistry of each reaction using Table 27.4.

a. A [6 + 4] thermal cycloaddition involves five electron pairs, making the reaction suprafacial.

b. A photochemical electrocyclic ring closure of 1,3,5,7,9-decapentaene involves five electron pairs, making the reaction conrotatory.

c. A [4 + 4] photochemical cycloaddition involves four electron pairs, making the reaction suprafacial.

d. A thermal [5,5] sigmatropic rearrangement involves five electron pairs, making the reaction suprafacial.

27.26 Use the rules found in Answers 27.6 and 27.8.

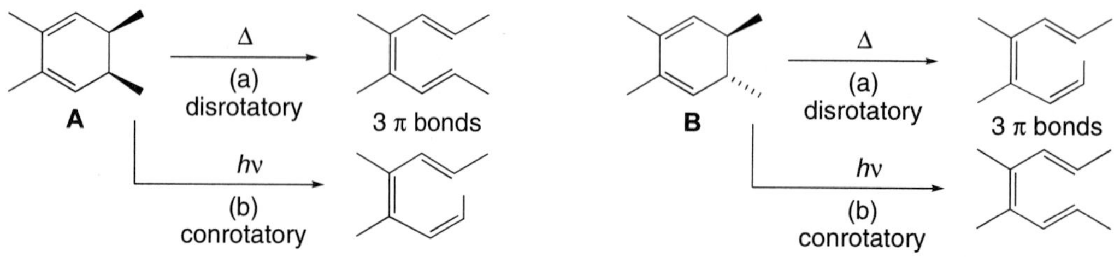

27.27 Draw the product of [3,3] sigmatropic rearrangement of each compound.

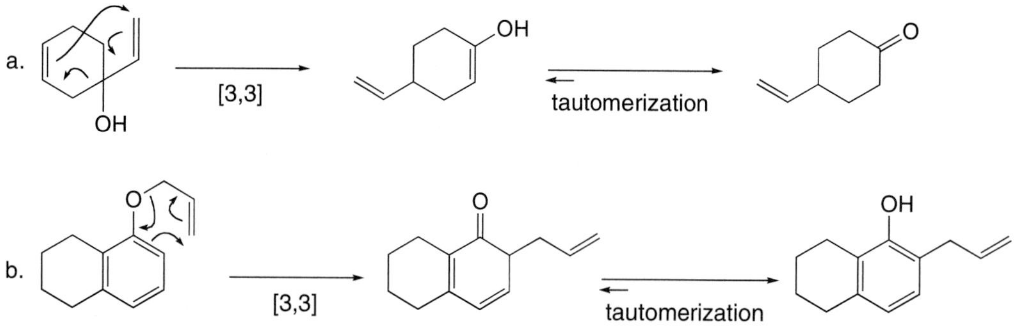

27.28 An electrocyclic reaction forms a product with one more or one fewer π bond than the starting material. A cycloaddition forms a ring with two new σ bonds. A sigmatropic rearrangement forms a product with the same number of π bonds, but the π bonds are rearranged. Use Table 27.4 to determine the stereochemistry.

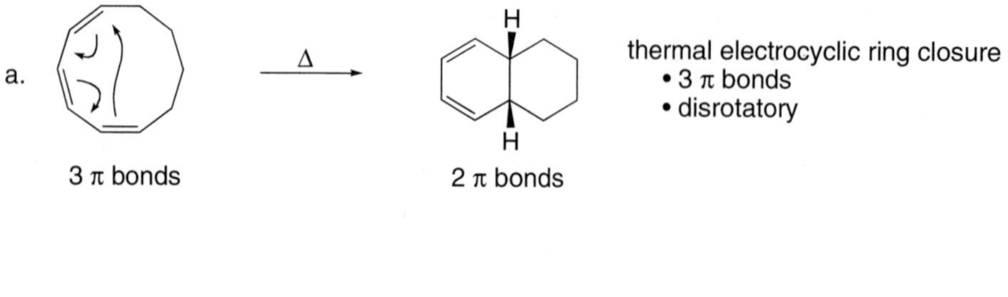

b.

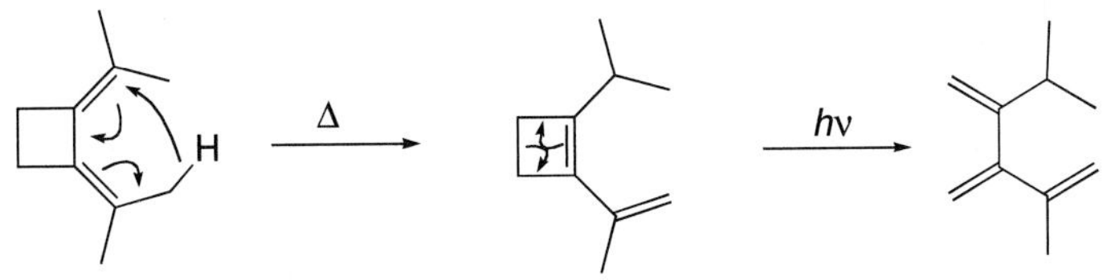
H
Δ
hν

2 π bonds — 2 π bonds — 3 π bonds

thermal [1,5] sigmatropic rearrangement
- 3 electron pairs (2 π + 1 σ)
- suprafacial

photochemical electrocyclic ring opening
- 2 π bonds in diene formed
- disrotatory

c.

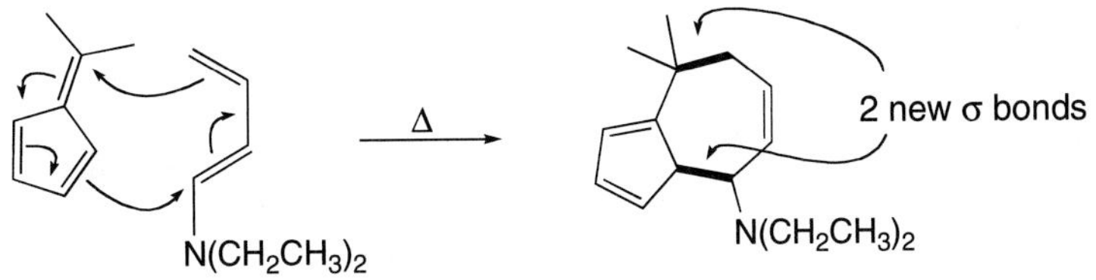
Δ
2 new σ bonds
N(CH2CH3)2
N(CH2CH3)2

thermal [6 + 4] cycloaddition
- 5 π bonds
- suprafacial

27.29 Use the rules for thermal electrocyclic reactions found in Answer 27.6.

a.

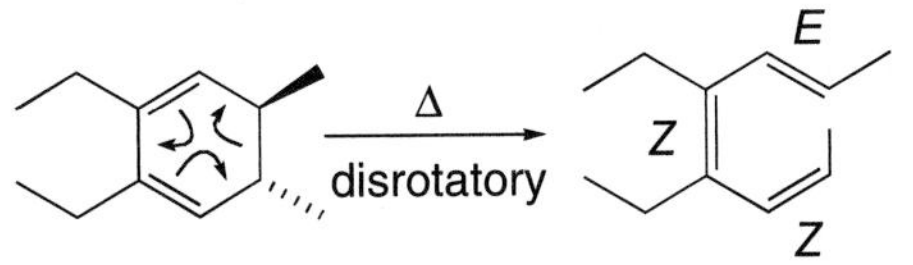
Δ
disrotatory
E
Z
Z

3 π bonds

b.

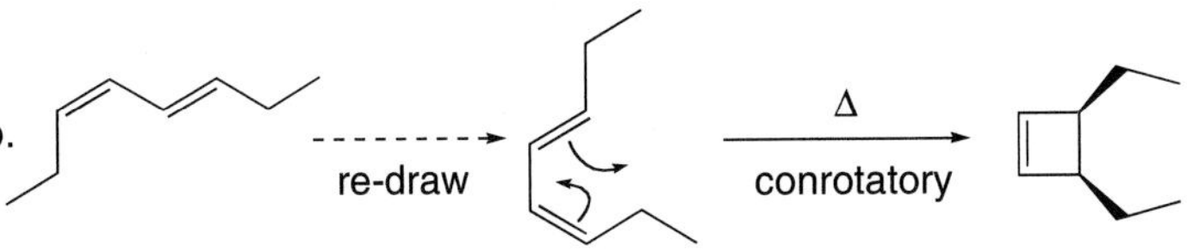
re-draw
Δ
conrotatory

2 π bonds

27.30 Use the rules for photochemical electrocyclic reactions found in Answer 27.8.

a.

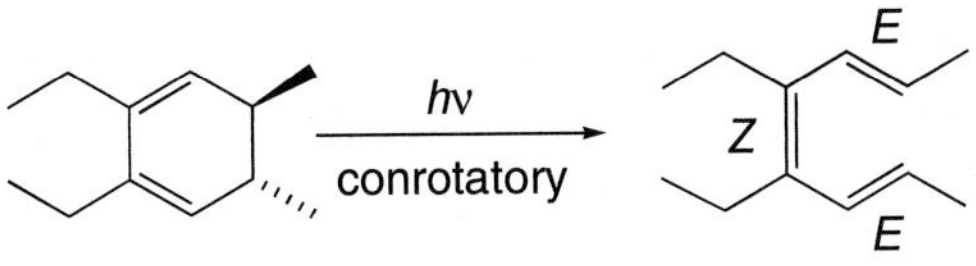
hν
conrotatory
E
Z
E

3 π bonds

Although conrotatory ring opening could also form, at least in theory, an all-(*Z*) triene, steric hindrance during ring opening would cause the terminal CH_3's to crash into one another, making this process unlikely.

b.

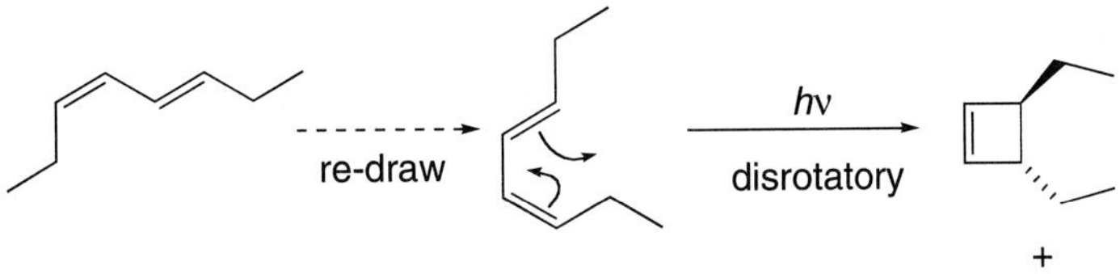
re-draw
hν
disrotatory

+
enantiomer

27.31 Use the rules found in Answer 27.8.

a.

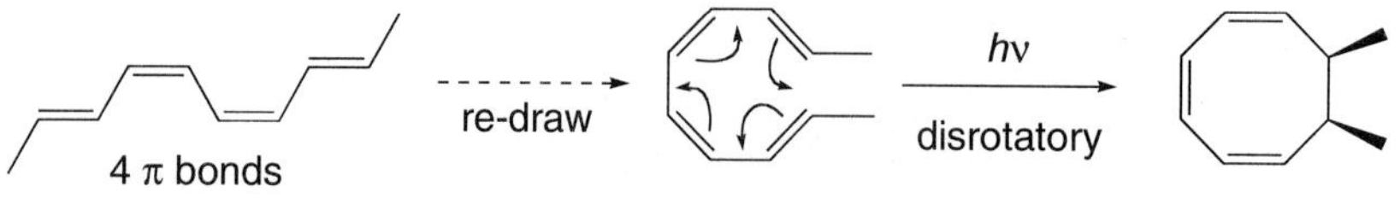
4 π bonds
re-draw
hν
disrotatory

b.

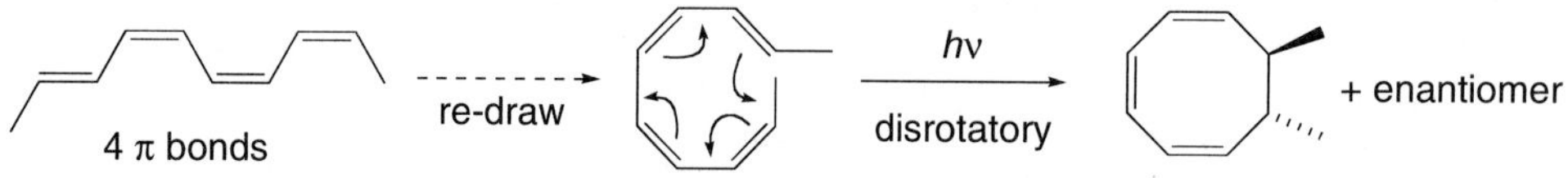
4 π bonds
re-draw
hν
disrotatory
+ enantiomer

27.32 Use the rules found in Answers 27.6 and 27.8.

a, b.

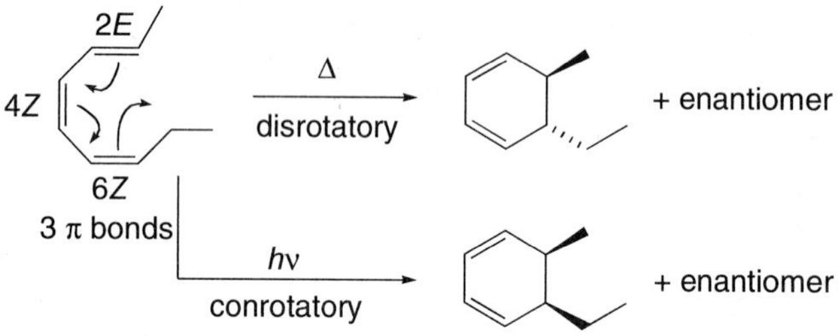
2E
4Z
6Z
3 π bonds
Δ
disrotatory
+ enantiomer
hν
conrotatory
+ enantiomer

c.

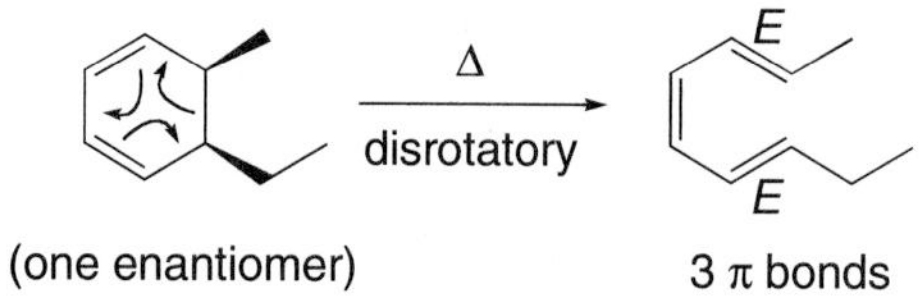
Δ
disrotatory
E
E
(one enantiomer)
3 π bonds

d.

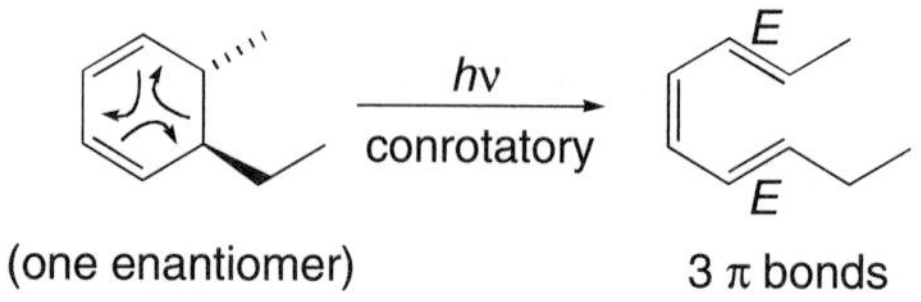
hν
conrotatory
E
E
(one enantiomer)
3 π bonds

27.33 The trans product is indicative of a disrotatory ring closure from the cyclic triene with the given stereochemistry at the double bonds. A disrotatory ring closure with a polyene having three π bonds must occur under thermal conditions.

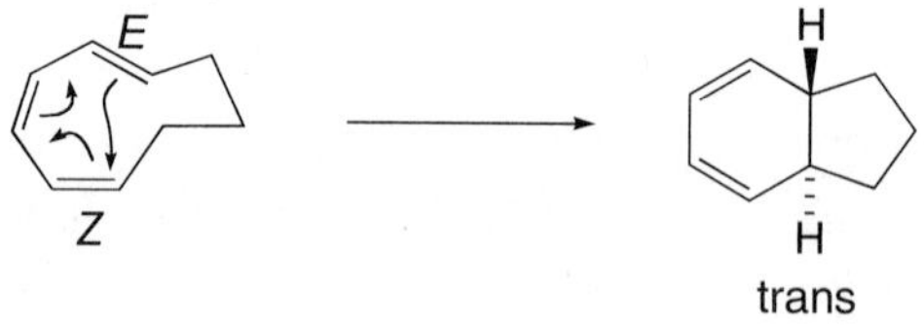
E
Z
H
H
trans

27.34 A disrotatory cyclization of a reactant with an even number of π bonds must occur under photochemical conditions.

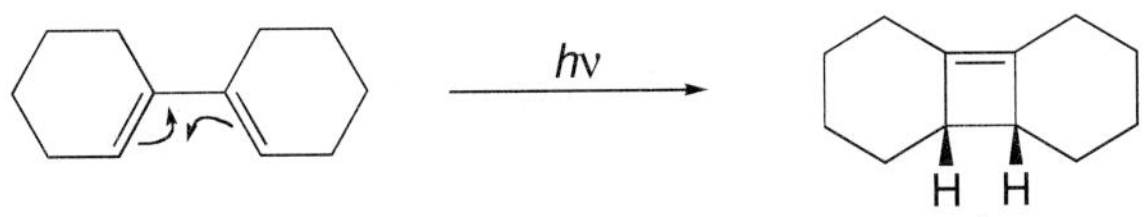
hν
H H
cis

M
2 π bonds

27.35 Use the rules found in Answers 27.6 and 27.8.

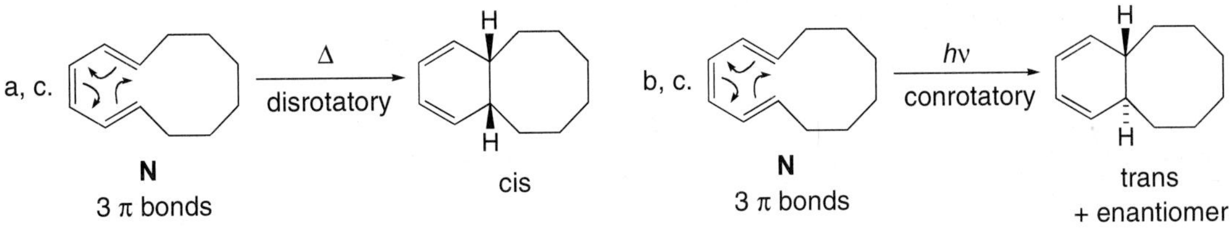
a, c.
Δ
disrotatory
H
H
N
3 π bonds
cis
b, c.
hν
conrotatory
H
H
N
3 π bonds
trans
+ enantiomer

27.36 Use the rules found in Answers 27.6 and 27.8.

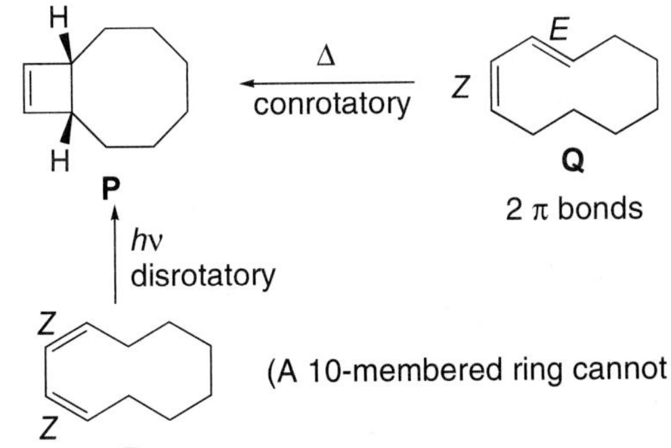
H
H
P
Δ
conrotatory
E
Z
Q
2 π bonds
hν
disrotatory
Z
Z
R

(A 10-membered ring cannot contain two *E* double bonds.)

27.37 Since the reaction involves three π bonds in one reactant and two π bonds in the second reactant, the reaction is a [6 + 4] cycloaddition. A suprafacial cycloaddition with five π bonds must proceed under thermal conditions.

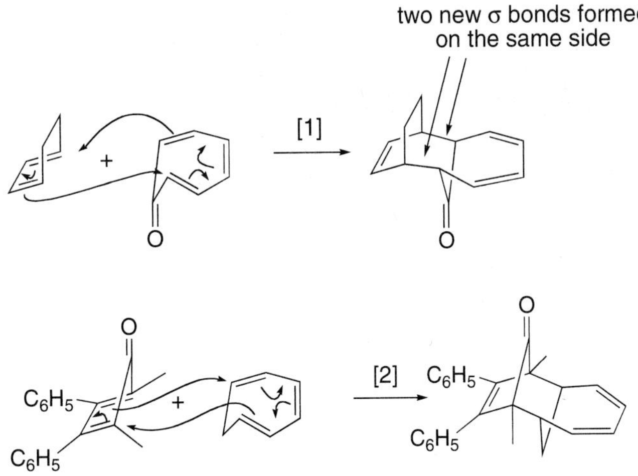
two new σ bonds formed
on the same side
+
[1]
O
O
+
[2]
C_6H_5
C_6H_5
C_6H_5
C_6H_5
O
O

27.38 The Diels–Alder reaction is a thermal, suprafacial [4 + 2] cycloaddition.

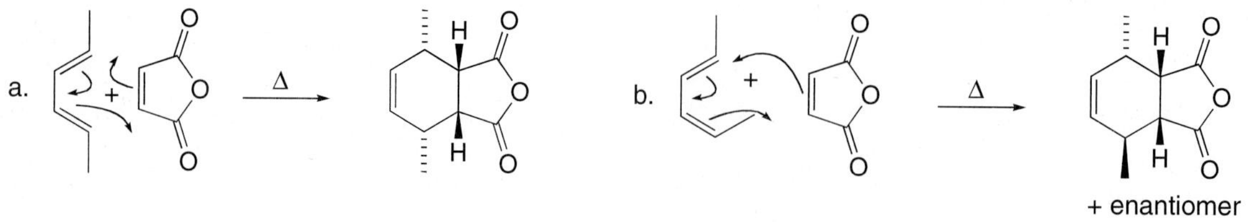

27.39 A photochemical [2 + 2] cycloaddition is suprafacial.

27.40 A thermal [4 + 2] cycloaddition is suprafacial.

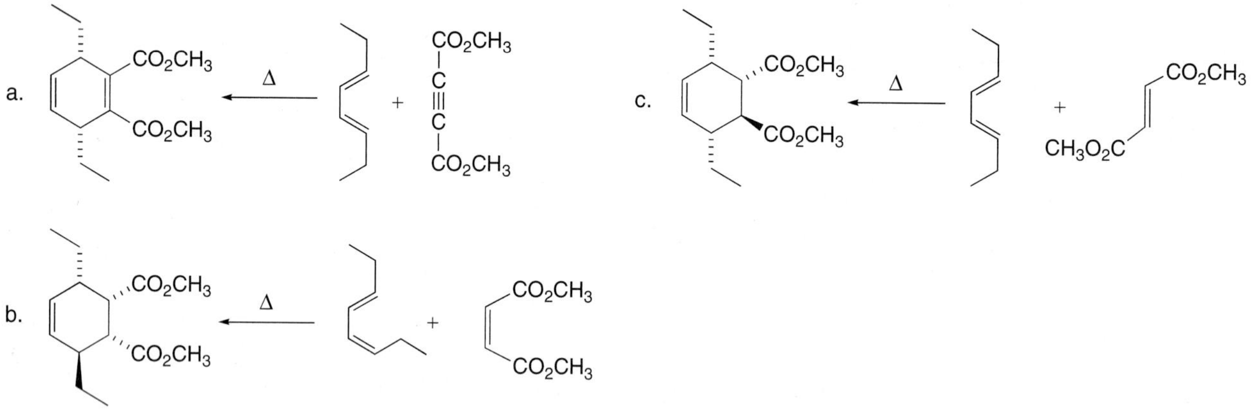

27.41 1,3-Butadiene can react with itself in a symmetry-allowed thermal [4 + 2] cycloaddition to form 4-vinylcyclohexene.

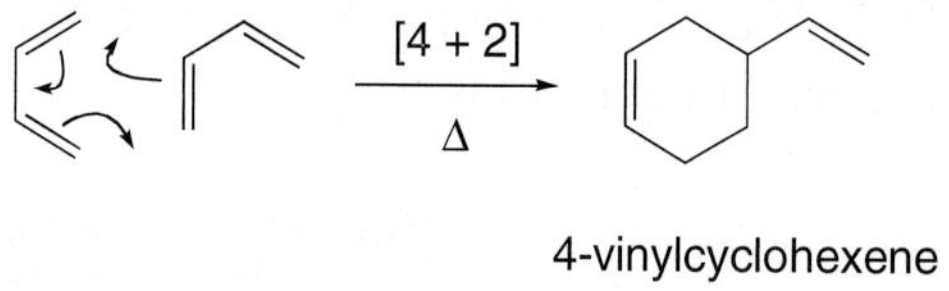

1,5-Cyclooctadiene would have to be formed from 1,3-butadiene by a [4 + 4] cycloaddition, which is not allowed under thermal conditions.

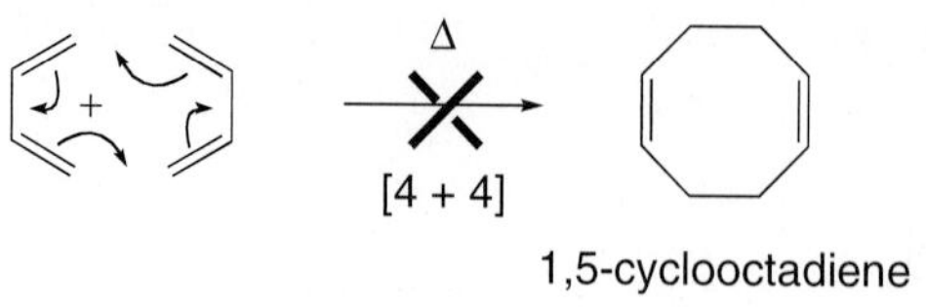

27.42 A series of three [2 + 2] cycloadditions with *E* alkenes forms **X.**

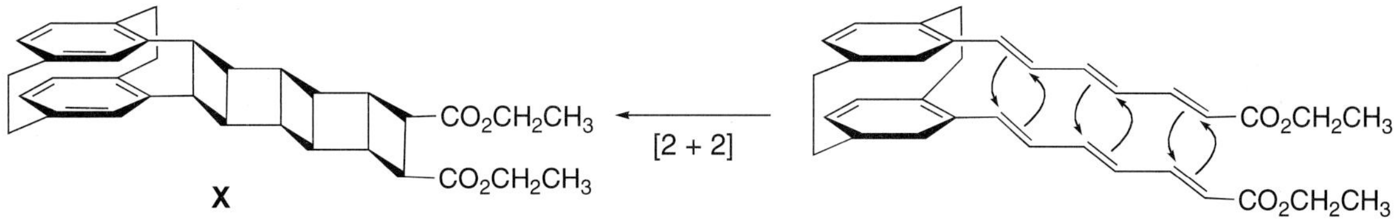

27.43 Re-draw the reactant and product to more clearly show the relative location of the bonds broken and formed.

a.

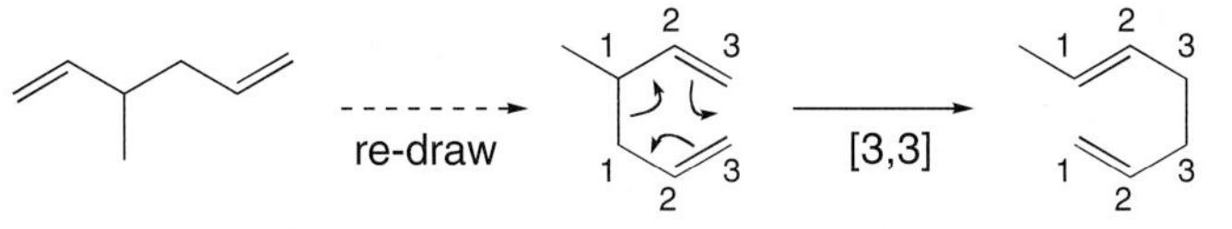

b.

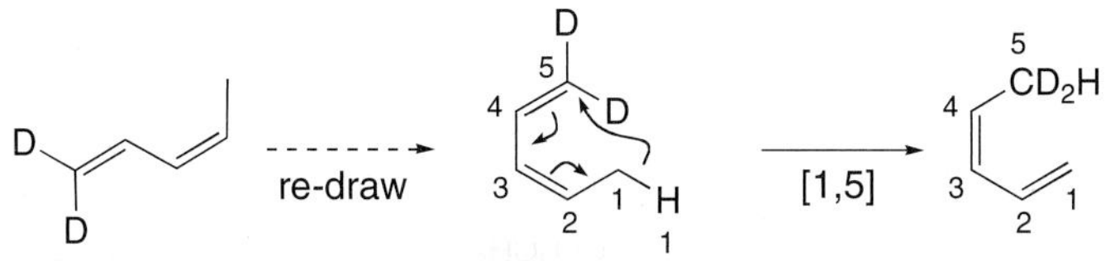

c.

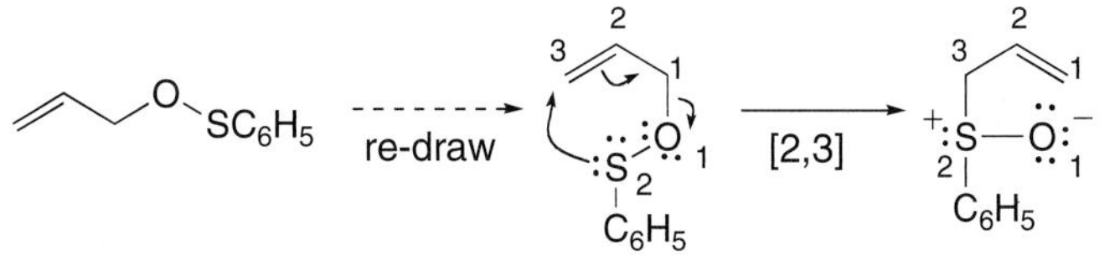

27.44 Draw the products of each reaction.

a.

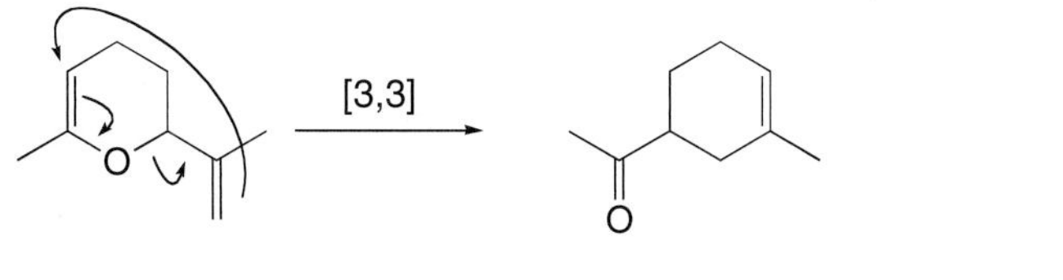

c.

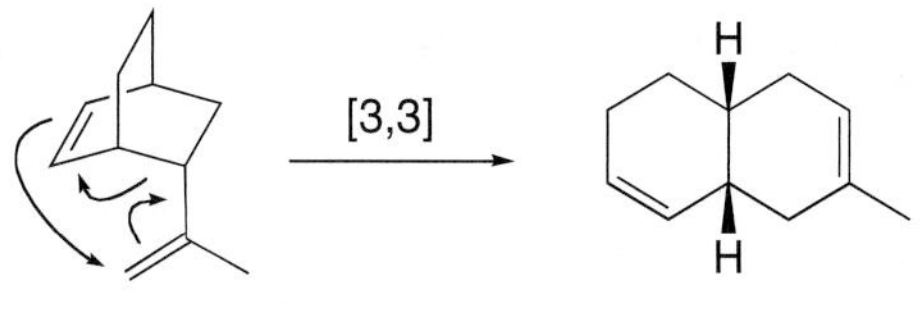

b.

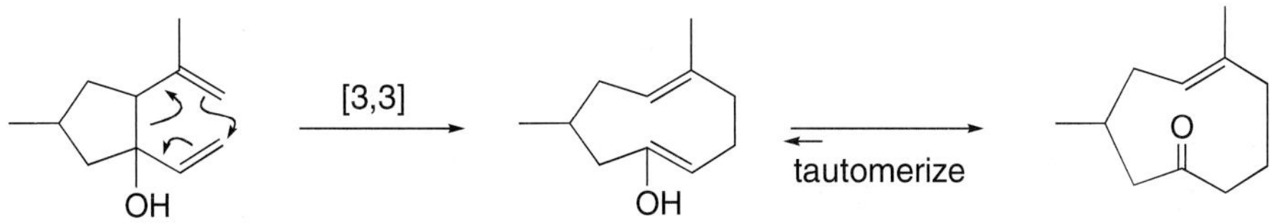

27.45 a. Two [1,5] sigmatropic rearrangements occur.

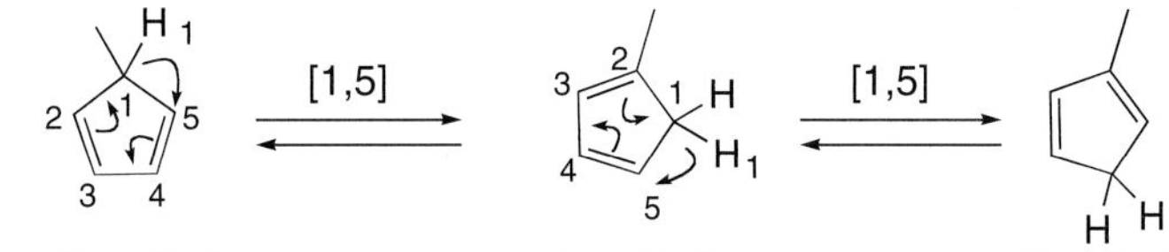

5-methyl-1,3-cyclopentadiene   1-methyl-1,3-cyclopentadiene   2-methyl-1,3-cyclopentadiene

b.

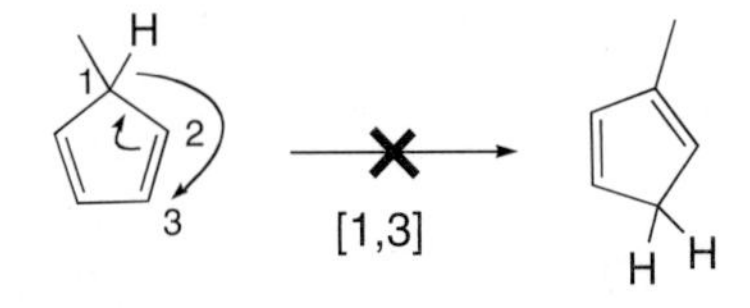

5-methyl isomer

2-methyl isomer

A [1,3] sigmatropic rearrangement requires photochemical conditions not thermal conditions, so 5-methyl-1,3-cyclopentadiene cannot rearrange directly to its 2-methyl isomer by a [1,3] shift.

27.46

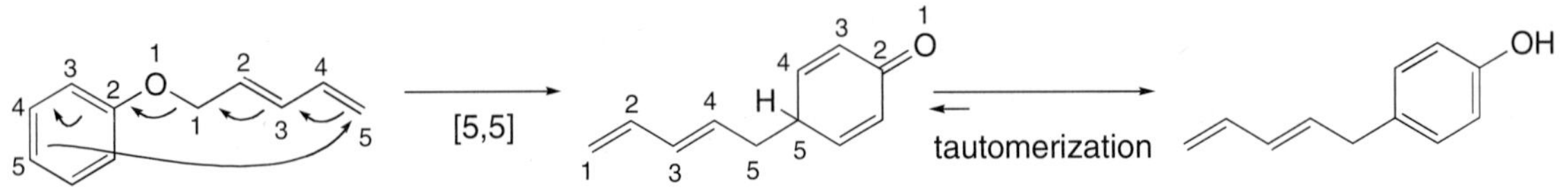

27.47

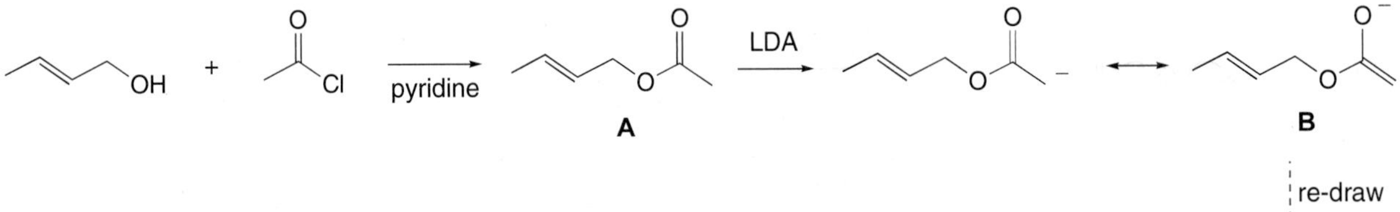

The conversion of **B** to **C** is a [3,3] sigmatropic rearrangement of an intermediate enolate.

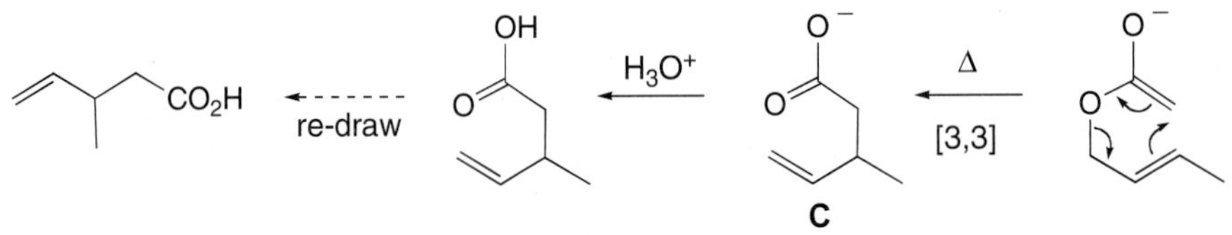

27.48 Use the definitions found in Answer 27.1.

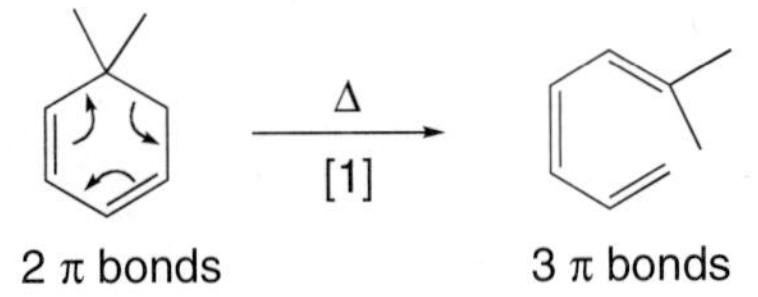

an electrocyclic ring opening

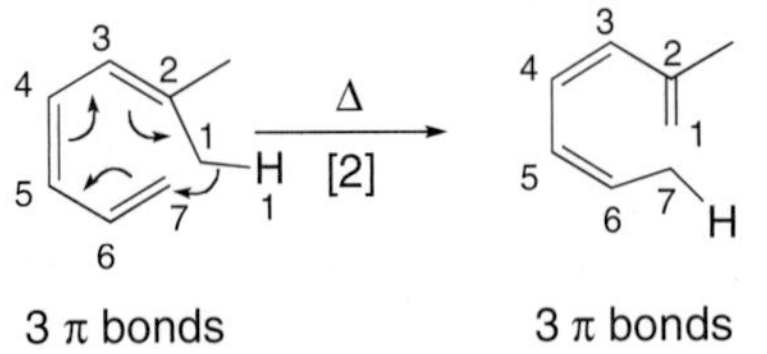

a [1,7] sigmatropic rearrangement

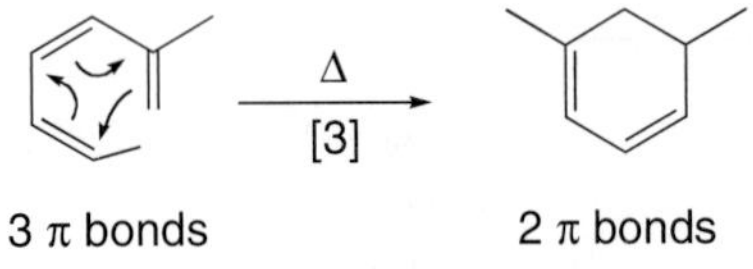

an electrocyclic ring closure

27.49

a. 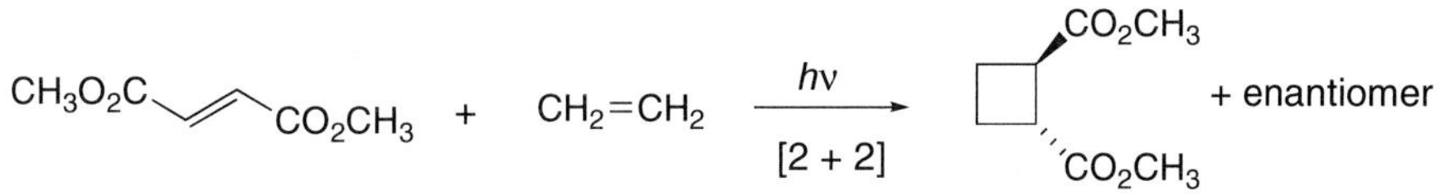

b. 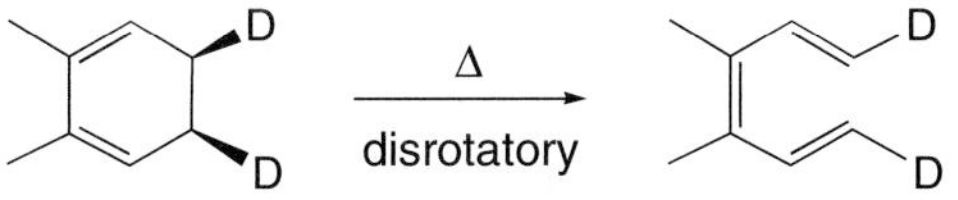

c. 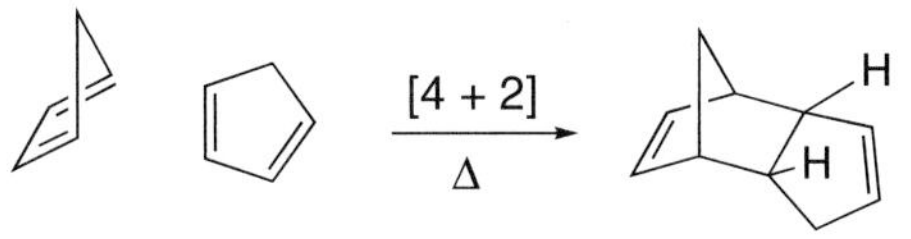

d. 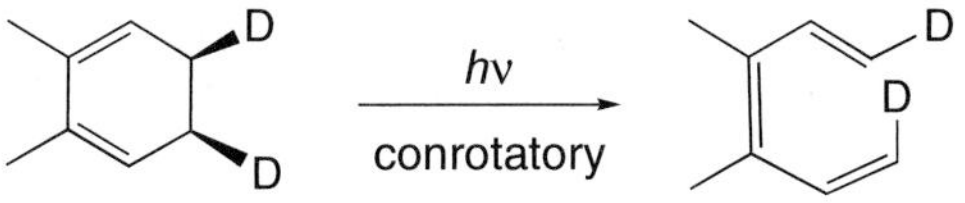

27.50

a. 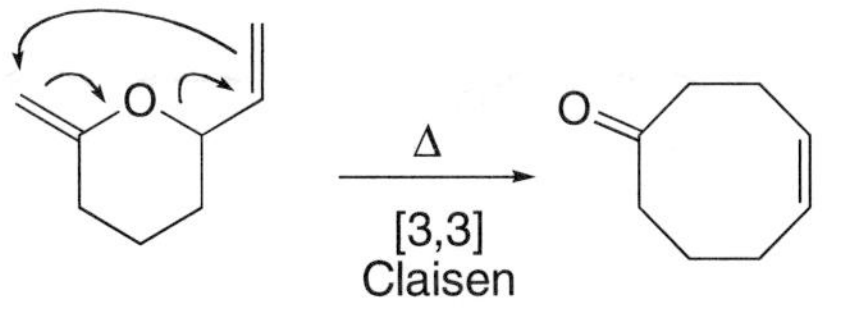

b. 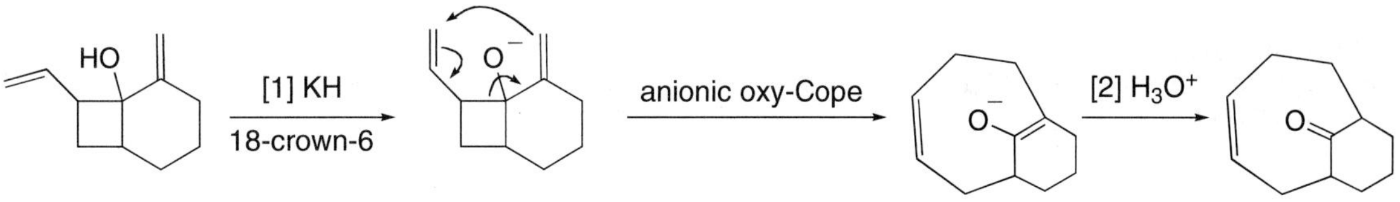

c. 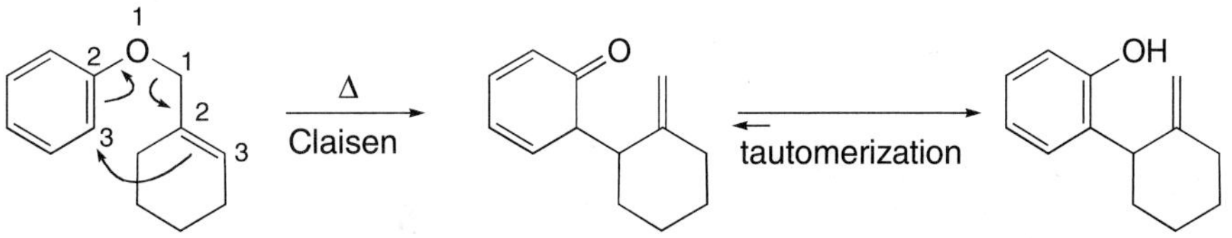

d. 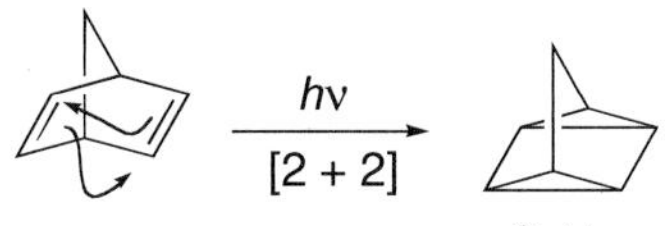

C_7H_8

27.51 The mechanism consists of sequential [3,3] sigmatropic rearrangements, followed by tautomerization.

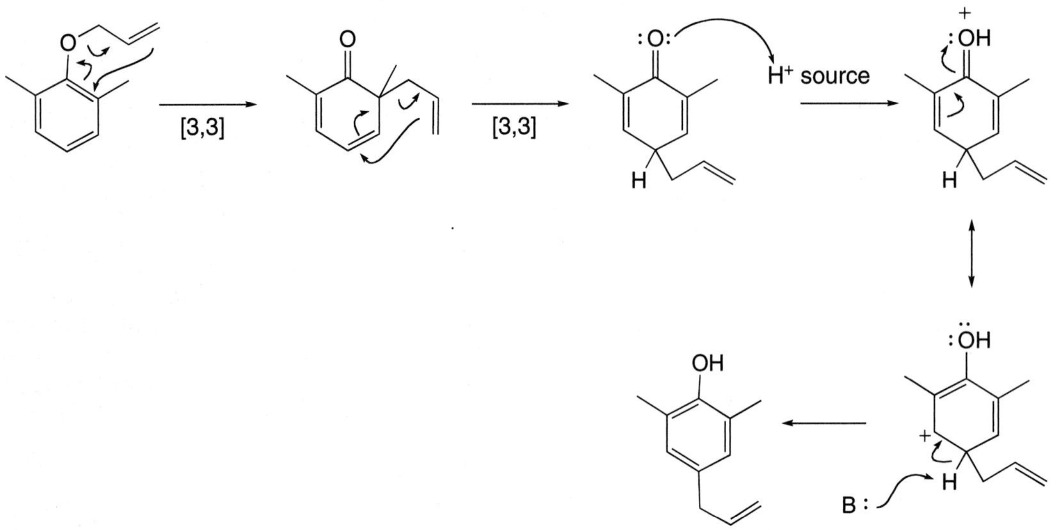

27.52

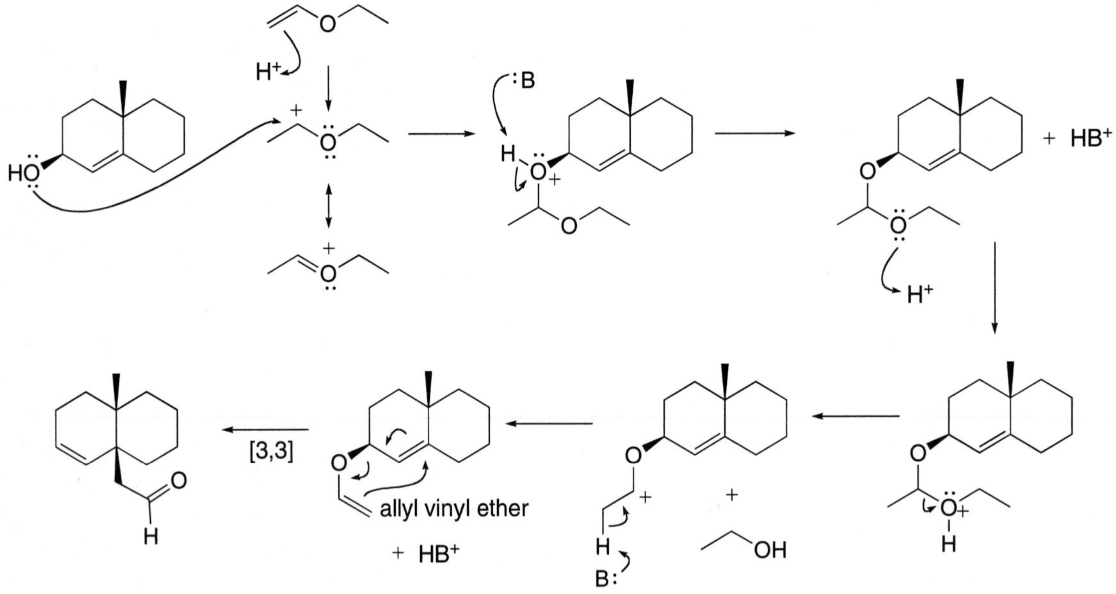

27.53

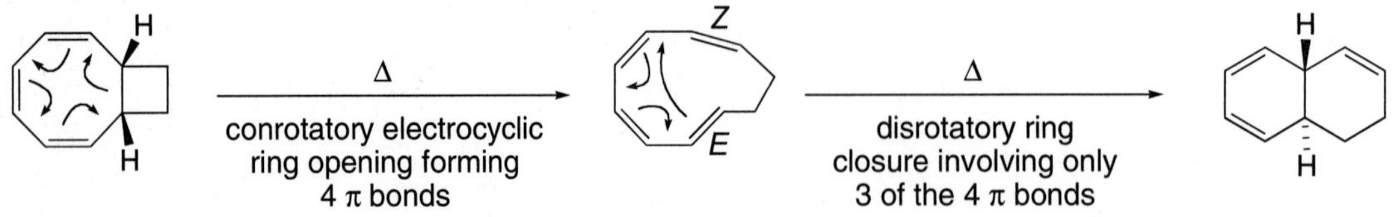

27.54

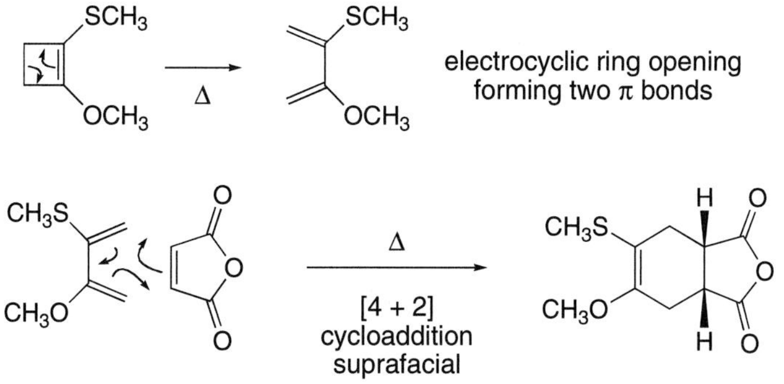
SCH3
OCH3
Δ
SCH3
OCH3
electrocyclic ring opening
forming two π bonds
CH3S
CH3O
O
O
O
Δ
[4 + 2]
cycloaddition
suprafacial
CH3S
CH3O
H
H
O
O
O

27.55 The mechanism consists of a [4 + 2] cycloaddition, followed by intramolecular imine formation.

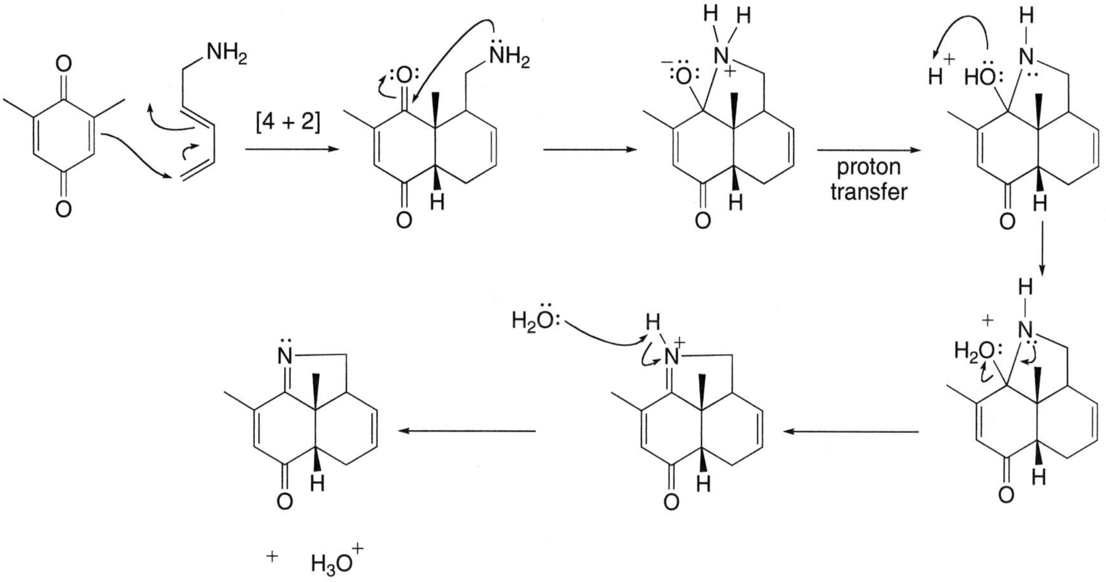
NH2
[4 + 2]
proton
transfer
H2O:
+ H3O+

27.56

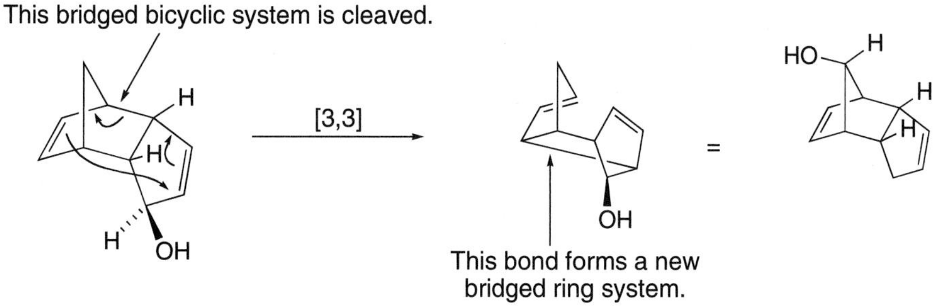
This bridged bicyclic system is cleaved.
[3,3]
OH
This bond forms a new
bridged ring system.
HO
H

27.57

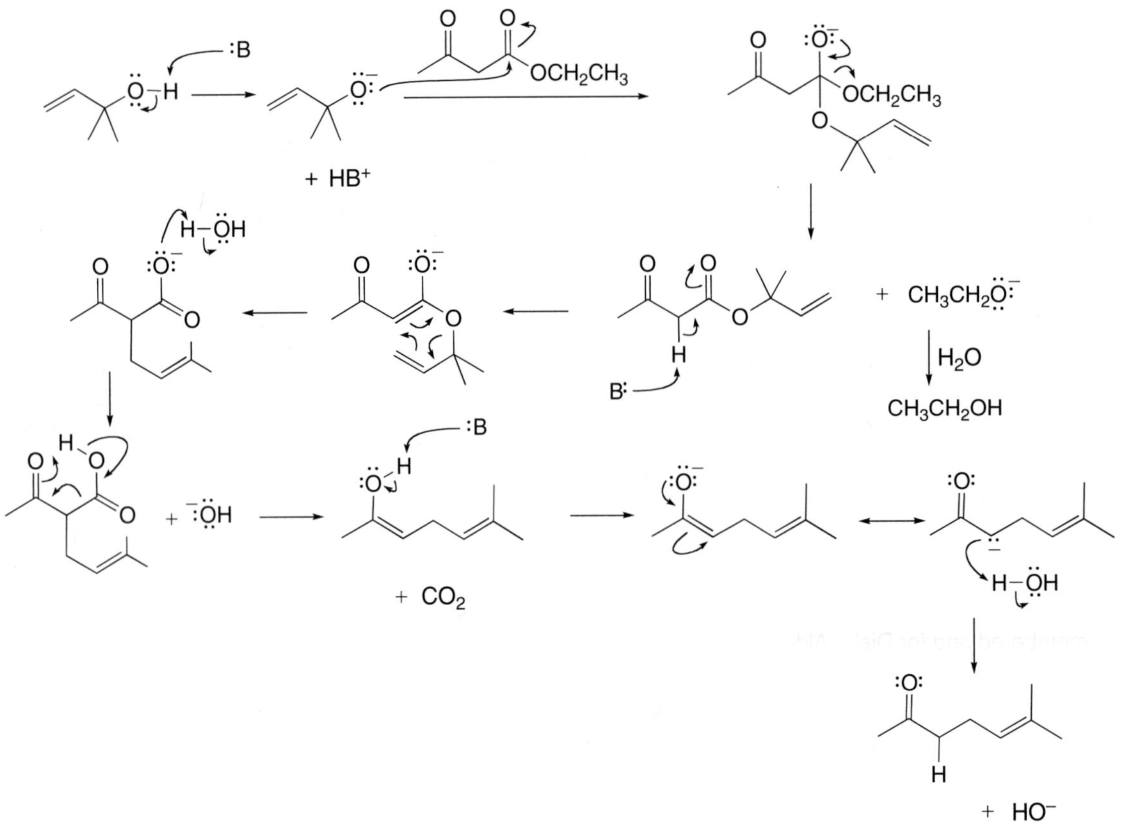

27.58 Conrotatory cyclization of **Y** using four π bonds forms **X.** Disrotatory ring closure of **X** can occur in two ways—on the top face or bottom face of the eight-membered ring to form diastereomers.

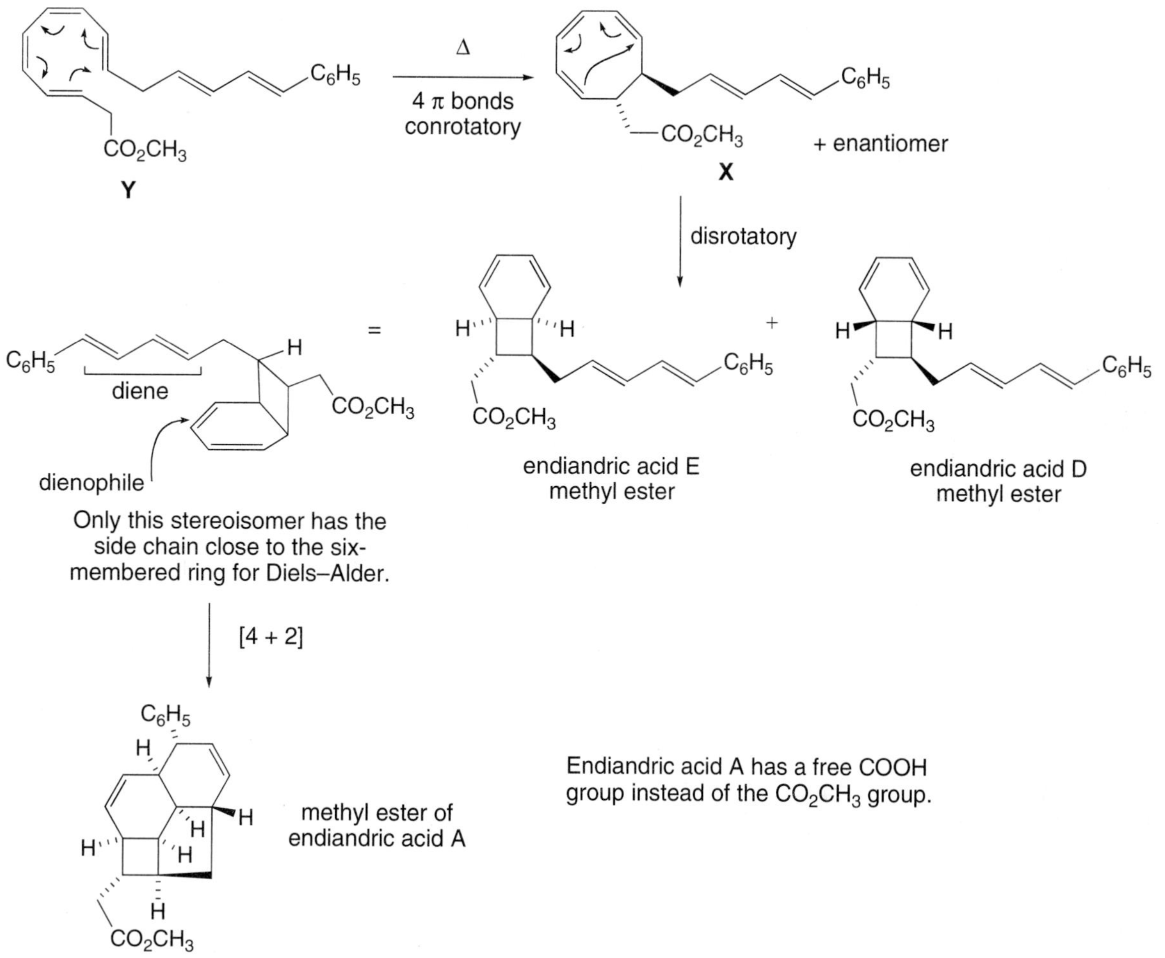
C_6H_5
Δ
4 π bonds
conrotatory
CO_2CH_3
Y
C_6H_5
CO_2CH_3
X
+ enantiomer
disrotatory
C_6H_5
H
diene
CO_2CH_3
dienophile
Only this stereoisomer has the side chain close to the six-membered ring for Diels–Alder.
=
H
H
C_6H_5
CO_2CH_3
endiandric acid E methyl ester
+
H
H
C_6H_5
CO_2CH_3
endiandric acid D methyl ester
[4 + 2]
C_6H_5
H
H
H
H
H
H
CO_2CH_3
methyl ester of endiandric acid A
Endiandric acid A has a free COOH group instead of the CO_2CH_3 group.

27.59

a.

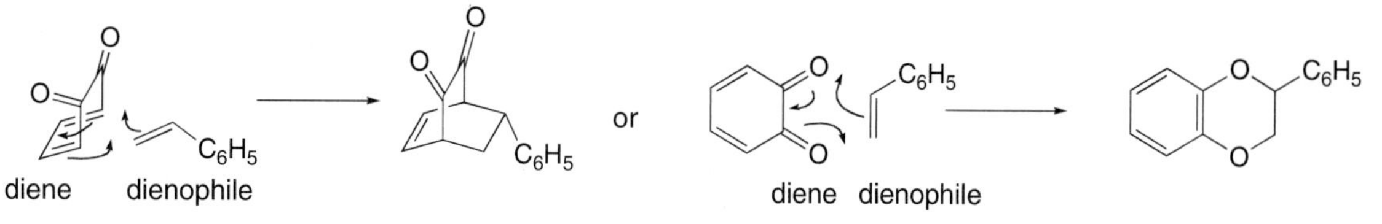
O
O
C_6H_5
diene
dienophile
O
O
C_6H_5
or
O
C_6H_5
O
diene
dienophile
O
C_6H_5
O

b.

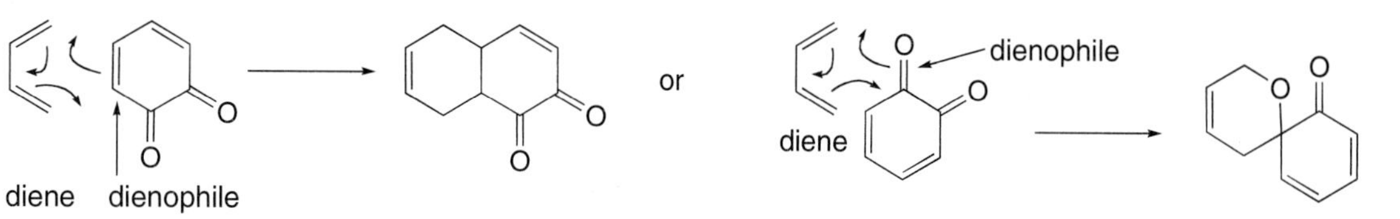
O
O
diene
dienophile
O
O
or
O
dienophile
O
diene
O
O

c. 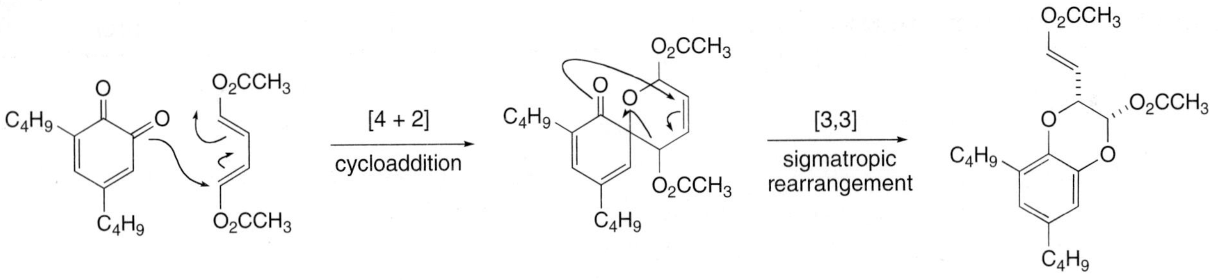
C_4H_9
O
O
O_2CCH_3
C_4H_9
O_2CCH_3
[4 + 2]
cycloaddition
C_4H_9
O
O
O_2CCH_3
O_2CCH_3
C_4H_9
[3,3]
sigmatropic
rearrangement
O_2CCH_3
O_2CCH_3
O
O
C_4H_9
C_4H_9

Chapter 28 Carbohydrates

Chapter Review

Important terms

- **Aldose** A monosaccharide containing an aldehyde (28.2)
- **Ketose** A monosaccharide containing a ketone (28.2)
- **D-Sugar** A monosaccharide with the O bonded to the stereogenic center farthest from the carbonyl group drawn on the right in the Fischer projection (28.2C)
- **Epimers** Two diastereomers that differ in configuration around one stereogenic center only (28.3)
- **Anomers** Monosaccharides that differ in configuration at only the hemiacetal OH group (28.6)
- **Glycoside** An acetal derived from a monosaccharide hemiacetal (28.7)

Acyclic, Haworth, and 3-D representations for D-glucose (28.6)

Haworth projection

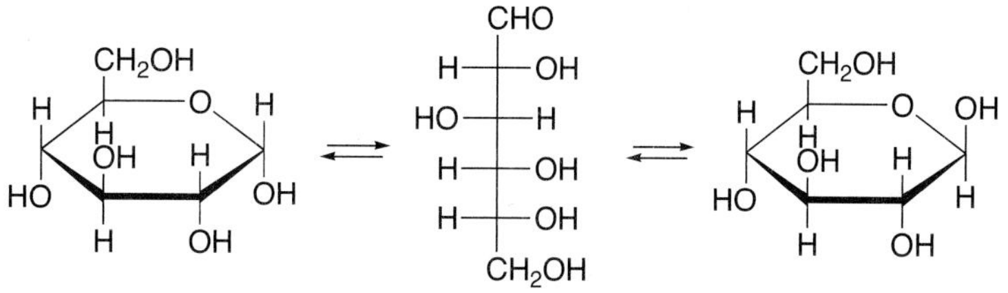

α anomer acyclic form β anomer

3-D representation

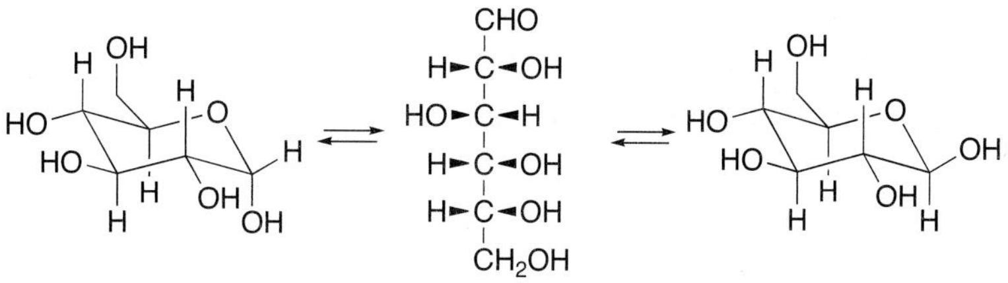

Reactions of monosaccharides involving the hemiacetal

[1] Glycoside formation (28.7A)

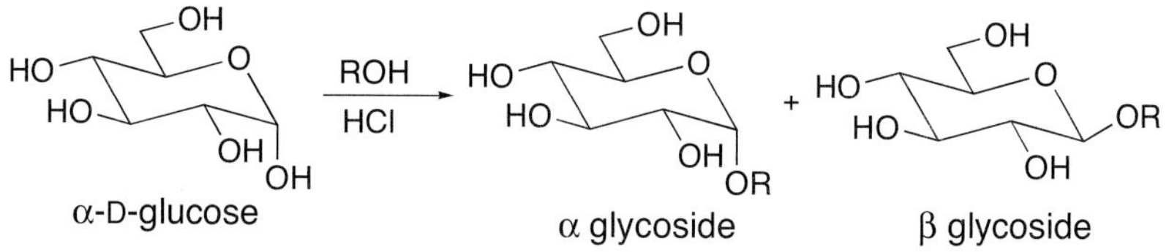

α-D-glucose α glycoside β glycoside

- Only the hemiacetal OH reacts.
- A mixture of α and β glycosides forms.

[2] Glycoside hydrolysis (28.7B)

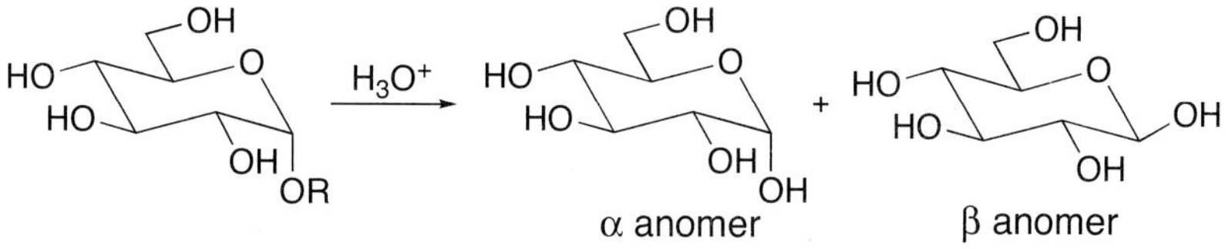

α anomer β anomer + ROH

- A mixture of α and β anomers forms.

Reactions of monosaccharides at the OH groups

[1] Ether formation (28.8)

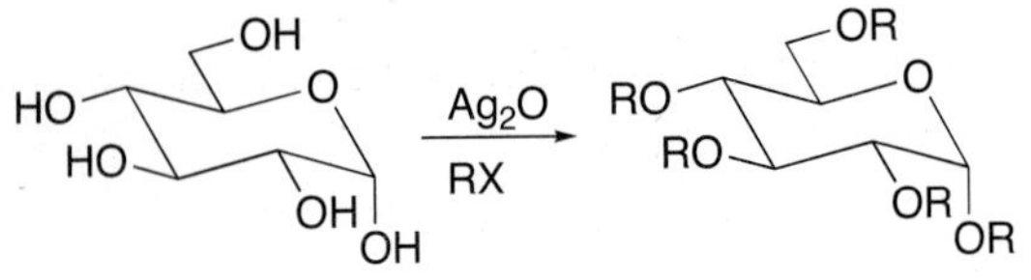
Ag2O
RX

- All OH groups react.
- The stereochemistry at all stereogenic centers is retained.

[2] Ester formation (28.8)

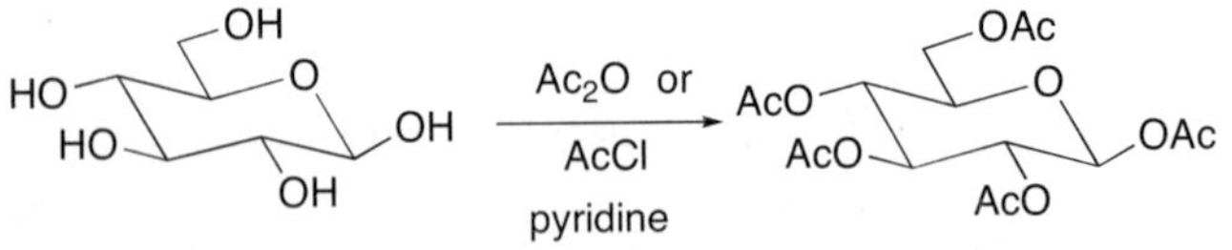
Ac2O or
AcCl
pyridine

- All OH groups react.
- The stereochemistry at all stereogenic centers is retained.

Reactions of monosaccharides at the carbonyl group

[1] Oxidation of aldoses (28.9B)

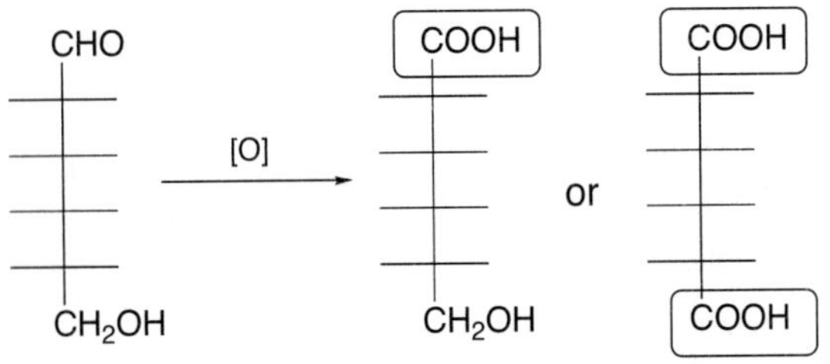
[O]
or

aldose — aldonic acid — aldaric acid

- Aldonic acids are formed using:
  - Ag_2O, NH_4OH
  - Cu^{2+}
  - Br_2, H_2O
- Aldaric acids are formed with HNO_3, H_2O.

[2] Reduction of aldoses to alditols (28.9A)

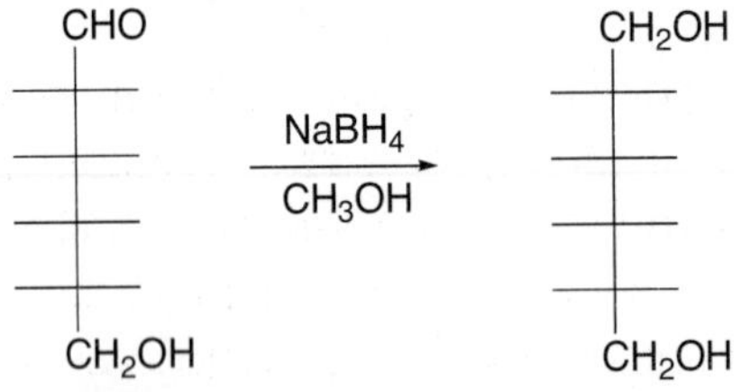
NaBH4
CH3OH

aldose — alditol

[3] Wohl degradation (28.10A)

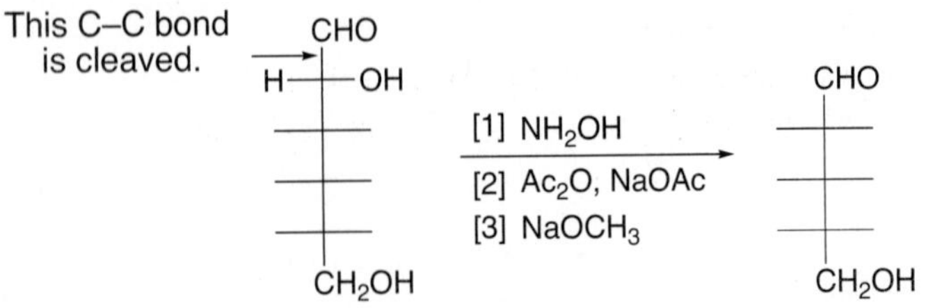
This C–C bond is cleaved.
[1] NH2OH
[2] Ac2O, NaOAc
[3] NaOCH3

- The C1–C2 bond is cleaved to shorten an aldose chain by one carbon.
- The stereochemistry at all other stereogenic centers is retained.
- Two epimers at C2 form the same product.

[4] Kiliani–Fischer synthesis (28.10B)

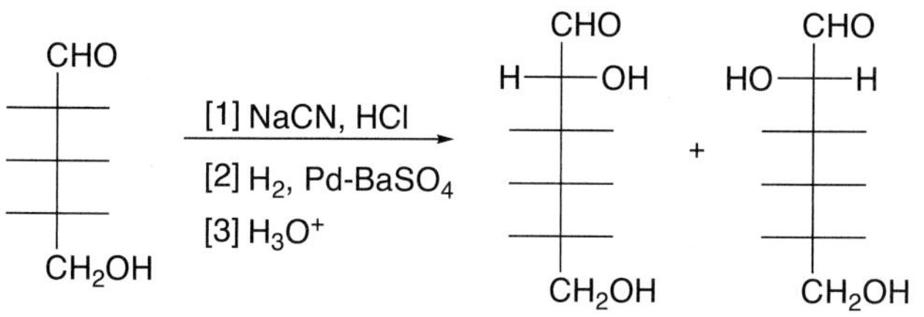
CHO
CH2OH
[1] NaCN, HCl
[2] H2, Pd-BaSO4
[3] H3O+
CHO
H OH
CH2OH
+
CHO
HO H
CH2OH

- One carbon is added to the aldehyde end of an aldose.
- Two epimers at C2 are formed.

Other reactions

[1] Hydrolysis of disaccharides (28.12)

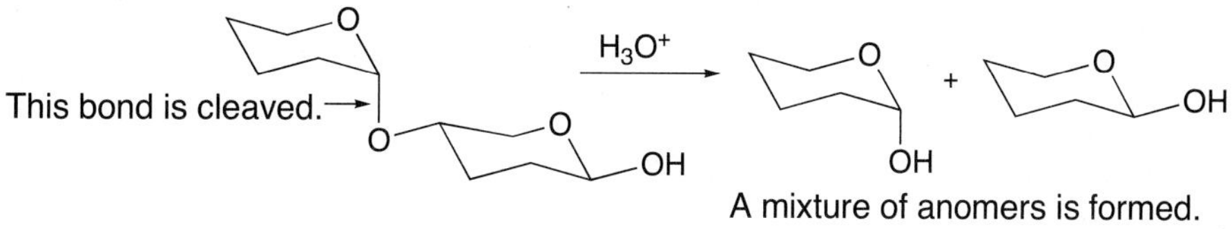
This bond is cleaved.
O
O
O
OH
H3O+
O
OH
+
O
OH
A mixture of anomers is formed.

[2] Formation of *N*-glycosides (28.14B)

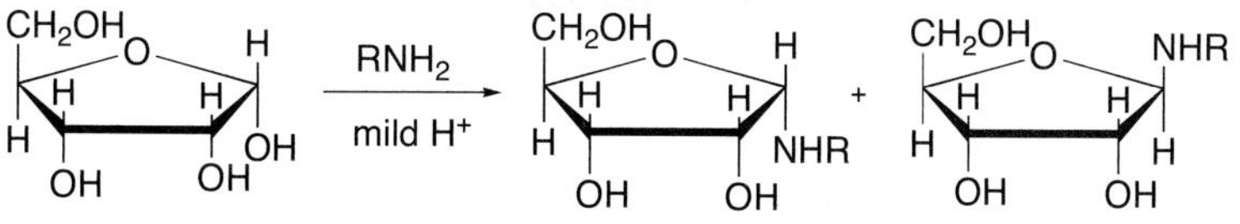
CH2OH
O
H
H
H
H
OH
OH
OH
RNH2
mild H+
NHR
+
NHR

- Two anomers are formed.

Practice Test on Chapter Review

1. a. How are the following two representations related to each other?

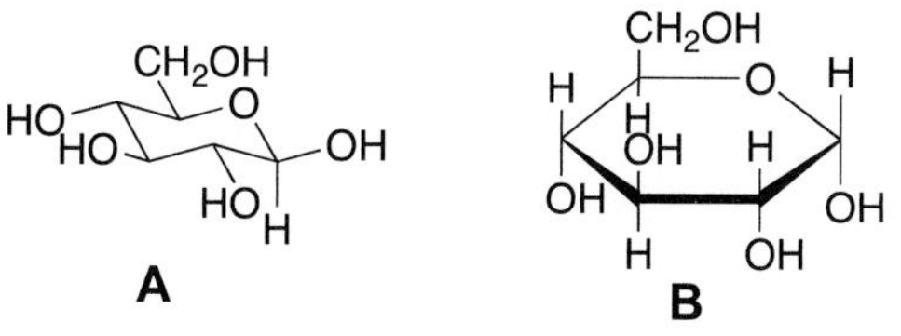
CH2OH
HO
HO
O
OH
HO
H
A
CH2OH
O
H
H
OH
H
OH
OH
H
OH
B

1. **A** and **B** are anomers of each other.
2. **A** and **B** are epimers of each other.
3. **A** and **B** are diastereomers of each other.
4. Statements [1] and [2] are both true.
5. Statements [1], [2], and [3] are all true.

b. Which of the following statements is (are) true about monosaccharide **C**?

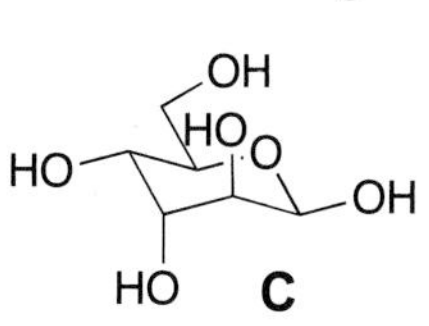
OH
HO
O
HO
OH
HO
C

1. **C** is a D-sugar.
2. The β anomer is drawn.
3. **C** is an aldohexose.
4. Statements [1] and [2] are both true.
5. Statements [1], [2], and [3] are all true.

c. Which of the following are different representations for monosaccharide **D?**

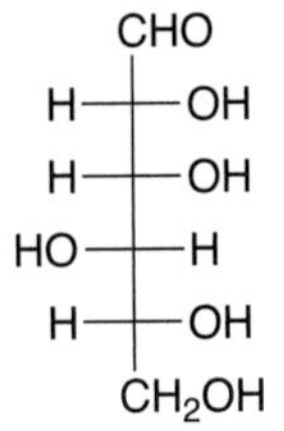

D

1. 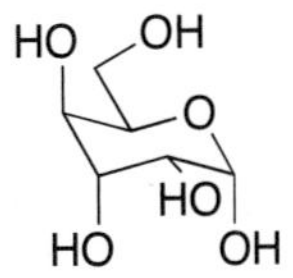
2. 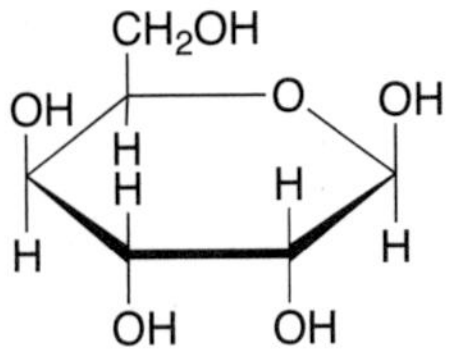
3. 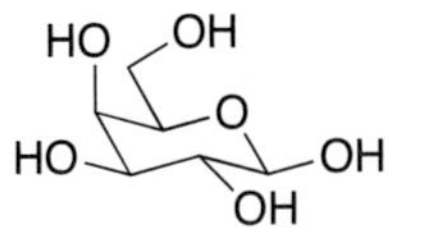
4. Both [1] and [2] are representations for **D.**
5. Compounds [1], [2], and [3] all represent **D.**

d. Which aldoses give an optically active compound upon reaction with $NaBH_4$ in CH_3OH?

1. 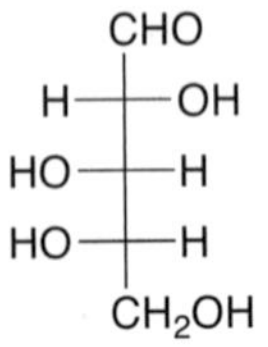
2. 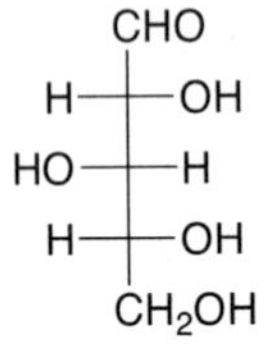
3. 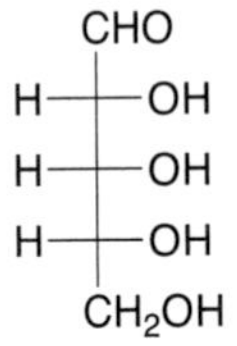
4. Both [1] and [2] give an optically active product.
5. Compounds [1], [2], and [3] all give optically active products.

2. Answer each question about monosaccharide **D** as True (T) or False (F).

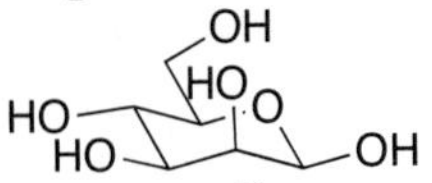

D

a. **D** is a D-sugar.
b. **D** is drawn as an α anomer.
c. **D** is an aldohexose.
d. Reduction of **D** with $NaBH_4$ in CH_3OH forms an optically inactive alditol.
e. Oxidation of **D** with Br_2, H_2O forms an optically active aldonic acid.
f. Oxidation of **D** with HNO_3 forms an optically active aldaric acid.
g. C2 has the *R* configuration.
h. Treatment of **D** with CH_3OH, HCl forms two products.
i. Treatment of **D** with Ag_2O, and CH_3I (excess) forms two products.
j. An epimer of **D** at C3 has an axial OH group.

3. Answer the following questions about the three monosaccharides (**A**–**C**) drawn below.

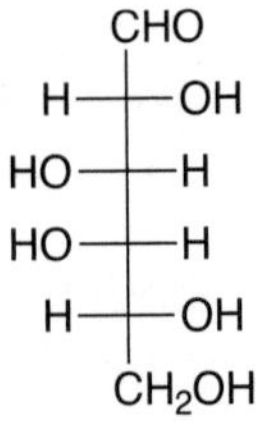

A

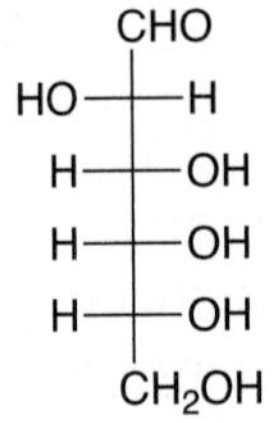

B

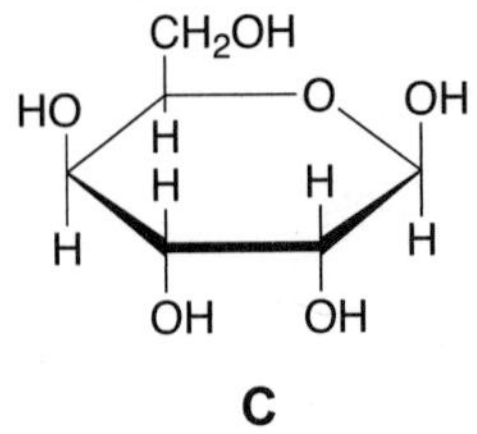

C

a. Draw the α anomer of **A** in a Haworth projection.
b. Draw the β anomer of **B** in a three-dimensional representation using a chair conformation.
c. Convert **C** into the acyclic form of the monosaccharide using a Fischer projection.
d. What two aldoses yield **A** in a Wohl degradation?

4. Draw the product of each reaction with the starting material D-xylose.

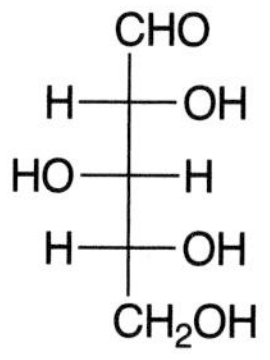
D-xylose

a. CH_3OH, HCl
b. $NaBH_4$, CH_3OH
c. Br_2, H_2O
d. [1] NaCN, HCl; [2] H_2, Pd-$BaSO_4$; [3] H_3O^+
e. Ac_2O, pyridine

Answers to Practice Test

1. a. 5
   b. 5
   c. 4
   d. 1

2. a. T
   b. F
   c. T
   d. F
   e. T
   f. T
   g. F
   h. T
   i. F
   j. T

3.

a. 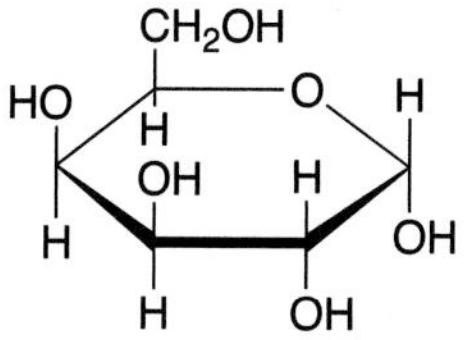

b. 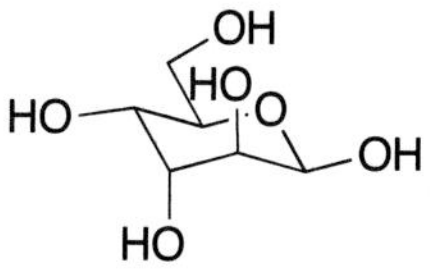

c. 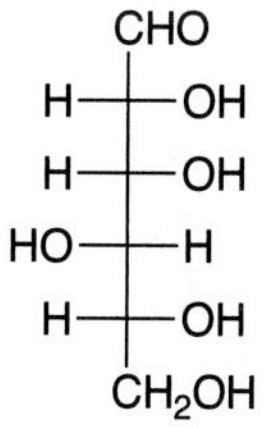

d. 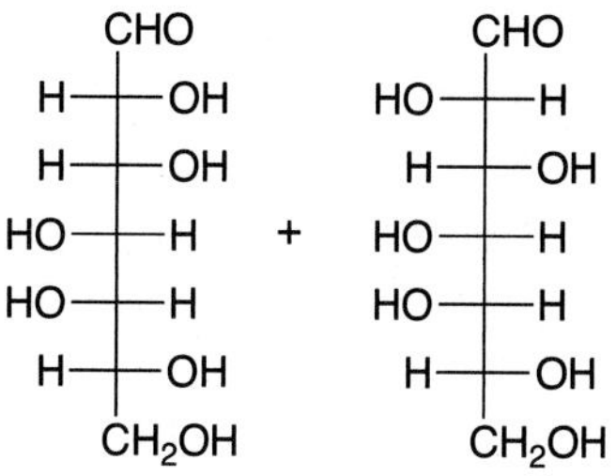

4.

a. 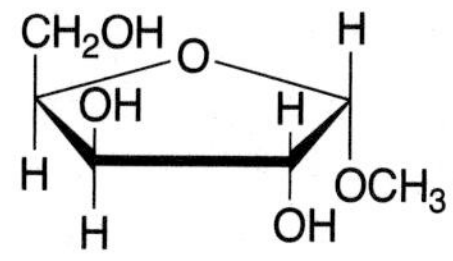
+ β anomer

b. 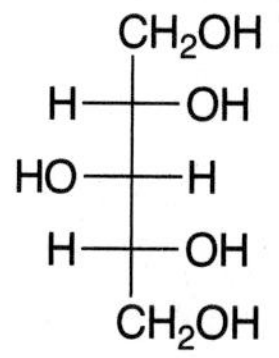

c. 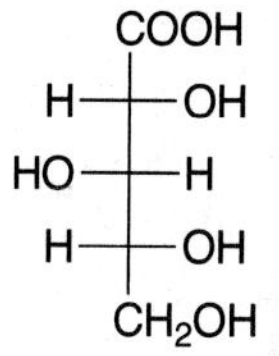

d. 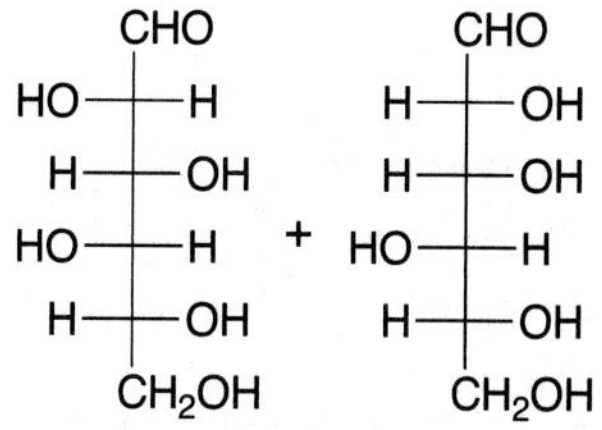

e. 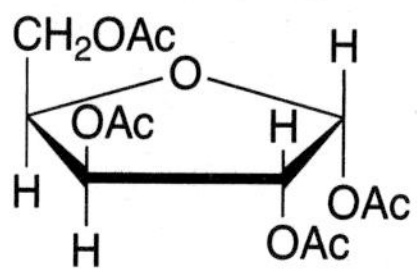
+ β anomer

Answers to Problems

28.1 A *ketose* is a monosaccharide containing a ketone. An *aldose* is a monosaccharide containing an aldehyde. A monosaccharide is called: a *triose* if it has three C's; a *tetrose* if it has four C's; a *pentose* if it has five C's; a *hexose* if it has six C's, and so forth.

a. a ketotetrose 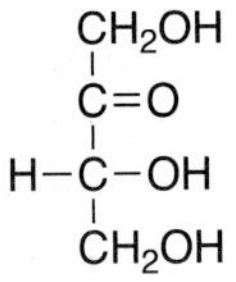

b. an aldopentose 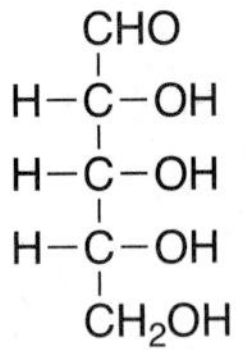

c. an aldotetrose 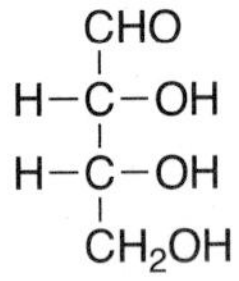

28.2 Rotate and re-draw each molecule to place the horizontal bonds in front of the plane and the vertical bonds behind the plane. Then use a cross to represent the stereogenic center in a Fischer projection formula.

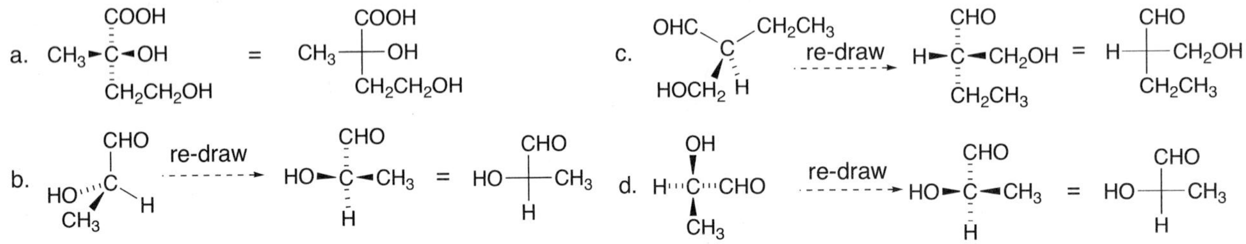

28.3 For each molecule:

[1] Convert the Fischer projection formula to a representation with wedges and dashes.

[2] Assign priorities (Section 5.6).

[3] Determine *R* or *S* in the usual manner. Reverse the answer if priority group [4] is oriented forward (on a wedge).

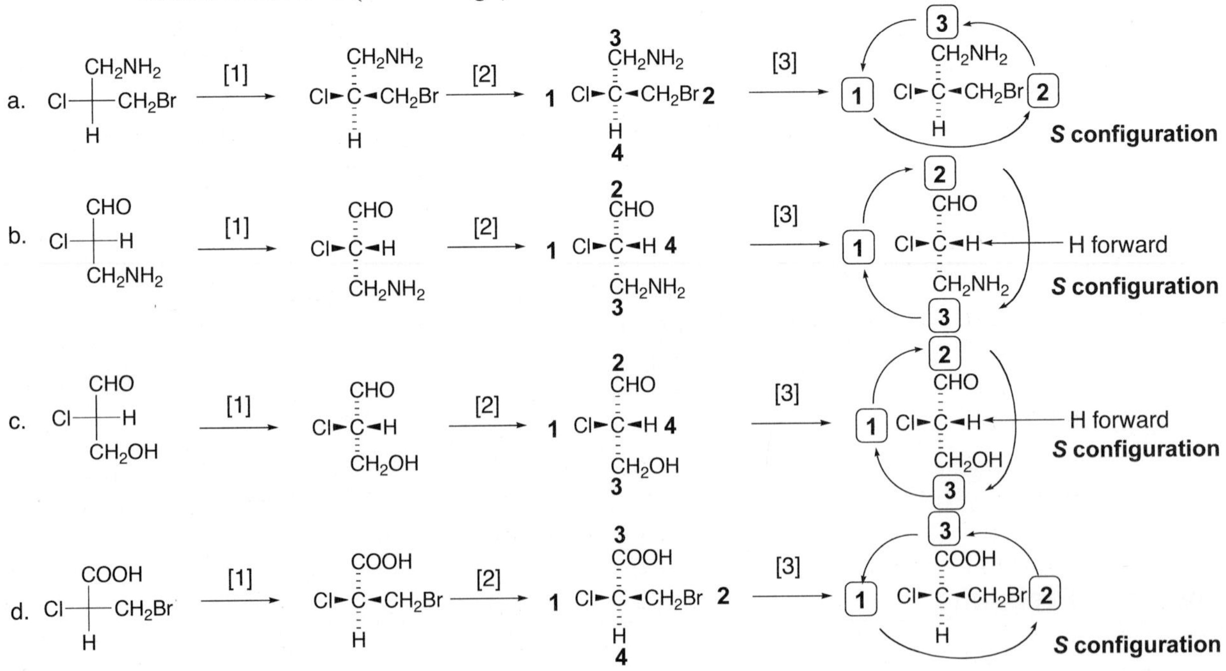

28.4

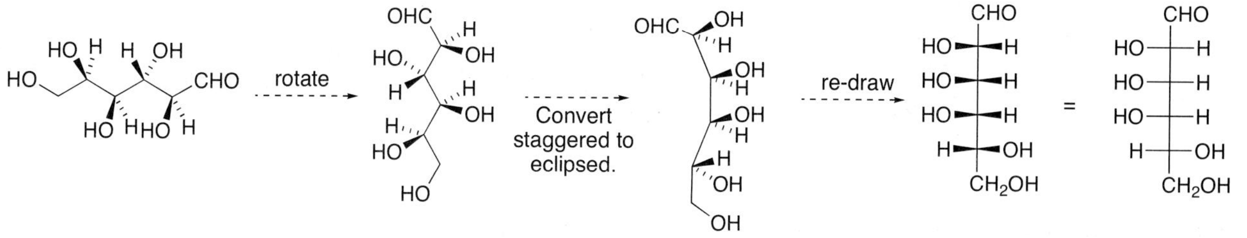

28.5

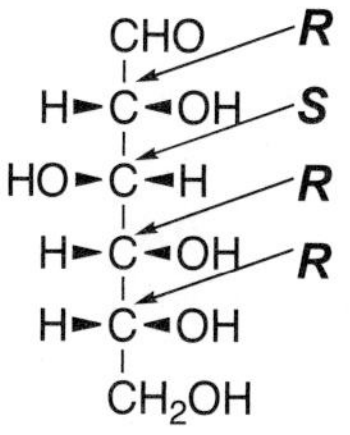

D-glucose

28.6 A D sugar has the OH group on the stereogenic center farthest from the carbonyl on the right. An L sugar has the OH group on the stereogenic center farthest from the carbonyl on the left.

a.

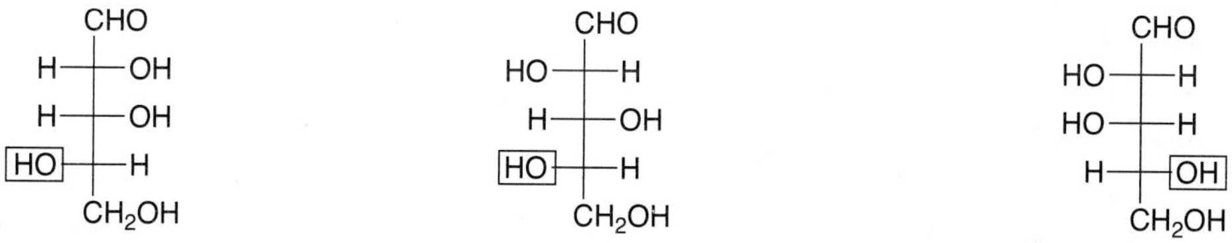

A OH group on the left: **L sugar**

B OH group on the left: **L sugar**

C OH group on the right: **D sugar**

b. **A** and **B** are diastereomers.
A and **C** are enantiomers.
B and **C** are diastereomers.

28.7 There are 32 aldoheptoses; 16 are D sugars.

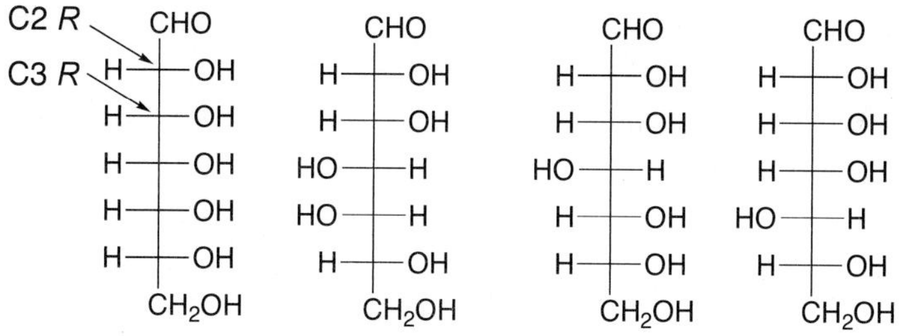

28.8 *Epimers* are two diastereomers that differ in the configuration around only one stereogenic center.

epimers

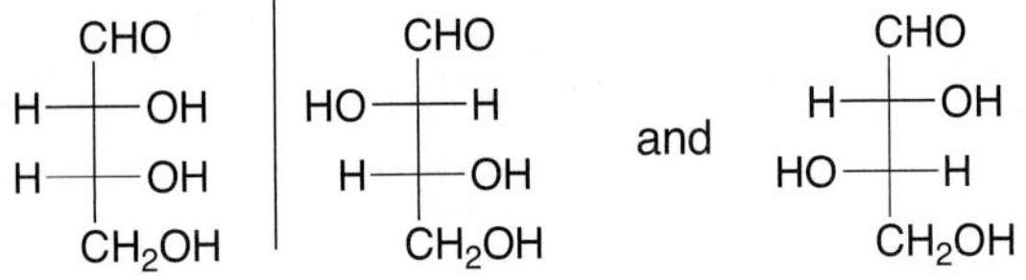

D-erythrose D-threose and L-threose

28.9
a. D-allose and L-allose: **enantiomers**
b. D-altrose and D-gulose: **diastereomers** but not epimers
c. D-galactose and D-talose: **epimers**
d. D-mannose and D-fructose: **constitutional isomers**
e. D-fructose and D-sorbose: **diastereomers** but not epimers
f. L-sorbose and L-tagatose: **epimers**

28.10

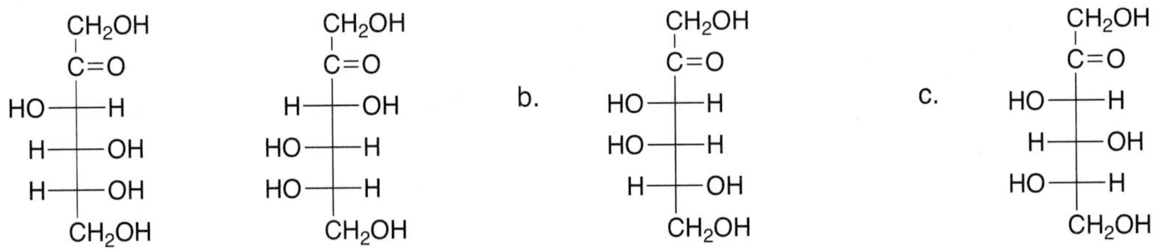

a. D-fructose L-fructose — **enantiomers**

b. D-tagatose

c. L-sorbose

28.11

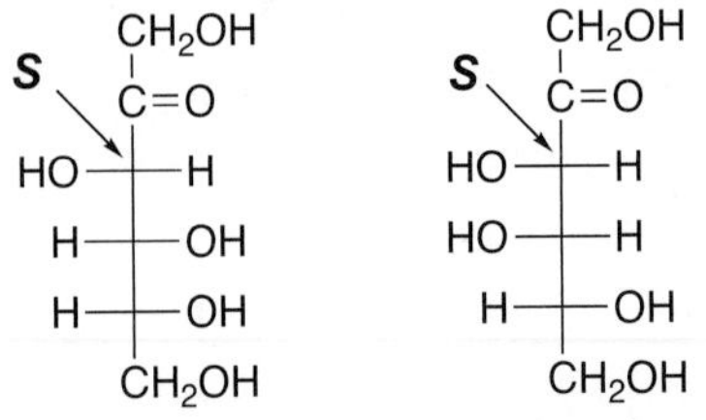

D-fructose **D-tagatose**

28.12 Step [1]: Place the O atom in the upper right corner of a hexagon, and add the CH_2OH group on the first carbon counterclockwise from the O atom.
Step [2]: Place the anomeric carbon on the first carbon clockwise from the O atom.
Step [3]: Add the substituents at the three remaining stereogenic centers, clockwise around the ring.

a. Draw the α anomer of:

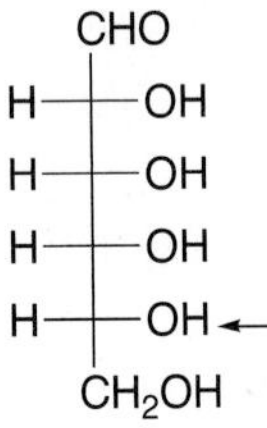

farthest away C, OH on right = D sugar

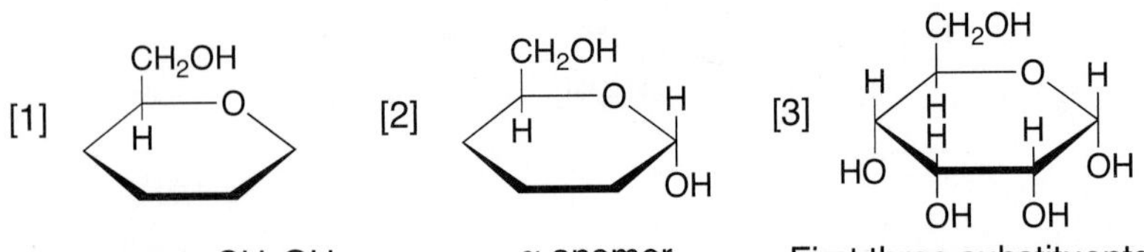

[1] D sugar, CH_2OH is drawn up.

[2] α anomer OH is down for a D sugar.

[3] First three substituents are on the right so they are drawn down.

b. Draw the α anomer of:

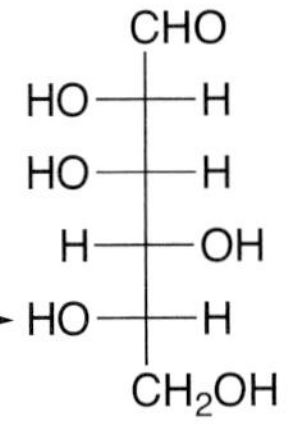
CHO
HO—H
HO—H
H—OH
HO—H
CH2OH

farthest away C,
OH on left
= L sugar

[1]
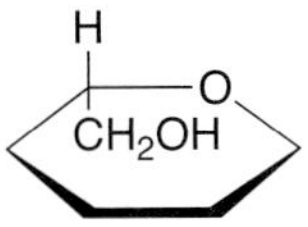
H
O
CH2OH

L sugar, CH_2OH is drawn down.

[2]
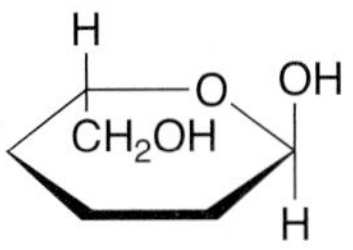
H
O
OH
CH2OH
H

The α anomer has the OH and CH_2OH trans. In an L sugar, the OH must be drawn up.

[3]
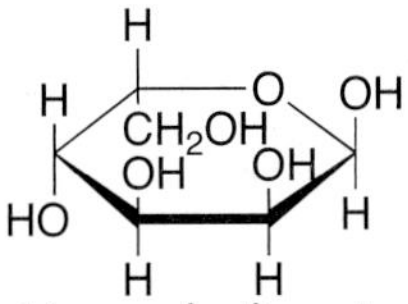
H
H
O
OH
CH2OH
OH
OH
HO
H
H
H

The first two substituents are on the left so they are drawn up. The third is on the right, drawn down.

c. Draw the β anomer of:

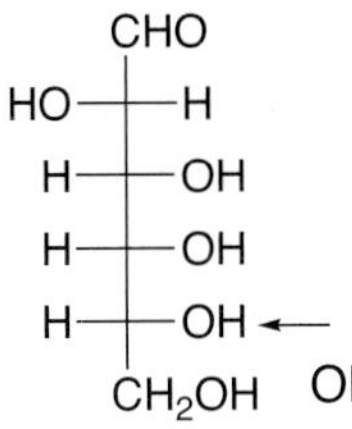
CHO
HO—H
H—OH
H—OH
H—OH
CH2OH

farthest away C,
OH on right = D sugar

[1]
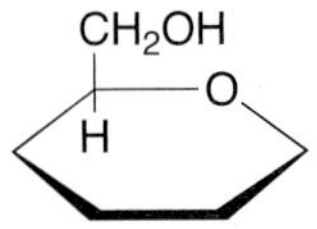
CH2OH
O
H

D sugar, CH_2OH is drawn up.

[2]
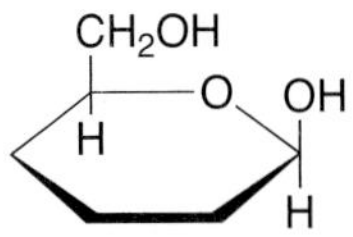
CH2OH
O
OH
H
H

β anomer OH is up for a D sugar.

[3]
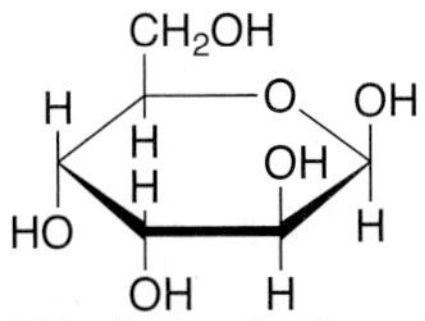
CH2OH
O
OH
H
H
H
OH
HO
H
OH
H

The first substituent is on the left so it is drawn up. The other two are on the right, drawn down.

28.13 To convert each Haworth projection into its acyclic form:

[1] Draw the C skeleton with the CHO on the top and the CH_2OH on the bottom.

[2] Draw in the OH group farthest from the C=O.

A CH_2OH group drawn up means a D sugar; a CH_2OH group drawn down means an L sugar.

[3] Add the three other stereogenic centers, counterclockwise around the ring.

"Up" groups go on the left, and "down" groups go on the right.

a.

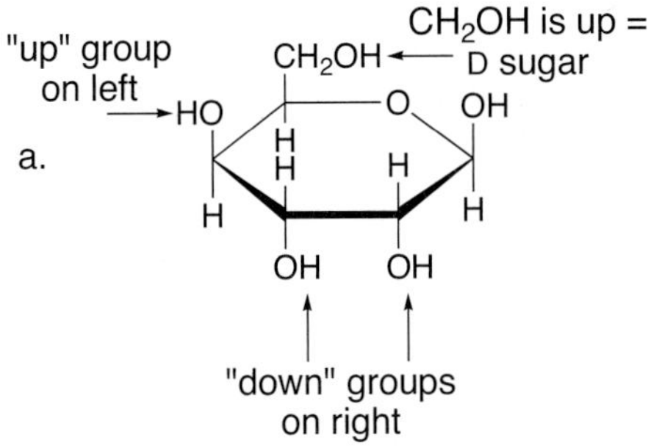
"up" group
on left
HO
CH2OH
CH2OH is up =
D sugar
O
OH
H
H
H
H
H
OH
OH
"down" groups
on right

[1]
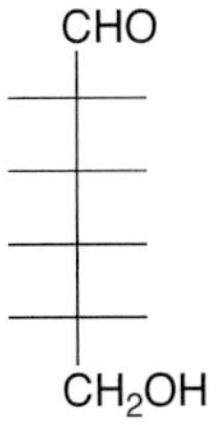
CHO
CH2OH

[2]
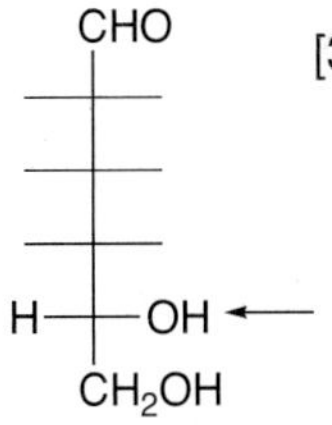
CHO
H—OH
CH2OH

OH on right =
D sugar

[3]
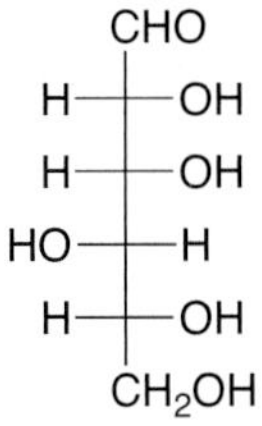
CHO
H—OH
H—OH
HO—H
H—OH
CH2OH

b.

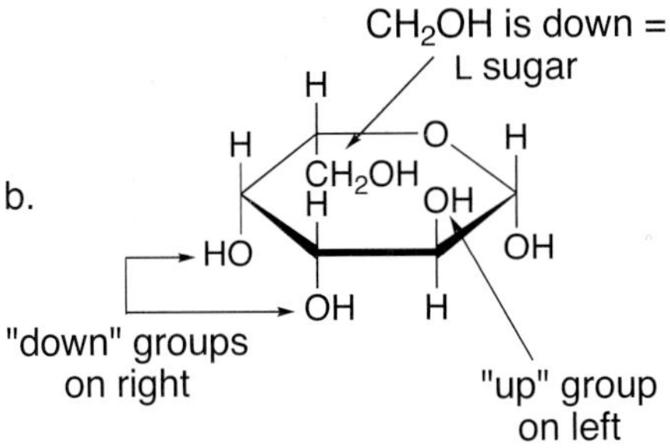
CH2OH is down =
L sugar
H
H
O
H
CH2OH
H
OH
HO
OH
OH
H
"down" groups
on right
"up" group
on left

[1]
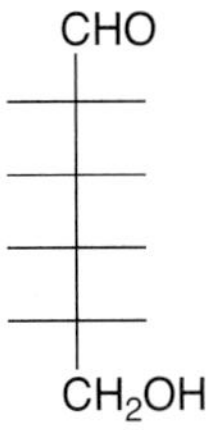
CHO
CH2OH

[2]
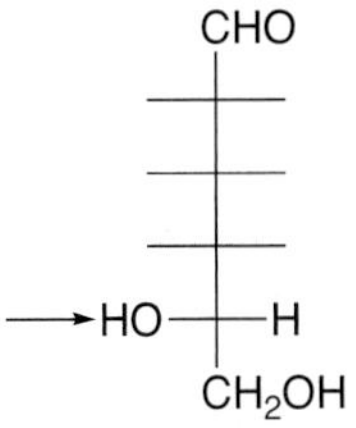
CHO
HO—H
CH2OH

OH on left =
L sugar

[3]
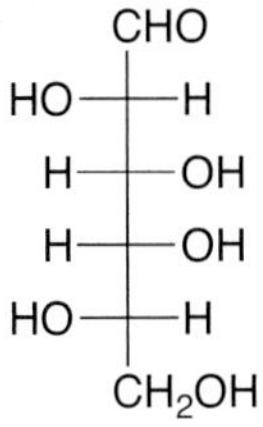
CHO
HO—H
H—OH
H—OH
HO—H
CH2OH

28.14 To convert a Haworth projection into a 3-D representation with a chair cyclohexane:
[1] Draw the pyranose ring as a chair with the O as an "up" atom.
[2] Add the substituents around the ring.

a. 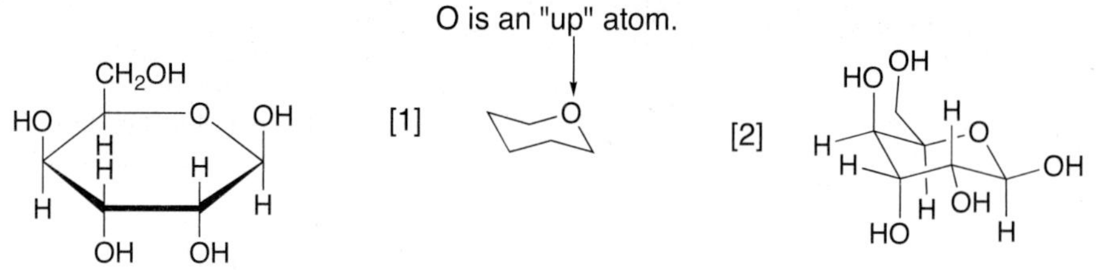
O is an "up" atom.
[1]
[2]

b. 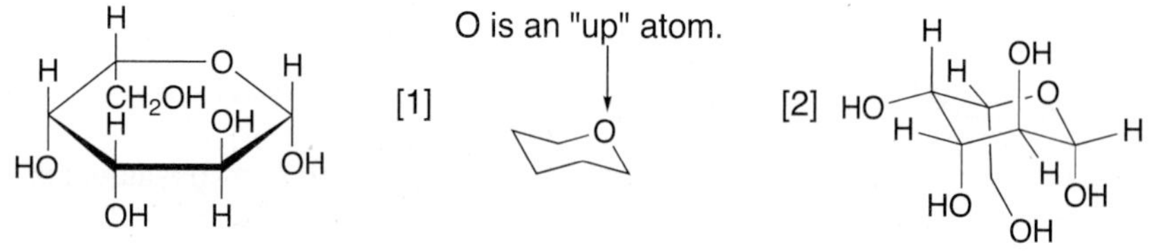
O is an "up" atom.
[1]
[2]

With so many axial groups, this is not the more stable conformation of this sugar.

28.15 Cyclization always forms a new stereogenic center at the anomeric carbon, so two different anomers are possible.

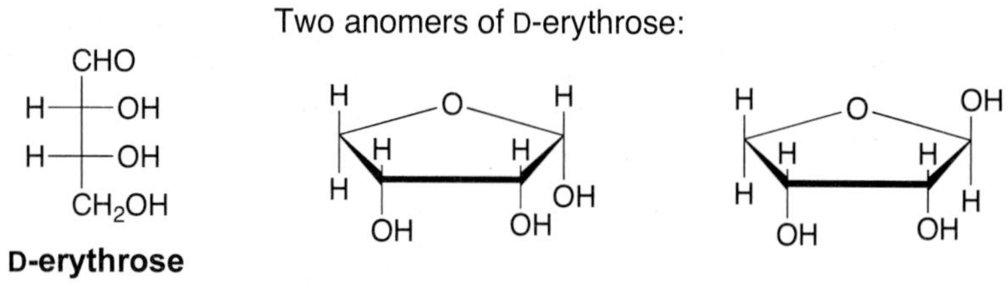
Two anomers of D-erythrose:
D-erythrose

28.16

a. 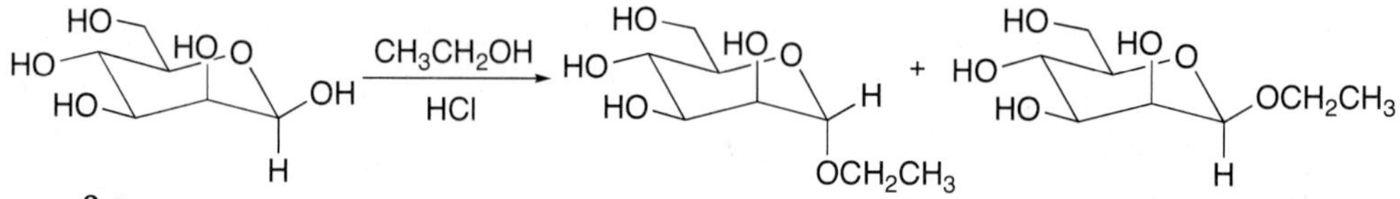
CH_3CH_2OH
HCl

β-D-mannose

b. 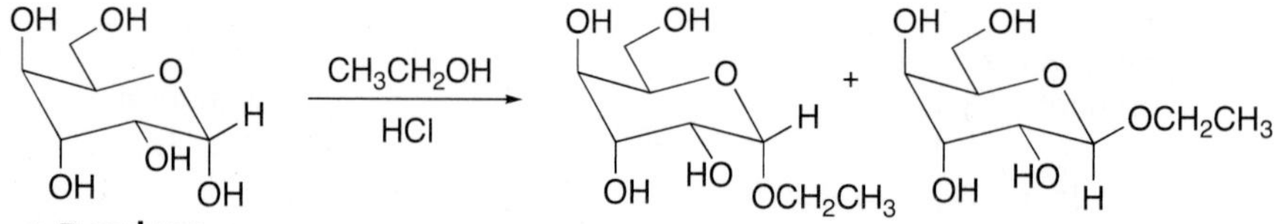
CH_3CH_2OH
HCl

α-D-gulose

c. 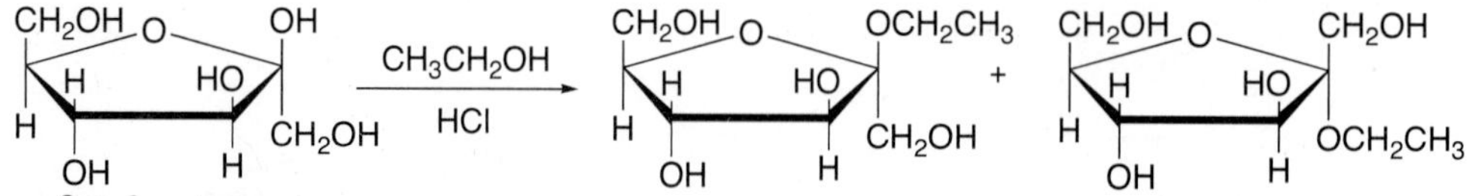
CH_3CH_2OH
HCl

β-D-fructose

28.17

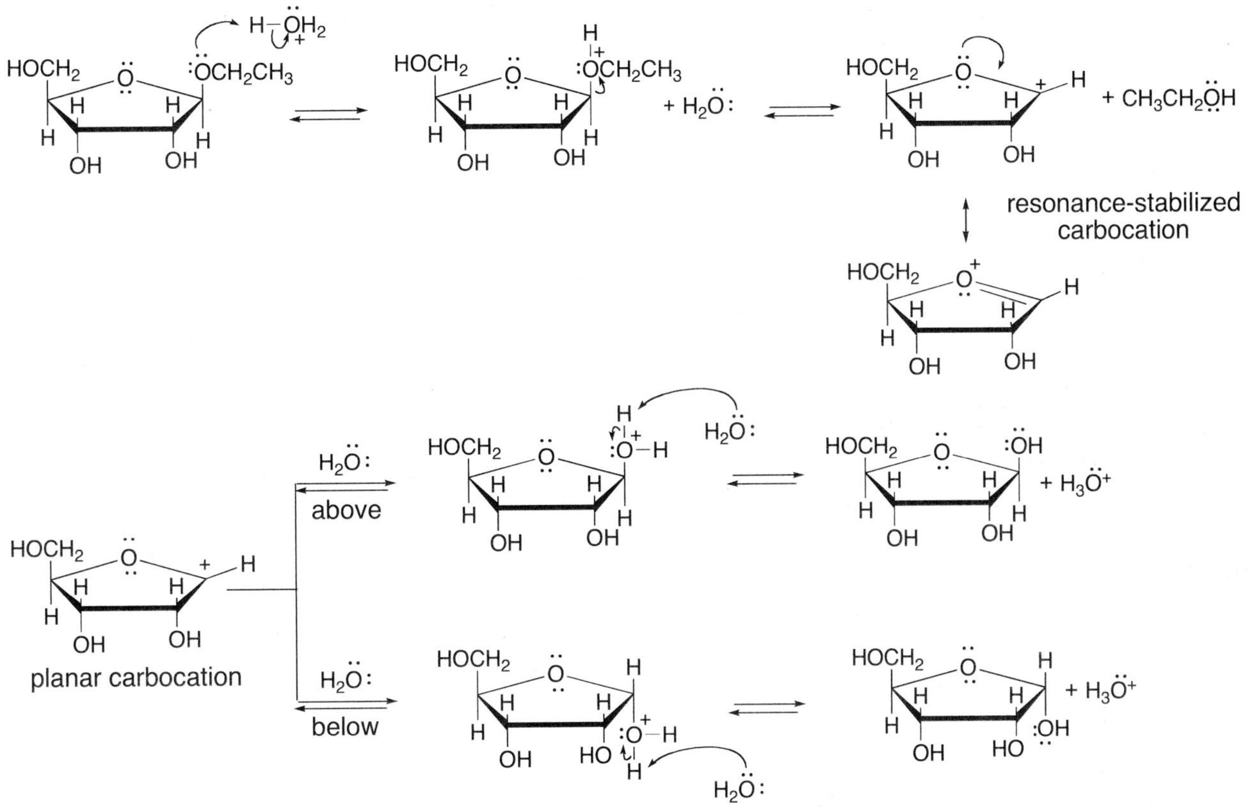

28.18

a. All circled O atoms are part of a glycoside.

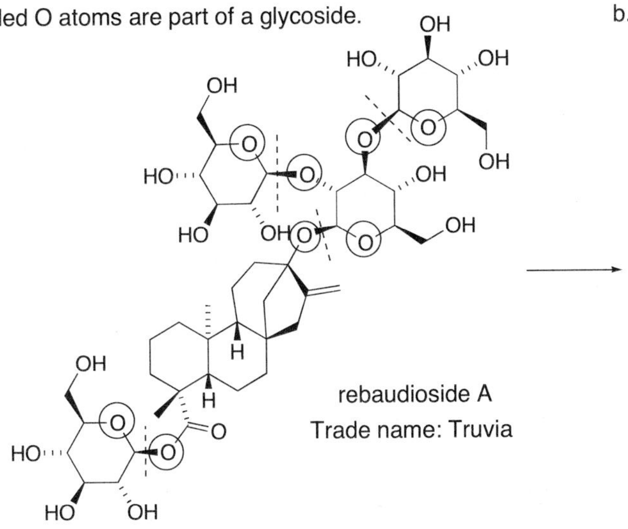

b. Hydrolysis of rebaudioside A breaks each bond indicated with a dashed line and forms four molecules of glucose and the aglycon drawn.

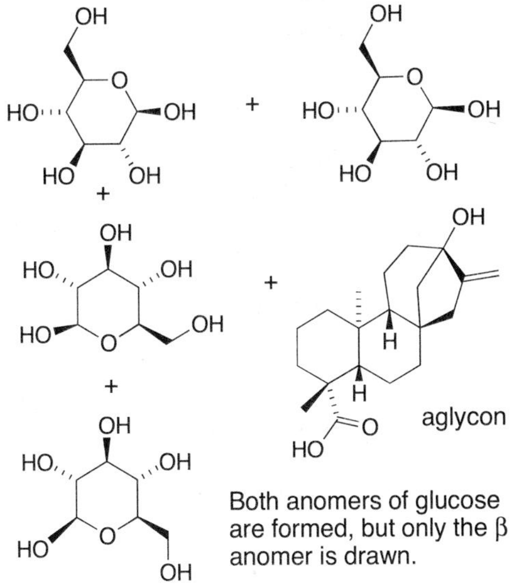

Both anomers of glucose are formed, but only the β anomer is drawn.

28.19

a.
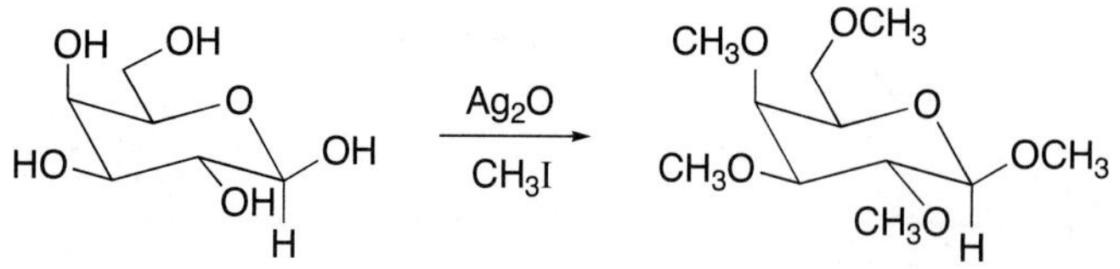

b.
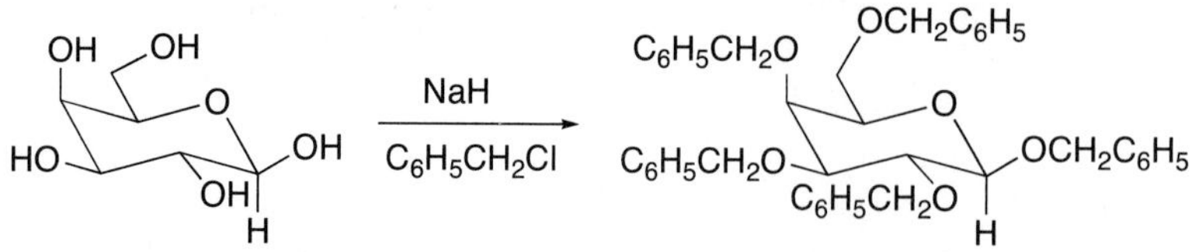

c.
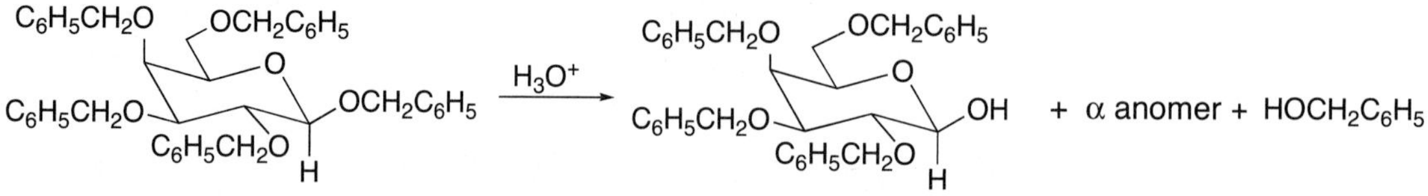

d.
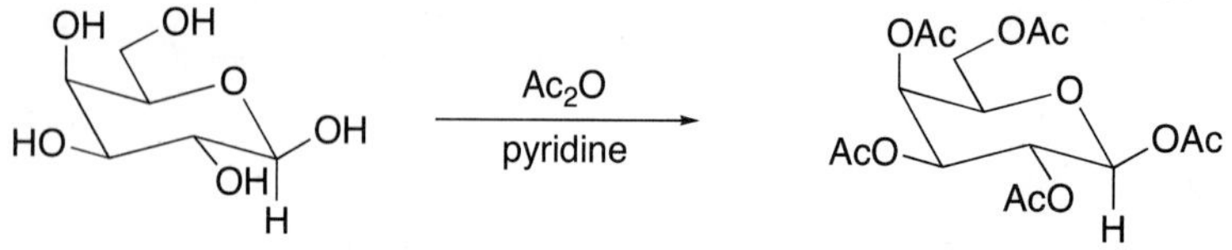

e.
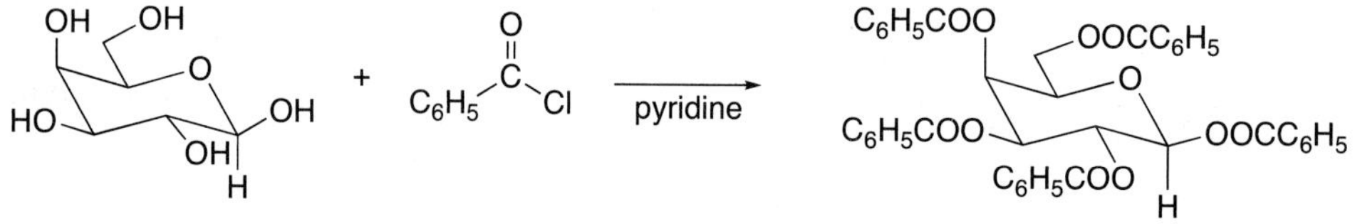

f.
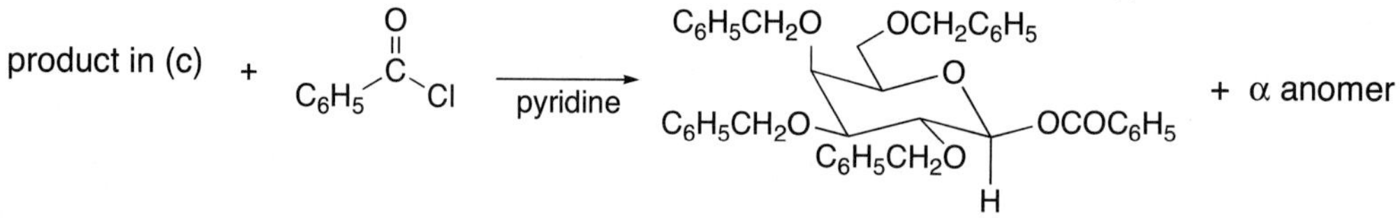

28.20

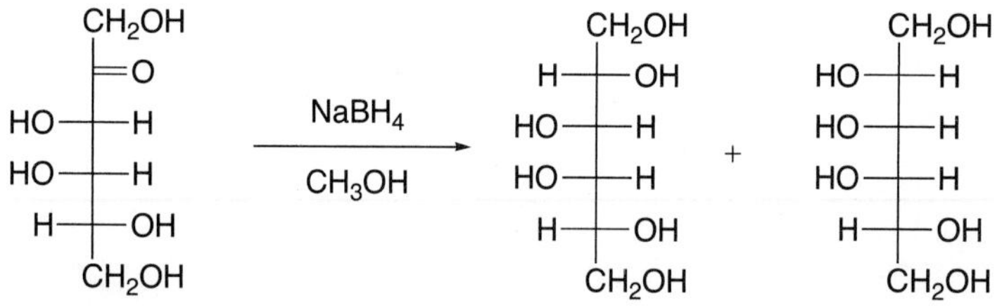

D-tagatose **D-galactitol** **D-talitol**

28.21 Carbohydrates containing a hemiacetal are in equilibrium with an acyclic aldehyde, making them reducing sugars. Glycosides are acetals, so they are not in equilibrium with any acyclic aldehyde, making them nonreducing sugars.

a.
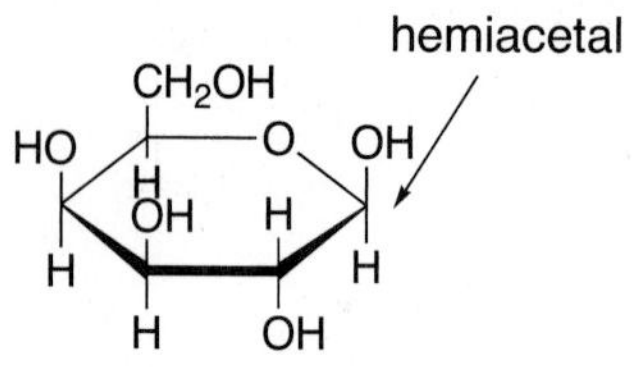

reducing sugar

b.
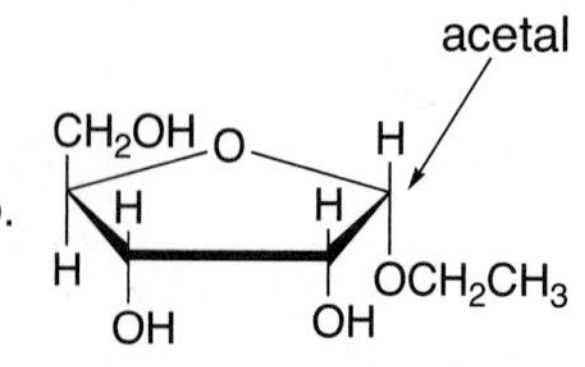

nonreducing sugar

c.
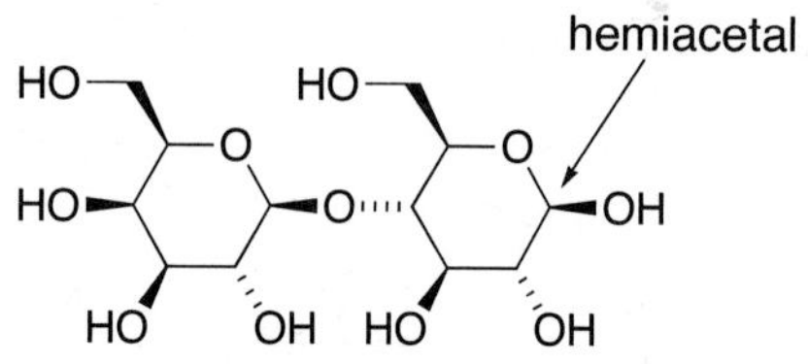

lactose
reducing sugar

28.22

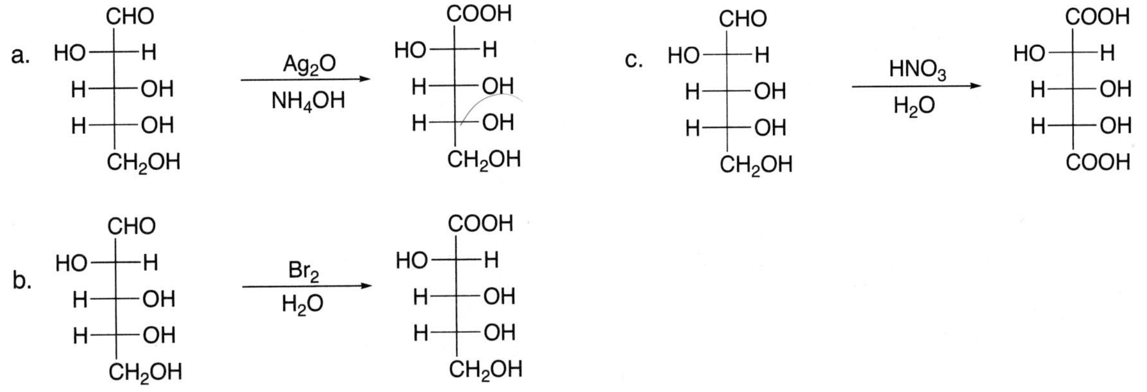
a.
Ag_2O
NH_4OH
b.
Br_2
H_2O
c.
HNO_3
H_2O

28.23 Molecules with a plane of symmetry are optically inactive.

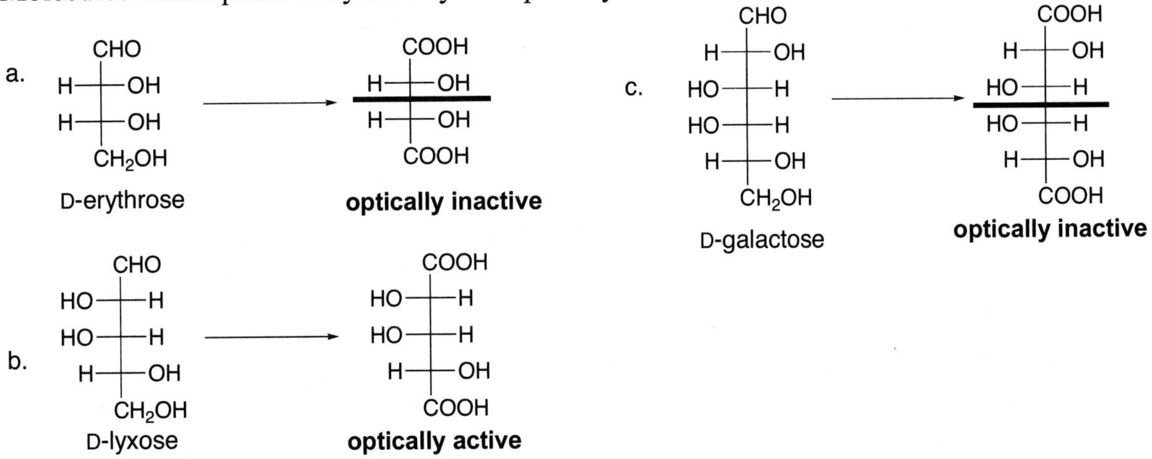
a.
D-erythrose
optically inactive
b.
D-lyxose
optically active
c.
D-galactose
optically inactive

28.24

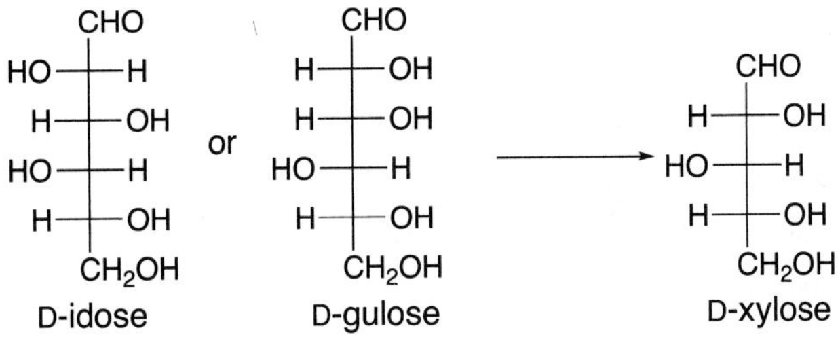
or
D-idose
D-gulose
D-xylose

28.25

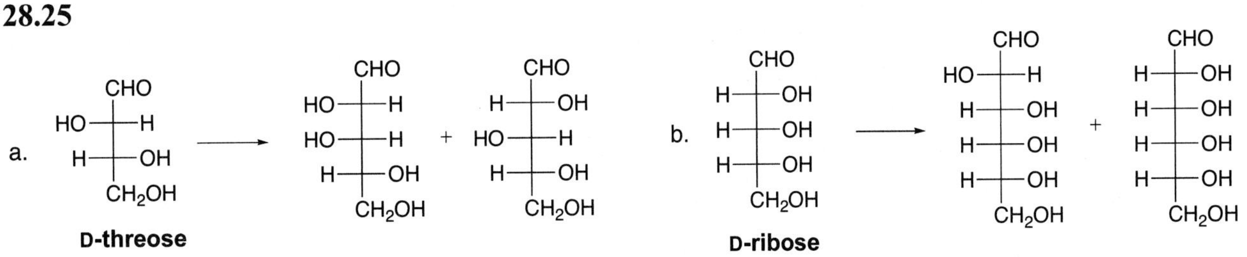
a.
D-threose
b.
D-ribose

c. 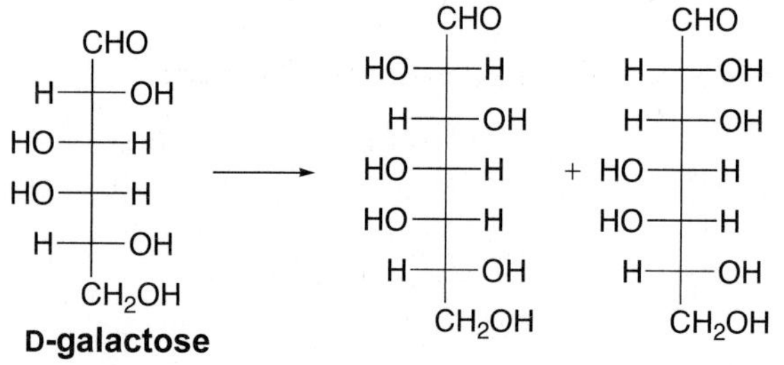
CHO
H—OH
HO—H
HO—H
H—OH
CH2OH
D-galactose
CHO
HO—H
H—OH
HO—H
HO—H
H—OH
CH2OH
+
CHO
H—OH
H—OH
HO—H
HO—H
H—OH
CH2OH

28.26

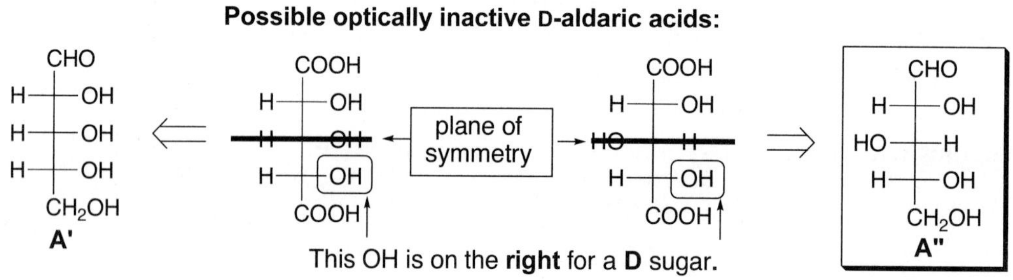
Possible optically inactive D-aldaric acids:
CHO
H—OH
H—OH
H—OH
CH2OH
A'
COOH
plane of symmetry
This OH is on the right for a D sugar.
CHO
H—OH
HO—H
H—OH
CH2OH
A"

There are two possible structures for the D-aldopentose (**A'** and **A"**), and the Wohl degradation determines which structure corresponds to **A.**

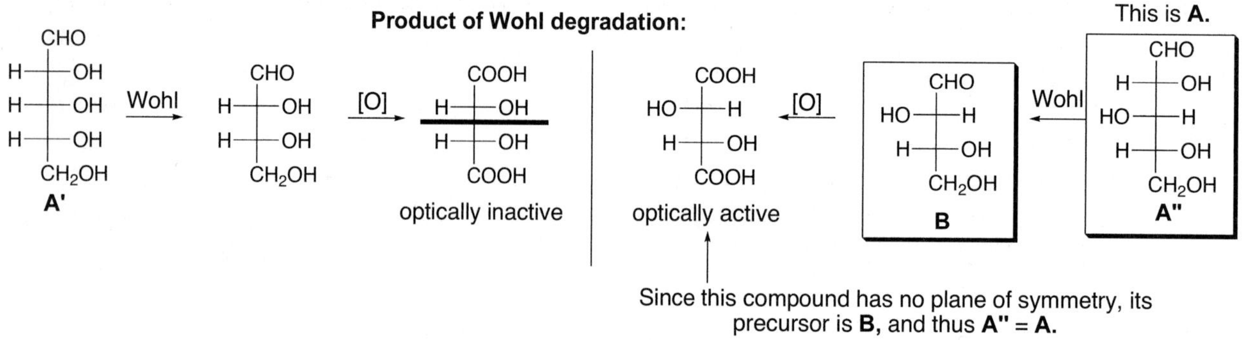
Product of Wohl degradation:
This is A.
A'
Wohl
[O]
optically inactive
optically active
B
A"
Since this compound has no plane of symmetry, its precursor is B, and thus A" = A.

28.27

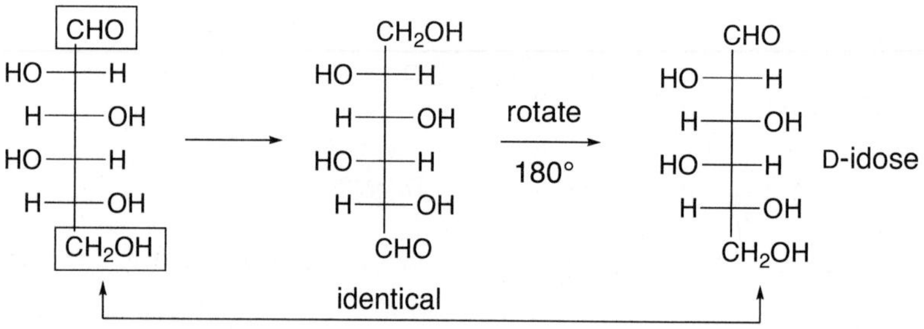
CHO
CH2OH
rotate
180°
D-idose
identical

28.28

Optically inactive alditols formed from $NaBH_4$ reduction of a D-aldohexose.

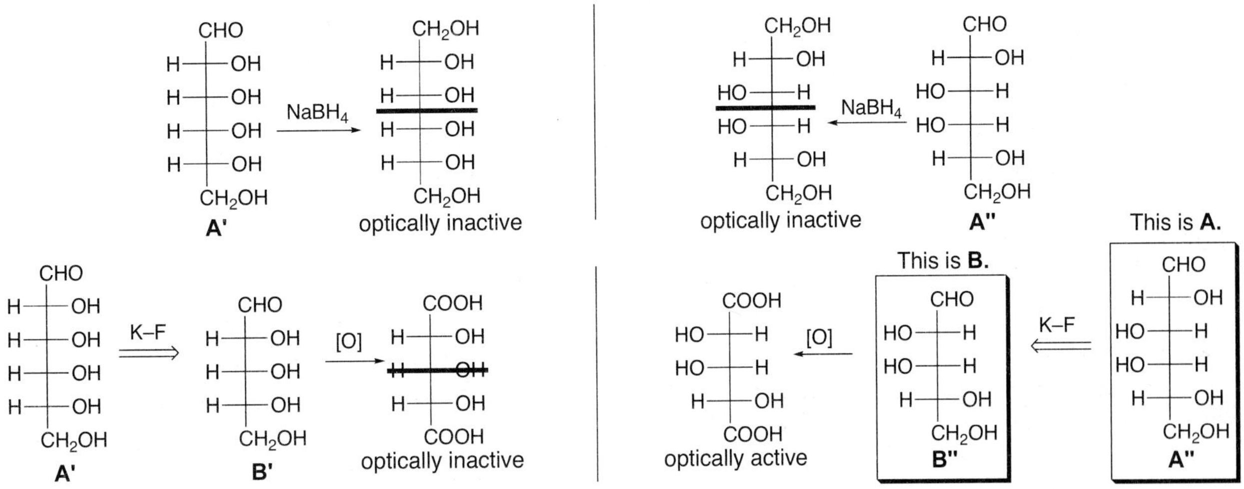

Two D-aldohexoses (**A'** and **A''**) give optically inactive alditols on reduction. **A''** is formed from **B''** by Kiliani–Fischer synthesis. Since **B''** affords an optically active aldaric acid on oxidation, **B''** is **B** and **A''** is **A.** The alternate possibility (**A'**) is formed from an aldopentose **B'** that gives an optically inactive aldaric acid on oxidation.

28.29

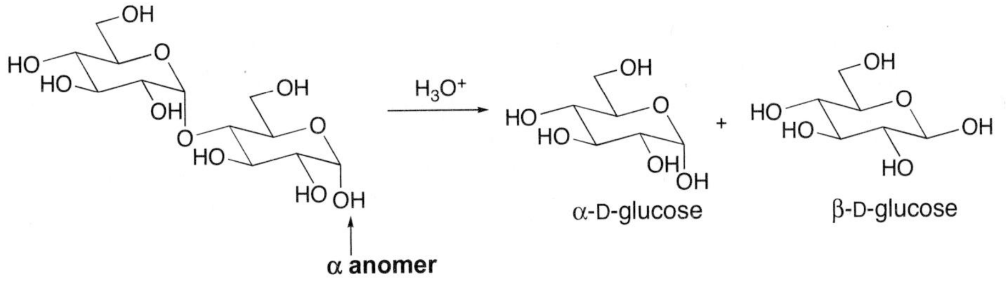

The same products are formed on hydrolysis of the α and β anomers of maltose.

28.30

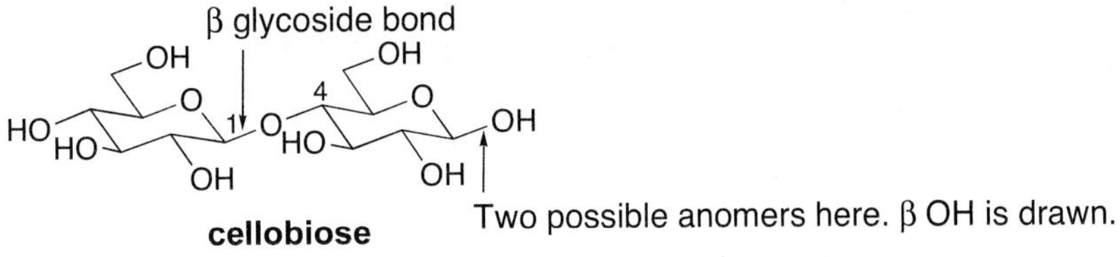

28.31

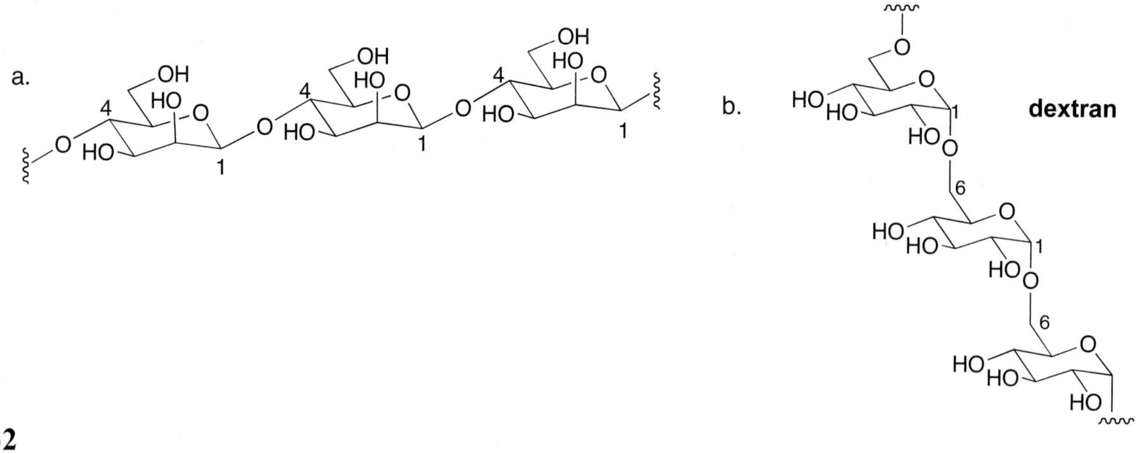
a.
b.
dextran

28.32

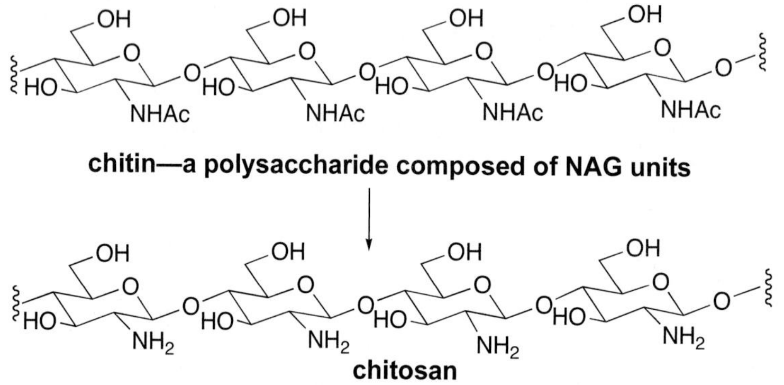
chitin—a polysaccharide composed of NAG units
chitosan

28.33

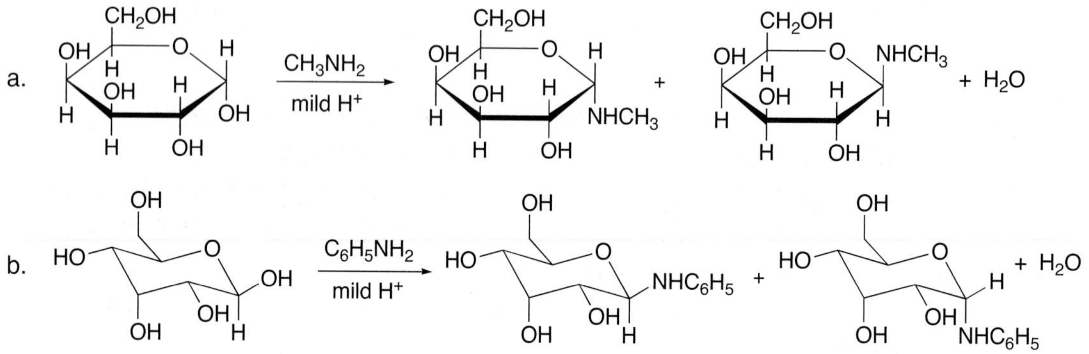
a.
CH_3NH_2
mild H^+
$+ H_2O$
b.
$C_6H_5NH_2$
mild H^+
$+ H_2O$

28.34

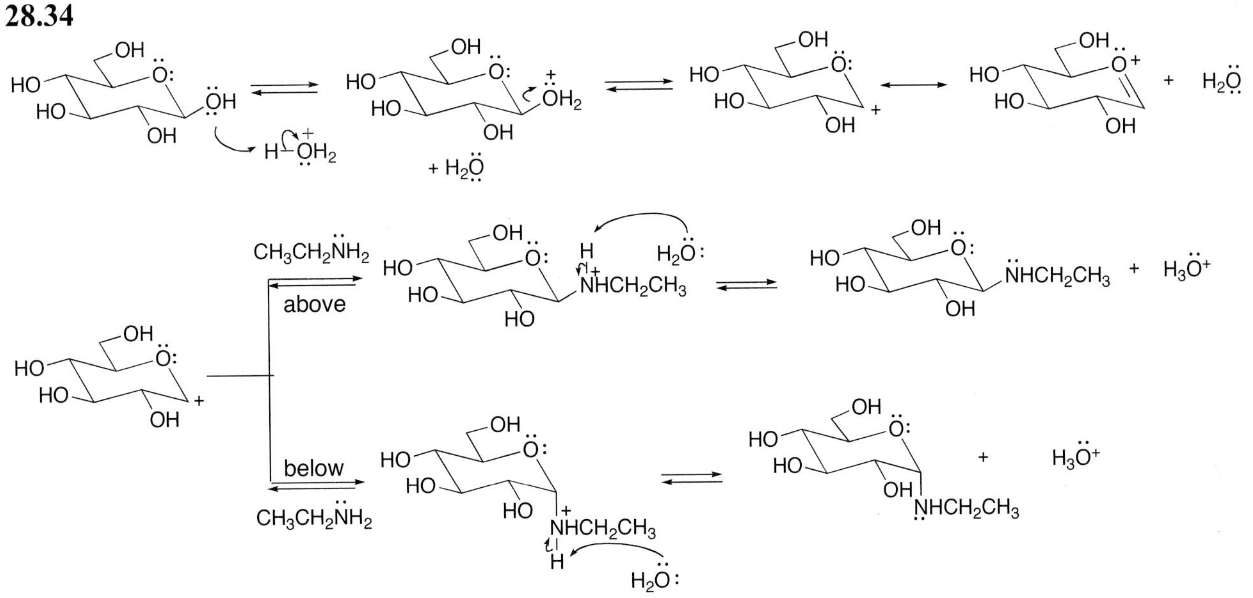

28.35

a.

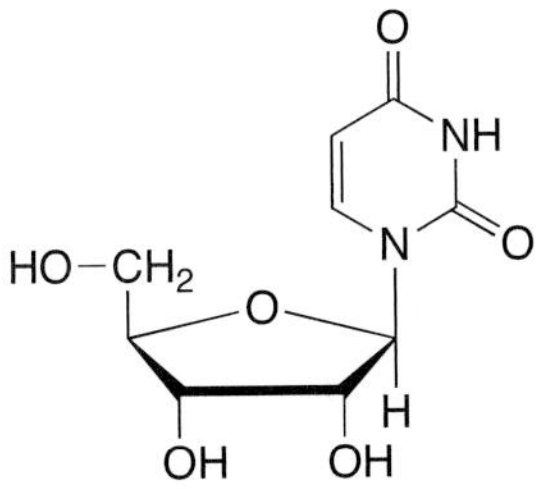

b.

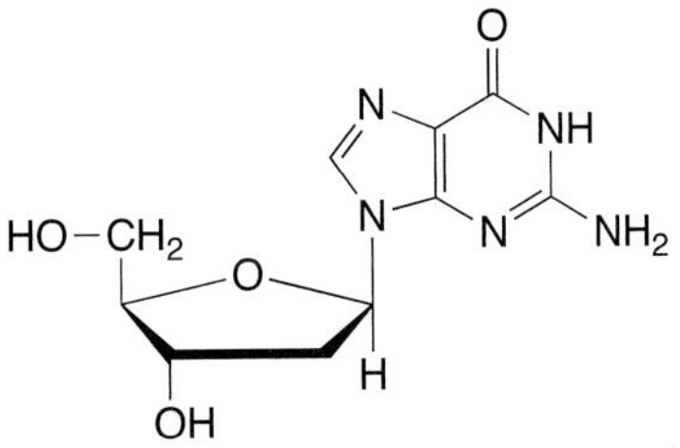

28.36

a. Two purine bases (A and G) are both bicyclic bases. Therefore they are too big to hydrogen bond to each other on the inside of the DNA double helix.

b. Hydrogen bonding between guanine and cytosine has three hydrogen bonds, whereas between guanine and thymine there are only two. This makes hydrogen bonding between guanine and cytosine more favorable.

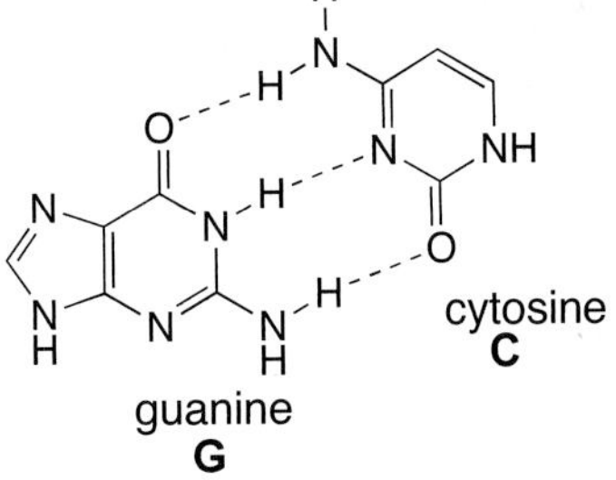

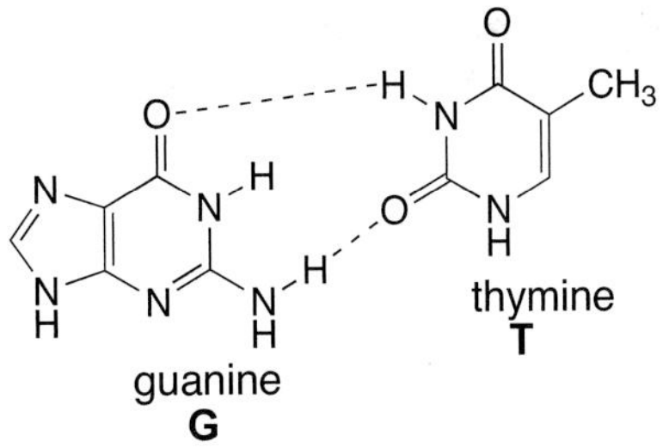

28.37

a.

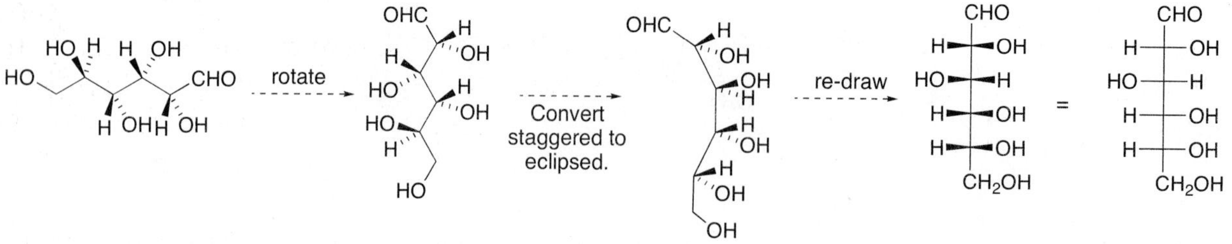

b.

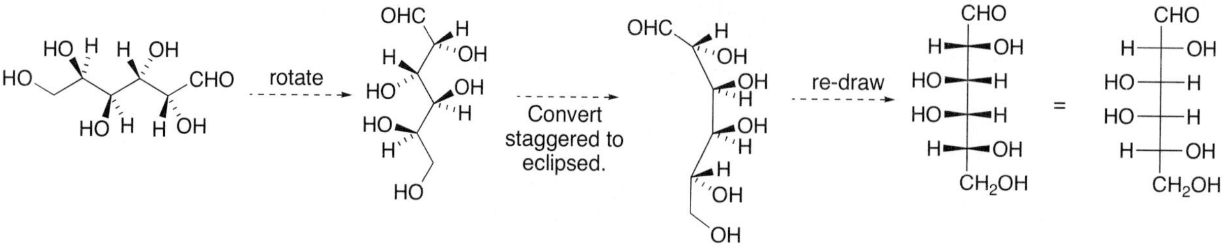

28.38

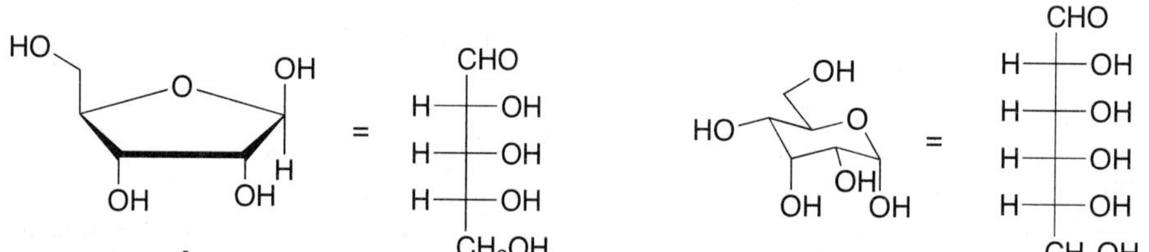

A β anomer = **D-ribose**

B α anomer = **D-allose**

28.39 Label the compounds with *R* or *S* and then classify.

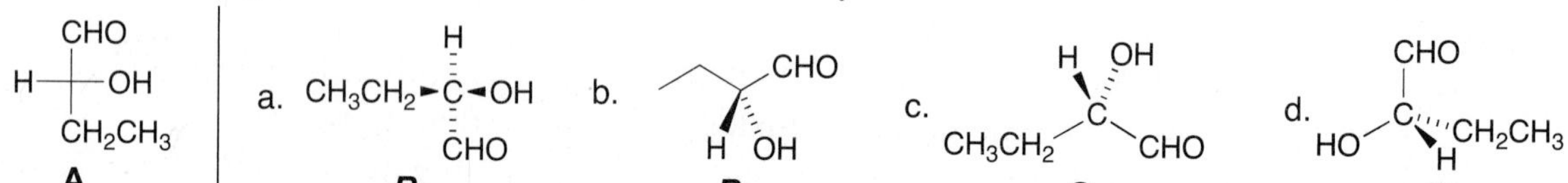

A ***R*** | a. ***R*** **identical** | b. ***R*** **identical** | c. ***S*** **enantiomer** | d. ***S*** **enantiomer**

28.40 Use the directions from Answer 28.2 to draw each Fischer projection.

a.

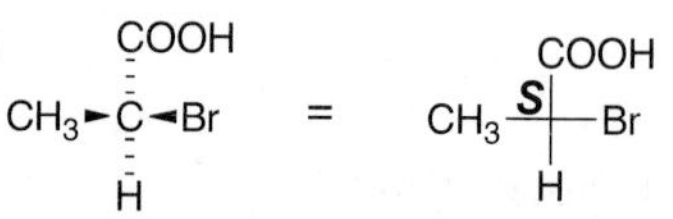

d.

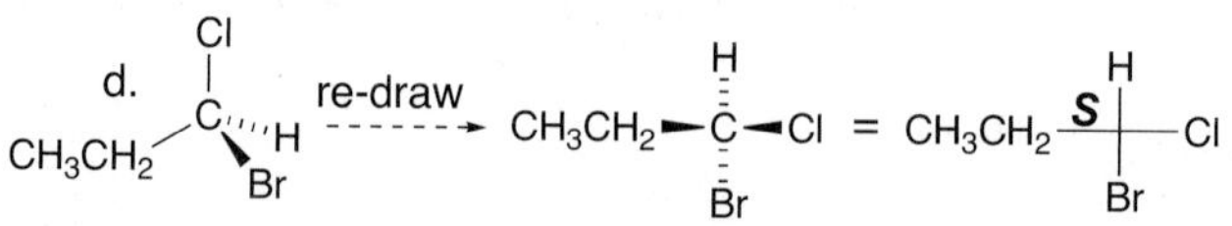

b.

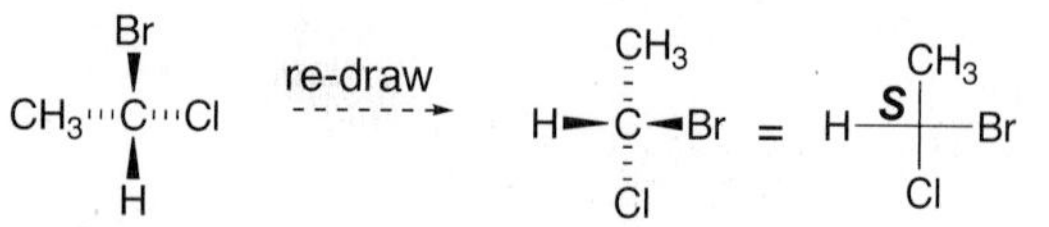

e.

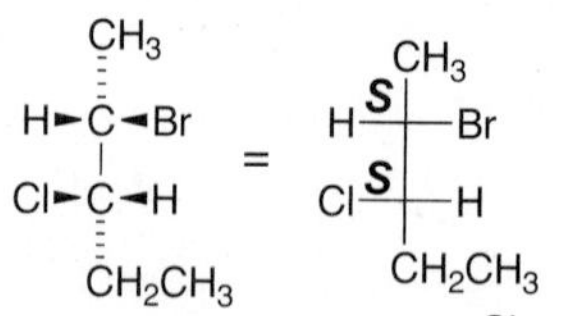

c.

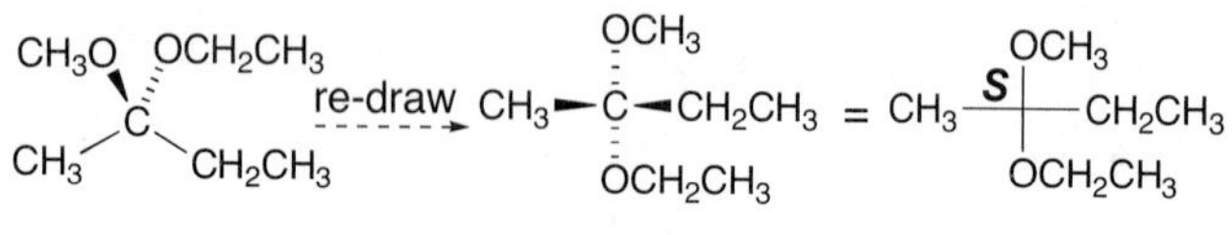

f.

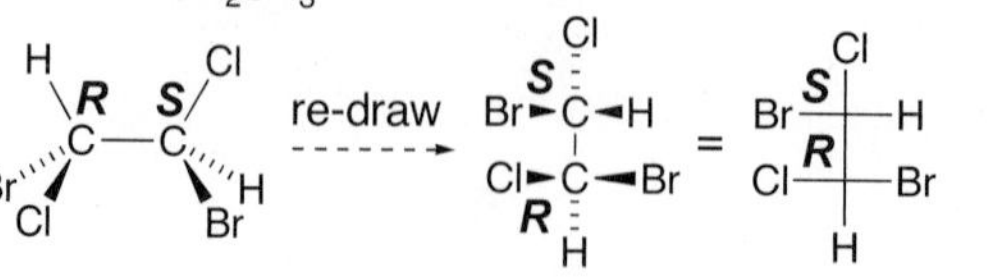

g. 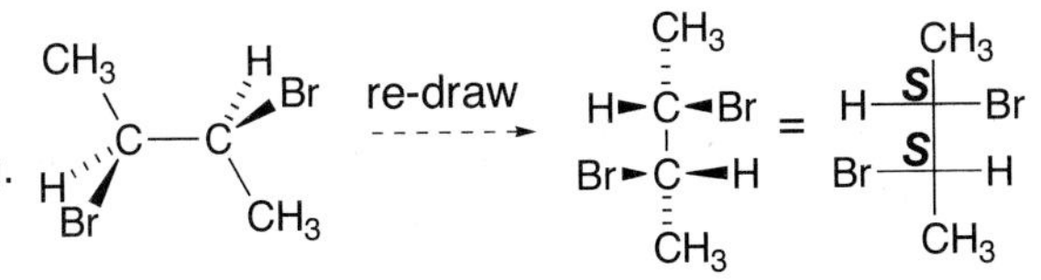

h. 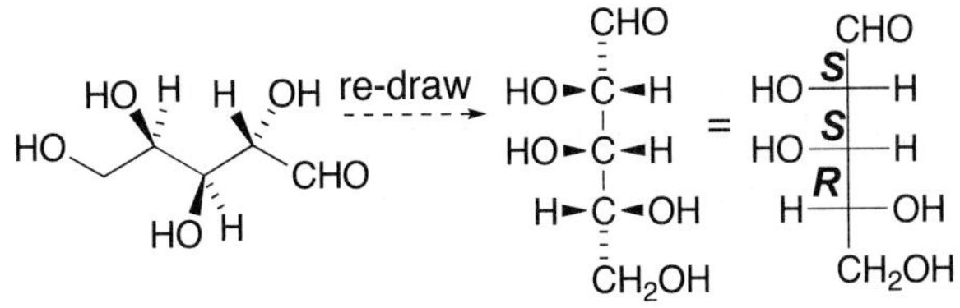

28.41 *Epimers* are two diastereomers that differ in the configuration around only one stereogenic center.

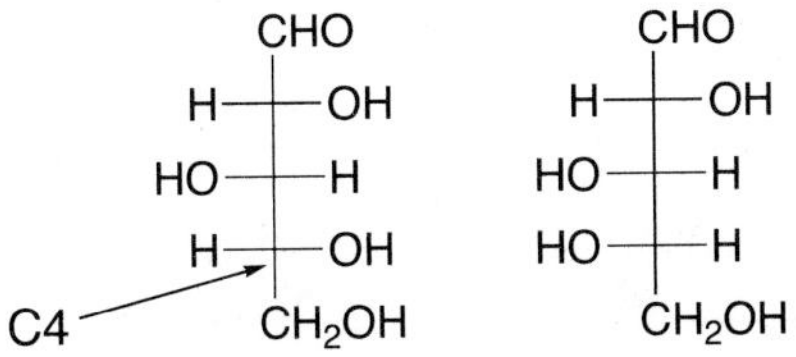

D-xylose **L-arabinose**

28.42

a. 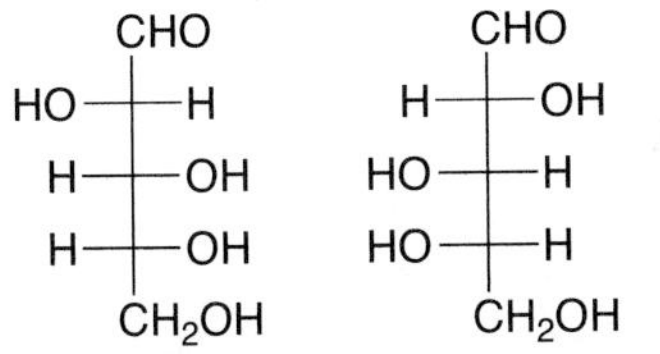

D-arabinose **enantiomer**

b. 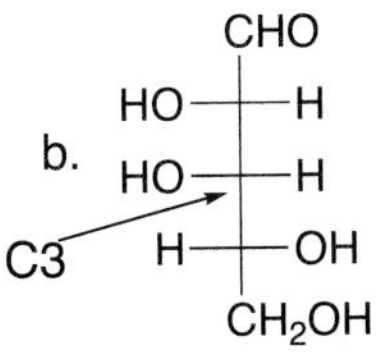

epimer

c. 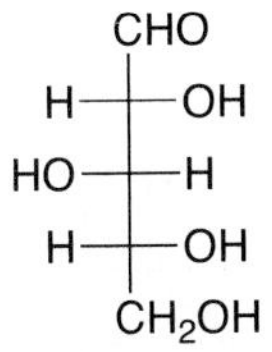

diastereomer (but not epimer)

d. 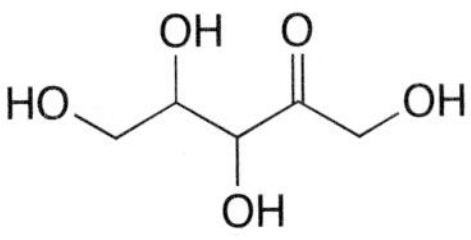

constitutional isomer

28.43

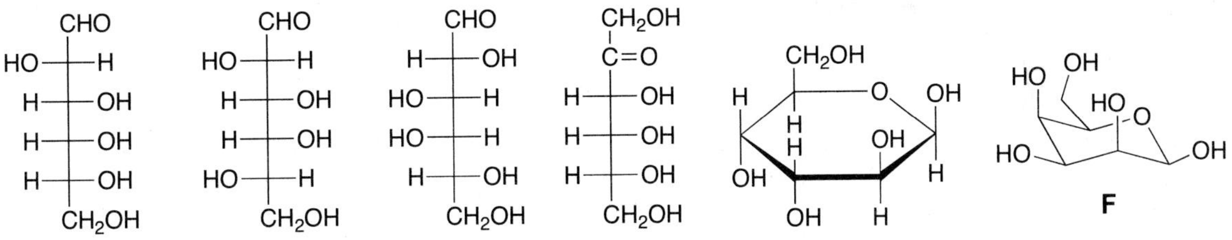

A **B** **C** **D** **E** **F**

a. **A** and **B** **epimers**
b. **A** and **C** **diastereomers**
c. **B** and **C** **enantiomers**
d. **A** and **D** **constitutional isomers**
e. **E** and **F** **diastereomers**

28.44

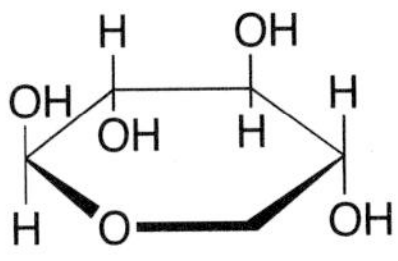

A

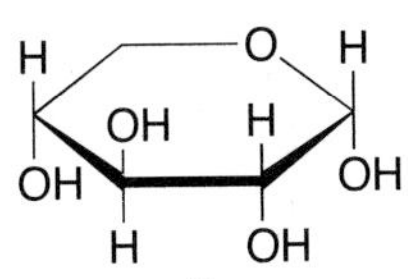

B

a. anomers, epimers, diastereomers, reducing sugars

b. 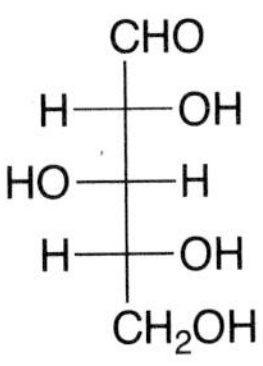

D-xylose

This is the acyclic form of both **A** and **B.**

28.45 Use the directions from Answer 28.12.

a. β-D-talopyranose

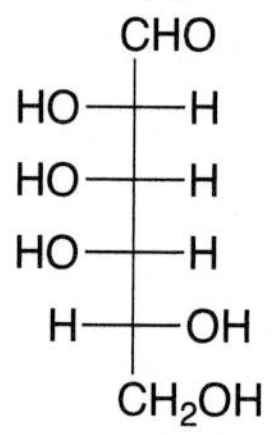
farthest away C, OH on right = D sugar

D-talose

[1]
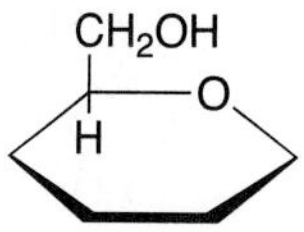
D sugar, CH_2OH is drawn up.

[2]
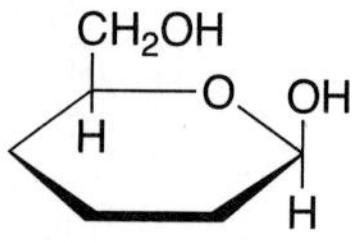
β anomer OH is up for a D sugar.

[3]
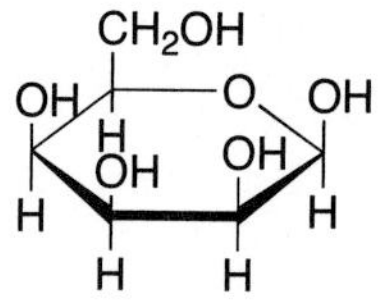

b. β-D-mannopyranose

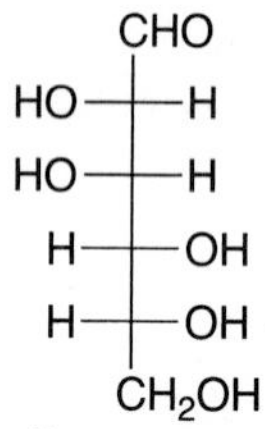
farthest away C, OH on right = D sugar

D-mannose

[1]
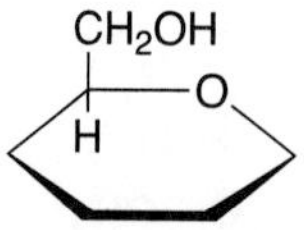
D sugar, CH_2OH is drawn up.

[2]
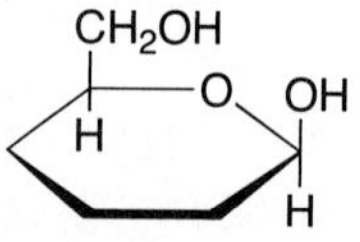
β anomer OH is up for a D sugar.

[3]
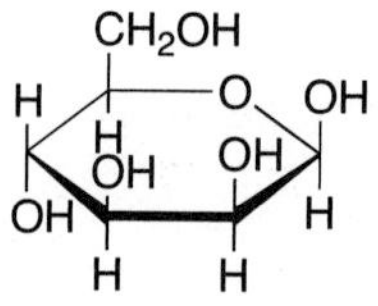

c. α-D-galactopyranose

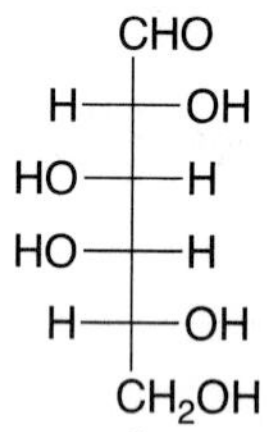
farthest away C, OH on right = D sugar

D-galactose

[1]
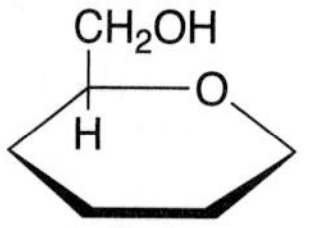
D sugar, CH_2OH is drawn up.

[2]
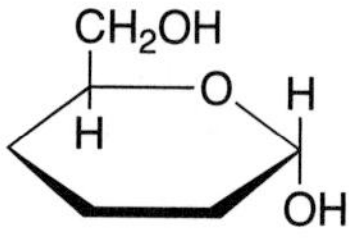
α anomer OH is down.

[3]
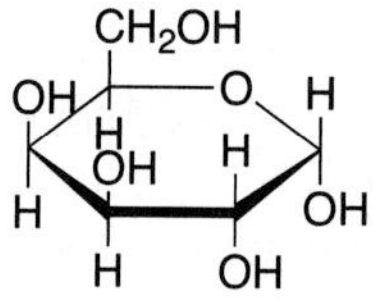

d. α-D-ribofuranose

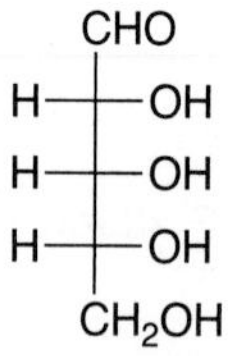
farthest away C, OH on right = D sugar

D-ribose

[1]
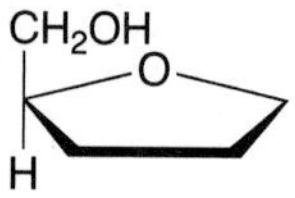
D sugar, CH_2OH is drawn up.

[2]
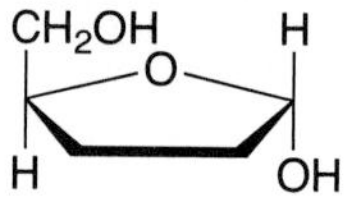
α anomer OH is down.

[3]
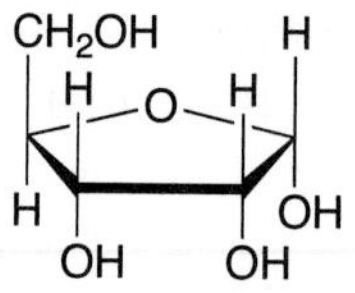

e. α-D-tagatofuranose

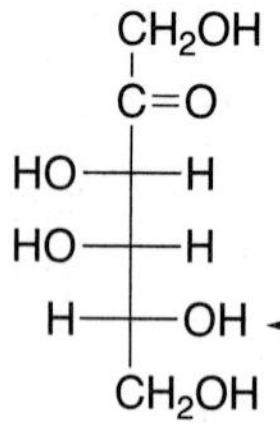
farthest away C, OH on right = D sugar

D-tagatose

[1]
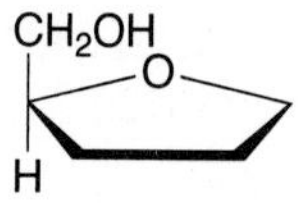
D sugar, CH_2OH is drawn up.

[2]
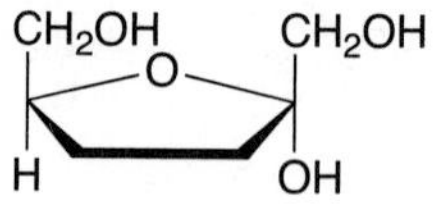
α anomer OH is down.

[3]
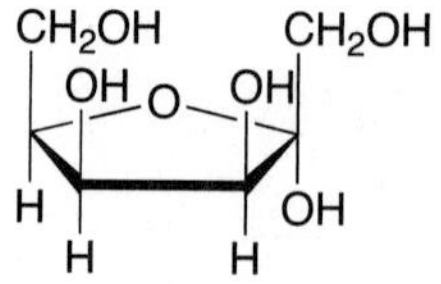

28.46

a.

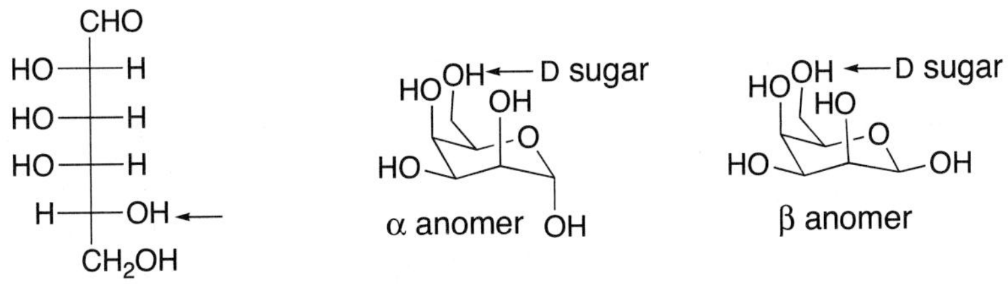
CHO
HO—H
HO—H
HO—H
H—OH
CH$_2$OH
D sugar
α anomer
D sugar
β anomer

farthest away C,
OH on right = D sugar

b.

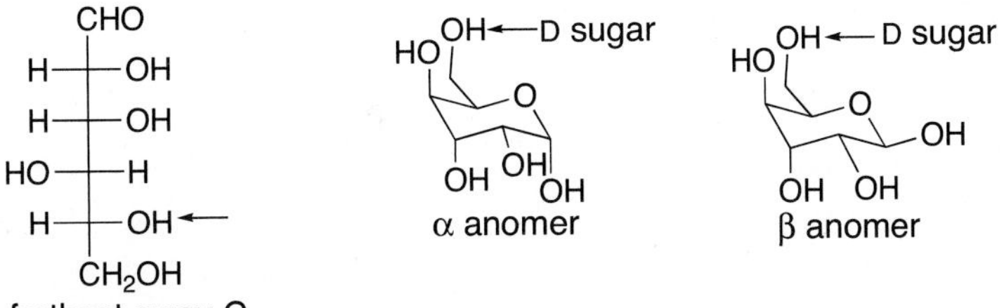
CHO
H—OH
H—OH
HO—H
H—OH
CH$_2$OH
D sugar
α anomer
D sugar
β anomer

farthest away C,
OH on right = D sugar

c.

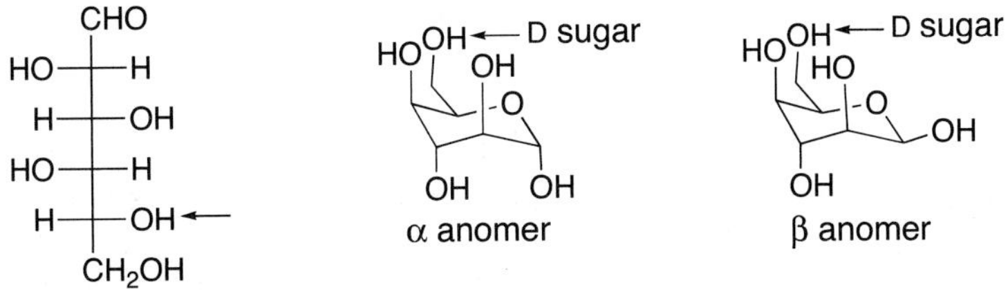
CHO
HO—H
H—OH
HO—H
H—OH
CH$_2$OH
D sugar
α anomer
D sugar
β anomer

farthest away C,
OH on right = D sugar

28.47 Use the directions from Answer 28.13.

a.

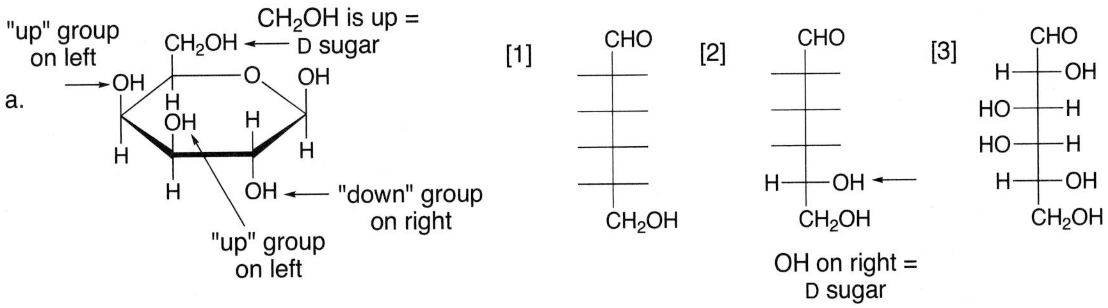
"up" group on left
CH$_2$OH is up = D sugar
"down" group on right
"up" group on left
[1]
[2]
OH on right = D sugar
[3]
CHO
H—OH
HO—H
HO—H
H—OH
CH$_2$OH

b.

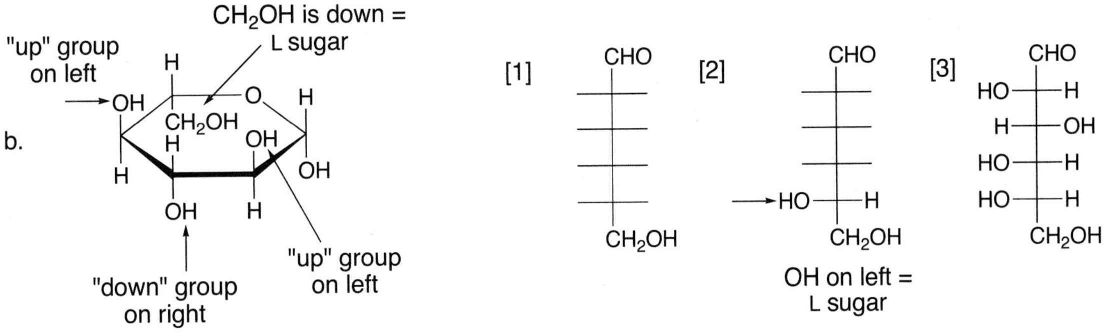
"up" group on left
CH$_2$OH is down = L sugar
"down" group on right
"up" group on left
[1]
[2]
OH on left = L sugar
[3]
CHO
HO—H
H—OH
HO—H
HO—H
CH$_2$OH

c. 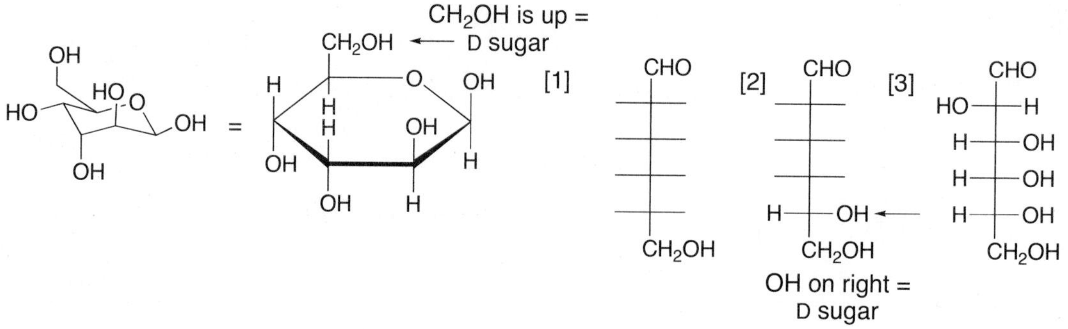
CH2OH is up =
D sugar
[1]
[2]
[3]
OH on right =
D sugar

d. 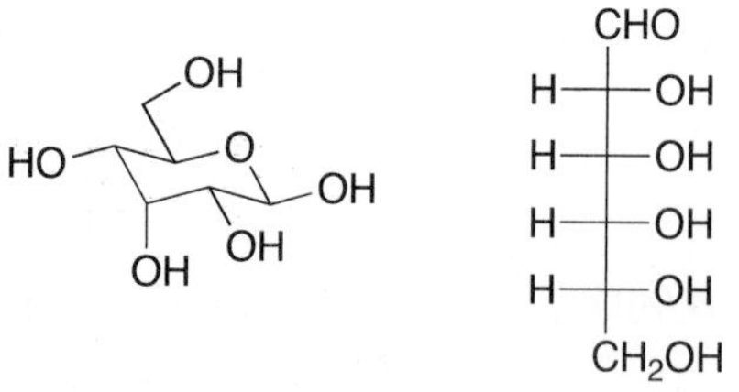

e. 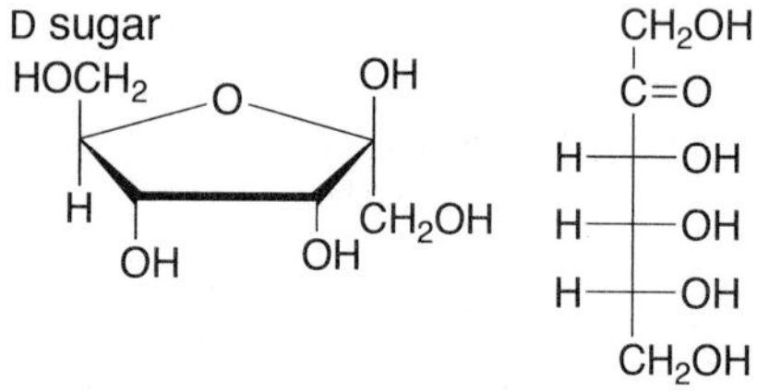
D sugar

f. 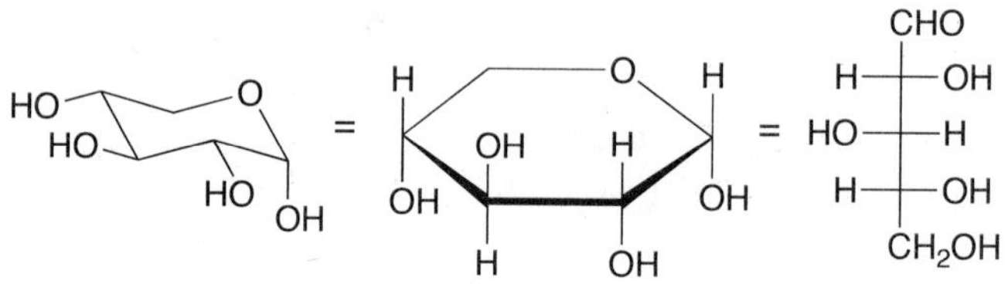

28.48

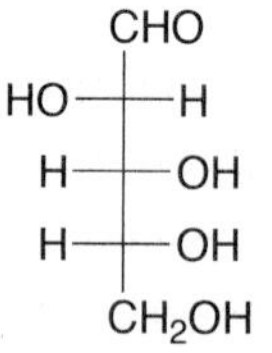

D-arabinose

a. 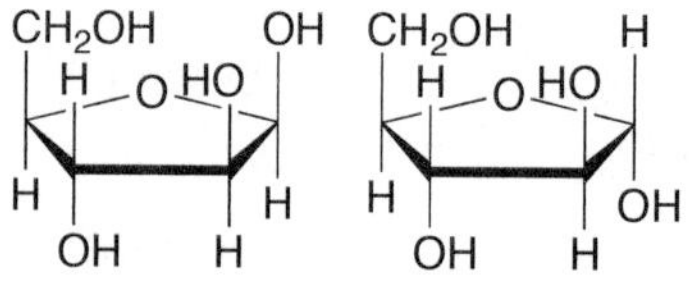

β anomer α anomer

b. 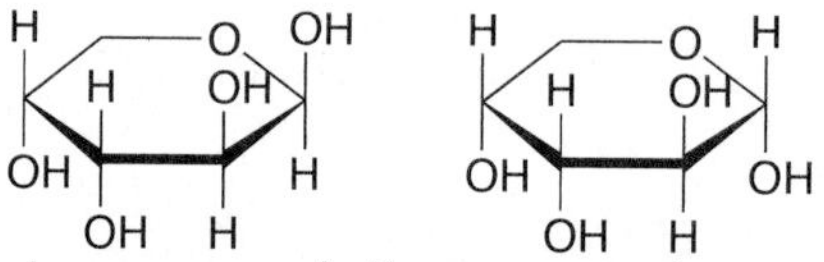

two anomers in the pyranose form

28.49

Two anomers of D-idose, as well as two conformations of each anomer:

α anomer 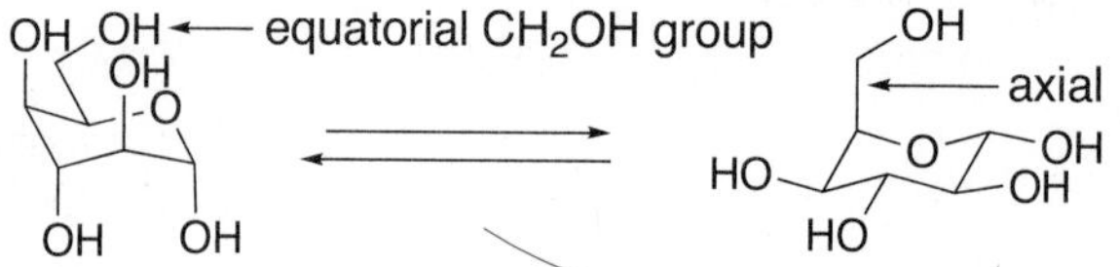
equatorial CH2OH group
axial

4 axial substituents

4 equatorial OH groups

More stable conformation for the α anomer—the CH_2OH is axial, but all other groups are equatorial.

β anomer 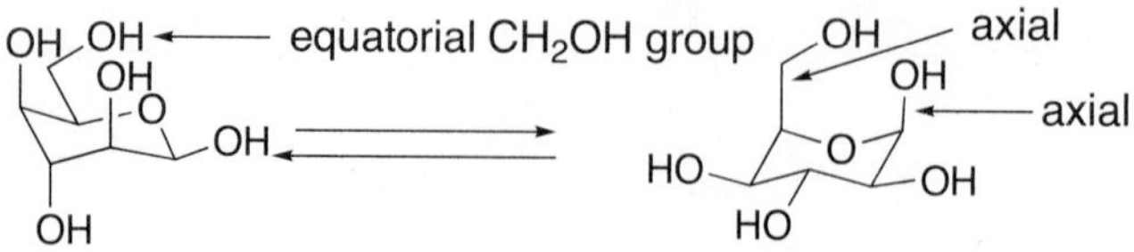
equatorial CH2OH group
axial
axial

3 axial substituents

3 equatorial OH groups

The more stable conformation for the β anomer—the CH_2OH is axial, as is the anomeric OH, but three other OH groups are equatorial.

28.50

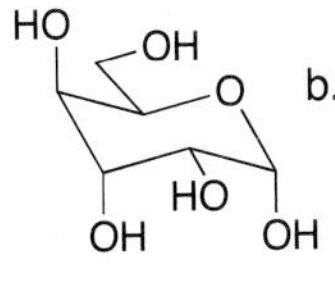

D-gulose

a. CH_3I, Ag_2O

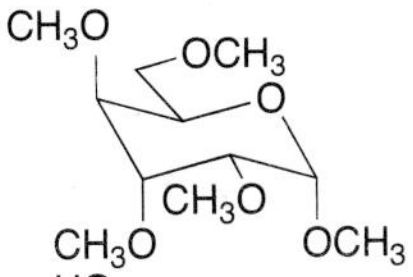

b. CH_3OH, HCl

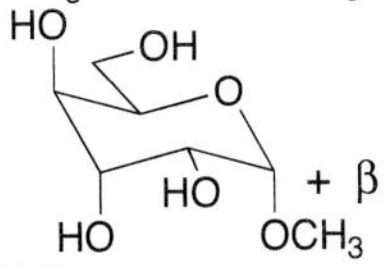

+ β anomer

c. $C_6H_5CH_2Cl$, Ag_2O

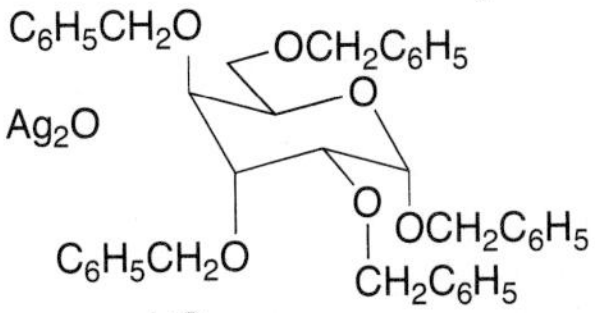

d. $C_6H_5CH_2OH$, HCl

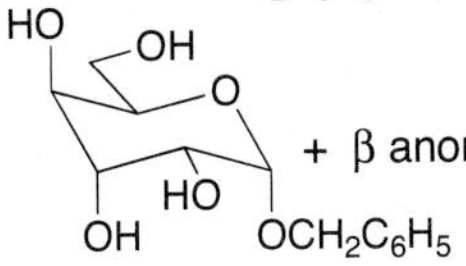

+ β anomer

e. Ac_2O, pyridine

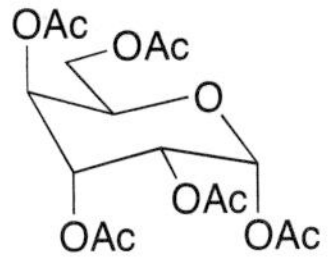

f. C_6H_5COCl, pyridine

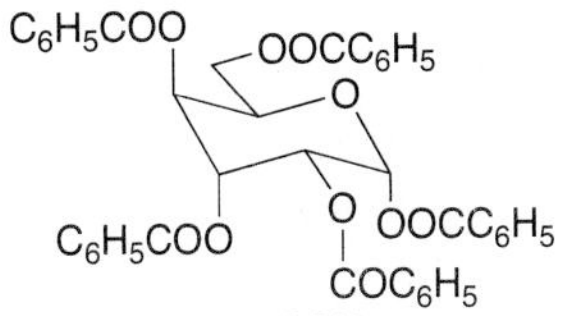

g. The product in (a), then H_3O^+

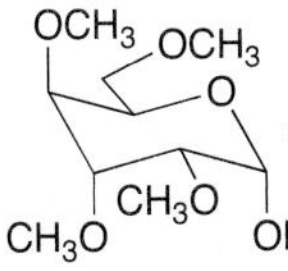

+ β anomer

h. The product in (b), then Ac_2O, pyridine

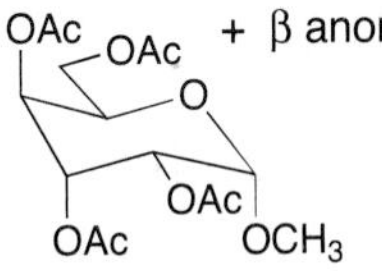

+ β anomer

i. The product in (g), then $C_6H_5CH_2Cl$, Ag_2O

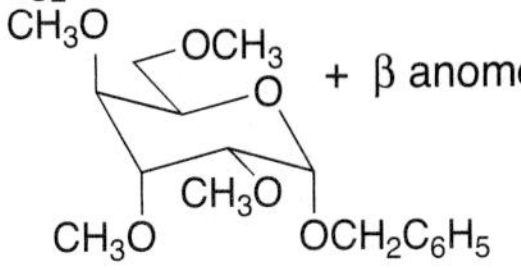

+ β anomer

j. The product in (d), then CH_3I, Ag_2O

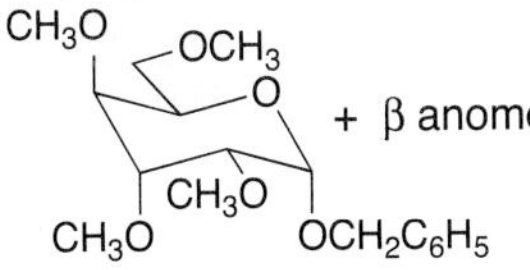

+ β anomer

28.51

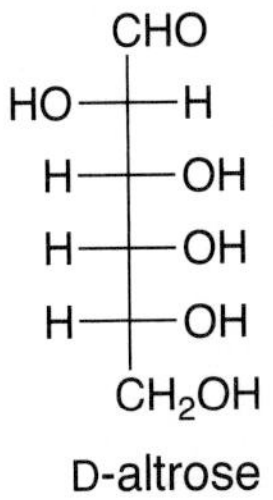

D-altrose

a. CH_3OH, HCl

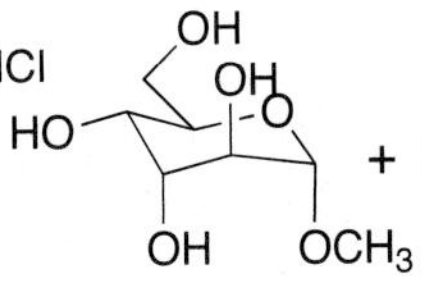

+ β anomer

b. $(CH_3)_2CHOH$, HCl

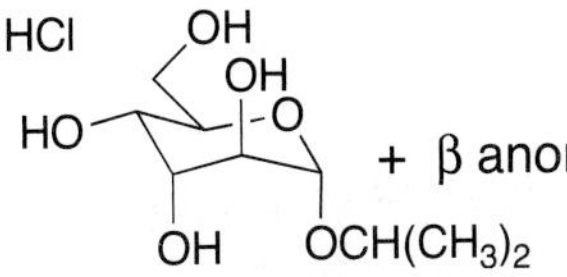

+ β anomer

c. $NaBH_4$, CH_3OH

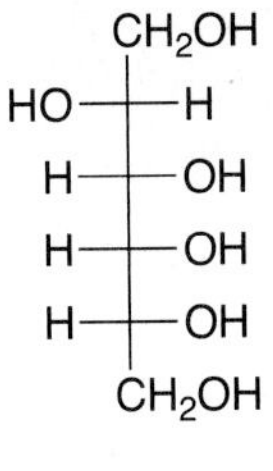

d. Br_2, H_2O

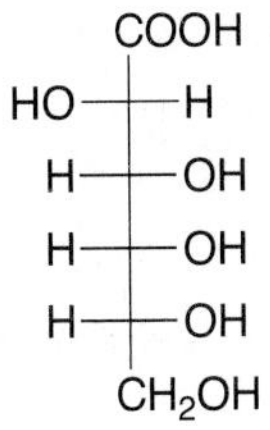

e. HNO_3, H_2O

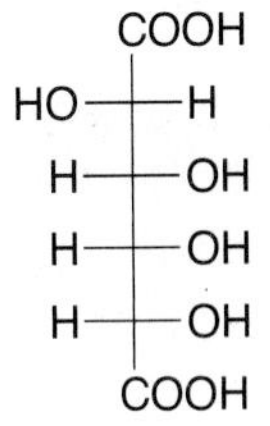

f. [1] NH_2OH
[2] $(CH_3CO)_2O$, $NaOCOCH_3$
[3] $NaOCH_3$

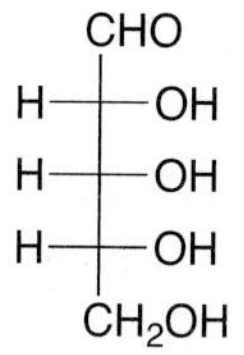

h. CH_3I, Ag_2O

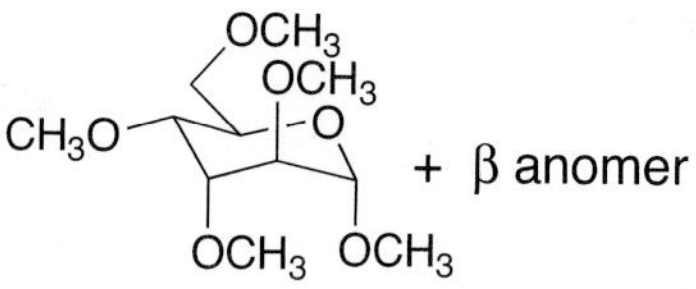
+ β anomer

g. [1] NaCN, HCl
[2] H_2, Pd-$BaSO_4$
[3] H_3O^+

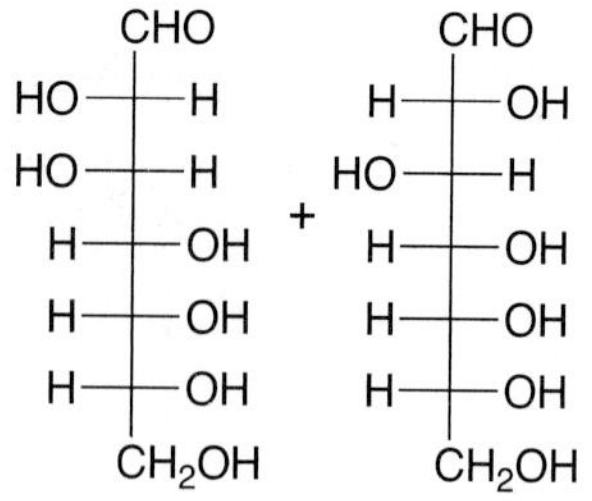

i. Ac_2O, pyridine

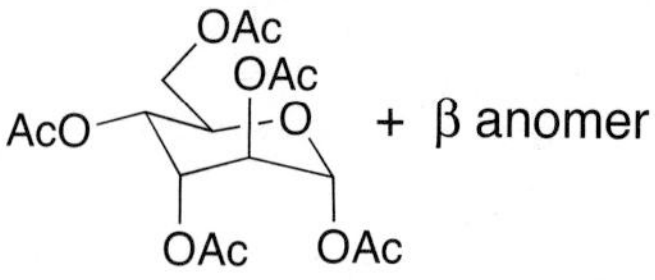
+ β anomer

j. $C_6H_5CH_2NH_2$, mild H^+

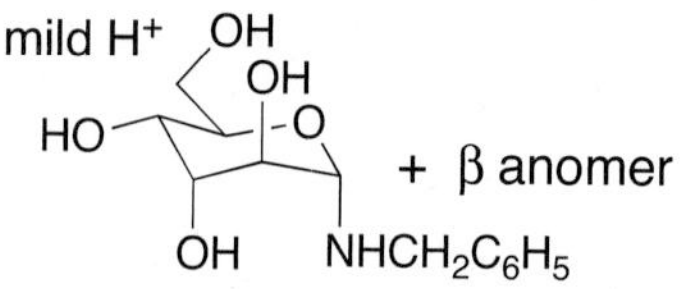
+ β anomer

28.52

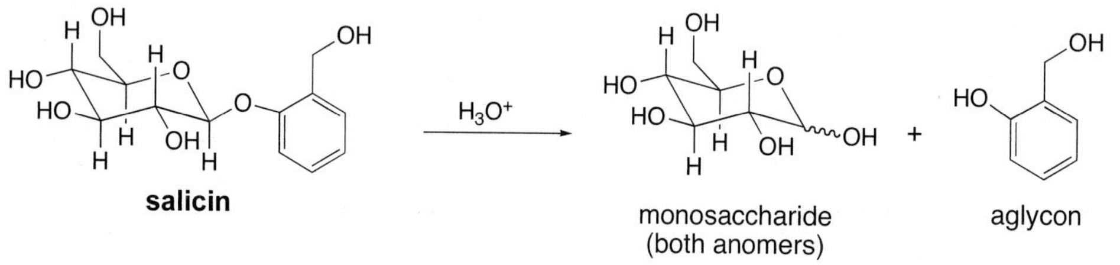
H3O+
salicin
monosaccharide
(both anomers)
aglycon

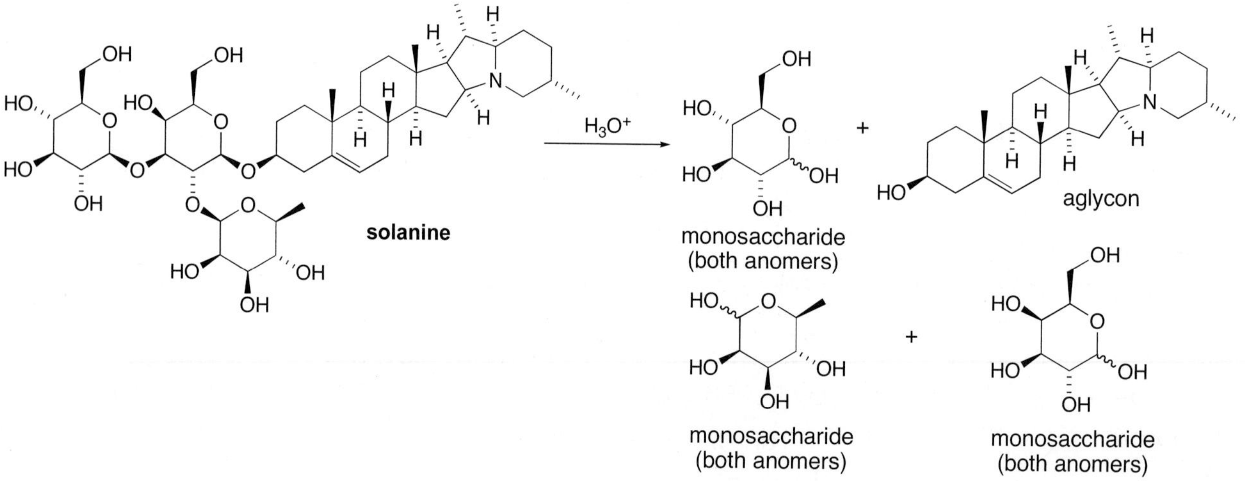
solanine
H3O+
monosaccharide
(both anomers)
aglycon
monosaccharide
(both anomers)
monosaccharide
(both anomers)

28.53

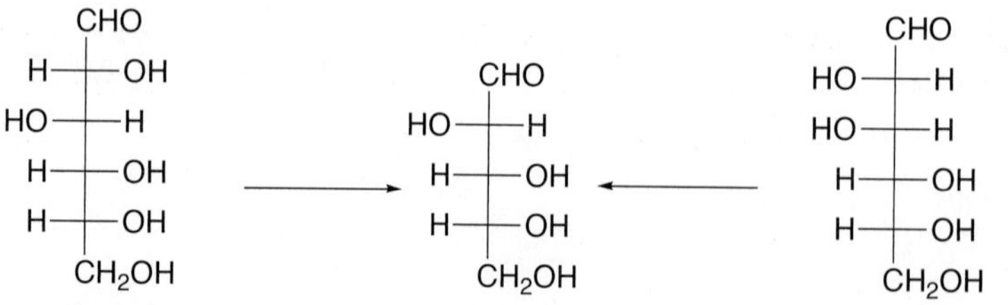

D-glucose D-arabinose D-mannose

28.54

a.

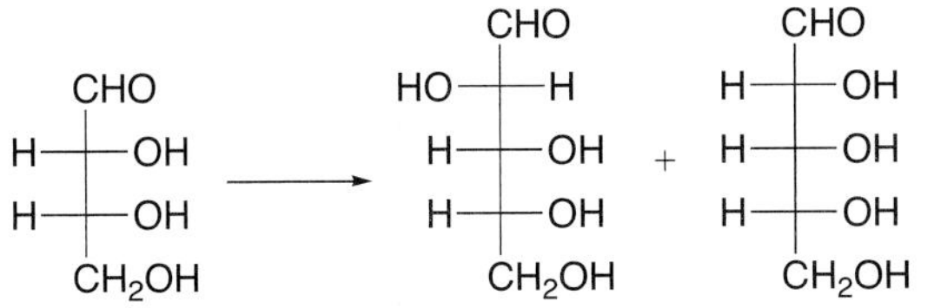

b.

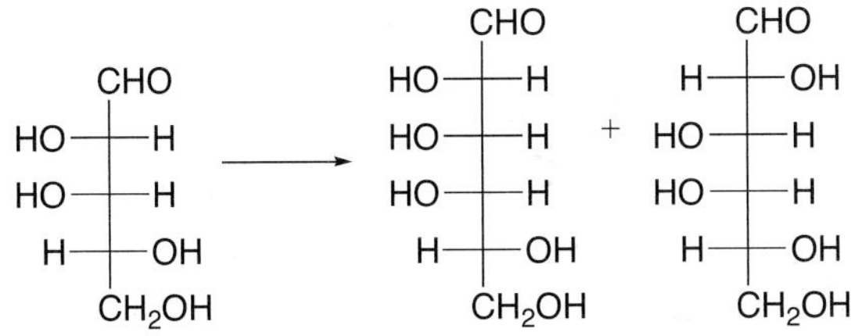

c.

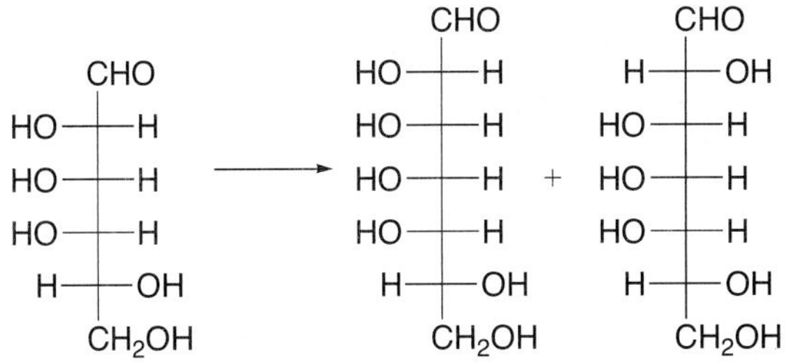

28.55

a.

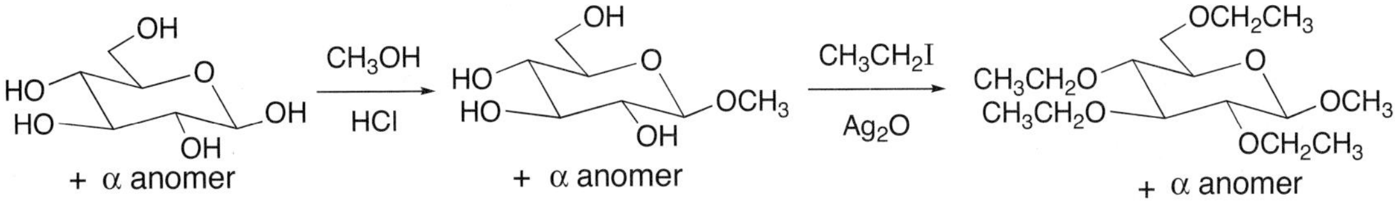

b.

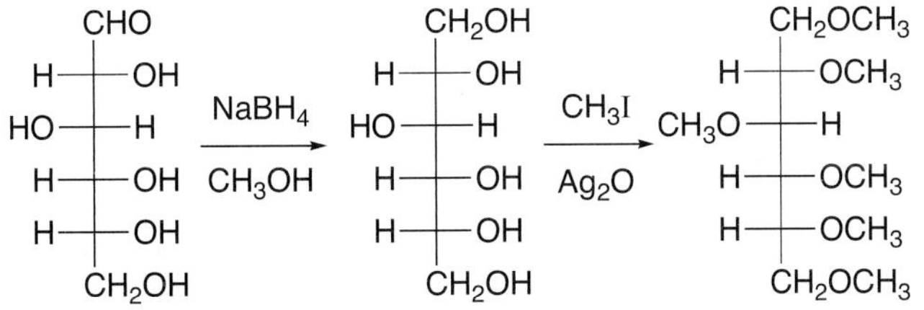

c.

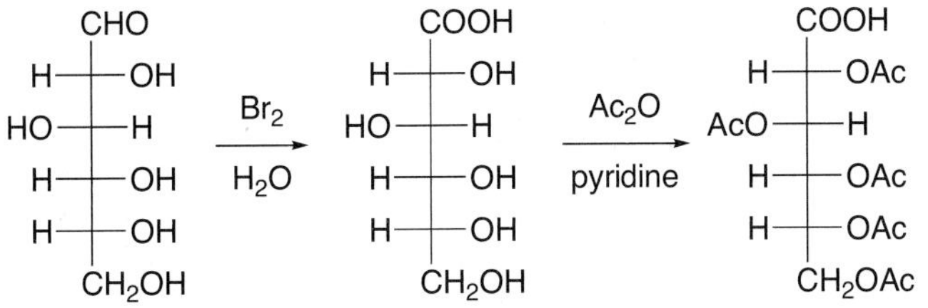

28.56 Molecules with a plane of symmetry are optically inactive.

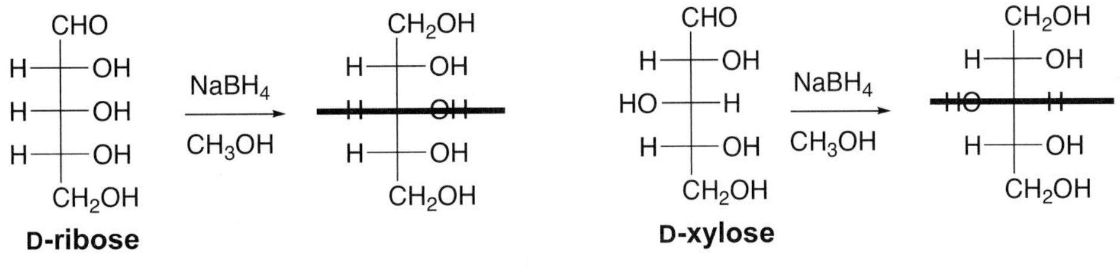

28.57

a.

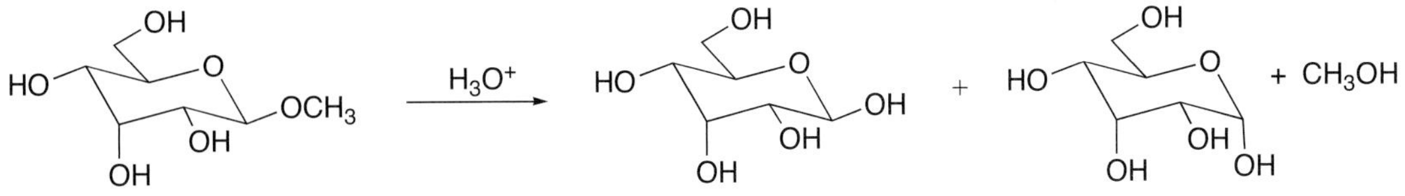

b.

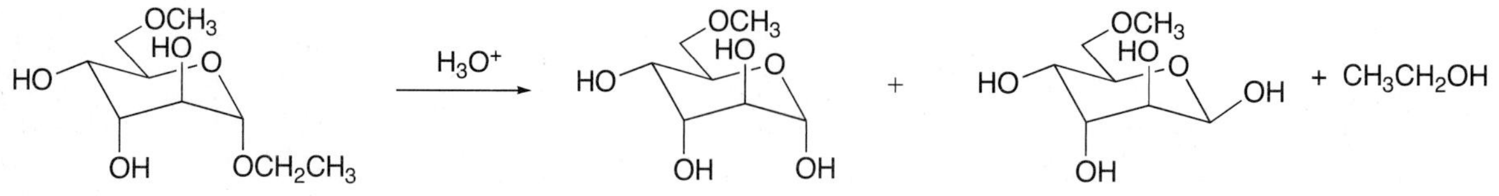
H_3O^+
+ CH_3CH_2OH

c.

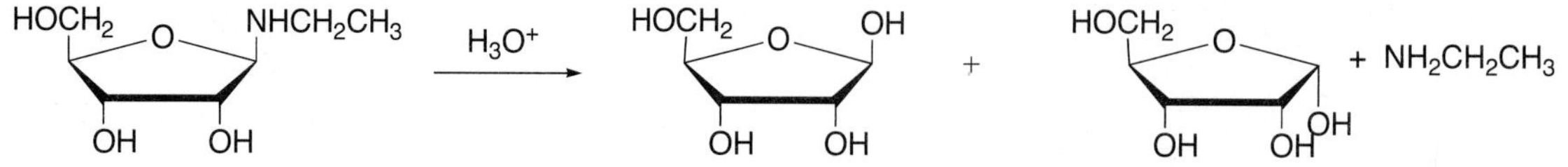
H_3O^+
+ $NH_2CH_2CH_3$

28.58

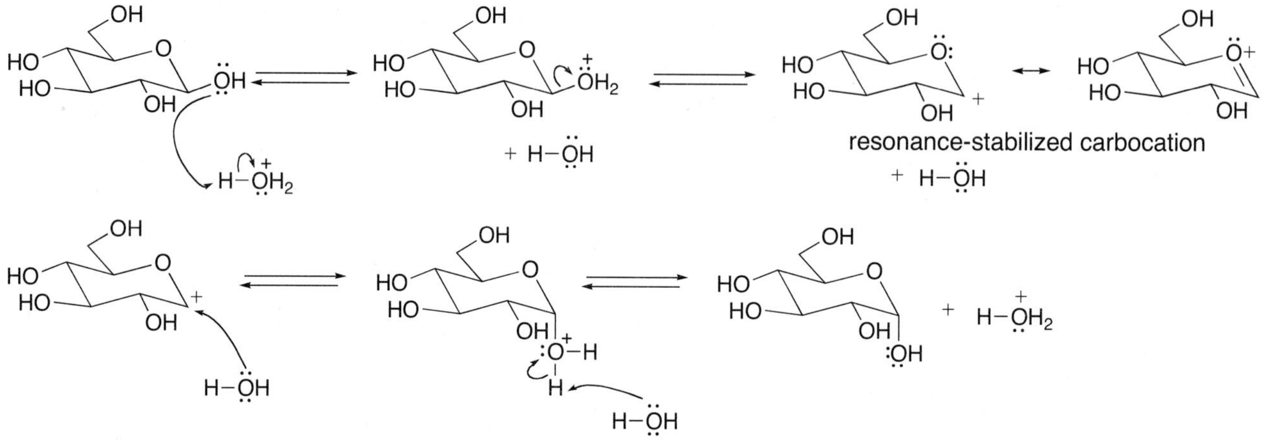
resonance-stabilized carbocation

28.59

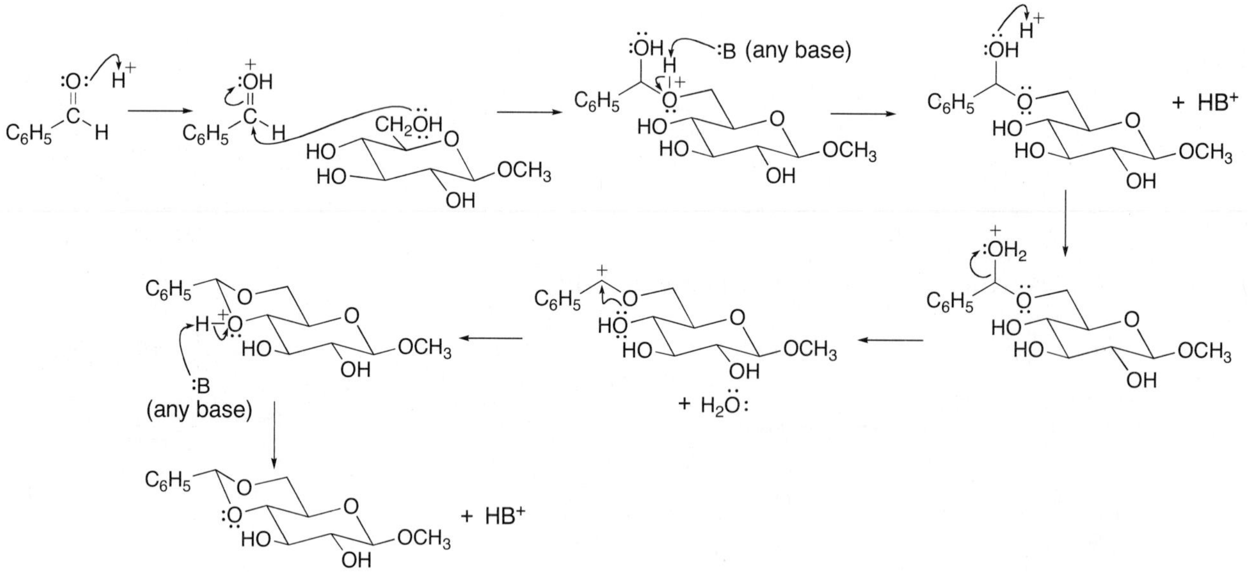
:B (any base)
+ HB^+
(any base)

28.60

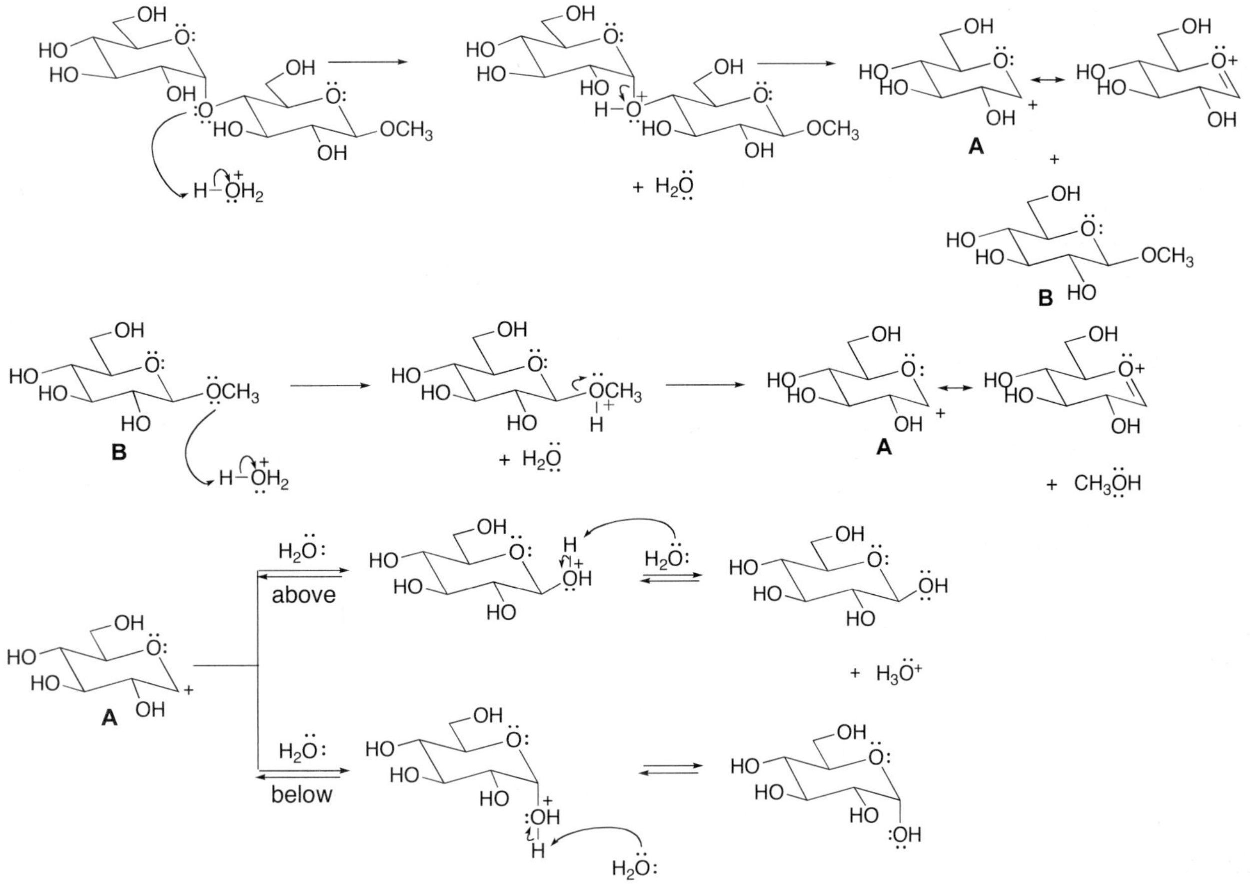

28.61

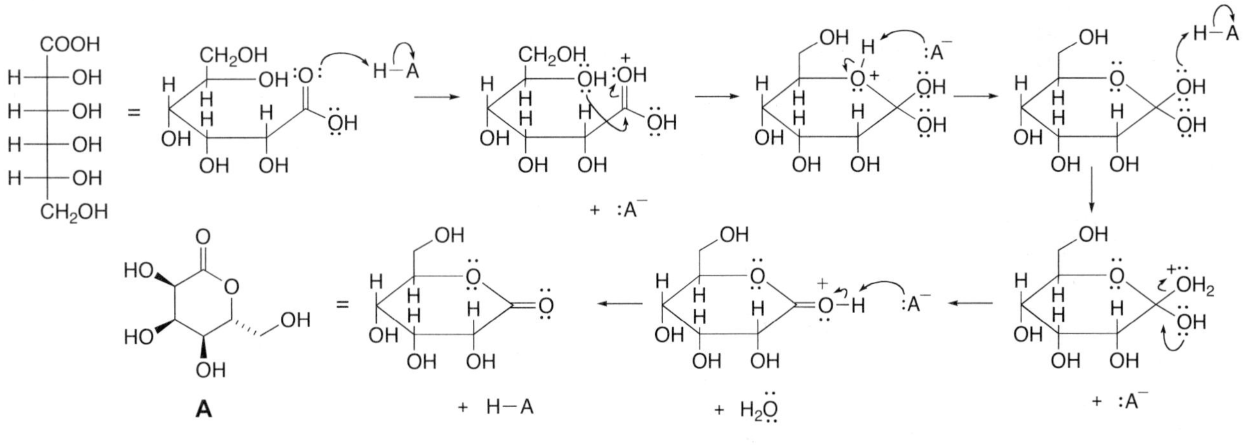

28.62

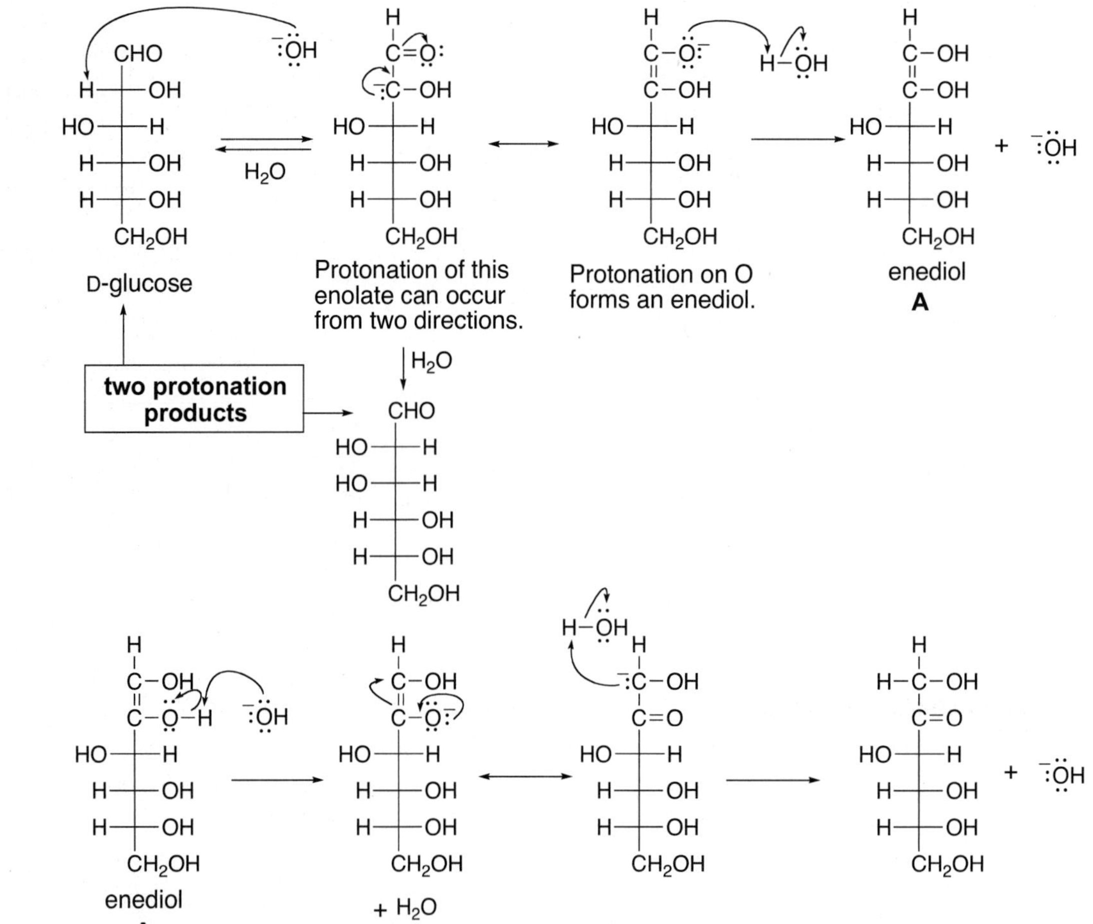

Deprotonation of the OH at C2 of the enediol forms a new enolate that goes on to form the ketohexose.

28.63

Two D-aldopentoses (**A**' and **A**") yield optically active aldaric acids when oxidized.

Optically active D-aldaric acids:

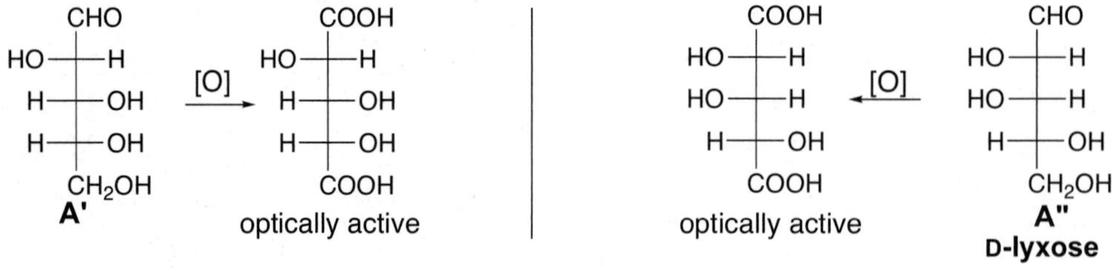

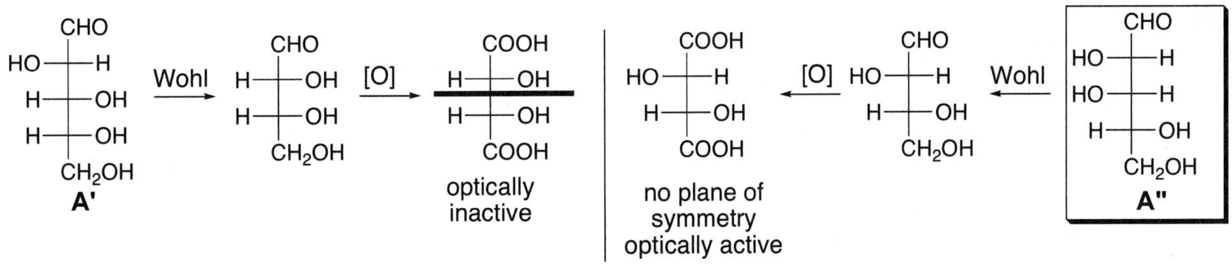

Only **A''** undergoes Wohl degradation to an aldotetrose that is oxidized to an optically active aldaric acid, so **A''** is the structure of the D-aldopentose in question.

28.64

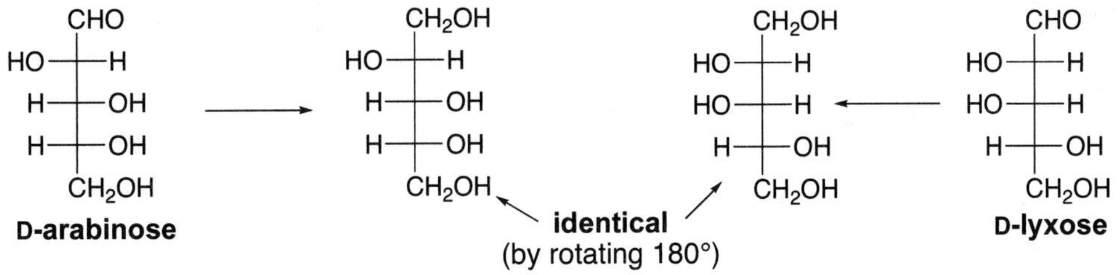

28.65

Only two D-aldopentoses (**A'** and **A''**) yield optically inactive aldaric acids (**B'** and **B''**).

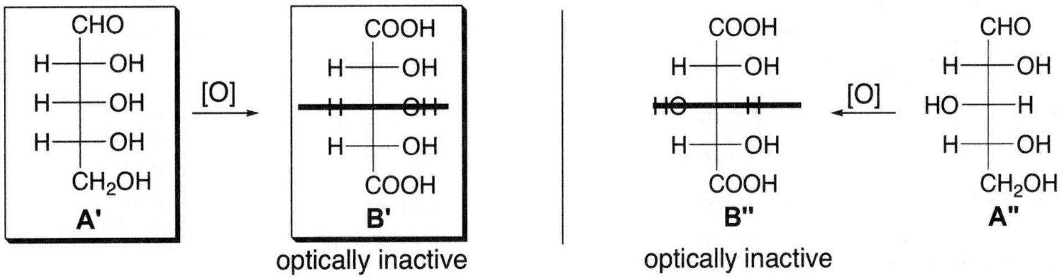

Product of Kiliani–Fischer synthesis:

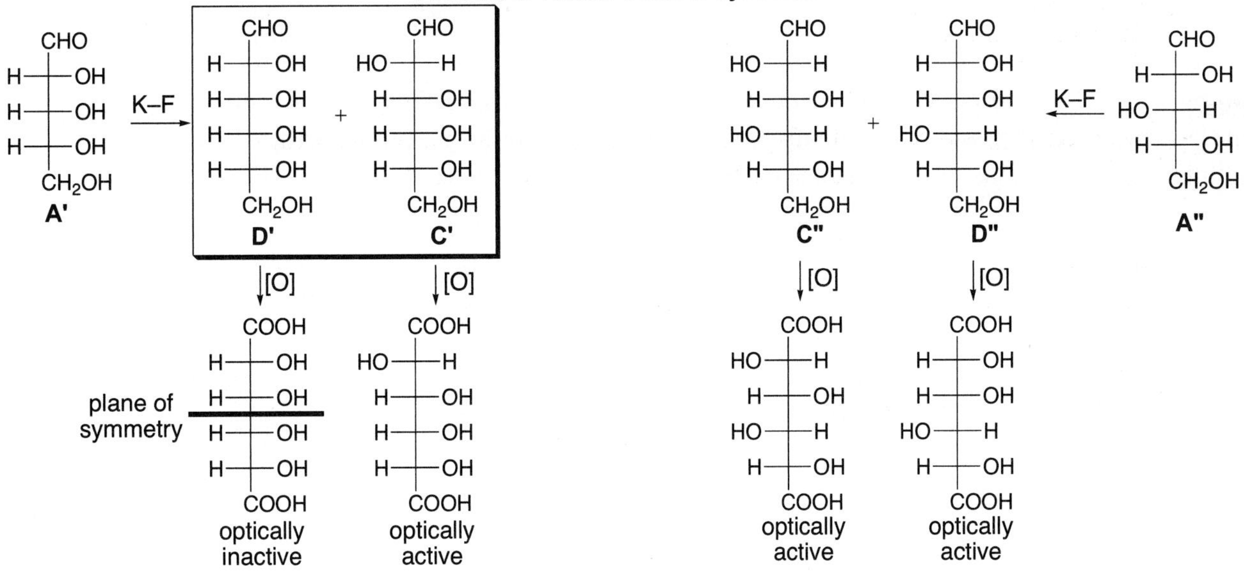

Only **A'** fits the criteria. Kiliani–Fischer synthesis of **A'** forms **C'** and **D'**, which are oxidized to one optically active and one optically inactive aldaric acid. A similar procedure with **A''** forms two optically active aldaric acids. Thus, the structures of **A–D** correspond to the structures of **A'–D'**.

28.66

Only two D-aldopentoses (**A'** and **A''**) are reduced to optically active alditols.

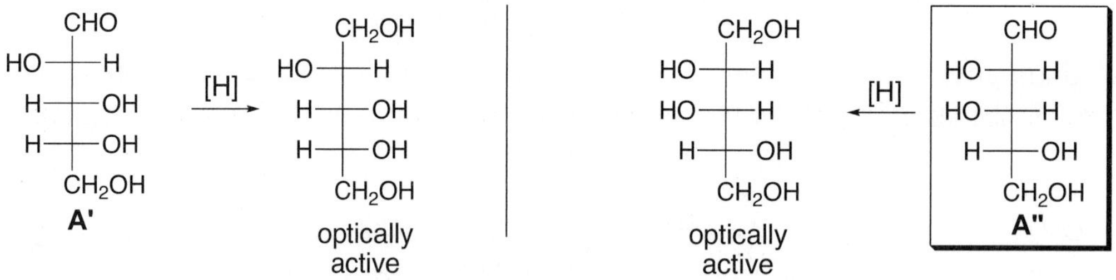

Product of Kiliani–Fischer synthesis:

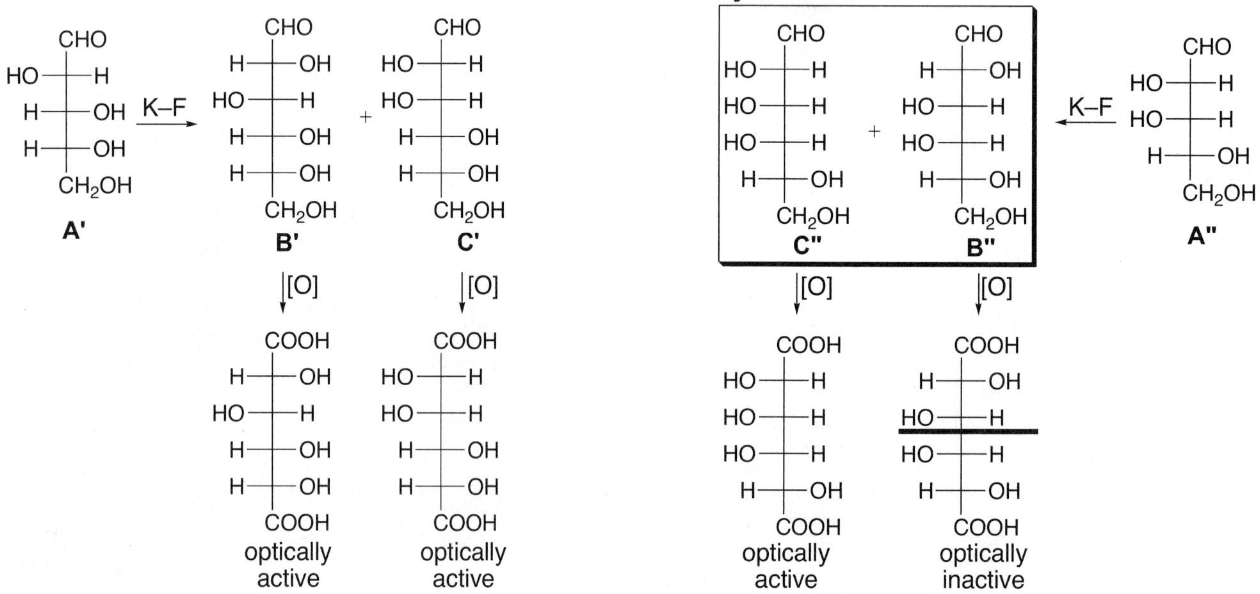

Only **A''** fits the criteria. Kiliani–Fischer synthesis of **A''** forms **B''** and **C''**, which are oxidized to one optically inactive and one optically active diacid. A similar procedure with **A'** forms two optically active diacids. Thus, the structures of **A–C** correspond to **A''–C''**.

28.67

D-gulose

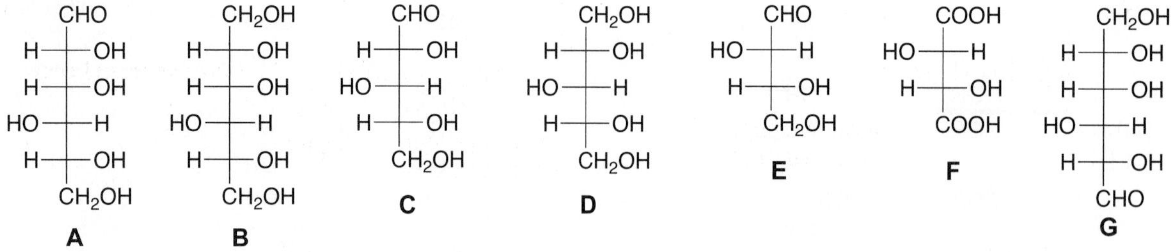

28.68 A disaccharide formed from two galactose units in a 1→4-β-glycosidic linkage:

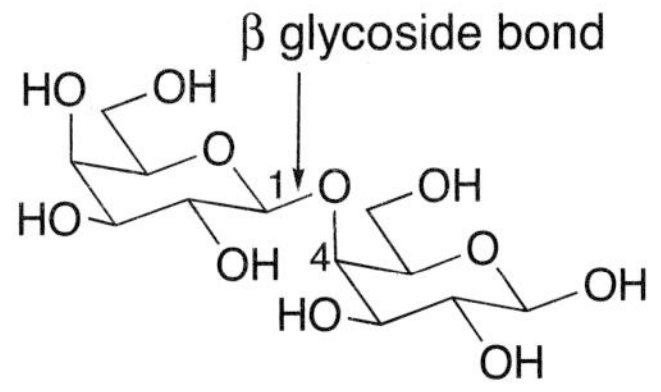
β glycoside bond

28.69 A disaccharide formed from two mannose units in a 1→4-α-glycosidic linkage:

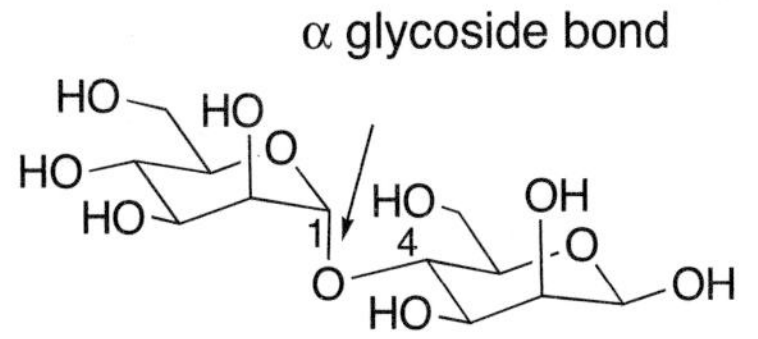
α glycoside bond

28.70

a.

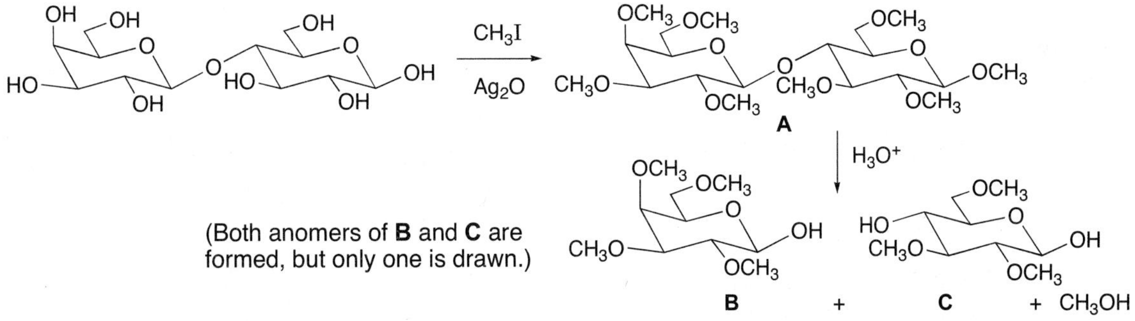
CH_3I
Ag_2O
A
H_3O^+
(Both anomers of **B** and **C** are formed, but only one is drawn.)
B + C + CH_3OH

b.

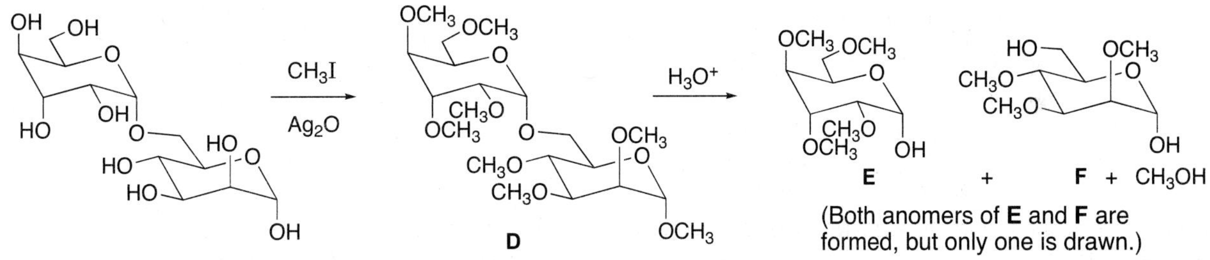
CH_3I
Ag_2O
D
H_3O^+
E + F + CH_3OH
(Both anomers of **E** and **F** are formed, but only one is drawn.)

28.71

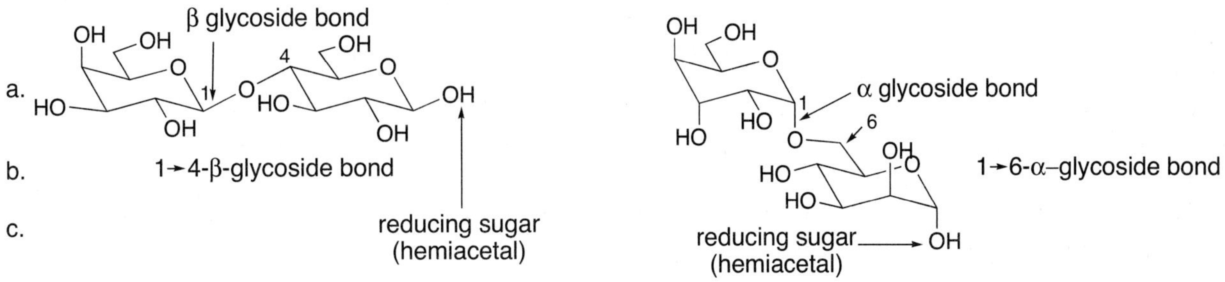
a.
β glycoside bond
b.
1→4-β-glycoside bond
c.
reducing sugar (hemiacetal)
α glycoside bond
1→6-α–glycoside bond
reducing sugar (hemiacetal)

28.72

a, b.

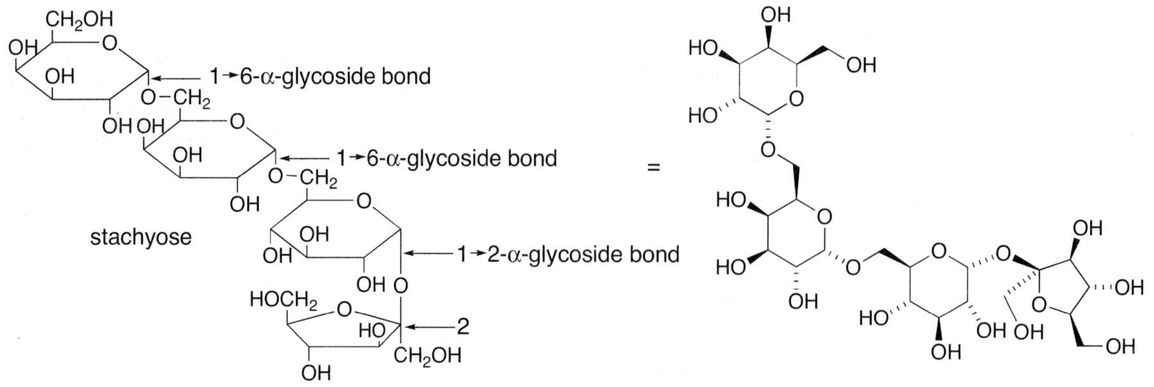
1→6-α-glycoside bond
1→6-α-glycoside bond
1→2-α-glycoside bond
stachyose
2
=

c.

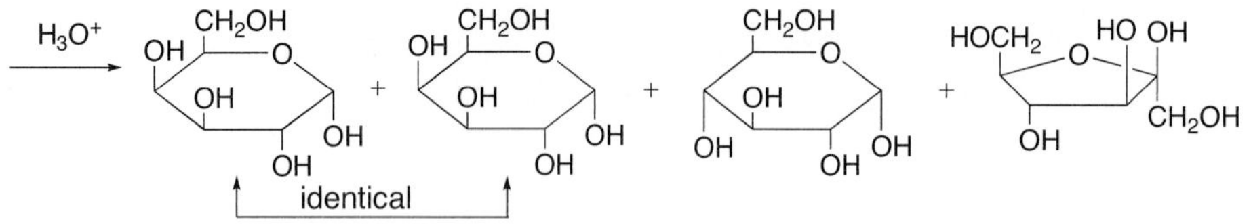
H3O+
identical

Two anomers of each monosaccharide are formed, but only one anomer is drawn.

d. Stachyose is not a reducing sugar since it contains no hemiacetal.

e.

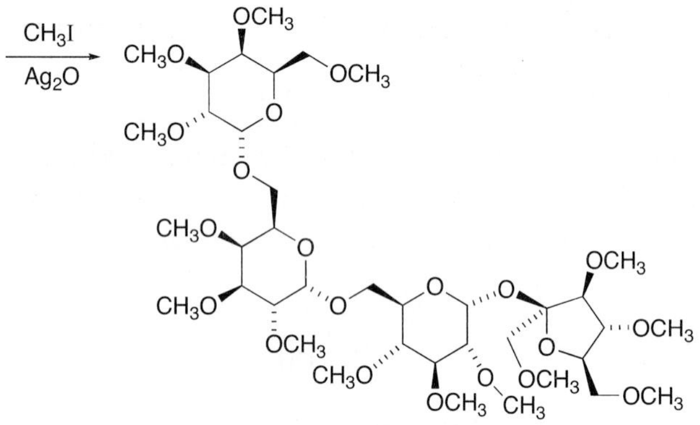
CH3I
Ag2O

f.

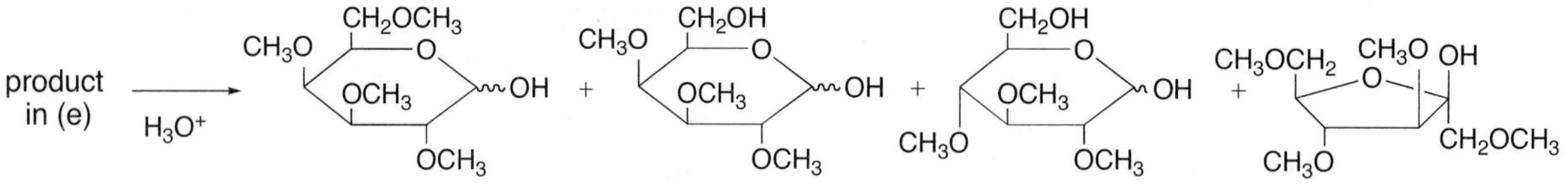
product in (e)
H3O+

Two anomers of each monosaccharide are formed.

28.73

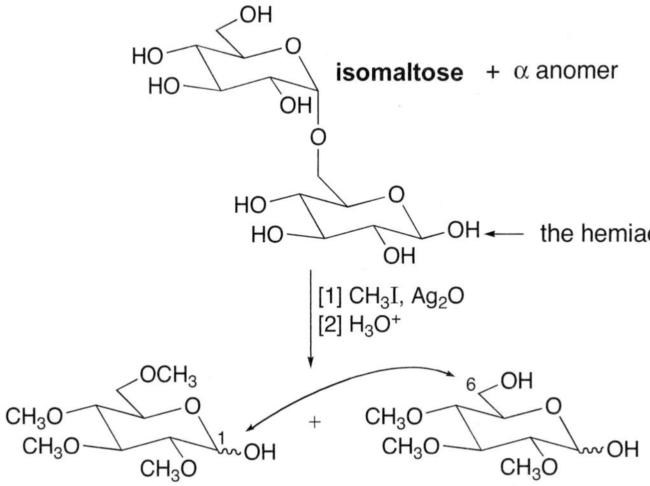
isomaltose
+ α anomer
[1] CH3I, Ag2O
[2] H3O+

Isomaltose must be composed of two glucose units in an α-glycosidic linkage. Since it is a reducing sugar it contains a hemiacetal. The free OH groups in the hydrolysis products show where the two monosaccharides are joined.

the hemiacetal

(Both anomers are present.)

28.74

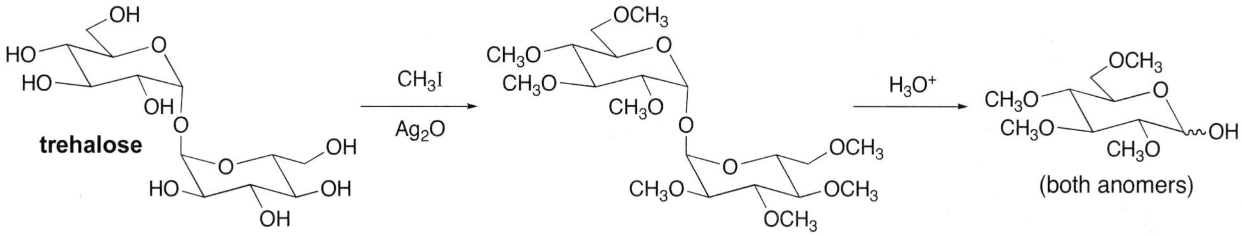
trehalose
CH3I
Ag2O
H3O+
(both anomers)

Trehalose must be composed of D-glucose units only, joined in an α-glycosidic linkage. Since trehalose is nonreducing it contains no hemiacetal. Since there is only one product formed after methylation and hydrolysis, the two anomeric C's must be joined.

28.75

a.

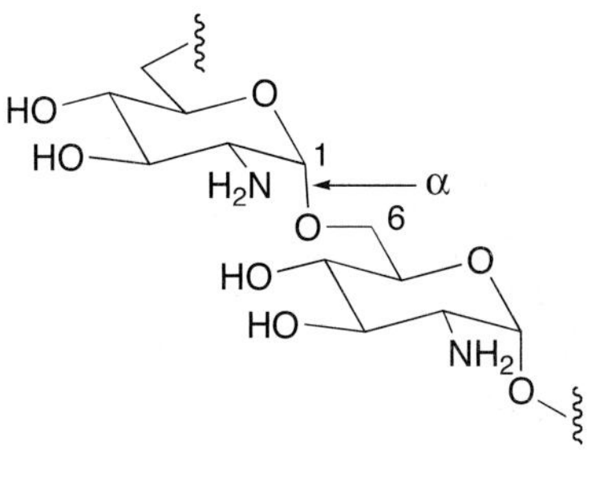
α

c.

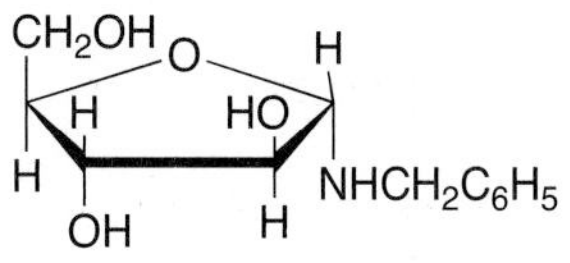

b.

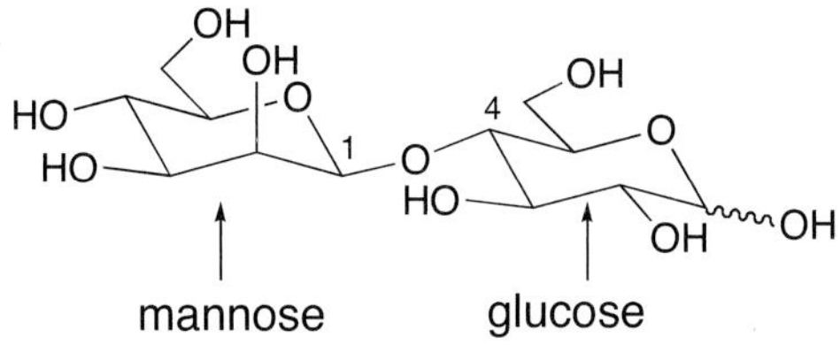
mannose
glucose

d.

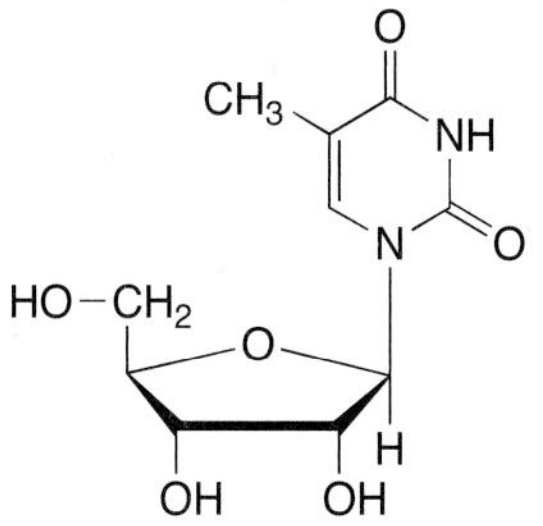

28.76

a.

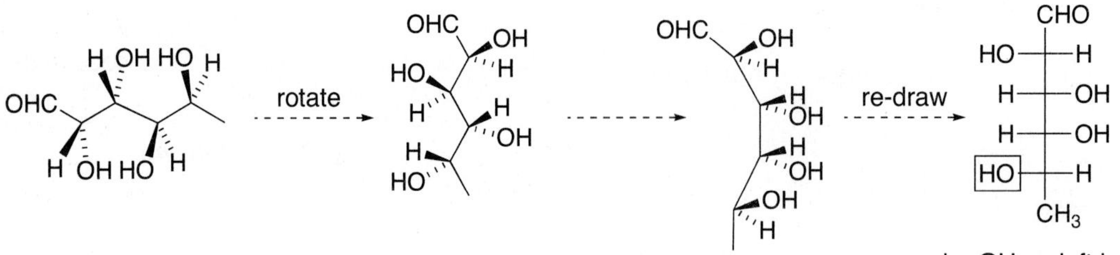

b. OH on left in Fischer
L-monosaccharide

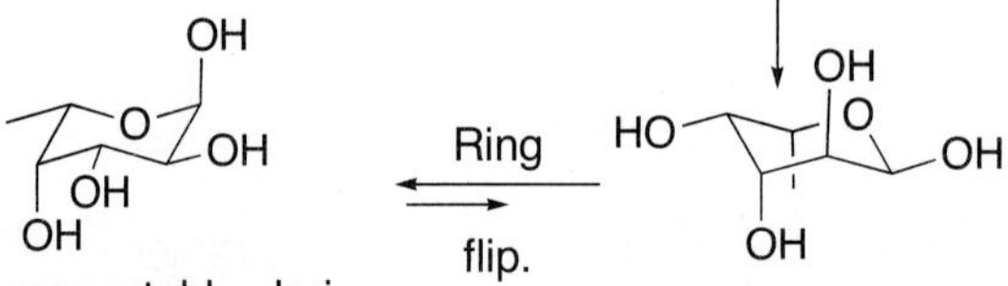

more stable chair

The α anomer has the CH_3 on C5 and the anomeric OH trans.

c. Fucose is unusual because it is an L-monosaccharide and it contains a CH_3 group rather than a CH_2OH group on its terminal carbon.

28.77

a.

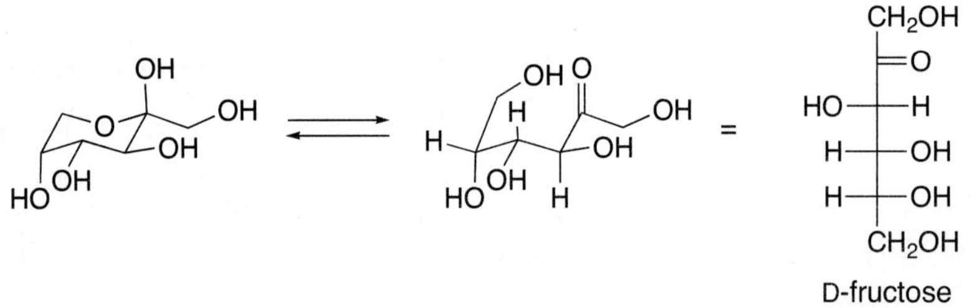

D-fructose

b.

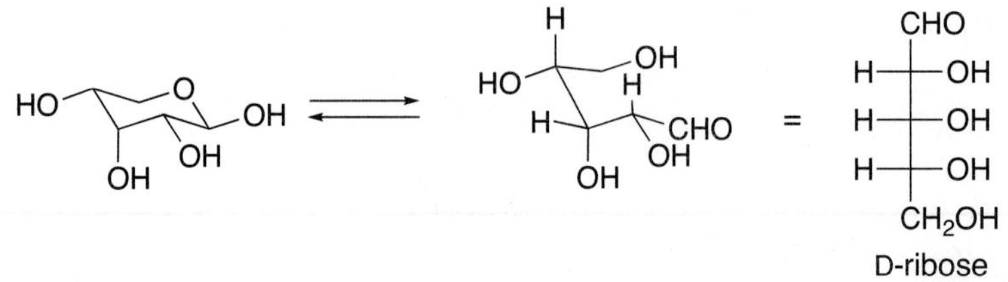

D-ribose

c.

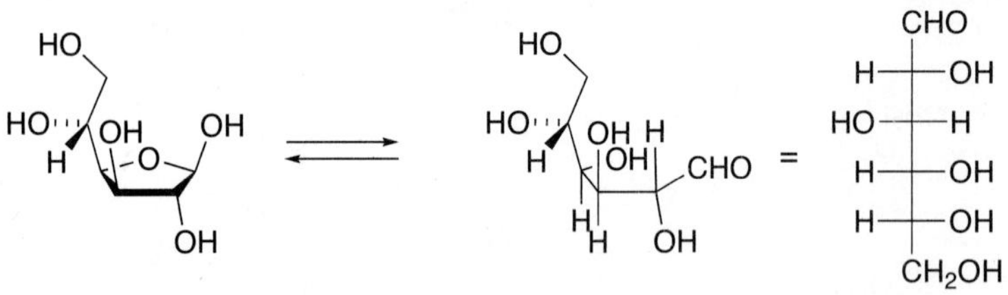

D-glucose

d.

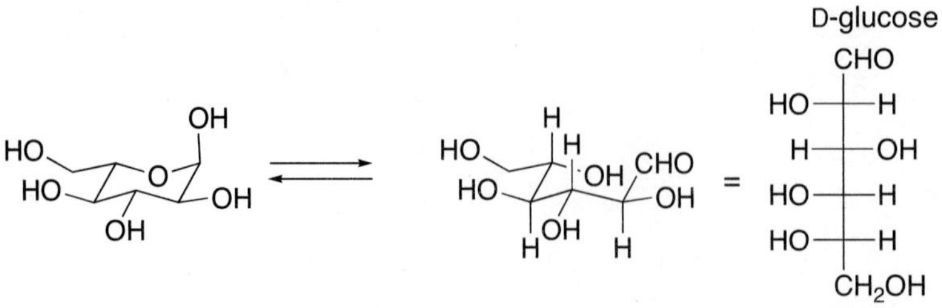

L-glucose

28.78

Ignoring stereochemistry along the way:

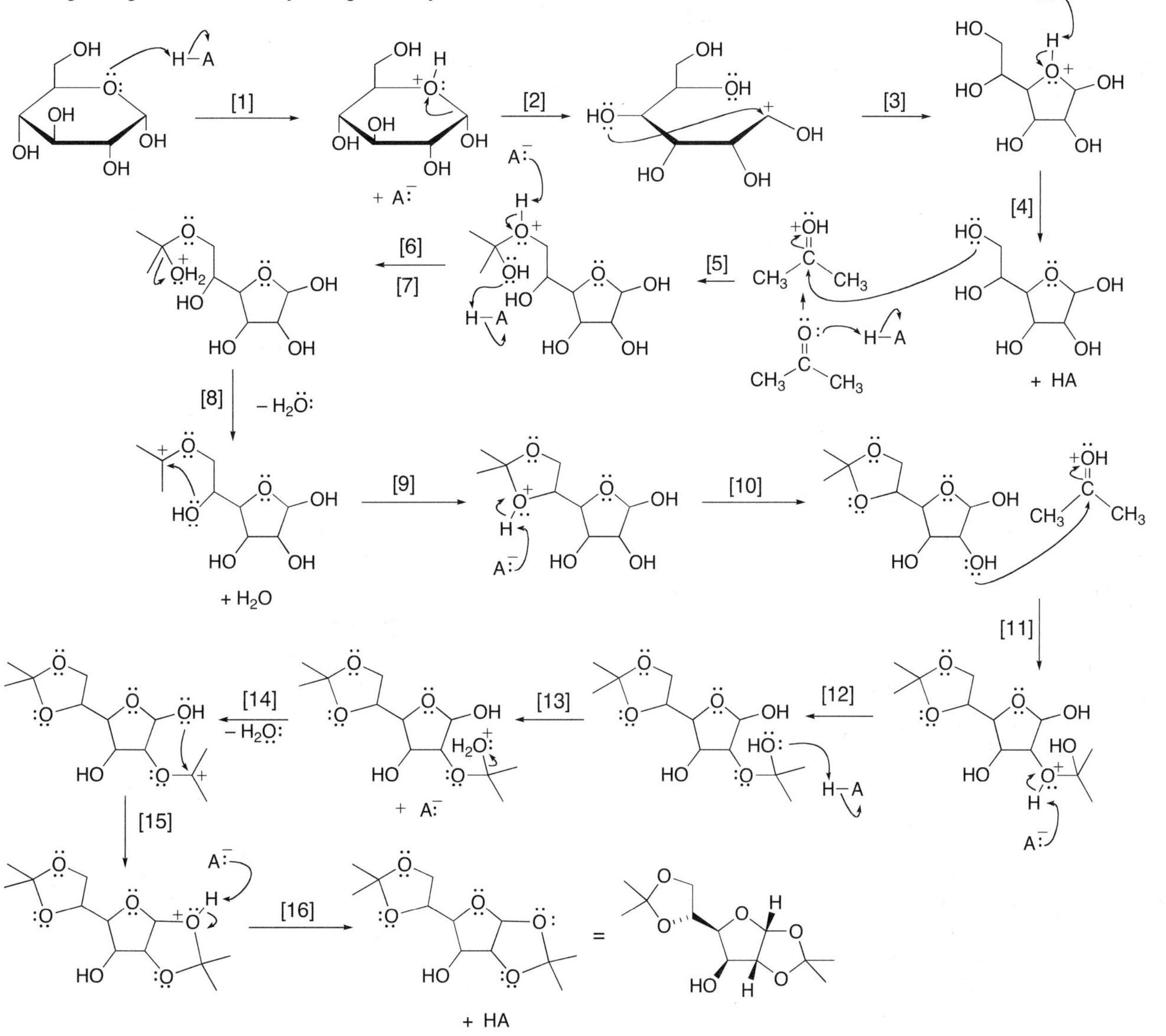

28.79 The hydrolysis data suggest that the trisaccharide has D-galactose on one end and D-fructose on the other. D-Galactose must be joined to its adjacent sugar by a β-glycosidic linkage. D-Fructose must be joined to its adjacent sugar by an α-glycosidic linkage.

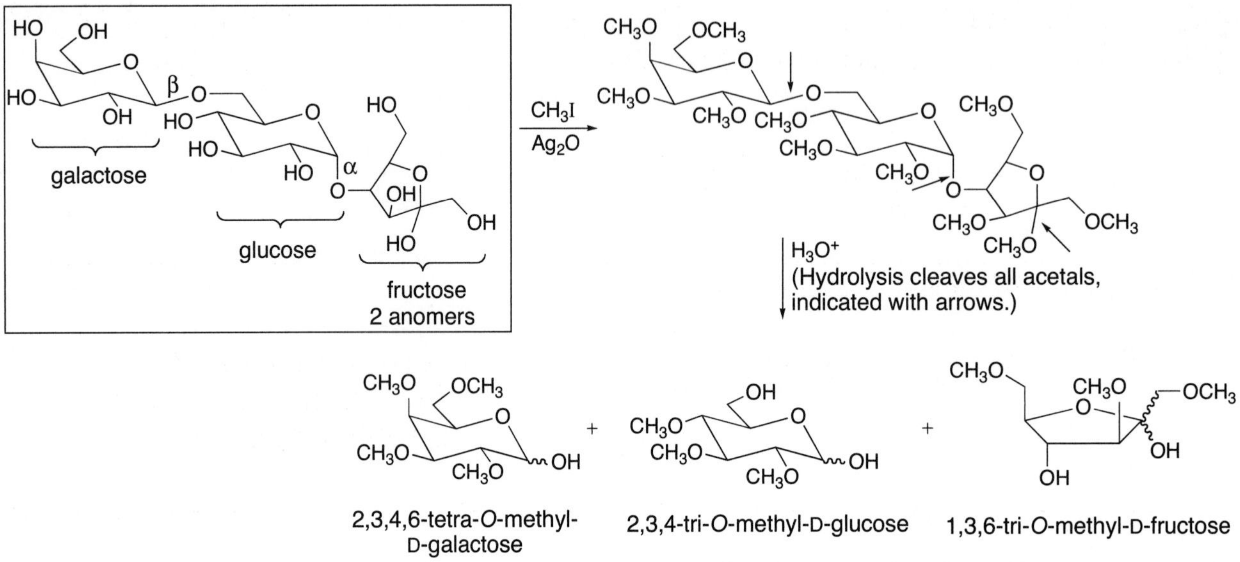
galactose
glucose
fructose
2 anomers
CH3I
Ag2O
H3O+
(Hydrolysis cleaves all acetals, indicated with arrows.)
2,3,4,6-tetra-O-methyl-D-galactose
2,3,4-tri-O-methyl-D-glucose
1,3,6-tri-O-methyl-D-fructose

(Both anomers of each compound are formed.)

Chapter 29 Amino Acids and Proteins

Chapter Review

Synthesis of amino acids (29.2)

[1] From α-halo carboxylic acids by S_N2 reaction

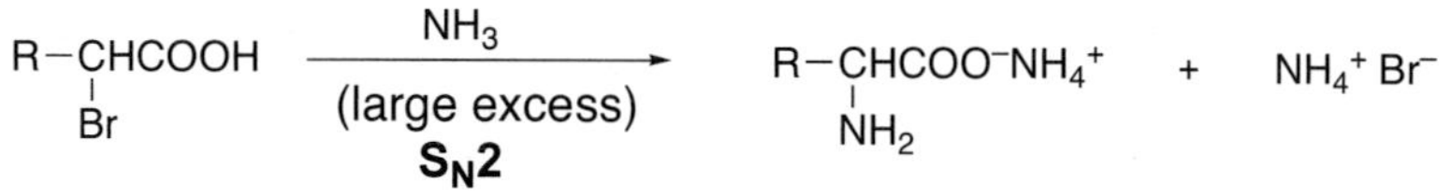
R–CHCOOH
Br
NH3
(large excess)
SN2
R–CHCOO⁻NH4⁺
NH2
+
NH4⁺ Br⁻

[2] By alkylation of diethyl acetamidomalonate

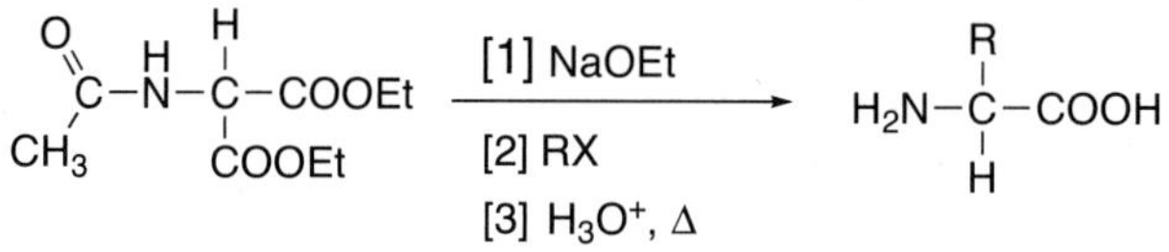
COOEt
CH3
[1] NaOEt
[2] RX
[3] H3O⁺, Δ
H2N–C–COOH

- Alkylation works best with unhindered alkyl halides—that is, with CH_3X and RCH_2X.

[3] Strecker synthesis

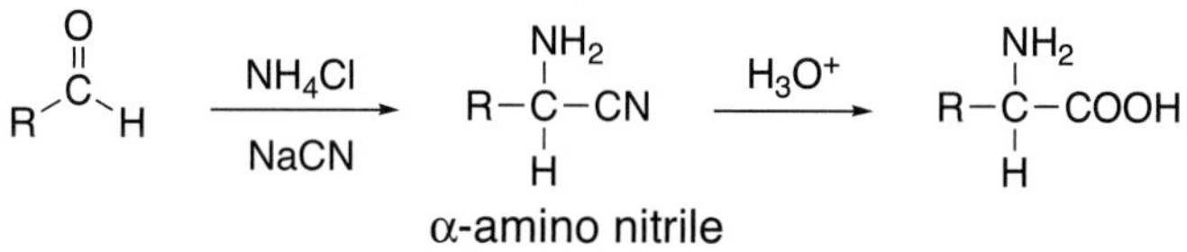
NH4Cl
NaCN
R–C–CN
H3O⁺
R–C–COOH
α-amino nitrile

Preparation of optically active amino acids

[1] Resolution of enantiomers by forming diastereomers (29.3A)

- Convert a racemic mixture of amino acids into a racemic mixture of *N*-acetyl amino acids [(*S*)- and (*R*)-$CH_3CONHCH(R)COOH$].
- React the enantiomers with a chiral amine to form a mixture of diastereomers.
- Separate the diastereomers.
- Regenerate the amino acids by protonation of the carboxylate salt and hydrolysis of the *N*-acetyl group.

[2] Kinetic resolution using enzymes (29.3B)

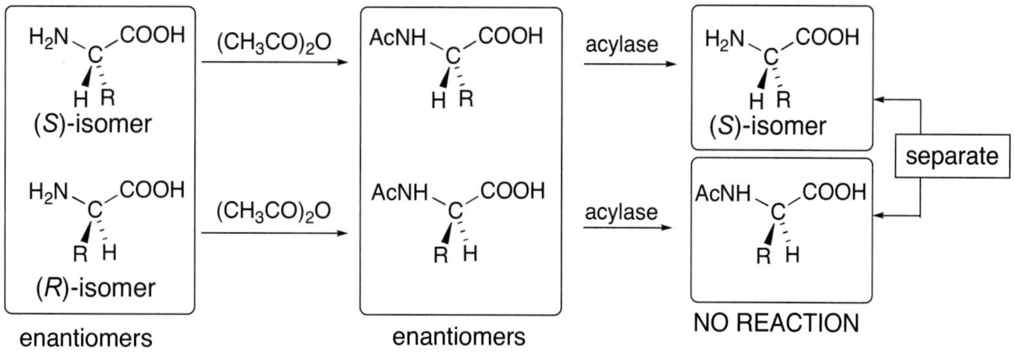
(S)-isomer
(R)-isomer
enantiomers
(CH3CO)2O
(CH3CO)2O
enantiomers
acylase
acylase
(S)-isomer
separate
NO REACTION

[3] By enantioselective hydrogenation (29.4)

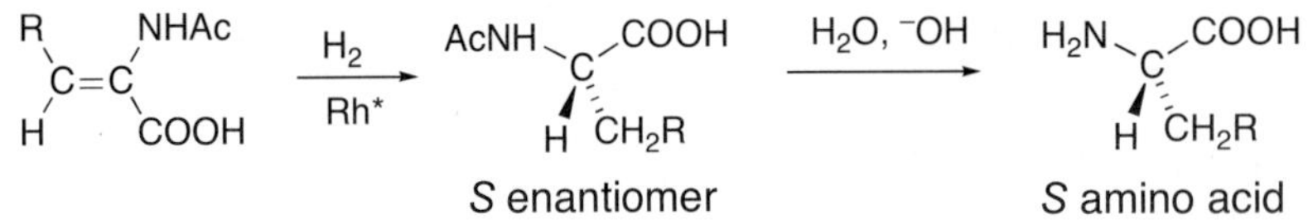

Rh* = chiral Rh hydrogenation catalyst

Summary of methods used for peptide sequencing (29.6)

- Complete hydrolysis of all amide bonds in a peptide gives the identity and amount of the individual amino acids.
- Edman degradation identifies the N-terminal amino acid. Repeated Edman degradations can be used to sequence a peptide from the N-terminal end.
- Cleavage with carboxypeptidase identifies the C-terminal amino acid.
- Partial hydrolysis of a peptide forms smaller fragments that can be sequenced. Amino acid sequences common to smaller fragments can be used to determine the sequence of the complete peptide.
- Selective cleavage of a peptide occurs with trypsin and chymotrypsin to identify the location of specific amino acids (Table 29.2).

Adding and removing protecting groups for amino acids (29.7)

[1] Protection of an amino group as a Boc derivative

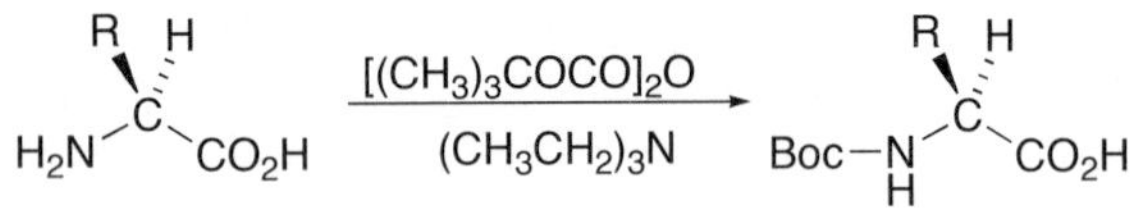

[2] Deprotection of a Boc-protected amino acid

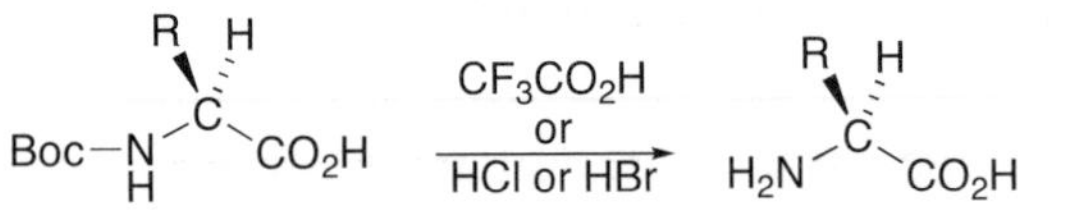

[3] Protection of an amino group as an Fmoc derivative

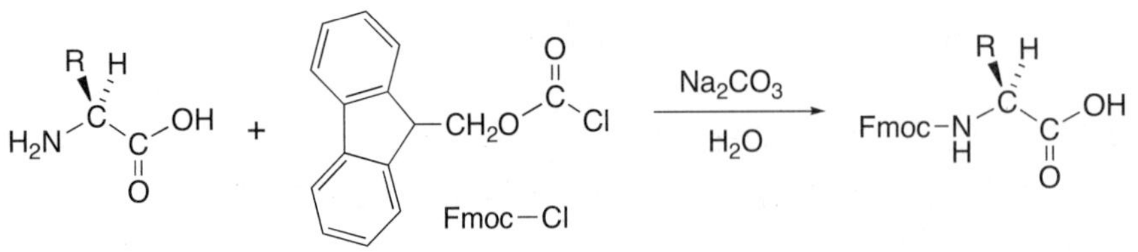

[4] Deprotection of an Fmoc-protected amino acid

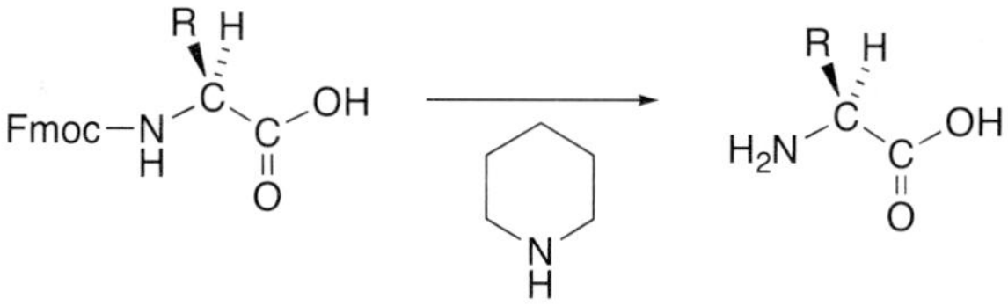

[5] Protection of a carboxy group as an ester

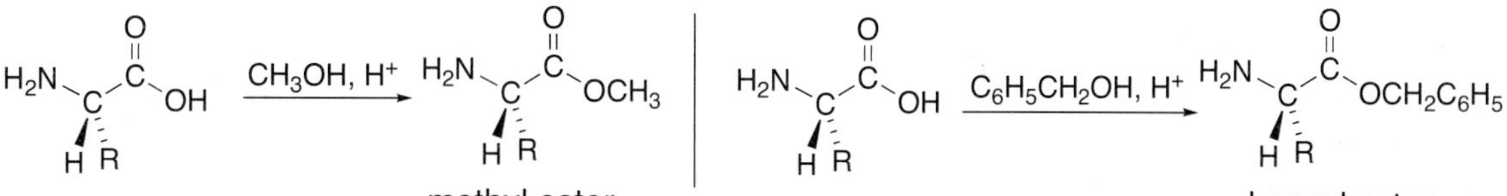

methyl ester | benzyl ester

[6] Deprotection of an ester group

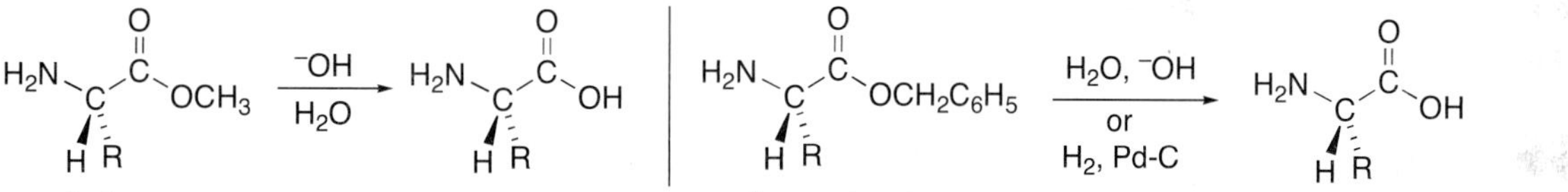

methyl ester | benzyl ester

Synthesis of dipeptides (29.7)

[1] Amide formation with DCC

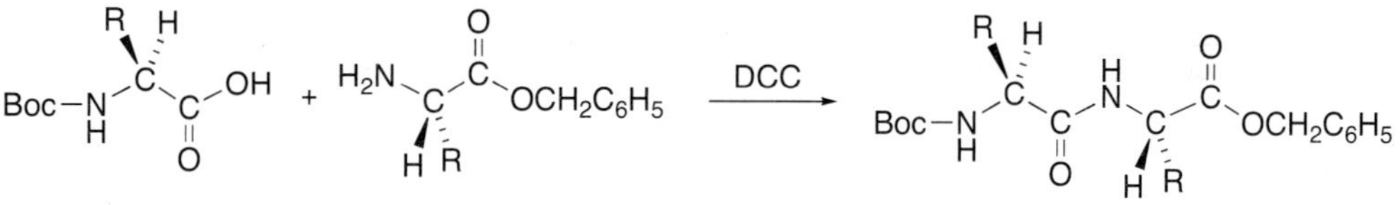

[2] Four steps are needed to synthesize a dipeptide:

a. **Protect** the amino group of one amino acid using a Boc or Fmoc group.
b. **Protect** the carboxy group of the second amino acid using an ester.
c. Form the amide bond with **DCC.**
d. **Remove both protecting groups** in one or two reactions.

Summary of the Merrifield method of peptide synthesis (29.8)

[1] Attach an Fmoc-protected amino acid to a polymer derived from polystyrene.
[2] Remove the Fmoc protecting group.
[3] Form the amide bond with a second Fmoc-protected amino acid using DCC.
[4] Repeat steps [2] and [3].
[5] Remove the protecting group and detach the peptide from the polymer.

Practice Test on Chapter Review

1. a Which statement is true about the peptide Ala–Gly–Tyr–Phe?
   1. The N-terminal amino acid is Ala.
   2. The N-terminal amino acid is Phe.
   3. The peptide contains four peptide bonds.
   4. Statements [1] and [3] are true.
   5. Statements [2] and [3] are true.

   b. Which of the following peptides is hydrolyzed by trypsin?
   1. Glu–Ser–Gly–Arg
   2. Arg–Gln–Trp–Asp
   3. Glu–Val–Leu–Lys
   4. Peptides [1] and [2] are hydrolyzed.
   5. Peptides [1], [2], and [3] are all hydrolyzed.

   c. In which types of protein structure is hydrogen bonding observed?
   1. α-helix
   2. β-pleated sheet
   3. 3° structure
   4. Hydrogen bonding is present in [1] and [2].
   5. Hydrogen bonding is present in [1], [2], and [3].

2. Answer the following questions about peptides.

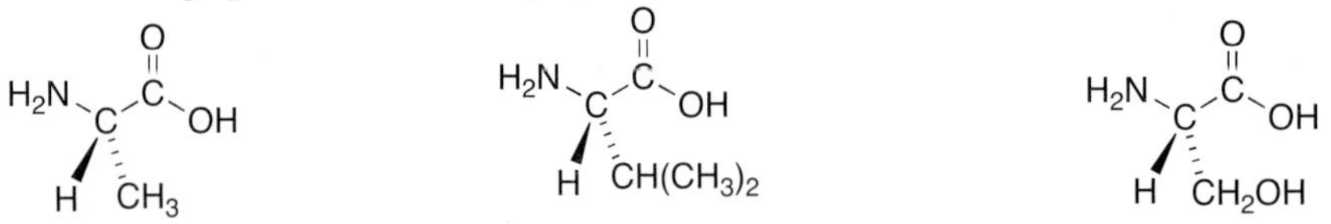

Ala Val Ser

   a. Draw the structure of the following tripeptide: Val–Ser–Ala.
   b. Give the three-letter abbreviation for the N-terminal amino acid.
   c. Give the three-letter abbreviation for the C-terminal amino acid.

3. Answer the following questions about the amino acid leucine (2-amino-4-methylpentanoic acid), which has pK_a's of 2.33 and 9.74 for its ionizable functional groups.
   a. Draw a Fischer projection for L-leucine and label the stereogenic center as *R* or *S*.
   b. What is the p*I* of leucine?
   c. Draw the structure of the predominant form of leucine at its isoelectric point.
   d. Draw the structure of the predominant form of leucine at pH 10.
   e. Is leucine an acidic, basic, or neutral amino acid?

4. What product is formed when the amino acid phenylalanine is treated with each reagent?
   a. $PhCH_2OH$, H^+
   b. Ac_2O, pyridine
   c. PhCOCl, pyridine
   d. $(Boc)_2O$
   e. $C_6H_5N{=}C{=}S$

5. Draw the amino acids and peptide fragments formed when the octapeptide Tyr–Gly–Ala–Lys–Val–Ser–Phe–Met is treated with each reagent or enzyme:
   a. chymotrypsin
   b. trypsin
   c. carboxypeptidase
   d. $C_6H_5N{=}C{=}S$

Answers to Practice Test

1. a. 1
   b. 2
   c. 5
2. a

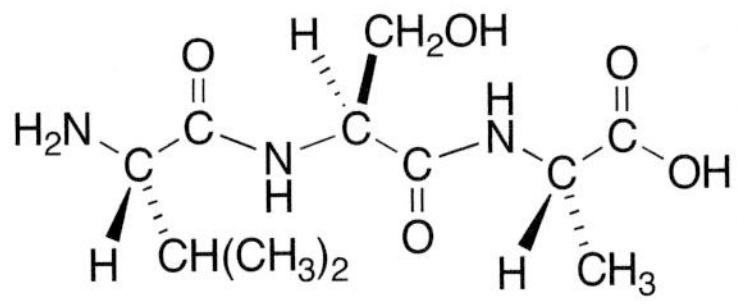

Val Ser Ala

   b. Val
   c. Ala
3.
   a. 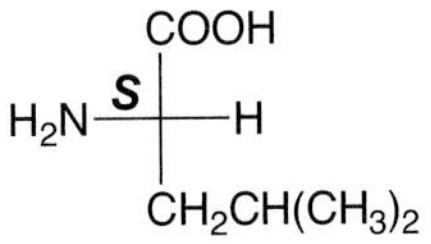

   b. 6.04

   c. 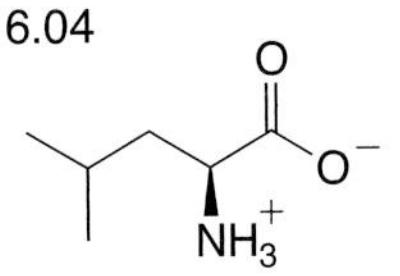

   d. 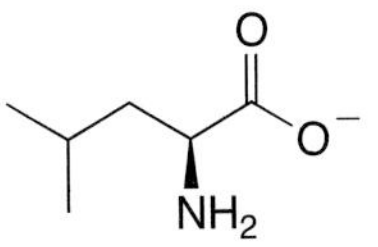

   e. neutral

4.
   a. 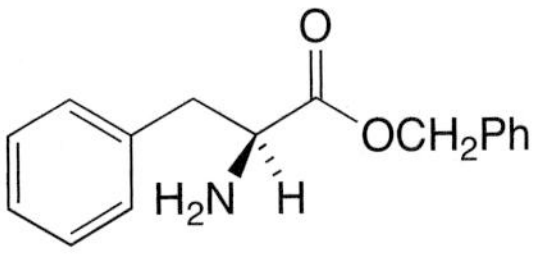

   b. 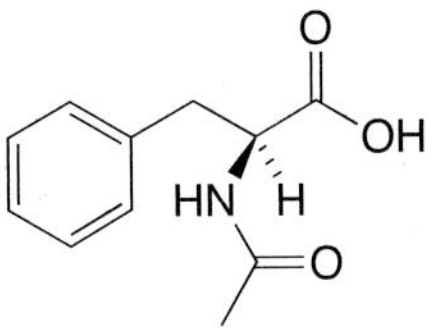

   c. 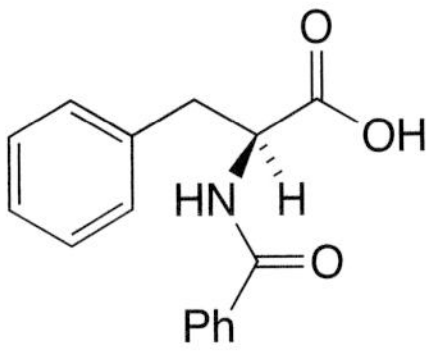

   d. 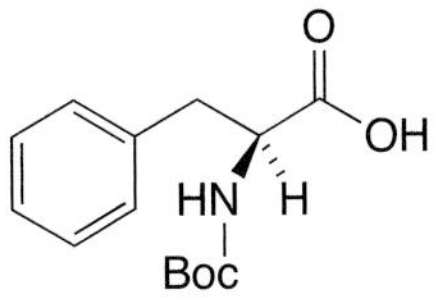

   e. 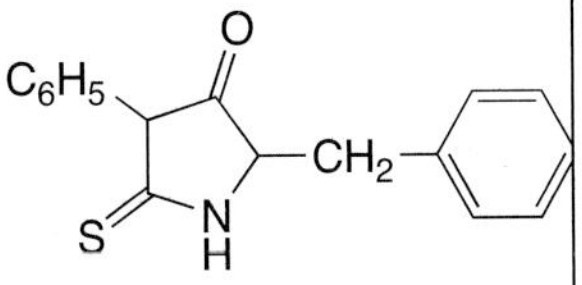

5.a. Tyr, Gly–Ala–Lys–Val–Ser–Phe, Met
b. Tyr–Gly–Ala–Lys, Val–Ser–Phe– Met
c. Tyr–Gly–Ala–Lys–Val–Ser–Phe, Met
d. Tyr, Gly–Ala–Lys–Val–Ser–Phe–Met

Answers to Problems

29.1

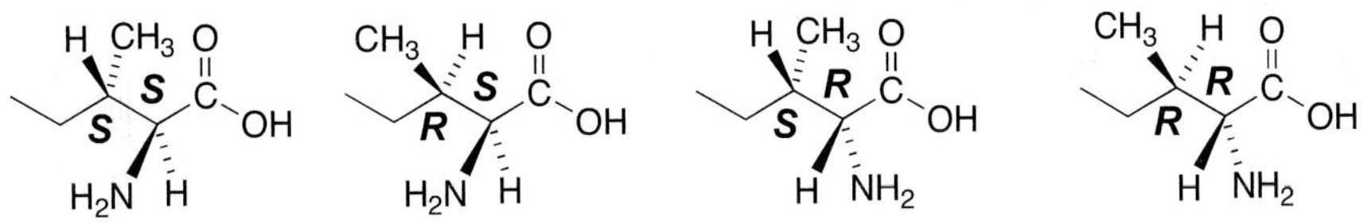

L-isoleucine

29.2

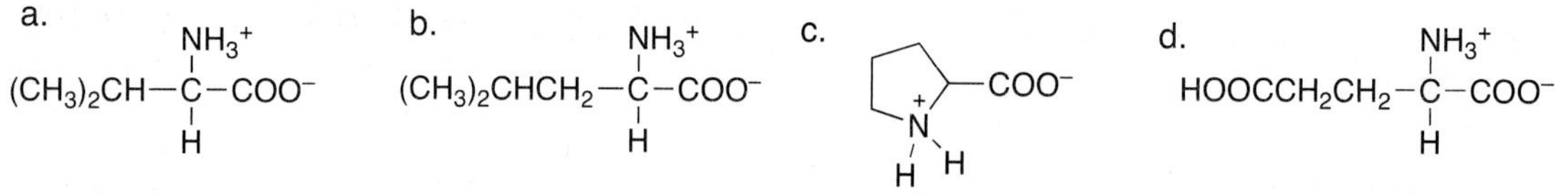

29.3 In an amino acid, the electron-withdrawing carboxy group destabilizes the ammonium ion ($–NH_3^+$), making it more readily donate a proton; that is, it makes it a stronger acid. Also, the electron-withdrawing carboxy group removes electron density from the amino group ($–NH_2$) of the conjugate base, making it a weaker base than a 1° amine, which has no electron-withdrawing group.

29.4 The most direct way to synthesize an α-amino acid is by **S_N2 reaction of an α-halo carboxylic acid with a large excess of NH_3.**

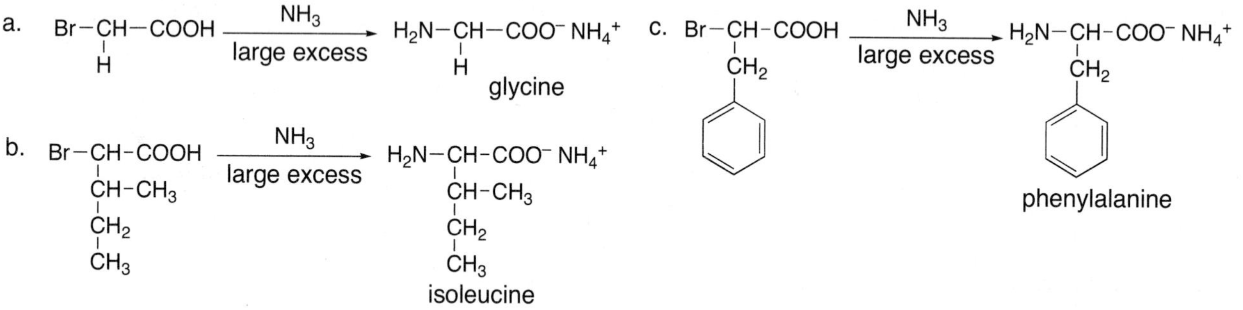
a.
large excess
glycine
b.
large excess
isoleucine
c.
large excess
phenylalanine

29.5

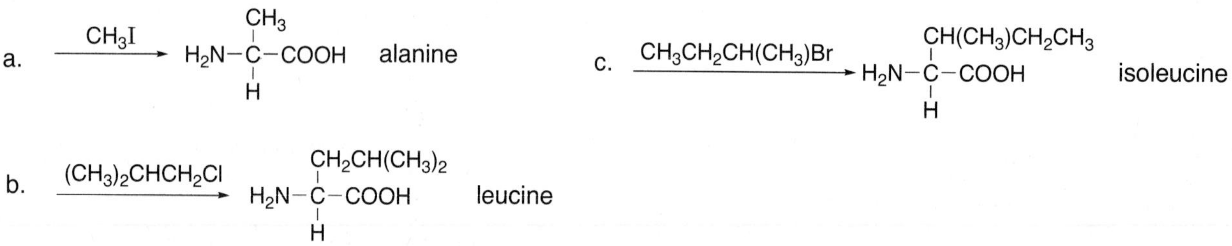
a.
alanine
b.
leucine
c.
isoleucine

29.6

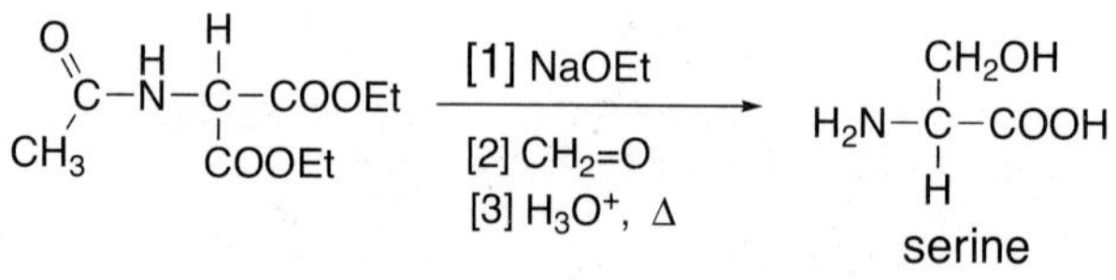
[1] NaOEt
[2] CH2=O
[3] H3O+, Δ
serine

29.7

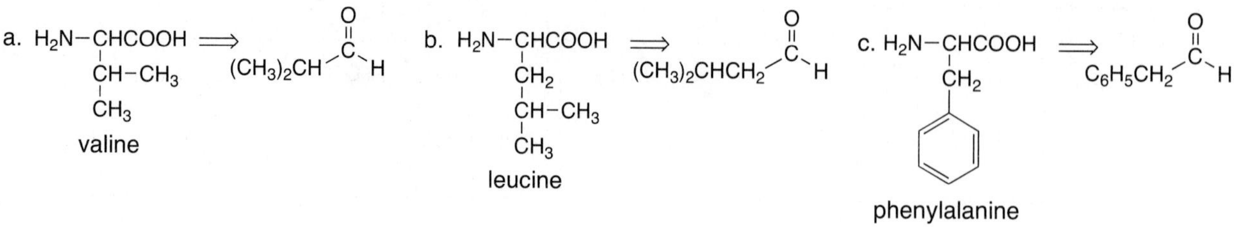
a.
valine
b.
leucine
c.
phenylalanine

29.8

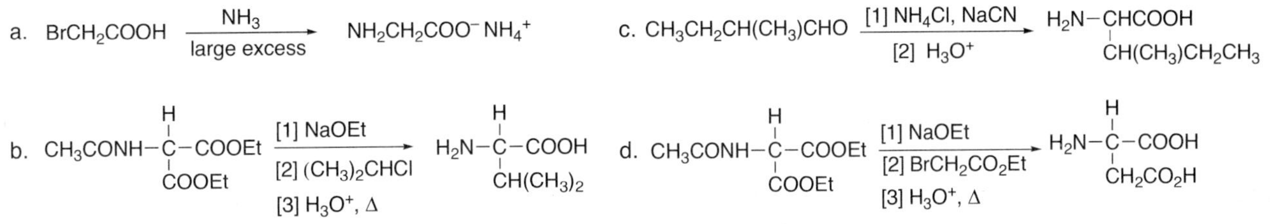
a. BrCH2COOH
NH3
large excess
NH2CH2COO− NH4+
b. CH3CONH–C–COOEt
[1] NaOEt
[2] (CH3)2CHCl
[3] H3O+, Δ
H2N–C–COOH
CH(CH3)2
c. CH3CH2CH(CH3)CHO
[1] NH4Cl, NaCN
[2] H3O+
H2N–CHCOOH
CH(CH3)CH2CH3
d. CH3CONH–C–COOEt
[1] NaOEt
[2] BrCH2CO2Et
[3] H3O+, Δ
H2N–C–COOH
CH2CO2H

29.9 A chiral amine must be used to resolve a racemic mixture of amino acids.

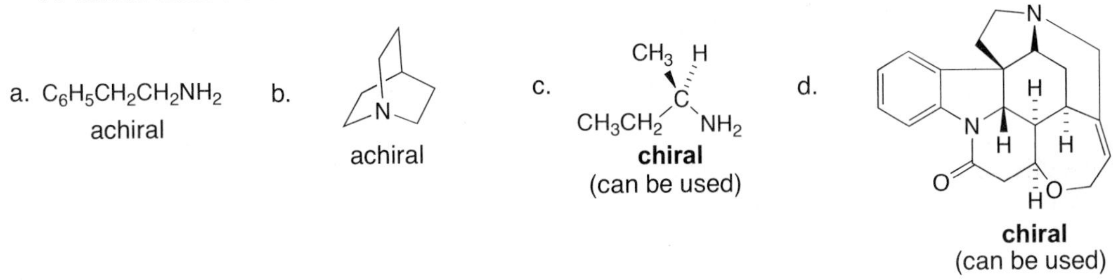
a. C6H5CH2CH2NH2
achiral
b.
achiral
c.
CH3CH2
NH2
chiral
(can be used)
d.
chiral
(can be used)

29.10

To begin:
Convert the amino acids into *N*-acetyl amino acids (two enantiomers).

Step [1]:
React both enantiomers with the *R* isomer of the chiral amine.

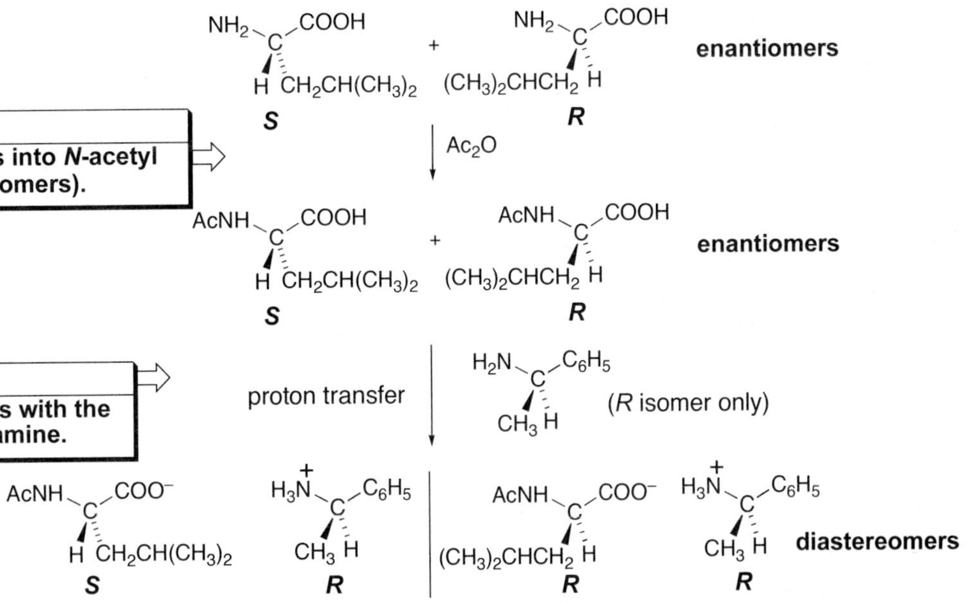
enantiomers
S
R
Ac2O
AcNH
enantiomers
proton transfer
(R isomer only)
diastereomers

These salts have the *same* configuration around one stereogenic center, but the *opposite* configuration about the other stereogenic center.

Step [2]:
Separate the diastereomers.

separate

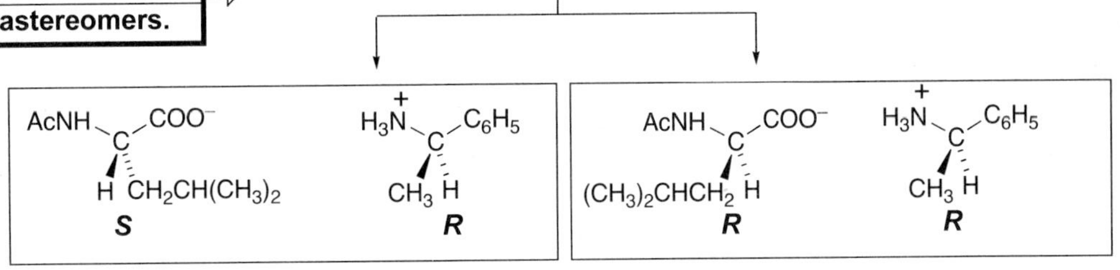
S
R
R
R

Step [3]: **Regenerate the amino acid by hydrolysis of the amide.**

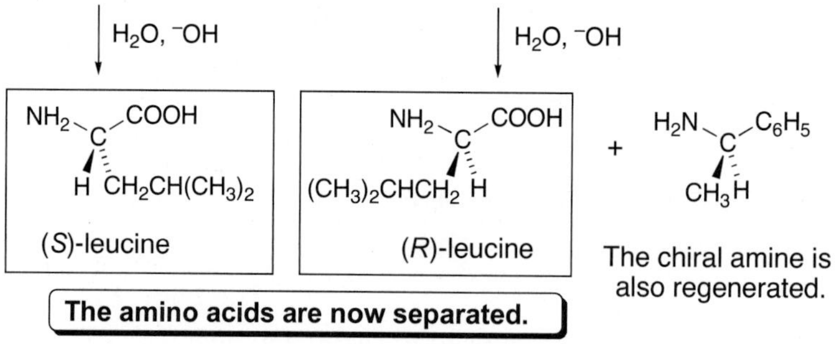
H2O, −OH
H2O, −OH
(S)-leucine
(R)-leucine
The chiral amine is also regenerated.
The amino acids are now separated.

29.11

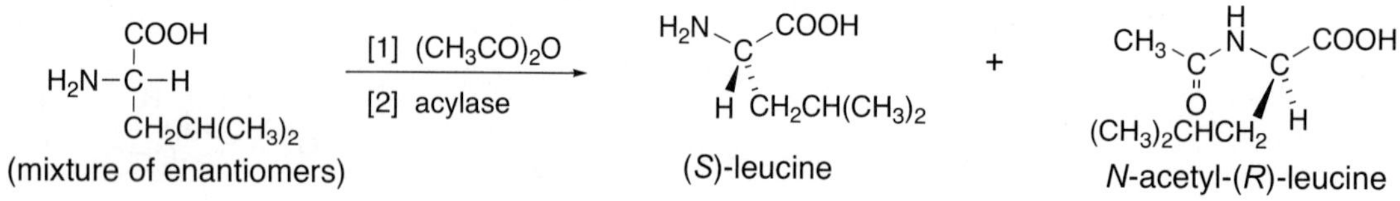
(mixture of enantiomers)
[1] (CH3CO)2O
[2] acylase
(S)-leucine
N-acetyl-(R)-leucine

29.12

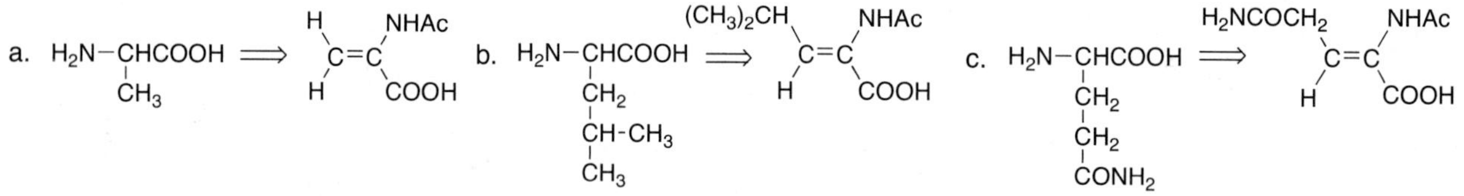
a.
b.
c.

29.13

Draw the peptide by joining adjacent COOH and NH_2 groups in amide bonds.

a.

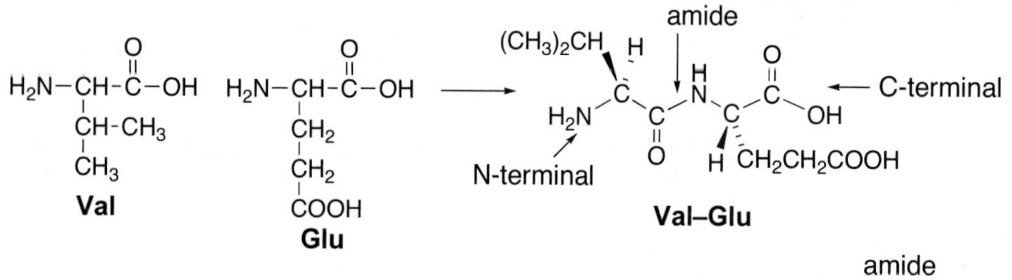
Val
Glu
amide
C-terminal
N-terminal
Val–Glu

b.

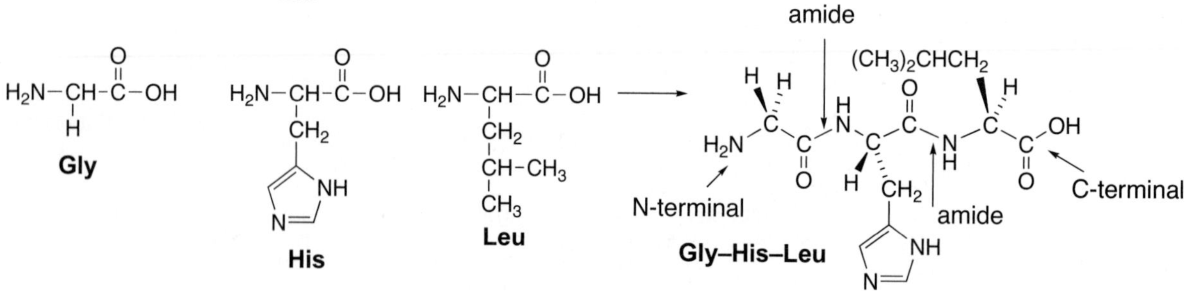
Gly
His
Leu
amide
amide
N-terminal
C-terminal
Gly–His–Leu

c. 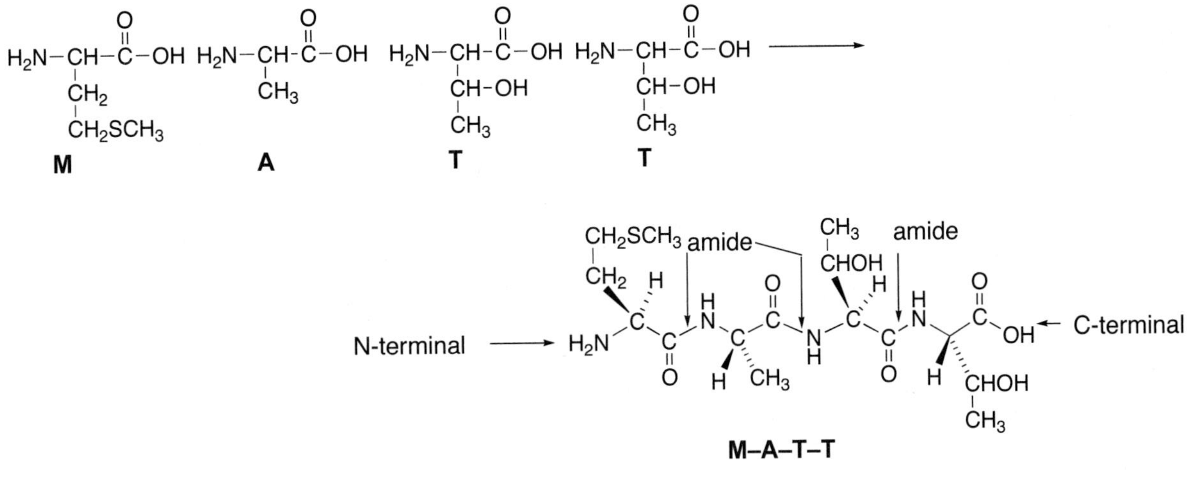
M
A
T
T
amide
amide
N-terminal
C-terminal
M–A–T–T

29.14

a. 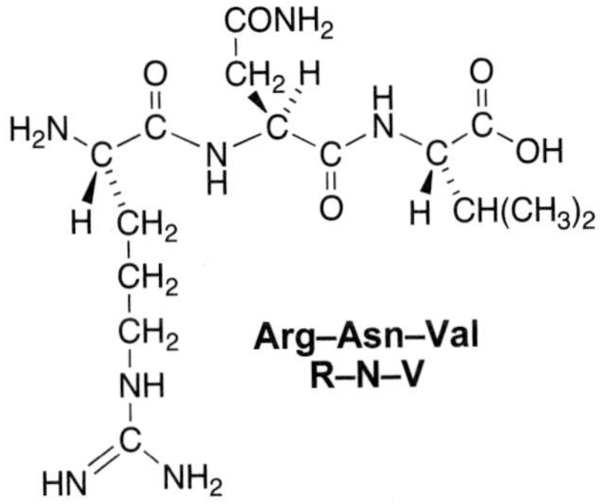
Arg–Asn–Val
R–N–V

b. 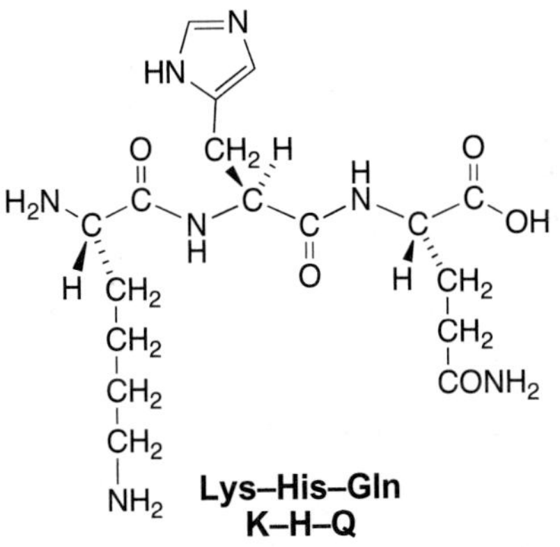
Lys–His–Gln
K–H–Q

29.15 There are six different tripeptides that can be formed from three amino acids (A, B, C): A–B–C, A–C–B, B–A–C, B–C–A, C–A–B, and C–B–A.

29.16

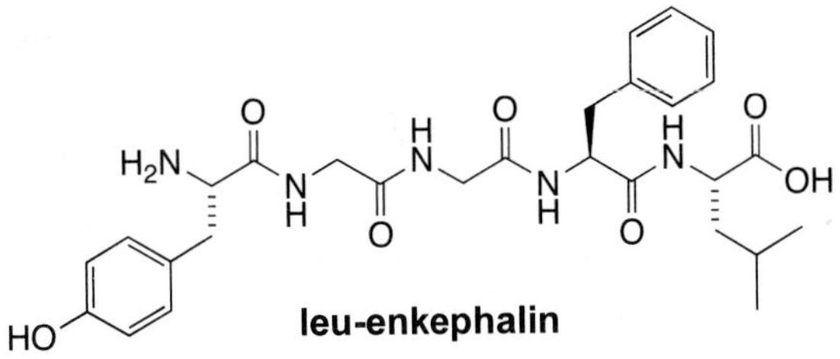
leu-enkephalin

29.17

a. 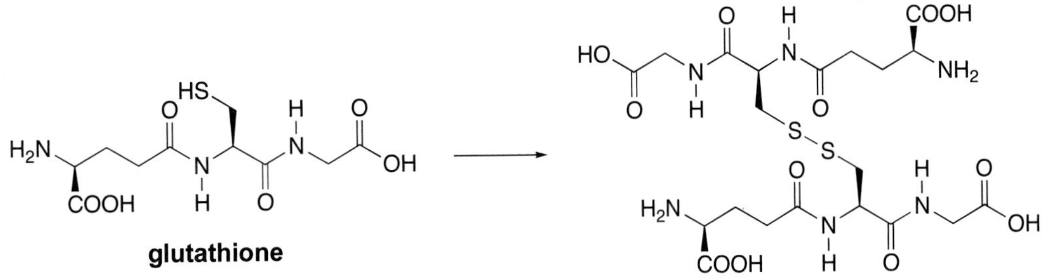
glutathione

b.

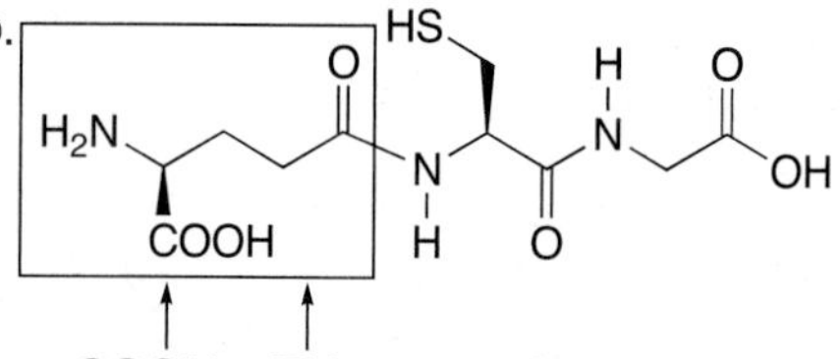

The peptide bond beween glutamic acid and its adjacent amino acid (cysteine) is formed from the COOH in the R group of glutamic acid, not the α COOH.

α COOH This comes from the amino acid glutamic acid.

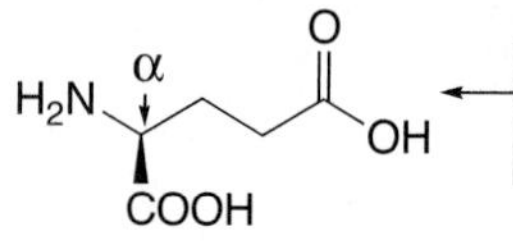

glutamic acid

This carboxy group is used to form the amide bond in the peptide, not the α COOH, as is usual. That's what makes glutathione's structure unusual.

29.18

a.

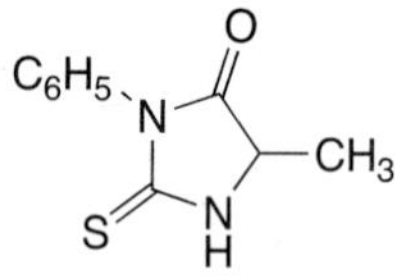

from Ala

b.

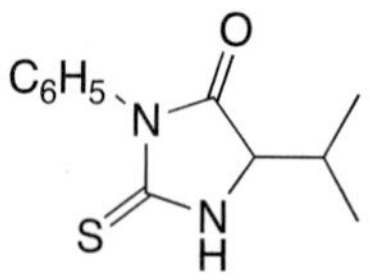

from Val

29.19 Determine the sequence of the octapeptide as in Sample Problem 29.2. Look for overlapping sequences in the fragments.

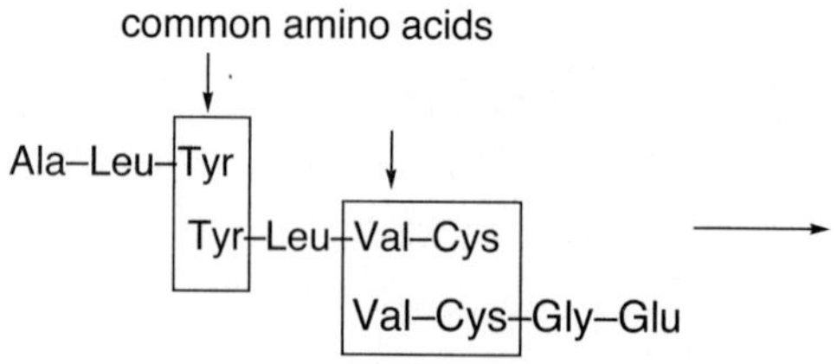
common amino acids
Ala–Leu–Tyr
Tyr–Leu–Val–Cys
Val–Cys–Gly–Glu

Answer:

Ala–Leu–Tyr–Leu–Val–Cys–Gly–Glu

29.20 Trypsin cleaves peptides at amide bonds with a carbonyl group from Arg and Lys. Chymotrypsin cleaves at amide bonds with a carbonyl group from Phe, Tyr, and Trp.

a. [1] Gly–Ala–Phe–Leu–Lys + Ala
   [2] Phe–Tyr–Gly–Cys–Arg + Ser
   [3] Thr–Pro–Lys + Glu–His–Gly–Phe–Cys–Trp–Val–Val–Phe

b. [1] Gly–Ala–Phe + Leu–Lys–Ala
   [2] Phe + Tyr + Gly–Cys–Arg–Ser
   [3] Thr–Pro–Lys–Glu–His–Gly–Phe + Cys–Trp + Val–Val–Phe

29.21

Edman degradation gives N-terminal amino acid: → Leu–___–___–___–___–___–___

Carboxypeptidase identifies the C-terminal amino acid: → Leu–___–___–___–___–___–Glu

Partial hydrolysis common amino acids

↓

Ala–Ser–Arg

Gly–Ala–Ser

↓

Gly–Ala–Ser–Arg → Leu–Gly–Ala–Ser–Arg–___–Glu

or

Leu–___–Gly–Ala–Ser–Arg–Glu

Cleavage by trypsin is after Arg and yields a dipeptide; therefore, this must be the peptide: → Leu–Gly–Ala–Ser–Arg–Phe–Glu

29.22

a.

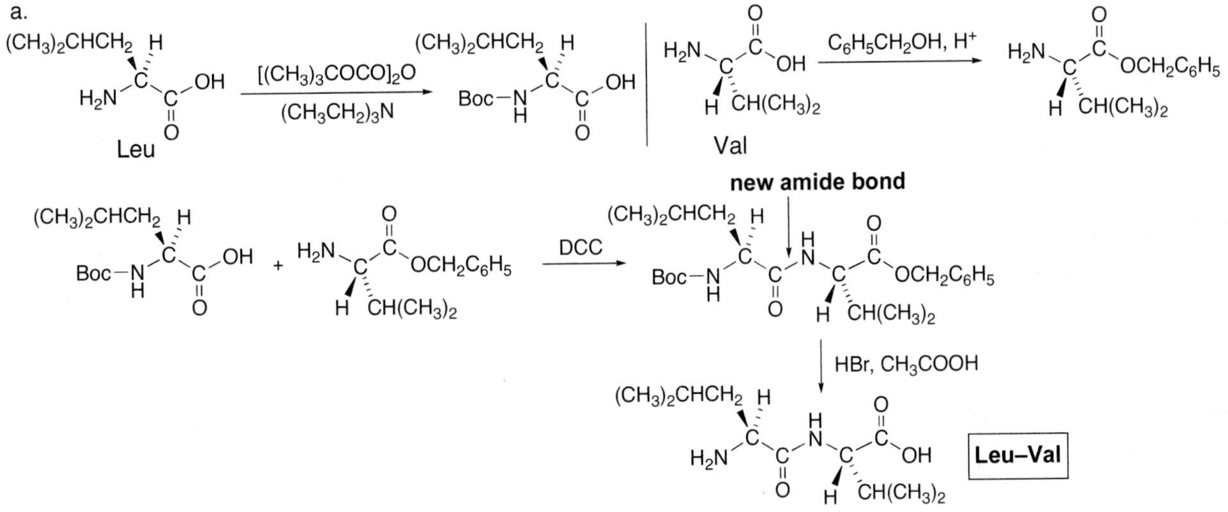

b.

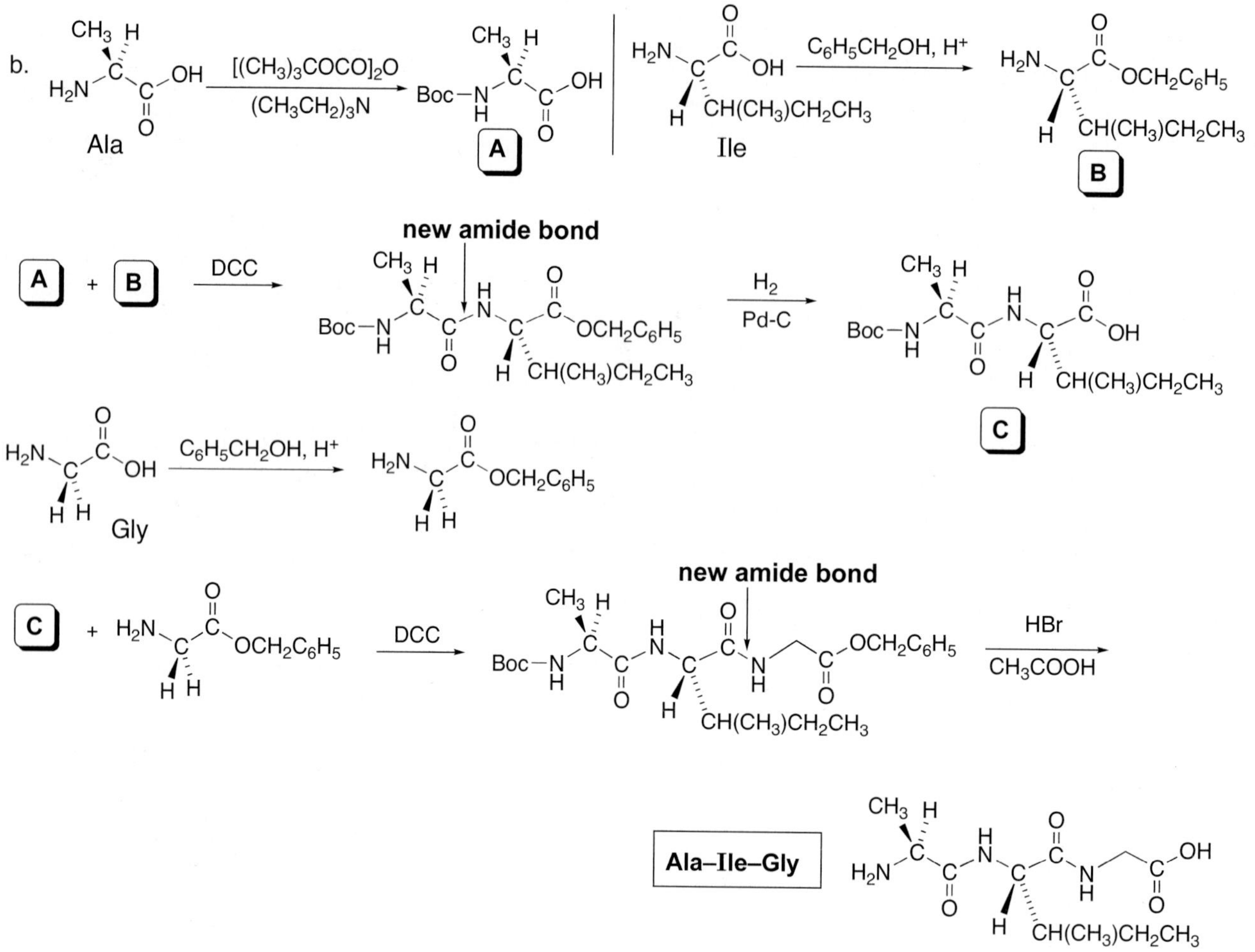
Ala
[(CH3)3COCO]2O
(CH3CH2)3N
A
Ile
C6H5CH2OH, H+
B
DCC
new amide bond
H2
Pd-C
C
Gly
C6H5CH2OH, H+
DCC
new amide bond
HBr
CH3COOH
Ala–Ile–Gly

c.

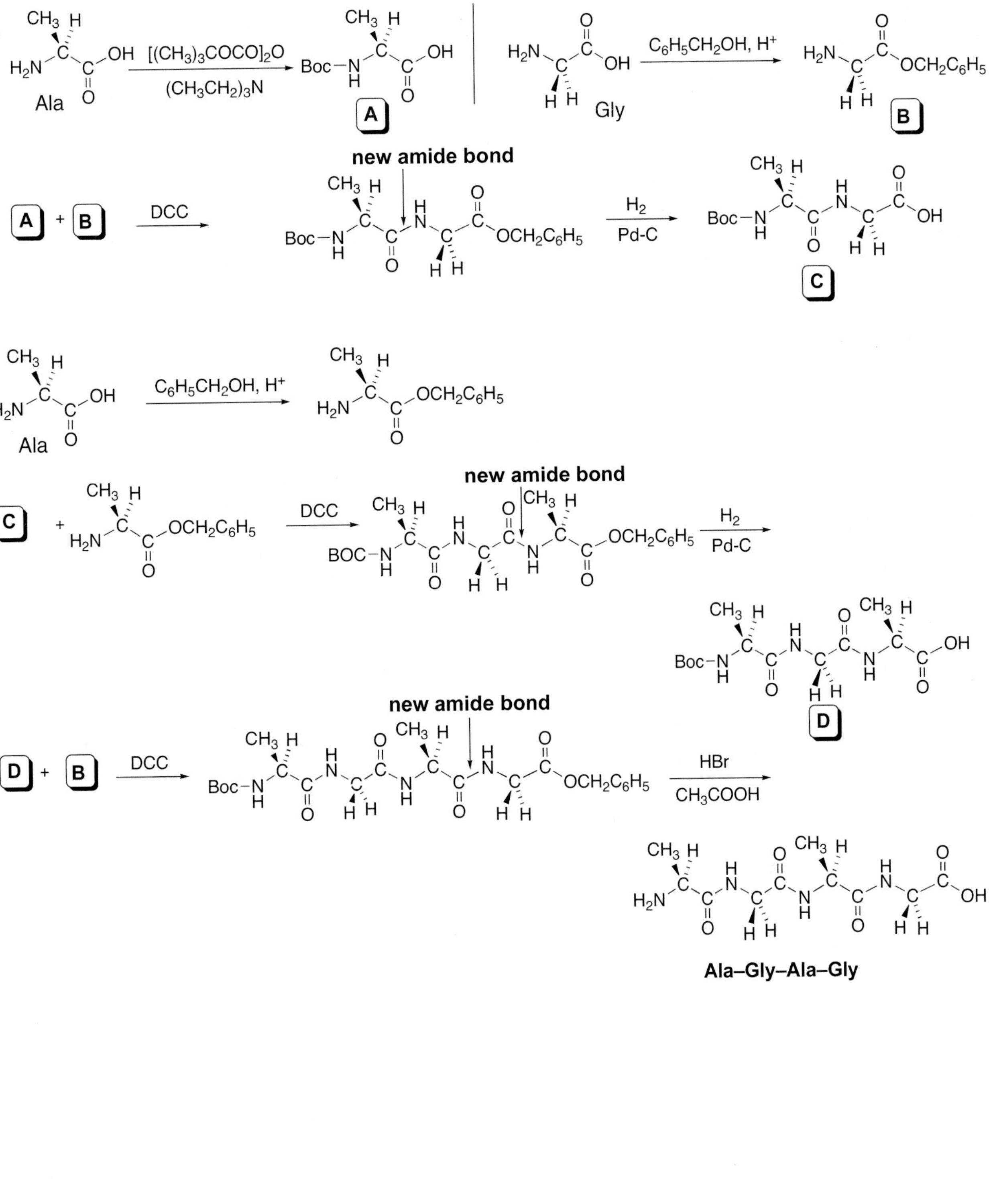
Ala
[(CH3)3COCO]2O
(CH3CH2)3N
A
Gly
C6H5CH2OH, H+
B
new amide bond
DCC
H2
Pd-C
C
Ala
C6H5CH2OH, H+
new amide bond
DCC
H2
Pd-C
D
new amide bond
DCC
HBr
CH3COOH
Ala–Gly–Ala–Gly

29.23 The dipeptide depicted in the 3-D model has alanine as the N-terminal amino acid and cysteine as the C-terminal amino acid.

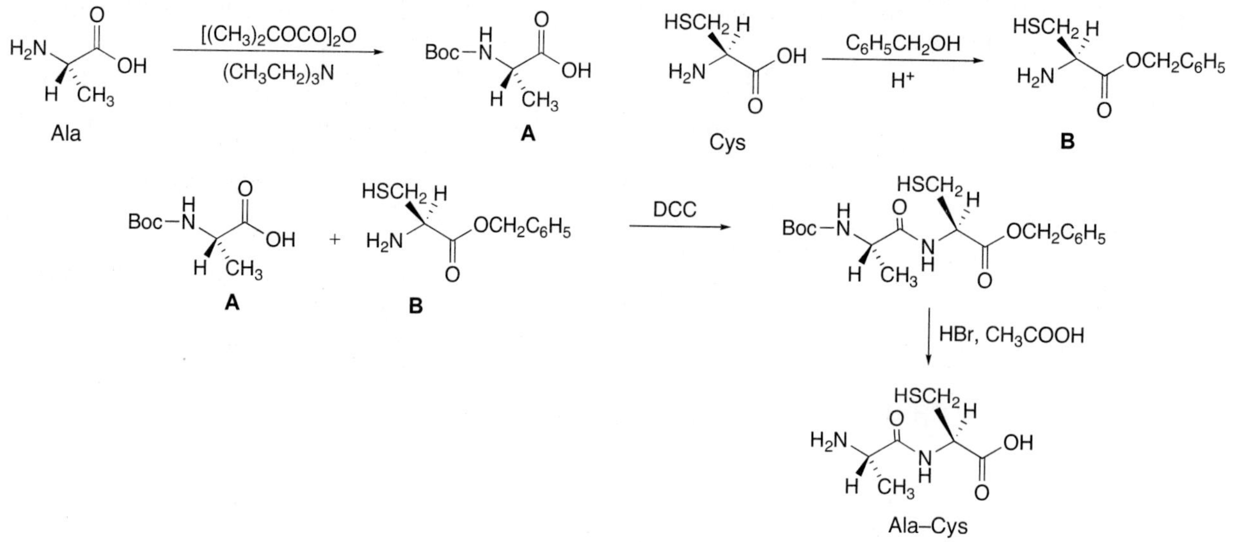

29.24

All Fmoc-protected amino acids are made by the following general reaction:

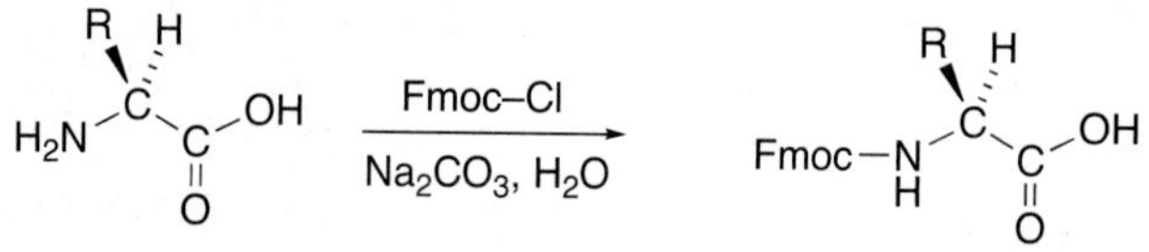

The steps:

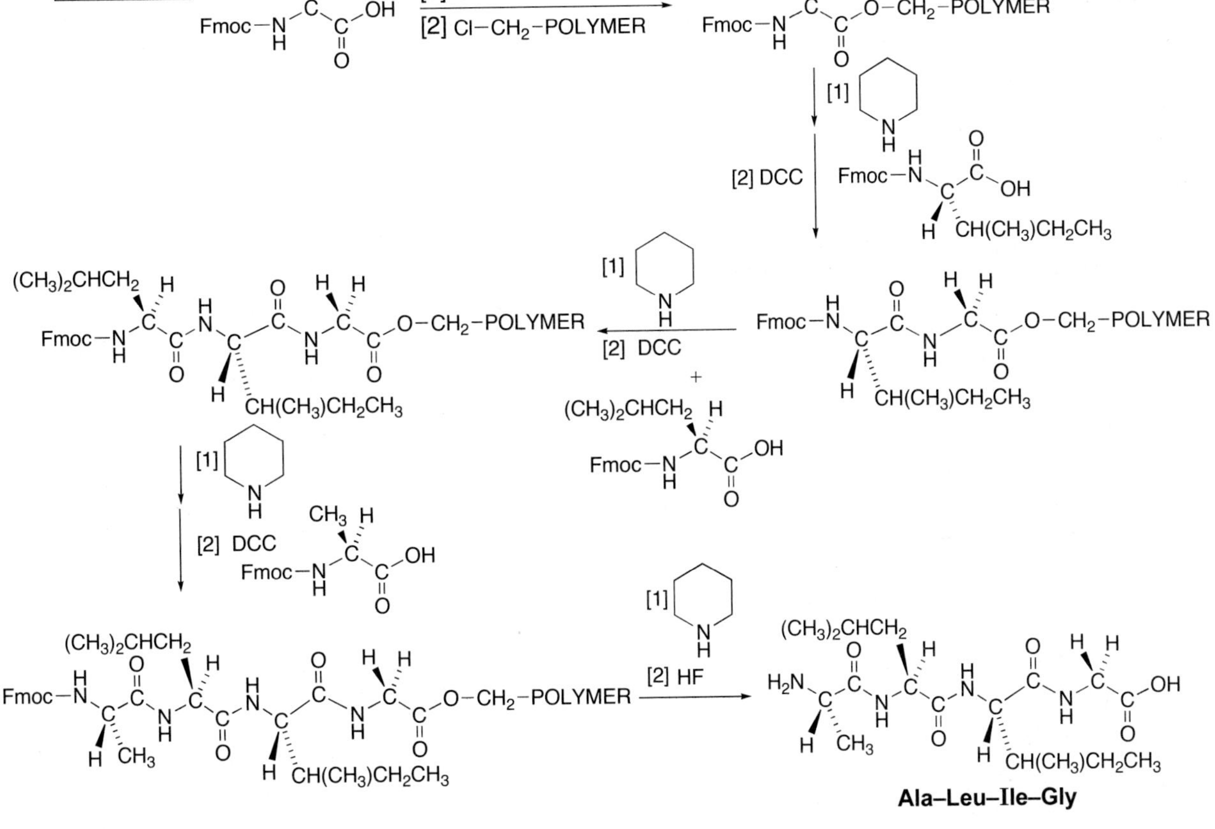

29.25 In a *parallel* β-pleated sheet, the strands run in the *same* direction from the N- to C-terminal amino acid. In an *antiparallel* β-pleated sheet, the strands run in the *opposite* direction.

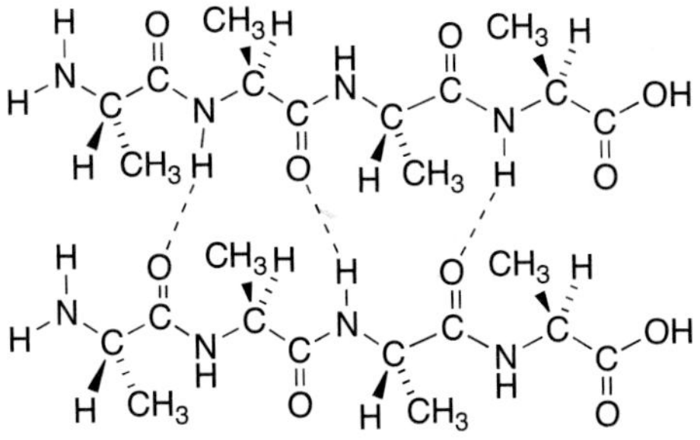

parallel

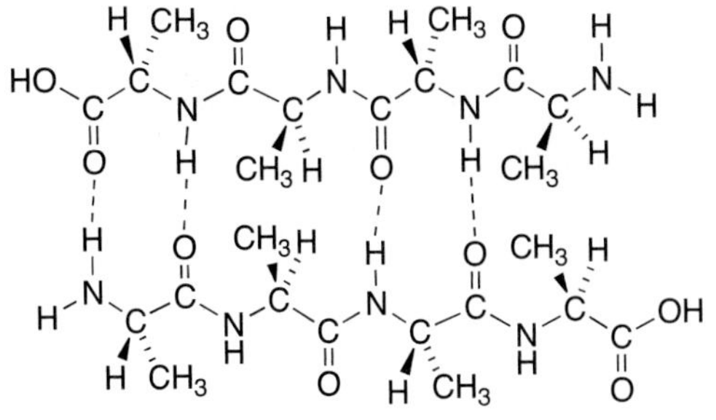

antiparallel

29.26

a. Ser and Tyr

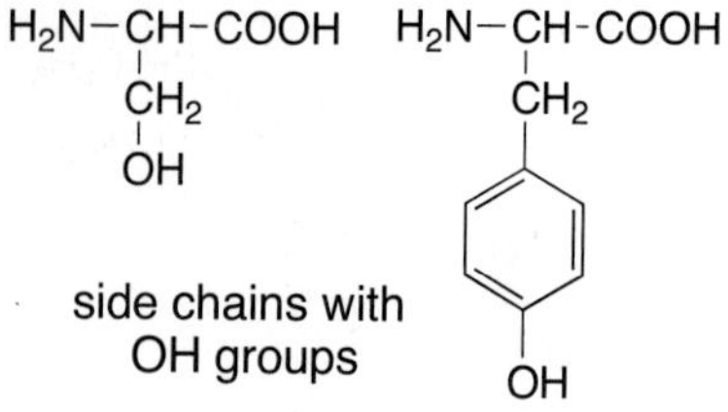
H2N–CH–COOH
CH2
OH
H2N–CH–COOH
CH2
OH

side chains with OH groups

hydrogen bonding

b. Val and Leu

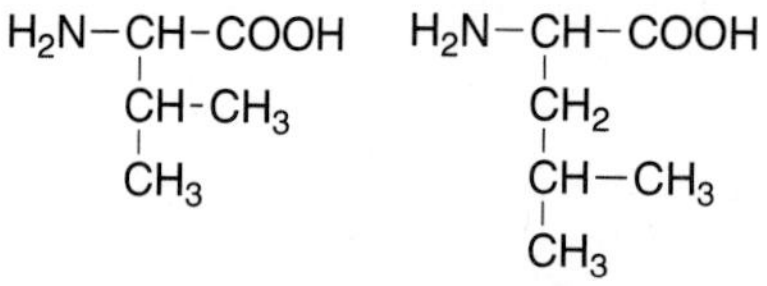
H2N–CH–COOH
CH–CH3
CH3
H2N–CH–COOH
CH2
CH–CH3
CH3

side chains with only C–C and C–H bonds

van der Waals forces

c. 2 Phe residues

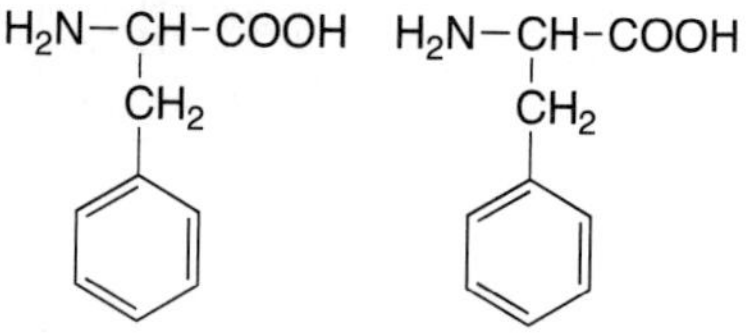
H2N–CH–COOH
CH2
H2N–CH–COOH
CH2

van der Waals forces

29.27 a. The R group for glycine is a hydrogen. The R groups must be small to allow the β-pleated sheets to stack on top of each other. With large R groups, steric hindrance prevents stacking.

b. Silk fibers are water insoluble because most of the polar functional groups are in the interior of the stacked sheets. The β-pleated sheets are stacked one on top of another, so few polar functional groups are available for hydrogen bonding to water.

29.28

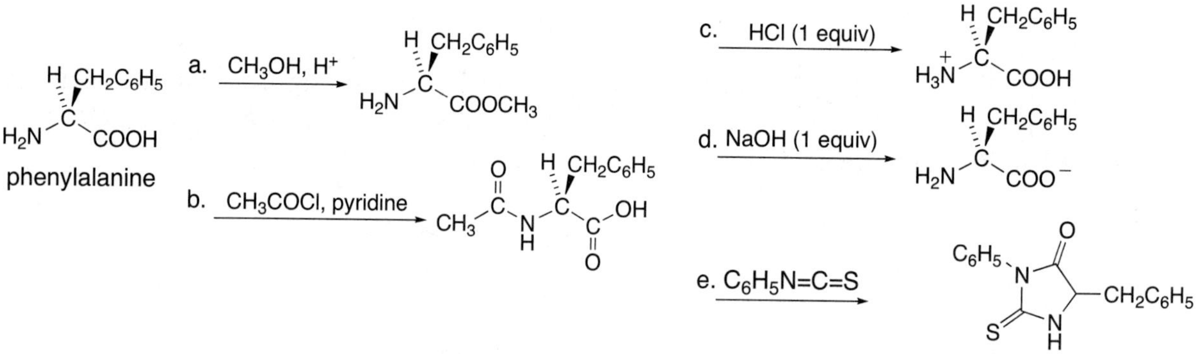
phenylalanine
a. CH3OH, H+
b. CH3COCl, pyridine
c. HCl (1 equiv)
d. NaOH (1 equiv)
e. C6H5N=C=S
H CH2C6H5
H2N COOH
H2N COOCH3
H3N COOH
H2N COO−
CH3 OH
C6H5
CH2C6H5

29.29

a. N-terminal amino acid: alanine
C-terminal amino acid: serine

b. A–Q–C–S

c. Amide bonds are **bold.**

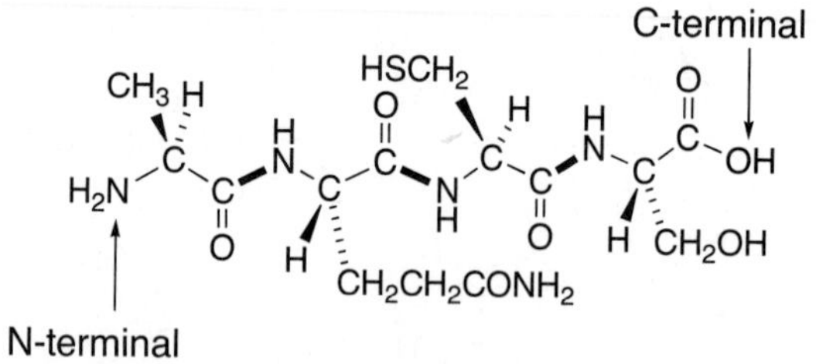
C-terminal
N-terminal
CH3 H
HSCH2
H2N
OH
H CH2OH
CH2CH2CONH2

Ala–Gln–Cys–Ser
A–Q–C–S

29.30 The dipeptide is composed of phenylalanine and leucine.

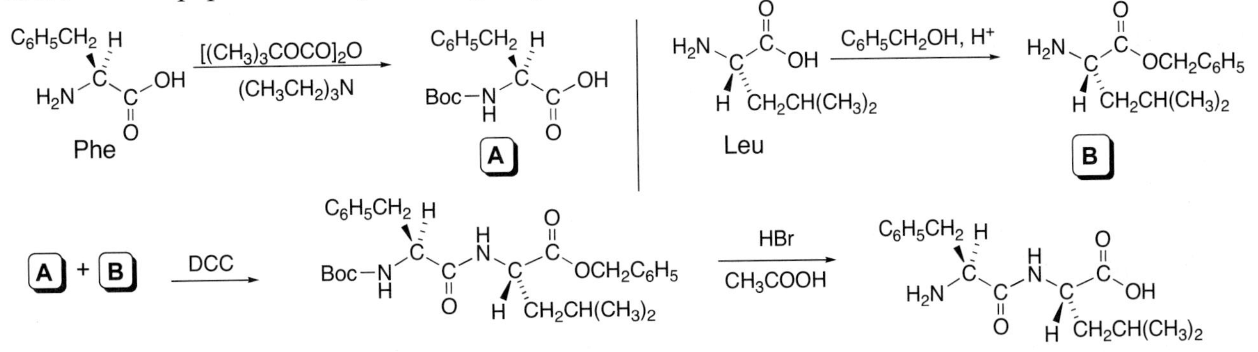
$[(CH_3)_3COCO]_2O$
$(CH_3CH_2)_3N$
Phe
A
Leu
$C_6H_5CH_2OH, H^+$
B
DCC
HBr
CH_3COOH

Phe–Leu

29.31

a.
b.

(R)-penicillamine (S)-penicillamine

29.32 Amino acids are insoluble in diethyl ether because amino acids are highly polar; they exist as salts in their neutral form. Diethyl ether is weakly polar, so amino acids are *not* soluble in it. *N*-Acetyl amino acids are soluble because they are polar but not salts.

amino acid, a salt
H_2O soluble and ether insoluble

N-acetyl amino acid
ether soluble

29.33 The electron pair on the N atom not part of a double bond is delocalized on the five-membered ring, making it less basic.

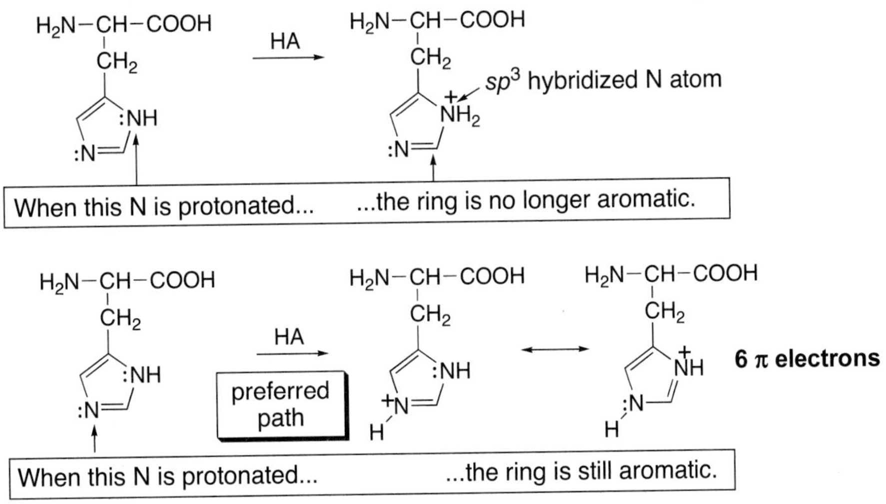
HA
sp^3 hybridized N atom
When this N is protonated...
...the ring is no longer aromatic.
HA
preferred path
6 π electrons
When this N is protonated...
...the ring is still aromatic.

29.34

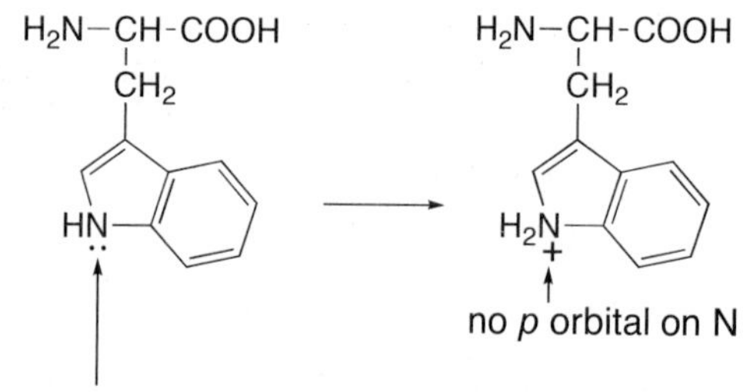
no p orbital on N

The ring structure on tryptophan is aromatic since each atom contains a *p* orbital. Protonation of the N atom would disrupt the aromaticity, making this a less favorable reaction.

This electron pair is delocalized on the bicyclic ring system (giving it 10 π electrons), making it less available for donation, and thus less basic.

29.35 At its isoelectric point, each amino acid is neutral.

a.
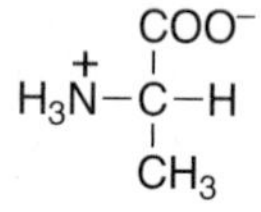
alanine

b.
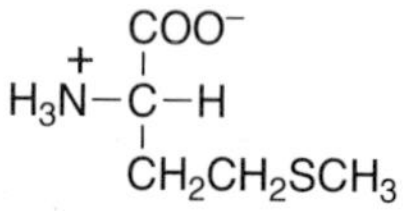
methionine

c.
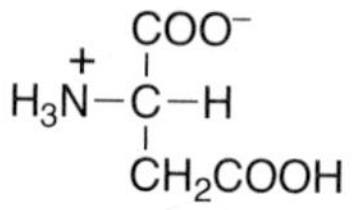
aspartic acid

d.
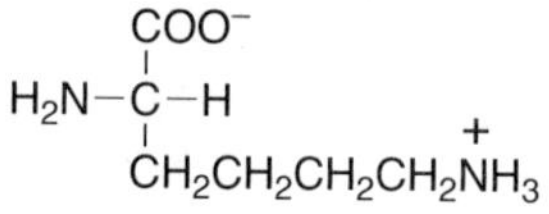
lysine

29.36

a. [1] glutamic acid: use the pK_a's 2.10 + 4.07
[2] lysine: use the pK_a's 8.95 + 10.53
[3] arginine: use the pK_a's 9.04 + 12.48

b. In general, the p*I* of an acidic amino acid is lower than that of a neutral amino acid.

c. In general, the p*I* of a basic amino acid is higher than that of a neutral amino acid.

29.37

a. **threonine**
p*I* = 5.06
(+1) charge at pH = 1

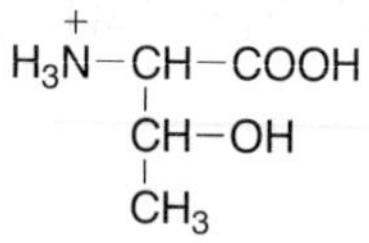

b. **methionine**
p*I* = 5.74
(+1) charge at pH = 1

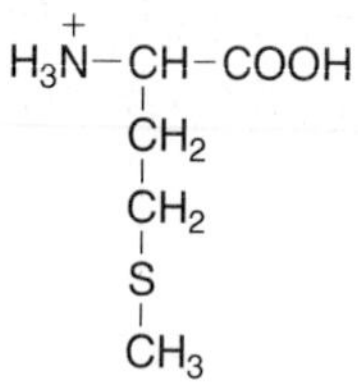

c. **aspartic acid**
p*I* = 2.98
(+1) charge at pH = 1

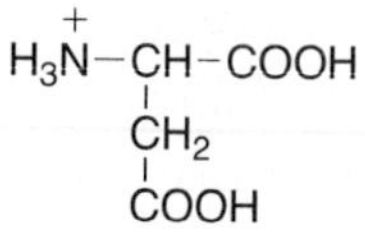

d. **arginine**
p*I* = 5.41
(+2) charge at pH = 1

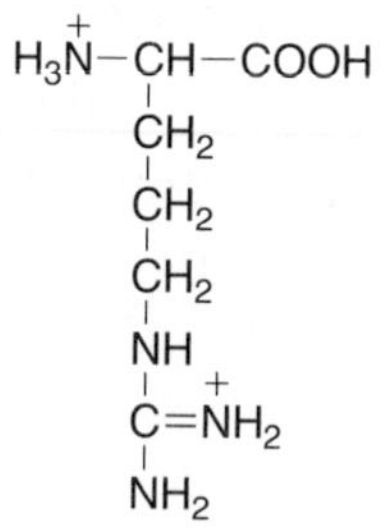

29.38

a. **valine**
pI = 6.00
(–1) charge
at pH = 11

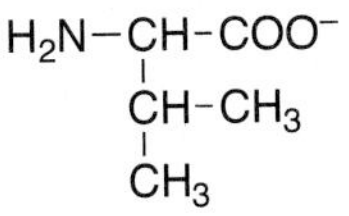

b. **proline**
pI = 6.30
(–1) charge
at pH = 11

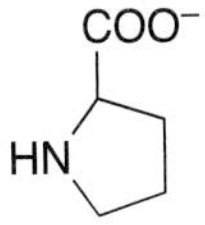

c. **glutamic acid**
pI = 3.08
(–2) charge
at pH = 11

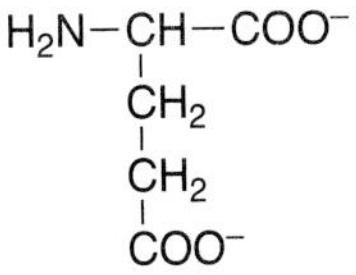

d. **lysine**
pI = 9.74
(–1) charge
at pH = 11

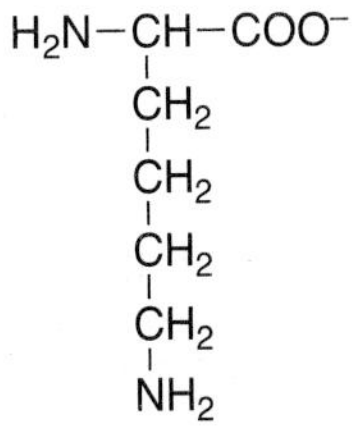

29.39 The terminal NH_2 and COOH groups are ionizable functional groups, so they can gain or lose protons in aqueous solution.

a. 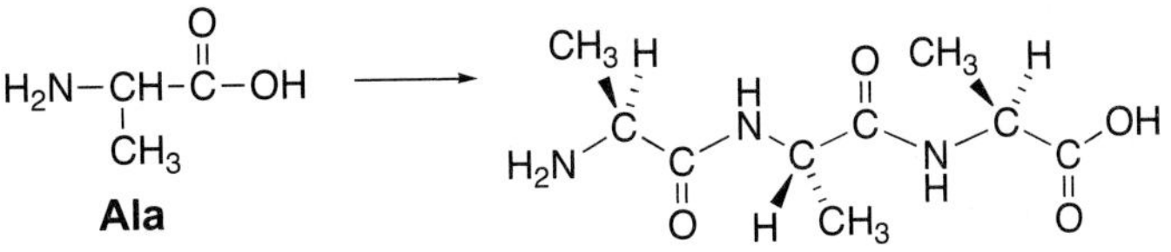

Ala

A–A–A

b. At pH = 1

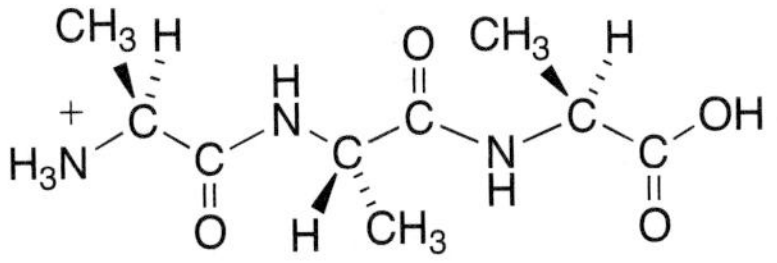

c. The pK_a of the COOH of the tripeptide is higher than the pK_a of the COOH group of alanine, making it less acidic. This occurs because the COOH group in the tripeptide is farther away from the $–NH_3^+$ group. The positively charged $–NH_3^+$ group stabilizes the negatively charged carboxylate anion of alanine more than the carboxylate anion of the tripeptide because it is so much closer in alanine. The opposite effect is observed with the ionization of the $–NH_3^+$ group. In alanine, the $–NH_3^+$ is closer to the COO^- group, so it is more difficult to lose a proton, resulting in a higher pK_a. In the tripeptide, the $–NH_3^+$ is farther away from the COO^-, so it is less affected by its presence.

29.40

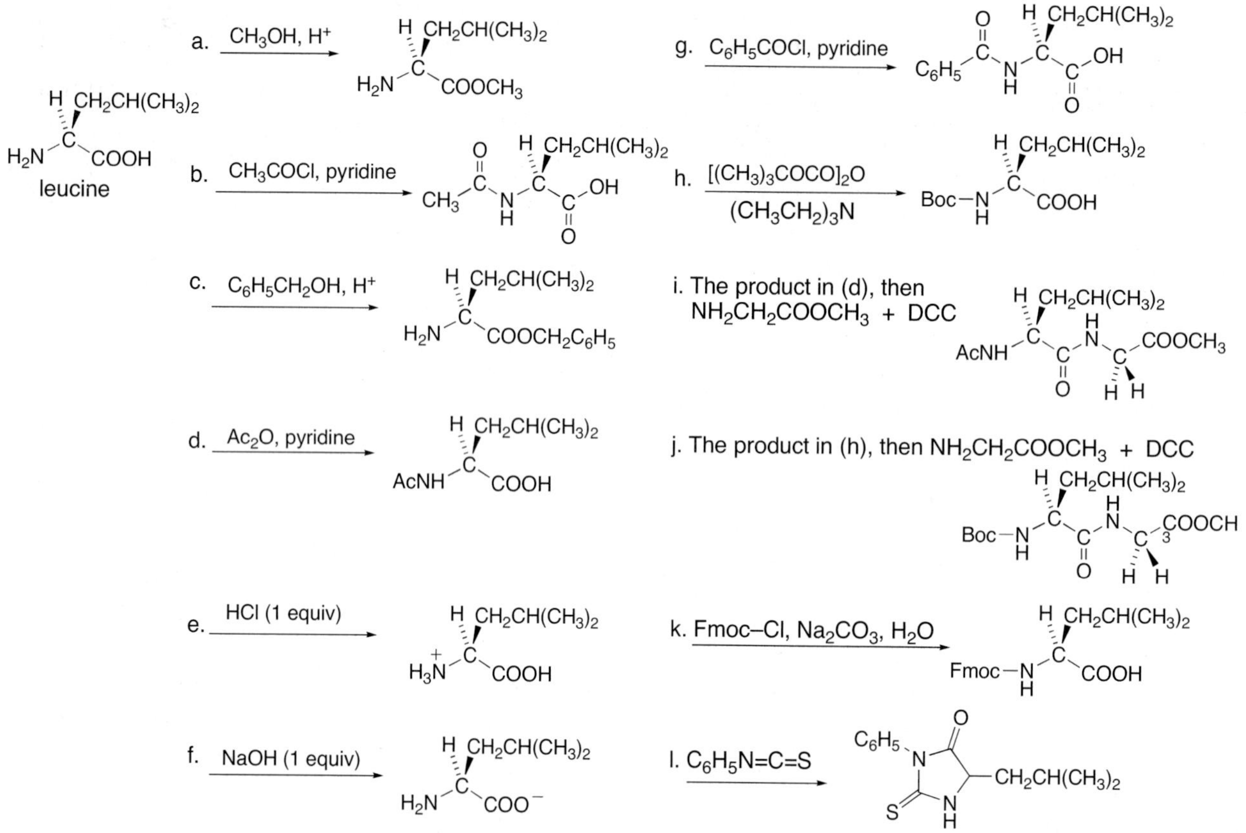
leucine
a. CH3OH, H+
b. CH3COCl, pyridine
c. C6H5CH2OH, H+
d. Ac2O, pyridine
e. HCl (1 equiv)
f. NaOH (1 equiv)
g. C6H5COCl, pyridine
h. [(CH3)3COCO]2O
(CH3CH2)3N
i. The product in (d), then
NH2CH2COOCH3 + DCC
j. The product in (h), then NH2CH2COOCH3 + DCC
k. Fmoc–Cl, Na2CO3, H2O
l. C6H5N=C=S

29.41

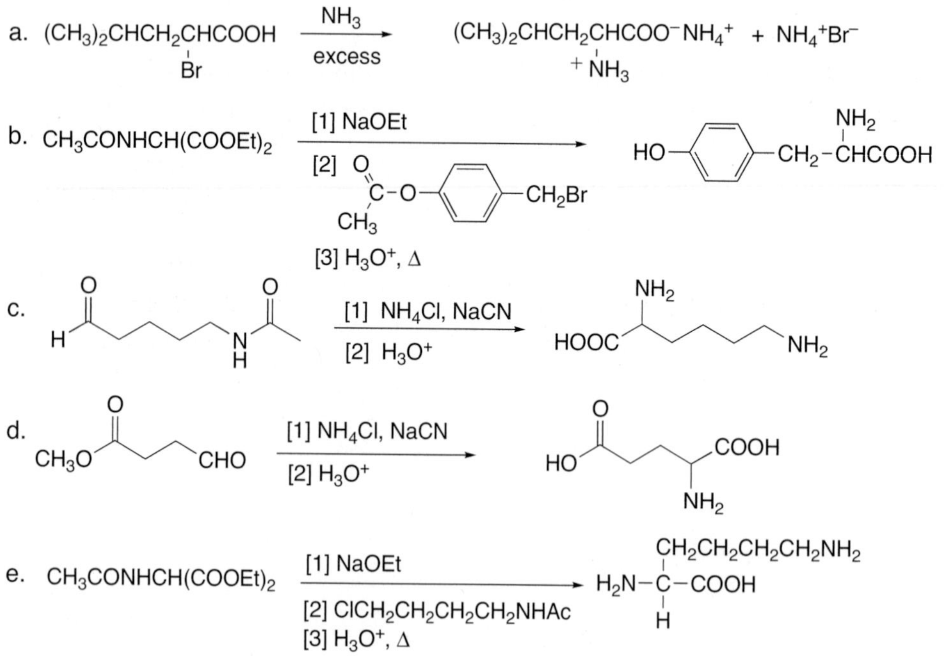
a. (CH3)2CHCH2CHCOOH
NH3
excess
(CH3)2CHCH2CHCOO−NH4+ + NH4+Br−
b. CH3CONHCH(COOEt)2
[1] NaOEt
[3] H3O+, Δ
c.
[1] NH4Cl, NaCN
[2] H3O+
d.
[1] NH4Cl, NaCN
[2] H3O+
e. CH3CONHCH(COOEt)2
[1] NaOEt
[2] ClCH2CH2CH2CH2NHAc
[3] H3O+, Δ

29.42

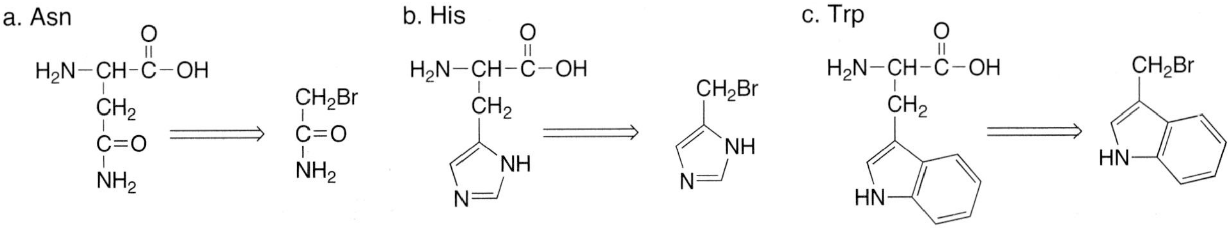

29.43

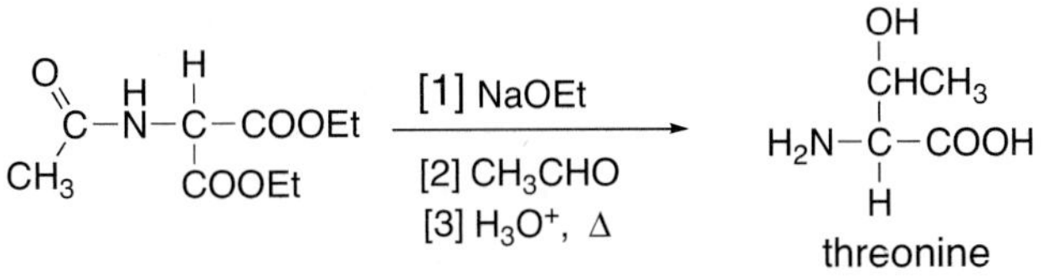

29.44

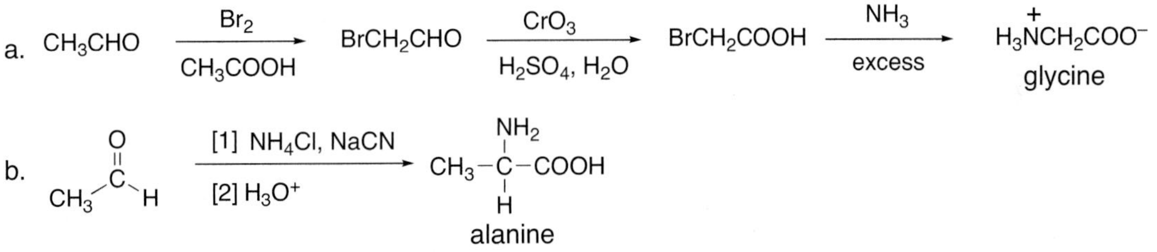

29.45

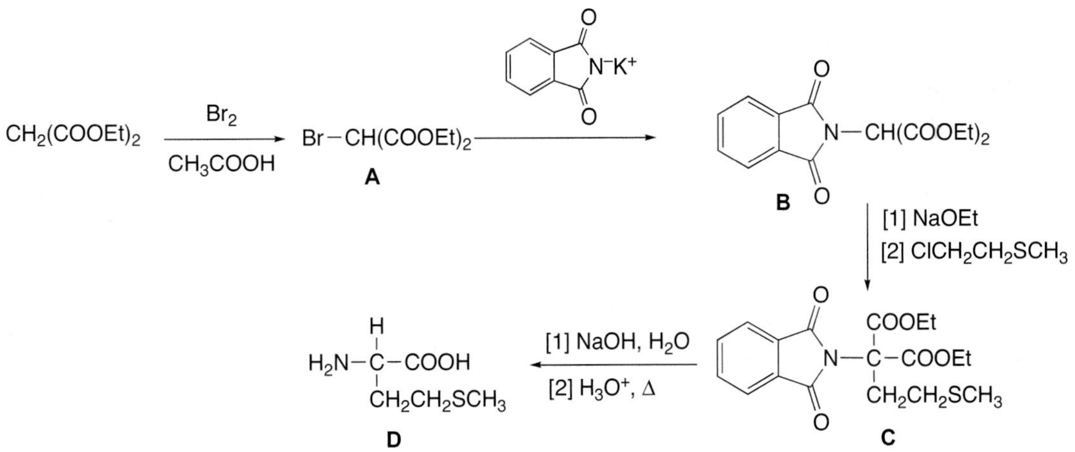

29.46

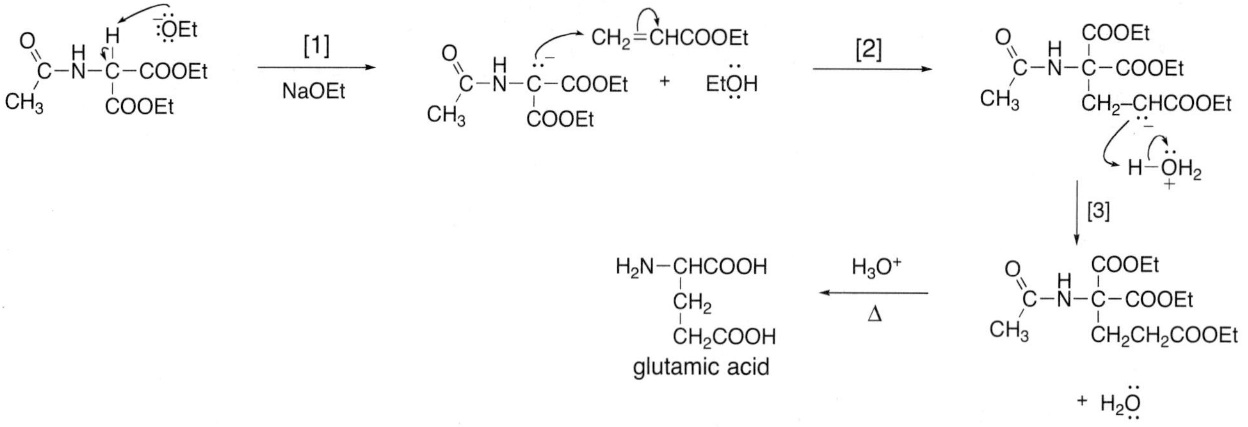

29.47

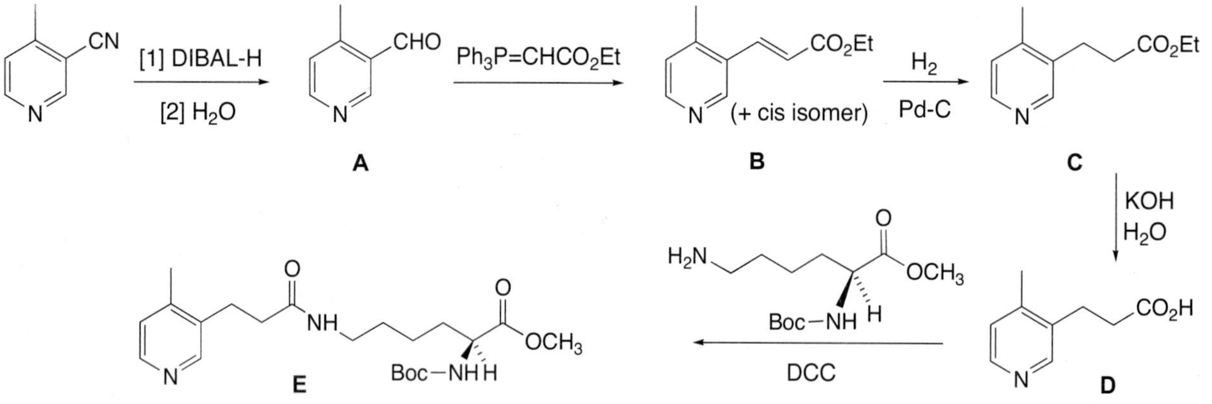

29.48

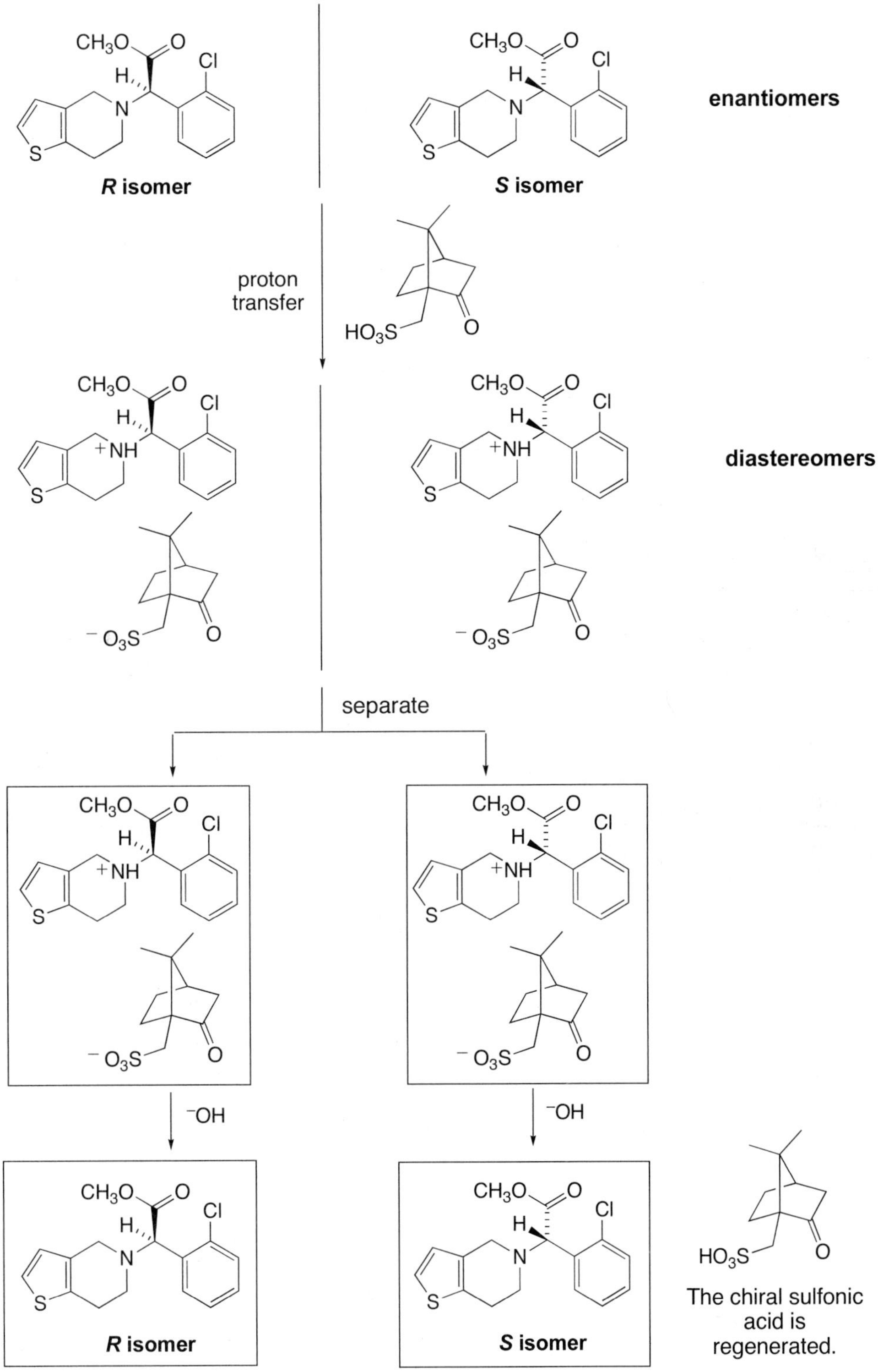

CH3O
O
Cl
H
N
S
R isomer
S isomer
enantiomers
proton transfer
HO3S
O
+NH
−O3S
diastereomers
separate
−OH
The chiral sulfonic acid is regenerated.

29.49

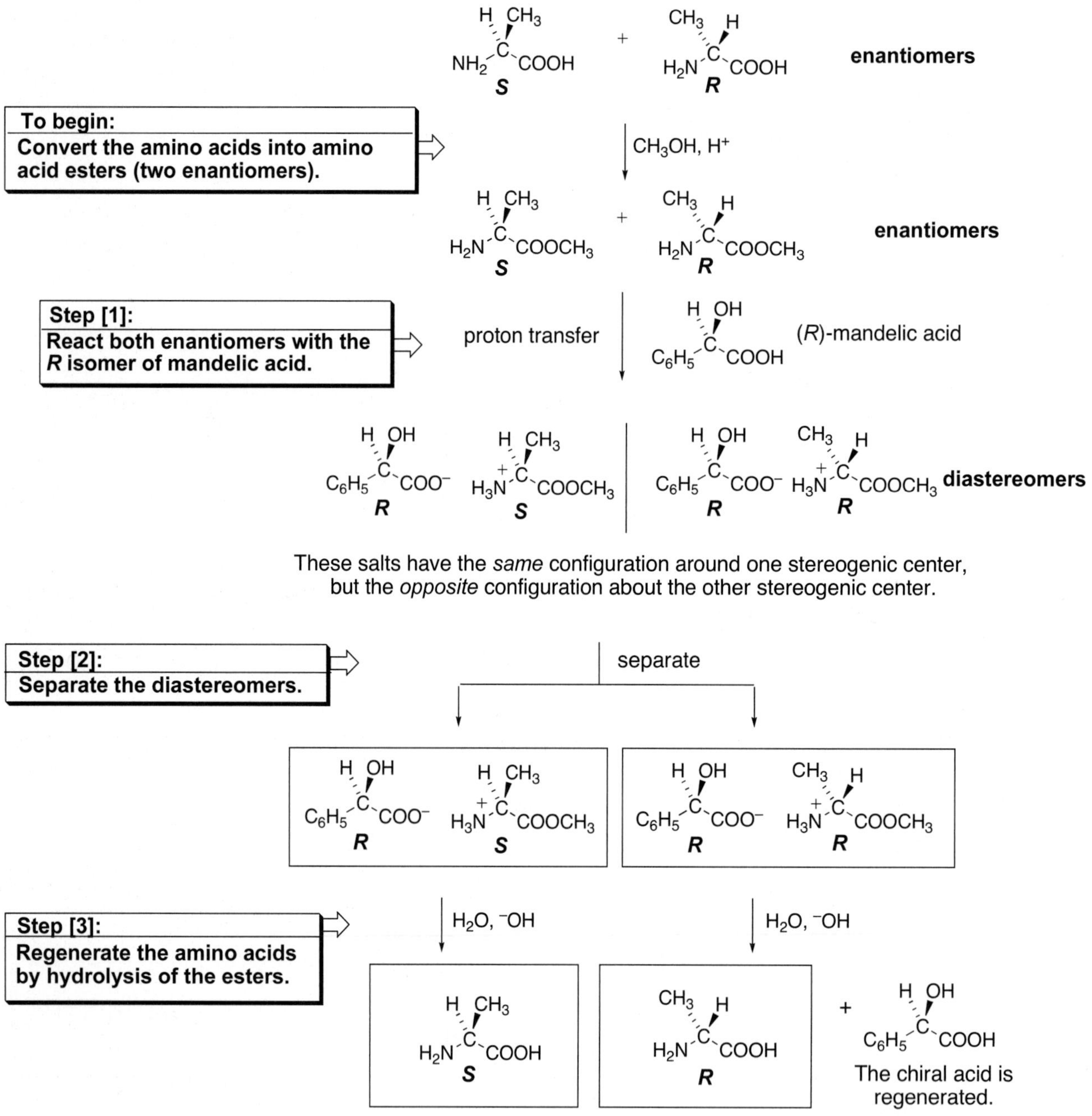
enantiomers
To begin:
Convert the amino acids into amino acid esters (two enantiomers).
CH3OH, H+
enantiomers
Step [1]:
React both enantiomers with the R isomer of mandelic acid.
proton transfer
(R)-mandelic acid
diastereomers
These salts have the same configuration around one stereogenic center, but the opposite configuration about the other stereogenic center.
Step [2]:
Separate the diastereomers.
separate
Step [3]:
Regenerate the amino acids by hydrolysis of the esters.
H2O, −OH
H2O, −OH
The chiral acid is regenerated.

29.50

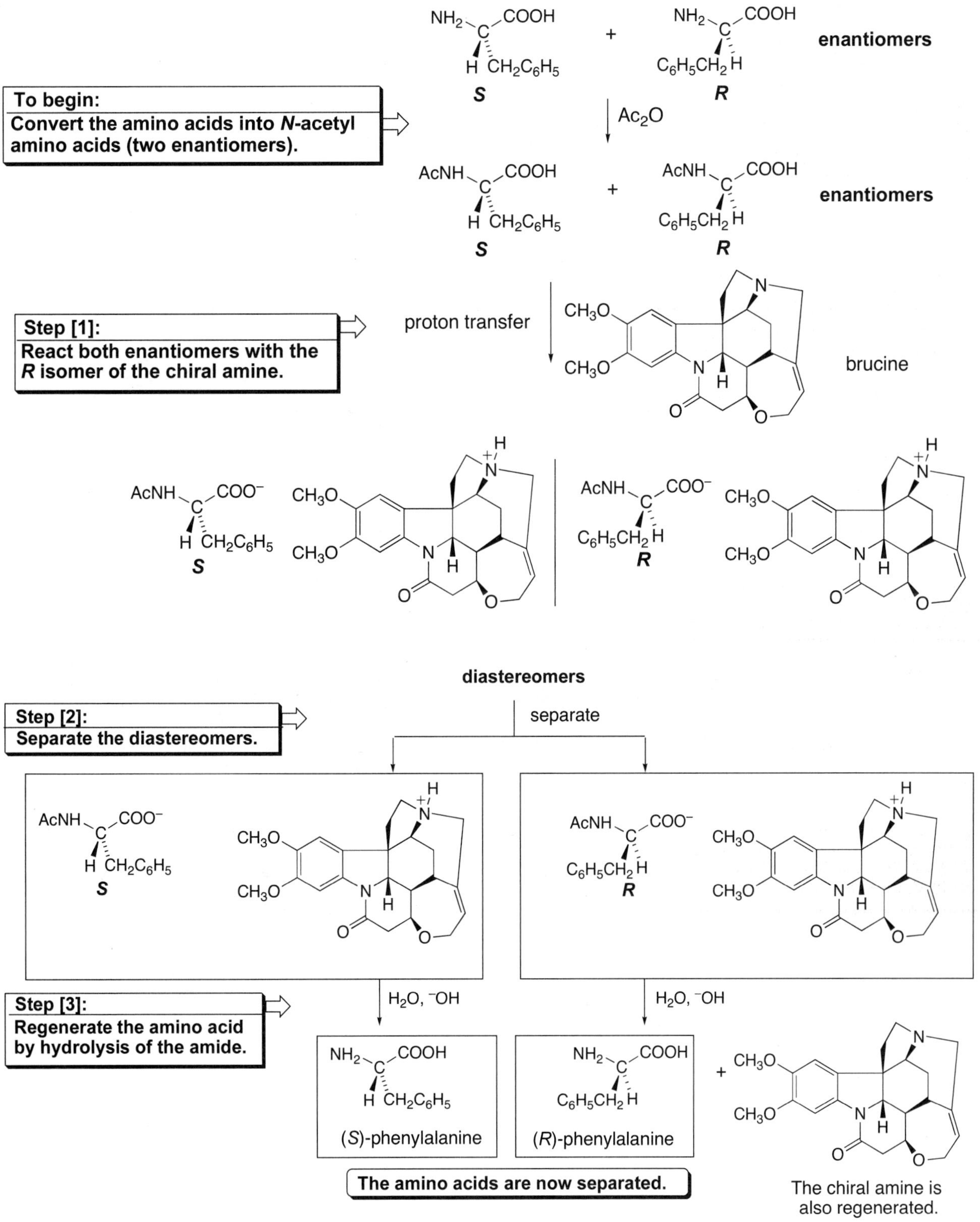
To begin:
Convert the amino acids into N-acetyl amino acids (two enantiomers).
NH2 COOH H CH2C6H5 S
+
NH2 COOH C6H5CH2 H R
enantiomers
Ac2O
AcNH COOH H CH2C6H5 S
+
AcNH COOH C6H5CH2 H R
enantiomers
Step [1]:
React both enantiomers with the R isomer of the chiral amine.
proton transfer
CH3O
CH3O
N
H
O
brucine
AcNH COO− H CH2C6H5 S
AcNH COO− C6H5CH2 H R
diastereomers
Step [2]:
Separate the diastereomers.
separate
Step [3]:
Regenerate the amino acid by hydrolysis of the amide.
H2O, −OH
H2O, −OH
(S)-phenylalanine
(R)-phenylalanine
The amino acids are now separated.
The chiral amine is also regenerated.

29.51

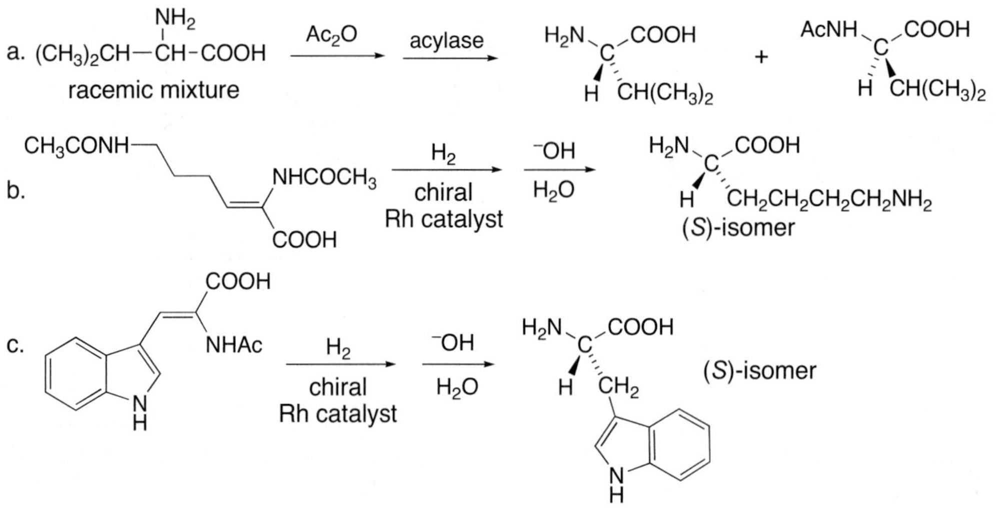

29.52

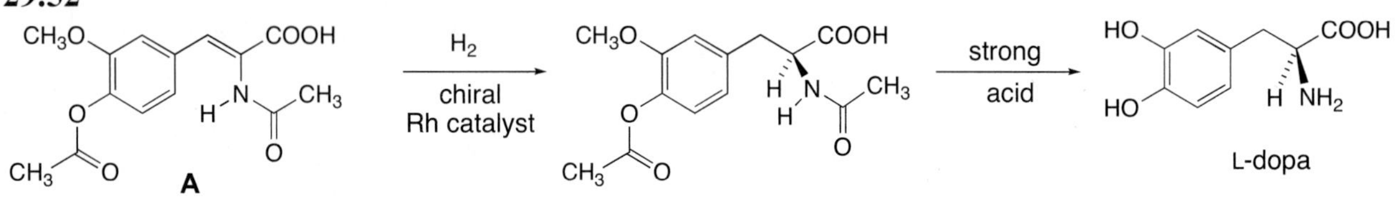

29.53

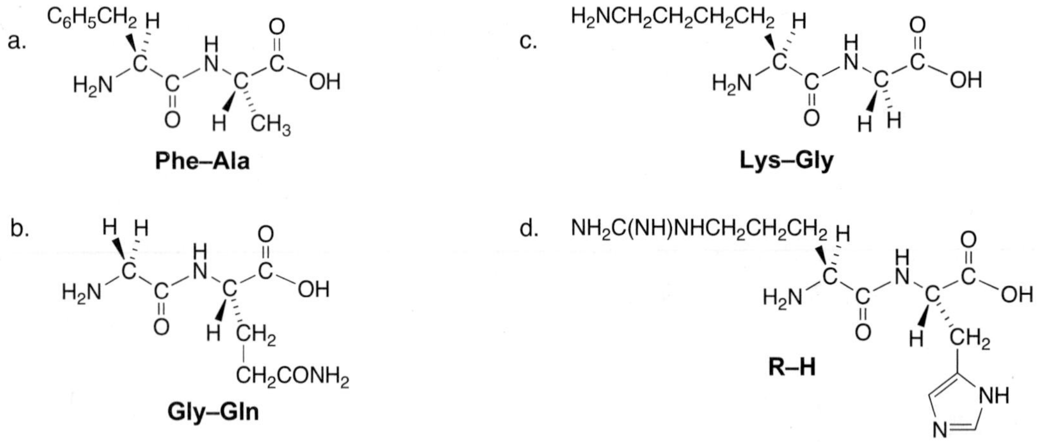

29.54 Amide bonds are bold lines (not wedges).

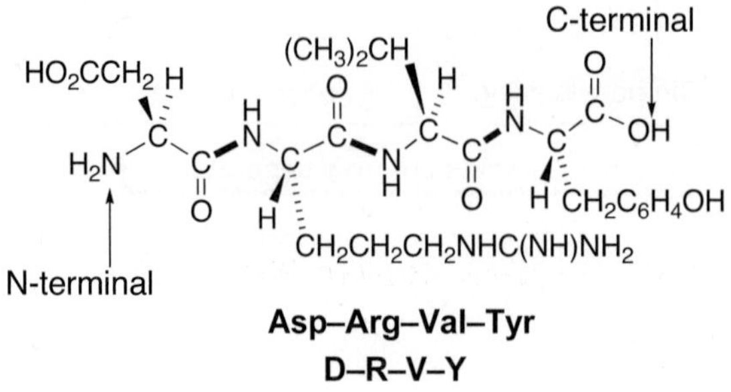
C-terminal
N-terminal
Asp–Arg–Val–Tyr
D–R–V–Y

29.55 Name a peptide from the N-terminal to the C-terminal end.

a.

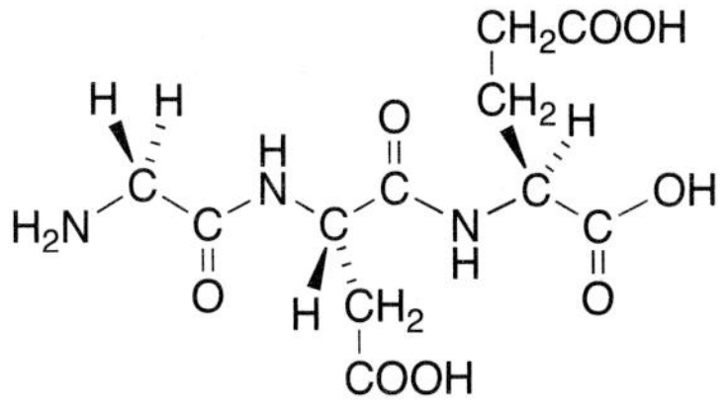

Gly–Asp–Glu
G–D–E

b.

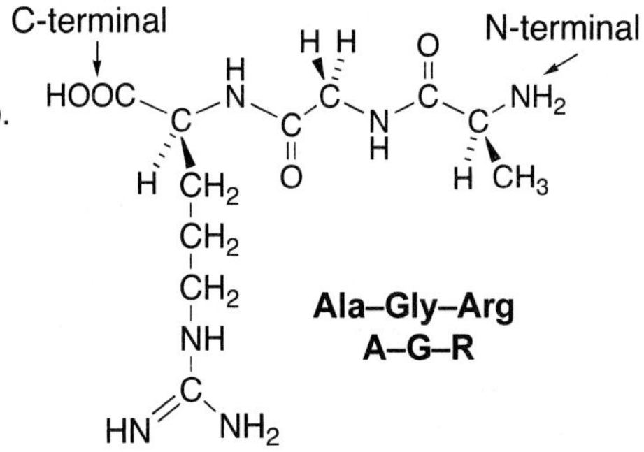
C-terminal
N-terminal

Ala–Gly–Arg
A–G–R

29.56 A peptide C–N bond is stronger than an ester C–O bond because the C–N bond has more double bond character due to resonance. Since N is more basic than O, an amide C–N bond is more stabilized by delocalization of the lone pair on N.

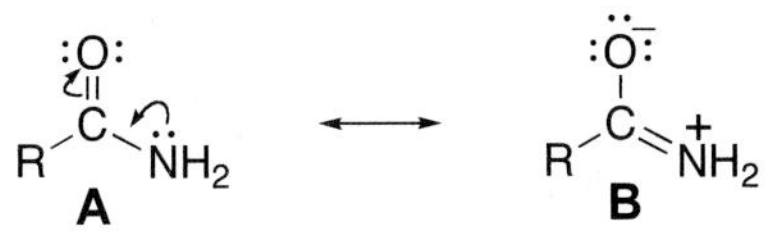

Structure **B** contributes greatly to the resonance hybrid and this shortens and strengthens the C–N bond.

29.57

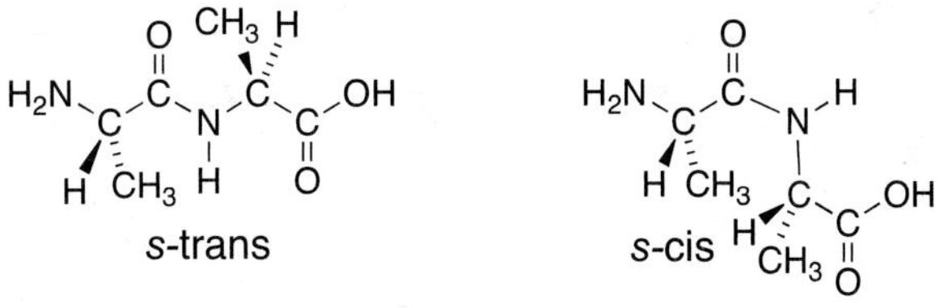
s-trans
s-cis

29.58

a. A–P–F + L–K–W + S–G–R–G
b. A–P–F–L–K + W–S–G–R + G
c. A–P–F–L–K–W–S–G–R + G
d. A + P–F–L–K–W–S–G–R–G

29.59

a.

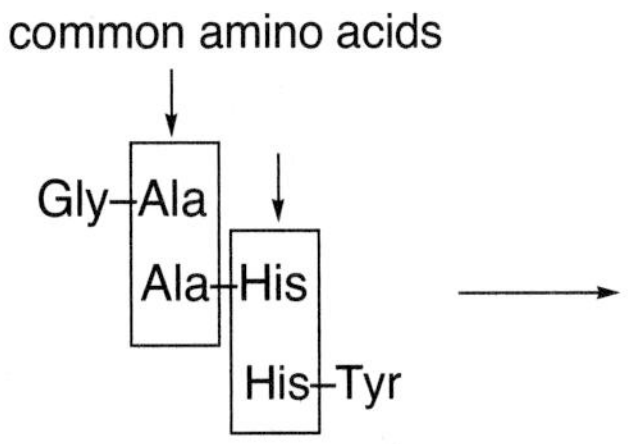
common amino acids
Gly–Ala
Ala–His
His–Tyr

Answer:

Gly–Ala–His–Tyr

b.

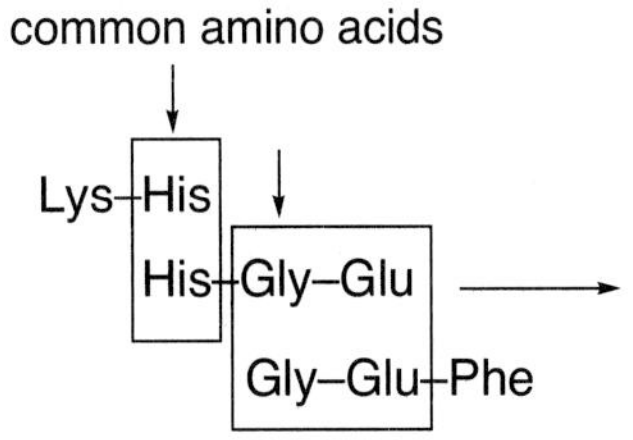
common amino acids
Lys–His
His–Gly–Glu
Gly–Glu–Phe

Answer:

Lys–His–Gly–Glu–Phe

29.60

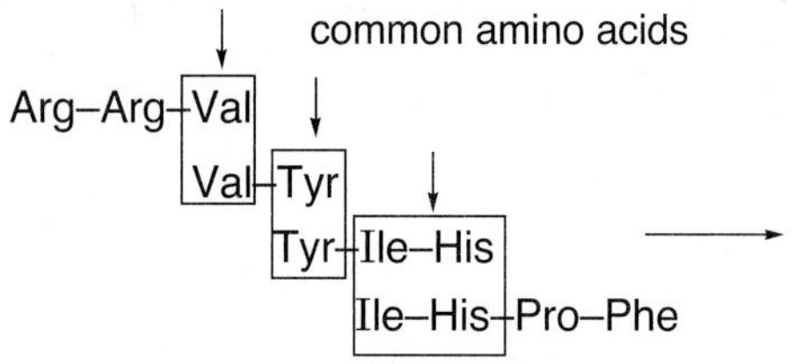
common amino acids
Arg–Arg–Val
Val–Tyr
Tyr–Ile–His
Ile–His–Pro–Phe

Answer:

Arg–Arg–Val–Tyr–Ile–His–Pro–Phe

29.61 Gly is the N-terminal amino acid (from Edman degradation), and Leu is the C-terminal amino acid (from treatment with carboxypeptidase). Partial hydrolysis gives the rest of the sequence.

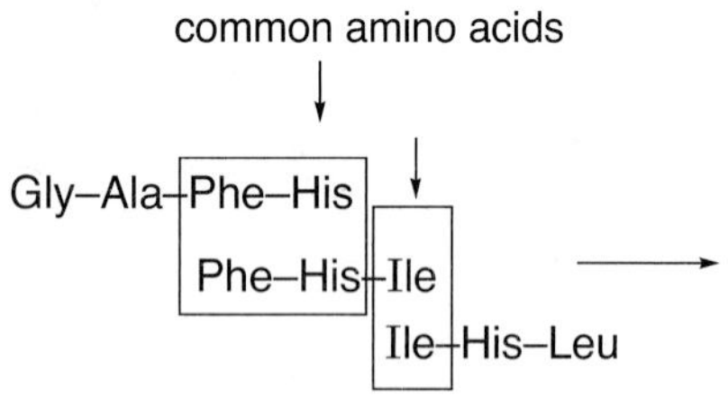
common amino acids
Gly–Ala–Phe–His
Phe–His–Ile
Ile–His–Leu

Answer:

Gly–Gly–Ala–Phe–His–Ile–His–Leu

29.62 Edman degradation data give the N-terminal amino acid for the octapeptide and all smaller peptides.

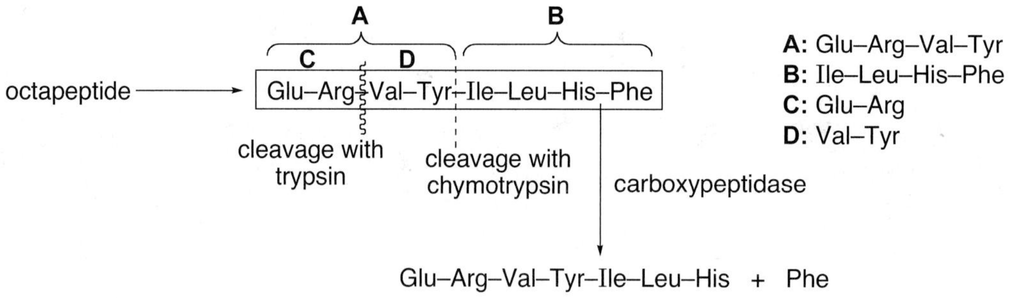
A
B
C
D
octapeptide
Glu–Arg–Val–Tyr–Ile–Leu–His–Phe
cleavage with trypsin
cleavage with chymotrypsin
carboxypeptidase
Glu–Arg–Val–Tyr–Ile–Leu–His + Phe
A: Glu–Arg–Val–Tyr
B: Ile–Leu–His–Phe
C: Glu–Arg
D: Val–Tyr

29.63 **A** and **B** can react to form an amide, or two molecules of **B** can form an amide.

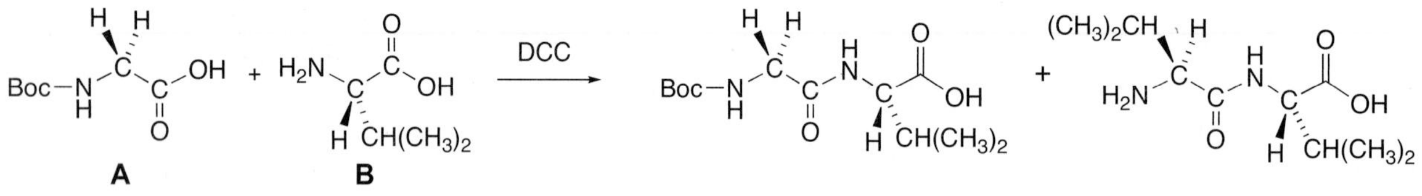
A
B
DCC

29.64

a.

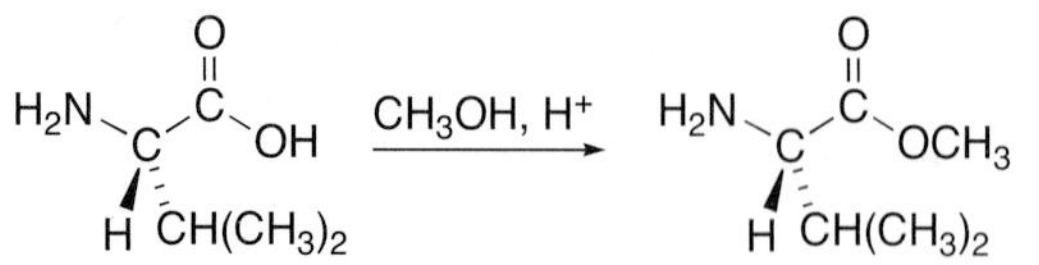
CH3OH, H+

b.

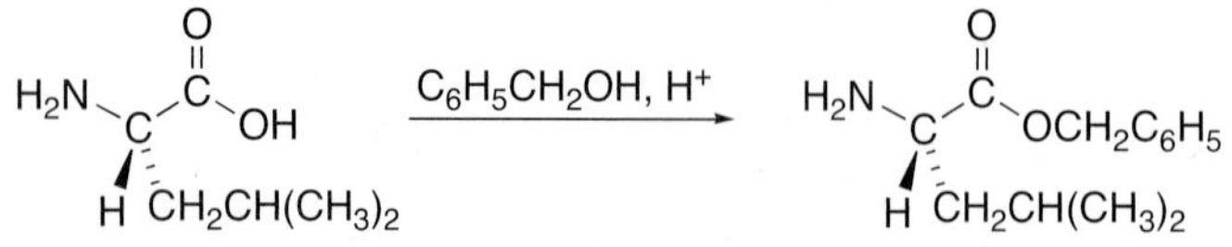
C6H5CH2OH, H+

c.

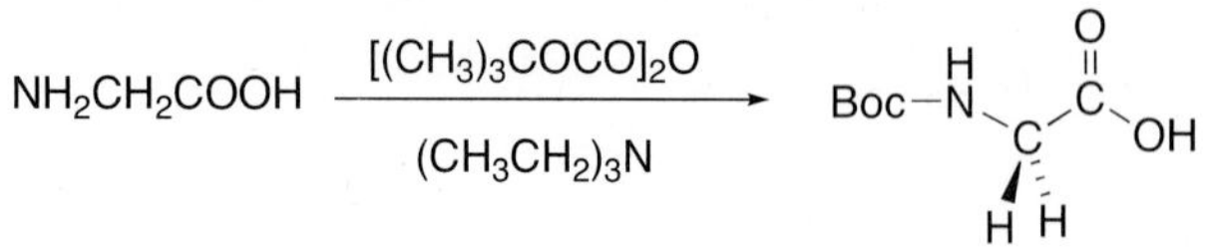
NH2CH2COOH
[(CH3)3COCO]2O
(CH3CH2)3N

d.
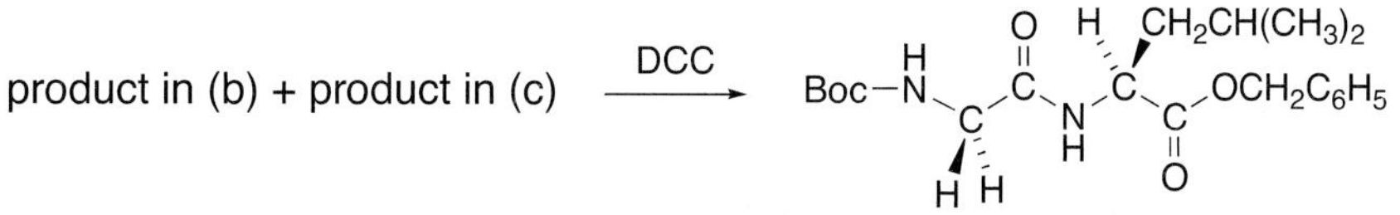
product in (b) + product in (c)
DCC
Boc–N
OCH2C6H5
CH2CH(CH3)2

e.
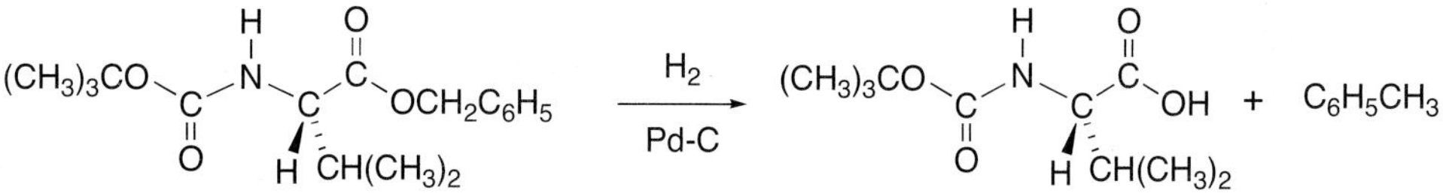
(CH3)3CO
OCH2C6H5
CH(CH3)2
H2
Pd-C
OH
+ C6H5CH3

f.
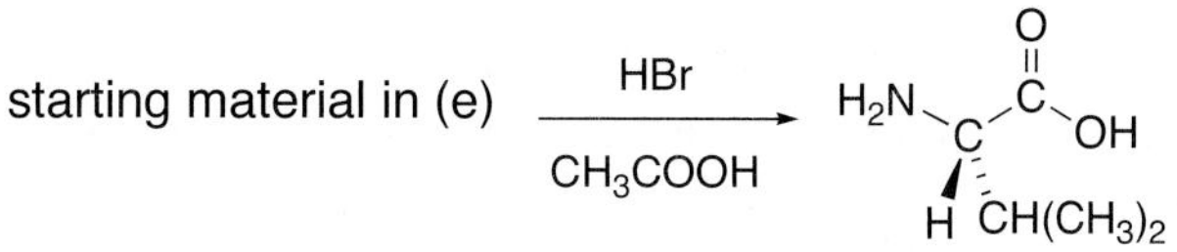
starting material in (e)
HBr
CH3COOH
H2N
OH
CH(CH3)2

g.
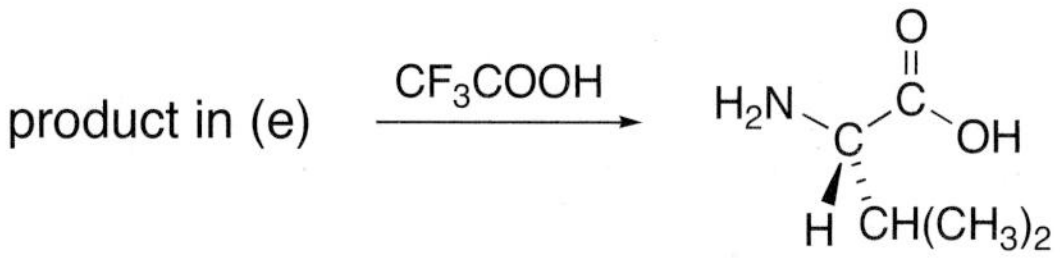
product in (e)
CF3COOH
H2N
OH
CH(CH3)2

h.
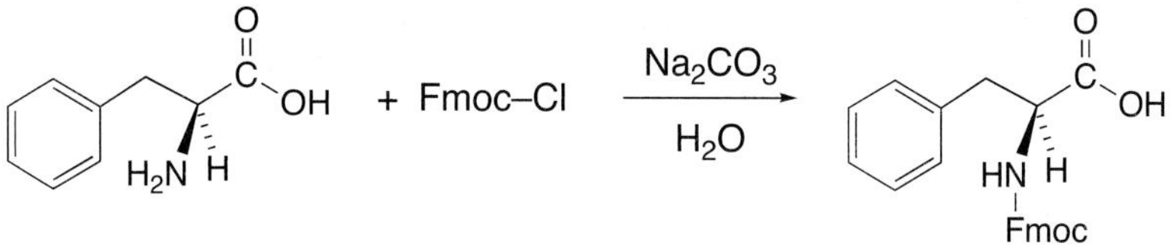
OH
H2N
+ Fmoc–Cl
Na2CO3
H2O
HN
Fmoc

29.65

a.
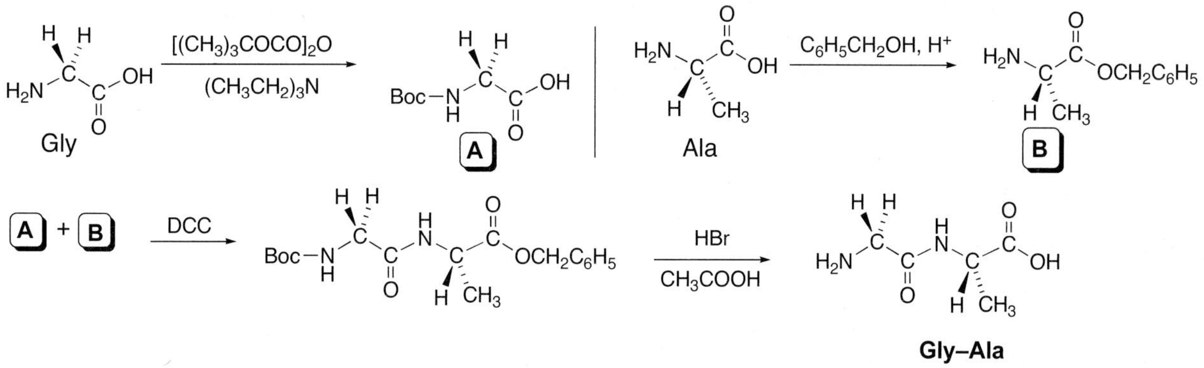
Gly
[(CH3)3COCO]2O
(CH3CH2)3N
Boc–N
A
Ala
C6H5CH2OH, H+
OCH2C6H5
B
A + B
DCC
HBr
CH3COOH
Gly–Ala

b.

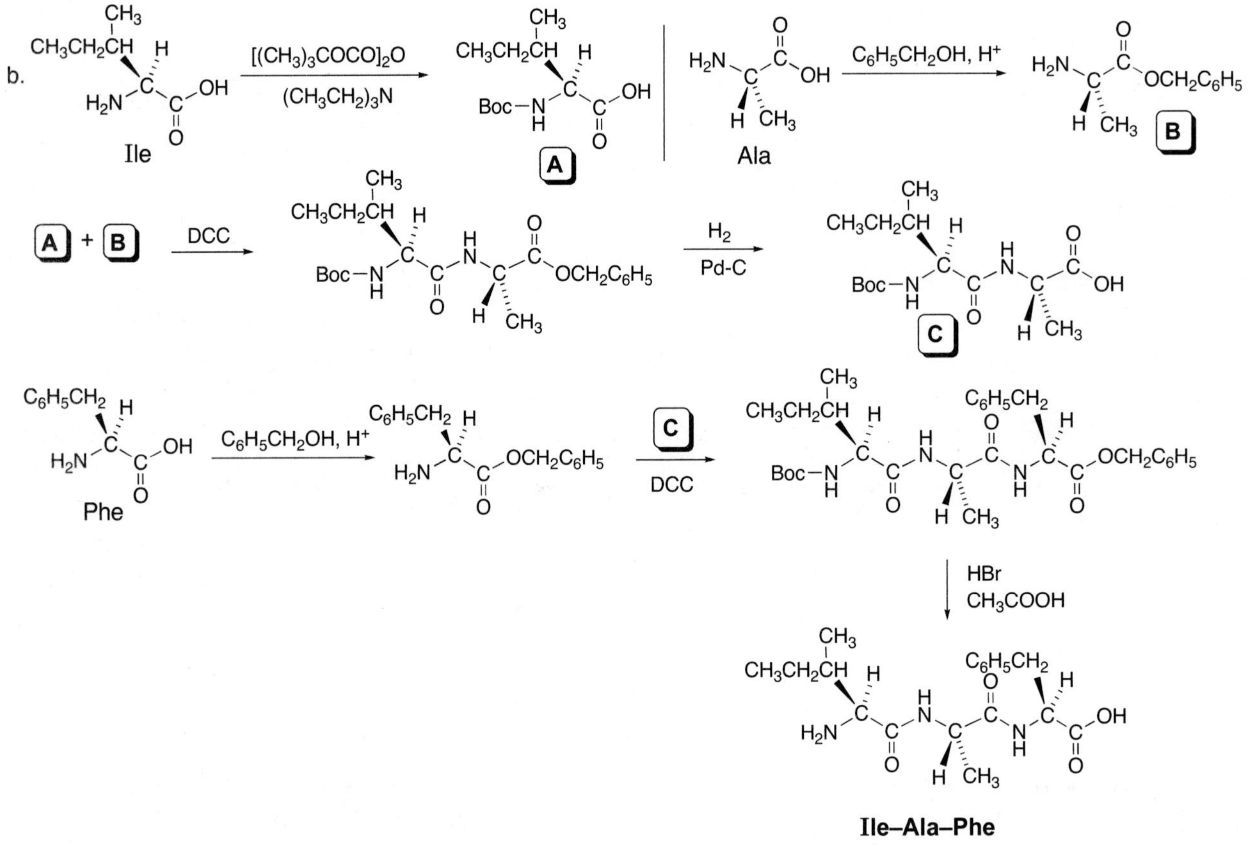

CH3
CH3CH2CH
H
H2N
C
OH
O
Ile
[(CH3)3COCO]2O
(CH3CH2)3N
Boc
A
Ala
C6H5CH2OH, H+
OCH2C6H5
CH3
B
DCC
H2
Pd-C
C
C6H5CH2
Phe
HBr
CH3COOH
Ile–Ala–Phe

29.66 Make all the Fmoc derivatives as described in Problem 29.24.

a.

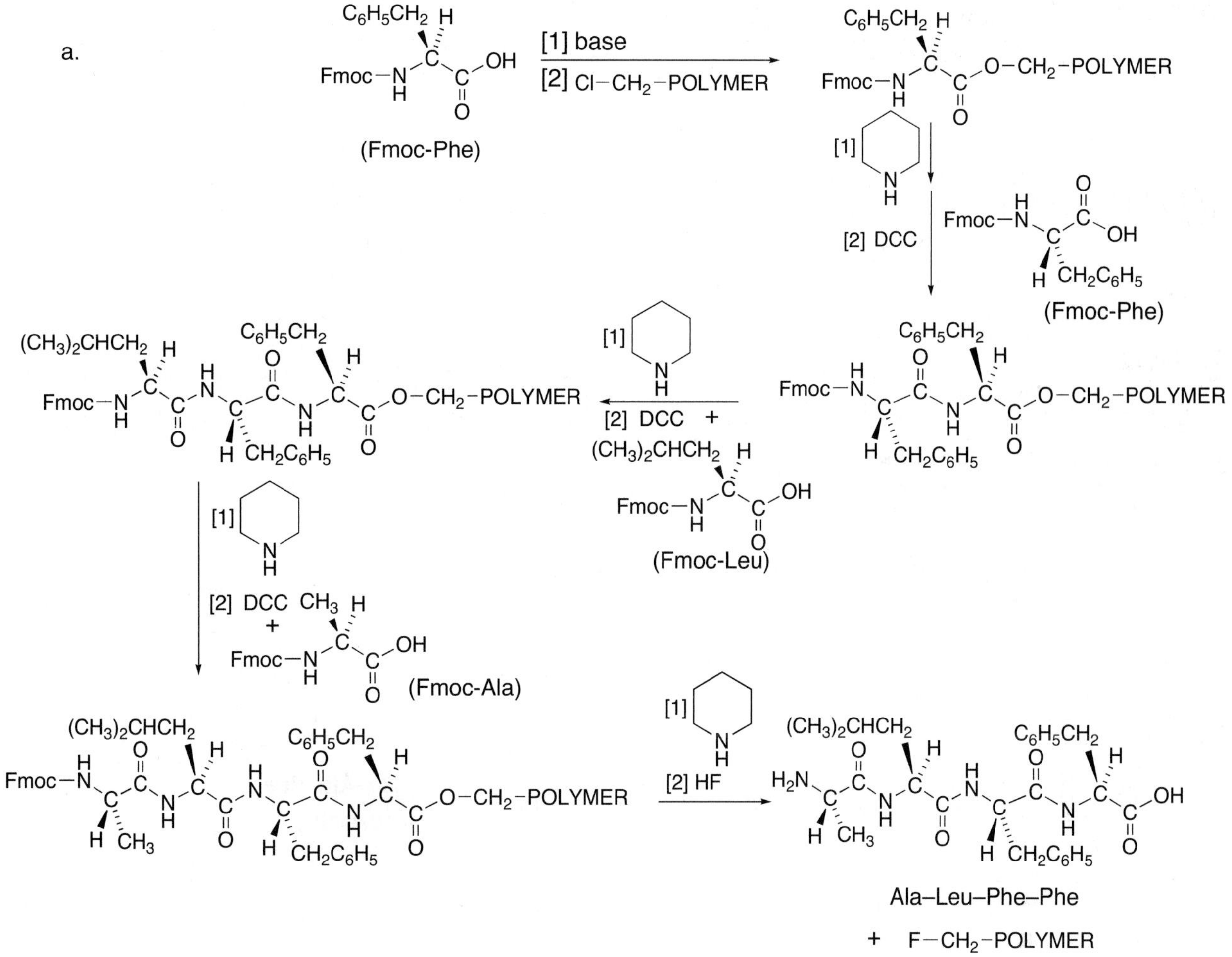

b.

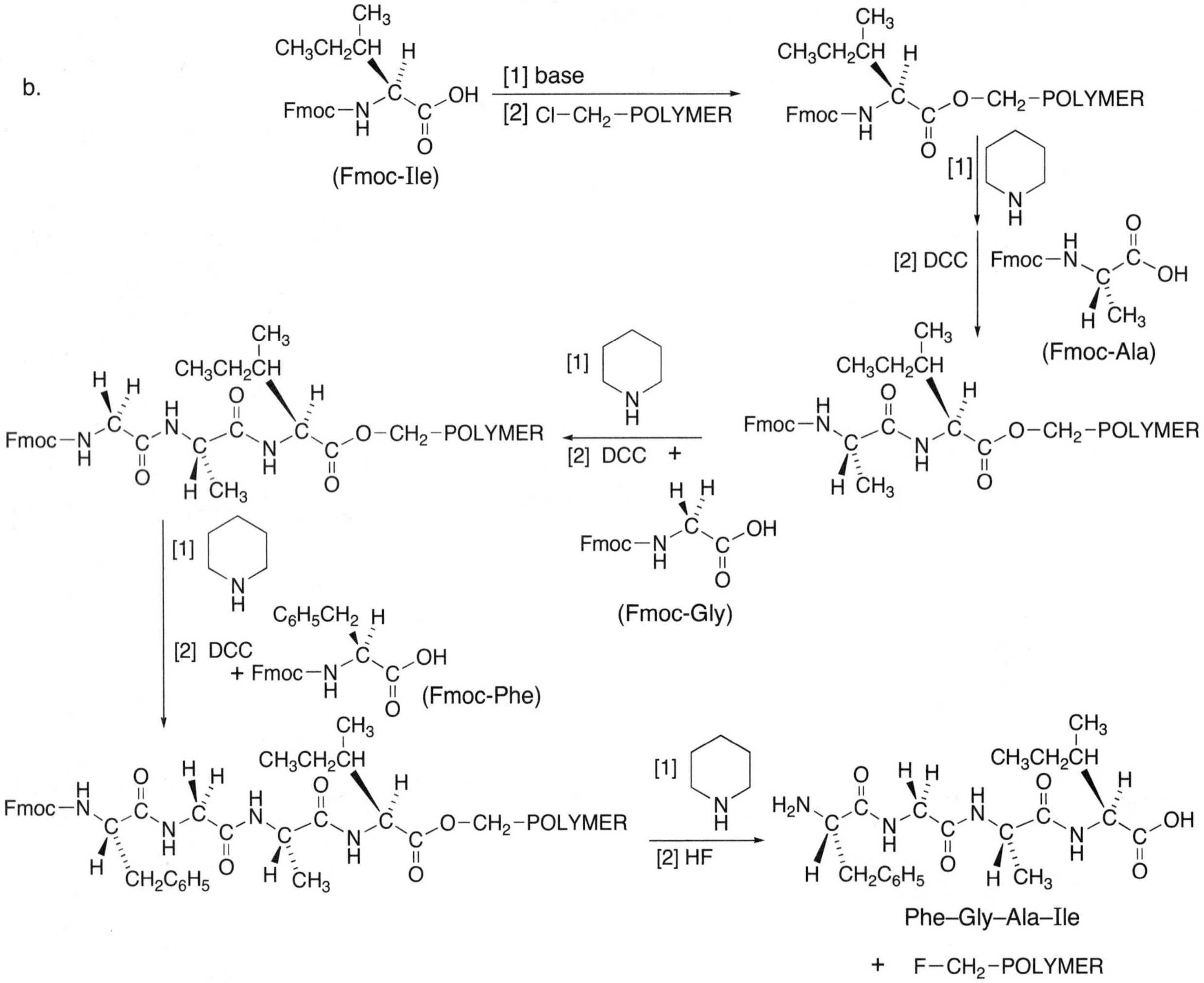

29.67

a. A *p*-nitrophenyl ester activates the carboxy group of the first amino acid to amide formation by converting the OH group into a good leaving group, the *p*-nitrophenoxide group, which is highly resonance stabilized. In this case the electron-withdrawing NO_2 group further stabilizes the leaving group.

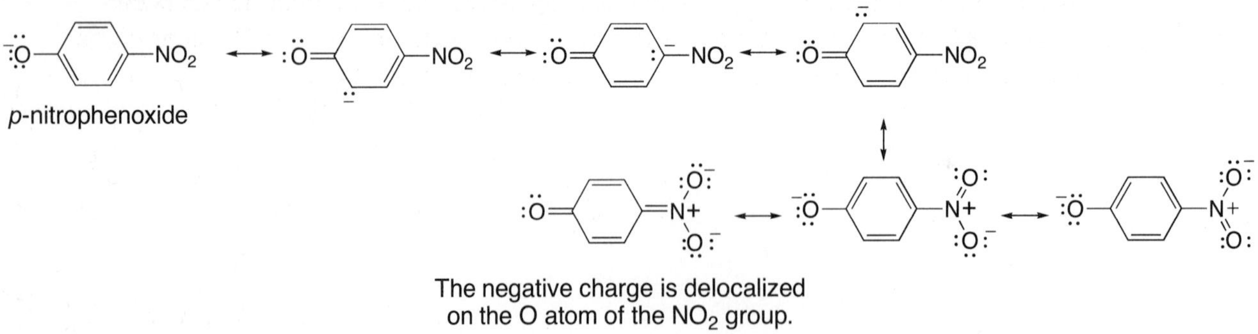

b. The *p*-methoxyphenyl ester contains an electron-donating OCH_3 group, making $CH_3OC_6H_4O^-$ a poorer leaving group than $NO_2C_6H_4O^-$, so this ester does not activate the amino acid to amide formation as much.

29.68

a. 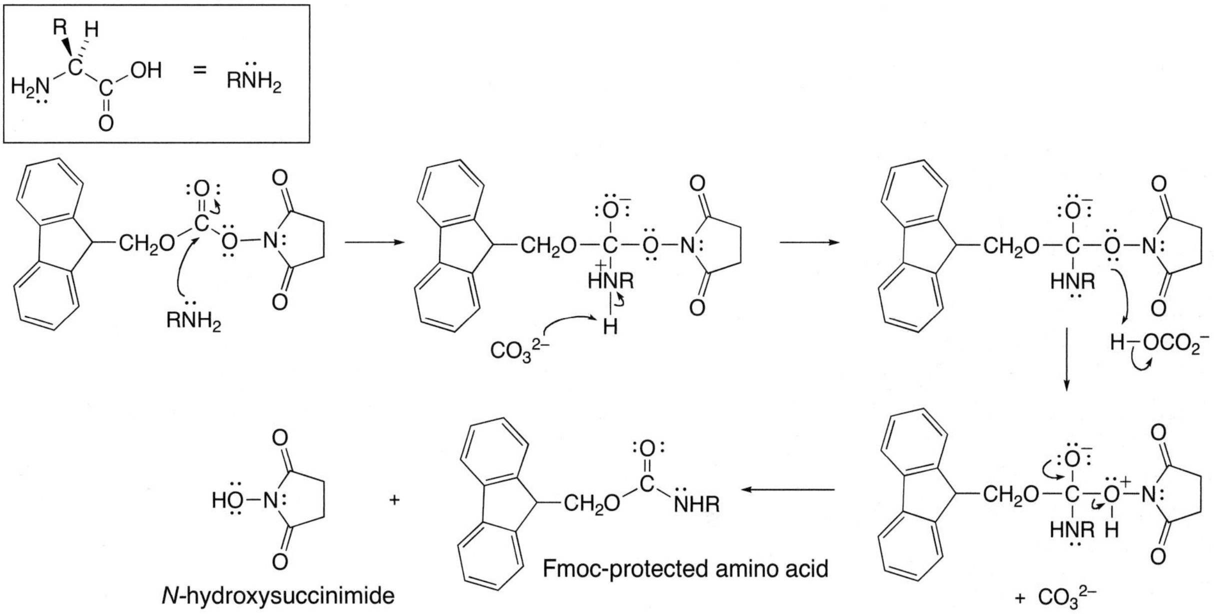

b. 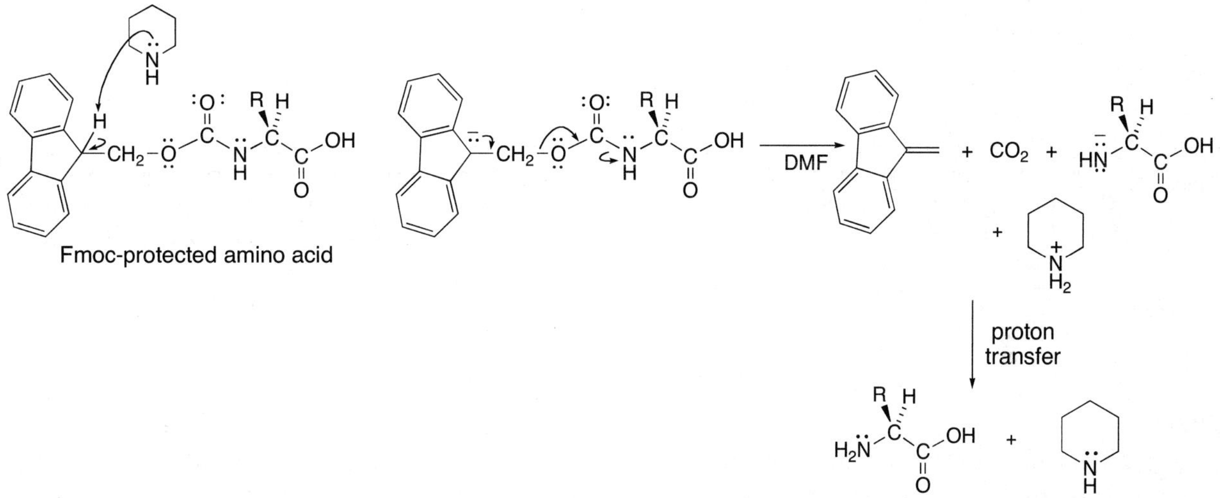

29.69 Reaction of the OH groups of the Wang resin with the COOH group of the Fmoc-protected amino acids would form esters by Fischer esterification. After the peptide has been synthesized, the esters can be hydrolyzed with aqueous acid or base, but the conditions cannot be too harsh to break the amide bond or cause epimerization.

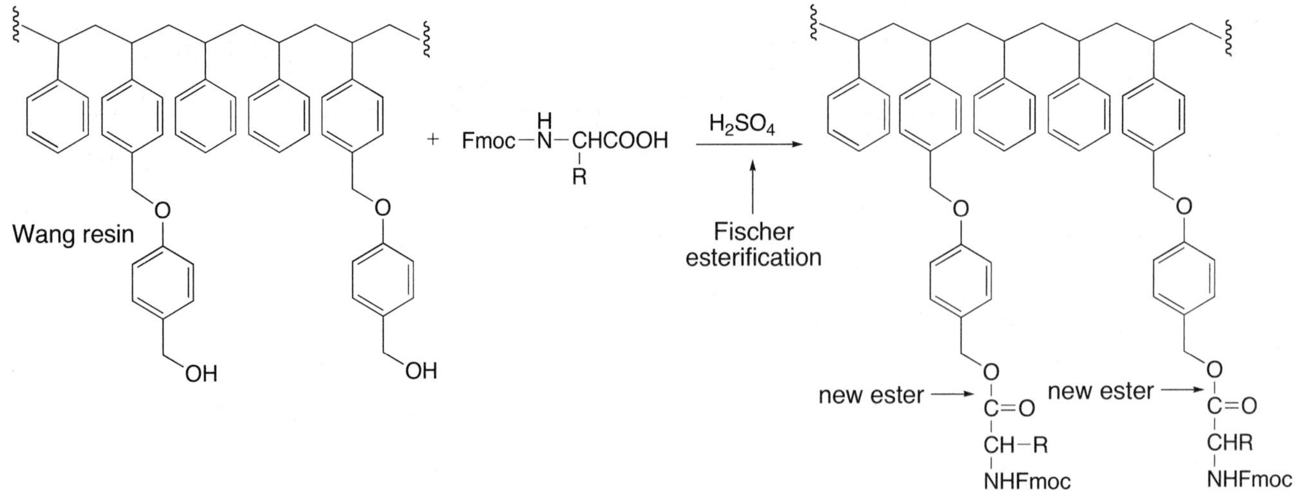

29.70 Amino acids commonly found in the interior of a globular protein have nonpolar or weakly polar side chains: isoleucine and phenylalanine. Amino acids commonly found on the surface have COOH, NH_2, and other groups that can hydrogen bond to water: aspartic acid, lysine, arginine, and glutamic acid.

29.71 The proline residues on collagen are hydroxylated to increase hydrogen bonding interactions.

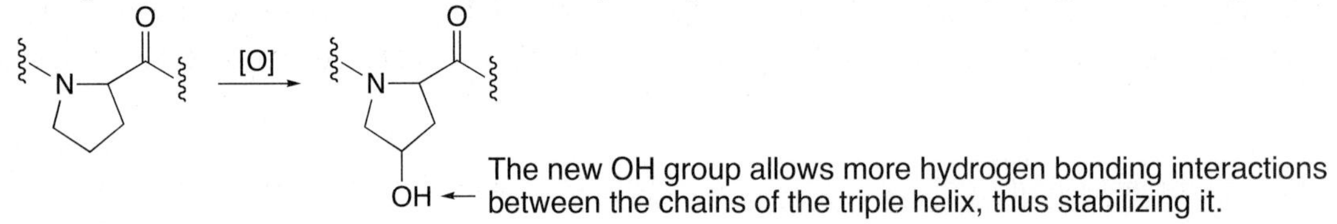

29.72

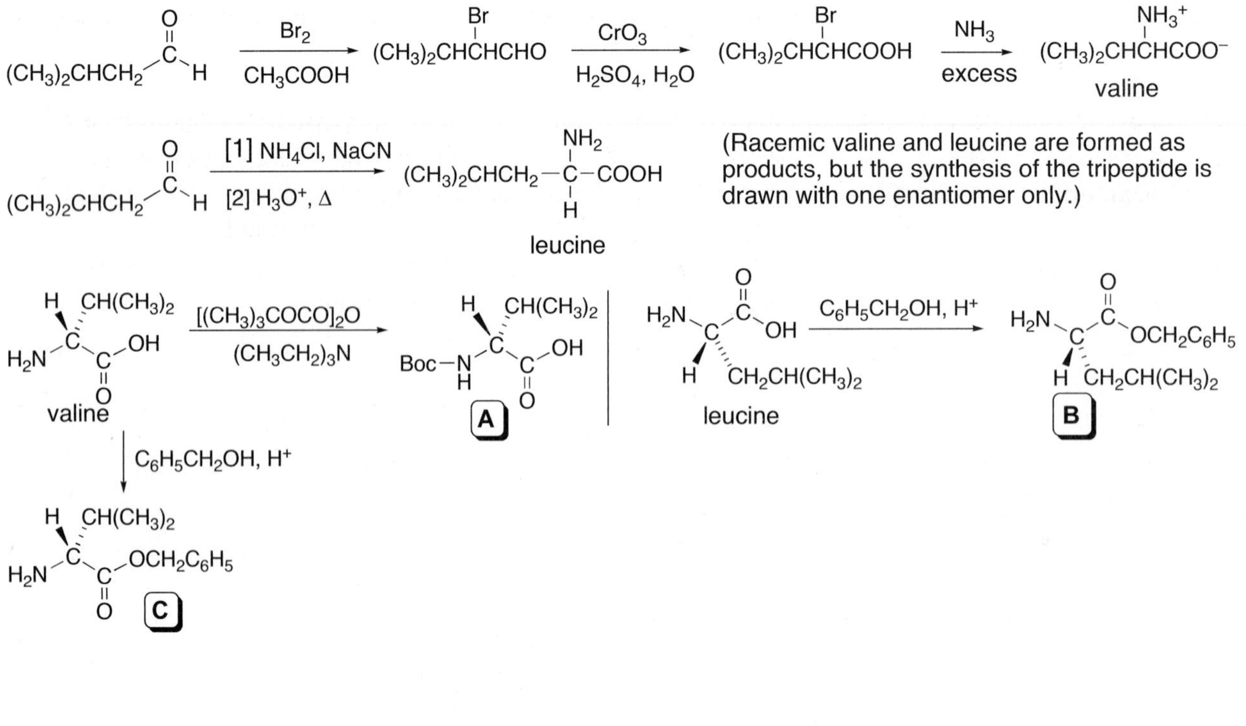

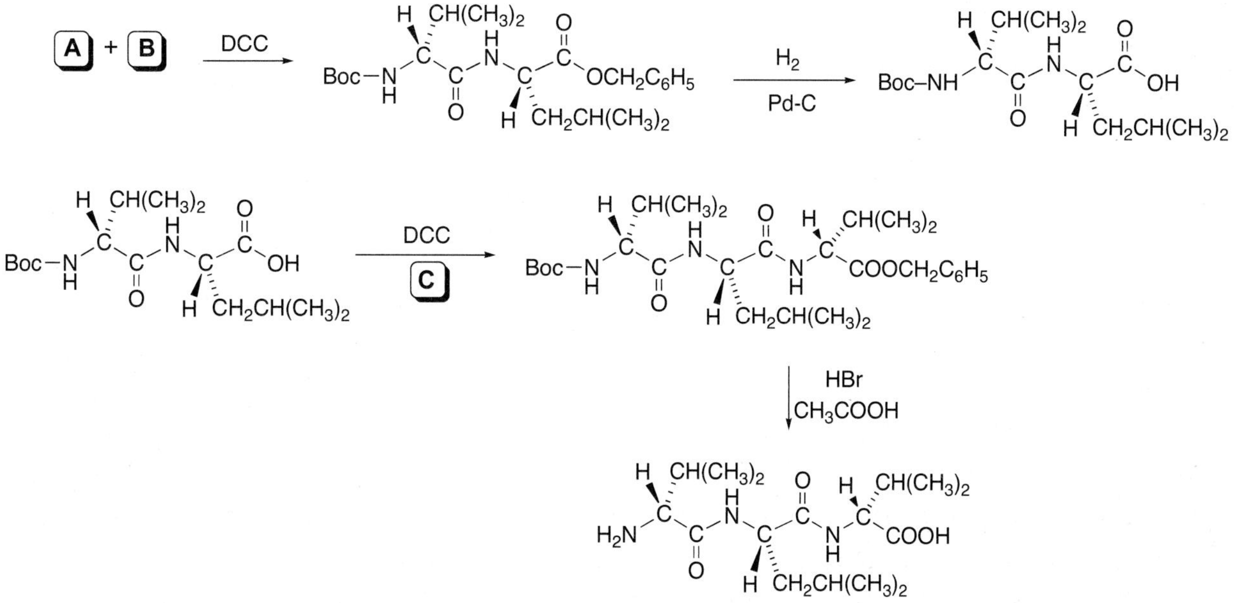

Val–Leu–Val

29.73 Perhaps using a chiral amine R*NH_2 (or related chiral nitrogen-containing compound) to make a chiral imine, will now favor formation of one of the amino nitriles in the Strecker synthesis. Hydrolysis of the CN group and removal of R* would then form the amino acid.

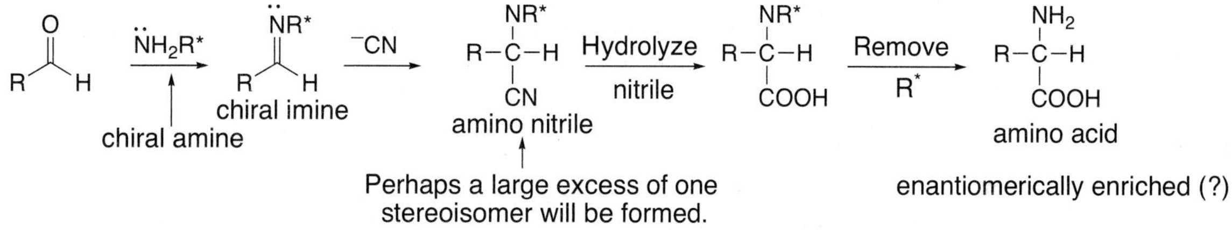

29.74 This reaction is similar to the reaction of penicillin with the glycopeptide transpeptidase enzyme discussed in Section 22.14. Serine has a nucleophilic OH, which can open the strained β-lactone to form a covalently bound, inactive enzyme.

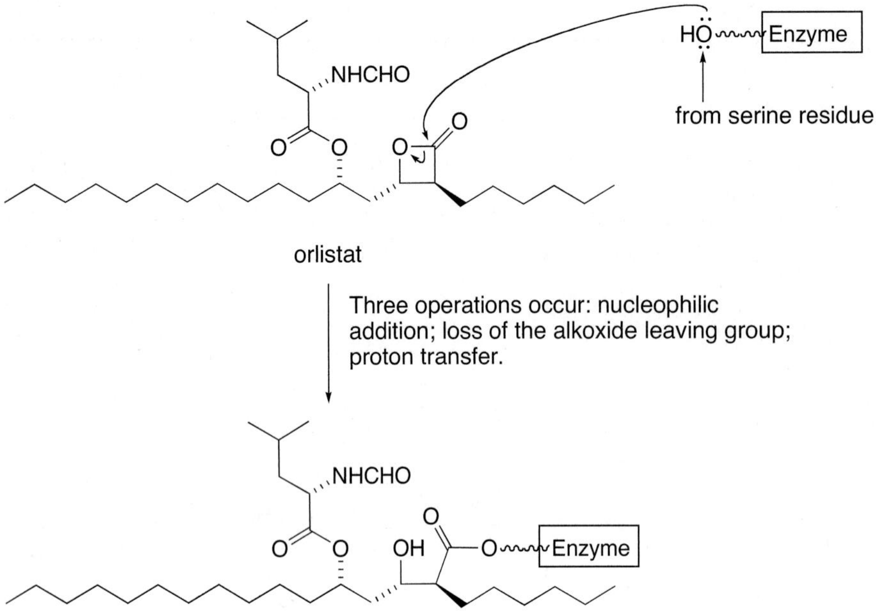
NHCHO
HO
Enzyme
from serine residue
orlistat
Three operations occur: nucleophilic addition; loss of the alkoxide leaving group; proton transfer.
NHCHO
OH
O
Enzyme

29.75

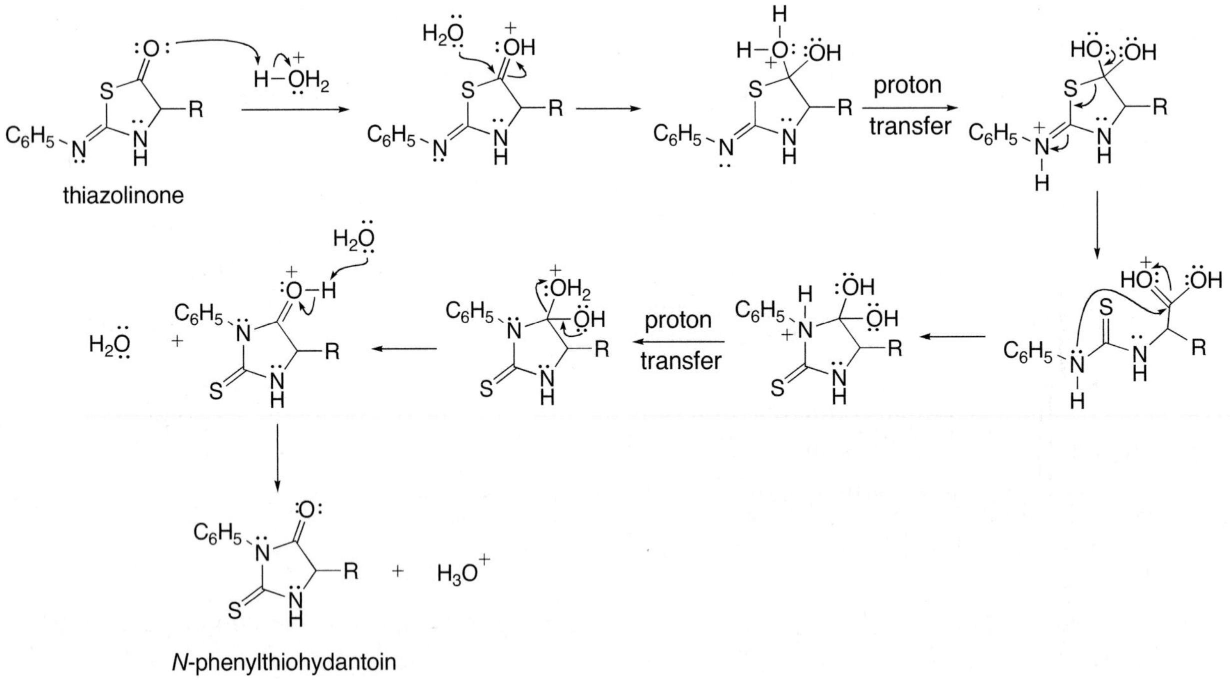
thiazolinone
proton
transfer
proton
transfer
N-phenylthiohydantoin

Chapter 30 Lipids

Chapter Review

Hydrolyzable lipids

[1] Waxes (30.2)—Esters formed from a long-chain alcohol and a long-chain carboxylic acid

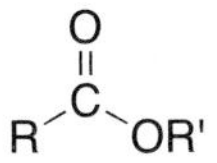

R, R' = long chains of C's

[2] Triacylglycerols (30.3)—Triesters of glycerol with three fatty acids

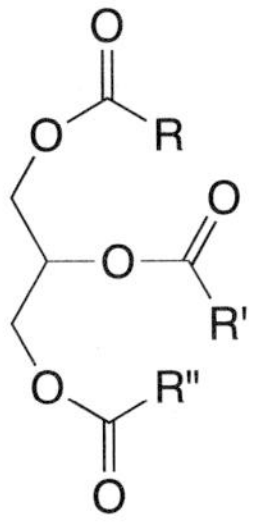

R, R', R" = alkyl groups with 11–19 C's

[3] Phospholipids (30.4)

[a] Phosphatidylethanolamine (cephalin)

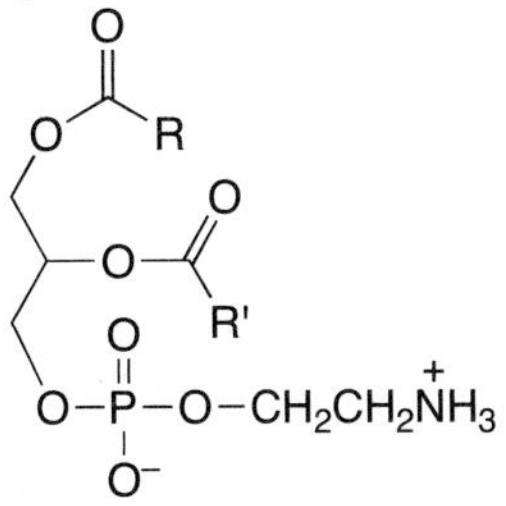

R, R' = long carbon chain

[b] Phosphatidylcholine (lecithin)

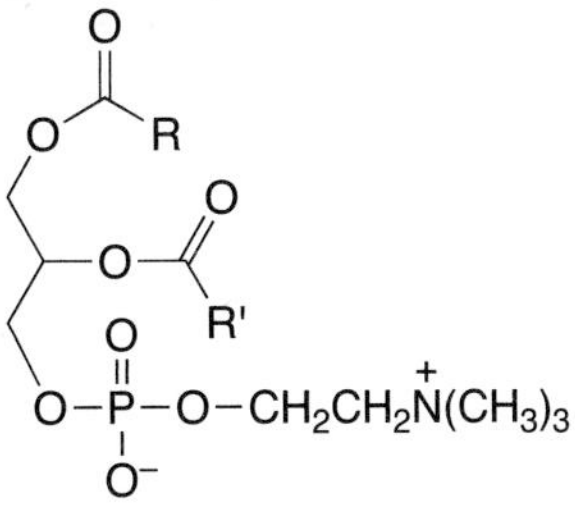

R, R' = long carbon chain

[c] Sphingomyelin

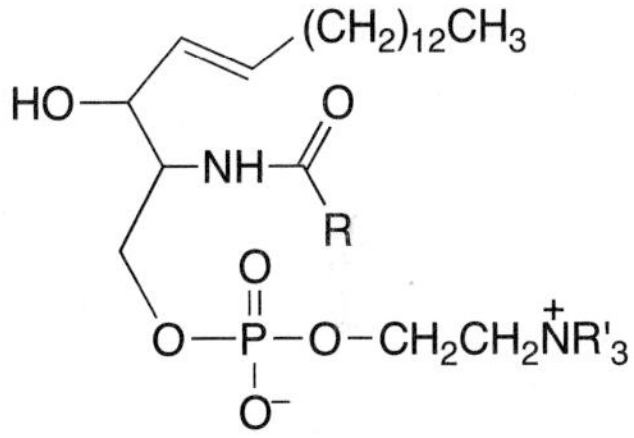

R = long carbon chain
R' = H or CH_3

Nonhydrolyzable lipids

[1] Fat-soluble vitamins (30.5)—Vitamins A, D, E, and K

[2] Eicosanoids (30.6)—Compounds containing 20 carbons derived from arachidonic acid. There are four types: prostaglandins, thromboxanes, prostacyclins, and leukotrienes.

[3] Terpenes (30.7)—Lipids composed of repeating five-carbon units called isoprene units

Isoprene unit	Types of terpenes			
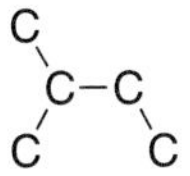	[1] monoterpene	10 C's	[4] sesterterpene	25 C's
	[2] sesquiterpene	15 C's	[5] triterpene	30 C's
	[3] diterpene	20 C's	[6] tetraterpene	40 C's

[4] Steroids (30.8)—Tetracyclic lipids composed of three six-membered and one five-membered ring

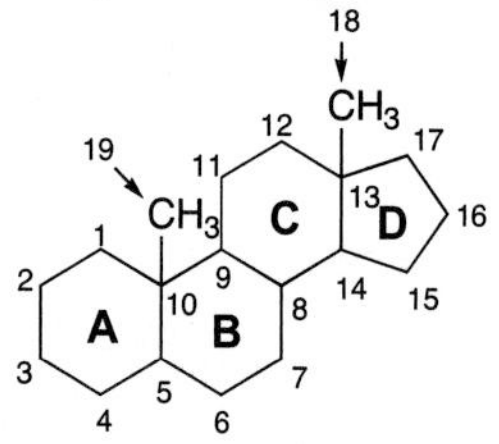

Practice Test on Chapter Review

1. a. Which of the following compounds contains an ester?
   1. a wax
   2. a cephalin
   3. a sphingomyelin
   4. Both [1] and [2] contain esters.
   5. Compounds [1], [2], and [3] all contain esters.

   b. Which of the following compounds is an eicosanoid?
   1. a leukotriene
   2. a thromboxane
   3. a prostaglandin
   4. Both [1] and [2] are eicosanoids.
   5. Compounds [1], [2], and [3] are all eicosanoids.

   c. Which of the following statements is (are) true about **A**?

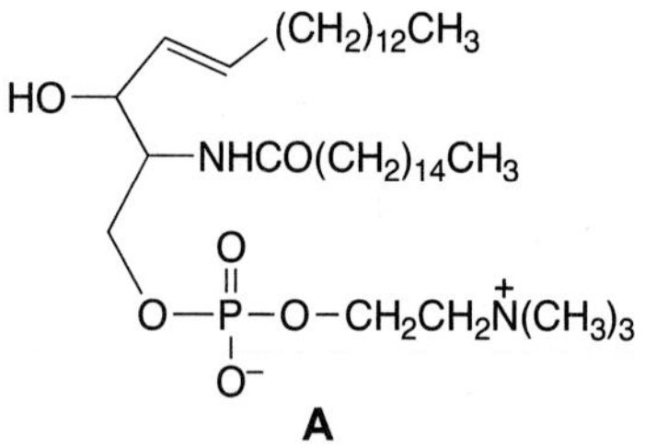

A

   1. **A** is a lecithin.
   2. **A** is a phosphoacylglycerol.
   3. **A** has two tetrahedral stereogenic centers.
   4. Both [1] and [2] are true.
   5. Statements [1], [2], and [3] are all true.

2. Label each compound as a (1) hydrolyzable or (2) nonhydrolyzable lipid.
   a. a triacylglycerol
   b. vitamin A
   c. cholesterol
   d. a lecithin
   e. oleic acid
   f. PGE_1
   g. a wax
   h. a phosphoacylglycerol

3. For each compound: How many isoprene units does the compound contain? Classify the compound as a monoterpene, sesquiterpenoid, etc.

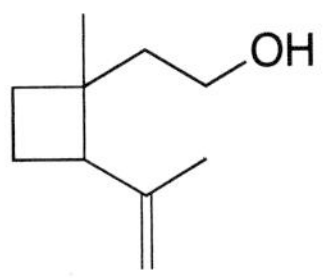

A

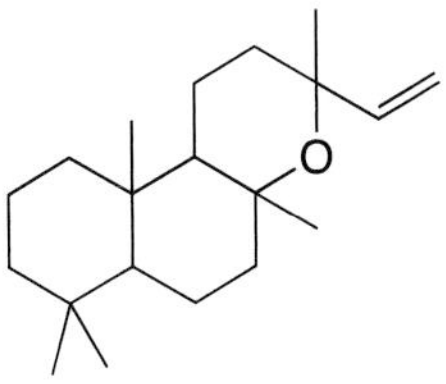

B

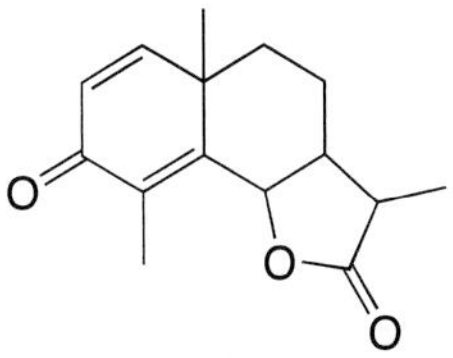

C

4. Answer True (T) or False (F) for each statement.
   a. Eicosanoids are biosynthesized from dimethylallyl diphosphate and isopentenyl diphosphate.
   b. Prostaglandins are biosynthesized from arachidonic acid.
   c. Fats have lower melting points than oils, and are generally solids at room temperature.
   d. A cephalin is one type of phosphoacylglycerol.
   e. Sphingomyelins possess a polar head and two nonpolar tails.
   f. A sesterterpene contains six isoprene units.
   g. The typical steroid skeleton has four six-membered rings joined with trans ring fusions.
   h. Waxes are high molecular weight lipids formed from a fatty acid and a long-chain amine.

5. Which terms describe each compound: (a) hydrolyzable lipid; (b) triacylglycerol; (c) phosphoacylglycerol; (d) phospholipid; (e) nonhydrolyzable lipid; (f) prostaglandin; (g) terpenoid? More than one term may apply to a compound.

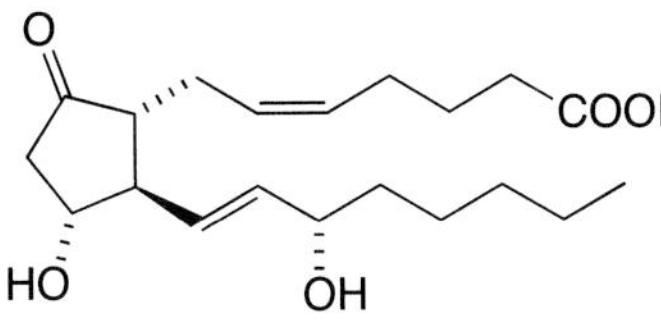

A

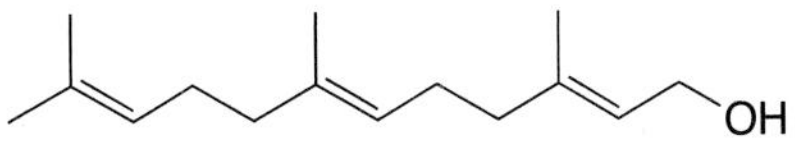

B

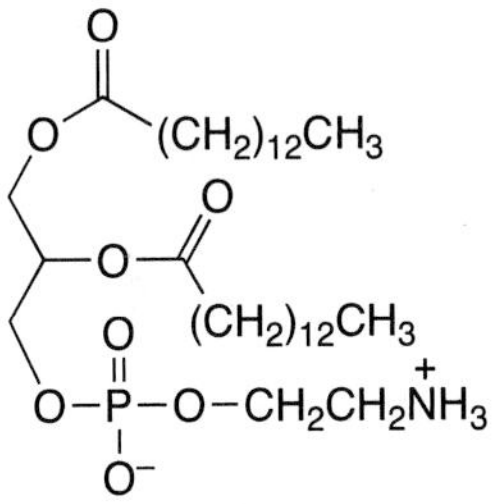

C

Answers to Practice Test

1. a. 4	2. a. 1	3. **A:** 2, monoterpenoid	4. a. F	5. **A:** e, f
b. 5	b. 2	**B:** 4, diterpenoid	b. T	**B:** e, g
c. 3	c. 2	**C:** 3, sesquiterpenoid	c. F	**C:** a, c, d
	d. 1		d. T	
	e. 2		e. T	
	f. 2		f. F	
	g. 1		g. F	
	h. 1		h. F	

Answers to Problems

30.1 Join the carboxylic acid and alcohol together to form an ester.

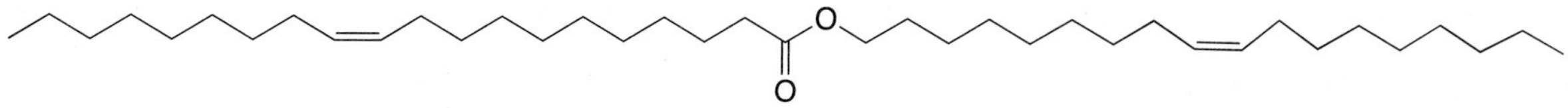

30.2 Eicosapentaenoic acid has 20 C's and 5 C=C's. Since an increasing number of double bonds decreases the melting point, eicosapentaenoic acid should have a melting point lower than arachidonic acid; that is, < –49 °C.

30.3

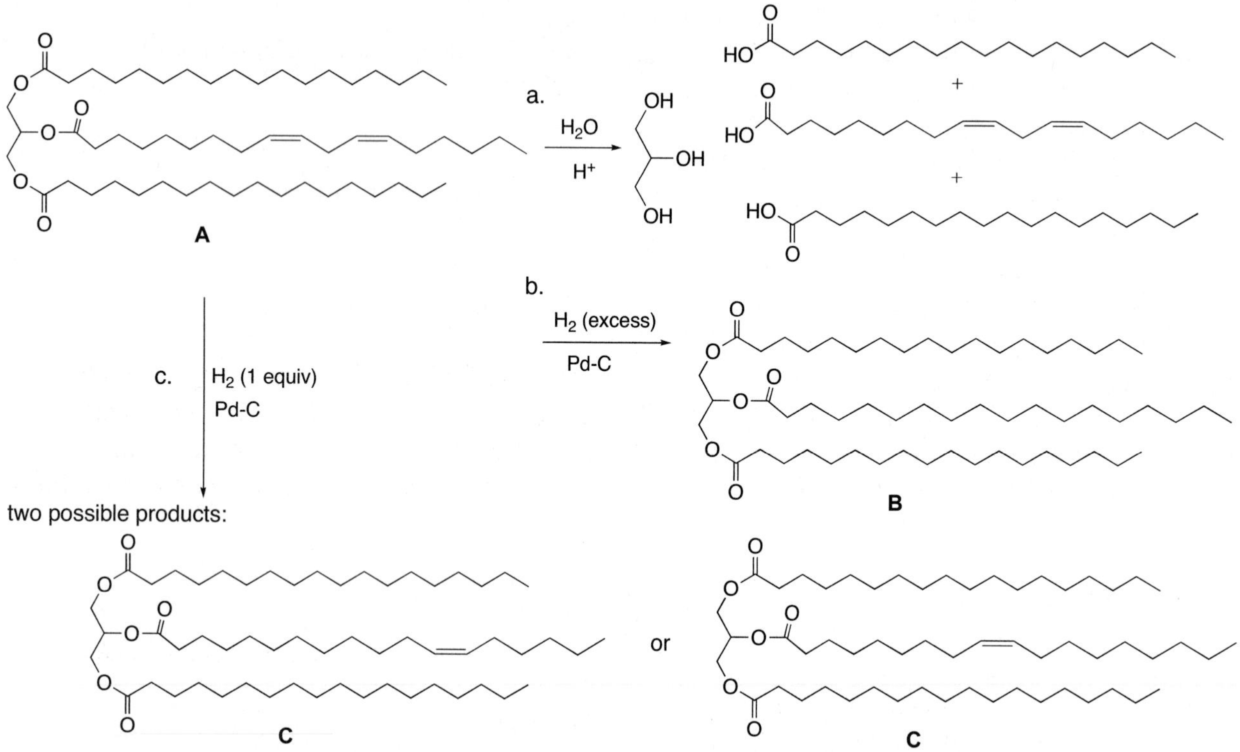

A	<	C	<	B
2 double bonds		1 double bond		0 double bonds
lowest melting point		**intermediate melting point**		**highest melting point**

30.4

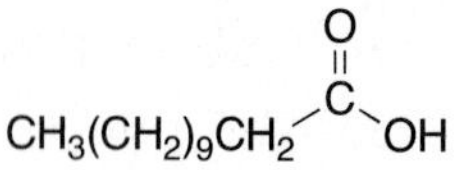

lauric acid

Lauric acid is a saturated fatty acid but has only 12 C's. The carbon chain is much shorter than palmitic acid (16 C's) and stearic acid (18 C's), making coconut oil a liquid at room temperature.

30.5

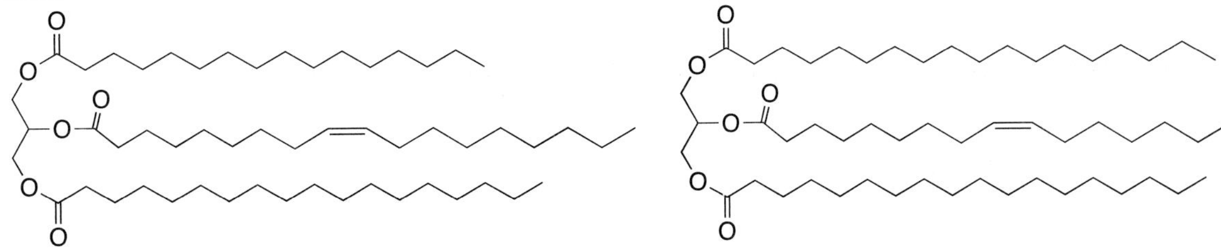

30.6 A lecithin is a type of phosphoacylglycerol. Two of the hydroxy groups of glycerol are esterified with fatty acids. The third OH group is part of a phosphodiester, which is also bonded to another low molecular weight alcohol.

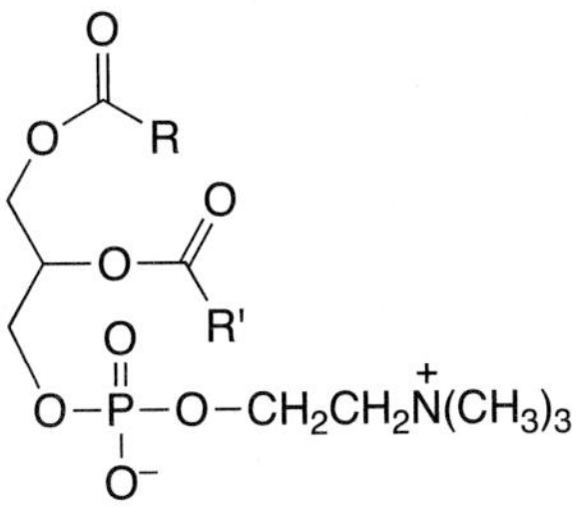

general structure
of a lecithin

one possibility:

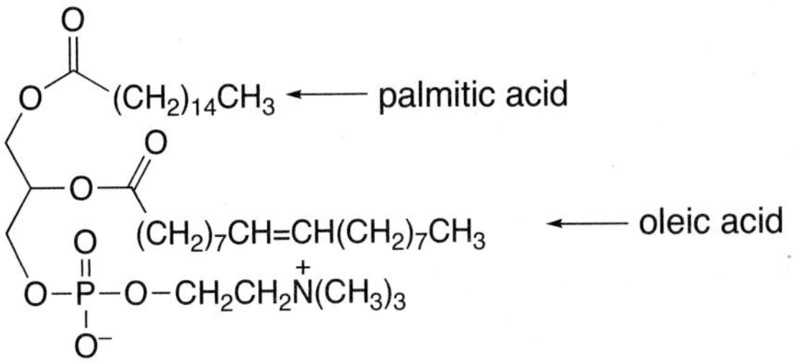

30.7 Soaps and phosphoacylglycerols have hydrophilic and hydrophobic components. Both compounds have an ionic "head" that is attracted to polar solvents like H_2O. This head is small in size compared to the hydrophobic region, which consists of one or two long hydrocarbon chains. These nonpolar chains consist of only C–C and C–H bonds and exhibit only van der Waals forces.

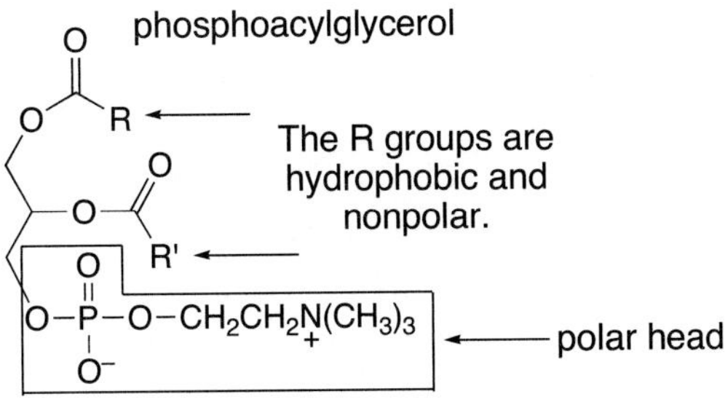

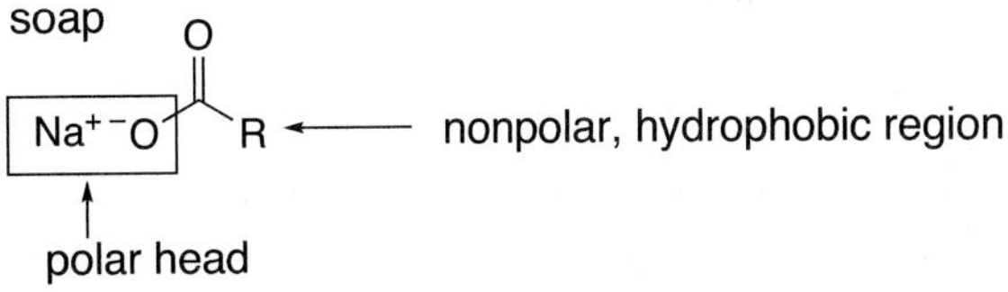

30.8 Phospholipids have a polar (ionic) head and two nonpolar tails. These two regions, which exhibit very different forces of attraction, allow the phospholipids to form a bilayer with a central hydrophobic region that serves as a barrier to agents crossing a cell membrane, while still possessing an ionic head to interact with the aqueous environment inside and outside the cell. Two different regions are needed in the molecule. Triacylglycerols have three polar, uncharged ester groups, but they are not nearly as polar as phospholipids. They do not have an ionic head with nonpolar tails and so they do not form bilayers. They are largely nonpolar C–C and C–H bonds so they are not attracted to an aqueous medium, making them H_2O insoluble.

30.9 Fat-soluble vitamins are hydrophobic and therefore are readily stored in the fatty tissues of the body. Water-soluble vitamins, on the other hand, are readily excreted in the urine, so large concentrations cannot build up in the body.

30.10

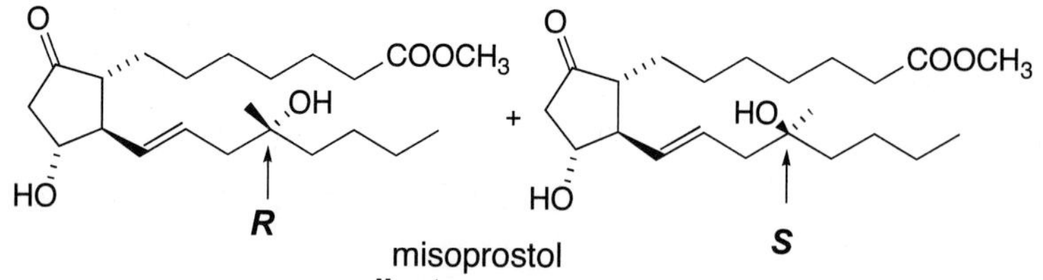

misoprostol

diastereomers

Only one tetrahedral stereogenic center is different in these two compounds.

30.11 Isoprene units are shown in bold.

a. 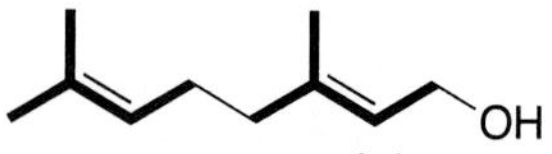

geraniol

c. 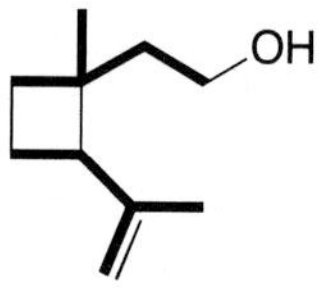

grandisol

b. 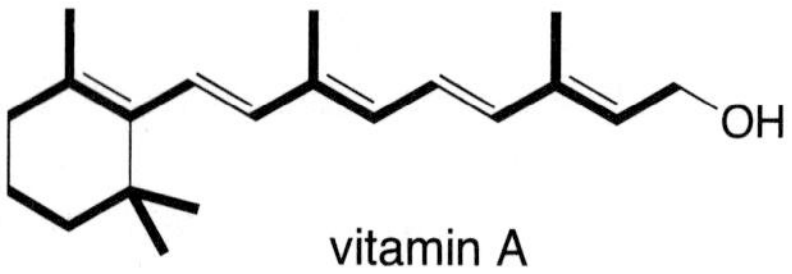

vitamin A

d. 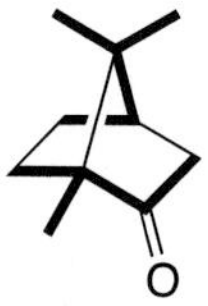

camphor

30.12

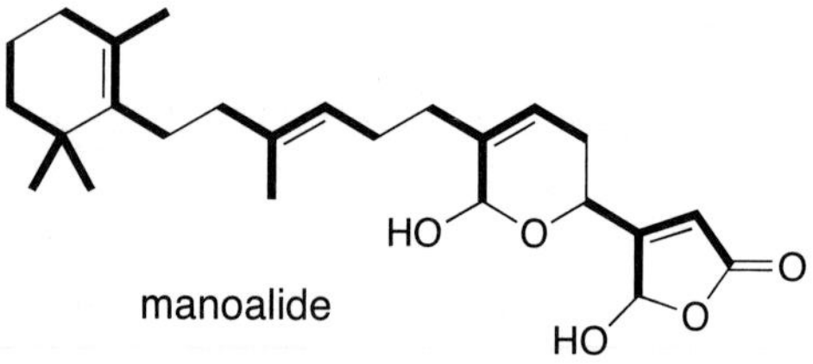

manoalide

30.13

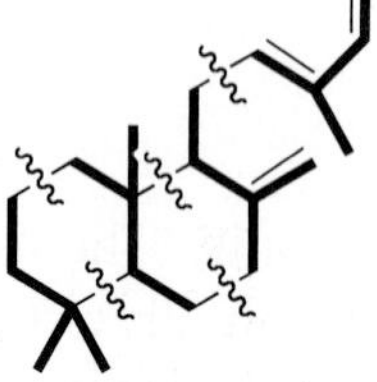

biformene

four isoprene units = diterpene

30.14

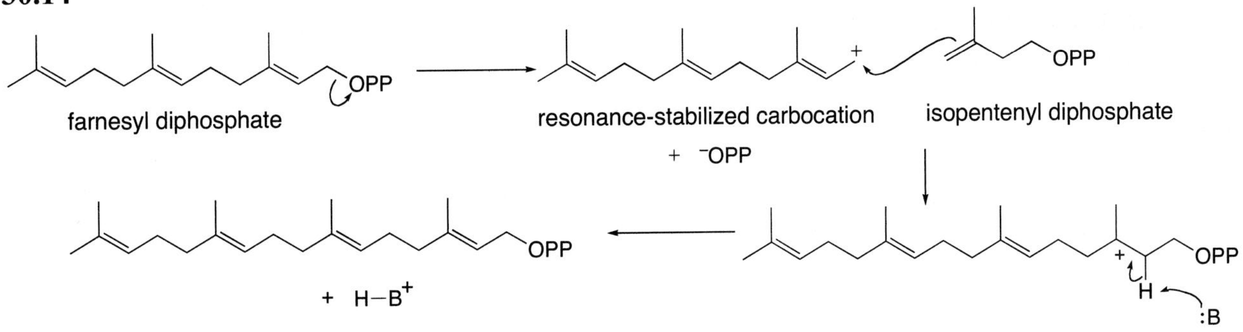
OPP
farnesyl diphosphate
+
OPP
resonance-stabilized carbocation
isopentenyl diphosphate
+ ⁻OPP
OPP
+ H–B⁺
+
OPP
H
:B

30.15

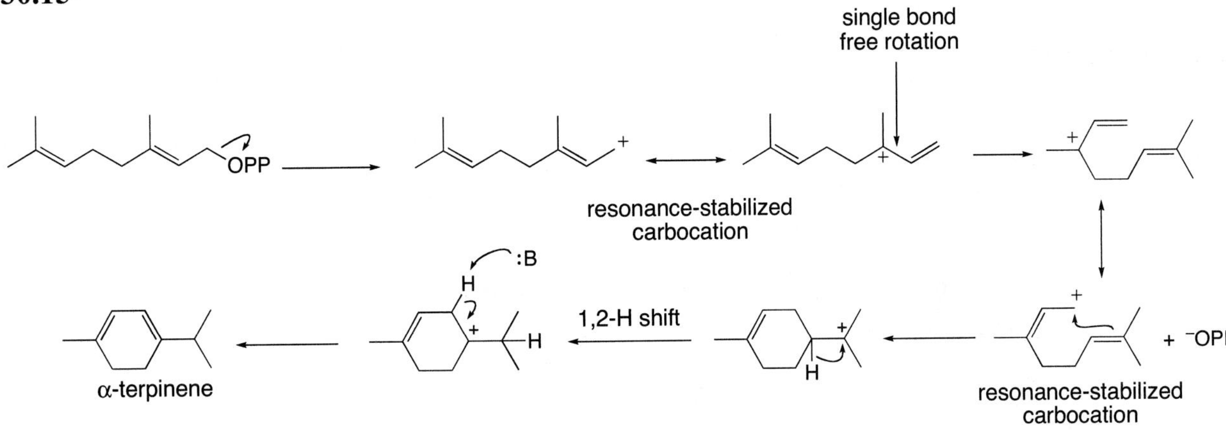
single bond
free rotation
OPP
+
+
resonance-stabilized
carbocation
+
:B
H
+
H
1,2-H shift
+
H
+
+ ⁻OPP
α-terpinene
resonance-stabilized
carbocation

30.16

a.

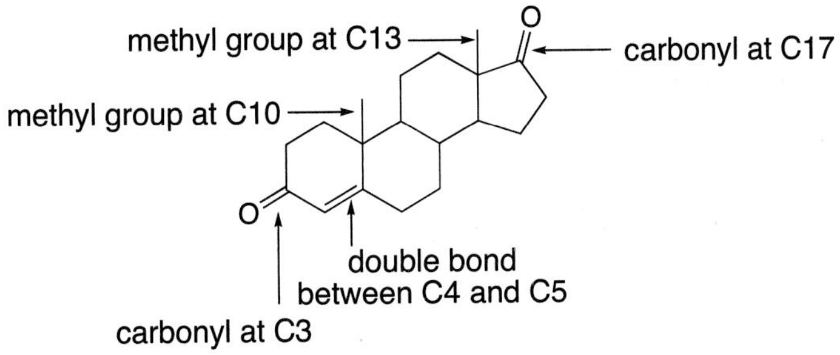
methyl group at C13
O
carbonyl at C17
methyl group at C10
O
double bond
between C4 and C5
carbonyl at C3

b.

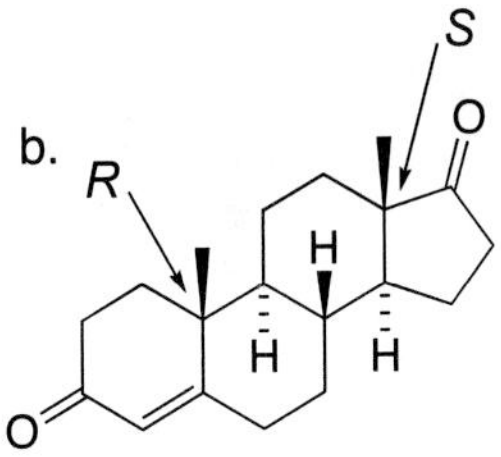
S
O
R
H
H
H
O

30.17

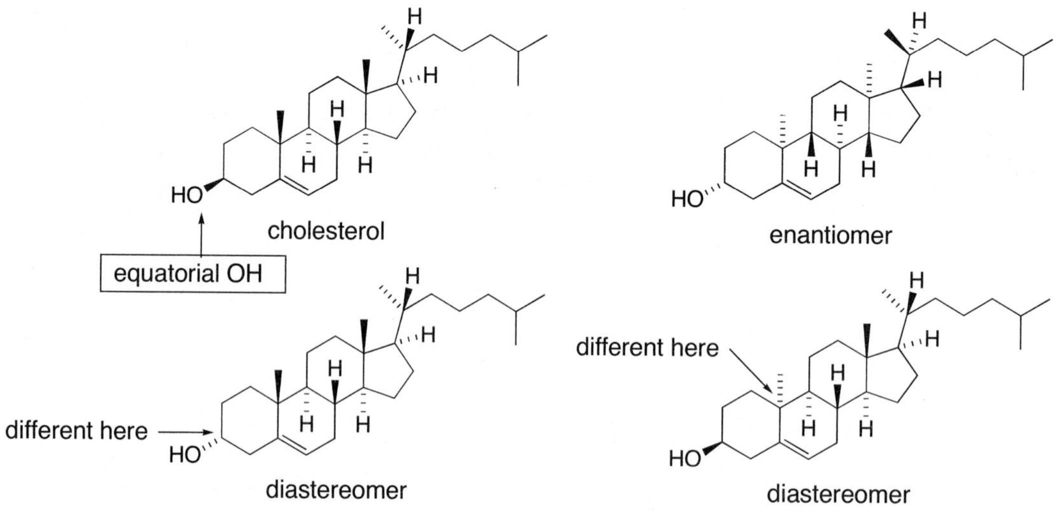
HO
cholesterol
equatorial OH
HO
enantiomer
different here
HO
diastereomer
different here
HO
diastereomer

30.18

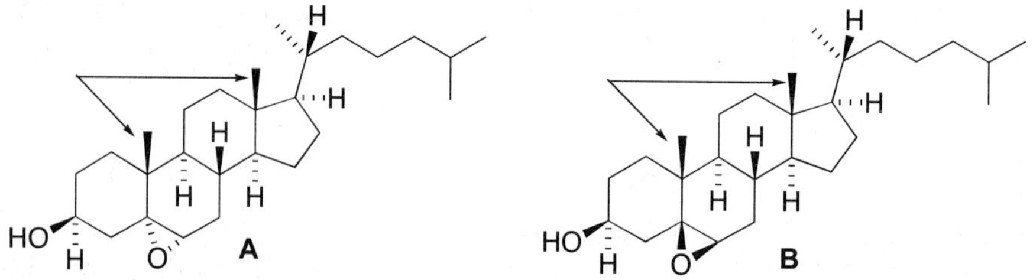
HO
O
A
HO
O
B

All four rings are in the same plane. The bulky CH_3 groups (arrows) are located above the plane. Epoxide **A** is favored, because it results from epoxidation below the plane, on the opposite side from the CH_3 groups that shield the top of the molecule somewhat to attack by reagents. In **B,** the epoxide ring is above the plane on the same side as the CH_3 groups. Formation of **B** would require epoxidation of the planar C=C from the less accessible, more sterically hindered side of the double bond. This path is thus disfavored.

30.19

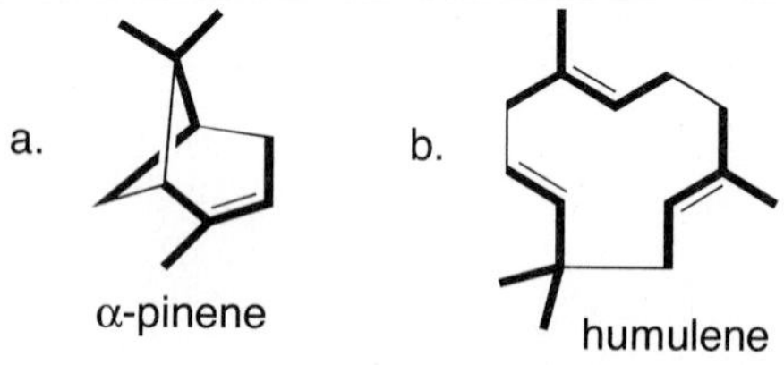
a.
α-pinene
b.
humulene

30.20

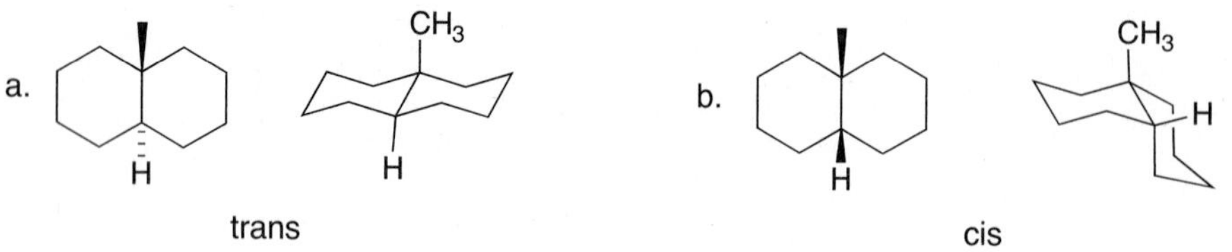
a.
H
CH_3
H
trans
b.
H
CH_3
H
cis

30.21

a. 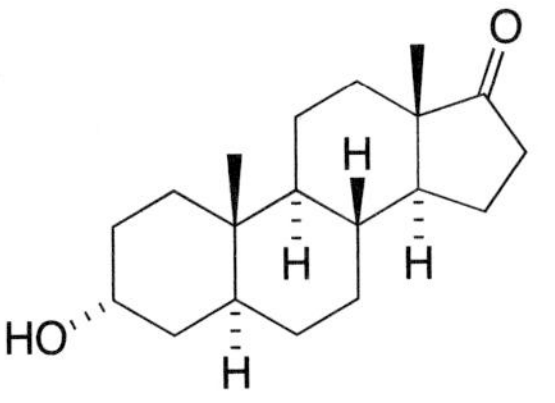

b. 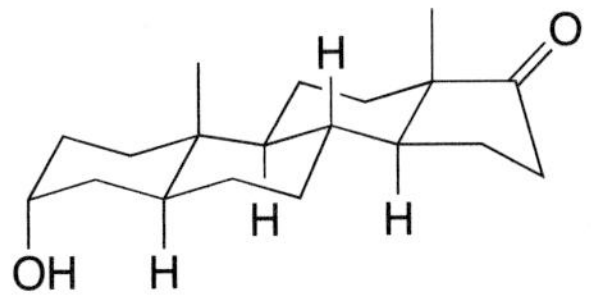

30.22

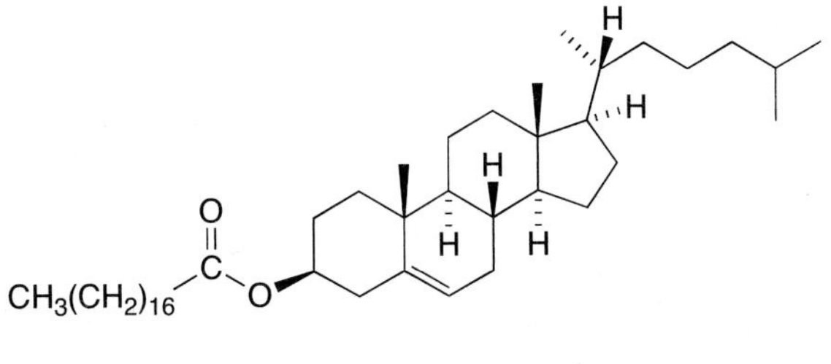

30.23 Each compound has one tetrahedral stereogenic center (circled), so there are two stereoisomers (two enantiomers) possible. All C=C's have the *Z* configuration.

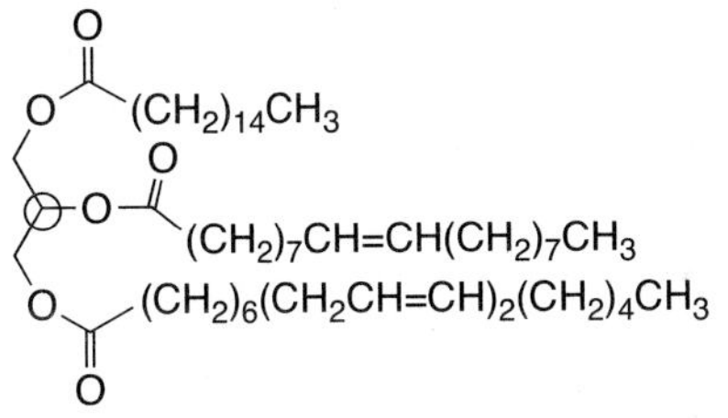

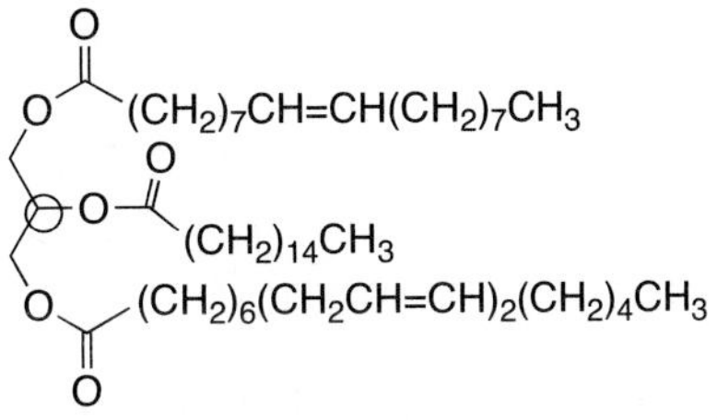

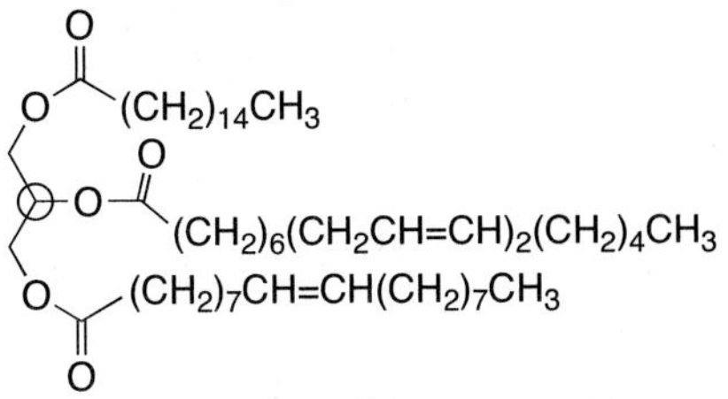

30.24

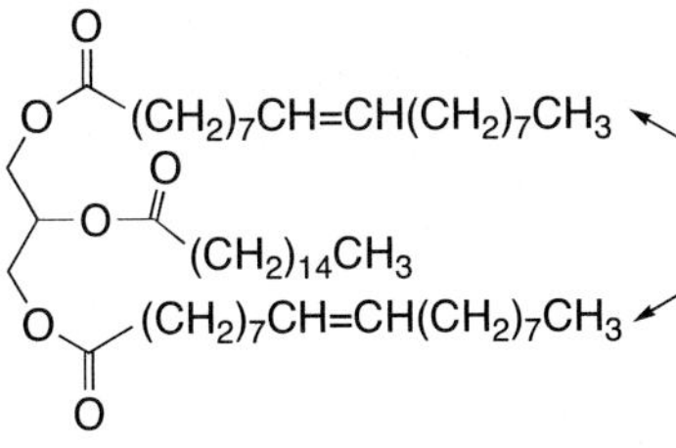

There is no stereogenic center in this triacylglycerol since these R groups are identical, making this triacylglycerol optically inactive.

30.25

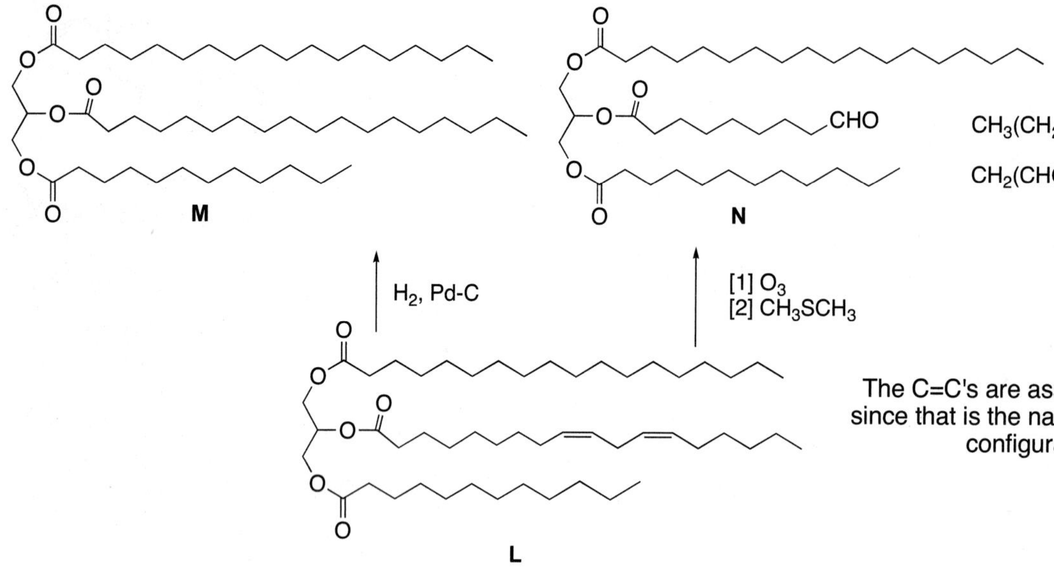
M
N
CHO
L
H2, Pd-C
[1] O3
[2] CH3SCH3

$CH_3(CH_2)_4CHO$ = **O**

$CH_2(CHO)_2$ = **P**

The C=C's are assumed to be *Z*, since that is the naturally occurring configuration.

30.26 When R" = $CH_2CH_2NH_3^+$, the compound is called a **phosphatidylethanolamine** or **cephalin.**

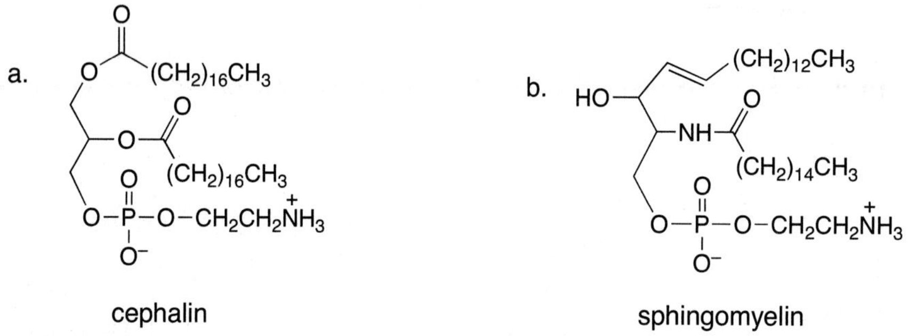
a.
(CH2)16CH3
(CH2)16CH3
O–P–O–CH2CH2NH3
O–
cephalin
b.
HO
(CH2)12CH3
NH
(CH2)14CH3
O–P–O–CH2CH2NH3
O–
sphingomyelin

30.27

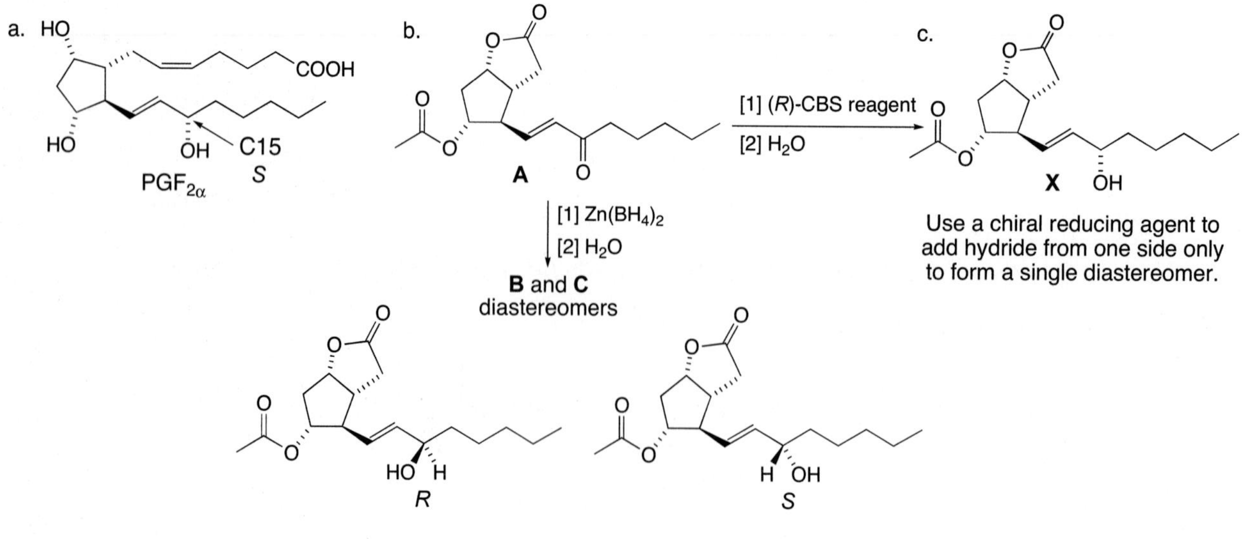
a. HO
COOH
HO
OH
C15
S
PGF2α
b.
A
[1] Zn(BH4)2
[2] H2O
B and C
diastereomers
HO H
R
H OH
S
c.
[1] (R)-CBS reagent
[2] H2O
X
OH

Use a chiral reducing agent to add hydride from one side only to form a single diastereomer.

30.28

a.

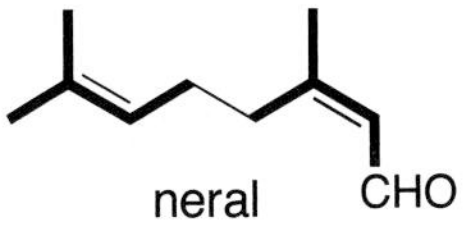

neral

e.

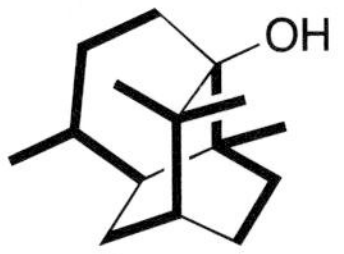

patchouli alcohol

g.

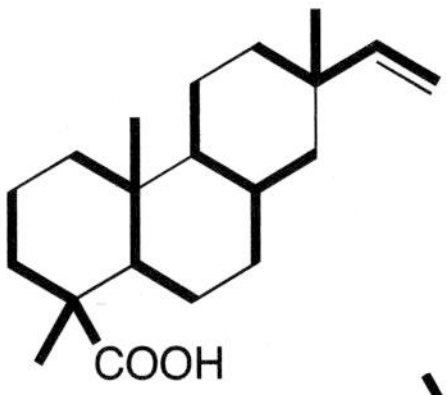

dextropimaric acid

b.

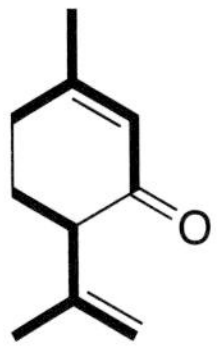

carvone

f.

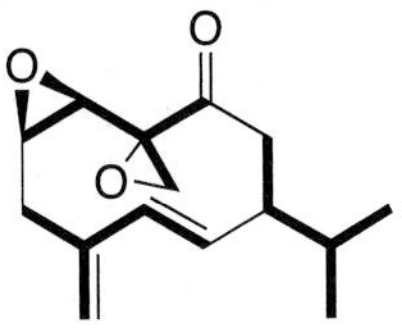

periplanone B

h.

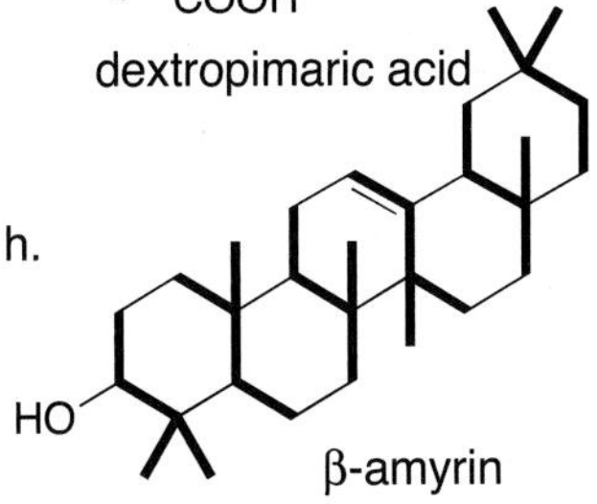

β-amyrin

c.

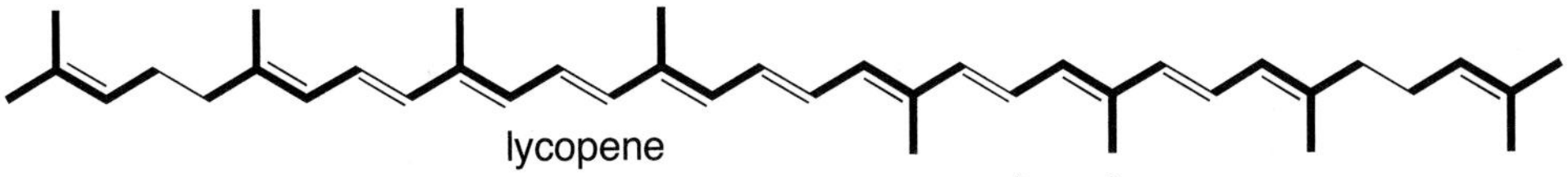

lycopene

d.

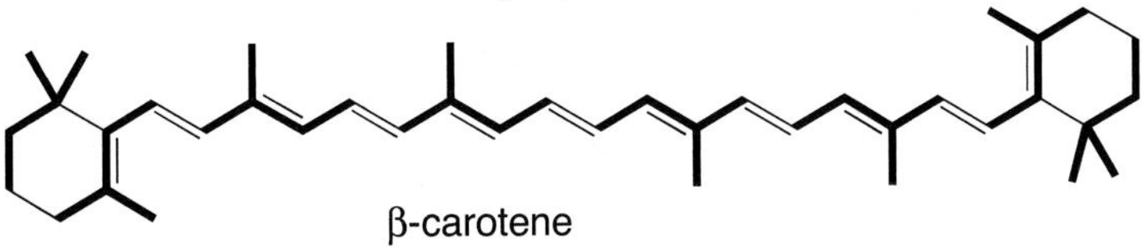

β-carotene

30.29 A ***monoterpene*** **contains 10 carbons** and two isoprene units; a ***sesquiterpene*** **contains 15 carbons** and three isoprene units, etc. See Table 30.5.

a.

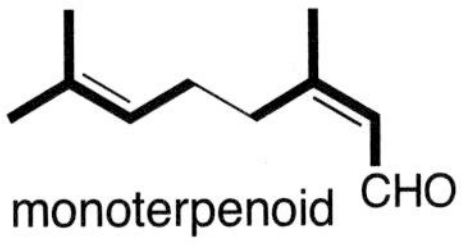

monoterpenoid

e.

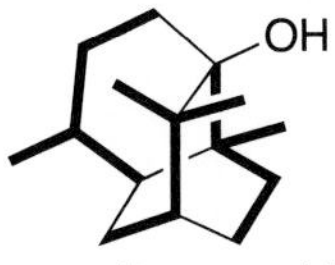

sesquiterpenoid

g.

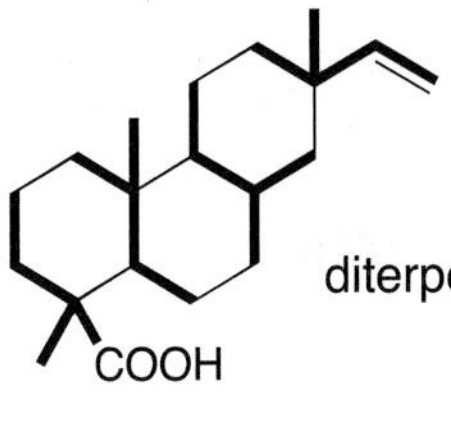

diterpenoid

b.

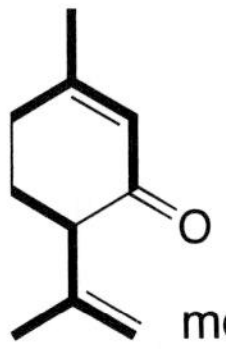

monoterpenoid

f.

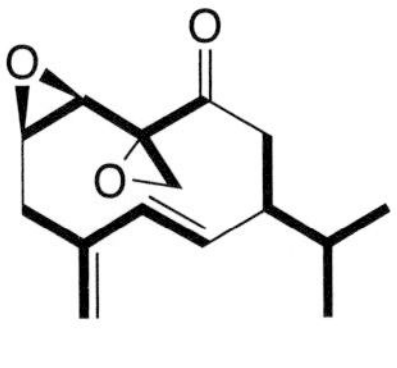

sesquiterpenoid

h.

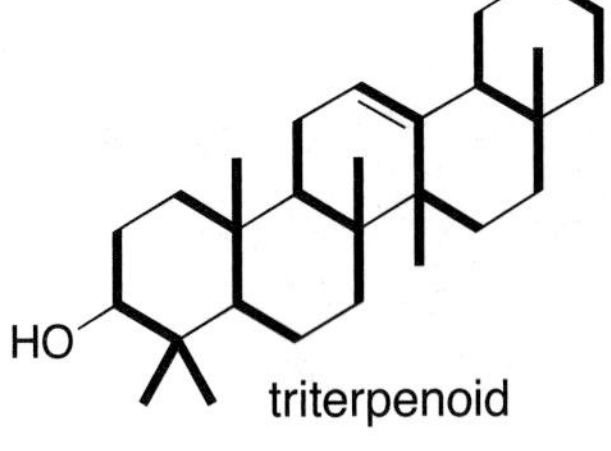

triterpenoid

c.

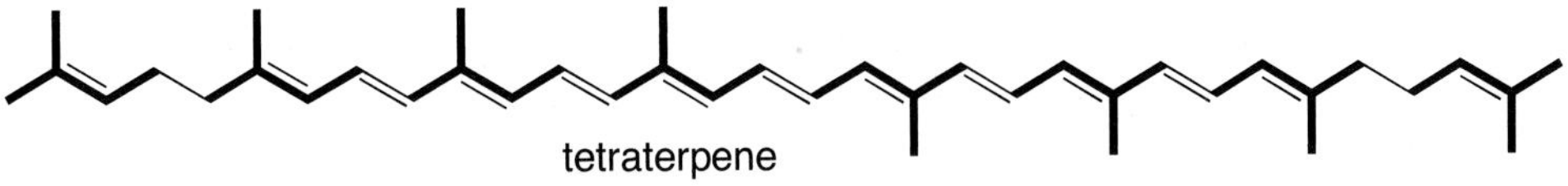

tetraterpene

d.

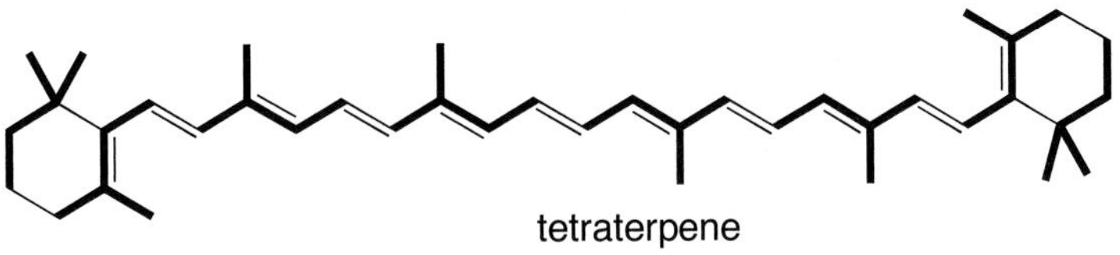

tetraterpene

30.30

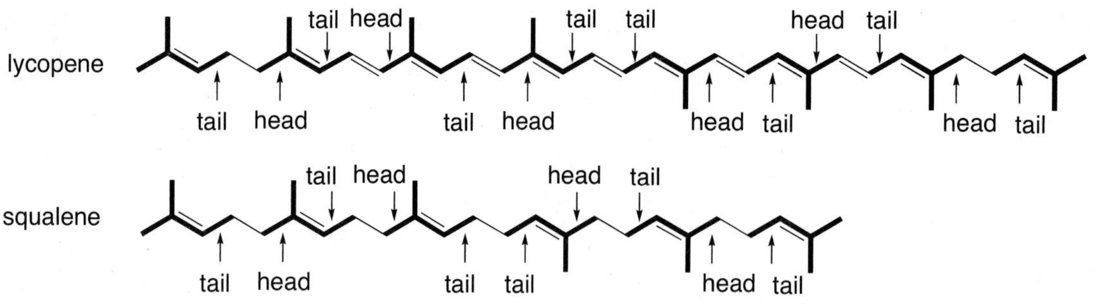

30.31

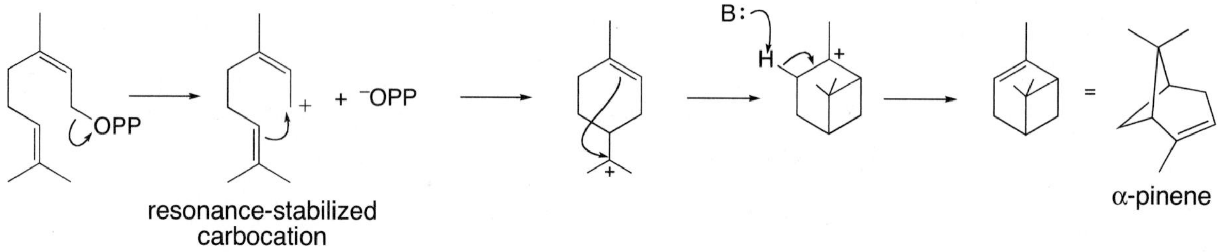

30.32 The unusual feature in the cyclization that forms flexibilene is that a 2° carbocation rather than a 3° carbocation is generated. Cyclization at the other end of the C=C would have given a 3° carbocation and formed a 14-membered ring. In addition, the 2° carbocation does not rearrange to form a 3° carbocation.

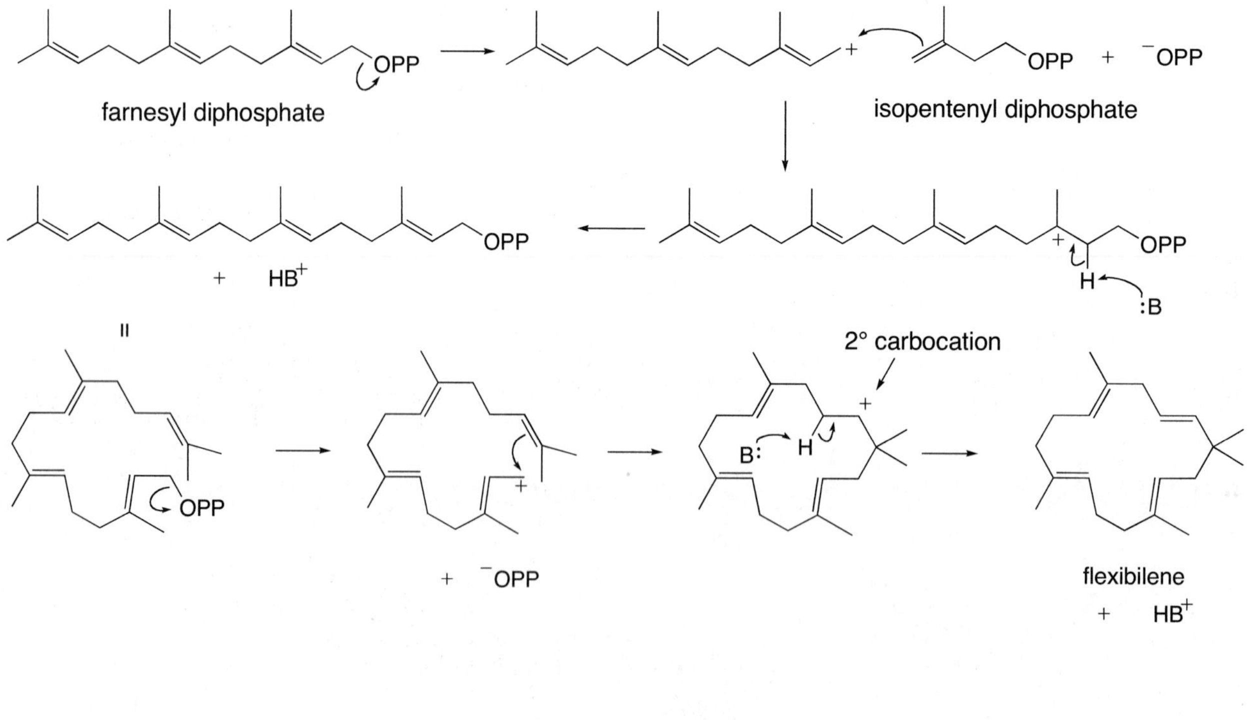

30.33

a.

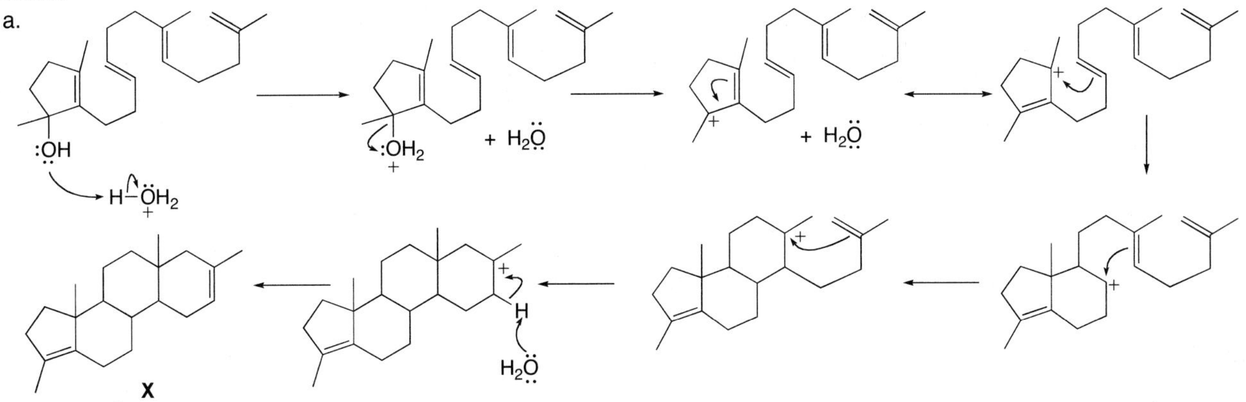
:OH
H–OH2
:OH2
+ H2O
+ H2O
H2O

X

b.

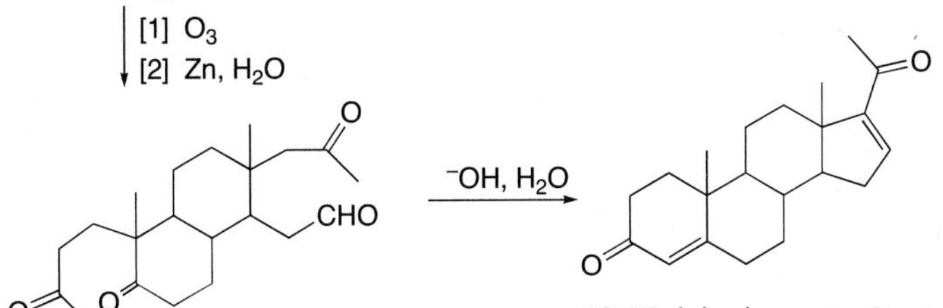
[1] O3
[2] Zn, H2O
CHO
–OH, H2O

16,17-dehydroprogesterone

30.34

a.

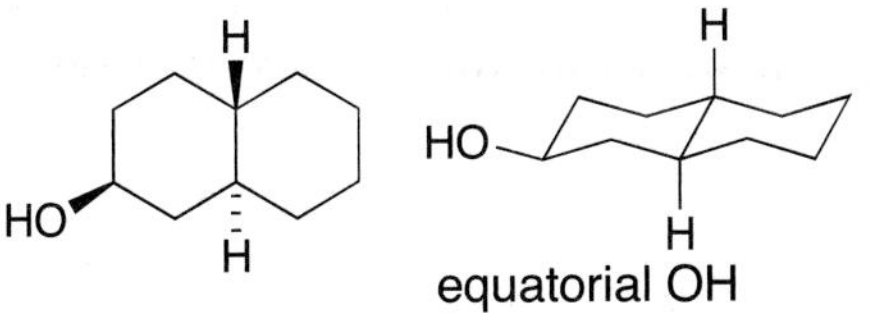

equatorial OH

c.

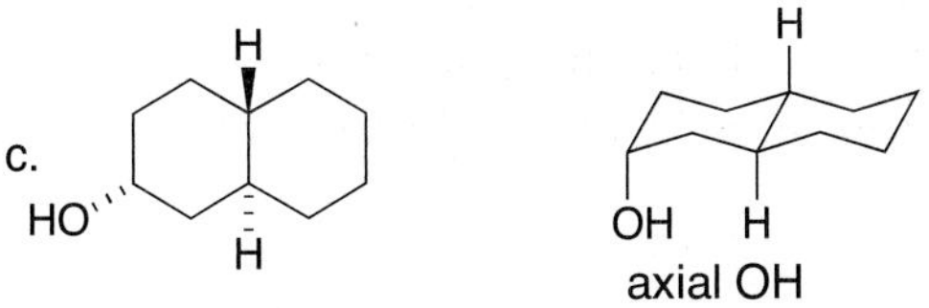

axial OH

b.

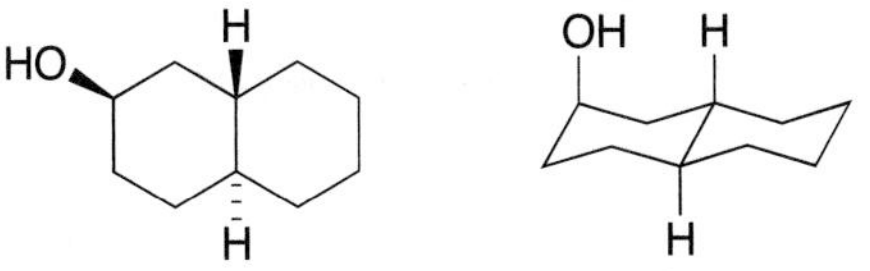

axial OH

d.

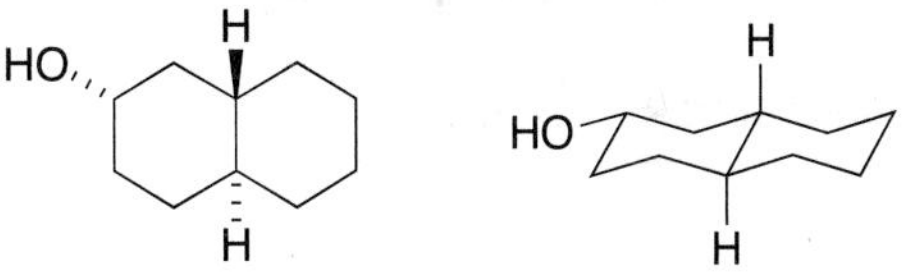

equatorial OH

30.35

a.

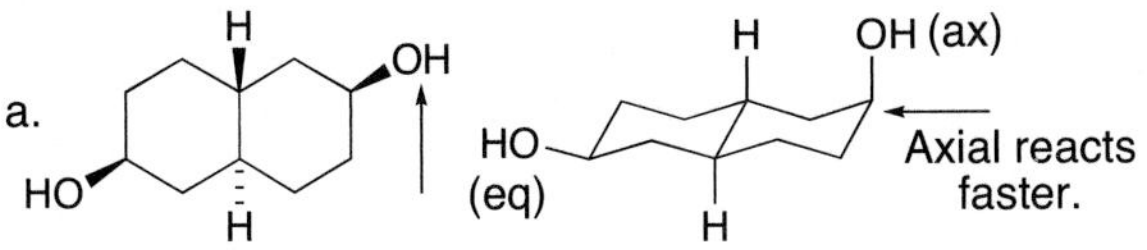
OH (ax)
HO
(eq)
Axial reacts
faster.

b.

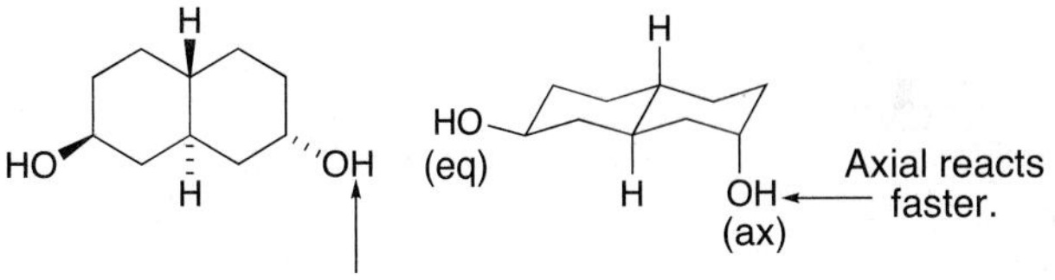
HO
(eq)
OH
(ax)
Axial reacts
faster.

30.36

a, b.

c.

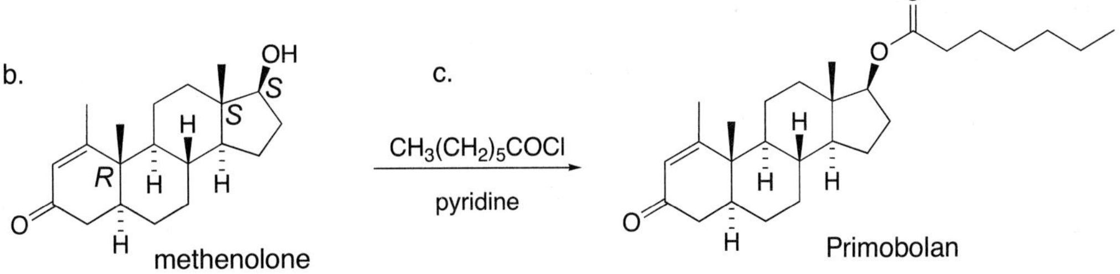
CH3(CH2)5COCl
pyridine

methenolone

Primobolan

30.37

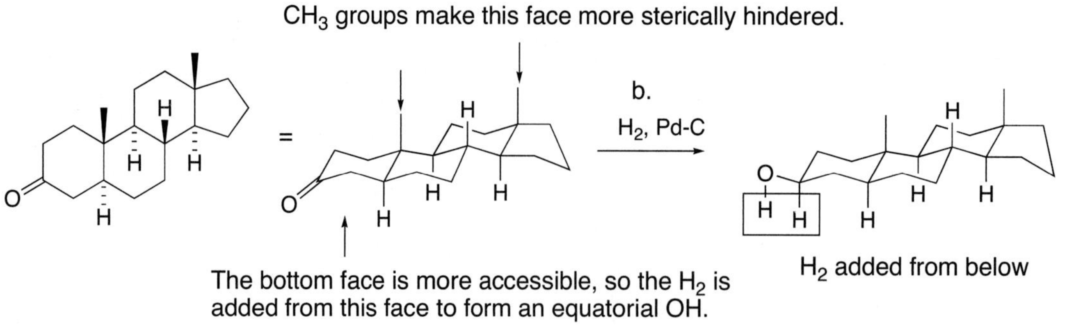
CH3 groups make this face more sterically hindered.
a.
b.
H2, Pd-C
The bottom face is more accessible, so the H2 is added from this face to form an equatorial OH.
H2 added from below

30.38

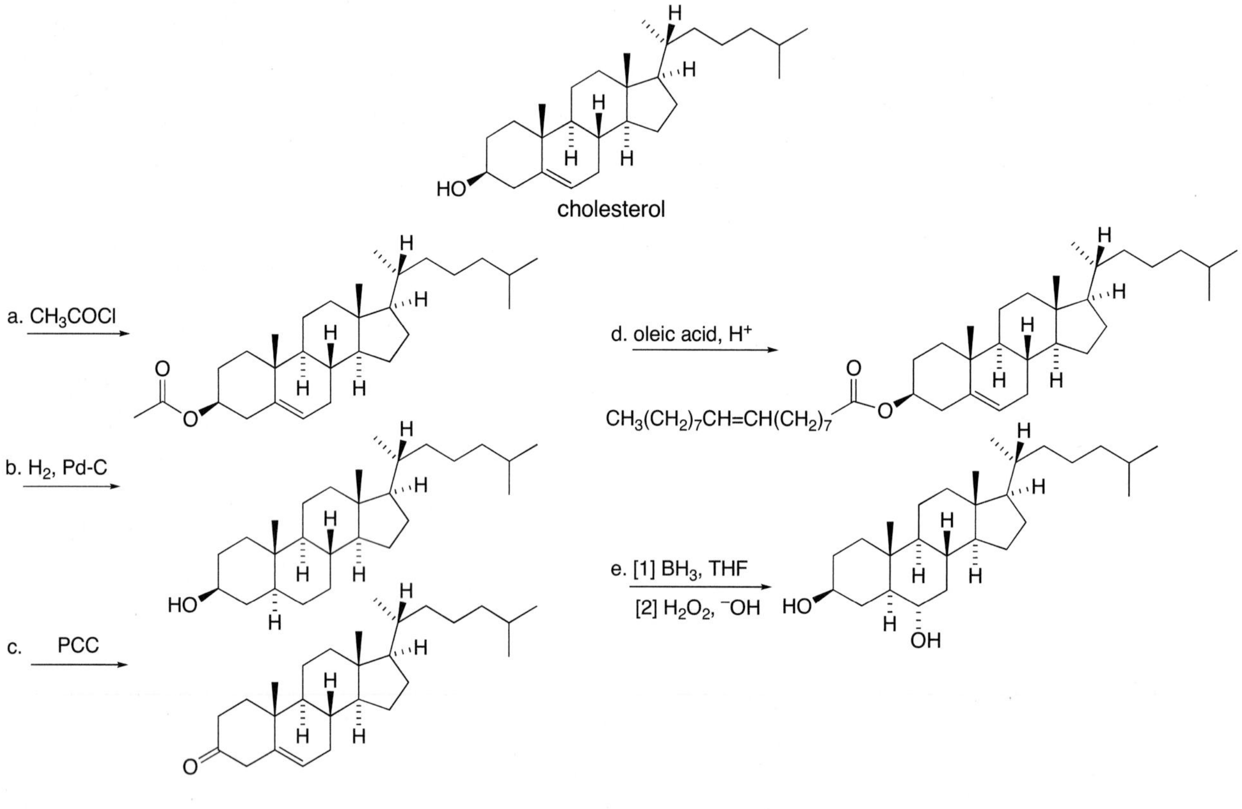
cholesterol
a. CH3COCl
b. H2, Pd-C
c. PCC
d. oleic acid, H+
CH3(CH2)7CH=CH(CH2)7
e. [1] BH3, THF
[2] H2O2, −OH

30.39

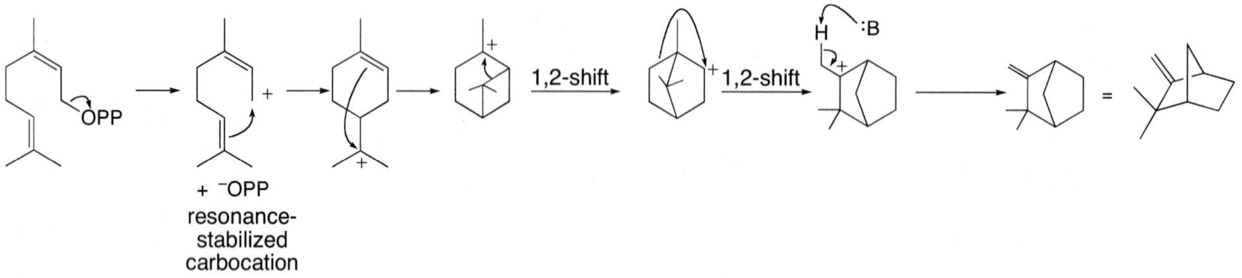
OPP
+ −OPP
resonance-stabilized carbocation
1,2-shift
1,2-shift
:B

30.40 Re-draw the starting material in a conformation that suggests the structure of the product.

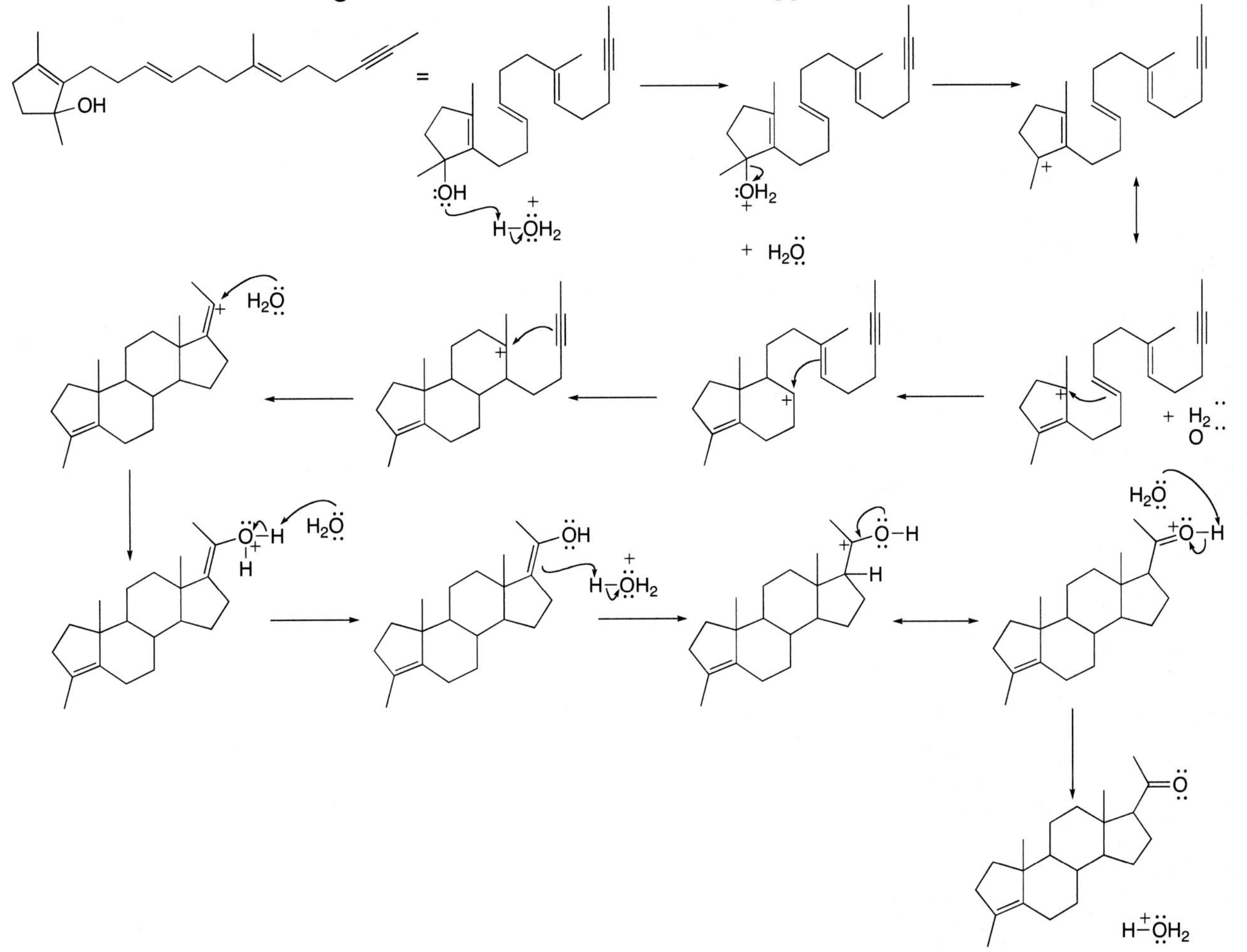

30.41

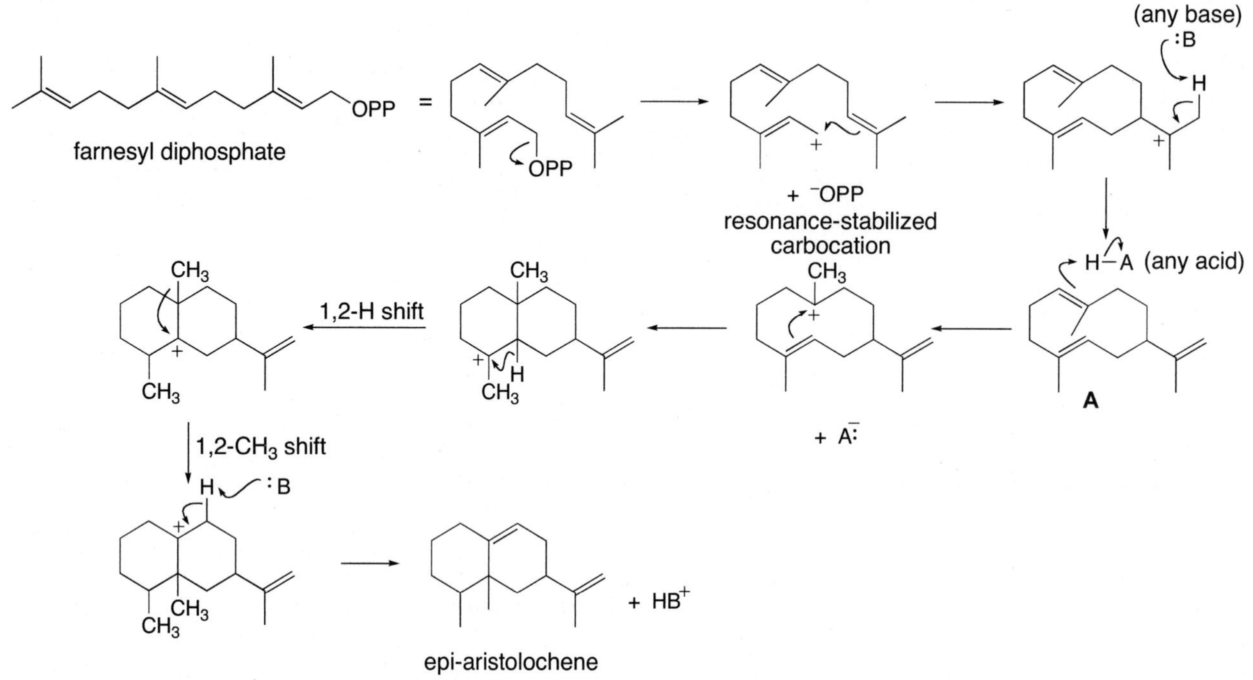

OPP
farnesyl diphosphate
=
OPP
+ ⁻OPP
resonance-stabilized
carbocation
(any base)
:B
H
H–A (any acid)
A
+ A:⁻
CH3
1,2-H shift
H
1,2-CH3 shift
H
:B
+ HB⁺
epi-aristolochene

Chapter 31 Synthetic Polymers

Chapter Review

Chain-growth polymers—Addition polymers

[1] Chain-growth polymers with alkene starting materials (31.2)

- General reaction:

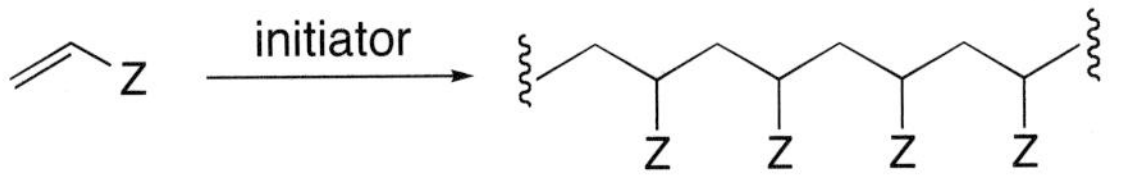

- Mechanism—three possibilities, depending on the identity of Z:

Type	Identity of Z	Initiator	Comments
[1] radical polymerization	Z stabilizes a radical. Z = R, Ph, Cl, etc.	A source of radicals (ROOR)	Termination occurs by radical coupling or disproportionation. Chain branching occurs.
[2] cationic polymerization	Z stabilizes a carbocation. Z = R, Ph, OR, etc.	H–A or a Lewis acid (BF_3 + H_2O)	Termination occurs by loss of a proton.
[3] anionic polymerization	Z stabilizes a carbanion. Z = Ph, COOR, COR, CN, etc.	An organolithium reagent (R–Li)	Termination occurs only when an acid or other electrophile is added.

[2] Chain-growth polymers with epoxide starting materials (31.3)

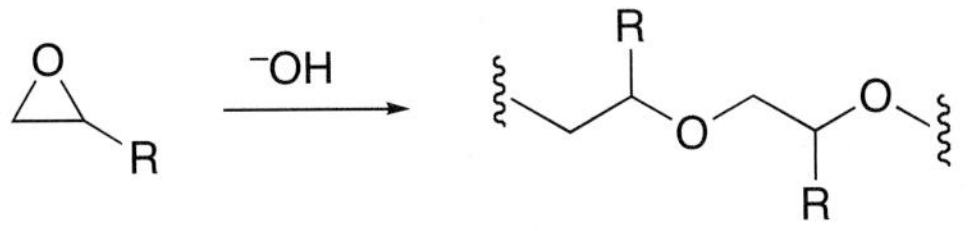

- The mechanism is S_N2.
- Ring opening occurs at the less substituted carbon of the epoxide.

Examples of step-growth polymers—Condensation polymers (31.6)

Polyamides

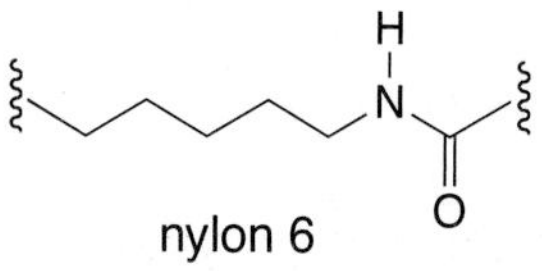

nylon 6

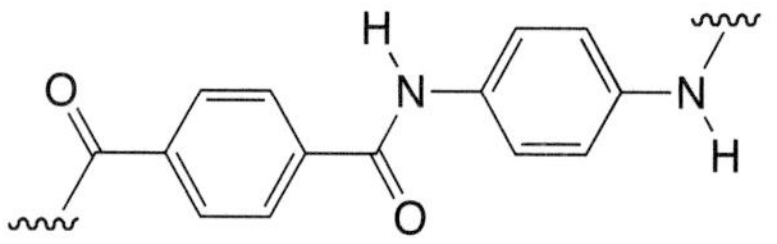

Kevlar

Polyesters

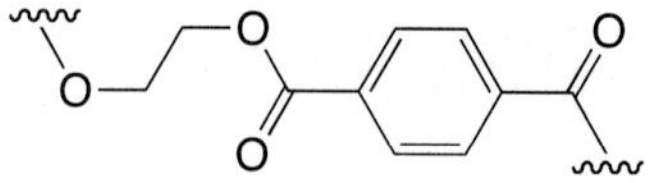

polyethylene terephthalate

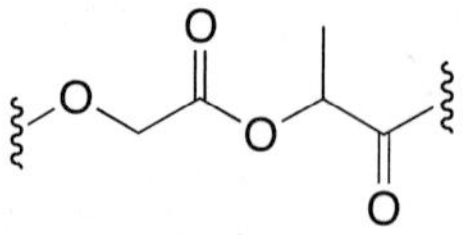

copolymer of
glycolic and lactic acids

Polyurethanes

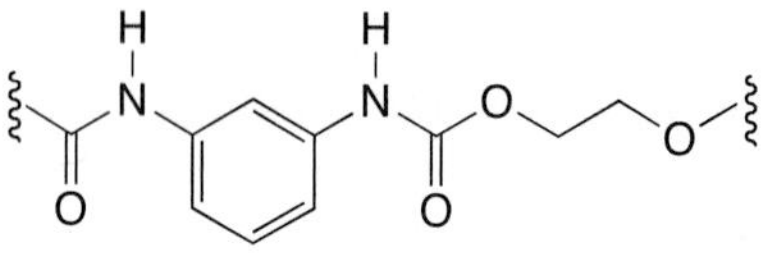

a polyurethane

Polycarbonates

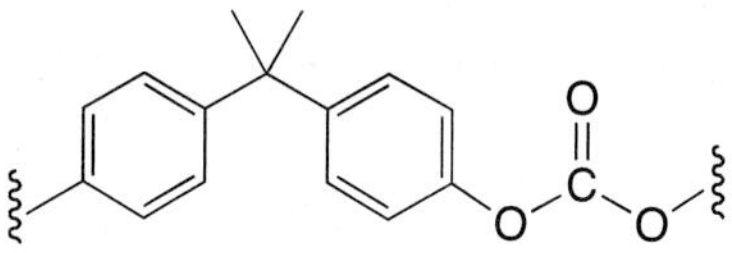

Lexan

Structure and properties

- Polymers prepared from monomers having the general structure $CH_2{=}CHZ$ can be **isotactic, syndiotactic,** or **atactic,** depending on the identity of Z and the method of preparation (31.4).
- **Ziegler–Natta catalysts** form polymers without significant branching. Polymers can be isotactic, syndiotactic, or atactic, depending on the catalyst. Polymers prepared from 1,3-dienes have the *E* or *Z* configuration, depending on the monomer (31.4, 31.5).
- Most polymers contain ordered crystalline regions and less ordered amorphous regions (31.7). The greater the crystallinity, the harder the polymer.
- **Elastomers** are polymers that stretch and can return to their original shape (31.5).
- **Thermoplastics** are polymers that can be molded, shaped, and cooled such that the new form is preserved (31.7).
- **Thermosetting polymers** are composed of complex networks of covalent bonds, so they cannot be melted to form a liquid phase (31.7).

Practice Test on Chapter Review

1. a. Which of the following statements is (are) true about chain-growth polymers?
    1. The reaction mechanism involves initiation, propagation, and termination.
    2. The reaction may occur with anionic, cationic, or radical intermediates.
    3. Epoxides can serve as monomers.
    4. Statements [1] and [2] are both true.
    5. Statements [1], [2], and [3] are all true.

b. Which of the following alkenes is likely to undergo anionic polymerization?
  1. $CH_2{=}CHCO_2CH_3$
  2. $CH_2{=}CHOCH_3$
  3. $CH_2{=}CHCH_2CO_2CH_3$
  4. Both [1] and [2] will react.
  5. Compounds [1], [2], and [3] will all react.

c. Which of the following compounds can serve as an initiator in cationic polymerization?
  1. butyllithium
  2. $(CH_3)3COOC(CH_3)_3$
  3. BF_3
  4. Both [1] and [2] can serve as initiators.
  5. Compounds [1], [2], and [3] can all serve as initiators.

d. Which of the following statements is (are) true about step-growth polymers?
  1. A small molecule such as H_2O or HCl is extruded during synthesis.
  2. Polycarbonates are an example of a step-growth polymer.
  3. Step-growth polymers are also called addition polymers.
  4. Statements [1] and [2] are both true.
  5. Statements [1], [2], and [3] are all true.

2. Label each statement as True (T) or False (F).
  a. A polyester is the most easily recycled polymer.
  b. Natural rubber is a polymer of repeating isoprene units in which all double bonds have the *E* configuration.
  c. A syndiotactic polymer has all Z groups bonded to the polymer chain on the same side.
  d. A polyether can be formed by anionic polymerization of an epoxide.
  e. An epoxy resin is a chain-growth polymer.
  f. A branched polymer is more amorphous, giving it a higher T_m.
  g. Polystyrene is a thermoplastic that can be melted and molded in shapes that are retained when the polymer is cooled.
  h. A polyurethane is a condensation polymer.
  i. Ziegler–Natta catalysts are used to form highly branched chain-growth polymers.
  j. Using a feedstock from a renewable source is one method of green polymer synthesis.

3. What monomer(s) are needed to synthesize each polymer?

a. 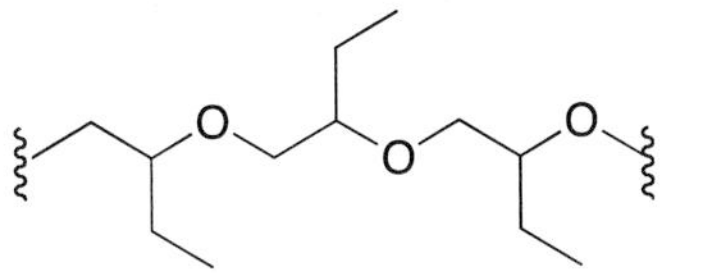

b. 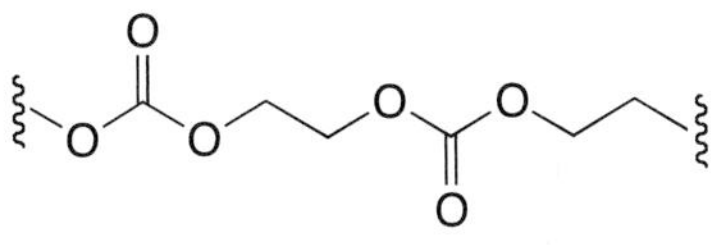

c. 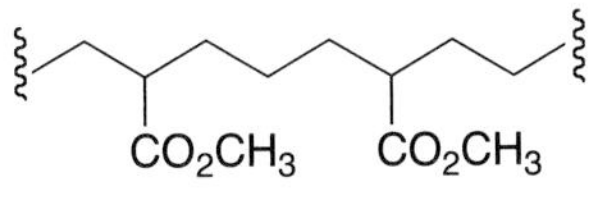

d. 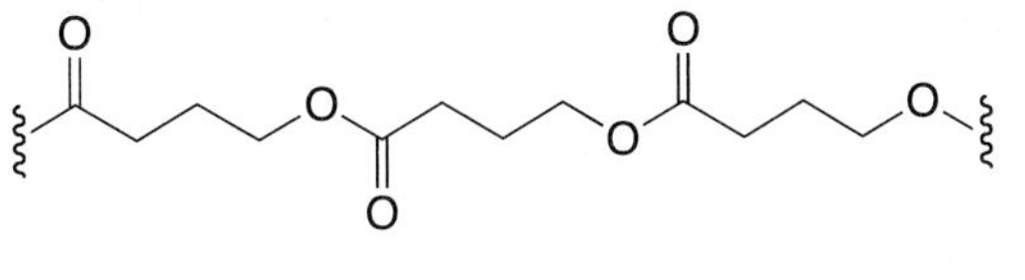

e. 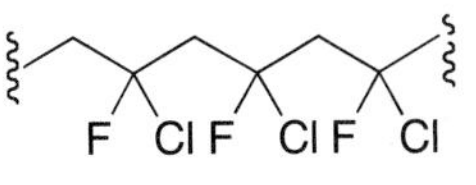

Answers to Practice Test

1. a. 5
   b. 1
   c. 3
   d. 4

2. a. T
   b. F
   c. F
   d. T
   e. F
   f. F
   g. T
   h. T
   i. F
   j. T

3.
a. 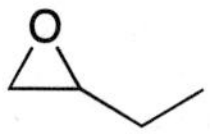

b. 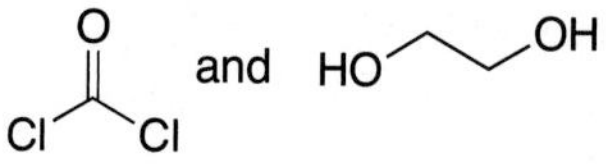
and

c. 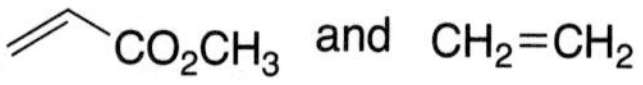
CO_2CH_3 and $CH_2=CH_2$

d. 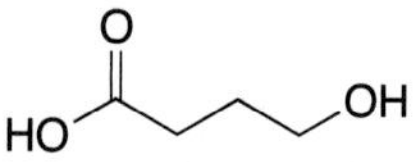

e. 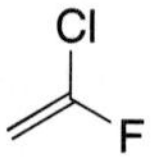

Answers to Problems

31.1 Place brackets around the repeating unit that creates the polymer.

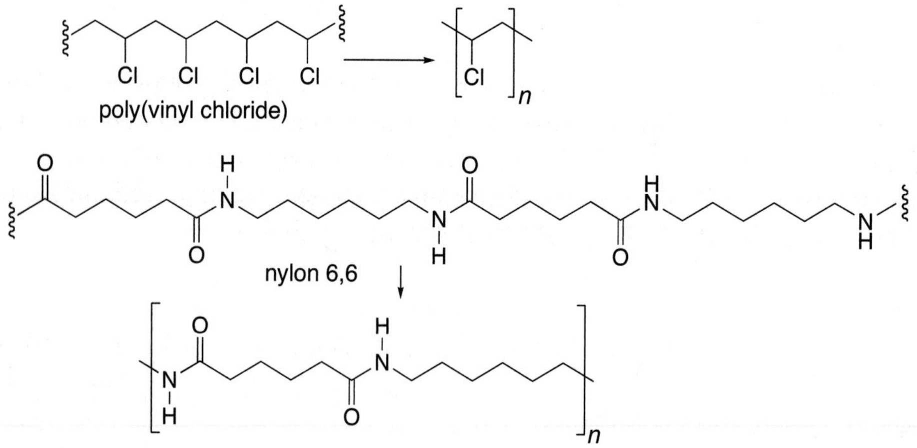
poly(vinyl chloride)
nylon 6,6

31.2 Draw each polymer formed by chain-growth polymerization.

a. 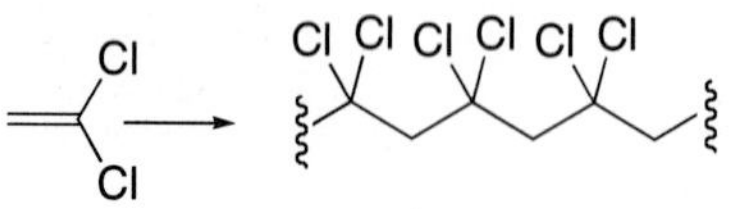

c. 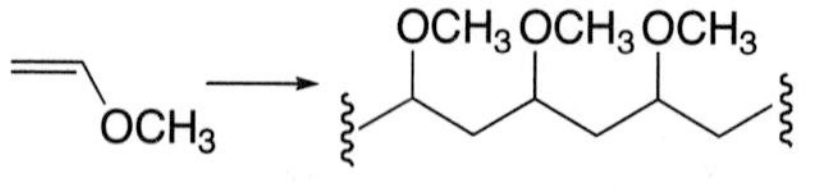

b. 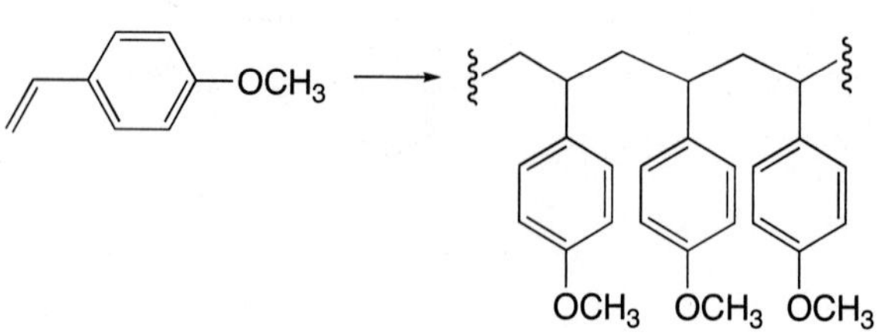

d. 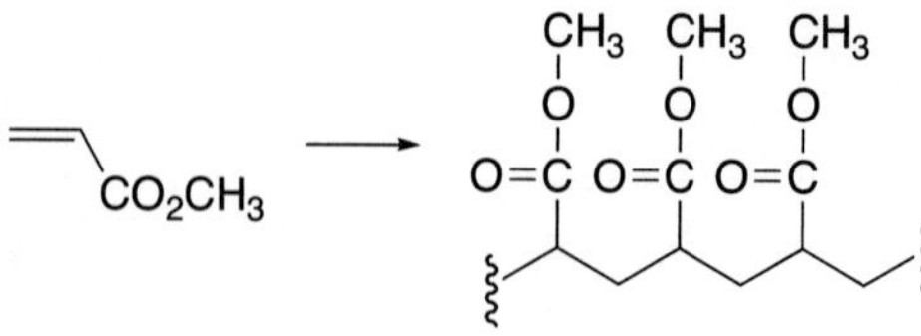

31.3 Draw each polymer formed by radical polymerization.

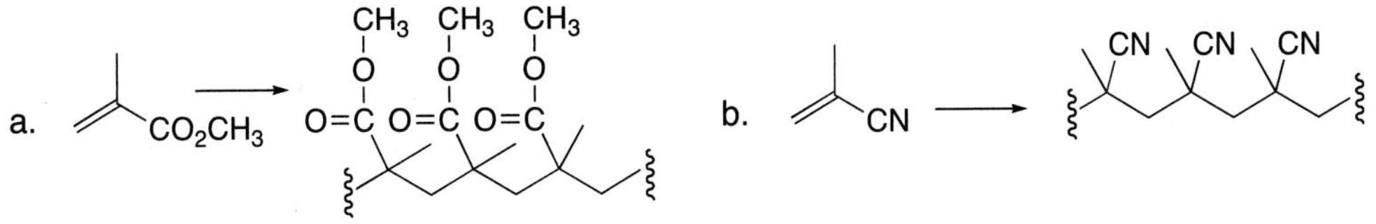

31.4 Use Mechanism 31.1 as a model of radical polymerization.

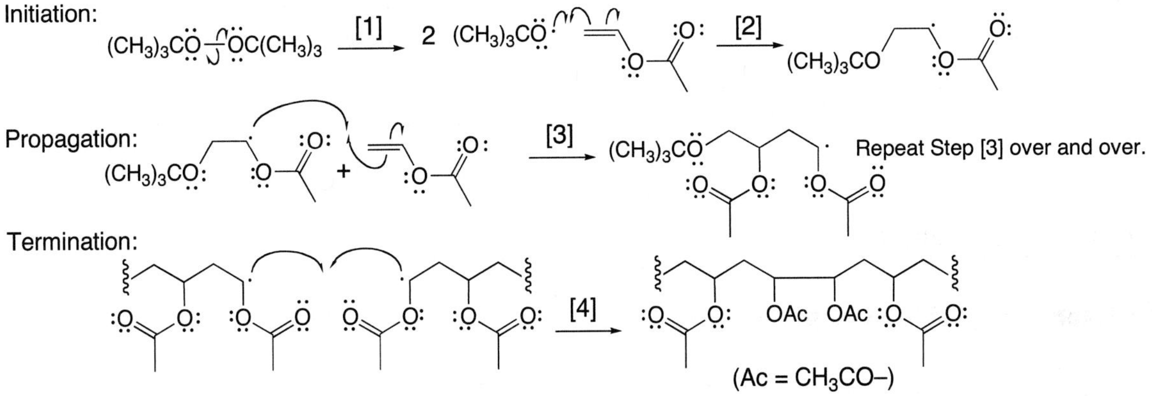

31.5 Radical polymerization forms a long chain of polystyrene with phenyl groups bonded to every other carbon. To form branches on this polystyrene chain, a radical on a second polymer chain abstracts a H atom. Abstraction of H_a forms a resonance-stabilized radical **A'**. The 2° radical **B'** (without added resonance stabilization) is formed by abstraction of H_b. Abstraction of H_a is favored, therefore, and this radical goes on to form products with 4° C's (**A**).

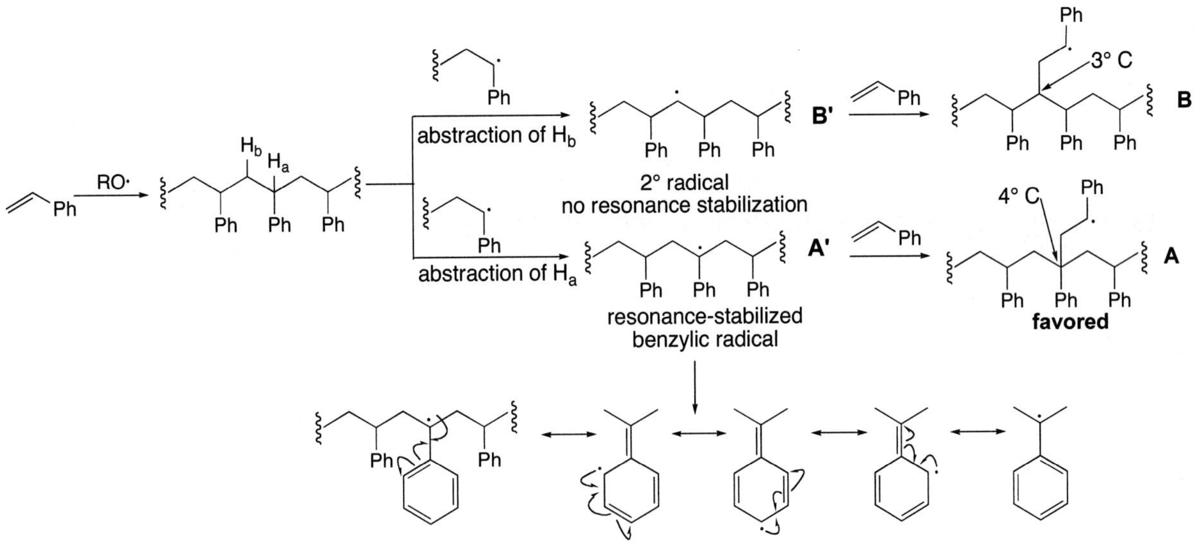

31.6 Cationic polymerization proceeds via a carbocation intermediate. Substrates that form more stable 3° carbocations react more readily in these polymerization reactions than substrates that form less stable 1° carbocations. $CH_2{=}C(CH_3)_2$ will form a more substituted carbocation than $CH_2{=}CH_2$.

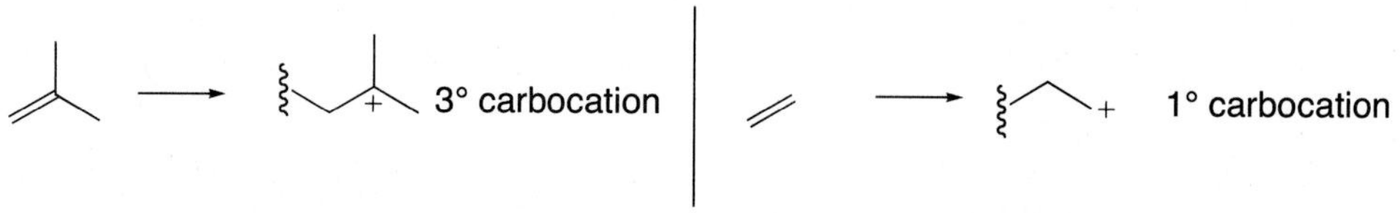
3° carbocation
1° carbocation

31.7 Cationic polymerization occurs with alkene monomers having substituents that can stabilize carbocations, such as alkyl groups and other electron-donor groups. Anionic polymerization occurs with alkene monomers having substituents that can stabilize a negative charge, such as COR, COOR, or CN.

a. $CH_2{=}C(CH_3)COOCH_3$ ↑ electron-withdrawing group **anionic polymerization**

b. $CH_2{=}CHCH_3$ ↑ alkyl group **cationic polymerization**

c. $CH_2{=}CHOC(CH_3)_3$ ↑ an electron-donating resonance effect **cationic polymerization**

d. $CH_2{=}CHCOCH_3$ ↑ electron-withdrawing group **anionic polymerization**

31.8 Use Mechanism 31.4 as a model of anionic polymerization.

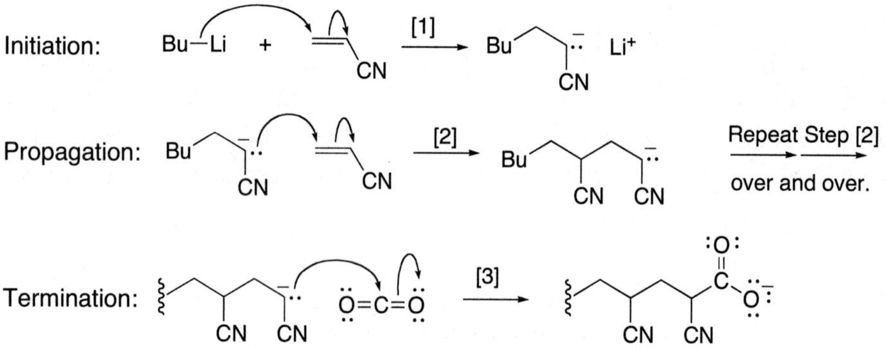
Initiation:
Bu–Li
CN
[1]
Bu
Li+
CN
Propagation:
Bu
CN
CN
[2]
Bu
CN CN
Repeat Step [2]
over and over.
Termination:
CN CN
O=C=O
[3]
O
C
O
CN CN

31.9 Styrene ($CH_2{=}CHPh$) can by polymerized by all three methods of chain-growth polymerization because a benzene ring can stabilize a radical, a carbocation, or a carbanion by resonance delocalization.

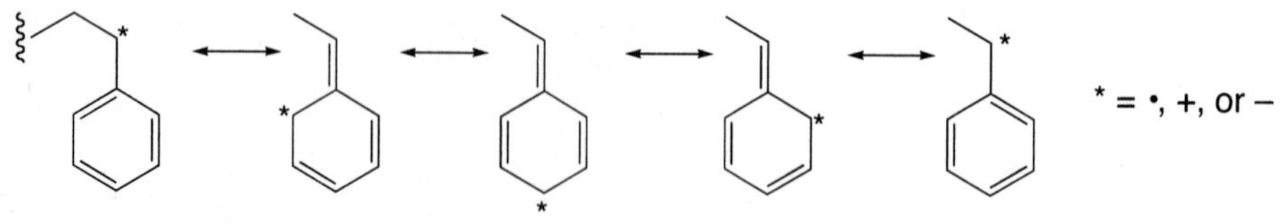
* = •, +, or –

31.10 Draw the copolymers formed in each reaction.

a. 
Ph
+
CN
Ph
CN
n

b.

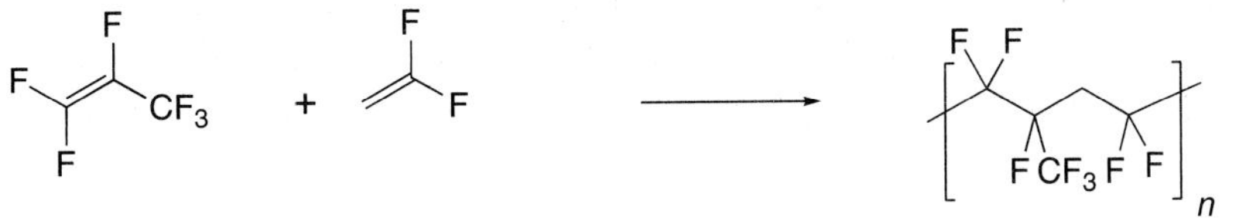

31.11

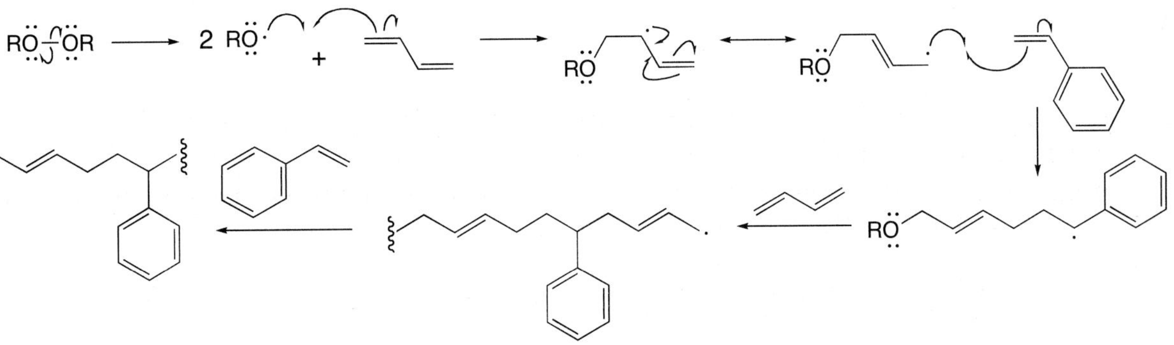

31.12

a.

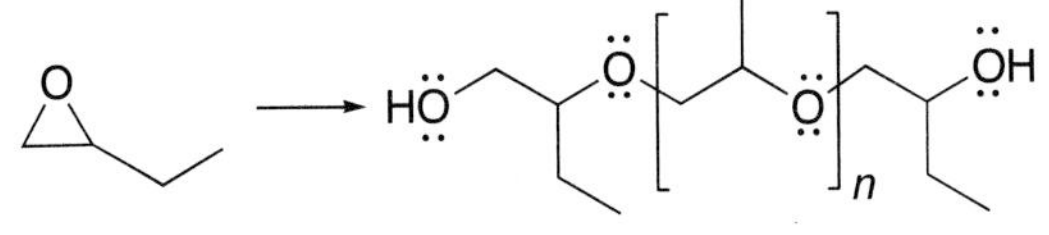

b.

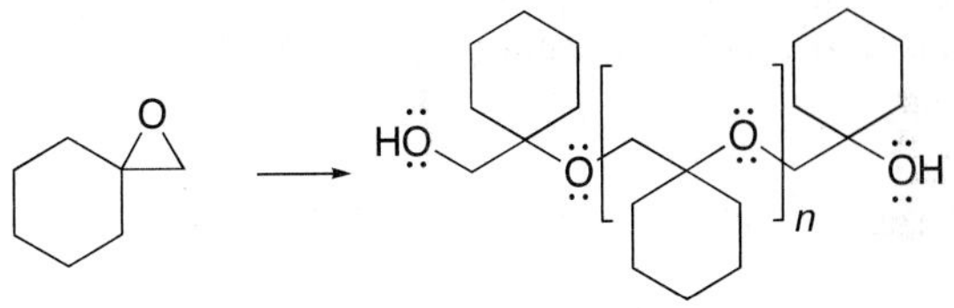

31.13

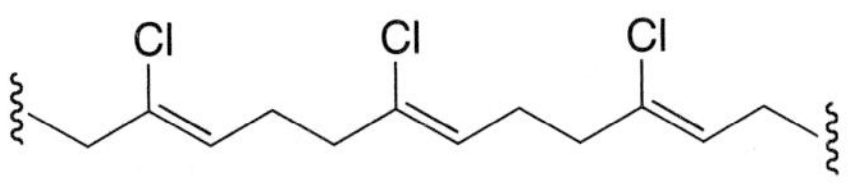

neoprene

All double bonds have the *Z* configuration.

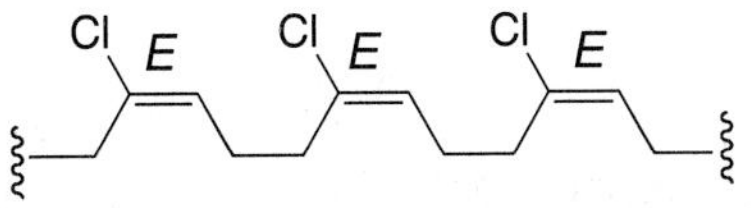

E configuration of each double bond

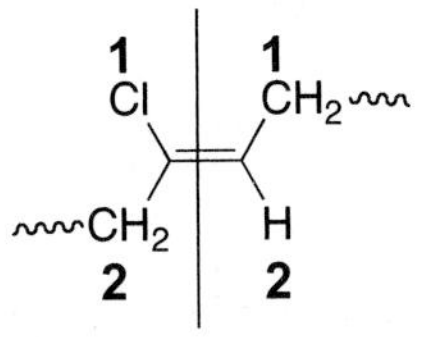

Two higher priority groups (1's) are on the same side of the double bond - - - > *Z* configuration.

31.14

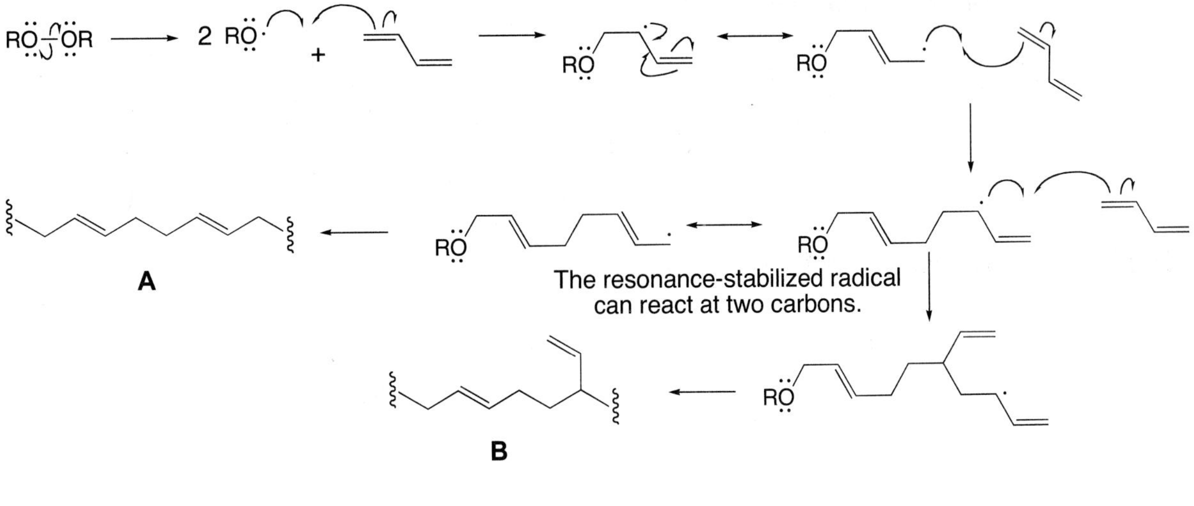

31.15

a.

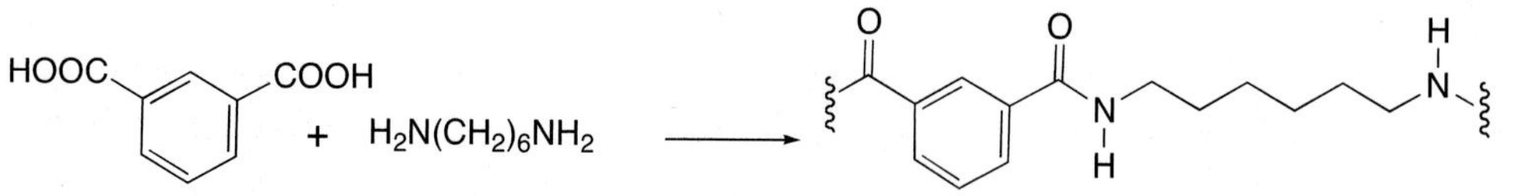

b.

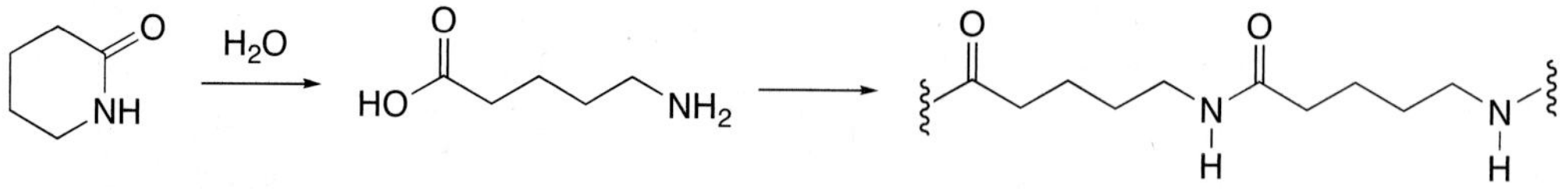

c.

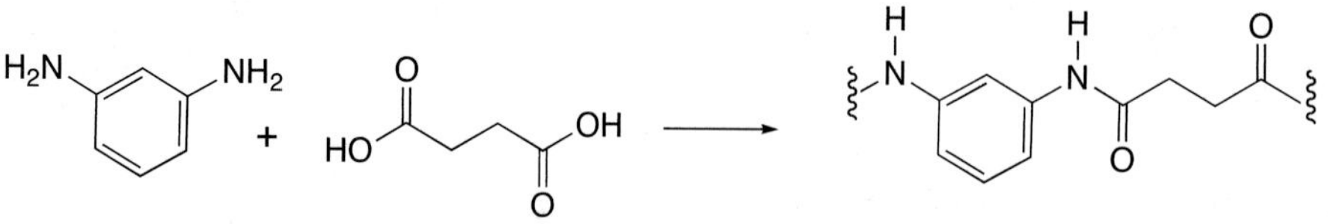

31.16

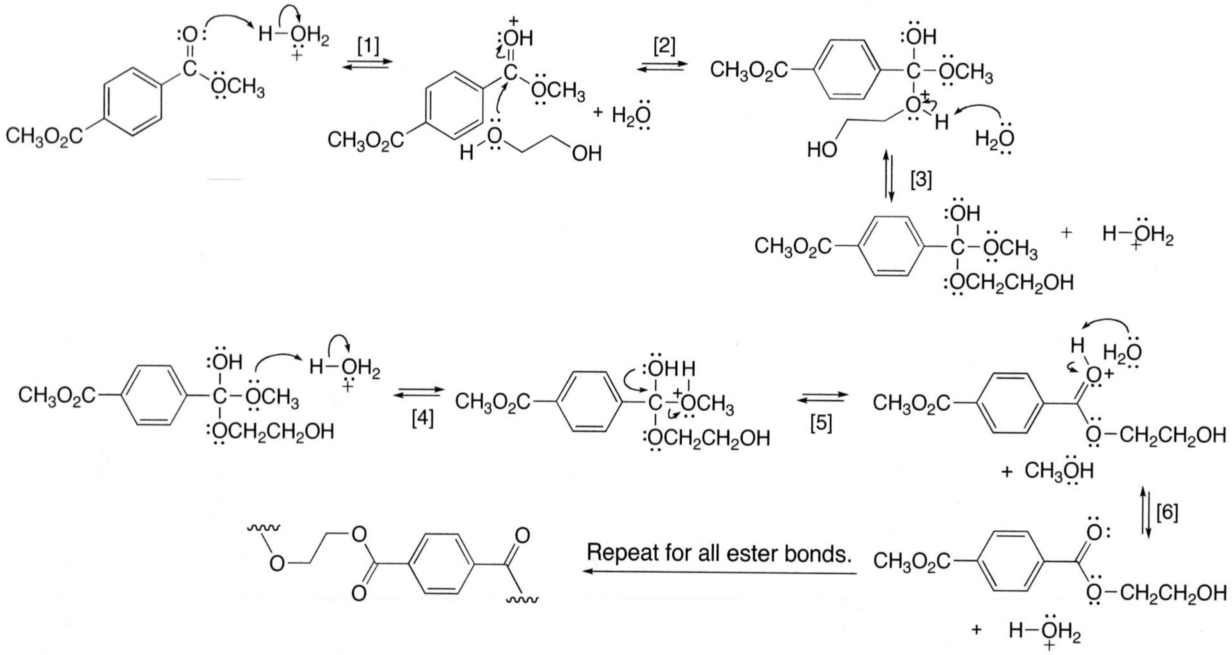

31.17

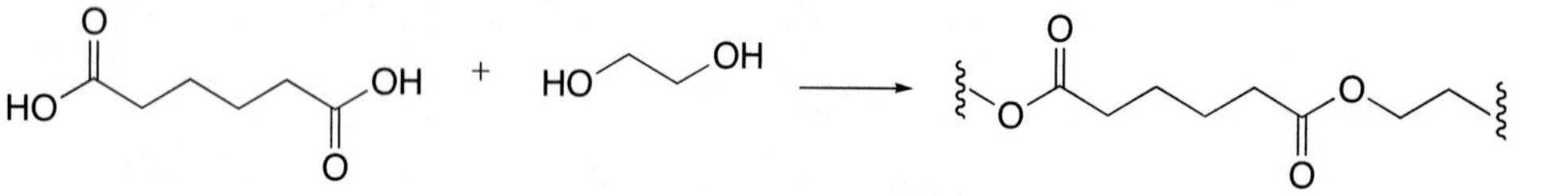

This compound is less suitable than either nylon 6,6 or PET for use in consumer products because esters are more easily hydrolyzed than amides, so this polyester is less stable than the polyamide nylon. This polyester has more flexible chains than PET, and this translates into a less strong fiber.

31.18

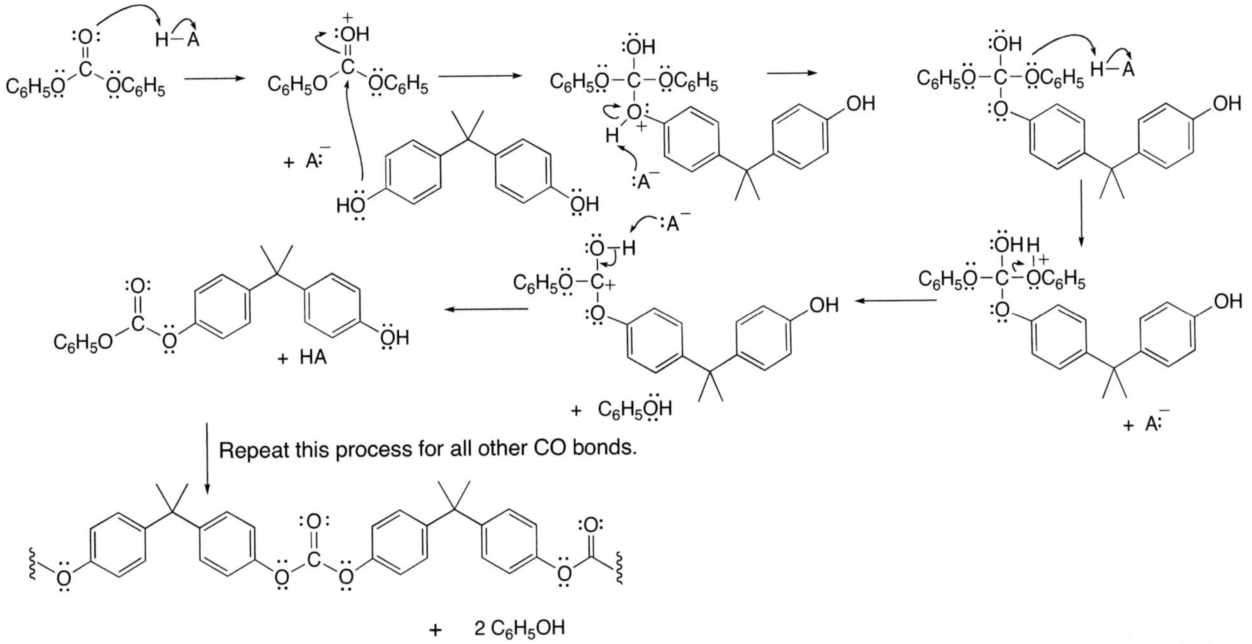
Repeat this process for all other CO bonds.
+ 2 C6H5OH

31.19

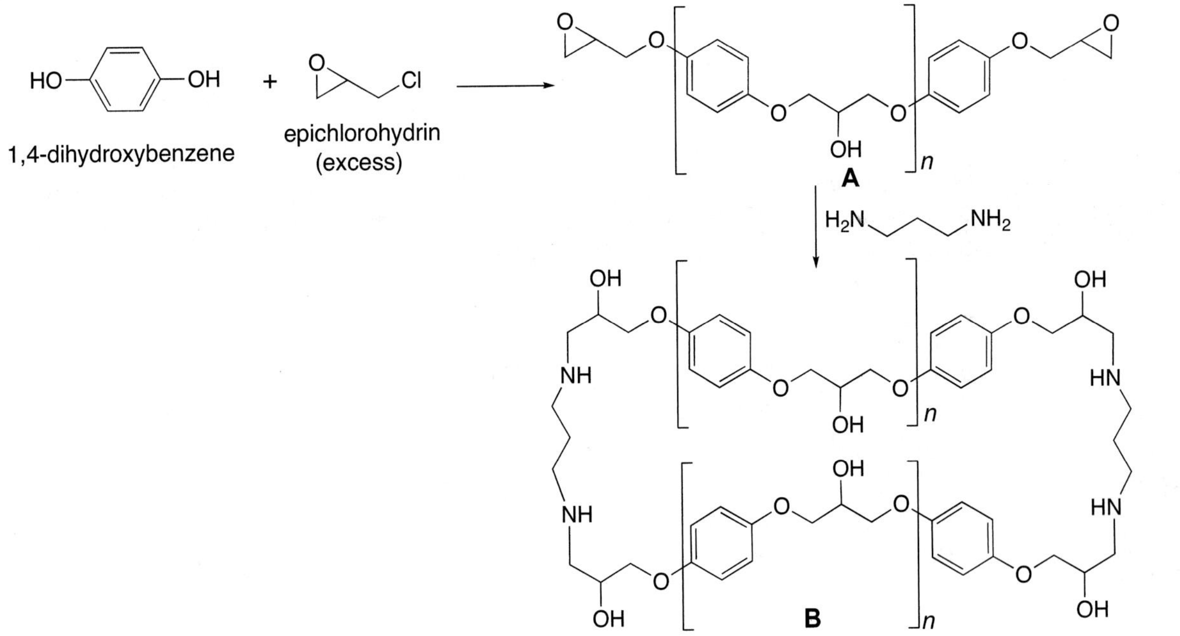
1,4-dihydroxybenzene
epichlorohydrin
(excess)
A
B

31.20

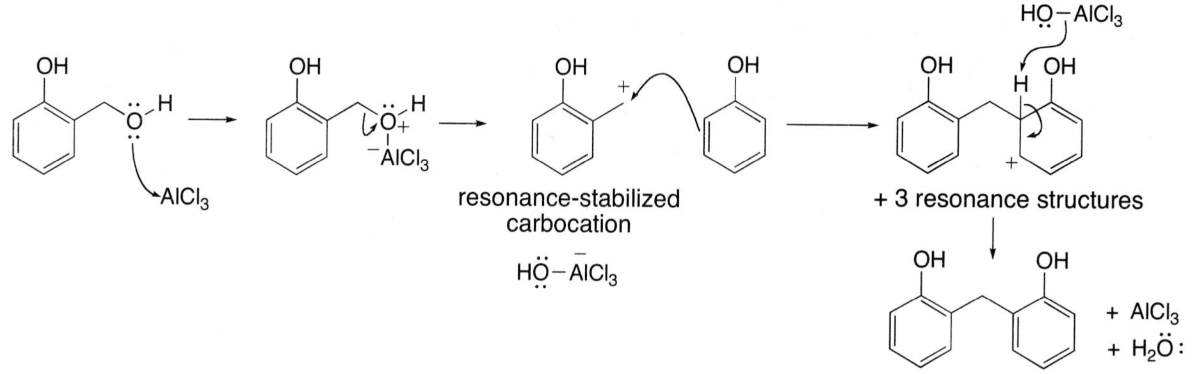
OH
AlCl3
resonance-stabilized carbocation
HÖ–AlCl3
+ 3 resonance structures
+ AlCl3
+ H2Ö:

31.21

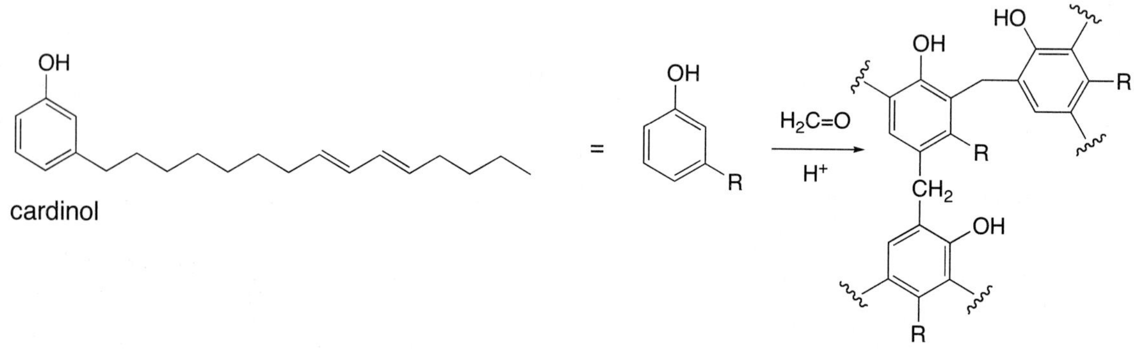
OH
cardinol
R
H2C=O
H+
HO
CH2

31.22 Chemical recycling of HDPE and LDPE is not easily done because these polymers are both long chains of CH_2 groups joined together in a linear fashion. Since there are only C–C bonds and no functional groups in the polymer chain, there are no easy methods to convert the polymers to their monomers. This process is readily accomplished only when the polymer backbone contains hydrolyzable functional groups.

31.23 a. Combustion of polyethylene forms $CO_2 + H_2O$.
b. Combustion of polyethylene terephthalate forms $CO_2 + H_2O$.
c. These reactions are exothermic.
d. HDPE and PET must be separated from poly(vinyl chloride) prior to incineration because combustion of hydrocarbons (like HDPE) and oxygen-containing organics (like PET) releases only $CO_2 + H_2O$ into the atmosphere. Poly(vinyl chloride) also contains Cl atoms bonded to a hydrocarbon chain. On combustion this forms HCl, which cannot be released directly into the atmosphere, making incineration of halogen-containing polymers more laborious and more expensive.

31.24

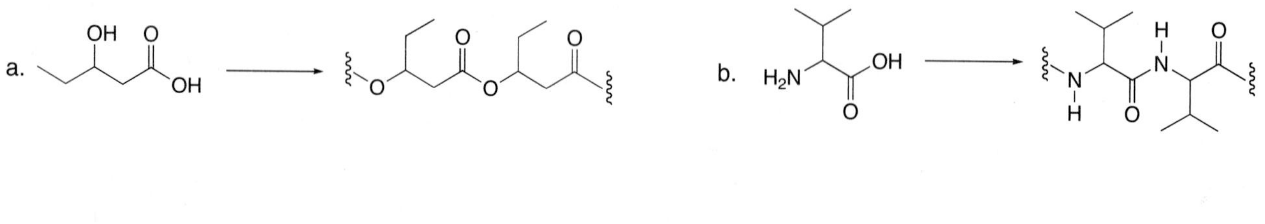
a.
b.
H2N
OH

31.25

a. 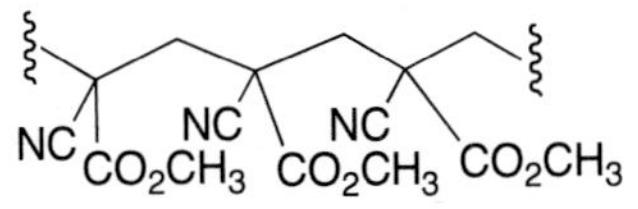

b. 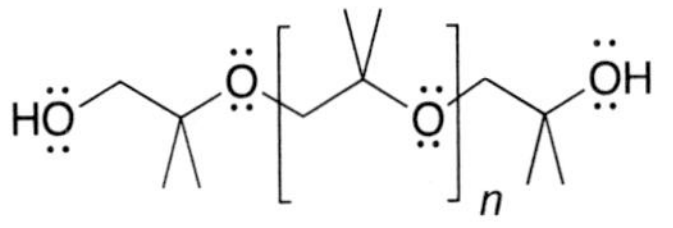

31.26

a. 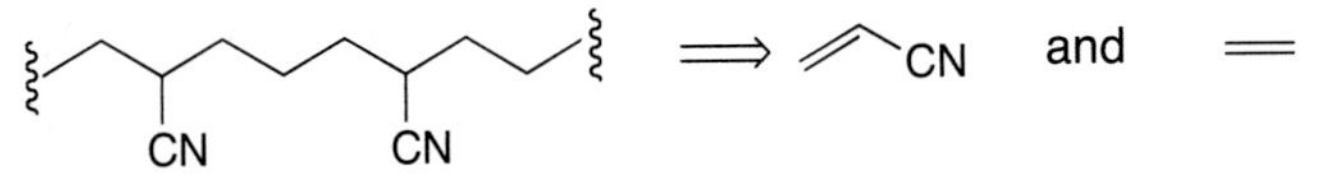

b. 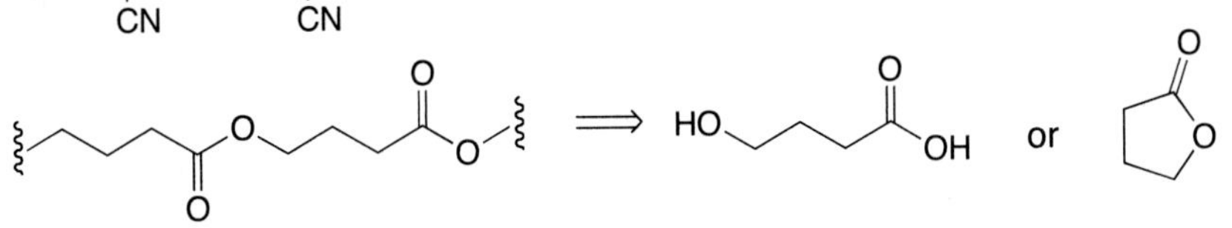

31.27

a. 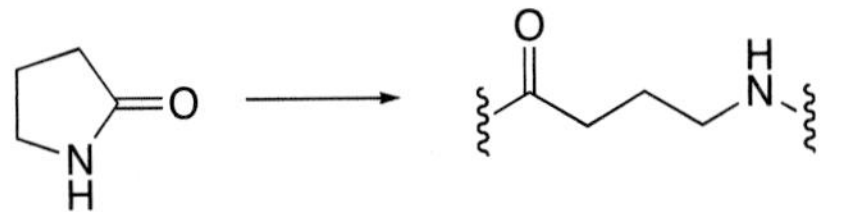

b. 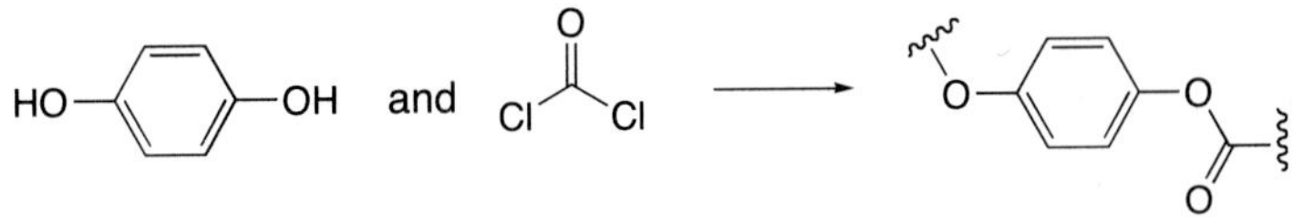

31.28 Draw the polymer formed by chain-growth polymerization as in Answer 31.2.

a. 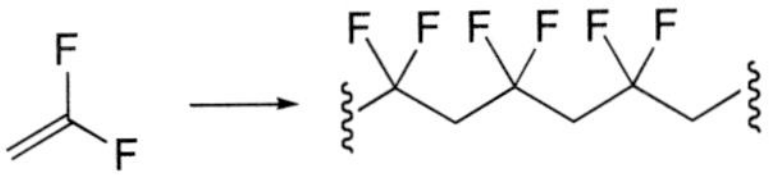

c. 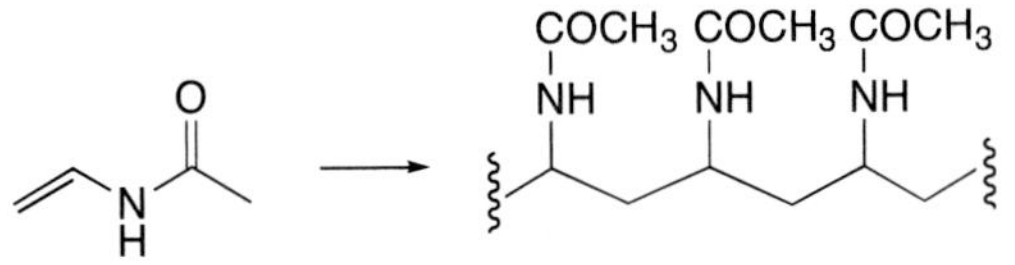

b. 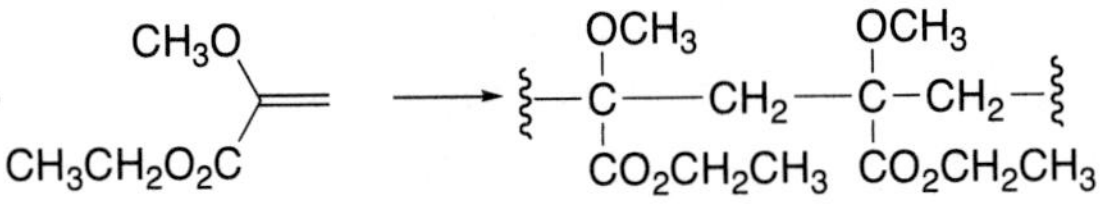

d. 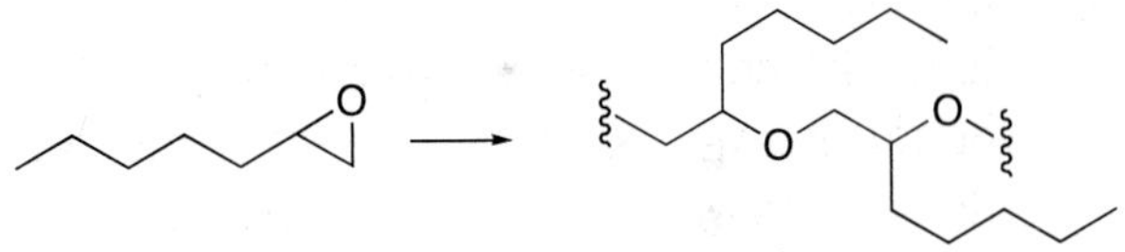

31.29 Draw the copolymers.

a. 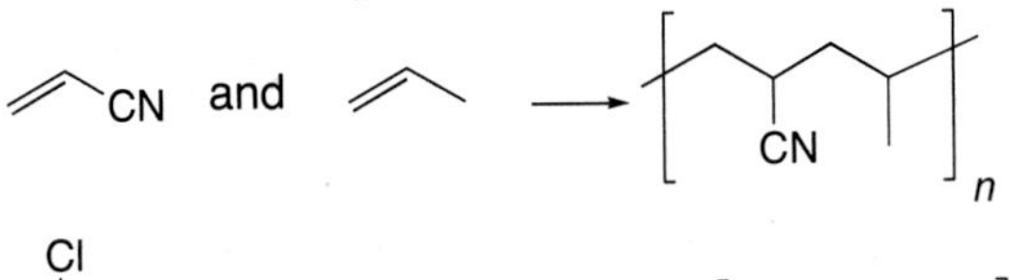

d. 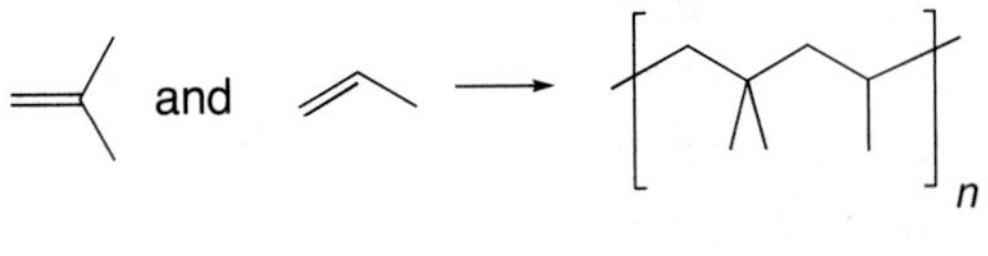

b. 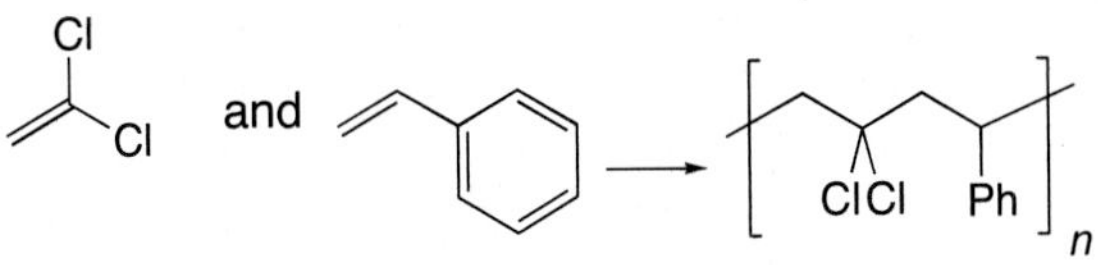

e. 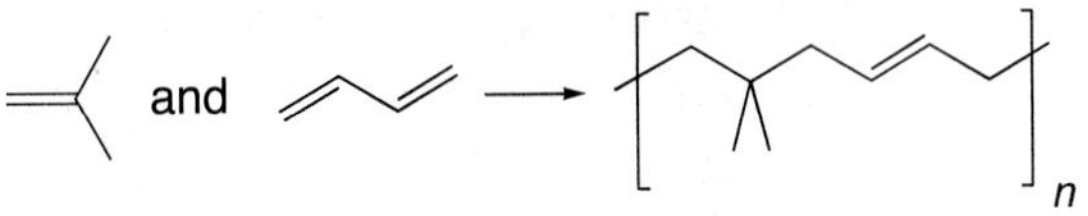

c. 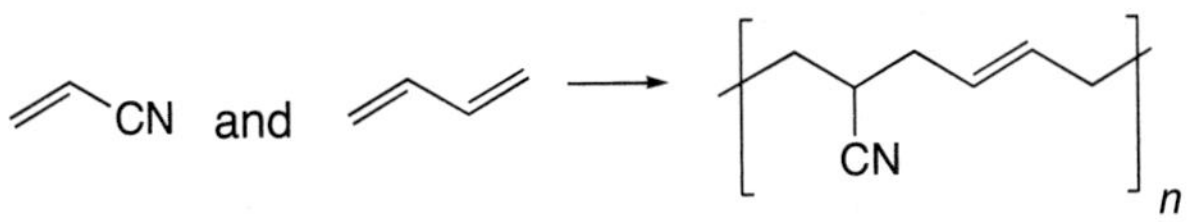

31.30

a. 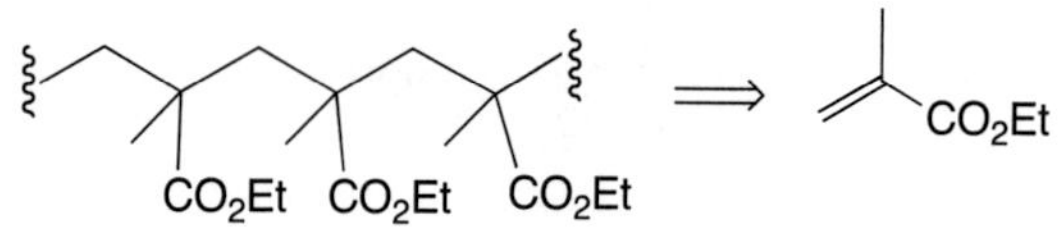

b. 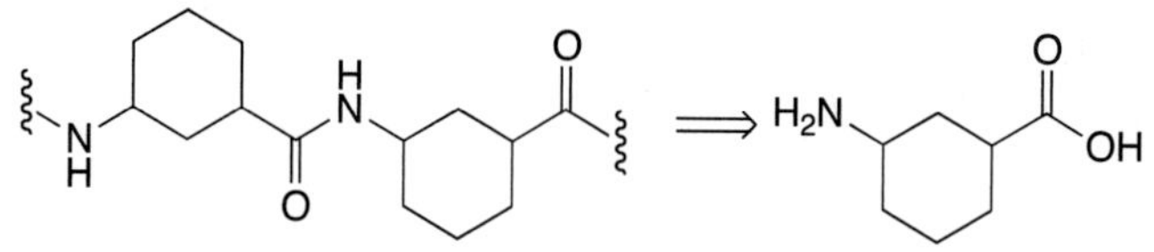

c. 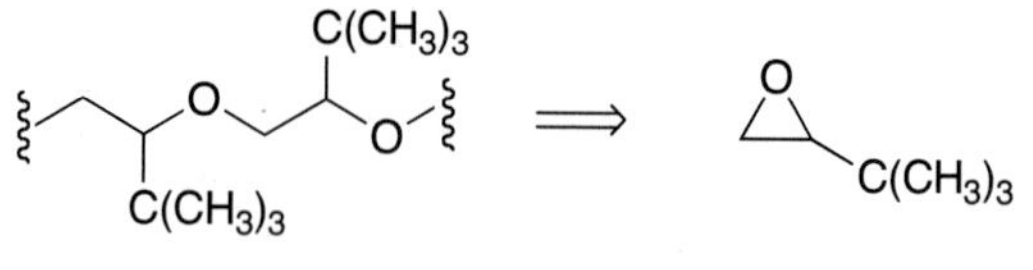

d. 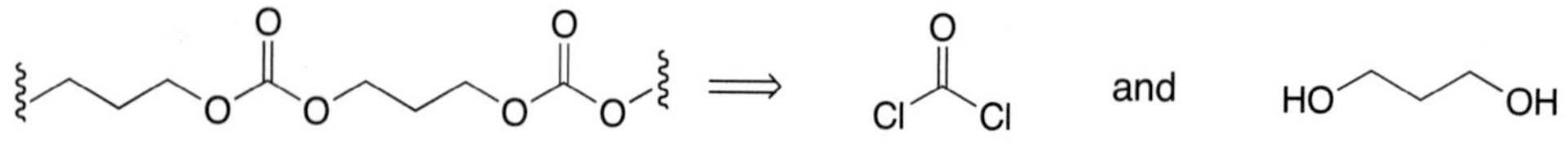

31.31

a. 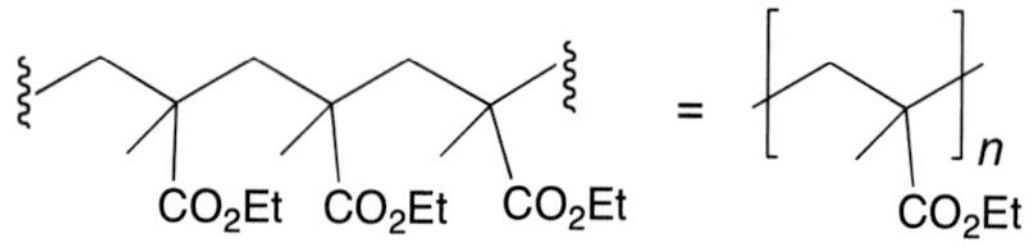

b. 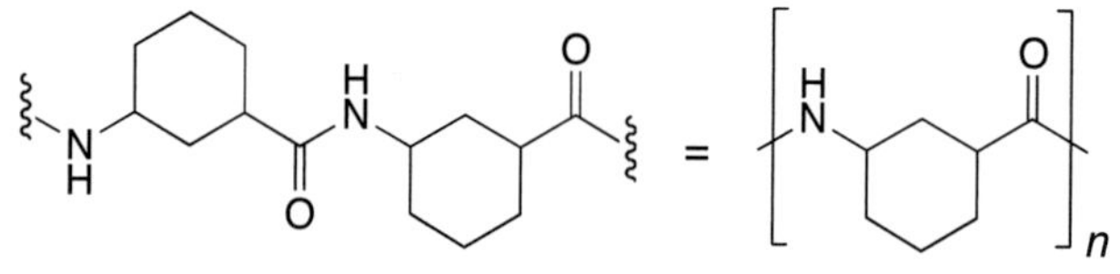

c. 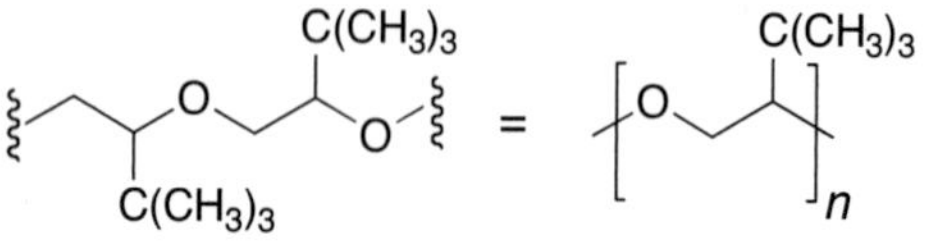

d. 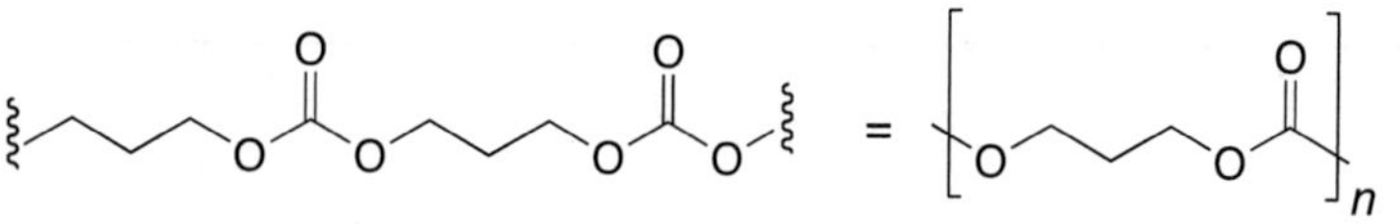

31.32 An **isotactic polymer** has all Z groups on the same side of the carbon backbone. A **syndiotactic polymer** has the Z groups alternating from one side of the carbon chain to the other. An **atactic polymer** has the Z groups oriented randomly along the polymer chain.

a. 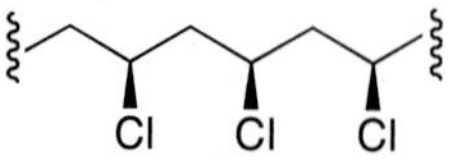

b. 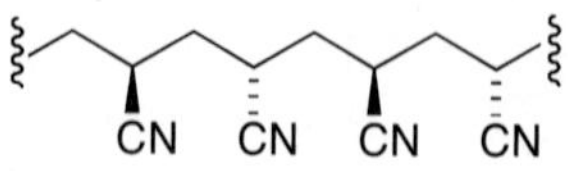

c. 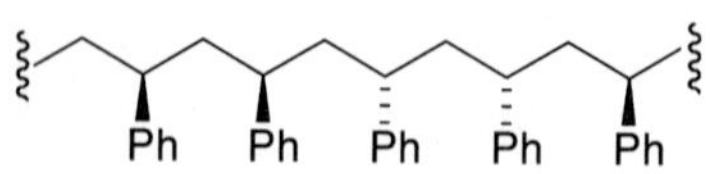

31.33

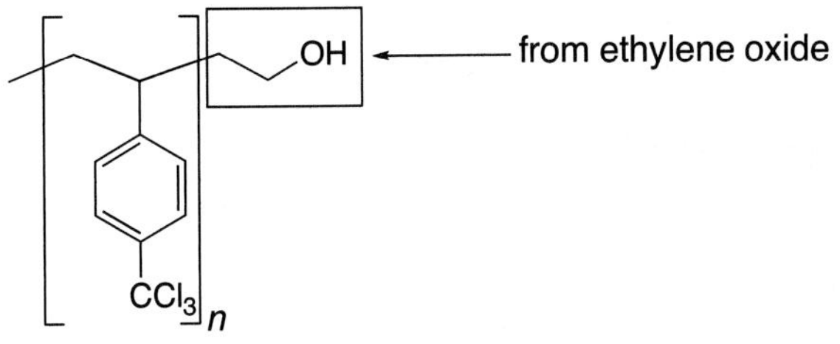

31.34

a.

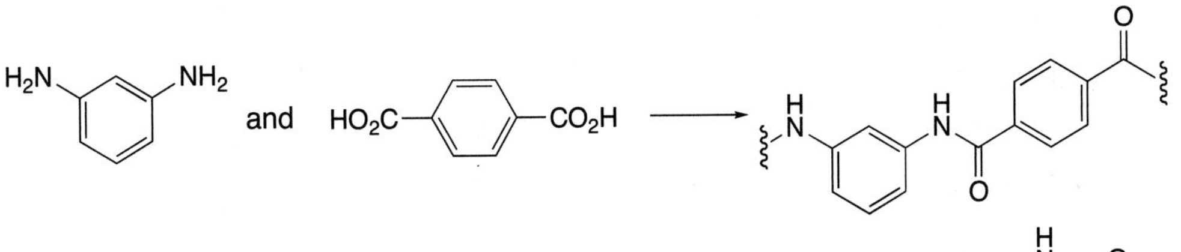

b.

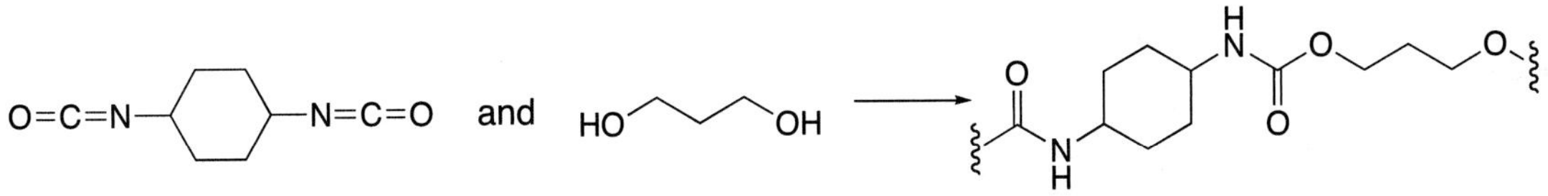

c.

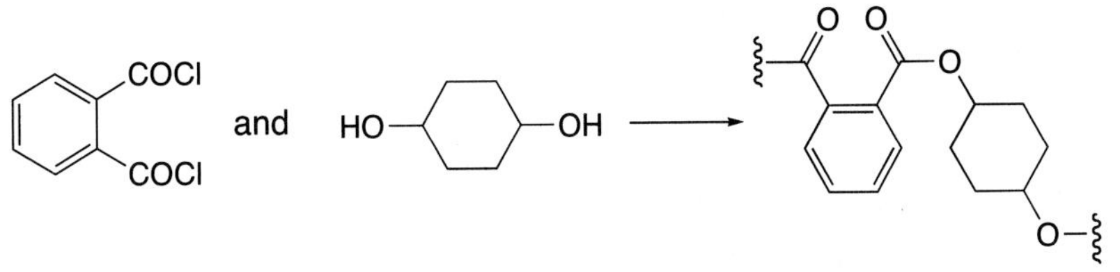

d.

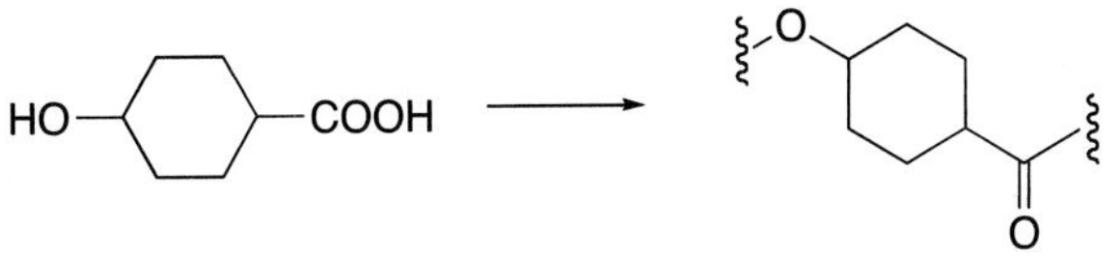

31.35

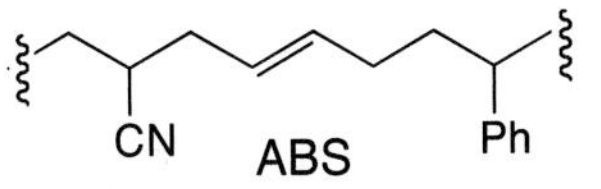

31.36

a.

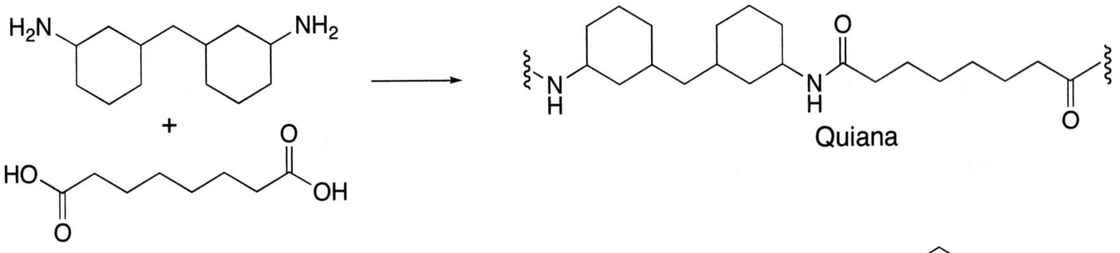

b.

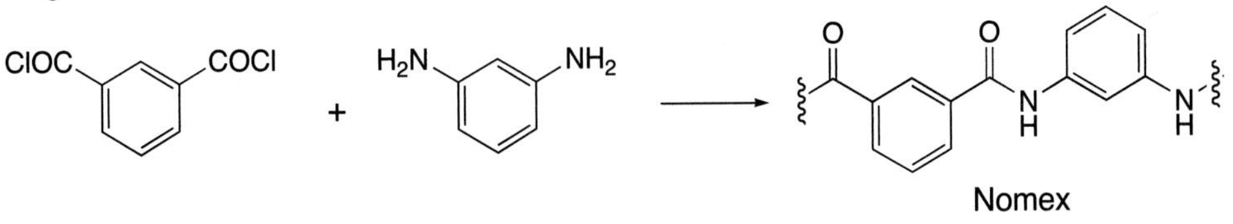

31.37

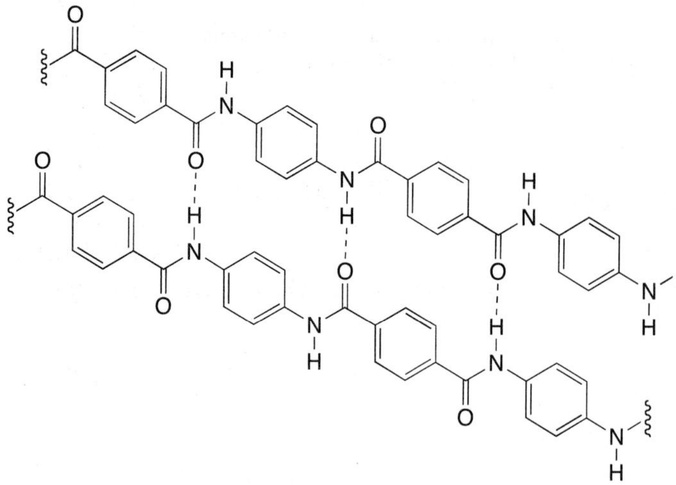

Kevlar

31.38

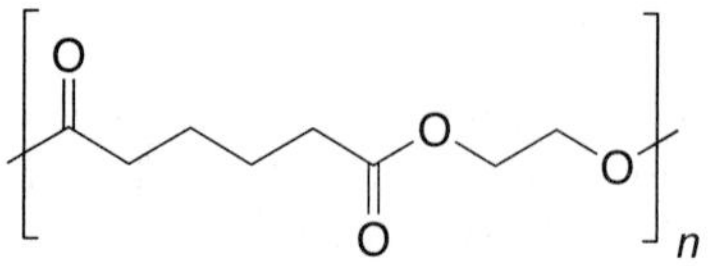

polyester **A**

T_g = < 0 °C
T_m = 50 °C

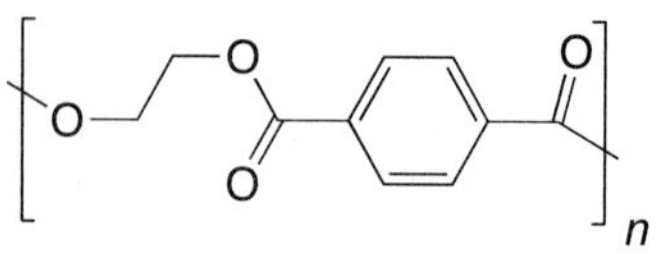

PET

T_g = 70 °C
T_m = 265 °C

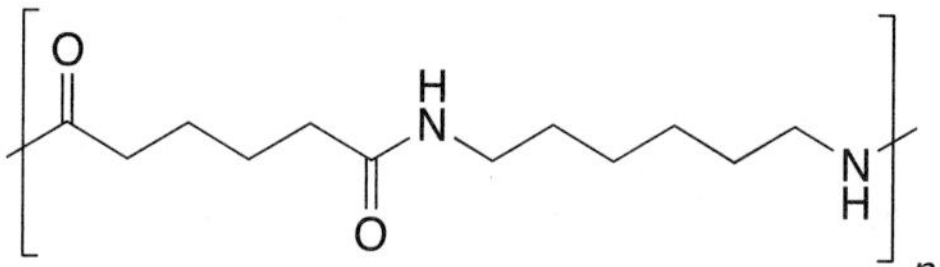

nylon 6,6

T_g = 53 °C
T_m = 265 °C

a. Polyester **A** has a lower T_g and T_m than PET because its polymer chain is more flexible. There are no rigid benzene rings, so the polymer is less ordered.
b. Polyester **A** has a lower T_g and T_m than nylon 6,6 because the N–H bonds of nylon 6,6 allow chains to hydrogen bond to each other, which makes the polymer more ordered.
c. The T_m for Kevlar would be higher than that of nylon 6,6, because in addition to extensive hydrogen bonding between chains, each chain contains rigid benzene rings. This results in a more ordered polymer.

31.39

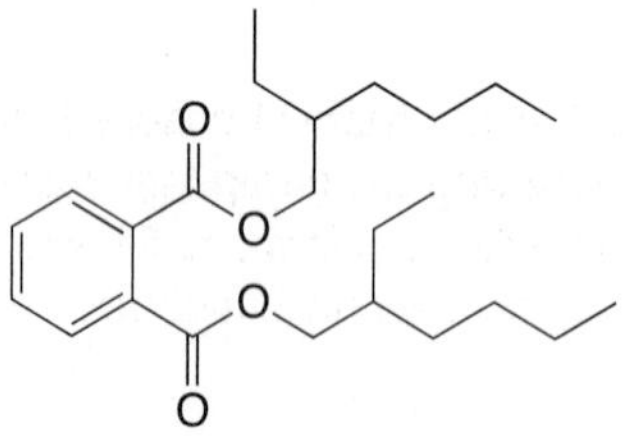

A

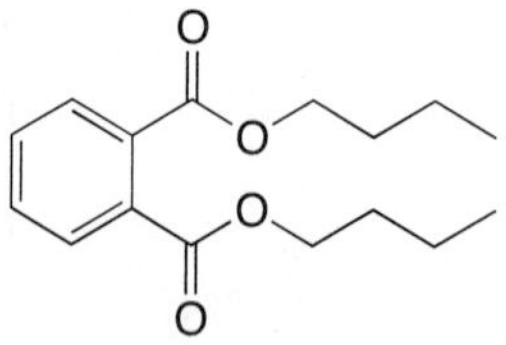

dibutyl phthalate

Diester **A** is often used as a plasticizer in place of dibutyl phthalate because it has a higher molecular weight, giving it a higher boiling point. **A** should therefore be less volatile than dibutyl phthalate, so it should evaporate from a polymer less readily.

31.40

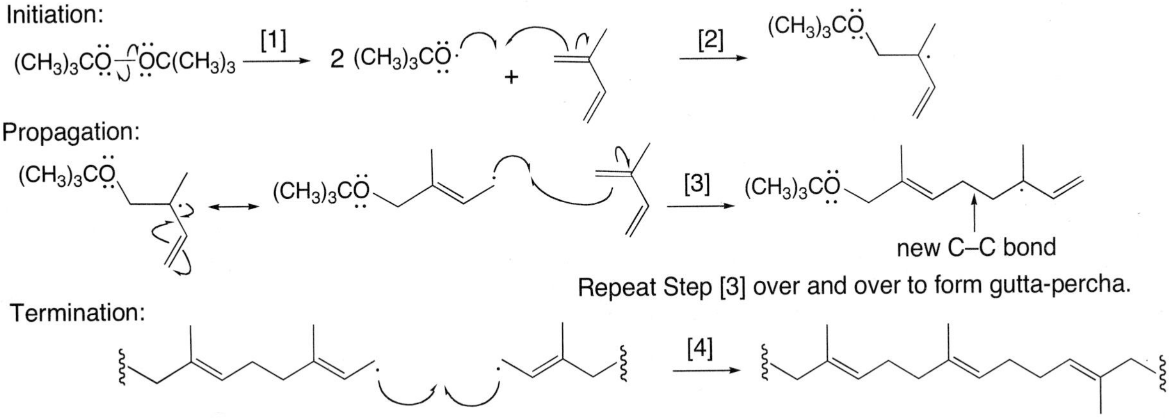
Initiation:
$(CH_3)_3CO{-}OC(CH_3)_3$
[1]
2 $(CH_3)_3CO\cdot$
+
[2]
$(CH_3)_3CO$
Propagation:
$(CH_3)_3CO$
$(CH_3)_3CO$
[3]
$(CH_3)_3CO$
new C–C bond
Repeat Step [3] over and over to form gutta-percha.
Termination:
[4]

31.41

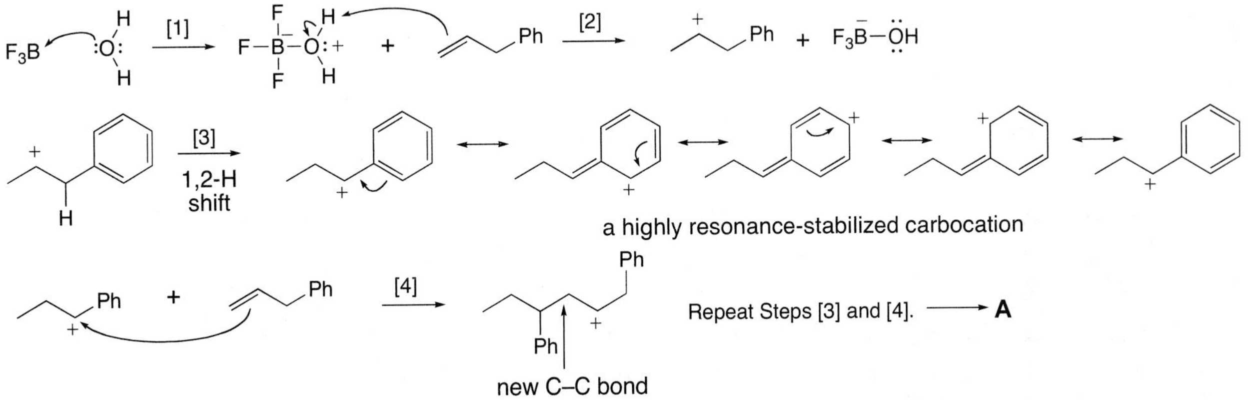
F_3B
[1]
+
Ph
[2]
Ph
+ $F_3\bar{B}{-}OH$
[3]
1,2-H shift
H
a highly resonance-stabilized carbocation
Ph
+
Ph
[4]
Ph
Repeat Steps [3] and [4]. → A
new C–C bond

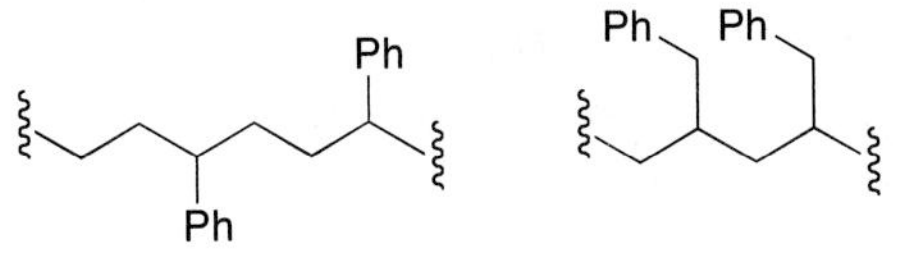
Ph
Ph
Ph
Ph

A
major product

B

A is the major product formed due to the 1,2-H shift (Step [3]) that occurs to form a resonance-stabilized carbocation.
B is the product that would form without this shift.

31.42

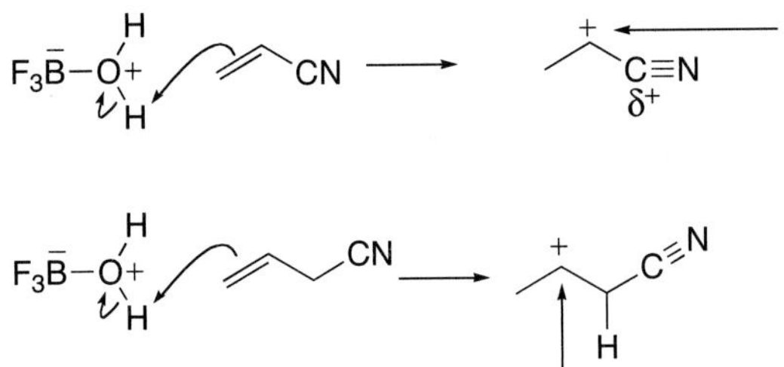
$F_3\bar{B}{-}O+$
CN
C≡N
δ^+
$F_3\bar{B}{-}O+$
CN
C≡N
H

This carbocation is unstable because it is located next to an electron-withdrawing CN group that bears a δ^+ on its C atom. This carbocation is difficult to form, so $CH_2{=}CHCN$ is only slowly polymerized under cationic conditions.

This 2° carbocation is more stable because it is not directly bonded to the electron-withdrawing CN group. As a result, it is more readily formed. Thus, cationic polymerization can occur more readily.

31.43

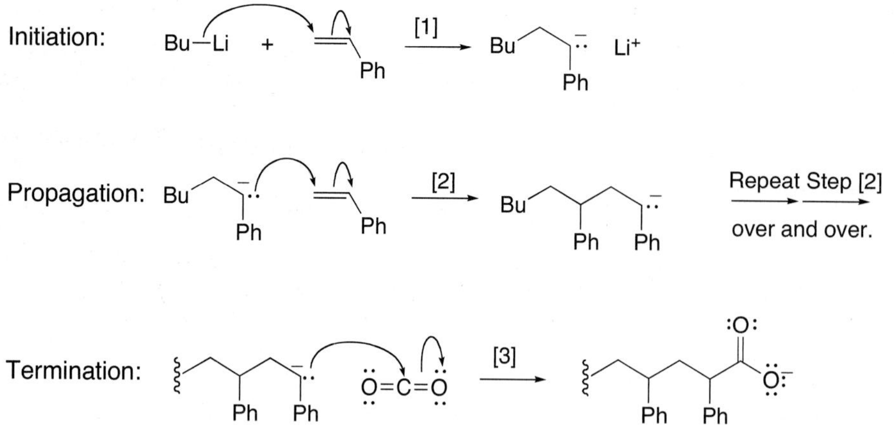
Initiation:
[1]
Propagation:
[2]
Repeat Step [2] over and over.
Termination:
[3]

31.44 The substituent on styrene determines whether cationic or anionic polymerization is preferred. When the substituent stabilizes a carbocation, cationic polymerization will occur. When the substituent stabilizes a carbanion, anionic polymerization will occur.

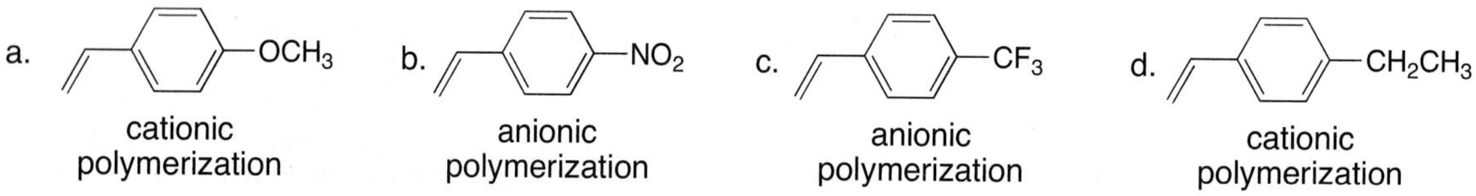
a. cationic polymerization
b. anionic polymerization
c. anionic polymerization
d. cationic polymerization

31.45 The rate of anionic polymerization depends on the ability of the substituents on the alkene to stabilize an intermediate carbanion: the better a substituent stabilizes a carbanion, the faster anionic polymerization occurs.

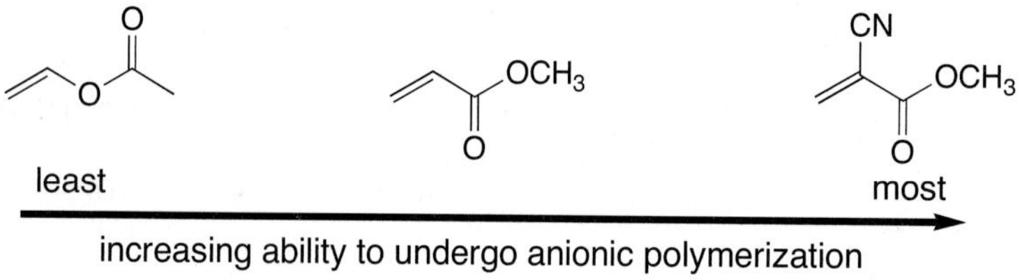
least
most
increasing ability to undergo anionic polymerization

31.46 The reason for this selectivity is explained in Figure 9.9. In the ring opening of an unsymmetrical epoxide under acidic conditions, nucleophilic attack occurs at the carbon atom that is more able to accept a δ^+ in the transition state; that is, nucleophilic attack occurs at the more substituted carbon. The transition state having a δ^+ on a C with an electron-donating CH_3 group is more stabilized (lower in energy), permitting a faster reaction.

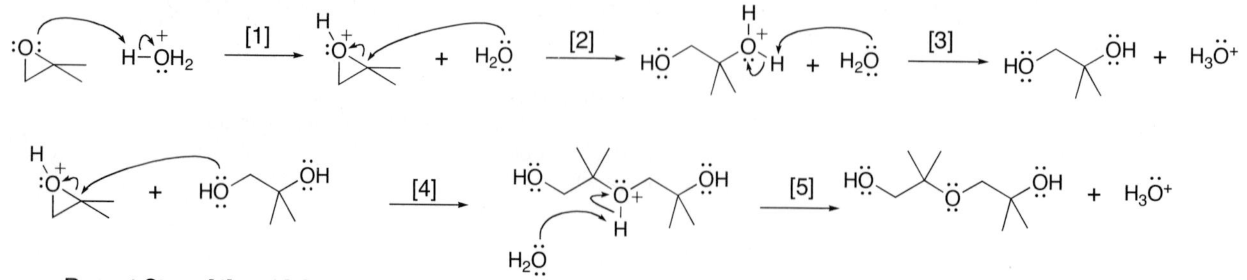

Repeat Steps [4] and [5] over and over.

31.47

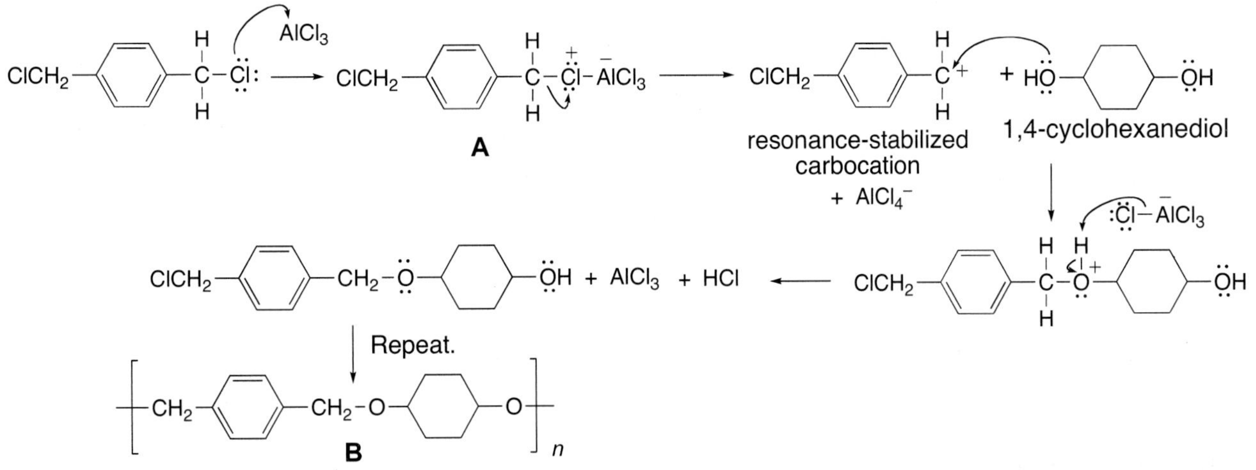

31.48

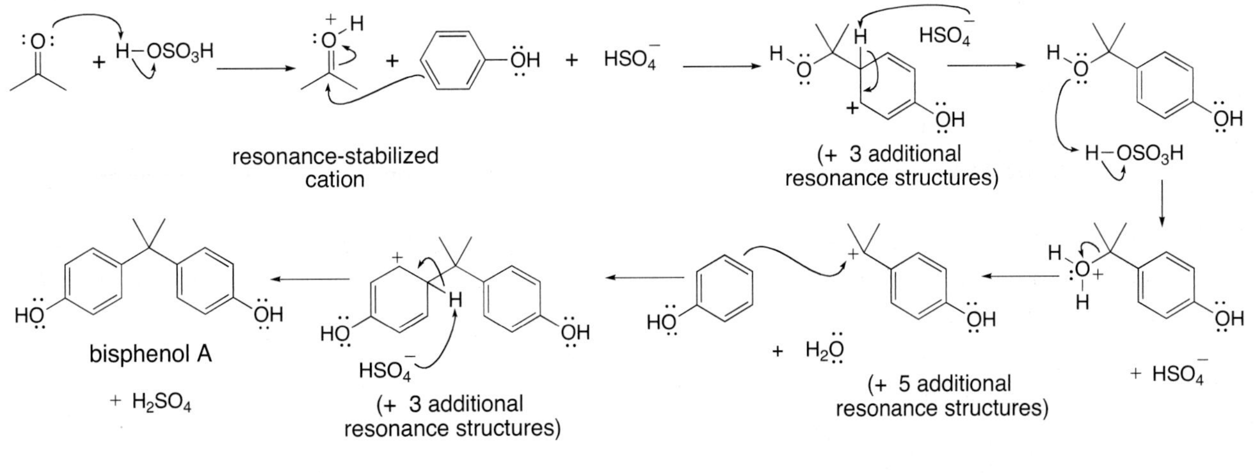

31.49

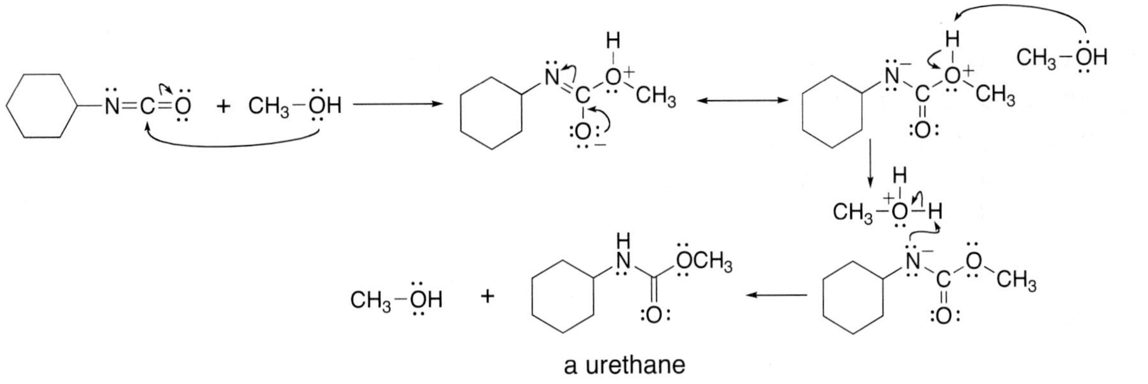

31.50

a. 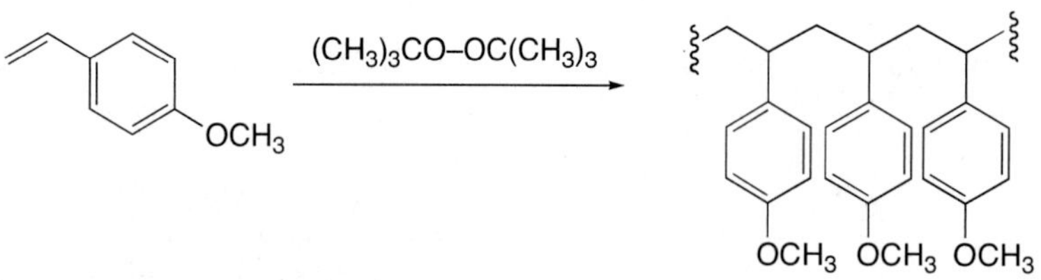

b. 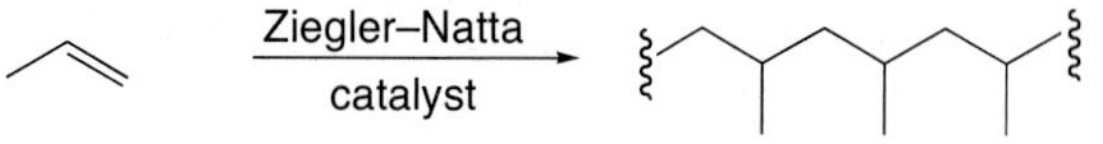

c. 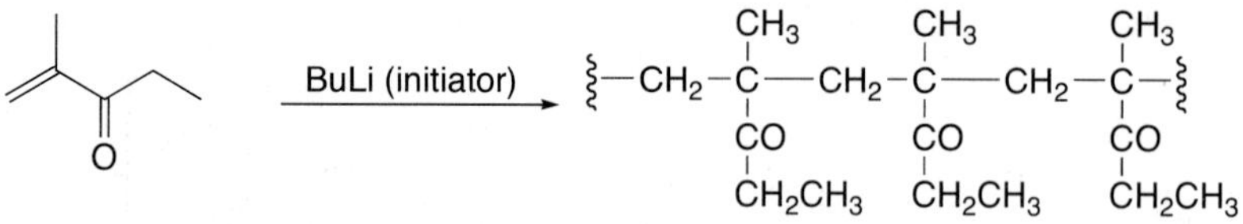

d. 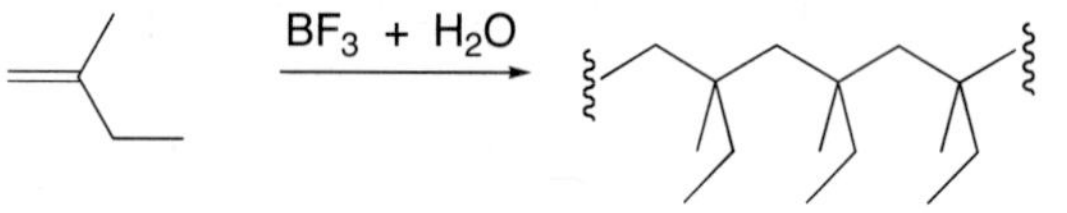

e. 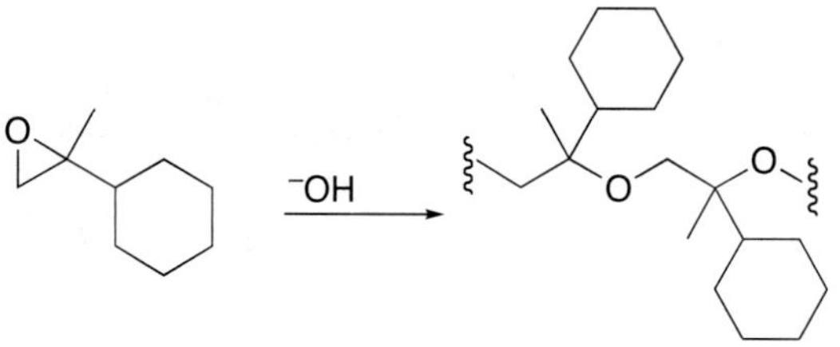

f. 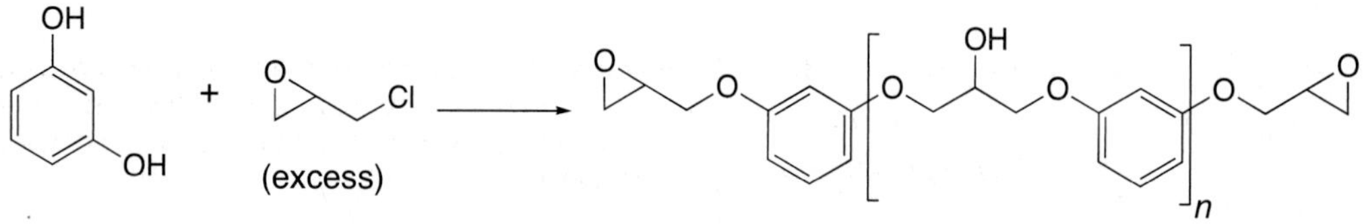

g. 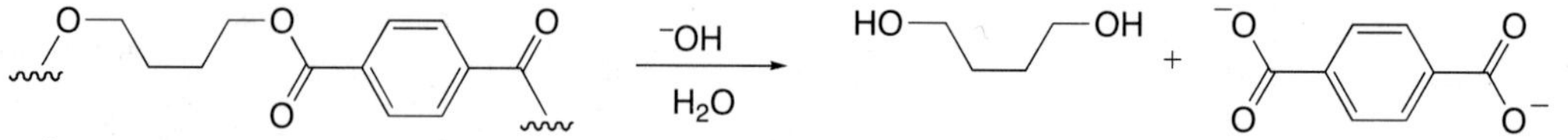

h. 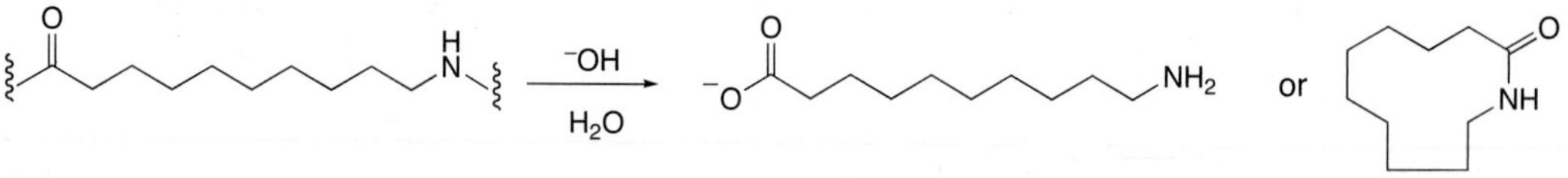

i. 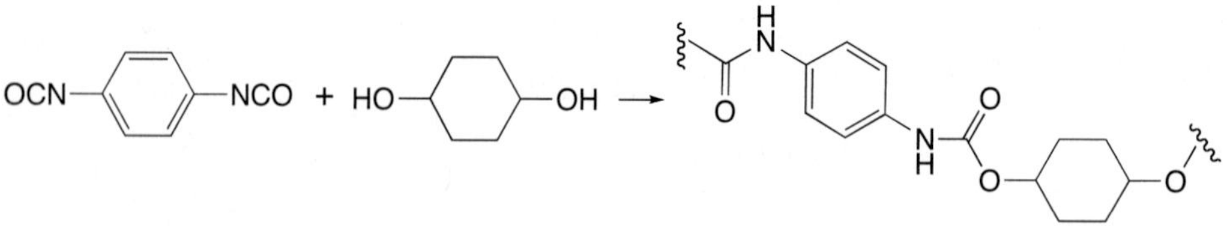

j. 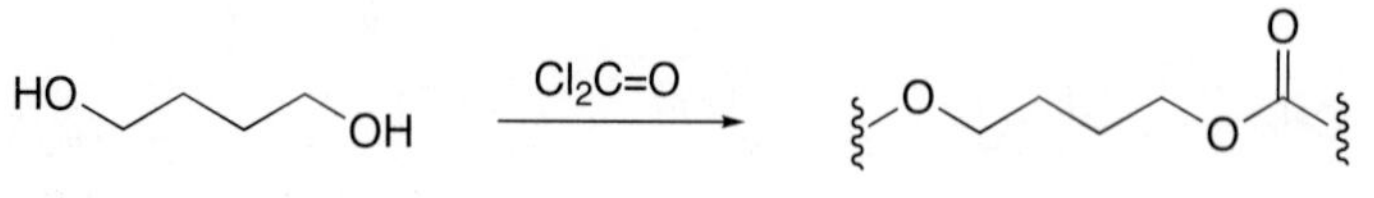

31.51 Polyethylene bottles are resistant to NaOH because they are hydrocarbons with no reactive sites. Polyester shirts and nylon stockings both contain functional groups. Nylon contains amides and polyester contains esters, two functional groups that are susceptible to hydrolysis with aqueous NaOH. Thus, the polymers are converted to their monomer starting materials, creating a hole in the garment.

31.52

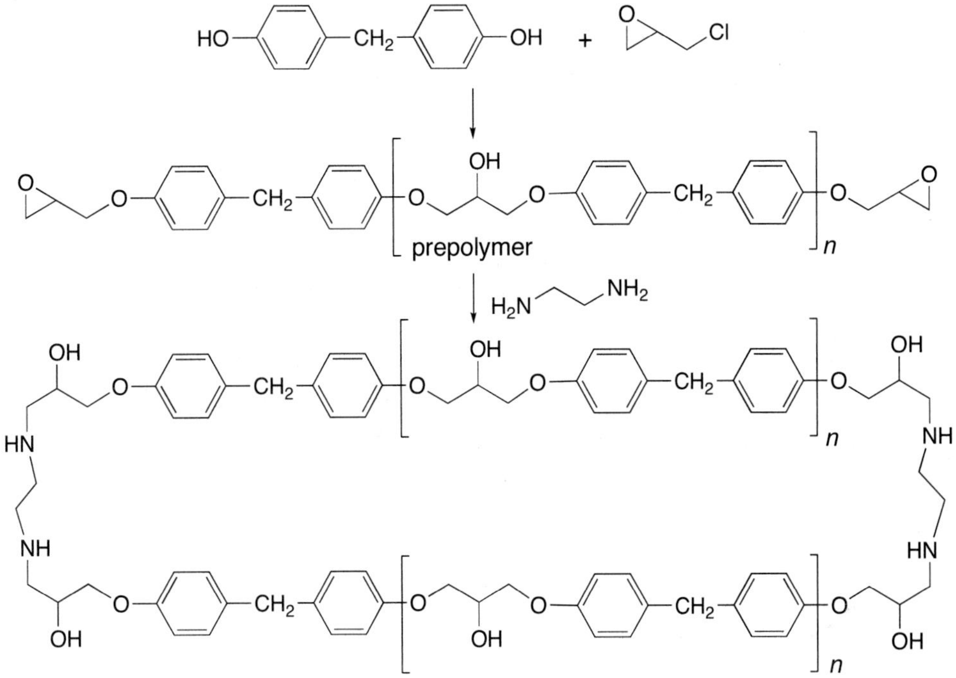
HO
CH2
OH
+
O
Cl
OH
O
CH2
O
O
CH2
O
prepolymer
n
H2N
NH2
OH
HN
NH
OH
n

31.53

a. 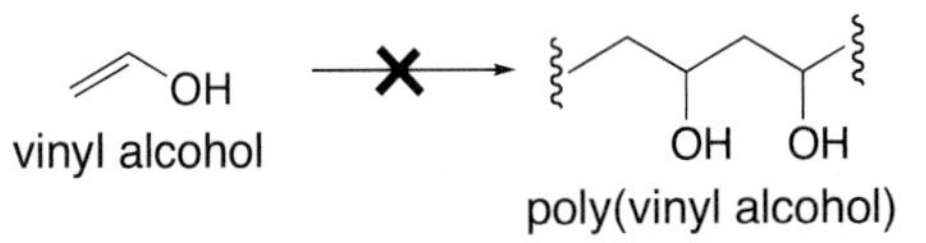
OH
vinyl alcohol
OH OH
poly(vinyl alcohol)

Poly(vinyl alcohol) cannot be prepared from vinyl alcohol because vinyl alcohol is not a stable monomer. It is the enol of acetaldehyde (CH_3CHO), and thus it can't be converted to poly(vinyl alcohol).

b. 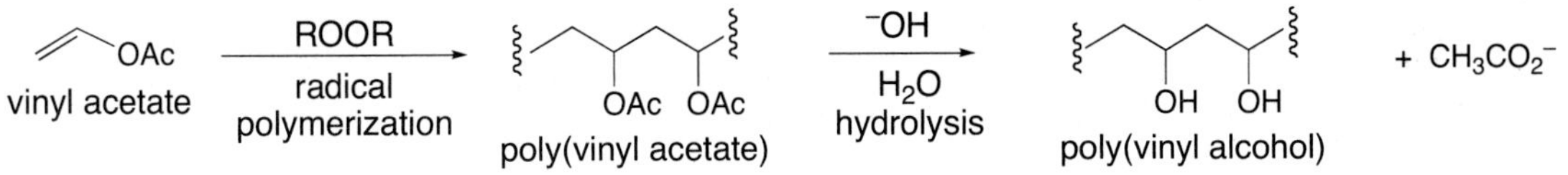
OAc
vinyl acetate
ROOR
radical polymerization
OAc OAc
poly(vinyl acetate)
⁻OH
H2O
hydrolysis
OH OH
poly(vinyl alcohol)
+ CH3CO2⁻

c. 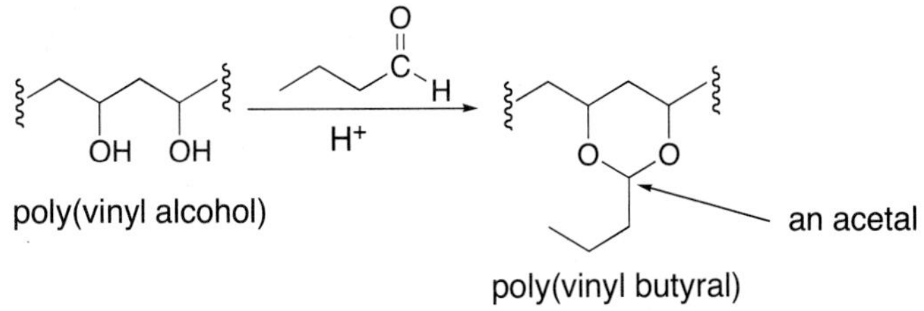
OH OH
poly(vinyl alcohol)
O
C
H
H+
O O
an acetal
poly(vinyl butyral)

31.54

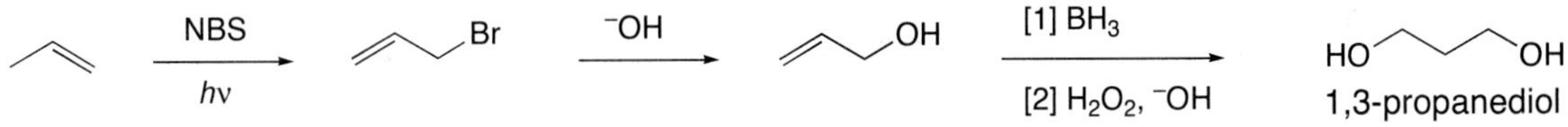
NBS
hν
Br
⁻OH
OH
[1] BH3
[2] H2O2, ⁻OH
HO
OH
1,3-propanediol

31.55

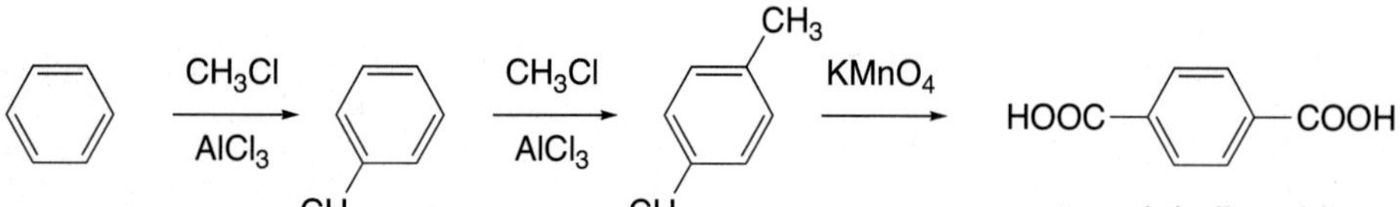

terephthalic acid

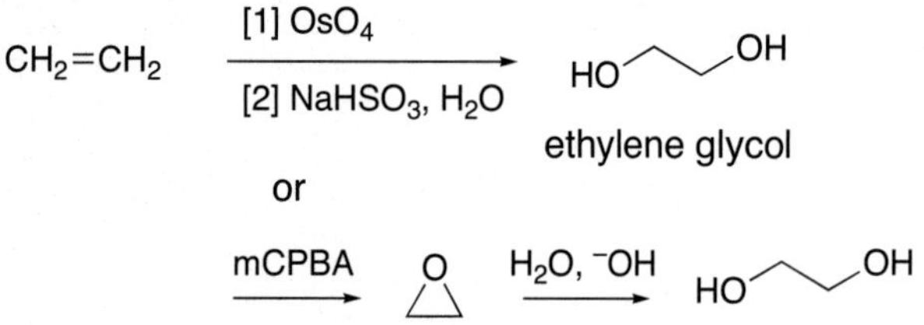

ethylene glycol

31.56

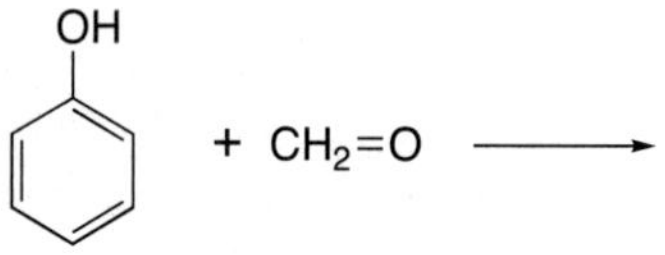

phenol

Since phenol has no substituents at any ortho or para position, an extensive network of covalent bonds can join the benzene rings together at all ortho and para positions to the OH groups.

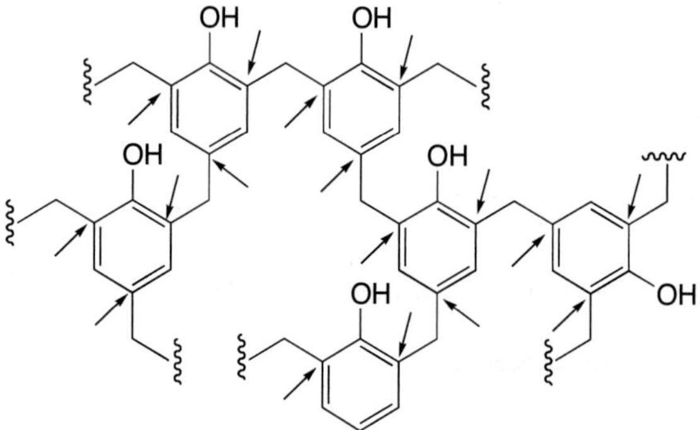

Bakelite

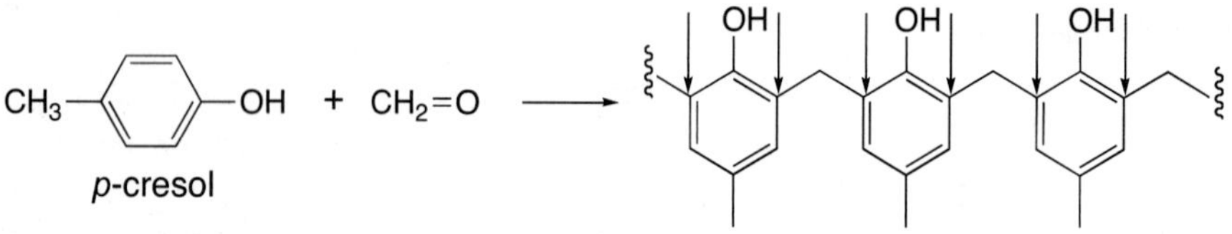

p-cresol

Since *p*-cresol has a CH_3 group at the para position to the OH group, new bonds can be formed only at two ortho positions, so that a less extensive three-dimensional network can form.

31.57

a. 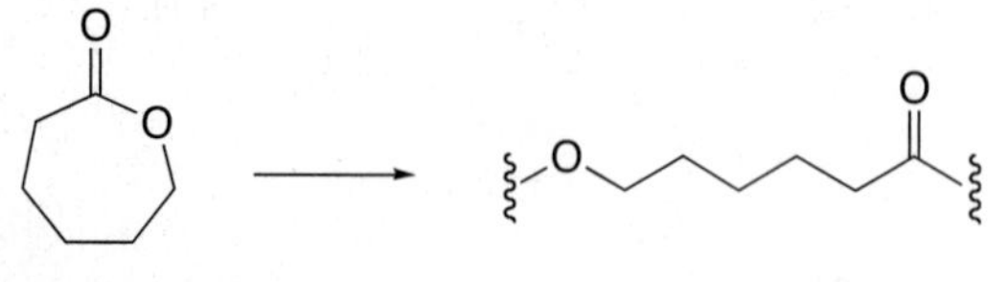

ε-caprolactone polycaprolactone

b. 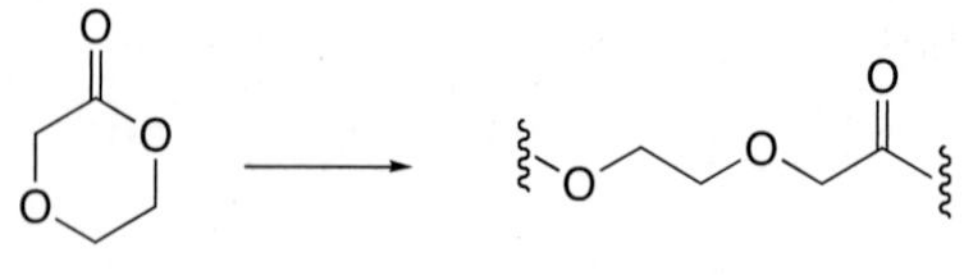

p-dioxanone polydioxanone

31.58

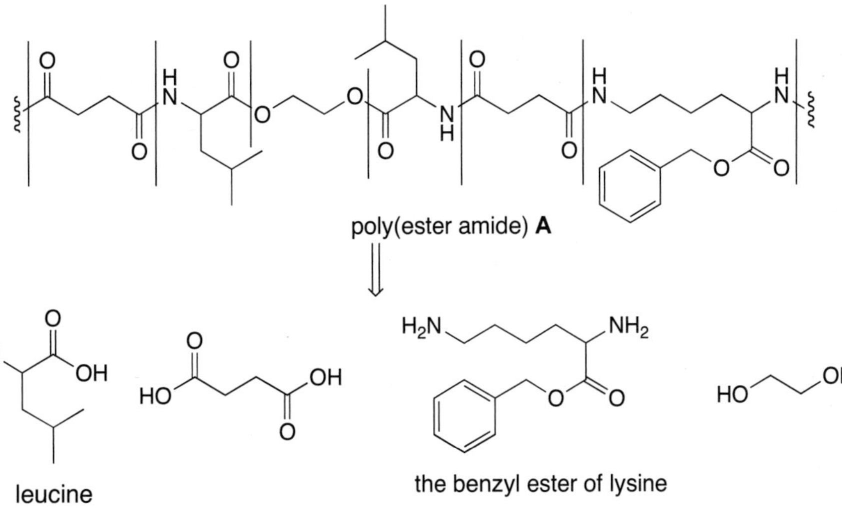
poly(ester amide) A
leucine
the benzyl ester of lysine

31.59

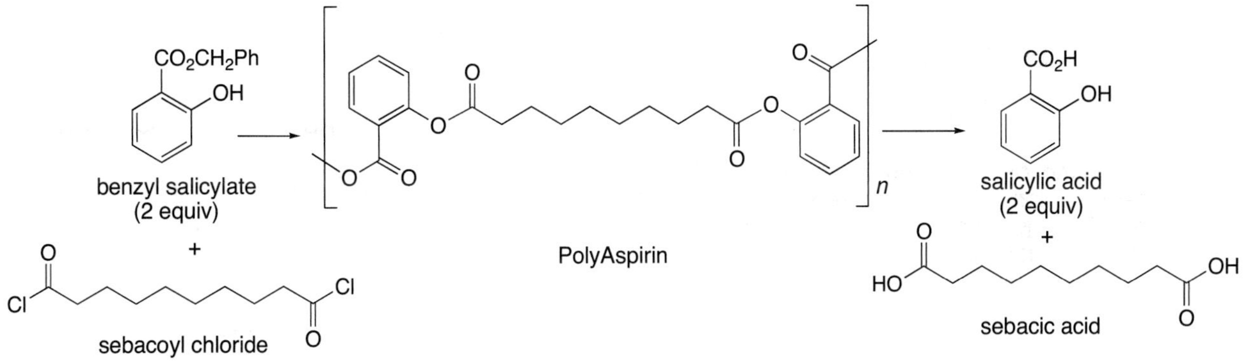
benzyl salicylate
(2 equiv)
+
sebacoyl chloride
PolyAspirin
salicylic acid
(2 equiv)
+
sebacic acid

31.60

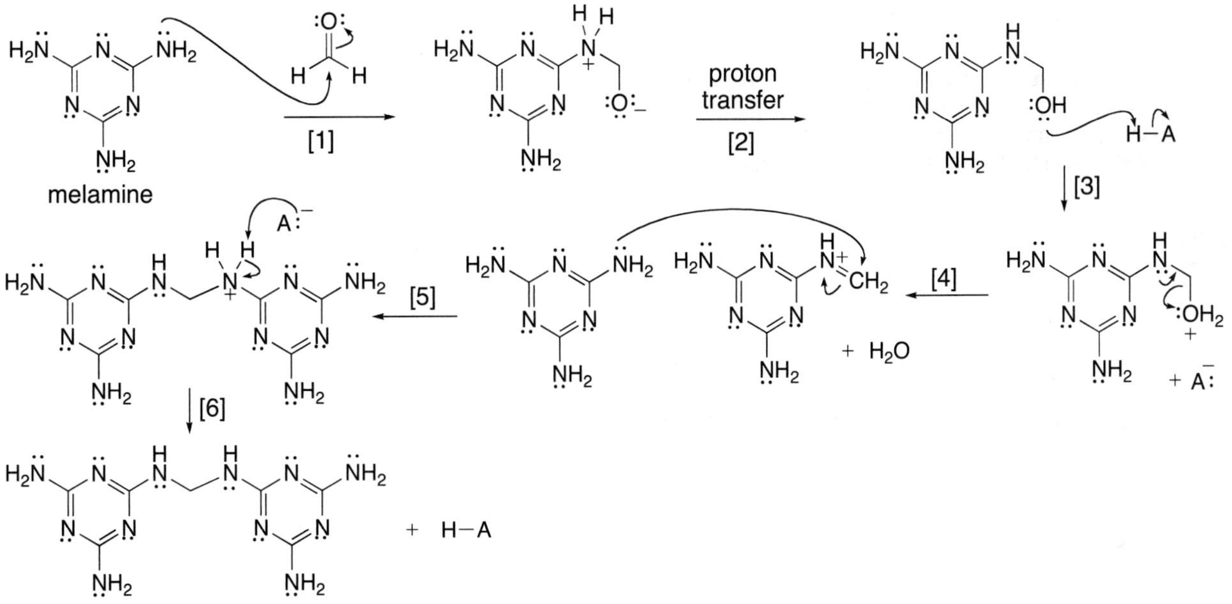
melamine
[1]
proton
transfer
[2]
[3]
[4]
[5]
[6]

31.61

a. 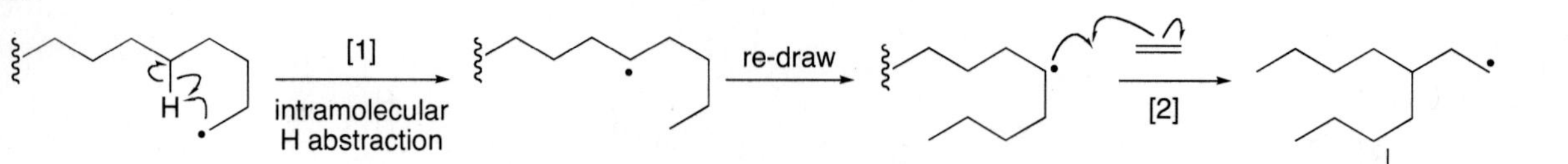
[1]
intramolecular
H abstraction
re-draw
[2]

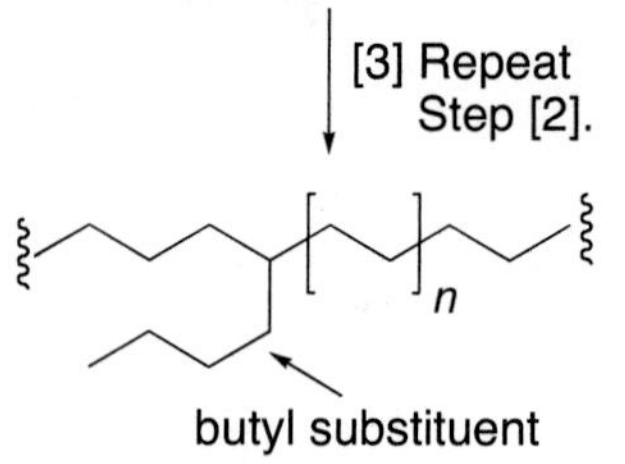
[3] Repeat
Step [2].
n
butyl substituent

b. Abstraction of the H is more facile than abstraction of the other H's because the H atom that is removed is six atoms from the radical. The transition state for this intramolecular reaction is cyclic, and resembles a six-membered ring, the most stable ring size. Other H's are too far away or the transition state would resemble a smaller, less stable ring.

31.62

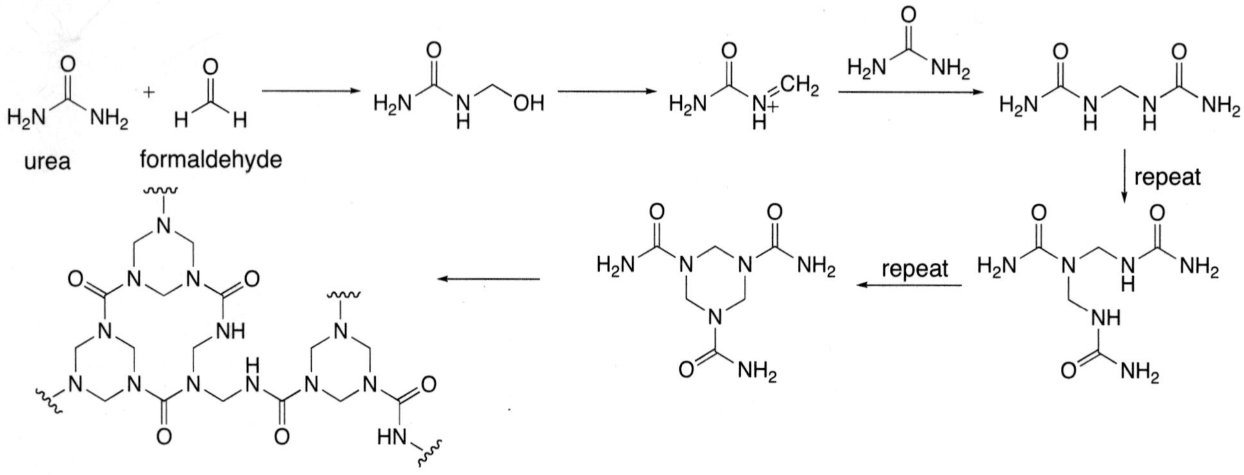
urea
formaldehyde
repeat
repeat

Notes

Notes

Notes

Notes

Notes

Notes